Hoover's MasterList of U.S. Companies

2020

Hoover's MasterList of U.S. Companies is intended to provide readers with accurate and authoritative information about the enterprises covered in it. The information contained herein is as accurate as we could reasonably make it. In many cases we have relied on third-party material that we believe to be trustworthy but were unable to independently verify. We do not warrant that the book is absolutely accurate or without error. Readers should not rely on any information contained herein in instances where such reliance might cause financial loss.

The publisher, the editors, and their data suppliers specifically disclaim all warranties, including the implied warranties of merchantability and fitness for a specific purpose. This book is sold with the understanding that neither the publisher, the editors, nor any content contributors are engaged in providing investment, financial, accounting, legal, or other professional advice.

Mergent Inc., provided financial data for most public companies in this book. For private companies and historical information on public companies prior to their becoming public, we obtained information directly from the companies or from third-party material that we believe to be trustworthy. Hoover's, Inc., is solely responsible for the presentation of all data.

Many of the names of products and services mentioned in this book are the trademarks or service marks of the companies manufacturing or selling them and are subject to protection under U.S. law. Space has not permitted us to indicate which names are subject to such protection, and readers are advised to consult with the owners of such marks regarding their use. Hoover's is a trademark of Hoover's, Inc.

Copyright © 2020 by Hoover's, Inc. All rights reserved. No part of this book may be reproduced or transmitted in any form or by any means, electronic or mechanical, including by photocopying, facsimile transmission, recording, rekeying, or using any information storage and retrieval system, without permission in writing from Hoover's, except that brief passages may be quoted by a reviewer in a magazine, in a newspaper, online, or in a broadcast review.

10 9 8 7 6 5 4 3 2 1

Publishers Cataloging-in-Publication Data

Hoover's MasterList of U.S. Companies 2020,

    Includes indexes.

    ISBN: 978-1-64141-564-4

    ISSN 1549-6457

    1. Business enterprises — Directories. 2. Corporations — Directories.

HF3010　338.7

U.S. AND WORLD BOOK SALES

Mergent Inc.
444 Madison Ave
New York, NY 10022
Phone: 704-559-6961

e-mail: skardon@ftserussell.com
Web: www.mergentbusinesspress.com

Mergent Inc.

Executive Managing Director: John Pedernales

Managing Director of Print Products and Publisher: Thomas Wecera

Director of Print Products: Charlot Volny

Quality Assurance Editor: Wayne Arnold

Production Research Assistant: Davie Christna

Data Manager: Jason Horvat

MERGENT CUSTOMER SERVICE-PRINT PRODUCTS
Support and Fulfillment Manager: Thomas Wecera 212-413-7726

ABOUT MERGENT, INC.

For over 100 years, Mergent, Inc. has been a leading provider of business and financial information on public and private companies globally. Mergent is known to be a trusted partner to corporate and financial institutions, as well as to academic and public libraries. Today we continue to build on a century of experience by transforming data into knowledge and combining our expertise with the latest technology to create new global data and analytical solutions for our clients. With advanced data collection services, cloud-based applications, desktop analytics and print products, Mergent and its subsidiaries provide solutions from top down economic and demographic information, to detailed equity and debt fundamental analysis. We incorporate value added tools such as quantitative Smart Beta equity research and tools for portfolio building and measurement. Based in the U.S., Mergent maintains a strong global presence, with offices in New York, Charlotte, San Diego, London, Tokyo, Kuching and Melbourne. Mergent, Inc. is a member of the London Stock Exchange plc group of companies. The Mergent business forms part of LSEG's Information Services Division, which includes FTSE Russell, a global leader in indexes.

Abbreviations

AFL-CIO – American Federation of Labor and Congress of Industrial Organizations
AMA – American Medical Association
AMEX – American Stock Exchange
ARM – adjustable-rate mortgage
ASP – application services provider
ATM – asynchronous transfer mode
ATM – automated teller machine
CAD/CAM – computer-aided design/computer-aided manufacturing
CD-ROM – compact disc – read-only memory
CD-R – CD-recordable
CEO – chief executive officer
CFO – chief financial officer
CMOS – complementary metal oxide silicon
COO – chief operating officer
DAT – digital audiotape
DOD – Department of Defense
DOE – Department of Energy
DOS – disk operating system
DOT – Department of Transportation
DRAM – dynamic random-access memory
DSL – digital subscriber line
DVD – digital versatile disc/digital video disc
DVD-R – DVD-recordable
EPA – Environmental Protection Agency
EPROM – erasable programmable read-only memory
EPS – earnings per share
ESOP – employee stock ownership plan
EU – European Union
EVP – executive vice president
FCC – Federal Communications Commission
FDA – Food and Drug Administration
FDIC – Federal Deposit Insurance Corporation
FTC – Federal Trade Commission
FTP – file transfer protocol
GATT – General Agreement on Tariffs and Trade
GDP – gross domestic product
HMO – health maintenance organization
HR – human resources
HTML – hypertext markup language
ICC – Interstate Commerce Commission
IPO – initial public offering
IRS – Internal Revenue Service
ISP – Internet service provider
kWh – kilowatt-hour
LAN – local-area network
LBO – leveraged buyout
LCD – liquid crystal display
LNG – liquefied natural gas
LP – limited partnership
Ltd. – limited
mips – millions of instructions per second
MW – megawatt
NAFTA – North American Free Trade Agreement
NASA – National Aeronautics and Space Administration
NASDAQ – National Association of Securities Dealers Automated Quotations
NATO – North Atlantic Treaty Organization
NYSE – New York Stock Exchange
OCR – optical character recognition
OECD – Organization for Economic Cooperation and Development
OEM – original equipment manufacturer
OPEC – Organization of Petroleum Exporting Countries
OS – operating system
OSHA – Occupational Safety and Health Administration
OTC – over-the-counter
PBX – private branch exchange
PCMCIA – Personal Computer Memory Card International Association
P/E – price to earnings ratio
RAID – redundant array of independent disks
RAM – random-access memory
R&D – research and development
RBOC – regional Bell operating company
RISC – reduced instruction set computer
REIT – real estate investment trust
ROA – return on assets
ROE – return on equity
ROI – return on investment
ROM – read-only memory
S&L – savings and loan
SCSI – Small Computer System Interface
SEC – Securities and Exchange Commission
SEVP – senior executive vice president
SIC – Standard Industrial Classification
SOC – system on a chip
SVP – senior vice president
USB – universal serial bus
VAR – value-added reseller
VAT – value-added tax
VC – venture capitalist
VP – vice president
VoIP – Voice over Internet Protocol
WAN – wide-area network
WWW – World Wide Web

CONTENTS

Volume 1

About Hoover's MasterList of
U.S. Companies 2020 vii

Company Lists 2a-16a
  Top 500 Companies By Sales 2a
  Top 500 Companies By Employer 7a
  Top 500 Companies by Net Profit 12a

Company Listings A – L 2

Volume 2

Company Listings M – Z 826

Indexes 1497
  By Company 1499
  By Headquarters Location 1537

Hoover's MasterList of U.S. Companies

Company Listings

M & F BANCORP INC   NBB: MFBP

2634 Durham Chapel Hill Blvd.
Durham, NC 27707
Phone: 919 687-7800
Fax: –
Web: www.mfbonline.com

CEO: James H Sills III
CFO: Randall C Hall
HR: –
FYE: December 31
Type: Public

M&F Bancorp strives to be the mother and father of lending in the Tar Heel State. It's the holding company for Mechanics and Farmers Bank (M&F Bank) which serves urban markets in central North Carolina from seven branch locations. Established in 1907 the bank provides standard products and services including savings and checking accounts IRAs and CDs. M&F Bank is a Community Development Financial Institution a US Treasury-designation for organizations that provide services to low-income communities. Its loan portfolio is dominated by real estate loans and mortgages largely written for faith-based and not-for-profit organizations. In 2016 the bank cut some 11% of its workforce to cut costs.

	Annual Growth	12/12	12/13	12/14	12/15	12/16
Assets ($ mil.)	(3.5%)	296.1	301.5	298.4	298.3	256.4
Net income ($ mil.)	–	0.3	0.4	1.0	0.3	(3.9)
Market value ($ mil.)	13.4%	5.2	6.6	9.6	6.5	8.6
Employees	(4.4%)	80	73	70	70	–

M & F WORLDWIDE CORP.   NYSE: MFW

35 E. 62nd St.
New York NY 10021
Phone: 212-572-8600
Fax: 214-981-0703
Web: www.energytransfer.com

CEO: Barry F Schwartz
CFO: –
HR: –
FYE: December 31
Type: Subsidiary

Check out M & F Worldwide. The holding company's Harland Clarke Corp. business manufactures checks and related products forms treasury supplies and delivery and fraud-prevention services. Its Harland Financial Solutions provides lending and mortgage applications risk management and business intelligence solutions and customer management software for commercial banks and credit unions. M & F's Scantron Corporation offers testing and assessment solutions to schools in North America while its Mafco Worldwide is one of the world's largest makers of licorice extract used primarily for flavoring tobacco and candy products. Diversified holding company MacAndrews & Forbes Holdings owns M & F.

M & H ENTERPRISES INC.

3030 S HIGHLAND DR
LAS VEGAS, NV 891091047
Phone: 702-385-5257
Fax: –
Web: www.martinharris.com

CEO: Frank E Martin
CFO: –
HR: –
FYE: December 31
Type: Private

What M & H Enterprises builds in Vegas stays in Vegas. Also known as Martin-Harris Construction the company provides design/build general construction and construction management services to commercial institutional and industrial projects throughout the Southwest. In addition to its home state Martin-Harris also provides general contracting services in New Mexico Texas Colorado and Utah. Martin-Harris has completed office retail hospitality entertainment high-rise condominium and public works projects for clients such as Neiman Marcus Embassy Suites and US Air Force. The company was founded in 1976 by president and CEO Frank Martin. It has offices in Las Vegas and Phoenix.

	Annual Growth	12/09	12/10*	11/11*	12/12	12/13
Sales ($ mil.)	4.3%	–	168.3	119.3	179.1	191.2
Net income ($ mil.)	6.0%	–	–	1.4	1.6	1.6
Market value ($ mil.)	–	–	–	–	–	–
Employees	–	–	–	–	–	140

*Fiscal year change

M & M MERCHANDISERS INC.

1923 BOMAR AVE
FORT WORTH, TX 761032102
Phone: 817-339-1400
Fax: –
Web: www.mmwholesale.com

CEO: Craig Harrison
CFO: Kirk Wensel
HR: Amy Odle
FYE: December 31
Type: Private

This M&M is sweet on pawn shops. M&M Merchandisers is a wholesale supplier of electronics musical instruments and accessories primarily to pawn shops in Texas and Georgia. It has expanded to serve several other industries including smaller music retailers and specializes in mobile audio video game accessories music surveillance tools and hardware sporting goods and jewelers supplies. The company distributes monthly newsletters and a semiannual catalog featuring its product offerings. M&M got its start in 1976 as a value added distributor with 150 SKUs; today it offers some 6000 SKUs. The business was founded by CEO Marty Stenzler and his father Mitch (hence the company name M&M).

	Annual Growth	12/04	12/05	12/06	12/07	12/08
Sales ($ mil.)	–	–	–	(49.0)	20.6	21.6
Net income ($ mil.)	612.2%	–	–	0.0	(0.2)	0.8
Market value ($ mil.)	–	–	–	–	–	–
Employees	–	–	–	–	–	78

M & T BANK CORP   NYS: MTB

One M & T Plaza
Buffalo, NY 14203
Phone: 716 635-4000
Fax: –
Web: www.mtb.com

CEO: René F. Jones
CFO: Darren J. King
HR: Janet M. Coletti
FYE: December 31
Type: Public

Bank holding company M&T Bank offers deposit loan trust investment brokerage mortgage and insurance services to individuals and small- and mid-sized businesses. With about $120 billion in total assets and $90 billion in deposits the bank operates some 750 branches and over 1800 ATMs in New York Pennsylvania other eastern states and Washington DC. Its lending is largely focused in those states but it originates its loans via offices in other states and Canada. The firm also manages a proprietary line of mutual funds through Wilmington Funds Management. M&T was founded in 1856 as Manufacturers and Traders Trust in Buffalo New York.

	Annual Growth	12/14	12/15	12/16	12/17	12/18
Assets ($ mil.)	5.6%	96,685.5	122,787.9	123,449.2	118,593.5	120,097.4
Net income ($ mil.)	15.8%	1,066.2	1,079.7	1,315.1	1,408.3	1,918.1
Market value ($ mil.)	3.3%	17,399.6	16,784.6	21,667.1	23,683.8	19,824.9
Employees	2.3%	15,782	17,476	16,973	16,794	17,267

M FINANCIAL HOLDINGS INCORPORATED

1125 NW Couch St. Ste. 900
Portland OR 97209
Phone: 503-232-6960
Fax: 503-238-1621
Web: www.mfin.com

CEO: –
CFO: –
HR: –
FYE: December 31
Type: Private

This company wants people who already have money to dial "M" for more. M Financial Holdings which does business as M Financial Group is an association of more than 125 financial services companies. Group members which are spread throughout the US offer a wide range of life insurance and other financial products and services geared toward ultra-wealthy individuals and leading business enterprises. M Financial Group provides product design marketing and securities-related services to its members which deal directly with customers. A subsidiary offers reinsurance (insurance for insurance products). M Financial Group is owned by its members.

M. B. KAHN CONSTRUCTION CO., INC.

101 FLINTLAKE RD
COLUMBIA, SC 292237851
Phone: 803-736-2950
Fax: –
Web: www.mbkahn.com

CEO: William H Neely
CFO: –
HR: –
FYE: December 31
Type: Private

One of the largest construction companies in the southeastern US M. B. Kahn Construction Co. works on commercial institutional and industrial projects including hospitals airports shopping centers and manufacturing plants. Additionally it is rated as one of the top builders in the nation's education market. The company provides general contracting and design/build delivery services as well as construction management and program management services. Russian immigrant Myron B. Kahn founded the company in 1927. It is now chaired by Alan Kahn his grandson. The group operates through divisions in South Carolina and Georgia.

	Annual Growth	12/11	12/12	12/13	12/14	12/15
Sales ($ mil.)	8.6%	–	251.6	225.9	225.9	322.7
Net income ($ mil.)	0.4%	–	7.0	5.8	5.8	7.1
Market value ($ mil.)	–	–	–	–	–	–
Employees	–	–	–	–	–	429

M. F. A. OIL COMPANY

1 RAY YOUNG DR
COLUMBIA, MO 652013506
Phone: 573-442-0171
Fax: –
Web: www.mfaoil.com

CEO: Jon Ihler
CFO: Robert Condron
HR: Beth Bartlett
FYE: August 31
Type: Private

Many farmers appreciate MFA Oil. The energy cooperative controlled by its 40000 farmer-members produces fuel and lubrication products and manages bulk petroleum and propane plants in the Central and Western US. Operating 140 propane plants the company sells more propane for farm use and home heating than any other company in Missouri. It also operates nearly 100 oil and lubricant bulk plants and serves customers in Arkansas Iowa Kansas and Oklahoma. Additionally the company operates 76 convenience stores under the Break Time brand (in Arkansas and Missouri) more than 160 Petro-Card 24 fueling locations and owns 10 Jiffy Lube and a dozen Big O Tire franchises.

	Annual Growth	08/14	08/15	08/16	08/17	08/18
Sales ($ mil.)	1.3%	–	1,045.1	800.3	900.0	1,086.7
Net income ($ mil.)	(24.7%)	–	48.1	24.7	8.3	20.5
Market value ($ mil.)	–	–	–	–	–	–
Employees	–	–	–	–	–	1,500

M.A. PATOUT & SON LIMITED, L.L.C.

3512 J PATOUT BURNS RD
JEANERETTE, LA 705447122
Phone: 337-276-4592
Fax: –
Web: www.mapatout.com

CEO: Craig Caillier
CFO: Randall K Romero
HR: –
FYE: July 31
Type: Private

For M. A. Patout & Son family tradition means processing sugarcane into raw sugar blackstrap molasses and cane syrup. Founded in 1825 the company is owned and operated by descendants of the founding Patout family. It operates the oldest working sugar mill in the US (the Enterprise Factory in Patoutville Louisiana) and is one of the oldest family-owned sugar businesses in the nation. The company also owns two additional factories in southern Louisiana (in the towns of Franklin and Raceland) through subsidiaries Sterling Sugars and Raceland Raw Sugars. The company owns 43000 acres of cane fields and its mills have the capacity to process approximately 4.6 million tons of cane per year.

	Annual Growth	07/04	07/05	07/15	07/16	07/18
Sales ($ mil.)	7.6%	–	117.5	–	288.8	306.0
Net income ($ mil.)	17.5%	–	3.4	–	11.6	27.6
Market value ($ mil.)	–	–	–	–	–	–
Employees	–	–	–	–	–	413

M.D.C. HOLDINGS, INC.   NYS: MDC

4350 South Monaco Street, Suite 500
Denver, CO 80237
Phone: 303 773-1100
Fax: –
Web: www.richmondamerican.com

CEO: Larry A. Mizel
CFO: Robert N Martin
HR: –
FYE: December 31
Type: Public

Operating through its Richmond American Homes subsidiary and several other units M.D.C. Holdings (MDC) is one of the largest homebuilders in Colorado and is active in about 10 other states in the western and eastern US. The homebuilder targets first-time and first-time move-up buyers with single-family detached homes that sell for an average price of around $480000. The company also constructs a limited number of luxury homes. Subsidiary HomeAmerican Mortgage provides loans to buyers of MDC's homes. MDC also has subsidiaries that offer home and title insurance.

	Annual Growth	12/15	12/16	12/17	12/18	12/19
Sales ($ mil.)	14.6%	1,909.0	2,326.8	2,577.6	3,065.2	3,293.3
Net income ($ mil.)	38.0%	65.8	103.2	141.8	210.8	238.3
Market value ($ mil.)	10.6%	1,597.5	1,605.7	1,994.9	1,759.0	2,387.9
Employees	7.8%	1,225	1,318	1,491	1,581	1,656

M/I HOMES INC   NYS: MHO

3 Easton Oval, Suite 500
Columbus, OH 43219
Phone: 614 418-8000
Fax: 614 418-8080
Web: www.mihomes.com

CEO: Robert H. Schottenstein
CFO: Phillip G. Creek
HR: Christy Morgan
FYE: December 31
Type: Public

M/I Homes sells single-family detached homes under the M/I Homes and Showcase Collection brands and to a lesser extent the Hans Hagen and Pinnacle Homes brands. It delivers more than 5800 homes a year to first-time move-up empty-nest and luxury buyers at prices ranging from about $180000 to $1.1 million (averaging $384000) and sizes ranging from 1400 to 5500 sq. ft. M/I Homes also builds attached townhomes in select markets. It caters to 16 markets throughout the Midwest Mid-Atlantic and South. Its M/I Financial mortgage banking subsidiary provides title and mortgage services.

	Annual Growth	12/14	12/15	12/16	12/17	12/18
Sales ($ mil.)	17.1%	1,215.2	1,418.4	1,691.3	1,962.0	2,286.3
Net income ($ mil.)	20.7%	50.8	51.8	56.6	72.1	107.7
Market value ($ mil.)	(2.2%)	631.8	603.2	692.9	946.6	578.4
Employees	10.7%	905	1,008	1,138	1,238	1,359

MABVAX THERAPEUTICS HOLDINGS INC   NAS: MBVX

11535 Sorrento Valley Road, Suite 400
San Diego, CA 92121
Phone: 858 259-9405
Fax: –
Web: www.mabvax.com

CEO: J David Hansen
CFO: Gregory P Hanson
HR: –
FYE: December 31
Type: Public

MabVax Therapeutics discovers new drugs focusing mainly on treatments for cancer. The clinical-stage biotech studies the body's immune response to repeated vaccinations. Its monoclonal antibody HuMab-5B1 has been studied in patients with pancreatic and similar cancers while its radioimmunotherapy product MVT-1075 is in early clinical study for the treatment of pancreatic colon and lung cancers. The company also has a diagnostic product ImmunoPET Imaging. MabVax partners with such organizations as Memorial Sloan Kettering Cancer Center and Rockefeller University.

	Annual Growth	12/12	12/13	12/14	12/15	12/16
Sales ($ mil.)	(31.4%)	–	–	0.3	1.3	0.1
Net income ($ mil.)	–	(8.0)	(5.2)	(7.9)	(18.1)	(17.7)
Market value ($ mil.)	–	–	–	–	–	7.1
Employees	9.6%	18	12	14	17	26

MAC BEATH HARDWOOD COMPANY

2150 OAKDALE AVE
SAN FRANCISCO, CA 941241516
Phone: 415-647-0782
Fax: –
Web: www.macbeath.com

CEO: George C Rothrock
CFO: Jonathan Macbeath
HR: –
FYE: July 31
Type: Private

This MacBeath doesn't want to get the spot out. MacBeath Hardwood Company specializes in spotted and striped specialty hardwoods from the US Mexico Panama India Brazil and several African nations. With wood from its 300000 board feet-capacity drying kiln the company makes furniture squares lumber veneer plywood maple countertops and specialty products like hand rails marine plywood and wood "blanks" to be used for baseball bats. MacBeath has five distribution centers in California Indiana and Utah; it also ships large loads worldwide. It also operates an online store. The company was founded in the early 1950s by K.E. MacBeath.

	Annual Growth	07/04	07/05	07/06	07/07	07/08
Sales ($ mil.)	(0.7%)	–	–	–	26.1	25.9
Net income ($ mil.)	(70.7%)	–	–	–	0.5	0.2
Market value ($ mil.)	–	–	–	–	–	–
Employees	–	–	–	–	–	90

MACALESTER COLLEGE

1600 GRAND AVE
SAINT PAUL, MN 551051899
Phone: 651-696-6000
Fax: –
Web: www.macalester.edu

CEO: –
CFO: David Wheaton
HR: –
FYE: May 31
Type: Private

Macalester College provides a private liberal arts education experience in St. Paul Minnesota. The four-year school serves about 2000 students. It offers more than 800 courses in 60 areas of study giving it about 40 major programs in fields including natural science social science fine arts and humanities. Macalester has a student-to-faculty ratio of 10:1 and a staff of about 170 full-time faculty members. It was founded in 1874 by the Rev. Edward Duffield as a Presbyterian-related but nonsectarian college and was named after Charles Macalester a prominent Philadelphia businessman and philanthropist.

	Annual Growth	05/14	05/15	05/16	05/17	05/18
Sales ($ mil.)	2.9%	–	106.8	111.0	117.4	116.3
Net income ($ mil.)	230.2%	–	0.9	(74.7)	53.9	31.3
Market value ($ mil.)	–	–	–	–	–	–
Employees	–	–	–	–	–	750

MACATAWA BANK CORP.

NMS: MCBC

10753 Macatawa Drive
Holland, MI 49424
Phone: 616 820-1444
Fax: –
Web: www.macatawabank.com

CEO: Ronald L Haan
CFO: Jon W Swets
HR: –
FYE: December 31
Type: Public

Macatawa Bank Corporation is the holding company for Macatawa Bank. Since its 1997 founding the company has grown into a network of more than 25 branches serving western Michigan's Allegan Kent and Ottawa counties. The bank provides standard services including checking and savings accounts CDs safe deposit boxes and ATM cards. It also offers investment services and products through an agreement with a third-party provider. With deposit funds the bank primarily originates commercial and industrial loans and mortgages which account for nearly 75% of its loan book. Macatawa Bank also originates residential mortgages and consumer loans.

	Annual Growth	12/14	12/15	12/16	12/17	12/18
Assets ($ mil.)	5.7%	1,583.8	1,729.6	1,741.0	1,890.2	1,975.1
Net income ($ mil.)	26.0%	10.5	12.8	16.0	16.3	26.4
Market value ($ mil.)	15.3%	185.2	206.0	354.4	340.5	327.5
Employees	(1.2%)	389	385	374	368	371

MACDONALD MOTT GROUP INC

111 WOOD AVE S STE 5
ISELIN, NJ 088302700
Phone: 973-379-3400
Fax: –
Web: www.mottmac.com

CEO: Nicholas DeNichilo
CFO: –
HR: –
FYE: December 31
Type: Private

Hatch Mott MacDonald (HMM) is the consulting engineering subsidiary of Mott MacDonald and offers planning project development analysis design construction management facility maintenance and facility management for all types of infrastructure projects to public and private clients across North America. It specializes in tunnels wastewater systems pipelines rail and transit systems buildings and utilities. Customers are both private companies and municipalities. HMM strategically acquires specialized engineering firms in new regions to expand its service offerings and geographic market reach. Formed in 1996 HHM now boasts a staff of 25000 and has more than 75 offices in the US and Canada.

	Annual Growth	12/08	12/09	12/10	12/11	12/12
Sales ($ mil.)	13.0%	–	–	374.2	440.6	478.0
Net income ($ mil.)	14.8%	–	–	20.7	25.4	27.2
Market value ($ mil.)	–	–	–	–	–	–
Employees	–	–	–	–	–	2,500

MACE SECURITY INTERNATIONAL, INC.

NBB: MACE

4400 Carnegie Avenue
Cleveland, OH 44103
Phone: 440 424-5321
Fax: 216 361-9555
Web: www.mace.com

CEO: Gary Medved
CFO: Mark Barrus
HR: –
FYE: December 31
Type: Public

Mace Security International (MSI) aims to secure your person and your property. The firm makes a variety of security products including electronic surveillance and access control products cameras monitors alarms and Kindergard brand childproof locks. It also sells Mace brand defense sprays for consumers and law enforcement officers as well as tear gas and animal repellents. While security products account for two-thirds of sales MSI also operates an e-commerce division that sells its own products and those of third parties. MSI is exiting the car wash business which at its peak operated some 60 car and truck washes to focus on its security and e-commerce activities. MSI was founded in 1993.

	Annual Growth	12/14	12/15	12/16	12/17	12/18
Sales ($ mil.)	10.2%	7.8	7.1	9.1	10.0	11.5
Net income ($ mil.)	–	(1.7)	(1.0)	0.3	(0.1)	(1.9)
Market value ($ mil.)	(7.3%)	24.0	24.6	25.9	24.1	17.7
Employees	–	–	–	34	–	–

MACERICH CO (THE)

NYS: MAC

401 Wilshire Boulevard, Suite 700
Santa Monica, CA 90401
Phone: 310 394-6000
Fax: –
Web: www.macerich.com

CEO: Arthur M. (Art) Coppola
CFO: Thomas E. (Tom) O'Hern
HR: –
FYE: December 31
Type: Public

Macerich provides the infrastructure that houses top retail shops throughout the US. The self-administered real estate investment trust (REIT) acquires develops leases and manages shopping and strip malls. Its portfolio consists of about 50 regional shopping centers and seven community shopping centers totaling more than 55 million sq. ft. of leasable space. The properties are located more than 25 states with top markets in Arizona California and the New York metropolitan area. Macerich's tenants include some of the country's leading retailersincluding L Brands Forever 21 The Gap Dick's Sporting Goods Sears and Best Buy to name a few.

	Annual Growth	12/14	12/15	12/16	12/17	12/18
Sales ($ mil.)	(3.5%)	1,105.2	1,288.1	1,041.3	993.7	960.4
Net income ($ mil.)	(55.3%)	1,499.0	487.6	517.0	146.1	60.0
Market value ($ mil.)	(15.1%)	11,779.3	11,395.2	10,004.1	9,275.4	6,112.1
Employees	(10.5%)	1,117	997	851	855	718

MACH 1 GLOBAL SERVICES, INC.

1530 W BROADWAY RD
TEMPE, AZ 852821131
Phone: 480-921-3900
Fax: –
Web: www.mach1global.com

CEO: –
CFO: –
HR: Jennifer Fischer
FYE: December 31
Type: Private

It doesn't ship goods at the speed of sound but Mach1 Global Services does like to think fast. The freight forwarder provides domestic and international air ground ocean and rail shipping services by buying transportation capacity from carriers and reselling it to customers. It also offers a variety of logistics services including project management and supply chain management. Most of Mach1's customers come from the retail automotive high-tech entertainment health care and manufacturing industries. The company has offices in the US Mexico and Asia (mostly China); it operates in other regions via network partners. CEO Michael Entzminger formed Mach1 in 1988.

	Annual Growth	12/03	12/04	12/05	12/06	12/08
Sales ($ mil.)	14.4%	–	57.1	69.7	86.1	97.8
Net income ($ mil.)	(29.6%)	–	1.2	3.1	1.8	0.3
Market value ($ mil.)	–	–	–	–	–	–
Employees	–	–	–	–	–	210

MACHADO/GARCIA-SERRA PUBLICIDAD INC.

1790 CORAL WAY FL 3
CORAL GABLES, FL 331452785
Phone: 305-444-4647
Fax: –
Web: www.mgscomm.com

CEO: –
CFO: –
HR: –
FYE: December 31
Type: Private

Machado|Garcia-Serra Publicidad provides integrated communications specializing in bridging the cultural gap between US consumer product manufacturers and the Hispanic market. The agency — which does business as Machado Garcia-Serra Communications or MGSCOMM — offers expertise in advertising public relations promotion and event marketing serving clients in the automotive health care and retail industries. The agency maintains three offices in Florida New York and Mexico. It was established in 2003 by public relations and advertising veterans Manual Machado and Al Garcia-Serra.

	Annual Growth	12/03	12/04	12/05	12/06	12/07
Sales ($ mil.)	82.3%	–	–	–	32.2	58.8
Net income ($ mil.)	(20.2%)	–	–	–	0.7	0.6
Market value ($ mil.)	–	–	–	–	–	–
Employees	–	–	–	–	–	22

MACK CALI REALTY CORP

Harborside 3, 210 Hudson St., Ste. 400
Jersey City, NJ 07311
Phone: 732 590-1010
Fax: –
Web: www.mack-cali.com

NYS: CLI
CEO: Michael J. DeMarco
CFO: Anthony Krug
HR: –
FYE: December 31
Type: Public

Mack-Cali Realty is a self-administered real estate investment trust (REIT) that owns develops leases and manages office and industrial buildings primarily in the Northeast. The REIT's portfolio consists primarily of Class A office and office/flex buildings but also includes industrial facilities warehouses stand-alone retail properties and land for development. Its holdings comprise some 280 properties totaling more than 31.5 million sq. ft. concentrated in suburban markets in New Jersey southern New York and eastern Pennsylvania. Recently Mack-Cali has been selling non-core office assets to fund its diversification into residential property.

	Annual Growth	12/14	12/15	12/16	12/17	12/18
Sales ($ mil.)	(4.5%)	636.8	594.9	613.4	616.2	530.6
Net income ($ mil.)	31.0%	28.6	(125.8)	117.2	23.2	84.1
Market value ($ mil.)	0.7%	1,721.5	2,109.0	2,621.1	1,947.3	1,769.4
Employees	(12.5%)	600	530	540	439	352

MACKINAC FINANCIAL CORP

130 South Cedar Street
Manistique, MI 49854
Phone: 888 343-8147
Fax: –

NAS: MFNC
CEO: Paul D Tobias
CFO: Jesse A Deering
HR: –
FYE: December 31
Type: Public

Mackinac Financial Corporation is the holding company for mBank which operates about a dozen branches in Michigan's Upper Peninsula and the northern part of the Lower Peninsula as well as suburban Detroit. Serving local consumers and business clients the bank provides traditional deposit products such as checking and savings accounts and CDs. Commercial real estate loans account for about three-quarters of the company's loan portfolio which also consists of agricultural business construction residential and consumer loans. mBank offers treasury management products and services to small and midsized businesses as well. Institutional investors own approximately half of Mackinac Financial's stock.

	Annual Growth	12/14	12/15	12/16	12/17	12/18
Assets ($ mil.)	15.4%	743.8	739.3	983.5	985.4	1,318.0
Net income ($ mil.)	48.9%	1.7	5.6	4.5	5.5	8.4
Market value ($ mil.)	3.6%	126.9	123.1	144.3	170.3	146.2
Employees	14.5%	171	173	222	221	294

MACOM TECHNOLOGY SOLUTIONS HOLDINGS INC

100 Chelmsford Street
Lowell, MA 01851
Phone: 978 656-2500
Fax: –
Web: www.macom.com

NMS: MTSI
CEO: John R. Croteau
CFO: Conrad Gagnon
HR: –
FYE: September 27
Type: Public

M/A-COM Technology Solutions (aka MACOM) has many components for all your semiconductor needs. The holding company makes analog semiconductors used in wireless and wireline applications across the radio-frequency (RF) microwave and millimeter wave spectrum. Its portfolio encompasses some 3500 standard and custom integrated circuits modules and subsystems across 40 product lines. MACOM's chips are used in such products as automotive navigation systems point-to-point radios radars CATV set-top boxes MRI systems and unmanned aerial vehicles. Cisco Motorola Solutions Ford Motor Nokia and Samsung are among its top customers. More than a third of sales come from customers in the US.

	Annual Growth	10/15*	09/16	09/17	09/18	09/19
Sales ($ mil.)	4.4%	420.6	544.3	698.8	570.4	499.7
Net income ($ mil.)	–	48.6	1.4	(169.5)	(140.0)	(383.8)
Market value ($ mil.)	(6.8%)	1,903.3	2,801.0	2,951.1	1,362.8	1,434.2
Employees	0.0%	1,100	1,400	1,800	1,400	1,100

*Fiscal year change

MACOMB OAKLAND REGIONAL CENTER INC

16200 19 MILE RD
CLINTON TOWNSHIP, MI 480381103
Phone: 586-263-8700
Fax: –
Web: www.morcinc.org

CEO: Gerald Provencal
CFO: Richard Stone
HR: –
FYE: September 30
Type: Private

Michigan's disabled citizens have more than a friend in MORC. The Macomb-Oakland Regional Center (MORC) advocates for adults and children with developmental physical or psychiatric disabilities hoping to improve the lives of its clients. In addition to finding homes and jobs and coordinating recreational activities for the disabled the not-for-profit organization helps connect customers with support services including psychology nursing and medical care. It also holds community education seminars and it provides home health visitation and rehabilitation therapy services through its MORC Home Care and MORC Rehab divisions. Founded in 1972 MORC serves over 4000 clients in the state.

	Annual Growth	09/11	09/12	09/13	09/14	09/17
Sales ($ mil.)	(2.3%)	–	193.9	198.3	198.3	172.6
Net income ($ mil.)	–	–	0.1	(0.2)	0.3	(0.0)
Market value ($ mil.)	–	–	–	–	–	–
Employees	–	–	–	–	–	300

MACQUARIE INFRASTRUCTURE CORP   NYS: MIC

125 West 55th Street
New York, NY 10019
Phone: 212 231-1000
Fax: –
Web: www.macquarie.com/mic

CEO: Christopher Frost
CFO: Liam Stewart
HR: –
FYE: December 31
Type: Public

If you've flown in a small plane or had a cold drink of water in a building in Chicago you may have done business with Macquarie Infrastructure Company. Its Atlantic Aviation Services unit provides fixed-base operations (FBO) including fueling and aircraft storage services at about 60 US airports. Another unit Hawaii Gas is Hawaii's only government franchised gas company. It also has a stake in District Energy a firm that provides chilled water in Chicago and heating and cooling to a casino complex in Las Vegas. The company holds a 50% stake in International-Matex Tank Terminals. Australia-based Macquarie Bank's Macquarie Infrastructure Management (USA) manages Macquarie Infrastructure Company.

	Annual Growth	12/14	12/15	12/16	12/17	12/18
Sales ($ mil.)	6.9%	1,350.9	1,639.3	1,651.7	1,814.7	1,761.5
Net income ($ mil.)	(39.8%)	1,042.0	(108.5)	156.4	451.2	136.5
Market value ($ mil.)	(15.3%)	6,099.5	6,229.1	7,009.9	5,508.4	3,136.9
Employees	(26.9%)	3,218	1,097	1,052	1,100	917

MACROGENICS, INC   NMS: MGNX

9704 Medical Center Drive
Rockville, MD 20850
Phone: 301 251-5172
Fax: –
Web: www.macrogenics.com

CEO: Scott Koenig
CFO: James (Jim) Karrels
HR: –
FYE: December 31
Type: Public

MacroGenics aims its enhanced antibodies at annihilating diseased cells. The clinical-stage biopharmaceutical company is focused on developing monoclonal antibody-based therapeutic treatments for cancer as well as autoimmune disorders and infectious diseases. MacroGenics has a handful of drug candidates in its pipeline and several others in pre-clinical development. Lead candidate margetuximab is being developed as an intravenous drug that would kill tumor cells in breast gastroesophageal and bladder cancer patients. Meanwhile antibody MGA271 is being tested for treating a variety of tumor types.

	Annual Growth	12/14	12/15	12/16	12/17	12/18
Sales ($ mil.)	5.9%	47.8	100.9	91.9	157.7	60.1
Net income ($ mil.)	–	(38.3)	(20.1)	(58.5)	(19.6)	(171.5)
Market value ($ mil.)	(22.4%)	1,485.3	1,311.7	865.7	804.7	537.9
Employees	14.6%	211	269	318	330	364

MADDEN (STEVEN) LTD.   NMS: SHOO

52-16 Barnett Avenue
Long Island City, NY 11104
Phone: 718 446-1800
Fax: –
Web: www.stevemadden.com

CEO: Edward R. (Ed) Rosenfeld
CFO: Arvind Dharia
HR: –
FYE: December 31
Type: Public

Steven Madden elevates chunky heels to new heights. It operates through five business segments: wholesale footwear wholesale accessories retail first cost and licensing. Its wholesale business boasts some 20-or-so brands such as Madden Girl Steven Steve Madden Men's Betsey Johnson and Stevies as well as Superga Kate Spade and Anne Klein under license. Its retail operation mainly consists of about 220 Steve Madden stores as well as two Steven and one Superga store along with several websites. Department stores such as Nordstrom and Dillard's also stock its shoes. Its First Cost segment designs and sources private-label footwear such as Candie's for mass merchants. Steven Madden shoes are sold in the US Canada and certain countries in Europe.

	Annual Growth	12/14	12/15	12/16	12/17	12/18
Sales ($ mil.)	5.5%	1,335.0	1,405.2	1,399.6	1,546.1	1,653.6
Net income ($ mil.)	3.7%	111.9	112.9	120.9	117.9	129.1
Market value ($ mil.)	(1.3%)	2,728.3	2,590.3	3,064.3	4,002.9	2,593.7
Employees	4.6%	3,256	3,578	3,925	3,884	3,900

MADISON AREA TECHNICAL COLLEGE DISTRICT

1701 WRIGHT ST
MADISON, WI 537042599
Phone: 608-246-6100
Fax: –
Web: www.madisoncollege.edu

CEO: –
CFO: –
HR: –
FYE: June 30
Type: Private

Madison Area Technical College (MATC) is a technical and community college that offers courses in liberal arts and sciences adult basic education and technical training. Students often enter careers in biotechnology broadcast captioning internet development mechanics or law enforcement. The college which is the largest member of the Wisconsin Technical College System provides education to more than 40000 students each year. Many students go on to transfer to the University of Wisconsin or other UW system schools. MATC has 10 college facilities spread among five campuses in south central Wisconsin.

	Annual Growth	06/09	06/10	06/11	06/16	06/17
Sales ($ mil.)	(5.8%)	–	108.2	115.3	77.4	71.4
Net income ($ mil.)	–	–	(0.8)	(0.4)	(2.9)	11.6
Market value ($ mil.)	–	–	–	–	–	–
Employees	–	–	–	–	–	3,500

MADISON ELECTRIC COMPANY

31855 VAN DYKE AVE
WARREN, MI 480931047
Phone: 586-825-0200
Fax: –
Web: www.madisonelectric.com

CEO: –
CFO: Benjamin Rosenthal
HR: –
FYE: January 31
Type: Private

Founded by Morris and Max Blumberg Madison Electric broke ground in a rented room in Detroit in 1914. The company has grown from pushing light bulbs fuses wire and conduit to rival the top 200 electrical and electronics distributors in the US. Joined by affiliate Standard Electric Co. Madison Electric distributes electrical supplies industrial automation commercial lighting and network communication components. Branches dotting Michigan cater to a swath of commercial industrial utility and defense activities. Supply options tout brands by 3M Brady Federal Signal Leviton Panduit Square D/ Schneider Electric and Thomas & Betts. The family-owned company is led by the Blumberg's fourth generation.

	Annual Growth	01/08	01/09	01/10	01/11	01/12
Sales ($ mil.)	692.8%	–	–	(920.5)	66.1	77.2
Net income ($ mil.)	–	–	–	0.0	(0.4)	1.0
Market value ($ mil.)	–	–	–	–	–	–
Employees	–	–	–	–	–	200

MADONNA REHABILITATION HOSPITAL

5401 SOUTH ST
LINCOLN, NE 685062150
Phone: 402-413-3000
Fax: –
Web: www.madonna.org

CEO: Paul Dongilli Jr
CFO: –
HR: –
FYE: June 30
Type: Private

Madonna Rehabilitation Hospital finds a rapt audience in recovering patients living in and around Lincoln Nebraska. The hospital has more than 250 beds and provides acute and long-term rehabilitation as well as subacute care. The hospital treats patients with a variety of orthopedic musculoskeletal and neurological conditions such as brain and spinal cord injury stroke cancer cerebral palsy arthritis and multiple sclerosis. Patients have access to a full team of physicians to help integrate and treat all symptoms. Madonna Rehabilitation Hospital was founded as a geriatric hospital by the Benedictine Sisters of Yankton South Dakota in 1958.

	Annual Growth	06/09	06/10	06/11	06/12	06/13
Sales ($ mil.)	3.8%	–	92.1	93.2	96.2	103.2
Net income ($ mil.)	14.7%	–	–	9.1	5.9	12.0
Market value ($ mil.)	–	–	–	–	–	–
Employees	–	–	–	–	–	1,400

MAGEE REHABILITATION HOSPITAL FOUNDATION

1513 RACE ST
PHILADELPHIA, PA 191021125
Phone: 215-587-3000
Fax: -
Web: www.mageerehab.org

CEO: Jack Carroll
CFO: Patricia Underwood
HR: -
FYE: June 30
Type: Private

Part of Pennsylvania's Jefferson Health System The Magee Memorial Hospital for Convalescents (operating as Magee Rehabilitation) is a not-for-profit health organization that provides inpatient and outpatient rehabilitative care to patients disabled by stroke arthritis spinal cord and brain injuries or other conditions. With 96 beds it also offers rehabilitation for patients recovering from amputation orthopedic surgery and joint replacements. In addition it provides wellness programs for muscular neurological and neurodegenerative disorders. Outpatient services include physical therapy speech therapy and emotional support.

	Annual Growth	06/08	06/09	06/14	06/15	06/16
Sales ($ mil.)	1.4%	-	54.7	64.7	59.3	60.2
Net income ($ mil.)	-	-	(7.0)	5.0	6.0	1.0
Market value ($ mil.)	-	-	-	-	-	-
Employees	-	-	-	-	-	600

MAGELLAN HEALTH INC.   NMS: MGLN

4800 N. Scottsdale Rd., Suite 4400
Scottsdale, AZ 85251
Phone: 602 572-6050
Fax: -
Web: www.magellanhealth.com

CEO: Barry M. Smith
CFO: Jonathan N. (Jon) Rubin
HR: Erin Kirchhardt
FYE: December 31
Type: Public

Magellan Health is one of the largest managed behavioral health care companies in the US. The company manages mental health plan employee assistance and work/life programs through its nationwide third-party provider network. Magellan also provides radiology benefits management specialty pharmaceutical management and Medicaid management. Overall it serves about 55 million members through contracts with federal and local government agencies insurance companies and employers. Magellan's Pharmacy Management segment's services include benefit management dispensing administration clinical programs medical pharmacy management and care coordination.

	Annual Growth	12/14	12/15	12/16	12/17	12/18
Sales ($ mil.)	18.1%	3,760.1	4,597.4	4,836.9	5,838.6	7,314.2
Net income ($ mil.)	(25.7%)	79.4	31.4	77.9	110.2	24.2
Market value ($ mil.)	(1.3%)	1,436.8	1,475.8	1,801.1	2,310.9	1,361.7
Employees	12.3%	6,600	6,900	9,700	10,700	10,500

MAGELLAN MIDSTREAM PARTNERS LP   NYS: MMP

One Williams Center, P.O.Box 22186
Tulsa, OK 74121-2186
Phone: 918 574-7000
Fax: -
Web: www.magellanlp.com

CEO: Michael N. (Mike) Mears
CFO: Aaron L. Milford
HR: Lisa J. Korner
FYE: December 31
Type: Public

Magellan Midstream Partners is discovering new opportunities in the world of midstream energy operations. The energy infrastructure company owns and operates assets to store transport and distribute refined products crude oil and marine fuels. Magellan Midstream Partners' portfolio includes nearly 12000 miles of pipeline more than 50 terminals and almost 85 million barrels of aggregate storage located mainly in the eastern half of the US. Magellan's upstream and downstream customers include Valero Marathon CVR Energy Kinder Morgan Phillips 66 and Shell.

	Annual Growth	12/14	12/15	12/16	12/17	12/18
Sales ($ mil.)	5.2%	2,303.7	2,188.5	2,205.4	2,507.7	2,826.6
Net income ($ mil.)	12.3%	839.5	819.1	802.8	869.5	1,333.9
Market value ($ mil.)	(8.8%)	18,862.6	15,499.0	17,258.4	16,188.2	13,020.8
Employees	4.5%	1,565	1,640	1,747	1,802	1,868

MAGMA DESIGN AUTOMATION INC.   NASDAQ: LAVA

1650 Technology Dr.
San Jose CA 95110
Phone: 408-565-7500
Fax: 408-565-7501
Web: www.magma-da.com

CEO: Rajeev Madhavan
CFO: Peter S Teshima
HR: -
FYE: April 30
Type: Public

Magma Design Automation has some hot design tips for chip engineers. The company provides electronic design automation (EDA) software used by engineers designing integrated circuits for electronic products such as cell phones Wi-Fi digital video and networking. Its Talus software products combine front- and back-end design processes into a single integrated workflow while its Quartz applications tackle sign-off and verification tasks. Customers have included Texas Instruments NEC Qualcomm and Samsung. The company also offers related services such as consulting training and maintenance. It gets about 60% of sales from North America. In 2012 Magma was acquired by key competitor Synopsys.

MAGNECO/METREL INC.

223 W INTERSTATE RD
ADDISON, IL 601014513
Phone: 630-543-6660
Fax: -
Web: www.magneco-metrel.com

CEO: -
CFO: Susan C Malloy
HR: -
FYE: December 31
Type: Private

Magneco/Metrel makes ceramics but you won't find any artistic pieces at this company's plant! Magneco/Metrel uses the world's largest blast furnace to produce high-temperature refractory ceramics. The lineup serves as a lining in pipes and molds carrying molten iron and steel. The heat of molten steel would erode the pipes and molds without the ceramic barrier. Magneco/Metrel also makes a spray-on nano-particulate refractory line that can be used to create a liner for constructing or repairing steel-making molds and pipe. Its ceramics line is sold largely to steel foundries; other applications include ironmaking glass and copper. Magneco/Metrel was established in 1979 and is owned by CEO Charles Connors.

	Annual Growth	12/07	12/08	12/10	12/11	12/12
Sales ($ mil.)	1.0%	-	63.4	62.0	66.4	65.9
Net income ($ mil.)	10.8%	-	-	2.3	3.4	2.8
Market value ($ mil.)	-	-	-	-	-	-
Employees	-	-	-	-	-	145

MAGNETEK, INC.   NMS: MAG

N49 W13650 Campbell Drive
Menomonee Falls, WI 53051
Phone: 262 783-3500
Fax: -
Web: www.magnetek.com

CEO: Peter M McCormick
CFO: Marty J Schwenner
HR: -
FYE: December 29
Type: Public

In the world of electrical equipment Magnetek is a power player. Among the largest the company makes digital power and motion-control systems. The systems comprise radio remote controls programmable drives and collision-avoidance devices used in overhead cranes and hoists. Its DC drives and integrated subsystems are used to control high rise high speed elevators. Magnetek also offers power inverters which direct AC power from generator to utility grid for wind turbines and other renewable energy projects. The company sells largely to North American OEMs of industrial cranes and hoists mining equipment and elevators as well as building and renewable energy contractors and systems integrators.

	Annual Growth	06/10*	07/11*	01/12*	12/12	12/13
Sales ($ mil.)	8.6%	80.6	109.8	58.7	114.3	103.3
Net income ($ mil.)	-	(5.1)	3.7	4.3	12.6	3.1
Market value ($ mil.)	175.4%	3.6	5.9	28.1	33.9	75.2
Employees	3.0%	300	311	330	350	328

*Fiscal year change

MAGNUM CONSTRUCTION MANAGEMENT, LLC

6201 SW 70TH ST FL 2
SOUTH MIAMI, FL 331434718
Phone: 305-541-0000
Fax: –
Web: www.mcm-us.com

CEO: –
CFO: Gil Ruizcalderon
HR: –
FYE: December 31
Type: Private

Munilla Construction Management (formerly Magnum Construction Management) was founded in 1983 and is owned by the Munilla family whose background in construction dates back more than five decades. MCM provides a range of design-build and construction management services to public- and private-sector clients in South Florida. The company contracts for a variety of construction projects including commercial institutional educational residential and health care facilities; airports; and such civil construction projects as roads and railway stations.

	Annual Growth	12/06	12/07	12/08	12/13	12/15
Sales ($ mil.)	–	–	–	0.0	0.0	251.0
Net income ($ mil.)	–	–	–	0.0	(0.2)	2.2
Market value ($ mil.)	–	–	–	–	–	–
Employees	–	–	–	–	–	500

MAGNUM HUNTER RESOURCES CORP (DE)   NBB: MAGH

909 Lake Carolyn Parkway, Suite 600
Irving, TX 75039
Phone: 832 369-6986
Fax: 832 369-6992
Web: www.magnumhunterresources.com

CEO: John K Reinhart
CFO: Joseph C Daches
HR: –
FYE: December 31
Type: Public

The treasure this hunter seeks is gold black gold. Magnum Hunter Resources acquires producing oil and natural gas leases conducts exploratory drilling and produces crude oil and natural gas liquids. It has proved reserves of about 75.9 million barrels of oil equivalent about half oil on properties located primarily in Texas Louisiana West Virginia and North Dakota. Most of the company's output comes from West Virginia where it also owns a 182-mile natural gas pipeline through its Triad Hunter subsidiary. Other subsidiaries include an oilfield drilling business and a natural gas wastewater disposal facility. The company filed for Chapter 11 bankruptcy protection in late 2015. It emerged in May 2016.

	Annual Growth	12/11	12/12	12/13	12/14	12/15
Sales ($ mil.)	4.5%	129.2	271.0	280.4	391.5	154.1
Net income ($ mil.)	–	(76.7)	(132.7)	(222.2)	(143.5)	(783.9)
Market value ($ mil.)	(76.6%)	1,404.0	1,039.3	1,904.1	817.9	4.2
Employees	3.4%	305	420	445	440	348

MAGYAR BANCORP INC   NMS: MGYR

400 Somerset Street
New Brunswick, NJ 08901
Phone: 732 342-7600
Fax: –
Web: www.magbank.com

CEO: John S Fitzgerald
CFO: Jon R Ansari
HR: –
FYE: September 30
Type: Public

Magyar doesn't mean "bank" in Hungarian it means "Hungarian" in Hungarian. Magyar Bancorp is the holding company for Magyar Bank which serves central New Jersey individuals and businesses through about a half-dozen offices. The bank offers standard deposit products including checking and savings accounts NOW accounts and CDs. It uses these funds to originate loans and invest in securities. Magyar Bank focuses on real estate lending including construction loans residential and commercial mortgages and home equity loans which altogether account for about 90% of its loan portfolio. Mutual holding company Magyar Bancorp MHC owns 56% of Magyar Bancorp.

	Annual Growth	09/15	09/16	09/17	09/18	09/19
Assets ($ mil.)	3.4%	550.6	584.4	603.0	624.0	630.3
Net income ($ mil.)	35.2%	0.9	1.1	1.4	2.0	3.0
Market value ($ mil.)	4.6%	57.0	58.7	71.3	70.8	68.3
Employees	2.9%	98	103	105	107	110

MAIMONIDES MEDICAL CENTER

4802 10TH AVE
BROOKLYN, NY 112192916
Phone: 718-581-0598
Fax: –
Web: www.maimonidesmed.org

CEO: Kenneth Gibbs
CFO: Robert Naldi
HR: Paul Stuart
FYE: December 31
Type: Private

Maimonides Medical Center a not-for-profit hospital offers emergency medicine surgical procedures psychiatric treatment and other traditional hospital services to patients in Brooklyn New York. It has more than 710 beds and more than 70 subspecialty treatment programs for a range of conditions including cancer cardiac stroke neurological pediatric and women's health ailments. It also operates outpatient family health and specialty clinics. Maimonides Medical Center is an independent teaching hospital that serves as a training facility for SUNY-Brooklyn St. George's University and other schools.

	Annual Growth	12/13	12/14	12/15	12/16	12/17
Sales ($ mil.)	2.7%	–	884.7	890.0	940.9	958.4
Net income ($ mil.)	23.2%	–	10.4	(2.0)	20.5	19.6
Market value ($ mil.)	–	–	–	–	–	–
Employees	–	–	–	–	–	6,382

MAIN LINE HEALTH INC.

130 S BRYN MAWR AVE
BRYN MAWR, PA 19010-3121
Phone: 484-337-3000
Fax: –
Web: www.mainlinehealth.org

CEO: –
CFO: –
HR: –
FYE: June 30
Type: Private

Part of the Jefferson Health System Main Line Health serves constituents in the Philadelphia area. The health system consists of four acute-care facilities (Bryn Mawr Hospital Lankenau Medical Center Paoli Hospital and Riddle Hospital) with a total of more than 1100 beds. It also operates physician practices a research institute a 150-bed rehabilitation hospital (Bryn Mawr Rehab Hospital) an addiction recovery facility (Mirmont Treatment Center) and various other facilities. Main Line Health provides home health care services and care for the elderly through senior programs. It operates several ambulatory-care centers and provides occupational health as well.

	Annual Growth	06/07	06/08	06/10	06/11	06/12
Sales ($ mil.)	4.8%	–	1,224.6	1,361.3	1,405.2	1,475.3
Net income ($ mil.)	13.1%	–	118.1	111.4	112.6	193.6
Market value ($ mil.)	–	–	–	–	–	–
Employees	–	–	–	–	–	5,840

MAIN LINE HEALTH SYSTEM

240 N RADNOR CHESTER RD
RADNOR, PA 190875170
Phone: 610-225-6200
Fax: –

CEO: Jack Lynch
CFO: –
HR: –
FYE: June 30
Type: Private

Main Line Health is a not-for-profit network that includes four acute care hospitals a drug and alcohol recovery treatment center home care outpatient centers a physician network and a biomedical research organization all serving the greater Philadelphia area. Its hospitals — Lankenau Medical Center Bryn Mawr Hospital Paoli Hospital and Riddle Hospital — are accredited as primary stroke care centers comprehensive breast centers and chest pain centers. Other specialties include diabetes and endocrinology orthopedics and cardiovascular care. Bryn Mawr Hospital offers residency programs in family practice radiology and surgical podiatry. Main Line Health was founded in 1985.

	Annual Growth	06/14	06/15	06/16	06/17	06/18
Sales ($ mil.)	3.2%	–	1,586.3	1,660.4	1,695.8	1,742.0
Net income ($ mil.)	30.2%	–	121.3	(130.8)	51.6	267.6
Market value ($ mil.)	–	–	–	–	–	–
Employees	–	–	–	–	–	17,485

MAIN LINE HOSPITALS, INC.

130 S BRYN MAWR AVE
BRYN MAWR, PA 190103121
Phone: 610-526-3000
Fax: –
Web: www.brynmawrurology.com

CEO: Leland I White
CFO: Michael J Buongiorno
HR: –
FYE: June 30
Type: Private

Bryn Mawr Hospital a member of the Main Line not-for-profit health network is an acute care facility providing a variety of inpatient and outpatient services in the western suburbs of Philadelphia. With some 320 beds Bryn Mawr Hospital is recognized nationally for its orthopedic program. Founded in 1893 by Dr. George Gerhard the teaching hospital also provides cancer cardiac surgical pediatric reproductive health diagnostic imaging psychiatric bariatric and wound care services. The hospital also operates the Main Line Health Center outpatient facility (which includes a comprehensive breast center) in Newtown Square.

	Annual Growth	06/13	06/14	06/15	06/16	06/18
Sales ($ mil.)	90.9%	–	–	–	327.6	1,193.6
Net income ($ mil.)	67.0%	–	–	–	36.1	100.8
Market value ($ mil.)	–	–	–	–	–	–
Employees	–	–	–	–	–	5,840

MAIN STREET AMERICA GROUP INC.

4601 Touchton Rd. E. Ste. 3400
Jacksonville FL 32246
Phone: 904-380-7281
Fax: 904-380-7244
Web: www.msagroup.com

CEO: –
CFO: –
HR: –
FYE: December 31
Type: Private - Mutual Com

Evoking tree- and shop-lined boulevards The Main Street America Group provides personal and commercial property/casualty products including insurance plans for small and midsized businesses and individual auto and homeowners plans through its NGM Insurance subsidiary and its regional subsidiaries and affiliates Grain Dealers Mutual and Spring Valley Mutual Insurance Company. Some 2000 independent agents sell group products in about 25 states. The firm also offers specialized surety bonds (in about 45 states) for contractors executors and public officials and fidelity bonds to protect businesses from employee dishonesty. The company is 99.6%-owned by Main Street America Group Mutual Holdings Incorporated.

MAIN STREET CAPITAL CORP

1300 Post Oak Boulevard, 8th floor
Houston, TX 77056
Phone: 713 350-6000
Fax: –
Web: www.mainstcapital.com

NYS: MAIN
CEO: Dwayne L Hyzak
CFO: Brent D Smith
HR: –
FYE: December 31
Type: Public

Main Street Capital doesn't care if its investments are on Main St. Manufacturing Blvd or Professional Services Pkwy. just as long as they are not too big and are (preferably) located in the southwestern US. As an investment firm Main Street provides long-term debt and equity capital to lower middle-market companies with annual revenues between $10 million and $100 million. Its portfolio includes more than 40 active investments in traditional and niche companies in the manufacturing technology restaurant business services and other sectors. Main Street tends to partner with business owners and management and provides capital to support buyouts recapitalizations growth financings and acquisitions.

	Annual Growth	12/13	12/14	12/15	12/16	12/17
Sales ($ mil.)	15.3%	116.5	140.8	164.6	178.3	205.7
Net income ($ mil.)	15.7%	75.4	95.5	107.1	115.8	135.4
Market value ($ mil.)	5.0%	1,917.6	1,715.2	1,705.9	2,157.0	2,330.6
Employees	11.9%	37	38	50	57	58

MAINE COAST REGIONAL HEALTH FACILITIES INC

50 UNION ST STE 2
ELLSWORTH, ME 046051534
Phone: 207-664-5311
Fax: –
Web: www.mcmhospital.org

CEO: Charlie Therrien
CFO: Kevin Sedgwick
HR: –
FYE: September 30
Type: Private

Maine Coast Memorial Hospital provides medical services to the residents of Ellsworth right on the Maine coastline. The community hospital has about 60 acute care beds. Its specialty service offerings include emergency medicine cancer treatment rehabilitation orthopedics surgery and mental health care. Maine Coast Memorial Hospital also operates a maternity and family birthing center senior services and a center for adolescent health as well as diagnostic and medical laboratory facilities. The hospital is part of Maine Coast Health Care.

	Annual Growth	06/13	06/14	06/15	06/16*	09/17
Sales ($ mil.)	1.5%	–	77.1	71.1	77.7	80.5
Net income ($ mil.)	–	–	(3.3)	(6.7)	(4.8)	(4.9)
Market value ($ mil.)	–	–	–	–	–	–
Employees	–	–	–	–	–	658

*Fiscal year change

MAINEGENERAL HEALTH

35 MEDICAL CENTER PKWY
AUGUSTA, ME 043308160
Phone: 207-626-1000
Fax: –

CEO: Charles Hays
CFO: Michael Koziol
HR: –
FYE: June 30
Type: Private

If you're aching or ailing within shouting distance of the Kennebec River in Maine then MaineGeneral Health is the place to head. The comprehensive health care organization features acute care hospitals outpatient clinics and physicians' practices long-term care centers and home health and hospice agencies. Its flagship facilities are the three main campuses (in state capital Augusta and Waterville farther north) of MaineGeneral Medical Center together featuring about 290 inpatient beds. MaineGeneral Health also runs nursing homes with some 270 beds in all as well as senior living apartments lab and imaging centers and inpatient rehabilitation and mental health facilities.

	Annual Growth	06/08	06/09	06/10	06/11	06/12
Sales ($ mil.)	(50.1%)	–	–	1,768.2	421.6	440.3
Net income ($ mil.)	–	–	–	0.0	46.1	(2.0)
Market value ($ mil.)	–	–	–	–	–	–
Employees	–	–	–	–	–	3,800

MAINEHEALTH

22 BRAMHALL ST
PORTLAND, ME 041023134
Phone: 207-662-0111
Fax: –
Web: www.mainehealth.org

CEO: Richard W. (Rich) Petersen
CFO: –
HR: –
FYE: September 30
Type: Private

Maine Medical Center (MMC) makes healing happen for the residents of northern New England. Part of MaineHealth the not-for-profit medical center consists of a tertiary care community hospital The Barbara Bush Children's Hospital and outpatient clinics. Specialty services include cancer care geriatrics emergency medicine cardiovascular care rehabilitation neurology orthopedics and women's health. Through its partnership with the Tufts University School of Medicine the 640-bed teaching hospital provides a variety of medical education and training programs. MMC also conducts research through the Maine Medical Center Research Institute. The medical center was founded in 1874 with 40 beds.

	Annual Growth	09/14	09/15	09/16	09/17	09/18
Sales ($ mil.)	35.1%	–	1,023.9	1,127.0	1,236.4	2,523.9
Net income ($ mil.)	–	–	(39.2)	3.1	152.9	205.9
Market value ($ mil.)	–	–	–	–	–	–
Employees	–	–	–	–	–	2,000

MAINSOURCE FINANCIAL GROUP INC   NMS: MSFG

2105 North State Road 3 Bypass   CEO: –
Greensburg, IN 47240   CFO: –
Phone: 812 663-6734   HR: –
Fax: 812 663-4812   FYE: December 31
Web: www.mainsourcebank.com   Type: Public

MainSource Financial wants to be the main source of financial services for residents and businesses in Indiana and beyond. It is the holding company of MainSource Bank which operates about 80 branches in the Hoosier State as well as neighboring portions of Ohio Illinois and Kentucky. The bank offers standard deposit and lending products in addition to trust and insurance services. Real estate loans account for the majority of MainSource Financial's lending portfolio which also includes other commercial and consumer loans. Through MainSource Insurance the company provides annuities and credit life insurance.

	Annual Growth	12/12	12/13	12/14	12/15	12/16
Assets ($ mil.)	10.2%	2,769.3	2,859.9	3,122.5	3,385.4	4,080.3
Net income ($ mil.)	8.9%	27.3	26.3	29.0	35.5	38.3
Market value ($ mil.)	28.4%	304.9	433.9	503.5	550.7	827.9
Employees	2.4%	808	772	801	841	888

MAINSTREET BANKSHARES INC   NBB: MREE

1075 Spruce Street   CEO: –
Martinsville, VA 24112   CFO: –
Phone: 276 632-8054   HR: –
Fax: –   FYE: December 31
Web: www.msbsinc.com   Type: Public

There is no exile on MainStreet BankShares (sorry Mick). The firm is the holding company for Franklin Community Bank which serves southern Virginia from about five offices. Chartered in 2002 Franklin offers such deposit products as checking and savings accounts money markets and CDs. The bank primarily uses funds from deposits to write real estate loans including commercial and residential mortgages construction loans and home equity loans. Franklin Community's market is centered in the rural communities of Virginia's Franklin County.

	Annual Growth	12/08	12/09	12/10	12/11	12/12
Assets ($ mil.)	(5.0%)	224.6	225.2	214.5	203.9	183.1
Net income ($ mil.)	35.4%	0.6	0.1	0.8	(0.1)	2.0
Market value ($ mil.)	(21.7%)	27.4	10.6	6.4	7.3	10.3
Employees	0.0%	53	54	51	50	53

MAKE-A-WISH FOUNDATION OF AMERICA

4742 N 24TH ST STE 400   CEO: –
PHOENIX, AZ 850164862   CFO: Trevor Vigfusson
Phone: 602-279-9474   HR: –
Fax: –   FYE: August 31
    Type: Private

The Make-A-Wish Foundation of America's mission is to grant the wishes of children with life-threatening medical conditions. The charitable organization grants wishes to ailing kids between the ages of two-and-a-half and 18 from more than 60 chapters in the US and its territories. Funded through donations in-kind contributions grants chapter fees and corporate donations the not-for-profit foundation boasts a volunteer network of some 25000 people and has granted more than 226000 wishes to children since its creation in 1980. The foundation was originally named the Chris Greicius Make-A-Wish Memorial after the first boy to receive his wish: becoming an honorary Arizona state trooper.

	Annual Growth	08/12	08/13	08/14	08/15	08/16
Sales ($ mil.)	12.1%	–	67.3	77.7	89.1	94.7
Net income ($ mil.)	–	–	(1.7)	2.7	(4.7)	4.4
Market value ($ mil.)	–	–	–	–	–	–
Employees	–	–	–	–	–	200

MALVERN BANCORP INC.   NASDAQ: MLVF

42 E. Lancaster Ave.   CEO: –
Paoli PA 19301   CFO: Joseph D Gangemi
Phone: 610-644-9400   HR: Maureen Wroblewski
Fax: 610-644-1943   FYE: September 30
Web: www.malvernfederal.com   Type: Public

Malvern Bancorp (formerly Malvern Federal Bancorp) was formed in 2008 to be the holding company for Malvern Federal Savings Bank which has been in business since 1887. The bank operates seven financial centers in Chester County in southeastern Pennsylvania west of Philadelphia. It offers standard deposit services such as checking and savings accounts certificates of deposit and retirement plans. The community-oriented institution has traditionally been a leading originator of residential home loans in Chester County but has been shifting its focus toward issuing more commercial real estate construction and consumer loans.

MAMMATECH CORPORATION   OTC: MAMM

930 NW 8th Ave.   CEO: Brenton Mix
Gainesville FL 32601   CFO: Brenton Mix
Phone: 352-375-0607   HR: –
Fax: 561-790-4332   FYE: August 31
Web: www.rangerconstruction.com   Type: Public

Mammatech Corporation wants to help doctors clinicians moms and other women keep an eye on breast cancer. The company manufactures a breast tumor detection training system designed to increase early detection of breast cancer and thus reduce patient deaths from the disease. Using models of a human female breast the MammaCare System trains individuals to perform manual breast exams to detect tumors. The system comes in different interactive training packages targeting medical professionals and individuals including those who are hearing or vision impaired. The company started as a research project in 1974 with support from the National Cancer Institute.

MANAGEMENT & TRAINING CORPORATION

500 N MARKET PLACE DR # 100   CEO: Scott Marquardt JD
CENTERVILLE, UT 840141711   CFO: Lyle J Parry
Phone: 801-693-2600   HR: Carol Westbroek
Fax: –   FYE: December 31
Web: www.mtctrains.com   Type: Private

Management & Training Corporation (MTC) prepares prison inmates for re-entry into society. It provides a variety of academic vocational and social-skills training in rehabilitation-oriented private prisons. Its holistic education model offers programs to help inmates avoid substance abuse as they also boost their engagement in community service find work and increase their cognitive skills. As part of its services MTC operates about two dozen correctional facilities in eight states through a contract with the Department of Labor. The company also operates Job Corps centers and provides healthcare-related services to correctional facilities.

	Annual Growth	12/11	12/12	12/13	12/15	12/17
Sales ($ mil.)	(1.1%)	–	704.1	735.4	753.8	667.7
Net income ($ mil.)	1.8%	–	45.7	50.7	30.1	49.8
Market value ($ mil.)	–	–	–	–	–	–
Employees	–	–	–	–	–	9,500

MANATEE MEMORIAL HOSPITAL, L.P.

206 2ND ST E
BRADENTON, FL 342081000
Phone: 941-746-5111
Fax: −
Web: www.manateememorial.com

CEO: Kevin Dilallo
CFO: Mark Tierney
HR: Anne Macdonald
FYE: December 31
Type: Private

Docile aquatic mammals will have to seek medical care elsewhere. Manatee Memorial Hospital provides general medical surgical and community health services to land-dwelling humans in southwestern Florida. The 320-bed hospital has about 400 affiliated physicians and offers acute primary and specialty care services including emergency cancer cardiovascular neurology rehabilitation and women's health care services. It also operates FirstCare urgent care clinics and provides community health screenings with partner Life Line Screenings. A subsidiary of Universal Health Services Manatee Memorial is part of the Manatee Healthcare System which also includes the 120-bed Lakewood Ranch Medical Center.

	Annual Growth	12/13	12/14	12/15	12/16	12/17
Sales ($ mil.)	7.0%	−	244.3	249.8	268.5	299.1
Net income ($ mil.)	42.4%	−	11.5	2.4	7.1	33.3
Market value ($ mil.)	−	−	−	−	−	−
Employees	−	−	−	−	−	1,450

MANER BUILDERS SUPPLY COMPANY, LLC

3787 MARTINEZ BLVD
MARTINEZ, GA 309072665
Phone: 706-863-0558
Fax: −
Web: www.maner.com

CEO: −
CFO: F Frank Chandler
HR: −
FYE: December 31
Type: Private

You can build a manor house with what Maner Builders Supply Company can offer. It sells and distributes building supplies such as cabinets designed closets doors engineered lumber fencing materials glass gypsum masonry roofing and premium windows through about a half dozen locations in Eastern Georgia and South Carolina. The company offers free quotes free delivery and warranty assistance for its customers which include home builders general contractors homeowners and public agencies. Maner Builders Supply carries products from manufacturers such as Bradley Buckley Rumford Fireplaces Ceco Door Makita Palmetto Brick Parex and Wellborn Cabinet. It was founded in 1951 as the Maner Hardware & Supply Company.

	Annual Growth	12/10	12/11	12/14	12/15	12/16
Sales ($ mil.)	8.2%	−	44.2	55.0	60.0	65.4
Net income ($ mil.)	45.0%	−	0.6	2.5	3.4	4.0
Market value ($ mil.)	−	−	−	−	−	−
Employees	−	−	−	−	−	325

MANGO CAPITAL INC.   OTC: MGOF-L

108 Village Sq. Ste. 315
Somers NY 10589
Phone: 914-669-5333
Fax: 866-277-3385
Web: www.mangosoft.com

CEO: Dennis M Goett
CFO: Sean M Gavin
HR: −
FYE: December 31
Type: Public

Mango Capital's software products are designed to improve the efficiency of Web-based business applications including online document delivery speed and remote file storage. Customers use the company's applications known as Mangomind to securely manage collaboration and file sharing with remote offices and trading partners. Mango Capital's clients come from a variety of industries and include small and midsized businesses workgroups and large enterprises. Founded in 1995 the company changed its name from MangoSoft to Mango Capital in 2011 to reflect the addition of financial services such as structured settlement to its business plan through its Aspyre Settlement Funding business.

MANHATTAN ASSOCIATES, INC.   NMS: MANH

2300 Windy Ridge Parkway, Tenth Floor
Atlanta, GA 30339
Phone: 770 955-7070
Fax: 770 995-0302
Web: www.manh.com

CEO: Eddie Capel
CFO: Linda C. Pinne
HR: −
FYE: December 31
Type: Public

Whether you're in New York or Kansas or points between or beyond Manhattan Associates keeps things moving with its supply chain management software and systems. The Atlanta-based company provides customers in retail distribution transportation and manufacturing with supply chain management software and related services. Its line of supply chain and inventory software includes warehouse transportation trading partner distributed order and reverse logistics management applications. Manhattan also offers performance management and radio-frequency identification tools designed to enhance the functionality of its other products and sells third-party hardware such as bar code scanners.

	Annual Growth	12/14	12/15	12/16	12/17	12/18
Sales ($ mil.)	3.2%	492.1	556.4	604.6	594.6	559.2
Net income ($ mil.)	6.3%	82.0	103.5	124.2	116.5	104.7
Market value ($ mil.)	1.0%	2,641.1	4,291.8	3,439.5	3,213.2	2,748.1
Employees	2.0%	2,770	2,930	3,020	2,790	3,000

MANHATTAN BRIDGE CAPITAL, INC.   NAS: LOAN

60 Cutter Mill Road
Great Neck, NY 11021
Phone: 516 444-3400
Fax: 212 779-2974
Web: www.manhattanbridgecapital.com

CEO: Assaf Ran
CFO: Vanessa KAO
HR: −
FYE: December 31
Type: Public

Manhattan Bridge Capital (formerly DAG Media) knew that when it came to a bridge it had to cross it. In 2008 it renamed itself when its DAG Funding Solutions commercial lending subsidiary which the company started in 2007 became its most profitable unit. The company offers short-term secured commercial loans to small businesses. It also offers an online service Nextyellow.com that lets consumers search for a product or service. The consumer's request is matched with appropriate businesses and the matched businesses then call or email the customer. Vendor partners pay the company monthly fees to be featured in the matching process.

	Annual Growth	12/14	12/15	12/16	12/17	12/18
Sales ($ mil.)	25.6%	2.9	4.0	4.6	5.9	7.2
Net income ($ mil.)	30.4%	1.5	2.2	2.8	3.4	4.2
Market value ($ mil.)	8.7%	38.9	42.4	73.4	57.4	54.3
Employees	7.5%	3	4	4	5	4

MANHATTAN COLLEGE CORP

4513 MNHTTAN COLLEGE PKWY
BRONX, NY 104714004
Phone: 718-862-8000
Fax: −
Web: www.engineering.manhattan.edu

CEO: −
CFO: Matthew S McManness
HR: −
FYE: June 30
Type: Private

A trip to Manhattan College doesn't take you to that well-known borough but instead to the Riverdale section of the Bronx. With its campus overlooking Van Cortlandt Park Manhattan College is a private Catholic university with about 3200 undergraduate and graduate students studying a wide range of topics from engineering to the arts to biotechnology. The school grants about 40 undergraduate degrees and graduate degrees in education and engineering. Founded in 1853 by the Brothers of the Christian Schools the college was originally located on Canal Street in Manhattan then later moved to a rural location at 131st Street and Broadway before settling into its present campus in 1922.

	Annual Growth	06/07	06/08	06/09	06/11	06/13
Sales ($ mil.)	11.9%	−	85.9	88.1	124.6	150.7
Net income ($ mil.)	57.7%	−	−	1.3	3.0	7.7
Market value ($ mil.)	−	−	−	−	−	−
Employees	−	−	−	−	−	496

MANHATTAN SCHOOL OF MUSIC INC

120 CLAREMONT AVE
NEW YORK, NY 100274698
Phone: 212-749-2802
Fax: –
Web: www.msmnyc.edu

CEO: –
CFO: Joanne Mandry
HR: –
FYE: June 30
Type: Private

Music is on the minds of students at the Manhattan School of Music in New York. The school is dedicated to the study of jazz and classical music. Majors range from orchestral instruments and voice to piano composition and jazz. It has more than 800 students and nearly 275 faculty. The school provides undergraduate graduate and doctoral programs. Manhattan School of Music also offers distance learning and a Global Conservatory which provides video conferencing to institutions throughout the world. Famous alumni include Harry Connick Jr. Herbie Hancock and Yusef Lateef. Pianist and philanthropist Janet D. Schenck founded the Manhattan School of Music as as the Neighborhood Music School in 1917.

	Annual Growth	06/12	06/13	06/15	06/16	06/17
Sales ($ mil.)	6.5%	–	47.6	47.9	56.7	61.2
Net income ($ mil.)	21.4%	–	2.1	(0.5)	3.1	4.6
Market value ($ mil.)	–	–	–	–	–	–
Employees	–	–	–	–	–	450

MANHATTANVILLE COLLEGE

2900 PURCHASE ST
PURCHASE, NY 105772132
Phone: 914-694-2200
Fax: –
Web: www.mville.edu

CEO: –
CFO: –
HR: –
FYE: June 30
Type: Private

Manhattanville College is a private liberal arts institution offering undergraduate and masters degree programs in more than 50 fields. Manhattanville is home to about 1700 undergraduate students and 1000 graduate students. In addition to college degree programs the school also offers in-house and on-site corporate training programs in such areas as business writing project management and diversity. Manhattanville was founded in 1841 in New York City by the Religious of the Sacred Heart. It relocated in 1847 to an area just north of New York City on a hill overlooking the village of Manhattanville. The school has been coeducational and non-denominational since 1971.

	Annual Growth	06/10	06/11	06/12	06/13	06/14
Sales ($ mil.)	(2.5%)	–	–	102.7	61.1	97.6
Net income ($ mil.)	(11.1%)	–	–	3.8	1.4	3.0
Market value ($ mil.)	–	–	–	–	–	–
Employees	–	–	–	–	–	420

MANITEX INTERNATIONAL INC

9725 Industrial Drive
Bridgeview, IL 60455
Phone: 708 430-7500
Fax: –
Web: www.manitexinternational.com

NAS: MNTX
CEO: Steve Filipov
CFO: Laura R Yu
HR: –
FYE: December 31
Type: Public

Manitex International makes products that are uplifting — literally. One of the largest manufacturers of lifting equipment in North America Manitex makes and sells boom trucks and sign cranes used in industrial jobs as well as energy exploration construction and commercial building. Through Liftking the company makes rough terrain forklifts heavy handling transports and military specialty vehicles. The Manitex family also includes Badger Equipment (cranes and material handling). A Crane & Machinery unit distributes Manitex Terex and Fuchs equipment.

	Annual Growth	12/14	12/15	12/16	12/17	12/18
Sales ($ mil.)	(2.1%)	264.1	386.7	289.0	213.1	242.1
Net income ($ mil.)	–	7.1	(5.4)	(35.2)	(8.1)	(13.2)
Market value ($ mil.)	(18.2%)	249.7	116.9	134.8	188.6	111.6
Employees	(1.7%)	663	961	709	561	619

MANNATECH INC

1410 Lakeside Parkway, Suite 200
Flower Mound, TX 75028
Phone: 972 471-7400
Fax: –
Web: www.mannatech.com

NMS: MTEX
CEO: Alfredo (Al) Bala
CFO: David Johnson
HR: –
FYE: December 31
Type: Public

Mannatech's nutritional products provide a sales mantra for independent entrepreneurs. The multi-level marketing company develops and sells nutritional supplements. Many of its proprietary products include Ambrotose a proprietary blend of monosaccharides (simple sugars) that is claimed to promote cell-to-cell communication and support the body's immune system. Its vitamins weight management products and skin care items are distributed through a network of more than 245000 independent salespeople. The company does not maintain its own manufacturing facilities and instead relies upon third-party contract manufacturers. In 2016 Mannatech opened a storefront at its Coppell Texas headquarters.

	Annual Growth	12/14	12/15	12/16	12/17	12/18
Sales ($ mil.)	(2.2%)	190.1	180.3	180.3	176.7	173.6
Net income ($ mil.)	–	6.5	5.8	(0.6)	(1.8)	(3.9)
Market value ($ mil.)	(8.4%)	63.5	44.9	48.3	35.7	44.8
Employees	(2.1%)	270	287	290	252	248

MANNING & NAPIER INC.

290 Woodcliff Drive
Fairport, NY 14450
Phone: 585 325-6880
Fax: –
Web: www.manning-napier.com

NYS: MN
CEO: Marc Mayer
CFO: James Mikolaichik
HR: –
FYE: December 31
Type: Public

Manning & Napier is in the business of making money for itself by making money for its investor clients. As a US-based independent financial services company it offers equity fixed income and blended-asset portfolios of collective investment trust funds mutual funds and separately managed accounts. With more than $25 billion in assets under management the firm serves high-net-worth individuals corporations endowments 401(k) plans pension plans Taft-Hartley plans and foundations. Manning & Napier offers its products through a direct sales force and through financial intermediaries and investment consultants. Formed in 1970 the company went public in 2011.

	Annual Growth	12/14	12/15	12/16	12/17	12/18
Sales ($ mil.)	(20.6%)	405.5	327.8	248.9	201.5	161.3
Net income ($ mil.)	(23.5%)	9.3	13.2	9.3	3.6	3.2
Market value ($ mil.)	(40.3%)	211.6	130.0	115.6	55.1	26.9
Employees	(8.6%)	525	474	468	433	366

MANNKIND CORP

30930 Russell Ranch Road, Suite 300
Westlake Village, CA 91362
Phone: 818 661-5000
Fax: –
Web: www.mannkindcorp.com

NMS: MNKD
CEO: Michael E. Castagna
CFO: Rose Alinaya
HR: –
FYE: December 31
Type: Public

MannKind seeks to improve the well-being of well mankind. The biopharmaceutical company focuses on developing and commercializing therapeutic products to treat diabetes and cancer. Its lead product AFREZZA (launched in the US in 2015) uses its Technosphere inhalation system technology to treat type 1 and type 2 diabetes. The system consists of a special inhaler that releases deep into the lungs a formula of dry powder insulin that could raise insulin levels more quickly and with less discomfort than other methods. The company is also developing therapeutic cancer vaccines that could be injected directly into a patient's lymph nodes.

	Annual Growth	12/14	12/15	12/16	12/17	12/18
Sales ($ mil.)	(60.1%)	–	–	174.8	11.7	27.9
Net income ($ mil.)	–	(198.4)	(368.4)	125.7	(117.3)	(87.0)
Market value ($ mil.)	(32.9%)	975.4	271.2	119.1	433.9	198.3
Employees	(5.9%)	287	192	153	250	225

MANTECH INTERNATIONAL CORP   NMS: MANT

2251 Corporate Park Drive   CEO: George J. Pedersen
Herndon, VA 20171   CFO: Judith L. (Judy) Bjornaas
Phone: 703 218-6000   HR: Cookie Perlmutter
Fax: –   FYE: December 31
Web: www.mantech.com   Type: Public

ManTech International is more than willing to lend a little high-tech staffing to ensure its country's security. ManTech provides security-focused IT services to 50 agencies primarily US government intelligence entities such as the Department of Defense (DoD) Homeland Security the FBI and the military. Its national security offerings include intelligence communications computer forensics and security systems development and support. The contractor also offers network design and installation and system testing and evaluation. ManTech is active in about 40 other countries but makes essentially all of its sales to US customers.

	Annual Growth	12/14	12/15	12/16	12/17	12/18
Sales ($ mil.)	2.5%	1,774.0	1,550.1	1,601.6	1,717.0	1,958.6
Net income ($ mil.)	14.8%	47.3	51.1	56.4	114.1	82.1
Market value ($ mil.)	14.7%	1,202.0	1,202.4	1,679.9	1,995.6	2,079.3
Employees	2.4%	7,100	7,200	7,000	7,600	7,800

MANUFACTURED HOUSING ENTERPRISES INC.

9302 US HIGHWAY 6   CEO: Mary Jane Fitzcharles
BRYAN, OH 435069516   CFO: –
Phone: 419-636-4511   HR: –
Fax: –   FYE: December 31
Web: www.mheinc.com   Type: Private

Manufactured Housing Enterprises builds modular sectional and singlewide homes as well as commercial and retail developments for clients in the Midwest. The company is the largest manufactured home builder in Ohio and among the 20 largest in the country. It offers more than 80 floor plans for singlewide homes as well as two-story homes of more than 3000 sq. ft. The company has delivered homes to Illinois Indiana Indiana Kentucky Michigan Missouri Tennessee West Virginia and Wisconsin. Manufactured Housing Enterprises was established in 1965 when being "mod" was fab.

	Annual Growth	12/09	12/10	12/11	12/12	12/13
Sales ($ mil.)	19.1%	–	7.4	8.0	13.1	12.5
Net income ($ mil.)	–	–	–	(0.1)	0.7	0.8
Market value ($ mil.)	–	–	–	–	–	–
Employees	–	–	–	–	–	1

MAR-JAC POULTRY, INC.

1020 AVIATION BLVD   CEO: J Pete Martin
GAINESVILLE, GA 305016839   CFO: Mirza M Yaqub
Phone: 770-531-5000   HR: –
Fax: –   FYE: April 27
Web: www.marjacpoultry.com   Type: Private

From farm to table Mar-Jac Poultry's business is "poultry in motion." The company is one of the major processors of chicken sold to the domestic fast-food restaurant and foodservice market. Its operations include a hatchery to raise birds and a feed mill that churns 8500 tons of feed a week for some 200 farmers in Georgia who contract with the company to grow its chicks and broilers. Mar-Jac's plant processes about two million chickens a week which are vacuum-packed in its cold storage facility prior to shipment to mostly local distributors in the US and some international export customers. Mar-Jac was started by brothers Marvin and Jackson McKibbon in 1954 and later acquired by a group of poultry farmers.

	Annual Growth	04/08	04/09	04/10	04/11	04/12
Sales ($ mil.)	3.9%	–	–	262.9	257.1	284.0
Net income ($ mil.)	(47.9%)	–	–	29.9	11.2	8.1
Market value ($ mil.)	–	–	–	–	–	–
Employees	–	–	–	–	–	1,200

MARATHON OIL CORP.   NYS: MRO

5555 San Felipe Street   CEO: Lee M. Tillman
Houston, TX 77056-2723   CFO: Dane E. Whitehead
Phone: 713 629-6600   HR: Deanna L. Jones
Fax: –   FYE: December 31
Web: www.marathonoil.com   Type: Public

In the long-running competition for success in the oil and gas industry Marathon Oil is keeping up a steady pace. It has proved reserves of more than 2.1 billion barrels of oil equivalent including 692 million barrels of synthetic oil derived from oil sands mining. It major focus of production is the US in the Gulf of Mexico Oklahoma Texas north Delaware and North Dakota. Its areas of production outside of the US include Europe (the UK); and Africa (Equatorial Guinea Gabon and Libya).

	Annual Growth	12/14	12/15	12/16	12/17	12/18
Sales ($ mil.)	(12.6%)	11,258.0	5,861.0	4,650.0	4,765.0	6,582.0
Net income ($ mil.)	(22.6%)	3,046.0	(2,204.0)	(2,140.0)	(5,723.0)	1,096.0
Market value ($ mil.)	(15.6%)	23,169.5	10,311.2	14,176.9	13,865.7	11,744.5
Employees	(7.9%)	3,330	2,611	2,117	2,300	2,400

MARATHON PETROLEUM CORP.   NYS: MPC

539 South Main Street   CEO: Gary R. Heminger
Findlay, OH 45840-3229   CFO: Timothy T. Griffith
Phone: 419 422-2121   HR: Rodney P. Nichols
Fax: –   FYE: December 31
Web: www.marathonpetroleum.com   Type: Public

Marathon Petroleum the former refining and marketing unit of Marathon Oil Corporation operates more than five refineries with the capacity to process about 1.9 million barrels of crude oil a day. Marathon Petroleum sells refined products through a nationwide network of branded gas stations. It also holds stakes in pipelines and is one of the largest asphalt and light oil product terminal operators in the US. The company distributes petroleum products wholesale to private-brand marketers and to large commercial and industrial consumers as well as to the spot market.

	Annual Growth	12/14	12/15	12/16	12/17	12/18
Sales ($ mil.)	(0.3%)	98,102.0	72,258.0	63,364.0	75,369.0	97,102.0
Net income ($ mil.)	2.4%	2,524.0	2,852.0	1,174.0	3,432.0	2,780.0
Market value ($ mil.)	(10.1%)	61,376.8	35,251.2	34,238.0	44,866.4	40,126.8
Employees	7.4%	45,340	45,440	44,460	43,800	60,350

MARCH OF DIMES INC.

1550 CRYSTAL DR STE 1300   CEO: –
ARLINGTON, VA 222024144   CFO: David Horne
Phone: 571-257-2324   HR: –
Fax: –   FYE: December 31
Web: www.marchofdimes.org   Type: Private

The March of Dimes Foundation has been on the march lending a hand since 1938. Established by President Franklin Roosevelt to fight polio the organization has evolved into an advocate for the prevention of birth defects and infant mortality. Its focus areas include genetic birth defects premature birth parent education and expanding access to health care. The foundation provides information and support services for professionals and the public and supports research efforts. Most of the foundation's revenue comes from contributions to its signature March for Babies event and other fundraisers.

	Annual Growth	12/08	12/09	12/13	12/14	12/16
Sales ($ mil.)	(3.3%)	–	214.7	202.8	195.9	169.3
Net income ($ mil.)	–	–	–	35.3	(9.7)	(7.9)	(8.7)
Market value ($ mil.)	–	–	–	–	–	–
Employees	–	–	–	–	–	1,200

MARCHEX INC
NMS: MCHX

520 Pike Street, Suite 2000
Seattle, WA 98101
Phone: 206 331-3300
Fax: –
Web: www.marchex.com

CEO: Ethan A. Caldwell
CFO: Michael A. (Mike) Arends
HR: –
FYE: December 31
Type: Public

This company marches to the beat of the telemarketing drummer. Marchex provides performance-based call advertising services. Advertisers pay Marchex a fee for each call they receive from an ad (online mobile or print) distributed by Marchex. Its Local Advertising Services include call distribution and call analytics services such as phone number and call tracking call mining and keyword tracking. Marchex distributes ads on its Publishing Network which includes more than 200000 owned and -operated websites as well as through search engines such as Google and Yahoo!. Its Publisher Network is focused on local products and services and includes domains such as chicagodoctors.com and bostonmortgage.com.

	Annual Growth	12/14	12/15	12/16	12/17	12/18
Sales ($ mil.)	(17.3%)	182.6	143.0	129.5	90.3	85.3
Net income ($ mil.)	–	(19.1)	26.7	(84.1)	(6.1)	(2.7)
Market value ($ mil.)	(12.8%)	192.9	163.5	111.4	135.7	111.4
Employees	(8.8%)	367	375	291	225	254

MARCUM LLP

750 3RD AVE FL 11
NEW YORK, NY 100172716
Phone: 212-485-5500
Fax: –
Web: www.marcumllp.com

CEO: –
CFO: Edward Scicchitano
HR: –
FYE: December 31
Type: Private

Marcum LLP (formerly MarcumStonefield) is making a mark on the world of accounting and consulting. With more than 20 offices in the US China and the Caribbean Marcum offers a full range of business and personal financial services including accounting auditing and tax and investment consulting. It also offers professional services such as mergers and acquisitions planning family office services forensic accounting and litigation support. The firm serves multiple industries such as construction health care real estate media and entertainment and financial services. Founded in 1951 Marcum is a member of the Marcum Group.

	Annual Growth	12/13	12/14	12/15	12/16	12/17
Sales ($ mil.)	10.7%	–	251.4	273.1	320.1	341.0
Net income ($ mil.)	(2.3%)	–	15.3	15.7	11.2	14.3
Market value ($ mil.)	–	–	–	–	–	–
Employees	–	–	–	–	–	1,434

MARCUS CORP. (THE)
NYS: MCS

100 East Wisconsin Avenue, Suite 1900
Milwaukee, WI 53202-4125
Phone: 414 905-1000
Fax: 414 905-2879
Web: www.marcuscorp.com

CEO: Gregory S. Marcus
CFO: Douglas A. Neis
HR: Fred Delmenhorst
FYE: December 27
Type: Public

With this company it's either showtime or bedtime. The Marcus Corporation operates movie theaters and hotels primarily in the Midwest. It owns or operates more than 55 theaters boastingsome 680 screens in Iowa Illinois Minnesota Nebraska North Dakota Ohio and Wisconsin. Its Marcus Hotels subsidiary owns and operates more than 10 hotels and resorts in Illinois Missouri Oklahoma and Wisconsin; it also manages 10 hotels for third parties in a handful of US states. Other holdings also include Funset Boulevard a family entertainment center adjacent to one of its Wisconsin theatres. Chairman Stephen Marcus and his sister Diane Marcus Gershowitz together control more than 75% of the firm.

	Annual Growth	05/15*	12/15	12/16	12/17	12/18
Sales ($ mil.)	13.2%	488.1	324.3	543.9	622.7	707.1
Net income ($ mil.)	30.6%	24.0	23.6	37.9	65.0	53.4
Market value ($ mil.)	25.1%	557.1	537.8	894.5	771.1	1,091.8
Employees	4.1%	7,100	7,000	7,900	7,800	8,000

*Fiscal year change

MARIAN UNIVERSITY, INC.

3200 COLD SPRING RD
INDIANAPOLIS, IN 462221960
Phone: 317-955-6000
Fax: –
Web: www.marian.edu

CEO: –
CFO: –
HR: –
FYE: June 30
Type: Private

Marian College is a Franciscan Catholic and liberal arts institution offering undergraduate and graduate programs through academic departments such as business nursing education and sport studies. The school has an enrollment of more than 2000 students and boasts a student-to-teacher ratio of just over 12 to 1. Marian College was founded in 1851 by the Sisters of St. Francis as a teacher training institution for German Catholics in southern Indiana.

	Annual Growth	06/13	06/14	06/15	06/17	06/18
Sales ($ mil.)	7.4%	–	79.5	98.8	95.9	105.7
Net income ($ mil.)	–	–	(2.6)	9.1	13.9	16.5
Market value ($ mil.)	–	–	–	–	–	–
Employees	–	–	–	–	–	305

MARIN GENERAL HOSPITAL

250 BON AIR RD
KENTFIELD, CA 949041784
Phone: 415-925-7000
Fax: –
Web: –

CEO: Lee Domanico
CFO: Theresa Daughton
HR: –
FYE: December 31
Type: Private

Serving Northern California's Marin County Marin General Hospital is the county's largest acute-care health care facility with some 235 beds. Opened in 1952 Marin General Hospital has been a member of Sutter Health since 1996. It operates the Marin Cancer Institute the Haynes Cardiovascular Institute the Surgery Center of Marin and The Institute for Health & Healing which provides holistic care within the hospital setting. Other services include adult psychiatric care a level III trauma center a family birthing center neonatal intensive care pediatrics and a cardiac catheterization lab.

	Annual Growth	12/14	12/15	12/16	12/17	12/18
Sales ($ mil.)	11.1%	–	342.4	350.3	371.0	470.1
Net income ($ mil.)	(41.6%)	–	20.7	6.5	17.8	4.1
Market value ($ mil.)	–	–	–	–	–	–
Employees	–	–	–	–	–	1,100

MARIN SOFTWARE INC
NMS: MRIN

123 Mission Street, 27th Floor
San Francisco, CA 94105
Phone: 415 399-2580
Fax: –
Web: www.marinsoftware.com

CEO: David A. (Dave) Yovanno
CFO: Stephen E. Kim
HR: –
FYE: December 31
Type: Public

Marin Software helps determine whether you're getting your money's worth from online advertising. The company's cloud-based digital advertising management software which it calls its Revenue Acquisition Management platform lets marketers measure the effectiveness of campaigns execute campaigns across publishers and channels and use analytics to fine tune campaigns in progress. Its software works with ad publishers Baidu Bing Google Facebook and Yahoo! and integrates with enterprise applications. Marin Software sells its software directly to advertisers and through ad agencies; it earns revenue based on the amount of ad spending customers manage. The company formed in 2006 and went public in 2013.

	Annual Growth	12/14	12/15	12/16	12/17	12/18
Sales ($ mil.)	(12.4%)	99.4	108.5	99.9	75.0	58.6
Net income ($ mil.)	–	(33.2)	(33.3)	(16.5)	(31.5)	(41.2)
Market value ($ mil.)	(11.0%)	50.2	21.3	14.0	65.0	31.5
Employees	(15.4%)	571	511	437	433	292

MARINA BIOTECH INC
NBB: MRNA

P.O. Box 1559
Bothell, WA 98041
Phone: 425-892-4322
Fax: 425-908-3101
Web: www.marinabio.com

CEO: Nancy R Phelan
CFO: –
HR: –
FYE: December 31
Type: Public

Marina Biotech is a clinical-stage drug discovery and development firm with a focus on rare diseases. company is developing treatments using gene silencing approaches such as RNA interference (RNAi) and messenger RNA (mRNA) blocking. It conducts clinical and preclinical tests on RNAi treatments for a variety of cancers and precancerous conditions. Marina Biotech has built up its holdings by licensing peptides with potential RNAi therapy applications from numerous pharmaceutical companies and universities including the University of Michigan. In late 2016 the struggling Marina Biotech merged with IthenaPharma a firm with a focus on pain arthritis hypertension and cancer.

	Annual Growth	12/11	12/12	12/13	12/14	12/15
Sales ($ mil.)	(25.7%)	2.2	4.2	2.1	0.5	0.7
Net income ($ mil.)	–	(29.4)	(9.5)	(1.6)	(6.5)	3.3
Market value ($ mil.)	(26.3%)	24.7	11.9	11.1	18.1	7.3
Employees	(45.1%)	11	1	1	1	1

MARINE PRODUCTS CORP
NYS: MPX

2801 Buford Highway, Suite 300
Atlanta, GA 30329
Phone: 404-321-7910
Fax: –
Web: www.marineproductscorp.com

CEO: Richard A. Hubbell
CFO: Ben M. Palmer
HR: Shannon Pope
FYE: December 31
Type: Public

A day on the water for you is a day at the office for Marine Products. The company builds recreational powerboats mainly though its Chaparral subsidiary. Its lineup includes fiberglass sterndrive and inboard deckboats cruisers and sport yachts ranging from 18 feet to 42 feet. Marine Products also makes a line of freshwater/saltwater sport fishing boats known for their "unsinkable hull" through subsidiary Robalo. Boats are sold to a network of about 230 independent dealers who then sell the lines to retail customers. The US generates the majority of the company's sales.

	Annual Growth	12/14	12/15	12/16	12/17	12/18
Sales ($ mil.)	14.9%	171.1	207.1	241.3	267.3	298.6
Net income ($ mil.)	33.7%	8.9	14.3	16.7	19.3	28.5
Market value ($ mil.)	19.0%	289.7	207.3	476.1	437.3	580.5
Employees	12.7%	605	767	823	891	976

MARINE TOYS FOR TOTS FOUNDATION

18251 QUANTICO GATEWAY DR
TRIANGLE, VA 221721776
Phone: 703-640-9433
Fax: –
Web: www.toysfortots.org

CEO: Robert M Shea
CFO: –
HR: –
FYE: December 31
Type: Private

The Marine Toys for Tots Foundation wears a Santa hat every year. A not-for-profit charity organized by the United States Marine Corps Toys for Tots collects and distributes new toys at Christmas to children in need. Campaigns in some 650 communities distributed more than 16.2 million toys to 7.6 million children in 2008. About 70 corporations are national sponsors collecting an average of $60 million in toys each year. Big Lots ESPN Starbucks Neopets and Ford Motor Company are among them. Major Bill Hendricks started Toys for Tots in 1947 after he couldn't find an organization to give away a Raggedy Ann doll that his wife had made for needy children.

	Annual Growth	12/02	12/03	12/04	12/08	12/16
Sales ($ mil.)	15.0%	–	44.7	187.4	235.5	274.3
Net income ($ mil.)	(1.3%)	–	2.6	183.5	0.0	2.2
Market value ($ mil.)	–	–	–	–	–	–
Employees	–	–	–	–	–	12

MARINEMAX INC
NYS: HZO

2600 McCormick Drive, Suite 200
Clearwater, FL 33759
Phone: 727-531-1700
Fax: –
Web: www.marinemax.com

CEO: William H. McGill
CFO: Michael H. (Mike) McLamb
HR: –
FYE: September 30
Type: Public

MarineMax aims to float your boat. The nation's largest recreational boat dealer has about 60 locations in around 16 states. Dealerships sell new and used pleasure boats fishing boats motor yachts ski boats and high-performance boats. Sales of new boats made by Brunswick including Sea Ray and Boston Whaler boats account for more than 40% of revenue. The company also sells boat engines trailers parts and accessories; arranges for financing and insurance; provides repair and maintenance; and offers boat brokerage and storage services. MarineMax is the exclusive dealer of Sea Ray in almost all the areas where it operates. Since its founding in 1998 MarineMax has acquired about 35 boat dealers.

	Annual Growth	09/15	09/16	09/17	09/18	09/19
Sales ($ mil.)	13.3%	751.4	942.1	1,052.3	1,177.4	1,237.2
Net income ($ mil.)	(7.1%)	48.3	22.6	23.5	39.3	36.0
Market value ($ mil.)	2.3%	301.3	446.7	352.9	453.1	330.1
Employees	8.0%	1,289	1,422	1,516	1,573	1,754

MARION COMMUNITY HOSPITAL INC

1431 SW 1ST AVE
OCALA, FL 344716500
Phone: 352-401-1000
Fax: –
Web: www.ocalahealthsystem.com

CEO: –
CFO: –
HR: –
FYE: August 31
Type: Private

With a giant like hospital operator HCA behind it residents of Marion County Florida can count on Ocala Regional Medical Center (ORMC) to be there to keep them healthy. The 200-bed acute care hospital and its sister facility the 94-bed West Marion Community Hospital provide a full spectrum of health care services to residents of the Sunshine State. ORMC specializes in bariatrics cancer care heart and vascular ailments neuroscience and women's care. West Marion operates a joint care center for orthopedic surgeries and physical therapy. Locals also have access to 24-hour health advice through HCA's Consult-A-Nurse telephone service.

	Annual Growth	09/02	09/03	09/04	09/05*	08/15
Sales ($ mil.)	81.0%	–	–	–	0.8	301.5
Net income ($ mil.)	145.5%	–	–	–	0.0	50.1
Market value ($ mil.)	–	–	–	–	–	–
Employees	–	–	–	–	–	1,100

*Fiscal year change

MARIST COLLEGE

3399 NORTH RD
POUGHKEEPSIE, NY 126011387
Phone: 845-575-3000
Fax: –
Web: www.marist.edu

CEO: –
CFO: Christopher M Capone
HR: Deborah Raikes
FYE: June 30
Type: Private

Marist College is a gem among small private US colleges. The liberal arts college has a enrollment of more than 6300 students and a student-faculty ratio of 16-to-1. It offers more than 40 bachelor's and a dozen master's programs as well as some 20 certificate programs. It seven schools specialize in communication and the arts computer science and math continuing education liberal arts management science and social and behavioral sciences. In addition to its main 210-acre campus along the shores of the Hudson River the college has several off-campus extension sites that mainly cater to adult students. Marist was founded in 1929 to train new members in the Marist Brothers order of Catholic priests.

	Annual Growth	06/12	06/13	06/15	06/17	06/18
Sales ($ mil.)	(1.0%)	–	228.9	239.3	202.1	217.4
Net income ($ mil.)	7.4%	–	33.7	21.2	57.6	48.2
Market value ($ mil.)	–	–	–	–	–	–
Employees	–	–	–	–	–	1,300

MARITZ HOLDINGS INC.

1375 N HIGHWAY DR
FENTON, MO 630990001
Phone: 636-827-4000
Fax: –
Web: www.maritz.com

CEO: W. Stephen (Steve) Maritz
CFO: Rick Ramos
HR: David Estes
FYE: March 31
Type: Private

Maritz Holdings designs employee incentive and reward programs including incentive travel rewards and customer loyalty programs. The company also plans corporate trade shows and events and offers traditional market research services such as the creation of product launch campaigns. Its programs are designed to help its clients improve workforce quality and customer satisfaction. The company operates through a number of subsidiaries including Maritz Motivation Solutions (services for marketing sales HR) MaritzCX (customer experience) Maritz Global Events (meeting and event industry professionals). The company is owned by Steve Maritz.

	Annual Growth	03/11	03/12	03/13	03/16	03/17
Sales ($ mil.)	1.1%	–	1,155.6	1,256.0	1,274.7	1,217.9
Net income ($ mil.)	–	–	47.3	42.1	(16.2)	(30.8)
Market value ($ mil.)	–	–	–	–	–	–
Employees	–	–	–	–	–	4,646

MARK IV LLC

501 John James Audubon Pkwy.
Amherst NY 14226-0810
Phone: 716-689-4972
Fax: 301-987-4438
Web: www.sodexousa.com

CEO: –
CFO: –
HR: –
FYE: February 28
Type: Private

Mark IV aims to make its mark in the auto industry through its assortment of components and belts. The company designs and manufactures power transmission components and an array of belts including timing belts poly-rib belts and raw edge belts. Its rigid components division manufacturers dampers idlers pulleys and tensioners. Mark IV sells to OEMs and aftermarket parts suppliers in the Americas Asia and Europe. The company traces its roots back to 1969 when Salvatore Alfiero and Clement Arrison founded Mark IV Homes as a Pennsylvania-based maker of mobile homes.

MARKEL CORP (HOLDING CO)   NYS: MKL

4521 Highwoods Parkway
Glen Allen, VA 23060-6148
Phone: 804 747-0136
Fax: –
Web: www.markelcorp.com

CEO: Thomas S. Gayner
CFO: Anne G. Waleski
HR: Mollie Stone
FYE: December 31
Type: Public

Have you ever thought about who insures the manicurist or an antique motorcycle? Specialty insurer Markel takes on the risks other insurers won't touch from amusement parks to thoroughbred horses to summer camps. Coverage is also available for one-time events such as golf tournaments and auto races. The company provides customized direct and facultative placements in the US and abroad as well as treaty reinsurance. Markel International provides specialty insurance internationally from its base in the UK while investment management is provided by Markel CATCo and Nephila Holdings. Subsidiary Markel Ventures invests in non-insurance companies.

	Annual Growth	12/14	12/15	12/16	12/17	12/18
Assets ($ mil.)	7.2%	25,200.4	24,941.3	25,875.3	32,805.0	33,306.3
Net income ($ mil.)	–	–	321.2	582.8	455.7	395.3	(128.2)
Market value ($ mil.)	11.0%	9,483.1	12,267.7	12,561.4	15,819.9	14,416.1
Employees	(33.3%)	8,600	10,600	10,900	15,600	1,700

MARKET & JOHNSON, INC.

2350 GALLOWAY ST
EAU CLAIRE, WI 547033441
Phone: 715-834-1213
Fax: –
Web: www.market-johnson.com

CEO: Dan Market
CFO: –
HR: –
FYE: December 31
Type: Private

Market & Johnson provides commercial construction and general contracting services in western Wisconsin. It offers a full range of services ranging from the planning and preliminary design stages through delivery and maintenance. The company operates in the industrial commercial government health care religion and education markets. Projects range from large buildings to small remodeling jobs. Juel Market and Milt Johnson founded the company as a home builder in 1948. Today Market & Johnson is owned by a group of five principal managers including CEO Dan Market.

	Annual Growth	12/09	12/10	12/11	12/12	12/13
Sales ($ mil.)	11.1%	–	–	84.6	107.3	104.4
Net income ($ mil.)	80.4%	–	–	1.5	6.2	5.0
Market value ($ mil.)	–	–	–	–	–	–
Employees	–	–	–	–	–	250

MARKET AMERICA, INC.

1302 PLEASANT RIDGE RD
GREENSBORO, NC 274099415
Phone: 336-605-0040
Fax: –
Web: www.marketamerica.com

CEO: –
CFO: –
HR: –
FYE: October 31
Type: Private

Calling itself a cross between Amazon and QVC Market America is an Internet marketer and broker of products and services from a variety of categories including apparel beauty and personal care electronics entertainment nutrition and sports. Market America sells more than 2500 of its own branded products (such as Isotonix Motives and Snap) and spotlights the offerings of more than 3000 other retailers (including Sears Staples and Wal-Mart) on its SHOP.COM web site (acquired in 2010). In addition the company manages UnFranchise a network marketing business with more than 180000 independent shopping consultants. The company was founded in 1992 by president and CEO James "JR" Ridinger.

	Annual Growth	12/06	12/07	12/08	12/09*	10/16
Sales ($ mil.)	7.3%	–	218.0	229.0	224.5	412.0
Net income ($ mil.)	391.3%	–	0.0	3.5	15.8	23.3
Market value ($ mil.)	–	–	–	–	–	–
Employees	–	–	–	–	–	650

*Fiscal year change

MARKETAXESS HOLDINGS INC.   NMS: MKTX

55 Hudson Yards, 15th Floor
New York, NY 10001
Phone: 212 813-6000
Fax: 212 813-6390
Web: www.marketaxess.com

CEO: Richard M. (Rick) McVey
CFO: Antonio L. (Tony) DeLise
HR: –
FYE: December 31
Type: Public

A little creative spelling never got in the way of a good bond trade. MarketAxess offers an electronic multi-dealer platform for institutional traders buying and selling US corporate high-yield and emerging market bonds as well as Eurobonds. Participating broker-dealers include some of the world's largest such as BNP Paribas Citigroup Deutsche Bank Goldman Sachs and Merrill Lynch. In all MarketAxess serves more than 1000 investment firms mutual funds insurance companies pension funds and other institutional investors. The company also provides real-time corporate bond price information through its Corporate BondTicker service.

	Annual Growth	12/14	12/15	12/16	12/17	12/18
Sales ($ mil.)	13.5%	262.8	303.1	369.9	397.5	435.6
Net income ($ mil.)	23.3%	74.8	96.0	126.2	148.1	172.9
Market value ($ mil.)	31.0%	2,699.2	4,200.2	5,530.1	7,593.9	7,953.7
Employees	10.6%	303	342	383	429	454

MARKETO INC

NMS: MKTO

901 Mariners Island Boulevard, Suite 500
San Mateo, CA 94404
Phone: 650 376-2300
Fax: –
Web: www.marketo.com

CEO: Steve Lucas
CFO: Mark Miller
HR: –
FYE: December 31
Type: Public

Marketo is making its mark among marketing professionals. The company's marketing automation software comprehensively manages marketing campaigns from email marketing and social media to event planning lead management and analytics to measure each campaign's effectiveness. Its software serves as a database to store current and potential customer data in order to track transactions and facilitate future sales. The software-as-a-service (SaaS) platform can be integrated into customer relationship management (CRM) programs such as salesforce.com Oracle and SAP. Marketo's products are designed to serve both small and large businesses. Founded in 2006 the company went public in 2013.

	Annual Growth	12/10	12/11	12/12	12/13	12/14
Sales ($ mil.)	80.8%	14.0	32.4	58.4	95.9	150.0
Net income ($ mil.)	–	(11.8)	(22.6)	(34.4)	(47.4)	(54.3)
Market value ($ mil.)	(11.7%)	–	–	–	1,537.7	1,357.3
Employees	38.5%	–	–	373	519	715

MARKWEST ENERGY PARTNERS L.P.

NYS: MWE

1515 Arapahoe Street, Tower 1, Suite 1600
Denver, CO 80202-2137
Phone: 303 925-9200
Fax: –

CEO: Frank M Semple
CFO: Nancy K Buese
HR: –
FYE: December 31
Type: Public

MarkWest Energy Partners marks its territory as an alpha dog in the US midstream markets. It has oil natural gas natural gas liquids and gathering and processing pipelines as well as storage terminals and fractionation plants. Its Northeast (Appalachia and Michigan) segment includes processing and storing plants and Southwest (Texas and Oklahoma) has port pipeline processing and treating facilities. MarkWest's Liberty segment operates natural gas processing fractionating storage and marketing facilities in the Marcellus Shale play while its Utica segment consists of a joint venture with The Energy & Minerals Group to develop natural gas infrastructure in the Utica Shale play in Ohio.

	Annual Growth	12/09	12/10	12/11	12/12	12/13
Sales ($ mil.)	22.5%	738.3	1,187.6	1,505.4	1,451.8	1,662.4
Net income ($ mil.)	–	(118.7)	0.5	60.7	220.4	38.1
Market value ($ mil.)	22.6%	5,085.1	7,524.2	9,565.6	8,862.0	11,488.8
Employees	21.7%	520	590	683	881	1,139

MARLIN BUSINESS SERVICES CORP

NMS: MRLN

300 Fellowship Road
Mount Laurel, NJ 08054
Phone: 888 479-9111
Fax: –
Web: www.marlincorp.com

CEO: Jeffrey A. Hilzinger
CFO: W. Taylor Kamp
HR: –
FYE: December 31
Type: Public

Marlin is hooked on equipment leasing. Marlin Business Services leases more than 100 categories of commercial equipment to about 68000 small and mid-sized businesses — and it provides the financing for the deals in part through its Marlin Business Bank subsidiary. The market is known in the equipment leasing field as the "small-ticket" segment. Copiers makes up about 30% of Marlin's lease portfolio but its customers also can get products as diverse as computer hardware and software security systems telecom equipment dental implant systems water filtration systems and restaurant equipment. The company primarily operates through its main subsidiary Marlin Leasing.

	Annual Growth	12/14	12/15	12/16	12/17	12/18
Sales ($ mil.)	10.9%	88.8	89.8	100.0	119.1	134.3
Net income ($ mil.)	6.6%	19.4	16.0	17.3	25.3	25.0
Market value ($ mil.)	2.1%	253.9	198.6	258.5	277.0	276.2
Employees	4.6%	285	314	318	330	341

MARQUETTE UNIVERSITY

1250 W WISCONSIN AVE
MILWAUKEE, WI 532332225
Phone: 414-288-7250
Fax: –
Web: www.marquette.edu

CEO: –
CFO: John C Lamb
HR: –
FYE: June 30
Type: Private

A member of the Association of Jesuit Colleges and Universities Marquette University provides undergraduate graduate and professional courses and programs. It specializes in business engineering arts and sciences nursing law dentistry and other fields. The university offers undergraduates some 75 majors and 65 minors and post-graduate students about 50 doctoral and master's degree programs. With an enrollment of more than 11700 students Marquette University boasts a student/faculty ratio of 14:1. Its student population consists of students from all 50 US states and nearly 70 countries. Founded in 1881 the university is named after French missionary explorer Father Jacques Marquette.

	Annual Growth	06/12	06/13	06/15	06/17	06/18
Sales ($ mil.)	3.4%	–	391.2	548.4	434.4	463.4
Net income ($ mil.)	9.2%	–	37.2	48.2	67.0	57.6
Market value ($ mil.)	–	–	–	–	–	–
Employees	–	–	–	–	–	3,000

MARRIOTT INTERNATIONAL, INC.

NMS: MAR

10400 Fernwood Road
Bethesda, MD 20817
Phone: 301 380-3000
Fax: –
Web: www.marriott.com

CEO: Arne M. Sorenson
CFO: Kathleen K. (Leeny) Oberg
HR: David A. Rodriguez
FYE: December 31
Type: Public

Marriott International is one of the world's leading hoteliers. The company operates or franchises some 6900 hotel residential and timeshare properties worldwide. Its hotel portfolio which comprises some 1.3 million guest rooms includes the premium Sheraton and Renaissance Hotels brands and its flagship Marriott Hotels & Resorts as well as the Ritz-Carlton W Hotels The Luxury Collection and St. Regis luxury brands. Additionally the company operates the select-service and extended-stay brands Courtyard and Fairfield Inn. It also manages about 80 golf courses. North America accounts for about 80% of Marriott International's revenue.

	Annual Growth	12/14	12/15	12/16	12/17	12/18
Sales ($ mil.)	10.8%	13,796.0	14,486.0	17,072.0	22,894.0	20,758.0
Net income ($ mil.)	26.2%	753.0	859.0	780.0	1,372.0	1,907.0
Market value ($ mil.)	8.6%	26,460.0	22,733.3	28,036.8	46,026.0	36,812.7
Employees	9.3%	123,500	127,500	226,500	177,000	176,000

MARRIOTT VACATIONS WORLDWIDE CORP.

NYS: VAC

6649 Westwood Blvd.
Orlando, FL 32821
Phone: 407 206-6000
Fax: –
Web: www.marriottvacationsworldwide.com

CEO: Stephen P. (Steve) Weisz
CFO: John E. Geller
HR: Michael E. (Mike) Yonker
FYE: December 31
Type: Public

Sometimes it pays to share. Marriott Vacations Worldwide formerly part of hotel giant Marriott International is one of the world's leading timeshare companies operating more than 100 timeshare resorts. Its properties are in prime vacation destinations in the US (such as California Colorado Florida Hawaii and Nevada) and a handful of other countries (Aruba France Spain St. Thomas the West Indies and Thailand). The villas are jointly owned by about 660000 people who have exclusive use of the properties for limited periods of time. Owners can also trade intervals for time at other Marriott Vacation Club resorts or for other rewards programs. Marriott spun off Marriott Vacations as a separately-traded company in 2011.

	Annual Growth	01/15	01/16*	12/16	12/17	12/18
Sales ($ mil.)	19.6%	1,736.0	1,830.5	1,811.2	1,951.9	2,968.0
Net income ($ mil.)	(12.1%)	81.0	122.8	137.3	226.8	55.0
Market value ($ mil.)	(1.7%)	3,418.6	2,619.3	3,902.5	6,218.7	3,242.9
Employees	32.0%	10,000	10,000	11,000	11,000	23,000

*Fiscal year change

MARRONE BIO INNOVATIONS INC   NAS: MBII

1540 Drew Avenue
Davis, CA 95618
Phone: 530 750-2800
Fax: -
Web: www.marronebioinnovations.com

CEO: Pamela G Marrone
CFO: James B Boyd
HR: -
FYE: December 31
Type: Public

Marrone Bio Innovations makes pesticide a little less poisonous. The company's biopesticides are made from eco-friendly ingredients such as plant extracts bacterium or fungus. Marrone Bio Innovations has three products on the market and three in development awaiting EPA approval. Its pesticide Grandevo contains bacteria that repels plant-eating insects and kills them if ingested. The company's plant extract-based fungicide Regalia is also used as a seed treatment for corn cotton and soybeans and Zequanox kills mussels found in water pipes. Its products are primarily sold to vegetable growers as alternatives to conventional agricultural chemicals. Marrone Bio Innovations went public in 2013.

	Annual Growth	12/14	12/15	12/16	12/17	12/18
Sales ($ mil.)	23.5%	9.1	9.8	14.0	18.2	21.2
Net income ($ mil.)	-	(51.7)	(43.7)	(31.1)	(30.9)	(20.2)
Market value ($ mil.)	(20.1%)	399.6	121.8	236.9	121.8	162.7
Employees	7.1%	86	86	97	103	113

MARS INCORPORATED

6885 Elm St.
McLean VA 22101-3810
Phone: 703-821-4900
Fax: 703-448-9678
Web: www.mars.com

CEO: -
CFO: Claus Aagaard
HR: -
FYE: December 31
Type: Private

Mars knows chocolate sales are nothing to snicker at. It makes such worldwide favorites as M&M's Snickers and the Mars bar. Other confections include 3 Musketeers Dove Milky Way Skittles and Twix. Its products portfolio also boasts Seeds of Change organic food the Klix and Flavia beverage systems Combos and Kudos snacks Uncle Ben's rice and pet food made under the Pedigree Sheba and Whiskas labels. Mars owns the world's largest chewing gum maker Wm. Wrigley Jr. Company as well. The Mars family — including siblings and chairman John Franklyn Mars VP Jacqueline Badger Mars and former CEO Forrest Mars Jr. — owns the highly secretive company making the family one of the wealthiest in the US.

MARSH & MCLENNAN COMPANIES INC.   NYS: MMC

1166 Avenue of the Americas
New York, NY 10036-2774
Phone: 212 345-5000
Fax: 212 345-4809
Web: www.mmc.com

CEO: Julio A. Portalatin
CFO: Mark C. McGivney
HR: Sarah Randall
FYE: December 31
Type: Public

One of the world's largest insurance brokers Marsh & McLennan Companies (MMC) is a heavyweight insurance middleman. Through core subsidiary Marsh the company provides a broad array of insurance-related brokerage consulting and risk management services to clients in more than 130 countries. Customers include large and small companies government entities and not-for-profit organizations. MMC's global reinsurance brokerage business is handled by subsidiary Guy Carpenter. The company also owns Mercer which provides human resources and financial consulting services to customers in about 45 nations worldwide; and Oliver Wyman which provides management consulting services.

	Annual Growth	12/14	12/15	12/16	12/17	12/18
Sales ($ mil.)	3.7%	12,951.0	12,893.0	13,211.0	14,024.0	14,950.0
Net income ($ mil.)	3.0%	1,465.0	1,599.0	1,768.0	1,492.0	1,650.0
Market value ($ mil.)	8.6%	28,839.6	27,937.8	34,054.4	41,007.3	40,181.0
Employees	3.3%	57,000	60,000	60,000	65,000	65,000

MARSH SUPERMARKETS INC.

9800 Crosspoint Blvd.
Indianapolis IN 46256
Phone: 317-594-2100
Fax: 715-926-5609
Web: www.marten.com

CEO: Frank Lazaran
CFO: Robert J Riesbeck
HR: -
FYE: March 31
Type: Private

Marsh Supermarkets is no backwater grocery chain. A leading retailer in Indianapolis (behind Kroger and Wal-Mart) Marsh operates about 95 supermarkets under the Marsh Supermarkets O'Malia's Food Markets and Main Street Markets banners in Indiana and Ohio. About 40% of the stores have pharmacy departments. Its floral business — Marsh Floral Fashions — operates floral and gift departments inside Marsh stores. Marsh abandoned self-distribution in 2011 and turned over the supply of all of its stores to C&S Wholesale Grocers. Founded in 1931 by the late Ermal Marsh the regional supermarket operator is owned by private equity firm Sun Capital Partners.

MARSH USA INC.

1166 Avenue of the Americas
New York NY 10036-2774
Phone: 212-345-6000
Fax: 212-345-4808
Web: www.marsh.com

CEO: Peter Zaffino
CFO: -
HR: -
FYE: December 31
Type: Subsidiary

Marsh is the flagship operation of Marsh & McLennan Companies (MMC) one of the world's largest insurance brokerages. The company brokers insurance and provides risk management and consulting services to corporate clients government agencies and other organizations big and small. Marsh has some 25000 agents and hundreds of brokerage locations in more than 100 countries. Marsh also provides risk financing insurance program design and underwriting management as well as claims administration and technological support services. MMC affiliate Guy Carpenter provides similar brokerage and risk management services to reinsurance companies; other MMC companies include consulting firms Mercer and Oliver Wyman.

MARSHALL UNIVERSITY

1 JOHN MARSHALL DR
HUNTINGTON, WV 257550003
Phone: 304-696-2385
Fax: -
Web: www.marshall.edu

CEO: -
CFO: -
HR: -
FYE: June 30
Type: Private

If "You Are Marshall" you know that Marshall University is a state-supported nonprofit educational institution serving about 14000 students including 3500 graduate and medical students. The university offers about 55 baccalaureate and more than 50 graduate programs through more than a dozen colleges and schools. It also offers two Associate Programs two Ed.S four Doctoral Degree Programs and three First Professional programs. Marshall students attend classes either at the university's main campus in Huntington West Virginia; at its regional campuses; or online.

	Annual Growth	06/12	06/13	06/16	06/17	06/18
Sales ($ mil.)	1.9%	-	175.8	189.6	192.5	192.9
Net income ($ mil.)	(27.8%)	-	26.2	(2.1)	7.4	5.1
Market value ($ mil.)	-	-	-	-	-	-
Employees	-	-	-	-	-	1,632

MARSHFIELD CLINIC HEALTH SYSTEM, INC.

1000 N OAK AVE
MARSHFIELD, WI 544495702
Phone: 715-387-5511
Fax: –
Web: www.marshfieldclinic.org

CEO: Susan L. Turney
CFO: Gordon T. Edwards
HR: Tami Friedrichsen
FYE: September 30
Type: Private

Marshfield Clinic Health System (MCHS) is a private group medical practice that operates more than 50 medical locations across Wisconsin. The network provides primary secondary and tertiary care through its more than 700 physicians who represent about 80 medical specialties. Through three hospitals — Marshfield Medical Center Flambeau Hospital and Lakeview Medical Center — and dozens of clinics MCHS annually serves hundreds of thousands of patients and handles millions of patient encounters. Other parts of the network include Marshfield Labs and Security Health Plan of Wisconsin as well as medical education and research organizations.

	Annual Growth	09/12	09/13	09/14	09/15	09/18
Sales ($ mil.)	1820.8%	–	–	–	0.3	2,430.7
Net income ($ mil.)	–	–	–	–	(3.1)	(3.9)
Market value ($ mil.)	–	–	–	–	–	–
Employees	–	–	–	–	–	363

MARTEN TRANSPORT LTD
NMS: MRTN

129 Marten Street
Mondovi, WI 54755
Phone: 715 926-4216
Fax: –
Web: www.marten.com

CEO: Randolph L. (Randy) Marten
CFO: James J. (Jim) Hinnendael
HR: Susan Detz
FYE: December 31
Type: Public

America's Dairyland-based Marten Transport hauls a lot more than cheese. The Wisconsin-based long-haul truckload carrier uses refrigerated and insulated trailers to convey a variety of food products and other temperature-sensitive materials; it also hauls dry freight. Marten Transport operates in 14 terminals throughout the US and also operates in Canada and Mexico; its average haul is about 600 miles. The company's fleet includes about 2420 tractors and 4265 trailers. In addition to freight transportation the company provides logistics services. In 2014 Marten Transport's largest customers were Wal-Mart and supply chain services provider Armada.

	Annual Growth	12/14	12/15	12/16	12/17	12/18
Sales ($ mil.)	4.0%	672.9	665.0	671.1	698.1	787.6
Net income ($ mil.)	16.5%	29.8	35.7	33.5	90.3	55.0
Market value ($ mil.)	(7.2%)	1,190.6	964.1	1,269.1	1,105.7	881.8
Employees	2.2%	3,292	3,577	3,622	3,492	3,589

MARTHA STEWART LIVING OMNIMEDIA, INC.
NYS: MSO

601 West 26th Street
New York, NY 10001
Phone: 212 827-8000
Fax: –
Web: www.marthastewart.com

CEO: Daniel W Dienst
CFO: Kenneth P West
HR: –
FYE: December 31
Type: Public

Martha Stewart Living Omnimedia (MSLO) seems to prove the old adage that all publicity is good publicity. Legendary lifestyle maven Martha Stewart and her company MSLO have embraced the media spotlight including Stewart's much ballyhooed sentence on federal criminal charges related to insider trading of stock. The domestic guru has her fingers in many revenue-generating pies that center around three business segments: publishing (magazines books websites) broadcasting (TV programs satellite radio) and merchandising. The majority of MSLO's business comes from publishing activities which are driven by its flagship magazine Martha Stewart Living.

	Annual Growth	12/09	12/10	12/11	12/12	12/13
Sales ($ mil.)	(10.0%)	244.8	230.8	221.4	197.6	160.7
Net income ($ mil.)	–	(14.6)	(9.6)	(15.5)	(56.1)	(1.8)
Market value ($ mil.)	(4.0%)	279.8	250.3	249.2	138.7	237.8
Employees	(10.1%)	620	615	582	497	405

MARTIN & BAYLEY, INC.

1311A W MAIN ST
CARMI, IL 628211389
Phone: 618-382-2334
Fax: –
Web: www.rovertown.com

CEO: –
CFO: Tom Logan
HR: Sheri Stevens
FYE: March 27
Type: Private

Martin & Bayley (dba Huck's Food and Fuel) operates 115 Huck's convenience stores and a number travel centers in mostly in Illinois and Indiana but also in Missouri Kentucky and Tennessee. Half of its outlets are in Illinois. The company operates a commissary at its warehouse in Carmi Illinois to supply sandwiches chicken and other food items to its stores. Some stores sell Godfather's Pizza. Family-owned since its inception Martin & Bayley became a 100% employee-owned firm when the Martin and Bayley families sold their stakes in the company.

	Annual Growth	03/08	03/09	03/10	03/11	03/18
Sales ($ mil.)	–	–	(1,579.4)	466.2	528.9	523.3
Net income ($ mil.)	193.4%	–	0.0	5.3	7.5	8.2
Market value ($ mil.)	–	–	–	–	–	–
Employees	–	–	–	–	–	1,500

MARTIN MIDSTREAM PARTNERS LP
NMS: MMLP

4200 Stone Road
Kilgore, TX 75662
Phone: 903 983-6200
Fax: –
Web: www.martinmidstream.com

CEO: Ruben S Martin
CFO: Robert D Bondurant
HR: –
FYE: December 31
Type: Public

Martin Midstream Partners moves petroleum products. The company gets most of its sales from the distribution of natural gas liquids (NGLs). Its NGL customers include retail propane distributors industrial processors and refiners. Martin Midstream owns more than 720 miles of natural gas gathering and transmission pipelines. Martin Midstream also manufactures sulfur and sulfur-based fertilizer products and provides marine transportation (through a fleet of more than 50 inland barges and push boats and four offshore tug barges) and the storage of liquid hydrocarbons (at about 50 terminals). The company an affiliate of Martin Resource Management operates primarily in the Gulf Coast region of the US.

	Annual Growth	12/14	12/15	12/16	12/17	12/18
Sales ($ mil.)	(12.3%)	1,642.1	1,036.8	827.4	946.1	972.7
Net income ($ mil.)	–	(11.7)	38.4	31.7	17.1	44.1
Market value ($ mil.)	(21.4%)	1,049.2	847.0	716.2	546.5	401.3
Employees	–	–	–	–	–	–

MARTIN RESOURCE MANAGEMENT CORPORATION

4200 STONE RD
KILGORE, TX 756626935
Phone: 903-983-6200
Fax: –

CEO: –
CFO: Bob Bondurant
HR: Melanie Mathews
FYE: December 31
Type: Private

Martin Resource Management likes to push around petroleum products. The employee-owned company's flagship affiliate Martin Midstream Partners offers transportation storage marketing and logistics management services for petroleum products including sulfur sulfur derivatives fuel oil liquefied petroleum gas asphalt and other bulk tank liquids primarily in the southern US. Martin Resource also manufactures and markets fertilizer and other processed sulfur products. Through its Martin Energy Services unit the company offers inland marine fuel supply and offshore support services. Other units include The Brimrock Group (sulfur) Cross Oil Refining & Marketing and Martin Asphalt.

	Annual Growth	12/07	12/08	12/09	12/11	12/15
Sales ($ mil.)	(2.1%)	–	2,903.0	1,537.6	2,985.1	2,493.9
Net income ($ mil.)	24.9%	–	5.8	23.2	37.7	27.3
Market value ($ mil.)	–	–	–	–	–	–
Employees	–	–	–	–	–	2,300

MARUBENI AMERICA CORPORATION

375 Lexington Ave.
New York NY 10017
Phone: 212-450-0100
Fax: 212-450-0700
Web: www.marubeni-usa.com

CEO: Hajime Kawamura
CFO: -
HR: Jen Grillo
FYE: December 31
Type: Subsidiary

For Marubeni America Corporation the trick of the trade is the trade. Marubeni America (MAC) is the primary US subsidiary of Japan-based manufacturing and trading company Marubeni; it acts as an independent trader an importer/exporter brokering deals for agricultural goods commodities consumer and energy products and natural resources. The company which was established in 1951 provides related services such as engineering financing insurance leasing marketing logistics and sales. Marubeni America has offices across the US Canada and Mexico. It also distributes crop protection chemicals through subsidiary Helena Chemical and exports wheat and barley through Columbia Grain.

MARVIN ENGINEERING CO., INC.

261 W BEACH AVE
INGLEWOOD, CA 903022904
Phone: 310-674-5030
Fax: -
Web: www.marvingroup.com

CEO: Gerald M Friedman
CFO: Leon Tsimmerman
HR: -
FYE: January 31
Type: Private

Marvin Engineering helps missiles get from Point A to Point B. The company manufactures missile launchers ejector racks test equipment and other hardware for military customers and companies in the aerospace and defense industries. Customers include branches of the US military and major US defense contractors as well as the governments of Australia Canada and Israel. Marvin Engineering is part of the Marvin Group which also includes Aerospace Dynamics International Flyer Defense Marvin Land Systems Geotest-Marvin Test Systems and Clean Water Technologies.

	Annual Growth	01/05	01/06	01/07	01/08	01/09
Sales ($ mil.)	8.0%	-	-	114.9	105.7	133.8
Net income ($ mil.)		-	-	22.8	0.6	(3.4)
Market value ($ mil.)		-	-	-	-	-
Employees		-	-	-	-	700

MARY KAY HOLDING CORPORATION

16251 Dallas Pkwy.
Addison TX 75001-6801
Phone: 972-687-6300
Fax: 972-687-1642
Web: www.marykay.com

CEO: David B Holl
CFO: Terry Smith
HR: -
FYE: December 31
Type: Holding Company

Mary Kay has been measuring its success by being in the pink rather than being in the red. Mary Kay Holding Corporation is a holding company for cosmetics direct-seller Mary Kay which makes and markets cosmetics women's and men's fragrances skin care and personal care products. It sells some 200 items through an independent sales force of more than 2 million consultants in some 35 global markets. The firm's products portfolio spans half a dozen categories such as body care color cosmetics facial skin care fragrance nail care and sun protection. Brand names include TimeWise Velocity Tribute Journey MKMen Stain Lips Indulge and others. The company was founded in Dallas by Mary Kay Ash in 1963.

MARY KAY INC.

16251 Dallas Pkwy.
Addison TX 75001
Phone: 972-687-6300
Fax: 972-687-1611
Web: www.marykay.com

CEO: David Holl
CFO: -
HR: -
FYE: December 31
Type: Private

Celebrating more than 40 years in business Mary Kay is in the pink as one of the top direct sellers of beauty products in the US. It offers more than 200 products in six categories: body care color cosmetics facial skin care fragrance nail care and sun protection. Some 2.4 million independent sales consultants demonstrate Mary Kay products in the US and about 35 other countries; the company also sells products through its website. Consultants vie for awards each year that range from jewelry to its trademark pink Cadillac (first awarded in 1969). The Mary Kay Ash Charitable Foundation funds cancer research and domestic violence programs. The family of founder Mary Kay Ash owns most of the company.

MARY WASHINGTON HEALTHCARE

2300 FALL HILL AVE # 418
FREDERICKSBURG, VA 224013343
Phone: 540-741-2507
Fax: -

CEO: Michael P McDermott
CFO: Sean T Barden
HR: -
FYE: March 31
Type: Private

Health care is Mary Washington Healthcare's realm in the Old Dominion State. The medical provider offers a comprehensive range of health services to residents of Fredericksburg and surrounding communities in central Virginia through its not-for-profit regional system of two hospitals and 28 healthcare facilities. The hub of this system is Mary Washington Hospital a 437-bed acute care medical center that provides services including emergency/trauma care and surgical procedures. The health system also includes outpatient care programs and facilities providing primary care and specialty care services for women seniors and children.

	Annual Growth	12/15	12/16	12/17	12/18*	03/19
Sales ($ mil.)	(33.6%)	-	610.2	635.0	673.4	178.5
Net income ($ mil.)	(12.9%)	-	43.5	53.2	(9.8)	28.8
Market value ($ mil.)		-	-	-	-	-
Employees		-	-	-	-	4,000

*Fiscal year change

MARYLAND AND VIRGINIA MILK PRODUCERS COOPERATIVE ASSOCIATION, INCORPORATED

1985 ISAAC NEWTON SQ W # 200
RESTON, VA 201905031
Phone: 703-742-6800
Fax: -
Web: www.mdvamilk.com

CEO: -
CFO: Jorge Gonzalez
HR: -
FYE: December 31
Type: Private

Milk is "Mar-VA-lous" for the members of the Maryland & Virginia Milk Producers Cooperative Association. Known as Maryland & Virginia the co-op processes and sells milk for nearly 1500 member/farmers with dairy herds in the southeastern US and mid-Atlantic region. Maryland & Virginia produces fluid milk ice cream and cultured dairy products for retail sale under the Marva Maid Maola and Valley Milk brands. Its butter condensed milk and milk-powder products are sold primarily to food manufacturers. As a co-op it also offers agricultural supplies to its members. Maryland & Virginia operates three fluid-milk processing plants a manufacturing plant and an equipment-supply warehouse.

	Annual Growth	12/08	12/09	12/10	12/11	12/12
Sales ($ mil.)	3.1%	-	-	1,219.2	1,362.5	1,296.4
Net income ($ mil.)	(20.4%)	-	-	8.7	(2.8)	5.5
Market value ($ mil.)		-	-	-	-	-
Employees		-	-	-	-	550

MARYLAND DEPARTMENT OF TRANSPORTATION

7201 CORPORATE CENTER DR — CEO: –
HANOVER, MD 210761415 — CFO: –
Phone: 410-865-1037 — HR: –
Fax: – — FYE: June 30
Type: Private

Traveling in Maryland? You can thank (or curse) the Maryland Department of Transportation (MDOT). MDOT is responsible for building operating and maintaining a safe and seamless transportation network that includes highway transit maritime and aviation facilities. The Department of Transportation is organized along various administrative groups including the Maryland Motor Vehicle Administration Transit Administration Port Administration Aviation Administration and Highway Administration. MDOT annual budget of about $1.5 billion is funded through the state's Transportation Trust Fund and federal aid.

	Annual Growth	06/13	06/14	06/16	06/17	06/18
Sales ($ mil.)	3.2%	–	3,890.8	4,170.7	4,491.0	4,407.9
Net income ($ mil.)	–	–	58.7	(232.8)	85.1	(189.5)
Market value ($ mil.)	–	–	–	–	–	–
Employees	–	–	–	–	–	1,000

MARYLAND SOUTHERN ELECTRIC COOPERATIVE INC

15035 BURNT STORE RD — CEO: –
HUGHESVILLE, MD 206372699 — CFO: Sonja M Cox
Phone: 301-274-3111 — HR: –
Fax: – — FYE: December 31
Web: www.smeco.coop — Type: Private

Historic Southern Maryland gets it power via the South Maryland Electric Cooperative (SMECO) which distributes electricity to about 154000 residential commercial and industrial customers in four counties via about 11360 miles of power line and 54 electric substations. One of the ten largest electric cooperatives in the US the member-owned enterprise gets its wholesale power supply through its membership in wholesale energy trading and risk management service company ACES Power Marketing. Overseen by a board of directors SMECO's single mission is to provide reliable competitively priced energy and related services to its members.

	Annual Growth	12/08	12/09	12/10	12/14	12/15
Sales ($ mil.)	(0.4%)	–	462.7	492.7	490.1	451.7
Net income ($ mil.)	5.6%	–	3.2	17.1	1.5	4.5
Market value ($ mil.)	–	–	–	–	–	–
Employees	–	–	–	–	–	375

MARYMOUNT MANHATTAN COLLEGE

221 E 71ST ST — CEO: –
NEW YORK, NY 100214532 — CFO: –
Phone: 212-517-0400 — HR: –
Fax: – — FYE: June 30
Web: www.mmm.edu — Type: Private

Marymount Manhattan College is a four-year undergraduate liberal arts college in the middle of New York City with an enrollment of more than 2000 students. Marymount Manhattan offers 17 major programs of study in fields including media technology and performing arts. The college has a student-to-teacher ratio of 12:1. It was originally was founded in 1936 by the Religious of the Sacred Heart of Mary in Tarrytown New York; it was independently chartered in 1961 as Marymount Manhattan College.

	Annual Growth	06/09	06/10	06/13	06/14	06/15
Sales ($ mil.)	6.2%	–	49.3	60.7	59.3	66.5
Net income ($ mil.)	16.9%	–	0.9	1.3	0.1	2.0
Market value ($ mil.)	–	–	–	–	–	–
Employees	–	–	–	–	–	630

MASCO CORP. — NYS: MAS

17450 College Parkway — CEO: Keith J. Allman
Livonia, MI 48152 — CFO: John G. Sznewajs
Phone: 313 274-7400 — HR: –
Fax: – — FYE: December 31
Web: www.masco.com — Type: Public

Masco Corporation doesn't mask its penchant for indoor style. It is a global leader in the design manufacturing and distribution of home improvement and building products. Well-known brands include Delta and Peerless (plumbing) KraftMaid (cabinetry) Behr (paints and stains) and Milgard (windows). It boasts a vast portfolio of diversified products ranging from storage containers to patio doors but its plumbing products account for half of all sales. Although most of its sales are within the US Masco has a major presence in the UK mainland Europe and China.

	Annual Growth	12/14	12/15	12/16	12/17	12/18
Sales ($ mil.)	(0.5%)	8,521.0	7,142.0	7,357.0	7,644.0	8,359.0
Net income ($ mil.)	(3.8%)	856.0	355.0	491.0	533.0	734.0
Market value ($ mil.)	3.8%	7,406.3	8,317.4	9,293.1	12,914.0	8,593.6
Employees	(5.1%)	32,000	25,000	26,000	26,000	26,000

MASCOMA CORPORATION

67 Etna Rd. Ste. 300 — CEO: –
Lebanon NH 03766 — CFO: –
Phone: 603-676-3320 — HR: –
Fax: 603-676-3321 — FYE: December 31
Web: www.mascoma.com — Type: Private

One man's trash is another man's brilliant idea. Mascoma Corporation's plan is to make a chemical used in cellulosic ethanol a renewable fuel made from the waste products of plants such as wood and agricultural by-products. The company invented genetically-modified yeasts and bacteria that aid in the fermentation of feedstocks and help turn it into biofuel and other chemicals. So far it has only produced test batches of its Mascoma Grain Technology (MGT) but Mascoma plans to begin selling it commercially to corn ethanol producers in 2012 as a less expensive alternative to other enzymes. The company filed a $100 million initial public offering in September 2011.

MASERGY COMMUNICATIONS INC.

2740 N. Dallas Pkwy. Ste. 260 — CEO: James Parker
Plano TX 75093-4834 — CFO: Rob Bodnar
Phone: 214-442-5700 — HR: –
Fax: 214-442-5756 — FYE: June 30
Web: www.masergy.com — Type: Private

Masergy Communications helps businesses manage vital communications. The company offers managed network and cloud communications services for clients in the financial health care entertainment broadcasting and manufacturing industries among others. Providing voice data and video network services and support across the globe its areas of expertise include Ethernet-based virtual private networks (VPNs) and wide area network (WANs). Masergy's cloud services include global cloud communications network and application management and hosted remote access. Its managed services focus on security and disaster recovery. The company is owned by private equity firm ABRY Partners.

MASIMO CORP.

NMS: MASI

52 Discovery
Irvine, CA 92618
Phone: 949 297-7000
Fax: –
Web: www.masimo.com

CEO: Joe E. Kiani
CFO: Mark P. de Raad
HR: Tracy Miller
FYE: December 29
Type: Public

As important as the blood running through your veins is the oxygen it carries. Masimo knows that and makes tools that monitor arterial blood-oxygen saturation levels and pulse rates in patients. The company's product range which is based on Signal Extraction Technology (SET) offers pulse oximeters in both handheld and stand-alone (bedside) form. Product benefits include the provision of real-time information and elimination of signal interference such as patient movements. In addition to general product sales Masimo licenses SET-based products to dozens of medical equipment manufacturers including Philips Atom Mindray North America GE Medical Medtronic Spacelabs and Zoll.

	Annual Growth	01/15	01/16*	12/16	12/17	12/18
Sales ($ mil.)	13.5%	586.6	630.1	694.6	798.1	858.3
Net income ($ mil.)	38.7%	72.5	83.3	300.7	131.6	193.5
Market value ($ mil.)	59.8%	1,373.8	2,203.6	3,577.9	4,501.6	5,603.7
Employees	7.7%	3,600	3,700	4,293	4,600	4,500

*Fiscal year change

MASSACHUSETTS HIGHER EDUCATION ASSISTANCE CORPORATION

33 ARCH ST STE 2100
BOSTON, MA 021101442
Phone: 617-728-4507
Fax: –
Web: www.asa.org

CEO: Paul Combe
CFO: Michael F Finn
HR: –
FYE: June 30
Type: Private

Don't know how you're going to pay for college? You might want to consult ASA ASAP. The Massachusetts Higher Education Assistance Corporation which does business as American Student Assistance (ASA) is a non-profit student loan collection agency that helps students understand finance and repay their higher education loans to prevent student loan default. Its SALT program boosts collection rates by offering students a variety of online tools to help them learn repayment options through blogs and videos track payment progress and find scholarships and careers/internships. Founded in 1956 ASA partners with 300-plus higher education institutions nonprofits and corporations nationwide serving over one million borrowers.

	Annual Growth	06/12	06/13	06/14	06/15	06/17
Assets ($ mil.)	11.8%	–	375.5	438.2	471.2	586.6
Net income ($ mil.)	(26.9%)	–	48.6	96.4	37.8	13.9
Market value ($ mil.)	–	–	–	–	–	–
Employees	–	–	–	–	–	580

MASSACHUSETTS INSTITUTE OF TECHNOLOGY

77 MASSACHUSETTS AVE
CAMBRIDGE, MA 021394307
Phone: 617-253-1000
Fax: –
Web: www.www-math.mit.edu

CEO: –
CFO: –
HR: Meg Regan
FYE: June 30
Type: Private

Massachusetts Institute of Technology (MIT) takes the prize for breeding ingenuity. A leading research institution the school is typically granted more patents annually than any other university and about 90 people associated with MIT are Nobel Prize recipients. Blending that science and engineering acumen with top business programs (including the Sloan School of Management) MIT graduates have started more than 30000 active companies. MIT has more than 11000 students more than 60% of whom attend graduate school. The faculty of the nearly three dozen academic departments includes more than 1000 professors. The school's student teacher ratio is 3:1 (undergraduates). Founded in 1865 MIT is privately endowed.

	Annual Growth	06/08	06/09	06/10	06/17	06/18
Sales ($ mil.)	9.2%	–	1,647.7	2,727.1	3,551.8	3,626.6
Net income ($ mil.)	–	–	0.0	(199.8)	2,196.0	2,391.7
Market value ($ mil.)	–	–	–	–	–	–
Employees	–	–	–	–	–	12,000

MASSACHUSETTS MEDICAL SOCIETY INC

860 WINTER ST
WALTHAM, MA 024511411
Phone: 781-893-4610
Fax: –
Web: www.massmed.org

CEO: –
CFO: –
HR: –
FYE: May 31
Type: Private

The Massachusetts Medical Society (MMS) is a professional organization of physicians and medical students with more than 24000 members. The organization an advocate for patients and physicians promotes a code of ethics for medical professions as well as the training research and continuing education of physicians and other health care professionals. It also helps to develop health care policy and publishes the New England Journal of Medicine a leading medical journal. The Massachusetts Medical Society was founded in 1781 and is the oldest continuously operating medical society in the nation.

	Annual Growth	05/09	05/10	05/11	05/13	05/16
Sales ($ mil.)	2.6%	–	–	118.9	118.5	135.2
Net income ($ mil.)	(8.8%)	–	–	19.6	12.2	12.4
Market value ($ mil.)	–	–	–	–	–	–
Employees	–	–	–	–	–	700

MASSACHUSETTS MUNICIPAL WHOLESALE ELECTRIC COMPANY

327 MOODY ST
LUDLOW, MA 010561246
Phone: 413-589-0141
Fax: –
Web: www.mmwec.org

CEO: Ronald Decurzio
CFO: –
HR: Peggy Bushey
FYE: December 31
Type: Private

A massive power resource Massachusetts Municipal Wholesale Electric Company (MMWEC) provides power supply services to its members — 23 of the state's 40 municipal utilities (28 utilities are also participants in MMWEC power supply projects). The power supplier has about 715 MW of generating capacity from interests in fossil-fueled and nuclear power plants in the northeastern US and it negotiates bulk electricity purchases from other generators for its members. MMWEC is the operator and principal owner of the Stony Brook Energy Center a 520 MW combined-cycle intermediate and peaking generating station in Ludlow Massachusetts.

	Annual Growth	12/03	12/04	12/06	12/07	12/18
Sales ($ mil.)	(0.5%)	–	283.7	354.5	362.0	264.6
Net income ($ mil.)	–	–	55.5	195.8	0.0	0.0
Market value ($ mil.)	–	–	–	–	–	–
Employees	–	–	–	–	–	70

MASSACHUSETTS MUTUAL LIFE INSURANCE COMPANY

1295 State St.
Springfield MA 01111-0001
Phone: 413-744-1000
Fax: 413-744-6005
Web: www.massmutual.com

CEO: Roger W Crandall
CFO: Michael Rollings
HR: –
FYE: December 31
Type: Private - Mutual Com

Massachusetts Mutual Life Insurance known affectionately as MassMutual brings a multitude of financial services to its membership base. A leading US mutual life insurer the firm provides life policies annuities money management and retirement planning to individuals and businesses in the US and abroad. Founded in 1851 MassMutual also offers disability income insurance long-term care insurance structured settlement annuities and trust services. Its subsidiaries include OppenheimerFunds (mutual funds) Baring Asset Management (international investment) and Babson Capital Management (investor services) with its Cornerstone Real Estate Advisors (real estate investment management) subsidiary.

MASSACHUSETTS PORT AUTHORITY

1 HARBORSIDE DR STE 200S
BOSTON, MA 021282905
Phone: 617-561-1600
Fax: –
Web: www.massport.com

CEO: Thomas P Glynn
CFO: John Pranckevicius
HR: –
FYE: June 30
Type: Private

Massachusetts Port Authority (Massport) operates three airports: Boston Logan International Hanscom Field and Worcester Regional. Logan is home to 50 airlines and is New England's largest airport and the first port of call for many international flights entering the US. (It accounts for the majority of Massport's revenues.) Hanscom Field operates as the region's main aviation airport and offers niche commercial services while Worcester Regional primarily supports commercial flight services. Massport also oversees various waterfront properties of the Port of Boston. The agency was created by the Commonwealth of Massachusetts in 1956. The governor of Massachusetts appoints the agency's board members.

	Annual Growth	06/12	06/13	06/14	06/15	06/16
Sales ($ mil.)	5.5%	–	–	–	662.9	699.5
Net income ($ mil.)	(2.0%)	–	–	–	107.4	105.3
Market value ($ mil.)	–	–	–	–	–	–
Employees	–	–	–	–	–	1,102

MAST INDUSTRIES INC.

2 Limited Pkwy.
Columbus OH 43230
Phone: 614-337-5600
Fax: 614-337-5080
Web: www.mast.com

CEO: Leslie H Wexner
CFO: –
HR: –
FYE: January 31
Type: Subsidiary

MAST makes clothes so its customers don't have to. MAST Industries (doing business as Mast Global Fashions) is one of the world's largest contract manufacturers importers and distributors of apparel including sportswear for hot brands such as Abercrombie & Fitch. Once a wholly owned subsidiary of Limited Brands a 51% stake in Mast was sold to private equity firm Sycamore Parters in November 2011 to establish it as a standalone company. Limited will continue to own Mast's separate sourcing operation for its Victoria's Secret La Senza and Bath & Body Works brands. Mast has manufacturing operations and joint ventures in more than a dozen countries including China Israel Mexico and Sri Lanka.

MASTEC INC. (FL)

800 S. Douglas Road, 12th Floor
Coral Gables, FL 33134
Phone: 305 599-1800
Fax: –
Web: www.mastec.com

NYS: MTZ
CEO: Jos © R. Mas
CFO: George L. Pita
HR: –
FYE: December 31
Type: Public

MasTec goes the last mile ? and the first mile and the miles in between ? to bring communications and energy to homes offices factories and other places. The company digs the trenches lays the cable and builds the towers that power communications and provide cell service and high-speed internet. The contractor plans and builds pipelines that transport natural gas and oil from wells to processing plants. It provides infrastructure construction to telecom vendors wireless providers cable TV operators and energy and utility companies. MasTec also builds electrical utility transmission and distribution and power generation wind and solar farms industrial infrastructure and water and sewer systems.

	Annual Growth	12/14	12/15	12/16	12/17	12/18
Sales ($ mil.)	10.6%	4,611.8	4,208.3	5,134.7	6,607.0	6,909.4
Net income ($ mil.)	22.3%	115.9	(79.1)	131.3	347.2	259.7
Market value ($ mil.)	15.7%	1,718.3	1,320.8	2,906.9	3,720.1	3,082.4
Employees	5.1%	15,550	15,900	15,400	17,300	19,000

MASTECH DIGITAL INC

1305 Cherrington Parkway, Building 210, Suite 400
Moon Township, PA 15108
Phone: 412 787-2100
Fax: –
Web: www.mastechdigital.com

ASE: MHH
CEO: –
CFO: John J Cronin Jr
HR: Vishwanath Shetty
FYE: December 31
Type: Public

Mastech provides outsourced staffing services primarily for businesses in need of contract information technology (IT) personnel. The company provides systems integrators and other IT staffing companies with temporary technical staff on a wholesale basis. It also serves companies in other industries directly. The company mainly serves customers in the US but it has international recruiting operations in India. Apart from finance clients come from such industries as consumer products health care retail technology and telecom. Formerly a subsidiary of IGATE Corporation Mastech was spun off to its parent company's shareholders in 2008.

	Annual Growth	12/14	12/15	12/16	12/17	12/18
Sales ($ mil.)	11.8%	113.5	123.5	132.0	147.9	177.2
Net income ($ mil.)	18.2%	3.4	2.8	2.5	1.6	6.7
Market value ($ mil.)	(12.2%)	116.7	80.4	74.9	110.6	69.3
Employees	16.9%	900	970	1,125	1,530	1,680

MASTERCARD INC

2000 Purchase Street
Purchase, NY 10577
Phone: 914 249-2000
Fax: –
Web: www.mastercard.com

NYS: MA
CEO: Ajaypal S. (Ajay) Banga
CFO: Martina Hund-Mejean
HR: Gs Ahluwalia
FYE: December 31
Type: Public

Surpassing Visa in market share — now that would be priceless. Serving financial institutions around the world Mastercard is the second largest payment system in the US. The company does not issue credit or its namesake cards; rather it markets the Mastercard Maestro and Cirrus brands provides a transaction authorization network and collects fees from members. The company provides its services in more than 210 countries and territories more than 150 currencies and its branded cards are accepted at millions of locations globally.

	Annual Growth	12/14	12/15	12/16	12/17	12/18
Sales ($ mil.)	12.1%	9,473.0	9,667.0	10,776.0	12,497.0	14,950.0
Net income ($ mil.)	12.8%	3,617.0	3,808.0	4,059.0	3,915.0	5,859.0
Market value ($ mil.)	21.6%	88,831.0	100,378.2	106,450.8	156,052.2	194,498.2
Employees	9.5%	10,300	11,300	11,900	13,400	14,800

MATADOR RESOURCES COMPANY

1 Lincoln Centre 5400 LBJ Freeway Ste. 1500
Dallas TX 75240
Phone: 972-371-5200
Fax: 972-371-5201
Web: www.matadorresources.com

NYSE: MTDR
CEO: –
CFO: –
HR: –
FYE: December 31
Type: Public

This Matador may be thriving in a bullish oil market but the company itself is more phoenix than bull. Matador Resources was founded by the former executives of Matador Petroleum which was bought by Tom Brown in 2003. Matador Resources focuses on natural gas exploration and production across about 75000 acres in South Texas Northwest Louisiana and East Texas and in the Permian Basin of West Texas and Southeast New Mexico. It reports estimated proved reserves of 154.8 billion cu. ft. of gas and an average daily production of 23.6 million cu. ft. per day. Matador Resources also has rights to another 135000 undeveloped acres in Idaho Utah and Wyoming. In 2011 the company filed an IPO seeking $150 million.

MATANUSKA TELEPHONE ASSOCIATION INCORPORATED

1740 S CHUGACH ST
PALMER, AK 996456796
Phone: 907-745-3211
Fax: –
Web: www.mtasolutions.com

CEO: –
CFO: Wanda Tankersley
HR: Matt Langhoff
FYE: December 31
Type: Private

One of the the largest telephone cooperatives in the largest state the Matanuska Telephone Association better known as MTA offers telecommunications services to the residents of south-central Alaska. Established in 1953 the co-op provides local and long-distance voice service and cell phone service (MTA Wireless) Internet access and digital cable television. It also offers telecommunications systems (provided by third-party companies such as Avaya) as well as Internet and wireless plans to businesses.

	Annual Growth	12/09	12/10	12/11	12/12	12/13
Sales ($ mil.)	(3.2%)	–	64.0	98.9	57.6	58.0
Net income ($ mil.)	–	–	–	3.7	5.0	(0.6)
Market value ($ mil.)	–	–	–	–	–	–
Employees	–	–	–	–	–	300

MATERIAL SCIENCES CORP.   NAS: MASC

2200 East Pratt Boulevard
Elk Grove Village, IL 60007
Phone: 847 439-2210
Fax: 847 439-0737
Web: www.matsci.com

CEO: Patrick Murley
CFO: James Todd
HR: –
FYE: February 28
Type: Public

Material Sciences Corporation known as MSC makes engineered materials as well as coated steel and electro-galvanized steel products. MSC has two primary product segments: acoustical (anti-noise and vibration products including the trademarked Quiet Steel reduced vibration metal) and coated (decorative and protective metal coatings). The company's products are used by the appliance automotive building systems computer construction furniture HVAC lighting and telecommunications industries. Automobile manufacturers are among the company's largest clients. MSC gets most of its sales in the US.

	Annual Growth	02/09	02/10	02/11	02/12	02/13
Sales ($ mil.)	(10.3%)	187.0	137.8	137.6	136.7	121.0
Net income ($ mil.)	–	(33.1)	(11.6)	12.0	28.5	9.0
Market value ($ mil.)	78.0%	10.3	19.5	74.7	88.3	103.5
Employees	(8.0%)	372	339	264	269	267

MATERION ADVANCED MATERIALS TECHNOLOGIES AND SERVICES INC

2978 Main St.
Buffalo NY 14214
Phone: 716-837-1000
Fax: 858-578-2344
Web: www.tsystemsinternational.com

CEO: –
CFO: –
HR: –
FYE: December 31
Type: Subsidiary

Materion Advanced Materials Technologies and Services (formerly Williams Advanced Materials) is the largest business segment of parent Materion Corp. Materion Advanced Materials also goes by Materion Microelectronics and Services. It makes vapor deposition targets frame lid assemblies clad and precious metal pre-forms high-temperature braze materials ultra-fine wire advanced chemicals optics performance coatings and microelectronic packages. The company's precious non-precious and specialty metal products are used in the magnetic and optical data storage markets as well as the solar/photovoltaic industry and the hybrid photonic semiconductor and wireless segments of the microelectronics industry.

MATERION CORP   NYS: MTRN

6070 Parkland Blvd.
Mayfield Heights, OH 44124
Phone: 216 486-4200
Fax: 216 383-4091
Web: www.materion.com

CEO: Jugal K. Vijayvargiya
CFO: Joseph P. Kelley
HR: Joseph Szafraniec
FYE: December 31
Type: Public

Materion (formerly Brush Engineered Materials) provides advanced engineered materials and services worldwide. It sells products to a number of markets including consumer electronics aerospace and defense industrial components telecommunications infrastructure automotive electronics and medical and appliance. It manufactures a variety of precious and specialty metal products including frame lid assemblies and clad and precious metal pre-forms high temperature braze materials and ultra-fine wire. Other products include precision optics and thin film coatings; inorganic chemicals and powders; specialty coatings; beryllium (which it mines in Utah) beryllium composites and beryllium alloys.

	Annual Growth	12/14	12/15	12/16	12/17	12/18
Sales ($ mil.)	1.7%	1,126.9	1,025.3	969.2	1,139.4	1,207.8
Net income ($ mil.)	(15.9%)	41.7	32.2	25.7	11.5	20.8
Market value ($ mil.)	6.3%	713.1	566.8	801.6	983.8	910.7
Employees	0.3%	2,671	2,450	2,550	2,700	2,700

MATRIX SERVICE CO.   NMS: MTRX

5100 East Skelly Drive, Suite 500
Tulsa, OK 74135
Phone: 918 838-8822
Fax: –
Web: www.matrixservicecompany.com

CEO: John R. Hewitt
CFO: Kevin S. Cavanah
HR: –
FYE: June 30
Type: Public

Matrix Service provides a range of construction repair and maintenance services mainly to petroleum and power companies in North America. Through four operating segments the company offers above-ground storage tanks to hold oil gas and specialty materials; provides engineering maintenance and repair services in the downstream and midstream petroleum sectors and to iron and steel companies; and constructs conducts upkeep for and repairs electrical infrastructure for investor-owned utilities. The company has operations in the US Canada South Korea and Australia; about 90% of its revenue derives from the US.

	Annual Growth	06/15	06/16	06/17	06/18	06/19
Sales ($ mil.)	1.3%	1,343.1	1,311.9	1,197.5	1,091.6	1,416.7
Net income ($ mil.)	13.0%	17.2	28.9	(0.2)	(11.5)	28.0
Market value ($ mil.)	2.6%	490.0	442.1	250.6	491.9	543.1
Employees	0.9%	4,826	3,560	4,001	4,650	5,000

MATRIXX INITIATIVES INC.

4742 N. 24th St. Ste. 455
Phoenix AZ 85016
Phone: 602-385-8888
Fax: 602-387-4112
Web: www.matrixxinc.com

CEO: Marc L Rovner
CFO: Sam Kamdar
HR: –
FYE: March 31
Type: Subsidiary

Matrixx Initiatives offers several ways to get its medicine up your nose without a rubber hose. The company makes oral and nasally delivered over-the-counter cold flu and allergy remedies marketed primarily under the Zicam name. Its Zicam Cold Remedy is a zinc-based product that claims to reduce the duration of cold symptoms. Zicam comes in a variety of delivery methods including nasal swabs cough lozenges chewable tablets and nasal and oral sprays. The company also produces Nasal Comfort a moisturizing nasal spray to treat congestion and Xcid an antacid cream. Major customers include Wal-Mart Walgreens and CVS. Matrixx is owned by an affiliate of investment firm H.I.G. Capital called Wonder Holdings.

MATSON INC
NYS: MATX

1411 Sand Island Parkway
Honolulu, HI 96819
Phone: 808 848-1211
Fax: –
Web: www.matson.com

CEO: Matthew J. (Matt) Cox
CFO: Joel M. Wine
HR: –
FYE: December 31
Type: Public

Matson transports freight between the continental US and ports in Hawaii Guam Micronesia and China. Containerships account for the majority of the company's more than 25-vessel fleet. Besides containerized freight cargo carried by Matson vessels includes automobiles packaged foods and beverages retail merchandise and building materials. Subsidiary Matson Logistics provides logistics and multimodal transportation services (arrangement of freight transportation by combinations of road rail and air). Other subsidiaries specialize in container stevedoring and related services for Matson and other carriers in Honolulu. The company traces its historical roots all the way back to 1882 when Captain William Matson sailed a schooner that transported goods from San Francisco to Hawaii.

	Annual Growth	12/14	12/15	12/16	12/17	12/18
Sales ($ mil.)	6.7%	1,714.2	1,884.9	1,941.6	2,046.9	2,222.8
Net income ($ mil.)	11.4%	70.8	103.0	80.5	232.0	109.0
Market value ($ mil.)	(1.9%)	1,474.0	1,820.3	1,511.2	1,274.2	1,367.3
Employees	17.4%	1,056	1,663	1,925	1,947	2,007

MATTEL INC
NMS: MAT

333 Continental Blvd.
El Segundo, CA 90245-5012
Phone: 310 252-2000
Fax: –
Web: www.mattel.com

CEO: Margaret H. (Margo) Georgiadis
CFO: Joseph J. (Joe) Euteneuer
HR: Richard R. Gros
FYE: December 31
Type: Public

Mattel is one of the largest toy makers in the world. Its products include Barbie and Polly Pocket dolls Fisher-Price and Thomas & Friends toys Hot Wheels and Matchbox cars and American Girl dolls and books. Mattel also sells action figures and toys based on Walt Disney Warner Bros. and NBCUniversal movies WWE Wrestling Nickelodeon characters and the popular Minecraft video game. Other products include games (UNO) educational toys and puzzles. Mattel is trying to reduce its reliance on its biggest customers — Walmart and Target — through internet sales and by branching into media licensing of its popular brands. The North America region accounts for nearly 65% of sales.

	Annual Growth	12/14	12/15	12/16	12/17	12/18
Sales ($ mil.)	(7.0%)	6,023.8	5,702.6	5,456.7	4,882.0	4,510.9
Net income ($ mil.)	–	498.9	369.4	318.0	(1,053.8)	(531.0)
Market value ($ mil.)	(24.6%)	10,685.3	9,381.8	9,513.0	5,310.7	3,449.5
Employees	(3.4%)	31,000	31,000	32,000	28,000	27,000

MATTERSIGHT CORP
NMS: MATR

200 W. Madison Street, Suite 3100
Chicago, IL 60606
Phone: 877 235-6925
Fax: –
Web: www.mattersight.com

CEO: Kelly D Conway
CFO: David B Mullen
HR: –
FYE: December 31
Type: Public

Mattersight has an eye for important data. The company (formerly eLoyalty) provides behavioral analytics software used by companies to collect and analyze customer data generated from sources including e-mail call centers as well as field sales and Internet channels. It also offers systems designed to measure financial and operating metrics associated with CRM programs and tools to help insurance companies banks and brokerages to identify instances of identity or financial fraud.

	Annual Growth	12/12	12/13	12/14	12/15	12/16
Sales ($ mil.)	5.6%	33.9	34.5	30.3	39.9	42.1
Net income ($ mil.)	–	(15.2)	(11.2)	(14.2)	(15.7)	(21.0)
Market value ($ mil.)	(7.1%)	132.3	127.5	166.4	174.6	98.5
Employees	3.6%	230	179	197	241	265

MATTESON-RIDOLFI INC.

14450 KING RD
RIVERVIEW, MI 481937939
Phone: 734-479-4500
Fax: –
Web: www.mattrid.com

CEO: –
CFO: –
HR: –
FYE: December 31
Type: Private

|Matteson-Ridolfi distributes chemicals such as catalysts pigments resins solvents surfactants and thickening agents to companies in the adhesives and sealants automotive glass and refractory paints and coatings pharmaceuticals pulp and paper and soaps and detergents industries. The company maintains facilities in Cleveland; Detroit; and Louisville Kentucky. Customers include Cabot and other major chemical manufacturers. The family of company president Scot Westerbeek owns Matteson-Ridolfi which was founded in 1932.

	Annual Growth	12/06	12/07	12/08	12/09	12/10
Sales ($ mil.)	–	–	–	(560.6)	28.7	34.4
Net income ($ mil.)	1261.7%	–	–	0.0	1.9	3.0
Market value ($ mil.)	–	–	–	–	–	–
Employees	–	–	–	–	–	18

MATTHEWS INTERNATIONAL CORP
NMS: MATW

Two Northshore Center
Pittsburgh, PA 15212-5851
Phone: 412 442-8200
Fax: –
Web: www.matw.com

CEO: Joseph C. Bartolacci
CFO: Steven F. Nicola
HR: –
FYE: September 30
Type: Public

Matthews International offers a host of branding products and services to help its customers better market their brands. These offerings include brand development and graphic design brand deployment such as in-store merchandising exhibits and consulting. The company is also one of the nation's leading makers of cremation equipment and urns bronze memorials metal and wood caskets and commemorative products; it builds mausoleums as well. Additionally Matthews International makes and sells marking and coding equipment industrial automation products and order fulfillment systems. The diverse company has operations in about two dozen countries across Asia Australia and Europe but North America accounts for about 65% of sales.

	Annual Growth	09/15	09/16	09/17	09/18	09/19
Sales ($ mil.)	1.9%	1,426.1	1,480.5	1,515.6	1,602.6	1,537.3
Net income ($ mil.)	–	63.4	66.7	74.4	107.4	(38.0)
Market value ($ mil.)	(7.8%)	1,535.1	1,904.7	1,951.4	1,572.1	1,109.4
Employees	1.7%	10,300	10,300	11,000	11,000	11,000

MATTINGLY FOODS, INC.

302 STATE ST
ZANESVILLE, OH 437013200
Phone: 740-454-0136
Fax: –
Web: www.mattinglycold.com

CEO: Rick Barnes
CFO: Rusty Deaton
HR: –
FYE: December 29
Type: Private

Mattingly Foods is a leading regional foodservice supplier that distributes food products and other goods to chain restaurant operators in more than a dozen states. It delivers a variety of dry goods along with frozen and refrigerated foods. In addition to its distribution business Mattingly Foods operates a cash & carry store where customers can purchase wholesale goods. Robert Mattingly started the family-owned business as Mattingly Seafood with his wife Bette in 1947.

	Annual Growth	12/03	12/04	12/05	12/06	12/07
Sales ($ mil.)	(5.2%)	–	309.2	301.3	290.9	263.4
Net income ($ mil.)	(11.0%)	–	1.6	3.1	1.0	1.1
Market value ($ mil.)	–	–	–	–	–	–
Employees	–	–	–	–	–	240

MATTRESS FIRM HOLDING CORP
NMS: MFRM

5815 Gulf Freeway
Houston, TX 77023
Phone: 713 923-1090
Fax: –
Web: www.mattressfirm.com

CEO: Kenneth E Murphy III
CFO: Alexander S Weiss
HR: –
FYE: February 3/
Type: Public

Mattress Firm Holding is soft on comfort. The bedding retailer owns and operates or franchises more than 2000 stores primarily under the Mattress Firm name in some 40 states. It sells conventional (Simmons) and specialty (Tempur Sealy) mattresses which together account for most of its sales in addition to other brands. The company also sells bed frames and bedding accessories. From its humble beginnings in 1986 when three friends pooled their resources to purchase a downtrodden spot in a Houston strip center the chain has grown into the top US bedding retailer. Since its 2011 IPO Mattress Firm has made multiple acquisitions to solidify its position as the nation's top mattress seller.

	Annual Growth	02/11*	01/12	01/13	01/14*	02/15
Sales ($ mil.)	38.1%	497.3	708.6	1,012.7	1,222.4	1,810.6
Net income ($ mil.)	235.6%	0.3	34.4	39.9	52.9	44.3
Market value ($ mil.)	20.1%	–	1,159.4	974.1	1,472.5	2,008.2
Employees	35.6%	2,040	2,230	3,340	3,861	6,900

*Fiscal year change

MATTSON TECHNOLOGY INC
NMS: MTSN

47131 Bayside Parkway
Fremont, CA 94538
Phone: 510 657-5900
Fax: –
Web: www.mattson.com

CEO: Fusen Chen
CFO: J Michael Dodson
HR: Carla Zhao
FYE: December 31
Type: Public

Mattson Technology has avoided being taken to the mat by the brutal fluctuations of the microchip industry. The company which has seen its business ebb and flow over the years makes several types of semiconductor manufacturing equipment including systems that deposit materials onto silicon wafers that prepare wafers for photoresist and that etch patterns onto wafers. Top customers TSMC (a contract manufacturer of semiconductors) and Samsung Electronics (an OEM) together account for more than two-thirds of sales.

	Annual Growth	12/10	12/11	12/12	12/13	12/14
Sales ($ mil.)	6.6%	138.3	184.9	126.5	119.4	178.4
Net income ($ mil.)	–	(33.4)	(18.0)	(19.3)	(11.0)	9.9
Market value ($ mil.)	3.2%	222.0	102.1	62.2	202.8	251.6
Employees	(5.9%)	379	382	323	264	297

MATTSON TECHNOLOGY, INC.
NMS: MTSN

47131 Bayside Parkway
Fremont, CA 94538
Phone: 510 657-5900
Fax: –
Web: www.mattson.com

CEO: Fusen Chen
CFO: J Michael Dodson
HR: Carla Zhao
FYE: December 31
Type: Public

Mattson Technology has avoided being taken to the mat by the brutal fluctuations of the microchip industry. The company which has seen its business ebb and flow over the years makes several types of semiconductor manufacturing equipment including systems that deposit materials onto silicon wafers that prepare wafers for photoresist and that etch patterns onto wafers. Top customers TSMC (a contract manufacturer of semiconductors) and Samsung Electronics (an OEM) together account for more than two-thirds of sales.

	Annual Growth	12/09	12/10	12/11	12/12	12/13
Sales ($ mil.)	29.3%	42.7	138.3	184.9	126.5	119.4
Net income ($ mil.)	–	(67.0)	(33.4)	(18.0)	(19.3)	(11.0)
Market value ($ mil.)	(6.4%)	211.4	177.6	81.7	49.7	162.2
Employees	(7.2%)	356	379	382	323	264

MAUI LAND & PINEAPPLE CO., INC.
NYS: MLP

200 Village Road, Lahaina
Maui, HI 96761
Phone: 808 877-3351
Fax: –
Web: www.mauiland.com

CEO: Warren H Haruki
CFO: Tim T Esaki
HR: –
FYE: December 31
Type: Public

Aloha! Maui Land & Pineapple (ML&P) invites you to live and play on its Hawaiian island — Maui. Through its Kapalua Land Company subsidiary the company operates the 1650-acre Kapalua Resort on Maui's northwest coast. The resort includes a minority-owned Ritz-Carlton hotel as well as tennis and spa facilities residential homes and condos and shops and restaurants. ML&P also develops residential and commercial property on its 23000 acres surrounding the resort. Its Kapalua Realty Company is a general brokerage real estate firm located within the resort. The company additionally owns forest and nature preserves on the island. Formerly one of Hawaii's largest pineapple producers the company exited that business in 2009.

	Annual Growth	12/14	12/15	12/16	12/17	12/18
Sales ($ mil.)	(24.0%)	33.0	22.8	47.4	24.4	11.0
Net income ($ mil.)	(59.0%)	17.6	6.8	21.8	10.9	0.5
Market value ($ mil.)	13.2%	115.7	104.4	137.7	330.9	189.7
Employees	(4.7%)	17	17	17	15	14

MAXIM HEALTHCARE SERVICES, INC.

7227 LEE DEFOREST DR
COLUMBIA, MD 210463236
Phone: 410-910-1500
Fax: –
Web: www.maximhealthcare.com

CEO: W. Bradley (Brad) Bennett
CFO: Raymond (Ray) Carbone
HR: Kelly Bart
FYE: December 31
Type: Private

Maxim Healthcare Services aims to promote good health by offering medical staffing and home health care as well as immunizations and other wellness services to clients nationwide. The company provides medical and administrative personnel for hospitals school systems nursing homes and correctional facilities. The company's staffing division offers contract per diem and travel assignments. Maxim Healthcare's consultants are available 24 hours a day seven days a week to provide assistance for clients. The company which operates from more than 360 locations nationwide was established in 1988.

	Annual Growth	12/12	12/13	12/14	12/15	12/17
Sales ($ mil.)	5.3%	–	1,226.9	1,269.3	1,382.9	1,510.6
Net income ($ mil.)	–	–	(1.4)	4.7	11.7	38.5
Market value ($ mil.)	–	–	–	–	–	–
Employees	–	–	–	–	–	35,000

MAXIM INTEGRATED PRODUCTS, INC.
NMS: MXIM

160 Rio Robles
San Jose, CA 95134
Phone: 408 601-1000
Fax: –
Web: www.maximintegrated.com

CEO: Tunc Doluca
CFO: Bruce E. Kiddoo
HR: –
FYE: June 29
Type: Public

Maxim Integrated Products makes linear analog and mixed-signal integrated circuits (ICs). The company's chips — which include amplifiers data converters and switching ICs — translate physical data such as temperature pressure and sound into signals for electronic processing. The company serves five major end-markets: automotive industrial data center and communications consumer and computing. Its ICs are used in products such as appliances telecommunications and networking gear automobiles medical devices instruments and utility meters. Maxim maintains a healthy R&D effort developing some 80% of its products in-house. International customers supply about 90% of the company's revenue.

	Annual Growth	06/15	06/16	06/17	06/18	06/19
Sales ($ mil.)	0.1%	2,306.9	2,194.7	2,295.6	2,480.1	2,314.3
Net income ($ mil.)	41.6%	206.0	227.5	571.6	467.3	827.5
Market value ($ mil.)	14.5%	9,446.9	9,542.0	12,483.4	15,946.8	16,262.2
Employees	(3.6%)	8,250	7,213	7,040	7,149	7,131

MAXIMUS INC.
NYS: MMS

1891 Metro Center Drive
Reston, VA 20190
Phone: 703 251-8500
Fax: −
Web: www.maximus.com

CEO: Bruce L. Caswell
CFO: Richard J. Nadeau
HR: −
FYE: September 30
Type: Public

MAXIMUS provides business services to help governments operate health and human services programs mostly at the state and national levels. The company's health services segment offers outsourced program management and administrative services mainly to government agencies responsible for health and human services programs. MAXIMUS's human services segment provides administrative and consulting support to welfare-to-work programs child support enforcement and higher education. A significant portion of the company's revenue comes from the US federal government directly or indirectly.

	Annual Growth	09/15	09/16	09/17	09/18	09/19
Sales ($ mil.)	8.3%	2,099.8	2,403.4	2,451.0	2,392.2	2,886.8
Net income ($ mil.)	11.2%	157.8	178.4	209.4	220.8	240.8
Market value ($ mil.)	6.7%	3,810.6	3,618.7	4,126.6	4,162.5	4,943.0
Employees	14.9%	17,000	18,800	20,400	21,051	29,600

MAXLINEAR INC
NYS: MXL

5966 La Place Court, Suite 100
Carlsbad, CA 92008
Phone: 760 692-0711
Fax: −
Web: www.maxlinear.com

CEO: Kishore Seendripu
CFO: Adam C. Spice
HR: −
FYE: December 31
Type: Public

MaxLinear provides integrated radio-frequency (RF) and mixed-signal semiconductor receivers used to receive and translate analog or digital radio television and broadband signals into images. Its products are used in cable TV set-top boxes transceivers and modems fiber-optic modules analog and digital TVs and mobile phones. The company sells to module makers OEMs distributors and original design manufacturers (ODMs) such as Arris Group and Technicolor. Nearly all sales are to Asian customers.

	Annual Growth	12/15	12/16	12/17	12/18	12/19
Sales ($ mil.)	1.4%	300.4	387.8	420.3	385.0	317.2
Net income ($ mil.)	−	(42.3)	61.3	(9.2)	(26.2)	(19.9)
Market value ($ mil.)	9.6%	1,059.5	1,568.1	1,900.4	1,266.0	1,526.4
Employees	8.7%	500	553	753	739	697

MAXOR NATIONAL PHARMACY SERVICES LLC

320 S POLK ST STE 900
AMARILLO, TX 791011429
Phone: 806-324-5400
Fax: −
Web: www.maxor.com

CEO: Michael Ellis
CFO: Jerry Havard
HR: −
FYE: December 31
Type: Private

Maxor National Pharmacy Services provides health care and pharmacy services including retail and mail order prescriptions (Maxor Pharmacies) pharmacy benefits management (MaxorPlus) pharmacy consulting (Maxor Pharmacy Consulting Services) and infusion and injection services (IVSolutions). The company operates about a dozen Maxor Pharmacy stores mostly in Texas and Washington but also in Colorado and New York. Its correctional division provides services to more than 330000 offenders in more than 250 correctional facilities in 26 states through direct management contracts or via its pharmacy services division. Founded in 1926 as a single pharmacy in Amarillo Maxor put itself up for sale in 2013.

	Annual Growth	12/04	12/05	12/06	12/07	12/09
Sales ($ mil.)	17.2%	−	118.5	0.0	176.3	223.9
Net income ($ mil.)	−	−	0.0	0.0	0.0	0.0
Market value ($ mil.)	−	−	−	−	−	−
Employees	−	−	−	−	−	481

MAXUS REALTY TRUST INC
NBB: MRTI

104 Armour Road, P.O. Box 34279
North Kansas City, MO 64116
Phone: 816 303-4500
Fax: 816 221-1829
Web: www.mrti.com

CEO: David L Johnson
CFO: John W Alvey
HR: −
FYE: December 31
Type: Public

Maxus Realty Trust believes in the value of maximizing housing space. The real estate investment trust (REIT) invests in income-producing properties primarily multifamily residential properties. It owns a portfolio of approximately 10 apartment communities in the Midwest US. Maxus Realty Trust was originally established to invest in office and light industrial facilities but switched gears and began focusing on residential real estate in 2000. The REIT de-registered with the SEC and stopped trading on the NASDAQ in 2008.

	Annual Growth	12/14	12/15	12/16	12/17	12/18
Sales ($ mil.)	19.6%	55.6	60.6	74.3	89.2	113.7
Net income ($ mil.)	(16.8%)	13.4	4.5	14.7	14.0	6.4
Market value ($ mil.)	36.8%	37.6	57.6	88.1	117.5	131.6
Employees	−	−	−	−	−	−

MAXWELL TECHNOLOGIES INC
NMS: MXWL

3888 Calle Fortunada
San Diego, CA 92123
Phone: 858 503-3200
Fax: −
Web: www.maxwell.com

CEO: Franz Fink
CFO: David Lyle
HR: −
FYE: December 31
Type: Public

Maxwell Technologies is more than capable of making products that store energy and deliver power you might even say ultracapable. The company makes ultracapacitors postage stamp-sized cells that are able to provide quick bursts of energy to meet power demands then recharge by capturing excess power that would otherwise be lost. Its ultracapacitors are used to provide additional power for hybrid cars electric trains and semi-trucks as well as in energy grid solid-state memory and other applications that need fast reliable power. Maxwell also makes high-voltage capacitors that protect power grid systems and radiation-shielded microelectronics for satellites and spacecraft. In 2019 Maxwell agreed to be acquired by Tesla Inc.

	Annual Growth	12/13	12/14	12/15	12/16	12/17
Sales ($ mil.)	(9.4%)	193.5	186.6	167.4	121.2	130.4
Net income ($ mil.)	−	6.3	(6.3)	(22.3)	(23.7)	(43.1)
Market value ($ mil.)	(7.2%)	289.0	339.3	265.6	190.5	214.3
Employees	0.7%	448	510	451	418	461

MAYER BROWN LLP

71 S. Wacker Dr.
Chicago IL 60606
Phone: 312-782-0600
Fax: 312-701-7711
Web: www.mayerbrown.com

CEO: −
CFO: −
HR: −
FYE: December 31
Type: Private - Partnershi

One of the world's largest law firms Mayer Brown (formerly Mayer Brown Rowe & Maw) represents many of the companies in the FORTUNE 100 and the FTSE 100 as well as a number of leading banks. Major practice areas include appellate corporate and securities finance litigation real estate and tax. Overall Mayer Brown has about 1800 lawyers in more than 20 offices in the Americas Europe and Asia. It significantly expanded its international reach in 2008 by combining with Hong Kong-based Johnson Stokes & Master (JSM) a 300-lawyer firm. Mayer Brown is made up of three partnerships — Mayer Brown LLP (located in the US) Mayer Brown International LLP (the UK) and JSM.

MAYER ELECTRIC SUPPLY COMPANY, INC.

3405 4TH AVE S
BIRMINGHAM, AL 352222300
Phone: 205-583-3500
Fax: –
Web: www.mayerelectric.com

CEO: Nancy Collat Goedecke
CFO: –
HR: Melissa Hill
FYE: December 30
Type: Private

Mayer Electric Supply helps to light up those southern nights. The company is one of the nation's largest distributors of electrical supplies with about 50 branch locations in the southeastern US. It offers some 40000 items made by leading manufacturers such as 3M GE Littelfuse and Schneider Electric. Products include conduit circuit breakers controls and switches fire and safety products LED and low-voltage lighting systems motors power tools transformers and wire and cable. Mayer Electric supplies customers in the construction datacomm government industrial and utility industries. The Collat family including CEO Nancy Collat Goedecke owns Mayer Electric.

	Annual Growth	12/13	12/14	12/15	12/16	12/17
Sales ($ mil.)	7.3%	–	737.3	811.3	812.6	911.4
Net income ($ mil.)	18.5%	–	6.7	7.4	5.9	11.2
Market value ($ mil.)	–	–	–	–	–	–
Employees	–	–	–	–	–	900

MAYFLOWER BANCORP INC.

30 S. Main St.
Middleboro MA 02346
Phone: 508-947-4343
Fax: 508-923-0864
Web: www.mayflowerbank.com

NASDAQ: MFLR
CEO: –
CFO: –
HR: –
FYE: April 30
Type: Public

Mayflower Bank (formerly Mayflower Co-operative Bank) has been proudly progressing like a pilgrim since 1889. It is the primary subsidiary of bank holding company Mayflower Bancorp and operates nearly 10 branches in southeastern Massachusetts. Serving individuals and local businesses Mayflower Bank provides standard fare such as checking and savings accounts money market accounts and certificates of deposit. It primarily uses funds from deposits to originate residential mortgages commercial real estate loans and home equity loans and lines of credit. To a far lesser extent Mayflower Bank also originates business consumer and construction loans.

MAYO CLINIC HEALTH SYSTEM-NORTHWEST WISCONSIN REGION, INC.

1221 WHIPPLE ST
EAU CLAIRE, WI 547035200
Phone: 715-838-3311
Fax: –

CEO: –
CFO: –
HR: –
FYE: December 31
Type: Private

Cheeseheads experiencing blocked arteries or high cholesterol have Luther Midelfort - Mayo Health System on their side. The organization serves western Wisconsin including Eau Claire and surrounding communities through its Luther Hospital Midelfort Clinic and other facilities. The health care system has been part of the Mayo Clinic since 1992. Luther Hospital founded in 1905 maintains more than 300 beds and specializes in comprehensive cardiac trauma and intensive care. The adjacent Midelfort Clinic houses more than 200 primary and specialty doctors' offices. The Luther Midelfort system also includes nearly a dozen community family care clinics and provides pharmacy and home health services.

	Annual Growth	12/06	12/07	12/08	12/12	12/13
Sales ($ mil.)	(9.8%)	–	–	514.6	253.5	307.7
Net income ($ mil.)	–	–	–	(4.4)	45.7	44.9
Market value ($ mil.)	–	–	–	–	–	–
Employees	–	–	–	–	–	1,290

MAYO CLINIC HOSPITAL-ROCHESTER

200 1ST ST SW
ROCHESTER, MN 559050002
Phone: 507-284-2511
Fax: –
Web: www.mayoclinic.org

CEO: –
CFO: Dennis Dahlen
HR: –
FYE: December 31
Type: Private

Multidisciplinary teamwork with coordinated care is Mayo Clinic's secret sauce. The not-for-profit Mayo Clinic provides health care most notably for complex medical conditions through its clinics in Rochester Minnesota Arizona and Florida. The clinics' multidisciplinary approach to care attracts more than a million patients a year from around the globe. For less specialized care the Mayo Clinic Health System operates a regional network of affiliated community hospitals and clinics in Minnesota Iowa and Wisconsin. Mayo Clinic also conducts research and trains physicians nurses and other health professionals. The Mayo Clinic is named for Dr. William Worrall Mayo who settled in Rochester in 1863.

	Annual Growth	12/13	12/14	12/15	12/16	12/17
Sales ($ mil.)	9.0%	–	–	–	10,998.0	11,993.0
Net income ($ mil.)	–	–	–	–	(480.0)	856.0
Market value ($ mil.)	–	–	–	–	–	–
Employees	–	–	–	–	–	32,271

MAYO CLINIC JACKSONVILLE (A NONPROFIT CORPORATION)

4500 SAN PABLO RD S
JACKSONVILLE, FL 322241865
Phone: 904-953-2000
Fax: –

CEO: Kent R Thielen
CFO: Mary J Hoffman
HR: –
FYE: December 31
Type: Private

With more than 370 doctors and scientists on staff Mayo Clinic Jacksonville offers a broad range of medical surgical and research services. The clinic part of the larger Mayo Clinic network and one of its four major campuses offers specialty services such as organ transplantation neurology and oncology therapy. Most patients provided care from the clinic are treated on an outpatient basis; those who require hospitalization are admitted to the adjacent Mayo Clinic Hospital a 214-bed acute care facility. The Jacksonville campus also includes the Birdsall Medical Research center and the Griffin Cancer Research building.

	Annual Growth	12/08	12/09	12/13	12/15	12/16
Sales ($ mil.)	6.2%	–	340.8	657.6	457.3	520.3
Net income ($ mil.)	–	–	(4.3)	(0.4)	65.3	94.8
Market value ($ mil.)	–	–	–	–	–	–
Employees	–	–	–	–	–	5,500

MAYS (J.W.), INC.

9 Bond Street
Brooklyn, NY 11201
Phone: 718 624-7400
Fax: 718 935-0378
Web: www.jwmays.com

NAS: MAYS
CEO: Lloyd J Shulman
CFO: –
HR: –
FYE: July 31
Type: Public

J. W. Mays can get you space in Brooklyn as long as you're interested in offices and not bridges. The company owns and leases about 10 properties in and around New York City — mostly former MAYS department stores — and a warehouse in central Ohio. It leases its properties to retail restaurant commercial and other tenants. The MAYS department store chain founded in 1924 by Russian immigrant Joe Weinstein closed in 1989 when management realized the New York real estate it occupied was worth more than the struggling discount retail business. Weinstein's descendants including CEO Lloyd Shulman control more than half of the company although relations among the heirs have not always been harmonious.

	Annual Growth	07/15	07/16	07/17	07/18	07/19
Sales ($ mil.)	2.0%	18.9	18.6	19.5	19.3	20.5
Net income ($ mil.)	(9.0%)	2.2	1.5	1.9	3.0	1.5
Market value ($ mil.)	(9.8%)	106.9	95.7	75.6	79.7	70.7
Employees	0.0%	29	30	30	30	29

MAYVILLE ENGINEERING CO INC

715 SOUTH ST
MAYVILLE, WI 530501823
Phone: 920-387-4500
Fax: –
Web: www.mecinc.com

CEO: –
CFO: Todd M Butz
HR: –
FYE: December 31
Type: Private

Sometimes it's all right to get loaded. Mayville Engineering Company (MEC) manufactures shotshell reloading machinery and equipment used by hunters sport shooting enthusiasts and sporting goods stores. MEC also provides coating welding riveting painting manufacturing prototyping and mechanical assembly services. Its operations are divided across the main divisions of MEC Tube MEC Coatings MEC Fabrication and MEC Shooting Sports. Overall these divisions cater to the agricultural construction military medical and industrial markets.

	Annual Growth	03/09	03/10*	12/10	12/11	12/18
Sales ($ mil.)	–	–	(1,003.0)	153.6	177.7	354.5
Net income ($ mil.)	342.5%	–	0.0	15.8	6.9	17.9
Market value ($ mil.)	–	–	–	–	–	–
Employees	–	–	–	–	–	3,100

*Fiscal year change

MB FINANCIAL INC

NMS: MBFI

800 West Madison Street
Chicago, IL 60607
Phone: 888 422-6562
Fax: –
Web: www.mbfinancial.com

CEO: Mitchell Feiger
CFO: Jill E York
HR: –
FYE: December 31
Type: Public

The "MB" in MB Financial doesn't stand for "Midsized Businesses" though that's its target market. The $16 billion-asset holding company owns MB Financial Bank which has about 80 branches in the Chicago area and one in Philadelphia. Commercial-related credits including mortgages operating loans lease financing and construction loans make up 85% of the bank's loan portfolio. In addition to serving small and middle-market businesses MB Financial provides retail banking and lending to consumers. The company also offers wealth management and trust services through its Cedar Hill Associates subsidiary and brokerage through Vision Investment Services. LaSalle Systems leases technology-related equipment to corporations.

	Annual Growth	12/13	12/14	12/15	12/16	12/17
Assets ($ mil.)	20.1%	9,641.4	14,602.1	15,585.0	19,302.3	20,086.9
Net income ($ mil.)	32.6%	98.5	86.1	158.9	174.1	304.0
Market value ($ mil.)	8.6%	2,690.4	2,757.5	2,716.4	3,963.4	3,736.0
Employees	19.1%	1,775	2,839	2,980	3,486	3,574

MBC HOLDINGS, INC.

1613 S DEFIANCE ST
ARCHBOLD, OH 435029488
Phone: 419-445-1015
Fax: –

CEO: –
CFO: –
HR: –
FYE: December 31
Type: Private

These are brothers heavy in the midwestern construction business. MBC Holdings is the parent company of heavy and civil construction firm Miller Bros. Construction (also known as Team Miller). The firm specializes in highway contracting commercial and industrial construction and paving as well as earthwork and excavation working primarily in Ohio Michigan Indiana and Kentucky. Other subsidiaries include aggregates specialists Cardinal Aggregate; and steel contractors Sawyer Steel Erectors Wymer Steel and DeWitt Rebar. Brothers Dale and Floyd Miller started the family-owned company in 1945.

	Annual Growth	12/03	12/04	12/05	12/06	12/09
Sales ($ mil.)	–	–	–	(563.7)	97.0	89.2
Net income ($ mil.)	–	–	–	0.0	6.0	(1.7)
Market value ($ mil.)	–	–	–	–	–	–
Employees	–	–	–	–	–	721

MBIA INC.

NYS: MBI

1 Manhattanville Road, Suite 301
Purchase, NY 10577
Phone: 914 273-4545
Fax: –
Web: www.mbia.com

CEO: William C. (Bill) Fallon
CFO: Anthony McKiernan
HR: –
FYE: December 31
Type: Public

MBIA does what it can to make sure that bonds get paid no matter what. The holding company's independent subsidiary National Public Finance Guarantee Corporation is a provider of insurance for municipal bonds and stable corporate bonds (such as utility bonds) in the US. Separately its MBIA Insurance Corporation provides global structured finance products and non-US public financial guarantees. Faced with a significant amount of default activity MBIA is currently not issuing new policies.

	Annual Growth	12/14	12/15	12/16	12/17	12/18
Assets ($ mil.)	(16.1%)	16,284.0	14,855.0	11,137.0	9,095.0	8,076.0
Net income ($ mil.)	–	569.0	180.0	(338.0)	(1,605.0)	(296.0)
Market value ($ mil.)	(1.7%)	856.9	582.0	961.1	657.5	801.2
Employees	(21.4%)	252	170	164	103	96

MBT FINANCIAL CORP.

NMS: MBTF

102 E. Front Street
Monroe, MI 48161
Phone: 734 241-3431
Fax: –
Web: www.mbandt.com

CEO: –
CFO: –
HR: –
FYE: December 31
Type: Public

MBT Financial is the holding company for Monroe Bank & Trust which operates some two dozen branches in southeastern Michigan. Serving residents and businesses in Monroe and Wayne counties the bank offers a range of services including checking and savings accounts CDs retirement accounts personal trust services employee benefit plans and investment management. More than 80% of the loans in MBT Financial's portfolio are secured by commercial or residential real estate. The bank also originates business agricultural and personal loans. In 2018 Indiana-based First Merchants Corp. agreed to acquire the bank for about $290.9 million.

	Annual Growth	12/13	12/14	12/15	12/16	12/17
Assets ($ mil.)	2.5%	1,222.7	1,278.7	1,342.3	1,357.3	1,347.4
Net income ($ mil.)	(19.7%)	25.5	7.3	12.1	14.5	10.6
Market value ($ mil.)	25.6%	97.6	114.3	156.5	260.0	242.8
Employees	(5.9%)	381	372	304	284	299

MC NEESE STATE UNIVERSITY

4205 RYAN ST
LAKE CHARLES, LA 706054500
Phone: 337-475-5000
Fax: –
Web: www.mcneese.edu

CEO: –
CFO: –
HR: –
FYE: June 30
Type: Private

Founded in 1938 as Lake Charles Junior College McNeese State is one of eight schools in the University of Louisiana System. Its more than 8000 enrolled students can choose from approximately 75 associate bachelor master and specialist degree programs offered at colleges of business education engineering and technology liberal arts nursing and science the Division of General and Basic Studies and the DorA© School of Graduate Studies. Its campus includes a 500-plus acre farm and nearly 1600 acres of donated farm property for research farming and ranching. The university is named for Louisiana educator John McNeese.

	Annual Growth	06/11	06/12	06/13	06/16	06/17
Sales ($ mil.)	4.1%	–	48.7	52.7	61.9	59.4
Net income ($ mil.)	106.7%	–	0.6	2.2	14.0	22.5
Market value ($ mil.)	–	–	–	–	–	–
Employees	–	–	–	–	–	894

MCAFEE INC.

2821 Mission College Blvd.
Santa Clara CA 95054
Phone: 972-963-8000
Fax: 408-970-9727
Web: www.mcafee.com

CEO: Christopher Young
CFO: Michael Berry
HR: –
FYE: December 31
Type: Subsidiary

McAfee puts a virtual padlock on IT resources. The company sells network security products that protect computers networks and mobile devices. Its software and hardware are used to guard against viruses spam and spyware as well as to manage data loss prevention mobile security host intrusion prevention encryption and e-mail security. McAfee gets a significant portion of its sales from follow-up service support and subscriptions to its software and managed services. The company sells directly and through resellers to corporations and consumers mainly in the US; its largest international market is Europe and it logs sales in Asia and Latin America. McAfee was acquired in 2011 by Intel for $7.68 billion.

MCCARTER & ENGLISH LLP

Four Gateway Center 100 Mulberry St.
Newark NJ 07102
Phone: 973-622-4444
Fax: 973-624-7070
Web: www.mccarter.com

CEO: –
CFO: Michael Leonardi
HR: –
FYE: December 31
Type: Private - Partnershi

McCarter & English wasn't around for the American Revolution but the law firm has been representing clients in the northeastern US since before the Civil War. Today's McCarter & English is made up of more than 400 lawyers who practice from several offices in the region's major business centers from Boston to New York to Philadelphia. The firm's practice areas include business and commercial litigation intellectual property and information technology and labor and employment law. Clients have come from the ranks of the FORTUNE 100 but also have included smaller companies and individuals. McCarter & English traces its roots to the 1840s.

MCCARTHY BUILDING COMPANIES, INC.

1341 N ROCK HILL RD
SAINT LOUIS, MO 631241441
Phone: 314-968-3300
Fax: –
Web: www.mccarthy.com

CEO: Michael D. (Mike) Bolen
CFO: Doug Audiffred
HR: –
FYE: December 31
Type: Private

A company that was in construction before Reconstruction McCarthy Building Companies is one of the oldest and largest privately-held builders in the US. The general contractor and construction manager ranks among the top builders of health care education and green building facilities in the country. Contracts include heavy construction projects (bridges and water- and waste-treatment plants) commercial projects (retail and office buildings) and institutional projects (airports schools and prisons). Subsidiary MC Industrial handles energy auto and other manufacturing projects. Founded by Timothy McCarthy in 1864 the company is 100% employee owned and generates $3 billion in annual revenues.

	Annual Growth	12/14	12/15	12/16	12/17	12/18
Sales ($ mil.)	12.3%	–	2,719.9	3,265.3	3,574.7	3,852.3
Net income ($ mil.)	–	–	0.0	0.0	0.0	0.0
Market value ($ mil.)	–	–	–	–	–	–
Employees	–	–	–	–	–	4,025

MCCLATCHY CO (THE)   ASE: MNI

2100 "Q" Street
Sacramento, CA 95816
Phone: 916 321-1844
Fax: –
Web: www.mcclatchy.com

CEO: Craig I. Forman
CFO: R. Elaine Lintecum
HR: Billie McConkey
FYE: December 30
Type: Public

The McClatchy Company is one of the top newspaper businesses in the US. McClatchy has about 30 daily papers with a combined circulation of about 3 million. Its portfolio includes The Kansas City Star The Miami Herald The Charlotte Observer The Sacramento Bee (California) and the Star-Telegram (Fort Worth Texas). In addition it has a 49.5% stake in The Seattle Times Company operates online news sites in conjunction with many of its papers and has stakes in other digital media companies. The company traces its roots back to the 1850s when James McClatchy co-founded The Bee his first newspaper.

	Annual Growth	12/14	12/15	12/16	12/17	12/18
Sales ($ mil.)	(8.4%)	1,146.6	1,056.6	977.1	903.6	807.2
Net income ($ mil.)	–	374.0	(300.2)	(34.2)	(332.4)	(79.8)
Market value ($ mil.)	24.1%	27.0	9.4	106.0	69.8	64.1
Employees	(13.3%)	6,200	5,600	5,400	4,200	3,500

MCCORMICK & CO INC   NYS: MKC

24 Schilling Road, Suite 1
Hunt Valley, MD 21031
Phone: 410 771-7301
Fax: 410 771-7462
Web: www.mccormickcorporation.com

CEO: Lawrence E. Kurzius
CFO: Michael R Smith
HR: –
FYE: November 30
Type: Public

McCormick & Company is more than just the flavor of the month. As one of the world's leading spice makers the company offers a broad assortment of herbs spices seasonings flavorings sauces and extracts. McCormick distributes and markets its products under brands including Lawry's Club House and McCormick as well as ethnic labels Zatarain's Thai Kitchen and Simply Asia and regional brands Ducros and Schwartz. Its products are sold to customers spanning the entire food industry from food retailers to food service businesses and industrial food manufacturers. McCormick operates in some 150 countries across North and Central America Europe the Asia/Pacific region and South Africa but generates about 60% of sales in the US.

	Annual Growth	11/15	11/16	11/17	11/18	11/19
Sales ($ mil.)	5.6%	4,296.3	4,411.5	4,834.1	5,408.9	5,347.4
Net income ($ mil.)	15.0%	401.6	472.3	477.4	933.4	702.7
Market value ($ mil.)	18.5%	11,418.8	12,120.5	13,579.7	19,935.0	22,493.3
Employees	5.5%	10,000	10,500	11,700	11,600	12,400

MCCORMICK & SCHMICK'S SEAFOOD RESTAURANTS INC.   NASDAQ: MSSR

1414 NW Northrup St. Ste. 700
Portland OR 97209
Phone: 503-226-3440
Fax: 503-228-5074
Web: www.mccormickandschmicks.com

CEO: William T Freeman
CFO: Michelle M Lantow
HR: –
FYE: December 31
Type: Private

McCormick & Schmick's Seafood Restaurants owns and operates about 80 upscale casual-dining spots that offer fish and other seafood dishes from its approximately 80-dish menu. Located in more than two dozen states the restaurants operate primarily under the McCormick & Schmick's Seafood Restaurant brand while other locations carry such names as M&S Grill McCormick's Fish House & Bar and Jake's Grill. Each restaurant offers a full-service bar. McCormick & Schmick's also owns about a half dozen Boathouse restaurants in Canada. The company was acquired by a subsidiary of Landry's Restaurants in late 2011.

MCCOY-ROCKFORD, INC.

6869 OLD KATY RD
HOUSTON, TX 770242105
Phone: 713-862-4600
Fax: –
Web: www.mccoy-rockford.com

CEO: –
CFO: David Barnett
HR: Rachel Crouchet
FYE: December 31
Type: Private

McCoy Workplace Solutions is the real McCoy when it comes to business furniture. It will sell it to you — then come and help arrange it in your office space. The company supplies everything you need to furnish an office — desks chairs tables cubicle systems lighting and even floor coverings. The company sells both new and used furniture from more than 200 manufacturers including Interface NuCraft and Steelcase. McCoy also provides services such as furniture rental installation maintenance project management and repairs. The company was established in 1972.

	Annual Growth	12/04	12/05	12/06	12/07	12/08
Sales ($ mil.)	14.4%	–	–	92.5	102.3	121.1
Net income ($ mil.)	29.9%	–	–	1.8	1.0	3.1
Market value ($ mil.)	–	–	–	–	–	–
Employees	–	–	–	–	–	275

MCDANIEL COLLEGE, INC

2 COLLEGE HL
WESTMINSTER, MD 211574303
Phone: 410-848-7000
Fax: –
Web: www.mcdaniel.edu

CEO: –
CFO: –
HR: –
FYE: June 30
Type: Private

McDaniel College's predecessor school was a true pioneer being the first coeducational institution south of the Mason-Dixon Line and among the first in the nation. McDaniel College is a four-year private university offering undergraduate and graduate studies in liberal arts and sciences. Its 1600 undergraduate students may choose from 23 majors and can even opt to study abroad at its campus in Budapest Hungary. McDaniel College has a faculty of 149 professors; 96% hold the most advanced degrees in their disciplines. Some 90% of undergraduate classes are taught by full-time faculty with Ph.D.s.

	Annual Growth	06/14	06/15	06/16	06/17	06/18
Sales ($ mil.)	5.1%	–	64.0	55.9	74.0	74.3
Net income ($ mil.)	–	–	(0.8)	(7.3)	9.5	10.2
Market value ($ mil.)	–	–	–	–	–	–
Employees	–	–	–	–	–	500

MCDERMOTT INTERNATIONAL INC (PANAMA)   NBB: MDRI Q

757 N. Eldridge Parkway
Houston, TX 77079
Phone: 281 870-5000
Fax: –
Web: www.mcdermott.com

CEO: David Dickson
CFO: Stuart Spence
HR: –
FYE: December 31
Type: Public

Under the sea is the place to be for McDermott International. The global engineering procurement construction and installation firm is focused on designing and building offshore oil and gas projects around the world. Subsidiary J. Ray McDermott builds deepwater and subsea oil and gas production and distribution facilities. McDermott's divides its business into geographic segments: Asia/Pacific Atlantic and the Middle East. Customers include major energy companies that operate in those areas. McDermott operates a fleet of marine vessels and has several fabrication facilities around the world.

	Annual Growth	12/14	12/15	12/16	12/17	12/18
Sales ($ mil.)	30.7%	2,300.9	3,070.3	2,636.0	2,984.8	6,705.0
Net income ($ mil.)	–	(76.0)	(18.0)	34.1	178.5	(2,687.0)
Market value ($ mil.)	22.4%	523.8	603.0	1,330.2	1,184.4	1,177.2
Employees	119.3%	1,380	10,600	12,400	11,800	31,900

MCDONALD'S CORP   NYS: MCD

110 North Carpenter Street
Chicago, IL 60607
Phone: 630 623-3000
Fax: –
Web: www.mcdonalds.com

CEO: Stephen J. (Steve) Easterbrook
CFO: Kevin M. Ozan
HR: –
FYE: December 31
Type: Public

Serving billions of hamburgers has put a shine on these arches. McDonald's has more than 38000 restaurants serving burgers and fries in about 100 countries. (There are roughly 14000 Golden Arches locations in the US.) The popular chain is well-known for its Big Macs Quarter Pounders and Chicken McNuggets. In addition to freestanding units with dine-in take-out and drive-through service McDonald's also has locations inside airports train stations malls and other high-traffic retail areas. More than 90% of the restaurants are run by franchisees or affiliates. More than half of revenues are generated outside the US.

	Annual Growth	12/14	12/15	12/16	12/17	12/18
Sales ($ mil.)	(6.4%)	27,441.3	25,413.0	24,621.9	22,820.4	21,025.2
Net income ($ mil.)	5.6%	4,757.8	4,529.3	4,686.5	5,192.3	5,924.3
Market value ($ mil.)	17.3%	71,877.3	90,625.2	93,371.4	132,033.3	136,213.9
Employees	(15.9%)	420,000	420,000	375,000	235,000	210,000

MCDONOUGH COUNTY HOSPITAL DISTRICT

525 E GRANT ST
MACOMB, IL 614553313
Phone: 309-833-4101
Fax: –
Web: www.mdh.org

CEO: Kenny Boyd
CFO: Bill Murdock
HR: Sara Robertson
FYE: June 30
Type: Private

It may be small but that doesn't keep McDonough District Hospital (MDH) from serving the health care needs of patients throughout west-central Illinois. The not-for-profit MDH is an acute care facility with 48 beds. The hospital provides general medical emergency and surgical services as well as specialty care including behavioral health cancer cardiopulmonary dialysis nutritional pediatric and women's health services. The hospital also offers home health and hospice programs. It has a medical staff of physicians representing a range of specialties. MDH opened its doors in 1958 with 25 beds.

	Annual Growth	06/07	06/08	06/09	06/15	06/16
Sales ($ mil.)	5.7%	–	50.5	54.9	72.2	78.7
Net income ($ mil.)	4.2%	–	4.7	6.2	4.4	6.5
Market value ($ mil.)	–	–	–	–	–	–
Employees	–	–	–	–	–	600

MCG CAPITAL CORP   NMS: MCGC

1001 19th Street North, 10th Floor
Arlington, VA 22209
Phone: 703 247-7500
Fax: –
Web: www.mcgcapital.com

CEO: –
CFO: –
HR: –
FYE: December 31
Type: Public

MCG Capital puts its money on the little guy. The closed-end investment firm lends money to and invests in lower middle-market US firms with annual sales of less than $50 million. As a business development company (BDC) MCG is required to invest at least 70% of its assets in private or thinly traded US public companies. It is an active investor working with companies' management teams to set and execute strategy. The company has invested more than $6 billion in more than 600 transactions since its 1999 founding. At the end of 2013 MCG's portfolio included mostly debt and some equity stakes in 34 companies with a combined fair value of about $369 million. MCG is buying back its shares and may liquidate.

	Annual Growth	12/09	12/10	12/11	12/12	12/13
Sales ($ mil.)	(15.7%)	99.8	89.6	85.7	61.0	50.5
Net income ($ mil.)	–	(51.1)	(13.1)	(93.1)	5.0	1.2
Market value ($ mil.)	0.5%	304.6	491.5	281.3	324.3	310.2
Employees	(28.2%)	64	66	37	21	17

MCGLADREY LLP

1 S. Wacker Dr. Ste. 800
Chicago IL 60606
Phone: 312-634-3400
Fax: 952-921-7702
Web: mcgladrey.com/

CEO: Joe Adams
CFO: –
HR: –
FYE: April 30
Type: Private - Partnershi

McGladrey LLP (formerly McGladrey & Pullen) pulls its weight while offering accounting auditing and consulting services. The certified public accountant serves primarily owner-managed midsized businesses from more than 75 offices across the US. Services include auditing financial statement preparation and public company reporting. Industry specializations include financial institutions not-for-profits and manufacturing concerns. The firm also works globally through its membership in RSM International. The accounting firm which traces its historical roots to 1926 changed its name to McGladrey LLP following the acquisition of RSM McGladrey marking its transition to a single partner-owned CPA firm.

MCGRATH RENTCORP

NMS: MGRC

5700 Las Positas Road
Livermore, CA 94551-7800
Phone: 925 606-9200
Fax: –
Web: www.mgrc.com

CEO: Joseph F Hanna
CFO: Keith E. Pratt
HR: –
FYE: December 31
Type: Public

McGrath RentCorp helps clients who are short on space. Through subsidiaries the company rents and sells commercial storage and electronic equipment. Its largest subsidiary is Mobile Modular which rents portable buildings used as classrooms field offices health care clinics or rest rooms. Other subsidiaries such as TRS-RenTelco rents and sells electronic test equipment used in the aerospace defense communications and manufacturing industries while Enviroplex makes and sells modular buildings used in California public schools. Adler Tank Rentals provides containers used for storing hazardous and nonhazardous materials. McGrath has most of its operations in California Texas and in Midwestern US states.

	Annual Growth	12/14	12/15	12/16	12/17	12/18
Sales ($ mil.)	5.1%	408.1	404.5	424.1	462.0	498.3
Net income ($ mil.)	14.8%	45.7	40.5	38.3	153.9	79.4
Market value ($ mil.)	9.5%	867.2	609.1	947.7	1,136.1	1,244.9
Employees	1.7%	995	1,016	1,071	1,073	1,066

MCKEE FOODS CORPORATION

10260 McKee Rd.
Collegedale TN 37315
Phone: 423-238-7111
Fax: 423-238-7127
Web: www.mckeefoods.com

CEO: Mike Kee
CFO: Andy Lang
HR: Jeanna Somers
FYE: June 30
Type: Private

Little Debbie smiles up from North American lunch bags. McKee Foods' Little Debbie is one of the nation's best-known brands of snack cakes named for and featuring the smiling face of the 4-year-old granddaughter of the company's late founders: O. D. and Ruth McKee. Founded in 1934 McKee also makes ready-to-eat breakfast cereals granola creme-filled cookies crackers and snack bars. It counts more than 160 varieties of Little Debbie-brand products. McKee's baked goods are available in the US Canada and Mexico. The bakery is still owned and operated by the McKee family including CEO Mike McKee and the real Little Debbie Debbie McKee-Fowler who is an EVP.

MCKESSON CORP

NYS: MCK

6555 State Highway 161
Irving, TX 75039
Phone: 972 446-4800
Fax: –
Web: www.mckesson.com

CEO: John H. Hammergren
CFO: James A. Beer
HR: Jorge L. Figueredo
FYE: March 31
Type: Public

McKesson is a top global pharmaceuticals distributor. The company delivers prescription and generic drugs as well as health and beauty care products to retail and institutional pharmacies worldwide. The company is also a major medical supplies wholesaler providing medical and surgical equipment to alternate health care sites such as doctors' offices surgery centers and long-term care facilities. In addition to distribution McKesson offers management consulting and technology services that help customers navigate supply chain clinical administrative and financial operations.

	Annual Growth	03/15	03/16	03/17	03/18	03/19
Sales ($ mil.)	4.6%	179,045.0	190,884.0	198,533.0	208,357.0	214,319.0
Net income ($ mil.)	(61.0%)	1,476.0	2,258.0	5,070.0	67.0	34.0
Market value ($ mil.)	(15.2%)	42,978.0	29,877.5	28,169.4	26,765.3	22,241.4
Employees	3.2%	70,400	68,000	78,000	78,000	80,000

MCKINSTRY CO. LLC

5005 3rd Ave. South
Seattle WA 98134
Phone: 206-762-3311
Fax: 206-762-2624
Web: www.mckinstry.com

CEO: Dean Allen
CFO: Bill Teplicky
HR: Janice Clusserath
FYE: December 31
Type: Private

McKinstry one of the top specialty contractors in the Pacific Northwest provides mechanical electrical and plumbing services in more than 15 US states throughout the West Midwest and Southwest. It designs and maintains complete building systems such as heating ventilation and air conditioning (HVAC) fire protection piping parking and solar panel and rain collection systems. The firm also provides design/build facilities management project management and maintenance services. McKinstry works on new buildings or retrofits existing facilities. It targets the commercial high-tech health care hospitality and industrial markets. The company was founded in 1960 by George Allen and Merrill McKinstry.

MCLANE COMPANY, INC.

4747 MCLANE PKWY
TEMPLE, TX 765044854
Phone: 254-771-7500
Fax: –
Web: www.mclaneco.com

CEO: W. Grady Rosier
CFO: –
HR: –
FYE: December 30
Type: Private

McLane Company is one of the largest wholesale suppliers of grocery and food products in the US serving some 50000 retail locations and 35000 restaurants across all 50 states. It delivers more than 50000 different consumer products to customers such as convenience and discount stores mass merchandisers wholesale clubs drug stores military bases and quick-service and casual dining restaurants. The company also distributes alcoholic beverages in the southeastern US and Colorado through subsidiaries. McLane is owned by Warren Buffett's Berkshire Hathaway and accounts for about a fifth of its revenue.

	Annual Growth	01/08	01/09*	12/12*	01/16*	12/16
Sales ($ mil.)	7.1%	–	29,800.4	37,389.6	48,144.7	48,016.1
Net income ($ mil.)	–	–	0.0	0.0	0.0	0.0
Market value ($ mil.)	–	–	–	–	–	–
Employees	–	–	–	–	–	20,128

*Fiscal year change

MCLAREN HEALTH CARE CORPORATION

1 MCLAREN PKWY
GRAND BLANC, MI 484397471
Phone: 810-342-1100
Fax: –

CEO: Philip A Incarnati
CFO: David Mazurkiewicz
HR: –
FYE: September 30
Type: Private

McLaren Health Care is where people in The Auto State go for repairs. The health care system includes some 300 facilities including a dozen regional hospitals and a network of cancer dialysis imaging and surgery centers across the state of Michigan. Combined its facilities have about 2900 beds and serve more than 50 counties. Through its subsidiaries McLaren manages a primary care physician network commercial and Medicaid HMOs and assisted living facilities and provides visiting nurse/home health care and hospice services. Its Great Lakes Cancer Institute provides cancer research and treatment with partner Michigan State University.

	Annual Growth	09/04	09/05	09/06	09/08	09/15
Sales ($ mil.)	(15.6%)	–	1,014.5	883.7	84.5	187.1
Net income ($ mil.)	(7.1%)	–	40.9	58.0	4.1	19.6
Market value ($ mil.)	–	–	–	–	–	–
Employees	–	–	–	–	–	10,003

MCMASTER-CARR SUPPLY COMPANY

600 N. County Line Rd.
Elmhurst IL 60126-2081
Phone: 630-600-3600
Fax: 630-834-9427
Web: www.mcmaster.com

CEO: Robert Delaney
CFO: –
HR: Colin Farinha
FYE: December 31
Type: Private

McMaster-Carr Supply is ready to fill your pipe pump power transmission and process control needs (and that's only in the P section of its extensive A to Z catalog). The company distributes more than 510000 mechanical electrical and utility products including air conditioners clamps drills exhaust fans generators light bulbs pipes pumps saws switches and valves. Family-owned McMaster-Carr operates through a handful of regional branches in the US that provide customer service sales warehousing and management. Customers order through an online catalog or through its traditional direct mail catalog.

MCNAUGHTON-MCKAY ELECTRIC CO.

1357 E LINCOLN AVE
MADISON HEIGHTS, MI 480714126
Phone: 248-399-7500
Fax: –
Web: www.mc-mc.com

CEO: –
CFO: John D Kuczmanski
HR: John D. Kuczmanski
FYE: December 31
Type: Private

Getting connected at work has a completely different meaning at McNaughton-McKay. Its more than 10000 customers can buy electrical supplies sensors and controls and automation and security software online or through 23 branches in five US states and two offices in Germany and Brazil. One of the largest employee-owned companies in the US McNaughton-McKay distributes some 300 product lines from manufacturers such as Hubbell GE Brady Belden Coleman Cable Leviton Thomas & Betts Cognex Specter Instruments and Rockwell Automation. It sells to the construction commercial government and industrial automation markets.

	Annual Growth	12/13	12/14	12/15	12/16	12/17
Sales ($ mil.)	6.1%	–	689.3	702.3	724.3	822.5
Net income ($ mil.)	–	–	0.0	0.0	0.0	0.0
Market value ($ mil.)	–	–	–	–	–	–
Employees	–	–	–	–	–	854

MCNEILUS COMPANIES INC.

524 County Rd. 34 East
Dodge Center MN 55927
Phone: 507-374-6321
Fax: 507-374-6394
Web: www.mcneiluscompanies.com

CEO: Charles Szews
CFO: –
HR: –
FYE: September 30
Type: Subsidiary

Talking trash (and transporting it) is big business at McNeilus Companies. The company manufactures garbage trucks (front side and rear loaders) concrete mixers and related heavy duty commercial construction vehicles and components. McNeilus also builds and erects concrete batch plants (machinery used to store and load concrete into concrete trucks) such as conveyors drums dust collectors material storage silos and bins rollers and water systems. The lineup is sold through a network of dealers to waste haulers and ready-mix companies and mining and construction businesses in the US and abroad. McNeilus Companies operates as a subsidiary of truck and vehicle maker Oshkosh.

MCNICHOLS COMPANY

2502 N ROCKY POINT DR # 750
TAMPA, FL 336071421
Phone: 877-884-4653
Fax: –
Web: www.mcnichols.com

CEO: –
CFO: Craig A Stein
HR: –
FYE: December 31
Type: Private

McNichols Company manufactures metal products that are full of holes ... by design. Its products include perforated and expanded metals wire mesh bar and plank gratings fiberglass grating floorings handrail components ladder rungs and mattings. Its perforated metal (aka "hole") products are sold under the brand names Eco-Mesh Grate-Lock Perf-O-Grip Safplate and Vinylmesh among many others. The company also provides custom fabrication services. McNichols operates is business through some 20 service centers nationwide. It was founded in 1952 by the late Robert McNichols grandfather of current president Scott McNichols. The McNichols family runs the firm based on Christian principles.

	Annual Growth	12/05	12/06	12/07	12/08	12/09
Sales ($ mil.)	(13.0%)	–	–	185.8	209.4	140.8
Net income ($ mil.)	–	–	–	7.8	3.7	0.0
Market value ($ mil.)	–	–	–	–	–	–
Employees	–	–	–	–	–	400

MCPHEE ELECTRIC, LTD

505 MAIN ST
FARMINGTON, CT 060322912
Phone: 860-677-9797
Fax: –
Web: www.mcpheeusa.com

CEO: Michael Mc Phee
CFO: John Conroy
HR: –
FYE: December 31
Type: Private

McPhee Electric is energized about its work. The company which is a unit of Phalcon provides electrical construction and data and communications installation services (including cellular towers) throughout New England. Services include conceptual planning feasibility studies budgeting design development installation maintenance and service. McPhee Electric's clients come from a wide variety of industries including education financial services government health care manufacturing pharmaceuticals retail and utilities. The company's projects include utility substations Foxwoods Resort Casino a Bristol-Myers Squibb research facility and Cordon Bleu Culinary Institute.

	Annual Growth	12/14	12/15	12/16	12/17	12/18
Sales ($ mil.)	(4.1%)	–	130.0	142.0	148.4	114.6
Net income ($ mil.)	20.1%	–	11.9	17.2	19.4	20.6
Market value ($ mil.)	–	–	–	–	–	–
Employees	–	–	–	–	–	500

MCRAE INDUSTRIES, INC.
NBB: MCRA A

400 North Main Street
Mount Gilead, NC 27306
Phone: 910 439-6147
Fax: 910 439-4190
Web: www.mcraeindustries.com

CEO: D Gary Mc Rae
CFO: Kelly Franklin
HR: –
FYE: July 28
Type: Public

McRae Industries has interests ranging from bar codes to boots. The company's footwear segment consisting of subsidiaries McRae Footwear and Dan Post Boot Co. makes combat boots for the US and foreign militaries Western boots and work boots. Dan Post Boot markets and distributes boot brands Laredo Dingo John Deere and Dan Post. A third subsidiary Compsee makes bar code readers printers and optical data-collection equipment. Compsee also licenses and sells computer software worldwide. McRae Industries makes most of its money from the Western and work boot segment. The McRae family controls more than 50% of the company's voting power.

	Annual Growth	08/14	08/15*	07/16	07/17	07/18
Sales ($ mil.)	(8.1%)	103.6	108.7	108.8	104.3	73.9
Net income ($ mil.)	(26.6%)	7.5	6.6	4.7	5.1	2.2
Market value ($ mil.)	0.0%	71.8	67.6	56.7	79.0	71.8
Employees	–	–	–	–	–	–

*Fiscal year change

MDC PARTNERS INC
NMS: MDCA

745 Fifth Avenue
New York, NY 10151
Phone: 646 429-1800
Fax: 212 937-4365
Web: www.mdc-partners.com

CEO: Miles S. Nadal
CFO: David B. Doft
HR: –
FYE: December 31
Type: Public

MDC Partners provides a wide range of marketing communications services through its vast network of subsidiaries. Advertising branding direct marketing public relations and sales promotion are provided through firms such as Allison & Partners Crispin Porter + Bogusky kirshenbaum bond senecal + partners Colle & McVoy Sloane & Company and Vitrorobertson. In addition specialized communication services are offered by Source Marketing and other affiliates and customer relationship management is provided via ACCENT Marketing Services. Major MDC clients have included Sprint Burger King and Volkswagen Group of America.

	Annual Growth	12/14	12/15	12/16	12/17	12/18
Sales ($ mil.)	4.8%	1,223.5	1,326.3	1,385.8	1,513.8	1,476.2
Net income ($ mil.)	–	(24.1)	(37.4)	(47.9)	241.8	(123.7)
Market value ($ mil.)	(41.8%)	1,306.9	1,249.4	376.6	560.8	150.1
Employees	3.5%	5,250	5,690	6,138	6,200	6,024

MDU RESOURCES GROUP INC
NYS: MDU

1200 West Century Avenue, P.O. Box 5650
Bismarck, ND 58506-5650
Phone: 701 530-1000
Fax: –
Web: www.mdu.com

CEO: Nicole A. Kivisto
CFO: Jason L. Vollmer
HR: Amanda Ross
FYE: December 31
Type: Public

MDU Resources has branched out from its roots as a regional utility to cover a range of natural resources businesses. Utility subsidiaries Montana-Dakota Utilities Wyoming Utilities Great Plains Natural Gas and Cascade Natural Gas deliver gas to more than 920000 customers and electricity to more than 142000 customers in 355 communities. MDU Resources' energy business is focused on natural gas transmission gathering and storage. The company also has an oil refinery business. Its construction materials and contracting division (including Knife River) mines and sells concrete gravel and other materials. MDU Resources' MDU Construction Services unit builds power lines pipelines and telecom systems.

	Annual Growth	12/14	12/15	12/16	12/17	12/18
Sales ($ mil.)	(0.8%)	4,670.6	4,191.5	4,128.8	4,443.4	4,531.6
Net income ($ mil.)	(2.2%)	298.2	(622.4)	64.4	281.2	272.3
Market value ($ mil.)	0.4%	4,606.6	3,591.2	5,639.7	5,269.2	4,673.3
Employees	8.7%	8,451	8,689	9,598	10,140	11,797

MEAD JOHNSON NUTRITION CO
NYS: MJN

2701 Patriot Blvd.
Glenview, IL 60026
Phone: 847 832-2420
Fax: –
Web: www.meadjohnson.com

CEO: Peter Kasper Jakobsen
CFO: Michel Cup
HR: –
FYE: December 31
Type: Public

Mead Johnson Nutrition helps babies grow up healthy. The company specializes in developing and manufacturing nutritional products for infants and children. It distributes its 70-plus products to more than 50 countries. Mead Johnson's Enfamil line of infant formulas is its most visible consumer brand. Other products in its portfolio include Sustagen and Lactum — two fortified beverages for children — and Nutramigen a nutritional supplement for children with dairy allergies. Besides babies the company markets nutritional supplements for use by pregnant and breastfeeding moms. Mead Johnson also produces specialty nutritional products for premature infants and infants with metabolic and digestive disorders. Reckitt Benckiser is buying Mead Johnson for $16.6 billion.

	Annual Growth	12/11	12/12	12/13	12/14	12/15
Sales ($ mil.)	2.6%	3,677.0	3,901.3	4,200.7	4,409.3	4,071.3
Net income ($ mil.)	6.5%	508.5	604.5	649.5	719.8	653.5
Market value ($ mil.)	3.5%	12,818.1	12,288.5	15,621.2	18,750.7	14,724.2
Employees	3.8%	6,600	6,800	7,200	7,700	7,660

MEADOWBROOK INSURANCE GROUP INC
NYS: MIG

26255 American Drive
Southfield, MI 48034
Phone: 248 358-1100
Fax: –
Web: www.meadowbrook.com

CEO: Robert S Cubbin
CFO: Karen M Spaun
HR: –
FYE: December 31
Type: Public

Meadowbrook Insurance puts its clients' liabilities and risks out to pasture. Through subsidiaries including Star Insurance Savers P&C Williamsburg National Ameritrust ProCentury and Century Surety the company writes a variety of specialty commercial property/casualty insurance policies including workers' compensation commercial auto and multi-peril liability policies. With coverage tailored to fit small to midsized businesses customers include self-insured companies trade groups and associations. Meadowbrook also offers brokering risk management consulting and insurance management services including claims handling and administrative services.

	Annual Growth	12/09	12/10	12/11	12/12	12/13
Assets ($ mil.)	8.5%	1,989.8	2,177.6	2,381.3	2,713.3	2,761.8
Net income ($ mil.)	–	52.7	59.7	43.6	11.7	(112.3)
Market value ($ mil.)	(1.5%)	369.2	511.3	532.8	288.3	347.2
Employees	1.0%	918	967	1,054	1,032	954

MEADWESTVACO CORP.
NYS: MWV

501 South 5th Street
Richmond, VA 23219-0501
Phone: 804 444-1000
Fax: –
Web: www.mwv.com

CEO: John A Luke Jr
CFO: Mark Rajkowski
HR: –
FYE: December 31
Type: Public

MeadWestvaco (MWV) has got your products covered — literally. MWV's packaging business — folding cartons corrugated boxes and printed plastics — serves many of the world's major brands. MWV wraps up health care personal and beauty care food and tobacco as well as home and garden goods. MWV also packages pharmaceuticals and manufactures packaging equipment for dairy and beverage OEMs. It operates through five segments: Food and Beverage; Specialty Chemicals; Home Health and Beauty; Industrial; and Community Development and Land Management.

	Annual Growth	12/09	12/10	12/11	12/12	12/13
Sales ($ mil.)	(2.8%)	6,049.0	5,693.0	6,060.0	5,459.0	5,389.0
Net income ($ mil.)	39.0%	225.0	106.0	246.0	205.0	839.0
Market value ($ mil.)	6.6%	4,994.3	4,563.4	5,224.6	5,559.5	6,442.2
Employees	(5.4%)	20,000	17,500	17,000	16,000	16,000

MEASUREMENT SPECIALTIES, INC. — NMS: MEAS

1000 Lucas Way
Hampton, VA 23666
Phone: 757 766-1500
Fax: –
Web: www.meas-spec.com

CEO: Frank D Guidone
CFO: Mark Thomson
HR: Martina Bartos
FYE: March 31
Type: Public

Sensing the pressure? Measurement Specialties would rather do that for you. The company's industrial product line includes sensors that measure such properties as fluid level and properties gas concentration and flow rate humidity torque pressure vibrations and more. Its sensors are used in aerospace consumer appliance environmental water monitoring industrial medical military test and measurement transportation and vehicle applications. The company's biggest customer Sensata Technologies (about 15% of sales) serves the automotive market. US customers account for one-thirds of sales; those in China make up nearly a quarter.

	Annual Growth	03/09	03/10	03/11	03/12	03/13
Sales ($ mil.)	14.2%	203.9	209.6	274.8	313.2	347.0
Net income ($ mil.)	59.5%	5.3	5.9	28.2	27.7	34.2
Market value ($ mil.)	76.6%	63.6	228.8	529.1	524.2	618.6
Employees	9.6%	2,184	2,520	2,923	3,235	3,154

MECHANICAL TECHNOLOGY, INC. — NBB: MKTY

325 Washington Avenue Extension
Albany, NY 12205
Phone: 518 218-2550
Fax: –
Web: www.mechtech.com

CEO: –
CFO: Frederick W Jones
HR: Patricia Phillips
FYE: December 31
Type: Public

Mechanical Technology Inc. (MTI) is warming up to the alternative energy market. The company's MTI Instruments Inc. subsidiary (MTII) specializes in the design manufacture and service of non-contact precision test and measurement equipment and makes computer-based aircraft engine balancing systems capacitance measuring systems and non-contact sensing instrumentation. MTII Instruments serves customers in the aerospace automotive bioengineering computer and semiconductor industries. MTI has diversified its offerings by investing in the alternative energy market. MTI was founded by two entrepreneurs in 1961.

	Annual Growth	12/14	12/15	12/16	12/17	12/18
Sales ($ mil.)	(2.1%)	8.8	6.3	7.1	7.1	8.1
Net income ($ mil.)	27.2%	0.7	(2.8)	(0.4)	0.6	1.9
Market value ($ mil.)	3.2%	6.7	8.9	13.7	9.5	7.6
Employees	(8.3%)	35	34	29	27	–

MECKLERMEDIA CORP — NBB: MECK

50 Washington Street, Suite 902
Norwalk, CT 06854
Phone: 212 389-2000
Fax: –

CEO: –
CFO: –
HR: –
FYE: December 31
Type: Public

If your brand isn't on the Web WebMediaBrands wants to help. The company provides digital content education job listings events and other resources for media creative and design professionals. Its flagship Mediabistro network of websites targets the media industry including digital and print publishing advertising television and public relations markets. Its AllCreativeWorld reaches creative and design professionals through websites such as Graphics.com and Creativebits. WebMediaBrands also offers community membership and e-commerce offerings such as a freelance listing service and a marketplace for designing and purchasing logos. Chairman and CEO Alan Meckler owns about 40% of WebMediaBrands.

	Annual Growth	12/10	12/11	12/12	12/13	12/14
Sales ($ mil.)	(20.7%)	9.0	12.4	14.0	12.5	3.6
Net income ($ mil.)	–	(3.0)	(11.9)	(8.7)	(5.7)	(3.8)
Market value ($ mil.)	(27.6%)	9.8	2.9	12.2	19.2	2.7
Employees	(28.5%)	69	74	121	94	18

MECO CORPORATION

1500 Industrial Rd.
Greeneville TN 37745
Phone: 423-639-1171
Fax: 423-639-2570
Web: www.meco.net

CEO: –
CFO: –
HR: –
FYE: June 30
Type: Private

Take a seat and then let MECO Corporation meet all of your changing lifestyle needs. The company specializes in manufacturing residential and commercial folding furniture including steel patio chairs heavy-duty banquet tables and covered swing sets. MECO designs and markets its furnishings under the Samsonite Innobella and SuddenComfort brands. It also produces barbecue grills and cooking accessories under the Aussie label. The company's products are available through retail stores nationwide.

MEDALLION FINANCIAL CORP — NMS: MFIN

437 Madison Avenue, 38th Floor
New York, NY 10022
Phone: 212 328-2100
Fax: –
Web: www.medallion.com

CEO: Alvin Murstein
CFO: Larry D Hall
HR: –
FYE: December 31
Type: Public

Medallion Financial turns taxicab licenses or "medallions" into gold. The specialty finance company makes loans for the purchase of medallions which are usually limited in number per city by law. It targets mainly New York City but also finances medallions in Boston and Cambridge Massachusetts; Chicago; and Newark New Jersey. (A NYC taxi medallion costs more than $1 million.) Subsidiary Medallion Bank funds its taxi and commercial lending activities by issuing certificates of deposit to clients; it also originates loans for boats trailers motorcycles and RVs. Other subsidiaries including Medallion Capital and Freshstart Venture Capital offer commercial loans ranging from $200000 to $5 million.

	Annual Growth	12/14	12/15	12/16	12/17	12/18
Assets ($ mil.)	21.6%	632.3	689.1	689.4	635.5	1,381.8
Net income ($ mil.)	–	15.1	16.8	0.1	(7.1)	(11.1)
Market value ($ mil.)	(17.3%)	244.6	172.0	73.8	86.3	114.6
Employees	2.7%	159	143	131	138	177

MEDASSETS INC — NMS: MDAS

100 North Point Center East, Suite 200
Alpharetta, GA 30022
Phone: 678 323-2500
Fax: –
Web: www.medassets.com

CEO: R Halsey Wise
CFO: Charles Garner
HR: –
FYE: December 31
Type: Public

MedAssets helps hospitals widen their profit margins — or at least not lose quite as much. The company's Spend and Clinical Resource Management (SCM) segment is its largest with almost 60% of sales. It operates a group purchasing organization (GPO) that negotiates lower prices on medical supplies and devices for hospitals and health systems. The company's Revenue Cycle Management (RCM) segment provides software and consulting services that help track and analyze a hospital's revenue stream. Such services aim to increase collections and reduce account balances. MedAssets' customers include more than 4200 hospitals and about 122000 non-acute health providers mainly in the US but also in Canada to a lesser extent.

	Annual Growth	12/09	12/10	12/11	12/12	12/13
Sales ($ mil.)	18.8%	341.3	391.3	578.3	640.1	680.4
Net income ($ mil.)	8.3%	19.9	(32.1)	(15.5)	(6.9)	27.4
Market value ($ mil.)	(1.7%)	1,309.5	1,246.5	571.1	1,035.4	1,224.3
Employees	9.8%	2,200	3,100	3,040	3,100	3,200

MEDIA GENERAL INC (NEW)   NYS: MEG

333 E. Franklin St.
Richmond, VA 23219
Phone: 804 887-5000
Fax: 804 649-6898
Web: www.mediageneral.com

CEO: –
CFO: –
HR: –
FYE: December 31
Type: Public

With interests in digital publishing and broadcasting this company generally has the media covered. Media General operates about 20 network-affiliated television stations. In addition Media General operates websites for every one of its television stations. Built through a series of acquisitions the company's collection of media properties is organized regionally making Media General a dominant voice in the southeastern US. In 2012 the company sold all of its newspapers and in 2016 Media General agreed to be acquired by Nexstar Broadcasting Group.

	Annual Growth	12/10	12/11	12/12	12/13	12/14
Sales ($ mil.)	(0.1%)	678.1	616.2	359.7	269.9	675.0
Net income ($ mil.)	–	(22.6)	(74.3)	(193.4)	6.1	53.5
Market value ($ mil.)	31.1%	735.4	554.8	558.7	2,936.5	2,173.8
Employees	3.3%	4,650	4,200	1,600	2,600	5,300

MEDIA SCIENCES INTERNATIONAL INC.   PINK SHEETS: MSII

8 Allerman Rd.
Oakland NJ 07463
Phone: 201-677-9311
Fax: 201-677-1440
Web: www.mediasciences.com

CEO: –
CFO: Denise Hawkins
HR: –
FYE: June 30
Type: Public

Media Sciences International supports the art science and business of printing. The company makes printing supplies for color business printers. Its products include solid ink sticks designed for printers from a variety of manufacturers including Brother Dell Konica Minolta Oki Data Ricoh Samsung Seiko Epson and Xerox. Through its INKlusive program Media Sciences supplies customers with color printers for a monthly fee that covers the price of ink supplies; the program requires a multiyear commitment. Media Sciences sells directly and through reseller channels primarily in the US.

MEDIA STORM, LLC

99 WASHINGTON ST STE 3
NORWALK, CT 068543080
Phone: 203-852-8001
Fax: –
Web: www.mediastorm.biz

CEO: –
CFO: Frank Connolly
HR: –
FYE: December 31
Type: Private

Media Storm is a rainmaker looking to bring a deluge. The company provides media planning and buying services for television radio print and interactive channels. Media Storm creates showers of customers primarily for clients in the entertainment industry; it specializes in audience acquisition for broadcasters cable networks pay-per-view companies and television program syndicators. Customers have included such big names as HBO NBCUniversal Food Network Twentieth Century Fox and the NFL. The company also drives traffic and memberships for e-commerce client Shopzilla. Managing partners Tim Williams and Craig Woerz created Media Storm in 2001.

	Annual Growth	12/03	12/04	12/05	12/06	12/07
Sales ($ mil.)	50.5%	–	36.5	80.9	114.4	124.3
Net income ($ mil.)	40.8%	–	3.8	7.1	10.1	10.6
Market value ($ mil.)	–	–	–	–	–	–
Employees	–	–	–	–	–	170

MEDIAMIND TECHNOLOGIES INC.

135 W. 18th St. 5th Fl.
New York NY 10011
Phone: 646-202-1320
Fax: 212-686-9208
Web: www.mediamind.com

CEO: Neil Nguyen
CFO: Sarit Firon
HR: –
FYE: December 31
Type: Subsidiary

MediaMind (formerly Eyeblaster) puts a lot of thought into online advertising. Advertisers and media agencies use the company's campaign management software to create and administer rich media content including online mobile and in-game advertisements. Its portfolio also includes tools for monitoring and measuring such metrics as display time and interaction rate. MediaMind offers services ranging from custom development and testing to data tracking and analysis. Its products have been used in advertisements for NIKE Sony Ford Toyota Vodafone MasterCard and McDonalds among others. The company went public in 2010; it was bought by Digital Generation (formerly DG FastChannel) for $418 million in 2011.

MEDICAL ACTION INDUSTRIES, INC.   NMS: MDCI

500 Expressway Drive South
Brentwood, NY 11717
Phone: 631 231-4600
Fax: –
Web: www.medical-action.com

CEO: Paul D Meringolo
CFO: –
HR: –
FYE: March 31
Type: Public

Medical Action Industries knows in advance that its products will end up in hospitals' waste bins. The company manufactures markets and distributes a wide range of single-use disposable medical products. Some of its main products include wash basins and bedpans IV start kits containment systems for medical waste sterilization products dressing and surgical sponges and laboratory products (such as Petri dishes and specimen containers). Though it sells primarily to hospitals Medical Action Industries also serves doctors dentists veterinary clinics outpatient centers and nursing homes.

	Annual Growth	03/09	03/10	03/11	03/12	03/13
Sales ($ mil.)	10.5%	296.1	290.1	362.5	437.3	441.6
Net income ($ mil.)	–	5.0	16.8	4.4	0.2	(54.9)
Market value ($ mil.)	(7.8%)	135.9	201.1	137.7	93.8	98.3
Employees	9.1%	854	831	1,289	1,210	1,210

MEDICAL INFORMATION TECHNOLOGY, INC.

MEDITECH CIR
WESTWOOD, MA 02090
Phone: 781-821-3000
Fax: –
Web: www.meditech.com

CEO: Howard Messing
CFO: Barbara A Manzolillo
HR: –
FYE: December 31
Type: Private

Medical Information Technology knows what to prescribe for the operational disorders of health care information systems. The company which does business as MEDITECH provides software used mainly by hospitals in the management of clinical and financial departments ambulatory care centers long-term care facilities nursing homes and home health care programs. Its applications include electronic health records (EHR) products tailored for patient identification and scheduling care management clinical data management long-term and ambulatory care behavioral health and financial and reimbursement management. The company's core market is the US but Canada accounts for nearly 10% of sales.

	Annual Growth	12/12	12/13	12/14	12/15	12/16
Sales ($ mil.)	(7.3%)	–	579.6	517.0	475.5	462.3
Net income ($ mil.)	(18.2%)	–	133.3	123.5	70.1	72.9
Market value ($ mil.)	–	–	–	–	–	–
Employees	–	–	–	–	–	4,000

MEDICAL PROPERTIES TRUST INC   NYS: MPW

1000 Urban Center Drive, Suite 501   CEO: Edward K. Aldag
Birmingham, AL 35242   CFO: R. Steven Hamner
Phone: 205 969-3755   HR: -
Fax: 205 969-3756   FYE: December 31
Web: www.medicalpropertiestrust.com   Type: Public

Hospitals trust Medical Properties to provide the leases under which their facilities operate. The self-advised real estate investment trust (REIT) invests in and owns more than 120 health care facilities including acute care hospitals inpatient rehabilitation hospitals and wellness centers in 25 US states and Germany. California and Texas combined account for nearly 50% of the REIT's annual revenue. It leases the facilities to more than 25 hospital operating companies under long-term triple-net leases where the tenant bears most of the operating costs. Prime Healthcare Services and Ernest Health are among the REIT's largest clients. Medical Properties Trust entered the European health care market in 2013.

	Annual Growth	12/14	12/15	12/16	12/17	12/18
Sales ($ mil.)	25.9%	312.5	441.9	541.1	704.7	784.5
Net income ($ mil.)	111.8%	50.5	139.6	225.0	289.8	1,016.7
Market value ($ mil.)	3.9%	5,107.4	4,266.0	4,558.8	5,107.4	5,959.8
Employees	14.4%	45	50	54	66	77

MEDICINE SHOPPE INTERNATIONAL INC.

1 Rider Trail Plaza Dr. Ste. 300   CEO: -
Earth City MO 63045   CFO: -
Phone: 314-993-6000   HR: -
Fax: 314-872-5500   FYE: June 30
Web: www.medicineshoppe.com   Type: Subsidiary

With locations spreading like the flu Medicine Shoppe International (MSI) is the nation's largest independent retail pharmacy franchisor. A subsidiary of Cardinal Health since 1995 MSI has more than 700 locations in about 45 US states and the Virgin Islands. Internationally MSI has more than 200 stores in Canada China Indonesia Japan and the Middle East. MSI pharmacies specialize in prescriptions (more than 97% of sales) and offer only health-related inventory including Medicine Shoppe-brand nonprescription products. Many locations offer free services such as immunizations and health screenings. The Medicine Shoppe was founded in 1968 by St. Louis pharmacist Michael Busch.

MEDICINES CO (THE)   NMS: MDCO

8 Sylvan Way   CEO: Clive A Meanwell
Parsippany, NJ 07054   CFO: Christopher J Visioli
Phone: 973 290-6000   HR: Patricia Vogt
Fax: -   FYE: December 31
Web: www.themedicinescompany.com   Type: Public

The Medicines Company will meet you at the hospital. The drug developer focuses on treatments used in acute care settings including the ER the surgical suite and the cardiac catheterization lab. It aims to be a leader in the areas of acute cardiovascular care and surgery and perioperative care. Its marketed products include Angiomax an anticoagulant used during coronary angioplasties; it also sells Brilinta. The Medicines Company has other compounds in various stages of development including cangrelor an anti-platelet agent with possible use during cardiac catheterization and antibiotic oritavancin.

	Annual Growth	12/13	12/14	12/15	12/16	12/17
Sales ($ mil.)	(49.5%)	687.9	724.4	309.0	167.8	44.8
Net income ($ mil.)	-	15.5	(32.2)	(352.8)	(119.1)	(708.4)
Market value ($ mil.)	(8.3%)	2,826.2	2,024.9	2,732.5	2,483.7	2,000.7
Employees	(26.1%)	571	727	614	410	170

MEDICINOVA INC   NMS: MNOV

4275 Executive Drive, Suite 650   CEO: Yuichi Iwaki
La Jolla, CA 92037   CFO: Carla Reyes
Phone: 858 373-1500   HR: -
Fax: -   FYE: December 31
Web: www.medicinova.com   Type: Public

MediciNova has medicine all over the map. The biopharmaceutical company has a diverse pipeline of products in development that aim to treat everything from asthma and cancer to anxiety and insomnia. Two of its core candidates are being clinically tested for use in the treatment of severe asthma and multiple sclerosis. Others are being developed for preterm labor interstitial cystitis (urinary frequency and bladder pain) and urinary incontinence. MediciNova has been building its development portfolio through licensing agreements acquiring product rights primarily from midsized Japanese pharmaceutical companies such as Kissei Pharmaceutical Kyorin Pharmaceutical and Mitsubishi Tanabe Pharma Corporation.

	Annual Growth	12/09	12/10	12/11	12/12	12/13
Sales ($ mil.)	648.0%	-	-	-	0.8	6.0
Net income ($ mil.)	-	(20.4)	(20.2)	(17.7)	(11.0)	(4.0)
Market value ($ mil.)	(25.8%)	158.4	106.0	38.2	36.9	48.1
Employees	(18.6%)	25	18	14	12	11

MEDICIS PHARMACEUTICAL CORPORATION   NYSE: MRX

7720 N. Dobson Rd.   CEO: Jonah Shacknai
Scottsdale AZ 85256-2740   CFO: Richard D Peterson
Phone: 602-808-8800   HR: -
Fax: 602-808-0822   FYE: December 31
Web: www.medicis.com   Type: Public

Medicis Pharmaceutical is a smooth operator when it comes to skin. It is a specialty pharmaceutical company that develops and markets branded prescription products for dermatological and aesthetic conditions. Major products include the Dysport injectable formulation for temporary improvement of frown lines Restalyne injectable gel for smoothing facial wrinkles Solodyn oral tablets for moderate to severe acne and Vanos topical cream for psoriasis and dermatitis. These products are marketed primarily to dermatologists and plastic surgeons in the US. Medicis was acquired for about $2.6 billion by Valeant Pharmaceuticals the largest publicly traded drug maker in Canada in December 2012.

MEDIDATA SOLUTIONS, INC.   NMS: MDSO

350 Hudson Street, 9th Floor   CEO: Tarek A Sherif
New York, NY 10014   CFO: Rouven Bergmann
Phone: 212 918-1800   HR: -
Fax: -   FYE: December 31
Web: www.mdsol.com   Type: Public

Medidata Solutions has electronic remedies to help clinical trials run smoothly. Founded in 1999 the company offers cloud-based applications that help biotechnology pharmaceutical and other life sciences companies conduct clinical trials and related research. Its products include hosted software for administering and managing clinical trials electronic data capture applications study management applications and patient diaries. The company also offers a variety of professional services such as consulting implementation integration and maintenance. Medidata operates in more than 115 countries but most of its sales come from the US.

	Annual Growth	12/13	12/14	12/15	12/16	12/17
Sales ($ mil.)	18.5%	276.8	335.1	392.5	463.4	545.5
Net income ($ mil.)	27.8%	16.7	6.1	13.2	29.0	44.4
Market value ($ mil.)	1.2%	3,545.8	2,798.5	2,888.7	2,911.0	3,713.9
Employees	23.3%	923	1,077	1,487	1,424	2,130

MEDIFAST INC
NYS: MED

100 International Drive
Baltimore, MD 21202
Phone: 410 581-8042
Fax: –
Web: www.medifastnow.com

CEO: Daniel R. (Dan) Chard
CFO: Timothy G. Robinson
HR: Jeanne M. City
FYE: December 31
Type: Public

Medifast tries to help people slim down and shape up... fast. The company develops and sells Medifast brand health and diet products including food and beverages (meal replacement shakes bars) as well as disease management products for diabetics. Until 2018 Medifast operated through two segments Medifast and Franchise Medifast Weight Control Centers (MWCC) and Wholesale. The Medifast segment included Direct (customers order Medifast products online) and OPTAVIA (formerly Take Shape For Life personal coaching division with independent contractor "health coaches") operations. MWCC and Wholesale covers franchised brick-and-mortar walk-in clinics.

	Annual Growth	12/14	12/15	12/16	12/17	12/18
Sales ($ mil.)	15.1%	285.3	272.8	274.5	301.6	501.0
Net income ($ mil.)	43.4%	13.2	20.1	17.8	27.7	55.8
Market value ($ mil.)	38.9%	398.2	360.5	494.1	828.5	1,483.7
Employees	(7.7%)	579	425	422	399	420

MEDIVATION INC
NMS: MDVN

525 Market Street, 36th Floor
San Francisco, CA 94105
Phone: 415 543-3470
Fax: 415 543-3411
Web: www.medivation.com

CEO: David T Hung
CFO: Jennifer Jarrett
HR: –
FYE: December 31
Type: Public

Medivation motivates medicine makers. The company acquires develops and sells (or partners with companies working on) biopharmaceuticals. Medivation initiates drug development programs seeking out candidates that address unmet medical needs and have the potential to rapidly enter clinical development and marketing stages. The firm typically develops its drug candidates through early-stage clinical trials and then determines whether to conduct further studies or to seek a partner or buyer to continue later-stage trials. Medivation's lead candidate XTANDI was approved by the FDA to treat certain forms of prostate cancer in 2012; the drug was developed in partnership with Astellas.

	Annual Growth	12/10	12/11	12/12	12/13	12/14
Sales ($ mil.)	83.6%	62.5	60.4	181.7	272.9	710.5
Net income ($ mil.)	–	(34.0)	(38.8)	(41.3)	(42.6)	276.5
Market value ($ mil.)	60.1%	2,370.1	7,204.0	7,993.0	9,970.9	15,562.5
Employees	51.5%	92	121	257	370	485

MEDIWARE INFORMATION SYSTEMS INC.
NASDAQ: MEDW

11711 W. 79th St.
Lenexa KS 66214
Phone: 913-307-1000
Fax: 913-307-1111
Web: www.mediware.com

CEO: Bill Miller
CFO: Robert Watkins
HR: –
FYE: June 30
Type: Private

Mediware Information Systems keeps blood banks' computers from becoming a bloody mess. The company offers data management systems for blood banks hospitals and pharmacies. Mediware is known for its clinical information systems which combine third-party and proprietary software to manage hospital departments. Products include the HCLL transfusion management system for tracking blood bank and transfusion facility inventories the WORx drug therapy management software for pharmacies and the InSight performance management software suite. In 2012 Mediware was acquired and taken private by private equity firm Thoma Bravo in a deal valued at about $195 million.

MEDLINE INDUSTRIES INC.

1 Medline Place
Mundelein IL 60060
Phone: 847-949-5500
Fax: 800-351-1512
Web: www.medline.com

CEO: Charles N Mills
CFO: –
HR: –
FYE: December 31
Type: Private

When health care supplies are on the line Medline Industries goes toe-to-toe with the big guys. With more than 125000 products the family-owned company's catalog includes hospital furnishings durable medical equipment housekeeping supplies and exam gloves and garments. The firm manufactures and distributes health care products to such customers as hospitals long-term care facilities physician practices and home health providers. It also acts as a distributor for other manufacturers' products. In addition Medline offers inventory and supply chain solutions for health care providers. Products are marketed by its more than 1100 sales representatives through some 50 distribution centers in 20 countries.

MEDNAX, INC.
NYS: MD

1301 Concord Terrace
Sunrise, FL 33323
Phone: 954 384-0175
Fax: –
Web: www.mednax.com

CEO: Roger J. Medel
CFO: Vivian Lopez-Blanco
HR: Cara Rhoads
FYE: December 31
Type: Public

MEDNAX is a multi-specialty medical group with a national focus. Through subsidiaries including Pediatrix Medical Group and American Anesthesiology the holding company operates a medical network composed of more than 4200 affiliated physicians specialty practitioners and subspecialists who focus on children's and women's health. It provides neonatal pediatric and obstetric care primarily in hospitals; it also operates a growing number of anesthesia and radiology practices. In addition MEDNAX conducts clinical research and offers practice administration services to physician members and hospital customers in the areas of billing compliance managed care contracting recruiting risk management and staffing.

	Annual Growth	12/14	12/15	12/16	12/17	12/18
Sales ($ mil.)	10.6%	2,438.9	2,780.0	3,183.2	3,458.3	3,647.1
Net income ($ mil.)	(4.1%)	317.3	336.3	324.9	320.4	268.6
Market value ($ mil.)	(15.9%)	5,805.8	6,293.2	5,854.1	4,693.1	2,898.1
Employees	3.9%	10,175	11,885	14,615	15,900	11,875

MEDSEEK INC.

3000 RIVERCHASE GALLERIA # 1500
HOOVER, AL 35244-2315
Phone: 205-982-5800
Fax: –
Web: www.medseek.com

CEO: Rupen Patel
CFO: Dave Morgan
HR: –
FYE: December 31
Type: Private

Hospitals searching for help with website development could find answers from MedSeek. The Web development company designs and manages websites and intranets for more than 1100 hospitals. It offers a propriety content management software called eHealth ecoSystem and also provides custom application design. Its Web portals feature physician directories and job boards and they provide secure access to clinical information and facilitate communication between doctors patients and hospitals. MedSeek was founded in 1996.

	Annual Growth	12/06	12/07	12/08	12/10	12/11
Sales ($ mil.)	21.6%	–	23.0	25.1	34.6	50.2
Net income ($ mil.)	94.6%	–	0.2	1.6	2.4	2.4
Market value ($ mil.)	–	–	–	–	–	–
Employees	–	–	–	–	–	50

MEDSTAR HEALTH, INC.

10980 GRANTCHESTER WAY WA
COLUMBIA, MD 210446097
Phone: 410-772-6500
Fax: –
Web: www.medstarhealth.org

CEO: Kenneth A. Samet
CFO: Susan K. Nelson
HR: –
FYE: June 30
Type: Private

Whether you're seeing stars or are just plain sickly MedStar Health can cater to you. The not-for-profit organization runs 10 hospitals and about 20 other health-related businesses across Maryland and the Washington DC area including Union Memorial and Georgetown University Hospital. With more than 3000 beds and 6000 affiliated physicians MedStar has a comprehensive service offering including acute and long-term sub-acute care emergency services home health care and rehabilitation. It also operates emergency clinics and assisted living and nursing homes maintains a primary care and specialist physician network (MedStar Physician Partners) and conducts research and medical education activities.

	Annual Growth	12/08	12/09*	06/11	06/13	06/18
Sales ($ mil.)	12.5%	–	1,936.5	4,011.7	4,217.2	5,604.0
Net income ($ mil.)	5.5%	–	200.8	271.0	311.4	324.6
Market value ($ mil.)	–	–	–	–	–	–
Employees		–	–	–	–	33,000

*Fiscal year change

MEDSTAR-GEORGETOWN MEDICAL CENTER, INC.

3800 RESERVOIR RD NW
WASHINGTON, DC 200072113
Phone: 202-444-2000
Fax: –
Web: www.medstargeorgetown.org

CEO: –
CFO: Pipper Williams
HR: Iman Mohammed
FYE: June 30
Type: Private

Medstar-Georgetown Medical Center (dba as Medstar Georgetown University Hospital as a part of MedStar Health) is a 609-bed acute care teaching hospital serving residents of the greater Washington DC area including Maryland and Virginia. The hospital's staff of more than 1100 physicians represents a wide range of medical specializations including cardiology oncology neurology/neurosurgery and surgical transplantation. Medstar Georgetown provides a comprehensive array of inpatient outpatient surgical and rehabilitative care services. The hospital is part of a local network of affiliated primary care providers.

	Annual Growth	06/09	06/10	06/11	06/15	06/16
Sales ($ mil.)	0.4%	–	782.5	809.1	774.6	801.8
Net income ($ mil.)	15.0%	–	45.4	43.7	98.1	104.8
Market value ($ mil.)	–	–	–	–	–	–
Employees		–	–	–	–	4,000

MEDTOX SCIENTIFIC INC.

NASDAQ: MTOX

402 W. County Rd. D
St. Paul MN 55112
Phone: 651-636-7466
Fax: 651-636-5351
Web: www.medtox.com

CEO: Richard J Braun
CFO: –
HR: –
FYE: December 31
Type: Public

Doctors depend on MEDTOX Scientific to gather up specimen cups and analyze the contents for any number of substances. Customers can either ship urine samples off to the company's central labs for testing or buy the company's diagnostic and screening tests for use at the point of collection. In addition to testing for drugs of abuse MEDTOX Laboratories specializes in clinical and forensic toxicology including heavy metals analysis and hazardous-materials exposure monitoring. The company's MEDTOX Diagnostics subsidiary develops and manufactures onsite drug testing kits for rapid detection. MEDTOX Scientific was acquired by diagnostics and laboratory services giant LabCorp in 2012.

MEDTRONIC SOFAMOR DANEK USA INC.

2600 Sofamor Danek Dr.
Memphis TN 38132
Phone: 901-396-3133
Fax: 901-344-0843
Web: www.medtronic.com/about-medtronic/business-ove

CEO: –
CFO: Gary Ellis
HR: –
FYE: May 31
Type: Subsidiary

Medtronic Sofamor Danek USA wants to help us all stand up straight and proud. It is the the lead business in Medtronic's Spinal unit and one of the world's biggest maker of spinal implants. It products treat degenerative diseases deformities and spine and cranium trauma. It manufactures both implanted devices and biologic bone graft products. It also develops minimally invasive surgical techniques and computer-assisted surgical instruments. The company's sister business Kyphon develops medical devices to help with spinal fractures caused by osteoporosis and cancer. Medtronic Sofamor Danek USA markets and distributes its products worldwide.

MEENAN OIL CO. L.P.

3020 Burns Ave.
Wantagh NY 11793-4407
Phone: 516-783-1000
Fax: 516-781-2332
Web: www.meenan.com

CEO: –
CFO: –
HR: –
FYE: June 30
Type: Subsidiary

"Me" may be at the beginning of Meenan Oil's name but it's the customer who comes first at the home heating oil company. Meenan Oil offers expert tank analysis heating and cooling services brand-name equipment and home security monitoring services to customers in New Jersey New York and Pennsylvania. The company's headquarters include a garage and repair shop installation equipment warehouses 12 loading and unloading stations and a 1.3 million gallon storage tank. Meenan Oil is a subsidiary of Star Gas Partners which is controlled by investment firm Kestrel Energy Partners LLC.

MEET GROUP INC (THE)

NAS: MEET

100 Union Square Drive
New Hope, PA 18938
Phone: 215 862-1162
Fax: –
Web: www.meetme.com

CEO: Geoffrey Cook
CFO: James Bugden
HR: –
FYE: December 31
Type: Public

MeetMe is all about making new friends. Formerly called Quepasa Corporation the company aims to connect people through social games and apps across iPhone Android Web and mobile Internet platforms. The company took its current shape after merging Quepasa (which targeted a Latin American audience) with Insider Guides (doing business as myYearbook.com) in 2011; it rebranded as MeetMe in 2012. The new name reflects a less regional focus as MeetMe is designed for a global audience. The company earns revenue mainly through display advertising on its site as well as selling virtual currency for its games.

	Annual Growth	12/14	12/15	12/16	12/17	12/18
Sales ($ mil.)	41.3%	44.8	56.9	76.1	123.8	178.6
Net income ($ mil.)	–	(4.0)	6.0	46.3	(64.6)	1.1
Market value ($ mil.)	31.9%	114.3	267.4	368.3	210.6	345.8
Employees	26.3%	121	112	131	298	308

MEI TECHNOLOGIES, INC.

18050 SATURN LN STE 300
HOUSTON, TX 770584502
Phone: 281-283-6200
Fax: –
Web: www.meitechinc.com

CEO: David Cazes
CFO: Karen Todd
HR: –
FYE: December 31
Type: Private

MEI Technologies helps companies with high aspirations. The engineering and IT services firm serves government agencies such as NASA and the Department of Defense and the aerospace industry with cyber services space access test and evaluation and human performance. Other high-tech services include launch vehicle and shuttle payload integration and operations mission safety program management and support and spacecraft systems engineering and design. The company was founded in 1992 as Muñiz Engineering Inc. (MEI) by former CEO Edelmiro Muñiz.

	Annual Growth	12/05	12/06	12/07	12/08	12/12
Sales ($ mil.)	3.4%	–	–	116.1	118.9	137.2
Net income ($ mil.)	15.4%	–	–	2.3	(0.9)	4.8
Market value ($ mil.)	–	–	–	–	–	–
Employees		–	–	–	–	721

MEIJER INC.

2929 Walker Ave. NW
Grand Rapids MI 49544-9424
Phone: 616-453-6711
Fax: 616-791-2572
Web: www.meijer.com

CEO: Gerald Melville
CFO: Dan Webb
HR: –
FYE: January 31
Type: Private

Meijer (pronounced "Meyer") is a giant of retailing in the Midwest. The company's huge combination grocery and general merchandise stores average 200000 to 250000 sq. ft. each (or about the size of four regular grocery stores) and stock about 120000 items including Meijer private-label products. Meijer operates some 200 locations; about half are in Michigan while the rest are in Illinois Indiana Kentucky and Ohio. Customers can choose from 40-plus departments including apparel electronics hardware and toys. Most stores also sell gasoline offer banking services and have multiple in-store restaurants. Founder Hendrik Meijer opened his first store in 1934; the business is still family owned and run.

MEINEKE CAR CARE CENTERS INC.

128 S. Tryon St. Ste. 900
Charlotte NC 28202
Phone: 704-377-8855
Fax: 704-377-1490
Web: www.meineke.com

CEO: Ken Walker
CFO: Mike Carlet
HR: –
FYE: June 30
Type: Private

Careful not to exhaust its options Meineke Car Care Centers (formerly Meineke Discount Mufflers) is thinking outside the muffler. Through 900-plus franchised stores in the US Canada Mexico Saudi Arabia South Korea and China Meineke repairs brakes aligns wheels installs tires and provides factory-scheduled maintenance among other services. From the company website customers can learn about vehicle maintenance and safety print coupons and apply for the Meineke credit card. Sam Meineke founded the company in Houston in 1972. Today it is owned by Driven Brands which also franchises the Maaco and Econo Lube 'N Tune brands among others.

MELINTA THERAPEUTICS INC

44 Whippany Road
Morristown, NJ 07960
Phone: 908 617-1309
Fax: –
Web: www.cempra.com

NBB: MLNT Q

CEO: David Zaccardelli
CFO: Mark W. Hahn
HR: –
FYE: December 31
Type: Public

Melinta has found a weak spot in bacteria's ribosomes. The biopharmaceutical drug discovery and development company is working to create new antibiotics to treat drug-resistant infections. Melinta's lead product Baxdela (delafloxacin) was FDA-approved in 2017 for the treatment of acute bacterial skin and skin structure infections caused by susceptible bacteria. The company also markets Vabomere for the treatment of urinary tract infections Orbactiv for the treatment of skin infections and Minocin injection for a variety of infections. Melinta's main pipeline candidate solithromycin is being developed for the treatment of community-acquired bacterial pneumonia. The company was founded by Susan Froshauer Peter Moore and Thomas Steitz who received the Nobel Prize in Chemistry for the ribosome science.

	Annual Growth	12/14	12/15	12/16	12/17	12/18
Sales ($ mil.)	58.7%	15.2	27.3	18.0	33.9	96.4
Net income ($ mil.)		(61.6)	(91.1)	(118.0)	(58.9)	(157.2)
Market value ($ mil.)	(57.1%)	263.4	348.8	31.4	177.0	8.9
Employees	51.5%	55	93	45	300	290

MEMORIAL HEALTH SERVICES

17360 BROOKHURST ST # 160
FOUNTAIN VALLEY, CA 927083720
Phone: 714-377-6748
Fax: –
Web: www.memorialcare.org

CEO: James Hobson
CFO: Cheryl Sadro
HR: –
FYE: June 30
Type: Private

Where do you go after you get sick riding the tea cups at Disneyland? Not-for-profit Memorial Health Services (known as MemorialCare) owns six hospitals in Southern California including Long Beach Memorial Medical Center Miller Children's Hospital Orange Coast Memorial Medical Center and Saddleback Memorial Medical Center. The facilities have a total of more than 1500 beds and offer a full spectrum of medical services including rehabilitation diagnostic/radiology and emergency services. MemorialCare also operates women's health facilities and other specialty and general practice clinics as well as home health and hospice programs. The organization was founded in 1907.

	Annual Growth	06/12	06/13	06/14	06/15	06/18
Sales ($ mil.)	117.8%	–	–	–	215.9	2,232.1
Net income ($ mil.)	56.3%	–	–	–	26.5	101.1
Market value ($ mil.)	–	–	–	–	–	–
Employees		–	–	–	–	6,000

MEMORIAL HEALTH SYSTEM

701 N 1ST ST
SPRINGFIELD, IL 627810001
Phone: 217-788-3000
Fax: –
Web: www.greathealthstartshere.com

CEO: Edgar J Curtis
CFO: –
HR: –
FYE: September 30
Type: Private

Memorial Health System provides the people of Central Illinois with health care services through three community-based not-for-profit hospitals as well as home health and primary care operations. Flagship facility Memorial Medical Center in Springfield with some 500 licensed beds provides comprehensive inpatient and outpatient acute-care services and conducts medical education and research programs. Two smaller hospitals — Taylorville Memorial Hospital and Abraham Lincoln Memorial Hospital — each with 25 beds serve the communities of Taylorville and Lincoln. Other operations include a hospice and home health care services provider a mental health organization and a primary care physician network.

	Annual Growth	09/13	09/14	09/15*	06/16*	09/16
Sales ($ mil.)	12.2%	–	67.4	955.9	753.1	84.9
Net income ($ mil.)	–	–	20.8	17.1	34.8	(28.9)
Market value ($ mil.)	–	–	–	–	–	–
Employees	–	–	–	–	–	2,400

*Fiscal year change

MEMORIAL HEALTH SYSTEM OF EAST TEXAS

1201 W FRANK AVE
LUFKIN, TX 759043357
Phone: 936-634-8111
Fax: –
Web: www.memorialhealth.us

CEO: Bryant H Krenek Jr
CFO: Ken Miller
HR: –
FYE: December 31
Type: Private

Memorial Health System of East Texas operates deep in the heart of East Texas. The system is anchored by the 270-bed Memorial Medical Center-Lufkin a full-service general acute care hospital offering everything from rehabilitative and diabetes care to specialized centers in heart disease and cancer treatment. The Lufkin hospital also includes Memorial Specialty Hospital a long-term ward for critically ill patients. In addition Memorial Health System of East Texas features two critical access hospitals with limited services including emergency care and diagnostic imaging; it also has a clinic network. It is part of non-profit health care systems operator Catholic Health Initiatives(CHI).

	Annual Growth	12/03	12/04	12/07	12/08	12/09
Sales ($ mil.)	13.5%	–	102.3	–	8.4	192.7
Net income ($ mil.)	–	–	–	–	0.0	22.3
Market value ($ mil.)	–	–	–	–	–	–
Employees	–	–	–	–	–	940

MEMORIAL HERMANN HEALTHCARE SYSTEM

929 GESSNER RD
HOUSTON, TX 770242515
Phone: 713-242-3000
Fax: –
Web: www.memorialhermann.org

CEO: Daniel J. Wolterman
CFO: Stacey Bevil
HR: –
FYE: June 30
Type: Private

Memorial Hermann Healthcare System is a Texas-sized operation. As Houston's largest not-for-profit health care system it includes 15 hospitals (including a children's hospital an orthopedic hospital and two rehabilitation hospitals) with more than 4000 beds and dozens of specialty treatment centers. The system also has joint ventures with four other hospitals in the Greater Houston metropolitan area (located in First Colony Kingwood and Tomball). Memorial Hermann provides medical training in affiliation with The University of Texas Health Science Center Medical School. Other services and programs include home health services air ambulances and imaging; it also offers health insurance coverage. In early 2019 Memorial Hermann canceled plans to merge with fellow Texas health care provider Baylor Scott & White Health.

	Annual Growth	06/04	06/05	06/06	06/07	06/08
Sales ($ mil.)	13.4%	–	–	–	2,506.6	2,841.3
Net income ($ mil.)	(92.3%)	–	–	–	209.9	16.3
Market value ($ mil.)	–	–	–	–	–	–
Employees	–	–	–	–	–	24,000

MEMORIAL HOSPITAL

1101 MICHIGAN AVE
LOGANSPORT, IN 469471596
Phone: 574-753-7541
Fax: –
Web: www.logansportmemorial.org

CEO: –
CFO: –
HR: –
FYE: December 31
Type: Private

If your Eel River boat has been sunk by a Wabash cannonball you're probably a short crawl from a hospital. Logansport Memorial Hospital is a 80-bed acute care regional medical center serving the residents of Cass County and the surrounding communities in north central Indiana. The hospital offers a full range of medical services and programs including primary and emergency care and specialized services in areas such as diabetes cardiac rehabilitation medical imaging respiratory therapy and mammography. Logansport Memorial Hospital has about 40 physicians on its active medical staff. The hospital opened in 1925 as the Cass County Hospital and changed its name to Memorial Hospital in 1947.

	Annual Growth	12/08	12/09	12/15	12/16	12/17
Sales ($ mil.)	3.1%	–	55.3	67.2	69.7	70.4
Net income ($ mil.)	10.1%	–	1.0	4.0	1.7	2.1
Market value ($ mil.)	–	–	–	–	–	–
Employees	–	–	–	–	–	507

MEMORIAL HOSPITAL CORPORATION

1400 E BOULDER ST
COLORADO SPRINGS, CO 809095599
Phone: 719-365-5000
Fax: –
Web: www.uchealth.org

CEO: Mike Scialdone
CFO: –
HR: Jerry Piard
FYE: June 30
Type: Private

Memorial Hospital tries to keep good health more than a memory for the patients in its care. The hospital is a 520-bed general hospital which provides a range of children's and adult health-care services and specialties including cardiac care cancer treatment trauma care women's services pediatric medicine and rehabilitation. The hospital has about 700 physicians on its medical staff. Memorial Hospital also includes the 100-bed Memorial Hospital North and Children's Hospital Colorado as well as outpatient clinics throughout the Colorado Springs area. In 2012 it became an affiliate of University of Colorado Health.

	Annual Growth	12/06	12/07*	06/14	06/15	06/16
Sales ($ mil.)	3.6%	–	503.2	–	612.1	693.8
Net income ($ mil.)	3.6%	–	18.7	–	34.5	25.7
Market value ($ mil.)	–	–	–	–	–	–
Employees	–	–	–	–	–	2,438

*Fiscal year change

MEMORIAL MEDICAL CENTER

701 N 1ST ST
SPRINGFIELD, IL 627810001
Phone: 217-788-3000
Fax: –
Web: www.memorialmedical.com

CEO: –
CFO: –
HR: –
FYE: September 30
Type: Private

If you've lost the spring in your step and need a little care Memorial Medical Center will be there. As the flagship facility for Memorial Health System in Springfield Illinois this acute care and teaching hospital provides a wide range of medical and surgical services as well as emergency medicine and outpatient care. Its myriad specialties include cardiovascular maternity cancer care behavioral health orthopedic rehabilitation and burn treatment services. The hospital which sees 25000 inpatients per year also has special surgical divisions for bariatric procedures and organ transplants. The 500-bed hospital is a teaching affiliate of the Southern Illinois University (SIU) School of Medicine.

	Annual Growth	09/13	09/14	09/15	09/16	09/17
Sales ($ mil.)	(28.3%)	–	1,850.6	667.8	699.3	682.2
Net income ($ mil.)	(6.9%)	–	78.9	(28.4)	12.8	63.7
Market value ($ mil.)	–	–	–	–	–	–
Employees	–	–	–	–	–	2,849

MEMORIAL SLOAN-KETTERING CANCER CENTER

1275 YORK AVE
NEW YORK, NY 100656007
Phone: 212-639-2000
Fax: –
Web: www.mskcc.org

CEO: Craig B. Thompson
CFO: Michael P. Gutnick
HR: Kerry Bessey
FYE: December 31
Type: Private

Memorial Sloan-Kettering Cancer Center (MSKCC) leads the way in cancer research and treatment. The center includes the 500-bed Memorial Hospital for Cancer and Allied Diseases providing pediatric and adult cancer care and the Sloan Kettering Institute for cancer research activities. Memorial Hospital specializes in bone-marrow transplants radiation therapy and chemotherapy. It also offers programs in cancer prevention diagnosis treatment research and education. The Sloan Kettering Institute conducts medical and clinical laboratory research on cancer genetics and therapeutics. In addition to the main cancer center and research facilities in New York City MSKCC operates clinics in New York New Jersey and Long Island.

	Annual Growth	12/05	12/06	12/09	12/13	12/17
Sales ($ mil.)	9.7%	–	1,623.0	2,105.6	582.7	4,499.1
Net income ($ mil.)	(0.2%)	–	320.6	(195.5)	1.0	314.4
Market value ($ mil.)	–	–	–	–	–	–
Employees	–	–	–	–	–	9,325

MEMRY CORPORATION

3 Berkshire Blvd.
Bethel CT 06801
Phone: 203-739-1100
Fax: 203-798-6606
Web: www.memry.com

CEO: Dean Tulumaris
CFO: Richard F Sowerby
HR: Jose Santana
FYE: June 30
Type: Subsidiary

Memry's products are designed to have a long memory. The company makes specialized metal and plastic products that are used primarily in medical devices. The company develops manufactures and sells components (wire tubing) and sub-assemblies made from nitinol a nickel-and-titanium-based "shape memory alloy" with more than 10 times the elasticity of normal metals. Nitinol is used in surgical instruments such as peripheral vascular and non-vascular stents guidewires and catheters. Medical applications account for more than 90% of Memry's sales. In 2008 Italian scientific equipment manufacturer SAES Getters bought the company for $78 million making Memry a wholly-owned subsidiary.

MENARD INC.

4777 Menard Dr.
Eau Claire WI 54703-9604
Phone: 715-876-5911
Fax: 715-876-2868
Web: www.menards.com

CEO: –
CFO: –
HR: –
FYE: January 31
Type: Private

If sticks and stones break bones what can two-by-fours and two-inch nails do? Menard's wondering that now that its biggest rivals (#1 home improvement giant The Home Depot and #2 Lowe's) are busy hammering away at its home turf. One of the Midwest's largest home improvement chains Menard boasts 270 stores in more than a dozen states including Illinois Indiana Iowa Kansas Kentucky Michigan Minnesota Missouri Nebraska North and South Dakota Ohio Wisconsin and Wyoming. Stores sell floor coverings hardware millwork paint and tools. Unlike competitors all the company's stores have full-service lumberyards. Menard is owned by president and CEO John Menard who founded the company in 1972.

MENASHA CORPORATION

1645 Bergstrom Rd.
Neenah WI 54956
Phone: 920-751-1000
Fax: 920-751-1236
Web: www.menasha.com

CEO: –
CFO: Thomas M Rettler
HR: –
FYE: December 31
Type: Private

Packaging giant Menasha definitely has "This End Up." Founded in 1849 as a woodenware business the holding company now manufactures packaging and paperboard returnable materials-handling systems product labels and promotional materials as well as offers logistics and marketing services. Its subsidiaries include Menasha Packaging (corrugated packaging and point-of-purchase displays) ORBIS Corporation (plastic reusable packaging) and LeveragePoint Media (in-store promotional services). Menasha is a family-owned business.

MENIL FOUNDATION INC.

1533 SUL ROSS ST
HOUSTON, TX 770064729
Phone: 713-525-9400
Fax: –
Web: www.menil.org

CEO: –
CFO: –
HR: –
FYE: June 30
Type: Private

The Menil Foundation controls the renowned art collection of the late John and Dominique de Menil. The collection was opened to the public in 1987 with the founding of a gallery in Houston. Key elements of the Menils' collection include African and tribal art Byzantine era pieces as well as 20th-century paintings (especially those done by surrealists including Max Ernst and Ren-© Magritte). The war chest for this impressive collection was funded mainly from stock in Schlumberger the oil services firm founded by Dominique's father. (The oil connection explains how the French-born couple found their way to Houston.)

	Annual Growth	06/06	06/07	06/08	06/10	06/13
Sales ($ mil.)	(43.2%)	–	1,782.8	12.2	49.6	59.8
Net income ($ mil.)	–	–	–	(8.0)	35.2	44.6
Market value ($ mil.)	–	–	–	–	–	–
Employees	–	–	–	–	–	70

MENNO TRAVEL SERVICE, INC.

104 LAKE ST
EPHRATA, PA 175222415
Phone: 717-733-4131
Fax: –
Web: www.raptim.org

CEO: Michael Bedient
CFO: Vickie Unruh
HR: –
FYE: September 30
Type: Private

For travelers with more of a mission than sipping fruit drinks poolside in some tropical locale there's Menno Travel Service which does business as MTS TRAVEL. The company provides travel and tour services to religious and not-for-profit groups through nine offices in the US. MTS focuses on supporting Christian organizations in carrying out their missions worldwide with airfare accommodations and other travel arrangements. It also books religious and pilgrimage tours for groups and individuals; standard vacation tours packages and cruises; and business and meeting travel. MTS was acquired by Raptim Travel a provider of missionary humanitarian and religious travel services in 2009.

	Annual Growth	09/03	09/04	09/05	09/06	09/07
Sales ($ mil.)	8.1%	–	95.2	101.6	111.7	120.2
Net income ($ mil.)	3.0%	–	0.2	0.0	(0.6)	0.2
Market value ($ mil.)	–	–	–	–	–	–
Employees	–	–	–	–	–	156

MENTOR GRAPHICS CORPORATION

8005 SW BOECKMAN RD
WILSONVILLE, OR 970707777
Phone: 503-685-7000
Fax: –
Web: www.mentor.com

CEO: Walden C. (Wally) Rhines
CFO: Gregory K Hinckley
HR: Paul Sale
FYE: January 31
Type: Private

Mentor Graphics lends a hand to guide engineers who design electronic components. The company is a leading global developer of electronic design automation (EDA) software and systems used by engineers to design simulate and test electronic components such as integrated circuits (IC's) wire harness systems and printed circuit boards (PCBs). Products include PADS (PCB design) Nucleus (operating system) and Calibre (IC design). Its software is used to design components for such products as computers and wireless handsets. Clients come from the aerospace IT telecommunications and increasingly transportation industries. Mentor Graphics was acquired by Siemens for $4.5 billion in 2017.

	Annual Growth	01/13	01/14	01/15	01/16	01/17
Sales ($ mil.)	3.5%	–	1,156.4	1,244.1	1,181.0	1,282.5
Net income ($ mil.)	0.3%	–	153.6	145.2	94.2	154.9
Market value ($ mil.)	–	–	–	–	–	–
Employees	–	–	–	–	–	5,700

MERA PHARMACEUTICALS INC.

PINK SHEETS: MRPI

73-4460 Queen Ka'ahumanu Hwy. Ste. 110
Kailua-Kona HI 96740
Phone: 808-326-9301
Fax: 808-326-9401
Web: www.merapharma.com

CEO: –
CFO: Charles G Spaniak Sr
HR: –
FYE: October 31
Type: Public

Algae... It's got to be good for something and Mera Pharmaceuticals aims to find out what that might be. The company has developed the technology to cultivate microalgae on a large scale and is working to identify and extract substances it hopes can be used in nutritional supplements vitamins pharmaceuticals and cosmetics. The company's nutritional supplement products AstaFactor and Salmon Essentials contain astaxanthin which acts as an antioxidant and anti-inflammatory agent. Mera Pharmaceuticals also provides private label and bulk astaxanthin sales.

MERCER INC.

1166 Avenue of the Americas
New York NY 10036
Phone: 212-345-7000
Fax: 212-345-7414
Web: www.mercer.com

CEO: –
CFO: –
HR: –
FYE: December 31
Type: Subsidiary

Mercer offers a wide range of human resources-related consulting investment management and outsourcing services for companies around the world. As a consultant the firm helps its clients design and manage retirement plans and health insurance programs of various types. Mercer's investment management business focuses on retirement plan assets. In addition the firm offers consulting services designed to help clients get the most from their employers. As an outsourcer Mercer administers benefits programs for its customers. The firm operates in more than 180 cities in 40 countries worldwide. Insurance giant Marsh & McLennan wholly owns the company which was established in 1959 as William M. Mercer.

MERCANTILE BANCORP INC.

NYSE AMEX: MBR

200 N. 33rd St.
Quincy IL 62306-3455
Phone: 217-223-7300
Fax: 217-223-8938
Web: www.mercbanx.com

CEO: –
CFO: Michael P McGrath
HR: –
FYE: December 31
Type: Public

If you want to sell the farm Mercantile Bancorp can help. The holding company owns Illinois-based Mercantile Bank (it also has a location in Indiana) Royal Palm Bank in Florida and Kansas' Heartland Bank. Through a total of about a dozen offices the community-oriented banks offer deposit and loan products asset management retail brokerage services and agricultural business management. The majority of the company's loan portfolio is related to real estate including farmland construction and commercial and residential mortgage loans. Mercantile Bancorp sold two Illinois-based banks in 2010 Marine Bank and Trust and Brown County State Bank.

MERCER INSURANCE GROUP INC.

10 N. Hwy. 31
Pennington NJ 08534
Phone: 609-737-0426
Fax: 609-737-8719
Web: https://www.unitedfiregroup.com

CEO: Andrew R Speaker
CFO: David B Merclean
HR: –
FYE: December 31
Type: Subsidiary

Mercer Insurance Group protects small businesses. With roots stretching back to 1844 the firm offers a range of property/casualty insurance policies through subsidiaries Mercer Insurance Company Mercer Insurance Company of New Jersey Franklin Insurance and Financial Pacific Insurance. The company focuses on commercial coverage for small to midsized businesses including multi-peril liability workers' compensation inland marine and commercial automobile as well as personal lines (homeowners auto). The company was acquired by United Fire for some $190 million in 2011.

MERCANTILE BANK CORP.

NMS: MBWM

310 Leonard Street N.W.
Grand Rapids, MI 49504
Phone: 616 406-3000
Fax: –
Web: www.mercbank.com

CEO: Robert B. Kaminski
CFO: Charles E. (Chuck) Christmas
HR: Tina Van Valkenburg
FYE: December 31
Type: Public

Mercantile Bank Corporation is the holding company for Mercantile Bank of Michigan (formerly Mercantile Bank of West Michigan) which boasts assets of nearly $3 billion and operates more than 50 branches in central and western Michigan around Grand Rapids Holland and Lansing. The bank targets local consumers and businesses offering standard deposit services such as checking and savings accounts CDs IRAs and health savings accounts. Commercial loans make up more than three-fourths of the bank's loan portfolio. Outside of banking subsidiary Mercantile Insurance Center sells insurance products.

	Annual Growth	12/14	12/15	12/16	12/17	12/18
Assets ($ mil.)	3.8%	2,893.4	2,903.6	3,082.6	3,286.7	3,363.9
Net income ($ mil.)	24.8%	17.3	27.0	31.9	31.3	42.0
Market value ($ mil.)	7.7%	347.6	405.8	623.3	584.8	467.3
Employees	(1.3%)	731	701	682	701	693

MERCHANTS BANCSHARES, INC. (BURLINGTON, VT)

NMS: MBVT

275 Kennedy Drive
South Burlington, VT 05403
Phone: 802 658-3400
Fax: –
Web: www.mbvt.com

CEO: –
CFO: –
HR: –
FYE: December 31
Type: Public

Merchants Bancshares hopes to provide the missing lynx in your financial chain. With a lynx emblazoned on its logo subsidiary Merchants Bank provides regional banking services in Vermont and western Massachusetts through about 35 branches. The bank provides standard retail products including checking money market and savings accounts; IRAs; and CDs. Commercial real estate business and construction loans account for more than 50% of its loan portfolio while agricultural and consumer loans make up the remainder. Subsidiary Merchants Trust offers trust and investment management services. Founded in 1849 the bank's assets exceed $1.8 billion. New York's Community Bank System is buying Merchants for $304 million.

	Annual Growth	12/11	12/12	12/13	12/14	12/15
Assets ($ mil.)	5.8%	1,611.9	1,708.6	1,725.5	1,723.5	2,021.2
Net income ($ mil.)	(3.6%)	14.6	15.2	15.1	12.1	12.6
Market value ($ mil.)	1.9%	200.2	183.5	229.7	210.0	215.9
Employees	(1.0%)	331	322	329	314	318

MERCK & CO INC — NYS: MRK

2000 Galloping Hill Road
Kenilworth, NJ 07033
Phone: 908 740-4000
Fax: 908 735-1500
Web: www.merck.com

CEO: Rasha Kelej
CFO: Robert M. Davis
HR: Mirian M. Graddick-Weir
FYE: December 31
Type: Public

A top 5 global drugmaker Merck makes medicines for an array of maladies ranging from hypertension to cancer. The pharmaceutical giant's top products include cancer drug Keytruda diabetes drugs Januvia and Janumet HPV vaccine Gardasil cholesterol combatants Vytorin and Zetia and HIV therapy Isentress. In addition Merck makes childhood and adult vaccines for such diseases as measles mumps pneumonia and shingles as well as veterinary pharmaceuticals through Merck Animal Health. In addition the company provides analytics and clinical services to the health care sector. The US market accounts for about 45% of sales.

	Annual Growth	12/14	12/15	12/16	12/17	12/18
Sales ($ mil.)	0.0%	42,237.0	39,498.0	39,807.0	40,122.0	42,294.0
Net income ($ mil.)	(15.0%)	11,920.0	4,442.0	3,920.0	2,394.0	6,220.0
Market value ($ mil.)	–	0.0	0.0	0.0	0.0	0.0
Employees	(0.4%)	70,000	68,000	68,000	69,000	69,000

MERCURY GENERAL CORP. — NYS: MCY

4484 Wilshire Boulevard
Los Angeles, CA 90010
Phone: 323 937-1060
Fax: –
Web: www.mercuryinsurance.com

CEO: Gabriel Tirador
CFO: Theodore R. Stalick
HR: –
FYE: December 31
Type: Public

Named after the Roman god of commerce and travel Mercury General hopes to combine the two and become the ultimate auto insurance provider. The company is the parent of a group of insurers including Mercury Casualty Company that write automobile insurance for all risk classifications in about a dozen states. Plain old private auto insurance accounts for a majority of premiums written. However Mercury General also sells commercial vehicle insurance and a bit of homeowners mechanical breakdown umbrella and fire insurance. The company is a leader in the California auto market and has significant operations in Florida.

	Annual Growth	12/14	12/15	12/16	12/17	12/18
Assets ($ mil.)	4.3%	4,600.3	4,628.6	4,788.7	5,101.3	5,433.7
Net income ($ mil.)	–	177.9	74.5	73.0	144.9	(5.7)
Market value ($ mil.)	(2.3%)	3,136.1	2,577.2	3,332.0	2,957.4	2,861.6
Employees	0.0%	4,400	4,300	4,200	4,300	4,400

MERCURY SYSTEMS INC — NMS: MRCY

50 Minuteman Road
Andover, MA 01810
Phone: 978 256-1300
Fax: –
Web: www.mrcy.com

CEO: Mark Aslett
CFO: Gerald M. (Gerry) Haines
HR: –
FYE: June 30
Type: Public

Mercury Systems (formerly Mercury Computer Systems) delivers digital signals faster than a wing-footed messenger. The company makes real-time digital signal processing (DSP) systems for the homeland security military and aerospace and telecommunications markets. Its military systems process radar sonar and other signals. It also makes specialized electronics used in semiconductor wafer inspection and airport baggage screeners. Mercury Systems acts as a subcontractor to prime contractors such as Northrop Grumman and Raytheon.

	Annual Growth	06/15	06/16	06/17	06/18	06/19
Sales ($ mil.)	29.2%	234.8	270.2	408.6	493.2	654.7
Net income ($ mil.)	45.7%	10.4	19.7	24.9	40.9	46.8
Market value ($ mil.)	48.1%	794.2	1,348.6	2,283.3	2,064.7	3,816.3
Employees	27.5%	629	965	1,159	1,320	1,661

MERCY CARE

4755 S 44TH PL
PHOENIX, AZ 850408895
Phone: 602-263-3000
Fax: –
Web: www.mercycareaz.org

CEO: Mark Fisher
CFO: –
HR: –
FYE: June 30
Type: Private

Mercy Care is a not-for-profit provider of managed health care services in Arizona. The Mercy Care Plan provides these services under a contract with the Arizona Health Care Cost Containment System the state of Arizona's Medicaid program. The plan provides health coverage and prescription drug benefits to some 300000 members. The company founded in 1985 is affiliated with St. Joseph's Hospital & Medical Center (which is part of Catholic Healthcare West) Dignity Health and Carondelet Health Network. The plan is administered by health care management firm Schaller Anderson.

	Annual Growth	06/09	06/10	06/11	06/12	06/14
Sales ($ mil.)	(1.3%)	–	1,904.2	1,939.8	1,747.6	1,808.9
Net income ($ mil.)	(3.8%)	–	49.0	58.3	28.3	41.9
Market value ($ mil.)	–	–	–	–	–	–
Employees	–	–	–	–	–	500

MERCY CHILDREN'S HOSPITAL

2401 GILLHAM RD
KANSAS CITY, MO 641084619
Phone: 816-234-3000
Fax: –
Web: www.childrensmercy.org

CEO: Randall L. O'Donnell
CFO: Sandra A. J. Lawrence
HR: –
FYE: June 30
Type: Private

Children's Mercy Kansas City is a not-for-profit health system providing care services for youngsters in and around Kansas City Missouri. The system has two hospitals three urgent care facilities and five campuses featuring primary care offices and more than 25 specialty clinics. Among its specialized services are diabetes and endocrinology genetics heart surgery neonatology and rehabilitation. Children's Mercy also offers medical training and research facilities. Founded in 1897 the system today has some 500000 patient visits annually.

	Annual Growth	06/10	06/11	06/13	06/15	06/16
Sales ($ mil.)	4.5%	–	816.8	9.1	978.1	1,020.2
Net income ($ mil.)	22.3%	–	13.2	(0.6)	79.2	36.0
Market value ($ mil.)	–	–	–	–	–	–
Employees	–	–	–	–	–	7,000

MERCY COLLEGE

555 BROADWAY FRNT
DOBBS FERRY, NY 105221189
Phone: 914-455-2650
Fax: –
Web: www.mercy.edu

CEO: –
CFO: –
HR: Anne Gilmartin
FYE: June 30
Type: Private

Mercy College is a private Catholic school founded by the Sisters of Mercy in 1950. The college provides higher education to some 9000 undergraduate and graduate students in the New York City area. Mercy College offers 90 degrees in fields including business accounting civic and cultural studies computer science education health professions literature language communication natural sciences and social sciences. The institution also provides some online courses as well as professional certification programs. Mercy College employs some 200 full-time faculty members.

	Annual Growth	06/09	06/10	06/15	06/17	06/18
Sales ($ mil.)	(0.6%)	–	154.1	190.2	151.5	146.7
Net income ($ mil.)	(3.9%)	–	28.2	38.2	38.1	20.6
Market value ($ mil.)	–	–	–	–	–	–
Employees	–	–	–	–	–	500

MERCY CORPS

45 SW ANKENY ST
PORTLAND, OR 972043500
Phone: 503-796-6800
Fax: –
Web: www.mercycorpsnw.org

CEO: –
CFO: Beth Dehamel
HR: Cameron Hall
FYE: June 30
Type: Private

Mercy Corps is dedicated to helping the poor and oppressed in developing countries. The not-for-profit organization offers emergency relief and economic support as well as assistance in building sustainable communities. It also develops curriculum guides to introduce students to various topics ranging from Kurdish history and Afghan henna art to the worldwide clean water campaign. Since its founding Mercy Corps programs have provided about $1.5 billion in assistance to people in 106 nations. Originally the organization was named Save the Refugees Fund when it was founded by Dan O'Neill in response to the plight of Cambodian refugees in 1979.

	Annual Growth	06/11	06/12	06/13	06/14	06/15
Sales ($ mil.)	12.2%	–	233.0	236.3	275.5	329.1
Net income ($ mil.)	–	–	(7.7)	(4.7)	(3.1)	3.0
Market value ($ mil.)	–	–	–	–	–	–
Employees	–	–	–	–	–	450

MERCY GWYNEDD UNIVERSITY

1325 SUMNEYTOWN PIKE
GWYNEDD VALLEY, PA 194370010
Phone: 215-646-7300
Fax: –
Web: www.gmercyu.edu

CEO: –
CFO: –
HR: –
FYE: June 30
Type: Private

Gwynedd-Mercy University (GMercyU formerly Gwynedd-Mercy College) is a private Catholic school founded in 1948 by the Sisters of Mercy. It offers about 40 associate and bachelor's degree programs at schools of allied health arts and sciences business education and nursing. The college also offers graduate programs in business education and nursing. GMercyU has an enrollment of nearly 3000 students and a student-to-faculty ratio of 13 to 1. In addition to its main campus the college operates centers for life-long learning (as part of its business school) in Philadelphia and Fort Washington Pennsylvania that cater to working adults. GMercyU was founded in 1948.

	Annual Growth	06/08	06/09	06/14	06/16	06/17
Sales ($ mil.)	5.6%	–	48.2	65.4	47.0	74.5
Net income ($ mil.)	–	–	0.0	7.0	(0.5)	3.0
Market value ($ mil.)	–	–	–	–	–	–
Employees	–	–	–	–	–	300

MERCY HEALTH

14528 SOUTH OUTER 40 RD # 100
CHESTERFIELD, MO 630175743
Phone: 314-579-6100
Fax: –

CEO: Lynn Britton
CFO: Shannon Sock
HR: –
FYE: June 30
Type: Private

Mercy Health formerly known as the Sisters of Mercy Health System provides a range of health care and social services through its network of facilities and service organizations. The organization operates some 35 acute care hospitals (including four specialty heart hospitals and two children's hospitals) with more than 4200 licensed beds as well as 700 clinics and outpatient facilities in four Midwestern states. Its hospital groups include facilities for nursing homes medical practices and outpatient centers. Mercy Health also operates Resource Optimization & Innovation (ROi) its industry-leading health care supply chain organization and health outreach organizations in Louisiana Mississippi and Texas.

	Annual Growth	03/08	03/09*	06/10	06/17	06/18
Sales ($ mil.)	8.8%	–	2,936.3	18.8	5,527.8	6,254.5
Net income ($ mil.)	–	–	(196.1)	7.2	558.1	243.9
Market value ($ mil.)	–	–	–	–	–	–
Employees	–	–	–	–	–	8,800

*Fiscal year change

MERCY HEALTH - ST. RITA'S MEDICAL CENTER, LLC

730 W MARKET ST
LIMA, OH 458014602
Phone: 419-227-3361
Fax: –
Web: www.mylivwell.org

CEO: –
CFO: John Renner
HR: –
FYE: December 31
Type: Private

St. Rita's Medical Center is all about healing. The general medical-surgical hospital serves west central Ohio. The not-for-profit facility provides health care services in a number of medical specialties including trauma and emergency care orthopedics cancer pediatrics women's health and cardiovascular disease. It also has physical rehabilitation mental health and outpatient care facilities and works to improve community health through disease screenings smoking cessation programs and other outreach initiatives. Established in 1918 by the Sisters of Mercy the hospital is a member of Catholic Healthcare Partners.

	Annual Growth	12/03	12/04	12/06	12/16	12/17
Sales ($ mil.)	3.5%	–	272.3	3,505.1	408.6	427.7
Net income ($ mil.)	13.7%	–	22.6	143.1	91.4	120.1
Market value ($ mil.)	–	–	–	–	–	–
Employees	–	–	–	–	–	2,850

MERCY HOSPITAL

144 STATE ST
PORTLAND, ME 041013795
Phone: 207-879-3000
Fax: –
Web: www.northernlighthealth.org

CEO: Eileen F Skinner
CFO: Stephen McDonnell
HR: –
FYE: September 24
Type: Private

Mercy Health System of Maine provides medical services to the people of Portland and other residents of Cumberland County. The health system operates two hospital campuses as well as primary and specialty care centers. It boasts a total of 230 beds. The system also operates a substance abuse treatment program a women's shelter a home health and hospice program and a hospitality home for families of patients undergoing treatment. Mercy Health System of Maine which includes Mercy Hospital and VNA Home Health Hospice is a part of Eastern Maine Healthcare Systems.

	Annual Growth	09/12	09/13	09/14	09/15	09/16
Sales ($ mil.)	14.6%	–	–	167.5	213.7	220.1
Net income ($ mil.)	–	–	–	4.4	(22.9)	(21.5)
Market value ($ mil.)	–	–	–	–	–	–
Employees	–	–	–	–	–	1,200

MERCY HOSPITAL AND MEDICAL CENTER

2525 S MICHIGAN AVE
CHICAGO, IL 606162332
Phone: 312-567-2201
Fax: –
Web: www.mercy-chicago.org

CEO: Carol L. Schneider
CFO: Tom Garvey
HR: –
FYE: June 30
Type: Private

Chicagoans in the loop know Mercy Hospital and Medical Center is the place to go for health care. The Catholic hospital located near Chicago's Loop (the historic downtown commercial district) has about 320 beds and operates a network of community clinics and occupational health facilities that provide employment-related services such as drug screening executive physicals and physical therapy. Other services include a cancer treatment center inpatient hospice care unit eye care center heart and vascular center diabetes treatment center stroke center and inpatient and outpatient chemical dependence recovery programs. Chicago's first teaching hospital it is owned by Ohio-based system Trinity Health.

	Annual Growth	06/12	06/13	06/14	06/15	06/18
Sales ($ mil.)	(2.1%)	–	265.7	273.4	278.1	238.4
Net income ($ mil.)	–	–	4.1	(6.0)	(7.5)	(66.4)
Market value ($ mil.)	–	–	–	–	–	–
Employees	–	–	–	–	–	1,550

MERCY HOSPITAL SOUTH

10010 KENNERLY RD
SAINT LOUIS, MO 631282106
Phone: 314-525-1000
Fax: –
Web: www.mercy.net

CEO: –
CFO: –
HR: –
FYE: June 30
Type: Private

St. Anthony's Medical Center applies its skills to medical cases in the Midwest. The hospital serves residents in the areas surrounding St. Louis Missouri as well as portions of southwestern Illinois. With about 770 beds and some 800 affiliated physicians the hospital provides a comprehensive offering including inpatient and outpatient medical surgical diagnostic and behavioral health care. The hospital operates a level II trauma center cancer and chest pain units and a pediatric emergency center as well as several urgent care facilities. It also offers home health hospice laboratory and pharmacy services. St. Anthony's Medical Center was founded in 1900 by the Franciscan Sisters of Germany.

	Annual Growth	06/12	06/13	06/14	06/15	06/17
Sales ($ mil.)	0.5%	–	443.8	424.0	482.5	452.0
Net income ($ mil.)	–	–	38.6	13.3	1.4	(43.4)
Market value ($ mil.)	–	–	–	–	–	–
Employees	–	–	–	–	–	3,900

MERCY HOSPITAL SPRINGFIELD

1235 E CHEROKEE ST
SPRINGFIELD, MO 658042203
Phone: 417-820-2000
Fax: –
Web: www.mercy.net

CEO: Lynn Britton
CFO: –
HR: –
FYE: June 30
Type: Private

Mercy Hospital Springfield is an 890-bed acute-care hospital in the Mercy Health system. The facility provides health care to southwestern Missouri and northwestern Arkansas and includes the Mercy Children's Hospital Springfield. Other hospital specialties include cardiology and stroke care as well as women's and seniors' health cancer emergency trauma burn neuroscience rehabilitation and sports medicine. In addition to its hospital in Springfield Mercy Hospital Springfield operates a number of community clinics and specialty care centers in the area.

	Annual Growth	06/12	06/13	06/14	06/15	06/16
Sales ($ mil.)	2.0%	–	965.6	964.4	948.2	1,024.7
Net income ($ mil.)	6.1%	–	87.7	42.6	93.4	104.7
Market value ($ mil.)	–	–	–	–	–	–
Employees	–	–	–	–	–	4,400

MERCY MEDICAL CENTER

1000 N VILLAGE AVE
ROCKVILLE CENTRE, NY 115701000
Phone: 516-594-6470
Fax: –

CEO: Dr Alan Guerci
CFO: William Armstrong
HR: –
FYE: December 31
Type: Private

Overlooking Long Island's Hempstead Lake State Park Mercy Medical Center offers healthcare services to patients just east of Manhattan. The not-for-profit Catholic hospital has expertise in weight loss and orthopedic surgeries mammograms and breast health and women's health services. It also provides outpatient services such as family and mental health care. With about 380 beds the medical center employs some 700 physicians who deliver about 1300 babies each year. Its acute care facilities include a suburban branch of Memorial Sloan-Kettering Cancer Center. Mercy Medical Center established in 1913 by the Sisters of the Congregation of the Infant Jesus is part of Catholic Health Services of Long Island.

	Annual Growth	12/12	12/13	12/14	12/15	12/17
Sales ($ mil.)	3.6%	–	203.3	185.9	195.3	234.0
Net income ($ mil.)	–	–	(3.6)	2.7	6.7	0.7
Market value ($ mil.)	–	–	–	–	–	–
Employees	–	–	–	–	–	1,610

MERCY MEDICAL CENTER, INC.

1320 MERCY DR NW
CANTON, OH 447082641
Phone: 330-489-1000
Fax: –
Web: www.cantonmercy.org

CEO: Thomas E Cecconi
CFO: David K Stewart
HR: –
FYE: December 31
Type: Private

Mercy Medical Center keeps patients doing the cancan in Canton. The facility is a 480-bed acute care hospital serving residents of five counties in southeastern Ohio. The Catholic medical center has 700 physicians and provides a comprehensive range of care including inpatient outpatient and rehabilitative services. It operates specialty care centers for cardiac vascular stroke and cancer treatment as well as trauma chest pain and rehabilitation units. Mercy Medical Center also operates outpatient health centers in the communities surrounding Canton Ohio. The facility is part of the Sisters of Charity Health System (SCHS) a not-for-profit ministry of the Sisters of Charity of St. Augustine.

	Annual Growth	12/13	12/14	12/15	12/16	12/17
Sales ($ mil.)	(0.1%)	–	301.1	298.3	309.1	299.8
Net income ($ mil.)	–	–	5.0	2.6	(1.1)	(14.3)
Market value ($ mil.)	–	–	–	–	–	–
Employees	–	–	–	–	–	80

MERCY SHIPS INTERNATIONAL

15862 STATE HIGHWAY 110 N
LINDALE, TX 757715932
Phone: 903-939-7000
Fax: –
Web: www.keithbrinkman.com

CEO: Myron E Ullman III
CFO: –
HR: –
FYE: December 31
Type: Private

Mercy Ships brings floating medical care to areas of the world that need it most. The Christian-based not-for-profit serves more than 50 developing nations around the world from its ship Africa Mercy which has six operating rooms and nearly 500 berths and a land-based clinic in Sierra Leone. Staff and volunteers perform cleft lip and cleft palate surgeries cataract and tumor removals and other medical procedures. The organization also distributes water purification kits prescription eyeglasses and prescriptions and offers a variety of training and education programs for local workers. Mercy Ships was founded in 1978 by Don and Deyon Stephens (who still serve as president and company VP respectively).

	Annual Growth	12/06	12/07	12/08	12/09	12/15
Sales ($ mil.)	2.0%	–	58.7	49.1	52.9	68.7
Net income ($ mil.)	14.0%	–	5.7	(1.0)	1.1	16.4
Market value ($ mil.)	–	–	–	–	–	–
Employees	–	–	–	–	–	650

MERGE HEALTHCARE INC

NMS: MRGE

350 North Orleans Street, 1st Floor
Chicago, IL 60654
Phone: 312 565-6868
Fax: –
Web: www.merge.com

CEO: –
CFO: Steven M Oreskovich
HR: Shelley Wyka
FYE: December 31
Type: Public

Merge Healthcare wants your imaging department to share the health. The company develops image and information exchange management software mainly for cardiology ophthalmology orthopedics radiology and clinical trials. Its products are available as traditional packaged software or hosted in the cloud. Its Merge iConnect suite lets users create information exchanges that enable sharing of diagnostic images and results within a facility and with other entities. The company also serves the business side of health care offering software to manage revenue cycle physician practices imaging centers and billing departments. It has customers in North America Europe and Asia.

	Annual Growth	12/09	12/10	12/11	12/12	12/13
Sales ($ mil.)	36.4%	66.8	140.3	232.4	248.9	231.7
Net income ($ mil.)	–	0.3	(11.5)	(5.5)	(28.8)	(39.0)
Market value ($ mil.)	(8.8%)	325.0	360.7	469.1	238.9	224.4
Employees	20.1%	385	750	925	860	800

MERIAL INC.

3239 Satellite Blvd. Bldg. 500
Duluth GA 30096-4640
Phone: 678-638-3000
Fax: 972-385-9887
Web: www.bb-armr.com

CEO: -
CFO: -
HR: -
FYE: December 31
Type: Subsidiary

Merial keeps animals merry. The company makes a variety of drugs and vaccines that treat and prevent disease in pets livestock and wildlife. Used by veterinarians farmers and pet owners in some 150 countries the company's lead products include Ivomec and Eprinex anti-parasitics for livestock; Frontline flea and tick treatments for cats and dogs; and heartworm prevention drug Heartgard. Merial focuses on four treatment areas: anti-infectious drugs pain medicines parasiticides and vaccines. The company sells its over-the-counter products wherever pet supplies are sold such as pet stores and online retailers and its prescription medications through veterinarians. The company is owned by Sanofi.

MERIDIAN BANCORP INC NMS: EBSB

67 Prospect Street
Peabody, MA 01960
Phone: 617 567-1500
Fax: -

CEO: Richard J. Gavegnano
CFO: Mark L. Abbate
HR: -
FYE: December 31
Type: Public

Meridian Bancorp is the holding company of East Boston Savings Bank which provides standard deposit and lending services to individuals and businesses in the greater Boston area. The bank writes single-family commercial and multifamily mortgages as well as construction and business loans and consumer loans. East Boston Savings operates about 30 branches in eastern Massachusetts. Mutual holding company Meridian Financial Services owns 59% of Meridian Bancorp.

	Annual Growth	12/14	12/15	12/16	12/17	12/18
Assets ($ mil.)	17.2%	3,278.5	3,524.5	4,436.0	5,299.5	6,178.7
Net income ($ mil.)	25.7%	22.3	24.6	34.2	42.9	55.8
Market value ($ mil.)	6.3%	600.7	754.9	1,011.9	1,103.0	766.7
Employees	4.2%	466	488	500	538	549

MERIDIAN BIOSCIENCE INC. NMS: VIVO

3471 River Hills Drive
Cincinnati, OH 45244
Phone: 513 271-3700
Fax: -
Web: www.meridianbioscience.com

CEO: Amy M. Winslow
CFO: Melissa A. Lueke
HR: -
FYE: September 30
Type: Public

Disease detection is the name of Meridian Bioscience's game. The company makes immunodiagnostic test kits and sample transport media for reference laboratories hospitals and doctors' offices. Its products analyze blood urine and other body fluid and tissue samples to diagnose such maladies as respiratory illness (pneumonia influenza) gastrointestinal disease (ulcers diarrhea) viruses (mononucleosis chicken pox) and parasitic diseases. The company's Life Science division makes and sells biological supplies including antigens antibodies and reagents used by research labs and other diagnostics firms; it also provides contract manufacturing of proteins and other biologics for drug developers.

	Annual Growth	09/15	09/16	09/17	09/18	09/19
Sales ($ mil.)	0.8%	194.8	196.1	200.8	213.6	201.0
Net income ($ mil.)	(9.0%)	35.5	32.2	21.6	23.8	24.4
Market value ($ mil.)	(13.7%)	730.4	823.9	610.8	636.4	405.3
Employees	3.3%	580	650	640	585	660

MERIT MEDICAL SYSTEMS, INC. NMS: MMSI

1600 West Merit Parkway
South Jordan, UT 84095
Phone: 801 253-1600
Fax: -
Web: www.merit.com

CEO: Fred P. Lampropoulos
CFO: Bernard Birkett
HR: Louise Bott
FYE: December 31
Type: Public

When it comes to medical devices this company believes its merits speak for themselves. Merit Medical Systems makes disposable medical products used during interventional and diagnostic cardiology radiology gastroenterology and pulmonary procedures. The company's products include catheters guide wires needles and tubing used in heart stent procedures pacemaker placement and angioplasties as well as products for endoscopy dialysis and other procedures. Merit Medical sells its products as stand-alone items or in custom-made kits to hospitals and other health care providers as well as to custom packagers and equipment makers worldwide.

	Annual Growth	12/14	12/15	12/16	12/17	12/18
Sales ($ mil.)	14.7%	509.7	542.1	603.8	727.9	882.8
Net income ($ mil.)	16.3%	23.0	23.8	20.1	27.5	42.0
Market value ($ mil.)	34.0%	951.3	1,020.5	1,454.7	2,371.4	3,063.6
Employees	16.8%	3,105	3,754	4,150	4,876	5,783

MERITAGE HOMES CORP NYS: MTH

8800 E. Raintree Drive, Suite 300
Scottsdale, AZ 85260
Phone: 480 515-8100
Fax: -
Web: www.meritagehomes.com

CEO: Steven J. (Steve) Hilton
CFO: Hilla Sferruzza
HR: Javier Feliciano
FYE: December 31
Type: Public

Meritage Homes builds houses in high-growth areas of the western eastern and central US. Targeting first- and second-time luxury and active senior homebuyers the builder constructs single-family homes in Arizona California Colorado Texas Florida Georgia North Carolina South Carolina and Tennessee. Sold under the Meritage Homes and luxury Monterey Homes brands its houses are priced from roughly $180000 to $1.3 million and at an average of $400000. Founded in 1985 about two-fifth of the builders' home sales are made in the western US.

	Annual Growth	12/14	12/15	12/16	12/17	12/18
Sales ($ mil.)	12.8%	2,179.8	2,579.5	3,041.7	3,241.0	3,528.6
Net income ($ mil.)	12.4%	142.2	128.7	149.5	143.3	227.3
Market value ($ mil.)	0.5%	1,370.2	1,294.1	1,324.9	1,949.3	1,398.0
Employees	5.6%	1,300	1,409	1,485	1,605	1,615

MERITAGE HOSPITALITY GROUP INC NBB: MHGU

45 Ottawa Ave SW, Suite 600
Grand Rapids, MI 49503
Phone: 616 776-2600
Fax: 616 776-2776
Web: www.meritagehospitality.com

CEO: Robert Schermer Jr
CFO: Tracey Smith
HR: -
FYE: December 30
Type: Public

This company is really big on the beef in Michigan. Meritage Hospitality Group is a leading franchisee of Wendy's fast food hamburger restaurants with about 70 locations operating mostly in western and southern Michigan. The units franchised from Wendy's/Arby's Group offer a menu of burgers and other sandwiches fries and other items. In addition to its quick-service operations Meritage runs four franchised O'Charley's casual dining restaurants in Michigan near Grand Rapids and Detroit. The company was founded in 1986 as Thomas Edison Inns. The family of chairman Robert Schermer Sr. including CEO Robert Schermer Jr. controls Meritage.

	Annual Growth	12/14*	01/16	01/17*	12/17	12/18
Sales ($ mil.)	28.4%	160.2	210.0	235.8	312.6	435.3
Net income ($ mil.)	47.4%	2.8	7.0	6.5	9.0	13.0
Market value ($ mil.)	37.0%	31.1	70.4	69.8	125.2	109.5
Employees	25.7%	4,000	5,100	5,700	6,800	10,000

*Fiscal year change

MERITER HEALTH SERVICES, INC.

202 S PARK ST
MADISON, WI 537151507
Phone: 608-417-5800
Fax: –
Web: www.meriter.com

CEO: Sue Erickson
CFO: Beth Erdman
HR: –
FYE: December 31
Type: Private

Meriter Health Services believes that the health concerns of its patients merits its careful attention. A teaching affiliate of the University of Wisconsin the Madison-based system serves residents of southern Wisconsin and northwestern Illinois. Its flagship facility is the 450-bed Meriter Hospital a not-for-profit community hospital providing general medical and surgical care as well as pediatric mental health services through its Child and Adolescent Psychiatric Hospital unit. Meriter Health Services also operates primary care clinics a home health care provider and clinical laboratories. It owns two-thirds of Physicians Plus Insurance a regional HMO.

	Annual Growth	12/08	12/09	12/10	12/11	12/12
Sales ($ mil.)	–	–	–	(1,872.1)	773.6	775.0
Net income ($ mil.)	20257.2%	–	–	0.0	(16.4)	12.8
Market value ($ mil.)	–	–	–	–	–	–
Employees	–	–	–	–	–	3,330

MERITOR INC

NYS: MTOR

2135 West Maple Road
Troy, MI 48084-7186
Phone: 248 435-1000
Fax: –
Web: www.meritor.com

CEO: Jeffrey A. (Jay) Craig
CFO: Kevin A. Nowlan
HR: Timothy J. Heffron
FYE: September 30
Type: Public

Meritor is a global supplier of drivetrain mobility braking and aftermarket solutions for commercial vehicle and industrial markets. It makes products such as axles brakes suspension systems and aftermarket transmissions for commercial and military vehicles including trucks and buses trailers and off-highway vehicles. Three of its largest customers are AB Volvo (primarily in Europe) Daimler and Paccar. The company divides its operations across two primary segments: Commercial Truck & Industrial and Aftermarket & Trailer. Meritor operates across North America Europe South America and the Asia/Pacific region. The US generates more than half its total revenue.

	Annual Growth	09/15	09/16	09/17	09/18	09/19
Sales ($ mil.)	5.8%	3,505.0	3,199.0	3,347.0	4,178.0	4,388.0
Net income ($ mil.)	46.0%	64.0	573.0	324.0	117.0	291.0
Market value ($ mil.)	14.9%	865.3	906.0	2,117.2	1,575.9	1,505.9
Employees	2.0%	8,400	8,000	8,200	8,600	9,100

MERITUS HEALTH INC.

11116 MEDICAL CAMPUS RD
HAGERSTOWN, MD 217426710
Phone: 301-790-8000
Fax: –
Web: www.meritushealth.com

CEO: –
CFO: –
HR: –
FYE: June 30
Type: Private

Meritus Health provides a wide range of medical services to patients living in western Maryland southern Pennsylvania and adjacent portions of West Virginia. The system's Meritus Medical Center has 250 beds and 40 bassinets and offers acute tertiary and long-term care including inpatient behavioral health services cardiac care obstetrics cancer treatment rehabilitation and trauma care. Meritus Health also operates the for-profit Meritus Enterprises a provider of outpatient health care including diagnostic imaging laboratory services and ambulatory surgery. In addition it provides general practice care at the Robinwood Professional Center.

	Annual Growth	06/09	06/10	06/11	06/12	06/13
Sales ($ mil.)	1112.5%	–	0.2	0.0	380.2	374.5
Net income ($ mil.)	–	–	–	0.0	7.5	17.6
Market value ($ mil.)	–	–	–	–	–	–
Employees	–	–	–	–	–	3,105

MERKLE GROUP INC.

7001 Columbia Gateway Dr.
Columbia MD 21046
Phone: 443-542-4000
Fax: 239-768-0711
Web: www.neogenomics.org

CEO: David S Williams
CFO: Rick Gross
HR: –
FYE: December 31
Type: Private

Has your company's marketing momentum moved from measurable to murky? Meet Merkle a customer relationship marketing agency that has counted enterprises such as Dell GEICO and the American Heart Association among its clients. Merkle helps clients market themselves by providing strategic consulting business intelligence and analytics media targeting and measurement and mail creation and production management services. The agency which manages more than 125 databases serves customers in a wide array of industries. It manages billions of direct mail pieces each year and owns a dozen offices throughout the US. Merkle was founded in 1971.

MERLE NORMAN COSMETICS, INC.

9130 BELLANCA AVE
LOS ANGELES, CA 900454772
Phone: 310-641-3000
Fax: –
Web: www.merlenorman.com

CEO: –
CFO: Michael Cassidy
HR: –
FYE: December 31
Type: Private

Merle Norman Cosmetics has built a foundation by offering samples to customers through its "try before you buy" concept. Founded by a young woman named Merle Nethercutt Norman the company opened its first shop in Santa Monica California in 1931. The family owned company makes and markets primarily skin care products and color cosmetics that are sold through some 2000 independently owned and operated retail outlets operating under the name Merle Norman Cosmetic Studios. Reaching from the US to Canada Mexico and the United Arab Emirates its studios are typically located in malls. Brand names include Automatic Definitive Inspirations Luxiva and Only Natural among others.

	Annual Growth	12/09	12/10	12/12	12/13	12/14
Sales ($ mil.)	(1.5%)	–	78.7	79.2	76.6	74.2
Net income ($ mil.)	(4.5%)	–	4.3	0.4	3.8	3.6
Market value ($ mil.)	–	–	–	–	–	–
Employees	–	–	–	–	–	529

MERRILL CORPORATION

1 MERRILL CIR
SAINT PAUL, MN 551085264
Phone: 651-646-4501
Fax: –
Web: www.merrillcorp.com

CEO: James (Rusty) Wiley
CFO: Thomas Donnelly
HR: –
FYE: January 31
Type: Private

Document services company Merrill is no relation to financial services giant Merrill Lynch but the companies do share an interest in SEC paperwork. Merrill Corporation is a provider of outsourced document management branded marketing services and other information management services. It helps clients gather organize and manage confidential and time-sensitive information for legal and financial transactions. In addition the company provides marketing and communication services such as document composition printing fulfillment and digital delivery as well as technology integration.

	Annual Growth	01/12	01/13	01/14	01/15	01/16
Sales ($ mil.)	(12.0%)	–	851.5	815.5	691.5	579.4
Net income ($ mil.)	–	–	(9.2)	24.6	64.5	78.1
Market value ($ mil.)	–	–	–	–	–	–
Employees	–	–	–	–	–	5,418

MERRILL LYNCH AND CO. INC.

Bank of America Corporate Center 100 N. Tryon St. CEO: –
Charlotte NC 28255 CFO: –
Phone: 704-386-5681 HR: –
Fax: 512-479-2553 FYE: December 31
  Type: Subsidiary

Economic crisis? Merrill Lynch cried bully on that. The Wall Street institution with the iconic bull logo is now the wealth management brokerage and investment banking arm of Bank of America. The retail banking giant acquired the distressed investment bank in 2009 in a move that greatly expanded its wealth management and international operations. Merrill Lynch is among the world's top brokerages with some $2.2 trillion in customer assets. The company also provides corporate finance investment banking and research services to institutional commercial and government clients. Merrill Lynch has offices in some 40 countries around the world.

MERRIMACK PHARMACEUTICALS INC   NMS: MACK

One Kendall Square, Suite B7201 CEO: –
Cambridge, MA 02139 CFO: Jean M Franchi
Phone: 617 441-1000 HR: –
Fax: – FYE: December 31
Web: www.merrimack.com Type: Public

Merrimack Pharmaceuticals takes a technological approach to fighting cancer. A biopharmaceutical company Merrimack develops oncology drugs using its proprietary Network Biology technology which combines biological data and computer-based modeling to discover and develop candidates. In 2015 it received US FDA approval and Taiwan FDA approval of ONIVYDE for the treatment of pancreatic cancer. The company has four additional candidates in clinical stage development; it also has additional candidates in its pipeline in pre-clinical stages of development. It is developing in vitro and in vivo diagnostics for use with its oncology candidates. Merrimack traces its roots back to the early 1990s.

	Annual Growth	12/12	12/13	12/14	12/15	12/16
Sales ($ mil.)	31.0%	48.9	47.8	102.8	89.3	144.3
Net income ($ mil.)	–	(91.3)	(130.9)	(83.3)	(148.0)	(151.7)
Market value ($ mil.)	(9.5%)	79.3	69.4	147.1	102.9	53.1
Employees	6.3%	230	254	306	426	294

MERRIMAN HOLDINGS INC.   NBB: MERR

250 Montgomery Street, 16th Floor CEO: D Jonathan Merriman
San Francisco, CA 94104 CFO: –
Phone: 415 248-5603 HR: –
Fax: – FYE: December 31
Web: www.merrimanco.com Type: Public

Merriman Holdings (formerly Merriman Curhan Ford Group) sees funds in its clients' futures. The company provides investment banking venture and corporate services asset management and investment research services with a focus on fast-growth sectors such as clean technology media and consumer services. Offerings include strategic advisory restructuring and private placements of stock warrants and convertibles. The company is also active in the emerging China market. Merriman Holdings has offices in New York City and San Francisco.

	Annual Growth	12/10	12/11	12/12	12/13	12/14
Sales ($ mil.)	(15.1%)	30.7	21.9	12.9	10.0	15.9
Net income ($ mil.)	–	(5.3)	(7.9)	(6.9)	(4.0)	(1.6)
Market value ($ mil.)	0.7%	9.9	1.9	0.3	0.6	10.2
Employees	(20.3%)	77	35	32	29	31

MERU NETWORKS INC.   NMS: MERU

894 Ross Drive CEO: Ken Xie
Sunnyvale, CA 94089 CFO: Andrew Del Matto
Phone: 408 215-5300 HR: –
Fax: – FYE: December 31
Web: www.merunetworks.com Type: Public

Meru Networks believes wireless networking should be a seamless experience for customers who don't want to worry about technology. The company develops networking equipment and software used to build wireless LANs. Its products include access points controllers and network management applications. Meru's products allow for the transmission of video voice and data over Wi-Fi connections. It targets customers in the education healthcare hospitality manufacturing and retail sectors among others. Meru has operations in Australia Canada China Germany India Japan Korea Singapore Sweden the UAE the UK and the US.

	Annual Growth	12/09	12/10	12/11	12/12	12/13
Sales ($ mil.)	11.1%	69.5	85.0	90.5	97.5	105.7
Net income ($ mil.)	–	(17.4)	(36.6)	(26.7)	(31.1)	(12.4)
Market value ($ mil.)	(34.6%)	–	353.7	94.7	60.8	98.9
Employees	14.7%	242	292	403	391	419

MERZ PHARMACEUTICALS INC.

4215 Tudor Ln. CEO: Bill Humphries
Greensboro NC 27410-8105 CFO: –
Phone: 336-856-2003 HR: –
Fax: 336-856-0107 FYE: June 30
Web: www.merzusa.com Type: Subsidiary

When the merciless sun has taken its toll on your skin Merz Pharmaceuticals will moisturize and replenish. Merz Pharmaceuticals the US subsidiary of German drugmaker Merz develops and distributes prescription and over-the-counter pharmaceutical treatments for skin and nail care. The company's products include Mederma which is used to reduce the appearance of scarring and Appearex which treats weak and brittle nails. It also makes Naftin a topical antifungal and the Aqua Glycolic line of skin cleansers and moisturizers. In addition Merz Pharmaceuticals distributes a handful of non-dermatology products developed by its parent company.

MESA AIR GROUP INC   NMS: MESA

410 North 44th Street, Suite 700 CEO: Jonathan G. Ornstein
Phoenix, AZ 85008 CFO: Michael J. Lotz
Phone: 602 685-4000 HR: –
Fax: – FYE: September 30
Web: www.mesa-air.com Type: Public

Mesa Air helps keep big carriers connected to many little places. Through its group of regional airline subsidiaries the company serves about 465-daily departures to nearly 100 cities across some 37 states Canada and Mexico via a fleet of almost 90 aircraft. Subsidiaries led by Mesa Airlines and Freedom Airlines operate under contract to provide connecting service for other airlines including US Airways and United Continental's United Airlines. The company also offers inter-island airline service in Hawaii as go!; consolidated passenger sales are largely attributable to operations on behalf of other airlines.

	Annual Growth	09/08	09/16	09/17	09/18	09/19
Sales ($ mil.)	(5.4%)	1,326.1	587.8	643.6	681.6	723.4
Net income ($ mil.)	–	(29.2)	14.9	32.8	33.3	47.6
Market value ($ mil.)	(51.3%)	–	–	–	435.4	211.9
Employees	(1.3%)	4,113	3,102	3,132	3,412	3,576

MESA LABORATORIES, INC.
NMS: MLAB

12100 West Sixth Avenue
Lakewood, CO 80228
Phone: 303 987-8000
Fax: –
Web: www.mesalabs.com

CEO: Gary M. Owens
CFO: John V. Sakys
HR: –
FYE: March 31
Type: Public

Mesa Laboratories measures its progress by the sales of its measurement devices. And so far it hasn't plateaued. The company makes niche-market electronic measurement testing and recording instruments for medical food processing electronics and aerospace applications. Mesa's products include sensors that record temperature humidity and pressure levels; flow meters for water treatment polymerization and chemical processing applications; and sonic concentration analyzers. The company also makes kidney dialysis treatment products including metering equipment and machines that clean dialyzers (or filters) for reuse. It also provides repair recalibration and certification services.

	Annual Growth	03/15	03/16	03/17	03/18	03/19
Sales ($ mil.)	9.7%	71.3	84.7	93.7	96.2	103.1
Net income ($ mil.)	(6.0%)	9.6	11.2	11.2	(3.0)	7.5
Market value ($ mil.)	33.7%	280.9	374.8	477.3	577.5	896.7
Employees	5.9%	276	367	381	366	347

MESA ROYALTY TRUST
NYS: MTR

601 Travis Street, Floor 16
Houston, TX 77002
Phone: 713 483-6020
Fax: –

CEO: –
CFO: –
HR: –
FYE: December 31
Type: Public

In oil and gas Enduro trusts. Enduro Royalty Trust is a Delaware trust formed in 2011 that owns royalty interests in oil and gas production properties in Texas Louisiana and New Mexico. The trust is entitled to receive 80% of net profits from the sale of oil and natural gas produced by privately held Enduro Sponsor at properties in the Permian Basin and in the East Texas/North Louisiana regions; it then makes monthly distributions to trust unitholders. Enduro Sponsor holds interests in more than 900 net producing wells that are operated by third-party oil and gas companies. Its properties have proved reserves of about 27 million barrels of oil equivalent. Enduro Royalty Trust filed to go public in 2011.

	Annual Growth	12/14	12/15	12/16	12/17	12/18
Sales ($ mil.)	(23.2%)	6.7	2.1	1.4	3.0	2.3
Net income ($ mil.)	(24.4%)	6.5	1.9	1.2	2.9	2.1
Market value ($ mil.)	(19.4%)	47.8	14.0	20.3	34.4	20.2
Employees		–	–	–	–	–

MESABI TRUST
NYS: MSB

c/o Deutsche Bank Trust Company Americas, Trust & Agency Services, 60 Wall Street, 24th Floor
New York, NY 10005
Phone: 904 271-2520
Fax: –
Web: www.mesabi-trust.com

CEO: –
CFO: –
HR: –
FYE: January 31
Type: Public

In the Iron Range of Mesabi the stockholders trust. Mesabi Trust collects royalties and bonuses from the sale of minerals that are shipped from Northshore Mining's Silver Bay Minnesota facility. The mining company is a wholly owned subsidiary of Cliffs a supplier of iron ore products to the steel industry. Northshore Mining pays royalties to Mesabi Trust based on production and sales of crude ore pulled from the trust's property; it has curtailed its extraction efforts citing lack of demand. Independent consultants track production and sales for Mesabi Trust. Deutsche Bank Trust Company Americas is the corporate trustee of Mesabi Trust.

	Annual Growth	01/15	01/16	01/17	01/18	01/19
Sales ($ mil.)	16.0%	26.1	9.7	10.7	34.6	47.3
Net income ($ mil.)	16.5%	24.8	8.6	9.6	33.5	45.6
Market value ($ mil.)	12.6%	224.1	57.7	179.7	325.4	360.0
Employees		–	–	–	–	–

MESIROW FINANCIAL HOLDINGS INC.

353 N. Clark St.
Chicago IL 60654
Phone: 312-595-6000
Fax: 312-595-4246
Web: www.mesirowfinancial.com

CEO: Richard S Price
CFO: Kristie Paskvan
HR: –
FYE: March 31
Type: Private

Mesirow Financial Holdings is an employee-owned company with nearly $380 million in equity investments and a global reach. Clients which are located in 38 countries include corporations public sector entities brokerages investment advisors and wealthy individuals and families. As part of its business Mesirow Financial manages some $61.7 billion in client assets; more than half ($35.4 billion) of this is invested in currencies and commodities. The company's operations span 18 offices located in metropolitan areas nationwide as well as in London. It was established in 1937 when Norman Mesirow purchased a seat on the New York Stock Exchange.

MESSER CONSTRUCTION CO.

643 W COURT ST
CINCINNATI, OH 452031511
Phone: 513-242-1541
Fax: –
Web: www.messer.com

CEO: Thomas M. (Tom) Keckeis
CFO: E. Paul Hitter
HR: –
FYE: September 30
Type: Private

From casinos and courthouses to laboratories and dormitories Messer Construction has built them all. The builder provides commercial construction services (including design/build and project management) for projects in Indiana Kentucky Ohio North Carolina and Tennessee. Messer completes over $830 million worth of projects each year for clients in the life sciences higher education senior living commercial manufacturing/industrial public and health care sectors among others. Its projects have included one of the US's only LEED-certified research buildings (at the University of Louisville) and the Newport Aquarium in Kentucky. Founded in 1932 employee-owned Messer boasts a return-customer rate of 80%.

	Annual Growth	09/12	09/13	09/14	09/15	09/17
Sales ($ mil.)	7.0%	–	831.7	1,029.8	1,167.1	1,092.0
Net income ($ mil.)	–	–	0.0	0.0	0.0	0.0
Market value ($ mil.)	–	–	–	–	–	–
Employees		–	–	–	–	900

MESSIAH COLLEGE

1 COLLEGE AVE
MECHANICSBURG, PA 170556805
Phone: 717-766-2511
Fax: –
Web: www.gomessiah.com

CEO: –
CFO: David Walker
HR: –
FYE: June 30
Type: Private

As its name implies Messiah College is a private Christian college that offers bachelor's degrees in the liberal and applied arts and sciences. Accredited by the Middle States Association of Colleges and Secondary Schools the institution serves more than 3000 students across more than 80 undergraduate majors. Messiah College with 200 full-time faculty members boasts a student/faculty ratio of 13:1. The institution's main campus located 12 miles southwest of Harrisburg Pennsylvania partners with a satellite campus in Philadelphia associated with Temple University. Previously named the Messiah Bible School and Missionary Training Home Messiah College was founded by the Brethren in Christ Church in 1909.

	Annual Growth	06/13	06/14	06/15	06/17	06/18
Sales ($ mil.)	(4.8%)	–	126.0	128.1	143.1	103.3
Net income ($ mil.)	131.2%	–	0.2	(0.5)	6.1	6.0
Market value ($ mil.)	–	–	–	–	–	–
Employees		–	–	–	–	800

MESTEK INC.
NBB: MCCK

260 North Elm Street
Westfield, MA 01085
Phone: 413 568-9571
Fax: –
Web: www.mestek.com

CEO: John E. Reed
CFO: –
HR: Joanne Berwald
FYE: December 31
Type: Public

Keeping the temperature just right is Mestek's main job. Through more than 35 subsidiaries Mestek makes heating ventilating and air-conditioning (HVAC) products such as hydronic heat-distribution units gas-fired heating and ventilating equipment louver and damper equipment boilers and refrigeration equipment. Mestek's Formtek family of companies designs builds and services metal-forming and fabricating systems. Its Embassy Industries arm makes radiant heating and plumbing products sold in North America and Europe. Mestek Technology provides computer software products that allow manufacturers to monitor equipment remotely.

	Annual Growth	12/14	12/15	12/16	12/17	12/18
Sales ($ mil.)	0.4%	345.5	347.1	311.0	329.3	350.7
Net income ($ mil.)	1.6%	17.4	18.0	16.0	15.0	18.5
Market value ($ mil.)	10.2%	146.4	157.6	180.2	218.4	216.1
Employees	–	–	–	–	–	–

META FINANCIAL GROUP INC
NMS: CASH

5501 South Broadband Lane
Sioux Falls, SD 57108
Phone: 605 782-1767
Fax: –
Web: www.metabank.com

CEO: J. Tyler Haahr
CFO: David W. Leedom
HR: Sheri Kamstra
FYE: September 30
Type: Public

Delivering financial products and services to Iowa and South Dakota is the calling of Meta Financial Group. The group's biggest component is MetaBank a 10-branch operation that offers standard banking solutions such as deposit accounts CDs home mortgages and student loans. Other subsidiaries provide prepaid card services insurance and a variety of tax related solutions. It holds a loan portfolio that exceeds $1 billion and deposits that surpass $3 billion.

	Annual Growth	09/15	09/16	09/17	09/18	09/19
Assets ($ mil.)	25.0%	2,529.7	4,006.4	5,228.3	5,835.1	6,182.9
Net income ($ mil.)	52.2%	18.1	33.2	44.9	51.6	97.0
Market value ($ mil.)	(6.0%)	1,579.2	2,291.5	2,964.1	3,124.8	1,232.9
Employees	16.8%	638	672	827	1,219	1,186

METALICO INC
ASE: MEA

186 North Avenue East
Cranford, NJ 07016
Phone: 908 497-9610
Fax: –
Web: www.metalico.com

CEO: Carlos E Aguero
CFO: Kevin Whalen
HR: –
FYE: December 31
Type: Public

No dude it's not a heavy metal band but Metalico is into metal — specifically scrap metal recycling and lead fabrication. The company collects ferrous and nonferrous metal at about 30 facilities in the eastern midwestern and southern US and recycles it into usable scrap. Recycled ferrous metal (iron and steel) is sold mainly to steelmakers including operators of electric arc furnace minimills and steel mills. Metalico's nonferrous scrap includes aluminum which is sold to makers of aluminum products. Metalico engages in lead fabrication at four US facilities. Its lead products include sheet (for roofing) and shot (for reloading).

	Annual Growth	12/09	12/10	12/11	12/12	12/13
Sales ($ mil.)	16.1%	291.7	553.3	660.9	573.6	530.0
Net income ($ mil.)	–	(3.4)	13.5	17.4	(13.1)	(34.8)
Market value ($ mil.)	(19.5%)	236.9	283.1	158.4	94.4	99.7
Employees	4.1%	658	782	768	766	774

METHES ENERGIES INTERNATIONAL LTD.
NBB: MEIL

3651 Lindell Road, Suite D-272
Las Vegas, NV 89103
Phone: 702 932-9964
Fax: –
Web: www.methes.com

CEO: –
CFO: Edward A Stoltenberg
HR: –
FYE: November 30
Type: Public

Methes Energies International lives and breathes biodiesel. Okay maybe the company doesn't breathe fuel but it resells biodiesel produced by third-party companies sells a line of biodiesel processors under the Denami brand and offers an array of services to biodiesel producers. The company also produces biodiesel through two facilities in Ontario and markets and sells its products throughout Canada and the US. Other offerings include selling feedstock (e.g. vegetable oils and animal fats used in biofuel production) installing and commissioning its Denami processors and licensing related proprietary software used to operate the processors. Founded in 2007 Methes Energies filed to go public in mid-2012.

	Annual Growth	11/10	11/11	11/12	11/13	11/14
Sales ($ mil.)	(1.2%)	5.7	11.8	6.5	8.9	5.5
Net income ($ mil.)	–	(1.0)	(0.8)	(4.0)	(5.7)	(6.3)
Market value ($ mil.)	(53.7%)	–	–	49.5	23.8	10.6
Employees	(7.4%)	–	29	33	44	23

METHODE ELECTRONICS INC
NYS: MEI

8750 West Bryn Mawr Avenue, Suite 1000
Chicago, IL 60631-3518
Phone: 708 867-6777
Fax: –
Web: www.methode.com

CEO: Donald W. Duda
CFO: John R. Hrudicka
HR: –
FYE: April 27
Type: Public

When it comes to making gear for manufacturers there's no madness in Methode Electronics' methods. Methode produces a wide variety of components especially electronic connectors and controls that are used by automotive manufacturers (products made for Ford and GM together account for more than half of sales) and in computers communications equipment industrial systems aircraft and spacecraft and consumer electronics. It also makes electrical bus systems and radio remote controls among other products.

	Annual Growth	05/15*	04/16	04/17	04/18	04/19
Sales ($ mil.)	3.2%	881.1	809.1	816.5	908.3	1,000.3
Net income ($ mil.)	(2.4%)	101.1	84.6	92.9	57.2	91.6
Market value ($ mil.)	(9.4%)	1,612.3	1,099.6	1,647.8	1,499.8	1,084.8
Employees	9.6%	4,295	4,345	4,464	5,056	6,187

*Fiscal year change

METHODIST HOSPITAL OF SOUTHERN CALIFORNIA

300 W HUNTINGTON DR
ARCADIA, CA 910073402
Phone: 626-898-8000
Fax: –
Web: www.methodisthospital.org

CEO: –
CFO: –
HR: John Peeples
FYE: December 31
Type: Private

If you're dehydrated in the Valley Methodist Hospital of Southern California can help. The hospital provides medical care to the residents of California's central San Gabriel Valley. The healthcare facility boasts some 600 beds and is part of Southern California Healthcare Systems. The not-for-profit hospital provides comprehensive acute care including surgical pediatric and intensive care units. It also offers a wide range of specialty services such as cardiology oncology neurology bariatrics and orthopedics. The hospital opened its doors in 1903 with five beds.

	Annual Growth	12/11	12/12	12/15	12/16	12/17
Sales ($ mil.)	1.3%	–	281.5	300.0	297.4	300.0
Net income ($ mil.)	81.5%	–	1.0	11.7	14.0	19.2
Market value ($ mil.)	–	–	–	–	–	–
Employees	–	–	–	–	–	2,200

METHODIST HOSPITALS OF DALLAS INC

1441 N BECKLEY AVE
DALLAS, TX 752031201
Phone: 877-637-4297
Fax: –
Web: www.methodisthealthsystem.org

CEO: Stephen L. (Steve) Mansfield
CFO: Michael J. Schaefer
HR: –
FYE: June 30
Type: Private

Methodist Hospitals of Dallas serves the health care needs of North Texas — from Mansfield to McKinney. The church-affiliated organization which does business as Methodist Health System operates 10 hospitals and more than two dozen family health centers and medical facilities in and around the area deemed by locals as Big D. The original hospital Methodist Dallas Medical Center opened in 1927. The 585-bed teaching and referral hospital boasts a Level I trauma center and an organ transplant program. Other facilities include the 317-bed Methodist Charlton Medical Center the 254-bed Methodist Mansfield Medical Center and the 334-bed Methodist Richardson Medical Center.

	Annual Growth	09/11	09/12	09/14*	06/15	06/16
Sales ($ mil.)	(18.3%)	–	969.2	1,096.9	411.4	431.7
Net income ($ mil.)	(31.9%)	–	165.3	137.0	21.9	35.6
Market value ($ mil.)	–	–	–	–	–	–
Employees	–	–	–	–	–	4,804

*Fiscal year change

METHODIST LE BONHEUR HEALTHCARE

1211 UNION AVE STE 700
MEMPHIS, TN 381046600
Phone: 901-516-7000
Fax: –
Web: www.methodisthealth.org

CEO: David G. Baytos
CFO: –
HR: Carol Shorb
FYE: December 31
Type: Private

Methodist Le Bonheur Healthcare (Methodist Healthcare) is happy to take care of sick people. The not-for-profit health care system serves the Memphis area with seven hospitals; multiple minor medical surgical and diagnostic health centers; and home health agencies. The system has about 1700 beds. In addition to traditional health services Methodist Healthcare offers extended care services sleep disorder centers and physical therapy. It also operates physician practices and a physician referral service. The system's flagship hospital Methodist University Hospital has more than 600 beds and is a teaching hospital affiliated with the University of Tennessee Health Science Center.

	Annual Growth	12/10	12/11	12/14	12/16	12/17
Sales ($ mil.)	3.0%	–	136.2	150.7	152.7	162.9
Net income ($ mil.)	–	–	7.1	9.5	(5.1)	(0.1)
Market value ($ mil.)	–	–	–	–	–	–
Employees	–	–	–	–	–	11,459

METLIFE INC

NYS: MET

200 Park Avenue
New York, NY 10166-0188
Phone: 212 578-9500
Fax: –
Web: www.metlife.com

CEO: Steven A. (Steve) Kandarian
CFO: John C. R. Hele
HR: Doris Jackson
FYE: December 31
Type: Public

While its name evolved from "metropolitan" MetLife's policies are found in villages towns and huge cities around the world. Its companies offer life accident and health insurance as well as retirement and savings products around the world. The group is a big force in Japan and growing in more than 50 other countries especially in Latin America. It distributes its products to retail corporate and government customers through agents third-party distributors including banks and brokers and direct marketing channels. About half of its revenue comes from the US but in mid-2017 MetLife split off much of its US life business.

	Annual Growth	12/14	12/15	12/16	12/17	12/18
Assets ($ mil.)	(6.6%)	902,337.0	877,933.0	898,764.0	719,892.0	687,538.0
Net income ($ mil.)	(5.1%)	6,309.0	5,310.0	800.0	4,010.0	5,123.0
Market value ($ mil.)	(6.7%)	51,851.4	46,214.8	51,659.7	48,467.5	39,360.7
Employees	(8.3%)	68,000	69,000	58,000	49,000	48,000

METRO BANCORP INC PA

NMS: METR

3801 Paxton Street
Harrisburg, PA 17111
Phone: 888 937-0004
Fax: –
Web: www.mymetrobank.com

CEO: –
CFO: –
HR: –
FYE: December 31
Type: Public

Metro Bancorp (formerly Pennsylvania Commerce Bancorp) is the holding company for Metro Bank (formerly Commerce Bank/Harrisburg) which has more than 30 branches in south-central Pennsylvania many of them with extended hours and open seven days a week. The bank provides standard services such as checking savings and money market accounts CDs IRAs and credit cards. Commercial loans including lines of credit and construction land development real estate and operating loans account for the majority of the bank's lending activities. It also originates consumer loans and residential mortgages.

	Annual Growth	12/09	12/10	12/11	12/12	12/13
Assets ($ mil.)	6.7%	2,147.8	2,234.5	2,421.2	2,634.9	2,781.1
Net income ($ mil.)	–	(1.9)	(4.3)	0.3	10.9	17.3
Market value ($ mil.)	14.4%	178.0	155.9	118.6	187.2	304.9
Employees	(1.6%)	1,043	959	957	919	978

METRO PACKAGING & IMAGING INC

5 HAUL RD
WAYNE, NJ 074706624
Phone: 973-709-9100
Fax: –
Web: www.metro-pi.com

CEO: –
CFO: –
HR: –
FYE: December 31
Type: Private

Metro gives its customers the full printing package. Metro Packaging and Imaging prints product packaging including folding cartons flexible packaging paper bags and curved cups as well as prints directly onto CDs. The company founded as Metro Litho in 1964-, uses gravure flexographic dry offset (letterpress) and silkscreen methods and offers a full range of digital imaging services.-, The company-, expanded its operations and menu of services in 2006 by adding full prepress capabilities. Metro's clients include Kraft Foods Revlon and Hartz. Metro Packaging boasts operations in California Georgia Minnesota New Jersey North Carolina and Ohio.

	Annual Growth	12/04	12/05	12/06	12/09	12/10
Sales ($ mil.)	(60.6%)	–	–	1,312.6	26.6	31.5
Net income ($ mil.)	609.3%	–	–	0.0	0.7	1.2
Market value ($ mil.)	–	–	–	–	–	–
Employees	–	–	–	–	–	120

METRO-NORTH COMMUTER RAILROAD CO INC

420 LEXINGTON AVE FL 12
NEW YORK, NY 101701200
Phone: 212-878-7000
Fax: –
Web: www.railroad.net

CEO: –
CFO: –
HR: –
FYE: December 31
Type: Private

Part of New York's Metropolitan Transportation Authority Metro-North Commuter Railroad carries passengers between New York City and its New York and Connecticut suburbs. The company known as MTA Metro-North Railroad or Metro-North covers 795 miles of track and serves a ridership of about 83 million. Three of the company's lines operate from Grand Central Terminal in New York City; the other two operate from Hoboken New Jersey. MTA Metro-North Railroad serves more than 120 stations in seven counties in New York State (Bronx Dutchess New York Orange Putnam Rockland and Westchester) and two in Connecticut (Fairfield and New Haven). The railroad 2014 operating annual budget was $1.4 billion.

	Annual Growth	12/03	12/04	12/05	12/06	12/08
Sales ($ mil.)	5.6%	–	433.1	470.2	490.5	538.6
Net income ($ mil.)	(6.7%)	–	247.0	226.4	152.6	186.9
Market value ($ mil.)	–	–	–	–	–	–
Employees	–	–	–	–	–	5,564

METROPLEX ADVENTIST HOSPITAL, INC.

2201 S CLEAR CREEK RD — CEO: Kevin Roberts
KILLEEN, TX 765494110 — CFO: Robert Brock
Phone: 254-526-7523 — HR: –
Fax: – — FYE: September 30
Web: www.adventhealth.com — Type: Private

Because the Texas towns of Belton Killeen and Lampasas aren't large they share a large health system between them. Metroplex Health System includes Metroplex Adventist Hospital with 148 beds in Killeen a behavioral health unit with 60 beds and Rollins Brook Community Hospital with 25 beds in Lampasas. The system part of Adventist Health System and served by Scott & White provides all the basics of general medical care including physician office buildings home health services and other outpatient services. Metroplex Adventist Hospital also serves the needs of nearby Ft. Hood making it the largest community healthcare provider to the military in the US.

	Annual Growth	12/13	12/14*	09/15	09/16	09/17
Sales ($ mil.)	(1.2%)	–	110.6	107.0	113.0	106.7
Net income ($ mil.)	4.8%	–	1.0	9.1	6.4	1.2
Market value ($ mil.)	–	–	–	–	–	–
Employees	–	–	–	–	–	779

*Fiscal year change

METROPOLITAN AIRPORTS COMMISSION

6040 28TH AVE S — CEO: Brian Ryks
MINNEAPOLIS, MN 554502701 — CFO: –
Phone: 612-726-8100 — HR: –
Fax: – — FYE: December 31
Web: www.metroairports.org — Type: Private

When you fly to the Twin Cities you'll most likely fly into a facility operated by the Metropolitan Airports Commission. The agency operates Minneapolis-St. Paul International Airport (MSP) along with six smaller reliever airports in the Twin Cities area. The smaller airports handle general aviation traffic and support military aircraft operations thus reducing potential congestion at MSP. The Metropolitan Airports Commission is considering other non-aeronautical uses for areas of the reliever airports such as business or commercial land development. The agency was created in 1943 by the Minnesota Legislature.

	Annual Growth	12/13	12/14	12/15	12/16	12/17
Sales ($ mil.)	5.9%	–	298.3	307.4	338.9	353.9
Net income ($ mil.)	33.1%	–	25.4	46.5	44.0	59.9
Market value ($ mil.)	–	–	–	–	–	–
Employees	–	–	–	–	–	575

METROPOLITAN EDISON COMPANY

76 S MAIN ST — CEO: –
AKRON, OH 443081812 — CFO: Mark T Clark
Phone: 800-736-3402 — HR: –
Fax: – — FYE: December 31
Web: www.firstenergycorp.com — Type: Private

Metropolitan Edison is an electric company and it knows a thing or two about serving cities and surrounding communities. The company a subsidiary of holding company FirstEnergy provides electric services to a population of 1.3 million in a 3300-sq. ml. service area in south central and eastern Pennsylvania. Metropolitan Edison or Met-Ed as it is sometimes referred to operates almost 16500 miles of power transmission and distribution lines. Although the company's primary source of electricity is derived from oil-and gas-fired units its York Haven Power Company generates hydroelectric power.

	Annual Growth	12/08	12/09	12/10	12/16	12/17
Sales ($ mil.)	(8.4%)	–	1,689.0	1,818.5	865.4	837.2
Net income ($ mil.)	7.3%	–	55.5	58.0	87.8	97.3
Market value ($ mil.)	–	–	–	–	–	–
Employees	–	–	–	–	–	678

METROPOLITAN HEALTH NETWORKS INC.   NYSE AMEX: MDF

777 Yamato Rd. Ste. 510 — CEO: John E Barger III
Boca Raton FL 33431 — CFO: Robert J Sabo
Phone: 561-805-8500 — HR: S Palmer
Fax: 404-236-2626 — FYE: December 31
Web: www.iss.net — Type: Public

Metropolitan Health Networks (MetCare) provides a way to keep Florida's senior citizens healthy. Through contracts with Humana and other health insurers the provider service network (PSN) operator provides health benefits to some 70000 members in Florida most of whom are part of Humana's Medicare Advantage and Medicare HMO plans. The company which offers health care services through its network of 30 primary care practices and 250 affiliated practices receives fees for services provided through contracts with insurers. It operates in 18 counties in Central and South Florida. MetCare doubled its network in 2011 by acquiring neighboring Continucare. It is owned by Humana.

METROPOLITAN OPERA ASSOCIATION, INC.

30 LINCOLN CENTER PLZ #1 — CEO: William Morris
NEW YORK, NY 100236980 — CFO: –
Phone: 212-799-3100 — HR: Anne Hackett
Fax: – — FYE: July 31
Web: www.metopera.org — Type: Private

Italians and Germans alike desire an American debut at the Met. Well their operas do anyway. The Metropolitan Opera Association manages The Metropolitan Opera company which presents more than 200 performances every year in its residence at the Lincoln Center for the Performing Arts. The Met is known for performing most works in their original languages and for producing regular Saturday radio broadcasts which are aired throughout North America and in South America Europe and the Asia/Pacific region. In association with sponsors the Met makes video and CD recordings of the performances and distributes them worldwide. The Met was founded in 1883.

	Annual Growth	07/04	07/05	07/08	07/09	07/15
Sales ($ mil.)	1.6%	–	286.8	309.4	223.5	335.3
Net income ($ mil.)	–	–	0.0	34.9	(71.2)	26.2
Market value ($ mil.)	–	–	–	–	–	–
Employees	–	–	–	–	–	1,500

METROPOLITAN SECURITY SERVICES, INC.

100 E 10TH ST STE 400 — CEO: Amy S Walden
CHATTANOOGA, TN 374024218 — CFO: –
Phone: 423-702-8200 — HR: Ian McCallum
Fax: – — FYE: December 31
Web: www.waldensecurity.com — Type: Private

Walden Security is something of a right-hand man — or in this case woman — to businesses and government. Majority owned and operated by women (the company is controlled by co-founder chairman and CEO Amy Walden) the security services contractor recruits trains and manages uniformed security professionals to guard such sites as airports auto dealerships manufacturing facilities museums office buildings residences schools and shopping malls. It is also contracted by the US General Services Administration to provide alarm monitors clerks court security officers and police officers. Walden Security has operations in about 15 states.

	Annual Growth	12/05	12/06	12/07	12/08	12/09
Sales ($ mil.)	–	–	–	(1,277.6)	85.7	95.9
Net income ($ mil.)	10535.9%	–	–	0.0	0.2	0.9
Market value ($ mil.)	–	–	–	–	–	–
Employees	–	–	–	–	–	2,500

METROPOLITAN ST. LOUIS SEWER DISTRICT

2350 MARKET ST STE 300
SAINT LOUIS, MO 631032555
Phone: 314-768-6200
Fax: -
Web: www.stlmsd.com

CEO: -
CFO: -
HR: Marnita Spight
FYE: June 30
Type: Private

Business is draining for The Metropolitan St. Louis Sewer District (MSD) which provides wastewater collection and treatment services for a population of about 1.3 million in the St. Louis area. The district operates nearly 10000 miles of sewer lines and seven wastewater treatment plants that process an average of 370 million gallons of sewage per day. MSD serves about 425000 residential and commercial/industrial customers. It has a budget of more than $470 million and is governed by a six-member board divided equally between appointees of the mayor of St. Louis and of the St. Louis County executive. The district was created by voters in 1954 and began operations two years later.

	Annual Growth	06/08	06/09	06/11	06/12	06/16
Sales ($ mil.)	3.6%	-	249.7	219.4	226.0	319.9
Net income ($ mil.)	(4.8%)	-	68.8	(10.6)	21.3	48.9
Market value ($ mil.)	-	-	-	-	-	-
Employees	-	-	-	-	-	976

METROPOLITAN STATE UNIVERSITY OF DENVER

890 AURARIA PKWY
DENVER, CO 802041806
Phone: 303-556-5740
Fax: -
Web: www.msudenver.edu

CEO: -
CFO: -
HR: -
FYE: June 30
Type: Private

Metropolitan State University of Denver serves students from the Mile High City and beyond. The public university offers bachelor's and master's degrees through its three schools: Business; Professional Studies; and Letters Arts and Sciences. It offers 55 major and 90 minor degree programs from its main Denver campus as well as satellite campuses in Northglenn and Greenwood Village. Students can take classes during the day at night on weekends or through correspondence or online. Some 23000 students attend MSU Denver which changed its name from Metropolitan State College of Denver (Metro State) in 2012.

	Annual Growth	06/01	06/02	06/03	06/05	06/16
Sales ($ mil.)	1.9%	-	121.9	66.1	2.1	157.8
Net income ($ mil.)	-	-	(81.6)	1.2	(0.5)	8.9
Market value ($ mil.)	-	-	-	-	-	-
Employees	-	-	-	-	-	2,300

METROPOLITAN TRANSIT AUTHORITY OF HARRIS COUNTY

1900 MAIN ST
HOUSTON, TX 770028130
Phone: 713-739-4834
Fax: -

CEO: -
CFO: -
HR: -
FYE: September 30
Type: Private

The Metropolitan Transit Authority of Harris County Texas (known as METRO in its hometown) provides bus transportation services for passengers in Houston and surrounding Harris County communities. The agency's fleet includes more than 1400 buses (including hybrids). METRO also provides transportation for people with disabilities (METROLift) who are unable to ride buses and oversees high-occupancy vehicle (HOV) lanes transit centers and park-and-ride lots. As an alternative to Houston's car-clogged streets METRO's 12.8 miles light rail system connects Houston's downtown midtown the museum district and the Texas Medical Center. Metro began operations in 1979.

	Annual Growth	09/03	09/04	09/05	09/16	09/17
Sales ($ mil.)	3.7%	-	45.6	50.1	72.1	72.8
Net income ($ mil.)	-	-	(61.8)	28.7	(175.5)	(134.5)
Market value ($ mil.)	-	-	-	-	-	-
Employees	-	-	-	-	-	3,916

METROPOLITAN TRANSPORTATION AUTHORITY

2 BROADWAY BSMT B
NEW YORK, NY 100043354
Phone: 212-878-7000
Fax: -

CEO: -
CFO: Robert E. (Bob) Foran
HR: -
FYE: December 31
Type: Private

The largest public transportation system in the US New York City's Metropolitan Transportation Authority (MTA) provides about 2.6 billion passenger trips and sees about 380 million vehicles travel its system annually. The MTA's largest agency the New York City Transit Authority operates about 8700 rail and subway cars that provide service across New York's five boroughs; it also runs a fleet of some 5900 buses. Other MTA units offer bus and rail service to Connecticut and Long Island and operate the Triborough system of toll bridges and tunnels.

	Annual Growth	12/14	12/15	12/16	12/17	12/18
Sales ($ mil.)	1.3%	-	8,408.0	8,527.0	8.7	8,736.0
Net income ($ mil.)	-	-	370.0	(271.0)	(0.5)	(145.0)
Market value ($ mil.)	-	-	-	-	-	-
Employees	-	-	-	-	-	67,457

METROPOLITAN UTILITIES DISTRICT

1723 HARNEY ST
OMAHA, NE 681021960
Phone: 402-554-6666
Fax: -
Web: www.mudomaha.com

CEO: -
CFO: Debra Schneider
HR: -
FYE: December 31
Type: Private

The Metropolitan Utilities District (MUD) distributes natural gas and water in the Omaha Nebraska metropolitan area. The company serves some 220000 natural gas customers and more than 200000 water customers. It also collects sewer and trash fees for municipalities. Customer-owned MUD which claims to be the fifth-largest public gas utility in the nation is a political subdivision of the State of Nebraska. Its board members are elected by residents of its service territory.

	Annual Growth	12/09	12/10	12/11	12/12	12/16
Sales ($ mil.)	(1.3%)	-	-	311.9	292.8	291.7
Net income ($ mil.)	15.8%	-	-	15.3	46.2	31.8
Market value ($ mil.)	-	-	-	-	-	-
Employees	-	-	-	-	-	852

METTLER-TOLEDO INTERNATIONAL, INC.

NYS: MTD

1900 Polaris Parkway
Columbus, OH 43240
Phone: 614 438-4511
Fax: 614 438-4646
Web: www.mt.com

CEO: Olivier A. Filliol
CFO: Shawn P. Vadala
HR: Mario Sanzo
FYE: December 31
Type: Public

Mettler-Toledo International measures up as one of the top suppliers of weighing instruments in the world. The company makes a range of bench and floor scales that precisely weigh materials as little as one ten-millionth of a gram to as much as several thousand kilograms. The company's main markets are laboratory industrial and food retail. Mettler-Toledo also makes analytical instruments and software for life science engineering and drug and chemical compound development. For grocery stores Mettler-Toledo offers labeling systems checkout scales receiving scales and data management software. The US accounts for about a third of the company's revenue.

	Annual Growth	12/15	12/16	12/17	12/18	12/19
Sales ($ mil.)	5.9%	2,395.4	2,508.3	2,725.1	2,935.6	3,008.7
Net income ($ mil.)	12.3%	352.8	384.4	376.0	512.6	561.1
Market value ($ mil.)	23.7%	8,181.6	10,097.9	14,946.1	13,644.8	19,138.1
Employees	4.7%	13,500	14,200	15,400	16,000	16,200

METWOOD INC
NBB: MTWD

819 Naff Road
Boones Mill, VA 24065
Phone: 540 334-4294
Fax: –

CEO: Keith M Thomas
CFO: –
HR: –
FYE: June 30
Type: Public

Metwood is shaping the future of construction. The company manufactures light-gauge steel building materials usually combined with wood for use in residential and commercial construction in lieu of conventional wood products. The combination increases load strength and structural integrity allowing for durable designs that can't be produced with wood alone. Products include girders and headers; floor joists; roof and floor trusses and rafters; metal framing; structural columns; and garage deck and porch concrete pour-over systems. The company primarily sells to lumber yards and home improvement stores mainly in Virginia. Affiliate Providence Engineering provides civil engineering services.

	Annual Growth	06/14	06/15	06/16	06/17	06/18
Sales ($ mil.)	0.1%	1.9	1.7	1.8	1.9	1.9
Net income ($ mil.)	–	(0.2)	(0.0)	(0.7)	(0.4)	(0.5)
Market value ($ mil.)	(25.8%)	8.9	11.5	5.3	1.8	2.7
Employees	0.0%	14	13	14	13	14

MEXCO ENERGY CORP.
ASE: MXC

415 West Wall Street, Suite 475
Midland, TX 79701
Phone: 432 682-1119
Fax: –
Web: www.mexcoenergy.com

CEO: Nicholas C Taylor
CFO: Tamala L McComic
HR: –
FYE: March 31
Type: Public

Mexco Energy gets most of its energy not from present day Mexico but from its close neighbor — what once was Old Mexico West Texas. The oil and gas exploration and production independent has proved reserves of 6.3 billion cu. ft. of natural gas and 659700 barrels of oil. While the company owns oil and gas properties in other states (including Louisiana New Mexico North Dakota and Oklahoma) the majority of its activities take place in Texas. Holly Frontier Refining & Marketing is Mexco Energy's top customer. Mexco Energy president Nicholas Taylor owns about 44% of the company.

	Annual Growth	03/15	03/16	03/17	03/18	03/19
Sales ($ mil.)	(5.6%)	3.4	2.4	2.5	2.7	2.7
Net income ($ mil.)	–	(0.3)	(4.0)	(0.7)	(0.3)	(0.0)
Market value ($ mil.)	(3.0%)	11.4	4.8	7.9	6.2	10.1
Employees	(4.5%)	6	7	6	6	5

MEXICAN AMERICAN OPPORTUNITY FOUNDATION

401 N GARFIELD AVE
MONTEBELLO, CA 906402901
Phone: 323-890-9600
Fax: –
Web: www.maof.org

CEO: –
CFO: Orlando M Sayson
HR: –
FYE: June 30
Type: Private

The Mexican American Opportunity Foundation (MAOF) works to increase and improve opportunities for the largest and fastest-growing Hispanic group in the US. One of the largest Latino not-for-profit organizations in the nation MAOF serves more than 100000 Californians. It provides funding for a wide variety of advocacy programs including nutrition and health awareness childcare centers and literacy initiatives. The East Los Angeles-based group also offers computer classes and other career training at no cost to qualified individuals. Sometimes referred to as an "urban Cesar Chavez" Dr. Dionicio Morales founded MAOF in 1963; Morales died in September 2008.

	Annual Growth	06/11	06/12	06/13	06/14	06/15
Sales ($ mil.)	11.6%	–	–	58.9	63.8	73.4
Net income ($ mil.)	–	–	–	(0.7)	0.1	0.8
Market value ($ mil.)	–	–	–	–	–	–
Employees	–	–	–	–	–	710

MEXICAN RESTAURANTS, INC.
NBB: CASA

12000 Aerospace Ave., Suite 400
Houston, TX 77034-5576
Phone: 832 300-5858
Fax: 832 300-5859
Web: www.mexicanrestaurantsinc.com

CEO: Marcus Jundt
CFO: Andrew J Dennard
HR: –
FYE: December 30
Type: Public

Mexican Restaurants gets the prize for the most straightforward name in the book. The company operates and franchises more than 70 casual-dining Mexican restaurants located primarily in Texas. Its flagship Casa Ole chain serves standard Mexican and Tex-Mex fare including burritos enchiladas and fajitas while its Monterey's Little Mexico and Monterey's Tex-Mex Cafe units offer a mix of more authentic Mexican cuisine. In addition the company operates a chain of half a dozen quick-casual restaurants under the Mission Burritos banner. Other brands include Crazy Jose's and Tortuga Coastal Cantina. More than 50 of the restaurants are company-owned while the rest are franchised.

	Annual Growth	12/08*	01/10	01/11	01/12*	12/12
Sales ($ mil.)	(4.5%)	81.9	72.0	66.2	66.9	68.1
Net income ($ mil.)	–	(4.0)	(0.8)	(5.5)	(0.5)	(0.0)
Market value ($ mil.)	(5.1%)	6.4	7.7	5.2	2.6	5.2
Employees	(9.4%)	2,378	1,950	–	–	–

*Fiscal year change

MEYER & WALLIS INC.

117 N JEFFERSON ST # 204
MILWAUKEE, WI 532026160
Phone: 414-224-0212
Fax: –
Web: www.meyerwallis.com

CEO: Robert L Meyer
CFO: Tod Kinunen
HR: –
FYE: December 31
Type: Private

Meyer & Wallis provides full service advertising and marketing for clients across the US. Services include strategic development advertising design public relations and interactive marketing with a strong background in serving retail clients. The agency also serves companies in health care and consumer products. Its portfolio includes work for such clients as the American Heart Association Quad/Graphics and Vectren Energy. The agency has offices in Indianapolis and Milwaukee. Meyer & Wallis was founded in 1967 by industry veteran CEO Bob Meyer.

	Annual Growth	12/04	12/05	12/06	12/07	12/08
Sales ($ mil.)	19.4%	–	9.8	9.8	17.3	16.7
Net income ($ mil.)	–	–	–	(0.1)	0.7	(0.1)
Market value ($ mil.)	–	–	–	–	–	–
Employees	–	–	–	–	–	27

MFA FINANCIAL, INC.
NYS: MFA

350 Park Avenue, 20th Floor
New York, NY 10022
Phone: 212 207-6400
Fax: 212 207-6420
Web: www.mfafinancial.com

CEO: Craig L Knutson
CFO: Stephen D Yarad
HR: –
FYE: December 31
Type: Public

MFA Financial (formerly MFA Mortgage Investments) has three good buddies: Fannie Freddie and Ginnie. This self-advised mortgage real estate investment trust (REIT) was incorporated in 1997 to invest in mortgage-backed securities and mortgages such as those guaranteed by government-related entities Fannie Mae Freddie Mac and Ginnie Mae. The REIT's investment portfolio mainly consists of agency mortgage-backed securities AAA-rated mortgage-backed securities corporate and government bonds and cash. MFA Financial buys its securities and loans from the banks savings and loans investment banks and mortgage banking institutions that originate them. Its portfolio weighs in at approximately $8 billion.

	Annual Growth	12/13	12/14	12/15	12/16	12/17
Sales ($ mil.)	(2.7%)	482.9	463.8	492.1	457.2	433.4
Net income ($ mil.)	1.6%	302.7	313.5	313.2	312.7	322.4
Market value ($ mil.)	2.9%	2,808.7	3,178.7	2,625.7	3,035.5	3,150.8
Employees	8.3%	40	43	53	52	55

MFA INCORPORATED

201 RAY YOUNG DR
COLUMBIA, MO 652013599
Phone: 573-874-5111
Fax: –
Web: www.mfa-inc.com

CEO: Bill Streeter
CFO: Ernie Verslues
HR: –
FYE: August 31
Type: Private

Agricultural cooperative MFA brings together 45000 farmers in Missouri and adjacent states. One of the US' oldest regional co-ops supplying its member/owners with agronomy distribution financing and purchasing services it runs more than 145 retail farm supply centers and works with independent dealers. MFA supplies animal feeds seed fertilizer and crop protection products. The co-op also provides its members with agronomy services animal-health products and farm supplies. It also offers marketing services and is the publisher of Today's Farmer. Agmo Corporation MFA's finance company provides co-op members longer credit terms for purchases made through MFA's retail outlets.

	Annual Growth	08/14	08/15	08/16	08/17	08/18
Sales ($ mil.)	(1.6%)	–	1,434.3	1,192.7	1,373.3	1,367.9
Net income ($ mil.)	(14.0%)	–	10.8	4.1	14.1	6.9
Market value ($ mil.)	–	–	–	–	–	–
Employees	–	–	–	–	–	1,393

MGC DIAGNOSTICS CORP

350 Oak Grove Parkway
Saint Paul, MN 55127-8599
Phone: 651 484-4874
Fax: –
Web: www.mgcdiagnostics.com

NAS: MGCD
CEO: Todd M Austin
CFO: –
HR: –
FYE: October 31
Type: Public

A good diagnosis for disease detection integrated care and wellness is key to the business model of MGC Diagnostics Corporation formerly Angeion. Through subsidiary Medical Graphics Corporation the company designs and sells cardiorespiratory diagnostic systems that analyze lung function and diagnose disease using a patient's breath. It sells systems under the MedGraphics brand to health care providers. The non-invasive MedGraphics devices analyze a patient's inhaled and exhaled breath to help detect emphysema asthma and heart disease among other things. Researchers also use MedGraphics' products in clinical trial studies.

	Annual Growth	10/12	10/13	10/14	10/15	10/16
Sales ($ mil.)	10.2%	27.2	31.6	30.0	37.5	40.0
Net income ($ mil.)	–	(0.0)	1.4	(1.1)	4.0	(3.8)
Market value ($ mil.)	4.0%	28.0	51.4	29.3	28.6	32.7
Employees	6.0%	123	121	158	165	155

MGE ENERGY INC

133 South Blair Street
Madison, WI 53788
Phone: 608 252-7000
Fax: –
Web: www.mgeenergy.com

NMS: MGEE
CEO: Gary J. Wolter
CFO: Jeffrey C. Newman
HR: –
FYE: December 31
Type: Public

MGE Energy warms folks during cold Wisconsin winters. The holding company distributes electricity to 140000 residential commercial and industrial customers in Dane County and natural gas to about 145000 customers in seven southern and western Wisconsin counties through its Madison Gas and Electric subsidiary. The utility has a generating capacity of more than 800 MW; the majority comes from fossil-fueled plants. The company's power-related but unregulated businesses include MGE Power (generating interests) MGE Construct (construction services) Central Wisconsin Development (business support services) and MAGAEL (property development).

	Annual Growth	12/14	12/15	12/16	12/17	12/18
Sales ($ mil.)	(2.5%)	619.9	564.0	544.7	563.1	559.8
Net income ($ mil.)	1.2%	80.3	71.3	75.6	97.6	84.2
Market value ($ mil.)	7.1%	1,581.2	1,608.6	2,263.8	2,187.6	2,078.7
Employees	0.2%	699	708	704	712	706

MGIC INVESTMENT CORP. (WI)

250 E. Kilbourn Avenue
Milwaukee, WI 53202
Phone: 414 347-6480
Fax: –
Web: www.mgic.com

NYS: MTG
CEO: Curt S. Culver
CFO: Timothy Mattke
HR: Kurt Thomas
FYE: December 31
Type: Public

Since a pinkie-promise isn't good enough for most lenders there's MGIC Investment's mortgage insurance to protect lenders from home buyers who don't hold up their end of the bargain. MGIC owns Mortgage Guaranty Insurance Corporation (MGIC) the largest provider of private mortgage insurance in the US Puerto Rico and Guam. Such coverage allows otherwise-qualified buyers who aren't able to scrape up the standard 20% down payment to get mortgages. MGIC writes primary insurance on individual loans; its customers include banks mortgage brokers credit unions and other residential mortgage lenders. In 2017 MGIC had $194.9 billion primary insurance in force covering 1 million mortgages.

	Annual Growth	12/14	12/15	12/16	12/17	12/18
Assets ($ mil.)	1.9%	5,266.4	5,879.5	5,734.5	5,619.5	5,677.8
Net income ($ mil.)	27.7%	251.9	1,172.0	342.5	355.8	670.1
Market value ($ mil.)	2.9%	3,312.1	3,137.9	3,621.2	5,014.3	3,717.2
Employees	(0.2%)	800	800	823	819	793

MGM RESORTS INTERNATIONAL

3600 Las Vegas Boulevard South
Las Vegas, NV 89109
Phone: 702 693-7120
Fax: –
Web: www.mgmresorts.com

NYS: MGM
CEO: James J. Murren
CFO: Daniel J. D'Arrigo
HR: Ashley Eddy
FYE: December 31
Type: Public

MGM Resorts International is one of the world's largest gaming firms. The company's properties include some of the biggest names on the Las Vegas Strip including MGM Grand The Mirage and the Monte Carlo as well as Luxor Bellagio Circus Circus New York-New York Mandalay Bay and the new T-Mobile Arena. MGM Resorts also operates regional properties in a handful of other US states including the MGM Grand Detroit and the Borgata in Atlantic City New Jersey among others. Internationally MGM Resorts operates in Macau an autonomous Chinese territory famed for gambling. Revenue comes from gambling room reservations food and drinks entertainment and retail operations.

	Annual Growth	12/14	12/15	12/16	12/17	12/18
Sales ($ mil.)	3.9%	10,082.0	9,190.1	9,455.1	10,773.9	11,763.1
Net income ($ mil.)	–	(149.9)	(447.7)	1,101.4	1,960.3	466.8
Market value ($ mil.)	3.2%	11,277.5	11,984.3	15,207.2	17,612.5	12,796.7
Employees	1.4%	68,100	59,500	69,000	68,000	72,000

MGT CAPITAL INVESTMENTS INC

512 S. Mangum Street, Suite 408
Durham, NC 27701
Phone: 914 630-7430
Fax: –
Web: www.mgtci.com

NBB: MGTI
CEO: John McAfee
CFO: Robert S Lowrey
HR: –
FYE: December 31
Type: Public

MGT Capital Investments is looking for ROI no matter if it's in American dollars or British sterling. The holding company is focused on medical imaging technology. It owns a 55% stake in Medicsight a publicly traded company that develops medical imaging software to help detect cancer. The company narrowed its investments in 2010 when it divested its holdings in Medicexchange XShares HipCricket and Eurindia. The following year it sold its stake in UK financial advisory firm Moneygate. Virtually all of MGT Capital's revenues now stem from Medicsight. Originally listed on the NYSE Amex in 1996 the company began trading on the London Stock Exchange's AIM exchange in 2011.

	Annual Growth	12/14	12/15	12/16	12/17	12/18
Sales ($ mil.)	17.7%	1.1	0.1	0.3	3.1	2.0
Net income ($ mil.)	–	(5.3)	(4.8)	(24.5)	(50.4)	(23.8)
Market value ($ mil.)	(45.7%)	67.8	25.5	81.1	528.7	5.9
Employees	(22.3%)	11	2	8	6	4

MIAMI JEWISH HEALTH SYSTEMS, INC.

5200 NE 2ND AVE
MIAMI, FL 331372706
Phone: 305-751-8626
Fax: –
Web: www.flmgma.com

CEO: Jeffrey P Freimark
CFO: –
HR: –
FYE: June 30
Type: Private

With age comes experience and Miami Jewish Health Systems is plenty experienced when it comes to geriatric care. The not-for-profit 460-bed nursing home and 30-bed hospital provides services to southern Florida residents of all ages with a focus on the elderly. It also operates independent and assisted-living centers for seniors as well as an ambulatory health center for general health care services. Its facilities provide a variety of services such as care for Alzheimer's patients assisted and independent living rehabilitation hospice and home health care.

	Annual Growth	06/12	06/13	06/14	06/15	06/17
Sales ($ mil.)	(6.0%)	–	83.5	70.9	70.8	65.3
Net income ($ mil.)	–	–	9.0	(0.9)	0.6	(2.0)
Market value ($ mil.)	–	–	–	–	–	–
Employees	–	–	–	–	–	1,100

MIAMI UNIVERSITY

501 E HIGH ST
OXFORD, OH 450561846
Phone: 513-529-1809
Fax: –
Web: www.miamioh.edu

CEO: –
CFO: –
HR: Dawn Fahner
FYE: June 30
Type: Private

Not that Miami the other one. Named for the Miami Indian Tribe that inhabited the area now known as the Miami Valley Region of Ohio Miami University emphasizes undergraduate study at its main campus in Oxford (35 miles north of Cincinnati) as well as at commuter campuses in Hamilton Middletown and West Chester Ohio and a European Center in Luxembourg. The school offers bachelors masters and doctoral programs in areas including business administration arts and sciences engineering and education. Its student body includes more than 15000 undergraduates on the Oxford campus; 2500 graduate students; and another 5700 students attending satellite campuses. Miami University was established in 1809.

	Annual Growth	06/11	06/12	06/16	06/17	06/18
Sales ($ mil.)	3.8%	–	440.5	522.2	544.6	551.7
Net income ($ mil.)	33.3%	–	32.9	65.1	83.7	184.5
Market value ($ mil.)	–	–	–	–	–	–
Employees	–	–	–	–	–	4,925

MIAMI VALLEY HOSPITAL

1 WYOMING ST
DAYTON, OH 454092711
Phone: 937-208-8000
Fax: –
Web: www.miamivalleyhospital.org

CEO: Bobbie Gerhart
CFO: Lisa Bishop
HR: Gretchen Long MBA
FYE: December 31
Type: Private

Don't go to Florida looking for this hospital! Miami Valley Hospital (MVH) is an acute care facility serving the residents of Dayton Ohio and surrounding areas through two campuses. MVH and MVH South have roughly 950 beds and offer 50 primary and specialty care practices through its Regional Adult Burn Center the MVH Cancer Center MVH Sports Medicine Center and behavioral health units for outpatient and inpatient chemical dependency therapy and other psychiatric services. MVH also offers Level I trauma services Level III-B NICU adult burn center an air ambulance program and blood marrow and kidney transplant services. The hospital is part of the Premier Health Partners network.

	Annual Growth	12/06	12/07	12/14	12/15	12/16
Sales ($ mil.)	3.0%	–	622.1	785.7	827.4	809.9
Net income ($ mil.)	(2.3%)	–	44.3	38.0	37.5	35.9
Market value ($ mil.)	–	–	–	–	–	–
Employees	–	–	–	–	–	6,000

MICHAEL FOODS GROUP INC.

301 Carlson Pkwy. Ste. 400
Minnetonka MN 55305
Phone: 952-258-4000
Fax: 973-790-3307
Web: www3.gehealthcare.com/en/products/categories/c

CEO: James E Dwyer Jr
CFO: –
HR: –
FYE: December 31
Type: Private

It's not meat and potatoes but poultry and potatoes and other foods at Michael Foods Group. The group operates through Michael Foods Inc. one of the top US producers and distributors of value-added egg products (frozen liquid pre-cooked and dried). Its Egg Products division comprised of four subsidiaries supplies egg products to foodservice retail grocery and food ingredient customers. The group's business includes Crystal Farms a distributor of cheese butter and other dairy case items to US groceries and Northern Star a supplier of refrigerated potato products to North American foodservice operators and grocery stores. GS Capital Partners and THL own 74% and 21% respectively of Michael Foods.

MICHELS CORPORATION

817 W. Main St.
Brownsville WI 53006-0128
Phone: 920-583-3132
Fax: 920-583-3429
Web: www.michels.us

CEO: Patrick D Michels
CFO: John Schroeder
HR: –
FYE: January 31
Type: Private

Michels Corporation is a utility engineering design and construction contractor. The family-owned company links systems for energy transportation distribution and communications customers in North America. It specializes in installing fiber optic networks for telephone broadband and cable providers. Through more than a dozen divisions Michels offers a variety of services including horizontal and directional drilling underground pipe repair tunneling engineering paving and materials production. The company also provides wind farm construction through a wind energy division.

MICHIGAN MILK PRODUCERS ASSOCIATION

41310 BRIDGE ST
NOVI, MI 483751302
Phone: 248-474-6672
Fax: –
Web: www.mimilk.com

CEO: John Dilland
CFO: Josep Barenys
HR: –
FYE: September 30
Type: Private

Ice cream and other dairy products might be missing a major ingredient without Michigan Milk Producers Association (MMPA). The dairy cooperative which serves more than 2100 farmers in Michigan Ohio Indiana and Wisconsin produces some 3.9 billion pounds of milk each year. Milk products include sweetened condensed milk instant nonfat milk and dried buttermilk as well as other items the likes of cream cheese butter and ice-cream mixes. With no consumer brands or products MMPA sells its products as ingredients to food makers who sell baby formulas candy ice cream and yogurt. Founded in 1916 the co-op operates a pair of Michigan plants and a merchandise facility.

	Annual Growth	09/07	09/08	09/09	09/10	09/11
Sales ($ mil.)	25.1%	–	–	556.7	698.8	870.9
Net income ($ mil.)	3.2%	–	–	6.0	6.8	6.4
Market value ($ mil.)	–	–	–	–	–	–
Employees	–	–	–	–	–	200

MICHIGAN STATE UNIVERSITY

426 AUDITORIUM RD
EAST LANSING, MI 488242600
Phone: 517-355-1855
Fax: –

CEO: –
CFO: –
HR: Chris Hanna
FYE: June 30
Type: Private

Remember the Spartans? You should if you graduated from a land-grant university in the US. Founded in 1855 Michigan State University (MSU) was the model of a land-grant institution made into law in 1862. Today MSU and its 50000 students cover a lot of land in East Lansing. The university offers more than 200 programs of study through 17 colleges. It has extensive programs in core fields including education physics psychology medicine and communications. It is also a leading research university with top-ranked international studies programs. As a highly ranked research university MSU is awarded millions of dollars in research grants each year from public and private entities.

	Annual Growth	06/12	06/13	06/16	06/17	06/18
Sales ($ mil.)	4.7%	–	1,578.4	1,811.1	1,931.6	1,986.9
Net income ($ mil.)	–	–	148.8	71.0	481.9	(246.3)
Market value ($ mil.)	–	–	–	–	–	–
Employees	–	–	–	–	–	11,100

MICHIGAN TECHNOLOGICAL UNIVERSITY

1400 TOWNSEND DR
HOUGHTON, MI 499311200
Phone: 906-487-1885
Fax: –
Web: www.mtu.edu

CEO: –
CFO: –
HR: –
FYE: June 30
Type: Private

Michigan Technological University trains techies in the Wolverine State. A premier research university the school affectionately known as Michigan Tech offers a range of programs in computing engineering technology business and technology forest resources and environmental science social work sciences and arts and non-departmental sponsored educational programs. Based in Houghton the school has an enrollment of about 7000 undergraduate and graduate students and a faculty of almost 480 instructors. The company is considered to be a discrete component unit of the State of Michigan because its Board of Control is appointed by the Governor.

	Annual Growth	06/10	06/11	06/13	06/17	06/18
Sales ($ mil.)	3.0%	–	147.5	155.4	173.7	181.2
Net income ($ mil.)	–	–	(0.9)	3.0	(1.9)	5.6
Market value ($ mil.)	–	–	–	–	–	–
Employees	–	–	–	–	–	1,939

MICREL, INC. NMS: MCRL

2180 Fortune Drive
San Jose, CA 95131
Phone: 408 944-0800
Fax: 408 944-0970
Web: www.micrel.com

CEO: –
CFO: –
HR: –
FYE: December 31
Type: Public

Micrel's semiconductors make their way into all sorts of electronic gear. The company makes around 3000 kinds of standard integrated circuits (ICs); its lineup includes high-performance analog power radio-frequency (RF) and mixed-signal ICs used in computers networking equipment industrial electronics and wireless phones and other telecom gear. The company also designs and manufactures custom ICs and provides contract wafer manufacturing (foundry) services for commercial and military customers that use Micrel-produced ICs in communications systems and transport aircraft. Customers in Asia account for more than 60% of sales.

	Annual Growth	12/09	12/10	12/11	12/12	12/13
Sales ($ mil.)	2.0%	218.9	297.4	259.0	250.1	237.1
Net income ($ mil.)	2.0%	16.3	50.7	34.0	12.3	17.6
Market value ($ mil.)	4.7%	462.8	733.2	570.6	536.2	557.1
Employees	(0.9%)	755	837	781	796	728

MICRO IMAGING TECHNOLOGY INC. OTC: MMTC

970 Calle Amanecer Ste. F
San Clemente CA 92673
Phone: 949-485-6000
Fax: 949-485-6005
Web: micro-imaging.com/

CEO: Jeffrey G Nunez
CFO: Victor A Hollander
HR: –
FYE: October 31
Type: Public

Micro Imaging Technology (formerly Electropure) is developing laser-based technology that detects microbes and microorganisms in water. Micro Imaging Technology hopes to commercialize its products for applications such as food inspection and water testing but the company hasn't had enough money to do so. In 2005 the company sold the assets of its Electropure EDI subsidiary a maker of ion-permeable membranes and deionization devices; Electropure then changed its name to Micro Imaging Technology effective 2006. In 2007 the company sold and installed two bacteria identification systems in Tokyo. Former US Postmaster General Anthony Frank owns a 45% stake in Micro Imaging Technology.

MICROBOT MEDICAL INC NAS: MBOT

25 Recreation Park Drive, Unit 108
Hingham, MA 02043
Phone: 781 875-3605
Fax: –
Web: www.microbotmedical.com

CEO: Harel Gadot
CFO: David Ben Naim
HR: –
FYE: December 31
Type: Public

For Microbot Medical (formerly StemCells) success stems from reinvention. Formerly focused on the discovery of cell-based therapies to treat diseases of the central nervous system (CNS) the company faced a major setback in mid-2016 when its unsuccessful Pathway Study in spinal cord injury was terminated. StemCells' initial response was to begin winding down operations. However within months the company merged with private firm Microbot. The merged company is now focused on the development of robotic medical devices such as a titanium miniature robot that can clean artificial drainage plants implanted in the body. It is hoped that those devices will eventually be used to clean plaque from blood vessels to prevent heart attack or stroke.

	Annual Growth	12/12	12/13	12/14	12/15	12/16
Sales ($ mil.)	–	1.4	1.2	1.0	0.1	0.0
Net income ($ mil.)	–	(28.5)	(26.4)	(32.7)	(36.4)	(9.7)
Market value ($ mil.)	39.1%	43.3	32.7	24.9	11.1	162.0
Employees	(38.5%)	49	58	69	74	7

MICROCHIP TECHNOLOGY INC NMS: MCHP

2355 W. Chandler Blvd.
Chandler, AZ 85224-6199
Phone: 480 792-7200
Fax: 480 792-7790
Web: www.microchip.com

CEO: Steve Sanghi
CFO: J. Eric Bjornholt
HR: Jennifer Myers
FYE: March 31
Type: Public

Microchip Technology's products are embedded in your car your copier and even your wallet. The semiconductor maker offers a variety of embedded devices including eight- 16- and 32-bit microcontrollers (it's a leading producer worldwide). It also makes specialty memory products such as electrically erasable programmable read-only memories (EEPROMs) and field programmable gate arrays (FPGA). Microchip's KeeLoq-brand code-hopping devices are used in keyless locks garage door openers and smart cards. Its chips have customers in the automotive consumer aerospace defense computing industrial and telecommunications markets. Microchip gets about 80% of sales from customers outside the US.

	Annual Growth	03/15	03/16	03/17	03/18	03/19
Sales ($ mil.)	25.6%	2,147.0	2,173.3	3,407.8	3,980.8	5,349.5
Net income ($ mil.)	(0.9%)	369.0	324.1	164.6	255.4	355.9
Market value ($ mil.)	14.1%	11,618.1	11,451.8	17,529.4	21,706.2	19,710.4
Employees	184.3%	280	9,766	12,656	14,234	18,286

MICROFINANCIAL, INC. NMS: MFI

16 New England Executive Park, Suite 200
Burlington, MA 01803
Phone: 781 994-4800
Fax: –
Web: www.microfinancial.com

CEO: –
CFO: James R Jackson Jr
HR: Cheryl Valera
FYE: December 31
Type: Public

MicroFinancial thinks big when it comes to leasing small-ticket commercial items to small and midsized businesses. Through subsidiary TimePayment MicroFinancial leases items that are generally valued between $500 and $15000. Although the "microticket" leaser provides financing for a variety of office and commercial equipment the majority of the contracts in its portfolio are for point-of-sale authorization systems for debit and credit cards. It doesn't lease and rent equipment directly but through a network of independent dealers across the US. Internet-based TimePaymentDirect processes applications and approves credit; Insta-Lease provides the same services via telephone fax and e-mail.

	Annual Growth	12/08	12/09	12/10	12/11	12/12
Sales ($ mil.)	10.7%	39.5	46.2	50.9	54.7	59.3
Net income ($ mil.)	12.0%	6.0	4.1	5.3	9.0	9.4
Market value ($ mil.)	37.8%	29.2	44.9	58.3	84.2	105.3
Employees	10.2%	103	111	118	135	152

MICRONETICS INC. NASDAQ: NOIZ

26 Hampshire Dr.
Hudson NH 03051
Phone: 603-883-2900
Fax: 603-882-8987
Web: www.mwireless.com

CEO: –
CFO: –
HR: –
FYE: March 31
Type: Public

Micronetics fights noise with noise. The company designs radio-frequency (RF) components and test equipment that help keep signals clear in cellular wireless cable satellite and radar systems worldwide. Products include RF controls for military radar and communications systems noise source components that test reception and transmission quality and other noise generators and frequency emulators. Micronetics sells primarily to military contractors like Northrop Grumman and Raytheon. ITT's Electronic Warfare Systems unit (22% of sales) is the company's top customer. Micronetics gets most of its sales in North America.

MICRON SOLUTIONS INC (DE) ASE: MICR

25 Sawyer Passway
Fitchburg, MA 01420
Phone: 978 345-5000
Fax: –
Web: www.arthrt.com

CEO: Salvatore Emma Jr
CFO: Derek T Welch
HR: –
FYE: December 31
Type: Public

It's all about heart for Arrhythmia Research Technology (ART). The company offers signal-averaging electrocardiographic (SAECG) software that collects data and analyzes electrical impulses of the heart in an effort to detect potentially lethal heart arrhythmias. The company plans to sell the products through licensing agreements with equipment makers. Until it finds a marketing partner however ART is relying on sales from its Micron Products subsidiary which makes snaps and sensors used in the manufacture and operation of disposable electrodes for electrocardiographic (ECG) equipment. Micron Products has acquired assets of several companies that enhance its metal and plastics molding capabilities.

	Annual Growth	12/14	12/15	12/16	12/17	12/18
Sales ($ mil.)	(5.0%)	24.1	21.5	19.6	20.1	19.6
Net income ($ mil.)	–	0.7	(0.4)	(0.7)	(1.4)	(1.1)
Market value ($ mil.)	(23.3%)	22.0	15.7	10.9	10.0	7.6
Employees	(7.3%)	119	108	107	95	88

MICROPAC INDUSTRIES, INC. NBB: MPAD

905 E. Walnut Street
Garland, TX 75040
Phone: 972 272-3571
Fax: –
Web: –

CEO: Mark King
CFO: Patrick S Cefalu
HR: –
FYE: November 30
Type: Public

Micropac Industries makes hybrid microelectronic circuits and optoelectronic components/assemblies as well as solid-state relays power controllers and amplifiers Hall-effect sensors light-emitting diodes (LEDs) and displays and high-temperature products. The company also offers contract manufacturing and packaging services with plants in Mexico and the US. Micropac's customers include industrial and medical markets as well as contractors for the US Department of Defense and NASA which account for more 70% of sales. Director Heinz-Werner Hempel owns more than three-quarters of the company. Micropac's products are marketed in the US and Europe.

	Annual Growth	11/14	11/15	11/16	11/17	11/18
Sales ($ mil.)	2.3%	19.1	20.0	17.6	19.7	21.0
Net income ($ mil.)	8.9%	1.0	1.5	0.2	1.4	1.4
Market value ($ mil.)	(0.5%)	21.0	23.2	21.9	18.7	20.6
Employees	1.5%	116	124	121	119	123

MICRON TECHNOLOGY INC. NMS: MU

8000 S. Federal Way
Boise, ID 83716-9632
Phone: 208 368-4000
Fax: –
Web: www.micron.com

CEO: Sanjay Mehrotra
CFO: Ernest E. (Ernie) Maddock
HR: –
FYE: August 29
Type: Public

Micron Technology is one of the largest memory chip makers in the world. It makes DRAM (Dynamic Random Access Memory) NAND Flash and NOR Flash memory and other memory technologies. The company sells to customers in networking and storage consumer electronics solid-state drives and mobile telecommunications but its largest concentration (about a quarter of sales) is the computer market. Micron's products are offered under the Micron Crucial and Ballistix brands as well as private labels. The US-based company generates about 90% of sales internationally. Besides being one of the biggest chipmakers Micron is one the most durable marking its 40th anniversary in 2018.

	Annual Growth	09/15	09/16*	08/17	08/18	08/19
Sales ($ mil.)	9.6%	16,192.0	12,399.0	20,322.0	30,391.0	23,406.0
Net income ($ mil.)	21.5%	2,899.0	(276.0)	5,089.0	14,135.0	6,313.0
Market value ($ mil.)	28.1%	18,348.5	18,403.8	35,358.8	58,352.6	49,405.0
Employees	3.9%	31,800	31,400	34,100	36,000	37,000

*Fiscal year change

MICROS SYSTEMS, INC. NMS: MCRS

7031 Columbia Gateway Drive
Columbia, MD 21046-2289
Phone: 443 285-6000
Fax: 443 285-0466
Web: www.micros.com

CEO: Peter A Altabef
CFO: Cynthia A Russo
HR: Carlos Echalar
FYE: June 30
Type: Public

MICROS' systems don't fold sheets bus tables or stock shelves but they do keep hotels restaurants and retail stores in order. MICROS Systems supplies point-of-sale terminals central reservation systems inventory and loss prevention systems and other hardware and software for the hospitality and retail industries. Customers include Hyatt Hotels InterContinental Hotels and Marriott International as well as IHOP Starbucks Wendy's Belk and The Jones Group. Additionally MICROS products are used in related settings such as casinos cruise ships sports arenas airport concourses and theme parks. The company generates more than half of its sales outside the US and Canada.

	Annual Growth	06/09	06/10	06/11	06/12	06/13
Sales ($ mil.)	8.6%	911.8	914.3	1,007.9	1,107.5	1,268.1
Net income ($ mil.)	14.6%	99.3	114.4	144.1	167.0	171.4
Market value ($ mil.)	14.3%	1,942.9	2,445.4	3,814.3	3,928.7	3,311.0
Employees	8.1%	4,757	4,646	4,953	6,383	6,506

MICROSEMI CORP
NMS: MSCC

One Enterprise
Aliso Viejo, CA 92656
Phone: 949 380-6100
Fax: –
Web: www.microsemi.com

CEO: James J Peterson
CFO: John W Hohener
HR: Sun M Kim
FYE: October 1/
Type: Public

Microsemi is on a power trip. The company makes power management semiconductors that regulate and condition electricity to make it more usable by electrical and electronic systems. Its products include discrete components such as diodes and rectifiers along with integrated circuits such as amplifiers and voltage regulators. Microsemi also makes devices for pacemakers GPS products LCD TVs and wireless networks. The company's high-reliability semiconductors go into jet engines missile systems oilfield equipment and satellites. Top customers have included big names like Boeing Dell Honeywell Medtronic Boston Scientific and Lockheed Martin. The company closed its $2.5 billion acquisition of PMC-Sierra in early 2016.

	Annual Growth	09/13	09/14	09/15*	10/16	10/17
Sales ($ mil.)	16.7%	975.9	1,138.3	1,245.6	1,655.0	1,811.8
Net income ($ mil.)	41.7%	43.7	23.1	84.6	(32.6)	176.3
Market value ($ mil.)	21.1%	2,781.9	2,916.8	3,749.5	4,882.3	5,987.1
Employees	9.8%	3,100	3,400	3,700	4,400	4,500

*Fiscal year change

MICROSTRATEGY INC.
NMS: MSTR

1850 Towers Crescent Plaza
Tysons Corner, VA 22182
Phone: 703 848-8600
Fax: 703 848-8610
Web: www.microstrategy.com

CEO: Michael J. Saylor
CFO: Phong Le
HR: –
FYE: December 31
Type: Public

MicroStrategy knows you need the details to make a good plan. The company's cloud-based business intelligence software addresses functions such as building reports and dashboards managing mobile applications and capitalizing on social media. Specific analytics modules include human resources management Web traffic analysis and sales and distribution. It sells to many of the world's largest companies such as Aetna and eBay as well as midsized companies and government agencies such as NASA and the US Army. MicroStrategy also offers consulting and support services. Founded in 1989 MicroStrategy has operations in about 25 countries.

	Annual Growth	12/14	12/15	12/16	12/17	12/18
Sales ($ mil.)	(3.7%)	579.8	529.9	512.2	504.5	497.6
Net income ($ mil.)	45.4%	5.0	105.9	90.9	17.6	22.5
Market value ($ mil.)	(5.8%)	1,719.3	1,898.1	2,089.9	1,390.1	1,352.5
Employees	0.6%	2,470	1,947	2,133	2,216	2,528

MICROTECHNOLOGIES LLC

8330 BOONE BLVD STE 600
VIENNA, VA 221822658
Phone: 703-891-1073
Fax: –
Web: www.microtech.net

CEO: Anthony R Jimenez
CFO: Lynn Wasylina
HR: –
FYE: December 31
Type: Private

MicroTechnologies is a US small business dishing up tech services to some big clients. Also known as MicroTech the Hispanic- and veteran-owned company delivers IT reseller products technical support systems integration and management consulting services to clients ranging from Fortune 500 companies to the federal government. It has added virtualization and cloud computing to its service portfolio. It also serves state city and local agencies. For the US General Services Administration it has provided and set up personal computers Web access data voice and video communications and teleconferencing systems for President Obama's staff.

	Annual Growth	12/05	12/06	12/07	12/08	12/10
Sales ($ mil.)	(64.7%)	–	–	2,124.0	39.0	93.5
Net income ($ mil.)	667.5%	–	–	0.0	2.5	7.4
Market value ($ mil.)	–	–	–	–	–	–
Employees	–	–	–	–	–	425

MICROVISION INC.
NMS: MVIS

6244 185th Avenue N.E., Suite 100
Redmond, WA 98052
Phone: 425 936-6847
Fax: –
Web: www.microvision.com

CEO: Perry M Mulligan
CFO: Stephen P Holt
HR: –
FYE: December 31
Type: Public

Microvision thinks tiny images have big potential. The company's PicoP display technology can be used to create high-quality video and image displays using an ultra-miniature projector that is embedded into mobile devices such as cell phones DVD players gaming devices and laptops. The projector enables users to display images and data onto a variety of surfaces from mobile products. Microvision's first product — the SHOWWX accessory projector — connects via cable to a video-out connection on a mobile device. It is sold directly and through distributors in Asia and Europe. The company also produces prototypes based on its light scanning technology under government and commercial development contracts.

	Annual Growth	12/14	12/15	12/16	12/17	12/18
Sales ($ mil.)	49.9%	3.5	9.2	14.8	10.9	17.6
Net income ($ mil.)	–	(18.1)	(14.5)	(16.5)	(24.2)	(27.3)
Market value ($ mil.)	(23.2%)	174.2	286.3	126.1	163.2	60.5
Employees	12.8%	66	67	81	113	107

MICROWAVE FILTER CO., INC.
NBB: MFCO

6743 Kinne Street
East Syracuse, NY 13057
Phone: 315 438-4700
Fax: 315 463-1467
Web: www.microwavefilter.com

CEO: Paul W Mears
CFO: Richard L Jones
HR: –
FYE: September 30
Type: Public

Microwave Filter Company (MFC) can improve your powers of reception. The company's electronic filters process TV radio and other signals and prevent unwanted signals from interfering with transmissions. Its Fastrap filters are used by cable TV operators either to allow or to prevent viewing of pay-per-view broadcasts and premium programming. MFC sells more than 1700 products to the broadcasting cable television defense and mobile radio industries. Subsidiary Niagara Scientific makes material handling equipment for the cosmetics food processing and pharmaceutical industries. Sales are primarily in the US.

	Annual Growth	09/14	09/15	09/16	09/17	09/18
Sales ($ mil.)	(2.0%)	3.6	3.5	3.5	3.0	3.3
Net income ($ mil.)	–	0.0	(0.2)	(0.0)	(0.3)	(0.0)
Market value ($ mil.)	5.7%	1.2	1.1	1.5	1.6	1.5
Employees	(3.1%)	42	44	42	36	37

MICROWAVE TRANSMISSION SYSTEMS, INC

1751 JAY ELL DR
RICHARDSON, TX 750811835
Phone: 972-669-0591
Fax: –
Web: www.mtsi.com

CEO: Preston David Spurling
CFO: –
HR: –
FYE: December 31
Type: Private

Microwave Transmission Systems (MTSI) constructs and maintains wireless communications transmitting and receiving facilities. In addition to building and erecting microwave towers and installing and testing cellular equipment the company's services include planning related to feasibility studies and FCC radio frequency licensing. It also provides site and project management services. Founded in 1987 MTSI has offices and subsidiaries in Florida New Mexico North Carolina Ohio Tennessee and Texas. Affiliated companies include Viper Communications and Site Communications.

	Annual Growth	12/13	12/14	12/15	12/16	12/17
Sales ($ mil.)	5.7%	–	53.9	49.5	40.8	63.6
Net income ($ mil.)	–	–	(1.1)	(1.2)	(2.0)	4.6
Market value ($ mil.)	–	–	–	–	–	–
Employees	–	–	–	–	–	656

MICRUS ENDOVASCULAR CORPORATION

821 Fox Ln.
San Jose CA 95131
Phone: 408-433-1400
Fax: 408-433-1401
Web: www.micruscorp.com

CEO: John T Kilcoyne
CFO: Gordon T Sangster
HR: –
FYE: March 31
Type: Subsidiary

Micrus makes microcoils to help prevent strokes. The company develops implantable and disposable medical devices specifically its microcoils and accessory products such as microcatheters and guidewires used to treat cerebral aneurysms and other cerebral vascular diseases. Physicians can use the microcoils to build scaffolds within an aneurysm to stabilize the blood flow to the brain. The catheterization procedure is less invasive and less expensive than other forms of surgery and aims to give patients a shorter recovery time. Micrus sells its products directly in North America and Europe and through distributors in other countries. The company was acquired by Johnson & Johnson in 2010.

MID AMERICA CLINICAL LABORATORIES LLC

2560 N SHADELAND AVE B
INDIANAPOLIS, IN 462191706
Phone: 877-803-1010
Fax: –
Web: www.maclonline.com

CEO: –
CFO: –
HR: Jane A Lloyd
FYE: December 31
Type: Private

Let's hope the Hoosiers at Mid America Clinical Laboratories don't suffer from test anxiety. The company operates more than 30 specimen collection and laboratory sites in Indianapolis and the surrounding central Indiana region. The company processes more than 4.5 million tests every year and its labs are equipped to perform a variety of medical testing including biopsies PAP tests urinalyses and blood tests. Mid America Clinical Laboratories is a joint venture company owned by Ascension Health's St. Vincent Hospital Community Hospital and Quest Diagnostics.

	Annual Growth	12/05	12/06	12/07	12/08	12/09
Sales ($ mil.)	5.8%	–	63.8	67.3	70.9	75.5
Net income ($ mil.)	4.7%	–	8.0	9.2	8.9	9.2
Market value ($ mil.)	–	–	–	–	–	–
Employees	–	–	–	–	–	525

MID PENN BANCORP INC   NMS: MPB

349 Union Street
Millersburg, PA 17061
Phone: 866 642-7736
Fax: –
Web: www.midpennbank.com

CEO: Rory G Ritrievi
CFO: Michael D Peduzzi
HR: –
FYE: December 31
Type: Public

Mid Penn Bancorp is the holding company for Mid Penn Bank which operates more than a dozen branches in central Pennsylvania's Cumberland Dauphin Northumberland and Schuylkill counties. The bank offers full-service commercial banking insurance and trust services. Its deposit products include checking savings money market and NOW accounts. Commercial real estate construction and land development loans account for nearly 80% of the company's loan portfolio; the bank also writes residential mortgages and business agricultural and consumer loans. Mid Penn is a descendant of Millersburg Bank founded in 1868. Trust company CEDE & Co. owns about a third of Mid Penn Bancorp.

	Annual Growth	12/14	12/15	12/16	12/17	12/18
Assets ($ mil.)	28.8%	755.7	931.7	1,032.6	1,170.4	2,078.0
Net income ($ mil.)	16.8%	5.7	6.5	7.8	7.1	10.6
Market value ($ mil.)	10.3%	131.6	136.2	201.6	280.0	194.7
Employees	18.9%	203	252	257	277	406

MID-AMERICA APARTMENT COMMUNITIES INC   NYS: MAA

6815 Poplar Avenue, Suite 500
Germantown, TN 38138
Phone: 901 682-6600
Fax: 901 682-6667
Web: www.maac.com

CEO: H. Eric Bolton
CFO: Albert M. (Al) Campbell
HR: Melanie Carter
FYE: December 31
Type: Public

For Mid-America Apartment Communities the Sunbelt is where it's at. Operating as MAA the firm is a self-administered self-managed real estate investment trust (REIT) that focuses solely on buying multifamily residences. MAA owns or has interests in approximately 79500 apartment units in 15 states primarily located in the West Southeast and south-central US. Its largest markets are California Florida Tennessee and Texas. MAA which has an average property occupancy rate of 95% targets large and midsized markets. MAA bought rival Colonial Properties in 2013 in an $8.6 billion deal. It is now buying Post Properties for $3.9 billion to become the nation's largest public apartment owner by unit number.

	Annual Growth	12/14	12/15	12/16	12/17	12/18
Sales ($ mil.)	12.3%	989.3	1,042.8	1,125.3	1,529.0	1,571.3
Net income ($ mil.)	10.8%	148.0	332.3	212.2	328.4	222.9
Market value ($ mil.)	6.4%	8,501.9	10,338.2	11,147.6	11,448.2	10,894.9
Employees	5.1%	2,090	1,989	2,528	2,464	2,552

MID-CON ENERGY PARTNERS LP   NAS: MCEP

2431 East 61st Street, Suite 850
Tulsa, OK 74136
Phone: 918 743-7575
Fax: –
Web: www.midconenergypartners.com

CEO: Jeffrey R Olmstead
CFO: Michael D Peterson
HR: –
FYE: December 31
Type: Public

Mid-Con Energy Partners is a Delaware limited partnership that owns operates and develops producing oil and natural gas properties in North America. With a focus on the Mid-Continent region of the US in particular Oklahoma and Colorado the company's operations primarily consist of enhancing the development of mature producing oil properties through an oil recovery method called waterflooding. It has total estimated proved reserves of about 8 million barrels of oil equivalent a majority of which is oil. Managed by Mid-Con Energy GP Mid-Con Energy Partners was formed in July 2011 and went public in December 2011.

	Annual Growth	12/14	12/15	12/16	12/17	12/18
Sales ($ mil.)	(12.9%)	126.3	96.3	43.9	57.0	72.8
Net income ($ mil.)	–	22.5	(95.5)	(24.8)	(27.3)	(18.3)
Market value ($ mil.)	(39.8%)	192.1	34.7	79.1	35.9	25.2
Employees	–	–	–	70	70	100

MIDAMERICAN ENERGY HOLDINGS COMPANY

666 Grand Ave. Ste. 500
Des Moines IA 50309-2580
Phone: 515-242-4300
Fax: 515-281-2389
Web: www.midamerican.com

CEO: William J Fehrman
CFO: Patrick J Goodman
HR: –
FYE: December 31
Type: Subsidiary

MidAmerican Energy Holdings reaches farther than its name implies. The company generates transmits and distributes electricity and natural gas to 7 million customers across the US and the UK primarily through subsidiaries MidAmerican Energy Company and PacifiCorp. UK regional distribution subsidiary Northern Powergrid serves about 3.8 million electricity customers. MidAmerican Energy Holdings also has independent power production operations as well as real estate (HomeServices of America) and gas exploration production and pipeline operations (Kern River Gas Transmission and Northern Natural Gas). It operates 38600 miles of natural gas pipeline.

MIDAS INC.

NYSE: MDS

1300 Arlington Heights Rd.
Itasca IL 60143
Phone: 630-438-3000
Fax: 630-438-3880
Web: www.midas.com

CEO: Alan D Feldman
CFO: -
HR: -
FYE: December 31
Type: Subsidiary

Midas hopes to apply a golden touch to the car repair business. In addition to focusing on brake and exhaust system services the company's facilities offer routine maintenance (oil changes fluid replacements) and work on suspensions shocks and struts. The Midas network includes about 1480 franchised and company-owned stores throughout the US and Canada as well as some 775 locations in more than a dozen other countries. (Midas' North American stores account for about 98% of total sales.) In addition to these the company has 160-plus quick-lube and maintenance shops operating under the SpeeDee Oil Change banner in the US and Mexico. Automotive company TBC Corporation owns Midas.

MIDASPLUS INC.

4801 E. Broadway Blvd. Ste. 335
Tucson AZ 85711
Phone: 520-296-7398
Fax: 520-886-4763
Web: www.midasplus.com

CEO: -
CFO: -
HR: -
FYE: June 30
Type: Subsidiary

This Midas turns medical records into gold. MidasPlus is a provider of healthcare management software (known as MIDAS+) that is used to provide HMOs hospitals and health systems with the ability to manage areas such as billing claims documents Medicaid services and patient care. The software can keep track of influenza immunization data or help an emergency room staff act quickly when a patient goes into decline. MidasPlus also provides related services such as consulting support and training. The company is a subsidiary of Xerox.

MIDCOAST ENERGY PARTNERS, L.P.

1100 LA ST STE 3300
HOUSTON, TX 77002
Phone: 713-821-2000
Fax: -

CEO: -
CFO: -
HR: -
FYE: December 31
Type: Private

Midcoast Energy Partners was formed by Enbridge Energy Partners in 2013 as an investment vehicle to own and grow its natural gas and NGL midstream business. It has minority stakes in Enbridge's network of natural gas and natural gas liquids (NGLs) gathering and transportation systems natural gas processing and treating facilities and NGL fractionation plants in Texas and Oklahoma. Organized as a limited partnership Midcoast Energy Partners is exempt from paying income tax as long as it distributes quarterly dividends to shareholders. It went public in 2013 raising $333 million. In 2017 Enbridge Energy Partners agreed to acquire control of Midcoast Energy Partners.

	Annual Growth	12/12	12/13	12/14	12/15	12/16
Sales ($ mil.)	(29.4%)	-	5,593.6	5,894.3	2,842.7	1,966.0
Net income ($ mil.)	-	-	53.9	144.3	(284.5)	(157.0)
Market value ($ mil.)	-	-	-	-	-	-
Employees	-	-	-	-	-	11

MIDCONTINENT INDEPENDENT SYSTEM OPERATOR, INC.

720 CITY CENTER DR
CARMEL, IN 460323826
Phone: 317-249-5400
Fax: -
Web: www.misoenergy.org

CEO: John R. Bear
CFO: Melissa A. Brown
HR: -
FYE: December 31
Type: Private

Midwest and more. Non-profit Midwest Independent Transmission System Operator (Midwest ISO) monitors and coordinates the operation of an electric transmission system with more than 49970 miles of transmission lines across 11 Midwestern states and Manitoba and more than 15810 miles across four southern US states. In 2012 it managed energy markets with $18.4 billion in gross energy transactions. The Regional Transmission Organization (RTO) ensures fair access to the grid and facilitates communication between its members which include investor-owned cooperative and municipal utilities as well as power marketers and independent transmission companies. Midwest ISO also provides wholesale electric service.

	Annual Growth	12/13	12/14	12/16	12/17	12/18
Sales ($ mil.)	5.6%	-	305.6	337.1	357.0	380.3
Net income ($ mil.)	-	-	(3.9)	0.0	0.0	0.0
Market value ($ mil.)	-	-	-	-	-	-
Employees	-	-	-	-	-	700

MIDDLE TENNESSEE STATE UNIVERSITY

1301 E MAIN ST
MURFREESBORO, TN 371320002
Phone: 615-898-2300
Fax: -
Web: www.mtsu.edu

CEO: -
CFO: -
HR: -
FYE: June 30
Type: Private

Middle Tennessee State University (MTSU) founded in 1911 as a school for teacher training offers bachelor's and master's degrees through its eight university colleges. The educational institution boasts basic and applied sciences business education and behavioral science honors liberal arts mass communication and graduate studies. The school bestows master's degrees in eight areas including business and education. MTSU also confers a Specialist in Education degree and doctorate degrees. It has an enrollment of more than 25000 students. MTSU is part of the State University and Community College System of Tennessee.

	Annual Growth	06/05	06/06	06/12	06/13	06/14
Sales ($ mil.)	54.2%	-	5.7	218.3	190.3	183.0
Net income ($ mil.)	-	-	0.0	18.4	46.8	35.0
Market value ($ mil.)	-	-	-	-	-	-
Employees	-	-	-	-	-	2,400

MIDDLEBURG FINANCIAL CORP

NAS: MBRG

111 West Washington Street
Middleburg, VA 20117
Phone: 703 777-6327
Fax: -

CEO: -
CFO: -
HR: -
FYE: December 31
Type: Public

Middleburg Financial Corp. (MFC) is the holding company for Middleburg Bank which serves individuals and businesses through about a dozen branches in northern Virginia. It offers standard deposit products such as checking and savings accounts money markets CDs and IRAs. Middleburg Bank focuses heavily on real estate lending: Real estate loans account for about 80% of its loan portfolio. Commercial loans account for about 18%. MFC also operates Middleburg Investment Group which offers investment products to the bank's customers. The 90-year-old bank has total assets of more than $1.2 billion. MFC is merging with Access National Corporation in a $233 million transaction.

	Annual Growth	12/11	12/12	12/13	12/14	12/15
Assets ($ mil.)	2.1%	1,192.9	1,236.8	1,227.8	1,222.9	1,294.9
Net income ($ mil.)	12.1%	5.0	5.5	6.2	7.6	7.8
Market value ($ mil.)	6.7%	101.0	125.1	127.8	127.6	130.9
Employees	(17.5%)	405	410	352	183	188

MIDDLEBY CORP
NMS: MIDD

1400 Toastmaster Drive
Elgin, IL 60120
Phone: 847 741-3300
Fax: –
Web: www.middleby.com

CEO: Selim A. Bassoul
CFO: Timothy J. (Tim) Fitzgerald
HR: –
FYE: December 29
Type: Public

Founded in 1888 Middleby makes a slew of commercial and institutional foodservice equipment for restaurants retailers and hotels worldwide. Middleby operates through three segments: Commercial Foodservice Equipment Food Processing Equipment and Residential Kitchen Equipment. The largest Foodservice makes machines for most types of cooking and warming activities. Products are sold under about 50 blue chip brands ? Anets Blodgett Southbend and TurboChef among them. Residential Kitchen makes ovens refrigerators dishwashers microwaves and other related products and Food Processing makes cooking mixing slicing and packaging machines. About two-thirds of sales come from the US and Canada.

	Annual Growth	01/15	01/16*	12/16	12/17	12/18
Sales ($ mil.)	18.5%	1,636.5	1,826.6	2,267.9	2,335.5	2,722.9
Net income ($ mil.)	17.9%	193.3	191.6	284.2	298.1	317.2
Market value ($ mil.)	0.8%	5,516.9	6,008.7	7,175.2	7,517.2	5,650.0
Employees	24.4%	4,860	7,800	8,026	8,493	9,346

*Fiscal year change

MIDDLEFIELD BANC CORP.
NAS: MBCN

15985 East High Street
Middlefield, OH 44062-0035
Phone: 440 632-1666
Fax: –

CEO: Thomas G Caldwell
CFO: Donald L Stacy
HR: –
FYE: December 31
Type: Public

Here's your cash stuck in the Middlefield Banc with you. The firm is the holding company for Middlefield Bank which has about 10 offices in northeast and central Ohio. The community bank offers standard deposit services such as checking and savings accounts CDs and IRAs. Investments insurance and brokerage services are offered through an agreement with UVEST a division of LPL Financial. Residential mortgage loans comprise more than 60% of the company's loan portfolio; commercial and industrial loans make up about 20%. The bank also offers commercial mortgages construction loans and consumer installment loans. Middlefield Banc is buying Liberty Bank which operates three branches in northeast Ohio.

	Annual Growth	12/14	12/15	12/16	12/17	12/18
Assets ($ mil.)	16.5%	677.5	735.1	787.8	1,106.3	1,248.4
Net income ($ mil.)	14.7%	7.2	6.9	6.4	9.5	12.4
Market value ($ mil.)	6.0%	218.1	210.2	251.1	312.8	275.3
Employees	9.5%	139	143	139	190	200

MIDDLESEX WATER CO.
NMS: MSEX

485C Route One South
Iselin, NJ 08830
Phone: 732 634-1500
Fax: –
Web: www.middlesexwater.com

CEO: Dennis W. Doll
CFO: A. Bruce O'Connor
HR: Lorrie P. Ginegaw
FYE: December 31
Type: Public

Like all gardens the Garden State needs water to thrive. Middlesex Water provides water and wastewater services to residential business and fire protection customers in New Jersey through its Middlesex Pinelands and Bayview systems. It also distributes water in Delaware through its Tidewater system. All told the utility's subsidiaries have more than 140000 customers and serve a retail population of 450000. The company also is engaged in municipal contract operations and public/private partnerships and provides line maintenance services. Middlesex Water's nonregulated Utility Service Affiliates (Perth Amboy) unit operates the municipal water and wastewater systems in Perth Amboy New Jersey.

	Annual Growth	12/14	12/15	12/16	12/17	12/18
Sales ($ mil.)	4.2%	117.1	126.0	132.9	130.8	138.1
Net income ($ mil.)	15.2%	18.4	20.0	22.7	22.8	32.5
Market value ($ mil.)	23.3%	378.3	435.3	704.3	654.6	875.1
Employees	4.0%	282	293	309	315	330

MIDLAND FINANCIAL CO.

501 NW Grand Blvd.
Oklahoma City OK 73118-6054
Phone: 405-840-7600
Fax: 405-767-5426
Web: www.midfirst.com

CEO: –
CFO: Todd A Dobson
HR: –
FYE: December 31
Type: Private

There's nothing middling about Midland Financial the holding company for MidFirst Bank and other financial services subsidiaries. One of the largest privately held banks in the US MidFirst Bank has more than 50 branches in Oklahoma and Arizona. Serving business and retail customers the bank offers standard services such as checking and savings accounts loans and mortgages CDs IRAs credit cards trust services and private banking. It maintains commercial real estate lending offices in Chicago Houston New York and Southern California. Affiliate Midland Mortgage acquires and services mortgages throughout the US.

MIDLAND STATES BANCORP INC
NMS: MSBI

1201 Network Centre Drive
Effingham, IL 62401
Phone: 217 342-7321
Fax: –
Web: www.midlandsb.com

CEO: Leon J. Holschbach
CFO: Kevin L. Thompson
HR: –
FYE: December 31
Type: Public

Born in rural Illinois Midland States Bancorp is now discovering banking life in new states. It is the $3 billion-asset holding company for Midland States Bank a community bank that operates more than 35 branches in central and northern Illinois and around 15 branches in the St. Louis metropolitan area. The bank offers traditional consumer and commercial banking products and services as well as merchant card services insurance and financial planning. Subsidiary Midland Wealth Management which boasts $1.2 billion-plus in assets under administration provides wealth management services while Heartland Business Credit offers commercial equipment leasing services. Midland States Bancorp went public in 2016.

	Annual Growth	12/14	12/15	12/16	12/17	12/18
Assets ($ mil.)	20.5%	2,676.6	2,884.8	3,233.7	4,412.7	5,637.7
Net income ($ mil.)	38.2%	10.8	24.3	31.5	16.1	39.4
Market value ($ mil.)	(21.4%)	–	–	859.3	771.5	530.6
Employees	16.3%	–	700	715	840	1,100

MIDSOUTH BANCORP, INC.
NYS: MSL

102 Versailles Boulevard
Lafayette, LA 70501
Phone: 337 237-8343
Fax: –
Web: www.midsouthbank.com

CEO: –
CFO: –
HR: –
FYE: December 31
Type: Public

For banking in the Deep South try MidSouth. MidSouth Bancorp is the holding company for MidSouth Bank which boasts roughly $2 billion in assets and around 60 branches across Louisiana and Texas. Targeting individuals and local business customers the bank offers such standard retail services as checking and savings accounts savings bonds investment accounts and credit card services. About 55% of its loan portfolio is made up of real estate mortgages while commercial loans make up more than 35%. Consumer and construction loans round out the rest of its lending activities.

	Annual Growth	12/13	12/14	12/15	12/16	12/17
Assets ($ mil.)	0.4%	1,851.2	1,936.7	1,927.7	1,943.3	1,881.2
Net income ($ mil.)	–	14.2	19.1	11.0	9.4	(11.8)
Market value ($ mil.)	(7.2%)	295.6	287.0	150.3	225.1	219.3
Employees	(6.2%)	604	549	536	535	467

MIDSTATE MEDICAL CENTER

435 LEWIS AVE
MERIDEN, CT 064512101
Phone: 203-694-8200
Fax: –
Web: www.midstatemedical.org

CEO: Lucille A Janatka
CFO: Ralph Becker
HR: –
FYE: September 30
Type: Private

MidState Medical Center serves patients across the Nutmeg State. The acute care hospital serves central Connecticut and has some 155 beds (including six psychiatric beds). It offers patients a range of services including cardiac emergency medicine and maternity care. MidState Medical Center also has centers dedicated to diabetes cancer treatment digestive health nutrition and women's health. The hospital manages satellite facilities in Cheshire Wallingford and Southington and it operates an emergency center and the MidState Medical Services Building for outpatient care. MidState Medical Center is part of the Hartford HealthCare network.

	Annual Growth	09/13	09/14	09/15	09/16	09/17
Sales ($ mil.)	0.5%	–	219.1	212.4	217.2	222.7
Net income ($ mil.)	1.9%	–	18.9	16.4	20.1	20.0
Market value ($ mil.)	–	–	–	–	–	–
Employees	–	–	–	–	–	900

MIDWEST ENERGY, INC.

1330 CANTERBURY DR
HAYS, KS 676012708
Phone: 785-625-3437
Fax: –
Web: www.mwenergy.com

CEO: –
CFO: –
HR: –
FYE: December 31
Type: Private

Some rural residents of the Sunflower State rely on Midwest Energy for their power and gas needs. The multi-utility serves approximately 48000 electricity customers and 42000 natural gas customers in central and western Kansas. It also has some power generation operations; it purchases most of its electric supply from wholesale marketers. The company's Midwest United Energy subsidiary is a competitive natural gas supplier in four states and its WestLand Energy unit sells propane to Kansas consumers. Midwest Energy has seen its power sales grow by 23% since 2006 and its natural gas sales by 17%.

	Annual Growth	12/14	12/15	12/16	12/17	12/18
Sales ($ mil.)	2.2%	–	205.8	208.8	208.4	219.6
Net income ($ mil.)	3.5%	–	15.9	12.9	15.0	17.6
Market value ($ mil.)	–	–	–	–	–	–
Employees	–	–	–	–	–	274

MIDWESTONE FINANCIAL GROUP, INC.   NMS: MOFG

102 South Clinton Street
Iowa City, IA 52240
Phone: 319 356-5800
Fax: –
Web: www.midwestone.com

CEO: Charles N. Funk
CFO: Katie A. Lorenson
HR: –
FYE: December 31
Type: Public

MidWestOne Financial Group is the holding company for MidWestOne Bank which operates about two dozen branches throughout central and east-central Iowa. The bank offers standard deposit products such as checking and savings accounts CDs and IRAs in addition to trust services credit cards insurance and brokerage and investment services. About two-thirds of MidWestOne Financial's loan portfolio consists of real estate loans including residential and commercial mortgages and farmland and construction loans. Founded in 1983 MidWestOne has total assets of $1.8 billion.

	Annual Growth	12/14	12/15	12/16	12/17	12/18
Assets ($ mil.)	16.3%	1,800.3	2,980.0	3,079.6	3,212.3	3,291.5
Net income ($ mil.)	13.1%	18.5	25.1	20.4	18.7	30.4
Market value ($ mil.)	(3.7%)	350.9	370.4	458.0	408.4	302.4
Employees	12.4%	374	648	587	610	597

MIKART INC.

1750 CHATTAHOOCHEE AVE NW
ATLANTA, GA 303182112
Phone: 404-352-0601
Fax: –
Web: www.mikart.com

CEO: Michael Kallelis
CFO: R Larry Gunnin
HR: –
FYE: December 31
Type: Private

In-, the art-, of making pills and capsules Mikart pays attention to the details. The company offers contract pharmaceutical manufacturing services specializing in oral capsule and tablet formulations. Tablets and capsules can be immediate or time-release; the company also makes liquid formulations and provides specialty packaging including laminated foil blister and pouches. Mikart's facilities have the capacity to produce-, everything from small pilot-scale-, batches all the way up to full-scale commercial production. Other services include drug development feasibility studies and product testing. Mikart will also walk customers through all the required regulatory processes.

	Annual Growth	06/04	06/05	06/06*	12/08	12/10
Sales ($ mil.)	(64.6%)	–	–	2,039.0	26.5	32.0
Net income ($ mil.)	862.5%	–	–	0.0	0.5	1.7
Market value ($ mil.)	–	–	–	–	–	–
Employees	–	–	–	–	–	165

*Fiscal year change

MILACRON LLC

3010 Disney St.
Cincinnati OH 45209
Phone: 513-487-5000
Fax: 513-487-5086
Web: www.milacron.com

CEO: Tom Goeke
CFO: Bruce Chalmers
HR: –
FYE: December 31
Type: Private

Milacron people are passionate for plastics. Once a machine toolmaker Milacron retooled in the '90s to focus on plastics processing technologies and industrial fluids. It leads five businesses. The largest a plastics machinery unit makes injection molding and extrusion processing equipment used to produce dashboards decking and other products. Other units include Uniloy (blow molding systems for consumer packaging) DME (parts such as mold bases for plastics machinery) Cimcool (coolants lubricants and cleaners for metal grinding machining and stamping) and Milacron Precision Machining Manufacturing (parts for wind power oil and gas and heavy equipment). North America is Milacron's core market.

MILAEGER"S INC.

4838 DOUGLAS AVE
RACINE, WI 534022447
Phone: 262-639-2040
Fax: –
Web: www.milaegerslandscape.com

CEO: –
CFO: –
HR: –
FYE: December 31
Type: Private

Milaeger's has the difficult task of keeping things green on the banks of Lake Michigan. The company operates two nurseries in Racine and Sturtevant Wisconsin selling seeds soil plants mulch as well as apparel Christmas collectibles figurines folk art outdoor furniture and home decor. It also offers landscape services including lawn tree and shrub care along with design services. Milaeger's regularly hosts shows by collectibles merchants local fashion shows and gardening workshops. The company's Java Garden Cafe onsite at both locations offers hot and cold beverages dessert and light lunch and dinner items. Milaeger's was founded in 1960 by Dan and Joan Milaeger.

	Annual Growth	12/09	12/10	12/11	12/12	12/13
Sales ($ mil.)	3.1%	–	11.5	11.5	12.3	12.6
Net income ($ mil.)	17.5%	–	–	0.1	0.3	0.1
Market value ($ mil.)	–	–	–	–	–	–
Employees	–	–	–	–	–	125

MILES HEALTH CARE, INC

35 MILES ST
DAMARISCOTTA, ME 045434047
Phone: 207-563-1234
Fax: –
Web: www.mainehealth.org

CEO: James Donavan
CFO: –
HR: –
FYE: September 30
Type: Private

Miles Health Care provides acute and specialty health care service to the residents of Maine's Lincoln County. The not-for-profit company operates Miles Memorial Hospital — known as LincolnHealth Miles Campus — a rural medical center with about 40 beds and has emergency intensive care surgery and birthing departments. In addition Miles Health Care operates outpatient and specialty practice clinics physician practice offices and home health rehabilitation and hospice programs. It also provides long-term senior care through its nursing assisted and independent living facilities. Miles Health Care is a member of Lincoln County Healthcare (LincolnHealth) which is part of the MaineHealth network.

	Annual Growth	09/04	09/05	09/06	09/08	09/09
Sales ($ mil.)	111.6%	–	52.0	59.0	14.2	1,043.0
Net income ($ mil.)	–	–	(0.3)	3.5	0.6	12.7
Market value ($ mil.)	–	–	–	–	–	–
Employees	–	–	–	–	–	800

MILESTONE SCIENTIFIC INC.

ASE: MLSS

220 South Orange Avenue
Livingston, NJ 07039
Phone: 973 535-2717
Fax: –
Web: www.milestonescientific.com

CEO: Leonard A Osser
CFO: Joseph D'Agostino
HR: –
FYE: December 31
Type: Public

Trips to the dentist might never be pain-free but they could be less painful if Milestone Scientific has its way. The company develops and markets dental injection devices (based on its CompuFlo technique) that cause less pain than a traditional syringe. Its primary product CompuDent and its accompanying accessory The Wand is a computer-controlled local anesthetic delivery unit that can be used in routine treatments including root canals crowns fillings and cleanings. CompuDent is also marketed as CompuMed to the medical industry for use in dermatology and orthopedics. Milestone sells its products through a global distributor network to dental and medical professionals in more than 25 countries.

	Annual Growth	12/14	12/15	12/16	12/17	12/18
Sales ($ mil.)	(1.8%)	10.3	9.5	10.5	11.3	9.6
Net income ($ mil.)	–	(1.7)	(5.5)	(5.9)	(5.2)	(7.4)
Market value ($ mil.)	(31.4%)	50.7	79.5	47.4	39.9	11.2
Employees	0.0%	16	15	17	14	16

MILFORD REGIONAL MEDICAL CENTER, INC.

14 PROSPECT ST
MILFORD, MA 017573003
Phone: 508-473-1190
Fax: –
Web: www.milfordregional.org

CEO: –
CFO: Jeanne Lynskey
HR: Alice D Hall
FYE: September 30
Type: Private

Medical treatment in south central Massachusetts and northern Rhode Island is the main affair of Milford Regional Medical Center. The 145-bed hospital provides acute medical services to the residents of Milford Massachusetts and surrounding areas. Specialty services include emergency medicine home health care diagnostic imaging physical therapy obstetrics and cancer treatment. It also has an affiliated physician practice group the Tri-County Medical Associates. The Medical Center which employs about 200 physicians is a teaching hospital affiliated with the University of Massachusetts.

	Annual Growth	09/13	09/14	09/15	09/16	09/17
Sales ($ mil.)	3.6%	–	184.1	195.2	195.6	204.6
Net income ($ mil.)	21.9%	–	4.5	5.9	(1.6)	8.2
Market value ($ mil.)	–	–	–	–	–	–
Employees	–	–	–	–	–	1,159

MILKEN FAMILY FOUNDATION

1250 4TH ST FL 1
SANTA MONICA, CA 904011418
Phone: 310-570-4800
Fax: –
Web: www.mff.org

CEO: –
CFO: Susan Fox
HR: –
FYE: November 30
Type: Private

Former investor Michael Milken is behind the foundation that helps to give back. The Milken Family Foundation funds awards and grants in the areas of education and medical research. Its $25000 Milken Educator Award is given to up to 80 teachers specialists and principals annually. Other initiatives include the Teacher Advancement Program a teacher recruitment and development program and the Milken Festival for Youth which funds community service opportunities for primarily disadvantaged students. Brothers Lowell Milken (the organization's chairman) and Michael Milken (a trustee; also famously indicted on racketeering charges in 1989 after amassing a fortune on junk bonds) started the foundation in 1982.

	Annual Growth	10/07	10/08	10/09*	11/09	11/13
Sales ($ mil.)	258.1%	–	–	0.7	13.1	115.3
Net income ($ mil.)	–	–	–	(2.5)	0.2	95.5
Market value ($ mil.)	–	–	–	–	–	–
Employees	–	–	–	–	–	200

*Fiscal year change

MILLENNIAL MEDIA INC

NYS: MM

2400 Boston Street, Suite 201
Baltimore, MD 21224
Phone: 410 522-8705
Fax: –
Web: www.millennialmedia.com

CEO: Michael G Barrett
CFO: Andrew Jeanneret
HR: –
FYE: December 31
Type: Public

There's an app for that is music to the ears of Millennial Media. Using a proprietary data and technology platform called MYDAS the independent mobile advertising company connects app developers and major advertisers by buying space in apps to display highly targeted banner and video ads. MYDAS gives developers a way to deliver ads from Warner Bros Patagonia Porsche GM and others to more than 7000 different types of mobile devices. Supported apps come from small developers content providers (New York Times CBS Interactive) and major developers (Zynga Pandora). Millennial Media the nation's second largest mobile advertiser was formed in 2006 and went public in 2012.

	Annual Growth	12/09	12/10	12/11	12/12	12/13
Sales ($ mil.)	99.9%	16.2	47.8	103.7	177.7	259.2
Net income ($ mil.)	–	(7.6)	(7.1)	(0.3)	(5.4)	(15.1)
Market value ($ mil.)	(42.0%)	–	–	–	1,332.1	772.9
Employees	64.4%	–	–	222	348	600

MILLENNIUM PRIME INC

NBB: MLMN

6538 Collins Avenue, Suite 262
Miami Beach, FL 33041
Phone: 786 347-9309
Fax: –
Web: www.millenniumprime.com

CEO: –
CFO: –
HR: –
FYE: September 30
Type: Public

Genio Group has decided that playing cards just isn't in the cards. Until 2005 the company designed and marketed entertainment products including the Genio Cards card collection which consisted of 360 cards spanning 30 different educational categories such as endangered animals man-made landmarks and space travel. The game-playing cards used popular Marvel super heroes to promote learning. Citing lack of sufficient funding Genio Group exited that business. Steven Horowitz succeeded Matthew Cohen as CEO in mid-2006. The firm is currently searching for new operations.

	Annual Growth	09/07	09/08	09/09	09/13	09/14
Sales ($ mil.)	–	–	0.0	–	0.1	0.1
Net income ($ mil.)	–	(0.3)	(0.3)	(0.8)	(0.2)	(0.3)
Market value ($ mil.)	76.6%	0.3	0.2	0.6	3.9	16.1
Employees	–	–	–	–	–	–

MILLER (HERMAN) INC
NMS: MLHR

855 East Main Avenue, PO Box 302
Zeeland, MI 49464-0302
Phone: 616 654-3000
Fax: -
Web: www.hermanmiller.com

CEO: Brian C. Walker
CFO: Jeffrey M. (Jeff) Stutz
HR: -
FYE: June 01
Type: Public

Desk jockeys can ride Herman Miller's products all the way up the corporate ladder and home again. A top US maker of office furniture it's known for developing designs for corporate government home office leisure and health care environments. Herman Miller's products include ergonomic devices filing and storage systems freestanding furniture seating textiles and wooden casegoods. It makes products in the US UK China Brazil and India and sells them worldwide through its sales staff and dealer network as well as through independent dealers and online. Most of the company?s revenue are generated in the US.

	Annual Growth	05/15	05/16*	06/17	06/18	06/19
Sales ($ mil.)	4.6%	2,142.2	2,264.9	2,278.2	2,381.2	2,567.2
Net income ($ mil.)	13.3%	97.5	136.7	123.9	128.1	160.5
Market value ($ mil.)	6.4%	1,628.6	1,860.2	1,922.6	1,931.4	2,086.6
Employees	1.6%	7,510	7,607	7,478	7,681	8,000

*Fiscal year change

MILLER ELECTRIC COMPANY

6805 SOUTHPOINT PKWY
JACKSONVILLE, FL 322166220
Phone: 904-388-8000
Fax: -
Web: www.mecojax.com

CEO: Henry K Brown
CFO: Susan A Walden
HR: -
FYE: September 30
Type: Private

Miller Electric Company flips the switch for projects primarily in the Southeast. The Florida-based electrical contractor provides services including construction installation renovation and maintenance of electrical systems. Industries the company serves include: communications construction health care and transportation. Outside of Florida the company has offices in Alabama Arizona Arkansas Georgia North Carolina Virginia Tennessee Texas and Wisconsin. Clients have included Anheuser Busch Bank of America Blue Cross and Blue Shield EverBank Field and the University of North Florida. Miller Electric was founded by Henry G. Miller in 1928 and remains a family business.

	Annual Growth	09/14	09/15	09/16	09/17	09/18
Sales ($ mil.)	8.9%	-	260.6	249.1	296.2	336.4
Net income ($ mil.)	14.5%	-	7.7	8.2	11.7	11.5
Market value ($ mil.)	-	-	-	-	-	-
Employees	-	-	-	-	-	691

MILLER ELECTRIC CONSTRUCTION INC

4377 WILLIAM FLYNN HWY
ALLISON PARK, PA 151011432
Phone: 412-487-1044
Fax: -
Web: www.millerelectric.com

CEO: Richard R Miller
CFO: -
HR: -
FYE: June 30
Type: Private

If you're looking for an electrical contractor then it could be Miller Electric Construction time for you. Miller Electric Construction specializes in industrial and commercial electrical construction projects in western Pennsylvania and nearby portions of Ohio and West Virginia. The company constructs lighting data communication and power distribution systems for general construction contractors construction managers and area businesses institutions and attractions. Dick Miller founded the company in the early 1960s.

	Annual Growth	06/06	06/07	06/08	06/09	06/10
Sales ($ mil.)	(88.5%)	-	-	1,947.1	34.1	26.0
Net income ($ mil.)	4142.6%	-	-	0.0	0.4	0.2
Market value ($ mil.)	-	-	-	-	-	-
Employees	-	-	-	-	-	150

MILLER ENERGY RESOURCES, INC.
NBB: MILL Q

9721 Cogdill Road, Suite 302
Knoxville, TN 37932
Phone: 865 223-6575
Fax: 865 691-8209
Web: www.millerenergyresources.com

CEO: Carl F Giesler Jr
CFO: Phillip G Elliott
HR: -
FYE: April 30
Type: Public

This Miller's tale is all about oil and gas in the Appalachian region. Miller Energy Resources has been exploring and producing in the southern Appalachian region since 1967. It operates oil and gas wells organizes joint drilling ventures with partners and rebuilds and sells oil field equipment (including compressors oil field trailers and drilling rigs). Active in drilling and production in eastern Tennessee in 2008 Miller had total proved reserves of 1.8 billion cu. ft. of natural gas and 74413 barrels of crude oil. It is developing more than 43490 acres of oil and gas leases. Diversifying in 2009 it acquired Alaskan oil explorer Cook Inlet Energy.

	Annual Growth	04/10	04/11	04/12	04/13	04/14
Sales ($ mil.)	86.2%	5.9	22.8	35.4	34.8	70.6
Net income ($ mil.)	-	249.5	(4.4)	(18.7)	(20.4)	(28.6)
Market value ($ mil.)	(4.4%)	264.5	264.0	248.5	173.9	220.5
Employees	15.6%	47	71	70	79	84

MILLER INDUSTRIES INC. (TN)
NYS: MLR

8503 Hilltop Drive
Ooltewah, TN 37363
Phone: 423 238-4171
Fax: 423 238-5371
Web: www.millerind.com

CEO: Jeffrey I. (Jeff) Badgley
CFO: J. Vincent Mish
HR: -
FYE: December 31
Type: Public

This body builder wants to pump up your chassis. Miller Industries makes bodies for light- and heavy-duty wreckers along with car carriers and multi-vehicle trailers. It serves as the official recovery team at some of the NASCAR races (including Talladega) as well as the Indy 500 races. Miller makes its recovery and towing vehicles at plants in the US and Europe. Its multi-vehicle transport trailers can carry as many as eight vehicles and loads up to 75 tons. Miller Industries' US brand names include Century Challenger Champion Chevron Eagle Holmes Titan and Vulcan. The company's European brands are Jige (France) and Boniface (UK). Miller and rival Jerr-Dan dominate the US market for wrecker bodies.

	Annual Growth	12/14	12/15	12/16	12/17	12/18
Sales ($ mil.)	9.6%	492.8	541.0	601.1	615.1	711.7
Net income ($ mil.)	22.7%	14.9	16.0	19.9	23.0	33.7
Market value ($ mil.)	6.8%	236.9	248.2	301.4	294.0	307.7
Employees	8.6%	890	990	1,103	1,120	1,240

MILLER TRANSPORTATION SERVICES, INC.

5500 HIGHWAY 80 W
JACKSON, MS 392093507
Phone: 601-856-6526
Fax: -
Web: www.millert.com

CEO: -
CFO: -
HR: -
FYE: December 31
Type: Private

No beer here. Tank truck carrier Miller Transporters hauls bulk commodities such as chemicals and petroleum products from a network of more than 20 terminals in the eastern half of the US. The company operates a fleet of some 500 tractors and 1100 trailers and carries cargo domestically as well as between the US and Canada and Mexico. A sister company Miller Intermodal Logistics arranges the transportation of liquid bulk cargo worldwide. The company that became Miller Transporters was founded in 1942 by Harold Dewey Miller. Its founder's family still owns Miller Transporters.

	Annual Growth	12/13	12/14	12/15	12/16	12/17
Sales ($ mil.)	3.0%	-	108.2	102.0	104.2	118.2
Net income ($ mil.)	292.4%	-	0.1	0.3	1.0	4.2
Market value ($ mil.)	-	-	-	-	-	-
Employees	-	-	-	-	-	1,000

MILLERCOORS LLC

250 S. Wacker Ste.800
Chicago IL 60606
Phone: 312-496-2700
Fax: 203-425-9562
Web: www.mxenergy.com

CEO: Gavin Hattersley
CFO: Tracey Joubert
HR: –
FYE: December 31
Type: Joint Venture

MillerCoors is proof that beer can make old foes new friends. Long-time rivals UK-based SABMiller and US-based Molson Coors put aside their differences to merge their operations in the US and Puerto Rico in a joint venture MilllerCoors. The #2 brewer in the US operates eight breweries and enjoys some 30% of the domestic beer market. Its flagship brews are sold under the Coors Light and Miller Lite labels and import brews under Peroni and Molson Canadian. A division the Tenth and Blake Beer Company offers craft and import brews such as Blue Moon Foster's and many others. MillerCoors also makes Sparks a line of brand malt-based beverages. The company is 58%-owned by SABMiller with Molson Coors holding 42%.

MILLS-PENINSULA HEALTH SERVICES

1501 TROUSDALE DR
BURLINGAME, CA 940104506
Phone: 650-696-5400
Fax: –
Web: www.mills-peninsula.org

CEO: –
CFO: –
HR: –
FYE: December 31
Type: Private

With health facilities south of San Francisco Mills-Peninsula Health Services provides care to communities in and around Burlingame California. The not-for-profit health care group includes the 240-bed Mills-Peninsula Medical Center an acute-care hospital in Burlingame; Mills Health Center an outpatient diagnostic surgery and rehabilitation facility in San Mateo; and physician practice offices in surrounding areas. The facilities provide specialty services such as cancer care cardiovascular therapy behavioral health radiology respiratory care and senior services. Mills-Peninsula Health Services is part of the Sutter Health network.

	Annual Growth	12/00	12/01	12/02	12/09	12/13
Sales ($ mil.)	3.6%	–	398.5	274.0	533.8	609.9
Net income ($ mil.)	172.8%	–	0.0	18.0	56.7	54.5
Market value ($ mil.)	–	–	–	–	–	–
Employees	–	–	–	–	–	2,200

MINDEN BANCORP INC.   OTC: MDNB

100 MBL Bank Drive
Minden, LA 71055
Phone: 318 371-4156
Fax: –
Web: www.mblminden.com

CEO: –
CFO: –
HR: –
FYE: December 31
Type: Public

You might not mind Minden Bancorp minding your business. The institution is the holding company for MBL Bank (formerly Minden Building and Loan) which has two branches in the northwestern Louisiana town of Minden. Serving local consumers and businesses the bank provides standard deposit services including checking and savings accounts NOW and money market accounts certificates of deposit and individual retirement accounts. MBL Bank's lending activities primarily consist of one-to-four family residential mortgages and consumer loans but it provides business services such as commercial real estate and operating loans as well. Minden Mutual Holding Company owns a majority of Minden Bancorp's stock.

	Annual Growth	12/10	12/11	12/12	12/13	12/14
Assets ($ mil.)	5.7%	247.8	264.6	276.5	288.9	309.4
Net income ($ mil.)	14.9%	2.3	2.6	3.0	3.4	3.9
Market value ($ mil.)	8.7%	–	35.3	37.4	41.6	45.3
Employees	(1.1%)	31	32	31	30	–

MINDWIRELESS

6300 Bridgepoint Pkwy. Bldg. 1 Ste. 560
Austin TX 78730
Phone: 512-615-7600
Fax: 866-777-1456
Web: www.mindwireless.com

CEO: –
CFO: –
HR: –
FYE: December 31
Type: Private

mindWireless doens't want your mind occupied with mundane tasks such as trying to manage wireless billing. The company provides services and software that help companies manage their wireless program billing. Looking to reduce the costs and hassles associated with wireless communications programs mindWireless uses its analytical software applications to gather data about corporate wireless expenses calculate and compare costs and manage wireless vendor relationships and billing processes. Founded in 2000 the company offers its wireless billing management services throughout the US.

MINERALS TECHNOLOGIES, INC.   NYS: MTX

622 Third Avenue
New York, NY 10017-6707
Phone: 212 878-1800
Fax: –
Web: www.mineralstech.com

CEO: Douglas T. (Doug) Dietrich
CFO: Matthew E. Garth
HR: Thomas J. Meek
FYE: December 31
Type: Public

Minerals Technologies one of the top producers of bentonite and precipitated calcium carbonate (PCC) supplies a broad range of specialty mineral and synthetic products to primarily the paper foundry steel construction environmental energy polymer and consumer products industries. With more than 1600 trademarks the company's technologically advanced product lines include Fulfill New Yield Volclay Additrol Hotcrete and Lacam. Majority of company sales are generated in the US.

	Annual Growth	12/14	12/15	12/16	12/17	12/18
Sales ($ mil.)	1.2%	1,725.0	1,797.6	1,638.0	1,675.7	1,807.6
Net income ($ mil.)	16.3%	92.4	107.9	133.4	195.1	169.0
Market value ($ mil.)	(7.3%)	2,444.0	1,613.8	2,718.5	2,422.9	1,806.7
Employees	(4.5%)	4,464	3,868	3,583	3,657	3,720

MINERS INCORPORATED

5065 MILLER TRUNK HWY
HERMANTOWN, MN 558111442
Phone: 218-729-5882
Fax: –
Web: www.superonefoods.com

CEO: James A Miner Sr
CFO: –
HR: –
FYE: June 24
Type: Private

Miner's is a family-owned chain of about 30 grocery stores in Michigan North Dakota northern Minnesota and Wisconsin. Most of the company's stores fly the Super One Foods banner but there are a few under the U-Save Foods and Marketplace Foods names. Following the acquisition of seven Jubilee and Festival Foods stores in Minnesota from Plaza Holding Co. Miner's converted the stores to its Super One Foods banner most of which are located in Minnesota. Miner's also has a wholesale grocery operation in Duluth. Miner's was founded by Anton and Ida Miner who started out selling groceries out of their tavern in Grand Rapids Michigan in the 1930s. In 1943 they built the family's first store Miner's Market.

	Annual Growth	06/09	06/10	06/11	06/12	06/17
Sales ($ mil.)	2.4%	–	463.6	475.6	501.5	548.9
Net income ($ mil.)	(0.5%)	–	27.1	30.2	31.8	26.1
Market value ($ mil.)	–	–	–	–	–	–
Employees	–	–	–	–	–	2,300

MINES MANAGEMENT, INC.

905 W. Riverside Avenue, Suite 311
Spokane, WA 99201
Phone: 509-838-6050
Fax: –
Web: www.minesmanagement.com

ASE: MGN
CEO: Glenn M Dobbs
CFO: Nicole Altenburg
HR: –
FYE: December 31
Type: Public

Mines Management explores and develops silver and copper properties in the US. The company's primary property is the Montanore project in northwestern Montana which was operated between 1988 and 2002 by Falconbridge. Mines Management would like to further develop the Montanore property and the company is working to complete the required environmental and engineering studies and to determine an economically viable way to conduct mining operations. Its preparation of the property for study was expedited in 2006 and underground testing has taken up most of 2007 through 2009. Silver Wheaton owns an 11% stake in Mines Management while US Global Investors owns just over 7%.

	Annual Growth	12/10	12/11	12/12	12/13	12/14
Sales ($ mil.)	3.8%	0.0	0.0	0.0	0.0	0.0
Net income ($ mil.)	–	(10.7)	(5.6)	(8.2)	(7.4)	(6.5)
Market value ($ mil.)	(42.1%)	124.6	59.6	30.7	17.9	14.0
Employees	(8.9%)	16	15	13	11	11

MINISTRY HEALTH CARE INC.

11925 W LAKE PARK DR # 100
MILWAUKEE, WI 53224-3002
Phone: 414-359-1060
Fax: –
Web: www.hyhc.com

CEO: Nicholas F Desien
CFO: –
HR: –
FYE: September 30
Type: Private

Part of the Marian Health System Ministry Health Care is a network of hospitals clinics and other health facilities serving all of Wisconsin and eastern Minnesota. The network includes 15 acute and tertiary care hospitals (such as the 500-bed Saint Joseph's Hospital of Marshfield) as well as about 50 physician clinics long-term and assisted living facilities home health agencies hospices and other community health programs and services. Ministry Health Care's flagship facility was founded in 1890 by the Sisters of the Sorrowful Mother as a Catholic health care system to contribute to the well-being of the community. Ministry Health Care and Marian Health System merged with Ascension Health in 2013.

	Annual Growth	09/01	09/02	09/03	09/06	09/07
Sales ($ mil.)	–	–	–	(709,296.1)	39.3	58.7
Net income ($ mil.)	122.6%	–	–	0.5	2.7	11.1
Market value ($ mil.)	–	–	–	–	–	–
Employees	–	–	–	–	–	5,000

MINITAB INC.

1829 PINE HALL RD
STATE COLLEGE, PA 168013008
Phone: 814-238-3280
Fax: –
Web: www.minitab.com

CEO: Barbara F Ryan
CFO: William J Vesnesky
HR: –
FYE: December 31
Type: Private

Minitab knows it's no small feat to work in a world of numbers and percentages. The company develops software that enables companies to analyze statistical data for quality improvement training and consulting purposes. It also markets to colleges and universities which use the company's applications in the classroom to instruct statistics students. Clients have included BASF DuPont Toyota Cisco and ExxonMobil. Minitab's original software was created in 1972 by three statistics instructors at Penn State including company CEO Barbara Ryan.

	Annual Growth	12/05	12/06	12/07	12/08	12/09
Sales ($ mil.)	–	–	–	(1,048.8)	63.6	53.7
Net income ($ mil.)	31213.8%	–	–	0.0	3.8	2.8
Market value ($ mil.)	–	–	–	–	–	–
Employees	–	–	–	–	–	321

MINN-DAK FARMERS COOPERATIVE

7525 Red River Rd.
Wahpeton ND 58075
Phone: 701-642-8411
Fax: 701-642-6814
Web: www.mdfarmerscoop.com

CEO: Kurt Wickstrom
CFO: Rick Kasper
HR: –
FYE: August 31
Type: Private - Cooperativ

Minn-Dak Farmers Cooperative walks the beat for the sugar beet. Minn-Dak serves sugar beet growers in the Red River Valley of Minnesota North Dakota and South Dakota. Located in Wahpeton North Dakota the co-op processes the sugar beets into sugar and products such as molasses and beet pulp pellets (used in animal feed); the products are then marketed through agents worldwide. The co-op's Minn-Dak Yeast segment produces fresh bakers' yeast. Minn-Dak Farmers Cooperative is owned by its farmer/members a group of some 480 sugar beet growers. Founded in 1972 its customers include industrial users such as confectioners breakfast-cereal manufacturers and bakeries.

MINNESOTA VIKINGS FOOTBALL CLUB L.L.C.

9520 Viking Dr.
Eden Prairie MN 55344
Phone: 952-828-6500
Fax: 952-828-6540
Web: www.vikings.com

CEO: –
CFO: –
HR: –
FYE: January 31
Type: Private

These Norsemen are looking to plunder their gridiron competition. The Minnesota Vikings Football Club joined the National Football League in 1961 and won its only league championship in 1969; however the team has been unsuccessful in four attempts to win the Super Bowl. Minnesota's roster has included such Hall of Fame players as Warren Moon Alan Page and Fran Tarkenton as well as former head coach Bud Grant. Vikings fans cheer the trumpeting Gjallarhorn at Mall of America Field at the Hubert H. Humphrey Metrodome in Minneapolis. The team has been owned since 2005 by a group headed by New Jersey real estate developer Zygmunt (Zygi) Wilf.

MINNKOTA POWER COOPERATIVE, INC.

5301 32ND AVE S
GRAND FORKS, ND 582013312
Phone: 701-795-4000
Fax: –
Web: www.minnkota.com

CEO: Robert McLennan
CFO: –
HR: –
FYE: December 31
Type: Private

The Minnkota Power Cooperative keeps the juice flowing to power users in northwestern Minnesota and eastern North Dakota. The generation and transmission cooperative supplies electricity to its 11 member-owner distribution cooperatives and as operating agent for the Northern Municipal Power Agency to 12 municipal systems to serve more than 118000 retail customers in a 34500-sq.-mi. region. Minnkota owns and operates the 235 MW lignite coal-fired generation Unit 1 of the Milton R. Young plant in Center North Dakota and 30% of the 400 MW lignite coal-fired Coyote Station near Beulah. The company also has wind power assets.

	Annual Growth	12/13	12/14	12/15	12/16	12/17
Sales ($ mil.)	41.8%	–	145.8	159.5	149.5	415.4
Net income ($ mil.)	129.6%	–	2.4	2.6	2.8	29.4
Market value ($ mil.)	–	–	–	–	–	–
Employees	–	–	–	–	–	355

MINTZ LEVIN COHN FERRIS GLOVSKY AND POPEO P.C.

1 Financial Center
Boston MA 02111
Phone: 617-542-6000
Fax: 617-542-2241
Web: www.mintz.com

CEO: –
CFO: –
HR: –
FYE: March 31
Type: Private - Partnershi

The lawyers of Mintz Levin Cohn Ferris Glovsky and Popeo specialize in such areas as antitrust communications employment and labor and intellectual property law. Overall the firm has about 450 lawyers in more than half a dozen offices in the US and the UK. Clients range from individual entrepreneurs to governmental agencies to FORTUNE 500 companies. Along with its law practices the firm has established affiliated consulting practices (ML Strategies and Mintz Levin Financial Advisors) that counsel clients on project management technology outsourcing financial planning and investment banking and government relations.

MIRAMAX FILM CORP.

Watergarden Complex Ste. 2000 1601 Cloverfield Blvd.
Santa Monica CA 90404
Phone: 310-409-4321
Fax: 212-466-7888
Web: www.sandleroneill.com

CEO: –
CFO: –
HR: –
FYE: September 30
Type: Private

Miramax Film Corp. depends on the independent. The company is known for its critically-acclaimed indie films that also perform well at the box office such as and Pulp Fiction and Shakespeare in Love. More recent hits include The Queen and No Country for Old Men. Miramax was formed in 1979 by brothers Bob and Harvey Weinstein. They sold the company to media giant Walt Disney in 1993. After a falling out with the corporate parent in 2005 the Weinsteins left to form their own production business The Weinstein Company. In 2010 Disney closed Miramax. Later that year it sold the label to a group of investors known as Filmyard Holdings who plan to focus on distributing the Miramax library of 700 titles.

MINUTEMAN PRESS INTERNATIONAL INC.

61 EXECUTIVE BLVD
FARMINGDALE, NY 117354710
Phone: 631-694-2614
Fax: –
Web: www.minutemanpress.com

CEO: Robert Titus
CFO: Stanley M Katz
HR: Kevin McDermott
FYE: December 31
Type: Private

Minuteman Press International wants to be the first in line for your printing business. The company franchises full-service quick printing centers offering graphic design typesetting and printing. It provides franchisees with equipment supplies training marketing services and site selection as well as start-up financing options. Minuteman Press International has more than 950 printing centers worldwide with locations in Australia Canada South Africa the UK and the US. The company was founded by Roy Titus in 1973. His son Bob leads the firm as president.

	Annual Growth	12/04	12/05	12/07	12/12	12/13
Assets ($ mil.)	(0.3%)	–	16.3	16.5	14.0	15.9
Net income ($ mil.)	3.5%	–	–	3.0	1.2	3.6
Market value ($ mil.)	–	–	–	–	–	–
Employees	–	–	–	–	–	120

MIRAPOINT SOFTWARE INC.

1215 Bordeaux Dr.
Sunnyvale CA 94089
Phone: 408-720-3700
Fax: 408-720-3725
Web: www.mirapoint.com

CEO: –
CFO: –
HR: –
FYE: January 31
Type: Private

Mirapoint wants you to get the message — but not the virus that could come with it. The company makes network appliances designed to route store and process incoming and outgoing e-mail. Its appliances and software also protect against viruses and spam. Combining messaging and server software with hardware the company's messaging tools are designed to work with a variety of mail formats and to integrate with existing e-mail applications wireless devices and Web-based systems. Founded in 1997 Mirapoint has received backing from Amerindo Investment Advisors Goldman Sachs MKS Ventures and Worldview Technology Partners. The company agreed to be acquired by Critical Path in 2010.

MIRACLE SOFTWARE SYSTEMS INC.

45625 GRAND RIVER AVE
NOVI, MI 483741309
Phone: 248-233-1100
Fax: –
Web: www.miraclesoft.com

CEO: Prasad Lokam
CFO: –
HR: Geetha Jampana
FYE: June 30
Type: Private

For businesses who feel that it might take divine intervention to solve their IT problems Miracle Software Systems offers a more down-to-Earth alternative. The company provides IT services such as enterprise application development and integration consulting network design legacy systems migration and training. The service-oriented architecture (SOA) specialist primarily installs customizes and supports software from IBM but it also offers products from Oracle and SAP among others. Customers have included businesses in the health care (Pfizer) insurance (Premera Blue Cross) finance logistics (Menlo Worldwide) manufacturing (John Deere) and retail (Target) industries.

	Annual Growth	06/08	06/09	06/10	06/11	06/17
Sales ($ mil.)	13.0%	–	29.9	26.0	27.0	79.6
Net income ($ mil.)	–	–	(0.3)	(0.0)	(0.0)	3.0
Market value ($ mil.)	–	–	–	–	–	–
Employees	–	–	–	–	–	435

MIRATI THERAPEUTICS INC

NAS: MRTX

9363 Towne Centre Drive, Suite 200
San Diego, CA 92121
Phone: 858 332-3410
Fax: 514 337-0550
Web: www.methylgene.com

CEO: –
CFO: –
HR: –
FYE: December 31
Type: Public

MethylGene's endeavors in the field of medicine may earn it a good look. The company is developing enzyme inhibitors to treat cancer and various infectious diseases. It develops product candidates for treatments for ailments such as solid tumors and hematological malignancies. MethylGene has also researched therapies to battle conditions including fungal infections and antibiotic resistance. The company forms licensing and collaboration agreements with other pharmaceutical firms to further its development programs.

	Annual Growth	12/08	12/09	12/10	12/11	12/12
Sales ($ mil.)	(90.4%)	24.0	2.9	2.4	3.0	0.0
Net income ($ mil.)	–	(7.3)	(22.5)	(14.7)	(9.5)	(20.4)
Market value ($ mil.)	–	–	–	–	–	–
Employees	(15.9%)	72	–	–	28	36

MIRENCO INC.
OTC: MREOE

206 May St.
Radcliffe IA 50230
Phone: 515-899-2164
Fax: 515-899-2147
Web: www.mirenco.com/

CEO: Dwayne L Fosseen
CFO: Glynis M Hendrickson
HR: –
FYE: December 31
Type: Public

MIRENCO would like to see bus fumes consigned to the scrap heap of history. The company's signature product D-Max is an electronic throttle control for heavy-duty start-and-stop vehicles such as buses and garbage trucks that is designed to improve fuel efficiency and reduce environmental emissions. MIRENCO's HydroFire product adds technology to reduce nitrogen-oxide emissions to the D-Max system. The company's EconoCruise product uses GPS technology to read the road ahead and adjusts the vehicle's cruise control to better manage throttle and emissions. Chairman and CEO Dwayne Fosseen owns about 35% of MIRENCO.

MISSION HOSPITAL, INC.

509 BILTMORE AVE
ASHEVILLE, NC 288014601
Phone: 828-213-1111
Fax: –
Web: www.missionhealth.org

CEO: Chad Patrick
CFO: –
HR: Teresa McCarthy
FYE: September 30
Type: Private

Its mission is clear and bold: Improve the health of all in western North Carolina. Mission Hospital is a 760-bed regional referral center serving the western quarter of North Carolina and portions of adjoining states. A not-for-profit community hospital system Mission is located in Asheville on two adjoining campuses: Memorial and St. Joseph's. It provides tertiary-level services in neurosciences cardiac care trauma care surgery pediatric medicine and women's services and has a medical staff of more than 540. It also includes the Mission Children's Hospital. Mission Hospital is the flagship hospital of Mission Health System which is being acquired by HCA Healthcare for $1.5 billion.

	Annual Growth	09/11	09/12	09/13	09/14	09/15
Sales ($ mil.)	5.8%	–	861.0	942.3	936.2	1,019.5
Net income ($ mil.)	2.0%	–	86.3	71.9	64.8	91.5
Market value ($ mil.)	–	–	–	–	–	–
Employees	–	–	–	–	–	10,000

MISONIX, INC.
NMS: MSON

1938 New Highway
Farmingdale, NY 11735
Phone: 631 694-9555
Fax: –
Web: www.misonix.com

CEO: Stavros G Vizirgianakis
CFO: Joseph P Dwyer
HR: –
FYE: June 30
Type: Public

Did you hear that Misonix is on the cutting edge of ultrasonic medical equipment? The development and manufacturing company makes ultrasonic devices to cut bone remove tumors and clean wounds. Its LySonix system is used to remove soft tissue during liposuction surgery. Subsidiary Hearing Innovations is developing devices to treat deafness and tinnitus. In addition to its therapeutic products Misonix manufactures the Aura line of fume hoods used in scientific and forensic laboratories. The company manufactures its products at its facility in Farmington New York. Misonix markets its products in the US and internationally through a direct sales force and wholesale distributors.

	Annual Growth	06/15	06/16	06/17	06/18	06/19
Sales ($ mil.)	15.0%	22.2	23.1	27.3	36.7	38.8
Net income ($ mil.)	–	5.6	(1.2)	(1.7)	(7.6)	(7.4)
Market value ($ mil.)	27.9%	91.6	49.9	92.1	119.6	245.2
Employees	11.8%	80	85	92	118	125

MISSION PHARMACAL COMPANY

10999 W INTERSTATE 10 # 1000
SAN ANTONIO, TX 782301300
Phone: 210-696-8400
Fax: –
Web: www.missionpharmacal.com

CEO: Neill B Walsdorf Sr
CFO: Tom Dooley
HR: –
FYE: April 30
Type: Private

Mission Pharmacal's purpose objective and undertaking if you will is to make you feel better. The company makes prescription and over-the-counter (OTC) remedies for infection kidney stones and arthritis as well as nutritional supplements. Mission's products include kidney stone preventer Urocit-K dermatitis ointment Texacort bacterial infection fighter Tindamax and CitraNatal prescription prenatal vitamins. The company also offers third-party OTC nutritional and prescription manufacturing packaging and inventory management to pharmaceutical companies. Mission is owned and run by the founding Walsdorf family.

	Annual Growth	04/13	04/14	04/15	04/16	04/17
Sales ($ mil.)	5.9%	–	152.0	157.2	138.4	180.5
Net income ($ mil.)	–	–	(1.6)	7.6	0.9	(0.8)
Market value ($ mil.)	–	–	–	–	–	–
Employees	–	–	–	–	–	495

MISSION COMMUNITY BANCORP
NBB: MISN

3380 S. Higuera St.
San Luis Obispo, CA 93401
Phone: 805 782-5000
Fax: –
Web: www.missioncommunitybank.com

CEO: –
CFO: –
HR: –
FYE: December 31
Type: Public

Mission Community Bancorp is on a mission to provide traditional community banking services and foster economic revitalization and community development. Subsidiary Mission Community Bank offers standard checking savings products money market accounts and certificates of deposit. It also focuses on agribusiness commercial construction and consumer loans. The bank has about 10 offices in San Luis Obispo and Santa Barbara counties. In late 2011 Mission Community Bancorp bought Santa Lucia Bancorp in a deal that added four branches in central California. The Carpenter Community BancFund owns about a quarter of Mission Community Bancorp.

	Annual Growth	12/08	12/09	12/10	12/11	12/12
Assets ($ mil.)	19.2%	215.5	193.1	217.8	462.2	435.2
Net income ($ mil.)	–	(3.8)	(6.9)	(6.7)	(3.0)	0.9
Market value ($ mil.)	(23.8%)	82.0	51.0	30.6	27.3	27.7
Employees	16.6%	60	56	64	139	111

MISSISSIPPI COUNTY ELECTRIC COOPERATIVE, INC.

510 N BROADWAY ST
BLYTHEVILLE, AR 723152732
Phone: 870-763-4563
Fax: –
Web: www.mceci.com

CEO: –
CFO: –
HR: –
FYE: December 31
Type: Private

Like much of the rest of the state of Arkansas people in Mississippi County get their electricity from a cooperative. Mississippi County Electric Cooperative (MCEC) serves customers in the northeast corner of Arkansas about 60 miles north of Memphis. The area is home to two steel mills owned by Nucor Corporation that are powered by MCEC power; most customers are industrial or agricultural. The coop also offers Internet service via rural satellite broadband provider WildBlue and provides its customers with energy audits and information on saving energy. It is a member of Touchstone Energy a national alliance of electric cooperatives in nearly 40 states. MCEC was formed in 1938.

	Annual Growth	12/13	12/14	12/15	12/16	12/17
Sales ($ mil.)	0.2%	–	160.6	133.8	144.0	161.5
Net income ($ mil.)	–	–	0.3	(0.7)	(1.6)	(1.6)
Market value ($ mil.)	–	–	–	–	–	–
Employees	–	–	–	–	–	16

MISSISSIPPI POWER CO
NYS: MP PRD

2992 West Beach Boulevard
Gulfport, MS 39501
Phone: 228 864-1211
Fax: –
Web: www.mississippipower.com

CEO: G Edison Holland Jr
CFO: Moses H Feagin
HR: –
FYE: December 31
Type: Public

Mississippi Power provides electric services to about 186680 residential commercial and industrial customers in the Magnolia State. The utility operates more than 6890 miles of transmission and distribution lines and it generates nearly 3160 MW of capacity from its power plants (of which 1450 MWs are coal-fired). Mississippi Power also sells wholesale electricity to several Florida municipal and cooperative utilities and it offers energy conservation services and sells electrical appliances. Mississippi Power is a subsidiary of utility holding firm Southern Company.

	Annual Growth	12/14	12/15	12/16	12/17	12/18
Sales ($ mil.)	0.4%	1,242.6	1,138.0	1,163.0	1,187.0	1,265.0
Net income ($ mil.)	–	(326.9)	(6.0)	(48.0)	(2,588.0)	236.0
Market value ($ mil.)	0.3%	28.5	29.7	29.3	28.8	–
Employees	(8.1%)	1,478	1,478	1,484	1,242	1,053

MISSISSIPPI STATE UNIVERSITY

245 BARR AVE MCRTHUR HL MCARTHUR HALL
MISSISSIPPI STATE, MS 39762
Phone: 662-325-2302
Fax: –
Web: www.msstate.edu

CEO: –
CFO: –
HR: –
FYE: June 30
Type: Private

While agriculture is at its roots Mississippi State University's (MSU) is today a four-year university offering approximately 150 undergraduate majors and pre-professional programs as well as master's educational specialist and doctorate degree programs at a dozen colleges and schools. It confers more than 4300 degrees annually and has an enrollment of more than 20870 students at its main campus in Starkville and a regional campus in Meridian. More than three-quarters of its student body hail from Mississippi. MSU was created by the Mississippi Legislature in 1878 as The Agricultural and Mechanical College of the State of Mississippi.

	Annual Growth	06/12	06/13	06/14	06/16	06/17
Sales ($ mil.)	5.6%	–	371.5	392.8	462.1	461.5
Net income ($ mil.)	(7.9%)	–	25.7	64.5	48.3	18.5
Market value ($ mil.)	–	–	–	–	–	–
Employees	–	–	–	–	–	4,500

MISSOURI HIGHER EDUCATION LOAN AUTHORITY

633 SPIRIT DR
CHESTERFIELD, MO 630051243
Phone: 636-733-3700
Fax: –
Web: www.mohela.com

CEO: –
CFO: Scott Gailes
HR: –
FYE: June 30
Type: Private

From the "Show Me" state comes Missouri Higher Education Loan Authority one of the country's top holders and servicers of student loans. The not-for-profit organization helps borrowers obtain education financing such as Federal Stafford alternative or supplemental and consolidation loans through lending institutions such as Bank of America and U.S. Bancorp. It also offers a "Rate Relief" program that can lower a borrower's interest rate by up to 3% as well as deferment and forbearance options that either postpone or reduce a borrower's monthly payment. The authority also manages loan servicing for lending institutions nationwide.

	Annual Growth	06/02	06/03	06/16	06/17	06/18
Assets ($ mil.)	(4.3%)	–	3,345.0	2,208.0	1,971.4	1,727.5
Net income ($ mil.)	(1.6%)	–	24.2	9.0	20.5	18.9
Market value ($ mil.)	–	–	–	–	–	–
Employees	–	–	–	–	–	550

MISSOURI STATE UNIVERSITY

901 S NATIONAL AVE
SPRINGFIELD, MO 658970001
Phone: 417-836-5000
Fax: –
Web: www.missouristate.edu

CEO: –
CFO: –
HR: –
FYE: June 30
Type: Private

When Missouri students say "show me" Missouri State University happily obliges. It is the state's second-largest university (after University of Missouri) with an enrollment of 23800 students. The school offers about 85 undergraduate majors 133 undergraduate minors and 50 graduate majors including 14 masters 3 doctoral degrees (audiology physical therapy and nurse practitioner) and one specialist degree. The university' coursework includes accounting biology criminology and physical geography. Missouri State awarded almost 4000 degrees in 2013. It also hosted some 16 NCAA Division One sports teams that year.

	Annual Growth	06/14	06/15	06/16	06/17	06/18
Sales ($ mil.)	4.3%	–	196.9	215.4	216.2	223.4
Net income ($ mil.)	–	–	17.0	18.8	(16.0)	(7.0)
Market value ($ mil.)	–	–	–	–	–	–
Employees	–	–	–	–	–	2,066

MISTRAS GROUP INC
NYS: MG

195 Clarksville Road
Princeton Junction, NJ 08550
Phone: 609 716-4000
Fax: –
Web: www.mistrasgroup.com

CEO: –
CFO: Jonathan H. (Jon) Wolk
HR: Julie Marini
FYE: December 31
Type: Public

Mistras could be all that stands between you and a massive oil refinery explosion nuclear facility meltdown or big bridge collapse. The engineering services company conducts non-destructive testing on critical equipment and processes used by petroleum aerospace infrastructure power generation and chemical manufacturing companies worldwide. It checks plant infrastructure for defects and problems without interrupting production; inspections take place during facility design build maintenance and operation phases. Mistras works from about 75 offices in 15 nations to serve clients that include Alcan Honeywell Bechtel BP Dow Chemical Airbus and federal and state governments.

	Annual Growth	05/15	05/16*	12/16	12/17	12/18
Sales ($ mil.)	1.4%	711.3	719.2	404.2	701.0	742.4
Net income ($ mil.)	(24.8%)	16.1	24.7	9.6	(2.2)	6.8
Market value ($ mil.)	(8.1%)	528.7	708.6	733.5	670.4	410.7
Employees	0.0%	5,700	5,700	5,600	6,000	5,700

*Fiscal year change

MITCHAM INDUSTRIES INC
NMS: MIND P

2002 Timberloch Place, Suite 400
The Woodlands, TX 77380
Phone: 936 291-2277
Fax: –
Web: www.mitchamindustries.com

CEO: Robert P Capps
CFO: Robert P Capps
HR: –
FYE: January 31
Type: Public

Here's a shocker: Mitcham Industries has few rivals that can match 'em when it comes to the leasing and sales of seismic equipment to the global seismic industry. The company's equipment offerings include channel boxes geophones earth vibrators various cables and other peripheral equipment. Through short-term leasing (three to nine months) from Mitcham Industries oil and gas companies - a major customer group — can improve their chances of drilling a productive well and reduce equipment costs. The company also manufactures marine seismic equipment under the Seamap brand.

	Annual Growth	01/15	01/16	01/17	01/18	01/19
Sales ($ mil.)	(15.2%)	83.1	51.8	41.0	48.3	42.9
Net income ($ mil.)	–	(9.2)	(38.7)	(33.2)	(21.1)	(19.8)
Market value ($ mil.)	(8.2%)	68.0	33.1	58.8	45.6	48.2
Employees	0.8%	187	210	199	197	193

MITCHELL SILBERBERG & KNUPP LLP

11377 W OLYMPIC BLVD FL 2
LOS ANGELES, CA 900641683
Phone: 310-312-2000
Fax: –
Web: www.msk.com

CEO: –
CFO: –
HR: –
FYE: December 31
Type: Private

Legally representing folks from the entertainment industry may not sound like your cup of tea but somebody's got to do the job — turns out Mitchell Silberberg & Knupp is up for the challenge. Founded in 1908 the law firm provides a variety of business law services with an emphasis on intellectual property and the entertainment industry. Other practice areas include technology; immigration; corporate law and homeland security; tax trust and estates; and international trade. Mitchell Silberberg & Knupp employs about 125 attorneys with three US offices located in Los Angeles New York and Washington D.C.

	Annual Growth	09/07	09/08	09/09	09/10*	12/10
Sales ($ mil.)	–	–	–	0.0	0.2	68.3
Net income ($ mil.)	200518.3%	–	–	0.0	0.0	32.9
Market value ($ mil.)	–	–	–	–	–	–
Employees	–	–	–	–	–	300

*Fiscal year change

MITEK SYSTEMS, INC.
NAS: MITK

600 B Street, Suite 100
San Diego, CA 92101
Phone: 619 269-6800
Fax: –
Web: www.miteksystems.com

CEO: James B Debello
CFO: Jeffrey Davison
HR: –
FYE: September 30
Type: Public

Mitek Systems is a company with character. Its automated document recognition (ADR) software known as ImageNet uses character recognition technology to digitally convert electronically scanned documents into digital form. While Mitek's products are used primarily to process financial documents the ImageNet suite of products also enables the processing and analysis of digitized still and moving images (Photo & Video) and reading coded print data such as bar codes (DataCapture). The company's FraudProtect group of products is used to detect forgeries and verify the authenticity of checks.

	Annual Growth	09/15	09/16	09/17	09/18	09/19
Sales ($ mil.)	35.1%	25.4	34.7	45.4	63.6	84.6
Net income ($ mil.)	–	2.5	2.0	14.1	(11.8)	(0.7)
Market value ($ mil.)	31.9%	128.8	334.6	383.5	284.6	389.5
Employees	35.2%	85	117	141	308	284

MKS INSTRUMENTS INC
NMS: MKSI

2 Tech Drive, Suite 201
Andover, MA 01810
Phone: 978 645-5500
Fax: –
Web: www.mksinst.com

CEO: Gerald G. Colella
CFO: Seth H. Bagshaw
HR: Sally Bouley
FYE: December 31
Type: Public

MKS Instruments makes systems that analyze and control gases during semiconductor manufacturing and other thin film industrial processes such as those used to make flat panel displays LEDs solar cells and data storage media. Top customers include chip equipment heavyweights Applied Materials and Lam Research. Other applications include medical equipment pharmaceutical manufacturing energy generation and environmental monitoring. MKS Instruments generates more than half its revenue from customers in the US. In 2019 the company acquired Electro Scientific Industries for about $1 billion.

	Annual Growth	12/14	12/15	12/16	12/17	12/18
Sales ($ mil.)	27.7%	780.9	813.5	1,295.3	1,916.0	2,075.1
Net income ($ mil.)	35.7%	115.8	122.3	104.8	339.1	392.9
Market value ($ mil.)	15.3%	1,977.8	1,945.4	3,209.9	5,106.7	3,491.5
Employees	19.6%	2,371	2,181	4,667	4,923	4,851

MKTG, INC.
NBB: CMKG

75 Ninth Avenue
New York, NY 10011
Phone: 212 366-3400
Fax: –
Web: www.mktg.com

CEO: Charles Horsey
CFO: Paul Trager
HR: –
FYE: March 31
Type: Public

Who needs vowels? 'mktg inc.' provides a menu of integrated marketing services primarily for manufacturers of packaged goods and consumer products. Services provided by 'mktg' include strategic consulting direct marketing sales promotion (sampling and sweepstakes) event marketing multicultural marketing and interactive services. Owning main offices in Chicago Cincinnati London Los Angeles New York and San Francisco it designs and coordinates displays artwork and sales campaigns on a local regional and national level. Its U.S. Concepts subsidiary provides experiential marketing campaigns featuring concerts tours and festivals.

	Annual Growth	03/09	03/10	03/11	03/12	03/13
Sales ($ mil.)	8.0%	96.2	78.0	117.9	125.5	130.8
Net income ($ mil.)	–	(2.8)	(0.8)	(0.1)	5.4	1.2
Market value ($ mil.)	10.0%	8.0	3.2	7.2	8.0	11.7
Employees	9.4%	4,750	5,750	6,275	6,900	6,800

MMA CAPITAL HOLDINGS INC
NAS: MMAC

3600 O'Donnell Street, Suite 600
Baltimore, MD 21224
Phone: 443 263-2900
Fax: –
Web: www.mmacapitalmanagement.com

CEO: Michael L Falcone
CFO: David C Bjarnason
HR: –
FYE: December 31
Type: Public

Municipal Mortgage & Equity (MuniMae) invests in tax-free municipal bonds issued by state and local governments. Those bonds are typically used to build multifamily housing including units for low-income families students and the elderly. The disruption in world credit markets coupled with a deterioration in the tax-exempt bond market hurt MuniMae. The commercial real estate market also tanked driving down the values of the company's assets. The company was forced to drastically reduce the size of its business cut its workforce by 80% and sell off assets at a loss in order to stay afloat. MuniMae continues to look for ways to reduce debt and raise capital.

	Annual Growth	12/14	12/15	12/16	12/17	12/18
Sales ($ mil.)	(29.0%)	41.6	27.4	28.6	35.0	10.6
Net income ($ mil.)	36.7%	17.5	17.8	42.4	19.4	61.0
Market value ($ mil.)	28.1%	54.1	83.5	109.8	140.4	145.6
Employees	–	49	55	63	216	–

MMODAL INC.
NASDAQ: MEDH

9009 Carothers Pkwy.
Franklin TN 37067
Phone: 615-261-1740
Fax: 866-796-5127
Web: mmodal.com

CEO: –
CFO: –
HR: –
FYE: December 31
Type: Public

MModal Inc. (formerly MedQuist Holdings) helps transcribe and analyze doctors' spoken and written notes. The company is a leading provider of integrated clinical documentation products and outsourced medical transcription services to the US health care industry. Its offerings include mobile voice capture devices speech recognition software web-based workflow platforms and a global network of more than 4000 medical transcriptionists and editors primarily in the US and India. Its customer base consists of more than 2400 hospitals clinics and multifacility health care organizations mostly in the US. MedQuist Holdings adopted the name MModal Inc. in 2012.

MMR GROUP, INC.

15961 AIRLINE HWY
BATON ROUGE, LA 708177412
Phone: 225-756-5090
Fax: –
Web: www.mmrgrp.com

CEO: –
CFO: –
HR: –
FYE: December 31
Type: Private

That murmur you hear could be the gentle hum of a properly functioning power system. MMG Group provides electrical and instrumentation construction maintenance management and technical services for clients in the oil and gas manufacturing chemical and power generation industries around the world. It also offers services in offshore marine and platform environments. Its Power Solutions division constructs onsite power-generation systems in industrial plants and other facilities. The group primarily operates in the Gulf of New Mexico. Founded in 1990 MMG is 100% management owned and has served such clients as Chevron Shell BP Merck Air Liquide DuPont and 3M.

	Annual Growth	12/14	12/15	12/16	12/17	12/18
Sales ($ mil.)	10.4%	–	585.1	608.3	618.5	786.6
Net income ($ mil.)	(10.8%)	–	24.9	15.0	9.5	17.7
Market value ($ mil.)	–	–	–	–	–	–
Employees	–	–	–	–	–	4,000

MMRGLOBAL INC

4401 Wilshire Blvd., Suite 200
Los Angeles, CA 90010
Phone: 310 476-7002
Fax: –
Web: www.mymedicalrecords.com

NBB: MMRF

CEO: –
CFO: –
HR: –
FYE: December 31
Type: Public

MMRGlobal aims to ride the worldwide digitizing wave as more physicians and consumers switch to digital medical record systems. Its products in development include online professional record storage systems and personal document management systems under the brands MyMedicalRecords Pro and MyEsafeDepositBox. The company's technology allows patient information to be stored securely but be shared with physicians pharmacies or insurance providers through the Internet. Previously operating as a biopharmaceutical development company in early 2009 the company completed a reverse merger with privately held MyMedicalRecords.com eventually changing its name to MMRGlobal in 2010.

	Annual Growth	12/11	12/12	12/13	12/14	12/15
Sales ($ mil.)	(39.4%)	1.4	0.8	0.6	2.6	0.2
Net income ($ mil.)	–	(8.9)	(5.9)	(7.6)	(2.2)	(3.0)
Market value ($ mil.)	(51.5%)	9.0	3.9	7.0	2.3	0.5
Employees	(46.3%)	48	19	19	17	4

MNP CORPORATION

44225 UTICA RD
UTICA, MI 483175464
Phone: 586-254-1320
Fax: –
Web: www.mnp.com

CEO: –
CFO: Craig L Stormer
HR: Randall Allison
FYE: November 30
Type: Private

If you are fascinated with fasteners then MNP will galvanize your senses. MNP manufactures a plethora of precision fasteners and cold formed components including screws rivets washers small stampings as well as screw machine parts. Its services range from plating to annealing flat-rolling pickling hot-dip galvanizing and coatings. General Fasteners Cadon Plating & Coatings Marathon Metals and Ohio Pickling & Processing are a few of MNP's affiliated companies that produce a medley of metal parts and jointly operate the GFC/MNP Engineering Center in Michigan. The company serves the automotive heavy truck military and industrial markets.

	Annual Growth	11/14	11/15	11/16	11/17	11/18
Sales ($ mil.)	6.5%	–	192.4	203.0	211.7	232.7
Net income ($ mil.)	6.9%	–	18.5	35.3	31.1	22.6
Market value ($ mil.)	–	–	–	–	–	–
Employees	–	–	–	–	–	746

MOBILE AREA NETWORKS INC

2772 Depot Street
Sanford, FL 32773
Phone: 407 333-2350
Fax: –
Web: www.mobilan.com

NBB: MANW

CEO: –
CFO: –
HR: –
FYE: December 31
Type: Public

Mobile enough to move from wireless to plastic Mobile Area Networks provides custom plastic injection molding services. The company originally installed wireless LANs in hotels office buildings and convention centers but in 2002 it moved into plastics manufacturing. Mobile Area Networks focuses on developing proprietary products and custom molding. The company makes air conditioner parts archery bow parts consumer and novelty products high-tech military parts irrigation devices non-invasive medical device parts roofing construction items snow ski equipment parts sporting rifle parts and other specialty applications. CEO George Wimbish controls Mobile Area Networks.

	Annual Growth	12/09	12/10	12/11	12/12	12/13
Sales ($ mil.)	(75.7%)	0.3	0.3	0.2	0.0	0.0
Net income ($ mil.)	–	(0.3)	(0.4)	(0.3)	0.3	(0.1)
Market value ($ mil.)	10.7%	0.2	1.0	1.5	0.4	0.3
Employees	(26.9%)	7	6	4	2	2

MOBILE MINI, INC.

4646 E. Van Buren Street, Suite 400
Phoenix, AZ 85008
Phone: 480 894-6311
Fax: –

NMS: MINI

CEO: Erik Olsson
CFO: Van A. Welch
HR: Mark Krivoruchka
FYE: December 31
Type: Public

Storing stuff is the stuff of big business for Mobile Mini. The company manufactures leases and sells portable storage containers and mobile buildings. Mobile Mini's lineup features steel and wood containers and residential and office units in various sizes including a selection of 100 different shelving wiring and locking options. Customers are consumer service and retail businesses construction companies and to a lesser degree distributors film producers military and municipal agencies schools and hospitals. Mobile Mini also refurbishes oceangoing containers for storage. The company's leasing arm comprising a fleet of 213500 portable containers and offices represents about 92% of sales.

	Annual Growth	12/15	12/16	12/17	12/18	12/19
Sales ($ mil.)	3.7%	530.8	508.6	533.5	593.2	612.6
Net income ($ mil.)	96.9%	5.6	47.2	122.2	(8.1)	83.7
Market value ($ mil.)	5.0%	1,374.5	1,335.6	1,523.2	1,401.8	1,673.8
Employees	0.7%	1,982	1,998	2,008	2,049	2,042

MOBITV INC.

6425 Christie Ave. 5th Fl.
Emeryville CA 94608
Phone: 510-450-5000
Fax: 510-450-5001
Web: www.mobitv.com

CEO: Charlie Nooney
CFO: Terri Stevens
HR: –
FYE: December 31
Type: Private

MobiTV turns mobile phones into media centers. The company provides technology that allows television broadcasts and other media content to be delivered to mobile devices. Its subscribers can access content — including on-demand and live television as well as digital music and satellite services — from ABC CBS NBC ESPN and other networks. MobiTV offers its technology as a managed service; it also licenses the server technology to carriers. MobiTV counts the leading US carriers among its partners. Other customers include broadband service providers content providers and handset manufacturers. The company filed an IPO in August 2011 but withdrew it a year later.

MOCON INC.
NMS: MOCO

7500 Mendelsohn Avenue North
Minneapolis, MN 55428
Phone: 763 493-6370
Fax: -
Web: www.mocon.com

CEO: Robert L Demorest
CFO: Elissa Lindsoe
HR: -
FYE: December 31
Type: Public

MOCON makes precision instruments that help you look before you leak. Its products include permeation and packaging instruments that measure the rate at which oxygen carbon dioxide and water vapor penetrate packaging. The company also makes materials analyzers that measure the thickness of coatings and thin films. Such products are used by packagers in the food and beverage pharmaceuticals and chemical industries and by paper plastics and coatings manufacturers. MOCON also makes pharmaceutical capsule and tablet weighing and sorting devices automatic sample preparation systems and offers related consulting and development services. More than half of sales come from outside the US.

	Annual Growth	12/11	12/12	12/13	12/14	12/15
Sales ($ mil.)	13.1%	37.4	49.9	57.1	64.5	61.2
Net income ($ mil.)	(14.1%)	5.5	2.0	3.5	1.5	3.0
Market value ($ mil.)	(2.2%)	92.7	83.4	91.5	103.6	84.8
Employees	14.3%	150	250	250	260	256

MODEL N, INC
NYS: MODN

777 Mariners Island Boulevard, Suite 300
San Mateo, CA 94404
Phone: 650 610-4600
Fax: -
Web: www.modeln.com

CEO: Zack Rinat
CFO: David Barter
HR: -
FYE: September 30
Type: Public

Model N develops revenue management software primarily for the worldwide life sciences and technology industries. Its product suite which is available on premise and via the cloud supports the entire revenue life cycle including pricing contracting compliance settlements channel management and business intelligence and analytics. Model N counts more than 70 customers ranging from multi-national corporations to smaller firms. The company also offers such services as consulting maintenance training and support. It was founded in 1999 and went public in March 2013.

	Annual Growth	09/15	09/16	09/17	09/18	09/19
Sales ($ mil.)	10.8%	93.8	107.0	131.2	154.6	141.2
Net income ($ mil.)	-	(19.6)	(33.1)	(39.5)	(28.2)	(19.3)
Market value ($ mil.)	29.0%	330.3	366.6	493.3	523.0	915.9
Employees	0.4%	721	814	864	782	733

MODERN WOODMEN OF AMERICA

1701 1ST AVE
ROCK ISLAND, IL 612018779
Phone: 309-793-5537
Fax: -
Web: www.modernwoodmen.org

CEO: -
CFO: -
HR: -
FYE: December 31
Type: Private

No need to pitch a tent to have Modern Woodmen in your camp. One of the largest fraternal benefit societies in the US Modern Woodmen of America provides annuities life insurance and other financial savings products to more than 770000 members through some 1600 agents. The group founded in 1883 is organized into "camps" (or chapters) that provide financial social recreational and service benefits to members. Founder Joseph Cullen Root chose the society's name to compare pioneering woodmen clearing forests to men using life insurance to remove the financial burdens their families could face upon their deaths.

	Annual Growth	12/03	12/04	12/05	12/06	12/07
Assets ($ mil.)	4.9%	-	-	-	7,928.9	8,318.2
Net income ($ mil.)	(2.6%)	-	-	-	99.2	96.6
Market value ($ mil.)	-	-	-	-	-	-
Employees	-	-	-	-	-	480

MODESTO IRRIGATION DISTRICT (INC)

1231 11TH ST
MODESTO, CA 953540701
Phone: 209-526-7337
Fax: -
Web: www.mid.org

CEO: -
CFO: -
HR: -
FYE: December 31
Type: Private

Modesty notwithstanding Modesto Irrigation District (MID) does much more than irrigate almost 58000 acres of land in and around Modesto California. The state-owned not-for-profit utility also generates transmits and distributes electricity. In 2012 the company reported that it distributed electricity in a 260-sq.-ml. area to about 94120 residential and 12265 commercial and industrial customers and some 7547 other customers. MID also markets wholesale power and treats and provides drinking water to the city of Modesto for distribution purposes. In 2012 the organization had 103733 irrigated acres (and more than 3100 customer accounts) in its service area.

	Annual Growth	12/14	12/15	12/16	12/17	12/18
Sales ($ mil.)	(1.0%)	-	425.0	413.8	384.4	412.3
Net income ($ mil.)	10.1%	-	42.7	36.5	18.3	56.9
Market value ($ mil.)	-	-	-	-	-	-
Employees	-	-	-	-	-	440

MODINE MANUFACTURING CO
NYS: MOD

1500 DeKoven Avenue
Racine, WI 53403
Phone: 262 636-1200
Fax: 262 636-1424
Web: www.modine.com

CEO: Thomas A. (Tom) Burke
CFO: Michael B. Lucareli
HR: Brian Agen
FYE: March 31
Type: Public

Modine Manufacturing designs and manufactures highly engineered heat transfer systems and components for a range of customers worldwide: automotive OEMs agricultural and construction machinery OEMs heating and cooling equipment OEMs construction contractors and wholesalers of plumbing and heating equipment. Products include heat transfer modules coils fuel and oil coolers radiators condensers and charge air coolers. With manufacturing operations in some 15 countries and technical centers in the US Germany and Italy more than half of Modine's revenues are generated outside of the US. The company was founded in 1916. In early 2019 Modine announced it was looking for strategic alternatives for its automotive business including a possible sale.

	Annual Growth	03/15	03/16	03/17	03/18	03/19
Sales ($ mil.)	10.3%	1,496.4	1,352.5	1,503.0	2,103.1	2,212.7
Net income ($ mil.)	40.4%	21.8	(1.6)	14.2	22.2	84.8
Market value ($ mil.)	0.7%	682.9	558.2	618.5	1,072.3	703.2
Employees	15.3%	6,900	7,100	11,200	11,700	12,200

MODSYS INTERNATIONAL LTD
NBB: MDSY F

6600 LBJ Freeway, Suite 210
Dallas, TX 75240
Phone: 206 395-4152
Fax: -
Web: www.modernsystems.com

CEO: -
CFO: -
HR: -
FYE: December 31
Type: Public

BluePhoenix Solutions hopes to help your legacy systems rise to new modern heights. The company provides legacy modernization products that are used to manage IT systems and resources integrate software applications and migrate legacy systems and data to new platforms. BluePhoenix also offers application development tools as well as products for updating and modernizing data for tasks such as Euro conversion and for managing UPC and EAN compliance. The company merged with Liraz Systems (which primarily operated through its BluePhoenix Solutions subsidiary) and renamed itself BluePhoenix Solutions as a result. BluePhoenix gets nearly half of its sales in Europe.

	Annual Growth	12/13	12/14	12/15	12/16	12/17
Sales ($ mil.)	6.7%	8.5	7.2	9.8	11.0	11.1
Net income ($ mil.)	-	(4.0)	(3.4)	(5.8)	(12.2)	0.2
Market value ($ mil.)	-	-	-	-	-	-
Employees	(11.6%)	100	77	58	69	-

MOHAWK INDUSTRIES, INC.   NYS: MHK

160 S. Industrial Blvd.
Calhoun, GA 30701
Phone: 706 629-7721
Fax: –
Web: www.mohawkind.com

CEO: Jeffrey S. Lorberbaum
CFO: Frank H. Boykin
HR: –
FYE: December 31
Type: Public

Mohawk Industries is the world's largest maker of commercial and residential flooring products. The company manufactures carpets and rugs ceramic and stone tile and laminate wood and vinyl flooring. It produces a range of broadloom carpets and rugs under such names as Mohawk Aladdin Durkan Karastan and Leoline. Mohawk's ceramic tile and stone flooring products are marketed under the popular Daltile brand and Unilin and Pergo laminate and wood flooring and other wood products round out Mohawk's operations. The company sells its products worldwide. Most of its revenue is generated in the US and it has a strong market position in Brazil.

	Annual Growth	12/14	12/15	12/16	12/17	12/18
Sales ($ mil.)	6.4%	7,803.4	8,071.6	8,959.1	9,491.3	9,983.6
Net income ($ mil.)	12.8%	532.0	615.3	930.4	971.6	861.7
Market value ($ mil.)	(6.9%)	11,233.6	13,694.2	14,438.3	19,949.5	8,457.0
Employees	6.8%	32,300	34,100	37,800	38,800	42,100

MOHEGAN TRIBAL GAMING AUTHORITY

1 MOHEGAN SUN BLVD
UNCASVILLE, CT 063821355
Phone: 860-862-8000
Fax: –
Web: www.mohegansun.com

CEO: Mario C Kontomerkos
CFO: Drew M Kelley
HR: –
FYE: September 30
Type: Private

The sun also rises at Mohegan Sun a gaming and entertainment complex run by the Mohegan Tribal Gaming Authority for the Mohegan Indian tribe of Connecticut. The Native American-themed Mohegan Sun complex includes three casinos (Casino of the Earth Casino of the Sky and Casino of the Wind) that feature slot machines game tables horse race wagering an arena a cabaret stores restaurants and a luxury hotel. The company also owns Pocono Downs a horse racetrack in Pennsylvania. Gambling revenues go to the Mohegan Tribe and are used for cultural and educational programs. The tribe has lived as a community for hundreds of years in what is today southeastern Connecticut and has about 1900 members.

	Annual Growth	09/14	09/15	09/16	09/17	09/18
Sales ($ mil.)	1.6%	–	1,291.6	1,334.8	1,380.0	1,355.6
Net income ($ mil.)	12.6%	–	92.1	133.1	76.4	131.6
Market value ($ mil.)	–	–	–	–	–	–
Employees	–	–	–	–	–	8,640

MOLECULAR TEMPLATES INC   NAS: MTEM

9301 Amberglen Blvd, Suite 100
Austin, TX 78729
Phone: 512 869-1555
Fax: –
Web: www.mtem.com

CEO: Eric E Poma
CFO: Adam D Cutler
HR: –
FYE: December 31
Type: Public

By targeting next-generation immunotoxins Molecular Templates (formerly Threshold Pharmaceuticals) hopes to develop drugs that are effective at fighting cancer. These immunotoxins called Engineered Toxin Bodies (ETBs) are able to forcefully enter cells and can target cancer cells for direct attack. The company's MT-3724 candidate is being studied for the treatment of leukemia and lymphoma while Evofosfamide is in trials to treat solid tumors and bone marrow cancer. In mid-2017 Threshold Pharmaceuticals merged with Austin TX-based Molecular Templates.

	Annual Growth	12/14	12/15	12/16	12/17	12/18
Sales ($ mil.)	(2.5%)	14.7	76.9	–	3.4	13.3
Net income ($ mil.)	–	(21.6)	43.8	(24.1)	(23.1)	(30.3)
Market value ($ mil.)	6.2%	116.8	17.6	16.2	368.1	148.4
Employees	2.8%	61	26	15	38	68

MOLINA HEALTHCARE INC   NYS: MOH

200 Oceangate, Suite 100
Long Beach, CA 90802
Phone: 562 435-3666
Fax: 562 437-1335
Web: www.molinahealthcare.com

CEO: Joseph M. Zubretsky
CFO: Joseph W. White
HR: –
FYE: December 31
Type: Public

Molina Healthcare is dedicated to helping low-income Americans receive health and behavioral health coverage as well as primary care services. The company's Health Plan segment arranges for the delivery of health services to some 4.5 million people who receive their care through Medicaid Medicare and other government-funded programs in about a dozen states and Puerto Rico. Its Medicaid Solutions segment provides business process outsourcing (BPO) solutions to Medicaid agencies in six states for their Medicaid Management Information Systems (MMIS) the tool used to support administration of state health care entitlement programs. The family of founder C. David Molina controls the company through holdings and trusts.

	Annual Growth	12/14	12/15	12/16	12/17	12/18
Sales ($ mil.)	18.2%	9,666.6	14,178.0	17,782.0	19,883.0	18,890.0
Net income ($ mil.)	83.6%	62.2	143.0	52.0	(512.0)	707.0
Market value ($ mil.)	21.4%	3,318.9	3,728.1	3,364.1	4,754.2	7,205.6
Employees	1.2%	10,500	21,000	21,000	20,000	11,000

MOLLER INTERNATIONAL INC.   OTC: MLER

1222 Research Park Dr.
Davis CA 95616
Phone: 530-756-5086
Fax: 530-756-5179
Web: www.moller.com

CEO: –
CFO: –
HR: –
FYE: June 30
Type: Public

Meet George Jetson...well not quite but Moller International is working on a Vertical Take-off and Landing (VTOL) aircraft that bears more than a passing resemblance to George's daily ride. The company is testing a prototype of its M400 Skycar in preparation for seeking FAA certification. The forecasted specs on the Skycar are intended to make traffic-jam veterans giddy: four passengers (including the pilot) maximum speed of 375 mph cruising speed of 275 mph and a range of 750 miles. No Skycars have been sold though and the resulting lack of revenue has caused Moller International's auditors to question whether the company can stay in business.

MOLLOY COLLEGE

1000 HEMPSTEAD AVE
ROCKVILLE CENTRE, NY 115701135
Phone: 516-678-5733
Fax: –
Web: www.molloy.edu

CEO: –
CFO: –
HR: –
FYE: June 30
Type: Private

Molloy College is a Catholic school on the South Shore of Long Island. In addition to a variety of undergraduate majors the college offers graduate degrees in business criminal justice education nursing and social work. Molloy College has an enrollment of 3500 undergraduate and 1000 graduate students. About 45% of incoming freshmen are first-generation college students. More than 68% of the educational institution's full-time faculty have doctoral degrees. Through its global learning program Molloy College students have studied abroad in a wide variety of locations including Australia Belgium China Italy France India Thailand and the UK.

	Annual Growth	06/13	06/14	06/15	06/17	06/18
Sales ($ mil.)	0.3%	–	117.3	121.1	118.4	118.9
Net income ($ mil.)	(4.1%)	–	7.2	4.6	9.8	6.1
Market value ($ mil.)	–	–	–	–	–	–
Employees	–	–	–	–	–	700

MOLSON COORS BREWING COMPANY
NYSE: TAP

1225 17th St. Ste. 3200
Denver CO 80202
Phone: 303-927-2337
Fax: 617-499-3361
Web: www.amagpharma.com

CEO: Gavin D K Hattersley
CFO: Tracey I Joubert
HR: –
FYE: December 31
Type: Public

Molson Coors Brewing Company (MCBC) drinks with the big boys: the company is one of the world's largest beer makers by volume. Operating through its subsidiaries MCBC produces some 19 million hectoliters (502 million US gallons) of beer a year. The beer maker's portfolio of brands led by Molson Canadian and Coors Light dominates the Canadian market accounting for 40% of the beer sold in that country. In the US MCBC does business through MillerCoors a joint venture 58%-owned by SABMiller. MillerCoors the second-largest US brewer by volume markets Coors Coors Light and Molson brands. In addition to Canada and the US MCBC operates in the UK and as Molson Coors International (MCI) in developing markets.

MOLYCORP INC. (DE)
NBB: MCPI Q

5619 Denver Tech Center Parkway, Suite 1000
Greenwood Village, CO 80111
Phone: 303 843-8040
Fax: 303 843-8082
Web: www.molycorp.com

CEO: Geoffrey R Bedford
CFO: Michael F Doolan
HR: Diane Braaton
FYE: December 31
Type: Public

Don't look for any mollycoddling of the earth here. Molycorp is an advanced material manufacturer that both controls a world-class rare earth resource and can produce high-purity custom engineered rare earth products to meet increasingly stringent customer specifications. Molycorp mines and produces lanthanide and molybdenum compounds concentrates and oxides using open-pit mining techniques. Lanthanides (which include cerium lanthanum and yttrium) are used in everything from cell phones and computers to X-ray film and television glass. The company is staking its future on the production of rare earth oxides (REOs). Molycop filed for bankruptcy in 2015.

	Annual Growth	12/10	12/11	12/12	12/13	12/14
Sales ($ mil.)	91.8%	35.2	396.8	528.9	554.4	475.6
Net income ($ mil.)	–	(49.1)	117.5	(449.6)	(374.4)	(604.9)
Market value ($ mil.)	(63.6%)	12,965.6	6,230.8	2,452.8	1,460.3	228.8
Employees	102.1%	150	920	2,700	2,580	2,500

MOMENTA PHARMACEUTICALS INC
NMS: MNTA

301 Binney Street
Cambridge, MA 02142
Phone: 617 491-9700
Fax: 617 621-0431
Web: www.momentapharma.com

CEO: Craig A. Wheeler
CFO: Scott M. Storer
HR: Jo-Ann Beltramello
FYE: December 31
Type: Public

Biotech Momenta Pharmaceuticals specializes in unpacking and engineering complex molecules in order to copy existing biologic drugs develop complex generic drugs and discover new drugs. Momenta's primary product is Glatopa an approved generic version of biotech multiple sclerosis treatment Copaxone (marketed by Sanofi and Teva).The company also co-developed Enoxaparin a generic version of Sanofi's heparin drug Lovenox with Sandoz (which also markets the drug). Enoxaparin is used to treat patients with deep-vein thrombosis and acute coronary syndromes.

	Annual Growth	12/14	12/15	12/16	12/17	12/18
Sales ($ mil.)	9.7%	52.3	89.7	109.6	138.9	75.6
Net income ($ mil.)	–	(98.6)	(83.3)	(21.0)	(88.1)	(176.1)
Market value ($ mil.)	(2.1%)	1,185.5	1,461.2	1,481.9	1,373.6	1,087.0
Employees	(15.4%)	256	258	290	279	131

MOMENTIVE PERFORMANCE MATERIALS INC.

22 Corporate Woods Blvd. 2nd Fl.
Albany NY 12211-2374
Phone: 518-533-4600
Fax: 785-296-0287
Web: www.ksdot.org

CEO: John G Boss
CFO: Erick R Asmussen
HR: –
FYE: December 31
Type: Private

Gathering momentum on a global scale Momentive Performance Materials is ready to take on the world. The company manufactures silicone quartz and ceramic products for everything from adhesive labels to hair care products to pesticides. Silicone is used in a vast array of products because of its ability to provide resistance to heat UV rays chemical reactions and friction while allowing for different levels of adhesion. Formed in 2006 after General Electric sold its Advanced Materials unit to Apollo Management Momentive became a subsidiary of Momentive Performance Materials Holdings in 2010. It operates 23 production plants around the world and serves customers in more than 100 countries.

MONARCH CASINO & RESORT, INC.
NMS: MCRI

3800 S. Virginia St.
Reno, NV 89502
Phone: 775 335-4600
Fax: –
Web: www.monarchcasino.com

CEO: John Farahi
CFO: Ron Rowan
HR: –
FYE: December 31
Type: Public

Monarch Casino & Resort hopes high rollers will rediscover Atlantis. The company's tropical-themed Atlantis Casino Resort Spa in Reno Nevada includes nearly 825 hotel rooms a 61000-sq.-ft. casino restaurants a health club retail outlets and a family entertainment center. The company also owns and operates the Monarch Casino Black Hawk in Black Hawk Colorado. Casino operations which account for more than half of revenue include gaming tables slot and video poker machines keno and a race and sports book. The family of founder David Farahi — including John Bob and Ben Farahi — own more than half of the company.

	Annual Growth	12/14	12/15	12/16	12/17	12/18
Sales ($ mil.)	6.4%	187.8	202.2	217.0	230.7	240.3
Net income ($ mil.)	24.5%	14.2	20.7	24.6	25.5	34.1
Market value ($ mil.)	23.1%	297.3	407.1	462.0	803.1	683.4
Employees	1.2%	2,100	2,100	2,100	2,200	2,200

MONARCH CEMENT CO.
NL:

P.O. Box 1000
Humboldt, KS 66748-0900
Phone: 620 473-2222
Fax: 620 473-2447
Web: www.monarchcement.com

CEO: –
CFO: Debra P Roe
HR: Emily Baughn
FYE: December 31
Type: Public

Monarch's chrysalis is made of stone. The Monarch Cement Company quarries clay limestone and gypsum near its Kansas plant to make portland cement ready-mixed concrete and other building materials. It can produce more than 1 million tons of cement annually and serves customers in Kansas Iowa southeast Nebraska western Missouri northwest Arkansas and northern Oklahoma. Its Monarch-brand portland cement is used in the production of ready-mixed concrete for constructing highways bridges and buildings. Chairman and president Walter Wulf Jr. and vice chair Byron Radcliff respectively control about 9% and 10% of the company.

	Annual Growth	12/14	12/15	12/16	12/17	12/18
Sales ($ mil.)	4.3%	146.9	147.9	165.2	168.1	173.9
Net income ($ mil.)	9.1%	11.3	18.3	21.2	21.7	16.0
Market value ($ mil.)	25.0%	104.2	116.6	181.5	274.1	254.8
Employees	–	–	–	–	–	–

MONARCH COMMUNITY BANCORP INC   NBB: MCBF

375 North Willowbrook Road   CEO: –
Coldwater, MI 49036   CFO: –
Phone: 517 278-4566   HR: –
Fax: –   FYE: December 31
Web: www.monarchcb.com   Type: Public

Monarch Community Bancorp emerged from its chrysalis in 2002 when it was organized to be the holding company for Monarch Community Bank (formerly Branch County Federal Savings and Loan Association). The bank operates more than five branches in southern Michigan's Branch Calhoun and Hillsdale counties. Its lending activities mainly consist of one- to four-family residential mortgages (about half of its loan portfolio) commercial mortgages and home equity loans. To fund its lending the bank offers such deposit products as checking savings and money market accounts CDs and IRAs. It provides insurance mutual funds annuities and financial planning services through an agreement with Prudential Financial.

	Annual Growth	12/09	12/10	12/11	12/12	12/13
Assets ($ mil.)	(11.9%)	283.2	256.9	208.1	190.3	171.0
Net income ($ mil.)	–	(19.4)	(10.9)	(0.4)	(0.4)	(2.2)
Market value ($ mil.)	0.0%	23.4	10.5	9.4	6.7	23.4
Employees	(1.9%)	94	68	79	106	87

MONARCH FINANCIAL HOLDINGS INC   NAS: MNRK

1435 Crossways Blvd.   CEO: –
Chesapeake, VA 23320   CFO: –
Phone: 757 389-5111   HR: –
Fax: –   FYE: December 31
Web: www.monarchbank.com   Type: Public

Money rules at Monarch Financial Holdings. The holding company serves the South Hampton Roads area of southeastern Virginia through Monarch Bank Monarch Mortgage Monarch Capital Monarch Investment and OBXBank. With nearly a dozen branches Monarch Bank offers standard services including savings and checking accounts IRAs and CDS. Bank subsidiary Monarch Mortgage formed in 2007 has about a dozen offices. Other divisions sell insurance title and investment products. Single-family mortgages make up the largest share of the bank's loan portfolio which also includes commercial construction and land development loans. Monarch Bank division OBX Bank operates in North Carolina's Outer Banks area. TowneBank agreed to buy Monarch in late 2015.

	Annual Growth	12/10	12/11	12/12	12/13	12/14
Assets ($ mil.)	6.6%	825.6	908.5	1,215.6	1,016.7	1,066.7
Net income ($ mil.)	17.2%	5.9	7.1	12.8	11.1	11.2
Market value ($ mil.)	15.2%	91.4	90.1	96.3	144.2	161.1
Employees	4.6%	527	579	663	634	631

MONDELEZ INTERNATIONAL INC   NMS: MDLZ

Three Parkway North   CEO: Dirk Van de Put
Deerfield, IL 60015   CFO: Brian T. Gladden
Phone: 847 943-4000   HR: Karen J. May
Fax: –   FYE: December 31
Web: www.mondelezinternational.com   Type: Public

One of the world's largest snack companies Mondelez International owns a pantry of billion-dollar brands such as Cadbury and Milka chocolates; LU BelVita and Oreo biscuits; Trident gum; and Tang powdered beverages. The company's portfolio includes global national and regional brands many of which are more than 100 years old. Biscuits (cookies crackers and salted snacks) and chocolate account for most of the company's sales. Mondelez which operates in more than 80 countries and sells its products in some 150 generates most of its revenue outside the US.

	Annual Growth	12/15	12/16	12/17	12/18	12/19
Sales ($ mil.)	(3.3%)	29,636.0	25,923.0	25,896.0	25,938.0	25,868.0
Net income ($ mil.)	(14.6%)	7,267.0	1,659.0	2,922.0	3,381.0	3,870.0
Market value ($ mil.)	5.3%	64,345.7	63,613.8	61,418.3	57,443.3	79,040.1
Employees	(5.2%)	99,000	90,000	90,000	80,000	80,000

MONEYGRAM INTERNATIONAL INC   NMS: MGI

2828 N. Harwood St., 15th Floor   CEO: W. Alexander (Alex) Holmes
Dallas, TX 75201   CFO: Lawrence Angelilli
Phone: 214 999-7552   HR: Steven (Steve) Piano
Fax: –   FYE: December 31
Web: www.moneygram.com   Type: Public

MoneyGram International has just the ticket to move money around the world. Operating through primary subsidiary MoneyGram Payment Systems the firm sells MoneyGram-branded cash transfers and money orders at some 335000 locations around the globe and is a leading provider of money orders in the US. Wal-Mart is MoneyGram's largest money-transfer and money order agent accounting for more than 20% of the company's revenues. MoneyGram also offers in-person and electronic bill payment services letting users pay everything from mortgages to utilities and processes official checks for financial institutions. Thomas H. Lee Partners (THL) owns more than half of MoneyGram.

	Annual Growth	12/14	12/15	12/16	12/17	12/18
Sales ($ mil.)	(0.1%)	1,454.9	1,434.7	1,630.4	1,602.1	1,447.6
Net income ($ mil.)	–	72.1	(76.9)	16.3	(29.8)	(24.0)
Market value ($ mil.)	(31.5%)	505.6	348.7	656.8	733.0	111.2
Employees	(2.8%)	2,727	1,215	2,916	2,936	2,436

MONMOUTH MEDICAL CENTER INC.

300 2ND AVE   CEO: Eric Carney
LONG BRANCH, NJ 077406395   CFO: David McClung
Phone: 732-222-5200   HR: –
Fax: –   FYE: December 31
Web: www.rwjbh.org   Type: Private

Monmouth Medical Center is a 530-bed tertiary care teaching hospital providing comprehensive health care to residents of central New Jersey. The not-for-profit medical center offers services ranging from orthopedics diagnostics and obstetric care to surgery dentistry and geriatric services. The medical center campus also includes a children's hospital a cancer center a neuroscience institute an outpatient care clinic and hospice and home health facilities. Monmouth Medical Center is a major teaching affiliate of the Drexel University College of Medicine in Philadelphia. The hospital is an affiliate of the Saint Barnabas Healthcare System.

	Annual Growth	12/13	12/14	12/16	12/17	12/18
Sales ($ mil.)	9.8%	–	375.9	399.7	529.8	546.9
Net income ($ mil.)	3.4%	–	38.3	46.1	53.0	43.8
Market value ($ mil.)	–	–	–	–	–	–
Employees	–	–	–	–	–	2,400

MONMOUTH REAL ESTATE INVESTMENT CORP   NYS: MNR

101 Crawfords Corner Road, Suite 1405   CEO: Michael P. Landy
Holmdel, NJ 07733   CFO: Kevin S. Miller
Phone: 732 577-9996   HR: –
Fax: –   FYE: September 30
Web: www.mreic.reit   Type: Public

Monmouth specializes in mammoth industrial properties particularly warehouses and distribution centers. The real estate investment trust (REIT) owns about 80 industrial buildings and a single New Jersey shopping center comprising some 10.7 million sq. ft. in more than 25 states mostly in the East and Midwest. Most are net-leased (in which tenants pay insurance taxes and maintenance costs) under long-term leases. The REIT's two largest tenants FedEx and Milwaukee Electric Tool together account for half of its revenue. The firm also invests in REIT securities. Founded in 1968 Monmouth is one of the oldest public equity REITs in the nation.

	Annual Growth	09/15	09/16	09/17	09/18	09/19
Sales ($ mil.)	19.4%	78.0	94.9	113.5	139.4	158.5
Net income ($ mil.)	3.9%	25.6	32.5	40.3	56.0	29.8
Market value ($ mil.)	10.3%	939.9	1,375.6	1,560.7	1,611.8	1,389.1
Employees	3.2%	15	14	15	15	17

MONMOUTH UNIVERSITY INC

400 CEDAR AVE
WEST LONG BRANCH, NJ 077641898
Phone: 732-571-3400
Fax: -
Web: www.monmouth.edu

CEO: -
CFO: -
HR: -
FYE: June 30
Type: Private

Students looking for a monumental education might want to head to Monmouth University. The private institution offers more than 30 undergraduate and 20 graduate programs through eight schools that include business administration education humanities and social sciences and nursing and health sciences as well as graduate and honors schools. Founded in 1933 as the Monmouth Junior College Monmouth University has an enrollment of roughly an 6500 graduate and undergraduate students. The school's student-teacher ratio is about 14:1.

	Annual Growth	06/07	06/08	06/10	06/13	06/15
Sales ($ mil.)	4.6%	-	166.4	145.2	162.3	227.9
Net income ($ mil.)	(1.7%)	-	14.9	18.3	14.4	13.2
Market value ($ mil.)	-	-	-	-	-	-
Employees	-	-	-	-	-	1,000

MONOGRAM FOOD SOLUTIONS, LLC

530 OAK COURT DR STE 400
MEMPHIS, TN 381173735
Phone: 901-685-7167
Fax: -
Web: www.monogramfoods.com

CEO: -
CFO: -
HR: -
FYE: December 29
Type: Private

Monogram Food Solutions is focused on M E A and T. As a manufacturer of meat and meat snack products the company produces beef jerky sausage hot dogs bacon and other processed food items. Its brands include Circle B King Cotton and Trail's Best Meat Snacks. Through several special licensing agreements Monogram Food Solutions also sells Jeff Foxworthy Jerky Products NASCAR Jerky and Steak Strips and Bass Pro Uncle Buck's Licensed Products. The company which distributes its products nationwide operates facilities in Minnesota Indiana and Virginia. Founded in 2004 Monogram Food Solutions was formed through the merger of assets (King Cotton and Circle B) previously owned by Sara Lee Corp.

	Annual Growth	01/15	01/16*	12/16	12/17	12/18
Sales ($ mil.)	24.3%	-	419.2	565.6	640.8	647.8
Net income ($ mil.)	285.8%	-	0.7	12.4	2.6	11.1
Market value ($ mil.)	-	-	-	-	-	-
Employees	-	-	-	-	-	790

*Fiscal year change

MONOLITHIC POWER SYSTEMS INC   NMS: MPWR

4040 Lake Washington Blvd. NE, Suite 201
Kirkland, WA 98033
Phone: 425 296-9956
Fax: -
Web: www.monolithicpower.com

CEO: Michael R. Hsing
CFO: Bernie Blegen
HR: -
FYE: December 31
Type: Public

Monolithic Power Systems (MPS) sends out mixed signals and that's a good thing. The fabless semiconductor company offers mixed-signal and analog microchips — especially DC-to-DC converters for powering flat-panel TVs wireless communications equipment notebook computers set-top boxes and other consumer electronic devices. MPS outsources production of its chips to three silicon foundries in China. The company's products are incorporated into electronic gear from tech heavyweights such as Dell Hewlett-Packard Samsung Electronics and Sony. The company was founded in 1997.

	Annual Growth	12/14	12/15	12/16	12/17	12/18
Sales ($ mil.)	19.8%	282.5	333.1	388.7	470.9	582.4
Net income ($ mil.)	31.2%	35.5	35.2	52.7	65.2	105.3
Market value ($ mil.)	23.6%	2,114.2	2,708.0	3,482.4	4,775.9	4,941.2
Employees	10.2%	1,178	1,260	1,417	1,534	1,737

MONONGAHELA POWER COMPANY

5001 NASA BLVD
FAIRMONT, WV 265548248
Phone: 800-686-0022
Fax: -
Web: www.firstenergycorp.com

CEO: Paul J Evanson
CFO: Jeffrey David Serkes
HR: -
FYE: December 31
Type: Private

Electricity flows from Monongahela Power (Mon Power) just like the river the utility was named after. The company services approximately 388000 residential and commercial customers in a service area of 13000 sq. mi. in West Virginia. Mon Power along with West Penn Power and Potomac Edison comprise the Allegheny Power arm of Allegheny Energy which is now part of FirstEnergy. In 2013 Mon Power owned or controlled 3580 MW of generating capacity. The company is contractually obligated to supply Potomac Edison with sufficient power to meet that company's power load obligations in West Virginia.

	Annual Growth	12/13	12/14	12/15	12/16	12/17
Sales ($ mil.)	0.3%	-	-	-	1,613.9	1,619.0
Net income ($ mil.)	4.5%	-	-	-	66.0	69.0
Market value ($ mil.)	-	-	-	-	-	-
Employees	-	-	-	-	-	4,000

MONOTYPE IMAGING HOLDINGS INC   NMS: TYPE

600 Unicorn Park Drive
Woburn, MA 01801
Phone: 781 970-6000
Fax: -
Web: www.monotypeimaging.com

CEO: Scott E Landers
CFO: Christopher Brooks
HR: -
FYE: December 31
Type: Public

Monotype Imaging may be the one to thank if you're reading this whether it's on a portable electronic device or a printed page. With most sales going to device manufacturers (OEMs) the company's text imaging software is integrated into applications and embedded in electronics ranging from mobile phones to laser printers automotive displays and digital cameras as well as navigation tools set-top boxes and Internet of Things devices. Its applications manage compression scaling color and layout. Providing customers access to thousands of typefaces OEM sales are complemented by about 46% of revenue coming from licenses to creative professionals mostly commercial clients. Customers have included Apple Google Sony and Microsoft.

	Annual Growth	12/13	12/14	12/15	12/16	12/17
Sales ($ mil.)	9.1%	166.6	184.5	192.4	203.4	235.8
Net income ($ mil.)	(21.9%)	31.1	32.5	26.2	14.9	11.6
Market value ($ mil.)	(6.7%)	1,329.2	1,202.8	986.2	828.1	1,005.4
Employees	20.0%	354	435	494	762	734

MONRO INC   NMS: MNRO

200 Holleder Parkway
Rochester, NY 14615
Phone: 585 647-6400
Fax: 585 647-0945
Web: www.monro.com

CEO: Brett Ponton
CFO: Brian J. DÂ'Ambrosia
HR: -
FYE: March 30
Type: Public

If you can't stop point your car toward Monro Muffler Brake and coast on in. The company provides a full range of brake tire exhaust system suspension and steering and alignment services at more than 800 automotive repair shops. Its operations span nearly 20 states in the Northeast and Midwest and include Monro Muffler Brake & Service Mr. Tire Tread Quarters Autotire Car Care Center and Tire Warehouse. Along with under-car work the company offers air conditioning maintenance state inspections and scheduled maintenance services including fleet maintenance. Tire replacements and service account for more than 35% of sales. Monro Muffler Brake services more than 4.4 million vehicles annually.

	Annual Growth	03/15	03/16	03/17	03/18	03/19
Sales ($ mil.)	7.6%	894.5	943.7	1,021.5	1,127.8	1,200.2
Net income ($ mil.)	6.6%	61.8	66.8	61.5	63.9	79.8
Market value ($ mil.)	7.4%	2,153.5	2,310.0	1,728.8	1,776.9	2,868.2
Employees	5.6%	6,577	6,725	7,535	7,878	8,183

MONSANTO CO
NYS: MON

800 North Lindbergh Blvd.
St. Louis, MO 63167
Phone: 314 694-1000
Fax: 314 694-1057
Web: www.monsanto.com

CEO: Brett Begemann
CFO: –
HR: –
FYE: August 31
Type: Public

Monsanto is something of a growth stalk in helping farmers grow corn and other crops. The company applies its biotechnology and genomics know-how to develop seeds and herbicides to help farmers produce corn (43% of revenue) cotton oilseeds and vegetables. It produces genetically altered seeds that tolerate Roundup (its flagship product and the world's #1 herbicide) and resist bugs. The company also produces Asgrow DEKALB Deltapine and Seminis seeds. About 60% of sales are in the US. Monsanto agreed to be bought by Bayer in a landmark $66 billion deal reached in September 2016.

	Annual Growth	08/13	08/14	08/15	08/16	08/17
Sales ($ mil.)	(0.4%)	14,861.0	15,855.0	15,001.0	13,502.0	14,640.0
Net income ($ mil.)	(2.3%)	2,482.0	2,740.0	2,314.0	1,336.0	2,260.0
Market value ($ mil.)	4.6%	43,030.3	50,837.2	42,924.8	46,815.1	51,518.6
Employees	(2.9%)	26,200	27,000	25,500	24,100	23,300

MONSTER WORLDWIDE INC
NYS: MWW

133 Boston Post Road, Building 15
Weston, MA 02493
Phone: 978 461-8000
Fax: –
Web: www.about-monster.com

CEO: Mark Stoever
CFO: –
HR: –
FYE: December 31
Type: Public

Finding a new job or a new employee can be a monstrous task but Monster Worldwide aims to help. Its network of online career services is led by Monster.com a job search website operating in local markets globally across 40 countries. Most of Monster's revenue comes from employers who pay to post job listings and search the site's database of resumes. Job seekers can post resumes and search listings free of charge. Monster also generates revenue by selling advertising on its websites which include offerings aimed at students and military personnel.

	Annual Growth	12/11	12/12	12/13	12/14	12/15
Sales ($ mil.)	(10.5%)	1,040.1	890.4	807.6	770.0	666.9
Net income ($ mil.)	8.2%	53.8	(258.7)	(0.5)	(289.3)	73.6
Market value ($ mil.)	(7.8%)	708.1	501.8	636.7	412.6	511.7
Employees	(11.4%)	6,000	5,000	4,000	4,000	3,700

MONTAGE RESOURCE CORP
NYS: MR

122 West John Carpenter Freeway, Suite 300
Irving, TX 75039
Phone: 469 444-1647
Fax: –
Web: www.montageresources.com

CEO: Benjamin W. Hulburt
CFO: Matthew R. DeNezza
HR: Jen Mitchell
FYE: December 31
Type: Public

Looking to eclipse its oil and gas rivals Eclipse Resources is an independent exploration and production company active in the Appalachian Basin. It has 227230 net acres in Eastern Ohio including 96240 net acres in the most prolific and economic area of the Utica Shale fairway (Utica Core Area) with 25740 net acres targeted as a highly liquids-rich area in the Marcellus Shale in Eastern Ohio (Marcellus Project Area). Eclipse operates 81% of its net acreage within the Utica Core and Marcellus Project areas. In 2014 the company reported estimated proved reserves of 109.6 billion cu. ft. equivalent and 18.3 million barrels of oil equivalent. It went public in June of that year.

	Annual Growth	12/14	12/15	12/16	12/17	12/18
Sales ($ mil.)	39.0%	137.8	255.3	235.0	383.7	515.1
Net income ($ mil.)	–	(183.2)	(971.4)	(203.8)	8.5	18.8
Market value ($ mil.)	(37.8%)	141.8	36.7	53.9	48.4	21.2
Employees	(8.5%)	227	210	138	171	159

MONTANA STATE UNIVERSITY, INC

901 W GARFIELD ST
BOZEMAN, MT 59717
Phone: 406-994-4361
Fax: –
Web: www.montana.edu

CEO: –
CFO: –
HR: –
FYE: June 30
Type: Private

Montana State University helps develop young minds in Big Sky Country. The university located in Bozeman serves more than 14500 students most of whom are undergraduates from Montana. The school offers baccalaureate degrees in 60 fields master's degrees in 45 fields and doctoral degrees in about 20 fields. The school offers primarily a liberal arts education though it is also strong in agriculture and the fine arts. The university provides courses in fields ranging from English to political science to engineering. It has a teaching staff of more than 1150 including 781 full-time and 373 part-time faculty and department heads. Tuition and fees for a resident student is $6705; a non-resident $20062.

	Annual Growth	06/14	06/15	06/16	06/17	06/18
Sales ($ mil.)	3.8%	–	349.6	361.6	66.4	391.1
Net income ($ mil.)	33.5%	–	9.8	22.2	21.4	23.3
Market value ($ mil.)	–	–	–	–	–	–
Employees	–	–	–	–	–	2,500

MONTCLAIR STATE UNIVERSITY

1 NORMAL AVE
MONTCLAIR, NJ 070431624
Phone: 973-655-4000
Fax: –
Web: www.montclair.edu

CEO: –
CFO: –
HR: Jerry Cutler
FYE: June 30
Type: Private

With its roots as a teaching college it's fitting that today Montclair State University (MSU) is one of a handful of universities in the US offering a doctorate in pedagogy (the art and science of teaching). For more than 100 years MSU has provided a comprehensive curriculum for future educators as well as other students studying a variety of subjects. With an enrollment of some 20000 students MSU operates through six schools and colleges: College of the Arts College of Education and Human Services College of Humanities and Social Sciences College of Science and Mathematics School of Business and the Graduate School.

	Annual Growth	06/05	06/06	06/07	06/08	06/12
Sales ($ mil.)	8.2%	–	–	179.4	200.6	266.5
Net income ($ mil.)	4.8%	–	–	23.3	24.9	29.4
Market value ($ mil.)	–	–	–	–	–	–
Employees	–	–	–	–	–	2,000

MONTEFIORE MEDICAL CENTER

111 E 210TH ST
BRONX, NY 104672401
Phone: 718-920-4321
Fax: –

CEO: Steven M. Safyer
CFO: Joel A. Perlman
HR: –
FYE: December 31
Type: Private

The primary teaching hospital of the Albert Einstein College of Medicine Montefiore Medical Center attends to the health care needs of residents of the Bronx and nearby Westchester County. The health system operates four main hospitals with about 1500 beds (and 93000 annual admissions) more than 100 ambulatory care offices a children's hospital and Centers of Excellence in cancer care cardiovascular services transplantation and neurosciences. Additionally it operates a home health care agency as well as outpatient facilities that provide ambulatory and diagnostic services. Montefiore also offers medical education programs in partnership with the Albert Einstein College of Medicine.

	Annual Growth	12/13	12/14	12/15	12/16	12/17
Sales ($ mil.)	39.9%	–	–	–	2,690.3	3,762.8
Net income ($ mil.)	2.7%	–	–	–	42.2	43.4
Market value ($ mil.)	–	–	–	–	–	–
Employees	–	–	–	–	–	11,000

MONUMENTAL SPORTS & ENTERTAINMENT

601 F St. NW
Washington DC 20004
Phone: 202-628-3200
Fax: 202-661-5063
Web: www.verizoncenter.com

CEO: Ted Leonsis
CFO: –
HR: –
FYE: June 30
Type: Private

You might say that professional sports is a big thing with this company. Monumental Sports & Entertainment is a holding company that controls three sports franchises in Washington DC including the Washington Wizards professional basketball team the Washington Capitals hockey club and the Washington Mystics women's basketball franchise. The company also owns and operates the city's Verizon Center an all-purpose venue that serves as home for all three sports teams. In addition Monumental Sports manages the Patriot Center at George Mason University in Fairfax Virginia. Chairman and majority owner Ted Leonsis formed the company when he acquired the Washington Wizards in 2010.

MOODY'S CORP.

NYS: MCO

7 World Trade Center, 250 Greenwich Street
New York, NY 10007
Phone: 212 553-0300
Fax: –
Web: www.moodys.com

CEO: Raymond W. (Ray) McDaniel
CFO: Linda S. Huber
HR: –
FYE: December 31
Type: Public

Moody's influential credit ratings can trigger mood swings in company directors across the globe. Moody's Corporation provides credit ratings research credit risk management and other services through its two primary segments: Moody's Investors Service (MIS) and Moody's Analytics. MIS publishes credit ratings on commercial and government entities in some 135 countries. Moody's Analytics sells credit risk management tools and provides portfolio management and training services for financial institutions. The company's famous letter ratings (ranging from "Aaa" to "C") were invented by John Moody in 1909 and are still used today.

	Annual Growth	12/14	12/15	12/16	12/17	12/18
Sales ($ mil.)	7.4%	3,334.3	3,484.5	3,604.2	4,204.1	4,442.7
Net income ($ mil.)	7.3%	988.7	941.3	266.6	1,000.6	1,309.6
Market value ($ mil.)	10.0%	18,328.8	19,195.4	18,034.2	28,238.3	26,790.2
Employees	7.0%	9,900	10,400	10,600	12,000	13,000

MOOG INC

NYS: MOG A

400 Jamison Rd, East Aurora
New York, NY 14052-0018
Phone: 716 652-2000
Fax: –
Web: www.moog.com

CEO: John R. Scannell
CFO: Donald R. Fishback
HR: John Grabon
FYE: September 28
Type: Public

Moog (rhymes with "rogue") makes precision-control components and systems used in aerospace products industrial machinery and marine and medical equipment. Servoactuators Moog's core product receive electrical signals from computers and then perform specific actions. Using its servoactuators Moog builds flight and control systems for commercial and military aircraft as well as hydraulic and electrical controls for automated industrial machinery wind turbines and control systems for satellites and spacecraft launch vehicles and missiles. It also makes infusion therapy pumps slip rings for CT scanners and motors used in devices for sleep apnea. Customers in the US make up more than half its sales.

	Annual Growth	10/15	10/16*	09/17	09/18	09/19
Sales ($ mil.)	3.6%	2,525.5	2,411.9	2,497.5	2,709.5	2,904.7
Net income ($ mil.)	8.0%	131.9	126.7	141.3	96.5	179.7
Market value ($ mil.)	10.6%	1,891.2	2,065.7	2,894.6	2,982.7	2,834.9
Employees	4.6%	10,691	10,497	10,675	11,787	12,809

*Fiscal year change

MOOREFIELD CONSTRUCTION, INC.

600 N TUSTIN AVE STE 210
SANTA ANA, CA 927053781
Phone: 714-972-0700
Fax: –
Web: www.moorefieldconstruction.com

CEO: Ann Moorefield
CFO: –
HR: –
FYE: September 30
Type: Private

Moorefield Construction wants to be more than just another big-box store builder. The company provides general contracting services for retail projects throughout Arizona California Colorado Idaho Nevada New Mexico Oregon Utah and Washington. Clients have included Lowe's Best Buy and Walgreen. The company operates from offices in Santa Ana and Sacramento. Moorefield Construction was founded in 1957 by the late Harold Moorefield and continues to be owned and operated by his family including his wife Ann (CEO) and their sons Mike (president) Larry (VP) and Hal (VP).

	Annual Growth	09/12	09/13	09/14	09/15	09/16
Sales ($ mil.)	17.2%	–	70.0	118.5	112.8	112.7
Net income ($ mil.)	62.4%	–	0.1	0.1	0.2	0.3
Market value ($ mil.)	–	–	–	–	–	–
Employees	–	–	–	–	–	95

MORAVIAN COLLEGE

1200 MAIN ST
BETHLEHEM, PA 180186650
Phone: 610-861-1300
Fax: –
Web: www.moravian.edu

CEO: –
CFO: –
HR: –
FYE: June 30
Type: Private

Moravian College America's sixth-oldest college was founded in Pennsylvania by the Moravian Church in 1742. The private school offers undergraduate coursework in the liberal arts and sciences with more than 50 programs including the arts chemistry business music and physics. It enrolls about 1600 students from 24 states and 14 countries with a student to teacher ratio of 11:1. Moravian College also includes the Moravian Theological Seminary an ecumenical graduate school offering master's degrees in divinity pastoral counseling and theological studies. Tuition and fees for the college total about $35000 per year.

	Annual Growth	06/14	06/15	06/16	06/17	06/18
Sales ($ mil.)	9.6%	–	54.6	74.6	69.0	71.9
Net income ($ mil.)	–	–	(0.2)	11.7	9.4	5.0
Market value ($ mil.)	–	–	–	–	–	–
Employees	–	–	–	–	–	450

MOREDIRECT INC.

1001 Yamato Rd. Ste. 200
Boca Raton FL 33431-4403
Phone: 561-237-3300
Fax: 561-237-3390
Web: www.moredirect.com

CEO: –
CFO: –
HR: –
FYE: December 31
Type: Subsidiary

MoreDirect provides a straightforward approach to technology purchases. The company serves the computer software and hardware procurement needs of corporate and government customers with its proprietary online software which enables them to search many distribution sources compare prices customize and place orders and track shipping in real time. MoreDirect provides its customers with access to information on products from about 2000 distributors and manufacturers including Apple Cisco Systems IBM Dell Hewlett-Packard Microsoft and Samsung Electronics. MoreDirect is a subsidiary of direct marketer PC Connection.

MOREHEAD MEMORIAL HOSPITAL INC

117 E KINGS HWY
EDEN, NC 272885201
Phone: 336-623-9711
Fax: –
Web: www.morehead.org

CEO: W Carl Martin
CFO: –
HR: Tom Stevens
FYE: September 30
Type: Private

Morehead Memorial Hospital is a not-for-profit community hospital that provides health care services to residents of North Carolina's Rockingham County. The hospital has about 110 acute care beds and provides general medical-surgical care including emergency services obstetrical care outpatient surgery and cancer treatment. It also provides home health care services and operates several ancillary facilities such as a freestanding diagnostic imaging facility and a physical rehabilitation center. The hospital's main campus (built in 1960) includes Morehead Nursing Center a long-term care facility with about 120 beds. Morehead Memorial Hospital traces its origin back to 1924.

	Annual Growth	09/13	09/14	09/15	09/16	09/17
Sales ($ mil.)	(4.8%)	–	81.2	77.6	72.5	70.1
Net income ($ mil.)	–	–	(7.1)	(6.0)	(6.7)	(5.8)
Market value ($ mil.)	–	–	–	–	–	–
Employees	–	–	–	–	–	850

MOREHOUSE COLLEGE (INC.)

830 WESTVIEW DR SW
ATLANTA, GA 303143776
Phone: 404-681-2800
Fax: –
Web: www.morehouse.edu

CEO: John Silvanus Wilson Jr
CFO: Gwendolyn Sykes
HR: –
FYE: June 30
Type: Private

Morehouse College is the largest private liberal arts college for African-American men. Located three miles from downtown Atlanta the college has an enrollment of more than 2500 students. Facilities include the Leadership Center at Morehouse College Morehouse Research Institute and Andrew Young Center for International Affairs. The school has courses of study in business and economics humanities and social sciences and science and mathematics. It also offers a degree in engineering in conjunction with Georgia Institute of Technology. Notable alumni include civil rights activist Dr. Martin Luther King Jr. filmmaker Shelton "Spike" Lee and actor Samuel L. Jackson.

	Annual Growth	06/07	06/08*	04/10*	06/10	06/15
Sales ($ mil.)	–	–	0.0	93.5	99.2	105.4
Net income ($ mil.)	–	–	0.0	30.9	16.1	(2.1)
Market value ($ mil.)	–	–	–	–	–	–
Employees	–	–	–	–	–	700

*Fiscal year change

MORGAN LEWIS & BOCKIUS LLP

1701 Market St.
Philadelphia PA 19103
Phone: 215-963-5000
Fax: 215-963-5001
Web: www.morganlewis.com

CEO: –
CFO: James M Diasio
HR: –
FYE: September 30
Type: Private - Partnershi

Long a leading Philadelphia law firm Morgan Lewis & Bockius these days extends its reach well beyond the City of Brotherly Love. The firm is home to some 1400 lawyers in about 25 offices throughout the US Europe and Asia. Morgan Lewis & Bockius also employs about 200 other legal professionals such as patent agents employee benefits advisors regulatory scientists and other specialists. The firm's multiple practice areas include business and finance intellectual property environmental law labor and employment real estate taxes and litigation. It provides services to clients of all sizes. Morgan Lewis & Bockius was founded in 1873 by Charles Morgan Jr. and Francis Lewis.

MORGAN PROPERTIES TRUST

160 Clubhouse Rd.
King of Prussia PA 19406
Phone: 610-265-2800
Fax: 610-265-5889
Web: www.morgan-properties.com

CEO: –
CFO: –
HR: –
FYE: December 31
Type: Private

Morgan Properties Trust wants to hand you the keys to a new apartment. The real estate investment trust (REIT) buys and manages middle-income apartments in the suburbs of Philadelphia New York the Baltimore/Washington DC area and other regions with high barriers to entry due to significant supply constraints. Its 90-plus properties contain more than 21500 apartments; its 30 properties in suburban Philly make up about 40% of revenue. To keep residents happy and living in its apartments Morgan offers newly renovated kitchens and bathrooms and Facebook and Twitter pages for each of its properties. In 2011 CEO Mitchell Morgan formed the company from his real estate business and filed to take it public.

MORGAN STANLEY

NYS: MS

1585 Broadway
New York, NY 10036
Phone: 212 761-4000
Fax: –
Web: www.morganstanley.com

CEO: James P. Gorman
CFO: Jonathan Pruzan
HR: Christine Discola
FYE: December 31
Type: Public

One of the world's top investment banks Morgan Stanley serves up a smorgasbord of financial services. It offers everything from advising corporate clients on mergers & acquisitions to raising capital for large companies to managing real estate investments for wealthy individuals. It boasts one of the largest financial advisor networks which works with clients to pursue their investment goals. Morgan Stanley has more than $470 billion of assets under management. The investment bank is a global enterprise with a presence in more than 40 nations serving corporate institutional government and individual clients.

	Annual Growth	12/14	12/15	12/16	12/17	12/18
Assets ($ mil.)	1.6%	801,510.0	787,465.0	814,949.0	851,733.0	853,531.0
Net income ($ mil.)	26.0%	3,467.0	6,127.0	5,979.0	6,111.0	8,748.0
Market value ($ mil.)	0.5%	65,953.4	54,071.6	71,817.8	89,190.0	67,398.2
Employees	2.0%	55,802	56,218	55,311	57,633	60,348

MORGAN STANLEY SMITH BARNEY LLC

2000 Westchester Ave.
Purchase NY 10577
Phone: 914-225-5510
Fax: 914-225-6770
Web: www.morganstanleysmithbarney.com

CEO: James P Gorman
CFO: Ruth Porat
HR: –
FYE: December 31
Type: Joint Venture

Sometimes it takes a complicated family tree to create stellar lineage. Morgan Stanley Smith Barney (doing business as Morgan Stanley Wealth Management or MSWM) formed in 2009 as a joint venture between Morgan Stanley and Citigroup. MSWM is one of the world's largest retail brokerages boasting $1.7 trillion under management and a network of almost 17000 financial advisors. It serves individuals businesses and institutions including brokerage and investment advisory services financial and wealth planning credit and lending cash management annuities and insurance and retirement and trust services. Morgan Stanley upped its stake from 51% to 65% in 2012 as a prelude to acquiring the company outright.

MORGAN'S FOODS, INC.
NBB: MRFD

4829 Galaxy Parkway, Suite S
Cleveland, OH 44128
Phone: 216 359-9000
Fax: –

CEO: –
CFO: Kenneth L Hignett
HR: –
FYE: March 3/
Type: Public

Fried chicken rules the roost at this restaurant company. Morgan's Foods is a leading operator of fast food restaurants franchised from YUM! Brands with nearly 100 locations in six states. Most of the company's estate more than 70 restaurants consists of KFC fried chicken outlets. Morgan's Foods also operates Taco Bell units and about 20 co-branded locations that combine two YUM! concepts (KFC Taco Bell Pizza Hut and A&W) in one building. Most of the company's eateries are located in Pennsylvania. Chairman and CEO Leonard Stein-Sapir owns more than 25% of the company.

	Annual Growth	03/09*	02/10	02/11	02/12*	03/13
Sales ($ mil.)	(1.6%)	92.5	90.5	89.9	82.2	86.9
Net income ($ mil.)	–	(1.4)	0.4	(1.0)	(1.7)	(0.1)
Market value ($ mil.)	–	0.0	0.0	0.0	2.6	5.1
Employees	(10.2%)	2,294	1,981	1,722	1,679	1,495

*Fiscal year change

MORGANS HOTEL GROUP CO
NMS: MHGC

475 Tenth Avenue
New York, NY 10018
Phone: 212 277-4100
Fax: –
Web: www.morganshotelgroup.com

CEO: Sam Nazarian
CFO: Richard T Szymanski
HR: –
FYE: December 31
Type: Public

Morgans Hotel Group (MHG) is part of a growing trend of staying in boutiques rather than shopping in them. The company owns (wholly or partially) and/or manages more than a dozen luxury boutique hotels in high profile markets. MHG also manages hotels in Isla Verde Puerto Rico and Playa del Carmen Mexico. The design of each location reflects its environs and all feature upscale restaurants and bars. Hotel brands include Delano Clift Hudson Mondrian and Royalton while restaurant and bar brands consist of Asia de Cuba and Skybar among others. The company developed its first property Morgans on Madison Avenue in New York in 1984.

	Annual Growth	12/10	12/11	12/12	12/13	12/14
Sales ($ mil.)	(0.1%)	236.4	207.3	189.9	236.5	235.0
Net income ($ mil.)	–	(81.4)	(85.4)	(55.7)	(44.2)	(50.7)
Market value ($ mil.)	(3.6%)	311.8	202.8	190.5	279.5	269.5
Employees	(13.3%)	4,600	4,500	5,000	4,400	2,600

MORNINGSTAR INC
NMS: MORN

22 West Washington Street
Chicago, IL 60602
Phone: 312 696-6000
Fax: –
Web: www.morningstar.com

CEO: Kunal Kapoor
CFO: Jason Dubinsky
HR: Bevin Desmond
FYE: December 31
Type: Public

Morningstar offers investment management services and research to individual professional and institutional investors via software tools and cloud technology platforms. The company provides information on investment products (including stocks and mutual funds) and real-time global market data on equities indexes futures options and commodities. Its Morningstar Style Box?which provides a visual summary of a mutual fund's underlying investment style?and Morningstar Ratings?which rate past performance based on risk- and cost-adjusted returns?have become fixtures of the investment landscape. The United States is the company's largest market; it provides around three-fourths of its revenue.

	Annual Growth	12/14	12/15	12/16	12/17	12/18
Sales ($ mil.)	7.6%	760.1	788.8	798.6	911.7	1,019.9
Net income ($ mil.)	23.6%	78.3	132.6	161.0	136.9	183.0
Market value ($ mil.)	14.1%	2,758.2	3,427.4	3,135.4	4,133.3	4,681.8
Employees	9.6%	3,760	3,930	4,595	4,920	5,416

MORO CORP.
NBB: MRCR

994 Old Eagle School Road, Suite 1000
Wayne, PA 19087
Phone: 484 367-0300
Fax: 484 667-9915
Web: www.morocorp.com

CEO: –
CFO: –
HR: –
FYE: December 31
Type: Public

The Moro Corporation is an industrial holding company that owns multiple construction businesses that provide a range of materials and services for the commercial construction industry. Its J.M. Ahle J&J Sheet Metal and Whaling City Iron subsidiaries fabricate and distribute sheet metal products and reinforcing and structural steel in addition to other construction accessories. Titchener Iron Works specializes in architectural and ornamental metal. Its Rado Enterprises and Appolo Heating units provide plumbing and HVAC services while Rondout Electric provides electrical contracting services.

	Annual Growth	12/14	12/15	12/16	12/17	12/18
Sales ($ mil.)	(6.4%)	71.3	58.9	59.9	59.2	54.7
Net income ($ mil.)	–	(0.7)	0.1	0.8	1.0	0.8
Market value ($ mil.)	14.5%	3.9	2.4	2.8	5.4	6.7
Employees	–	–	–	–	–	–

MOROSO PERFORMANCE PRODUCTS INC.

80 Carter Dr.
Guilford CT 06437-2116
Phone: 203-453-6571
Fax: 203-453-6906
Web: www.moroso.com

CEO: –
CFO: –
HR: –
FYE: September 30
Type: Private

Need more horsepower? Need more chrome bling under the hood? You may need more Moroso. Moroso Performance Products makes a wide range of automotive parts for motorsport racing and street-legal car enthusiasts. The company's lineup includes air cleaners chassis and suspension equipment fuel system equipment ignition wire and ignition components oil pans and oiling systems and valve covers. Moroso sells its products through independent distributors. The company was founded in 1968 by Dick Moroso featured by Hot Rod magazine as one of the 100 most influential people in the history of drag racing. His son Rick Moroso leads the company.

MORRIS BUSINESS DEVELOPMENT CO
NBB: MBDE

220 Nice Lane #108
Newport Beach, CA 92663
Phone: 949 444-9090
Fax: –
Web: www.morrisbdc.com

CEO: –
CFO: George Morris
HR: –
FYE: March 31
Type: Public

Morris Business Development hopes to get more out of life as an investment firm. The company formerly Electronic Media Central previously provided CD and DVD replication duplication and packaging services. However in 2007 the firm changed its name to Morris Business Development and became a managed investment company providing early stage capital strategic guidance and operational support to other businesses.

	Annual Growth	03/10	03/11	03/12	03/13	03/14
Sales ($ mil.)	11.5%	0.0	0.0	0.0	0.0	0.0
Net income ($ mil.)	–	(0.0)	(0.0)	(0.0)	(0.0)	(0.0)
Market value ($ mil.)	17.2%	0.9	0.3	0.4	0.9	1.7
Employees	–	–	–	1	1	–

MORRIS HOSPITAL

150 W HIGH ST
MORRIS, IL 604501497
Phone: 815-942-2932
Fax: –
Web: www.morrishospital.org

CEO: Mark Steadham
CFO: –
HR: –
FYE: December 31
Type: Private

Feeling a little green in Grundy? Morris Hospital & Healthcare Centers will fix you right up! The system operates the 90 bed Morris Hospital as well as a handful of primary care physician practices and eight health care centers (the Braidwood Channahon Dwight Gardner Marseilles Minooka Morris and Newark Healthcare Centers) scattered throughout Grundy and four neighboring counties in northwest Illinois. Specialized services at Morris Hospital include neurology oncology pediatrics rehabilitation pain management and occupational health. It has a level II trauma center and a level II obstetrical unit. Not-for-profit Morris Hospital employs some 200 physicians across most medical specialties.

	Annual Growth	12/12	12/13	12/15	12/16	12/17
Sales ($ mil.)	8.8%	–	119.4	153.6	157.1	167.1
Net income ($ mil.)	6.0%	–	8.0	11.8	9.8	10.1
Market value ($ mil.)	–	–	–	–	–	–
Employees	–	–	–	–	–	525

MORRIS PUBLISHING GROUP LLC

725 Broad St.
Augusta GA 30901
Phone: 706-724-0851
Fax: 816-325-7012
Web: www.ci.independence.mo.us

CEO: William S Morris IV
CFO: Delinda Fogel
HR: –
FYE: December 31
Type: Subsidiary

No news would be bad news for Morris Publishing Group. The newspaper company has a portfolio of about a dozen daily newspapers serving small and midsized markets. Papers include The Augusta Chronicle (Georgia) The Florida Times-Union (Jacksonville) and The Topeka Capital-Journal (Kansas). The company also publishes several non-daily papers shoppers and regional interest magazines. Morris Publishing is controlled by the family of chairman William Morris through their Shivers Trading & Operating Company. The Morris family also owns affiliate Morris Communications which has book publishing outdoor advertising and radio broadcasting operations. Morris Publishing emerged from bankruptcy in 2010.

MORROW-MEADOWS CORPORATION

231 BENTON CT
CITY OF INDUSTRY, CA 91789-5213
Phone: 909-598-7700
Fax: –
Web: www.morrow-meadows.com

CEO: –
CFO: Tim Langley
HR: –
FYE: October 31
Type: Private

Today and tomorrow Morrow-Meadows Corp. provides electrical contracting services including work on data communications and power distribution systems for commercial and industrial facilities in the western US primarily in California and Oregon. Its divisions include Oregon-based Cherry City Electric and Morrow-Meadows Corp. Northern California. The company provides project development design engineering and construction services on a range of projects such as shopping malls office buildings medical centers hotels parking garages theme parks and water treatment plants. The company counts among its customers Disney Intel Stanford University Hewlett-Packard and Kaiser Permanente.

	Annual Growth	10/0-1	10/00	10/01	10/04	10/11
Sales ($ mil.)	6.4%	–	158.5	201.3	177.5	312.1
Net income ($ mil.)	–	–	4.0	4.9	1.0	0.0
Market value ($ mil.)	–	–	–	–	–	–
Employees	–	–	–	–	–	1,200

MORSE OPERATIONS, INC.

2850 S FEDERAL HWY
DELRAY BEACH, FL 334833216
Phone: 561-276-5000
Fax: –
Web: www.edmorsesawgrass.com

CEO: Dennis M Macinnes
CFO: Carmine Colella
HR: –
FYE: December 31
Type: Private

Morse Operations (dba Ed Morse Automotive Group) has been selling cars and trucks long enough to know the code of the road. It owns about a dozen new car dealerships across Florida most of them operating under the Ed Morse name. Dealerships house more than 15 franchises and 10 domestic and import car brands including Cadillac Fiat Chevrolet Buick GMC Scion Honda Mazda and Toyota. The company's Bayview Cadillac in Fort Lauderdale is one of the world's largest volume sellers of Cadillacs. Morse Operations also sells used cars provides parts and service and operates a fleet sales division. Founder and auto magnate the late Ed Morse entered the automobile business in 1946 with a 20-car rental fleet.

	Annual Growth	12/14	12/15	12/16	12/17	12/18
Sales ($ mil.)	(8.2%)	–	–	1,334.8	1,019.2	1,125.5
Net income ($ mil.)	–	–	–	9.4	4.4	(0.7)
Market value ($ mil.)	–	–	–	–	–	–
Employees	–	–	–	–	–	925

MORTON'S RESTAURANT GROUP INC.

NYSE: MRT

1510 W. Loop South
Houston TX 77027
Phone: 713-850-1010
Fax: 800-552-6379
Web: www.mortons.com

CEO: Christopher Artinian
CFO: Ronald M Dinella
HR: –
FYE: December 31
Type: Public

Morton's Restaurant Group offers eateries with an aura the Rat Pack would have loved. The company operates about 65 upscale Morton's The Steakhouse locations that serve steak lobster and veal in an upscale setting featuring dark wood interiors and background music by Sinatra. In addition to fine food the chain is well-known for offering an extensive wine list and providing quality service. The restaurants are found in about 25 states and a handful of international markets. Morton's also operates an upscale Italian restaurant concept called Trevi within the Caesars Palace resort complex in Las Vegas. Landry's owner Tilman Fertitta formed Fertitta Morton's Restaurants Inc. to acquire Morton's in early 2012.

MOSAIC

4980 S 118TH ST
OMAHA, NE 681372200
Phone: 402-896-3884
Fax: –

CEO: –
CFO: Cindy Schroeder
HR: Paula Burton
FYE: June 30
Type: Private

Mosaic creates color in the lives of the disadvantaged. The not-for-profit organization provides individualized support and advocacy services living facilities education and employment for people with disabilities. The Christian organization serves some 3500 clients through 40 agencies across the US as well as select international locations. Services include case management foster care vocational training and supervised living arrangements. Mosaic also offers senior independent living services and support at select facilities. The organization is affiliated with the Evangelical Lutheran Church in America.

	Annual Growth	06/14	06/15	06/16	06/17	06/18
Sales ($ mil.)	(0.6%)	–	240.8	242.7	238.4	236.4
Net income ($ mil.)	241.7%	–	0.1	2.5	2.3	3.9
Market value ($ mil.)	–	–	–	–	–	–
Employees	–	–	–	–	–	5,000

MOSAIC CO (THE)   NYS: MOS

101 East Kennedy Blvd, Suite 2500   CEO: James (Joc) O'Rourke
Tampa, FL 33602   CFO: Richard L. (Rich) Mack
Phone: 918 918-8270   HR: Kerrie Campbell
Fax: 763 577-2990   FYE: December 31
Web: www.mosaicco.com   Type: Public

Big pieces of the global agricultural chemical industry come together to form The Mosaic Co. It ranks as one of the world's largest producers of phosphate and potash which are used for crop nutrition and as input to animal feed. In North America Mosaic accounts for about 75% of annual phosphate production and about 40% of potash production. In the rest of the world the company holds significant market share about 15% of phosphate and 15% of potash production. The raw materials of its products are mined from locations in Canada and the US. About 70% of Mosaic's sales are from international customers.

	Annual Growth	12/14	12/15	12/16	12/17	12/18
Sales ($ mil.)	1.4%	9,055.8	8,895.3	7,162.8	7,409.4	9,587.3
Net income ($ mil.)	(17.8%)	1,028.6	1,000.4	297.8	(107.2)	470.0
Market value ($ mil.)	(10.6%)	17,596.7	10,635.1	11,305.8	9,891.2	11,259.6
Employees	9.1%	9,100	8,900	8,700	8,500	12,900

MOSAIC LIFE CARE

5325 FARAON ST   CEO: Mark Laney
SAINT JOSEPH, MO 645063488   CFO: –
Phone: 816-271-6000   HR: –
Fax: –   FYE: June 30
Web: www.mymosaiclifecare.org   Type: Private

Heartland Regional Medical Center strives for healthy hearts minds and bodies in the US heartland. The acute care hospital a subsidiary of Heartland Health provides medical services to residents of St. Joseph Missouri and some 20 surrounding counties in northwest Missouri southeast Nebraska and northeast Kansas. Heartland Regional Medical Center encompasses specialty centers for trauma and long-term care acute rehabilitation cancer heart disease and birthing. As part of the services provided by the medical center Heartland Regional Medical Center offers services such as arthritis pain and wound treatments as well as home health and hospice care.

	Annual Growth	06/14	06/15	06/16	06/17	06/18
Sales ($ mil.)	4.3%	–	563.2	562.9	606.0	639.1
Net income ($ mil.)	46.0%	–	20.7	(5.5)	26.9	64.4
Market value ($ mil.)	–	–	–	–	–	–
Employees	–	–	–	–	–	2,600

MOSYS INC   NAS: MOSY

2309 Bering Drive   CEO: Leonard C. (Len) Perham
San Jose, CA 95131   CFO: James W. (Jim) Sullivan
Phone: 408 418-7500   HR: –
Fax: –   FYE: December 31
Web: www.mosys.com   Type: Public

MoSys (formerly Monolithic System Technology) works to keep its licensing mojo workin.' The company knows it can't match the Goliaths of the memory market so rather than spend a lot of time and money on development it focuses on licensing the designs of its embedded memory chips for the high-speed networking communications storage and computing markets. The fabless semiconductor company licenses its 1T-SRAM technology to manufacturers which in turn make the chips and embed them in communications and consumer electronics devices. The 1T-SRAM products are sold under the Bandwidth Engine brand. Other products are in the company's LineSpeed line integrated circuits.

	Annual Growth	12/14	12/15	12/16	12/17	12/18
Sales ($ mil.)	32.5%	5.4	4.4	6.0	8.8	16.6
Net income ($ mil.)	–	(32.7)	(31.5)	(32.0)	(10.7)	(11.4)
Market value ($ mil.)	(43.8%)	4.0	2.3	0.5	2.4	0.4
Employees	(34.8%)	116	104	63	24	21

MOTHER MURPHY'S LABORATORIES, INC.

2826 S ELM EUGENE ST   CEO: –
GREENSBORO, NC 274064435   CFO: Timothy Hansen
Phone: 336-273-1737   HR: Melissa Rumbley
Fax: –   FYE: October 31
Web: www.mothermurphys.com   Type: Private

This Mother Murphy does her cooking in an industrial-strength kitchen. Mother Murphy's Laboratories develops and manufactures dry and liquid natural and synthetic flavorings and extracts for the bakery beverage dairy tobacco confectionery pharmaceutical tobacco pet product confectionery and snack food industries. The company specializes in vanilla and vanilla variations offering a wide array of product types of everyone's favorite baking flavoring. Family owned and operated Mother Murphy's Laboratories was founded in 1945 by Kermit Murphy Sr. who named the company after his mother. Murphy died in 2008.

	Annual Growth	10/14	10/15	10/16	10/17	10/18
Sales ($ mil.)	33.2%	–	44.6	50.9	63.9	105.3
Net income ($ mil.)	83.5%	–	7.4	11.6	17.2	46.0
Market value ($ mil.)	–	–	–	–	–	–
Employees	–	–	–	–	–	120

MOTION INDUSTRIES INC.

1605 Alton Rd.   CEO: Timothy P Breen
Birmingham AL 35201   CFO: –
Phone: 205-956-1122   HR: –
Fax: 713-237-3777   FYE: December 31
Web: www.iwilson.com   Type: Subsidiary

Power transmission products may not be on anyone's Christmas list but Santa's workshop couldn't groove without the parts that Motion Industries sells. A subsidiary of Genuine Parts the company drives Genuine's industrial parts business segment by distributing a slew of bearings hoses material handling and linear motion products. Its short list of offerings includes electrical (motors and drives) and mechanical (belts clutches and chains) as well as fluid (pneumatic and hydraulic) power transmission replacement parts supplied by big brands like Bosch Rexroth Eaton NSK and Timken. Motion Industries sells 4.3 million parts and serves its customers through about 550 locations across North America.

MOTORCAR PARTS OF AMERICA INC   NMS: MPAA

2929 California Street   CEO: Selwyn Joffe
Torrance, CA 90503   CFO: David Lee
Phone: 310 212-7910   HR: –
Fax: –   FYE: March 31
Web: www.motorcarparts.com   Type: Public

Motorcar Parts of America (MPA) is always ready for a fresh start. The company manufactures remanufactures and distributes alternators and starters for cars and all-weight trucks. MPA sells the remanufactured products to retailers and warehouse distributors which sell to do-it-yourself (DIY) consumers and to repair shops (DIFM or do-it-for-me) primarily in the US and Canada. Some of its top customers include retail chains AutoZone (almost 50% of sales) Advance Genuine Parts Pep Boys and O'Reilly Automotive. Although most of MPA's products are sold under its customers' private labels (about 90%) the company does market alternators and starters with its Quality-Built Reliance and Xtreme brands.

	Annual Growth	03/15	03/16	03/17	03/18	03/19
Sales ($ mil.)	11.9%	301.7	369.0	421.3	428.1	472.8
Net income ($ mil.)	–	11.5	10.6	37.6	16.3	(7.8)
Market value ($ mil.)	(9.2%)	522.9	714.7	578.3	403.3	355.1
Employees	13.1%	2,362	2,663	2,817	2,996	3,868

MOTOROLA MOBILITY HOLDINGS INC.   NYSE: MMI

600 N. US Hwy. 45   CEO: Dennis Woodside
Libertyville IL 60048   CFO: Vanessa Wittman
Phone: 847-523-5000   HR: –
Fax: 515-296-3520   FYE: December 31
Web: www.linkp.com   Type: Public

Motorola Mobility has a rich wireless heritage thanks to former parent Motorola Solutions (formerly Motorola). An early developer of mobile device technology Motorola Solutions spun off its handset business into the stand-alone company known as Motorola Mobility in early 2011. Motorola Mobility's products include handsets and smartphones tablets wireless accessories set-top boxes and video distribution products. Top customers include telecom carriers Verizon and Sprint. Though it has operations in some 40 countries more than half of sales comes from the US. Google acquired Motorola Mobility for about $12.5 billion in 2012.

MOTOROLA SOLUTIONS INC   NYS: MSI

500 West Monroe Street   CEO: Gregory Q. (Greg) Brown
Chicago, IL 60661   CFO: Gino A. Bonanotte
Phone: 847 576-5000   HR: –
Fax: 847 576-3477   FYE: December 31
Web: www.motorolasolutions.com   Type: Public

Do you copy? and "Roger that" might be snippets of conversation heard over two-way radios and other devices made by Motorola Solutions. The company's radios and wireless broadband products are used by government public safety and first-responder agencies for communications and personnel deployment. Commercial and industrial customers use products from Motorola to stay in touch with mobile work forces. Besides two-way radios the company makes vehicle-mounted radios body cameras headsets and other devices and develops software systems to connect them. Some 60% of sales are to customers in the US. Motorola Solutions goes back to the late 1920s when the company made radios for police cars.

	Annual Growth	12/14	12/15	12/16	12/17	12/18
Sales ($ mil.)	5.7%	5,881.0	5,695.0	6,038.0	6,380.0	7,343.0
Net income ($ mil.)	(7.1%)	1,299.0	610.0	560.0	(155.0)	966.0
Market value ($ mil.)	14.4%	10,967.6	11,191.6	13,552.5	14,770.6	18,809.0
Employees	1.6%	15,000	14,000	14,000	15,000	16,000

MOTORSPORTS AUTHENTICS LLC

6301 Performance Dr.   CEO: –
Concord NC 28027   CFO: –
Phone: 704-454-4000   HR: –
Fax: 704-454-4006   FYE: September 30
Web: www.motorsports-authentics.com   Type: Joint Venture

Motorsports Authentics is in a racy business. The company designs and markets collector-quality die-cast miniature replicas of NASCAR and other racing vehicles. The firm also sells licensed motorsports apparel (T-shirts hats and jackets) and souvenirs and manages race car drivers' fan clubs. Its merchandise is sold in about 45 countries through some 10000 retailers 30 trackside stores and its goracing.com website. Through an exclusive agreement with QVC Motorsports Authentics sells directly to its collectors club. The company changed its name from Action Performance when it was acquired by 50:50 partners International Speedway and Speedway Motorsports for $245 million.

MOUNT CARMEL HEALTH SYSTEM

6150 E BROAD ST   CEO: Michael Englehart
COLUMBUS, OH 432131574   CFO: –
Phone: 614-234-6000   HR: –
Fax: –   FYE: June 30
Web: www.mountcarmelhealth.com   Type: Private

Mount Carmel Health System cares for the sick in the greater Columbus area and central Ohio. The health care system boasts 1500 physicians at three general hospitals and a specialty surgical hospital offering a comprehensive range of medical and surgical services including cardiovascular care. Mount Carmel Health also operates outpatient centers including primary care and specialty physicians' practices and it offers home health care services. The hospital group is part of Trinity Health one of the largest Catholic health care systems in the US.

	Annual Growth	06/12	06/13	06/14	06/15	06/18
Sales ($ mil.)	9.8%	–	1,195.8	1,223.6	1,267.3	1,911.4
Net income ($ mil.)	11.9%	–	89.4	94.4	131.3	157.2
Market value ($ mil.)	–	–	–	–	–	–
Employees	–	–	–	–	–	8,000

MOUNT CLEMENS REGIONAL MEDICAL CENTER

1000 HARRINGTON ST   CEO: Thomas M Brisse
MOUNT CLEMENS, MI 480432920   CFO: –
Phone: 586-493-8000   HR: –
Fax: –   FYE: September 30
Web: www.mclaren.org   Type: Private

Mount Clemens Regional Medical Center (doing business as McLaren Medical Center-Macomb) is an general acute care hospital serving the Macomb County area of suburban Detroit. With about 290 beds the hospital offers such specialties as cardiac and cancer care family practice services home and hospice care and emergency care. The McLaren Health Care-controlled company also operates three prompt care centers in nearby townships as well as a wound treatment clinic. Of the more than 420 physicians on staff at the hospital more than 100 are family medicine and internal medicine specialists who provide primary care.

	Annual Growth	09/08	09/09	09/13	09/14	09/15
Sales ($ mil.)	1.6%	–	277.8	303.6	312.2	305.8
Net income ($ mil.)	(4.9%)	–	11.7	18.6	18.8	8.6
Market value ($ mil.)	–	–	–	–	–	–
Employees	–	–	–	–	–	2,249

MOUNT SINAI MEDICAL CENTER OF FLORIDA, INC.

4300 ALTON RD   CEO: Steven D. Sonenreich
MIAMI BEACH, FL 331402948   CFO: Alex Mendez
Phone: 305-674-2121   HR: Jennifer Foreman
Fax: –   FYE: December 31
Web: www.msmc.com   Type: Private

Mount Sinai Medical Center of Florida is a not-for-profit acute care teaching hospital providing a wide range of health services to residents of South Florida. The medical center which boasts more than 670 beds provides general medical and surgical care as well as specialty care in cardiology (Mount Sinai Heart Institute) neuroscience oncology orthopedics pulmonology radiology and other fields. It also participates in clinical research studies and drug trials with an emphasis on cancer heart and lung conditions It maintains an inpatient behavioral health unit and houses the Wien Center for Alzheimer's disease and memory disorders diagnosis and research the largest such facillility in the region.

	Annual Growth	12/12	12/13	12/14	12/15	12/16
Sales ($ mil.)	(1.4%)	–	584.7	531.0	533.0	560.3
Net income ($ mil.)	(22.9%)	–	42.8	17.1	38.6	19.7
Market value ($ mil.)	–	–	–	–	–	–
Employees	–	–	–	–	–	3,225

MOUNTAIN VALLEY SPRING COMPANY LLC

150 Central Ave.
Hot Springs National Park AR 7
Phone: 501-624-1635
Fax: 501-623-5135
Web: www.mountainvalleyspring.com

CEO: Jim Waldeck
CFO: –
HR: –
FYE: December 31
Type: Private

In a world of bottled water hope springs eternal for Mountain Valley Spring. Through its Mountain Valley Spring Water division the company bottles and sells natural spring water collected from three neighboring natural springs via such brands as Mountain Valley Spring Water Mountain Valley Sparkling Water and Diamond Spring Water. The company uses both glass and PET (polyethylene terephthalate resin) bottles. Its Veriplas division makes and sells preforms and finished PET bottles ranging in sizes from 10 ounces to 4 gallons. The company sells its bottled water through grocers such as H-E-B Sprouts Farmers Market and Whole Foods Market. Mountain Valley Spring filed to go public in late 2011.

MOUNTAIRE CORPORATION

204 E 4th St
North Little Rock AR 72114-540
Phone: 501-372-6524
Fax: 501-372-3972
Web: mountaire.com

CEO: –
CFO: Dabbs Cavin
HR: –
FYE: October 31
Type: Private

These birds breathe the mountain air: Mountaire is a leading supplier of private-label chicken and value-added chicken products to supermarkets and foodservice customers worldwide. The company's chicken production business (Mountaire Farms) maintains breeding and chicken-processing facilities in Delaware Maryland and North Carolina. The company sells its products under names such as Black Label (aimed at the foodservice market) Blue Label (wholesale) and Bo-San Roasters (Asian market in the US). Mountaire Grain and Feed produces poultry feeds and operates grain elevators for corn soybeans wheat and barley. Mountaire was founded in 1971 but the company's roots in the feed business date back to 1914.

MOVADO GROUP, INC.

NYS: MOV

650 From Road, Ste. 375
Paramus, NJ 07652-3556
Phone: 201 267-8000
Fax: –
Web: www.movadogroup.com

CEO: Efraim Grinberg
CFO: Sallie A. DeMarsilis
HR: –
FYE: January 31
Type: Public

Movado Group knows that time is of the essence. Its watch brands — including namesake Movado Concord and Ebel as well as the licensed Coach Tommy Hilfiger Hugo Boss Lacoste and Juicy Couture lines — are sold worldwide. While its watches range in price from about $75 to $10000 for luxury designs the watch maker is focused on the middle market. Movado sells its watches to major jewelry store and department store chains (including Nordstrom and Macy's) as well as to independent jewelers (such as Zale Corp.). The company operates a growing chain of more than 35 outlet stores across the US. The family of the late Gerry Grinberg who founded Movado controls about 70% of the company's voting power.

	Annual Growth	01/15	01/16	01/17	01/18	01/19
Sales ($ mil.)	3.7%	587.0	594.9	552.8	568.0	679.6
Net income ($ mil.)	4.4%	51.8	45.1	35.1	(15.2)	61.6
Market value ($ mil.)	7.4%	553.2	591.6	625.0	704.4	735.5
Employees	0.7%	1,110	1,100	1,100	1,000	1,140

MOVE INC

NMS: MOVE

10 Almaden Blvd, Suite 800
San Jose, CA 95113
Phone: 408 558-7100
Fax: –
Web: www.move.com

CEO: Steven H Berkowitz
CFO: Rachel C Glaser
HR: –
FYE: December 31
Type: Public

For Move real estate is more about location on the Web. The company provides real estate and move-related information and services through its flagship Move.com REALTOR.com and Moving.com websites. Its REALTOR.com lists some 4 million homes for sale. In addition its Top Producer produce is a customer relationship management application for real estate agents. Revenue primarily comes from advertising (cost-per-click text link and display ads) and software sales. The company attracts visitors via agreements with partners such as the National Association of Realtors (REALTOR.com is the official website of NAR). Move is a portfolio company of private equity firm Elevation Partners.

	Annual Growth	12/08	12/09	12/10	12/11	12/12
Sales ($ mil.)	(4.8%)	242.1	212.0	197.5	191.7	199.2
Net income ($ mil.)	–	(27.6)	(6.9)	(15.5)	7.3	5.6
Market value ($ mil.)	47.5%	63.0	65.3	101.1	248.7	297.9
Employees	(5.5%)	1,181	951	966	889	943

MOZILLA FOUNDATION

331 E EVELYN AVE
MOUNTAIN VIEW, CA 940411550
Phone: 650-903-0800
Fax: –
Web: www.mozilla.org

CEO: Mark Surman
CFO: –
HR: –
FYE: December 31
Type: Private

Microsoft's Internet Explorer (IE) may have subdued Netscape in the "browser wars" of the 1990s but Mozilla's Firefox rose from the ashes with renewed vigor. Firefox has clawed market share away from IE over the years (now at about 25%) only to now be harassed itself by the meteoric rise of Google's Chrome being overtaken by the browser in usage share at the end of 2011. The Mozilla Foundation was created in 2003 to carry on the open-source development work of the mozilla.org project (spun off from Netscape in 1998). For-profit subsidiary Mozilla Corporation (spun off in 2005) oversees product development marketing and distribution.

	Annual Growth	12/11	12/12	12/13	12/14	12/15
Sales ($ mil.)	2081.7%	–	–	–	19.3	421.3
Net income ($ mil.)	1553.4%	–	–	–	3.5	57.1
Market value ($ mil.)	–	–	–	–	–	–
Employees	–	–	–	–	–	588

MPHASE TECHNOLOGIES INC.

NBB: XDSL

587 CONNECTICUT AVE.
NORWALK, CT 06854-1711
Phone: 203 838-2741
Fax: –
Web: www.mphasetech.com

CEO: Anshu Bhatnagar
CFO: Christopher Cutchen
HR: –
FYE: June 30
Type: Public

mPhase Technologies has lots of plans for potential profits. mPhase a development-stage company designed broadband communications equipment that lets telephone companies provide television over DSL lines. It has since shifted its development to middleware that allows telephone companies to deliver voice Internet and television service over Internet protocol (IP). It plans to market its systems to phone companies in areas with relatively little multi-channel television access such as international markets and the rural US. It is also developing power cells that utilize nanotechnology through its AlwaysReady subsidiary.

	Annual Growth	06/11	06/12	06/13	06/14	06/15
Sales ($ mil.)	119.5%	0.0	0.0	0.0	0.6	1.1
Net income ($ mil.)	–	(0.5)	(8.8)	(0.3)	(5.9)	(1.1)
Market value ($ mil.)	–	0.0	0.0	0.0	0.0	0.0
Employees	38.4%	6	5	5	6	22

MPLX LP
NYS: MPLX

200 E. Hardin Street
Findlay, OH 45840
Phone: 419 421-2414
Fax: –
Web: www.mplx.com

CEO: Gary R Heminger
CFO: –
HR: –
FYE: December 31
Type: Public

MPLX is a diversified master limited partnership formed in 2012 by Marathon Petroleum Corporation (MPC) to own operate develop and acquire midstream energy infrastructure assets. It gathers processes and transports natural gas; gathers transports fractionates stores and markets natural gas liquids (NGLs); and transports stores and distributes crude oil and refined petroleum products. Headquartered in Findlay Ohio MPLX's assets consist of a network of crude oil and products pipeline assets located in the Midwest and Gulf Coast regions of the United States. It owns and operates light-product terminals an inland marine business storage caverns crude oil and product storage facilities (tank farms) a barge dock facility and gathering and processing assets. MPLX went public in 2012.

	Annual Growth	12/14	12/15	12/16	12/17	12/18
Sales ($ mil.)	85.0%	548.3	703.0	2,590.0	3,867.0	6,425.0
Net income ($ mil.)	96.8%	121.3	156.0	256.0	830.0	1,818.0
Market value ($ mil.)	(19.9%)	58,357.6	31,231.5	27,491.4	28,166.4	24,060.9
Employees	–	–	–	–	–	–

MPW INDUSTRIAL SERVICES GROUP INC.

9711 Lancaster Rd. SE
Hebron OH 43025
Phone: 800-827-8790
Fax: 315-685-3361
Web: www.welchallyn.com

CEO: Monte R Black
CFO: Sarah D Pemberton
HR: Heather Paul
FYE: June 30
Type: Private

MPW Industrial Services Group knows it takes more than a bar of soap to clean a chemical plant. MPW provides industrial-strength cleaning services for the foul deposits and caustic corrosion created by such processing facilities as well as those in the automotive energy manufacturing and refining industries. The company offers facility maintenance container cleaning and water treatment services; procedures include dry and wet vacuuming power washing water blasting and cryojetic (dry ice) cleaning. Its water unit provides deionization filtration and reverse osmosis for pollution control and chemical cleaning applications. MPW has a network of 40 offices in the US and also serves customers in Canada.

MRC GLOBAL INC
NYS: MRC

Fulbright Tower, 1301 McKinney Street, Suite 2300
Houston, TX 77010
Phone: 877 294-7574
Fax: –
Web: www.mrcglobal.com

CEO: Andrew R. (Andy) Lane
CFO: James E. (Jim) Braun
HR: –
FYE: December 31
Type: Public

MRC Global Inc. is the world's top distributor of pipes valves fittings (PVF) and other infrastructure products catering primarily to the energy industry. Its 200000 PVF and other oilfield products help oil and gas companies in the construction and maintenance of complex equipment that are used in extreme operating conditions (pressure temperature corrosion). MRC Global's customers include oil exploration and production companies natural gas utilities crude oil refiners and petrochemical manufacturers. It also provides services likes multiple deliveries and zone store management. With 300 service locations the company serves some 15000 customers around the world though most of its sales comes from the US.

	Annual Growth	12/14	12/15	12/16	12/17	12/18
Sales ($ mil.)	(8.4%)	5,933.2	4,528.6	3,041.0	3,646.0	4,172.0
Net income ($ mil.)	(15.3%)	144.1	(331.6)	(83.0)	50.0	74.0
Market value ($ mil.)	(5.2%)	1,296.9	1,104.3	1,734.4	1,448.5	1,047.0
Employees	(7.4%)	4,900	4,100	3,500	3,450	3,600

MRI INTERVENTIONS INC
NAS: MRIC

5 Musick
Irvine, CA 92618
Phone: 949 900-6833
Fax: –
Web: www.mriinterventions.com

CEO: Francis P Grillo
CFO: Harold A Hurwitz
HR: –
FYE: December 31
Type: Public

SurgiVision designs products with surgical focus. A medical devices company SurgiVision develops imaging technologies and precision instruments (i.e. needles that deliver radiation) designed for surgeons performing minimally invasive procedures by way of MRI (magnetic resonance imaging) scanners. The company received FDA approval for its first commercial product the ClearPoint system for use in neurological procedures in 2010. It also has candidates in earlier stages of development including its ClearTrace and SafeLead products which are designed for cardiac procedures. SurgiVision was established in 1998; it filed to go public through an IPO in 2009.

	Annual Growth	12/14	12/15	12/16	12/17	12/18
Sales ($ mil.)	19.5%	3.6	4.6	5.7	7.4	7.4
Net income ($ mil.)	–	(4.5)	(8.4)	(8.1)	(7.2)	(6.2)
Market value ($ mil.)	17.1%	9.2	4.2	37.5	30.3	17.3
Employees	0.7%	37	33	33	15	38

MRIGLOBAL

425 VOLKER BLVD
KANSAS CITY, MO 641102241
Phone: 816-753-7600
Fax: –
Web: www.mriglobal.org

CEO: Thomas M Sack
CFO: Thomas Fleener
HR: –
FYE: September 30
Type: Private

MRIGlobal provides contract research services for government and private-sector clients in fields such as agricultural and food safety analytical chemistry biological sciences energy engineering environment health sciences information technology and national defense. The institute operates laboratories and agricultural research centers in Florida Kansas Maryland Missouri North Carolina and Washington DC. MRIGlobal also manages the US Department of Energy's National Renewable Energy Laboratory in Golden Colorado. Work related to biological and chemical defense accounts for most of MRIGlobal's sales. The not-for-profit organization was founded in 1944.

	Annual Growth	06/12	06/13*	09/13	09/14	09/15
Sales ($ mil.)	(57.3%)	–	497.6	–	466.8	90.7
Net income ($ mil.)	–	–	2.0	–	1.6	(4.4)
Market value ($ mil.)	–	–	–	–	–	–
Employees	–	–	–	–	–	2,547

*Fiscal year change

MRV COMMUNICATIONS, INC.
NAS: MRVC

20520 Nordhoff St
Chatsworth, CA 91311
Phone: 818 773-0900
Fax: –
Web: www.mrv.com

CEO: –
CFO: –
HR: –
FYE: December 31
Type: Public

MRV Communications puts the buzz in optical communications. MRV supplies the switching routing Ethernet optical transport and console management equipment used in voice data and video traffic by telecommunications carriers data centers and labs. It also provides network system design services as well as integrated network products and services. It sells to cable operators networking services providers Internet and telecom companies and governments worldwide. About two-thirds of sales are outside the US mostly in Europe.

	Annual Growth	12/11	12/12	12/13	12/14	12/15
Sales ($ mil.)	(24.2%)	266.8	151.7	166.2	172.1	88.2
Net income ($ mil.)	–	–	(6.8)	5.7	(6.8)	(12.2)	(7.2)
Market value ($ mil.)	94.2%	6.0	71.9	74.8	69.3	85.3
Employees	(20.7%)	678	414	420	445	268

MSB FINANCIAL CORP
NMS: MSBF

1902 Long Hill Road
Millington, NJ 07946-0417
Phone: 908 647-4000
Fax: –
Web: www.millingtonsb.com

CEO: –
CFO: –
HR: –
FYE: June 30
Type: Public

MSB Financial Corp. is the holding company for Millington Savings Bank a five-branch bank located in north central New Jersey. Millington Savings Bank offers checking savings money market and CD accounts as well as traditional and Roth IRAs to individuals. For small businesses the bank offers checking accounts and courier service. It does not offer credit cards. More than half of its loan portfolio is made up of residential mortgages while home equity loans account for about 20%. Commercial mortgages construction loans and business and consumer loans round out its portfolio. MSB Financial Corp. was founded in 2004; Millington Savings Bank traces it roots back to 1911 when it was founded as Millington Building and Loan.

	Annual Growth	06/10	06/11	06/12	06/13	06/14
Assets ($ mil.)	(1.0%)	358.7	349.5	347.3	352.6	345.2
Net income ($ mil.)	5.2%	0.8	0.7	0.5	(1.4)	1.0
Market value ($ mil.)	0.6%	39.5	27.4	27.6	36.8	40.5
Employees	1.0%	51	52	53	65	53

MSC INDUSTRIAL DIRECT CO INC
NYS: MSM

75 Maxess Road
Melville, NY 11747
Phone: 516 812-2000
Fax: 516 349-7096
Web: www.mscdirect.com

CEO: Erik Gershwind
CFO: Rustom F. Jilla
HR: –
FYE: August 31
Type: Public

MSC Industrial Direct is more than 75 years old and is one of the largest distributors of metalworking and maintenance repair and overhaul (MRO) products in the US. It distributes fasteners and measuring instruments cutting tools and plumbing supplies to customers in the US Canada and the UK and also offers inventory management and supply chain solutions. MSC Industrial stocks about 1.6 million products from approximately 3000 suppliers. Its customers include a broad range of companies from individual machine shops to Fortune 100 companies as well as the US government.

	Annual Growth	08/15*	09/16	09/17	09/18*	08/19
Sales ($ mil.)	3.7%	2,910.4	2,863.5	2,887.7	3,203.9	3,363.8
Net income ($ mil.)	5.7%	231.3	231.2	231.4	329.2	288.9
Market value ($ mil.)	0.1%	3,724.7	4,095.8	3,819.1	4,720.3	3,734.1
Employees	0.2%	6,642	6,462	6,563	6,657	6,700

*Fiscal year change

MSCI INC
NYS: MSCI

7 World Trade Center, 250 Greenwich Street, 49th Floor
New York, NY 10007
Phone: 212 804-3900
Fax: –
Web: www.msci.com

CEO: Henry A. Fernandez
CFO: Kathleen A. Winters
HR: Michelle Davidson
FYE: December 31
Type: Public

MSCI formerly Morgan Stanley Capital International manages more than 145000 daily equity fixed income and hedge fund indices for use by large asset management firms. MSCI is organized through two business segments. Its Performance and Risk business provides equity indices portfolio risk and performance analytics credit analytics and environmental social and governance (ESG) products under brands such as MSCI RiskMetrics and Barra. Its Governance business provides corporate governance and specialized financial research and analysis. MSCI has about 7500 clients across more than 80 countries.

	Annual Growth	12/14	12/15	12/16	12/17	12/18
Sales ($ mil.)	9.5%	996.7	1,075.0	1,150.7	1,274.2	1,434.0
Net income ($ mil.)	15.6%	284.1	223.6	260.9	304.0	507.9
Market value ($ mil.)	32.8%	3,993.2	6,071.5	6,631.2	10,651.4	12,409.8
Employees	1.6%	2,926	2,926	2,862	3,038	3,112

MSG NETWORK INC
NYS: MSGN

11 Pennsylvania Plaza
New York, NY 10001
Phone: 212 465-6400
Fax: –
Web: www.msgnetworks.com

CEO: David E. Dibble
CFO: Donna M. Coleman
HR: –
FYE: June 30
Type: Public

MSG Networks owns the legendary Madison Square Garden Arena. The company also owns or operates Radio City Music Hall the Chicago Theatre the Beacon Theater and the Forum near Los Angeles. MSG also owns sports teams the New York Knicks of the NBA and the NHL's New York Rangers which operate as part of the company's MSG Sports segment. Its MSG Media unit distributes television programming through cable. The company owns regional sports networks MSG MSG+ and streaming platform MSG Go offering games for basketball's Knicks and New York Liberty and hockey's Rangers New York Islanders New Jersey Devils and Buffalo Sabres.

	Annual Growth	06/15	06/16	06/17	06/18	06/19
Sales ($ mil.)	(18.3%)	1,621.6	658.2	675.4	696.7	720.8
Net income ($ mil.)	(7.5%)	254.7	7.6	167.3	288.9	186.2
Market value ($ mil.)	(29.4%)	6,251.4	1,148.6	1,681.0	1,793.3	1,552.9
Employees	(45.5%)	9,300	1,009	788	790	820

MSGI TECHNOLOGY SOLUTIONS INC.
OTC: MSGI

NASA Ames Research Center Bldg. 19
Moffett Field CA 94035
Phone: 212-605-0245
Fax: 212-605-0222
Web: msgisecurity.com

CEO: J Jeremy Barbera
CFO: –
HR: –
FYE: June 30
Type: Public

MSGI Technology Solutions Solutions (formerly Security Solutions) invests in companies that make equipment and software for security safety and surveillance applications. It typically acquires controlling interests in early-stage early growth technology and software development businesses. Majority-owned Innalogic develops software applications that combine biometric sensor text and/or video data for wireless mobile devices to aid in emergency response. The company's Future Developments America subsidiary makes audio and video electronic surveillance equipment. MSGI Technology Solutions has licensing agreements with Hyundai Syscomm and Apro Media through which it aggregates and configures security systems.

MTGE INVESTMENT CORP
NMS: MTGE

2 Bethesda Metro Center, 12th Floor
Bethesda, MD 20814
Phone: 301 968-9220
Fax: –
Web: www.mtge.com

CEO: Anthony Green
CFO: Peter J Federico
HR: –
FYE: December 31
Type: Public

When reading its name it's not difficult to figure out what MTGE Investment (formerly American Capital Mortgage Investment) does. The newly formed real estate investment trust (REIT) invests in and manages a portfolio of residential mortgage-backed securities mostly fixed-rate pass-through certificates guaranteed by Fannie Mae Freddie Mac or Ginnie Mae. The company which is externally-managed by American Capital MTGE Management also plans to invest in adjustable-rate mortgages (ARMs) and collateralized mortgage obligations (CMOs). American Capital Mortgage was formed and went public in 2011.

	Annual Growth	12/12	12/13	12/14	12/15	12/16
Sales ($ mil.)	(14.2%)	288.1	(11.6)	274.5	93.7	156.3
Net income ($ mil.)	(35.4%)	250.2	(84.5)	159.2	(38.4)	43.7
Market value ($ mil.)	(9.7%)	1,079.5	799.6	862.8	639.3	719.0
Employees				250	270	330	18

MTM TECHNOLOGIES, INC.

4 MANHATTANVILLE RD # 106
PURCHASE, NY 105772119
Phone: 866-383-2867
Fax: –
Web: www.mtm.com

CEO: Marcus Holloway
CFO: Rosemarie Milano
HR: –
FYE: March 31
Type: Private

When it comes to business technology MTM Technologies has all sorts of technological bases covered. The company provides a wide variety of information technology services and products for Global 2000 and midsized companies. Among MTM Technologies' specialties are virtualization mobile computing endpoint management unified communications network infrastructure storage and managed services. The company handles products from a variety of suppliers including Cisco Systems Citrix EMC VMware Microsoft and NetApp. Columbia Partners an investment firm bought MTM in 2015.

	Annual Growth	03/05	03/06	03/07	03/07	03/08
Sales ($ mil.)	(11.7%)	–	–	275.0	275.0	242.7
Net income ($ mil.)	–	–	–	(32.0)	(32.0)	(14.4)
Market value ($ mil.)	–	–	–	–	–	–
Employees	–	–	–	–	–	250

MTR GAMING GROUP, INC.
NMS: MNTG

State route 2 South, P.O. Box 356
Chester, WV 26034
Phone: 304 387-8000
Fax: –
Web: www.mtrgaming.com

CEO: Gary L Carano
CFO: Robert M Jones
HR: –
FYE: December 31
Type: Public

Gamblers looking beyond casino games can climb the summit of MTR Gaming Group. The company operates three regional casino hotels in the US. Its Mountaineer Racetrack and Gaming Resort in Chester West Virginia includes horse racing and wagering in addition to some 2500 slot machines 25 poker tables and approximatelu 60 additional table games. The Mountaineer resort also boasts a hotel and convention center as well as a fitness center a theater and several restaurants. Its Presque Isle Downs & Casino in Erie Pennsylvania also has horse racing and wagering as well as about 2000 slot machines 50 table games and dining options. MTR also owns Scioto Downs the operator of a harness racetrack in Ohio.

	Annual Growth	12/08	12/09	12/10	12/11	12/12
Sales ($ mil.)	1.0%	470.9	444.2	424.9	428.1	490.0
Net income ($ mil.)	–	(17.7)	(22.5)	(5.1)	(50.4)	(5.7)
Market value ($ mil.)	25.5%	46.5	36.0	56.2	51.8	115.5
Employees	(2.7%)	2,900	2,300	2,500	2,600	2,600

MTS SYSTEMS CORP
NMS: MTSC

14000 Technology Drive
Eden Prairie, MN 55344
Phone: 952 937-4000
Fax: –
Web: www.mts.com

CEO: Jeffrey A. (Jeff) Graves
CFO: Brian T. Ross
HR: –
FYE: September 28
Type: Public

In this world nothing is certain but death and taxes — and those things tested by MTS Systems. The company produces testing systems that simulate repeated or harsh conditions to determine mechanical behavior of materials products and structures. Its systems are used worldwide in infrastructure markets from inspecting steel to locomotive rails. MTS caters to auto makers with road simulators while in aerospace its equipment tests aircraft fatigue. Services include maintenance and training. MTS also supplies industrial sensors to increase machine efficiency and safety. International customers generate more than two-thirds of the company's revenue.

	Annual Growth	10/15	10/16*	09/17	09/18	09/19
Sales ($ mil.)	12.2%	563.9	650.1	788.0	778.0	892.5
Net income ($ mil.)	(1.3%)	45.5	27.5	25.1	61.3	43.1
Market value ($ mil.)	(1.1%)	1,104.0	880.3	1,022.2	1,047.0	1,057.0
Employees	9.9%	2,400	3,500	3,500	3,400	3,500

*Fiscal year change

MUELLER (PAUL) CO
NBB: MUEL

1600 West Phelps Street
Springfield, MO 65802
Phone: 417 575-9000
Fax: 417 575-9669
Web: www.paulmueller.com

CEO: David T. Moore
CFO: Kenneth E. Jeffries
HR: –
FYE: December 31
Type: Public

Paul Mueller Company is in the "moo-d" for more than milk. The company manufactures stainless-steel industrial storage tanks and processing equipment and is a world-leading producer of dairy farm equipment such as pasteurizers. Paul Mueller's industrial equipment unit makes processing equipment for brewery food chemical and pharmaceutical applications. Mueller Field Operations the company's field fabrication subsidiary builds storage tanks that are too large to be manufactured and shipped from the factory. Its Mueller Transportation unit delivers the company's products and components. Operating in more than 100 countries Paul Mueller makes about 45% of its sales in international markets.

	Annual Growth	12/14	12/15	12/16	12/17	12/18
Sales ($ mil.)	0.1%	200.7	178.6	168.0	168.0	201.2
Net income ($ mil.)	(21.3%)	6.9	8.6	(2.3)	(2.3)	2.6
Market value ($ mil.)	(15.0%)	57.4	32.3	33.3	46.7	29.9
Employees	(0.2%)	976	954	918	928	967

MUELLER INDUSTRIES INC
NYS: MLI

150 Schilling Boulevard, Suite 100
Collierville, TN 38017
Phone: 901 753-3200
Fax: –
Web: www.muellerindustries.com

CEO: Gregory L. (Greg) Christopher
CFO: Jeffrey A. Martin
HR: –
FYE: December 29
Type: Public

Mueller Industries manufactures copper tubes and fittings bars and rods forgings extrusions pipes and valves. Mueller also resells a myriad of products from brass and plastic plumbing valves to faucets and malleable iron fittings. Its operations are divided among three divisions: Piping Systems Industrial Metals and Climate. The company's products are used in a wide range of applications including plumbing HVAC refrigeration automotive process industry machinery and construction. Most of Muller Industries' sales are generated within the US. The company traces its historical roots back to 1917.

	Annual Growth	12/14	12/15	12/16	12/17	12/18
Sales ($ mil.)	1.5%	2,364.2	2,100.0	2,055.6	2,266.1	2,507.9
Net income ($ mil.)	0.7%	101.6	87.9	99.7	85.6	104.5
Market value ($ mil.)	(9.0%)	1,938.1	1,587.7	2,265.9	2,009.0	1,327.4
Employees	7.5%	3,850	4,104	4,244	4,125	5,134

MUELLER WATER PRODUCTS INC
NYS: MWA

1200 Abernathy Road N.E., Suite 1200
Atlanta, GA 30328
Phone: 770 206-4200
Fax: –
Web: www.muellerwaterproducts.com

CEO: J. Scott Hall
CFO: Evan L. Hart
HR: –
FYE: September 30
Type: Public

Mueller Water Products knows how to keep the water flowing. The company is one of the largest manufacturers and marketers of hydrants as well as valves and pipe fittings in North America. Its flow control products are used in new and upgraded municipal infrastructure industrial and residential and non-residential construction projects such as water distribution networks water and wastewater treatment facilities fire protection systems gas distribution and HVAC. Mueller operates through three segments: Mueller Co. Mueller Technologies and Anvil International. It also is a wholesale distributor of its own products and those made by other companies. The US accounts for most of Mueller's sales.

	Annual Growth	09/15	09/16	09/17	09/18	09/19
Sales ($ mil.)	(4.5%)	1,164.5	1,138.5	826.0	916.0	968.0
Net income ($ mil.)	19.9%	30.9	63.9	123.3	105.6	63.8
Market value ($ mil.)	10.1%	1,206.2	1,976.1	2,015.5	1,812.4	1,769.9
Employees	(6.8%)	4,100	3,900	2,600	2,700	3,100

MULESOFT, INC.

50 FREMONT ST STE 300
SAN FRANCISCO, CA 941052231
Phone: 415-229-2009
Fax: –

CEO: Greg Schott
CFO: Matt Langdon
HR: –
FYE: December 31
Type: Private

MuleSoft Inc.'s name describes what it does ? if you know that IT workers call the drudgery of connecting company networks "donkey work." The company replaced donkey with mule and began selling software that uses application programming interfaces (APIs) to connect applications data and devices into a network of applications. MuleSoft's Anypoint Platform enables an infrastructure so companies can conduct business using mobile cloud software-as-a-service and Internet of Things technologies. When a purchase is made with a mobile app MuleSoft makes sure it is connected to a company's supply chain software and other pertinent functions. MuleSoft raised about $120 million in a 2017 IPO. Then in 2018 it agreed to be bought by Salesforce.com for about $6.5 billion.

	Annual Growth	12/13	12/14	12/15	12/16	12/17
Sales ($ mil.)	57.9%	–	–	–	187.7	296.5
Net income ($ mil.)	–	–	–	–	(49.6)	(80.0)
Market value ($ mil.)	–	–	–	–	–	–
Employees	–	–	–	–	–	841

MULTI-COLOR CORP.   NMS: LABL

4053 Clough Woods Dr.
Batavia, OH 45103
Phone: 513 381-1480
Fax: –
Web: www.mcclabel.com

CEO: Michael J Henry
CFO: Sharon E Birkett
HR: –
FYE: March 31
Type: Public

Multi-Color Corporation's labels aren't just black and white and red all over. The company produces printed labels for product makers in markets such as home and personal care wine and spirit food and beverage and specialty consumer goods. Multi-Color serves customers in North and South America Europe the Asia/Pacific region and South Africa. The company prints and affixes heat transfer re-sealable shrink wrap pressure sensitive and other label types to glass and plastic containers. Multi-Color also offers gravure printing and injection in-mold labels. Over the years the company has counted Procter & Gamble and Miller Brewing among its biggest customers. Multi-Color traces its roots to 1916.

	Annual Growth	03/14	03/15	03/16	03/17	03/18
Sales ($ mil.)	16.5%	706.4	810.8	870.8	923.3	1,300.9
Net income ($ mil.)	26.4%	28.2	45.7	47.7	61.0	72.0
Market value ($ mil.)	17.2%	715.6	1,417.5	1,090.8	1,451.7	1,350.5
Employees	26.8%	3,250	3,550	5,000	5,450	8,400

MULTI-FINELINE ELECTRONIX INC   NMS: MFLX

8659 Research Drive
Irvine, CA 92618
Phone: 949 453-6800
Fax: –
Web: www.mflex.com

CEO: Reza Meshgin
CFO: Tom Kampfer
HR: –
FYE: December 31
Type: Public

Multi-Fineline Electronix offers a multitude of fine electronic parts. The WBL Corporation-controlled company which does business as MFLEX manufactures a variety of flexible printed circuit boards (PCBs) and circuit assemblies. These devices are used to connect other components in various kinds of electronics such as mobile phones smartphones laptop computers medical devices and portable bar code scanners. Directly and through subcontractors MFLEX sells to three major customers that combined accounted for 90% of the company's 2013 sales.

	Annual Growth	09/12	09/13	09/14*	12/14	12/15
Sales ($ mil.)	(8.1%)	818.9	787.6	633.2	210.0	636.6
Net income ($ mil.)	15.2%	29.5	(65.5)	(84.5)	16.0	45.1
Market value ($ mil.)	(2.8%)	551.6	396.8	228.7	274.7	505.9
Employees	(32.7%)	23,470	17,310	11,570	9,140	7,170

*Fiscal year change

MULTICARE HEALTH SYSTEM

316 M L KING JR WAY # 314
TACOMA, WA 984054252
Phone: 253-403-1000
Fax: –

CEO: William G. (Bill) Robertson
CFO: Anna Loomis
HR: –
FYE: December 31
Type: Private

MultiCare Health System is a not-for-profit health system that serves the residents of four counties in the southern Puget Sound region and southwestern Washington. Altogether the system's five hospitals have more than 1100 beds. The largest facility Tacoma General boasts about 440 beds and provides specialized cancer cardiac orthopedic and trauma care in addition to general medical and surgical care. Other medical centers include Good Samaritan Hospital (with 286 beds) Allenmore Hospital (130 beds) Auburn Regional Medical Center (195 beds) and Mary Bridge Children's Hospital (82 beds).

	Annual Growth	12/10	12/11	12/16	12/17	12/18
Sales ($ mil.)	11.3%	–	1,384.3	1,927.1	2,416.1	2,923.0
Net income ($ mil.)	3.2%	–	27.6	180.7	347.5	34.4
Market value ($ mil.)	–	–	–	–	–	–
Employees	–	–	–	–	–	6,510

MULTICELL TECHNOLOGIES INC   NBB: MCET

68 Cumberland Street, Suite 301
Woonsocket, RI 02895
Phone: 401 762-0045
Fax: –
Web: www.multicelltech.com

CEO: –
CFO: –
HR: –
FYE: November 30
Type: Public

MultiCell Technologies is working on multiple therapeutics but still sells liver cells on the side to help pay the rent. It is developing drug candidates to treat degenerative neurological diseases. Its MCT-125 candidate is being developed as a treatment for the fatigue that comes with multiple sclerosis while MCT-175 is intended to slow the progression of the disease. Two other candidates are targeting breast and cervical cancers. MultiCell also produces liver cells (hepatocytes) and a serum-free culture medium for research. Larger firms including Corning and Pfizer have licensed the company's liver cell lines.

	Annual Growth	11/10	11/11	11/12	11/13	11/14
Sales ($ mil.)	(16.0%)	0.1	0.0	0.0	0.0	0.0
Net income ($ mil.)	–	(1.2)	(1.8)	(1.3)	(1.2)	(0.4)
Market value ($ mil.)	–	0.0	0.0	0.0	0.0	0.0
Employees	0.0%	2	2	2	2	2

MULTIMEDIA GAMES HOLDING COMPANY, INC.   NMS: MGAM

206 Wild Basin Road South, Building B
Austin, TX 78746
Phone: 515 334-7500
Fax: –
Web: www.multimediagames.com

CEO: –
CFO: –
HR: –
FYE: September 30
Type: Public

You might say this company's games help casinos hit the jackpot. Multimedia Games is a leading manufacturer of slot machines and other gaming systems used by both commercial casinos and by establishments in the Native American gaming industry. It makes both video reel and mechanical reel games as well as multi-terminal games that allow gamblers to compete for jackpots. In addition to its proprietary gaming machines Multimedia Games licenses games from third parties such as WMS Industries and Aristocrat Technologies. The company also makes casino management systems that monitor gaming machine performance and tracking player activity as well as video lottery terminals and charitable gaming systems.

	Annual Growth	09/09	09/10	09/11	09/12	09/13
Sales ($ mil.)	10.5%	127.2	117.9	127.9	156.2	189.4
Net income ($ mil.)	–	(44.8)	2.6	5.7	28.2	34.9
Market value ($ mil.)	61.2%	150.5	108.7	118.7	462.3	1,015.3
Employees	6.4%	412	397	410	471	528

MUNICIPAL ELECTRIC AUTHORITY OF GEORGIA

1470 RIVEREDGE PKWY
ATLANTA, GA 303284640
Phone: 770-563-0300
Fax: –
Web: www.meagpower.org

CEO: James E Fuller
CFO: –
HR: –
FYE: December 31
Type: Private

With more juice than a ripe Georgia peach the Municipal Electric Authority of Georgia (MEAG Power) supplies wholesale electric power. The authority has a generating capacity of 2069 MW through its interests in nuclear and fossil-fueled plants. Some 49% of the energy MEAG Power delivered in 2012 came from its nuclear plants. MEAG Power transmits electricity to 48 municipal and one county distribution systems across Georgia that in turn serve some 600000 consumers. It utilizes a transmission network that is co-owned by all the power suppliers in Georgia although it is considering joining a regional transmission organization (RTO) to further defray costs.

	Annual Growth	12/14	12/15	12/16	12/17	12/18
Sales ($ mil.)	2.0%	–	643.0	661.4	623.2	681.3
Net income ($ mil.)	–	–	(131.3)	(110.5)	0.0	(4.1)
Market value ($ mil.)	–	–	–	–	–	–
Employees	–	–	–	–	–	150

MUNROE REGIONAL MEDICAL CENTER, INC.

1500 SW 1ST AVE
OCALA, FL 344716559
Phone: 352-351-7200
Fax: –
Web: www.munroeregional.com

CEO: –
CFO: –
HR: –
FYE: September 30
Type: Private

Munroe Regional Health System operates the Munroe Regional Medical Center and affiliated facilities serving residents of north central Florida's Marion County and surrounding areas. Munroe Regional Medical Center is a 500-bed acute care hospital that offers comprehensive medical surgical and emergency care along with programs devoted to cardiovascular care stroke prevention and care orthopedics and women's health. The system also provides home health services and operates outpatient clinics providing primary care diagnostic and rehabilitation therapy services. Adventist Health System subsidiary Florida Hospital acquired the hospital's lease and operations from Community Health Systems in mid-2018.

	Annual Growth	09/05	09/06	09/08	09/09	09/17
Sales ($ mil.)	(0.3%)	–	263.0	312.1	313.6	254.5
Net income ($ mil.)	–	–	4.1	(3.3)	(7.4)	(19.3)
Market value ($ mil.)	–	–	–	–	–	–
Employees	–	–	–	–	–	2,179

MUNSON HEALTHCARE

1105 SIXTH ST
TRAVERSE CITY, MI 496842345
Phone: 800-252-2065
Fax: –
Web: www.munsonhealthcare.org

CEO: Ed Ness
CFO: –
HR: –
FYE: June 30
Type: Private

Munson Healthcare is a not-for-profit health care system serving residents in northern Michigan. Its flagship facility is Munson Medical Center in Traverse City a regional referral hospital with about 390 beds offering specialty services including cancer treatment behavioral health cardiac care and orthopedics. Munson Healthcare also has management agreements and other types of affiliations with about a dozen other hospitals in the region. In addition Munson Healthcare operates urgent care and community clinics home health care and hospice agencies an ambulance service and the Northern Michigan Supply Alliance a supply chain management group co-owned with Trinity Health.

	Annual Growth	06/12	06/13	06/15	06/17	06/18
Sales ($ mil.)	175.3%	–	6.6	8.1	940.8	1,039.2
Net income ($ mil.)	–	–	(3.7)	(7.0)	161.0	142.6
Market value ($ mil.)	–	–	–	–	–	–
Employees	–	–	–	–	–	4,000

MURPHY COMPANY MECHANICAL CONTRACTORS AND ENGINEERS

1233 N PRICE RD
SAINT LOUIS, MO 631322303
Phone: 314-997-6600
Fax: –
Web: www.murphynet.com

CEO: James J Murphy Jr
CFO: Robert L Koester
HR: –
FYE: March 31
Type: Private

Keeping Murphy's Law from plaguing construction projects is a task handled by Murphy Company Mechanical Contractors and Engineers. One of the nation's top mechanical contractors Murphy Company provides energy HVAC plumbing piping and design/build services to the commercial industrial heavy industrial and institutional markets. Its projects range from new and retrofit construction to clean manufacturing (for biotechnology or microelectronics clients). The company which offers 24-hour service became LEED-certified in mid-2011. Clients have included Harrah's and Pfizer. The Murphy Company was founded in 1907 and continues to be controlled and managed by members of the founding family.

	Annual Growth	03/05	03/06	03/07	03/08	03/15
Sales ($ mil.)	–	–	0.0	0.0	233.0	212.3
Net income ($ mil.)	–	–	0.0	0.0	0.0	0.0
Market value ($ mil.)	–	–	–	–	–	–
Employees	–	–	–	–	–	550

MURPHY OIL CORP

NYS: MUR

300 Peach Street
El Dorado, AR 71730-7000
Phone: 870 862-6411
Fax: 870 864-3673
Web: www.murphyoilcorp.com

CEO: Roger W Jenkins
CFO: John W. Eckart
HR: –
FYE: December 31
Type: Public

Murphy Oil Corporation is a pure-play upstream company. It explores for and produces oil and gas — crude oil and condensate natural gas and natural gas liquids — primarily in the US Canada and Malaysia. The company partially or wholly owns around 1400 oil wells and some 415 gas wells worldwide with proved reserves of 685 million barrels of oil equivalent. Murphy Oil's major holdings include fields in the Eagle Ford Shale area the deepwater Gulf of Mexico and the Western Canadian Sedimentary Basin as well as in Sarawak Malaysia.

	Annual Growth	12/14	12/15	12/16	12/17	12/18
Sales ($ mil.)	(17.2%)	5,476.1	3,033.1	1,874.1	2,225.1	2,570.6
Net income ($ mil.)	(17.9%)	905.6	(2,270.8)	(276.0)	(311.8)	411.1
Market value ($ mil.)	(17.5%)	8,742.9	3,885.2	5,387.3	5,373.5	4,047.8
Employees	(10.3%)	1,712	1,258	1,294	1,128	1,108

MURPHY OIL USA INC.

200 Peach St.
El Dorado AR 71730
Phone: 870-862-6411
Fax: 870-864-6373
Web: www.murphyusa.com

CEO: –
CFO: –
HR: –
FYE: December 31
Type: Subsidiary

It may not be the biggest but Murphy Oil USA (MOUSA) is no mouse in the gas station market. A wholly owned subsidiary of Murphy Oil MOUSA markets refined products through its network of branded gasoline stations and convenience stores customers and unbranded wholesale customers in 23 southern and Midwestern US states. The company's 1130 retail gas stations (more than 1000 of which in Wal-Mart Supercenter parking lots) sell gas under the Murphy USA brand. In 2011 the company owned the land underlying about 900 of the more than 1000 gas stations located in Wal-Mart parking lots and rented the rest.

MURPHY USA INC

NYS: MUSA

200 Peach Street
El Dorado, AR 71730-5836
Phone: 870 875-7600
Fax: –
Web: www.murphyusa.com

CEO: R. Andrew Clyde
CFO: Mindy K. West
HR: –
FYE: December 31
Type: Public

It may not be the biggest but Murphy USA is flexing its muscles in the US gas station market. Murphy USA (a former operating unit of Murphy Oil) markets refined products through its network of branded gasoline stations and convenience stores customers and unbranded wholesale customers in more than 25 Southern and Midwestern US states to more than 1.6 million customers. The company's more than 1400 retail gas stations (more than 1150 of which are in Wal-Mart Supercenter parking lots) sell gas under the Murphy USA brand. It also operates about 300 Murphy Express locations and sells some 4 billion gallons of motor fuel through retail outlets.

	Annual Growth	12/14	12/15	12/16	12/17	12/18
Sales ($ mil.)	(4.4%)	17,209.9	12,699.4	11,594.6	12,826.6	14,362.9
Net income ($ mil.)	(3.3%)	243.9	176.3	221.5	245.3	213.6
Market value ($ mil.)	2.7%	2,221.5	1,959.6	1,983.1	2,592.5	2,472.5
Employees	0.1%	9,450	9,800	9,100	9,600	9,500

MURPHY-BROWN LLC

2822 Hwy. 24 West
Warsaw NC 28398
Phone: 910-293-3434
Fax: 910-289-6400
Web: www.murphybrownllc.com

CEO: –
CFO: –
HR: –
FYE: April 30
Type: Subsidiary

When it comes to work Murphy-Brown goes 'whole hog.' The livestock production subsidiary of pork-processing giant Smithfield Foods is the world's largest hog producer. Murphy-Brown maintains some 827000 breeding sows (more than 90% of which are genetic lines that produce the leanest hogs possible) and brings to market more than 16 million hogs annually. It operates about 450 company-owned farms in a dozen states. The company extends its hog production through partnerships with more than 1500 independent farmers and contract growers in the US. More than 75% of Murphy-Brown's revenues are attributable to hogs sold to Smithfield Foods' fresh pork and packaged meats subsidiaries including John Morrell.

MUSCULAR DYSTROPHY ASSOCIATION, INC.

222 S RIVERSIDE PLZ # 1500
CHICAGO, IL 606066000
Phone: 520-529-2000
Fax: –
Web: www.mda.org

CEO: Kristine Welker
CFO: Julie Faber
HR: –
FYE: December 31
Type: Private

The Muscular Dystrophy Association (MDA) is a not-for-profit health agency that supports research into more than 40 neuromuscular diseases including including muscular dystrophy and Lou Gehrig's disease (also known as ALS). MDA believes more than one million Americans have some form of muscular dystrophy. The organization operates more than 200 health care clinics across the US runs summer camps for kids provides funding for research publishes educational materials and engages in national advocacy. It also sponsors more than 200 hospital-affiliated clinics and funds some 330 research projects globally. Founded in 1950 MDA is funded by private contributions.

	Annual Growth	12/11	12/12	12/13	12/14	12/15
Sales ($ mil.)	(7.5%)	–	159.0	153.0	139.8	126.0
Net income ($ mil.)	–	–	(11.9)	19.7	(15.0)	5.2
Market value ($ mil.)	–	–	–	–	–	–
Employees	–	–	–	–	–	950

MUSEUM OF FINE ARTS

465 HUNTINGTON AVE
BOSTON, MA 021155597
Phone: 617-267-9300
Fax: –
Web: www.mfa.org

CEO: –
CFO: –
HR: –
FYE: June 30
Type: Private

In a city known for its erudite inhabitants the The Museum of Fine Arts (MFA) Boston seeks to entertain and educate. The MFA offers a wide range of collections such as Art of Americas Art of Europe Art of the Ancient World Contemporary Art Textile and Fashion Arts and Musical Instruments. The museum also provides public programs for children and adults including art classes and workshops. With approximately 72000 member households the MFA attracts some 1.2 million visitors annually. Founded in 1870 the museum through a partnership opened the Nagoya/Boston Museum of Fine Arts in 1999.

	Annual Growth	06/08	06/09	06/10	06/13	06/15
Sales ($ mil.)	13.9%	–	69.2	122.8	131.5	151.0
Net income ($ mil.)	–	–	(49.8)	7.2	(8.9)	13.8
Market value ($ mil.)	–	–	–	–	–	–
Employees	–	–	–	–	–	1,000

MUSTANG FUEL CORPORATION

9800 N OKLAHOMA AVE
OKLAHOMA CITY, OK 731147406
Phone: 405-884-2092
Fax: –
Web: www.mustangfuel.com

CEO: Carey Joullian IV
CFO: –
HR: –
FYE: December 31
Type: Private

Like a good mustang Mustang Fuel is independent — an independent oil and gas exploration production transportation and marketing company that is. The company owns and operates 200 properties and owns non-operated interests in more than 1300 other properties. It also controls more than 100000 net undeveloped leasehold acres in a four-state service region. Mustang Fuel also owns natural gas gathering and transporting pipelines operates one of the largest gas processing facilities in Oklahoma and has a fleet of trucks that transports petroleum products. It also markets gas. Subsidiaries include Mustang Fuel Marketing Company and Mustang Gas Products LLC.

	Annual Growth	12/03	12/04	12/05	12/08	12/09
Sales ($ mil.)	(5.2%)	–	313.7	441.4	482.2	240.7
Net income ($ mil.)	52.7%	–	1.7	24.6	43.4	13.7
Market value ($ mil.)	–	–	–	–	–	–
Employees	–	–	–	–	–	124

MUTUAL OF AMERICA LIFE INSURANCE COMPANY

320 Park Ave.
New York NY 10022-6839
Phone: 212-224-1600
Fax: 212-224-2539
Web: www.mutualofamerica.com

CEO: John R Greed
CFO: Manfred Altstadt
HR: –
FYE: December 31
Type: Private - Mutual Com

Mutual of America Life Insurance provides retirement savings and employee benefit plans to small to midsized companies and to not-for-profit organizations. As part of its business the company typically serves those involved in the health and social services fields. In addition to group pension and insurance plans Mutual of America Life Insurance offers IRAs annuities and life and disability coverage to individual investors and about 35 separate account investment funds that leverage equity fixed-income retirement asset allocation and balanced strategies. Founded in 1945 Mutual of America Life Insurance operates throughout the US through a network of some 35 regional field offices and a pair of satellite offices in Alaska and Hawaii.

MUTUAL OF ENUMCLAW INSURANCE COMPANY

1460 Wells St.
Enumclaw WA 98022
Phone: 360-825-2591
Fax: 360-825-6885
Web: www.mutualofenumclaw.com

CEO: Eric Nelson
CFO: —
HR: —
FYE: December 31
Type: Private - Mutual Com

Mutual of Enumclaw Insurance Company provides commercial and personal property/casualty insurance in four western states (Idaho Oregon Utah and Washington). Mutual of Enumclaw Insurance Company and Enumclaw Property and Casualty Insurance Company comprise Enumclaw Insurance Group. The group writes a variety of lines including auto homeowners liability and umbrella insurance. Enumclaw also offers specialty package policies for churches farms and business owners. Farmers' Mutual Insurance the group's Washington-based predecessor was founded in 1898.

MUTUAL OF OMAHA INSURANCE CO. (NE)

Mutual Of Omaha Plaza
Omaha, NE 68175
Phone: 402 342-7600
Fax: —
Web: www.mutualofomaha.com

CEO: Daniel P Neary
CFO: David A Diamond
HR: —
FYE: December 31
Type: Public

In the wild kingdom that is today's insurance industry Mutual of Omaha Insurance Company wants to distinguish itself from the pack. The company provides individual group and employee benefits products through a range of affiliated companies. It offers Medicare supplement disability illness and long-term care coverage as well as life insurance and annuities through its United of Omaha Life Insurance unit. Its Mutual of Omaha Investor Services offers brokerage services pension plans and mutual funds while the Mutual of Omaha Bank operates regionally. Mutual of Omaha is owned by its policyholders.

	Annual Growth	12/11	12/12	12/13	12/14	12/15
Assets ($ mil.)	5.1%	29,198.4	30,993.1	5,795.4	6,426.8	35,629.4
Net income ($ mil.)	26.5%	130.1	283.8	105.8	30.4	333.0
Market value ($ mil.)	—	—	—	—	—	—
Employees	—	—	—	—	—	—

MUTUALFIRST FINANCIAL INC   NMS: MFSF

110 E. Charles Street
Muncie, IN 47305-2419
Phone: 765 747-2800
Fax: —

CEO: David W Heeter
CFO: Christopher D Cook
HR: —
FYE: December 31
Type: Public

Before you bank anywhere else this company wants you to head to MutualFirst. MutualFirst Financial is the holding company for MutualFirst Bank which has more than 30 financial centers and trust offices in northern Indiana and a loan production office in southern Michigan. The bank offers standard products and services such as checking and savings accounts CDs IRAs and credit cards. More than 40% of the company's loan portfolio is devoted to residential mortgages. Consumer loans including auto boat RV home equity and home improvement loans account for about 25%. Business loans also make up about a quarter of MutualFirst's loan portfolio.

	Annual Growth	12/14	12/15	12/16	12/17	12/18
Assets ($ mil.)	9.5%	1,424.2	1,478.3	1,553.1	1,588.9	2,049.3
Net income ($ mil.)	14.9%	10.8	12.3	13.2	12.3	18.9
Market value ($ mil.)	5.0%	188.2	213.4	284.8	331.7	228.6
Employees	4.8%	438	445	442	422	528

MV OIL TRUST   NYS: MVO

The Bank of New York Mellon Trust Company, N.A., Trustee, Global Corporate Trust, 601 Travis Street, Floor 16
Houston, TX 77002
Phone: 512 236-6599
Fax: —

CEO: —
CFO: —
HR: —
FYE: December 31
Type: Public

Call it what you will black gold Texas tea or the black blood of the earth MV Oil Trust is wringing out the value from each drop and distributing it to shareholders. MV Oil Trust receives royalty interests from the mature oil and gas properties of MV Partners located in Kansas and Colorado. The properties have proved reserves of 9.5 million barrels of oil from 922 net wells. The trust receives royalties based on the amount of oil (and gas) produced and sold and then distributes virtually all of the proceeds to shareholders on a regular basis. MV Partners a private company engaged in the exploration production gathering aggregation and sale of oil and natural gas has the rights to 80% of net proceeds.

	Annual Growth	12/14	12/15	12/16	12/17	12/18
Sales ($ mil.)	(19.0%)	39.9	15.5	5.5	9.1	17.2
Net income ($ mil.)	(19.6%)	39.0	14.7	4.6	8.3	16.3
Market value ($ mil.)	(16.8%)	167.6	56.0	71.6	96.6	80.5
Employees						

MV TRANSPORTATION, INC.

2711 N HASKELL AVE
DALLAS, TX 752042911
Phone: 214-265-3400
Fax: —
Web: www.mvtransit.com

CEO: Thomas A Egan
CFO: Erin Niewinski
HR: Jarrett Andrews
FYE: December 31
Type: Private

Need to supply transportation by bus? MV Transportation will run your bus system so you don't have to. The company operates more than 200 contracts to offer fixed-route and shuttle bus services as well as paratransit (transportation of people with disabilities) and transportation of Medicaid beneficiaries. Its customers consist primarily of transit authorities and other state and local government agencies responsible for public transportation. MV Transportation operates in more than 130 locations spanning 28 US states and in British Columbia Canada and Saudi Arabia; overall the company maintains a fleet of about 7000 vehicles. MV Transportation was founded in 1975.

	Annual Growth	12/05	12/06	12/07	12/08	12/09
Sales ($ mil.)	29.3%	—	—	422.6	646.0	706.5
Net income ($ mil.)		—	—	0.0	(3.0)	23.5
Market value ($ mil.)		—	—	—	—	—
Employees		—	—	—	—	224

MVP HEALTH PLAN, INC.

625 STATE ST
SCHENECTADY, NY 123052260
Phone: 518-370-4793
Fax: —
Web: www.mvphealthcare.com

CEO: Denise V. Gonick
CFO: Mark Fish
HR: —
FYE: December 31
Type: Private

MVP Health Plan also know as MVP Health Care provides health insurance and employee benefits to its more than 700000 members in upstate New York New Hampshire and Vermont. MVP a not-for-profit organization offers a variety of plans including HMO PPO and indemnity coverage as well as dental plans health accounts and Medicare Advantage plans. Subsidiary MVP Select Care provides third-party administration (TPA) services for self-insured employers. MVP Health Care was founded in 1983 as Mohawk Valley Physicians' Health Plan.

	Annual Growth	12/11	12/12	12/13	12/14	12/15
Assets ($ mil.)	9.2%	—	—	—	540.3	589.9
Net income ($ mil.)		—	—	—	(26.3)	11.1
Market value ($ mil.)		—	—	—	—	—
Employees		—	—	—	—	1,500

MWH GLOBAL, INC.

370 INTERLOCKEN BLVD # 300
BROOMFIELD, CO 800218009
Phone: 303-533-1900
Fax: –
Web: www.stantec.com

CEO: Alan J. Krause
CFO: David G. Barnes
HR: Shannon Aguilar
FYE: January 01
Type: Private

MWH Global is an environmental engineering construction and management firm that specializes in water-related projects or "wet infrastructure." The company's typical projects include building water treatment or desalination plants water transmission systems or storage facilitates. MWH also provides general building services for transportation energy mining ports and waterways and industrial projects. The company is active in some 35 countries and serves governments public utilities and private sector clients. Affiliates of the employee-owned company include software provider Innovyze and business and government relations firm mCapitol. Canadian Engineering firm Stantec acquired MWH Global for $795 million in May 2016.

	Annual Growth	12/00	12/01*	01/03*	12/05*	01/16
Sales ($ mil.)	3.6%	–	774.5	975.9	946.0	1,318.2
Net income ($ mil.)	4.0%	–	19.8	942.3	0.0	35.9
Market value ($ mil.)	–	–	–	–	–	–
Employees	–	–	–	–	–	6,700

*Fiscal year change

MWI VETERINARY SUPPLY INC   NMS: MWIV

3041 W. Pasadena Dr.
Boise, ID 83705
Phone: 208 955-8930
Fax: –
Web: www.mwivet.com

CEO: James F Cleary Jr
CFO: Richard Dubois
HR: –
FYE: September 30
Type: Public

While MWI could stand for Mastiff Weimaraner and Irish Setter MWI Veterinary Supply is actually named after founder and veterinarian Millard Wallace Ickes. The veterinary products distributor supplies drugs diagnostics equipment and other medical supplies for companion animals and livestock. It serves veterinary practices from about a dozen distribution centers across the US and in the UK. The firm offers 41000 products from more than 700 vendors. In addition to medical supplies and equipment MWI distributes pet food and nutritional products. The company in business since 1976 offers customers online ordering tools to manage inventory consultation for equipment and pet cremation services.

	Annual Growth	09/10	09/11	09/12	09/13	09/14
Sales ($ mil.)	24.8%	1,229.3	1,565.3	2,075.1	2,347.5	2,981.0
Net income ($ mil.)	21.1%	33.4	42.6	53.5	62.8	72.0
Market value ($ mil.)	26.6%	745.3	888.6	1,377.5	1,928.5	1,916.1
Employees	15.8%	1,179	1,273	1,629	1,732	2,121

MYERS INDUSTRIES INC.   NYS: MYE

1293 South Main Street
Akron, OH 44301
Phone: 330 253-5592
Fax: 330 761-6156
Web: www.myersindustries.com

CEO: R. David Banyard
CFO: Matteo Anversa
HR: Kevin Gehrt
FYE: December 31
Type: Public

Myers Industries' Material Handling segment (74% of sales) manufacturers plastic reusable containers and pallets plastic organizational products and plastic carts. Products are used to make material handling and product transport more efficient in industries ranging from food processing to wholesale. Other Material Handling offerings include portable plastic fuel tanks and water containers and storage totes. Meyers' Distribution segment (26% of sales) includes the Myers Tire Supply Myers Tire Supply International and Patch Rubber Company brands which offer a range of tools and equipment used to service tires wheels and related components. The US accounts for more than 90% of sales.

	Annual Growth	12/14	12/15	12/16	12/17	12/18
Sales ($ mil.)	(2.4%)	623.6	601.5	558.1	547.0	566.7
Net income ($ mil.)	–	(8.7)	17.8	1.1	(9.9)	(3.3)
Market value ($ mil.)	(3.7%)	622.6	471.2	505.6	689.8	534.5
Employees	(13.7%)	3,241	2,360	2,200	1,900	1,800

MYR GROUP INC   NMS: MYRG

1701 Golf Road, Suite 3-1012
Rolling Meadows, IL 60008
Phone: 847 290-1891
Fax: –
Web: www.myrgroup.com

CEO: Richard S. (Rick) Swartz
CFO: Betty R. Johnson
HR: Doreen Keller
FYE: December 31
Type: Public

MYR Group's work can be electrifying. The specialty contractor builds and maintains electric delivery infrastructure systems for utilities and commercial clients. MYR Group constructs transmission and distribution lines for the oil and gas power and telecommunications industries. The company also installs and maintains electrical wiring in commercial and industrial facilities and traffic and rail systems. The group operates nationwide through subsidiaries including The L.E. Myers Co. Harlan Electric Hawkeye Construction Sturgeon Electric MYR Transmission Services and Great Southwestern Construction. MYR's transmission and distribution segment accounts for about three-fourths of the group's revenues.

	Annual Growth	12/14	12/15	12/16	12/17	12/18
Sales ($ mil.)	12.9%	944.0	1,061.7	1,142.5	1,403.3	1,531.2
Net income ($ mil.)	(4.0%)	36.5	27.3	21.4	21.2	31.1
Market value ($ mil.)	0.7%	453.9	341.4	624.2	591.9	466.6
Employees	10.8%	3,650	4,075	4,600	5,275	5,500

MYREXIS INC.   NASDAQ: MYRX

305 Chipeta Way
Salt Lake City UT 84108
Phone: 801-214-7800
Fax: 801-214-7992
Web: www.myrexis.com

CEO: –
CFO: –
HR: –
FYE: June 30
Type: Public

Myrexis hoped to convince cancer cells to stop dividing and die with the destabilizing agent drugs in its pipeline. The pharmaceutical development firm's pipeline consisted of oncology compounds in clinical and preclinical R&D stages including drugs aiming to treat solid tumors and relapsed cancers. However the company restructured its operations and slashed its workforce in 2011 after deciding to halt clinical trials on its leading candidate Azixa (a metastatic tumor drug) in order to focus on its more promising early stage development compounds. Then in early 2012 it halted all remaining development activities and began exploring strategic alternatives. In November 2012 Myrexis announced plans to liquidate.

MYRIAD GENETICS, INC.   NMS: MYGN

320 Wakara Way
Salt Lake City, UT 84108
Phone: 801 584-3600
Fax: –
Web: www.myriad.com

CEO: Mark C. Capone
CFO: R. Bryan Riggsbee
HR: Jayne B. Hart
FYE: June 30
Type: Public

Myriad Genetics is working to detect which diseases folks might develop based on their genes. The company develops and sells molecular diagnostic tests in three main areas: predictive medicine (to assess a patient's risk for developing disease) personalized medicine (to identify likelihood of drug response to therapies) and prognostic medicine (to assess risk of disease progression or recurrence). Its biggest revenue maker BRAC Analysis helps determine risk for breast or ovarian cancer. Myriad Genetics markets its products in the US through its own sales force and uses collaborations to sell them elsewhere.

	Annual Growth	06/15	06/16	06/17	06/18	06/19
Sales ($ mil.)	4.2%	723.1	753.8	771.4	772.6	851.1
Net income ($ mil.)	(51.1%)	80.2	125.3	21.8	131.1	4.6
Market value ($ mil.)	(4.9%)	2,498.3	2,249.1	1,899.2	2,746.7	2,041.8
Employees	6.3%	2,038	2,206	2,400	2,400	2,600

N-VIRO INTERNATIONAL CORP
NBB: NVIC

2254 Centennial Road
Toledo, OH 43617
Phone: 419 535-6374
Fax: –
Web: www.nviro.com

CEO: Timothy R Kasmoch
CFO: James K McHugh
HR: –
FYE: December 31
Type: Public

Wastewater sludge smells like money to N-Viro International. The company's patented process converts sludge and other bio-organic waste into a better-quality soil by treating it with alkaline byproducts. The treated N-Viro Soil is used in agriculture and as a landfill cover material among other applications. N-Viro has licensed its recycling process to more than 25 wastewater treatment plants around the world. Outside the US the company's process is marketed through a network of agents. N-Viro International itself manages two facilities that use the process under a contract with the City of Toledo Ohio and another in Florida.

	Annual Growth	12/11	12/12	12/13	12/14	12/15
Sales ($ mil.)	(32.1%)	5.6	3.6	3.4	1.3	1.2
Net income ($ mil.)	–	(1.6)	(1.6)	(1.6)	(1.8)	(2.3)
Market value ($ mil.)	(10.9%)	10.0	8.2	11.8	23.3	6.3
Employees	(22.7%)	28	18	19	12	10

NACCO INDUSTRIES INC
NYS: NC

5875 Landerbrook Drive, Suite 220
Cleveland, OH 44124-4069
Phone: 440 229-5151
Fax: –
Web: www.nacco.com

CEO: J. C. Butler
CFO: –
HR: Dana Portwood
FYE: December 31
Type: Public

NACCO Industries has a knack for coal mining housewares and specialty retail. The holding company conducts these businesses through three main independent operating subsidiaries. North American Coal (NACoal) mines and markets coal for power generation and steel production through developed mines located in North Dakota Texas Mississippi Louisiana and Alabama. On the housewares side Hamilton Beach Brands designs small kitchen appliances such as meat grinders blenders and juicers while Kitchen Collection (KC) operates Kitchen Collection and Le Gourmet Chef retail stores in factory outlet and traditional malls across the US.

	Annual Growth	12/14	12/15	12/16	12/17	12/18
Sales ($ mil.)	(37.7%)	896.8	915.9	856.4	104.8	135.4
Net income ($ mil.)	–	(38.1)	22.0	29.6	30.3	34.8
Market value ($ mil.)	(13.1%)	410.9	292.1	626.7	260.6	234.6
Employees	(7.3%)	3,250	3,600	2,000	2,300	2,400

NALCO HOLDING COMPANY
NYSE: NLC

1601 W. Diehl Rd.
Naperville IL 60563-1198
Phone: 630-305-1000
Fax: 630-305-2900
Web: www.nalco.com

CEO: J Erik Fyrwald
CFO: Kathryn A Mikells
HR: –
FYE: December 31
Type: Subsidiary

Dirty water? Wastewater? Process-stream water? Nalco treats them all. The company is the world's largest maker of chemicals used in water treatment for industrial processes (ahead of #2 GE Water and Process Technologies). Nalco's Energy Services segment is also #1 worldwide ahead of Baker Petrolite; it provides fuel additives oilfield chemicals and flow assurance services to energy companies. The company's chemicals help clarify water conserve energy prevent pollution separate liquids from solids and prevent corrosion in cooling systems and boilers. In 2011 cleaning products firm Ecolab acquired Nalco in a $5.4 billion cash and stock deal.

NAN YA PLASTICS CORPORATION U.S.A.

9 PEACH TREE HILL RD
LIVINGSTON, NJ 070395702
Phone: 973-992-1775
Fax: –
Web: www.npcusa.com

CEO: –
CFO: –
HR: –
FYE: December 31
Type: Private

Where do artificial Christmas trees come from? It's Nan Ya business. More specifically it's Nan Ya Plastics Corporation USA's business. A subsidiary of Taiwanese firm Nan Ya Plastics— itself a unit of Formosa Plastics Corporation— the company produces rigid PVC film that is used in the making of such products as artificial trees packaging material stationery water treatment panels and baffles and shrink wrap. Established in 1983 Nan Ya Plastics Corporation USA is based in New Jersey and also operates a PVC manufacturing plant in Wharton Texas.

	Annual Growth	12/13	12/14	12/15	12/16	12/17
Sales ($ mil.)	(3.3%)	–	124.9	120.3	116.7	113.1
Net income ($ mil.)	(25.2%)	–	4.9	7.0	10.3	2.0
Market value ($ mil.)	–	–	–	–	–	–
Employees	–	–	–	–	–	1,300

NANOPHASE TECHNOLOGIES CORP.
NBB: NANX

1319 Marquette Drive
Romeoville, IL 60446
Phone: 630 771-6708
Fax: –
Web: www.nanophase.com

CEO: –
CFO: Jess A Jankowski
HR: –
FYE: December 31
Type: Public

Nanophase Technologies sweats the small stuff. The company is commercializing its nanocrystalline materials (molecular-size ceramic and metallic materials in powder form) for applications in advanced materials technology such as conductive and antistatic coatings for computer monitors. It also develops abrasion-resistant coatings (with uses from coated vinyl flooring to contact lenses) environmental catalysts health care products (sunscreen) and advanced ceramics (cutting tools and ceramic bearings). Chemicals maker BASF accounts for more than half of Nanophase's sales.

	Annual Growth	12/14	12/15	12/16	12/17	12/18
Sales ($ mil.)	9.3%	9.9	10.3	10.8	12.5	14.2
Net income ($ mil.)	–	(1.7)	(1.2)	(1.3)	(0.8)	(2.1)
Market value ($ mil.)	16.2%	13.6	13.6	24.4	17.6	24.8
Employees	8.5%	39	40	46	48	54

NANOSPHERE INC
NAS: NSPH

4088 Commercial Avenue
Northbrook, IL 60062
Phone: 847 400-9000
Fax: –
Web: www.nanosphere.us

CEO: Michael McGarrity
CFO: –
HR: –
FYE: December 31
Type: Public

Nanosphere offers molecular diagnostics for the masses: Its molecular testing system is intended for use in hospital-based laboratories that don't have the money or expertise to maintain the complex genomic testing equipment often reserved for reference labs and research centers. The company's diagnostic Verigene System is a compact and simple workstation designed to perform multiple genomic and protein tests simultaneously on a single sample. Nanosphere also sells Verigene-compatible tests including hematology cystic fibrosis and influenza diagnostic assays and has several other tests including HPV (the virus that causes cervical cancer) in the works.

	Annual Growth	12/10	12/11	12/12	12/13	12/14
Sales ($ mil.)	63.0%	2.0	2.5	5.1	10.0	14.3
Net income ($ mil.)	–	(40.6)	(35.4)	(32.9)	(34.6)	(39.1)
Market value ($ mil.)	(45.3%)	25.6	8.6	16.9	13.4	2.3
Employees	10.1%	115	131	151	165	169

NANOSTRING TECHNOLOGIES INC
NMS: NSTG

530 Fairview Avenue North
Seattle, WA 98109
Phone: 206 378-6266
Fax: –
Web: www.nanostring.com

CEO: R. Bradley (Brad) Gray
CFO: James A. Johnson
HR: Deborah Krogman
FYE: December 31
Type: Public

NanoString Technologies helps unspool the mystery of the human genome for research and diagnostic purposes. The company makes a complex genomic analysis device that can be used onsite at clinical laboratories instead of shipping samples offsite for study. Called the nCounter Analysis System the device uses tissue extracted from a tumor to analyze up to 800 genes in a single experiment. These tests can help researchers understand the molecular basis of some diseases such as cancer. The company makes about 75% of its sales in US. Customers include Merck Medivation and Astellas.

	Annual Growth	12/14	12/15	12/16	12/17	12/18
Sales ($ mil.)	22.4%	47.6	62.7	86.5	114.9	106.7
Net income ($ mil.)	–	(50.0)	(45.6)	(47.1)	(43.6)	(77.4)
Market value ($ mil.)	1.6%	430.6	454.7	689.4	230.9	458.4
Employees	14.6%	276	307	407	467	476

NAPCO SECURITY TECHNOLOGIES, INC.
NMS: NSSC

333 Bayview Avenue
Amityville, NY 11701
Phone: 631 842-9400
Fax: –
Web: www.napcosecurity.com

CEO: –
CFO: –
HR: –
FYE: June 30
Type: Public

Crime pays for Napco Security Technologies. If you're trying to prevent it Napco manufactures a slew of security products used in commercial and residential buildings as well as government and institutional facilities. Products include burglary and fire alarm systems exit alarm-locks and digital-access control locks video surveillance systems such as cameras and monitors and emergency communications systems. Napco also buys and resells security devices made by third-party manufacturers. The company sells its products worldwide mainly through independent distributors dealers and installers of security equipment.

	Annual Growth	06/15	06/16	06/17	06/18	06/19
Sales ($ mil.)	7.3%	77.8	82.5	87.4	91.7	102.9
Net income ($ mil.)	26.0%	4.8	5.8	5.6	7.6	12.2
Market value ($ mil.)	50.9%	105.9	117.5	173.7	270.7	548.4
Employees	1.5%	1,013	984	1,101	1,081	1,076

NARUS INC.

570 Maude Ct.
Sunnyvale CA 94085
Phone: 408-215-4300
Fax: 408-215-4301
Web: www.narus.com

CEO: –
CFO: –
HR: –
FYE: January 31
Type: Subsidiary

Narus wants to give you insight into the inner workings of your Internet protocol (IP) network. The company provides software used by telecommunications services providers to optimize their IP platforms. Narus' products are used to protect networks against malicious attacks analyze network traffic flow and monitor network activity. The company also offers professional services such as consulting installation training maintenance and support. The company's customers have included Korea Telecom KDDI Telecom Egypt and KPN. Narus was acquired by Boeing in 2010.

NASB FINANCIAL INC
NBB: NASB

12498 South 71 Highway
Grandview, MO 64030
Phone: 816 765-2200
Fax: –
Web: www.nasb.com

CEO: –
CFO: Rhonda Nyhus
HR: Christine M Schaben
FYE: September 30
Type: Public

NASB Financial is the holding company for North American Savings Bank which operates about 15 branches and loan offices in the Kansas City and Springfield Missouri areas. Established in 1927 the bank offers standard deposit products to retail and commercial customers including checking and savings accounts and CDs. Mortgages secured by residential or commercial properties make up most of the bank's lending activities; it also originates business consumer and construction loans. Subsidiary Nor-Am sells annuities mutual funds and credit life and disability insurance. Chairman David Hancock and his wife Linda who is also a member of the company's board of directors own about 45% of NASB Financial.

	Annual Growth	09/15	09/16	09/17	09/18	09/19
Assets ($ mil.)	14.2%	1,530.6	1,949.7	2,062.3	2,060.4	2,605.2
Net income ($ mil.)	19.0%	21.6	22.4	29.4	29.1	43.2
Market value ($ mil.)	11.1%	213.9	248.9	266.3	299.4	326.0
Employees	–	–	–	–	–	–

NASDAQ INC
NMS: NDAQ

151 W. 42nd Street
New York, NY 10036
Phone: 212 401-8700
Fax: –
Web: www.ir.nasdaq.com

CEO: Adena T. Friedman
CFO: Michael S. Ptasznik
HR: –
FYE: December 31
Type: Public

Buy low and sell high on the NASDAQ. Nasdaq Inc. is a holding company whose most recognizable business is the US-based NASDAQ stock market upon which such tech-titans as Apple Cisco Google (aka Alphabet) Amazon and Facebook are listed. The holding company operates dozens of exchanges around the world including in the US Sweden Iceland Denmark and Finland. Nasdaq Inc. (formerly NASDAQ OMX) is a leader in floorless exchanges and has challenged NYSE Euronext as the world's largest stock exchange. NASDAQ-powered exchanges trade more than 3900 companies worth more than $13.0 trillion in market value through instruments such as exchange-traded funds (ETFs) equities options futures derivatives commodities and structured products. International business accounts for a bit more than 20% revenue.

	Annual Growth	12/14	12/15	12/16	12/17	12/18
Sales ($ mil.)	5.1%	3,500.0	3,403.0	3,705.0	3,965.0	4,277.0
Net income ($ mil.)	2.6%	414.0	428.0	108.0	734.0	458.0
Market value ($ mil.)	14.2%	7,921.3	9,607.7	11,085.9	12,689.6	13,472.5
Employees	2.7%	3,687	3,824	4,325	4,734	4,099

NASSAU HEALTH CARE CORPORATION

2201 HEMPSTEAD TPKE
EAST MEADOW, NY 115541859
Phone: 516-572-0123
Fax: –
Web: www.numc.edu

CEO: –
CFO: Richard Perrotti
HR: –
FYE: December 31
Type: Private

Nassau Health Care (NuHealth) keeps residents healthy in the suburbs of the Big Apple. The health system operates Nassau University Medical Center which has some 530 beds as well as the A. Holly Patterson Extended Care Facility a skilled nursing center with 590 beds. Other operations include about a half-dozen community family health centers and a home health care agency serving the people of Long Island. Nassau University Medical Center's specialized services include trauma burn care orthopedics psychiatry and obstetrics. NuHealth is a public benefit company governed by a representative board appointed by state and county officials.

	Annual Growth	12/13	12/14	12/15	12/16	12/17
Sales ($ mil.)	2.8%	–	392.0	363.4	375.5	425.5
Net income ($ mil.)	42.8%	–	5.4	(80.2)	(62.8)	15.8
Market value ($ mil.)	–	–	–	–	–	–
Employees	–	–	–	–	–	3,500

NATHAN'S FAMOUS, INC.
NMS: NATH

One Jericho Plaza, Second Floor - Wing A
Jericho, NY 11753
Phone: 516 338-8500
Fax: –
Web: www.nathansfamous.com

CEO: Eric Gatoff
CFO: Ronald G Devos
HR: –
FYE: March 31
Type: Public

Patrons of this restaurateur are in the dog house. Nathan's Famous is a leading franchisor of quick-service restaurants with a chain of about 300 Nathan's outlets known for all-beef frankfurters served with a variety of toppings. The eateries located in about 25 states and a half dozen other countries also serve hamburgers crinkle-cut fries and breakfast sandwiches. More than 50 Nathan's units also feature fish and chips under the Arthur Treacher's brand. In addition to restaurants the company sells Nathan's branded products through vending machines Subway units at Wal-Mart stores and Auntie Anne's pretzel shops. Specialty Foods Group makes Nathan's hot dogs for retail sale under a licensing deal.

	Annual Growth	03/15	03/16	03/17	03/18	03/19
Sales ($ mil.)	0.7%	99.1	100.9	96.7	104.2	101.8
Net income ($ mil.)	16.4%	11.7	6.1	7.5	2.6	21.5
Market value ($ mil.)	(1.8%)	308.6	176.3	254.4	302.4	286.9
Employees	(10.1%)	228	237	180	205	149

NATIONAL ACADEMY OF RECORDING ARTS & SCIENCES INC

3030 OLYMPIC BLVD
SANTA MONICA, CA 904045073
Phone: 310-392-3777
Fax: –
Web: www.grammy.com

CEO: Neil Portnow
CFO: Wayne J Zahner
HR: Gaetano Frizzi
FYE: July 31
Type: Private

The National Academy of Recording Arts and Sciences better known as The Recording Academy provides arts advocacy outreach and education and support services to professionals in the recording industry. The membership organization boasts some 18000 members served by a dozen regional chapters throughout the US. The Recording Academy acknowledges outstanding work by musicians producers engineers and recording professionals with its annual GRAMMY Awards ceremonies. Its first international venture The Latin Academy of Recording Arts & Sciences (which produces The Latin GRAMMY Awards) was formed in 1997. The Recording Academy was established in 1957.

	Annual Growth	07/07	07/08	07/09	07/14	07/15
Sales ($ mil.)	3.4%	–	65.8	55.3	77.6	83.0
Net income ($ mil.)	8.3%	–	5.1	(4.8)	7.1	8.8
Market value ($ mil.)	–	–	–	–	–	–
Employees	–	–	–	–	–	110

NATIONAL ALLIANCE TO END HOMELESSNESS INC.

1518 K St. NW Ste. 410
Washington DC 20005
Phone: 202-638-1526
Fax: 202-638-4664
Web: www.naeh.org

CEO: –
CFO: –
HR: –
FYE: June 30
Type: Private - Not-for-Pr

This group wants to put roofs over the heads of the estimated 675000 people who are homeless in America each night. The National Alliance to End Homelessness is dedicated to solving the problem of homelessness in every community. The organization works with around 5000 public private and not-for-profit sectors in its plan to end homelessness in 10 years (or by 2010). The Alliance lobbies government supports local assistance groups and educates the public about the causes effects and solutions to homelessness. It also promotes best practices by sharing the programs that are working in communities. The Alliance was founded in 1983 as homelessness began to be a problem in the US.

NATIONAL AMERICAN UNIVERSITY HOLDINGS INC.
NBB: NAUH

5301 Mt. Rushmore Road
Rapid City, SD 57701
Phone: 605 721-5200
Fax: –
Web: www.national.edu

CEO: Ronald L Shape
CFO: Thomas Bickart
HR: –
FYE: May 31
Type: Public

National American University Holdings believes in the power of continuing education. Through subsidiary Dlorah the for-profit company owns National American University (NAU) which has more than 20 campuses in eight states and offers classes online. Some locations are considered hybrids offering both in-class and online courses. Targeting working adults and other non-traditional students NAU offers associate's bachelor's and master's degrees as well as certification in business criminal justice and health care disciplines. The university was founded in 1941 as the National School of Business; the holding company which was formed in 2007 to acquire an education company purchased Dlorah in 2009.

	Annual Growth	05/15	05/16	05/17	05/18	05/19
Sales ($ mil.)	(25.0%)	117.9	96.1	86.6	77.2	37.3
Net income ($ mil.)	–	6.7	(5.3)	(6.3)	(12.2)	(25.1)
Market value ($ mil.)	(59.6%)	75.4	49.9	64.3	28.0	2.0
Employees	(10.8%)	740	870	880	739	469

NATIONAL ASSOCIATION OF BROADCASTERS

1771 N ST NW
WASHINGTON, DC 200362800
Phone: 202-429-5300
Fax: –
Web: www.nab.org

CEO: –
CFO: Ken Almgrem
HR: –
FYE: March 31
Type: Private

The National Association of Broadcasters (NAB) represents on-the-air talkers ranging from local radio reporters to TV network news anchors. The trade group serves as its members' eyes ears and of course voice before Congress the courts and federal regulatory agencies in Washington DC. NAB priorities have included spectrum management retransmission consent political advertising rates and limiting content regulation. The NAB predates television and goes back to the early days of radio — the organization was founded in 1923.

	Annual Growth	03/12	03/13	03/14	03/15	03/17
Sales ($ mil.)	5.6%	–	57.0	57.9	64.1	70.9
Net income ($ mil.)	13.6%	–	5.8	4.5	(15.3)	9.7
Market value ($ mil.)	–	–	–	–	–	–
Employees	–	–	–	–	–	173

NATIONAL AUDUBON SOCIETY, INC.

225 VARICK ST FL 7
NEW YORK, NY 100144396
Phone: 212-979-3000
Fax: –
Web: www.audubon.org

CEO: David Yarnold
CFO: Mary Beth Henson
HR: –
FYE: June 30
Type: Private

Audubon has gone to the birds. The National Audubon Society is a not-for-profit organization dedicated to preserving birds and other wildlife and their habitats by conserving and restoring their natural ecosystems. The society operates programs and educational centers in every US state and in several South American and Caribbean countries to encourage grassroots conservation and promote environmental public policy reform. Projects have included saving habitats in the Everglades Arctic Wildlife Refuge Long Island Sound and Mississippi River basin. Audubon also publishes Audubon Magazine . A precursor to the society formed in 1886 but disbanded when it grew too quickly. The current society began in 1905.

	Annual Growth	06/08	06/09	06/10	06/16	06/18
Sales ($ mil.)	5.2%	–	74.0	80.1	102.6	116.7
Net income ($ mil.)	–	–	0.0	(1.8)	(19.2)	24.3
Market value ($ mil.)	–	–	–	–	–	–
Employees	–	–	–	–	–	600

NATIONAL AUTOMOBILE DEALERS ASSOCIATION

8400 WESTPARK DR STE 1
MC LEAN, VA 221023522
Phone: 703-821-7000
Fax: –
Web: www.nadafrontpage.com

CEO: –
CFO: Joseph Cowden
HR: –
FYE: December 31
Type: Private

The National Automobile Dealers Association (N.A.D.A.) has been around almost as long as there have been cars. Founded in 1917 N.A.D.A. represents more than 16000 new car and truck dealers in the US and abroad. Through its more than 32500 franchises N.A.D.A. offers a range of services including: government relations (lobbying of Congress education of dealers) legal and public affairs dealership operations and other courses through N.A.D.A University insurance and retirement benefits IT training and convention and exposition support. N.A.D.A. also publishes AutoExec magazine (it sold The N.A.D.A. Official Used Car Guide). Membership is open to any dealer with a new car or truck sales and service franchise.

	Annual Growth	12/01	12/02	12/05	12/09	12/12
Sales ($ mil.)	5.9%	–	59.4	43.0	35.4	105.8
Net income ($ mil.)	24.7%	–	–	4.2	(0.9)	20.0
Market value ($ mil.)	–	–	–	–	–	–
Employees	–	–	–	–	–	500

NATIONAL BANCSHARES CORP. (OHIO)   NBB: NBOH

112 West Market Street, P.O. Box 57
Orrville, OH 44667
Phone: 330 682-1010
Fax: –
Web: www.discoverfirstnational.com

CEO: –
CFO: –
HR: –
FYE: December 31
Type: Public

Bank on the fact that National Bancshares is the holding company for First National Bank which serves northeastern Ohio through about 15 branch locations. Operating in Wayne Medina and Stark counties the bank offers traditional retail products and services such as deposit accounts CDs and credit cards. It mainly uses funds from deposits to originate commercial and consumer loans and mortgages. Real estate loans account for 85% of its loan book. First National Bank also owns 49% of title insurance agency First Kropf Title; National Bancshares chairman John Kropf is a partner of the title company's majority stakeholder law firm Kropf Wagner Hohenberger & Lutz.

	Annual Growth	12/09	12/10	12/11	12/12	12/13
Assets ($ mil.)	6.5%	370.2	374.1	406.1	440.8	476.2
Net income ($ mil.)	26.5%	1.6	1.3	2.6	2.8	4.1
Market value ($ mil.)	11.4%	31.7	28.9	32.5	33.8	48.8
Employees	2.6%	101	113	115	113	112

NATIONAL BANK HOLDINGS CORP   NYS: NBHC

7800 East Orchard Road, Suite 300
Greenwood Village, CO 80111
Phone: 303 892-8715
Fax: –
Web: www.nationalbankholdings.com

CEO: G. Timothy (Tim) Laney
CFO: Brian F. Lilly
HR: –
FYE: December 31
Type: Public

National Bank Holdings is the holding company for NBH Bank which operates nearly 100 branches in four south and central US states under various brands including: Bank Midwest in Kansas and Missouri Community Banks of Colorado in Colorado and Hillcrest Bank in Texas. Targeting small to medium-sized businesses and consumers the banks offer traditional checking and savings accounts as well as commercial and residential mortgages agricultural loans and commercial loans. The bank boasted $4.7 billion in assets at the end of 2015 including $2.6 billion in loans and $3.8 billion in deposits. Over 80% of its total revenue is made up of interest income.

	Annual Growth	12/14	12/15	12/16	12/17	12/18
Assets ($ mil.)	4.2%	4,819.6	4,683.9	4,573.0	4,843.5	5,676.7
Net income ($ mil.)	60.9%	9.2	4.9	23.1	14.6	61.5
Market value ($ mil.)	12.3%	597.2	657.5	981.2	997.8	949.8
Employees	6.0%	1,056	1,042	1,004	926	1,332

NATIONAL BANKSHARES INC. (VA)   NAS: NKSH

101 Hubbard Street, P.O. Box 90002
Blacksburg, VA 24062-9002
Phone: 540 951-6300
Fax: –
Web: www.nationalbankshares.com

CEO: James G. (Jim) Rakes
CFO: David K. Skeens
HR: –
FYE: December 31
Type: Public

National Bankshares is the holding company for National Bank of Blacksburg (National Bank for short) which serves consumers and small business in southwest Virginia through some two dozen branches. The community bank's services include deposit accounts credit cards and personal and corporate trust services. Commercial mortgages including loans secured by college housing and professional office buildings account for more than half of National Bankshares' loan portfolio; residential mortgages make up more than a quarter. To a lesser extent the bank also writes business construction and consumer loans. Another subsidiary National Bankshares Financial Services provides investments and insurance.

	Annual Growth	12/14	12/15	12/16	12/17	12/18
Assets ($ mil.)	2.1%	1,154.7	1,199.7	1,233.9	1,256.8	1,256.0
Net income ($ mil.)	(1.1%)	16.9	15.8	14.9	14.1	16.2
Market value ($ mil.)	4.6%	211.5	247.3	302.3	316.2	253.5
Employees	90.1%	18	225	229	228	235

NATIONAL BEVERAGE CORP.   NMS: FIZZ

8100 SW Tenth Street, Suite 4000
Fort Lauderdale, FL 33324
Phone: 954 581-0922
Fax: –
Web: www.nationalbeverage.com

CEO: Nick A. Caporella
CFO: –
HR: –
FYE: April 27
Type: Public

National Beverage makes and distributes the popular LaCroix sparkling water brand including a variety flavors. National Beverage also makes the Shasta and Faygo brands of flavored soft drinks (both of which were launched more than a century ago) the ClearFruit flavored waters Everfresh and Mr. Pure juice and juice-added drinks Rip It energy drink and Ohana lemonades and teas. Customers include national and regional grocers convenience stores and foodservice distributors. National Beverage operates a dozen facilities located in ten US states. Founded in 1985 chairman and CEO Nick Caporella owns 74% of the business.

	Annual Growth	05/15*	04/16	04/17	04/18	04/19
Sales ($ mil.)	11.9%	645.8	704.8	826.9	975.7	1,014.1
Net income ($ mil.)	30.0%	49.3	61.2	107.0	149.8	140.9
Market value ($ mil.)	26.5%	1,045.8	2,180.2	4,132.3	4,187.8	2,682.1
Employees	8.1%	1,200	1,200	1,300	1,500	1,640

*Fiscal year change

NATIONAL CABLE SATELLITE CORP

400 N CAPITOL ST NW # 650
WASHINGTON, DC 200011550
Phone: 202-737-3220
Fax: –
Web: www.c-span.org

CEO: Robert Kennedy
CFO: –
HR: –
FYE: March 31
Type: Private

National Cable Satellite Corporation is a political junkie. The company (better known as C-SPAN which stands for Cable Satellite Public Affairs Network) is a not-for-profit created in 1979 by the cable industry as a public service to provide live coverage of the US House of Representatives. The corporation's C-SPAN C-SPAN2 and C-SPAN3 air public proceedings such as congressional sessions White House press briefings and speeches British House of Commons sessions and other political and public affairs programs. C-SPAN also runs a radio network with content similar to its TV broadcasts and publishes more than 15 Web sites. The company gets its funds from license fees paid by cable and satellite systems.

	Annual Growth	03/13	03/14	03/15	03/16	03/17
Sales ($ mil.)	(2.7%)	–	73.2	69.7	68.5	67.4
Net income ($ mil.)	9.7%	–	9.8	11.9	(0.6)	13.0
Market value ($ mil.)	–	–	–	–	–	–
Employees	–	–	–	–	–	260

NATIONAL CINEMEDIA INC

NMS: NCMI

6300 S. Syracuse Way, Suite 300
Centennial, CO 80111
Phone: 303 792-3600
Fax: –
Web: www.ncm.com

CEO: Thomas F Lesinski
CFO: Katie Scherping
HR: –
FYE: December 27
Type: Public

National CineMedia (NCM) puts on its show before the real show starts at the movies (and even before the previews of coming attractions). Through its NCM Cinema Network the company distributes in-theater advertising on about 20150 movie screens across the US. NCM also produces and distributes FirstLook a pre-show entertainment program and entertainment industry infomercial. Additionally the company provides advertising to theater lobbies on its Lobby Entertainment Network (LEN). Major NCM shareholders include theater operators Regal Entertainment AMC Entertainment and Cinemark.

	Annual Growth	01/15*	12/15	12/16	12/17	12/18
Sales ($ mil.)	3.9%	394.0	446.5	447.6	426.1	441.4
Net income ($ mil.)	30.5%	13.4	15.4	25.4	2.5	29.8
Market value ($ mil.)	(24.0%)	1,106.2	1,209.3	1,126.9	521.9	485.0
Employees	(3.4%)	595	634	615	572	536

*Fiscal year change

NATIONAL COLLEGIATE ATHLETIC ASSOCIATION

700 W WASHINGTON ST
INDIANAPOLIS, IN 462042710
Phone: 317-917-6222
Fax: –
Web: www.ncaa.org

CEO: –
CFO: –
HR: –
FYE: August 31
Type: Private

The National Collegiate Athletic Association (NCAA) supports the intercollegiate sports activities of around 1000 member colleges and universities. A not-for-profit organization the NCAA administers scholarship and grant programs enforces conduct and eligibility rules and works to support and promote the needs of student athletes. The association is known for its lucrative branding and television deals such as those surrounding the popular "March Madness" tournament for Division I men's basketball. Seeking reform of athletics rules and regulations officials from 13 schools formed the Intercollegiate Athletic Association of the United States in 1906. The organization took its current name in 1910.

	Annual Growth	08/14	08/15	08/16	08/17	08/18
Sales ($ mil.)	3.8%	–	952.1	995.9	1,061.4	1,064.4
Net income ($ mil.)	(14.5%)	–	43.3	(403.9)	104.8	27.1
Market value ($ mil.)	–	–	–	–	–	–
Employees	–	–	–	–	–	508

NATIONAL COUNCIL OF YOUNG MEN'S CHRISTIAN ASSOCIATIONS OF THE UNITED STATES OF AMERICA

101 N WACKER DR STE 1600
CHICAGO, IL 606067310
Phone: 312-419-8456
Fax: –
Web: www.ymca.net

CEO: –
CFO: –
HR: Jackie Gordon
FYE: December 31
Type: Private

A venerable not-for-profit community service organization YMCA of the USA (Y-USA) assists the more than 2700 individual YMCAs across the country and represents them on both national and international levels. Although YMCA stands for Young Men's Christian Association the organization's programs are open to all. Local YMCAs are leading providers of child care in the US. The facilities also offer programs in aquatics arts and humanities education of new immigrants health and fitness and teen leadership. Overall YMCAs serve about 21 million people in some 10000 neighborhoods across the US which includes about 9 million children under the age of 17.

	Annual Growth	09/07	09/08*	12/08	12/13	12/14
Sales ($ mil.)	105.7%	–	1.5	0.5	119.0	114.2
Net income ($ mil.)	–	–	(0.0)	0.0	17.6	3.1
Market value ($ mil.)	–	–	–	–	–	–
Employees	–	–	–	–	–	350

*Fiscal year change

NATIONAL EDUCATION ASSOCIATION OF THE UNITED STATES

1201 16TH ST NW STE 410
WASHINGTON, DC 200363290
Phone: 202-833-4000
Fax: –
Web: www.nea.org

CEO: –
CFO: –
HR: –
FYE: August 31
Type: Private

The National Education Association (NEA) is dedicated to promoting the cause of public education and the teaching profession. The organization boasts a membership of 3 million elementary and secondary teachers support professionals administrators higher education faculty and student teachers. It operates in all US states through affiliates. The group's key issues include the No Child Left Behind Act professional pay education funding minority community outreach dropout prevention achievement gaps and other matters facing America's schools. Founded in 1857 the NEA also hosts Read Across America a one-day reading event held on Dr. Seuss' birthday.

	Annual Growth	08/07	08/08*	12/08*	08/10	08/14
Sales ($ mil.)	(0.4%)	–	392.9	0.6	376.6	384.2
Net income ($ mil.)	14.7%	–	18.1	0.0	16.1	41.2
Market value ($ mil.)	–	–	–	–	–	–
Employees	–	–	–	–	–	735

*Fiscal year change

NATIONAL FOOTBALL LEAGUE PLAYERS ASSOCIATION

1133 20TH ST NW FRNT 1
WASHINGTON, DC 200363449
Phone: 202-756-9100
Fax: –
Web: www.nflpa.com

CEO: –
CFO: –
HR: –
FYE: February 28
Type: Private

The National Football League Players Association (NFLPA) represents the interests of people who go to work in helmets and shoulder pads. The union oversees its members' collective bargaining agreement with the National Football League negotiates and monitors retirement and insurance benefits and works to promote the image of the players through marketing and licensing subsidiary NFL PLAYERS (formerly PLAYERS INC). A member of the AFL-CIO the NFLPA represents both active and retired players. It is governed by a board of player representatives who are chosen by their teammates. The union was established in 1956 more than 35 years after the NFL was organized.

	Annual Growth	02/08	02/09	02/12	02/14	02/15
Sales ($ mil.)	5.2%	–	62.7	81.3	65.9	84.8
Net income ($ mil.)	26.0%	–	11.5	(36.2)	26.0	46.0
Market value ($ mil.)	–	–	–	–	–	–
Employees	–	–	–	–	–	89

NATIONAL FROZEN FOODS CORPORATION

1600 FRVIEW AVE E STE 200
SEATTLE, WA 98102
Phone: 206-322-8900
Fax: –
Web: www.nffc.com

CEO: –
CFO: –
HR: –
FYE: August 30
Type: Private

Cool Beans! National Frozen Foods has made a name for itself as one of the nation's largest private-label frozen vegetable producers. The family-owned company's products which include peas sweet corn carrots squash and beans (green Italian lima and wax) as well as vegetable blends organic veggies and pureed items are available in grocery stores worldwide. National Frozen Foods also provides bulk and custom-packaging services. The company operates four processing plants in Washington and Oregon that offer a combined cold storage capacity for nearly 200 million pounds of frozen vegetables.

	Annual Growth	04/10	04/11	04/12*	08/13	08/14
Sales ($ mil.)	4.4%	–	178.1	197.2	18.2	202.6
Net income ($ mil.)	41.3%	–	6.2	13.6	5.8	17.6
Market value ($ mil.)	–	–	–	–	–	–
Employees	–	–	–	–	–	1,009

*Fiscal year change

NATIONAL FUEL GAS CO. (NJ)   NYS: NFG

6363 Main Street
Williamsville, NY 14221
Phone: 716 857-7000
Fax: –
Web: www.nationalfuelgas.com

CEO: Ronald J. (Ron) Tanski
CFO: Karen M Camiolo
HR: Nathan Barnes
FYE: September 30
Type: Public

Though not quite national in its reach National Fuel Gas explores for produces stores transmits and distributes natural gas in the Northeast US. It serves around 743500 customers in New York and Pennsylvania and engages in energy marketing and some timber processing. Its oil and gas subsidiary Seneca Resources has proved reserves of 1.9 billion cu. ft. of natural gas and 30.2 million barrels of oil.

	Annual Growth	09/15	09/16	09/17	09/18	09/19
Sales ($ mil.)	(1.0%)	1,760.9	1,452.4	1,579.9	1,592.7	1,693.3
Net income ($ mil.)	–	(379.4)	(291.0)	283.5	391.5	304.3
Market value ($ mil.)	(1.6%)	4,314.0	4,667.1	4,886.3	4,838.8	4,049.9
Employees	(0.2%)	2,125	2,080	2,100	2,105	2,107

NATIONAL GALLERY OF ART

6TH AND CNSTTUTION AVE NW
WASHINGTON, DC 205650001
Phone: 202-737-4215
Fax: –
Web: www.nga.gov

CEO: –
CFO: –
HR: –
FYE: September 30
Type: Private

The National Gallery of Art one of the world's pre-eminent art museums owns more than 100000 works of art dating from the Middle Ages to the present. Its collection of European and American art is comprised of works by some 10000 artists including Leonardo da Vinci Claude Monet and Pablo Picasso. The gallery is located on the National Mall in two buildings and an adjacent sculpture garden; its Web site offers virtual collection tours and in-depth study tours as well as the ability to search the entire collection by artist title or style. The National Gallery of Art was established by Congress as an affiliate of the Smithsonian Institution in 1937; some 6 million people visit each year. The idea of a national art museum was the passion of former secretary of state Andrew Mellon who began collecting works of art for the project in the 1930s.

	Annual Growth	09/06	09/07	09/08	09/09	09/15
Sales ($ mil.)	(1.2%)	–	–	226.8	138.2	207.7
Net income ($ mil.)	(12.9%)	–	–	60.0	(43.2)	22.8
Market value ($ mil.)	–	–	–	–	–	–
Employees	–	–	–	–	–	1,000

NATIONAL GRAPE CO-OPERATIVE ASSOCIATION, INC.

80 STATE ST
WESTFIELD, NY 14787
Phone: 716-326-5200
Fax: –
Web: www.welchs.com

CEO: –
CFO: –
HR: –
FYE: August 31
Type: Private

Well of course grape growers want to hang out in a bunch! The more than 1090 grower/owner-members of the National Grape Cooperative harvest Concord and Niagara grapes from almost 50000 acres of vineyards. The plucked produce supplies the coop's wholly owned subsidiary Welch Foods. Welch Foods makes and sells fruit-based juices jams jellies and spreads under the Welch's and Bama brands in the US and nearly 50 other countries. Offerings include fresh eating grapes distributed by C.H. Robinson Worldwide as well as dried fruit and frozen juice pops. The grape growers own vineyards in Pennsylvania Michigan New York Ohio Washington and Ontario Canada which produce some 300000 tons of grapes annually.

	Annual Growth	08/08	08/09	08/10	08/11	08/12
Sales ($ mil.)	(0.7%)	–	–	658.7	640.9	649.5
Net income ($ mil.)	(5.1%)	–	–	82.7	74.2	74.4
Market value ($ mil.)	–	–	–	–	–	–
Employees	–	–	–	–	–	1,325

NATIONAL HEAD START ASSOCIATION

1651 Prince St.
Alexandria VA 22314
Phone: 703-739-0875
Fax: 703-739-0878
Web: www.nhsa.org

CEO: –
CFO: –
HR: –
FYE: June 30
Type: Private - Not-for-Pr

These children aren't cheating they are getting a head start. National Head Start Association (NHSA) is a nonprofit that provides low-income families with education health nutrition and parental support services. The membership organization represents more than 1 million children and 2600 Head Start programs in the US. In addition NHSA provides Head Start's more than 200000 staff with professional development and training. The organization publishes research on early childhood education through the periodicals NHSA Dialog and Children and Families. Formed in the 1970s NHSA was an advocacy group for the Head Start community in Congress. The Head Start program got its start in 1965.

NATIONAL HEALTH INVESTORS, INC.   NYS: NHI

222 Robert Rose Drive
Murfreesboro, TN 37129
Phone: 615 890-9100
Fax: –
Web: www.nhireit.com

CEO: D. Eric Mendelsohn
CFO: John L Spaid
HR: –
FYE: December 31
Type: Public

National Health Investors has a financial investment in the nation's health. The real estate investment trust (REIT) owns or makes mortgage investments in health care properties primarily long-term care facilities. With more than 180 properties in over 30 states its holdings also include residences for people with developmental disabilities assisted-living complexes medical office buildings retirement centers and an acute care hospital. About one-third of National Health Investors' properties are leased to its largest tenant National HealthCare Corporation; half are leased to regional health care providers. A majority of the REIT's facilities are located in Florida Texas and Tennessee.

	Annual Growth	12/14	12/15	12/16	12/17	12/18
Sales ($ mil.)	13.5%	177.5	229.0	248.5	278.7	294.6
Net income ($ mil.)	11.0%	101.6	148.9	151.5	159.4	154.3
Market value ($ mil.)	1.9%	2,987.3	2,599.2	3,167.1	3,218.8	3,225.6
Employees	7.5%	12	12	15	16	16

NATIONAL HEALTHCARE CORP.   ASE: NHC

100 E. Vine Street
Murfreesboro, TN 37130
Phone: 615 890-2020
Fax: 615 890-0123
Web: www.nhccare.com

CEO: Stephen F. (Steve) Flatt
CFO: –
HR: –
FYE: December 31
Type: Public

National HealthCare (NHC) provides long-term care to those who have had long-term lives. Through its subsidiaries NHC manages some 75 skilled nursing homes in 10 states mainly in the southeastern US. Of its facilities the company owns or leases about 55 facilities and manages the other 20 for third-party organizations; together its facilities house about 9400 beds. In addition to its nursing homes NHC manages more than 35 home health programs and about 25 independent and assisted-living facilities. The company provides a number of health services through its facilities including hospice rehabilitation Alzheimer's care and institutional pharmacy services.

	Annual Growth	12/14	12/15	12/16	12/17	12/18
Sales ($ mil.)	3.0%	871.7	906.6	926.6	967.0	980.3
Net income ($ mil.)	2.5%	53.4	53.1	50.5	56.2	59.0
Market value ($ mil.)	5.7%	958.6	941.2	1,156.2	929.6	1,196.8
Employees	3.4%	13,050	13,225	14,450	14,850	14,891

NATIONAL HERITAGE ACADEMIES INC.

3850 Broadmoor Ave. SE Ste. 201 CEO: Brian Britton
Grand Rapids MI 49512 CFO: Stephen Conley
Phone: 616-222-1700 HR: Jenny Delessio
Fax: 616-575-6801 FYE: June 30
Web: www.heritageacademies.com Type: Private

The traditions at National Heritage Academies (NHA) may not be that old but they are already a part of many families' heritage. The company operates charter schools which are state-funded public schools operated by government-approved independent entities; charter schools are given operational autonomy while being held accountable to state and local regulations. NHA operates some 57 charter schools that enroll some 35000 students in kindergarten through eighth grades. The schools offer a rigorous curriculum character development and strong parental involvement. NHA was founded in 1995 by J.C. Huizenga a cousin of Wayne Huizenga founder of Waste Management and Blockbuster.

NATIONAL HOLDINGS CORP NAS: NHLD

200 Vesey Street, 25th Floor CEO: Michael A Mullen
New York, NY 10281 CFO: Glenn C Worman
Phone: 212 417-8000 HR: –
Fax: – FYE: September 30
Web: www.nhldcorp.com Type: Public

National Holdings helps investors manage their holdings. Through National Securities Corporation and vFinance the firm provides brokerage services to individual and institutional investors in the US. Products include stocks options bonds mutual funds and annuities. Its subsidiaries also provide investment banking services to growth companies. The group employs more than 800 advisors and brokers most of whom are independent contractors. National Holdings provides its representatives with research materials order execution trade processing and compliance support as well as higher-than-average commissions. Fortress Biotech acquired National Holdings in mid-2016.

	Annual Growth	09/15	09/16	09/17	09/18	09/19
Sales ($ mil.)	6.9%	163.0	174.1	189.9	211.1	212.9
Net income ($ mil.)	–	0.3	(5.6)	12.5	(11.5)	(0.8)
Market value ($ mil.)	(0.1%)	36.2	42.6	34.1	42.1	36.1
Employees	(4.2%)	1,152	1,150	1,070	1,020	970

NATIONAL INSTRUMENTS CORP. NMS: NATI

11500 North MoPac Expressway CEO: Alexander (Alex) Davern
Austin, TX 78759 CFO: Karen Rapp
Phone: 512 683-0100 HR: –
Fax: 512 683-9300 FYE: December 31
Web: www.ni.com Type: Public

National Instruments (NI) makes a measurable difference virtually in the lab. The company?s products help create virtual instruments that can observe measure and control electrical signals and physical attributes such as voltage and pressure. The company's flagship LabView product allows users to create graphical interfaces for controlling instruments and capturing and analyzing data as well as set up automated functions. In addition NI provides programming tools software applications and hardware products. Its hardware and software products can be used in a modular fashion depending on a customer?s needs. The Americas accounts for around 40% of sales. The company was founded in 1976.

	Annual Growth	12/14	12/15	12/16	12/17	12/18
Sales ($ mil.)	2.2%	1,243.9	1,225.5	1,228.2	1,289.4	1,359.1
Net income ($ mil.)	5.3%	126.3	95.3	82.7	52.4	155.1
Market value ($ mil.)	9.9%	4,124.3	3,805.9	4,088.5	5,522.5	6,019.9
Employees	0.6%	7,084	7,441	7,552	7,412	7,263

NATIONAL INTERSTATE CORP NMS: NATL

3250 Interstate Drive CEO: Anthony J Mercurio
Richfield, OH 44286-9000 CFO: Julie A McGraw
Phone: 330 659-8900 HR: –
Fax: 330 659-8909 FYE: December 31
Web: www.natl.com Type: Public

National Interstate stands behind you when you get on the bus! The specialty property/casualty insurer concentrates on the transportation market. One of the nation's largest insurers of truck and passenger transportation fleets the company also provides insurance to moving companies and personal lines of coverage for recreational vehicles. Additionally National Interstate offers general commercial insurance for small businesses in Alaska and Hawaii. The company distributes its products throughout the US. American Financial Group spun off National Interstate in 2005 but continues to control the company through a 52% stake held by its Great American Insurance Company.

	Annual Growth	12/10	12/11	12/12	12/13	12/14
Assets ($ mil.)	4.2%	1,488.6	1,525.1	1,570.2	1,623.8	1,754.7
Net income ($ mil.)	(27.3%)	39.5	35.6	34.3	17.6	11.0
Market value ($ mil.)	8.6%	423.8	488.3	570.4	455.2	589.8
Employees	6.7%	494	532	546	580	641

NATIONAL LIFE INSURANCE COMPANY

1 National Life Dr. CEO: Mehran Assadi
Montpelier VT 05604-0001 CFO: Edward Bonach
Phone: 802-229-3333 HR: –
Fax: 802-229-9281 FYE: December 31
Web: https://www.nationallife.com Type: Private - Mutual Com

One nation under insurance with financial security for all. National Life Group the marketing name for National Life Insurance Company and its affiliated companies is a mutually owned insurer dating back to 1848. Today National Life Group offers a range of insurance and investment products throughout the US through its namesake National Life Insurance Company and other subsidiaries including Equity Services (financial products broker/dealer) Life Insurance Company of the Southwest (insurance and annuities) National Retirement Plan Advisors (a third-party administrator) and Sentinel Investments (mutual funds retirement plans and institutional investment accounts).

NATIONAL MULTIPLE SCLEROSIS SOCIETY

733 3RD AVE FL 3 CEO: Cyndi Zagieboylo
NEW YORK, NY 100173211 CFO: Tami Caesar
Phone: 212-463-9791 HR: –
Fax: – FYE: September 30
Web: nationalmssociety.org/chapters/nyn Type: Private

The National Multiple Sclerosis Society funds research intended to find the cause and cure of MS. For people affected by the disease it offers counseling education and equipment assistance. The Society also works to promote public policies and professional education that serve the estimated 500000 people in the US who have MS and more than 2 million worldwide. The Society operates through its national office and a 50-state network of chapters. It generates most of its revenue through fundraising and counts some 16000 federal MS activists. The Society was founded in 1946 after Sylvia Lawry ran a classified ad in The New York Times looking for anyone who had recovered from the disease her brother was battling.

	Annual Growth	09/05	09/06	09/08	09/09	09/15
Sales ($ mil.)	–	–	0.0	5.2	2.9	113.6
Net income ($ mil.)	–	–	0.0	(0.2)	0.0	(3.7)
Market value ($ mil.)	–	–	–	–	–	–
Employees	–	–	–	–	–	1,200

NATIONAL PARK FOUNDATION (INC)

1110 VERMONT AVE NW # 200　　　　　　　　　　CEO: Will Shafroth
WASHINGTON, DC 200053563　　　　　　　　　CFO: Mandeep Singh
Phone: 202-796-2500　　　　　　　　　　　　　　　　HR: –
Fax: –　　　　　　　　　　　　　　　　　　　　FYE: September 30
Web: www.nationalparks.org　　　　　　　　　　　　Type: Private

Chartered by Congress in 1967 the National Park Foundation is a not-for-profit organization responsible for raising funds establishing grants and increasing public awareness of national parks in the US. About 70% of funds raised each year are used for programs which include education community involvement and volunteerism. The National Park Foundation works with the National Park Service to educate the public about the parks and recruit volunteers to maintain the parks. Each year more than 150000 volunteers contribute to preserving about 400 national parks in the US.

	Annual Growth	09/13	09/14	09/15	09/16	09/17
Sales ($ mil.)	10.2%	–	–	75.8	160.9	92.0
Net income ($ mil.)	(23.3%)	–	–	27.2	25.0	16.0
Market value ($ mil.)	–	–	–	–	–	–
Employees	–	–	–	–	–	78

NATIONAL PENN BANCSHARES INC.　　　　　　NASDAQ: NPBC

Philadelphia and Reading Avenues　　　　　　　　　　　CEO: –
Boyertown PA 19512　　　　　　　　　　　　　　　　CFO: –
Phone: 610-367-6001　　　　　　　　　　　　　　　　HR: –
Fax: 610-369-6118　　　　　　　　　　　　　　FYE: December 31
Web: www.natpennbank.com　　　　　　　　　　　Type: Public

Pennies or Benjamins it's all good to National Penn Bancshares the holding company for National Penn Bank which operates about 120 branches in eastern and central Pennsylvania and one in Maryland. Originally chartered in 1874 the bank courts small to midsized businesses with annual sales of less than $100 million. Business loans leases and lines of credit make up nearly half of the bank's loan portfolio which also includes commercial real estate loans (around 20%) residential mortgages home equity loans and lines of credit and consumer loans. Other units offer trust investment insurance wealth management retirement plan consulting and health care advisory services.

NATIONAL PRESTO INDUSTRIES, INC.　　　　　　　NYS: NPK

3925 North Hastings Way　　　　　　　　　　　　CEO: Maryjo Cohen
Eau Claire, WI 54703-3703　　　　　　　　　　　CFO: Randy F. Lieble
Phone: 715 839-2121　　　　　　　　　　　　　　　HR: –
Fax: –　　　　　　　　　　　　　　　　　　FYE: December 31
Web: www.gopresto.com　　　　　　　　　　　　　Type: Public

The heat is on at National Presto Industries but it's thermostatically controlled for even-cooking on nonstick surfaces. Under the Presto brand the company makes and distributes small appliances and housewares including pressure cookers fry pans deep fryers griddles coffeemakers can openers electric knives and pizza ovens. The company pours itself into defense work too supplying ammo; cartridge cases; electromechanical assemblies; and Load Assemble and Pack (LAP) setup for regulated goods. Adding to the bottom line its absorbent products unit makes private label and Presto brand diapers and incontinence supplies. The diversified company counts the US government among its largest customers.

	Annual Growth	12/14	12/15	12/16	12/17	12/18
Sales ($ mil.)	(5.9%)	412.4	427.7	341.9	333.6	323.3
Net income ($ mil.)	10.8%	26.5	40.5	44.6	53.0	39.9
Market value ($ mil.)	19.1%	405.2	578.5	742.8	694.3	816.2
Employees	(2.3%)	1,043	1,090	1,138	982	949

NATIONAL PUBLIC RADIO, INC.

1111 N CAPITOL ST NE　　　　　　　　　　　　CEO: John Lansing
WASHINGTON, DC 200027502　　　　　　　　　CFO: Debbie Cullen
Phone: 202-513-2000　　　　　　　　　　　HR: Barbara Sheppard
Fax: –　　　　　　　　　　　　　　　　　　FYE: September 30
Web: www.npr.org　　　　　　　　　　　　　　　Type: Private

This company helps keep radio listeners informed and entertained without commercial interruptions. National Public Radio (NPR) is a privately supported not-for-profit organization that produces and syndicates radio programming to 900 independently operated noncommercial radio stations including about 750 NPR member stations. Its shows include news programs Morning Edition and All Things Considered as well as cultural programs (Fresh Air) and entertainment shows (Car Talk; Wait Wait … Don't Tell Me!). Founded in 1970 NPR is funded through private donations member station dues and grants from organizations such as the Corporation for Public Broadcasting and the National Science Foundation.

	Annual Growth	09/14	09/15	09/16	09/17	09/18
Sales ($ mil.)	9.5%	–	196.5	208.0	219.7	258.1
Net income ($ mil.)	–	–	(6.4)	1.7	25.6	5.8
Market value ($ mil.)	–	–	–	–	–	–
Employees	–	–	–	–	–	741

NATIONAL RAILROAD PASSENGER CORPORATION

60 MASSACHUSETTS AVE NW　　　　　　　CEO: Richard H Anderson
WASHINGTON, DC 20001　　　　　　　　　　　　　　CFO: –
Phone: 202-906-3000　　　　　　　　　　　　　　　　HR: –
Fax: –　　　　　　　　　　　　　　　　　　FYE: September 30
Web: www.amtrak.com　　　　　　　　　　　　　Type: Private

National Railroad Passenger Corporation better known as Amtrak has been riding the rails for more than 40 years. Amtrak is the US' intercity passenger rail provider and its only high-speed rail operator. More than 30 million passengers travel on Amtrak every year on more than 300 daily trains. It connects 46 states Washington DC and three provinces in Canada. Its network consists of about 21000 route miles of track most of which is owned by freight railroads. Amtrak also operates commuter rail systems on behalf of several states and transit agencies. Owned by the US government through the US Department of Transportation Amtrak depends on subsidies from the federal government to operate.

	Annual Growth	09/07	09/08	09/14	09/16	09/17
Sales ($ mil.)	122.7%	–	2.5	0.0	3,240.6	3,305.7
Net income ($ mil.)	–	–	(1.1)	0.0	(1,080.5)	(968.7)
Market value ($ mil.)	–	–	–	–	–	–
Employees	–	–	–	–	–	18,650

NATIONAL RESEARCH CORP　　　　　　　　　　　NMS: NRC

1245 Q Street　　　　　　　　　　　　　　　　CEO: Michael D Hays
Lincoln, NE 68508　　　　　　　　　　　　　　　CFO: Kevin Karas
Phone: 402 475-2525　　　　　　　　　　　　　　　HR: –
Fax: –　　　　　　　　　　　　　　　　　　FYE: December 31
Web: www.nationalresearch.com　　　　　　　　　Type: Public

The ultimate father figure National Research Corporation (NRC) is there to let you know when you're not measuring up. Founded in 1981 NRC offers performance measurement and analysis services to clients within the health care industry including hospitals HMOs home care hospice and regulatory groups. The company's performance tracking system uses individualized questionnaires to better determine an organization's satisfaction rating and the NRC Healthcare Market Guide provides industry statistics allowing clients to compare their services to those of competitors. Founder and CEO Michael Hays owns more than 65% of the company.

	Annual Growth	12/14	12/15	12/16	12/17	12/18
Sales ($ mil.)	4.9%	98.8	102.3	109.4	117.6	119.7
Net income ($ mil.)	13.4%	18.2	17.6	20.5	22.9	30.0
Market value ($ mil.)	28.5%	347.0	397.8	471.2	925.1	945.9
Employees	3.7%	397	375	404	458	459

NATIONAL RESTAURANTS MANAGEMENT INC.

560 5th Ave.   CEO: Dennis Riese
New York NY 10036   CFO: -
Phone: 212-563-7440   HR: -
Fax: 212-613-1929   FYE: April 30
Web: www.rieserestaurants.com   Type: Private

Without this organization New Yorkers might go hungry. National Restaurants Management which does business as The Riese Organization is among the largest multiple-franchise restaurant operators in New York City. Its portfolio of about 80 eateries includes quick-service outlets (Tim Hortons KFC and Pizza Hut) and chain restaurants (T.G.I. Friday's and Houlihan's); Riese also operates upscale Manhattan night spots such as Charley O's and Times Square Grill. In addition to restaurants the Riese Organization manages several real-estate holdings through a separate division. The company founded by brothers Murray and Irving Riese in 1940 is controlled by CEO Dennis Riese (Murray's son).

NATIONAL RETAIL FEDERATION, INC.

1101 NEW YORK AVE NW # 1200   CEO: Matthew Shay
WASHINGTON, DC 200054348   CFO: -
Phone: 202-626-8155   HR: -
Fax: -   FYE: February 28
Web: www.nrf.com   Type: Private

The National Retail Federation (NRF) wants everyone to shop 'til they drop. The group is a trade association representing the retail industry that works through four divisions addressing technology in retail chain restaurants advertising and marketing and online retail. It functions as both an advocacy group and an informational network for its members lobbying government hosting conferences and seminars and publishing newsletters and books. The NRF magazine Stores is published monthly. NRF includes more than 100 US national state and international retail associations and more than 1.6 million US retailers with about 42 million employees.

	Annual Growth	02/14	02/15	02/16	02/17	02/18
Sales ($ mil.)	5.7%	-	56.3	58.6	60.8	66.4
Net income ($ mil.)	8.9%	-	1.1	(3.4)	9.1	1.5
Market value ($ mil.)	-	-	-	-	-	-
Employees	-	-	-	-	-	135

NATIONAL RETAIL PROPERTIES INC   NYS: NNN

450 South Orange Avenue, Suite 900   CEO: Julian E. (Jay) Whitehurst
Orlando, FL 32801   CFO: Kevin B. Habicht
Phone: 407 265-7348   HR: -
Fax: 407 423-2894   FYE: December 31
Web: www.nnnreit.com   Type: Public

For National Retail Properties good things come in big boxes. The self-administered real estate investment trust (REIT) acquires develops and manages freestanding retail properties in heavily traveled commercial and residential areas. Its portfolio includes more than 2250 properties with some 25 million sq. ft. of leasable space in almost all 50 states concentrated in Texas the Southeast and the Midwest. National Retail Properties also invests in mortgages operates some of its retail properties and develops properties to sell them later for a profit. More than 30% of its rental income comes from convenience store and restaurant operators with its top clients being Sunoco Mister Car Wash LA Fitness The Pantry and Camping World.

	Annual Growth	12/14	12/15	12/16	12/17	12/18
Sales ($ mil.)	9.4%	434.8	482.9	533.6	584.9	622.7
Net income ($ mil.)	11.3%	190.6	197.8	239.5	265.0	292.4
Market value ($ mil.)	5.4%	6,358.4	6,468.2	7,138.5	6,965.6	7,834.5
Employees	1.5%	64	62	65	66	68

NATIONAL RIFLE ASSOCIATION OF AMERICA

11250 WAPLES MILL RD # 1   CEO: -
FAIRFAX, VA 220309400   CFO: Wilson H Phillips
Phone: 703-267-1000   HR: -
Fax: -   FYE: December 31
Web: www.nraila.org   Type: Private

The NRA believes in the right to bear arms. With more than 5 million members The National Rifle Association (NRA) is the staunch defender of Second Amendment rights. It's a major player in the political arena and stands firm in its resolve to protect the right to keep and bear arms. The NRA offers a variety of educational and gun safety programs and publishes magazines (America's 1st Freedom American Hunter Women's Outlook). It also caters to more than one million youth through its shooting sports events and affiliated programs with the likes of 4-H the Boy Scouts of America and others. It also sells NRA merchandise. Union army veterans William Church and George Wingate founded the NRA in 1871.

	Annual Growth	12/08	12/09	12/13	12/14	12/16
Sales ($ mil.)	6.4%	-	237.5	348.0	310.5	366.9
Net income ($ mil.)	-	-	1.2	57.4	(35.1)	(45.8)
Market value ($ mil.)	-	-	-	-	-	-
Employees	-	-	-	-	-	500

NATIONAL RURAL ELECTRIC COOPERATIVE ASSOCIATION

4301 WILSON BLVD STE 1   CEO: Glenn L English Jr
ARLINGTON, VA 222031867   CFO: -
Phone: 703-907-5500   HR: -
Fax: -   FYE: December 31
Web: www.electric.coop   Type: Private

Would it shock you to learn that consumer-owned cooperatives provide electricity to more than 42 million people in the US? The National Rural Electric Cooperative Association (NRECA) is the cooperatives' voice in politics and policymaking. It publishes a monthly magazine and a weekly newspaper sponsors conferences and seminars and represents about 900 rural electric co-ops (from 47 states) in the US Congress and state legislatures. As the nation embraces investor-owned utilities NRECA has been lobbying hard for more moderate approaches to deregulation in order to protect consumers from potential monopolies. The association also provides power assistance and technical advice to developing nations.

	Annual Growth	12/07	12/08	12/12	12/13	12/14
Sales ($ mil.)	6.0%	-	162.7	208.7	194.5	230.5
Net income ($ mil.)	47.1%	-	0.2	4.5	(8.1)	2.0
Market value ($ mil.)	-	-	-	-	-	-
Employees	-	-	-	-	-	885

NATIONAL RURAL UTILITIES COOPERATIVE FINANCE CORP   NL:

20701 Cooperative Way   CEO: Sheldon C Petersen
Dulles, VA 20166   CFO: J Andrew Don
Phone: 703 467-1800   HR: -
Fax: 703 709-6779   FYE: May 31
Web: www.nrucfc.coop   Type: Public

Cooperation may work wonders on Sesame Street but in the real world it takes money to pay the power bill. The National Rural Utilities Cooperative Finance Corporation provides financing and investment services for rural electrical and telephone projects throughout the US. The group is owned by some 1500 member electric utility and telecommunications systems. National Rural supplements the government loans that traditionally have fueled rural electric utilities by selling commercial paper medium-term notes and collateral trust bonds to fund its loan programs. National Rural was formed in 1969 by the National Rural Electric Cooperative Association a lobby representing the nation's electric co-ops.

	Annual Growth	05/15	05/16	05/17	05/18	05/19
Sales ($ mil.)	4.0%	672.6	717.7	1,149.5	1,326.7	787.7
Net income ($ mil.)	-	(19.0)	(49.7)	309.9	455.2	(149.2)
Market value ($ mil.)	-	-	-	-	-	-
Employees	2.6%	232	243	248	254	257

NATIONAL SAFETY COUNCIL

1121 SPRING LAKE DR
ITASCA, IL 601433201
Phone: 630-285-1121
Fax: -
Web: www.nsc.org

CEO: Lorraine M Martin
CFO: Patrick Phelam
HR: -
FYE: June 30
Type: Private

What are the odds of crashing while driving and talking on a cell phone? This is a question the National Safety Council (NSC) can answer. The NSC is a not-for-profit organization dedicated to educating Americans on safety and health to stop as many of the millions of preventable injuries a year as possible. NSC and its about 60 local chapters comprise members from more than 50000 business academic government community and labor organizations as well as individuals. It provides information and training to its members (and members' employees) on injury statistics and prevention. The group also offers consulting services on safety program development incident investigation and hazard recognition.

	Annual Growth	06/12	06/13	06/15	06/16	06/17
Sales ($ mil.)	3.5%	-	51.6	55.0	59.7	59.2
Net income ($ mil.)	(8.4%)	-	7.4	5.0	6.9	5.2
Market value ($ mil.)	-	-	-	-	-	-
Employees	-	-	-	-	-	350

NATIONAL SECURITY GROUP, INC

NMS: NSEC

661 East Davis Street
Elba, AL 36323
Phone: 334 897-2273
Fax: -
Web: www.nationalsecuritygroup.com

CEO: W L Brunson Jr
CFO: Brian R McLeod
HR: -
FYE: December 31
Type: Public

This National Security Group is keeping homeowners safe in the South. The company's subsidiaries Omega One Insurance and National Security Fire and Casualty sell property/casualty insurance in about a dozen southern states. Most of National Security Group's revenues are generated by its residential premiums from homeowners and mobile homeowners policies. The unit also offers personal nonstandard automobile insurance. Its life insurance subsidiary National Security Insurance offers basic life health and accident insurance. Alabama and Mississippi together account for about half of the company's sales.

	Annual Growth	12/14	12/15	12/16	12/17	12/18
Assets ($ mil.)	(0.1%)	144.9	148.1	148.6	146.4	144.2
Net income ($ mil.)	(43.4%)	7.6	4.7	3.1	(1.2)	0.8
Market value ($ mil.)	(0.8%)	34.0	38.5	44.9	41.3	32.9
Employees	(2.9%)	91	85	84	81	81

NATIONAL TRUST FOR HISTORIC PRESERVATION IN THE UNITED ST

1785 Massachusetts Ave. NW
Washington DC 20036-2117
Phone: 202-588-6000
Fax: 202-588-6038
Web: www.nationaltrust.org/index.html

CEO: -
CFO: Carla Washinko
HR: -
FYE: September 30
Type: Private - Not-for-Pr

National Trust for Historic Preservation wants to ensure that historic America is protected against destruction and negligence. The not-for-profit organization was founded in 1949 and educates advocates and provides resources for the preservation of historic buildings and land (not to be confused with the National Register of Historical Places which designates buildings and neighborhoods as historic). The group also operates about 30 historic sites across the US. National Trust which boasts about 270000 members operates out of a Washington DC headquarters and nine regional and field offices. It also works with thousands of preservation groups in all 50 states.

NATIONAL UNIVERSITY

11355 N TORREY PINES RD
LA JOLLA, CA 920371013
Phone: 858-642-8000
Fax: -
Web: www.nu.edu

CEO: -
CFO: -
HR: -
FYE: June 30
Type: Private

National University is the flagship school of the National University System. The institution offers more than 150 undergraduate and graduate degrees and teacher credential and certificate programs. A not-for-profit institution National University programs range across fields including business engineering education media and human services. The university enrolls 23000 students at multiple locations in California and Nevada; it also offers about 70 online degree programs. The school conducts research through the National University Community Research Institute (NUCRI). National University was founded in 1971.

	Annual Growth	06/08	06/09	06/10	06/11	06/15
Sales ($ mil.)	8.1%	-	165.0	178.6	203.3	263.8
Net income ($ mil.)	37.7%	-	5.2	18.5	25.2	35.3
Market value ($ mil.)	-	-	-	-	-	-
Employees	-	-	-	-	-	1,954

NATIONAL VAN LINES, INC.

2800 W ROOSEVELT RD
BROADVIEW, IL 601553771
Phone: 708-450-2900
Fax: -

CEO: Maureen Beal
CFO: -
HR: Sharon Cutta
FYE: April 30
Type: Private

National Van Lines provides moving services for households and businesses. The company which operates through a national network of some 400 agents can arrange international as well as domestic moves. Besides consumers and businesses National Van Lines has a dedicated unit National Forwarding Company to serve customers including government agencies such as the US Department of Defense to move military families. CEO Maureen Beal owns National Van Lines which was founded in 1929 by her grandfather F.J. McKee.

	Annual Growth	04/06	04/07	04/08	04/09	04/10
Sales ($ mil.)	-	-	-	(1,696.8)	89.4	80.7
Net income ($ mil.)	27674.5%	-	-	0.0	3.5	2.2
Market value ($ mil.)	-	-	-	-	-	-
Employees	-	-	-	-	-	135

NATIONAL WESTERN LIFE INSURANCE CO. (AUSTIN, TX)

NMS: NWLI

850 East Anderson Lane
Austin, TX 78752-1602
Phone: 512 836-1010
Fax: 512 836-6980
Web: www.nationalwesternlife.com

CEO: Robert L Moody
CFO: Brian M Pribyl
HR: -
FYE: December 31
Type: Public

National Western Life Insurance sells life insurance and annuity products including individual universal whole and term plans. The company operates throughout the US except in New York and internationally in Central and South America the Caribbean Eastern Europe Asia and the Pacific Rim. Annuities sold by independent agents make up most of its US sales. Some two-thirds of its life insurance premiums come from outside the US where the company targets wealthy individuals. Investments mainly in fixed debt securities account for some 70% of revenues.

	Annual Growth	12/09	12/10	12/11	12/12	12/13
Assets ($ mil.)	9.6%	7,518.7	8,773.9	9,728.0	10,263.9	10,830.4
Net income ($ mil.)	20.6%	45.5	72.9	55.6	92.6	96.2
Market value ($ mil.)	6.5%	631.1	606.0	494.9	573.3	812.6
Employees	(1.3%)	294	292	278	280	279

NATIONAL WILDLIFE FEDERATION INC

11100 WILDLIFE CENTER DR
RESTON, VA 201905362
Phone: 703-438-6000
Fax: –
Web: www.nwf.org

CEO: Collin O'Mara
CFO: –
HR: April Bowen
FYE: August 31
Type: Private

The National Wildlife Federation (NWF) works to educate the public about conservation of wildlife and other natural resources. The non-profit organization with some four million members organizes efforts on an educational and political front. Conservation projects include restoring gray wolves to Yellowstone protecting the Everglades preserving wetlands flood plain management and fighting effects of climate change. It also conducts wildlife tours and publishes a number of magazines including National Wildlife Ranger Rick Your Big Backyard and Animal Baby and produces film and television programs on conservation. The NWF was founded in 1936.

	Annual Growth	08/13	08/14	08/15	08/16	08/17
Sales ($ mil.)	2.6%	–	86.3	75.3	79.7	93.3
Net income ($ mil.)	32.6%	–	5.6	(5.3)	7.4	13.2
Market value ($ mil.)	–	–	–	–	–	–
Employees	–	–	–	–	–	350

NATIONSTAR MORTGAGE HOLDINGS INC

NYS: NSM

8950 Cypress Waters Blvd.
Coppell, TX 75019
Phone: 469 549-2000
Fax: –
Web: www.nationstarholdings.com

CEO: Jay Bray
CFO: Amar R Patel
HR: –
FYE: December 31
Type: Public

Nationstar Mortgage helps turn home ownership into more than just a wish upon a star. The company is one of the largest servicers of residential mortgage loans in the US with a servicing portfolio comprising more than 2.9 million loans that total in excess of $470 billion in unpaid principal balances. Nationstar also originates loans (primarily government- and agency-backed mortgages) which it typically sells or securitizes within one month of origination; mortgage sales make up one-third of its total revenue. The company serves consumers directly through its call centers and also offers its products through wholesalers. Its Xome subsidiary offers ancillary real estate services.

	Annual Growth	12/12	12/13	12/14	12/15	12/16
Sales ($ mil.)	18.1%	984.3	2,087.0	1,973.1	1,988.6	1,915.0
Net income ($ mil.)	(44.8%)	205.3	217.1	220.7	38.8	19.0
Market value ($ mil.)	(12.6%)	3,020.5	3,603.5	2,748.4	1,303.5	1,760.8
Employees	13.5%	4,672	6,984	5,500	6,740	7,750

NATIONSTAR MORTGAGE HOLDINGS INC.

NYSE: NSM

350 Highland Dr.
Lewisville TX 75067
Phone: 469-549-2000
Fax: 952-853-1410
Web: www.nathcompanies.com/

CEO: –
CFO: –
HR: –
FYE: December 31
Type: Public

Nationstar Mortgage helps turn home ownership into more than just a wish upon a star. The company services residential mortgage loans throughout the US. Its servicing portfolio comprises more than 1.8 million loans that total in excess of $300 billion in unpaid principal balances. Nationstar also originates loans primarily government- and agency-backed mortgages which it typically sells or securitizes within one month of origination. The company serves consumers directly through its Texas-based call center; it also offers its products through wholesalers. The firm has seen rapid growth as a result of its expanding servicing portfolio. Nationstar went public in 2012.

NATIONWIDE CHILDREN'S HOSPITAL

700 CHILDRENS DR
COLUMBUS, OH 432052639
Phone: 614-722-2000
Fax: –
Web: www.nationwidechildrens.org

CEO: Steve Allen
CFO: Timothy C. Robinson
HR: –
FYE: December 31
Type: Private

Buckeye babies toddlers and teens don't have to travel the country to find pediatric care with Nationwide Children's Hospital at their disposal. The Columbus Ohio health care provider is one of the largest pediatric care centers in the US. The hospital has some 430 licensed beds and offers services in areas such as behavioral health cardiology hospice orthopedics and surgery. It has roughly 1100 health care providers on its medical staff and its emergency department treats more than 83000 patients each year. The hospital also operates outpatient and specialty clinics in the area and a research institute which is investigating gene therapy.

	Annual Growth	12/13	12/14	12/15	12/16	12/17
Sales ($ mil.)	21.8%	–	1,282.2	1,386.9	1,385.4	2,317.0
Net income ($ mil.)	24.8%	–	332.7	285.7	330.5	647.4
Market value ($ mil.)	–	–	–	–	–	–
Employees	–	–	–	–	–	12,000

NATIONWIDE MUTUAL INSURANCE COMPANY

1 Nationwide Plaza
Columbus OH 43215-2220
Phone: 614-249-7111
Fax: 914-681-6949
Web: www.nypa.gov

CEO: Steve Rasmussen
CFO: Mark R Thresher
HR: Lorie Kuyoth
FYE: December 31
Type: Private - Mutual Com

Call it truth in advertising — Nationwide Mutual Insurance Company has offices throughout the US. The company is a leading US property/casualty insurer that also provides life insurance and retirement products through its Nationwide Financial Services subsidiary. Its property/casualty products range from general personal and commercial coverage to such specialty lines as professional liability workers' compensation agricultural insurance and loss-control pet insurance and other coverage. The company sells its products and provides services through Allied Group Harleysville Group Nationwide Agribusiness Insurance GatesMcDonald Scottsdale Insurance and other subsidiaries.

NATIVE ENVIRONMENTAL L.L.C.

3250 S 35TH AVE
PHOENIX, AZ 850096734
Phone: 602-254-0122
Fax: –
Web: www.nativeaz.com

CEO: –
CFO: –
HR: –
FYE: December 31
Type: Private

Removal of mold lead and asbestos is not a foreign concept at Native Environmental L.L.C. The Phoenix-based industrial cleaning and environmental contracting company serves Arizona New Mexico and thirty other states. Native Environmental focuses on mold remediation lead-based paint removal and removal of asbestos. The company contracts with customers like hospitals governmental entities and demolition companies and has short and long-term contracts that range in size from small commercial projects to large industrial projects. Founded by CEO Jon W. Riggs Native Environmental has been in business since 2000.

	Annual Growth	12/08	12/09	12/10	12/11	12/12
Sales ($ mil.)	9.9%	–	7.3	9.6	10.2	9.6
Net income ($ mil.)	–	–	–	1.6	1.0	(0.1)
Market value ($ mil.)	–	–	–	–	–	–
Employees	–	–	–	–	–	100

NATURAL ALTERNATIVES INTERNATIONAL, INC. — NMS: NAII

1535 Faraday Ave
Carlsbad, CA 92008
Phone: 760 744-7700
Fax: –
Web: www.nai-online.com

CEO: Mark A Ledoux
CFO: Michael E Fortin
HR: –
FYE: June 30
Type: Public

Natural Alternatives International (NAI) is a natural alternative for nutritional supplement marketers who want to outsource manufacturing. The company provides private-label manufacturing of vitamins minerals herbs and other customized nutritional supplements. Its main customers are direct sellers such as Mannatech and NSA International for whom it makes JuicePlus+ chewables capsules and powdered products. NAI also makes some branded products for sale in the US: the Pathway to Healing brand of nutritional supplements promoted by doctor and evangelist Reginald B. Cherry.

	Annual Growth	06/15	06/16	06/17	06/18	06/19
Sales ($ mil.)	14.8%	79.5	114.2	121.9	132.4	138.3
Net income ($ mil.)	18.2%	3.3	9.5	7.2	5.1	6.5
Market value ($ mil.)	19.8%	40.9	79.8	71.9	73.3	84.2
Employees	16.9%	167	285	227	266	312

NATURAL GAS SERVICES GROUP INC — NYS: NGS

404 Veterans Airpark Ln., Ste 300
Midland, TX 79705
Phone: 432 262-2700
Fax: –
Web: www.ngsgi.com

CEO: Stephen C. Taylor
CFO: G. Larry Lawrence
HR: –
FYE: December 31
Type: Public

The pressure is on to enhance oil and gas well production. Natural Gas Services Group (NGS) manufactures and leases natural gas compressors used to boost oil and gas well production primarily in non-conventional plays such as coal bed methane tight gas and oil and gas shales. The company also provides flare tip burners ignition systems and components used to combust waste gases before entering the atmosphere. It offers products and services to exploration and production companies operating in Colorado Kansas Michigan New Mexico North Dakota Ohio Oklahoma Pennsylvania Texas Utah West Virginia and Wyoming. The company has more than 2500 natural gas compressors in rental fleet totaling some 370000 horsepower.

	Annual Growth	12/14	12/15	12/16	12/17	12/18
Sales ($ mil.)	(9.4%)	97.0	95.9	71.7	67.7	65.5
Net income ($ mil.)	(58.3%)	14.1	10.1	6.5	19.9	0.4
Market value ($ mil.)	(8.1%)	299.6	290.0	418.1	340.7	213.8
Employees	(6.2%)	353	263	217	235	273

NATURAL GROCERS BY VITAMIN COTTAGE INC — NYS: NGVC

12612 West Alameda Parkway
Lakewood, CO 80228
Phone: 303 986-4600
Fax: –
Web: www.naturalgrocers.com

CEO: –
CFO: Sandra M. Buffa
HR: –
FYE: September 30
Type: Public

Natural Grocers by Vitamin Cottage is riding the wave of increased consumer interest in wellness and nutrition. The fast-growing company (both in sales and store count) operates about 140 stores in some 20 US states that sell natural and organic food including fresh produce meat frozen food and non-perishable bulk food; vitamins and dietary supplements; personal care products; pet care products; and books. The company uses United Natural Foods as its primary supplier and it also runs a bulk food repackaging facility and distribution center in its home state of Colorado. Founded by Margaret and Philip Isely in 1958 Natural Grocers by Vitamin Cottage is run by members of the Isely family.

	Annual Growth	09/15	09/16	09/17	09/18	09/19
Sales ($ mil.)	9.7%	624.7	705.5	769.0	849.0	903.6
Net income ($ mil.)	(12.7%)	16.2	11.5	6.9	12.7	9.4
Market value ($ mil.)	(18.5%)	509.7	250.7	125.3	379.4	224.4
Employees	6.8%	2,830	3,074	3,270	3,598	3,681

NATURAL RESOURCE PARTNERS LP — NYS: NRP

1201 Louisiana Street, Suite 3400
Houston, TX 77002
Phone: 713 751-7507
Fax: –
Web: www.nrplp.com

CEO: Corbin J Robertson Jr
CFO: Christopher J Zolas
HR: –
FYE: December 31
Type: Public

Natural Resource Partners (NRP) makes money from coal without getting its hands dirty. Rather than mining the coal itself NRP leases properties to coal producers. The company's properties — mainly in Appalachia but also in the Northern Powder River Basin and the Illinois Basin — contain proved and probable reserves of about 2.4 billion tons of coal. NRP was formed as a partnership between WPP Group (Western Pocahontas Properties New Gauley Coal and Great Northern Properties) and Arch Coal. Arch Coal has sold its stake in NRP but remains one of the company's top lessees along with Alpha Natural Resources. Chairman and CEO Corbin Robertson controls about 35% of NRP primarily through WPP Group.

	Annual Growth	12/14	12/15	12/16	12/17	12/18
Sales ($ mil.)	(8.6%)	399.8	488.8	400.1	378.0	278.5
Net income ($ mil.)	6.4%	108.8	(571.7)	96.9	88.7	139.5
Market value ($ mil.)	42.6%	113.3	15.6	395.7	318.5	468.4
Employees	–	–	–	284	307	57

NATURAL RESOURCES DEFENSE COUNCIL INC.

40 W 20TH ST
NEW YORK, NY 100114211
Phone: 212-727-2700
Fax: –
Web: www.nrdc.org

CEO: Gina McCarthy
CFO: Lawrence Levine
HR: –
FYE: June 30
Type: Private

Natural Resource Defense Council (NRDC) may be Mother Nature's strongest advocate. It is a nonprofit environmental action organization comprising 1.4-million members dedicated to preserving wildlife and the wilderness. To that end the NRDC's mission takes aim at curbing global warming; creating a future fueled by clean energy; restoring the Earth's oceans; saving endangered wildlife and wild places; stemming the tide of pollutants that endanger heath; and accelerating the greening of communities. In addition press releases and blog posts it publishes Nature's Voice a bulletin on environmental campaigns; O nEarth its quarterly magazine; and periodic NRDC Reports on specific issues.

	Annual Growth	06/09	06/10	06/13	06/14	06/15
Sales ($ mil.)	9.9%	–	97.0	116.0	121.6	155.2
Net income ($ mil.)	29.0%	–	8.0	13.5	5.9	28.4
Market value ($ mil.)	–	–	–	–	–	–
Employees	–	–	–	–	–	500

NATURE'S SUNSHINE PRODUCTS, INC. — NAS: NATR

2901 W Bluegrass Boulevard, Suite 100
Lehi, UT 84043
Phone: 801 341-7900
Fax: –
Web: www.natr.com

CEO: Gregory L. (Greg) Probert
CFO: Joseph W. (Joe) Baty
HR: –
FYE: December 31
Type: Public

If you're in need of some Vitamin D you can stand in the sunshine or visit Nature's Sunshine Products. The company is one of the nation's largest manufacturers and marketers of supplementary health care products. It makes more than 700 products including herbal supplements (available in capsule tablet and liquid form) and vitamins. Nature's Sunshine Products also sells essential oils and personal care items. The company has operations and distribution agreements in Asia Europe and North and South America. Its Synergy Worldwide multi-level marketing division sells the company's products in the US and selected Asian and European countries.

	Annual Growth	12/14	12/15	12/16	12/17	12/18
Sales ($ mil.)	(0.1%)	366.4	324.7	341.2	342.0	364.8
Net income ($ mil.)	–	10.0	14.7	2.1	(12.9)	(0.9)
Market value ($ mil.)	(13.9%)	284.6	194.3	288.1	221.8	156.5
Employees	(1.6%)	964	901	972	911	905

NATUS MEDICAL INC.
NMS: NTUS

6701 Koll Center Parkway, Suite 120
Pleasanton, CA 94566
Phone: 925 223-6700
Fax: –
Web: www.natus.com

CEO: James B. Hawkins
CFO: Jonathan A. Kennedy
HR: –
FYE: December 31
Type: Public

Natus Medical designs and manufactures audiological and neurological diagnostic and screening products. While the company's focus has historically been on infants (newborn hearing screening neonatal monitoring) it has expanded its product line to include an array of screening and diagnostic systems for use with children and adults. Its systems detect such neurological conditions as epilepsy and balance and sleep disorders. Natus also manufactures newborn and infant care products to diagnose and treat brain injury and jaundice neurosurgery products such as shunts and dural graft implants and hearing aid fitting tools. The company sells its wares worldwide through a direct sales force and distributors; its largest market is the US.

	Annual Growth	12/14	12/15	12/16	12/17	12/18
Sales ($ mil.)	10.5%	355.8	375.9	381.9	501.0	530.9
Net income ($ mil.)	–	32.5	37.9	42.6	(20.3)	(22.9)
Market value ($ mil.)	(1.4%)	1,218.3	1,624.3	1,176.4	1,291.3	1,150.4
Employees	16.2%	948	1,067	1,160	1,726	1,729

NAUGATUCK VALLEY FINANCIAL CORPORATION
NASDAQ: NVSL

333 Church St.
Naugatuck CT 06770
Phone: 203-720-5000
Fax: 203-720-5016
Web: www.nvsl.com

CEO: –
CFO: –
HR: –
FYE: December 31
Type: Public

Naugatuck Valley Financial Corporation (NVFC) owns Naugatuck Valley Savings and Loan a community-oriented thrift serving southwestern Connecticut. Operating from more than a half-dozen locations the bank provides traditional retail banking offerings such as checking and savings accounts CDs and IRAs. Naugatuck Valley Savings and Loan concentrates on residential lending. It also writes construction multifamily and commercial real estate loans. NVFC and Southern Connecticut Bancorp called off plans to merge in 2010. Naugatuck Valley Mutual Holding Company owned around 60% of NVFC's stock until the firm converted to a wholly public company in 2011.

NAUTICA APPAREL INC.

40 W. 57th St.
New York NY 10019
Phone: 212-541-5757
Fax: 212-887-8136
Web: www.nautica.com

CEO: –
CFO: –
HR: –
FYE: February 28
Type: Subsidiary

Explorers once sailed the ocean blue unmindful that their legacy would live on in a global apparel brand. Launched under the spinnaker logo in 1983 Nautica designs makes and retails men's sportswear outerwear underwear swimwear and sleepwear. It also licenses the Nautica name in the US for women's and children's clothing and nonapparel (fragrances footwear furniture). Nautica which is owned by brand behemoth V.F. Corporation is marketed to department store and boutique wholesale customers as well as sold through some 80 VF-operated Nautica retail outlets and website. Independent licensees sell the lineup through some 150 Nautica stores mostly in Asia the Middle East and North and South America.

NAUTILUS INC
NYS: NLS

17750 S.E. 6th Way
Vancouver, WA 98683
Phone: 360 859-2900
Fax: –
Web: www.nautilusinc.com

CEO: Bruce M. Cazenave
CFO: Sid Nayar
HR: –
FYE: December 31
Type: Public

Nautilus wants to pump you up. The company makes and markets cardio and strength-building fitness equipment for home use. Its products include home gyms free weights and benches treadmills exercise bikes and elliptical machines that are sold under the popular brand names Bowflex Nautilus Schwinn Fitness and Universal. Nautilus sells its fitness equipment directly to consumers through its variety of brand websites and catalogs as well as through TV commercials. The company also markets its gear through specialty retailers in the US and Canada. Nautilus exited the commercial fitness category in recent years so that it could focus entirely on providing gear that consumers can use at home.

	Annual Growth	12/14	12/15	12/16	12/17	12/18
Sales ($ mil.)	9.7%	274.4	335.8	406.0	406.2	396.8
Net income ($ mil.)	(6.0%)	18.8	26.6	34.2	26.3	14.7
Market value ($ mil.)	(8.0%)	448.5	494.0	546.6	394.4	322.0
Employees	7.8%	340	470	469	491	460

NAVARRO RESEARCH AND ENGINEERING INC.

669 EMORY VALLEY RD
OAK RIDGE, TN 378307758
Phone: 865-220-9650
Fax: –
Web: www.navarro-inc.com

CEO: Susana Navarro-Valenti PHD
CFO: –
HR: –
FYE: December 31
Type: Private

It's primary mission is about nuclear fission and making sure that it does not happen. Navarro Research and Engineering provides environmental remediation and related services throughout the US. Specialties include nuclear safety and environmental safety and health. Navarro Research and Engineering's offices tend to be located near sites overseen by the US Department of Energy where nuclear materials have been stored. The company had employees in 14 offices and 23 project locations across the country. Navarro Research and Engineering works on projects for the US Department of Energy and the National Nuclear Security Administration and their primary contractors.

	Annual Growth	12/05	12/06	12/07	12/08	12/09
Sales ($ mil.)	(78.2%)	–	–	1,254.8	49.6	59.6
Net income ($ mil.)	199591.0%	–	–	0.0	2.5	4.0
Market value ($ mil.)	–	–	–	–	–	–
Employees	–	–	–	–	–	327

NAVIDEA BIOPHARMACEUTICALS INC
ASE: NAVB

4995 Bradenton Avenue, Suite 240
Dublin, OH 43017-3552
Phone: 614 793-7500
Fax: 614 793-7520
Web: www.navidea.com

CEO: Jed A Latkin
CFO: Jed A Latkin
HR: –
FYE: December 31
Type: Public

Navidea Biopharmaceuticals is tracking down cancer with targeting agents. The biopharmaceutical company specializes in diagnostics therapeutics and radiopharmaceutical agents. It has several radiopharmaceutical products in development designed to help surgeons detect disease. The firm's targeted products and platforms include Manocept and NAV4694. Its Lymphoseek product part of the Manocept platform gained FDA approval in 2013 (and European approval in 2014) and is marketed in the US to detect cancerous tissues. Other candidates aim to detect cancer and neurological conditions including Parkinson's disease and Alzheimer's disease. Customers include diagnostic laboratories physicians and patients.

	Annual Growth	12/14	12/15	12/16	12/17	12/18
Sales ($ mil.)	(34.3%)	6.3	13.2	22.0	1.8	1.2
Net income ($ mil.)	–	(35.7)	(27.6)	(14.3)	74.9	(16.1)
Market value ($ mil.)	(52.0%)	18.9	13.3	6.4	3.6	1.0
Employees	(23.0%)	54	57	28	24	19

NAVIENT CORP NMS: NAVI

123 Justison Street
Wilmington, DE 19801
Phone: 302 283-8000
Fax: –
Web: www.navient.com

CEO: John F. (Jack) Remondi
CFO: Christian Lown
HR: Jon Kroehler
FYE: December 31
Type: Public

Navient is a new name for an old business — namely the loan management servicing and asset recovery unit of SLM Corp. (aka Sallie Mae). Navient services a $300 billion student loan portfolio composed of federal and private education loans issued to around 12 million customers. In addition to serving indebted former students Navient provides asset recovery services (collections) to the government higher education institutions and business clients. Navient manages the largest portfolio of Federal Family Education Loan Program (FFELP) loans as well as the largest portfolio of private education loans. Navient began life as an independent company through a strategic divestiture from Sallie Mae which still exists and continues to provide consumer loans.

	Annual Growth	12/14	12/15	12/16	12/17	12/18
Assets ($ mil.)	(8.1%)	146,352.0	134,112.0	121,136.0	114,991.0	104,176.0
Net income ($ mil.)	(23.4%)	1,149.0	997.0	681.0	292.0	395.0
Market value ($ mil.)	(20.1%)	5,347.1	2,833.2	4,065.4	3,295.9	2,179.9
Employees	1.2%	6,200	7,300	6,773	6,700	6,500

NAVIGANT CONSULTING, INC. NYS: NCI

150 North Riverside Plaza, Suite 2100
Chicago, IL 60606
Phone: 312 573-5600
Fax: 312 573-5675
Web: www.navigant.com

CEO: Scott McIntyre
CFO: –
HR: –
FYE: December 31
Type: Public

Navigant Consulting aims to help its clients navigate troubled business waters. A significant portion of the firm's practice is devoted to issues related to business disputes litigation and regulatory compliance. Navigant Consulting also offers operational strategic and technical management consulting services. Employing about 1825 consultants it targets customers in regulated industries such as construction energy financial services health care and insurance; in addition the firm works with government agencies and companies involved in product liability cases. Navigant Consulting was formed in 1996 under the name The Metzler Group.

	Annual Growth	12/13	12/14	12/15	12/16	12/17
Sales ($ mil.)	5.4%	835.6	859.6	919.5	1,034.5	1,032.3
Net income ($ mil.)	9.5%	52.2	(36.4)	60.3	58.1	75.0
Market value ($ mil.)	0.3%	871.4	697.6	728.9	1,188.2	880.9
Employees	22.3%	2,743	3,559	5,507	5,768	6,130

NAVIGATORS GROUP INC (THE) NMS: NAVG

400 Atlantic Street
Stamford, CT 06901
Phone: 203 905-6090
Fax: –
Web: www.navg.com

CEO: Christopher J Swift
CFO: –
HR: –
FYE: December 31
Type: Public

The Navigators Group writes specialty lines of insurance and reinsurance to clients whom it hopes are good navigators themselves. The company's various subsidiaries write marine liability and other lines of business primarily in the US and the UK. Its Navigators Insurance and Navigators Underwriting Agency (NUA) units specialize in ocean marine insurance including hull energy and cargo insurance as well as property insurance for inland marine and onshore energy concerns. Navigators Specialty primarily provides excess and surplus (high risk) lines. The firm's subsidiaries are also involved in professional liability especially directors' and officers' coverage as well as general liability for contractors. The Hartford Financial Services Group is buying Navigators for $2.1 billion.

	Annual Growth	12/13	12/14	12/15	12/16	12/17
Assets ($ mil.)	5.8%	4,169.5	4,464.2	4,584.0	4,814.0	5,224.6
Net income ($ mil.)	(10.6%)	63.5	95.3	81.1	82.7	40.5
Market value ($ mil.)	(6.3%)	1,863.7	2,164.0	2,531.4	3,474.4	1,437.0
Employees	5.3%	596	651	675	683	732

NAVISITE INC.

400 Minuteman Rd.
Andover MA 01810
Phone: 978-682-8300
Fax: 978-688-8100
Web: www.navisite.com

CEO: Arthur Becker
CFO: –
HR: –
FYE: July 31
Type: Subsidiary

NaviSite helps enterprises manage their IT resources. The company provides managed cloud and software hosting and management services and it specializes in setting up and supporting enterprise applications from such vendors as Microsoft Dynamics and Oracle. NaviSite also provides Web hosting and collocation server management and other outsourced data and network services. The company has about 10 data centers in the US and the UK; as well as operations centers in India Japan and Singapore. Mainly targeting middle-market enterprises in the US NaviSite serves such industries as financial services health care and manufacturing. The company was acquired in 2011 by Time Warner Cable (TWC) for $530 million.

NAVY FEDERAL CREDIT UNION

820 Follin Ln.
Vienna VA 22180-4907
Phone: 703-255-8000
Fax: 703-255-8741
Web: https://www.navyfederal.org

CEO: –
CFO: Debbie Freeman
HR: –
FYE: December 31
Type: Private - Not-for-Pr

"Once a member always a member" promises Navy Federal Credit Union (NFCU). This policy has helped NFCU become one of the nation's largest credit unions claiming more than four million members who can retain their credit union privileges even after discharge from the armed services. Formed in 1933 NFCU provides a variety of financial services to all Department of Defense uniformed personnel reservists National Guard personnel civilian employees and contractors as well as their families. The credit union has more than 220 branch locations in the US and overseas many of them on or near military bases.

NB&T FINANCIAL GROUP, INC. NAS: NBTF

48 N. South Street
Wilmington, OH 45177
Phone: 937 382-1441
Fax: –

CEO: –
CFO: –
HR: –
FYE: December 31
Type: Public

NB&T Financial is the holding company for National Bank and Trust which serves southwestern and central Ohio from some two-dozen branches. The bank offers standard deposit products and services including checking and savings accounts CDs and IRAs. Its Really Awesome Dollars (RAD) accounts target the 16-and younger set; a minimum deposit of $1.00 is required. Residential mortgages account for about a third of all loans; commercial loans and mortgages make up another 40%. The bank also offers asset management and retirement planning services. NB&T acquired Community National another Ohio-based community bank in late 2009. The following year it sold subsidiary NB&T Insurance Agency to its management.

	Annual Growth	12/09	12/10	12/11	12/12	12/13
Assets ($ mil.)	(0.4%)	649.3	690.6	675.6	651.1	638.3
Net income ($ mil.)	1.3%	4.0	8.8	3.8	3.9	4.2
Market value ($ mil.)	4.4%	55.9	92.8	67.5	58.4	66.3
Employees	(5.5%)	241	217	211	203	192

NBCUNIVERSAL MEDIA LLC

30 Rockefeller Plaza
New York NY 10112
Phone: 212-664-4444
Fax: 212-664-4085
Web: www.nbcuni.com

CEO: Stephen B Burke
CFO: –
HR: –
FYE: December 31
Type: Joint Venture

Television movies and more fill the vastness of this entertainment company. NBCUniversal Media is a leading media conglomerate anchored by its broadcast network NBC with more than 200 affiliate stations (including 10 that are company-owned) and its Universal Studios feature film division. Other broadcasting operations owned by NBCUniversal include Spanish-language network Telemundo and a portfolio of cable TV channels that includes Bravo E! Entertainment Syfy G4 USA Network Oxygen and news channel MSNBC. It also owns online portal iVillage and has a stake in video site Hulu. Comcast the country's #1 cable systems operator owns 51% of NBCUniversal and has agreed to acquire General Electric's 49% stake.

NBHX TRIM USA CORPORATION

1020 7 MILE RD NW
COMSTOCK PARK, MI 493219542
Phone: 616-785-9400
Fax: –
Web: www.nbhx-trim.com

CEO: –
CFO: –
HR: –
FYE: December 31
Type: Private

NBHX Trim (formerly Behr Industries) manufactures interior wood trim components for OEM automotive heavy-duty truck and marine suppliers across North America. It is the only US-based full-service wood component supplier with a domestic production plant. The Michigan-based facility neighbors the Detroit Big Three production plants. NBHX Trim has captured more than 70% of the US market for center consoles instrument panels side door panels and similar wood components. Its fortunes have been closely tied to those of GM's.

	Annual Growth	12/11	12/12	12/13	12/14	12/15
Sales ($ mil.)	24.6%	–	49.6	59.9	64.7	96.1
Net income ($ mil.)	103.1%	–	1.3	2.1	3.9	11.0
Market value ($ mil.)	–	–	–	–	–	–
Employees	–	–	–	–	–	425

NBL PERMIAN LLC

1001 NOBLE ENERGY WAY
HOUSTON, TX 770701435
Phone: 281-872-3100
Fax: –
Web: www.nblenergy.com

CEO: Clayton W. Williams
CFO: Jaime R. Casas
HR: –
FYE: December 31
Type: Private

Former Texas gubernatorial candidate Clayton Williams once devoted his energy to politics. Now he's devoted to the independent oil and gas firm that he founded. Clayton Williams Energy explores for oil and gas deposits primarily in Louisiana New Mexico and Texas and exploits those resources. The company has estimated proved reserves of 75.4 million barrels of oil equivalent located mainly in the Permian Basin and South Texas. It has 951000 gross undeveloped acres. It also operates gas pipeline and a small natural gas processing infrastructure in Louisiana Mississippi New Mexico and Texas and offers contract drilling services. In 2017 the company was acquired by Noble Energy for $2.7 billion.

	Annual Growth	12/12	12/13	12/14	12/15	12/16
Sales ($ mil.)	(12.3%)	–	429.2	468.5	232.4	289.4
Net income ($ mil.)	–	–	(24.9)	43.9	(98.2)	(292.2)
Market value ($ mil.)	–	–	–	–	–	–
Employees	–	–	–	–	–	253

NBT BANCORP. INC.

52 South Broad Street
Norwich, NY 13815
Phone: 607 337-2265
Fax: 607 336-7538
Web: www.nbtbancorp.com

NMS: NBTB
CEO: John H. Watt
CFO: Michael J. Chewens
HR: Catherine M. Scarlett
FYE: December 31
Type: Public

NBT Bancorp is the holding company for NBT Bank which operates about 155 branches mainly in suburban and rural areas of central and northern New York northeastern Pennsylvania western Massachusetts southern New Hampshire and northwestern Vermont. The bank offers traditional deposit accounts and trust services and specializes in making business and commercial real estate loans. NBT also holds two main financial services subsidiaries: the EPIC Advisors unit administers retirement plans while Mang Insurance Agency sells personal and commercial coverage. NBT Capital provides venture funding to growing area businesses.

	Annual Growth	12/14	12/15	12/16	12/17	12/18
Assets ($ mil.)	5.2%	7,797.9	8,262.6	8,867.3	9,136.8	9,556.4
Net income ($ mil.)	10.7%	75.1	76.4	78.4	82.2	112.6
Market value ($ mil.)	7.1%	1,147.3	1,217.6	1,829.0	1,607.2	1,510.6
Employees	(0.7%)	1,840	1,721	1,704	1,733	1,791

NBTY INC.

2100 Smithtown Ave.
Ronkonkoma NY 11779
Phone: 631-200-2000
Fax: 801-342-4305
Web: www.naturessunshine.com

CEO: Paul Sturman
CFO: Ted McCormick
HR: –
FYE: September 30
Type: Private

NBTY draws upon nature's bounty to cash in on the market for preventive and alternative health care. As the largest vertically integrated source of nutritional supplements in the US the company manufactures wholesales and retails more than 25000 products including vitamins minerals herbs and sports drinks. Brands include Ester-C Nature's Bounty Solgar and Sundown. NBTY has manufacturing facilities in Canada China the UK and the US and is able to produce and package capsules tablets powders and liquids. The Carlyle Group-owned company sells its goods through pharmacies wholesalers supermarkets and health food stores around the world.

NCH CORPORATION

2727 CHEMSEARCH BLVD
IRVING, TX 750626454
Phone: 972-438-0211
Fax: –
Web: www.nch.com

CEO: –
CFO: Christopher T Sortwell
HR: –
FYE: April 30
Type: Private

NCH has been cleaning up for years and like everyone else it's been using soaps and detergents to do so. The company makes and sells about 450 chemical maintenance repair and supply products including all kinds of cleaners for customers in more than 50 countries throughout the world. NCH markets its products through a direct sales force to companies in the agricultural home-improvement industrial recreational and utility markets. Other products include fasteners welding supplies pet care supplies plumbing parts lubricants and metal-working fluids.

	Annual Growth	04/09	04/10	04/11	04/12	04/16
Sales ($ mil.)	0.9%	–	–	952.5	1,045.1	996.6
Net income ($ mil.)	(52.6%)	–	–	6.7	6.8	0.2
Market value ($ mil.)	–	–	–	–	–	–
Employees	–	–	–	–	–	8,500

NCH HEALTHCARE SYSTEM INC.

350 7TH ST N
NAPLES, FL 34102-5754
Phone: 239-436-5000
Fax: –
Web: www.nchmd.org

CEO: Phil Dutcher
CFO: Vicki Hale Orr
HR: –
FYE: September 30
Type: Private

NCH Healthcare System provides a comprehensive range of health care services to residents in southwest Florida. The system includes two acute care hospitals (NCH Downtown Naples Hospital and NCH North Naples Hospital) with a combined 715-bed capacity and regional institutes which specialize in orthopedics and the treatment of cancer heart ailments and women's and children's health issues. NCH also operates an area network of outpatient and ambulatory care facilities that provide services ranging from diagnostics to rehabilitative care to surgery and emergency care.

	Annual Growth	09/05	09/06	09/07	09/08	09/11
Sales ($ mil.)	0.3%	–	475.3	524.7	456.4	483.1
Net income ($ mil.)	(27.2%)	–	35.5	49.6	25.4	7.3
Market value ($ mil.)	–	–	–	–	–	–
Employees	–	–	–	–	–	3,500

NCI INC

NMS: NCIT

11730 Plaza America Drive
Reston, VA 20190-4764
Phone: 703 707-6900
Fax: 703 707-6901
Web: www.nciinc.com

CEO: Paul A Dillahay
CFO: Lucas J Narel
HR: –
FYE: December 31
Type: Public

NCI isn't the newest hit show on CBS but an IT services provider primarily for US federal government agencies. Among its services are enterprise systems management and integration health IT cybersecurity and information assurance network design and engineering logistics program management and lifecycle support training and simulation and application development. Defense and intelligence agency clients (which account for about 75% of sales) include the Army Air Force USSOCOM and the National Guard. The company also serves federal civilian agencies such as NASA the Department of Energy and the Senate.

	Annual Growth	12/11	12/12	12/13	12/14	12/15
Sales ($ mil.)	(12.1%)	558.3	368.4	332.3	317.0	333.1
Net income ($ mil.)	(1.9%)	13.2	(86.8)	7.7	8.5	12.2
Market value ($ mil.)	4.0%	156.8	63.1	89.1	137.4	183.7
Employees	(6.3%)	2,600	2,200	1,900	1,800	2,000

NCS TECHNOLOGIES, INC.

7669 LIMESTONE DR STE 130
GAINESVILLE, VA 201554038
Phone: 703-743-8500
Fax: –
Web: www.ncst.com

CEO: –
CFO: –
HR: –
FYE: December 31
Type: Private

NCS Technologies makes enterprise computing needs personal. The company makes and supplies PC products to clients large and small. NCS Technologies offers personal computers mobile computing thin client computing servers and Internet appliances to clients in the government educational and private sectors. Products include desktops notebooks rugged tablets and servers. In addition to providing built-to-order hardware the company also provides software customizations and installation and technical support services. Founded in 1996 the company's single facility in Washington DC serves clients from across the world.

	Annual Growth	09/04	09/05	09/06*	12/09	12/10
Sales ($ mil.)	35.1%	–	–	35.2	80.0	117.5
Net income ($ mil.)	(12.2%)	–	–	1.1	1.3	0.7
Market value ($ mil.)	–	–	–	–	–	–
Employees	–	–	–	–	–	108

*Fiscal year change

NEACE LUKENS INC.

2305 River Rd.
Louisville KY 40206-1010
Phone: 502-894-2100
Fax: 502-894-8602
Web: www.neacelukens.com

CEO: –
CFO: –
HR: –
FYE: December 31
Type: Private

Neace Lukens is a regional insurance broker in the south-central US with offices in Arizona Georgia Indiana Kentucky Michigan Ohio and Tennessee. The company offers personal and commercial insurance policies such as property/casualty (general and professional liability auto insurance and workers' compensation) employee benefits (health and life insurance) and industry-specific insurance for school districts nursing homes contractors truck drivers manufacturing facilities and lumber yards. Founded in 1991 by chairman John Neace and president Joseph Lukens Neace Lukens was acquired by Florida-based private equity firm AssuredPartners in September 2011.

NEBRASKA BOOK COMPANY INC.

4700 S. 19th St.
Lincoln NE 68501-0529
Phone: 402-421-7300
Fax: 800-869-0399
Web: www.nebook.com

CEO: Rick Bunka
CFO: John Macieo
HR: –
FYE: March 31
Type: Private

If books are engines of change Nebraska Book Company (NBC) is transforming college students across the US. One of the largest textbook distributors in the US NBC sells 6 million-plus books annually. It serves some 2500 booksellers and operates nearly 250 bookstores on or adjacent to college campuses that sell and rent textbooks and other merchandise. NBC also supplies educational materials to private high schools nontraditional colleges and corporate and correspondence classes as well as store management and e-commerce software. Founded in 1915 as a bookstore near The University of Nebraska NBC emerged from Chapter 11 bankruptcy protection in 2012. It is owned by holding company Neebo Inc.

NEBRASKA PUBLIC POWER DISTRICT

1414 15TH ST
COLUMBUS, NE 686015226
Phone: 877-275-6773
Fax: –
Web: www.nppd.com

CEO: Patrick Pope
CFO: Traci Bender
HR: –
FYE: December 31
Type: Private

Nebraska Public Power District (NPPD) electrifies the Cornhusker State. The government-owned electric utility the largest in the state provides power in 86 of the state's 93 counties. The firm has a generating capacity of about 3130 MW and operates more than 5200 miles of transmission lines. NPPD distributes electricity to about 89000 retail customers in 81 cities and towns; it also provides power to about 1 million customers through wholesale power contracts with more than 50 towns and 25 public power districts. In addition NPPD purchases electricity from the federally owned Western Area Power Administration and operates a surface water irrigation system.

	Annual Growth	12/14	12/15	12/16	12/17	12/18
Sales ($ mil.)	1.4%	–	1,097.2	1,154.0	1,101.6	1,144.9
Net income ($ mil.)	(3.2%)	–	91.1	82.9	71.3	82.7
Market value ($ mil.)	–	–	–	–	–	–
Employees	–	–	–	–	–	1,900

NEENAH INC
NYS: NP

3460 Preston Ridge Road
Alpharetta, GA 30005
Phone: 678 566-6500
Fax: –
Web: www.neenah.com

CEO: John ODonnell
CFO: Bonnie Lind
HR: –
FYE: December 31
Type: Public

Neenah makes filtration media and fine paper and packaging products. The company's Technical Products division (55% of sales) makes air fuel and oil filtration media for automotive suppliers that serve OEMs and the automotive aftermarket. Other Technical Products include filtration media for water and other industrial markets specialty backing for pressure sensitive tapes abrasive backings and labels. Neenah's Fine Paper and Packaging segment (43% of sales) offers printing papers and envelopes as well as food and beverage labels folding cartons and box wrap. Paper and packaging customers include distributors converters and retailers. The US accounts for about 70% of sales.

	Annual Growth	12/14	12/15	12/16	12/17	12/18
Sales ($ mil.)	3.5%	902.7	887.7	941.5	979.9	1,034.9
Net income ($ mil.)	(14.7%)	68.7	51.1	73.0	80.3	36.4
Market value ($ mil.)	(0.6%)	1,016.1	1,052.5	1,436.4	1,528.3	993.3
Employees	7.2%	2,000	2,340	2,303	2,612	2,641

NEFFS BANCORP INC.
NBB: NEFB

5629 PA Route 873, P.O. Box 10
Neffs, PA 18065-0010
Phone: 610 767-3875
Fax: –
Web: www.neffsnatl.com

CEO: John J Remaley
CFO: –
HR: –
FYE: December 31
Type: Public

Eneff with the megabanks already! Neffs Bancorp is the holding company for The Neffs National Bank an independent bank that has been serving eastern Pennsylvania's Lehigh County since 1923. The bank operates a single office in the village of Neffs north of Allentown. Targeting consumers and local businesses it provides a variety of deposit products including checking and savings accounts CDs and IRAs. The bank is mainly a real estate lender with residential mortgages home equity loans and commercial mortgages comprising some 90% of its portfolio. Business consumer and construction loans round out its lending activities. The Neffs National Bank also offers tax estate and investment planning.

	Annual Growth	12/11	12/12	12/13	12/14	12/15
Assets ($ mil.)	3.4%	286.5	294.2	303.8	309.9	327.5
Net income ($ mil.)	3.8%	3.7	4.2	4.2	4.0	4.3
Market value ($ mil.)	2.1%	42.2	42.2	43.2	43.8	45.8
Employees	–	–	–	–	–	–

NEIGHBORHOOD REINVESTMENT CORPORATION

999 N CAPITOL ST NE # 900
WASHINGTON, DC 200026096
Phone: 202-760-4000
Fax: –
Web: www.neighborworks.org

CEO: Marietta Rodriguez
CFO: Michael L. Forster
HR: –
FYE: September 30
Type: Private

Neighborhood Reinvestment Corporation (now dba NeighborWorks America) wants to be your neighbor. The not-for-profit organization supports more than 240 independent local organizations in suburban urban and rural communities across the country. Programs include building multi-family dwellings and helping low and middle income families with financing and insurance as well as job creation community facilities and economic development in rural areas. The organization also offers training for community leaders and would-be homeowners on community planning green building and financing among others. NeighborWorks America is funded by Congress private donations and corporate support.

	Annual Growth	09/09	09/10	09/13	09/14	09/15
Sales ($ mil.)	(7.8%)	–	312.4	248.0	261.3	208.0
Net income ($ mil.)	–	–	2.5	11.3	22.1	(16.2)
Market value ($ mil.)	–	–	–	–	–	–
Employees	–	–	–	–	–	260

NEKTAR THERAPEUTICS
NMS: NKTR

455 Mission Bay Boulevard South
San Francisco, CA 94158
Phone: 415 482-5300
Fax: –
Web: www.nektar.com

CEO: Howard W. Robin
CFO: Gil M. Labrucherie
HR: –
FYE: December 31
Type: Public

Nektar Therapeutics has pegged its fortunes to making drugs more effective. The clinical-stage drug development firm uses its PEGylation technology (based upon polyethylene glycol) to improve the delivery and efficacy of existing drugs. Nektar's pipeline includes about 20 drugs focused on anti-infectives and anti-virals immunology oncology and pain treatments. Its lead candidates are NKTR-118 for opioid-induced constipation and NKTR-102 to treat breast cancer. Nektar receives royalties on about a dozen approved products including Neulasta Somavert and Macugen as well as its surgical and imaging technology. The company's development partners include Roche AstraZeneca Amgen and Pfizer.

	Annual Growth	12/14	12/15	12/16	12/17	12/18
Sales ($ mil.)	56.2%	200.7	230.8	165.4	307.7	1,193.3
Net income ($ mil.)	–	(53.9)	(81.2)	(153.5)	(96.7)	681.3
Market value ($ mil.)	20.7%	2,689.7	2,924.0	2,129.2	10,363.2	5,703.9
Employees	9.0%	438	425	468	509	618

NELNET INC
NYS: NNI

121 South 13th Street, Suite 100
Lincoln, NE 68508
Phone: 402 458-2370
Fax: –
Web: www.nelnetinvestors.com

CEO: Jeffrey R. (Jeff) Noordhoek
CFO: James D. (Jim) Kruger
HR: –
FYE: December 31
Type: Public

Got Ivy League tastes on a community college budget? Nelnet may be able to help. The education planning and financing company helps students and parents plan and pay for college educations. Nelnet is mostly known for servicing federal student loans. The firm manages about $76 billion in student loan assets most of which are government loans. However in light of regulatory changes to the student lending market Nelnet is increasingly expanding its fee-based education services. It serves the K-12 and higher education marketplace providing long-term payment plans college enrollment services and software and technology services. It acquired in 2018 Great Lakes Educational Loan Services for $150 million. The firm is part of financial holding company Farmers & Merchants Investment.

	Annual Growth	12/14	12/15	12/16	12/17	12/18
Assets ($ mil.)	(4.3%)	30,098.1	30,485.9	27,180.1	23,964.4	25,221.0
Net income ($ mil.)	(7.2%)	307.6	268.0	256.8	173.2	227.9
Market value ($ mil.)	3.1%	1,865.2	1,351.5	2,043.1	2,205.3	2,107.1
Employees	18.9%	3,100	3,400	3,700	4,300	6,200

NEMOURS FOUNDATION

10140 CENTURION PKWY N
JACKSONVILLE, FL 322560532
Phone: 904-697-4100
Fax: –
Web: www.nemours.org

CEO: –
CFO: –
HR: –
FYE: December 31
Type: Private

Even if their offspring are fanatical about Finding Nemo parents of sick children may prefer finding Nemours. The Nemours Foundation operates the Nemours/Alfred I. duPont Hospital for Children in Wilmington Delaware; the Nemours Children's Hospital in Orlando Florida; and dozens of pediatric clinics in Delaware Florida New Jersey and Pennsylvania that treat acutely and chronically ill children. Specialties include orthopedics cardiology neurology and oncology. Nemours also has extensive research programs and it operates a clinic in Delaware that serves low-income elderly residents. The not-for-profit foundation was created in 1936 through the will of chemicals pioneer Alfred I. duPont.

	Annual Growth	12/05	12/06	12/07	12/08	12/17
Sales ($ mil.)	7.8%	–	578.7	635.0	160.4	1,317.5
Net income ($ mil.)	2.1%	–	29.3	53.9	(81.0)	36.7
Market value ($ mil.)	–	–	–	–	–	–
Employees	–	–	–	–	–	4,400

NEOGEN CORP
NMS: NEOG

620 Lesher Place
Lansing, MI 48912
Phone: 517 372-9200
Fax: –
Web: www.neogen.com

CEO: John E. Adent
CFO: Steven J. (Steve) Quinlan
HR: Melissa Marciniak
FYE: May 31
Type: Public

Bacteriophobes have a friend in Neogen a maker of products for the food safety and animal health markets. Its food safety testing products are used by the food industry to make sure our edibles are clean unspoiled and free of toxins pathogens and allergens. In core markets in the Americas and Europe Neogen reaches end users (including dairies meat processors and animal feed producers) through a direct sales force; it uses distributors elsewhere. On the animal health front Neogen produces drugs vaccines diagnostics and instruments for the veterinary market; it also makes rat poisons and disinfectants used in animal production plants and diagnostic products for research laboratories.

	Annual Growth	05/15	05/16	05/17	05/18	05/19
Sales ($ mil.)	10.0%	283.1	321.3	361.6	402.3	414.2
Net income ($ mil.)	15.7%	33.5	36.6	43.8	63.1	60.2
Market value ($ mil.)	4.8%	2,440.6	2,577.9	3,304.8	3,953.3	2,942.4
Employees	12.2%	1,062	1,235	1,413	1,546	1,682

NEOGENOMICS INC
NAS: NEO

12701 Commonwealth Drive, Suite 9
Fort Myers, FL 33913
Phone: 239 768-0600
Fax: 239 690-4237
Web: www.neogenomics.com

CEO: Douglas M. VanOort
CFO: George A. Cardoza
HR: Erin Johnson
FYE: December 31
Type: Public

NeoGenomics is a fortune teller of sorts. The company offers genetic and molecular testing in five categories to determine a person's genetic predisposition to certain cancers and other diseases. Testing methods include immunohistochemisty cytogenetics flourescence in-situ hybridization (FISH) flow cytometry and molecular genetic testing. Its Path Labs (dba PathLogic) unit provides specialized anatomic pathology services primarily in Northern California. NeoGenomics serves customers including community-based oncologists pathologists urologists hospitals and other health care facilities through its labs located across the US.

	Annual Growth	12/14	12/15	12/16	12/17	12/18
Sales ($ mil.)	33.5%	87.1	99.8	244.1	258.6	276.7
Net income ($ mil.)	23.6%	1.1	(2.5)	(5.7)	(0.8)	2.6
Market value ($ mil.)	31.9%	393.9	743.4	809.6	837.0	1,191.2
Employees	34.7%	455	880	968	1,030	1,500

NEOMAGIC CORPORATION
PINK SHEETS: NMGC

3250 Jay St.
Santa Clara CA 95054
Phone: 408-988-7020
Fax: 408-988-7036
Web: www.neomagic.com

CEO: Syed Zaidi
CFO: –
HR: –
FYE: January 31
Type: Public

NeoMagic is trying to deliver chip magic for everything from smart phones to electronic toll collection systems. The company develops and markets semiconductors including a family of system-on-chip (SoC) processors sold under the MiMagic brand and software for audio video imaging graphics and television. It also provides design services on system and software development that help OEMs bring their products to market. NeoMagic sells through distributors and representatives in the US the UK and Asia. Among the company's customers is California-based startup ViV Systems a home theater developer and manufacturer.

NEOMEDIA TECHNOLOGIES, INC.
NBB: NEOM

1515 Walnut Street, Suite 100
Boulder, CO 80302
Phone: 303 546-7946
Fax: –
Web: www.neom.com

CEO: Laura A Marriott
CFO: Barry S Baer
HR: –
FYE: December 31
Type: Public

NeoMedia Technologies has a new approach to mobile marketing. The company develops hardware and software that allows camera-enabled mobile phones to read and transmit data from bar codes embedded in advertisements. Marketers use the technology to link phone users to targeted URLs. It also offers mobile ticketing and coupon systems. The company also generates revenue by licensing its technology and from designing and implementing mobile marketing campaigns. NeoMedia has undergone significant restructuring in recent years including the divestiture of a number of business lines.

	Annual Growth	12/10	12/11	12/12	12/13	12/14
Sales ($ mil.)	23.2%	1.5	2.3	2.3	5.0	3.5
Net income ($ mil.)	–	35.1	(0.8)	(19.4)	(214.1)	(2.5)
Market value ($ mil.)	–	0.0	0.0	0.0	0.0	0.0
Employees	(14.9%)	21	27	14	18	11

NEOPHOTONICS CORP
NYS: NPTN

2911 Zanker Road
San Jose, CA 95134
Phone: 408 232-9200
Fax: –
Web: www.neophotonics.com

CEO: Timothy S. (Tim) Jenks
CFO: Elizabeth (Beth) Eby
HR: –
FYE: December 31
Type: Public

NeoPhotonics wants its clients to see communications in a new light. The company develops and manufactures optical network components using laser-reactive deposition. Its products include photonic integrated circuits (PICs) amplifiers glass substrates laser modules passive optical components photodiodes and transceivers. NeoPhotonics' chips and components are used in optical networking equipment for data communications and passive optical networks that enable fiber-to-the-home broadband access among other functions. It has a portfolio of more than 40 product families including ones that enable data transmission at more than 100 gigabits per second.

	Annual Growth	12/14	12/15	12/16	12/17	12/18
Sales ($ mil.)	1.3%	306.2	339.4	411.4	292.9	322.5
Net income ($ mil.)	–	(19.7)	3.7	(0.2)	(53.3)	(43.6)
Market value ($ mil.)	17.7%	156.8	503.7	501.3	305.2	300.5
Employees	(8.7%)	2,541	2,304	2,401	1,783	1,769

NEPHROS INC
NAS: NEPH

380 Lackawanna Place
South Orange, NJ 07079
Phone: 201 343-5202
Fax: –
Web: www.nephros.com

CEO: Daron Evans
CFO: Andrew Astor
HR: –
FYE: December 31
Type: Public

Nephros develops and makes medical devices that are used to treat irreversible loss of kidney function associated with End Stage Renal Disease or ESRD. ESRD is often the result of other health problems such as diabetes and high blood pressure. The company's products are designed to replace a patient's kidney function with the device system. Nephros is positioning its therapeutic devices as an alternative to hemodialysis the most common form of renal replacement therapy. The company's products use a process called "hemodiafiltration" (HDF) combining hemodialysis with hemofiltration to clean the patient's blood.

	Annual Growth	12/14	12/15	12/16	12/17	12/18
Sales ($ mil.)	34.3%	1.7	1.9	2.3	3.8	5.7
Net income ($ mil.)	–	(7.4)	(3.1)	(3.0)	(0.8)	(3.4)
Market value ($ mil.)	(7.9%)	5.7	1.5	2.6	3.2	4.1
Employees	15.8%	10	11	10	15	18

NES RENTALS HOLDINGS, INC.

8420 W BRYN MAWR AVE # 300
CHICAGO, IL 606313436
Phone: 773-695-3999
Fax: –
Web: www.nesrentals.com

CEO: –
CFO: –
HR: –
FYE: December 31
Type: Private

Forklifts and other lifts lift the revenues of NES Rentals formerly National Equipment Services. The company offers industrial and construction customers a range of aerial rental equipment from scissor and boom lifts to rough terrain and truck-mounted cranes. It also supplies specialty equipment including bulldozers trenchers and skid steers as well as scaffolding systems. In addition to equipment rentals and repair and maintenance services for nonresidential construction customers NES sells new and used pieces by OEMs including BMC JLG SkyJack Sala Doosan and Terex. In mid-2017 NES was acquired by rival United Rentals for $965 million.

	Annual Growth	12/07	12/08	12/09	12/13	12/14
Sales ($ mil.)	(2.6%)	–	406.3	300.6	317.0	347.0
Net income ($ mil.)	–	–	(18.3)	(17.6)	(25.8)	(1.7)
Market value ($ mil.)	–	–	–	–	–	–
Employees	–	–	–	–	–	1,100

NESTLE WATERS NORTH AMERICA INC.

900 Long Ridge Rd. Bldg. 2
Stamford CT 06902-1138
Phone: 203-531-4100
Fax: 312-926-8283
Web: www.nmh.org

CEO: Fernando Merce
CFO: Bill Pearson
HR: –
FYE: December 31
Type: Subsidiary

Jack and Jill went up a hill to fetch a pail of water; Nestle Waters North America (NWNA) offers an easier alternative. The company entered the US and Canada by selling Perrier Sparkling Mineral Water in 1976; it has grown to represent about one-third of the bottled water market. Its portfolio boasts national top seller Nestle Pure Life and a dozen or so international and regional water brands: Acqua Panna Deer Park Ozarka Poland Spring and S. Pellegrino to name a few. Non-sparking waters generate some 90% of its sales. NWNA also added tea with the purchase of Sweet Leaf Tea. In addition to selling water via retail outlets the company provides home and office delivery. NWNA is a division of Nestle Waters.

NET MEDICAL XPRESS SOLUTIONS INC   NBB: NMXS

5021 Indian School Road, Suite 100
Albuquerque, NM 87110
Phone: 505 255-1999
Fax: –
Web: www.nmxs.com

CEO: Richard F Govatski
CFO: –
HR: –
FYE: December 31
Type: Public

NMXS.com has a clear image of what good document management looks like. The company provides software and services for archiving and retrieving documents and images primarily to health care and medical providers. Its customers have come from fields including health care government and entertainment as well as not-for-profit organizations. NMSC.com's products are made available under the Software-As-a-Service model.

	Annual Growth	12/14	12/15	12/16	12/17	12/18
Sales ($ mil.)	(17.7%)	4.6	4.2	3.0	2.8	2.1
Net income ($ mil.)	–	(0.5)	0.2	(0.3)	0.1	(0.0)
Market value ($ mil.)	54.3%	0.3	0.5	2.2	1.0	1.7
Employees	(4.1%)	25	22	23	–	–

NETEZZA CORPORATION

26 Forest St.
Marlborough MA 01752
Phone: 508-382-8200
Fax: 508-382-8300
Web: www.netezza.com

CEO: –
CFO: –
HR: –
FYE: January 31
Type: Subsidiary

Netezza understands that there's no point in storing your data if you can't find it again. The company provides data warehouse network appliances used to manage large databases. Tailored for toward government agencies and companies in data-intensive fields such as financial services and health care its network devices integrate database server and storage functions enabling the analysis of huge amounts of data. Netezza's TwinFin appliance is its core product. The Skimmer device is geared for small and midsized clients with less data to manage as well as for testing and development environments. Netezza sells its products directly worldwide. The company was acquired by IBM in 2010 for about $1.8 billion.

NETFLIX INC   NMS: NFLX

100 Winchester Circle
Los Gatos, CA 95032
Phone: 408 540-3700
Fax: –
Web: www.netflix.com

CEO: –
CFO: Spencer Neumann
HR: Barbie Graver
FYE: December 31
Type: Public

Netflix and chill? More like Netflix and bill the increasing numbers of global viewers who subscribe to the video streaming service. The world's leading internet streaming company distributes movies and TV shows in a variety of genres and languages to a whopping 139 million monthly (and growing) paid subscribers in more than 190 countries. Netflix creates its own content and strikes deals with other producers for the rights to distribute programming. To keep viewers binging it deploys sophisticated algorithms to predict viewer preferences and make recommendations on what to watch. Netflix still sends DVDs to US customers through the mail though the legacy business gets smaller every year.

	Annual Growth	12/15	12/16	12/17	12/18	12/19
Sales ($ mil.)	31.3%	6,779.5	8,830.7	11,692.7	15,794.3	20,156.4
Net income ($ mil.)	97.5%	122.6	186.7	558.9	1,211.2	1,866.9
Market value ($ mil.)	29.7%	50,190.7	54,324.3	84,233.3	117,451.0	141,984.7
Employees	23.5%	3,700	4,700	5,500	7,100	8,600

NETGEAR INC   NMS: NTGR

350 East Plumeria Drive
San Jose, CA 95134
Phone: 408 907-8000
Fax: –
Web: www.netgear.com

CEO: Patrick C.S. Lo
CFO: Christine M. Gorjanc
HR: Tamesa Rogers
FYE: December 31
Type: Public

NETGEAR keeps consumers and small businesses wired — and wireless. The company designs a range of networking equipment — adapters hubs routers switches media servers and interfaces — for connecting PCs in home and small business settings to each other and the Internet. (Manufacturing is outsourced to contractors in Asia.) NETGEAR also supplies network-attached storage (NAS) systems VPN firewalls and digital media receivers. It sells through distributors including Ingram Micro and Tech Data and to retailers such as Amazon.com Best Buy Fry's Electronics JB HiFi and RadioShack. The company generates about 40% of its sales from international markets.

	Annual Growth	12/14	12/15	12/16	12/17	12/18
Sales ($ mil.)	(6.6%)	1,393.5	1,300.7	1,328.3	1,406.9	1,058.8
Net income ($ mil.)	–	8.8	48.6	75.9	19.4	(9.2)
Market value ($ mil.)	10.0%	1,123.0	1,322.8	1,715.4	1,854.3	1,642.2
Employees	(5.2%)	1,038	963	945	1,008	837

NETIQ CORPORATION

1233 West Loop South Park Towers North Ste. 810
Houston TX 77027
Phone: 713-548-1700
Fax: 713-548-1771
Web: www.netiq.com

CEO: –
CFO: –
HR: –
FYE: June 30
Type: Subsidiary

NetIQ thinks it can help you intelligently manage your IT assets. The company a unit of Attachmate provides enterprise software used to test migrate secure and analyze distributed computer systems. Its products include performance and availability management applications that customers use to diagnose and analyze systems running Windows UNIX and Linux. The unit's security and systems management products encompass a variety of hardware and software including servers databases and VoIP networks. Its products are used by 12000-plus customers — which have included ExxonMobil Ford the Mayo Clinic NASA and Nasdaq — in more than 60 countries and are marketed through resellers worldwide.

NETLIST INC

175 Technology Drive, Suite 150
Irvine, CA 92618
Phone: 949 435-0025
Fax: –
Web: www.netlist.com

NBB: NLST
CEO: Chun K Hong
CFO: Gail Sasaki
HR: –
FYE: December 29
Type: Public

Netlist designs manufactures and markets high-performance memory subsystems for the OEM market. Its line of board-level memory products are used in IT infrastructure equipment such as servers data centers and other high-performance computing and communications markets. Netlist designs manufactures and sells a variety of memory circuits with dynamic random access memory (DRAM) and NAND flash memory as well as a hybrid of both. The company targets applications in which the preservation of data stored in memory is important such as cloud computing big data and online banking. Key customers include Dell and IBM.

	Annual Growth	12/14*	01/16*	12/16	12/17	12/18
Sales ($ mil.)	15.0%	19.2	8.0	19.7	38.3	33.5
Net income ($ mil.)	–	(15.4)	(20.5)	(11.2)	(13.4)	(17.1)
Market value ($ mil.)	(14.5%)	98.9	122.6	142.1	42.8	52.9
Employees	(9.1%)	114	110	95	82	78

*Fiscal year change

NETSCOUT SYSTEMS INC

310 Littleton Road
Westford, MA 01886
Phone: 978 614-4000
Fax: –
Web: www.netscout.com

NMS: NTCT
CEO: Anil K. Singhal
CFO: Jean A. Bua
HR: Skip Maloney
FYE: March 31
Type: Public

NetScout Systems products ride out on computer networks looking for trouble. The company?s monitoring appliances placed throughout a network allow administrators to collect information about traffic flow and to optimize application and network performance. NetScout?s nGenius Service Assurance Solution monitors systems ranging from VoIP communications to customer relationship management applications. NetScout sells directly and through resellers and distributors to corporate and government customers. The US supplies about 60% of revenue.

	Annual Growth	03/15	03/16	03/17	03/18	03/19
Sales ($ mil.)	19.0%	453.7	955.4	1,162.1	986.8	909.9
Net income ($ mil.)	–	61.2	(28.4)	33.3	79.8	(73.3)
Market value ($ mil.)	(10.6%)	3,403.2	1,782.7	2,945.3	2,045.0	2,178.5
Employees	24.7%	1,069	3,144	3,113	3,019	2,585

NETSOL TECHNOLOGIES INC

23975 Park Sorrento, Suite 250
Calabasas, CA 91302
Phone: 818 222-9195
Fax: 818 222-9197
Web: www.netsoltech.com

NAS: NTWK
CEO: Najeeb Ghauri
CFO: Roger Almond
HR: –
FYE: June 30
Type: Public

NetSol Technologies is sold on the power of IT. The company provides information technology services and software for the banking financial services automotive leasing and financing and healthcare industries. NetSol's LeaseSoft software for asset-based lending organizations automates such tasks as credit valuation financial comparisons wholesale finance management and services tracking. NetSol also offers a hospital management information product. The company's services include assistance with SAP information security business intelligence project management maintenance and testing. NetSol Technologies was founded in 1997.

	Annual Growth	06/15	06/16	06/17	06/18	06/19
Sales ($ mil.)	7.4%	51.0	64.6	65.4	60.9	67.8
Net income ($ mil.)	–	(5.5)	3.4	(5.0)	4.3	8.6
Market value ($ mil.)	2.1%	60.1	68.1	46.1	64.7	65.2
Employees	(3.8%)	1,590	1,630	1,461	1,356	1,360

NETSUITE INC

2955 Campus Drive, Suite 100
San Mateo, CA 94403-2511
Phone: 650 627-1000
Fax: –
Web: www.netsuite.com

NYS: N
CEO: –
CFO: –
HR: –
FYE: December 31
Type: Public

NetSuite is set on helping customers manage their core business processes in a single system. The company's main offering is cloud-based business management software called NetSuite. It automates operations and streamlines processes in accounting customer relationship management (CRM) e-commerce enterprise resource planning (ERP) human resources and inventory. In addition to NetSuite the company offers OneWorld and NetSuite CRM+ designed for use by most types of businesses. OpenAir is designed for professional services businesses. The company serves midsized companies and divisions of large corporations in the consulting distribution manufacturing retail and software industries among others.

	Annual Growth	12/10	12/11	12/12	12/13	12/14
Sales ($ mil.)	30.3%	193.1	236.3	308.8	414.5	556.3
Net income ($ mil.)	–	(27.5)	(32.0)	(35.2)	(70.4)	(100.0)
Market value ($ mil.)	44.6%	1,925.8	3,123.6	5,184.2	7,935.8	8,409.6
Employees	32.7%	1,084	1,265	1,778	2,434	3,357

NETWORK ENGINES INC.

25 Dan Rd.
Canton MA 02021-2817
Phone: 781-332-1000
Fax: 781-770-2000
Web: www.nei.com

NASDAQ: NEI
CEO: Corry Hong
CFO: –
HR: –
FYE: September 30
Type: Public

Network Engines revs up hardware and software integration for many a technology provider. The company doing business as NEI designs and builds server appliances and provides software integration services. Its integration services are used by software vendors and equipment manufacturers who resell and support the finished appliances under their own brands. NEI also offers platform management software and support services. The company targets the communications storage and security sectors. Customers include EMC (60% of sales) Tektronix (10%) ArcSight Juniper Networks and Sophos. In 2012 NEI agreed to be acquired by UNICOM Systems in a deal valued at about $63 million.

NETWORK MANAGEMENT RESOURCES INC.

15000 CONFERENCE CEN DR
CHANTILLY, VA 201513819
Phone: 703-229-1055
Fax: –
Web: www.nmrconsulting.com

CEO: –
CFO: –
HR: –
FYE: December 31
Type: Private

Network Management Resources believes there's a lot to be said for a clear descriptive name. The company designs installs and maintains information technology (IT) equipment. Services include help desk support network administration application development software engineering and training. Its customers (which include both public and private sector organizations) come from a range of industries including financial services manufacturing and health care.

	Annual Growth	12/09	12/10	12/11	12/12	12/13
Sales ($ mil.)	7.6%	–	17.2	21.5	11.7	21.4
Net income ($ mil.)	(31.7%)	–	–	3.1	(1.1)	1.5
Market value ($ mil.)	–	–	–	–	–	–
Employees	–	–	–	–	–	131

NETWORKFLEET INC.

6363 Greenwich Dr. Ste. 200
San Diego CA 92122
Phone: 858-450-3245
Fax: 858-450-3246
Web: www.networkfleet.com

CEO: –
CFO: –
HR: Stephanie Glover
FYE: December 31
Type: Subsidiary

Networkfleet keeps its eyes on the street. A subsidiary of HUGHES Telematics the company provides wireless networking systems that monitor the performance and location of business fleet vehicles. Its products provide Global Positioning System (GPS) tracking confirm driver deliveries and collect preventive maintenance data on engine diagnostics and repairs. Customers include commercial and government fleets including city state and federal agencies. It serves fleets ranging from a few automobiles to thousands of vehicles. Formerly called Networkcar the company changed its name in 2008 to reflect its focus on commercial and government fleets.

NEUMANN SYSTEMS GROUP INC.

890 ELKTON DR STE 101
COLORADO SPRINGS, CO 809073554
Phone: 719-593-7848
Fax: –
Web: www.neumannsystemsgroup.com

CEO: Todd Tiahrt
CFO: Diane Neumann
HR: –
FYE: December 31
Type: Private

If you direct a lot of energy to one place you get a beam. At least that's the plan at Neumann Systems Group doing business as Directed Energy Solutions (DES). The company makes lasers and other optical devices used in research remote sensing communication medical and military applications. It also works on chemical and biological decontamination products that could be used to sterilize medical equipment and improve indoor air quality. DES which operates from its 20000-sq.-ft. research production and development facility in Colorado counts various agencies and branches of the US government including the Army and Air Force and Raytheon as customers. CEO David Neumann formed the company in 1999.

	Annual Growth	12/09	12/10	12/11	12/12	12/13
Sales ($ mil.)	0.3%	–	–	22.1	25.7	22.2
Net income ($ mil.)	(5.7%)	–	–	1.9	2.2	1.7
Market value ($ mil.)	–	–	–	–	–	–
Employees	–	–	–	–	–	60

NEUROCRINE BIOSCIENCES, INC.

NMS: NBIX

12780 El Camino Real
San Diego, CA 92130
Phone: 858 617-7600
Fax: –
Web: www.neurocrine.com

CEO: Kevin C Gorman
CFO: Matthew C Abernethy
HR: –
FYE: December 31
Type: Public

For Neurocrine Biosciences drug development is all about body chemistry. The development-stage biotech develops treatments for neurological and endocrine hormone-related diseases such as insomnia depression and menstrual pain. Lead drug candidate Elagolix is designed to treat endometriosis which causes pain and irregular menstrual bleeding in women. Second in line is NBI-98854 a treatment for movement disorders. Neurocrine Biosciences works in additional therapeutic areas including anxiety cancer epilepsy and diabetes. The company has about a dozen drug candidates in various stages of research and clinical development through both internal programs and collaborative agreements with partners.

	Annual Growth	12/14	12/15	12/16	12/17	12/18
Sales ($ mil.)	183.7%	–	19.8	15.0	161.6	451.2
Net income ($ mil.)	–	(60.5)	(88.9)	(141.1)	(142.5)	21.1
Market value ($ mil.)	33.7%	2,028.4	5,136.4	3,513.8	7,044.9	6,483.8
Employees	57.9%	94	120	196	400	585

NEUROMETRIX INC

NAS: NURO

1000 Winter Street
Waltham, MA 02451
Phone: 781 890-9989
Fax: 781 890-1556
Web: www.neurometrix.com

CEO: Shai N Gozani
CFO: Thomas T Higgins
HR: –
FYE: December 31
Type: Public

NeuroMetrix makes medical devices and consumables that detect diagnose and monitor diabetic neuropathies (DPNs) and neurological conditions affecting the peripheral nerves and spine. The company makes two FDA-approved products: a noninvasive NC-stat DPNCheck system designed for endocrinologists podiatrists and primary care doctors and its ADVANCE system used by specialists. Its systems allow doctors to distinguish between pain caused by nerve root compression and pain caused by less-serious factors. NeuroMetrix's pipeline includes the SENSUS device designed to treat painful DPNs and the ADVANCE CTS device for diagnosing and evaluating carpal tunnel syndrome. CEO Shai Gozani founded the company in 1996.

	Annual Growth	12/15	12/16	12/17	12/18	12/19
Sales ($ mil.)	6.2%	7.3	12.0	17.1	16.1	9.3
Net income ($ mil.)	–	(9.2)	(14.9)	(12.9)	0.0	(3.8)
Market value ($ mil.)	21.0%	2.8	1.0	2.4	1.1	6.0
Employees	(16.8%)	48	44	41	42	23

NEUSTAR, INC.

NYS: NSR

21575 Ridgetop Circle
Sterling, VA 20166
Phone: 571 434-5400
Fax: –
Web: www.neustar.biz

CEO: Charles Gottdiener
CFO: Carolyn Ullerick
HR: Marjorie R Bailey
FYE: December 31
Type: Public

Neustar shines as a key provider of registry and clearinghouse services used in telecommunications and internet networks. The company manages the registry of North American area codes and telephone numbers and the database used by telecom carriers (Verizon AT&T) and cable companies (Comcast Cox Communications) to route phone calls. It is also a leading provider of operations support systems (OSS) clearinghouse services that provide ordering service provisioning billing and customer service functions. In addition Neustar operates an Internet registry supporting domain addresses and provides a host of other registry domain name system and IP services. In June 2016 Neustar said it would split into two public companies.

	Annual Growth	12/11	12/12	12/13	12/14	12/15
Sales ($ mil.)	14.1%	620.5	831.4	902.0	963.7	1,050.0
Net income ($ mil.)	2.2%	160.8	156.1	162.8	163.7	175.5
Market value ($ mil.)	(8.5%)	1,828.7	2,244.0	2,668.4	1,487.8	1,282.8
Employees	9.3%	1,488	1,543	1,623	1,576	2,125

NEUTRON ENERGY INC.

9000 E. Nichols Ave. Ste. 225
Englewood CO 80112
Phone: 303-531-0470
Fax: +86-10-8456-4234
Web: www.21vianet.com

CEO: –
CFO: –
HR: –
FYE: December 31
Type: Private

Unlike most of mankind Neutron Energy actually wants to dig up lots of radioactive material. The exploration stage company searches for uranium perhaps because one kilogram of uranium can produce as much energy as 3000 metric tons of coal. Neutron energy has more than 63000 acres of land in New Mexico South Dakota and Wyoming. Its primary focus is on confirming uranium at its Cibola and Ambrosia Lake Projects. The company also holds mineral interests in previously owns properties in Arizona and South Dakota. In 2012 the company was acquired by Uranium Resources in a deal valued at $38 million.

NEVADA STATE BANK

750 E. Warm Springs Rd.
Las Vegas NV 89119
Phone: 702-855-4530
Fax: 702-914-4512
Web: www.nsbank.com

CEO: –
CFO: –
HR: –
FYE: December 31
Type: Subsidiary

Believe it or not there's a business in Las Vegas that helps you keep your money. A subsidiary of Zions Bancorporation Nevada State Bank operates more than 50 branches in Sin City and the rest of the state. Serving consumers professionals and small and midsized businesses the bank provides standard services such as checking and savings accounts certificates of deposit and check and credit cards. It also offers financial planning investment management and trust services. Nevada State Bank is mainly a real estate lender with one- to four family residential mortgages commercial real estate loans and construction and land development loans making up most of its portfolio.

NEVADA GOLD & CASINOS, INC.

133 E.Warm Springs Road, Suite 102
Las Vegas, NV 89119
Phone: 702 685-1000
Fax: –
Web: www.nevadagold.com

ASE: UWN
CEO: Michael P Shaunnessy
CFO: James D Meier
HR: –
FYE: April 30
Type: Public

Nevada Gold & Casinos knows there's gold in them thar casinos. The company owns about 10 small casinos in Washington State. Three of these casinos — the Crazy Moose-Pasco Crazy Moose-Mountlake Terrace and Coyote Bob-Kennewick — are in close proximity to Seattle while the remaining properties are located in western Washington. It also owns AG Trucano Son & Grandsons a slot machine route in Deadwood South Dakota. It acquired AG Trucano which runs the only authorized commercialized gambling location South Dakota in 2012 for about $5.2 million adding some 900 slots and 20 sites to Nevada Gold's portfolio.

	Annual Growth	04/14	04/15	04/16	04/17	04/18
Sales ($ mil.)	4.4%	62.8	64.3	70.3	74.6	74.6
Net income ($ mil.)	31.1%	0.4	1.8	1.3	0.6	1.3
Market value ($ mil.)	16.2%	19.2	28.3	34.5	37.4	35.0
Employees	0.4%	1,240	1,140	1,280	1,280	1,260

NEVADA SYSTEM OF HIGHER EDUCATION

2601 ENTERPRISE RD
RENO, NV 895121666
Phone: 775-784-4901
Fax: –
Web: www.nevada.edu

CEO: Daniel Klaich
CFO: –
HR: –
FYE: June 30
Type: Private

You can gamble on a solid academic foundation with The Nevada System of Higher Education (NSHE). The system oversees Nevada's public colleges and institutions. NSHE encompasses eight institutions: the University of Nevada Las Vegas; the University of Nevada Reno; Nevada State College; community colleges Truckee Meadows Great Basin College College of Southern Nevada and Western Nevada College; and environmental research arm Desert Research Institute (DRI). The system which enrolls some 106000 students is governed by the Nevada Board of Regents consisting of 13 members elected for six-year terms.

	Annual Growth	06/06	06/07	06/16	06/17	06/18
Sales ($ mil.)	3.1%	–	685.1	1,055.1	1,116.0	953.8
Net income ($ mil.)	(0.0%)	–	116.4	49.0	140.3	116.4
Market value ($ mil.)	–	–	–	–	–	–
Employees	–	–	–	–	–	8,000

NEVADA POWER CO.

6226 West Sahara Avenue
Las Vegas, NV 89146
Phone: 702 402-5000
Fax: –
Web: www.nvenergy.com

NL:
CEO: Michael W. Yackira
CFO: Jonathan S. Halkyard
HR: –
FYE: December 31
Type: Public

Those famous bright city lights of gamblers' paradise (Las Vegas) are lit by Nevada Power a subsidiary of NV Energy (owned by Berkshire Hathaway Energy). The utility transmits and distributes electricity to 892000 customers in southern Nevada including in "Sin City" North Las Vegas Henderson Searchlight Laughlin and adjoining areas including Nellis Air Force Base and the US Department of Energy's Nevada Test Site in Nye County. Nevada Power's 44 gas and coal generating units produces more than 5500 MW of fossil-fueled capacity; it also buys power from the Hoover Dam and elsewhere and markets excess wholesale power. It is also pursuing the development of renewable energy power sources.

	Annual Growth	12/14	12/15	12/16	12/17	12/18
Sales ($ mil.)	(1.7%)	2,337.0	2,402.0	2,083.0	2,206.0	2,184.0
Net income ($ mil.)	(0.1%)	227.0	288.0	279.0	255.0	226.0
Market value ($ mil.)	–	–	–	–	–	–
Employees	0.0%	1,400	1,400	1,400	1,400	1,400

NEW BRAUNFELS UTILITIES

263 MAIN PLZ
NEW BRAUNFELS, TX 781305135
Phone: 830-608-8867
Fax: –
Web: www.nbutexas.com

CEO: Paula J Difonzo
CFO: –
HR: –
FYE: July 31
Type: Private

New Braunfels Utilities is its namesake city's most powerful entity. The utility provides electric water and sewage services to New Braunfels Texas and nearby communities. Its electric system serves more than 28200 customers via 700 miles of overhead and underground distribution lines. New Braunfels Utilities' water and sewer systems serve more than 21600 water and almost 20000 wastewater customers. The water system operates six groundwater wells over the Edwards Aquifer as well as an 8 million gallon per day surface water plant on the Guadalupe River. New Braunfels Utilities' three wastewater treatment plants have a total daily capacity of 8.4 million gallons.

	Annual Growth	07/06	07/07	07/16	07/17	07/18
Sales ($ mil.)	4.4%	–	89.9	135.4	132.8	144.3
Net income ($ mil.)	(0.7%)	–	17.3	23.4	26.2	16.1
Market value ($ mil.)	–	–	–	–	–	–
Employees	–	–	–	–	–	210

NEW BRIDGE MEDICAL CENTER

230 E RIDGEWOOD AVE
PARAMUS, NJ 076524142
Phone: 201-967-4000
Fax: –
Web: www.newbridgehealth.org

CEO: –
CFO: Connie Magdangal
HR: –
FYE: December 31
Type: Private

Bergen Regional Medical Center (BRMC) is not just the biggest hospital in Paramus New Jersey — it's one of the biggest in the state. BRMC provides acute care long-term care and behavioral health care services to the residents of northeastern New Jersey. The not-for-profit medical center with approximately 1190 beds also offers specialized services including orthopedics cardiology neurology emergency medicine and surgery as well as substance abuse treatment and hospice services. About half of the facility is devoted to long-term nursing care; and about 325 beds serve behavioral health patients.

	Annual Growth	12/05	12/06	12/07	12/08	12/15
Sales ($ mil.)	5.1%	–	–	–	146.2	207.5
Net income ($ mil.)	–	–	–	–	(78.9)	(8.4)
Market value ($ mil.)	–	–	–	–	–	–
Employees	–	–	–	–	–	1,856

NEW CAM COMMERCE SOLUTIONS LLC

17075 Newhope St. Ste. A
Fountain Valley CA 92708
Phone: 714-241-9241
Fax: 714-241-9893
Web: www.camcommerce.com

CEO: –
CFO: –
HR: Andrea Grassi
FYE: September 30
Type: Private

New CAM Commerce Solutions doesn't want you missing a single sale or losing a single inventory item. The company's point-of-sale software automates many functions of a retail business from sales transactions and inventory management to loyalty programs reporting and integrated e-commerce features. The company primarily serves specialty retailers including clothing shoe pet sporting good hardware pharmacy and liquor stores. It offers technical support training and Web store design services. In 2008 CAM Commerce was taken private by Great Hill Partners in a deal valued at $180 million. Great Hill Partners sold the majority of CAM Commerce to Robertson Piper Software Group in 2010.

NEW CONCEPT ENERGY, INC.

ASE: GBR

1603 LBJ Freeway, Suite 800
Dallas, TX 75234
Phone: 972 407-8400
Fax: 972 407-8421
Web: www.newconceptenergy.com

CEO: –
CFO: Gene S Bertcher
HR: –
FYE: December 31
Type: Public

New Concept Energy is exploring possibilities in natural resources while keeping one foot planted in the long-term care industry. The firm owns a residential community for senior citizens in Oregon that provides support services for about 115 independent living units. New Concept Energy also has oil and gas production assets in the midwestern US including about 100 producing wells and 120 non-producing wells with a total proved reserves of some 7.6 million cu. ft. of natural gas. The company has gone through a number of industries over the years; it has divested most of its former assisted living communities and all of its cable and retail shopping assets and it is seeking to grow its energy operations.

	Annual Growth	12/14	12/15	12/16	12/17	12/18
Sales ($ mil.)	(37.1%)	4.4	3.8	0.8	0.8	0.7
Net income ($ mil.)	–	(0.8)	(2.6)	0.0	(3.2)	(0.5)
Market value ($ mil.)	(1.7%)	7.7	5.5	11.1	8.0	7.2
Employees	(40.8%)	49	46	41	6	6

NEW ENGLAND REALTY ASSOCIATES L.P.

ASE: NEN

39 Brighton Avenue
Allston, MA 02134
Phone: 617 783-0039
Fax: –

CEO: –
CFO: Andrew Bloch
HR: –
FYE: December 31
Type: Public

New England Realty Associates invests in develops operates and sells residential and commercial real estate primarily in the Boston area. The company's portfolio includes more than 2300 apartment and condominium units and about 85000 sq. ft. of commercial space that includes a shopping center and mixed-use properties. It also has a 50% stake in a portfolio of about 10 commercial properties. New England Realty Associates is managed by general partner NewReal which in turn is owned by company officers and brothers Ronald and Harold Brown. Harold Brown also owns The Hamilton Company which manages the partnership's properties.

	Annual Growth	12/14	12/15	12/16	12/17	12/18
Sales ($ mil.)	8.0%	42.6	45.5	49.6	52.8	58.0
Net income ($ mil.)	42.0%	1.0	3.8	5.0	6.9	4.2
Market value ($ mil.)	3.5%	6.1	6.3	7.6	9.1	7.0
Employees	–	–	–	–	68	–

NEW HAMPSHIRE ELECTRIC COOPERATIVE INC

579 TENNEY MOUNTAIN HWY
PLYMOUTH, NH 032643147
Phone: 603-536-8824
Fax: –
Web: www.nhec.com

CEO: –
CFO: –
HR: Brenda Boisvert
FYE: December 31
Type: Private

The granite in the Granite State won't keep the folks in New Hampshire warm in winter but New Hampshire Electric Cooperative will. The utility provides electricity to about 80000 residential and business customers (who are also member-owners of the cooperative) in 115 New Hampshire towns and cities. The enterprise operates 5400 miles of distribution lines and is seeking to become a complete energy solutions organization offering energy saving options such as equipment retrofits at local schools and selling energy-efficient compact fluorescent light bulbs. Most of New Hampshire Electric Cooperative's revenues comes from residential customers and the balance form small businesses.

	Annual Growth	12/13	12/14	12/15	12/16	12/17
Sales ($ mil.)	1.0%	–	135.5	139.0	128.9	139.5
Net income ($ mil.)	6.3%	–	5.7	9.5	8.8	6.8
Market value ($ mil.)	–	–	–	–	–	–
Employees	–	–	–	–	–	199

NEW HAMPSHIRE THRIFT BANCSHARES, INC.

NMS: NHTB

9 Main Street, P.O. Box 9
Newport, NH 03773
Phone: 603 863-0886
Fax: –
Web: www.nhthrift.com

CEO: –
CFO: –
HR: –
FYE: December 31
Type: Public

New Hampshire Thrift Bancshares is the holding company for Lake Sunapee Bank which operates nearly 30 branches in western and central New Hampshire and western Vermont. Targeting individuals and local businesses the bank mainly uses funds from deposits to originate a variety of loans mainly residential and commercial mortgages. It also offers investment insurance and trust services. New Hampshire Thrift Bancshares expanded into Vermont with the 2007 acquisition of First Brandon National Bank which now operates as a division of Lake Sunapee Bank. The company bought insurance agency McCrillis & Eldredge in 2011. It now plans to buy the single-branch Nashua Bank.

	Annual Growth	12/09	12/10	12/11	12/12	12/13
Assets ($ mil.)	10.3%	962.6	995.1	1,041.8	1,270.5	1,423.9
Net income ($ mil.)	6.3%	6.6	7.9	7.7	7.8	8.4
Market value ($ mil.)	12.0%	79.6	103.1	92.8	104.4	125.3
Employees	12.3%	240	249	274	304	382

NEW HANOVER REGIONAL MEDICAL CENTER

2131 S 17TH ST
WILMINGTON, NC 284017407
Phone: 910-343-7001
Fax: –
Web: www.nhrmc.org

CEO: Kathy Batchelor
CFO: Ed Ollie
HR: –
FYE: December 31
Type: Private

Those living in the Cape Fear area need not fear when it comes to accessing good medical care. Integrated health system New Hanover Regional Medical Center (NHRMC) serves the Wilmington and Cape Fear area of North Carolina through its flagship 855-bed New Hanover Regional Medical Center the 130-bed Cape Fear Hospital and the 85-bed Pender Memorial Hospital. NHRMC also operates a rehabilitation center a behavioral health facility and a women's and children's hospital as well as home health hospice EMS transport physician practice and outpatient care clinic locations. The not-for-profit health network is affiliated with the UNC-Chapel Hill School of Medicine.

	Annual Growth	12/13	12/14*	06/15*	12/15	12/16
Sales ($ mil.)	8.3%	–	200.8	601.5	246.6	235.5
Net income ($ mil.)	(8.3%)	–	26.3	83.8	22.7	22.1
Market value ($ mil.)	–	–	–	–	–	–
Employees	–	–	–	–	–	3,692

*Fiscal year change

NEW JERSEY HOUSING AND MORTGAGE FINANCE AGENCY

637 S CLINTON AVE
TRENTON, NJ 086111811
Phone: 609-278-7400
Fax: –
Web: www.nj-hmfa.com

CEO: John Mu
CFO: –
HR: –
FYE: December 31
Type: Private

So you're from Jersey? What exit? Regardless of where on the turnpike you live or want to live New Jersey Housing and Mortgage Finance Agency can help you find fund and maintain affordable housing. The agency offers low interest mortgage loans to low- and moderate-income families; construction loans and other programs to assist developers with the production of low-cost rental properties and affordable houses; reverse mortgages for seniors; homeownership counseling; and various programs to promote homeownership among its state's disabled homeless and adopting families.

	Annual Growth	12/06	12/07	12/08	12/09	12/11
Assets ($ mil.)	0.1%	–	–	–	4,362.1	4,370.4
Net income ($ mil.)	–	–	–	–	(21.2)	(56.2)
Market value ($ mil.)	–	–	–	–	–	–
Employees	–	–	–	–	–	250

NEW JERSEY INSTITUTE OF TECHNOLOGY

323 DR MARTIN LUTHER KING
NEWARK, NJ 071021824
Phone: 973-596-3000
Fax: –
Web: www.njit.edu

CEO: –
CFO: Edward J Bishof
HR: Theodore Johnson
FYE: June 30
Type: Private

A public research university New Jersey Institute of Technology (NJIT) offers about 100 undergraduate and graduate programs including about 20 doctoral programs in fields including architecture engineering computer science and liberal arts. The school also offers continuing education and distance courses. With some 500 full-time faculty members NJIT boasts a student-faulty ratio of 16:1. Its Albert Dorman Honors College provides students with individualized curricula and honors colloquia including travel and featured speakers. About 10000 students attend the NJIT which operates a single campus in Newark. NJIT was founded in 1881 as the Newark Technical School.

	Annual Growth	06/12	06/13	06/16	06/17	06/18
Sales ($ mil.)	6.2%	–	210.7	263.2	275.5	284.9
Net income ($ mil.)	–	–	17.4	5.8	24.2	(0.5)
Market value ($ mil.)	–	–	–	–	–	–
Employees	–	–	–	–	–	1,047

NEW JERSEY MINING CO.

201 N. Third Street
Coeur d'Alene, ID 83814
Phone: 208 625-9001
Fax: –
Web: www.newjerseymining.com

NBB: NJMC
CEO: Delbert W Steiner
CFO: –
HR: –
FYE: December 31
Type: Public

No product of the Garden State New Jersey Mining seeks out gold silver and base metals in the Coeur d'Alene mining district of northern Idaho and western Montana. The development and exploration company maintains two Idaho-based joint ventures one with Marathon Gold at the Golden Chest gold mine and another with United Mining Group involved in ore processing. The company also holds rights to several mineral properties including the Niagara copper-silver deposit Toboggan gold exploration project (formerly a JV with Newmont Mining) and Silver Strand mine. President Fred Brackebusch controls about a quarter of New Jersey Mining.

	Annual Growth	12/14	12/15	12/16	12/17	12/18
Sales ($ mil.)	150.3%	0.1	1.9	0.5	4.3	3.6
Net income ($ mil.)	–	(1.4)	(0.2)	(1.4)	0.0	0.8
Market value ($ mil.)	20.6%	9.3	11.1	14.8	18.8	19.7
Employees	9.0%	17	7	16	16	24

NEW JERSEY NATURAL GAS COMPANY

1415 Wyckoff Rd.
Wall NJ 07719
Phone: 732-938-7977
Fax: 732-938-2134
Web: www.njng.com

CEO: Lawrence M Downes
CFO: –
HR: –
FYE: September 30
Type: Subsidiary

It's not just the tourists that appreciate the services of New Jersey Natural Gas it's the locals too. The gas utility provides gas distribution service to 500100 residential commercial and industrial customers in New Jersey's vacationland — Monmouth and Ocean counties and parts of Morris and Middlesex counties. The company is the principal subsidiary of publicly traded regional utility New Jersey Resources and operates 6700 miles of distribution pipeline. Sister company NJR Retail Holdings offers appliance installation repair and maintenance service to about 150000 homes and businesses in its service region.

NEW JERSEY RESOURCES CORP

1415 Wyckoff Road
Wall, NJ 07719
Phone: 732 938-1000
Fax: –
Web: www.njresources.com

NYS: NJR
CEO: Laurence M. (Larry) Downes
CFO: Patrick Migliaccio
HR: –
FYE: September 30
Type: Public

New Jersey Resources (NJR) shows its resourcefulness by distributing natural gas to some 539000 customers in New Jersey. Beyond gas distribution the company also provides energy storage and transportation services to industrial customers across several Northeast US states as well as HVAC & solar installation services to some 110000 households in its home state. The company also invests in clean energy like solar projects and midstream assets. Northern and central New Jersey is the heart of NJR's customer base. NJR serves customers like regulated natural gas distribution companies industrial companies electric generators natural gas/liquids processors retail aggregators wholesale marketers and natural gas producers.

	Annual Growth	09/15	09/16	09/17	09/18	09/19
Sales ($ mil.)	(1.3%)	2,734.0	1,880.9	2,268.6	2,915.1	2,592.0
Net income ($ mil.)	(1.6%)	181.0	131.7	132.1	233.4	169.5
Market value ($ mil.)	10.8%	2,702.7	2,957.4	3,793.4	4,148.9	4,069.7
Employees	2.8%	991	1,034	1,052	1,068	1,108

NEW JERSEY TURNPIKE AUTHORITY INC

1 TURNPIKE PLZ
WOODBRIDGE, NJ 070955195
Phone: 732-750-5300
Fax: -
Web: www.state.nj.us

CEO: -
CFO: -
HR: -
FYE: December 31
Type: Private

The New Jersey Turnpike Authority operates two toll-supported highways the New Jersey Turnpike and the Garden State Parkway. The New Jersey Turnpike runs for 148 miles from the Delaware River Bridge at the southern end of the state to the George Washington Bridge that connects New Jersey with New York. The turnpike includes about 10 rest stops or service areas named for former New Jersey residents such as Alexander Hamilton Vince Lombardi and Walt Whitman. The Garden State Parkway runs for 173 miles and spans the length of New Jersey's Atlantic coastline.

	Annual Growth	12/12	12/13	12/14	12/16	12/17
Sales ($ mil.)	3.1%	-	-	1,549.7	1,689.4	1,698.6
Net income ($ mil.)	7.5%	-	-	265.1	260.0	329.7
Market value ($ mil.)	-	-	-	-	-	-
Employees	-	-	-	-	-	2,400

NEW MEXICO STATE UNIVERSITY

2850 WEDDELL ST RM 210
LAS CRUCES, NM 880031245
Phone: 575-646-4030
Fax: -
Web: www.nmsu.edu

CEO: Andy Burke
CFO: -
HR: -
FYE: June 30
Type: Private

New Mexico State University (NMSU) aims to spice things up for its 30000 students. The university provides education services from five main campuses one satellite learning center and extension offices in every New Mexico county. The university offers certificate associate bachelor's master's and doctoral degrees through six academic colleges focused on agriculture arts and sciences business administration education engineering and health and social services as well as an honors college and a graduate school. It also provides distance education services and operates about a dozen research and science centers.

	Annual Growth	06/14	06/15	06/16	06/17	06/18
Sales ($ mil.)	(4.2%)	-	-	226.4	221.7	207.9
Net income ($ mil.)	-	-	-	18.6	(4.0)	(83.3)
Market value ($ mil.)	-	-	-	-	-	-
Employees	-	-	-	-	-	5,000

NEW MILFORD HOSPITAL INC.

21 ELM ST
NEW MILFORD, CT 067762993
Phone: 860-355-2611
Fax: -
Web: www.newmilfordhospital.org

CEO: John M Murphy
CFO: -
HR: -
FYE: September 30
Type: Private

Residents of New Milford Connecticut naturally turn to New Milford Hospital for emergency care. Established in 1921 the acute care hospital has some 85 beds and offers cardiology cancer care pediatric and surgical services. The not-for-profit facility also has family birthing sleep disorder treatment and cancer research facilities. Affiliate New Milford Visiting Nurse Association provides home health services. New Milford Hospital exited its membership in the NewYork-Presbyterian Healthcare System in 2010. It then formed a new affiliation with Danbury Hospital and the two hospitals now operate under the administrative umbrella of Western Connecticut Healthcare (formerly Danbury Health Systems).

	Annual Growth	09/09	09/10	09/11	09/12	09/13
Sales ($ mil.)	(8.8%)	-	91.9	93.4	78.1	69.7
Net income ($ mil.)	-	-	-	(4.3)	(6.5)	(3.2)
Market value ($ mil.)	-	-	-	-	-	-
Employees	-	-	-	-	-	400

NEW MOUNTAIN FINANCE CORP

787 Seventh Avenue, 48th Floor
New York, NY 10019
Phone: 212 720-0300
Fax: 212 582-2277
Web: www.newmountainfinance.com

NYS: NMFC
CEO: Robert A Hamwee
CFO: Shiraz Y Kajee
HR: -
FYE: December 31
Type: Public

Investment firm New Mountain Finance Corporation won't make its portfolio companies climb over too many hills for a loan. The affiliate of private equity firm New Mountain Capital makes investments of $10 million-$50 million in middle-market companies (those with annual revenues of less than $200 million). Its portfolio is made up of senior secured first-lien and second-lien term loans and subordinated debt. Organized as a business development company (BDC) New Mountain Finance pays little in income taxes as long as it distributes 90% of its profits back to shareholders. It is externally managed by New Mountain Finance Advisers BDC L.L.C. The company went public in 2011.

	Annual Growth	12/13	12/14	12/15	12/16	12/17
Sales ($ mil.)	21.5%	90.9	135.6	153.9	168.1	197.8
Net income ($ mil.)	19.3%	50.5	80.1	82.5	88.1	102.2
Market value ($ mil.)	(2.6%)	1,142.1	1,134.5	988.7	1,070.7	1,028.9
Employees	-	-	-	-	-	-

NEW PRIME, INC.

2740 N MAYFAIR AVE
SPRINGFIELD, MO 658035084
Phone: 800-321-4552
Fax: -
Web: www.primeinc.com

CEO: Robert E. Low
CFO: Dean Hoedl
HR: -
FYE: March 31
Type: Private

Specialized carrier New Prime (which does business simply as Prime) provides refrigerated flatbed tanker and intermodal trucking services throughout North America through more than 10000 remotely monitored temperature-controlled trailers. The company operates in the US and Canada and serves Mexico through arrangements with other carriers. A subsidiary Prime Floral uses the parent company's refrigerated equipment and facilities to serve the flower industry. In addition to its freight-hauling operations Prime provides logistics services including freight brokerage.

	Annual Growth	04/10	04/11*	03/12*	04/16*	03/17
Sales ($ mil.)	9.8%	-	941.4	1,022.2	1,598.5	1,653.6
Net income ($ mil.)	16.2%	-	47.4	61.0	133.3	116.6
Market value ($ mil.)	-	-	-	-	-	-
Employees	-	-	-	-	-	5,000

*Fiscal year change

NEW SOURCE ENERGY CORPORATION

914 N. Broadway Suite 230
Oklahoma City OK 73102
Phone: 405-272-3028
Fax: 310-788-1990
Web: www.ilfc.com

CEO: -
CFO: Antranik Armoudian
HR: -
FYE: December 31
Type: Private

New Source Energy is actually looking for the same old energy source - oil and gas - but in a new way. The company formed in July 2011 plans to comb over mature oil and natural gas reservoirs a second time to hunt for leftover deposits. Right away it bought the rights to working interests in about 54000 net acres across the Hunton formation in Oklahoma. The company estimates the properties' net proved reserves to be 19 million barrels of oil equivalent made up of about 60% oil and natural gas liquids and 40% natural gas. New Source Energy filed an IPO in 2011 but withdrew it in 2012.

NEW SOURCE ENERGY PARTNERS LP

NBB: NSLP

914 North Broadway, Suite 230
Oklahoma City, OK 73102
Phone: 405 272-3028
Fax: 405 272-3034
Web: www.newsource.com

CEO: –
CFO: –
HR: –
FYE: December 31
Type: Public

If at first you don't succeed try try again. That's the ethos behind New Source Energy Partners L.P. a company formed in October 2012 in the hopes of becoming a publicly traded entity. A previous incarnation New Source Energy Corporation formed in July 2011 filed an IPO but withdrew it in May 2012. Should New Source Energy Partners successfully go public it will have working interests across more than 30000 net acres in the Hunton formation in Oklahoma. Those properties produce about 170 barrels of oil per day 6 million cu. ft. of natural gas and almost 2000 barrels per day of natural gas liquids (NGLs). New Source Energy Partners filed an IPO in January 2013 seeking to raise up to $106 million.

	Annual Growth	10/11	10/12*	12/12	12/13	12/14
Sales ($ mil.)	–	0.0	–	–	50.7	165.6
Net income ($ mil.)	–	0.0	–	–	26.6	(42.3)
Market value ($ mil.)	–	–	–	–	432.8	133.3
Employees	630.6%	–	8	9	136	427

*Fiscal year change

NEW TANGRAM, LLC

9200 SORENSEN AVE
SANTA FE SPRINGS, CA 906702645
Phone: 562-365-5000
Fax: –
Web: www.tangraminteriors.com

CEO: –
CFO: Nick Greenko
HR: –
FYE: December 31
Type: Private

Tangram Interiors keeps it all on the inside. The company is an office furniture manufacturer and dealer specializing in Steelcase products. Other brands include Brayton Vecta Metro and Lightolier. The company with two showrooms in southern California offers asset management furniture rental network installation remanufacturing and moving and relocation assistance. Tangram sells an "acoustic privacy system" that allows workplace conversations to remain private by broadcasting a signal that scrambles speech patterns into white noise. The company's Tangram Studio provides design services project management and custom architectural elements. Tangram is part of Steelcase family of companies.

	Annual Growth	12/08	12/09	12/10	12/11	12/12
Sales ($ mil.)	7.7%	–	–	84.9	92.4	98.5
Net income ($ mil.)	(63.1%)	–	–	1.7	1.8	0.2
Market value ($ mil.)	–	–	–	–	–	–
Employees	–	–	–	–	–	50

NEW YORK BLOOD CENTER, INC.

310 E 67TH ST
NEW YORK, NY 100656273
Phone: 212-570-3010
Fax: –
Web: www.nybloodcenter.org

CEO: Christopher D. Hillyer
CFO: Elizabeth C. Gibson
HR: Doriane Gloria
FYE: March 31
Type: Private

New York Blood Center (NYBC) holds a very literal interpretation of the meaning of life. It is a not-for-profit blood distribution and research organization serving New York City and its environs in New York State and New Jersey as well as parts of Connecticut and Pennsylvania. As one of the largest blood centers in the US NYBC provides nearly 1 million blood components to some 200 hospitals each year. The center's facilities collect blood from more than 2000 donors each day. It also operates the nation's oldest and largest public cord blood bank. In addition its Kimball Research Institute includes more than a dozen research laboratories which study the prevention and treatment of blood-related illnesses.

	Annual Growth	03/12	03/13	03/14	03/15	03/18
Sales ($ mil.)	13.4%	–	–	–	320.3	466.7
Net income ($ mil.)	–	–	–	–	(0.9)	48.4
Market value ($ mil.)	–	–	–	–	–	–
Employees	–	–	–	–	–	1,600

NEW YORK CITY HEALTH AND HOSPITALS CORPORATION

125 WORTH ST RM 514
NEW YORK, NY 100134006
Phone: 212-788-3321
Fax: –

CEO: Alan D. Aviles
CFO: Marlene Zurack
HR: –
FYE: June 30
Type: Private

New York City Health and Hospitals Corporation (NYC H+H) operates health care facilities in all five boroughs of New York City. As one of the largest municipal health service systems in the US HHC serves 1 million New Yorkers including more than 500000 who are uninsured. It operates a network of around 10 acute care hospitals (including Bellevue the nation's oldest public hospital) large diagnostic and treatment centers skilled nursing centers long-term care facilities and a home health care agency. NYC H+H also operates more than 70 community-based clinics and provides medical services to New York City's correctional facilities. In addition it operates MetroPlus a managed health care plan.

	Annual Growth	06/0-1	06/00	06/01	06/02	06/17
Sales ($ mil.)	5.1%	–	4,083.8	4,288.0	4,285.3	9,550.9
Net income ($ mil.)	–	–	9.3	(71.9)	(118.9)	(193.6)
Market value ($ mil.)	–	–	–	–	–	–
Employees	–	–	–	–	–	35,700

NEW YORK CITY TRANSIT AUTHORITY

2 BROADWAY FL 18
NEW YORK, NY 100043357
Phone: 718-330-1234
Fax: –

CEO: –
CFO: –
HR: –
FYE: December 31
Type: Private

New York City Transit Authority has your ticket to ride in the Big Apple. Known as MTA New York City Transit it provides subway and bus transportation throughout New York City's five boroughs. It is the primary agency of the MTA and the largest public transportation system in North America. Its subway system — which includes more than 6300 subway cars 468 stations and 660 miles of track — serves more than 5.5 million passengers a day day on 238 local six select bus service and 61 express routes in the five boroughs. Its more than 5700 buses transport some 2.6 million riders each day. The agency also operates the Staten Island Railway system.

	Annual Growth	12/14	12/15	12/16	12/17	12/18
Sales ($ mil.)	(0.4%)	–	–	–	4,911.6	4,892.7
Net income ($ mil.)	–	–	–	–	(287.6)	985.8
Market value ($ mil.)	–	–	–	–	–	–
Employees	–	–	–	–	–	47,956

NEW YORK CITY TRANSITIONAL FINANCE AUTHORITY

75 Park Place 6th Fl.
New York NY 10007
Phone: 212-788-5877
Fax: 212-788-9197
Web: www.nyc.gov/html/tfa/home.html

CEO: –
CFO: –
HR: –
FYE: June 30
Type: Government Agency

The New York City Transitional Finance Authority (TFA) won't sell you the Brooklyn Bridge but it will let you invest in repairs. The quasi-independent government agency sells municipal bonds to finance the Big Apple's capital improvement projects — public buildings roads bridges etc. The authority was created in 1997 to circumvent state constitutional limitations on the amount of debt the city could take on. With the authority to issue up to $11.5 billion in bonds the agency proved to be even more useful than anticipated selling $2 billion in bonds for recovery costs following the September 11 attacks that destroyed the World Trade Center. The TFA's bond limit has since been raised to $13.5 billion.

NEW YORK COMMUNITY BANCORP INC.

NYS: NYCB

615 Merrick Avenue
Westbury, NY 11590
Phone: 516 683-4100
Fax: -
Web: www.mynycb.com

CEO: Joseph R. Ficalora
CFO: Thomas R. (Tom) Cangemi
HR: Patricia King
FYE: December 31
Type: Public

It's big banking in the Big Apple and beyond. New York Community Bancorp is the holding company for one of the largest thrifts in the US New York Community Bank as well as New York Commercial Bank (also dba Atlantic Bank) and seven other banking divisions. In its home state New York Community Bank operates through Queens County Savings Bank Richmond County Savings Bank Roosevelt Savings Bank and Roslyn Savings Bank. It serves customers in New Jersey through its Garden State Community Bank division. New York Community Bank also does business as AmTrust Bank which operates in Arizona and Florida and Ohio Savings Bank. Altogether New York Community Bancorp has about 275 bank branches in five states.

	Annual Growth	12/14	12/15	12/16	12/17	12/18
Assets ($ mil.)	1.7%	48,559.2	50,317.8	48,926.6	49,124.2	51,899.4
Net income ($ mil.)	(3.4%)	485.4	(47.2)	495.4	466.2	422.4
Market value ($ mil.)	(12.4%)	7,576.6	7,728.1	7,534.0	6,165.4	4,456.0
Employees	(3.9%)	3,416	3,448	3,487	3,096	2,913

NEW YORK CONVENTION CENTER OPERATING CORPORATION

655 W 34TH ST
NEW YORK, NY 100011114
Phone: 212-216-2000
Fax: -
Web: www.javitscenter.com

CEO: Alan E Steel
CFO: Melanie McManus
HR: -
FYE: March 31
Type: Private

The New York Convention Center Operating Corporation may be able to claim that it has the whole world in its hand since it's the manager and operator of the "marketplace for the world" (also know as the Jacob K. Javits Convention Center in Manhattan). The center serves as host each year for myriad conventions fashion shows association meetings trade shows and more. The center features such amenities as restaurants and cocktail lounges temporary private office rentals and concierge service. The New York Convention Center Operating Corporation (also known as NYCCOC) was established in 1979 to manage the Javits Center.

	Annual Growth	03/07	03/08	03/15	03/17	03/18
Sales ($ mil.)	3.7%	-	143.1	170.0	200.6	206.4
Net income ($ mil.)	-	-	(8.8)	1.1	6.7	8.9
Market value ($ mil.)	-	-	-	-	-	-
Employees	-	-	-	-	-	3,500

NEW YORK FOOTBALL GIANTS INC.

Giants Stadium
East Rutherford NJ 07073
Phone: 201-935-8111
Fax: 201-935-8493
Web: www.giants.com

CEO: Preston R Tisch
CFO: -
HR: -
FYE: February 28
Type: Private

It only seems natural that the Big Apple would have a big football team. New York Football Giants owns and operates the New York Giants professional football team one of the oldest and most storied franchises in the National Football League. Started in 1925 the team has played for the league championship a record 19 times winning eight titles including four Super Bowl championships. The Giants roster has included such Hall of Fame players as Frank Gifford Sam Huff Lawrence Taylor and Y.A. Tittle. The team plays host at New Meadowlands Stadium in New Jersey which it shares with the New York Jets. Tim Mara paid $500 to found the franchise; the Mara and Tisch families continue to control the team.

NEW YORK JETS LLC

1 Jets Dr.
Florham Park NJ 07932
Phone: 973-549-4800
Fax: 510-864-5160
Web: www.raiders.com

CEO: -
CFO: -
HR: -
FYE: February 28
Type: Private

These Jets begin boarding at the start of every football season. A storied franchise in the National Football League the New York Jets claim just one Super Bowl title but its victory over the favored Baltimore Colts (now the Indianapolis Colts) in 1969 was one of the more famous matches in the history of championship. The franchise founded by broadcaster Harry Wismer as the Titans was a founding member of the American Football League in 1960 and joined the NFL when the leagues merged in 1970. Robert Johnson IV whose family founded pharmaceutical giant Johnson & Johnson has owned the team since 2000.

NEW YORK LIFE INSURANCE COMPANY

51 Madison Ave.
New York NY 10010
Phone: 212-576-7000
Fax: 914-681-6949
Web: www.nypa.gov

CEO: Ted Mathas
CFO: Michael E Sproule
HR: -
FYE: December 31
Type: Private - Mutual Com

New York Life Insurance has been providing life insurance policies in the Big Apple since it was a tiny seed. While the top mutual life insurer in the US has branched out a bit it retains its core business: life insurance and annuities. Its products include long-term care insurance and special group policies sold through AARP and other affinity groups and professional associations. New York Life Investments' offerings include mutual funds for individuals and investment management services for institutional investors. Through New York Life International the firm provides life policies in overseas markets. Founded in 1841 New York Life is owned by its policyholders.

NEW YORK MEDICAL COLLEGE

40 SUNSHINE COTTAGE RD
VALHALLA, NY 105951524
Phone: 914-594-4100
Fax: -
Web: www.nyctg.com

CEO: -
CFO: -
HR: -
FYE: June 30
Type: Private

It doesn't take a brain surgeon to figure out this school's specialty. New York Medical College (NYMC) confers advanced degrees to those preparing for careers in the medical and health professions. The institution's three divisions — the School of Medicine the School of Public Health and the Graduate School of Basic Medical Sciences — offer programs in more than 20 disciplines. NYMC has an enrollment of more than 1400 students who practice at nearby Westchester Medical Center and the Manhattan location of Saint Vincent Catholic Medical Centers. Founded in 1860 the medical college has been affiliated with the Archdiocese of New York since 1978. NYMC is part of Touro College.

	Annual Growth	06/09	06/10	06/13	06/14	06/15
Sales ($ mil.)	(9.2%)	-	215.3	145.4	151.1	133.0
Net income ($ mil.)	-	-	(1.2)	6.0	4.6	(3.8)
Market value ($ mil.)	-	-	-	-	-	-
Employees	-	-	-	-	-	1,100

NEW YORK MORTGAGE TRUST INC   NMS: NYMT

90 Park Avenue
New York, NY 10016
Phone: 212 792-0107
Fax: –
Web: www.nymtrust.com

CEO: Steven R. Mumma
CFO: Kristine R. Nario
HR: –
FYE: December 31
Type: Public

New York Mortgage Trust is a self-advised real estate investment trust (REIT) that invests in mortgage-related real estate assets and some financial assets. It mostly invests in residential mortgage loans including multi-family commercial mortgage-backed securities (CMBS) distressed residential mortgage loans and direct financing to multi-family property owners through mezzanine loans and preferred equity investments. More than 60% of its revenue comes from interest on multi-family loans held in securitization trusts though the REIT's fortunes depend heavily on security gains and losses. New York Mortgage Trust was formed in 2003 and is headquartered in New York City.

	Annual Growth	12/14	12/15	12/16	12/17	12/18
Sales ($ mil.)	1.9%	486.0	384.0	359.7	439.4	523.5
Net income ($ mil.)	(6.8%)	136.2	78.0	67.6	92.0	102.9
Market value ($ mil.)	(6.5%)	1,199.6	829.3	1,026.9	960.0	916.4
Employees	50.6%	7	7	19	19	36

NEW YORK POWER AUTHORITY

123 MAIN ST
WHITE PLAINS, NY 106013104
Phone: 914-681-6200
Fax: –
Web: www.nypa.gov

CEO: Gil C. Quiniones
CFO: Robert F. Lurie
HR: –
FYE: December 31
Type: Private

The hydropower generated by the mighty Niagara Falls is the real authority behind the New York Power Authority (NYPA). More than 70% of the power that NYPA produces is from hydropower resources. The company generates and transmits more than 20% of New York's electricity making it the largest state-owned public power provider in the US. It is also New York's only statewide electricity supplier. NYPA owns hydroelectric and fossil-fueled generating facilities (16 in total) that produce about 5700 MW of electricity and it operates more than 1400 circuit-miles of transmission lines. NYPA is owned by the State of New York.

	Annual Growth	12/13	12/14	12/15	12/16	12/17
Sales ($ mil.)	(6.8%)	–	3,175.0	2,625.0	2,421.0	2,573.0
Net income ($ mil.)	(24.1%)	–	272.0	74.0	22.0	119.0
Market value ($ mil.)	–	–	–	–	–	–
Employees	–	–	–	–	–	2,237

NEW YORK PUBLIC RADIO

160 VARICK ST FL 7
NEW YORK, NY 100131270
Phone: 646-829-4400
Fax: –
Web: www.nypublicradio.org

CEO: Laura R Walker
CFO: –
HR: –
FYE: June 30
Type: Private

If you want the NPR in NYC turn your radio dial to WNYC. With more than one million listeners per week WNYC is the most popular public radio station in the country. The stations broadcasts on FM and AM and produces and airs original programming including daily news reports talk shows and music shows including The Brian Lehrer Show   Radio Lab   and   Studio 360   . It also features shows from affiliate National Public Radio (NPR) stations (including   All Things Considered   and   Morning Edition   ) and Public Radio International. Listeners can also access WYNC's Web site to read the news download podcasts and hear recently broadcasted shows. The radio station one of the oldest in the US began broadcasting on AM in 1922.

	Annual Growth	06/07	06/08	06/13	06/15	06/17
Sales ($ mil.)	7.6%	–	46.7	61.3	68.0	90.2
Net income ($ mil.)	(17.1%)	–	11.1	1.0	(1.8)	2.0
Market value ($ mil.)	–	–	–	–	–	–
Employees	–	–	–	–	–	120

NEW YORK STATE CATHOLIC HEALTH PLAN, INC.

9525 QUEENS BLVD
REGO PARK, NY 113744510
Phone: 888-343-3547
Fax: –
Web: www.fideliscare.org

CEO: Rev Patrick J Frawley
CFO: Thomas Halloran
HR: –
FYE: December 31
Type: Private

Fidelis Care hopes for always faithful health plan members. The New York State Catholic Health Plan which does business as Fidelis Care serves more than 921000 residents in some 60 counties across the state including the New York City area. The church-sponsored plan's provider network includes more than 63000 physicians hospitals and other health care professionals and facilities. Fidelis Care provides managed Medicaid Medicare and state-sponsored family and children's Health Plus plans as well as long-term care and behavioral health coverage.

	Annual Growth	12/07	12/08	12/09	12/10	12/14
Sales ($ mil.)	30.6%	–	1,068.2	1,435.2	1,921.0	5,304.8
Net income ($ mil.)	103.1%	–	3.9	27.9	51.4	271.7
Market value ($ mil.)	–	–	–	–	–	–
Employees	–	–	–	–	–	1,625

NEW YORK STATE LOTTERY

1 Broadway Center
Schenectady NY 12301-7500
Phone: 518-388-3300
Fax: 518-388-3403
Web: www.nylottery.org

CEO: –
CFO: –
HR: –
FYE: March 31
Type: Government-owned

Winning the New York State Lottery could make you king of the hill top of the heap. The New York State Lottery is one of the largest and oldest state lotteries in the US (only New Hampshire's lottery is older). It runs three jackpot five daily and about a dozen scratch-off games through retailers and online outlets. About a third of the lottery's revenue or some $2 billion a year goes to support New York State education. It also awards Leaders of Tomorrow scholarships to one eligible graduating senior from every public and private school in the state (provided they attend New York universities). The New York Lottery was established by the new state constitution passed in 1966.

NEW YORK STATE TEACHERS' RETIREMENT SYSTEM

10 Corporate Woods Dr.
Albany NY 12211-2395
Phone: 518-447-2900
Fax: 518-447-2875
Web: www.nystrs.org

CEO: George Philip
CFO: Arthur Hewig
HR: –
FYE: June 30
Type: Government Agency

The New York State Teachers' Retirement System known as NYSTRS for short provides retirement death and disability benefits to more than 280000 public school teachers and administrators as well as to some 140000 retirees and beneficiaries. Eligible retirees are guaranteed monthly benefits payments for life. The system which was established by the state in 1921 serves public school educators in the Empire State excluding New York City. Employees of New York State community colleges boards of cooperative educational services The State University of New York system and some charter school employees have the option of participating as well.

NEW YORK TIMES CO.
NYS: NYT

620 Eighth Avenue
New York, NY 10018
Phone: 212 556-1234
Fax: –
Web: www.nytco.com

CEO: Mark Thompson
CFO: James M. Follo
HR: –
FYE: December 30
Type: Public

All the News That's Fit to Print and Post Online would be a more accurate motto for this media titan. The New York Times Company (The Times Co.) publishes The New York Times. The iconic newspaper known to many as The Grey Lady is one of the world's most respected sources of news. The paper boasts a weekday circulation of about 500000 and 1.1 million on Sundays. The Times Co. owns The Boston Globe among other big city newspapers and distributes news online through NYTimes.com and other sites. Chairman Arthur Sulzberger and his family control the firm through a trust.

	Annual Growth	12/14	12/15	12/16	12/17	12/18
Sales ($ mil.)	2.4%	1,588.5	1,579.2	1,555.3	1,675.6	1,748.6
Net income ($ mil.)	39.4%	33.3	63.2	29.1	4.3	125.7
Market value ($ mil.)	13.3%	2,241.9	2,266.7	2,245.2	3,054.2	3,698.0
Employees	4.8%	3,588	3,560	3,710	3,790	4,320

NEW YORK UNIVERSITY

70 WASHINGTON SQ S
NEW YORK, NY 100121019
Phone: 212-998-1212
Fax: –

CEO: Robert I. Grossman
CFO: –
HR: Robert White
FYE: August 31
Type: Private

Higher education is at the core of this Big Apple institution. The setting and heritage of New York University (NYU) make it one of the nation's most popular educational institutions. With more than 50000 students attending its 18 schools and colleges NYU is among the largest private schools in the US. Its Tisch School of the Arts is well-regarded and its law school and Leonard N. Stern School of Business are among the foremost in the country. NYU occupies five major centers in Manhattan; its Washington Square campus is in the heart of Greenwich Village. The school was founded in 1831. Notable alumni include former Federal Reserve Chairman Alan Greenspan and film producer Oliver Stone.

	Annual Growth	08/04	08/05	08/06	08/11	08/16
Sales ($ mil.)	14.7%	–	–	2,148.1	5,172.2	8,500.2
Net income ($ mil.)	(1.0%)	–	–	195.6	563.7	177.5
Market value ($ mil.)	–	–	–	–	–	–
Employees	–	–	–	–	–	21,000

NEW YORK YANKEES PARTNERSHIP

Yankee Stadium E. 161st St. and River Ave.
Bronx NY 10451
Phone: 718-293-4300
Fax: 718-293-8431
Web: newyork.yankees.mlb.com

CEO: –
CFO: –
HR: –
FYE: December 31
Type: Private

These Yanks are a big hit with New York baseball fans. New York Yankees Partnership owns and operates the New York Yankees professional baseball team one of the most storied and popular clubs in Major League Baseball. The franchise boasts a record 27 World Series titles and 40 American League pennants making it the most successful professional sports team in history. Along with that success the Yankees organization has been associated with such sports icons as Babe Ruth Lou Gehrig Joe DiMaggio and Mickey Mantle. Once known as the Highlanders the team has represented New York City since 1903. The Steinbrenner family led by Hal Steinbrenner has controlled the Yanks since 1973.

NEWARK BETH ISRAEL MEDICAL CENTER INC.

201 LYONS AVE
NEWARK, NJ 071122027
Phone: 973-926-7000
Fax: –
Web: www.rwjbh.org

CEO: Paul Mertz
CFO: Veronica Zichner
HR: –
FYE: December 31
Type: Private

Part of the Saint Barnabas Health Care System Newark Beth Israel Medical Center is a 670-bed acute-care regional referral hospital. The facility serves residents of Newark and surrounding areas in northern New Jersey. The hospital offers services including primary diagnostic emergency surgical and rehabilitative care. It is home to specialized programs such as kidney transplantation cancer care dentistry sleep disorders geriatrics and women's health services. Newark Beth Israel Medical Center also houses the Children's Hospital of New Jersey and the Saint Barnabas Heart Center. The research and teaching hospital has a medical staff of more than 800 physicians.

	Annual Growth	12/14	12/15	12/16	12/17	12/18
Sales ($ mil.)	6.0%	–	542.0	539.7	545.4	645.5
Net income ($ mil.)	(19.8%)	–	38.6	28.0	35.6	19.9
Market value ($ mil.)	–	–	–	–	–	–
Employees	–	–	–	–	–	3,000

NEWARK CORPORATION

300 S RIVERSIDE PLZ # 2200
CHICAGO, IL 606066765
Phone: 773-784-5100
Fax: –
Web: www.premierfarnell.com

CEO: –
CFO: –
HR: –
FYE: February 01
Type: Private

Newark offers all sorts of electronic goods in one place and in places all across the Americas. The company doing business as Newark element14 distributes some 4.4 million electronic components and supplies including semiconductors passive devices electrical equipment connectors wire and cable optoelectronics test and measurement instruments and tools. It is also a source for companies needing parts compliant with the Restrictions of Hazardous Substances order in the European Union. Customers are electronics design engineers maintenance technicians and other electronics buyers. Newark element14 is a subsidiary of Premier Farnell a top UK electronic and industrial parts supplier.

	Annual Growth	02/11	02/12	02/13	02/14	02/15
Sales ($ mil.)	(3.2%)	–	–	580.8	541.1	544.0
Net income ($ mil.)	9.6%	–	–	20.3	23.7	24.4
Market value ($ mil.)	–	–	–	–	–	–
Employees	–	–	–	–	–	834

NEWAYS INC.

2089 Neways Dr.
Springville UT 84663
Phone: 801-418-2000
Fax: 702-589-7213
Web: www.allegiantair.com

CEO: Asma Ishaq
CFO: Shane Ware
HR: –
FYE: December 31
Type: Private

Neways helps its consumers find new ways to live clean healthy lives. The company designs and makes products that are free of more than 3000 harmful ingredients for wellness (nutritional supplements weight management) beauty (cosmetics hair treatments) and household care (automotive laundry supplies). The consumer products company distributes its products to about 30 countries worldwide. Neways boasts corporate offices in Australia Israel Japan and the US among other countries. The company was established in 1987 by Tom and Dee Mower veterans of the chemical industry.

NEWBRIDGE BANCORP
NMS: NBBC

1501 Highwoods Boulevard, Suite 400
Greensboro, NC 27410
Phone: 336 369-0900
Fax: -
Web: www.newbridgebank.com

CEO: -
CFO: -
HR: -
FYE: December 31
Type: Public

Bridging the gap between its community banks and North Carolinians NewBridge Bancorp is the holding company that owns NewBridge Bank which operates about 40 branches plus a handful of loan production offices located primarily in the state's Piedmont Triad Region. Boasting more than $2.5 billion in total assets the community bank offers personal and business banking products and services including checking and savings accounts and loans as well as wealth management services including investment and asset management and estate planning. Real estate-secured loans make up nearly 90% of the bank's $1.6 billion loan portfolio. Raleigh-based Yadkin Bank agreed to buy NewBridge in late 2015.

	Annual Growth	12/10	12/11	12/12	12/13	12/14
Assets ($ mil.)	8.7%	1,807.2	1,734.6	1,708.7	1,965.2	2,520.2
Net income ($ mil.)	42.6%	3.4	4.7	(25.3)	20.8	14.0
Market value ($ mil.)	16.7%	174.8	143.9	172.2	276.2	324.0
Employees	(0.5%)	497	442	442	449	487

NEWEGG INC.

17560 ROWLAND ST
CITY OF INDUSTRY, CA 917481114
Phone: 626-271-9700
Fax: -
Web: www.newegg.com

CEO: Danny Lee
CFO: David King
HR: -
FYE: December 31
Type: Private

Newegg is a leading online-only distributor of consumer electronics and computing products with about 25 million registered users in the US Canada and China. It sells desktop and laptop computers along with all the related components to build or repair one yourself. Newegg also stocks cell phones digital cameras home appliances networking devices peripherals DVDs accessories and software. Its websites (including its B2B site NeweggBusiness.com) carry products made by vendors including Apple ATi Canon Sony Toshiba and Viewsonic. Founded in 2001 Newegg is extending its reach to Europe.

	Annual Growth	12/10	12/11	12/12	12/13	12/14
Sales ($ mil.)	(6.5%)	-	-	-	2,738.2	2,559.4
Net income ($ mil.)	(95.3%)	-	-	-	5.1	0.2
Market value ($ mil.)	-	-	-	-	-	-
Employees	-	-	-	-	-	1,072

NEWELL BRANDS INC
NMS: NWL

6655 Peachtree Dunwoody Road,
Atlanta, GA 30328
Phone: 770 418-7000
Fax: -
Web: www.newellrubbermaid.com

CEO: Michael B. (Mike) Polk
CFO: Ralph J. Nicoletti
HR: Fiona Laird
FYE: December 31
Type: Public

Newell Brands is the company behind such household names as Rubbermaid storage boxes Calphalon cookware Graco pushchairs and Sharpie pens. Newell Brands' customers are mainly mass retailers such as Target and home and office supply stores such as Staples in the US which accounts for some two-thirds of total sales. Newell's footprint spans 70 factories and some 120 warehouses and distribution centers. The megabucks acquisition of consumer products giant Jarden brought products such as Bicycle Playing Cards Mr. Coffee Coleman Jostens Oster Rawlings Sunbeam and Yankee Candle under its umbrella.

	Annual Growth	12/14	12/15	12/16	12/17	12/18
Sales ($ mil.)	10.8%	5,727.0	5,915.7	13,264.0	14,742.2	8,630.9
Net income ($ mil.)	-	377.8	350.0	527.8	2,748.8	(6,917.9)
Market value ($ mil.)	(16.4%)	16,104.5	18,637.0	18,878.0	13,064.5	7,859.9
Employees	20.8%	17,400	17,200	53,400	49,000	37,000

NEWESCO INC.

1500 ARTHUR AVE STE 200
ELK GROVE VILLAGE, IL 600075744
Phone: 847-437-7050
Fax: -
Web: www.amertranslogistics.com

CEO: John R Westerberg
CFO: Lawrence Cap
HR: -
FYE: December 31
Type: Private

An agent of leading mover Atlas Van Lines (part of Atlas World Group) Nelson Westerberg specializes in handling household moves for employees who are being transferred by their companies. It also offers office and industrial moving services and household moves for individuals. (As an agent the company handles moves within its assigned geographic territory and cooperates with other agents on interstate moves.) Major corporate clients have included Sara Lee and Walgreen. Founded in 1904 by Swedish immigrants Fred Nelson and Oscar Westerberg the company started out in Chicago hauling coal ice and furniture with a horse-drawn wagon. Company chairman and CEO John Westerberg is Oscar's grandson.

	Annual Growth	12/04	12/05	12/06	12/07	12/08
Sales ($ mil.)	-	-	-	(806.2)	61.9	55.8
Net income ($ mil.)	38004.0%	-	-	0.0	5.6	3.6
Market value ($ mil.)	-	-	-	-	-	-
Employees	-	-	-	-	-	400

NEWFIELD EXPLORATION CO
NYS: NFX

4 Waterway Square Place, Suite 100
The Woodlands, TX 77380
Phone: 281 210-5100
Fax: 281 210-5101
Web: www.newfield.com

CEO: Lee K Boothby
CFO: Sherri A Brillon
HR: -
FYE: December 31
Type: Public

Newfield Exploration likes to depend on good old resource plays. The Texas-based energy company explores for crude oil natural gas and natural gas liquids mostly onshore in the US with some activity offshore China. Its prime asset is the Anadarko and Arkoma plays in Oklahoma further supported by the Williston in North Dakota and Uinta in Utah. Its estimated proved reserves currently stand at 700 MBoe with 120 net development wells. In November 2018 the company was bought out by Canada's Encana for US$5.5 billion in a flurry of mergers in the sector.

	Annual Growth	12/13	12/14	12/15	12/16	12/17
Sales ($ mil.)	(0.3%)	1,789.0	2,288.0	1,557.0	1,472.0	1,767.0
Net income ($ mil.)	30.6%	147.0	900.0	(3,362.0)	(1,230.0)	427.0
Market value ($ mil.)	6.4%	4,918.7	5,416.0	6,502.4	8,088.0	6,296.7
Employees	(10.1%)	1,548	1,331	1,111	994	1,010

NEWGISTICS INC.

2700 Via Fortuna Ste. 300
Austin TX 78746
Phone: 512-225-6000
Fax: 512-225-6001
Web: www.newgistics.com

CEO: William Razzouk
CFO: Michael Twomey
HR: -
FYE: December 31
Type: Private

Newgistics steps in when that new gizmo you ordered turns out to be not what you wanted. The company provides returns management services for direct retailers manufacturers distributors and other fulfillment businesses; customers have included Victoria's Secret QVC and Neiman Marcus. Shoppers who return purchases attach a label with a bar code provided by Newgistics and mail the package. Postage is deducted from the refund. The Newgistics SmartLabel system is intended to make the return process easier for both customer and company. Newgistics arranges transportation and warehousing for its customers through third-parties. Austin Ventures owns 63% of Newgistics.

NEWLINK GENETICS CORP
NMS: NLNK

2503 South Loop Drive
Ames, IA 50010
Phone: 515 296-5555
Fax: –
Web: www.newlinkgenetics.com

CEO: Charles J. Link
CFO: John B. (Jack) Henneman
HR: –
FYE: December 31
Type: Public

NewLink Genetics is hoping to give a boost to the immune systems of cancer patients. A biopharmaceutical company focused on discovering cancer treatments NewLink develops and commercializes small-molecule immunotherapy therapies that stimulate patients' immune systems. NewLink's HyperAcute Cellular Immunotherapy technology is under evaluation with the company reducing its investment in related candidates and having no plans to conduct future clinical trials. Its pancreatic cancer immunotherapy candidate algenpantucel-L was in late-stage clinical development but was dropped in 2016. The company is now steering away from studying treatments for advanced melanoma and pancreatic cancer.

	Annual Growth	12/14	12/15	12/16	12/17	12/18
Sales ($ mil.)	(48.2%)	172.6	68.5	35.8	28.7	12.5
Net income ($ mil.)	–	102.9	(40.4)	(85.2)	(72.0)	(53.6)
Market value ($ mil.)	(55.8%)	1,480.7	1,355.6	382.9	302.1	56.6
Employees	(19.3%)	130	210	122	76	55

NEWLY WEDS FOODS INC.

4140 W. Fullerton Ave.
Chicago IL 60639
Phone: 773-489-7000
Fax: 773-292-3809
Web: www.newlywedsfoods.com

CEO: –
CFO: –
HR: Bert Rodriguez
FYE: December 31
Type: Private

Don't let the name fool you Newly Weds Foods doesn't bake wedding cakes. But it might just make that cake tastier. The company makes seasonings marinades glazes sauces batters breadings binders and fillers for the food processing and food-service industries in some 70 countries throughout the world. Newly Weds uses its proprietary database FlavorTrak to monitor restaurant trends and then develop flavors it hopes will appeal to the most consumers. Newly Weds boasts that it has expertise in providing ingredients for more than 45 cuisines. Based in Chicago the company owns and operates about 25 production plants and 20 laboratories.

NEWMARK & COMPANY REAL ESTATE, INC.

125 PARK AVE
NEW YORK, NY 100175529
Phone: 212-372-2000
Fax: –
Web: www.ngkf.com

CEO: Barry M Gosin
CFO: Michael J Rispoli
HR: –
FYE: December 31
Type: Private

Whether you're talking cubicle cities or corner offices Newmark & Company Real Estate (dba Newmark Knight Frank or NKF) makes its mark on commercial real estate. As one of the world's top commercial real estate advisory firms it provides property brokerage development and management services to investors corporations and property owners. Newmark also offers facility management services overseeing a portfolio of properties across the globe. Together with its London-based partner Knight Frank NKF operates more than 370 offices across six continents. NKF comprises parent company BGC Partners' Real Estate Services segment which made up 40% of the parent company's total revenue in 2014.

	Annual Growth	12/12	12/13	12/14	12/15	12/16
Assets ($ mil.)	91.7%	–	–	234.3	694.6	860.6
Net income ($ mil.)	–	–	–	0.0	139.4	53.8
Market value ($ mil.)	–	–	–	–	–	–
Employees	–	–	–	–	–	2,250

NEWMARKET CORP
NYS: NEU

330 South Fourth Street
Richmond, VA 23219-4350
Phone: 804 788-5000
Fax: –
Web: www.newmarket.com

CEO: Thomas E. (Teddy) Gottwald
CFO: Brian D. Paliotti
HR: –
FYE: December 31
Type: Public

NewMarket is the holding entity for two petroleum additive subsidiaries: Afton Chemical (its primary business) and Ethyl Corporation. Afton manufactures petroleum additives used to improve the performance of gasoline diesel and other fuels and as a lubricant in motor oil fluids and grease. Ethyl's main product is the anti-knock additive tetraethyl lead though the compound has lost substantial ground in markets where unleaded gas is preferred or required. About 70% of the holding company's sales come from outside of US. NewMarket precursor company Albemarle Paper Manufacturing was founded in Richmond Virginia in 1887.

	Annual Growth	12/14	12/15	12/16	12/17	12/18
Sales ($ mil.)	(0.5%)	2,335.4	2,140.8	2,049.5	2,198.4	2,289.7
Net income ($ mil.)	0.2%	233.3	238.6	243.4	190.5	234.7
Market value ($ mil.)	0.5%	4,513.3	4,258.3	4,740.4	4,444.6	4,609.0
Employees	2.9%	1,866	1,979	1,998	2,223	2,089

NEWMARKET TECHNOLOGY INC.
PINK SHEETS: NWMT

14860 Montfort Dr. Ste. 210
Dallas TX 75254
Phone: 972-386-3372
Fax: 972-386-8165
Web: www.newmarkettechnology.com

CEO: –
CFO: –
HR: –
FYE: December 31
Type: Public

NewMarket Technology is all about growing into new markets. The holding company invests in development-stage tech firms located in emerging markets outside the US. It has a handful of subsidiaries in its portfolio — China Crescent Enterprises RKM Suministros (Venezuela) and UniOne Consulting (Brazil) — that provide systems integration software development and telecommunications hardware. It also has equity stakes in other companies including mobile payment services company Alternet Systems and wireless broadband operator RedMoon. NewMarket's customers have included international giants such as Siemens ExxonMobil Visa and Bayer; customers in China account for most of the company's sales however.

NEWMONT CORP
NYS: NEM

6363 South Fiddlers Green Circle
Greenwood Village, CO 80111
Phone: 303 863-7414
Fax: 303 837-5877
Web: www.newmont.com

CEO: Gary J. Goldberg
CFO: Nancy K. Buese
HR: William N. (Bill) MacGowan
FYE: December 31
Type: Public

Newmont goes for the gold. Producing close to 6 million ounces of gold annually Newmont Goldcorp Corporation (formerly Newmont Mining Corporation) is one of the top three gold producers in the world. The company has significant operations in the US Australia Peru Ghana and Suriname. Its gold reserves are close to 70 million ounces spread across 23000 square miles of its own land. Newmont also produces some copper principally through Boddington in Australia and Phoenix in the US. Although Newmont makes almost all its sales from refined gold the end-product of its operations is dor- © bars an alloy consisting primarily of gold but also containing silver and other metals. In 2019 Newmont Mining acquired Goldcorp for $10 billion to create the newly rebranded Newmont Goldcorp Corporation.

	Annual Growth	12/14	12/15	12/16	12/17	12/18
Sales ($ mil.)	(0.1%)	7,292.0	7,729.0	6,711.0	7,348.0	7,253.0
Net income ($ mil.)	(9.5%)	508.0	220.0	(627.0)	(98.0)	341.0
Market value ($ mil.)	16.4%	10,073.7	9,588.7	18,159.3	19,998.2	18,468.5
Employees	15.3%	13,700	15,600	12,400	24,658	24,200

NEWPAGE GROUP INC.

8540 Gander Creek Dr.   CEO: –
Miamisburg OH 45342   CFO: –
Phone: 937-242-9345   HR: –
Fax: 203-393-1684   FYE: December 31
Web: www.laticrete.com   Type: Private

After struggling through several financially challenging years for the coated paper making industry NewPage would like to do jus that turn over a new page. Through subsidiary NewPage Corp. the company is one of the largest makers of coated and specialty paper in North America. From mills in the Eastern and Midwestern US NewPage churns out about 3.5 million tons of paper annually. Its papers are often used to produce annual reports magazines and catalogs. Customers include xpedx Advance Magazine Publishers (dba Conde Nast) McGraw-Hill Time Inc. and Avery Dennison. NewPage Corp. filed for Chapter 11 bankruptcy in late 2011.

NEWPARK RESOURCES, INC.   NYS: NR

9320 Lakeside Boulevard, Suite 100   CEO: Paul L. Howes
The Woodlands, TX 77381   CFO: Gregg Piontek
Phone: 281 362-6800   HR: –
Fax: –   FYE: December 31
Web: www.newpark.com   Type: Public

Oil and gas activity means money for oil field support services company Newpark Resources. The company provides drilling fluid and engineering services to oil and gas drillers. Newpark Resources also supplies prefab work platforms and provides DuraBase brand composite mats used to make temporary access roads and provide related wellsite services and equipment (through its Newpark Mats & Integrated Services unit). In 2014 the industrial services company sold its Environmental Services business which had historically operated as Newpark Resources' third segment.

	Annual Growth	12/14	12/15	12/16	12/17	12/18
Sales ($ mil.)	(4.1%)	1,118.4	676.9	471.5	747.8	946.5
Net income ($ mil.)	(25.0%)	102.3	(90.8)	(40.7)	(6.1)	32.3
Market value ($ mil.)	(7.9%)	866.5	479.6	681.2	781.2	624.0
Employees	0.2%	2,478	1,980	1,800	2,400	2,500

NEWPORT CORPORATION

1791 DEERE AVE   CEO: Robert J. Phillippy
IRVINE, CA 926064814   CFO: Charles F. (Chuck) Cargile
Phone: 949-863-3144   HR: –
Fax: –   FYE: January 03
Web: www.newport.com   Type: Private

Newport helps all sorts of customers take a measured approach. The company makes lasers precision components and automated assembly measurement and test equipment. It makes products that are used around the world in such fields as fiber-optic communications health care life sciences military/aerospace scientific research and semiconductor manufacturing. Industrial and scientific components include lenses and other devices for vibration and motion control. Newport also offers automated systems used to make fiber-optic components and photonics. More than 60% of sales come from outside the US. In 2016 Newport was acquired by MKS Instruments.

	Annual Growth	12/10	12/11	12/12	12/13*	01/15
Sales ($ mil.)	0.5%	–	–	595.3	560.1	605.2
Net income ($ mil.)	–	–	–	(90.0)	15.7	35.2
Market value ($ mil.)	–	–	–	–	–	–
Employees	–	–	–	–	–	2,480

*Fiscal year change

NEWS AMERICA MARKETING FSI LLC

1185 Avenue of the Americas 27th Fl.   CEO: –
New York NY 10036   CFO: Ajay Singh
Phone: 212-782-8000   HR: –
Fax: 212-575-5845   FYE: June 30
Web: www.newsamerica.com   Type: Business Segment

News America Marketing a subsidiary of global media giant News Corp. provides marketing services primarily through newspaper inserts and in-store coupon displays. The company publishes SmartSource Magazine the largest newspaper insert in the US (it reaches nearly 70 million households in more than 1500 newspapers); its SmartSource Price Pop Guaranteed offers shoppers coupons on the shelf near a product; overall the SmartSource brands reaches more than 150 million consumers each week. News America Marketing's other services include promotional products merchandising database marketing tools and online promotions. It owns 12 offices throughout North America and one in New Zealand.

NEWS CORP (NEW)   NMS: NWSA

1211 Avenue of the Americas   CEO: Brian Murray
New York, NY 10036   CFO: Susan Panuccio
Phone: 212 416-3400   HR: Katie Perdomo
Fax: –   FYE: June 30
Web: www.newscorp.com   Type: Public

News Corp is one of the biggest news organizations in the world publishing well-known mastheads such as The Wall Street Journal and New York Post Australia's Herald Sun and The Sun and The Times in the UK. The company owns the Dow Jones and Factiva information services as well as book publisher HarperCollins. In TV News Corp has a majority stake in Foxtel in Australia and owns the Australian News Channel. Other properties are the real estate websites REA Group and Motive. North America supplies about 45% of News Corp's revenue.

	Annual Growth	06/15	06/16	06/17	06/18	06/19
Sales ($ mil.)	3.9%	8,633.0	8,292.0	8,139.0	9,024.0	10,074.0
Net income ($ mil.)	–	(147.0)	179.0	(738.0)	(1,514.0)	155.0
Market value ($ mil.)	(1.9%)	8,538.2	6,642.1	8,017.4	9,070.8	7,894.5
Employees	2.9%	25,000	24,000	26,000	28,000	28,000

NEWSMAX MEDIA, INC.

750 PARK OF COMMERCE DR # 100   CEO: Christopher Ruddy
BOCA RATON, FL 334873650   CFO: Darryle Burnham
Phone: 561-686-1165   HR: –
Fax: –   FYE: December 31
Web: www.newsmax.com   Type: Private

NewsMax Media serves up the news with a conservative slant. The company publishes alternative news and opinion content through its monthly magazine News-Max and corresponding Web site. Columnists include Reed Irvine (founder of conservative watchdog group Accuracy In Media) and national broadcasting hosts and analysts Bill O'Reilly Ed Koch and Dick Morris. The company generates sales from advertising as well as from politically oriented merchandise (clothing posters books) showcasing stars of the Republican Party. Former New York Post reporter Christopher Ruddy the company's CEO founded NewsMax Media in 1998.

	Annual Growth	12/07	12/08	12/11	12/12	12/16
Sales ($ mil.)	–	–	(1,957.2)	54.6	83.3	93.9
Net income ($ mil.)	–	–	0.0	1.2	12.0	5.0
Market value ($ mil.)	–	–	–	–	–	–
Employees	–	–	–	–	–	181

NEWSTAR FINANCIAL INC — NMS: NEWS

500 Boylston Street, Suite 1250
Boston, MA 02116
Phone: 617-848-2500
Fax: –
Web: www.newstarfin.com
CEO: Timothy J Conway
CFO: John K Bray
HR: –
FYE: December 31
Type: Public

No hot air here: NewStar Financial is in the business of providing middle-market companies with the capital they need to create a spark. The commercial financier provides a variety of loans (primarily secured senior debt) for refinancing acquisitions consolidations and commercial real estate and equipment purchases to clients in the retail and consumer health care media and information and energy industries among others. Its loans typically range from $10 million to $50 million. Newstar also offers investment advisory and asset management services to institutional investors through managed credit funds that invest in its originated loans.

	Annual Growth	12/11	12/12	12/13	12/14	12/15
Assets ($ mil.)	20.4%	1,946.4	2,157.1	2,606.9	2,811.0	4,092.1
Net income ($ mil.)	4.5%	14.1	24.0	24.6	10.6	16.9
Market value ($ mil.)	(3.1%)	473.2	651.8	826.8	595.5	417.8
Employees	8.5%	88	104	101	98	122

NEWTEK BUSINESS SERVICES CORP — NMS: NEWT

1981 Marcus Avenue, Suite 130
Lake Success, NY 11042
Phone: 212-356-9500
Fax: –
Web: www.newtekone.com
CEO: Barry Sloane
CFO: –
HR: –
FYE: December 31
Type: Public

Newtek Business Services provides a suite of business and financial services to small to midsized businesses including electronic merchant payment processing website hosting Small Business Administration (SBA) loans data storage insurance accounts receivable financing and payroll management. The company serves more than 100000 business accounts throughout the US. Newtek also has investments in certified capital companies (Capcos) which are authorized in eight states and Washington DC. It has stakes in about a dozen Capcos that traditionally have issued debt and equity securities to insurance firms then used the funds to mainly invest in small and midsized financial and business services firms.

	Annual Growth	12/14	12/15	12/16	12/17	12/18
Sales ($ mil.)	123.7%	2.0	26.1	31.0	38.9	49.5
Net income ($ mil.)	–	(2.5)	(6.2)	(9.3)	(7.9)	(7.5)
Market value ($ mil.)	4.3%	279.2	270.9	300.8	349.8	329.9
Employees	(15.0%)	335	123	137	162	175

NEWTON MEMORIAL HOSPITAL INC

175 HIGH ST
NEWTON, NJ 078601099
Phone: 973-383-2121
Fax: –
Web: www.nmhnj.org
CEO: –
CFO: –
HR: –
FYE: December 31
Type: Private

The folks at Newton Medical Center want to cure what ails you or help you slip into slumber. With about 150 beds and numerous clinical specialties Newton Memorial provides medical care to residents at the crux of northwestern New Jersey southwestern New York and eastern Pennsylvania. Established in 1932 the acute-care hospital offers specialized services such as emergency care pediatrics home health cardiac care respiratory care and aesthetic surgery. The not-for-profit hospital also has a sleep lab and inpatient clinics for orthopedics stroke care cancer treatment and rehabilitation. It is part of Atlantic Health System.

	Annual Growth	12/05	12/06	12/07	12/08	12/09
Sales ($ mil.)	4.4%	–	121.4	122.1	111.3	138.0
Net income ($ mil.)	(10.3%)	–	5.2	(0.5)	(5.9)	3.7
Market value ($ mil.)	–	–	–	–	–	–
Employees	–	–	–	–	–	805

NEWTON WELLESLEY HOSPITAL CORP

2014 WASHINGTON ST
NEWTON, MA 024621607
Phone: 617-243-6000
Fax: –
Web: www.nwh.org
CEO: –
CFO: Jeffrey P. (Jeff) Dion
HR: –
FYE: September 30
Type: Private

Newton-Wellesley Hospital provides the Greater Boston area with a full range of medical surgical and diagnostic services. The hospital which boasts more than 260 beds offers a variety of programs including a full-service diagnostic imaging department a multiple sclerosis clinic cancer center joint reconstruction surgery physical and occupational therapy and inpatient psychiatric care. In addition the Partners Reproductive Medicine Center offers infertility treatment in collaboration with two other area hospitals. Part of the Partners HealthCare family Newton-Wellesley is a teaching hospital for Tufts University's School of Medicine and the Massachusetts College of Pharmacy and Health Sciences..

	Annual Growth	09/13	09/14	09/15	09/16	09/17
Sales ($ mil.)	2.4%	–	405.2	422.9	414.8	435.6
Net income ($ mil.)	–	–	12.2	22.0	(5.2)	(1.0)
Market value ($ mil.)	–	–	–	–	–	–
Employees	–	–	–	–	–	2,500

NEWYORK-PRESBYTERIAN/BROOKLYN METHODIST

506 6TH ST
BROOKLYN, NY 112153609
Phone: 718-780-3000
Fax: –
CEO: –
CFO: –
HR: –
FYE: December 31
Type: Private

New York Methodist Hospital is a not-for-profit acute-care teaching hospital serving Brooklyn residents. Established in 1881 as the Methodist Episcopal Hospital the facility has more than 650 licensed beds. It offers a full range of medical services including primary and emergency care as well as specialty services such as women's health cancer cardiovascular pediatric geriatric and behavioral health. The hospital also operates satellite clinics in surrounding areas. A member of New York-Presbyterian Healthcare System New York Methodist is a teaching hospital affiliated with Cornell University's Weill Medical College.

	Annual Growth	12/13	12/14	12/15	12/16	12/17
Sales ($ mil.)	14.0%	–	687.7	732.9	788.1	1,018.1
Net income ($ mil.)	26.7%	–	68.9	88.9	145.6	139.9
Market value ($ mil.)	–	–	–	–	–	–
Employees	–	–	–	–	–	4,929

NEWYORK-PRESBYTERIAN/QUEENS

5645 MAIN ST
FLUSHING, NY 113555045
Phone: 718-670-2000
Fax: –
CEO: –
CFO: Kevin Ward
HR: Helen Lavas
FYE: December 31
Type: Private

The New York Hospital Medical Center of Queens aims to provide care that's fit for royalty. Better known as the New York Hospital Queens the acute care hospital has about 520 beds and provides both primary and tertiary care. Specialist services include cancer cardiovascular pediatric obstetric surgical and dental care. The medical center also operates about a dozen outpatient clinics and care centers that offer such services as family health kidney dialysis rehabilitation and dental care as well as home health care services. New York Hospital Queens is part of the NewYork-Presbyterian Healthcare System.

	Annual Growth	12/02	12/03	12/05	12/14	12/17
Sales ($ mil.)	5.7%	–	389.5	457.9	670.0	846.5
Net income ($ mil.)	(2.5%)	–	7.2	10.6	14.1	5.1
Market value ($ mil.)	–	–	–	–	–	–
Employees	–	–	–	–	–	2,380

NEXSAN CORPORATION

555 St. Charles Dr. Ste. 202
Thousand Oaks CA 91360
Phone: 805-418-2700
Fax: 805-418-2799
Web: www.nexsan.com

CEO: Philip Black
CFO: Gene Spies
HR: –
FYE: June 30
Type: Private

Nexsan makes hoarding so much easier (and cleaner). With space and energy limitations in mind the company provides SAN NAS and unified hybrid storage systems for midsized businesses and mid-level deployments in larger enterprises. Its storage and archiving systems are suitable for a broad range of data including e-mail medical images web content digital video and CAD and other reference materials. Nexsan sells through distributors original equipment manufacturers resellers and systems integrators. The company which has sold more than 28000 systems across 60 countries serves clients in such industries as financial services technology media healthcare and public sector.

NEXSTAR MEDIA GROUP INC NMS: NXST

545 E. John Carpenter Freeway, Suite 700
Irving, TX 75062
Phone: 972 373-8800
Fax: –
Web: www.nexstar.tv

CEO: Perry A. Sook
CFO: Thomas E. (Tom) Carter
HR: –
FYE: December 31
Type: Public

Star light star bright Nexstar Broadcasting wishes for you to tune in tonight. The company is the nation's leading television station operator with nearly 200 full power owned or serviced television stations in 115 markets reaching approximately 43 million or nearly 40% of all US TV households. Its portfolio includes affiliates of ABC CBS FOX NBC and The CW. It has television duopolies (two or more stations) in many of its markets. Nexstar in 2019 acquired Tribune Media for $7.2 billion creating the biggest broadcaster in the US. The deal added more than 40 TV stations including Chicago's WGN cable channel WGN America and 31% ownership of TV Food Network to its mix of holdings.

	Annual Growth	12/14	12/15	12/16	12/17	12/18
Sales ($ mil.)	44.7%	631.3	896.4	1,103.2	2,432.0	2,766.7
Net income ($ mil.)	56.7%	64.6	77.7	91.5	475.0	389.5
Market value ($ mil.)	11.0%	2,363.0	2,678.3	2,888.1	3,568.0	3,588.0
Employees	26.8%	3,464	4,422	4,527	9,113	8,959

NEXTEC GROUP

1111 North Loop West Ste. 810
Houston TX 77008
Phone: 713-957-8350
Fax: 713-957-4259
Web: www.nextecgroup.com

CEO: –
CFO: –
HR: –
FYE: June 30
Type: Private

NexTec Group is on the lookout for technology products that might improve efficiency for its middle-market business clients. The information technology consulting company evaluates installs and customizes accounting financial and management information software. It also offers training and technical support services. NexTec specializes in enterprise software made by Microsoft and Sage among others. The company serves clients in a variety of industries such as energy financial services manufacturing and health care. It serves clients from satellite offices in California New Jersey New York Ohio and Washington. NexTec was founded in 1994 by president Eric Frank and VP's Russell Harper and Alan Subel.

NEXTERA ENERGY INC NYS: NEE PRO

700 Universe Boulevard
Juno Beach, FL 33408
Phone: 561 694-4000
Fax: 561 694-4620
Web: www.nexteraenergy.com

CEO: James L. (Jim) Robo
CFO: Rebecca J Kujawa
HR: Deborah H. Caplan
FYE: December 31
Type: Public

NextEra Energy (NEE) owns and operates two businesses: Florida Power & Light (FPL) Florida's largest electric company and NextEra Energy Resources (NEER) one of the world's largest generators of renewable energy. FPL generates more than 24000 MW of electricity and delivers it to more than 5 million mostly residential customers in the state. NEER generates more than 20000 MW of energy via wind and solar sources. NEE operates one of the largest nuclear power fleets in the US with eight commercial nuclear power units in Florida New Hampshire Iowa and Wisconsin. All total the company has assets in nearly 30 US states four Canadian provinces and one province in Spain.

	Annual Growth	12/14	12/15	12/16	12/17	12/18
Sales ($ mil.)	(0.4%)	17,021.0	17,486.0	16,155.0	17,195.0	16,727.0
Net income ($ mil.)	28.0%	2,465.0	2,762.0	2,912.0	5,378.0	6,638.0
Market value ($ mil.)	13.1%	50,806.6	49,659.4	57,101.9	74,658.8	83,086.0
Employees	0.7%	13,800	13,800	14,200	13,900	14,200

NEXTGEN HEALTHCARE INC NMS: NXGN

18111 Von Karman Avenue, Suite 800
Irvine, CA 92612
Phone: 949 255-2600
Fax: –
Web: www.nextgen.com

CEO: Rusty Frantz
CFO: James R. (Jamie) Arnold
HR: Babs Stewart
FYE: March 31
Type: Public

Quality Systems can't help doctors' with the legibility of their signatures but it knows how to insure the integrity of their digital records. The company develops data management software for medical and dental practices and a variety of other health care businesses. Its NextGen subsidiary (more than 75% of sales) makes electronic records and practice management software tailored for patient data scheduling billing and claims handling. Its RCM unit focuses on electronic claims submission remittance and payments services. The company's QSI Dental division makes practice and clinical management software for dentists.

	Annual Growth	03/15	03/16	03/17	03/18	03/19
Sales ($ mil.)	1.9%	490.2	492.5	509.6	531.0	529.2
Net income ($ mil.)	(2.7%)	27.3	5.7	18.2	2.4	24.5
Market value ($ mil.)	1.3%	1,036.1	988.1	988.1	885.0	1,091.2
Employees	(2.5%)	2,939	2,987	2,791	2,830	2,660

NFINANSE INC. OTC: NFSE

3923 Coconut Palm Dr. Ste. 107
Tampa FL 33619
Phone: 813-367-4400
Fax: 256-386-0234
Web: www.johnsoncont.com

CEO: –
CFO: –
HR: –
FYE: December 31
Type: Public

Through nFinanSe Card the company provides stored value cards or SVCs. It offers reloadable Discover-branded spending cards (for consumers without bank cards or credit cards) gift cards payroll cards and corporate reward cards; cards issued by nFinanSe bear a logo in the form of a Discover Financial Services hologram. Customers can purchase load and reload cards at more than 70000 locations that are part of the nFinanSe Network; most load stations are found inside Western Union and MoneyGram locations. Formerly named Morgan Beaumont the company has agreed to be purchased by AccountNow provider of general purpose reloadable prepaid cards in the direct-to-consumer sales channel.

NFP CORP.

340 MADISON AVE FL 21　　　　　　　　CEO: Jessica M. Bibliowicz
NEW YORK, NY 101730401　　　　　　　　CFO: Brett Schneider
Phone: 212-301-4000　　　　　　　　　　HR: –
Fax: –　　　　　　　　　　　　　　　　FYE: December 31
Web: www.nfp.com　　　　　　　　　　　Type: Private

Through a network of subsidiaries and affiliates NFP provides commercial and personal insurance corporate benefits products and wealth management services to businesses and individuals in the US Canada and the UK. The consultancy and brokerage runs three professional advisor organizations: corporate benefits arm Benefits Partners; Partners Financial a network of independent life insurance and financial professionals; and the Retirement Plan Advisory Group (RPAG) which provides due diligence fiduciary compliance business consulting and other services through 2000 retirement plan advisors. NFP a Madison Dearborn Partners portfolio company is one of the largest retirement plan aggregators and privately owned brokers in the US.

	Annual Growth	12/07	12/08	12/09	12/10	12/11
Assets ($ mil.)	(16.6%)	–	1,543.3	970.4	893.1	894.2
Net income ($ mil.)	35.5%	–	14.8	(493.4)	42.6	36.9
Market value ($ mil.)	–	–	–	–	–	–
Employees	–	–	–	–	–	4,700

NGAS RESOURCES INC.

120 Prosperous Place Ste. 201　　　　　CEO: –
Lexington KY 40509-1844　　　　　　　CFO: Michael P Windisch
Phone: 859-263-3948　　　　　　　　　HR: Clarence Smith
Fax: 859-263-4228　　　　　　　　　　FYE: December 31
Web: www.ngas.com　　　　　　　　　Type: Subsidiary

In gas we trust could be the motto of NGAS Resources. The company searches for and produces gas in the Appalachian and Illinois basins. In 2010 NGAS Resources reported proved reserves of 63.1 billion cu. ft. of natural gas equivalent. In the Appalachian basin it holds more than 330000 net acres and stakes in about 1350 gross wells. Through partnerships the company also acts as a contract driller in its core areas. NGAS Resources owns and operates the gas gathering infrastructure for its Illinois Basin acreage and operates the gas gathering system for its Appalachian assets. To boost its Appalachian holdings in 2011 Magnum Hunter Resources acquired debt-laden NGAS Resources in a $98 million deal.

NGL ENERGY PARTNERS LP　　　　　　NYS: NGL

6120 South Yale Avenue, Suite 805　　　CEO: H. Michael Krimbill
Tulsa, OK 74136　　　　　　　　　　　CFO: Robert W. (Trey) Karlovich
Phone: 918 481-1119　　　　　　　　　HR: –
Fax: –　　　　　　　　　　　　　　　FYE: March 31
Web: www.nglenergypartners.com　　　Type: Public

All hail NGL for providing a secured energy trail. This Master Limited Partnership (MLP) provides transportation storage blending and marketing services for crude oil natural gas refined products and renewables in the US. With the Grand Mesa pipeline seven storage terminals and some 5.5 MMbbls of storage capacity to its name NGL buys refined petroleum in the Gulf Coast Southeast and Midwest regions transports them through the Colonial Plantation Magellan and NuStar pipelines and ultimately sells them to industrial end users or independent retailers and distributors. In addition the company provides water solutions that treats processes and disposes wastewater and solids generated from oil and natural gas production. The company also has a fleet of 160 trucks and 260 trailers as well as 10 tows and 19 barges.

	Annual Growth	03/15	03/16	03/17	03/18	03/19
Sales ($ mil.)	9.3%	16,802.1	11,742.1	13,022.2	17,282.7	24,016.9
Net income ($ mil.)	115.6%	16.7	(198.9)	137.0	(70.9)	360.0
Market value ($ mil.)	(14.5%)	3,269.1	937.2	2,816.7	1,371.0	1,748.6
Employees	(19.5%)	3,100	3,200	2,700	2,400	1,300

NHL ENTERPRISES, INC.

1185 AVE OF THE AMERICAS　　　　　　CEO: –
NEW YORK, NY 100362601　　　　　　　CFO: –
Phone: 212-789-2000　　　　　　　　　HR: –
Fax: –　　　　　　　　　　　　　　　FYE: June 30
Web: www.nhl.com　　　　　　　　　　Type: Private

Hockey is more than a cool sport for serious fans. The National Hockey League is one of the four major professional sports associations in North America boasting 30 professional ice hockey franchises in the US and Canada. The NHL governs the game sets and enforces rules regulates team ownership and collects licensing fees for merchandise. It also negotiates fees for national broadcasting rights. (Each team controls the rights to regional broadcasts.) In addition five minor and semi-pro hockey leagues also fly under the NHL banner. The league was organized in Canada in 1917.

	Annual Growth	06/04	06/05	06/06	06/09	06/14
Sales ($ mil.)	15.1%	–	35.2	17.4	74.4	124.4
Net income ($ mil.)	–	–	(1.8)	4.9	(1.3)	(8.5)
Market value ($ mil.)	–	–	–	–	–	–
Employees	–	–	–	–	–	200

NHS HUMAN SERVICES, INC.

620 GERMANTOWN PIKE　　　　　　　CEO: –
LAFAYETTE HILL, PA 194441810　　　　CFO: Derek Yacovelli
Phone: 610-260-4600　　　　　　　　　HR: –
Fax: –　　　　　　　　　　　　　　　FYE: June 30
　　　　　　　　　　　　　　　　　　Type: Private

Northwestern Human Services (operating as NHS Human Services) exists to lend a helping hand to humans throughout the Northeast. Founded in 1967 the organization primarily offers a variety of behavioral health care services that include mental health and drug and alcohol rehabilitation mental retardation services juvenile justice autism special education foster care and elder care. The not-for-profit organization provides programs for nearly 40000 adults and children at more than 675 facilities in more than half a dozen eastern US states. NHS' programs are offered through its specialty care facilities mobile clinics and on an independent case management basis.

	Annual Growth	06/09	06/10	06/14	06/15	06/16
Sales ($ mil.)	62.1%	–	28.9	44.4	49.4	524.0
Net income ($ mil.)	40.5%	–	0.7	3.9	1.3	5.2
Market value ($ mil.)	–	–	–	–	–	–
Employees	–	–	–	–	–	6,500

NIC INC.　　　　　　　　　　　　　　NMS: EGOV

25501 West Valley Parkway, Suite 300　　CEO: Harry H Herington
Olathe, KS 66061　　　　　　　　　　　CFO: Stephen M. (Steve) Kovzan
Phone: 877 234-3468　　　　　　　　　HR: –
Fax: –　　　　　　　　　　　　　　　FYE: December 31
Web: www.egov.com　　　　　　　　　Type: Public

So people can do business with government agencies NIC helps government agencies plug in to the Internet. The company is a leading provider of outsourced Web portal services for federal state and local governments. It designs implements and operates websites under contracts with more than 3500 government agencies. NIC generates much of its revenue from transaction fees for such services as online license renewals and for providing data on motor vehicle titles and business licenses to insurance companies lenders and other authorized organizations.

	Annual Growth	12/14	12/15	12/16	12/17	12/18
Sales ($ mil.)	6.1%	272.1	292.4	317.9	336.5	344.9
Net income ($ mil.)	10.5%	39.1	42.0	55.8	51.6	58.3
Market value ($ mil.)	(8.7%)	1,197.6	1,310.1	1,591.0	1,105.0	830.8
Employees	3.0%	818	859	929	950	920

NICE-PAK PRODUCTS INC.

2 Nice-Pak Park
Orangeburg NY 10962-1376
Phone: 845-365-1700
Fax: 845-365-1729
Web: www.nicepak.com

CEO: Robert Julius
CFO: –
HR: –
FYE: June 30
Type: Private

Nice-Pak Products wipes up the competition. The company makes and markets premoistened wipes including baby wipes antibacterial towelettes cloths for cleaning lenses and removing makeup and wipes for surface cleaning and industrial uses. The company's brand names include Grime Boss Hygea Nice'n Clean PDI Sani-Cloth Tar-Off and Wet Nap. The company also offers custom-packaged towelettes for mass marketers and retailers. Arthur Julius founded the family-owned firm in 1957. His son Robert Julius is Nice-Pak's chairman.

NICHOLAS FINANCIAL INC (BC) NMS: NICK

2454 McMullen Booth Road, Building C
Clearwater, FL 33759
Phone: 727 726-0763
Fax: –
Web: www.nicholasfinancial.com

CEO: –
CFO: Kelly M Malson
HR: –
FYE: March 31
Type: Public

Nickel-less? No problem. Nicholas Financial can still get you behind the wheel of a car. The company buys new and used car loans from some 2300 car dealers in the Southeast and Midwest US and conducts its automobile finance business through more than 65 offices in more than 15 states. In addition to its indirect lending activities Nicholas Financial offers and finances extended warranties roadside assistance plans and credit life accident and health insurance to its borrowers. Nicholas also makes some direct consumer loans primarily to customers whose car loans it has bought and serviced.

	Annual Growth	03/15	03/16	03/17	03/18	03/19
Sales ($ mil.)	(4.8%)	86.8	90.7	90.5	83.9	71.3
Net income ($ mil.)	–	16.9	12.4	5.4	(1.1)	(3.6)
Market value ($ mil.)	(10.5%)	110.8	85.3	84.1	71.7	71.2
Employees	(4.4%)	334	333	306	299	279

NICOLON CORPORATION

365 S HOLLAND DR
PENDERGRASS, GA 305674625
Phone: 706-693-2226
Fax: –

CEO: –
CFO: –
HR: –
FYE: December 31
Type: Private

TenCate Geosynthetics North America (formerly Nicolon Corporation) the commercial division of fabric giant Royal Ten Cate manufactures and distributes a variety of industrial fabrics and geosynthetic textiles used for infrastructure and civil engineering agriculture and recreation applications. The company's branded fabrics include Nicolon (truck covers and tennis windscreens); Permatron (trampoline fabric); Aquagrid (fish farming nets); Geotube (dewatering and shoreline protection); GeoDetect (soil reinforcement monitoring system); Mirafi NT (water storage liner for erosion control); and Miragrid (soil reinforcement). Other products include geogrids paving products and drainage composites.

	Annual Growth	12/09	12/10	12/11	12/12	12/13
Sales ($ mil.)	(5.6%)	–	–	178.9	150.6	159.4
Net income ($ mil.)	–	–	–	0.0	0.0	0.0
Market value ($ mil.)	–	–	–	–	–	–
Employees	–	–	–	–	–	402

NII HOLDINGS INC. NL:

12110 Sunset Hills Road, Suite 600
Reston, VA 20190
Phone: 703 390-5100
Fax: –
Web: www.nii.com

CEO: Steven M. Shindler
CFO: Daniel E. (Dan) Freiman
HR: –
FYE: December 31
Type: Public

NII Holdings brings the Nextel brand to Brazil where it has about 3.2 million consumer and business users. The company's customers are concentrated in the country's urban areas including Rio de Janeiro and São Paulo. The company offers mobile telephone voice and wireless data services; international voice and data roaming services; application-based radio connection; and streaming capabilities. NII was to wind down its legacy iDEN network in 2018 offering those subscribers access to its WCDMA network. The company is based in Reston Virginia.

	Annual Growth	06/15*	12/15	12/16	12/17	12/18
Sales ($ mil.)	(3.2%)	683.7	529.4	985.0	869.8	620.7
Net income ($ mil.)	–	1,740.5	(274.0)	(1,553.9)	(301.0)	(143.1)
Market value ($ mil.)	(4.4%)	–	511.7	217.8	43.0	446.8
Employees	(2.8%)	–	2,875	2,645	2,288	2,640

*Fiscal year change

NIMBLE STORAGE, INC.

211 RIVER OAKS PKWY
SAN JOSE, CA 951341913
Phone: 408-432-9600
Fax: –
Web: www.hpe.com

CEO: Suresh Vasudevan
CFO: Anup V. Singh
HR: Paul Whitney
FYE: January 31
Type: Private

In a mashup of Jack be nimble and Jumpin' Jack Flash Nimble Storage offers data storage systems that are a hybrid between a hard disk drive and a flash memory device. Its CS200 Series is designed for midsize IT organizations while its CS400 Series is geared for larger-scale deployments. The company even offers data analytics through its InfoSight service. Nimble Storage counts more than 2330 customers including cloud-based service providers government agencies and financial services health care manufacturing and technology companies. Nimble was bought by Hewlett Packard Enterprise for about $1.1 billion in April 2017.

	Annual Growth	01/13	01/14	01/15	01/16	01/17
Sales ($ mil.)	47.4%	–	125.7	227.7	322.2	402.6
Net income ($ mil.)	–	–	(43.1)	(98.8)	(120.1)	(158.3)
Market value ($ mil.)	–	–	–	–	–	–
Employees	–	–	–	–	–	1,300

NINTENDO OF AMERICA INC.

4600 150th Ave. NE
Redmond WA 98052
Phone: 425-882-2040
Fax: 425-882-3585
Web: www.nintendo.com

CEO: –
CFO: –
HR: –
FYE: March 31
Type: Subsidiary

Good hand/eye coordination serves those who play Nintendo of America games well. Serving as the Western Hemisphere distribution headquarters for Japan's Nintendo the company makes the #1 home game console Wii (pronounced "we") which is motion controlled and able to access Netflix. It also makes the #1 handheld game console Nintendo DS which features two screens and intuitive touch controls. On those consoles users can access and play such classic games as "Mario Bros. Donkey Kong Pokemon" and Zelda. Nintendo of America is also well known for legacy systems NES and Game Boy. Nintendo of America serves the US Canada Mexico and Brazil.

NINYO & MOORE GEOTECHNICAL & ENVIRONMENTAL SCIENCES CONSULTANTS

5710 RUFFIN RD
SAN DIEGO, CA 921231013
Phone: 858-576-1000
Fax: –
Web: www.ninyoandmoore.com

CEO: Avram Ninyo
CFO: –
HR: –
FYE: December 31
Type: Private

Need more engineering services than are immediately at your disposal? Ninyo & Moore provides geological and technical engineering and consulting services for public and private projects throughout the western US. Its offerings include earthquake and fault studies hydrogeologic and geologic hazard evaluations air quality services and environmental consultations for site developments. The company serves a variety of clients including school districts property developers transportation agencies and the military. Past projects include the Las Vegas monorail and the Emporium redevelopment project in San Francisco. Ninyo & Moore was founded in 1986 and today operates about a dozen offices.

	Annual Growth	12/09	12/10	12/11	12/12	12/13
Sales ($ mil.)	(1.1%)	–	52.7	55.0	54.2	50.9
Net income ($ mil.)	(52.1%)	–	–	4.0	3.0	0.9
Market value ($ mil.)	–	–	–	–	–	–
Employees		–	–	–	–	350

NISOURCE INC. (HOLDING CO.) — NYS: NI

801 East 86th Avenue
Merrillville, IN 46410
Phone: 877 647-5990
Fax: –
Web: www.nisource.com

CEO: Joseph (Joe) Hamrock
CFO: Donald E. Brown
HR: Teresa Smith
FYE: December 31
Type: Public

Energy holding company NiSource manages rate-regulated natural gas and electric utility companies serving nearly 4 million customers in seven US states making it one the nation's largest natural gas distributors. Its principal subsidiaries include NiSource Gas Distribution Group and NIPSCO. It owns 60000 miles of natural gas pipelines reaching Indiana Ohio Pennsylvania Virginia Kentucky Maryland and Massachusetts. NiSource assets also include power plants that generate close to 3300 MW of electricity annually serving some 479000 customers in northern Indiana.

	Annual Growth	12/14	12/15	12/16	12/17	12/18
Sales ($ mil.)	(5.7%)	6,470.6	4,651.8	4,492.5	4,874.6	5,114.5
Net income ($ mil.)	–	530.0	286.5	331.5	128.5	(50.6)
Market value ($ mil.)	(12.1%)	15,795.7	7,264.8	8,244.1	9,558.6	9,439.4
Employees	(2.6%)	8,982	7,596	8,007	8,175	8,087

NIXON PEABODY LLP

1300 Clinton Sq.
Rochester NY 14604
Phone: 585-263-1000
Fax: 585-263-1600
Web: www.nixonpeabody.com

CEO: –
CFO: –
HR: –
FYE: January 31
Type: Private - Partnershi

Nixon Peabody no relation to the former US president is a full-service law firm that has about 700 attorneys working in more than 20 major practice areas. Specialties include corporate law intellectual property litigation and representation of parties involved in private equity investments. Nixon Peabody operates from about 20 offices mainly in the northeast US and California. The firm also has four international offices. Nixon Peabody was formed through the 1999 merger of Nixon Hargrave Devans & Doyle and Peabody & Brown. Since then Nixon Peabody has grown by absorbing firms such as Sixbey Friedman Leedom & Ferguson and Hutchins Wheeler & Dittmar.

NL INDUSTRIES, INC. — NYS: NL

5430 LBJ Freeway, Suite 1700
Dallas, TX 75240-2620
Phone: 972 233-1700
Fax: –

CEO: Robert D. Graham
CFO: Gregory M. (Greg) Swalwell
HR: –
FYE: December 31
Type: Public

NL Industries is looking to paint a bright future. The company owns 30% of Kronos Worldwide one of the world's largest suppliers of titanium dioxide (TiO 2) which maximizes the whiteness opacity and brightness of paints plastics paper fibers and ceramics. Kronos produces more than 40 different grades of titanium dioxide. Majority-owned (87%) subsidiary CompX International makes components such as security products (locking systems) ball bearing slides and ergonomic computer support systems. Valhi which is 94%-owned by Contran Corporation in turn owns 83% of NL Industries. Through trusts billionaire Harold C. Simmons controls Contran Valhi and NL Industries.

	Annual Growth	12/14	12/15	12/16	12/17	12/18
Sales ($ mil.)	3.3%	103.8	109.0	108.9	112.0	118.2
Net income ($ mil.)	–	28.5	(23.9)	15.3	116.1	(41.0)
Market value ($ mil.)	(20.1%)	419.1	148.1	397.1	694.4	171.0
Employees	(34.7%)	3,017	2,792	2,776	2,765	547

NMI HEALTH INC — NBB: NANM

50 West Liberty Street, Suite 880
Reno, NV 89501
Phone: 209 275-9270
Fax: –
Web: www.nmihealth.com

CEO: Edward Suydam
CFO: Michael J Marx
HR: –
FYE: December 31
Type: Public

NMI Health formerly Nano Mask aims to block out germs. The company develops and markets advanced antimicrobial and filtration materials. Its products include the Nano-Zyme enzymatic detergents used for instrument reprocessing and antimicrobial textiles used in hospital apparel and supplies. Its CPR and environmental masks and filters use a proprietary advanced dual filtration system designed to remove infectious bacteria and viruses from air flow systems. Its products are designed to be used by health care providers and emergency response workers.

	Annual Growth	12/08	12/09	12/10	12/11	12/12
Sales ($ mil.)	363.8%	–	–	–	0.1	0.5
Net income ($ mil.)	–	(0.8)	(0.6)	(0.8)	(0.6)	(0.8)
Market value ($ mil.)	(24.0%)	0.3	1.2	0.3	0.2	0.1
Employees	0.0%	5	5	5	5	5

NMI HOLDINGS INC — NMS: NMIH

2100 Powell Street
Emeryville, CA 94608
Phone: 855 530-6642
Fax: –
Web: www.nationalmi.com

CEO: Bradley M. (Brad) Shuster
CFO: Glenn Farrell
HR: –
FYE: December 31
Type: Public

NMI Holdings provides mortgage insurance through two primary subsids – National Mortgage Insurance Corp (NMIC) and National Mortgage Reinsurance Inc. One (Re One). NMIC is its primary insurance subsidiary approved to write coverage in all 50 states and Washington DC. Re One provides reinsurance to NMIC on insured loans with coverage levels in excess of 25%. The company also provides outsourced loan review services to mortgage loan originators through NMI Services. Mortgage insurance protects lenders and investors from default-related losses.

	Annual Growth	12/14	12/15	12/16	12/17	12/18
Assets ($ mil.)	23.9%	463.3	662.5	841.7	894.8	1,092.0
Net income ($ mil.)	–	(48.9)	(27.8)	65.8	22.1	107.9
Market value ($ mil.)	18.2%	605.5	449.0	706.3	1,127.4	1,183.8
Employees	12.6%	189	243	276	299	304

NN, INC
NMS: NNBR

6210 Ardrey Kell Road
Charlotte, NC 28277
Phone: 980 264-4300
Fax: -
Web: www.nninc.com

CEO: Richard D. Holder
CFO: Thomas C. Burwell
HR: -
FYE: December 31
Type: Public

Hardly an unknown or no name ("NN") supplier NN produces a slew of precision metal components and assemblies for a highly diverse global market. Operating through three manufacturing units NN makes precision steel balls and rollers for bearing makers; carmakers; drilling bit makers whose products extract water oil and gas and minerals; and OEMs of stainless steel valves and pumps. It also churns out precision bearing seals metal and plastic retainers for ball and roller bearings and molded plastic products for automotive electronic instrument and fluid control industries.

	Annual Growth	12/14	12/15	12/16	12/17	12/18
Sales ($ mil.)	12.1%	488.6	667.3	833.5	619.8	770.7
Net income ($ mil.)	-	8.2	(7.4)	7.9	163.1	(264.5)
Market value ($ mil.)	(24.4%)	865.7	671.1	802.1	1,162.1	282.5
Employees	9.2%	4,220	5,313	5,299	4,407	5,991

NOBEL LEARNING COMMUNITIES INC.

1615 West Chester Pike Ste. 200
West Chester PA 19382-6233
Phone: 484-947-2000
Fax: 484-947-2004
Web: www.nobellearning.com

CEO: George H Bernstein
CFO: -
HR: -
FYE: June 30
Type: Private

This Nobel prizes a strong foundation built on education. Nobel Learning Communities operates more than 180 private schools across 15 states and the District of Columbia. These range from preschools (including six Montessori schools) and elementary schools to middle schools and private high schools. Operating under such brands as Paladin Academy Laurel Springs School and Houston Learning Academy Nobel's schools offer standard curriculum as well as programs for students with mild learning disabilities and online programs. Nobel's Links to Learning pre-K curriculum is designed to prepare children from ages six weeks to five years for school. Founded in 1984 Nobel Learning is owned by Leeds Equity Partners.

NOBILITY HOMES, INC.
NBB: NOBH

3741 S.W. 7th Street
Ocala, FL 34474
Phone: 352 732-5157
Fax: -
Web: www.nobilityhomes.com

CEO: Terry E Trexler
CFO: Thomas W Trexler
HR: -
FYE: November 02
Type: Public

Florida's prince of prefab Nobility Homes is a leading player in the state's competitive manufactured-home market. Nobility has built and sold about 50000 homes through about 20 retail Prestige Home Centers Majestic Homes retail sales centers and on a wholesale basis to independent dealers and residential communities. Nobility offers some 100 models that range in price from about $30000 to more than $100000 and in sizes from about 700 sq. ft. to 2650 sq. ft. The company also provides financing mortgage lending and brokerage and insurance services. Founder and president Terry Trexler and his family control nearly two-thirds of the company.

	Annual Growth	10/15*	11/16	11/17	11/18	11/19
Sales ($ mil.)	13.6%	27.8	34.1	37.5	42.8	46.3
Net income ($ mil.)	31.8%	2.9	6.0	3.3	5.0	8.8
Market value ($ mil.)	17.8%	47.1	56.8	62.3	84.3	90.7
Employees	1.9%	129	140	147	149	139

*Fiscal year change

NOBLE ENERGY INC
NMS: NBL

1001 Noble Energy Way
Houston, TX 77070
Phone: 281 872-3100
Fax: 281 872-3111
Web: www.nobleenergyinc.com

CEO: David L. Stover
CFO: Kenneth M. (Ken) Fisher
HR: Lee Robison
FYE: December 31
Type: Public

Noble Energy explores and produces crude oil and natural gas in the US and internationally. The company's properties are located onshore and offshore and the firm seeks to acquire exploration rights and conduct exploration activities in various geographic areas of interest. Its US operations are focused on the Delaware Basin Denver-Julesburg (DJ) Basin and Eagle Ford Shale. Its international operations are focused on offshore conventional basins in the Mediterranean Sea and off the west coast of Africa. Noble reports proved reserves of about 1.9 billion barrels of oil equivalent. The company has been engaged in crude oil NGL and natural gas exploration and development activities in the US since 1932.

	Annual Growth	12/14	12/15	12/16	12/17	12/18
Sales ($ mil.)	(0.6%)	5,101.0	3,133.0	3,491.0	4,256.0	4,986.0
Net income ($ mil.)	-	1,214.0	(2,441.0)	(998.0)	(1,118.0)	(66.0)
Market value ($ mil.)	(20.7%)	22,870.9	15,878.9	18,352.6	14,051.4	9,046.1
Employees	(3.9%)	2,735	2,395	2,274	2,277	2,330

NOBLE ROMAN'S, INC.
NBB: NROM

6612 E. 75th Street, Suite 450
Indianapolis, IN 46250
Phone: 317 634-3377
Fax: -
Web: www.nobleromans.com

CEO: A Scott Mobley
CFO: Paul W Mobley
HR: -
FYE: December 31
Type: Public

This patrician gives a thumbs-up to quick-service pizza. Noble Roman's operates a chain of about 820 franchised quick-service restaurants located mostly in high-traffic areas such as shopping malls college campuses and military bases. Operating primarily under the names Noble Roman's Pizza Noble Roman's Express and Noble Roman's Pizza & Subs the eateries offer a limited menu of pizzas pasta and sandwiches. Noble Roman's also has some restaurants operating under the Tuscano's Italian Style Subs brand as well as a self-service concept designed for convenience stores. The company's restaurants operate in about 45 states and in Canada Guam and Italy.

	Annual Growth	12/14	12/15	12/16	12/17	12/18
Sales ($ mil.)	12.0%	7.9	7.7	7.8	9.8	12.4
Net income ($ mil.)	-	1.6	0.8	(0.9)	(3.4)	(3.1)
Market value ($ mil.)	(34.8%)	47.7	22.2	8.6	12.9	8.6
Employees	35.4%	36	28	79	159	121

NOBLIS, INC.

2002 EDMUND HALLEY DR
RESTON, VA 201913436
Phone: 703-610-2000
Fax: -
Web: www.noblis.org

CEO: Amr A. ElSawy
CFO: Mark A. Simione
HR: David Webb
FYE: September 30
Type: Private

Noblis' noble pursuit is through its offering of science-related strategic and technology consulting services. The not-for-profit company which pledges to serve the public interest helps various government entities and other clients evaluate technology options and vendors as well as solve complex technical problems. Noblis provides strategic planning decision analysis and acquisition support services. The company addresses problems in areas such as environment and energy intelligence health care homeland security public safety enterprise engineering and transportation. Noblis has worked with such clients as the US Air Force Army Navy and Departments of Commerce and Defense.

	Annual Growth	10/14	10/15*	09/16	09/17	09/18
Sales ($ mil.)	(1.0%)	-	314.3	320.2	319.2	305.1
Net income ($ mil.)	36.7%	-	12.0	19.0	13.1	30.7
Market value ($ mil.)	-	-	-	-	-	-
Employees	-	-	-	-	-	1,000

*Fiscal year change

NOCOPI TECHNOLOGIES, INC. NBB: NNUP

480 Shoemaker Road, Suite 104
King of Prussia, PA 19406
Phone: 610 834-9600
Fax: –
Web: www.nocopi.com

CEO: –
CFO: Rudolph A Lutterschmidt
HR: –
FYE: December 31
Type: Public

Nocopi Technologies dogs copycats. The company makes anti-counterfeiting and anti-diversion technologies that prevent the unauthorized photocopying of sensitive documents. Offerings include Copimark which allows information to be printed invisibly on certain areas of a document as well as document security products such as its line of printed forms containing areas that can't be copied legibly. Another Nocopi technology Rub-it & Color enables publishers to create children's activity books in which colors appear when a page is rubbed. The company also has a licensing agreement with Elmer's Products which incorporates Nocopi's technologies in its Giddy Up and Color Loco activity book products.

	Annual Growth	12/14	12/15	12/16	12/17	12/18
Sales ($ mil.)	37.9%	0.9	1.0	1.4	1.6	3.3
Net income ($ mil.)	282.9%	0.0	(0.0)	0.3	0.4	1.7
Market value ($ mil.)	43.2%	0.5	0.4	1.5	2.3	2.1
Employees	0.0%	5	5	5	5	5

NON-INVASIVE MONITORING SYSTEMS INC. NBB: NIMU

4400 Biscayne Blvd., Suite 180
Miami, FL 33137
Phone: 305 575-4200
Fax: 305 575-4201
Web: www.nims-inc.com

CEO: Jane H Hsiao
CFO: James J Martin
HR: –
FYE: July 31
Type: Public

Non-Invasive Monitoring Systems (NIMS) believes being rocked in a cradle is good for grown-ups too. The company has developed a moving bed-style device that is intended to improve circulation and joint mobility and possibly to relieve minor aches and pains. Originally tagged as AT-101 the device was sold in Japan and the US until the FDA required the company to get regulatory approval for it. NIMS halted sales and marketing efforts on AT-101 and is seeking FDA approval for a similar but less costly device known as the Exer-Rest intended for home and clinic use.

	Annual Growth	07/13	07/14	07/15	07/16	07/17
Sales ($ mil.)	(51.6%)	0.1	0.0	0.0	0.0	0.0
Net income ($ mil.)	–	(0.5)	(0.4)	(0.4)	(0.7)	(0.5)
Market value ($ mil.)	(3.3%)	14.2	12.6	19.0	10.3	12.4
Employees	–	1	1	–	–	–

NONPAREIL CORPORATION

40 N. 400 West
Blackfoot ID 83221-5632
Phone: 208-785-5880
Fax: 208-785-3656
Web: www.nonparl.com

CEO: Chris Abend
CFO: John Fullmer
HR: –
FYE: August 31
Type: Private

One potato two potato — you know how the rest of the ditty goes and so does Nonpareil. The company grows and ships fresh potatoes and manufactures value-added potato products such as hash browns mashed potatoes and potato flakes which it distributes to US foodservice operators. Nonpareil also supplies ingredients including flavor additives made from potatoes to other food manufacturers. The company's potatoes are grown on a 10000 acres in Nebraska and 3000 acres in Idaho. The Nonpareil Corporation was founded in 1946 by Harold and Robert Abend; it continues to be owned and managed by members of the Abend family.

NOODLES & CO NMS: NDLS

520 Zang Street, Suite D
Broomfield, CO 80021
Phone: 720 214-1900
Fax: –
Web: www.noodles.com

CEO: Dave Boennighausen
CFO: Ken Kuick
HR: –
FYE: January 01
Type: Public

Noodles & Company operates and franchises more than 480 quick-casual restaurants in about 30 states that specialize in noodle entrees. Its restaurants feature menu items ranging in style from American to Asian to Mediterranean including noodle and vegetable bowls soups and green salads with pasta. Founder Aaron Kennedy a former brand manager at PepsiCo who opened the first Noodles & Company location in Denver in 1995 owned the company with a group of private investors until the company went public in 2013. Most of Noodles & Company's eateries are company-owned.

	Annual Growth	12/14	12/15*	01/17	01/18	01/19
Sales ($ mil.)	2.5%	403.7	455.5	487.5	456.5	457.8
Net income ($ mil.)	–	11.4	(13.8)	(71.7)	(37.5)	(8.4)
Market value ($ mil.)	(23.3%)	1,158.9	463.5	177.9	228.4	307.1
Employees	(0.2%)	9,500	10,600	10,900	9,600	9,400

*Fiscal year change

NORANDA ALUMINUM HOLDING CORP NBB: NORN Q

801 Crescent Centre Drive, Suite 600
Franklin, TN 37067
Phone: 615 771-5700
Fax: –
Web: www.norandaaluminum.com

CEO: Layle K Smith
CFO: Dale W Boyles
HR: –
FYE: December 31
Type: Public

Noranda Aluminum succeeds by keeping its operations — and profits — all under the same corporate roof. The company a vertically integrated aluminum producer starts the process by producing bauxite in a Jamaican mining project refining it into alumina in a Louisiana smelter and then using the alumina to make primary aluminum metal products at its processing facility in Missouri and aluminum coils at four flat rolling facilities in the Southeast. Noranda's primary aluminum products include aluminum rods extruded billets and foundry ingots. The downstream business segment manufactures foil and light sheet metal.

	Annual Growth	12/11	12/12	12/13	12/14	12/15
Sales ($ mil.)	(5.8%)	1,559.8	1,394.9	1,343.5	1,355.1	1,228.1
Net income ($ mil.)	–	140.9	49.5	(47.6)	(26.6)	(259.6)
Market value ($ mil.)	(55.6%)	82.5	61.1	32.9	35.2	3.2
Employees	(3.1%)	2,500	2,500	2,350	1,600	2,200

NORDSTROM, INC. NYS: JWN

1617 Sixth Avenue
Seattle, WA 98101
Phone: 206 628-2111
Fax: –
Web: www.nordstrom.com

CEO: Steven C. Mattics
CFO: Anne L. Bramman
HR: Christine F. Deputy
FYE: February 02
Type: Public

Service with a smile is a part of Nordstrom's corporate culture. One of the nation's largest upscale apparel and shoe retailers Nordstrom sells clothes shoes and accessories through about 115 Nordstrom full-line stores and about 240 off-price outlet stores (Nordstrom Rack) in about 40 states and online. It also operates six full-line and six Rack stores in Canada three Jeffrey luxury boutiques six Trunk Club personal clothing service clubhouses three Nordstrom Local hubs two "Last Chance" clearance stores and online private sale site HauteLook. With its easy-return policy and touches such as thank-you notes from employees Nordstrom has earned a reputation for top-notch customer service. Nordstrom family members who own about 30% of the retailer's stock closely supervise the chain.

	Annual Growth	01/15	01/16	01/17*	02/18	02/19
Sales ($ mil.)	4.1%	13,506.0	14,437.0	14,757.0	15,478.0	15,860.0
Net income ($ mil.)	(5.9%)	720.0	600.0	354.0	437.0	564.0
Market value ($ mil.)	(12.2%)	12,009.1	7,738.2	6,750.0	7,541.2	7,144.0
Employees	1.5%	67,000	72,500	72,500	72,500	71,000

*Fiscal year change

NORFOLK SOUTHERN CORP

NYS: NSC

Three Commercial Place
Norfolk, VA 23510-2191
Phone: 757 629-2680
Fax: –
Web: www.norfolksouthern.com

CEO: James A. (Jim) Squires
CFO: Cynthia C. (Cindy) Earhart
HR: Annie Adams
FYE: December 31
Type: Public

Norfolk Southern Corporation's main subsidiary Norfolk Southern Railway transports freight over a network consisting of about 20000 route miles in 20-plus states (plus DC) in the eastern southeastern and Midwestern US. The rail system is made up of nearly 20000 route miles owned by Norfolk Southern and about 8000 route miles of trackage rights which allow the company to use tracks owned by other railroads. Norfolk Southern transports coal and general merchandise including automotive products and chemicals.

	Annual Growth	12/15	12/16	12/17	12/18	12/19
Sales ($ mil.)	1.8%	10,511.0	9,888.0	10,551.0	11,458.0	11,296.0
Net income ($ mil.)	15.0%	1,556.0	1,668.0	5,404.0	2,666.0	2,722.0
Market value ($ mil.)	23.1%	21,816.2	27,871.8	37,370.4	38,567.1	50,067.1
Employees	(5.2%)	30,456	28,044	27,110	26,662	24,587

NORFOLK STATE UNIVERSITY

700 PARK AVE
NORFOLK, VA 235048090
Phone: 757-823-8600
Fax: –
Web: www.nsu.edu

CEO: –
CFO: Marry Weaver
HR: –
FYE: June 30
Type: Private

Founded in 1935 during the Great Depression Norfolk State University (NSU) is one of the nation's largest predominately black institutions of higher education. NSU is a four-year state-supported Virginia university offering undergraduate degrees in about 30 disciplines. The school also offers more than 15 master's and three doctoral degree programs. NSU boasts an enrollment of 7000-plus students at its main campus and at its satellite centers in nearby Virginia cities Portsmouth and Virginia Beach. Some 6400 of students are undergraduates; the remainder are pursuing graduate degrees. Most of the degrees conferred by the school are in liberal arts followed by science and technology and business.

	Annual Growth	06/13	06/14	06/15	06/16	06/17
Sales ($ mil.)	15.8%	–	–	–	60.2	69.7
Net income ($ mil.)	3529.9%	–	–	–	0.9	34.2
Market value ($ mil.)	–	–	–	–	–	–
Employees	–	–	–	–	–	1,095

NORKUS ENTERPRISES, INC.

505 RICHMOND AVE
POINT PLEASANT BEACH, NJ 087422552
Phone: 732-899-8485
Fax: –

CEO: –
CFO: –
HR: –
FYE: April 25
Type: Private

They sell pasta shells by the Jersey sea shore. Norkus Enterprises operates grocery stores under the Foodtown and Super Foodtown banners in Monmouth County and Ocean County New Jersey. The regional grocery chain also offers online shopping and home delivery. It was founded when Francis Norkus opened his first grocery store called Table Talk in Freehold New Jersey in 1935. Norkus Enterprises is a member of the Foodtown Supermarket cooperative. The company also owns four Max's Beer Wine & Liquor stores located in New Jersey. In 2011 Norkus sold five of its six Foodtown stores — located in Freehold Township Manalapan Neptune City Point Pleasant Beach and Long Branch — to The Stop & Shop Supermarket Company.

	Annual Growth	04/05	04/06	04/07	04/08	04/09
Sales ($ mil.)	2.0%	–	148.6	153.2	157.7	157.6
Net income ($ mil.)	29.4%	–	0.3	0.9	1.1	0.6
Market value ($ mil.)	–	–	–	–	–	–
Employees	–	–	–	–	–	1,000

NORMAN REGIONAL HOSPITAL AUTHORITY

901 N PORTER AVE
NORMAN, OK 730716482
Phone: 405-307-1000
Fax: –
Web: www.normanregional.com

CEO: –
CFO: Ken Hopkins
HR: Sharon K Goff
FYE: June 30
Type: Private

NORM! Perhaps that's how locals refer to Norman Regional Health System when they are headed there for health care. The system operates in and around Norman Oklahoma through the full service 325-bed Norman Regional Hospital and affiliated health centers including Moore Medical Center Services and the HealthPlex a 136-bed specialty hospital focused on cardiology orthopedic and spine and women's and children's services. Moore Medical Center's services include include acute care and surgery diagnostic and outpatient health care services. The organization's programs include behavioral medicine rehabilitation a women's center and a sleep disorder clinic. The hospital which employs more than 350 physicians was established in 1946.

	Annual Growth	06/10	06/11	06/12	06/14	06/17
Sales ($ mil.)	(13.6%)	–	921.7	324.5	347.2	382.6
Net income ($ mil.)	476.1%	–	0.0	8.0	24.8	18.7
Market value ($ mil.)	–	–	–	–	–	–
Employees	–	–	–	–	–	3,500

NORTECH SYSTEMS INC.

NAS: NSYS

7550 Meridian Circle N., Suite #150
Maple Grove, MN 55369
Phone: 952 345-2244
Fax: –
Web: www.nortechsys.com

CEO: Richard G. (Rich) Wasielewski
CFO: Paula M. Graff
HR: –
FYE: December 31
Type: Public

If you design it Nortech will come. The company offers outsourced electronics and cable assembly manufacturing to a variety of industries such as aerospace automotive medical and military contracting. Products include wire harnesses printed circuit boards electronic subassemblies components and more. A bevy of services includes design testing prototyping and supply chain management. Most revenue comes from products following customer design specificacations. One customer accounts for more than a quarter of revenue.

	Annual Growth	12/14	12/15	12/16	12/17	12/18
Sales ($ mil.)	0.3%	112.0	115.2	116.6	112.3	113.4
Net income ($ mil.)	(34.1%)	0.9	(0.6)	0.0	(2.4)	0.2
Market value ($ mil.)	(10.9%)	15.1	10.3	10.4	10.3	9.5
Employees	0.2%	813	841	904	800	819

NORTEK INC

NMS: NTK

500 Exchange Street
Providence, RI 02903-2699
Phone: 401 751-1600
Fax: –
Web: www.nortekinc.com

CEO: Michael J Clarke
CFO: –
HR: –
FYE: December 31
Type: Public

Nortek delivers a breath of fresh air. The company makes and distributes residential and commercial air conditioning and heating systems (HVAC) residential ventilation products and home technology products. In addition to HVAC systems Nortek's wares include range hoods and other ventilation products indoor air-quality systems lighting controls and home entertainment and security system equipment. Products which are sold primarily in North America and Europe bear the Nortek name along with other brands including Broan-NuTone as well as such licensed names as Frigidaire and Maytag. Speaker brands include Niles SpeakerCraft and Xantech.

	Annual Growth	12/10	12/11	12/12	12/13	12/14
Sales ($ mil.)	7.6%	1,899.3	2,140.5	2,201.3	2,287.9	2,546.1
Net income ($ mil.)	–	–	(13.4)	(55.9)	9.5	(8.3)	(45.6)
Market value ($ mil.)	22.6%	585.1	425.2	1,076.8	1,212.6	1,322.0
Employees	4.2%	9,500	9,300	9,400	9,600	11,200

NORTH AMERICAN ELECTRIC RELIABILITY CORPORATION

3353 PEACHTREE RD NE # 600 — CEO: James Robb
ATLANTA, GA 303261063 — CFO: –
Phone: 404-446-2560 — HR: –
Fax: – — FYE: December 31
Web: www.nerc.com — Type: Private

Working to keep the lights on the North American Electric Reliability Corp. (NERC) sets standards for the operation of the continent's power grid. The NERC monitors wholesale activities on the grid and provides assessment training tools and services in coordination with regional councils to ensure reliability. It is a self-regulatory organization overseen by the US Federal Energy Regulatory Commission and the Canadian government. The NERC has worked with the FERC to establish legally enforceable reliability standards for the US bulk power system that took effect in 2007. The NERC was formed in 1968 three years after one of the largest blackouts in American history.

	Annual Growth	12/12	12/13	12/14	12/15	12/16
Sales ($ mil.)	9.5%	–	50.5	58.7	63.3	66.3
Net income ($ mil.)	–	–	(3.9)	4.1	1.0	2.6
Market value ($ mil.)	–	–	–	–	–	–
Employees	–	–	–	–	–	175

NORTH AMERICAN LIGHTING, INC.

2275 S MAIN ST — CEO: Takashi Ohtake
PARIS, IL 619442963 — CFO: –
Phone: 217-465-6600 — HR: –
Fax: – — FYE: December 31
Web: www.nal.com — Type: Private

North American Lighting offers travelers a beacon of safety through the fog. The company is an independent manufacturer of vehicle lighting products in North America. Operating through four assembly plants and one technology center the company produces a line-up of headlamps signal lamps and fog lamps. Its forward-lighting products include mercury-free high intensity discharge (HID) headlamps and the Adaptive Front Lighting System (AFS). Among its signal lamps are rear-combo and license plate lamps. Its products are tailored to the designs of large auto makers and local Japanese automakers. Founded in 1983 North American Lighting is a subsidiary of Japan-based KOITO MANUFACTURING.

	Annual Growth	12/08	12/09	12/10	12/11	12/17
Sales ($ mil.)	25.6%	–	–	297.4	297.4	1,466.4
Net income ($ mil.)	35.6%	–	–	13.2	13.2	111.3
Market value ($ mil.)	–	–	–	–	–	–
Employees	–	–	–	–	–	2,200

NORTH BROWARD HOSPITAL DISTRICT

1800 NW 49TH ST — CEO: –
FORT LAUDERDALE, FL 333093092 — CFO: Robert Martin
Phone: 954-473-7010 — HR: Melanie Hatcher
Fax: – — FYE: June 30
Web: www.browardhealth.org — Type: Private

North Broward Hospital District which operates as Broward Health takes care of shark bites and more. The taxpayer-supported not-for-profit health system serves the coastal city of Fort Lauderdale and the northern two-thirds of Broward County Florida with four acute care hospitals and a host of community-based centers. Flagship hospital Broward General Medical Center has more than 700 beds and features the Chris Evert Children's Hospital; all of the hospitals together have more than 1500 beds. Broward Health boasts about 30 additional facilities including family health and surgery centers and home health and hospice programs.

	Annual Growth	06/07	06/08	06/16	06/17	06/18
Sales ($ mil.)	(2.5%)	–	1,335.1	1,014.6	1,025.3	1,035.6
Net income ($ mil.)	6.0%	–	67.4	(12.9)	33.5	120.2
Market value ($ mil.)	–	–	–	–	–	–
Employees	–	–	–	–	–	7,000

NORTH CAROLINA ELECTRIC MEMBERSHIP CORPORATION

3400 SUMNER BLVD — CEO: Joe Brannon
RALEIGH, NC 276162950 — CFO: Lark James
Phone: 919-872-0800 — HR: –
Fax: – — FYE: December 31
Web: www.ncelectriccooperatives.com — Type: Private

It's a cooperative effort: North Carolina Electric Membership Corporation (NCEMC) generates and transmits electricity to the state's 26 electric cooperatives (more than 2.5 million people) in 93 of 100 North Carolina counties. The co-op owns more than 600 MW of generating capacity through four primarily natural gas peak load generators plus a 61.5% stake in Catawba Nuclear Station Unit 1 and a 31% stake in the Catawba Nuclear Station in South Carolina. It also buys power from Progress Energy American Electric Power and other for-profit utilities. NCEMC's member cooperatives serve more than 950000 metered businesses and homes in North Carolina. The wholesale co-op also operates an energy operations center.

	Annual Growth	12/07	12/08	12/16	12/17	12/18
Sales ($ mil.)	1.7%	–	1,006.5	1,022.7	1,018.0	1,188.9
Net income ($ mil.)	17.2%	–	6.1	25.5	23.0	30.0
Market value ($ mil.)	–	–	–	–	–	–
Employees	–	–	–	–	–	150

NORTH CENTRAL BANCSHARES INC.   NASDAQ: FFFD

825 Central Ave. — CEO: David M Bradley
Fort Dodge IA 50501 — CFO: Jane M Funk
Phone: 515-576-7531 — HR: –
Fax: 515-576-3398 — FYE: December 31
Web: www.firstfederaliowa.com — Type: Public

North Central Bancshares is the holding company for First Federal Savings Bank of Iowa which serves north-central and southeastern portions of the Hawkeye State through about a dozen branches. Offering standard retail deposit products the bank uses funds gathered to write a variety of loans; residential and commercial mortgages account for about three-fourths of the company's loan portfolio. Subsidiaries of the bank offer insurance annuities title services and investment services. The company converted First Federal Savings from a federal thrift to a state-chartered commercial bank in 2011. Great Western Bancorporation is acquiring North Central Bancshares.

NORTH CENTRAL FARMERS ELEVATOR

12 5TH AVE — CEO: –
IPSWICH, SD 574517700 — CFO: –
Phone: 605-426-6021 — HR: –
Fax: – — FYE: December 31
Web: www.ncfe.coop — Type: Private

North Central Farmers Elevator's mission is to give its members a lift. The full-service member-owned agricultural cooperative located in South Dakota offers farm-support goods and services including feed seed and other farm supplies along with agronomy energy and marketing services. In conjunction with LOL Farmland Feeds and South Dakota Wheat Growers North Central Farmers Elevator owns Dakotaland Feeds which makes and markets feed to producers. It also has a marketing alliance with South Dakota Oilseed Processors to sell its member/farmer's soybean crops. The coop's 21 locations serve more than 2500 producer-members in north central South Dakota and south central North Dakota.

	Annual Growth	12/03	12/04	12/05	12/06	12/07
Sales ($ mil.)	19.2%	–	–	198.2	135.1	281.5
Net income ($ mil.)	1.1%	–	–	2.7	(1.2)	2.7
Market value ($ mil.)	–	–	–	–	–	–
Employees	–	–	–	–	–	200

NORTH DAKOTA MILL & ELEVATOR ASSOCIATION

1823 MILL RD
GRAND FORKS, ND 582031535
Phone: 701-795-7000
Fax: –
Web: www.ndmill.com

CEO: –
CFO: –
HR: –
FYE: June 30
Type: Private

When bakeries need flour North Dakota Mill & Elevator rises to the occasion. The mill is a producer of wheat flour used specifically in breads and other baked goods like cookies and crackers. It processes more than 78000 bushels of wheat a day and ships most of its flour in bulk to wholesalers. It offers semolina flour as well as specialty products such as wholegrain wheat flour wheat germ and corn flour for tortillas. The mill also sells pancake mixes bread machine mixes and wholewheat all-purpose and bread flours under the Dakota Maid brand to consumers through its online store. Owned by the State of North Dakota it contributes 50% of its profits to the North Dakota State General Fund.

	Annual Growth	06/13	06/14	06/15	06/16	06/18
Sales ($ mil.)	1.4%	–	256.1	247.9	216.1	270.6
Net income ($ mil.)	(22.5%)	–	9.2	12.4	4.4	3.3
Market value ($ mil.)	–	–	–	–	–	–
Employees	–	–	–	–	–	120

NORTH DAKOTA STATE UNIVERSITY

1919 UNIVERSITY DR N # 102
FARGO, ND 581021843
Phone: 701-231-7015
Fax: –
Web: www.ndsu.edu

CEO: –
CFO: –
HR: –
FYE: June 30
Type: Private

The state's leading research institution North Dakota State University (NDSU) has an enrollment of more than 14600 students. The university offers more than 100 undergraduate degree programs some 60 master's degree programs and more than 40 doctoral and professional programs. Historically NDSU's strengths have been agriculture and the applied sciences but the school also offers courses of study in business liberal arts engineering architecture mathematics and education. NDSU is a land-grant college; its extension service offers education and outreach programs throughout North Dakota in agriculture health and nutrition and community leadership. NDSU which was established in 1890 is part of the North Dakota University System.

	Annual Growth	06/15	06/16*	12/16*	06/17	06/18
Sales ($ mil.)	1.3%	–	253.8	42.2	258.7	260.3
Net income ($ mil.)	(62.4%)	–	44.3	13.4	28.8	6.3
Market value ($ mil.)	–	–	–	–	–	–
Employees	–	–	–	–	–	4,500

*Fiscal year change

NORTH EUROPEAN OIL ROYALTY TRUST

5 N. Lincoln Street
Keene, NH 03431
Phone: 732 741-4008
Fax: 732 741-3140
Web: www.neort.com

NYS: NRT
CEO: –
CFO: John R Van Kirk
HR: –
FYE: October 31
Type: Public

North European Oil Royalty Trust isn't owned by the crowned oil barons of Europe. The passive fixed investment trust receives royalties based on its interests in natural gas (97% of revenues) oil and sulfur producing properties in the former state of Oldenburg and portions of northwest Germany. Royalties are generated by the sale of crude oil natural gas distillate and sulfur mined by Exxon Mobil Royal Dutch Shell and their subsidiaries; the trust then distributes the royalties to shareholders on a quarterly basis. As a grantor trust North European Oil is exempt from paying income taxes; shareholders however are not.

	Annual Growth	10/15	10/16	10/17	10/18	10/19
Sales ($ mil.)	(9.4%)	12.4	7.0	7.8	7.2	8.4
Net income ($ mil.)	(10.1%)	11.6	6.1	7.0	6.4	7.6
Market value ($ mil.)	(11.4%)	91.0	71.3	61.2	66.1	56.2
Employees	0.0%	2	2	2	2	2

NORTH FLORIDA REGIONAL MEDICAL CENTER, INC.

6500 W NEWBERRY RD
GAINESVILLE, FL 326054309
Phone: 352-333-4100
Fax: –
Web: www.nfrmc.com

CEO: –
CFO: –
HR: –
FYE: February 28
Type: Private

North Florida Regional Medical Center (NFRMC) part of the HCA health services network is a 445-bed acute care community hospital serving Gainesville Florida and more than a dozen surrounding counties. The hospital boasts specialty centers for diabetes senior care obesity surgery and sleep disorders. It also provides emergency services cancer care heart care imaging services orthopedics neurological care physical therapy and wound therapy. NFRMC was founded in 1972 by HCA and a group of physicians. As part of HCA's North Florida Regional Healthcare network it has affiliates including physician practices and express care clinics.

	Annual Growth	12/95	12/96	12/97*	02/09	02/17
Sales ($ mil.)	6.2%	–	–	133.3	331.2	443.9
Net income ($ mil.)	7.4%	–	–	26.7	61.8	110.7
Market value ($ mil.)	–	–	–	–	–	–
Employees	–	–	–	–	–	2,000

*Fiscal year change

NORTH MEMORIAL HEALTH CARE

3300 OAKDALE AVE N
MINNEAPOLIS, MN 554222900
Phone: 763-520-5200
Fax: –
Web: www.northmemorial.com

CEO: Andy Cochrane
CFO: Todd Ostendorf
HR: –
FYE: December 31
Type: Private

North Memorial Health Care fights illness in the Twin Cities. Established in 1939 as Victory Hospital the health care network is home to North Memorial Medical Center a 520-bed hospital that features a Level I trauma center and the Humphrey Cancer Center. The hospital also operates specialty centers for cardiovascular care orthopedics pediatrics and women's health as well as an emergency vehicle fleet of more than 125 ambulances and nearly 10 helicopters. The adjacent outpatient center provides oncology radiation and imaging services. North Memorial Health Care also has a network of primary and specialty care clinics in the Twin Cities region and it provides home health and hospice services.

	Annual Growth	12/11	12/12	12/13	12/16	12/17
Sales ($ mil.)	2.8%	–	566.0	735.7	721.9	651.3
Net income ($ mil.)	–	–	(4.6)	51.5	(0.1)	(28.7)
Market value ($ mil.)	–	–	–	–	–	–
Employees	–	–	–	–	–	5,180

NORTH MISSISSIPPI HEALTH SERVICES, INC.

830 S GLOSTER ST
TUPELO, MS 388014934
Phone: 662-377-3000
Fax: –
Web: www.nmhs.net

CEO: –
CFO: Sharon Nobles
HR: Mark Pittman
FYE: September 30
Type: Private

North Mississippi Health Services (NMHS) isn't contained by its name: The health system also provides health care to residents of northwestern Alabama. NMHS includes half a dozen community hospitals including its flagship North Mississippi Medical Center in Tupelo. North Mississippi Medical Clinics a regional network of more than 30 primary and specialty clinics; and nursing homes. Combined the facilities have nearly 1000 beds designated for acute long term and nursing care. Specialty services include home health and long-term care inpatient and outpatient behavioral health and treatment centers for cancer and digestive disorders. NMHS also operates outpatient care and wellness clinics in the region.

	Annual Growth	09/13	09/14	09/15	09/16	09/17
Sales ($ mil.)	4.9%	–	779.4	860.0	893.0	898.8
Net income ($ mil.)	–	–	(14.4)	19.2	30.5	26.5
Market value ($ mil.)	–	–	–	–	–	–
Employees	–	–	–	–	–	6,000

NORTH MISSISSIPPI MEDICAL CENTER, INC.

830 S GLOSTER ST
TUPELO, MS 388014934
Phone: 662-377-3000
Fax: –
Web: www.nmhs.net

CEO: –
CFO: –
HR: –
FYE: September 30
Type: Private

At North Mississippi Medical Center you might get some Mississippi Mud ice cream after your tonsils are removed. The full-service 650-bed regional referral hospital in Tupelo Mississippi is part of the North Mississippi Health Services system an affiliation of hospitals and clinics serving northern Mississippi northwestern Alabama and parts of Tennessee. It's the largest private not-for-profit hospital in Mississippi and the largest non-metropolitan hospital in America. Specialty services at the medical center include cancer treatment women's health care cardiology and behavioral health care. The hospital also operates a skilled-nursing facility and home health and hospice organizations.

	Annual Growth	09/11	09/12	09/13	09/14	09/15
Sales ($ mil.)	0.4%	–	620.8	537.6	633.9	627.5
Net income ($ mil.)	–	–	(6.4)	2.5	52.5	46.0
Market value ($ mil.)	–	–	–	–	–	–
Employees	–	–	–	–	–	6,000

NORTH PACIFIC PAPER COMPANY, LLC

3001 INDUSTRIAL WAY
LONGVIEW, WA 986321057
Phone: 360-636-6400
Fax: –
Web: www.norpacpaper.com

CEO: Craig Anneberg
CFO: –
HR: –
FYE: December 31
Type: Private

The old adage "all the news fit to print" might not be possible without North Pacific Paper Corporation (NORPAC). The firm a joint venture between Weyerhaeuser and Nippon Paper produces newsprint for newspaper publishers and commercial printers. NORPAC manufactures a variety of paper grades including standard and lightweight newsprint and super- and ultra-lightweight stocks especially for the Japanese market. It produces more than 250000 tons of newsprint annually at its manufacturing facility in Longview Washington. Its products are sent via truck and train to customers in the western US or are shipped by boat to customers in Japan. Weyerhaeuser is selling its stake in NORPAC to One Rock Capital Partners.

	Annual Growth	12/04	12/05	12/06	12/07	12/08
Sales ($ mil.)	3.5%	–	–	499.0	474.7	534.4
Net income ($ mil.)	7.4%	–	–	19.3	(3.8)	22.2
Market value ($ mil.)	–	–	–	–	–	–
Employees	–	–	–	–	–	410

NORTH PARK UNIVERSITY

2543 W CULLOM AVE
CHICAGO, IL 606181501
Phone: 773-244-6200
Fax: –
Web: www.northpark.edu

CEO: –
CFO: –
HR: –
FYE: June 30
Type: Private

North Park University is a Christian university that is located on Chicago's north side and enrolls more than 3200 undergraduate and graduate students. The school specializes in liberal arts business the health sciences and education and also offers seminary degree programs. North Park offers more than 40 majors and pre-professional programs. Undergraduate classes average less than 20 students. Some 87% of North Park full time faculty hold earned PhD's or the highest degree in their field. Founded in 1891 by the Evangelical Covenant Church the university also has three satellite campuses in the Chicago metropolitan area.

	Annual Growth	06/11	06/12	06/13	06/14	06/15
Sales ($ mil.)	18.4%	–	54.1	53.4	94.4	89.8
Net income ($ mil.)	697.4%	–	0.0	0.0	1.6	5.6
Market value ($ mil.)	–	–	–	–	–	–
Employees	–	–	–	–	–	375

NORTH SHORE MEDICAL CENTER, INC.

81 HIGHLAND AVE
SALEM, MA 019702768
Phone: 978-741-1200
Fax: –
Web: www.nsmc.partners.org

CEO: –
CFO: Sally Mason Boemer
HR: –
FYE: September 30
Type: Private

This health system strives to cast a spell of salubriousness over Salem Massachusetts. The North Shore Medical Center (NSMC) provides medical care to the residents of several cities north of Boston including Salem (aka The Witch City) Lynn and Peabody. The network is home to two acute care hospitals children's and rehabilitation hospitals a heart institute a women's center and a number of community health centers. It also boasts more than 600 physicians and other health care professionals in its North Shore Physician Group. Its flagship the NSMC Salem Hospital is a nearly 250-bed teaching hospital providing adult and pediatric services. The not-for-profit system is part of Partners HealthCare System.

	Annual Growth	09/13	09/14	09/15	09/16	09/17
Sales ($ mil.)	1.0%	–	395.2	403.9	408.8	407.2
Net income ($ mil.)	–	–	(21.5)	(35.2)	(48.7)	(58.0)
Market value ($ mil.)	–	–	–	–	–	–
Employees	–	–	–	–	–	5,000

NORTH SHORE UNIVERSITY HOSPITAL

300 COMMUNITY DR
MANHASSET, NY 110303876
Phone: 516-562-0100
Fax: –

CEO: –
CFO: Robert S. (Bob) Shapiro
HR: –
FYE: December 31
Type: Private

North Shore University Hospital (NSUH) knows you shouldn't have to leave the island for quality health care. The Long Island hospital has more than 800 beds devoted to adult and pediatric medicine rehabilitation stroke care women's health orthopedics urology wound healing dentistry and trauma emergency services among other areas. The hospital is home to specialist institutes for cancer care and cardiology. It also serves as a campus for the Hofstra Northwell Shool of Medicine. NSUH is part of Northwell Health.

	Annual Growth	12/13	12/14	12/15	12/16	12/17
Sales ($ mil.)	6.9%	–	1,495.4	1,617.9	1,795.4	1,826.9
Net income ($ mil.)	31.1%	–	84.9	37.3	171.6	191.0
Market value ($ mil.)	–	–	–	–	–	–
Employees	–	–	–	–	–	5,000

NORTH VALLEY BANCORP (REDDING, CA)   NMS: NOVB

300 Park Marina Circle
Redding, CA 96001
Phone: 530 226-2900
Fax: –
Web: www.novb.com

CEO: –
CFO: –
HR: –
FYE: December 31
Type: Public

NVB wants to be the MVP of banks in Northern California. North Valley Bancorp is the holding company for North Valley Bank (NVB) which operates some two dozen branches in about 10 Northern California counties. The bank offers commercial and retail services such as checking savings money market and NOW accounts and certificates of deposit. Real estate loans dominate the bank's lending portfolio including commercial and residential mortgages and construction loans. NVB has an agreement with Essex National Securities which provides brokerage services and investment advice to the bank's customers.

	Annual Growth	12/08	12/09	12/10	12/11	12/12
Assets ($ mil.)	0.6%	879.6	884.4	884.9	905.0	902.3
Net income ($ mil.)	–	(1.8)	(25.9)	(6.2)	3.0	6.3
Market value ($ mil.)	39.6%	25.6	14.3	61.2	65.7	97.3
Employees	(6.9%)	437	341	346	334	329

NORTH WIND INC.
1425 HIGHAM ST
IDAHO FALLS, ID 834021513
Phone: 505-661-4290
Fax: –
Web: www.northwindinc.com

CEO: –
CFO: –
HR: Andrew Henderson
FYE: December 31
Type: Private

The North wind doth blow and we shall have.... clean air and water. North Wind works to keep the air clean the ground fresh and the water clear in North America. The environmental consulting firm's services include site assessment soil and groundwater remediation geographic information system (GIS) data hazardous and nonhazardous waste management and project engineering and construction. North Wind has expanded by buying South Carolina-based Pinnacle Consulting Group which offers engineering environmental and information technology consulting services.

	Annual Growth	12/06	12/07	12/08	12/09	12/10
Sales ($ mil.)	(66.2%)	–	–	750.6	120.2	85.5
Net income ($ mil.)	146601.7%	–	–	0.0	6.3	4.3
Market value ($ mil.)	–	–	–	–	–	–
Employees	–	–	–	–	–	86

NORTHEAST BANK (ME)
500 Canal Street
Lewiston, ME 04240
Phone: 207 786-3245
Fax: –
Web: www.northeastbank.com

NMS: NBN
CEO: –
CFO: –
HR: –
FYE: June 30
Type: Public

Northeast Bancorp is the holding company for Northeast Bank which operates about a dozen branches in western and southern Maine. Founded in 1872 the bank offers standard retail services such as checking and savings accounts NOW and money market accounts CDs and trust services as well as financial planning and brokerage. Residential mortgages account for about a third of all loans; commercial mortgages and consumer loans each make up about 25%. The bank also writes business and construction loans. Newly created investment entity FHB Formation acquired a 60% stake in Northeast Bancorp in 2010. The deal brought in $16 million in capital. The 2011 sale of insurance agency Varney added another $8.4 million.

	Annual Growth	06/15	06/16	06/17	06/18	06/19
Assets ($ mil.)	7.9%	850.8	986.2	1,076.9	1,157.7	1,153.9
Net income ($ mil.)	18.1%	7.1	7.6	12.3	16.2	13.9
Market value ($ mil.)	29.0%	90.0	101.7	184.0	197.1	249.4
Employees	(1.1%)	191	203	195	185	183

NORTHEAST COMMUNITY BANCORP INC
325 Hamilton Avenue
White Plains, NY 10601
Phone: 914 684-2500
Fax: –
Web: www.necommunitybank.com

NBB: NECB
CEO: Kenneth A Martinek
CFO: Donald S Hom
HR: –
FYE: December 31
Type: Public

Northeast Community Bancorp is the holding company for Northeast Community Bank which serves consumers and businesses in the New York metropolitan area and Massachusetts. Through about a half-dozen branches the thrift offers traditional deposit services like checking and savings accounts as well as a variety of lending products such as commercial and multi-family real estate loans home equity construction and secured loans. While its deposit services are confined to New York and Massachusetts it markets its loan products throughout the northeastern US. The bank offers investment and financial planning services through Hayden Wealth Management. Northeast Community Bank's roots date back to 1934.

	Annual Growth	12/13	12/14	12/15	12/16	12/17
Assets ($ mil.)	15.5%	458.2	515.4	593.6	734.5	814.8
Net income ($ mil.)	63.1%	1.1	1.7	2.3	5.0	8.1
Market value ($ mil.)	8.8%	88.0	88.0	86.8	96.3	123.2
Employees	(7.7%)	104	96	–	–	–

NORTHEAST GEORGIA HEALTH SYSTEM, INC.
743 SPRING ST NE
GAINESVILLE, GA 305013715
Phone: 770-219-9000
Fax: –
Web: www.nghs.com

CEO: Carol Burrell
CFO: Brian Steines
HR: Judy Canaday
FYE: September 30
Type: Private

Northeast Georgia Health System (NGHS) is a not-for-profit health system that serves nearly 1 million residents in about 20 counties in Georgia. Its Northeast Georgia Medical Center operates three hospital campuses — its flagship location in Gainesville and two additional locations in Barrow County and Greater Braselton. The medical center is home to a heart center with more than 25 cardiologists making it the largest such practice in the region. The system also offers urgent care primary care rehabilitation services and long-term care. Its Northeast Georgia Physicians Group (NGPG) includes some 250 doctors with more than 20 specializations. NGHS was founded in 1951.

	Annual Growth	09/08	09/09	09/13	09/14	09/15
Sales ($ mil.)	40.0%	–	8.8	33.4	50.4	65.9
Net income ($ mil.)	–	–	(7.6)	9.9	10.0	0.1
Market value ($ mil.)	–	–	–	–	–	–
Employees	–	–	–	–	–	8,000

NORTHEAST HEALTH SYSTEMS INC.
85 HERRICK ST
BEVERLY, MA 019151777
Phone: 978-922-3000
Fax: –
Web: www.nhs-healthlink.org

CEO: Dennis S Conroy
CFO: –
HR: –
FYE: September 30
Type: Private

If a particularly beastly Nor'easter wreaks havoc on your immune system you might want to turn to Northeast Health System (NHS) for a little TLC. The organization provides a continuum of health services to residents of Massachusetts' North Shore communities through its network of hospitals outpatient care facilities and behavioral health and senior care centers. NHS' hospitals include Addison Gilbert Hospital a 60-bed full-service acute care facility; the 60-bed BayRidge Hospital a mental health and drug rehab facility; and Beverly Hospital with more than 220 beds. The company is a part of the Lahey Health System.

	Annual Growth	09/07	09/08	09/09	09/10	09/11
Sales ($ mil.)	(49.9%)	–	–	1,733.6	0.1	434.8
Net income ($ mil.)	–	–	–	0.0	(0.6)	(12.6)
Market value ($ mil.)	–	–	–	–	–	–
Employees	–	–	–	–	–	5,100

NORTHEAST INDIANA BANCORP INC
648 North Jefferson Street
Huntington, IN 46750
Phone: 260 356-3311
Fax: 260 358-0035
Web: www.firstfedindiana.com

NBB: NIDB
CEO: Michael S Zahn
CFO: Randy J Sizemore
HR: –
FYE: December 31
Type: Public

Northeast Indiana Bancorp is the holding company for First Federal Savings Bank which operates three branches in Huntington and another in Warsaw. First Federal offers checking savings credit cards money market accounts CDs and health savings accounts. Its subsidiary Innovative Financial Services division offers investments financial planning and insurance to individuals and corporate clients can set up retirement plans for employees.

	Annual Growth	12/14	12/15	12/16	12/17	12/18
Assets ($ mil.)	4.9%	276.2	284.2	301.0	314.2	334.2
Net income ($ mil.)	7.4%	3.1	3.8	3.6	3.4	4.2
Market value ($ mil.)	19.7%	21.7	21.7	21.7	42.4	44.6
Employees	–	–	–	–	–	–

NORTHEASTERN SUPPLY, INC.

8323 PULASKI HWY
BALTIMORE, MD 212372941
Phone: 410-574-0010
Fax: –
Web: www.northeastern.com

CEO: Stephen D Cook
CFO: –
HR: –
FYE: December 31
Type: Private

Northeastern Supply keeps its little corner of the world cozy. Through more than 30 locations in Delaware Maryland Pennsylvania Virginia and West Virginia the company distributes air conditioning heating plumbing ventilation and water system equipment along with fixtures and hardware to contractors and other building professionals. Major suppliers include American Standard Bradford White Delta Elkay Jacuzzi and Moen. Northeastern also offers online credit applications electronic funds transfers and e-mail invoicing to its customers. It operates through some 30 locations plus an 175000 sq. ft. distribution center.

	Annual Growth	12/06	12/07	12/08	12/09	12/11
Sales ($ mil.)	(2.1%)	–	–	113.6	100.9	106.5
Net income ($ mil.)	(20.8%)	–	–	2.2	2.6	1.1
Market value ($ mil.)	–	–	–	–	–	–
Employees	–	–	–	–	–	285

NORTHEASTERN UNIVERSITY

360 HUNTINGTON AVE
BOSTON, MA 021155000
Phone: 617-373-2000
Fax: –
Web: www.northeastern.edu

CEO: Philomena V. Mantella
CFO: –
HR: –
FYE: June 30
Type: Private

Since 1898 Northeastern University has been educating students in Boston and beyond. The school enrolls roughly 24000 students and employs 1600 faculty members. Its nine colleges offer 100 undergraduate programs and 160 graduate programs in areas such as the arts business engineering and law. Northeastern has a student-to-teacher ratio of about 13:1. Its highly-regarded experiential education program integrates classroom learning with real-world experience; students typically alternate between school and paid full-time work and leave with up to two years of professional experience. Northeastern started out as a night school housed in a YMCA facility.

	Annual Growth	06/12	06/13	06/16	06/17	06/18
Sales ($ mil.)	6.6%	–	947.4	1,106.4	1,161.6	1,306.5
Net income ($ mil.)	2.0%	–	147.7	3.2	169.1	163.3
Market value ($ mil.)	–	–	–	–	–	–
Employees	–	–	–	–	–	4,175

NORTHERN ARIZONA HEALTHCARE CORPORATION

1200 N BEAVER ST
FLAGSTAFF, AZ 860013118
Phone: 928-779-3366
Fax: –
Web: www.nahealth.com

CEO: Chris Bavasi
CFO: Gregory D Kuzma
HR: –
FYE: June 30
Type: Private

Northern Arizona Healthcare (NAH) is an integrated health care system serving residents of northern and central Arizona. It features two acute care hospitals: Flagstaff Medical Center (FMC) with about 270 beds; and Verde Valley Medical Center in Cottonwood with about 100 beds. NAH also operates several area outpatient clinics that provide emergency and primary care services as well as physical therapy cancer treatments and other services. Additionally it operates home health hospice and pharmacy divisions as well as a cardiovascular physician practice and a childhood obesity program. NAH serves more than 167000 patients annually and employs some 300 physicians.

	Annual Growth	06/08	06/09	06/10	06/11	06/15
Sales ($ mil.)	5.6%	–	49.4	50.3	53.7	68.5
Net income ($ mil.)	–	–	(0.6)	(0.6)	(0.8)	(3.8)
Market value ($ mil.)	–	–	–	–	–	–
Employees	–	–	–	–	–	2,500

NORTHERN ARIZONA UNIVERSITY

601 S KNOLES DR ROOM 220
FLAGSTAFF, AZ 860110001
Phone: 928-523-9011
Fax: –
Web: www.azk12.org

CEO: –
CFO: –
HR: –
FYE: June 30
Type: Private

Located a stone's throw from the Grand Canyon Northern Arizona University (NAU) has been educating students to see forever for more than a century. About 20000 students attend the school which is dominated by a mountainous landscape. Founded in 1899 NAU offers roughly 100 baccalaureate about 50 master's and a handful of doctoral programs. Undergraduate majors include exercise science hotel and restaurant management and visual communication. It's home to the High Altitude Sports Training Complex a multi-sport training center used by athletes to prepare for different environments and enhance performance. NAU's Extended Campuses provide access to higher education for students in their own communities.

	Annual Growth	06/14	06/15	06/16	06/17	06/18
Sales ($ mil.)	5.2%	–	308.9	321.7	351.7	359.6
Net income ($ mil.)	(18.5%)	–	10.1	(8.7)	5.2	5.4
Market value ($ mil.)	–	–	–	–	–	–
Employees	–	–	–	–	–	3,863

NORTHERN INDIANA PUBLIC SERVICE COMPANY

801 E 86TH AVE
MERRILLVILLE, IN 464106271
Phone: 800-464-7726
Fax: –
Web: www.nipsco.com

CEO: –
CFO: Pete Disser
HR: –
FYE: December 31
Type: Private

Northern Indiana Public Service Company (NIPSCO) can shine a little light on the topic of Hoosiers. The largest subsidiary of utility holding company NiSource NIPSCO has more than 457000 electricity customers and more than 786000 natural gas customers. The utility has three coal-fired power plants with 2540 MW of generating capacity. On the power side of the business NIPSCO generates transmits and distributes electricity to the northern part of Indiana and engages in electric wholesale and transmission transactions. The company operates approximately 13000 miles of electric transmission and distribution lines and 16000 miles of gas mains.

	Annual Growth	12/05	12/06	12/15	12/16	12/17
Sales ($ mil.)	0.8%	–	2,209.6	–	2,252.0	2,418.2
Net income ($ mil.)	3.3%	–	157.9	–	178.3	226.0
Market value ($ mil.)	–	–	–	–	–	–
Employees	–	–	–	–	–	3,096

NORTHERN INYO HEALTHCARE DISTRICT

150 PIONEER LN
BISHOP, CA 935142556
Phone: 760-873-5811
Fax: –
Web: www.nih.org

CEO: Victoria Alexander-Lane
CFO: –
HR: –
FYE: June 30
Type: Private

Northern Inyo Hospital provides general medical services for the region north of Los Angeles California. Its staff of physicians specialize in areas such as emergency medicine obstetrics urology ophthalmology and pediatrics. The company's Rural Health Clinic offers immunizations wound care women's and children's health exams and sports physicals.

	Annual Growth	06/11	06/12	06/13	06/15	06/16
Sales ($ mil.)	6.3%	–	59.8	0.1	73.4	76.3
Net income ($ mil.)	(3.5%)	–	1.1	0.0	0.8	1.0
Market value ($ mil.)	–	–	–	–	–	–
Employees	–	–	–	–	–	402

NORTHERN NATURAL GAS COMPANY

1111 S 103RD ST
OMAHA, NE 681241072
Phone: 877-654-0646
Fax: –
Web: www.northernnaturalgas.com

CEO: Mark A. Hewett
CFO: –
HR: Norma Hasenjager
FYE: December 31
Type: Private

Northern Natural Gas (NNG) keeps the pipes gassed up. The company operates 14700 miles of natural gas pipeline (6300 miles of transmission line and 8400 miles of branch and lateral lines) stretching from the Permian Basin in Texas to the Great Lakes in the Midwest. It also provides transportation and storage services to almost 80 utilities and a number of other customers in the Upper Midwest. The company has a 5.5 billion cu. ft. per day market area peak capacity and its five natural gas storage facilities have a total capacity of 73 billion cu. ft. including 4 billion cu. ft. of liquefied natural gas (LNG). NNG which was formed in 1930 is an indirect subsidiary of Berkshire Hathaway Energy.

	Annual Growth	12/05	12/06	12/07	12/16	12/17
Sales ($ mil.)	0.8%	–	633.6	664.0	636.4	693.4
Net income ($ mil.)	1.7%	–	142.4	161.1	159.4	170.6
Market value ($ mil.)	–	–	–	–	–	–
Employees	–	–	–	–	–	1,055

NORTHERN OIL & GAS INC (MN)   ASE: NOG

601 Carlson Pkwy, Suite 990
Minnetonka, MN 55305
Phone: 952 476-9800
Fax: –
Web: www.northernoil.com

CEO: Thomas W. Stoelk
CFO: –
HR: –
FYE: December 31
Type: Public

If there is an oil & gas acquisition exploration and development activity going on in North Dakota and Montana you can bet Northern Oil and Gas wants a piece of it. But there is a twist: the company has its eye only on non-operated working interests in wells drilled and completed by third parties. Avoiding development agreement contracts to a significant extent the company diversifies by claiming small stakes in many wells. Currently it has interests in more than 3260 wells in the Bakken and Three Forks formations (an average interest of 7%) with proven reserves of around 76000 MBoe.

	Annual Growth	12/14	12/15	12/16	12/17	12/18
Sales ($ mil.)	3.4%	595.0	275.1	144.9	209.3	678.9
Net income ($ mil.)	(3.2%)	163.7	(975.4)	(293.5)	(9.2)	143.7
Market value ($ mil.)	(20.5%)	2,137.6	1,460.4	1,040.4	775.6	855.0
Employees	(3.4%)	23	20	19	18	20

NORTHERN STATES FINANCIAL CORP. (WAUKEGAN, IL)   NBB: NSFC

1601 North Lewis Avenue
Waukegan, IL 60085
Phone: 847 244-6000
Fax: 847 244-7853
Web: www.nsfc.com

CEO: –
CFO: –
HR: –
FYE: December 31
Type: Public

Northern States Financial is the holding company for NorStates Bank which serves individuals and businesses in northeastern Illinois and southeastern Wisconsin through 8 branches. With more than $400 million in assets it provides retail services like savings checking money market accounts CDs and IRAs. The company uses deposits to originate commercial mortgages (accounting for about half of its portfolio) as well as residential mortgages commercial loans construction loans and consumer loans. NorStates Bank was founded in 2005 when Northern States merged its Bank of Waukegan and First State Bank of Round Lake (founded in 1949 and acquired in 2004) subsidiaries.

	Annual Growth	12/11	12/12	12/14	12/15	12/16
Assets ($ mil.)	1.1%	463.0	413.3	422.0	485.3	490.0
Net income ($ mil.)	–	(6.7)	(12.6)	0.2	23.1	2.1
Market value ($ mil.)	4.2%	–	56.0	58.7	52.9	65.9
Employees	(8.8%)	125	114	–	–	–

NORTHERN TECHNOLOGIES INTERNATIONAL CORP.   NMS: NTIC

4201 Woodland Road
Circle Pines, MN 55014
Phone: 763 225-6600
Fax: –
Web: www.ntic.com

CEO: G Patrick Lynch
CFO: David Bonczek
HR: –
FYE: August 31
Type: Public

Northern Technologies International (NTIC) keeps rust away with its proprietary corrosion-inhibiting packaging. Its ZERUST product line features special packaging that emits corrosion-inhibiting molecules and compounds; the packaging comes in films and bags liquids and coatings rust removers and cleaners vapor capsules and pipe strips for residue-free protection of pipes thermal spray coatings and cathodic protection technologies. NTIC's customers include automotive electronics power generation and metal processing firms. The company makes about 85% of its sales in North America.

	Annual Growth	08/15	08/16	08/17	08/18	08/19
Sales ($ mil.)	16.4%	30.3	32.9	39.6	51.4	55.8
Net income ($ mil.)	30.6%	1.8	(0.9)	3.4	6.7	5.2
Market value ($ mil.)	(8.4%)	141.6	126.2	159.9	330.8	99.5
Employees	(12.2%)	123	121	71	136	73

NORTHERN TIER ENERGY INC.   NYSE: NTI

38C Grove St. Ste. 100
Ridgefield CT 06877
Phone: 203-244-6550
Fax: 203-431-7672
Web: www.ntenergy.com

CEO: –
CFO: –
HR: –
FYE: December 31
Type: Private

Northern Tier Energy will make your gas and sell it too. The company formed in late 2010 owns one of only two oil refineries in Minnesota and about 230 SuperAmerica gas stations across Minnesota and Wisconsin. Its oil refinery produces 74000 barrels per day of gasoline diesel jet fuel and asphalt. The company also owns storage and transportation assets including terminals storage tanks rail loading and unloading facilities and a dock on the Mississippi River. In addition Northern Tier Energy owns a 17% stake in the 300-mile Minnesota Pipeline (Koch Industries owns the rest) that transports crude oil to its refinery. The company went public with a $200 million IPO in 2012.

NORTHERN TIER ENERGY LP   NYS: NTI

1250 W. Washington Street, Suite 300
Tempe, AZ 85281
Phone: 602 302-5450
Fax: –
Web: www.ntenergy.com

CEO: Dave L Lamp
CFO: Karen B Davis
HR: –
FYE: December 31
Type: Public

Northern Tier Energy makes gasoline and sells it too. The company owns one of only two oil refineries in Minnesota and more than 260 SuperAmerica gas stations across Minnesota and Wisconsin. Its oil refinery produces 97800 barrels per day of gasoline diesel jet fuel and asphalt. The company also owns storage and transportation assets including terminals storage tanks rail loading and unloading facilities and a dock on the Mississippi River. In addition Northern Tier Energy owns a 17% stake in the 300-mile Minnesota Pipeline (Koch Industries owns the rest) that transports crude oil to its refinery.

	Annual Growth	12/10	12/11	12/12	12/13	12/14
Sales ($ mil.)	100.3%	344.9	4,280.8	4,653.9	4,979.2	5,556.0
Net income ($ mil.)	76.7%	24.8	28.3	197.6	231.1	241.6
Market value ($ mil.)	(6.7%)	–	–	2,358.6	2,280.7	2,052.7
Employees	3.4%	–	2,667	2,893	2,896	2,950

NORTHERN TIER ENERGY LP

38C GROVE ST STE 1
RIDGEFIELD, CT 068774667
Phone: 203-244-6550
Fax: –
Web: www.ntenergy.com

CEO: Dave L Lamp
CFO: Karen B Davis
HR: –
FYE: December 31
Type: Private

Northern Tier Energy makes gasoline and sells it too. The company owns one of only two oil refineries in Minnesota and more than 260 SuperAmerica gas stations across Minnesota and Wisconsin. Its oil refinery produces 97800 barrels per day of gasoline diesel jet fuel and asphalt. The company also owns storage and transportation assets including terminals storage tanks rail loading and unloading facilities and a dock on the Mississippi River. In addition Northern Tier Energy owns a 17% stake in the 300-mile Minnesota Pipeline (Koch Industries owns the rest) that transports crude oil to its refinery.

	Annual Growth	12/10	12/11	12/12	12/13	12/14
Sales ($ mil.)	9.3%	–	–	4,653.9	4,979.2	5,556.0
Net income ($ mil.)	10.6%	–	–	197.6	231.1	241.6
Market value ($ mil.)	–	–	–	–	–	–
Employees	–	–	–	–	–	642

NORTHERN TRUST CORP

NMS: NTRS

50 South LaSalle Street
Chicago, IL 60603
Phone: 312 630-6000
Fax: –
Web: www.northerntrust.com

CEO: Michael G. O'Grady
CFO: Stephen B. (Biff) Bowman
HR: S. Gillian Pembleton
FYE: December 31
Type: Public

Through its flagship subsidiary The Northern Trust Company Northern Trust provides wealth management brokerage securities lending asset servicing and management and banking and trust services. The firm addresses institutional clients and affluent individuals through around 80 offices in some 20 states and about 20 countries. Operating two main segments?Corporate and Institutional Services (C&IS) and Wealth Management?Northern Trust has approximately $10.1 trillion in assets under custody/administration roughly $7.6 trillion under custody and greater than $1 trillion under direct management. About 65% of company's total revenue comes from the US.

	Annual Growth	12/14	12/15	12/16	12/17	12/18
Assets ($ mil.)	4.7%	109,946.5	116,749.6	123,926.9	138,590.5	132,212.5
Net income ($ mil.)	17.7%	811.8	973.8	1,032.5	1,199.0	1,556.4
Market value ($ mil.)	5.5%	14,761.4	15,788.6	19,503.0	21,877.1	18,307.2
Employees	5.1%	15,400	16,200	17,100	18,100	18,800

NORTHERN UTAH HEALTHCARE CORPORATION

1200 E 3900 S
SALT LAKE CITY, UT 841241300
Phone: 801-268-7111
Fax: –
Web: www.stmarkshospital.com

CEO: John Hanshaw
CFO: Brian McKenley
HR: –
FYE: June 30
Type: Private

St. Mark's Hospital provides a variety of health care services in Salt Lake City and surrounding areas of northern Utah. The medical center has a capacity of some 320 beds and provides acute care and specialty services including cardiology orthopedics oncology women's services pain management general surgery and emergency care. It also offers family practice and specialist services. Established in 1872 St. Mark's Hospital is part of HCA's MountainStar Healthcare Network which operates hospitals and other health care facilities in Alaska Idaho and Utah.

	Annual Growth	05/0-1	05/00*	12/05*	06/15	06/16
Sales ($ mil.)	5.9%	–	140.3	0.3	341.7	352.9
Net income ($ mil.)	11.8%	–	17.5	0.1	110.5	103.9
Market value ($ mil.)	–	–	–	–	–	–
Employees	–	–	–	–	–	1,600

*Fiscal year change

NORTHERN VIRGINIA ELECTRIC COOPERATIVE

10323 LOMOND DR
MANASSAS, VA 201093113
Phone: 703-335-0500
Fax: –
Web: www.novec.com

CEO: –
CFO: Wilbur Rollins
HR: Marlane Parsons
FYE: December 31
Type: Private

NOVEC is no novice when it comes to electricity distribution. Northern Virginia Electric Cooperative (NOVEC) is a member-owned not-for profit utility that serves more than 150000 residential commercial industrial and government customers in a 651-sq. ml. service area in northern Virginia. NOVEC which has more than 6790 miles of power lines receives its power supply from the PJM Interconnection marketplace. The company also markets natural gas to retail customers in Virginia and Maryland through its NOVEC Energy Solutions unit. Subsidiary NOVEC Solutions sells gas and electric water heaters and other energy appliances and provides optical data networking service for large businesses and government agencies.

	Annual Growth	12/08	12/09	12/13	12/14	12/15
Sales ($ mil.)	2.0%	–	419.4	397.0	433.1	472.0
Net income ($ mil.)	(14.2%)	–	51.0	23.9	20.5	20.3
Market value ($ mil.)	–	–	–	–	–	–
Employees	–	–	–	–	–	275

NORTHFIELD BANCORP INC.

NASDAQ: NFBK

581 Main St. Suite 810
Woodbridge NJ 07095
Phone: 732-499-7200
Fax: +86-755-8298-1111
Web: www.visionchina.cn

CEO: Steven M Klein
CFO: William R Jacobs
HR: –
FYE: December 31
Type: Public

Northfield Bancorp is the holding company for Northfield Bank which offers checking savings and retirement accounts; CDs; mortgage and home equity loans; life insurance; and credit cards. Its commercial offerings include checking and money market accounts commercial lending and business credit cards. Founded in 1887 Northfield Bank operates some 20 branches in New York and New Jersey. It added a pair of branches in New Jersey through the FDIC-assisted transaction of First State Bank in 2011. And in late 2012 Northfield Bancorp expanded its presence in Brooklyn through its acquisition of Flatbush Federal Bancorp.

NORTHRIM BANCCORP INC

NMS: NRIM

3111 C Street
Anchorage, AK 99503
Phone: 907 562-0062
Fax: –
Web: www.northrim.com

CEO: Joe Schierhorn
CFO: Latosha M Frye
HR: –
FYE: December 31
Type: Public

Can you get banking services at the north rim of the world? Of course! Northrim BanCorp formed in 2001 to be the holding company for Northrim Bank provides a full range of commercial and retail banking services and products through some 10 banking offices in Alaska's Anchorage Fairbanks North Star and Matanuska Susitna counties. Division offices that provide short-term capital to customers also are located in Washington and Oregon. The bank offers standard deposit products including checking savings and money market accounts; CDs; and IRAs. It uses funds from deposits to write commercial loans (40% of loan portfolio) and real estate term loans (nearly 35%) as well as construction and consumer loans.

	Annual Growth	12/14	12/15	12/16	12/17	12/18
Assets ($ mil.)	0.9%	1,449.3	1,499.5	1,526.5	1,519.1	1,503.0
Net income ($ mil.)	3.5%	17.4	17.8	14.4	13.2	20.0
Market value ($ mil.)	5.8%	180.6	183.1	217.5	233.0	226.3
Employees	0.2%	426	441	451	429	430

NORTHROP GRUMMAN CORP
NYS: NOC

2980 Fairview Park Drive
Falls Church, VA 22042
Phone: 703-280-2900
Fax: –
Web: www.northropgrumman.com

CEO: Wesley G. (Wes) Bush
CFO: Kenneth L. Bedingfield
HR: Heidi Hendrix
FYE: December 31
Type: Public

Northrop Grumman's major military systems include manned and autonomous aircraft such as the Global Hawk drone a next-generation B-21 Raider bomber and fuselage sections for the F-35 Lightening. Other products and services include various command control communications computer intelligence surveillance and reconnaissance (C4ISR) systems that support the military from the ground the air and space. The company also offers software and services in support of national security for the US and its allies. The 2018 acquisition of Orbital ATK added space vehicles satellites ammunition and missile propulsion systems. The US government accounts for more than 80% of Northrop Grumman's sales.

	Annual Growth	12/15	12/16	12/17	12/18	12/19
Sales ($ mil.)	9.5%	23,526.0	24,508.0	25,803.0	30,095.0	33,841.0
Net income ($ mil.)	3.1%	1,990.0	2,200.0	2,015.0	3,229.0	2,248.0
Market value ($ mil.)	16.2%	31,691.5	39,038.2	51,514.4	41,106.1	57,734.8
Employees	8.5%	65,000	67,000	70,000	85,000	90,000

NORTHSHORE UNIVERSITY HEALTHSYSTEM

1301 CENTRAL ST
EVANSTON, IL 602011613
Phone: 847-570-5295
Fax: –
Web: www.northshore.org

CEO: Gerald (J.P.) Gallagher
CFO: Gary E. Weiss
HR: Bill Leuhes
FYE: September 30
Type: Private

NorthShore University HealthSystem provides care to residents of Chicago's north side and its suburbs. The health system operates four hospitals a home care organization and a Medical Group with some 970 primary and specialty care physicians. With about 355 beds the organization's flagship Evanston Hospital has teaching and research programs as well as capabilities for trauma cancer and cardiology. The system also includes Glenbrook Hospital (about 175 beds) Highland Park Hospital (140 beds) and Skokie Hospital (more than 120 beds). The health care system is affiliated with the University of Chicago Pritzker School of Medicine.

	Annual Growth	09/04	09/05	09/08	09/09	09/18
Sales ($ mil.)	5.6%	–	1,061.0	26.2	1,085.3	2,153.7
Net income ($ mil.)	9.1%	–	64.1	0.1	(71.4)	197.8
Market value ($ mil.)	–	–	–	–	–	–
Employees	–	–	–	–	–	9,000

NORTHSIDE HOSPITAL

6000 49TH ST N
SAINT PETERSBURG, FL 337092145
Phone: 727-521-4411
Fax: –
Web: www.northsidehospital.com

CEO: Valerie Stafford
CFO: Gary Searls
HR: Tammy Rodriguez
FYE: September 30
Type: Private

Hurting hearts aren't the only thing Northside Hospital can treat. The acute care facility which houses the Tampa Bay Heart Institute has some 290 beds and provides a gamut of medical services to the residents of Pinellas County Florida. The Heart Institute offers surgical diagnostic and rehabilitation services for cardiac patients. In addition to its cardiovascular expertise Northside Hospital offers specialized treatment for patients with spine disorders and chronic pain conditions as well as diagnostic imaging orthopedics rehabilitation urology outpatient surgery. Northside Hospital is part of the HCA family.

	Annual Growth	09/03	09/04	09/05	09/13	09/14
Sales ($ mil.)	–	–	–	0.0	120.3	140.7
Net income ($ mil.)	–	–	–	0.0	(2.0)	10.8
Market value ($ mil.)	–	–	–	–	–	–
Employees	–	–	–	–	–	340

NORTHSIDE HOSPITAL, INC.

1000 JOHNSON FERRY RD
ATLANTA, GA 303421611
Phone: 404-851-8000
Fax: –
Web: www.northside.com

CEO: Robert Putnam
CFO: Peggy Gatliff
HR: Barbara Schipani
FYE: September 30
Type: Private

Northside Hospital is no one-trick pony — it actually operates three hospitals serving Atlanta and surrounding areas. Also known as the Northside Healthcare Delivery System the Northside Hospital network includes some 840 licensed beds and more than 2500 physicians on multiple campuses with a host of outpatient health facilities including physician office parks and specialized cancer centers. All of Northside's hospitals are full-service acute-care facilities that provide specialty care including cancer care surgery radiology and women's health. Northside Hospital which opened in 1970 is merging with Gwinnett Health System.

	Annual Growth	09/12	09/13	09/15	09/16	09/17
Sales ($ mil.)	12.4%	–	1,253.5	1,733.0	1,897.7	2,002.9
Net income ($ mil.)	28.9%	–	109.1	223.3	157.6	301.4
Market value ($ mil.)	–	–	–	–	–	–
Employees	–	–	–	–	–	8,000

NORTHSTAR AEROSPACE INC.
TORONTO: NAS

6006 W. 73rd St.
Bedford Park IL 60638
Phone: 708-728-2000
Fax: 708-728-2009
Web: www.nsaero.com

CEO: –
CFO: –
HR: –
FYE: December 31
Type: Private

If you're sighting this Northstar you're probably an aerospace mechanic. Northstar Aerospace manufactures complex machined components for airplanes and helicopters. Primary products include helicopter transmissions helicopter rotor heads and shafts accessory gearboxes and components for auxiliary power units. Northstar also provides machining and fabrication services and maintenance repair and overhaul services (MRO). Clients include Boeing Sikorsky GE Aviation and Rolls-Royce. Northstar Aerospace voluntarily filed for Chapter 11 bankruptcy protection in 2012 and was acquired by affiliates of private equity firm Wynnchurch Capital for $70 million.

NORTHSTAR REALTY FINANCE CORP
NYS: NRF

399 Park Avenue, 18th Floor
New York, NY 10022
Phone: 212-547-2600
Fax: –
Web: www.nrfc.com

CEO: –
CFO: –
HR: –
FYE: December 31
Type: Public

Let NorthStar guide you to higher dividends. A real estate investment trust (REIT) NorthStar Realty manages a portfolio of commercial properties related securities and debt secured by commercial real estate. It largely funds its investments by issuing collateralized debt obligations (CDOs) under its N-Star brand. The REIT also manages and controls a fund it created in 2007 through which it conducts its securities investment activities; assets include mortgage-backed securities and fixed-income securities and equity issued by REITs. NorthStar invests in real estate throughout the US — mostly manufactured housing communities and healthcare properties that together account for more than 70% of its holdings.

	Annual Growth	12/10	12/11	12/12	12/13	12/14
Sales ($ mil.)	21.2%	453.7	527.8	504.7	596.6	978.4
Net income ($ mil.)	–	(389.6)	(242.5)	(273.1)	(87.9)	(321.1)
Market value ($ mil.)	38.7%	716.5	719.5	1,061.9	2,028.8	2,651.8
Employees	(28.3%)	91	107	124	155	24

NORTHWAY FINANCIAL, INC.   NBB: NWYF

9 Main Street   CEO: William J Woodward
Berlin, NH 03570   CFO: Richard P Orsillo
Phone: 603 752-1171   HR: –
Fax: –   FYE: December 31
                                      Type: Public

For managing finances way up north try Northway Financial. Northway Financial is the holding company for Northway Bank which operates about 20 branches in New Hampshire. The community-oriented bank serves individuals and local business customers by offering deposit products such as checking and savings accounts NOW and money market accounts CDs and IRAs. Lending activities mainly consist of residential and commercial mortgages which together account for about three-quarters of the company's loan portfolio; other offerings include construction business and consumer loans. The bank offers investments insurance and retirement services through an agreement with a third-party provider Infinex Financial.

	Annual Growth	12/14	12/15	12/16	12/17	12/18
Assets ($ mil.)	0.0%	925.7	933.6	889.6	884.1	926.9
Net income ($ mil.)	(21.8%)	7.9	6.5	4.0	7.3	2.9
Market value ($ mil.)	8.4%	56.3	59.2	73.8	86.7	77.6
Employees	–	–	–	–	–	–

NORTHWEST BANCORPORATION INC   NBB: NBCT

421 W. Riverside Ave.   CEO: –
Spokane, WA 99201-0403   CFO: –
Phone: 509 456-8888   HR: –
Fax: 509 742-6669   FYE: December 31
Web: www.inb.com   Type: Public

Who needs a map? Northwest Bancorporation is the holding company for Inland Northwest Bank which is proud to give directions within its name. The bank has some 16 locations in eastern Washington and the Idaho panhandle that serve individuals professionals and small to midsized businesses. It offers standard services such as checking and savings accounts money market accounts CDs and credit cards. The bank focuses on commercial lending mainly commercial mortgages construction loans business operating loans and lines of credit. It also writes residential mortgage auto home improvement and land loans.

	Annual Growth	12/12	12/13	12/14	12/15	12/16
Assets ($ mil.)	12.4%	398.9	394.2	421.8	610.8	636.5
Net income ($ mil.)	38.9%	1.4	3.3	3.3	3.1	5.1
Market value ($ mil.)	17.0%	35.3	47.8	55.5	62.6	66.1
Employees	(1.3%)	120	–	117	–	–

NORTHWEST BANCSHARES INC.   NASDAQ: NWBI

100 Liberty St.   CEO: William J Wagner
Warren PA 16365   CFO: William W Harvey Jr
Phone: 814-726-2140   HR: –
Fax: 814-728-7716   FYE: December 31
Web: www.northwestsavingsbank.com   Type: Public

Northwest Bancshares is the holding company for Northwest Savings Bank which operates about 170 branches mostly in Pennsylvania but also in northern Maryland western New York and eastern Ohio. Founded in 1896 the bank offers checking and savings accounts CDs credit cards and trust and investment management services. It mainly uses funds from deposits to write a variety of loans and to invest in mortgage-backed securities and municipal bonds. Real estate loans including one- to four-family residential mortgages home equity loans and commercial mortgages make up nearly 90% of the company's loan portfolio.

NORTHWEST BIOTHERAPEUTICS INC   NBB: NWBO

4800 Montgomery Lane, Suite 800   CEO: Linda F Powers
Bethesda, MD 20814   CFO: –
Phone: 240 497-9024   HR: –
Fax: –   FYE: December 31
Web: www.nwbio.com   Type: Public

Northwest Biotherapeutics is a development-stage drug company. Its DCVax vaccine platform uses dendritic cells (a type of white blood cell) obtained from a patient's blood to program that patient's own T cells to kill cancer cells. Northwest Biotherapeutics' two DCVax product candidates are being targeted to treat brain and prostate cancer. Both candidates are in late-stage clinical trials. If successful the therapies could work in conjunction with more traditional cancer treatments. Toucan Capital holds over 85% of the company's shares. Toucan's Cognate Therapeutics subsidiary manufactures the DCVax products and provides additional services to Northwest Biotherapeutics.

	Annual Growth	12/14	12/15	12/16	12/17	12/18
Sales ($ mil.)	(27.0%)	1.5	1.7	0.6	0.3	0.4
Net income ($ mil.)	–	(135.6)	(114.7)	(80.2)	(73.1)	(35.8)
Market value ($ mil.)	(56.0%)	2,877.8	2,877.8	182.1	123.1	107.5
Employees	3.9%	12	12	16	16	14

NORTHWEST COMMUNITY HOSPITAL INC

800 W CENTRAL RD   CEO: Stephen O. Scogna
ARLINGTON HEIGHTS, IL 600052349   CFO: Marsha Liu
Phone: 847-618-1000   HR: –
Fax: –   FYE: September 30
Web: www.nch.org   Type: Private

Northwest Community Healthcare (NCH) has captured the hearts of northern Illinois. Located in Chicago's northwest suburbs the not-for-profit health system includes the not-for-profit Northwest Community Hospital a regional leader in providing all kinds of cardiac care including open-heart surgery cardiac catheterization and rehabilitation services. Along with cardiac care the nearly 500-bed hospital offers a comprehensive range of acute medical and surgical care. NCH also operates NCH Medical Group which has more than 150 primary and specialty physicians in more than 20 medical offices. Other offerings include an ambulatory surgery center a handful of urgent care centers and a behavioral health center. NCH has more than 1200 physicians on its staff.

	Annual Growth	09/13	09/14	09/15	09/16	09/17
Sales ($ mil.)	1.5%	–	422.4	432.9	446.7	441.9
Net income ($ mil.)	–	–	25.1	24.3	15.8	(7.8)
Market value ($ mil.)	–	–	–	–	–	–
Employees	–	–	–	–	–	2,800

NORTHWEST DAIRY ASSOCIATION

5601 6TH AVE S STE 300   CEO: Jim Werkhoven
SEATTLE, WA 981082544   CFO: –
Phone: 206-284-7220   HR: –
Fax: –   FYE: March 31
Web: www.darigold.com   Type: Private

Northwest Dairy Association (NDA) members milk a lot of cows. The dairy cooperative's 550-plus member/farmers ship 7.2 billion pounds of milk annually which is processed by the co-op's subsidiary Darigold and packaged and sold under the Darigold label. NDA produces fluid and cultured dairy products including milk butter cottage cheese sour cream and yogurt that altogether generate some $2 billion in sales. It also makes bulk butter and cheese milk powder and whey products. The co-op caters to several sectors nationwide. Its customers include food retailers and wholesalers as well as foodservice and food-manufacturing companies. The association's membership spans half a dozen US states.

	Annual Growth	03/02	03/03	03/04	03/07	03/08
Sales ($ mil.)	14.1%	–	1,140.2	1,297.3	1,450.2	2,207.3
Net income ($ mil.)	107.0%	–	2.3	(6.4)	12.8	87.4
Market value ($ mil.)	–	–	–	–	–	–
Employees	–	–	–	–	–	1,300

NORTHWEST FARM CREDIT SERVICES

2001 S FLINT RD
SPOKANE, WA 992249198
Phone: 509-838-2429
Fax: –
Web: www.northwestfcs.com

CEO: –
CFO: Tom Nakano
HR: Alice Hardin
FYE: December 31
Type: Private

Customer-owned financial cooperative Northwest Farm Credit Services is an agricultural lender that provides financial services to farmers ranchers agribusinesses commercial fishermen timber producers and rural home owners in Alaska Idaho Montana Oregon and Washington. The company has a network of around 45 branches and offers a broad range of flexible loan programs to meet the needs of people in the agriculture business. Northwest Farm Credit also provides leasing services appraisal services and life mortgage disability and crop insurance as well as legal advocacy and assistance to customers in need. It is part of the Farm Credit System a network of lenders serving the US agriculture industry.

	Annual Growth	12/10	12/11	12/12	12/13	12/14
Assets ($ mil.)	5.6%	–	8,696.7	9,471.2	9,604.7	10,252.7
Net income ($ mil.)	12.7%	–	159.2	187.3	236.9	228.1
Market value ($ mil.)	–	–	–	–	–	–
Employees	–	–	–	–	–	500

NORTHWEST INDIANA BANCORP
NBB: NWIN

9204 Columbia Avenue
Munster, IN 46321
Phone: 219 836-4400
Fax: –
Web: www.ibankpeoples.com

CEO: –
CFO: Robert T Lowry
HR: –
FYE: December 31
Type: Public

NorthWest Indiana Bancorp is the holding company for Peoples Bank which serves individuals and businesses customers through about 10 branches in northwest Indiana's Lake County. The savings bank offers traditional deposit services such as checking and savings accounts money market accounts and CDs. It primarily uses the funds collected to originate loans secured by single-family residences and commercial real estate; it also makes construction consumer and business loans. The bank's Wealth Management Group provides retirement and estate planning investment accounts land trusts and profit-sharing and 401(k) plans.

	Annual Growth	12/14	12/15	12/16	12/17	12/18
Assets ($ mil.)	9.1%	775.0	864.9	913.6	927.3	1,096.2
Net income ($ mil.)	6.0%	7.4	7.9	9.1	9.0	9.3
Market value ($ mil.)	12.9%	80.3	93.3	117.7	134.8	130.3
Employees	9.1%	195	215	216	217	276

NORTHWEST NATURAL HOLDING CO
NYS: NWN

220 N.W. Second Avenue
Portland, OR 97209
Phone: 503 226-4211
Fax: –
Web: www.nwnatural.com

CEO: David H. Anderson
CFO: Brody J. Wilson
HR: –
FYE: December 31
Type: Public

Warmth in the Pacific Northwest comes naturally for Northwest Natural Gas which does business as NW Natural. The company provides natural gas to some 668800 residential 68000 commercial and 1000 industrial customers in Oregon and southwestern Washington through its 20000 miles of transmission and distribution mains and service lines. Responding to increased demand NW Natural is looking to expand its gas transportation and storage services through Gill Ranch Storage. It also owns pipeline investment company NNG Financial Corporation.

	Annual Growth	12/14	12/15	12/16	12/17	12/18
Sales ($ mil.)	(1.6%)	754.0	723.8	676.0	762.2	706.1
Net income ($ mil.)	2.4%	58.7	53.7	58.9	(55.6)	64.6
Market value ($ mil.)	4.9%	1,441.1	1,461.6	1,727.0	1,722.7	1,746.1
Employees	1.4%	1,103	1,076	1,123	1,160	1,167

NORTHWEST PIPE CO.
NMS: NWPX

201 NE Park Plaza Drive, Suite 100
Vancouver, WA 98684
Phone: 360 397-6250
Fax: 360 397-6257
Web: www.nwpipe.com

CEO: Scott J. Montross
CFO: Robin A. Gantt
HR: –
FYE: December 31
Type: Public

Northwest Pipe goes with the flow. It makes welded-steel water transmission lines that form the circulatory systems of water suppliers. Its transmission pipes are made to transport water under pressure and sold primarily to water utilities. Northwest Pipe also makes tubular products from 1.5 inches to 16 inches in diameter for the construction agriculture and energy markets. The Water Transmission Group is a top supplier of high pressure highly engineered steel pipe products. The Tubular Products Group operates three technologically-advanced Electric Resistance Weld (ERW) mill facilities. The Fabricated Products segment fabricates pressure vessels tanks steel pipe and miscellaneous metals products.

	Annual Growth	12/14	12/15	12/16	12/17	12/18
Sales ($ mil.)	(19.2%)	403.3	236.6	156.3	132.8	172.1
Net income ($ mil.)	–	(17.9)	(29.4)	(9.3)	(10.2)	20.3
Market value ($ mil.)	(6.2%)	293.2	108.9	167.6	186.3	226.7
Employees	(7.5%)	943	676	583	–	691

NORTHWEST TEXAS HEALTHCARE SYSTEM, INC.

1501 S COULTER ST
AMARILLO, TX 791061770
Phone: 806-354-1000
Fax: –
Web: www.nwths.com

CEO: Moody Chisholm
CFO: –
HR: –
FYE: December 31
Type: Private

Northwest Texas Healthcare has a (pan)handle on the medical problems of the state's northernmost region. Part of the Universal Health Services (UHS) health system Northwest Texas Healthcare System features the Northwest Texas Hospital and its related facilities and programs which serve residents in and around the Texas Panhandle city of Amarillo. The hospital is a 490-bed academic medical center features a behavioral health pavilion and provides emergency trauma diagnostic surgery and general inpatient care as well as about 50 medical specialties. Northwest Texas Healthcare operates various outpatient treatment and health awareness programs and services.

	Annual Growth	12/12	12/13	12/14	12/15	12/16
Sales ($ mil.)	6.1%	–	–	246.5	270.5	277.6
Net income ($ mil.)	–	–	–	12.2	23.4	(4.9)
Market value ($ mil.)	–	–	–	–	–	–
Employees	–	–	–	–	–	1,798

NORTHWESTERN CORP.
NYS: NWE

3010 W. 69th Street
Sioux Falls, SD 57108
Phone: 605 978-2900
Fax: –
Web: www.northwesternenergy.com

CEO: Robert C. (Bob) Rowe
CFO: Brian B. Bird
HR: Bobbi L. Schroeppel
FYE: December 31
Type: Public

NorthWestern once a holding company for several energy-related businesses is now blowing in one direction only — providing power and gas through regulated utilities. Through its NorthWestern Energy subsidiary the company provides electricity and natural gas to about 678200 customers in Montana Nebraska and South Dakota. In Montana it delivers electricity to approximately 344500 customers in 187 communities and surrounding rural areas 15 rural electric cooperatives and in Wyoming to Yellowstone National Park. NorthWestern delivers gas to 184300 customers in 105 Montana communities. It also distributes natural gas to 86700 customers in 60 Nebraska communities and four South Dakota communities.

	Annual Growth	12/14	12/15	12/16	12/17	12/18
Sales ($ mil.)	(0.3%)	1,204.9	1,214.3	1,257.2	1,305.7	1,192.0
Net income ($ mil.)	13.0%	120.7	151.2	164.2	162.7	197.0
Market value ($ mil.)	1.2%	2,847.3	2,730.1	2,861.9	3,004.3	2,991.2
Employees	(1.2%)	1,604	1,279	1,552	1,557	1,528

NORTHWESTERN LAKE FOREST HOSPITAL

660 N WESTMORELAND RD
LAKE FOREST, IL 600451696
Phone: 847-234-0945
Fax: –
Web: www.nm.org

CEO: Dean Harrison
CFO: –
HR: –
FYE: August 31
Type: Private

Northwestern Lake Forest Hospital brings good health to Illinois residents. The hospital is licensed for 117 acute care beds 40 skilled nursing care beds and 44 long-term care beds and provides acute long-term and other health care services to the residents of northeastern Illinois. It offers specialties as cancer and cardiovascular care speech therapy behavioral health and the Hunter Family Center for Women's Health. The hospital includes Westmoreland Nursing Home (senior and hospice care); it also operates a child care center a home health organization and several outpatient clinics. Northwestern Lake Forest Hospital is part of the Northwestern Memorial HealthCare system.

	Annual Growth	08/12	08/13	08/14	08/15	08/16
Sales ($ mil.)	7.2%	–	–	–	226.8	243.1
Net income ($ mil.)	67.0%	–	–	–	12.9	21.5
Market value ($ mil.)	–	–	–	–	–	–
Employees	–	–	–	–	–	1,700

NORTHWESTERN MEMORIAL HEALTHCARE

251 E HURON ST STE 3-710
CHICAGO, IL 606112908
Phone: 312-926-2000
Fax: –
Web: www.nm.org

CEO: Dean Harrison
CFO: –
HR: –
FYE: August 31
Type: Private

If you get blown over in the Windy City Northwestern Memorial HealthCare (NMHC) can get you upright again. Its primary facility Northwestern Memorial Hospital (NMH) is a teaching hospital serving residents of the Chicago area offering virtually every medical specialty. The hospital has more than 890 beds and is affiliated with Northwestern University's Feinberg School of Medicine. NMHC also operates the 200-bed Northwestern Lake Forest Hospital ambulatory surgery centers physicians' practices community clinics a home hospice program and health and wellness centers. Other subsidiaries of the NMHC health system include a philanthropic foundation an insurance company and a managed care contracts provider.

	Annual Growth	08/09	08/10	08/11	08/12	08/14
Sales ($ mil.)	108.0%	–	22.5	27.1	1,701.5	421.3
Net income ($ mil.)	184.3%	–	0.6	1.9	145.5	37.4
Market value ($ mil.)	–	–	–	–	–	–
Employees	–	–	–	–	–	20,000

NORTHWESTERN UNIVERSITY

633 CLARK ST
EVANSTON, IL 602080001
Phone: 847-491-3741
Fax: –

CEO: –
CFO: –
HR: Mikenzie Steffens
FYE: August 31
Type: Private

With its main campus in the Chicago suburb of Evanston Northwestern University (NU) serves its 21000 students through about a dozen schools and colleges such as the Medill School of Journalism and the McCormick School of Engineering and Applied Sciences. Its Chicago campus houses the schools of law and medicine as well as several hospitals of the McGaw Medical Center. With a faculty of more than 3300 the school has a student-to-teacher ratio of about 6:1. NU is home to several research centers and community outreach programs; it also has a branch in Qatar. It is the only private member of the Big 10 conference; varsity sports include baseball football basketball and fencing.

	Annual Growth	08/14	08/15	08/16	08/17	08/18
Sales ($ mil.)	6.7%	–	–	–	2,310.0	2,464.5
Net income ($ mil.)	(16.2%)	–	–	–	669.0	560.5
Market value ($ mil.)	–	–	–	–	–	–
Employees	–	–	–	–	–	5,954

NORTON COMMUNITY HOSPITAL AUXILIARY INC.

100 15TH ST NW
NORTON, VA 242731616
Phone: 276-679-9600
Fax: –
Web: www.nch.org

CEO: –
CFO: –
HR: –
FYE: September 30
Type: Private

Norton Community Hospital provides medical surgical and therapeutic services in southwest Virginia and southeast Kentucky. Established in 1949 as a hospital for miners Norton Community Hospital has grown to an acute care facility with some 130 beds. Specialized services include emergency medicine diagnostics pulmonary health orthopedics obstetrics cardiology psychiatry and oncology. The hospital which is an affiliate of the Mountain States Health Alliance also provides home health services through affiliate Community Home Care and it operates outpatient and family medicine clinics.

	Annual Growth	09/04	09/05*	06/07	06/08*	09/12
Sales ($ mil.)	–	–	(407.2)	–	39.4	53.4
Net income ($ mil.)	38.4%	–	–	–	2.6	9.4
Market value ($ mil.)	–	–	–	–	–	–
Employees	–	–	–	–	–	460

*Fiscal year change

NORTONLIFELOCK INC

NMS: NLOK

60 E. Rio Salado Parkway, Suite 1000
Tempe, AZ 85281
Phone: 650 527-8000
Fax: –
Web: www.symantec.com

CEO: Gregory (Greg) Clark
CFO: Nicholas R. (Nick) Noviello
HR: Amy Cappelanti-Wolf
FYE: March 29
Type: Public

Symantec offers security software for companies and consumers that protects against viruses detects attempted intrusions reduces spam and filters unwanted content. The company's Norton Security and LifeLock Identity Theft Protection products help consumers protect their devices identities online privacy and home networks. For commercial customers Symantec's Enterprise products offer similar protections on a grander scale as well as others such as network security and cloud security and threat intelligence. The company counts as customers some 350000 corporations and organizations and more than 50 million consumers. In 2019 Symantec agreed to sell its enterprise security business and its name to Broadcom for $10.7 billion.

	Annual Growth	04/15	04/16*	03/17	03/18	03/19
Sales ($ mil.)	(7.7%)	6,508.0	3,600.0	4,019.0	4,834.0	4,731.0
Net income ($ mil.)	(56.7%)	878.0	2,488.0	(106.0)	1,138.0	31.0
Market value ($ mil.)	(0.6%)	14,836.5	11,598.3	19,328.4	16,285.5	14,483.7
Employees	(11.0%)	19,000	11,000	13,000	11,800	11,900

*Fiscal year change

NORWEGIAN CRUISE LINE HOLDINGS LTD.

NASDAQ: NCLH

7665 Corporate Center Dr.
Miami FL 33126
Phone: 305-436-4000
Fax: 503-557-4501
Web: www.nortek-inc.com/cleanpak.html

CEO: Frank J Del Rio
CFO: Wendy Beck
HR: –
FYE: December 31
Type: Private

Norwegian Cruise Line Holdings is always ready to set sail on its next adventure. Incorporated in Bermuda but headquartered in Miami the holding company is a global cruise line operator through its subsidiaries with a fleet of about a dozen vessels and more than 26000 berths. Itineraries originate from 17 ports 10 of which are in North America. The company offers tours to such locales as Alaska the Bahamas Hawaii and South America. Norwegian Cruise Line markets a "freestyle cruising" concept which allows guests to casually roam eat and mingle at their leisure. After several failed attempts the company finally went public in 2013 with an offering worth $447 million.

NORWICH UNIVERSITY

158 HARMON DR
NORTHFIELD, VT 056631035
Phone: 802-485-2000
Fax: –
Web: www.norwich.edu

CEO: –
CFO: Richard E Rebmann
HR: –
FYE: May 31
Type: Private

Whether military man or regular old citizen Norwich University could be the perfect place to learn the ropes. As both a traditional and a military college Norwich accepts military and civilian students. The coeducational school has an undergraduate enrollment of about 2300. It offers 30 on-campus bachelor's programs a teacher lincensure program and four ROTC programs. Its five colleges include the College of Professional Schools and the College of Science and Mathematics. The university is the birthplace of the nation's Reserve Officers' Training Corps (ROTC) program. The oldest private military college in the US Norwich was founded in 1819 by Captain Alden Partridge.

	Annual Growth	05/14	05/15	05/16	05/17	05/18
Sales ($ mil.)	2.1%	–	101.2	103.7	108.0	107.8
Net income ($ mil.)	11.1%	–	13.3	(15.0)	20.3	18.2
Market value ($ mil.)	–	–	–	–	–	–
Employees	–	–	–	–	–	510

NORWOOD FINANCIAL CORP.   NMS: NWFL

717 Main Street
Honesdale, PA 18431
Phone: 570 253-1455
Fax: –
Web: www.waynebank.com

CEO: Lewis J Critelli
CFO: William S Lance
HR: –
FYE: December 31
Type: Public

Norwood Financial not Batman owns Wayne Bank. The bank serves individuals and local businesses through about 30 branches in northeastern Pennsylvania. It offers standard deposit products and services including checking and savings accounts money market savings accounts CDs and IRAs. Mortgages account for about 80% of Wayne Bank's loan portfolio. The bank also runs a trust and wealth management division; subsidiary Norwood Investment provides annuities and mutual funds; Norwood Settlement (70%-owned) offers title and settlement services. Norwood Financial bought Delaware Bancshares and its National Bank of Delaware County subsidiary in mid-2016; the purchase nearly doubled its branch network.

	Annual Growth	12/14	12/15	12/16	12/17	12/18
Assets ($ mil.)	13.6%	711.6	750.5	1,111.2	1,132.9	1,184.6
Net income ($ mil.)	15.6%	7.7	5.9	6.7	8.2	13.7
Market value ($ mil.)	3.2%	182.8	180.9	208.5	207.7	207.7
Employees	10.5%	141	145	215	214	210

NOTIFY TECHNOLOGY CORPORATION   OTC: NTFY

1054 S. De Anza Blvd. Ste. 105
San Jose CA 95129
Phone: 408-777-7920
Fax: 408-996-7405
Web: www.notifycorp.com

CEO: –
CFO: –
HR: –
FYE: September 30
Type: Public

Notify Technology is betting its future on wireless. Formerly a provider of messaging applications to telecommunications carriers the company has shifted efforts to developing products for the enterprise wireless market. Its NotifyLink application allows mobile employees to connect to their company's email server using wireless handhelds including Blackberry and iPhone devices. The product can be used with Novell GroupWise and Microsoft Exchange e-mail software as well as with offerings from Google Sun and Oracle. Director David Brewer controls about 56% of the company's outstanding shares.

NOVA SOUTHEASTERN UNIVERSITY, INC.

3301 COLLEGE AVE
DAVIE, FL 333147796
Phone: 954-262-7300
Fax: –
Web: www.nova.edu

CEO: George L. Hanbury
CFO: Alyson Silva
HR: Robert Pietrykowski
FYE: June 30
Type: Private

Nova Southeastern University (NSU) gives a whole new meaning to "school of sharks." NSU whose mascot is the deep sea predator has an enrollment of more than 27000 students and offers a variety of undergraduate graduate and professional academic programs. NSU offers degrees in several medical disciplines (osteopathic medicine pharmacy optometry nursing) marine biology business law education and computer sciences. The not-for-profit independent school operates four campuses in the Miami-Fort Lauderdale area several health centers and an oceanographic center. Founded in 1964 Nova University merged with Southeastern University of the Health Sciences in 1994 to become Nova Southeastern University.

	Annual Growth	06/08	06/09	06/10	06/12	06/15
Sales ($ mil.)	2.1%	–	–	612.4	689.2	678.2
Net income ($ mil.)	15.2%	–	–	22.5	48.9	45.6
Market value ($ mil.)	–	–	–	–	–	–
Employees	–	–	–	–	–	2,500

NOVABAY PHARMACEUTICALS INC   ASE: NBY

2000 Powell Street, Suite 1150
Emeryville, CA 94608
Phone: 510 899-8800
Fax: –
Web: www.novabay.com

CEO: Justin Hall
CFO: Jason Raleigh
HR: –
FYE: December 31
Type: Public

NovaBay Pharmaceuticals aims to keep the "bed bugs" away. The clinical-stage biopharmaceutical company develops antimicrobial compounds (known as Aganocide compounds) for the treatment and prevention of infections in hospital and non-hospital environments. Aganocide compounds destroy bacteria by attacking multiple sites and aim to treat and prevent bacterial fungal and viral infections. The compounds are intended to prevent infections resulting from surgical or other hospital procedures such as nasal surgery urinary tract catheterization and wound care as well as for use on patients with infections of the eyes ears sinuses or skin.

	Annual Growth	12/14	12/15	12/16	12/17	12/18
Sales ($ mil.)	85.6%	1.1	4.4	11.9	18.2	12.5
Net income ($ mil.)	–	(15.2)	(19.0)	(13.2)	(7.4)	(6.5)
Market value ($ mil.)	5.1%	10.8	34.5	56.4	65.8	13.2
Employees	17.3%	37	26	78	86	70

NOVANT HEALTH, INC.

2085 FRONTIS PLAZA BLVD
WINSTON SALEM, NC 271035614
Phone: 336-277-1404
Fax: –

CEO: Carl S. Armato
CFO: Fred M. Hargett
HR: Janet Smith-Hill
FYE: December 31
Type: Private

With 14 hospitals and about 2600 beds Novant Health certainly has what it takes to keep denizens along the Eastern Seaboard in tip-top condition. The not-for-profit health system provides medical care to residents in more than 30 counties throughout North and South Carolina Georgia and Virginia. Its largest facilities include the 920-bed Forsyth Medical Center in Winston-Salem North Carolina and the 600-bed Presbyterian Hospital in Charlotte North Carolina. It also operates about 340 physician clinics outpatient surgery and diagnostic imaging centers. Additionally Novant is home to nursing homes rehabilitation and community outreach programs and philanthropic foundations.

	Annual Growth	12/13	12/14	12/16	12/17	12/18
Sales ($ mil.)	–	–	0.0	4,340.1	167.6	4,985.9
Net income ($ mil.)	–	–	0.0	559.6	(142.3)	109.0
Market value ($ mil.)	–	–	–	–	–	–
Employees	–	–	–	–	–	13,800

NOVANTA INC

NMS: NOVT

125 Middlesex Turnpike
Bedford, MA 01730
Phone: 781 266-5700
Fax: 781 266-5114
Web: www.gsig.com

CEO: Matthijs Glastra
CFO: Robert Buckley
HR: –
FYE: December 31
Type: Public

Novanta's business is laser focused. The company uses its expertise in laser and motion control technologies to design and manufacture sets of products that are geared to the medical and healthcare and advanced industrial markets. Sealed CO2 lasers ultrafast lasers and optical light engines are sold primarily to the industrial and scientific markets. Novanta supplies lasers optics encoders and air bearing spindles to the healthcare and medical markets as well as the aerospace market for high-precision cutting drilling marking and measuring. The company changed its name to Novanta from GSI Group in mid-2016. International customers account for about 60% of sales.

	Annual Growth	12/14	12/15	12/16	12/17	12/18
Sales ($ mil.)	13.9%	364.7	373.6	384.8	521.3	614.3
Net income ($ mil.)	–	(24.3)	35.6	22.0	60.1	49.1
Market value ($ mil.)	43.8%	513.5	475.1	732.6	1,744.3	2,197.8
Employees	10.7%	1,418	1,355	1,269	2,034	2,133

NOVATION COMPANIES INC

NBB: NOVC

9229 Ward Parkway, Suite 340
Kansas City, MO 64114
Phone: 816 237-7000
Fax: –
Web: www.novationcompanies.com

CEO: Jeffrey E Eberwein
CFO: Carolyn K Campbell
HR: –
FYE: December 31
Type: Public

NovaStar Financial is forging a new life for itself — one with as little to do with subprime mortgages as possible. The firm bought originated serviced and securitized subprime mortgages until that sector experienced its own flameout. After exiting the lending business NovaStar began investing in other businesses to reinvent itself. In 2008 it acquired a majority of StreetLinks National Appraisal which provides property appraisals to residential mortgage lenders. The next year it bought a majority of Advent Financial Services a startup firm that provides banking services to low- and moderate-income consumers. NovaStar bought 51% of mortgage banking software provider Corvisa in late 2010.

	Annual Growth	12/14	12/15	12/16	12/17	12/18
Sales ($ mil.)	46.2%	12.1	6.1	5.1	28.0	55.1
Net income ($ mil.)	(33.3%)	30.9	(28.7)	5.2	(10.9)	6.1
Market value ($ mil.)	(47.0%)	27.8	12.6	4.6	6.7	2.2
Employees	91.4%	169	115	5	1,999	2,269

NOVAVAX, INC.

NMS: NVAX

20 Firstfield Road
Gaithersburg, MD 20878
Phone: 240 268-2000
Fax: –
Web: www.novavax.com

CEO: Stanley C. Erck
CFO: Barclay A. (Buck) Phillips
HR: –
FYE: December 31
Type: Public

Out to ax the dreaded flu is Novavax a producer of novel next-generation vaccines designed to prevent life-threatening infectious diseases such as the influenza virus. The clinical-stage company uses its own virus-like particle (VLP) technology that unlike traditional vaccines which are grown in chicken eggs use recombinant proteins grown from insect cell lines. Its manufacturing process is also faster and more flexible than traditional manufacturing methods — a fact that might help the vaccines succeed in combating fast-changing strains of pandemic influenza. Candidates in the company's pipeline include vaccines for seasonal and pandemic influenza Respiratory Syncytial virus (RSV) Varicella Zoster (shingles) and HIV.

	Annual Growth	12/14	12/15	12/16	12/17	12/18
Sales ($ mil.)	2.8%	30.7	36.3	15.4	31.2	34.3
Net income ($ mil.)	–	(82.9)	(156.9)	(280.0)	(183.8)	(184.7)
Market value ($ mil.)	(25.4%)	114.0	161.3	24.2	23.8	35.4
Employees	5.3%	308	443	355	347	379

NOVELIS INC.

3560 Lenox Rd. Ste. 2000
Atlanta GA 30326
Phone: 404-760-4000
Fax: 512-442-9342
Web: www.artzribhouse.com/

CEO: Steven Fisher
CFO: Devinder Ahuja
HR: –
FYE: March 31
Type: Subsidiary

Nothing can foil Novelis because it has the art of rolling aluminum in the can — the aluminum can that is. It is a global leader in aluminum rolled products and can recycling. A 2005 spinoff of what is now Rio Tinto Alcan it manufactures aluminum rolled semi-finished products used by the construction and industrial foil products transportation and beverage and food can industries. The rolled aluminum is made with alloy mixtures in a range of hardnesses thicknesses and widths with various coatings and finishes designed specifically for its end-use segments. The company also recycles more than 35 billion beverage cans annually. India's Hindalco Industries part of the Aditya Birla Group owns Novelis.

NPC INTERNATIONAL INC.

7300 W. 129th St.
Overland Park KS 66213
Phone: 913-327-5555
Fax: 913-327-5850
Web: www.npcinternational.com

CEO: –
CFO: Troy D Cook
HR: –
FYE: December 31
Type: Private

NPC International is the prince of pepperoni in a pizza empire. The world's largest franchisee of Pizza Hut restaurants NPC owns and operates more than 1230 pizza restaurants and delivery kitchens in about 30 states. The quick-service eateries located mostly in such southern states as Alabama Florida Georgia and Tennessee serve a variety of pizza styles as well as such items as buffalo wings and pasta. The pizza parlors are franchised from YUM! Brands the world's largest fast-food restaurant company. NPC was founded in 1962 by former chairman Gene Bicknell who was one of the first Pizza Hut franchisees. The company was acquired by private equity group NPC International Holdings in late 2011.

NPC RESTAURANT HOLDINGS, LLC

7300 W 129TH ST
OVERLAND PARK, KS 662132631
Phone: 913-327-5555
Fax: –
Web: www.npcinternational.com

CEO: –
CFO: Troy D Cook
HR: –
FYE: December 27
Type: Private

NPC International is the prince of pepperoni in a pizza empire. The world's largest franchisee of Pizza Hut restaurants NPC owns and operates more than 1275 pizza restaurants and delivery kitchens in about 30 states. The quick-service eateries located mostly in such southern states as Alabama Florida Georgia and Tennessee serve a variety of pizza styles as well as such items as buffalo wings and pasta. The pizza parlors are franchised from YUM! Brands the world's largest fast-food restaurant company. NPC was founded in 1962 by former chairman Gene Bicknell who was one of the first Pizza Hut franchisees. The company was acquired by private equity group NPC International Holdings in late 2011.

	Annual Growth	12/12	12/13	12/14	12/15	12/16
Sales ($ mil.)	4.2%	–	1,094.0	1,179.9	1,223.3	1,236.6
Net income ($ mil.)	(33.5%)	–	29.7	1.7	6.7	8.7
Market value ($ mil.)	–	–	–	–	–	–
Employees	–	–	–	–	–	29,000

NPS PHARMACEUTICALS INC.
NMS: NPSP

550 Hills Drive
Bedminster, NJ 07921
Phone: 908 450-5300
Fax: –
Web: www.npsp.com

CEO: Flemming Ornskov
CFO: –
HR: –
FYE: December 31
Type: Public

Those suffering from intestinal failure are rooting for NPS Pharmaceuticals. The drug development company has a handful of candidates in development for gastrointestinal and endocrine disorders focusing on rare conditions with few available treatment options. Lead candidates Gattex (teduglutide) is a treatment for short bowel syndrome a rare gastrointestinal disorder. Another Natpara is being studied as a treatment for a hormone deficiency disorder known as hyperparathyroidism. The company outsources much of its research; it also often partners with or licenses candidates to larger firms to help fund late-stage development and commercialization efforts. Shire is buying NPS Pharma for $5.2 billion.

	Annual Growth	12/09	12/10	12/11	12/12	12/13
Sales ($ mil.)	16.6%	84.1	89.4	101.6	130.6	155.6
Net income ($ mil.)	–	(17.9)	(31.4)	(36.3)	(18.7)	(13.5)
Market value ($ mil.)	72.9%	348.9	810.6	676.2	933.8	3,115.4
Employees	40.6%	53	63	86	149	207

NRG ENERGY INC
NYS: NRG

804 Carnegie Center
Princeton, NJ 08540
Phone: 609 524-4500
Fax: –
Web: www.nrgenergy.com

CEO: Mauricio Gutierrez
CFO: Kirkland B. Andrews
HR: –
FYE: December 31
Type: Public

NRG Energy is a leading power producer with a generating capacity of 28000 MW (including 1600 MW of solar power assets). The vast majority of NRG's power plants are in North America but it also has one in Australia and one in Turkey. Its portfolio includes 50 power plants. It also markets natural gas oil and other commodities. NRG's retail units (including Reliant Energy and Green Mountain Energy) distribute power to about 3 million customers across the US.

	Annual Growth	12/14	12/15	12/16	12/17	12/18
Sales ($ mil.)	(12.1%)	15,868.0	14,674.0	12,351.0	10,629.0	9,478.0
Net income ($ mil.)	18.9%	134.0	(6,382.0)	(774.0)	(2,153.0)	268.0
Market value ($ mil.)	10.1%	7,644.4	3,338.6	3,477.5	8,078.4	11,232.5
Employees	(16.1%)	9,806	10,468	8,763	5,940	4,862

NSTAR ELECTRIC CO
NBB: NSAR O

800 Boylston Street
Boston, MA 02199
Phone: 800 286-5000
Fax: –
Web: www.nstar.com

CEO: Leon J Olivier
CFO: James J Judge
HR: –
FYE: December 31
Type: Public

NSTAR Electric plays a starring role in bringing electric power to Boston. The NSTAR company's electric transmission and distribution utility serves 1.1 million residential commercial and industrial customers in Beantown and about 80 surrounding communities (including Cambridge New Bedford and Plymouth). NSTAR Electric also sells wholesale power to municipal utilities in the area and it provides standard offer and default supply services to retail customers who choose not to purchase energy from competitive suppliers in the state's deregulated power market. Subsidiary Harbor Electric Energy distributes power to a Massachusetts Water Resources Authority wastewater treatment facility in Boston.

	Annual Growth	12/14	12/15	12/16	12/17	12/18
Sales ($ mil.)	5.3%	2,536.7	2,681.3	2,557.9	2,980.6	3,112.9
Net income ($ mil.)	6.0%	303.1	344.5	292.7	374.7	383.1
Market value ($ mil.)	–	0.0	0.0	0.0	0.0	0.0
Employees	(1.5%)	1,717	1,240	1,627	1,922	1,618

NTELOS HOLDINGS CORP
NMS: NTLS

1154 Shenandoah Village Drive
Waynesboro, VA 22980
Phone: 540 946-3500
Fax: –
Web: www.ntelos.com

CEO: –
CFO: Adele Skolits
HR: –
FYE: December 31
Type: Public

NTELOS communicates over the hills and through the woods of the Virginias (and in other US states). The company serves more than 460000 wireless subscribers in Virginia and West Virginia as well as portions of Maryland North Carolina Ohio and Pennsylvania. Wireless operations include its FRAWG and nTelos-branded retail business as well as a wholesale business it operates under a contract with Sprint. In 2013 the company had 1444 cell sites in operation of which 120 sites were company owned. It conducts its business through NTELOS-branded retail operations which sell products and services via direct and indirect distribution channels and provides network access to other telecommunications carriers most notably through an arrangement with Sprint.

	Annual Growth	12/10	12/11	12/12	12/13	12/14
Sales ($ mil.)	(2.8%)	545.7	422.6	454.0	491.9	487.8
Net income ($ mil.)	–	44.8	(23.7)	18.4	24.7	(53.6)
Market value ($ mil.)	(31.5%)	411.8	440.5	283.4	437.3	90.6
Employees	(14.5%)	1,600	975	960	970	854

NTN BUZZTIME INC
ASE: NTN

1800 Aston Avenue, Suite 100
Carlsbad, CA 92008
Phone: 760 438-7400
Fax: 760 438-7470
Web: www.buzztime.com

CEO: Allen Wolff
CFO: Allen Wolff
HR: –
FYE: December 31
Type: Public

NTN Buzztime doesn't see its knowledge contests as mere trivial pursuits. The company distributes interactive trivia and sports games to almost 4000 bars and restaurants in the US and Canada through its Buzztime Network. Players use wireless game controllers or mobile phones to play along with the Buzztime games displayed on television screens. The majority of the company's revenue comes from recurring subscription fees paid by hospitality firms. About 35% of the company's Buzztime Network subscribers are national chains including Hooters and Buffalo Wild Wings. NTN has promotional and marketing partnerships with some of its biggest customers and generates revenue through advertising and marketing services.

	Annual Growth	12/14	12/15	12/16	12/17	12/18
Sales ($ mil.)	(2.7%)	26.0	24.5	22.3	21.3	23.3
Net income ($ mil.)	–	(5.0)	(7.2)	(2.9)	(1.1)	(0.3)
Market value ($ mil.)	44.1%	1.3	0.5	24.4	12.1	5.6
Employees	(7.0%)	375	357	402	446	281

NTS INC
ASE: NTS

1220 Broadway
Lubbock, TX 79401
Phone: 806 771-5212
Fax: –
Web: www.ntscom.com

CEO: Brad D Worthington
CFO: –
HR: –
FYE: December 31
Type: Public

Xfone USA offers alternative local and long-distance services to residential and business customers in the south eastern US. The company is certified as a competitive local-exchange carrier in Louisiana Texas and its home state of Mississippi. In addition to traditional phone services Xfone USA offers cable TV and broadband Internet access. Commercial clients include planned communities and apartment buildings. The company also provides such business-oriented services as Web design and hosting as well as data network maintenance and support. Xfone USA is a subsidiary of Texas-based Xfone Inc.

	Annual Growth	12/08	12/09	12/10	12/11	12/12
Sales ($ mil.)	(9.8%)	90.3	85.0	58.9	57.7	59.9
Net income ($ mil.)	–	2.0	(22.2)	(4.6)	(1.2)	(0.5)
Market value ($ mil.)	3.1%	31.3	28.8	50.7	16.5	35.4
Employees	(12.3%)	391	372	294	310	231

NTS REALTY HOLDINGS LTD PARTNERSHIP — ASE: NLP

600 North Hurstbourne Parkway, Suite 300
Louisville, KY 40222
Phone: 502 426-4800
Fax: 502 426-4994
Web: www.ntsdevelopment.com

CEO: Brian F Lavin
CFO: Gregory A Wells
HR: –
FYE: December 31
Type: Public

NTS Realty Holdings invests in develops and manages commercial real estate in the Southeast and Midwest. The company's portfolio includes some 25 properties including about 15 dozen apartment communities about a half-dozen office centers and three retail properties in Kentucky Florida Indiana Tennessee Virginia and Georgia. Chairman J.D. Nichols owns about 60% of NTS Realty Holdings; he and president Brian Lavin control the company's managing general partner NTS Realty Capital. The firm's properties are managed by NTS Development Company an affiliate of NTS Realty Capital. Established in 2004 NTS Realty Holdings is the result of the merger of several property companies and partnerships.

	Annual Growth	12/08	12/09	12/10	12/11	12/12
Sales ($ mil.)	8.3%	41.6	44.5	47.9	54.6	57.3
Net income ($ mil.)	–	7.7	(17.2)	(11.4)	(12.0)	(12.0)
Market value ($ mil.)	19.5%	38.9	49.6	39.7	36.2	79.4
Employees	–	–	–	–	–	–

NU HORIZONS ELECTRONICS CORP.

70 Maxess Rd.
Melville NY 11747
Phone: 631-396-5000
Fax: 631-396-5050
Web: www.nuhorizons.com

CEO: Martin Kent
CFO: Kurt Freudenberg
HR: –
FYE: February 28
Type: Subsidiary

Nu Horizons sees new electronic components on the horizon. The company distributes semiconductors display lighting and power components from manufacturers that include Atmel Connect Tech IXYS Marvell Micron Renesas Silicon Image GE Energy and LG Display. It targets the audio/visual (broadcast consumer surveillance) energy (generation distribution alternative building automation smart metering) and medical (home health imaging patient monitoring instruments) industries. Nu Horizons also value-added services that include device programming materials management packaging tape and reel and display integration. Rival Arrow Electronics bought the company for about $161 million in 2011.

NU SKIN ENTERPRISES, INC. — NYS: NUS

75 West Center Street
Provo, UT 84601
Phone: 801 345-1000
Fax: –
Web: www.nuskin.com

CEO: Ritch N. Wood
CFO: Mark H. Lawrence
HR: –
FYE: December 31
Type: Public

Nu Skin Enterprises offers more than 200 personal care products such as cleansers toners and anti-aging skin care products through a global network of independent distributors sales reps and preferred customers. It also sells cosmetics fragrances hair care items and mouthwash. Nu Skin has its foot in the door in 50-plus global markets including China. Its Pharmanex unit sells LifePak nutritional supplements. In addition the company has introduced its new ageLOC Youth nutritional supplement and ageLOC Me customized skin care system to its markets. Nu Skin was founded in 1984 by its former chairman Blake Roney.

	Annual Growth	12/14	12/15	12/16	12/17	12/18
Sales ($ mil.)	1.0%	2,569.5	2,247.0	2,207.8	2,279.1	2,679.0
Net income ($ mil.)	(10.4%)	189.2	133.0	143.1	129.4	121.9
Market value ($ mil.)	8.8%	2,421.0	2,099.1	2,647.0	3,779.9	3,397.7
Employees	(0.5%)	5,000	4,800	4,650	4,700	4,900

NUANCE COMMUNICATIONS INC — NMS: NUAN

1 Wayside Road
Burlington, MA 01803
Phone: 781 565-5000
Fax: –
Web: www.nuance.com

CEO: Paul A. Ricci
CFO: Daniel D. (Dan) Tempesta
HR: Mike Gmiterek
FYE: September 30
Type: Public

Nuance Communications helps machines navigate the subtleties of human speech. The company develops speech recognition systems for applications in customer service consumer electronics healthcare financial services and automotive. It employs artificial intelligence cognitive science and machine learning in developing its products with some 2100 language experts on staff. Nuance has customers worldwide although most of its revenue comes from the US. In 2018 Nuance began to sell or spin off non-core businesses to focus on AI-powered speech and cloud technologies. Nuance technologies conduct about 16 billion self-service transactions a year.

	Annual Growth	09/15	09/16	09/17	09/18	09/19
Sales ($ mil.)	(1.4%)	1,931.1	1,948.9	1,939.4	2,051.7	1,823.1
Net income ($ mil.)	–	(115.0)	(12.5)	(151.0)	(159.9)	213.8
Market value ($ mil.)	(0.1%)	4,680.7	4,146.0	4,494.8	4,952.3	4,663.5
Employees	(12.0%)	13,500	13,200	11,600	10,400	8,100

NUCO2 INC.

2800 SE Market Place
Stuart FL 34997
Phone: 772-221-1754
Fax: 772-781-3500
Web: www.nuco2.com

CEO: –
CFO: –
HR: Elizabeth Amber
FYE: June 30
Type: Private

NuCO2 puts tiny bubbles in the soda. The company supplies liquid carbon dioxide (bulk CO2) for carbonating and dispensing fountain drinks which differs from the traditional method of carbonation that uses high-pressure CO2. Its more than 130000 customers include restaurants (Pizza Hut) retailers (Costco) convenience stores (7-Eleven) movie theaters (Loews Cineplex) and stadiums and arenas (Madison Square Garden). NuCO2's services include system installation and maintenance product delivery and technical support. Its products are used by 30 million consumers a day. In 2013 Praxair acquired NuCO2 Inc. for $1.1 billion.

NUCOR CORP. — NYS: NUE

1915 Rexford Road
Charlotte, NC 28211
Phone: 704 366-7000
Fax: 704 362-4208
Web: www.nucor.com

CEO: John J. Ferriola
CFO: James D. (Jim) Frias
HR: –
FYE: December 31
Type: Public

Nucor Corporation is a leading manufacturer trader and seller of steel and steel products in the US. It is also North America's largest recycler of scrap metal and a leading scrap broker. The company produces rolled sheets bars and beams used in the energy automotive transportation and heavy equipment industries. Its other steel products including steel joists electrical conduits and metal building systems are sold to fabricators distributors and metal manufacturers. Subsidiary Harris Steel fabricates rebar for highways and bridges and other construction projects. Another unit the David J. Joseph Company processes and brokers metals pig iron hot briquetted iron and direct reduced iron (DRI).

	Annual Growth	12/14	12/15	12/16	12/17	12/18
Sales ($ mil.)	4.4%	21,105.1	16,439.3	16,208.1	20,252.4	25,067.3
Net income ($ mil.)	34.8%	713.9	357.7	796.3	1,318.7	2,360.8
Market value ($ mil.)	1.4%	14,989.3	12,315.4	18,188.8	19,429.5	15,832.7
Employees	2.7%	23,600	23,700	23,900	25,100	26,300

NUO THERAPEUTICS INC
NBB: AURX

8285 El Rio, Suite 150
Houston, TX 77054
Phone: 240 499-2680
Fax: –
Web: www.nuot.com

CEO: David E Jorden
CFO: David E Jorden
HR: –
FYE: December 31
Type: Public

Here's a concept — using the body's own faculties to heal wounds. Nuo Therapeutics has developed and markets an autologous platelet therapy which uses a patient's own blood plasma to promote healing. Its AutoloGel System includes a centrifuge and blood draw kit. The centrifuge is used to separate key blood components including platelets and growth factors which are then combined with reagents to make a topical gel. When applied to a wound the gel spurs the body's own healing process. AutoloGel has received FDA approval to treat chronic exuding wounds such as diabetic ulcers. Other products in Nuo's pipeline include an anti-inflammatory peptide that may help treat such diseases as rheumatoid arthritis.

	Annual Growth	12/15*	05/16*	12/16	12/17	12/18
Sales ($ mil.)	(50.8%)	11.5	1.7	0.5	0.7	1.4
Net income ($ mil.)	–	(52.8)	28.2	(5.7)	(15.0)	(1.5)
Market value ($ mil.)	(71.0%)	–	–	–	3.1	0.9
Employees	(29.5%)	20	–	19	15	7

*Fiscal year change

NUSTAR ENERGY LP
NYS: NS

19003 IH-10 West
San Antonio, TX 78257
Phone: 210 918-2000
Fax: –
Web: www.nustarenergy.com

CEO: Bradley C. (Brad) Barron
CFO: Thomas R. (Tom) Shoaf
HR: Bob Grimes
FYE: December 31
Type: Public

NuStar Energy is following its pipelines to terminals in pursuit of energy profits. The company is one of the largest independent pipeline and terminal operators in the US managing about 9800 miles of refined products pipelines more than 2000 miles of anhydrous ammonia pipelines and some 2000 miles of crude oil pipelines. The pipelines generally deliver their contents to about 75 terminals and storage facilities. Overall NuStar has about 74 million barrels of storage capacity at its terminals. The company which generates more than three-quarters of its revenue in the US also has operations in Mexico and Canada.

	Annual Growth	12/14	12/15	12/16	12/17	12/18
Sales ($ mil.)	(10.6%)	3,075.1	2,084.0	1,756.7	1,814.0	1,961.8
Net income ($ mil.)	(0.6%)	210.8	306.7	150.0	148.0	205.8
Market value ($ mil.)	(22.4%)	6,192.3	4,299.7	5,339.8	3,211.4	2,244.2
Employees	5.4%	1,227	1,644	1,661	1,694	1,517

NUSTAR GP HOLDINGS LLC
NYS: NSH

19003 IH-10 West
San Antonio, TX 78257
Phone: 210 918-2000
Fax: –
Web: www.nustargpholdings.com

CEO: Bradley C Barron
CFO: Thomas R Shoaf
HR: –
FYE: December 31
Type: Public

NuStar GP Holdings owns a 2% general-partner interest and a 17% limited-partner interest in NuStar Energy which operates terminals and petroleum-liquids pipeline systems primarily in the US. NuStar Energy has 7480 miles of refined product and ammonia pipelines 940 miles of crude oil pipelines 96 refined product terminal facilities a crude oil storage facility and two asphalt refineries. It also has terminals in Canada Mexico the Netherlands Turkey and the UK. Valero GP Holdings was controlled by Valero Energy. Following Valero GP Holdings' 2006 IPO Valero Energy sold its interest in both Valero L.P. and Valero GP Holdings. In 2007 Valero GP Holdings changed its name to NuStar GP Holdings LLC.

	Annual Growth	12/12	12/13	12/14	12/15	12/16
Sales ($ mil.)	–	(4.6)	(6.7)	65.4	79.7	56.1
Net income ($ mil.)	125.5%	2.1	(11.0)	61.4	72.2	55.1
Market value ($ mil.)	1.1%	1,189.3	1,206.5	1,478.4	908.4	1,241.3
Employees	(5.4%)	1,478	1,221	1,227	1,251	–

NUTRA PHARMA CORP
NBB: NPHC

12538 West Atlantic Blvd.
Coral Springs, FL 33071
Phone: 954 509-0911
Fax: –
Web: www.nutrapharma.com

CEO: Rik J Deitsch
CFO: Jason Barry
HR: –
FYE: December 31
Type: Public

Nutra Pharma is a biotechnology holding company active in several areas. The company's ReceptoPharm subsidiary holds a pipeline of drug candidates that may eventually treat HIV/AIDS rabies and other viral and neurological diseases as well as pain. Another subsidiary NanoLogix develops diagnostic test kits to identify infectious diseases while its Designer Diagnostics subsidiary markets and sells the test kits. One product in development as a possible therapy for MS was based upon cobra venom. That product was then reformulated and launched commercially as an over-the-counter topical analgesic for chronic pain under the brand name Cobroxin.

	Annual Growth	12/13	12/14	12/15	12/16	12/17
Sales ($ mil.)	(0.3%)	0.1	0.6	0.3	0.2	0.1
Net income ($ mil.)	–	(4.3)	(2.5)	(5.4)	(3.4)	(4.0)
Market value ($ mil.)	(44.9%)	15.2	11.6	112.8	16.7	1.4
Employees	7.5%	3	5	4	4	4

NUTRACEUTICAL INTERNATIONAL CORP.
NMS: NUTR

1400 Kearns Boulevard, 2nd Floor
Park City, UT 84060
Phone: 435 655-6106
Fax: –
Web: www.nutraceutical.com

CEO: Frank W Gay II
CFO: Cory J McQueen
HR: –
FYE: September 30
Type: Public

Nutraceutical International manufactures markets and even retails a world of nutritional supplements vitamins minerals body care products and diet and energy products in the US and abroad. Its branded products include such names as KAL Herbs for Kids Nature's Life Solaray Sunny Green and VegLife. Its company-owned US retail stores include Cornucopia Community Market Granola's and The Real Food Company while its Au Naturel unit markets the company's brands in about 70 other countries. Nutraceutical International also publishes natural health books under the Woodland name. The acquisitive company is actively buying up and integrating smaller firms.

	Annual Growth	09/12	09/13	09/14	09/15	09/16
Sales ($ mil.)	3.8%	200.4	208.4	214.5	216.5	233.0
Net income ($ mil.)	4.3%	15.8	17.0	15.9	15.3	18.7
Market value ($ mil.)	18.6%	145.1	218.5	192.5	217.3	287.5
Employees	0.8%	862	832	913	845	890

NUTRISYSTEM INC
NMS: NTRI

Fort Washington Executive Center, 600 Office Center Drive
Fort Washington, PA 19034
Phone: 215 706-5300
Fax: –
Web: www.nutrisystem.com

CEO: Dawn M Zier
CFO: Michael P Monahan
HR: –
FYE: December 31
Type: Public

Nutrisystem helps its customers trim their waistline morning noon and night. It promotes weight loss by selling prepared meals and grocery items that are delivered directly to US consumers. Customers order monthly food packages consisting of 28 days of portion-controlled items such as a breakfast lunch dinner and dessert supplemented with fruits and vegetables. It also offers individualized calorie plans one-on-one diet counseling behavior modification and exercise education and maintenance plans. Nutrisystem also sells its weight-management products through a partnership with TV marketer QVC (3% of revenue) and club retailers the likes of Costco. Tivity Health is buying Nutrisystem for $1.4 billion.

	Annual Growth	12/13	12/14	12/15	12/16	12/17
Sales ($ mil.)	18.1%	358.1	403.1	462.6	545.5	697.0
Net income ($ mil.)	67.4%	7.4	19.3	26.1	35.5	57.9
Market value ($ mil.)	33.7%	494.0	587.5	650.3	1,041.2	1,580.6
Employees	9.0%	430	417	451	487	606

NUTRITION 21 LLC
OTC: NXXI

4 Manhattanville Rd.
Purchase NY 10577-2197
Phone: 914-701-4500
Fax: 914-696-0860
Web: www.nutrition21.com

CEO: –
CFO: –
HR: –
FYE: June 30
Type: Private

Nutrition 21 believes in the power of chromium picolinate. The company primarily makes and sells this and other ingredients used in dietary supplement products. It supplies some 80% of the chromium picolinate (sold as Chromax) used in US dietary supplements. Other ingredient products include manganese selenium and zinc all of which are stirred into dietary supplements. In addition to selling ingredients the company supports the health claims for its products with clinical trials. After struggling under a debt burden in mid-2011 Nutrition 21 filed for Chapter 11 bankruptcy protection. In late 2011 the company's assets were purchased by a private investment group.

NUTRITION MANAGEMENT SERVICES COMPANY
PINK SHEETS: NMSCA

725 Kimberton Rd.
Kimberton PA 19442
Phone: 610-935-2050
Fax: 610-935-8287
Web: www.nmsc.com

CEO: Joseph V Roberts
CFO: –
HR: Barb Preston
FYE: June 30
Type: Public

Nutrition Management Services is a regional foodservices operator that provides retirement communities hospitals and other health care facilities with food management services. It offers supervision of dietary operations through onsite management cost and quality controls and dietary staff training. In addition the company operates a conference center and banquet facility used for training. Chairman and CEO Joseph Roberts controls nearly 75% of Nutrition Management Services.

NUTROGANICS INC
NBB: NUTT Q

20270 Goldenrod Lane
Germantown, MD 20876-4070
Phone: 301 540-5500
Fax: 301 540-5557
Web: www.mlog.com

CEO: Richard E Meccariella
CFO: –
HR: –
FYE: December 31
Type: Public

Microlog develops software that helps businesses and other organizations keep track of the tiny details involved in providing a good customer service experience. The company's ServiceFirst and Tereleminder-branded applications provide a single software environment for managing customer contact via voice email Web and fax. It also offers consulting training and technical support services. Microlog serves such industries as health care and education as well as state and local government agencies. Clients have included the US Department of Homeland Security the University of New Mexico and Walter Reed Army Medical Center.

	Annual Growth	10/03*	12/12	12/13	12/14	12/15
Sales ($ mil.)	7.0%	5.1	0.9	2.1	7.5	11.4
Net income ($ mil.)	–	(0.4)	(0.5)	(0.2)	(1.1)	(3.3)
Market value ($ mil.)	(3.8%)	14.8	7.9	15.1	6.5	9.3
Employees	–	23	–	–	–	–

*Fiscal year change

NUVASIVE INC
NMS: NUVA

7475 Lusk Boulevard
San Diego, CA 92121
Phone: 858 909-1800
Fax: 800 475-9134
Web: www.nuvasive.com

CEO: Gregory T. Lucier
CFO: Rajesh J. (Raj) Asarpota
HR: Carol Cox
FYE: December 31
Type: Public

When a back is seriously out of whack NuVasive has some options. The company makes and markets medical devices for the surgical treatment of spinal disorders. NuVasive's products are primarily used in spinal restoration and fusion surgeries. Its minimally disruptive Maximum Access Surgery (MAS) platform enables surgeons to access the spine from the side of the body instead of from the front or back helping them to avoid hitting nerves. NuVasive also features a line of biologic bone grafting materials — both allograft and synthetic — and has a cervical disc replacement system in development. The company sells its FDA-approved products through a network of exclusive sales agents supported by an in-house sales team.

	Annual Growth	12/14	12/15	12/16	12/17	12/18
Sales ($ mil.)	9.6%	762.4	811.1	962.1	1,029.5	1,101.7
Net income ($ mil.)	–	(16.7)	66.3	37.1	83.0	12.5
Market value ($ mil.)	1.2%	2,671.5	3,065.2	3,815.8	3,313.3	2,807.5
Employees	14.7%	1,500	1,600	2,200	2,600	2,600

NUVEEN INVESTMENTS INC.

333 W. Wacker Dr.
Chicago IL 60606
Phone: 312-917-7700
Fax: 312-917-8049
Web: www.nuveen.com

CEO: John P Amboian
CFO: –
HR: –
FYE: December 31
Type: Private

Chicago-based Nuveen Investments once financed the growth of its hometown and other cities by underwriting and trading municipal bonds. Nuveen has since parlayed its investment banking experience into a career as a money manager specializing in municipal bond and stock portfolios for high-net-worth and institutional investors in the US. Offering more than 100 mutual funds about 120 closed-end funds as well as separate accounts and managed accounts the company sells its products through banks brokerages insurance agents and other financial services providers. It has more than $210 billion of assets under management. An investor group led by private equity firm Madison Dearborn Partners owns Nuveen.

NUVERA COMMUNICATIONS INC
NBB: NUVR

27 North Minnesota Street
New Ulm, MN 56073
Phone: 507 354-4111
Fax: –
Web: www.nuvera.net

CEO: Glenn Zerbe
CFO: Curtis O Kawlewski
HR: –
FYE: December 31
Type: Public

New Ulm Telecom operates three incumbent local-exchange carriers (ILECs) serving southern Minnesota and northern Iowa: an ILEC serving New Ulm Minnesota and surrounding communities; subsidiary Western Telephone operating in the Springfield Minnesota area; and Peoples Telephone serving portions of Cherokee and Buena Vista counties in Iowa. Operating under the common NU-Telecom brand they make up New Ulm's Telecom Segment and provide traditional phone services such as local exchange access and long-distance as well as cable TV and Internet access. The company's Phonery division provides customer premise equipment (CPE) offers transport services and resells long distance toll services.

	Annual Growth	12/14	12/15	12/16	12/17	12/18
Sales ($ mil.)	9.1%	40.0	41.7	42.3	46.9	56.7
Net income ($ mil.)	29.7%	2.7	2.7	2.9	10.0	7.8
Market value ($ mil.)	25.8%	37.8	37.8	50.1	91.7	94.7
Employees	3.8%	148	146	145	134	172

NUVILEX INC.

PINK SHEETS: NVLX

1971 Old Cuthbert Rd.
Cherry Hill NJ 08034
Phone: 856-354-0707
Fax: 856-354-1077
Web: www.nuvilex.com

CEO: Kenneth L Waggoner
CFO: Carlos A Trujillo
HR: –
FYE: April 30
Type: Public

Nuvilex is out to fill niche markets with its products. The company makes and sells a handful of items that can be classified as a couple of parts nutraceutical a part dermatological and a little bit environmental. Nuvilex's products are sold worldwide and include nutritional supplements Cinnergen and Cinnechol tattoo ink Infinitink and scar cream Talysn. Nuvilex has also developed an environmentally safe germicidal topical spray that kills some of the most frequent bacterial pathogens. The company is also developing a sporicidal to kill anthrax and has formulated Citroxin a product designed to knock out avian flu viruses.

NV5 GLOBAL INC

NAS: NVEE

200 South Park Road, Suite 350
Hollywood, FL 33021
Phone: 954 495-2112
Fax: –
Web: www.nv5.com

CEO: Dickerson Wright
CFO: Michael P. Rama
HR: Eileen Heller
FYE: December 29
Type: Public

NV5 Global wants the world to envy its engineering services. It offers infrastructure engineering support and consulting services as well as construction quality assurance and asset management. Customers include government agencies along with quasi-public and private firms in education health care and energy. NV5's enviable projects have included the international terminal at Philadelphia International Airport UC Santa Barbara's Marine Center the New Jersey Devils Arena San Diego's Manchester Grand Hyatt and a wind turbine manufacturing plant in Colorado. The company works from about 20 offices in California Colorado Florida New Jersey and Utah. It was formed in 2011 and filed to go public in 2013.

	Annual Growth	12/14	12/15	12/16	12/17	12/18
Sales ($ mil.)	40.1%	108.4	154.7	223.9	333.0	418.1
Net income ($ mil.)	53.1%	4.9	8.5	11.6	24.0	26.9
Market value ($ mil.)	45.5%	163.2	275.9	419.2	679.6	731.0
Employees	38.4%	649	975	1,532	2,023	2,384

NVE CORP

NAS: NVEC

11409 Valley View Road
Eden Prairie, MN 55344
Phone: 952 829-9217
Fax: –
Web: www.nve.com

CEO: Daniel A. Baker
CFO: Curt A Reynders
HR: –
FYE: March 31
Type: Public

NVE is definitely a spin zone and one with a certain magnetism. The company develops sensors incorporating spintronic (short for spin-based electronic) materials called giant magnetoresistors (GMR). Spintronics differ from conventional electronics in that they use the spin – rather than the charge – of electrons to store and transmit data. The company's sensors are used in aerospace automotive currency verification and factory automation applications. In addition to analog and digital GMR sensors NVE offers magnetic couplers magnetic random-access memory (MRAM) and custom-designed modules. Customers include the US government Broadcom Limited St. Jude Medical and Digi-Key.

	Annual Growth	03/15	03/16	03/17	03/18	03/19
Sales ($ mil.)	(3.5%)	30.6	27.7	28.3	29.9	26.5
Net income ($ mil.)	0.2%	14.4	12.3	12.9	13.9	14.5
Market value ($ mil.)	9.2%	334.0	273.9	401.2	402.8	474.4
Employees	(0.5%)	49	47	51	45	48

NVIDIA CORP

NMS: NVDA

2788 San Tomas Expressway
Santa Clara, CA 95051
Phone: 408 486-2000
Fax: –
Web: www.nvidia.com

CEO: Jen-Hsun Huang
CFO: Colette M. Kress
HR: Shelly Cerio
FYE: January 27
Type: Public

NVIDIA is racking up points in computer games logging miles in driverless cars and going deep into data centers. The Santa Clara California-based company's graphics processing units (GPUs) are used to generate computer game images in many PCs and game consoles in the gaming market. What's more its GPUs work well in applications for autonomous vehicles and deep learning a branch of artificial intelligence. NVIDIA's GPU brands are GeForce for games Quadro for designers and digital artists and Tesla and DGX for scientists and researchers. Its Tegra line of system-on-a-chip devices is for mobile gaming and entertainment as well as autonomous robots drones and cars. In 2019 NVIDIA agreed to buy chipmaker Mellanox for $6.9 billion.

	Annual Growth	01/15	01/16	01/17	01/18	01/19
Sales ($ mil.)	25.8%	4,681.5	5,010.0	6,910.0	9,714.0	11,716.0
Net income ($ mil.)	60.1%	630.6	614.0	1,666.0	3,047.0	4,141.0
Market value ($ mil.)	66.8%	12,550.3	17,749.7	67,732.6	147,458.0	97,050.9
Employees	9.5%	9,228	6,566	10,299	11,528	13,277

NVR INC.

NYS: NVR

11700 Plaza America Drive, Suite 500
Reston, VA 20190
Phone: 703 956-4000
Fax: –
Web: www.nvrinc.com

CEO: Paul C. Saville
CFO: Daniel D. Malzahn
HR: Juanita Maat
FYE: December 31
Type: Public

From finished lot to signed mortgage NVR offers homebuyers everything?including the kitchen sink. The company builds single-family detached homes townhomes and condominiums?mainly for first-time and move-up buyers?primarily in the eastern US. NVR's houses range in size from 1000 sq. ft. to 9500 sq. ft. and sell for an average price of around $380000. The company's brands include Ryan Homes Heartland Homes and NVHomes. Its largest markets are the Washington DC and Baltimore areas; together they account for around 40% of sales. Its subsidiary NVR Mortgage Finance offers mortgage and title services. The builder was founded in 1980 as NVHomes.

	Annual Growth	12/14	12/15	12/16	12/17	12/18
Sales ($ mil.)	12.7%	4,453.1	5,169.6	5,834.6	6,322.3	7,189.7
Net income ($ mil.)	29.7%	281.6	382.9	425.3	537.5	797.2
Market value ($ mil.)	17.6%	4,562.9	5,878.4	5,971.4	12,551.8	8,719.1
Employees	9.2%	3,942	4,300	4,900	5,200	5,600

NXSTAGE MEDICAL INC

NMS: NXTM

350 Merrimack Street
Lawrence, MA 01843
Phone: 978 687-4700
Fax: –
Web: www.nxstage.com

CEO: William Valle
CFO: –
HR: –
FYE: December 31
Type: Public

NxStage Medical helps patients suffering from end-stage renal disease. The medical device firm operates through three segments: System One In-Center and Services. The System One segment features NxStage Medical's lead product the System One portable hemodialysis machine which can be used by patients at home or by professionals in a hospital setting. The device is also marketed to hospitals for critical care and to dialysis clinics that want to create or expand their services to home-based patients. The In-Center segment sells NxStage Medical's blood tubing sets and needles to dialysis clinics primarily through distributor relationships while the Services segment comprises the company's kidney dialysis centers. NxStage Medical is being acquired by Fresenius Medical Care for some $2 billion.

	Annual Growth	12/13	12/14	12/15	12/16	12/17
Sales ($ mil.)	10.6%	263.4	301.5	336.1	366.4	393.9
Net income ($ mil.)	–	(18.6)	(23.9)	(15.3)	(4.8)	(14.0)
Market value ($ mil.)	24.8%	662.9	1,188.7	1,452.5	1,737.6	1,606.3
Employees	4.4%	3,200	3,400	3,600	3,400	3,800

NYACK HOSPITAL FOUNDATION, INC.

160 N MIDLAND AVE
NYACK, NY 109601998
Phone: 845-348-2000
Fax: –
Web: www.montefiorenyack.org

CEO: Mark Geller
CFO: –
HR: –
FYE: December 31
Type: Private

Nyack Hospital rocks when it comes to providing medical services in New York's Rockland and Bergen counties. The not-for-profit hospital is a 375-bed acute care medical and surgical facility with a staff of more than 650 doctors and surgeons. Nyack Hospital houses specialty centers for cancer care stroke pediatrics joint replacement sleep studies wound care and women's wellness. In partnership with Touro College of Osteopathic Medicine it also provides training programs for medical students. Nyack Hospital is a member of the New York-Presbyterian Healthcare System and is affiliated with the Columbia University College of Physicians and Surgeons.

	Annual Growth	12/13	12/14	12/15	12/16	12/17
Sales ($ mil.)	3.6%	–	206.7	216.2	224.1	229.9
Net income ($ mil.)	–	–	(4.3)	(2.8)	(8.8)	(11.3)
Market value ($ mil.)	–	–	–	–	–	–
Employees	–	–	–	–	–	1,300

NYPRO INC.

101 UNION ST
CLINTON, MA 01510-2935
Phone: 978-365-9721
Fax: –
Web: www.nypro.com

CEO: –
CFO: Gregory G Adams
HR: Anna Wellman
FYE: June 30
Type: Private

Nypro is a real pro when it comes to injection molding. The company makes plastic parts used in devices that range from cell phones and electric razors to inkjet printer cartridges and personal computers. Nypro's three global units include Consumer & Electronics Packaging and Healthcare (medical devices such as single-use fluid and drug management components). Although custom-precision plastic-injection molding is Nypro's core business the company also offers assembly services to other manufacturers. Major customers include Dell Nokia and Procter & Gamble. Established in 1955 Nypro agreed to be acquired by electronics manufacturing services provider Jabil Circuit in early 2013.

	Annual Growth	06/08	06/09*	07/10	07/11*	06/12
Sales ($ mil.)	1.6%	–	1,089.6	1,234.2	1,169.7	1,144.2
Net income ($ mil.)	–	–	2.6	30.0	9.8	(6.0)
Market value ($ mil.)	–	–	–	–	–	–
Employees	–	–	–	–	–	16,000

*Fiscal year change

O P I PRODUCTS INC.

13034 Saticoy St.
North Hollywood CA 91605
Phone: 818-759-2400
Fax: 661-257-5856
Web: www.starnail.com

CEO: Jules Kaufman
CFO: –
HR: –
FYE: June 30
Type: Subsidiary

OPI Products knows some women like to make a statement with their 20 collective finger and toe nails. The family-owned company is well known for whimsical nail polish names such as Not So Bora-Bora-ing Pink I'm Not Really A Waitress Got A Date To-Knight! and Who the Shrek Are You? The firm offers 200 nail colors among its product portfolio. In addition to nail polish OPI also makes and markets nail care and skin care products. The company peddles its products primarily through salons and specialty beauty stores throughout the US and in about 70 foreign countries. The company's brands include Nail Envy Avoplex Feet Garden Party Avojuice and Nicole. OPI was acquired by fragrance giant Coty.

O'BRIEN & GERE LIMITED

333 W WASHINGTON ST # 400
SYRACUSE, NY 132025253
Phone: 315-437-6100
Fax: –
Web: www.mass-awma.net

CEO: James A Fox
CFO: Joseph M McNulty
HR: –
FYE: December 30
Type: Private

O'Brien & Gere provides a range of engineering consulting and project management services throughout the US including wastewater management and water resources environmental compliance and remediation civil and facilities engineering and utility services. It also provides contract operations and maintenance. Employee-owned O'Brien & Gere serves municipal environmental manufacturing and federal clients. The company which employs hundreds of scientists engineers construction and other personnel operates nearly 30 offices in about a dozen states.

	Annual Growth	12/05	12/06	12/11	12/15	12/17
Sales ($ mil.)	7.3%	–	125.4	188.0	189.2	271.4
Net income ($ mil.)	5.5%	–	1.4	2.8	3.2	2.5
Market value ($ mil.)	–	–	–	–	–	–
Employees	–	–	–	–	–	800

O'CHARLEY'S INC.

NASDAQ: CHUX

3038 Sidco Dr.
Nashville TN 37204
Phone: 615-256-8500
Fax: 615-782-5044
Web: www.ocharleysinc.com

CEO: –
CFO: R Jeffrey Williams
HR: Jeffrey Campbell
FYE: December 31
Type: Private

O'Charley's is a leading full-service restaurant company with about 360 locations in 25 states. Its flagship casual-dining chain serves mostly traditional American fare including beef chicken and seafood entrees along with burgers sandwiches and a selection of starters. It boasts more than 230 company-owned outposts in the Southeast and Midwest. O'Charley's also owns Ninety Nine Restaurants a pub-style chain with more than 100 locations in Massachusetts and a handful of other New England states. In addition the company operates about a dozen upscale steakhouses under the name Stoney River Legendary Steaks. Fidelity National Financial acquired the company in 2012 and merged it with American Blue Ribbon.

O'MELVENY & MYERS LLP

400 S. Hope St.
Los Angeles CA 90071-2899
Phone: 213-430-6000
Fax: 213-430-6407
Web: www.omm.com

CEO: –
CFO: –
HR: –
FYE: January 31
Type: Private - Partnershi

O'Melveny & Myers has gotten used to playing the role of legal guardian angel. The firm is one of the oldest in Los Angeles and over the years it has developed strong ties to the media and entertainment industries. Among its clients have been such leading players as Walt Disney Sony Pictures Entertainment and Time Warner. Besides entertainment and media law O'Melveny & Myers' practice areas include labor and employment intellectual property and technology and venture capital litigation. The firm has some 900 lawyers located in more than a dozen offices worldwide. O'Melveny & Myers was founded in 1885.

O'NEIL INDUSTRIES, INC.

1245 W WASHINGTON BLVD
CHICAGO, IL 606071929
Phone: 773-755-1611
Fax: –
Web: www.weoneil.com

CEO: Brian Ramsay
CFO: –
HR: Andrea Boisseau
FYE: December 31
Type: Private

A family of construction companies O'Neil Industries has also built W.E. O'Neil Construction Company. The employee-owned company operates in Arizona California Colorado and Illinois providing general contracting construction management design/build and structural concrete services for commercial projects in the US and Canada. O'Neil Industries has worked on corporate offices manufacturing and distribution facilities and mixed-use centers for clients in the education gaming health care hospitality and retail industries. The company also serves the residential and senior living sectors. Clients have included Boeing DePaul University and The Nature Conservancy.

	Annual Growth	12/13	12/14	12/15	12/16	12/17
Sales ($ mil.)	0.0%	–	605.3	605.3	605.3	605.3
Net income ($ mil.)	0.0%	–	5.1	5.1	5.1	5.1
Market value ($ mil.)	–	–	–	–	–	–
Employees	–	–	–	–	–	400

O'REILLY AUTOMOTIVE, INC.

233 South Patterson Avenue
Springfield, MO 65802
Phone: 417 862-6708
Fax: –
Web: www.oreillyauto.com

NMS: ORLY
CEO: Gregory L. (Greg) Henslee
CFO: Thomas G. (Tom) McFall
HR: –
FYE: December 31
Type: Public

O'Reilly Automotive has its foot on the gas. The company is the nation's #1 provider of automotive aftermarket parts (both new and remanufactured) maintenance supplies professional service equipment tools and accessories. It also offers customers a range of services including oil and battery recycling battery testing paint mixing and tool rental. O'Reilly operates through a fast-growing network of some 5200 stores across the US as well as online. The family-founded and -operated company wheels and deals with automotive professionals as well as DIY (do-it-yourself) customers.

	Annual Growth	12/14	12/15	12/16	12/17	12/18
Sales ($ mil.)	7.2%	7,216.1	7,966.7	8,593.1	8,977.7	9,536.4
Net income ($ mil.)	14.2%	778.2	931.2	1,037.7	1,133.8	1,324.5
Market value ($ mil.)	15.6%	15,225.4	20,031.3	22,006.6	19,013.2	27,217.2
Employees	3.9%	67,926	71,943	74,715	75,289	79,174

O-I GLASS INC

One Michael Owens Way
Perrysburg, OH 43551
Phone: 567 336-5000
Fax: –
Web: www.o-i.com

NYS: OI
CEO: Andres A. Lopez
CFO: Jan A. Bertsch
HR: Avril Fisher
FYE: December 31
Type: Public

Owens-Illinois (O-I) is one of the world's largest makers of glass containers touting a leading market presence with more than 49000 customers in 85 countries around the world. O-I offers more than 10000 types of glass containers such as bottles in a wide range of shapes sizes and colors used to hold beer wine liquor as well as soft drinks juice and other beverages. It also makes glass containers for foods such as soups salad dressings and dairy products and for pharmaceuticals. Some of its products are made using recycled glass. Major customers have included such heavy hitters as Anheuser-Busch InBev Coca-Cola Diageo H.J. Heinz and Nestle.

	Annual Growth	12/14	12/15	12/16	12/17	12/18
Sales ($ mil.)	0.3%	6,784.0	6,156.0	6,702.0	6,869.0	6,877.0
Net income ($ mil.)	36.1%	75.0	(74.0)	209.0	180.0	257.0
Market value ($ mil.)	(10.6%)	4,201.2	2,711.6	2,710.0	3,450.9	2,683.6
Employees	5.9%	21,100	27,000	27,000	26,500	26,500

O. C. TANNER COMPANY

1930 S STATE ST
SALT LAKE CITY, UT 841152311
Phone: 801-486-2430
Fax: –
Web: www.octanner.com

CEO: –
CFO: Scott Archibald
HR: Karen Erickson
FYE: December 31
Type: Private

O.C. Tanner recognizes that it's nice to be appreciated. The company designs and helps implement employee recognition programs for customers around the world. Related services intended to help customers take full advantage of their investment in employee recognition include communication consulting research leadership training and social programs. The company which operates from offices in the US Canada and the UK has shipped awards to clients in about 150 countries. Over the years O.C. Tanner has counted numerous Fortune 100 companies among its clients.

	Annual Growth	12/13	12/14	12/16	12/17	12/18
Sales ($ mil.)	2.4%	–	344.1	351.2	342.0	378.8
Net income ($ mil.)	(12.2%)	–	19.4	16.8	9.6	11.5
Market value ($ mil.)	–	–	–	–	–	–
Employees	–	–	–	–	–	1,700

O.F. MOSSBERG & SONS INC.

7 Grasso Ave.
North Haven CT 06473
Phone: 203-230-5300
Fax: 203-230-5420
Web: www.mossberg.com

CEO: A Iver Mossberg Jr
CFO: –
HR: –
FYE: September 30
Type: Private

Whatever the game whatever the season O.F. Mossberg & Sons is riding shotgun in the small firearms manufacturing industry. The oldest family-owned firearms maker in America and the largest pump-action shotgun maker in the world Mossberg has more than 100 design and utility patents to its name. Shotguns are the company's specialty but it also produces rifles; accessories such as barrels choke tubes and magazines; and hunting apparel. In addition to its guns for hunting home protection and target shooting Mossberg manufactures exclusive firearms for US military and law enforcement agencies. The company is a subsidiary of Mossberg Corporation which also owns shotgun maker Maverick Arms.

OAK VALLEY BANCORP

125 N. 3rd Ave.
Oakdale CA 95361
Phone: 209-848-2265
Fax: 209-848-1929
Web: www.ovcb.com

NASDAQ: OVLY
CEO: Ronald C Martin
CFO: Rick McCarty
HR: –
FYE: December 31
Type: Public

Oak Valley Bancorp was formed in 2008 to be the holding company for Oak Valley Community Bank which serves individuals and local businesses through about 10 branches in California's Central Valley. Eastern Sierra Community Bank a division of Oak Valley has three locations. The banks provide standard deposit products such as savings checking and retirement accounts and CDs. Their lending activities consist of commercial real estate loans (more than half of their combined loan portfolio) and business real estate construction agricultural residential mortgage and consumer loans. Investment products and services are offered through an agreement with PrimeVest Financial Services.

OAK VALLEY BANCORP (OAKDALE, CA) — NAS: OVLY

125 N. Third Ave.
Oakdale, CA 95361
Phone: 209 848-2265
Fax: –
Web: www.ovcb.com

CEO: Christopher M Courtney
CFO: Jeffrey A Gall
HR: –
FYE: December 31
Type: Public

Oak Valley Bancorp was formed in 2008 to be the holding company for Oak Valley Community Bank which serves individuals and local businesses through about 10 branches in California's Central Valley. Eastern Sierra Community Bank a division of Oak Valley has three locations. The banks provide standard deposit products such as savings checking and retirement accounts and CDs. Their lending activities consist of commercial real estate loans (more than half of their combined loan portfolio) and business real estate construction agricultural residential mortgage and consumer loans. Investment products and services are offered through an agreement with PrimeVest Financial Services.

	Annual Growth	12/14	12/15	12/16	12/17	12/18
Assets ($ mil.)	9.9%	749.7	897.0	1,002.1	1,034.9	1,094.9
Net income ($ mil.)	12.8%	7.1	4.9	7.7	9.1	11.5
Market value ($ mil.)	15.8%	83.3	85.2	102.8	160.1	150.0
Employees	4.3%	157	167	169	175	186

OAKLAND UNIVERSITY

2200 N SQUIRREL RD
ROCHESTER, MI 483094401
Phone: 248-370-2100
Fax: –
Web: www.oakland.edu

CEO: –
CFO: –
HR: –
FYE: June 30
Type: Private

Oakland University is the OU of the North. The Michigan public university serves a student body of more than 20000 offering about 130 baccalaureate degree programs and more than 100 graduate degree and certificate programs. It boasts a student-to-faculty ratio of 22-to-1. In addition to academic and specialty programs in areas ranging from business and technology to nursing and athletics its faculty members also coordinate hands-on research projects for graduate students. The main university campus spans some 1400 acres that house seven academic schools and colleges in Rochester Michigan. Oakland University also has satellite campuses in Macomb County and a law school in Auburn Hills.

	Annual Growth	06/14	06/15	06/16	06/17	06/18
Sales ($ mil.)	4.9%	–	227.4	254.0	263.5	262.2
Net income ($ mil.)	(2.5%)	–	20.3	9.7	22.2	18.9
Market value ($ mil.)	–	–	–	–	–	–
Employees	–	–	–	–	–	2,650

OAKRIDGE ENERGY INC. — OTC: OAKR

4613 Jacksboro Hwy.
Wichita Falls TX 76302
Phone: 940-322-4772
Fax: 940-322-9452
Web: oakridgeenergy.com

CEO: –
CFO: –
HR: –
FYE: February 28
Type: Public

Despite the radioactive connotations of this company's name Oakridge Energy is engaged in the exploration and production of more benign natural resources — oil and gas with some gravel thrown into the product mix. The oil and gas independent's assets are primarily in North Texas but Oakridge Energy also receives lease and royalty income from gravel deposits in Colorado and holds real estate assets in that state. Oakridge Energy has proved reserves of 675700 barrels of oil and 234000 million cu. ft. of natural gas. President Sandra Pautsky owns 56% of the company. Due in part to the ill health of its president Oakridge Energy has decided to sell its real estate development project.

OAKRIDGE GLOBAL ENERGY SOLUTIONS INC — NBB: OGES

3520 Dixie Highway NE
Palm Bay, FL 32905
Phone: 321 610-7959
Fax: –

CEO: Stephen J Barber
CFO: Tami L Tharp
HR: –
FYE: December 31
Type: Public

Oak Ridge Micro-Energy is hoping to provide macro-power. The development-stage company makes thin-film lithium batteries with consumer industrial and military applications. Oak Ridge Micro-Energy licensed the thin-film battery technology from Oak Ridge National Laboratory (ORNL) on a non-exclusive basis. Mark Meriwether president and CEO owns 20% of Oak Ridge; John Bates (CTO and former CEO) holds about one-quarter of the company. Dr. Bates worked at ORNL for nearly 30 years developing the technology that is being commercialized by Oak Ridge Micro-Energy. The company is moving into the third phase of its strategic plan focusing on commercial licensing and marketing of its technology.

	Annual Growth	12/11	12/12	12/13	12/14	12/15
Sales ($ mil.)	–	0.0	–	–	0.1	0.0
Net income ($ mil.)	–	(0.1)	(0.7)	(5.1)	(8.6)	11.5
Market value ($ mil.)	36.0%	65.3	54.4	81.6	125.1	223.1
Employees	169.8%	1	6	18	14	53

OAKRIDGE HOLDINGS INC — NBB: OKRG Q

400 West Ontario Street
Chicago, IL 60654
Phone: 312 505-9267
Fax: –
Web: www.oakridgeholdingsinc.com

CEO: Robert C Harvey
CFO: Tim Thompson
HR: Jane Jacobus
FYE: June 30
Type: Public

In a unique arrangement of business services Oakridge Holdings can offer customers support and service whether they are flying high or lying low above the ground or below it. Through two subsidiaries (Oakridge Cemetery and Glen Oak Cemetery) it buries human remains and through another (Stinar Corporation) it makes aviation ground support equipment (lifts truck mounted stairways water and catering trucks). Oakridge provides its customers internment burial plots crypts and cremation as well as stairways for loading aircraft and lavatory water cabin cleaning and catering trucks for servicing airplanes.

	Annual Growth	06/12	06/13	06/14	06/15	06/16
Sales ($ mil.)	(23.6%)	13.3	12.8	5.3	5.6	4.5
Net income ($ mil.)	–	(0.5)	(2.0)	2.5	(0.8)	(0.5)
Market value ($ mil.)	(24.0%)	0.6	0.6	0.5	0.3	0.2
Employees	(25.1%)	124	72	48	39	39

OAKTREE CAPITAL GROUP LLC — NYS: OAK

333 South Grand Avenue, 28th Floor
Los Angeles, CA 90071
Phone: 213 830-6300
Fax: –
Web: www.oaktreecapital.com

CEO: Jay S Wintrob
CFO: David M Kirchheimer
HR: –
FYE: December 31
Type: Public

Oaktree Capital Group knows money doesn't grow on trees but it often grows on alternative investments. The global investment manager specializes in credit and contrarian value-oriented investments such as distressed debt corporate debt convertible securities real estate private equity (or control investing) and listed equities. Founded in 1995 Oaktree Capital boasts $97 billion of assets under management on behalf of institutional investors such as pension funds corporations government entities universities endowments foundations and private clients. The firm has more than 15 offices in the US Asia and Europe.

	Annual Growth	12/13	12/14	12/15	12/16	12/17
Sales ($ mil.)	65.7%	194.9	193.9	201.9	1,125.7	1,469.8
Net income ($ mil.)	1.1%	222.0	126.3	71.3	194.7	231.5
Market value ($ mil.)	(8.0%)	9,195.9	8,100.3	7,458.0	5,860.7	6,579.6
Employees	3.5%	809	927	924	939	930

OAKTREE SPECIALTY LENDING CORP
NMS: OCSL

333 South Grand Avenue, 28th Floor
Los Angeles, CA 90071
Phone: 213 830-6300
Fax: –
Web: www.fifthstreetfinance.com

CEO: Edgar Lee
CFO: Mel Carlisle
HR: –
FYE: September 30
Type: Public

Fifth Street Finance works to put the companies it lends money to on easy street. A business development firm Fifth Street lends capital to and invests in small and midsized firms with annual revenues between $25 million and $250 million. The company typically invests $10 million to $100 million in the form of senior debt or equity per transaction. It favors established firms over start-ups and prefers to participate actively in its investments as advisors. Fifth Street's portfolio comprises more than 85 companies many of which operate in the health care manufacturing IT services and business services sectors. Formed in 2007 the specialty finance company boasts about $2 billion in assets under management.

	Annual Growth	09/14	09/15	09/16	09/17	09/18
Sales ($ mil.)	(17.1%)	294.0	265.5	247.9	178.0	138.7
Net income ($ mil.)	(19.4%)	142.6	114.9	106.7	72.7	60.0
Market value ($ mil.)	(14.3%)	1,294.0	869.7	819.0	771.1	699.2
Employees						

OAKWOOD HEALTHCARE INC.

18101 OAKWOOD BLVD
DEARBORN, MI 48124-4089
Phone: 313-593-7000
Fax: –
Web: www.oakwood.org

CEO: Brain Connolly
CFO: –
HR: –
FYE: December 31
Type: Private

Oakwood Healthcare stands proud as a regional health care provider in southeastern Michigan. It offers a range of health services to residents in more than 35 communities. At the center of the system are four hospitals with a total of more than 1200 beds: Oakwood Hospital & Medical Center a full-service teaching hospital; Oakwood Annapolis Hospital a community hospital; Oakwood Heritage Hospital a tertiary care hospital; and Oakwood Southshore Medical Center a community hospital. Founded in 1953 the system also includes community health and diagnostic facilities retirement and nursing communities rehabilitative care centers and specialty care centers for women children and seniors.

	Annual Growth	12/0-1	12/00	12/01	12/02	12/09
Sales ($ mil.)	4.7%	–	658.3	666.3	744.7	997.0
Net income ($ mil.)		–	(9.9)	(4.2)	(4.2)	10.3
Market value ($ mil.)	–	–	–	–	–	–
Employees	–	–	–	–	–	9,200

OASIS PETROLEUM INC.
NAS: OAS

1001 Fannin Street, Suite 1500
Houston, TX 77002
Phone: 281 404-9500
Fax: –
Web: www.oasispetroleum.com

CEO: Thomas B. (Tommy) Nusz
CFO: Michael H. Lou
HR: Jennifer Pratt
FYE: December 31
Type: Public

Oasis Petroleum is combing the northern US for watering holes made of oil. The independent exploration and production company acquires and develops primarily oil and some gas resources in the fertile oilfields of Williston Basin of Montana and North Dakota specifically in the Bakken and Three Forks formation. Oasis has net reserves of more than 320 million barrels of oil equivalent and more than 430000 net acres of land holdings. The company also reported an average daily production of more than 82000 barrels of oil equivalent from some 880 net producing wells. It provides midstream activities such as water gas and oil gathering to its own upstream operations as well as third-parties'.

	Annual Growth	12/14	12/15	12/16	12/17	12/18
Sales ($ mil.)	13.7%	1,390.2	789.7	704.7	1,248.4	2,321.9
Net income ($ mil.)		506.9	(40.2)	(243.0)	123.8	(35.3)
Market value ($ mil.)	(24.0%)	5,266.0	2,346.4	4,820.2	2,677.6	1,760.6
Employees	6.8%	558	535	477	585	727

OBA FINANCIAL SERVICES INC
NAS: OBAF

20300 Seneca Meadows Parkway
Germantown, MD 20876
Phone: 301 916-0742
Fax: –
Web: www.obabank.com

CEO: –
CFO: –
HR: –
FYE: June 30
Type: Public

Don't get OBA Financial Services started on new money vs. old money. OBA Financial Services is the holding company for OBA Bank a community bank that traces its roots back to 1861. OBA Bank serves Montgomery and Howard County Maryland from five branches (it sold its sixth branch in Washington DC to Eagle Bancorp in January 2011). The bank's loan portfolio is made up of residential mortgages (45%) commercial mortgages (30%) home equity loans (15%) and commercial business loans (10%). OBA stands for the Oriental Building Association a 19th century savings and loan that catered to German immigrants. OBA Financial Services went public in January 2010 raising $46.3 million in its initial public offering.

	Annual Growth	06/09	06/10	06/11	06/12	06/13
Assets ($ mil.)	1.3%	362.5	374.1	386.4	392.1	381.6
Net income ($ mil.)		(0.6)	(0.7)	0.9	0.3	1.1
Market value ($ mil.)	18.3%	–	45.1	59.9	60.1	74.7
Employees	3.8%	62	62	69	69	72

OBERLIN COLLEGE

173 W LORAIN ST
OBERLIN, OH 440741073
Phone: 440-775-8121
Fax: –
Web: www.oberlin.edu

CEO: –
CFO: –
HR: –
FYE: June 30
Type: Private

Founded in 1833 Oberlin College was the first college in the US to enroll women on an equal basis with men. The school has a College of Arts and Sciences (about 2300 enrollees) but may be best known for its Conservatory of Music (about 600 enrollees) the oldest such institution in the US. The College of Arts and Sciences offers nearly 50 undergraduate majors the Conservatory about 10. Students can earn bachelor's degrees in either program but can also earn a five-year double-degree in both. In addition Oberlin offers master's degrees in opera theater conducting performance historical performance historical instruments music teaching and education. It has two-year certificate programs as well.

	Annual Growth	06/14	06/15	06/16	06/17	06/18
Sales ($ mil.)	0.2%	–	184.7	184.5	184.7	185.6
Net income ($ mil.)		–	(3.6)	(71.1)	77.2	74.2
Market value ($ mil.)	–	–	–	–	–	–
Employees	–	–	–	–	–	1,140

OCATA THERAPEUTICS INC
NBB: OCAT

33 Locke Drive
Marlborough, MA 01752
Phone: 508 756-1212
Fax: –
Web: www.advancedcell.com/

CEO: Paul Wotton
CFO: Edward Myles
HR: –
FYE: December 31
Type: Public

No need to choose between embryonic and adult stem cells — Advanced Cell Technology (ACT) works with both to develop cellular therapies designed to regenerate human tissue. The company has developed three product platforms based on stem-cell technology. They are retinal pigment epithelial therapy (RPE) for the treatment of degenerative retinal disease; myoblast stem cell therapy to treat chronic heart failure and other heart problems; and the hemangioblast platform (HG) for the treatment of blood and cardiovascular diseases. Though the company is focused on bringing the clinical-stage technologies to market it is also continuing to conduct research for other regenerative medicine treatments.

	Annual Growth	12/09	12/10	12/11	12/12	12/13
Sales ($ mil.)	(36.9%)	1.4	0.7	0.5	0.5	0.2
Net income ($ mil.)		(36.8)	(54.4)	(72.8)	(28.5)	(31.0)
Market value ($ mil.)	(9.6%)	2.4	5.5	2.2	1.5	1.6
Employees	28.4%	14	22	30	36	38

OCCIDENTAL COLLEGE

1600 CAMPUS RD
LOS ANGELES, CA 900413314
Phone: 323-259-2500
Fax: –
Web: www.oxy.edu

CEO: –
CFO: –
HR: Martin Cozyn
FYE: June 30
Type: Private

It's no accident that Occidental College is a liberal arts school. With more than 2000 students an average class size of 19 and a 10:1 student-to-faculty ratio the school (nicknamed "Oxy") offers a hands-on approach to higher education. Its campus located in Eagle Rock is surrounded by the metropolis of Los Angeles. The college has 180 faculty members and offers about 30 majors including a number of interdisciplinary programs. Occidental students can also take classes at Caltech or the Art Center College of Design and earn joint degrees at Columbia University Keck Graduate Institute and Caltech. Occidental students can also participate in service-learning and study abroad programs.

	Annual Growth	06/13	06/14	06/15	06/16	06/17
Sales ($ mil.)	(13.6%)	–	188.7	182.6	162.3	121.9
Net income ($ mil.)	11.3%	–	37.7	26.0	(7.7)	52.0
Market value ($ mil.)	–	–	–	–	–	–
Employees	–	–	–	–	–	610

OCCIDENTAL PETROLEUM CORP

NYS: OXY

5 Greenway Plaza, Suite 110
Houston, TX 77046
Phone: 713 215-7000
Fax: –
Web: www.oxy.com

CEO: Vicki A. Hollub
CFO: Cedric W. Burgher
HR: –
FYE: December 31
Type: Public

Harnessing its heritage of Western technical know-how Occidental Petroleum engages in oil and gas exploration and production and makes basic chemicals plastics and petrochemicals. It boasts proved reserves of 2.8 billion barrels of oil equivalent primarily from assets in the US the Middle East North Africa and Latin America. Subsidiary Occidental Chemical (OxyChem) produces acids chlorine and specialty products and owns Oxy Vinyls the #1 maker of polyvinyl chloride (PVC) resin in North America. Occidental Petroleum's midstream and marketing units gather treat process transport store trade and market crude oil natural gas NGLs condensate and CO2 and generate and market power. In 2019 it acquired Anadarko for $55 billion.

	Annual Growth	12/14	12/15	12/16	12/17	12/18
Sales ($ mil.)	(3.6%)	21,947.0	12,699.0	10,398.0	13,274.0	18,934.0
Net income ($ mil.)	60.9%	616.0	(7,829.0)	(574.0)	1,311.0	4,131.0
Market value ($ mil.)	(6.6%)	60,408.3	50,666.2	53,379.0	55,200.0	45,997.5
Employees	(1.5%)	11,700	11,100	11,000	11,000	11,000

OCEAN BEAUTY SEAFOODS LLC

1100 W EWING ST
SEATTLE, WA 981191321
Phone: 206-285-6800
Fax: –
Web: www.oceanbeauty.com

CEO: Mark Palmer
CFO: Tony Ross
HR: –
FYE: December 31
Type: Private

Prefer your piscatory purchase to be fresh frozen or canned? Ocean Beauty Seafoods has it covered. Doing no fishing of its own the company buys seafood from commercial fishermen and then processes sells and distributes its seafood products in Alaska and across the continental US. Founded in 1910 the company also exports seafood to Mexico Europe Asia Africa and the Middle East. Ocean Beauty's specialty products include smoked salmon smoked salmon spreads pickled and marinated herring shrimp cocktail caviar and lobster p- -t-©. Nonprofit Bristol Bay Economic Development Corporation owns 50% of Ocean Beauty; individual investors own the rest.

	Annual Growth	12/12	12/13*	01/15	01/16*	12/16
Sales ($ mil.)	2.1%	–	426.0	439.4	437.8	453.9
Net income ($ mil.)	–	–	11.1	4.6	(4.6)	(27.2)
Market value ($ mil.)	–	–	–	–	–	–
Employees	–	–	–	–	–	2,500

*Fiscal year change

OCEAN BIO-CHEM, INC.

NAS: OBCI

4041 SW 47 Avenue
Fort Lauderdale, FL 33314
Phone: 954 587-6280
Fax: –
Web: www.oceanbiochem.com

CEO: Peter G Dornau
CFO: Jeffrey S Barocas
HR: –
FYE: December 31
Type: Public

Ocean Bio-Chem provides everything but the elbow grease to scrub down boats planes RVs and automobiles. The company makes and distributes Star Brite and StarTron brand maintenance and appearance products. Its marine and automotive lines include waxes lubricants and coolants and its recreational vehicle and power sports equipment offerings primarily consist of polishes and cleaners. Ocean Bio-Chem's products are sold by both national retailers and specialty stores including Wal-Mart West Marine and Bass Pro Shops. The company handles its manufacturing in-house through its Alabama-based Kinpak subsidiary which also provides contract services. President and CEO Peter Dornau owns about 70% of the company.

	Annual Growth	12/14	12/15	12/16	12/17	12/18
Sales ($ mil.)	5.4%	33.9	34.0	36.2	38.9	41.8
Net income ($ mil.)	8.1%	2.0	0.5	2.1	2.6	2.8
Market value ($ mil.)	(7.7%)	42.2	20.0	35.1	40.5	30.6
Employees	5.4%	123	123	128	142	152

OCEAN DUKE CORPORATION

21250 HAWTHORNE BLVD # 500
TORRANCE, CA 905035514
Phone: 310-326-3198
Fax: –

CEO: –
CFO: Alice Lin
HR: –
FYE: March 31
Type: Private

Ocean Duke maintains a regal demeanor in a fishy environment. The company is a seafood wholesaler offering a variety of frozen raw fish shrimp mollusks and crustaceans. Ocean Duke also sells breaded fish shrimp and squid. The company imports its products and serves foodservice food processing distribution and wholesale companies throughout the US.

	Annual Growth	03/0-1	03/00	03/01	03/02	03/11
Sales ($ mil.)	–	–	0.0	196.8	191.3	158.3
Net income ($ mil.)	–	–	0.0	1.1	0.9	2.2
Market value ($ mil.)	–	–	–	–	–	–
Employees	–	–	–	–	–	25

OCEAN POWER TECHNOLOGIES INC

NAS: OPTT

28 Engelhard Drive, Suite B
Monroe Township, NJ 08831
Phone: 609 730-0400
Fax: –
Web: www.oceanpowertechnologies.com

CEO: George H Kirby III
CFO: Matthew T Shafer
HR: –
FYE: April 30
Type: Public

Harnessing the motion of the ocean is what Ocean Power Technologies (OPT) is all about. The company with offices in the US and UK uses a proprietary system called PowerBouy to generate electricity using the mechanical energy produced when offshore waves move the anchored buoys up and down. OPT offers a buoy system that connects to power grids as well as an autonomous one that can be used in remote locations and for tsunami monitoring oceanographic data collection and offshore aquaculture. Customers include the US Navy Spanish power producer Iberdrola and Spanish energy firm TOTAL. It has a contract with Lockheed Martin to build a large power generation system off the west coast of the US.

	Annual Growth	04/15	04/16	04/17	04/18	04/19
Sales ($ mil.)	(37.4%)	4.1	0.7	0.8	0.5	0.6
Net income ($ mil.)	–	(13.1)	(13.1)	(9.5)	(10.2)	(12.2)
Market value ($ mil.)	49.8%	3.0	10.2	7.8	6.0	15.1
Employees	4.3%	33	30	30	35	39

OCEAN SHORE HOLDING CO

NMS: OSHC

1001 Asbury Avenue
Ocean City, NJ 08226
Phone: 609 399-0012
Fax: –
Web: www.ochome.com

CEO: –
CFO: –
HR: –
FYE: December 31
Type: Public

That soothing noise you hear in South Jersey isn't waves lapping or gulls flapping it's the sweet sound of money. Ocean Shore Holding owns Ocean City Home Bank a community thrift serving New Jersey's Atlantic and Cape May counties where gaming and tourism thrive. Through about a dozen locations the bank offers individuals businesses and government entities such standard fare as checking and savings accounts CDs and money market accounts. Residential mortgages including loans secured by second homes and rental properties account for more than 80% of the company's loan portfolio. Subsidiary Seashore Financial sells investment and insurance products. Ocean Shore Holding bought rival Select Bank in 2011.

	Annual Growth	12/10	12/11	12/12	12/13	12/14
Assets ($ mil.)	5.1%	839.9	994.7	1,045.5	1,020.0	1,024.8
Net income ($ mil.)	3.7%	5.4	5.1	5.0	5.3	6.3
Market value ($ mil.)	5.8%	73.2	65.6	94.6	87.3	91.6
Employees	2.7%	168	206	196	188	187

OCEAN SPRAY CRANBERRIES, INC.

1 OCEAN SPRAY DR
MIDDLEBORO, MA 023490001
Phone: 508-946-1000
Fax: –
Web: www.oceanspray.com

CEO: Bobby J Chacko
CFO: Joseph Vanderstelt
HR: –
FYE: August 31
Type: Private

Ocean Spray Cranberries has transformed that ubiquitous Thanksgiving side dish into a big business with beverages cereals and snacks. Known for its blue-and-white wave logo Ocean Spray is a top US maker of canned bottled and shelf-stable juice drinks. Structured as a cooperative Ocean Spray is owned by more than 700 cranberry and grapefruit growers in North America. It produces juice drinks by blending cranberries with other fruits typically ranging from apples to blueberries at around 20 processing facilities. Its other products include fresh and dried cranberries sauces and trail mixes along with fresh citrus fruits. Ocean Spray sells its products through food retailers foodservice providers and food makers worldwide.

	Annual Growth	08/11	08/12	08/13	08/14	08/15
Sales ($ mil.)	1.1%	–	1,662.7	1,658.9	1,655.3	1,719.3
Net income ($ mil.)	(2.2%)	–	338.7	389.7	289.9	317.3
Market value ($ mil.)	–	–	–	–	–	–
Employees	–	–	–	–	–	2,000

OCEANEERING INTERNATIONAL, INC.

NYS: OII

11911 FM 529
Houston, TX 77041
Phone: 713 329-4500
Fax: –
Web: www.oceaneering.com

CEO: Roderick A. (Rod) Larson
CFO: Alan R. Curtis
HR: Holly Kriendler
FYE: December 31
Type: Public

Oceaneering International is one of the world's largest underwater service contract providers. It caters primarily to the oil and gas industry by manufacturing remotely operated vehicles (ROVs) and specialty subsea hardware that are used to control hydrocarbon flow from subsea wellheads. The company also offers services ranging from subsea hardware installation and repair to third-party asset safety inspections. Oceaneering also provides advanced engineering services to US governmental agencies and the commercial theme park industry. It is primarily active in the US but also has operations in Angola Brazil India and Australia.

	Annual Growth	12/14	12/15	12/16	12/17	12/18
Sales ($ mil.)	(15.0%)	3,659.6	3,062.8	2,271.6	1,921.5	1,909.5
Net income ($ mil.)	–	428.3	231.0	24.6	166.4	(212.3)
Market value ($ mil.)	(32.7%)	5,795.1	3,697.2	2,779.8	2,083.1	1,192.3
Employees	(8.7%)	12,400	11,000	9,300	8,200	8,600

OCEANFIRST FINANCIAL CORP

NMS: OCFC

110 West Front Street
Red Bank, NJ 07701
Phone: 732 240-4500
Fax: –
Web: www.oceanfirst.com

CEO: Christopher D. Maher
CFO: Michael J. Fitzpatrick
HR: Anne Johnson
FYE: December 31
Type: Public

Ask the folks at OceanFirst Bank for a home loan and they might say "shore." The subsidiary of holding company OceanFirst Financial operates 25 branches in the coastal New Jersey counties of Middlesex Monmouth and Ocean. The community-oriented bank caters to individuals and small to midsized businesses in the Jersey Shore area offering standard products such as checking and savings accounts CDs and IRAs. It uses funds from deposits mainly to invest in mortgages loans and securities. One- to four-family residential mortgages make up more than half of Ocean-First Financial's loan portfolio which also includes commercial real estate (about 30%) business construction and consumer loans.

	Annual Growth	12/14	12/15	12/16	12/17	12/18
Assets ($ mil.)	33.6%	2,356.7	2,593.1	5,167.1	5,416.0	7,516.2
Net income ($ mil.)	37.9%	19.9	20.3	23.0	42.5	71.9
Market value ($ mil.)	7.1%	821.9	960.5	1,440.0	1,258.7	1,079.4
Employees	24.1%	376	393	797	684	892

OCERA THERAPEUTICS INC

NMS: OCRX

525 University Avenue, Suite 610
Palo Alto, CA 94301
Phone: 650 475-0158
Fax: –
Web: www.ocerainc.com

CEO: –
CFO: –
HR: –
FYE: December 31
Type: Public

Tranzyme has a gut feeling about its therapies. A drug discovery and development company Tranzyme is developing therapies to treat acute and chronic gastrointestinal (GI) disorders. Its lead candidate ulimorelin is an intravenously-administered treatment for GI motility problems that occur after abdominal surgery. If commercialized the therapy (which is in late clinical stages of development) could be used by hospitals to quickly restore normal intestinal function to patients. The company also has other candidates in earlier stages of development including a mid-stage oral therapy to treat chronic GI motility caused by diabetes. Founded in 1998 Tranzyme went public through a $48 million IPO in 2011.

	Annual Growth	12/11	12/12	12/13	12/14	12/15
Sales ($ mil.)	(66.2%)	10.2	8.4	0.1	0.3	0.1
Net income ($ mil.)	–	(22.2)	(22.8)	(17.5)	(23.4)	(26.5)
Market value ($ mil.)	1.9%	59.8	11.2	268.8	131.8	64.6
Employees	(19.2%)	47	29	14	16	20

OCI PARTNERS LP

NYS: OCIP

5470 N. Twin City Highway
Nederland, TX 77627
Phone: 409 723-1900
Fax: –
Web: www.ocipartnerslp.com

CEO: Ahmed K El-Hoshy
CFO: Beshoy Guirguis
HR: –
FYE: December 31
Type: Public

OCI Partners is bringing methanol production back to the good ol' US of A. The company reopened a methanol and ammonia plant in Beaumont Texas in 2012. (It's actually the largest methanol plant in the US; currently most of the country's methanol is imported from Trinidad.) The plant (shut down by Terra Industries in 2004) has an annual production capacity of 730000 tons of methanol and 265000 tons of ammonia. OCI Partners sells the methanol and ammonia to customers such as Koch Industries Methanex and Transammonia who use it to create other chemicals. OCI Partners is affiliated with Egypt-based Orascom Construction Industries (OCI). It went public in 2013.

	Annual Growth	12/12	12/13	12/14	12/15	12/16
Sales ($ mil.)	3.5%	224.6	428.0	402.8	309.4	258.2
Net income ($ mil.)	–	51.8	154.4	119.4	52.0	(50.6)
Market value ($ mil.)	(32.9%)	–	2,401.1	1,392.0	620.3	726.4
Employees	–	–	–	–	–	–

OCLARO INC
NMS: OCLR

225 Charcot Avenue
San Jose, CA 95131
Phone: 408-383-1400
Fax: –
Web: www.oclaro.com

CEO: Greg Dougherty
CFO: Pete Mangan
HR: –
FYE: July 1/
Type: Public

And you thought splitting hairs was tedious. Oclaro (a combination of the words "optical" and "clarity") integrates the light-processing functions of optical networking components onto silicon chips which it then puts into communications products such as transceivers transponders transmitters receivers and modulators. Typical devices for dividing wavelengths of light combine several components such as tunable lasers lenses and filters. Oclaro sells its optical components to telecommunications and data communications systems and components vendors; other customers come from the laser systems life sciences industrial printing and consumer electronics industries.

	Annual Growth	06/13	06/14	06/15*	07/16	07/17
Sales ($ mil.)	0.6%	586.0	390.9	341.3	407.9	601.0
Net income ($ mil.)	–	(122.7)	17.8	(56.7)	8.6	127.9
Market value ($ mil.)	67.7%	197.8	360.4	378.9	803.0	1,565.7
Employees	(9.4%)	2,782	1,294	1,233	1,689	1,876

*Fiscal year change

OCLC, INC.

6565 KILGOUR PL
DUBLIN, OH 430173395
Phone: 614-764-6000
Fax: –
Web: www.oclc.org

CEO: David A Prichard
CFO: –
HR: –
FYE: June 30
Type: Private

Working to reduce the cost of information OCLC Online Computer Library Center is a membership cooperative that provides access to the world's information. The group offers services and tools to some 74000 member libraries in about 170 countries. Services include computer-based cataloging preservation and library management. OCLC additionally facilitates interlibrary loan services administers the Dewey Decimal Classification system and operates the WorldCat database an online resource for finding library materials. OCLC was founded in 1967 by presidents of the colleges and universities in Ohio. OCLC which stands for Ohio College Library Center opened its first location in Ohio State's main library.

	Annual Growth	06/13	06/14	06/15	06/16	06/17
Sales ($ mil.)	(0.8%)	–	213.6	202.8	203.4	208.4
Net income ($ mil.)	(14.0%)	–	21.9	(17.1)	(9.8)	13.9
Market value ($ mil.)	–	–	–	–	–	–
Employees	–	–	–	–	–	1,227

OCONEE REGIONAL HEALTH SYSTEMS, INC.

821 N COBB ST
MILLEDGEVILLE, GA 310612343
Phone: 478-454-3500
Fax: –
Web: www.oconeeregional.com

CEO: –
CFO: –
HR: –
FYE: September 30
Type: Private

Oconee Regional Health Systems (ORHS) helps people return to their natural healthy state though sometimes using unnatural methods to do so. Oconee Regional Health Systems serves the residents of Baldwin County in central Georgia. Its Oconee Regional Medical Center founded in 1957 has some 140 beds. Other facilities include Jasper Memorial Hospital (almost 20 beds) Primary Care Center of Monticello The Retreat Nursing Home and the ConvenientCare after-hours care center. Specialty services include behavioral medicine cancer treatment emergency care hospice pediatrics and physical therapy.

	Annual Growth	09/09	09/10	09/12	09/13	09/15
Sales ($ mil.)	280.1%	–	0.1	75.4	0.1	59.5
Net income ($ mil.)	–	–	0.0	(1.0)	0.0	(6.5)
Market value ($ mil.)	–	–	–	–	–	–
Employees	–	–	–	–	–	750

OCWEN FINANCIAL CORPORATION
NYSE: OCN

2002 Summit Blvd. 6th Fl.
Atlanta GA 30319
Phone: 561-682-8000
Fax: 561-682-8177
Web: www.ocwen.com

CEO: Glen A Messina
CFO: June C Campbell
HR: –
FYE: December 31
Type: Public

Oc-what? Oc-who? Ocwen. Ocwen Financial and its subsidiaries service residential and commercial mortgages for third parties. The company also offers special servicing and asset management services. Its main Ocwen Loan Servicing subsidiary is licensed to service loans in all 50 states and two US territories. The company which has offices and call centers in the US South America and India earns fees from the owners of mortgages or foreclosed real estate for which it collects. Clients include banks and other financial institutions including Credit Suisse Deutsche Bank Freddie Mac Goldman Sachs and Morgan Stanley. Ocwen no longer originates subprime loans.

OCZ TECHNOLOGY GROUP INC
NBB: OCZT Q

6373 San Ignacio Avenue
San Jose, CA 95119
Phone: 408-733-8400
Fax: –
Web: www.ocztechnology.com

CEO: –
CFO: –
HR: –
FYE: February 28
Type: Public

You down with OCZ? You should be because OCZ Technology's solid-state drives (SSDs) and related products are performing in PCs servers data centers and industrial gear around the world. The company designs manufactures and sells high-performance SSDs which use flash memory chips and are a smaller faster more reliable and more energy-efficient storage device than traditional hard disk drives. OCZ offers some 200 products to more than 400 customers in 60 countries. It sells directly to OEMs and large company and to other end users through systems integrators online retailers such as Amazon and computer distributors that include Memoryworld GmbH (10% of sales).

	Annual Growth	02/09	02/10	02/11	02/12	02/13
Sales ($ mil.)	21.0%	156.0	144.0	190.1	365.8	334.0
Net income ($ mil.)	–	(11.7)	(13.5)	(30.0)	(17.7)	(125.8)
Market value ($ mil.)	(30.9%)	–	357.5	515.5	585.3	117.8
Employees	24.1%	–	312	422	708	597

ODOM CORPORATION

11400 SE 8TH ST STE 300
BELLEVUE, WA 980046409
Phone: 425-456-3535
Fax: –
Web: www.odomcorp.com

CEO: –
CFO: Dana Leslie
HR: –
FYE: December 31
Type: Private

The Odom Corporation wants you to drink up if you happen to be in the Pacific Northwest. The company distributes beer wine and spirits as well as sodas energy drinks and bottled waters from more than 500 domestic and foreign suppliers including Coca-Cola Diageo E. & J. Gallo MillerCoors and Pernod Ricard. The company serves retail customers throughout the northwestern US including those in Alaska Idaho Oregon and Washington. It also runs Odom-Southern Holdings a joint venture with Southern Glazer's Wine and Spirits the #1 distributor of alcoholic beverages in the US. Milt Odom founded the company in 1933.

	Annual Growth	12/02	12/03	12/04	12/06	12/07
Sales ($ mil.)	22.1%	–	151.9	211.0	304.6	337.9
Net income ($ mil.)	4.4%	–	2.5	3.8	1.8	2.9
Market value ($ mil.)	–	–	–	–	–	–
Employees	–	–	–	–	–	1,500

ODYSSEY MARINE EXPLORATION, INC. NAS: OMEX

205 S. Hoover Blvd., Suite 210
Tampa, FL 33609
Phone: 813 876-1776
Fax: –
Web: www.odysseymarine.com

CEO: Mark D Gordon
CFO: Jay A Nudi
HR: Donna Fernandez
FYE: December 31
Type: Public

Gone are the days when one-eyed peg-legged buccaneers counted their steps to where X marked the spot of lost treasure. Odyssey Marine Exploration a new breed of treasure hunter uses sonar magnetometers and remotely operated vehicles (ROVs) to locate and excavate shipwrecks as well as for subsea mineral exploration. The company focuses on deepwater projects where the booty is less susceptible to damage and less likely to have been salvaged. Odyssey Marine Exploration surveys and maps seabeds too; its experience covers more than 10000 sq. mi. The company sells artifacts (coins bullion) salvaged from shipwrecks but also in recent years generates revenue from expedition charter services.

	Annual Growth	12/14	12/15	12/16	12/17	12/18
Sales ($ mil.)	25.4%	1.3	5.3	4.7	1.2	3.3
Net income ($ mil.)	–	(26.5)	(18.2)	(6.3)	(7.8)	(5.2)
Market value ($ mil.)	37.5%	8.6	2.5	31.5	34.8	30.7
Employees	(18.2%)	38	22	19	17	17

OEC BUSINESS INTERIORS INC.

900 N CHURCH RD
ELMHURST, IL 60126-1014
Phone: 630-589-5500
Fax: –
Web: www.oecbusinessinteriors.com

CEO: –
CFO: –
HR: –
FYE: September 30
Type: Private

Success at OEC Business Interiors is an inside job. The company supplies office equipment in the Chicago area and throughout the Midwest. Products include furniture panel systems floor coverings and textiles from major manufacturers as well as a wide range of services such as remanufacturing rentals brokerage warehouse storage and physical asset management. OEC Business Interiors was founded in 1955 by president Raymond Riha his wife and two partners as Riha Petersen & Vail. In 1961 the company purchased Office Equipment Company which had been in business since 1929.

	Annual Growth	09/08	09/09	09/09	09/11	09/12
Sales ($ mil.)	(0.9%)	–	55.2	47.8	54.7	53.7
Net income ($ mil.)	–	–	(0.1)	(0.4)	0.2	0.0
Market value ($ mil.)	–	–	–	–	–	–
Employees	–	–	–	–	–	135

OFFICE DEPOT, INC. NMS: ODP

6600 North Military Trail
Boca Raton, FL 33496
Phone: 561 438-4800
Fax: 561 265-4406
Web: www.officedepot.com

CEO: Gerry P. Smith
CFO: Joseph T. (Joe) Lower
HR: –
FYE: December 29
Type: Public

Paper and pens have made room for PC repair and point-of-sale services at office products giant Office Depot (#2 worldwide behind Staples). The office supply chain operates nearly 1400 retail stores under the Office Depot and OfficeMax names through which it sells a wide selection of office and school supplies furniture printers and breakroom and cleaning products. It has also moved into IT support and other business-to-business services which it offers through CompuCom and other brands. After divesting all its international holdings Office Depot operates entirely in North America.

	Annual Growth	12/14	12/15	12/16	12/17	12/18
Sales ($ mil.)	(9.0%)	16,096.0	14,485.0	11,021.0	10,240.0	11,015.0
Net income ($ mil.)	–	(354.0)	8.0	529.0	181.0	104.0
Market value ($ mil.)	(26.9%)	4,807.5	3,045.5	2,458.1	1,925.2	1,370.5
Employees	(5.9%)	56,000	49,000	38,000	45,000	44,000

OFFICE PROPERTIES INCOME TRUST NMS: OPI

Two Newton Place, 255 Washington Street, Suite 300
Newton, MA 02458-1634
Phone: 617 219-1440
Fax: –
Web: www.opireit.com

CEO: –
CFO: Mark L. Kleifges
HR: –
FYE: December 31
Type: Public

If Government Properties Income Trust had one request of Uncle Sam it would be this: "I want you to lease our properties." As a real estate investment trust (REIT) Government Properties Income Trust invests in properties that are leased to government tenants. It owns nearly 11 million sq. ft. of leasing space across more than 70 properties across the US. The company leases mostly to federal agencies (such as the FBI IRS and FDA) but it does lease to some state-run agencies and the United Nations as well. It also makes some equity investments. Government Properties Income Trust went public in 2009.

	Annual Growth	12/14	12/15	12/16	12/17	12/18
Sales ($ mil.)	14.2%	251.0	248.5	258.2	316.5	426.6
Net income ($ mil.)	–	56.5	(210.0)	57.8	12.1	(21.9)
Market value ($ mil.)	(26.1%)	1,106.4	763.1	916.7	891.5	330.3
Employees	–	–	–	–	–	–

OFFICIAL PAYMENTS HOLDINGS INC. NASDAQ: TIER

10780 Parkridge Blvd. 4th Fl.
Reston VA 20191
Phone: 571-382-1000
Fax: 571-382-1002
Web: www.officialpayments.com

CEO: Alex P Hart
CFO: –
HR: –
FYE: September 30
Type: Public

Official Payments Holdings helps the tax man get what's coming to him. Formerly Tier Technologies the company provides electronic payments services (EPS) services for federal state and local government entities as well as utilities colleges and universities and commercial clients. Through its main subsidiary Official Payments the company processes more than 20 million transactions each year for payment of federal and state income taxes business and property taxes court fees and fines and utility bills among others. It handles more than $8 billion annually. Payments can be made online by phone or mobile device or at the point-of-sale.

OGE ENERGY CORP. NYS: OGE

321 North Harvey, P.O. Box 321
Oklahoma City, OK 73101-0321
Phone: 405 553-3000
Fax: –
Web: www.oge.com

CEO: R. Sean Trauschke
CFO: Stephen E. (Steve) Merrill
HR: –
FYE: December 31
Type: Public

OGE Energy is the holding company for the largest electric utility in Oklahoma. Its regulated utility Oklahoma Gas and Electric (OG&E) generates transmits and sells electricity to about 850000 customers in Oklahoma and a slice of western Arkansas. It generates about 6600 MW of power through its coal- and gas-fired power plants and increasingly wind and solar resources. OGE Energy also owns roughly 25% of a natural gas gathering processing and transport operation Enable Midstream Partners.

	Annual Growth	12/14	12/15	12/16	12/17	12/18
Sales ($ mil.)	(1.9%)	2,453.1	2,196.9	2,259.2	2,261.1	2,270.3
Net income ($ mil.)	1.8%	395.8	271.3	338.2	619.0	425.5
Market value ($ mil.)	2.5%	7,085.4	5,250.1	6,680.0	6,572.1	7,826.2
Employees	(8.9%)	3,329	2,586	2,453	2,413	2,292

OGLETHORPE POWER CORP

2100 East Exchange Place
Tucker, GA 30084-5336
Phone: 770 270-7600
Fax: –
Web: www.opc.com

CEO: Michael L. Smith
CFO: Elizabeth Bush (Betsy) Higgins
HR: –
FYE: December 31
Type: Public

Much ogled for its robust energy supply not-for-profit Oglethorpe Power Corporation is one of the largest electricity cooperatives in the US with contracts to supply wholesale power to 38 member/owners (making up most of Georgia's electric distribution cooperatives) until 2050. Oglethorpe's member/owners which also operate as not-for-profits serve 1.8 million residential commercial and industrial customers (or about 4.2 million people). The company has a generating capacity of more than 7700 MW from fossil-fueled nuclear and hydroelectric power plants. Oglethorpe has stakes in 31 generating units. In addition the company purchases power from other suppliers and it markets power on the wholesale market.

	Annual Growth	12/14	12/15	12/16	12/17	12/18
Sales ($ mil.)	1.3%	1,408.2	1,349.8	1,507.2	1,434.2	1,480.1
Net income ($ mil.)	2.4%	46.6	48.3	50.3	51.3	51.2
Market value ($ mil.)	–	–	–	–	–	–
Employees	1.5%	265	273	278	278	281

OHIO EDISON COMPANY

76 S MAIN ST BSMT
AKRON, OH 443081817
Phone: 800-736-3402
Fax: –
Web: www.firstenergycorp.com

CEO: –
CFO: James F Pearson
HR: –
FYE: December 31
Type: Private

Ohio Edison has taken a shine to the folks in the Buckeye state. The company distributes electricity to a population of about 2.3 million (more than 1 million customers) in a 7000 sq. ml. area of central and northeastern Ohio. Ohio Edison a unit of FirstEnergy also has 5955 MW of generating capacity from interests in primarily fossil-fueled and nuclear generation facilities and it sells excess power to wholesale customers. The utility's power plants are operated by sister companies FirstEnergy Nuclear and FirstEnergy Generation. Subsidiary Pennsylvania Power Company provides electric service to communities in a 1100 sq. ml. area of western Pennsylvania which has a population of approximately 400000.

	Annual Growth	12/08	12/09	12/10	12/11	12/16
Sales ($ mil.)	(8.1%)	–	2,516.9	1,836.1	1,633.0	1,394.9
Net income ($ mil.)	3.0%	–	122.4	157.2	128.0	151.0
Market value ($ mil.)	–	–	–	–	–	–
Employees	–	–	–	–	–	1,190

OHIO LEGACY CORP

600 South Main Street
North Canton, OH 44720
Phone: 330 499-1900
Fax: –
Web: www.ohiolegacycorp.com

NBB: OLCB
CEO: –
CFO: –
HR: –
FYE: December 31
Type: Public

Ohio Legacy Corp is the holding company for Premier Bank & Trust (formerly Ohio Legacy Bank) which serves northeastern Ohio's Stark and Wayne counties through about five branches. Operating since 2000 the bank offers standard deposit products and services including checking and savings accounts CDs IRAs cash management and safe deposit box facilities. It added trust services in 2010 and changed its name to reflect its new focus. Commercial multifamily and residential mortgages account for some two-thirds of all loans. United Community Financial is buying Ohio Legacy for some $40.3 million.

	Annual Growth	12/11	12/12	12/13	12/14	12/15
Assets ($ mil.)	21.7%	146.6	174.7	229.9	266.2	321.4
Net income ($ mil.)	(10.8%)	1.8	0.1	0.9	4.9	1.2
Market value ($ mil.)	76.1%	2.1	12.3	14.8	18.7	20.2
Employees	11.3%	53	59	–	–	–

OHIO LIVING

1001 KINGSMILL PKWY
COLUMBUS, OH 432291129
Phone: 614-888-7800
Fax: –
Web: www.ohioliving.org

CEO: Laurence Gumina
CFO: Robert Stillman
HR: –
FYE: June 30
Type: Private

Ohio Presbyterian Retirement Service (OPRS) operates a network of continuing care retirement communities in Ohio. The company offers services through about a dozen senior living communities across the state and serves about 7000 residents. The centers include skilled nursing assisted living and independent living residences. Through its Senior Independence program the not-for-profit organization also provides independent-living services to about 90000 seniors in Ohio including adult day care home health hospice and community health clinics. OPRS was established in 1922.

	Annual Growth	06/09	06/10	06/15	06/17	06/18
Sales ($ mil.)	–	–	0.0	2.3	226.4	228.3
Net income ($ mil.)	–	–	0.0	1.8	18.8	7.3
Market value ($ mil.)	–	–	–	–	–	–
Employees	–	–	–	–	–	3,100

OHIO POWER COMPANY

NL:

1 Riverside Plaza
Columbus, OH 43215-2373
Phone: 614 716-1000
Fax: –
Web: www.aep.com

CEO: Nicholas K Akins
CFO: Brian X Tierney
HR: –
FYE: December 31
Type: Public

To access electricity across the state of Ohio residents and businesses turn to Ohio Power which in tandem with Wheeling Power does business as part of AEP Ohio. AEP Ohio serves 1.5 million retail customers. The company one of American Electric Power's largest utility subsidiaries operates more than 31260 miles of transmission and distribution lines. The utility also generates more than 8500 MW of capacity from primarily hydroelectric and fossil-fueled power plants (the bulk from coal-fired plants) and it sells wholesale electricity to other power companies.

	Annual Growth	12/14	12/15	12/16	12/17	12/18
Sales ($ mil.)	(2.4%)	3,376.9	3,148.7	2,953.9	2,883.9	3,063.4
Net income ($ mil.)	10.7%	216.4	232.7	282.2	323.9	325.5
Market value ($ mil.)	–	–	–	–	–	–
Employees	3.0%	1,516	1,552	1,582	1,654	1,704

OHIO TURNPIKE AND INFRASTRUCTURE COMMISSION

682 PROSPECT ST
BEREA, OH 440172711
Phone: 440-234-2081
Fax: –
Web: www.ohioturnpike.org

CEO: Randy Cole
CFO: Martin S Seekely
HR: –
FYE: December 31
Type: Private

The Ohio Turnpike Commission operates the 241-mile James W. Shocknessy Ohio Turnpike and its service plazas. The turnpike spans the width of the state. It begins near the Michigan border in the northwest corner of Ohio and passes just south of the Toledo and Cleveland metropolitan areas before terminating east of Youngstown. The turnpike connects with other toll roads in Indiana and Pennsylvania. The Ohio legislature established the turnpike commission in 1949 and the toll road was opened to traffic in 1955. The Ohio Turnpike Commission is governed separately from the state's primary highway agency the Ohio Department of Transportation.

	Annual Growth	12/09	12/10	12/16	12/17	12/18
Sales ($ mil.)	3.6%	–	251.7	313.2	321.9	333.0
Net income ($ mil.)	–	–	54.6	(230.3)	(66.8)	(0.4)
Market value ($ mil.)	–	–	–	–	–	–
Employees	–	–	–	–	–	953

OHIO VALLEY BANC CORP
NMS: OVBC

420 Third Avenue
Gallipolis, OH 45631
Phone: 740 446-2631
Fax: –
Web: www.ovbc.com

CEO: Thomas E Wiseman
CFO: Scott W Shockey
HR: –
FYE: December 31
Type: Public

Ohio Valley Banc Corp. (OVBC) knows when you go to buy groceries you'll probably need some cabbage. That's why this holding company likes to operate its Ohio Valley Bank branches inside supermarkets. The bank has some 20 branches in Ohio and West Virginia about half of which are in Wal-Marts and other stores. The bank accepts deposits in checking savings time and money market accounts and offers standard banking services such as safe deposit boxes and wire transfers. Commercial and residential real estate loans combine to make up almost three-quarters of the bank's loan portfolio. Business and consumer loans make up the remainder. Also part of OVBC is life insurance agency Ohio Valley Financial Services.

	Annual Growth	12/14	12/15	12/16	12/17	12/18
Assets ($ mil.)	7.3%	778.7	796.3	954.6	1,026.3	1,030.5
Net income ($ mil.)	10.3%	8.1	8.6	6.9	7.5	11.9
Market value ($ mil.)	9.6%	116.3	116.4	128.9	191.5	167.8
Employees	3.2%	264	248	297	305	300

OHIO VALLEY ELECTRIC CORPORATION

3932 US RTE 23
PIKETON, OH 45661
Phone: 740-289-7200
Fax: –

CEO: –
CFO: –
HR: –
FYE: June 30
Type: Private

Down by the banks of the Ohio Ohio Valley Electric and its subsidiary Indiana-Kentucky Electric generate power for customers across the Ohio River Valley. It operates two coal-fired plants which collectively have about 2290 MW of generating capacity. Ohio Valley Electric's Kyger Creek Plant (Cheshire Ohio) and Indiana-Kentucky Electric's Clifty Creek Plant (Madison Indiana) are linked by 705 miles of transmission lines. Most of Ohio Valley Electric's power goes to its shareholders (a dozen investor-owned utilities utility holding entities led by American Electric Power and units of generation and transmission rural electric cooperatives). It also supplies energy to the Department of Energy.

	Annual Growth	09/14	09/15*	12/15*	03/16*	06/16
Sales ($ mil.)	(39.2%)	–	436.6	565.3	119.9	265.3
Net income ($ mil.)	(36.2%)	–	0.7	0.8	0.4	0.4
Market value ($ mil.)	–	–	–	–	–	–
Employees	–	–	–	–	–	428

*Fiscal year change

OHIO VALLEY GENERAL HOSPITAL

25 HECKEL RD
MC KEES ROCKS, PA 151361651
Phone: 412-777-6161
Fax: –
Web: www.ohiovalleyhospital.org

CEO: Norman F Mitry
CFO: –
HR: –
FYE: June 30
Type: Private

Ohio Valley General Hospital is a full-service 140-bed medical center serving western Pennsylvania residents. The not-for-profit community hospital's staff of about 250 doctors (representing about 35 medical specialties) provides emergency acute diagnostic and specialty care and a variety of inpatient and outpatient care services. Ohio Valley General Hospital's programs include cardiology occupational medicine pain treatment orthopedics rehabilitation sleep disorder diagnosis geriatric psychiatry and wound care. The hospital also offers assisted living for seniors. Ohio Valley General began serving patients in 1906.

	Annual Growth	06/14	06/15	06/16	06/17	06/18
Sales ($ mil.)	8.4%	–	58.5	67.9	72.1	74.5
Net income ($ mil.)	–	–	(1.0)	(13.9)	3.1	(5.0)
Market value ($ mil.)	–	–	–	–	–	–
Employees	–	–	–	–	–	570

OHIO VALLEY MEDICAL CENTER INCORPORATED

2000 EOFF ST
WHEELING, WV 260033823
Phone: 304-234-0123
Fax: –
Web: www.ovmc-eorh.com

CEO: Lex Reddy
CFO: –
HR: –
FYE: December 31
Type: Private

Ohio Valley Medical Center (OVMC) is a Wheeling West Virginia-based medical provider that administers a variety of acute care primary care and other health services to patients through a 200-bed hospital. The facility established in 1890 as City Hospital specializes in intermediate care physical rehabilitation and skilled nursing. Other services include cardiology cancer care emergency care gynecology neurology oncology and psychiatry as well as home health care. OVMC also operates the Peterson Rehabilitation Center and two-year hospital based education program OVMC School of Radiologic Technology. It partners with nearby East Ohio Regional Hospital to provide 340 total beds.

	Annual Growth	12/06	12/07	12/09	12/14	12/16
Sales ($ mil.)	1.5%	–	94.7	106.4	103.2	108.2
Net income ($ mil.)	(16.2%)	–	6.0	(1.8)	4.0	1.2
Market value ($ mil.)	–	–	–	–	–	–
Employees	–	–	–	–	–	1,275

OHIOHEALTH CORPORATION

3430 OHHALTH PKWY FL 5 FLR 5
COLUMBUS, OH 43202
Phone: 614-788-8860
Fax: –

CEO: David P. Blom
CFO: Vinson M. Yates
HR: –
FYE: June 30
Type: Private

Operating throughout the central part of the state OhioHealth aims to keep Buckeyes healthy. The not-for-profit system runs eight acute care hospitals and is affiliated with another 11 community hospitals and area health systems. All told OhioHealth has about 2000 staffed beds in and around Columbus. Additional facilities offer urgent care physical rehabilitation diagnostic imaging and sleep diagnostics services. Subsidiary HomeReach provides home health care and hospice care. Its WorkHealth program offers workers' compensation care management and occupational rehabilitation services. OhioHealth Group OhioHealth's joint venture with The Medical Group of Ohio operates the HealthReach PPO.

	Annual Growth	06/10	06/11	06/14	06/17	06/18
Sales ($ mil.)	8.2%	–	2,328.4	2,179.6	3,792.7	4,045.7
Net income ($ mil.)	3.3%	–	413.0	354.3	631.5	519.0
Market value ($ mil.)	–	–	–	–	–	–
Employees	–	–	–	–	–	15,000

OIL STATES INTERNATIONAL, INC.
NYS: OIS

Three Allen Center, 333 Clay Street, Suite 4620
Houston, TX 77002
Phone: 713 652-0582
Fax: –

CEO: –
CFO: Lloyd A. Hajdik
HR: Lias J. (Jeff) Steen
FYE: December 31
Type: Public

Oil States International is an oilfield services company with a leading market position as a manufacturer of products for deepwater production facilities and certain drilling equipment as well as a provider of completion services and land drilling services to the oil and gas industry and oil and gas perforation systems and downhole tools. The company provides well site services including subsea pipeline products. It also offers offshore products including flex-element technology and deepwater mooring systems. Oil States International focuses on supporting explorers in major producing regions throughout the world. About 80% of its revenue comes from the US.

	Annual Growth	12/14	12/15	12/16	12/17	12/18
Sales ($ mil.)	(12.1%)	1,819.6	1,100.0	694.4	670.6	1,088.1
Net income ($ mil.)	–	179.0	28.6	(46.4)	(84.9)	(19.1)
Market value ($ mil.)	(26.5%)	2,932.5	1,634.2	2,338.8	1,697.1	856.4
Employees	(7.2%)	5,290	3,586	2,821	3,077	3,926

OIL-DRI CORP. OF AMERICA
NYS: ODC

410 North Michigan Avenue, Suite 400
Chicago, IL 60611-4213
Phone: 312 321-1515
Fax: 312 321-9525
Web: www.oildri.com

CEO: Daniel S Jaffee
CFO: Daniel T Smith
HR: –
FYE: July 31
Type: Public

Oil-Dri Corporation (ODC) of America keeps cat lovers' homes from stinking to high heaven. The company produces sorbent products for the consumer industrial automotive agricultural and fluid-purification markets. It makes and sells traditional coarse and scoopable cat litters under its own Cat's Pride and Jonny Cat brands. ODC manufactures the Fresh Step brand exclusively for Clorox as well as private label cat litters for others. Its litters are sold by mass merchants (Wal-Mart) supermarkets pet stores wholesale clubs and other retailers. ODC also makes sorbents for oil grease and water; bleaching and clarification clays; agricultural and sports fields; and animal health and nutrition products.

	Annual Growth	07/15	07/16	07/17	07/18	07/19
Sales ($ mil.)	1.5%	261.4	262.3	262.3	266.0	277.0
Net income ($ mil.)	2.6%	11.4	13.6	10.8	8.2	12.6
Market value ($ mil.)	7.8%	199.8	285.0	314.7	322.3	269.6
Employees	0.1%	797	767	783	775	801

OILTANKING PARTNERS LP
NYS: OILT

333 Clay Street, Suite 2400
Houston, TX 77002
Phone: 281 457-7900
Fax: –
Web: www.oiltankingpartners.com

CEO: Laurie H Argo
CFO: Donna Y Hymel
HR: Lisa Cargile
FYE: December 31
Type: Public

What do Germany and Houston have in common? Not much besides Oiltanking Partners. The limited partnership formed in March 2011 by Oiltanking Holding Americas a subsidiary of Oiltanking GmbH the world's second-largest independent storage provider for crude oil liquid chemicals and gases. (Oiltanking GmbH is in turn owned by private German conglomerate Marquard & Bahls). Oiltanking Partners owns and operates pipeline terminals with about 135 tanks in Houston and Beaumont that have a storage capacity of about 18 million barrels. Customers include oil and companies marketers and distributors. Oiltanking Partners raised $215 million in its 2011 initial public offering.

	Annual Growth	12/08	12/09	12/10	12/11	12/12
Sales ($ mil.)	–	0.0	100.8	116.5	117.4	135.5
Net income ($ mil.)	–	0.0	25.1	37.8	62.4	62.6
Market value ($ mil.)	–	0.0	–	–	1,086.1	1,472.7
Employees	–	–	–	–	–	–

OKEECHOBEE HOSPITAL, INC.

1796 US HIGHWAY 441 N
OKEECHOBEE, FL 349721918
Phone: 863-763-2151
Fax: –
Web: www.raulersonhospital.com

CEO: –
CFO: Bob Risch
HR: –
FYE: April 30
Type: Private

Raulerson Hospital part of HCA is an acute care hospital with some 100 beds. The facility serves the community of Okeechobee and surrounding areas in eastern Florida. The hospital provides a variety of general medical services including diagnostic imaging laparoscopic surgery intensive care neurology orthopedics rehabilitation and physical therapy. Specialty units include a cardiopulmonary department a sleep disorder lab a diabetes education unit and outpatient testing and surgery centers. Raulerson Hospital is part of HCA's East Florida division.

	Annual Growth	04/10	04/11	04/12	04/13	04/15
Sales ($ mil.)	2.7%	–	–	–	70.4	74.4
Net income ($ mil.)	7.0%	–	–	–	17.1	19.6
Market value ($ mil.)	–	–	–	–	–	–
Employees	–	–	–	–	–	350

OKLAHOMA STATE UNIVERSITY

401 WHITEHURST HALL
STILLWATER, OK 740781030
Phone: 405-744-5000
Fax: –
Web: www.okstate.com

CEO: –
CFO: –
HR: –
FYE: June 30
Type: Private

Oooooklahoma where the... students come to learn! Oklahoma State University is the flagship campus of its namesake (OSU) system which also includes OSU-Tulsa OSU-Oklahoma City OSU-Okmulgee the OSU Center for Health Sciences in Tulsa the OSU College of Veterinary Medicine and the Oklahoma Agricultural Experiment Station. OSU offers courses in a variety of disciplines and confers undergraduate graduate doctoral and professional degrees in everything from agriculture and the arts to business and engineering. Altogether the system boasts an enrollment of about 36000 students across its five campuses; its student-teacher ratio is about 17:1.

	Annual Growth	06/14	06/15	06/16	06/17	06/18
Sales ($ mil.)	(1.5%)	–	–	–	815.1	802.9
Net income ($ mil.)	(77.8%)	–	–	–	40.3	9.0
Market value ($ mil.)	–	–	–	–	–	–
Employees	–	–	–	–	–	8,882

OLD DOMINION ELECTRIC COOPERATIVE

4201 Dominion Boulevard
Glen Allen, VA 23060
Phone: 804 747-0592
Fax: –
Web: www.odec.com

CEO: –
CFO: –
HR: –
FYE: December 31
Type: Public

Ol' Virginny and neighboring states get power from Old Dominion Electric Cooperative which generates and purchases electricity for its 11 member distribution cooperatives. These in turn serve more than 550000 customer meters in four northeastern states. The member-owned power utility has more than 2000 MW of generating capacity from nuclear hydro and fossil-fueled power plants and diesel generators; it purchases the remainder of its power from neighboring utilities and power marketers. Old Dominion transmits power to its members through the systems of utilities and transmission operators in the region. It also provides power to TEC Trading a wholesale company owned by the distribution cooperatives.

	Annual Growth	12/14	12/15	12/16	12/17	12/18
Sales ($ mil.)	(0.5%)	951.6	1,020.0	877.9	753.1	932.6
Net income ($ mil.)	9.9%	9.1	11.9	17.6	26.6	13.3
Market value ($ mil.)	–	–	–	–	–	–
Employees	6.0%	111	137	136	136	140

OLD DOMINION FREIGHT LINE, INC.
NMS: ODFL

500 Old Dominion Way
Thomasville, NC 27360
Phone: 336 889-5000
Fax: –
Web: www.odfl.com

CEO: David S. Congdon
CFO: Adam N. Satterfield
HR: –
FYE: December 31
Type: Public

Old Dominion Freight Line is a trucking company specializing in less-than-truckload (LTL) shipments (freight from multiple shippers consolidated into a single truckload). It operates a fleet of some 8000 tractors and more than 30500 trailers from more than 225 service centers. In addition to its core LTL services Old Dominion offers its customers a broad range of logistics services including ground and air transportation supply chain consulting container delivery and warehousing and household moving. The company traces its historical roots back to 1934.

	Annual Growth	12/14	12/15	12/16	12/17	12/18
Sales ($ mil.)	9.7%	2,787.9	2,972.4	2,991.5	3,358.1	4,043.7
Net income ($ mil.)	22.7%	267.5	304.7	295.8	463.8	605.7
Market value ($ mil.)	12.3%	6,306.8	4,798.3	6,968.8	10,686.0	10,031.2
Employees	6.7%	16,443	17,931	17,543	19,183	21,279

OLD LINE BANCSHARES INC   NAS: OLBK

1525 Pointer Ridge Place   CEO: –
Bowie, MD 20716   CFO: –
Phone: 301 430-2500   HR: –
Fax: –   FYE: December 31
Web: www.oldlinebank.com   Type: Public

Old Line Bancshares is the holding company for Old Line Bank serving consumers businesses and wealthy individuals in the Old Line State and in the Washington DC area. With some 20 branch offices and total assets in excess of $1.2 billion the bank offers standard retail products including deposit accounts CDs and credit cards. Commercial and industrial and commercial real estate loans make up 75% of the bank's loan portfolio though it also offers consumer loans and luxury boat financing. The company also owns 50% of real estate firm Pointer Ridge Office Investment.

	Annual Growth	12/13	12/14	12/15	12/16	12/17
Assets ($ mil.)	15.9%	1,167.2	1,227.5	1,510.1	1,709.0	2,105.6
Net income ($ mil.)	19.5%	7.8	7.1	10.5	13.2	16.0
Market value ($ mil.)	19.4%	181.4	197.9	219.8	299.9	368.2
Employees	1.6%	254	228	248	234	271

OLD NATIONAL BANCORP (EVANSVILLE, IN)   NMS: ONB

One Main Street   CEO: Robert G. (Bob) Jones
Evansville, IN 47708   CFO: Christopher A. (Chris) Wolking
Phone: 800 731-2265   HR: Ann Claspell
Fax: –   FYE: December 31
Web: www.oldnational.com   Type: Public

Old National Bank is old but it's not quite national. Founded in 1834 the main subsidiary of Old National Bancorp operates about 200 bank centers across Indiana Kentucky Michigan and Illinois. The bank serves consumers and business customers offering standard checking and savings accounts credit cards and loans. Its treasury segment manages investments for bank and commercial clients. Business loans commercial and residential mortgages and consumer loans account for most of Old National's lending activity. The company also sells insurance manages wealth for high-net-worth clients and offers investment and retirement services through third-party provider LPL Financial.

	Annual Growth	12/14	12/15	12/16	12/17	12/18
Assets ($ mil.)	14.1%	11,647.6	11,991.5	14,860.2	17,518.3	19,728.4
Net income ($ mil.)	16.5%	103.7	116.7	134.3	95.7	190.8
Market value ($ mil.)	0.9%	2,606.1	2,374.9	3,178.8	3,056.2	2,697.2
Employees	(0.4%)	2,938	2,652	2,733	2,801	2,892

OLD NAVY INC.

2 Folsom St.   CEO: Sonia Syngal
San Francisco CA 94105   CFO: John J Lenk
Phone: 650-952-4400   HR: –
Fax: 773-714-4595   FYE: January 31
Web: www.wilson.com   Type: Business Segment

Old Navy commands a fleet of more than 1025 family clothing stores throughout the US and Canada offering items under its own brand name at discounted prices. (The apparel retailer also operates a Web-based store at oldnavy.com.) Products include men's women's and children's (even dogs') apparel and accessories. Founded in 1994 Old Navy is owned by the king of casual apparel Gap Inc. and is known for advertising that plays up the kitsch factor of various celebrities. Old Navy which has suffered from sales declines in recent years appears to be back on track and has extended its brand to include maternity and women's plus-size apparel as well as accessories and personal care products.

OLD POINT FINANCIAL CORP   NAS: OPOF

1 West Mellen Street   CEO: Robert F Shuford Sr
Hampton, VA 23663   CFO: Laurie D Grabow
Phone: 757 728-1200   HR: –
Fax: –   FYE: December 31
Web: www.oldpoint.com   Type: Public

Community banking and wealth management is the point at Old Point Financial. It is the holding company for Old Point National Bank of Phoebus which has more than 20 branches in the Hampton Roads region of southeastern Virginia. Founded in 1923 the bank serves area businesses and consumers offering such services as checking and savings accounts money market accounts and CDs. With these funds the bank mainly originates commercial and residential mortgages which account for a majority of its loans. Subsidiary Old Point Trust & Financial Services provides investment management and tax estate and retirement planning services. Old Point National Bank also owns 49% of Old Point Mortgage.

	Annual Growth	12/14	12/15	12/16	12/17	12/18
Assets ($ mil.)	4.3%	876.3	896.8	903.0	981.8	1,038.2
Net income ($ mil.)	4.6%	4.1	3.6	3.8	(0.0)	4.9
Market value ($ mil.)	9.8%	77.8	89.0	129.6	154.2	113.2
Employees	0.0%	301	296	280	301	301

OLD REPUBLIC INTERNATIONAL CORP.   NYS: ORI

307 North Michigan Avenue   CEO: Aldo C. (Al) Zucaro
Chicago, IL 60601   CFO: Karl W. Mueller
Phone: 312 346-8100   HR: –
Fax: –   FYE: December 31
Web: www.oldrepublic.com   Type: Public

Old Republic International keeps pace with changing financial times. With about 140 subsidiaries across North America Old Republic's primary operations are conducted through the Old Republic General Insurance division which offers commercial liability and property/casualty insurance (mostly commercial trucking workers' compensation and general liability policies). In addition the company's Title Insurance group specializes in naturally issuing title insurance to property owners and lenders. Its Old Republic National Title subsidiary is one of the US's oldest and largest title insurance companies with offices throughout the US.

	Annual Growth	12/14	12/15	12/16	12/17	12/18
Assets ($ mil.)	3.3%	16,988.1	17,110.5	18,591.6	19,403.5	19,327.1
Net income ($ mil.)	(2.5%)	409.7	422.1	466.9	560.5	370.5
Market value ($ mil.)	8.9%	4,428.7	5,639.6	5,751.6	6,472.0	6,226.8
Employees	3.0%	8,000	8,200	8,500	8,700	9,000

OLD SECOND BANCORP., INC. (AURORA, ILL.)   NMS: OSBC

37 South River Street   CEO: James L. Eccher
Aurora, IL 60507   CFO: J. Douglas Cheatham
Phone: 630 892-0202   HR: Robert Dicosola
Fax: –   FYE: December 31
Web: www.oldsecond.com   Type: Public

Old Second won't settle for a silver finish when it comes to community banking around Chicago. Old Second Bancorp is the holding company for Old Second National Bank which serves the Chicago metropolitan area through 25 branches in Kane Kendall DeKalb DuPage LaSalle Will and Cook counties. The bank provides standard services such as checking and savings accounts credit and debit cards CDs mortgages loans and trust services to consumers and business clients. Subsidiary River Street Advisors offers investment management and advisory services. Another unit Old Second Affordable Housing Fund provides home-buying assistance to lower-income customers.

	Annual Growth	12/14	12/15	12/16	12/17	12/18
Assets ($ mil.)	6.7%	2,061.8	2,077.9	2,251.2	2,383.4	2,676.0
Net income ($ mil.)	35.3%	10.1	15.4	15.7	15.1	34.0
Market value ($ mil.)	24.7%	159.8	233.3	328.9	406.3	386.9
Employees	1.7%	485	450	467	450	518

OLD TIME POTTERY INC.

480 RIVER ROCK BLVD
MURFREESBORO, TN 37128-4804
Phone: 615-890-6060
Fax: –
Web: www.oldtimepotteryindianapolis.com

CEO: Scott Peterson
CFO: Robert Sharp
HR: –
FYE: December 31
Type: Private

You won't find any dusty crocks or cracked pots at Old Time Pottery. The chain markets discounted closeout and overstock housewares silk flowers hanging baskets framed art linens rugs craft supplies seasonal merchandise and more. Its network of more than 30 stores spans some 10 states in the nation's South and Midwest. Old Time Pottery sources its inventory which the retailer displays in a warehouse-type setting from the canceled orders and excess stock of manufacturers. To its benefit the specialty retailer can accommodate lots of inventory as stores average about 2 acres in size. Founded in 1986 Old Time Pottery is controlled by the Peterson family.

	Annual Growth	12/04	12/05	12/06	12/11	12/12
Sales ($ mil.)	(2.8%)	–	188.9	208.5	146.7	154.4
Net income ($ mil.)	9.5%	–	4.1	1.1	6.6	7.8
Market value ($ mil.)	–	–	–	–	–	–
Employees	–	–	–	–	–	3,000

OLDCASTLE INC.

375 Northridge Rd. Ste. 350
Atlanta GA 30350
Phone: 770-804-3363
Fax: 402-537-9847
Web: www.isecuretrac.com

CEO: Mark S Towe
CFO: Michael G O'Driscoll
HR: –
FYE: December 31
Type: Subsidiary

Oldcastle has the materials to build your modern castle. The North American arm of CRH makes architectural and construction building products in the US and Canada. It operates through six product groups including Oldcastle Materials which produces and sells aggregates asphalt and ready-mix concrete and provides paving services. Masonry products are made by Oldcastle Architectural. Meanwhile Oldcastle Precast provides precast concrete and Oldcastle BuildingEnvelope provides curtain walls and architectural windows and doors. Its distribution arm Allied Building Products delivers to specialty contractors. Oldcastle Construction Accessories sells fencing concrete reinforcements and anchoring systems.

OLE' MEXICAN FOODS, INC.

6585 CRESCENT DR
NORCROSS, GA 300712901
Phone: 770-582-9200
Fax: –
Web: www.olemex.com

CEO: Veronica Moreno
CFO: –
HR: –
FYE: December 31
Type: Private

Its a wrap at Ol-© Mexican Foods. The company makes Mexican-American foods inducing tortillas and taco shells under brand names La Banderita La Centroamericana Ol-© and Verol-©. The company also produces salsa sour cream Mexican cheeses and sausages tostadas and tortilla chips among other items. Its customers include retail food outlets and food service operations. Headquartered in Norcross Georgia the company has about a dozen distribution centers across the US. It serves customers across the continental US and Alaska as well as in Puerto Rico.

	Annual Growth	12/01	12/02	12/03	12/13	12/14
Sales ($ mil.)	14.6%	–	52.7	65.1	242.7	269.1
Net income ($ mil.)	5.1%	–	3.6	5.8	12.5	6.6
Market value ($ mil.)	–	–	–	–	–	–
Employees	–	–	–	–	–	920

OLIN CORP.

NYS: OLN

190 Carondelet Plaza, Suite 1530
Clayton, MO 63105
Phone: 314 480-1400
Fax: –
Web: www.olin.com

CEO: John E. Fischer
CFO: Todd A. Slater
HR: Dolores Ennico
FYE: December 31
Type: Public

The making of bleach and bullets is all in a day's work for Olin Corporation. The company manufactures chemicals used to make bleach water purification and swimming pool chemicals pulp and paper processing agents and PVC plastics. Olin Chlor Alkali Products is one of the top chlor-alkali producers in North America along with OxyChem. Olin also distributes caustic soda vinyls epoxies chlorinated organics hydrochloric acid and bleach. In addition in a quite divergent business the company's Winchester Ammunition unit makes branded sporting ammunition reloading components small caliber military ammunition and components and industrial cartridges.

	Annual Growth	12/14	12/15	12/16	12/17	12/18
Sales ($ mil.)	32.7%	2,241.2	2,854.4	5,550.6	6,268.4	6,946.1
Net income ($ mil.)	32.7%	105.7	(1.4)	(3.9)	549.5	327.9
Market value ($ mil.)	(3.1%)	3,763.9	2,853.1	4,233.3	5,881.4	3,324.2
Employees	13.6%	3,900	6,200	6,400	6,400	6,500

OLMSTED MEDICAL CENTER

210 9TH ST SE STE 1
ROCHESTER, MN 559046400
Phone: 507-288-3443
Fax: –
Web: www.olmmed.org

CEO: Tim Weir
CFO: –
HR: –
FYE: December 31
Type: Private

Olmsted Medical Center (OMC) provides general medical and surgical care to the Rochester Minnesota area. The not-for-profit hospital also partners with regional schools to provide medical nursing and technical training and it engages in clinical research programs. Specialty services include pediatrics neurology occupational medicine and orthopedics. In addition to its hospital OMC also operates several urgent care specialty and general practice clinics in the region. OMC was formed through the merger of Olmsted Community Hospital and Olmsted Medical Group in 1996.

	Annual Growth	12/01	12/02	12/08	12/09	12/16
Sales ($ mil.)	(10.0%)	–	896.6	0.3	144.2	205.3
Net income ($ mil.)	125.4%	–	0.0	0.0	12.3	21.5
Market value ($ mil.)	–	–	–	–	–	–
Employees	–	–	–	–	–	1,200

OLYMPIC PIPE LINE COMPANY

2319 LIND AVE SW
RENTON, WA 980573347
Phone: 425-235-7736
Fax: –
Web: –

CEO: –
CFO: –
HR: –
FYE: December 31
Type: Private

Olympic Pipe Line is going for the gold (you know black gold or Texas tea). The company owned by Enbridge (65%) and integrated oil giant BP p.l.c. (35%) operates a 400-mile interstate pipeline system used for the transportation of refined petroleum products including aviation jet fuel diesel and gasoline from Washington to Oregon; through joint ventures the company has operations in 30 US states. Its systems are capable of moving about 285000 barrels of refined petroleum products per day. In 2006 Enbridge paid BP nearly $100 million for a controlling share in Olympic Pipe Line. BP is the pipeline operator.

	Annual Growth	12/13	12/14	12/15	12/16	12/17
Sales ($ mil.)	18.4%	–	–	–	66.1	78.3
Net income ($ mil.)	495.7%	–	–	–	10.1	59.9
Market value ($ mil.)	–	–	–	–	–	–
Employees	–	–	–	–	–	82

OLYMPIC STEEL INC.

NMS: ZEUS

22901 Millcreek Boulevard, Suite 650
Highland Hills, OH 44122
Phone: 216 292-3800
Fax: 216 682-4065
Web: www.olysteel.com

CEO: Michael D. Siegal
CFO: Richard T. Marabito
HR: –
FYE: December 31
Type: Public

A metals service center Olympic Steel processes and distributes flat-rolled sheet coil and plate steel products to manufacturers and metal fabricators including companies operating in the construction automobile manufacturing mining and other industries. Through its Olympic Steel Lafayette and other subsidiaries the company offers cutting-to-length slitting and shearing as well as blanking laser welding and precision machining. It also makes tubular and pipe products through its Chicago Tube and Iron (CTI) subsidiary. Olympic Steel operates more than 30 processing and distribution facilities throughout the southern eastern and midwestern US.

	Annual Growth	12/14	12/15	12/16	12/17	12/18
Sales ($ mil.)	4.5%	1,436.3	1,175.5	1,055.1	1,330.7	1,715.1
Net income ($ mil.)	–	(19.1)	(26.8)	(1.1)	19.0	33.8
Market value ($ mil.)	(5.4%)	195.5	127.3	266.4	236.3	156.9
Employees	0.1%	1,810	1,740	1,660	1,670	1,820

OM GROUP, INC.

NYS: OMG

950 Main Avenue, Suite 1300
Cleveland, OH 44113-7210
Phone: 216 781-0083
Fax: –
Web: www.omgi.com

CEO: Joseph Scaminace
CFO: Christopher M Hix
HR: –
FYE: December 31
Type: Public

Mmmmetals is the mantra for OM Group. The company uses unrefined cobalt and other metals to make specialty products and is one of the world's largest refiners of cobalt. It serves markets that include battery materials semiconductors ceramics chemical and defense. It also makes magnetic technologies products for electronic equipment auto and alternative energy markets. Its specialty chemicals segment develops chemicals and products for computer components coating and inks tires and other industries. EaglePicher Technologies makes up its battery technologies segment which serves the defense aerospace and medical markets.

	Annual Growth	12/09	12/10	12/11	12/12	12/13
Sales ($ mil.)	7.3%	871.7	1,196.6	1,514.5	1,637.8	1,157.5
Net income ($ mil.)	–	(17.9)	83.4	37.9	(38.9)	(84.0)
Market value ($ mil.)	3.8%	988.1	1,212.2	704.8	698.8	1,146.1
Employees	30.9%	2,007	2,806	7,067	6,800	5,900

OMAGINE INC.

OTC: AHDS

350 5th Ave. Ste. 1103
New York NY 10118
Phone: 212-563-4141
Fax: 212-563-3355
Web: www.omagine.com

CEO: Frank J Drohan
CFO: Frank J Drohan
HR: –
FYE: December 31
Type: Public

Omagine wants you to imagine investing in beachfront abodes in the Middle East and North Africa (MENA). Formerly Alfa International Omagine repositioned and rebranded itself in 2007 as it exited the apparel business. The company's Journey of Light subsidiary now intends to tap into the high-margin real estate development and luxury travel markets in MENA. In 2008 Journey of Light was granted initial approval to develop the Omagine Project a $1.6 billion government-sponsored entertainment retail commercial residential and hotel real estate development in Oman. Omagine will also provide property management services.

OMAHA PUBLIC POWER DISTRICT

444 S 16TH ST
OMAHA, NE 681022247
Phone: 402-636-2000
Fax: –
Web: www.oppd.com

CEO: W. Gary Gates
CFO: Edward E. Easterlin
HR: Ron Miller
FYE: December 31
Type: Private

Thirteen's the lucky number for Omaha Public Power District (OPPD). A subdivision of the Nebraska state government OPPD generates and distributes electricity to residents and businesses in 13 counties in southeastern Nebraska. It operates and maintains its facilities without tax revenues and raises money for major construction through bonds. OPPD serves more than 356000 customers in an area covering 5000 sq. mi. The utility has a generating capacity of more than 3235 MW which is powered by primarily nuclear coal oil and natural gas sources. It sells wholesale power to other utilities and offers energy consulting and management services.

	Annual Growth	06/14	06/15*	12/15	12/16	12/17
Sales ($ mil.)	0.4%	–	1,096.6	1,131.2	1,126.5	1,104.3
Net income ($ mil.)	116.6%	–	16.5	34.6	(933.8)	77.2
Market value ($ mil.)	–	–	–	–	–	–
Employees	–	–	–	–	–	2,300

*Fiscal year change

OMEGA FLEX INC

NMS: OFLX

451 Creamery Way
Exton, PA 19341
Phone: 610 524-7272
Fax: 610 524-7282
Web: www.omegaflex.com

CEO: Kevin R. Hoben
CFO: Paul J. Kane
HR: –
FYE: December 31
Type: Public

Like a reed in a stream Grasshopper sometimes the flexible withstand pressure better than the rigid. That's certainly a concept that Omega Flex can get behind: The company makes corrugated metal and flexible tubular and braided metal (stainless steel bronze) hoses and reinforcements for construction and industrial customers to use in liquid and gas transportation. Its products are designed to deal with high pressure motion extreme temperatures harsh liquids or gases and abrasion. Other applications include cryogenics and propane and natural gas installations. The estate of John Reed and his son chairman Stewart Reed own a majority of Omega Flex which was spun off from Mestek in 2005.

	Annual Growth	12/14	12/15	12/16	12/17	12/18
Sales ($ mil.)	6.2%	85.2	93.3	94.1	101.8	108.3
Net income ($ mil.)	10.6%	13.5	15.8	14.4	15.7	20.1
Market value ($ mil.)	9.4%	381.6	333.1	562.7	720.7	545.7
Employees	1.9%	140	132	144	142	151

OMEGA HEALTHCARE INVESTORS, INC.

NYS: OHI

303 International Circle, Suite 200
Hunt Valley, MD 21030
Phone: 410 427-1700
Fax: 410 427-8800
Web: www.omegahealthcare.com

CEO: C. Taylor Pickett
CFO: Robert O. Stephenson
HR: –
FYE: December 31
Type: Public

Omega Healthcare Investors can put an end to the burdens of real-estate management. The self-administered real estate investment trust (REIT) invests in health care facilities throughout the US. It owns some 900 properties primarily long-term care facilities in more than 40 states. The REIT specializes in sales/leaseback transactions in which it purchases properties owned by health care providers and leases them back to those companies (thereby freeing the health care companies from the responsibilities of real estate management). The REIT's properties are operated by third-party health care operating companies including Genesis HealthCare System and CommuniCare Health Services.

	Annual Growth	12/14	12/15	12/16	12/17	12/18
Sales ($ mil.)	15.0%	504.8	743.6	900.8	908.4	881.7
Net income ($ mil.)	6.2%	221.3	224.5	366.4	100.4	281.6
Market value ($ mil.)	(2.6%)	7,905.7	7,078.1	6,325.3	5,572.6	7,112.5
Employees	17.2%	27	58	60	59	51

OMEGA PROTEIN CORP.　　　　　　　　　　　　　　NYS: OME

2105 City West Blvd., Suite 500　　　　　　　　　CEO: Bret D Scholtes
Houston, TX 77042-2838　　　　　　　　　CFO: Andrew C Johannesen
Phone: 713 623-0060　　　　　　　　　　　　　　　　　　　　HR: –
Fax: –　　　　　　　　　　　　　　　　　　　　FYE: December 31
Web: www.omegaprotein.com　　　　　　　　　　　　　Type: Public

Omega Protein is the alpha dog of the fish-meal market. With a handful of US processing plants a fleet of some 40 fishing vessels and 30-plus spotter aircraft the company is the largest US producer of fish meal and fish oil derived from menhaden (an inedible fish found in the Gulf of Mexico and along the East Coast). Animal-feed makers and livestock ranchers use Omega Protein's fish meal for protein additives in feed; the fish oil is used in Europe in margarine and for industrial ends. Rich in Omega-3 fatty acids (linked to health benefits) fish oil is also used as a human food supplement. Through subsidiaries Omega Protein provides nutraceutical ingredients and compounds including Omega-3 fish oils.

	Annual Growth	12/11	12/12	12/13	12/14	12/15
Sales ($ mil.)	11.2%	235.2	235.6	244.3	308.6	359.3
Net income ($ mil.)	(8.5%)	34.2	4.1	30.5	18.5	24.0
Market value ($ mil.)	32.8%	158.4	136.0	273.1	234.9	493.3
Employees	6.1%	495	500	450	657	627

OMEROS CORP　　　　　　　　　　　　　　NMS: OMER

201 Elliott Avenue West　　　　　　　　　CEO: Gregory A. Demopulos
Seattle, WA 98119　　　　　　　　　　　　　　　　　　　　CFO: –
Phone: 206 676-5000　　　　　　　　　　　　　　　　　　　HR: –
Fax: –　　　　　　　　　　　　　　　　　　　　FYE: December 31
Web: www.omeros.com　　　　　　　　　　　　　　　　Type: Public

Omeros doesn't claim to soothe the soul but it may be able to tame inflammation caused by surgery. The biopharmaceutical company is developing products based on its PharmacoSurgery platform a combination of low-dose therapeutic agents applied directly to a surgical site to inhibit inflammation. Its first marketed product is Omidria for use in cataract surgery. Omidria was launched in early 2015. Another candidate OMS103HP is in trials for its ability to improve joint function and reduce pain following ACL knee reconstruction surgery and arthroscopic meniscectomy (removal of knee cartilage tears). In addition to inflammation Omeros maintains programs focused on blood clot issues and the central nervous system (CNS).

	Annual Growth	12/14	12/15	12/16	12/17	12/18
Sales ($ mil.)	172.8%	0.5	13.5	41.6	64.8	29.9
Net income ($ mil.)	–	(73.7)	(75.1)	(66.7)	(53.5)	(126.8)
Market value ($ mil.)	(18.1%)	1,214.5	771.0	486.2	952.3	546.0
Employees	23.0%	103	162	154	173	236

OMNI CABLE CORPORATION

2 HAGERTY BLVD　　　　　　　　　CEO: William J. (Jeff) Siegfried
WEST CHESTER, PA 193827594　　　　　　　　CFO: Steve Glinski
Phone: 610-701-0100　　　　　　　　　　　　　　　　　　　HR: –
Fax: –　　　　　　　　　　　　　　　　　　　　FYE: December 31
Web: www.omnicable.com　　　　　　　　　　　　　Type: Private

Omni Cable has it down to the wire. The company distributes electrical and electronic cables to wholesale customers in the US through 12 warehouses and distribution centers. Omni Cable also offers custom bundling coloring striping lashing twisting and imprinting of wires and cables. The employee-owned company was founded in 1977. Omni Cable has locations in Atlanta Boston Chicago Denver Houston Los Angeles Philadelphia Seattle St. Louis San Francisco and Tampa. It expended its presence in the Pacific Northwest in 2016 through the opening of its Seattle branch.

	Annual Growth	12/13	12/14	12/15	12/16	12/17
Sales ($ mil.)	0.0%	–	258.8	234.7	221.9	258.9
Net income ($ mil.)	(17.1%)	–	15.1	16.2	10.9	8.6
Market value ($ mil.)	–	–	–	–	–	–
Employees	–	–	–	–	–	216

OMNIAMERICAN BANCORP, INC.　　　　　　　　　　　　NMS: OABC

1320 S. University Drive　　　　　　　　　　　　　CEO: Tim Carter
Fort Worth, TX 76107　　　　　　　　　CFO: Deborah B Wilkinson
Phone: 817 367-4640　　　　　　　　　　　　　　　　　　　HR: –
Fax: –　　　　　　　　　　　　　　　　　　　　FYE: December 31
Web: www.omniamerican.com　　　　　　　　　　　　Type: Public

You might say this institution is omnipresent in the Dallas-Fort Worth metroplex. OmniAmerican Bancorp is the holding company for OmniAmerican Bank which provides deposit and lending services through more than 15 offices. OmniAmerican Bank caters to businesses and individuals. The company also offers wealth management services such as money market and high yield checking accounts and financial planning. OmniAmerican Bank started in 1956 as a small financial institution serving the Carswell Air Force Base military community and converted from a credit union to a thrift in 2006.

	Annual Growth	12/08	12/09	12/10	12/11	12/12
Assets ($ mil.)	4.2%	1,067.9	1,133.9	1,108.4	1,336.7	1,257.3
Net income ($ mil.)	72.5%	0.6	0.7	1.7	4.0	5.7
Market value ($ mil.)	30.6%	–	–	155.1	179.7	264.7
Employees	(2.0%)	372	348	320	334	343

OMNICARE INC.　　　　　　　　　　　　　　　NYS: OCR

900 Omnicare Center, 201 E. Fourth Street　　　　　CEO: Nitin Sahney
Cincinnati, OH 45202　　　　　　　　　　　　CFO: Robert O Kraft
Phone: 513 719-2600　　　　　　　　　　　　　　　　　　　HR: –
Fax: –　　　　　　　　　　　　　　　　　　　　FYE: December 31
Web: www.omnicare.com　　　　　　　　　　　　　　Type: Public

Omnicare strives to be omnipresent in US nursing homes. The firm is the country's largest institutional pharmacy services provider dispensing drugs to nursing homes assisted-living centers and other long-term care (LTC) facilities in the US and parts of Canada. In addition it provides clinical and financial software consulting and billing services to LTC facilities as well as infusion respiratory and chronic disease therapy products and services for nursing home residents and hospice patients. It also provides some services to drugmakers. The company has pharmacy and distribution locations across the US and it serves LTC facility customers with a combined capacity of some 1 million patient beds.

	Annual Growth	12/09	12/10	12/11	12/12	12/13
Sales ($ mil.)	(0.6%)	6,166.2	6,146.2	6,182.9	6,160.4	6,013.4
Net income ($ mil.)	–	211.9	(106.1)	86.9	194.9	(43.4)
Market value ($ mil.)	25.7%	2,432.7	2,554.5	3,466.0	3,632.0	6,072.8
Employees	(2.2%)	15,200	15,200	14,600	14,400	13,900

OMNICELL INC　　　　　　　　　　　　　　　NMS: OMCL

590 East Middlefield Road　　　　　　　　　CEO: Randall A. Lipps
Mountain View, CA 94043　　　　　　　　　　CFO: Peter Kuipers
Phone: 650 251-6100　　　　　　　　　　　　HR: Susan Moriconi
Fax: –　　　　　　　　　　　　　　　　　　　　FYE: December 31
Web: www.omnicell.com　　　　　　　　　　　　　　Type: Public

Omnicell wants to be indispensable when it comes to dispensing drugs. The company makes systems that automate delivery of drugs to patients in hospitals homes long-term care centers and other medical healthcare settings. Pharmacies and medical facilities use its mobile cabinets and workstations to automatically dispense doses of medication and surgical supplies to help reduce errors and increase patient safety. More than 4000 hospitals use automation and analytics products such as the Omnicell XT Automated Dispensing Cabinet and Singlepointe software. Omnicell's medications adherence products that include specific-count blister packs help patients take the drugs they're supposed to when they're supposed to.

	Annual Growth	12/14	12/15	12/16	12/17	12/18
Sales ($ mil.)	15.6%	440.9	484.6	692.6	716.2	787.3
Net income ($ mil.)	5.4%	30.5	30.8	0.6	20.6	37.7
Market value ($ mil.)	16.6%	1,335.9	1,253.6	1,367.4	1,956.2	2,470.1
Employees	19.0%	1,236	1,451	2,444	2,350	2,480

OMNICOM GROUP, INC.

NYS: OMC

437 Madison Avenue
New York, NY 10022
Phone: 212 415-3600
Fax: 212 415-3393
Web: www.omnicomgroup.com

CEO: Dennis E. Hewitt
CFO: Philip J. Angelastro
HR: –
FYE: December 31
Type: Public

Omnicom Group creates advertising that is omnipresent. The company ranks as the world's #1 corporate media services conglomerate with 1500 agencies across 100-plus countries conducting advertising marketing and public relations operations. It serves global clients through its agency networks BBDO Worldwide DDB Worldwide and TBWA Worldwide. Agencies such as OMD PHD and Hearts & Science comprise the Omnicom Media Group which provides end-to-end data-driven media services. Omnicom's Diversified Agency Services division includes 200 companies providing customer relationship management (CRM) as well as branding and research events and public relations. The US accounts for about 50% of sales.

	Annual Growth	12/14	12/15	12/16	12/17	12/18
Sales ($ mil.)	(0.0%)	15,317.8	15,134.4	15,416.9	15,273.6	15,290.2
Net income ($ mil.)	4.7%	1,104.0	1,093.9	1,148.6	1,088.4	1,326.4
Market value ($ mil.)	(1.4%)	17,345.5	16,940.3	19,056.1	16,306.6	16,398.4
Employees	(1.2%)	74,000	74,900	78,500	77,300	70,400

OMNICOMM SYSTEMS INC

NBB: OMCM

2101 W. Commercial Blvd., Suite 3500
Fort Lauderdale, FL 33309
Phone: 954 473-1254
Fax: –
Web: www.omnicomm.com

CEO: Marc Eigner
CFO: Thomas E Vickers
HR: –
FYE: December 31
Type: Public

Computers can't catch the kind of viruses that OmniComm Systems handles. The company's Web-based software helps pharmaceutical and biotechnology companies clinical research organizations and academic research institutions manage data collected during clinical trials. Its TrialMaster software enables researchers to collect validate and analyze data for clinical trials to speed up the process of developing drugs and medical devices. The eClinical Suite combines a clinical data management system (CDMS) and a clinical trial management system (CTMS) to manage all phases of a clinical trial. OmniComm counts almost 100 customers including Boston Scientific and Johnson & Johnson. The majority of its sales are in the US.

	Annual Growth	12/13	12/14	12/15	12/16	12/17
Sales ($ mil.)	17.1%	14.3	16.5	20.7	25.4	27.0
Net income ($ mil.)	–	(3.2)	(4.5)	2.6	0.1	3.0
Market value ($ mil.)	12.3%	25.3	43.1	35.7	35.7	40.3
Employees	6.7%	108	119	112	130	140

OMNIVISION TECHNOLOGIES INC

NMS: OVTI

4275 Burton Drive
Santa Clara, CA 95054
Phone: 408 567-3000
Fax: –
Web: www.ovt.com

CEO: Shaw Hong
CFO: Anson Chan
HR: Charis Wong
FYE: April 30
Type: Public

OmniVision Technologies gets the big picture with a single chip. The fabless semiconductor company designs semiconductor image sensors (CameraChips) that capture and convert images for cameras mobile phones notebooks webcams surveillance equipment and medical imaging systems among other applications. Its CameraCubeChip device combines the company's image sensors with wafer-level optics for a complete camera module. OmniVision outsources manufacturing chores to silicon foundries (contract semiconductor manufacturers) primarily Taiwan Semiconductor Manufacturing Company (TSMC). Most sales are from Asia predominantly China.

	Annual Growth	04/10	04/11	04/12	04/13	04/14
Sales ($ mil.)	24.6%	603.0	956.5	897.7	1,407.9	1,453.9
Net income ($ mil.)	93.9%	6.7	124.5	65.8	42.9	95.0
Market value ($ mil.)	2.7%	984.7	1,883.8	1,033.0	752.1	1,095.3
Employees	8.5%	1,450	1,465	1,796	2,057	2,008

OMNOVA SOLUTIONS INC

NYS: OMN

25435 Harvard Road
Beachwood, OH 44122-6201
Phone: 216 682-7000
Fax: –
Web: www.omnova.com

CEO: Anne P. Noonan
CFO: Paul F. DeSantis
HR: Michael A Quinn
FYE: November 30
Type: Public

OMNOVA makes emulsion polymers specialty chemicals and other products used for commercial industrial and residential applications. Its products which include specialty coatings laminates and films are used by manufacturers to make plastics paper carpet coated fabrics and other products. Although the majority of the company sales come from the US OMNOVA generates revenue from customers in Europe China and Thailand as well. In 2019 UK-based specialty chemicals company Synthomer plc agreed to acquire OMNOVA.

	Annual Growth	11/15	11/16	11/17	11/18	11/19
Sales ($ mil.)	(3.2%)	838.0	759.9	783.1	769.8	736.2
Net income ($ mil.)	–	(17.8)	(0.4)	(87.8)	20.7	(22.4)
Market value ($ mil.)	7.7%	336.9	430.1	479.4	365.1	453.4
Employees	(4.6%)	2,235	2,100	1,800	1,900	1,850

ON SEMICONDUCTOR CORP

NMS: ON

5005 E. McDowell Road
Phoenix, AZ 85008
Phone: 602 244-6600
Fax: 602 244-6071
Web: www.onsemi.com

CEO: Keith D. Jackson
CFO: Bernard Gutmann
HR: Colleen McKeown
FYE: December 31
Type: Public

ON Semiconductor's products manage power use and handle dozens of other functions in an array of electronics. The company designs and manufactures energy efficient low-cost high-volume analog logic and discrete semiconductors ? some 84000 products in all. ON's devices perform power and signal control and interface functions in electronic gear ranging from networking routers and wireless phones and digital cameras to household appliances and electronically controlled operations in vehicles. ON sells directly to manufacturers and to distributors such as Avnet and Arrow Electronics. More than half of ON's sales come from the Asia/Pacific region.

	Annual Growth	12/14	12/15	12/16	12/17	12/18
Sales ($ mil.)	16.8%	3,161.8	3,495.8	3,906.9	5,543.1	5,878.3
Net income ($ mil.)	34.9%	189.7	206.2	182.1	810.7	627.4
Market value ($ mil.)	13.0%	4,192.0	4,055.6	5,280.5	8,665.7	6,832.4
Employees	9.9%	24,500	24,500	32,000	34,000	35,700

ON-SITE FUEL SERVICE, INC.

1089 OLD FANNIN RD STE A
BRANDON, MS 390479201
Phone: 601-353-4142
Fax: –

CEO: Kevin T French
CFO: Margaret Wong
HR: Pam Welborn
FYE: December 31
Type: Private

When it comes down to gassing up the fleet On-Site Fuel Service delivers. The company specializes in dispensing fuel (diesel or regular) to corporate fleets in the most efficient location available. For most customers this means fueling their vehicles once the workday is complete (and eliminating fueling time from the workday). But the company also offers mobile fueling services allowing vehicles to be refueled in the field or at remote job sites. On-Site Fuel Service dispenses the fuel directly into each vehicle and also provides fueling data and reports for each vehicle (to comply with regulatory requirements when necessary). Its operations extend south from North Carolina to Florida and west to Arizona.

	Annual Growth	12/00	12/01	12/02	12/06	12/07
Sales ($ mil.)	–	–	–	0.0	113.1	119.7
Net income ($ mil.)	–	–	–	0.0	(0.1)	(0.4)
Market value ($ mil.)	–	–	–	–	–	–
Employees	–	–	–	–	–	120

ONCOLOGIX TECH INC
NBB: OCLG

P.O. Box 8832
Grand Rapids, MI 49518-8832
Phone: 616 977-9933
Fax: –
Web: www.oclghealth.com

CEO: Roy Wayne Erwin
CFO: Michael A Kramarz
HR: –
FYE: August 31
Type: Public

Oncologix Tech (formerly BestNet Communications) has changed gears. The company which had developed a system using the Internet and text messaging networks to manage voice communications over public phone networks merged with JDA Medical Technologies and sold off most of its telephone business assets to Interactive Media Technologies. Oncologix then became a development-stage medical device firm focused on developing microsphere (particle) technology to treat liver and other soft tissue cancers; however the company licensed out most of its development operations in 2009 to a third party.

	Annual Growth	08/13	08/14	08/15	08/16	08/17
Sales ($ mil.)	84.8%	0.2	3.7	4.9	4.0	2.9
Net income ($ mil.)	–	(0.7)	(1.3)	(2.6)	(1.8)	(2.4)
Market value ($ mil.)	(60.2%)	8.0	4.4	0.7	0.1	0.2
Employees	12.4%	170	191	–	–	–

ONCOMED PHARMACEUTICALS INC.
NMS: OMED

800 Chesapeake Drive
Redwood City, CA 94063
Phone: 650 995-8200
Fax: –
Web: www.oncomed.com

CEO: Denise Scots-Knight
CFO: –
HR: –
FYE: December 31
Type: Public

OncoMed Pharmaceuticals is a development-stage biotech company working to produce pharmaceuticals targeting cancer cells. Like a growing group of pharma firms its work is focused on cancer stem cells (CSCs) which are believed to be the root cause of cancer tumors. Traditional chemotherapy may kill the tumors but leaves the CSCs to grow more tumors. OncoMed's antibody drugs target both CSCs and the tumors they produce. The company has three candidates in development; it has strategic alliances with major pharma companies Celgene GSK and Bayer in conjunction with its product development. OncoMed is merging with UK-based rare disease specialist Mereo BioPharma.

	Annual Growth	12/13	12/14	12/15	12/16	12/17
Sales ($ mil.)	0.2%	37.8	39.6	25.9	25.2	38.2
Net income ($ mil.)	–	(26.1)	(50.0)	(85.4)	(103.1)	(39.1)
Market value ($ mil.)	(38.9%)	1,128.0	831.5	861.3	294.6	156.7
Employees	(11.4%)	91	108	122	122	56

ONCONOVA THERAPEUTICS INC
NAS: ONTX

375 Pheasant Run
Newtown, PA 18940
Phone: 267 759-3680
Fax: –
Web: www.onconova.com

CEO: Steven Fruchtman
CFO: Mark P Guerin
HR: –
FYE: December 31
Type: Public

Onconova Therapeutics is taking a novel approach to oncology. The biopharmaceutical company is developing small molecule drug candidates to treat cancer and protect against certain side effects of radiation. Onconova has three clinical-stage product candidates and six preclinical ones. Its leading drug candidate rigosertib is being tested to higher risk myelodysplastic syndromes (MDS) pancreatic cancer and head and neck cancers. Onconova has revenue-generating collaboration agreements with Baxter in Europe and SymBio in Japan and Korea. The company which was formed in 1998 went public in mid-2013 raising $78 million in its IPO. It will use the proceeds to further develop its drug candidates.

	Annual Growth	12/14	12/15	12/16	12/17	12/18
Sales ($ mil.)	11.3%	0.8	11.5	5.5	0.8	1.2
Net income ($ mil.)	–	(63.7)	(24.0)	(19.7)	(24.1)	(20.6)
Market value ($ mil.)	(10.5%)	18.7	5.4	12.9	8.5	12.0
Employees	(15.9%)	50	36	23	25	25

ONCOR ELECTRIC DELIVERY CO LLC

1616 Woodall Rodgers Freeway
Dallas, TX 75202
Phone: 214 486-2000
Fax: –
Web: www.oncor.com

CEO: Robert S. (Bob) Shapard
CFO: David M. Davis
HR: Deborah Dennis
FYE: December 31
Type: Public

Oncor Electric Delivery serves miles and miles of Texas' vast energy market. The company operates the regulated power assets of parent Energy Future Holdings which include about 120000 miles of transmission and distribution lines serving more than 400 cities and 91 counties situated in the eastern north-central and western portions of the state. The company provides power to more than 3.2 million meters in homes and businesses. Oncor Electric Delivery maintains streetlights in its service territory. The utility also provides services to competitive retail electric providers. As an outcome of parent company EFH's bankruptcy Oncor received buyout offers from Berkshire-Hathaway and eventual winner Sempra Energy in 2017.

	Annual Growth	12/14	12/15	12/16	12/17	12/18
Sales ($ mil.)	1.8%	3,822.0	3,878.0	3,920.0	3,958.0	4,101.0
Net income ($ mil.)	4.9%	450.0	432.0	431.0	419.0	545.0
Market value ($ mil.)	–	–	–	–	–	–
Employees	4.2%	3,410	3,520	3,730	3,965	4,015

ONCOTHYREON INC.
NASDAQ: ONTY

2601 4th Ave. Ste. 500
Seattle WA 98121
Phone: 206-801-2100
Fax: 206-801-2101
Web: www.oncothyreon.com

CEO: –
CFO: –
HR: –
FYE: December 31
Type: Public

Beating cancer is Oncothyreon's sole goal. The biotechnology company is developing synthetic vaccines and small-molecule (chemical) drugs that aim to battle the dread disease. Oncothyreon's vaccine candidates stimulate cancer-fighting elements in patients' immune systems. Lead candidate Stimuvax is a potential vaccine for non-small cell lung cancer that the company has licensed to Germany's Merck KGaA. Oncothyreon's traditional drug candidates work to inhibit certain cancer-specific proteins; candidates being developed by the company include potential treatments for pancreatic and metastatic cancer.

ONE GAS, INC.
NYS: OGS

15 East Fifth Street
Tulsa, OK 74103
Phone: 918 947-7000
Fax: –
Web: www.onegas.com

CEO: Pierce H. Norton
CFO: Curtis L. Dinan
HR: Rhonda Mayhan
FYE: December 31
Type: Public

ONE Gas consists of former ONEOK natural gas utilities: Kansas Gas Service Oklahoma Natural Gas Company and Texas Gas Service. One of the largest publicly traded natural gas utilities in the US ONE Gas serves more than 2 million customers in three states. Kansas Gas Service has more than 13500 miles of distribution mains and service lines and serves more than 635000 customers; Oklahoma Natural Gas Company has more than 19100 miles of distribution mains and service lines and serves about 861000 customers; while Texas Gas Service has more than 10900 miles of distribution mains and service lines and serves about 644000 customers. ONEOK spun off ONE Gas in early 2014.

	Annual Growth	12/14	12/15	12/16	12/17	12/18
Sales ($ mil.)	(2.6%)	1,818.9	1,547.7	1,427.2	1,539.6	1,633.7
Net income ($ mil.)	11.9%	109.8	119.0	140.1	163.0	172.2
Market value ($ mil.)	17.9%	2,166.7	2,637.2	3,362.1	3,850.9	4,184.2
Employees	1.5%	3,300	3,400	3,400	3,500	3,500

ONE LIBERTY PROPERTIES, INC.　　　　　NYS: OLP

60 Cutter Mill Road　　　　　　　　　　　CEO: Patrick J Callan Jr
Great Neck, NY 11021　　　　　　　　　　CFO: David W. Kalish
Phone: 516 466-3100　　　　　　　　　　HR: –
Fax: –　　　　　　　　　　　　　　　　　FYE: December 31
Web: www.onelibertyproperties.com　　　　Type: Public

One Liberty Properties may own the space where lovebirds shop for loveseats. Or bird food. The self-managed and self-administered real estate investment trust (REIT) invests in retail industrial and office properties throughout the US. It owns or co-owns over 100 properties totaling more than 8 million sq. ft. of space; more than half of its portfolio is leased to retailers including Haverty Furniture PetSmart and Giant Food Stores. The REIT also owns warehouses fitness centers and a movie theater. One Liberty Properties targets net-leased properties minimizing its responsibilities for taxes maintenance and other operating costs. The firm is controlled by the family of its chairman.

	Annual Growth	12/14	12/15	12/16	12/17	12/18
Sales ($ mil.)	7.0%	60.5	65.7	70.6	75.9	79.1
Net income ($ mil.)	(1.7%)	22.1	20.5	24.4	24.1	20.7
Market value ($ mil.)	0.6%	443.5	402.1	470.6	485.6	453.8
Employees	0.0%	9	9	8	9	9

ONE STOP SYSTEMS INC.

2235 ENTP ST STE 110　　　　　　　　　CEO: Steve Cooper
ESCONDIDO, CA 92029　　　　　　　　　CFO: John W Morrison Jr
Phone: 760-737-0122　　　　　　　　　　HR: –
Fax: –　　　　　　　　　　　　　　　　　FYE: December 31
Web: www.onestopsystems.com　　　　　Type: Private

One Stop Systems designs and manufactures industrial computing systems and components including backplanes enclosures filler panels input/output boards and power supplies. One Stop's catalog includes a number of products built around the CompactPCI industry standard an interconnect technology intended for industrial environments that is also being used for military computers and other rugged electronics. The company also makes single-board computers and a variety of custom CPU and I/O boards enclosures and systems. One Stop Systems was founded in 1998. CEO Steve Cooper is the majority shareholder of the company. With Cooper VP Mark Gunn is a co-founder of One Stop Systems.

	Annual Growth	12/08	12/09	12/10	12/11	12/12
Sales ($ mil.)	4.6%	–	9.9	13.3	13.8	11.4
Net income ($ mil.)	(51.3%)	–	–	0.6	0.2	0.1
Market value ($ mil.)	–	–	–	–	–	–
Employees	–	–	–	–	–	35

ONEBEACON INSURANCE GROUP LTD.　　NYSE: OB

601 Carlson Pkwy.　　　　　　　　　　　CEO: Mike Miller
Minnetonka MN 55305　　　　　　　　　CFO: –
Phone: 952-852-2431　　　　　　　　　　HR: –
Fax: 888-656-1213　　　　　　　　　　　FYE: December 31
Web: www.onebeacon.com　　　　　　　Type: Public

OneBeacon Insurance Group shines its light on several insurance options for its customers across the US. OneBeacon provides specialty property/casualty insurance policies including marine travel professional liability medical malpractice data privacy umbrella property and even tuition coverage for when a student is forced to leave school unexpectedly. Products are sold to businesses and individuals through a network of 2900 independent agents and brokers across the US. Holding company White Mountains Insurance owns a controlling stake in OneBeacon.

ONEIDA LTD.

163-181 Kenwood Ave.　　　　　　　　　CEO: –
Oneida NY 13421-2899　　　　　　　　　CFO: –
Phone: 315-361-3000　　　　　　　　　　HR: –
Fax: 315-361-3700　　　　　　　　　　　FYE: January 31
Web: www.oneida.com　　　　　　　　　Type: Private

Oneida knows its place at the table. Once one of the world's largest makers of stainless steel and silver-plated flatware Oneida now designs and supplies flatware dinnerware and crystal for both consumers and the foodservice and institutional markets. Its facilities dot the US Canada Mexico the UK and China. Flatware accounts for more than half of sales. Other tabletop items are cutlery and kitchen utensils and gadgets as well as baby keepsake gifts. Subsidiary Kenwood Silver operates about 15 Oneida outlet stores. Overwhelmed by debt Oneida filed for Chapter 11 bankruptcy protection in 2006 emerging later that year backed by a group of investors. Private equity Monomoy Capital bought Oneida in 2011.

ONEMAIN HOLDINGS INC　　　　　　　　NYS: OMF

601 N.W. Second Street　　　　　　　　CEO: Jay N. Levine
Evansville, IN 47708　　　　　　　　　　CFO: Scott T. Parker
Phone: 812 424-8031　　　　　　　　　　HR: Angela Celestin
Fax: –　　　　　　　　　　　　　　　　　FYE: December 31
Web: www.onemainfinancial.com　　　　Type: Public

With more than $21 billion in total assets consumer finance company OneMain Holdings (formerly known as Springleaf Holdings) offers auto loans and personal loans primarily to non-prime customers who have limited access to credit from banks credit card companies and other lenders through more than 1600 branches in around 45 states. It also provides credit insurance non-credit insurance and related products through subsidiaries Merit Life Insurance AHL and Triton. Tracing its roots back to 1920 Springleaf renamed itself in late 2015 after acquiring OneMain Financial.

	Annual Growth	12/14	12/15	12/16	12/17	12/18
Assets ($ mil.)	16.1%	11,057.9	21,056.0	18,123.0	19,433.0	20,090.0
Net income ($ mil.)	(3.0%)	504.6	(242.0)	215.0	183.0	447.0
Market value ($ mil.)	(9.5%)	4,913.1	5,642.5	3,007.3	3,530.3	3,299.4
Employees	19.3%	5,030	11,400	10,100	10,100	10,200

ONEOK INC　　　　　　　　　　　　　　NYS: OKE

100 West Fifth Street　　　　　　　　　CEO: –
Tulsa, OK 74103　　　　　　　　　　　　CFO: Derek S. Reiners
Phone: 918 588-7000　　　　　　　　　　HR: Amber Waid
Fax: 918 588-7273　　　　　　　　　　　FYE: December 31
Web: www.oneok.com　　　　　　　　　Type: Public

ONEOK ("one oak") is having a gas pursuing its pipeline dreams. ONEOK is an Oklahoma-based midstream natural gas corporation that plays a key role in transforming and transporting natural gas from exploration & producer (E&P) businesses to downstream customers such as refiners and petrochemical companies. Through its primary subsidiary ONEOK Partners its operations include a 38000-mile integrated network of natural gas and natural gas liquid (NGL) pipelines processing plants fractionators and storage facilities in the Mid-Continent Williston Permian and Rocky Mountain regions.

	Annual Growth	12/14	12/15	12/16	12/17	12/18
Sales ($ mil.)	0.8%	12,195.1	7,763.2	8,920.9	12,173.9	12,593.2
Net income ($ mil.)	38.4%	314.1	245.0	352.0	387.8	1,151.7
Market value ($ mil.)	2.0%	20,490.2	10,148.4	23,626.1	21,996.4	22,202.2
Employees	4.3%	2,269	2,364	2,384	2,470	2,684

ONEOK PARTNERS, L.P.

100 W 5TH ST STE LL
TULSA, OK 741034298
Phone: 918-588-7000
Fax: –
Web: www.oneokpartners.com

CEO: Terry K Spencer
CFO: Walter S Hulse III
HR: –
FYE: December 31
Type: Private

For ONEOK Partners it's OK to have three businesses: natural gas pipelines; gas gathering and processing; and natural gas liquids (NGLs). Its pipelines include Midwestern Gas Transmission Guardian Pipeline Viking Gas Transmission and OkTex Pipeline. The ONEOK affiliate operates 17100 miles of gas-gathering pipeline and 7600 miles of transportation pipeline as well as gas processing plants and storage facilities (with 52 billion cu. ft. of capacity). It also owns one of the US's top natural NGL systems (more than 7200 miles of pipeline). In 2017 41%-owner ONEOK agreed to buy the stock of ONEOK Partners that it did not already own for $9.3 billion in a stock deal. Operations ONEOK Partners operates in three business segments: natural gas gathering and processing; natural gas pipelines; and natural gas liquids.

	Annual Growth	12/12	12/13	12/14	12/15	12/16
Sales ($ mil.)	(14.5%)	–	–	12,191.7	7,761.1	8,918.5
Net income ($ mil.)	8.5%	–	–	911.3	597.9	1,072.3
Market value ($ mil.)	–	–	–	–	–	–
Employees	–	–	–	–	–	2,364

ONESPAN INC

121 West Wacker Drive, Suite 2050
Chicago, IL 60601
Phone: 312 766-4001
Fax: –

NAS: OSPN

CEO: Scott M. Clements
CFO: Mark S. Hoyt
HR: –
FYE: December 31
Type: Public

VASCO Data Security International holds the key to electronic banking. Its hardware and software lines include authentication platforms security tokens handheld devices and related applications used for authenticating a person's identity on computer networks. The company's products incorporate authentication and digital signature security technologies and can be used to secure intranets extranets and LANs. In addition to banking VASCO's products are used to provide remote workers with secure access to corporate networks; other applications include e-commerce transactions. It counts more than 10000 customers including some 1700 financial institutions such as Citibank BNP-Paribas and HSBC.

	Annual Growth	12/14	12/15	12/16	12/17	12/18
Sales ($ mil.)	1.3%	201.5	241.4	192.3	193.3	212.3
Net income ($ mil.)	(41.8%)	33.5	42.2	10.5	(22.4)	3.8
Market value ($ mil.)	(17.7%)	1,134.7	673.0	549.1	559.1	520.9
Employees	18.5%	371	545	613	611	732

ONLINE VACATION CENTER HOLDINGS CORP

2307 West Broward Boulevard, Suite 400
Fort Lauderdale, FL 33312
Phone: 954 377-6400
Fax: 954 377-6368
Web: www.onlinevacationcenter.com

NBB: ONVC

CEO: Edward B Rudner
CFO: John Stunson
HR: –
FYE: December 31
Type: Public

Online Vacation Center Holdings has quit the cigar business and is spending its future traveling. Previously called Alec Bradley Cigar Corporation the company was known for importing and selling cigars wholesale. In 2006 the firm completed a reverse merger with Online Vacation Center Holdings. It shuttered its cigar operations and changed its name to reflect its new adventure as an online retailer of vacation packages. The company specializes in cruise deals. Its subsidiaries include Online Vacation Center and Dunhill Vacations. Chairman CEO president and CFO Edward Rudner owns about 60% of Online Vacation Center Holdings.

	Annual Growth	12/14	12/15	12/16	12/17	12/18
Sales ($ mil.)	6.7%	14.1	14.3	16.1	16.4	18.2
Net income ($ mil.)	5.1%	1.0	0.6	1.0	0.5	1.3
Market value ($ mil.)	33.7%	4.5	12.4	11.4	12.4	14.4
Employees	–	74	–	–	–	–

ONSTREAM MEDIA CORP

1291 SW 29 Avenue
Pompano Beach, FL 33069
Phone: 954 917-6655
Fax: –
Web: www.onstreammedia.com

NBB: ONSM

CEO: Randy S Selman
CFO: Robert E Tomlinson
HR: Andrea Polack
FYE: September 30
Type: Public

If a picture says a thousand words then Onstream Media Corporation speaks volumes about corporate communication and digital asset management. The company's Digital Media Services Group provides video and audio Webcasting to corporate clients and produces Internet-based multimedia streaming promotional videos for hotels and resorts. The group also includes DMSP (Digital Media Services Platform) and UGC (User Generated Content) divisions which provide encoding storage search retrieval and reuse of photos audio files Web pages and other digital files. Onstream's Audio & Web Conferencing Services Group includes conferencing provider Infinite and audio and video networking services provider EDNet.

	Annual Growth	09/11	09/12	09/13	09/14	09/15
Sales ($ mil.)	(2.3%)	17.7	18.2	17.2	16.9	16.1
Net income ($ mil.)	–	(5.2)	(2.6)	(7.2)	(1.7)	(8.6)
Market value ($ mil.)	(26.7%)	16.6	11.0	6.2	3.7	4.8
Employees	(3.1%)	93	102	88	86	82

ONTO INNOVATION INC

16 Jonspin Road
Wilmington, MA 01887
Phone: 978 253-6200
Fax: –
Web: www.nanometrics.com

NYS: ONTO

CEO: Timothy J. Stultz
CFO: Jeffrey (Jeff) Andreson
HR: Dawn Laplante
FYE: December 29
Type: Public

Nanometrics works on a nano scale for electronics manufacturers that need their goods to measure up. The company provides thin-film metrology and inspection systems used by makers of precision electronic gear. These stand-alone integrated and tabletop measurement devices gauge the thickness and consistency of film materials used in making semiconductors LEDs data storage components and power management components. Its systems are used throughout the fabrication process from substrate manufacturing to advanced wafer-scale packaging. Top customers include Samsung Electronics Intel and SK Hynix. Nanometrics generates most of its sales in Asia. Nanometrics and Rudolph Technologies agreed to merge in 2019.

	Annual Growth	12/14	12/15	12/16	12/17	12/18
Sales ($ mil.)	18.2%	166.4	187.4	221.1	258.6	324.5
Net income ($ mil.)	–	(31.1)	2.9	44.0	30.2	57.6
Market value ($ mil.)	13.6%	404.3	384.8	610.8	607.4	673.9
Employees	7.5%	525	518	532	592	701

ONVIA INC

509 Olive Way, Suite 400
Seattle, WA 98101
Phone: 206 282-5170
Fax: –

NAS: ONVI

CEO: Russell Mann
CFO: Cameron S Way
HR: –
FYE: December 31
Type: Public

Onvia aims to help companies win government contracts and government agencies find suppliers by providing a database of business leads. The company identifies purchasing behavior and bid opportunities from some 86000 federal state and local government agencies as well as more than 400000 private-sector enterprises and delivers notices of those opportunities to its subscribers. Its Onvia database includes data on millions of current and historical contracting opportunities in markets such as construction consulting and information technology. Subscriptions account for the bulk of the company's sales; It also generates revenues by licensing its content to other companies. Onvia was established in 2000.

	Annual Growth	12/11	12/12	12/13	12/14	12/15
Sales ($ mil.)	0.5%	23.2	22.0	22.0	22.6	23.6
Net income ($ mil.)	–	1.6	1.5	(2.7)	(0.7)	(0.5)
Market value ($ mil.)	6.8%	20.4	26.2	35.3	35.8	26.5
Employees	(0.7%)	141	132	130	136	137

OP-TECH ENVIRONMENTAL SERVICES INC.
PINK SHEETS: OPST

6392 Deere Rd.
Syracuse NY 13206
Phone: 315-463-1643
Fax: 315-463-9764
Web: www.op-tech.us

CEO: Charles Morgan
CFO: –
HR: –
FYE: December 31
Type: Public

More than 1000 private industrial and municipal clients opt for OP-TECH Environmental Services which provides spill cleanup remediation and industrial cleaning services including lead abatement. The company also offers transportation and management of hazardous and nonhazardous wastes. OP-TECH Environmental Services provides rapid response to hazardous and nonhazardous spills primarily in New Jersey New York Ohio Pennsylvania and New England. Other services include building demolition and removal and health and safety training classes for clients. Director Richard Messina owns 33% of the company.

OPEN SOLUTIONS INC.

455 Winding Brook Dr.
Glastonbury CT 06033
Phone: 860-815-5000
Fax: 510-444-3580
Web: www.scilearn.com

CEO: –
CFO: –
HR: –
FYE: December 31
Type: Private

Open Solutions' software helps run the till for small and midsized banks and credit unions. The company's processing systems manage customer service payroll processing and year-end reporting. It also offers hosted software that enables banks to provide online services such as account information and management electronic bill payment and funds transfer. The firm also offers tools that integrate with its core systems including applications for online procurement business intelligence check imaging financial accounting and interactive voice response. Open Solutions sells directly and via partnerships with distributors and systems integrators. The company is owned by Fiserv which acquired it in 2013.

OPENLINK FINANCIAL LLC

800 RXR PLZ FL 8
UNIONDALE, NY 115563810
Phone: 516-227-6600
Fax: –

CEO: Rich Grossi
CFO: –
HR: –
FYE: December 31
Type: Private

OpenLink Financial develops risk management trading portfolio management and operations processing software for more than 550 clients in the financial services commodities and energy industries. Its products sold worldwide link and automate front- and back-office applications for banks corporate treasury departments energy marketers and insurance companies. OpenLink also provides professional services (consulting maintenance support and training) as well as complementary niche products through subsidiaries such as dbcSMARTsoftware (software for agricultural commodities) and iRM (energy trade processing software). Founded in 1992 the company is owned by Ion Investment Group.

	Annual Growth	12/03	12/04	12/05	12/06	12/08
Sales ($ mil.)	35.7%	–	–	73.4	83.6	183.6
Net income ($ mil.)	23.6%	–	–	9.1	0.4	17.2
Market value ($ mil.)	–	–	–	–	–	–
Employees	–	–	–	–	–	1,300

OPENTABLE INC.
NMS: OPEN

One Montgomery Street, 7th Floor
San Francisco, CA 94104
Phone: 415 344-4200
Fax: –
Web: www.opentable.com

CEO: Christa Quarles
CFO: I Duncan Robertson
HR: –
FYE: December 31
Type: Public

Even if your favorite restaurant is closed for the day you can still try to reserve a table through OpenTable. The firm provides online reservations at about 27000 upscale restaurants around the world. The service is free to diners but OpenTable charges participating restaurants an installation and monthly license fee for its Electronic Reservation Book (ERB) a computerized reservation system. It also provides training and support for ERB and charges a fee for tables booked through Connect a Web-based solution for reservations with less functionality than ERB. Since its founding in 1998 OpenTable has seated more than 200 million diners.

	Annual Growth	12/08	12/09	12/10	12/11	12/12
Sales ($ mil.)	30.4%	55.8	68.6	99.0	139.5	161.6
Net income ($ mil.)	–	(1.0)	5.1	14.1	21.6	24.0
Market value ($ mil.)	24.2%	–	583.0	1,613.9	896.0	1,117.4
Employees	17.5%	304	198	493	558	580

OPERATING ENGINEERS FUNDS INC.

100 E. Corson St.
Pasadena CA 91103
Phone: 626-356-1000
Fax: 626-356-1065
Web: www.oefunds.org

CEO: Mike Roddy
CFO: Chuck Killian
HR: Kelli Magdaleno
FYE: June 30
Type: Private - Not-for-Pr

The Operating Engineers Funds are in fact for operating engineers — not the kind who run trains but those who operate other large machinery. The company administers employee benefits including pensions health welfare vacation and holiday benefit for more than 35000 active or retired members of the International Union of Operating Engineers (I.U.O.E.) Local 12 as well as their beneficiaries and dependents. The union consists of individuals in construction-related trades including heavy equipment operators soil testers concrete pumpers inspectors and surveyors.

OPERATION SMILE, INC.

3641 FACULTY BLVD
VIRGINIA BEACH, VA 234538000
Phone: 888-677-6453
Fax: –
Web: www.operationsmile.org

CEO: Magee Jr DDS MD William P
CFO: –
HR: –
FYE: June 30
Type: Private

Operation Smile's mission is simple: Make the children of the world grin. The not-for-profit volunteer group provides reconstructive surgery and health-care services to children and young adults suffering from facial deformities such as cleft lips cleft palates burns and tumors. Operation Smile has assisted more than 120000 patients in 25 developing countries and the US. The organization also provides educational fellowship programs in craniofacial surgery and runs a physician training program. Operation Smile was founded in 1982 by Dr. William Magee and his wife Kathleen a nurse and clinical social worker. A plan to merge with Smile Train in 2011 is being called off due to donor opposition.

	Annual Growth	06/13	06/14	06/15	06/16	06/17
Sales ($ mil.)	2.3%	–	58.5	66.3	61.5	62.6
Net income ($ mil.)	–	–	(11.0)	9.5	(5.1)	0.6
Market value ($ mil.)	–	–	–	–	–	–
Employees	–	–	–	–	–	128

OPKO HEALTH INC   NMS: OPK

4400 Biscayne Blvd.
Miami, FL 33137
Phone: 305 575-4100
Fax: –
Web: www.opko.com

CEO: Phillip Frost
CFO: Adam Logal
HR: Yifat Philip
FYE: December 31
Type: Public

OPKO Health operates clinical laboratories and develops tests and medicines for a range of health indications. The company's BioReference Laboratories unit is one of the largest clinical lab groups in the US. The subsidiary offers routine and esoteric services including molecular diagnostics oncology women's health and genetic testing. OPKO's commercial biopharmaceutical offerings include Rayaldee for hyperparathyroidism in kidney disease patients; R&D candidates address endocrine renal and metabolic disorders. OPKO Health sells prescription drugs and over-the-counter products in Spain Ireland Chile and Mexico and it makes pharmaceutical ingredients in Israel. The US market accounts for most of sales.

	Annual Growth	12/14	12/15	12/16	12/17	12/18
Sales ($ mil.)	81.6%	91.1	491.7	1,221.7	1,067.5	990.3
Net income ($ mil.)	–	(171.7)	(30.0)	(25.1)	(308.9)	(153.0)
Market value ($ mil.)	(25.9%)	5,857.5	5,892.6	5,452.9	2,873.0	1,764.9
Employees	70.5%	674	5,936	6,041	6,030	5,690

OPLINK COMMUNICATIONS INC.   NMS: OPLK

46335 Landing Parkway
Fremont, CA 94538
Phone: 510 933-7200
Fax: –
Web: www.oplink.com

CEO: Joseph Y Liu
CFO: Shirley Yin
HR: –
FYE: June 30
Type: Public

Oplink Communications has its eye on network connections. The company makes fiber-optic components that increase the capacity of communications networks. Oplink's dense wavelength division multiplexers transmit several light signals simultaneously over a single glass fiber. Other products provide signal functions such as amplification wavelength performance monitoring and preservation redirection connectivity and transmission and reception. Telecommunications equipment makers including Huawei and Tellabs (each more than 10% of sales) incorporate Oplink's components into gear used to build networks both interoffice and international. Customers in Asia primarily in China and Japan account for about a third of sales.

	Annual Growth	06/09	06/10	06/11*	07/12*	06/13
Sales ($ mil.)	6.3%	143.7	138.8	198.8	174.9	183.4
Net income ($ mil.)	–	(13.8)	11.1	48.5	(2.6)	13.4
Market value ($ mil.)	11.1%	218.2	274.3	356.2	259.0	332.5
Employees	13.5%	2,260	3,821	3,570	3,454	3,744

*Fiscal year change

OPNEXT INC.   NASDAQ: OPXT

46429 Landing Pkwy.
Fremont CA 94538
Phone: 510-580-8828
Fax: 503-223-0182
Web: www.tripwire.com

CEO: Harry L Bosco
CFO: Robert J Nobile
HR: –
FYE: March 31
Type: Public

Stay tuned: light-speed communication is Opnext. The company makes optoelectronic components used to assemble fiber-optic data and voice communications networks. These laser diode modules transmitter/receiver devices and transceivers are incorporated by other equipment makers into larger multiplexing and digital cross-connect systems used in data communications and telecommunications. Opnext has a limited number of customers. Alcatel-Lucent Cisco Systems and Huawei Technologies together account for about 45% of sales. Other customers include Nokia Siemens Networks and Ciena Corporation. The company gets 40% of sales in North America. In 2012 it was bought by rival Oclaro.

OPPENHEIMER HOLDINGS INC   NYS: OPY

85 Broad Street
New York, NY 10004
Phone: 212 668-8000
Fax: –
Web: www.opco.com

CEO: James P. Carley
CFO: Jeffery J. Alfano
HR: –
FYE: December 31
Type: Public

J. Robert Oppenheimer dealt in mushroom clouds but Oppenheimer Holdings helps mushroom finances. Through subsidiaries Oppenheimer & Co. Oppenheimer Asset Management and Oppenheimer Trust it provides a range of financial services including brokerage investment banking asset management lending and research. Its Private Client segment which offers retail brokerage wealth management and margin lending to affluent and business clients in the US and Latin America makes up the bulk of sales. The group also has operations in the UK Israel and Hong Kong. It has more than $25 billion of client assets under management. The firm is not affiliated with OppenheimerFunds a unit of MassMutual Financial Group.

	Annual Growth	12/14	12/15	12/16	12/17	12/18
Sales ($ mil.)	(1.2%)	1,004.5	928.4	857.8	920.3	958.2
Net income ($ mil.)	34.5%	8.8	2.0	(1.2)	22.8	28.9
Market value ($ mil.)	2.4%	303.2	226.7	242.6	349.5	333.2
Employees	(3.5%)	3,434	3,290	3,098	2,992	2,976

OPTICAL CABLE CORP.   NMS: OCC

5290 Concourse Drive
Roanoke, VA 24019
Phone: 540 265-0690
Fax: –
Web: www.occfiber.com

CEO: –
CFO: Tracy G Smith
HR: Phil Peters
FYE: October 31
Type: Public

Optical Cable Corporation (OCC) wants to keep you connected with a little help from its products of course. The company makes fiber-optic cable and copper data communications connectivity equipment and systems. Its high-bandwidth cables transmit data video and audio over distances of up to 10 miles. OCC's fiber-optic cables which are suitable for indoor and outdoor use are used in local-area networks (LANs) for schools hospitals manufacturing plants and business facilities. OCC also produces security cables for use with surveillance cameras and specialty fiber-optic cables for military tactical field applications. Customers include electrical contractors OEMs systems resellers and distributors.

	Annual Growth	10/15	10/16	10/17	10/18	10/19
Sales ($ mil.)	(0.8%)	73.6	64.6	64.1	87.8	71.3
Net income ($ mil.)	–	(4.3)	(1.8)	(1.7)	1.1	(5.7)
Market value ($ mil.)	(1.4%)	23.3	20.9	18.3	35.4	22.0
Employees	1.7%	342	331	356	376	366

OPTIMUMBANK HOLDINGS INC   NAS: OPHC

2477 East Commercial Boulevard
Fort Lauderdale, FL 33308
Phone: 954 900-2800
Fax: –
Web: www.optimumbank.com

CEO: Timothy Terry
CFO: David Edgar
HR: –
FYE: December 31
Type: Public

OptimumBank Holdings is the holding company for OptimumBank which operates three branches in the communities of Plantation Fort Lauderdale and Deerfield Beach in South Florida. The bank is mainly a real estate lender with commercial mortgages representing the largest portion of its loan portfolio followed by residential mortgages land and construction loans and multifamily residential mortgages. It also offers other standard services such as checking and savings accounts CDs credit cards and personal loans. OptimumBank was founded in 2000 by chairman Albert Finch and president Richard Browdy. As a group executive officers and directors of OptimumBank Holdings own more than 40% of the company.

	Annual Growth	12/14	12/15	12/16	12/17	12/18
Assets ($ mil.)	(5.2%)	124.5	127.5	119.7	95.9	100.4
Net income ($ mil.)	(16.1%)	1.6	(0.2)	(0.4)	(0.6)	0.8
Market value ($ mil.)	29.4%	2.0	0.7	7.0	8.7	5.6
Employees	2.8%	17	17	16	16	19

OPTION CARE HEALTH INC
NMS: OPCH

3000 Lakeside Dr. Suite 300N
Bannockburn, IL 60015
Phone: 312 940-2443
Fax: –
Web: www.bioscrip.com

CEO: Richard M. (Rick) Smith
CFO: Jeffrey M. Kreger
HR: Bet Rosa
FYE: December 31
Type: Public

Option Care Health (formerly BioScrip) gets specialty medications and home health services to the people who need them. The company provides infusion services so that chronic care patients can skip a visit to the hospital and instead receive their medicine at specialty pharmacies in physicians' offices or at home. Option Care Health's nurses administer the medicines to treat hemophilia cancer pain management or even simply hydration. The company also offers pharmacy benefit management (PBM) services for customers such as managed care organizations government agencies and self-funded employer groups. The former BioScrip merged with another infusion services firm Option Care Enterprises in 2019 to form Option Care Health.

	Annual Growth	12/14	12/15	12/16	12/17	12/18
Sales ($ mil.)	(7.9%)	984.1	982.2	935.6	817.2	708.9
Net income ($ mil.)	–	(147.5)	(299.7)	(41.5)	(64.2)	(51.7)
Market value ($ mil.)	(15.5%)	895.3	224.1	133.2	372.7	457.2
Employees	(4.8%)	2,490	2,286	2,540	2,154	2,043

OPTIONSXPRESS HOLDINGS INC.

311 W. Monroe St. Ste. 1000
Chicago IL 60606
Phone: 312-630-3300
Fax: 312-629-5256
Web: www.optionsxpress.com

CEO: David A Fisher
CFO: Adam J Dewitt
HR: –
FYE: December 31
Type: Subsidiary

In a hurry to do some options trading? optionsXpress is an online brokerage that provides a customized interface for trading options futures stocks and other products. The company is one of the few online brokerages offering futures and options which together account for about 80% of its trading activity. optionsXpress has grown from some 162000 customer accounts to around 400000 accounts since 2005. It averages approximately 45000 trades per day. The company also offers investor education products and services through Optionetics which it acquired in 2009. optionsXpress was acquired by Charles Schwab in 2011.

OPTUMRX INC.

2300 Main St.
Irvine CA 92614-9731
Phone: 949-221-9974
Fax: 403-213-3648
Web: www.vereseninc.com

CEO: Mark Thierer
CFO: Jeffrey Grosklags
HR: –
FYE: December 31
Type: Subsidiary

OptumRx (previously Prescription Solutions) has the Rx for insurance providers reeling from high drug costs. The company provides pharmacy benefit management (PBM) services to health insurers managed care organizations employers unions and other clients representing more than 10 million members nationwide. Its services range from formulary management and benefit design to pharmacy network management online reporting and claims processing and tracking. OptumRx also operates mail-order pharmacies and provides specialty pharmacy services for high-cost biotech drugs. Founded in 1993 the business is a subsidiary of UnitedHealth and accounts for about 20% of its parent company's revenues.

ORAGENICS INC
ASE: OGEN

4902 Eisenhower Blvd., Suite 125
Tampa, FL 33634
Phone: 813 286-7900
Fax: 813 286-7904
Web: www.oragenics.com

CEO: Alan F Joslyn
CFO: Michael Sullivan
HR: –
FYE: December 31
Type: Public

Oragenics wants to get the beneficial microflora in your mouth to bloom. The biotechnology company is developing an oral topical treatment that could provide life-long protection from most forms of tooth decay. It is also researching an antibiotic that could kill harmful bacteria in the mouth such as drug-resistant Staphylococcus. It is also developing a weight-loss product. Oragenics aims to turn from product development to commercialization through alliances and partnerships. In 2016 the company sold its Consumer Probiotic Business (including the ProBiora3 and Evora brands to promote oral and periodontal health) to ProBiora Health for $1.7 million.

	Annual Growth	12/11	12/12	12/13	12/14	12/15
Sales ($ mil.)	(5.0%)	1.4	1.3	1.0	0.9	1.2
Net income ($ mil.)	–	(7.7)	(13.1)	(16.1)	(5.8)	(11.7)
Market value ($ mil.)	10.4%	40.3	105.2	112.0	35.5	59.8
Employees	1.6%	15	10	10	13	16

ORANGE AND ROCKLAND UTILITIES INC

1 BLUE HILL PLZ STE 20
PEARL RIVER, NY 109653100
Phone: 845-352-6000
Fax: –
Web: www.oru.com

CEO: –
CFO: –
HR: –
FYE: December 31
Type: Private

Orange and Rockland Utilities (O&R) operates under the auspices of its big city cousin holding company Consolidated Edison (Con Edison). O&R's subsidiaries Rockland Electric and Pike County Power & Light operate in southeastern New York and adjacent portions of New Jersey and Pennsylvania. The utilities distribute electricity to more than 301800 customers in about 100 communities in those three states and deliver natural gas more than to 128000 customers in New York and Pennsylvania. O&R's transmission and distribution facilities include 5550 miles of overhead and underground power distribution lines 560 miles of transmission lines and more than 1850 miles of gas pipeline.

	Annual Growth	12/02	12/03	12/04	12/05	12/16
Sales ($ mil.)	(0.8%)	–	727.0	703.0	824.0	653.5
Net income ($ mil.)	2.1%	–	45.0	46.0	50.0	59.2
Market value ($ mil.)	–	–	–	–	–	–
Employees	–	–	–	–	–	1,060

ORANGE COUNTY TRANSPORTATION AUTHORITY

550 S MAIN ST
ORANGE, CA 928684506
Phone: 714-636-7433
Fax: –
Web: www.octa.net

CEO: Darrell Johnson
CFO: –
HR: –
FYE: June 30
Type: Private

Public transportation in sunny Orange County California is overseen by the Orange County Transportation Authority (OCTA). The OCTA is the main provider of bus services in its 800-sq.-mi. territory which is home to more than 3 million people. In cooperation with the Southern California Regional Rail Authority the OCTA oversees Metrolink commuter rail service in Orange County. The agency also operates a 10-mile toll road and issues permits to taxi operators. Revenue from a half-cent local sales tax allows the agency to pay for road improvement and mass transit projects.

	Annual Growth	06/14	06/15	06/16	06/17	06/18
Sales ($ mil.)	1.5%	–	607.7	600.2	611.9	634.8
Net income ($ mil.)	–	–	43.8	67.5	54.8	(53.2)
Market value ($ mil.)	–	–	–	–	–	–
Employees	–	–	–	–	–	1,050

ORASURE TECHNOLOGIES INC.   NMS: OSUR

220 East First Street   CEO: Douglas A. Michels
Bethlehem, PA 18015   CFO: Ronald H. Spair
Phone: 610 882-1820   HR: Ayesha Herrera
Fax: –   FYE: December 31
Web: www.orasure.com   Type: Public

When it comes to diagnostic tests OraSure is certain it can deliver results. The oral specimen kits and other diagnostic tests developed by OraSure Technologies are designed to detect drug use and certain infectious diseases namely HIV and hepatitis C. Its OraSure products use oral specimens rather than traditional blood or urine based methods to test for HIV. The Intercept line uses oral samples to test for marijuana cocaine opiates PCP and amphetamines. OraSure has also developed a rapid HIV blood diagnostic testing method and it has entered the genetic testing market through its DNAG subsidiary. OraSure sells its products in the US and internationally to health care facilities and medical laboratories.

	Annual Growth	12/14	12/15	12/16	12/17	12/18
Sales ($ mil.)	14.3%	106.5	119.7	128.2	167.1	181.7
Net income ($ mil.)	–	(4.6)	8.2	19.7	30.9	20.4
Market value ($ mil.)	3.6%	621.3	394.6	538.0	1,155.7	715.7
Employees	5.6%	320	326	325	377	398

ORBCOMM INC   NMS: ORBC

395 W. Passaic Street   CEO: Marc J. Eisenberg
Rochelle Park, NJ 07662   CFO: Robert G. Costantini
Phone: 703 433-6300   HR: Michele Coniglio
Fax: –   FYE: December 31
Web: www.orbcomm.com   Type: Public

ORBCOMM uses its fleet of 41 low-Earth-orbit (LEO) satellites to help businesses keep an eye on their earthbound assets. The company machine-to-machine (M2M) communications and telematics services that help clients keep track of mobile assets from ships to trucks to heavy equipment. ORBCOMM has joined the move to Internet of Things offerings offering its satellites and complementary networks to keep companies and assets connected and directed. Key clients include heavy equipment makers Caterpillar Komatsu and Hitachi. The company also serves government customers with Automatic Identification System (AIS) data services for marine vessel tracking.

	Annual Growth	12/14	12/15	12/16	12/17	12/18
Sales ($ mil.)	30.1%	96.2	178.3	186.7	254.2	276.1
Net income ($ mil.)	–	(4.7)	(13.3)	(23.5)	(61.3)	(26.2)
Market value ($ mil.)	6.0%	516.5	571.8	653.2	804.0	652.4
Employees	36.7%	225	462	542	785	785

ORBIT INTERNATIONAL CORP.   NBB: ORBT

80 Cabot Court   CEO: Mitchell Binder
Hauppauge, NY 11788   CFO: David Goldman
Phone: 631 435-8300   HR: –
Fax: –   FYE: December 31
Web: www.orbitintl.com   Type: Public

Orbit International is at home in the world — on land in the air or at sea. The company's core electronics group is comprised of its instrument division and its Tulip and ICS subsidiaries. It specializes in customized display terminals intercommunication panels and keyboards for military ships and aircraft as well as rugged computing hardware for commercial customers. Orbit's power unit led by subsidiary Behlman Electronics makes electrical AC power supplies and frequency converters; it also reconfigures obsolete military equipment and does repairs for the US Air Force and Navy. Orbit primarily serves the US government and defense contractors such as BAE SYSTEMS.

	Annual Growth	12/14	12/15	12/16	12/17	12/18
Sales ($ mil.)	6.5%	19.2	20.1	20.7	20.9	24.7
Net income ($ mil.)	–	(2.0)	0.9	1.4	1.8	2.2
Market value ($ mil.)	14.8%	11.3	11.6	14.3	19.5	19.6
Employees	–	–	–	–	–	–

ORBIT/FR, INC.   NBB: ORFR

506 Prudential Road   CEO: Per Iversen
Horsham, PA 19044   CFO: Relland Winand
Phone: 215 674-5100   HR: –
Fax: –   FYE: December 31
Web: www.orbitfr.com   Type: Public

ORBIT/FR's business revolves around microwave test and measurement. The company manufactures automated hardware and software systems for evaluating microwave signal performance in devices such as cell phones radio transmitters Global Positioning System (GPS) receivers military antennas and guided missiles. Other products include microwave receivers and antennas and anechoic foam (an echo-free microwave-absorbing material). ORBIT/FR designs systems for product manufacturers in the aerospace and defense satellite wireless communications and automotive industries. Customers include BT Group Ford IBM Lufthansa Northrop Grumman Samsung UCLA and the US military.

	Annual Growth	12/12	12/13	12/14	12/15	12/16
Sales ($ mil.)	4.1%	34.1	38.2	39.4	34.5	40.0
Net income ($ mil.)	–	0.7	0.5	0.8	(2.4)	(1.5)
Market value ($ mil.)	40.5%	4.7	14.5	14.8	20.8	18.3
Employees	–	–	–	–	–	–

ORBITAL ATK INC   NYS: OA

45101 Warp Drive   CEO: –
Dulles, VA 20166   CFO: Heather Crofford
Phone: 703 406-5000   HR: Mandi Couch
Fax: –   FYE: December 31
Web: www.orbitalatk.com   Type: Public

Through several operating segments Orbital ATK is a leading manufacturer of mission-critical products including launch vehicles and related propulsion systems; satellites and associated components and services; composite aerospace structures; tactical missiles subsystems and defense electronics; and precision weapons armament systems and ammunition. Its operations are divided across the three segments of Flight Systems Defense Systems and Space Systems. In late 2017 Orbital ATK agreed to be bought by Northrop Grumman for about $7.8 billion in cash.

	Annual Growth	03/13	03/14	03/15*	12/15	12/16
Sales ($ mil.)	0.7%	4,362.1	4,775.1	3,174.0	3,399.1	4,455.0
Net income ($ mil.)	2.5%	271.8	340.9	202.5	182.4	293.0
Market value ($ mil.)	6.6%	4,163.8	8,171.8	4,405.3	5,135.9	5,043.4
Employees	(3.2%)	14,000	16,000	12,300	12,300	12,700

*Fiscal year change

ORBITAL SCIENCES CORP.   NYS: ORB

45101 Warp Drive   CEO: David W Thompson
Dulles, VA 20166   CFO: Garrett E Pierce
Phone: 703 406-5000   HR: –
Fax: –   FYE: December 31
Web: www.orbital.com   Type: Public

Orbital Sciences maintains that what goes up doesn't have to come down — at least not for a long time. The company makes low-Earth-orbit satellites and other spacecraft for communications science and technology research and national security purposes. Orbital Sciences also manufactures satellite launch vehicles as well as interceptors (to stop missile attacks) and target launch vehicles that test missile defense systems. Its advanced space programs division develops and supports human space flight space exploration and launch systems and satellites primarily used for national security programs. The US government and its contractors account for about 71% of the company's sales.

	Annual Growth	12/08	12/09	12/10	12/11	12/12
Sales ($ mil.)	5.3%	1,168.6	1,125.3	1,294.6	1,345.9	1,436.8
Net income ($ mil.)	(0.1%)	61.3	36.6	47.5	67.4	61.0
Market value ($ mil.)	(8.4%)	1,164.3	909.8	1,021.2	866.2	820.9
Employees	0.7%	3,400	3,100	3,400	3,500	3,500

ORBITZ WORLDWIDE INC

NYS: OWW

500 W. Madison Street, Suite 1000
Chicago, IL 60661
Phone: 312 894-5000
Fax: –
Web: www.orbitz.com

CEO: Barney Harford
CFO: Michael Randolfi
HR: Mike Goldwasser
FYE: December 31
Type: Public

Orbiting within the universe among the celestial "big four" giants of online travel (the other three being Expedia Travelocity and Priceline) Orbitz Worldwide offers an assortment of travel products and services to both consumers and professionals. The online travel agency offers plane tickets (from some 400 airlines) lodging (at more than 80000 hotels) rental car services cruises and vacation packages. Its portfolio of brands includes CheapTickets ebookers HotelClub RatesToGo Orbitz for Business and the Away Network. Hotel services are offered through partners such as Hilton Marriott and Hyatt. Orbitz is a division of travel conglomeratge Travelport Limited owned by The Blackstone Group.

	Annual Growth	12/09	12/10	12/11	12/12	12/13
Sales ($ mil.)	3.5%	738.0	757.5	766.8	778.8	847.0
Net income ($ mil.)	–	(337.0)	(58.2)	(37.3)	(301.7)	165.1
Market value ($ mil.)	(0.6%)	795.5	605.8	407.5	294.8	778.1
Employees	(1.8%)	1,400	1,400	1,329	1,328	1,300

ORCA BAY SEAFOODS, INC.

2729 6TH AVE S 200
SEATTLE, WA 981342101
Phone: 425-204-9100
Fax: –
Web: www.orcabayseafoods.com

CEO: –
CFO: –
HR: –
FYE: February 28
Type: Private

Orca Bay Seafoods is a leading supplier of fresh frozen seafood sourcing products from oceans all over the world. The company buys flash-frozen fish from suppliers and keeps it frozen as it cuts individual portions for sale to foodservice companies supermarkets club stores and restaurants across the US. Its products include Ahi tuna Alaskan cod Pacific Ocean pearch sockeye salmon mahi mahi and tilapia as well as Mexican white shrimp. Orca Bay was founded by Mike Samsel in 1985; the giant Japanese seafood company Maruha Nichiro owns a minority interest in the company; Japanese conglomerate Tokusui Corporation owns the controlling interest.

	Annual Growth	02/06	02/07	02/08	02/09	02/10
Sales ($ mil.)	(10.8%)	–	–	–	157.0	140.0
Net income ($ mil.)	(36.6%)	–	–	–	1.4	0.9
Market value ($ mil.)	–	–	–	–	–	–
Employees	–	–	–	–	–	180

ORCHID CELLMARK INC.

NASDAQ: ORCH

4390 US Rte. 1
Princeton NJ 08540
Phone: 609-750-2200
Fax: 609-750-6400
Web: www.orchid.com

CEO: Thomas A Bologna
CFO: James F Smith
HR: –
FYE: December 31
Type: Subsidiary

Orchid Cellmark can prove who the baby daddy is and determine if suspects were at the scene of a crime. The company is a leading provider of forensic genetic testing services to criminal justice agencies in the UK and US. It tests DNA found at crime scenes or taken from suspects in custody; it also contributes DNA profiles to law enforcement databases. The company also performs paternity testing (mainly for child support enforcement agencies family-law firms and individuals). Most of its work is through contracts with government agencies. The company was acquired by LabCorp in a deal worth about $84 million.

ORCHID ISLAND CAPITAL, INC.

NYS: ORC

3305 Flamingo Drive
Vero Beach, FL 32963
Phone: 772 231-1400
Fax: –
Web: www.orchidislandcapital.com

CEO: Robert E. Cauley
CFO: G. Hunter Haas
HR: –
FYE: December 31
Type: Public

No REIT is an island unless your name is Orchid Island Capital. The company which is seeking to become a real estate investment trust invests in residential mortgage-backed securities (RMBS) that are guaranteed by the US government or federally sponsored entities like Fannie Mae Freddie Mac and Ginnie Mae. Its portfolio and principal investment targets consist of pass-through agency RMBS and structured agency RMBS including fixed-rate mortgages adjustable-rate mortgages (ARMs) and hybrid ARMs as well as collateralized mortgage obligations. Formed by mortgage REIT Bimini Capital Management in 2010 Orchid Island Capital filed to go public for the second time in October 2012.

	Annual Growth	12/14	12/15	12/16	12/17	12/18
Assets ($ mil.)	19.6%	1,657.8	2,241.8	3,138.7	4,023.3	3,395.6
Net income ($ mil.)	–	24.5	1.1	2.0	2.0	(44.4)
Market value ($ mil.)	(16.3%)	641.2	487.9	532.1	455.9	314.0
Employees	–	–	–	–	–	–

ORCHIDS PAPER PRODUCTS CO. (DE)

NBB: TISU Q

4826 Hunt Street
Pryor, OK 74361
Phone: 918 825-0616
Fax: –
Web: www.orchidspaper.com

CEO: Jeffrey S. Schoen
CFO: Rodney D. Gloss
HR: –
FYE: December 31
Type: Public

Orchids Paper Products hopes to leave its end users smelling like a rose. The company makes bulk tissue paper and converts it into bathroom tissue paper napkins and paper towels for the consumer market. Most of the company's products are sold as private-label items by discount retailers; Orchids Paper products also are sold under the company's Colortex and Velvet brands. Dollar General is Orchids Paper's largest customer; other big customers include Family Dollar and Wal-Mart. Orchids Paper sells most of its products within a 500-mile radius of its manufacturing plant in northeastern Oklahoma.

	Annual Growth	12/14	12/15	12/16	12/17	12/18
Sales ($ mil.)	6.9%	142.7	168.4	164.5	162.5	186.7
Net income ($ mil.)	–	9.5	13.6	12.8	6.7	(37.7)
Market value ($ mil.)	(57.6%)	310.6	329.9	279.3	136.6	10.0
Employees	11.3%	313	352	406	472	481

OREGON HEALTH & SCIENCE UNIVERSITY

3181 SW SAM JACKSON PK RD
PORTLAND, OR 972393011
Phone: 503-494-8311
Fax: –
Web: www.ohsu.edu

CEO: –
CFO: Lawrence J. Furnstahl
HR: E F Keeling
FYE: June 30
Type: Private

Oregon Health & Science University (OHSU) is the state's sole institution providing doctoral degrees in medicine dentistry and nursing. Its other two schools are science and engineering and in partnership with Oregon State University pharmacy. OHSU has about 2900 students. The university is also home to two hospitals (one a children's hospital) as well as specialty and primary care clinics research and interdisciplinary centers and community service programs. OHSU traces its roots to 1867 when members of the medical department at Willamette University began the first formal medical education program in Oregon.

	Annual Growth	06/11	06/12	06/13	06/17	06/18
Sales ($ mil.)	7.5%	–	1,975.6	2,169.5	2,846.5	3,050.1
Net income ($ mil.)	22.0%	–	78.6	221.2	222.4	259.7
Market value ($ mil.)	–	–	–	–	–	–
Employees	–	–	–	–	–	19,500

OREGON STATE LOTTERY

500 AIRPORT RD SE
SALEM, OR 973015068
Phone: 503-540-1000
Fax: –
Web: www.oregonlottery.org

CEO: –
CFO: –
HR: –
FYE: June 30
Type: Private

The Oregon State Lottery operates the Beaver State's lottery and other state-run games of chance. It offers traditional lotto numbers games and instant-win tickets and it operates video lottery and video poker machines. Oregon also takes part in the multistate Powerball drawing. About 65% of the lottery's profits are channeled into public education programs while the rest is used to fund economic development projects state parks and other government programs. Oregon created its lottery in 1984.

	Annual Growth	06/13	06/14	06/15	06/16	06/18
Sales ($ mil.)	2.9%	–	–	–	1,230.2	1,302.9
Net income ($ mil.)	–	–	–	–	61.3	(14.4)
Market value ($ mil.)	–	–	–	–	–	–
Employees	–	–	–	–	–	420

OREGON STATE UNIVERSITY

308 KERR ADM BLDG
CORVALLIS, OR 97331
Phone: 541-737-2198
Fax: –
Web: www.coas.oregonstate.edu

CEO: –
CFO: –
HR: –
FYE: June 30
Type: Private

Oregon State University (OSU) offers about 200 undergraduate and more than 80 graduate degree programs at about a dozen colleges and schools including nationally recognized programs in engineering environmental sciences forestry and pharmacy. The university is also home to centers of marine science and gene research and biotechnology a wave research laboratory and the Linus Pauling Institute. It also offers professional certificate non-degree and extension programs as well as precollege programs for elementary and high school students. In addition to its main campus in Corvallis the university operates OSU-Cascades in Bend Oregon. OSU has an annual enrollment of more than 18000 students.

	Annual Growth	06/02	06/03	06/04	06/05	06/12
Sales ($ mil.)	(0.7%)	–	377.4	78.5	78.5	354.8
Net income ($ mil.)	–	–	5.7	33.7	26.9	(22.6)
Market value ($ mil.)	–	–	–	–	–	–
Employees	–	–	–	–	–	8,188

OREXIGEN THERAPEUTICS INC   NMS: OREX

3344 North Torrey Pines Court, Suite 200
La Jolla, CA 92037
Phone: 858 875-8600
Fax: –
Web: www.orexigen.com

CEO: –
CFO: –
HR: –
FYE: December 31
Type: Public

Orexigen Therapeutics thinks it has the skinny on how to stay trim. The company is developing drugs under the names Contrave and Empatic (formerly Excalia) intended for use by obese people who are trying to get a grip on the urge to overeat. The products are designed to control appetite from the central nervous system; they contain some of the same chemicals used in drugs approved for the treatment of smoking alcoholism and opiate addiction. The development-stage company is conducting late-stage clinical trials on its top two drug candidates. Orexigen was formed in 2002 and went public in 2012.

	Annual Growth	12/12	12/13	12/14	12/15	12/16
Sales ($ mil.)	77.1%	3.4	3.4	55.5	24.5	33.7
Net income ($ mil.)	–	(90.1)	(77.7)	(37.5)	(68.7)	(24.5)
Market value ($ mil.)	(24.1%)	76.7	82.3	88.6	25.1	25.4
Employees	32.4%	43	51	50	67	132

ORGANICALLY GROWN COMPANY

1800 PRAIRIE RD STE B
EUGENE, OR 974029722
Phone: 541-689-5320
Fax: –
Web: www.organicgrown.com

CEO: Josh Hinerfeld
CFO: Robbie Vasilinda
HR: –
FYE: December 30
Type: Private

Started by health-conscious Oregon farmers Organically Grown is exactly what its name says it is. The company grows and sells certified organic fruits vegetables and herbs produced by small to medium family-owned farmers located throughout the US's Pacific Northwest. Its line of more than 100 seasonal produce items are sold under the LADYBUG brand to customers including independent retailers supermarket chains restaurants home-delivery services and wholesalers. Organically Grown which is owned by its employees and growers was founded in 1978.

	Annual Growth	12/13	12/14	12/15	12/16	12/17
Sales ($ mil.)	(0.1%)	–	163.8	176.4	180.2	163.3
Net income ($ mil.)	(83.1%)	–	2.3	3.1	1.6	0.0
Market value ($ mil.)	–	–	–	–	–	–
Employees	–	–	–	–	–	189

ORION ENERGY SYSTEMS INC   NAS: OESX

2210 Woodland Drive
Manitowoc, WI 54220
Phone: 920 892-9340
Fax: –
Web: www.orionlighting.com

CEO: Michael W Altschaefl
CFO: William T Hull
HR: Nancy McPhail
FYE: March 31
Type: Public

Orion Energy Systems wants customers to see the light ... high intensity fluorescent (HIF) lighting systems that is. Orion designs manufactures and installs energy management systems that include HIF lighting and intelligent lighting controls. Its Apollo Light Pipe product collects and focuses daylight without consuming electricity. The firm estimates its HIF lineup can help cut customers' lighting-related electricity costs by up to 50% boost quantity and quality of light and reduce related carbon-dioxide emissions. In addition its engineered systems division makes solar photovoltaic products that allow customers to convert sunlight into electricity.

	Annual Growth	03/15	03/16	03/17	03/18	03/19
Sales ($ mil.)	(2.3%)	72.2	67.6	70.2	60.3	65.8
Net income ($ mil.)	–	(32.1)	(20.1)	(12.3)	(13.1)	(6.7)
Market value ($ mil.)	(27.1%)	92.9	41.1	58.6	25.2	26.2
Employees	12.8%	198	263	264	214	321

ORION GROUP HOLDINGS INC   NYS: ORN

12000 Aerospace Avenue, Suite 300
Houston, TX 77034
Phone: 713 852-6500
Fax: –
Web: www.orionmarinegroup.com

CEO: Mark R. Stauffer
CFO: Christopher J. DeAlmeida
HR: –
FYE: December 31
Type: Public

As Poseidon's son the Greek god Orion could walk on water. That's about the only thing Orion Group Holdings (formerly Orion Marine) doesn't do when it comes to water. Through operating subsidiaries the company provides civil construction and maintenance services for marine infrastructure including pipelines bridges waterways and port and other transportation facilities. It also performs dredging surveying inspections excavation and demolition services. Orion Marine serves government commercial and industrial clients; government projects account for some three-fourths of its revenues. The company operates in the Gulf Coast Atlantic Seaboard West Coast Pacific Northwest and Caribbean Basin regions.

	Annual Growth	12/14	12/15	12/16	12/17	12/18
Sales ($ mil.)	7.8%	385.8	466.5	578.2	578.6	520.9
Net income ($ mil.)	–	6.9	(8.1)	(3.6)	0.4	(94.4)
Market value ($ mil.)	(21.1%)	319.4	120.5	287.6	226.3	124.0
Employees	20.0%	1,200	1,200	2,250	2,625	2,487

ORLANDO HEALTH, INC.

52 W UNDERWOOD ST
ORLANDO, FL 328061110
Phone: 407-841-5111
Fax: –

CEO: David W. Strong
CFO: Bernadette Spong
HR: –
FYE: September 30
Type: Private

It's not Disney World but for Floridians needing health care it is a prime destination. Orlando Health is a not-for-profit organization with a network of community and specialty hospitals with nearly 2300 beds in Central Florida. Its flagship facility the Orlando Regional Medical Center features a Level 1 trauma center and provides comprehensive acute care services in a range of specialties. Orlando Health also operates several community hospitals. Its specialty hospitals include the Arnold Palmer Hospital for Children and the Winnie Palmer Hospital for Women and Babies. It also operates the renowned M. D. Anderson Cancer Center Orlando (the first affiliate of Houston-based M. D. Anderson center).

	Annual Growth	09/08	09/09	09/10	09/13	09/14
Sales ($ mil.)	(0.6%)	–	–	1,700.7	1,576.9	1,663.4
Net income ($ mil.)	26.1%	–	–	91.4	115.9	231.5
Market value ($ mil.)	–	–	–	–	–	–
Employees	–	–	–	–	–	23,000

ORLANDO UTILITIES COMMISSION

100 W. Anderson St.
Orlando FL 32801
Phone: 407-423-9100
Fax: 407-236-9616
Web: www.ouc.com

CEO: Kenneth P Ksionek
CFO: –
HR: –
FYE: September 30
Type: Government-owned

Orlando Utilities Commission (OUC) has a simple mission — to provide electricity and water services to customers in and around Orlando Florida. In 2010 the utility was serving 221380 residential and business accounts (51% electric only 33% electric and water customers and 16% water only). In addition it operates fossil-fueled power plants and markets wholesale power. OUC also provides district cooling chilled water and commercial lighting services and advises customers on power and water conservation measures. In 2010 OUC delivered 24.9 billion gallons of water and 7.4 million MW of power.

ORMAT TECHNOLOGIES INC

6140 Plumas Street
Reno, NV 89519-6075
Phone: 775 356-9029
Fax: –
Web: www.ormat.com

NYS: ORA

CEO: Isaac Angel
CFO: Doron Blachar
HR: –
FYE: December 31
Type: Public

Ormat Technologies is on an environmentally safe power trip building plants for geothermal energy recovered energy and solar power. The company set up by Israel-based Ormat Industries also sells power units for both types of plants and sells fossil fuel-powered turbo-generators with a capacity of between 200W and 5000W. Ormat operates power plants in Guatemala Kenya Guadeloupe Island Honduras and the US. The company's largest market is the US accounting for 45% of annual revenue.

	Annual Growth	12/14	12/15	12/16	12/17	12/18
Sales ($ mil.)	6.5%	559.5	594.6	662.6	692.8	719.3
Net income ($ mil.)	16.0%	54.2	119.6	93.9	155.5	98.0
Market value ($ mil.)	17.8%	1,378.0	1,849.0	2,718.5	3,242.8	2,651.6
Employees	5.3%	1,095	1,060	1,180	1,303	1,346

ORRSTOWN FINANCIAL SERVICES, INC.

77 East King Street, P.O. Box 250
Shippensburg, PA 17257
Phone: 717 532-6114
Fax: –
Web: www.orrstown.com

NAS: ORRF

CEO: Thomas R Quinn Jr
CFO: Thomas R Brugger
HR: –
FYE: December 31
Type: Public

Orrstown Financial Services keeps both paddles in the money pool. The institution is the holding company for Orrstown Bank which operates some 20 branches in Pennsylvania's Cumberland Perry and Franklin counties as well as in Maryland's Washington County. In addition to traditional retail deposit offerings Orrstown also provides investment management services including retirement planning and investment analysis. Real estate mortgages account for about 40% of the bank's lending portfolio followed by commercial construction and consumer loans. Orrstown is growing its mortgage lending capabilities. It launched an online application system in order to increase mortgage origination sales.

	Annual Growth	12/14	12/15	12/16	12/17	12/18
Assets ($ mil.)	12.9%	1,190.4	1,292.8	1,414.5	1,558.8	1,934.4
Net income ($ mil.)	(18.6%)	29.1	7.9	6.6	8.1	12.8
Market value ($ mil.)	1.7%	160.3	168.2	211.2	238.1	171.7
Employees	5.5%	312	306	327	338	386

ORTHOLOGIC CORP.

1275 W. Washington St.
Tempe AZ 85281
Phone: 602-286-5520
Fax: 216-755-1500
Web: www.ddrc.com

NASDAQ: CAPS

CEO: –
CFO: Les M Taeger
HR: –
FYE: December 31
Type: Public

OrthoLogic doing business as Capstone Therapeutics is trying to make sense of scarred skin and damaged hearts with its biopharmaceutical products designed to repair the body's tissues. The biotechnology company is focused on a couple of synthetic peptide technologies that may accelerate healing. Its Chrysalin program has yielded several potential therapies including TP508 which the company is evaluating as a treatment for vascular diseases as well as diabetic foot ulcers. OrthoLogic acquired another candidate AZX100 in 2006 and has begun clinical testing on the drug as a treatment for dermal scarring.

OSAGE BANCSHARES INC.

239 E. Main St.
Pawhuska OK 74056
Phone: 918-287-2919
Fax: 918-287-2974
Web: www.osagefed.com

OTC: OSBK

CEO: Mark S White
CFO: Sue Allen Smith
HR: –
FYE: June 30
Type: Public

Osage Bancshares is the holding company for Osage Federal Bank which provides deposit and lending services to consumers and businesses in Osage and Washington counties in northern Oklahoma. The bank's offerings include checking savings and retirement accounts such as IRAs and CDs as well as consumer commercial construction and real estate loans. One- to four-family real estate loans make up about two-thirds of Osage Federal's total loan portfolio; other real estate loans include multi-family commercial and land. The bank operates a handful of branches in the cities of Pawhuska Bartlesville and Barnsdall. Its roots date back to 1918.

OSBORN & BARR COMMUNICATIONS INC.

914 SPRUCE ST
SAINT LOUIS, MO 631021118
Phone: 314-726-5511
Fax: –
Web: www.osborn-barr.com

CEO: Michael Turley
CFO: Rhonda Ries
HR: –
FYE: December 31
Type: Private

You can take the ad agency out of the country but well you know. Osborn & Barr Communications has built its reputation on its work in the agriculture rural-lifestyle and outdoors markets but its portfolio also includes work in government finance and leisure industries. The agency offers advertising public relations brand management creative services social marketing digital marketing media services and strategic marketing for clients across North America. Clients have included Michelin the USDA Intervet and Monsanto. Founded in 1989 Osborn & Barr has offices in St. Louis; Kansas City Missouri; and Des Moines.

	Annual Growth	12/04	12/05	12/06	12/07	12/08
Sales ($ mil.)	2.7%	–	61.2	67.8	56.3	66.3
Net income ($ mil.)	(10.5%)	–	–	1.6	1.5	1.3
Market value ($ mil.)	–	–	–	–	–	–
Employees	–	–	–	–	–	160

OSC SPORTS, INC.

5 BRADLEY DR
WESTBROOK, ME 040922013
Phone: 207-854-2794
Fax: –
Web: www.olympiasports.net

CEO: –
CFO: Woodbury Sanders
HR: –
FYE: September 30
Type: Private

Olympia Sports may not make you an Olympian but the company carries the gear to help you go for gold. The sporting goods retailer offers sports equipment fitness gear and apparel athletic shoes casual wear and sports accessories under such brands as Columbia Louisville Slugger Bauer PUMA Reebok and Teva. It sells merchandise through its website and via more than 225 banner stores across the Northeast and Mid-Atlantic states. In addition to its retail business the company oversees the private nonprofit Olympia Sports Foundation which runs a clothing bank and collaborates on projects with local charities and schools within its retail region. Founder and CEO Ed Manganello owns Olympia.

	Annual Growth	09/05	09/06	09/07	09/08	09/09
Sales ($ mil.)	(2.0%)	–	–	172.7	191.0	165.8
Net income ($ mil.)	(70.1%)	–	–	3.1	4.4	0.3
Market value ($ mil.)	–	–	–	–	–	–
Employees	–	–	–	–	–	2,000

OSCAR DE LA RENTA, LLC

11 W 42ND ST FL 24
NEW YORK, NY 100368002
Phone: 212-282-0500
Fax: –
Web: www.odlr.com

CEO: Alexander L Bolen
CFO: Giuseppe Celio
HR: –
FYE: December 31
Type: Private

Women navigate toward the Oscar de la Renta style. The late designer's namesake firm designs couture and ready-to-wear apparel for men and women and licenses its name for a number of products including jewelry eyewear lingerie home furnishings luggage swimwear fragrance and furs. Other collections made by the company are sold under the OSCAR by Oscar de la Renta and Pink Label brands (the latter licensed to apparel marketer Kellwood). Oscar de la Renta sells its products in upscale department stores and specialty shops worldwide. Its apparel is made in the US and Italy. Dominican Republic-born designer Oscar de la Renta and partner Ben Shaw (both now deceased) founded the company in 1966.

	Annual Growth	12/11	12/12	12/13	12/14	12/15
Sales ($ mil.)	8.0%	–	–	–	112.0	121.0
Net income ($ mil.)	212.7%	–	–	–	1.6	5.1
Market value ($ mil.)	–	–	–	–	–	–
Employees	–	–	–	–	–	250

OSF HEALTHCARE SYSTEM

800 NE GLEN OAK AVE
PEORIA, IL 616033200
Phone: 309-655-2850
Fax: –
Web: www.osfhealthcare.org

CEO: Robert Sehring
CFO: –
HR: –
FYE: September 30
Type: Private

OSF Healthcare helps patients who are feeling oh-so-frail in northern Illinois and southwestern Michigan. OSF Healthcare system includes 11 acute care hospitals and one long-term care facility that combined are home to more than 1500 beds and offer a full spectrum of inpatient and outpatient medical and surgical services. The system's primary care physician network consists of about 650 physicians at more than 105 locations throughout its service area. Subsidiary OSF Home Care provides hospice home visit and equipment services and OSF Saint Francis provides ambulance pharmacy and health care management services. The not-for-profit system is a subsidiary of the Sisters of The Third Order of St. Francis.

	Annual Growth	09/14	09/15	09/16	09/17	09/18
Sales ($ mil.)	220.1%	–	86.2	2,422.9	2,561.4	2,826.1
Net income ($ mil.)	100.6%	–	19.2	99.2	144.8	155.4
Market value ($ mil.)	–	–	–	–	–	–
Employees	–	–	–	–	–	4,000

OSI GROUP LLC

1225 Corporate Blvd.
Aurora IL 60504
Phone: 630-851-6600
Fax: 630-692-2340
Web: www.osigroup.com

CEO: Sheldon Lavin
CFO: Bill Weimer
HR: –
FYE: December 31
Type: Private

You might say a steady diet of red meat has made this company big and strong. OSI Industries (doing business as OSI Group) is one of the largest suppliers of meat products to US foodservice operators. Through its operating companies OSI boasts a bulging menu that includes a variety of beef pork and poultry products including beef patties hot dogs sausages bacon and chicken nuggets. It has long been a supplier of beef to #1 fast-food chain McDonald's. As part of its business OSI also offers contract manufacturing packaging services and supply chain management for other food processors; it has more than 50 production facilities in 17 countries.

OSI SYSTEMS, INC. (DE)

NMS: OSIS

12525 Chadron Avenue
Hawthorne, CA 90250
Phone: 310 978-0516
Fax: –
Web: www.osi-systems.com

CEO: Deepak Chopra
CFO: Alan I. Edrick
HR: Sandy Davis
FYE: June 30
Type: Public

OSI Systems is keeping a close scan on transportation security and health care worldwide. The company's security division manufactures specialized inspection equipment under the Rapiscan Systems name used to screen everything from baggage and people to cargo and vehicles at airports ports and borders. Its Spacelabs Healthcare subsidiary makes patient monitoring cardiac monitoring and clinical networking systems primarily for hospitals. A third division makes optoelectronic devices (OSI Optoelectronics) for aerospace/defense electronics industrial automation security medical diagnostics and other applications. That division also offers contract electronics manufacturing services (OSI Electronics).

	Annual Growth	06/15	06/16	06/17	06/18	06/19
Sales ($ mil.)	5.4%	958.2	829.7	961.0	1,089.3	1,182.1
Net income ($ mil.)	(0.1%)	65.2	26.2	21.1	(29.1)	64.8
Market value ($ mil.)	12.3%	1,286.0	1,056.0	1,365.3	1,404.9	2,046.2
Employees	3.5%	5,810	5,847	5,763	6,087	6,667

OSIRIS THERAPEUTICS INC
NMS: OSIR

7015 Albert Einstein Drive
Columbia, MD 21046-1707
Phone: 443 545-1800
Fax: –
Web: www.osiris.com

CEO: Samson Tom
CFO: –
HR: –
FYE: December 31
Type: Public

Unlike the Eygptian god this Osiris seeks to keep people out of the afterlife. The biotech company researches develops and markets cellular regenerative drug candidates. It engages in stem cell research bioengineering and the development of tissue-based products. Its marketed products include treatments in the areas of orthopedics sports medicine and wound care Bone repair and regeneration allograft Bio4 is a viable bone matrix and alternative to autografts (the transfer of tissue from one part of the body to another). Other products include allograft Cartiform placental membrane Grafix skin allograft TruSkin and placental allograft Stravix.

	Annual Growth	12/13	12/14	12/15	12/16	12/17
Sales ($ mil.)	48.6%	24.3	59.9	79.7	109.4	118.5
Net income ($ mil.)	(32.2%)	41.6	(1.8)	(35.8)	(3.7)	8.8
Market value ($ mil.)	(21.8%)	555.2	552.1	358.4	169.5	207.2
Employees	47.0%	75	217	–	–	350

OTELCO INC
NAS: OTEL

505 Third Avenue East
Oneonta, AL 35121
Phone: 205 625-3574
Fax: –
Web: www.otelcoinc.com

CEO: Robert J Souza
CFO: Curtis L Garner Jr
HR: –
FYE: December 31
Type: Public

Otelco makes sure rural areas enjoy all the modern communications conveniences. The company operates six incumbent rural local-exchange carriers (RLECs) that provide local and long-distance phone services. Other services include high-speed and dial-up Internet access as well as cable television. Otelco has four RLECs in north central Alabama one in central Missouri and one adjacent to Bangor Maine. It maintains more than 69000 access lines and has more than 4000 cable-TV customers. Otelco has made a business of acquiring RLECs including assets from Oneonta Telephone that were used to create Otelco Telephone in 1999.

	Annual Growth	12/14	12/15	12/16	12/17	12/18
Sales ($ mil.)	(2.8%)	73.9	71.1	68.9	68.5	66.1
Net income ($ mil.)	17.1%	5.0	7.5	5.1	12.1	9.5
Market value ($ mil.)	35.0%	16.5	23.8	21.5	45.2	54.8
Employees	(4.2%)	241	228	222	222	203

OTSUKA AMERICA INC

1 EMBARCADERO CTR # 2020
SAN FRANCISCO, CA 94111-3750
Phone: 415-986-5300
Fax: –
Web: www.otsuka-america.com

CEO: Hiromi Yoshikawa
CFO: –
HR: Masami Travis
FYE: December 31
Type: Private

Otsuka America is the holding company for the US operations of Japan's Otsuka Pharmaceutical. Otsuka America oversees pharmaceutical research and development marketing and distribution of both prescription drugs and over-the-counter (OTC) medicines. The company's pharmaceutical subsidiaries include Otsuka America Pharmaceutical (prescription drug marketing) Otsuka Maryland Medicinal Laboratories (research) Cambridge Isotope Laboratories (chemical ingredients) and Pharmavite (nutritionals). To help wash down its pills Otsuka America also holds consumer beverage makers Crystal Geyser (bottled water) Ridge Vineyards (wine) and Soma Beverage Company (specialty bottled water).

	Annual Growth	12/00	12/01	12/02	12/03	12/07
Sales ($ mil.)	30.1%	–	567.7	612.8	1,066.7	2,755.3
Net income ($ mil.)	–	–	(56.1)	153.2	56.3	51.7
Market value ($ mil.)	–	–	–	–	–	–
Employees	–	–	–	–	–	2,065

OTTER PRODUCTS, LLC

209 S MELDRUM ST
FORT COLLINS, CO 805212603
Phone: 855-688-7269
Fax: –
Web: www.otterbox.com

CEO: Jim Parke
CFO: Gerald Chen
HR: –
FYE: December 31
Type: Private

Otter Products' products keep your precious electronic devices safe and dry. The company which goes by OtterBox makes more than 250 models of protective cases for cell phones smart phones tablet computers and other portable electronics from Apple LG Corp BlackBerry Samsung and other manufacturers. It outsources production and sells its impact and water resistant Defender Reflex Commuter and Impact cases and watertight boxes at Best Buy Target and other retailers. OtterBox was formed in 1998 by CEO Curt Richardson and his wife Nancy who came up with the name after being inspired by otters' water-repellent skin and playful and creative attitudes.

	Annual Growth	12/06	12/07	12/08	12/09	12/10
Sales ($ mil.)	309.6%	–	–	10.1	48.6	168.9
Net income ($ mil.)	837.9%	–	–	0.7	15.4	60.4
Market value ($ mil.)	–	–	–	–	–	–
Employees	–	–	–	–	–	320

OTTER TAIL CORP.
NMS: OTTR

215 South Cascade Street, P.O. Box 496
Fergus Falls, MN 56538-0496
Phone: 866 410-8780
Fax: –
Web: www.ottertail.com

CEO: Chuck MacFarlane
CFO: Kevin G. Moug
HR: –
FYE: December 31
Type: Public

Like the broad end of its furry namesake Otter Tail covers a swath of businesses from electric services and construction to manufacturing equipment and plastics. The electric utility (Otter Tail Power Corporation) is the company's core business; it keeps the lights on for more than 129000 residential commercial and industrial customers in Minnesota and the Dakotas. The company also makes PVC pipes (Northern Pipe Products and Vinyltech Corporation) manufactures parts and trays (BTD Manufacturing and T.O. Plastics) and provides construction services (Foley Company and Aevenia).

	Annual Growth	12/14	12/15	12/16	12/17	12/18
Sales ($ mil.)	3.5%	799.3	779.8	803.5	849.4	916.4
Net income ($ mil.)	9.3%	57.7	59.3	62.3	72.4	82.3
Market value ($ mil.)	12.5%	1,228.0	1,056.3	1,618.3	1,763.1	1,969.0
Employees	5.2%	1,893	2,005	2,054	2,097	2,321

OUR LADY OF LOURDES MEDICAL CENTER, INC

1600 HADDON AVE
CAMDEN, NJ 081033101
Phone: 856-757-3500
Fax: –
Web: www.lourdesnet.org

CEO: Dennis Pullin
CFO: –
HR: –
FYE: June 30
Type: Private

Our Lady of Lourdes Medical Center tends to the sick of southern New Jersey. The hospital is a general acute care facility with about 325 inpatient beds. In addition to general medical emergency and surgical care the hospital specializes in organ transplantation joint replacement rehabilitation dialysis treatment cardiac care and birthing care. The hospital also offers nursing and other medical training programs and it operates area clinics and provides community health and outreach services. Our Lady of Lourdes Medical Center part of Catholic Health East's Lourdes Health System was purchased by Virtua Health in 2019.

	Annual Growth	06/11	06/12	06/13	06/14	06/15
Sales ($ mil.)	3.5%	–	–	–	298.1	308.5
Net income ($ mil.)	99.9%	–	–	–	14.1	28.1
Market value ($ mil.)	–	–	–	–	–	–
Employees	–	–	–	–	–	3,000

OUR LADY OF LOURDES REGIONAL MEDICAL CENTER, INC.

4801 AMBSSDOR CFFERY PKWY — CEO: –
LAFAYETTE, LA 705086917 — CFO: –
Phone: 337-470-2000 — HR: Jennifer Trahan
Fax: – — FYE: June 30
Web: www.lourdesrmc.com — Type: Private

Established in 1949 as part of the not-for-profit Franciscan Missionaries of Our Lady Health System Our Lady of Lourdes Regional Medical Center is a hospital that provides medical care in southern Louisiana. The facility cares for denizens of the bayou with a medical staff of more than 400 physicians representing some 50 specialties including cardiology neurology and oncology. The medical center also offers oupatient care and urgent care as well as a general family practice and pediatric care. Our Lady of Lourdes extends its reach outside the facility into the Acadiana regional community by offering primary care physicians' offices home health care programs and occupational medicine.

	Annual Growth	06/09	06/10	06/15	06/16	06/18
Sales ($ mil.)	7.7%	–	162.9	197.2	229.0	294.8
Net income ($ mil.)	–	–	(9.2)	(38.3)	(24.9)	2.8
Market value ($ mil.)	–	–	–	–	–	–
Employees	–	–	–	–	–	1,700

OUR LADY OF THE LAKE HOSPITAL, INC.

7777 HENNESSY BLVD — CEO: K Scott Wester
BATON ROUGE, LA 708084300 — CFO: –
Phone: 225-765-6565 — HR: –
Fax: – — FYE: June 30
Web: www.ololrmc.com — Type: Private

Our Lady of the Lake Regional Medical Center reaches out to Baton Rouge residents with a helping hand. Participating in teaching programs for LSU and Tulane medical schools the medical center has some 800 inpatient beds and includes trauma emergency surgery general medical and specialty care centers for conditions including heart disease cancer orthopedics and ENT (ear nose and throat) disorders. Our Lady of the Lake also includes a Children's Hospital two nursing homes and an independent-living facility and it offers outpatient services at its main campus and at satellite facilities throughout the greater Baton Rouge area.

	Annual Growth	06/13	06/14	06/15	06/16	06/18
Sales ($ mil.)	7.3%	–	946.5	984.6	895.7	1,254.6
Net income ($ mil.)	16.0%	–	57.0	21.1	(89.4)	103.3
Market value ($ mil.)	–	–	–	–	–	–
Employees	–	–	–	–	–	1,800

OUR LADY OF THE LAKE UNIVERSITY OF SAN ANTONIO

411 SW 24TH ST — CEO: –
SAN ANTONIO, TX 782074617 — CFO: –
Phone: 210-432-8904 — HR: –
Fax: – — FYE: May 31
Web: www.ollusa.edu — Type: Private

Our Lady of the Lake University was founded in 1895 by the Sisters of the Congregation of Divine Providence not   that   lady of the lake. The Catholic college offers undergraduate and graduate education courses at its main campus in San Antonio Texas as well as satellite locations in Houston and the Rio Grande Valley. It offers night and weekend classes as well as online programs. Altogether its 2700 students may choose from a variety of liberal arts and science subject areas including business information technology education social work and psychology.

	Annual Growth	05/12	05/13	05/15	05/16	05/17
Sales ($ mil.)	13.0%	–	46.0	51.3	73.6	74.9
Net income ($ mil.)	20.2%	–	1.4	(2.2)	1.8	3.0
Market value ($ mil.)	–	–	–	–	–	–
Employees	–	–	–	–	–	504

OURPET'S COMPANY
NBB: OPCO

1300 East Street — CEO: Steven Tsengas
Fairport Harbor, OH 44077 — CFO: Scott R Mendes
Phone: 440 354-6500 — HR: –
Fax: – — FYE: December 31
Web: www.ourpets.com — Type: Public

OurPet's is counting on its customers' pets being spoiled rotten. The company makes some 400 pet products (such as feeders toys litter and natural and nutritional pet supplements and treats) for dogs cats and domestic and wild birds. Besides its namesake brands OurPet's makes its items under brand names Flappy Pet Zone SmartScoop Ecopure Naturals Play-N-Squeak Durapet Go! Cat Go and DockDogs. The firm's products are sold through suppliers including PetSmart and Wal-Mart (its two biggest customers accounting for about 43% of sales). Chairman president and CEO Dr. Steven Tsengas and his wife control about 27% of the company's voting shares.

	Annual Growth	12/13	12/14	12/15	12/16	12/17
Sales ($ mil.)	7.0%	21.6	22.8	23.8	27.1	28.3
Net income ($ mil.)	13.0%	1.1	0.8	1.3	2.1	1.7
Market value ($ mil.)	11.6%	18.0	16.8	17.8	18.5	27.9
Employees	(4.1%)	59	56	54	53	50

OUTERWALL INC
NMS: OUTR

1800 114th Avenue SE — CEO: James H Gaherity
Bellevue, WA 98004 — CFO: Kevin McColly
Phone: 425 943-8000 — HR: –
Fax: – — FYE: December 31
Web: www.outerwall.com — Type: Public

Outerwall (formerly Coinstar) takes its name from the previously underutilized "fourth wall" area between the cash registers and the front door in retail stores. Once known for its coin-counting Coinstar kiosks the company's Redbox kiosk business which vends DVD and Blu-Ray rentals now generates more than 80% of Outerwall's sales. Redbox operates some 43680 DVD rental kiosks located at supermarkets malls big-box retailers drug and convenience stores and restaurants across North America. The fast-growing company changed its name to Outerwall in 2013 to reflect its evolution from coin counting to an operator of various automated retail businesses.

	Annual Growth	12/11	12/12	12/13	12/14	12/15
Sales ($ mil.)	4.4%	1,845.4	2,202.0	2,306.3	2,303.0	2,193.2
Net income ($ mil.)	(19.2%)	103.9	150.2	174.8	106.6	44.3
Market value ($ mil.)	(5.4%)	758.0	863.8	1,117.2	1,249.2	606.8
Employees	(0.1%)	2,676	2,927	2,900	2,760	2,670

OVERLAKE HOSPITAL MEDICAL CENTER

1035 116TH AVE NE — CEO: –
BELLEVUE, WA 980044687 — CFO: –
Phone: 425-688-5000 — HR: Lisa Brock
Fax: – — FYE: June 30
Web: www.overlakehospital.org — Type: Private

Over the lake and through the sound to Overlake Hospital Medical Center we go! The not-for-profit hospital provides health care services to residents of Bellevue Washington in the Puget Sound region. The nearly 350-bed facility provides comprehensive inpatient and outpatient services ranging from cancer care and surgery to specialized senior care. Overlake also operates a number of outpatient clinics providing primary care urgent care and specialty care such as weight loss surgery. The organization also provides patients with health and wellness programs addressing issues like women's and children's health.

	Annual Growth	06/13	06/14	06/15	06/16	06/18
Sales ($ mil.)	5.4%	–	450.1	485.8	502.5	555.4
Net income ($ mil.)	(10.0%)	–	59.9	17.0	21.6	39.4
Market value ($ mil.)	–	–	–	–	–	–
Employees	–	–	–	–	–	2,450

OVERLAND CONTRACTING INC.

600 N GREENFIELD PKWY
GARNER, NC 275296947
Phone: 800-790-2149
Fax: –
Web: www.overlandcontracting.com

CEO: –
CFO: Jeffrey J Stamm
HR: –
FYE: December 31
Type: Private

With the extent of work the company does Overland Contracting could be called Overall Contracting. The company a wholly-owned subsidiary of Black & Veatch offers engineering procurement and construction services on electric utility substations power plants water and wastewater facilities telecommunications sites and gas oil and chemical facilities throughout the US. From testing to laying the foundation the company is involved in nearly every part of the building process. Headquartered in Georgia the company also has regional offices in Alabama Florida Kansas Michigan and North Carolina. Customers have included Florida Power & Light Company and T-Mobile.

	Annual Growth	12/05	12/06	12/07	12/08	12/09
Sales ($ mil.)	6.1%	–	318.3	486.1	324.0	380.6
Net income ($ mil.)	–	–	22.8	35.4	11.0	(51.5)
Market value ($ mil.)	–	–	–	–	–	–
Employees	–	–	–	–	–	15

OVERLAND STORAGE, INC.

9112 Spectrum Center Boulevard
San Diego, CA 92123
Phone: 858 571-5555
Fax: –

NAS: OVRL
CEO: Eric L Kelly
CFO: Kurt L Kalbfleisch
HR: –
FYE: June 30
Type: Public

Overland Storage has your backup. The company sells data storage systems software and related media to businesses of all sizes. Its most popular line the tape-based NEO Series of products protects data with nonstop operation remote library management and other features. SnapServer provides network-attached storage (NAS) and storage-area network (SAN) data management for remote offices and distributed enterprises while the REO family of products offers backup and recovery. With more than 450000 installations the company sells to distributors resellers retailers and manufacturers worldwide. Its distribution partners include Ingram Micro and SYNNEX.

	Annual Growth	06/09	06/10	06/11	06/12	06/13
Sales ($ mil.)	(17.9%)	105.6	77.7	70.2	59.6	48.0
Net income ($ mil.)	–	(18.0)	(13.0)	(14.5)	(16.2)	(19.6)
Market value ($ mil.)	24.8%	14.3	61.4	84.5	57.2	34.7
Employees	(6.1%)	229	190	197	187	178

OVERSEAS SHIPHOLDING GROUP INC (NEW)

302 Knights Run Avenue
Tampa, FL 33602
Phone: 813 209-0600
Fax: –
Web: www.osg.com

NYS: OSG
CEO: Samuel H Norton
CFO: Richard Trueblood
HR: –
FYE: December 31
Type: Public

Overseas Shipholding Group (OSG) flies the flags of many nations. The marine transportation company's fleet made up mainly of crude oil tankers and product carriers includes vessels registered in the US and in a number of other countries. Through both long-term and spot market contracts the company charters its fleet to commercial shippers and government agencies. Overall the OSG fleet consists of about 110 vessels with a capacity of about 11 million deadweight tons (DWT). Transportation of crude oil and refined petroleum products accounts for the bulk of the company's business but OSG also transports liquefied natural gas (LNG). In late 2012 OSG filed for Chapter 11 bankruptcy. It emerged in 2014.

	Annual Growth	12/14	12/15	12/16	12/17	12/18
Sales ($ mil.)	(21.4%)	957.4	964.5	462.4	390.4	366.2
Net income ($ mil.)	–	(152.3)	284.0	(293.6)	56.0	13.5
Market value ($ mil.)	(16.3%)	–	240.1	324.9	232.4	140.8
Employees	4.5%	890	890	882	1,123	1,061

OVERSTOCK.COM INC (DE)

799 West Coliseum Way
Midvale, UT 84047
Phone: 801 947-3100
Fax: –
Web: www.overstock.com

NMS: OSTK
CEO: Patrick M. Byrne
CFO: Robert P Hughes
HR: –
FYE: December 31
Type: Public

Overstock.com allows you to shop an online bazaar of clothes housewares music books and more. The discount retailer hawks brand-name merchandise including furniture electronics jewelry travel and insurance at low cost through its websites. Most of its inventory comes from manufacturers stuck with overproduction older models or some color that wasn't as popular as the designer had envisioned. The company also generates a small portion of sales from owned inventory primarily current-run books magazines and music. Furniture is Overstock's leading product line accounting for about a third of sales. It serves customers primarily in the US. Entirely separate from Overstock's retail business Medici Ventures and its main subsid tZERO work to develop blockchain technologies.

	Annual Growth	12/14	12/15	12/16	12/17	12/18
Sales ($ mil.)	5.0%	1,497.1	1,657.8	1,800.0	1,744.8	1,821.6
Net income ($ mil.)	–	8.9	2.4	12.5	(109.9)	(206.1)
Market value ($ mil.)	(13.5%)	780.8	394.8	562.6	2,054.1	436.5
Employees	4.9%	1,700	1,900	1,800	1,800	2,060

OWENS & MINOR, INC.

9120 Lockwood Boulevard
Mechanicsville, VA 23116
Phone: 804 723-7000
Fax: 804 723-7100
Web: www.owens-minor.com

NYS: OMI
CEO: P. Cody Phipps
CFO: Richard A. (Randy) Meier
HR: –
FYE: December 31
Type: Public

Owens & Minor (O&M) is a leading distributor of medical and surgical supplies. The company carries products from about 1100 manufacturers; those products include surgical dressings endoscopic and intravenous products needles syringes sterile procedure trays gowns gloves and sutures. The firm also provides kitting consulting and other services to help customers manage their supplies. O&M primarily serves hospitals and health systems and the purchasing organizations that serve them. It delivers products to roughly 3000 health care providers across the US (where most of its sales are made).

	Annual Growth	12/14	12/15	12/16	12/17	12/18
Sales ($ mil.)	1.0%	9,440.2	9,772.9	9,723.4	9,318.3	9,838.7
Net income ($ mil.)	–	66.5	103.4	108.8	72.8	(437.0)
Market value ($ mil.)	(34.8%)	2,187.1	2,241.3	2,198.4	1,176.1	394.3
Employees	33.1%	5,700	8,100	7,900	6,200	17,900

OWENS CORNING

One Owens Corning Parkway
Toledo, OH 43659
Phone: 419 248-8000
Fax: –
Web: www.owenscorning.com

NYS: OC
CEO: Michael H. (Mike) Thaman
CFO: Michael C McMurray
HR: Paula Russell
FYE: December 31
Type: Public

Owens Corning (OC) operates in the PINK. Famous for its Pink Panther mascot and its trademarked PINK glass fiber insulation the company is a top global maker of building and composite material systems. The building materials company makes insulation roofing fiber-based glass reinforcements and other materials for the residential and commercial markets. Its composite products business makes glass fiber reinforcement materials for the transportation industrial infrastructure marine wind energy and consumer markets.

	Annual Growth	12/14	12/15	12/16	12/17	12/18
Sales ($ mil.)	7.5%	5,276.0	5,350.0	5,677.0	6,384.0	7,057.0
Net income ($ mil.)	24.6%	226.0	330.0	393.0	289.0	545.0
Market value ($ mil.)	5.3%	3,921.2	5,149.8	5,645.8	10,067.4	4,815.8
Employees	9.3%	14,000	15,000	16,000	17,000	20,000

OWENSBORO MUNICIPAL UTILITIES ELECTRIC LIGHT & POWER SYSTEM

2070 TAMARACK RD
OWENSBORO, KY 423016876
Phone: 270-926-3200
Fax: –
Web: www.omu.org

CEO: –
CFO: –
HR: –
FYE: May 31
Type: Private

Owensboro Kentucky (named after Abraham Owen a Shelby County legislator killed in the Battle of Tippecanoe) is served by Owensboro Municipal Utilities which provides power to almost 26000 customers and water to 24500. The city-owned utility operates water treatment facilities and a power plant that uses coal and used tires for fuel. Its operating divisions are Elmer Smith power plant Engineering & Operations Water Production and Customer Service Center. It also offers telecommunications services. Owensboro Municipal Utilities is overseen by the five-member Owensboro Utility Commission which is appointed by the mayor of Owensboro.

	Annual Growth	05/14	05/15	05/16	05/17	05/18
Sales ($ mil.)	2.4%	–	139.8	140.8	147.5	150.2
Net income ($ mil.)	–	–	(0.3)	2.6	8.8	8.6
Market value ($ mil.)	–	–	–	–	–	–
Employees	–	–	–	–	–	235

OXBOW CORPORATION

1601 Forum Pl. Ste. 1400
West Palm Beach FL 33401
Phone: 561-697-4300
Fax: 561-640-8740
Web: www.oxbow.com

CEO: William I Koch
CFO: William D Parmelee
HR: –
FYE: December 31
Type: Private

Oxbow's founder and CEO William Koch is bullish on coke and other energy commodities. The diversified firm's Oxbow Carbon unit markets and distributes coke coal petroleum and carbon products and other commodities to power producers refineries and industrial manufacturers. Oxbow is the world's top marketer of petroleum coke which is used in power generation cement kilns sugar mills and aluminum manufacturing. The company also trades in products that include gypsum anthracite and activated carbon. Oxbow owns a coal mine in Colorado that produces 5 million tons of coal annually.

OXFORD GLOBAL RESOURCES INC.

100 Cummings Center Ste. 206L
Beverly MA 01915
Phone: 978-236-1182
Fax: 978-236-1077
Web: www.oxfordcorp.com

CEO: Theodore Hanson
CFO: Jim Brill
HR: Tracy McBride
FYE: December 31
Type: Subsidiary

Need a high-level information technology consultant? Looking for an engineering expert? Oxford Global Resources can fill the void. The company provides IT and engineering consultants for clients in a wide range of industries. It delivers IT consultants and managers in fields such as ERP business intelligence customer relationship management application development and project management; it offers engineers for functions such as software hardware mechanical electrical and regulatory and compliance. The company operates from more than 20 locations across the US plus one in Ireland. Founded in 1984 Oxford Global Resources is a subsidiary of professional staffing specialist On Assignment.

OXFORD INDUSTRIES, INC.
NYS: OXM

999 Peachtree Street, N.E., Suite 688
Atlanta, GA 30309
Phone: 404 659-2424
Fax: –

CEO: Thomas C. Chubb
CFO: K. Scott Grassmyer
HR: Christine Cole
FYE: February 02
Type: Public

No longer all buttoned up Oxford has embraced the island life. It's a top US maker of brand name and private-label clothing including golf attire as well as a retailer in the US and UK. Its Tommy Bahama unit makes branded men's and women's casual attire and owns more than 155 stores and restaurants in the US. Lanier Clothes offers men's suits sportcoats and slacks under such brands as Dockers Geoffrey Beene and Kenneth Cole. Oxford's newest lifestyle brand is colorful Lilly Pulitzer. Oxford's customers include national and regional specialty stores direct retailers and department stores. Macy's Nordstrom and Debenhams are some of its biggest customers.

	Annual Growth	01/15	01/16	01/17*	02/18	02/19
Sales ($ mil.)	2.6%	997.8	969.3	1,022.6	1,086.2	1,107.5
Net income ($ mil.)	9.7%	45.8	30.6	52.5	65.1	66.3
Market value ($ mil.)	8.4%	948.7	1,184.8	917.0	1,343.2	1,310.1
Employees	3.1%	5,400	5,500	5,800	5,900	6,100

*Fiscal year change

OXFORD UNIVERSITY PRESS INC.

198 MADISON AVE FL 8
NEW YORK, NY 10016-4308
Phone: 212-726-6000
Fax: –
Web: www.oup.com

CEO: –
CFO: –
HR: –
FYE: March 31
Type: Private

Pick a word any word. Chances are good you'll find it in one of the many books published by the Oxford University Press Inc. The publisher known as OUP USA is affiliated the world's largest university publisher UK-based Oxford University Press (OUP UK) itself a department of the venerable and prestigious University of Oxford. OUP USA publishes some 500 titles a year including scholarly works reference publications Bibles and school texts. Revenues from the not-for-profit Oxford University Press are used to support the University of Oxford.

	Annual Growth	03/02	03/03	03/04*	07/05*	03/09
Sales ($ mil.)	(46.7%)	–	–	2,000.0	1.4	86.3
Net income ($ mil.)	762.8%	–	–	0.0	(0.0)	7.0
Market value ($ mil.)	–	–	–	–	–	–
Employees	–	–	–	–	–	530

*Fiscal year change

OXIGENE, INC.
NAS: OXGN

701 Gateway Boulevard, Suite 210
South San Francisco, CA 94080
Phone: 650 635-7000
Fax: –
Web: www.oxigene.com

CEO: –
CFO: Matthew M Loar
HR: –
FYE: December 31
Type: Public

OXiGENE starves cancer to death. The company's drug candidate Zybrestat works by disrupting the functioning of blood vessels that deliver oxygen to tumors. Zybrestat is being investigated as a treatment for patients with ovarian cancer and other forms of cancer. OXiGENE is also working on a second-generation version of its oxygen-starving technology. OXiGene's strategy is to identify and license compounds from academic research centers and then shepherd the compounds through clinical trials. However it has limited its in-house drug development operations instead sponsoring research at academic and other research institutions or using contract research organizations.

	Annual Growth	12/09	12/10	12/11	12/12	12/13
Sales ($ mil.)	(39.1%)	–	–	–	0.2	0.1
Net income ($ mil.)	–	(24.7)	(23.8)	(9.7)	(8.1)	(8.3)
Market value ($ mil.)	21.8%	6.4	1.3	5.5	29.9	14.1
Employees	(31.7%)	46	22	11	10	10

OXIS INTERNATIONAL INC.
NBB: OXIS

100 South Ashley Drive, Suite 600
Tampa, FL 33602
Phone: 800 304-9888
Fax: -
Web: www.oxis.com

CEO: Anthony J Cataldo
CFO: Steven Weldon
HR: -
FYE: December 31
Type: Public

Don't stress out — call OXIS International. The company specializes in researching and treating conditions related to oxidative stress in which low antioxidant levels throw off metabolic balance at the cellular level. OXIS is focused on the development of nutritional and cosmeceutical products including formulations for use in OTC food supplements and skin products. Its ERGO (L-Ergothioneine) antioxidant product line treats anti-inflammatory ailments and other health conditions. OXIS also licenses out compounds to biotech and pharmaceutical companies.

	Annual Growth	12/11	12/12	12/13	12/14	12/15
Sales ($ mil.)	0.9%	0.0	0.3	0.4	0.1	0.0
Net income ($ mil.)	-	(3.7)	(5.2)	(0.5)	(23.5)	(32.7)
Market value ($ mil.)	-	-	-	-	-	7.7
Employees	18.9%	1	2	2	2	2

OZARKS ELECTRIC COOPERATIVE CORPORATION

3641 W WEDINGTON DR
FAYETTEVILLE, AR 727045742
Phone: 479-521-2900
Fax: -
Web: www.ozarksecc.com

CEO: -
CFO: Todd Townsend
HR: Dena Reeves
FYE: December 31
Type: Private

Even people living up in the Ozark Mountains need power and Ozarks Electric Cooperative aims to deliver. The member-owned not-for-profit cooperative serves more than 62000 customers in about a dozen counties spread across northwest Arkansas and northeast Oklahoma. Its 350 miles of line reach industrial commercial residential and agricultural power users. Ozarks Electric provides its customers with energy audits and information on saving energy as well as energy efficient water heaters and surge protectors. It is a member of Touchstone Energy a national alliance of electric cooperatives in nearly 40 states. The coop was formed in 1938.

	Annual Growth	12/13	12/14	12/15	12/16	12/17
Sales ($ mil.)	3.6%	-	123.0	123.2	129.7	137.0
Net income ($ mil.)	4.8%	-	6.1	6.3	6.0	7.0
Market value ($ mil.)	-	-	-	-	-	-
Employees	-	-	-	-	-	190

P & F INDUSTRIES, INC.
NMS: PFIN

445 Broadhollow Road, Suite 100
Melville, NY 11747
Phone: 631 694-9800
Fax: -
Web: www.pfina.com

CEO: Richard A Horowitz
CFO: Joseph A Molino Jr
HR: -
FYE: December 31
Type: Public

P&F Industries helps craftsmen use less muscle. The company operates through two primary subsidiaries: Continental Tool Group and Countrywide Hardware. Continental Tool Group sells air-powered tools including sanders drills and saws through its Florida Pneumatic Manufacturing and Hy-Tech Machine units. Florida Pneumatic's Berkley Tool division makes pipe-cutting tools and wrenches for machinery for Sears and Home Depot. Countrywide Hardware through its Nationwide Industries unit produces and imports hardware for doors gates fences windows kitchens and bathrooms as well as stair parts. In mid-2010 the company ceased operating through its WM Coffman unit.

	Annual Growth	12/14	12/15	12/16	12/17	12/18
Sales ($ mil.)	(3.5%)	75.0	81.7	57.3	59.0	65.0
Net income ($ mil.)	(19.9%)	2.1	3.5	6.9	(0.9)	0.9
Market value ($ mil.)	(0.7%)	28.6	31.8	29.7	30.1	27.8
Employees	2.5%	163	164	115	171	180

P&G-CLAIROL INC.

1 Procter & Gamble Plaza
Cincinnati OH 45202
Phone: 513-983-1100
Fax: 515-643-5350
Web: www.mercyhealthnetwork.com/

CEO: -
CFO: -
HR: -
FYE: June 30
Type: Subsidiary

Clairol is big on hair care — mostly focused on covering up the gray and helping to keep non-blondes blond. A unit of consumer products behemoth Procter & Gamble P&G-Clairol specializes in making and marketing hair-coloring products hair spray shampoo conditioner and hair-styling items. Some of its brands include Nice 'n Easy Hydrience Natural Instincts and Perfect Lights. Besides all-over color the beauty company also sells highlighting products for touches of hair color. Clairol markets its products in the US Australia Canada and the UK. One of P&G's larger acquisitions (behind Gillette) P&G-Clairol is part of its beauty segment which generated 24% of revenue in 2011.

P.A.M. TRANSPORTATION SERVICES, INC.
NMS: PTSI

297 West Henri De Tonti
Tontitown, AR 72770
Phone: 479 361-9111
Fax: -
Web: www.pamtransport.com

CEO: Daniel H. Cushman
CFO: Allen W. West
HR: Tyler Majors
FYE: December 31
Type: Public

Pretty Awesome Mileage that's the goal! Through its subsidiaries truckload carrier P.A.M. Transportation Services moves freight over the road throughout the US and in parts of Canada; the company offers service in Mexico via arrangements with other carriers. It has a fleet of more than 1760 trucks including 4920 trailers. Most of the company's sales come from automakers and suppliers to the auto industry; General Motors represents 20%. For large accounts P.A.M. provides a dedicated fleet in which drivers and equipment are assigned to a particular customer or route long-term. The company also offers brokerage/logistics services such as carrier selection transportation scheduling and routing.

	Annual Growth	12/14	12/15	12/16	12/17	12/18
Sales ($ mil.)	6.7%	410.9	417.1	432.9	437.8	533.3
Net income ($ mil.)	15.5%	13.5	21.4	11.1	38.9	24.0
Market value ($ mil.)	(6.6%)	308.8	164.3	154.8	205.1	234.7
Employees	(1.4%)	2,911	3,049	2,463	2,409	2,748

P.F. CHANG'S CHINA BISTRO INC.
NASDAQ: PFCB

7676 E. Pinnacle Peak Rd.
Scottsdale AZ 85255
Phone: 480-888-3000
Fax: 480-888-3001
Web: www.pfcb.com

CEO: Michael Osanloo
CFO: -
HR: Danna Acevedo
FYE: December 31
Type: Private

The ancient Chinese secret behind P.F. Chang's success is upscale American service. P.F. Chang's China Bistro owns and operates about 200 full-service Asian-style bistro restaurants in about 40 states that offer lunch and dinner menus inspired by five culinary regions of China. The chain's restaurants offer stylish dining areas display kitchens and narrative murals based on ancient Chinese designs. The company also owns and operates 170 quick-casual outlets under the name Pei Wei Asian Diner. The Pei Wei locations offer a limited menu with an emphasis on carry-out service. In 2012 the company was acquired by Centerbridge Partners.

P10 HOLDINGS INC
NBB: PIOE

8214 Westchester Drive, Suite 950
Dallas, TX 75225
Phone: 214 999-0149
Fax: –

CEO: Mark A Ascolese
CFO: James A. (Jay) Powers
HR: –
FYE: December 31
Type: Public

Active Power keeps the juices flowing. The company's UPS (uninterruptible power system) products use a flywheel that stores kinetic energy by spinning converting the kinetic energy into electricity when power quality problems are detected. It was developed in partnership with heavy equipment maker Caterpillar which markets the product with its generator sets. Active Power also makes PowerHouse a continuous power system that combines the company's flywheel UPS products with switchgear and a generator which is sold primarily for military utility and data center applications. Customers in North America account for about 70% of sales.

	Annual Growth	12/14	12/15	12/16	12/17	12/18
Sales ($ mil.)	(9.4%)	49.1	57.4	–	4.3	33.1
Net income ($ mil.)	–	(12.8)	(6.5)	(15.9)	1.1	6.0
Market value ($ mil.)	(4.3%)	–	–	–	72.7	69.6
Employees	(78.6%)	204	219	2	2	–

PABST BREWING COMPANY

10635 Santa Monica Blvd. Ste. 305
Los Angeles CA 90025
Phone: 310-470-0962
Fax: 248-299-8514
Web: www.saturnee.com

CEO: Joseph Michel Schulmann
CFO: –
HR: –
FYE: July 31
Type: Private

The Pabst Brewing Company is a 19th-century brewer retooled for the 21st century. The company founded in Milwaukee in 1844 today is something of a "virtual" brewer. Pabst owns no breweries but instead it contracts with MillerCoors to actually manufacture its beers while Pabst retains the brand ownership of and does the marketing for its stable of blue-collar brands (including Pabst Blue Ribbon Blatz Pearl Lone Star Old Milwaukee Old Style Schlitz and Colt 45). Pabst Brewing was owned by the Kalmanovitz Charitable Foundation until June 2010 when it sold the company to former food executive and billionaire investor C. Dean Metropoulos.

PACCAR INC.
NMS: PCAR

777 - 106th Ave. N.E.
Bellevue, WA 98004
Phone: 425 468-7400
Fax: –
Web: www.paccar.com

CEO: Ronald E. (Ron) Armstrong
CFO: Harrie C.A.M. Schippers
HR: –
FYE: December 31
Type: Public

PACCAR (named for former rail car manufacturer Pacific Car and Foundry Company) is one of the world's leading designers and manufacturers of big rig diesel trucks. Its lineup of light- medium- and heavy-duty trucks includes the Kenworth Peterbilt and DAF nameplates. The company also manufactures and distributes aftermarket truck parts for these brands. PACCAR's other products include Braden Carco and Gearmatic industrial winches. PACCAR typically sells its trucks and parts through independent dealers. Its PACCAR Financial Services arm offers vehicle financing and its PacLease subsidiary handles truck leasing.

	Annual Growth	12/14	12/15	12/16	12/17	12/18
Sales ($ mil.)	5.5%	18,997.0	19,115.1	17,033.3	19,456.4	23,495.7
Net income ($ mil.)	12.7%	1,358.8	1,604.0	521.7	1,675.2	2,195.1
Market value ($ mil.)	(4.3%)	23,572.3	16,428.8	22,147.7	24,636.3	19,804.7
Employees	4.7%	23,300	23,000	23,000	25,000	28,000

PACE UNIVERSITY

1 PACE PLZ
NEW YORK, NY 100381598
Phone: 212-346-1956
Fax: –
Web: www.pace.edu

CEO: –
CFO: Robert C Almon
HR: Matt Renna
FYE: June 30
Type: Private

Students can learn at their own pace at Pace University which offers certificate programs as well as undergraduate graduate and doctoral degrees through half a dozen schools: arts and sciences business computer science and information systems education law and nursing. Altogether the school is home to 100 undergraduate majors offering roughly 30 undergraduate and graduate degrees 50 master's programs and four doctoral programs. Nearly 13000 students attend the university's three New York campuses (Lower Manhattan Pleasantville-Briarcliff and White Plains). Pace was founded in 1906 by the brothers Homer and Charles Pace as a co-educational business school called Pace Institute.

	Annual Growth	06/11	06/12	06/13	06/14	06/16
Sales ($ mil.)	6.1%	–	310.4	326.4	493.0	393.7
Net income ($ mil.)	–	–	(15.9)	20.3	26.6	14.7
Market value ($ mil.)	–	–	–	–	–	–
Employees	–	–	–	–	–	1,862

PACER INTERNATIONAL INC
NMS: PACR

6805 Perimeter Drive
Dublin, OH 43016
Phone: 614 923-1400
Fax: –
Web: www.pacer.com

CEO: John T Hickerson
CFO: John J Hardig
HR: –
FYE: December 31
Type: Public

Pacer International wants to move freight at the right pace. The logistics provider's flagship business Pacer Stacktrain arranges intermodal transportation (movement of containerized freight by road and rail). Stacktrain's largely leased fleet includes rail cars that carry containers stacked two high along with the chassis used to transport containers on the road. Sister company Pacer Cartage provides local road transportation of the containers in major markets while Pacer Transportation Solutions arranges door-to-door rail and trucking service. The company's logistics segment provides services such as freight brokerage freight forwarding and supply chain management for shippers.

	Annual Growth	12/08	12/09	12/10	12/11	12/12
Sales ($ mil.)	(9.3%)	2,087.7	1,574.2	1,502.8	1,478.5	1,415.0
Net income ($ mil.)	–	(16.6)	(174.1)	0.9	13.9	4.3
Market value ($ mil.)	(19.3%)	324.2	110.9	240.0	187.7	137.2
Employees	(13.2%)	1,601	1,042	1,060	1,010	908

PACIFIC BIOSCIENCES OF CALIFORNIA INC
NMS: PACB

1305 O'Brien Drive
Menlo Park, CA 94025
Phone: 650 521-8000
Fax: –
Web: www.pacb.com

CEO: Michael Hunkapiller
CFO: Susan K. Barnes
HR: –
FYE: December 31
Type: Public

In the past it took years to sequence the human and other genomes but Pacific Biosciences of California (PacBio) has introduced a third-generation DNA sequencing technology that can map an organism's genome in minutes. The biotechnology company develops proprietary technology known as SMRT (single-molecule real-time) that performs fast and inexpensive DNA sequencing. The technology performs highly accurate reads of ultra-long sequences with the ability to simultaneously detect epigenetic changes. PacBio' sequencing machines are designed for use by clinical commercial and institutional research laboratories. Nearly half of the company's revenues come from the US. Genetic sequencing rival Illumina is buying PacBio for $1.2 billion.

	Annual Growth	12/14	12/15	12/16	12/17	12/18
Sales ($ mil.)	6.7%	60.6	92.8	90.7	93.5	78.6
Net income ($ mil.)	–	(66.2)	(31.7)	(74.4)	(92.2)	(102.6)
Market value ($ mil.)	(1.4%)	1,177.9	1,972.7	570.9	396.6	1,111.8
Employees	3.9%	344	394	438	456	401

1009

PACIFIC BUILDING GROUP

9752 ASPEN CREEK CT # 100
SAN DIEGO, CA 921261081
Phone: 858-552-0600
Fax: –
Web: www.pacificbuildinggroup.com
CEO: Gregory A Rogers
CFO: Lisa Hitt
HR: –
FYE: December 31
Type: Private

Pacific Building Group pacifies its clients by taking care of their property construction needs. The general contractor provides services including pre-construction evaluation facility design/build tenant improvements and facilities maintenance. It is known for its work on health care facilities including laboratories and medical office buildings; the company also provides services for corporate hospitality and industrial clients. Pacific Building Group has handled major projects for such customers as IBM Sharp HealthCare Sony and United Airlines. The company operates mainly in Southern California primarily in San Diego County. CEO and owner Greg Rogers founded the group in 1984.

	Annual Growth	12/09	12/10	12/11	12/12	12/13
Sales ($ mil.)	15.0%	–	43.6	51.1	74.9	66.2
Net income ($ mil.)	70.5%	–	–	0.2	1.9	0.6
Market value ($ mil.)	–	–	–	–	–	–
Employees	–	–	–	–	–	190

PACIFIC COAST PRODUCERS

631 N CLUFF AVE
LODI, CA 952400756
Phone: 209-367-8800
Fax: –
Web: www.pacificcoastproducers.com
CEO: –
CFO: Mark Wahlman
HR: Richard Ehrler
FYE: May 31
Type: Private

Fruits seafood sauces and organic tomato puree — rather than movies — are the creative output of this particular group of Pacific Coast Producers. The cooperative markets the apricots grapes peaches pears and tomatoes grown by its approximately 160 California-based members. It turns the produce into private-label canned fruit sauces and juices and sells them to the retail and foodservice industries. Pacific Coast Producers typically serves retailers the likes of Albertson's Aldi Kroger Safeway SUPERVALU Whole Foods and Wal-Mart as well as the US Department of Agriculture. The company founded in 1971 operates three production sites and one distribution center in California.

	Annual Growth	05/14	05/15	05/16	05/17	05/18
Sales ($ mil.)	2.3%	–	623.4	630.7	607.9	668.1
Net income ($ mil.)	(9.4%)	–	30.6	30.5	26.9	22.8
Market value ($ mil.)	–	–	–	–	–	–
Employees	–	–	–	–	–	1,000

PACIFIC CONTINENTAL CORP   NMS: PCBK

111 West 7th Avenue
Eugene, OR 97401
Phone: 541 686-8685
Fax: –
CEO: –
CFO: –
HR: –
FYE: December 31
Type: Public

Pacific Continental Corporation is the holding company for Pacific Continental Bank which has about 15 branches across the metropolitan areas of Eugene and Portland Oregon and Seattle. It offers standard banking deposit products and specializes in commercial and residential real estate loans. The bank's services for commercial clients also include credit card transaction processing and business credit cards. About 60% of the bank's loan portfolio is secured by commercial and residential real estate while the rest is made up of business construction and consumer loans.

	Annual Growth	12/11	12/12	12/13	12/14	12/15
Assets ($ mil.)	10.7%	1,270.2	1,373.5	1,449.7	1,504.3	1,909.5
Net income ($ mil.)	36.9%	5.3	12.7	13.8	16.0	18.8
Market value ($ mil.)	13.9%	173.5	190.7	312.5	278.0	291.7
Employees	5.1%	264	268	290	291	322

PACIFIC DENTAL SERVICES INC.

2860 Michelle Dr. 2nd Fl.
Irvine CA 92606
Phone: 714-508-3600
Fax: 714-508-6400
Web: www.pacificdentalservices.com
CEO: Stephen E Thorne IV
CFO: Brady Aase
HR: –
FYE: December 31
Type: Private

Pacific Dental Services (PDS) brings smiles to dentists' faces. The growing company provides management administration and IT services to affiliated dental practices so that dentists can focus on fixing smiles rather than managing the minutiae of business. Established in 1994 PDS does everything from helping dentists choose practice sites to facilitating the design and staffing of offices. The company also negotiates managed health care contracts and asset management. More than 275 dental practices throughout Arizona California Colorado Nevada New Mexico and Texas make use of PDS' services. The company incorporates close to 4000 team members and affiliated dentists in its business.

PACIFIC ETHANOL INC   NAS: PEIX

400 Capitol Mall, Suite 2060
Sacramento, CA 95814
Phone: 916 403-2123
Fax: 916 446-3937
Web: www.pacificethanol.com
CEO: Neil M. Koehler
CFO: Bryon T. McGregor
HR: –
FYE: December 31
Type: Public

Pacific Ethanol hopes that the fuel alternative it produces will bring some peace of mind to customers worried about the US' fossil fuel dependency. The company is a leading producer of low-carbon renewable fuels in the Western US. Pacific Ethanol buys and sells ethanol to a number of large energy companies that blend it into gasoline. It also sells co-products such as wet distillers grain (WDG) a nutritional animal feed. Serving integrated oil companies and gasoline marketers who blend ethanol into gasoline Pacific Ethanol provides transportation storage and delivery of ethanol through third-party service providers in the Western US. It acquired Aventine Renewable Energy in 2015.

	Annual Growth	12/14	12/15	12/16	12/17	12/18
Sales ($ mil.)	8.2%	1,107.4	1,191.2	1,624.8	1,632.3	1,515.4
Net income ($ mil.)	–	21.3	(18.8)	1.4	(35.0)	(60.3)
Market value ($ mil.)	(46.3%)	472.8	218.8	434.8	208.3	39.4
Employees	29.7%	180	465	500	560	510

PACIFIC FINANCIAL CORP.   NBB: PFLC

1216 Skyview Drive
Aberdeen, WA 98520-5244
Phone: 360 533-8873
Fax: –
Web: www.bankofthepacific.com
CEO: Dennis A Long
CFO: Douglas N Biddle
HR: –
FYE: December 31
Type: Public

Pacific Financial Corporation is the holding company for The Bank of the Pacific which has more than 15 branches in southwestern and northwestern portions of Washington as well as neighboring parts of Oregon. Serving small to midsized businesses and professionals the bank offers traditional deposit services including checking and savings accounts NOW and money market accounts CDs and IRAs. Commercial mortgages dominate the bank's loan portfolio which also includes business construction consumer residential farmland and credit card loans. The bank offers investments and financial planning through an agreement with third-party provider Elliott Cove Capital Management.

	Annual Growth	12/14	12/15	12/16	12/17	12/18
Assets ($ mil.)	5.1%	744.8	824.6	891.4	895.0	907.9
Net income ($ mil.)	23.1%	4.9	5.6	6.6	7.0	11.3
Market value ($ mil.)	14.3%	69.6	74.0	104.1	108.9	118.9
Employees	–	234	–	–	–	–

PACIFIC HIDE & FUR DEPOT

5 RIVER DR S
GREAT FALLS, MT 594051872
Phone: 406-771-7222
Fax: –
Web: www.pacific-steel.com

CEO: –
CFO: Tim Culliton
HR: –
FYE: August 28
Type: Private

Pacific Steel & Recycling sells at one end of the steel mill and buys at the other. The company's Pacific Recycling unit supplies steel mills with scrap metal a key raw material. It operates about 46 recycling centers in the northwestern US and Canada that also handle cardboard and scrap paper in addition to metals. The company's Pacific Steel unit buys steel products and resells them from steel service centers and distribution centers in the northwestern US. Pacific Steel's facilities handle items such as bar products and structurals flat-rolled products reinforcing bar and tubing and pipe. The company offers a variety of processing services.

	Annual Growth	08/05	08/06	08/07	08/08	08/10
Sales ($ mil.)	(0.0%)	–	–	301.9	241.4	301.6
Net income ($ mil.)	(16.7%)	–	–	60.3	2.9	34.9
Market value ($ mil.)	–	–	–	–	–	–
Employees	–	–	–	–	–	780

PACIFIC MERCANTILE BANCORP

NMS: PMBC

949 South Coast Drive, Suite 300
Costa Mesa, CA 92626
Phone: 714 438-2500
Fax: 714 438-1059
Web: www.pmbank.com

CEO: –
CFO: Curt A Christianssen
HR: Kathleen Wiesinger
FYE: December 31
Type: Public

Pacific Mercantile is banking on southern California businesses. Pacific Mercantile Bancorp is the holding company for Pacific Mercantile Bank which operates more than a dozen branches in southern California's Los Angeles Orange San Bernardino and San Diego counties. Serving area consumers and businesses the bank provides standard services including checking savings and money market accounts CDs and IRAs as well as online banking and bill payment. It uses deposits primarily to fund business loans including commercial mortgages which account for some 65% of the bank's loan portfolio. The bank also offers residential mortgages construction land development and consumer loans.

	Annual Growth	12/14	12/15	12/16	12/17	12/18
Assets ($ mil.)	5.2%	1,099.6	1,062.4	1,140.7	1,322.6	1,349.3
Net income ($ mil.)	195.8%	0.4	12.4	(34.6)	10.4	27.3
Market value ($ mil.)	0.4%	154.3	156.3	160.0	191.8	156.7
Employees	(1.2%)	168	160	169	168	160

PACIFIC MUTUAL HOLDING CO.

700 Newport Center Drive
Newport Beach, CA 92660-6397
Phone: 949 219-3011
Fax: –
Web: www.pacificmutual.com

CEO: Thomas C Sutton
CFO: –
HR: –
FYE: December 31
Type: Public

Life insurance is "alive and whale" at Pacific Mutual Holding. The company's primary operating subsidiary Pacific Life Insurance (whose logo is a breaching whale) is a top California-based life insurer. Lines of business include a variety of life insurance products for individuals and businesses; annuities and mutual funds geared to individuals and small businesses; management of stable value funds fixed income investments and other investments for institutional clients and pension plans; and real estate investing. Additionally its Aviation Capital Group subsidiary provides commercial jet aircraft leasing. The company is owned by its Pacific Life shareholders.

	Annual Growth	12/11	12/12	12/13	12/14	12/15
Assets ($ mil.)	4.1%	116,811.0	123,697.0	129,921.0	137,048.0	137,279.0
Net income ($ mil.)	(0.7%)	679.0	460.0	720.0	540.0	661.0
Market value ($ mil.)	–	–	–	–	–	–
Employees	–	–	–	–	–	–

PACIFIC NATIONAL GROUP

2392 BATEMAN AVE
DUARTE, CA 910103312
Phone: 626-357-4400
Fax: –
Web: www.pacific-inc.com

CEO: –
CFO: Arden L Boren
HR: –
FYE: December 31
Type: Private

Pacific National Group (PNG) performs general contracting and construction management services in Arizona and Southern California. The company tackles a range of projects including commercial and industrial complexes medical buildings high-tech and aerospace centers and sports and recreation facilities. The company offers pre-construction through post-construction services as well as site supervision. Its Modulex division manufactures aluminum door frames and glazing systems. PNG's client roster includes Northrop Grumman Cedars-Sinai Medical Center Universal Studios and the Jet Propulsion Laboratory in Pasadena California. The company was founded in 1959 as Pacific Luminaire.

	Annual Growth	12/11	12/12	12/15	12/16	12/17
Sales ($ mil.)	8.9%	–	110.4	113.0	125.7	169.2
Net income ($ mil.)	14.5%	–	1.7	2.8	2.4	3.2
Market value ($ mil.)	–	–	–	–	–	–
Employees	–	–	–	–	–	25

PACIFIC NORTHWEST NATIONAL LABORATORY

902 Battelle Blvd.
Richland WA 99352
Phone: 509-375-2121
Fax: 509-375-6550
Web: www.pnl.gov

CEO: –
CFO: –
HR: –
FYE: September 30
Type: Government-owned

Pacific Northwest National Laboratory (PNNL) provides basic and applied scientific research services and facilities to both government agencies and private industries. The laboratory specializes in research about such areas as energy and the environment fundamental and computer sciences and national security. PNNL has about 4900 scientists engineers and staff members. The lab is funded and managed by the US Department of Energy but it is operated by Battelle Memorial Institute. PNNL was established in 1965. Since its inception it has received more than 1600 patents.

PACIFIC OFFICE PROPERTIES TRUST INC

NBB: PCFO

841 Bishop Street, Suite 1700
Honolulu, HI 96813
Phone: 808 521-7444
Fax: –
Web: www.pacificofficeproperties.com

CEO: –
CFO: Lawrence J Taff
HR: –
FYE: December 31
Type: Public

Like the mythical phoenix rising out of the ashes Arizona Land Income gained new life as Pacific Office Properties Trust. The real estate investment trust (REIT) largely languished in inactivity for years but in 2008 joined forces with private commercial property owner Shidler Group. The combined company owns more than 20 commercial properties with some 4.7 million sq. ft. of leasable space in the western US. The REIT is the largest office building owner in Honolulu. Chairman Jay Shidler who founded Shidler Group and has had success with other REITS including Corporate Office Properties Trust and First Industrial Realty Trust owns 94% of Pacific Office Properties Trust.

	Annual Growth	12/13	12/14	12/15	12/16	12/17
Sales ($ mil.)	0.1%	45.3	44.1	44.1	44.8	45.5
Net income ($ mil.)	–	(4.4)	(2.9)	(2.2)	(2.2)	(2.2)
Market value ($ mil.)	0.0%	1.0	1.0	5.4	0.7	1.0
Employees	–	–	–	–	–	–

PACIFIC SANDS INC
NBB: PFSD

4611 Green Bay Road
Kenosha, WI 53144
Phone: 262 925-0123
Fax: -
Web: www.pacificsands.biz

CEO: Michael D Michie
CFO: -
HR: -
FYE: June 30
Type: Public

Not a company that caters to resort-goers but one that cares about clean water Pacific Sands makes and markets nontoxic liquid and powder cleaning laundry and water-treatment products under the Natural Choices (cleaning and laundry products) and ecoone (pool and spa water-management systems) brands. The company incorporated in 1994 serves the industrial and consumer products industries. It acquired Natural Choices Home Safe Products in early 2008 to further improve its standing as an environmentally friendly products maker. Natural Choices' best known brand is Oxy-Boost cleaning products. Pacific Sands' products are available online and through dealers in the US and internationally.

	Annual Growth	06/11	06/12	06/13	06/14	06/15
Sales ($ mil.)	8.5%	1.6	1.9	2.0	2.9	2.2
Net income ($ mil.)	-	0.1	(0.0)	(0.1)	(0.3)	(1.3)
Market value ($ mil.)	(28.8%)	11.7	8.7	4.5	3.6	3.0
Employees	8.7%	11	12	13	-	-

PACIFIC SUNWEAR OF CALIFORNIA, INC.
NMS: PSUN

3450 East Miraloma Avenue
Anaheim, CA 92806
Phone: 714 414-4000
Fax: -
Web: www.pacsun.com

CEO: -
CFO: -
HR: -
FYE: January 31
Type: Public

Pacific Sunwear of California (PacSun) knows that teens aspire to the "swag" of the board sports world. The company operates more than 600 mall-based apparel stores (down from a peak of 950) in all 50 US states and Puerto Rico under the names Pacific Sunwear and PacSun and an e-commerce site. It courts the young and active consumer by representing brands associated with surfing skateboarding and snowboarding including apparel by Billabong Volcom and Quicksilver as well as footwear by DC Shoes and others. PacSun also sells its own private-label merchandise (Bullhead Black Poppy Kirra and Nollie). Amid a steep decline in sales the teen-focused chain is closing hundreds of stores.

	Annual Growth	01/11	01/12*	02/13	02/14*	01/15
Sales ($ mil.)	(2.9%)	929.5	833.8	803.1	797.8	826.8
Net income ($ mil.)	-	(96.6)	(106.4)	(52.1)	(48.7)	(29.4)
Market value ($ mil.)	(10.4%)	295.8	139.9	139.9	199.5	190.5
Employees	(6.5%)	11,500	9,100	8,200	10,300	8,777

*Fiscal year change

PACIFIC THEATRES CORPORATION

120 N. Robertson Blvd.
Los Angeles CA 90048
Phone: 310-657-8420
Fax: 310-657-6813
Web: www.pacifictheatres.com

CEO: -
CFO: -
HR: -
FYE: June 30
Type: Private

Pacific Theatres Corporation brings a tidal wave of entertainment to moviegoers in California. The company has about 15 theaters housing some 100 movie screens in the Los Angeles area including properties in the ArcLight Cinemas theater chain. Its portfolio consists of theaters such as the Paseo in Pasadena the Culver Stadium in Culver City the Grove in Los Angeles and the ArcLight Cinema in Sherman Oaks. The Forman family founded Pacific Theatres in 1946 and continues to own and operate the company through its Decurion Corp. It has transitioned over the last 50 years from a drive-in theater business to a high-end multi- and megaplex exhibitor.

PACIFIC WEBWORKS, INC.
NBB: PWEB

230 West 400 South, 1st Floor
Salt Lake City, UT 84101
Phone: 801 578-9020
Fax: -
Web: www.pacificwebworks.com

CEO: -
CFO: -
HR: -
FYE: December 31
Type: Public

Pacific WebWorks wants to ensure that you have the power of the Web working for you. Through its subsidiaries the company targets small and midsized businesses with a number of Web page design applications and consulting and training services; it also provides Web site hosting for its customers as well as hosted versions of its products. Customers use the company's products to build Web sites manage e-commerce transactions create online storefronts and track Web site visitor behavior.

	Annual Growth	12/10	12/11	12/12	12/13	12/14
Sales ($ mil.)	(6.4%)	8.6	1.7	1.1	1.7	6.6
Net income ($ mil.)	-	0.0	(1.0)	(0.8)	(3.7)	(0.5)
Market value ($ mil.)	(26.9%)	3.5	2.4	0.3	0.8	1.0
Employees	7.5%	6	8	7	8	8

PACIFICHEALTH LABORATORIES INC.
OTC: PHLI

100 Matawan Rd. Ste. 420
Matawan NJ 07747
Phone: 732-739-2900
Fax: 732-739-4360
Web: www.pacifichealthlabs.com

CEO: Fred Duffner
CFO: Stephen P Kuchen
HR: -
FYE: December 31
Type: Public

PacificHealth Laboratories plans to go the distance with its dietary supplements. The firm develops sports enhancement and weight-loss products as well as treatments for diabetes using its proprietary protein-based technologies. It sells sports drinks Endurox and Accelerade to retail outlets including GNC health clubs and Internet retailers and it launched weight-loss drink Satiatrim in 2007. The company is also working on products for oral rehydration post-surgical muscle recovery and glucose regulation. PacificHealth sold its Endurox and Accelerade lines to Mott's in 2006 but it continues to sell the products under a royalty-free license. The firm sells its products internationally using distributors.

PACIFICORP
NBB: PPWL M

825 N.E. Multnomah Street
Portland, OR 97232
Phone: 888 221-7070
Fax: -
Web: www.pacificorp.com

CEO: Gregory E. (Greg) Abel
CFO: Douglas K. (Doug) Stuver
HR: Ellene Gurtov-Smith
FYE: December 31
Type: Public

PacifiCorp's core businesses are regulated utilities Pacific Power and Rocky Mountain Power which together provide electricity to 1.9 million customers in six western states. The subsidiaries operate about 16500 miles of transmission lines 64000 miles of distribution lines and 900 substations. PacifiCorp owns or has stakes in about 50 thermal hydroelectric and renewable generation facilities that supply its utilities with about 10900 MW of net capacity. It also purchases and sells power in wholesale markets to subsidize its supply offload excess output or obtain lower prices. The company is a unit of Berkshire Hathaway Energy.

	Annual Growth	12/14	12/15	12/16	12/17	12/18
Sales ($ mil.)	(1.1%)	5,252.0	5,232.0	5,201.0	5,237.0	5,026.0
Net income ($ mil.)	1.4%	698.0	695.0	763.0	768.0	738.0
Market value ($ mil.)	(2.2%)	38,020.5	39,984.0	39,984.0	62,475.0	34,718.3
Employees	(2.2%)	5,900	5,700	5,600	5,500	5,400

PACIRA BIOSCIENCES INC
NMS: PCRX

5 Sylvan Way, Suite 300
Parsippany, NJ 07054
Phone: 973-254-3560
Fax: –
Web: www.pacira.com

CEO: David M. (Dave) Stack
CFO: Charles A. Reinhart
HR: –
FYE: December 31
Type: Public

Pacira BioSciences (formerly Pacira Pharmaceuticals) develops pain management products that don't involve opioids. The company develops sustained-release therapies based on DepoFoam an injectable drug delivery technology that allows both immediate and sustained release. Pacira's primary drug EXPAREL is an injectable local anesthetic. The company is conducting development and licensing programs on other DepoFoam candidates as well. Through the 2019 acquisition of MyoScience (now Pacira CryoTech) Pacira gained another commercial product the iovera pain management system. The iovera system is a handheld device that delivers precise doses of cold temperature to targeted nerves.

	Annual Growth	12/14	12/15	12/16	12/17	12/18
Sales ($ mil.)	14.3%	197.7	249.0	276.4	286.6	337.3
Net income ($ mil.)	–	(13.7)	1.9	(37.9)	(42.6)	(0.5)
Market value ($ mil.)	(16.5%)	3,654.8	3,165.5	1,331.5	1,881.8	1,773.4
Employees	3.8%	447	487	503	489	518

PACKAGING CORP OF AMERICA
NYS: PKG

1 North Field Court
Lake Forest, IL 60045
Phone: 847-482-3000
Fax: –
Web: www.packagingcorp.com

CEO: Mark W. Kowlzan
CFO: Robert P. (Bob) Mundy
HR: –
FYE: December 31
Type: Public

One of the largest containerboard manufacturers in the US Packaging Corporation of America (PCA) produces about 3.9 million tons of containerboard a year most of which is converted into corrugated boxes and ships about 56 billion square feet of corrugated products. PCA's mills also churn out about a million tons of semi-chemical corrugating medium. The company's corrugated packaging includes shipping containers for manufactured goods multi-color boxes and displays for retail locations and honeycomb protective packaging. Its packaging materials also contain food and beverages and other consumer and industrial products. PCA operates manufacturing plants throughout the US.

	Annual Growth	12/14	12/15	12/16	12/17	12/18
Sales ($ mil.)	4.6%	5,852.6	5,741.7	5,779.0	6,444.9	7,014.6
Net income ($ mil.)	17.1%	392.6	436.8	449.6	668.6	738.0
Market value ($ mil.)	1.7%	7,375.5	5,958.0	8,015.2	11,391.6	7,886.7
Employees	1.7%	14,000	13,000	14,000	14,600	15,000

PACWEST BANCORP
NMS: PACW

9701 Wilshire Blvd., Suite 700
Beverly Hills, CA 90212
Phone: 310-887-8500
Fax: –
Web: www.pacwestbancorp.com

CEO: Matthew P. (Matt) Wagner
CFO: Patrick J. (Pat) Rusnak
HR: Christopher D. Blake
FYE: December 31
Type: Public

PacWest Bancorp is the holding company for Pacific Western Bank which operates about 80 branches mostly in southern and central California plus an additional branch in Durham North Carolina. The $21 billion-asset bank caters to small and midsized businesses and their owners and employees offering traditional deposit and loan products and services. Commercial real estate mortgages make up more than 30% of its loan portfolio while cash flow- and asset-based business loans make up another 40%. The bank also originates residential mortgage real estate construction and land loans venture capital equipment finance and consumer loans. PacWest offers investment services and international banking through agreements with correspondent banks.

	Annual Growth	12/14	12/15	12/16	12/17	12/18
Assets ($ mil.)	12.2%	16,234.8	21,288.5	21,869.8	24,994.9	25,731.4
Net income ($ mil.)	28.8%	168.9	299.6	352.2	357.8	465.3
Market value ($ mil.)	(7.5%)	5,600.2	5,309.5	6,706.5	6,208.8	4,099.8
Employees	6.2%	1,443	1,670	1,669	1,786	1,833

PAETEC HOLDING CORP.

1 PAETEC Plaza 600 Willowbrook Office Park
Fairport NY 14450
Phone: 585-340-2500
Fax: 585-340-2801
Web: www.paetec.com

CEO: –
CFO: –
HR: –
FYE: December 31
Type: Subsidiary

PAETEC gets its paycheck from enterprise users of voice and data communication services. Operating through subsidiary PAETEC Communications the company provides services for local long-distance and Internet-based (VoIP) voice; cloud and data center functions and data access and transport for more than 54000 businesses in about 90 of the largest metropolitan areas of the US. It also provides enterprise telecommunications management software under the PINNACLE brand and it offers premises equipment installation as well as network engineering consulting. Customers include US federal agencies such as the DISA DoD and the FAA. PAETEC was acquired by Windstream in 2011 for about $2.3 billion.

PAGE SOUTHERLAND PAGE L.L.P.

1100 LOUISIANA ST STE 1
HOUSTON, TX 770025246
Phone: 713-871-8484
Fax: –

CEO: James M Wright
CFO: –
HR: –
FYE: December 31
Type: Private

Page Southerland Page performs pre-design planning architectural engineering historic preservation interior design and sustainable design services in Texas and far beyond. Also known as Page since a 2013 rebranding the company boasts a portfolio of projects that includes corporate education healthcare hospitality government sports and science and technology facilities. Page takes on projects in more than 80 countries worldwide including the UK and the Middle East. The construction firm traces its beginnings to a two-person office in Austin Texas established by brothers Charles and Louis Page in 1898; Louis Southerland joined the firm during the 1930s.

	Annual Growth	12/06	12/07	12/08	12/09	12/11
Sales ($ mil.)	127.6%	–	–	5.2	57.2	61.1
Net income ($ mil.)	6824.7%	–	–	0.0	6.7	10.0
Market value ($ mil.)	–	–	–	–	–	–
Employees	–	–	–	–	–	450

PAID INC
NBB: PAYD

225 Cedar Hill Street
Marlborough, MA 01752
Phone: 617-861-6050
Fax: –
Web: www.paid-corp.com

CEO: Allan Pratt
CFO: W Austin Lewis IV
HR: –
FYE: December 31
Type: Public

Paid Inc. (formerly Sales Online Direct) hopes celebrities and fans will pay it some attention. The company's celebrity services division offers merchandising brand building marketing online ticketing services and it hosts Web-based fan clubs for clients. Its AuctionInc technology processes and calculates transactions for website owners. The company also auctions collectibles sports memorabilia and celebrity-related items through the Internet. Paid Inc. makes its money on collectibles and through related services (such as appraisals and its own auction management software).

	Annual Growth	12/14	12/15	12/16	12/17	12/18
Sales ($ mil.)	84.6%	0.8	0.3	0.5	7.6	9.3
Net income ($ mil.)	–	(1.7)	(1.3)	(0.3)	(0.6)	(11.5)
Market value ($ mil.)	165.9%	0.1	0.2	0.7	5.6	5.0
Employees	35.8%	5	6	8	16	17

PAIN THERAPEUTICS INC
NMS: PTIE

7801 N. Capital of Texas Highway, Suite 260
Austin, TX 78731
Phone: 512 501-2444
Fax: -
Web: www.paintrials.com

CEO: Remi Barbier
CFO: Eric Schoen
HR: -
FYE: December 31
Type: Public

Pain Therapeutics is providing opiates for the masses. The development-stage pharmaceutical company is working on abuse-resistant painkillers including Remoxy a version of the frequently abused Oxycontin. Pain Therapeutics is developing Remoxy in partnership with Pfizer which holds all of the commercialization rights to the drug except in Australia and New Zealand. In addition to its chronic pain candidates Pain Therapeutics has other development products in early stages. Because many of its drug candidates already contain FDA-approved components the firm hopes for a faster approval process for its lead candidate.

	Annual Growth	12/09	12/10	12/11	12/12	12/13
Sales ($ mil.)	18.9%	20.6	16.8	11.5	10.9	41.1
Net income ($ mil.)	-	(3.5)	(12.0)	(2.6)	(3.4)	31.5
Market value ($ mil.)	(2.4%)	243.9	307.2	172.9	123.3	221.2
Employees	(26.2%)	27	18	10	8	8

PALATIN TECHNOLOGIES INC
ASE: PTN

4B Cedar Brook Drive
Cranbury, NJ 08512
Phone: 609 495-2200
Fax: -
Web: www.palatin.com

CEO: Carl Spana
CFO: Stephen T Wills
HR: -
FYE: June 30
Type: Public

Palatin Technologies fights the perils of poor health with protein and peptide-based therapies. The company researches and develops drugs that target melanocortin (MC) receptors and natriuretic receptors in the brain. Its lead candidate Vyleesi (bremelanotide) was approved for marketing in the US to treat sexual dysfunction in women in 2019; the drug is licensed to and marketed by AMAG Pharmaceuticals. Other MC-targeted drug candidates aim to treat inflammatory and autoimmune conditions such as dry eye disease and inflammatory bowel disease. Natriuretic (a type of peptide) focused treatments are being studied for the treatment of heart failure acute asthma and other cardiovascular diseases.

	Annual Growth	06/15	06/16	06/17	06/18	06/19
Sales ($ mil.)	46.9%	13.0	-	44.7	67.1	60.3
Net income ($ mil.)	-	(17.7)	(51.7)	(13.3)	24.7	35.8
Market value ($ mil.)	6.8%	201.9	100.1	97.5	220.0	263.1
Employees	0.0%	18	22	22	19	18

PALL CORP.
NYS: PLL

25 Harbor Park Drive
Port Washington, NY 11050
Phone: 516 484-5400
Fax: 516 484-3649
Web: www.pall.com

CEO: Rainer Blair
CFO: -
HR: -
FYE: July 31
Type: Public

With operations around the globe Pall is not small. The company is a leading supplier of filtration separation and purification technologies. Its products are used to remove solid liquid and gaseous contaminants from a variety of liquids and gases. It operates two businesses globally: Life Sciences and Industrial. The Life Sciences business group is focused on developing manufacturing and selling products to customers in the Medical BioPharmaceuticals and Food & Beverage markets. The Industrial business group is focused on developing manufacturing and selling products to customers in the Process Technologies Aerospace and Microelectronics markets.

	Annual Growth	07/10	07/11	07/12	07/13	07/14
Sales ($ mil.)	3.8%	2,401.9	2,740.9	2,671.7	2,648.1	2,789.1
Net income ($ mil.)	10.8%	241.2	315.5	319.3	574.9	364.0
Market value ($ mil.)	19.3%	4,200.5	5,446.2	5,866.9	7,684.9	8,509.8
Employees	0.0%	10,400	10,900	10,800	9,800	10,400

PALLADIUM EQUITY PARTNERS LLC

Rockefeller Center 1270 Avenue of the Americas Ste. 2200
New York NY 10020
Phone: 212-218-5150
Fax: 212-218-5155
Web: www.palladiumequity.com

CEO: -
CFO: -
HR: -
FYE: December 31
Type: Private

In the mining world palladium is a rare and precious metal; in the investment world however Palladium is an investment firm known to mine for companies that serve the US Hispanic population. Formed in 1997 Palladium Equity Partners focuses on companies that are in a position to target the Hispanic market which the company deems to be a fast-growing and profitable market segment. It invests in various industries including financial services food retail business services health care manufacturing and media. Palladium has offices in New York and Los Angeles.

PALMETTO BANCSHARES, INC. (SC)
NAS: PLMT

306 East North Street
Greenville, SC 29601
Phone: 800 725-2265
Fax: -
Web: www.palmettobank.com

CEO: -
CFO: -
HR: -
FYE: December 31
Type: Public

Since the palmetto is the official state tree of South Carolina does that make Palmetto Bancshares the state's official bank? Palmetto Bancshares is the holding company for The Palmetto Bank which operates about 40 full- and limited-service branches mostly in upstate South Carolina. Its offerings include checking savings and money market accounts; IRAs; and CDs. Loans secured by commercial real estate account for the largest portion of its loan portfolio with single-family residential mortgages at a distant second. The Palmetto Bank also provides financial planning trust and brokerage services plus bond mutual fund and annuity sales. It's been serving South Carolinians since 1906.

	Annual Growth	12/09	12/10	12/11	12/12	12/13
Assets ($ mil.)	(6.7%)	1,436.0	1,355.2	1,203.2	1,145.5	1,090.2
Net income ($ mil.)	-	(40.1)	(60.2)	(23.4)	(1.9)	27.7
Market value ($ mil.)	12.8%	102.3	38.4	65.3	106.5	165.7
Employees	(7.5%)	413	394	352	323	302

PALMETTO HEALTH

1301 TAYLOR ST STE 8A
COLUMBIA, SC 292012955
Phone: 803-296-2100
Fax: -

CEO: Charles D Beaman Jr
CFO: Paul Duane
HR: -
FYE: September 30
Type: Private

Palmetto Health provides health care in the Palmetto State. The not-for-profit organization administers a comprehensive range of medical services to residents of Columbia South Carolina and surrounding areas through a network of hospitals and other medical providers. The 1140-bed system includes a 650-bed teaching hospital Palmetto Health Richland which is affiliated with the University of South Carolina Medical School. Palmetto also operates the 490-bed Palmetto Health Baptist Columbia hospital as well as Baptist Health Easley a 110-bed general acute-care community hospital in the Appalachian highlands which it operates with Greenville Hospital System University Medical Center. Palmetto Health is merging with Greenville Health System to create South Carolina's largest health care system.

	Annual Growth	09/04	09/05	09/06	09/07	09/08
Sales ($ mil.)	5.0%	-	-	-	1,131.7	1,188.7
Net income ($ mil.)	-	-	-	-	41.2	0.0
Market value ($ mil.)	-	-	-	-	-	-
Employees	-	-	-	-	-	10,200

PALMS WEST HOSPITAL LIMITED PARTNERSHIP

13001 SOUTHERN BLVD
LOXAHATCHEE, FL 334709203
Phone: 561-798-3300
Fax: –
Web: www.palmswesthospital.com

CEO: Eric Goldsmann
CFO: –
HR: –
FYE: May 31
Type: Private

Palms West Hospital part of the HCA system of healthcare providers is a 200-bed acute care hospital that serves western Palm Beach County Florida. The hospital's specialized care programs include cardiopulmonary services diabetes education a birthing center diagnostics and rehabilitation. Its pediatric department boasts an emergency clinic and intensive care unit. The medical campus includes physician offices and an outpatient surgery center (Palms West Surgicenter). Palms West Hospital is part of the HCA East Florida division. Affiliate Integrated Regional Laboratories provides medical testing for Palms West and other area facilities.

	Annual Growth	05/12	05/13	05/14	05/15	05/16
Sales ($ mil.)	1.9%	–	–	–	167.7	170.9
Net income ($ mil.)	(17.1%)	–	–	–	34.7	28.8
Market value ($ mil.)	–	–	–	–	–	–
Employees	–	–	–	–	–	850

PALO ALTO MEDICAL FOUNDATION FOR HEALTH CARE RESEARCH AND EDUCAT

795 EL CAMINO REAL AMES B
PALO ALTO, CA 94301
Phone: 650-321-4121
Fax: –
Web: www.pamf.org

CEO: Jeff Gerard
CFO: –
HR: –
FYE: December 31
Type: Private

The Palo Alto Medical Foundation (PAMF) is a not-for-profit multi-specialty physicians group providing medical and outpatient care mostly in the San Francisco Bay Area. It operates through three divisions serving distinct geographical areas: the Palo Alto Medical Clinic and the Camino Medical Group serve Silicon Valley and the East Bay; and the Santa Cruz Medical Foundation operates farther south in and around Santa Cruz. An affiliate of Sutter Health the organization has some 1100 doctors covering dozens of medical specialties; its facilities also provide outpatient surgery diagnostic imaging and women's services. Additionally PAMF houses a Research Institute that performs medical research.

	Annual Growth	08/98	08/99*	12/00	12/01	12/11
Sales ($ mil.)	–	–	0.0	–	322.0	1,434.0
Net income ($ mil.)	–	–	0.0	–	5.0	3.0
Market value ($ mil.)	–	–	–	–	–	–
Employees	–	–	–	–	–	1,168

*Fiscal year change

PALO ALTO NETWORKS, INC

3000 Tannery Way
Santa Clara, CA 95054
Phone: 408 753-4000
Fax: –
Web: www.paloaltonetworks.com

NYS: PANW
CEO: Mark D. McLaughlin
CFO: Steffan C. Tomlinson
HR: Wendy Barnes
FYE: July 31
Type: Public

Palo Alto Networks is a leading cyber security company offering enterprise-wide internet security (including security measures for mobile devices) to protect companies from breaches in their corporate networks and cloud computing environments. Its hardware and software security products identify network traffic in detail and provide the ability to control access by user. Palo Alto Networks designs its products to identify and manage threats rather than just block access. It sells products outright as well as through a growing subscription business. Competitors include Juniper Networks and Cisco Systems. The US accounts for about two-thirds of sales.

	Annual Growth	07/15	07/16	07/17	07/18	07/19
Sales ($ mil.)	33.0%	928.1	1,378.5	1,761.6	2,273.1	2,899.6
Net income ($ mil.)	–	(165.0)	(225.9)	(216.6)	(147.9)	(81.9)
Market value ($ mil.)	5.1%	17,988.3	12,670.2	12,756.3	19,191.6	21,929.1
Employees	27.7%	2,637	3,795	4,562	5,348	7,014

PALOMAR HEALTH

456 E GRAND AVE
ESCONDIDO, CA 920253319
Phone: 442-281-5000
Fax: –
Web: www.palomarhealth.org

CEO: –
CFO: –
HR: Tracey Creese
FYE: June 30
Type: Private

Palomar Health (formerly Palomar Pomerado Health) packs a medical punch in northern San Diego. The not-for-profit public health care district's Palomar Medical Center (PMC) is a 290-bed acute care hospital (able to hold 650 beds) that provides inpatient care and surgical emergency trauma and rehabilitation and interventional services; its Palomar Health Downtown Campus is a 320-bed specialty hospital for women's and children's health rehabilitation behavioral health and urgent care services. The system also operates the 110-bed acute care Pomerado Hospital skilled nursing centers outpatient facilities and a home health care unit. Palomar Health has its roots in a 13-bed hospital founded in 1933.

	Annual Growth	06/10	06/11	06/12	06/13	06/14
Sales ($ mil.)	7.8%	–	490.0	552.2	657.5	614.2
Net income ($ mil.)	–	–	44.8	19.6	(45.7)	(33.7)
Market value ($ mil.)	–	–	–	–	–	–
Employees	–	–	–	–	–	3,000

PAMIDA STORES OPERATING COMPANY LLC

8800 F St.
Omaha NE 68127
Phone: 402-339-2400
Fax: 402-596-7330
Web: www.pamida.com

CEO: –
CFO: –
HR: –
FYE: January 31
Type: Private

Pamida Stores Operating Co. offers more small-town values to small town communities. The rural retailer operates some 195 Pamida general merchandise discount stores in more than 15 states mostly in the Midwest. The stores are located in small towns (5500 people on average) most of which are not served by mass merchandisers such as Wal-Mart. Pamida's stores sell brand-name and private-label apparel jewelry health and beauty aids housewares electronics and lawn and garden supplies. Most stores also sell groceries and two-thirds have in-store pharmacies. In 2012 Pamida merged with Shopko; both retailers are portfolio companies of private equity Sun Capital Partners.

PANAVISION INC.

6219 De Soto Ave.
Woodland Hills CA 91367-2602
Phone: 818-316-1000
Fax: 818-316-1111
Web: www.panavision.com

CEO: Kimberly Snyder
CFO: John Suh
HR: –
FYE: June 30
Type: Private

Without Panavision Iron Man and Batman: The Dark Knight wouldn't be much to look at. The company manufactures and rents out cameras lenses and lighting equipment and related accessories to movie and TV production studios. Subsidiary Lee Filters sells lighting color-correction and diffusion filters. Other subsidiaries supply lighting systems and develop digital image sensor chips. Panavision has provided the camera system for every James Bond film ever made. It also supplies camera equipment to popular TV series such as Glee Modern Family and Two and a Half Men. All total it has a global network of about 40 facilities and 20 independent distributors.

PANDORA MEDIA INC
NYS: P

2101 Webster Street, Suite 1650
Oakland, CA 94612
Phone: 510 451-4100
Fax: 510 451-4286
Web: www.pandora.com/about

CEO: Roger Lynch
CFO: Naveen Chopra
HR: –
FYE: December 31
Type: Public

This Pandora's box is filled with music. The Internet radio station generates playlists based on a user's favorite artist or song. As part of the company's Music Genome Project songs are analyzed according to musical features — including details of instrumentation harmony lyrics melody rhythm and vocals. Users enter the name of a song and Pandora creates a playlist of songs with similar characteristics. Pandora's service free to its more than 175 million registered users and available only in the US is supported by local and national advertising. Chief strategy officer Tim Westergren founded the company in 2000; Pandora went public in 2011.

	Annual Growth	01/13*	12/13	12/14	12/15	12/16
Sales ($ mil.)	48.0%	427.1	600.2	920.8	1,164.0	1,384.8
Net income ($ mil.)	–	(38.1)	(27.0)	(30.4)	(169.7)	(343.0)
Market value ($ mil.)	4.2%	2,709.1	6,255.3	4,193.0	3,153.5	3,066.5
Employees	49.8%	740	1,069	1,414	2,219	2,488

*Fiscal year change

PANDUIT CORP.

18900 PANDUIT DR
TINLEY PARK, IL 604873600
Phone: 708-532-1800
Fax: –

CEO: John E. (Jack) Caveney
CFO: –
HR: Tim Dee
FYE: December 31
Type: Private

Panduit's got your cables covered connected and enclosed. The company's electrical components tie together the communications computing power and security systems of a building or physical location. Products include cabling connectors copper wire fiber-optic components cabinets and racks grounding systems outlets terminals and other electrical components. It also offers software used to integrate and manage separate building functions. Panduit's products are used in data centers office buildings industrial plants processing lines and other settings. The privately held company has customers in more than 100 countries. Among its customers are Noosa Yogurt Iveco and Purdue University.

	Annual Growth	12/12	12/13	12/14	12/15	12/16
Sales ($ mil.)	(1.9%)	–	–	973.7	924.5	937.5
Net income ($ mil.)	–	–	–	0.0	0.0	0.0
Market value ($ mil.)	–	–	–	–	–	–
Employees	–	–	–	–	–	5,110

PANERA BREAD CO
NMS: PNRA

3630 South Geyer Road, Suite 100
St. Louis, MO 63127
Phone: 314 984-1000
Fax: –
Web: www.panerabread.com

CEO: Ronald M Shaich
CFO: Michael J Bufano
HR: –
FYE: December 29
Type: Public

Panera Bread Company is a leader in the quick-casual restaurant business. The company operates about 2000 bakery-cafes located throughout the US and Ontario Canada. Its locations which operate under the banners Panera Bread Saint Louis Bread Co. and Paradise Bakery & Café offer made-to-order sandwiches using a variety of artisan breads including Asiago cheese bread focaccia and its classic sourdough bread. The chain's menu also features soups salads and gourmet coffees. In addition Panera sells its bread bagels and pastries to go. About 900 of its locations are company-operated and roughly 1100 locations are run by franchisees.

	Annual Growth	12/11	12/12	12/13	12/14	12/15
Sales ($ mil.)	10.1%	1,822.0	2,130.1	2,385.0	2,529.2	2,681.6
Net income ($ mil.)	2.4%	136.0	173.4	196.2	179.3	149.3
Market value ($ mil.)	8.7%	3,486.9	3,915.4	4,369.2	4,324.7	4,873.4
Employees	9.7%	32,600	36,300	40,100	45,400	47,200

PANHANDLE EASTERN PIPE LINE COMPANY, LP

8111 WESTCHESTER DR # 600
DALLAS, TX 752256142
Phone: 214-981-0700
Fax: –

CEO: Kelcy L Warren
CFO: Martin Salinas Jr
HR: –
FYE: December 31
Type: Private

From the oilfield to the burner under a frying pan Panhandle Eastern Pipe Line can move the gas. The company operates 10000 miles of interstate pipelines (Panhandle Eastern — 6000 miles Trunkline — 3000 miles and Sea Robin — 1000 miles) that can transport 6.4 billion cu. ft. of natural gas a day primarily to markets in the Midwest and Great Lakes regions of the US. It also provides terminalling services through nearly 50 compressor stations and five gas storage fields capable of holding 68.1 billion cu. ft. of natural gas. The company also has liquefied natural gas (LNG) terminalling assets. Panhandle Eastern Pipe Line operates as part of Energy Transfer Equity's Southern Union's Panhandle Energy unit.

	Annual Growth	12/12	12/13	12/14	12/15	12/16
Sales ($ mil.)	(5.9%)	–	–	581.0	548.0	514.0
Net income ($ mil.)	–	–	–	(3.0)	125.0	(646.0)
Market value ($ mil.)	–	–	–	–	–	–
Employees	–	–	–	–	–	562

PANHANDLE OIL & GAS INC
NYS: PHX

Grand Centre, Suite 300, 5400 N. Grand Blvd.
Oklahoma City, OK 73112
Phone: 405 948-1560
Fax: 405 948-2038
Web: www.panhandleoilandgas.com

CEO: Paul F. Blanchard
CFO: Robb P. Winfield
HR: –
FYE: September 30
Type: Public

This is not your conventional Panhandler. Panhandle Oil & Gas takes pride in owning non-operated oil and natural gas properties in unconventional plays in Arkansas Oklahoma and Texas. Assets include mineral acreage leasehold acreage and working or royalty interests in producing wells. The company does not operate on its own properties and engages business partners mostly well operators in drilling management and sales & marketing of energy products. It has proven reserves of 2.2 million barrels of oil 1.5 million barrels of NGL and 88 million Mcf of natural gas.

	Annual Growth	09/15	09/16	09/17	09/18	09/19
Sales ($ mil.)	(1.8%)	70.9	39.1	46.3	45.0	66.0
Net income ($ mil.)	–	9.3	(10.3)	3.5	14.6	(40.7)
Market value ($ mil.)	(3.6%)	264.0	286.4	388.9	301.5	228.4
Employees	1.2%	21	20	21	20	22

PANTRY INC. (THE)
NMS: PTRY

P.O. Box 8019, 305 Gregson Drive
Cary, NC 27511
Phone: 919 774-6700
Fax: –
Web: www.thepantry.com

CEO: –
CFO: –
HR: –
FYE: September 25
Type: Public

If you've ever passed through the Carolinas on business or made the drive to Disney World chances are The Pantry has provided fuel for your car and body. The company is the leading convenience store operator in the southeastern US with some 1500 shops in more than a dozen states. (Florida accounts for about a quarter of all sales.) Most of the company's stores do business under the Kangaroo Express banner; other names include Bean Street Coffee Celeste and Aunt M's. Branded fuel is sold under such names as Marathon BP and ExxonMobil. The stores sell cigarettes beverages candy gasoline magazines among other items. In 2014 the company agreed to be acquired by Alimentation Couche-Tard for $860 million.

	Annual Growth	09/10	09/11	09/12	09/13	09/14
Sales ($ mil.)	1.0%	7,265.3	8,138.5	8,253.2	7,822.0	7,545.7
Net income ($ mil.)	–	(165.6)	9.8	(2.5)	(3.0)	13.2
Market value ($ mil.)	(4.3%)	565.3	300.6	346.3	273.1	474.3
Employees	1.2%	14,419	13,928	13,709	14,903	15,140

PAPA JOHN'S INTERNATIONAL, INC. NMS: PZZA

2002 Papa John's Boulevard | CEO: Stephen M (Steve) Ritchie
Louisville, KY 40299-2367 | CFO: Lance F Tucker
Phone: 502 261-7272 | HR: –
Fax: – | FYE: December 30
Web: www.papajohns.com | Type: Public

Papa John's International makes a lot of dough — pizza dough that is. The company operates the world's #3 pizza chain (behind YUM! Brands' Pizza Hut brand and Domino's) with around 4893 pizzerias across the US and in about 39 international markets. Its restaurants offer several different pizza styles and topping choices as well as a few specialty pies such as The Works and The Meats. Papa John's locations typically offer delivery and carry-out service only. The company owns and operates more than 752 locations while the rest are franchised. Founder and CEO John Schnatter owns more than 20% of the chain.

	Annual Growth	12/14	12/15	12/16	12/17	12/18
Sales ($ mil.)	(0.4%)	1,598.1	1,637.4	1,713.6	1,783.4	1,573.3
Net income ($ mil.)	(61.3%)	73.3	75.7	102.8	102.3	1.6
Market value ($ mil.)	(7.7%)	1,744.9	1,736.1	2,728.7	1,760.3	1,268.4
Employees	(4.6%)	21,700	22,350	23,100	22,400	18,000

PAPER CONVERTING MACHINE COMPANY

2300 S ASHLAND AVE | CEO: –
GREEN BAY, WI 543045213 | CFO: –
Phone: 920-494-5601 | HR: Mike Kwaterski
Fax: – | FYE: September 30
Web: www.pcmc.com | Type: Private

An empire built on paper: The Paper Converting Machine Company (PCMC) does just that — manufactures machinery for the converting packaging printing and laminating of paper. PCMC makes and sells equipment for tissue converting and packaging; wide-web flexo printing coating and laminating; coaters; roll engraving; and non-woven converting. Its equipment is used by manufacturers of flexible packaging non-woven disposable products (wet wipes) and sanitary tissues. PCMC is a division of manufacturing technology supplier Barry-Wehmiller Companies.

	Annual Growth	09/04	09/05	09/06	09/10	09/11
Sales ($ mil.)	2.1%	–	–	194.1	196.9	215.1
Net income ($ mil.)	–	–	–	0.0	0.0	0.0
Market value ($ mil.)	–	–	–	–	–	–
Employees	–	–	–	–	–	1,304

PAPERWORKS INDUSTRIES INC.

5000 Flat Rock Rd. | CEO: C Anderson Bolton
Philadelphia PA 19127 | CFO: Mark Schlei
Phone: 215-984-7000 | HR: –
Fax: 215-984-7181 | FYE: December 31
Web: www.paperworksindustries.com | Type: Private

PaperWorks Industries is knee deep in paper and that's the way it likes it. With mills in Pennsylvania and Indiana it is a North American producer of coated recycled paperboard (CRB) manufacturing about 300000 tons of it annually. Its MasterWorks product line includes everything from freezer-enhanced CRB to uncoated eco-friendly paperboard. End-use markets for CRB include beverages dry and frozen foods household goods and oral care products. In addition to its CRB offerings PaperWorks produces specialized folding cartons. The current iteration of PaperWorks Industries was formed when it merged with Specialized Packaging Group (SPG) in 2009. It is controlled by investment firm Sun Capital Partners.

PAR PACIFIC HOLDINGS INC NYS: PARR

825 Town & Country Lane, Suite 1500 | CEO: William C. (Bill) Pate
Houston, TX 77024 | CFO: William (Will) Monteleone
Phone: 281 899-4800 | HR: –
Fax: – | FYE: December 31
Web: www.parpacific.com | Type: Public

Supplying oil and gas to Hawaii is par for the course for Par Pacific. The company owns and operates a 94000 barrels per day refinery with related logistics and a retail network across the major Hawaiian islands. It owns an equity investment in Laramie Energy LLC which has natural gas production and reserves located in the Piceance Basin of Colorado. In addition Par Pacific also transports markets and distributes crude oil from the Western US and Canada to refining hubs in the Midwest Gulf Coast East Coast and to Hawaii.

	Annual Growth	12/14	12/15	12/16	12/17	12/18
Sales ($ mil.)	2.4%	3,108.0	2,066.3	1,865.0	2,443.1	3,410.7
Net income ($ mil.)	–	(47.0)	(39.9)	(45.8)	72.6	39.4
Market value ($ mil.)	(3.4%)	763.5	1,106.0	683.1	905.9	666.2
Employees	22.2%	577	744	863	905	1,285

PAR PHARMACEUTICAL COMPANIES INC. NYSE: PRX

300 Tice Blvd. | CEO: –
Woodcliff Lake NJ 07677 | CFO: –
Phone: 201-802-4000 | HR: –
Fax: 201-802-4600 | FYE: December 31
Web: www.parpharm.com | Type: Private

Generic drugs are par for the course for Par Pharmaceutical Companies. The company markets about 55 generic drugs with a focus on central nervous system cardiovascular and anti-inflammatory medications as well as infectious disease. The generic division manufactures some of its own products but it also distributes drugs manufactured by strategic partners. The company's Strativa division develops updated versions of off-patent branded drugs. Par markets product through its internal sales force mainly to wholesalers retail pharmacy and grocery chains and distributors across the US. Par Pharmaceutical was taken private by investment firm TPG in 2012.

PAR TECHNOLOGY CORP. NYS: PAR

PAR Technology Park, 8383 Seneca Turnpike | CEO: Donald H. (Don) Foley
New Hartford, NY 13413-4991 | CFO: Bryan Menar
Phone: 315 738-0600 | HR: Darla Haas
Fax: – | FYE: December 31
Web: www.partech.com | Type: Public

PAR Technology is POS for fast food giants such as McDonald's and Yum! Brands. The company makes point-of-sale (POS) systems that are used to input and display orders by more than 75000 restaurants in some 110 countries. Through its PAR Government Systems unit the company designs data processing systems and develops software for advanced radar and other detection systems used by the US Department of Defense (DOD) and other federal and state agencies. Most sales come from customers in the US.

	Annual Growth	12/14	12/15	12/16	12/17	12/18
Sales ($ mil.)	(3.7%)	233.6	229.0	229.7	232.6	201.2
Net income ($ mil.)	–	(3.7)	(0.9)	1.8	(3.4)	(24.1)
Market value ($ mil.)	37.1%	99.5	108.8	90.2	151.2	351.7
Employees	(4.9%)	1,221	1,010	1,002	1,137	1,000

PARADIGM HOLDINGS INC.
OTC: PDHO

9715 Key West Ave. 3rd Fl.
Rockville MD 20850
Phone: 301-468-1200
Fax: 301-468-1201
Web: www.paradigmsolutions.com

CEO: J P London
CFO: –
HR: –
FYE: December 31
Type: Public

Paradigm Holdings serves the big guns of big government. Through subsidiary Paradigm Solutions the company provides IT and database services including consulting systems integration network design project management and technical support. Additionally Paradigm offers custom software and database development and data center and facilities management services. Its key areas of focus are enterprise optimization enterprise solutions mission support and assurance and mission critical infrastructure. Public sector customers have included Homeland Security the State Dept. Defense Dept. Justice Dept. and the Treasury. Paradigm was acquired in 2011 by CACI for $61.5 million.

PARADISE VALLEY HOSPITAL

2400 E 4TH ST
NATIONAL CITY, CA 919502098
Phone: 619-470-4100
Fax: –
Web: www.paradisevalleyhospital.net

CEO: –
CFO: –
HR: –
FYE: December 31
Type: Private

Paradise Valley Hospital aims to elevate patient care to a divine level. Established in 1904 the medical center serves residents in the San Diego area. This acute-care facility has more than 300 beds as well as 300 general care and specialty physicians. Paradise Valley Hospital's range of services include health and wellness programs respiratory therapy and same-day surgery. Specialty divisions include rehabilitation behavioral health cardiac care and geriatric services. Paradise Valley Hospital is a subsidiary of Prime Healthcare Services which acquired the hospital from former parent Adventist Health in 2007.

	Annual Growth	12/13	12/14	12/15	12/16	12/17
Sales ($ mil.)	(5.3%)	–	–	134.1	143.7	120.4
Net income ($ mil.)	–	–	–	(9.8)	(7.6)	(22.7)
Market value ($ mil.)	–	–	–	–	–	–
Employees	–	–	–	–	–	1,200

PARADISE, INC.
NBB: PARF

1200 W. Dr. Martin Luther King, Jr., Blvd.
Plant City, FL 33563
Phone: 813 752-1155
Fax: –
Web: www.paradisefruitco.com

CEO: Randy S. Gordon
CFO: Jack M. Laskowitz
HR: –
FYE: December 31
Type: Public

Paradise and fruitcakes are holiday traditions right up there with visiting in-laws. The company is the largest US maker and seller of glac-© fruits a mainstay ingredient in fruitcakes. It sells its dried and candied fruits to home bakers through supermarkets and other retail stores and less so to commercial bakers and foodservice operators under brands Paradise Mor-Fruit and White Swan (licensed) among several. Wal-Mart is one the company's biggest customers; most sales are generated during September October and November. The company also makes molded plastic packaging for its products and for third parties through subsidiary Paradise Plastics. Chairman and CEO Melvin Gordon control the company.

	Annual Growth	12/14	12/15	12/16	12/17	12/18
Sales ($ mil.)	(5.4%)	25.2	23.7	23.2	22.0	20.1
Net income ($ mil.)	–	0.5	0.5	1.1	0.6	(0.6)
Market value ($ mil.)	10.7%	11.4	12.2	13.9	14.6	17.1
Employees	(14.1%)	275	195	195	195	150

PARAGON DEVELOPMENT SYSTEMS, INC.

13400 BISHOPS LN STE 190
BROOKFIELD, WI 530056237
Phone: 262-569-5300
Fax: –
Web: www.pdsit.net

CEO: Craig Schiefelbein
CFO: Thomas Mount
HR: –
FYE: December 31
Type: Private

Paragon Development Systems (PDS) brings Midwestern roots and a nationwide reach to the technology services market. The company offers services ranging from procurement to systems integration reselling and supporting PCs networking equipment printers servers software and storage systems as part of its business. Its supplier list includes Cisco Systems Fujitsu Hewlett-Packard IBM and Microsoft. Paragon also builds and markets its own PCs under the Infinity Vector and Vision brand names. Founded in 1986 PDS partners with US-based medium and large enterprises in a variety of markets such as healthcare corporate government and education.

	Annual Growth	12/04	12/05	12/06	12/07	12/08
Sales ($ mil.)	13.3%	–	94.4	91.1	113.0	137.2
Net income ($ mil.)	144.4%	–	0.5	(0.3)	2.3	6.9
Market value ($ mil.)	–	–	–	–	–	–
Employees	–	–	–	–	–	290

PARAGON REAL ESTATE EQUITY & INVESTMENT TRUST
NBB: PRLE

10011 Valley Forge Drive
Houston, TX 77042
Phone: 440 283-6319
Fax: –
Web: www.prgreit.com

CEO: James C Mastandrea
CFO: John J Dee
HR: –
FYE: December 31
Type: Public

Ideally Paragon Real Estate Equity and Investment Trust would be the very model of real estate investing but it merely is a corporate shell company. The firm is seeking investment opportunities in land development joint ventures other real estate companies and retail office industrial and hospitality properties. In 2008 it began investing in stock of publicly traded real estate investment trusts (REITs). Entities associated with CEO James Mastandrea control more than three-quarters of Paragon which has expressed doubts about its ability to continue as a going concern and may seek additional investors or sell its corporate shell.

	Annual Growth	12/09	12/10	12/11	12/12	12/13
Sales ($ mil.)	(54.7%)	0.0	0.0	0.0	0.0	0.0
Net income ($ mil.)	–	(0.1)	(0.0)	(0.0)	(0.1)	(0.1)
Market value ($ mil.)	–	0.0	0.0	0.1	0.1	0.3
Employees	0.0%	2	2	2	2	2

PARAGON TECHNOLOGIES INC
NBB: PGNT

101 Larry Holmes Drive, Suite 500
Easton, PA 18042
Phone: 610 252-3205
Fax: 610 252-3102
Web: www.pgntgroup.com

CEO: Hesham M. Gad
CFO: Deborah Mertz
HR: Diana Maglio
FYE: December 31
Type: Public

Paragon Technologies produces automated order picking systems and other order fulfilling products used by manufacturing assembly and order distribution customers. Also known by its major brand name SI Systems the company supplies customers with horizontal transportation and conveyor systems related computer software and other products and services used for improving productivity. Customers are located primarily in the US and have included Caterpillar engine giant Cummins General Motors and contact lens manufacturer Vistakon (a subsidiary of Johnson & Johnson). The company was founded in 1958.

	Annual Growth	12/14	12/15	12/16	12/17	12/18
Sales ($ mil.)	88.9%	6.7	11.6	8.6	64.6	85.1
Net income ($ mil.)	–	(0.4)	0.8	(1.1)	2.7	1.0
Market value ($ mil.)	3.2%	1.5	3.4	2.0	2.0	1.7
Employees						

PARAMOUNT GOLD & SILVER CORP ASE: PZG

665 Anderson Street
Winnemucca, NV 89445
Phone: 775 625-3600
Fax: –
Web: www.paramountgold.com

CEO: Christopher Crupi
CFO: Carlo A Buffone
HR: –
FYE: June 30
Type: Public

Paramount Gold and Silver is all about the bling. The development-stage company explores for gold silver and other metals in Mexico and Nevada gold-producing regions. Through subsidiary Paramount Gold de Mexico the company owns 100% of a 450000-acre property in Chihuahua that includes seven advanced stage gold mines. It also owns the Sleeper project in Nevada a 30-square mile site that produced gold and silver from 1986 to 1996. The company is conducting exploration drilling and geological surveys but has no proved reserves. Paramount also holds several earlier stage smaller claims in Nevada and inactive subsidiaries in Mexico and Peru. CEO Christopher Crupi founded the company in 2005.

	Annual Growth	06/10	06/11	06/12	06/13	06/14
Sales ($ mil.)	41.1%	0.0	0.3	0.1	4.5	0.1
Net income ($ mil.)	–	(5.4)	(28.5)	(12.1)	(13.5)	(11.1)
Market value ($ mil.)	(7.3%)	206.9	518.9	382.0	189.4	152.8
Employees	(9.6%)	30	40	40	20	20

PARATEK PHARMACEUTICALS INC NMS: PRTK

75 Park Plaza
Boston, MA 02116
Phone: 617 807-6600
Fax: 650 228-1088
Web: www.transcept.com

CEO: Michael F. Bigham
CFO: Douglas W. Pag ̌n
HR: Regina Paglia
FYE: December 31
Type: Public

Paratek Pharmaceuticals is determined to fight the problem of antibiotic-resistant infections. A clinical-stage biopharmaceutical firm Paratek focuses on developing tetracycline-based therapeutics which have the potential to be an innovative class of antibiotics. Its two primary product candidates are omadacycline for the treatment of skin infections and community-acquired bacterial pneumonia and sarecycline for the treatment of acne. Paratek's first commercial product Intermezzo is a quick-acting low-dosage medication for treating insomnia that occurs in the middle of the night. However Intermezzo (approved in 2011) never cracked the insomnia market. Paratek contracts with third parties for manufacturing and sales.

	Annual Growth	12/14	12/15	12/16	12/17	12/18
Sales ($ mil.)	40.9%	4.3	–	0.0	12.6	17.1
Net income ($ mil.)	–	(17.8)	(70.9)	(111.6)	(89.1)	(112.4)
Market value ($ mil.)	(39.6%)	1,243.6	612.0	496.8	577.4	165.5
Employees	68.2%	13	41	50	83	104

PARATEK PHARMACEUTICALS INC.

75 Kneeland St.
Boston MA 02111-1901
Phone: 617-275-0040
Fax: 617-275-0039
Web: www.paratekpharm.com

CEO: –
CFO: –
HR: –
FYE: December 31
Type: Private

Paratek Pharmaceuticals wants to teach an old drug new tricks. The development-stage company is working to create new forms of antibiotic compound tetracycline that will be effective against newly resistant strains of bacteria. Its lead antibiotic candidate omadacycline is in clinical trials for the treatment of complicated bacterial skin infections pneumonia and urinary tract infections in the hospital setting. The company also has preclinical and clinical research programs on potential treatments for certain inflammatory and neurodegenerative conditions such as acne rosacea multiple sclerosis and rheumatoid arthritis. Paratek filed to go public in 2012.

PARATURE INC.

13625 Dulles Technology Dr. Ste. B
Herndon VA 20171
Phone: 703-564-7758
Fax: 703-564-7757
Web: www.parature.com

CEO: Ching Ho Fung
CFO: Daniel Yoo
HR: –
FYE: December 31
Type: Private

Parature just wants to help you help your customers. The company develops help desk and customer service support software used to manage internal and external technical support and other customer support functions. Its software includes applications for help desk tracking customer self servicing managing online discussion boards and forums and conducting online surveys. Parature's customers include educational institutions government agencies and businesses; Office Depot Sage Software Florida State University and Blackboard have all been clients of the company. Parature also offers professional services including consulting support implementation and training.

PAREXEL INTERNATIONAL CORPORATION

195 WEST ST
WALTHAM, MA 024511146
Phone: 781-487-9900
Fax: –
Web: www.parexel.com

CEO: Josef H. von Rickenbach
CFO: Simon N. R. Harford
HR: Michael Brandt
FYE: June 30
Type: Private

PAREXEL International excels in pharmaceutical development services. A top contract research organization (CRO) the firm counts among its clients some of the world's largest drug biotech diagnostics and medical device firms. Its core Clinical Research Services (CRS) segment provides clinical trial and data management study design patient recruitment biostatistical analysis clinical pharmacology and industry training and publishing. Its PAREXEL Consulting Services (PC) segment handles the non-clinical aspects of drug development regulatory affairs and new product launches. Finally the PAREXEL Informatics (PI) segment offers patient technology solutions and regulatory and clinical solutions. PAREXEL was taken private by Pamplona Capital Management for $4.5 billion in 2017.

	Annual Growth	06/13	06/14	06/15	06/16	06/17
Sales ($ mil.)	2.5%	–	2,266.3	2,330.3	2,426.3	2,441.5
Net income ($ mil.)	(6.0%)	–	129.1	147.8	154.9	107.3
Market value ($ mil.)	–	–	–	–	–	–
Employees	–	–	–	–	–	18,900

PARK AEROSPACE CORP NYS: PKE

1400 Old Country Road
Westbury, NY 11590
Phone: 631 465-3600
Fax: –
Web: www.parkelectro.com

CEO: Brian E. Shore
CFO: P. Matthew Farabaugh
HR: –
FYE: March 03
Type: Public

Printed circuit board manufacturer Park Electrochemical has parked its manufacturing facilities where it can reach its niche market customers — in Asia Europe and North America. The company's Nelco brand of copper-clad laminates and reinforced composite materials are used to make printed circuit boards and other components for laptop computers cellular phones satellite switching systems and other electronics. Park also makes engineered materials including composites for electronics aerospace and industrial markets. About half of Park's sales come from Asia and Europe. In July 2018 the company agreed to sells its electronics business to Tokyo Japan-based AGC Inc. It will retain its aerospace business manufacturing composite materials for the global aeropace markets.

	Annual Growth	03/15*	02/16	02/17	02/18*	03/19
Sales ($ mil.)	(25.1%)	162.1	145.9	114.6	111.2	51.1
Net income ($ mil.)	54.3%	20.0	18.0	9.3	20.6	113.5
Market value ($ mil.)	(5.4%)	444.8	289.7	393.3	351.5	356.5
Employees	(29.8%)	461	451	426	387	112

*Fiscal year change

PARK BANCORP, INC.
NBB: PFED

5400 South Pulaski Road
Chicago, IL 60632
Phone: 773 582-8616
Fax: –
Web: www.parkfed.com

CEO: David A Remijas
CFO: Victor E Caputo
HR: –
FYE: December 31
Type: Public

Looking for a place to park your money? Try Park Bancorp the holding company for Park Federal Savings Bank. The community-oriented bank serves Chicago and Westmont Illinois through about five offices. It offers deposit products such as checking and savings accounts CDs and IRAs. Its lending activities focus on residential mortgages (one- to two-family residential mortgages account for nearly 60% of its loan portfolio and multifamily mortgages represent more than 15%). Other loan products include commercial real estate mortgages and land construction and consumer loans. Chicago-based Royal Financial Inc. agreed to buy Park Bancorp for $240 thousand in early 2016.

	Annual Growth	12/10	12/11	12/12	12/13	12/14
Assets ($ mil.)	(7.3%)	211.8	198.4	188.6	173.6	156.1
Net income ($ mil.)	–	(5.4)	(3.9)	(4.3)	(2.0)	(2.3)
Market value ($ mil.)	(36.5%)	4.3	2.4	1.6	1.5	0.7
Employees		57				

PARK CITY GROUP INC
NAS: PCYG

5282 South Commerce Drive, Suite D292
Murray, UT 84107
Phone: 435 645-2000
Fax: –
Web: www.parkcitygroup.com

CEO: Randall K. (Randy) Fields
CFO: Edward L. Clissold
HR: –
FYE: June 30
Type: Public

Park City Group understands that managing complex retail operations is no picnic. The company supplies retailers with operation management software used to optimize supply chains. Park City sells to supermarkets convenience stores and specialty retailers. Its software packages include Fresh Market Manager Supply Chain Profit Link and ActionManager. The company counts Circle K The Home Depot Williams-Sonoma and L Brands among its customers. Park City was founded by chairman and CEO Randy Fields who also co-founded Mrs. Fields Cookies. Fields controls almost half of Park City Group's stock.

	Annual Growth	06/15	06/16	06/17	06/18	06/19
Sales ($ mil.)	11.6%	13.6	14.0	18.9	22.0	21.2
Net income ($ mil.)	–	(3.8)	0.7	3.8	3.4	3.9
Market value ($ mil.)	(18.9%)	245.2	177.5	240.5	156.4	106.1
Employees	2.1%	68	66	77	77	74

PARK NATIONAL CORP (NEWARK, OH)
ASE: PRK

50 North Third Street, P.O. Box 3500
Newark, OH 43058-3500
Phone: 740 349-8451
Fax: –
Web: www.parknationalcorp.com

CEO: David L. Trautman
CFO: Brady T. Burt
HR: –
FYE: December 31
Type: Public

Customers can park their money with Park National. The holding company owns Park National Bank which operates more than 120 branches in Ohio and northern Kentucky through 11 community banking divisions. The banks provide an array of consumer and business banking services including traditional savings and checking accounts and CDs. Business loans including commercial leases and mortgages operating loans and agricultural loans account for about 35% of Park National's loan portfolio. The banks also originate consumer residential real estate and construction loans. Park National's nonbank units include consumer finance outfit Guardian Finance Scope Aircraft Finance and Park Title Agency.In 2018 it acquired Charlotte NC-based NewDominion Bank for some $75 million.

	Annual Growth	12/14	12/15	12/16	12/17	12/18
Assets ($ mil.)	2.7%	7,003.3	7,311.4	7,467.6	7,537.6	7,804.3
Net income ($ mil.)	7.0%	84.1	81.0	86.1	84.2	110.4
Market value ($ mil.)	(1.0%)	1,389.0	1,420.4	1,878.4	1,632.6	1,333.6
Employees	(0.3%)	1,801	1,793	1,726	1,746	1,782

PARK NICOLLET HEALTH SERVICES

3800 Park Nicollet Blvd.
Minneapolis MN 55416
Phone: 952-993-9900
Fax: 952-993-1392
Web: www.parknicollet.com

CEO: David K Wessner
CFO: David J Cooke
HR: –
FYE: December 31
Type: Private - Not-for-Pr

Park Nicollet Health Services helps Twin Cities medical patients get back on their feet and onto the playground. Park Nicollet operates Methodist Hospital a 425-bed acute care facility that offers a full range of medical and surgical care. It also runs about 30 Park Nicollet Clinic facilities in the Minneapolis/St. Paul metropolitan area that provide primary and specialty care services including cancer treatment and outpatient surgery. Additionally Park Nicollet Health Services operates the Park Nicollet Institute which performs medical research. In 2012 Park Nicollet agreed to merge with HealthPartners a Twin Cities health plan and hospital network operator.

PARK NICOLLET METHODIST HOSPITAL

6500 EXCELSIOR BLVD
SAINT LOUIS PARK, MN 554264702
Phone: 952-993-5000
Fax: –

CEO: David J. Abelson
CFO: David J. Cooke
HR: –
FYE: December 31
Type: Private

Park Nicollet Methodist Hospital helps keep residents swimmingly healthy in the City of Lakes. Operating as Methodist Hospital the acute care facility serves the greater Minneapolis area. It has some 430 beds and provides such specialized care programs as cancer treatment cardiovascular health emergency care obstetrics therapy for eating disorders and neurological rehabilitation. The facility is home to the Struthers Parkinson's Center which is devoted to helping patients with Parkinson's disease and their families to cope with the disease. Methodist Hospital is owned by Minnesota-based not-for-profit health care organization HealthPartners.

	Annual Growth	12/00	12/01	12/02*	06/05*	12/14
Sales ($ mil.)	(3.1%)	–	734.5	301.7	1.2	490.0
Net income ($ mil.)	150.8%	–	0.0	11.5	0.7	47.1
Market value ($ mil.)	–	–	–	–	–	–
Employees	–	–	–	–	–	2,503

*Fiscal year change

PARK STERLING CORP
NMS: PSTB

1043 E. Morehead Street, Suite 201
Charlotte, NC 28204
Phone: 704 716-2134
Fax: –
Web: www.parksterlingbank.com

CEO: –
CFO: –
HR: –
FYE: December 31
Type: Public

Park Sterling Corporation owns Park Sterling Bank which offers traditional deposit accounts and loans to individuals as well as small and midsized businesses through more than 55 branches mostly in North and South Carolina but also in northern Georgia and in Virginia. Commercial real estate and commercial and industrial business loans account for more than 70% of its loan portfolio while residential mortgages and home equity loans make up another 25%. The first Park Sterling Bank opened in 2006. Boasting over $3 billion in assets it is the largest community bank based in Charlotte North Carolina.

	Annual Growth	12/11	12/12	12/13	12/14	12/15
Assets ($ mil.)	22.6%	1,113.2	2,032.6	1,960.8	2,359.2	2,514.3
Net income ($ mil.)	–	(8.4)	4.3	15.3	12.9	16.6
Market value ($ mil.)	15.7%	183.0	234.6	320.3	329.7	328.3
Employees	16.2%	270	482	490	534	493

PARK-OHIO HOLDINGS CORP.   NMS: PKOH

6065 Parkland Boulevard   CEO: Edward F. Crawford
Cleveland, OH 44124   CFO: Patrick W. Fogarty
Phone: 440 947-2000   HR: –
Fax: –   FYE: December 31
Web: www.pkoh.com   Type: Public

Park-Ohio Holdings troubleshoots industrial supply chain logistics issues and makes a slew of fasteners and other industrial components. The company straddles three business segments: Supply Technologies sources and procures production components for OEMs in industries ranging from automotive to aerospace; Engineered Products produces specialized systems and parts used in such industrial applications as coatings forging oil and gas and rail; and the Assembly Components unit casts and machines metal parts — knuckles oil pans cylinders — used by auto agricultural construction and marine OEMs.

	Annual Growth	12/14	12/15	12/16	12/17	12/18
Sales ($ mil.)	4.7%	1,378.7	1,463.8	1,276.9	1,412.9	1,658.1
Net income ($ mil.)	4.1%	45.6	48.1	31.7	28.6	53.6
Market value ($ mil.)	(16.5%)	795.8	464.4	537.9	580.2	387.5
Employees	5.0%	6,000	6,000	5,900	6,100	7,300

PARKDALE MILLS INCORPORATED

531 Cotton Blossom Cir.   CEO: Anderson W Warlick
Gastonia NC 28054-5245   CFO: Cecelia Meade
Phone: 704-874-5000   HR: Ashley Cockerham
Fax: 704-874-5175   FYE: September 30
Web: www.parkdalemills.com   Type: Private

In an industry where margins are thread-thin Parkdale Mills spins cotton into cash. The North Carolina-based company is the largest privately owned yarn spinner in the US. It manufactures cotton and cotton-polyester blend yarns and specializes in spun yarn that winds up in such goods as sheets towels underwear and jeans. Parkdale Mills' global slate of customers include Jockey International Lands' End L.L. Bean and Springmaid. The company operates and owns 66% of Parkdale America a joint venture with polyester and nylon yarn maker Unifi. The company has about two dozen plants in the US Colombia and Mexico and a fiber research center. Its cotton consumption represents 30% of total US cotton demand.

PARKE BANCORP INC   NAS: PKBK

601 Delsea Drive   CEO: Vito S Pantilione
Washington Township, NJ 08080   CFO: John F Hawkins
Phone: 856 256-2500   HR: –
Fax: –   FYE: December 31
Web: www.parkebank.com   Type: Public

Community banking is a walk in the park for Parke Bancorp holding company for Parke Bank which has three branches in the New Jersey communities of Sewell and Northfield as well as two loan production offices in the Philadelphia area. The bank provides such traditional products as checking and savings accounts money market and individual retirement accounts and certificates of deposit. Parke Bank has a strong focus on business lending — including operating loans commercial mortgages and construction loans — which accounts for about 90% of the company's loan portfolio. The bank also writes residential real estate and consumer loans.

	Annual Growth	12/14	12/15	12/16	12/17	12/18
Assets ($ mil.)	15.6%	821.7	885.1	1,016.2	1,137.5	1,467.4
Net income ($ mil.)	24.1%	10.5	10.7	18.5	11.9	24.8
Market value ($ mil.)	12.8%	123.2	133.1	215.0	219.2	199.7
Employees	8.8%	70	84	86	91	98

PARKER DRILLING CO   NBB: PKDC

5 Greenway Plaza, Suite 100   CEO: Gary G. Rich
Houston, TX 77046   CFO: Jon-Al Duplantier
Phone: 281 406-2000   HR: –
Fax: –   FYE: December 31
                                                           Type: Public

Parker Drilling parks its oil rigs off the beaten path. Its helicopter-transportable rigs allow drillers to work in otherwise inaccessible desert mountain and remote jungle locations. Its barge rigs allow the company to drill in transition zones (such as bays and marshes). Parker Drilling owns 22 international land rigs and 18 US-based barge drilling rigs in the Gulf of Mexico and two land rigs in Alaska. Subsidiary Quail Tools provides rental tools for oil and gas drilling and workover activities with operations in the Gulf Coast the Rocky Mountains and West Texas regions. Parker Drilling also has project management and drilling rig construction units. In 2019 the company emerged from bankruptcy after filing for Chapter 11 bankruptcy protection the previous year.

	Annual Growth	12/14	12/15	12/16	12/17	12/18
Sales ($ mil.)	(16.1%)	968.7	712.2	427.0	442.5	480.8
Net income ($ mil.)	–	23.5	(95.1)	(230.8)	(118.7)	(165.7)
Market value ($ mil.)	–					
Employees	(8.4%)	3,443	2,567	2,199	2,266	2,425

PARKER HANNIFIN CORP   NYS: PH

6035 Parkland Boulevard   CEO: Thomas L. (Tom) Williams
Cleveland, OH 44124-4141   CFO: Catherine A. (Cathy) Suever
Phone: 216 896-3000   HR: Mark J. Hart
Fax: –   FYE: June 30
Web: www.parker.com   Type: Public

Parker-Hannifin is a leading global manufacturer of motion and control technologies including fluid power systems for the manufacturing and processing industries. It additionally makes hydraulic fuel pneumatic and electromechanical systems and components for the aerospace/defense industry; and motion and control systems for the heating ventilation air conditioning and refrigeration (HVACR) and transportation industries. It owns some 330 manufacturing plants and operates through the two business segments of Diversified Industrial and Aerospace. The company traces its historical roots back to 1918.

	Annual Growth	06/15	06/16	06/17	06/18	06/19
Sales ($ mil.)	3.0%	12,711.7	11,360.8	12,029.3	14,302.4	14,320.3
Net income ($ mil.)	10.6%	1,012.1	806.8	983.4	1,060.8	1,512.4
Market value ($ mil.)	10.0%	14,946.1	13,882.3	20,533.7	20,023.6	21,842.9
Employees	0.4%	54,754	48,950	56,690	57,170	55,610

PARKERVISION INC   NBB: PRKR

7915 Baymeadows Way, Suite 400   CEO: Jeffrey L Parker
Jacksonville, FL 32256   CFO: Cynthia L Poehlman
Phone: 904 732-6100   HR: –
Fax: –   FYE: December 31
Web: www.parkervision.com   Type: Public

Parkervision is more about sound than sight. The company develops radio frequency integrated circuits (RFICs) for use in wireless networking. The company has produced limited numbers of its chips through contract manufacturers but it has not recorded a sale in recent years. If it did the chips could be in mobile handsets tablets data cards femtocells machine-to-machine communications embedded applications even military radios and cable modems. ParkerVision was founded in 1989 by CEO Jeffery Parker. In 2014 it retained advisory firm 3LP Advisors to help execute a licensing strategy and get its business off the ground.

	Annual Growth	12/14	12/15	12/16	12/17	12/18
Sales ($ mil.)	–	0.0	0.0	4.1	0	0.1
Net income ($ mil.)	–	(23.6)	(17.1)	(21.5)	(19.3)	(20.9)
Market value ($ mil.)	(37.0%)	26.1	6.7	52.8	30.4	4.1
Employees	(24.4%)	49	23	25	50	16

1021

PARKRIDGE MEDICAL CENTER, INC.

2333 MCCALLIE AVE
CHATTANOOGA, TN 374043258
Phone: 423-698-6061
Fax: -
Web: www.parkridgehealth.com

CEO: -
CFO: Jay St Pierre
HR: Carole Hoffman
FYE: March 31
Type: Private

Parkridge Medical Center provides health care services in southern Tennessee. The hospital also operates two satellite facilities: Parkridge East Hospital another acute care facility and Parkridge Valley Hospital an adult and pediatric behavior health care facility. The hospitals combined have some 520 beds. Specialty services include cardiac surgery orthopedics and diagnostic imaging. The Sarah Cannon Cancer Center provides oncology therapeutics. Parkridge Medical Center is a subsidiary of HCA and is part of HCA's TriStar Health System.

	Annual Growth	03/06	03/07	03/08	03/09	03/17
Sales ($ mil.)	5.1%	-	-	-	216.0	322.4
Net income ($ mil.)	14.9%	-	-	-	24.7	74.7
Market value ($ mil.)	-	-	-	-	-	-
Employees	-	-	-	-	-	1,364

PARKWAY PROPERTIES INC.

NYS: PKY

Bank of America Center, 390 North Orange Avenue, Suite 2400
Orlando, FL 32801
Phone: 407 650-0593
Fax: -
Web: www.pky.com

CEO: -
CFO: -
HR: -
FYE: December 31
Type: Public

Parkway Properties knows its way around office spaces. The self-administered real estate investment trust (REIT) acquires owns and operates office properties throughout the Sunbelt region. Parkway owns or has an interest in more than 40 office properties with 10 million sq. ft. of leasable space in 10 states. Nearly a third of its portfolio is held through discretionary funds and joint venture partnerships through which the REIT receives fees for providing asset property and construction management. These services are offered through its subsidiary Parkway Realty Services which manages and leases offices for both its parent and third-parties.

	Annual Growth	12/10	12/11	12/12	12/13	12/14
Sales ($ mil.)	15.5%	256.3	165.9	226.5	291.6	456.7
Net income ($ mil.)	-	-	(2.6)	(126.9)	(39.4)	(19.7)	42.9
Market value ($ mil.)	1.2%	2,020.8	1,137.3	1,613.6	2,224.9	2,121.1
Employees	5.9%	256	341	286	326	322

PARKWEST MEDICAL CENTER

9352 PARK WEST BLVD
KNOXVILLE, TN 379234387
Phone: 865-373-1000
Fax: -
Web: www.treatedwell.com

CEO: -
CFO: Scott Hamilton
HR: Randall Carr
FYE: August 31
Type: Private

Parkwest Medical Center is a wholly-owned subsidiary of Covenant Health and the largest medical center in West Knoxville. Parkwest has more than 285 beds and provides health care services to patients of Knox County Tennessee. Its various specialties include cardiology orthopedics neurology and spine care women's services and bariatric surgery. Other services include cardiac rehabilitation diagnostic services outpatient surgery and senior health care. Parkwest's facilities include a 40-bed emergency care center a 30-bed critical care unit and a 20-suite childbirth center. The medical center also has a diabetes center and provides dental care.

	Annual Growth	12/04	12/05	12/13*	08/15	08/16
Sales ($ mil.)	5.5%	-	172.8	337.2	290.1	311.2
Net income ($ mil.)	21.0%	-	5.4	29.6	35.8	43.9
Market value ($ mil.)	-	-	-	-	-	-
Employees	-	-	-	-	-	1,300

*Fiscal year change

PARLUX FRAGRANCES LLC

NASDAQ: PARL

5900 N. Andrews Ave. Ste. 500
Fort Lauderdale FL 33309
Phone: 954-316-9008
Fax: 954-316-9152
Web: www.parlux.com

CEO: Frederick E Purches
CFO: Raymond J Balsys
HR: Fina Talpeer
FYE: January 31
Type: Subsidiary

If scents could speak Parlux Fragrances (from the French verb parler) might be its lexicon. The fragrance and beauty products designer and manufacturer owns and licenses to third-party manufacturers the perfumes and beauty-related products of a handful of celeb brand names including Paris Hilton Jessica Simpson Marc Ecko Nicole Miller Queen Latifah Rhianna and others. Parlux markets designer and other fragrance blends that are sold primarily through national department stores (Belk Macy's Boscov's) and 340 Perfumania retail stores in the US. Distributors from Canada to the Caribbean cater to retailers mainly perfumeries in 80 countries. Partner fragrance purveyor Perfumania acquired Parlux in 2012.

PARMA COMMUNITY GENERAL HOSPITAL

7007 POWERS BLVD
PARMA, OH 441295437
Phone: 440-743-3000
Fax: -
Web: www.uhhospitals.org

CEO: Patricia A Ruflin
CFO: Barry Franklin
HR: -
FYE: December 31
Type: Private

Parma Community General Hospital aka University Hospitals Parma Medical Center cares for residents of Ohio's Cuyahoga County and surrounding areas along the northern Lake Erie shoreline. The 332-bed acute care medical center has a staff of more than 500 physicians representing some 30 medical specialties. It offers a broad range of inpatient care services including cardiology oncology orthopedics and rehabilitation. Its outpatient and community outreach programs include home health hospice senior care diagnostic labs and various community health clinics. The hospital was founded in 1961.

	Annual Growth	12/11	12/12	12/13	12/15	12/16
Sales ($ mil.)	(0.6%)	-	183.6	180.5	180.9	179.2
Net income ($ mil.)	(4.0%)	-	2.5	(0.2)	3.8	2.1
Market value ($ mil.)	-	-	-	-	-	-
Employees	-	-	-	-	-	2,000

PARRON-HALL CORPORATION

7700 RONSON RD STE 100
SAN DIEGO, CA 921111553
Phone: 858-268-1212
Fax: -
Web: www.parronhall.com

CEO: -
CFO: -
HR: -
FYE: December 31
Type: Private

This company can outfit your conference room waiting area and hall. Parron-Hall which does business as Parron Hall Office Interiors sells office furniture to customers in the San Diego area. The company's inventory includes products manufactured by such companies as Kimball and Knoll as well as HON Humanscale and izzydesign. Parron Hall also offers space planning installation warehousing and maintenance services. Customers include California Highway Patrol Anheuser-Busch Garden Fresh Restaurant Corp. and Qualcomm. The company was founded in 1947 but grew out of a business founded in the 1880s by the great great grandfather of company president James Herr.

	Annual Growth	12/09	12/10	12/11	12/12	12/13
Sales ($ mil.)	(7.2%)	-	38.8	40.2	29.0	31.0
Net income ($ mil.)	(46.9%)	-	-	1.2	0.3	0.3
Market value ($ mil.)	-	-	-	-	-	-
Employees	-	-	-	-	-	49

PARSONS ENVIRONMENT & INFRASTRUCTURE GROUP INC.

4701 HEDGEMORE DR
CHARLOTTE, NC 282093281
Phone: 704-529-6246
Fax: -
Web: www.parsons.com

CEO: -
CFO: Leslie Bradley
HR: Debra Fiori
FYE: July 29
Type: Private

A unit of Parsons Corporation Parsons Commercial Technology Group (PARCOMM) provides project management engineering construction design maintenance and related services for industrial and commercial projects. The company's clients include firms in the telecommunications health care manufacturing defense petroleum and chemical industries. PARCOMM also completes projects for schools colleges and government entities. Specialized services include industrial environmental remediation factory modernization and developing state vehicle inspection and compliance programs. PARCOMM operates throughout the US and the world.

	Annual Growth	12/09	12/10	12/11	12/12*	07/14
Sales ($ mil.)	15.6%	-	-	443.1	684.1	684.1
Net income ($ mil.)	-	-	-	(57.2)	(12.0)	(12.0)
Market value ($ mil.)	-	-	-	-	-	-
Employees	-	-	-	-	-	1,205

*Fiscal year change

PARTNERS HEALTHCARE SYSTEM, INC.

800 BOYLSTON ST STE 1150
BOSTON, MA 021998123
Phone: 617-278-1000
Fax: -

CEO: Peter L. Slavin
CFO: Peter K. Markell
HR: -
FYE: September 30
Type: Private

Partners HealthCare operates two large acute-care medical centers — Brigham and Women's Hospital and Massachusetts General Hospital — and about 15 community hospitals in Boston and surrounding communities. The not-for-profit system also provides primary and specialty care through clinics physician offices rehabilitation centers long-term care facilities and home health and hospice agencies. Subsidiary MassHealth provides medical insurance to state residents. Partners HealthCare also provides medical training and research through an affiliation with Harvard. The organization has additional partnerships with health research and educational organizations around the globe.

	Annual Growth	09/06	09/07	09/08	09/10	09/15
Sales ($ mil.)	54.7%	-	-	551.0	8.1	11,665.6
Net income ($ mil.)	-	-	-	(44.1)	(0.1)	(916.1)
Market value ($ mil.)	-	-	-	-	-	-
Employees	-	-	-	-	-	67,000

PASADENA AREA COMMUNITY COLLEGE DISTRICT

1570 E COLORADO BLVD
PASADENA, CA 911062003
Phone: 626-585-7123
Fax: -
Web: www.pasadena.edu

CEO: -
CFO: -
HR: -
FYE: June 30
Type: Private

Pasadena City College (PCC) wants to hand out passes to higher education. PCC is a junior college offering associate's degree and vocational programs to more than 30000 students a year (including 1200 international students from more than 90 countries). Among its 60 academic programs are architecture computer science journalism and physics. The college also offers occupational training in 76 areas such as bookkeeping construction inspection hospitality and nursing. PCC also provides community enrichment programs through its Extended Learning Center which offers non-credit workshops and classes. The college staff includes about 400 faculty librarians counselors and administrators.

	Annual Growth	06/03	06/04	06/05	06/06	06/07
Sales ($ mil.)	(55.9%)	-	-	769.9	52.3	149.7
Net income ($ mil.)	72214.0%	-	-	0.0	3.0	89.4
Market value ($ mil.)	-	-	-	-	-	-
Employees	-	-	-	-	-	1,607

PASADENA HOSPITAL ASSOCIATION, LTD.

100 W CALIFORNIA BLVD
PASADENA, CA 911053010
Phone: 626-397-5000
Fax: -

CEO: Stephen A Ralph
CFO: Steven L Mohr
HR: -
FYE: December 31
Type: Private

No need to hunt for medical care if you're near Huntington Hospital. The not-for-profit Pasadena Hospital Association which does business as Huntington Hospital provides health care to residents of the San Gabriel Valley in Southern California. The hospital boasts some 625 beds and offers acute medical and surgical care and community services in a number of specialties including cardiology gastroenterology women's and children's health orthopedics and neurology. It engages in clinical cancer research (as well as diagnosis and treatment) through the Huntington Cancer Center. The hospital is also a teaching facility for the University of Southern California (USC) Keck School of Medicine.

	Annual Growth	12/13	12/14	12/15	12/16	12/17
Sales ($ mil.)	5.0%	-	-	593.6	695.7	654.4
Net income ($ mil.)	678.3%	-	-	0.3	8.5	15.2
Market value ($ mil.)	-	-	-	-	-	-
Employees	-	-	-	-	-	2,800

PASSUR AEROSPACE, INC.

NBB: PSSR

One Landmark Square, Suite 1900
Stamford, CT 06901
Phone: 203 622-4086
Fax: -
Web: www.passur.com

CEO: James T Barry
CFO: Louis J Petrucelly
HR: -
FYE: October 31
Type: Public

Anxious to arrive at your destination? PASSUR Aerospace's radar network provides arrival and departure information to airline pilots. Such information is displayed through various data management software used by airports and airlines to track landing and weather conditions. The company's FlightNews Live software displays information to passengers while FlightPerform gives pilots accurate estimated time of arrival and graphical flight positioning and OPSnet Airport Communicator incorporates messaging tools. Chairman and former CEO G.S. Beckwith Gilbert owns about 66% of the company.

	Annual Growth	10/15	10/16	10/17	10/18	10/19
Sales ($ mil.)	4.7%	12.5	14.9	13.9	14.8	15.0
Net income ($ mil.)	-	0.3	0.4	(3.5)	(5.5)	(3.8)
Market value ($ mil.)	(19.9%)	23.1	27.3	20.7	11.2	9.5
Employees	5.7%	44	49	62	56	55

PATAPSCO BANCORP INC.

OTC: PATD

1301 Merritt Boulevard
Dundalk, MD 21222-2194
Phone: 410 285-1010
Fax: -
Web: www.patapscobank.com

CEO: -
CFO: -
HR: -
FYE: June 30
Type: Public

Patapsco Bancorp deserves a pat on the back for its financial services. It is the holding company for The Patapsco Bank which serves the Baltimore area through about a half dozen branches. The bank provides personal and commercial services and products including checking and savings accounts CDs money market accounts and a variety of loans. Residential mortgages account for about a third of the bank's lending portfolio which also includes construction consumer and commercial real estate loans. Another Baltimore-area bank Bradford Bancorp announced plans to buy Patapsco in 2007 but later called off the deal after it could not secure adequate funding.

	Annual Growth	06/08	06/09	06/10	06/11	06/12
Assets ($ mil.)	(0.7%)	261.3	268.4	269.7	264.6	254.4
Net income ($ mil.)	-	1.4	(5.5)	(2.3)	(2.9)	(1.6)
Market value ($ mil.)	(46.1%)	14.2	6.7	4.9	1.5	1.2
Employees	(7.9%)	86	81	73	70	62

PATELCO CREDIT UNION

156 2nd St.
San Francisco CA 94105
Phone: 415-442-6200
Fax: 415-442-6245
Web: www.patelco.com

CEO: Erin Mendez
CFO: Sue Gruber
HR: –
FYE: December 31
Type: Private - Not-for-Pr

Just as communication from afar has progressed from smoke signals and carrier pigeons to today's World Wide Web Patelco Credit Union has evolved as well. Founded in 1936 it has grown from a five-member organization with $500 in assets serving employees of Pacific Telephone and Telegraph to a nearly 270000-member credit union serving employees with assets now totaling more than $3.6 billion. A telephone company credit union until 1983 Patelco Credit Union provides deposit lending insurance and investment services as well as credit cards debit cards and online banking. It operates through 40 branches in Northern California.

PATHEON INC.

4721 Emperor Blvd. Ste. 200
Durham NC 27703
Phone: 919-226-3200
Fax: 416-926-5410
Web: www.manulife.com

TORONTO: PTI
CEO: –
CFO: –
HR: –
FYE: October 31
Type: Public

Patheon makes the production path for pharmaceutical companies a little easier to tread. With facilities in North America and Europe the company provides contract development and manufacturing services to pharmaceutical biotechnology and specialty drug companies worldwide. It develops drug candidates at pre-formulation stage through final stages of launch commercialization and production. On the manufacturing services side it makes mainly prescription drugs in a wide variety of dosage forms — from solids to sprays. Customers include 18 of the top 20 largest pharmaceutical companies in the world.

PATHFINDER BANCORP, INC.

214 West First Street
Oswego, NY 13126
Phone: 315 343-0057
Fax: –

NAS: PBHC
CEO: –
CFO: –
HR: –
FYE: December 31
Type: Public

This bank wants customers beating a path to its door. Pathfinder Bancorp is the holding company for Pathfinder Bank which operates seven branches serving upstate New York's Oswego County and surrounding areas. Founded in 1859 the bank provides standard services such as checking and savings accounts money market accounts IRAs CDs and credit cards. It primarily originates residential real estate loans which account for the majority of the company's loan portfolio. The bank's Pathfinder Investment Services division provides mutual funds insurance brokerage and financial advisory services. Mutual holding company Pathfinder Bancorp M.H.C. owns nearly two-thirds of the company.

	Annual Growth	12/08	12/09	12/10	12/11	12/12
Assets ($ mil.)	7.9%	352.8	371.7	408.5	443.0	477.8
Net income ($ mil.)	63.8%	0.4	1.6	2.5	2.3	2.6
Market value ($ mil.)	13.3%	16.4	14.7	22.3	23.3	27.0
Employees	2.5%	107	109	116	119	118

PATHFINDER CELL THERAPY INC.

12 Bow Street
Cambridge, MA 02138
Phone: 617 245-0289
Fax: –

NBB: PFND
CEO: Richard L Franklin
CFO: John Benson
HR: –
FYE: December 31
Type: Public

Pathfinder Cell Therapy (formerly SyntheMed) keeps surgery patients and disease sufferers off the path towards scarring and organ damage. The company develops polymers aimed at preventing or reducing post-operative adhesions (scar tissue) for a variety of surgical procedures. Its REPEL-CV product used to prevent the formation of scar tissue in open heart surgeries is marketed internationally and is approved for use in pediatric cardiac surgeries in the US. The firm added development-stage tissue regeneration products for diabetics and others at risk of organ damage through its 2011 merger with biotech firm Pathfinder LLC; its name changed from SyntheMed to Pathfinder Cell Therapy following the merger.

	Annual Growth	12/10	12/11	12/12	12/13	12/14
Sales ($ mil.)	–	0.3	0.1	0.1	0.1	0.0
Net income ($ mil.)	–	(2.1)	(11.3)	(2.2)	(1.7)	(1.4)
Market value ($ mil.)	(75.3%)	133.4	33.4	13.3	9.3	0.5
Employees	18.9%	1	2	2	2	2

PATHFINDER INTERNATIONAL

9 GALEN ST STE 217
WATERTOWN, MA 024724523
Phone: 617-924-7200
Fax: –
Web: www.pathfinder.org

CEO: –
CFO: Mike Zeitouny
HR: Lee Gelb
FYE: June 30
Type: Private

Pathfinder International finds a way to provide reproductive health and family planning information and services to people in developing nations. The organization works in some 25 countries in Africa Asia Latin America and the Caribbean. It partners with local governments and other groups to provide access to sexual health and family planning information HIV/AIDS prevention and treatment advocacy for reproductive health policies worldwide abortion support where it's legal and post care where it isn't. Pathfinder also publishes newsletters resource lists guides and training information. Founded in 1957 it gets support from the US and European governments the United Nations and private sources.

	Annual Growth	06/12	06/13	06/14	06/15	06/16
Sales ($ mil.)	9.2%	–	99.9	102.9	107.8	130.2
Net income ($ mil.)	–	–	(1.1)	(1.7)	(3.1)	(2.3)
Market value ($ mil.)	–	–	–	–	–	–
Employees	–	–	–	–	–	628

PATHMARK STORES INC.

2 Paragon Dr.
Montvale NJ 07645
Phone: 201-573-9700
Fax: 201-505-3054
Web: www.pathmark.com/

CEO: Eric Claus
CFO: Frank Vitrano
HR: –
FYE: February 28
Type: Private

Pathmark Stores hopes it's finally on the upward path. The largest banner belonging to long-struggling grocery operator A&P Pathmark operates about 110 supermarkets under the Pathmark and Pathmark Sav-A-Center banners in densely populated areas in four states: Delaware New Jersey New York and Pennsylvania. Many of its stores are Pathmark Super Centers which offer an expanded selection of general merchandise and foods nearly all have pharmacies and more than half have in-store banks. Pathmark's owner A&P in 2012 emerged after 15 months in Chapter 11 bankruptcy as a private company following a financial restructuring and the closure of many stores including about half a dozen Pathmark locations.

PATIENT SAFETY TECHNOLOGIES INC. OTC: PSTX

27555 Ynez Rd. Ste. 330
Temecula CA 92591
Phone: 951-587-6201
Fax: 310-895-7751
Web: www.patientsafetytechnologies.com

CEO: –
CFO: –
HR: –
FYE: December 31
Type: Public

Patient Safety Technologies wants to give you one less thing to worry about on your next trip to the operating room. Its SurgiCount Medical subsidiary develops and markets the Safety-Sponge System which uses hand-held barcode scanning technology to help keep track of sponges and towels used during surgeries so that they don't go home inside patients. Hospitals and surgical centers first invest in the system and then must keep ordering the coded products. Cardinal Health is the exclusive distributor of SurgiCount Medical products. China-based A Plus International is the exclusive supplier of its bar-coded surgical dressings.

PATRICK CUDAHY INCORPORATED

1 Sweet Apple-Wood Ln.
Cudahy WI 53110
Phone: 414-744-2000
Fax: 414-744-4213
Web: www.patrickcudahy.com

CEO: –
CFO: –
HR: –
FYE: April 30
Type: Subsidiary

Patrick Cudahy established in 1888 calls itself the "Home of Sweet Apple Wood Smoked Flavor" and that says it all. The company makes sliced ham salami and specialty Italian and deli meats for sandwich shops delicatessens and fast-food operators. Its retail products include sausage bacon boneless hams lean ham and turkey products and sliced luncheon meats. The company has expanded its products to include Hispanic and Latino specialties including such items as chorizo salami higueral salchichon servecero and more. Patrick Cudahy also makes foodservice products and oils for industrial and institutional use. Patrick Cudahy is owned by US pork giant Smithfield Foods which purchased it in 1984.

PATRICK INDUSTRIES INC NMS: PATK

107 West Franklin Street, P.O. Box 638
Elkhart, IN 46515
Phone: 574 294-7511
Fax: –
Web: www.patrickind.com

CEO: Todd M. Cleveland
CFO: Joshua A. Boone
HR: Courtney A. Blosser
FYE: December 31
Type: Public

A recreational vehicle is just an empty motor home until Patrick Industries adds the finishing interior touches. The company makes and distributes a range of building materials and prefinished products primarily for the manufactured home (MH) recreational vehicle (RV) and marine industries. Patrick Industries manufactures decorative paper and vinyl panels moldings countertops doors and cabinet and slotwall components. In addition to these the firm distributes roofing siding flooring drywall ceiling and wall panels household electronics electrical and plumbing supplies and adhesives. Founded in 1959 the company operates more 100 manufacturing plants and more than 40 distribution centers and warehouses in about two dozen US states China Canada and the Netherlands.

	Annual Growth	12/14	12/15	12/16	12/17	12/18
Sales ($ mil.)	32.4%	735.7	920.3	1,221.9	1,635.7	2,263.1
Net income ($ mil.)	40.6%	30.7	42.2	55.6	85.7	119.8
Market value ($ mil.)	(9.4%)	1,034.7	1,023.4	1,795.1	1,634.0	696.6
Employees	30.5%	2,799	3,542	4,497	6,721	8,113

PATRIOT COAL CORP NBB: PATC A

12312 Olive Boulevard, Suite 400
St. Louis, MO 63141
Phone: 314 275-3600
Fax: –
Web: www.patriotcoal.com

CEO: –
CFO: –
HR: –
FYE: December 31
Type: Public

Patriot Coal Corporation is engaged in what many see as a patriotic US tradition — mining for metallurgical and thermal coal. With 11 mining complexes in Appalachia and the Illinois Basin Patriot Coal mines coal used for domestic and international electricity generation (about three-quarters of its production) and steel manufacturing in the eastern US. The company's operations include company-managed mines joint ventures and numerous contractor-operated mines placing about 1.8 billion tons of proved and probable coal reserves in 2013 under Patriot's control.

	Annual Growth	12/09	12/10	12/11	12/12	12/13
Sales ($ mil.)	(8.0%)	2,045.3	2,035.1	2,402.5	1,922.7	1,462.1
Net income ($ mil.)	(9.4%)	127.2	(48.0)	(115.5)	(730.6)	85.8
Market value ($ mil.)	–	–	–	–	–	–
Employees	3.4%	3,500	3,700	4,300	4,100	4,000

PATRIOT NATIONAL BANCORP INC NMS: PNBK

900 Bedford Street
Stamford, CT 06901
Phone: 203 324-7500
Fax: –
Web: www.pnbdirectonline.com

CEO: –
CFO: –
HR: Fred Staudmyer
FYE: December 31
Type: Public

What's red white blue and green? Why Patriot National Bancorp of course. It's the holding company for Patriot National Bank which operates about a dozen branches in affluent southwestern Connecticut and a handful more in neighboring New York. Serving consumers professionals and small to midsized businesses the bank offers checking savings and money market accounts as well as CDs IRAs and health savings accounts. Real estate loans including commercial mortgages residential mortgages and construction loans dominate its lending activities. To a far lesser extent the bank also originates business and consumer loans. PNBK Holdings acquired control of Patriot National Bancorp in 2010.

	Annual Growth	12/14	12/15	12/16	12/17	12/18
Assets ($ mil.)	10.7%	632.6	653.5	756.7	852.1	951.7
Net income ($ mil.)	(32.8%)	15.7	2.1	1.9	4.1	3.2
Market value ($ mil.)	71.8%	6.4	56.9	54.9	69.8	55.7
Employees	6.4%	92	101	99	109	118

PATRIOT SCIENTIFIC CORPORATION OTC: PTSC

6183 Paseo Del Norte Ste. 180
Carlsbad CA 92011
Phone: 760-547-2700
Fax: 760-547-2705
Web: www.ptsc.com

CEO: Carlton M Johnson Jr
CFO: Clifford L Flowers
HR: –
FYE: May 31
Type: Public

Patriot Scientific proudly designs microprocessors for licensing to other parties. Advanced Micro Devices which has an equity investment in the company licenses Patriot's microprocessor patent portfolio. AMD also has the rights to manufacture and sell Patriot's Ignite 32-bit stack microprocessor. Patriot is in litigation over patented microprocessor technology with other MPU suppliers. CASIO COMPUTER Fujitsu Hewlett-Packard Hoya NEC Nokia Philips Sharp and Sony among others have licensed technology from Patriot. The company also owns part of Scripps Secured Data Inc. (SSDI) and Talis Data Systems both network security software suppliers.

1025

PATTERN ENERGY GROUP INC
NMS: PEGI

1088 Sansome Street
San Francisco, CA 94111
Phone: 415 283-4000
Fax: –
Web: www.patternenergy.com

CEO: Michael M. Garland
CFO: Michael J. Lyon
HR: –
FYE: December 31
Type: Public

Pattern Energy wants to be the wind power beneath your energy wings. The company has eight wind power projects (six operating two under construction) in the US Canada and Chile with a generation capacity of more than 1000MW. Nearly all of the company's capacity is contracted to be sold under long-term agreements. Pattern Energy named for the patterns the company says it uses to maximize both production and profits was formed in late 2012 by Pattern Energy Group (PEG) to take over that company's power operations while it focuses on development. Pattern went public in 2013; it intends to use its $352 million in IPO proceeds to repay PEG which still controls it and for general corporate purposes.

	Annual Growth	12/14	12/15	12/16	12/17	12/18
Sales ($ mil.)	16.1%	265.5	329.8	354.1	411.3	483.0
Net income ($ mil.)	–	(31.3)	(32.5)	(17.1)	(17.9)	142.0
Market value ($ mil.)	(6.8%)	2,418.0	2,050.3	1,862.0	2,107.1	1,825.7
Employees	31.9%	69	116	140	210	209

PATTERSON COMPANIES INC
NMS: PDCO

1031 Mendota Heights Road
St. Paul, MN 55120
Phone: 651 686-1600
Fax: –
Web: www.pattersoncompanies.com

CEO: Mark S. Walchirk
CFO: Ann B. Gugino
HR: –
FYE: April 27
Type: Public

Patterson Companies' catalogs are like wish lists for veterinary and dental practices. The company operates through two primary segments — wholesalers Patterson Animal Health and Patterson Dental. Patterson Animal Health distributes animal supplies including pharmaceuticals parasiticides and equipment in the US Canada and the UK. Patterson Dental distributes products including X-ray film and machines hand instruments sterilization products dental chairs and lights and diagnostic equipment. Patterson Dental serves the US and Canada; some 85% of its sales come from the US.

	Annual Growth	04/15	04/16	04/17	04/18	04/19
Sales ($ mil.)	6.2%	4,375.0	5,386.7	5,593.1	5,465.7	5,574.5
Net income ($ mil.)	(21.8%)	223.3	187.2	170.9	201.0	83.6
Market value ($ mil.)	(17.9%)	4,591.2	4,130.0	4,238.7	2,263.7	2,086.5
Employees	2.7%	7,000	7,000	7,500	7,700	7,800

PATTERSON-UTI ENERGY INC.
NMS: PTEN

10713 W. Sam Houston Pkwy. N., Suite 800
Houston, TX 77064
Phone: 281 765-7100
Fax: –
Web: www.patenergy.com

CEO: William A. (Andy) Hendricks
CFO: C. Andrew (Andy) Smith
HR: –
FYE: December 31
Type: Public

Patterson-UTI Energy's pattern of activity is to drill for oil and gas. The company provides onshore contract drilling for oil and natural gas producers and operates 221 land-based rigs and a fleet of support vehicles. It has one of the largest land-based drilling fleets in North America behind that of Nabors Industries. Patterson-UTI complements its contract drilling business in Canada and across the US (Patterson-UTI Drilling) by providing pressure pumping services for oil and natural gas operators. Patterson-UTI's marketable drilling rigs have depth capabilities ranging from 10000 ft. to 25000 ft. and a total of 1 million hydraulic horsepower. In late 2016 the company agreed to buy Seventy Seven Energy.

	Annual Growth	12/14	12/15	12/16	12/17	12/18
Sales ($ mil.)	1.1%	3,182.3	1,891.3	915.9	2,356.7	3,327.0
Net income ($ mil.)	–	162.7	(294.5)	(318.6)	5.9	(321.4)
Market value ($ mil.)	(11.1%)	3,543.9	3,221.3	5,750.5	4,915.3	2,210.9
Employees	0.3%	7,900	3,400	3,600	8,000	8,000

PAUL HASTINGS JANOFSKY & WALKER LLP

515 S. Flower St. 25th Fl.
Los Angeles CA 90071-2371
Phone: 213-683-6000
Fax: 213-627-0705
Web: www.paulhastings.com

CEO: –
CFO: –
HR: –
FYE: January 31
Type: Private - Partnershi

Paul Hastings Janofsky & Walker has built a solid reputation in employment law and over the years companies such as United Parcel Service and Hughes Aircraft have turned to the firm for its expertise in the field. With about 900 attorneys Paul Hastings also practices in such areas as intellectual property litigation mergers and acquisitions and real estate. Paul Hastings operates from about 20 offices not only in the US but also in Europe and the Asia/Pacific region. The firm was founded in 1951; it adopted its current name in 1962.

PAVILION ENERGY RESOURCES INC.
PINK SHEETS: PVRE

261 S. Robertson Blvd.
Beverly Hills CA 90211
Phone: 310-288-4585
Fax: 713-706-6201
Web: www.americanspectrum.com

CEO: –
CFO: –
HR: –
FYE: June 30
Type: Public

Pavilion Energy Resources (formerly Energetics Holdings and before that formerly Global Business Services) has gone from the mailbox to the oil patch. In 2007 the company acquired Energetics a Texas-based oil and gas development company that holds an oil lease in Louisiana. In conjunction with the deal executives from Energetics took over at Global Business Services which then changed its name to Energetics Holdings. The next year the company again changed its name and the two groups rescinded the 2007 agreement to sell the company. Pavilion Energy Resources also holds oil and gas assets in Tennessee and Kentucky.

PAXTON MEDIA GROUP, LLC

100 TELEVISION LN
PADUCAH, KY 420037905
Phone: 270-575-8630
Fax: –

CEO: –
CFO: Richard Paxton
HR: –
FYE: December 28
Type: Private

Paxton Media Group owns about 30 daily newspapers in the Midwest and South including its flagship The Paducah Sun (Kentucky) and The Herald-Sun (Durham North Carolina). The company also owns several dozen weekly papers and more than 100 free papers as well as a television station in Paducah Kentucky. W.F. Paxton launched The Paducah Sun in 1896; his family led by CEO David Paxton continues to run the publishing business.

	Annual Growth	12/02	12/03	12/05	12/06	12/08
Sales ($ mil.)	–	–	0.0	0.0	204.5	188.2
Net income ($ mil.)	–	–	0.0	0.0	0.0	0.0
Market value ($ mil.)	–	–	–	–	–	–
Employees	–	–	–	–	–	2,000

PAYBOX CORP
NBB: PBOX

500 East Broward Boulevard, Suite 1550
Fort Lauderdale, FL 33394
Phone: 954 510-3750
Fax: 954 846-8841
Web: www.gopaybox.com

CEO: Matthew Oakes
CFO: –
HR: –
FYE: December 31
Type: Public

Direct Insite helps give its customers insight into their customers. The company's hosted software and services provide data mining and analysis reporting electronic invoice management and electronic bill presentment and payment functions. Its products are used to manage such functions as customer service workflows order processing dispute resolution and accounts payable and receivable. Direct Insite serves clients in more than 60 countries with its applications available in 15 languages and all major currencies. IBM is responsible for 51% of the company's sales while EDS accounts for 46%.

	Annual Growth	12/12	12/13	12/14	12/15	12/16
Sales ($ mil.)	(7.3%)	8.8	9.0	8.3	8.0	6.5
Net income ($ mil.)	–	0.5	0.2	0.1	0.6	(1.5)
Market value ($ mil.)	–	–	–	–	–	–
Employees	(4.8%)	45	46	38	33	37

PAYCHEX INC
NMS: PAYX

911 Panorama Trail South
Rochester, NY 14625-2396
Phone: 585 385-6666
Fax: 585 383-3428
Web: www.paychex.com

CEO: Martin Mucci
CFO: Efrain Rivera
HR: –
FYE: May 31
Type: Public

Paychex began as a payroll processing firm but has since expanded to offer a variety of human resources-related services. The company provides payroll services through its SurePayroll online application while its Paychex Flex platform integrates payroll processing with HR management employee benefits administration time tracking and employee performance management. Paychex processes the payrolls of more than 670000 clients making it the second-largest payroll accounting firm in the US after Automatic Data Processing. The company focuses on small and mid-sized businesses and serves clients throughout the US and Europe.

	Annual Growth	05/15	05/16	05/17	05/18	05/19
Sales ($ mil.)	8.3%	2,739.6	2,951.9	3,151.3	3,380.9	3,772.5
Net income ($ mil.)	11.3%	674.9	756.8	817.3	933.7	1,034.4
Market value ($ mil.)	14.8%	17,753.0	19,481.2	21,281.3	23,562.9	30,824.3
Employees	4.7%	13,000	13,500	13,700	14,300	15,600

PAYMENT ALLIANCE INTERNATIONAL INC.

One Paragon Centre 6060 Dutchmans Ln. Ste. 320
Louisville KY 40205-3277
Phone: 502-212-4000
Fax: 502-212-4004
Web: paymentallianceintl.com

CEO: David Dove
CFO: –
HR: –
FYE: December 31
Type: Private

Who carries cash anymore? Fewer and fewer people these days which is good news for Payment Alliance International (PAI). The company provides electronic payment processing and related services including electronic check authorization services and credit and debit card processing for merchants and banks. The company's ATM Services Group helps merchants outfit their stores with ATMs providing hardware software and maintenance services. It operates the largest ATM network in the US totaling more than 45000 machines. PAI also helps clients create gift card and loyalty programs. CEO John Leehy and COO Greg Sahrmann co-founded PAI in 2005.

PAYPAL INC.
CEO: Daniel H Schulman

2211 N. First St.
San Jose CA 95131
Phone: 408-967-1000
Fax: 408-376-7514
Web: www.paypal.com

CFO: –
HR: –
FYE: December 31
Type: Subsidiary

PayPal wants to be your best bud in the electronic payments industry. The company which is a subsidiary of eBay allows individuals and merchants to transfer money via personal computer or Web-enabled mobile phone with transactions charged to the customer's bank account credit card or PayPal account. The company earns fees mainly from payment transactions foreign exchange and withdrawals from foreign bank accounts as well as on its customer balances and PayPal-branded credit and debit cards. PayPal has about 80 million users in 190 markets and 25 currencies around the world. PayPal revenues account for about 40% of eBay's total sales.

PBF ENERGY INC
NYS: PBF

One Sylvan Way, Second Floor
Parsippany, NJ 07054
Phone: 973 455-7500
Fax: –
Web: www.pbfenergy.com

CEO: Thomas J. Nimbley
CFO: C. Erik Young
HR: Denise Guillory
FYE: December 31
Type: Public

Established US oil refiners meet the new kid on the block. Formed in the first decade of 21st century PBF Energy's five oil refineries are located in California Delaware Louisiana New Jersey and Ohio and have a combined production capacity of about 900000 barrels per day making the company the fourth-largest refiner in the US. PBF's refineries produce gasoline ultra-low-sulfur diesel heating oil jet fuel lubricants petrochemicals and asphalt for the Midwestern and Northeastern US. The company indirectly owns the general partner and approximately 44.2% of the limited partnership interest of PBF Logistics LP. PBF Energy is majority-owned by investment firms The Blackstone Group and First Reserve.

	Annual Growth	12/14	12/15	12/16	12/17	12/18
Sales ($ mil.)	8.2%	19,828.2	13,123.9	15,920.4	21,786.6	27,186.1
Net income ($ mil.)	–	(38.2)	146.4	170.8	415.5	128.3
Market value ($ mil.)	5.2%	3,193.4	4,412.6	3,342.1	4,249.5	3,916.3
Employees	17.5%	1,714	2,270	3,165	3,165	3,266

PBF ENERGY INC.
NYSE: PBF

1 Sylvan Way
Parsippany NJ 07054
Phone: 973-455-7500
Fax: 605-965-2203
Web: www.poet.com

CEO: Thomas J Nimbley
CFO: C Erik Young
HR: –
FYE: December 31
Type: Private

Oil refiners meet the new kid on the block. PBF Energy formed in 2008 and has since spent almost $1 billion buying three oil refineries from Valero and Sunoco. Its refineries located in Delaware New Jersey and Ohio have a combined production capacity of about 540000 barrels per day. The refineries produce gasoline ultra-low-sulfur diesel heating oil jet fuel lubricants petrochemicals and asphalt for the midwestern and northeastern US. PBF Energy which is majority-owned by investment firms The Blackstone Group and First Reserve went public in 2012 with an IPO that raised $429 million.

PC CONNECTION, INC.
NMS: CNXN

730 Milford Road
Merrimack, NH 03054
Phone: 603 683-2000
Fax: -
Web: www.connection.com

CEO: Timothy J. McGrath
CFO: William Schulze
HR: Richard P Saporito
FYE: December 31
Type: Public

You won't see a store on every street corner but PC Connection is just a click away. Doing business as Connection the company is a leading direct marketer of computer products and IT solutions in the US selling hardware software networking devices services and peripherals. It offers more than 425000 items from manufacturers such as Apple HP and Microsoft as well as a range of IT services. Through its websites catalogs and direct sales force Connection targets small and midsized businesses large corporations government agencies and educational institutions as well as individual consumers. The company dropped "PC" from its tradestyle in 2016 to reflect its mission of connecting people to technology and its range of products.

	Annual Growth	12/15	12/16	12/17	12/18	12/19
Sales ($ mil.)	2.3%	2,574.0	2,692.6	2,911.9	2,699.5	2,820.0
Net income ($ mil.)	15.1%	46.8	48.1	54.9	64.6	82.1
Market value ($ mil.)	21.7%	596.5	740.0	690.5	783.2	1,308.3
Employees	4.9%	2,155	2,501	2,505	2,513	2,609

PC GROUP INC.
PINK SHEETS: PCGR

450 Commack Rd.
Deer Park NY 11729-4510
Phone: 631-667-1200
Fax: 631-667-1203
Web: www.pcgrpinc.com

CEO: -
CFO: -
HR: -
FYE: December 31
Type: Public

PC Group (formerly Langer) wants feet and hands to be soft and comfortable. The firm makes a range of personal care products including soaps lotions and acne creams as well as gel-based therapeutic products. Its Silipos subsidiary makes gel-based foot and hand care products (such as bandages and wraps) for the consumer market as well as orthopedic supports and prosthetic liners for medical devices. PC Group's other main operating unit specialty soap maker Twincraft creates personal care products for mass marketers and specialty retailers including Bath & Body Works.

PC-TEL INC
NMS: PCTI

471 Brighton Drive
Bloomingdale, IL 60108
Phone: 630 372-6800
Fax: -
Web: www.pctel.com

CEO: David A Neumann
CFO: Kevin J McGowan
HR: Les Sgnilek
FYE: December 31
Type: Public

PCTEL wants to help its customers find the right connections. The company provides scanning receiver and antenna products to public and private telecom carriers and wireless infrastructure providers. Its products include a broad line of antennas (Bluewave MAXRAD) scanning receivers (SeeGull) and interference management products (CLARIFY). The company also generates a small portion of revenues from licensing intellectual property related to its discontinued modem business. The company sells directly and through resellers distributors and OEM equipment providers. PCTEL serves a variety of markets in addition to telecommunications such as transportation public safety health care energy and agriculture.

	Annual Growth	12/14	12/15	12/16	12/17	12/18
Sales ($ mil.)	(6.2%)	107.2	106.6	96.7	91.4	83.0
Net income ($ mil.)	-	4.6	(1.6)	(17.7)	3.8	(12.9)
Market value ($ mil.)	(16.1%)	158.2	83.1	98.3	134.7	78.4
Employees	(0.6%)	465	491	503	484	454

PCL CONSTRUCTION ENTERPRISES, INC.

2000 S COLORADO BLVD 2-500
DENVER, CO 802227908
Phone: 303-365-6500
Fax: -
Web: www.pcl.com

CEO: -
CFO: -
HR: -
FYE: October 31
Type: Private

PCL Construction Enterprises is the contractor to call on for commercial and civil construction concerns. The company serves as the parent to half a dozen US construction companies: PCL Construction Services PCL Civil Constructors PCL Construction PCL Industrial Services PCL Industrial Construction and Nordic PCL Construction. The companies serve as the operating entities for PCL one of Canada's largest general contracting groups. Having completed projects in nearly every US state PCL Construction Enterprises is active in the commercial institutional multi-family residential heavy industrial and civil construction sectors. PCL first entered the US construction market in 1975.

	Annual Growth	10/06	10/07	10/08	10/09	10/10
Sales ($ mil.)	(16.4%)	-	-	2,315.5	2,182.8	1,616.8
Net income ($ mil.)	(47.2%)	-	-	84.9	52.9	23.6
Market value ($ mil.)	-	-	-	-	-	-
Employees	-	-	-	-	-	3,300

PCM, INC
NMS: PCMI

1940 E. Mariposa Avenue
El Segundo, CA 90245
Phone: 310 354-5600
Fax: -
Web: www.pcm.com

CEO: -
CFO: Glynis A Bryan
HR: -
FYE: December 31
Type: Public

PCM markets and sells computer hardware software and services to corporate government and educational customers. The company offers products and services from the world's top technology vendors — including Apple Cisco Dell HP and Microsoft — and adds value by packaging multiple offerings into a comprehensive solution. Software is its largest product segment accounting for nearly 30% of sales; other products include desktops and notebooks displays and servers. PCM sells through websites and catalogs as well as a direct sales force. It generates most of its sales in the US.

	Annual Growth	12/13	12/14	12/15	12/16	12/17
Sales ($ mil.)	11.4%	1,424.2	1,356.4	1,661.9	2,250.6	2,193.4
Net income ($ mil.)	(21.5%)	8.1	5.5	(18.3)	17.6	3.1
Market value ($ mil.)	(0.9%)	121.0	112.1	117.0	265.0	116.6
Employees	9.3%	2,920	2,708	3,739	3,645	4,162

PCRE L.L.C

860 N. Main St.
Wallingford CT 06492
Phone: 860-571-7000
Fax: 860-571-7410
Web: www.prudentialct.com

CEO: -
CFO: -
HR: -
FYE: December 31
Type: Private

Prudential Connecticut Realty helps people buy and sell houses in the Constitution State home to some of the highest-priced homes in the US. The company has more than 60 sales offices throughout the state and some 1800 sales professionals. In addition to residential brokerage services Prudential Connecticut Realty provides relocation services referrals for renters and commercial real estate services. The company also has affiliates that provide financing escrow and insurance services. Chairman CEO and owner Peter G. Helie founded Prudential Connecticut Realty an independent member of Prudential Real Estate Affiliates in 1997.

PCS EDVENTURES! INC
NBB: PCSV

11915 W. Executive Dr., Ste. 101
Boise, ID 83713
Phone: 208 343-3110
Fax: –
Web: www.edventures.com

CEO: Robert O Grover
CFO: –
HR: –
FYE: March 31
Type: Public

PCS Edventures!.com provides science and engineering-based educational software for elementary and high school children. The company's software offerings include its Academy of Engineering Lab program which helps students understand simple machines gear systems and power transfer systems; Edventures! Lab which uses Lego materials for online engineering learning; Academy of Robotics Lab which teaches logic engineering and problem-solving skills; and Edventures in Language Arts which offers literacy learning activities for children.

	Annual Growth	03/14	03/15	03/16	03/17	03/18
Sales ($ mil.)	15.4%	1.9	2.9	3.3	2.3	3.3
Net income ($ mil.)	–	(1.0)	(1.4)	(0.4)	(1.8)	(0.9)
Market value ($ mil.)	(18.2%)	6.7	3.3	8.9	5.6	3.0
Employees	10.9%	13	13	16	–	–

PDC ENERGY INC
NMS: PDCE

1775 Sherman Street, Suite 3000
Denver, CO 80203
Phone: 303 860-5800
Fax: –
Web: www.pdce.com

CEO: Barton R. (Bart) Brookman
CFO: David W. (Dave) Honeyfield
HR: –
FYE: December 31
Type: Public

PDC Energy is an independent energy company that acquires explores and develops crude oil natural gas and NGL assets primarily in the Wattenberg Field in Colorado and the Delaware Basin in Texas. The company owns interests in approximately 2300 net wells and reported net proved reserves of nearly 1200 billion cu. ft. of natural gas equivalent.

	Annual Growth	12/14	12/15	12/16	12/17	12/18
Sales ($ mil.)	16.0%	856.2	595.3	382.9	921.6	1,548.7
Net income ($ mil.)	(66.2%)	155.4	(68.3)	(245.9)	(127.5)	2.0
Market value ($ mil.)	(7.8%)	2,728.1	3,528.6	4,797.8	3,407.0	1,967.2
Employees	15.0%	343	362	395	–	600

PDF SOLUTIONS INC.
NMS: PDFS

2858 De La Cruz Blvd.
Santa Clara, CA 95050
Phone: 408 280-7900
Fax: 408 280-7915
Web: www.pdf.com

CEO: John K. Kibarian
CFO: Gregory C. Walker
HR: Pamela Fong
FYE: December 31
Type: Public

PDF Solutions can solve chip design and manufacturing inefficiencies. The company provides software and services that help integrated circuit makers get more working chips out of a production batch. PDF's products are used to simulate model and analyze the chip design and manufacturing processes. As part of the Design-to-Silicon-Yield program PDF also receives a portion of customers' cost savings called gain share. The Exensio data analytics platform (in on-premise or cloud versions) helps customers draw information from manufacturing process data. Two customers — GLOBALFOUNDRIES and Samsung Electronics— collectively account for about 53% of sales. PDF Solutions generates about 54% of sales outside the US.

	Annual Growth	12/14	12/15	12/16	12/17	12/18
Sales ($ mil.)	(3.8%)	100.2	98.0	107.5	101.9	85.8
Net income ($ mil.)	–	18.5	12.4	9.1	(1.3)	(7.7)
Market value ($ mil.)	(13.2%)	481.2	351.0	730.2	508.4	273.0
Employees	0.4%	359	390	441	417	365

PDL BIOPHARMA INC
NMS: PDLI

932 Southwood Boulevard
Incline Village, NV 89451
Phone: 775 832-8500
Fax: –
Web: www.pdl.com

CEO: John P McLaughlin
CFO: Peter S. (Pete) Garcia
HR: –
FYE: December 31
Type: Public

If your body starts fighting you PDL BioPharma hopes to help you fight back. The company's antibody (protein) humanization technology makes it possible to alter mouse monoclonal antibodies (MAbs) for use in human therapies such as preventing and treating autoimmune diseases and cancer. The firm has licensed its technology to such companies as Genentech (a Roche subsidiary) Biogen and Chugai Pharmaceutical. PDL derives nearly all of its revenues from royalties on products including Genentech's cancer medications Herceptin and Avastin and Biogen's multiple sclerosis drug Tysabri.

	Annual Growth	12/14	12/15	12/16	12/17	12/18
Sales ($ mil.)	(23.6%)	581.2	590.4	244.3	320.1	198.1
Net income ($ mil.)	–	322.2	332.8	63.6	110.7	(68.9)
Market value ($ mil.)	(21.7%)	1,046.7	480.6	287.8	372.0	393.7
Employees	18.9%	10	10	11	14	20

PDS TECH, INC.

300 E JOHN CARPENTER FWY # 700
IRVING, TX 750622383
Phone: 214-647-9600
Fax: –
Web: www.pdstech.com

CEO: –
CFO: –
HR: Lorri Bloom
FYE: December 31
Type: Private

Need an IT pro to assist with your company's computer needs? PDS Tech wants to help. The company provides temporary technical industrial and general staffing services through more than 30 offices across the US with a concentration in Texas and on the East Coast. PDS Tech's specialties include aviation architecture engineering information technology administration and maritime staffing. Its PDS Engineering division handles engineering placement for the aerospace mechanical and structural engineering industries while the Information Services division offers technical consulting services in the IT and telecommunication industries. The company was founded in 1977 by aerospace engineer Art Janes.

	Annual Growth	12/13	12/14	12/15	12/16	12/17
Sales ($ mil.)	(8.2%)	–	339.6	321.4	287.8	262.5
Net income ($ mil.)	(69.5%)	–	0.4	0.7	0.3	0.0
Market value ($ mil.)	–	–	–	–	–	–
Employees	–	–	–	–	–	4,000

PEABODY ENERGY CORP (NEW)
NYS: BTU

701 Market Street
St. Louis, MO 63101-1826
Phone: 314 342-3400
Fax: –
Web: www.peabodyenergy.com

CEO: Glenn L. Kellow
CFO: Amy B. Schwetz
HR: Gregg Heaton
FYE: December 31
Type: Public

Peabody likes to be at the pinnacle of the coal industry. One of the world's leading pure-play coal companies Peabody supplies some 190 million tons of coal to major power and steel customers in some 25 countries. With a leading position in the US Powder River and Illinois basins Peabody sits on 5.2 billion tons of coal reserves across 23 mines. US customers primarily power companies account for most of Peabody's sales. Major operations (mainly in the US and Australia) include coal trading and brokering coalbed methane production transportation-related services and development of coal-based generating plants. Facing regulatory pressure and a down market Peabody sought Chapter 11 bankruptcy protection in 2016 from which it emerged in 2017.

	Annual Growth	12/15	12/16*	04/17*	12/17	12/18
Sales ($ mil.)	(0.2%)	5,609.2	4,715.3	1,326.2	4,252.6	5,581.8
Net income ($ mil.)	–	(1,996.0)	(739.8)	(216.5)	678.1	646.9
Market value ($ mil.)	(22.6%)	–	–	–	4,346.4	3,365.0
Employees	(0.9%)	7,600	6,700	–	7,100	7,400

*Fiscal year change

PEACEHEALTH

1115 SE 164TH AVE # 328
VANCOUVER, WA 986838003
Phone: 360-788-6841
Fax: –
Web: www.peacehealth.org

CEO: Liz Dunne
CFO: Kimberly Hodgkinson
HR: Amy Smith
FYE: June 30
Type: Private

PeaceHealth provides patients with a tranquil place to recover. Make that several tranquil places to recover. PeaceHealth serves residents in southeastern Alaska coastal regions of Washington and central portions of Oregon. Its medical centers include PeaceHealth Ketchikan Medical Center PeaceHealth St. Joseph Medical Center PeaceHealth St. John Medical Center Sacred Heart Medical Center (two campuses) Cottage Grove Community Hospital Peace Harbor Hospital PeaceHealth Peace Island Medical Center and PeaceHealth Southwest Medical Center. Other operations include physician practices community clinics hospices chemical dependency rehabilitation clinics and other outpatient facilities and services.

	Annual Growth	06/04	06/05	06/06	06/09	06/14
Sales ($ mil.)	10.0%	–	–	1,048.7	1,372.1	2,249.9
Net income ($ mil.)	1.3%	–	–	103.2	(88.9)	114.5
Market value ($ mil.)	–	–	–	–	–	–
Employees	–	–	–	–	–	6,690

PEAK RESORTS INC

17409 Hidden Valley Drive
Wildwood, MO 63025
Phone: 636 938-7474
Fax: –
Web: www.peakresorts.com

NMS: SKIS
CEO: Timothy D Boyd
CFO: Christopher J Bub
HR: Greg Fisher
FYE: April 30
Type: Public

If you can't fly to Aspen Peak Resorts offers a closer alternative for weekend skiers and snowboarders in the Midwest and Northeast. The company operates 14 ski resorts in 7 states - Indiana Missouri New Hampshire New York Ohio Pennsylvania and Vermont. Its two largest are Mount Snow in Vermont and Attitash in New Hampshire. The Mount Snow resort also has two hotels the Grand Summit and Snow Lake Lodge and Attitash offers a Grand Summit hotel. The company's resorts are open seasonally generally from December to April. In 2016 Peak Resorts acquired Hunter Mountain the Catskills' premier winter resort destination for $36.8 million.

	Annual Growth	04/14	04/15	04/16	04/17	04/18
Sales ($ mil.)	5.8%	105.2	104.9	95.7	123.2	131.7
Net income ($ mil.)	–	(1.5)	(1.9)	(3.2)	1.2	1.4
Market value ($ mil.)	(11.4%)	–	93.5	44.9	78.3	65.0
Employees	12.8%	–	450	630	600	646

PEAPACK-GLADSTONE FINANCIAL CORP.

500 Hills Drive, Suite 300
Bedminster, NJ 07921-0700
Phone: 908 234-0700
Fax: –
Web: www.pgbank.com

NMS: PGC
CEO: Douglas L. Kennedy
CFO: Jeffrey J. Carfora
HR: –
FYE: December 31
Type: Public

Peapack-Gladstone Financial is the $3.4 billion-asset holding company for the near-century-old Peapack-Gladstone Bank which operates more than 20 branches in New Jersey's Hunterdon Morris Somerset Middlesex and Union counties. Founded in 1921 the bank provides traditional deposit accounts credit cards and loans to individuals and small businesses as well as trust and investment management services through its PGB Trust and Investments unit. Multifamily residential mortgages represent nearly 50% of the company's loan portfolio while commercial mortgages make up around 15%. The bank also originates construction consumer and business loans.

	Annual Growth	12/14	12/15	12/16	12/17	12/18
Assets ($ mil.)	14.3%	2,702.4	3,364.7	3,878.6	4,260.5	4,617.9
Net income ($ mil.)	31.2%	14.9	20.0	26.5	36.5	44.2
Market value ($ mil.)	7.9%	358.9	398.7	597.1	677.2	486.9
Employees	7.5%	306	316	338	384	409

PEBBLEBROOK HOTEL TRUST

4747 Bethesda Avenue 1100
Bethesda, MD 20814
Phone: 240 507-1300
Fax: –
Web: www.pebblebrookhotels.com

NYS: PEB
CEO: Jon E. Bortz
CFO: Raymond D. Martz
HR: –
FYE: December 31
Type: Public

Pebblebrook Hotel Trust wants the term staycation to take a vacation. The self-managed real estate investment trust (REIT) acquires and manages upscale hotels in the US targeting mostly full-service and select-service luxury properties that don't need major renovation in major US gateway cities. The REIT owns more than 30 hotels (with 7400 rooms) across 11 states and has a 49% interest in six more hotels spanning nearly 1800 rooms through its Manhattan Collection joint venture. Nearly 70% of its revenue comes from room fees while the remainder comes from food and beverage services. Pebblebrook Hotel Trust is the brainchild of CEO Jon Bortz who also founded LaSalle Hotel Properties.

	Annual Growth	12/14	12/15	12/16	12/17	12/18
Sales ($ mil.)	8.5%	598.8	770.9	816.4	769.3	828.7
Net income ($ mil.)	(34.5%)	72.9	94.7	73.7	99.9	13.4
Market value ($ mil.)	(11.2%)	5,946.1	3,651.3	3,876.8	4,843.7	3,689.1
Employees	16.7%	27	27	26	28	50

PEDERNALES ELECTRIC COOPERATIVE, INC.

201 S AVENUE F
JOHNSON CITY, TX 786364827
Phone: 830-868-7155
Fax: –
Web: www.pec.coop

CEO: John Hewa
CFO: –
HR: –
FYE: December 31
Type: Private

Created by Texas ranchers and business owners Pedernales Electric Cooperative provides electricity services in the Texas Hill Country. The company the largest electric cooperative in the US purchases its electricity from wholesale providers primarily the Lower Colorado River Authority (LCRA) and transmits and distributes it to about 209350 cooperative members (or more than 247810 individual customer meters). Pedernales Electric Cooperative operates more than 17450 miles of power line and maintains 290000 wooden utility poles in its service area.

	Annual Growth	12/07	12/08	12/09	12/10	12/11
Sales ($ mil.)	0.9%	–	–	578.7	550.8	589.1
Net income ($ mil.)	(66.5%)	–	–	57.6	53.7	6.5
Market value ($ mil.)	–	–	–	–	–	–
Employees	–	–	–	–	–	741

PEDEVCO CORP

575 N. Dairy Ashford, Suite 210
Houston, TX 77079
Phone: 713 221-1768
Fax: –
Web: www.pacificenergydevelopment.com

ASE: PED
CEO: Simon Kukes
CFO: –
HR: –
FYE: December 31
Type: Public

Blast Energy Services (formerly Verdisys) is having a blast helping its customers keep pumping out oil from mature fields. Using specially fabricated mobile drilling rigs the company provides a range of oil and gas services including lateral drilling and well production enhancement. The company which emerged from Chapter 11 bankruptcy protection in 2008 acquired $1.2 million of oil and gas properties in Matagorda County Texas in 2010 as a way to expand its revenue base and to fund the development of its proprietary Applied Fluid Jetting drilling activity. To raise cash in 2011 it sold its oilfield satellite telecommunications services unit to GlobaLogix.

	Annual Growth	12/14	12/15	12/16	12/17	12/18
Sales ($ mil.)	(1.5%)	4.8	5.3	4.0	3.0	4.5
Net income ($ mil.)	–	(29.9)	(21.3)	(19.6)	(36.4)	53.6
Market value ($ mil.)	14.0%	7.1	4.6	1.8	5.1	12.0
Employees	(1.7%)	15	11	6	6	14

PEDIATRIC SERVICES OF AMERICA INC.

310 Technology Pkwy.
Norcross GA 30092-2929
Phone: 770-441-1580
Fax: 770-263-9340
Web: www.psahealthcare.com

CEO: Daniel J Kohl
CFO: James M McNeill
HR: –
FYE: September 30
Type: Private

Pediatric Services of America (doing business as PSA Healthcare) knows there's no place like home especially when you're a sick kid. The pediatric home health care company provides in-home nursing and related services for infants and children through locations in about 17 states. It also provides limited in-home nursing services for adults with severe conditions. The company offers some outpatient rehabilitation and nursing through pediatric day treatment centers in Florida and Georgia. Additionally PSA Healthcare offers discharge planning services that arrange for the transfer of patients from hospital to home and the supply of medical equipment. The company is owned by private investment firm Portfolio Logic.

PEERLESS SYSTEMS CORP.

1055 Washington Blvd., 8th Floor
Stamford, CT 06901
Phone: 203 350-0040
Fax: –
Web: www.peerless.com

NAS: PRLS
CEO: Anthony Bonid
CFO: Yi Tsai
HR: –
FYE: January 31
Type: Public

Peerless Systems lets you peer at digitally produced images more easily. Peerless proffers software-based imaging systems embedded in printers copiers scanners and other digital devices. Its products include designs for application-specific integrated circuits (ASICs) printer drivers and network interfaces that let digital document companies like Adobe and Ricoh incorporate networking support or multifunction features into equipment. Peerless also offers related engineering services. Top customers include Konica Minolta Kyocera Mita Novell and Seiko Epson which together account for more than three-quarters of sales. About 90% of the company's revenues comes from customers in Japan.

	Annual Growth	01/09	01/10	01/11	01/12	01/13
Sales ($ mil.)	(30.0%)	10.4	4.8	6.2	3.7	2.5
Net income ($ mil.)	(43.7%)	17.6	7.2	4.1	1.4	1.8
Market value ($ mil.)	17.1%	5.7	8.0	10.7	12.3	10.7
Employees	(24.0%)	9	5	6	5	3

PEET'S COFFEE & TEA INC.

1400 Park Ave.
Emeryville CA 94608-3520
Phone: 510-594-2100
Fax: 510-594-2180
Web: www.peets.com

NASDAQ: PEET
CEO: David Burwick
CFO: –
HR: –
FYE: December 31
Type: Private

Peet's Coffee & Tea enjoys the daily grind. The company owns and operates about 195 coffee shops in California and half a dozen other states offering java lovers about 25 types of whole bean and fresh ground coffee including about 15 blends. Its teas run the spectrum from India black to herbal blends. The stores also offer freshly brewed coffee biscotti and other pastries along with mugs and brewing equipment. In addition to its retail operation Peet's sells coffee through retail grocery chains such as Safeway and Whole Foods and through its own online mail order operation. The company which also supplies coffee to foodservice operators was acquired in 2012 by privately-held Joh. A. Benckiser.

PEGASYSTEMS INC

One Rogers Street
Cambridge, MA 02142-1209
Phone: 617 374-9600
Fax: –
Web: www.pega.com

NMS: PEGA
CEO: Alan Trefler
CFO: Ken Stillwell
HR: Jeff Yanagi
FYE: December 31
Type: Public

Pegasystems helps companies fly through business changes without being reined in by their old processes. The company provides a range of enterprise software applications that include customer relationship management business process management business rules management systems and more. The company's Pega Platform serves as the base for its software development and is licensed to customers for their development needs. Pegasystems targets companies in the financial services insurance and health care industries. Established in 1983 Pegasystems also offers cloud-based systems software maintenance consulting and training. International customers account for about 45% of the company's revenue.

	Annual Growth	12/14	12/15	12/16	12/17	12/18
Sales ($ mil.)	10.9%	590.0	682.7	750.3	840.6	891.6
Net income ($ mil.)	(24.8%)	33.3	36.3	27.0	32.9	10.6
Market value ($ mil.)	23.2%	1,631.0	2,159.5	2,826.9	3,702.5	3,755.9
Employees	11.9%	2,970	3,333	3,908	4,237	4,650

PEN INC

701 Brickell Ave., Suite 1550
Florida, MI 33131
Phone: 844 273-6462
Fax: –
Web: www.appliednanotech.net

NBB: PENC
CEO: Scott E Rickert
CFO: –
HR: –
FYE: December 31
Type: Public

Applied Nanotech Holdings hopes to make it big by thinking small. The company conducts research on carbon nanotubes — molecular-sized cylindrical structures that could be used in making electronic displays and other products. Applied Nanotech derives most of its revenues from contracts with agencies of the US government or by doing research on a contract basis with other entities. The company is developing nanomaterials for use in epoxies glass fibers and nylons. Other applications of carbon nanotube technology are in conductive inks (used in communications instrumentation flexible electronics printed circuit boards and radio-frequency identification tags) sensors and thermal management.

	Annual Growth	12/14	12/15	12/16	12/17	12/18
Sales ($ mil.)	(18.8%)	10.0	9.7	8.1	7.9	4.3
Net income ($ mil.)	–	(2.4)	(1.9)	(0.6)	(0.7)	(0.1)
Market value ($ mil.)	41.4%	0.2	0.0	6.4	4.7	0.8
Employees	(21.4%)	34	38	27	15	13

PENDRELL CORP

2300 Carillon Point
Kirkland, WA 98033
Phone: 425 278-7100
Fax: –
Web: www.pendrell.com

NBB: PCOA
CEO: Lee E Mikles
CFO: Steven A Ednie
HR: –
FYE: December 31
Type: Public

Pendrell is an asset management company of the intellectual property (IP) kind. It gathers up patents (it holds about 1200) and licenses them to technology companies thus receiving a cut when a technology is used. Its patent holdings center on technologies for tablets smart phones and other consumer electronics devices. Besides licensing IP Pendrell also develops technologies though none generate revenue yet. Companies that license IP from Pendrell include Casio Hitachi LG Electronics Microsoft Nokia Technicolor and Xerox.

	Annual Growth	12/13	12/14	12/15	12/16	12/17
Sales ($ mil.)	34.4%	13.1	42.5	43.5	59.0	42.8
Net income ($ mil.)	–	(55.1)	(51.0)	(109.7)	17.8	19.1
Market value ($ mil.)	–	0.0	0.0	0.0	0.0	0.6
Employees	(36.3%)	73	57	16	14	12

PENFORD CORP.
NMS: PENX

7094 South Revere Parkway
Centennial, CO 80112-3932
Phone: 303 649-1900
Fax: –
Web: www.penx.com

CEO: Thomas D Malkoski
CFO: Steven O Cordier
HR: –
FYE: August 31
Type: Public

Penford Corporation doesn't mind its reputation for being stiff and starchy — that's how it makes its money. The company makes carbohydrate-based specialty starches used by the paper packaging and food industries. Paper and packaging manufacturers use the specialty starches and film-forming ingredients from Penford's industrial ingredients segment to improve the strength and quality of containers and magazine and catalog paper. The division also produces and sells ethanol from corn. The company's food ingredients segment makes starches and dextrins that improve the crispness texture and shelf life of various food products (including pet food and treats). Penford generates most of its sales in the US.

	Annual Growth	08/10	08/11	08/12	08/13	08/14
Sales ($ mil.)	14.9%	254.3	315.4	361.4	467.3	443.9
Net income ($ mil.)	3.8%	6.7	(5.1)	(9.6)	4.0	7.8
Market value ($ mil.)	29.1%	62.4	70.0	93.1	172.6	173.5
Employees	7.6%	330	333	396	403	443

PENGUIN COMPUTING, INC.

45800 NORTHPORT LOOP W
FREMONT, CA 945386413
Phone: 415-954-2800
Fax: –
Web: www.penguincomputing.com

CEO: Tom Coull
CFO: Lisa Cummins
HR: –
FYE: December 31
Type: Private

Penguin Computing hopes to save the world from the cold clutches of monopolistic operating systems. The company builds and customizes Linux-based workstations servers and clustered computing systems. It also offers third-party storage and peripheral equipment. The company's Scyld Software subsidiary which it acquired in 2003 develops clustered computing software including its Scyld Beowulf operating system. Penguin's customers have included Brookhaven National Laboratory CACI International Caterpillar Duke University Genentech the National Institutes of Health Northrop Grumman and Stanford University. Penguin was founded in 1998.

	Annual Growth	12/01	12/02	12/03	12/04	12/17
Sales ($ mil.)	–	–	(847.1)	17.9	21.9	166.5
Net income ($ mil.)	104.9%	–	0.0	(0.5)	(2.5)	5.7
Market value ($ mil.)	–	–	–	–	–	–
Employees	–	–	–	–	–	175

PENN NATIONAL GAMING INC
NMS: PENN

825 Berkshire Blvd., Suite 200
Wyomissing, PA 19610
Phone: 610 373-2400
Fax: 610 376-2842
Web: www.pngaming.com

CEO: Timothy J. (Tim) Wilmott
CFO: William J. (BJ) Fair
HR: Chris Mcgivern
FYE: December 31
Type: Public

Penn National Gaming is a leading regional gaming company that operates or has ownership interests in 42 casinos racing facilities and video gaming terminals across the US. Its holdings feature about 51000 gaming machines more than 1300 table games and 9000 hotel rooms. Many of its properties operate under the Hollywood and Argosy brands. Other facilities include the Tropicana on the Las Vegas Strip; racetracks (horseracing and greyhounds) in Florida New Jersey and Texas; and riverboat and dockside casinos mostly in the Midwest and the South. The firm also offers online gaming through Penn Interactive Ventures. Penn gained 12 properties through its $2.8 billion acquisition of Pinnacle Entertainment in 2018.

	Annual Growth	12/14	12/15	12/16	12/17	12/18
Sales ($ mil.)	8.5%	2,590.3	2,838.4	3,034.4	3,148.0	3,587.9
Net income ($ mil.)	–	(233.2)	0.7	109.3	473.5	93.5
Market value ($ mil.)	8.2%	1,602.1	1,869.3	1,609.1	3,655.8	2,197.2
Employees	11.5%	16,650	18,204	18,808	18,754	25,750

PENN VIRGINIA CORP (NEW)
NMS: PVAC

16285 Park Ten Place, Suite 500
Houston, TX 77084
Phone: 713 722-6500
Fax: –
Web: www.pennvirginia.com

CEO: John A Brooks
CFO: Russell T Kelley Jr
HR: –
FYE: December 31
Type: Public

Incorporated in Virginia and based in Pennsylvania Penn Virginia is an oil and gas exploration and production company operating primarily in South Texas (Eagle Ford Shale). It also has assets in the Mid-Content Mississippi and to a much lesser extent in Appalachia (Marcellus Shale). In 2014 it reported proved reserves of 115 million barrels of oil equivalent of which 77% were oil and natural gas liquids (NGLs) and 40% were proved developed. That year some 83% of the company's proved reserves were located in Texas. Sales of crude oil from the Eagle Ford play accounted for the bulk of Penn Virginia's total revenues in 2014. Denbury Resources announced plans to acquire Penn Virginia for approximately $1.7 billion in 2018.

	Annual Growth	12/15*	09/16*	12/16	12/17	12/18
Sales ($ mil.)	13.0%	305.3	94.3	39.0	160.1	440.8
Net income ($ mil.)	–	(1,583.0)	1,054.6	(5.3)	32.7	224.8
Market value ($ mil.)	5.0%	–	–	738.9	589.8	815.3
Employees	(5.3%)	112	–	59	80	95

*Fiscal year change

PENNANTPARK INVESTMENT CORPORATION
NASDAQ: PNNT

590 Madison Ave. 15th Fl.
New York NY 10022
Phone: 212-905-1000
Fax: 212-905-1075
Web: www.pennantpark.com

CEO: Arthur H Penn
CFO: Aviv Efrat
HR: –
FYE: September 30
Type: Public

PennantPark Investment believes that the higher the leverage the greater the reward. A business development company and closed-end investment firm PennantPark makes debt and equity investments primarily in highly-leveraged (companies with more debt than equity) middle market firms. It invests in senior secured loans mezzanine debt and equity investments and it typically contributes between $10 million and $50 million per transaction. The firm's portfolio comprises 45 companies that operate in a wide range of industries including business services aerospace and defense health care education hospitality and chemicals. Formed in 2007 PennantPark is externally managed by PennantPark Investment Advisers.

PENNEY (J.C.) CO.,INC. (HOLDING CO.)
NYS: JCP

6501 Legacy Drive
Plano, TX 75024-3698
Phone: 972 431-1000
Fax: –
Web: www.jcpenney.com

CEO: Marvin R. Ellison
CFO: Jeffrey (Jeff) Davis
HR: Brynn L. Evanson
FYE: February 02
Type: Public

J. C. Penney Company is a holding company for department store operator J. C. Penney Corp. One of the largest department store and e-commerce retailers in the US J. C. Penney Corp. operates more than 860 JCPenney department stores across the country and in Puerto Rico. Its stores are mostly found in suburban shopping malls and sell clothing for men women and children as well as footwear accessories homeware and curtains and drapes. Some stores contain styling salons optical centers and portrait studios as well as shop-in-shops such as Sephora cosmetics. J. C. Penney Corp. has been closing stores amid a tough retail environment.

	Annual Growth	01/15	01/16	01/17*	02/18	02/19
Sales ($ mil.)	(0.5%)	12,257.0	12,625.0	12,547.0	12,506.0	12,019.0
Net income ($ mil.)	–	(771.0)	(513.0)	1.0	(116.0)	(255.0)
Market value ($ mil.)	(34.7%)	2,298.0	2,294.9	2,038.8	1,119.0	417.3
Employees	(4.5%)	114,000	105,000	106,000	98,000	95,000

*Fiscal year change

PENNICHUCK CORPORATION   NASDAQ: PNNW

25 Manchester St.   CEO: Duane C Montopoli
Merrimack NH 03054   CFO: Thomas C Leonard
Phone: 603-882-5191   HR: –
Fax: 603-882-4125   FYE: December 31
Web: www.pennichuck.com   Type: Government-owned

How much water would Pennichuck pump if Pennichuck could pump water? Well Pennichuck does pump water to about 33200 customers (about 120000 people) in New Hampshire and Massachusetts. Its water utility subsidiaries — Pennichuck Water Works Pennichuck East Utility and Pittsfield Aqueduct — distribute water in more than 30 communities including the city of Nashua. Most of the company's water comes from a system of ponds. Nonregulated subsidiary The Southwood Corporation develops and sells real estate and Pennichuck Water Service offers contract maintenance testing and billing services. In 2012 the company was acquired by the City of Nashua.

PENNONI ASSOCIATES INC.

1900 MARKET ST FL 3   CEO: –
PHILADELPHIA, PA 191033511   CFO: Stacey M McPeak
Phone: 215-222-3000   HR: –
Fax: –   FYE: December 31
                                         Type: Private

Design consulting and engineering firm Pennoni Associates specializes in the creation of civil infrastructure projects. The company offers construction services planning surveys transportation planning lab testing environmental engineering landscape architecture site design and other services. Pennoni serves East Coast clients including government entities and private companies. Affiliate Pennoni Engineering and Surveying of New York specializes in heating ventilation and air conditioning systems electrical plumbing and fire protection engineering. The employee-owned company was established by chairman Celestino "Chuck" Pennoni in 1966.

	Annual Growth	12/12	12/13	12/14	12/16	12/17
Sales ($ mil.)	11.2%	–	127.6	146.2	180.2	195.3
Net income ($ mil.)	57.8%	–	1.2	1.6	1.5	7.2
Market value ($ mil.)	–	–	–	–	–	–
Employees	–	–	–	–	–	900

PENNS WOODS BANCORP, INC. (JERSEY SHORE, PA)   NMS: PWOD

300 Market Street, P.O. Box 967   CEO: Richard A. Grafmyre
Williamsport, PA 17703-0967   CFO: Brian L. Knepp
Phone: 570 322-1111   HR: –
Fax: –   FYE: December 31
Web: www.jssb.com   Type: Public

Penns Woods Bancorp (PWB) is the holding company for Jersey Shore State Bank (named for the Pennsylvania town not the coastal vacation spot) which serves north central Pennsylvania through about a dozen branches. The bank accepts deposits from individuals and local businesses offering checking and savings accounts money market and NOW accounts and CDs. Residential real estate loans and commercial mortgages make up the majority of the bank's loan portfolio. The bank's lending activities are rounded out by agricultural commercial and consumer loans. PWB also owns Luzerne Bank which operates eight branch offices providing financial services in Pennsylvania.

	Annual Growth	12/14	12/15	12/16	12/17	12/18
Assets ($ mil.)	7.9%	1,245.0	1,320.1	1,348.6	1,474.5	1,684.8
Net income ($ mil.)	0.2%	14.6	13.9	12.5	9.8	14.7
Market value ($ mil.)	(4.9%)	346.7	298.8	355.4	327.8	283.2
Employees	3.7%	284	308	296	319	328

PENNSYLVANIA - AMERICAN WATER COMPANY

800 W HERSHEY PARK DR   CEO: –
HERSHEY, PA 170332400   CFO: –
Phone: 717-533-5000   HR: –
Fax: –   FYE: December 31
                                         Type: Private

Pennsylvania-American Water distributes water and provides wastewater services to a population of more than 2 million people in some 390 communities across Pennsylvania. The company serves 635000 water customers and 17500 wastewater customers. It operates about 35 water treatment plants six wastewater facilities and 9800 miles of pipeline. Pennsylvania-American Water's service territory covers some three dozen Pennsylvania counties. The utility the largest regulated water and wastewater service provider in Pennsylvania is a subsidiary of New Jersey-based American Water Works.

	Annual Growth	12/12	12/13*	03/14*	06/14*	12/17
Sales ($ mil.)	3.7%	–	571.2	584.0	589.8	661.1
Net income ($ mil.)	7.1%	–	122.1	128.2	127.8	160.7
Market value ($ mil.)	–	–	–	–	–	–
Employees	–	–	–	–	–	1,007

*Fiscal year change

PENNSYLVANIA ELECTRIC COMPANY

76 S MAIN ST BSMT   CEO: Charles E Jones
AKRON, OH 443081817   CFO: Mark T Clark
Phone: 800-545-7741   HR: Josh Martin
Fax: –   FYE: December 31
Web: www.firstenergycorp.com   Type: Private

Pennsylvania Electric (Penelec) has elected to provide power to the people of the Keystone State. The company distributes power to a population of 1.6 million in a 17600-square-mile portion of northern western and south-central Pennsylvania. The utility operates more than 20170 miles of distribution and more than 2700 transmission lines. The Waverly Electric Light & Power Company a subsidiary of Penelec provides electric services to a population of about 8400 in Waverly New York. Penelec is an operating subsidiary of regional utility power player FirstEnergy.

	Annual Growth	12/08	12/09	12/10	12/16	12/17
Sales ($ mil.)	(5.9%)	–	1,448.9	1,539.9	904.8	893.8
Net income ($ mil.)	4.9%	–	65.4	59.5	88.4	95.5
Market value ($ mil.)	–	–	–	–	–	–
Employees	–	–	–	–	–	896

PENNSYLVANIA HIGHER EDUCATION ASSISTANCE AGENCY

1200 N. 7th St.   CEO: James L Preston
Harrisburg PA 17102   CFO: –
Phone: 717-720-2700   HR: Tom Rineer
Fax: 717-720-3901   FYE: June 30
Web: www.pheaa.org   Type: Private - Not-for-Pr

Understanding how Pennsylvania Higher Education Assistance Agency (PHEAA) is set up may require a higher education. The government-related financial aid agency does business under the name American Education Services. It's one of the nation's top guarantors of the US Department of Education's Federal Family Education Loan Program (FFELP) as well as one of the largest student loan servicers and one of the largest student loan holders. PHEAA uses the funds it generates to improve higher education opportunities lower the cost of financial assistance and streamline the financial aid process.

PENNSYLVANIA HOUSING FINANCE AGENCY

211 N FRONT ST
HARRISBURG, PA 171011406
Phone: 717-780-3800
Fax: –
Web: www.phfa.org

CEO: –
CFO: –
HR: Arlene Frontz
FYE: June 30
Type: Private

Pennsylvania Housing Finance Agency (PHFA) helps residents of the Keystone State obtain keys to their dream homes. The government-owned agency provides financing for low-income homebuyers including the elderly and disabled and participates in rental housing development initiatives. It generates funding from state and federal grants interest earned on investments and loans and the sale of its own securities to private investors. The agency is run by a board which includes Pennsylvania's secretary of banking secretary of community and economic development secretary of public welfare and the state treasurer. The PHFA has funded more than 130000 houses and 54000 apartment units since its founding in 1972.

	Annual Growth	06/09	06/10	06/11	06/12	06/18
Assets ($ mil.)	(4.4%)	–	6,265.4	6,051.3	5,593.4	4,367.0
Net income ($ mil.)	(2.2%)	–	24.6	39.4	10.6	20.6
Market value ($ mil.)	–	–	–	–	–	–
Employees	–	–	–	–	–	250

PENNSYLVANIA POWER COMPANY INC

76 S MAIN ST BSMT
AKRON, OH 443081817
Phone: 800-720-3600
Fax: –
Web: www.papowerswitch.com

CEO: Anthony J Alexander
CFO: –
HR: –
FYE: December 31
Type: Private

Although this Penn is mighty indeed powerful is a more apt description. Organized in 1930 Pennsylvania Power (Penn Power) serves 164000 customers in a 1100 square mile region of western Pennsylvania. The company's 1200 MW of power is primarily generated at its fossil-fueled (Bruce Mansfield and W.H. Sammis) and nuclear (Beaver Valley and Perry) power plants. Penn Power maintains nearly 13540 miles of distribution lines. The company is owned by Ohio Edison Company (which itself is a wholly-owned subsidiary of utility holding company FirstEnergy).

	Annual Growth	12/04	12/05	12/15	12/16	12/17
Sales ($ mil.)	(6.4%)	–	540.6	–	251.2	243.8
Net income ($ mil.)	(6.0%)	–	65.9	–	21.9	31.3
Market value ($ mil.)	–	–	–	–	–	–
Employees	–	–	–	–	–	610

PENNSYLVANIA REAL ESTATE INVESTMENT TRUST   NYS: PEI

200 South Broad Street
Philadelphia, PA 19102
Phone: 215 875-0700
Fax: –
Web: www.preit.com

CEO: Joseph F. (Joe) Coradino
CFO: Robert F. McCadden
HR: Brenda Shanholtz
FYE: December 31
Type: Public

Pennsylvania Real Estate Investment Trust (PREIT) owns either outright or through partnerships about three dozen enclosed shopping malls and six strip and power centers as well as several retail properties under development. The REIT's portfolio contains more than 30 million sq. ft. of retail space in a dozen states concentrated in the mid-Atlantic region with a focus on Pennsylvania. The company also provides construction management development leasing marketing and property management services. It counts retailers such as Foot Locker J.C. Penney The Gap Macy's and Sears among its largest tenants. Founded in 1960 PREIT was one of the first publicly traded REITs in the US.

	Annual Growth	12/14	12/15	12/16	12/17	12/18
Sales ($ mil.)	(4.3%)	432.7	425.4	399.9	367.5	362.4
Net income ($ mil.)	–	(13.8)	(116.7)	(11.3)	(29.3)	(110.3)
Market value ($ mil.)	(29.1%)	1,653.8	1,541.7	1,336.6	838.2	418.7
Employees	(10.6%)	429	397	347	297	274

PENNYMAC FINANCIAL SERVICES INC (NEW)   NYS: PFSI

3043 Townsgate Road
Westlake Village, CA 91361
Phone: 818 224-7442
Fax: –
Web: www.pennymacusa.com

CEO: David A. Spector
CFO: Andrew S. Chang
HR: –
FYE: December 31
Type: Public

If you're thinking residential mortgage this company has more than a penny for your thoughts. The parent of investment management loan services and investment trust companies PennyMac Financial Services (PennyMac) focuses on the US residential mortgage market offering loans and investment management services. Through its Private National Mortgage Acceptance Company the company's PennyMac Loan Services (PLS) originates home loans in 45 states and DC and services loans in 49 states DC and the US Virgin Islands. PLS's counterpart PNMAC Capital Management acts as investment manager and advisor. The companies service and advise PennyMac Mortgage Investment Trust (PMT). PennyMac went public in 2013.

	Annual Growth	12/14	12/15	12/16	12/17	12/18
Assets ($ mil.)	31.4%	2,507.1	3,505.3	5,133.9	7,368.1	7,478.6
Net income ($ mil.)	24.2%	36.8	47.2	66.1	100.8	87.7
Market value ($ mil.)	5.3%	1,340.7	1,190.3	1,290.3	1,732.0	1,647.5
Employees	17.5%	1,816	2,509	3,038	3,189	3,460

PENNYMAC MORTGAGE INVESTMENT TRUST   NYS: PMT

3043 Townsgate Road
Westlake Village, CA 91361
Phone: 818 224-7442
Fax: –
Web: www.pennymacmortgageinvestmenttrust.com

CEO: Stanford L. Kurland
CFO: Anne D. McCallion
HR: –
FYE: December 31
Type: Public

PennyMac Mortgage Investment Trust trusts in its ability to acquire distressed US residential mortgage loans. The company seeks to acquire primarily troubled home mortgage loans and mortgage-backed securities from FDIC liquidations of failed banks US Treasury Legacy Loans Program auctions and direct acquisitions from mortgage and insurance companies and foreign banks. PennyMac is managed by investment adviser PNMAC Capital Management and offers primary and special loan servicing through PennyMac Loan Services. The company is held by Private National Mortgage Acceptance Company (PNMAC).

	Annual Growth	12/14	12/15	12/16	12/17	12/18
Sales ($ mil.)	4.4%	442.3	373.5	421.9	469.3	526.2
Net income ($ mil.)	(5.9%)	194.5	90.1	75.8	117.7	152.8
Market value ($ mil.)	(3.1%)	1,285.5	930.1	997.8	979.5	1,134.9
Employees	–	–	–	3	3	3

PENSION BENEFIT GUARANTY CORPORATION

1200 K St. NW
Washington DC 20005-4026
Phone: 202-326-4000
Fax: 202-326-4042
Web: www.pbgc.gov

CEO: –
CFO: –
HR: –
FYE: September 30
Type: Government Agency

Underfunded pension plans give PBGC the heebie-jeebies. The Pension Benefit Guaranty Corporation or PBGC — itself operating at a multi-billion-dollar deficit — was set up to promote the growth of defined-benefit pension plans provide payment of retirement benefits and keep pension premiums as low as possible. The government agency protects the pensions of more than 34 million workers and monitors employers to ensure that plans are adequately funded. The agency receives no tax funds; its income is generated by insurance premiums paid by employers investments and assets recovered from terminated plans. The corporation was created by the Employee Retirement Income Security Act of 1974.

PENSKE AUTOMOTIVE GROUP INC   NYS: PAG

2555 Telegraph Road   CEO: Roger S. Penske
Bloomfield Hills, MI 48302-0954   CFO: John D Carlson Jr
Phone: 248 648-2500   HR: Claude H. (Bud) Denker
Fax: 248 648-2525   FYE: December 31
Web: www.penskeautomotive.com   Type: Public

Penske Automotive Group has lots of lots. The US' #2 publicly traded auto dealer behind AutoNation Penske operates about 155 auto franchises from California to New Jersey and Puerto Rico and another 190 franchises abroad mainly in the UK. It sells more than 40 car brands. Non-US brands including AUDI BMW Land Rover Mercedez-Benz and Porsche generate more than 70% of sales. Penske also sells used vehicles provides financing and runs more than 35 collision repair centers. UK subsidiary Sytner Group operates more than 145 franchises selling 20 brands of mostly high-end models. Additionally Penske holds a nearly 30% stake in Penske Truck Leasing (PTL) known for commercial leasing and contract maintenance. The company is named after its Chairman Roger Penske.

	Annual Growth	12/14	12/15	12/16	12/17	12/18
Sales ($ mil.)	7.3%	17,177.2	19,284.9	20,118.5	21,386.9	22,785.1
Net income ($ mil.)	13.2%	286.7	326.1	342.9	613.3	471.0
Market value ($ mil.)	(4.8%)	4,148.7	3,579.7	4,382.9	4,045.6	3,408.9
Employees	5.1%	22,100	22,000	24,000	26,000	27,000

PENTAGON FEDERAL CREDIT UNION

2930 Eisenhower Ave.   CEO: Christopher J Flynn
Alexandria VA 22314   CFO: Denise McGlone
Phone: 703-838-1000   HR: –
Fax: 800-557-7328   FYE: December 31
Web: www.penfed.org   Type: Private - Not-for-Pr

Pentagon Federal Credit Union (PenFed) is one of the largest credit unions in the US with about a dozen branches in the Washington DC area and a dozen others on military bases in the US and internationally. The credit union has more than 1 million members primarily employees of the Department of Defense and the Department of Homeland Security; members of the Army Navy Air Force Coast Guard and other uniformed services; employees of defense-related companies; Veterans of Foreign Wars; and their families. PenFed - which provides standard retail financial services such as checking and savings accounts; home mortgages; credit cards; and auto student and personal loans — has more than $15 billion in assets.

PENTAIR LTD.   NYSE: PNR

5500 Wayzata Blvd. Ste. 800   CEO: John L Stauch
Minneapolis MN 55416-1261   CFO: Mark C Borin
Phone: 763-545-1730   HR: –
Fax: 763-656-5402   FYE: December 31
Web: www.pentair.com   Type: Public

Pentair is pumped about water! Water & Fluid Solutions the company's largest segment manufactures water flow and filtration products for the residential and commercial construction projects and municipal markets. Pentair's Technical Products segment makes custom enclosures (under brands Hoffman and Schroff) that house and protect sensitive electronics as well as thermal management systems used in industrial communications electronics and energy industries. Products are sold to a network of distributors OEMs water treatment facilities retailers and pool and electrical contractors. In 2012 Pentair merged its operations with Tyco Flow Control a unit owned by security products maker Tyco International.

PEOPLE FOR THE ETHICAL TREATMENT OF ANIMALS, INC.

501 FRONT ST   CEO: –
NORFOLK, VA 235101009   CFO: –
Phone: 757-622-7382   HR: –
Fax: –   FYE: July 31
Web: www.peta.org   Type: Private

Talk about a watchdog! People for the Ethical Treatment of Animals (PETA) works to raise public awareness concerning animal rights and issues; its high-profile campaigns promote vegetarianism and veganism cruelty-free products and alternatives to animal experimentation. PETA's Domestic Animal Issues & Abuse Department investigates reports of cruelty towards animals; Caring Consumer 101 publishes lists of companies and charities that do and don't perform animal testing as well as Animal Times and Grrr! (for kids) magazines. the international not-for-profit organization has some 2 million members and affiliates in Europe and Asia. PETA is funded primarily by member contributions.

	Annual Growth	07/12	07/13	07/14	07/15	07/16
Sales ($ mil.)	21.6%	–	34.7	42.9	42.8	62.4
Net income ($ mil.)	–	–	(0.0)	4.5	0.1	16.3
Market value ($ mil.)	–	–	–	–	–	–
Employees	–	–	–	–	–	14

PEOPLE'S UNITED FINANCIAL INC   NMS: PBCT

850 Main Street   CEO: John P. (Jack) Barnes
Bridgeport, CT 06604   CFO: R. David Rosato
Phone: 203 338-7171   HR: David K. Norton
Fax: 203 338-2545   FYE: December 31
Web: www.peoples.com   Type: Public

People's United Financial is the holding company for People's United Bank (formerly People's Bank) which boasts more than 400 traditional branches supermarket branches commercial banking offices investment and brokerage offices and equipment leasing offices across New England and eastern New York. In addition to retail and commercial banking services the bank offers trust wealth management brokerage and insurance services. Its lending activities consist mainly of commercial mortgages (more than a third of its loan portfolio) commercial and industrial loans (more than a quarter) residential mortgages equipment financing and home equity loans. Founded in 1842 the bank has $36 billion in assets.

	Annual Growth	12/14	12/15	12/16	12/17	12/18
Assets ($ mil.)	7.4%	35,997.1	38,877.4	40,609.8	44,453.4	47,877.3
Net income ($ mil.)	16.8%	251.7	260.1	281.0	337.2	468.1
Market value ($ mil.)	(1.3%)	5,727.4	6,093.4	7,304.5	7,055.5	5,444.4
Employees	2.3%	5,397	5,139	5,173	5,584	5,920

PEOPLES BANCORP INC (AUBURN, IN)   NBB: PBNI

212 West Seventh Street, P.O. Box 231   CEO: –
Auburn, IN 46706   CFO: –
Phone: 260 925-2500   HR: –
Fax: 260 925-8303   FYE: September 30
Web: www.peoplesfed.com/peoples-bancorp.htm   Type: Public

Peoples Bancorp is the holding company for Peoples Federal Savings Bank of DeKalb County which operates about 15 branches in northeastern Indiana and southern Michigan. Targeting area individuals and small to midsized business customers the bank offers such standard products as checking savings and NOW accounts; CDs; IRAs; and credit cards. One- to four-family residential mortgages make up most of the company's loan portfolio which is rounded out by multifamily real estate commercial real estate land acquisition and development and consumer loans.

	Annual Growth	09/09	09/10	09/11	09/12	09/13
Assets ($ mil.)	(2.0%)	487.8	472.5	480.6	484.3	450.8
Net income ($ mil.)	(4.2%)	3.1	3.3	3.8	3.0	2.6
Market value ($ mil.)	15.7%	30.8	33.0	38.2	46.3	55.2
Employees	–	–	148	–	–	–

PEOPLES BANCORP INC (MARIETTA, OH)   NMS: PEBO

138 Putnam Street, P.O. Box 738
Marietta, OH 45750
Phone: 740 373-3155
Fax: –
Web: www.peoplesbancorp.com

CEO: Charles W. Sulerzyski
CFO: John C. Rogers
HR: –
FYE: December 31
Type: Public

Peoples Bancorp offers banking for the people by the people and of the people. The holding company owns Peoples Bank which has about 50 branches in rural and small urban markets in Ohio Kentucky and West Virginia. The bank offers traditional services such as checking and savings accounts CDs loans and trust services. Commercial and agricultural loans including those secured by commercial real estate account for the majority of the bank's lending activities. Its Peoples Financial Advisors division offers investment management services while Peoples Insurance sells life health and property/casualty coverage.

	Annual Growth	12/14	12/15	12/16	12/17	12/18
Assets ($ mil.)	11.7%	2,567.8	3,259.0	3,432.3	3,581.7	3,991.5
Net income ($ mil.)	29.0%	16.7	10.9	31.2	38.5	46.3
Market value ($ mil.)	3.8%	506.2	367.8	633.7	636.8	587.6
Employees	5.7%	699	817	782	774	871

PEOPLES BANCORP OF NORTH CAROLINA INC   NMS: PEBK

518 West C. Street
Newton, NC 28658
Phone: 828 464-5620
Fax: –
Web: www.peoplesbanknc.com

CEO: Lance A Sellers
CFO: A Joseph Lampron Jr
HR: –
FYE: December 31
Type: Public

Peoples Bancorp of North Carolina owns Peoples Bank which serves the Catawba Valley region of North Carolina through about 20 locations. It also runs Banco de la Gente ("Peoples Bank" in Spanish) which serves the area's Latino community. The banks offer standard services such as checking and savings accounts; CDs; mortgage construction development and other real estate loans (combined some 90% of its loan portfolio); and business and consumer loans. Peoples Bank has two subsidiaries: Peoples Investment Services which provides financial planning and investment products through an agreement with Raymond James Financial and Real Estate Advisory Services a real estate brokerage and appraisal services firm.

	Annual Growth	12/14	12/15	12/16	12/17	12/18
Assets ($ mil.)	1.2%	1,040.5	1,038.5	1,088.0	1,092.2	1,093.3
Net income ($ mil.)	9.3%	9.4	9.6	9.2	10.3	13.4
Market value ($ mil.)	8.0%	107.9	115.9	150.3	184.0	146.6
Employees	2.1%	317	324	331	335	345

PEOPLES BANCORP, INC. (MD)   NBB: PEBC

P.O. Box 210, 100 Spring Avenue
Chestertown, MD 21620
Phone: 410 778-3500
Fax: –

CEO: –
CFO: –
HR: –
FYE: December 31
Type: Public

People who need Peoples Bancorp may or may not be the luckiest people but they are Peoples Bancorp customers. The firm is the holding company for Peoples Bank of Kent County which operates more than five branches in eastern Maryland. Serving local consumers and businesses the bank provides standard deposit products such as checking and savings accounts money market accounts CDs and IRAs. Commercial real estate loans make up the largest portion of the company's lending portfolio which also includes residential mortgages and business loans as well as a lesser amount of construction and consumer loans. Peoples Bancorp also owns insurance agency Fleetwood Athey Macbeth & McCown.

	Annual Growth	12/11	12/14	12/15	12/16	12/17
Assets ($ mil.)	(0.2%)	253.2	234.7	239.9	254.7	250.3
Net income ($ mil.)	–	(2.0)	0.6	1.0	1.3	1.5
Market value ($ mil.)	(8.2%)	33.5	10.8	13.1	14.0	20.1
Employees	–	–	70	–	–	–

PEOPLES EDUCATIONAL HOLDINGS, INC.   NBB: PEDH

299 Market Street
Saddle Brook, NJ 07663
Phone: 201 712-0090
Fax: –
Web: www.peopleseducation.com;www.epathknowledge.com

CEO: Brian T Beckwith
CFO: Michael L Demarco
HR: –
FYE: May 31
Type: Public

Peoples Educational Holdings wants to help make sure your student measures up — to state standards. Its subsidiary Peoples Education develops and publishes test preparation and supplementary educational materials for students in grades pre-K through 12 focusing on preparation materials for state-specific standardized tests. Its customized Measuring Up products are available in a dozen states. The company also publishes college preparation materials for high school students. Peoples Educational Holdings distributes its own print and electronic publications as well as titles from other publishers. Subjects covered include language arts mathematics science and social studies.

	Annual Growth	05/08	05/09	05/10	05/11	05/12
Sales ($ mil.)	(10.5%)	40.0	36.9	34.9	31.3	25.6
Net income ($ mil.)	–	(0.8)	(1.1)	0.3	(0.5)	(9.3)
Market value ($ mil.)	0.0%	31.3	31.3	31.3	31.3	31.3
Employees	(6.2%)	110	82	91	91	85

PEOPLES FEDERAL BANCSHARES, INC.   NAS: PEOP

435 Market Street
Brighton, MA 02135
Phone: 617 254-0707
Fax: –
Web: www.pfsb.com

CEO: –
CFO: –
HR: –
FYE: September 30
Type: Public

Peoples Federal Bancshares is the holding company for Peoples Federal Savings Bank a seven-branch bank in the greater Boston area. Peoples Federal Savings Bank offers traditional checking and NOW accounts; savings accounts include money market and CDs. The bank offers MasterCard debit cards but does not issue credit cards. It originates loans from retail deposits and advances from the Federal Home Loan Bank of Boston; in 2013 66% of its loan portfolio consisted one-to four-family residential mortgages. Peoples Federal Bancshares was incorporated in 2010 to convert from a mutual holding company to a stock company. The bank itself traces its roots bank to 1888.

	Annual Growth	09/10	09/11	09/12	09/13	09/14
Sales ($ mil.)	(1.4%)	23.0	22.3	22.2	21.2	21.7
Net income ($ mil.)	–	(0.2)	3.1	1.7	2.3	1.5
Market value ($ mil.)	16.8%	67.1	80.1	107.8	108.7	124.8
Employees	1.6%	75	82	83	87	80

PEOPLES FINANCIAL CORP (BILOXI, MS)   NBB: PFBX

Lameuse and Howard Avenues
Biloxi, MS 39533
Phone: 228 435-5511
Fax: –
Web: www.thepeoples.com

CEO: –
CFO: Lauri A Wood
HR: Doreen Moffat
FYE: December 31
Type: Public

Peoples Financial helps people with their money. The company owns The Peoples Bank which operates more than 15 branches along the Mississippi Gulf Coast. The bank offers traditional checking and savings products. Real estate mortgages make up about nearly 65% of its loan portfolio which also includes business construction and personal loans. Other offerings include fixed-rate mortgages and asset management and trust services. Peoples caters to individuals and middle-market businesses in industries such as seafood retail hospitality gaming and construction. Chairman and CEO Chevis Swetman owns about 16% of the bank; his family has had an interest in the bank since its inception in 1896.

	Annual Growth	12/14	12/15	12/16	12/17	12/18
Assets ($ mil.)	(2.0%)	668.9	641.0	688.0	650.4	616.8
Net income ($ mil.)	–	(10.0)	(4.6)	0.2	2.8	0.6
Market value ($ mil.)	(2.0%)	61.5	44.5	79.8	64.3	56.8
Employees	(3.1%)	176	173	168	166	155

PEOPLES FINANCIAL SERVICES CORP NMS: PFIS

150 North Washington Avenue
Scranton, PA 18503
Phone: 570 346-7741
Fax: –

CEO: Alan W. Dakey
CFO: Scott Seasock
HR: –
FYE: December 31
Type: Public

Power to the Peoples Financial Services. The firm is the holding company for Peoples Security Bank and Trust Company (formerly Peoples National Bank) which operates about 25 branches across northeastern Pennsylvania and neighboring Broome County in New York. Established in 1905 the bank offers standard retail products and services including checking and savings accounts CDs and credit cards to local businesses and individuals. Commercial loans including mortgages construction loans and operating loans make up the greatest portion (40%) of the company's loan book followed by residential mortgages (25%) and consumer loans. The company's Peoples Advisors subsidiary provides investment and brokerage services.

	Annual Growth	12/14	12/15	12/16	12/17	12/18
Assets ($ mil.)	7.1%	1,741.7	1,819.1	1,999.4	2,169.0	2,289.0
Net income ($ mil.)	9.0%	17.6	17.7	19.6	18.5	24.9
Market value ($ mil.)	(3.0%)	367.6	281.8	360.3	344.6	326.0
Employees	2.5%	354	348	364	388	390

PEOPLES-SIDNEY FINANCIAL CORP. NBB: PPSF

101 East Court Street
Sidney, OH 45365-3021
Phone: 937 492-6129
Fax: 937 498-4554

CEO: Douglas Stewart
CFO: Debra Geuy
HR: –
FYE: June 30
Type: Public

Peoples-Sidney Financial Corporation is the holding company for Peoples Federal Savings and Loan Association of Sidney which operates primarily in western Ohio's Shelby County through five branches. Founded in 1886 the bank targets area individuals and small to midsized businesses offering standard retail services like checking and savings accounts CDs and IRAs. Lending activities consist mostly of one- to four-family residential mortgages which make up approximately 70% of the bank's loan portfolio. In addition Peoples Federal Savings and Loan originates agricultural construction commercial consumer and land loans.

	Annual Growth	06/13	06/14	06/15	06/16	06/17
Assets ($ mil.)	(2.1%)	119.9	118.2	111.7	111.3	110.1
Net income ($ mil.)	(2.8%)	0.6	(0.1)	0.5	0.4	0.5
Market value ($ mil.)	(3.8%)	13.1	9.8	9.7	10.7	11.2
Employees	–	–	–	–	–	–

PEP BOYS-MANNY, MOE & JACK NYS: PBY

3111 West Allegheny Avenue
Philadelphia, PA 19132
Phone: 215 430-9000
Fax: –
Web: www.pepboys.com

CEO: William Inhken
CFO: –
HR: –
FYE: February 1/
Type: Public

An automotive paradise for do-it-yourselfers The Pep Boys - Manny Moe & Jack hears the cries of "Do it for me!" too. The company sells brand name and private label auto parts and provides select services through some 800 stores in 35 states and Puerto Rico. Pep Boys stock about 25000 car parts and accessories including tires and combined operate more than 7500 service bays for vehicle repairs inspections and parts installations. It also offers credit and parts delivery to commercial customers such as repair shops fleet operators schools and municipalities. The Pep Boys was founded in 1921 by Philadelphians Manny Moe and Jack.

	Annual Growth	01/10	01/11	01/12*	02/13	02/14
Sales ($ mil.)	2.0%	1,910.9	1,988.6	2,063.6	2,090.7	2,066.6
Net income ($ mil.)	(26.1%)	23.0	36.6	28.9	12.8	6.9
Market value ($ mil.)	9.4%	444.2	743.7	642.6	585.7	635.2
Employees	1.6%	17,718	18,279	19,123	19,441	18,914

*Fiscal year change

PEPCO HOLDINGS INC. NYS: POM

701 Ninth Street, N.W.
Washington, DC 20068
Phone: 202 872-2000
Fax: –
Web: www.pepcoholdings.com

CEO: David M Velazquez
CFO: Donna J Kinzel
HR: –
FYE: December 31
Type: Public

Pepco Holdings (PHI) arguably has more power in the US capital than most politicians. The holding company distributes electricity and natural gas through its Potomac Electric Power (Pepco) Delmarva Power & Light and Atlantic City Electric utilities to about 2.3 million customers in Delaware Maryland New Jersey and Washington DC. None of the company's three utilities have power generation plants. Nonregulated operations include energy efficiency consultation and renewable energy services for institutional and government clients through the company's Pepco Energy Services unit. In a major industry consolidation move in 2014 PHI agreed to be bought by rival Exelon for $6.8 billion.

	Annual Growth	12/10	12/11	12/12	12/13	12/14
Sales ($ mil.)	(8.8%)	7,039.0	5,920.0	5,081.0	4,666.0	4,878.0
Net income ($ mil.)	65.8%	32.0	257.0	285.0	(212.0)	242.0
Market value ($ mil.)	10.2%	4,612.3	5,130.4	4,956.0	4,834.7	6,806.0
Employees	0.5%	5,014	5,104	5,040	5,025	5,125

PEPPER CONSTRUCTION GROUP, LLC

643 N ORLEANS ST
CHICAGO, IL 606543690
Phone: 312-266-4700
Fax: –
Web: www.pepperconstruction.com

CEO: –
CFO: Chris Averill
HR: –
FYE: September 30
Type: Private

Pepper Construction Group spices up the construction business with a little of this and a pinch of that. The company provides general contracting and construction management services for commercial office education entertainment health care and institutional clients as well as waterworks projects. (Health care projects account for about 50% of Pepper's revenue.) Its client list includes UBS Northwestern University University of Notre Dame Texas Heart Institute Loyola University Medical Center and NASA. Pepper Construction Group has divisions in Illinois Indiana Ohio and Texas. Stanley F. Pepper founded the company in Chicago in 1927. The group is owned by his family and employees of the firm.

	Annual Growth	09/10	09/11	09/15	09/16	09/17
Sales ($ mil.)	3.5%	–	911.8	1,110.4	1,179.1	1,119.6
Net income ($ mil.)	5.2%	–	15.6	9.6	23.1	21.1
Market value ($ mil.)	–	–	–	–	–	–
Employees	–	–	–	–	–	1,100

PEPPERDINE UNIVERSITY

24255 PACIFIC COAST HWY # 5000
MALIBU, CA 902635000
Phone: 310-506-4000
Fax: –
Web: www.pepperdine.edu

CEO: Andrew K. Benton
CFO: Paul B. Lasiter
HR: Angi Ibrahim
FYE: July 31
Type: Private

Pepperdine University offers undergraduate and graduate programs to some 7300 students. Affiliated with Churches of Christ the university boasts five colleges and schools: Seaver College of Letters Arts and Sciences; the Graziadio School of Business and Management; the School of Law; the School of Public Policy; and the Graduate School of Education and Psychology. Pepperdine whose 830-acre main campus overlooks the Pacific Ocean in Malibu California has half a dozen additional campuses in California as well as international campuses in Argentina Italy Germany and the UK. The university was founded in 1937 by Christian businessman George Pepperdine who also founded the Western Auto Supply Company.

	Annual Growth	07/11	07/12	07/15	07/17	07/18
Sales ($ mil.)	4.7%	–	291.2	437.6	361.3	383.6
Net income ($ mil.)	–	–	(8.8)	31.8	105.6	70.6
Market value ($ mil.)	–	–	–	–	–	–
Employees	–	–	–	–	–	1,500

PEPSI-COLA BOTTLING CO OF CENTRAL VIRGINIA

1150 PEPSI PL
CHARLOTTESVILLE, VA 229012865
Phone: 434-978-2140
Fax: -
Web: www.pepsicva.com

CEO: -
CFO: -
HR: Katie Cole
FYE: December 31
Type: Private

Pepsi-Cola Bottling Co. of Central Virginia (PCBCCV) operates four soda and water bottling plants and distribution centers throughout the state of Virginia. They are located in Charlottesville Virginia Beach Warrenton and Weyer's Cave. In addition to providing some 18 Virginia counties with Pepsi Gatorade Tropicana and other PepsiCo products the company also distributes Dr Pepper Snapple Group products such as Snapple 7UP and Canada Dry. PCBCCV is the holder of the oldest written franchise (1908) on record with PepsiCo. Founded by Samuel Ambrose Jessup that same year it is still owned and operated by his descendents.

	Annual Growth	12/12	12/13	12/14	12/15	12/16
Sales ($ mil.)	-	-	0.0	106.3	111.1	114.8
Net income ($ mil.)	10.0%	-	5.0	6.0	6.3	6.7
Market value ($ mil.)	-	-	-	-	-	-
Employees	-	-	-	-	-	370

PEPSICO INC

NMS: PEP

700 Anderson Hill Road
Purchase, NY 10577
Phone: 914 253-2000
Fax: -
Web: www.pepsico.com

CEO: Indra K. Nooyi
CFO: Hugh F. Johnston
HR: Cynthia M. Trudell
FYE: December 29
Type: Public

PepsiCo butts heads with its eternal rival The Coca-Cola Company for the title of world's biggest soft drinks maker. PepsiCo's beverage brands include Pepsi Mountain Dew Tropicana Gatorade and Aquafina water. The company also owns Frito-Lay the world's #1 snack maker with offerings such as Lay's Ruffles Doritos and Cheetos. The Quaker Foods unit makes breakfast cereals (Quaker oatmeal Life) Rice-A-Roni and Near East side dishes. Pepsi products are available in 200-plus countries although the US accounts for nearly 60% of total sales. The company operates about half of its bottling plants and distribution facilities.

	Annual Growth	12/14	12/15	12/16	12/17	12/18
Sales ($ mil.)	(0.8%)	66,683.0	63,056.0	62,799.0	63,525.0	64,661.0
Net income ($ mil.)	17.7%	6,513.0	5,452.0	6,329.0	4,857.0	12,515.0
Market value ($ mil.)	3.3%	136,743.5	141,660.9	147,423.7	168,967.3	155,497.2
Employees	(0.4%)	271,000	263,000	264,000	263,000	267,000

PERCEPTRON, INC.

NMS: PRCP

47827 Halyard Drive
Plymouth, MI 48170-2461
Phone: 734 414-6100
Fax: 734 414-4700
Web: www.perceptron.com

CEO: Jay W Freeland
CFO: David L Watza
HR: -
FYE: June 30
Type: Public

Perceptron has a multidimensional view of what constitutes quality assurance for carmakers and building tradesmen. The company's proprietary image-processing systems provide 3-D scanning non-contact measurement and robot guidance systems for the automotive industry. Automakers use Perceptron's products to detect abnormalities and prevent variations — such as metal or paint defects — on formed parts. Perceptron also offers services such as consulting maintenance repair work upgrades and training. General Motors VW BMW and Snap-on are among its top customers. Roughly half of sales come from the Americas primarily the US.

	Annual Growth	06/15	06/16	06/17	06/18	06/19
Sales ($ mil.)	0.8%	74.4	69.1	77.9	84.7	76.8
Net income ($ mil.)	-	(0.5)	(22.1)	(0.2)	3.7	(6.8)
Market value ($ mil.)	(19.4%)	102.0	45.2	70.3	101.9	43.0
Employees	(1.4%)	346	323	327	337	327

PERDOCEO EDUCATION CORP

NMS: PRDO

231 N. Martingale Road
Schaumburg, IL 60173
Phone: 847 781-3600
Fax: -
Web: www.careered.com

CEO: Todd S. Nelson
CFO: Andrew J Cederoth
HR: Maureen Cahill
FYE: December 31
Type: Public

Career Education Corporation (CEC) has made a career of handing out diplomas. The for-profit company owns and operates almost 90 US campuses (a third of which are slated for closure) and online programs that offer post-secondary education to about 53700 enrolled students. CEC offers certificate and degree programs in areas including information technology health education business studies culinary arts and visual communication and design. The group's operating names include Colorado Technical University (CTU) Sanford-Brown Institutes Le Cordon Bleu and American InterContinental University (AIU). CEC schools offers non-degree certificates as well as associate bachelor's master's and doctoral degrees.

	Annual Growth	12/14	12/15	12/16	12/17	12/18
Sales ($ mil.)	(5.9%)	741.4	847.3	704.4	596.4	581.3
Net income ($ mil.)	-	(178.2)	51.9	(18.7)	(31.9)	55.2
Market value ($ mil.)	13.2%	485.6	253.3	704.0	842.9	796.8
Employees	(15.0%)	8,127	7,251	5,149	4,462	4,244

PEREGRINE SEMICONDUCTOR CORPORATION

NASDAQ: PSMI

9380 Carroll Park Dr.
San Diego CA 92121-5201
Phone: 858-731-9400
Fax: 858-731-9499
Web: www.psemi.com

CEO: Sumit Tomar
CFO: Takaki Muratajay C Biskupski
HR: -
FYE: December 31
Type: Private

Peregrine Semiconductor's chips are made to take flight. The fabless company designs radio-frequency integrated circuits (RFICs) used in the wireless infrastructure broadband mobile wireless device aerospace and test and measurement markets. Its UltraCMOS technology combines standard complementary metal oxide semiconductor (CMOS) with a synthetic sapphire substrate that provides enhanced power and performance over silicon substrates. Other products include attenuators mixers and synthesizers. Founded in 1990 Peregrine Semi went public in a 2012 IPO.

PEREZ TRADING COMPANY, INC.

3490 NW 125TH ST
MIAMI, FL 331672412
Phone: 305-769-0761
Fax: -
Web: www.pereztrading.com

CEO: -
CFO: -
HR: -
FYE: December 31
Type: Private

No matter how you say it paper or el papel Perez Trading has it. From its Miami warehouse the company distributes more than 15000 tons of paper and paperboard inventory including corrugated box equipment napkin paper printing paper and other printing and shipping equipment and supplies. Customers include commercial printers converters distributors and packaging manufacturers. Perez Trading imports and exports to nearly 30 countries encompassing the Caribbean Islands Central and South America Mexico and the US. Perez Trading has been family owned and operated since 1947.

	Annual Growth	12/10	12/11	12/12	12/13	12/14
Sales ($ mil.)	(5.1%)	-	-	570.5	527.0	514.3
Net income ($ mil.)	(26.3%)	-	-	20.3	16.9	11.0
Market value ($ mil.)	-	-	-	-	-	-
Employees	-	-	-	-	-	140

PERFECTION BAKERIES INC.

350 Pearl St.
Fort Wayne IN 46802
Phone: 260-424-8245
Fax: 260-424-1477
Web: www.auntmillies.com

CEO: John F Popp
CFO: Jay E Miller
HR: –
FYE: September 30
Type: Private

You might say Perfection Bakeries strives for excellence in baking. A leading producer of baked goods the company makes such products as bread hamburger and hotdog buns and English muffins for the retail market under its flagship Aunt Millie's brand. It also supplies baked goods and mixes to the foodservice industry. Perfection Bakeries has operations in Illinois Indiana Kentucky Michigan and Ohio and its products are distributed primarily throughout the Great Lakes region. The family-owned company was founded in 1901 by John Franke as the Wayne Biscuit Company.

PERFICIENT INC
NMS: PRFT

555 Maryville University Drive, Suite 600
Saint Louis, MO 63141
Phone: 314 529-3600
Fax: –
Web: www.perficient.com

CEO: Jeffrey S. (Jeff) Davis
CFO: Paul E. Martin
HR: –
FYE: December 31
Type: Public

Perficient is proficient in helping its customers use technology to their advantage. The IT consultancy provides software development systems integration and technical support. It specializes in developing middleware applications used to integrate and modernize legacy computer hardware and software. Its expertise also encompasses content management systems ERP and CRM applications business process integration service oriented architectures business intelligence e-commerce and wireless communication. Perficient integrates and supports applications from vendors including IBM Oracle Salesforce and Magento.

	Annual Growth	12/14	12/15	12/16	12/17	12/18
Sales ($ mil.)	2.2%	456.7	473.6	487.0	485.3	498.4
Net income ($ mil.)	1.5%	23.2	23.0	20.5	18.6	24.6
Market value ($ mil.)	4.5%	591.9	543.9	555.7	605.9	707.2
Employees	10.2%	2,074	2,678	2,728	3,024	3,060

PERFORMANCE FOOD GROUP INC.

12650 E. Arapahoe Rd. Bldg. D
Centennial CO 80112-3901
Phone: 303-662-7100
Fax: 303-662-7565
Web: www.vistar.com

CEO: –
CFO: –
HR: –
FYE: February 28
Type: Subsidiary

Performance Food builds its fortune on snack-food. Doing business as Vistar it distributes more than 3000 snacks quick-serve foods and other impulse items nationwide. In addition to candy savory and sweet bites and beverages it offers equipment including vending machines coffee brewers and hot dog rollers. Vistar also sells its lines through about a dozen Merchant's Mart a vending wholesaler with a handful of cash and carry outlets. Vistar's customers include foodservice vendors office coffee services theater concessions and convenience stores. Formed in 1997 the company operates through some 20 hubs. Vistar is a subsidiary of distribution foodservice giant Performance Food Group Company (PFG).

PERFORMANCE TECHNOLOGIES, INC.
NMS: PTIX

140 Canal View Blvd.
Rochester, NY 14623
Phone: 585 256-0200
Fax: –
Web: www.pt.com

CEO: John M Slusser
CFO: Dorrance W Lamb
HR: –
FYE: December 31
Type: Public

Performance Technologies (PT) contributes to communications convergence. The company makes networking equipment used to integrate traditional telephone and Internet protocol (IP) data networks. Its products include gateways routers and embedded IP switches designed for carrier-grade telecommunication providers. PT also sells related adapters and software. Most of its sales come from equipment manufacturers and systems integrators; it also sells products through distributors. The company's 125-plus customers include Alcatel-Lucent Leap Wireless/Cricket Raytheon and Metaswitch Networks. Recently rebranded as PT the company gets more than half of its sales outside the US.

	Annual Growth	12/08	12/09	12/10	12/11	12/12
Sales ($ mil.)	(12.9%)	40.5	29.5	27.9	36.2	23.3
Net income ($ mil.)	–	1.7	(10.1)	(11.2)	(1.2)	(7.1)
Market value ($ mil.)	(29.6%)	37.1	31.0	18.2	20.1	9.1
Employees	(13.6%)	228	201	172	146	127

PERFORMANT FINANCIAL CORP
NMS: PFMT

333 North Canyons Parkway
Livermore, CA 94551
Phone: 925 960-4800
Fax: –
Web: www.performantcorp.com

CEO: Lisa C Im
CFO: –
HR: –
FYE: December 31
Type: Public

For most of us it is best if we have never heard from or about Performant Financial. The company specializes in collecting debts owed mostly to government entities such as the US Department of Education's delinquent student loans improper Medicare payments from the US Department of Health and Human Services and taxes overdue to the US Department of the Treasury and various state governments. The financial firm operates its business nationwide. A relatively small part of Performant Financial's business involves recovering funds for private clients. The company began operations in 1976 but took its present name in 2005. Performant Financial went public in mid-2012.

	Annual Growth	12/14	12/15	12/16	12/17	12/18
Sales ($ mil.)	(5.5%)	195.4	159.4	141.4	132.0	155.7
Net income ($ mil.)	–	9.4	(1.8)	(11.5)	(12.7)	(8.0)
Market value ($ mil.)	(23.7%)	352.4	94.9	124.5	87.4	119.2
Employees	6.3%	1,484	1,218	1,211	1,260	1,892

PERFUMANIA HOLDINGS INC
NAS: PERF

35 Sawgrass Drive, Suite 2
Bellport, NY 11713
Phone: 631 866-4100
Fax: –
Web: www.perfumaniaholdingsinc.com

CEO: Michael W Katz
CFO: Michael Nofi
HR: Sophie Cardone
FYE: January 30
Type: Public

Perfumania Holdings makes dollars with scents. The holding company owns scent-seller Perfumania which numbers about 330 stores in 40 states (about a third are located in California Florida and Texas) Puerto Rico and the US Virgin Islands offering some 2000 fragrance products at discounted prices for men and women. Perfumania also sells cosmetics skin care and bath and body products. The company sells perfume online through perfumania.com and operates Scents of Worth which sells fragrances in retail stores (including Kmart) on consignment. Perfumania Holdings which own fragrance manufacturer Parlux is also a wholesale supplier of fragrances to other retailers through its Quality King Fragrance unit.

	Annual Growth	01/12*	02/13	02/14*	01/15	01/16
Sales ($ mil.)	2.4%	493.5	534.8	575.9	584.0	542.0
Net income ($ mil.)	–	4.1	(56.0)	(12.5)	2.6	(11.7)
Market value ($ mil.)	(30.9%)	152.3	99.2	96.9	89.1	34.7
Employees	0.2%	2,025	2,269	2,287	2,154	2,040

*Fiscal year change

PERICOM SEMICONDUCTOR CORP.   NMS: PSEM

1545 Barber Lane
Milpitas, CA 95035
Phone: 408 232-9100
Fax: –
Web: www.pericom.com

CEO: Alex Chiming Hui
CFO: Kevin S Bauer
HR: Elaine Liao
FYE: June 28
Type: Public

Interface chips are hardly peripheral to Pericom Semiconductor's business. The fabless company provides high-performance analog digital mixed-signal interface integrated circuits (ICs) and frequency control products (FCPs) which control the routing and transfer of data among a system's microprocessor memory and peripherals. Targeting the computer networking and telecom markets Pericom offers various chip product lines: interfaces for data transfer switches for digital and analog signals clock management chips and telecommunications switches and component bridges. Most sales come from customers located outside the US primarily in the Asia/Pacific region.

	Annual Growth	07/10	07/11*	06/12	06/13	06/14
Sales ($ mil.)	(3.4%)	146.9	166.3	137.1	129.3	128.1
Net income ($ mil.)	(21.4%)	10.8	13.5	(2.1)	(21.6)	4.1
Market value ($ mil.)	(0.1%)	201.1	195.1	197.8	156.5	200.0
Employees	2.0%	869	991	976	990	940

*Fiscal year change

PERKINELMER, INC.   NYS: PKI

940 Winter Street
Waltham, MA 02451
Phone: 781 663-6900
Fax: 781 663-6052
Web: www.perkinelmer.com

CEO: Robert F. (Rob) Friel
CFO: Frank A. (Andy) Wilson
HR: Andrew Foster
FYE: December 30
Type: Public

PerkinElmer makes tools to find out what's in you and your environment. It develops and sells equipment that researchers use to identify and treat diseases and to analyze food products as well as air water and soil to identify impurities and contaminants. The company which distributes its offerings in more than 180 countries generates most of its sales from laboratory products and other offerings. Prenatal and newborn testing and screenings in emerging markets such as China and India are fast growing areas for the company. The US is PerkinElmer's biggest market but most of its sales are to international customers. The company can trace its roots to 1931 when it started as an innovator in high-speed photography.

	Annual Growth	12/14*	01/16	01/17*	12/17	12/18
Sales ($ mil.)	5.6%	2,237.2	2,262.4	2,115.5	2,257.0	2,778.0
Net income ($ mil.)	10.8%	157.8	212.4	234.3	292.6	237.9
Market value ($ mil.)	15.1%	4,874.0	5,924.7	5,767.6	8,086.9	8,548.0
Employees	12.9%	7,700	8,000	8,000	11,000	12,500

*Fiscal year change

PERKINS COIE LLP

1201 3rd Ave. Ste. 4900
Seattle WA 98101-3099
Phone: 206-359-8000
Fax: 206-359-9000
Web: www.perkinscoie.com

CEO: –
CFO: Trevor W Varnes
HR: –
FYE: December 31
Type: Private - Partnershi

Fueled by longtime client Boeing and newer clients from the high-tech arena Perkins Coie is one of the largest law firms in the Northwest. Founded in 1912 the firm has more than 850 lawyers specializing in such areas as antitrust and trade regulation intellectual property and labor and employment. Perkins Coie's clients include individuals government agencies and not-for-profit organizations as well as international companies. The company has about 20 offices across the United States and in China. It has been listed on "FORTUNE"'s "The 100 Best Companies to Work for in America" for nine consecutive years.

PERMA-FIX ENVIRONMENTAL SERVICES, INC.   NAS: PESI

8302 Dunwoody Place, Suite 250
Atlanta, GA 30350
Phone: 770 587-9898
Fax: –

CEO: Mark Duff
CFO: Ben Naccarato
HR: –
FYE: December 31
Type: Public

Perma-Fix Environmental Services fixes its focus on nuclear waste management and related services. It operates four nuclear waste treatment plants. Its activities include the treatment of radioactive and mixed waste treatment and disposal for customers such as federal agencies nuclear utilities and hospitals and research labs. The company's services segment helps customers address regulatory compliance and other environmental concerns such as permitting and water sampling. Perma-Fix is also involved in researching and developing new ways to process low-level radioactive and mixed waste.

	Annual Growth	12/14	12/15	12/16	12/17	12/18
Sales ($ mil.)	(3.5%)	57.1	62.4	51.2	49.8	49.5
Net income ($ mil.)	–	(1.2)	(1.1)	(13.4)	(3.7)	(1.4)
Market value ($ mil.)	(14.2%)	51.9	44.4	46.6	43.6	28.1
Employees	(2.1%)	281	262	253	246	258

PERMA-PIPE INTERNATIONAL HOLDINGS INC   NMS: PPIH

6410 W. Howard Street
Niles, IL 60714
Phone: 847 966-1000
Fax: –
Web: www.permapipe.com

CEO: David J Mansfield
CFO: D Bryan Norwood
HR: –
FYE: January 31
Type: Public

MFRI's motto could be: "Pipe down and take a deep breath." The company makes piping systems and air filter elements through subsidiaries Perma-Pipe and Midwesco Filter respectively. It makes pre-insulated specialty piping systems for oil and gas gathering district heating and cooling as well as other applications. The company also makes custom-designed industrial filtration products to remove particulates from air and other gas streams. Perma-Pipe's specialty piping systems are used on college campuses military bases and other large sites. Midwesco provides products and services for industrial air filtration. Its Filtration Products segment supplies filter elements to more than 4000 user locations.

	Annual Growth	01/15	01/16	01/17	01/18	01/19
Sales ($ mil.)	(9.8%)	194.9	122.7	98.8	105.2	129.0
Net income ($ mil.)	–	(0.3)	(4.4)	(11.7)	(10.0)	(0.5)
Market value ($ mil.)	11.9%	43.8	50.3	68.7	71.1	68.6
Employees	(9.4%)	1,040	998	710	665	701

PERMIAN BASIN ROYALTY TRUST   NYS: PBT

Royalty Trust Management, Simmons Bank, 2911 Turtle Creek Boulevard, Suite 850
Dallas, TX 75219
Phone: 855 588-7839
Fax: 214 209-2431
Web: www.pbt-permian.com

CEO: –
CFO: –
HR: –
FYE: December 31
Type: Public

Permian Basin Royalty Trust is a tax-deferred pipeline for Texas oil money. Formed in 1980 the trust derives royalties from the sale of certain oil and gas assets produced by ConocoPhillips in mature oil fields in Texas including property that's part of the Waddell Ranch. The trust distributes royalties to shareholders monthly based on the amount of oil and gas produced and sold. The company owns royalty interests on proved reserves of 5.5 million barrels of oil and 18.4 billion cu. ft. of natural gas. It also has interests in 1300 gross wells and more than 76900 gross acres of land. U.S. Trust Bank of America Private Wealth Management acts as Trustee.

	Annual Growth	12/14	12/15	12/16	12/17	12/18
Sales ($ mil.)	(10.0%)	49.0	17.8	21.1	30.6	32.1
Net income ($ mil.)	(10.4%)	47.7	16.0	19.3	29.3	30.8
Market value ($ mil.)	(11.3%)	445.1	235.8	359.4	413.4	275.0
Employees						

PERNIX GROUP INC
NBB: PRXG

151 E. 22nd Street
Lombard, IL 60148
Phone: 630 620-4787
Fax: –
Web: www.pernixgroup.com

CEO: Nidal Zayed
CFO: Marco A Martinez
HR: –
FYE: December 31
Type: Public

Pernix Group (formerly Telesource International) provides engineering and construction services and operates independent power generation projects in the Pacific region and in the US. The group offers project development and management specialized construction and engineering and utility and plant operations. It also brokers goods and services. While its previous focus had been on Fiji and other islands in the Pacific Pernix Group has shifted its business model to emphasize offering construction services and working on power plant projects in North America.

	Annual Growth	12/11	12/12	12/13	12/14	12/15
Sales ($ mil.)	29.3%	69.8	120.0	73.8	85.3	195.5
Net income ($ mil.)	–	1.9	0.5	(4.6)	(1.4)	(18.8)
Market value ($ mil.)	147.6%	0.5	23.5	25.3	32.9	18.8
Employees	28.4%	175	105	115	148	475

PERSEON CORP
NBB: PRSN

460 West 50 North
Salt Lake City, UT 84101
Phone: 801 972-5555
Fax: –
Web: www.bsdmedical.com

CEO: Clinton E Carnell Jr
CFO: William S Barth
HR: –
FYE: December 31
Type: Public

BSD Medical has developed equipment to provide hyperthermia treatment specifically for treating cancer (including melanoma breast cancer brain cancer and cervical cancer). Its systems are used in tandem with chemotherapy and radiation therapy or as a stand-alone treatment. BSD Medical was the first to develop an approvable hyperthermia system which uses focused radio frequencies and microwaves to heat cancer cells until they die. The company's devices are designed to target superficial tumors as well as tumors located deep within a patient's body. Its products are sold to clinics hospitals and other cancer-treatment institutions through its sales force and external distributors.

	Annual Growth	08/11	08/12	08/13	08/14*	12/14
Sales ($ mil.)	(28.4%)	3.0	2.1	3.7	5.3	1.1
Net income ($ mil.)	–	(5.3)	(8.0)	(8.3)	(7.1)	(3.8)
Market value ($ mil.)	(50.6%)	11.6	6.9	6.0	2.6	1.4
Employees	6.1%	41	50	48	52	49

*Fiscal year change

PERSIAN ARTS SOCIETY INCORPORATED

12021 Wilshire Blvd. #420
Los Angeles CA 90025
Phone: 424-253-4726
Fax: +91-20-4012-2100
Web: www.suzlon.com

CEO: –
CFO: –
HR: –
FYE: December 31
Type: Private - Not-for-Pr

If your idea of Persian art is an intricately woven rug this organization has something to teach you. The not-for-profit group formed in 1993 works to promote and preserve traditional Persian art including music dance cinema and other visual and decorative arts in the US. It hosts lectures performances and exhibitions and offers a variety of classes; it hosts many performers and teachers who are living in Iran and other countries. While covering all the traditional arts Persian Arts Society focuses on music. It formed the first school of Persian music in the US in 2000 and regularly schedules concerts featuring Persian music a combination of vocals instruments and poetry.

PERVASIP CORP
NBB: PVSP

430 North Street
White Plains, NY 10605
Phone: 914 750-9339
Fax: –
Web: www.canalytix.com

CEO: Paul H Riss
CFO: Paul H Riss
HR: –
FYE: November 30
Type: Public

As the popularity of computer telephony spreads Pervasip (formerly eLEC Communications) hopes to cash in on convergence. Through its VoX Communications subsidiary the company provides wholesale Voice-over-Internet Protocol (VoIP) service to cable network operators ISPs competitive local exchange carriers (CLECs) and other resellers. Its customers in turn provide private or co-branded VoIP services to the residential and small business markets. VoX's service packages include such features as call return voicemail caller ID and call waiting.

	Annual Growth	11/11	11/12	11/13	11/14	11/15
Sales ($ mil.)	(17.3%)	1.3	1.0	0.9	0.5	0.6
Net income ($ mil.)	–	(4.4)	3.2	0.1	(0.5)	0.5
Market value ($ mil.)	–	0.0	0.0	0.0	0.0	0.0
Employees	(21.7%)	8	8	4	5	3

PET SUPERMARKET INC.

1100 INTL PKWY STE 200
SUNRISE, FL 33323
Phone: 954-351-0834
Fax: –
Web: www.petsupermarket.com

CEO: Richard Maltsbarger
CFO: James Grady
HR: –
FYE: December 31
Type: Private

Pet Supermarket has it all for your furry and feathered friends. The company sells more than 10000 pet care products including food toys medicine and clothing through its website and more than 135 stores in a dozen states primarily Florida. Stores also offer vaccinations for dogs cats and ferrets and sell a variety of small animals such as hamsters guinea pigs rabbits and tropical fish. In addition Pet Supermarket works with area organizations to host adoptions and related events for cats and dogs. Like its pet superstore competitors customers can take their pets shopping with them. Founded in 1973 by Chuck West as Pet Circus the family-owned company became Pet Supermarket in 1986.

	Annual Growth	12/08	12/09	12/09	12/11	12/12
Sales ($ mil.)	13.5%	–	168.0	171.1	198.7	245.6
Net income ($ mil.)	–	–	9.4	0.0	0.0	0.0
Market value ($ mil.)	–	–	–	–	–	–
Employees	–	–	–	–	–	1,000

PETCO ANIMAL SUPPLIES INC.

9125 Rehco Rd.
San Diego CA 92121
Phone: 858-453-7845
Fax: 949-255-2605
Web: www.qsii.com

CEO: Ron Coughlin
CFO: Michael M Nuzzo
HR: –
FYE: January 31
Type: Private

PETCO Animal Supplies is a holding company for PETCO Animal Supplies Stores the second-largest US retailer of specialty pet supplies (behind PetSmart). The company boasts about 1150 stores in all 50 states and the District of Columbia making it the only pet store to cover the entire US market. The chain sells more than 10000 pet-related products for dogs cats fish reptiles birds and other small animals. PETCO Animal Supplies holding company was formed to create a foundation for the firm's upcoming growth strategies. Founded in 1965 PETCO Animal Supplies is owned by Texas Pacific Groupand Leonard Green & Partners which took it private in a deal worth $1.8 billion.

PETER KIEWIT SONS', INC.

3555 FARNAM ST STE 1000
OMAHA, NE 681313374
Phone: 402-342-2052
Fax: -
Web: www.kiewit.com

CEO: Bruce E. Grewcock
CFO: Michael J. Piechoski
HR: -
FYE: December 29
Type: Private

A heavyweight in the heavy construction industry Kiewit is one of North America's largest construction and engineering firms. The company is active in building industrial mining oil gas chemicals power transportation water and wastewater. It builds everything from roads and dams to high-rise office towers and power plants. The company focuses on projects located throughout the US Canada and Mexico. Affiliate Kiewit Mining owns or manages coal mines in Texas and Wyoming and manages a phosphate operation in southeast Idaho. Founded in 1884 Kiewit is owned by employees and Kiewit family members.

	Annual Growth	12/08	12/09	12/10	12/11	12/12
Sales ($ mil.)	6.3%	-	-	9,938.0	10,381.0	11,220.0
Net income ($ mil.)	(19.2%)	-	-	789.0	790.0	515.0
Market value ($ mil.)	-	-	-	-	-	-
Employees	-	-	-	-	-	14,700

PETER PAN BUS LINES INC.

1776 MAIN ST STE 1
SPRINGFIELD, MA 011031025
Phone: 413-781-2900
Fax: -
Web: www.peterpanbus.com

CEO: Peter A Picknelly
CFO: -
HR: -
FYE: December 31
Type: Private

The Boy Who Wouldn't Grow Up has given up midnight flights to Neverland for the more mundane bus routes of the northeastern and mid-Atlantic US. Peter Pan Bus Lines provides scheduled service to more than 100 cities in about 10 states along the Boston-to-Washington DC corridor. It transports packages as well as passengers on its scheduled routes; in addition the company offers charter and tour bus services in the US and Canada. Overall the company and its subsidiaries which include Arrow Line and Bonanza Bus Lines operate a fleet of about 300 buses. Peter Pan Bus Lines was founded in 1933 by Peter C. Picknelly grandfather of company president Peter A. Picknelly. The Picknelly family owns the company.

	Annual Growth	12/03	12/04	12/05	12/06	12/08
Sales ($ mil.)	2.9%	-	51.9	52.6	53.9	58.2
Net income ($ mil.)	(12.1%)	-	-	3.2	2.7	2.1
Market value ($ mil.)	-	-	-	-	-	-
Employees	-	-	-	-	-	750

PETMED EXPRESS INC

420 South Congress Avenue
Delray Beach, FL 33445
Phone: 561 526-4444
Fax: -
Web: www.1800petmeds.com

NMS: PETS
CEO: Menderes Akdag
CFO: Bruce S. Rosenbloom
HR: -
FYE: March 31
Type: Public

Convenience is king to PetMed Express which bills itself as America's largest pet pharmacy. Through 1-800-PetMeds and 1800petmeds.com as well as a catalog with hundreds of items PetMed Express offers prescription and nonprescription medicines and other pet care supplies for your calico collie or colt. Founded in 1996 the company purchases its products at wholesale prices and ships directly to customers. The company makes 81% of its sales via its website. Most sales come from previous customers. It also offers pet health information on a separate site PetHealth101.com which it sponsors.

	Annual Growth	03/15	03/16	03/17	03/18	03/19
Sales ($ mil.)	5.4%	229.4	234.7	249.2	273.8	283.4
Net income ($ mil.)	21.3%	17.5	20.6	23.8	37.3	37.7
Market value ($ mil.)	8.4%	341.5	370.3	416.4	863.1	471.0
Employees	2.3%	182	178	187	187	199

PETRO HOLDINGS INC.

2187 Atlantic St.
Stamford CT 06902
Phone: 203-325-5400
Fax: 203-328-7422
Web: www.petrohp.com

CEO: -
CFO: -
HR: -
FYE: September 30
Type: Subsidiary

When it's chilly in the East residents have warm spots in their hearts for Petro Holdings (formerly Petroleum Heat & Power). The company is a leading retail distributor of home heating oil in the US and sells provides more than 351 million gallons of heating oil a year to approximately 402000 customers and propane to 7000 customers in Connecticut Maryland Massachusetts New Jersey New York Pennsylvania Rhode Island and Virginia. A unit of Star Gas Partners' Star/Petro subsidiary Petro Holdings also sells home heating oil gasoline and diesel to some 28000 customers on a delivery-only basis. Other activities include HVAC equipment repair and home security and plumbing services to 11000 customers.

PETRO STAR INC.

3900 C ST STE 802
ANCHORAGE, AK 995035963
Phone: 907-339-6600
Fax: -
Web: www.petrostar.com

CEO: -
CFO: -
HR: -
FYE: December 31
Type: Private

Petro Star is an oil refining and fuel marketing shining star that brings heating fuel and energy (diesel gasoline and aviation and marine fuel)s to the citizens of the communities in the vast cold and lonely expanses of the US' largest state Alaska. It operates refineries at North Pole and Valdez and distributes fuels and lubricants throughout Interior Alaska Dutch Harbor Kodiak and Valdez. Started in 1984 by a group of petroleum industry veterans the company built its first refinery operations along the Trans-Alaska Pipeline at North Pole Alaska. Petro Star is a subsidiary of Arctic Slope Regional Corp..

	Annual Growth	12/00	12/01	12/02	12/03	12/08
Sales ($ mil.)	19.9%	-	279.2	267.8	291.0	992.1
Net income ($ mil.)	-	-	3.0	1.9	3.6	0.0
Market value ($ mil.)	-	-	-	-	-	-
Employees	-	-	-	-	-	300

PETROCELLI ELECTRIC CO. INC.

2209 QUEENS PLZ N
LONG ISLAND CITY, NY 11101-4003
Phone: 718-752-2200
Fax: -

CEO: -
CFO: -
HR: -
FYE: March 31
Type: Private

Petrocelli Electric keeps the city that never sleeps wired. Founded in 1933 the contractor installs and maintains electrical communications and lighting systems for commercial institutional and public sector clients in the New York City metropolitan area. Its activities include project management electrical engineering and design-build services such as developing electrical distribution and communications systems installing generators and fiber-optic cables and laying underground feeder cables. In 2009 former owner Santo Petrocelli Sr. pleaded guilty to charges that he made illegal payments to a union official.

	Annual Growth	03/01	03/02	03/03	03/07	03/09
Sales ($ mil.)	(4.2%)	-	159.1	162.1	147.2	118.0
Net income ($ mil.)	(1.1%)	-	0.6	0.1	0.6	0.5
Market value ($ mil.)	-	-	-	-	-	-
Employees	-	-	-	-	-	300

PETROHAWK ENERGY CORPORATION

1000 Louisiana Ste. 5600
Houston TX 77002
Phone: 832-204-2700
Fax: 832-204-2800
Web: www.petrohawk.com

CEO: –
CFO: –
HR: –
FYE: December 31
Type: Subsidiary

Petrohawk Energy (formerly Beta Oil & Gas) is riding rising oil prices to higher profits. The independent company's activities include the exploration development and production of crude oil and natural gas in the Anadarko Arkoma East Texas/North Louisiana Gulf Coast Permian Basin and South Texas regions. Petrohawk Energy has estimated proved reserves of about 2.8 trillion cu. ft. of natural gas equivalent. The company is concentrating its efforts on developing key shale plays including the Haynesville Shale the Lower Bossier Shale and the Eagle Ford Shale. In a move to boost its US shale assets in 2011 BHP Billiton acquired Petrohawk Energy for $12.1 billion.

PETROLOGISTICS LP

909 Fannin St. Ste. 2630
Houston TX 77010
Phone: 713-255-5990
Fax: 919-872-1645
Web: www.ateb.com

NYSE: PDH
CEO: –
CFO: –
HR: –
FYE: December 31
Type: Public

PetroLogistics thinks it's perfectly logical to focus on making one petrochemical at a time. The company operates a 67-acre propane dehydrogenation (PDH) plant in Houston that turns propane into propylene a chemical used in the production of polypropylene. PetroLogistics sells its propylene to three major polypropylene manufacturers — Dow INEOS and TOTAL which use it to make petrochemical-based consumer and industrial products such as coatings paints plastic parts reusable containers ropes and textiles. The plant which began production in 2010 has an annual production capacity of 1.2 billion pounds of propylene. The company filed a $600 million IPO in June 2011 and went public in 2012.

PETROLEUM MARKETERS INCORPORATED

3000 OGDEN RD
ROANOKE, VA 24018-8857
Phone: 540-772-4900
Fax: –
Web: www.petroleummarketers.com

CEO: –
CFO: –
HR: –
FYE: June 30
Type: Private

No fancy name for this company. It is what it says it is. Petroleum Marketers is a full-service petroleum company serving customers in Kentucky Maryland North Carolina Tennessee West Virginia and Virginia. The company's PM Terminals unit supplies gasoline diesel fuel motor oil and antifreeze to customers in its service area from eight bulk fuel storage facilities in Virginia. PMI Lubricants operates a fleet of bulk transport trucks while PM Transport offers for-hire tanker truckers for the transportation of petroleum products. The company also runs a chain of about 70 convenience stores/gas stations in Virginia under the banner Stop In Food Stores.

	Annual Growth	06/09	06/10	06/10	06/12	06/13
Sales ($ mil.)	9.3%	–	797.3	945.1	1,081.4	1,040.6
Net income ($ mil.)	(37.4%)	–	4.6	2.0	2.0	1.1
Market value ($ mil.)	–	–	–	–	–	–
Employees	–	–	–	–	–	1,500

PETROQUEST ENERGY INC (NEW)

400 E. Kaliste Saloom Road, Suite 6000
Lafayette, LA 70508
Phone: 337 232-7028
Fax: –
Web: www.petroquest.com

NBB: QWST
CEO: Charles T Goodson
CFO: J Bond Clement
HR: –
FYE: December 31
Type: Public

Independent oil and gas exploration and production company PetroQuest Energy once focused its quest for petroleum on the hydrocarbon-rich and high margin Gulf Coast Basin but in the last decade in order to diversify its reserve base and allow it more financial flexibility it has looked to grow its assets in long-lived lower risk basins onshore. PetroQuest estimates its 2018 production was a little more than 21 billion cubic feet equivalent (bcfe) of gas (about 75% of production) oil (9%) and natural gas liquids (16%). PetroQuest Energy filed for Chapter 11 bankruptcy protection in late 2018 and emerged early the following year.

	Annual Growth	12/14	12/15	12/16	12/17	12/18
Sales ($ mil.)	(21.1%)	225.0	116.0	66.7	108.3	87.1
Net income ($ mil.)	–	31.2	(294.8)	(90.9)	(6.6)	(9.5)
Market value ($ mil.)	(82.0%)	95.7	12.8	84.7	48.4	0.1
Employees	(21.3%)	141	119	64	65	54

PETROLEUM TRADERS CORPORATION

7120 POINTE INVERNESS WAY
FORT WAYNE, IN 468047928
Phone: 260-432-6622
Fax: –
Web: www.petroleumtraders.com

CEO: Michael Himes
CFO: Linda Stephens
HR: Jen Bynum
FYE: June 30
Type: Private

Petroleum Traders Corporation barters with fuel. The company provides wholesale gasoline diesel fuel and heating oil to fuel distributors government agencies and other large consumers of fuel such as businesses with vehicle fleets. The largest pure wholesale fuel distributor in the country Petroleum Traders operates and trades in 44 US states. It supplies #1 and #2 low sulfur diesel fuels biodiesel high sulfur heating oil and kerosene and conventional ethanol and reformulated blends of gasoline in regular midgrade and premium octane ratings.

	Annual Growth	06/14	06/15	06/16	06/17	06/18
Sales ($ mil.)	(5.2%)	–	2,128.0	1,667.4	1,606.4	1,815.8
Net income ($ mil.)	(43.6%)	–	64.0	38.3	19.0	11.5
Market value ($ mil.)	–	–	–	–	–	–
Employees	–	–	–	–	–	150

PETSMART, INC.

19601 North 27th Avenue
Phoenix, AZ 85027
Phone: 623 580-6100
Fax: 623 395-6517
Web: www.petsmart.com

NMS: PETM
CEO: –
CFO: –
HR: –
FYE: February 2/
Type: Public

PetSmart is the top dog and the cat's meow in its industry. The #1 US specialty retailer of pet food and supplies operates about 1350 stores in the US Canada and Puerto Rico. The retailer offers a noteworthy 11000 products which range from scratching posts to iguana harnesses. Products which are also sold through the PetSmart website are marketed under national brands and its own private labels. Unique to PetSmart its stores provide in-store PetsHotel boarding facilities grooming services and obedience training. The company's 20%-owned vet services firm Medical Management International (known as Banfield) offers its services in about 850 stores. Investment company BC Partners is buying PetSmart.

	Annual Growth	01/10	01/11	01/12*	02/13	02/14
Sales ($ mil.)	6.7%	5,336.4	5,693.8	6,113.3	6,758.2	6,916.6
Net income ($ mil.)	20.6%	198.3	239.9	290.2	389.5	419.5
Market value ($ mil.)	25.1%	2,591.9	4,043.4	5,387.2	6,440.1	6,341.5
Employees	4.2%	45,000	47,000	50,000	52,000	53,000

*Fiscal year change

PFIZER INC
NYS: PFE

235 East 42nd Street
New York, NY 10017
Phone: 212 733-2323
Fax: –
Web: www.pfizer.com

CEO: Ian C. Read
CFO: Frank A. D'Amelio
HR: Charles H. (Chuck) Hill
FYE: December 31
Type: Public

Pfizer is one of the world's largest research-based pharmaceuticals firms producing medicines for ailments in fields including cardiovascular health metabolism oncology and inflammation and immunology. Its top prescription products include cholesterol-lowering Lipitor pain management drugs Celebrex and Lyrica pneumonia vaccine Prevnar and erectile dysfunction treatment Viagra as well as arthritis drug Enbrel antibiotic Zyvox and high-blood-pressure therapy Norvasc. The firm also makes and sells generic drugs and consumer health products. Pfizer operates around the world but gets half of its revenues from the US.

	Annual Growth	12/14	12/15	12/16	12/17	12/18
Sales ($ mil.)	2.0%	49,605.0	48,851.0	52,824.0	52,546.0	53,647.0
Net income ($ mil.)	5.1%	9,135.0	6,960.0	7,215.0	21,308.0	11,153.0
Market value ($ mil.)	–	0.0	0.0	0.0	0.0	0.0
Employees	4.2%	78,300	97,900	96,500	90,200	92,400

PFSWEB INC
NAS: PFSW

505 Millennium Drive
Allen, TX 75013
Phone: 972 881-2900
Fax: –
Web: www.pfsweb.com

CEO: Michael C. (Mike) Willoughby
CFO: Thomas J. Madden
HR: Latrice Bryant-robinson
FYE: December 31
Type: Public

PFSweb is all in when it comes to outsourcing. The company is an international business process outsourcing (BPO) provider of e-commerce services. Through its End2End eCommerce platform it offers such services as customer care digital marketing financial management logistics and fulfillment and order management. These services support both direct-to-consumer (DTC) and business-to-business (B2B) sales initiatives from developing new products to implementing new business strategies. PFSweb serves major brand name companies across a range of industries including toys (LEGO) consumer goods (Procter & Gamble) cosmetics (L'Or-©al) and the US Mint.

	Annual Growth	12/14	12/15	12/16	12/17	12/18
Sales ($ mil.)	7.2%	247.0	288.3	334.6	326.8	326.2
Net income ($ mil.)	–	(4.6)	(7.9)	(7.5)	(4.0)	1.2
Market value ($ mil.)	(20.2%)	243.8	247.9	163.7	143.1	98.8
Employees	7.8%	1,700	2,100	2,500	25,500	2,300

PG&E CORP (HOLDING CO)
NYS: PCG

77 Beale Street, P.O. Box 770000
San Francisco, CA 94177
Phone: 415 973-1000
Fax: 415 267-7265
Web: www.pgecorp.com

CEO: –
CFO: David S. Thomason
HR: Dinyar B. Mistry
FYE: December 31
Type: Public

Pacific Gas and Electric Company one of the largest public utility providers in California supplies electricity and natural gas to residential commercial industrial and agricultural customers in northern and central California. It reaches 5.4 million electric customers via 107000 miles of electric distribution lines and 4.5 million gas customers via 43100 miles of gas distribution lines. The company sources its electric and natural gas supply from owned generation facilities (135 electric plants) and through third-party agreements. The utility along with its parent PG&E Corporation filed for Chapter 11 bankruptcy protection in January 2019 as it faced up to $30 billion in damage liabilities related to California wildfires in 2017 and 2018.

	Annual Growth	12/14	12/15	12/16	12/17	12/18
Sales ($ mil.)	(0.5%)	17,090.0	16,833.0	17,666.0	17,135.0	16,759.0
Net income ($ mil.)	–	1,450.0	888.0	1,407.0	1,660.0	(6,837.0)
Market value ($ mil.)	(18.3%)	27,702.8	27,676.8	31,621.0	23,326.8	12,358.0
Employees	1.5%	22,581	23,000	24,000	23,000	24,000

PGA TOUR, INC.

100 PGA TOUR BLVD
PONTE VEDRA BEACH, FL 320823046
Phone: 904-285-3700
Fax: –
Web: www.golfexperiences.com

CEO: –
CFO: Charles L Zink
HR: Tom Perry
FYE: December 31
Type: Private

It takes the ferocity of a Tiger to get to the top of this membership organization. The PGA TOUR which includes Tiger Woods and golf's other top players puts on more than 100 official events per year that offer more than $350 million in prize money. Its major championships are the Masters US Open British Open and PGA Championship. The group also oversees the Champions Tour for players 50 and older and the Nationwide Tour for emerging players. The PGA TOUR is separate from the PGA of America which consists mostly of club pros although most tour players maintain membership in both groups. The PGA TOUR was formed in 1968 by a splinter faction of the PGA of America.

	Annual Growth	12/03	12/04	12/05	12/06	12/13
Sales ($ mil.)	3.3%	–	802.2	875.8	894.0	1,075.0
Net income ($ mil.)	29.4%	–	3.4	4.5	3.1	34.6
Market value ($ mil.)	–	–	–	–	–	–
Employees	–	–	–	–	–	3,563

PGT INNOVATIONS INC
NYS: PGTI

1070 Technology Drive
North Venice, FL 34275
Phone: 941 480-1600
Fax: –
Web: www.pgtinnovations.com

CEO: Rodney (Rod) Hershberger
CFO: Bradley (Brad) West
HR: Debbie L Lapinska
FYE: December 29
Type: Public

PGT helps Floridians weather their storms. The company makes and sells WinGuard and PremierVue impact-resistant doors and windows for the residential market. The energy-efficient customizable doors and windows are made of aluminum or vinyl with laminated glass and are designed to withstand hurricane-strength winds. PGT also makes Eze-Breeze porch enclosure panels and garage door screens SpectraGuard vinyl replacement windows and PGT Architectural Systems windows for high-rises. The company has two manufacturing facilities in Florida and North Carolina. PGT sells its products through some 1200 window distributors dealers and contractors in the Southeastern US Canada Central America and the Caribbean.

	Annual Growth	01/15	01/16*	12/16	12/17	12/18
Sales ($ mil.)	31.6%	306.4	389.8	458.6	511.1	698.5
Net income ($ mil.)	48.7%	16.4	23.6	23.7	39.8	53.9
Market value ($ mil.)	17.2%	566.9	661.5	665.0	978.7	913.0
Employees	16.4%	1,900	2,300	2,600	2,700	3,000

*Fiscal year change

PH GLATFELTER CO
NYS: GLT

96 South George Street, Suite 520
York, PA 17401
Phone: 717 850-0170
Fax: 717 846-7208
Web: www.glatfelter.com

CEO: Dante C. Parrini
CFO: John P. Jacunski
HR: William T Yanavitch
FYE: December 31
Type: Public

In business for more than 150 years P. H. Glatfelter is a global manufacturer of specialty papers and engineered products. The company's largest business unit Specialty Papers produces products such as carbonless and book publishing papers envelopes and engineered paper for digital imaging (the company has agreed to sell its Specialty Papers business in 2018). Its Germany-based Composite Fibers unit makes products like coffee and tea filter paper and self-adhesive labeling paper while the Advanced Airlaid Materials business focuses on nonwoven fabric-like materials used in feminine hygiene products diapers cleaning pads and wipes. More than half of the company's total sales are generated in the US.

	Annual Growth	12/14	12/15	12/16	12/17	12/18
Sales ($ mil.)	(16.8%)	1,810.3	1,666.7	1,610.9	1,596.4	866.3
Net income ($ mil.)	–	69.2	64.6	21.6	7.9	(177.6)
Market value ($ mil.)	(21.4%)	1,124.0	810.6	1,050.2	942.5	429.0
Employees	(13.3%)	4,610	4,375	4,346	4,175	2,600

PHARMACEUTICAL PRODUCT DEVELOPMENT INC.
NASDAQ: PPDI

929 N. Front St.
Wilmington NC 28401
Phone: 910-251-0081
Fax: 910-762-5820
Web: www.ppdi.com

CEO: David Simmons
CFO: Robert Hureau
HR: –
FYE: December 31
Type: Private

Pharmaceutical Product Development (PPD) is on the hunt for newfangled drugs. One of the world's largest contract research organizations (CROs) PPD provides global research and development services to pharmaceutical biotech and medical device companies seeking regulatory approval for their products. The CRO offers a broad range of services from toxicology testing in the earliest phases of drug research to the management of large multi-site clinical trials in which drug compounds are tested on human subjects. Its customers have included most of the world's top 50 pharma companies. PPD was acquired in 2011 for some $3.9 billion by private investors The Carlyle Group and Hellman & Friedman.

PHARMACYCLICS, INC.
NMS: PCYC

995 E. Arques Avenue
Sunnyvale, CA 94085-4521
Phone: 408 774-0330
Fax: 408 774-0340
Web: www.pharmacyclics.com

CEO: –
CFO: –
HR: –
FYE: December 31
Type: Public

Pharmacyclics wants to help cancer and other diseases cycle right out of your body. The clinical-stage company develops small-molecule drugs to fight cancer and auto-immune diseases. Its key product Imbruvica is approved in the US to treat mantle cell lymphoma a rare cancer and in testing for three other cancers. Pharmacyclis has two other cancer treatments and an autoimmune disease cure in its pipeline. The company has licensing and development agreements with Janssen Biotech Les Laboratories Servier and Novo Nordisk. It sells its products to specialty pharmacies whose customers are individuals and to specialty distributors whose customers are hospital pharmacies. Pharmacyclics was formed in 1991.

	Annual Growth	06/10	06/11	06/12*	12/12	12/13
Sales ($ mil.)	203.5%	9.3	8.2	82.0	160.7	260.2
Net income ($ mil.)	–	(15.0)	(35.2)	12.0	117.5	67.0
Market value ($ mil.)	151.4%	494.0	774.3	4,050.3	4,285.4	7,845.4
Employees	102.8%	58	77	150	224	484

*Fiscal year change

PHARMERICA CORP
NYS: PMC

1901 Campus Place
Louisville, KY 40299
Phone: 502 627-7000
Fax: –
Web: www.pharmerica.com

CEO: Gregory S Weishar
CFO: Robert E Dries
HR: –
FYE: December 31
Type: Public

The only time you'll see PharMerica's products is when a nurse hands you a pill in a paper cup. As the country's second-largest institutional pharmacy operator (behind Omnicare) the firm provides purchasing packaging and dispensing of drugs to hospitals nursing homes assisted living facilities and other long-term care settings. PharMerica operates about 100 institutional pharmacies including 15 focused on infusion therapies and five for oncology medications from which it packages and delivers medications in unit doses (rather than in bulk) to customers in 45 states. It also provides consulting and monitoring services of drug usage to help care facilities comply with government regulations.

	Annual Growth	12/11	12/12	12/13	12/14	12/15
Sales ($ mil.)	(0.6%)	2,081.1	1,832.6	1,757.9	1,894.5	2,028.5
Net income ($ mil.)	10.7%	23.4	22.9	18.9	6.8	35.1
Market value ($ mil.)	23.2%	462.4	433.8	654.9	630.8	1,066.1
Employees	(0.4%)	5,900	6,100	5,800	6,000	5,800

PHARMOS CORPORATION
PINK SHEETS: PARS

99 Wood Ave. South Ste. 311
Iselin NJ 08830
Phone: 732-452-9556
Fax: 732-452-9557
Web: www.pharmoscorp.com

CEO: –
CFO: –
HR: –
FYE: December 31
Type: Public

Drug developer Pharmos has focused its attention on the central nervous system. Its stable of drug candidates aim to treat conditions such as pain inflammation and autoimmune conditions. It gained its lead candidate dextofisopam when it acquired Vela Pharmaceuticals; the compound is a potential treatment for irritable bowel syndrome a condition associated with the "brain-gut axis" or the connection between the nervous system and the intestines. Pharmos has also discovered several compounds in-house using its expertise in cannabinoid compounds (the kind without psychotropic effects). It is investigating several such compounds as treatments for pain and inflammation.

PHELPS DUNBAR L.L.P.

365 CANAL ST STE 2000
NEW ORLEANS, LA 70130-6534
Phone: 504-566-1311
Fax: –
Web: www.phelpsdunbar.com

CEO: Jeffrey M Baudier
CFO: –
HR: –
FYE: December 31
Type: Private

A leading regional law firm Phelps Dunbar has more than 280 attorneys overall. The firm has represented public and private companies educational institutions governmental agencies health care systems estates and individuals. Clients have included T3 Technologies Louisiana Wholesale Drug Co. and Deutsche Schiffsbank. Among Phelps Dunbar's practice areas are admiralty; bankruptcy; commercial litigation; intellectual property; oil and gas; and product liability. Phelps Dunbar is especially focused on clients operating in the oil gas and energy industries.

	Annual Growth	12/07	12/08	12/09	12/10	12/11
Sales ($ mil.)	3.9%	–	98.0	98.6	109.5	109.8
Net income ($ mil.)	7.3%	–	36.5	36.4	46.4	45.1
Market value ($ mil.)	–	–	–	–	–	–
Employees	–	–	–	–	–	611

PHELPS MEMORIAL HOSPITAL ASSOCIATION

701 N BROADWAY
SLEEPY HOLLOW, NY 105911096
Phone: 914-366-3000
Fax: –
Web: www.phelpshospital.org

CEO: –
CFO: Vincent Desantis
HR: Jake Maijala
FYE: December 31
Type: Private

If you happen to spot the headless horseman in Sleepy Hollow it's possible he's on his way to Phelps Memorial Hospital for some medical treatment. The 240-bed hospital provides both physical and mental health care services to residents of Sleepy Hollow and Westchester County New York. Specialized services include cardiology emergency care orthopedics and psychiatry. It also includes a satellite location of the Memorial Sloan-Kettering Cancer Center and it provides geriatric health services through a partnership with Mount Sinai Hospital and operates a senior retirement community with Kendal Corporation. Phelps Memorial is one of four hospitals that make up the Stellaris Health Network.

	Annual Growth	12/13	12/14	12/15	12/16	12/17
Sales ($ mil.)	2.2%	–	224.8	230.0	220.4	240.2
Net income ($ mil.)	13.9%	–	12.0	3.1	21.0	17.8
Market value ($ mil.)	–	–	–	–	–	–
Employees	–	–	–	–	–	1,200

PHH CORP
NYS: PHH

3000 Leadenhall Road
Mt. Laurel, NJ 08054
Phone: 856 917-1744
Fax: –
Web: www.phh.com

CEO: Robert B Crowl
CFO: Michael R Bogansky
HR: –
FYE: December 31
Type: Public

Through its primary PHH Mortgage segment PHH Corporation offers mortgage-related activities such as originating purchasing selling and servicing mortgage loans. It caters primarily to financial institutions and real estate brokers in the US. PHH Corporation makes nearly 70% of its revenue through mortgage origination service fees and in selling its mortgage loans on the secondary market and another 25% from its mortgage servicing business. The company's former Vehicle Management segment a provider of commercial fleet management services in the US and Canada was sold to Element Financial Corporation in 2014. Its top clients include Fannie Mae Freddie Mac and Ginnie Mae.

	Annual Growth	12/12	12/13	12/14	12/15	12/16
Sales ($ mil.)	(31.0%)	2,743.0	2,842.0	639.0	790.0	622.0
Net income ($ mil.)	–	34.0	135.0	81.0	(145.0)	(202.0)
Market value ($ mil.)	(9.6%)	1,219.4	1,305.1	1,284.2	868.3	812.6
Employees	(15.0%)	6,700	6,000	4,100	3,800	3,500

PHI GROUP INC.
NBB: PHIL

5348 Vegas Drive,#237
Las Vegas, NV 89108
Phone: 702 475-5430
Fax: –
Web: www.phiglobal.com

CEO: –
CFO: Henry D Fahman
HR: –
FYE: June 30
Type: Public

PHI Group rolls a variety of business into one. The holding company focuses its attention on consulting and financial services real estate investment and natural resources and energy. At the center of PHI Group's offerings is PHI Vietnam and PHI Capital which provide assistance to Vietnamese companies that go public in the US. Other PHI Group holdings include PHI Gold Corporation which invests in gold mines around the world. Real estate arm PHILAND Ranch develops industrial residential and hospitality properties in southeast Asia.

	Annual Growth	06/14	06/15	06/16	06/17	06/18
Sales ($ mil.)	115.6%	0.1	0.1	0.3	0.1	1.7
Net income ($ mil.)	–	(0.3)	(1.4)	(0.0)	(1.6)	(2.0)
Market value ($ mil.)	(47.1%)	62.8	28.5	92.7	3.7	4.9
Employees	–	–	–	–	–	–

PHI INC
NMS: PHII K

2001 S.E. Evangeline Thruway
Lafayette, LA 70508
Phone: 337 235-2452
Fax: 337 235-1357
Web: www.phihelico.com

CEO: Lance F Bospflug
CFO: Trudy P McConnaughhay
HR: –
FYE: December 31
Type: Public

Whirlybird wizard PHI transports people and equipment mainly for oil and gas companies. One of the world's top commercial helicopter operators PHI maintains a fleet of more than 270 aircraft and provides contract transportation services across the US and in Africa primarily for the oil and gas industry. Its fleet is primarily made up of helicopters but also includes fixed-wing aircraft. The company is a leading provider of helicopter transport services in the Gulf of Mexico. In addition to its energy-related operations PHI provides air transportation services to hospitals and other medical facilities and overhauls and maintains airframes engines and components.

	Annual Growth	12/13	12/14	12/15	12/16	12/17
Sales ($ mil.)	(9.3%)	856.5	836.3	804.2	634.1	579.5
Net income ($ mil.)	(40.2%)	59.0	32.7	26.9	(26.7)	7.5
Market value ($ mil.)	(28.1%)	685.9	591.0	259.3	284.8	182.8
Employees	(2.5%)	2,791	2,844	2,694	2,472	2,521

PHIBRO ANIMAL HEALTH CORPORATION

Glenpoint Centre East Frank W. Burr Blvd. 3rd Fl 300
Teaneck NJ 07666-6712
Phone: 201-329-7300
Fax: 201-329-7399
Web: www.pahc.com

CEO: Jack C Bendheim
CFO: Richard G Johnson
HR: Lisa A Escudero
FYE: June 30
Type: Private

Phibro Animal Health makes feeding time down on the farm a happy occasion. The company's Animal Health and Nutrition segment produces animal feed additives including trace minerals vitamins and antibiotics for livestock poultry and aquaculture markets worldwide. Phibro's Performance Products segment manufactures specialty chemicals for agricultural and industrial uses including ingredients for the ethanol coatings and adhesives metal and personal care industries. Phibro also supplies antimicrobials used in ethanol production. Chairman and president Jack Bendheim owns a majority stake in Phibro Animal Health.

PHILADELPHIA CONSOLIDATED HOLDING CORP.

1 BALA PLZ STE 100
BALA CYNWYD, PA 190041401
Phone: 610-617-7900
Fax: –
Web: www.phly.com

CEO: –
CFO: –
HR: Laura Boylan
FYE: December 31
Type: Private

Because each industry has its own unique set of risks Philadelphia Insurance Companies and its subsidiaries specialize in designing and underwriting commercial property/casualty insurance. Its niche clients include rental car companies (for that insurance they always want to sell you at the counter) not-for-profits health and fitness centers and day-care facilities. Its specialty lines include loss-control policies and liability coverage for such professionals as lawyers doctors accountants dog groomers and even insurance claims adjusters. Philadelphia Insurance Companies is a subsidiary of Tokio Marine Holdings.

	Annual Growth	12/12	12/13	12/14	12/15	12/16
Assets ($ mil.)	7.4%	–	–	–	9,047.4	9,719.4
Net income ($ mil.)	7.5%	–	–	–	323.2	347.5
Market value ($ mil.)	–	–	–	–	–	–
Employees	–	–	–	–	–	1,374

PHILADELPHIA NORTH HEALTH SYSTEM

801 W GIRARD AVE
PHILADELPHIA, PA 191224212
Phone: 215-787-9001
Fax: –
Web: www.nphs.com

CEO: George Walmsley III
CFO: –
HR: –
FYE: June 30
Type: Private

Too many Philly cheesesteaks got you feeling down? The North Philadelphia Health System (NPHS) is there to help. The system is composed of two health care facilities serving some of Philadelphia's poorest neighborhoods. The Girard Medical Center provides long-term care outpatient mental health services and general medical and surgical care; while Goldman Clinic treats substance abuse. After losing money for two years NPHS shut down its St. Joseph's Hospital facility in 2016. At the end of that year NPHS filed for Chapter 11 bankruptcy protection.

	Annual Growth	06/10	06/11	06/12	06/13	06/15
Sales ($ mil.)	2.5%	–	–	–	101.8	107.0
Net income ($ mil.)	–	–	–	–	(1.8)	(0.5)
Market value ($ mil.)	–	–	–	–	–	–
Employees	–	–	–	–	–	900

PHILADELPHIA WORKFORCE DEVELOPMENT CORPORATION

1617 JFK BLVD STE 1300
PHILADELPHIA, PA 191031813
Phone: 215-963-2100
Fax: –
Web: www.philaworks.org

CEO: Mark Edwards
CFO: Dale Porter
HR: –
FYE: June 30
Type: Private

The Philadelphia Workforce Development Corporation (PWDC) wants Philadelphians to get a job. A tax-exempt not-for-profit PWDC has served the city's workforce since 1982. For businesses it offers employee recruitment development and retention services; assessment and testing; job fair coordination; wage subsidies; and tax credits. It trains job seekers (including ex-offenders the homeless workers with disabilities and unemployed adults) in areas such as skills development resume writing interviewing and salary negotiations. The agency also funnels state and federal dollars to agencies that provide workforce training. Philadelphia area employers that have partnered with PWDC include ARAMARK and IKEA.

	Annual Growth	06/07	06/08	06/09	06/10	06/11
Sales ($ mil.)	4.4%	–	–	110.5	112.8	120.3
Net income ($ mil.)	–	–	–	(0.2)	0.0	(0.2)
Market value ($ mil.)	–	–	–	–	–	–
Employees	–	–	–	–	–	100

PHILIP MORRIS INTERNATIONAL INC   NYS: PM

120 Park Avenue
New York, NY 10017
Phone: 917 663-2000
Fax: 917 663-5372
Web: www.pmi.com

CEO: André Calantzopoulos
CFO: Martin G. King
HR: –
FYE: December 31
Type: Public

Philip Morris is quitting smoking: The cigarette company is on the long path to a smoke-free product portfolio. In the meantime however Philip Morris International (PMI) is still one of the world's biggest cigarette manufacturers making six of the world's top 15 tobacco brands and laying claim to more than 15% of the cigarette market outside the US. Despite being US-based its sales presence is entirely non-US. Its biggest brands are Marlboro (the world's #1-selling cigarette) which accounts for about a third of PMI's total shipment volume L&M and Bond Street. Top local brands include Fortune Belmont and Dji Sam Soe. PMI was formed when its former parent Altria spun off its international operations.

	Annual Growth	12/15	12/16	12/17	12/18	12/19
Sales ($ mil.)	2.7%	26,794.0	26,685.0	28,748.0	29,625.0	29,805.0
Net income ($ mil.)	1.1%	6,873.0	6,967.0	6,035.0	7,911.0	7,185.0
Market value ($ mil.)	(0.8%)	136,778.7	142,348.8	164,380.3	103,871.5	132,391.1
Employees	(2.2%)	80,200	79,500	80,600	77,400	73,500

PHILIPS ELECTRONICS NORTH AMERICA CORPORATION

3000 Minuteman Rd.
Andover MA 01810
Phone: 800-223-1828
Fax: 310-952-2199
Web: www.pioneerelectronics.com

CEO: Vitor Rocha
CFO: –
HR: –
FYE: December 31
Type: Subsidiary

Whether you need an early morning shave or a late night TV fix Philips Electronics North America has got the goods. The US arm of Dutch company Royal Philips Electronics the company oversees Philips operations in the US Canada and Mexico. Its divisions include Philips Healthcare (imaging patient information systems home healthcare products clinical management and equipment financing) Consumer Lifestyle (consumer electronics home appliances personal care) and Lighting (home industrial and municipal light bulbs fixtures and systems). Philips Electronics North America's Corporate Technologies group conducts R&D and partners with outside groups to feed the development pipeline for the other units.

PHILLIPS 66   NYS: PSX

2331 CityWest Blvd.
Houston, TX 77042
Phone: 281 293-6600
Fax: –
Web: www.phillips66.com

CEO: Greg C. Garland
CFO: Kevin J. Mitchell
HR: –
FYE: December 31
Type: Public

Phillips 66 is a leading marketer of gas aviation fuels crude oil and other refined petroleum products as well as specialty products such as oils waxes solvents and lubricants. It markets in the US under the Phillips 66 Conoco and 76 brands and internationally under the JET and Coop brands. One of the largest crude oil refiners the company processes transports and markets natural gas and natural gas liquids as well as liquefied petroleum gas. It produces olefins and polyolefins and other products through CPChem a joint venture with Chevron. Phillips 66 operates primarily in the US and Europe.

	Annual Growth	12/14	12/15	12/16	12/17	12/18
Sales ($ mil.)	(8.7%)	164,093.0	100,949.0	85,777.0	104,622.0	114,217.0
Net income ($ mil.)	4.1%	4,762.0	4,227.0	1,555.0	5,106.0	5,595.0
Market value ($ mil.)	4.7%	32,707.1	37,314.3	39,417.3	46,141.1	39,298.7
Employees	0.4%	14,000	14,000	14,800	14,600	14,200

PHILLIPS 66 COMPANY   NYSE: PSX

600 N. Dairy Ashford
Houston TX 77079
Phone: 281-293-6600
Fax: 775-284-4426
Web: argonautgoldinc.com

CEO: Greg C Garland
CFO: –
HR: Cesar Reyes
FYE: December 31
Type: Public

Phillips 66 is one of the largest independent refiners in the US and the world by sales (though rival Valero Energy leads it by capacity). The company has global refining and marketing midstream and chemical operations. It has a crude processing capacity of more than 2.2 million barrels per day and it sells fuel at about 10000 retail outlets in the US and Europe under such brands as 76 Conoco JET and Phillips 66. Its midstream business handles natural gas gathering and processing partly through DCP Midstream a joint venture with Spectra Energy. Phillips 66's chemicals business is conducted through CPChem a joint venture with Chevron. Phillips 66 was spun off by ConocoPhillips in 2012.

PHILLIPS 66 PARTNERS LP   NYS: PSXP

2331 CityWest Blvd.
Houston, TX 77042
Phone: 855 283-9237
Fax: –
Web: www.phillips66partners.com

CEO: Greg C Garland
CFO: –
HR: –
FYE: December 31
Type: Public

How many ways can you break up an oil and gas company? The ConocoPhillips and Phillips 66 family of companies may be trying to find out. Phillips 66 Partners is the mid-stream component owning and acquiring crude oil refined petroleum and natural gas liquids pipelines terminals and storage facilities in the US. The company has capacity for about 650 million barrels a day and its assets include 135 miles of pipeline terminals and docks connected to Phillips 66 refineries in Texas Louisiana and Illinois. Phillips 66 Partners earns revenue from fees it charges for transportation and storage of petroleum. In 2017 it bought mid-stream assets from its general partner Phillips 66 for a total transaction value of $2.4 billion.

	Annual Growth	12/14	12/15	12/16	12/17	12/18
Sales ($ mil.)	59.6%	229.1	348.1	873.0	1,169.0	1,486.0
Net income ($ mil.)	59.0%	124.4	194.2	408.0	524.0	796.0
Market value ($ mil.)	(11.6%)	8,725.4	7,772.3	6,157.1	6,626.7	5,330.5
Employees	–	–	–	–	–	–

PHILLIPS AND JORDAN, INCORPORATED

10201 PARKSIDE DR STE 300　　　　　　　CEO: William T Phillips Jr
KNOXVILLE, TN 379221983　　　　　　　　CFO: –
Phone: 865-688-8342　　　　　　　　　　　HR: –
Fax: –　　　　　　　　　　　　　　　　　　FYE: December 31
Web: www.pandj.com　　　　　　　　　　　Type: Private

While some like to clear the air Phillips and Jordan (P&J) prefers to clear the land. Founded in 1952 as a small land clearing firm P&J is a general and specialty contractor that still provides land clearing services in addition to industrial commercial and residential site development and heavy civil construction on dams highways bridges railroads and waterways. P&J also performs reclamation landfill and disaster recovery services. The latter includes handling some of the nation's worst disaster cleanups including hurricanes floods toxic spills and land and rock slides. P&J operates about a dozen offices in eight states. The Phillips family owns and runs the company.

	Annual Growth	12/11	12/12	12/13	12/14	12/18
Sales ($ mil.)	6.9%	–	284.5	215.2	340.9	425.1
Net income ($ mil.)	11.9%	–	11.3	4.5	14.5	22.2
Market value ($ mil.)	–	–	–	–	–	–
Employees	–	–	–	–	–	650

PHILLIPS-MEDISIZE CORPORATION

1201 Hanley Rd.　　　　　　　　　　　　CEO: Matthew J Jennings
Hudson WI 54555-5401　　　　　　　　　CFO: –
Phone: 715-386-4320　　　　　　　　　　HR: –
Fax: 715-381-3291　　　　　　　　　　　FYE: June 30
Web: www.phillipsmedisize.com　　　　Type: Private

Phillips-Medisize Corporation injects itself into the competitive world of molded products. The manufacturing company is a custom injection molder of plastic and metal creating end products that range from calculators to fishing reels to radios. It even makes molded parts for firearms. The company's tooling department offers market-entry design production and prototype tooling services. Phillips-Medisize serves customers primarily in the automotive consumer electronics defense and medical markets. The company has 14 locations throughout China Europe and the US in addition to design centers in California and Wisconsin. It is owned by private equity firm Kohlberg & Co.

PHOEBE PUTNEY MEMORIAL HOSPITAL, INC.

417 W 3RD AVE　　　　　　　　　　　　CEO: Joel Wernick
ALBANY, GA 317011943　　　　　　　　　CFO: Kerry Loudermilk
Phone: 229-312-1000　　　　　　　　　　HR: –
Fax: –　　　　　　　　　　　　　　　　　FYE: July 31
　　　　　　　　　　　　　　　　　　　　Type: Private

Phoebe Putney Memorial Hospital provides health care services to residents of southwest Georgia. With more than 650 beds and some 300 physicians the acute-care hospital provides emergency and inpatient services as well as cardiology oncology psychiatric women's health and pediatric specialty care. It's one of Georgia's largest comprehensive regional medical centers. Founded in 1911 it is part of the Phoebe Putney Health System which also includes the 25-bed Phoebe Worth Medical Center and several satellite community health centers that provide outpatient primary health laboratory and surgical services. The health system is governed by the Albany-Dougherty County Hospital Authority.

	Annual Growth	07/07	07/08	07/09	07/15	07/16
Sales ($ mil.)	(0.0%)	–	500.6	513.7	490.6	498.9
Net income ($ mil.)	–	–	15.2	19.6	32.3	(13.5)
Market value ($ mil.)	–	–	–	–	–	–
Employees	–	–	–	–	–	3,000

PHOENIX CHILDREN'S HOSPITAL, INC.

1919 E THOMAS RD　　　　　　　　　　CEO: Robert L. Meyer
PHOENIX, AZ 850167710　　　　　　　　CFO: Douglas T. Myers
Phone: 602-546-1000　　　　　　　　　　HR: Tom Diederich
Fax: –　　　　　　　　　　　　　　　　　FYE: December 31
Web: www.phoenixchildrens.org　　　　Type: Private

Phoenix Children's Hospital (PCH) invests in the health of the next generation. Founded in 1983 the hospital provides a comprehensive range of medical services specifically for children and adolescents in the greater Phoenix area. The hospital has about 385 beds and provides care in a number of pediatric sub-specialties including childhood cancers hematology neuroscience heart disease trauma and orthopedics. It also operates a newborn intensive care unit (NICU) at its main campus. PCH has several pediatric outpatient care centers in surrounding Phoenix suburbs.

	Annual Growth	12/08	12/09	12/11	12/13	12/14
Sales ($ mil.)	10.1%	–	408.2	498.7	655.2	661.6
Net income ($ mil.)	(24.1%)	–	106.4	(5.1)	31.9	26.9
Market value ($ mil.)	–	–	–	–	–	–
Employees	–	–	–	–	–	3,000

PHOENIX COMPANIES, INC. (THE)　　　　　　　NYS: PNX

One American Row　　　　　　　　　　CEO: Phillip J Gass
Hartford, CT 06102-5056　　　　　　　CFO: Ernest McNeill Jr
Phone: 860 403-5000　　　　　　　　　HR: –
Fax: –　　　　　　　　　　　　　　　　FYE: December 31
Web: www.phoenixwm.com　　　　　　　Type: Public

Fiscal firestorms might reduce assets to ashes but The Phoenix Companies gives its customers a chance to rise again. The holding company's primary subsidiary Phoenix Life Insurance offers life insurance annuities and a hybrid of the two it calls "alternative retirement solutions." Historically the company targeted wealthy individuals and institutions but it is newly focused on the merely secure. The Phoenix Companies' distribution arm Saybrus Partners wholesales its products which are sold through third-party agents brokers and financial planning firms. Phoenix has about $5.5 billion in funds under management.

	Annual Growth	12/10	12/11	12/12	12/13	12/14
Assets ($ mil.)	0.8%	21,076.9	21,439.9	21,629.8	21,624.6	21,745.9
Net income ($ mil.)	–	(12.6)	8.1	(168.5)	5.1	(213.2)
Market value ($ mil.)	128.3%	14.7	9.7	143.4	356.1	399.4
Employees	0.6%	625	600	600	620	640

PHOENIX FOOTWEAR GROUP, INC.　　　　　　　NBB: PXFG

2236 Rutherford Road, Suite 113　　　CEO: James R Riedman
Carlsbad, CA 92008　　　　　　　　　　CFO: Dennis Nelson
Phone: 760 602-9688　　　　　　　　　　HR: –
Fax: 760 602-9619　　　　　　　　　　　FYE: December 29
Web: www.phoenixfootwear.com　　　　Type: Public

Phoenix Footwear is a well-shod bird. The company manufactures comfort footwear under the Trotters and SoftWalk names for women and H.S. Trask for men. Trotters products include sandals boots and dress and casual footwear. Focused on comfort the SoftWalk brand boasts clogs slings and casual styles. Its Western-inspired footwear H.S. Trask comprises boots oxfords moccasins and slippers. Phoenix Footwear's products are manufactured overseas — primarily in Brazil and China — and are sold through some 1155 US retailers including mass merchants major department stores mail order companies and specialty shoe retailers. Founded in 1882 as Daniel Green Company the shoemaker changed its name in 2001.

	Annual Growth	01/15	01/16*	12/16	12/17	12/18
Sales ($ mil.)	(0.6%)	22.0	21.7	20.2	18.7	21.6
Net income ($ mil.)	7.6%	0.3	(1.0)	(1.2)	(1.0)	0.4
Market value ($ mil.)	(43.8%)	11.8	4.2	3.9	2.4	2.1
Employees	–	–	–	–	–	–

*Fiscal year change

PHOENIX TECHNOLOGIES LTD.

915 Murphy Ranch Rd.
Milpitas CA 95035
Phone: 408-570-1000
Fax: 408-570-1001
Web: www.phoenix.com

CEO: Rich Geruson
CFO: Brian Stein
HR: –
FYE: September 30
Type: Private

Phoenix Technologies' fortunes rise every time a computer maker decides to employ its software to fire up their PCs. The company develops basic input/output systems (BIOS) — the software that loads a computer's operating system (OS) each time it is turned on. BIOS software also manages the settings and connections between the OS and basic hardware such as the keyboard and monitor. Core system software (CSS) is the modern form of BIOS software that the company provides primarily through its Phoenix SecureCore SecureCore Tiano and Embedded BIOS products. Phoenix Technologies also makes similar software for manufacturers of other computer peripherals and electronics.

PHOTRONICS, INC.

NMS: PLAB

15 Secor Road
Brookfield, CT 06804
Phone: 203 775-9000
Fax: –
Web: www.photronics.com

CEO: Peter S. Kirlin
CFO: John P. Jordan
HR: Laurie Conley
FYE: October 31
Type: Public

Photronics is a company behind the photomasks. The company is the biggest maker of high-precision quartz photomasks a key tool in the process for manufacturing integrated circuits (ICs) and flat-panel displays (FPDs) for TVs computer displays and mobile phones. Photomasks carry microscopic images of electronic circuits and are used as stencils to transfer circuit patterns onto semiconductor wafers during the manufacture of ICs and FPDs. Photronics also provides maintenance for etching systems as well as research and consulting in techniques for wafer cleaning and etching. About 70% of the company's sales are from customers in Asia.

	Annual Growth	11/15*	10/16	10/17	10/18	10/19
Sales ($ mil.)	1.2%	524.2	483.5	450.7	535.3	550.7
Net income ($ mil.)	(9.6%)	44.6	46.2	13.1	42.1	29.8
Market value ($ mil.)	5.3%	629.1	646.1	626.4	638.9	774.0
Employees	3.4%	1,550	1,530	1,475	1,575	1,775

*Fiscal year change

PHYSICIANS FORMULA HOLDINGS INC.

NASDAQ: FACE

1055 W. 8th St.
Azusa CA 91702
Phone: 626-334-3395
Fax: 626-812-9462
Web: www.physiciansformula.com

CEO: Ingrid Jackel
CFO: –
HR: –
FYE: December 31
Type: Private

Physicians Formula Holdings (PFH) boasts the professional formula for skin imperfections. It develops and makes prestige cosmetics products focusing on face and eye makeup. Physicians Formula label includes facial powders bronzers concealers blushes foundations eye shadows eye liners brow makeup and mascaras. It sells its products through 25000 stores including mass merchandisers (Wal-Mart and Target) drugstores (CVS and Rite Aid) and specialty cosmetics shops (Ulta). PFH caters to the US but also sells its beauty aids in Canada Australia and beyond. Founded in 2003 PFH is owned by Markwins International.

PHYSICIANS REALTY TRUST

NYS: DOC

309 N. Water Street, Suite 500
Milwaukee, WI 53202
Phone: 414 367-5600
Fax: –
Web: www.docreit.com

CEO: John T. Thomas
CFO: Jeff Theiler
HR: –
FYE: December 31
Type: Public

Physicians Realty Trust doesn't make house calls. The real estate investment trust (REIT) owns and invests in doctor's offices and other health care properties that are leased to hospitals and medical groups. A self-managed REIT its portfolio consists of more than 25 medical office buildings in about a dozen states. Tenants include Fresenius Dialysis Hackley Hospital and Piedmont Hospital. Physicians Realty Trust was formed in 2013 with properties owned by investment bank B.C. Ziegler & Company. As a REIT it is exempt from paying federal income tax as long as it distributes 90% of profits back to shareholders. Physicians Realty Trust went public in 2013 raising $120 million.

	Annual Growth	12/14	12/15	12/16	12/17	12/18
Sales ($ mil.)	67.8%	53.3	129.4	241.0	343.6	422.6
Net income ($ mil.)	–	(4.0)	11.8	30.0	38.1	56.2
Market value ($ mil.)	(0.9%)	3,028.1	3,075.5	3,458.6	3,281.7	2,924.1
Employees	49.5%	14	25	41	63	70

PICO HOLDINGS INC.

NMS: PICO

3480 GS Richards Blvd, Suite 101
Carson City, NV 89703
Phone: 775 885-5000
Fax: –
Web: www.picoholdings.com

CEO: Maxim C. W. Webb
CFO: John T. Perri
HR: –
FYE: December 31
Type: Public

For PICO Holdings the pick o' the litter might look like a diamond in the rough. The holding company invests in what it believes to be undervalued businesses involved in real estate water resources and storage and other industries. Its majority-owned UCP homebuilding business constructs Benchmark Communities branded single-family homes and acquires and develops finished and unfinished residential lots in select markets including the Puget Sound Area in Washington California North Carolina South Carolina and Tennessee. PICO also owns Vidler Water Company which acquires and develops water resources and water storage operations in the American Southwest.

	Annual Growth	12/14	12/15	12/16	12/17	12/18
Sales ($ mil.)	(56.2%)	354.9	266.7	362.6	36.3	13.1
Net income ($ mil.)	–	(52.4)	(81.9)	(21.9)	0.5	(3.3)
Market value ($ mil.)	(16.6%)	390.7	213.9	314.0	265.3	189.4
Employees	(50.4%)	281	220	234	21	17

PIEDMONT ATHENS REGIONAL MEDICAL CENTER, INC.

1199 PRINCE AVE
ATHENS, GA 306062797
Phone: 706-475-7000
Fax: –

CEO: Charles Peck
CFO: Wendy J Cook
HR: –
FYE: September 30
Type: Private

Piedmont Athens Regional Medical Center (formerly Athens Regional Medical Center) is a full-service health care facility with 360 beds serving 17 counties in northeastern Georgia. The regional hospital provides general medical surgical and diagnostic services as well as a wide range of specialty care in such areas as oncology rehabilitation pediatrics and radiology. Piedmont Athens Regional is part of the not-for-profit Piedmont Healthcare which operates eight hospitals some 20 urgent care centers and around 100 physician practice locations across Georgia.

	Annual Growth	09/11	09/12	09/13	09/14	09/15
Sales ($ mil.)	8.6%	–	–	–	361.7	392.9
Net income ($ mil.)	–	–	–	–	(17.9)	20.5
Market value ($ mil.)	–	–	–	–	–	–
Employees	–	–	–	–	–	3,000

PIEDMONT HOSPITAL, INC.

1968 PEACHTREE RD NW
ATLANTA, GA 303091285
Phone: 404-605-5000
Fax: –
Web: www.piedmont.org

CEO: Sid Kirschner
CFO: Michael McAnder
HR: –
FYE: June 30
Type: Private

Those feeling ill in Atlanta can count on Piedmont Healthcare for help. Founded in 1905 the not-for-profit organization's flagship facility is Piedmont Atlanta an acute care hospital with more than 485 beds. Piedmont Atlanta provides general and advanced medical-surgical care including open-heart surgery organ transplantation and neurosurgery. Also part of the Piedmont family are Piedmont Fayette Hospital with more than 170 beds; Piedmont Mountainside Hospital a 52-bed community hospital north of Atlanta; and the Piedmont Physicians Group a network of more than 150 primary care physicians operating in dozens of offices throughout metropolitan Atlanta.

	Annual Growth	12/08	12/09*	06/10	06/15	06/16
Sales ($ mil.)	156.0%	–	–	1.3	690.0	857.5	918.1
Net income ($ mil.)	–	–	–	(0.0)	75.7	67.0	60.0
Market value ($ mil.)	–	–	–	–	–	–	–
Employees	–	–	–	–	–	–	6,419

*Fiscal year change

PIEDMONT MUNICIPAL POWER AGENCY

121 VILLAGE DR
GREER, SC 296511291
Phone: 864-877-9632
Fax: –
Web: www.pmpa.com

CEO: –
CFO: Steven Ruark
HR: –
FYE: December 31
Type: Private

Piedmont Municipal Power Agency (Piedmont Power) generates purchases and transmits wholesale electricity on behalf of its 10 member municipal utilities which distribute the power to nearly 95000 retail customers in northwestern South Carolina. These ten utilities serve the cities of Abbeville Clinton Easley Gaffney Greer Laurens Newberry Rock Hill Union and Westminster. Piedmont Power was created to buy an ownership interest in the Catawba Nuclear Station in York County South Carolina in order to secure a reliable source of electric generation for its member utilities. The agency owns a 25% stake in the Catawba plant.

	Annual Growth	12/12	12/13	12/14	12/15	12/16
Sales ($ mil.)	5.7%	–	219.9	237.5	250.6	259.9
Net income ($ mil.)	32.5%	–	9.4	19.9	4.7	21.9
Market value ($ mil.)	–	–	–	–	–	–
Employees	–	–	–	–	–	11

PIEDMONT NATURAL GAS CO INC   NYS: PNY

4720 Piedmont Row Drive
Charlotte, NC 28210
Phone: 704 364-3120
Fax: –
Web: www.piedmontng.com

CEO: Lynn J Good
CFO: Steven K Young
HR: –
FYE: October 31
Type: Public

Piedmont Natural Gas seeks to fulfill the burning desires of natural gas users in a wide part of the Southeast. The utility distributes natural gas to more than 1 million residential commercial and industrial customers (including 53000 wholesale customers) in the Carolinas and Tennessee. It also has gas transportation and storage operations and sells residential and commercial gas appliances in Tennessee. Piedmont Natural Gas is involved in unregulated energy supply through its 15% stake in SouthStar Energy Services which serves gas customers in Georgia and through other joint ventures.

	Annual Growth	10/11	10/12	10/13	10/14	10/15
Sales ($ mil.)	(1.1%)	1,433.9	1,122.8	1,278.2	1,470.0	1,371.7
Net income ($ mil.)	4.8%	113.6	119.8	134.4	143.8	137.0
Market value ($ mil.)	15.1%	2,644.1	2,577.7	2,761.3	3,074.4	4,635.4
Employees	2.2%	1,782	1,752	1,795	1,879	1,943

PIEDMONT NATURAL GAS CO., INC.   NYS: PNY

4720 Piedmont Row Drive
Charlotte, NC 28210
Phone: 704 364-3120
Fax: –
Web: www.piedmontng.com

CEO: Lynn J Good
CFO: Steven K Young
HR: –
FYE: October 31
Type: Public

Piedmont Natural Gas seeks to fulfill the burning desires of natural gas users in a wide part of the Southeast. The utility distributes natural gas to more than 1 million residential commercial and industrial customers (including 53000 wholesale customers) in the Carolinas and Tennessee. It also has gas transportation and storage operations and sells residential and commercial gas appliances in Tennessee. Piedmont Natural Gas is involved in unregulated energy supply through its 15% stake in SouthStar Energy Services which serves gas customers in Georgia and through other joint ventures.

	Annual Growth	10/10	10/11	10/12	10/13	10/14
Sales ($ mil.)	(1.4%)	1,552.3	1,433.9	1,122.8	1,278.2	1,470.0
Net income ($ mil.)	0.3%	142.0	113.6	119.8	134.4	143.8
Market value ($ mil.)	6.6%	2,315.9	2,567.2	2,502.8	2,681.0	2,985.0
Employees	1.2%	1,788	1,782	1,752	1,795	1,879

PIEDMONT OFFICE REALTY TRUST INC   NYS: PDM

5565 Glenridge Connector, Ste. 450
Atlanta, GA 30342
Phone: 770 418-8800
Fax: –
Web: www.piedmontreit.com

CEO: Donald A Miller
CFO: Robert E Bowers
HR: –
FYE: December 31
Type: Public

Piedmont Office Realty Trust provides office space for life in the big city. A self-managed and self-administered real estate investment trust (REIT) the company invests in develops and manages primarily Class A office buildings in major US markets. One of the nation's largest office REITs Piedmont owns or partially owns about 75 office and industrial properties comprising some 21 million sq. ft. of leasable space. Many of its properties are located in Chicago the New York Metro area and Washington DC. Piedmont's holdings include Chicago's Aon Center and the headquarters buildings for US Bancorp and Nestl-© USA.

	Annual Growth	12/14	12/15	12/16	12/17	12/18
Sales ($ mil.)	(1.8%)	566.3	584.8	555.7	574.2	526.0
Net income ($ mil.)	31.7%	43.3	173.0	107.9	133.6	130.3
Market value ($ mil.)	(2.5%)	2,378.0	2,383.0	2,639.2	2,475.1	2,150.8
Employees	0.8%	130	143	137	136	134

PIER 1 IMPORTS INC.   NYS: PIR

100 Pier 1 Place
Fort Worth, TX 76102
Phone: 817 252-8000
Fax: 817 252-8174
Web: www.pier1.com

CEO: Alasdair James
CFO: Nancy A. Walsh
HR: Gregory S. (Greg) Humenesky
FYE: March 02
Type: Public

When shoppers fish for home decor Pier 1 Imports wants to be sure they catch something. The company sells thousands of items (imported from dozens of countries) through more than 970 Pier 1 Imports stores in the US and Canada as well as online. Its stores offer a wide selection of indoor and outdoor furniture lamps vases baskets ceramics dinnerware candles and other decorative accessories. In addition the company supplies merchandise to stores in Mexico owned by Grupo Sanborns. Pier 1 which has been closing stores is struggling amid intense competition and falling retail foot traffic

	Annual Growth	02/15	02/16	02/17*	03/18	03/19
Sales ($ mil.)	(4.5%)	1,865.8	1,892.2	1,828.4	1,798.5	1,552.9
Net income ($ mil.)	–	75.2	39.6	30.1	11.6	(198.8)
Market value ($ mil.)	(41.4%)	51.6	20.4	29.4	13.5	6.1
Employees	(6.9%)	24,000	22,000	20,500	18,500	18,000

*Fiscal year change

PIERCE MANUFACTURING INC.

2600 American Dr.
Appleton WI 54912
Phone: 920-832-3000
Fax: 920-832-3084
Web: www.piercemfg.com

CEO: Wilson Jone
CFO: David Sagehorn
HR: Jodi Mueller
FYE: September 30
Type: Subsidiary

If you were to call "Jim Dandy to the Rescue" odds are the R&B music hero would wheel up in a vehicle made by Pierce Manufacturing. The company is a subsidiary of Oshkosh Corporation's Fire & Emergency business and the top North American maker of custom fire apparatus. Its lineup includes aerials commercial pumpers elliptical tankers and rescue trucks. The company also builds homeland security apparatus designed to help police and emergency crews better respond to terrorist events. Many vehicle bodies are assembled on major commercial chassis brands to meet customer needs such as the US Army's. Its innovations include the industry's first side roll protection and frontal airbag systems for fire apparatus.

PILGRIMS PRIDE CORP.
NMS: PPC

1770 Promontory Circle
Greeley, CO 80634-9038
Phone: 970 506-8000
Fax: -
Web: www.pilgrims.com

CEO: Don Jackson
CFO: Fabio Sandri
HR: Doug Schult
FYE: December 30
Type: Public

As one of the world's top chicken processors Pilgrim's Pride has a lot to crow about. The company sells fresh frozen and value-added poultry products under a host of brands (Pilgrim's Pride Gold Kist and Moy Park among them) primarily in North America and Europe. Vertically integrated Pilgrim's Pride is involved in breeding hatching raising processing and distributing chicken; it produces some 11 billion pounds of chicken products annually. The company — which serves more than 6000 retail food outlets distributors and food service operators — is majority owned by Brazil's JBS.

	Annual Growth	12/14	12/15	12/16	12/17	12/18
Sales ($ mil.)	6.2%	8,583.4	8,180.1	7,931.1	10,767.9	10,937.8
Net income ($ mil.)	(23.2%)	711.6	645.9	440.5	718.1	247.9
Market value ($ mil.)	(17.8%)	8,482.2	5,599.2	4,735.3	7,732.9	3,881.4
Employees	10.5%	35,000	38,850	39,600	51,300	52,100

PIKE CORP
NYS: PIKE

100 Pike Way
Mount Airy, NC 27030
Phone: 336 789-2171
Fax: -
Web: www.pike.com

CEO: J Eric Pike
CFO: Richard Wimmer
HR: -
FYE: June 30
Type: Public

Pike Electric helps its customers stay current. The electrical services contractor (also known as Pike Energy Solutions) provides services for more than 200 public municipal and cooperative utility companies primarily in the eastern and southern US. Activities include the planning design engineering construction maintenance and repair of electric substations and transmission lines including renewable energy systems. Pike Electric owns a fleet of more than 4700 pieces of motorized equipment including trucks trailers cranes backhoes and generators. The company is active in some 40 states.

	Annual Growth	06/09	06/10	06/11	06/12	06/13
Sales ($ mil.)	10.6%	613.5	504.1	593.9	685.2	918.7
Net income ($ mil.)	3.5%	31.6	(13.5)	1.4	10.9	36.2
Market value ($ mil.)	0.5%	382.2	298.8	280.4	244.9	390.1
Employees	6.1%	4,500	4,500	4,600	5,400	5,700

PILKINGTON NORTH AMERICA, INC.

811 MADISON AVE FL 3
TOLEDO, OH 436045688
Phone: 419-247-3731
Fax: -
Web: www.pilkington.com

CEO: -
CFO: -
HR: Spencer Harris
FYE: March 31
Type: Private

Pilkington North America has a clear view of the US glass market. The company manufactures and markets glass and glazing products primarily for the automotive and building industries. Benefits of its glass include fire protection noise control solar heat control and thermal insulation. A majority of its sales come from automotive glass sold to the original equipment and replacement markets. More than a quarter of sales are made from building glass geared at homeowners and architects. A small but growing part of its business focuses on specialty glass used in solar energy conversion. Pilkington North America is a subsidiary of Pilkington plc which operates as part of Japanese glass giant Nippon Sheet Glass.

	Annual Growth	03/02	03/03	03/04	03/07	03/08
Sales ($ mil.)	1.0%	-	-	931.8	913.4	967.9
Net income ($ mil.)	-	-	-	32.0	(17.2)	(11.4)
Market value ($ mil.)	-	-	-	-	-	-
Employees	-	-	-	-	-	3,747

PIKEVILLE MEDICAL CENTER, INC.

911 BYPASS RD
PIKEVILLE, KY 415011689
Phone: 606-218-3500
Fax: -
Web: www.pikevillehospital.org

CEO: Walter E May
CFO: Michelle Hagey
HR: -
FYE: September 30
Type: Private

Taking a nasty fall while hiking the rugged Appalachians will likely land you at Pikeville Medical Center (PMC). Serving patients in eastern Kentucky the hospital boasts more than 260 beds and provides a full range of inpatient outpatient and surgical services. PMC's centers and departments handle a number of specialties such as diagnostic imaging echocardiogram neurosurgery cancer care and bariatric surgery. Employing some 350 physicians PMC also operates a rehabilitation hospital a home health agency and outpatient family practice and specialty clinics as well as a physician residency program. PMC first opened on Christmas Day in 1924.

	Annual Growth	09/13	09/14	09/15	09/16	09/18
Sales ($ mil.)	9.3%	-	367.2	381.5	489.6	524.1
Net income ($ mil.)	-	-	8.9	9.7	29.1	(14.2)
Market value ($ mil.)	-	-	-	-	-	-
Employees	-	-	-	-	-	2,527

PILOT CORPORATION

5508 LONAS DR
KNOXVILLE, TN 379093221
Phone: 865-588-7488
Fax: -
Web: www.pilotflyingj.com

CEO: -
CFO: Mitchell D Steenrod
HR: Gary Price
FYE: December 31
Type: Private

Pilot offers a salve to those suffering from white-line fever. Its Pilot Flying J a joint venture between Pilot and CVC Capital Partners runs more than 650 travel centers that sell fuel and food across North America. Its truck stops feature restaurant chains such as Subway Pizza Hut and Taco Bell and offer hot showers. Pilot has fuel islands large enough to service several 18-wheelers. Pilot Truck Care Centers provide TLC (tender loving care) for big rigs while some 45 Pilot Food Marts (all in Tennessee) keep drivers fed. James Haslam II got Pilot off the ground in 1958 as a gas station that sold cigarettes and soft drinks; now his son CEO James Haslam III runs the firm. The Haslam family owns the company.

	Annual Growth	12/07	12/08	12/09	12/10	12/11
Sales ($ mil.)	(3.2%)	-	-	-	415.1	402.0
Net income ($ mil.)	(2.0%)	-	-	-	373.2	365.7
Market value ($ mil.)	-	-	-	-	-	-
Employees	-	-	-	-	-	51,337

PINE GROVE MANUFACTURED HOMES INC.

2 PLEASANT VALLEY RD
PINE GROVE, PA 179639563
Phone: 570-345-2011
Fax: –
Web: www.pinegrovehomes.com

CEO: Wayne A Fanelli
CFO: Joseph Gallagher
HR: –
FYE: October 28
Type: Private

Pine Grove Manufactured Homes designs and builds manufactured homes in the mid-Atlantic and northeastern regions of the US. Its single-section homes range in width from 12 ft. to 16 ft.; its multi-section homes range from 20 ft. to 32 ft. in width and can be built up to 76 ft. in length. Special features offered include gourmet kitchens and spa baths. Sister company Pleasant Valley Modular Homes manufactures ranch split-level and two-story residences as well as log-sided homes and duplexes in a variety of styles ranging in size from around 1000 sq. ft. to 3000 sq. ft. Pine Grove markets its homes through independent retailers and developers. Privately held Pine Grove was established in 1982.

	Annual Growth	10/03	10/04	10/05	10/06	10/07
Sales ($ mil.)	–	–	–	(1,460.1)	42.5	31.9
Net income ($ mil.)	1281.9%	–	–	0.0	5.5	3.1
Market value ($ mil.)	–	–	–	–	–	–
Employees	–	–	–	–	–	100

PINEY WOODS HEALTHCARE SYSTEM, L.P.

505 S JOHN REDDITT DR
LUFKIN, TX 759043120
Phone: 936-634-8311
Fax: –
Web: www.woodlandheights.net

CEO: Casey Robertson
CFO: –
HR: –
FYE: December 31
Type: Private

Piney Woods Healthcare does business as Woodland Heights Medical Center and while it's not in the woods and it's not located on a mountain top it is a full service hospital in Lufkin Texas. Established in 1918 the medical center has about 150 beds and provides a comprehensive range of inpatient outpatient surgical and emergency services. Specialized treatment programs including cardiac care maternity care sports and occupational medicine physical therapy and rehabilitation. Woodland Heights also offers community services including its Healthy Woman program designed to educate the public on women's health issues and Senior Circle which offers senior discounts activities and events exercise and wellness classes. The company is part of Community Health Systems.

	Annual Growth	12/13	12/14	12/15	12/16	12/17
Sales ($ mil.)	(8.3%)	–	122.5	99.7	93.5	94.6
Net income ($ mil.)	(13.2%)	–	10.0	15.5	4.4	6.5
Market value ($ mil.)	–	–	–	–	–	–
Employees	–	–	–	–	–	600

PINNACLE BANCSHARES, INC.   NBB: PCLB

1811 Second Avenue
Jasper, AL 35501
Phone: 205 221-4111
Fax: –
Web: www.pinnaclebancshares.com

CEO: Robert B Nolen Jr
CFO: –
HR: –
FYE: December 31
Type: Public

Pinnacle is on top of Alabama's banking needs. Pinnacle Bancshares is the holding company for Pinnacle Bank which serves central and northwestern Alabama through more than a half-dozen offices. The bank provides consumer and business banking services including checking and money market accounts as well as a variety of consumer and commercial loans. Real estate lending dominates the loan portfolio with one- to four-family residential mortgages making up the largest percentage followed by commercial mortgages business loans and construction and land development loans. The bank also makes consumer and farm loans.

	Annual Growth	12/13	12/14	12/15	12/16	12/17
Assets ($ mil.)	(0.3%)	220.4	219.0	219.5	216.6	217.8
Net income ($ mil.)	4.3%	1.9	2.0	2.2	2.3	2.3
Market value ($ mil.)	11.3%	15.1	17.9	21.1	23.7	23.2
Employees	–	–	–	–	–	–

PINNACLE BANKSHARES CORP   NBB: PPBN

622 Broad Street
Altavista, VA 24517
Phone: 434 369-3000
Fax: –
Web: www.bankstreetpartners.com

CEO: Aubrey H Hall III
CFO: Bryan M Lemley
HR: –
FYE: December 31
Type: Public

Pinnacle Bankshares is always looking for the high point. The firm is the holding company for the First National Bank which operates about 10 branches and loan production centers in central Virginia. Serving individuals and businesses in the area the bank offers standard products and services including checking and savings accounts IRAs and merchant bankcard processing. The company uses funds from deposit accounts to originate real estate loans consumer loans and business loans. The company which traces its roots to 1908 also has two real estate subsidiaries First Properties and FNB Property Corp.

	Annual Growth	12/14	12/15	12/16	12/17	12/18
Assets ($ mil.)	6.8%	362.2	371.3	440.1	443.9	470.6
Net income ($ mil.)	18.0%	2.1	2.7	3.0	2.7	4.2
Market value ($ mil.)	11.5%	27.4	30.3	44.5	45.4	42.3
Employees	–	110	–	–	–	–

PINNACLE DATA SYSTEMS INC.   NYSE AMEX: PNS

6600 Port Rd.
Groveport OH 43125
Phone: 614-748-1150
Fax: 614-409-1269
Web: www.pinnacle.com

CEO: –
CFO: –
HR: –
FYE: December 31
Type: Subsidiary

Pinnacle Data Systems Inc. (PDSi) has a custom approach to computing. The company builds and services made-to-order UNIX-based servers and other application-specific computer systems used in the medical telecommunications and process control industries as well as in government markets. PDSi combines third-party equipment — including processors from AMD Intel and Oracle — with its own custom parts to create its systems. The company provides its build and repair services to manufacturers that include Hewlett-Packard and Silicon Graphics International. PDSi gets most of its revenues in the US. The company was acquired by electronic components distributor Avnet in early 2012.

PINNACLE ENTERTAINMENT INC   NMS: PNK

3980 Howard Hughes Parkway
Las Vegas, NV 89169
Phone: 702 541-7777
Fax: –
Web: www.pnkinc.com

CEO: –
CFO: –
HR: –
FYE: December 31
Type: Public

Pinnacle Entertainment realizes most gamblers don't know when they've reached their peak. The Las Vegas-based gaming company actually has no casinos in Vegas; instead the regional casino operator owns 15 casinos in other locations. Pinnacle also owns the Retama Park Horse Racetrack located near San Antonio Texas. Three of Pinnacle's casinos operate under the Boomtown banner. Its L'Auberge du Lac Hotel & Casino property in Lake Charles Louisiana is the company's largest casino resort. In St. Louis the company owns Lumière Place (including the Lumière Place Casino the Pinnacle-owned Four Seasons Hotel St. Louis and HoteLumière) and the River City Casino.

	Annual Growth	12/10	12/11	12/12	12/13	12/14
Sales ($ mil.)	19.1%	1,098.4	1,141.2	1,197.1	1,487.8	2,210.5
Net income ($ mil.)	–	(23.4)	(2.5)	(31.8)	(255.9)	43.8
Market value ($ mil.)	12.2%	840.9	609.4	949.5	1,558.9	1,334.6
Employees	18.3%	7,533	7,463	8,479	14,569	14,738

PINNACLE FINANCIAL PARTNERS INC   NMS: PNFP

150 Third Avenue South, Suite 900   CEO: M. Terry Turner
Nashville, TN 37201   CFO: Harold R. Carpenter
Phone: 615 744-3700   HR: -
Fax: -   FYE: December 31
Web: www.pnfp.com   Type: Public

Pinnacle Financial Partners works to be at the top of the community banking mountain in central Tennessee. It's the holding company for Tennessee-based Pinnacle Bank which has grown to some 40 branches in the Nashville and Knoxville areas since its founding in 2000. Serving consumers and small- to mid-sized business the $9 billion financial institution provides standard services such as checking and savings accounts CDs credit cards and loans and mortgages. The company also offers investment and trust services through Pinnacle Asset Management while its insurance brokerage subsidiary Miller Loughry Beach specializes in property/casualty policies. Pinnacle agreed to merge with North Carolina-based BNC Bancorp in 2017.

	Annual Growth	12/14	12/15	12/16	12/17	12/18
Assets ($ mil.)	42.8%	6,018.2	8,715.4	11,194.6	22,205.7	25,031.0
Net income ($ mil.)	50.3%	70.5	95.5	127.2	174.0	359.4
Market value ($ mil.)	3.9%	3,063.7	3,979.6	5,369.6	5,137.2	3,572.0
Employees	31.6%	767	1,065	1,180	2,132	2,297

PINNACLE FOODS FINANCE LLC

1 Bloomfield Ave.   CEO: Robert J Gamgort
Mountain Lakes NJ 07046   CFO: Craig Steeneck
Phone: 973-541-6620   HR: -
Fax: 901-345-8511   FYE: December 31
Web: www.elvis.com   Type: Subsidiary

Pinnacle Foods holds a mouthful of big-name brands. The company makes markets and distributes such North American grocery store staples as Duncan Hines baking mix and frosting Armour canned meat Vlasic pickles and Comstock pie and pastry filling. It owns Birds Eye Foods' lineup acquired in 2009 of frozen breakfast (Aunt Jemima) vegetable (Birds Eye) dinner (Hungry Man) seafood (Mrs. Paul's) and pizza (Celeste) brand products. A specialty foods unit supplies snacks as well as distributes frozen products to foodservice operators and makes private label food products. Pinnacle has grown by buying and expanding upon the lines of name brands. The company is owned by private equity The Blackstone Group.

PINNACLE FOODS INC.   NYS: PF

399 Jefferson Road   CEO: -
Parsippany, NJ 07054   CFO: Craig Steeneck
Phone: 973 541-6620   HR: -
Fax: -   FYE: December 25
Web: www.pinnaclefoods.com   Type: Public

Pinnacle Foods' grocery products enjoy a bird's-eye view from store shelves across the US and Canada. Pinnacle Foods is the holding company of Pinnacle Foods Finance which manufactures markets and distributes the Birds Eye frozen food line Duncan Hines line of baking mixes and frostings Snyder of Berlin snack foods Nalley Hungry ? Man Boulder Brands healthy foods and other grocery brands. The company also offers food service and private-label services. Its product lines sold predominantly through major US retailers like Wal-Mart and top grocery-store chains hold top market-share positions across several food product categories. Pinnacle Foods went public in 2013.

	Annual Growth	12/12	12/13	12/14	12/15	12/16
Sales ($ mil.)	6.0%	2,478.5	2,463.8	2,591.2	2,655.8	3,127.9
Net income ($ mil.)	41.6%	52.5	89.3	248.4	212.5	211.1
Market value ($ mil.)	25.0%	-	3,217.8	4,205.3	5,058.2	6,290.3
Employees	8.4%	3,700	3,700	4,000	4,300	5,100

PINNACLE FRAMES AND ACCENTS INC.

12201 Technology Blvd. Ste. 1200   CEO: -
Austin TX 78727   CFO: -
Phone: 512-506-3900   HR: -
Fax: 512-506-3933   FYE: June 30
Web: www.pinnacleframe.com   Type: Private

Pinnacle Frames and Accents has plenty of frames but what it needs is a prettier picture. Once home to nearly 20 retailing and manufacturing companies the company now makes and markets photo frames and albums under its own brand name and private labels in addition to other decor. The firm's Gallery Solutions brand features matted wall frames in mix-and-match styles while its Snap collection targeted to cost-conscious digital photographers consists of clear and magnetic frames key chains and coasters. Pinnacle's products are available at major retail stores in the US and Canada including Wal-Mart and Target. The company formerly named Tandycrafts is owned by investment firm Newcastle Partners.

PINNACLE HEALTH SYSTEM

409 S 2ND ST STE 2B   CEO: Philip W Guarneschelli
HARRISBURG, PA 17104-1612   CFO: -
Phone: 717-231-8245   HR: -
Fax: -   FYE: June 30
Web: www.pinnaclehealth.org   Type: Private

PinnacleHealth helps central Pennsylvanians reach the peaks of wellness. PinnacleHealth System provides a continuum of care through its four hospitals that have a combined total of about 600 beds. Together Community General Hospital Harrisburg Hospital Polyclinic Hospital and the Helen M. Simpson Rehab Hospital provide general and specialty services in areas such as oncology cardiovascular medicine neurology mental health physical therapy women's health and orthopedics. PinnacleHealth is also home to a network of community health diagnostic ambulatory surgery and outpatient centers. Additionally the system administers home care and hospice care programs.

	Annual Growth	06/06	06/07	06/08	06/09	06/11
Sales ($ mil.)	5.9%	-	486.9	578.6	0.0	612.8
Net income ($ mil.)	3.8%	-	32.9	(23.5)	(2.6)	38.2
Market value ($ mil.)	-	-	-	-	-	-
Employees	-	-	-	-	-	4,837

PINNACLE WEST CAPITAL CORP   NYS: PNW

400 North Fifth Street, P.O. Box 53999   CEO: Donald E. (Don) Brandt
Phoenix, AZ 85072-3999   CFO: James R. (Jim) Hatfield
Phone: 602 250-1000   HR: Donna Easterly
Fax: 602 379-2625   FYE: December 31
Web: www.pinnaclewest.com   Type: Public

Pinnacle West Capital is on top of power use in Arizona. It is the holding company for the state's largest electric utility Arizona Public Service which transmits and distributes electricity to more than 1.2 million residential commercial and industrial customers throughout most of the state. The power distribution utility also has 6200 MW of regulated generating capacity and has a mix of both long-term and short-term purchased power agreements for additional capacity including a range of agreements for the purchase of energy from renewable sources.

	Annual Growth	12/14	12/15	12/16	12/17	12/18
Sales ($ mil.)	1.4%	3,491.6	3,495.4	3,498.7	3,565.3	3,691.2
Net income ($ mil.)	6.5%	397.6	437.3	442.0	488.5	511.0
Market value ($ mil.)	5.7%	7,657.7	7,228.3	8,747.3	9,548.8	9,551.1
Employees	(0.4%)	6,366	6,407	6,339	6,292	6,259

PIONEER BANKSHARES INC.   OTC: PNBI

263 E. Main St.   CEO: Thomas R Rosazza
Stanley VA 22851   CFO: Lori G Hassett
Phone: 540-778-2294   HR: –
Fax: 540-778-5140   FYE: December 31
Web: www.pioneerbks.com   Type: Public

Although you don't get a coonskin cap when you open an account Pioneer Bankshares likes to maintain that pioneer spirit. The financial institution is the holding company for Pioneer Bank which serves northeastern Virginia through about a half dozen branches. It provides standard retail products and services to individuals and small to midsized businesses. Lending activities are focused on real estate loans and mortgages: Loans secured by real estate account for some 80% of its total loan book. The company also offers business and consumer loans. The bank has two subsidiaries Pioneer Financial Services (insurance and investment products) and Pioneer Special Assets (foreclosures with added liabilities).

PIONEER RAILCORP   NBB: PRRR

1318 S. Johanson Road   CEO: Alex Yeros
Peoria, IL 61607   CFO: Carrie Genualdi
Phone: 309 697-1400   HR: –
Fax: 309 697-5387   FYE: December 31
Web: www.pioneer-railcorp.com   Type: Public

Although Pioneer Railcorp doesn't often chart new territory the company's multiple railroad subsidiaries cover a lot of ground. Pioneer's short-line freight railroads travel 600-plus miles of track in about a dozen states neighboring Indiana Illinois and Michigan. More than half operate as interline carriers with major railroads. They haul such freight as lumber pulpboard fertilizer grain and plastic. Subsidiary Pioneer Railroad Equipment owns a fleet of some 600 railcars that are used by the company's railroads and leased to other rail carriers. Illinois businessman Guy Brenkman founded Pioneer Railcorp in 1986. Shortly after his retirement in 2006 the company switched from the NASDAQ to OTC markets.

	Annual Growth	12/13	12/14	12/15	12/16	12/17
Sales ($ mil.)	1.3%	21.6	20.8	24.1	23.2	22.8
Net income ($ mil.)	(2.7%)	4.5	2.0	2.0	2.4	4.1
Market value ($ mil.)	(1.5%)	39.5	37.5	28.9	32.1	37.2
Employees	–	–	–	–	–	–

PIONEER ENERGY SERVICES CORP   NBB: PESX

1250 N.E. Loop 410, Suite 1000   CEO: William S. (Stacy) Locke
San Antonio, TX 78209   CFO: Lorne E. Phillips
Phone: 855 884-0575   HR: –
Fax: –   FYE: December 31
Web: www.pioneeres.com   Type: Public

Pioneer Energy Services (formerly Pioneer Drilling) digs down deep to make money from beneath the land where Texas pioneers used to roam as well as in other locations. The company provides contract drilling services primarily to oil and gas companies in Texas and to a lesser degree in the Rockies and in Colombia. Pioneer Energy Services owns 64 land drilling rigs that can reach depths of 8000-18000 feet. In addition the company's Pioneer Production Services Division provides workover rig services wireline services and fishing and rental services to US-based oil and gas producers.

	Annual Growth	12/14	12/15	12/16	12/17	12/18
Sales ($ mil.)	(13.5%)	1,055.2	540.8	277.1	446.5	590.1
Net income ($ mil.)	–	(38.0)	(155.1)	(128.4)	(75.1)	(49.0)
Market value ($ mil.)	(31.4%)	433.3	169.7	535.8	238.6	96.2
Employees	(8.3%)	3,400	1,700	1,800	2,300	2,400

PIPER SANDLER COMPANIES   NYS: PIPR

800 Nicollet Mall, Suite 1000   CEO: Andrew S. Duff
Minneapolis, MN 55402   CFO: Debbra L. Schoneman
Phone: 612 303-6000   HR: Esete Bekele
Fax: –   FYE: December 31
Web: www.piperjaffray.com   Type: Public

Investment bank Piper Jaffray Companies specializes in supplying clients with mergers and acquisitions advice financing and industry research. The bank's Capital Markets business comprises its investment banking operations equity and fixed income brokerage merchant banking for late-stage private companies and alternative asset funds. Its Asset Management segment boasts some $5.8 billion in assets under management primarily master limited partnerships energy infrastructure and equity strategies. Piper Jaffray targets a variety of clients including corporations government entities not-for-profits and middle-market companies across the consumer financial services healthcare technology and industrial sectors. In 2019 the company agreed to acquire investment bank Sandler O'Neill + Partners..

	Annual Growth	12/14	12/15	12/16	12/17	12/18
Sales ($ mil.)	4.4%	673.2	696.3	769.9	895.2	801.0
Net income ($ mil.)	(2.5%)	63.2	52.1	(22.0)	(61.9)	57.0
Market value ($ mil.)	3.2%	754.9	525.0	942.2	1,120.9	855.6
Employees	4.6%	1,055	1,192	1,315	1,301	1,262

PIONEER NATURAL RESOURCES CO   NYS: PXD

5205 N. O'Connor Blvd., Suite 200   CEO: Timothy L. (Tim) Dove
Irving, TX 75039   CFO: Richard P. (Rich) Dealy
Phone: 972 444-9001   HR: –
Fax: 972 969-3587   FYE: December 31
Web: www.pxd.com   Type: Public

Pioneer Natural Resources Company explores for and produces oil gas and NGLs in the Midland Basin of West Texas. With some 680000 net acres containing proved reserves of 1050 million barrels of oil equivalent this independent energy company is one the biggest energy producers in the Midland Basin. Pioneer's production comes mostly from its Spraberry/Wolfcamp oil field which consists of oil (65% of total output) gas (20%) and NGLs (15%). The company reports around 6940 net producing wells. Additionally the company owns interests in two gas processing systems (plants and pipelines) in Texas. Its major customers include Sunoco Logistics Partners Occidental Energy Marketing and Plains Marketing.

	Annual Growth	12/14	12/15	12/16	12/17	12/18
Sales ($ mil.)	16.8%	5,055.0	4,825.0	3,824.0	5,455.0	9,415.0
Net income ($ mil.)	1.3%	930.0	(273.0)	(556.0)	833.0	978.0
Market value ($ mil.)	(3.0%)	25,229.9	21,251.8	30,521.7	29,297.9	22,292.5
Employees	(6.0%)	4,075	3,732	3,604	3,836	3,177

PISMO COAST VILLAGE, INC.

165 South Dolliver Street   CEO: –
Pismo Beach, CA 93449   CFO: Wayne Hardesty
Phone: 805 773-5649   HR: –
Fax: –   FYE: September 30
Web: www.pismocoastvillage.com   Type: Public

Pismo Coast Village will prove that half the fun of owning an RV is parking it. The company runs a full-service recreational vehicle (RV) resort on more than 25 acres in Pismo Beach California that accommodates up to 400 RVs. Vacationers have access to an onsite general store heated swimming pool laundry facilities mini-golf course recreation hall video arcade wireless Internet and several playgrounds. Pismo Coast's recreation department aims to keep kids and families busy by renting out sports equipment and planning activities such as arts and crafts mini-golf tournaments pet costume contests and scavenger hunts. The resort also offers an RV repair shop.

	Annual Growth	09/15	09/16	09/17	09/18	09/19
Sales ($ mil.)	2.7%	7.6	8.0	8.2	8.5	8.5
Net income ($ mil.)	11.4%	1.0	0.9	1.1	1.6	1.5
Market value ($ mil.)	–	–	–	–	–	–
Employees	0.4%	62	64	63	62	63

PISTON AUTOMOTIVE L.L.C.

12723 TELEGRAPH RD STE 1
REDFORD, MI 48239-1489
Phone: 313-541-8689
Fax: –
Web: www.pistongroup.com

CEO: –
CFO: Amit Singhi
HR: –
FYE: December 31
Type: Private

Surprisingly there are no pistons on the workbenches and pallets of Piston Automotive. Less surprisingly a former Detroit Pistons player Vinnie "the Microwave" Johnson leads it as chairman. Piston Automotive specializes in the supply of powertrain systems front-end and powertrain cooling systems chassis systems and interior systems for the automotive industry. The company was formed in 1995 by Johnson to serve major automotive makers and related OEM suppliers in the greater Detroit area. A year later Piston Automotive began suspension module assembly and sequencing operations.

	Annual Growth	12/07	12/08	12/09	12/10	12/11
Sales ($ mil.)	42.9%	–	162.3	0.0	326.4	473.8
Net income ($ mil.)	424.6%	–	0.1	0.0	9.7	10.2
Market value ($ mil.)	–	–	–	–	–	–
Employees	–	–	–	–	–	380

PITNEY BOWES INC   NYS: PBI

3001 Summer Street
Stamford, CT 06926
Phone: 203 356-5000
Fax: 203 351-7336
Web: www.pb.com

CEO: Marc B. Lautenbach
CFO: Stanley J. (Stan) Sutula
HR: Johnna G. Torsone
FYE: December 31
Type: Public

Known as the world's largest producer of postage meters (1.1 million installed worldwide) Pitney Bowes Inc. has moved into other areas of getting information from point A to point B. For sure sending mail and packages is a big part of its business with services like pre-sort label printing and logistics among its offerings. But Pitney Bowes has integrated digital capabilities with its physical mail services and expanded into other digital areas. The company offers software-as-a-service and cloud-based services for e-commerce that facilitate cross-border shipping enabling its clients to provide their customers with the complete cost of the transaction at checkout. The US accounts for about 80% of sales.

	Annual Growth	12/14	12/15	12/16	12/17	12/18
Sales ($ mil.)	(2.0%)	3,821.5	3,578.1	3,406.6	3,549.9	3,522.4
Net income ($ mil.)	(9.5%)	333.8	407.9	92.8	261.3	223.7
Market value ($ mil.)	(29.8%)	4,573.6	3,875.5	2,850.8	2,098.2	1,109.2
Employees	(3.3%)	15,200	14,800	14,200	14,700	13,300

PITT COUNTY MEMORIAL HOSPITAL, INCORPORATED

2100 STANTONSBURG RD
GREENVILLE, NC 278342832
Phone: 252-847-4100
Fax: –
Web: www.vidanthealth.com

CEO: –
CFO: –
HR: Charlene Wilson
FYE: September 30
Type: Private

Vidant Medical Center is an acute health services facility that serves the vibrant community of Greenville North Carolina and surrounding areas. The 909-bed regional referral hospital's specialty divisions include Vidant Children's Hospital East Carolina Heart Institute a rehabilitation center and the outpatient Vidant SurgiCenter. Other services include oncology transplant women's health orthopedic behavioral care and home health and hospice care units. The center also serves as a teaching facility for East Carolina University's Brody School of Medicine. Vidant Medical Center (formerly Pitt County Memorial Hospital) is a member of University Health Systems of Eastern Carolina (dba Vidant Health).

	Annual Growth	09/12	09/13	09/14	09/15	09/18
Sales ($ mil.)	3.1%	–	1,031.7	1,025.4	1,066.2	1,201.3
Net income ($ mil.)	7.4%	–	91.9	79.9	79.8	131.5
Market value ($ mil.)	–	–	–	–	–	–
Employees	–	–	–	–	–	15,000

PITT-OHIO EXPRESS, LLC

15 27TH ST
PITTSBURGH, PA 152224729
Phone: 412-232-3015
Fax: –
Web: www.pittohio.com

CEO: –
CFO: Scott Sullivan
HR: –
FYE: December 31
Type: Private

Primarily a regional less-than-truckload (LTL) freight carrier Pitt Ohio operates a fleet of about 1000 tractors and 3100 trailers. (LTL carriers consolidate freight from multiple shippers into a single truckload.) It maintains straight trucks and vans in its fleet. Pitt Ohio additionally provides truckload (TL) transportation through ECM Transport. It operates a network of about 20 terminals primarily in the Midwest and Mid-Atlantic US. Beyond freight hauling Pitt Ohio provides specialized logistics services for shippers. The family of Charles Hammel III owns Pitt Ohio which has grown from a business established by Hammel's grandfather in 1919.

	Annual Growth	12/01	12/02	12/04	12/06	12/07
Sales ($ mil.)	5.0%	–	205.6	221.4	243.7	261.8
Net income ($ mil.)	(22.2%)	–	65.9	22.2	24.7	18.8
Market value ($ mil.)	–	–	–	–	–	–
Employees	–	–	–	–	–	3,000

PIXELWORKS INC   NMS: PXLW

226 Airport Parkway, Suite 595
San Jose, CA 95110
Phone: 408 200-9200
Fax: –
Web: www.pixelworks.com

CEO: Todd A Debonis
CFO: Elias Nader
HR: –
FYE: December 31
Type: Public

Pixelworks' chips put the sizzle in digital displays. The company's display controller integrated circuits (ICs) power visual displays in PCs TVs and other electronic devices. Its ImageProcessor system-on-chip ICs combine microprocessor memory software and digital signal processor components onto a single device. Distributor Tokyo Electron Device (TED) accounts for about 44% of sales; distributors are behind more than 60% of Pixelworks' sales. Other customers include SANYO Electric Seiko Epson and Hitachi which each account for 10% of sales. About 90% of the company's sales come from customers in Asia primarily Japan.

	Annual Growth	12/14	12/15	12/16	12/17	12/18
Sales ($ mil.)	5.9%	60.9	59.5	53.4	80.6	76.6
Net income ($ mil.)	–	(10.0)	(10.6)	(11.1)	(4.2)	(4.6)
Market value ($ mil.)	(10.7%)	168.4	87.9	103.4	233.8	107.1
Employees	(0.6%)	220	215	166	215	215

PJM INTERCONNECTION, L.L.C.

2750 MONROE BLVD
NORRISTOWN, PA 194032429
Phone: 610-666-8980
Fax: –
Web: www.pjm.com

CEO: Terry Boston
CFO: –
HR: –
FYE: December 31
Type: Private

Interdependence is a given at PJM Interconnection which oversees a 62555-mile section of the North American power transmission grid that spans 13 northeastern and midwestern states and the District of Columbia. The regional transmission organization monitors and coordinates the movement of wholesale electricity in its service territory; its 850 members have a combined generating capacity of 185600 MW. Sanctioned by the Federal Energy Regulatory Commission PJM is charged with ensuring fair competition among power purchasers sellers and traders; it also is responsible for the reliable delivery of distributed electricity to 61 million consumers in its territory.

	Annual Growth	12/04	12/05	12/06	12/08	12/16
Sales ($ mil.)	1.7%	–	–	274.9	241.3	324.8
Net income ($ mil.)	(15.4%)	–	–	0.5	0.7	0.1
Market value ($ mil.)	–	–	–	–	–	–
Employees	–	–	–	–	–	600

PLACID REFINING COMPANY LLC

2101 CEDAR SPRINGS RD # 600
DALLAS, TX 752012104
Phone: 214-880-8479
Fax: –
Web: www.placidrefining.com

CEO: –
CFO: –
HR: –
FYE: December 31
Type: Private

A calm presence in the volatile oil and gas industry Placid Refining owns and operates the Port Allen refinery in Louisiana which converts crude oil into a number of petroleum products including diesel ethanol gasoline liquid petroleum gas jet fuel and fuel oils. Placid Refining's refinery has the capacity to process 80000 barrels of crude oil per day. The company is one of the largest employers and taxpayers in West Baton Rouge Parish. Placid Refining which is controlled by Petro-Hunt distribute fuels across a dozen states in the southeastern US from Texas to Virginia and is a major supplier of jet fuel to the US military.

	Annual Growth	12/05	12/06	12/10	12/11	12/13
Sales ($ mil.)	7.7%	–	2,925.7	3,686.1	4,699.6	4,929.2
Net income ($ mil.)	(13.1%)	–	128.5	39.3	4.2	47.9
Market value ($ mil.)	–	–	–	–	–	–
Employees	–	–	–	–	–	200

PLAINS ALL AMERICAN PIPELINE LP

NYS: PAA

333 Clay Street, Suite 1600
Houston, TX 77002
Phone: 713 646-4100
Fax: –
Web: www.plainsallamerican.com

CEO: Greg L. Armstrong
CFO: Al Swanson
HR: –
FYE: December 31
Type: Public

Plains All American Pipeline L.P. owns and operates an extensive network of midstream energy infrastructure that provides logistical and transportation services to oil and gas companies in the US and Canada. With 30 million barrels of active above-ground storage capacity the limited partnership is engaged in the transportation storage terminaling and marketing of crude oil natural gas liquids (NGLs) and natural gas products. Its portfolio includes some 18000 miles of pipelines and a fleet of 830 trailers 50 barges and 20 transport tugs. Plains All American Pipeline has a presence in the major energy market hubs including California Oklahoma Texas and Alberta. Its prominent customers include ExxonMobil and Phillips 66.

	Annual Growth	12/14	12/15	12/16	12/17	12/18
Sales ($ mil.)	(5.9%)	43,464.0	23,152.0	20,182.0	26,223.0	34,055.0
Net income ($ mil.)	12.5%	1,384.0	903.0	726.0	856.0	2,216.0
Market value ($ mil.)	(20.9%)	37,276.9	16,779.0	23,454.2	14,992.1	14,556.3
Employees	(1.9%)	5,300	5,400	5,100	4,850	4,900

PLAINS COTTON COOPERATIVE ASSOCIATION

3301 E 50TH ST
LUBBOCK, TX 794044331
Phone: 806-763-8011
Fax: –
Web: www.pcca.com

CEO: Kevin Brinkley
CFO: –
HR: –
FYE: June 30
Type: Private

Plainly speaking most of the US cotton used by textile mills worldwide starts with the Plains Cotton Cooperative Association (PCCA). The farmer-owned co-op markets millions of bales annually for members in Oklahoma Kansas and Texas. To obtain a competitive price for their cotton PCCA takes advantage of Telmark LP's access to The Seam an online cotton marketplace that continually updates cotton prices buyer data and more. The co-op operates cotton warehouses in Texas Oklahoma and Kansas. PCCA sold its textile and apparel operations in 2014 to focus exclusively on cotton marketing and warehousing. Formed in 1953 PCCA's customers include Replay Urban Outfitters and Abercrombie & Fitch.

	Annual Growth	06/13	06/14	06/15	06/16	06/17
Sales ($ mil.)	13.2%	–	947.5	975.5	892.1	1,373.4
Net income ($ mil.)	–	–	(37.0)	25.8	23.8	45.2
Market value ($ mil.)	–	–	–	–	–	–
Employees	–	–	–	–	–	170

PLANAR SYSTEMS INC.

NMS: PLNR

1195 NW Compton Drive
Beaverton, OR 97006
Phone: 503 748-1100
Fax: –
Web: www.planar.com

CEO: –
CFO: Cindy Bai
HR: –
FYE: September 26
Type: Public

Planar Systems has no qualms about making a public display. The company makes custom embedded and video wall displays used in such applications as vehicle dashboards instrumentation security monitoring and retail systems. Planar also sells desktop monitors and home theater systems. Its products — marketed under the Planar Clarity and Runco brands — include matrix and mosaic LCD systems flat-panel displays rear-project cube displays touch monitors and theater front-projection systems. The company serves consumers as well as clients in the retail industrial transportation and education industries among others. It generates most of its sales in the US.

	Annual Growth	09/10	09/11	09/12	09/13	09/14
Sales ($ mil.)	0.5%	175.7	186.5	171.4	166.8	179.0
Net income ($ mil.)	–	(5.1)	(4.7)	(16.2)	(6.5)	3.8
Market value ($ mil.)	14.4%	47.0	43.1	29.3	39.5	80.4
Employees	(8.0%)	429	471	422	298	308

PLANET PAYMENT, INC.

NAS: PLPM

670 Long Beach Boulevard
Long Beach, NY 11561
Phone: 516 670-3200
Fax: 516 670-3520
Web: www.planetpayment.com

CEO: Carl J Williams
CFO: Raymond D'Aponte
HR: –
FYE: December 31
Type: Public

Planet Payment may not be able to break language barriers but its systems can break currency barriers. Through its Pay in Your Currency and other services Planet Payment provides point-of-sale and e-commerce payment processing services that allow merchants to accept Visa MasterCard and American Express credit and debit card payments in multiple currencies. The company's services also help merchants set up pricing in different currencies. It operates at more than 60000 merchant locations in 20-plus counties in the Asia Pacific region and North America. Customers include hotels restaurants and retailers operating in international business and tourist centers. Chairman Philip Beck founded Planet Payment in 1999.

	Annual Growth	12/11	12/12	12/13	12/14	12/15
Sales ($ mil.)	6.0%	41.9	43.6	46.6	47.4	52.8
Net income ($ mil.)	44.4%	2.4	(4.5)	0.0	3.2	10.4
Market value ($ mil.)	2.5%	145.1	183.0	146.2	109.4	160.4
Employees	(4.5%)	–	201	205	167	175

PLANGRAPHICS INC.

OTC: PGRA

112 E. Main St.
Frankfort KY 40601
Phone: 502-223-1501
Fax: 502-223-1235
Web: www.plangraphics.com

CEO: –
CFO: –
HR: –
FYE: September 30
Type: Public

PlanGraphics can do more than read a map. The company provides IT services for geographic information systems (GIS) computer-based mapping applications used with database management software to analyze customer demographics mineral exploration military surveillance crop forecasting and other data. PlanGraphics' customers include government entities utilities and corporations such as Entergy and the US Army Corps of Engineers. In 2009 Integrated Freight Corp. a Florida-based transportation company acquired a majority stake in PlanGraphics which then acquired Integrated Freight. The merged company then sold PlanGraphics' operating subsidiary to CEO John Antenucci.

PLANNED PARENTHOOD FEDERATION OF AMERICA, INC.

123 WILLIAM ST FL 10
NEW YORK, NY 100383844
Phone: 212-541-7800
Fax: –
Web: www.pplafoodfare.com

CEO: –
CFO: Wallace D'Sousa
HR: Carolyn Harvey
FYE: June 30
Type: Private

He who fails to plan plans to fail could refer to parenting. No fear the Planned Parenthood Federation Of America provides sexual health information as well as reproductive healthcare through 800 affiliated health centers to more than 5 million people each year. PPFA also lobbies for reproductive rights and reproductive health issues and works to extend access to family planning services for all. The not-for-profit organization is supported by private and corporate donations and patient fees as well as government grants. Founded in 1916 by Margaret Sanger PPFA has grown to 84 affiliates in all 50 US states and the District of Columbia and is part of the International Planned Parenthood Federation.

	Annual Growth	06/11	06/12	06/13	06/14	06/15
Sales ($ mil.)	7.3%	–	159.5	139.4	176.6	196.9
Net income ($ mil.)	–	–	34.0	1.5	28.4	(3.5)
Market value ($ mil.)	–	–	–	–	–	–
Employees	–	–	–	–	–	530

PLANTATION PIPE LINE COMPANY

1000 WINDWARD CONCOURSE # 450
ALPHARETTA, GA 300055474
Phone: 770-751-4000
Fax: –
Web: www.kindermorgan.com

CEO: –
CFO: Park Shaper
HR: –
FYE: December 31
Type: Private

The only green from this company's crop is the cash it gets from its petroleum products transport business. Plantation Pipe Line one of the largest petroleum products pipeline companies in the US delivers gasoline jet fuel diesel and heating oils through its 3100 mile pipeline network which serves oil refiners and fuel wholesalers through connection points in Atlanta Birmingham Charlotte Washington DC and other destinations in the Southeast. Plantation Pipe Line delivers more than 600000 barrels per day to more than 30 delivery points. Kinder Morgan Energy Partners owns a 51% interest in the company which was founded in 1940. Exxon Mobil owns the rest.

	Annual Growth	12/04	12/05	12/06	12/16	12/17
Sales ($ mil.)	4.3%	–	170.5	174.5	273.9	281.7
Net income ($ mil.)	8.8%	–	30.0	15.3	71.7	82.2
Market value ($ mil.)	–	–	–	–	–	–
Employees	–	–	–	–	–	279

PLANTE & MORAN PLLC

27400 Northwestern Hwy.
Southfield MI 48034
Phone: 248-352-2500
Fax: 248-352-0018
Web: www.plantemoran.com

CEO: –
CFO: Jerry Smith
HR: Jill Chateau
FYE: May 31
Type: Private

Plante & Moran is planted firmly in the upper Midwest. With some 20 offices in Michigan Ohio and Illinois the firm provides a variety of accounting and management consulting services. Its offerings include tax preparation employee benefits consulting technology assessment and planning and wealth management. The firm has expertise in several industries ranging from retail and dealerships to health care financial services and manufacturing. It also serves the not-for-profit and public sectors. Plante & Moran which is affiliated with international accounting alliance Praxity also has offices in Mexico India and China. The company was founded by Elorion Plante in 1924.

PLANTRONICS, INC.

NYS: PLT

345 Encinal Street
Santa Cruz, CA 95060
Phone: 831 426-5858
Fax: 831 426-6098
Web: www.poly.com

CEO: Joseph (Joe) Burton
CFO: Pamela (Pam) Strayer
HR: Pat Wadors
FYE: March 31
Type: Public

Plantronics is a leading provider of business and consumer communications tools that range from lightweight headsets to desktop phones to video conferencing equipment. It also offers cloud computing and analytics software for managing its systems. Plantronics sells its products through distributors manufacturers and communications service providers. Product lines include Backbeat Savi Voyager and Calisto. The company gets about 45% of its sales from US customers. In 2018 Plantronics bought Polycom for about $2 billion expanding its product portfolio and nearly doubling its revenue. The combined company was rebranded as Poly.

	Annual Growth	03/15	03/16	03/17	03/18	03/19
Sales ($ mil.)	18.0%	865.0	856.9	881.2	856.9	1,674.5
Net income ($ mil.)	–	112.3	68.4	82.6	(0.9)	(135.6)
Market value ($ mil.)	(3.4%)	2,092.5	1,548.7	2,138.3	2,385.7	1,822.2
Employees	21.9%	3,397	3,398	3,852	4,003	7,490

PLANVIEW INC.

8300 N MO PAC EXPY # 300
AUSTIN, TX 78759-8330
Phone: 512-346-8600
Fax: –
Web: www.planview.com

CEO: Gregory Gilmore
CFO: –
HR: Tammy Sullivan
FYE: December 31
Type: Private

This company's plan is to stay on the lookout for clients in need of a good IT strategy. PlanView develops enterprise software that helps large and midsized companies make the most of their information technology processes and related assets (including software computers printers and servers). Its applications combine tools for business process management (Process Builder) and resource project and portfolio management (Enterprise). The company offers a comprehensive portfolio management solutions in the industry to enable better decision making and business accountability.

	Annual Growth	12/04	12/05	12/06	12/07	12/08
Sales ($ mil.)	(81.6%)	–	–	1,988.8	70.0	67.1
Net income ($ mil.)	70246.3%	–	–	0.0	1.8	2.0
Market value ($ mil.)	–	–	–	–	–	–
Employees	–	–	–	–	–	262

PLASTIPAK PACKAGING INC.

41605 Ann Arbor Rd.
Plymouth MI 48170
Phone: 734-455-3600
Fax: 734-354-7391
Web: www.plastipak.com

CEO: William C Young
CFO: Michael Plotzke
HR: Jessica Short
FYE: October 31
Type: Private

Plastipak likes to keep things bottled up. Plastipak Packaging produces more than 8 billion plastic containers a year for consumer products' manufacturers. Containers are used to hold beverages (soft drinks water juice beer) cleansers (laundry soap household cleaners) processed foods (coffee creamer salad dressing) hygiene (mouthwash perfume) and industrial and automotive goods (motor oil windshield washer fluid). The company has served established companies such as Kraft Foods Kroger Procter & Gamble Reckitt Benckiser and Pepsico. Plastipak operates in the US Europe and South America. Founded in 1967 it is owned and led by the Young family.

PLATINUM ENERGY SOLUTIONS INC.

2100 West Loop South Ste. 1601
Houston TX 77027
Phone: 713-622-7731
Fax: 832-553-7431
Web: www.platinumenergysolutions.com

CEO: -
CFO: -
HR: -
FYE: December 31
Type: Private

Platinum Energy Solutions (PES) is a regular frack of all trades. The oilfield services company provides hydraulic fracturing (fracking) coiled tubing and other onshore pressure pumping services to three customers Petrohawk Energy Encana Oil & Gas and El Paso E&P Company. (Fracking is a somewhat controversial method to extract oil and natural gas by pumping pressurized chemicals into the ground to break it up). PES formed in 2010 and began fracking services the next year. PES also filed a $300 million initial public offering in September 2011 but withdrew it in January 2013 citing unfavorable market conditions.

PLATTE RIVER POWER AUTHORITY (INC)

2000 E HORSETOOTH RD
FORT COLLINS, CO 805255721
Phone: 970-229-5332
Fax: -
Web: www.prpa.org

CEO: -
CFO: David D Smalley
HR: -
FYE: December 31
Type: Private

Delivering power not platitudes Platte River Power Authority supplies wholesale electricity to four municipalities (Estes Park Fort Collins Longmont and Loveland) in northern Colorado which in turn serve about 146500 residences and businesses. The utility which is a political subdivision of the state of Colorado has interests in fossil-fueled and wind-powered generation facilities; it also operates transmission assets and acts as a wholesale electric utility acquiring constructing and operating generation capacity and supplying electric energy on an as needed basis. Platte River Power Authority evolved from the Platte River Municipal Power Association a consortium of 31 municipalities.

	Annual Growth	12/13	12/14	12/16	12/17	12/18
Sales ($ mil.)	2.7%	–	199.9	205.3	213.3	222.1
Net income ($ mil.)	18.8%	–	16.5	17.8	14.0	32.7
Market value ($ mil.)	–	–	–	–	–	–
Employees	–	–	–	–	–	172

PLAYERS NETWORK (THE)

1771 E. Flamingo Road, #201-A
Las Vegas, NV 89119
Phone: 702 840-3270
Fax: -

NBB: PNTV
CEO: Mark Bradley
CFO: -
HR: -
FYE: December 31
Type: Public

Players Network acquires produces and distributes video content focused on Las Vegas gaming and nightlife. It has a library of more than 1000 videos including instructional programs on gambling and features on Las Vegas casinos and nightspots as well as videos featuring Vegas entertainers and other personalities. Players Network distributes its programming primarily through cable and satellite video-on-demand (VOD) services and through content partnerships with online video sites including Google. CEO Mark Bradley and president Michael Berk (who helped create the TV series Baywatch) together own about 30% of the company.

	Annual Growth	12/13	12/14	12/15	12/16	12/17
Sales ($ mil.)	173.7%	0.0	0.0	0.0	0.1	0.1
Net income ($ mil.)	–	(1.7)	(3.3)	(2.1)	(1.7)	(14.0)
Market value ($ mil.)	43.0%	18.0	11.6	1.2	8.5	75.2
Employees	82.1%	2	2	1	1	22

PLEXUS CORP.

One Plexus Way
Neenah, WI 54957
Phone: 920 969-6000
Fax: 920 751-5395
Web: www.plexus.com

NMS: PLXS
CEO: Todd P. Kelsey
CFO: Patrick J. (Pat) Jermain
HR: -
FYE: September 28
Type: Public

Plexus flexes its manufacturing muscles in doing contract work for customers in a wide range of businesses. The company develops and manufactures electronic products for companies in the telecommunications medical industrial and defense markets. Plexus does product design assembly and testing of printed circuit boards (PCBs) and other electronic components. The company also offers prototyping materials procurement warehousing and distribution and other support services. Major customers include General Electric and ARRIS Group. Plexus gets most of its sales from customers in Malaysia. The Neenah Wisconsin-based company was founded in 1979.

	Annual Growth	10/15	10/16*	09/17	09/18	09/19
Sales ($ mil.)	4.5%	2,654.3	2,556.0	2,528.1	2,873.5	3,164.4
Net income ($ mil.)	3.6%	94.3	76.4	112.1	13.0	108.6
Market value ($ mil.)	13.3%	1,102.2	1,356.8	1,626.5	1,697.0	1,814.5
Employees	7.9%	14,000	14,000	16,000	18,000	19,000

*Fiscal year change

PLUG POWER INC

968 Albany Shaker Road
Latham, NY 12110
Phone: 518 782-7700
Fax: 518 782-9060
Web: www.plugpower.com

NAS: PLUG
CEO: Andrew J. (Andy) Marsh
CFO: Paul B. Middleton
HR: -
FYE: December 31
Type: Public

Plug Power wants to give alternative power sources a lift. The company develops on-site power generation systems used in forklifts and material handling equipment and in remote power applications. Plug Power uses proton exchange membrane (PEM) fuel cells to generate electricity from hydrogen gas without combustion. The company's GenDrive product is sold to large distribution centers as a replacement for lead-acid batteries in lift trucks including pallet trucks and narrow-aisle reach trucks. Plug Power caters primarily to the US market; customers have included big names like SYSCO Wal-Mart Central Grocers Whole Foods and FedEx Freight.

	Annual Growth	12/14	12/15	12/16	12/17	12/18
Sales ($ mil.)	28.4%	64.2	103.3	85.9	103.3	174.6
Net income ($ mil.)	–	(88.5)	(55.7)	(57.5)	(127.1)	(78.1)
Market value ($ mil.)	(19.8%)	657.5	462.4	263.0	517.2	271.8
Employees	25.0%	326	439	486	644	795

PLUM CREEK TIMBER CO., INC.

601 Union Street, Suite 3100
Seattle, WA 98101-1374
Phone: 206 467-3600
Fax: 206 467-3795
Web: www.plumcreek.com

NYS: PCL
CEO: -
CFO: -
HR: -
FYE: December 31
Type: Public

Plum Creek Timber is not only one of the largest timber companies in the US it is also one of the country's largest private landowners. The real estate investment trust (REIT) which owns and manages some 6.8 million acres of timberlands in 19 states harvests old- and new-growth timber and sells logs to sawmills and pulp and paper mills around the country. Plum Creek's manufacturing operations include two softwood lumber mills two medium-density fiberboard (MDF) plants two plywood plants and two lumber manufacturing facilities in Idaho and Montana. Major customers include Evergreen Packaging Georgia-Pacific Graphic Packaging and West Fraser. Forest products company Weyerhaeuser agreed to purchase Plum Creek for $8.4 billion in late 2015.

	Annual Growth	12/10	12/11	12/12	12/13	12/14
Sales ($ mil.)	5.5%	1,190.0	1,167.0	1,339.0	1,340.0	1,476.0
Net income ($ mil.)	0.1%	213.0	193.0	203.0	214.0	214.0
Market value ($ mil.)	3.4%	6,587.5	6,430.9	7,804.7	8,181.1	7,526.8
Employees	2.5%	1,202	1,192	1,223	1,308	1,325

PLUMAS BANCORP INC   NAS: PLBC

35 South Lindan Avenue
Quincy, CA 95971
Phone: 530 283-7305
Fax: –
Web: www.plumasbank.com

CEO: Andrew J Ryback
CFO: Richard L Belstock
HR: –
FYE: December 31
Type: Public

Plumas Bancorp is the holding company for Plumas Bank which serves individuals and businesses in the northeastern corner of California from Lake Tahoe to the Oregon border. Through more than a dozen branches the bank offers deposit products such as checking savings and retirement accounts and certificates of deposit. Loans secured by real estate account for more than half of Plumas Bank's loan portfolio; combined commercial and agricultural loans make up about a quarter. The bank writes consumer loans as well. It also provides access to investment products and services such as financial planning mutual funds and annuities.

	Annual Growth	12/14	12/15	12/16	12/17	12/18
Assets ($ mil.)	11.2%	538.9	599.3	658.0	745.4	824.4
Net income ($ mil.)	31.1%	4.7	5.8	7.5	8.2	14.0
Market value ($ mil.)	29.9%	41.0	44.6	97.6	119.2	116.7
Employees	2.9%	155	151	155	161	174

PLUMB SUPPLY COMPANY

1622 NE 51ST AVE
DES MOINES, IA 503132194
Phone: 515-262-9511
Fax: –
Web: www.plumbsupply.com

CEO: –
CFO: –
HR: –
FYE: December 31
Type: Private

Plumb Supply is plum tickled with the plumbing and HVAC business. Through about 20 locations in Iowa Plumb Supply distributes plumbing heating cooling and bathroom products to builders and contractors. In addition to air conditioners and heaters the company sells pipes valves fittings and about 200 other product lines from Bemis Manufacturing Honeywell Kohler Mueller Industries and Whirlpool. About 10 stores feature Water Concepts Galleries which showcase kitchen and bathroom fixtures from major brands. The company was founded in 1946 and purchased by Templeton Coal in 1965.

	Annual Growth	12/09	12/10	12/11	12/12	12/13
Sales ($ mil.)	–	–	–	0.0	0.0	97.9	97.9
Net income ($ mil.)	–	–	–	–	0.0	3.3	3.3
Market value ($ mil.)	–	–	–	–	–	–
Employees	–	–	–	–	–	215

PLUS THERAPEUTICS INC   NAS: PSTV

3020 Callan Road
San Diego, CA 92121
Phone: 858 458-0900
Fax: –
Web: www.cytori.com

CEO: –
CFO: –
HR: Lisa Hellmann Rhodes
FYE: December 31
Type: Public

Cytori Therapeutics focuses on the development of regenerative and oncology treatments using its cell therapy and nanoparticle platforms. Its Cytori Cell Therapy treatment has shown evidence of improving blood flow and modulating the body's immune system as well as promoting wound care. The company is investigating its effectiveness in the treatment of a number of diseases particularly those that have unmet medical needs. Its newest arm Cytori Nanomedicine was established in early 2017 when the firm acquired assets of Azaya Therapeutics including a proprietary liposomal nanoparticle that expanded its existing pipeline.

	Annual Growth	12/14	12/15	12/16	12/17	12/18
Sales ($ mil.)	(7.2%)	5.0	4.8	4.7	2.7	3.7
Net income ($ mil.)	–	(37.4)	(18.7)	(22.0)	(22.7)	(12.6)
Market value ($ mil.)	0.0%	0.1	0.1	0.4	0.1	0.1
Employees	(17.0%)	78	80	65	37	37

PLX TECHNOLOGY INC   NMS: PLXT

870 W. Maude Avenue
Sunnyvale, CA 94085
Phone: 408 774-9060
Fax: –
Web: www.plxtech.com

CEO: Hock Tan
CFO: Anthony Maslowski
HR: –
FYE: December 31
Type: Public

PLX Technology's devices handle complex traffic inside electronic gear. PLX makes input/output accelerators and other chips used to manage data transfer between the microprocessor memory and peripheral chips within an embedded system. It also sells hardware and software development kits used to design subsystems that employ its chips. Its chips are compatible with communications processors made by industry leaders such as Broadcom. OEMs use the company's industry-standard PCI interconnect chips in products such as digital TVs media servers cable modems printers and video surveillance equipment.

	Annual Growth	12/08	12/09	12/10	12/11	12/12
Sales ($ mil.)	5.5%	81.1	82.8	116.6	115.8	100.2
Net income ($ mil.)	–	(56.5)	(18.8)	(3.3)	(24.8)	(32.6)
Market value ($ mil.)	20.5%	77.6	145.7	162.8	129.4	163.7
Employees	(0.3%)	158	197	260	205	156

PLY GEM HOLDINGS, INC.

5020 WESTON PKWY STE 400
CARY, NC 275132322
Phone: 919-677-3900
Fax: –
Web: www.plygem.com

CEO: Gary E. Robinette
CFO: Shawn K. Poe
HR: David N. Schmoll
FYE: December 31
Type: Private

Ply Gem brings out a new side of homes. The company makes and supplies exterior building materials used in home construction and renovation primarily in the US. Its products — vinyl siding aluminum windows and doors stone veneer and fencing — are supplied to home center retailers distributors construction companies and contractors in North America. Subsidiaries include Variform (vinyl siding) Napco (vinyl and metal exterior siding and trim) Kroy Building Products (vinyl fencing) and Great Lakes Window (energy-efficient vinyl windows and patio doors). Ply Gem Holdings was founded in 2004; it was acquired by Clayton Dubilier & Rice in 2018.

	Annual Growth	12/13	12/14	12/15	12/16	12/17
Sales ($ mil.)	9.5%	–	1,566.6	1,839.7	1,911.8	2,056.3
Net income ($ mil.)	–	–	(31.3)	32.3	75.5	68.3
Market value ($ mil.)	–	–	–	–	–	–
Employees	–	–	–	–	–	9,000

PMC-SIERRA INC.   NMS: PMCS

1380 Bordeaux Drive
Sunnyvale, CA 94089
Phone: 408 239-8000
Fax: –
Web: www.pmcs.com

CEO: –
CFO: John W Hohener
HR: –
FYE: December 28
Type: Public

For PMC-Sierra success is all about networking. The company develops and markets some 700 semiconductor products designed to support the Internet infrastructures of corporations and enterprise clients as well as the communications networking equipment industry. Its controllers mappers multiplexers processors switches and transceivers are used in laser and multifunction printers servers and storage devices communications infrastructure equipment and fiber-to-the-home equipment. OEM customers include Alcatel-Lucent Cisco EMC HP Huawei Nokia Siemens and ZTE. PMC-Sierra sells products directly and through distributors. It gets more than three-quarters of its sales in the Asia/Pacific region.

	Annual Growth	12/09	12/10	12/11	12/12	12/13
Sales ($ mil.)	0.6%	496.1	635.1	654.3	531.0	508.0
Net income ($ mil.)	–	46.9	83.2	84.7	(336.2)	(32.3)
Market value ($ mil.)	(7.0%)	1,666.1	1,650.6	1,071.2	995.4	1,244.3
Employees	7.6%	1,079	1,449	1,564	1,546	1,448

PMFG, INC.
NMS: PMFG

14651 North Dallas Parkway, Suite 500
Dallas, TX 75254
Phone: 214 357-6181
Fax: 214 351-0194
Web: www.peerlessmfg.com

CEO: -
CFO: -
HR: -
FYE: June 28
Type: Public

Even though its name has changed PMFG (formerly Peerless Mfg.) is still without peer when it comes to making products that remove contaminants. It operates through two segments: environmental systems and process products. Its process products include separation filtration systems that remove solid and liquid contaminants from natural gas and saltwater aerosols from the air intakes of marine gas turbine and diesel engines. The segment also makes industrial noise control and heat transfer products. PMFG's environmental systems unit makes air pollution abatement products primarily catalytic reduction systems used to convert nitrogen oxide produced by the burning of fossil fuels into nitrogen and water vapor.

	Annual Growth	06/10*	07/11*	06/12	06/13	06/14
Sales ($ mil.)	2.8%	116.8	121.8	135.3	133.9	130.7
Net income ($ mil.)	-	(4.2)	5.7	(1.0)	(2.1)	(38.4)
Market value ($ mil.)	(24.3%)	319.1	421.7	164.5	145.8	104.7
Employees	5.7%	400	400	500	450	500

*Fiscal year change

PNM RESOURCES INC
NYS: PNM

414 Silver Ave. SW
Albuquerque, NM 87102-3289
Phone: 505 241-2700
Fax: -
Web: www.pnmresources.com

CEO: Patricia K. (Pat) Vincent-Collawn
CFO: Charles N. (Chuck) Eldred
HR: -
FYE: December 31
Type: Public

Most glowing lights in New Mexico are lit by PNM Resources. The company's primary utility Public Service Company of New Mexico (PNM Electric) distributes power to residential commercial and industrial customers in the state. PNM Resources has (or purchases power from) plants with 2707 MW of generating capacity and markets energy to wholesale customers in the western US. Its Texas-New Mexico Power Company (TNMP) unit provides transmission and distribution services at regulated rates to retail electricity providers. PNM Resources' two regulated utilities serve 753000 residential commercial and industrial customers and end-users of electricity in New Mexico and Texas.

	Annual Growth	12/14	12/15	12/16	12/17	12/18
Sales ($ mil.)	0.0%	1,435.9	1,439.1	1,363.0	1,445.0	1,436.6
Net income ($ mil.)	(7.3%)	116.8	16.2	117.4	80.4	86.2
Market value ($ mil.)	8.5%	2,360.1	2,435.0	2,732.1	3,222.0	3,273.0
Employees	(16.0%)	1,881	1,868	1,814	1,699	938

POAGE BANKSHARES INC
NAS: PBSK

1500 Carter Avenue
Ashland, KY 41101
Phone: 606 324-7196
Fax: -
Web: www.hfsl.com

CEO: -
CFO: -
HR: -
FYE: December 31
Type: Public

Poage Bankshares is the holding company for Home Federal Savings and Loan Association a small bank with six branches in northeast Kentucky located along the Ohio and West Virginia state line. Home Federal caters to area individuals and small businesses offering checking and savings accounts; NOW COD and money market accounts; retirement accounts; and Visa debit and credit cards. Its loan portfolio primarily consists of fixed-rate residential mortgages followed by nonresidential real estate loans home equity loans and lines of credit auto and personal loans and commercial business loans. Home Federal traces its history back to 1889 when it was founded as Home and Saving Fund Association.

	Annual Growth	09/13*	12/13	12/14	12/15	12/16
Assets ($ mil.)	16.4%	291.0	289.2	414.7	435.1	458.5
Net income ($ mil.)	(5.9%)	2.2	(0.2)	1.8	3.2	1.8
Market value ($ mil.)	9.2%	53.5	51.9	55.1	63.4	69.6
Employees	13.3%	79	82	120	120	115

*Fiscal year change

POCONO HEALTH SYSTEM

206 E. Brown St.
East Stroudsburg PA 18301
Phone: 570-421-4000
Fax: 570-476-3469
Web: www.poconohealthsystem.org

CEO: -
CFO: -
HR: -
FYE: June 30
Type: Private - Not-for-Pr

The Poconos may be a popular destination among honeymooners but they probably don't have the Pocono Health System on their lists of must-sees. Nevertheless the health care provider can treat whatever ails visitors and residents of eastern Pennsylvania. The system's Pocono Medical Center is an acute care community hospital with some 200 beds. The system also operates a community health center for children a surgical center and specialty care centers for cancer and heart disease. Its medical staff includes more than 200 physicians and it has more than 1800 staff members. Subsidiaries include Pocono Medical Center Pocono Healthcare Management Pocono Healthcare Partners Pocono Ambulatory Services and Pocono Health Foundation

POINT LOMA NAZARENE UNIVERSITY

3900 LOMALAND DR
SAN DIEGO, CA 921062899
Phone: 619-221-2200
Fax: -
Web: www.pointloma.edu

CEO: -
CFO: -
HR: Jeff Herman
FYE: June 30
Type: Private

Point Loma Nazarene University (PLNU) intends to provide a rounded education for Christian students. PLNU offers liberal arts and professional programs in more than 60 areas of study on its main campus in San Diego and select graduate and professional programs at regional centers in the California towns of Bakersfield and Mission Valley (San Diego). Areas of study include art science business administration teaching medicine and ministry. About 3500 undergraduate and graduate students are enrolled at the school which boasts a 14-to-1 faculty-student ratio. PLNU dates back to 1902 when it was established by Dr. Phineas F. Bresee one of the founders of the Church of the Nazarene.

	Annual Growth	06/14	06/15	06/16	06/17	06/18
Sales ($ mil.)	7.3%	-	95.5	102.8	135.8	118.0
Net income ($ mil.)	49.0%	-	5.4	7.4	13.6	17.9
Market value ($ mil.)	-	-	-	-	-	-
Employees	-	-	-	-	-	688

POINT.360 (NEW)
NBB: PTSX Q

2701 Media Center Drive
Los Angeles, CA 90065
Phone: 323 987-9400
Fax: -
Web: www.point360.com

CEO: Haig S Bagerdjian
CFO: Alan R Steel
HR: Mary Berg
FYE: June 30
Type: Public

Just how do the latest movie trailers make it to a theater near you? The answer is simple: Point.360. The company provides audio video and film management and post-production services (including color correction editing and animation) for TV programming feature films and movie trailers. Clients include film studios ad agencies TV networks and production firms. Point.360 also offers editing mastering reformatting archiving and electronic distribution services for commercials press kits and corporate training. In addition the company rents and sells DVDs and video games directly to consumers through its MovieQ retail stores. Chairman and CEO Haig Bagerdjian owns more than 50% of Point.360.

	Annual Growth	06/12	06/13	06/14	06/15	06/16
Sales ($ mil.)	1.8%	35.0	30.9	25.7	21.6	37.6
Net income ($ mil.)	-	0.4	(1.2)	(2.7)	(2.9)	(1.8)
Market value ($ mil.)	3.1%	7.6	12.9	4.6	3.4	8.6
Employees	12.2%	240	231	201	179	380

POKERTEK INC
NAS: PTEK

1150 Crews Road, Suite F
Matthews, NC 28105
Phone: 704 849-0860
Fax: –
Web: www.pokertek.com

CEO: –
CFO: –
HR: –
FYE: December 31
Type: Public

PokerTek is bringing technology to the poker table. The company's electronic poker table automatically tracks bets and the outcome of hands as players pit their poker skills against each other. The PokerTek technology — currently available at casinos in the US Canada Macau Panama Germany Australia South Africa and several major cruise lines — can increase revenue for casino operators because PokerTek says more hands can be played with an automated dealer; casinos earn money from poker tables by taking a percentage of all bets made — also known as the rake.

	Annual Growth	12/08	12/09	12/10	12/11	12/12
Sales ($ mil.)	(22.6%)	14.4	6.7	5.9	6.5	5.2
Net income ($ mil.)	–	(7.6)	(5.7)	(4.0)	(1.8)	(0.8)
Market value ($ mil.)	0.2%	11.2	6.0	6.1	8.2	11.3
Employees	(18.6%)	57	35	32	30	25

POLARIS INC
NYS: PII

2100 Highway 55
Medina, MN 55340
Phone: 763 542-0500
Fax: –
Web: www.polaris.com

CEO: Scott W. Wine
CFO: Michael T. (Mike) Speetzen
HR: –
FYE: December 31
Type: Public

One of the world's top makers of off-road vehicles Polaris Industries makes and sells all-terrain vehicles (ATVs) and side-by-side recreational and utility RANGER-brand vehicles. It also manufactures snowmobiles on-road vehicles such as the Victory and Indian brands motorcycle and small electric vehicles (SEVs). Offerings include replacement parts accessories (covers windshields backrests) garments and riding gear (bags and helmets). Polaris' lineup is sold through dealers and distributors in North America Western Europe and Australia.

	Annual Growth	12/14	12/15	12/16	12/17	12/18
Sales ($ mil.)	7.9%	4,479.6	4,719.3	4,516.6	5,428.5	6,078.5
Net income ($ mil.)	(7.3%)	454.0	455.4	212.9	172.5	335.3
Market value ($ mil.)	(15.6%)	9,209.0	5,233.5	5,016.7	7,549.8	4,669.0
Employees	14.4%	7,000	8,100	8,600	11,000	12,000

POLARITYTE INC
NAS: PTE

123 Wright Brothers Drive
Salt Lake City, UT 84116
Phone: 800 560-3983
Fax: –
Web: www.polarityte.com

CEO: Denver Lough
CFO: Paul E Mann
HR: –
FYE: December 31
Type: Public

PolarityTE (formerly Majesco Entertainment) has put the games away to focus on regenerative medicine and tissue engineering. Formerly a video game developer Majesco acquired the intellectual property of PolarityTE in early 2017 and began developing technology that could allow it to regenerate the body's skin bone muscle cartilage fat nerves and blood vessels. Its first product SkinTE is in development as the first platform to regenerate skin in the case of burn. If successful PolarityTE hopes to expand into other markets including the acute wound scar and hair revision markets. Other technologies in development include OsteoTE (bone) AngioTE (vascular tissue) MyoTE (muscle) CartTE (cartilage) NeuralTE (nerves) and AdiposeTE (fat).

	Annual Growth	10/15	10/16	10/17	10/18*	12/18
Sales ($ mil.)	(53.5%)	6.7	1.5	–	1.6	0.7
Net income ($ mil.)	–	(3.8)	(4.6)	(130.8)	(65.4)	(18.4)
Market value ($ mil.)	120.5%	27.0	76.8	554.8	326.9	289.3
Employees	214.8%	5	4	33	123	156

*Fiscal year change

POLYCOM INC.
NMS: PLCM

6001 America Center Drive
San Jose, CA 95002
Phone: 408 586-6000
Fax: –
Web: www.polycom.com

CEO: Joe Burton
CFO: Chuck Boynton
HR: –
FYE: December 31
Type: Public

Polycom's vision is a world united by video. The company makes video-conferencing and immersive telepresence (which combines digital audio video and content sharing) systems that let users collaborate as if they were in the same room. Its products combine camera microphone network connection and external audio and video devices. The company also offers PC-based phones that transmit both voice and video. Polycom's software enables users to manage conferencing locations and connect with them using ISDN and Internet protocol connections. It partners with the likes of Microsoft and IBM to develop open standards-based products. Polycom gets more than half of its sales from outside the US.

	Annual Growth	12/10	12/11	12/12	12/13	12/14
Sales ($ mil.)	2.5%	1,218.5	1,495.8	1,392.6	1,368.4	1,345.2
Net income ($ mil.)	(11.5%)	68.4	135.8	9.8	(18.1)	42.1
Market value ($ mil.)	(23.3%)	5,270.3	2,203.8	1,414.2	1,518.4	1,825.3
Employees	2.2%	3,230	3,839	3,747	3,774	3,525

POLYMER GROUP INC.

9335 Harris Corners Pkwy. Ste. 300
Charlotte NC 28269
Phone: 704-697-5100
Fax: 704-697-5116
Web: www.polymergroupinc.com

CEO: J Joel Hackney Jr
CFO: Dennis Norman
HR: –
FYE: December 31
Type: Private

Polymer Group Inc.'s (PGI) business is interwoven with nonwovens. Rivaling Ahlstrom and E.I. du Pont de Nemours the company is a leading developer and maker of nonwoven textiles and other engineered materials used by consumer and industrial product manufacturers. Its absorbent and disposable fabrics go into baby wipes diapers and other hygiene and medical products. On the industrial side they are incorporated into filtration insulation and automotive acoustics products. PGI operates more than a dozen manufacturing and converting facilities worldwide. In 2011 the company was acquired by Scorpio Acquisition an affiliate of private equity group Blackstone Capital Partners.

POLYONE CORP.
NYS: POL

33587 Walker Road
Avon Lake, OH 44012
Phone: 440 930-1000
Fax: –
Web: –

CEO: Robert M Patterson
CFO: Bradley C. Richardson
HR: –
FYE: December 31
Type: Public

PolyOne Corp. a top North American plastics compounder and resins distributor has a single focus — providing specialized polymer products and services. The company's Performance Products and Solutions unit produces custom-made compounded plastics and custom-formulated colorants for plastics manufacturers throughout North America and Europe. Other units include Color Additives and Inks; Specialty Engineered Materials; and PolyOne Distribution which distributes more than 4000 thermoplastic resins and compounds from more than 25 major material suppliers. The US accounts for around 55% of sales.

	Annual Growth	12/14	12/15	12/16	12/17	12/18
Sales ($ mil.)	(2.0%)	3,835.5	3,377.6	3,339.8	3,229.9	3,533.4
Net income ($ mil.)	19.2%	79.2	144.6	165.2	(57.7)	159.8
Market value ($ mil.)	(6.8%)	2,945.6	2,467.8	2,489.5	3,380.0	2,222.2
Employees	(1.1%)	6,900	6,900	7,000	6,300	6,600

POLYPORE INTERNATIONAL INC

NYS: PPO

11430 North Community House Road, Suite 350
Charlotte, NC 28277
Phone: 704 587-8409
Fax: –
Web: www.polypore.net

CEO: Shgeki Takayama
CFO: –
HR: –
FYE: December 28
Type: Public

Polypore International believes in separation of states — mainly liquid from materials such as ions gases and particles. The company develops and manufactures polymer-based membranes containing millions of pores per square inch that are used in separation and filtration processes. Through its Energy Storage segment Polypore sells membrane separators that help the performance of lead-acid batteries used in electronic drive vehicles (EDVs) and lithium batteries used in a variety of consumer electronics from laptops to mobile phones. Its Separations Media segment makes membranes for health care applications (hemodialysis and blood oxygenation) and specialty applications (ultra-pure water filtration and degasification).

	Annual Growth	01/10	01/11*	12/11	12/12	12/13
Sales ($ mil.)	7.2%	516.9	616.6	763.1	717.4	636.3
Net income ($ mil.)	–	(117.3)	63.6	105.2	71.0	81.6
Market value ($ mil.)	47.3%	534.5	1,829.5	1,975.9	2,072.0	1,707.3
Employees	8.1%	1,900	2,200	2,500	2,700	2,400

*Fiscal year change

POLYVISION CORPORATION

3970 Johns Creek Ct. Ste. 325
Suwanee GA 30024
Phone: 678-542-3100
Fax: 678-542-3200
Web: www.polyvision.com

CEO: Peter Lewchanin
CFO: –
HR: –
FYE: February 28
Type: Subsidiary

No presentation is complete without visual displays so PolyVision wants all eyes on its boards. The company makes static and electronic whiteboards writing slates and other visual communication products for schools offices and public places. Its brands include eno and the TS Series. The firm also markets educational software and projectors from such makers as 3M and Hitachi that operate in conjunction with its products. Polyvision runs manufacturing facilities in Oklahoma and Oregon and its lines are sold by audiovisual equipment dealers throughout the US as well as Europe. Founded in 1954 the company has been owned by office furniture maker Steelcase since 2002.

POMONA COLLEGE

550 N COLLEGE AVE
CLAREMONT, CA 917114434
Phone: 909-621-8135
Fax: –
Web: www.pomona.edu

CEO: David Oxtoby
CFO: –
HR: –
FYE: June 30
Type: Private

Looking to get an education in sunny California? You might want to consider Pomona College. The school offers about 50 academic programs in areas such as art humanities biology psychology computer science and English. It also has research and interdisciplinary study opportunities. The liberal arts college enrolls about 1600 students. Formed in 1887 Pomona College is the founding member of The Claremont Colleges an affiliated group of seven independent colleges located on adjoining campuses in Claremont California. The affiliated campuses are coordinated by one of the member institutions the Claremont University Consortium.

	Annual Growth	06/13	06/14	06/15	06/16	06/17
Sales ($ mil.)	(11.1%)	–	275.5	281.0	193.1	193.5
Net income ($ mil.)	34.9%	–	86.0	82.7	(125.3)	211.3
Market value ($ mil.)	–	–	–	–	–	–
Employees	–	–	–	–	–	500

POMP'S TIRE SERVICE, INC.

1123 CEDAR ST
GREEN BAY, WI 543014703
Phone: 920-435-8301
Fax: –
Web: www.pompstire.com

CEO: –
CFO: –
HR: –
FYE: December 31
Type: Private

If by circumstance you have a flat tire in the Midwest limp on over to Pomp's Tire Service. The company sells tires for agricultural commercial and industrial vehicles as well as everyday cars and trucks from more than 75 locations in eight Midwestern states. (More than half are located in Wisconsin and Illinois.) Its brands include Bridgestone Goodrich Goodyear and Michelin among others. Pomp's Tire Service also offers 24-hour truck roadside assistance retread and auto repair services and has federal contracts with the US Army for vehicle parts. Originally called Pomprowitz Tire Co. the company was founded in 1939 by Andrew "Sparky" Pomprowitz. It is owned by the family of Roger Wochinske who bought the firm in 1964.

	Annual Growth	12/07	12/08	12/09	12/10	12/11
Sales ($ mil.)	18.3%	–	–	284.8	342.4	398.2
Net income ($ mil.)	11.5%	–	–	10.2	11.1	12.7
Market value ($ mil.)	–	–	–	–	–	–
Employees	–	–	–	–	–	1,200

POOL CORP

NMS: POOL

109 Northpark Boulevard
Covington, LA 70433-5001
Phone: 985 892-5521
Fax: 985 892-2438
Web: www.poolcorp.com

CEO: Manuel J. Perez de la Mesa
CFO: Mark W. Joslin
HR: –
FYE: December 31
Type: Public

Pool Corporation swims laps around its competitors as the world's largest wholesale distributor of swimming pool supplies. It operates about 370 service centers throughout the Americas Europe and Australia serving some 120000 wholesale customers such as pool builders and remodelers retail pool stores and pool repair and service companies. Pool Corporation's more than 180000 products include private-label and name-brand pool maintenance items (chemicals cleaners) equipment (pumps filters) accessories (heaters lights) and packaged pool kits. Founded in 1993 as SCP Holding Pool Corporation generates most of its sales in the US.

	Annual Growth	12/14	12/15	12/16	12/17	12/18
Sales ($ mil.)	7.5%	2,246.6	2,363.1	2,570.8	2,788.2	2,998.1
Net income ($ mil.)	20.6%	110.7	128.3	149.0	191.6	234.5
Market value ($ mil.)	23.7%	2,506.3	3,191.3	4,122.1	5,122.0	5,872.6
Employees	2.0%	3,700	3,800	3,900	4,000	4,000

POPE RESOURCES LP

NAS: POPE

19950 7th Avenue NE, Suite 200
Poulsbo, WA 98370
Phone: 360 697-6626
Fax: 360 697-1156
Web: www.poperesources.com

CEO: Thomas M Ringo
CFO: Daemon P Repp
HR: –
FYE: December 31
Type: Public

More earthly than divine Pope Resources owns or manages more than 150000 acres of timberland and development property in Washington. Its holdings include the 70000-acre Hood Canal and 44000-acre Columbia tree farms in Washington. It sells its Douglas fir and other timber products mainly in the US Japan China and Korea; Weyerhaeuser and Simpson Investment Company are major customers. Pope Resources also invests in and manages two timberland investment funds and provides investment management and consulting services to third-party timberland owners and managers in Washington Oregon and California. Its real estate unit acquires develops resells and rents residential and commercial real estate.

	Annual Growth	12/14	12/15	12/16	12/17	12/18
Sales ($ mil.)	4.3%	87.5	78.0	80.4	99.8	103.6
Net income ($ mil.)	(13.9%)	12.4	10.9	5.9	17.9	6.8
Market value ($ mil.)	0.7%	274.4	276.3	286.0	300.8	282.5
Employees	2.0%	60	66	65	70	65

POPEYES LOUISIANA KITCHEN, INC.

5505 BLUE LAGOON DR
MIAMI, FL 331262029
Phone: 404-459-4450
Fax: –

CEO: –
CFO: –
HR: –
FYE: December 25
Type: Private

This company's recipe for success features fried chicken and biscuits. A leading fast-food company Popeyes Louisiana Kitchen (formerly AFC Enterprises) operates the Popeyes restaurant chain the #2 quick-service chain specializing in chicken behind YUM! Brands' KFC. The chain boasts more than 2300 locations in the US and in more than 25 other countries. The restaurants feature Cajun-style fried chicken and seafood that is typically served with buttermilk biscuits and a variety of sides including Cajun rice coleslaw mashed potatoes or french fries. Restaurant Brands International acquired the company for $1.8 billion 2017.

	Annual Growth	12/12	12/13	12/14	12/15	12/16
Sales ($ mil.)	9.3%	–	206.0	235.6	259.0	268.9
Net income ($ mil.)	7.9%	–	34.1	38.0	44.1	42.8
Market value ($ mil.)	–	–	–	–	–	–
Employees	–	–	–	–	–	1,000

POPLAR BLUFF REGIONAL MEDICAL CENTER, INC.

3100 OAK GROVE RD
POPLAR BLUFF, MO 639011573
Phone: 573-785-7721
Fax: –

CEO: Kenneth James
CFO: Mark Johnson
HR: –
FYE: December 31
Type: Private

Poplar Bluff Regional Medical Center part of Health Management Associates serves southeastern Missouri with general and acute care services. The hospital's offerings range from cardiology and pediatrics to home care and maternity services. It also has centers devoted to such areas as cancer care pain management and rehabilitation. The two-campus hospital has about 425 beds.

	Annual Growth	12/07	12/08	12/15	12/16	12/17
Sales ($ mil.)	2.8%	–	156.0	215.1	208.8	199.8
Net income ($ mil.)	2.2%	–	20.8	28.8	33.9	25.2
Market value ($ mil.)	–	–	–	–	–	–
Employees	–	–	–	–	–	19

POPULAR INC.

NMS: BPOP

Popular Center Building, 209 Munoz Rivera Avenue, Hato Rey
San Juan, PR 00918
Phone: 787 765-9800
Fax: –
Web: www.popular.com

CEO: Ignacio Ívarez
CFO: Carlos J. V ´zquez
HR: –
FYE: December 31
Type: Public

Founded in 1893 Popular is the holding company for Banco Popular de Puerto Rico the largest bank in Puerto Rico with some 170 branches (and around 10 more on the Virgin Islands). In addition to commercial and retail banking services Popular owns subsidiaries that offer vehicle financing and leasing (Popular Auto) insurance (Popular Insurance) financial advisory and brokerage services (Popular Securities) and mortgages (Popular Mortgage). Popular also owns Banco Popular North America (BPNA) which serves the US Hispanic population from about 50 Popular Community Bank branches in New York Florida and New Jersey.

	Annual Growth	12/14	12/15	12/16	12/17	12/18
Assets ($ mil.)	9.5%	33,096.7	35,769.5	38,661.6	44,277.3	47,604.6
Net income ($ mil.)	–	(313.5)	895.3	216.7	107.7	618.2
Market value ($ mil.)	8.5%	3,403.1	2,832.4	4,379.5	3,547.0	4,719.3
Employees	2.3%	7,752	7,810	7,828	7,784	8,474

POPULATION SERVICES INTERNATIONAL

1120 19TH ST NW STE 600
WASHINGTON, DC 200363605
Phone: 202-785-0072
Fax: –
Web: www.psi.org

CEO: Karl Hofmann
CFO: –
HR: –
FYE: December 31
Type: Private

Population Services International (PSI) goes far beyond the scope of its name. Founded in 1970 to promote global family planning PSI has established social programs that use local networks in low-income regions to distribute such lifelines as insecticide-treated mosquito nets iodized salt snake boots and insect repellent along with condoms contraceptives and pregnancy test kits. The group prides itself on using business principals to confront health issues in more than 65 countries worldwide. It reportedly has averted 4.2 million unintended pregnancies some 29 million malaria cases and provided 1.8-plus million clients with of HIV testing and counseling. PSI is also active ensuring safe water supplies.

	Annual Growth	12/0-2	12/0-1	12/00	12/01	12/13
Sales ($ mil.)	14.8%	–	–	96.8	121.7	584.0
Net income ($ mil.)	2.9%	–	–	3.2	(0.8)	4.7
Market value ($ mil.)	–	–	–	–	–	–
Employees	–	–	–	–	–	417

PORT OF CORPUS CHRISTI AUTHORITY OF NUECES COUNTY, TEXAS

222 POWER ST
CORPUS CHRISTI, TX 784011529
Phone: 361-882-5633
Fax: –
Web: www.portofcc.com

CEO: –
CFO: –
HR: Angie Ramirez
FYE: December 31
Type: Private

The Port of Corpus Christi Authority of Nueces County Texas owns and operates docks and freight handling facilities at the Port of Corpus Christi which is on the Gulf of Mexico about 150 miles north of the US-Mexico border. The port has terminals designed to handle general refrigerated and liquid and dry bulk cargo. Port facilities are served by rail carriers and highways as well as by the Gulf Intracoastal Waterway. The agency was created by Nueces County voters in 1922 as Nueces County Navigation District No. 1; it became the Port of Corpus Christi Authority of Nueces County Texas by an act of the Texas Legislature in 1981. Commissioners appointed by local government entities oversee the agency.

	Annual Growth	12/14	12/15	12/16	12/17	12/18
Sales ($ mil.)	4.2%	–	93.4	82.7	95.3	105.8
Net income ($ mil.)	12.5%	–	34.7	34.0	35.9	49.3
Market value ($ mil.)	–	–	–	–	–	–
Employees	–	–	–	–	–	146

PORT OF HOUSTON AUTHORITY

111 EAST LOOP N
HOUSTON, TX 770294326
Phone: 713-670-2662
Fax: –

CEO: –
CFO: –
HR: –
FYE: December 31
Type: Private

Houston is too far inland to be a port city by the strictest of definitions but don't try to tell that to the Port of Houston Authority. The agency manages the Port of Houston complex including the Barbours Cut Container Terminal one of the busiest in the US. Port of Houston facilities are arrayed along the Houston Ship Channel which connects Houston with Galveston Bay and the Gulf of Mexico and with intracoastal waterways. The Port of Houston Authority itself operates more than 40 cargo wharves; however most of the terminal facilities along the ship channel are managed by private companies. The ship channel was opened in 1914; the Port of Houston Authority was created by the Texas Legislature in 1927.

	Annual Growth	12/13	12/14	12/15	12/16	12/17
Sales ($ mil.)	8.0%	–	263.9	293.7	290.2	332.9
Net income ($ mil.)	14.2%	–	69.2	85.5	57.9	103.1
Market value ($ mil.)	–	–	–	–	–	–
Employees	–	–	–	–	–	595

PORT OF NEW ORLEANS

1350 PORT OF NEW ORLEANS
NEW ORLEANS, LA 701301805
Phone: 504-522-2551
Fax: –
Web: www.portno.com

CEO: Gary Lagrange
CFO: –
HR: –
FYE: June 30
Type: Private

The Port of New Orleans has played a major part of American history — after all the US purchased Louisiana to ensure control of it. By virtue of its location at the mouth of the Mississippi River on the Gulf of Mexico the port connects the Midwestern US with the world. One of the busiest US ports the Port of New Orleans handles export cargo such as grain and steel that arrives via the US inland waterway system. The port also is served by six major railroads. Import cargo handled at the port includes coffee plywood rubber and steel. The Port of New Orleans is governed by a seven-member board appointed by the governor of Louisiana; board members represent New Orleans and two neighboring parishes.

	Annual Growth	06/13	06/14	06/15	06/16	06/17
Sales ($ mil.)	7.1%	–	–	–	61.0	65.3
Net income ($ mil.)	–	–	–	–	(6.3)	(11.8)
Market value ($ mil.)	–	–	–	–	–	–
Employees	–	–	–	–	–	380

PORT OF SEATTLE

2711 ALASKAN WAY PIER 69
SEATTLE, WA 981211107
Phone: 206-728-3000
Fax: –
Web: www.portseattle.org

CEO: Dave Soike
CFO: Dan Thomas
HR: Alma Harrell
FYE: December 31
Type: Private

The Port of Seattle oversees both an airport (Seattle-Tacoma International also known as Sea-Tac) and a seaport. The agency's aviation division sees more than 33.2 million passengers a year. The seaport division serves more than 18 container steamship lines that import and export containerized and bulk cargo. It also handles calls from cruise ships. In addition the seaport division oversees commercial fishing marinas and portside commercial properties. Most of the agency's revenue comes from airport operations. The Port of Seattle is run by a five-member commission elected by King County voters.

	Annual Growth	12/13	12/14	12/15	12/16	12/17
Sales ($ mil.)	5.7%	–	534.5	558.9	598.5	632.0
Net income ($ mil.)	15.1%	–	131.2	20.0	41.4	199.8
Market value ($ mil.)	–	–	–	–	–	–
Employees	–	–	–	–	–	1,515

PORTAGE INC.

1075 S UTAH AVE STE 200
IDAHO FALLS, ID 83402-3320
Phone: 208-528-6608
Fax: –
Web: www.portageinc.com

CEO: –
CFO: –
HR: –
FYE: December 31
Type: Private

Portage Environmental helps carry the load for customers needing environmental engineering services. The firm's offerings include environmental remediation process and project engineering and decontamination and decommissioning services. Portage Environmental counts US government agencies (such as the Department of Defense and the Department of Energy) and Native American tribes among its clients and has conducted projects in 20 US states as well as in Afghanistan Guam Iraq Japan Kuwait Qatar and South Korea. The firm operates from some two dozen offices throughout the US. President and CEO Michael Spry helped found Portage Environmental in 1992.

	Annual Growth	12/03	12/04	12/05	12/06	12/10
Sales ($ mil.)	46.4%	–	24.9	29.9	33.4	245.3
Net income ($ mil.)	68.4%	–	0.3	1.9	1.9	6.4
Market value ($ mil.)	–	–	–	–	–	–
Employees	–	–	–	–	–	300

PORTION PAC INC.

7325 Snider Rd.
Mason OH 45040
Phone: 513-398-0400
Fax: 513-459-5300
Web: www.portionpac.com

CEO: –
CFO: –
HR: –
FYE: April 30
Type: Subsidiary

Who actually makes those little white cups that hold the honey you drizzle on your morning bagel? Or the foil-topped grape jelly containers the waitperson brings you at the local breakfast joint? Portion Pac that's who. A subsidiary of Heinz Foodservice Portion Pac manufactures and markets shelf-stable portion-control food products for the catering fast-food restaurant and vending-machine industries. Its national licensed products include cream cheese jams jellies ketchup mustard salad dressings steak sauce salsa syrup and more. They're marketed under popular name brands such as Welch's Log Cabin Musselman's Mrs. Butterworths and ReaLemon.

PORTLAND GENERAL ELECTRIC CO.

NYS: POR

121 SW Salmon Street
Portland, OR 97204
Phone: 503 464-8000
Fax: 503 464-2676
Web: www.portlandgeneral.com

CEO: Maria M. Pope
CFO: James F. Lobdell
HR: Anne Mersereau
FYE: December 31
Type: Public

Portland General Electric (PGE) keeps many Birkenstock-shod feet warm by providing power to about 885000 retail customers in Oregon. The company generates transmits and distributes electricity in more than 50 cities in the state including Portland and Salem. It owns power plants with about 3900 MW of fossil-fueled and renewable generating capacity and buys a further 1000 MW via power purchase agreements. The company runs a market-leading voluntary renewable energy program for customers.

	Annual Growth	12/14	12/15	12/16	12/17	12/18
Sales ($ mil.)	1.2%	1,900.0	1,898.0	1,923.0	2,009.0	1,991.0
Net income ($ mil.)	4.9%	175.0	172.0	193.0	187.0	212.0
Market value ($ mil.)	4.9%	3,377.0	3,246.7	3,868.0	4,068.8	4,092.9
Employees	3.4%	2,600	2,646	2,752	2,906	2,967

PORTLAND STATE UNIVERSITY

1600 SW 4TH AVE
PORTLAND, OR 972015522
Phone: 503-725-4444
Fax: –
Web: www.pdx.edu

CEO: –
CFO: –
HR: –
FYE: June 30
Type: Private

Portland State University (PSU) is one of seven institutions of higher learning in the Oregon University System. It offers nearly 100 bachelor's 90 master's and 40 doctoral degrees as well as graduate certificates and continuing education programs. PSU has eight schools and colleges devoted to liberal arts and sciences; engineering and computer science; fine and performing arts; urban and public affairs; business administration; social work; and education. It also has a school dedicated to extended studies including distance learning continuing education and professional development. Student enrollment exceeds 29000 (80% undergrads) and the student to faculty ratio is 19:1. PSU was established in 1946.

	Annual Growth	06/13	06/14	06/15	06/16	06/17
Sales ($ mil.)	0.3%	–	350.0	351.8	357.4	353.1
Net income ($ mil.)	9.2%	–	36.4	181.7	(4.1)	47.4
Market value ($ mil.)	–	–	–	–	–	–
Employees	–	–	–	–	–	4,000

PORTOLA PHARMACEUTICALS, INC.
NMS: PTLA

270 E. Grand Avenue
South San Francisco, CA 94080
Phone: 650 246-7000
Fax: –
Web: www.portola.com

CEO: William Lis
CFO: Mardi C. Dier
HR: –
FYE: December 31
Type: Public

Portola Pharmaceuticals is putting blood sweat and tears into developing new medications for blood disorders. The company has three drug candidates in the works that if approved will treat thrombosis (blood clots). Its lead candidate Betrixaban is an oral medication that would prevent certain types of blood clots in seriously ill patients. Betrixaban is currently in Phase 3 study. Another medication in development PRT4445 would help with uncontrolled bleeding episodes after surgery and PRT2070 is being developed for hematologic or blood cancers and inflammatory disorders. Another version of PRT2070 is being developed with Biogen. Founded in 2003 Portola Pharmaceuticals went public in 2013.

	Annual Growth	12/14	12/15	12/16	12/17	12/18
Sales ($ mil.)	42.9%	9.6	12.1	35.5	22.5	40.1
Net income ($ mil.)	–	(137.1)	(226.5)	(269.0)	(286.1)	(350.2)
Market value ($ mil.)	(8.9%)	1,886.6	3,427.5	1,494.9	3,243.0	1,300.4
Employees	34.5%	99	137	446	252	324

PORTSMOUTH SQUARE, INC.
NBB: PRSI

12121 Wilshire Boulevard, Suite 610
Los Angeles, CA 90025
Phone: 310 889-2500
Fax: 310 899-2525
Web: www.intgla.com

CEO: John V Winfield
CFO: Danfeng Xu
HR: –
FYE: June 30
Type: Public

Investments are a square deal for Portsmouth Square which owns a 50% partnership interest in Justice Investors a property investment firm based in San Francisco. Justice Investors owns and operates the Hilton San Francisco Financial District a hotel property that includes more than 500 individual units a health and beauty spa a Chinese cultural center and an underground parking garage. Portsmouth Square has an investment portfolio valued at some $3 million that includes consumer financial material and communications equities. Through Santa Fe Financial and other entities CEO John Winfield controls more than 80% of Portsmouth Square.

	Annual Growth	06/15	06/16	06/17	06/18	06/19
Sales ($ mil.)	1.3%	56.8	58.6	54.3	57.1	59.9
Net income ($ mil.)	–	(1.8)	(4.8)	0.2	3.6	2.6
Market value ($ mil.)	13.2%	36.7	39.6	51.4	51.4	60.2
Employees	(71.7%)	314	278	277	2	2

POSITIVEID CORP
NBB: PSID

1690 South Congress Avenue, Suite 201
Delray Beach, FL 33445
Phone: 561 805-8000
Fax: –
Web: www.positiveidcorp.com

CEO: –
CFO: William J Caragol
HR: –
FYE: December 31
Type: Public

Who knew something the size of a grain of rice could protect so much? PositiveID formerly VeriChip knows it well. The firm provides implantable radio frequency identification (RFID) microchips for humans and animals. The chip is inserted under the skin and has a unique verification number used to access a subscriber-supplied database providing information when scanned. While its implantable technology has made headlines most of its business comes from wearable and attachable ID tags as well as vibration monitoring systems used to monitor and protect people and assets. In 2009 the company changed its name from VeriChip to PositiveID to reflect a new focus on electronic health records.

	Annual Growth	12/13	12/14	12/15	12/16	12/17
Sales ($ mil.)	78.3%	–	0.9	2.9	5.6	5.4
Net income ($ mil.)	–	(4.3)	(7.2)	(11.4)	(13.1)	(8.6)
Market value ($ mil.)	–	0.0	0.0	0.0	0.0	0.0
Employees	3.0%	8	9	32	29	9

POSITRON CORP
NBB: POSC

530 Oakmont Lane
Westmont, IL 60559
Phone: 317 576-0183
Fax: –
Web: www.positron.com

CEO: –
CFO: Corey N Conn
HR: –
FYE: December 31
Type: Public

Positron is positive that its imaging systems can figure out what's wrong with you. The company makes positron emission tomography (PET) scanners under the POSICAM and mPower trade names. The scanners are primarily used to detect coronary artery disease but also have applications in neurology and oncology. Medical centers such as the University of Texas Health Science Center at Houston and the Heart Center of Niagara use the system; the company has an installed base of about 30 systems in the US and abroad. Subsidiary IS2 Medical Systems (acquired in 2006) makes nuclear imaging devices including the PulseCDC cardiac gamma camera.

	Annual Growth	12/10	12/11	12/12	12/13	12/14
Sales ($ mil.)	(25.0%)	4.6	6.7	2.8	1.6	1.5
Net income ($ mil.)	–	(10.9)	(6.1)	(8.0)	(7.1)	(2.6)
Market value ($ mil.)	–	0.7	0.1	0.1	0.1	0.0
Employees	(8.4%)	27	32	26	22	19

POSITRON CORP.
NBB: POSC

530 Oakmont Lane
Westmont, IL 60559
Phone: 317 576-0183
Fax: –
Web: www.positron.com

CEO: –
CFO: Corey N Conn
HR: –
FYE: December 31
Type: Public

Positron is positive that its imaging systems can figure out what's wrong with you. The company makes positron emission tomography (PET) scanners under the POSICAM and mPower trade names. The scanners are primarily used to detect coronary artery disease but also have applications in neurology and oncology. Medical centers such as the University of Texas Health Science Center at Houston and the Heart Center of Niagara use the system; the company has an installed base of about 30 systems in the US and abroad. Subsidiary IS2 Medical Systems (acquired in 2006) makes nuclear imaging devices including the PulseCDC cardiac gamma camera.

	Annual Growth	12/09	12/10	12/11	12/12	12/13
Sales ($ mil.)	3.0%	1.4	4.6	6.7	2.8	1.6
Net income ($ mil.)	–	(5.7)	(10.9)	(6.1)	(8.0)	(7.1)
Market value ($ mil.)	(48.8%)	101.7	72.6	12.9	12.3	7.0
Employees	1.2%	21	27	32	26	22

POST HOLDINGS INC
NYS: POST

2503 S. Hanley Road
St. Louis, MO 63144
Phone: 314 644-7600
Fax: –
Web: www.postholdings.com

CEO: Richard R. Koulouris
CFO: Jeff A. Zadoks
HR: –
FYE: September 30
Type: Public

Breakfast food company Post Holdings has a healthy appetite. The maker of Grape-Nuts Golden Puffs Honey Bunches of Oats Raisin Bran Shredded Wheat Pebbles and Alpha-Bits Post is the third-best-selling breakfast cereal brand in the US (behind Kellogg and General Mills). As well as cereal the company also makes egg products potato products and cheese pasta and other dairy-based products. More recently it has moved beyond the breakfast table by adding snacks active nutrition products and pasta through a series of major acquisitions. It also manufactures nut butters and cereals for private labels. The company has warehouses manufacturing facilities and distribution facilities located throughout the US and Canada.

	Annual Growth	09/15	09/16	09/17	09/18	09/19
Sales ($ mil.)	5.1%	4,648.2	5,026.8	5,225.8	6,257.2	5,681.1
Net income ($ mil.)	–	(115.3)	(3.3)	48.3	467.3	124.7
Market value ($ mil.)	15.7%	4,261.1	5,564.0	6,364.3	7,068.7	7,631.1
Employees	4.4%	8,500	8,700	11,410	11,550	10,100

POST PROPERTIES, INC.
NYS: PPS

4401 Northside Parkway, Suite 800
Atlanta, GA 30327
Phone: 404 846-5000
Fax: –

CEO: –
CFO: –
HR: –
FYE: December 31
Type: Public

Post Properties offers Southerners a place to hang their hats but has also started showing Yankees some down-home hospitality. A self-administered and self-managed real estate investment trust (REIT) Post Properties owns develops and manages primarily upscale multi-family apartment communities. Operating through Post Apartment Homes it owns some 60 properties with about 22500 apartment units. Its primary markets are Atlanta Dallas Tampa and Washington DC with additional holdings in New York North Carolina and other markets in Florida and Texas. Post Properties also acts as a property manager and provides furnished short-term corporate apartments in several markets.

	Annual Growth	12/10	12/11	12/12	12/13	12/14
Sales ($ mil.)	7.3%	285.1	305.3	334.9	362.7	377.8
Net income ($ mil.)	–	(7.0)	25.5	83.9	110.5	215.1
Market value ($ mil.)	12.8%	1,978.7	2,383.1	2,722.7	2,465.4	3,203.5
Employees	(0.1%)	597	609	625	635	594

POSTROCK ENERGY CORP
NBB: PSTR

210 Park Avenue
Oklahoma City, OK 73102
Phone: 405 600-7704
Fax: –
Web: www.pstr.com

CEO: –
CFO: –
HR: –
FYE: December 31
Type: Public

PostRock Energy (formerly Quest Resource) is looking to create a rock solid energy company specializing in oil and gas exploration and production and the transportation of natural gas. Its exploration and drilling efforts are focused in the Cherokee Basin of southeastern Kansas and northeastern Oklahoma and the Appalachian Basin where it is accumulating leasehold acreage. PostRock Energy has net proved reserves of 192.2 billion cu. ft. of net proved reserves (the bulk of which is coal bed methane gas) and operates more than 2200 miles of gas gathering pipeline in Kansas and Oklahoma. It also operates more than 1100 miles of interstate natural gas transmission pipelines in the region.

	Annual Growth	12/10	12/11	12/12	12/13	12/14
Sales ($ mil.)	0.3%	82.4	96.3	55.0	72.3	83.5
Net income ($ mil.)	(46.0%)	45.2	20.0	(47.6)	(9.0)	3.9
Market value ($ mil.)	(44.2%)	23.8	17.7	9.1	7.4	2.3
Employees	(9.8%)	300	233	216	209	199

POTBELLY CORP
NMS: PBPB

111 N. Canal Street, Suite 850
Chicago, IL 60606
Phone: 312 951-0600
Fax: –
Web: www.potbelly.com

CEO: Alan Johnson
CFO: Michael W. (Mike) Coyne
HR: –
FYE: December 30
Type: Public

Potbelly is a quick-service sandwich shop chain. The company owns almost 400 quick-service restaurants that specialize in fresh-made sandwiches in 28 states and Washington DC. Potbelly's franchisees operate 24 shops domestically 11 in the Middle East and one location in London UK. The chain's menu features a variety of sandwich styles including such specialty items as its four-meat stacker called A Wreck. The eateries also serve salads soup and chili as well as homemade cookies ice cream and smoothies. In 2013 Potbelly went public raising $105 million.

	Annual Growth	12/14	12/15	12/16	12/17	12/18
Sales ($ mil.)	6.6%	327.0	372.8	407.1	428.1	422.6
Net income ($ mil.)	–	4.4	5.6	8.2	(7.0)	(8.9)
Market value ($ mil.)	(10.0%)	294.8	289.7	329.5	297.0	193.6
Employees	0.0%	7,000	7,000	7,400	7,300	7,000

POTLATCHDELTIC CORP
NMS: PCH

601 West First Avenue, Suite 1600
Spokane, WA 99201
Phone: 509 835-1500
Fax: –
Web: www.potlatch.com

CEO: Michael J. Covey
CFO: Jerald W. (Jerry) Richards
HR: –
FYE: December 31
Type: Public

Potlatch is Chinook for giving but you'll have to pay for Potlatch's wood products. The real estate investment trust (REIT) harvests timber from some 1.6 million acres of hardwood and softwood forestland in Alabama Arkansas Idaho Mississippi and Minnesota; it claims to be the largest private landowner in Idaho. Potlatch operates sawmills in five states that produce logs and fiber and lumber and panels. Beyond wood product sales the company generates revenue by leasing its land for hunting recreation mineral rights biomass production and carbon sequestration. It also sells real estate through Potlatch TRS. In 2018 it completed its acquisition of Arkansas-based Deltic Timber Corporation.

	Annual Growth	12/14	12/15	12/16	12/17	12/18
Sales ($ mil.)	12.6%	607.0	575.3	599.1	678.6	974.6
Net income ($ mil.)	8.1%	89.9	31.7	10.9	86.5	122.9
Market value ($ mil.)	(6.8%)	2,829.1	2,043.3	2,814.3	3,371.7	2,137.9
Employees	13.5%	887	927	953	963	1,471

POTOMAC BANCSHARES, INC.
NBB: PTBS

111 East Washington Street, P.O. Box 906
Charles Town, WV 25414-0906
Phone: 304 725-8431
Fax: 304 725-0059
Web: www.bankatbct.com

CEO: Arch Moore III
CFO: Dean Cognetti
HR: –
FYE: December 31
Type: Public

Potomac Bancshares is the holding company for Bank of Charles Town which serves eastern West Virginia and neighboring parts of Maryland and Virginia. Through about five offices the bank provides standard deposit products such as checking and savings accounts CDs and IRAs as well as trust services investments and financial planning. It uses funds from deposits primarily to write real estate loans. Residential mortgages account for the largest portion of the company's loan portfolio followed by construction land development and commercial real estate loans. Consumer business and farm loans round out the bank's lending activities. Bank of Charles Town opened in 1871.

	Annual Growth	12/14	12/15	12/16	12/17	12/18
Assets ($ mil.)	10.9%	320.9	351.8	383.7	425.5	484.6
Net income ($ mil.)	12.0%	2.2	2.6	2.2	3.8	3.4
Market value ($ mil.)	14.7%	33.7	35.6	39.5	58.9	58.3
Employees	–	–	–	–	–	–

POTOMAC HOSPITAL CORPORATION OF PRINCE WILLIAM

2300 OPITZ BLVD
WOODBRIDGE, VA 221913399
Phone: 703-523-1000
Fax: –

CEO: David L Bernd
CFO: –
HR: –
FYE: December 31
Type: Private

Potomac Hospital Corporation of Prince William — operating as Sentara Northern Virginia Medical Center — provides a variety of medical surgical and therapeutic services in northern Virginia. The not-for-profit medical center has more than 180 beds and provides emergency medicine diagnostic imaging and surgery services as well as specialized care in fields including cancer treatment women's health cardiology urology and pediatrics. It also offers health education programs and operates two outpatient care clinics. Sentara Northern Virginia Medical Center is part of the Sentara Healthcare network.

	Annual Growth	12/13	12/14	12/15	12/16	12/17
Sales ($ mil.)	(2.2%)	–	242.9	214.3	222.5	227.5
Net income ($ mil.)	–	–	26.4	10.7	0.8	(4.2)
Market value ($ mil.)	–	–	–	–	–	–
Employees	–	–	–	–	–	1,300

POUDRE VALLEY HEALTH CARE, INC.

2315 E HARMONY RD STE 200
FORT COLLINS, CO 805288620
Phone: 970-495-7000
Fax: –

CEO: Rulon Stacey
CFO: –
HR: –
FYE: June 30
Type: Private

Providing health care is what this Poudre Valley is all about. The not-for-profit Poudre Valley Health System (PVHS) cares for residents of Colorado western Nebraska and southern Wyoming through the Poudre Valley Hospital and the Medical Center of the Rockies. With a total of about 440 beds the two hospitals offer general medical and surgical services and trauma care. They also offer treatment centers for specialties including cancer heart brain and spine disorders. PVHS is home to the Mountain Crest Behavioral Healthcare Center which administers mental health and substance abuse treatment. PVHS is part of the Health District of Northern Larimer County; it is also part of University of Colorado Health.

	Annual Growth	06/12	06/13	06/14	06/15	06/16
Sales ($ mil.)	4.7%	–	–	478.3	480.4	523.9
Net income ($ mil.)	56.2%	–	–	38.1	98.8	93.0
Market value ($ mil.)	–	–	–	–	–	–
Employees	–	–	–	–	–	2,800

POWELL ELECTRONICS INC.

200 COMMODORE DR
SWEDESBORO, NJ 080851270
Phone: 856-241-8000
Fax: –
Web: www.powell.com

CEO: Ernest Schilling Jr
CFO: Schawn E Beatty
HR: –
FYE: December 31
Type: Private

Powell Electronics distributes switches sensors connectors relays and other electronic components. The company stocks more than 100000 parts from such manufacturers as 3M Amphenol AVX Emerson Network Power EnerSys Honeywell ITT RF Industries Winchester Electronics and TE Connectivity. It also manufactures custom assemblies and offers several services including bar coding special packaging materials management and wire cutting. Powell Electronics was founded in 1946 by the late Harold Powell who started selling components from his garage after World War II. His family continues to own the company.

	Annual Growth	03/08	03/09	03/10*	12/10	12/11
Sales ($ mil.)	390.4%	–	–	22.4	98.8	109.8
Net income ($ mil.)	651.2%	–	–	0.5	3.7	3.7
Market value ($ mil.)	–	–	–	–	–	–
Employees	–	–	–	–	–	205

*Fiscal year change

POWELL INDUSTRIES, INC.

NMS: POWL

8550 Mosley Road
Houston, TX 77075-1180
Phone: 713 944-6900
Fax: –
Web: www.powellind.com

CEO: Brett A. Cope
CFO: Don R. Madison
HR: Latasha Stoker
FYE: September 30
Type: Public

Powell Industries manufactures equipment that monitors and controls the flow of electricity in industrial and government facilities. Products include power control room substations switchgear (units that manage the flow of electricity to motors transformers and other equipment); bus ducts (insulated power conductors housed in a metal enclosure); medium-voltage circuit breakers; monitoring and control communications systems; and motor control centers. Powell sells to customers that use large amounts of electricity for industrial processes including oil and gas producers and pipelines refineries utilities pulp and paper mills and petrochemical plants. About 75% of the company's sales are generated in the US.

	Annual Growth	09/15	09/16	09/17	09/18	09/19
Sales ($ mil.)	(6.0%)	661.9	565.2	395.9	448.7	517.2
Net income ($ mil.)	1.2%	9.4	15.5	(9.5)	(7.2)	9.9
Market value ($ mil.)	6.8%	348.2	463.2	346.9	419.4	452.8
Employees	(4.7%)	2,803	2,323	18,411	1,985	2,312

POWELL'S BOOKS INC.

7 NW 9th Ave.
Portland OR 97209
Phone: 503-228-0540
Fax: 503-228-1142
Web: www.powells.com

CEO: Miriam Sontz
CFO: –
HR: –
FYE: June 30
Type: Private

Powell's may not be the big dog when it comes to books but its dog-eared volumes keep it near the front of the pack. The book retailer maintains more than a handful of stores in the Portland Oregon area including its flagship City of Books store which covers a city block and contains more than 1 million volumes. It sells new used out-of-print and rare books; it even sells books that are returned to online bookseller Amazon.com. The company operates specialty stores for cookbooks and gardening technical books and travel books; it also features author readings and book discussion groups and sells books online. President Michael Powell whose father Walter opened City of Books in 1971 owns the firm.

POWER CONSTRUCTION COMPANY LLC

2360 PALMER DR
SCHAUMBURG, IL 60173-3824
Phone: 847-925-1300
Fax: –
Web: www.powerconstruction.net

CEO: –
CFO: –
HR: –
FYE: December 31
Type: Private

The Midwest is the best for Power Construction Company a general contractor operating in the Chicago area for nearly 90 years. The company provides customers with preconstruction planning construction management and design/build services. It serves several markets such as health care education hotel and corporate projects. Power Construction is engaged in new building construction as well as buildouts expansions and renovations. More than 90% of the firm's business comes from repeat customers which have included Astellas Pharma US Federal Express and Walgreen. Jerome Goldstein founded the company which is still owned by management in 1926.

	Annual Growth	12/07	12/08	12/09	12/10	12/11
Sales ($ mil.)	106.6%	–	29.4	0.0	259.5	259.5
Net income ($ mil.)	–	–	0.0	0.0	9.9	9.9
Market value ($ mil.)	–	–	–	–	–	–
Employees	–	–	–	–	–	185

POWER INTEGRATIONS INC.

NMS: POWI

5245 Hellyer Avenue
San Jose, CA 95138
Phone: 408 414-9200
Fax: 408 414-9201
Web: www.power.com

CEO: Balu Balakrishnan
CFO: Sandeep Nayyar
HR: –
FYE: December 31
Type: Public

Power Integrations develops high-voltage analog integrated circuits (ICs) that convert alternating current (AC) to lower-voltage direct current (DC). The fabless company's high-voltage analog semiconductors which account for virtually all of its sales are used in PCs cell phones cable boxes and other consumer and industrial electronics. The TOPSwitch line features products made with its environmentally friendly EcoSmart technology which reduces energy waste. Power Integrations sells its chips to electronics manufacturers and distributors such as ATM Electronic and Burnon. It makes nearly all of its sales overseas.

	Annual Growth	12/14	12/15	12/16	12/17	12/18
Sales ($ mil.)	4.5%	348.8	344.0	387.4	431.8	416.0
Net income ($ mil.)	4.1%	59.5	39.1	47.9	27.6	70.0
Market value ($ mil.)	4.2%	1,494.7	1,404.9	1,960.1	2,124.8	1,761.6
Employees	2.9%	590	595	626	646	662

POWERFLEET INC
NMS: PWFL

123 Tice Boulevard
Woodcliff Lake, NJ 07677
Phone: 201 996-9000
Fax: -
Web: www.id-systems.com

CEO: Chris Wolfe
CFO: Ned Mavrommatis
HR: Lindsay Estelle
FYE: December 31
Type: Public

I.D. Systems has taken its tracking business on the road. The company's products track analyze and control the movements of objects such as packages and vehicles. Its systems use radio-frequency identification (RFID) technology and tiny computers attached to the object to be monitored and users can access tracking data via the Internet. The company is focused on vehicle management rental car package tracking and airport ground security applications. Customers include 3M the FAA Ford Hallmark Cards Target the US Postal Service (42% of sales) and Wal-Mart Stores (41%).

	Annual Growth	12/14	12/15	12/16	12/17	12/18
Sales ($ mil.)	3.8%	45.6	41.8	36.8	41.0	53.1
Net income ($ mil.)	-	(11.6)	(10.0)	(6.4)	(3.9)	(5.8)
Market value ($ mil.)	(4.4%)	121.5	83.6	98.5	126.1	101.5
Employees	2.9%	123	101	100	117	138

POWERTECH URANIUM CORP.
TORONTO: PWE

5575 DTC Parkway Ste. 140
Greenwood Village CO 80111
Phone: 303-790-7528
Fax: 303-790-3885
Web: www.powertechuranium.com

CEO: -
CFO: -
HR: -
FYE: March 31
Type: Public

Powertech Uranium has traded stainless steel and boilers for something a little more radioactive. The company formerly called Powertech Industries sold off subsidiary Gasmaster Industries — a maker of stainless steel products condensing boilers and water heaters — in 2005. In 2006 the company acquired Denver Uranium Company a uranium-exploration firm focused exclusively on the Dewey Burdock deposit in South Dakota. In 2007 Powertech Uranium's uranium holdings covered more than 59000 acres in the western US.

POWERSECURE INTERNATIONAL, INC.
NYS: POWR

1609 Heritage Commerce Court
Wake Forest, NC 27587
Phone: 919 556-3056
Fax: 919 556-3596
Web: www.powersecure.com

CEO: -
CFO: -
HR: -
FYE: December 31
Type: Public

PowerSecure International helps its utility energy and water customers stay on top of what is going on with their gas electricity and water. Its Energy & Smart Grid Solutions segment offers distributed generation electricity systems to industrial and commercial users which help to monitor and more efficiently dispatch the flow of electricity. It also provides management consulting and utility engineering planning design and construction services as well energy efficiency products (such as LED lighting). In order to focus on its core smart grid segment in mid-2011 the company sold its WaterSecure subsidiary which operated water processing facilities in northeastern Colorado.

	Annual Growth	12/10	12/11	12/12	12/13	12/14
Sales ($ mil.)	27.4%	97.5	130.0	162.0	270.2	256.7
Net income ($ mil.)	-	3.5	24.1	3.1	4.4	(7.0)
Market value ($ mil.)	10.6%	174.0	110.7	174.7	384.1	260.6
Employees	18.8%	415	516	654	753	827

POWERVERDE INC
NBB: PWVI

9300 S. Dadeland Blvd, Suite 600
Miami, FL 33156
Phone: 305 670-3370
Fax: -
Web: www.powerverdeenergy.com

CEO: Richard H Davis
CFO: John Hofmann
HR: -
FYE: December 31
Type: Public

PowerVerde (formerly known as Vyrex) has abandoned its quest for a molecular fountain of youth. These days it's only interested in power. The development-stage biotech company had been researching antioxidants to develop cures for respiratory cardiovascular and neurodegenerative diseases and other conditions related to aging. Unable to continue funding its activities however Vyrex executed a reverse merger with PowerVerde which has designed a power system that generates electricity with zero emissions. The system created by the company's founders George Konrad and Fred Barker uses solar-heated water to power an environmentally friendly motor.

	Annual Growth	12/14	12/15	12/16	12/17	12/18
Sales ($ mil.)	(18.4%)	0.4	0.5	0.6	0.9	0.2
Net income ($ mil.)	-	(0.6)	(0.4)	(0.1)	0.4	(0.7)
Market value ($ mil.)	(28.2%)	6.4	3.8	4.1	3.8	1.7
Employees	(24.0%)	3	2	2	1	1

POWERSOUTH ENERGY COOPERATIVE

2027 E THREE NOTCH ST
ANDALUSIA, AL 364212427
Phone: 334-427-3000
Fax: -
Web: www.powersouth.com

CEO: Gary Smith
CFO: Rick Kyle
HR: -
FYE: December 31
Type: Private

Several hundred thousand Alabamans and Floridians get their electric power courtesy of the work of PowerSouth Energy Cooperative which provides wholesale power to its member-owners (16 electric cooperatives and four municipal distribution utilities). Its distribution members provide electric services to almost 417200 customer meters in central and southern Alabama and western Florida. PowerSouth operates a more than 2200-mile power transmission system and has more than 2000 MW of generating capacity from interests in six fossil-fueled and hydroelectric power plants.

	Annual Growth	12/13	12/14	12/15	12/16	12/17
Sales ($ mil.)	(4.5%)	-	675.9	622.9	596.4	588.6
Net income ($ mil.)	(17.0%)	-	16.8	17.1	13.3	9.6
Market value ($ mil.)	-	-	-	-	-	-
Employees	-	-	-	-	-	640

PPG INDUSTRIES INC
NYS: PPG

One PPG Place
Pittsburgh, PA 15272
Phone: 412 434-3131
Fax: -
Web: www.ppg.com

CEO: Michael H. McGarry
CFO: Vincent J. Morales
HR: -
FYE: December 31
Type: Public

Thanks to its extensive range of paints and coatings you won't catch PPG Industries painting itself into a corner. The company?s Performance and Industrial coatings offerings include paints stains adhesives and sealants for automotive aerospace marine architectural and industrial applications. Well-known paint brands include Glidden Olympic and PPG Pittsburg Paints. Other products include packaging coatings used for the protection and decoration of metal cans closures and plastic tubes. PPG's specialty coatings are used in lighting and lens materials and label substrates. In recent years the company has shed its fiber glass and flat glass businesses to focus on its core coatings operations.

	Annual Growth	12/14	12/15	12/16	12/17	12/18
Sales ($ mil.)	0.0%	15,360.0	15,330.0	14,751.0	14,750.0	15,374.0
Net income ($ mil.)	(10.6%)	2,102.0	1,406.0	877.0	1,591.0	1,341.0
Market value ($ mil.)	(18.5%)	54,519.4	23,307.8	22,350.2	27,553.3	24,112.1
Employees	(11.0%)	44,400	46,600	47,000	47,200	27,800

PPL CORP
NYS: PPL

Two North Ninth Street
Allentown, PA 18101-1179
Phone: 610 774-5151
Fax: –
Web: www.pplweb.com

CEO: Victor A. Staffieri
CFO: Vincent (Vince) Sorgi
HR: Thomas Lynch
FYE: December 31
Type: Public

PPL Corporation is one of the largest utility companies in the world delivering electricity to more than 10 million customers through its regulated utility subsidiaries in Kentucky Pennsylvania and Virginia as well as in the UK. It also delivers natural gas to customers in Kentucky Operating as Western Power Distribution in the UK it holds four of the UK's 14 power distribution licenses. The company has more than 8000 MW of electric generating capacity about 220000 miles of electric lines and gas transmission mains and storage fields. PPL was incorporated in 1994.

	Annual Growth	12/14	12/15	12/16	12/17	12/18
Sales ($ mil.)	(9.3%)	11,499.0	7,669.0	7,517.0	7,447.0	7,785.0
Net income ($ mil.)	1.3%	1,737.0	682.0	1,902.0	1,128.0	1,827.0
Market value ($ mil.)	(6.0%)	26,169.3	24,584.6	24,527.0	22,294.0	20,406.8
Employees	(8.0%)	17,391	12,799	12,689	12,512	12,444

PPL ELECTRIC UTILITIES CORP
NL:

Two North Ninth Street
Allentown, PA 18101-1179
Phone: 610 774-5151
Fax: 610 774-4198

CEO: –
CFO: –
HR: –
FYE: December 31
Type: Public

PPL Electric Utilities pulls its weight in Pennsylvania's power market. The company which transmits and distributes electricity to 1.4 million customers in 29 counties in eastern and central portions of the state is a subsidiary of PPL Corporation. The regulated utility operates more than 48000 miles of overhead and underground power distribution lines and it is a member of the PJM Interconnection regional transmission organization (RTO). Under the state's Customer Choice Act PPL Electric also acts as the Provider of Last Resort for customers who don't choose an alternative supplier.

	Annual Growth	12/14	12/15	12/16	12/17	12/18
Sales ($ mil.)	2.7%	2,044.0	2,124.0	2,156.0	2,195.0	2,277.0
Net income ($ mil.)	13.1%	263.0	252.0	340.0	362.0	430.0
Market value ($ mil.)	–					
Employees	(5.8%)	2,122	1,935	1,837	1,755	1,674

PRA GROUP INC
NMS: PRAA

120 Corporate Boulevard
Norfolk, VA 23502
Phone: 888 772-7326
Fax: –
Web: www.pragroup.com

CEO: Steven D. (Steve) Fredrickson
CFO: Peter M. (Pete) Graham
HR: Angie S Trunzo
FYE: December 31
Type: Public

When times are tough businesses find the going a little easier with PRA Group. The company specializes in consumer debt collection on behalf of clients (including banks credit unions consumer and auto finance companies and retail merchants) in the US and Scotland. PRA also buys charged-off and bankrupt consumer debt portfolios and then collects the debts on its own behalf. The company operates through its subsidiaries which specialize in location and skip tracing (PRA Location Services) class action claims monitoring (Claims Compensation Bureau or CCB) and government accounts receivable management (PRA Government Services).

	Annual Growth	12/14	12/15	12/16	12/17	12/18
Sales ($ mil.)	0.8%	881.0	942.0	830.6	813.6	908.3
Net income ($ mil.)	(21.9%)	176.5	167.9	85.1	162.3	65.6
Market value ($ mil.)	(19.5%)	2,624.5	1,571.6	1,771.4	1,504.1	1,104.1
Employees	8.4%	3,900	3,799	4,019	5,154	5,377

PRAIRIE FARMS DAIRY, INC.

3744 STAUNTON RD
EDWARDSVILLE, IL 620256936
Phone: 618-659-5700
Fax: –
Web: www.prairiefarms.com

CEO: Fletcher Gourley
CFO: Tom Weber
HR: Kayla Samuelson
FYE: September 30
Type: Private

Prairie Farms Dairy is very cooperative. With some 700 dairy farmer/members the cooperative offers a full line of retail and food service dairy products. It turns raw milk into fresh fluid cultured and frozen dairy products under the Prairie Farms label. It also makes juices and ice cream novelties. The company's customers include food drug and convenience stores mass merchandisers schools restaurants and other food service operators. Located in Carlinville Illinois it is the managing partner for joint ventures with smaller regional dairies. It makes its products at 24 Prairie Farms-owned plants and 13 joint-venture plants which are located throughout the midwestern and southern areas of the US.

	Annual Growth	09/09	09/10	09/11	09/12	09/13
Sales ($ mil.)	3.5%	–	–	1,607.2	1,649.9	1,721.3
Net income ($ mil.)	(28.9%)	–	–	28.0	38.8	14.2
Market value ($ mil.)	–	–	–	–	–	–
Employees	–	–	–	–	–	1,965

PRAIRIE VIEW A&M UNIVERSITY

100 UNIVERSITY DR
PRAIRIE VIEW, TX 77445
Phone: 936-261-3311
Fax: –
Web: www.pvamu.edu

CEO: –
CFO: –
HR: –
FYE: August 31
Type: Private

A historically African American institution of higher learning Prairie View A&M University offers its 8400 students baccalaureate degrees in about 50 academic majors nearly 40 graduate degree programs and four doctoral programs through nine colleges and schools. Its main campus in southeast Texas home to the university's nine colleges and schools is about 40 miles outside of Houston; its nursing college maintains a branch in that city's Texas Medical Center. Part of The Texas A&M University System Prairie View A&M was founded in 1876 and was originally known as Alta Vista Agricultural and Mechanical College of Texas for Colored Youth.

	Annual Growth	08/14	08/15	08/16	08/17	08/18
Sales ($ mil.)	3.9%	–	88.0	88.1	91.3	98.8
Net income ($ mil.)	15.8%	–	28.8	46.1	64.2	44.7
Market value ($ mil.)	–	–	–	–	–	–
Employees	–	–	–	–	–	965

PRATT INDUSTRIES, INC.

1800 SARASOTA BUSIN STE C
CONYERS, GA 300135775
Phone: 770-918-5678
Fax: –
Web: www.prattindustries.com

CEO: Brian McPheely
CFO: Stephen Ward
HR: –
FYE: June 30
Type: Private

Pratt Industries (USA) doesn't mill around when it comes to recycling and caring for the environment. The company rivals the world's largest manufacturers of recycled paper and packaging and claims to be the 5th largest box manufacturer in the US and the world's largest privately-held 100% recycled paper and packaging company. Pratt has a handful of operating divisions: recycling mills corrugating converting displays packaging systems and national accounts. Its products which include container board and corrugated sheets are sold to clients such as Rubbermaid and Pringles.

	Annual Growth	06/03	06/04	06/05	06/06	06/18
Sales ($ mil.)	13.1%	–	446.8	0.5	713.2	2,498.6
Net income ($ mil.)	–	–	(15.2)	(0.0)	(4.5)	200.8
Market value ($ mil.)	–	–	–	–	–	–
Employees	–	–	–	–	–	5,890

PRECIGEN INC
NMS: PGEN

20374 Seneca Meadows Parkway
Germantown, MD 20876
Phone: 301 556-9900
Fax: –
Web: www.dna.com

CEO: Helen Sabzevari
CFO: Rick Sterling
HR: –
FYE: December 31
Type: Public

One man's frankenfood is another man's solution to world hunger. Intrexon is developing technology that uses synthetic biology or biological engineering to make advances in everything from pharmaceuticals to genetically modified plants and animals. The company has development agreements with AmpliPhi (antibacterial medication) AquaBounty (genetically modified salmon) BioLife (genetic disease) Eli Lilly (animal medication) Fibrocell (dermatology medication) Genopaver (pharmaceutical ingredients) Oragenics (antibiotics) Soligenix (antibiotics) Synthetic Biologics (antibiotics) and ZIOPHARM (cancer medicine). Intrexon went public in 2013 raising $160 million in its IPO.

	Annual Growth	12/14	12/15	12/16	12/17	12/18
Sales ($ mil.)	22.2%	71.9	173.6	190.9	231.0	160.6
Net income ($ mil.)	–	(81.8)	(84.5)	(186.6)	(117.0)	(509.3)
Market value ($ mil.)	(30.2%)	4,405.4	4,824.6	3,888.5	1,843.4	1,046.5
Employees	15.1%	558	734	935	1,006	979

PRECIPIO INC
NAS: PRPO

4 Science Park
New Haven, CT 06511
Phone: 203 787-7888
Fax: –
Web: www.precipiodx.com

CEO: Paul Kinnon
CFO: Paul Kinnon
HR: –
FYE: December 31
Type: Public

Precipio (formerly Transgenomic) travels the uncharted frontiers of the human genome. Its clinical laboratories arm specializes in molecular diagnostics for cardiology neurology mitochondrial disorders and oncology. Precipio's diagnostic tools arm produces equipment reagents and other consumables for clinical and research applications in molecular testing and cytogenetics. The proprietary WAVE System is used for genetic variation detection in molecular genetic research and molecular diagnostics. The company also operates a contract research laboratory that supports all phases of pre-clinical and clinical trials for oncology drugs in development. Transgenomic changed its name when it merged with Precipio Diagnostics in 2017.

	Annual Growth	12/14	12/15	12/16	12/17	12/18
Sales ($ mil.)	(43.0%)	27.1	1.7	1.6	1.7	2.9
Net income ($ mil.)	–	(13.9)	(33.0)	(7.6)	(20.7)	(15.7)
Market value ($ mil.)	(85.7%)	–	–	–	2.8	0.4
Employees	(26.2%)	152	37	19	33	45

PRECISION AUTO CARE, INC.
NBB: PACI

748 Miller Drive, S.E.
Leesburg, VA 20175
Phone: 703 777-9095
Fax: 703 771-7108
Web: www.precisiontune.com

CEO: Robert R Falconi
CFO: Mark P Francis
HR: –
FYE: June 30
Type: Public

If it's in a car Precision Auto Care can lube flush or grease it. The company franchises about 380 Precision Tune Auto Care centers in the US and half a dozen other countries. The centers provide general maintenance and repair services including brake service engine tune-ups oil and fluid changes tire rotation and wheel alignments. Precision Auto Care was founded in 1976 by Bill Childs in Beaumont Texas. Former director Arthur Kellar owns about 40% of the company; chairman Louis Brown owns about 15%.

	Annual Growth	06/12	06/13	06/14	06/15	06/16
Sales ($ mil.)	0.8%	26.7	26.0	25.4	25.4	27.6
Net income ($ mil.)	29.3%	0.4	0.6	1.0	0.6	1.1
Market value ($ mil.)	26.2%	5.2	5.8	7.3	10.8	13.2
Employees	(2.0%)	171	–	–	–	158

PRECISION CASTPARTS CORP.

4650 SW MCDAM AVE STE 300
PORTLAND, OR 97239
Phone: 503-946-4800
Fax: –
Web: www.precast.com

CEO: Mark Donegan
CFO: Shawn R. Hagel
HR: –
FYE: January 03
Type: Private

Precision Castparts Corp. (PCC) is a maker of investment castings and forged and airframe products that have applications in industries from aerospace and energy to machinery and medical implants. Products include metal components for aircraft engines industrial gas turbines (IGT) medical implants unmanned aerial vehicles (UAVs) and other industrial applications. The company also makes metal forgings including seamless pipe used in power plants downhole casings and tubing pipe for oil and gas production and aerospace and defense applications. PCC is also a leading manufacturer of fasteners and fastening systems used in the aerospace construction automotive machinery and energy industries. The aerospace sector accounts for most of PCC's sales. The company is a subsidiary of Berkshire Hathaway.

	Annual Growth	03/12	03/13	03/14	03/15*	01/16
Sales ($ mil.)	(5.8%)	–	8,377.8	9,616.0	10,005.0	7,002.0
Net income ($ mil.)	(17.0%)	–	1,429.1	1,784.0	1,533.0	817.0
Market value ($ mil.)	–	–	–	–	–	–
Employees	–	–	–	–	–	30,100

*Fiscal year change

PRECISION OPTICS CORP INC (MA)
NBB: PEYE

22 East Broadway
Gardner, MA 01440-3338
Phone: 978 630-1800
Fax: –
Web: www.poci.com

CEO: Joseph N Forkey
CFO: Donald A Major
HR: –
FYE: June 30
Type: Public

Precision Optics plays it up close and personal. The company makes specialized video cameras and stereo endoscopes for use in minimally invasive surgery. Its other products include laparoscopes (for abdominal surgery) and arthroscopes (for joint surgery) as well as sterilizable image couplers and beamsplitters that connect endoscopes to video cameras. The US is Precision Optics' biggest market accounting for almost all sales although the company has received regulatory approval to sell its products in Europe. In 2019 Precision Optics acquired Ross Optical for $200 million.

	Annual Growth	06/15	06/16	06/17	06/18	06/19
Sales ($ mil.)	14.8%	3.9	3.9	3.2	4.0	6.8
Net income ($ mil.)	–	(1.2)	(1.0)	(1.0)	(0.4)	(0.6)
Market value ($ mil.)	11.0%	9.1	6.4	7.2	6.4	13.8
Employees	13.0%	38	33	27	30	62

PRECYSE SOLUTIONS LLC

1275 Drummers Ln. Ste. 200
Wayne PA 19087
Phone: 610-688-2464
Fax: 610-688-1798
Web: www.precyse.com

CEO: Christopher A Powell
CFO: James Matas
HR: –
FYE: December 31
Type: Private

Precyse Solutions pays attention to the details so health care organizations can focus on helping patients get well. The company provides a wide range of health information management (HIM) and medical transcription services and software to hospitals health networks and physician practices throughout the US. Precyse Solutions offers consulting business process outsourcing medical coding software electronic health record (EHR) platforms oncology data management customized projects and compliance and regulatory services. Founded in 1999 as Capital MT the firm has since grown through acquisitions. Private equity firms Altaris Capital Partners and NewSpring Capital own Precyse Solutions.

PREFERRED APARTMENT COMMUNITIES INC.   NYS: APTS

3284 Northside Parkway N.W., Suite 150 — CEO: Daniel M Dupree
Atlanta, GA 30327 — CFO: John A Isakson
Phone: 770 818-4100 — HR: –
Fax: – — FYE: December 31
Web: www.pacapts.com — Type: Public

Preferred Apartment Communities prefers to own retail properties with multifamily ones. The real estate investment trust (REIT) owns nearly 20 multifamily communities with 6100-plus units as well as some 20 grocery-anchored retail shopping centers with some 2 million sq. ft. of leasable space in major metro areas including Atlanta Austin Dallas Houston Nashville Orlando and Philadelphia. Its largest retail tenants include Publix Kroger and Tom Thumb. The REIT also buys senior mortgage loans or mezzanine debt and membership or partnership interests in multifamily properties. Preferred Apartment Communities was formed in 2009 and went public in 2011.

	Annual Growth	12/14	12/15	12/16	12/17	12/18
Sales ($ mil.)	62.8%	56.5	109.3	200.1	294.0	397.3
Net income ($ mil.)	113.5%	2.1	(2.4)	(9.5)	27.7	43.5
Market value ($ mil.)	11.5%	380.2	546.4	622.9	846.0	587.4
Employees	–	–	–	–	–	–

PREFERRED BANK (LOS ANGELES, CA)   NMS: PFBC

601 S. Figueroa Street, 48th Floor — CEO: Li Yu
Los Angeles, CA 90017 — CFO: Edward J. Czajka
Phone: 213 891-1188 — HR: Karen Cangey
Fax: – — FYE: December 31
Web: www.preferredbank.com — Type: Public

Preferred Bank wants to be the bank of choice of Chinese-Americans in Southern California. Employing a multilingual staff the bank provides international banking services to companies doing business in the Asia/Pacific region. It targets middle-market businesses typically manufacturing service distribution and real estate firms as well as entrepreneurs professionals and high-net-worth individuals through about a dozen branches in Los Angeles Orange and San Francisco Counties. Preferred Bank offers standard deposit products such as checking accounts savings money market and NOW accounts. Specialized services include private banking and international trade finance.

	Annual Growth	12/14	12/15	12/16	12/17	12/18
Assets ($ mil.)	19.7%	2,054.2	2,598.8	3,221.6	3,769.9	4,216.4
Net income ($ mil.)	30.3%	24.6	29.7	36.4	43.4	71.0
Market value ($ mil.)	11.7%	427.0	505.5	802.5	899.8	663.6
Employees	12.7%	163	205	218	238	263

PREFORMED LINE PRODUCTS CO.   NMS: PLPC

660 Beta Drive — CEO: Robert G. Ruhlman
Mayfield Village, OH 44143 — CFO: Michael A. Weisbarth
Phone: 440 461-5200 — HR: –
Fax: 440 442-8816 — FYE: December 31
Web: www.preformed.com — Type: Public

Masterful "preformances" are expected from Preformed Line Products (PLP) by its audience in the energy and communications industries. The company designs and manufactures components and systems used by utility crews and others to construct repair and maintain overhead and underground networks for energy communications and broadband network companies. It provides formed wire products (for maintenance and repair of aging plant infrastructures) protective fiber-optic closures and splice cases solar hardware and data communication interconnect devices and enclosures for data communications networks.

	Annual Growth	12/14	12/15	12/16	12/17	12/18
Sales ($ mil.)	2.0%	388.2	354.7	336.6	378.2	420.9
Net income ($ mil.)	19.9%	12.9	6.7	15.3	12.7	26.6
Market value ($ mil.)	(0.2%)	274.3	211.4	291.8	356.7	272.4
Employees	(0.9%)	2,744	2,645	2,579	2,762	2,650

PREMIER AG CO-OP, INC.

811 W 2ND ST — CEO: Harold Cooper
SEYMOUR, IN 472742711 — CFO: –
Phone: 812-522-4911 — HR: –
Fax: – — FYE: July 31
Web: www.premierag.com — Type: Private

Premier AG Co-Op provides the agricultural communities in Bartholomew Decatur and Johnson counties of south-central Indiana with farming supplies services and marketing assistance. It operates four grain elevators that handle corn soybeans and wheat. The co-op operates CountryMark gas stations as well as one Countrymart store in Greensburg Indiana. The store sells seed fertilizer and chemical treatments lawn and garden products hardware apparel pet food and supplies animal feed and plants (in season). Premier also owns Premier Energy and Heyob Energy suppliers of propane and home heating oil.

	Annual Growth	07/11	07/12	07/13	07/14	07/15
Sales ($ mil.)	(7.3%)	–	–	141.7	139.8	121.7
Net income ($ mil.)	(12.6%)	–	–	4.5	4.8	3.4
Market value ($ mil.)	–	–	–	–	–	–
Employees	–	–	–	–	–	100

PREMIER ENTERTAINMENT III, LLC

1131 N DUPONT HWY — CEO: George Papanier
DOVER, DE 199012008 — CFO: Stephen Capp
Phone: 302-674-4600 — HR: –
Fax: – — FYE: December 31
Web: www.doverdowns.com — Type: Private

Dover Downs Gaming & Entertainment is betting on being the first stop for gamblers in the First State. The company operates three facilities all in Dover Delaware adjacent to Dover Motorsports' Dover Downs International Speedway. Dover Downs Casino a 165000 square-foot facility has more than 2700 video slot machines; Dover Downs Hotel and Conference Center is a 500-room luxury hotel featuring ballroom concert hall banquet dining meeting room and spa facilities; and Dover Downs Raceway features harness racing and simulcast horse race betting. Dover Downs' video slot operations are operated and administered by the Delaware State Lottery Office. Twin River Worldwide Holdings acquired the company in 2019.

	Annual Growth	12/14	12/15	12/16	12/17	12/18
Sales ($ mil.)	(0.6%)	–	182.9	182.3	176.9	179.9
Net income ($ mil.)	(74.8%)	–	1.9	0.8	(1.1)	0.0
Market value ($ mil.)	–	–	–	–	–	–
Employees	–	–	–	–	–	1,388

PREMIER EXHIBITIONS INC   NBB: PRXI Q

3340 Peachtree Road, N.E., Suite 900 — CEO: Daoping Bao
Atlanta, GA 30326 — CFO: Jerome Henshall
Phone: 404 842-2600 — HR: Shone Thomas
Fax: – — FYE: February 28
Web: www.prxi.com — Type: Public

The Titanic was on her maiden trip when an iceberg hit the ship and Premier Exhibitions is here to tell the tale. The company owns RMS Titanic which salvages and displays artifacts from the doomed Titanic ocean liner runs a touring Titanic exhibit and sells Titanic merchandise. It is considered the salvor-in-possession or owner of the wrecked ship. Premier's other exhibits include "Bodies...The Exhibition" and "Bodies Revealed" (preserved bodies and organs) and "Dialog in the Dark" (exploring a world without sight). Premier was created as a holding company in 2004 when it spun off RMS Titanic. The company has announced plans to sell its Titanic holdings to focus on other touring exhibits.

	Annual Growth	02/11	02/12	02/13	02/14	02/15
Sales ($ mil.)	(10.0%)	44.8	31.7	39.5	29.3	29.4
Net income ($ mil.)	–	(12.5)	(5.8)	2.0	(0.7)	(10.5)
Market value ($ mil.)	(32.4%)	8.6	12.0	11.3	4.3	1.8
Employees	(5.9%)	222	201	191	196	174

PREMIER FINANCIAL BANCORP, INC.
NMS: PFBI

2883 Fifth Avenue
Huntington, WV 25702
Phone: 304 525-1600
Fax: –

CEO: Robert W Walker
CFO: Brien M Chase
HR: –
FYE: December 31
Type: Public

Premier Financial Bancorp is the holding company for Citizens Deposit Bank and Premier Bank rural and small-town banks with locations across Kentucky Virginia Ohio Maryland West Virginia and the District of Columbia. Altogether the banks have about 40 branches that offer standard deposit trust and lending services. Premier bought the $245-milion First National Bankshares along with its six First National Bank branch locations in early 2016 boosting Premier's total assets by nearly 20% to $1.5 billion while expanding its presence in Greenbrier Valley in West Virgnia and into Covington Virginia. The firm entered the DC area with the 2009 purchase of Adams National Bank for some $11 million.

	Annual Growth	12/14	12/15	12/16	12/17	12/18
Assets ($ mil.)	7.8%	1,252.8	1,244.7	1,496.2	1,493.4	1,690.1
Net income ($ mil.)	11.3%	13.2	12.4	12.2	14.8	20.2
Market value ($ mil.)	(1.1%)	227.8	240.4	293.9	293.7	218.0
Employees	(0.2%)	366	344	356	354	363

PREMIER HEALTH PARTNERS

110 N MAIN ST STE 450
DAYTON, OH 454023712
Phone: 937-499-9596
Fax: –
Web: www.premierhealth.com

CEO: James R Pancoast
CFO: Thomas M Duncan
HR: –
FYE: December 31
Type: Private

There may not be any red carpets but this Premier does feature good health. Premier Health Partners is a multi-hospital health system operating in the Dayton Ohio area. It includes Miami Valley Hospital and Good Samaritan Hospital both in Dayton; Atrium Medical Center in nearby Middletown; and Upper Valley Medical Center in Troy. Collectively the hospitals house about 1800 inpatient beds. The health system also operates about 65 other facilities including outpatient health centers a primary care physician group (Premier HealthNet) home health care psychiatric care and health outreach programs that provide health screenings education and smoking cessation programs.

	Annual Growth	12/11	12/12	12/13	12/14	12/15
Sales ($ mil.)	4.1%	–	–	–	340.1	354.1
Net income ($ mil.)	37.5%	–	–	–	11.4	15.7
Market value ($ mil.)	–	–	–	–	–	–
Employees	–	–	–	–	–	5,336

PREMIERE GLOBAL SERVICES INC
NYS: PGI

3280 Peachtree Road N.E., The Terminus Building, Suite 1000
Atlanta, GA 30305
Phone: 404 262-8400
Fax: –
Web: www.pgi.com

CEO: Don Joos
CFO: Kevin J McAdams
HR: Francoise Caraguel
FYE: December 31
Type: Public

Premiere Global Services (PGi) knows you don't actually have to meet to have a meeting. The company provides cloud-based software services that enable small and midsized businesses as well as larger corporate clients to collaborate virtually using audio video and Web-based communications. Its conferencing services — provided primary through iMeet and GlobalMeet - include audio and video conferencing operator-assisted event conferencing social networking and file sharing. PGi serves some 45000 clients in about 25 countries but does about two-thirds of its business in North America.

	Annual Growth	12/09	12/10	12/11	12/12	12/13
Sales ($ mil.)	(3.3%)	601.5	441.8	473.8	505.3	526.9
Net income ($ mil.)	7.7%	13.6	4.8	21.4	27.6	18.3
Market value ($ mil.)	8.9%	398.8	328.7	409.4	472.7	560.2
Employees	(2.2%)	2,250	1,700	1,700	1,830	2,060

PREMIO, INC.

918 RADECKI CT
CITY OF INDUSTRY, CA 917481132
Phone: 626-839-3100
Fax: –
Web: www.premioinc.com

CEO: –
CFO: –
HR: –
FYE: December 31
Type: Private

Premio can sell you one of its computers or build one of your own design. The company provides contract manufacturing services including the design and assembly testing and support of products ranging from computer servers and displays to medical equipment. The company markets its own line of built-to-order desktop and notebooks PCs servers workstations along with third-party peripherals. It sells to customers in the education medical government security and surveillance markets. Customers have included Sourcefire and Rapiscan Systems. Founded in 1989 by CEO Crystal Wu and Tom Tsao Premio is owned by its officers.

	Annual Growth	12/10	12/11	12/12	12/13	12/14
Sales ($ mil.)	9.8%	–	58.9	64.5	63.5	77.9
Net income ($ mil.)	(17.7%)	–	0.5	0.4	0.3	0.3
Market value ($ mil.)	–	–	–	–	–	–
Employees	–	–	–	–	–	140

PREMIUM BEERS OF OKLAHOMA, L.L.C.

9537 N KELLEY AVE STE A
OKLAHOMA CITY, OK 731312444
Phone: 405-608-6881
Fax: –

CEO: –
CFO: –
HR: –
FYE: December 31
Type: Private

Premium Beers of Oklahoma is the leading beer distributor in the Sooner State and one of the top Anheuser-Busch distributorships in the country. The company supplies such brands as Budweiser Michelob and Busch from distribution facilities in Ardmore Clinton and Lawton. It also distributes Mexican beers from Grupo Modelo such as Corona Corona Light and Modelo Especial as well as BACARDI Silver branded malt beverages Rolling Rock and Stella Artois beers non-alcoholic O'Doul's beverages and Monster energy drinks. Premium Beers serves customers primarily in central and south-central Oklahoma. Denny Cresap started the company in 1968 as a one-person one-route delivery service.

	Annual Growth	12/03	12/04	12/05	12/06	12/07
Sales ($ mil.)	5.5%	–	114.8	114.5	121.7	134.7
Net income ($ mil.)	(52.3%)	–	24.3	5.6	4.6	2.6
Market value ($ mil.)	–	–	–	–	–	–
Employees	–	–	–	–	–	300

PRESIDENT & TRUSTEES OF BATES COLLEGE

2 ANDREWS RD
LEWISTON, ME 042406020
Phone: 207-786-6255
Fax: –
Web: www.bates.edu

CEO: –
CFO: –
HR: –
FYE: June 30
Type: Private

Bates College is a selective private co-educational liberal arts college granting bachelor of arts and bachelor of science degrees. The institute of higher leatning's more than 1750 students can choose from 30 majors the most popular of which include history environmental studies political science English biology economics and psychology. Students enjoy a 10-to-1 student to faculty ratio. Bates' endowment is an estimated $150 million. With tuition and fees hitting almost $59000 most students receive financial aid. The college has about 220 faculty members.

	Annual Growth	06/11	06/12	06/13	06/14	06/15
Sales ($ mil.)	4.2%	–	97.3	98.8	101.3	110.0
Net income ($ mil.)	–	–	(15.3)	19.4	38.9	2.3
Market value ($ mil.)	–	–	–	–	–	–
Employees	–	–	–	–	–	720

PRESIDENT & TRUSTEES OF WILLIAMS COLLEGE

880 MAIN ST FL 1
WILLIAMSTOWN, MA 012672600
Phone: 413-597-4412
Fax: –
Web: www.williams.edu

CEO: –
CFO: –
HR: –
FYE: June 30
Type: Private

Liberals need apply. Liberal arts majors that is! Williams College is a private liberal arts school with an enrollment of more than 2000 students at its main campus in the Berkshires of northwestern Massachusetts. It also offers programs in England (Williams-Exeter Programme at Oxford) Connecticut (Williams-Mystic Program) and Williams in New York. The majority of its students come from New York followed by Massachusetts and California. Williams College offers more than 30 undergraduate majors in three academic divisions: humanities sciences and social sciences. Founded in 1793 by Colonel Ephraim Williams the school also confers master's degrees in the history of art and in policy economics.

	Annual Growth	06/07	06/08	06/09	06/10	06/11
Sales ($ mil.)	(10.5%)	–	–	187.3	146.9	150.0
Net income ($ mil.)	–	–	–	(419.6)	92.4	245.3
Market value ($ mil.)	–	–	–	–	–	–
Employees	–	–	–	–	–	950

PRESIDENT AND BOARD OF TRUSTEES OF SANTA CLARA COLLEGE

500 EL CAMINO REAL
SANTA CLARA, CA 950504345
Phone: 408-554-4000
Fax: –
Web: www.scu.edu

CEO: –
CFO: –
HR: –
FYE: June 30
Type: Private

Santa Clara University wants its students to achieve clarity. The Jesuit Catholic school California's oldest higher-education institution offers degrees in more than 40 disciplines. Its variety of graduate programs include business engineering law pastoral ministries counseling psychology and education. With more than 8000 students Santa Clara University boasts a student/faculty ratio of 12:1 and support from a $760 million endowment. The university occupies a 106-acre campus and has more than 520 full-time and more than 360 part-time faculty members.

	Annual Growth	06/12	06/13	06/14	06/16	06/17
Sales ($ mil.)	–	–	0.0	458.0	460.0	363.0
Net income ($ mil.)	37.8%	–	29.0	65.5	16.2	104.8
Market value ($ mil.)	–	–	–	–	–	–
Employees	–	–	–	–	–	1,431

PRESIDENT AND FELLOWS OF MIDDLEBURY COLLEGE

38 COLLEGE ST
MIDDLEBURY, VT 05753
Phone: 802-443-5000
Fax: –
Web: www.middlebury.edu

CEO: –
CFO: –
HR: –
FYE: June 30
Type: Private

President and Fellows of Middlebury College operates Middlebury College a private liberal arts school in Vermont that offers courses of study in the arts humanities literature foreign languages social sciences and natural sciences. About 2450 undergraduates are enrolled at the educational institution. Founded in 1800 it is home to the Bread Loaf School of English known for its summer graduate courses in literature as well as instruction in creative writing and theatre. Bread Loaf is located in the Green Mountains a dozen miles east of Middlebury. Every summer Middlebury College also opens the Language Schools from which the college provides instruction in 10 languages to more than 2000 students.

	Annual Growth	06/04	06/05	06/06	06/08	06/12
Sales ($ mil.)	4.2%	–	–	182.0	278.5	233.4
Net income ($ mil.)	–	–	–	79.8	50.9	(24.7)
Market value ($ mil.)	–	–	–	–	–	–
Employees	–	–	–	–	–	1,000

PRESIDENTIAL LIFE CORPORATION   NASDAQ: PLFE

69 Lydecker St.
Nyack NY 10960
Phone: 845-358-2300
Fax: 845-353-0273
Web: www.presidentiallife.com

CEO: Donald L Barnes
CFO: Paul B Pheffer
HR: –
FYE: December 31
Type: Public

Do you need a new annuity? Presidential Life Corporation is the parent of Presidential Life Insurance which focuses on individual annuities. The company sells single-premium and flexible-premium annuity products. It also offers short-term disability contracts in New York and medical stop loss coverage to employers. Most of its life insurance business was placed in run-off in 2004 so although the company still services its existing policies it does not write new business. The firm does offer some more limited graded-benefit and simplified-issue life policies. Presidential Life distributes its products through independent agents and brokers. The company agreed to be acquired by Athene Annuity & Life in 2012.

PRESIDENTIAL REALTY CORP.   NBB: PDNL B

1430 Broadway, Suite 503
New York, NY 10018
Phone: 914 948-1300
Fax: 914 948-1327
Web: www.presrealty.com

CEO: Nickolas W Jekogian III
CFO: Alexander Ludwig
HR: –
FYE: December 31
Type: Public

This president may have been elected for a second term. Presidential Realty is a real estate investment trust (REIT) that invests in commercial real estate loans secured by real estate and other property-related assets. Its portfolio includes stakes in a handful of properties in Massachusetts and Puerto Rico including office and industrial properties. Faced with ongoing revenue declines in the turbulent economy the REIT began liquidating itself in 2011. Later that year it terminated the liquidation instead coming to an investment agreement with new CEO Nickolas Jekogian through Signature Community Investment Group.

	Annual Growth	12/12	12/13	12/14	12/15	12/16
Sales ($ mil.)	4.8%	0.8	0.8	0.9	0.9	0.9
Net income ($ mil.)	–	(1.8)	1.0	(0.9)	(0.5)	(0.8)
Market value ($ mil.)	(19.1%)	0.7	0.9	0.1	0.0	0.3
Employees	(13.1%)	7	7	6	4	4

PRESONUS AUDIO ELECTRONICS INC.

7257 FLORIDA BLVD
BATON ROUGE, LA 70806-4634
Phone: 225-216-7887
Fax: –
Web: www.presonus.com

CEO: –
CFO: Chris Elliott
HR: –
FYE: December 31
Type: Private

PreSonus Audio Electronics makes digital audio equipment for amateur musicians and professionals alike. Its product lineup (designed for the purposes of broadcasting live sound reinforcement live streaming of audio and recording) includes items such as preamplifiers processors and equalizers. PreSonus sells through more than 800 specialty music retailers (Guitar Center Hermes) in the US as well as internationally. The company was founded in 1995.

	Annual Growth	12/01	12/02	12/10	12/11	12/12
Sales ($ mil.)	–	–	0.0	28.1	43.4	50.3
Net income ($ mil.)	–	–	0.0	1.1	4.5	3.6
Market value ($ mil.)	–	–	–	–	–	–
Employees	–	–	–	–	–	115

PRESSTEK INC.

NASDAQ: PRST

55 Executive Dr.
Hudson NH 03051
Phone: 603-595-7000
Fax: 800-447-1231
Web: www.presstek.com

CEO: Yuval Dubois
CFO: Rebecca Itkin Duffy
HR: -
FYE: December 31
Type: Public

Image is everything at Presstek which combines printing press and computer technologies in its PEARL direct imaging (DI) systems. These systems produce color printing plates and non-photosensitive films and also transfer images from computer to press. The PEARLdry process results in high-resolution plates without chemical processing or hazardous byproducts. Presstek markets its products through 30 graphic arts dealers worldwide. Heidelberger Druckmaschinen AG Harold M. Pitman and Eastman Kodak are Presstek's leading customers as well as competitors. Presstek is being acquired by MAI Holdings an affiliate of American Industrial Partners Capital Fund IV.

PRESSURE BIOSCIENCES INC

NBB: PBIO

14 Norfolk Avenue
South Easton, MA 02375
Phone: 508 230-1828
Fax: -
Web: www.pressurebiosciences.com

CEO: Richard T Schumacher
CFO: Joseph L Damasio Jr
HR: -
FYE: December 31
Type: Public

Pressure BioSciences knows how to strong-arm at the molecular level. Using its pressure cycling technology (PCT) which uses cycles of hydrostatic pressure to control molecular interactions the company has developed the PCT Sample Preparation System for life science research. The system which consists of the Barocycler instrument and related consumables helps researchers extract DNA or other molecules from plant and animal tissues for further study. Pressure BioSciences is working on other applications for PCT such as protein purification diagnostics DNA sequencing and enzyme reaction control.

	Annual Growth	12/14	12/15	12/16	12/17	12/18
Sales ($ mil.)	15.6%	1.4	1.8	2.0	2.2	2.5
Net income ($ mil.)	-	(4.6)	(7.4)	(2.7)	(10.7)	(9.7)
Market value ($ mil.)	(35.6%)	-	-	-	5.9	3.8
Employees	11.3%	15	14	13	19	23

PRESTIGE CONSUMER HEALTHCARE INC

NYS: PBH

660 White Plains Road
Tarrytown, NY 10591
Phone: 914 524-6800
Fax: -
Web: www.prestigeconsumerhealthcare.com

CEO: Ronald M. (Ron) Lombardi
CFO: Christine (Chris) Sacco
HR: -
FYE: March 31
Type: Public

Prestige Brands is a lifesaver in the business of resuscitating offloaded consumer brands. The company acquires develops and markets over-the-counter (OTC) drugs and household cleaning products. Its portfolio includes Chloraseptic Clear Eyes Comet Compound W Doctor's Nightguard Little Remedies PediaCare Murine Monistat New Skin and many other big-name brands. Prestige Brands contracts out manufacturing of its products which are sold through mass merchandisers and retail stores primarily in North America. The company was formed in 1996 to acquire and revitalize leading but neglected consumer brands divested by major consumer companies such as Procter & Gamble.

	Annual Growth	03/15	03/16	03/17	03/18	03/19
Sales ($ mil.)	8.1%	714.6	806.2	882.1	1,041.2	975.8
Net income ($ mil.)	-	78.3	99.9	69.4	339.6	(35.8)
Market value ($ mil.)	(8.6%)	2,221.7	2,765.5	2,878.0	1,746.7	1,549.3
Employees	29.1%	187	259	530	530	520

PRESTIGE TRAVEL INC

6175 SPRING MOUNTAIN RD 2C
LAS VEGAS, NV 891468899
Phone: 702-248-1300
Fax: -
Web: www.prestigecruises.com

CEO: -
CFO: Leo Falkensammer
HR: Kris Hagan
FYE: December 31
Type: Private

What happens in Vegas may stay in Vegas but if you don't want to stay in Vegas Prestige Travel can help you out. The company provides leisure and corporate travel services — serving the US Southwest — through about 15 Las Vegas-area locations. Prestige Travel's TripRes.com subsidiary allows visitors to book airfare hotel car cruise and package arrangements as well as Vegas shows. However the company's specialty is low-roller rates in high-roller Vegas hotels and casinos. Prestige Travel an affiliate of American Express was founded in 1980 by president and CEO Kathy Falkensammer.

	Annual Growth	09/00	09/01	09/02	09/03*	12/09
Sales ($ mil.)	(19.1%)	-	-	342.7	82.3	77.9
Net income ($ mil.)	-	-	-	0.0	(0.1)	(0.5)
Market value ($ mil.)	-	-	-	-	-	-
Employees	-	-	-	-	-	170

*Fiscal year change

PRETIUM PACKAGING LLC

15450 S Outer 40 Ste 120
Chesterfield MO 63017-2062
Phone: 314-727-8200
Fax: 314-727-0249
Web: www.pvcc.com

CEO: -
CFO: Mike Alger
HR: Melissa Babyak
FYE: June 30
Type: Private

Content with containment Pretium Packaging (formerly NOVAPAK) makes blow-molded plastic bottles and containers using polyvinyl chloride (PVC) compounds high-density polyethylene (HDPE) and polyethylene terephthalate (PET) resins. It caters to a high-margin niche comprised of small to medium orders for custom containers. Pretium is joined by sister companies Airopak and Marpac in turning out an array of specialty designed plastics. Its industrial and consumer customers include General Mills Colgate-Palmolive Proctor & Gamble and Spectrum Brands. In 2010 Pretium in partnership with Castle Harlan merged with the former NOVAPAK and its parent PVC Container Corp. as part of a double-barrel transaction.

PRGX GLOBAL, INC.

NMS: PRGX

600 Galleria Parkway, Suite 100
Atlanta, GA 30339-5986
Phone: 770 779-3900
Fax: -
Web: www.prgx.com

CEO: Ronald E Stewart
CFO: Kurt J Abkemeier
HR: -
FYE: December 31
Type: Public

PRGX helps clients get every bit of bang from their buck. The firm provides recovery audit services to organizations with high volumes of payment transactions including retail and wholesale businesses manufacturers health care providers and government agencies. It uses proprietary tools to mine clients' books and identify erroneous overpayments which over time can represent a significant loss of money (sometimes to the annual aggregate tune of more than $1 billion). PRGX charges a percentage of the savings realized. The company does business in more than 30 countries around the world: the US accounts for about 60% of its revenue.

	Annual Growth	12/14	12/15	12/16	12/17	12/18
Sales ($ mil.)	1.1%	164.2	138.3	140.8	161.6	171.8
Net income ($ mil.)	-	(7.5)	(3.2)	0.9	3.2	4.6
Market value ($ mil.)	13.4%	132.6	86.3	136.8	164.6	219.6
Employees	1.6%	1,500	1,460	1,500	1,500	1,600

PRICESMART INC
NMS: PSMT

9740 Scranton Road
San Diego, CA 92121
Phone: 858 404-8800
Fax: –
Web: www.pricesmart.com

CEO: Jose L. Laparte
CFO: John M. Heffner
HR: –
FYE: August 31
Type: Public

PriceSmart is wise in the ways of members-only club retailing. The retailer runs about 40 membership stores with about three million cardholders under the PriceSmart name in about a dozen countries in Latin America the Caribbean and one US territory. It sells low-cost food drugs and basic consumer items while charging an annual fee to consumer and business members. In each store nearly half of the merchandise comes from the US and around the world and the other half is sourced locally. PriceSmart stores at 50000-60000 sq. ft. are typically smaller than wholesale clubs in the US. Chairman and former CEO Robert Price (individually and through The Price Group) owns 25% of PriceSmart.

	Annual Growth	08/15	08/16	08/17	08/18	08/19
Sales ($ mil.)	3.6%	2,802.6	2,905.2	2,996.6	3,166.7	3,223.9
Net income ($ mil.)	(4.8%)	89.1	88.7	90.7	74.3	73.2
Market value ($ mil.)	(8.2%)	2,596.1	2,550.9	2,481.3	2,652.3	1,845.5
Employees	4.3%	7,592	7,835	7,903	8,680	9,000

PRICEWATERHOUSECOOPERS LLP

300 Madison Ave. 24th Fl.
New York NY 10017
Phone: 646-471-4000
Fax: 925-355-1591
Web: www.pixion.com

CEO: –
CFO: –
HR: –
FYE: June 30
Type: Private - Partnershi

What price accounting? Perhaps the better question is what PricewaterhouseCoopers accounting? PricewaterhouseCoopers LLP is the US arm of Big Four accounting firm PricewaterhouseCoopers International (which formally rebranded itself PwC in 2010). The accountancy's offerings include auditing and human resources tax-related and other advisory services. Focus industries include consumer products and services; industrial products and services; financial services; entertainment; utilities; and technology. PricewaterhouseCoopers also has a practice area geared specifically to private companies. It has about 80 offices in more than 30 states and accounts for 35% of its parent company's revenue.

PRIDGEON & CLAY, INC

50 COTTAGE GROVE ST SW
GRAND RAPIDS, MI 495071685
Phone: 616-241-5675
Fax: –
Web: www.pridgeonandclay.com

CEO: –
CFO: –
HR: Elizabeth Hanning
FYE: December 31
Type: Private

A moving target not a sitting duck Pridgeon & Clay (P&C) takes on all rivals within the metal forming industry. An independent manufacturer and supplier of stamped and fine blanked components the family-owned company designs and produces an array of parts for auto assembly plants across the US. Its lineup includes steering column lock nuts brackets for headlights to engines control arms flanges exhaust parts and muffler shields. Stamping equipment runs from fine blanking presses to high tonnage and progressive presses. P&C also makes blanks for equipment in other industries. The company touts hand assembly spot welding and tapping services along with a global sales force.

	Annual Growth	12/08	12/09	12/10	12/11	12/12
Sales ($ mil.)	15.6%	–	–	220.5	267.6	294.8
Net income ($ mil.)	(66.8%)	–	–	9.7	5.0	1.1
Market value ($ mil.)	–	–	–	–	–	–
Employees	–	–	–	–	–	600

PRIME HEALTHCARE SERVICES - GARDEN CITY, LLC

6245 INKSTER RD
GARDEN CITY, MI 481354001
Phone: 734-458-3300
Fax: –
Web: www.gch.org

CEO: Saju George
CFO: Gina Butcher
HR: –
FYE: December 31
Type: Private

Garden City Hospital provides health care services and medical education in western Wayne County Michigan. With about 320 licensed beds the community hospital offers emergency inpatient and surgical care in a variety of general and specialist fields including cardiology women's health and sports rehabilitation. Some of its more unusual services include clinical hypnotherapy and a massage clinic. Garden City Hospital also provides residency and internship programs through partnerships with universities and medical schools.

	Annual Growth	12/12	12/13	12/14	12/15	12/16
Sales ($ mil.)	5.5%	–	–	–	150.7	159.0
Net income ($ mil.)	13.9%	–	–	–	17.4	19.8
Market value ($ mil.)	–	–	–	–	–	–
Employees	–	–	–	–	–	1,200

PRIME HEALTHCARE SERVICES - SHASTA, LLC

1100 BUTTE ST
REDDING, CA 960010852
Phone: 530-244-5400
Fax: –
Web: www.shastaregional.com

CEO: Cyndy Gordon
CFO: –
HR: –
FYE: December 31
Type: Private

Shasta Regional Medical Center serves counties in northern California. The medical center offers a variety of services in areas such as surgical and critical care emergency and trauma and cardiac care. It has a capacity of about 250 beds. Specialty units include the complex's Chest Pain Center Vascular Wellness Center and Cardiovascular Catheterization Laboratory. Other services include diabetes care neurosciences orthopedics radiology and oncology. Shasta Regional is operated by hospital management firm Prime Healthcare Services.

	Annual Growth	12/05	12/06	12/07	12/08	12/15
Sales ($ mil.)	174.1%	–	–	–	0.1	152.3
Net income ($ mil.)	–	–	–	–	0.0	8.2
Market value ($ mil.)	–	–	–	–	–	–
Employees	–	–	–	–	–	850

PRIMEENERGY RESOURCES CORP
NAS: PNRG

9821 Katy Freeway
Houston, TX 77024
Phone: 713 735-0000
Fax: –
Web: www.primeenergy.com

CEO: –
CFO: Beverly A Cummings
HR: –
FYE: December 31
Type: Public

PrimeEnergy hopes to keep the pump primed with its oil and gas exploration and production activities which take place primarily in Colorado Louisiana New Mexico Oklahoma Texas West Virginia and the Gulf of Mexico. The company has proved reserves of 87 billion cu. ft. of natural gas equivalent. It operates 1500 wells and owns interests in 850 non-operating wells. Its PrimeEnergy Management unit is the managing general partner of 18 oil and gas limited partnerships and two trusts. Subsidiary Southwest Oilfield Construction provides site preparation and construction services for PrimeEnergy and third parties. CEO Charles Drimal owns 32% of the firm.

	Annual Growth	12/14	12/15	12/16	12/17	12/18
Sales ($ mil.)	(4.9%)	144.6	79.1	56.8	89.3	118.1
Net income ($ mil.)	(14.4%)	27.0	(12.8)	3.4	42.0	14.5
Market value ($ mil.)	(0.9%)	148.4	108.1	110.2	105.1	142.9
Employees	(12.8%)	270	182	155	144	156

PRIMEX INTERNATIONAL TRADING CORP

5777 W CENTURY BLVD # 1485
LOS ANGELES, CA 90045-5600
Phone: 310-568-8855
Fax: –
Web: www.primex-usa.com

CEO: Ali Amin
CFO: Andrik Sarkesians
HR: –
FYE: December 31
Type: Private

Primex International Trading is a leading exporter and international trader that specializes in dried fruits and nuts. Through affiliate offices located around the world the company ships such products as almonds hazelnuts and pecans as well as apricots figs and raisins. Primex also has its own pistachio orchards and a processing plant in California. The company was founded in 1989 by Ali Amin whose family has been involved in producing pistachios for four generations. It first started planting pistachio orchards in 1990. In 2008 the company shipped about 30 million pounds of pistachios and more than 40 million pounds of almonds.

	Annual Growth	12/98	12/99	12/00	12/01	12/11
Sales ($ mil.)	–	–	(836.8)	47.8	57.2	262.9
Net income ($ mil.)	153.4%	–	0.0	0.2	0.2	2.0
Market value ($ mil.)	–	–	–	–	–	–
Employees	–	–	–	–	–	31

PRIMO WATER CORP

NMS: PRMW

101 North Cherry Street, Suite 501
Winston-Salem, NC 27101
Phone: 336 331-4000
Fax: –
Web: www.primowater.com

CEO: –
CFO: Mark Castaneda
HR: –
FYE: December 31
Type: Public

Among the amenities of today's home a water dispenser appears near indispensable. Serving the growing trend of household purified water dispensers Primo Water provides water dispensers along with three- and five-gallon purified bottled water and carbonating beverage appliances. The company's products are sold through US and Canadian retailers such as Lowe's Wal-Mart Kroger HEB Grocery and Walgreen. Empty bottles are exchanged at retail locations with Primo Water recycling centers (where consumers receive a discount toward buying a new Primo bottle) or refilled at a self-serve filtered drinking water display. Started in 2005 Primo expanded quickly and went public in both 2010 and 2011.

	Annual Growth	12/14	12/15	12/16	12/17	12/18
Sales ($ mil.)	29.8%	106.3	127.0	142.5	286.1	302.1
Net income ($ mil.)	–	(13.5)	1.9	(5.9)	(6.4)	(54.8)
Market value ($ mil.)	34.3%	166.2	308.5	473.6	484.8	540.3
Employees	50.6%	117	135	627	625	602

PRIMORIS SERVICES CORP

NMS: PRIM

2300 N. Field Street, Suite 1900
Dallas, TX 75201
Phone: 214 740-5600
Fax: –
Web: www.prim.com

CEO: Randy Kessler
CFO: Peter J. Moerbeek
HR: –
FYE: December 31
Type: Public

Primoris Services provides construction engineering and maintenance services including underground pipeline replacement and repair industrial plant upgrades and maintenance concrete structures design and buildings and water and wastewater facility construction. It also engineers industrial machinery used in oil refineries petrochemical plants and other facilities. Founded as ARB in 1960 the firm primarily operates in the US. Primoris' largest clients are public and private gas and electric utilities state Departments of Transportation pipeline operators and chemical and energy producers. Its customers have included Chevron Sempra and Kinder Morgan.

	Annual Growth	12/14	12/15	12/16	12/17	12/18
Sales ($ mil.)	9.0%	2,086.2	1,929.4	1,996.9	2,380.0	2,939.5
Net income ($ mil.)	5.2%	63.2	36.9	26.7	72.4	77.5
Market value ($ mil.)	(4.7%)	1,178.6	1,117.3	1,155.3	1,379.0	970.2
Employees	11.9%	6,757	7,011	7,926	7,102	10,600

PRIMUS BUILDERS INC.

8294 HIGHWAY 92 STE 210
WOODSTOCK, GA 301893672
Phone: 770-928-7120
Fax: –
Web: www.primusbuilders.com

CEO: Richard A O'Connell
CFO: –
HR: –
FYE: December 31
Type: Private

Primus Builders is proud of leaving its customers in the cold. The design/build firm makes refrigerated frozen and ambient storage processing and distribution facilities and other industrial buildings. It offers turnkey services as well as planning and design construction and construction management a la carte. Primus Builders specializes in restaurants condominiums health clubs office buildings and retail centers. The company's Primus Properties leases office park space to businesses. Primus Builders shares work and officers with SubZero Constructors but the two do not share any corporate linkage.

	Annual Growth	12/01	12/02	12/05	12/06	12/07
Sales ($ mil.)	–	–	0.0	16.2	85.3	66.3
Net income ($ mil.)	112.4%	–	–	0.4	2.5	1.7
Market value ($ mil.)	–	–	–	–	–	–
Employees	–	–	–	–	–	88

PRINCETON COMMUNITY HOSPITAL ASSOCIATION, INC.

122 12TH ST
PRINCETON, WV 247402312
Phone: 304-487-7000
Fax: –
Web: www.pchonline.org

CEO: Wayne Griffith
CFO: Frank Sinicrope
HR: Heather Poff
FYE: June 30
Type: Private

Princeton Community Hospital serves the residents of southern West Virginia. The health care facility provides acute care home health care services physical therapy behavioral medicine laboratory and other health care services. Specialty medical divisions include cardiovascular and cancer care organ transplants radiology sleep disorder diagnostics and women's health. The hospital has about 190 beds and a medical staff of more than 100 physicians. Affiliates include the Athens Family Practice and Mercer Medical Group outpatient clinics and the Princeton Health Care Center nursing home. Princeton Community Hospital was founded in 1970.

	Annual Growth	06/05	06/06	06/15	06/17	06/18
Sales ($ mil.)	3.2%	–	93.5	129.1	144.4	135.7
Net income ($ mil.)	–	–	5.4	8.6	9.6	(6.8)
Market value ($ mil.)	–	–	–	–	–	–
Employees	–	–	–	–	–	1,000

PRINCIPAL FINANCIAL GROUP INC

NMS: PFG

711 High Street
Des Moines, IA 50392
Phone: 515 247-5111
Fax: –
Web: www.principal.com

CEO: Daniel J. (Dan) Houston
CFO: Deanna Strable
HR: –
FYE: December 31
Type: Public

Founded in 1879 Principal Financial Group (Principal) is a top administrator of employer-sponsored retirement plans offering pension products and services as well as mutual funds annuities asset management trust services and investment advice. Its insurance segment provides group and individual life and disability insurance and group dental and vision coverage. PFG serves 25 million customers and has more than $625 billion in assets under management. Principal operates offices in nearly 25 countries and serves clients in more than 85 countries.

	Annual Growth	12/14	12/15	12/16	12/17	12/18
Assets ($ mil.)	2.6%	219,087.0	218,685.9	228,014.3	253,941.2	243,036.1
Net income ($ mil.)	7.8%	1,144.1	1,234.0	1,316.5	2,310.4	1,546.5
Market value ($ mil.)	(4.0%)	14,517.2	12,571.9	16,171.9	19,721.5	12,345.5
Employees	2.6%	14,873	14,895	14,854	15,378	16,475

PRINCIPAL GLOBAL INVESTORS LLC

801 Grand Ave.
Des Moines IA 50392-0490
Phone: 515-247-6582
Fax: 866-850-4024
Web: www.principalglobal.com

CEO: James P McCaughan
CFO: Gerald Hipner
HR: –
FYE: December 31
Type: Subsidiary

Principal Global Investors is the institutional asset management division of Principal Financial Group (aka The Principal). The firm manages approximately $230 billion of assets mainly for retirement plans and other institutional clients such as foundations endowments insurance companies investment banks and government entities. A majority of assets under management are invested in fixed income securities but the company also focuses on equities real estate and alternative investments. Principal Global Investors and its affiliates have more than a dozen offices in the US Brazil Europe Asia and Australia.

PRIORITY AVIATION INC

NBB: PJET

15 Maiden Lane, Suite 408
New York, NY 10038
Phone: 646 783-7507
Fax: –
Web: www.priorityonejets.com

CEO: –
CFO: –
HR: –
FYE: December 31
Type: Public

NuMobile formerly Phoenix Interests is a development stage company that is looking to build a portfolio of software applications and services aimed at the mobile computing and smartphone markets. It plans to use a series of acquisitions targeting technology and infrastructure businesses in order to fulfill its new strategy. The company acquired Stonewall Networks a security software maker for mobile networks and network security specialist Enhance Network Communication in 2009. NuMobile previously focused on gaming and entertainment technologies.

	Annual Growth	12/12	12/13	12/14	12/15	12/16
Sales ($ mil.)	(4.8%)	6.8	6.3	6.5	5.6	5.6
Net income ($ mil.)	155.6%	0.0	(0.5)	(3.6)	(1.1)	0.7
Market value ($ mil.)	–	0.0	0.0	1.4	0.5	0.2
Employees	–	–	–	–	–	–

PRIORITY HEALTH MANAGED BENEFITS INC.

1231 E. Beltline NE
Grand Rapids MI 49525-4501
Phone: 616-942-0954
Fax: 616-942-5651
Web: www.priority-health.com

CEO: Joan Budden
CFO: Greg Hawkins
HR: –
FYE: June 30
Type: Private - Not-for-Pr

Priority Health Managed Benefits' chief concern is its members' wellbeing. A subsidiary of Spectrum Health the health insurance provider serves some 600000 members throughout the state of Michigan. The company offers managed care plans to about 12000 employer groups; it also provides individual coverage. It contracts with a network of some 100 acute care hospitals and more than 16000 health care providers including primary care doctors and specialists. Health plan offerings include HMO POS PPO Medicaid and Medicare plans. Priority Health also offers health savings accounts (HSAs) and provides administrative services for companies with self-funded plans.

PRISMA HEALTH-UPSTATE

701 GROVE RD
GREENVILLE, SC 296054210
Phone: 864-455-7000
Fax: –
Web: www.ghs.org

CEO: Michael C. Riordan
CFO: Terri T. Newsom
HR: Mary Martin
FYE: September 30
Type: Private

From education and research to primary care and surgery Upstate Affiliate Organization (dba Prisma Health-Upstate formerly Greenville Hospital System) is out to keep residents of the "Golden Strip" (the corridor connecting Charlotte North Carolina and Atlanta) healthy. Originally founded in 1912 the system encompasses eight inpatient hospitals and more than 100 outpatient facilities. Its flagship facility is Prisma Health Greenville Memorial Hospital a referral and academic medical center with more than 800 beds; other facilities include several smaller community hospitals a nursing home and a long-term acute care hospital. Greenville Hospital System merged with Palmetto Health in 2017; the combined system rebranded as Prisma Health in early 2019.

	Annual Growth	09/02	09/03	09/04	09/05	09/13
Sales ($ mil.)	2.9%	–	754.3	789.1	789.1	1,001.1
Net income ($ mil.)	4.4%	–	52.6	21.1	21.1	80.9
Market value ($ mil.)	–	–	–	–	–	–
Employees	–	–	–	–	–	7,200

PRISON REHABILITATIVE INDUSTRIES AND DIVERSIFIED ENTERPRISES, INC.

223 MORRISON RD
BRANDON, FL 335114835
Phone: 813-324-8700
Fax: –
Web: www.pride-enterprises.org

CEO: –
CFO: Peter J Radanovich
HR: –
FYE: December 31
Type: Private

Even convicted felons can take PRIDE in their work. Prison Rehabilitative Industries and Diversified Enterprises (PRIDE Enterprises) a not-for-profit corporation enables inmates in some 20 Florida prisons to learn job skills. PRIDE operates in about 40 industries employing inmates in activities such as furniture making license plate embossing meat processing and eyewear production. Customers such as schools local governments and nonprofits buy the products made by the inmates. PRIDE also offers labor outsourcing to private businesses. The group's revenue is dedicated to inmate room and board inmate wages and transition services and victim restitution. PRIDE was founded in 1981.

	Annual Growth	12/10	12/11	12/12	12/15	12/16
Sales ($ mil.)	4.0%	–	63.1	64.4	75.6	76.9
Net income ($ mil.)	157.3%	–	0.0	4.1	5.2	2.8
Market value ($ mil.)	–	–	–	–	–	–
Employees	–	–	–	–	–	250

PRIVATEBANCORP INC

NMS: PVTB

120 South LaSalle Street
Chicago, IL 60603
Phone: 312 564-2000
Fax: –
Web: www.pvtb.com

CEO: –
CFO: –
HR: –
FYE: December 31
Type: Public

It's your private banker a banker for money and any old teller won't do. PrivateBancorp is the holding company for The PrivateBank and Trust Co which provides commercial and community banking real estate lending investments and money management services to middle-market companies commercial real estate professionals small business owners executives and wealthy individuals and their families. The bank boasts over $15.6 billion in assets around 25 branches in the Chicago area and 10 branches across Atlanta Cleveland Denver Des Moines Detroit Milwaukee Minneapolis Kansas City and St. Louis. PrivateBancorp is being acquired by Canada's CIBC for $3.8 billion.

	Annual Growth	12/11	12/12	12/13	12/14	12/15
Assets ($ mil.)	8.6%	12,416.9	14,057.5	14,085.7	15,603.4	17,259.4
Net income ($ mil.)	43.0%	44.4	77.9	122.9	153.1	185.3
Market value ($ mil.)	39.0%	868.5	1,211.8	2,288.3	2,641.8	3,244.5
Employees	3.9%	1,045	1,105	1,116	1,168	1,219

PRO-DEX INC. (CO)
NAS: PDEX

2361 McGaw Avenue
Irvine, CA 92614
Phone: 949 769-3200
Fax: –
Web: www.pro-dex.com

CEO: Richard L Van Kirk
CFO: Alisha K Charlton
HR: –
FYE: June 30
Type: Public

Pro-Dex is responsible for that high-pitched whirring sound at the dentist's office. The company designs and manufactures rotary drive systems used in the dental and medical instrument industries. Its motors are used in instruments for arthroscopic cranial dental orthopedic and spinal surgery. It also markets its own line of dental handpieces under the Micro Motors brand. Pro-Dex also develops motion control systems for industrial manufacturing and scientific research industries under the Oregon Micro Systems brand. In addition to manufacturing Pro-Dex also offers repair services on its products.

	Annual Growth	06/15	06/16	06/17	06/18	06/19
Sales ($ mil.)	19.4%	13.4	20.2	21.9	22.5	27.2
Net income ($ mil.)	–	(0.4)	0.8	5.1	1.6	4.1
Market value ($ mil.)	53.3%	9.5	22.5	24.8	26.9	52.4
Employees	10.7%	66	104	81	81	99

PROASSURANCE CORP
NYS: PRA

100 Brookwood Place
Birmingham, AL 35209
Phone: 205 877-4400
Fax: –
Web: www.proassurance.com

CEO: W. Stancil (Stan) Starnes
CFO: Edward L. (Ned) Rand
HR: –
FYE: December 31
Type: Public

ProAssurance protects professional health associates — the doctors dentists and nurses of the US. One of the largest medical liability insurance providers in the nation ProAssurance is the holding company for ProAssurance Indemnity ProAssurance Casualty and other subsidiaries that sell liability coverage for health care providers primarily in the South and Midwest. Its customers include individual doctors in private practice as well as large physician groups clinics and hospitals. Its ProAssurance Specialty Insurance subsidiary writes excess and surplus (higher risk) lines of medical professional liability insurance. ProAssurance Casualty also provides some coverage for legal professionals.

	Annual Growth	12/14	12/15	12/16	12/17	12/18
Assets ($ mil.)	(2.9%)	5,169.2	4,908.2	5,065.2	4,929.2	4,600.7
Net income ($ mil.)	(30.1%)	196.6	116.2	151.1	107.3	47.1
Market value ($ mil.)	(2.6%)	2,421.7	2,603.0	3,014.4	3,065.4	2,175.5
Employees	0.6%	967	938	965	994	991

PROBUILD HOLDINGS INC.

7595 Technology Way 5th Fl.
Denver CO 80237
Phone: 303-262-8500
Fax: +55-11-2162-0630
Web: www.vcimentos.com.br

CEO: Robert Marchbank
CFO: Jeff Pinkerman
HR: John O' Loughlin
FYE: December 31
Type: Private

ProBuild Holdings is where the pros go for building supplies. The company is one of the nation's largest suppliers of building materials to professional builders contractors and project-oriented consumers serving customers through 10 regional brands. ProBuild boasts more than 470 locations where it operates lumber and building product manufacturing sites and distribution centers. It supplies lumber millwork windows doors roofing insulation engineered wood siding and trim and gypsum. Its specialty building products business line provides hardware fasteners tools for residential and light commercial construction. Dixieline ProBuild and Stober Building Supply are among ProBuild's regional holdings.

PROCERA NETWORKS INC
NMS: PKT

47448 Fremont Boulevard
Fremont, CA 94538
Phone: 510 230-2777
Fax: –
Web: www.proceranetworks.com

CEO: Lyndon Cantor
CFO: Charles Constanti
HR: –
FYE: December 31
Type: Public

Procera Networks makes it easier for broadband and mobile service providers to run a tight ship. The company's deep packet inspection (DPI) devices are sold under the brand name PacketLogic. As network management equipment it monitors network traffic optimizes bandwidth identifies security threats and manages application usage. Customers also use PacketLogic to differentiate service levels. Procera sells directly and through resellers distributors and systems integrators worldwide. Its customers include cable phone and Internet service providers as well as businesses and schools that manage their own networks. The company was established in 2003.

	Annual Growth	12/09	12/10	12/11	12/12	12/13
Sales ($ mil.)	38.8%	20.1	20.3	44.4	59.6	74.7
Net income ($ mil.)	–	(7.4)	(2.9)	3.8	5.3	(16.3)
Market value ($ mil.)	141.6%	9.1	12.8	321.8	383.1	310.2
Employees	44.4%	52	70	96	151	226

PROCESSA PHARMACEUTICALS INC
NBB: PCSA

7380 Coca Cola Drive, Suite 106
Hanover, MD 21076
Phone: 443 776-3133
Fax: –
Web: www.heatwurx.com

CEO: David Young
CFO: James Stanker
HR: –
FYE: December 31
Type: Public

Heatwurx provides a way to fix cracks and potholes in the roadway not by just laying more asphalt but by repairing them through the use of plenty of heat. The company manufactures machinery that recycles broken asphalt at temperatures above 300° F. with infrared heating equipment that is electrically powered. Heatwurx claims it is an environmentally friendly method by virtue of its reuse of distressed pavement and the lack of need to transport material from asphalt plants. It incorporated in early 2011 and is a development-stage company with negligible sales. In late 2012 Heatwurx filed an IPO initially aiming to raise $7.6 million.

	Annual Growth	12/12	12/13	12/14	12/15	12/16
Sales ($ mil.)	(59.8%)	0.2	0.3	0.2	0.1	0.0
Net income ($ mil.)	–	(2.4)	(3.1)	(4.5)	(3.4)	(0.3)
Market value ($ mil.)	(57.7%)	–	5.3	3.5	0.6	0.4
Employees	(38.5%)	7	8	9	1	1

PROCTER & GAMBLE COMPANY (THE)
NYS: PG

One Procter & Gamble Plaza
Cincinnati, OH 45202
Phone: 513 983-1100
Fax: –
Web: www.pg.com

CEO: David S. Taylor
CFO: Jon R. Moeller
HR: Giorgio Siracusa
FYE: June 30
Type: Public

The Procter & Gamble Company (P&G) boasts billion-dollar brands for home and health. The world's largest maker of consumer packaged goods divides its business into five global segments that comprise its vast portfolio of hair skin and personal oral family feminine and baby care product lines. Its dozens of brands include Ace Bounce Crest Gillette Pampers Pepto Bismol Puffs Old Spice Swiffer and Tide. Fabric and home care is P&G's leading product category accounting for about a third of sales. The company sells products in 180-plus countries although the US is its largest market.

	Annual Growth	06/15	06/16	06/17	06/18	06/19
Sales ($ mil.)	(2.9%)	76,279.0	65,299.0	65,058.0	66,832.0	67,684.0
Net income ($ mil.)	(13.7%)	7,036.0	10,508.0	15,326.0	9,750.0	3,897.0
Market value ($ mil.)	–	0.0	0.0	0.0	0.0	0.0
Employees	(3.1%)	110,000	105,000	95,000	92,000	97,000

PROCYON CORPORATION
OTC: PCYN

1300 S. Highland Ave.
Clearwater FL 33756
Phone: 727-443-0530
Fax: 727-447-5617
Web: www.amerigel.com

CEO: Regina W Anderson
CFO: James B Anderson
HR: –
FYE: June 30
Type: Public

Procyon sees past people's scars — though it tries to rid the world of scarring altogether. Through subsidiary Amerx Health Care Procyon Corporation makes medical products used to treat pressure ulcers inflammation dermatitis and other wounds and skin problems. Amerx makes the AmeriGel wound dressing used by many podiatrists. The company's skin treatment products are sold primarily to distributors doctors pharmacies and end-users. Procyon's Sirius Medical Supply division is a mail-order diabetic medical supply distributor selling mostly to Medicare customers. The founding Anderson family including CEO Regina Anderson owns about 40% of the company.

PRODUCERS RICE MILL, INC.

518 E HARRISON ST
STUTTGART, AR 721603700
Phone: 870-673-4444
Fax: –
Web: www.producersrice.com

CEO: –
CFO: –
HR: Kimberley Meek
FYE: July 31
Type: Private

These producers aren't just milling about they're about milling. Producers Rice Mill dries mills and markets more than 50 million bushels of rice each year which it sells both domestically and overseas. The growers' cooperative is one of the largest private-label producers of rice in the US packaging more than 100 brands for the foodservice retail private label export and industrial industries. Its brands include ParExcellence LeGourment Golden Harvest Classic Grains Granada Mandalay Bamboo 103 Calrose and Thai Orchard. It also processes rice for animal feeds such as Buck Grub deer feed and Equi-Jewel horse feed.

	Annual Growth	07/14	07/15	07/16	07/17	07/18
Sales ($ mil.)	(3.6%)	–	488.2	415.0	420.3	436.7
Net income ($ mil.)	(9.8%)	–	354.7	275.1	276.3	260.3
Market value ($ mil.)	–	–	–	–	–	–
Employees	–	–	–	–	–	650

PRODUCTION TOOL SUPPLY COMPANY, LLC

8655 E 8 MILE RD
WARREN, MI 480894030
Phone: 586-755-2200
Fax: –

CEO: –
CFO: –
HR: –
FYE: December 31
Type: Private

Production Tool Supply totes the tools of the trade — and it distributes them to customers worldwide. With nine showrooms in Michigan and Ohio the company (PTS) distributes brand-name discount industrial tools and machinery. It markets approximately 235000 products through a 1700-page catalog on the Internet and through independent distributors. Products include cutting tools carbide tools abrasives measuring tools clamps and vises power tools tool safety products and power machinery by blue chip OEMs such as Bosch Porter-Cable and Sandvik. D. Dan Kahn founded PTS in 1951 to serve small factories and shops in the Detroit area. The Kahn family still controls the company.

	Annual Growth	10/07	10/08	10/09	10/10*	12/13
Sales ($ mil.)	18.2%	–	–	117.2	129.1	228.5
Net income ($ mil.)	21.7%	–	–	10.7	15.0	23.5
Market value ($ mil.)	–	–	–	–	–	–
Employees	–	–	–	–	–	357

*Fiscal year change

PROFESSIONAL DIVERSITY NETWORK INC
NAS: IPDN

801 W. Adams Street, Suite 600
Chicago, IL 60607
Phone: 312 614-0950
Fax: –
Web: www.prodivnet.com

CEO: Maoji Wang
CFO: Jiangping Xiao
HR: –
FYE: December 31
Type: Public

Birds of a feather can build careers together at Professional Diversity Network (PDN). An online professional networking company PDN operates minority-focused websites that facilitate professional networking within ethnic and social communities. Its websites include iHispano.com which serves Hispanic-American professionals and AMightyRiver.com which caters to African-Americans. The company also operates sites that serve other societal subsets including women Asian-Americans gays and lesbians and enlisted and veteran military personnel. Together its websites have 1.8 million members and provide access to job listings a social network professional groups and mentoring. PDN went public in 2013.

	Annual Growth	12/14	12/15	12/16	12/17	12/18
Sales ($ mil.)	(7.7%)	11.6	38.6	26.2	22.1	8.5
Net income ($ mil.)	–	(3.7)	(35.8)	(4.1)	(22.3)	(15.1)
Market value ($ mil.)	(32.5%)	23.6	2.4	53.0	19.9	4.9
Employees	(34.6%)	515	355	253	167	94

PROFESSIONAL GOLFERS ASSOCIATION OF AMERICA INC

100 AVENUE OF CHAMPIONS
PALM BEACH GARDENS, FL 334183653
Phone: 561-624-8400
Fax: –
Web: www.nepga.com

CEO: Jim L Awtrey
CFO: –
HR: –
FYE: June 30
Type: Private

The Professional Golfers' Association of America (PGA) is the world's largest professional sports organization with more than 28000 members. PGA members are primarily club pros but most touring professionals are also members in addition to holding membership in the separate PGA TOUR organization. The PGA conducts some 40 tournaments and runs four major golf competitions: the Ryder Cup the PGA Championship the Senior PGA Championship and the PGA Grand Slam of Golf. It also operates the PGA Learning Center a golf instruction school in Port St. Lucie Florida. Rodman Wanamaker a Philadelphia department store tycoon organized the PGA in 1916.

	Annual Growth	06/09	06/10	06/13	06/14	06/15
Sales ($ mil.)	13.9%	–	56.4	91.1	82.3	108.2
Net income ($ mil.)	–	–	(10.6)	12.4	(8.3)	(2.0)
Market value ($ mil.)	–	–	–	–	–	–
Employees	–	–	–	–	–	270

PROFESSIONAL PROJECT SERVICES INC.

1100 BETHEL VALLEY RD
OAK RIDGE, TN 378308073
Phone: 865-220-4300
Fax: –
Web: www.p2s.trademarkads.org

CEO: Dr L Barry Goss
CFO: Mike Webster
HR: –
FYE: December 31
Type: Private

Pro2Serve Professional Project Services lives to serve. The contractor provides technical and engineering services that support the security of infrastructures in the US defense energy and environmental markets. Pro2Serve designs high-level security systems to protect national laboratories government facilities and US nuclear weapons. Its work with the US Department of Energy's National Nuclear Security Administration aims to secure nuclear sites and dangerous radiological materials around the world. The company also offers environmental services which include facility planning compliance consulting remediation and waste management. Founded by president Barry Goss Pro2Serve is privately held.

	Annual Growth	12/06	12/07	12/08	12/09	12/10
Sales ($ mil.)	–	–	–	(983.8)	50.5	58.0
Net income ($ mil.)	8575.1%	–	–	0.0	1.7	2.8
Market value ($ mil.)	–	–	–	–	–	–
Employees	–	–	–	–	–	340

PROGENICS PHARMACEUTICALS, INC.   NMS: PGNX

One World Trade Center, 47th Floor
New York, NY 10007
Phone: 646 975-2500
Fax: –
Web: www.progenics.com

CEO: Mark R. Baker
CFO: Patrick Fabbio
HR: –
FYE: December 31
Type: Public

Progenics develops biotech drugs with oncology applications as well as therapeutics used in clinical settings. Its pipeline includes prostate cancer treatments as well as drugs targeting viral and infectious diseases. Progenics' sole commercial product Relistor blocks the side effects of opioids without lessening their pain-killing power and is approved as an injectable treatment for opioid-induced constipation in seriously ill patients. The firm has licensed out marketing rights for Relistor to third parties in order to focus on its R&D activities. Progenics' EXINI Bone BSI (bone scan index) product acquired in 2015 is a tool to help physicians analyze bone scan images. It is marketed in Europe and Japan.

	Annual Growth	12/14	12/15	12/16	12/17	12/18
Sales ($ mil.)	(23.0%)	44.4	8.7	69.4	11.7	15.6
Net income ($ mil.)	–	4.4	(39.1)	10.8	(51.0)	(67.7)
Market value ($ mil.)	(13.7%)	639.1	518.2	730.4	503.0	355.1
Employees	8.5%	57	66	58	64	79

PROGINET CORPORATION

200 Garden City Plaza Ste. 220
Garden City NY 11530
Phone: 516-535-3600
Fax: 516-535-3601
Web: www.proginet.com

CEO: –
CFO: –
HR: –
FYE: July 31
Type: Subsidiary

Proginet had a secure grasp on enterprise data. The company provided software that businesses use to create encrypted documents — including text graphics and executable files — so that they can safely be sent over public networks. The company also offers identity management process automation software as well as password management tools that eliminate the need for users to remember multiple access codes. Its service portfolio ranges from installation and support to project management requirements analysis and security assessments. Proginet was acquired in 2010 by TIBCO Software in an all-cash deal valued at about $20 million.

PROGRESS ENERGY INC.   NYSE: PGN

410 S. Wilmington St.
Raleigh NC 27601-1748
Phone: 919-546-6111
Fax: 919-546-2920
Web: www.progress-energy.com

CEO: Lynn J Good
CFO: Steven K Young
HR: –
FYE: December 31
Type: Public

Without progress millions of people would be without energy. Progress Energy provided electricity to 3.1 million customers. It serves customers in North and South Carolina through utility Carolina Power & Light (dba Progress Energy Carolinas) and in Florida through Florida Power (or Progress Energy Florida). The company generated most of its energy from nuclear and fossil-fueled plants and has a total capacity of about 23000 MW. Progress Energy had been seeking to improve its operational efficiency while expanding its alternative energy power sources in order to reduce its greenhouse gas emissions. In 2012 the debt-laden company was acquired by Duke Energy in a $32 billion transaction.

PROGRESS SOFTWARE CORP   NMS: PRGS

14 Oak Park
Bedford, MA 01730
Phone: 781 280-4000
Fax: 781 280-4095
Web: www.progress.com

CEO: Yogesh Gupta
CFO: Paul Jalbert
HR: –
FYE: November 30
Type: Public

Progress Software can help you make significant headway when managing and deploying business applications. The company's platform-as-a-service PaaS) software is used for tasks such as business process management application integration data management and analysis and application development and deployment. Progress' products encompass desktops servers mainframes and data centers and can be implemented in a variety of computing environments such as Linux Unix and Windows. Progress serves about 140000 organizations in more than 180 countries with clients coming from industries such as financial services health care manufacturing and technology.

	Annual Growth	11/15	11/16	11/17	11/18	11/19
Sales ($ mil.)	2.3%	377.6	405.3	397.6	397.2	413.3
Net income ($ mil.)	–	(8.8)	(55.7)	37.4	63.5	26.4
Market value ($ mil.)	15.0%	1,080.4	1,331.7	1,861.8	1,583.5	1,892.0
Employees	(3.4%)	1,766	1,912	1,470	1,412	1,538

PROGRESSIVE CORP. (OH)   NYS: PGR

6300 Wilson Mills Road
Mayfield Village, OH 44143
Phone: 440 461-5000
Fax: 440 446-7168
Web: www.progressive.com

CEO: S. Patricia (Tricia) Griffith
CFO: John P. Sauerland
HR: –
FYE: December 31
Type: Public

The Progressive Corporation offers personal lines insurance as well as commercial lines and property insurance. Personal auto insurance is Progressive's largest business; it also offers personal-use vehicle policies for motorcycles RVs snowmobiles and other specialty vehicles. The company's commercial policies cover vans and light to heavy trucks. Most of its commercial lines policies are sold to small business owners. The property insurance business writes residential property insurance for homeowners and offers renters insurance. Progressive markets directly to consumers online and by phone and through more than 35000 independent agents.

	Annual Growth	12/14	12/15	12/16	12/17	12/18
Assets ($ mil.)	15.9%	25,787.6	29,819.3	33,427.5	38,701.2	46,575.0
Net income ($ mil.)	19.5%	1,281.0	1,267.6	1,031.0	1,592.2	2,615.3
Market value ($ mil.)	22.3%	15,740.6	18,545.8	20,703.6	32,845.8	35,184.5
Employees	9.0%	26,501	28,580	31,721	33,656	37,346

PROHEALTH CARE INC

725 AMERICAN AVE
WAUKESHA, WI 531885031
Phone: 262-928-1000
Fax: –

CEO: Donald W Fundingsland
CFO: –
HR: –
FYE: September 30
Type: Private

That cheddar-and-beer diet take a toll on your health? Might be time to turn your health over to the pros. ProHealth Care provides health care services to southeastern Wisconsin through a network of three hospitals (Waukesha Memorial Oconomowoc Memorial and the Rehabilitation Hospital of Wisconsin) about two dozen clinics assisted living facilities (Regency Senior Communities) a rehabilitation partnership home health care services and a hospice facility. The community-based organization's specialized services include advanced cancer care cardiology orthopedic and obstetrical and neonatal intensive care.

	Annual Growth	09/14	09/15	09/16	09/17	09/18
Sales ($ mil.)	3.1%	–	748.3	747.2	765.3	820.6
Net income ($ mil.)	–	–	(20.8)	74.6	127.2	111.2
Market value ($ mil.)	–	–	–	–	–	–
Employees	–	–	–	–	–	3,000

PROJECT ENHANCEMENT CORP

20300 CENTURY BLVD # 175　　　　　　　　　　　　CEO: Ricardo Martinez
GERMANTOWN, MD 208741132　　　　　　　　　　　CFO: –
Phone: 240-686-3059　　　　　　　　　　　　　　　HR: –
Fax: –　　　　　　　　　　　　　　　　　　　　　FYE: May 31
Web: www.projectenhancement.com　　　　　　　　Type: Private

Project Enhancement offers a variety of environmental services including hazardous waste management nuclear plant decommissioning and stabilization and disposition of nuclear materials. The company serves customers throughout the US from offices in Maryland Tennessee and Washington state. Clients have included several US Department of Energy nuclear sites as well a range of industrial manufacturing companies and utilties including Bechtel British Nuclear Fuels Commonwealth Edison Fluor Lockheed Martin Morrison Knudsen and Science Applications International.

	Annual Growth	05/10	05/11	05/12	05/13	05/14
Sales ($ mil.)	(18.0%)	–	19.7	14.5	12.4	10.9
Net income ($ mil.)	58.0%	–	–	0.2	0.3	0.4
Market value ($ mil.)	–	–	–	–	–	–
Employees	–	–	–	–	–	45

PROJECT LEADERSHIP ASSOCIATES INC.

120 S. LaSalle St. Ste. 1200　　　　　　　　　　　CEO: Lee Hovermale
Chicago IL 60603　　　　　　　　　　　　　　　　CFO: –
Phone: 312-441-0077　　　　　　　　　　　　　　　HR: –
Fax: 312-441-0088　　　　　　　　　　　　　　　　FYE: December 31
Web: www.projectleadership.net　　　　　　　　　Type: Private

Project Leadership Associates (PLA) may not be leading the market but it is fast rising among the pantheon of business consulting firms. The employee-owned company has been profitable every year since its founding in 1998 advising small middle-market and large US companies on strategy performance and merger and acquisition integration. It also advises on complementary IT matters helping clients assess which software applications and infrastructures are best suited for their operations. Industries it serves include financial services health care insurance legal manufacturing and utilities. The company works with partners such as Citrix Microsoft and Symantec to deliver its services.

PROLOGIS INC　　　　　　　　　　　　　　　　　NYS: PLD

Pier 1, Bay 1　　　　　　　　　　　　　　　CEO: Eugene F. (Gene) Reilly
San Francisco, CA 94111　　　　　　　　　　CFO: Thomas S. (Tom) Olinger
Phone: 415 394-9000　　　　　　　　　　　　HR: –
Fax: 415 394-9001　　　　　　　　　　　　　FYE: December 31
Web: www.prologis.com　　　　　　　　　　　Type: Public

Prologis does its part for the ever-expanding ever-quickening global supply chain. It owns and manages an $80 billion real estate portfolio of more than 680 million sq.ft. of warehouse and distribution space in nearly 20 countries. Organized as an industrial real estate investment trust (REIT) Prologis acquires and develops facilities for some 5000 clients including Amazon FedEx DHL Nippon Express BMW and Keuhne + Nagel. The company tends to more than 3300 properties in the Americas Europe and Asia. Prologis selectively manages its portfolio and usually only develops new properties when lease terms are in place for it.

	Annual Growth	12/14	12/15	12/16	12/17	12/18
Sales ($ mil.)	12.3%	1,760.8	2,197.1	2,533.1	2,618.1	2,804.4
Net income ($ mil.)	26.9%	636.2	869.4	1,209.9	1,652.3	1,649.4
Market value ($ mil.)	8.1%	27,092.4	27,023.1	33,237.4	40,616.5	36,971.1
Employees	1.8%	1,505	1,555	1,530	1,565	1,617

PROMEGA CORPORATION

2800 WOODS HOLLOW RD　　　　　　　　　CEO: William A. (Bill) Linton
FITCHBURG, WI 537115399　　　　　　　　　CFO: John Leblanc
Phone: 608-274-4330　　　　　　　　　　　　HR: –
Fax: –　　　　　　　　　　　　　　　　　　FYE: March 31
Web: www.promega.com　　　　　　　　　　Type: Private

Promega provides tools to help researchers delve into the life sciences. The company sells more than 3500 products that allow scientists to conduct various experiments in gene protein and cellular research. Its offerings fall into more than two dozen categories including DNA and RNA purification genotype analysis protein expression and analysis and DNA sequencing. Promega has branches in 15 countries around the world. The firm sells its products directly and through about 50 distributors. Customers include academic pharmaceutical and clinical labs as well as government agencies and energy and chemical companies.

	Annual Growth	03/14	03/15	03/16	03/17	03/18
Sales ($ mil.)	6.6%	–	–	370.1	386.1	420.9
Net income ($ mil.)	24.1%	–	–	44.8	55.0	69.0
Market value ($ mil.)	–	–	–	–	–	–
Employees	–	–	–	–	–	1,487

PROMETHEUS LABORATORIES INC.

9410 Carroll Park Dr.　　　　　　　　　　　CEO: Warren Cresswell
San Diego CA 92121　　　　　　　　　　　　CFO: Peter Westlake
Phone: 858-824-0895　　　　　　　　　　　　HR: –
Fax: 858-824-0896　　　　　　　　　　　　　FYE: December 31
Web: www.prometheuslabs.com　　　　　　　Type: Private

If you've got fire in your belly Prometheus Laboratories can help put it out. The pharmaceutical company markets several drugs that treat gastrointestinal disorders such as irritable bowel syndrome gout and kidney stones as well as certain cancers and other medical conditions. Prometheus Laboratories markets its products mainly to US gastroenterologists and oncologists. It also pairs its drug offerings with a diagnostic testing products and services that helps doctors diagnose and treat gastrointestinal and oncology conditions. The company was acquired by Nestle in mid-2011.

PROMISE TECHNOLOGY INC.　　　　　　　　　TAIWAN: 3057

580 Cottonwood Dr.　　　　　　　　　　　　CEO: Tung-Hsu Lin
Milpitas CA 95035　　　　　　　　　　　　　CFO: –
Phone: 408-228-1400　　　　　　　　　　　　HR: –
Fax: 408-228-0730　　　　　　　　　　　　　FYE: December 31
Web: www.promise.com　　　　　　　　　　　Type: Public

Promise Technology keeps data storage under control. The company makes storage controller cards and other products supporting cloud storage A/V postproduction virtual tape libraries and surveillance storage. Its products are powered by RAID (redundant array of independent disks) technology interfacing through the Parallel Advanced Technology Attachment standard as well as the newer Serial ATA. Promise Technology serves the enterprise small and medium business small office/home office and consumer markets worldwide. The company partners with hard-disk drive makers such as Seagate and Western Digital as well as Dell Gateway Fujitsu and other computer makers.

PROOFPOINT INC   NMS: PFPT

892 Ross Drive
Sunnyvale, CA 94089
Phone: 408 517-4710
Fax: –
Web: www.proofpoint.com

CEO: Gary L. Steele
CFO: Paul R. Auvil
HR: –
FYE: December 31
Type: Public

Proofpoint is like a bouncer for your computer - it needs to see some proof of ID. The company provides security for e-mails instant messages and other communications. Its Proofpoint Protection Server and Messaging Security Gateway defend against computer viruses hacker attacks on networks and spam. Clients come from the health care financial services government education retail and technology sectors; customers include HCA Bank of America the Dept. of Agriculture the University of North Carolina at Charlotte PETCO and T-Mobile. It has offices across the US Europe Asia/Pacific and Latin America. Founded in 2002 by chairman Eric Hahn Proofpoint went public in 2012.

	Annual Growth	12/14	12/15	12/16	12/17	12/18
Sales ($ mil.)	38.4%	195.6	265.4	375.5	515.3	717.0
Net income ($ mil.)	–	(64.2)	(106.5)	(111.2)	(84.3)	(103.7)
Market value ($ mil.)	14.8%	2,659.8	3,585.2	3,896.3	4,897.8	4,622.0
Employees	32.1%	859	1,203	1,573	2,047	2,613

PROPHASE LABS INC   NAS: PRPH

621 N. Shady Retreat Road
Doylestown, PA 18901
Phone: 215 345-0919
Fax: 215 345-5920
Web: www.prophaselabs.com

CEO: Ted Karkus
CFO: Monica Brady
HR: –
FYE: December 31
Type: Public

ProPhase Labs wants cold sufferers to put away their tissues and tonics and take Cold-EEZE lozenges instead. The firm contends that its Cold-EEZE remedy (a zinc-based nutritional formula available in lozenge tablet liquid and gum forms) lessens the length and severity of the common cold. ProPhase markets its products primarily in the US market. The company's Pharmaloz Manufacturing subsidiary makes Cold-EEZE lozenges and provides contract manufacturing of lozenges for other firms. In early 2017 ProPhase agreed to sell its Cold-EEZE assets to Mylan for some $50 million. It will continue to manufacture the products for Mylan. ProPhase is also conducting research and development programs into potential new OTC medicines.

	Annual Growth	12/14	12/15	12/16	12/17	12/18
Sales ($ mil.)	(12.2%)	22.1	20.6	21.0	9.9	13.1
Net income ($ mil.)	–	(7.8)	(3.6)	(2.9)	41.8	(1.7)
Market value ($ mil.)	21.1%	16.9	17.3	23.1	25.1	36.4
Employees	(2.4%)	55	54	53	46	50

PROPHOTONIX LTD   NBB: STKR

13 Red Roof Lane, Suite 200
Salem, NH 03079
Phone: 603 893-8778
Fax: 603 893-5604
Web: www.prophotonix.com

CEO: Mark W Blodgett
CFO: Timothy P Losik
HR: –
FYE: December 31
Type: Public

ProPhotonix (formerly StockerYale) lights the way with lasers and LEDs. The company makes light-emitting diode (LED) modules used in semiconductor manufacturing machine vision biomedical and other applications. It also makes custom LED modules for OEMs systems integrators and end users with unique lighting needs. Its Photonic Products Ltd. (PPL) subsidiary makes custom laser modules and other electro-optical subassemblies and optoelectronic components based on semiconductor laser diode technology. It also distributes precision optical lenses from Panasonic to OEMs in the industrial medical scientific and defense markets. ProPhotonix has operations in Ireland the UK and the US.

	Annual Growth	12/14	12/15	12/16	12/17	12/18
Sales ($ mil.)	(0.0%)	16.4	14.4	16.2	17.7	16.4
Net income ($ mil.)	–	(1.3)	0.3	1.3	2.0	(1.3)
Market value ($ mil.)	21.6%	2.7	1.9	5.8	9.3	5.9
Employees	–	–	–	–	–	–

PROS HOLDINGS INC   NYS: PRO

3100 Main Street, Suite 900
Houston, TX 77002
Phone: 713 335-5151
Fax: –
Web: www.pros.com

CEO: Andres D. Reiner
CFO: Stefan B. Schulz
HR: –
FYE: December 31
Type: Public

PROS Holdings can help you squeeze the most out of every single penny. The company provides price and revenue optimization software that customers use for tasks such as forecasting demand optimizing inventory allocation modeling price elasticity and monitoring transaction profitability. PROS' customers come from the distribution manufacturing services and travel industries. Some 800 companies such as airline Deutsche Lufthansa paper mill NewPage and industrial conglomerate Honeywell. It also offers professional services such as consulting support maintenance and implementation. PROS was founded in 1985.

	Annual Growth	12/14	12/15	12/16	12/17	12/18
Sales ($ mil.)	1.5%	185.8	168.2	153.3	168.8	197.0
Net income ($ mil.)	–	(36.6)	(65.8)	(75.2)	(77.9)	(64.2)
Market value ($ mil.)	3.4%	1,021.0	856.1	799.6	982.8	1,166.7
Employees	3.2%	1,011	1,033	1,018	1,066	1,145

PROSEK PARTNERS

1552 Post Rd.
Fairfield CT 06824
Phone: 203-254-1300
Fax: 203-254-1330
Web: www.prosek.com

CEO: –
CFO: Mike Del Vecchio
HR: –
FYE: December 31
Type: Private

Public relations firm Prosek Partners is positively pleased to provide financial communications and investor relations. It also offers traditional and digital media relations corporate advisory editorial public affairs and graphic and Web design services. Customers include energy professional services financial services insurance and technology companies. Prosek Partners serves regional national and international clients through offices in London; New York; and Fairfield Connecticut. Formerly Cubitt Jacobs & Prosek Communications the public relations agency is a minority- and women-owned business; it changed its name to Prosek Partners in 2012.

PROSPECT CAPITAL CORPORATION   NMS: PSEC

10 East 40th Street, 42nd Floor
New York, NY 10016
Phone: 212 448-0702
Fax: –
Web: www.prospectstreet.com

CEO: John F Barry III
CFO: Kristin Van Dask
HR: –
FYE: June 30
Type: Public

Prospect Capital is a closed-end investment fund with holdings in the consumer food health care and manufacturing sectors among others. The company targets privately held middle-market firms with annual revenues of less than $750 million; it also considers thinly traded public companies or turnaround situations. Prospect's portfolio includes interests in more than 100 companies mainly through senior loans and mezzanine debt. The company also makes equity and secured debt investments. Typically investing from $5 million to $250 million per transaction Prospect is a long-term investor that maintains regular contact with its portfolio company's management and participates in their board meetings.

	Annual Growth	06/13	06/14	06/15	06/16	06/17
Assets ($ mil.)	8.5%	4,448.2	6,477.3	6,798.1	6,276.7	6,172.8
Net income ($ mil.)	(1.5%)	324.9	357.2	362.7	371.1	306.1
Market value ($ mil.)	(6.9%)	3,888.8	3,825.8	2,653.8	2,815.8	2,923.8
Employees	–	–	–	–	–	–

PROSPECT MEDICAL HOLDINGS INC.

10780 Santa Monica Blvd. Ste. 400 — CEO: Samuel S Lee
Los Angeles CA 90025 — CFO: Mike Heather
Phone: 310-943-4500 — HR: –
Fax: 310-943-4501 — FYE: September 30
Web: www.prospectmedicalholdings.com — Type: Private

Prospect Medical Holdings sees synergies between hospitals and managed health care. The company owns and manages seven hospitals and about a dozen independent physicians associations (IPAs) in Southern California and Texas. Its hospital segment which includes the majority owned Brotman Medical Center has a total of about 1050 beds and provide acute care and specialty medical services. The firm's medical group segment provides administrative management services to about 7000 IPA member physicians which in turn provide health care to 181000 HMO enrollees for fixed monthly fees paid by the managed care organization to which they belong. Prospect is owned by private equity firm Leonard Green & Partners.

PROSPECT WATERBURY, INC.

64 ROBBINS ST — CEO: –
WATERBURY, CT 067082613 — CFO: –
Phone: 203-573-6000 — HR: –
Fax: – — FYE: December 31
 — Type: Private

Where do broken hearts go? Waterbury Hospital hopes it's to its cardiologists. The community teaching hospital serving western Connecticut has been named one of the top hospitals in the nation for cardiac intervention. Of course hearts aren't the only body parts Waterbury Hospital treats; the full-service facility has nearly 370 beds and offers services that include behavioral health care an orthopedic center and an outpatient surgery center. Waterbury Hospital founded in 1890 forms the cornerstone of the Greater Waterbury Health Network which provides a range of outpatient health services from nursing care to hospice imaging and lab services. Prospect Medical Holdings is buying Waterbury Hospital.

	Annual Growth	09/13	09/14	09/15	09/16*	12/17
Sales ($ mil.)	6.7%	–	–	–	206.9	220.8
Net income ($ mil.)	–	–	–	–	(3.8)	49.9
Market value ($ mil.)	–	–	–	–	–	–
Employees	–	–	–	–	–	1,625

*Fiscal year change

PROSPERITY BANCSHARES INC.   NYS: PB

Prosperity Bank Plaza, 4295 San Felipe — CEO: David Zalman
Houston, TX 77027 — CFO: David Hollaway
Phone: 281 269-7199 — HR: –
Fax: – — FYE: December 31
Web: www.prosperitybankusa.com — Type: Public

Prosperity Bancshares reaches banking customers across the Lone Star State. The holding company for Prosperity Bank operates about 230 branches across Texas and about 15 more in Oklahoma. Serving consumers and small to midsized businesses the bank offers traditional deposit and loan services in addition to wealth management retail brokerage and mortgage banking investment services. Prosperity Bank focuses on real estate lending: Commercial mortgages make up the largest segment of the company's loan portfolio (33%) followed by residential mortgages (24%). Credit cards business auto consumer home equity loans round out its lending activities.

	Annual Growth	12/14	12/15	12/16	12/17	12/18
Assets ($ mil.)	1.4%	21,507.7	22,037.2	22,331.1	22,587.3	22,693.4
Net income ($ mil.)	2.0%	297.4	286.6	274.5	272.2	321.8
Market value ($ mil.)	3.0%	3,866.7	3,342.9	5,013.6	4,894.2	4,351.5
Employees	(0.5%)	3,096	3,037	3,035	3,035	3,036

PROTALEX INC   NBB: PRTX

131 Columbia Turnpike, Suite 1 — CEO: –
Florham Park, NJ 07932 — CFO: Kirk M Warshaw
Phone: 215 862-9720 — HR: –
Fax: – — FYE: May 31
Web: www.protalex.com — Type: Public

Protalex is developing a technique called bioregulation to make drugs that control a disease instead of treating the symptoms after the disease has wreaked havoc on the body. The company's development programs target autoimmune diseases and inflammatory ailments. Lead drug candidate PRTX-100 is in early stage trials to target rheumatoid arthritis and idiopathic thrombocytopenic purpura (ITP) an autoimmune disorder characterized by excessive bleeding. Other potential disease targets include skin diseases psoriasis and pemphigus inflammatory bowel condition Crohn's disease and autoimmune disorders multiple sclerosis and lupus.

	Annual Growth	05/11	05/12	05/13	05/14	05/15
Sales ($ mil.)	–	0.0	0.0	0.0	0.0	0.0
Net income ($ mil.)	–	(3.4)	(4.4)	(6.3)	(11.9)	(11.6)
Market value ($ mil.)	33.2%	50.3	28.8	69.0	236.5	158.2
Employees	0.0%	3	3	3	3	3

PROTECTIVE INSURANCE CORP   NMS: PTVC B

111 Congressional Boulevard — CEO: W. Randall Birchfield
Carmel, IN 46032 — CFO: William C. Vens
Phone: 317 636-9800 — HR: –
Fax: – — FYE: December 31
Web: www.protectiveinsurance.com — Type: Public

Baldwin & Lyons (B&L) insures truckers bus drivers and other types of drivers. The company's Protective Insurance subsidiary licensed in the US and Canada writes property/casualty insurance for large to midsized trucking fleets and public transportation fleets. It also covers independent contractors in the trucking industry. B&L's Sagamore Insurance subsidiary provides insurance to high-risk private auto drivers throughout most of the US through a network of independent agents. It also markets physical-damage insurance and liability insurance for small trucking fleets and for large and midsized bus fleets. Founded in 1930 B&L also provides property/casualty reinsurance and brokerage services.

	Annual Growth	12/14	12/15	12/16	12/17	12/18
Assets ($ mil.)	6.8%	1,144.2	1,085.8	1,154.1	1,357.0	1,490.1
Net income ($ mil.)	–	29.7	23.3	28.9	18.3	(34.1)
Market value ($ mil.)	(10.3%)	383.3	357.3	374.7	356.1	247.6
Employees	5.9%	425	438	455	528	535

PROTECTIVE LIFE CORP.   NYS: PL

2801 Highway 280 South — CEO: John D Johns
Birmingham, AL 35223 — CFO: Richard J Bielen
Phone: 205 268-1000 — HR: –
Fax: – — FYE: December 31
Web: www.protective.com — Type: Public

Protective Life wants to cushion its customers from the nasty blows of life and death. The company primarily sells life insurance products through its Life Marketing business segment including universal term and bank-owned life insurance coverage; Protective Life also brings in and manages blocks of life insurance policies sold elsewhere through its Acquisitions segment. The firm's Asset Protection unit sells extended service contracts and credit life insurance while its Annuities division offers fixed and variable annuities. The Stable Value Products unit sells guaranteed funding agreements for financial instruments such as municipal bonds and the ProEquities brokerage serves independent financial advisors.

	Annual Growth	12/08	12/09	12/10	12/11	12/12
Assets ($ mil.)	9.7%	39,572.4	42,311.6	47,562.8	52,932.1	57,384.7
Net income ($ mil.)	–	(41.9)	271.5	260.2	339.1	302.5
Market value ($ mil.)	18.8%	1,121.3	1,293.2	2,081.6	1,762.8	2,233.2
Employees	(0.9%)	2,372	2,317	2,315	2,332	2,284

PROTECTIVE LIFE INSURANCE CO

2801 Highway 280 South
Birmingham, AL 35223
Phone: 205 268-1000
Fax: –
Web: www.protective.com

CEO: John D. Johns
CFO: Steven G. Walker
HR: –
FYE: December 31
Type: Public

Protective Life & Annuity markets and sells financial security in the form of term and universal life insurance policies and fixed and variable annuity products. Although the company is based in Alabama and licensed to sell insurance throughout the US it exclusively serves clients in New York. Sister companies include West Coast Life Insurance (life insurance and annuities) MONY Life Insurance (ditto) and Lyndon Insurance (specialty coverage). Protective Life & Annuity is a unit of Protective Life Insurance which is part of Dai-Ichi Life Holdings subsidiary Protective Life Corporation.

	Annual Growth	01/15*	12/15	12/16	12/17	12/18
Assets ($ mil.)	9.5%	–	68,031.9	74,465.1	79,113.7	89,383.1
Net income ($ mil.)	29.9%	88.5	179.7	352.6	1,182.4	193.9
Market value ($ mil.)	–	–	–	–	–	–
Employees	5.2%	–	2,541	2,719	2,773	2,957

*Fiscal year change

PROTESTANT MEMORIAL MEDICAL CENTER, INC.

4500 MEMORIAL DR
BELLEVILLE, IL 622265360
Phone: 618-233-7750
Fax: –
Web: www.memhosp.com

CEO: –
CFO: –
HR: John Ziegler
FYE: December 31
Type: Private

With more than 315 beds Memorial Hospital has plenty of space to take care of Prairie Staters. The Bellevue Illinois-based hospital is owned and operated by Protestant Memorial Medical Center a community-based not-for-profit organization. Memorial Hospital provides general medical surgical and emergency care as well as pediatric home health and cardiovascular care. Specialty services include treatment for sleep disorders and women's health. The hospital also operates Memorial Convalescent Center a nearly 110-bed skilled nursing facility and the Belleville Health and Sports Center which provides fitness facilities to promote community health.

	Annual Growth	12/13	12/14	12/15	12/16	12/17
Sales ($ mil.)	(3.2%)	–	261.5	281.8	240.7	237.4
Net income ($ mil.)	–	–	23.3	35.9	(11.7)	(9.3)
Market value ($ mil.)	–	–	–	–	–	–
Employees	–	–	–	–	–	2,344

PROTEXT MOBILITY INC

22 S.E. 2nd Avenue
Delray Beach, FL 33444
Phone: 800 215-4212
Fax: –
Web: www.protextmobility.net

NBB: TXTM
CEO: Roger Baylis-Duffield
CFO: –
HR: –
FYE: December 31
Type: Public

Echo Metrix (formerly SearchHelp) makes sure children are always under a watchful eye. The company provides parental control software designed to monitor the activity of children while they surf the Web send instant messages or chat online. Its Sentry At Home software alerts parents via e-mail or mobile phone when established usage guidelines are violated. The company's Sentry Remote software allows parents to monitor their children's online activities in real-time and remotely shut down their computers. Echo Metrix also developed an application for tracking registered sex offenders but it decided to discontinue that line in 2008.

	Annual Growth	12/09	12/10	12/11	12/12	12/13
Sales ($ mil.)	(62.2%)	0.0	0.0	0.0	0.0	0.0
Net income ($ mil.)	–	(4.5)	(5.7)	(3.6)	(2.2)	(1.4)
Market value ($ mil.)	–	0.1	0.3	0.0	0.0	0.0
Employees	(38.5%)	7	5	4	1	1

PROTO LABS INC

5540 Pioneer Creek Drive
Maple Plain, MN 55359
Phone: 763 479-3680
Fax: –
Web: www.protolabs.com

NYS: PRLB
CEO: Victoria M. (Vicki) Holt
CFO: John A. Way
HR: –
FYE: December 31
Type: Public

Proto Labs creates custom parts in quick turnaround for prototypes and short-run production. The company's web-based interface allows customers to upload a 3D CAD file and Proto Labs' software can quickly quote a price. The Injection Molded division (47% of sales) produces aluminum molds for production of plastic and rubber injection-molded parts. Proto Labs' CNC Machining segment (35% of sales) uses milling machinery to produce custom products. The 3D Printing division (12% of sales) makes plastic and metal parts. The company's Sheet Metal segment (6% of sales) can produce between one and 500 precision metal products. The US accounts for about 80% of Proto Labs' sales.

	Annual Growth	12/14	12/15	12/16	12/17	12/18
Sales ($ mil.)	20.8%	209.6	264.1	298.1	344.5	445.6
Net income ($ mil.)	16.5%	41.6	46.5	42.7	51.8	76.6
Market value ($ mil.)	13.8%	1,812.3	1,718.7	1,385.7	2,779.4	3,043.6
Employees	23.3%	1,077	1,549	1,700	2,266	2,487

PROVECTUS PHARMACEUTICALS INC.

7327 Oak Ridge Hwy. Ste. A
Knoxville TN 37931
Phone: 865-769-4011
Fax: 865-769-4013
Web: www.pvct.com

OTC: PVCT
CEO: –
CFO: John Glass
HR: –
FYE: December 31
Type: Public

Provectus prospects the death of cancer. Provectus Pharmaceuticals designs pharmaceuticals for the treatment of cancer and various skin problems. Its Provectus Pharmatech division is developing prescription drugs for the treatment of eczema psoriasis and acne as well as therapeutics targeting breast liver and prostate cancers and melanoma. In addition the company develops laser-based medical devices and anti-cancer vaccines through its Provectus Devicetech and Provectus Biotech divisions respectively. Provectus also has over-the-counter drug assets through its Pure-ific division. Together CEO Craig Dees president Timothy Scott and EVP Eric Wachter control about 16% of the company's shares.

PROVIDE COMMERCE INC.

5005 Wateridge Vista Dr.
San Diego CA 92121
Phone: 858-638-4900
Fax: 858-638-4708
Web: www.providecommerce.com

CEO: Chris Shimojima
CFO: Adam Fischer
HR: –
FYE: June 30
Type: Subsidiary

Provide Commerce keeps the perishable goods and gift markets fresh. The majority of the e-tailer's sales are generated by ProFlowers.com and ProPlants.com which ship flowers plants and wreaths directly from growers to residential and corporate clients. The Internet florist also offers chocolate popcorn and fruit and cheese baskets. Provide Commerce's Cherry Moon Farms and Sharis Berries virtual shops offer hand-picked fruits hand-dipped sweets and wine. In addition to gourmet perishables the company operates RedEnvelope (acquired in 2008) and Personal Creations (acquired in 2010) which sell upscale and personalized gifts and jewelry. Founded in 1998 Provide Commerce is owned Liberty Interactive.

PROVIDENCE & WORCESTER RAILROAD CO. NMS: PWX

75 Hammond Street
Worcester, MA 01610
Phone: 508 755-4000
Fax: -
Web: www.pwrr.com

CEO: -
CFO: Daniel T Noreck
HR: -
FYE: December 31
Type: Public

Giving an island its link Providence and Worcester Railroad (P&W) stands as Rhode Island's sole interstate freight carrier. The regional freight railroad operates over a network of about 545 miles of track in Connecticut Massachusetts New York and Rhode Island. It hauls such goods as chemicals and plastics construction aggregate food and forest and paper products for more than 160 customers. Major customers include Cargill Dow Chemical Frito-Lay International Paper and GDF SUEZ Energy. P&W interchanges freight traffic with CSX the New England Central Railroad the New York and Atlantic Railroad and Pan Am Railways (formerly Springfield Terminal Railway).

	Annual Growth	12/10	12/11	12/12	12/13	12/14
Sales ($ mil.)	3.5%	29.9	33.7	30.0	33.3	34.3
Net income ($ mil.)	-	(0.3)	0.9	3.5	1.4	3.2
Market value ($ mil.)	1.9%	81.4	55.4	67.8	95.0	87.9
Employees	0.2%	137	147	147	141	138

PROVIDENCE COLLEGE

1 CUNNINGHAM SQ
PROVIDENCE, RI 029187001
Phone: 401-865-1000
Fax: -
Web: www.providence.edu

CEO: -
CFO: -
HR: Kathleen Alvino
FYE: June 30
Type: Private

Students don't need divine intervention to get into Providence College they just need good grades and an interest in liberal arts. The Catholic institution of higher education offers undergraduate and graduate degrees at its four schools: Arts and Sciences Business Continuing Education and Professional Studies. It offers degrees in about 50 academic disciplines including biology business education marketing politics and psychology. It has a student-to-faculty ratio of 12:1 with students primarily coming from New England and the Midwest and Mid-Atlantic regions. Providence College was founded in 1917 by the Dominican Friars of the Province of St. Joseph and the Diocese of Providence.

	Annual Growth	06/10	06/11	06/12	06/13	06/15
Sales ($ mil.)	6.1%	-	-	-	237.6	267.4
Net income ($ mil.)	3.3%	-	-	-	22.4	23.9
Market value ($ mil.)	-	-	-	-	-	-
Employees	-	-	-	-	-	800

PROVIDENCE RESOURCES INC. OTC: PVRS

5300 Bee Caves Rd. Bldg. 1 Ste. 240
Austin TX 78746
Phone: 512-970-2888
Fax: 501-666-4741
Web: www.cdicon.com

CEO: Nora Coccaro
CFO: Nora Coccaro
HR: -
FYE: December 31
Type: Public

Guided perhaps by Providence Providence Resources (formerly Healthbridge a development-stage company that had plans to market medical waste sterilization and disposal systems) changed course in 2006 and acquired Providence Exploration a company that drills for oil and natural gas and provides drilling services in Texas. It has interests in approximately 6272 acres of oil and gas leases in Comanche and Hamilton Counties and holds 12832 acres of oil and gas leases in Val Verde County. Providence Resources also provides drilling services through its PDX Drilling I LLC subsidiary. Company director Markus Mueller owns 14% of Providence Resources.

PROVIDENCE SERVICE CORP NMS: PRSC

1275 Peachtree Street, Sixth Floor
Atlanta, GA 30309
Phone: 404 888-5800
Fax: 520 747-6605
Web: www.prscholdings.com

CEO: Carter Pate
CFO: David Shackelton
HR: -
FYE: December 31
Type: Public

Social services firm Providence Service Corporation operates through two primary segments: Non-Emergency Transportation Services (NET Services also known as LogistiCare) and Workforce Development Services (WD Services). Through these segments the company provides provide non-emergency transportation to people in home and community-based settings manages foster care systems provides correctional support such as probation supervision offers job training and provides substance abuse treatment. Providence operates in about 40 states and in about 10 countries abroad.

	Annual Growth	12/14	12/15	12/16	12/17	12/18
Sales ($ mil.)	(1.7%)	1,481.2	1,695.4	1,578.9	1,623.9	1,385.0
Net income ($ mil.)	-	20.3	83.7	91.9	53.4	(19.0)
Market value ($ mil.)	13.3%	467.0	601.3	487.6	760.4	769.1
Employees	(26.5%)	13,700	9,072	7,590	7,100	4,000

PROVIDENT COMMUNITY BANCSHARES, INC. NBB: PCBS

2700 Celanese Road
Rock Hill, SC 29732
Phone: 803 325-9400
Fax: -
Web: www.providentonline.com

CEO: -
CFO: -
HR: -
FYE: December 31
Type: Public

Provident Community Bancshares (formerly Union Financial Bancshares) is the holding company for Provident Community Bank which operates about 10 branches in Laurens Union Fairfield Greenville and York counties in northern South Carolina. The bank attracts deposits from local consumers and businesses by offering checking and savings accounts money market and NOW accounts CDs and IRAs. Its lending activities mainly consist of business loans commercial mortgages and consumer and installment loans. The bank also offers investments brokerage services retirement planning and credit cards.

	Annual Growth	12/08	12/09	12/10	12/11	12/12
Assets ($ mil.)	(5.3%)	434.2	457.0	408.7	376.6	349.9
Net income ($ mil.)	-	(0.4)	(7.4)	(13.8)	(0.2)	(0.1)
Market value ($ mil.)	(59.1%)	17.9	4.2	1.2	0.2	0.5
Employees	(3.8%)	84	79	77	74	72

PROVIDENT FINANCIAL HOLDINGS, INC. NMS: PROV

3756 Central Avenue
Riverside, CA 92506
Phone: 951 686-6060
Fax: -
Web: www.myprovident.com

CEO: Craig G Blunden
CFO: Donavon P Ternes
HR: -
FYE: June 30
Type: Public

Provident Financial Holdings is the holding company for Provident Savings Bank which operates more than a dozen branches in Southern California's Riverside and San Bernardino counties. Catering to individuals and small to midsized businesses the bank offers such standard retail products as checking and savings accounts money market accounts and CDs as well as retirement planning services. Real estate loans including single-family multifamily and commercial mortgages and construction loans make up essentially all of the company's loan portfolio. Single-family residential mortgages make up more than half of all loans.

	Annual Growth	06/15	06/16	06/17	06/18	06/19
Assets ($ mil.)	(2.0%)	1,174.6	1,171.4	1,200.6	1,175.5	1,084.9
Net income ($ mil.)	(18.1%)	9.8	7.5	5.2	2.1	4.4
Market value ($ mil.)	5.8%	125.3	137.0	144.1	142.8	157.1
Employees	(22.9%)	528	522	464	376	187

PROVIDENT FINANCIAL SERVICES INC   NYS: PFS

239 Washington Street
Jersey City, NJ 07302
Phone: 732 590-9200
Fax: –
Web: www.providentnj.com

CEO: Christopher P. Martin
CFO: Thomas M. Lyons
HR: Janet D. Krasowski
FYE: December 31
Type: Public

Provident wants to be a prominent force in the New Jersey banking scene. Provident Financial Services owns The Provident Bank which serves individuals businesses and families from 85 branches across more than 10 northern and central New Jersey counties. Founded in 1839 the $8.5 billion-bank offers traditional deposit and lending products as well as wealth management and trust services. About 50% of its revenue comes from real estate loan interest while another 25% comes from interest on commercial and consumer loans. Construction loans round out its lending activities. The company's Provident Investment Services subsidiary sells life and health insurance and investment products.

	Annual Growth	12/14	12/15	12/16	12/17	12/18
Assets ($ mil.)	3.4%	8,523.4	8,911.7	9,500.5	9,845.3	9,725.8
Net income ($ mil.)	12.6%	73.6	83.7	87.8	93.9	118.4
Market value ($ mil.)	7.5%	1,197.8	1,336.5	1,877.0	1,788.8	1,600.4
Employees	0.6%	1,021	1,064	1,057	1,054	1,044

PRUDENTIAL ANNUITIES LIFE ASSURANCE CORP   NL:

One Corporate Drive
Shelton, CT 06484
Phone: 203 926-1888
Fax: –
Web: www.investor.prudential.com

CEO: Robert F O'Donnell
CFO: Yanela C Frias
HR: –
FYE: December 31
Type: Public

Prudential Annuities Life Assurance has a name that fits — the company is the annuities business unit of life insurance giant Prudential Financial. It offers variable and fixed annuities and other retirement and long-term investment products and services. Prudential Annuities Life Assurance's products are distributed through independent financial planners brokers and banks. It holds the lead position in the US variable annuities market; its variable annuities are distributed by Prudential Annuities Distributors. The company which is part of Prudential Financial's US Retirement Solutions and Investment Management Division targets US residents with a household income level of above $100000.

	Annual Growth	12/14	12/15	12/16	12/17	12/18
Assets ($ mil.)	1.0%	52,472.8	47,254.7	59,822.2	59,960.9	54,677.8
Net income ($ mil.)	60.9%	250.8	173.2	(1,090.1)	(83.5)	1,682.7
Market value ($ mil.)	–	–	–	–	–	–
Employees	–	–	–	–	–	–

PRUDENTIAL FINANCIAL INC   NYS: PRU

751 Broad Street
Newark, NJ 07102
Phone: 973 802-6000
Fax: –
Web: www.investor.prudential.com

CEO: John R. Strangfeld
CFO: Robert M. Falzon
HR: Sharon C. Taylor
FYE: December 31
Type: Public

Prudential Financial wants to make sure its position near the top of the life insurance summit is set in stone. Prudential known for its Rock of Gibraltar logo is one of the top US life insurers and one of the largest life insurance companies worldwide. The firm is perhaps best known for its individual life insurance though it also sells group life and disability insurance as well as annuities. Prudential also offers investment products and services including asset management services mutual funds and retirement planning. In Asia the company operates through its Gibraltar Life Insurance and Life Planner units. Prudential has some $1.4 trillion in assets under management.

	Annual Growth	12/14	12/15	12/16	12/17	12/18
Assets ($ mil.)	1.5%	766,655.0	757,388.0	783,962.0	831,921.0	815,078.0
Net income ($ mil.)	31.1%	1,381.0	5,642.0	4,368.0	7,863.0	4,074.0
Market value ($ mil.)	(2.6%)	37,153.0	33,436.1	42,738.7	47,223.7	33,493.6
Employees	1.1%	48,331	49,384	49,739	49,705	50,492

PRUDENTIAL OVERALL SUPPLY

1661 ALTON PKWY
IRVINE, CA 926064877
Phone: 949-250-4855
Fax: –
Web: www.prudentialuniforms.com

CEO: Dan Clark
CFO: –
HR: –
FYE: December 31
Type: Private

Prudential works to outfit every member of your organization. From uniforms to career apparel Prudential Overall Supply rents sells and leases workwear to those in food service health care manufacturing and the government. The company also rents and sells industrial-grade products (entrance and logo mats) and janitorial supplies (dust mops paper towels and cleansers). In addition to its products Prudential offers industrial cleaning and laundering services. The company operates about 30 branches in the US more than half of which are located in California and sells its products online and through catalogs. Prudential has been family-owned and -operated since its founding in 1932.

	Annual Growth	12/07	12/08	12/10	12/11	12/14
Sales ($ mil.)	–	–	0.0	139.9	141.0	158.2
Net income ($ mil.)	–	–	0.0	1.3	4.3	7.6
Market value ($ mil.)	–	–	–	–	–	–
Employees	–	–	–	–	–	1,457

PRWT SERVICES, INC.

1835 MARKET ST STE 800
PHILADELPHIA, PA 191032919
Phone: 215-563-7698
Fax: –
Web: www.prwt.com

CEO: Malik Majeed
CFO: Don Peloso
HR: –
FYE: December 31
Type: Private

Vowels are overrated. PRWT Services provides outsourced customer support services to a variety of industries. Services include payment processing call center services document processing claims administration mailroom operations and other technical support services. PRWT also provides toll operations services for Delaware River Authority and fulfillment of stationary forms envelopes business cards and other business supplies. PRWT's subsidiaries include U.S. Facilities (facilities maintenance and management) and Cherokee Pharmaceuticals (pharmaceutical ingredients manufacturer). PRWT considered forming a subsidiary and merging with KBL Healthcare Acquisition Corp. but the deal fell through in July 2009.

	Annual Growth	12/03	12/04	12/05	12/06	12/10
Sales ($ mil.)	–	–	–	(563.3)	66.5	89.8
Net income ($ mil.)	869.8%	–	–	0.0	0.2	7.7
Market value ($ mil.)	–	–	–	–	–	–
Employees	–	–	–	–	–	1,312

PS BUSINESS PARKS INC   NYS: PSB PRZ

701 Western Avenue
Glendale, CA 91201-2349
Phone: 818 244-8080
Fax: 818 242-0566
Web: www.psbusinessparks.com

CEO: Maria R. Hawthorne
CFO: Edward A Stokx
HR: –
FYE: December 31
Type: Public

Pssst! Know where a fella can find some spare flex space? PS Business Parks does. The company is a self-managed real estate investment trust (REIT) that owns develops and operates industrial office and flex (combined industrial and office) properties. The REIT owns assets in eight states with concentrations in California Virginia Florida and Texas. Its portfolio includes some 27 million sq. ft. of multi-tenant industrial and office space including light manufacturing plants warehouses distribution centers and research and development facilities. The company also manages more than 1 million sq. ft. of properties owned by self-storage giant Public Storage which owns some 23% of PS Business Parks.

	Annual Growth	12/14	12/15	12/16	12/17	12/18
Sales ($ mil.)	2.3%	376.9	373.7	387.4	402.2	413.5
Net income ($ mil.)	6.8%	174.0	130.5	128.0	155.0	226.7
Market value ($ mil.)	–	–	–	–	–	–
Employees	(1.8%)	168	142	157	158	156

PSB HOLDINGS INC
NAS: PSBH

40 Main Street
Putnam, CT 06260
Phone: 860 928-6501
Fax: 860 928-2147
Web: www.putnambank.com

CEO: –
CFO: –
HR: –
FYE: June 30
Type: Public

PSB Holdings thinks it offers Pretty Smart Banking for the businesses and individuals of Connecticut's Windham and New London counties. The holding company owns Putnam Savings Bank a thrift with about 10 bank branches and lending offices. Putnam Savings Bank offers standard deposit products and services including checking and savings accounts merchant and check cards CDs and IRAs. It largely uses funds from deposits to write real estate loans: Residential and commercial mortgages together account for about 95% of the bank's loan portfolio. Mutual holding company Putnam Bancorp owns a majority stake in PSB Holdings.

	Annual Growth	06/10	06/11	06/12	06/13	06/14
Assets ($ mil.)	(1.5%)	489.4	472.5	452.3	454.4	461.0
Net income ($ mil.)	(5.6%)	1.3	1.1	1.1	1.3	1.0
Market value ($ mil.)	8.6%	31.6	34.0	27.3	36.7	44.0
Employees	0.0%	121	120	122	118	121

PSCU INCORPORATED

560 CARILLON PKWY
SAINT PETERSBURG, FL 337161294
Phone: 727-572-8822
Fax: –
Web: www.pscu.com

CEO: Michael J. (Mike) Kelly
CFO: Brian Caldarelli
HR: Lynn Heckler
FYE: September 30
Type: Private

Credit unions turn to PSCU to provide key card services. As one of the nation's largest credit union service organizations PSCU (short for Payment Systems for Credit Unions) provides credit debit ATM and prepaid card servicing as well as electronic banking bill payment risk management specialized marketing and contact center services to credit unions across the US. The not-for-profit cooperative serves more than 1300 institutions nationwide which combined represent more than 18 million cardholder accounts and one million online bill payment subscribers. PSCU is owned by about 800 member credit unions.

	Annual Growth	12/10	12/11	12/12*	09/16	09/18
Sales ($ mil.)	1.8%	–	425.2	377.0	458.8	481.7
Net income ($ mil.)	(12.7%)	–	29.3	38.6	28.1	11.4
Market value ($ mil.)	–	–	–	–	–	–
Employees	–	–	–	–	–	1,850

*Fiscal year change

PSEG POWER LLC
NYS: PEG 31

80 Park Plaza
Newark, NJ 07102
Phone: 973 430-7000
Fax: –
Web: www.pseg.com

CEO: Ralph Izzo
CFO: Daniel J Cregg
HR: –
FYE: December 31
Type: Public

Power player PSEG Power does not play with power it markets it for profit. The company is the independent power production and energy marketing subsidiary of Public Service Enterprise Group (PSEG). The unit owns and/or manages about 25 power stations in Connecticut New Jersey New York and Pennsylvania. It oversees PSEG Nuclear LLC (which operates the Salem and Hope Creek generating stations in New Jersey and owns 50% of the Peach Bottom plant in Pennsylvania) and PSEG Fossil LLC (which has gas oil coal and natural gas power plants). PSEG Power has installed capacity of more than 13466 MW. Its PSEG Energy Resources and Trade unit buys and sells wholesale power natural gas and other energy commodities.

	Annual Growth	12/14	12/15	12/16	12/17	12/18
Sales ($ mil.)	(6.5%)	5,434.0	4,928.0	4,023.0	3,930.0	4,146.0
Net income ($ mil.)	(16.8%)	760.0	856.0	18.0	479.0	365.0
Market value ($ mil.)	–	–	–	–	–	–
Employees	(8.1%)	2,973	2,939	2,714	2,367	2,122

PSYCHEMEDICS CORP.
NAS: PMD

289 Great Road
Acton, MA 01720
Phone: 978 206-8220
Fax: –
Web: www.psychemedics.com

CEO: Raymond C Kubacki
CFO: –
HR: –
FYE: December 31
Type: Public

Beware of giving a lock of hair as a keepsake — it could end up at Psychemedics which provides drug testing services through the analysis of hair samples. Its tests which it markets under the brand name RIAH (or Radioimmunoassay of Hair) not only reveal that a substance has been consumed but also detect patterns of use over time; the tests look for cocaine marijuana PCP Ecstasy and opiates. The company's primary market is employers who use the service for pre-employment screening as well as random testing of current employees. Psychemedics also sells its service to hundreds of schools nationwide (and in some foreign countries) and offers a service to parents worried that their kids might be on drugs.

	Annual Growth	12/14	12/15	12/16	12/17	12/18
Sales ($ mil.)	9.9%	29.2	27.0	39.0	39.7	42.7
Net income ($ mil.)	9.3%	3.2	1.5	6.7	6.1	4.6
Market value ($ mil.)	1.2%	83.4	55.8	135.9	113.2	87.4
Employees	12.5%	156	154	206	231	250

PTC INC
NMS: PTC

121 Seaport Boulevard
Boston, MA 02210
Phone: 781 370-5000
Fax: –
Web: www.ptc.com

CEO: James E. (Jim) Heppelmann
CFO: Andrew D. Miller
HR: –
FYE: September 30
Type: Public

PTC's offerings in CAD PLM the IoT and AR help customers digitize operations and collaborate. In computer aided design (CAD) its Creo offering is used to create 3D computer models for products ranging from engines to phones. PTC's Windchill software suite for product lifecycle management (PLM) enables collaborative content and process management over the internet. With ThingWorx PTC provides a platform for developing applications for the Internet of Things (IoT). The augmented reality (AR) product Vuforia Studio overlays digital information such as repair instructions onto the view of physical objects and processes. The Americas and Europe each account for about 40% of PTC's revenue.

	Annual Growth	09/15	09/16	09/17	09/18	09/19
Sales ($ mil.)	0.0%	1,255.2	1,140.5	1,164.0	1,241.8	1,255.6
Net income ($ mil.)	–	47.6	(54.5)	6.2	52.0	(27.5)
Market value ($ mil.)	21.1%	3,646.9	5,091.2	6,466.5	12,201.1	7,833.8
Employees	0.3%	5,982	5,800	6,041	6,110	6,055

PTC THERAPEUTICS INC
NMS: PTCT

100 Corporate Court
South Plainfield, NJ 07080
Phone: 908 222-7000
Fax: –
Web: www.ptcbio.com

CEO: Stuart W. Peltz
CFO: Shane Kovacs
HR: Martin Rexroad
FYE: December 31
Type: Public

PTC Therapeutics has some real GEMS in its pipeline. The firm uses a proprietary technology called GEMS to screen for small molecules that modulate post-transcriptional control mechanisms which regulate protein synthesis and thereby offer potential control over certain diseases. PTC is targeting these mechanisms to develop oral drugs designed to treat various genetic disorders infectious diseases and cancers. Lead drug candidate ataluren (Translarna) is licensed in Europe and South Korea for Duchenne muscular dystrophy; it is also being tested for the treatment of cystic fibrosis. Candidates in earlier stages of development address spinal muscular atrophy chemo-resistant cancers and HIV.

	Annual Growth	12/14	12/15	12/16	12/17	12/18
Sales ($ mil.)	80.0%	25.2	36.8	82.7	194.4	264.7
Net income ($ mil.)	–	(93.8)	(170.4)	(142.1)	(79.0)	(128.1)
Market value ($ mil.)	(9.8%)	2,619.9	1,639.6	552.1	844.1	1,736.8
Employees	27.9%	193	320	304	373	517

PUBLIC BROADCASTING SERVICE

2100 CRYSTAL DR STE 100
ARLINGTON, VA 222023784
Phone: 703-739-5000
Fax: –
Web: www.pbs.org

CEO: Paula A. Kerger
CFO: Barbara L. Landes
HR: –
FYE: June 30
Type: Private

You might say these shows get a lot of public support. Public Broadcasting Service (PBS) is a non-profit organization that provides educational and public interest programming to more than 350 member public TV stations in the US. In addition to such programs as NOVA This Old House and Downton Abbey it provides related services such as distribution fundraising support and technology development. PBS gets its revenue from underwriting membership dues federal funding (including grants from the not-for-profit Corporation for Public Broadcasting) royalties license fees and product sales. The organization was founded in 1969 to provide cultural and educational programming.

	Annual Growth	06/08	06/09	06/10	06/14	06/15
Sales ($ mil.)	(1.0%)	–	502.6	505.6	539.6	473.3
Net income ($ mil.)	–	–	(80.6)	28.2	89.9	(46.9)
Market value ($ mil.)	–	–	–	–	–	–
Employees	–	–	–	–	–	507

PUBLIC COMMUNICATIONS SERVICES, INC.

11859 WILSHIRE BLVD # 600
LOS ANGELES, CA 900256621
Phone: 310-231-1000
Fax: –
Web: www.teampcs.com

CEO: Paul Jennings
CFO: Dennis Komai
HR: –
FYE: December 31
Type: Private

Public Communications Services (PCS) designs and installs inmate telephone systems for state federal and county correctional facilities across the US. Its systems feature collect pre-paid and debit calling as well as automated call processing and security features like blocking of certain phone numbers. Clients can also use the company's proprietary systems management software called SOPHIA to run reports on inmate usage and to monitor and record conversations. Customers include the Ventura County California Sheriff's Department and the Federal Bureau of Prisons.

	Annual Growth	12/02	12/03	12/04	12/07	12/08
Sales ($ mil.)	10.1%	–	49.2	34.7	80.5	79.7
Net income ($ mil.)	21.2%	–	1.8	2.8	3.8	4.8
Market value ($ mil.)	–	–	–	–	–	–
Employees	–	–	–	–	–	150

PUBLIC HEALTH SOLUTIONS

40 WORTH ST FL 5
NEW YORK, NY 100132955
Phone: 646-619-6400
Fax: –
Web: www.healthsolutions.org

CEO: Ellen Rautenberg
CFO: –
HR: –
FYE: December 31
Type: Private

Public Heath Solutions (formerly Medical and Health Research Association of New York City) is here to help. Public Health Solutions (PHS) is a not-for-profit organization that works with the NYC Department of Health to create and administer projects aimed at providing better healthcare to the city's low-income at-risk population. It helps about 200000 people a year with studies like the Human Papillomavirus Screening Project and others looking at disease awareness and prevention in minority groups. Services include women's and children's health HIV/AIDS health care smoking cessation counseling and access to health care. The organization was founded in 1957 to conduct health research projects.

	Annual Growth	12/05	12/06	12/07	12/13	12/15
Sales ($ mil.)	(0.4%)	–	214.2	225.6	202.0	207.0
Net income ($ mil.)	–	–	(2.1)	7.4	2.9	0.4
Market value ($ mil.)	–	–	–	–	–	–
Employees	–	–	–	–	–	650

PUBLIC HEALTH TRUST OF MIAMI DADE COUNTY

1611 NW 12TH AVE
MIAMI, FL 331361005
Phone: 305-585-1111
Fax: –

CEO: Carlos A. Migoya
CFO:
HR: –
FYE: September 30
Type: Private

Jackson Memorial Hospital is the flagship facility of the Jackson Health System (JHS). It has roughly 2450 beds and offers a wide variety of services including burn treatment trauma pediatrics rehabilitation obstetrics and transplants. It is also a teaching facility for the University of Miami School of Medicine. JHS also operates Holtz Children's Hospital a rehabilitation hospital a mental health hospital primary and specialty care centers two long-term care nursing facilities six corrections health clinics and two community hospitals. Jackson Memorial Hospital and JHS are overseen by The Public Health Trust of Miami-Dade County.

	Annual Growth	09/02	09/03*	06/05*	09/15	09/17
Sales ($ mil.)	1.4%	–	960.1	0.0	883.0	1,160.2
Net income ($ mil.)	–	–	(26.8)	0.0	200.3	184.6
Market value ($ mil.)	–	–	–	–	–	–
Employees	–	–	–	–	–	11,000

*Fiscal year change

PUBLIC SERVICE COMPANY OF OKLAHOMA

NBB: PSOK

1 Riverside Plaza
Columbus, OH 43215-2373
Phone: 614 716-1000
Fax: –

CEO: Nicholas K Akins
CFO: Brian X Tierney
HR: –
FYE: December 31
Type: Public

Where the wavin' wheat can sure smell sweet Public Service Company of Oklahoma helps its customers to beat the heat. The utility serves approximately 540000 homes and businesses in eastern and southwestern Oklahoma. The American Electric Power (AEP) subsidiary operates more than 22080 miles of electric transmission and distribution lines in eastern and southwestern Oklahoma. The utility also has about 4230 MW of capacity from interests in fossil-fueled power plants and it markets wholesale electricity to other utilities and energy companies in the region. it also has wind energy assets.

	Annual Growth	12/14	12/15	12/16	12/17	12/18
Sales ($ mil.)	3.4%	1,351.6	1,339.2	1,249.8	1,427.2	1,547.3
Net income ($ mil.)	(1.1%)	86.9	92.5	100.0	72.0	83.2
Market value ($ mil.)	–	–	–	–	–	–
Employees	(0.2%)	1,133	1,134	1,110	1,141	1,125

PUBLIC SERVICE ENTERPRISE GROUP INC

NYS: PEG

80 Park Plaza
Newark, NJ 07102
Phone: 973 430-7000
Fax: –
Web: www.pseg.com

CEO: Ralph Izzo
CFO: Daniel J. (Dan) Cregg
HR: –
FYE: December 31
Type: Public

In the Garden State Public Service Enterprise Group's (PSEG) diversified business model has it smelling like a rose. Regulated subsidiary Public Service Electric and Gas (PSE&G) transmits and distributes electricity to 2.2 million customers and natural gas to 1.8 million customers in New Jersey. Subsidiary PSEG Power operates power generating plants and sells its energy wholesale to PSE&G and others. PSEG Power's 11800-MW generating capacity comes mostly from nuclear and fossil-fuel plants in the US Northeast and Mid-Atlantic regions.

	Annual Growth	12/14	12/15	12/16	12/17	12/18
Sales ($ mil.)	(2.9%)	10,886.0	10,415.0	9,061.0	9,084.0	9,696.0
Net income ($ mil.)	(1.3%)	1,518.0	1,679.0	887.0	1,574.0	1,438.0
Market value ($ mil.)	5.9%	20,870.6	19,499.8	22,115.5	25,956.0	26,233.2
Employees	0.9%	12,689	13,025	13,065	12,945	13,145

PUBLIC STORAGE
NYS: PSA

701 Western Avenue
Glendale, CA 91201-2349
Phone: 818 244-8080
Fax: 818 244-0581
Web: www.publicstorage.com

CEO: Ronald L. Havner
CFO: John Reyes
HR: Candace Krol
FYE: December 31
Type: Public

If the attic and garage are stuffed with stuff you can't bear to toss out it might be time to call Public Storage. The real estate investment trust (REIT) is one of the largest self-storage companies in the US. It operates nearly 2400 storage facilities under the Public Storage brand comprising some 160 million sq. ft. of storage space in the US and about 220 facilities in Europe under the Shurgard brand. The firm's self-storage properties located in densely populated areas generate about 95% of the company's sales. Public Storage which was founded in 1980 also sells moving supplies such as locks boxes and packing supplies. The company owns part of publicly traded PS Business Parks an office building REIT.

	Annual Growth	12/14	12/15	12/16	12/17	12/18
Sales ($ mil.)	5.8%	2,195.4	2,381.7	2,560.5	2,668.5	2,754.3
Net income ($ mil.)	10.6%	1,144.2	1,311.2	1,453.6	1,442.2	1,711.0
Market value ($ mil.)	2.3%	32,188.1	43,132.2	38,918.3	36,393.4	35,245.8
Employees	1.4%	5,300	5,300	5,500	5,600	5,600

PUBLIC UTILITIES BOARD OF THE CITY OF BROWNSVILLE

1425 ROBINHOOD ST
BROWNSVILLE, TX 785214230
Phone: 956-983-6100
Fax: –
Web: www.brownsville-pub.com

CEO: –
CFO: Leandro G Garcia
HR: –
FYE: September 30
Type: Private

This PUB has no beer. Brownsville Public Utilities Board (Brownsville PUB) is a municipally-owned utility company providing electric water and wastewater services to residential and commercial customers in Brownsville Texas. Brownsville PUB serves 46000 with electric service and 47000 with water and wastewater service. The utility's two water treatment plants have the capacity to provide 40 million gallons of treated water per day. It gets its water supply from the Rio Grande. The utility's wastewater system has 174 lift stations and two treatment plants.

	Annual Growth	09/14	09/15	09/16	09/17	09/18
Sales ($ mil.)	2.7%	–	203.0	202.7	216.2	219.6
Net income ($ mil.)	(38.6%)	–	31.4	7.2	5.3	7.3
Market value ($ mil.)	–	–	–	–	–	–
Employees	–	–	–	–	–	604

PUBLIC UTILITY DISTRICT 1 OF CLARK COUNTY

1200 FORT VANCOUVER WAY
VANCOUVER, WA 986633527
Phone: 360-992-3000
Fax: –
Web: www.clarkpublicutilities.com

CEO: Wayne Nelson
CFO: –
HR: –
FYE: December 31
Type: Private

There are no "we're No 1" signs waving at this publicly minded company's head office. Public Utility District No. 1 of Clark County (Clark Public Utilities) provides utility services to residents and businesses in Clark County Washington. Clark Public Utilities transmits and distributes electricity to more than 184100 customers; the company operates a 250-MW gas-fired power plant but purchases the bulk of its power from the Bonneville Power Administration. Clark Public Utilities also distributes water to more than 30640 customers and collects and treats wastewater for the City of La Center Washington.

	Annual Growth	12/04	12/05	12/16	12/17	12/18
Sales ($ mil.)	0.3%	–	463.3	486.9	502.1	481.7
Net income ($ mil.)	23.6%	–	2.4	35.5	45.7	38.1
Market value ($ mil.)	–	–	–	–	–	–
Employees	–	–	–	–	–	325

PUBLIC UTILITY DISTRICT 1 OF SNOHOMISH COUNTY

2320 CALIFORNIA ST
EVERETT, WA 982013750
Phone: 425-257-9288
Fax: –
Web: www.snopud.com

CEO: –
CFO: –
HR: –
FYE: December 31
Type: Private

Keeping its customers satisfied is priority No. 1 at Public Utility District No. 1 of Snohomish County Washington (Snohomish County PUD) which distributes electricity to 332516 commercial industrial and residential customers in Washington State. The utility the largest PUD in the state with a 2200 sq. ml. service area purchases most of its power supply from third parties (Bonneville Power Administration and other producers. It operates hydroelectric and fossil-fueled power plants and participates in wholesale power transactions to balance its supply load. Snohomish County PUD also serves more than 20000 water utility customers in a 205 sq. ml. service territory via about 375 miles of pipe.

	Annual Growth	12/14	12/15	12/16	12/17	12/18
Sales ($ mil.)	3.5%	–	626.9	658.0	686.6	695.8
Net income ($ mil.)	15.5%	–	52.1	60.4	76.0	80.3
Market value ($ mil.)	–	–	–	–	–	–
Employees	–	–	–	–	–	879

PUBLIC UTILITY DISTRICT NO 1 OF COWLITZ COUNTY

961 12TH AVE
LONGVIEW, WA 986322507
Phone: 360-577-7507
Fax: –
Web: www.cowlitzpud.org

CEO: –
CFO: Royce Hagelstein
HR: Teedara Garn
FYE: December 31
Type: Private

Being Number One is old hat for Public Utility District No. 1 of Cowlitz County Washington (or Cowlitz County Public Utility District) a Depression era institution that provides electric utility services to 47400 customers (including 42400 residential customers and 5200 commercial clients) in its service territory. The municipal utility also serves more than 3800 Longview-Kelso area water utility customers. Like 27 other PUDs in Washington state Cowlitz County Public Utility District has the authority to offer electric water wastewater and wholesale telecommunication service.

	Annual Growth	12/09	12/10	12/15	12/16	12/17
Sales ($ mil.)	3.5%	–	220.3	138.9	278.7	279.9
Net income ($ mil.)	3.5%	–	2.1	(2.4)	3.8	2.6
Market value ($ mil.)	–	–	–	–	–	–
Employees	–	–	–	–	–	170

PUBLIC UTILITY DISTRICT NO. 1 OF CHELAN COUNTY

327 N WENATCHEE AVE
WENATCHEE, WA 988012011
Phone: 509-663-8121
Fax: –
Web: www.chelanpud.org

CEO: –
CFO: –
HR: –
FYE: December 31
Type: Private

It's Number One! Public Utility District No. 1 of Chelan County Washington (Chelan County PUD) provides power and water to residents of the county located in the middle of the Evergreen State. The utility operates three hydroelectric generation facilities on or near the Columbia River that have a combined capacity of 1988 MW. About 30% of the district's electricity goes to its more than 48000 residential commercial and industrial customers; the rest is sold wholesale to other utilities operating in the northwestern US. Chelan County PUD also provides water and wastewater services to about 5900 customers. The company's major power purchasers serve 7 million homes and businesses in the Northwest.

	Annual Growth	12/14	12/15	12/16	12/17	12/18
Sales ($ mil.)	3.2%	–	–	362.8	372.9	386.5
Net income ($ mil.)	4.9%	–	–	95.7	105.0	105.3
Market value ($ mil.)	–	–	–	–	–	–
Employees	–	–	–	–	–	841

PUBLIX SUPER MARKETS, INC.
NL:

3300 Publix Corporate Parkway
Lakeland, FL 33811
Phone: 863 688-1188
Fax: –
Web: www.publix.com

CEO: Randall T. (Todd) Jones
CFO: David P. Phillips
HR: –
FYE: December 29
Type: Public

Publix Super Markets tops the list of privately owned grocery operators in the US. By emphasizing service and a family-friendly image over price Publix has outgrown and outperformed its regional rivals. Some two-thirds of its nearly 1200 stores are in Florida but it also operates in half a dozen other southeastern states. Publix makes some of its own bakery deli dairy goods and fresh prepared foods at its own manufacturing plants in Florida and Georgia. Many stores also house pharmacies and banks. Founder George Jenkins began offering stock to Publix employees in 1930; employees own more than a quarter of the company.

	Annual Growth	12/14	12/15	12/16	12/17	12/18
Sales ($ mil.)	4.3%	30,802.5	32,618.8	34,274.1	34,836.8	36,395.7
Net income ($ mil.)	8.2%	1,735.3	1,965.0	2,025.7	2,291.9	2,381.2
Market value ($ mil.)	–	–	10,552.8	–	–	–
Employees	3.7%	175,000	180,000	191,000	193,000	202,000

PUBLIX SUPER MARKETS, INC.

3300 PUBLIX CORP PKWY
LAKELAND, FL 338113311
Phone: 863-688-1188
Fax: –
Web: www.publix.com

CEO: Randall T. (Todd) Jones
CFO: David P. Phillips
HR: –
FYE: December 31
Type: Private

Publix Super Markets tops the list of privately owned grocery operators in the US. By emphasizing service and a family-friendly image over price Publix has outgrown and outperformed its regional rivals. Some two-thirds of its nearly 1200 stores are in Florida but it also operates in half a dozen other southeastern states. Publix makes some of its own bakery deli dairy goods and fresh prepared foods at its own manufacturing plants in Florida and Georgia. Many stores also house pharmacies and banks. Founder George Jenkins began offering stock to Publix employees in 1930; employees own more than a quarter of the company.

	Annual Growth	12/11	12/12	12/14	12/15	12/16
Sales ($ mil.)	5.5%	–	27,706.8	30,802.5	32,618.8	34,274.1
Net income ($ mil.)	6.9%	–	1,552.3	1,735.3	1,965.0	2,025.7
Market value ($ mil.)	–	–	–	–	–	–
Employees	–	–	–	–	–	193,000

PUERTO RICO ELECTRIC POWER AUTHORITY

Avenida Ponce de Leon 17 1/2
Santurce PR 00909
Phone: 787-289-3434
Fax: 787-289-4120
Web: www.prepa.com

CEO: Jose Ortiz
CFO: –
HR: –
FYE: June 30
Type: Government-owned

Puerto Rico Electric Power Authority (PREPA) is prepared to serve an entire island nation. The government-owned utility is the sole electricity distributor for Puerto Rico where it serves more than 1.4 million residential and business customers. PREPA owns five primarily fossil-fueled power plants that with private cogenerators and purchased power give it nearly 5840 MW of generating capacity and it has about 33900 miles of transmission and distribution lines. In order to provide cheaper options for power production the Puerto Rican government has allowed independent power producers to build cogeneration plants on the island to sell power to PREPA.

PUGET ENERGY, INC.

10885 NE 4TH ST STE 1200
BELLEVUE, WA 980045591
Phone: 425-454-6363
Fax: –
Web: www.pugetenergy.com

CEO: Kimberly J Harris
CFO: Daniel A Doyle
HR: –
FYE: December 31
Type: Private

A sound investment Puget Energy is the holding company for one of Washington State's largest utilities Puget Sound Energy. The utility provides electricity to more than 1.1 million customers and natural gas to some 814600 customers in about 10 counties in western Washington. Puget Sound Energy owns fossil-fueled and hydroelectric plants as well as wind farms with a cumulative total of 4887 power transmission lines and 20430 miles of distribution lines. Puget Sound Energy also has about 12190 miles of gas mains and about 13655 miles of gas service lines.

	Annual Growth	12/12	12/13	12/14	12/15	12/16
Sales ($ mil.)	(0.2%)	–	3,187.3	3,113.2	3,092.7	3,164.3
Net income ($ mil.)	3.1%	–	285.7	171.8	241.2	312.9
Market value ($ mil.)	–	–	–	–	–	–
Employees	–	–	–	–	–	2,700

PULASKI FINANCIAL CORP
NMS: PULB

12300 Olive Boulevard
St. Louis, MO 63141-6434
Phone: 314 878-2210
Fax: –
Web: www.pulaskibank.com

CEO: –
CFO: –
HR: –
FYE: September 30
Type: Public

Community-oriented banking is the push at Pulaski. Pulaski Financial is the holding company for Pulaski Bank which provides financial services to residents and businesses from about a dozen branches throughout the St. Louis and Kansas City metropolitan areas. The bank offers standard deposit products including checking and savings accounts NOW accounts and money market accounts. Pulaski's loan portfolio includes primarily commercial and residential mortgages as well as home equity and construction loans. Through subsidiaries the bank offers title insurance annuities and insurance and fixed-income investment and trading. Illinois-based First Busey Corporation holder of Busey Bank agreed to buy Pulaski for nearly $211 million in late 2015.

	Annual Growth	09/11	09/12	09/13	09/14	09/15
Assets ($ mil.)	3.8%	1,309.2	1,347.5	1,275.9	1,380.1	1,521.7
Net income ($ mil.)	15.0%	8.1	9.8	9.8	11.0	14.1
Market value ($ mil.)	19.9%	77.4	97.5	121.9	136.0	160.2
Employees	5.6%	410	416	454	441	509

PULASKI FINANCIAL CORP.
NMS: PULB

12300 Olive Boulevard
St. Louis, MO 63141-6434
Phone: 314 878-2210
Fax: –
Web: www.pulaskibank.com

CEO: –
CFO: –
HR: –
FYE: September 30
Type: Public

Community-oriented banking is the push at Pulaski. Pulaski Financial is the holding company for Pulaski Bank which provides financial services to residents and businesses from about a dozen branches throughout the St. Louis and Kansas City metropolitan areas. The bank offers standard deposit products including checking and savings accounts NOW accounts and money market accounts. Pulaski's loan portfolio includes primarily commercial and residential mortgages as well as home equity and construction loans. Through subsidiaries the bank offers title insurance annuities and insurance and fixed-income investment and trading.

	Annual Growth	09/10	09/11	09/12	09/13	09/14
Assets ($ mil.)	(1.3%)	1,452.8	1,309.2	1,347.5	1,275.9	1,380.1
Net income ($ mil.)	35.3%	3.3	8.1	9.8	9.8	11.0
Market value ($ mil.)	13.6%	80.6	76.5	96.4	120.5	134.4
Employees	(0.9%)	457	410	416	454	441

PULSE ELECTRONICS CORP — NBB: PULS

12220 World Trade Drive
San Diego, CA 92128
Phone: 858 674-8100
Fax: –
Web: www.pulseelectronics.com

CEO: Mark C J Twaalfhoven
CFO: –
HR: Kimerbly Gillette
FYE: December 27
Type: Public

Pulse Electronics (formerly Technitrol) pulses with the desire to control electronic impulses. The company makes a variety of electronic components used in network power and wireless devices. Network products include passive magnetic components including chokes filters transformers and splitters. Power components include current and voltage sensors ignition coils power transformers and magnetic devices. Its wireless devices are primarily antennas and mounting devices for handsets. Pulse Electronics has manufacturing facilities in China and the US. The company gets around 85% of its sales from outside the US.

	Annual Growth	12/09	12/10	12/11	12/12	12/13
Sales ($ mil.)	(2.8%)	398.8	432.5	369.3	373.2	355.7
Net income ($ mil.)	–	(193.2)	(38.4)	(53.4)	(32.0)	(27.1)
Market value ($ mil.)	(9.9%)	34.0	42.3	22.3	2.2	22.4
Employees	(15.3%)	19,400	16,100	14,000	12,000	10,000

PULTEGROUP INC — NYS: PHM

3350 Peachtree Road N.E., Suite 150
Atlanta, GA 30326
Phone: 404 978-6400
Fax: –
Web: www.pultegroupinc.com

CEO: Ryan R. Marshall
CFO: Robert T. (Bob) O'Shaughnessy
HR: James R. (Jim) Ellinghausen
FYE: December 31
Type: Public

PulteGroup targets a cross-section of home buyers nationwide by buying or optioning land to build single-family houses duplexes townhouses and condominiums. Its Centex brand is marketed to entry-level buyers while Pulte Homes aims to capture customers looking to trade up. PulteGroup also builds Del Webb retiree communities for the growing number of buyers in the 55-plus age range. The company sells its homes in some 45 markets across roughly 25 states. Its homes go for an average price of $425000. PulteGroup became one of the top homebuilders in the US by buying rivals John Wieland Homes and Centex Homes.

	Annual Growth	12/15	12/16	12/17	12/18	12/19
Sales ($ mil.)	14.3%	5,982.0	7,668.5	8,573.3	10,188.3	10,213.0
Net income ($ mil.)	19.8%	494.1	602.7	447.2	1,022.0	1,016.7
Market value ($ mil.)	21.5%	4,815.6	4,966.9	8,985.3	7,023.4	10,485.1
Employees	3.7%	4,542	4,623	4,810	5,086	5,245

PURADYN FILTER TECHNOLOGIES INC — NBB: PFTI

2017 High Ridge Road
Boynton Beach, FL 33426
Phone: 561 547-9499
Fax: –
Web: www.puradyn.com

CEO: Edward S Vittoria
CFO: –
HR: –
FYE: December 31
Type: Public

Check your oil? Puradyn Filter Technologies would like to. The company has developed a bypass oil filtration system that can be used in internal combustion engines and pieces of hydraulic equipment that rely on lubricating oil. The Puradyn system works in conjunction with a standard oil filter to remove solids as small as a micron (1/39 millionth of an inch) along with liquid and gaseous contaminants. Puradyn markets its filtration systems worldwide; target customers include OEMs commercial trucking fleets and operators of construction machinery. Puradyn has not been profitable however and the company's auditors have questioned whether it can stay in business.

	Annual Growth	12/14	12/15	12/16	12/17	12/18
Sales ($ mil.)	7.8%	3.1	2.0	1.9	2.3	4.2
Net income ($ mil.)	–	(1.2)	(1.4)	(1.4)	(1.2)	(0.2)
Market value ($ mil.)	(27.8%)	15.1	2.6	5.5	0.9	4.1
Employees	(1.2%)	21	21	20	21	20

PURDUE UNIVERSITY

401 S GRANT ST
WEST LAFAYETTE, IN 479072024
Phone: 765-494-8000
Fax: –
Web: www.purduesports.com

CEO: –
CFO: Kevin Popa
HR: –
FYE: June 30
Type: Private

Purdue University enrolls more than 70000 undergraduate graduate and continuing education students at its flagship West Lafayette campus four regional campuses and 10 satellite College of Technology locations. The university offers undergraduate and graduate programs from about a dozen colleges including agriculture education nursing veterinary medicine and family sciences; its College of Technology provides industrial courses (applicable towards associate's or bachelor's degrees) in conjunction with Indiana communities. The student-faculty ratio is 12:1. Through the newly established Purdue University Global (formerly Kaplan University) the institution provides coursework for another 30000 students.

	Annual Growth	06/06	06/07	06/12	06/13	06/17
Sales ($ mil.)	3.9%	–	1,038.7	1,429.6	1,450.1	1,529.4
Net income ($ mil.)	(5.5%)	–	302.0	136.1	227.5	172.1
Market value ($ mil.)	–	–	–	–	–	–
Employees	–	–	–	–	–	18,715

PURE BIOSCIENCE INC — NBB: PURE

9669 Hermosa Avenue
Rancho Cucamonga, CA 91730
Phone: 619 596-8600
Fax: 619 596-8790
Web: www.purebio.com

CEO: Tom Y Lee
CFO: Mark Elliott
HR: –
FYE: July 31
Type: Public

PURE Bioscience is all about killing what's on the surface. The company makes and markets a patented low-toxicity disinfectant (Axenohl in its concentrated form Axen Axen30 or Axen50 in diluted form) approved for use in hospitals restaurants and schools among other commercial and industrial locations. PURE's consumer sanitation products for home use are sold under the PureGreen 24 label. The company is also working to develop consumer products and drug treatments using the disinfectant's base compound silver dihydrogen citrate which it also sells as a product ingredient to other manufacturers. PURE Bioscience's products are marketed in countries around the globe.

	Annual Growth	07/15	07/16	07/17	07/18	07/19
Sales ($ mil.)	27.2%	0.7	1.3	1.8	1.8	1.9
Net income ($ mil.)	–	(7.6)	(14.4)	(6.3)	(7.4)	(6.6)
Market value ($ mil.)	(15.1%)	48.0	77.5	95.9	43.0	24.9
Employees	0.0%	11	13	13	11	11

PURE CYCLE CORP. — NAS: PCYO

34501 E. Quincy Avenue, Building 34
Watkins, CO 80137
Phone: 303 292-3456
Fax: –
Web: www.purecyclewater.com

CEO: Mark W Harding
CFO: Mark W Harding
HR: –
FYE: August 31
Type: Public

Struggling to survive in the barren waste without a trace of water is no longer the fate of inhabitants of the Lowry Range thanks to Pure Cycle. The water utility has the exclusive right to provide water and wastewater services to about 24000 acres of the Lowry Range near Denver. Pure Cycle generates revenues from three sources: water and wastewater fees; construction fees; and monthly service fees. In 2009 it served 247 single-family water connections and 157 wastewater connections in the southeastern Denver area. It also has 60000 acre-feet of water rights in the Arkansas River basin in Southern Colorado. In 2010 Pure Cycle acquired the 931-acre Sky Ranch Property near Denver for $7 million.

	Annual Growth	08/15	08/16	08/17	08/18	08/19
Sales ($ mil.)	72.1%	2.3	0.5	1.2	7.0	20.4
Net income ($ mil.)	–	(23.1)	(1.3)	(1.7)	0.4	4.8
Market value ($ mil.)	21.4%	119.1	115.3	172.7	268.0	258.5
Employees	42.7%	7	6	11	19	29

PURPLE COMMUNICATIONS, INC.

595 MENLO DR
ROCKLIN, CA 957653708
Phone: 888-600-4780
Fax: –
Web: www.purplevrs.com

CEO: Sherri Turpin
CFO: Michael Flanagan
HR: –
FYE: December 31
Type: Private

Purple Communications (formerly GoAmerica) provides a colorful alternative to traditional phone services for the hearing impaired. It offers telecommunications relay services such as text relay video relay and Internet Protocol text relay whereby hard of hearing subscribers can video chat send and receive text telephone messages faxes and e-mail over computers or wireless devices. Purple Communications maintains 15 call centers in the US to facilitate the calls. The company also offers on-site live interpreting services in a dozen US cities and via video across the country. Clearlake Capital Group owns nearly all of the company's stock.

	Annual Growth	12/04	12/05	12/06	12/07	12/08
Sales ($ mil.)	219.1%	–	–	12.8	18.6	130.1
Net income ($ mil.)	–	–	–	(2.0)	(3.7)	(5.0)
Market value ($ mil.)	–	–	–	–	–	–
Employees	–	–	–	–	–	1,000

PVH CORP

200 Madison Avenue
New York, NY 10016
Phone: 212 381-3500
Fax: –
Web: www.pvh.com

NYS: PVH
CEO: Emanuel (Manny) Chirico
CFO: Gene Gosselin
HR: David F. (Dave) Kozel
FYE: February 03
Type: Public

PVH has the buttoned-up look down. A top global apparel player PVH is the world's largest dress shirt and neckwear company. The company owns three titans of the apparel industry: Calvin Klein Tommy Hilfiger and Heritage Brands. The former two are multi-billion dollar global lifestyle brands while Heritage Brands is a luxury apparel wholesaler that owns the brands Van Heusen IZOD ARROW Warner's Olga and True&Co. PVH is also has licenses for third-party brands such as DKNY Speedo Kenneth Cole Reaction Michael Kors Collection and others. The company generates sales from multiple channels including about 1700 company-operated retail stores 1500 concession stands retail partners and licensees. It also charges royalty and advertising fees.

	Annual Growth	02/15*	01/16	01/17*	02/18	02/19
Sales ($ mil.)	4.0%	8,241.2	8,020.3	8,203.1	8,914.8	9,656.8
Net income ($ mil.)	14.2%	439.0	572.4	549.0	537.8	746.4
Market value ($ mil.)	(0.3%)	8,314.0	5,533.1	6,808.9	11,391.2	8,200.9
Employees	2.7%	34,100	34,200	44,500	36,500	38,000

*Fiscal year change

PVR PARTNERS LP

Three Radnor Corporate Center, Suite 301, 100 Matsonford Road
Radnor, PA 19087
Phone: 610 975-8200
Fax: –

NYS: PVR
CEO: –
CFO: –
HR: –
FYE: December 31
Type: Public

Penn Virginia Resource Partners (PVR) owns and manages a variety of natural resources including coal reserves and natural gas midstream pipelines and processing plants. It leases mining rights on its properties to third-party mine operators collecting royalties based on the amount of coal produced and the price at which it is sold. Its land contains nearly 900 million tons of proven or probable reserves (mostly low-sulfur bituminous coal). However most of PVR's revenue comes from natural gas processing and collection. The company operates seven processing facilities and more than 4400 miles of pipeline in Oklahoma Pennsylvania and Texas.

	Annual Growth	12/08	12/09	12/10	12/11	12/12
Sales ($ mil.)	3.4%	881.6	656.7	864.1	1,160.0	1,007.8
Net income ($ mil.)	–	104.5	65.2	68.5	97.0	(70.6)
Market value ($ mil.)	22.9%	1,458.6	2,765.8	3,633.0	3,275.1	3,332.9
Employees	18.1%	157	167	210	250	305

PVS TECHNOLOGIES INC.

10900 HARPER AVE
DETROIT, MI 482133364
Phone: 313-571-1100
Fax: –
Web: www.pvschemicals.com

CEO: James B Nicholson
CFO: Candee Saferian
HR: –
FYE: December 31
Type: Private

When it comes to making chemicals for wastewater treatment and manufacturing PVS Chemicals is in its element. The company's product list includes sulfuric and hydrochloric acids liquid caustic soda ferric chloride and ammonium thiosulfate. These chemicals are used in applications such as water treatment (wastewater process and municipal) electronics manufacture (including semiconductor etching) gold and copper mining and food and aluminum production. PVS Chemicals' subsidiaries include PVS Technologies (water treatment) Dynecol (transportation analysis treatment and recycling of chemicals) and PVS Nolwood (chemical distribution).

	Annual Growth	12/09	12/10	12/11	12/12	12/13
Sales ($ mil.)	14.8%	–	35.2	45.0	48.3	53.3
Net income ($ mil.)	(17.2%)	–	–	4.1	2.7	2.8
Market value ($ mil.)	–	–	–	–	–	–
Employees	–	–	–	–	–	60

PYCO INDUSTRIES, INC.

2901 AVENUE A
LUBBOCK, TX 794042231
Phone: 806-747-3434
Fax: –
Web: www.pycoindustriesinc.com

CEO: –
CFO: –
HR: –
FYE: September 30
Type: Private

Ginning up business is the secret to this vegetable oil producer's success. PYCO Industries is said to be the largest cotton seed co-op to serve the southern US. The Texas-based cooperative comprising more than 60-member gins processes cottonseed for a broad market through two cottonseed oil mills. Its cottonseed oil is shipped to food manufacturers and other foodservice customers across the country. The co-op also markets whole cottonseed as well as the by-products of crushing cottonseed such as cottonseed hulls and cottonseed meal for beef and dairy cattle feed. Cottonseed linters another byproduct are used by manufacturers of mattresses and upholstery padding paper and plastics and other products.

	Annual Growth	09/14	09/15	09/16	09/17	09/18
Sales ($ mil.)	11.3%	–	161.0	201.5	185.6	222.2
Net income ($ mil.)	(7.4%)	–	30.5	23.8	9.8	24.2
Market value ($ mil.)	–	–	–	–	–	–
Employees	–	–	–	–	–	160

PYXUS INTERNATIONAL INC

8001 Aerial Center Parkway
Morrisville, NC 27560
Phone: 919 379-4300
Fax: –
Web: www.aointl.com

NYS: PYX
CEO: J. Pieter Sikkel
CFO: Joel L. Thomas
HR: Laura D. Jones
FYE: March 31
Type: Public

Alliance One International keeps one eye on the world's tobacco farmers and the other eye on the cigarette makers. The company is a leading global leaf-tobacco merchant behind its slightly larger rival Universal Corporation. Alliance One purchases leaf tobacco from producers in more than 45 countries which it packs stores and ships to cigarette manufacturers worldwide. It also processes flue-cured burley and oriental tobaccos and sells them to large multinational cigarette and cigar manufacturers including Philip Morris International (PMI) and Japan Tobacco in some 90 countries. Alliance One was formed by the merger of tobacco processor DIMON and Standard Commercial.

	Annual Growth	03/15	03/16	03/17	03/18	03/19
Sales ($ mil.)	(3.4%)	2,065.9	1,904.6	1,714.8	1,846.0	1,801.6
Net income ($ mil.)	–	(15.4)	65.5	(62.9)	52.4	(70.5)
Market value ($ mil.)	115.7%	10.9	173.5	127.0	257.4	236.1
Employees	0.5%	3,281	3,299	3,277	3,450	3,347

PZENA INVESTMENT MANAGEMENT INC — NYS: PZN

320 Park Avenue
New York, NY 10022
Phone: 212 355-1600
Fax: –
Web: www.pzena.com

CEO: Richard S. Pzena
CFO: Jessica R Doran
HR: –
FYE: December 31
Type: Public

It takes money to make money and Pzena Investment Management has made plenty. The firm serves corporate institutional and high-net-worth individual clients in the US and abroad and has about $21 billion in assets under management. Through a dozen funds Pzena makes long-term investments in domestic and international companies — particularly financial services firms. Pzena also acts as a sub-investment adviser for about two dozen mutual funds and offshore funds. The firm is the sole managing member of its operating company Pzena Investment Management LLC. The employee-owned firm was founded by chairman and CEO Richard Pzena in 1995.

	Annual Growth	12/14	12/15	12/16	12/17	12/18
Sales ($ mil.)	8.1%	112.5	116.6	108.3	141.3	153.6
Net income ($ mil.)	14.2%	8.1	7.7	16.2	6.9	13.8
Market value ($ mil.)	(2.2%)	658.9	599.0	773.8	743.2	602.5
Employees	7.0%	81	88	100	105	106

Q.E.P. CO., INC. — NBB: QEPC

1001 Broken Sound Parkway N.W.
Boca Raton, FL 33487
Phone: 561 994-5550
Fax: 561 241-2830
Web: www.qepcorporate.com

CEO: Lewis Gould
CFO: Richard A. Brooke
HR: –
FYE: February 28
Type: Public

Q.E.P. brings flooring to life. The company makes and distributes hardwood flooring and flooring installation tools (including adhesives trowels wet saws and carpet trimmers) for professionals and do-it-yourselfers. It sells more than 7000 flooring and flooring-related products mainly for installing marble carpet ceramic tile and drywall under the QEP Capitol ROBERTS Elastiment and Ludell brands among others. Q.E.P. makes about 25% of its products and acquires the rest from some 200 suppliers. Its customers include retailers and distributors to the home improvement hardware and construction trades primarily in the US. The family-run company was founded by chairman and CEO Lewis Gould in 1979.

	Annual Growth	02/14	02/15	02/16	02/17	02/18
Sales ($ mil.)	1.6%	302.7	297.7	309.2	310.1	322.4
Net income ($ mil.)	(16.2%)	16.1	1.9	4.0	7.4	7.9
Market value ($ mil.)	11.2%	60.5	56.0	48.1	66.8	92.6
Employees	–	–	–	–	–	–

QAD, INC. — NMS: QADA

100 Innovation Place
Santa Barbara, CA 93108
Phone: 805 566-6000
Fax: –
Web: www.qad.com

CEO: Karl F. Lopker
CFO: Daniel Lender
HR: –
FYE: January 31
Type: Public

QAD tries to keep factories running smoothly. More than 2000 manufacturers use the company's enterprise resource planning (ERP) and supply chain software to streamline production processes by automating the management of manufacturing as well as related distribution customer relationships and financial applications. QAD's customers cluster in the automotive food and beverage life sciences and high-tech industries. The company increasingly emphasizes it cloud-based subscription software while maintaining a large base of customers that deploy QAD software on their own servers. The company which also offers related maintenance and consulting services generates more than half of sales outside North America.

	Annual Growth	01/15	01/16	01/17	01/18	01/19
Sales ($ mil.)	3.1%	295.1	277.9	278.0	305.0	333.0
Net income ($ mil.)	(5.3%)	12.9	8.9	(15.5)	(9.1)	10.4
Market value ($ mil.)	21.5%	379.6	363.3	567.2	845.9	827.5
Employees	4.5%	1,650	1,680	1,710	1,870	1,970

QC HOLDINGS INC — NBB: QCCO

9401 Indian Creek Parkway, Suite 1500
Overland Park, KS 66210
Phone: 913 234-5000
Fax: –
Web: www.qcholdings.com

CEO: Darrin J Andersen
CFO: Douglas E Nickerson
HR: –
FYE: December 31
Type: Public

Need cash PDQ? Cue QC. QC Holdings runs about 500 payday loan stores operating mostly as Quik Cash or National Quik Cash but also under about a half-dozen other brands including California Budget Finance Express Check Advance of South Carolina First Payday Loans Nationwide Budget Finance and QC Financial Services. Targeting working-class individuals its stores provide short-term loans ranging from $100 to $500 for a fee typically between 15% to 20% per each $100 of the loan. The company also offers check cashing services title loans and Western Union money orders and transfers. It is active in nearly two dozen states; Missouri California Illinois and Kansas are its largest markets.

	Annual Growth	12/10	12/11	12/12	12/13	12/14
Sales ($ mil.)	(5.0%)	188.1	187.5	180.6	152.0	153.1
Net income ($ mil.)	(18.2%)	11.9	10.2	5.4	(14.0)	5.3
Market value ($ mil.)	(18.6%)	64.8	69.6	56.1	31.0	28.4
Employees	(7.3%)	1,681	1,593	1,563	1,347	1,244

QCR HOLDINGS INC — NMS: QCRH

3551 7th Street
Moline, IL 61265
Phone: 309 736-3580
Fax: –
Web: www.qcrh.com

CEO: Douglas M. (Doug) Hultquist
CFO: Todd A. Gipple
HR: Cathie Whiteside
FYE: December 31
Type: Public

Quad City is muscling in on the community banking scene in the Midwest. QCR Holdings is the holding company for Quad City Bank & Trust Cedar Rapids Bank & Trust Rockford Bank & Trust and Community State Bank. Together the banks have about 20 offices serving the Quad City area of Illinois and Iowa as well as the communities of Cedar Rapids Iowa; Rockford Illinois; and Milwaukee. The banks offer traditional deposit products and services and concentrate their lending activities on local businesses: Commercial real estate loans make up about half of the loan portfolio; commercial loans and leases make up another third.

	Annual Growth	12/14	12/15	12/16	12/17	12/18
Assets ($ mil.)	18.3%	2,525.0	2,593.2	3,301.9	3,982.7	4,949.7
Net income ($ mil.)	30.3%	15.0	16.9	27.7	35.7	43.1
Market value ($ mil.)	15.8%	280.7	381.8	680.6	673.5	504.4
Employees	16.6%	409	406	572	641	755

QEP RESOURCES INC — NYS: QEP

1050 17th Street, Suite 800
Denver, CO 80265
Phone: 303 672-6900
Fax: –
Web: www.qepres.com

CEO: Charles B. (Chuck) Stanley
CFO: Richard J. Doleshek
HR: –
FYE: December 31
Type: Public

QEP Resources has the resources to conduct exploration and production gas gathering processing and storage and energy trading operations in North Carolina Wyoming Utah Texas and Louisiana. Its QEP Energy unit acquires and develops gas and oil properties generates and drills prospects and develops gas reserves. Natural gas accounts for over 50% of total production although the gap to oil and NGL (natural gas liquids) has closed in recent years. QEP has estimated proved reserves of 731.4 MMboe. QEP Energy also conducts its own and third-party marketing. It markets equity and third-party gas and oil owns and operates an underground gas storage reservoir and provides risk-management services. In January 2019 QEP received an unsolicited proposal to be acquired by hedge fund Elliott Management for around $2.07 billion.

	Annual Growth	12/14	12/15	12/16	12/17	12/18
Sales ($ mil.)	(13.3%)	3,414.3	2,018.6	1,377.1	1,622.9	1,932.6
Net income ($ mil.)	–	784.4	(149.4)	(1,245.0)	269.3	(1,011.6)
Market value ($ mil.)	(27.4%)	4,786.1	3,171.8	4,357.6	2,265.2	1,332.6
Employees	(11.7%)	765	693	656	656	465

QHG OF SOUTH CAROLINA, INC.

805 PAMPLICO HWY
FLORENCE, SC 295056047
Phone: 843-674-5000
Fax: –
Web: www.carolinashospital.com

CEO: Darcy Craven
CFO: –
HR: –
FYE: June 30
Type: Private

QHG of South Carolina (dba Carolinas Hospital System) provides acute health care services in the Palmetto State town of Florence. The hospital has some 420 inpatient beds and employs about 300 specialized physicians. In addition to emergency trauma general medicine and surgeries service specialties at the medical campus include cancer care diagnostics women's health cardiology pediatrics urology orthopedics rehabilitation and behavioral health. It also includes affiliated medical emergency clinics outpatient centers and doctor's offices. Carolinas Hospital System is a subsidiary of Community Health Systems (CHS).

	Annual Growth	06/12	06/13	06/14	06/15	06/16
Sales ($ mil.)	(25.3%)	–	–	–	261.6	195.4
Net income ($ mil.)	(55.1%)	–	–	–	17.9	8.1
Market value ($ mil.)	–	–	–	–	–	–
Employees	–	–	–	–	–	1,500

QLIK TECHNOLOGIES INC.   NMS: QLIK

150 N. Radnor Chester Road, Suite E220
Radnor, PA 19087
Phone: 888 828-9768
Fax: –
Web: www.qlikview.com

CEO: Mike Capone
CFO: –
HR: –
FYE: December 31
Type: Public

Qlik Technologies (QlikTech) puts important business data just a click away. The company provides its QlikView business intelligence (BI) software that gives clients the tools to search and query business data in a variety of ways; reports are displayed in a visual format that can be explored and analyzed further. QlikTech serves midsized and large enterprises throughout the world; its approximately 34000 customers have included Campbell Soup Company Colonial Life Hertz Kraft Foods the UK National Health Service and QUALCOMM. The company was founded in Sweden in 1993.

	Annual Growth	12/10	12/11	12/12	12/13	12/14
Sales ($ mil.)	25.2%	226.5	320.6	388.5	470.5	556.8
Net income ($ mil.)	–	13.5	9.0	3.8	(10.0)	(24.6)
Market value ($ mil.)	4.5%	2,350.4	2,198.6	1,973.3	2,419.4	2,806.4
Employees	27.1%	780	1,054	1,425	1,721	2,038

QLOGIC CORP.   NMS: QLGC

26650 Aliso Viejo Parkway
Aliso Viejo, CA 92656
Phone: 949 389-6000
Fax: –
Web: www.qlogic.com

CEO: –
CFO: –
HR: –
FYE: March 29
Type: Public

QLogic keeps its customers on a steady diet of Fibre…Channel. The company designs server and storage system networking products including switches adapters and storage routers. QLogic's products are primarily Fibre Channel and Ethernet-based but can also operate as Internet Small Computer System Interface (iSCSI) products or as a combination of technologies. The company also provides controllers for embedded applications. QLogic uses contract manufacturers to build its products which are sold directly to server and workstation manufacturers and through distributors. Customers include Hewlett-Packard (more than a quarter of sales) Dell (17%) and IBM (15%).

	Annual Growth	04/11	04/12*	03/13	03/14	03/15
Sales ($ mil.)	(3.4%)	597.2	558.6	484.5	460.9	520.2
Net income ($ mil.)	(22.3%)	139.1	229.4	73.1	(18.3)	50.6
Market value ($ mil.)	(5.7%)	1,583.9	1,549.0	1,011.8	1,089.4	1,250.3
Employees	(5.2%)	1,147	1,121	1,229	1,044	927

*Fiscal year change

QNB CORP.   NBB: QNBC

15 North Third Street, P.O. Box 9005
Quakertown, PA 18951-9005
Phone: 215 538-5600
Fax: –
Web: www.qnbbank.com

CEO: David W Freeman
CFO: Janice S McCracken Erkes
HR: –
FYE: December 31
Type: Public

QNB Corp. is the holding company for QNB Bank which provides commercial banking services through 11 branches serving Bucks Lehigh and Montgomery counties in southeastern Pennsylvania. QNB offers standard banking services including checking savings and money market accounts; IRAs; and CDs. It uses funds from deposits to originate business loans residential mortgages and consumer loans. Commercial loans and mortgages account for more than half of its lending portfolio. Unlike many of its peers QNB Bank does not directly offer trust services or full-service insurance. The company was founded in 1877.

	Annual Growth	12/14	12/15	12/16	12/17	12/18
Assets ($ mil.)	4.7%	977.1	1,020.9	1,063.1	1,152.3	1,175.5
Net income ($ mil.)	5.9%	9.0	8.2	8.9	8.3	11.3
Market value ($ mil.)	7.8%	99.3	109.7	124.7	154.7	134.1
Employees	0.8%	185	186	186	181	191

QORVO INC   NMS: QRVO

7628 Thorndike Road
Greensboro, NC 27409-9421
Phone: 336 664-1233
Fax: –
Web: www.qorvo.com

CEO: Robert A. (Bob) Bruggeworth
CFO: Mark J. Murphy
HR: Ralph E Knupp
FYE: March 30
Type: Public

The result of the 2015 combination of RF Micro Devices and TriQuint Qorvo develops makes and sells a wide range of radio frequency (RF) technologies that enable devices big and small to communicate with each other. Its products are made for mobile devices (from phones to cell towers) infrastructure applications (smart meters and Wi-Fi base stations) and aerospace and defense systems (radar and satellites). Major customers include Apple and Samsung. Unlike many other chip companies Qorvo operates its own foundry where RF devices can be made to specifications. It has operations in the US Costa Rica Singapore China and Germany.

	Annual Growth	03/15*	04/16	04/17*	03/18	03/19
Sales ($ mil.)	15.9%	1,711.0	2,610.7	3,032.6	2,973.5	3,090.3
Net income ($ mil.)	(9.3%)	196.3	(28.8)	(16.6)	(40.3)	133.1
Market value ($ mil.)	(2.5%)	9,439.3	6,050.8	8,163.0	8,388.0	8,540.4
Employees	4.9%	6,700	7,300	8,600	8,300	8,100

*Fiscal year change

QR ENERGY LP   NYS: QRE

5 Houston Center, 1401 McKinney Street, Suite 2400
Houston, TX 77010
Phone: 713 452-2200
Fax: 713 452-2202
Web: www.qrenergylp.com

CEO: –
CFO: –
HR: –
FYE: December 31
Type: Public

QR Energy has the power to make quick profits for its shareholders. The company owns mature land-based oil and natural gas reservoirs in the south central US. Its holdings include total proved reserves of 30 million barrels of oil equivalent about 70% of which is oil and natural gas liquids with options on other similar properties. QR Energy's properties are located in the oil producing regions of Permian Basin (Texas) Ark-La-Tex Mid-Continent (Kansas to Texas including Arkansas and Louisiana) and along the Gulf Coast. Quantum Resource Funds formed the limited partnership in 2010; it receives administrative and operational services from Quantum Resources Management. QR Energy went public in 2010.

	Annual Growth	12/08	12/09	12/10	12/11	12/12
Sales ($ mil.)	–	0.0	0.0	3.0	259.9	372.0
Net income ($ mil.)	–	0.0	0.0	(7.1)	61.1	79.8
Market value ($ mil.)	–	0.0	0.0	1,176.9	1,179.3	969.9
Employees	17.8%	–	–	211	250	293

QTS REALTY TRUST INC
NYS: QTS

12851 Foster Street
Overland Park, KS 66213
Phone: 913 312-5503
Fax: –
Web: www.qtsdatacenters.com

CEO: Chad L. Williams
CFO: William H. (Bill) Schafer
HR: –
FYE: December 31
Type: Public

In the world of server farms QTS Realty sows a lot of concrete. The company owns secure office buildings that house data centers — where companies keep their computer equipment. QTS (which stands for Quality Technology Services) owns and operates 10 data centers across seven states totaling 3.8 million sq. ft. It counts almost 900 corporations and government agencies as customers. Organized as a real estate investment trust (REIT) QTS is exempt from paying federal income tax as long as it makes quarterly distributions to shareholders. It went public in 2013 raising $257 million which it will use to pay down debt as well as buy and renovate more data centers.

	Annual Growth	12/14	12/15	12/16	12/17	12/18
Sales ($ mil.)	19.9%	217.8	311.1	402.4	446.5	450.5
Net income ($ mil.)	–	15.1	20.3	21.5	1.3	(4.5)
Market value ($ mil.)	2.3%	1,730.0	2,306.2	2,538.3	2,768.8	1,894.1
Employees	7.1%	460	720	780	818	606

QUAD/GRAPHICS, INC.
NYS: QUAD

N61 W23044 Harry's Way
Sussex, WI 53089-3995
Phone: 414 566-6000
Fax: –
Web: www.qg.com

CEO: J. Joel Quadracci
CFO: David J. (Dave) Honan
HR: –
FYE: December 31
Type: Public

Trading as Quad Quad/Graphics Inc is one of the largest printing company in the US producing catalogs magazines books direct mail and other commercial materials. The company's services include production design photography binding wrapping and distribution. The company has printing facilities located around the world. With print media in structural decline Quad/Graphics has been acquiring integrated new media marketing companies including Periscope Rise Interactive and Ivie. Having nothing to do with the number four Quad takes its name from Harry Quadracci who founded the company in 1971. His youngest son Joel runs the company today as Chairman and CEO.

	Annual Growth	12/14	12/15	12/16	12/17	12/18
Sales ($ mil.)	(3.6%)	4,862.4	4,677.7	4,329.5	4,131.4	4,193.7
Net income ($ mil.)	(17.8%)	18.6	(641.9)	44.9	107.2	8.5
Market value ($ mil.)	(14.4%)	1,184.7	479.9	1,387.0	1,166.2	635.7
Employees	(3.8%)	24,100	22,500	22,600	21,100	20,600

QUAKER CHEMICAL CORPORATION
NYSE: KWR

1 Quaker Park 901 E. Hector St.
Conshohocken PA 19428-2380
Phone: 610-832-4000
Fax: 610-832-8682
Web: www.quakerchem.com

CEO: Michael F Barry
CFO: Mary Dean Hall
HR: –
FYE: December 31
Type: Public

Rolling lubricants like rolled oats have a Quaker as a maker. This Quaker — Quaker Chemical — rolls out specialty chemicals for industrial and manufacturing processes. Its rolling lubricants are used in making rolled aluminum products and hot- and cold-rolled steel products. Quaker Chemical also makes corrosion preventives metal finishing compounds hydraulic fluids and machining grinding and forming compounds. Other products and services include aerospace milling compounds metal and concrete coatings and chemical management services. Quaker Chemical's subsidiaries and joint ventures operate worldwide although it sells primarily to the steel auto and appliance industries in the US and Europe.

QUAKER VALLEY FOODS, INC.

2701 RED LION RD
PHILADELPHIA, PA 191541038
Phone: 215-992-0900
Fax: –
Web: www.quakervalleyfoods.com

CEO: –
CFO: Pat Veasey
HR: –
FYE: January 02
Type: Private

Quaker Valley Foods (QVF) is known by friends high and low for its take-out fresh and frozen staples. The food distributor makes daily deliveries of meat and other provisions to foodservice customers across the Northeast US. QVF a member of the UNIPRO Foodservice coop offers beef pork poultry frozen seafood imported meats (mutton and goat) cheeses salads and other items from its Philadelphia warehouse. Customers range from wholesalers and jobbers to independent retail and wholesale groceries and major supermarket chains. Its vendors include Hormel Swift Packerland Carolina Turkey Tyson Alpine Lace and Land O' Lakes. QVF was started by two brothers-in-law in 1975 and is led by its founders' sons.

	Annual Growth	01/09	01/10	01/11*	12/11*	01/16
Sales ($ mil.)	6.9%	–	160.6	177.3	195.5	239.5
Net income ($ mil.)	22.0%	–	0.6	0.4	0.4	2.0
Market value ($ mil.)	–	–	–	–	–	–
Employees	–	–	–	–	–	145

*Fiscal year change

QUALCOMM ATHEROS INC.

1700 Technology Dr.
San Jose CA 95110
Phone: 408-773-5200
Fax: 408-773-9940
Web: www.qca.qualcomm.com

CEO: Steve Mollenkopf
CFO: –
HR: –
FYE: December 31
Type: Subsidiary

Qualcomm Atheros (formerly Atheros Communications) builds high-speed connections right through the ether. Its radio-frequency (RF) transceiver chipsets combine features such as a radio power amplifier low-noise amplifier and a media access control processor onto just two or three chips eliminating the need for bulkier components in wireless networking gear. Customers have included Apple Dell Fujitsu HP Hon Hai Microsoft Nintendo and Sony. The fabless chip company was started by faculty members from Stanford and Berkeley. Most of its sales are to customers in Asia principally in Taiwan and China. In 2011 QUALCOMM bought Atheros Communications in a deal valued at around $3 billion and changed its name.

QUALCOMM INC
NMS: QCOM

5775 Morehouse Dr.
San Diego, CA 92121-1714
Phone: 858 587-1121
Fax: –
Web: www.qualcomm.com

CEO: Steven M. (Steve) Mollenkopf
CFO: George S. Davis
HR: Michelle Sterling
FYE: September 29
Type: Public

QUALCOMM is a leading designer and supplier of computer chips that mobile phone and wireless carriers depend on to get signals straight. The company pioneered the commercialization of the code-division multiple access (CDMA) technology used in digital wireless communications equipment and satellite ground stations mainly in North America. It generates most of its sales through the development and marketing of semiconductor chips such as its Snapdragon line and system software based on CDMA and other technologies. Its biggest customers have been suppliers to mobile phone makers Samsung and Apple. In 2018 QUALCOMM ended its $47 billion bid to buy NXP Semiconductors after the Chinese government failed to approve the deal.

	Annual Growth	09/15	09/16	09/17	09/18	09/19
Sales ($ mil.)	(1.0%)	25,281.0	23,554.0	22,291.0	22,732.0	24,273.0
Net income ($ mil.)	(4.5%)	5,271.0	5,705.0	2,466.0	(4,864.0)	4,386.0
Market value ($ mil.)	9.5%	60,936.9	71,848.8	59,643.1	82,474.4	87,741.4
Employees	2.9%	33,000	30,500	33,800	35,400	37,000

QUALITY DISTRIBUTION INC (FL) — NMS: QLTY

4041 Park Oaks Boulevard, Suite 200
Tampa, FL 33610
Phone: 813 630-5826
Fax: –
Web: www.qualitydistribution.com

CEO: Gary Enzor
CFO: Joseph Troy
HR: –
FYE: December 31
Type: Public

As far as North American bulk chemicals carriers go Quality Distribution is the bulkiest. Through subsidiary Quality Carriers Inc. (QCI) the company operates the largest chemical bulk tank truck network running through the US Canada and Mexico. It transports both liquid and dry bulk chemicals (including plastics) and provides logistics services through about 30 independent affiliates with 90 trucking terminals and three company-operated trucking terminals. Quality Distribution is also the largest provider of intermodal tank container and depot services in North America through subsidiary Boasso America. Key customers include BASF Dow DuPont Exxon Mobil Procter & Gamble and PPG Industries.

	Annual Growth	12/09	12/10	12/11	12/12	12/13
Sales ($ mil.)	10.9%	613.6	686.6	746.0	842.1	929.8
Net income ($ mil.)	–	(180.5)	(7.4)	23.4	50.1	(42.0)
Market value ($ mil.)	34.1%	108.0	247.3	306.0	163.2	349.0
Employees	(1.4%)	810	752	2,741	2,001	765

QUALITY FOOD CENTERS INC.

10116 NE 8th St.
Bellevue WA 98004
Phone: 425-455-3761
Fax: 425-462-2146
Web: www.qfconline.com

CEO: –
CFO: –
HR: –
FYE: January 31
Type: Subsidiary

If you're sleepless — and hungry — in Seattle consider Quality Food Centers (QFC). The grocery chain operates about 70 stores (most open 24 hours) primarily in the Puget Sound region of Washington (including Seattle) but also including about a half a dozen supermarkets in Portland Oregon. QFC stores offer more than just groceries: Seattle's Best Coffee and Cinnabon serve up goodies at some locations and many stores offer services such as catering video rental in-store banking pharmacies floral departments and film developing. Founded more than 60 years ago QFC is a division of grocery giant Kroger.

QUALITY OIL COMPANY, LLC

1540 SILAS CREEK PKWY
WINSTON SALEM, NC 271273705
Phone: 336-722-3441
Fax: –
Web: www.qualityoilnc.com

CEO: –
CFO: –
HR: –
FYE: December 31
Type: Private

With more services than your average oil company Quality Oil helps its customers get fueled up cooled off and well rested. And they can smoke if they want to. The company distributes fuel oil and propane to customers in the Winston-Salem area of North Carolina. Quality Oil provides air conditioning and heating equipment service operates 47 convenience stores (Quality Marts) and about 20 service stations and owns hotels in five southern states. In addition the company operates 60 Quality Plus locations at which drivers can buy cigarettes at discount prices. The company also provides Right-a-Way oil change services at many of its gas stations.

	Annual Growth	12/05	12/06	12/07	12/08	12/09
Sales ($ mil.)	5.4%	–	542.2	619.7	806.4	634.8
Net income ($ mil.)	(8.1%)	–	15.2	10.9	27.6	11.8
Market value ($ mil.)	–	–	–	–	–	–
Employees	–	–	–	–	–	1,000

QUALSERV CORPORATION

7400 S 28TH ST
FORT SMITH, AR 72908-7800
Phone: 479-646-8386
Fax: –
Web: www.qualservcorp.com

CEO: Larry D Hughes
CFO: Peter Duff
HR: –
FYE: December 31
Type: Private

QualServ serves up quality by providing everything to turn an empty building into a functioning restaurant. The turnkey company brings together everything — from design and construction to millwork equipment furniture and fixtures — for opening a restaurant or a wide variety of other businesses and institutions. QualServ also serves up installation maintenance and repair services. Don't need a complete restaurant? Customers may also order a la carte from QualServ's menu of products and services. QualServ's clientele has included the likes of Chipotle Mexican Grill Extended Stay America Papa John's and Red Robin Gourmet Burgers. QualServ partners with Direct Capital Corporation to offer financing.

	Annual Growth	12/07	12/08	12/09	12/10	12/11
Sales ($ mil.)	(1.0%)	–	–	69.8	68.4	68.4
Net income ($ mil.)	–	–	–	(1.0)	(0.3)	(0.3)
Market value ($ mil.)	–	–	–	–	–	–
Employees	–	–	–	–	–	192

QUALSTAR CORP — NAS: QBAK

1267 Flynn Road
Camarillo, CA 93012
Phone: 805 583-7744
Fax: –
Web: www.qualstar.com; www.n2power.com

CEO: Steven N Bronson
CFO: Louann L Negrete
HR: –
FYE: December 31
Type: Public

People often refer to 'tape' when speaking about digital video. But Qualstar means it when it talks about tape especially when storing archival information on tape library systems. The company's products — tape drives and tape library data storage systems — house retrieve and manage large amounts of data in computer networks. Its other business is power supplies that convert AC voltage to DC. Qualstar's systems are compatible with a variety of operating systems and with storage management software from companies such as Symantec. The company which incorporates tape drives and media from Quantum and Sony into its libraries sells mainly to manufacturers and resellers. Two customers account for a combined quarter of revenues.

	Annual Growth	06/15*	12/15	12/16	12/17	12/18
Sales ($ mil.)	(1.8%)	12.9	4.9	9.4	10.6	12.2
Net income ($ mil.)	–	(1.3)	(1.9)	(1.2)	0.6	1.5
Market value ($ mil.)	64.6%	2.4	1.6	5.9	17.1	10.7
Employees	(19.3%)	38	32	22	20	20

*Fiscal year change

QUALYS, INC. — NMS: QLYS

919 E. Hillsdale Boulevard, 4th Floor
Foster City, CA 94404
Phone: 650 801-6100
Fax: –
Web: www.qualys.com

CEO: Philippe F. Courtot
CFO: Melissa Fisher
HR: –
FYE: December 31
Type: Public

Qualys tries to calm customers' qualms about cybersecurity. The Qualys Cloud Platform is a cloud security and compliance management software suite of about 20 applications that automates security weakness detection and network security asset auditing. Its biggest product Vulnerability Management includes continuous monitoring threat protection and IT asset tracking through a cloud agent. Its products keep watch over networks with hardware and software sensors. The company counts more than 12200 customers in some 130 countries. Qualys reaches many customers through partnerships with managed service providers consultants and resellers including IBM Fujitsu Optiv and Verizon Communications.

	Annual Growth	12/14	12/15	12/16	12/17	12/18
Sales ($ mil.)	20.2%	133.6	164.3	197.9	230.8	278.9
Net income ($ mil.)	17.3%	30.2	15.9	19.2	40.4	57.3
Market value ($ mil.)	18.6%	1,472.8	1,291.0	1,234.8	2,315.5	2,916.0
Employees	29.0%	431	510	684	869	1,194

QUANEX BUILDING PRODUCTS CORP
NYS: NX

1800 West Loop South, Suite 1500
Houston, TX 77027
Phone: 713 961-4600
Fax: –
Web: www.quanex.com

CEO: William C. (Bill) Griffiths
CFO: Brent L. Korb
HR: Cheryl Roettger
FYE: October 31
Type: Public

Quanex Building Products (QBP) makes engineered materials and components for OEMs of building products. Its Engineered Products and Aluminum Sheet Products operations serve the new home building and remodeling markets in North America and lesser so in Asia and Europe. QBP produces aluminum flat-rolled products used in exterior home trims screens and gutters. It also churns out window and door components insulating glass spacers solar panel sealants and extruded vinyl and composite framing material for fenestration OEMs. QBP generates around 80% of its total sales in the US.

	Annual Growth	10/15	10/16	10/17	10/18	10/19
Sales ($ mil.)	8.5%	645.5	928.2	866.6	889.8	893.8
Net income ($ mil.)	–	16.1	(1.9)	18.7	26.3	(46.7)
Market value ($ mil.)	0.6%	623.1	538.3	724.8	489.4	637.0
Employees	7.8%	2,693	4,138	3,954	3,818	3,632

QUANTA SERVICES, INC.
NYS: PWR

2800 Post Oak Boulevard, Suite 2600
Houston, TX 77056
Phone: 713 629-7600
Fax: –
Web: www.quantaservices.com

CEO: Earl C. (Duke) Austin
CFO: Derrick A. Jensen
HR: –
FYE: December 31
Type: Public

Quanta Services is a specialty contractor that designs installs repairs and maintains network infrastructure across North America and abroad. The company serves the electric power oil and natural gas and communication industries mainly in the US Canada and Australia. Capabilities include pylon construction distribution infrastructure and emergency response among much more. Its oil and gas business offers onshore and offshore services. Quanta's other services include outsource management and other specialty work such as installing traffic and light rail control systems directional drilling and constructing wind and solar power facilities. The company was founded in 1997.

	Annual Growth	12/14	12/15	12/16	12/17	12/18
Sales ($ mil.)	9.2%	7,851.3	7,572.4	7,651.3	9,466.5	11,171.4
Net income ($ mil.)	(0.3%)	296.7	310.9	198.4	315.0	293.3
Market value ($ mil.)	1.5%	4,019.7	2,867.2	4,934.4	5,537.6	4,261.9
Employees	12.4%	24,600	24,500	28,100	32,800	39,200

QUANTUM CORP
NMS: QMCO

224 Airport Parkway, Suite 550
San Jose, CA 95110
Phone: 408 944-4000
Fax: –
Web: www.quantum.com

CEO: Jon W. Gacek
CFO: Fuad Ahmad
HR: –
FYE: March 31
Type: Public

Quantum Corp. provides hardware and software used for data archiving backup and recovery. Its software-defined storage products include non-volatile memory express (NVMe) to solid-state drives (SSD) hard disk drives (HDD) tape and the cloud. Some of the company's products facilitate the storage and accessing of video and are used by broadcasters studios post-production companies sports franchises and corporations. Quantum sells its products through resellers and distributors and to computing equipment makers such as Dell EMC HP IBM and Oracle. The San Jose California-based company relies on five customers for about a third of its sales. About 55% of revenue comes from customers in the US.

	Annual Growth	03/15	03/16	03/17	03/18	03/19
Sales ($ mil.)	(7.6%)	553.1	476.0	505.3	437.7	402.7
Net income ($ mil.)	–	16.8	(74.7)	3.6	(43.3)	(42.8)
Market value ($ mil.)	10.4%	57.7	22.0	31.4	131.2	85.8
Employees	(10.6%)	1,250	1,200	1,150	–	800

QUANTUM FUEL SYSTEMS TECHNOLOGIES WORLDWIDE INC.
NAS: QTWW

25242 Arctic Ocean Drive
Lake Forest, CA 92630
Phone: 949 399-4500
Fax: 949 399-4600
Web: www.qtww.com

CEO: W Brian Olson
CFO: Bradley J Timon
HR: –
FYE: December 31
Type: Public

If you're ready to make a quantum leap to a new fuel source then Quantum Fuel Systems Technologies Worldwide is the place to land. Quantum makes fuel storage delivery devices and electronic control systems for alternative-fueled vehicles. It serves the military with its branded HyHauler Plus a transportable hydrogen refueling station that powers battlefield vehicles. Fisker Automotive a joint venture between Quantum and Fisker Coachbuild is developing the Karma an environmentally friendly luxury sports sedan using Quantum's plug-in-hybrid engine technology. Its customer base also includes aerospace and government entities.

	Annual Growth	04/11*	12/11	12/12	12/13	12/14
Sales ($ mil.)	18.9%	20.3	24.5	22.7	31.9	34.1
Net income ($ mil.)	–	(11.0)	(38.5)	(30.9)	(23.0)	(14.9)
Market value ($ mil.)	(6.8%)	60.1	17.0	15.9	181.6	48.6
Employees	15.4%	112	123	122	147	172

*Fiscal year change

QUEEN OF THE VALLEY MEDICAL CENTER

1000 TRANCAS ST
NAPA, CA 945582906
Phone: 707-252-4411
Fax: –
Web: www.thequeen.org

CEO: –
CFO: Don Miller
HR: Ron Scott
FYE: June 30
Type: Private

The Queen of the Valley Medical Center reigns over the whole of Napa Valley. The 190-bed hospital provides acute and tertiary care to the residents of California's Napa County. It operates a level III trauma center and provides emergency surgery and wound care services as well as specialty family work health nutritional and rehabilitation services. "The Queen" as it is known colloquially operates regional cancer orthopedic women's and heart centers as well as the Napa Valley Imaging Center and the Napa Valley Women's Healthcare Center. Queen of the Valley Medical Center is part of St. Joseph Health.

	Annual Growth	06/13	06/14	06/15	06/16	06/17
Sales ($ mil.)	2.4%	–	249.9	243.6	242.9	268.2
Net income ($ mil.)	–	–	(4.0)	(1.6)	(2.0)	13.5
Market value ($ mil.)	–	–	–	–	–	–
Employees	–	–	–	–	–	1,070

QUEST DIAGNOSTICS, INC.
NYS: DGX

500 Plaza Drive
Secaucus, NJ 07094
Phone: 973 520-2700
Fax: –
Web: www.questdiagnostics.com

CEO: Stephen H. (Steve) Rusckowski
CFO: Mark J. Guinan
HR: –
FYE: December 31
Type: Public

Quest Diagnostics is one of the largest clinical labs in the US. The company performs diagnostics on some 150 million specimens each year including routine clinical tests such as cholesterol checks Pap smears and HIV screenings. Quest Diagnostics also performs esoteric testing (such as genetic screening) and anatomic pathology testing (such as tissue biopsies for cancer testing). Its Quest Diagnostic Nichols Institute develops new diagnostics. In all the company serves about half of the physicians and hospitals and about a third of the adult population in the US per year. Quest Diagnostics has more than 2200 patient service centers where samples are collected.

	Annual Growth	12/14	12/15	12/16	12/17	12/18
Sales ($ mil.)	0.3%	7,435.0	7,493.0	7,515.0	7,709.0	7,531.0
Net income ($ mil.)	7.3%	556.0	709.0	645.0	772.0	736.0
Market value ($ mil.)	5.6%	9,053.1	9,603.9	12,406.5	13,296.2	11,241.5
Employees	0.6%	45,000	44,000	43,000	45,000	46,000

QUEST MEDIA & SUPPLIES, INC.

9000 FTHILLS BLVD STE 100
ROSEVILLE, CA 95747
Phone: 916-338-7070
Fax: –
Web: www.questsys.com

CEO: Timothy Burke
CFO: Francine Walrath
HR: Doreen Salvage
FYE: December 31
Type: Private

Quest wants to help guide clients in their technology journeys. Quest Media & Supplies provides a wide range of IT consulting and management services to Fortune 5000 firms as well as educational institutions government agencies and small and midsized companies across the US. Its offerings include cloud hosting application development networking security and disaster recovery data storage telecommunications and transport services and technology staffing. Quest is Gold Certified in the US for Cisco Systems and also supplies products from Blue Coat Dell Hitachi IBM Microsoft Polycom VMware and Xerox among other vendors. The company was founded in 1982 by CEO Tim Burke with his wife Cindy.

	Annual Growth	12/11	12/12	12/13	12/14	12/16
Sales ($ mil.)	7.7%	–	118.4	118.3	168.0	159.5
Net income ($ mil.)	18.8%	–	2.1	3.9	1.2	4.2
Market value ($ mil.)	–	–	–	–	–	–
Employees	–	–	–	–	–	130

QUEST SOFTWARE INC.

NASDAQ: QSFT

5 Polaris Way
Aliso Viejo CA 92656
Phone: 949-754-8000
Fax: 949-754-8999
Web: www.quest.com

CEO: Mike Kohlsdorf
CFO: –
HR: Amada Zapatagill
FYE: December 31
Type: Public

Quest Software has made enterprise systems management its personal mission. The company's software is designed to improve application performance manage transitions to new software platforms and monitor the delivery of data over corporate networks and the Internet. Its applications which are compatible with Oracle Microsoft and IBM database systems are used for diagnostics network monitoring application deployment and data replication in the event of system failures. Quest also offers virtualization software and provides a range of application database and other IT services. Customers come from the telecom manufacturing energy and public sectors. In 2012 Quest was acquired by Dell for $2.4 billion.

QUESTAR CORP.

NYS: STR

333 South State Street, P.O. Box 45433
Salt Lake City, UT 84145-0433
Phone: 801 324-5900
Fax: –
Web: www.questar.com

CEO: –
CFO: –
HR: –
FYE: December 31
Type: Public

Questar is on a quest for natural gas — finding it producing it and transporting storing and distributing it. The integrated energy company operates through three major units. Public utility Questar Gas its largest unit distributes natural gas to more than 900000 customers in Utah southwestern Wyoming and southeastern Idaho. Questar Pipeline operates a 2640-mile natural gas transportation system and gas storage facilities in Colorado Utah and Wyoming. Its exploration activities are led by its Wexpro business. In 2014 the company reported proved reserves of 566.1 billion cu. ft. of natural gas equivalent.

	Annual Growth	12/10	12/11	12/12	12/13	12/14
Sales ($ mil.)	1.4%	1,123.6	1,194.4	1,098.9	1,220.0	1,189.3
Net income ($ mil.)	(9.6%)	339.2	207.9	212.0	161.2	226.5
Market value ($ mil.)	9.8%	3,053.7	3,483.4	3,465.9	4,032.4	4,434.1
Employees	0.6%	1,705	1,730	1,738	1,725	1,745

QUESTAR GAS CO.

333 South State Street, P.O. Box 45433
Salt Lake City, UT 84145
Phone: 801 324-5000
Fax: –
Web: www.questar.com

CEO: Ronald W Jibson
CFO: Kevin W Hadlock
HR: –
FYE: December 31
Type: Public

Questar Gas's quest is to distribute natural gas to almost 919230 customers throughout Utah and in southeastern Idaho and southwestern Wyoming. The regulated utility which a subsidiary of integrated energy concern Questar Corporation operates more than 27000 miles of gas distribution mains and service lines. The company is regulated by the Public Service Commission of Utah and the Wyoming Public Service Commission. With an efficient and low-cost gas supply and a low ratio of customers to employees rates paid by Questar Gas customers are among the lowest in the US.

	Annual Growth	12/13	12/14	12/15	12/16	12/17
Sales ($ mil.)	(1.0%)	985.8	960.9	917.6	921.3	947.0
Net income ($ mil.)	6.3%	52.8	55.2	64.3	57.2	67.5
Market value ($ mil.)	–	–	–	–	–	–
Employees	(0.5%)	917	1,745	930	900	900

QUESTCOR PHARMACEUTICALS INC

NMS: QCOR

1300 North Kellogg Drive, Suite D
Anaheim, CA 92807
Phone: 714 786-4200
Fax: –
Web: www.questcor.com

CEO: Don M Bailey
CFO: Juergen Hermann
HR: –
FYE: December 31
Type: Public

Questcor Pharmaceuticals is on a journey for better health for patients and some good profitability for itself to boot. The company makes and develops drugs for neurological conditions and kidney treatments. Most of its revenue comes from the sale of H.P. Acthar Gel (or Acthar). Acthar is approved for the treatment of nearly 20 indications but the company receives the majority of its income from sales related to three of those: multiple sclerosis nephrotic syndrome and infantile spasms (a rare form of pediatric epilepsy). Questcor also sells insomnia treatment Doral. The company's BioVectra subsidiary provides contract manufacturing to other pharma firms.

	Annual Growth	12/08	12/09	12/10	12/11	12/12
Sales ($ mil.)	52.1%	95.2	88.3	115.1	218.2	509.3
Net income ($ mil.)	48.6%	40.5	26.6	35.1	79.6	197.7
Market value ($ mil.)	30.2%	545.0	278.1	862.4	2,434.3	1,564.3
Employees	86.5%	46	77	152	206	557

QUICK-MED TECHNOLOGIES INC.

OTC: QMDT

902 NW 4th St.
Gainesville FL 32601
Phone: 888-835-2211
Fax: 616-392-2438
Web: www.russells-tech.com

CEO: –
CFO: –
HR: –
FYE: June 30
Type: Public

Quick-Med Technologies hopes to be floating on a cloud — but not a cloud of mustard gas. The life sciences development company is working with the US Army to develop a therapy to treat people exposed to mustard gas. The underlying technology for the potential therapy MultiStat is also the basis for wound care products and cosmetic ingredient applications. A second technology NIMBUS (Novel Intrinsically Micro-Bonded Utility Substrate) uses bio-engineered antimicrobial polymers to protect wounds from infection and industrial and consumer goods from harmful microscopic pests.

QUICKEN LOANS INC.

1 Campus Martius Compuware Bldg. 1050 Woodward Ave.
Detroit MI 48226
Phone: 313-373-3000
Fax: 734-947-7931
Web: www.unitedroad.com

CEO: Matt Cullen
CFO: Julie Booth
HR: –
FYE: July 31
Type: Private

People searching for a loan quick click on Quicken Loans. A leading online mortgage lender Quicken Loans offers residential mortgages in all 50 states and provides such financing options as fixed- and adjustable-rate mortgages reverse mortgages and refinancing through its interactive website. The company also has loan centers in Michigan Ohio and Arizona. Affiliate Title Source offers title insurance property valuations and closing services. Its San Diego-based One Reverse Mortgage unit handles FHA-backed reverse mortgage programs. Another division In-House Realty includes a network of 4000 real estate agents. Rock Holdings which is led by founder and chairman Dan Gilbert owns Quicken Loans.

QUICKLOGIC CORP

NAS: QUIK

2220 Lundy Avenue
San Jose, CA 95131-1816
Phone: 408 990-4000
Fax: 408 990-4040
Web: www.quicklogic.com

CEO: Brian C Faith
CFO: Suping Cheung
HR: –
FYE: December 30
Type: Public

QuickLogic is quick to get embed. The company designs and sells logic chips that can be programmed by OEMs as well as low-power customizable chips used to add features to and extend the battery life of mobile consumer and business electronics. It also offers related hardware and software plus custom programming services. The fabless company — it uses contract manufacturers to produce its chips — targets smartphone tablet and access card manufacturers. Customers for its logic chips come from the aerospace instrumentation and military industries among others. Honeywell (15% of sales) is a top customer.

	Annual Growth	12/14*	01/16	01/17*	12/17	12/18
Sales ($ mil.)	(17.9%)	27.8	19.0	11.4	12.1	12.6
Net income ($ mil.)	–	(13.1)	(17.8)	(19.1)	(14.1)	(13.8)
Market value ($ mil.)	(30.1%)	21.8	7.7	9.5	11.9	5.2
Employees	(4.4%)	98	91	76	89	82

*Fiscal year change

QUICKSILVER PRODUCTION PARTNERS LP

801 Cherry St. Ste. 3700 Unit 19
Fort Worth TX 76102
Phone: 817-665-5000
Fax: 214-302-5980
Web: www.redmangousa.com

CEO: –
CFO: –
HR: –
FYE: December 31
Type: Private

Silver is nowhere to be found on Quicksilver Production Partners' production radar. An oil and gas exploration and development company Quicksilver Production owns and operates mature properties in the Barnett Shale in north Texas. Its assets which produce primarily natural gas and natural gas liquids (NGLs) have total proved reserves of some 430 billion of cubic feet equivalent. The company uses hydraulic fracturing to extract gas and NGLs from its wells which are found in terrain that makes extracting resources difficult or impossible to do using conventional methods. Quicksilver Production Partners was formed in late 2011 by Quicksilver Resources; it filed to go public in early 2012.

QUICKSILVER RESOURCES, INC.

NBB: KWKA Q

801 Cherry Street, Suite 3700, Unit 19
Fort Worth, TX 76102
Phone: 817 665-5000
Fax: 817 665-5008
Web: www.qrinc.com

CEO: Glenn Darden
CFO: Vanessa Gomez Lagatta
HR: –
FYE: December 31
Type: Public

With mercurial speed Quicksilver Resources seeks to turn oil and gas finds into profits. The independent oil and gas company acquires explores for develops and produces onshore oil and gas in North America. Its US and Canadian producing properties are primarily located in Colorado Montana Texas and Wyoming as well as Alberta with a focus on the Barnett Shale Horn River and Horseshoe Canyon basins. The company also has oil exploration opportunities in the Midland and Delaware basins in West Texas and Sand Wash basin in northwestern Colorado. In 2012 Quicksilver Resources had total proved reserves of 1.5 trillion cubic feet of natural gas equivalent.

	Annual Growth	12/10	12/11	12/12	12/13	12/14
Sales ($ mil.)	(11.5%)	928.3	943.6	709.0	561.6	569.4
Net income ($ mil.)	–	435.1	90.0	(2,352.6)	161.6	(103.1)
Market value ($ mil.)	(66.0%)	2,658.5	1,210.2	515.8	553.7	35.7
Employees	(10.3%)	452	477	417	338	293

QUIDEL CORP.

NMS: QDEL

12544 High Bluff Drive, Suite 200
San Diego, CA 92130
Phone: 858 552-1100
Fax: –
Web: www.quidel.com

CEO: Douglas C. (Doug) Bryant
CFO: Randall J. (Randy) Steward
HR: –
FYE: December 31
Type: Public

Is it the flu or are you pregnant? Quidel can tell you quickly enough. The company makes rapid diagnostic in vitro test products used at the point-of-care (POC) usually at a doctor's office or other outpatient setting. Unlike tests sent off to a lab POC tests can be read on the spot. Quidel's leading products are diagnostics for infectious diseases (such as influenza and strep throat) and reproductive health sold under the QuickVue D3 Direct Detection and Thyretain brands. The company also makes diagnostics for streptococci chlamydia and the ulcer-causing H. pylori bacterium as well as Sofia a next generation rapid immunofluorescence-based point-of-care diagnostic test system.

	Annual Growth	12/14	12/15	12/16	12/17	12/18
Sales ($ mil.)	30.0%	182.6	196.1	191.6	277.7	522.3
Net income ($ mil.)	–	(7.1)	(6.1)	(13.8)	(8.2)	74.2
Market value ($ mil.)	14.0%	1,139.0	835.0	843.6	1,707.4	1,922.8
Employees	19.0%	610	624	627	1,193	1,224

QUIKTRIP CORPORATION

4705 S. 129th East Ave.
Tulsa OK 74134
Phone: 918-615-7700
Fax: 918-615-7377
Web: www.quiktrip.com

CEO: Chet Cadieux
CFO: Sandra J Westbrook
HR: –
FYE: April 30
Type: Private

QuikTrip provides a quick fix for those on the go. QuikTrip (QT) owns and operates more than 615 gasoline/convenience stores in nearly a dozen mostly in the central US. QT stores which average 4600 sq. ft. feature the company's own QT brand of gas and diesel fuel as well as brand-name beverages candy and tobacco and QT's Quik 'n Tasty and HOTZI lines of sandwiches. QT's 15-plus travel centers offer scales food fuel showers and other services for truckers. The firm's FleetMaster program offers commercial trucking companies detailed reports showing drivers' product purchases amounts spent and odometer readings. QT was co-founded in 1958 by chairman Chester Cadieux. His son Chet runs the firm.

QUILL CORPORATION

100 Schelter Rd.
Lincolnshire IL 60069-3621
Phone: 847-634-6690
Fax: 847-821-2347
Web: www.quill.com

CEO: –
CFO: –
HR: –
FYE: January 31
Type: Subsidiary

Not quite as old-fashioned as its name suggests Quill distributes office products to about 1 million small and midsized US businesses. To compete with office supply superstores Quill markets some 50000 products under the Quill brand as well as under the Bic Hewlett-Packard Mead Papermate and Xerox names. It sells office supplies and furniture including technology products (cameras monitors) through a catalog and the company's website. Quill also equips medical professionals with workplace goods through its Medical Arts Press business. Jack Miller founded Quill in 1956. It was acquired in 1998 by office retailer Staples which counts Quill among its North American delivery segment.

QUINN EMANUEL URQUHART & SULLIVAN LLP

865 S. Figueroa St. 10th Fl.
Los Angeles CA 90017
Phone: 213-443-3000
Fax: 213-443-3100
Web: www.quinnemanuel.com

CEO: –
CFO: –
HR: –
FYE: December 31
Type: Private - Partnershi

Business litigation specialist Quinn Emanuel Urquhart & Sullivan has about 600 lawyers working out of a dozen offices. The firm organizes its trial practices into areas such as antitrust and trade regulation class actions construction health care intellectual property real estate and white-collar crime. Quinn Emanuel was founded in 1986. In March 2010 it added Kathleen Sullivan as a partner and as the head of its appellate practice; the firm updated its name from Quinn Emanuel Urquhart Oliver & Hedges to Quinn Emanuel Urquhart & Sullivan at that time.

QUINNIPIAC UNIVERSITY

275 MOUNT CARMEL AVE
HAMDEN, CT 065181908
Phone: 203-582-8200
Fax: –
Web: www.qu.edu

CEO: –
CFO: –
HR: –
FYE: June 30
Type: Private

At Quinnipiac University the first thing you may have to learn is how to pronounce it (for the record it's KWIN-uh-pe-ack). The private university offers a variety of liberal arts undergraduate programs as well as graduate programs in selected professional fields (business education health sciences communications arts and sciences nursing and law) to some 9000 students with a student-to-faculty ration of 16 to 1. It often appears on lists of top colleges including those published by U.S. News & World Report. The university known to political junkies and others for its polling operation includes eight schools and colleges across three Connecticut campuses (Mount Carmel York Hill and North Haven).

	Annual Growth	06/09	06/10	06/13	06/15	06/17
Sales ($ mil.)	2.4%	–	290.8	376.5	416.3	343.7
Net income ($ mil.)	14.1%	–	45.3	46.0	29.7	114.2
Market value ($ mil.)	–	–	–	–	–	–
Employees	–	–	–	–	–	900

QUINSTREET, INC.

950 Tower Lane, 6th Floor
Foster City, CA 94404
Phone: 650 587-7700
Fax: –
Web: www.quinstreet.com

NMS: QNST
CEO: Douglas (Doug) Valenti
CFO: Gregory Wong
HR: –
FYE: June 30
Type: Public

QuinStreet connects companies with potential customers through the information superhighway. The online direct marketing company uses proprietary technologies to provide leads to companies. Clients use the leads as the targets of their direct marketing campaigns. As a sign of its confidence in its quality QuinStreet has adopted a pay-for-performance model of pricing in which customers are charged based on lead performance. Catering mainly to the education and financial services sectors its customers have included big organizations such as DeVry and ADT. QuinStreet has offices in the US Brazil and India. The company was founded in 1999.

	Annual Growth	06/15	06/16	06/17	06/18	06/19
Sales ($ mil.)	12.7%	282.1	297.7	299.8	404.4	455.2
Net income ($ mil.)	–	(20.0)	(19.4)	(12.2)	15.9	62.5
Market value ($ mil.)	25.2%	325.8	179.3	210.7	641.6	800.7
Employees	(0.0%)	638	601	469	506	637

QUMU CORP

510 1st Avenue North, Suite 305
Minneapolis, MN 55403
Phone: 612 638-9100
Fax: –
Web: www.qumu.com

NAS: QUMU
CEO: Vern Hanzlik
CFO: Peter J. Goepfrich
HR: –
FYE: December 31
Type: Public

Qumu has ditched the disc and punched play on video. The company provides services that help companies create manage secure distribute and measure the reach of their videos. It divested its business tied to CDs DVDs and Blu-ray Discs to concentrate on products and service surrounding digital video. Qumu targets businesses that use video for meetings communications sales training and other purposes. Following an industry trend the company is moving from an on-premise video product to cloud-based model. Users can play Qumu videos on any device. The company counts IBM Safeway Barclays AT&T and Bayer as customers.

	Annual Growth	12/14	12/15	12/16	12/17	12/18
Sales ($ mil.)	(1.5%)	26.5	34.5	31.7	28.2	25.0
Net income ($ mil.)	–	(8.5)	(28.7)	(11.2)	(11.7)	(3.6)
Market value ($ mil.)	(38.9%)	131.6	26.1	22.9	22.8	18.3
Employees	(18.7%)	222	192	150	121	97

QURATE RETAIL INC

12300 Liberty Boulevard
Englewood, CO 80112
Phone: 720 875-5300
Fax: –
Web: www.qurateretail.com

NMS: QRTE A
CEO: Gregory B. (Greg) Maffei
CFO: Mark D. Carleton
HR: –
FYE: December 31
Type: Public

Liberty Interactive Corp. stands by your right to shop at home and online. The company owns and operates market-leading home shopping channel QVC which sells 770 products each week across the home apparel beauty and accessories jewelry and electronics categories. QVC also sells online. Liberty Interactive also runs online businesses including Zulily and online invitation site Evite. It also holds equity stakes in FTD Companies HSN Interval Leisure and LendingTree among others. Liberty Interactive acquired the long-standing rival of its QVC business HSN Inc. for around $2.1 billion in 2017. Liberty Interactive Corp. was formed in 2011 when its predecessor restructured and split off its Liberty Capital and Liberty Starz businesses as Liberty Media.

	Annual Growth	12/14	12/15	12/16	12/17	12/18
Sales ($ mil.)	7.6%	10,499.0	9,989.0	10,647.0	10,404.0	14,070.0
Net income ($ mil.)	14.3%	537.0	869.0	1,235.0	2,441.0	916.0
Market value ($ mil.)	(9.7%)	12,919.8	11,997.6	8,774.2	10,724.0	8,572.2
Employees	7.9%	20,078	22,080	21,080	28,255	27,226

QVC, INC.

1200 WILSON DR
WEST CHESTER, PA 193804262
Phone: 484-701-1000
Fax: –
Web: www.qvc.com

CEO: Michael A George
CFO: Jeffrey A Davis
HR: Roger Tegtmeyer
FYE: December 31
Type: Private

The phones are ringing off the hook at television home shopping company QVC. QVC (its name stands for "quality value and convenience") offers about 1000 items each week to TV-tied consumer shoppers. Merchandise includes apparel cosmetics electronics housewares jewelry and toys. It broadcasts 24 hours a day; viewers call in their orders to one of its three US call centers. If you can't find what you're shopping for on the tube it also sells online at QVC.com through mobile apps and some half dozen outlet stores in four states. The company has shopping channels in Germany Japan Italy and the UK. QVC is a subsidiary of shopping and travel site operator Liberty Interactive.

	Annual Growth	12/12	12/13	12/14	12/15	12/16
Sales ($ mil.)	0.2%	–	8,623.0	8,801.0	8,743.0	8,682.0
Net income ($ mil.)	0.5%	–	633.0	633.0	662.0	642.0
Market value ($ mil.)	–	–	–	–	–	–
Employees	–	–	–	–	–	17,700

R. E. MICHEL COMPANY, LLC

1 RE MICHEL DR
GLEN BURNIE, MD 210606408
Phone: 410-760-4000
Fax: –
Web: www.remichel.com

CEO: –
CFO: –
HR: –
FYE: December 31
Type: Private

Blowing hot and cold is good for R.E. Michel. The company is one of the nation's largest wholesale distributors of heating air-conditioning and refrigeration (HVAC-R) equipment parts and supplies. The family-owned and operated firm offers more than 16000 items through about 2 sales offices located across the Southern Mid-Atlantic and Northeastern regions of the country. R.E. Michel ships more than 20000 items each day from its 900000-sq.-ft. distribution center in Maryland. Its Exclusive Supplier Partnership (ESP) program offers customers inventory control advertising and marketing support. R.E. Michel was founded in 1935 as a supplier to the home heating oil burner industry.

	Annual Growth	12/09	12/10	12/11	12/12	12/13
Sales ($ mil.)	4.9%	–	593.1	607.0	611.7	685.1
Net income ($ mil.)	41.2%	–	11.2	8.4	3.9	31.5
Market value ($ mil.)	–	–	–	–	–	–
Employees	–	–	–	–	–	1,960

R. L. JORDAN OIL COMPANY OF NORTH CAROLINA, INC.

1451 FERNWOOD GLENDALE RD
SPARTANBURG, SC 293073044
Phone: 864-585-2784
Fax: –
Web: www.hotspotcstore.com

CEO: Wilton Jordan
CFO: –
HR: Elizabeth Gladson
FYE: September 30
Type: Private

R. L. Jordan Oil Company takes gas from hot spots and sells it — and lots more — at Hot Spots. The company operates a chain of more than 50 convenience stores and gas stations under the Hot Spots banner as well as about 10 fast food restaurants under the Hardee's and Subway names. It operates in the Carolinas. About 75% of the company's stores are located in South Carolina. The family-owned and operated company was founded by its namesake and former chairman in 1950 the late R. L. Jordan. As part of its operations the Jordan family also owns a real estate business Jordan Properties which operates several hotels and properties in North Carolina.

	Annual Growth	09/03	09/04	09/05	09/06	09/07
Sales ($ mil.)	12.3%	–	–	221.0	271.0	278.6
Net income ($ mil.)	–	–	–	(0.9)	(1.7)	(0.3)
Market value ($ mil.)	–	–	–	–	–	–
Employees	–	–	–	–	–	900

R.C. WILLEY HOME FURNISHINGS

2301 S 300 W
SALT LAKE CITY, UT 841152516
Phone: 801-461-3900
Fax: –
Web: www.rcwilley.com

CEO: –
CFO: Curtis Child
HR: Dan Pessetto
FYE: December 31
Type: Private

R.C. Willey Home Furnishings does its best to be top dog. The company drives traffic by giving away some 600000 hot dogs a year at about a dozen stores in Utah Nevada California and Idaho. Despite Sunday store closures and operations in only four states R.C. Willey is one of the nation's largest furniture retailers. It sells furniture (La-Z-Boy Flexsteel) appliances (GE Maytag) electronics (Sony Panasonic) and flooring. The company also sells mattresses (Serta Spring Air Simmons). In 1932 Rufus Call (R.C.) Willey sold appliances door-to-door; today the company he founded is run by his son-in-law chairman Bill Child and grandsons. Berkshire Hathaway purchased the company in 1995.

	Annual Growth	12/12	12/13	12/14	12/16	12/17
Sales ($ mil.)	5.0%	–	664.6	713.0	800.9	807.7
Net income ($ mil.)	6.3%	–	15.4	17.4	26.7	19.6
Market value ($ mil.)	–	–	–	–	–	–
Employees	–	–	–	–	–	2,700

R.S. HUGHES COMPANY, INC.

1162 SONORA CT
SUNNYVALE, CA 940865378
Phone: 408-739-3211
Fax: –
Web: www.rshughes.com

CEO: Peter Biocini
CFO: Thomas Smith
HR: –
FYE: September 30
Type: Private

R.S. Hughes distributes the stuff that holds the world together — duct tape that is — plus a lot more. Established in 1954 the employee-owned company maintains some 45 warehouse locations in the US and Mexico. It supplies adhesives (epoxies aerosols hot glues silicones) electrical specialties (tubing terminals films tape and barriers) safety products (glasses ear plugs masks) tapes (masking foam vinyl cloth foil duct joining) and abrasives (roll disc brush wheel belt and air tools). R.S. Hughes also distributes labels and signs (printable labels and tags safety signs) and aerosols and coatings (WD-40 paints lubricants oils cleaners).

	Annual Growth	09/14	09/15*	10/16	10/17*	09/18
Sales ($ mil.)	6.6%	–	323.7	329.5	351.7	392.4
Net income ($ mil.)	8.4%	–	16.4	16.6	17.1	20.9
Market value ($ mil.)	–	–	–	–	–	–
Employees	–	–	–	–	–	505

*Fiscal year change

R1 RCM INC

NMS: RCM

401 North Michigan Avenue, Suite 2700
Chicago, IL 60611
Phone: 312 324-7820
Fax: –
Web: www.r1rcm.com

CEO: Joseph G. (Joe) Flanagan
CFO: Christopher Ricaurte
HR: Mike Shearin
FYE: December 31
Type: Public

R1 RCM provides revenue cycle management (RCM) services to health care providers. It handles patient registration benefits verification medical coding billing and other tasks for clients. The company specializes in enhancing efficiencies and quality while reducing costs. It provides technology solutions process workflows and administrative personnel to improve back-office operations. Typical customers are not-for-profit and for-profit hospital systems such as Ascension Health and Intermountain Health as well as independent medical centers physician groups and EMS organizations. The company operates more than 25 offices in the US and seven offices overseas.

	Annual Growth	12/14	12/15	12/16	12/17	12/18
Sales ($ mil.)	42.6%	210.1	117.2	592.6	449.8	868.5
Net income ($ mil.)	–	(79.6)	(84.3)	177.1	(58.8)	(45.3)
Market value ($ mil.)	3.8%	758.3	353.7	248.7	487.5	878.8
Employees	57.4%	3,030	3,258	6,644	9,965	18,600

RABOBANK N.A.

1448 Main St.
El Centro CA 92243
Phone: 760-337-3200
Fax: 508-634-3394
Web: www.seracare.com

CEO: –
CFO: –
HR: –
FYE: December 31
Type: Subsidiary

Rabobank N.A. is the primary US subsidiary of Netherlands-based Rabobank Group. It operates about 120 bank branches agricultural field offices and financial service centers in Central and Southern California that offer commercial and consumer loans; checking savings and time deposits; trust and investment services; Visa credit cards; and more. Rabobank Group entered the US in 2005 when it bought Valley Independent Bank which was founded more than twenty years earlier by local farmers and business owners to serve agricultural concerns. The strategy mirrors that of Rabobank Group which was founded by Dutch farmers in the 1890s.

RACETRAC PETROLEUM, INC.

3225 CUMBERLAND BLVD SE # 100
ATLANTA, GA 303396407
Phone: 770-850-3491
Fax: –
Web: www.racetrac.com

CEO: Carl E Bolch Jr
CFO: Robert J Dumbacher
HR: –
FYE: December 31
Type: Private

RaceTrac Petroleum hopes it's a popular pit stop for gasoline and snacks in the South. The company operates more than 600 gas stations and convenience stores in 10 southern US states under the RaceTrac and RaceWay names. (RaceWay stores are operated by independent contractors.) The chain plans to grow by expanding its store count by about 10% a year. Carl Bolch founded RaceTrac in Missouri in 1934. His son chairman Carl Bolch Jr. moved the company into high-volume gas stations with long self-service islands that can serve as many as two dozen vehicles at one time. RaceTrac's convenience stores sell fresh deli food and offer some fast-food fare. The Bolch family owns and runs the company.

	Annual Growth	12/11	12/12	12/13	12/14	12/15
Sales ($ mil.)	–	–	0.0	8,843.3	9,101.5	7,501.8
Net income ($ mil.)	24.3%	–	56.0	122.2	161.0	107.6
Market value ($ mil.)	–	–	–	–	–	–
Employees	–	–	–	–	–	3,479

RACKSPACE HOSTING INC
NYS: RAX

1 Fanatical Place, City of Windcrest
San Antonio, TX 78218
Phone: 210 312-4000
Fax: –
Web: www.rackspace.com

CEO: Kevin Jones
CFO: Karl Pichler
HR: –
FYE: December 31
Type: Public

Looking for server rack space to host your company's data network needs? Well look no further than Rackspace Hosting. The company provides a range of web hosting and managed network services for businesses. It offers traditional hosting services with dedicated servers but is expanding into cloud hosting which lets customers use pooled server resources on an on-demand basis. Its cloud computing services include public private and hybrid cloud hosting which provides a combination of dedicated hosting and cloud computing. Founded in 1998 Rackspace has more than 200000 business customers in 120 countries.

	Annual Growth	12/10	12/11	12/12	12/13	12/14
Sales ($ mil.)	23.1%	780.6	1,025.1	1,309.2	1,534.8	1,794.4
Net income ($ mil.)	24.3%	46.4	76.4	105.4	86.7	110.6
Market value ($ mil.)	10.5%	4,427.1	6,062.1	10,468.0	5,515.2	6,597.6
Employees	16.1%	3,262	4,040	4,852	5,651	5,936

RADIAN GROUP, INC.
NYS: RDN

1500 Market Street
Philadelphia, PA 19102
Phone: 215 231-1000
Fax: –
Web: www.radian.biz

CEO: Richard G. (Rick) Thornberry
CFO: J. Franklin (Frank) Hall
HR: Karen L Chung
FYE: December 31
Type: Public

Radian Group is glowing from a conflagration of private mortgage insurance claims. Through subsidiaries Radian Guaranty Radian Mortgage Assurance and Radian Insurance Radian Group provides traditional private mortgage insurance coverage to protect lenders from defaults by borrowers who put down a deposit of less than 20% when buying a home. Such coverage provides protection on individual loans and covers unpaid loan principal and delinquent interest. Its pool insurance covers limited exposure on groups of loans. Radian still insures municipal bonds written before 2008 through its financial guaranty business. Radian Group's customers include mortgage bankers commercial banks and savings institutions.

	Annual Growth	12/14	12/15	12/16	12/17	12/18
Assets ($ mil.)	(2.0%)	6,860.0	5,642.1	5,863.2	5,900.9	6,314.7
Net income ($ mil.)	(10.9%)	959.5	286.9	308.3	121.1	606.0
Market value ($ mil.)	(0.5%)	3,569.3	2,858.4	3,838.2	4,399.7	3,492.4
Employees	3.4%	1,702	1,881	1,971	1,887	1,942

RADIANT LOGISTICS, INC.
ASE: RLGT

405 114th Ave S.E., Third Floor
Bellevue, WA 98004
Phone: 425 943-4599
Fax: 425 462-0768
Web: www.radiantdelivers.com

CEO: Bohn H. Crain
CFO: Todd E. Macomber
HR: –
FYE: June 30
Type: Public

When companies need someone to transport their freight Radiant Logistics delivers. Operating through its Airgroup and Adcom Worldwide subsidiaries the company offers logistics services such as domestic and international air ocean and ground freight forwarding (Radiant purchases transportation capacity from carriers and resells to its customers). In addition Radiant provides supply chain management services such as warehousing order fulfillment and inventory management. Government and automotive sectors (e.g. US Transportation Command Ford and General Motors) make up the company's customer base. Radiant operates through more than 100 offices located throughout North America.

	Annual Growth	06/15	06/16	06/17	06/18	06/19
Sales ($ mil.)	15.4%	502.7	782.5	777.6	842.4	890.5
Net income ($ mil.)	29.2%	5.9	(3.5)	4.9	10.2	16.3
Market value ($ mil.)	(4.3%)	362.5	148.8	266.8	193.9	304.5
Employees	(1.8%)	760	640	758	728	708

RADIANT SYSTEMS INC.

3925 Brookside Pkwy.
Alpharetta GA 30022
Phone: 770-576-6000
Fax: 770-754-7790
Web: www.radiantsystems.com

CEO: John Bruno
CFO: Mark E Haidet
HR: –
FYE: December 31
Type: Subsidiary

Radiant Systems helps businesses provide shining service. The company's point-of-sale (POS) systems combine hardware and software to manage centralized merchandising functions like ordering and scheduling customer access and visibility across an enterprise. Its touchscreen-based POS systems are used largely in the US hospitality industry; other clients include retail businesses like gas stations and cinemas. Radiant has historically gotten about half of its revenues from sales of maintenance subscription transaction and other services. The company markets directly and through resellers. Clients have included 7-Eleven Exxon Mobil and The Home Depot. Radiant was acquired by NCR for $1.2 billion in 2011.

RADISYS CORP.

NMS: RSYS

5435 N.E. Dawson Creek Drive
Hillsboro, OR 97124
Phone: 503 615-1100
Fax: –
Web: www.radisys.com

CEO: Brian Bronson
CFO: Jonathan Wilson
HR: –
FYE: December 31
Type: Public

RadiSys makes hardware and software that help its customers run their networks more efficiently. Its products help route video and audio traffic to systems that will process it most effectively in terms of quality and cost. Radisys' offerings include application-specific systems board-level modules and chip-level components. The company also offers system integration software training and repair services. RadiSys sells its products to companies that make telecommunications products automated manufacturing devices gaming machines cars medical instruments and test and measurement tools. Customers range from Aastra and AT&T to Verint Systems and West Corp.

	Annual Growth	12/12	12/13	12/14	12/15	12/16
Sales ($ mil.)	(7.2%)	286.1	237.9	192.7	184.6	212.4
Net income ($ mil.)	–	(43.5)	(49.4)	(27.6)	(14.7)	(10.3)
Market value ($ mil.)	10.4%	114.8	88.2	90.1	106.7	170.6
Employees	(4.8%)	976	984	859	710	800

RADIUS HEALTH INC

NMS: RDUS

950 Winter Street
Waltham, MA 02451
Phone: 617 551-4000
Fax: –
Web: www.radiuspharm.com

CEO: Robert E. (Bob) Ward
CFO: Jose (Pepe) Carmona
HR: –
FYE: December 31
Type: Public

Radius Health would like to banish the fear of Grandma falling and breaking a hip. The biopharmaceutical company targets osteoporosis and other women's health concerns through the development of new drugs. Its leading candidate is a synthetic version of a naturally occurring human bone-building protein. Administered via injection or transdermal patch the drug could be used to promote new bone growth and restore bone density in patients with osteoporosis. The company's pipeline also contains a treatment for hot flashes and one for age-related weigh loss frailty and muscle loss; 3M Lonza and Vetter Pharma make its drugs. Radius Health became a public company in mid-2015.

	Annual Growth	12/14	12/15	12/16	12/17	12/18
Sales ($ mil.)	348.8%	–	–	–	22.1	99.2
Net income ($ mil.)	–	(62.5)	(101.5)	(182.8)	(254.2)	(221.3)
Market value ($ mil.)	(19.3%)	1,772.9	2,804.0	1,732.8	1,447.6	751.3
Employees	105.6%	26	75	237	561	465

RADNET INC

NMS: RDNT

1510 Cotner Avenue
Los Angeles, CA 90025
Phone: 310 478-7808
Fax: –
Web: www.radnet.com

CEO: Howard G. Berger
CFO: Mark D. Stolper
HR: –
FYE: December 31
Type: Public

Image is everything at RadNet. The company owns and/or manages more than 300 centers that offer a variety of diagnostic imaging services including magnetic resonance imaging (MRI) computed tomography (CT) PET scanning X-ray ultrasound and mammography. Its facilities are typically organized in regional clusters around urban hubs. RadNet contracts with groups of radiologists and other third parties to provide the actual medical services while it runs the administration of the facilities and takes a cut of the revenues plus a management fee. It also develops and sells radiology software and provides teleradiology interpretation services.

	Annual Growth	12/14	12/15	12/16	12/17	12/18
Sales ($ mil.)	8.0%	717.6	809.6	884.5	922.2	975.1
Net income ($ mil.)	120.0%	1.4	7.7	7.2	0.1	32.2
Market value ($ mil.)	4.5%	418.3	302.7	315.9	494.7	498.1
Employees	5.5%	6,361	7,384	7,360	7,525	7,869

RADY CHILDREN'S HOSPITAL-SAN DIEGO

3020 CHILDRENS WAY
SAN DIEGO, CA 921234223
Phone: 858-576-1700
Fax: –
Web: www.rchsd.org

CEO: Stephen Kingsmore
CFO: –
HR: –
FYE: June 30
Type: Private

Rady Children's Hospital-San Diego handles the big injuries of pint-sized patients. Serving as the region's only pediatric trauma center the nonprofit hospital boasts more than 520 beds. As part of its services Rady Children's Hospital-San Diego offers comprehensive pediatric care including surgical services convalescent care a neonatal intensive care unit and orthopedic services. Across its service area the hospital also operates about 25 satellite centers that provide such primary and specialized care services as physical therapy and hearing diagnostics. Rady Children's Hospital a teaching hospital affiliated with the University of California San Diego Medical School was founded in 1954.

	Annual Growth	06/08	06/09	06/10	06/14	06/15
Sales ($ mil.)	1.0%	–	490.9	619.9	838.7	522.0
Net income ($ mil.)	–	–	(56.5)	42.6	82.6	104.9
Market value ($ mil.)	–	–	–	–	–	–
Employees	–	–	–	–	–	2,313

RAE SYSTEMS INC.

3775 N. 1st St.
San Jose CA 95134
Phone: 408-952-8200
Fax: 408-952-8480
Web: www.raesystems.com

CEO: –
CFO: Michael Hansen
HR: –
FYE: December 31
Type: Private

You may not learn who dealt it but the detection and monitoring instruments of RAE Systems will confirm the presence of gas and detail its chemical composition. The company went from being a supplier of stand-alone analytical instruments to providing networked instrumentation that can be used in many locales from factories to spills of hazardous materials and even to find those pesky missing weapons of mass destruction. RAE Systems counts the US Departments of Homeland Security Justice and State among its customers along with many sports facilities in the US. Customers in Asia account for about 40% of sales. In 2011 Vector Capital took RAE Systems private in a deal valued at about $138 million.

RAILAMERICA INC.

NYSE: RA

7411 Fullerton St. Ste. 300
Jacksonville FL 32256
Phone: 904-999-5000
Fax: 716-854-8480
Web: www.randcapital.com

CEO: John E Giles
CFO: Clyde Preslar
HR: –
FYE: December 31
Type: Public

Piece by piece RailAmerica has assembled an extensive rail transportation network. The company operates short-line railroads (generally less than 350 miles long) and regional freight lines in the US and Canada. RailAmerica owns interests in more than 40 railroads that operate over a network of about 7500 miles of track. RailAmerica has about 1500 customers and transports such items as coal lumber and forest products chemicals and agricultural products. RailAmerica's real estate division handles track and land leases and handles road and other access requests. In late 2012 the company was acquired by rival Genesee & Wyoming.

RAINMAKER SYSTEMS INC. — NBB: RMKR

900 East Hamilton Avenue, Suite 400
Campbell, CA 95008
Phone: 408 626-3800
Fax: 408 369-0910
Web: www.rainmakersystems.com

CEO: -
CFO: -
HR: -
FYE: December 31
Type: Public

Rainmaker Systems is tapping into the power of the cloud. The company is a global provider of cloud-based business-to-business (B2B) selling services designed to help companies boost buying activity among their customers online. Its Rainmaker Revenue Delivery Platform provides a hosted technology portal for clients to sell and renew product and service contracts. It allows Rainmaker to resell subscriptions software licenses and warranties on behalf of its clients. Additionally it aids in sales lead development and in selling training services. Operating from offices in the US Europe and Asia Rainmaker primarily serves clients in computer hardware and software telecommunications and financial services.

	Annual Growth	12/09	12/10	12/11	12/12	12/13
Sales ($ mil.)	(22.0%)	47.8	42.8	37.0	25.4	17.7
Net income ($ mil.)	-	(8.3)	(10.0)	(11.0)	(10.3)	(21.0)
Market value ($ mil.)	(36.6%)	61.8	58.8	33.9	30.3	10.0
Employees	(37.0%)	950	1,450	1,050	130	150

RAIT FINANCIAL TRUST — NBB: RASL Q

Two Logan Square, 100 N. 18th Street, 23rd Floor
Philadelphia, PA 19103
Phone: 215 207-2100
Fax: -
Web: www.rait.com

CEO: Scott L. N. Davidson
CFO: Paul W. Kopsky
HR: -
FYE: December 31
Type: Public

RAIT Financial Trust is a real estate investment trust (REIT) that specializes in originating commercial real estate loans and acquiring and managing commercial real estate properties. Its loan portfolio is made up of mezzanine and short-term bridge financing mainly secured by multifamily office and retail properties. RAIT also provides loan servicing commercial property and asset management and asset repositioning and sales services for other real estate firms. Subsidiary Taberna Realty Finance provides long-term real estate capital while Independence Realty Trust (IRT) owns apartment properties in opportunistic US markets. RAIT filed for Chapter 11 bankruptcy protection in 2019.

	Annual Growth	12/14	12/15	12/16	12/17	12/18
Assets ($ mil.)	(32.4%)	3,513.5	4,447.3	2,406.8	1,791.8	733.8
Net income ($ mil.)	-	(289.5)	40.0	25.3	(151.9)	(123.5)
Market value ($ mil.)	(46.4%)	46.1	35.1	39.3	23.3	3.8
Employees	(57.9%)	794	870	226	223	25

RALCORP FROZEN BAKERY PRODUCTS INC.

3250 Lacey Rd. Ste. 600
Downers Grove IL 60515
Phone: 630-455-5200
Fax: 630-455-5202
Web: www.ralcorpfrozen.com

CEO: -
CFO: -
HR: -
FYE: September 30
Type: Subsidiary

Go ahead bask in the applause; Ralcorp Frozen Bakery Products makes you the chef. The company manufactures frozen food products from ready-to-eat and thaw-and-sell to toastable and microwaveable baked goods. Products are sold under private- and global name brands such as Bakery Chef (biscuits) Krusteaz (pancakes) and Lofthouse (cookies). It also makes breakfast items for McDonald's. Ralcorp Frozen a division of private-brand food giant Ralcorp accounts for some 20% of its parent's revenues selling to in-store bakeries but also retail groceries and industrial and institutional food service operators. To puff up its frozen offerings Ralcorp acquired Sara Lee's refrigerated dough business in 2011.

RALEY'S

500 W CAPITOL AVE
WEST SACRAMENTO, CA 956052696
Phone: 916-373-3333
Fax: -
Web: www.raleys.com

CEO: Michael J. (Mike) Teel
CFO: Ken Mueller
HR: -
FYE: June 30
Type: Private

Raley's has to stock plenty of fresh fruit and great wines — it sells to the people that produce them. The company operates about 130 supermarkets and superstores in California and Nevada. In addition to about 80 flagship Raley's Superstores the company operates about 20 Bel Air Markets (in the Sacramento area) and Nob Hill Foods (an upscale Bay Area chain with some 20 locations). Raley's stores typically offer groceries natural foods and liquor as well as in-store pharmacies. Founded during the Depression by Thomas Porter Raley the company is still owned and run by the Raley family.

	Annual Growth	06/07	06/08	06/09	06/10	06/12
Sales ($ mil.)	-	-	-	0.0	3,064.4	3,162.3
Net income ($ mil.)	-	-	-	0.0	0.0	(1.3)
Market value ($ mil.)	-	-	-	-	-	-
Employees	-	-	-	-	-	14,000

RALPH LAUREN CORP — NYS: RL

650 Madison Avenue
New York, NY 10022
Phone: 212 318-7000
Fax: -
Web: www.ralphlauren.com

CEO: Patrice J. L. Louvet
CFO: Jane H. Nielsen
HR: Dean Dellantonia
FYE: March 30
Type: Public

Ralph Lauren Corporation is galloping at a faster clip than when its namesake founder first entered the arena over 45 years ago. With golden mallet brands such as Polo by Ralph Lauren Chaps RRL Club Monaco and RLX Ralph Lauren the company designs and markets apparel and accessories home furnishings and fragrances. Its collections are available at more than 13000 retail locations worldwide including many upscale and mid-tier department stores (Macy's contributes 25% to RL's wholesale revenue). It operates 465-plus Ralph Lauren and Club Monaco retail stores worldwide as well as 615-plus concession-based shops-within-shops and 10 e-commerce sites.

	Annual Growth	03/15*	04/16	04/17*	03/18	03/19
Sales ($ mil.)	(4.6%)	7,620.0	7,405.0	6,652.8	6,182.3	6,313.0
Net income ($ mil.)	(11.5%)	702.0	396.0	(99.3)	162.8	430.9
Market value ($ mil.)	(0.3%)	10,248.3	7,596.0	6,374.5	8,731.6	10,128.0
Employees	(0.7%)	25,000	26,000	23,300	23,500	24,300

*Fiscal year change

RAMBUS INC. (DE) — NMS: RMBS

1050 Enterprise Way, Suite 700
Sunnyvale, CA 94089
Phone: 408 462-8000
Fax: -
Web: www.rambus.com

CEO: Ronald D. (Ron) Black
CFO: Rahul Mathur
HR: -
FYE: December 31
Type: Public

While Rambus sits around and thinks of new semiconductor technologies other companies put its designs to work. Rambus licenses its intellectual property designs for computer memory — called Rambus DRAM or RDRAM — that speeds the exchange of signals between a computer's memory and logic chips. RDRAM chips are used in PCs video game consoles and other electronic systems. Rambus' leading licensees include AMD Fujitsu NEC Panasonic and Toshiba. It also licenses LCD lighting product designs. The company holds more than 1800 patents and has some 700 patent applications pending.

	Annual Growth	12/14	12/15	12/16	12/17	12/18
Sales ($ mil.)	(6.0%)	296.6	296.3	336.6	393.1	231.2
Net income ($ mil.)	-	26.2	211.4	6.8	(22.9)	(158.0)
Market value ($ mil.)	(8.8%)	1,209.0	1,263.5	1,501.2	1,550.2	836.2
Employees	12.0%	505	495	540	570	796

RAMTRON INTERNATIONAL CORPORATION NASDAQ: RMTR

1850 Ramtron Dr.
Colorado Springs CO 80921
Phone: 719-481-7000
Fax: 719-481-9294
Web: www.ramtron.com

CEO: Eric A Balzer
CFO: Gery E Richards
HR: –
FYE: December 31
Type: Public

Ramtron International provides the F-RAM needed to watch Tron in the palm of your hand. Ramtron designs ferroelectric random-access memories (F-RAMs) which it touts as providing better performance than other kinds of memory chips and which are used in products such as power meters laser printers and handheld devices. It partners with Fujitsu Infineon and Toshiba among others. The company sells directly and through distributors including Future Electronics Mouser (a subsidiary of TTI) and Tokyo Electron Device. Most of Ramtron's sales come from outside the US. In 2012 the company agreed to be acquired by Cypress Semiconductor in a $3.10 per share deal with a total value of around $110 million.

RAND LOGISTICS INC NBB: RLOG Q

333 Washington Street, Suite 201
Jersey City, NJ 07302
Phone: 212 863-9427
Fax: –
Web: www.randlogisticsinc.com

CEO: Peter Coxon
CFO: Mark S Hiltwein
HR: –
FYE: March 31
Type: Public

Rand Logistics hauls dry bulk cargo across the Great Lakes calling on ports in the US and Canada. Through subsidiaries Lower Lakes Towing (Canadian ports) Lower Lakes Transportation (US ports) and Grand River Navigation the company operates a fleet of more than a dozen vessels consisting mainly of self-unloading bulk carriers. (Self-unloading vessels don't require land-based assistance so they can arrive at a dock and unload any time.) Conventional bulk carriers and an integrated tug/barge unit make up the rest of Rand Logistics' fleet. Cargo carried by the company includes construction aggregates coal grain iron ore and salt. Mainly to eliminate about $90 million in outstanding debt Rand Logistics agreed to be acquired by American Industrial Partners a New York-based private equity firm in late 2017.

	Annual Growth	03/13	03/14	03/15	03/16	03/17
Sales ($ mil.)	(7.3%)	156.6	155.8	153.0	148.4	115.5
Net income ($ mil.)	–	(3.8)	(4.5)	(9.4)	(4.2)	(18.2)
Market value ($ mil.)	(43.2%)	114.1	128.6	60.6	17.7	11.9
Employees	(1.5%)	543	504	515	498	512

RANDOM HOUSE INC.

1745 Broadway
New York NY 10019
Phone: 212-782-9000
Fax: 919-554-4361
Web: www.thebodyshop.com

CEO: –
CFO: –
HR: –
FYE: December 31
Type: Subsidiary

Its not-so-random acts of publishing have transformed Random House into the world's largest trade book publisher. The book publishing subsidiary of media giant Bertelsmann Random House operates its eponymous imprint and some 200 others such as Alfred A. Knopf Ballantine Bantam Dell and Doubleday. Its top-sellers include Dan Brown's The Da Vinci Code and its stable of authors includes Elmore Leonard Toni Morrison and Dr. Seuss. In addition the company publishes Fodor's popular travel books audio products and electronic books. Outside the US Random House oversees publishers such as McClelland & Stewart (Canada) and Plaza & Janes (Spain). In 2012 it announced plans to combine with The Penguin Group.

RANGE RESOURCES CORP NYS: RRC

100 Throckmorton Street, Suite 1200
Fort Worth, TX 76102
Phone: 817 870-2601
Fax: –

CEO: Jeffrey L. (Jeff) Ventura
CFO: Roger S. Manny
HR: –
FYE: December 31
Type: Public

Range Resources is an independent natural gas NGLs and oil company engaged in the exploration development and acquisition of natural gas and oil properties primarily in the Marcellus Shale of Pennsylvania with some operations in the Lower Cotton Valley formation of Louisiana. The company has more than 15 Tcfe of proved reserves (70% of which is natural gas) with average production of 2000 Mmcfe per day from around 5120 net producing wells.

	Annual Growth	12/14	12/15	12/16	12/17	12/18
Sales ($ mil.)	4.9%	2,711.7	1,598.1	1,099.9	2,611.0	3,282.6
Net income ($ mil.)	–	634.4	(713.7)	(521.4)	333.1	(1,746.5)
Market value ($ mil.)	(35.0%)	13,336.3	6,140.4	8,573.2	4,256.6	2,387.8
Employees	(5.3%)	990	744	762	773	796

RAPID CITY REGIONAL HOSPITAL, INC.

353 FAIRMONT BLVD
RAPID CITY, SD 577017393
Phone: 605-719-1000
Fax: –

CEO: Charles Hart
CFO: –
HR: Jeremy Weaver
FYE: June 30
Type: Private

Mt. Rushmore sightseers bikers and locals alike can seek medical care at Rapid City Regional Hospital. The medical facility is a general and psychiatric hospital with some 330 acute care beds and 50 psychiatric beds located in the Black Hills region of western South Dakota. In addition to emergency and acute care the not-for-profit hospital also offers a behavioral health center a rehabilitation facility a cancer care institute and women's and children's departments. Rapid City Regional Hospital is part of Regional Health a network of regional hospitals medical clinics and senior care centers.

	Annual Growth	06/12	06/13	06/14	06/15	06/16
Sales ($ mil.)	(1.6%)	–	489.9	517.9	437.5	467.4
Net income ($ mil.)	(17.2%)	–	50.0	56.7	39.4	28.3
Market value ($ mil.)	–	–	–	–	–	–
Employees	–	–	–	–	–	4,200

RAPPAHANNOCK ELECTRIC COOPERATIVE

247 INDUSTRIAL CT
FREDERICKSBURG, VA 224082443
Phone: 540-898-8500
Fax: –
Web: www.myrec.coop

CEO: Kent D Farmer
CFO: –
HR: Patricia Hatcher
FYE: December 31
Type: Private

Like the river it's named after the Rappahannock Electric Cooperative (REC) keeps the power running smoothly. The consumer-owned cooperative provides electricity to homes businesses and industries in parts of 22 counties from the Blue Ridge Mountains to the mouth of the Rappahannock River in eastern Virginia. REC supplies power to more than 157000 members over more than 16000 miles of power line. REC offers surge protection internet services and home security plans to entice customers as competition from other suppliers arrives. Once rural in nature the cooperative's territory has seen large pockets of suburban growth.

	Annual Growth	12/14	12/15	12/16	12/17	12/18
Sales ($ mil.)	(1.1%)	–	461.9	418.2	373.8	446.7
Net income ($ mil.)	11.8%	–	15.3	15.0	17.8	21.3
Market value ($ mil.)	–	–	–	–	–	–
Employees	–	–	–	–	–	423

RAPTOR NETWORKS TECHNOLOGY INC.　　　　OTC: RPTN

1508 S. Grand Ave.　　　　　　　　　　　　　CEO: Dmitriy Nikitin
Santa Ana CA 92705　　　　　　　　　　　　CFO: Carlos Gonzalez
Phone: 949-623-9300　　　　　　　　　　　　HR: -
Fax: 949-623-9400　　　　　　　　　　　　FYE: December 31
Web: www.raptor-networks.com　　　　　　　Type: Public

Raptor Networks Technology preys on network latency. The company develops switching hardware and software for enterprise networks. Its core and edge switching products are designed specifically for high-bandwidth applications such as Internet Protocol television (IPTV) and Voice over Internet Protocol (VoIP). The company also offers network interface cards (NICs) for PCs and servers. It targets the education financial services government health care and telecommunications markets. Raptor sells directly and through resellers; the company is also pursuing an OEM channel strategy. The company has a systems integration partnership with government IT contractor CACI.

RAPTOR PHARMACEUTICALS CORP.　　　　NMS: RPTP

7 Hamilton Landing, Suite 100　　　　　　　CEO: Timothy P Walbert
Novato, CA 94949　　　　　　　　　　　　　CFO: Paul W Hoelscher
Phone: 415 408-6200　　　　　　　　　　　　HR: -
Fax: -　　　　　　　　　　　　　　　　　　FYE: December 31
Web: www.raptorpharma.com　　　　　　　　Type: Public

Raptor Pharmaceuticals (formerly TorreyPines Therapeutics) can help you calm your nerves. The drug company is developing small molecule therapies to treat central nervous system disorders specifically migraines and chronic pain. Its lead candidate tezampanel is undergoing clinical testing as a treatment for migraines and muscle spasms; the compound was licensed from Eli Lilly. Other discovery and development programs target neuropathic pain (pain caused by nerve damage) dry mouth Alzheimer's disease and cognitive impairment associated with schizophrenia. In mid-2009 the former TorreyPines was acquired by Raptor Pharmaceuticals.

	Annual Growth	08/11	08/12*	12/12	12/13	12/14
Sales ($ mil.)	-	-	0.0	0.0	16.9	69.5
Net income ($ mil.)	-	-	(37.2)	(38.6)	(19.3)	(69.4)	(52.5)
Market value ($ mil.)	30.5%	325.7	342.2	402.8	896.6	724.4
Employees	106.3%	14	38	42	72	123

*Fiscal year change

RARITAN BAY MEDICAL CENTER, A NEW JERSEY NONPROFIT CORPORATION

530 NEW BRUNSWICK AVE　　　　　　　　　CEO: -
PERTH AMBOY, NJ 088613685　　　　　　　　CFO: Thomas Shanahan
Phone: 732-442-3700　　　　　　　　　　　　HR: Brian McCauley
Fax: -　　　　　　　　　　　　　　　　　　FYE: December 31
Web: www.rbmc.org　　　　　　　　　　　　Type: Private

Health care is not rare at Raritan Bay Medical Center (RBMC). The not-for-profit center operates two hospitals in central New Jersey: Its Perth Amboy campus has about 390 beds and its Old Bridge campus has more than 110 beds. RBMC provides acute care and emergency services as well as ambulatory care through its outpatient clinics. Its Perth Amboy location provides specialized care in fields including women's and children's health. RBMC is affiliated with the University of Medicine and Dentistry of New Jersey- Robert Wood Johnson Medical School as well as the Cancer Institute of New Jersey.

	Annual Growth	12/05	12/06	12/08	12/13	12/15
Sales ($ mil.)	(0.2%)	-	232.3	228.6	228.2	227.7
Net income ($ mil.)	-	-	3.5	(6.9)	0.2	(9.3)
Market value ($ mil.)	-	-	-	-	-	-
Employees	-	-	-	-	-	1,970

RARITAN VALLEY COMMUNITY COLLEGE

118 LAMINGTON RD　　　　　　　　　　　　CEO: -
BRANCHBURG, NJ 088763315　　　　　　　　CFO: -
Phone: 908-526-1200　　　　　　　　　　　　HR: -
Fax: -　　　　　　　　　　　　　　　　　　FYE: June 30
Web: www.rvccathletics.com　　　　　　　　Type: Private

Raritan Valley Community College offers more than 90 associate degree and certification programs to residents in central New Jersey's Somerset and Hunterdon counties. The school offers nine academic departments including Business and Public Service; Communication & Languages; Computer Science; English; Health Science Education; Humanities; Social Science & Education; Mathematics; Science & Engineering; and Visual and Performing Arts. The college which boasts some 1400 courses also provides customized training programs and non-credit courses as well as job and career counseling services. More than 8400 students take classes at Raritan Valley Community College which was founded in 1965.

	Annual Growth	06/05	06/06	06/08	06/10	06/13
Sales ($ mil.)	-	-	(1,421.9)	56.5	61.4	62.6
Net income ($ mil.)	-	-	-	3.6	0.7	(0.6)
Market value ($ mil.)	-	-	-	-	-	-
Employees	-	-	-	-	-	550

RAVE RESTAURANT GROUP INC　　　　　NAS: RAVE

3551 Plano Parkway　　　　　　　　　　　　CEO: Brandon L Solano
The Colony, TX 75056　　　　　　　　　　　CFO: Timothy E Mullany
Phone: 469 384-5000　　　　　　　　　　　　HR: -
Fax: -　　　　　　　　　　　　　　　　　　FYE: June 30
Web: www.pizzainn.com　　　　　　　　　　Type: Public

Pizza is the in thing for this company. Pizza Inn operates a chain of franchised quick-service pizza restaurants with more than 300 locations in the US and the Middle East. The eateries feature a menu of pizzas pastas and sandwiches along with salads and desserts. Most locations offer buffet-style and table service while other units are strictly delivery and carryout units. The chain also has limited-menu express carryout units in convenience stores and airport terminals and on college campuses. Pizza Inn's domestic locations are concentrated in more than 15 southern states with about half located in Texas and North Carolina. Chairman Mark Schwarz owns more than 35% of the company.

	Annual Growth	06/15	06/16	06/17	06/18	06/19
Sales ($ mil.)	(28.9%)	48.2	60.8	57.1	15.1	12.3
Net income ($ mil.)	-	(1.8)	(8.9)	(12.5)	1.9	(0.8)
Market value ($ mil.)	(30.8%)	202.2	59.6	27.6	19.9	46.5
Employees	(46.7%)	557	558	353	51	45

RAVEN INDUSTRIES, INC.　　　　　　　　NMS: RAVN

205 East 6th Street, P.O. Box 5107　　　　　CEO: -
Sioux Falls, SD 57117-5107　　　　　　　　　CFO: Steven E Brazones
Phone: 605 336-2750　　　　　　　　　　　　HR: Jan Matthiesen
Fax: -　　　　　　　　　　　　　　　　　　FYE: January 31
Web: www.ravenind.com　　　　　　　　　　Type: Public

Quoth the Raven "Balloons (and more) evermore!" Raven Industries is a diversified technology company that caters to the industrial agricultural energy construction military and aerospace sectors. The company's Aerostar division sells high-altitude research balloons as well as parachutes and protective wear used by US agencies while its Engineered Films Division makes reinforced plastic sheeting for various applications. The Applied Technology Division manufactures high-tech agricultural aids from global positioning system (GPS)-based steering devices and chemical spray equipment to field computers.

	Annual Growth	01/15	01/16	01/17	01/18	01/19
Sales ($ mil.)	1.8%	378.2	258.2	277.4	377.3	406.7
Net income ($ mil.)	13.0%	31.7	8.5	20.2	41.0	51.8
Market value ($ mil.)	14.6%	770.9	539.7	900.7	1,386.1	1,330.0
Employees	2.1%	1,200	910	941	1,157	1,304

RAYBURN COUNTRY ELECTRIC COOPERATIVE, INC

980 SIDS RD
ROCKWALL, TX 750326512
Phone: 972-771-1336
Fax: –
Web: www.rayburnelectric.com

CEO: –
CFO: Loretto Martin
HR: –
FYE: December 31
Type: Private

This is indeed Sam Rayburn country. Rayburn Country Electric Cooperative (Rayburn Electric) operates in the old stomping grounds of the legendary Texas politician and former speaker of the US House of Representatives. Rayburn Electric is a power generation and transmission organization that supplies wholesale power to five rural distribution cooperatives operating in 16 counties in north central and northeastern Texas. Five distribution cooperatives (Fannin County Electric Coop Farmers Electric Coop Grayson-Collin Electric Coop Lamar Electric Coop and Trinity Valley Electric Coop) collectively own the company.

	Annual Growth	12/09	12/10	12/11	12/13	12/14
Sales ($ mil.)	9.3%	–	238.6	316.0	301.3	340.2
Net income ($ mil.)	(71.7%)	–	1.6	0.0	0.0	0.0
Market value ($ mil.)	–	–	–	–	–	–
Employees	–	–	–	–	–	8

RAYMOND JAMES & ASSOCIATES INC

880 CARILLON PKWY
SAINT PETERSBURG, FL 337161100
Phone: 727-567-1000
Fax: –
Web: www.raymondjames.com

CEO: Paul Reilly
CFO: Jeffrey P Julien
HR: –
FYE: September 30
Type: Private

Does everybody love Raymond James & Associates (RJA)? Raymond James Financial hopes so. RJA is that company's primary subsidiary and one of the largest retail brokerages in the US. The unit provides brokerage financial planning investments and related services to consumers. It performs equity and fixed income sales trading and research for institutional clients in North America and Europe. Its investment banking group provides corporate and public finance debt underwriting and mergers and acquisitions advice. RJA also makes markets for approximately 1000 stocks including thinly traded issues. Planning Corporation of America a wholly-owned subsidiary of RJA sells insurance and annuities.

	Annual Growth	09/13	09/14	09/15	09/16	09/17
Assets ($ mil.)	12.6%	–	6,955.6	7,893.9	10,689.2	9,917.5
Net income ($ mil.)	2.8%	–	182.7	167.8	145.8	198.5
Market value ($ mil.)	–	–	–	–	–	–
Employees	–	–	–	–	–	10,000

RAYMOND JAMES FINANCIAL, INC.

NYS: RJF

880 Carillon Parkway
St. Petersburg, FL 33716
Phone: 727 567-1000
Fax: –
Web: www.raymondjames.com

CEO: Dennis W. Zank
CFO: Jeffrey P. (Jeff) Julien
HR: Michael Girolamo
FYE: September 30
Type: Public

Diversified financial services company Raymond James Financial offers financial advice to retail clients and corporations alike. The brokerage house has more than 7800 advisors and nearly $800 billion in total client assets held in about 3 million client accounts. Raymond James offers investment and asset management services for retail and institutional clients; underwriting distribution trading and brokerage of equity and debt securities; sale of mutual funds and other investment products; corporate and retail banking services; and trust services. It has an extended geographic reach with more than 3100 locations in the US Canada and Europe although the US accounts for most of revenue.

	Annual Growth	09/15	09/16	09/17	09/18	09/19
Sales ($ mil.)	10.9%	5,308.2	5,520.3	6,524.9	7,475.8	8,023.0
Net income ($ mil.)	19.8%	502.1	529.4	636.2	856.7	1,034.0
Market value ($ mil.)	13.5%	6,841.1	8,023.8	11,624.2	12,688.4	11,366.4
Employees	6.2%	14,850	15,900	17,000	18,550	18,910

RAYMOURS FURNITURE COMPANY, INC.

7248 MORGAN RD
LIVERPOOL, NY 130904535
Phone: 315-453-2500
Fax: –
Web: www.raymourflanigan.com

CEO: –
CFO: James Poole
HR: –
FYE: December 29
Type: Private

Raymours Furniture is heating up the oft-chilly Northeast doing business as Raymour & Flanigan. The company operates in several states through 94 retail stores including nearly a dozen clearance centers. It sells furniture for just about every room in the house (bedroom dining room home office living room) offering such pieces as bookcases entertainment centers headboards mattresses nightstands recliners sofas and tables. Brands such as Broyhill La-Z-Boy Natuzzi and Tempur Sealy are represented. Raymours is run by founding Goldberg family.

	Annual Growth	12/03	12/04	12/05	12/06	12/07
Sales ($ mil.)	16.0%	–	–	655.5	780.6	881.8
Net income ($ mil.)	20.2%	–	–	21.0	23.4	30.4
Market value ($ mil.)	–	–	–	–	–	–
Employees	–	–	–	–	–	4,400

RAYONIER INC.

NYS: RYN

1 Rayonier Way
Wildlight, FL 32097
Phone: 904 357-9100
Fax: –
Web: www.rayonier.com

CEO: David L. (Dave) Nunes
CFO: Mark D. McHugh
HR: Shelby Pyatt
FYE: December 31
Type: Public

Timber is at the root of Rayonier's business. The real estate investment trust (REIT) owns and manages timberlands grows and sells timber and manufactures Southern pine lumber specialty cellulose fibers and fluff pulp used in absorbent consumer products. The company owns leases or manages about 2.4 million acres of timberland and real estate in the US in addition to some 300000 acres in New Zealand through a joint venture. Rayonier operates two cellulose fiber mills and lumber sawmills in Georgia and Florida. The firm also ships wood pulp to China and Japan. Founded in 1926 as a pulp and paper manufacturer the name Rayonier is derived from rayon (a manufactured cellulose fiber) and Mount Rainier.

	Annual Growth	12/14	12/15	12/16	12/17	12/18
Sales ($ mil.)	7.8%	603.5	544.9	788.3	819.6	816.1
Net income ($ mil.)	0.7%	99.3	46.2	212.0	148.8	102.2
Market value ($ mil.)	(0.2%)	3,617.9	2,874.6	3,444.4	4,095.7	3,585.5
Employees	2.2%	320	325	315	334	349

RAYTHEON APPLIED SIGNAL TECHNOLOGY INC.

460 W. California Ave.
Sunnyvale CA 94086
Phone: 408-749-1888
Fax: 408-522-2800
Web: www.appsig.com

CEO: John R Treichler
CFO: James E Doyle
HR: –
FYE: October 31
Type: Subsidiary

Eavesdropping is big business at Raytheon Applied Signal Technology (AST). The company makes reconnaissance systems — including receivers processors and software — used by the US government and its contractors to collect and process electronic communications. Its products are used to scan and filter cell phone ship-to-shore microwave and military transmissions and evaluate them for relevant information. Others are designed to collect and process radar signals for weapons systems. The company sells mostly to intelligence and military agencies but it has some commercial clients. Formerly known simply as Applied Signal Technology the company was acquired by top military contractor Raytheon in 2011 for $490 million.

RAYTHEON CO. NYS: RTN

870 Winter Street
Waltham, MA 02451
Phone: 781 522-3000
Fax: –
Web: www.raytheon.com

CEO: John D. Harris
CFO: Anthony F. O'Brien
HR: James Cronin
FYE: December 31
Type: Public

Raytheon Company regularly places among the Pentagon's top ten prime contractors. Its air land sea space and cyber defense offerings include reconnaissance targeting and navigation systems as well as missile systems (Patriot Sidewinder and Tomahawk) unmanned ground and aerial systems sensing technologies and radars. Additionally Raytheon makes systems for communications (satellite) and intelligence radios cybersecurity and air traffic control. The company serves both domestic and international customers primarily as a prime contractor or subcontractor on a broad portfolio of defense and related programs for government customers. The US government accounts for about 70% of sales. In early 2019 Raytheon agreed to merge with leading aerospace and defense giant United Technologies Corporation (UTC).

	Annual Growth	12/14	12/15	12/16	12/17	12/18
Sales ($ mil.)	4.3%	22,826.0	23,247.0	24,069.0	25,348.0	27,058.0
Net income ($ mil.)	6.7%	2,244.0	2,074.0	2,211.0	2,024.0	2,909.0
Market value ($ mil.)	9.1%	30,503.9	35,117.5	40,044.0	52,973.7	43,244.7
Employees	2.4%	61,000	61,000	63,000	64,000	67,000

RAYTHEON TECHNICAL SERVICES COMPANY LLC

22265 Pacific Blvd.
Dulles VA 20166
Phone: 571-250-3000
Fax: 903-457-4413
Web: www.l-3com.com/is

CEO: –
CFO: –
HR: –
FYE: December 31
Type: Subsidiary

Some people talk about supporting the troops but this company really does. Raytheon Technical Services Company (RTSC) is a leading provider of logistical operational engineering and technical support services for the US Department of Defense (DoD) and other agencies of the federal government. It offers project and program management services in support of equipment and installations as well as base operations support and maintenance services. RTSC also provides engineering services for design and development of avionics communications systems and surveillance equipment as well as such IT services as systems integration and software development. RTSC is a business segment of defense contractor Raytheon.

RB RUBBER PRODUCTS INC.

904 NE 10th Ave.
McMinnville OR 97128
Phone: 503-472-4691
Fax: 503-434-4455
Web: www.rbrubber.com

CEO: –
CFO: –
HR: –
FYE: April 30
Type: Subsidiary

When tires are too tired to be functional RB Rubber Products recycles them. The company produces rubber matting which can be found in horse and livestock trailers as well as gym weight rooms. Secondary product lines include truck bed liners roof pads anti-fatigue mats and drain tiles. RB Rubber's Waste Recovery subsidiary operates a tire collection and processing facility that shreds tires to form tire chips used to make the company's products. RB Rubber sells its products to distributors retailers and OEMs and directly to consumers. Dash Multi-Corp — whose president Marvin Wool was RB Rubber's chairman — acquired the company in early 2003.

RBC BEARINGS INC NMS: ROLL

One Tribology Center
Oxford, CT 06478
Phone: 203 267-7001
Fax: –
Web: www.rbcbearings.com

CEO: Michael J. Hartnett
CFO: Daniel A. (Dan) Bergeron
HR: –
FYE: March 30
Type: Public

RBC Bearings keeps businesses on a roll. The company makes an array of plain roller and ball bearing products. It specializes in regulated bearings used by OEMs and their aftermarkets of commercial/military aircraft automobiles and commercial trucks industrial/agricultural machinery as well as air turbines. Targeting high-end markets its precision lineup satisfies thousands of applications from engine controls to radar systems mining tools and gear pumps. RBC's top customers include Boeing GE Lockheed Martin and the US Department of Defense. RBC Bearings has grown since 1919 to some 30 manufacturing facilities in Europe and North America.

	Annual Growth	03/15*	04/16	04/17*	03/18	03/19
Sales ($ mil.)	12.1%	445.3	597.5	615.4	674.9	702.5
Net income ($ mil.)	15.9%	58.2	63.9	70.6	87.1	105.2
Market value ($ mil.)	13.9%	1,878.5	1,830.5	2,413.1	3,086.9	3,160.7
Employees	10.9%	2,490	3,277	3,401	3,466	3,764

*Fiscal year change

RBC LIFE SCIENCES INC NBB: RBCL

2301 Crown Court
Irving, TX 75038
Phone: 972 893-4000
Fax: 972 893-4111
Web: www.rbclifesciences.com

CEO: Clinton H Howard
CFO: Steven E Brown
HR: –
FYE: December 31
Type: Public

RBC Life Sciences offers really big changes to its clients' bodies. RBC markets and distributes more than 75 nutritional weight loss and personal care products under the RBC Life brand. The company's leading product Microhydrin is touted to increase energy and slow the effects of aging. The company relies on a multi-level marketing network of some 10000 independent distributors in the US and Canada. It also markets and distributes wound care pain management and cancer care products used in clinical settings and sold under the MPM Medical brand.

	Annual Growth	12/12	12/13	12/14	12/15	12/16
Sales ($ mil.)	0.6%	25.2	25.5	28.3	24.4	25.8
Net income ($ mil.)	–	(0.4)	(0.5)	(0.6)	(0.7)	(0.8)
Market value ($ mil.)	36.8%	0.2	3.4	2.9	0.6	0.7
Employees	8.2%	76	76	89	–	–

RBS GLOBAL INC.

4701 W. Greenfield Ave.
Milwaukee WI 53214
Phone: 414-643-3000
Fax: 414-643-3078
Web: www.rexnord.com

CEO: Todd A Adams
CFO: Mark W Peterson
HR: –
FYE: March 31
Type: Private

RBS Global is the parent company of Rexnord LLC whose subsidiaries serve the company's two main segments. Process Motion Control (formerly Power Transmission) makes gear drives couplings bearings and chains and conveying equipment for use in the aerospace construction energy mining marine and petrochemical industries. Its Water Management segment is supported by three primary companies: Zurn Industries GA Industries and Rodney Hunt. It designs and makes water-related products for conservation quality drainage safety and flow control. The US accounts for about three-quarters of the company's sales. RBS Global is owned by Rexnord Corporation which began trading in 2012 after filing an IPO in 2011.

RC2 CORPORATION

1111 W. 22nd St. Ste. 320
Oak Brook IL 60523
Phone: 630-573-7200
Fax: 630-573-7575
Web: www.rc2corp.com

CEO: Peter Henseler
CFO: –
HR: –
FYE: March 31
Type: Subsidiary

RC2 is tackling the Learning Curve of selling playthings. The company designs child care products and toys for infants toddlers and preschool-aged children and markets them through its Learning Curve unit whose brand portfolio includes The First Years Lamaze and JJ Cole. For bigger kids it offers plastic and die-cast collectibles such as Ertl agricultural vehicle replicas and Johnny Lightning vintage cars and trucks. The firm also holds licensing agreements to make products under such names as Thomas & Friends Bob the Builder and John Deere. Its goods are sold at toy and discount stores in the US and more than 60 other countries. In early 2011 RC2 was acquired by TOMY for about $640 million in cash.

RCI HOSPITALITY HOLDINGS INC
NMS: RICK

10737 Cutten Road
Houston, TX 77066
Phone: 281 397-6730
Fax: –
Web: www.rcihospitality.com

CEO: Eric S Langan
CFO: Phillip Marshall
HR: –
FYE: September 30
Type: Public

Far from Casablanca these night clubs offer topless entertainment as part of the floor show. Rick's Cabaret International operates more than 30 adult night clubs in Arizona Florida Minnesota New York North Carolina and Texas. Most of the gentlemen's clubs are run under the Rick's Cabaret name while others operate under such banners as Club Onyx and XTC. Rick's caters to highbrow patrons with dough to blow: It offers VIP memberships for individual and corporate clients that can cost hundreds of dollars annually. In addition to its night clubs Rick's operates adult websites and an auction site for adult entertainment products.

	Annual Growth	09/14	09/15	09/16	09/17	09/18
Sales ($ mil.)	6.4%	129.2	144.7	134.9	144.9	165.7
Net income ($ mil.)	17.9%	11.2	9.3	11.1	8.3	21.7
Market value ($ mil.)	28.0%	107.1	101.3	112.1	240.5	287.8
Employees	4.0%	1,750	2,150	2,000	2,130	2,050

RCM TECHNOLOGIES, INC.
NMS: RCMT

2500 McClellan Avenue, Suite 350
Pennsauken, NJ 08109-4613
Phone: 856 356-4500
Fax: –
Web: www.rcmt.com

CEO: Rocco Campanelli
CFO: Kevin D. Miller
HR: –
FYE: December 29
Type: Public

Whether you need brains in people form or of the digital persuasion RCM Technologies has it covered. The company is an IT services and engineering firm that performs design and implementation of technology and software systems project management and engineering analysis services. Recently it has become more of an engineering services firm primarily to the energy industry. It also provides specialty health care staffing for therapists nurses and caregivers. The company mainly targets midsized firms and federal government agencies; clients have included the Treasury Department and its largest client United Technologies.

	Annual Growth	01/15	01/16*	12/16	12/17	12/18
Sales ($ mil.)	1.1%	193.8	185.7	176.4	186.7	200.4
Net income ($ mil.)	(26.4%)	6.8	6.0	1.8	2.0	2.7
Market value ($ mil.)	(22.0%)	87.9	70.2	81.1	79.7	41.7
Employees	17.4%	2,059	2,360	2,370	3,245	3,335

*Fiscal year change

RCS CAPITAL CORP
NBB: RCAP Q

405 Park Avenue, 14th Floor
New York, NY 10022
Phone: 866 904-2988
Fax: –
Web: www.rcscapital.com

CEO: –
CFO: –
HR: –
FYE: December 31
Type: Public

RCS Capital is a holding company with its fingers in a variety of financial services businesses namely securities brokering investment banking and securities record-keeping services. Its Realty Capital Securities is a wholesale broker and dealer specializing in REIT investments. RCS Advisory Services is a company that provides financing and consulting to clients served by the brokerage. Finally American National Stock Transfer among other services registers the securities with the SEC. RCS Capital is affiliated with American Realty Capital which has accumulated $7 billion of real estate in the US. RCS Capital filed for Chapter 11 bankruptcy protection in January 2016 to reduce its debt.

	Annual Growth	12/10	12/11	12/12	12/13	12/14
Sales ($ mil.)	107.2%	114.1	174.7	287.5	886.5	2,102.2
Net income ($ mil.)	–	(2.4)	3.7	7.4	98.4	(119.6)
Market value ($ mil.)	(33.3%)	–	–	–	1,295.0	863.8
Employees	215.2%	–	–	198	183	1,967

RDO EQUIPMENT CO.

700 7TH ST S
FARGO, ND 581032704
Phone: 701-239-8700
Fax: –

CEO: Christi Offutt
CFO: Steven Dewald
HR: –
FYE: January 31
Type: Private

RDO Equipment has built a business herding Deere in a big way. The company sells and rents new and used trucks and heavy equipment to customers in the agriculture and construction industries. As the largest independent dealer of John Deere equipment RDO Equipment operates 70 locations in nearly 10 states. Of these 10 locations are dedicated Vermeer dealerships while its RDO Truck Centers offer heavy-duty Volvo GMC Isuzu and Mack trucks. RDO Integrated Controls is the company's acquisitive positioning division. RDO also supplies lawn and garden equipment and provides maintenance and repair services and replacement parts. Ronald Offutt founded the family owned and operated company in 1968.

	Annual Growth	01/12	01/13	01/14	01/15	01/16
Sales ($ mil.)	0.0%	–	1,650.3	1,698.4	1,762.4	1,651.6
Net income ($ mil.)	(20.0%)	–	82.2	82.9	53.3	42.1
Market value ($ mil.)	–	–	–	–	–	–
Employees	–	–	–	–	–	1,500

REACHLOCAL INC.
NMS: RLOC

21700 Oxnard Street, Suite 1600
Woodland Hills, CA 91367
Phone: 818 274-0260
Fax: –
Web: www.reachlocal.com

CEO: Sharon T Rowlands
CFO: Ross G Landsbaum
HR: –
FYE: December 31
Type: Public

When looking to broaden their online presence local business owners can get a hand from ReachLocal. Targeting small to midsized businesses ReachLocal offers Internet-based advertising and marketing services including search engine marketing (for preferred placement of a company's listing on Yahoo! or Google's search results pages) marketing analytics and display advertising. The company serves mostly US businesses through a network of locally based marketing consultants that use among other tools the company's proprietary technology platform to create advertising and marketing campaigns. ReachLocal was founded in 2003; it launched an initial public offering in mid-2010.

	Annual Growth	12/10	12/11	12/12	12/13	12/14
Sales ($ mil.)	13.0%	291.7	375.2	455.4	514.1	474.9
Net income ($ mil.)	–	(11.1)	(10.2)	(0.2)	(2.5)	(45.0)
Market value ($ mil.)	(35.5%)	582.7	180.9	377.9	372.0	100.7
Employees	8.3%	1,381	1,668	1,900	2,100	1,900

READING HOSPITAL

420 S 5TH AVE
READING, PA 196112143
Phone: 484-628-8000
Fax: –

CEO: David Clint Matthews
CFO: –
HR: Lori Fiddler
FYE: June 30
Type: Private

No it's not a square on the game of Monopoly but The Reading Hospital and Medical Center does treat patients in Berks County Pennsylvania and the surrounding area. Operating as Reading Health System the not-for-profit 735-bed medical center provides acute care and rehabilitation programs as well as behavioral and occupational health services. Specialty units include cancer cardiovascular weight management diabetes orthopedic trauma (level II) and women's health centers. In addition to the main hospital the Reading Health System includes Reading Health Rehabilitation Hospital and medical centers in nearby communities as well as laboratory imaging and outpatient centers throughout its region.

	Annual Growth	06/04	06/05	06/06	06/08	06/09
Sales ($ mil.)	–	–	–	(783.4)	640.6	675.7
Net income ($ mil.)	–	–	–	0.0	50.1	42.0
Market value ($ mil.)	–	–	–	–	–	–
Employees	–	–	–	–	–	5,500

READING INTERNATIONAL INC

NAS: RDI

5995 Sepulveda Boulevard, Suite 300
Culver City, CA 90230
Phone: 213 235-2240
Fax: –
Web: www.readingrdi.com

CEO: Ellen M. Cotter
CFO: Devasis (Dev) Ghose
HR: –
FYE: December 31
Type: Public

Reading International is all about the show not the book. The company owns about 60 movie theaters in Australia New Zealand and the US. Cinemas operate under brands such as Reading and Rialto. Its Angelika Film Center & Caf-© in New York (50%) and Dallas show art house films. Reading also has real estate operations that develop and rent entertainment commercial retail space. Holdings include three live theaters in New York (the Union Square Orpheum and Minetta Lane) and one in Chicago (the Royal George) as well as the Australia Newmarket shopping center. Chairman and CEO James Cotter owns about 70% of the voting stock of the firm which is descended from Reading Railroad of Monopoly fame.

	Annual Growth	12/14	12/15	12/16	12/17	12/18
Sales ($ mil.)	5.0%	254.7	257.3	270.5	279.7	309.4
Net income ($ mil.)	(13.5%)	25.7	22.8	9.4	31.0	14.4
Market value ($ mil.)	2.3%	303.3	299.9	379.5	382.0	332.6
Employees	3.2%	2,596	2,712	2,793	2,585	2,944

READY CAPITAL CORP

NYS: RC

1251 Avenue of the Americas, 50th Floor
New York, NY 10020
Phone: 212 257-4600
Fax: –
Web: www.readycapital.com

CEO: Thomas E Capasse
CFO: Frederick C Herbst
HR: –
FYE: December 31
Type: Public

ZAIS is a REIT that invests in RMBS. As a real estate investment trust ZAIS Financial aims to put its money in residential mortgage-backed securities primarily of the non-agency variety meaning ones that are not issued or guaranteed by such government-sponsored entities as Fannie Mae Freddie Mac and Ginnie Mae. The company also invests in such real estate and financial assets as mortgage servicing rights (MSRs) asset-backed securities (ABS) and commercial mortgage-backed securities (CMBS). Formed in mid-2011 the company now plans to merge with private REIT Sutherland Asset Management.

	Annual Growth	12/14	12/15	12/16	12/17	12/18
Sales ($ mil.)	45.8%	65.3	72.7	171.5	211.5	295.2
Net income ($ mil.)	22.0%	26.7	(1.3)	49.2	43.3	59.3
Market value ($ mil.)	(5.4%)	553.8	484.1	431.8	486.4	444.0
Employees	(63.1%)	216	246	–	–	4

REAL GOODS SOLAR INC

NBB: RGSE

110 16th Street, Suite 300
Denver, CO 80202
Phone: 303 222-8300
Fax: –
Web: www.rgsenergy.com

CEO: Dennis Lacey
CFO: Alan Fine
HR: –
FYE: December 31
Type: Public

Real Goods Solar enjoys its time in the sun. The company which got its start as a small seller of solar panels in 1978 designs and installs solar power systems for homes and small businesses across the US. In addition to design and installation Real Goods Solar also provides permitting grid connection financing referrals and warranty services. The company does not manufacture its own solar panels or equipment but procures supplies from other companies such as Sharp SunPower Sanyo and Kyocera Solar.

	Annual Growth	12/14	12/15	12/16	12/17	12/18
Sales ($ mil.)	(34.9%)	70.8	45.5	17.4	15.2	12.7
Net income ($ mil.)	–	(57.1)	(10.8)	(25.3)	(17.7)	(42.1)
Market value ($ mil.)	2.0%	44.4	57.9	22.1	136.0	48.1
Employees	(27.0%)	246	179	160	140	70

REALD INC.

NYS: RLD

100 North Crescent Drive, Suite 200
Beverly Hills, CA 90210
Phone: 310 385-4000
Fax: 310 385-4001
Web: www.reald.com

CEO: Michael V Lewis
CFO: Andrew A Skarupa
HR: –
FYE: March 31
Type: Public

Thanks to RealD a new era of 3-D movies is upon us. The new crop of feature films projected by RealD's three-dimensional digital projection equipment is dispelling the schlocky image of such 1950s fare as It Came from Outer Space. Recent films that have used RealD's 3-D technology include Kung Fu Panda 2 Toy Story 3 and Despicable Me. The firm has outfitted more than 15000 movie screens in some 60 countries with its 3-D systems. Its products are also used by engineers industrial designers and scientific researchers for applications such as consumer electronics education aerospace defense and health care. (RealD has even helped pilot the Mars Rover.) The company filed an IPO in 2010.

	Annual Growth	03/11	03/12	03/13	03/14	03/15
Sales ($ mil.)	(9.7%)	246.1	246.6	215.6	199.2	163.5
Net income ($ mil.)	–	(6.8)	37.0	(9.9)	(11.2)	(23.7)
Market value ($ mil.)	(14.2%)	1,192.8	659.7	655.6	563.3	645.0
Employees	9.2%	114	129	163	148	162

REALOGY HOLDINGS CORP

NYS: RLGY

175 Park Avenue
Madison, NJ 07940
Phone: 973 407-2000
Fax: –
Web: www.realogy.com

CEO: Richard A. Smith
CFO: Anthony E. (Tony) Hull
HR: Sunita Holzer
FYE: December 31
Type: Public

Realogy Holdings is one of the largest franchisors of residential real estate offices in the world with about 16600 offices in around 115 countries. Its brands include Century 21 Coldwell Banker ERA Better Homes and Gardens Real Estate and Sotheby's. In addition to franchising the company owns and operates about 760 offices under those brands and the Corcoran Group and Citi Habitats labels. It also provides relocation title and settlement services and mortgages. The company derives almost all its revenue from its US operations.

	Annual Growth	12/14	12/15	12/16	12/17	12/18
Sales ($ mil.)	3.4%	5,328.0	5,706.0	5,810.0	6,114.0	6,079.0
Net income ($ mil.)	(1.1%)	143.0	184.0	213.0	431.0	137.0
Market value ($ mil.)	(24.2%)	5,099.5	4,203.1	2,949.2	3,037.4	1,682.6
Employees	1.6%	10,700	11,400	11,800	11,800	11,400

REALPAGE INC
NMS: RP

2201 Lakeside Blvd.
Richardson, TX 75082-4305
Phone: 972 820-3000
Fax: –
Web: www.realpage.com

CEO: Stephen T. (Steve) Winn
CFO: W. Bryan Hill
HR: –
FYE: December 31
Type: Public

RealPage's keeps real estate operations on the same page for property managers. The company's on-demand software platform is designed to make the property management process more efficient enabling owners and managers of single- and multifamily rental properties to oversee their accounting leasing marketing pricing and screening operations from a single shared database. The centralized system helps with managing incoming and outgoing residents and overseeing property functions from hiring plumbers to training staff. Its customers include all of the top 10 largest multifamily property management companies in the US.

	Annual Growth	12/14	12/15	12/16	12/17	12/18
Sales ($ mil.)	21.1%	404.6	468.5	568.1	671.0	869.5
Net income ($ mil.)	–	(10.3)	(9.2)	16.7	0.4	34.7
Market value ($ mil.)	21.7%	2,056.6	2,102.4	2,809.5	4,148.7	4,513.0
Employees	12.5%	3,875	4,122	4,400	5,400	6,200

REALTY INCOME CORP
NYS: O

11995 El Camino Real
San Diego, CA 92130
Phone: 858 284-5000
Fax: –
Web: www.realtyincome.com

CEO: John P. Case
CFO: Paul M. Meurer
HR: –
FYE: December 31
Type: Public

Retail real estate is a reality for Realty Income Corporation. The self-administered real estate investment trust (REIT) acquires owns and manages primarily free-standing highly-occupied single-tenant properties which it leases to regional and national consumer retail and service chains. Realty Income owns more than 4320 (mostly retail) properties spanning some 71 million sq. ft. of leasable space across every US state except Hawaii though nearly half of the REIT's rental revenue comes from its properties in Texas California Florida Minnesota Georgia Illinois and Virginia. Realty Income's top five tenants include Walgreens FedEx Dollar General LA Fitness and Family Dollar.

	Annual Growth	12/14	12/15	12/16	12/17	12/18
Sales ($ mil.)	9.2%	933.5	1,023.3	1,103.2	1,215.8	1,327.8
Net income ($ mil.)	7.7%	270.6	283.8	315.6	318.8	363.6
Market value ($ mil.)	7.2%	14,491.5	15,682.2	17,459.1	17,319.4	19,147.9
Employees	7.2%	125	132	146	152	165

RECALL CORPORATION

1 Recall Center 180 Technology Pkwy.
Norcross GA 30092
Phone: 770-776-1000
Fax: 770-776-1001
Web: www.recall.com

CEO: –
CFO: –
HR: –
FYE: June 30
Type: Subsidiary

It's not necessary to memorize your documents: this company can Recall them for you. Recall Corporation is one of the world's largest information management companies helping some 80000 customers store and protect (and sometimes destroy) important documents and data. Recall's services include physical and electronic document storage and retrieval protection of computer backup data and destruction of sensitive documents. The company operates about 300 facilities in more than 20 countries on five continents. Recall was established in 1977. Today it is a subsidiary of Australian industrial conglomerate Brambles Group.

RECOLOGY INC.

50 California St. 24th Fl.
San Francisco CA 94111
Phone: 415-875-1000
Fax: 415-875-1124
Web: www.recology.com

CEO: Michael J Sangiacomo
CFO: Mark R Lomele
HR: –
FYE: September 30
Type: Private

San Francisco's trash collector since 1921 Recology (formerly Norcal Waste Systems) cleans up in California Nevada Oregon and Washington. Through its subsidiaries Recology handles garbage collection recycling and other waste management services for more than 670000 residential customers and 95000 commercial customers. The employee-owned company operates landfills transfer stations and hundreds of recycling programs. Recology's recycling operations include materials-recovery facilities recycling of construction and demolition debris and composting of food and other organic waste.

RECTOR & VISITORS OF THE UNIVERSITY OF VIRGINIA

1001 EMMET ST N
CHARLOTTESVILLE, VA 229034833
Phone: 434-924-0311
Fax: –
Web: www.virginia.edu

CEO: –
CFO: Yoke San L Reynolds
HR: –
FYE: June 30
Type: Private

The nation's third president Thomas Jefferson founded the University of Virginia in 1819. Named Rector and Visitors of the University of Virginia the university is known as UVa today. It is said to be Jefferson's proudest achievement and boasts an enrollment of more than 22000 students throughout its 12 graduate and undergraduate schools. One of the most prestigious public universities in the US the school has been noted for its law program English department and its more than 160-year-old student-enforced conduct code (the Honor System). The school also includes the University of Virginia Health System which trains future doctors and other health care workers at its Medical Center hospital.

	Annual Growth	06/06	06/07	06/08	06/10	06/11
Sales ($ mil.)	(2.6%)	–	2,121.5	2,181.3	524.6	1,910.0
Net income ($ mil.)	(5.0%)	–	1,114.4	312.9	97.8	909.3
Market value ($ mil.)	–	–	–	–	–	–
Employees	–	–	–	–	–	13,300

RECYCLENET CORPORATION
OTC: GARM

175 E. 400 South Ste. 900
Salt Lake City UT 84111
Phone: 801-531-0404
Fax: 801-531-0707
Web: www.recyclenet.com

CEO: –
CFO: –
HR: –
FYE: December 31
Type: Public

You can even use the Internet to reduce re-use and recycle. RecycleNet Corporation owns a network of Web sites that acts as an online trading system for scrap. Buyers and sellers of recyclable materials (glass metal rubber paper wood and plastic) are brought together at the company's electronic exchange system which uses a buy/sell/trade and bid/ask order matching system. RecycleNet earns money by charging a subscription fee for access to its service. Google pay-per-click advertising accounts for about 20% of revenue.

RED BLOSSOM SALES, INC.

400 W VENTURA BLVD # 140
CAMARILLO, CA 930109139
Phone: 805-686-4747
Fax: –
Web: www.redblossom.com

CEO: Craig A Casca
CFO: –
HR: –
FYE: December 31
Type: Private

Red Blossom Sales is berry enthusiastic about its market. The company is one of California's leading strawberry producers with more than 1200 acres across the cities of Baja Irvine Oxnard Santa Maria and Salinas/Watsonville. It contracts a hefty chunk of its production to growers in California and Mexico and ships a total of about 8 million cartons of field-packed strawberries throughout the US every year. Red Blossom's products are sold in large retail grocery stores nationwide including Costco Safeway and Vons; it also exports some to Canada and Hong Kong. Established in 2004 the company took on its current moniker when Red Blossom Farms merged with ASG Produce in 2008.

	Annual Growth	12/13	12/14	12/15	12/16	12/17
Sales ($ mil.)	7.7%	–	124.1	141.5	171.8	154.8
Net income ($ mil.)	(9.6%)	–	1.2	5.5	5.6	0.9
Market value ($ mil.)	–	–	–	–	–	–
Employees	–	–	–	–	–	1,046

RED GOLD INC.

120 E. Oak St.
Orestes IN 46063
Phone: 765-754-7527
Fax: 765-754-3230
Web: www.redgold.com

CEO: –
CFO: –
HR: –
FYE: December 31
Type: Private

Red Gold uses a vegetable-patch-colored pallet to produce the perfect mix of red and gold in its tomato sauces. It makes its own brand and private-label canned and bottled tomato products including ketchup tomato juice diced and crushed tomatoes salsa and pasta sauces under the Red Gold Redpack Sacramento and Tuttorosso labels. It operates three manufacturing sites in Indiana where it makes products for retail food service and private-label distribution. Products are available nationwide and in more than 15 countries. In its third-generation of family ownership Red Gold was founded in 1942 by Grover Hutcherson. The Reicharts now own and operate Red Gold and employ more than a dozen family members.

RED HAT INC

100 East Davie Street
Raleigh, NC 27601
Phone: 919 754-3700
Fax: –
Web: www.redhat.com

NYS: RHT
CEO: –
CFO: Laurie Krebs
HR: –
FYE: February 28
Type: Public

Red Hat flips its lid for open-source computing tools. The company dominates the market for Linux the open-source computer operating system (OS) for enterprise computing infrastructure and applications. In addition to its Red Hat Enterprise Linux OS the company's product line includes database content and collaboration management applications; server and embedded operating systems; and software development tools. Red Hat also provides consulting custom application development support and training services. The company's business model is a mix of providing free open-source software paired with subscription-based support training and integration services. In 2018 Red Hat agreed to be acquired by IBM for about $34 billion.

	Annual Growth	02/14	02/15	02/16	02/17	02/18
Sales ($ mil.)	17.5%	1,534.6	1,789.5	2,052.2	2,411.8	2,920.5
Net income ($ mil.)	9.8%	178.3	180.2	199.4	253.7	258.8
Market value ($ mil.)	25.7%	10,445.6	12,239.3	11,571.8	14,663.5	26,100.7
Employees	17.2%	6,300	7,300	8,800	10,500	11,870

RED LIONS HOTELS CORP

1550 Market St. #350
Denver, CO 80202
Phone: 509 459-6100
Fax: 509 325-7324
Web: www.rlhco.com

NYS: RLH
CEO: Roger Bloss
CFO: Douglas L. Ludwig
HR: Elizabeth Norberg
FYE: December 31
Type: Public

Red Lion Hotels wants to be the leader of the pack when it comes to hotel franchising. The company franchises and owns more than 1100 hotels with nearly 70000 rooms operating under the Red Lion Hotels Red Lion Inn & Suites Hotel RL Settle Inn Americas Best Value Inn Canadas Best Value Inn and other brands. Its properties which range from economy to upscale hotels are located primarily in the US with locations in Canada and select international markets as well. Red Lion owns and leases about 20 hotels and franchises the rest. Until recently the hotel company was also in the ticket-selling business; in 2017 it sold its WestCoast Entertainment and TicketsWest businesses.

	Annual Growth	12/14	12/15	12/16	12/17	12/18
Sales ($ mil.)	(1.7%)	145.4	142.9	164.1	171.9	135.8
Net income ($ mil.)	(4.0%)	2.3	2.7	(4.7)	0.6	2.0
Market value ($ mil.)	6.6%	155.8	172.2	205.2	242.0	201.5
Employees	(29.1%)	1,622	1,783	1,752	1,580	410

RED RIVER COMMODITIES, INC.

501 42ND ST N
FARGO, ND 581023952
Phone: 701-282-2600
Fax: –
Web: www.redriv.com

CEO: –
CFO: Randall C Wigen
HR: Audrey Opgrand
FYE: March 31
Type: Private

Red River Commodities' products may include sunflower seeds but they're not just for the birds. The company manufactures and markets standard and organic grain and seed products including oils to be used for consumption as food for people and as bird food. Its products include in-shell sunflower seeds sunflower kernels millet flax soybeans kidney beans poppy seeds and caraway seeds. Red River Commodities also makes butter from sunflower seeds. Its bird food products are sold under the Valley Splendor brand. Red River Commodities boasts production facilities in North Dakota Kansas Minnesota and Texas. The seed producer also owns a plant in the Netherlands.

	Annual Growth	03/04	03/05	03/06	03/07	03/08
Sales ($ mil.)	–	–	–	(882.0)	92.5	105.7
Net income ($ mil.)	1452.4%	–	–	0.0	11.3	3.9
Market value ($ mil.)	–	–	–	–	–	–
Employees	–	–	–	–	–	250

RED RIVER COMPUTER CO. INC.

21 Water St. Ste. 500
Claremont NH 03743
Phone: 603-448-8880
Fax: 603-448-8844
Web: www.redriver.com

CEO: –
CFO: –
HR: –
FYE: December 31
Type: Private

Red River Computer helps its customers get data flowing. The company is a computer and communications hardware software and peripherals reseller that provides related support services such as installation network design and network engineering. Other areas of specialty include data storage and network security. Red River primarily serves government agencies (GSA NASA and NIH) and acts as a subcontractor for major defense contractors. It also counts other commercial enterprises such as health care companies and universities among its clients. Founded in 1995 the company is owned by its management team. FusionStorm Global offered to buy Red River for $12.5 million in 2011.

RED ROBIN GOURMET BURGERS INC   NMS: RRGB

6312 S. Fiddler's Green Circle, Suite 200 N   CEO: Pattye L. Moore
Greenwood Village, CO 80111   CFO: Lynn S. Schweinfurth
Phone: 303 846-6000   HR: –
Fax: –   FYE: December 30
Web: www.redrobin.com   Type: Public

Hamburger fans are chirping about Red Robin Gourmet Burgers. The company operates a chain of about 515 casual-dining restaurants that specialize in high-end hamburgers. Its menu features more than 20 different twists on the American classic including the Banzai Burger (marinated in teriyaki) Bleu Ribbon Burger and the jalape- ±o-charged Burnin' Love Burger. The signature Royal Red Robin Burger features bacon and a fried egg on top of the beef. Red Robin also serves chicken seafood and turkey burgers as well as vegetarian alternatives. Non-burger entr-©es include salads pasta seafood and fajitas.

	Annual Growth	12/14	12/15	12/16	12/17	12/18
Sales ($ mil.)	4.0%	1,146.1	1,257.6	1,296.4	1,380.9	1,338.6
Net income ($ mil.)	–	32.6	47.7	11.7	30.0	(6.4)
Market value ($ mil.)	(23.1%)	991.2	802.1	732.2	731.6	346.6
Employees	(0.2%)	27,543	28,933	29,293	29,349	27,283

REDMOND PARK HOSPITAL, LLC

501 REDMOND RD NW   CEO: John Quinlivan
ROME, GA 301651483   CFO: Kenneth Metteauer
Phone: 706-291-0291   HR: Patsy Adams
Fax: –   FYE: June 30
Web: www.redmondregional.com   Type: Private

Redmond Regional is deeply involved with administering health to those living in the deep South. Serving northwest Georgia and portions of Alabama Redmond Regional Medical Center houses some 230 beds and employs about 250 physicians in more than 30 areas of specialization. The acute-care facility specializes in cardiology (it's the only dedicated chest pain center in the region) general surgery orthopedic care uruology and vascular care. Redmond Regional Medical Center also provides emergency oncology radiology rehabilitation and women's health services. It has centers dedicated to diabetes treatment family care and sleep disorders. Founded in 1972 the Rome-based hospital is owned by HCA.

	Annual Growth	06/96	06/97	06/14	06/15	06/16
Sales ($ mil.)	–	–	0.0	–	188.0	187.2
Net income ($ mil.)	–	–	0.0	–	21.1	7.8
Market value ($ mil.)	–	–	–	–	–	–
Employees	–	–	–	–	–	1,000

REDNER'S MARKETS, INC.

3 QUARRY RD   CEO: –
READING, PA 196059787   CFO: –
Phone: 610-926-3700   HR: Robert McDonough
Fax: –   FYE: October 01
Web: www.rednersmarkets.com   Type: Private

Redner's Markets operates about 45 warehouse club-style supermarkets under the Redner's Warehouse Markets banner and more than a dozen Quick Shoppe convenience stores. Most of the company's stores are located in eastern Pennsylvania but the regional grocer also operates several locations in Maryland and Delaware having closed its one New York supermarket. Redner's Warehouse Markets house bakery deli meat produce and seafood departments as well as in-store banks. The employee-owned company was founded by namesake Earl Redner in 1970. It is still operated by the Redner family including chairman and CEO Richard and COO Ryan Redner.

	Annual Growth	09/12	09/13	09/14	09/15*	10/16
Sales ($ mil.)	(1.1%)	–	892.5	902.6	884.9	864.2
Net income ($ mil.)	1.8%	–	4.6	1.6	6.1	4.8
Market value ($ mil.)	–	–	–	–	–	–
Employees	–	–	–	–	–	4,800

*Fiscal year change

REDPOINT BIO CORPORATION   OTC: RPBC

7 Graphics Dr.   CEO: –
Ewing NJ 08628   CFO: Scott M Horvitz
Phone: 609-637-9700   HR: –
Fax: 609-637-0126   FYE: December 31
Web: www.redpointbio.com   Type: Public

Redpoint Bio believes a spoonful of sugar helps the medicine go down. So the development stage biotechnology company is developing compounds that make foul medicines foods and drinks a thing of the bitter past. The company is working on developing bitter blockers compounds that will prevent taste buds from sensing bitter flavors in pharmaceutical products. It is also developing flavor enhancers which will amplify sweet savory and salty taste sensations in foods and beverages and possibly make processed foods and drinks healthier. Redpoint Bio was founded in 1995 by Robert Margolskee to capitalize on a taste-specific protein he discovered four years earlier.

REDWOOD TRUST INC   NYS: RWT

One Belvedere Place, Suite 300   CEO: Martin S. (Marty) Hughes
Mill Valley, CA 94941   CFO: Collin Cochrane
Phone: 415 389-7373   HR: –
Fax: –   FYE: December 31
Web: www.redwoodtrust.com   Type: Public

Redwood Trust is cultivating a forest of real estate mortgage assets. The real estate investment trust (REIT) finances manages and invests in residential real estate mortgages and securities backed by such loans. It also invests in commercial real estate loans and securities. Redwood acquires assets throughout the US but has a concentration of credit risk in California Texas Massachusetts Florida and New York which hold some of the US' most active real estate markets. Redwood Trust slowed loan origination acquisition and securitization during the most recent recession but has picked up those activities as the economy has recovered.

	Annual Growth	12/14	12/15	12/16	12/17	12/18
Assets ($ mil.)	19.2%	5,919.0	6,231.0	5,483.5	7,039.8	11,937.4
Net income ($ mil.)	4.4%	100.6	102.1	131.3	140.4	119.6
Market value ($ mil.)	(6.5%)	1,672.2	1,120.5	1,291.1	1,258.0	1,279.2
Employees	(9.4%)	221	211	125	120	149

REED & BARTON CORPORATION

144 W. Britannia St.   CEO: –
Taunton MA 02780   CFO: Charles Daly
Phone: 508-824-6611   HR: –
Fax: 508-822-7269   FYE: January 31
Web: www.reedandbarton.com   Type: Private

Reed & Barton has built a business out of setting an exquisite table. Founded in 1824 Reed & Barton is one of the nation's oldest privately-held silversmiths that designs and manufactures high-quality flatware gifts and household collectibles. The company's brands include Reed & Barton Miller Rogaska Crystal by Reed & Barton The Sheffield Collection R&B EveryDay Belleek Fine Parian China and Aynsley Fine English Bone China. Reed & Barton sells its products in regional specialty shops jewelry stores and department stores including Belk Dillard's Macy's and Neiman Marcus. The company also operates about 10 retail stores located primarily in outlet centers.

REEDS INC
NAS: REED

201 Merritt 7
Norwalk, CT 06851
Phone: 800 997-3337
Fax: –
Web: www.reedsinc.com

CEO: John Bello
CFO: Thomas J Spisak
HR: –
FYE: December 31
Type: Public

Everybody needs a Reed's. The company makes two dozen all-natural soft drinks such as Original Ginger Brew and Virgil's Root Beer as well as ginger candy and three ginger-flavored ice creams. Reed's brews its drinks from roots herbs spices and fruits in a manner similar to how beer is brewed from malt and hops (without alcohol though — carbonation is added to Reed's drinks separately). The company also owns the China Cola brand which contains an herbal mixture designed to help digestion. Reed's products are sold in some 10500 natural food and traditional supermarkets as well as specialty stores and restaurants throughout North America. It also makes private-label products for retailers.

	Annual Growth	12/14	12/15	12/16	12/17	12/18
Sales ($ mil.)	(3.2%)	43.4	45.9	42.5	37.7	38.1
Net income ($ mil.)	–	(0.8)	(4.0)	(5.0)	(18.4)	(10.3)
Market value ($ mil.)	(23.1%)	152.1	138.4	105.5	39.9	53.3
Employees	(11.6%)	82	76	62	52	50

REFAC OPTICAL GROUP

1 Bridge Plaza Ste. 550
Fort Lee NJ 07024-7102
Phone: 856-228-0077
Fax: 856-228-5577
Web: www.refacopticalgroup.com

CEO: –
CFO: –
HR: –
FYE: January 31
Type: Private

Refac Optical Group keeps its eye on the business of vision care. The company manages more than 700 U.S. Vision and OptiCare retail optical stores in the US and Canada. Shops carry designer and private-label frames sunglasses contact lenses and accessories as well as offer optometric services. Brands have included Armani Exchange Calvin Klein Revlon and Vera Wang. In addition to its retail operations Refac operates two surgical centers and two manufacturing laboratories. Founded in 1952 Refac Optical Group is owned by private equity firm ACON Investments.

REGAL BELOIT CORP
NYS: RBC

200 State Street
Beloit, WI 53511
Phone: 608 364-8800
Fax: –
Web: www.regal-beloit.com

CEO: Mark J. Gliebe
CFO: Charles A. (Chuck) Hinrichs
HR: Terry R. Colvin
FYE: December 29
Type: Public

Regal Beloit (now known as just Regal) makes a range of electric motors mechanical motion control and power generation products that move mechanical equipment around the world. The company serves residential commercial and industrial OEM customers in a range of industries including HVAC automotive aerospace and oil and gas. It makes electric motors used for heating and air conditioning generators for prime and standby power electronic variable speed controls and blowers and mechanical power transmissions and gear drives. About 65% of Regal Beloit's sales comes from the US.

	Annual Growth	01/15	01/16*	12/16	12/17	12/18
Sales ($ mil.)	3.8%	3,257.1	3,509.7	3,224.5	3,360.3	3,645.6
Net income ($ mil.)	95.4%	31.0	143.3	203.4	213.0	231.2
Market value ($ mil.)	(2.4%)	3,225.8	2,504.7	2,963.9	3,278.5	2,997.7
Employees	0.7%	24,100	26,200	23,000	23,600	24,600

*Fiscal year change

REGAL ENTERTAINMENT GROUP

101 E BLOUNT AVE STE 100
KNOXVILLE, TN 379201605
Phone: 865-922-1123
Fax: –
Web: www.regmovies.com

CEO: Amy E. Miles
CFO: David H. Ownby
HR: Jackie McClure
FYE: December 31
Type: Private

Regal Entertainment Group hopes to create loyal subjects out of fickle moviegoers. The largest theater owner and exhibitor in the US has around 560 theaters with some 7300 screens in 40-plus states through its Regal Cinemas Edwards Theatres United Artists Theatre Company Great Escapes Theatres and Hollywood Theatres brands. Its theaters house an average of 12.9 screens and more than 75% of its screens are in theaters with stadium seating. Regal Entertainment co-owns National CineMedia a joint venture that sells in-theater ads and operates a video network that distributes digital content to theaters. Regal Entertainment Group was formed in 2002. It was acquired by UK-based Cineworld in a $3.6 billion reverse takeover in 2018.

	Annual Growth	01/14	01/15*	12/15	12/16	12/17
Sales ($ mil.)	2.9%	–	2,990.1	3,127.3	3,197.1	3,163.0
Net income ($ mil.)	3.3%	–	105.2	153.2	170.5	112.3
Market value ($ mil.)	–	–	–	–	–	–
Employees	–	–	–	–	–	25,359

*Fiscal year change

REGENCY CENTERS CORP
NMS: REG

One Independent Drive, Suite 114
Jacksonville, FL 32202
Phone: 904 598-7000
Fax: –
Web: www.regencycenters.com

CEO: Martin E. (Hap) Stein
CFO: Lisa Palmer
HR: –
FYE: December 31
Type: Public

Regency Centers' bread and butter comes from grocery stores. A real estate investment trust (REIT) the firm owns manages and develops neighborhood shopping centers in about two dozen states and Washington DC many of them anchored by a Kroger Publix or Safeway supermarket. Other tenants include retailers restaurants and professional services firms. The REIT wholly owns or has interests in about 330 properties measuring more than 44 million sq. ft. of leaseable space. The REIT focuses on high-growth areas in states including California Florida Texas Georgia and Colorado home to the majority of its wholly-owned holdings.

	Annual Growth	12/14	12/15	12/16	12/17	12/18
Sales ($ mil.)	20.2%	537.9	569.8	614.4	984.3	1,121.0
Net income ($ mil.)	7.4%	187.4	150.1	164.9	176.1	249.1
Market value ($ mil.)	(2.1%)	10,684.1	11,411.1	11,550.1	11,588.6	9,829.7
Employees	4.8%	370	371	371	446	446

REGENCY ENERGY PARTNERS LP
NYS: RGP

2001 Bryan Street, Suite 3700
Dallas, TX 75201
Phone: 214 750-1771
Fax: 214 750-1749
Web: www.regencygasservices.com

CEO: Michael J Bradley
CFO: Thomas E Long
HR: –
FYE: December 31
Type: Public

Midstream is the decisive choice of Regency Energy Partners. The independent energy partnership focuses on the gathering processing marketing and transportation of natural gas and natural gas liquids (NGLs) in Arkansas Kansas Louisiana and Texas. Its gathering and processing unit moves natural gas from the wellhead through gathering systems primarily for producers. Regency's gathering and processing assets include 8 gas treating/processing plants and 5260 miles of related gathering and pipeline infrastructure. Its transportation segment ships natural gas across Louisiana. The company also offers natural gas compression services and provides treating services to gas producers and pipeline companies.

	Annual Growth	05/10*	12/10	12/11	12/12	12/13
Sales ($ mil.)	70.9%	505.1	716.6	1,433.9	1,339.0	2,521.0
Net income ($ mil.)	–	(5.4)	(6.1)	72.4	46.0	19.0
Market value ($ mil.)	6.7%	4,751.1	5,996.1	5,468.2	4,768.7	5,776.1
Employees	14.4%	–	793	729	781	1,187

*Fiscal year change

REGENERON PHARMACEUTICALS, INC.   NMS: REGN

777 Old Saw Mill River Road   CEO: Leonard S. Schleifer
Tarrytown, NY 10591-6707   CFO: Robert E. Landry
Phone: 914 847-7000   HR: –
Fax: –   FYE: December 31
Web: www.regeneron.com   Type: Public

Regeneron is fighting some serious enemies. Regeneron Pharmaceuticals develops protein-based drugs used to battle a variety of diseases and conditions including cancer high cholesterol inflammatory ailments and eye diseases. The biotechnology company has a handful of products on the market including eye disease treatment EYLEA (aflibercept) cholesterol lowering drug Praluent rare inflammatory disease treatment ARCALYST rheumatoid arthritis drug Kevzara and cancer treatment ZALTRAP. Regeneron has 15 more candidates in clinical development.

	Annual Growth	12/15	12/16	12/17	12/18	12/19
Sales ($ mil.)	17.7%	4,103.7	4,860.4	5,872.2	6,710.8	7,863.4
Net income ($ mil.)	35.1%	636.1	895.5	1,198.5	2,444.4	2,115.8
Market value ($ mil.)	(8.8%)	59,866.0	40,481.6	41,459.7	41,188.4	41,406.8
Employees	17.2%	4,300	5,400	6,200	7,400	8,100

REGENERX BIOPHARMACEUTICALS INC   NBB: RGRX

15245 Shady Grove Road, Suite 470   CEO: J J Finkelstein
Rockville, MD 20850   CFO: Dane Saglio
Phone: 301 208-9191   HR: –
Fax: –   FYE: December 31
Web: www.regenerx.com   Type: Public

RegeneRx Biopharmaceuticals may not care about the state of your soul but it does want to help damaged bodily tissue be born again. The firm's main drug candidate called Thymosin beta 4 ("T--4") is undergoing clinical trials for use in accelerating wound healing and for treating other medical problems such as certain kinds of ulcers and ophthalmic conditions. The company operates using an outsourcing business model contracting most of its research and manufacturing operations to third-parties. It has research and licensing agreements with the National Institutes of Health and George Washington University.

	Annual Growth	12/14	12/15	12/16	12/17	12/18
Sales ($ mil.)	4.8%	–	0.1	0.1	0.1	0.1
Net income ($ mil.)	–	(2.8)	(5.3)	0.2	0.3	(2.0)
Market value ($ mil.)	1.8%	18.5	56.5	40.7	21.8	19.9
Employees	(27.7%)	11	12	12	3	3

REGENTS OF THE UNIVERSITY OF IDAHO

875 PERIMETER DR MS3020   CEO: Lee Ostrom
MOSCOW, ID 838449803   CFO: –
Phone: 208-885-6174   HR: –
Fax: –   FYE: June 30
Web: www.uidaho.edu   Type: Private

You won't have to learn Russian to attend school in Moscow. The University of Idaho — located in Moscow Idaho — has more than 900 faculty members and an enrollment of more than 12000 students. It offers undergraduate degree programs in subjects ranging from agriculture and art to natural resources and science. The University of Idaho also offers master's degrees and doctoral degrees in a broad range of subjects including law. In addition to its main campus University of Idaho has locations in Boise Coeur d'Alene Idaho Falls and Twin Falls as well dozens of extension offices statewide. The university was founded in 1889.

	Annual Growth	06/11	06/12	06/15	06/16	06/18
Sales ($ mil.)	(0.2%)	–	216.1	214.8	212.6	214.0
Net income ($ mil.)	–	–	1.2	24.5	20.9	(21.1)
Market value ($ mil.)	–	–	–	–	–	–
Employees	–	–	–	–	–	3,350

REGENTS OF THE UNIVERSITY OF MICHIGAN

503 THOMPSON ST   CEO: Marschall S. Runge
ANN ARBOR, MI 481091340   CFO: Kevin P. Hegarty
Phone: 734-764-1817   HR: Donna Lartigue
Fax: –   FYE: June 30
Web: www.umich.edu   Type: Private

Ranking among the top US public universities Regents of the University of Michigan (or simply University of Michigan) boasts more than 60000 students and about 8000 faculty members in southeast Michigan. Its three campuses in Ann Arbor Dearborn and Flint offer more than 260 undergraduate and graduate degree programs in fields including architecture education law medicine music and social work. The university has a student to faculty ratio of 15:1. The vast University of Michigan Health System which includes four hospitals and numerous outpatient centers provides about half of annual revenue. The university is supported by an $11.9 billion endowment.

	Annual Growth	06/13	06/14	06/16	06/17	06/18
Sales ($ mil.)	7.8%	–	5,534.9	6,278.0	7,079.7	7,466.9
Net income ($ mil.)	(12.6%)	–	1,574.9	(294.6)	1,275.9	920.4
Market value ($ mil.)	–	–	–	–	–	–
Employees	–	–	–	–	–	34,624

REGIONAL HEALTH PROPERTIES INC   ASE: RHE

454 Satellite Boulevard NW, Suite 100   CEO: –
Suwanee, GA 30024   CFO: –
Phone: 678 869-5116   HR: –
Fax: –   FYE: December 31
Web: www.regionalhealthproperties.com   Type: Public

Retirement keeps AdCare Health Systems working. The company buys leases and manages some 50 nursing homes assisted-living facilities and independent retirement communities in Alabama Arkansas Georgia Missouri North Carolina Ohio and Oklahoma with a total of more than 4800 beds in service. It owns all or part of about half of its facilities including the Hearth & Home assisted living facilities. Services include Alzheimer's and subacute care. AdCare also operates a home health care business Assured Health Care which offers nursing therapy and living assistance services as well as administrative services for insurance coordination and caregiver hiring.

	Annual Growth	12/14	12/15	12/16	12/17	12/18
Sales ($ mil.)	(41.9%)	193.3	18.4	27.3	25.1	22.0
Net income ($ mil.)	–	(13.6)	(23.5)	(7.5)	(1.0)	(11.9)
Market value ($ mil.)	(58.6%)	6.8	4.2	2.5	0.3	0.2
Employees	(73.8%)	3,414	31	19	16	16

REGIONAL MANAGEMENT CORP   NYS: RM

979 Batesville Road, Suite B   CEO: Peter R. Knitzer
Greer, SC 29651   CFO: Donald E. (Don) Thomas
Phone: 864 448-7000   HR: –
Fax: –   FYE: December 31
Web: www.regionalmanagement.com   Type: Public

Regional Management is looking to give credit where credit is due. Consumer finance company Regional Management provides secured personal loans (up to $27500) auto loans and furniture and appliance loans to consumers who may otherwise have limited access to credit through banks and other traditional lenders. The company which operates under the Regional Finance RMC Financial Services Anchor Finance and Sun Finance banners among others has some 265 branch locations in eight states in the south and southwest. It also provides loans through pre-screened live check mailings auto dealerships and its e-commerce site. Founded in 1987 Regional Management went public via an IPO in 2012.

	Annual Growth	12/14	12/15	12/16	12/17	12/18
Assets ($ mil.)	15.9%	530.3	629.1	712.2	829.5	956.4
Net income ($ mil.)	24.3%	14.8	23.4	24.0	30.0	35.3
Market value ($ mil.)	11.1%	186.2	182.2	309.5	309.9	283.2
Employees	1.6%	1,443	1,421	1,363	1,448	1,535

REGIONAL TRANSPORTATION DISTRICT

1660 BLAKE ST
DENVER, CO 802021324
Phone: 303-628-9000
Fax: –
Web: www.rtd-denver.com

CEO: –
CFO: –
HR: –
FYE: December 31
Type: Private

The Regional Transportation District (RTD) offers mass transit services via bus and light rail in the Denver area. The agency services almost 3 million people across six counties covering approximately 2348 square miles. The agency's bus system operates a fleet of approximately 1000 buses but leases about 425 of them to private operators. It provides almost 75 park-n-ride facilities to riders. RTD's light rail system includes almost 35 stations spread over some 35 miles of track. The agency's service territory encompasses all of Boulder Broomfield Denver and Jefferson counties along with parts of Adams Arapahoe Weld and Douglas counties. The agency was established by the Colorado legislature in 1969.

	Annual Growth	12/13	12/14	12/15	12/16	12/17
Sales ($ mil.)	5.7%	–	124.9	125.9	140.4	147.4
Net income ($ mil.)	(23.5%)	–	203.6	182.2	145.4	91.2
Market value ($ mil.)	–	–	–	–	–	–
Employees	–	–	–	–	–	2,700

REGIONS FINANCIAL CORP (NEW)   NYS: RF

1900 Fifth Avenue North
Birmingham, AL 35203
Phone: 205 581-7890
Fax: –
Web: www.regions.com

CEO: –
CFO: David J. Turner
HR: Ellie Long
FYE: December 31
Type: Public

The holding company for Alabama-chartered Regions Bank Regions Financial boasts around $125 billion in total assets. With some 1500 branches and more than 1900 ATMs across 15 states in the South Midwest and Texas Regions offers banking services for large corporations middle market companies and real estate investors on top of its main business of standard banking products for retail customers and small businesses. The company's smaller wealth and asset management operations target affluent private individuals. Formed in 1971 as First Alabama Bancshares Regions was Alabama's first multibank holding company.

	Annual Growth	12/14	12/15	12/16	12/17	12/18
Assets ($ mil.)	1.2%	119,679.0	126,050.0	125,968.0	124,294.0	125,688.0
Net income ($ mil.)	11.1%	1,155.0	1,062.0	1,163.0	1,263.0	1,759.0
Market value ($ mil.)	6.1%	10,822.2	9,838.3	14,716.5	17,709.0	13,712.2
Employees	(4.2%)	23,723	23,916	22,166	21,714	19,969

REGIONS HOSPITAL FOUNDATION

640 JACKSON ST
SAINT PAUL, MN 551012595
Phone: 651-254-3456
Fax: –
Web: www.healthpartners.com

CEO: –
CFO: Greg Klugherz
HR: –
FYE: December 31
Type: Private

If you live around the Twin Cities Regions Hospital can help with your medical needs. The not-for-profit hospital has more than 450 beds and provides acute medical and emergency care services as well as specialty programs in areas including behavioral health rehabilitation burn care cancer cardiovascular orthopedic pediatrics and women's care. Regions Hospital is one of a handful of level I trauma centers in Minnesota and is also a teaching and residency center for the University of Minnesota Medical School. Regions Hospital is part of HealthPartners which operates a network of medical centers and a health plan in the Twin Cities area.

	Annual Growth	12/03	12/04	12/05	12/06	12/12
Sales ($ mil.)	71.3%	–	7.9	430.7	413.9	582.0
Net income ($ mil.)	320.5%	–	0.0	12.1	4.0	36.6
Market value ($ mil.)	–	–	–	–	–	–
Employees	–	–	–	–	–	3,000

REGIS CORP   NYS: RGS

7201 Metro Boulevard
Edina, MN 55439
Phone: 952 947-7777
Fax: –
Web: www.regiscorp.com

CEO: Hugh E. Sawyer
CFO: Andrew H. Lacko
HR: Carmen D. Thiede
FYE: June 30
Type: Public

Regis is a global leader in beauty salons with about 8100 locations worldwide that it owns or franchises. Its salons operate under the banners Regis Salons SmartStyle (located in Walmart Supercenters) Supercuts MasterCuts Sassoon Style America and Cost Cutters. Hair care services ? cutting coloring styling ? generate some 75% of its sales and geographically the US accounts for more than 90% of revenue. Other revenue comes from hair care products that include its own Regis DESIGNLINE line as well as PaulMitchell Biolage and Redken. About 155 million customers visit the company's salons a year.

	Annual Growth	06/15	06/16	06/17	06/18	06/19
Sales ($ mil.)	(12.7%)	1,837.3	1,790.9	1,691.9	1,214.1	1,069.0
Net income ($ mil.)	–	(33.8)	(11.3)	(16.1)	8.7	(14.2)
Market value ($ mil.)	1.3%	581.1	459.0	378.6	609.8	612.0
Employees	(19.2%)	47,000	45,000	41,000	27,000	20,000

REI SYSTEMS, INC.

14325 WILLARD RD STE 200
CHANTILLY, VA 201512110
Phone: 703-230-0011
Fax: –
Web: www.reisystems.com

CEO: Veer Bhartiya
CFO: –
HR: –
FYE: December 31
Type: Private

No they don't sell hiking boots or kayaks. REI Systems provides information technology services and develops custom Web-based software used to automate the management of internal business communications contracts customer relationships and grants. Its Electronic Handbooks application is used to manage a variety of data collection and reporting functions; MaintenanceMax is an organizational tool for equipment maintenance providers. The company's IT services include database design software integration and network security. REI Systems' clientele is made up largely of US government agencies such as the Department of Energy and the Department of Defense; commercial clients have included Raytheon.

	Annual Growth	12/10	12/11	12/12	12/13	12/14
Sales ($ mil.)	4.3%	–	66.6	73.3	69.1	75.4
Net income ($ mil.)	(8.4%)	–	4.3	2.0	0.6	3.3
Market value ($ mil.)	–	–	–	–	–	–
Employees	–	–	–	–	–	311

REINSURANCE GROUP OF AMERICA, INC.   NYS: RGA

16600 Swingley Ridge Road
Chesterfield, MO 63017
Phone: 636 736-7000
Fax: –
Web: www.rgare.com

CEO: Mark E. Showers
CFO: Todd C. Larson
HR: Gay Burns
FYE: December 31
Type: Public

Just what is reinsurance? Here hold this pile of insurance risk while we explain that holding company Reinsurance Group of America (RGA) is one of the largest life reinsurers in the US. RGA provides insurance companies with reinsurance on the risks they've taken on allowing them to reduce their liability and increase their business volume. Its operations are organized into two large groups: Traditional and Financial Solutions. Traditional reinsurance includes individual and group life and health disability and critical illness coverage while Financial Solutions includes longevity financial and asset-intensive products. RGA operates in more than 25 countries in the Americas the Asia/Pacific region Europe and South Africa. The US and Latin America account for some 55% of RGA's total sales.

	Annual Growth	12/14	12/15	12/16	12/17	12/18
Assets ($ mil.)	9.6%	44,679.6	50,383.2	53,097.9	60,514.8	64,535.2
Net income ($ mil.)	1.1%	684.0	502.2	701.4	1,822.2	715.8
Market value ($ mil.)	12.5%	5,503.8	5,373.8	7,903.9	9,794.6	8,808.5
Employees	7.5%	2,070	2,201	2,482	2,640	2,767

REIS, INC
NMS: REIS

1185 Avenue of the Americas
New York, NY 10036
Phone: 212 921-1122
Fax: 212 921-2533
Web: www.reis.com

CEO: Lloyd Lynford
CFO: Mark P Cantaluppi
HR: –
FYE: December 31
Type: Public

Reis knows how to get below the surface of real estate. The company provides commercial real estate market information through online databases containing information on apartment retail office and industrial properties in several US metropolitan markets. Its flagship product Reis SE offers trend and forecast analysis as well as information on rent vacancy rates lease terms sale prices and new construction listings. Reis also furnishes data to small businesses through its Reis-Reports product. Its databases are used by real estate investors lenders and brokers to make buying selling and financing decisions. Customers access Reis' data through subscription or by purchasing reports individually.

	Annual Growth	12/12	12/13	12/14	12/15	12/16
Sales ($ mil.)	11.1%	31.2	34.7	41.3	50.9	47.5
Net income ($ mil.)	–	(4.3)	17.6	4.0	10.3	2.8
Market value ($ mil.)	14.3%	146.9	216.8	295.0	267.5	250.8
Employees	11.1%	190	208	205	272	289

RELAX THE BACK CORPORATION

6 Centerpointe Dr. Ste. 350
La Palma CA 90623
Phone: 714-523-2870
Fax: 714-523-2980
Web: www.relaxtheback.com

CEO: Richard W Palfreyman
CFO: –
HR: –
FYE: January 31
Type: Private

Relax the Back tries to take the "ERRRGG!" out of ergonomic injuries and chronic back pain. The firm offers muscle-soothing products for the office home and gym including back and neck supports custom and Tempur-Pedic mattresses desk chairs educational books and DVDs exercise and therapy equipment massage loungers and recliners. Doctors and therapists advise the company on decisions about products many of which are supplied by manufacturing unit BackSaver Products. Relax the Back sells through catalogs and the Internet as well as through more than 100 stores in 30 states in the US and Canada that it owns or franchises. Dominion Ventures owns Relax the Back; it was founded in 1986 by an osteopath.

RELIABILITY INCORPORATED
OTC: REAL

410 Park Ave. 15th Fl.
New York NY 91362
Phone: 212-231-8359
Fax: 503-331-2734
Web: www.rentrak.com

CEO: –
CFO: Mark Speck
HR: –
FYE: December 31
Type: Public

Reliability wanted integrated circuit (IC) manufacturers to rely on its testing systems but after a number of moves it is looking for a new line of business. The company designed manufactured and supported testing and conditioning equipment that helped detect defects in ICs. Running low on cash and needing to repay debt in 2006 Reliability sold its headquarters closed its Singapore burn-in and testing services operations and sold the assets of its Power Sources division (which made DC-to-DC converters) to Reliability Power an unaffiliated firm. The company in 2007 acquired Medallion Electric a Florida-based electrical contractor but sold it back six months later.

RELIANCE STEEL & ALUMINUM CO.
NYS: RS

350 South Grand Avenue, Suite 5100
Los Angeles, CA 90071
Phone: 213 687-7700
Fax: –
Web: www.rsac.com

CEO: Gregg J. Mollins
CFO: Karla R. Lewis
HR: Don Prebola
FYE: December 31
Type: Public

Reliance Steel & Aluminum shows its mettle as North America's largest metals service center company. Operating in the US (about 300 service centers in 40 states) and a dozen other countries it processes and distributes more than 100000 metal products (bars beams pipes tubes plates coils etc.) to 125000-plus customers in industries like aerospace energy construction manufacturing semiconductor and electronics and transportation. Carbon steel is its top product; Reliance also markets alloy stainless and specialty steel as well as aluminum brass copper and titanium products. The company's trade names include Earle M. Jorgensen Metals USA and Precision Strip.

	Annual Growth	12/14	12/15	12/16	12/17	12/18
Sales ($ mil.)	2.5%	10,451.6	9,350.5	8,613.4	9,721.0	11,534.5
Net income ($ mil.)	14.3%	371.5	311.5	304.3	613.4	633.7
Market value ($ mil.)	3.8%	4,097.9	3,873.1	5,319.8	5,737.8	4,760.0
Employees	1.2%	14,900	14,000	14,500	14,900	15,600

RELIV' INTERNATIONAL INC
NAS: RELV

136 Chesterfield Industrial Boulevard
Chesterfield, MO 63005
Phone: 636 537-9715
Fax: 636 537-9753
Web: www.reliv.com

CEO: Ryan A Montgomery
CFO: Steven D Albright
HR: –
FYE: December 31
Type: Public

Reliv' International is offering its customers more than a beverage it's offering a way of life. Reliv' develops manufactures and sells powdered nutritional supplements weight-management products sports nutrition drinks and skin care products. Top seller Reliv' Classic and Reliv NOW are vegetarian beverage powders that contains vitamins minerals and soy protein. Other products include Innergize! sports drink and high-fiber supplement FibRestore. The company uses a multi-level marketing system selling its products through more than 57000 independent distributors primarily in the US but also in Canada Mexico Europe and the Pacific Rim.

	Annual Growth	12/14	12/15	12/16	12/17	12/18
Sales ($ mil.)	(10.9%)	57.3	51.8	45.5	41.8	36.1
Net income ($ mil.)	–	0.7	(1.2)	(0.6)	(0.7)	(1.9)
Market value ($ mil.)	37.2%	2.2	1.1	8.6	8.8	7.8
Employees	(5.4%)	195	189	161	160	156

REMY INTERNATIONAL INC.
PINK SHEETS: REMYI

600 Corporation Dr.
Pendleton IN 46064
Phone: 765-778-6499
Fax: 561-241-4628
Web: www.pwg-inc.com

CEO: John J Pittas
CFO: –
HR: –
FYE: December 31
Type: Private

Remy International (formerly Delco Remy International) revs up cars and light- and heavy-duty trucks. The manufacturer and distributor offers starter motors alternators hybrid electric motors and transmission components. Most parts are sold under the Delco Remy brand which debuted in 1918. The company holds the top spot for remanufacturing starters and alternators for the automotive aftermarket in North America. Its roster of customers includes OEMs (General Motors is largest customer generating almost 25% of annual sales) and aftermarket businesses such as Advance Auto Parts and AutoZone. Fidelity National a title insurance company owns 49% of Remy which filed to go public in 2011.

RENAISSANCE LEARNING INC.

2911 Peach St.
Wisconsin Rapids WI 54495
Phone: 715-424-3636
Fax: 715-424-4242
Web: www.renlearn.com
CEO: Chris Bauleke
CFO: Mary T Minch
HR: –
FYE: December 31
Type: Private

Renaissance Learning offers a technical approach to education. The company's educational software designed for grades pre-K through 12 is used by schools in North America. Offered on CD-ROMs and on a hosted basis its software includes its flagship Accelerated Reader program as well as applications for writing math language acquisition and early literacy. Renaissance also markets portable computing devices pre-loaded with software to improve writing skills. Husband and wife Terrance Paul (chairman) and Judith Paul (vice chairman) who founded the company in 1986 together owned 54% of Renaissance before it was acquired in 2011 by London-based private equity firm Permira Funds for about $440 million.

RENASANT CORP
NMS: RNST

209 Troy Street
Tupelo, MS 38804-4827
Phone: 662 680-1001
Fax: –
Web: www.renasant.com
CEO: E. Robinson (Robin) McGraw
CFO: Kevin D. Chapman
HR: Atonya Smith
FYE: December 31
Type: Public

Those who are cognizant of their finances may want to do business with Renasant Corporation. The holding company owns Renasant Bank which serves consumers and local business through about 80 locations in Alabama Georgia Mississippi and Tennessee. The bank offers standard products such as checking and savings accounts CDs credit cards and loans and mortgages as well as trust retail brokerage and retirement plan services. Its loan portfolio is dominated by residential and commercial real estate loans. The bank also offers agricultural business construction and consumer loans and lease financing. Subsidiary Renasant Insurance sells personal and business coverage.Shareholders approved a merger with Metropolitan Bank in mid-2017.

	Annual Growth	12/14	12/15	12/16	12/17	12/18
Assets ($ mil.)	22.2%	5,805.1	7,926.5	8,699.9	9,830.0	12,934.9
Net income ($ mil.)	25.3%	59.6	68.0	90.9	92.2	146.9
Market value ($ mil.)	1.1%	1,693.7	2,014.6	2,471.8	2,394.0	1,766.9
Employees	12.5%	1,471	1,996	1,965	2,102	2,359

RENESAS ELECTRONICS AMERICA INC.

1001 MURPHY RANCH RD
MILPITAS, CA 950357912
Phone: 408-432-8888
Fax: –
Web: www.renesas.com
CEO: Necip Sayiner
CFO: Richard D. (Rick) Crowley
HR: –
FYE: January 01
Type: Private

Intersil makes transfer of power an orderly process at least in electronics. Its line of semiconductor devices for power management include power regulators converters and controllers power modules amplifiers and buffers proximity and light sensors data converters video decoders and interfaces. Its products are components in data centers computers smartphones autos and a range of other applications. Almost three-quarters of its sales are to customers in Asia. In 2017 Intersil was bought by Renesas Electronics for $3.2 billion.

	Annual Growth	01/12	01/13	01/14	01/15	01/16
Sales ($ mil.)	(4.8%)	–	–	575.2	562.6	521.6
Net income ($ mil.)	58.7%	–	–	2.9	54.8	7.2
Market value ($ mil.)	–	–	–	–	–	–
Employees	–	–	–	–	–	1,027

RENEWABLE ENERGY GROUP INC.
NASDAQ: REGI

416 S. Bell Ave.
Ames IA 50010
Phone: 515-239-8000
Fax: 515-239-8009
Web: www.regfuel.com
CEO: –
CFO: –
HR: Brenda Brown
FYE: December 31
Type: Public

Renewable Energy Group or REG wants alternative fuel to become a regular thing for its customers. The company sells SoyPOWER brand biodiesel throughout the US controlling about 40% of US sales. Biodiesel is a clean burning fuel made from waste including vegetable oil corn grain and soybeans. REG owns four and manages five plants that make more than 300 million gallons of biofuel per year; that fuel is sold to fleet operators the military and mining agriculture and home-heating companies. In addition to its production and distribution activities REG also builds biodiesel production plants for other firms. The company was formed in 2003 by West Central Cooperative. REG went public in 2011 with an IPO.

RENEWABLE ENERGY GROUP, INC.
NMS: REGI

416 South Bell Avenue
Ames, IA 50010
Phone: 515 239-8000
Fax: –
Web: www.regi.com
CEO: Daniel J. Oh
CFO: Chad Stone
HR: –
FYE: December 31
Type: Public

Renewable Energy Group (REG) is North America's largest advanced biofuels producers converting natural fats oils and greases into lower carbon intensive products such as heating oil ultra-low sulfur diesel and blended fuel. The company sells some 650 million gallons of biofuels yearly through some 15 refineries in the US and Germany. REG is also working to develop renewable chemicals from fatty acids and other raw materials. Vertically integrated REG sells to municipalities transportation fleets fuel wholesalers and convenience stores and industries like mining and agriculture. The company generates nearly all its revenue in the US.

	Annual Growth	12/14	12/15	12/16	12/17	12/18
Sales ($ mil.)	17.0%	1,273.8	1,387.3	2,041.2	2,158.2	2,383.0
Net income ($ mil.)	37.2%	82.6	(151.4)	44.3	(79.1)	292.3
Market value ($ mil.)	27.5%	362.4	346.7	362.0	440.4	959.1
Employees	14.1%	502	597	703	727	850

RENFRO CORPORATION

661 LINVILLE RD
MOUNT AIRY, NC 270303101
Phone: 336-719-8000
Fax: –
Web: www.renfro.com
CEO: Stan Jewell
CFO: David Dinkins
HR: Cathleen Allred
FYE: January 29
Type: Private

For those who tend to misplace their socks Renfro can foot the bill. The company designs and manufacturers hundreds of styles of socks and legwear products and markets them in North America through department stores specialty stores and e-commerce sites. Renfro's products are sold under several brands including Carhartt Fruit of the Loom Dr. Scholl's Copper Sole Polo Work King and Wrangler among others. The company also sells its owns brands K. Bell and Hot Sox. The clothing company's customers include well-known retailers such as Costco Kmart J.C. Penney Target and Wal-Mart.

	Annual Growth	01/06	01/07	01/08	01/10	01/11
Sales ($ mil.)	(0.1%)	–	–	391.7	375.6	390.1
Net income ($ mil.)	(29.8%)	–	–	28.0	11.7	9.7
Market value ($ mil.)	–	–	–	–	–	–
Employees	–	–	–	–	–	4,200

RENNOVA HEALTH INC   NBB: RNVA

931 Village Boulevard, Suite 905   CEO: Seamus Lagan
West Palm Beach, FL 33409   CFO: Marlene McLennan
Phone: 561 855-1626   HR: –
Fax: –   FYE: December 31
Web: www.collabrx.com   Type: Public

Rennova Health (formerly CollabRx) is collaborating between data and health care. The company provides data analytics through its products including Medytox Diagnostics HIPAA-compliant tracking software Advantage lab data management software Clinlab electronic health record Medical Mime cancer analytics platform CollabRx revenue cycle management tool Medical Billing Choices; it also provides access to lending services through Platinum Financial Solutions. Customers include Life Technologies Inc. and Everyday Health Inc.

	Annual Growth	03/15*	12/15	12/16	12/17	12/18
Sales ($ mil.)	208.0%	0.5	18.4	5.2	4.6	14.5
Net income ($ mil.)	–	(5.2)	(34.7)	(32.6)	(55.2)	(14.0)
Market value ($ mil.)	(88.7%)	140.1	173.6	10.7	4.1	0.2
Employees	187.5%	13	198	116	155	309

*Fiscal year change

RENO CONTRACTING INC.

1450 FRAZEE RD STE 100   CEO: –
SAN DIEGO, CA 921084341   CFO: –
Phone: 619-220-0224   HR: –
Fax: –   FYE: October 31
Web: www.renocon.com   Type: Private

Reno Contracting is building on its commercial state of mind in the southern part of the Golden State. The general contractor specializes in commercial construction projects primarily in its home region of San Diego County California. Projects include office retail and hospitality construction biotech and industrial facilities and hospitals. Reno develops properties from the ground up and also performs interior tenant improvements. Clients have included Diversa Corporation Biosite and Bridgepoint Education. Reno's green building division Reno ESP utilizes energy efficient products and technology in the construction process. The company was founded in 1993 by CEO Matt Reno.

	Annual Growth	10/05	10/06	10/07	10/08	10/10
Sales ($ mil.)	(59.1%)	–	–	884.1	213.7	60.5
Net income ($ mil.)	5313.5%	–	–	0.0	1.4	1.0
Market value ($ mil.)	–	–	–	–	–	–
Employees	–	–	–	–	–	32

RENSSELAER POLYTECHNIC INSTITUTE

110 8TH ST   CEO: –
TROY, NY 121803522   CFO: –
Phone: 518-276-6000   HR: –
Fax: –   FYE: June 30
Web: www.rpi.edu   Type: Private

Rensselaer Polytechnic Institute (RPI) feeds scientific minds. The university offers about 150 bachelor's master's and doctoral degree programs primarily in scientific research and technology fields. With some 7000 undergraduate and graduate students and a student-to-faculty ratio of 15:1 RPI strives to provide interdisciplinary education programs through its five schools (Architecture; Engineering; Humanities Arts and Social Sciences; Management and Technology; and Science). The institute was founded in 1824 and is one of the oldest engineering schools in the country. RPI's main campus is in Troy New York but the institute also has a location in Hartford Connecticut that caters to working professionals.

	Annual Growth	06/06	06/07	06/08	06/10	06/17
Sales ($ mil.)	0.7%	–	–	390.2	391.9	414.1
Net income ($ mil.)	–	–	–	(96.7)	(13.1)	77.7
Market value ($ mil.)	–	–	–	–	–	–
Employees	–	–	–	–	–	1,500

RENT-A-CENTER INC.   NMS: RCII

5501 Headquarters Drive   CEO: Mitchell E. (Mitch) Fadel
Plano, TX 75024   CFO: Maureen B Short
Phone: 972 801-1100   HR: –
Fax: 972 701-0360   FYE: December 31
Web: www.rentacenter.com   Type: Public

Rent-A-Center (RAC) the #1 rent-to-own chain nationwide owns and operates some 2465 company-owned stores throughout the US Mexico and Puerto Rico under the Rent-A-Center Get It Now and Home Choice names. It also franchises more than 225 stores through subsidiary Rent-A-Center Franchising International (formerly ColorTyme). The stores rent name-brand home electronics furniture accessories appliances and computers. While customers have the option to eventually own their rented items only about 25% ever do. The company's Acceptance Now business operates from kiosks on the premises of other retailers. RAC is being taken private by investment firm Vintage Capital Management.

	Annual Growth	12/14	12/15	12/16	12/17	12/18
Sales ($ mil.)	(4.2%)	3,157.8	3,278.4	2,963.3	2,702.5	2,660.5
Net income ($ mil.)	(45.5%)	96.4	(866.6)	(105.2)	6.7	8.5
Market value ($ mil.)	(18.3%)	1,944.6	801.5	602.3	594.3	866.8
Employees	(10.9%)	22,200	24,300	21,600	18,300	14,000

RENTECH INC   NBB: RTKH Q

1000 Potomac Street NW, 5th Floor   CEO: Keith Forman
Washington, DC 20007   CFO: Paul M Summers
Phone: 202 791-9040   HR: –
Fax: –   FYE: December 31
Web: www.rentechinc.com   Type: Public

Rentech owns and operates wood fiber processing and nitrogen fertilizer manufacturing businesses. It also owns the intellectual property including patents pilot and demonstration data and engineering designs for a number of clean energy technologies designed to produce certified synthetic fuels and renewable power when integrated with third-party technologies. Originally a clean energy business that rented (licensed) its alternative energy technology (hence "rent-tech") the company now gets most of its revenues from its fertilizers and wood fiber processing operations.

	Annual Growth	12/12	12/13	12/14	12/15	12/16
Sales ($ mil.)	(12.9%)	261.9	374.9	472.7	295.8	150.7
Net income ($ mil.)	–	(14.0)	(1.5)	(32.0)	(114.6)	169.3
Market value ($ mil.)	(1.5%)	61.0	40.6	29.2	81.7	57.5
Employees	15.8%	347	760	891	939	625

RENTRAK CORP.   NMS: RENT

7700 NE Ambassador Place   CEO: William P Livek
Portland, OR 97220   CFO: David I Chemerow
Phone: 503 284-7581   HR: –
Fax: –   FYE: March 31
Web: www.rentrak.com   Type: Public

What a bargain movie matinee is to parents Rentrak strives to be to mom-and-pop video rental stores: a lower-priced necessity. Rentrak provides content to regional and independent video entertainment rental outlets in the US and Canada via its Pay-Per-Transaction (PPT) system. This system enables retailers to lease content such as movies TV and games at lower distribution costs in return for a cut of the rental revenue. Rentrak also provides nearly real-time viewer transaction measurement services to the entertainment and advertising industries reporting consumer viewing behavior for on-demand TV Internet and theatrical release content. Customers include Starcom MediaVest and Fisher Communications.

	Annual Growth	03/10	03/11	03/12	03/13	03/14
Sales ($ mil.)	(4.5%)	91.1	97.1	91.1	99.2	75.6
Net income ($ mil.)	–	0.6	(0.8)	(6.4)	(22.6)	(4.3)
Market value ($ mil.)	29.3%	263.2	328.8	277.2	268.4	736.2
Employees	8.2%	382	423	448	471	524

REPLACEMENT PARTS, INC.

1901 E ROOSEVELT RD
LITTLE ROCK, AR 722062533
Phone: 501-375-1215
Fax: –

CEO: Bill Schlatterer
CFO: –
HR: Martha Harper
FYE: December 31
Type: Private

Replacement Parts works Bumper to Bumper. The company's subsidiary Crow-Burlingame operates about 160 stores under the Bumper To Bumper banner in Arkansas Louisiana Mississippi Missouri Oklahoma and Texas. Replacement Parts also distributes auto parts through three Parts Warehouses in Arkansas Louisiana and Oklahoma. The company was founded in 1919 by grocer J.G. Burlingame and candy salesman William Robert Crow grandfather of president Fletcher Lord Jr. The duo first entered the auto business by purchasing new cars in St. Louis and driving them around Little Rock to attract buyers. Employees own about 15% of the company through its stock ownership program.

	Annual Growth	12/02	12/03	12/04	12/06	12/07
Sales ($ mil.)	47.0%	–	40.1	149.4	179.0	187.3
Net income ($ mil.)	17.7%	–	1.6	2.8	5.1	3.1
Market value ($ mil.)	–	–	–	–	–	–
Employees	–	–	–	–	–	1,200

REPLACEMENTS, LTD.

1089 KNOX RD
MC LEANSVILLE, NC 273019228
Phone: 336-697-3000
Fax: –
Web: www.replacements.com

CEO: –
CFO: –
HR: –
FYE: September 30
Type: Private

Face it the good china is going to get chipped. While throwing it all out is always an option Replacements offers a cheaper solution. The company offers new and previously-owned china crystal flatware and collectibles from its facilities spanning some 500000 sq. ft. Its inventory consists of nearly 14 million pieces in more than 340000 patterns. In addition to its bridal and gift registry Replacements' website features a dinnerware knowledge base place-setting guides pattern identification tools and showroom tour. Customers can place their orders by mail phone fax e-mail or in person at the company's store in Greensboro North Carolina. Replacements was founded by CEO Bob Page in 1981.

	Annual Growth	09/14	09/15	09/16	09/17	09/18
Sales ($ mil.)	0.7%	–	81.6	83.7	81.8	83.3
Net income ($ mil.)	1.8%	–	9.3	9.1	9.3	9.8
Market value ($ mil.)	–	–	–	–	–	–
Employees	–	–	–	–	–	400

REPLIGEN CORP.

NMS: RGEN

41 Seyon Street, Bldg. 1, Suite 100
Waltham, MA 02453
Phone: 781 250-0111
Fax: 781 250-0115
Web: www.repligen.com

CEO: Tony J. Hunt
CFO: Jon K. Snodgres
HR: Kelly Capra
FYE: December 31
Type: Public

Repligen supplies bio-engineered drug ingredients to the pharmaceutical industry. The company's bioprocessing business develops and commercializes proteins and other agents used in the production of biopharmaceuticals. Repligen is a major supplier of Protein A a recombinant protein used in the production of monoclonal antibodies and other biopharmaceutical manufacturing applications. Its product portfolio also includes filtration products and chromatography devices. Repligen's largest customer is GE Healthcare with which it has a multi-year supply agreement. The US accounts for about half of the company's total revenue.

	Annual Growth	12/14	12/15	12/16	12/17	12/18
Sales ($ mil.)	32.2%	63.5	83.5	104.5	141.2	194.0
Net income ($ mil.)	19.4%	8.2	9.3	11.7	28.4	16.6
Market value ($ mil.)	27.8%	869.6	1,242.4	1,353.5	1,593.3	2,316.2
Employees	41.7%	136	168	236	476	548

REPRO MED SYSTEMS, INC.

NAS: KRMD

24 Carpenter Road
Chester, NY 10918
Phone: 845 469-2042
Fax: 845 469-5518
Web: www.rmsmedicalproducts.com

CEO: –
CFO: Karen Fisher
HR: –
FYE: December 31
Type: Public

Repro-Med Systems (aka RMS Medical Products) doesn't want to repo your medical devices it wants to supply you with them! The company manufactures portable medical devices for respiratory and infusion therapy. Most of RMS' products are designed for simplicity and do not require batteries or electricity. The company's biggest seller is a hand-powered airway suction device (RES-Q-VAC) used in emergency situations in hospitals and ambulances. Its other key product is a portable self-powered infusion system (FREEDOM60) for ambulatory home and hospital use. The company also has a line of gynecological instruments. Founder CEO Andrew Sealfon owns 20% of the company he established in 1980.

	Annual Growth	02/15	02/16	02/17*	12/17	12/18
Sales ($ mil.)	15.6%	11.2	12.2	12.3	13.3	17.4
Net income ($ mil.)	6.5%	0.8	0.8	(0.5)	0.9	0.9
Market value ($ mil.)	60.3%	15.3	21.8	16.2	47.7	63.0
Employees	0.4%	75	55	69	–	76

*Fiscal year change

REPROS THERAPEUTICS INC

NAS: RPRX

2408 Timberloch Place, Suite B-7
The Woodlands, TX 77380
Phone: 281 719-3400
Fax: 281 363-8796
Web: www.reprosrx.com

CEO: –
CFO: –
HR: –
FYE: December 31
Type: Public

Repros Therapeutics focuses on reproductive health. The pharmaceutical firm develops small-molecule drugs to treat hormonal and reproductive system disorders. Its lead candidate Proellex is a possible therapy for uterine fibroids endometriosis and associated anemia. The company is developing an orally delivered version as well as a vaginally delivered one. Repros' second candidate Androxal may treat testosterone deficiencies in men particularly when the deficiency is caused by obesity. The company was formed in 1987 and went public in mid-2013.

	Annual Growth	12/11	12/12	12/13	12/14	12/15
Sales ($ mil.)	53.1%	0.0	0.0	0.0	0.0	0.0
Net income ($ mil.)	–	(12.5)	(18.2)	(27.7)	(32.5)	(29.2)
Market value ($ mil.)	(29.2%)	117.2	383.0	445.0	242.5	29.4
Employees	18.9%	13	21	25	28	26

REPUBLIC AIRWAYS HOLDINGS INC

NBB: RJET Q

8909 Purdue Road, Suite 300
Indianapolis, IN 46268
Phone: 317 484-6000
Fax: –
Web: www.rjet.com

CEO: Bryan K Bedford
CFO: Joseph P Allman
HR: –
FYE: December 31
Type: Public

Many US airlines pledge allegiance to Republic Airways. The airline holding company's subsidiaries Chautauqua Airlines Republic Airlines and Shuttle America offer passenger flight service to major airports and smaller markets as well as regional service under code-sharing agreements with American Continental Delta United and US Airways. (Code-sharing allows airlines to sell tickets on one another's flights and extend their network.) The company maintains a fleet of about 240 aircraft and offer scheduled passenger service with more than 1250 flights daily to 100 cities. Republic made headlines in early 2016 when it filed for Chapter 11 bankruptcy protection.

	Annual Growth	12/11	12/12	12/13	12/14	12/15
Sales ($ mil.)	(17.2%)	2,864.5	2,810.9	1,346.5	1,375.4	1,344.0
Net income ($ mil.)	–	(151.8)	51.3	26.7	64.3	(27.1)
Market value ($ mil.)	3.5%	174.8	289.4	544.6	743.3	200.2
Employees	(12.3%)	9,420	9,140	5,821	5,935	5,581

REPUBLIC BANCORP, INC. (KY)
NMS: RBCA A

601 West Market Street
Louisville, KY 40202
Phone: 502 584-3600
Fax: –
Web: www.republicbank.com

CEO: Steven E. (Steve) Trager
CFO: Kevin Sipes
HR: –
FYE: December 31
Type: Public

As one of the top five bank holding companies based in Kentucky $4 billion-asset Republic Bancorp is the parent of Republic Bank & Trust (formerly First Commercial Bank) which offers deposit accounts loans and mortgages credit cards private banking and trust services through more than 30 branches in across Kentucky and around 10 more in southern Indiana Nashville Tampa and Cincinnati Ohio. About one-third of the bank's $3 billion-loan portfolio is tied to residential real estate while another 25% is made up of commercial real estate loans. Warehouse lines of credit home equity loans and commercial and industrial loans make up most of the rest. The company also offers short-term consumer loans and tax refund loans.

	Annual Growth	12/14	12/15	12/16	12/17	12/18
Assets ($ mil.)	8.7%	3,747.0	4,230.3	4,816.3	5,085.4	5,240.4
Net income ($ mil.)	28.2%	28.8	35.2	45.9	45.6	77.9
Market value ($ mil.)	11.9%	516.3	551.6	825.9	794.2	808.8
Employees	9.7%	735	799	954	1,009	1,064

REPUBLIC FIRST BANCORP, INC.
NMS: FRBK

50 South 16th Street
Philadelphia, PA 19102
Phone: 215 735-4422
Fax: –
Web: www.myrepublicbank.com

CEO: –
CFO: Frank A Cavallaro
HR: Janine Zangrilli
FYE: December 31
Type: Public

Republic First Bancorp is the holding company for Republic Bank which serves the Greater Philadelphia area and southern New Jersey from more than 15 branches. Boasting over $1 billion in assets the bank targets individuals and small to midsized businesses offering standard deposit products including checking and savings accounts money market accounts IRAs and CDs. Commercial mortgages account for more than 70% of the company's loan portfolio which also includes consumer loans business loans and residential mortgages. Republic has been transitioning from a commercial bank into a major regional retail and commercial bank.

	Annual Growth	12/14	12/15	12/16	12/17	12/18
Assets ($ mil.)	22.7%	1,214.6	1,439.4	1,923.9	2,322.3	2,753.3
Net income ($ mil.)	37.1%	2.4	2.4	4.9	8.9	8.6
Market value ($ mil.)	12.3%	220.5	254.6	490.9	496.8	351.0
Employees	22.6%	235	277	306	448	531

REPUBLIC SERVICES INC
NYS: RSG

18500 North Allied Way
Phoenix, AZ 85054
Phone: 480 627-2700
Fax: –
Web: www.republicservices.com

CEO: Donald W. (Don) Slager
CFO: Charles F Serianni
HR: –
FYE: December 31
Type: Public

Republic Services is the second-largest nonhazardous waste management provider in the US behind leader Waste Management in terms of revenue and geographic coverage. Republic provides waste disposal services for commercial industrial municipal and residential customers through its network of 350 collection firms. It owns or operates some 190 solid waste landfills more than 200 transfer stations and about 90 recycling centers. Other assets include seven treatment recovery and disposal facilities and 10 salt water disposal wells. It also has about 75 landfill-to-gas and a handful of other renewable energy projects.

	Annual Growth	12/14	12/15	12/16	12/17	12/18
Sales ($ mil.)	3.4%	8,788.3	9,115.0	9,387.7	10,041.5	10,040.9
Net income ($ mil.)	17.3%	547.6	749.9	612.6	1,278.4	1,036.9
Market value ($ mil.)	15.7%	12,980.6	14,186.8	18,398.6	21,804.2	23,249.0
Employees	3.8%	31,000	33,000	33,000	35,000	36,000

RES-CARE INC.

9901 Linn Station Rd.
Louisville KY 40223
Phone: 502-394-2100
Fax: 502-394-2206
Web: www.rescare.com

CEO: Jon Rousseau
CFO: David W Miles
HR: –
FYE: December 31
Type: Private

Through its residential training and support services ResCare offers RESpect and CARE to people with physical and mental disabilities. ResCare has residential and nonresidential facilities in more than 40 states and some international locations. The company operates through four primary segments: ResCare HomeCare Services ResCare Residential Services ResCare Workforce Services and ResCare Youth Services. The segments provide in-home personal care and training in social vocational and functional skills as well as counseling and therapy programs. Additionally Res-Care runs correctional and care programs for at-risk youth and assistance for adults. The company is owned by investment firm Onex.

RESEARCH FRONTIERS INC.
NAS: REFR

240 Crossways Park Drive
Woodbury, NY 11797-2033
Phone: 516 364-1902
Fax: –
Web: www.smartglass.com

CEO: Joseph M Harary
CFO: Seth L Van Voorhees
HR: –
FYE: December 31
Type: Public

Research Frontiers is exploring smart light frontiers. The company's suspended-particle device (SPD) technology controls the flow of light. When microscopic particles in a liquid suspension or film are electrically excited they align. By varying voltage the amount of light transmitted can be controlled. Applications include "smart windows" that control light transmission eyewear auto sunroofs and mirrors and flat-panel displays for computers and other electronic devices. Research Frontiers licenses its technologies to such manufacturers as Asahi Glass Dainippon Ink and Chemicals General Electric Hitachi Chemical and Polaroid.

	Annual Growth	12/14	12/15	12/16	12/17	12/18
Sales ($ mil.)	(1.8%)	1.6	2.0	1.2	1.5	1.5
Net income ($ mil.)	—	(4.4)	(4.3)	(4.2)	(2.4)	(2.7)
Market value ($ mil.)	(25.7%)	141.6	144.1	50.4	28.8	43.2
Employees	(8.8%)	13	12	11	7	9

RESEARCH INCORPORATED

7128 Shady Oak Rd.
Eden Prairie MN 55344-3517
Phone: 952-949-9009
Fax: 952-949-9559
Web: www.researchinc.com

CEO: –
CFO: –
HR: –
FYE: September 30
Type: Private

Research Inc. keeps the heat on its customers. The company makes reflow ovens drying systems and heating devices used in the graphic arts semiconductor and plastics industries. Its ink-drying products provide precise heat control in printing processes (such as ink-jet printing). The company's reflow ovens are used in surface-mount applications such as semiconductor production and printed circuit board assembly and its heating devices produce items such as silicone tubing and plastic bottles. Research Inc. markets its integrated heating systems to the graphic arts and print media markets under the Speed-Dri Roll-Dri and Web-Dri brands. In 2007 the company was acquired by Precison Control Systems Inc.

RESEARCH TRIANGLE INSTITUTE INC

3040 CORNWALLIS RD
DURHAM, NC 277090155
Phone: 919-541-6000
Fax: –
Web: www.rti.org

CEO: E. Wayne Holden
CFO: Michael H. (Mike) Kaelin
HR: –
FYE: September 30
Type: Private

The scientists at Research Triangle Institute address the problems of a sphere (the planet). Operating mainly under its trade name RTI International (RTI) the not-for-profit enterprise conducts research in such areas as advanced technologies environmental resources and medicine. It provides such services as certification and materials testing as well as software used in laboratories and research projects. Serving the US federal government other governments nonprofits and for-profit companies RTI offers analytical perspectives on public policy and has researchers working in offices around the world.

	Annual Growth	09/13	09/14	09/15	09/16	09/17
Sales ($ mil.)	7.2%	–	788.2	831.5	884.7	972.3
Net income ($ mil.)	(10.4%)	–	31.8	40.6	16.0	22.9
Market value ($ mil.)	–	–	–	–	–	–
Employees	–	–	–	–	–	3,117

RESERVE PETROLEUM CO.   NBB: RSRV

6801 Broadway Ext., Suite 300
Oklahoma City, OK 73116-9037
Phone: 405 848-7551
Fax: –
Web: www.reserve-petro.com

CEO: Cameron R McLain
CFO: –
HR: –
FYE: December 31
Type: Public

The Reserve Petroleum Company has petroleum reserves of about 266870 barrels of oil. It also has 1.6 billion cu. ft. of natural gas reserves. In 2008 the oil and gas exploration and production company owned non-producing properties of more than 262000 gross acres (90330 net acres) located in nine states. About 64800 net acres of this land asset are in Oklahoma South Dakota and Texas. About 53% of Reserve Petroleum's oil production in 2008 was derived from royalty interests. The company has royalty interests in 33 gross (1.1 net) wells that were drilled and completed as producing wells. President Mason McLain owns about 10% of Reserve Petroleum.

	Annual Growth	12/14	12/15	12/16	12/17	12/18
Sales ($ mil.)	(20.8%)	21.2	8.5	6.3	6.3	8.3
Net income ($ mil.)	(23.5%)	6.8	(1.9)	(0.1)	0.7	2.3
Market value ($ mil.)	(13.8%)	56.1	34.6	30.9	34.6	31.0
Employees	0.0%	9	9	8	9	9

RESHAPE LIFESCIENCES INC   NBB: RSLS

1001 Calle Amanecer
San Clemente, CA 92673
Phone: 949 429-6680
Fax: –
Web: www.reshapelifesciences.com

CEO: Dan W. Gladney
CFO: Scott P. Youngstrom
HR: –
FYE: December 31
Type: Public

ReShape Lifesciences (formerly EnteroMedics) is a medical device company that develops and sells weight loss devices. The company's flagship Lap-Band System is a silicone band that is surgically placed around the top of the stomach to simulate to the patient a sensation of fullness when eating. This sensation is intended to curb food consumption and ultimately lead to weight loss. The ReShape Vest is another company weight-loss product in development that serves the same function as the Lap-Band System but with a vest-like design that wraps around the stomach. ReShape Lifesciences which traces its root back to 2002 acquired the FDA-approved Lap-Band System from Apollo Endosurgery in late 2018.

	Annual Growth	12/14	12/15	12/16	12/17	12/18
Sales ($ mil.)	27.6%	–	0.3	0.8	1.3	0.6
Net income ($ mil.)	–	(26.1)	(25.5)	(23.4)	(33.8)	(81.2)
Market value ($ mil.)	–	0.1	0.1	0.1	0.1	0.0
Employees	11.3%	28	37	32	83	43

RESMED INC.   NYS: RMD

9001 Spectrum Center Blvd.
San Diego, CA 92123
Phone: 858 836-5000
Fax: –
Web: www.resmed.com

CEO: Michael J Farrell
CFO: Brett Sandercock
HR: –
FYE: June 30
Type: Public

ResMed develops makes and distributes medical equipment used to diagnose and treat respiratory disorders that occur during sleep such as sleep apnea. Most of its products treat obstructive sleep apnea (OSA) a condition in which a patient's air flow is periodically obstructed causing multiple disruptions during sleep that can lead to daytime sleepiness and other conditions such as high blood pressure. Its products include air-flow generators face masks diagnostic products and accessories. ResMed sells directly and through distributors worldwide to home health equipment dealers sleep clinics and hospitals. ResMed was founded in Australia in 1989 by Peter C. Farrell who remains chairman.

	Annual Growth	06/15	06/16	06/17	06/18	06/19
Sales ($ mil.)	11.6%	1,678.9	1,838.7	2,066.7	2,340.2	2,606.6
Net income ($ mil.)	3.5%	352.9	352.4	342.3	315.6	404.6
Market value ($ mil.)	21.3%	8,097.8	9,083.3	11,186.4	14,879.8	17,530.2
Employees	(35.7%)	4,340	5,250	6,080	5,940	740

RESOLUTE ENERGY CORP   NYS: REN

1700 Lincoln Street, Suite 2800
Denver, CO 80203
Phone: 303 534-4600
Fax: –
Web: www.resoluteenergy.com

CEO: –
CFO: –
HR: –
FYE: December 31
Type: Public

With determined resolve Resolute Energy searches for oil and gas. The company reports net proved reserves of 78.8 million barrels of oil equivalent from assets across five US states. The company's assets include water and carbon dioxide injected wells on land in the Greater Aneth Field (its primary asset) in Utah. It shares ownership of the oil field with Navajo Nation Oil and Gas Company (NNOG) since the Aneth Field sits on reservation land. In recent years Resolute Energy has expanded its operations to also include conventional and unconventional oil and gas assets in a New Mexico North Dakota Texas and Wyoming. In 2017 the company acquired 4600 net acres in the Delaware Basin (Texas) for $160 million.

	Annual Growth	12/13	12/14	12/15	12/16	12/17
Sales ($ mil.)	(3.5%)	349.8	329.4	154.6	164.5	303.5
Net income ($ mil.)	–	(113.8)	(21.9)	(742.3)	(161.7)	(1.2)
Market value ($ mil.)	36.6%	203.4	29.7	19.6	927.9	708.9
Employees	(16.4%)	262	265	226	206	128

RESOURCE AMERICA, INC.   NMS: REXI

One Crescent Drive, Suite 203, Navy Yard Corporate Center
Philadelphia, PA 19112
Phone: 215 546-5005
Fax: –
Web: www.resourceamerica.com

CEO: Jonathan Z Cohen
CFO: Thomas C Elliott
HR: –
FYE: December 31
Type: Public

Resource America's resource of choice is real estate investment. The company manages a series of funds that invest in real estate-related debt commercial mortgages and other real estate assets as well as trust-preferred securities and asset-backed securities. Its financial fund management operations finance structure and manage investments in bank loans securities bonds and other instruments. Through its Trapeza Capital Management and Ischus Capital Management divisions and other ventures the company focuses on financial funds for collateralized debt and loan obligations. Resource America and its affiliates manage some $17.8 billion in assets.

	Annual Growth	09/10	09/11	09/12*	12/13	12/14
Sales ($ mil.)	17.5%	88.7	86.0	64.4	153.7	169.3
Net income ($ mil.)	–	(16.7)	(7.4)	26.2	52.0	68.4
Market value ($ mil.)	12.3%	129.1	102.5	155.4	212.7	205.4
Employees	3.0%	656	737	602	655	737

*Fiscal year change

RESOURCES CONNECTION INC   NMS: RECN

17101 Armstrong Avenue
Irvine, CA 92614
Phone: 714 430-6400
Fax: –
Web: www.rgp.com

CEO: Kate W. Duchene
CFO: Jennifer Ryu
HR: –
FYE: May 25
Type: Public

Resources Connection doing business as Resources Global Professional (RGP) is a global consulting firm. The company assists clients with enterprise functions across practice areas such as Business Transformation Governance Risk and Compliance and Technology and Digital Innovation. It primarily conducts business on a project-by-project basis positioning itself as a flexible alternative to traditional accounting consulting and law firms for certain tasks. RGP has more than 3800 professionals that serve some 2400 clients from some 70 offices in 20 countries across the world. Most revenues come from North America (82%) followed by Europe and the Asia/Pacific region.

	Annual Growth	05/15	05/16	05/17	05/18	05/19
Sales ($ mil.)	5.4%	590.6	598.5	583.4	654.1	729.0
Net income ($ mil.)	3.4%	27.5	30.4	18.7	18.8	31.5
Market value ($ mil.)	(0.2%)	495.6	489.9	399.6	516.5	491.5
Employees	4.6%	3,258	3,283	3,301	4,153	3,896

RESPIRERX PHARMACEUTICALS INC   NBB: RSPI

126 Valley Road, Suite C
Glen Rock, NJ 07452
Phone: 201 444-4947
Fax: –
Web: www.respirerx.com

CEO: Arnold S Lippa
CFO: Jeff E Margolis
HR: –
FYE: December 31
Type: Public

Cortex Pharmaceuticals develops drugs to treat brain-controlled breathing disorders. It has several compounds designed to prevent or reverse drug-induced respiratory depression and to reduce obstructive sleep apnea in Phase 2 clinical studies. Its leading compounds include CX1739 which targets opiate-induced respiratory depression and central sleep apnea and dronabinol a compound being studied in obstructive sleep apnea patients in an National Institutes of Health-funded study. Cortex hopes to obtain orphan drug designation on its compounds which would give it a relatively quick regulatory pathway and a period of exclusive marketing rights. Cortex merged Pier Pharmaceuticals into its operations in 2012.

	Annual Growth	12/11	12/12	12/13	12/14	12/15
Sales ($ mil.)	(59.1%)	3.1	0.0	–	0.1	0.1
Net income ($ mil.)	–	(2.3)	(7.6)	(1.2)	(2.7)	(6.0)
Market value ($ mil.)	–	0.1	0.0	0.0	0.1	0.0
Employees	(4.5%)	6	2	3	6	5

RESTAURANT TECHNOLOGIES INC.

2250 Pilot Knob Rd. Ste. 100
Mendota Heights MN 55120
Phone: 651-796-1600
Fax: 651-379-4082
Web: www.rti-inc.com

CEO: Jeffrey R Kiesel
CFO: Robert E Weil
HR: –
FYE: December 31
Type: Private

Restaurant Technologies Inc. (RTI) regularly strikes oil. It provides oil-management equipment and supplies to restaurants and other foodservice operations specializing in its MaxLife system for handling and disposing of used cooking oil. It also offers oil-disposal services to cart away used frying oil. RTI's Global Tier division markets equipment for monitoring restaurant kitchen equipment such as walk-in coolers and fryers. The company distributes clean cooking oil and other supplies to more than 17000 customers from facilities in about 35 metropolitan areas. In mid-2011 Swedish investor EQT Infrastructure acquired the company from Parthenon Capital Partners and ABS Capital Partners.

RESTORGENEX CORP   NBB: RESX

1800 Century Park East, 6th Floor
Los Angeles, CA 90067
Phone: 805 229-1829
Fax: 313 995-6337
Web: www.stratusmediagroup.com

CEO: David G Kalergis
CFO: William Hornung
HR: –
FYE: December 31
Type: Public

This company wants you to get your head out of the clouds and into the bleachers. Stratus Media Group provides marketing and management services for live entertainment and sporting events including action sports automotive shows and trade shows and expositions. The company makes money through corporate sponsorships TV and broadcast fees tickets event merchandise concessions and consulting services. Specific events have included the Core Tour (action sports) the Freedom Bowl (college football) the Napa Jazz Festival and the Long Beach Marathon. Stratus Media also offers talent representation services to athletes and is buying motor sports promoter Hot Import Nights.

	Annual Growth	12/09	12/10	12/11	12/12	12/13
Sales ($ mil.)	21.3%	–	0.0	0.6	0.4	0.1
Net income ($ mil.)	–	(3.4)	(8.4)	(15.8)	(6.8)	(2.5)
Market value ($ mil.)	(64.8%)	13.1	3.7	2.9	1.1	0.2
Employees	–	–	–	–	13	–

RETAIL OPPORTUNITY INVESTMENTS CORP   NMS: ROIC

11250 El Camino Real, Suite 200
San Diego, CA 92130
Phone: 858 677-0900
Fax: –
Web: www.roireit.net

CEO: Stuart A. Tanz
CFO: Michael B. (Mike) Haines
HR: –
FYE: December 31
Type: Public

For this company opportunity knocking sounds a lot like a neighborhood shopping center. Retail Opportunity Investments (ROIC) true to its name invests in owns leases and manages shopping centers. It targets densely populated middle and upper class markets and looks for centers anchored by large grocery or drug stores. The self-managed real estate investment trust (REIT) owns more than 50 shopping centers comprising 5.5 million sq. ft. in Oregon Washington and California. It makes money from rent management expenses and mortgage interest. ROIC was formed in 2007 as an acquisition company. It purchased NRDC Capital Management in 2009 and took its current name in 2010.

	Annual Growth	12/14	12/15	12/16	12/17	12/18
Sales ($ mil.)	17.4%	155.9	192.7	237.2	273.3	295.8
Net income ($ mil.)	20.5%	20.3	23.9	32.8	38.5	42.7
Market value ($ mil.)	(1.4%)	1,913.9	2,040.5	2,408.7	2,274.2	1,810.2
Employees	2.2%	65	69	71	73	71

RETAIL PROPERTIES OF AMERICA INC   NYS: RPAI

2021 Spring Road, Suite 200
Oak Brook, IL 60523
Phone: 630 634-4200
Fax: –
Web: www.rpai.com

CEO: Steven P Grimes
CFO: Julie M Swinehart
HR: –
FYE: December 31
Type: Public

You could say Retail Properties of America (formerly Inland Western Retail Real Estate Trust) is a bit of a shopaholic. The self-managed real estate investment trust (REIT) buys owns and operates one of the largest retail shopping center portfolios in the US with more than 225 wholly or partially owned properties that include power centers community centers and lifestyle centers. Among its tenants are big-box stores such as Best Buy Ross Stores and TJX Cos. It also has about 20 property management offices to serve its diverse client base with leasing asset management and property management services. The company went public in 2012. It was formerly sponsored by an affiliate of The Inland Group.

	Annual Growth	12/14	12/15	12/16	12/17	12/18
Sales ($ mil.)	(5.3%)	600.6	604.0	583.1	538.1	482.5
Net income ($ mil.)	15.7%	43.3	125.1	166.8	251.5	77.6
Market value ($ mil.)	(10.2%)	3,557.9	3,148.6	3,268.0	2,865.1	2,313.0
Employees	(4.5%)	254	240	237	220	211

RETAILMENOT INC   NMS: SALE

301 Congress Avenue, Suite 700
Austin, TX 78701
Phone: 512 777-2970
Fax: –
Web: www.retailmenot.com

CEO: Marissa Tarleton
CFO: J Scott Di Valerio
HR: –
FYE: December 31
Type: Public

Do an Internet search for "coupon code" and you've got this company's formula for success. RetailMeNot is a leading provider of digital coupons that allow consumers to obtain discounts on retailers' websites and in-store purchases. E-tail is big business and promo codes are incentives that appeal to both retailers and consumers. RetailMeNot has its flagship US website retailmenot.com as well as deals2buy.com which features sale items from selected retailers. Its international brand portfolio includes VoucherCodes.co.uk in the UK Web.Bons-de-Reduction.com and Poulpeo.com in France Actiepagina.nl in the Netherlands and Deals.com in Germany. RetailMeNot became a public company in 2013.

	Annual Growth	12/11	12/12	12/13	12/14	12/15
Sales ($ mil.)	32.7%	80.4	144.7	209.8	264.7	249.1
Net income ($ mil.)	(8.6%)	17.0	26.0	31.5	27.0	11.8
Market value ($ mil.)	(41.3%)	–	–	1,470.9	747.0	506.8
Employees	16.4%	–	331	444	527	522

RETRACTABLE TECHNOLOGIES INC   ASE: RVP

511 Lobo Lane
Little Elm, TX 75068-5295
Phone: 972 294-1010
Fax: –
Web: www.retractable.com

CEO: Thomas J Shaw
CFO: Douglas W Cowan
HR: Stefanie Perry
FYE: December 31
Type: Public

Retractable Technologies knows you can't be too safe when you work around needles all day. The company develops makes and markets safety syringes and other injection technologies for the health care industry. Its flagship VanishPoint syringe retracts after injection reducing the risk of both syringe reuse and accidental needlesticks (both are means of transmitting HIV and other infectious diseases). Retractable also makes blood collection needles and IV catheters using the VanishPoint technology which was invented by Thomas Shaw the company's founder CEO and majority owner. The firm sells to hospitals and other care providers in the US and abroad both directly and through distributors.

	Annual Growth	12/14	12/15	12/16	12/17	12/18
Sales ($ mil.)	(0.9%)	34.5	29.6	29.8	34.5	33.3
Net income ($ mil.)	–	(2.4)	4.3	(3.7)	(3.7)	(1.3)
Market value ($ mil.)	(41.3%)	163.3	101.3	30.4	22.2	19.4
Employees	(1.4%)	132	136	135	150	125

REVAL HOLDINGS INC.

420 Fifth Ave. 5th Fl.
New York NY 10018
Phone: 212-393-1313
Fax: 212-901-9797
Web: www.reval.com

CEO: Jiro Okochi
CFO: Dino Ewing
HR: Henry Janssen
FYE: December 31
Type: Private

Reval wants you to revel in their products and revile all rivals. The company makes cloud-based software used by CFOs finance managers and treasurers for treasury and risk management. Its products let customers examine and analyze cash liquidity and risk across an enterprise and incorporate hedging accounting and compliance. Reval's software-as-a-service (SaaS) is deployed so that the company can seamlessly and automatically push out updates every six months to reflect changing financial regulations. Reval has more than 550 clients including Tiffany & Co Microsoft Starbucks Ford and Visa in 20 countries and claims a 90% customer retention rate. Formed in 1999 Reval filed to go public in 2012.

REVANCE THERAPEUTICS INC   NMS: RVNC

7555 Gateway Boulevard
Newark, CA 94560
Phone: 510 742-3400
Fax: –
Web: www.revance.com

CEO: L. Daniel (Dan) Browne
CFO: Lauren P. Silvernail
HR: Justin Ford
FYE: December 31
Type: Public

Revance Therapeutics wants to rev up the revenue engine with poison. The company's candidates include a topical application of botulinum toxin the deadly toxin that causes botulism and a longer-acting injectable form. Though Botox has made aesthetic uses well known Revance also wants it for medical reasons including as a cure for excessive sweating (hyperhidrosis) and migraines. Current treatment requires up to 30 shots compared to Revance's single-application gel. Once its candidates are approved the company will do its own manufacturing and sales. Revance was formed in 1999 and went public in 2014. It raised $96 million which it plans to use to fund R&D and clinical trials and to pay debt.

	Annual Growth	12/14	12/15	12/16	12/17	12/18
Sales ($ mil.)	76.6%	0.4	0.3	0.3	0.3	3.7
Net income ($ mil.)	–	(62.9)	(73.5)	(89.3)	(120.6)	(142.6)
Market value ($ mil.)	4.4%	626.4	1,263.1	765.4	1,321.9	744.3
Employees	19.6%	83	103	106	134	170

REVETT MINING CO INC   ASE: RVM

11115 East Montgomery, Suite G
Spokane Valley, WA 99206
Phone: 509 921-2294
Fax: 509 891-8901
Web: www.revettminerals.com

CEO: –
CFO: –
HR: –
FYE: December 31
Type: Public

Revett gets revved up over minerals in Montana. The mining company produces copper and silver at the state's Troy Mine. Its holdings there include proved and probable reserves of 10.5 tons of minerals. Troy has produced 6.4 million ounces of silver and 44 million pounds of copper with estimated future annual production of 1.3 million ounces of silver and 11 million pounds of copper. Revett also owns the Rock Creek Project an exploratory property in northwestern Montana with inferred resources of about 230 million ounces of silver and 2 billion pounds of copper. Revett Silver the company's operating subsidiary was formed in 1999 to buy the Troy and Rock Creek mines. Revett Minerals was created in 2004.

	Annual Growth	12/09	12/10	12/11	12/12	12/13
Sales ($ mil.)	(77.7%)	29.5	47.0	70.1	59.2	0.1
Net income ($ mil.)	–	(5.0)	4.4	13.5	4.1	(11.6)
Market value ($ mil.)	22.1%	11.4	169.1	163.3	97.6	25.3
Employees	(23.4%)	186	198	194	209	64

REVLON INC   NYS: REV

One New York Plaza
New York, NY 10004
Phone: 212 527-4000
Fax: –
Web: www.revloninc.com

CEO: Fabian T. Garcia
CFO: Christopher (Chris) Peterson
HR: Patty Assatly-huet
FYE: December 31
Type: Public

Revlon has the look of a leader in the US mass-market cosmetics business alongside L'Or-©al's Maybelline and Procter & Gamble's Cover Girl. Aside from its Almay and Revlon brands of makeup and beauty tools the company makes Revlon ColorSilk hair color Mitchum antiperspirants and deodorants Charlie and Jean Nat-© fragrances and Natural Honey and Gatineau skincare products. It also owns Elizabeth Arden a maker of prestige fragrance brands. Revlon's beauty aids are distributed in more than 150 countries with more than half of its revenue generated outside the US. Revlon products are primarily sold by mass merchandisers and drugstores such as CVS Target Shoppers Drug Mart A.S. Watson Boots and Wal-Mart. Charles Revson founded Revlon in 1931.

	Annual Growth	12/14	12/15	12/16	12/17	12/18
Sales ($ mil.)	7.2%	1,941.0	1,914.3	2,334.0	2,693.7	2,564.5
Net income ($ mil.)	–	40.9	56.1	(21.9)	(183.2)	(294.2)
Market value ($ mil.)	(7.3%)	1,845.4	1,504.0	1,574.8	1,177.7	1,360.8
Employees	6.9%	5,600	5,700	7,300	7,800	7,300

REVOLUTION LIGHTING TECHNOLOGIES INC   NBB: RVLT

177 Broad Street, 12th Floor
Stamford, CT 06901
Phone: 203 504-1111
Fax: –
Web: www.rvlti.com
CEO: Robert V Lapenta
CFO: Joan Nano
HR: –
FYE: December 31
Type: Public

Because you can't have a revolution without light. Revolution Lighting Technologies (formerly Nexxus Lighting) designs produces and sells light-emitting diode (LED) replacement light bulbs. Its products which include multiple-color temperatures and optic/lens options are marketed for their energy savings improved lighting and reliability as well as eco-friendly benefits. It also makes Hyperion R-Lite and Lumeon 360 LED-based signage systems for decorative lighting strips through subsidiary Lumificient Corp. In late 2012 Nexxus Lighting changed its name to Revolution Lighting Technologies to reflect what it believes is the new change taking place — LED technology — in the lighting industry.

	Annual Growth	12/13	12/14	12/15	12/16	12/17
Sales ($ mil.)	55.5%	26.1	76.8	129.7	172.1	152.3
Net income ($ mil.)	–	(16.8)	(5.2)	(2.4)	(0.5)	(53.9)
Market value ($ mil.)	(1.0%)	73.1	28.8	17.0	117.4	70.2
Employees	27.2%	103	209	238	300	270

REX AMERICAN RESOURCES CORP   NYS: REX

7720 Paragon Road
Dayton, OH 45459
Phone: 937 276-3931
Fax: –
Web: www.rexamerican.com
CEO: Zafar Rizvi
CFO: Douglas L. Bruggeman
HR: –
FYE: January 31
Type: Public

REX American Resources believes that a key American energy resource is renewables. REX American has stakes in six ethanol entities; its two majority owned facilities (NuGen Energy and One Earth Energy) each have a design capacity of 100 million gallons of ethanol. The company had operated through two segments: alternative energy and real estate (the legacy of its earlier retail appliances business) but REX American sold its remaining real estate assets in 2014 and 2015. REX American derives almost all of its revenues from ethanol and related byproducts.

	Annual Growth	01/15	01/16	01/17	01/18	01/19
Sales ($ mil.)	(4.0%)	572.2	436.5	453.8	452.6	486.7
Net income ($ mil.)	(22.4%)	87.3	31.4	32.3	39.7	31.6
Market value ($ mil.)	7.1%	348.2	335.2	520.8	512.2	457.5
Employees	4.6%	106	116	114	120	127

REX ENERGY CORP   NBB: REXX Q

366 Walker Drive
State College, PA 16801
Phone: 814 278-7267
Fax: –
Web: www.rexenergy.com
CEO: Thomas C Stabley
CFO: Curtis J Walker
HR: –
FYE: December 31
Type: Public

Though it isn't exactly the T. Rex of the oil and gas industry Rex Energy is taking a bite out of available hydrocarbon assets. The exploration and production company has estimated proved reserves of In fiscal 2012 the company reported estimated proved reserves of 618.1 billion cu. ft. of natural gas equivalent (42% proved developed) primarily from two regions: the Illinois Basin (in Illinois and Indiana) and the Appalachian Basin (Pennsylvania and West Virginia). The company's Lawrence Field ASP (alkaline-surfactant-polymer) Flood Project uses ASP technology which washes residual oil from reservoir rock improving the existing waterflow's ability to sweep the residual oil and increasing oil recoveries.

	Annual Growth	12/13	12/14	12/15	12/16	12/17
Sales ($ mil.)	(3.6%)	237.9	298.0	172.0	139.0	205.3
Net income ($ mil.)	–	(2.1)	(46.7)	(363.3)	(176.7)	(64.2)
Market value ($ mil.)	(48.6%)	201.9	52.2	10.8	4.8	14.1
Employees	(23.0%)	298	320	274	104	105

REX HEALTHCARE, INC.

4420 LAKE BOONE TRL
RALEIGH, NC 276077505
Phone: 919-784-3100
Fax: –
Web: www.rexhealth.com
CEO: Gary Park
CFO: Bernadette Spong
HR: –
FYE: June 30
Type: Private

Part of the UNC HealthCare System UNC REX Healthcare is a not-for-profit health care provider that serves residents of Raleigh and the rest of Wake County North Carolina. Founded in 1894 UNC REX Healthcare includes the more than 430-bed acute-care Rex Hospital and two nursing homes with nearly 230 beds as well as primary and specialty care clinics throughout the area. Specialty centers and clinics provide services such as birthing cancer treatment same-day surgery heart and vascular care pain management and sleep disorder therapy. UNC REX also provides home health and mobile emergency medical services. UNC HealthCare also includes affiliate UNC Hospitals.

	Annual Growth	06/09	06/10	06/11	06/12	06/13
Sales ($ mil.)	7.9%	–	–	628.6	719.9	731.4
Net income ($ mil.)	(64.1%)	–	–	69.1	34.7	8.9
Market value ($ mil.)	–	–	–	–	–	–
Employees	–	–	–	–	–	5,500

REXAHN PHARMACEUTICALS INC.   NYSE AMEX: RNN

15245 Shady Grove Rd. Ste. 455
Rockville MD 20850
Phone: 240-268-5300
Fax: 240-268-5310
Web: www.rexahn.com
CEO: Douglas J Swirsky
CFO: –
HR: –
FYE: December 31
Type: Public

Rexahn Pharmaceuticals has its R&D sights set on difficult-to-treat cancers and central nervous system (CNS) disorders. A biopharmaceutical company Rexahn has three drug candidates in clinical stages of development including its lead candidate and pancreatic cancer treatment Archexin (designed to inhibit a protein involved in cancer cell proliferation); Serdaxin a depression and Parkinson's disease drug; and Zoraxel a treatment for erectile dysfunction. The company also has seven cancer drugs in preclinical development. It develops its candidates through its own R&D arm and through partnerships with pharmaceutical and biopharmaceutical companies like Teva Pharmaceutical and TheraTarget.

REXFORD INDUSTRIAL REALTY INC   NYS: REXR

11620 Wilshire Boulevard, Suite 1000
Los Angeles, CA 90025
Phone: 310 966-1680
Fax: –
Web: www.rexfordindustrial.com
CEO: Howard Schwimmer
CFO: Adeel Khan
HR: –
FYE: December 31
Type: Public

Rexford Industrial Realty knows that there's more to business in Southern California than moviemaking and fashion. A real estate investment trust or REIT Rexford Industrial owns and manages a portfolio of nearly 70 industrial properties in Los Angeles County and surrounding areas. Its portfolio comprises about 7.6 million sq. ft. of warehouse distribution and light manufacturing space that's leased to small and midsized businesses. It manages 20 more properties — altogether comprising 1.2 million sq. ft. of rentable space. A self-administered and self-managed REIT Rexford Industrial was formed in 2013 from the assets of its predecessor. In mid-2013 the company went public.

	Annual Growth	12/14	12/15	12/16	12/17	12/18
Sales ($ mil.)	33.7%	66.6	93.9	126.2	161.4	212.5
Net income ($ mil.)	168.0%	0.9	1.9	25.1	40.7	46.2
Market value ($ mil.)	17.0%	1,520.9	1,583.8	2,245.0	2,823.0	2,853.0
Employees	22.5%	48	70	90	98	108

REXFORD INDUSTRIAL REALTY, INC.

11620 WILSHIRE BLVD # 1000
LOS ANGELES, CA 900256821
Phone: 310-966-1680
Fax: –
Web: www.rexfordindustrial.com

CEO: Howard Schwimmer
CFO: Adeel Khan
HR: –
FYE: December 31
Type: Private

Rexford Industrial Realty knows that there's more to business in Southern California than moviemaking and fashion. A real estate investment trust or REIT Rexford Industrial owns and manages a portfolio of nearly 70 industrial properties in Los Angeles County and surrounding areas. Its portfolio comprises about 7.6 million sq. ft. of warehouse distribution and light manufacturing space that's leased to small and midsized businesses. It manages 20 more properties — altogether comprising 1.2 million sq. ft. of rentable space. A self-administered and self-managed REIT Rexford Industrial was formed in 2013 from the assets of its predecessor. In mid-2013 the company went public.

	Annual Growth	12/12	12/13	12/14	12/15	12/16
Assets ($ mil.)	39.8%	–	554.7	932.8	1,153.3	1,515.0
Net income ($ mil.)	–	–	(0.7)	1.0	2.0	25.9
Market value ($ mil.)	–	–	–	–	–	–
Employees	–	–	–	–	–	40

REXNORD CORP (NEW)

511 West Freshwater Way
Milwaukee, WI 53204
Phone: 414 643-3739
Fax: –
Web: www.rexnordcorporation.com

NYS: RXN
CEO: Todd A. Adams
CFO: Mark W. Peterson
HR: –
FYE: March 31
Type: Public

Industrial company Rexnord designs and manufactures two categories of products process and motion control (PMC) and water management. PMC makes things like gears couplings bearings industrial chains and other highly engineered mechanical components under brand names such as Rexnord Rex Falk FlatTop and Link-Belt. Its customers are diverse active in food and drink aerospace mining energy and cement among others. The Water management business makes products used in commercial plumbing water control and treatment and wastewater markets with names such as Zurn Wilkins Green Turtle and World Dryer. While it has operations spread across the globe Wisconsin-based Rexnord racks up most of its sales in the US.

	Annual Growth	03/15	03/16	03/17	03/18	03/19
Sales ($ mil.)	0.0%	2,050.2	1,923.8	1,918.2	2,066.0	2,050.9
Net income ($ mil.)	(20.0%)	83.8	67.9	74.1	75.9	34.3
Market value ($ mil.)	(1.5%)	2,798.2	2,119.9	2,419.8	3,111.7	2,635.7
Employees	(4.3%)	8,000	7,700	8,000	8,300	6,700

REYNOLDS AMERICAN INC

401 North Main Street
Winston-Salem, NC 27101
Phone: 336 741-2000
Fax: 336 728-8888
Web: www.reynoldsamerican.com

NYS: RAI
CEO: Ricardo Oberlander
CFO: Tony Hayward
HR: –
FYE: December 31
Type: Public

They say there's no smoke without fire and Reynolds American Inc. (RAI) the #2 US cigarette manufacturer is giving off plenty of heat. Reynolds American owns cigarette manufacturer RJR Tobacco which produces many of the top-selling cigarette brands – Camel Doral Eclipse Pall Mall and Newport – and smokeless tobacco maker American Snuff. American Snuff offers moist snuff under the value-priced Grizzly and premium Kodiak brands. Vuse the company's e-cigarette brand is the market leader. Other businesses include Santa Fe Natural Tobacco and Lorillard the former #3 cigarette company in the US which it bought for $27 billion in 2015. Reynolds American is 42% owned by British American Tobacco; in late 2016 British American Tobacco agreed to acquire the remaining shares for $47 billion.

	Annual Growth	12/12	12/13	12/14	12/15	12/16
Sales ($ mil.)	10.8%	8,304.0	8,236.0	8,471.0	10,675.0	12,503.0
Net income ($ mil.)	47.8%	1,272.0	1,718.0	1,470.0	3,253.0	6,073.0
Market value ($ mil.)	7.8%	59,071.9	71,277.0	91,637.8	65,801.8	79,903.2
Employees	2.4%	5,050	5,290	5,400	5,700	5,550

RF INDUSTRIES LTD.

7610 Miramar Road, Building 6000
San Diego, CA 92126
Phone: 858 549-6340
Fax: –
Web: www.rfindustries.com

NMS: RFIL
CEO: Robert D Dawson
CFO: Mark Turfler
HR: –
FYE: October 31
Type: Public

RF Industries (RFI) helps keep the world connected. The company's core business is conducted by its RF Connector division which makes coaxial connectors used in radio-frequency (RF) communications and computer networking equipment. Its Neulink Division makes wireless digital transmission devices such as modems and antennas used to link wide-area computer networks and global positioning systems. Through its Bioconnect division RF Industries also makes cable assemblies including electric cabling and interconnect products used in medical monitoring applications. Customers in the US account for more than 80% of sales. In 2019 RF Industries bought C Enterprises a maker of connectivity tools sold to telecommunications and data communications distributors.

	Annual Growth	10/15	10/16	10/17	10/18	10/19
Sales ($ mil.)	14.0%	32.8	30.2	31.0	50.2	55.3
Net income ($ mil.)	37.2%	1.0	(4.1)	0.4	5.8	3.5
Market value ($ mil.)	7.1%	42.7	16.6	23.2	73.4	56.2
Employees	5.6%	226	189	195	186	281

RF MICRO DEVICES, INC.

7628 Thorndike Road
Greensboro, NC 27409-9421
Phone: 336 664-1233
Fax: –
Web: www.rfmd.com

NMS: RFMD
CEO: –
CFO: –
HR: –
FYE: March 30
Type: Public

RF Micro Devices was raised on radio — high-performance radio-frequency (RF) components that is. RFMD makes a variety of RF devices and compound semiconductor technologies for markets that include cellular handsets wireless infrastructure wireless local area networks (WLAN or WiFi) cable television broadband and advanced metering for Smart Energy. Many of the company's chips are made from gallium arsenide (GaAs) — a material valued for wireless applications because of its speed and efficiency. RFMD's top customer is Nokia which accounts for nearly 40% of the company's sales. Customers in Asia represent more than 75% of sales.

	Annual Growth	03/09*	04/10	04/11*	03/12	03/13
Sales ($ mil.)	2.1%	886.5	978.4	1,051.8	871.4	964.1
Net income ($ mil.)	–	(898.6)	71.0	124.6	0.9	(53.0)
Market value ($ mil.)	40.4%	383.8	1,406.4	1,790.2	1,395.2	1,490.5
Employees	0.6%	4,095	3,687	3,726	3,986	4,191

*Fiscal year change

RF MONOLITHICS INC.

4441 Sigma Rd.
Dallas TX 75244-4589
Phone: 972-233-2903
Fax: 972-387-8148
Web: www.rfm.com

NASDAQ: RFMI
CEO: Farlin A Halsey
CFO: Harley E Barnes III
HR: –
FYE: August 31
Type: Public

RF Monolithics (RFM) says welcome to the machine. The company designs and sells wireless connectivity products for machine-to-machine communications. Its wireless solutions group provides surface acoustic wave (SAW) and radio-frequency (RF) integrated circuit short-range radios RF modules and stand-alone radio systems. Its wireless components unit covers communications products that include frequency control filters oscillators and optical timing products. RFM markets its wares to distributors and OEMs worldwide. Customers include Delphi Flextronics GE and Avnet. RFM gets two-thirds of its sales outside North America. In 2012 the company was acquired by Murata Electronics North America.

RGC RESOURCES, INC.

NMS: RGCO

519 Kimball Avenue, N.E.
Roanoke, VA 24016
Phone: 540 777-4427
Fax: 540 777-2636
Web: www.rgcresources.com

CEO: John S D'Orazio
CFO: Paul W Nester
HR: –
FYE: September 30
Type: Public

RGC Resources is not only sticking to its knitting (the regulated distribution of natural gas) it is also staying close to home (Roanoke Virginia). RGC's Roanoke Gas unit distributes natural gas to 56000 customers in Roanoke. The holding company's Application Resources provides information system services for the utility industry. RGC Resources has taken the proceeds from the sale of its noncore operation to reinvest in its core gas distribution business. In 2008 it installed nine miles of plastic mains and replaced 684 steel main-to-meter service lines with modern plastic service lines (a 40% increase over 2007).

	Annual Growth	09/15	09/16	09/17	09/18	09/19
Sales ($ mil.)	(0.1%)	68.2	59.1	62.3	65.5	68.0
Net income ($ mil.)	14.3%	5.1	5.8	6.2	7.3	8.7
Market value ($ mil.)	9.7%	163.1	191.3	230.7	215.6	236.1
Employees	(5.3%)	133	132	109	112	107

RH

NYS: RH

15 Koch Road, Suite K
Corte Madera, CA 94925
Phone: 415 924-1005
Fax: –
Web: www.restorationhardware.com

CEO: Gary G. Friedman
CFO: Karen Boone
HR: –
FYE: February 02
Type: Public

RH (formerly Restoration Hardware Holdings) puts vintage American fixtures and fittings into homes old and new. The company sells upscale home and outdoor furnishings garden products hardware bathware lighting textiles baby and child products and more through about 115 retail and outlet stores under the Restoration Hardware RH and Waterworks names. Furniture accounts for more than 60% of total revenue. In addition to stores RH markets products through its catalogs (called Source Books) and e-commerce sites which together account for just less than half of overall sales. The company operates primarily in the US with stores in some 30 states as well as in Canada and the UK.

	Annual Growth	01/15	01/16	01/17*	02/18	02/19
Sales ($ mil.)	7.6%	1,867.4	2,109.0	2,134.9	2,440.2	2,505.7
Net income ($ mil.)	13.4%	91.0	91.1	5.4	2.2	150.6
Market value ($ mil.)	11.2%	1,792.4	1,261.8	534.3	1,884.8	2,736.7
Employees	6.8%	4,000	4,600	5,800	5,200	5,200

*Fiscal year change

RHE HATCO INC.

601 Marion Dr.
Garland TX 75042
Phone: 972-494-0511
Fax: 972-494-2369
Web: www.stetsonhat.com

CEO: –
CFO: –
HR: –
FYE: June 30
Type: Private

RHE Hatco has built a business topping off Western wear for dress or work and doing it with style to boot. The company makes and markets western hats for men and women under iconic names such as Stetson Resistol and Charlie 1 Horse; it makes dress hats under the Dobbs label. In August 2009 the hat manufacturer was acquired by an affiliate of Pro Equine Group whose expertise lies in other cowboy accoutrements such as saddles ropes and protective legwear for horses. Previous owner Arena Brands had been shedding its stable of products such as Imperial Headwear and Montana Silversmiths when Pro Equine picked up the longtime hat makers.

RHINO RESOURCE PARTNERS LP

NBB: RHNO

424 Lewis Hargett Circle, Suite 250
Lexington, KY 40503
Phone: 859 389-6500
Fax: –
Web: www.rhinolp.com

CEO: Richard A Boone
CFO: Wendell S Morris
HR: –
FYE: December 31
Type: Public

Rhino Resource Partners is looking to take the coal industry by the horn. The company operates both surface and underground mines in Colorado Kentucky Ohio West Virginia and Utah. Rhino Energy controls more than 309 million tons of proved and probable coal reserves of which about three-quarters is used for electricity generation by utilities and industrial customers. It produces approximately 4 million tons annually. Subsidiary Rhino Trucking hauls much of that production to preparation plants. The company operated as CAM Holdings until 2006. Hoping the third time is a charm Rhino went public in 2010 with an initial public offering (IPO).

	Annual Growth	12/14	12/15	12/16	12/17	12/18
Sales ($ mil.)	0.8%	239.1	206.7	170.8	218.7	247.0
Net income ($ mil.)	–	49.0	(55.2)	(130.8)	(18.8)	(16.0)
Market value ($ mil.)	(18.1%)	32.0	4.1	62.0	48.4	14.4
Employees	(0.5%)	715	551	570	635	701

RHODE ISLAND HOUSING

44 WASHINGTON ST
PROVIDENCE, RI 029031731
Phone: 401-457-1234
Fax: –
Web: www.rihousing.com

CEO: –
CFO: Tom Hogg
HR: –
FYE: June 30
Type: Private

The State of Rhode Island wants to help you become a homeowner. Rhode Island Housing assists low- to moderate-income Rhode Islanders buy homes by offering low interest mortgages. Income limits are $77300 for one or two person households and $88950 for households of three or more. The organization also offers home equity loans construction loans to real estate developers reverse mortgages for older homeowners homebuyer education and other programs. Rhode Island Housing receives no state funding; instead it sells taxable and tax-exempt bonds on the capital markets to fund its activities. Since its inception in the early 1970s the organization has helped some 175000 families fund affordable homes.

	Annual Growth	06/04	06/05	06/06	06/07	06/18
Sales ($ mil.)	2.3%	–	90.3	88.5	102.2	121.3
Net income ($ mil.)	3.5%	–	8.3	17.2	11.7	13.0
Market value ($ mil.)	–	–	–	–	–	–
Employees	–	–	–	–	–	170

RHODE ISLAND SCHOOL OF DESIGN INC

2 COLLEGE ST
PROVIDENCE, RI 029032717
Phone: 401-454-6100
Fax: –
Web: www.risd.edu

CEO: –
CFO: –
HR: –
FYE: June 30
Type: Private

The Rhode Island School of Design (RISD pronounced RIZ-dee) is among the highest-rated fine arts colleges in the US. The private school enrolls about 2400 undergraduate and graduate students. It offers about 20 fine arts and design programs including art history apparel design architecture jewelry industrial design film printmaking textiles and painting. The college also offers continuing education through classes lectures workshops gallery talks and a six-week pre-college program designed for high schoolers. Notable alumni include David Byrne Tina Weymouth and Chris Frantz of the Talking Heads. RISD was founded in 1877.

	Annual Growth	06/08	06/09	06/10	06/13	06/15
Sales ($ mil.)	7.7%	–	101.6	150.8	142.8	158.5
Net income ($ mil.)	–	–	(27.7)	27.6	1.7	2.7
Market value ($ mil.)	–	–	–	–	–	–
Employees	–	–	–	–	–	1,142

RHODES COLLEGE

244 N LAUDERDALE ST # 105   CEO: –
MEMPHIS, TN 381053663   CFO: –
Phone: 901-843-3000   HR: –
Fax: –   FYE: June 30
Web: www.rhodes.edu   Type: Private

Rhodes College helps its students get further down the road to edification. A private liberal arts school in historic downtown Memphis Rhodes College enrolls about 1700 students in academic majors including biology English international studies and business administration. Rhodes College's students come from about 45 states and 15 countries. It additionally offers a Master's degree in accounting. In total Rhodes College offers more than 30 majors and 35 minors. The school also provides continuing education courses to the community. Founded in 1848 the college is supported by an endowment of more than $230 million. The student-to-faculty ratio is about 10:1 and the average class size is just 13.

	Annual Growth	06/12	06/13	06/14	06/15	06/16
Sales ($ mil.)	5.3%	–	70.7	76.9	78.9	82.5
Net income ($ mil.)	–	–	26.4	51.2	19.4	(19.6)
Market value ($ mil.)	–	–	–	–	–	–
Employees	–	–	–	–	–	400

RIB-X PHARMACEUTICALS INC.

300 George St. Ste. 301   CEO: Jennifer Sanfilippo
New Haven CT 06511-6663   CFO: Paul Estrem
Phone: 203-624-5606   HR: –
Fax: 203-624-5627   FYE: December 31
Web: www.rib-x.com   Type: Private

Rib-X Pharmaceuticals has found a weak spot in bacteria's ribosomes. The biopharmaceutical drug discovery and development company is working to create new antibiotics to treat drug-resistant infections. Rib-X's leading drug candidates are delafloxacin for the treatment of methicillin-resistant Staphylococcus aureus (MRSA) and radezolid to treat community acquired bacterial pneumonia (CABP). Its research targets binding sites on bacterial ribosomes to interrupt cell reproduction. The company was founded by Susan Froshauer Peter Moore and Thomas Steitz who received the Nobel Prize in Chemistry for the ribosome science that is the basis for the company's research. Rib-X withdrew its IPO in 2012.

RICE ENERGY INC   NYS: RICE

2200 Rice Drive   CEO: –
Canonsburg, PA 15317   CFO: –
Phone: 724 271-7200   HR: –
Fax: –   FYE: December 31
Web: www.riceenergy.com   Type: Public

Rice Energy is engaged in the purchasing of and exploration and development of natural gas and oil properties in the Appalachian Basin. It has holdings in the Marcellus Shale in southwestern Pennsylvania and the Utica Shale in southeastern Ohio. The company holds more than 43350 net acres in the southwestern core of the Marcellus Shale primarily in Washington County. Rice Energy operates a majority of its acreage. In fiscal 2013 the company's pro forma estimated proved reserves stood at 552 billion cu. ft. of natural gas equivalent all of which were in southwestern Pennsylvania. Rice Energy completed an IPO in 2014. In 2016 it agreed to buy Vantage Energy LLC and Vantage Energy II LLC for $2.7 billion.

	Annual Growth	12/11	12/12	12/13	12/14	12/15
Sales ($ mil.)	144.8%	14.0	27.2	88.6	390.9	502.1
Net income ($ mil.)	–	(0.9)	(19.3)	(35.8)	218.5	(291.3)
Market value ($ mil.)	(48.0%)	–	–	–	2,860.0	1,486.6
Employees	63.4%	–	–	139	290	371

RICEBRAN TECHNOLOGIES   NAS: RIBT

1330 Lake Robbins Drive, Suite 250   CEO: Brent R Rystrom
The Woodlands, TX 77380   CFO: Dennis A Dykes
Phone: 281 675-2421   HR: –
Fax: –   FYE: December 31
Web: www.ricebrantech.com   Type: Public

RiceBran Technologies (formerly NutraCea) hopes that one person's trash really can be another person's treasure. The company uses one of the world's largest wasted food resources rice bran — a rice by-product containing oil protein carbohydrates vitamins minerals fibers and antioxidants — to make and enhance the nutritional value of consumer products such as dietary and food supplements and animal feed. Its products are used by food manufacturers nutraceutical makers and petfood and feed manufacturers. Following a strategic change in focus from a multidivisional company to one focused solely on rice bran bio-refining the company in 2012 changed its name to RiceBran Technologies.

	Annual Growth	12/14	12/15	12/16	12/17	12/18
Sales ($ mil.)	(22.1%)	40.1	39.9	39.4	13.4	14.8
Net income ($ mil.)	–	(23.0)	(8.3)	(8.5)	(4.5)	(8.1)
Market value ($ mil.)	(7.8%)	121.0	55.3	30.0	43.1	87.3
Employees	(23.3%)	295	264	227	65	102

RICELAND FOODS, INC.

2120 S PARK AVE   CEO: Danny Kennedy
STUTTGART, AR 721606822   CFO: Sandra Morgan
Phone: 870-673-5500   HR: –
Fax: –   FYE: July 31
Web: www.riceland.com   Type: Private

Handling more than 125 million bushels of grain a year Riceland Foods is ingrained in its business. The agricultural cooperative processes and markets the rice soybeans and wheat grown by its 9000 member/owners who farm in Arkansas Louisiana Mississippi Missouri and Texas. One of the world's largest rice millers it sells white and brown rice plus flavored rices and meal kits under the Riceland and private-label brands. The co-op sells to food retailers and food service and food manufacturing companies worldwide. Riceland also makes cooking oils and processes soybeans bran and lecithin and offers rice bran and hulls to pet food makers and livestock farmers as feed and bedding.

	Annual Growth	07/13	07/14	07/15	07/16	07/17
Sales ($ mil.)	(6.4%)	–	1,148.1	1,122.5	1,007.7	941.1
Net income ($ mil.)	(54.4%)	–	2.6	9.6	5.6	0.2
Market value ($ mil.)	–	–	–	–	–	–
Employees	–	–	–	–	–	1,646

RICH PRODUCTS CORPORATION

1 ROBERT RICH WAY   CEO: William G. (Bill) Gisel
BUFFALO, NY 142131701   CFO: James R. (Jim) Deuschle
Phone: 716-878-8000   HR: –
Fax: –   FYE: December 31
  Type: Private

Starting in 1945 with "the miracle cream from the soya bean" Rich Products has grown from a niche maker of soy-based whipped toppings and frozen desserts to a leading global US frozen foods maker. The family-owned business has developed other products such as toppings and icings and Coffee Rich (nondairy coffee creamer). It has expanded its product line to include frozen bakery and pizza doughs and ingredients for the food service and in-store bakery markets plus appetizers and snacks (Farm Rich) baked goods frozen ice cream cakes (Carvel) seafood (SeaPak) meatballs and barbecue meat. Rich Products markets more than 4000 food items that are sold in more than 100 countries; it has operations around the world on six continents.

	Annual Growth	12/08	12/09	12/10	12/11	12/12
Sales ($ mil.)	7.7%	–	–	2,465.0	2,736.3	2,858.5
Net income ($ mil.)	–	–	–	0.0	0.0	0.0
Market value ($ mil.)	–	–	–	–	–	–
Employees	–	–	–	–	–	10,536

RICHARD J. CARON FOUNDATION

243 N GALEN HALL RD
WERNERSVILLE, PA 195659331
Phone: 610-678-2332
Fax: –
Web: www.caron.org

CEO: Brian J Boon
CFO: –
HR: –
FYE: June 30
Type: Private

Caron cares — about addiction to drinking and drugs. The Richard J. Caron Foundation is a not-for-profit organization that runs clinical treatment centers for substance abuse in Pennsylvania New York Florida and Bermuda. It tailors its services gender specifically (under the idea that men and women respond to treatment differently) and serves adolescents adults seniors and families. The foundation offers addiction assessment as well as residential treatment extended care and outpatient counseling. To complement its medical and psychological programs Caron offers self-development workshops and pastoral services for those wanting to participate in meditation journal writing and other exercises.

	Annual Growth	06/12	06/13	06/14	06/15	06/17
Sales ($ mil.)	(4.5%)	–	103.3	90.8	68.9	85.9
Net income ($ mil.)	(23.4%)	–	21.0	13.1	(8.7)	7.2
Market value ($ mil.)	–	–	–	–	–	–
Employees	–	–	–	–	–	500

RICHARDSON ELECTRONICS LTD

NMS: RELL

40W267 Keslinger Road, P.O. Box 393
LaFox, IL 60147-0393
Phone: 630 208-2200
Fax: 630 208-2550
Web: www.rell.com

CEO: –
CFO: Robert J Ben
HR: –
FYE: June 01
Type: Public

Richardson Electronics runs the kind of superstore that isn't open to the public. The company distributes electronics products including electron devices semiconductor manufacturing equipment and video display equipment from suppliers that include GE Thales TE Connectivity and Vishay. Richardson also sells its own products under such the National Electronics brand and provides components customized to its customers' specifications. The company primarily sells to the alternative energy avionics broadcast and communication marine medical and semiconductor markets. Chairman and CEO Edward Richardson has about 64% voting control of the company.

	Annual Growth	05/15	05/16	05/17*	06/18	06/19
Sales ($ mil.)	5.0%	137.0	142.0	136.9	163.2	166.7
Net income ($ mil.)	–	(5.6)	(6.8)	(6.9)	3.8	(7.3)
Market value ($ mil.)	(12.5%)	113.0	67.8	79.1	126.6	66.3
Employees	3.0%	338	373	366	421	380

*Fiscal year change

RIDGE TOOL COMPANY

400 Clark St.
Elyria OH 44035-2023
Phone: 440-323-5581
Fax: 440-329-4551
Web: www.ridgid.com

CEO: –
CFO: –
HR: –
FYE: September 30
Type: Subsidiary

Business for Ridge Tool customers is wrenching and draining. The company manufactures the RIDGID brand of tools which includes 300 types of professional products in more than 4000 models and sizes for a variety of industries. The usual run of hand tools including more than 60 kinds of wrenches bear the RIDGID name in addition to such power tools as band saws drill presses lathes planers and sanders. Plumbing tools and equipment made under the RIDGID brand include drain cleaners pipe cutters sump pumps and tube wrenches. The brand also includes tools for workers in mechanical pipe fitting construction HVAC and facility maintenance. Ridge Tool is a subsidiary of Emerson Electric.

RIDGEWOOD SAVINGS BANK

71-02 Forest Ave.
Ridgewood NY 11385
Phone: 718-240-4800
Fax: 860-638-2969
Web: www.liberty-bank.com

CEO: Leonard Sekol
CFO: Leonard Sekol
HR: –
FYE: December 31
Type: Private

Serving the New York City metropolitan area and Long Island Ridgewood Savings Bank is New York State's largest mutually owned bank with $4.8 billion in assets. The financial institution operates about 40 branches and loan centers in Brooklyn the Bronx Manhattan and Queens as well as in Nassau Suffolk and Westchester counties. It provides standard retail and commercial deposits including checking and savings accounts CDs and IRAs. It services loans for residential real estate — mainly for one- to four-family homes — but also multifamily housing. Loans comprise nearly 90% of the bank's portfolio. Ridgewood Savings Bank was founded in 1921.

RIGEL PHARMACEUTICALS INC

NMS: RIGL

1180 Veterans Blvd.
South San Francisco, CA 94080
Phone: 650 624-1100
Fax: 650 624-1101
Web: www.rigel.com

CEO: Raul R. Rodriguez
CFO: Ryan D. Maynard
HR: –
FYE: December 31
Type: Public

When immune systems attack Rigel Pharmaceuticals wants to be there. The drug discovery and development firm focuses its research and development efforts on inflammatory/autoimmune muscle and immuno-oncology-related diseases. Drugs in development include candidates for treating rheumatoid arthritis psoriasis muscle wasting multiple sclerosis and transplant rejection. Rigel Pharmaceuticals prefers to collaborate with larger pharmaceutical companies in the development of its drug candidates. The company has more than 90 pending patent applications and more than 230 issued patents in the US as well as corresponding pending foreign patent applications and issued foreign patents.

	Annual Growth	12/14	12/15	12/16	12/17	12/18
Sales ($ mil.)	52.4%	8.3	28.9	20.4	4.5	44.5
Net income ($ mil.)	–	(90.9)	(51.5)	(69.2)	(78.0)	(70.5)
Market value ($ mil.)	0.3%	379.5	506.5	397.9	648.6	384.5
Employees	5.6%	127	126	77	103	158

RIGNET INC

NMS: RNET

15115 Park Row Blvd, Suite 300
Houston, TX 77084-4947
Phone: 281 674-0100
Fax: –
Web: www.rig.net

CEO: Steven E. (Steve) Pickett
CFO: Charles E. (Chip) Schneider
HR: –
FYE: December 31
Type: Public

Because no one wants to be stranded on a desert island much less an offshore oil rig there's RigNet. A telecommunications company that caters mainly to the oil and gas drilling industry it provides voice data video and networking and real-time data management to remote offshore and land-based locations. It serves drilling rigs and production platforms throughout the world. RigNet's 500 customers operate more than 1000 remote sites in about 50 countries. Customers outside the US make up most of sales.

	Annual Growth	12/14	12/15	12/16	12/17	12/18
Sales ($ mil.)	(7.8%)	330.2	271.3	220.6	204.9	238.9
Net income ($ mil.)	–	15.6	(17.0)	(11.5)	(16.2)	(62.5)
Market value ($ mil.)	(25.5%)	798.6	402.7	450.6	291.0	246.0
Employees	(3.6%)	698	546	508	503	604

RINGCENTRAL INC
NYS: RNG

20 Davis Drive
Belmont, CA 94002
Phone: 650 472-4100
Fax: -
Web: www.ringcentral.com

CEO: Vladimir (Vlad) Shmunis
CFO: Clyde R. Hosein
HR: -
FYE: December 31
Type: Public

RingCentral provides cloud-based communications services that connect multiple users over multiple devices. With its hosted platform workers no longer need settle for simply having their office lines forwarded to a mobile device. Businesses use RingCentral to connect smartphones tablets PCs and desk phones from various locations and allow for communication across multiple channels including voice text and fax. The company rings up more than 300000 businesses from small to enterprise-sized across a wide range of industries including advertising finance and legal and technology. RingCentral was founded in 1999.

	Annual Growth	12/14	12/15	12/16	12/17	12/18
Sales ($ mil.)	32.3%	219.9	296.2	379.7	501.5	673.6
Net income ($ mil.)	-	(48.3)	(32.1)	(29.3)	(26.1)	(26.2)
Market value ($ mil.)	53.3%	1,209.2	1,911.1	1,669.5	3,922.6	6,681.4
Employees	1.7%	1,751	2,108	2,583	3,298	1,871

RIO HOLDINGS, INC.

600 CONGRESS AVE STE 200
AUSTIN, TX 787012995
Phone: 512-917-1742
Fax: -

CEO: Michael Wilfrey
CFO: -
HR: -
FYE: December 31
Type: Private

Grande Communications' big idea is to become a bigger player in Texas telecommunications. Through operating subsidiary Grande Communications Networks the company provides bundled telephone services Internet access and cable television to about 140000 residential and business customers over its own fiber-optic network. It also offers wholesale communications services to other telecoms and ISPs through its Grande Networks division. While its core Central Texas service area includes Austin San Marcos and San Antonio it also provides service in Corpus Christi Dallas Midland Odessa and Waco. Grande Communications is controlled by Boston-based private equity firm ABRY Partners.

	Annual Growth	12/04	12/05	12/06	12/07	12/08
Sales ($ mil.)	4.0%	-	-	189.9	197.1	205.3
Net income ($ mil.)	-	-	-	(141.6)	(50.5)	(50.4)
Market value ($ mil.)	-	-	-	-	-	-
Employees	-	-	-	-	-	10

RIOT BLOCKCHAIN INC
NAS: RIOT

202 6th Street, Suite 401
Castle Rock, CO 80104
Phone: 303 794-2000
Fax: -
Web: www.bioptix.com

CEO: Jeff McGonegal
CFO: Robby Chang
HR: -
FYE: December 31
Type: Public

Riot Blockchain (formerly Bioptix) has ditched the drug diagnostic machinery business for the digital currency trade. The company invests in cryptocurrency entities such as Canadian exchange Coinsquare blockchain accounting and audit technology firm Verady and payment platform developer Tesspay. It has also launched its own bitcoin mining firm. In 2017 Bioptix changed its course of business (it was developing a platform for the detection of molecular interactions to help determine if a drug will be effective) to focus on the cryptocurrency industry; it sold its biotech-focused patents and intellectual property as part of the change.

	Annual Growth	12/14	12/15	12/16	12/17	12/18
Sales ($ mil.)	161.8%	0.2	0.1	0.0	0.2	7.8
Net income ($ mil.)	-	(10.4)	(8.8)	(4.3)	(19.8)	(58.0)
Market value ($ mil.)	(3.9%)	25.7	4.4	55.8	412.3	21.9
Employees	(30.0%)	25	5	8	9	6

RIP GRIFFIN TRUCK SERVICE CENTER, INC.

4710 4TH ST
LUBBOCK, TX 794164900
Phone: 806-795-8785
Fax: -
Web: www.ripgriffin.com

CEO: -
CFO: Don Hayden
HR: Darci Aaron
FYE: December 31
Type: Private

Rip Griffin Truck Service Center tries to make sure you never go hungry again (in Scarlett O'Hara's words) at least when you're driving on the highways of North Texas. Rip Griffin's network of about 10 travel centers offers truckers tour buses and other travelers a smorgasbord of features such as convenience stores fuel game rooms laundry facilities restaurants and showers. Locations also offer truck maintenance and repair services. In addition to its travel center business Rip Griffin sells Freightliner trucks through two Texas dealerships and provides fuel transportation services. In 2004 CEO Rip Griffin sold the company to Ohio-based TravelCenters of America.

	Annual Growth	12/13	12/14	12/15	12/16	12/17
Sales ($ mil.)	(8.9%)	-	213.7	145.8	104.3	161.7
Net income ($ mil.)	9.3%	-	3.5	1.5	0.1	4.6
Market value ($ mil.)	-	-	-	-	-	-
Employees	-	-	-	-	-	88

RISK GEORGE INDUSTRIES INC
NBB: RSKI A

802 South Elm St.
Kimball, NE 69145
Phone: 308 235-4645
Fax: -
Web: www.grisk.com

CEO: -
CFO: Stephanie Risk-Mcelroy
HR: -
FYE: April 30
Type: Public

George Risk Industries (GRI) wants customers to be able to manage risks. The company makes burglar alarm components and systems including panic buttons (for direct access to alarm monitoring centers). In addition to security products GRI manufactures pool alarms which are designed to sound alerts when a pool or spa area has been entered. The company also makes thermostats specialty computer keyboards and keypads custom-engraved key caps and push-button switches. Chairman President and CEO Stephanie Risk-McElroy granddaughter of founder George Risk and daughter of former CEO Ken Risk controls the company.

	Annual Growth	04/15	04/16	04/17	04/18	04/19
Sales ($ mil.)	4.4%	11.9	11.2	10.9	11.9	14.1
Net income ($ mil.)	1.0%	3.2	3.1	2.4	2.5	3.3
Market value ($ mil.)	(0.2%)	41.2	35.0	42.1	42.4	40.9
Employees	1.5%	165	145	130	175	175

RITE AID CORP
NYS: RAD

30 Hunter Lane
Camp Hill, PA 17011
Phone: 717 761-2633
Fax: 717 975-5905
Web: www.riteaid.com

CEO: John T. Standley
CFO: Darren W. Karst
HR: Ken Black
FYE: March 02
Type: Public

While Rite Aid ranks a distant third (behind Walgreen and CVS) in the US retail drugstore business it nevertheless boasts a formidable presence with nearly 2500 drugstores in almost 20 states and the District of Columbia. Rite Aid stores generate roughly 70% of their sales from filling prescriptions while the rest comes from selling health and beauty aids convenience foods greeting cards and more including Rite Aid brand private-label products. Some 60% of all Rite Aid stores are free-standing more than half have drive-through pharmacies and more than 60% have a GNC store within them. Rite Aid sold some 1900 stores to Walgreens in 2018 for around $4 billion.

	Annual Growth	02/15	02/16*	03/17	03/18	03/19
Sales ($ mil.)	(5.0%)	26,528.4	30,736.7	32,845.1	21,529.0	21,639.6
Net income ($ mil.)	-	2,109.2	165.5	4.1	943.5	(422.2)
Market value ($ mil.)	(45.0%)	431.0	430.7	294.4	103.2	39.4
Employees	(12.1%)	89,000	88,000	87,000	59,000	53,100

*Fiscal year change

RIVER VALLEY BANCORP   NAS: RIVR

430 Clifty Drive   CEO: -
Madison, IN 47250   CFO: -
Phone: 812 273-4949   HR: -
Fax: 812 273-4944   FYE: December 31
Web: www.rvfbank.com   Type: Public

This River wants to help manage your revenue stream. River Valley Bancorp is the holding company for River Valley Financial Bank a thrift serving southeast Indiana and neighboring communities in Kentucky from about 10 branches. The bank offers standard deposit products including checking and savings accounts CDs NOW accounts and IRAs. It uses funds from deposits to write a variety of commercial and consumer loans; single-family mortgages make up about half of its loan portfolio. River Valley Financial also invests in government bonds municipal securities and mortgage-backed securities. The bank's wealth management arm offers brokerage trust and advisory services. German American Bancorp agreed to buy the bank in 2015 for $83.5 million.

	Annual Growth	12/10	12/11	12/12	12/13	12/14
Assets ($ mil.)	7.1%	386.6	406.6	472.9	482.8	509.5
Net income ($ mil.)	19.9%	2.3	1.8	4.0	4.4	4.8
Market value ($ mil.)	7.3%	40.2	39.0	44.4	65.4	53.2
Employees	8.4%	92	96	125	128	127

RIVERBED TECHNOLOGY INC   NMS: RVBD

680 Folsom Street   CEO: -
San Francisco, CA 94107   CFO: -
Phone: 415 247-8800   HR: -
Fax: 415 247-8801   FYE: December 31
Web: www.riverbed.com   Type: Public

Riverbed Technology keeps data flowing. The company develops hardware and software that improves the performance of software shared over wide area networks (WANs) and reduce network traffic. Its Steelhead network appliances and software tools are designed for small businesses and global enterprises. Riverbed's other products enable mobile access to business software and data facilitate online data storage (Whitewater) and manage network performance (Cascade). Customers have included Carhartt OMV and Tatts Group. The company makes most of its sales through resellers distributors and systems integrators. Riverbed sells worldwide but it does more than half of its business in the US.

	Annual Growth	12/09	12/10	12/11	12/12	12/13
Sales ($ mil.)	27.5%	394.1	551.9	726.5	836.9	1,041.0
Net income ($ mil.)	-	7.1	34.2	63.8	54.6	(12.4)
Market value ($ mil.)	(5.8%)	3,671.6	5,621.7	3,756.4	3,152.1	2,890.0
Employees	26.0%	1,013	1,244	1,610	2,566	2,556

RIVERSIDE HEALTHCARE ASSOCIATION, INC.

701 TOWN CENTER DR # 1000   CEO: -
NEWPORT NEWS, VA 236064283   CFO: -
Phone: 757-534-7000   HR: -
Fax: -   FYE: December 31
Web: www.riversideonline.com   Type: Private

Extra! Extra! Read all about it! Residents of Newport News (and about a dozen other cities in Eastern Virginia) Turn to Riverside Health for Medical Care. The not-for-profit health care provider administers general emergency and specialty medical services from five hospitals Riverside Regional Medical Center Riverside Walter Reed Hospital Riverside Tappahannock Hospital and Riverside Shore Memorial Hospital and Riverside Doctors Hospital as well as a psychiatric hospital a physical rehabilitation facility and retirement communities. Riverside also operates physician offices and medical training facilities. Specialty centers provide home and hospice care cancer treatment and dialysis.

	Annual Growth	12/11	12/12	12/13	12/14	12/15
Sales ($ mil.)	6.6%	-	948.0	1,017.5	1,059.2	1,149.8
Net income ($ mil.)	(20.3%)	-	41.7	102.0	(86.5)	21.1
Market value ($ mil.)	-	-	-	-	-	-
Employees	-	-	-	-	-	8,000

RIVERSIDE HOSPITAL, INC.

500 J CLYDE MORRIS BLVD   CEO: William B Downey
NEWPORT NEWS, VA 236011929   CFO: -
Phone: 757-594-2000   HR: -
Fax: -   FYE: December 31
Web: www.riversideonline.com   Type: Private

Riverside Hospital operates as Riverside Regional Medical Center a 450-bed acute-care facility that serves the residents of Newport News Virginia. Founded in 1916 the hospital moved to its current 72-acre campus in 1963 providing more than 30 medical specialties including cancer treatment cardiology birthing and diagnostic imaging. It specializes in cardiovascular and neurological surgeries and provides radiosurgery (radiation surgery) through a partnership with the University of Virginia Health System. Its emergency department is a 42-room Level II Trauma Center that treats more than 57000 patients each year. Riverside Hospital is part of the Riverside Health System.

	Annual Growth	12/09	12/10	12/11	12/16	12/17
Sales ($ mil.)	5.2%	-	429.7	466.1	636.7	611.3
Net income ($ mil.)	15.5%	-	20.8	36.2	65.3	57.2
Market value ($ mil.)	-	-	-	-	-	-
Employees	-	-	-	-	-	8,000

RIVERVIEW BANCORP, INC.   NMS: RVSB

900 Washington St., Ste. 900   CEO: Kevin J Lycklama
Vancouver, WA 98660   CFO: David Lam
Phone: 360 693-6650   HR: -
Fax: -   FYE: March 31
Web: www.riverviewbank.com   Type: Public

Riverview Bancorp is the holding company for Riverview Community Bank which operates about 20 branches located primarily in the Columbia River Gorge area of Washington State and Oregon. Serving consumers and local businesses the bank offers such standard retail banking services as checking and savings accounts money market accounts NOW accounts and CDs. Commercial construction and commercial real estate loans account for nearly 90% of its lending portfolio which also includes residential mortgages residential construction loans and other consumer loans. Trust and investment services are provided through the company's Riverview Asset Management Corp. Riverview Community Bank was founded in 1923.

	Annual Growth	03/15	03/16	03/17	03/18	03/19
Assets ($ mil.)	7.7%	858.8	921.2	1,133.9	1,151.5	1,156.9
Net income ($ mil.)	40.0%	4.5	6.4	7.4	10.2	17.3
Market value ($ mil.)	12.9%	101.7	95.0	161.6	211.2	165.3
Employees	2.0%	231	229	260	258	250

RIVERVIEW HOSPITAL

395 WESTFIELD RD   CEO: -
NOBLESVILLE, IN 460601434   CFO: -
Phone: 317-773-0760   HR: -
Fax: -   FYE: December 31
Web: www.riverview.org   Type: Private

Riverview Hospital (which changed its operating name to Riverside Health in 2014) provides general medical and surgical care to residents in central Indiana. With about 155 beds and 300 physicians representing more than 35 medical specialties the hospital is a full-service facility that offers specialty care in a number of areas including heart disease cancer women's health and orthopedics. Besides its main campus Riverview operates several outpatient facilities including an occupational health center a community health clinic and several rehab and fitness centers.

	Annual Growth	12/13	12/14	12/15	12/16	12/17
Sales ($ mil.)	3.8%	-	160.7	162.2	171.6	179.7
Net income ($ mil.)	14.9%	-	5.7	1.3	1.9	8.6
Market value ($ mil.)	-	-	-	-	-	-
Employees	-	-	-	-	-	949

RIVIERA HOLDINGS CORPORATION

2901 Las Vegas Blvd. South
Las Vegas NV 89109
Phone: 702-734-5110
Fax: 702-794-9442
Web: www.rivierahotel.com

CEO: –
CFO: –
HR: –
FYE: December 31
Type: Private

It may not be the south of France but gamblers at the more than 50-year-old Riviera Holdings' Riviera Hotel & Casino probably don't care. The casino located on the Las Vegas Strip has about 900 slot machines 35 gaming tables a keno lounge poker room a sports-betting club and bingo. The Riviera also has a 2100-room hotel with bars restaurants a convention center and entertainment such as An Evening at La Cage (a female impersonation show). The Riviera opened in 1955. The company filed for Chapter 11 in 2010 and exited bankruptcy in 2011.

RLI CORP   NYS: RLI

9025 North Lindbergh Drive
Peoria, IL 61615
Phone: 309 692-1000
Fax: 309 692-1068
Web: www.rlicorp.com

CEO: Jonathan E. Michael
CFO: Thomas L. Brown
HR: –
FYE: December 31
Type: Public

You might wonder what folks in Illinois know about earthquake insurance but as a specialty property/casualty insurer Peoria-based RLI knows how to write such policies. Through its subsidiaries the company mainly offers coverage for US niche markets — risks that are hard to place in the standard market and are otherwise underserved. It focuses on public and private companies as well as non-profit organizations. RLI's commercial property/casualty lines include products liability property damage marine cargo directors and officers liability medical malpractice and general liability. It also writes commercial surety bonds and a smattering of specialty personal insurance.

	Annual Growth	12/14	12/15	12/16	12/17	12/18
Assets ($ mil.)	2.8%	2,775.5	2,736.6	2,777.6	2,947.2	3,105.1
Net income ($ mil.)	(17.0%)	135.4	137.5	114.9	105.0	64.2
Market value ($ mil.)	8.7%	2,198.5	2,748.1	2,809.5	2,699.6	3,070.3
Employees	0.8%	882	902	943	902	912

ROADRUNNER TRANSPORTATION SERVICES HOLDINGS INC.   NYSE: RRTS

4900 S. Pennsylvania Ave.
Cudahy WI 53110-8903
Phone: 414-615-1500
Fax: 414-615-1513
Web: www.rrts.com

CEO: –
CFO: –
HR: –
FYE: December 31
Type: Public

Running your cargo down the road is Roadrunner Transportation Services' (RRTS) business. The company offers less-than-truckload (LTL) freight transportation which combines freight from multiple shippers into a single truckload. In addition it arranges the transportation of truckload freight as well as provides logistics services. RRTS caters to small and mid-size shippers and some large national accounts throughout the US via a network of 15-plus service centers. Rather than owning trucks and trailers the company relies on a network of independent contractors and on purchased transportation capacity. Investment firm Thayer Hidden Creek owns a majority of RRTS.

ROADRUNNER TRANSPORTATION SYSTEMS INC   NYS: RRTS

1431 Opus Place, Suite 530
Downers Grove, IL 60515
Phone: 414 615-1500
Fax: –

CEO: Curtis W. (Curt) Stoelting
CFO: Terence R. (Terry) Rogers
HR: –
FYE: December 31
Type: Public

Roadrunner Transportation Systems (RRTS) offers a host of freight transportation and logistics services. The company's truckload (TL) operations serve customers throughout North America with a focus on the automotive industrial consumer product and food and beverage industries. RRTS also offers on-demand express transportation through its fleet of trucks and cargo aircraft. The company's logistics services include truckload brokerage LTL shipment execution international freight forwarding and customs brokerage. RRTS' less-than-truckload (LTL) freight transportation operations combine freight from multiple shippers into a single truckload and serve customers across the US and parts of Canada. General Motors accounts for more than 10% of the company's revenue.

	Annual Growth	12/14	12/15	12/16	12/17	12/18
Sales ($ mil.)	4.3%	1,872.8	1,995.0	2,033.2	2,091.3	2,216.1
Net income ($ mil.)	–	52.0	48.0	(360.3)	(91.2)	(165.6)
Market value ($ mil.)	(61.5%)	36.3	14.7	16.2	12.0	0.8
Employees	3.3%	4,045	4,502	4,645	4,600	4,600

ROAN RESOURCES INC   NYS: ROAN

14701 Herts Quail Springs Parkway
Oklahoma, OK 73134
Phone: 405 896-8050
Fax: –
Web: www.linnenergy.com

CEO: –
CFO: –
HR: –
FYE: December 31
Type: Public

Linn Energy is all in when it comes to drilling for oil and natural gas across the US although in recent years the company has narrowed its focus to exploiting assets in the Mid-Continent California and the Permian Basin. The company has proved reserves of 3.5 trillion cu. ft. of natural gas equivalent. The company operates about 60% of its more than 23000 gross productive wells. In addition to its core oil and gas activities Linn Energy pursues an aggressive hedging strategy to reduce the effects of oil price volatility on its annual income. However hurt by years of low commodity prices in 2016 the company filed for Chapter 11 bankruptcy protection from which it emerged in 2017.

	Annual Growth	12/14	12/15	12/16*	02/17*	12/17
Sales ($ mil.)	(45.1%)	4,983.3	2,883.3	917.7	298.1	826.7
Net income ($ mil.)	–	(451.8)	(4,759.8)	(2,171.9)	2,397.1	432.9
Market value ($ mil.)	–	–	–	–	–	3,364.2
Employees	(18.6%)	1,800	1,760	1,500	–	970

*Fiscal year change

ROBERT BOSCH LLC

2800 S 25TH AVE
BROADVIEW, IL 601554532
Phone: 248-876-1000
Fax: –
Web: www.boschtechinfo.com

CEO: Berend Bracht
CFO: Maximiliane Straub
HR: Michael Mckenna
FYE: December 31
Type: Private

Robert Bosch LLC is your one-stop shop for German-engineered auto parts appliances and power tools. The North American subsidiary of German giant Robert Bosch GmbH Bosch LLC makes and markets automotive original equipment and aftermarket products industrial drive and control technology packaging technology power tools home appliances security and communication systems thermotechnology and software solutions. Robert Bosch LLC's biggest area Mobility Solutions makes products aimed at the next generation of automobiles particularly around connectivity automation and electrification. Active since 1906 Bosch LLC has grown to around 70 primary North American locations.

	Annual Growth	12/07	12/08	12/09	12/10	12/14
Sales ($ mil.)	13.9%	–	–	5,464.0	6,810.0	10,474.0
Net income ($ mil.)	25.1%	–	–	59.0	326.0	181.0
Market value ($ mil.)	–	–	–	–	–	–
Employees	–	–	–	–	–	12,986

ROBERT HALF INTERNATIONAL INC.

NYS: RHI

2884 Sand Hill Road, Suite 200 — CEO: Harold M. Messmer
Menlo Park, CA 94025 — CFO: M. Keith Waddell
Phone: 650 234-6000 — HR: –
Fax: – — FYE: December 31
Web: www.roberthalf.com — Type: Public

Robert Half International carries the full load of personnel services. The company places temporary and permanent staff through eight divisions: Accountemps Robert Half Finance and Accounting Robert Half Legal OfficeTeam (general administrative) Robert Half Technology (information technology) Robert Half Management Resources (senior level professionals) and The Creative Group (advertising marketing and Web design). The firm also publishes job reports and surveys on the latest employment trends and annual salary guides to track pay trends and has an internal audit and risk consulting division in Protiviti. The US accounts for three-quarters of sales.

	Annual Growth	12/14	12/15	12/16	12/17	12/18
Sales ($ mil.)	5.4%	4,695.0	5,094.9	5,250.4	5,266.8	5,800.3
Net income ($ mil.)	9.2%	305.9	357.8	343.4	290.6	434.3
Market value ($ mil.)	(0.5%)	6,951.8	5,613.4	5,808.6	6,613.6	6,811.3
Employees	0.7%	225,000	236,000	231,400	228,600	231,600

ROBERT MORRIS UNIVERSITY

6001 UNIVERSITY BLVD — CEO: –
CORAOPOLIS, PA 151081189 — CFO: –
Phone: 412-397-3000 — HR: –
Fax: – — FYE: May 31
Web: www.rmu.edu — Type: Private

Robert Morris University is a private four-year institution located in suburban Pittsburgh. It offers more than 30 undergraduate degree programs and nearly 20 master's and doctoral degree programs as well as adult and continuing education programs. The school has an enrollment of more than 5000 students. Named for a Pennsylvanian patriot who helped finance the Revolutionary War and signed the Declaration of Independence Robert Morris University was founded in 1921. Formerly Robert Morris College the institution gained university status in 2002.

	Annual Growth	05/08	05/09	05/10	05/16	05/18
Sales ($ mil.)	3.1%	–	105.1	112.6	173.3	137.8
Net income ($ mil.)	–	–	0.0	2.8	5.9	8.4
Market value ($ mil.)	–	–	–	–	–	–
Employees	–	–	–	–	–	500

ROBERT W. BAIRD & CO. INCORPORATED

777 E WISCONSIN AVE FL 29 — CEO: Steven G. (Steve) Booth
MILWAUKEE, WI 532025391 — CFO: Terrance P. (Terry) Maxwell
Phone: 414-765-3500 — HR: –
Fax: – — FYE: December 31
Web: www.rwbaird.com — Type: Private

Employee-owned Robert W. Baird & Co. brings midwestern sensibility to the high-flying world of investment banking. The company offers brokerage asset management and investment banking services to middle-market corporations institutional clients and wealthy individuals and families. Its investment banking activities include underwriting and distributing corporate securities mergers and acquisition advisory and institutional sales and trading. The company also conducts equity research on more than 600 US firms. Baird manages more than $97 billion in client assets.

	Annual Growth	12/05	12/06	12/07	12/08	12/09
Assets ($ mil.)	9.8%	–	–	1,712.8	1,080.5	2,063.9
Net income ($ mil.)	(8.6%)	–	–	50.2	36.6	41.9
Market value ($ mil.)	–	–	–	–	–	–
Employees	–	–	–	–	–	5,215

ROBERT WOOD JOHNSON UNIVERSITY HOSPITAL AT RAHWAY

865 STONE ST — CEO: –
RAHWAY, NJ 070652742 — CFO: –
Phone: 732-381-4200 — HR: –
Fax: – — FYE: December 31
Web: www.rwjbh.org — Type: Private

Robert Wood Johnson University Hospital at Rahway (RWJUHR) has the people of Rahway cheering for it. Providing health care services for Rahway and 15 other communities of eastern New Jersey the hospital has 265 beds. Founded in 1917 RWJUHR offers patients ambulatory cardiac geriatric psychiatric pulmonary rehabilitation and surgical services. The hospital has specialty divisions for wound healing balance sleep and pain care and it has hospice and long-term stay units. Part of the Robert Wood Johnson Health System and Network since 2003 RWJUH is also affiliated with The University of Medicine and Dentistry of New Jersey's Robert Wood Johnson Medical School.

	Annual Growth	12/14	12/15	12/16	12/17	12/18
Sales ($ mil.)	1.6%	–	109.8	115.1	115.3	115.3
Net income ($ mil.)	34.4%	–	9.8	10.4	23.8	23.8
Market value ($ mil.)	–	–	–	–	–	–
Employees	–	–	–	–	–	700

ROBERT WOOD JOHNSON UNIVERSITY HOSPITAL, INC.

1 ROBERT WOOD JOHNSON PL — CEO: –
NEW BRUNSWICK, NJ 089011928 — CFO: John Gantner
Phone: 732-828-3000 — HR: Martin Everhart
Fax: – — FYE: December 31
Web: www.rwjbh.org — Type: Private

Robert Wood Johnson University Hospital (RWJUH) is the flagship facility of the Robert Wood Johnson Health System and Network. The medical center offers patients acute and tertiary care including cardiovascular services organ and tissue transplantation pediatric care (at The Bristol-Myers Squibb Children's Hospital) Level I trauma care cancer treatment (at the Cancer Hospital of New Jersey) women's health and emergency medicine. Founded in 1884 the 965-bed facility serves as a teaching center for the Robert Wood Johnson Medical School (RWJMS). The Robert Wood Johnson Health System plans to merge with fellow New Jersey hospital system Barnabas Health.

	Annual Growth	12/14	12/15	12/16	12/17	12/18
Sales ($ mil.)	1.9%	–	1,264.0	–	1,249.6	1,337.1
Net income ($ mil.)	–	–	8.4	–	(59.8)	(3.0)
Market value ($ mil.)	–	–	–	–	–	–
Employees	–	–	–	–	–	4,674

ROBERTS DAIRY COMPANY, LLC

2901 CUMING ST — CEO: –
OMAHA, NE 681312108 — CFO: –
Phone: 402-344-4321 — HR: Tim Nelson
Fax: – — FYE: September 30
Web: www.hilanddairy.com — Type: Private

Holy cow! Roberts Dairy Foods is a leading producer of fluid cultured and frozen dairy products. It offers milk yogurt sour cream cottage cheese and other dairy products. A division of Hiland Dairy the firm operates production plants in Omaha and Kansas City and 10 distribution centers located in the Midwest. The company markets its products under the Roberts and Hiland-Dairy brands; it also provides private-label services and school milk. Through a joint venture named Hiland-Roberts the company makes ice cream products from a facility in Norfolk Nebraska. Founded as a milk route by J.R. Roberts in 1906 Roberts Dairy Foods serves retail food and food service customers throughout the Midwest.

	Annual Growth	09/04	09/05	09/06	09/07	09/08
Sales ($ mil.)	17.7%	–	–	259.5	319.7	359.7
Net income ($ mil.)	(27.8%)	–	–	1.6	2.2	0.9
Market value ($ mil.)	–	–	–	–	–	–
Employees	–	–	–	–	–	320

ROBINSON (C.H.) WORLDWIDE, INC.   NMS: CHRW

14701 Charlson Road
Eden Prairie, MN 55347
Phone: 952 937-8500
Fax: 952 937-6714
Web: www.chrobinson.com

CEO: John P. Wiehoff
CFO: Andrew C. Clarke
HR: –
FYE: December 31
Type: Public

C.H. Robinson Worldwide (CHRW) keeps merchandise moving. A third-party logistics (3PL) provider the company contracts with more than 73000 carriers including trucks trains ships and airplanes to arrange freight transportation for its 120000-plus customers in the the food and beverage manufacturing and retail industries. Using its proprietary Navisphere platform CHRW can handle more than 45 million digital transaction per month and close to 20 million shipments per year. Besides transportation the company also offers logistics supply chain management and transportation management services. C.H. Robinson operates worldwide but generates about 90% of total revenue in the US.

	Annual Growth	12/14	12/15	12/16	12/17	12/18
Sales ($ mil.)	5.4%	13,470.1	13,476.1	13,144.4	14,869.4	16,631.2
Net income ($ mil.)	10.3%	449.7	509.7	513.4	504.9	664.5
Market value ($ mil.)	2.9%	10,281.2	8,514.4	10,057.4	12,230.6	11,544.2
Employees	7.3%	11,521	13,159	14,125	15,074	15,262

ROBINSON HEALTH SYSTEM, INC.

6847 N CHESTNUT ST
RAVENNA, OH 442663929
Phone: 330-297-0811
Fax: –
Web: www.uhhospitals.org

CEO: –
CFO: –
HR: –
FYE: December 31
Type: Private

Robinson Health System operates the Portage Medical Center a 300-bed medical facility serving communities in northeast Ohio. In addition to a Level III trauma center the hospital offers programs in pediatrics women's health home health care and oncology. It also operates outpatient facilities including urgent care clinics a freestanding surgery center an occupational health center and several physician practices. Robinson Memorial Hospital has nearly 400 physicians representing more than 40 medical specialties. Robinson Health is part of the University Hospitals Health System.

	Annual Growth	12/06	12/07	12/08	12/09	12/14
Sales ($ mil.)	1.8%	–	141.4	146.8	6.9	160.6
Net income ($ mil.)	11.8%	–	10.1	10.1	(0.1)	22.0
Market value ($ mil.)	–	–	–	–	–	–
Employees	–	–	–	–	–	26,000

ROBINSON OIL CORPORATION

955 MARTIN AVE
SANTA CLARA, CA 950502608
Phone: 408-327-4300
Fax: –
Web: www.rottenrobbie.com

CEO: –
CFO: Stephen F White
HR: –
FYE: December 31
Type: Private

Like Hamlet 's Denmark something's rotten in the state of Robinson Oil. The company owns and operates Rotten Robbie a regional brand of independent gas stations that caters to consumer and commercial motorists. The chain consists of some 35 stops in Northern California mainly around the San Francisco Bay Area. Some stops are kiosks; about half are larger with Mrs. Robbie's Markets a food store and several offer commercial fleet fueling services affiliated with Pacific Pride and other cardlock networks. Diesel is available at all locations and at certain stores kerosene propane and biodiesel. Founded in the 1930s as a private-label fuel retailer Robinson Oil is a fourth-generation family-owned business.

	Annual Growth	12/07	12/08	12/09	12/12	12/16
Sales ($ mil.)	(20.1%)	–	2,048.5	292.4	464.2	339.7
Net income ($ mil.)	352.3%	–	0.0	8.2	10.7	20.9
Market value ($ mil.)	–	–	–	–	–	–
Employees	–	–	–	–	–	250

ROCHESTER GAS AND ELECTRIC CORPORATION

89 EAST AVE
ROCHESTER, NY 146490002
Phone: 800-295-7323
Fax: –

CEO: –
CFO: –
HR: –
FYE: December 31
Type: Private

Upstate New York residents count on Rochester Gas and Electric (RG&E) to keep the lights turned on. The regulated utility provides electricity to about 370000 customers and natural gas to 306000 customers. RG&E operates 22500 miles of power transmission and distribution lines and has a generating capacity of approximately 400 MW from interests in fossil-fueled and hydroelectric power plants. RG&E and sister utility company New York State Electric & Gas (NYSEG) are subsidiaries of regional power and gas distribution player Avangrid.

	Annual Growth	12/08	12/09	12/10	12/16	12/17
Sales ($ mil.)	(2.0%)	–	–	982.5	1,042.2	850.7
Net income ($ mil.)	6.3%	–	–	54.3	80.7	83.2
Market value ($ mil.)	–	–	–	–	–	–
Employees	–	–	–	–	–	865

ROCHESTER INSTITUTE OF TECHNOLOGY (INC)

1 LOMB MEMORIAL DR
ROCHESTER, NY 146235698
Phone: 585-475-2411
Fax: –
Web: www.rit.edu

CEO: –
CFO: –
HR: Judy Bender
FYE: June 30
Type: Private

The Rochester Institute of Technology (RIT) is a privately endowed university with nine colleges focused on providing career-oriented education to about 18600 students. The school which has a student-faculty ratio of about 14:1 offers more than 90 bachelor's degree programs in art and design business engineering science and hotel management. RIT also confers master's and doctorate degrees. The university's National Technical Institute for the Deaf is the first and largest technological college for learners who suffer from hearing loss. RIT which traces its roots back to 1829 counts among its alumni the CEOs of Kodak and The Associated Press.

	Annual Growth	06/05	06/06	06/12	06/17	06/18
Sales ($ mil.)	3.8%	–	370.7	490.3	560.2	579.3
Net income ($ mil.)	13.4%	–	45.1	16.8	74.2	203.8
Market value ($ mil.)	–	–	–	–	–	–
Employees	–	–	–	–	–	3,300

ROCK CREEK PHARMACEUTICALS INC   NMS: RCPI

2040 Whitfield Ave., Suite 300
Sarasota, FL 34243
Phone: 844 727-0727
Fax: –

CEO: –
CFO: –
HR: –
FYE: December 31
Type: Public

Rock Creek Pharmaceuticals (formerly Star Scientific) has a new name and business strategy focused on the development of drugs to treat chronic inflammatory conditions and neurological disorders. The company has adopted the name of its Rock Creek Pharmaceuticals subsidiary (founded in 2007) which makes nutraceuticals using alkaloids found in tobacco and other plants. Its core products are Anatabloc to reduce inflammation and CigRx a tobacco alternative. (Both products are the subject of warning letters from the US Food and Drug Administration.) Formerly a seller of discount cigarettes the emerging drug development company has since exited the cigarette and dissolvable tobacco businesses.

	Annual Growth	12/09	12/10	12/11	12/12	12/13
Sales ($ mil.)	89.6%	0.7	0.8	1.7	6.2	9.1
Net income ($ mil.)	–	(22.8)	(28.3)	(38.0)	(22.9)	(32.8)
Market value ($ mil.)	13.5%	120.7	336.1	375.8	462.0	200.0
Employees	(5.2%)	31	31	39	23	25

ROCK ENERGY RESOURCES INC.   OTC: RCKE.PK

10375 Richmond Ste. 2100 — CEO: -
Houston TX 77042 — CFO: -
Phone: 713-954-3600 — HR: -
Fax: 916-649-3594 — FYE: December 31
Web: www.casepower.com — Type: Public

Rock Energy Resources is pushing to release oil and gas energy from the rocks in which they are trapped. The former Hanover Gold Company is in the business of natural gas and crude oil production in Texas and California. In 2008 not long after changing its name and its business focus Rock Energy Resources doubled its ownership interest in the Orcutt project in California. It plans to continue drilling more wells and increase its overall reserve base. In 2010 after a hiatus during which the company sought to obtain more capital it recommenced work on its Garwood Wilcox properties in Colorado County Texas.

ROCK-TENN CO.   NYS: RKT

504 Thrasher Street — CEO: Steven C Voorhees
Norcross, GA 30071 — CFO: Ward H Dickson
Phone: 770 448-2193 — HR: -
Fax: - — FYE: September 30
Web: www.rocktenn.com — Type: Public

A rock-solid reputation? You betcha. One of North America's containerboard giants Rock-Tenn produces packaging for food hardware apparel and other consumer goods. With approximately 9.4 million tons of mill capacity the company's lineup includes recycled and bleached paperboard containerboard consumer and corrugated packaging and point-of-purchase displays. Specialty paperboard is also converted into book cover and laminated paperboard and sold to other manufacturers for such applications as furniture storage and automotive components. Rock-Tenn traces its roots back to 1936 and operates through 240 locations worldwide.

	Annual Growth	09/10	09/11	09/12	09/13	09/14
Sales ($ mil.)	34.7%	3,001.4	5,399.6	9,207.6	9,545.4	9,895.1
Net income ($ mil.)	20.8%	225.6	141.1	249.1	727.3	479.7
Market value ($ mil.)	(1.1%)	6,973.4	6,815.2	10,105.2	14,177.8	6,661.2
Employees	26.5%	10,400	26,600	26,300	25,800	26,600

ROCKET FUEL INC   NMS: FUEL

1900 Seaport Boulevard, Pacific Shores Center — CEO: Mark Grether
Redwood City, CA 94063 — CFO: Stephen Snyder
Phone: 650 595-1300 — HR: -
Fax: - — FYE: December 31
Web: www.rocketfuel.com — Type: Public

Rocket Fuel employs data science not rocket science to help its customers keep pace with the escape velocity of digital advertising. The company's proprietary software uses big data and artificial intelligence to simultaneously run more than 1000 online ad campaigns for customers ranging from UCLA and Kraft Foods to Choice Hotels and Johns Manville with 130% revenue retention. Its program learns from customers' behavior and adjusts individual campaigns on the fly to follow the clicks faster than human analysis would allow. Rocket Fuel was formed in 2008 and went public in 2013 raising $116 million for general corporate purposes.

	Annual Growth	12/11	12/12	12/13	12/14	12/15
Sales ($ mil.)	79.3%	44.7	106.6	240.6	408.6	461.6
Net income ($ mil.)	-	(4.3)	(10.3)	(20.9)	(64.3)	(210.5)
Market value ($ mil.)	(76.2%)	-	-	2,678.9	702.3	152.0
Employees	27.1%	-	465	619	1,123	954

ROCKVIEW DAIRIES, INC.

7011 STEWART AND GRAY RD — CEO: Egbert Jim Degroot
DOWNEY, CA 902414347 — CFO: Joe Valadez
Phone: 562-927-5511 — HR: Diana Trujillo
Fax: - — FYE: March 31
— Type: Private

Got organic milk? Rockview Dairies does. Doing business as Rockview Farms the company produces milk and other dairy products under brand names Rockview Farms and Good Heart Organic Milk. Bucking modern trends the dairy owns its own farms and cows which have not been treated with bovine growth hormones. Rockview Dairies processes packages and distributes its own milk. It also offers eggs dressings fruit drinks and desserts. The company wholesales its products to food retailers and foodservice operators and as a bonus offers home-delivery service. Established in 1927 by Bob Hops Rockview Dairies serves Southern California. It has been owned and operated by the DeGroot family since 1965.

	Annual Growth	03/04	03/05	03/06	03/07	03/08
Sales ($ mil.)	15.3%	-	-	251.2	265.2	333.7
Net income ($ mil.)	21.4%	-	-	5.5	4.0	8.1
Market value ($ mil.)	-	-	-	-	-	-
Employees	-	-	-	-	-	250

ROCKWELL COLLINS INC   NYS: COL

400 Collins Road N.E. — CEO: Kelly Ortberg
Cedar Rapids, IA 52498 — CFO: -
Phone: 319 295-1000 — HR: -
Fax: - — FYE: September 30
Web: www.rockwellcollins.com — Type: Public

Rockwell Collins makes aviation electronics and communication equipment for commercial and military aircraft. The company also provides flight simulation and training MRO services navigation and surveillance systems. It has three primary segments: commercial systems (avionics and in-flight entertainment systems for commercial aircraft); government systems (airborne/ground/shipboard communication systems with military applications and overhaul services); and information management services business (communications systems integration and security solutions). In 2017 Rockwell Collins agreed to be acquired by diversified manufacturing giant United Technologies for $23 billion.

	Annual Growth	09/13	09/14	09/15	09/16	09/17
Sales ($ mil.)	10.3%	4,610.0	4,979.0	5,244.0	5,259.0	6,822.0
Net income ($ mil.)	2.8%	632.0	604.0	686.0	728.0	705.0
Market value ($ mil.)	17.8%	11,054.4	12,787.7	13,331.7	13,739.0	21,292.7
Employees	12.2%	18,300	20,000	19,500	19,000	29,000

ROCKWELL MEDICAL, INC   NMS: RMTI

411 Hackensack Avenue, Suite 501 — CEO: Robert L Chioini
Hackensack, NJ 07601 — CFO: Thomas E. Klema
Phone: 248 960-9009 — HR: -
Fax: - — FYE: December 31
Web: www.rockwellmed.com — Type: Public

Rockwell Medical (formerly Rockwell Medical Technologies) specializes in hemodialysis products. The company makes hemodialysis concentrates (in liquid and dry powder form) dialysis kits and other related products for treatment of end-stage renal disease (chronic kidney failure). Its lead Triferic drug is the only FDA-approved iron product for dialysate delivery for the treatment of anemia in the hemodialysis patient population. The company markets and distributes its products directly to hemodialysis providers across the US as well as through independent distributors abroad. To expand its product range Rockwell Medical is also developing new renal drug therapies.

	Annual Growth	12/14	12/15	12/16	12/17	12/18
Sales ($ mil.)	4.0%	54.2	55.4	53.3	57.3	63.4
Net income ($ mil.)	-	(21.3)	(14.4)	(19.8)	(25.9)	(32.1)
Market value ($ mil.)	(31.5%)	586.3	584.0	373.6	331.9	128.9
Employees	(1.3%)	283	300	300	300	269

ROCKWOOD HOLDINGS INC
NYS: ROC

100 Overlook Center
Princeton, NJ 08540
Phone: 609 514-0300
Fax: –
Web: www.rockwoodspecialties.com

CEO: Seifi Ghasemi
CFO: Robert J Zatta
HR: –
FYE: December 31
Type: Public

Rockwood Holdings which operates as Rockwood Specialties manages a portfolio of world-class specialty chemicals and advanced materials businesses. Its specialty chemicals operations (which the company restructured in 2012) include lithium compounds metal treatments and performance additives such as wood preservation chemicals and iron oxide pigments. Other products include titanium dioxide advanced ceramics an performance additives. A leader in most of its niches Rockwood serves the construction paper and water treatment industries. Sales to Germany outpace those to any other region including the US.

	Annual Growth	12/08	12/09	12/10	12/11	12/12
Sales ($ mil.)	0.9%	3,380.1	2,962.9	3,191.6	3,669.3	3,506.9
Net income ($ mil.)	–	(588.4)	21.1	239.4	411.3	383.5
Market value ($ mil.)	46.3%	847.4	1,848.7	3,069.6	3,089.2	3,880.9
Employees	0.0%	10,200	9,500	9,600	9,700	10,200

ROCKY BRANDS INC
NMS: RCKY

39 East Canal Street
Nelsonville, OH 45764
Phone: 740 753-9100
Fax: –
Web: www.rockybrands.com

CEO: Jason Brooks
CFO: Thomas Robertson
HR: –
FYE: December 31
Type: Public

Rocky is a sole survivor. Rocky Brands makes and sells men's and women's footwear and apparel. Its footwear brands include Rocky Georgia Boot Creative Recreation Durango Lehigh and licensed brand Michelin. The company targets six markets: outdoor duty work military lifestyle and western. (Its Rocky brand is sold to the US military.) A wholesaler and retailer the company's products are sold in the US and Canada through more than 10000 retail stores such as sporting goods and outdoor stores (Bass Pro Shops Cabela's) mass merchandisers and farm store chains. It also sells Lehigh-brand footwear online and through mobile and outlet stores. Brothers William and F. M. Brooks founded Rocky in 1932.

	Annual Growth	12/14	12/15	12/16	12/17	12/18
Sales ($ mil.)	(3.1%)	286.2	269.3	260.3	253.2	252.7
Net income ($ mil.)	10.3%	9.8	6.6	(2.1)	9.6	14.6
Market value ($ mil.)	18.0%	98.9	85.2	85.1	139.3	191.6
Employees	(6.4%)	2,714	2,447	2,407	2,079	2,087

ROCKY MOUNTAIN CHOCOLATE FACTORY INC (DE)
NMS: RMCF

265 Turner Drive
Durango, CO 81303
Phone: 970 259-0554
Fax: –
Web: www.rmcf.com; www.sweetfranchise.com; www.u-swirl.com

CEO: Bryan J Merryman
CFO: –
HR: –
FYE: February 28
Type: Public

Rocky Mountain Chocolate Factory knows that tourists often leave their diets at home. That's why many of its candy stores are intentionally placed in factory outlet malls regional malls and tourist areas. The company and its franchisees operate about 300 chocolate stores and another 55 co-branded stores in in 40 US states Canada Japan and the United Arab Emirates. Its majority-owned subsidiary U-Swirl operates more than 65 self-serve frozen yogurt stores. The chocolate maker's products are also wholesaled and sold through fundraising programs and a company website. Most of the retailer's sales come from its 300 factory-made premium chocolates and confections; the remainder comes from franchise fees.

	Annual Growth	02/15	02/16	02/17	02/18	02/19
Sales ($ mil.)	(4.5%)	41.5	40.5	38.3	38.1	34.5
Net income ($ mil.)	(13.2%)	3.9	4.4	3.5	3.0	2.2
Market value ($ mil.)	(11.2%)	91.0	61.4	64.8	72.7	56.5
Employees	(6.3%)	300	300	280	285	231

ROFIN SINAR TECHNOLOGIES INC.
NMS: RSTI

40984 Concept Drive
Plymouth, MI 48170
Phone: 734 455-5400
Fax: –
Web: www.rofin.com

CEO: John R Ambroseo
CFO: –
HR: –
FYE: September 30
Type: Public

Any way you slice it ROFIN-SINAR Technologies is one of the world's leading makers of industrial lasers. The company designs manufactures and markets lasers primarily used for cutting welding and marking a wide range of materials. Its macro (cutting and welding) line is targeted at the machine tool and automotive markets while its laser marking and micro (fine cutting and welding) product lines are principally geared toward the semiconductor electronics and photovoltaic markets. ROFIN sells directly to OEMs systems integrators and industrial end users that integrate its lasers into their own systems. Europe (mainly Germany) is its largest market followed by Asia and North America.

	Annual Growth	09/11	09/12	09/13	09/14	09/15
Sales ($ mil.)	(3.4%)	597.8	540.1	560.1	530.1	519.6
Net income ($ mil.)	(8.9%)	60.0	34.5	34.8	25.2	41.3
Market value ($ mil.)	7.8%	541.1	556.0	682.3	649.9	730.8
Employees	1.4%	2,108	2,213	2,265	2,270	2,231

ROGERS CORP.
NYS: ROG

2225 W. Chandler Blvd.
Chandler, AZ 85224-6155
Phone: 480 917-6000
Fax: –
Web: www.rogerscorp.com

CEO: Bruce D. Hoechner
CFO: Janice E. Stipp
HR: –
FYE: December 31
Type: Public

Rogers Corp. makes and sell specialty materials used for connecting and cushioning as well as managing power in electronic industrial and consumer products. The company's connectivity products are circuit materials used in telecommunications infrastructure automotive applications and consumer electronics. Its polyurethane and silicone products provide cushioning sealing and vibration management in smart phones automotive and aerospace applications and shoes. Its ceramic substrate materials are used in power-related applications like variable frequency drives vehicle electrification and renewable energy. International customers generate about 70% of the Chandler Arizona-based company's revenue.

	Annual Growth	12/14	12/15	12/16	12/17	12/18
Sales ($ mil.)	9.5%	610.9	641.4	656.3	821.0	879.1
Net income ($ mil.)	13.5%	52.9	46.3	48.3	80.5	87.7
Market value ($ mil.)	5.0%	1,498.1	948.6	1,412.9	2,978.5	1,822.2
Employees	7.2%	2,800	2,800	3,100	3,400	3,700

ROLLINS COLLEGE

1000 HOLT AVE 2718
WINTER PARK, FL 327894409
Phone: 407-646-2000
Fax: –
Web: www.rollins.edu

CEO: –
CFO: –
HR: –
FYE: May 31
Type: Private

Students get rolling at Rollins College. The school is a liberal arts college with an enrollment of some 3200 undergraduate students seeking associate bachelor and master's degrees. Rollins' core arts and sciences and professional studies programs offer about 30 majors. In addition its Crummer Graduate School of Business offers an MBA program and its Hamilton Holt School provides undergraduate and graduate evening degree and outreach programs in 10 major fields. The college has 200 faculty members and a student-to-teacher ratio of 10:1. Rollins was founded in 1885 by New England Congregationalists and is the oldest college in Florida. It is named for Chicago businessman and philanthropist Alonzo Rollins.

	Annual Growth	05/11	05/12	05/13	05/16	05/17
Sales ($ mil.)	6.0%	–	105.1	154.5	141.1	140.9
Net income ($ mil.)	–	–	(27.3)	2.2	(26.3)	20.0
Market value ($ mil.)	–	–	–	–	–	–
Employees	–	–	–	–	–	645

ROLLINS, INC.

NYS: ROL

2170 Piedmont Road, N.E.
Atlanta, GA 30324
Phone: 404 888-2000
Fax: –
Web: www.rollins.com

CEO: Gary W. Rollins
CFO: Paul E. (Eddie) Northen
HR: Jerry Gahlhoff
FYE: December 31
Type: Public

If Rollins has anything to do with it you'll sleep tight and the bed bugs won't bite. Rollins is a solid leader in the pest control industry offering an array of residential and commercial pest control and termite control services. With a total of more than 500 company-owned and franchised locations operating under various brands Rollins offers inspections baits traps and crack and crevice treatments. Subsidiaries led by famous bug killer Orkin serve more than 2 million customers which mainly reside in the Americas. International operations Primarily in Asia and in the Middle East account for less than 10% of revenues. Other Rollins brands include and HomeTeam Pest Defense and IFC.

	Annual Growth	12/14	12/15	12/16	12/17	12/18
Sales ($ mil.)	6.6%	1,411.6	1,485.3	1,573.5	1,674.0	1,821.6
Net income ($ mil.)	13.9%	137.7	152.1	167.4	179.1	231.7
Market value ($ mil.)	2.2%	10,833.9	8,477.3	11,056.5	15,229.6	11,815.8
Employees	5.9%	10,936	11,268	12,153	13,126	13,734

RONCO ACQUISITION CORPORATION

110 Wall St. 21st Fl. Ste. C
New York NY 10005
Phone: 646-378-4044
Fax: 646-378-4090
Web: www.ronco.com

CEO: –
CFO: –
HR: –
FYE: June 30
Type: Private

Operators are standing by so have your credit card ready. Ronco's former head huckster (and inventor) Ron Popeil is by his 1995 autobiographical account "The Salesman of the Century". Ronco uses TV infomercials (and the Internet) to sell food dehydrators rotisseries cutlery flavor injectors inside-the-shell egg scramblers pasta makers and GLH (great looking hair) a hair-in-a-can remedy for baldness. The company went public in mid-2005 through a $50-million reverse merger with Fi-Tek. Popeil divested his interest that year. Ronco filed for Chapter 11 bankruptcy protection in mid-2007. By August it emerged from bankruptcy headed by industry veteran Larry Nusbaum and Marlin Equity Partners.

RONILE, INC.

701 ORCHARD AVE
ROCKY MOUNT, VA 241511848
Phone: 540-483-0261
Fax: –

CEO: Phillip C Essig
CFO: –
HR: –
FYE: June 30
Type: Private

Ronile can spin a yarn — a textile one that is. The company manufactures custom-dyed accent yarns including twisted space-dyed air-ply and heatset yarns. Ronile's slew of finished yarn goods include nylon polyester acrylic and other wool fibers which are marketed to carpet rug home furnishings craft and automotive markets. Ronile also operates through subsidiary Bacova Guild Ltd. a manufacturer and supplier of printed accent rugs room-size rugs and bath ensembles to US retail chains and Gulistan a division supplying broadloom carpet. Employee-owned the company is led by its founder's son Phillip Essig.

	Annual Growth	07/03	07/04	07/05	07/06*	06/07
Sales ($ mil.)	1.3%	–	–	226.5	245.5	232.4
Net income ($ mil.)	–	–	–	0.0	0.0	0.0
Market value ($ mil.)	–	–	–	–	–	–
Employees	–	–	–	–	–	1,383

*Fiscal year change

ROOFING WHOLESALE CO., INC.

1918 W GRANT ST
PHOENIX, AZ 850095991
Phone: 602-258-3794
Fax: –
Web: www.rwc.org

CEO: –
CFO: Stephen K Rold
HR: –
FYE: December 31
Type: Private

Business at Roofing Wholesale doesn't have to be complicated but it should be over your head. Roofing Wholesale Company (RWC) distributes residential and commercial roofing stone flooring and stucco to contractors builders and do-it-yourself home owners through ten locations in Arizona California Nevada and New Mexico. It also operates an online store. Products include asphalt shingles cedar shakes and shingles clay tiles fasteners marble floors and slate roofs. John Lisherness father of current president Harley Lisherness founded the family-owned company in 1958.

	Annual Growth	12/11	12/12	12/13	12/14	12/15
Sales ($ mil.)	4.7%	–	–	106.9	106.9	117.1
Net income ($ mil.)	31.1%	–	–	4.8	7.8	8.2
Market value ($ mil.)	–	–	–	–	–	–
Employees	–	–	–	–	–	225

ROOMLINX INC

NBB: MTWO

433 Hackensack Avenue 6th Floor, Continental Place
Hackensack, NJ 07601
Phone: 201 968-9797
Fax: –
Web: www.roomlinx.com

CEO: Robert B Machinist
CFO: Christopher Broderick
HR: –
FYE: December 31
Type: Public

Roomlinx believes high-speed networking should be a standard hotel amenity. The company provides wireless and wired Internet installation and support services primarily to customers in the hospitality industry. Roomlinx's services are used to provide access in hotel rooms convention centers corporate apartments and for special events. The company has serviced more than 140 hotels equipping more than 24000 rooms. The company is also moving into the in-room entertainment market offering a system that includes a flat-panel display and a media console for distributing movies advertising and other content.

	Annual Growth	12/11	12/12	12/13	12/14	12/15
Sales ($ mil.)	14.3%	6.2	13.6	9.4	7.4	10.6
Net income ($ mil.)	–	(2.7)	(7.4)	(4.1)	(2.7)	(81.5)
Market value ($ mil.)	(48.1%)	394.5	278.8	15.0	9.5	28.6
Employees	(10.3%)	51	59	39	43	33

ROOT LEARNING INC.

5470 Main St.
Sylvania OH 43560
Phone: 419-874-0077
Fax: 419-874-4801
Web: www.rootinc.com

CEO: Jim Haudan
CFO: –
HR: –
FYE: December 31
Type: Private

Root Learning wants to ensure your employees aren't just learning by rote. The company provides teaching tools facilitator training and consultative services including leadership alignment and strategy clarification for businesses. Services help clients create training content implement learning programs and measure results. Root also offers software for learning visualization game-based education and knowledge management as well as off-the-shelf courseware that addresses subjects such as workplace diversity emotional literacy branding and business process mapping. Major clients have included Delta and Pepsi. The company was founded in 1993 by former president Randall Root.

ROOT9B HOLDINGS INC NBB: RTNB
102 N. Cascade Avenue, Suite 220 — CEO: –
Colorado Springs, CO 80903 — CFO: William Hoke
Phone: 719 358-8735 — HR: –
Fax: – — FYE: December 31
Web: www.root9bholdings.com — Type: Public

First and foremost Premier Alliance Group looks to be a business and technology ally to its customers. Premier Alliance provides technology consulting and professional services to organizations in the education financial health care utility and other sectors. Core consulting services include systems implementation and architecture information management business intelligence and analysis. It also offers expertise in key professional areas such as risk management compliance and finance. Founded in 1995 Premier Alliance has counted Duke Energy Bank of America and a handful of other large companies as among its key customers. In 2012 it acquired environmental consulting firm GreenHouse Holdings.

	Annual Growth	12/12	12/13	12/14	12/15	12/16
Sales ($ mil.)	(14.8%)	19.5	26.4	20.2	29.4	10.2
Net income ($ mil.)	–	(9.5)	(6.1)	(24.4)	(8.3)	(30.5)
Market value ($ mil.)	97.5%	4.6	3.5	9.5	8.4	70.0
Employees	(1.0%)	160	151	215	224	154

ROPER TECHNOLOGIES INC NYS: ROP
6901 Professional Parkway East, Suite 200 — CEO: Brian D. Jellison
Sarasota, FL 34240 — CFO: Robert Crisci
Phone: 941 556-2601 — HR: –
Fax: – — FYE: December 31
Web: www.ropertech.com — Type: Public

Roper Technologies is an industrial manufacturer and technology company providing a diverse set of offerings such as industrial controls water meter reading products and measurement instrumentation as well as application management software. Its business segments include RF Technology (toll and traffic systems RFID card readers and software) Medical and Scientific Imaging (digital imaging products and software) Industrial Technology (pumps leak testing fluid measurement) and Energy Systems and Controls (controls and sensors testing and inspection equipment). Roper's lines are used in niche markets engaged in RF (radio frequency) water energy research and medical education transportation and security applications. The company targets end-markets seeking value-added engineered products. About 80% of total sales is US.

	Annual Growth	12/14	12/15	12/16	12/17	12/18
Sales ($ mil.)	10.0%	3,549.5	3,582.4	3,789.9	4,607.5	5,191.2
Net income ($ mil.)	10.0%	646.0	696.1	658.6	971.8	944.4
Market value ($ mil.)	14.3%	16,166.6	19,624.3	18,930.5	26,780.6	27,558.2
Employees	11.4%	10,137	10,806	14,155	14,236	15,611

ROSE ACRE FARMS INC.
Rural Rte. 5 — CEO: –
Seymour IN 47274 — CFO: Greg Marshall
Phone: 812-497-2557 — HR: –
Fax: 812-497-3311 — FYE: July 31
Web: www.roseacre.com — Type: Private

Pity the poor rooster; Rose Acre Farms relies instead on millions of hens to produce its profits. Among the largest egg suppliers in the US the business farms and sells fresh chicken eggs under the Rose Acre Farm and Eggland's Best brand. It offers eggs from pen-kept hens and free-roaming cage-free hens both of which peck on a natural hormone-free feed made in the farm's own feed mill. Rose Acre also makes dried egg products such as egg white protein used in animal feed and nutritional supplements for athletes. The company's operations are supported by a fleet of refrigerated Rose Acre semi-trailers that deliver the eggs to retailers or distributors. The founding Rust family owns and operates the farm.

ROSE INTERNATIONAL, INC.
16401 SWINGLEY RIDGE RD — CEO: Himanshu Bhatia
CHESTERFIELD, MO 630170757 — CFO: –
Phone: 636-812-4000 — HR: –
Fax: – — FYE: December 31
Web: www.roseit.com — Type: Private

Rose International keep its customers' tech gardens in bloom. The company provides outsourced IT services including database performance optimization application development and project management to businesses and government agencies in the US. Other services include vendor management payroll processing training and staffing and call center operations. Rose — its name is an acronym for "reliable open systems engineering" — serves customers in the financial services energy technology telecommunications and health care industries. Its software development activities in Missouri and India are overseen by subsidiary Rose I.T. Solutions.

	Annual Growth	12/13	12/14	12/15	12/16	12/17
Sales ($ mil.)	(2.5%)	–	293.5	248.9	233.5	271.7
Net income ($ mil.)	(12.1%)	–	7.2	5.2	2.6	4.9
Market value ($ mil.)	–	–	–	–	–	–
Employees	–	–	–	–	–	6,000

ROSE PAVING CO.
7300 W 100TH PL — CEO: –
BRIDGEVIEW, IL 604552414 — CFO: Jim Muckerheide
Phone: 708-430-1100 — HR: –
Fax: – — FYE: December 31
Web: www.rosepaving.com — Type: Private

A rose by this name smells of hot tar and asphalt. Rose Paving a pavement maintenance contractor provides site evaluation installation management and maintenance of asphalt and concrete parking lots throughout the US. Its activities include pavement removal resurfacing repair and installation lot marking seal coating crack sealing storm sewer repair and installation and installation and repair of concrete curbs walks and pads. The company tailors its services for specific regional situations and circumstances. Clients include commercial and industrial customers in the retail real estate hospitality health care industries as well as homeowner associations schools and religious institutions.

	Annual Growth	12/03	12/04	12/05	12/07	12/08
Sales ($ mil.)	–	–	0.0	25.0	18.3	30.4
Net income ($ mil.)	–	–	–	0.0	0.2	1.5
Market value ($ mil.)	–	–	–	–	–	–
Employees	–	–	–	–	–	120

ROSE ROCK MIDSTREAM L P NYS: RRMS
Two Warren Place, 6120 South Yale Avenue, Suite 700 — CEO: –
Tulsa, OK 74136-4216 — CFO: –
Phone: 918 524-7700 — HR: –
Fax: – — FYE: December 31
Web: www.rrmidstream.com — Type: Public

A rose by any other name would smell as sweet or so says Rose Rock Midstream the new name for SemCrude L.P. Rose Rock Midstream was established in 2011 to take over the assets of SemCrude the storage and pipeline division of SemGroup. Rose Rock Midstream's new assets include SemCrude's crude oil storage terminal in Cushing Oklahoma; its gathering and transportation system in Kansas and Oklahoma; its Bakken Shale operations and its Platteville Colorado crude oil unloading facility. The only midstream operation Rose Rock won't handle is the White Cliffs Pipeline which will continue to be 51%-owned by SemCrude Pipeline L.L.C. In 2014 Rose Rock Midstream acquired trucking assets from a unit of Chesapeake Energy.

	Annual Growth	12/10	12/11	12/12	12/13	12/14
Sales ($ mil.)	57.8%	208.1	431.3	620.4	766.5	1,290.6
Net income ($ mil.)	23.6%	23.5	23.2	24.0	36.7	54.8
Market value ($ mil.)	30.2%	–	673.4	1,029.7	1,266.3	1,487.1
Employees	65.1%	–	80	80	230	360

ROSE'S SOUTHWEST PAPERS, INC.

1701 2ND ST SW
ALBUQUERQUE, NM 871024505
Phone: 505-842-0134
Fax: -
Web: www.rosessouthwestpapers.com

CEO: Roberto E Espat
CFO: -
HR: -
FYE: December 31
Type: Private

Roses Southwest Papers has bloomed in the desert Southwest by manufacturing napkins tissue paper and paper bags used in fast food restaurants and other places of business. The company's tissue products include bathroom tissue center pull towels facial tissue fold towels kitchen roll towels jumbo roll tissue and roll towels. Roses Southwest Papers also provides custom converting and private labeling services. The company counts McDonald's and Burger King among its major clients. Roses Southwest Papers is owned and operated by CEO Roberto Espat and other members of the Espat family.

	Annual Growth	12/03	12/04	12/05	12/06	12/07
Sales ($ mil.)	12.0%	-	66.9	76.7	79.9	94.0
Net income ($ mil.)	(2.3%)	-	2.5	1.2	1.2	2.3
Market value ($ mil.)	-	-	-	-	-	-
Employees	-	-	-	-	-	225

ROSEN HOTELS AND RESORTS INC.

8990 INTL DR STE 200
ORLANDO, FL 328199321
Phone: 407-996-1706
Fax: -
Web: www.rosenhotels.com

CEO: -
CFO: -
HR: -
FYE: January 31
Type: Private

Want to make your Florida stay a little rosy? Rosen Hotels & Resorts owns and operates seven hotels in Orlando collectively totaling more than 6300 rooms and suites. Its properties are located near major area attractions such as Disney World (from Walt Disney Parks) and Universal Studios Orlando (from Universal Parks & Resorts). Its portfolio consists of hotels such as the Rosen Plaza Hotel and Rosen Inn. Three of its hotels are home to major Orlando convention centers: Rosen Plaza Rosen Centre and Rosen Shingle Creek. In addition subsidiary Millennium Technology Group manages computer systems for its hotels. The family-owned Rosen Hotels & Resorts was founded by president Harris Rosen in 1974.

	Annual Growth	01/10	01/11	01/12	01/13	01/14
Sales ($ mil.)	216.0%	-	8.5	8.5	268.8	268.8
Net income ($ mil.)	-	-	-	0.0	76.6	76.6
Market value ($ mil.)	-	-	-	-	-	-
Employees	-	-	-	-	-	3,420

ROSEN'S DIVERSIFIED INC.

1120 Lake Ave.
Fairmont MN 56031
Phone: 507-238-6001
Fax: 507-238-6086
Web: rosensdiversifiedinc.com

CEO: Thomas J Rosen
CFO: Robert A Hovde
HR: -
FYE: September 30
Type: Private

Rosen's Diversified (RDI) has the goods to make the grass greener for its cash cows. The agricultural holding company's subsidiaries cover agricultural chemicals pet food and treats (Performance Pet) beef processing trucking and marketing (Light Inc.). The slaughtering operations of American Foods Group consist of nine meat-packing plants with the capacity to handle 4 million pounds of beef a day. America's Service Line delivers the meat to restaurants and food manufacturers in the US; RDI also ships to nearly 40 countries worldwide. Rosen's Inc. distributes agricultural chemicals and fertilizer. RDI was founded in 1946 by brothers Elmer and Ludwig Rosen and is still controlled by the Rosen family.

ROSETTA RESOURCES, INC.

NMS: ROSE

1111 Bagby Street, Suite 1600
Houston, TX 77002
Phone: 713 335-4000
Fax: -
Web: www.rosettaresources.com

CEO: -
CFO: -
HR: -
FYE: December 31
Type: Public

Rosetta Resources is hoping that its hard work translates into oil and natural gas discoveries. The company which was built onCalpine Corporation's former domestic oil and natural gas exploration assets primarily focuses on developing acreage and production and Texas. In 2012 the company reported estimated proved reserves of 201 million barrels of which 37% was proved developed. Calpine (which spun off its US oil and gas business in 2005) accounted for 12% of Rosetta Resources' revenues in 2012. The company's management is largely made up of former Calpine employees.

	Annual Growth	12/09	12/10	12/11	12/12	12/13
Sales ($ mil.)	29.0%	294.0	308.4	446.2	613.5	814.0
Net income ($ mil.)	-	(219.2)	19.0	100.5	159.3	199.4
Market value ($ mil.)	24.6%	1,221.2	2,307.6	2,666.9	2,778.5	2,945.2
Employees	5.6%	203	168	165	183	252

ROSETTA STONE INC

NYS: RST

1621 North Kent Street, Suite 1200
Arlington, VA 22209
Phone: 703 387-5800
Fax: -
Web: www.rosettastone.com

CEO: A. John Hass
CFO: Thomas Pierno
HR: -
FYE: December 31
Type: Public

Rosetta Stone holds itself out as the key to common language — at least to understanding another language. The provides language-learning software via digital download online subscriptions and CD-ROM. It's Rosetta Stone Language Library combines images text and audio without the traditional translation or grammar explanations to mimic the way children learn their native languages. With consumer and institutional customers in more than 150 countries Rosetta Stone offers software for about 30 languages. Its products are available through direct sales channels and at selected retailers such as Amazon.com Barnes & Noble and Staples.

	Annual Growth	12/14	12/15	12/16	12/17	12/18
Sales ($ mil.)	(9.8%)	261.9	217.7	194.1	184.6	173.6
Net income ($ mil.)	-	(73.7)	(46.8)	(27.6)	(1.5)	(21.5)
Market value ($ mil.)	13.9%	228.6	156.7	208.7	292.1	384.2
Employees	(5.3%)	1,292	1,148	1,012	992	1,040

ROSS STORES INC

NMS: ROST

5130 Hacienda Drive
Dublin, CA 94568-7579
Phone: 925 965-4400
Fax: -
Web: www.rossstores.com

CEO: Barbara Rentler
CFO: Michael J. Hartshorn
HR: Deon Riley
FYE: February 02
Type: Public

Ross wants you to dress for less. A leading off-price apparel retailer (behind TJX Cos. and Kohl's) Ross operates some 1340 Ross Dress for Less and more than 190y 200 dd's Discounts stores that sell closeout merchandise including men's women's and children's clothing at prices well below those of department and specialty stores. While apparel accounts for more than half of sales it also sells small furnishings toys and games luggage and jewelry. Featuring the Ross "Dress for Less" trademark the chain targets 18- to 54-year-old white-collar shoppers from primarily middle-income households. Ross and dd's stores are located in strip malls in over 35 states and mostly in the western US and Guam.

	Annual Growth	01/15	01/16	01/17*	02/18	02/19
Sales ($ mil.)	7.9%	11,041.7	11,940.0	12,866.8	14,134.7	14,983.5
Net income ($ mil.)	14.5%	924.7	1,020.7	1,117.7	1,362.8	1,587.5
Market value ($ mil.)	0.0%	33,771.5	20,717.3	24,057.2	29,120.6	33,778.8
Employees	5.4%	71,400	77,800	78,600	82,700	88,100

*Fiscal year change

ROSS-SIMONS OF WARWICK INC.

9 Ross-Simons Dr.
Cranston RI 02920
Phone: 401-463-3100
Fax: 401-463-8599
Web: www.ross-simons.com

CEO: Darrell Ross
CFO: David Pawlak
HR: –
FYE: January 31
Type: Private

Look no further than Ross-Simons of Warwick for the perfect wedding gift. Bringing a little taste of luxury to the masses the multi-channel retailer sells jewelry (estate jewelry diamond pieces) tableware (fine china sterling silver flatware) collectibles (Lladro figurines Swarovski crystal) and home decor at discounted prices. It also markets supermodel Christie Brinkley's signature jewelry collection. Ross-Simons mails at least 20 million catalogs annually and operates about 15 retail and outlet stores in seven East Coast states. The company also sells jewelry through QVC. Ross-Simons opened its first retail store in 1952 added catalog sales in the early '80s and has a thriving Internet business.

ROTARY INTERNATIONAL

1 ROTARY CTR
EVANSTON, IL 602014422
Phone: 847-866-3000
Fax: –
Web: www.rotary.org

CEO: John Hewko
CFO: Lori O Carlson
HR: –
FYE: June 30
Type: Private

The rotary phone may be a thing of the past but Rotary International (founded in 1905 and now with more than 1.2 million members) is still going strong. The service organization with a motto of Service Above Self comprises 34000-plus clubs in more than 200 countries and territories. Rotary service projects are intended to alleviate problems such as hunger illiteracy poverty and violence. Grants from the Rotary Foundation support its efforts. Along with its service projects Rotary aims to promote high ethical standards in the workplace. Membership in Rotary clubs is by invitation. Each club strives to include representatives from major businesses professions and institutions in its community.

	Annual Growth	06/10	06/11	06/12	06/16	06/18
Sales ($ mil.)	2.2%	–	433.5	90.6	356.0	503.4
Net income ($ mil.)	(11.5%)	–	168.4	(1.0)	(17.8)	71.9
Market value ($ mil.)	–	–	–	–	–	–
Employees	–	–	–	–	–	800

ROTH CAPITAL PARTNERS LLC

24 Corporate Plaza
Newport Beach CA 92660
Phone: 949-720-5700
Fax: 949-720-7215
Web: www.rothcp.com

CEO: Byron Roth
CFO: –
HR: –
FYE: June 30
Type: Private

ROTH Capital Partners is an investment banking firm with a focus on small-cap companies. The employee-owned company offers its clients a full spectrum of investment banking services including capital raising research coverage trading and market making merger and acquisition advisory services and investor conferences. Activities include IPO underwriting and strategic advice. ROTH which operates in the US and China has investment banking teams devoted to the business services energy industrial consumer financial services gaming health care media technology and consumer sectors.

ROTH PRODUCE CO.

3882 AGLER RD
COLUMBUS, OH 432193607
Phone: 614-337-2825
Fax: –

CEO: –
CFO: –
HR: –
FYE: December 31
Type: Private

|Roth Produce provides fresh produce herbs exotic vegetables dairy products and frozen breads to foodservice customers in the greater Columbus Ohio area. The company distributes to caterers country clubs hotels and other fine dining establishments as well as to local eateries pizza parlors and schools. Roth Produce's gift basket division Bensoni's Baskets makes custom gift baskets and fruit baskets.

	Annual Growth	09/07	09/08	09/09	09/10*	12/11
Sales ($ mil.)	–	–	–	0.0	17.6	20.6
Net income ($ mil.)	–	–	–	0.0	(0.0)	0.0
Market value ($ mil.)	–	–	–	–	–	–
Employees	–	–	–	–	–	45

*Fiscal year change

ROTH STAFFING COMPANIES, L.P.

450 N STATE COLLEGE BLVD
ORANGE, CA 928681708
Phone: 714-939-8600
Fax: –
Web: www.rothstaffing.com

CEO: Ben Roth
CFO: –
HR: Edmarie Garcia
FYE: December 31
Type: Private

Roth Staffing offers temporary and temp-to-hire staffing and permanent placement services through its specialized business lines. Ultimate Staffing Services specializes in administrative customer service clerical manufacturing & production positions. Ledgent Finance & Accounting focuses on accounting and finance professionals while Ledgent Technology & Engineering concentrates on professionals in those fields. Adams & Martin Group recruits legal professionals. The company serves clients in 21 US states and Washington DC through more than 100 branches and a number of on-premise locations.

	Annual Growth	12/09	12/10	12/11	12/12	12/16
Sales ($ mil.)	9.3%	–	202.1	244.4	244.4	344.4
Net income ($ mil.)	–	–	–	0.0	0.0	0.0	7.1
Market value ($ mil.)	–	–	–	–	–	–
Employees	–	–	–	–	–	610

ROUNDY'S INC.

875 E. Wisconsin Ave.
Milwaukee WI 53202
Phone: 414-231-5000
Fax: 414-231-7939
Web: www.roundys.com

NYSE: RNDY
CEO: –
CFO: –
HR: –
FYE: December 31
Type: Public

If you live in Wisconsin you can probably find one of these grocery stores right 'round the corner. Roundy's owns and operates about 160 grocery stores in Milwaukee the Twin Cities area of Minnesota and now greater Chicago under five banners: Pick 'n Save Copps Food Centers Rainbow Foods Metro Market and its newest format Mariano's Fresh Market (launched in 2010). About 100 of the supermarkets have in-store pharmacies. Once a major food distributor to independent grocery stores in the Midwest Roundy's shed its wholesale operations to concentrate on its growing retail businesses. Founded in Milwaukee in 1872 Roundy's went public in 2012 in a offering worth $163 million.

ROUSE PROPERTIES, INC.

NYS: RSE

1114 Avenue of the Americas, Suite 2800
New York, NY 10036
Phone: 212 608-5108
Fax: –
Web: www.rouseproperties.com

CEO: Brian L Harper
CFO: –
HR: –
FYE: December 31
Type: Public

Rouse Properties wants to keep the shopping mall a part of life in small town America. The real estate investment trust (REIT) owns and manages about 35 regional malls in more than 20 states across the country. Rouse Properties' malls are located in secondary and tertiary markets where they are often the only mall in the area. With more than 23 million sq. ft. of space the company's malls house big retail names such as American Eagle Footlocker Old Navy Target and Victoria's Secret as well as sit-down restaurants (Buffalo Wild Wings Red Robin) and food court standbys (Panda Express and Starbucks). Rouse Properties was spun off from General Growth Properties in 2012.

	Annual Growth	12/10	12/11	12/12	12/13	12/14
Sales ($ mil.)	69.3%	35.5	234.8	234.0	243.5	292.1
Net income ($ mil.)	–	(2.9)	(27.0)	(68.7)	(54.7)	(51.8)
Market value ($ mil.)	4.6%	–	–	977.0	1,281.3	1,069.4
Employees	13.7%	–	225	284	269	331

ROWAN COMPANIES INC.

NYSE: RDC

2800 Post Oak Blvd. Ste. 5450
Houston TX 77056-6189
Phone: 713-621-7800
Fax: 713-960-7660
Web: www.rowancompanies.com

CEO: –
CFO: –
HR: –
FYE: December 31
Type: Public

Where does a gorilla drill for oil? Anywhere it wants if it is one of Rowan Companies' Gorilla-class heavy-duty offshore drilling rigs. Rowan performs contract drilling of oil and gas wells. Its fleet consists of more than 30 jack-up rigs. The company performs contract drilling primarily in the US (which accounts for more than one-quarter of revenues) as well as the Middle East Mexico and the North Sea. Rowan seeks to maintain its competitive edge by beefing up its current fleet of drilling rigs. It has rigs with a drilling capacity of 35000 feet in water of 550 feet depth although the new ultra-deepwater rigs will drill down to 40000 feet in water depths of 12000 feet.

ROWAN REGIONAL MEDICAL CENTER, INC.

612 MOCKSVILLE AVE
SALISBURY, NC 281442799
Phone: 704-210-5000
Fax: –

CEO: Carl Armato
CFO: –
HR: –
FYE: December 31
Type: Private

Rowan Regional Medical Center oversees medical care for residents of central North Carolina. The acute care facility has about 270 beds and provides general emergency and surgical inpatient services. It also includes a host of centers dedicated to specialty fields such as cancer care cardiac rehabilitation behavioral health pain management sleep medicine and women's health. Founded in 1936 Rowan Regional also has specialized physical and respiratory rehabilitation units and home health and hospice organizations. Rowan Regional is part of the Novant Health network.

	Annual Growth	12/13	12/14	12/15	12/16	12/17
Sales ($ mil.)	2.4%	–	187.8	197.0	207.9	201.5
Net income ($ mil.)	(13.7%)	–	16.3	21.6	22.6	10.5
Market value ($ mil.)	–	–	–	–	–	–
Employees	–	–	–	–	–	1,196

ROWLAND COFFEE ROASTERS INC.

5605 NW 82nd Ave.
Miami FL 33166
Phone: 305-594-9062
Fax: 305-594-7603
Web: www.rowlandcoffee.com

CEO: Jose Enrique Souto
CFO: –
HR: –
FYE: April 30
Type: Subsidiary

There's a rich aroma coming from Florida home of Rowland Coffee Roasters. One of North America's largest producers of coffee products the company is known for espresso. Rowland roasts some 80% of all espresso sold in the US and owns the top two Hispanic brands: Cafe Bustelo and Pilon. The company also markets European and Cabana blends (such as Cafe Estrella El Pico and Medaglia D'Oro) specialty mixes and canned coffee drinks. In addition to wholesale operations the company sells coffee online through its Java Cabana website. Established in Cuba in 1865 the previously family-run company is part of the Folgers and Kava coffee brand empire owned by J. M. Smucker which acquired the business in 2011.

ROYAL BANCSHARES OF PENNSYLVANIA INC

NMS: RBPA A

One Bala Plaza, Suite 522, 231 St. Asaph's Road
Bala Cynwyd, PA 19004
Phone: 610 668-4700
Fax: –
Web: www.royalbankamerica.com

CEO: –
CFO: –
HR: –
FYE: December 31
Type: Public

Frederick the Great never did business with this bank even though it serves a town named after him. Royal Bancshares of Pennsylvania is the holding company of Royal Bank America which operates about 15 branches in southeastern Pennsylvania (including Philadelphia and its King of Prussia suburb) and another in New Jersey. It offers products such as checking and savings accounts CDs loans and credit cards. Royal Bancshares has other units devoted to equipment leasing (Royal Leasing) commercial finance (Royal Investments America) and lender financing (RAB Capital).

	Annual Growth	12/11	12/12	12/13	12/14	12/15
Assets ($ mil.)	(1.8%)	848.4	773.7	732.3	732.6	788.3
Net income ($ mil.)	–	(8.6)	(15.6)	2.1	5.1	11.0
Market value ($ mil.)	13.7%	37.2	35.7	41.1	47.9	62.2
Employees	(5.9%)	152	152	115	117	119

ROYAL CARIBBEAN CRUISES LTD

NYS: RCL

1050 Caribbean Way
Miami, FL 33132
Phone: 305 539-6000
Fax: –
Web: www.royalcaribbean.com

CEO: Richard D. Fain
CFO: Jason Liberty
HR: Victoria Tuffy
FYE: December 31
Type: Public

Royal Caribbean Cruises is the world's second-largest cruise line (behind the combined Carnival Corporation and Carnival plc behemoth) the company operates around 60 ships with more than 135000 berths overall. Its four main brands — Royal Caribbean Celebrity Cruises Azamara Club Criuses and Silversea Cruises — carry more than 6 million passengers a year to 1000-plus ports in some 125 countries on every continent. Its other brands include Pullmantur CDF Croisi-"res de France and a 50% joint venture interest in TUI Cruises. In addition Royal Caribbean operates land-based tours and expeditions through Royal Celebrity Tours. It generates revenue from tickets and on-board goods while more than half its sales come from customers in the US.

	Annual Growth	12/14	12/15	12/16	12/17	12/18
Sales ($ mil.)	4.1%	8,073.9	8,299.1	8,496.4	8,777.8	9,493.8
Net income ($ mil.)	24.1%	764.1	665.8	1,283.4	1,625.1	1,811.0
Market value ($ mil.)	–	–	–	–	–	–
Employees	4.6%	64,300	66,100	66,100	66,100	77,100

ROYAL GOLD INC
NMS: RGLD

1144 15th Street, Suite 2500
Denver, CO 80202
Phone: 303 573-1660
Fax: –
Web: www.royalgold.com

CEO: Tony Jensen
CFO: Stefan L. Wenger
HR: –
FYE: June 30
Type: Public

Royal Gold loves royalties. Rather than operating gold mines the company buys the right to collect royalties and stream finance (a purchase arrangement that provides in exchange for an upfront deposit the right to purchase metal production from a mine at a price determined for the term of the agreement) from mine operators. This approach allows Royal Gold to minimize its exposure to the costs of mineral exploration and development. It owns interests in more than 190 properties (including producing exploration and development-stage projects) on six continents. Its operations in Chile accounts for about 15% of the company's revenues; operations in Canada 35%.

	Annual Growth	06/15	06/16	06/17	06/18	06/19
Sales ($ mil.)	11.1%	278.0	359.8	440.8	459.0	423.1
Net income ($ mil.)	15.9%	52.0	(77.1)	101.5	(113.1)	93.8
Market value ($ mil.)	13.6%	4,030.5	4,713.0	5,115.5	6,075.5	6,707.0
Employees	3.6%	20	21	23	23	23

ROYALE ENERGY INC
NBB: ROYL

1870 Cordell Court, Suite 210
El Cajon, CA 92020
Phone: 619 383-6600
Fax: –
Web: www.royl.com

CEO: –
CFO: Stephen M Hosmer
HR: –
FYE: December 31
Type: Public

The geological basins of Northern California are getting the Royale treatment. Using modern computer-aided exploration technologies Royale Energy concentrates its exploration and production efforts in the Sacramento and San Joaquin basins. The company pursues a strategy of acquiring stakes in oil and gas reserves via private joint ventures. It also owns leasehold interests in Louisana Texas and Utah. Royale Energy has estimated proved reserves of 4 billion cu. ft. of natural gas equivalent. CEO Donald Hosmer CFO Stephen Hosmer and their father and company chairman Harry Hosmer together own approximately 36% of Royale Energy. The company made a bid to buy privately held Matrix Oil in 2016.

	Annual Growth	12/14	12/15	12/16	12/17	12/18
Sales ($ mil.)	0.5%	3.2	1.7	1.2	1.0	3.3
Net income ($ mil.)	–	(2.2)	(2.0)	(4.1)	(2.4)	(23.5)
Market value ($ mil.)	(50.0%)	104.3	17.7	30.6	17.5	6.5
Employees	(13.9%)	20	15	11	11	11

RPC, INC.
NYS: RES

2801 Buford Highway, Suite 300
Atlanta, GA 30329
Phone: 404 321-2140
Fax: –
Web: www.rpc.net

CEO: Richard A. Hubbell
CFO: Ben M. Palmer
HR: –
FYE: December 31
Type: Public

RPC helps to grease the wheels of oil and gas production through a number of business units. Through its Cudd Energy Services division the company provides oil industry consulting and technical services including snubbing coiled tubing nitrogen services and well control. Another unit Patterson Services rents specialized tools and equipment such as drill pipe tubing and blowout preventers. RPC also provides maintenance emergency services and storage and inspection services for offshore and inland vessels. The company operates in most of the world's major oil producing regions.

	Annual Growth	12/14	12/15	12/16	12/17	12/18
Sales ($ mil.)	(7.4%)	2,337.4	1,263.8	729.0	1,595.2	1,721.0
Net income ($ mil.)	(8.0%)	245.2	(99.6)	(141.2)	162.5	175.4
Market value ($ mil.)	(6.7%)	2,797.6	2,563.8	4,250.1	5,477.3	2,117.5
Employees	(5.4%)	4,500	3,100	2,500	3,500	3,600

RPM INTERNATIONAL INC (DE)
NYS: RPM

P.O. Box 777, 2628 Pearl Road
Medina, OH 44258
Phone: 330 273-5090
Fax: 330 225-8743
Web: www.rpminc.com

CEO: Frank C. Sullivan
CFO: Russell L. Gordon
HR: –
FYE: May 31
Type: Public

RPM International's products like Rust-Oleum Zinsser and DAP are familiar sites on shelves of home improvement stores and consumers' workshops. Its products also are used by industrial manufacturers and contractors for bigger jobs. The company's consumer brands include do-it-yourself caulks and sealants rust preventatives and general-purpose paints repair products personal care items and hobby paints. Beyond those consumer-related products RPM offers industrial-grade products for waterproofing corrosion resistance floor maintenance and wall finishing. RPM also offers industrial cleaners restoration services equipment and colorants. The company gets two-thirds of its sales from US customers.

	Annual Growth	05/15	05/16	05/17	05/18	05/19
Sales ($ mil.)	4.9%	4,594.6	4,813.6	4,958.2	5,321.6	5,564.6
Net income ($ mil.)	2.7%	239.5	354.7	181.8	337.8	266.6
Market value ($ mil.)	1.7%	6,553.7	6,574.6	7,103.9	6,484.3	7,010.9
Employees	3.8%	12,864	13,394	14,318	14,540	14,957

RPT REALTY
NYS: RPT

19 West 44th Street, Suite 1002
New York, NY 10036
Phone: 212 221-1261
Fax: –
Web: www.rgpt.com

CEO: Dennis E. Gershenson
CFO: Geoffrey Bedrosian
HR: Karen Childress-Newberger
FYE: December 31
Type: Public

Ramco-Gershenson Properties Trust makes no bones about horning in on the retail world. A self-administered real estate investment trust (REIT) it owns develops and manages a property portfolio of about 90 shopping centers in about a dozen states east of the Mississippi River. The REIT's properties contain approximately 20 million sq. ft. of leasable space in the Midwest mid-Atlantic and Southeast. Nearly all of its assets are community shopping centers in metropolitan areas anchored by grocery or big-box stores. The REIT also owns one enclosed regional mall and one single-tenant property and has a handful of projects under development.

	Annual Growth	12/14	12/15	12/16	12/17	12/18
Sales ($ mil.)	4.5%	218.4	251.8	260.9	265.1	260.6
Net income ($ mil.)	–	(2.4)	65.1	59.7	69.1	17.6
Market value ($ mil.)	(10.6%)	1,494.2	1,324.4	1,322.0	1,174.5	952.8
Employees	(4.9%)	116	120	117	122	95

RPX CORP
NMS: RPXC

One Market Plaza, Suite 1100
San Francisco, CA 94105
Phone: 866 779-7641
Fax: –
Web: www.rpxcorp.com

CEO: Dan McCurdy
CFO: Robert H Heath
HR: –
FYE: December 31
Type: Public

In our litigious society RPX Corporation helps keep technology companies out of the courtroom. RPX owns a portfolio of more than 2500 intellectual property patents that it licenses to customers in order to prevent patent infringement lawsuits. (So one company can't sue another over a patent since it's RPX that owns the patent). Its patent portfolio spans six industries — consumer electronics software media content mobile communications and devices networking and semiconductors. RPX counts more than 250 clients including Cisco Google Sharp Sony and Verizon and earns one-third of its revenues from Asian firms. Founded in 2008 RPX launched an IPO in 2011.

	Annual Growth	12/12	12/13	12/14	12/15	12/16
Sales ($ mil.)	13.9%	197.7	237.5	259.3	291.9	333.1
Net income ($ mil.)	(17.3%)	39.0	40.8	39.3	29.1	18.2
Market value ($ mil.)	4.6%	440.9	824.3	672.1	536.5	526.8
Employees	24.3%	125	137	152	161	298

RSA SECURITY LLC

174 Middlesex Tpke.
Bedford MA 01730
Phone: 781-515-5000
Fax: 781-515-5010
Web: www.rsasecurity.com

CEO: Joseph M Tucci
CFO: –
HR: –
FYE: December 31
Type: Subsidiary

RSA Security wants everyone to show ID. The company provides software and hardware used to protect monitor and manage access to computer networks and enterprise software. A subsidiary of data storage systems maker EMC it offers Web access and digital certificate management software as well as development tools for creating encryption tools. The company's growing services segment offers data security consulting systems design and integration maintenance and training. RSA sells directly and through resellers distributors and manufacturers. Customers come from a variety of industries including telecommunications health care and financial services.

RSM MCGLADREY INC.

3600 American Blvd. West 3rd Fl.
Bloomington MN 55431
Phone: 952-921-7700
Fax: 952-921-7702
Web: www.rsmmcgladrey.com

CEO: Joseph Adams
CFO: Doug Opheim
HR: –
FYE: April 30
Type: Subsidiary

RSM McGladrey will gladly service your business if you happen to be a midsized company. The firm created in 1999 when H&R Block acquired it from McGladrey & Pullen has some 90 offices in about 25 states. The RSM McGladrey group of companies offer such services as tax consulting investment banking retirement planning wealth management and international business services to clients in industries including construction health care and manufacturing. In December 2011 RSM McGladrey was reunited with McGladrey & Pullen when its former parent bought back RSM McGladrey to reorganize itself into a more robust partnership structure capable of offering a wide array of consulting services.

RSP PERMIAN INC   NYS: RSPP

3141 Hood Street, Suite 500
Dallas, TX 75219
Phone: 214 252-2700
Fax: –
Web: www.rsppermian.com

CEO: Steven Gray
CFO: Scott McNeill
HR: –
FYE: December 31
Type: Public

RSP Permian is looking to be a permanent fixture in the US's energy supply. The company explores for and produces hard-to-find oil natural gas and natural gas liquids in the Permian Basin of West Texas. It drills horizontal wells (the better to find deeply buried natural resources) and has working interests in about 325 producing wells. RSP Permian reports estimated proved oil and natural gas reserves of 52 million barrels of oil equivalent (MBoe) (62% oil 21% natural gas liquids and 17% natural gas). It has an average daily production of about 5000 MBoe. Formed in 2010 the company went public in 2014 raising $390 million.

	Annual Growth	12/12	12/13	12/14	12/15	12/16
Sales ($ mil.)	35.7%	104.4	–	281.9	284.0	353.9
Net income ($ mil.)	–	35.9	–	2.5	(18.3)	(24.9)
Market value ($ mil.)	33.2%	–	–	3,568.0	3,461.5	6,332.6
Employees	34.6%	35	36	79	99	115

RTI INTERNATIONAL METALS, INC.   NYS: RTI

Westpointe Corporate Center One, 5th Floor, 1550 Coraopolis Heights Road
Pittsburgh, PA 15108-2973
Phone: 412 893-0026
Fax: 330 544-7876
Web: www.rtiintl.com

CEO: –
CFO: –
HR: –
FYE: December 31
Type: Public

RTI International Metals has titanium on the cranium. Through its Titanium Group the company produces ingots bars plates sheets strips pipes wire and welded tubing used primarily by the aerospace industry to make bulkheads tail sections engine components and wing supports. Fabrication and Distribution groups operate through subsidiary RTI Energy Systems making pipe and tubing for offshore oil and gas exploration and production as well as geothermal energy production. RTI caters to commercial aerospace and defense industries which represent almost 80% of sales and a growing number of industrial and consumer customers.

	Annual Growth	12/09	12/10	12/11	12/12	12/13
Sales ($ mil.)	17.7%	408.0	431.8	529.7	738.6	783.3
Net income ($ mil.)	–	(67.2)	3.4	6.6	23.5	14.1
Market value ($ mil.)	8.0%	770.0	825.4	710.1	843.2	1,046.6
Employees	13.3%	1,478	1,534	1,729	2,362	2,437

RTI SURGICAL HOLDINGS INC   NMS: RTIX

520 Lake Cook Road, Suite 315
Deerfield, IL 60015
Phone: 877 343-6832
Fax: –
Web: www.rtix.com

CEO: Robert P. (Rob) Jordheim
CFO: Wy Louw
HR: Paul Montague
FYE: December 31
Type: Public

When it comes to surgical implants RTI Surgical (formerly RTI Biologics) recommends the natural alternative. The firm develops products made from human and animal tissue that are used in orthopedic dental and other surgeries to repair fractures spinal disorders sports injuries breast reconstruction and other procedures. Using its BioCleanse Cancelle SP and Tutoplast processes the company sterilizes tissue — including bone tendons and skin — that is then used in surgeries. RTI Surgical sells its allografts (made from human tissue) and xenografts (made from animals) in the US and more than 50 countries around the globe. Its direct sales force targets the sports medicine and general orthopedic markets.

	Annual Growth	12/14	12/15	12/16	12/17	12/18
Sales ($ mil.)	1.7%	262.8	282.3	272.9	279.6	280.9
Net income ($ mil.)	–	2.7	14.9	(14.4)	6.3	(1.3)
Market value ($ mil.)	(8.2%)	330.0	252.0	206.3	260.2	234.8
Employees	(5.2%)	1,102	1,169	1,140	942	891

RTW RETAILWINDS INC   NYS: RTW

330 West 34th Street, 9th Floor
New York, NY 10001
Phone: 212 884-2000
Fax: –
Web: www.nyandcompany.com

CEO: Gregory (Greg) Scott
CFO: Sheamus Toal
HR: Faeth Bradley
FYE: February 02
Type: Public

RTW Retailwinds (formerly New York & Company) caters to working women ages 25 to 49 looking for moderately priced apparel (jeans dresses and coordinates) and accessories (sunglasses jewelry and handbags). It offers proprietary branded fashions at more than 400 stores in about three dozen US states and online. The company sells merchandise under the New York & Company and Fashion to Figure names and has collaborations with celebrities such as Eva Mendes Gabrielle Union and Kate Hudson. RTW Retailwinds was founded in 1918 and changed its name from New York & Company in late 2018.

	Annual Growth	01/15	01/16	01/17*	02/18	02/19
Sales ($ mil.)	(0.8%)	923.3	950.1	929.1	926.9	893.2
Net income ($ mil.)	–	(16.9)	(10.1)	(17.3)	5.7	4.2
Market value ($ mil.)	8.1%	149.1	142.6	138.7	195.8	203.5
Employees	(4.8%)	6,400	6,282	5,885	6,789	5,255

*Fiscal year change

1143

RUBICON TECHNOLOGY INC
NAS: RBCN

900 East Green Street
Bensenville, IL 60106
Phone: 847 295-7000
Fax: –
Web: www.rubicon-es2.com

CEO: Timothy Brog
CFO: Inga A Slavutsky
HR: –
FYE: December 31
Type: Public

Sapphires are the jewel in Rubicon Technology's crown. Using proprietary crystal growth technology Rubicon makes sapphire materials wafers and components for a variety of products. In the field of optoelectronics the vertically integrated company makes sapphire components for light-emitting diodes (LEDs) used in cell phones video screens and other items. Rubicon's sapphire materials also are used for compound semiconductor manufacturing and laser imaging. In the telecom sector the company's silicon materials are in demand for the silicon-on-sapphire (SOS) components of cellular and fiber-optics products. The majority of its sales are to customers in Asia.

	Annual Growth	12/14	12/15	12/16	12/17	12/18
Sales ($ mil.)	(46.0%)	45.7	23.8	19.6	5.0	3.9
Net income ($ mil.)	–	(44.0)	(77.8)	(62.9)	(17.9)	1.0
Market value ($ mil.)	14.7%	12.5	3.1	1.6	21.8	21.6
Employees	(51.2%)	283	244	53	21	16

RUBY TUESDAY, INC.
NYS: RT

150 West Church Avenue
Maryville, TN 37801
Phone: 865 379-5700
Fax: –
Web: www.rubytuesday.com

CEO: Ray Blanchette
CFO: Sue Briley
HR: –
FYE: May 31
Type: Public

The patrons of this US restaurant chain are hopefully well fed when it's time to say good bye. Ruby Tuesday (RTI) which takes its name from the song by the Rolling Stones operates a nationwide chain of casual-dining restaurants. There are about 550 company-owned Ruby Tuesday locations in the US. The company also has 18 franchised locations in the US and 50 franchised international outposts. The full-service eateries offer a menu of American and ethnic foods including burgers fajitas pasta ribs seafood steak and a variety of appetizers.

	Annual Growth	06/12	06/13	06/14	06/15*	05/16
Sales ($ mil.)	(4.8%)	1,325.8	1,251.5	1,168.7	1,126.6	1,091.2
Net income ($ mil.)	–	(0.2)	(39.4)	(64.3)	(3.2)	(50.7)
Market value ($ mil.)	(13.1%)	408.9	571.3	462.5	370.4	233.3
Employees	(5.5%)	36,300	34,100	33,000	32,100	28,900

*Fiscal year change

RUCKUS WIRELESS INC
NYS: RKUS

350 West Java Drive
Sunnyvale, CA 94089
Phone: 650 265-4200
Fax: –
Web: www.ruckuswireless.com

CEO: Ken Cheng
CFO: Jean Furter
HR: Kathleen Swift
FYE: December 31
Type: Public

When a crowd of Internet users generates a ruckus of signals Ruckus Wireless aims to smooth the commotion and get everyone connected. Ruckus makes network gateways controllers and access points used to provide and manage large-scale Wi-Fi access in office buildings hospitals stadiums and the Internet of Things. Its Smart-branded products help Internet and telecom providers extend range and reliability and offer scalability for rapidly growing companies. Ruckus sells worldwide through a network of more than 5300 resellers and distributors to about 48000 customers in a variety of industries. Its customers have included Bright House Networks Time Warner Cable Sky plc and KDDI. The company formed in 2002 as Sceos Technologies and went public in late 2012.

	Annual Growth	12/10	12/11	12/12	12/13	12/14
Sales ($ mil.)	44.3%	75.5	120.0	214.7	263.1	326.9
Net income ($ mil.)	–	(4.4)	4.2	31.7	1.8	8.2
Market value ($ mil.)	(27.0%)	–	–	1,917.5	1,208.6	1,023.0
Employees	15.8%	–	606	669	824	940

RUDOLPH AND SLETTEN, INC.

2 CIRCLE STAR WAY FL 4
SAN CARLOS, CA 940706200
Phone: 650-216-3600
Fax: –

CEO: Martin B Sisemore
CFO: Terry Huie
HR: –
FYE: December 31
Type: Private

Rudolph and Sletten ... the little-known tenth reindeer? More like the elves who built Santa's workshop. The firm is a mainstay of the California construction scene especially Silicon Valley. It has built corporate campuses for Apple Microsoft and Wells Fargo as well as Lucasfilm's Skywalker Ranch production facility. Rudolph and Sletten is one of the US' largest general building contractors with site selection design/build and construction management capabilities. Key projects also include biotech labs hospitals and schools. Onslow "Rudy" Rudolph founded the company in 1959 and was joined by partner Kenneth Sletten in 1962. Rudolph and Sletten is a subsidiary of Tutor Perini Corporation .

	Annual Growth	12/12	12/13	12/14	12/15	12/16
Sales ($ mil.)	25.2%	–	666.0	637.1	940.4	1,307.8
Net income ($ mil.)	–	–	–	(0.0)	3.2	7.0	14.9
Market value ($ mil.)	–	–	–	–	–	–
Employees	–	–	–	–	–	700

RUDOLPH TECHNOLOGIES, INC.
NYS: RTEC

16 Jonspin Road
Wilmington, MA 01887
Phone: 978 253-6200
Fax: –
Web: www.rudolphtech.com

CEO: Michael P Plisinski
CFO: Steven R Roth
HR: –
FYE: December 31
Type: Public

Rudolph Technologies' inspection and metrology systems lead the way to better yields for chip makers. To create semiconductors manufacturers deposit precise layers of conducting and insulating materials on silicon wafers. Rudolph's process control metrology equipment monitors these layers to ensure that the material doesn't get too thick or too thin. Its inspection equipment (around half of sales) looks for defects not obvious to the human eye such as tiny scratches or gouges in the surface of a silicon wafer. The company also makes a range of data analysis and process control software. Rudolph gets about two-thirds of sales from customers outside the US.

	Annual Growth	12/13	12/14	12/15	12/16	12/17
Sales ($ mil.)	9.7%	176.2	181.2	221.7	232.8	255.1
Net income ($ mil.)	75.6%	3.5	(4.6)	18.0	37.0	32.9
Market value ($ mil.)	19.5%	371.0	323.3	449.4	738.0	755.3
Employees	(0.9%)	615	586	572	579	592

RUMSEY ELECTRIC COMPANY

15 COLWELL LN
CONSHOHOCKEN, PA 194281878
Phone: 610-832-9000
Fax: –
Web: www.rumsey.com

CEO: Gerald M. (Jerry) Lihota
CFO: Scott M. Cutler
HR: –
FYE: December 31
Type: Private

Rumsey Electric distributes electrical construction equipment utility products and services and systems for relay and power and lighting for retailers. Operating through one central distribution facility and a dozen branches the company caters to construction and industrial businesses and utilities as well as OEMs institutions and commercial Mid-Atlantic markets. It is the authorized distributor of Rockwell Automation a large industrial automation firm. The company operates through its 135000 sq. ft. central distribution facility and 11 branch locations primarily located in Delaware Pennsylvania and New Jersey. Employee-owned Rumsey Electric has been in business for over 110 years.

	Annual Growth	12/14	12/15	12/16	12/17	12/18
Sales ($ mil.)	(0.4%)	–	223.1	218.2	211.8	220.6
Net income ($ mil.)	9.3%	–	8.0	7.2	11.7	10.5
Market value ($ mil.)	–	–	–	–	–	–
Employees	–	–	–	–	–	284

RUSH ENTERPRISES INC.
NMS: RUSH A

555 I.H. 35 South, Suite 500
New Braunfels, TX 78130
Phone: 830 302-5200
Fax: –
Web: www.rushenterprises.com

CEO: W. M. (Rusty) Rush
CFO: Steven L. (Steve) Keller
HR: –
FYE: December 31
Type: Public

Rush Enterprises has been truckin' along as a heavy-duty commercial vehicle dealer since 1965. The company operates a growing network of more than 100 commercial vehicle and service dealerships under the name Rush Truck Centers in some 21 states. It is one of the largest Peterbilt truck dealers in the US but it also sells trucks manufactured by Blue Bird Ford Isuzu Hino Mitsubishi Fuso and IC Bus. Additionally Rush offers aftermarket parts and services such as body shop repairs insurance and third-party financing and rentals and leasing. Founded in 1965 Rush's reach has spread as far as California and Florida. Late chairman W. Marvin Rush's family control the rapidly growing company.

	Annual Growth	12/14	12/15	12/16	12/17	12/18
Sales ($ mil.)	3.9%	4,727.4	4,979.7	4,214.6	4,713.9	5,506.2
Net income ($ mil.)	14.8%	80.0	66.1	40.6	172.1	139.1
Market value ($ mil.)	1.8%	1,185.8	809.9	1,180.3	1,880.0	1,275.8
Employees	3.5%	6,297	6,700	6,180	6,825	7,214

RUSH-COPLEY MEDICAL CENTER, INC.

2000 OGDEN AVE
AURORA, IL 605045893
Phone: 630-978-6200
Fax: –
Web: www.rushcopley.com

CEO: John Diederich
CFO: –
HR: –
FYE: June 30
Type: Private

People in a rush to get healthy can find help at Rush-Copley Medical Center. A member of the Rush System for Health family the medical center serves Illinois' Fox Valley area. The hospital has about 210 beds and provides acute and tertiary medical services including cardiac care cancer treatment neurology women's services neonatal care and health education programs. Its Rush-Copley Surgery Center performs both day surgeries and inpatient procedures while its nearby Rush-Copley Healthcare Center houses doctors' offices and offers outpatient diagnostic imaging services. Other programs include a neuroscience center a home health care agency and its Healthplex fitness center.

	Annual Growth	06/09	06/10	06/11	06/12	06/13
Sales ($ mil.)	–	–	–	(624.0)	296.8	319.9
Net income ($ mil.)	4919.1%	–	–	0.0	17.7	41.3
Market value ($ mil.)	–	–	–	–	–	–
Employees	–	–	–	–	–	2,000

RUSSELL SIGLER, INC.

9702 W TONTO ST
TOLLESON, AZ 853539703
Phone: 623-388-5100
Fax: –
Web: www.siglers.com

CEO: –
CFO: Robert D Osborne
HR: –
FYE: December 31
Type: Private

Russell Sigler has built a business providing a rather cool service in a hot region. Through about 30 offices located primarily in California and Arizona (but also in Idaho Nevada New Mexico and Texas) the company provides commercial and residential air conditioning contractors with equipment parts supplies and technical support. Its brands include Carrier Bryant and Payne. Russell Sigler has distributed Carrier products for more than 60 years. As part of its business the company also operates a residential and commercial distribution joint venture with industry giant Carrier. Russell Sigler owns a 60% stake while Carrier holds 40%.

	Annual Growth	12/07	12/08	12/09	12/13	12/14
Sales ($ mil.)	19.4%	–	176.9	140.2	488.7	513.4
Net income ($ mil.)	38.4%	–	1.5	(0.5)	6.6	10.2
Market value ($ mil.)	–	–	–	–	–	–
Employees	–	–	–	–	–	550

RUTH'S HOSPITALITY GROUP INC
NMS: RUTH

1030 W. Canton Avenue, Suite 100
Winter Park, FL 32789
Phone: 407 333-7440
Fax: –
Web: www.rhgi.com

CEO: Michael P. O'Donnell
CFO: Arne G. Haak
HR: –
FYE: December 30
Type: Public

High end and "chain restaurant" are not mutually exclusive terms for this company. Ruth's Hospitality Group is one of the largest upscale dining operators in the country with some 160 restaurants anchored by the Ruth's Chris Steak House chain. Boasting about 140 restaurants in 30 states and some international markets Ruth's Chris is the largest high-end steak house chain in terms of number of locations. Its menu features a variety of steak cuts along with lamb veal and fresh seafood. About 65 of the restaurants are company-owned and 95 are franchised. In 2014 Ruth's Hospitality agreed to sell its Mitchell's Fish Market restaurants to Landry's.

	Annual Growth	12/14	12/15	12/16	12/17	12/18
Sales ($ mil.)	6.9%	346.1	373.4	385.9	414.8	452.3
Net income ($ mil.)	26.2%	16.5	30.0	30.5	30.1	41.7
Market value ($ mil.)	11.8%	421.2	469.8	534.2	633.7	657.1
Employees	5.6%	4,342	4,350	4,728	4,915	5,408

RUTHERFORD ELECTRIC MEMBERSHIP CORPORATION

186 HUDLOW RD
FOREST CITY, NC 280432575
Phone: 704-245-1621
Fax: –
Web: www.remc.com

CEO: –
CFO: –
HR: –
FYE: December 31
Type: Private

Through a kind of power sharing "brotherhood" Rutherford Electric Membership Corporation provides power to more than 67000 members located in 10 counties (Burke Catawba Caldwell Cleveland Gaston Lincoln McDowell Mitchell Polk and Rutherford) in the Southwestern Piedmont region of North Carolina. The cooperative (which had a membership of only 394 in 1938 but grew rapidly after WWII) owns and maintains about 7000 miles of power line. Rutherford Electric has total assets of more than $300 million. The cooperative is a member of the Touchstone Energy Cooperatives network.

	Annual Growth	12/08	12/09	12/14	12/15	12/16
Sales ($ mil.)	2.3%	–	118.4	134.3	136.9	138.4
Net income ($ mil.)	(48.0%)	–	10.4	(2.1)	(0.5)	0.1
Market value ($ mil.)	–	–	–	–	–	–
Employees	–	–	–	–	–	178

RVUE HOLDINGS INC
NBB: RVUE

17W220 22nd Street, Suite 200
Oakbrook Terrace, IL 60181
Phone: 855 261-8370
Fax: –
Web: www.rvue.com

CEO: –
CFO: –
HR: –
FYE: December 31
Type: Public

rYou ready to reach your target audience? rVue brings advertisers and consumers together. Through its flagship rVue platform the company helps agencies and advertisers plan media campaigns by delivering proprietary advertising content directly to retail outlets (where people are ready to buy) and other venues for its advertising clients. rVue partners with companies that provide digital signage networks installed across the US playing ads infotainment and other programming aimed at increasing sales. Content is tweaked based on performance reports and sales figures reported by stores.

	Annual Growth	12/11	12/12	12/13	12/14	12/15
Sales ($ mil.)	14.3%	0.6	0.6	0.7	1.3	1.1
Net income ($ mil.)	–	(3.6)	(3.8)	(2.1)	(0.9)	(1.4)
Market value ($ mil.)	(37.3%)	43.4	12.1	15.6	18.2	6.7
Employees	(15.9%)	14	7	9	9	7

RW STEARNS INC.

201 Mission St. Ste. 2030
San Francisco CA 94105
Phone: 415-593-1000
Fax: 415-593-1001
Web: www.rwstearns.com

CEO: Jay M Stearns
CFO: -
HR: -
FYE: December 31
Type: Private

RW Stearns puts the "hunt" in executive head-hunting — researching information for corporate recruiting sales leads or comparisons with competitors. Utilizing its proprietary database of more than 1 million names titles and organizational structures the company furnishes custom research reports and offers profiling services to businesses ranging from startups to the FORTUNE 1000. Over the years the company has increased its competitive intelligence services offering benchmarking strategic recruiting and mapping competitors' organizational and employment structures. RW Stearns serves all industries but has roots in the high-tech biotech and pharmaceutical sectors. The company was founded in 1984.

RYAN BUILDING GROUP, INC.

2700 PATRIOT BLVD STE 430
GLENVIEW, IL 600268078
Phone: 847-995-8700
Fax: -
Web: www.williamryanhomes.com

CEO: -
CFO: John Rushin
HR: -
FYE: December 31
Type: Private

Ryan Building Group understands that there's no place like home there's no place like home there's no place like home. Doing business as William Ryan Homes the company builds and sells single-family homes townhouses and duplexes in Arizona Florida Illinois Texas and Wisconsin. Its homes have from two to five bedrooms and range in size from 1400 sq. ft. to about 3500 sq. ft. The company also offers mortgages and insurance through affiliates. CEO William Ryan (part of the building family that also spawned the Ryland Group) founded Ryan Building Group in 1992.

	Annual Growth	12/04	12/05	12/06	12/07	12/08
Sales ($ mil.)	(78.7%)	-	-	1,831.8	214.2	83.4
Net income ($ mil.)	-	-	-	0.0	(0.5)	(19.3)
Market value ($ mil.)	-	-	-	-	-	-
Employees	-	-	-	-	-	85

RYAN, LLC

13155 NOEL RD STE 100
DALLAS, TX 752405050
Phone: 972-934-0022
Fax: -
Web: www.ryan.com

CEO: G. Brint Ryan
CFO: Kandis Thompson
HR: -
FYE: December 31
Type: Private

Ryan is the largest tax services and software provider in the world that is focused solely focused on business taxes. The company provides tax advice preparation and planning for major corporations and other businesses. The firm specializes in consulting services such as audit defense dispute resolution strategic planning tax process efficiencies and tax recovery. Headquartered in Dallas Ryan addresses a wide range of industries including blockchain and cryptocurrency business services construction food services healthcare manufacturing energy real estate and retail. It has roughly 50 offices in more than 30 US states and 40 countries across North America the Asia-Pacific region and Europe.

	Annual Growth	12/10	12/11	12/12	12/13	12/14
Sales ($ mil.)	20.6%	-	225.3	242.0	382.6	394.7
Net income ($ mil.)	(10.6%)	-	25.2	9.9	39.6	18.0
Market value ($ mil.)	-	-	-	-	-	-
Employees	-	-	-	-	-	1,598

RYDER SYSTEM, INC.   NYS: R

11690 N.W., 105th Street
Miami, FL 33178
Phone: 305 500-3726
Fax: -
Web: www.ryder.com

CEO: Robert E. Sanchez
CFO: Art A. Garcia
HR: Amparo Bared
FYE: December 31
Type: Public

When it comes to commercial vehicles and distribution Ryder System wants to be the designated driver. The company's Fleet Management Solutions (FMS) segment acquires manages and maintains fleet vehicles for commercial customers. Similarly the Supply Chain Solutions (SCS) segment provides logistics and supply chain services from industrial start to finish?raw material supply to product distribution. SCS also offers dedicated contract carriage service by supplying trucks drivers and management and administrative services to customers on a contract basis. Ryder's worldwide fleet of more than 270000 vehicles ranges from tractor-trailers to light-duty trucks and more recently electric trucks. The majority of its revenue comes from the US.

	Annual Growth	12/14	12/15	12/16	12/17	12/18
Sales ($ mil.)	6.1%	6,638.8	6,571.9	6,787.0	7,329.6	8,409.2
Net income ($ mil.)	5.7%	218.6	304.8	262.5	790.6	273.3
Market value ($ mil.)	(15.1%)	4,931.9	3,018.6	3,954.0	4,470.8	2,557.6
Employees	6.7%	30,600	33,100	34,500	36,100	39,600

RYERSON HOLDING CORP   NYS: RYI

227 W. Monroe St., 27th Floor
Chicago, IL 60606
Phone: 312 292-5000
Fax: -
Web: www.ir.ryerson.com

CEO: Edward J. (Eddie) Lehner
CFO: Erich S. Schnaufer
HR: -
FYE: December 31
Type: Public

Aspiring to be the one-stop shop for all your metal needs Ryerson is a leading industrial metal processor and distributor in North America with some 70000 products to its name. Majority of its revenue comes from buying bulk metals in sheets and bar forms and processing them to meet client specifications. Products range from pipes and valves to roofing flooring and grating tools. Ryerson is also well known for providing fabrication services with 100 locations across the US Mexico Canada and China. Its 40000 customers include various machinery manufacturers fabricators and shops.

	Annual Growth	12/14	12/15	12/16	12/17	12/18
Sales ($ mil.)	5.0%	3,622.2	3,167.2	2,859.7	3,364.7	4,408.4
Net income ($ mil.)	-	(25.7)	(0.5)	18.7	17.1	106.0
Market value ($ mil.)	(10.6%)	371.8	174.9	499.9	389.4	237.4
Employees	4.2%	3,650	6,800	3,000	3,300	4,300

RYLAND GROUP, INC.   NYS: RYL

3011 Townsgate Road, Suite 200
Westlake Village, CA 91361-3027
Phone: 805 367-3800
Fax: -
Web: www.ryland.com

CEO: -
CFO: -
HR: -
FYE: December 31
Type: Public

Building the American dream is home sweet home for The Ryland Group. The homebuilder founded by James Ryan and Bob Gaw in 1967 constructs single-family detached homes as well as attached condominiums for entry-level first- and second-time move-up and retired buyers. Ryland has constructed more than 300000 homes in hundreds of communities around the US. The average price for a Ryland Home is around $260000. The company offers services that span the homeownership process. Homebuyers can select custom home finishes at a My Style Design Center. The group also provides mortgage financing title and escrow and insurance services.

	Annual Growth	12/09	12/10	12/11	12/12	12/13
Sales ($ mil.)	13.6%	1,283.6	1,063.9	890.7	1,308.5	2,140.8
Net income ($ mil.)	-	(162.5)	(85.1)	(50.8)	40.4	379.2
Market value ($ mil.)	21.8%	910.8	787.4	728.7	1,687.6	2,007.1
Employees	8.2%	1,019	991	922	1,100	1,395

RYMAN HOSPITALITY PROPERTIES INC — NYS: RHP

One Gaylord Drive
Nashville, TN 37214
Phone: 615-316-6000
Fax: –
Web: www.rymanhp.com
CEO: Colin V. Reed
CFO: Mark Fioravanti
HR: Shawn Smith
FYE: December 31
Type: Public

Ryman Hospitality Properties (formerly Gaylord Entertainment) may be hollerin' for attention in the hospitality game but it's no corporate hayseed. Its properties consist of resort hotels tethered closely to attractions that appeal to the meetings and conventions market. They include the Gaylord Opryland Resort & Convention Center in Nashville the Gaylord Palms Resort in Florida (close to Disney World) the Gaylord Texan Resort near Dallas and the Gaylord National Resort and Convention Center in the Washington DC area. Ryman's hotels are managed by hotel giant Marriott. In 2012 the company changed its name convered to a REIT and sold its hotel brand and management business to Marriott.

	Annual Growth	12/14	12/15	12/16	12/17	12/18
Sales ($ mil.)	5.2%	1,041.0	1,092.1	1,149.2	1,184.7	1,275.1
Net income ($ mil.)	20.3%	126.5	111.5	159.4	176.1	264.7
Market value ($ mil.)	6.0%	2,707.5	2,651.0	3,234.7	3,543.2	3,423.6
Employees	13.0%	682	746	807	899	1,113

RYMAN HOSPITALITY PROPERTIES, INC.

1 GAYLORD DR
NASHVILLE, TN 372141207
Phone: 615-316-6000
Fax: –
Web: www.rymanhp.com
CEO: Colin V. Reed
CFO: Mark Fioravanti
HR: Shawn Smith
FYE: December 31
Type: Private

Ryman Hospitality Properties (formerly Gaylord Entertainment) may be hollerin' for attention in the hospitality game but it's no corporate hayseed. Its properties consist of resort hotels tethered closely to attractions that appeal to the meetings and conventions market. They include the Gaylord Opryland Resort & Convention Center in Nashville the Gaylord Palms Resort in Florida (close to Disney World) the Gaylord Texan Resort near Dallas and the Gaylord National Resort and Convention Center in the Washington DC area. Ryman's hotels are managed by hotel giant Marriott. In 2012 the company changed its name convered to a REIT and sold its hotel brand and management business to Marriott.

	Annual Growth	12/12	12/13	12/14	12/15	12/16
Assets ($ mil.)	(0.3%)	–	2,424.6	2,413.1	2,331.4	2,405.8
Net income ($ mil.)	12.0%	–	113.5	126.5	111.5	159.4
Market value ($ mil.)	–	–	–	–	–	–
Employees	–	–	–	–	–	1,000

S & B ENGINEERS AND CONSTRUCTORS, LTD.

7825 PARK PLACE BLVD
HOUSTON, TX 770874697
Phone: 713-645-4141
Fax: –
Web: www.sbec.com
CEO: –
CFO: –
HR: Ralph Morales
FYE: December 31
Type: Private

S & B Engineers and Constructors makes it possible for others to burn the midnight oil. The employee-owned company specializes in engineering procurement and construction of process plants in the chemical petrochemical refining power generation infrastructure and pulp and paper industries. S&B also flexes its engineering muscle on transportation waste and wastewater and environmental and telecommunications projects for public sector clients. Founded in 1967 by James Slaughter and William Brookshire to serve refineries and other process plants along the Texas and Louisiana gulf coasts the company has expanded services globally with two offices in India.

	Annual Growth	12/12	12/13	12/16	12/17	12/18
Sales ($ mil.)	–	–	0.0	950.2	679.5	679.5
Net income ($ mil.)	–	–	0.0	0.0	0.0	0.0
Market value ($ mil.)	–	–	–	–	–	–
Employees	–	–	–	–	–	2,400

S & T BANCORP INC (INDIANA, PA) — NMS: STBA

800 Philadelphia Street
Indiana, PA 15701
Phone: 800-325-2265
Fax: –
Web: www.stbancorp.com
CEO: Todd D. Brice
CFO: Mark Kochvar
HR: –
FYE: December 31
Type: Public

S&T Bancorp is the bank holding company for S&T Bank which boasts nearly $5 billion in assets and serves customers from some 60 branch offices in western Pennsylvania. Targeting individuals and local businesses the bank offers such standard retail products as checking savings and money market accounts CDs and credit cards. Business loans including commercial mortgages make up more than 80% of the company's loan portfolio. The bank also originates residential mortgages construction loans and consumer loans. Through subsidiaries S&T Bank sells life disability and commercial property/casualty insurance provides investment management services and advises the Stewart Capital Mid Cap Fund.

	Annual Growth	12/13	12/14	12/16	12/17	12/18
Assets ($ mil.)	9.9%	4,533.2	4,964.7	6,943.1	7,060.3	7,252.2
Net income ($ mil.)	15.8%	50.5	57.9	71.4	73.0	105.3
Market value ($ mil.)	8.4%	877.8	1,033.9	1,354.1	1,380.8	1,312.4
Employees	1.9%	948	945	1,080	1,080	1,040

S&ME, INC.

2724 DISCOVERY DR STE 120
RALEIGH, NC 276161940
Phone: 919-872-2660
Fax: –
Web: www.smeinc.com
CEO: –
CFO: Bruce L Altstaetter
HR: –
FYE: December 31
Type: Private

This is not your S&ME old engineering company. S&ME which services both public and private entities focuses on environmental and engineering services. The company's main areas of expertise are: geotechnical engineering; environmental engineering; natural and cultural resource preservation; occupational health and safety; constructional materials engineering and testing; and water resources and solid waste engineering. The employee-owned company which mainly serves clients in the Southeast operates from more than 26 offices in nine US states.

	Annual Growth	12/12	12/13	12/14	12/16	12/17
Sales ($ mil.)	7.1%	–	121.8	133.6	174.2	160.5
Net income ($ mil.)	28.9%	–	1.6	2.8	2.6	4.5
Market value ($ mil.)	–	–	–	–	–	–
Employees	–	–	–	–	–	1,115

S&P GLOBAL INC — NYS: SPGI

55 Water Street
New York, NY 10041
Phone: 212-438-1000
Fax: –
Web: www.spglobal.com
CEO: Douglas L. (Doug) Peterson
CFO: Ewout L. Steenbergen
HR: France M. Gingras
FYE: December 31
Type: Public

Say "AAA!". One of the big-three credit ratings agencies S&P Global (formerly McGraw-Hill Financial) assigns companies local governments and countries its well-known credit scores ranging from D (lowest) to AAA (highest). It also assigns ratings to corporate or municipal bonds and other individual debt issues. S&P Global's other businesses include S&P Global Market Intelligence S&P Dow Jones Indices and S&P Global Platts. Its largest market is the US which generates around 60% of the company's revenue. After it sold its education and construction businesses in 2016 the company changed its name from McGraw-Hill Financial to S&P Global.

	Annual Growth	12/15	12/16	12/17	12/18	12/19
Sales ($ mil.)	6.0%	5,313.0	5,661.0	6,063.0	6,258.0	6,699.0
Net income ($ mil.)	16.4%	1,156.0	2,106.0	1,496.0	1,958.0	2,123.0
Market value ($ mil.)	29.0%	24,053.5	26,239.8	41,333.6	41,465.4	66,624.2
Employees	2.5%	20,400	20,000	20,400	21,200	22,500

S&W SEED CO.
NAS: SANW

2101 Ken Pratt Blvd, Suite 201
Longmont, CO 80501
Phone: 559 884-2535
Fax: –
Web: www.swseedco.com

CEO: Mark W Wong
CFO: Matthew K Szot
HR: –
FYE: June 30
Type: Public

S&W Seed breeds seeds of the alfalfa variety. The agricultural company contracts locally grown alfalfa seeds from farmers in California's San Joaquin Valley processes them at its production facility and sells them to agribusinesses and farmers worldwide for use in growing animal feed — particularly alfalfa hay — for dairy and beef cattle horses and other livestock. About 50% of its certified seeds are sold to customers in the Middle East and Latin America since the varieties it produces are better suited for warmer climates. S&W Seed also produces wheat on occasion and supplies PureCircle with stevia a natural no-calorie sweetener. The company went public in May 2010.

	Annual Growth	06/15	06/16	06/17	06/18	06/19
Sales ($ mil.)	7.8%	81.2	96.0	75.4	64.1	109.7
Net income ($ mil.)	–	(3.2)	0.4	(11.8)	(4.7)	(9.3)
Market value ($ mil.)	(14.2%)	162.4	145.1	138.1	108.2	87.9
Employees	15.0%	72	77	78	84	126

S. D. WARREN COMPANY

255 State St.
Boston MA 02109
Phone: 617-423-7300
Fax: +82-2-3777-3428
Web: www.lge.com

CEO: –
CFO: Annette Luchene
HR: –
FYE: September 30
Type: Subsidiary

There's nothing sticky about Sappi. Sappi Fine Paper North America (SFPNA) the dba for S.D. Warren Company produces fine paper for use in annual reports magazines and high-end advertising. SFPNA's high-end paper includes coated specialty and uncoated fine papers marketed under multiple brands including the mill-branded LOE (Lustro Offset Environmental) paper the first premium sheet to use 30% post-consumer waste content. It also produces graphic and packaging paper and bleached chemical pulp. Since 1995 SFPNA has operated as a subsidiary of South Africa-based Sappi Limited. It touts a production capacity of 1.3 million tons a year.

S.C. JOHNSON & SON INC.

1525 Howe St.
Racine WI 53403-5011
Phone: 262-260-2000
Fax: 262-260-6004
Web: www.scjohnson.com

CEO: H Fisk Johnson
CFO: –
HR: –
FYE: June 30
Type: Private

S.C. Johnson & Son has helped to make the flyswatter a thing of the past with its pest control in a can. It's one of the world's largest makers of consumer chemical products boasting big brands such as Raid OFF! Glade Mr. Muscle Pledge Drano fantastik Scrubbing Bubbles Shout Vanish Windex and Ziploc among others. S.C. Johnson founded in 1886 sells its products in more than 70 countries. The founder's great-grandson and once one of the richest men in the US Samuel Johnson died in 2004. His immediate family owns about 60% of the company; descendants of the founder's daughter own about 40%. Chairman Dr. Fisk Johnson assumed the title of CEO when president and CEO Bill Perez left for NIKE in 2004.

SABINE ROYALTY TRUST
NYS: SBR

Simmons Bank, Park Place, 2911 Turtle Creek Boulevard, Suite 850
Dallas, TX 75219
Phone: 855 588-7839
Fax: 214 508-2431
Web: www.sbr-sabine.com

CEO: –
CFO: –
HR: –
FYE: December 31
Type: Public

Sabine Royalty Trust owns royalty interests in oil and gas properties located on about 2.1 million gross acres (216551 net) in Florida Louisiana Mississippi New Mexico Oklahoma and Texas. The trust which was formed in 1983 receives royalties based on the amount of oil and gas produced and sold and distributes them on a monthly basis to shareholders. Although royalty trusts distribute essentially all royalties received to shareholders (at substantial tax advantage) their profitability depends on the price of oil and gas and the continued productivity of the properties. Sabine Royalty Trust's properties have proved reserves of about 5.3 million barrels of oil and 35.6 billion cu. ft. of natural gas.

	Annual Growth	12/14	12/15	12/16	12/17	12/18
Sales ($ mil.)	(3.7%)	61.1	48.4	30.0	37.2	52.5
Net income ($ mil.)	(4.0%)	58.7	46.0	27.5	34.7	49.9
Market value ($ mil.)	1.0%	521.6	382.9	512.5	650.2	543.5
Employees	–	–	–	–	–	–

SABRA HEALTH CARE REIT INC
NMS: SBRA

18500 Von Karman Avenue, Suite 550
Irvine, CA 92612
Phone: 888 393-8248
Fax: –
Web: www.sabrahealth.com

CEO: Richard K. Matros
CFO: Harold W. Andrews
HR: –
FYE: December 31
Type: Public

Sabra Health Care REIT doesn't mind a little healthy competition in the real estate sector. The company invests in income-producing health care facilities in the US. The REIT's investment portfolio includes about 180 properties most of which are skilled nursing/post-acute centers. It also invests in assisted living and independent living facilities and hospitals. Sabra's facilities house more than 18300 beds and are located in 35-plus states. Substantially all of the properties are leased to and operated by subsidiaries of Sun Healthcare Group which spun off its real estate assets to form Sabra Health Care REIT in 2010. In mid-2017 Sabra acquired Care Capital Properties for approximately $2.1 billion more than doubling the REIT's size.

	Annual Growth	12/14	12/15	12/16	12/17	12/18
Sales ($ mil.)	35.8%	183.5	238.9	260.5	405.6	623.4
Net income ($ mil.)	56.1%	47.0	79.4	70.3	158.4	279.1
Market value ($ mil.)	(14.2%)	5,415.2	3,607.1	4,354.2	3,346.8	2,938.5
Employees	29.6%	11	13	14	61	31

SABRE INDUSTRIES INC.

1120 Welsh Rd. Ste. 210
North Wales PA 19454
Phone: 267-263-1300
Fax: 267-263-1301
Web: www.sabreindustriesinc.com

CEO: Peter Sandore
CFO: Timothy Rossetti
HR: –
FYE: April 30
Type: Private

Sabre Industries designs and builds steel towers poles shelters and other utility structures for the wireless communications and electric transmission and distribution (T&D) industries. It also offers tower parts and accessories and provides a full range of services such as pole and structure testing turnkey construction site development interior integration and field maintenance. Customers include wireless service providers tower management companies utilities and government agencies. The company which is owned by private equity firm Kohlberg & Co operates primarily in the US.

SACRAMENTO MUNICIPAL UTILITY DISTRICT

6201 S ST
SACRAMENTO, CA 958171818
Phone: 916-452-3211
Fax: –
Web: www.smud.org

CEO: Arlen Orchard
CFO: Jim Tracy
HR: Nancy Evans
FYE: December 31
Type: Private

The Sacramento Municipal Utility District (SMUD) doesn't want its name to be mud. One of the largest locally owned electric utilities in the US SMUD serves more than 624770 residential and commercial customer meters (a service area population of 1.4 million) in California's Sacramento and Placer counties. The utility generates about 70% of its electricity (its 1300-MW capacity is derived primarily from hydroelectric and cogeneration power plants) and buys the rest. SMUD also sells power to wholesale customers andhas one of the largest solar energy distribution systems in the US.

	Annual Growth	12/14	12/15	12/16	12/17	12/18
Sales ($ mil.)	2.7%	–	1,474.2	1,494.8	1,559.3	1,595.5
Net income ($ mil.)	17.5%	–	129.0	195.3	181.4	209.1
Market value ($ mil.)	–	–	–	–	–	–
Employees	–	–	–	–	–	2,213

SACRED HEART HEALTH SYSTEM, INC.

5151 N 9TH AVE
PENSACOLA, FL 325048721
Phone: 850-416-1600
Fax: –
Web: www.sacred-heart.org

CEO: Laura S Kaiser
CFO: Buddy Elmore
HR: –
FYE: June 30
Type: Private

Part of Ascension Health the Sacred Heart Health System serves residents of Northwestern Florida primarily through the Sacred Heart Hospital of Pensacola. With more than 560 beds altogether the acute care medical center boasts the Sacred Heart Children's Hospital the Sacred Heart Women's Hospital and the Sacred Heart Regional Heart and Vascular Institute. Sacred Heart Hospital of Pensacola also specializes in trauma care heart disease cancer care weight loss stroke care neurology and orthopedics. It has an educational affiliation with Florida State University College of Medicine. Sacred Heart Health System operates additional acute long-term primary and specialty care centers in the region.

	Annual Growth	06/08	06/09	06/10	06/11	06/15
Sales ($ mil.)	145.9%	–	3.3	772.3	846.7	725.1
Net income ($ mil.)	217.8%	–	0.0	30.0	42.5	16.9
Market value ($ mil.)	–	–	–	–	–	–
Employees	–	–	–	–	–	1,100

SACRED HEART HOSPITAL OF ALLENTOWN

421 CHEW ST
ALLENTOWN, PA 181023406
Phone: 610-776-4500
Fax: –

CEO: –
CFO: Thomas Regner
HR: –
FYE: June 30
Type: Private

Hearts (and all other parts of the body) are sacred to Sacred Heart Hospital of Allentown. The acute care facility has some 230 beds and serves the residents of Pennsylvania's Lehigh Valley. Specialty services include pediatrics cardiology obstetrics weight-loss surgery orthopedics behavioral health and cancer treatment. Sacred Heart Hospital is part of the Sacred Heart Health System which also operates more than a dozen family practice clinics as well as specialty clinics long-term care facilities and imaging and rehabilitation centers. The hospital was founded by the Missionary Sisters of the Most Sacred Heart (a Catholic religious order) in 1912.

	Annual Growth	06/07	06/08	06/09	06/10	06/15
Sales ($ mil.)	–	–	(1,546.0)	107.1	106.8	101.2
Net income ($ mil.)	608.2%	–	0.0	0.0	0.8	8.9
Market value ($ mil.)	–	–	–	–	–	–
Employees	–	–	–	–	–	1,058

SACRED HEART HOSPITAL OF THE HOSPITAL SISTERS OF THE THIRD ORDER OF ST. FRANCIS

900 W CLAIREMONT AVE
EAU CLAIRE, WI 547015105
Phone: 715-717-3926
Fax: –

CEO: Julie Manas
CFO: –
HR: –
FYE: June 30
Type: Private

Sacred Heart Hospital not only cares for hearts that are holey but also for the rest of what ails residents of western Wisconsin. The more than 300-bed medical center provides specialized services that include cardiology cancer care pediatrics and emergency medicine. The hospital provides community-wide care through affiliations with the Marshfield Clinic (a provider network with more than 700 physicians) Oakleaf Medical Network (an organization of providers and clinics) and Infinity Healthcare and Pathology Services (supplies the hospital with medical x-ray professionals). Founded in 1889 by the Hospital Sisters of the Third Order of St. Francis the center is part of the Hospital Sisters Health System.

	Annual Growth	06/13	06/14	06/15	06/16	06/17
Sales ($ mil.)	(1.6%)	–	249.3	234.2	233.4	237.5
Net income ($ mil.)	(9.7%)	–	55.0	46.0	(0.6)	40.5
Market value ($ mil.)	–	–	–	–	–	–
Employees	–	–	–	–	–	1,010

SADDLEBACK MEMORIAL MEDICAL CENTER

24451 HEALTH CENTER DR # 1
LAGUNA HILLS, CA 926533689
Phone: 949-837-4500
Fax: –
Web: www.memorialcare.org

CEO: Steve Geidt
CFO: Adolfo Chanez
HR: –
FYE: June 30
Type: Private

Saddleback Memorial Medical Center part of Memorial Health Services (MHS) serves the residents of southern Orange County in California. With some 325 beds the not-for-profit medical center provides general medical and surgical services as well as specialty care in areas such as cancer heart disease and physical rehabilitation. It operates two campuses one in Laguna Hills and one in San Clemente. The medical center also features several facilities for women's health including the Saddleback Women's Hospital and the MemorialCare Breast Center. In addition Saddleback Memorial provides home health care and hospice services.

	Annual Growth	06/12	06/13	06/14	06/15	06/16
Sales ($ mil.)	3.5%	–	–	–	337.2	349.2
Net income ($ mil.)	16.9%	–	–	–	43.1	50.4
Market value ($ mil.)	–	–	–	–	–	–
Employees	–	–	–	–	–	1,209

SAFE RIDE SERVICES INC.

2001 W. Camelback Rd.
Phoenix AZ 85015
Phone: 602-627-6705
Fax: 602-627-6751
Web: www.saferideservices.com

CEO: –
CFO: –
HR: Monique Jordan
FYE: August 31
Type: Subsidiary

Safe Ride Services provides non-emergency medical transportation services in Arizona Colorado Florida Illinois Kansas Missouri New Mexico New York Oklahoma Texas Utah and Washington. The company offers its services through a fleet of vans configured to carry people in wheelchairs or on stretchers as well as those who are ambulatory. Safe Ride clients include Medicaid beneficiaries; the company also contracts with other health insurance programs. The company is part of the First Transit unit of FirstGroup America which itself is a subsidiary of UK-based bus and train operator FirstGroup. Safe Ride Services was founded in 1989.

SAFEGUARD SCIENTIFICS INC.   NYSE: SFE

435 Devon Park Dr. Building 800   CEO: Brian J Sisko
Wayne PA 19087-1945   CFO: Mark A Herndon
Phone: 610-293-0600   HR: –
Fax: 610-293-0601   FYE: December 31
Web: www.safeguard.com   Type: Public

Safeguard Scientifics' goal is to nurture investments not protect Poindexters in a lab. The firm invests in early-stage high-tech and life sciences ventures with prospects for growth. It focuses on companies involved in the development of diagnostics medical devices regenerative medicine specialty pharmaceuticals new media and financial services and health care information technology. Safeguard Scientifics has significant minority stakes in about a dozen companies; holdings include specialty pharmaceutical maker NuPathe biotechnology firm Tengion and Swap.com a web site that enables users to swap books and other media.

SAFENET INC.

4690 Millennium Dr.   CEO: Prakash Panjwani
Belcamp MD 21017   CFO: Jon McCabe
Phone: 410-931-7500   HR: –
Fax: 410-931-7524   FYE: December 31
Web: www.safenet-inc.com   Type: Private

SafeNet makes the digital world a safer place. The company provides security products that protect networks intellectual property software and personal identity. Its software and hardware systems employ encryption technology in USB identity tokens and smart cards virtual private networks (VPNs) and security appliances and software antipiracy and digital rights management products. Clients include financial institutions corporations and government agencies. SafeNet counts Citigroup Dell Starbucks Netflix Cisco and the US Defense Department among its blue-chip customers. Private equity firm Vector Capital took SafeNet private in 2007; the company filed for an IPO in 2010 but withdrew it in 2012.

SAFETY INSURANCE GROUP, INC.   NMS: SAFT

20 Custom House Street   CEO: George M. Murphy
Boston, MA 02110   CFO: William J. Begley
Phone: 617 951-0600   HR: –
Fax: 617 603-4837   FYE: December 31
Web: www.safetyinsurance.com   Type: Public

Buckle up Bostonians car safety first! Safety Insurance Group through subsidiaries Safety Insurance Safety Indemnity Insurance and Safety Property and Casualty sells property/casualty insurance exclusively in Massachusetts Maine and New Hampshire. It is one of the top private passenger automobile and commercial automobile insurers in the region controlling more than 10% of the markets in its home state. Safety Insurance also provides homeowners dwelling fire personal umbrella and business-owner policies; it cross-sells its non-auto property/casualty products to increase its share of the market. The firm sells its products through more than 920 independent agents and more than 1100 offices.

	Annual Growth	12/14	12/15	12/16	12/17	12/18
Assets ($ mil.)	2.6%	1,675.7	1,703.9	1,758.2	1,807.3	1,856.2
Net income ($ mil.)	8.8%	59.4	(13.9)	64.6	62.4	83.2
Market value ($ mil.)	6.3%	978.5	861.9	1,126.6	1,229.0	1,250.6
Employees	0.7%	610	622	643	623	627

SAFETY-KLEEN INC.

2600 N. Central Expressway Ste. 400   CEO: –
Richardson TX 75080   CFO: Jeff Richard
Phone: 972-265-2000   HR: Jean Lee
Fax: 972-265-2990   FYE: December 31
Web: www.safety-kleen.com   Type: Private

Safety-Kleen is a North American leader in oil re-refining and parts cleaning services. It provides these services to commercial industrial and automotive customers to meet their environmental needs. The company's Oil Re-refining segment processes about 160 million gallons of used oil annually to produce base and blended lubricating oils which are sold to distributors fleets government agencies railroads and retailers. Its Environmental Services segment collects about 200 million gallons of used oil; other services offered include containerized waste collection and parts cleaning. Safety-Kleen filed for a $400 million IPO in mid-2012. That year Clean Harbors offered to buy the company for $1.25 billion.

SAFEWAY INC.   NYS: SWY

5918 Stoneridge Mall Road   CEO: Robert L Edwards
Pleasanton, CA 94588-3229   CFO: –
Phone: 925 467-3000   HR: –
Fax: 925 467-3323   FYE: December 29
Web: www.safeway.com   Type: Public

For many Americans "going to Safeway" is synonymous with "going to the grocery store." Safeway is one of the nation's largest food retailers with some 1400 stores located mostly in the western Midwestern and mid-Atlantic regions of the US. It also operates regional supermarket companies including The Vons Companies (primarily in Southern California) Dominick's Finer Foods (Chicago) Carr-Gottstein Foods (Alaska's largest retailer) and Randall's Food Markets (Texas). Safeway owns grocery e-retailer GroceryWorks.com. Outside the US Safeway owns 49% of Casa Ley which operates about 195 food and variety stores in western Mexico. It exited the Canadian market in 2013.

	Annual Growth	01/09	01/10	01/11*	12/11	12/12
Sales ($ mil.)	0.1%	44,104.0	40,850.7	41,050.0	43,630.2	44,206.5
Net income ($ mil.)	(14.8%)	965.3	(1,097.5)	589.8	516.7	596.5
Market value ($ mil.)	(9.7%)	5,760.0	5,099.0	5,386.4	5,039.1	4,239.2
Employees	(4.6%)	197,000	186,000	180,000	178,000	171,000

*Fiscal year change

SAFRA NATIONAL BANK OF NEW YORK

546 5th Ave.   CEO: Simone Morato
New York NY 10036   CFO: Carlos Bertaco
Phone: 212-704-5500   HR: –
Fax: 212-704-5527   FYE: December 31
Web: www.safra.com   Type: Private

Rich folks are wild about Safra and Safra's wild about them. Private bank Safra National Bank of New York serves high-net-worth individuals local businesses and international corporations through branches in New York and Miami. It offers certificates of deposit investment funds money market instruments alternative investments and gold bullion. In addition to wealth management the bank also performs equity brokerage services bond trading and correspondent banking. Established in 1987 Safra National Bank is owned by the Safra family benefactors of hospitals synagogues and universities in the US and abroad.

SAGA COMMUNICATIONS INC
NMS: SGA

73 Kercheval Avenue
Grosse Pointe Farms, MI 48236
Phone: 313 886-7070
Fax: 313 886-7150
Web: www.sagacom.com

CEO: Edward K. (Ed) Christian
CFO: Samuel D. (Sam) Bush
HR: –
FYE: December 31
Type: Public

This company could spin a good tale about the radio and television industries. Saga Communications is a leading radio broadcaster with more than 90 stations serving about 25 markets in more than 15 states offering a variety of formats including sports talk and news as well as several music formats. Most of the stations serve small and midsized markets; the company typically has clusters of stations in each market allowing it to combine certain business functions. Saga also operates five regional radio networks. In addition the company owns a portfolio of four full-power and five low-power TV stations. Chairman and CEO Edward Christian has about two-thirds control of Saga.

	Annual Growth	12/14	12/15	12/16	12/17	12/18
Sales ($ mil.)	(1.8%)	134.0	132.9	142.6	118.1	124.8
Net income ($ mil.)	(2.1%)	14.9	13.4	18.2	54.7	13.7
Market value ($ mil.)	(6.5%)	258.8	228.9	299.4	240.8	197.8
Employees	(1.3%)	1,086	1,141	1,146	1,030	1,031

SAGARSOFT INC.

78 EASTERN BLVD STE 8
GLASTONBURY, CT 060334325
Phone: 860-633-2880
Fax: –
Web: www.sagarsoft.com

CEO: –
CFO: –
HR: –
FYE: March 31
Type: Private

|Sagarsoft hopes to take all of the hard work out of information technology. The company provides information technology (IT) services such as software development data warehousing and enterprise application integration. Additional offerings include project management network design systems architecture and support. Sagarsoft's clients have included Pfizer General Electric Sprint and CA. It has partnered with technology products providers including Microsoft Oracle Cisco and others. The company was founded in 1995

	Annual Growth	03/10	03/11	03/12	03/13	03/14
Sales ($ mil.)	(5.7%)	–	18.7	18.3	15.7	15.6
Net income ($ mil.)	(7.7%)	–	–	0.2	0.2	0.2
Market value ($ mil.)	–	–	–	–	–	–
Employees	–	–	–	–	–	95

SAGE SOFTWARE INC.

6561 Irvine Center Dr.
Irvine CA 92618-2301
Phone: 949-753-1222
Fax: 949-753-0374
Web: www.na.sage.com

CEO: Nancy Harris
CFO: Marc Scheipe
HR: –
FYE: September 30
Type: Subsidiary

Sage Software caters to businesses that appreciate the wisdom of planning. The company (which does business as Sage North America) is the North American subsidiary of UK-based software developer The Sage Group plc. Sage North America provides small and midsized companies with a variety of business management applications focused on such functions as accounting customer relationship management not-for-profit and government management human resources and fixed asset management and contact management. The company also provides industry-specific applications for customers in fields that include construction real estate and health care.

SAGENT PHARMACEUTICALS INC
NMS: SGNT

1901 North Roselle Road, Suite 700
Schaumburg, IL 60195
Phone: 847 908-1600
Fax: –
Web: www.sagentpharma.com

CEO: Peter Kaemmerer
CFO: Jonathon Singer
HR: –
FYE: December 31
Type: Public

Sagent Pharmaceuticals is imbued with a restorative spirit. Through its subsidiaries Sagent develops markets and sells a range of generic injectable products used by US hospitals and other health care organizations. Its products — which include anti-infection drugs chemotherapy drugs and critical care treatments used for anesthesia or to stabilize cardiac conditions like blood clotting and arrhythmia — consist of more than 30 ready-to-use pre-filled syringes single and multiple-dose vials and pre-mixed bags. Sagent develops its products using active pharmaceutical ingredients (APIs) and finished drugs supplied by partner pharmaceutical companies.

	Annual Growth	12/10	12/11	12/12	12/13	12/14
Sales ($ mil.)	40.5%	74.1	152.4	183.6	244.8	289.0
Net income ($ mil.)	–	(24.5)	(26.4)	(16.8)	29.6	39.9
Market value ($ mil.)	6.1%	–	671.5	514.5	811.6	802.9
Employees	53.0%	85	99	98	269	466

SAIA INC
NMS: SAIA

11465 Johns Creek Parkway, Suite 400
Johns Creek, GA 30097
Phone: 770 232-5067
Fax: –
Web: www.saia.com

CEO: Richard D. (Rick) O'Dell
CFO: Frederick J. Holzgrefe
HR: T Richard
FYE: December 31
Type: Public

Saia — you say it "sigh-ah" — is a holding company for less-than-truckload (LTL) carrier Saia Motor Freight Line. (LTL carriers consolidate freight from multiple shippers into a single truckload.) Saia Motor Freight specializes in regional and interregional services including time-definite and expedited transportation it also offers truckload freight hauling. The carrier operates a fleet of some 3900 tractors and 12370 trailers from a network of about 150 terminals. Saia's service territory spans about 35 states in the South Southwest Midwest as well as Pacific Northwest and West US. It offers coverage elsewhere in North America through partnerships with other carriers.

	Annual Growth	12/14	12/15	12/16	12/17	12/18
Sales ($ mil.)	6.8%	1,272.3	1,221.3	1,218.5	1,378.5	1,653.8
Net income ($ mil.)	19.2%	52.0	55.0	48.0	91.2	105.0
Market value ($ mil.)	0.2%	1,422.4	571.7	1,134.4	1,817.8	1,434.2
Employees	3.7%	8,900	8,700	8,900	9,800	10,300

SAINT AGNES MEDICAL CENTER

1303 E HERNDON AVE
FRESNO, CA 937203309
Phone: 559-450-3000
Fax: –
Web: www.samc.com

CEO: Jim Leonard
CFO: Phil Robinson
HR: –
FYE: June 30
Type: Private

Protecting and caring for the vulnerable Saint Agnes continues to ward off death for the patients at Saint Agnes Medical Center. The medical center provides health care to Valley residents of Fresno California through a 436-bed acute care hospital. Along with general surgery the hospital offers a variety of services including asthma management bariatric surgery (for which it has scored state-wide accolades) cardiac rehabilitation hospice care and home care. The facility also runs an internal medicine physician residency and a nurses' residency program. Saint Agnes is part of Trinity Health one of the largest Catholic health care systems in the US.

	Annual Growth	06/12	06/13	06/15	06/16	06/18
Sales ($ mil.)	0.4%	–	503.7	478.6	486.0	513.9
Net income ($ mil.)	13.3%	–	19.0	24.3	11.2	35.6
Market value ($ mil.)	–	–	–	–	–	–
Employees	–	–	–	–	–	2,400

SAINT ALPHONSUS REGIONAL MEDICAL CENTER, INC.

1055 N CURTIS RD
BOISE, ID 837061309
Phone: 208-367-2121
Fax: -
Web: www.saintalphonsus.org

CEO: -
CFO: Kenneth Fry
HR: Kelly Dally
FYE: June 30
Type: Private

Saint Alphonsus Regional Medical Center makes medical care its primary mission. The 384-bed hospital provides Boise Idaho and the surrounding region (including eastern Oregon and northern Nevada) with general acute and specialized health care services. Its facilities and operations include a level II trauma center an orthopedic spinal care unit an air transport service and a home health and hospice division. Saint Alphonsus Regional Medical Center is part of Trinity Health's four-hospital Saint Alphonsus Health System which serves Boise and Nampa in Idaho and Ontario and Baker City in Oregon. The Sisters of the Holy Cross founded the hospital in 1894.

	Annual Growth	06/09	06/10	06/13	06/14	06/15
Sales ($ mil.)	4.3%	-	450.0	545.1	572.4	556.2
Net income ($ mil.)	24.1%	-	13.8	43.1	46.0	40.5
Market value ($ mil.)	-	-	-	-	-	-
Employees	-	-	-	-	-	3,500

SAINT ANSELM COLLEGE

100 SAINT ANSELM DR
MANCHESTER, NH 031021310
Phone: 603-641-7000
Fax: -
Web: www.anselm.edu

CEO: -
CFO: -
HR: -
FYE: June 30
Type: Private

It may be named after a philosopher and theologian but students of all types are welcome at Saint Anselm College. The Benedictine Catholic liberal arts college offers degrees in more than 40 majors as well as over 20 certificate programs. With an enrollment of some 2000 and a full-time faculty of around 150 (90% of which hold a doctorate or other terminal degree) the school's student-teacher enrollment is 11:1 with an average class size of 18. Saint Anselm College's core curriculum includes classes in English humanities philosophy foreign language science and theology. Located on a hill overlooking Manchester New Hampshire Saint Anselm College was founded in 1889 by monks of the Benedictine order.

	Annual Growth	06/09	06/10	06/11	06/12	06/13
Sales ($ mil.)	(8.8%)	-	86.5	65.9	66.5	65.7
Net income ($ mil.)	(2.0%)	-	-	20.8	(12.0)	20.0
Market value ($ mil.)	-	-	-	-	-	-
Employees	-	-	-	-	-	700

SAINT EDWARD'S UNIVERSITY, INC.

3001 S CONGRESS AVE
AUSTIN, TX 787046489
Phone: 512-448-8400
Fax: -
Web: www.stedwards.edu

CEO: -
CFO: Rhonda Cartwright
HR: -
FYE: June 30
Type: Private

St. Edward's University is a private Catholic liberal arts university in Austin Texas. With an enrollment of more than 4600 students and a student-to-faculty ratio of 13:1 the university offers undergraduate degrees in more than 60 areas of study at schools of behavioral and social sciences management and business the humanities education and natural sciences. St. Edward's also has about ten master's degree programs in fields including accounting business administration information systems and counseling. It offers numerous study abroad programs in Europe Latin America and Asia as well as continuing education programs through its New College.

	Annual Growth	06/11	06/12	06/14	06/16	06/18
Sales ($ mil.)	1.8%	-	109.7	163.0	121.4	122.0
Net income ($ mil.)	(27.2%)	-	18.6	8.3	7.2	2.8
Market value ($ mil.)	-	-	-	-	-	-
Employees	-	-	-	-	-	964

SAINT ELIZABETH MEDICAL CENTER, INC.

1 MEDICAL VILLAGE DR
EDGEWOOD, KY 410173403
Phone: 859-301-2000
Fax: -
Web: www.stelizabeth.com

CEO: -
CFO: Lori Ritchey-Baldwin
HR: Linda D
FYE: December 31
Type: Private

It doesn't have much to do with the Holy Trinity except for the fact that St. Elizabeth Medical Center (operating as St. Elizabeth Healthcare) does business in a trinity of states. The system provides health care services to residents in Kentucky Ohio and West Virginia. St. Elizabeth Healthcare's programs include stroke and cardiac care hospice services and neurosurgery. The system is home to six hospitals with about 1200 beds and dozens of primary care offices. St. Elizabeth Healthcare was formed through a merger between St. Elizabeth Medical and nearby St. Luke Hospitals. The organization has one board of directors and one management structure and is sponsored by the Catholic Diocese of Covington.

	Annual Growth	12/05	12/06	12/08	12/13	12/14
Sales ($ mil.)	3.4%	-	484.0	623.7	984.4	633.6
Net income ($ mil.)	(1.0%)	-	49.2	(32.4)	124.9	45.3
Market value ($ mil.)	-	-	-	-	-	-
Employees	-	-	-	-	-	6,227

SAINT ELIZABETH REGIONAL MEDICAL CENTER

555 S 70TH ST
LINCOLN, NE 685102462
Phone: 402-219-5200
Fax: -
Web: www.chihealth.com

CEO: -
CFO: -
HR: -
FYE: June 30
Type: Private

Saint Elizabeth Regional Medical Center a Catholic Health Initiatives (CHI) affiliate is a 260-bed acute care hospital that serves the Lincoln Nebraska area. The not-for-profit hospital also known as CHI Health St. Elizabeth provides a variety of services such as obstetrics bariatrics cancer care burn and wound care and cardiac and pulmonary care. Some 430 physicians are affiliated with the facility. The hospital also operates community health clinics urgent care centers and physical therapy clinics as well as home health and hospice organizations. CHI Health St. Elizabeth was originally founded as a simple frontier hospital in 1889 by the Sisters of St. Francis of Perpetual Adoration.

	Annual Growth	06/09	06/10	06/13	06/14	06/15
Sales ($ mil.)	184.5%	-	1.1	268.1	254.3	212.5
Net income ($ mil.)	-	-	0.4	27.6	19.1	(9.3)
Market value ($ mil.)	-	-	-	-	-	-
Employees	-	-	-	-	-	1,825

SAINT FRANCIS HEALTH SYSTEM, INC.

6161 S YALE AVE
TULSA, OK 741361902
Phone: 918-494-2200
Fax: -
Web: www.sffcutulsa.org

CEO: Jake Henry Jr
CFO: Eric Schick
HR: -
FYE: June 30
Type: Private

If you have an ulcer in Tulsa or a broken arm in Broken Arrow you'll likely be visiting a Saint Francis Health System facility. The not-for-profit system serves Tulsa and northeastern Oklahoma through its hospitals clinics and home health services. Its largest facility is Saint Francis Hospital with about 920 beds and more than 700 doctors. Other facilities include Saint Francis Hospital at Broken Arrow The Children's Hospital at Saint Francis the Laureate Psychiatric Clinic and Hospital and the Saint Francis Heart Hospital. Its Warren Clinic consists of physicians offices in about a dozen cities providing primary and specialty health care.

	Annual Growth	06/08	06/09	06/10	06/11	06/15
Sales ($ mil.)	397.0%	-	-	0.4	0.4	1,167.9
Net income ($ mil.)	-	-	-	(6.3)	(4.1)	148.1
Market value ($ mil.)	-	-	-	-	-	-
Employees	-	-	-	-	-	8,200

SAINT FRANCIS HOSPITAL AND MEDICAL CENTER FOUNDATION, INC.

114 WOODLAND ST
HARTFORD, CT 061051208
Phone: 860-714-4006
Fax: –

CEO: –
CFO: Steven H Rosenberg
HR: Dennis Sparks
FYE: September 30
Type: Private

Saint Francis takes care of the hearts of Hartford Connecticut. The Saint Francis Hospital and Medical Center is a not-for-profit regional medical center with some 620 beds and 65 bassinets. The hospital specializes in cardiology oncology neurology orthopedics and women's and children's health services. It also offers behavioral health weight management trauma care and injury rehabilitation programs. Saint Francis serves as a teaching hospital affiliated with the University of Connecticut Schools of Medicine and Dentistry. It also operates laboratories a home health and hospice agency and other entities. Saint Francis is part of Catholic health care system Trinity Health.

	Annual Growth	09/08	09/09	09/10	09/14	09/17
Sales ($ mil.)	–	–	(1,321.8)	651.9	670.6	769.5
Net income ($ mil.)	314.7%	–	0.0	(10.8)	17.6	52.2
Market value ($ mil.)	–	–	–	–	–	–
Employees	–	–	–	–	–	3,270

SAINT FRANCIS UNIVERSITY

117 EVERGREEN DR
LORETTO, PA 159409704
Phone: 814-472-3000
Fax: –
Web: www.francis.edu

CEO: –
CFO: –
HR: –
FYE: June 30
Type: Private

Saint Francis University is a Catholic liberal arts college with more than 2500 full- and part-time students. The university offers undergraduate and graduate degree programs in areas such as business administration education medical science nursing and computer science. It also has doctorate programs in fields such as education and physical therapy. Its four schools cover arts and letters health sciences business and sciences. Saint Francis University was established when six Franciscan Friars from Ireland founded a boys' academy in the mountain hamlet of Loretto Pennsylvania in 1847. Now more than 60% of the student body is made up of women. The former St. Francis College gained university status in 2001.

	Annual Growth	06/09	06/10	06/12	06/13	06/15
Sales ($ mil.)	9.2%	–	59.8	84.5	90.8	93.1
Net income ($ mil.)	(16.2%)	–	6.5	5.2	9.4	2.7
Market value ($ mil.)	–	–	–	–	–	–
Employees	–	–	–	–	–	420

SAINT JOSEPH HOSPITAL, INC

1375 E 19TH AVE
DENVER, CO 802181114
Phone: 303-812-2000
Fax: –
Web: www.sclhealth.org

CEO: –
CFO: –
HR: –
FYE: December 31
Type: Private

The goal of Saint Joseph Hospital (formerly Exempla Saint Joseph Hospital) is to give residents of the Mile High City exemplary care. The Denver acute care facility has nearly 400 licensed beds and specializes in areas including cardiovascular disease cancer orthopedics pediatrics neurology diagnostics and high-risk labor and delivery. The Catholic not-for-profit hospital sees about 50000 emergency department visits annually and employs more than 1300 physicians. The hospital also offers residency programs in family practice internal medicine obstetrics and gynecology and general surgery. Catholic-sponsored Saint Joseph is part of SCL Health - Front Range.

	Annual Growth	12/10	12/11	12/12	12/13	12/14
Sales ($ mil.)	(4.9%)	–	–	–	490.0	465.8
Net income ($ mil.)	(50.2%)	–	–	–	51.6	25.7
Market value ($ mil.)	–	–	–	–	–	–
Employees	–	–	–	–	–	2,300

SAINT JOSEPH'S UNIVERSITY

5600 CITY AVE
PHILADELPHIA, PA 191311376
Phone: 610-660-1000
Fax: –
Web: www.sju.edu

CEO: –
CFO: Edward W Moneypenny
HR: –
FYE: May 31
Type: Private

Saint Joseph's University (SJU) has been educating Joes and Janes for more than 150 years. The Catholic Jesuit university provides higher education for about 8000 students a year from its campus on the outskirts of Philadelphia. It has more than 300 full-time faculty members and offers 50 undergraduate majors and 40 graduate and professional study areas including an Ed.D. in Educational Leadership. About 650 undergraduates attend its College of Professional and Liberal Studies; the remainder attend the College of Arts and Sciences and the Haub School of Business. SJU also conducts study abroad honors service and faith learning and other special study programs. It was founded in 1851 by the Society of Jesus.

	Annual Growth	05/14	05/15	05/16	05/17	05/18
Sales ($ mil.)	2.0%	–	–	–	229.1	233.6
Net income ($ mil.)	1132.7%	–	–	–	4.9	60.6
Market value ($ mil.)	–	–	–	–	–	–
Employees	–	–	–	–	–	1,138

SAINT LOUIS UNIVERSITY

1 N GRAND BLVD
SAINT LOUIS, MO 631032006
Phone: 314-977-2500
Fax: –
Web: www.slu.edu

CEO: –
CFO: David Heimburger
HR: –
FYE: June 30
Type: Private

This university gives students a SLU of opportunities. Saint Louis University (SLU) is a Jesuit Catholic school offering about 90 undergraduate 100 graduate and a host of professional degree programs through about a dozen schools and colleges including a school of medicine and a campus in Madrid Spain. Most programs require core classes in philosophy and theology. SLU has an enrollment of more than 8200 undergraduate and more than 4600 graduate and professional students. Its student-teacher ratio is 9:1. Saint Louis University was founded in 1818 by Reverend Louis William Du Bourg Catholic Bishop of Louisiana.

	Annual Growth	06/06	06/07	06/08	06/09	06/10
Sales ($ mil.)	8.9%	–	–	633.3	697.5	750.7
Net income ($ mil.)	–	–	–	(54.5)	0.0	28.5
Market value ($ mil.)	–	–	–	–	–	–
Employees	–	–	–	–	–	7,500

SAINT LUKE'S HEALTH SYSTEM, INC.

901 E 104TH ST
KANSAS CITY, MO 641314517
Phone: 816-932-2000
Fax: –

CEO: Julie L. Quirin
CFO: Chuck Robb
HR: –
FYE: December 31
Type: Private

Caring for the residents of Missouri's largest city is no mean feat but Saint Luke's Health System manages it through 10 area hospitals and a host of clinics located throughout Kansas City. The not-for-profit system's flagship facility is Saint Luke's Hospital which offers a Level I trauma center and internationally recognized cardiac and stroke care. Its Crittenton Children's Center is a behavioral health center serving children and their families on an inpatient and outpatient basis. Saint Luke's Health System is a network of almost 320 doctors providing primary and specialty care through clinics and other locations. The system is affiliated with the University of Missouri- Kansas City School of Medicine.

	Annual Growth	12/13	12/14	12/15	12/17	12/18
Sales ($ mil.)	91.8%	–	140.4	155.7	1,721.0	1,901.6
Net income ($ mil.)	–	–	(0.9)	(3.9)	89.0	42.3
Market value ($ mil.)	–	–	–	–	–	–
Employees	–	–	–	–	–	5,111

SAINT MARY'S UNIVERSITY OF MINNESOTA

700 TERRACE HTS 8
WINONA, MN 559871321
Phone: 507-457-1436
Fax: –
Web: www.smumn.edu

CEO: –
CFO: –
HR: –
FYE: May 31
Type: Private

Saint Mary's University of Minnesota is a private Roman Catholic institution that enrolls about 6000 students. About 20% of students are traditional undergraduates while the majority are adult learners in the Schools of Graduate and Professional Programs. The school which was founded in 1912 by Bishop Patrick R. Heffron has been administered by the Christian Brothers organization (under the De La Salle order) since 1933. It offers instruction in about 55 major minor and professional fields including arts science education and psychology.

	Annual Growth	05/14	05/15	05/16	05/17	05/18
Sales ($ mil.)	7.4%	–	–	77.4	85.2	89.3
Net income ($ mil.)	56.3%	–	–	5.4	14.4	13.2
Market value ($ mil.)	–	–	–	–	–	–
Employees	–	–	–	–	–	1,000

SAINT PETER'S UNIVERSITY HOSPITAL, INC.

254 EASTON AVE
NEW BRUNSWICK, NJ 089011766
Phone: 732-745-8600
Fax: –
Web: www.saintpetershcs.com

CEO: Ronald Rak
CFO: Garrick Stoldt
HR: –
FYE: December 31
Type: Private

Serving the central portions of the Garden State Saint Peter's University Hospital has about 480 beds. The facility is sponsored by the Roman Catholic Diocese of Metuchen New Jersey and provides patients with a staff of more than 900 physicians and dentists. Saint Peter's also offers one of the country's largest Neonatal Intensive Care Units minimally invasive surgical (MIS) procedures and specialized cancer diabetes and geriatric care. In affiliation with the Children's Hospital of Philadelphia Saint Peter's provides cardiac care for infants and children. The teaching hospital is also affiliated with the Drexel University College of Medicine.

	Annual Growth	12/12	12/13	12/15	12/16	12/17
Sales ($ mil.)	2.3%	–	403.1	405.8	447.1	440.8
Net income ($ mil.)	–	–	(2.7)	3.3	32.9	(7.2)
Market value ($ mil.)	–	–	–	–	–	–
Employees	–	–	–	–	–	3,000

SAINT TAMMANY PARISH HOSPITAL SERVICE DISTRICT 1

1202 S TYLER ST
COVINGTON, LA 704332330
Phone: 985-898-4000
Fax: –
Web: www.stph.org

CEO: Joan Coffman
CFO: Sandra Dipietrio
HR: –
FYE: December 31
Type: Private

St. Tammany Parish Hospital serves communities in St. Tammany Parish and Washington Parish along the northern shores of Lake Ponchartrain in eastern Louisiana. The not-for-profit hospital has about 240 beds and offers acute care diagnostic rehabilitation and community wellness services. It also includes centers and clinics specializing in surgery breast care cardiology and sleep disorders. In addition St. Tammany Parish Hospital operates a home health and hospice agency an outpatient services center and a primary care physicians' office. The company's facilities are served by doctors in St. Tammany Physicians Network.

	Annual Growth	12/10	12/11	12/14	12/16	12/17
Sales ($ mil.)	5.4%	–	223.1	246.9	293.6	306.6
Net income ($ mil.)	5.3%	–	16.9	20.0	21.4	23.1
Market value ($ mil.)	–	–	–	–	–	–
Employees	–	–	–	–	–	1,520

SAINT THOMAS RUTHERFORD HOSPITAL

1700 MEDICAL CENTER PKWY
MURFREESBORO, TN 371292245
Phone: 615-849-4100
Fax: –

CEO: Gordon B Ferguson
CFO: Ken Venuto
HR: –
FYE: June 30
Type: Private

Saint Thomas Rutherford Hospital (formerly Middle Tennessee Medical Center) is a 285-bed acute care hospital serving central Tennessee. In addition to general medical diagnostic and surgical services the not-for-profit hospital offers 30 medical specialties including centers devoted to cancer care pediatrics cardiology orthopedics neurology diabetes and women's health. Saint Thomas Rutherford established in 1927 is part of Saint Thomas Health which includes four additional area hospitals and is in turn is a member of Ascension Health.

	Annual Growth	06/07	06/08	06/09	06/14	06/15
Sales ($ mil.)	6.6%	–	178.4	189.9	249.0	279.5
Net income ($ mil.)	20.3%	–	13.2	13.5	35.4	48.0
Market value ($ mil.)	–	–	–	–	–	–
Employees	–	–	–	–	–	1,100

SAJAN INC.

NAS: SAJA

625 Whitetail Blvd.
River Falls, WI 54022
Phone: 715 426-9505
Fax: –
Web: www.sajan.com

CEO: Shannon Zimmerman
CFO: Thomas P Skiba
HR: –
FYE: December 31
Type: Public

Sajan wants to make sure nothing is lost in translation. Formerly known as MathStar Sajan offers global language services and software for document and translation management Web site localization and multilingual desktop publishing. The company's offerings which are supported by its Global Communication Management Systems (GCMS) Web-based platform allow companies to expand into untapped international markets by making their Web sites accessible and culturally suitable for target audiences. Sajan also adapts Web pages for images e-learning and search engine optimization. The company's Ireland-based subsidiary Sajan Software covers markets in Europe Africa and the Middle East.

	Annual Growth	12/11	12/12	12/13	12/14	12/15
Sales ($ mil.)	9.2%	20.9	20.5	24.0	28.3	29.7
Net income ($ mil.)	20.7%	0.1	(1.1)	0.0	0.2	0.1
Market value ($ mil.)	40.5%	4.6	2.2	6.9	27.0	17.9
Employees	5.6%	114	99	112	127	142

SAKS FIFTH AVENUE INC.

12 E. 49th St.
New York NY 10017
Phone: 212-753-4000
Fax: 703-684-3478
Web: www.salvationarmyusa.org

CFO: –
CFO: –
HR: –
FYE: January 31
Type: Business Segment

Saks Fifth Avenue is Saks Inc.'s most expensive accessory. A subsidiary of Saks Saks Fifth Avenue (SFA) operates about 45 upscale department stores in 20-plus states. The retailer is near the top of the line in fashion selling apparel cosmetics jewelry and shoes from top designers such as Burberry Chanel and Prada as well as Saks' own private label merchandise. SFA's fast-growing off-price sister chain Off 5th caters to thriftier customers and has overtaken SFA with more than 60 locations across the US. SFA also operates a catalog and an online store and runs smaller shops in chic vacation spots. The flagship store at 611 Fifth Ave. opened in 1924 rings up about 20% of SFA's total sales.

SALARY.COM INC.

160 Gould St.
Needham MA 02494
Phone: 781-464-7300
Fax: 781-726-7880
Web: www.salary.com

CEO: –
CFO: –
HR: –
FYE: March 31
Type: Subsidiary

Think you're grossly underpaid? Check out Salary.com to find out for sure. (Just refrain from doing so while you're at work.) The company's website provides the Salary Wizard which offers employee compensation data and analysis geared toward individuals managers and businesses. Other tools include a Cost of Living Wizard Benefits Wizard Performance Self Test and Job Assessor. The firm provides employer-reported data on more than 4000 job titles. Salary.com also operates Salary.com for Business (at http://business.salary.com) a separate site that offers articles tips and tools for companies. Most revenue comes from advertising. Salary.com is a division of human resources firm Kenexa Corporation.

SALEM HEALTH

890 OAK ST SE
SALEM, OR 973013905
Phone: 503-561-5200
Fax: –
Web: www.salemhealth.org

CEO: Cheryl Nester Wolfe
CFO: James Parr
HR: –
FYE: June 30
Type: Private

Salem Hospital serves the healthcare needs of residents in and around Oregon's Willamette Valley. The acute care hospital boasts about 455 beds and a medical staff of 440-plus physicians that represents some 45 specialty areas such as oncology joint replacement obstetrics diabetes weight loss and mental health among others. The not-for-profit hospital offers a range of services from emergency and critical care to rehabilitation and community wellness programs. Its Center for Outpatient Medicine provides cancer care outpatient surgery and imaging services and has a sleep disorders center. Salem Hospital is part of Salem Health which also includes West Valley Hospital and Willamette Health Partners.

	Annual Growth	09/11	09/12	09/13	09/14*	06/18
Sales ($ mil.)	7.8%	–	–	531.1	584.3	773.2
Net income ($ mil.)	10.1%	–	–	61.4	58.5	99.2
Market value ($ mil.)	–	–	–	–	–	–
Employees	–	–	–	–	–	3,400

*Fiscal year change

SALEM MEDIA GROUP, INC.

4880 Santa Rosa Road
Camarillo, CA 93012
Phone: 805 987-0400
Fax: –
Web: www.salemmedia.com

NMS: SALM
CEO: Edward G Atsinger III
CFO: Evan D Masyr
HR: –
FYE: December 31
Type: Public

His eye may be on the sparrow but Salem Media Group (formerly Salem Communications) hopes His ear is tuned to the radio. The leading Christian radio company operates about 100 stations serving more than 35 markets. Its stations offer Christian-themed talk shows Christian music country music and traditional talk radio. The company also produces and syndicates religious programming through the Salem Radio Network which boasts about 2000 affiliates. In addition Salem Media publishes books and magazines operates a radio advertising sales firm and operates the Salem Web Network a provider of online Christian content. Chairman Stuart Epperson CEO Edward Atsinger and other family members control about 85% of the company.

	Annual Growth	12/14	12/15	12/16	12/17	12/18
Sales ($ mil.)	(0.4%)	266.5	265.8	274.3	263.7	262.8
Net income ($ mil.)	–	5.5	11.2	8.9	24.6	(3.2)
Market value ($ mil.)	(28.1%)	204.8	130.4	163.7	117.8	54.7
Employees	(0.8%)	1,605	1,624	1,590	1,590	1,552

SALESFORCE.COM INC

Salesforce Tower, 415 Mission Street, 3rd Fl
San Francisco, CA 94105
Phone: 415 901-7000
Fax: –
Web: www.salesforce.com

NYS: CRM
CEO: Marc Benioff
CFO: Mark J. Hawkins
HR: –
FYE: January 31
Type: Public

Salesforce.com Inc. is the top developer and seller of customer relationship management software with more than 150000 users. The company offers cloud-based applications that manage customer relationships including Sales Cloud Marketing and Commerce Cloud and Service Cloud (for customer support) as well as the Salesforce Platform. Other products offer e-commerce analytics and social media tools through cloud-based applications. Salesforce's customers come from a variety of industries including financial services telecommunications manufacturing entertainment and government. It generates most of its revenue in the US. Salesforce bought Tableau for about $15.7 billion in 2019.

	Annual Growth	01/15	01/16	01/17	01/18	01/19
Sales ($ mil.)	25.4%	5,373.6	6,667.2	8,392.0	10,480.0	13,282.0
Net income ($ mil.)	–	(262.7)	(47.4)	179.6	127.5	1,110.0
Market value ($ mil.)	28.1%	43,466.5	52,406.2	60,907.0	87,710.7	117,016.9
Employees	21.6%	16,000	19,000	25,000	29,000	35,000

SALINAS VALLEY MEMORIAL HEALTHCARE SYSTEMS

450 E ROMIE LN
SALINAS, CA 939014029
Phone: 831-757-4333
Fax: –
Web: www.svmh.com

CEO: Pete Delgado
CFO: Agustine Lopez
HR: –
FYE: June 30
Type: Private

The primary facility of the Salinas Valley Memorial Healthcare System (a public hospital district) is Salinas Valley Memorial Hospital which opened in 1953 and has some 270 acute-care beds. The medical center includes a comprehensive cancer center joint replacement clinic regional heart and spine centers a level III neonatal intensive care unit and a women's and children's unit. Salinas Valley Memorial Healthcare System also operates the Summerville Harden Ranch an 80-bed assisted-living facility and a network of outpatient care clinics. The system has collaborative relationships with other area care providers as well as a partnership with NASA that allows earthbound physicians to assist astronauts with medical emergencies in space.

	Annual Growth	06/04	06/05	06/15	06/16	06/17
Sales ($ mil.)	4.7%	–	284.2	344.2	366.3	494.4
Net income ($ mil.)	11.1%	–	14.2	37.7	44.1	50.1
Market value ($ mil.)	–	–	–	–	–	–
Employees	–	–	–	–	–	1,800

SALINE MEMORIAL HOSPITAL AUXILIARY

1 MEDICAL PARK DR
BENTON, AR 720153353
Phone: 501-922-2619
Fax: –
Web: www.salinememorial.org

CEO: Bob Trautman
CFO: Carla Robertson
HR: –
FYE: June 30
Type: Private

Saline Memorial Hospital (SMH) is a not-for-profit medical facility serving the western region of Arkansas. The full-service hospital has about 167 beds and provides inpatient and outpatient care in the areas of cardiology neurology otolaryngology (ear nose and throat) ophthalmology pediatrics psychiatry and wound care among others. The hospital's campus also includes a sleep disorder laboratory two separate medical office buildings and a home health and hospice services center. In addition SMH operates two primary care clinics in nearby Bryant.

	Annual Growth	06/06	06/07	06/08	06/09	06/12
Sales ($ mil.)	(16.9%)	–	–	198.3	0.0	94.8
Net income ($ mil.)	–	–	–	(1.4)	0.0	2.4
Market value ($ mil.)	–	–	–	–	–	–
Employees	–	–	–	–	–	950

SALISBURY BANCORP, INC.   NAS: SAL

5 Bissell Street | CEO: Richard J Cantele Jr
Lakeville, CT 6039 | CFO: Donald E White
Phone: 860 435-9801 | HR: –
Fax: – | FYE: December 31
Web: www.salisburybank.com | Type: Public

Salisbury Bancorp has a stake in New England's financial market. The holding company owns the Salisbury Bank and Trust Company which operates seven branches in northwestern Connecticut southwestern Massachusetts and southeastern New York. With roots dating to 1848 the bank offers a variety of financial products and services including checking savings and money market accounts CDs credit cards and trust services. Residential real estate mortgages make up the largest portion of the bank's loan portfolio by far; commercial real estate construction land development business financial agricultural and consumer loans round out its lending activities.

	Annual Growth	12/14	12/15	12/16	12/17	12/18
Assets ($ mil.)	7.0%	855.4	891.2	935.4	987.0	1,121.6
Net income ($ mil.)	36.8%	2.5	8.5	6.7	6.3	8.8
Market value ($ mil.)	7.3%	76.7	94.0	105.3	125.3	101.5
Employees	2.1%	182	188	187	194	198

SALIX PHARMACEUTICALS LTD   NMS: SLXP

8510 Colonnade Center Drive | CEO: Joseph Papa
Raleigh, NC 27615 | CFO: –
Phone: 919 862-1000 | HR: –
Fax: – | FYE: December 31
Web: www.salix.com | Type: Public

Salix Pharmaceuticals is a finishing school for drugs. With a focus on treating gastrointestinal ailments the company prefers to acquire drug candidates nearing commercial viability. It then takes them through the final development stages and brings them to market. The company's marketed products include Xifaxan (an antibiotic for gastrointestinal troubles) Pepcid (gastric ulcers and acid reflux) and Apriso and Colazal (for ulcerative colitis). Other products include colonoscopy preparatory bowel purgatives MoviPrep OsmoPrep and Visicol. Its late-stage candidates include both new drugs and new uses for existing drugs.

	Annual Growth	12/09	12/10	12/11	12/12	12/13
Sales ($ mil.)	41.5%	232.9	337.0	540.5	735.4	933.8
Net income ($ mil.)	—	(43.6)	(27.1)	87.4	64.2	143.0
Market value ($ mil.)	37.2%	1,598.0	2,955.6	3,011.6	2,547.2	5,660.6
Employees	8.7%	395	390	490	525	552

SALLY BEAUTY HOLDINGS INC   NYS: SBH

3001 Colorado Boulevard | CEO: Christian A. (Chris) Brickman
Denton, TX 76210 | CFO: Donald T. (Don) Grimes
Phone: 940 898-7500 | HR: Michael Corso
Fax: – | FYE: September 30
Web: www.sallybeautyholdings.com | Type: Public

Sally Beauty Holdings (SBH) is one of the largest retailers and distributors of professional beauty supplies in the US. The company's segments Sally Beauty Supply stores and Beauty Systems Group sell more than 10500 hair skin and nail products in more than 5000 stores including franchised locations. Sally Beauty Supply's customers are consumers salons and salon professionals while the Beauty Systems Group focuses on salons and professionals. The latter segment operates Armstrong McCall a beauty supply distributor which sells through franchised stores. While the US accounts for most of its sales the company also has stores in Canada Europe and South America.

	Annual Growth	09/15	09/16	09/17	09/18	09/19
Sales ($ mil.)	0.3%	3,834.3	3,952.6	3,938.3	3,932.6	3,876.4
Net income ($ mil.)	3.7%	235.1	222.9	215.1	258.0	271.6
Market value ($ mil.)	(11.0%)	2,772.2	2,997.5	2,285.5	2,146.6	1,738.0
Employees	1.9%	28,330	29,665	29,475	29,970	30,500

SALON MEDIA GROUP INC.   NBB: SLNM

870 Market Street | CEO: Richard Macwilliams
San Francisco, CA 94102 | CFO: Trevor Calhoun
Phone: 415 870-7566 | HR: –
Fax: – | FYE: March 31
Web: www.salon.com | Type: Public

Salon Media Group (formerly Salon.com) hopes to satisfy sophisticated Web surfers weary of run-of-the-mill Internet schlock. The company that garnered attention for essays by the likes of Camille Paglia and Allen Barra has expanded from its original online magazine format. Salon.com's content includes news features interviews columns and blogs covering topics such as politics business technology books sports and arts and entertainment. Revenues come from advertising and subscription fees. Salon.com and its online communities (Table Talk and The Well) attract more than six million unique visitors a month.

	Annual Growth	03/13	03/14	03/15	03/16	03/17
Sales ($ mil.)	5.8%	3.6	6.0	4.9	7.0	4.6
Net income ($ mil.)	—	(3.9)	(2.2)	(3.9)	(2.0)	(9.6)
Market value ($ mil.)	(12.0%)	37.5	25.5	24.0	15.0	22.5
Employees	(2.2%)	48	44	49	53	44

SALT LAKE COMMUNITY COLLEGE

4600 S REDWOOD RD | CEO: –
SALT LAKE CITY, UT 841233145 | CFO: –
Phone: 801-957-4111 | HR: –
Fax: – | FYE: June 30
Web: www.slcc.edu | Type: Private

Salt Lake Community College (SLCC) provides day night and weekend courses for early risers and night owls alike. SLCC serves more than 60000 students and has a student-to-teacher ratio of 23:1. The two-year school has more than a dozen campuses and outreach centers in Salt Lake City Utah as well as online courses available to reach both traditional and non-traditional students. In addition to being a top US source of associate degrees in arts science applied science and pre-engineering the community college also has career and technical programs. SLCC was founded in 1948 to provide skilled workforce training for Utah residents.

	Annual Growth	06/12	06/13	06/14	06/15	06/16
Sales ($ mil.)	(3.6%)	–	94.1	92.6	85.4	84.4
Net income ($ mil.)	28.3%	–	3.9	55.2	11.2	8.2
Market value ($ mil.)	–	–	–	–	–	–
Employees	–	–	–	–	–	3,200

SALT RIVER PROJECT AGRICULTURAL IMPROVEMENT AND POWER DISTRICT

1500 N MILL AVE | CEO: Mark B. Bonsall
TEMPE, AZ 852811252 | CFO: Aidan McSheffrey
Phone: 602-236-5900 | HR: Karen A Krull
Fax: – | FYE: April 30
Web: www.srpnet.com | Type: Private

One of the US's largest government-owned utilities Salt River Project (SRP) provides Phoenix with two types of currents: electric and water. Electricity comes from the Salt River Project Agricultural Improvement and Power District a political subdivision of the State of Arizona that has a generating capacity of about 8300 MW and distributes power to more than 984000 homes and businesses. The district sells excess power to wholesale customers. Water comes from the Salt River Valley Water Users' Association a private firm that delivers 1 million acre-feet of water per year to residents and agricultural irrigators; the association also operates dams canals reservoirs and wells in its service area.

	Annual Growth	01/07	01/08	01/09	01/10*	04/17
Sales ($ mil.)	4.8%	–	–	–	2,217.5	3,084.7
Net income ($ mil.)	(10.0%)	–	–	–	517.4	247.8
Market value ($ mil.)	–	–	–	–	–	–
Employees	–	–	–	–	–	4,336

*Fiscal year change

SALVE REGINA UNIVERSITY

100 OCHRE POINT AVE
NEWPORT, RI 028404149
Phone: 401-847-6650
Fax: –
Web: www.salve.edu

CEO: –
CFO: –
HR: –
FYE: June 30
Type: Private

Salve Regina isn't just an anthem that Catholics sing near Christmas. It's also a college they attend in Rhode Island. Salve Regina (meaning Hail Holy Queen) is a Catholic university serving more than 2500 undergraduate and graduate students. The university offers degrees in more than 45 disciplines including accounting anthropology biology economics education and religious studies. Salve Regina offers associate baccalaureate and master's degrees a Certificate of Advanced Graduate Study and a Ph.D. in humanities. Salve Regina was founded by the Sisters of Mercy in 1934; it opened its doors in 1947.

	Annual Growth	06/13	06/14	06/15	06/16	06/17
Sales ($ mil.)	(0.1%)	–	–	–	67.9	67.8
Net income ($ mil.)	(18.6%)	–	–	–	8.4	6.8
Market value ($ mil.)	–	–	–	–	–	–
Employees	–	–	–	–	–	450

SAM ASH MUSIC CORPORATION

278 Duffy Ave.
Hicksville NY 11801
Phone: 516-932-6400
Fax: 201-825-3524
Web: www.okonite.com

CEO: D Richard Ash
CFO: Stuart Leibowitz
HR: Pat Reilly
FYE: August 31
Type: Private

Sam Ash Music (SAM) has been instrumental in selling the tools that make tunes. The nation's #2 musical instrument retailer (behind Guitar Center) SAM operates 45 stores in more than 15 states mostly in California New York and Florida. Besides instruments the company sells sheet music recording equipment lighting computers and music software. It also sells online. In addition SAM sells vintage guitars offers custom-built instruments and music clinics and buys used musical instruments. It runs a pro services and parts division Sam Ash Professional and an Educational Division serving schools. The company was founded in 1924 by Sam and Rose Ashkynase whose descendants still own and run the company.

SAM HOUSTON STATE UNIVERSITY

1806 AVE J
HUNTSVILLE, TX 77340
Phone: 936-294-1111
Fax: –
Web: www.shsu.edu

CEO: –
CFO: –
HR: –
FYE: August 31
Type: Private

Part of the Texas State University System Sam Houston University has an enrollment of nearly 18500 students. It consists of six schools: Business Administration Criminal Justice Education Fine Arts and Mass Communications Humanities and Social Sciences and Sciences. The university offers some 130 undergraduate and master programs as well as doctoral programs in counselor education criminal justice educational leadership reading and clinical psychology. It offers more than 20 undergraduate and graduate degrees entirely online. Sam Houston State was founded as Sam Houston Normal Institute in 1879 and is named after Texas hero General Sam Houston.

	Annual Growth	08/04	08/05	08/06	08/07	08/08
Sales ($ mil.)	–	–	–	(1,117.7)	128.8	136.5
Net income ($ mil.)	–	–	–	0.0	14.9	63.4
Market value ($ mil.)	–	–	–	–	–	–
Employees	–	–	–	–	–	2,200

SAM LEVIN INC.

301 FITZ HENRY RD
SMITHTON, PA 154798715
Phone: 724-872-2055
Fax: –
Web: www.levinfurniture.com

CEO: –
CFO: –
HR: Irene Fostyk
FYE: December 31
Type: Private

Founded in 1920 as a furniture and hardware store by the husband-and-wife team Sam and Jessie Levin Sam Levin (dba Levin Furniture) sells a wide variety of dining room bedroom living room and office furniture as well as mattresses at about a dozen retail locations in northeastern Ohio and southwestern Pennsylvania. It also operates a Sleep Center bedding store in Pennsylvania and a clearance outlet in Ohio. The family-owned-and run-company offers self-service kiosks in its showrooms and creative exhibits that include sports- and Wizard of Oz-themed displays. Robert Levin Sam and Jessie's grandson is president of the company.

	Annual Growth	12/12	12/13	12/14	12/15	12/16
Sales ($ mil.)	4.3%	–	188.0	188.8	202.7	213.2
Net income ($ mil.)	25.4%	–	7.2	12.2	16.2	14.1
Market value ($ mil.)	–	–	–	–	–	–
Employees	–	–	–	–	–	400

SAMARITAN REGIONAL HEALTH SYSTEM

1025 CENTER ST
ASHLAND, OH 448054097
Phone: 419-289-0491
Fax: –
Web: www.samaritanhospital.org

CEO: Danny L Boggs
CFO: Mary Griest
HR: –
FYE: December 31
Type: Private

Samaritan Regional Health System (SRHS) provides a wide range of inpatient and outpatient services to the residents of north central Ohio. Among its specialty services are emergency medicine orthopedics obstetrics rehabilitation cardiology gastrointestinal disease pediatrics and home health care. Its flagship facility Samaritan Hospital has about 110 licensed beds and is located in Ashland Ohio which is located between the Cleveland and Columbus metropolitan areas. The not-for-profit health system also includes outpatient general care diagnostic and specialty clinics. SRHS was founded in 1912 by philanthropists J.L. and Mary Clark.

	Annual Growth	12/12	12/13	12/14	12/15	12/16
Sales ($ mil.)	–	–	0.0	78.6	70.9	74.7
Net income ($ mil.)	62.7%	–	2.0	5.5	4.3	8.6
Market value ($ mil.)	–	–	–	–	–	–
Employees	–	–	–	–	–	650

SAMMONS ENTERPRISES INC.

5949 Sherry Ln. Ste. 1900
Dallas TX 75225
Phone: 214-210-5000
Fax: 214-210-5099
Web: www.sammonsenterprises.com

CEO: Heather Kreager
CFO: Pam Doeppe
HR: –
FYE: December 31
Type: Private

Sammons Enterprises summons its revenues from several sources. The diversified holding company's operations include the Sammons Financial Group (life insurance and financial services) and Briggs Equipment (heavy equipment sales and rentals). Its insurance and financial group includes Midland National Life Insurance North American Company for Life and Health Insurance and Sammons Annuity Group. The company's list of partially owned holdings runs the range from real estate investments to oilfield suppliers. It is owned by its employees and prefers to invest in companies with strong employee-ownership programs.

SAMSUNG C&T AMERICA, INC.

105 CHALLENGER RD FL 3
RIDGEFIELD PARK, NJ 076602100
Phone: 201-229-4000
Fax: –

CEO: Jeong Soo Kim
CFO: Know-Kook Park
HR: Billie Aliu
FYE: December 31
Type: Private

It is Samsung but instead of just making the stuff you see at the electronics store it buys and sells a wide range of consumer and industrial goods. Samsung C&T America (SCTA the C&T stands for construction and trading) is the US arm of the Korean commodities trading marketing and distribution and investment company Samsung C&T (a part of the Samsung& chaebol or industrial group). As a commodities trader SCTA deals in chemicals steel metals textiles and natural resources. The company's marketing and distribution efforts include consumer products ranging from health care products to FUBU clothing and US Polo Association footwear.

	Annual Growth	12/03	12/04	12/05	12/06	12/07
Sales ($ mil.)	–	–	–	0.0	1,356.0	437.8
Net income ($ mil.)	–	–	–	0.0	(16.9)	12.3
Market value ($ mil.)	–	–	–	–	–	–
Employees	–	–	–	–	–	250

SAMSUNG ELECTRONICS AMERICA INC.

85 Challenger Rd.
Ridgefield Park NJ 07660
Phone: 201-229-4000
Fax: 864-752-1632
Web: www.samsung.com/us

CEO: Yangkyu Kim
CFO: –
HR: –
FYE: December 31
Type: Subsidiary

Samsung Electronics America (SEA) sells everything Samsung from sea to shining sea. A subsidiary of electronics giant Samsung Electronics the company's Consumer Business division markets consumer electronics and household appliances including TVs Blu-ray disc players portable audio players home theater systems hard drives cameras and camcorders refrigerators and washers and dryers. It also sells printers monitors laptops digital signage and projectors through its Enterprise Business division. Formed in 1977 SEA also manages the North American operations of Samsung Semiconductor Inc. (a leading global chip maker) and Samsung Telecommunications America (mobile phones and telephony equipment).

SAMUELS JEWELERS

2914 Montopolis Dr. Ste. 200
Austin TX 78741
Phone: 512-369-1400
Fax: 512-369-1527
Web: www.samuelsjewelers.com

CEO: –
CFO: –
HR: –
FYE: May 31
Type: Subsidiary

In addition to diamonds and gemstones Samuels Jewelers knows something about millstones — the bankruptcy kind (it has been thrice drawn into bankruptcy court since the early 1990s). Samuels sells fine jewelry items through about 85 jewelry stores in California Texas and about 15 other states; stores are primarily located in regional shopping malls power centers and strip centers. Samuels also operates some stand-alone stores and sells jewelry online at SamuelsJewelers.com. Its stores operate under the Samuels Diamonds and Samuels Jewelers banners. Founded in 1891 Texas-based Samuels Jewelers was acquired by India's Gitanjali Gems Ltd. a jewelry maker and retailer in late 2006.

SAN ANTONIO WATER SYSTEM

2800 US HIGHWAY 281 N
SAN ANTONIO, TX 782123106
Phone: 210-704-7297
Fax: –
Web: www.saws.org

CEO: Robert R. Puente
CFO: Douglas (Doug) Evanson
HR: –
FYE: December 31
Type: Private

Wasting water is a sore point in drought-prone South Texas and San Antonio Water System (SAWS) seeks to husband this precious resource the best it can. The company serves about 460000 water and 411000 wastewater customers or about 1.6 million people in the San Antonio metropolitan area (including most of the city of San Antonio several suburban municipalities and adjacent parts of Bexar County). In addition to serving its own retail customers SAWS provides wholesale water supplies to several smaller utility systems in its service area. The utility is owned by the City of San Antonio.

	Annual Growth	12/10	12/11	12/12	12/16	12/17
Sales ($ mil.)	–	–	–	0.0	622.5	666.8
Net income ($ mil.)	–	–	–	0.0	213.4	240.9
Market value ($ mil.)	–	–	–	–	–	–
Employees	–	–	–	–	–	1,700

SAN DIEGO STATE UNIVERSITY FOUNDATION

5250 CAMPANILE DR MC1947
SAN DIEGO, CA 921821901
Phone: 619-594-1900
Fax: –
Web: www.sdsu.edu

CEO: –
CFO: Leslie Levinson
HR: –
FYE: June 30
Type: Private

San Diego State University (SDSU) with an enrollment of more than 31000 is one of the largest universities in California. It offers some 75 academic programs leading to about 90 bachelor's 80 master's and 22 joint-doctoral degrees. Its Imperial Valley campus on the Mexican border provides upper-division courses and exchange programs with Mexican universities in Baja California. More than one-fifth of SDSU's student population is Hispanic. It is part of the California State University System.

	Annual Growth	06/09	06/10	06/12	06/13	06/15
Sales ($ mil.)	(2.1%)	–	179.7	186.9	175.2	161.3
Net income ($ mil.)	–	–	4.8	6.3	5.3	(1.0)
Market value ($ mil.)	–	–	–	–	–	–
Employees	–	–	–	–	–	2,500

SAN DIEGO UNIFIED PORT DISTRICT

3165 PACIFIC HWY
SAN DIEGO, CA 921011128
Phone: 619-686-6200
Fax: –
Web: www.portofsandiego.org

CEO: John Bolduc
CFO: Robert Deangelis
HR: –
FYE: June 30
Type: Private

The San Diego Unified Port District (better known as the Port of San Diego) brings in cash from land and sea. The agency manages two marine cargo facilities as well as a terminal used by cruise ships. Its real estate operations include leasing and managing land around the port including almost 20 bayfront parks and commercial property. In addition the Port of San Diego is charged with protecting San Diego Bay and adjoining tidelands from pollution. The agency which was created in 1962 is governed by a seven-member board appointed by the city councils of San Diego and four neighboring cities.

	Annual Growth	06/14	06/15	06/16	06/17	06/18
Sales ($ mil.)	5.0%	–	149.6	160.3	170.4	172.9
Net income ($ mil.)	–	–	9.1	20.0	(14.3)	(9.2)
Market value ($ mil.)	–	–	–	–	–	–
Employees	–	–	–	–	–	604

SAN FRANCISCO BAY AREA RAPID TRANSIT DISTRICT

300 LAKESIDE DR
OAKLAND, CA 94604
Phone: 510-464-6000
Fax: –
Web: www.bart.gov

CEO: –
CFO: –
HR: –
FYE: June 30
Type: Private

If you're going to San Francisco — from Oakland Berkeley or another Bay Area community — San Francisco Bay Area Rapid Transit District (BART) can take you there. BART's trains carry about 365000 daily weekday riders from more than 45 stations over more than 100 miles of track including the 3.6 mile Transbay Tube under the San Francisco Bay that links the City by the Bay with Oakland and other East Bay communities. Directors elected from nine districts in Alameda Contra Costa and San Francisco counties oversee BART which operates with an annual budget of about $480 million. Construction on the rail system began in 1964 and BART carried its first passengers in 1972.

	Annual Growth	06/04	06/05	06/06	06/16	06/18
Sales ($ mil.)	–	–	0.0	275.1	545.8	605.7
Net income ($ mil.)	–	–	0.0	(2.7)	331.8	212.9
Market value ($ mil.)	–	–	–	–	–	–
Employees	–	–	–	–	–	3,347

SAN JOAQUIN REFINING CO. INC.

3129 STANDARD ST
BAKERSFIELD, CA 93308-6242
Phone: 661-327-4257
Fax: –
Web: www.sjr.com

CEO: –
CFO: –
HR: –
FYE: December 31
Type: Private

The late Buck Owens is not the only natural resource to come from Bakersfield. California's San Joaquin Valley serves as the backdrop for Bakersfield-based independent refiner San Joaquin Refining which refines locally produced heavy crude oil. The majority of its crude oil is derived from Kern County. San Joaquin Refining's refined products are used in the development of adhesives asphalt electrical insulation lubricants paints plastics printing inks rubber roofing materials and other items. The company also owns more than 90 storage tanks capable of storing 800000 barrels of crude oil.

	Annual Growth	12/03	12/04	12/05	12/06	12/11
Sales ($ mil.)	14.9%	–	215.4	288.8	371.9	567.8
Net income ($ mil.)	33.5%	–	3.4	16.5	26.3	25.4
Market value ($ mil.)	–	–	–	–	–	–
Employees	–	–	–	–	–	20

SAN JOSE WATER COMPANY

110 W TAYLOR ST
SAN JOSE, CA 951102131
Phone: 408-288-5314
Fax: –
Web: www.sjwater.com

CEO: W Richard Roth
CFO: Angela Yip
HR: –
FYE: December 31
Type: Private

Tapping into a number of water sources San Jose Water the primary subsidiary of SJW provides water utility services to approximately 225000 customers (about 1 million people) in California's Santa Clara County. To obtain its water supply San Jose Water taps wells and surface sources and buys water from the Santa Clara Valley Water District. It also collects local mountain surface water from the watershed in the Santa Cruz Mountains which is then treated at San Jose Water's two treatment plants. This local surface water accounts for about 7% of the water utility's total supply. Purchased water accounts for more than 40%.

	Annual Growth	12/98	12/99	12/00	12/16	12/17
Sales ($ mil.)	6.6%	–	115.7	0.0	318.1	366.9
Net income ($ mil.)	5.7%	–	16.7	12.8	44.0	45.5
Market value ($ mil.)	–	–	–	–	–	–
Employees	–	–	–	–	–	300

SAN JUAN BASIN ROYALTY TRUST

BBVA USA, 300 W. 7th Street, Suite B
Fort Worth, TX 76102
Phone: 866 809-4553
Fax: –
Web: www.sjbrt.com

NYS: SJT
CEO: –
CFO: –
HR: –
FYE: December 31
Type: Public

Trusting in the power of rising oil prices to keep investors happy has been a good strategy for San Juan Basin Royalty Trust. The trust owns working and royalty interests in oil and gas properties in the San Juan Basin of northwestern New Mexico. Carved from interests owned by Southland Royalty (now controlled by ConocoPhillips) San Juan Basin Royalty Trust's holdings consist of a 75% stake in about 151900 gross (119000 net) productive acres in San Juan Rio Arriba and Sandoval counties. The property contains 3823 gross producing wells with estimated proved reserves of 249000 barrels of oil and more than 156.3 billion cu. ft. of natural gas.

	Annual Growth	12/14	12/15	12/16	12/17	12/18
Sales ($ mil.)	(25.0%)	61.6	19.5	17.5	40.7	19.5
Net income ($ mil.)	(26.0%)	59.9	17.0	13.9	39.1	18.0
Market value ($ mil.)	(23.8%)	664.2	193.0	308.6	384.1	223.7
Employees	–	–	–	–	–	–

SANCHEZ ENERGY CORP.

1000 Main Street, Suite 3000
Houston, TX 77002
Phone: 713 783-8000
Fax: –
Web: www.sanchezenergycorp.com

NBB: SNEC Q
CEO: Antonio R. (Tony) Sanchez
CFO: Howard J. Thill
HR: –
FYE: December 31
Type: Public

The Sanchez family has been around South Texas almost as long as the oil found in the Eagle Ford Shale. Sanchez Energy is a spin off from Sanchez Oil & Gas Corporation (SOG) a private firm owned by the Sanchez family who trace their family history back to the founding of Laredo in 1755. Sanchez Energy was formed in 2011 to take over almost 39000 acres (about 60 sq. mi.) of land in the oil-rich Eagle Ford Shale in South Texas. In 2013 it had 140000 net acres in the Eagle Ford play and 40000 net acres in the Tuscaloosa Marine Shale in Louisiana. It also has undeveloped acreage in Montana. The company filed Chapter 11 in 2019.

	Annual Growth	12/14	12/15	12/16	12/17	12/18
Sales ($ mil.)	12.2%	666.1	475.8	431.3	740.3	1,056.9
Net income ($ mil.)	–	(21.8)	(1,454.6)	(257.0)	43.2	85.2
Market value ($ mil.)	(52.6%)	3,029.6	977.0	2,914.6	1,539.2	152.8
Employees	–	–	–	–	–	–

SANCHEZ MIDSTREAM PARTNERS LP

1000 Main Street, Suite 3000
Houston, TX 77002
Phone: 713 783-8000
Fax: –
Web: www.sanchezpp.com

ASE: SNMP
CEO: Gerald F Willinger
CFO: –
HR: –
FYE: December 31
Type: Public

Constellation Energy Partners' domain is decidedly more terrestrial than stellar. A spin off from Constellation Energy the company is a coalbed methane exploration and production company that operates in Alabama's Black Warrior Basin (one of the oldest and most lucrative coalbed methane basins in the US) the Cherokee Basin in Kansas and Oklahoma and the Woodford Shale in the Arkoma Basin in Oklahoma. In 2010 Constellation Energy Partners reported proved reserves of 221 billion cu. ft. of natural gas equivalent. That year the company operated 87% of the more than 2780 wells in which it held an interest.

	Annual Growth	12/14	12/15	12/16	12/17	12/18
Sales ($ mil.)	2.0%	77.3	68.4	70.7	88.1	83.6
Net income ($ mil.)	13.4%	9.5	(137.1)	19.2	(3.0)	15.7
Market value ($ mil.)	5.3%	23.1	234.4	194.5	183.0	28.4
Employees	(41.7%)	52	48	33	8	6

SANDERSON FARMS INC   NMS: SAFM

127 Flynt Road
Laurel, MS 39443
Phone: 601 649-4030
Fax: 601 426-1461
Web: www.sandersonfarms.com

CEO: Joseph F. (Joe) Sanderson
CFO: D. Michael (Mike) Cockrell
HR: –
FYE: October 31
Type: Public

Sanderson Farms roosts near the top of the poultry producing pecking order. As the third-largest poultry processor in the US it produces processes sells and distributes fresh chill-pack and frozen chicken under the Sanderson Farms label. In addition to buying chicks from some 225 breeders the company contracts with nearly 800 independent chicken farmers who raise the breeder flocks for Sanderson. Its prepared-foods business processes sells and distributes partially cooked or marinated chicken. Customers are food retailers distributors and restaurants and food-service operators. The company processes more than 600 million chickens annually.

	Annual Growth	10/15	10/16	10/17	10/18	10/19
Sales ($ mil.)	5.3%	2,803.5	2,816.1	3,342.2	3,236.0	3,440.3
Net income ($ mil.)	(29.5%)	216.0	189.0	279.7	61.4	53.3
Market value ($ mil.)	22.2%	1,543.4	1,997.9	3,321.0	2,184.6	3,437.4
Employees	8.6%	12,264	13,232	14,669	15,104	17,055

SANDIA NATIONAL LABORATORIES

1515 Eubank Blvd. SE
Albuquerque NM 87123
Phone: 505-845-0011
Fax: 505-844-1120
Web: www.sandia.gov

CEO: –
CFO: –
HR: –
FYE: September 30
Type: Government-owned

Sandia stands for national security. Established in 1949 as part of the Manhattan Project Sandia National Laboratories performs research and development related to national security and defense. Its focus is nuclear weapons systems research but the lab also performs nonproliferation assessments infrastructure assurance and research and development in such areas as energy and environmental security. Sandia's duties have expanded in recent years to combat terrorism aid homeland security and support the US military in Afghanistan and Iraq. Sandia which operates with a $2.5 billion annual budget is managed by Lockheed Martin for the US Department of Energy's National Nuclear Security Administration.

SANDISK CORP.   NMS: SNDK

951 SanDisk Drive
Milpitas, CA 95035
Phone: 408 801-1000
Fax: 408 542-0503
Web: www.sandisk.com

CEO: Sanjay Mehrotra
CFO: Judy Bruner
HR: –
FYE: January 3/
Type: Public

SanDisk is a top producer of data storage products based on flash memory which retains data even when power is interrupted. Its products — which are sold to four primary end-markets (mobile consumer electronics computing and enterprise and hyperscale data centers) — include removable and embedded memory cards used in digital cameras mobile phones digital audio/video players GPS devices tablets and other electronic gear as well as USB flash drives and solid-state drives (SSDs). It also licenses technologies from its portfolio of some 4700 US and international patents. SanDisk serves consumers and enterprises worldwide with most of its sales coming from outside the US. In 3Q 2015 SanDisk agreed to be bought by Western Digital the leading maker of disk drives. The value of the cash-and-stock transaction was set at $19 billion.

	Annual Growth	01/12*	12/12	12/13	12/14*	01/16
Sales ($ mil.)	(0.4%)	5,662.1	5,052.5	6,170.0	6,627.7	5,564.9
Net income ($ mil.)	(20.8%)	987.0	417.4	1,042.7	1,007.4	388.5
Market value ($ mil.)	11.5%	9,889.9	8,577.5	14,116.4	20,360.6	15,272.0
Employees	22.2%	3,939	4,636	5,459	8,696	8,790

*Fiscal year change

SANDRIDGE ENERGY INC   NYS: SD

123 Robert S. Kerr Avenue
Oklahoma City, OK 73102
Phone: 405 429-5500
Fax: –
Web: www.sandridgeenergy.com

CEO: James D. Bennett
CFO: Julian M. Bott
HR: –
FYE: December 31
Type: Public

Sandridge Energy has exploration and production activities in the US Mid-Continent and North Park Basin of Colorado. With four rigs 2100 net producing wells plus 643000 net well acres under lease the company has proved reserves of roughly 180 million barrels of oil equivalent with around 70% labeled developed.

	Annual Growth	12/15*	10/16*	12/16	12/17	12/18
Sales ($ mil.)	(23.1%)	768.7	293.8	98.5	357.3	349.4
Net income ($ mil.)	–	(3,697.5)	1,440.8	(334.0)	47.1	(9.1)
Market value ($ mil.)	(43.2%)	–	–	840.4	751.9	271.6
Employees	(35.7%)	1,165	–	509	476	310

*Fiscal year change

SANDSTON CORPORATION   OTC: SDON

40950 Woodward Ave. Ste. 304
Bloomfield Hills MI 48304
Phone: 248-723-3007
Fax: 212-622-7301
Web: www.aljregionalholdings.com

CEO: Daniel J Dorman
CFO: –
HR: –
FYE: December 31
Type: Public

Sandston had control issues. The company formerly known as Nematron is a public shell that is pursuing investment opportunities. In 2004 it sold the assets of its control systems business to a group of private investors and changed its name to Sandston. (The private investors continue to provide industrial workstations used to control factory equipment under the Nematron name.) Dorman Industries a company controlled by CEO Daniel Dorman owns about 49% of Sandston; Patricia Dorman his wife owns another 5%.

SANDY SPRING BANCORP INC   NMS: SASR

17801 Georgia Avenue
Olney, MD 20832
Phone: 301 774-6400
Fax: –
Web: www.sandyspringbank.com

CEO: Daniel J. (Dan) Schrider
CFO: Philip J. Mantua
HR: –
FYE: December 31
Type: Public

Sandy Spring Bancorp is the holding company for Sandy Spring Bank which operates around 50 branches in the Baltimore and Washington DC metropolitan areas. Founded in 1868 the bank is one of the largest and oldest headquartered in Maryland. It provides standard deposit services including checking and savings accounts money market accounts and CDs. Commercial and residential real estate loans account for nearly three-quarters of the company's loan portfolio; the remainder is a mix of consumer loans business loans and equipment leases. The company also offers personal investing services wealth management trust services insurance and retirement planning.

	Annual Growth	12/14	12/15	12/16	12/17	12/18
Assets ($ mil.)	17.0%	4,397.1	4,655.4	5,091.4	5,446.7	8,243.3
Net income ($ mil.)	27.5%	38.2	45.4	48.3	53.2	100.9
Market value ($ mil.)	4.7%	926.6	957.9	1,420.9	1,386.4	1,113.5
Employees	6.4%	727	737	752	754	932

SANFILIPPO (JOHN B) & SON INC   NMS: JBSS

1703 North Randall Road   CEO: Jeffrey T. Sanfilippo
Elgin, IL 60123-7820   CFO: Michael J. Valentine
Phone: 847-289-1800   HR: –
Fax: –   FYE: June 27
Web: www.jbssinc.com   Type: Public

John B. Sanfilippo & Son (JBSS) is one of the largest processors of peanuts almonds pecans walnuts cashews and other nuts in the US. It markets the nuts as snacks and baking ingredients under a number of private labels as well as its own name brands including Fisher Orchard Valley Harvest Squirrel and Sunshine Country. The company also produces and distributes other foods and snacks such as peanut butter dried fruit and trail mixes corn snacks sesame sticks and candy. JBSS's products are sold worldwide to consumers (via retailers) and less so to commercial ingredient channels (food service and industrial markets) and contract packagers.

	Annual Growth	06/15	06/16	06/17	06/18	06/19
Sales ($ mil.)	(0.3%)	887.2	952.1	846.6	888.6	876.2
Net income ($ mil.)	7.7%	29.3	30.4	36.1	32.4	39.5
Market value ($ mil.)	9.9%	619.6	485.5	712.7	861.7	904.3
Employees	0.3%	1,450	1,350	1,325	1,450	1,470

SANFORD

801 BROADWAY N   CEO: –
FARGO, ND 581023641   CFO: Joann Kunkel
Phone: 701-234-6000   HR: –
Fax: –   FYE: June 30
Web: www.sanfordhealth.org   Type: Private

Sanford is one of the largest not-for-profit integrated health care systems in the US. It primarily serves rural areas through its network of more than 40 regional and community hospitals in nine states including the Dakotas Iowa Minnesota and Nebraska. The organization operating as Sanford Health also operates local clinics and long-term care centers. In addition to primary care and general hospital services Sanford's medical centers and specialty outpatient practices provide care in fields including senior living cancer cardiology vascular health neurology orthopedics pediatrics virology and women's health. In early 2019 Sanford merged with Good Samaritan Society which specializes in senior care.

	Annual Growth	06/13	06/14	06/16	06/17	06/18
Sales ($ mil.)	486.1%	–	3.9	4,231.4	4,411.0	4,639.3
Net income ($ mil.)	–	–	–	(11.9)	108.1	175.4	117.5
Market value ($ mil.)	–	–	–	–	–	–
Employees	–	–	–	–	–	50,000

SANFORD BURNHAM PREBYS MEDICAL DISCOVERY INSTITUTE

10901 N TORREY PINES RD   CEO: Perry Nisen
LA JOLLA, CA 920371005   CFO: Gary F. Raisl
Phone: 858-795-5000   HR: Teddi Reilly
Fax: –   FYE: June 30
Web: www.sbpdiscovery.org   Type: Private

Founded in 1976 as the La Jolla Cancer Research Foundation the Sanford-Burnham Medical Research Institute is a nonprofit organization that performs biomedical research in areas such as cellular biology cancer genetics degenerative diseases and developmental neurobiology. Known for its stem cell research and drug discovery technologies Sanford-Burnham boasts a handful of research centers including its Cancer Center which has been supported by National Cancer Institute (part of the NIH) since 1981. Sanford-Burnham's other centers include the Sanford Children's Health Research Center and the Del E. Webb Neuroscience Aging and Stem Cell Research Center.

	Annual Growth	06/14	06/15	06/16	06/17	06/18
Sales ($ mil.)	(21.4%)	–	254.7	122.1	132.6	123.7
Net income ($ mil.)	–	–	100.6	(23.1)	(2.0)	(25.5)
Market value ($ mil.)	–	–	–	–	–	–
Employees	–	–	–	–	–	1,000

SANFORD HEALTH OF NORTHERN MINNESOTA

1300 Anne St. NW   CEO: –
Bemidji MN 56601   CFO: –
Phone: 218-751-5430   HR: –
Fax: 218-333-5880   FYE: September 30
Web: www.nchs.com   Type: Subsidiary

If ya have a run-in with a snowmobile up Bemidji then ya may need Sanford Health of Northern Minnesota doncha know. Formerly named North Country Health Services the system serves residents of the town of Bemidji and other parts of Beltrami County in northern Minnesota. Its flagship facility is Sanford Bemidji Medical Center (formerly North Country Regional Hospital) a 120-bed acute care hospital founded in 1898 providing general surgical psychiatric cardiac and other specialty services. The system also has home health and hospice agencies community clinics and assisted living facilities. It added the Sanford Bemidji Clinic when it joined the Sanford Health-Meritcare network in 2011.

SANMINA CORP   NMS: SANM

2700 N. First St.   CEO: Robert K. (Bob) Eulau
San Jose, CA 95134   CFO: David Anderson
Phone: 408-964-3500   HR: Alan M. Reid
Fax: –   FYE: September 28
Web: www.sanmina.com   Type: Public

Contract manufacturer Sanmina makes the boards and components that make up many an electronic device. Starting with the design stage the company makes assembles and tests printed circuit boards. It also makes backplanes cable assemblies radio frequency and optical components and modules and memory modules. Besides products Sanmina provides services such as engineering materials management and order fulfillment. Its customers are OEMs in the healthcare defense medical aerospace telecommunications and technology industries among others. Sanmina operates about 25 manufacturing facilities on six continents. The California-based company gets more than 80% of its sales from outside the US.

	Annual Growth	10/15	10/16*	09/17	09/18	09/19
Sales ($ mil.)	6.6%	6,374.5	6,481.2	6,868.6	7,110.1	8,233.9
Net income ($ mil.)	(21.7%)	377.3	187.8	138.8	(95.5)	141.5
Market value ($ mil.)	10.7%	1,489.9	1,984.9	2,590.1	1,924.3	2,239.4
Employees	(0.5%)	43,854	45,397	47,000	47,000	43,000

*Fiscal year change

SANOFI-AVENTIS U.S. LLC

55 Corporate Dr.   CEO: Christopher A Viehbacher
Bridgewater NJ 08807   CFO: –
Phone: 908-231-4000   HR: –
Fax: 415-466-2300   FYE: December 31
Web: www.intermune.com   Type: Subsidiary

Yes Sanofi-Aventis US is "just" a subsidiary but it's still one of the largest pharmaceutical companies in the country. As the US operations of global drugmaker Sanofi the company develops manufactures and markets pharmaceutical products for a range of ailments. Its principal therapeutic areas include cardiovascular disease central nervous system ailments internal medicine metabolic disorders oncology and ophthalmology. Some of its key products include injectable insulin Lantus cancer drug Taxotere thrombosis treatment Lovenox and blood thinner Plavix. Also known as simply Sanofi US the firm markets its parent's products in the US through its thousands of field sales professionals.

SANTA CRUZ SEASIDE COMPANY INC

400 BEACH ST
SANTA CRUZ, CA 950605416
Phone: 831-423-5590
Fax: –
Web: www.beachboardwalk.com

CEO: –
CFO: –
HR: Sabra Reyes
FYE: December 31
Type: Private

Santa Cruz Seaside Company has been making people scream laugh and spend money for more than a century. The company operates the Santa Cruz Boardwalk amusement park in California which has been touted the "Coney Island of the West". The park features about 35 rides 30 restaurants 15 retail shops arcades miniature golf bowling and conference and banquet facilities. The property is a State Historic Landmark while its Looff Carousel (1911) and Giant Dipper roller coaster (1924) are both National Historic Landmarks. In addition some arcade games date back to 1910. The Canfield family including chairman and president Charles own the company. The Boardwalk celebrated its 100th anniversary in 2007.

	Annual Growth	12/09	12/10	12/11	12/12	12/13
Sales ($ mil.)	6.9%	–	45.2	47.5	51.9	55.2
Net income ($ mil.)	38.7%	–	–	3.8	6.1	7.3
Market value ($ mil.)	–	–	–	–	–	–
Employees	–	–	–	–	–	1,000

SANTA FE FINANCIAL CORP. NBB: SFEF

12121 Wilshire Boulevard, Suite 610
Los Angeles, CA 90025
Phone: 310 889-2500
Fax: 310 889-2525
Web: www.intgla.com

CEO: John V Winfield
CFO: Danfeng Xu
HR: –
FYE: June 30
Type: Public

No Santa Fe Financial doesn't invest in the City Different but it does know its way around city living. Santa Fe Financial invests in residential and commercial real estate mostly in California. Its majority-owned Portsmouth Square jointly owns the land improvements and leaseholds for a Hilton hotel in San Francisco. It also owns a majority stake in a Los Angeles apartment complex and owns a smaller residential building through its Acanto Properties subsidiary. Portsmouth also invested in a residential development in Hawaii. Investments derived from Portsmouth along with rental income make up most of Santa Fe Financial's revenue. CEO John Winfield also serves as CEO of InterGroup and Portsmouth Square.

	Annual Growth	06/15	06/16	06/17	06/18	06/19
Sales ($ mil.)	1.2%	57.4	59.0	54.7	57.4	60.2
Net income ($ mil.)	–	(2.5)	(5.0)	(1.2)	1.5	3.3
Market value ($ mil.)	8.4%	31.0	37.9	43.5	44.7	42.8
Employees	(71.7%)	314	278	277	2	2

SANTA FE GOLD CORP NBB: SFEG

P.O. Box 25201
Albuquerque, NM 87125
Phone: 505 255-4852
Fax: –
Web: www.santafegoldcorp.com

CEO: Catalin Chiloflishi
CFO: Frank Mueller
HR: –
FYE: June 30
Type: Public

Santa Fe Gold hopes it has the Midas touch. The company controls the Summit silver and gold mining project and the Lordsburg mill in southwestern New Mexico. It has also been developing the Ortiz gold property in north-central New Mexico and holds the Black Canyon mica deposit and processing equipment near Phoenis. With an increased emphasis on those projects Santa Fe Gold has transformed itself into a precious metals miner. The company focuses on acquiring and developing gold silver copper and industrial mineral assets. Although it dropped its bid to acquire Columbus Silver in 2012 the company plans to buy some of that company's mineral properties.

	Annual Growth	06/12	06/13	06/14	06/15	06/16
Sales ($ mil.)	(84.7%)	11.5	14.6	2.1	0.1	0.0
Net income ($ mil.)	–	(4.2)	(10.4)	(11.6)	(9.6)	(4.8)
Market value ($ mil.)	(54.9%)	74.9	31.0	13.3	14.6	3.1
Employees	(59.0%)	71	65	5	5	2

SANTA MONICA COMMUNITY COLLEGE DISTRICT

1900 PICO BLVD
SANTA MONICA, CA 904051628
Phone: 310-434-4000
Fax: –
Web: www.smc.edu

CEO: –
CFO: –
HR: –
FYE: June 30
Type: Private

Talk about a (class)room with a view. Santa Monica Community College is a two-year school with about 34000 students. The beach-side college offers programs in more than 80 fields of study and leads California's junior colleges in transferring students to the University of California and University of Southern California. Its unique Academy of Entertainment and Technology offers courses in entertainment technology (animation game development editing visual effects) graphic design and interior architectural design. The school also provides career training in such fields as accounting automotive technology computer science fine arts and nursing. Santa Monica Community College was founded in 1929.

	Annual Growth	06/0-1	06/00	06/16	06/17	06/18
Sales ($ mil.)	(1.5%)	–	118.8	66.9	269.9	91.1
Net income ($ mil.)	–	–	8.6	19.1	2.6	(5.3)
Market value ($ mil.)	–	–	–	–	–	–
Employees	–	–	–	–	–	1,300

SANTANDER CONSUMER USA HOLDINGS INC NYS: SC

1601 Elm Street, Suite 800
Dallas, TX 75201
Phone: 214 634-1110
Fax: –
Web: www.santanderconsumerusa.com

CEO: Mahesh Aditya
CFO: Juan Carlos Alvarez
HR: –
FYE: December 31
Type: Public

This auto finance company aims to put credit-impaired car buyers in the driver's seat. Santander Consumer USA (SCUSA) makes subprime new and used vehicle loans to buyers at more than 14000 Chrysler Ford GM and Toyota dealerships throughout the US. The technology-driven company also originates loans through independent dealers such as CarMax banks and its direct-to-consumer website Roadloans.com. SCUSA also provides refinancing and cash-back refinancing services. While subprime loans make up more than 80% of its loan portfolio the company is looking to increase its prime loan business. Founded in 1995 SCUSA is owned by Spanish banking giant Banco Santander SA. The company went public in 2014.

	Annual Growth	12/14	12/15	12/16	12/17	12/18
Assets ($ mil.)	8.0%	32,342.2	36,570.4	38,539.1	39,422.3	43,959.9
Net income ($ mil.)	4.6%	766.3	827.3	766.5	1,187.6	915.9
Market value ($ mil.)	(2.7%)	6,908.7	5,584.0	4,756.1	6,559.9	6,197.0
Employees	3.0%	4,400	5,100	5,100	5,076	4,952

SANTANDER HOLDINGS USA INC. NYS: SOV PRC

75 State Street
Boston, MA 02109
Phone: 617 346-7200
Fax: –
Web: www.santanderus.com/us/investorshareholderrelations

CEO: Timothy Wennes
CFO: Juan Carlos Alvarez
HR: –
FYE: December 31
Type: Public

Santander Holdings USA is the parent company of Sovereign Bank which reigns in the Northeast with more than 700 branch locations. The bank caters to individuals and small to midsized businesses offering deposits credit cards insurance and investments as well as commercial loans and mortgages (which together account for nearly half of its total portfolio) and residential mortgages and home equity loans (more than a quarter). Santander Holdings also owns a majority of Santander Consumer USA which purchases and services subprime car loans made by auto dealerships and other companies. Spain-based banking giant Banco Santander acquired the rest of Sovereign Bancorp it didn't already own in 2009.

	Annual Growth	12/14	12/15	12/16	12/17	12/18
Sales ($ mil.)	(1.3%)	11,919.2	10,473.7	10,745.5	10,715.7	11,313.4
Net income ($ mil.)	(25.8%)	2,335.2	(1,454.6)	362.9	561.1	707.4
Market value ($ mil.)	0.2%	13,540.9	13,710.6	13,647.0	13,620.4	–
Employees	4.5%	14,000	15,150	16,500	17,000	16,700

SAP AMERICA INC.

3999 West Chester Pike
Newtown Square PA 19073
Phone: 610-661-1000
Fax: 919-832-8322
Web: fwv-us.com
CEO: William McDermott
CFO: Mark R White
HR: –
FYE: December 31
Type: Subsidiary

SAP America represents its German parent SAP in the US providing enterprise software and services for managing accounting distribution human resources and manufacturing functions. The company's products include business intelligence enterprise resource planning customer relationship management and supply chain management software. SAP America offers industry-specific applications for markets ranging from aerospace and defense to wholesale distribution. Its services include consulting and support as well as custom development and application hosting. SAP America accounts for more about one-quarter of SAP's sales and three-quarters of all the Americas.

SAPIENT CORP.
NMS: SAPE

131 Dartmouth St.
Boston, MA 02116
Phone: 617 621-0200
Fax: 617 621-1300
Web: www.sapient.com
CEO: Alan J Herrick
CFO: Joseph S Tibbetts Jr
HR: –
FYE: December 31
Type: Public

Sapient is no sap when it comes to helping businesses make the jump to the digital age. The company offers consulting software development digital marketing and other services that help clients transform their businesses to compete for a global digital audience. Its customers have included AT&T Mobility Unilever and the US government. Sapient has expertise in providing services for financial and commodity markets though it also targets global blue-chip customers in the consumer travel and automotive industries among others. It has more than 30 offices worldwide; about half of those are in North America.

	Annual Growth	12/08	12/09	12/10	12/11	12/12
Sales ($ mil.)	14.0%	687.5	666.7	863.5	1,062.2	1,161.5
Net income ($ mil.)	1.1%	62.5	88.1	43.8	73.6	65.2
Market value ($ mil.)	24.2%	612.8	1,141.4	1,670.0	1,739.0	1,457.5
Employees	13.9%	6,360	7,052	9,015	9,950	10,700

SAPP BROS. PETROLEUM INC.

9915 S 148TH ST STE 2
OMAHA, NE 681383876
Phone: 402-895-2202
Fax: –
Web: www.sappbrospetro.com
CEO: Allen Marsh
CFO: Tyler A Marsh
HR: –
FYE: October 31
Type: Private

There have been few poor saps in this family since the Sapp brothers made a go of their petroleum products business. Sapp Bros Petroleum distributes petroleum products such as fuels lubricants propane antifreeze absorbents additives and equipment through more than 10 locations in Nebraska and western Iowa. It has a sideline selling used computer parts such as modems processors and keyboards. The regional fuel distributor was founded by the four Sapp brothers in 1980 and is run by CEO Bill Sapp who also runs sister company Sapp Bros Truck Stops.

	Annual Growth	10/05	10/06	10/07	10/08	10/09
Sales ($ mil.)	–	–	–	(1,566.9)	922.3	564.0
Net income ($ mil.)	19890.6%	–	–	0.0	3.2	5.6
Market value ($ mil.)	–	–	–	–	–	–
Employees	–	–	–	–	–	285

SAPP BROS., INC.

9915 S 148TH ST
OMAHA, NE 681383876
Phone: 402-895-7038
Fax: –
Web: www.sappbros.net
CEO: Allen J Marsh
CFO: –
HR: –
FYE: September 30
Type: Private

Need air in those 18 wheels? Sapp Bros Travel Centers (formerly Sapp Bros Truck Stops) has the usual air gas food but also offers human conveniences such such as laundry rooms mailbox rentals private showers and TV lounges. The company operates a chain of some 15 truck stops — readily identifiable by the giant red-and-white coffeepot logo — along interstate highways from Utah to Pennsylvania; with a concentration in Nebraska. Half of the locations also operate service centers offering oil changes new tires and safety checks. Its sister company Sapp Bros Petroleum distributes fuels and lubricants to more than 200 retailers. The firm is run by CEO Bill Sapp one of the four founding Sapp brothers.

	Annual Growth	09/14	09/15	09/16	09/17	09/18
Sales ($ mil.)	3.7%	–	1,128.4	802.8	990.2	1,259.1
Net income ($ mil.)	(17.5%)	–	20.9	18.5	11.8	11.7
Market value ($ mil.)	–	–	–	–	–	–
Employees	–	–	–	–	–	1,700

SARAH BUSH LINCOLN HEALTH CENTER

1000 HEALTH CENTER DR
MATTOON, IL 619384644
Phone: 217-258-2525
Fax: –
Web: www.sarahbush.org
CEO: Jerry Esker
CFO: –
HR: –
FYE: June 30
Type: Private

With the moniker of the Illinois' favorite son's stepmother (Sarah Bush Lincoln) who wouldn't want to go to this health center? And apparently the locals agree since Sarah Bush Lincoln Health Center (SBLHC) has a market share of about 44% in its seven-county service area in east-central Illinois and an inpatient market share for Coles County of nearly 80%. SBLHC has 128 beds and provides a wide range of health care services including emergency medicine behavioral health care surgical services and cancer treatment. Its network also includes about 30 clinics doctors' offices and hospice centers. The hospital also offers support groups and continuing education classes.

	Annual Growth	06/10	06/11	06/14	06/15	06/16
Sales ($ mil.)	3.9%	–	195.7	252.7	223.9	237.2
Net income ($ mil.)	10.5%	–	14.0	28.3	37.8	23.1
Market value ($ mil.)	–	–	–	–	–	–
Employees	–	–	–	–	–	1,543

SARAH LAWRENCE COLLEGE

1 MEAD WAY
BRONXVILLE, NY 107085999
Phone: 914-337-0700
Fax: –
Web: www.sarahlawrence.edu
CEO: –
CFO: –
HR: –
FYE: May 31
Type: Private

Sarah Lawrence College (SLC) was founded in 1926 as an institution of higher education for young women. The private liberal arts school located on a 44-acre campus in suburban New York has been coeducational since 1968 and has an annual enrollment of some 1300 undergraduate and about 350 graduate students. Most of its courses are seminars limited to 14 students; the school has a student-to-faculty ratio of approximately 10-to-1 one of the lowest at any US university. SLC offers a wide range of academic concentrations including performing arts natural science history teaching and literature. It was founded by William Lawrence who named the school after his wife Sarah a supporter of women's suffrage.

	Annual Growth	05/14	05/15	05/16	05/17	05/18
Sales ($ mil.)	1.3%	–	73.4	71.8	131.4	76.4
Net income ($ mil.)	(27.3%)	–	16.6	(11.5)	19.6	6.4
Market value ($ mil.)	–	–	–	–	–	–
Employees	–	–	–	–	–	450

SARASOTA COUNTY PUBLIC HOSPITAL DISTRICT

1700 S TAMIAMI TRL
SARASOTA, FL 342393509
Phone: 941-917-9000
Fax: –
Web: www.smh.com

CEO: David Verinder
CFO: David Verinder
HR: –
FYE: September 30
Type: Private

Sarasota County Public Hospital Board which does business as the Sarasota Memorial Health Care System is a publicly owned hospital system serving residents in and around Sarasota on Florida's western coast. It operates Sarasota Memorial Hospital a not-for-profit acute-care facility with more than 800 beds (and more than 900 doctors) that provides general medical and surgical care as well as specialized care in areas such as heart disease cancer and neuroscience. The system also features a skilled nursing facility walk-in medical centers an outpatient surgical center and home health care operations. Additionally the hospital conducts clinical trials and has an educational affiliation with Florida State University.

	Annual Growth	09/13	09/14	09/15	09/16	09/17
Sales ($ mil.)	14.8%	–	524.7	590.8	12.5	793.1
Net income ($ mil.)	2.6%	–	92.5	131.7	0.5	99.9
Market value ($ mil.)	–	–	–	–	–	–
Employees	–	–	–	–	–	4,200

SARATOGA RESOURCES INC

9225 Katy Freeway, Suite 100
Houston, TX 77024
Phone: 713 458-1560
Fax: –
Web: www.saratogaresources.com

NBB: SARA Q
CEO: Thomas F Cooke
CFO: –
HR: –
FYE: December 31
Type: Public

Saratoga Resources (SRI) hopes to find more than springs underground. The independent oil and gas company explores for and produces oil and natural gas along the coast of Louisiana. The company's 13 oil fields are spread across more than 52000 acres with about 90 wells and have proved and probable reserves of about 342 million barrels of oil equivalent 46% of which is natural gas. SRI produces about 803400 barrels of oil equivalent per year about 75% of it oil. The company owns associated infrastructure assets on its oilfields including 100 miles of pipeline about 90 wellbores and 10 saltwater disposal wells which it uses and provides to third parties for a fee.

	Annual Growth	12/10	12/11	12/12	12/13	12/14
Sales ($ mil.)	(0.3%)	55.0	80.9	84.0	67.4	54.4
Net income ($ mil.)	–	(19.4)	20.8	(3.7)	(26.4)	(143.9)
Market value ($ mil.)	28.2%	69.7	188.4	188.4	188.4	188.4
Employees	1.6%	30	40	31	34	32

SAREPTA THERAPEUTICS INC

215 First Street, Suite 415
Cambridge, MA 02142
Phone: 617 274-4000
Fax: –
Web: www.sarepta.com

NMS: SRPT
CEO: Douglas S. Ingram
CFO: Sandesh (Sandy) Mahatme
HR: Joan Wood
FYE: December 31
Type: Public

Sarepta Therapeutics makes sense of antisense. The biopharmaceutical's investigational therapies are based on its RNA-based antisense drug technology which can halt disease processes at the genetic level. The commercial-stage company is working on drugs that could potentially be used in the treatment of a wide range of conditions including genetic and infectious diseases. In 2016 the FDA granted accelerated approval for Sarepta's first product Duchenne muscular dystrophy (DMD) drug EXONDYS 51 (eteplirsen). It was the first FDA approval of a treatment for that condition; the company has additional therapies for DMD in development. Sarepta also has research and development programs for targets including the Ebola and Marburg viruses dengue fever anthrax and pandemic influenza.

	Annual Growth	12/14	12/15	12/16	12/17	12/18
Sales ($ mil.)	135.7%	9.8	1.3	5.4	154.6	301.0
Net income ($ mil.)	–	(135.8)	(220.0)	(267.3)	(50.7)	(361.9)
Market value ($ mil.)	65.7%	1,028.4	2,742.0	1,949.5	3,954.4	7,756.1
Employees	25.1%	204	270	197	255	499

SARGENT ELECTRIC COMPANY

2767 LIBERTY AVE
PITTSBURGH, PA 152224703
Phone: 412-338-8480
Fax: –
Web: www.sargentelectric.com

CEO: Stephan H Dake
CFO: Elizabeth Lawrence
HR: –
FYE: December 31
Type: Private

Sargent Electric Company has earned its stripes providing electrical services for its customers. Founded in 1907 to serve Pittsburgh's steel industry the electrical contractor performs construction work for utilities foundries oil refineries chemical processing firms and steelmakers. Clients have included Allegheny Energy Duquesne Light General Electric and United States Steel. The company also provides electric service and maintenance services to residential commercial and government customers. Its service area encompasses about 20 states in the eastern half of the US. Sargent Electric is owned and managed by the Sargent family.

	Annual Growth	12/10	12/11	12/13	12/14	12/15
Sales ($ mil.)	2.6%	–	89.1	187.7	88.9	98.7
Net income ($ mil.)	63.2%	–	0.3	10.2	1.7	2.4
Market value ($ mil.)	–	–	–	–	–	–
Employees	–	–	–	–	–	400

SAS INSTITUTE INC.

100 SAS Campus Dr.
Cary NC 27513-2414
Phone: 919-677-8000
Fax: 919-677-4444
Web: www.sas.com

CEO: James H Goodnight
CFO: Wm David Davis
HR: –
FYE: December 31
Type: Private

Don't talk back to this company about business intelligence. SAS (pronounced "sass") specializes in software used for business analytics data warehousing and data mining activities employed by corporations to gather manage and analyze enormous amounts of data. Clients mainly financial services firms government agencies and telecom carriers use its applications to find patterns in customer data manage resources and target new business. SAS also offers software and support packages for other segments such as leisure manufacturing and retail. It has more than 400 offices in over 50 countries. Founder and CEO James Goodnight owns about two-thirds of the company; co-founder and EVP John Sall owns the rest.

SATMETRIX SYSTEMS INC.

1100 Park Place
San Mateo CA 94403
Phone: 650-227-8300
Fax: 650-227-8301
Web: www.satmetrix.com

CEO: Richard Owen
CFO: Raymond Yue
HR: –
FYE: June 30
Type: Private

Survey says Satmetrix Systems can help you know if your customers are satisfied. The company's software uses customer surveys to provide feedback on sales products training and support services. Survey results can be displayed in standard charts and graphs or in customized reports in a real-time Web-based environment. Satmetrix software can also integrate data from existing call tracking or customer relationship management systems. Customers come from a wide range of industries and have included firms such as AT&T eBay and Hewlett-Packard.

HOOVER'S MASTERLIST OF U.S. COMPANIES 2020

SATTERFIELD AND PONTIKES CONSTRUCTION, INC.

11750 KATY FWY STE 500
HOUSTON, TX 770791219
Phone: 713-996-1300
Fax: –
Web: www.satpon.com

CEO: George A Pontikes Jr
CFO: Angela Salinas
HR: Alicia Manlove
FYE: December 31
Type: Private

Satterfield & Pontikes Construction (S&P) provides general contracting consultation and construction management services primarily in the Gulf Coast region of Texas and Louisiana. The company often works on buildings for the commercial retail industrial educational entertainment and recreational sectors. High profile projects include the Texas A&M University Health Science Center and the expansion of the World War II Museum in New Orleans. S&P specializes in concrete work and early-stage site work as well as 3-D modeling and virtual design. The company was founded in 1989 and is headed by majority owner and CEO George Pontikes.

	Annual Growth	12/08	12/09	12/10	12/11	12/12
Sales ($ mil.)	–	–	–	(1,698.0)	388.8	377.3
Net income ($ mil.)	–	–	–	0.0	0.3	(8.9)
Market value ($ mil.)	–	–	–	–	–	–
Employees	–	–	–	–	–	400

SAUL CENTERS INC

NYS: BFS

7501 Wisconsin Avenue
Bethesda, MD 20814
Phone: 301 986-6200
Fax: –
Web: www.saulcenters.com

CEO: B. Francis Saul
CFO: Scott V. Schneider
HR: Ken Kovach
FYE: December 31
Type: Public

This company might say that with shopping properties it's "Saul" good. A self-managed and self-administered real estate investment trust (REIT) Saul Centers acquires develops and manages commercial real estate primarily in the Washington DC metropolitan area. The REIT owns about 50 strip malls and shopping centers anchored by big-box retailers and supermarkets along with half a dozen mixed-use properties. Altogether its properties comprise some 9.3 million sq. ft. of leasable space. Outside of its core market the company has properties in the Southeast and Midwest. Its major tenants include the likes of Giant Food Safeway Capital One Bank and the US government.

	Annual Growth	12/14	12/15	12/16	12/17	12/18
Sales ($ mil.)	2.4%	207.1	209.1	217.1	227.3	227.9
Net income ($ mil.)	1.9%	46.9	42.5	45.3	48.3	50.6
Market value ($ mil.)	(4.7%)	1,300.5	1,165.8	1,514.7	1,404.1	1,073.7
Employees	0.0%	65	61	58	65	65

SAVANNAH HEALTH SERVICES, LLC

4700 WATERS AVE
SAVANNAH, GA 314046220
Phone: 912-350-8000
Fax: –
Web: www.memorialhealth.com

CEO: Magaret Gill
CFO: –
HR: –
FYE: December 31
Type: Private

Memorial Health University Medical Center wants to provide memorable health care to residents of Savannah Georgia and surrounding areas. An affiliate of Mercer University School of Medicine the tertiary care facility provides such services as cardiac and trauma care and rehabilitation. Also known as Memorial University Medical Center (MUMC) the hospital has some 620 beds and includes the MUMC Children's Hospital. It also operates specialty cancer care and women's health centers as well as research programs. Founded in 1955 MUMC is the flagship facility in a broader system of entities known as Memorial Health which includes affiliated primary and specialty care clinics in the region.

	Annual Growth	12/07	12/08	12/13	12/14	12/15
Sales ($ mil.)	0.4%	–	453.3	547.2	469.4	466.2
Net income ($ mil.)	–	–	(29.4)	38.6	32.3	9.6
Market value ($ mil.)	–	–	–	–	–	–
Employees	–	–	–	–	–	4,700

SAVE THE CHILDREN FEDERATION, INC.

501 KINGS HWY E STE 400
FAIRFIELD, CT 068254861
Phone: 203-221-4000
Fax: –
Web: www.savethechildren.org

CEO: Carolyn Miles
CFO: –
HR: –
FYE: December 31
Type: Private

Save the Children helps poor and malnourished children in some 15 US states and nearly 120 countries focusing on such areas as health and nutrition economic development education child protection and HIV/AIDS. The humanitarian organization also participates in international disaster relief efforts focusing on children and their families. Save the Children spends about 90% of its budget on program services with the rest allocated to administration and fundraising. The group was founded in 1932 inspired by the international children's rights movement begun in the UK in 1919 by Eglantyne Jebb founder of the British Save the Children Fund. It is a member of the International Save the Children Alliance.

	Annual Growth	12/12	12/13	12/14	12/15	12/16
Sales ($ mil.)	(3.9%)	–	–	–	678.3	652.0
Net income ($ mil.)	–	–	–	–	(10.1)	(7.5)
Market value ($ mil.)	–	–	–	–	–	–
Employees	–	–	–	–	–	3,000

SAVIENT PHARMACEUTICALS INC

NBB: SVNT Q

400 Crossing Boulevard, 3rd Floor
Bridgewater, NJ 08807
Phone: 732 418-9300
Fax: –
Web: www.savient.com

CEO: Louis Ferrari
CFO: John P Hamill
HR: –
FYE: December 31
Type: Public

Savient Pharmaceuticals is a savant of gout management weight gain encouragement and joint pain relief commercializing niche drug products that address these conditions which it then sells to medical specialists. The biopharmaceutical company gets most of its revenues from KRYSTEXXA a treatment for chronic gout which it launched commercially in 2011. Savient's other marketed products are Oxandrin a synthetic derivative of testosterone used to treat involuntary weight loss caused by trauma surgery or disease (mainly HIV) and the the generic form of that drug known as Oxandrolone.

	Annual Growth	12/08	12/09	12/10	12/11	12/12
Sales ($ mil.)	54.3%	3.2	3.0	4.0	9.6	18.0
Net income ($ mil.)	–	(84.2)	(90.9)	(73.1)	(102.0)	(118.3)
Market value ($ mil.)	(34.8%)	423.2	994.7	814.1	163.0	76.7
Employees	13.7%	73	43	129	173	122

SAVVIS INC.

1 Savvis Pkwy.
Chesterfield MO 63017
Phone: 314-628-7000
Fax: 845-695-2699
Web: www.mediacomcc.com

CEO: –
CFO: –
HR: –
FYE: December 31
Type: Subsidiary

SAVVIS serves up a wide array of network services. The company primarily provides hosting services including data colocation and hosted software for businesses from its 32 data centers. It also provides managed network services such as network security and utility computing and it sells network bandwidth on a wholesale basis. SAVVIS markets directly to customers mainly in the Americas region but it also has clients and operations in Europe and Asia. The company targets large and midsized businesses and federal government entities. Customers have included Procter & Gamble Reuters and Virgin Entertainment. SAVVIS was acquired in 2011 by CenturyLink a leading US phone company for $2.5 billion.

1165

SAWNEE ELECTRIC MEMBERSHIP CORPORATION

543 ATLANTA RD
CUMMING, GA 300402701
Phone: 770-887-2363
Fax: –
Web: www.sawnee.com

CEO: Michael A Goodroe
CFO: Sandra Fraro
HR: –
FYE: December 31
Type: Private

Sawnee Electric Membership Corporation (Sawnee EMC) wasn't around on the night the lights went out in Georgia but it plans to make sure they stay on. The electric distribution cooperative serves about 152000 residential commercial and industrial meters in a seven-county area of northern Georgia comprised of Cherokee Dawson Forsyth Fulton Gwinnett Hall and Lumpkin counties. Residential customers in the area (which includes the sprawling Atlanta suburbs) account for two-thirds of electricity usage. While small and medium users must get their electricity from Sawnee potential customers with loads exceeding 900 kilowatts can shop around. Sawnee EMC distributes electricity over 9970 miles of power line.

	Annual Growth	12/12	12/13	12/14	12/15	12/16
Sales ($ mil.)	1.1%	–	335.6	346.7	337.2	346.9
Net income ($ mil.)	–	–	0.0	0.0	0.0	0.0
Market value ($ mil.)	–	–	–	–	–	–
Employees	–	–	–	–	–	300

SB FINANCIAL GROUP INC

NAS: SBFG

401 Clinton Street
Defiance, OH 43512
Phone: 419 783-8950
Fax: –
Web: www.yoursbfinancial.com

CEO: Mark A Klein
CFO: Anthony V Cosentino
HR: –
FYE: December 31
Type: Public

SB Financial Group (formerly Rurban Financial) is the holding company The State Bank and Trust Company (dba State Bank) which has more than 20 branches in northwestern Ohio and another in northeastern Indiana. The banks offer products including checking and savings accounts money market accounts credit cards IRAs and CDs. Commercial and agricultural loans account for approximately two-thirds of the company's loan portfolio; the bank also writes mortgage and consumer loans. State Bank Wealth Management (formerly Reliance Financial Services) a unit of State Bank offers trust and investment management services as well as brokerage services through an alliance with Raymond James.

	Annual Growth	12/14	12/15	12/16	12/17	12/18
Assets ($ mil.)	9.6%	684.2	733.1	816.0	876.6	986.8
Net income ($ mil.)	21.9%	5.3	7.6	8.8	11.1	11.6
Market value ($ mil.)	15.0%	61.1	72.4	104.4	120.2	107.0
Employees	7.1%	190	214	227	234	250

SB ONE BANCORP

NMS: SBBX

95 State Route 17
Paramus, NJ 07652
Phone: 844 256-7328
Fax: –
Web: www.sussexbank.com

CEO: Anthony Labozzetta
CFO: Steven M Fusco
HR: –
FYE: December 31
Type: Public

Sussex Bancorp is the holding company for Sussex Bank which operates about 10 branches in Sussex County New Jersey and two others in Orange County New York. Targeting individuals and local businesses the bank offers such standard retail products as checking and savings accounts NOW and money market accounts and certificates of deposit. It also provides trust and financial advisory and insurance services. Lending activities consist primarily of commercial mortgages (more than half of the company's loan portfolio) and residential mortgages (more than 20%). To a lesser extent the bank also writes construction land development business and consumer loans. The company agreed to merge with the Community Bank of Bergen County in 2017.

	Annual Growth	12/14	12/15	12/16	12/17	12/18
Assets ($ mil.)	31.8%	595.9	684.5	848.7	979.4	1,795.7
Net income ($ mil.)	39.8%	2.6	3.7	5.5	5.7	9.9
Market value ($ mil.)	19.0%	97.2	124.8	199.2	256.0	194.9
Employees	14.9%	136	139	148	156	237

SBA COMMUNICATIONS CORP (NEW)

NMS: SBAC

8051 Congress Avenue
Boca Raton, FL 33487
Phone: 561 995-7670
Fax: –
Web: www.sbasite.com

CEO: Jeffrey A. (Jeff) Stoops
CFO: Brendan T Cavanagh
HR: Jo Rutherford
FYE: December 31
Type: Public

SBA Communications wants to tower over the wireless communications industry. The company is a top independent owner and operator of wireless communications towers in the US. It leases antenna space to wireless service carriers and provides site development services including network design zoning and permit assistance and tower construction. SBA owns and operates more than 25.400 towers in North Central and America. It built most of the towers it operates often through build-to-suit arrangements with carriers. AT&T Mobility Sprint Nextel Verizon Wireless and T-Mobile are its four largest customers.

	Annual Growth	12/14	12/15	12/16	12/17	12/18
Sales ($ mil.)	5.1%	1,527.0	1,638.5	1,633.1	1,727.7	1,865.7
Net income ($ mil.)	–	(24.3)	(175.7)	76.2	103.7	47.5
Market value ($ mil.)	10.0%	12,453.1	11,813.3	11,609.8	18,367.1	18,201.8
Employees	1.7%	1,259	1,310	1,241	1,291	1,347

SC FUELS

1800 W. Katella Ste. 400
Orange CA 92863-4159
Phone: 714-744-7140
Fax: 714-922-7200
Web: www.scfuels.com

CEO: Frank P Greinke
CFO: Mimi Taylor
HR: –
FYE: September 30
Type: Private

Southern name Western beat. SC Fuels (formerly Southern Counties Oil) is the oldest and largest wholesale distributor of gasoline diesel fuel and lubricants to more than 35000 customers in the western US. SC Fuels delivers fuel and lubricants to commercial accounts in varied industries in Northern and Southern California. Clients include Costco and Albertsons. Through its Pacific Northwest Energy subsidiary SC Fuels provides heating oils propane delivery and heating and air conditioning repair services to residential construction industrial and fleet operating customers in Washington state.

SCAI HOLDINGS, LLC

510 LAKE COOK RD STE 400
DEERFIELD, IL 600154971
Phone: 847-236-0921
Fax: –
Web: www.scasurgery.com

CEO: Andrew P. Hayek
CFO: Peter Clemens
HR: –
FYE: December 31
Type: Private

SCAI Holdings (dba SCA or Surgical Care Affiliates) can stitch 'em up and move 'em out. The company operates one of the largest networks of outpatient surgery centers in the US. (Also known as ambulatory surgical centers or ASCs these facilities charge less than hospitals to perform routine surgeries.) SCA operates more than 200 surgery centers and surgical hospitals in about 35 states. The centers offer non-emergency day surgeries in orthopedics ophthalmology gastroenterology pain management otolaryngology (ear nose and throat) urology and gynecology. The company went public in 2013 but was acquired by insurance giant UnitedHealth in 2017 for some $2.3 billion.

	Annual Growth	12/12	12/13	12/14	12/15	12/16
Sales ($ mil.)	16.9%	–	802.0	864.7	1,051.5	1,281.4
Net income ($ mil.)	62.5%	–	52.7	157.1	273.6	226.3
Market value ($ mil.)	–	–	–	–	–	–
Employees	–	–	–	–	–	5,248

SCANA CORP   NYS: SCG

100 SCANA Parkway — CEO: P Rodney Blevins
Cayce, SC 29033 — CFO: James R Chapman
Phone: 803 217-9000 — HR: –
Fax: – — FYE: December 31
Web: www.scana.com — Type: Public

SCANA is a holding company for public utilities and unregulated wholesale gas operations in the Carolinas and Georgia. It serves nearly 700000 electricity customers and 900000 gas customers through utilities South Carolina Electric & Gas (SCE&G) and Public Service Company of North Carolina. SCE&G has electric generating capacity of 5200 MW derived from fossil-fueled power plants and hydroelectric and nuclear generation facilities. Unregulated operations through subsidiary SCANA Energy include retail and wholesale energy marketing and trading gas transportation and power plant management. SCANA is not an acronym but a play on the name of its headquarter state South CAroliNA.

	Annual Growth	12/12	12/13	12/14	12/15	12/16
Sales ($ mil.)	0.3%	4,176.0	4,495.0	4,951.0	4,380.0	4,227.0
Net income ($ mil.)	9.1%	420.0	471.0	538.0	746.0	595.0
Market value ($ mil.)	12.6%	6,522.0	6,706.3	8,631.2	8,644.0	10,471.7
Employees	0.3%	5,842	5,989	5,886	5,829	5,910

SCHAWK, INC.   NYS: SGK

1695 South River Road — CEO: David Schawk
Des Plaines, IL 60018 — CFO: –
Phone: 847 827-9494 — HR: –
Fax: – — FYE: December 31
Web: www.schawk.com — Type: Public

Schawk has designs on consumers' products. The company provides digital prepress and other graphic services primarily for consumer product packaging advertising and point-of-sale marketing. It offers digital imaging color separations electronic retouching and platemaking services for lithography gravure and flexography. Ultimately the company is responsible for manipulating images used to entice consumers to buy a product. The family of founder and chairman Clarence Schawk owns a controlling stake (more than 50%) in the company. It has been in operation since 1953.

	Annual Growth	12/08	12/09	12/10	12/11	12/12
Sales ($ mil.)	(1.7%)	494.2	452.4	460.6	455.3	460.7
Net income ($ mil.)	–	–	(60.0)	19.5	32.4	20.6	(23.4)
Market value ($ mil.)	3.5%	299.3	355.1	537.4	292.7	343.7
Employees	3.8%	3,100	3,100	3,200	3,600	3,600

SCHEID VINEYARDS INC.   NBB: SVIN

305 Hilltown Road — CEO: Scott D Scheid
Salinas, CA 93908 — CFO: Michael S Thomsen
Phone: 831 455-9990 — HR: –
Fax: – — FYE: February 28
Web: www.scheidvineyards.com — Type: Public

Scheid Vineyards hasn't shied away from the expensive and timely task of growing grapes for wine. The company works about 5300 acres of vineyards mainly located in Monterey County California. It has the capacity to process approximately 30000 tons of grapes every harvest. Its main business is producing bulk wine which it sells to other winemakers for blending. Scheid also makes its own wines under the Scheid Vineyards label; they are available in the Monterey area and through the company's Web site. The Scheid family including founder and chairman Alfred Scheid control a majority of the company.

	Annual Growth	02/15	02/16	02/17	02/18	02/19
Sales ($ mil.)	8.7%	41.9	49.1	62.3	57.3	58.5
Net income ($ mil.)	–	0.7	1.7	2.9	2.4	(7.9)
Market value ($ mil.)	27.8%	27.0	24.7	28.3	79.5	72.0
Employees	–	–	–	–	–	–

SCHEIN (HENRY) INC   NMS: HSIC

135 Duryea Road — CEO: James P. Breslawski
Melville, NY 11747 — CFO: Steven Paladino
Phone: 631 843-5500 — HR: –
Fax: – — FYE: December 29
Web: www.henryschein.com — Type: Public

From Poughkeepsie to Prague Henry Schein outfits dental offices around the world with everything they need. The company is a leading global distributor of dental supplies equipment and pharmaceuticals. Henry Schein provides everything from delicate hand-held tools up to X-ray equipment and patient chair accessories as well as office supplies and anesthetics. But the company isn't only interested in teeth: It also supplies doctors' offices and other office-based health care providers with diagnostic kits surgical tools drugs and vaccines. Other offerings include practice management software repair services and financing. The US accounts for about 65% of revenue.

	Annual Growth	12/14	12/15	12/16	12/17	12/18
Sales ($ mil.)	6.2%	10,371.4	10,629.7	11,571.7	12,461.5	13,202.0
Net income ($ mil.)	3.6%	466.1	479.1	506.8	406.3	535.9
Market value ($ mil.)	(13.2%)	20,800.3	23,783.7	22,969.1	10,579.9	11,797.2
Employees	0.7%	17,500	19,000	21,000	22,000	18,000

SCHEWEL FURNITURE COMPANY INCORPORATED

1031 MAIN ST — CEO: Marc A Schewel
LYNCHBURG, VA 245041800 — CFO: –
Phone: 434-522-0200 — HR: –
Fax: – — FYE: March 31
Web: www.schewels.com — Type: Private

Schewel Furniture Company operates about 50 retail furniture and bedding stores in Virginia West Virginia and North Carolina. In addition to home furnishings the chain sells appliances electronics carpeting and related accessories. Typical store units average 18000 sq. ft. and primarily target the lower- and middle-income markets. Newer stores are larger in the 40000-55000 square foot range. Customers can also browse furniture collections and other items available at Schewel stores through the company's Web site. The family-run company now in its fourth generation of management got its start in 1897 when Elias Schewel began selling small furniture pieces out of his horse-drawn wagon.

	Annual Growth	03/13	03/14	03/15	03/16	03/17
Sales ($ mil.)	(2.2%)	–	122.0	118.5	117.5	114.2
Net income ($ mil.)	(3.3%)	–	4.5	4.1	4.1	4.1
Market value ($ mil.)	–	–	–	–	–	–
Employees	–	–	–	–	–	650

SCHLUMBERGER LIMITED   NYSE: SLB

5599 San Felipe 17th Fl. — CEO: Paal Kibsgaard
Houston TX 77056 — CFO: Simon Ayat
Phone: 713-513-2000 — HR: –
Fax: 201-703-4205 — FYE: December 31
Web: www.sealedair.com — Type: Public

Schlumberger has the know-how to get oil and gas drillers out of a slump. One of the world's largest oilfield services companies it provides a full range of services including seismic surveys formation evaluation drilling technologies and equipment cementing well construction and completion and project management. Schlumberger also provides reservoir evaluation development and management services and is developing new technologies for reservoir optimization. Through its WesternGeco business the company provides seismic and other surveying services to customers worldwide. In a blockbuster deal valued at $11 billion Schlumberger acquired drilling services giant Smith International in 2010.

SCHMITT INDUSTRIES INC (OR)

NAS: SMIT

2765 N.W. Nicolai Street
Portland, OR 97210
Phone: 503 227-7908
Fax: 503 223-1258
Web: www.schmitt-ind.com

CEO: Michael R Zapata
CFO: Regina Walker
HR: -
FYE: May 31
Type: Public

What can we tell you about Schmitt? Schmitt Industries takes a balanced approach; most of its sales comes from its computerized balancing equipment which machine tool builders and grinding machine operators use to improve the efficiency of rotating devices. Customers incorporate the company's flagship Schmitt Dynamic Balance System into grinding machines. Subsidiary Schmitt Measurement Systems makes laser-based precision-measurement instruments for computer disk drive manufacturing and for military and industrial applications. Schmitt Industries has operations in the UK and the US. Customers in North America account for more than half of the company's sales.

	Annual Growth	05/15	05/16	05/17	05/18	05/19
Sales ($ mil.)	1.4%	13.1	11.7	12.4	13.9	13.8
Net income ($ mil.)	-	(0.1)	(1.5)	(1.1)	0.2	(1.2)
Market value ($ mil.)	(5.1%)	11.1	9.2	7.0	9.2	9.0
Employees	(3.2%)	57	54	50	56	50

SCHMITT MUSIC COMPANY

100 N. Sixth St. Ste. 850B
Minneapolis MN 55403-1505
Phone: 612-339-4811
Fax: 612-339-3574
Web: www.schmittmusic.com

CEO: Thomas M Schmitt
CFO: Robert Baker
HR: Beth Palmer
FYE: May 31
Type: Private

Schmitt Music is all for marching to the beat of a different drummer. Or any drummer really. The company operates about 15 retail music stores in Minnesota and about a half a dozen other midwestern states under the Schmitt Music Organ Center and Wells Music (keyboard) names. The stores offer musical instruments (guitars pianos organs band instruments) accessories and lessons. They also sell music books sheet music for piano competitions and guides to planning the music for church services. School band and orchestra members are Schmitt's biggest customer group. Fourth generation Schmitt family members Tom (president) and Doug (VP) run and own the company their grandfather founded in 1896.

SCHNITZER STEEL INDUSTRIES INC

NMS: SCHN

299 SW Clay Street, Suite 350
Portland, OR 97201
Phone: 503 224-9900
Fax: -
Web: www.schnitzersteel.com

CEO: Tamara L. Lundgren
CFO: Richard D. Peach
HR: -
FYE: August 31
Type: Public

Your old car could end up as part of a American on Asian office building if Schnitzer Steel Industries gets its steel jaws on it. The company processes scrap steel and iron which it obtains from sources such as auto salvage yards industrial manufacturers and metals brokers. The company scrap to steelmakers primarily in the US and Asia. Much of it goes to Schnitzer's own steelmaking business including Cascade Steel Rolling Mills which produces merchant bar steel reinforcing bar and other products at its mini-mill in Oregon. Schnitzer's Pick-N-Pull Auto Dismantlers unit operates auto salvage yards.

	Annual Growth	08/15	08/16	08/17	08/18	08/19
Sales ($ mil.)	2.7%	1,915.4	1,352.5	1,687.6	2,364.7	2,132.8
Net income ($ mil.)	-	(197.0)	(19.4)	44.5	156.5	56.3
Market value ($ mil.)	6.3%	461.6	500.7	717.3	702.6	590.3
Employees	3.3%	2,955	2,818	3,183	3,575	3,363

SCHNUCK MARKETS INC.

11420 Lackland Rd.
St. Louis MO 63146-6928
Phone: 314-994-9900
Fax: 614-449-0403

CEO: Scott C Schnuck
CFO: David Bell
HR: -
FYE: September 30
Type: Private

If you'll meet me in St. Louis chances are there'll be a Schnucks in sight. The region's largest food chain Schnuck Markets operates about 100 stores two-thirds of which are in the St. Louis area. The other stores are in Missouri Illinois Indiana Iowa and Wisconsin. All stores offer a full line of groceries and 95% have pharmacies. Other services include Redbox video rentals in-store banking and florist shops. Although most stores operate under the Schnucks banner the company also runs about half a dozen Logli supermarkets in Illinois and Wisconsin and a specialty pharmacy. Founded in 1939 the company is owned by the Schnuck family and run by CEO Scott Schnuck and president and COO Todd Schnuck.

SCHOLASTIC CORP

NMS: SCHL

557 Broadway
New York, NY 10012
Phone: 212 343-6100
Fax: -
Web: www.scholastic.com

CEO: Richard (Dick) Robinson
CFO: Maureen O'Connell
HR: -
FYE: May 31
Type: Public

Once upon a time a company grew up to become one of the world's leading children's book publishers. Scholastic Corporation sells books to children in more than 150 countries. It operates through three divisions: Children's Book Publishing and Distribution; Education; and International. Scholastic owns the rights to properties such as Goosebumps and The Baby-Sitters Club and is the US distributor of the Harry Potter books the best-selling children's series of all time. Known for its school book fairs Scholastic also publishes magazines textbooks and software for students and teachers and produces children's TV shows.

	Annual Growth	05/15	05/16	05/17	05/18	05/19
Sales ($ mil.)	0.3%	1,635.8	1,672.8	1,741.6	1,628.4	1,653.9
Net income ($ mil.)	(52.0%)	294.6	40.5	52.3	(5.0)	15.6
Market value ($ mil.)	(7.1%)	1,558.7	1,369.3	1,491.4	1,577.6	1,160.4
Employees	0.0%	8,900	8,900	9,000	9,000	8,900

SCHOOL EMPLOYEES RETIREMENT SYSTEM OF OHIO

300 E. Broad St. Ste. 100
Columbus OH 43215-3746
Phone: 614-222-5853
Fax: 614-340-1295
Web: www.ohsers.org

CEO: -
CFO: Virginia Briszendine
HR: -
FYE: June 30
Type: Government Agency

In retirement there's no free lunch - even for the lunch lady. That's where the School Employees Retirement System of Ohio comes in. The system also known as SERS manages pension health care retirement and other benefits for about 190000 non-teaching public school employees and retirees in the Buckeye State. More than half its portfolio consists of US and international stocks with the rest invested in bonds real estate private equity and short-term securities. The School Employees Retirement System of Ohio was established in 1937 and now manages more than $7 billion in plan assets. It pays out approximately $900 billion in benefits annually.

SCHOOLSFIRST FCU

2115 N. Broadway
Santa Ana CA 92706
Phone: 714-258-4000
Fax: 847-426-4630
Web: www.revcor.com

CEO: –
CFO: –
HR: Jodi Falco
FYE: December 31
Type: Private - Not-for-Pr

SchoolsFirst FCU formerly Orange County Teachers Federal Credit Union (OCT-FCU) serves more than 500000 members through nearly 30 branches and seven express centers located in Southern California. Founded in 1934 the credit union changed its name to better reflect its membership which is open to all school employees and their family members across 10 Southern California counties. As part of its business SchoolsFirst FCU offers traditional financial products such as checking and savings accounts and credit cards. It also provides members with financial advice insurance and retirement and college savings plans. Lending activities at SchoolsFirst FCU consist of home auto and personal loans.

SCHOTTENSTEIN REALTY TRUST INC.

4300 E. 5th Ave.
Columbus OH 43219
Phone: 614-445-8461
Fax: 214-303-4901
Web: www.isnetworld.com

CEO: –
CFO: –
HR: –
FYE: December 31
Type: Private

As long as US consumers are shopping Schottenstein Realty will do a little shopping of its own. A self-administered and self-managed real estate company Schottenstein Realty acquires and re-develops retail properties and shopping centers anchored by big-box stores. It prefers to acquire distressed or bankrupt properties in major metropolitan areas invest in expansion and redevelopment and then bring in large retailers like Wal-Mart Bed Bath & Beyond and T.J. Maxx as tenants. Upon its 2010 formation the company filed to go public and sought to qualify as a REIT (real estate investment trust). If all goes according to plan Schottenstein Realty will own interests in some 156 properties in 27 states.

SCHREIBER FOODS INC.

425 Pine St.
Green Bay WI 54301
Phone: 920-437-7601
Fax: 920-437-1617
Web: www.schreiberfoods.com

CEO: Michael J Haddad
CFO: Matt P Mueller
HR: –
FYE: September 30
Type: Private

Want cheese with that? That's Schreiber Foods. The company is a major supplier of cheese used in hamburgers and other dishes served by US fastfood chains and restaurants schools and universities hospitals and other foodservice operators. Schreiber produces some 575 private-label processed and natural cheeses as well as dairy ingredients for grocers club stores and wholesalers and food manufacturers. It offers a few of its own brands for retail sale including American Heritage and Cooper. The company has expanded its presence to more than 20 countries by acquiring or forming joint ventures with smaller cheese makers. Schreiber Foods is arguably the largest employee-owned dairy company in the world.

SCHULMAN (A) INC

NMS: SHLM

3637 Ridgewood Road
Fairlawn, OH 44333
Phone: 330 666-3751
Fax: 330 668-7204
Web: www.aschulman.com

CEO: Bhavesh V Patel
CFO: Thomas Aebischer
HR: –
FYE: August 31
Type: Public

A. Schulman is really into plastics. It is an international leader of designed and engineered plastic compounds composites color concentrates size reduction services and specialty molded parts. It provides products to end markets such as agriculture building & construction electronics mobility and packaging. End products that are built from its compounds include kitchen appliances gas tanks and kayaks. It operates more than 50 manufacturing locations worldwide and generates approximately 50% of its revenue in Europe Middle East & Africa (EMEA). It also serves as a distributor for polymer producers worldwide.

	Annual Growth	08/13	08/14	08/15	08/16	08/17
Sales ($ mil.)	3.6%	2,133.4	2,447.0	2,392.2	2,496.0	2,461.1
Net income ($ mil.)	6.1%	26.1	56.2	26.6	(357.1)	33.0
Market value ($ mil.)	3.0%	794.4	1,144.2	1,011.6	751.4	895.8
Employees	11.2%	3,200	3,900	5,000	4,800	4,900

SCHUMACHER ELECTRIC CORPORATION

801 E BUSINESS CENTER DR
MOUNT PROSPECT, IL 600562179
Phone: 847-385-1600
Fax: –
Web: www.batterychargers.com

CEO: Donald A. (Don) Schumacher
CFO: Daniel Frano
HR: –
FYE: December 31
Type: Private

Schumacher Electric gets a charge out of starting things up. The company makes and sells its own brand of battery starters and chargers including automatic manual wheel and bench battery chargers. The chargers rev up cars boats light trucks commercial trucks snowmobiles motorcycles recreational vehicles and farm vehicles and equipment. Schumacher Electric also makes power inverters and testers as well as welding machines and accessories and custom-built transformers. The specialty manufacturing company is run by veteran drag car racer Don Schumacher.

	Annual Growth	12/00	12/01	12/02	12/03	12/13
Sales ($ mil.)	–	–	0.0	0.0	85.3	142.6
Net income ($ mil.)	–	–	0.0	0.0	0.0	3.0
Market value ($ mil.)	–	–	–	–	–	–
Employees	–	–	–	–	–	125

SCHWAB (CHARLES) CORP (THE)

NYS: SCHW

211 Main Street
San Francisco, CA 94105
Phone: 415 667-7000
Fax: 415 627-8894
Web: www.aboutschwab.com

CEO: Walter W. (Walt) Bettinger
CFO: Peter Crawford
HR: Sarah Stanson
FYE: December 31
Type: Public

The once-rebellious Charles Schwab is all grown up: the discount broker now offers the same traditional brokerage services it shunned over three decades ago. Schwab manages more than $3.4 trillion in assets for some 13.8 million individual investors and institutional clients. Traders can access its services via telephone the internet-enabled devices and through more than 345 offices in 45-plus states as well as London Hong Kong Singapore and Australia. Besides discount brokerage the firm offers financial research advice and planning investment management and retirement and employee compensation plans.It also operates Charles Schwab Bank a federal savings bank and Charles Schwab Investment Management an investment advisor for Schwab's mutual finds and exchange-traded funds.

	Annual Growth	12/14	12/15	12/16	12/17	12/18
Sales ($ mil.)	15.6%	6,160.0	6,512.0	7,649.0	8,960.0	10,989.0
Net income ($ mil.)	27.6%	1,321.0	1,447.0	1,889.0	2,354.0	3,507.0
Market value ($ mil.)	8.3%	40,226.0	43,876.8	52,590.9	68,446.8	55,335.7
Employees	7.5%	14,600	15,300	16,200	17,600	19,500

SCHWEITZER-MAUDUIT INTERNATIONAL INC
NYS: SWM

100 North Point Center East, Suite 600
Alpharetta, GA 30022
Phone: 800 514-0186
Fax: -
Web: www.swmintl.com

CEO: Jeffrey Kramer
CFO: Allison Aden
HR: -
FYE: December 31
Type: Public

Business is smokin' at Schweitzer-Mauduit International (SWM) one of the world's leading suppliers of fine papers to the tobacco industry. About 90% of its sales come from tobacco-related products including cigarette wraps plug wraps (used to wrap filters) and tipping paper (used to join the filter to the rest of the cigarette) low ignition propensity (fire-safe) cigarettes as well as reconstituted tobacco leaf (RTL) — virgin tobacco blended by cigarette manufacturers. Non-tobacco lines comprise a mix of products from drinking-straw wrappers to lightweight printing paper and business forms. SWM markets its lineup in Europe the Americas and Asia garnering about 60% of its sales outside the US.

	Annual Growth	12/14	12/15	12/16	12/17	12/18
Sales ($ mil.)	7.0%	794.3	764.1	839.9	982.1	1,041.3
Net income ($ mil.)	1.3%	89.7	89.7	82.8	34.5	94.5
Market value ($ mil.)	(12.3%)	1,301.6	1,292.1	1,401.0	1,395.8	770.8
Employees	3.9%	3,000	3,100	3,000	3,600	3,500

SCICLONE PHARMACEUTICALS, INC.
NMS: SCLN

950 Tower Lane, Suite 900
Foster City, CA 94404
Phone: 650 358-3456
Fax: -
Web: www.sciclone.com

CEO: Friedhelm Blobel
CFO: Wilson W Cheung
HR: -
FYE: December 31
Type: Public

SciClone hopes its drug sales create a whirlwind in China. The drug firm's flagship product Zadaxin is approved for use in some 30 countries including China its primary market. Zadaxin treats hepatitis B as a vaccine adjuvant (to boost a vaccine's effectiveness) as well as certain cancers. The company also partners with other drug makers including Baxter International and Pfizer to market those companies' products in China. SciClone also maintains a pipeline of products that it is shepherding through the approval process in China. The company entered a strategic review process in early 2016 but in July announced that it was no longer continuing active discussions with potential acquirers.

	Annual Growth	12/11	12/12	12/13	12/14	12/15
Sales ($ mil.)	4.2%	133.6	156.3	127.1	134.8	157.3
Net income ($ mil.)	0.9%	28.5	9.6	11.0	25.2	29.5
Market value ($ mil.)	21.0%	212.5	213.5	249.7	433.9	455.7
Employees	(9.4%)	875	870	570	570	590

SCIENCE APPLICATIONS INTERNATIONAL CORP (NEW)
NYS: SAIC

12010 Sunset Hills Road
Reston, VA 20190
Phone: 703 676-4300
Fax: -
Web: www.saic.com

CEO: -
CFO: Charles A. Mathis
HR: Pat V Iannatti
FYE: February 01
Type: Public

Science Applications International Corporation (SAIC) helps federal agencies make the most of their information technologies. The company integrates IT systems that handle security logistics simulation and large-scale data processing and analysis. Based in the Washington DC area SAIC gets more than 60% of its revenue from the US Department of Defense. It also works with the Department of Homeland Security as well as the State Department the EPA and NASA. SAIC is one of the biggest pure-play technical services providers to the federal government the source of 98% of its revenue. Since spinning off from Leidos in 2013 SAIC has added capabilities through acquisitions.

	Annual Growth	01/15	01/16*	02/17	02/18	02/19
Sales ($ mil.)	4.6%	3,885.0	4,315.0	4,450.0	4,454.0	4,659.0
Net income ($ mil.)	(0.7%)	141.0	117.0	148.0	179.0	137.0
Market value ($ mil.)	8.5%	2,926.8	2,557.2	4,962.0	4,482.0	4,056.6
Employees	15.3%	13,000	15,000	15,500	15,000	23,000

*Fiscal year change

SCIENTIFIC INDUSTRIES INC
NBB: SCND

80 Orville Drive, Suite 102
Bohemia, NY 11716
Phone: 631 567-4700
Fax: -
Web: www.scientificindustries.com

CEO: Helena R Santos
CFO: -
HR: -
FYE: June 30
Type: Public

There's a whole lotta shakin' goin' on at Scientific Industries. The company manufactures research laboratory equipment featuring the Genie line of mixers particularly the Vortex-Genie mixer as well as orbital magnetic and microplate mixers and refrigerated and shaking incubators. The company's products are generally used by clinics hospitals and universities among other customers. In business for more than five decades Scientific Industries has distributors worldwide. The company also carries spinner flasks made by Bellco Biotechnology. Scientific Industries gets more than half of its sales outside the US.

	Annual Growth	06/15	06/16	06/17	06/18	06/19
Sales ($ mil.)	6.8%	7.8	9.6	8.1	8.5	10.2
Net income ($ mil.)	193.5%	0.0	0.2	(0.1)	(0.2)	0.6
Market value ($ mil.)	13.1%	4.1	4.3	4.8	4.6	6.7
Employees	4.3%	33	34	33	34	39

SCIENTIFIC LEARNING CORP.
NBB: SCIL

1956 Webster Street, Suite 200
Oakland, CA 94612
Phone: 888 665-9707
Fax: -
Web: www.scilearn.com

CEO: Robert C Bowen
CFO: Jane A Freeman
HR: -
FYE: December 31
Type: Public

Scientific Learning uses computers to help teach language reading and reading comprehension skills in public and private schools in the US and about 45 countries. Its flagship Fast ForWord software offers products to build language skills (elementary students) literacy skills (for students in middle and high school) and reading skills (all levels). The software is used in computer labs and the classroom in before and after school programs and during summer school. About 90% of sales come from some 117000 US schools; international sales are mostly to tutoring and learning centers professionals working with language-impaired children and ESL programs. The company also sells directly to parents.

	Annual Growth	12/14	12/15	12/16	12/17	12/18
Sales ($ mil.)	(3.3%)	19.2	17.7	15.9	16.4	16.7
Net income ($ mil.)	-	1.4	(0.2)	(1.4)	0.2	(0.9)
Market value ($ mil.)	42.1%	2.7	7.6	15.7	14.4	11.0
Employees	-	-	-	-	-	-

SCIENTIFIC RESEARCH CORP

2300 WINDY RIDGE PKWY SE 400S
ATLANTA, GA 303398431
Phone: 770-859-9161
Fax: -
Web: www.scires.com

CEO: Michael L. (Mike) Watt
CFO: Thomas L. Papst
HR: Sandra Holtzclaw
FYE: December 31
Type: Private

Scientific Research Corporation (SRC) doesn't limit its services to the laboratory. The government contractor provides a wide variety of engineering and research services including consulting systems engineering project management network design hardware and software development prototyping testing and evaluation systems integration and training. Its expertise encompasses communications and intelligence systems electronic warfare simulation and instrumentation systems. In some cases SRC works as a subcontractor for larger companies such as Booz Allen. SRC's clients include the US government and military state agencies and private sector businesses.

	Annual Growth	12/13	12/14	12/15	12/16	12/17
Sales ($ mil.)	(4.3%)	-	318.7	293.8	281.9	279.3
Net income ($ mil.)	(2.1%)	-	20.8	19.5	19.5	19.5
Market value ($ mil.)	-	-	-	-	-	-
Employees	-	-	-	-	-	1,006

SCIQUEST INC
NMS: SQI

3020 Carrington Mill Blvd., Suite 100
Morrisville, NC 27560
Phone: 919 659-2100
Fax: –
Web: www.sciquest.com

CEO: Robert Bonavito
CFO: Vic Chynoweth
HR: –
FYE: December 31
Type: Public

SciQuest is on a mission to help organizations take better control of their supplies. The company's on-demand procurement automation software helps customers manage costs by integrating with their suppliers. Its SciQuest Supplier Network enables clients to tap into a marketplace of more than 30000 different suppliers and includes tools for negotiating discounts automating orders and managing contracts. The SciQuest Supplier Network is available in tailored versions for specific industries: higher education life sciences health care and government. It can also be integrated with other existing enterprise software so that data can easily be shared when procurement accounting and settlement functions are managed.

	Annual Growth	12/10	12/11	12/12	12/13	12/14
Sales ($ mil.)	24.5%	42.5	53.4	66.5	90.2	101.9
Net income ($ mil.)	–	1.7	2.8	(1.2)	(4.7)	(0.1)
Market value ($ mil.)	2.7%	358.7	393.5	437.3	785.3	398.4
Employees	30.8%	192	265	479	538	562

SCL HEALTH - FRONT RANGE, INC.

8300 W 38TH AVE
WHEAT RIDGE, CO 800336005
Phone: 303-813-5000
Fax: –
Web: www.sclhealth.org

CEO: –
CFO: William Pack
HR: Darren Walker
FYE: December 31
Type: Private

Exempla aims to provide exemplary health care to residents in the Denver area. The Exempla medical network operating as Exempla Healthcare includes three hospitals: Exempla Saint Joseph Hospital (570 beds) Exempla Lutheran Medical Center (400 beds) and Good Samaritan Medical Center (more than 230 beds). It also operates the Exempla Physician Network a chain of primary care clinics. The company employs more than 2100 physicians. Among its specialties are cardiovascular services and surgeries rehabilitation cancer care orthopedics and women's and children's services. Exempla Healthcare is sponsored by the Catholic faith-based Sisters of Charity of Leavenworth Health System (SCL Health System).

	Annual Growth	12/01	12/02	12/04	12/05	12/09
Sales ($ mil.)	12.2%	–	267.6	335.0	472.4	597.8
Net income ($ mil.)	(16.2%)	–	27.0	37.5	30.5	7.8
Market value ($ mil.)	–	–	–	–	–	–
Employees	–	–	–	–	–	5,300

SCOTT & WHITE HEALTH PLAN

1206 WEST CAMPUS DR
TEMPLE, TX 765027124
Phone: 254-298-3000
Fax: –
Web: www.swhp.org

CEO: –
CFO: Stephen Bush
HR: Queen Greene
FYE: December 31
Type: Private

The Scott & White Health Plan (SWHP) works to keep its members Safe & Well. The not-for-profit company provides health insurance plans and related services to more than 200000 members across some 50 counties in and around Central Texas. Owned by the Scott & White network of hospitals and clinics SWHP has employer-sponsored plans (including HMO PPO and consumer choice options) as well as several choices for individuals and families. It also offers COBRA state-administered continuation plans the Young Texan Health Plan for children Medicare and dental and vision benefits. The company began offering its services in 1982. Owner Scott & White is exploring a merger with Baylor Health Care System.

	Annual Growth	12/05	12/06	12/07	12/08	12/09
Sales ($ mil.)	5.8%	–	557.5	586.3	621.2	660.1
Net income ($ mil.)	54.1%	–	3.6	8.2	(4.0)	13.3
Market value ($ mil.)	–	–	–	–	–	–
Employees	–	–	–	–	–	426

SCOTT EQUIPMENT COMPANY, L.L.C.

1000 M L KING JR DR J
MONROE, LA 71203
Phone: 318-387-4160
Fax: –
Web: www.scottcompanies.com

CEO: George J Bershen Sr
CFO: –
HR: –
FYE: December 31
Type: Private

Scott Equipment Company sells and rents construction and farm equipment through some 25 locations located in the South and Midwest. The company also offers parts and service financing and insurance. Scott Equipment is part of the Scott family of companies which also includes Scott Toyota Lift (material handling) Scott Irrigation (pivot irrigation systems) and Scott Truck (sales leasing and service). The company's beginnings date back to 1939 when Tom Scott founded Scott Truck & Tractor. It is operated by descendants of the founder. Scott Equipment has shut down several agricultural stores (Scott Tractor) to focus on its Construction Equipment division.

	Annual Growth	12/04	12/05	12/06	12/07	12/08
Sales ($ mil.)	6.1%	–	266.0	299.3	323.4	317.6
Net income ($ mil.)	56.8%	–	3.3	6.2	17.7	12.9
Market value ($ mil.)	–	–	–	–	–	–
Employees	–	–	–	–	–	525

SCOTT'S LIQUID GOLD, INC.
NBB: SLGD

4880 Havana Street, Suite 400
Denver, CO 80239
Phone: 303 373-4860
Fax: –
Web: www.slginc.com

CEO: Mark E Goldstein
CFO: Barry J Levine
HR: –
FYE: December 31
Type: Public

Known for its wood furniture cleaner Scott's Liquid Gold is banking on striking gold in skin care and cosmetics products. While the company generates 46% of its sales from its namesake cleaning product a growing portion of its business is from its Neoteric Cosmetics subsidiary which sells skin care products under the Alpha Hydrox and Diabetic Skin Care brand names. Scott's Liquid Gold also makes household items such as Touch of Scent air fresheners. The company sells its products through retailers in the US Canada and abroad; it also distributes Montagne Jeunesse sachets. The children of the late founder Jerome Goldstein (including president and CEO Mark Goldstein) own about a quarter of the company.

	Annual Growth	12/14	12/15	12/16	12/17	12/18
Sales ($ mil.)	11.1%	24.3	29.2	35.2	42.2	37.1
Net income ($ mil.)	1.6%	2.1	4.8	1.9	4.7	2.2
Market value ($ mil.)	28.2%	11.7	17.5	17.9	36.0	31.6
Employees	3.3%	65	67	61	66	74

SCOTTS MIRACLE-GRO CO (THE)
NYS: SMG

14111 Scottslawn Road
Marysville, OH 43041
Phone: 937 644-0011
Fax: 937 644-7614
Web: www.scotts.com

CEO: James (Jim) Hagedorn
CFO: Thomas R. (Randy) Coleman
HR: Denise S. Stump
FYE: September 30
Type: Public

Scotts Miracle-Gro is one of the world's leading producers of horticultural and turf materials. It sells grass seed plant food fertilizer weed control and pest control products. The company sells its products through major retailers like The Home Depot Lowe's and Walmart as well as through warehouse clubs nurseries garden centers and food and drug stores. Its leading brands include Scotts Turf Builder Nature's Care Miracle-Gro LiquaFeed and Tomcat. Scotts is also the exclusive agent of Monsanto's Roundup brand in the US and other countries. Primarily based in the US Scotts has a presence in Canada Mexico China and the Netherlands.

	Annual Growth	09/15	09/16	09/17	09/18	09/19
Sales ($ mil.)	1.1%	3,016.5	2,836.1	2,642.1	2,663.4	3,156.0
Net income ($ mil.)	30.3%	159.8	315.3	218.3	63.7	460.7
Market value ($ mil.)	13.7%	3,393.8	4,646.5	5,431.6	4,393.1	5,681.6
Employees	(8.2%)	7,900	3,300	4,700	5,150	5,600

SCOTTSDALE HEALTHCARE CORP.

8125 N HAYDEN RD
SCOTTSDALE, AZ 852582463
Phone: 480-882-4000
Fax: –
Web: www.honorhealth.com

CEO: Thomas J Sadvary
CFO: Todd LaPorte
HR: –
FYE: December 31
Type: Private

Scottsdale Healthcare a not-for-profit organization serves the health care needs of central Arizona residents. Its operations include three acute care hospitals that combined boast some 900 beds. Scottsdale Healthcare also operates other campuses that offer physician offices a cancer center home health and other health care services. It conducts clinical research through the Scottsdale Healthcare Research Institute. The group's Essential Touch Wellness Center and Boutique provides spa-like stress-reduction therapies. With nearly 2000 medical and surgical staff members the company offers some 35 medical specialties. Scottsdale Healthcare is an affiliate of Scottsdale Lincoln Health Network along with John C. Lincoln Health Network.

	Annual Growth	12/13	12/14	12/16	12/17	12/18
Sales ($ mil.)	117.3%	–	88.2	1,716.5	1,763.2	1,967.2
Net income ($ mil.)	67.2%	–	9.9	93.0	105.0	77.3
Market value ($ mil.)	–	–	–	–	–	–
Employees	–	–	–	–	–	17,000

SCRIPPS (EW) COMPANY (THE)   NMS: SSP

312 Walnut Street
Cincinnati, OH 45202
Phone: 513 977-3000
Fax: –
Web: www.scripps.com

CEO: Adam P. Symson
CFO: Timothy M. (Tim) Wesolowski
HR: Candace Anderson
FYE: December 31
Type: Public

You might say this media company tries to be appealing to both newspaper readers and television viewers. The E. W. Scripps Company is a venerable newspaper publisher with a portfolio of more than 15 dailies including The Commercial Appeal (Memphis Tennessee) the Knoxville News Sentinel (Tennessee) and the Ventura County Star (California). Scripps also owns some 60 local TV stations in 42 markets most of which are affiliated with ABC and NBC. Subsidiaries Scripps Howard News Service and United Media distribute syndicated content including news columns editorial cartoons and such comic strips Peanuts. The Scripps family controls the company through various trusts.

	Annual Growth	12/14	12/15	12/16	12/17	12/18
Sales ($ mil.)	8.6%	869.1	715.7	943.0	864.8	1,208.4
Net income ($ mil.)	18.0%	10.5	(82.5)	67.2	(13.1)	20.4
Market value ($ mil.)	(8.4%)	1,803.0	1,532.7	1,559.3	1,260.9	1,268.9
Employees	(4.8%)	4,800	3,800	4,100	4,100	3,950

SCRIPPS COLLEGE

1030 COLUMBIA AVE
CLAREMONT, CA 917113948
Phone: 909-621-8000
Fax: –
Web: www.scrippscollege.edu

CEO: –
CFO: –
HR: –
FYE: June 30
Type: Private

Scripps helps empower women through academic knowledge. Part of the Claremont University Consortium the all-women liberal arts college maintains an enrollment of fewer than 1000 students to encourage active participation in academic and campus life. Students participate in the Core Curriculum for their first three semesters at Scripps; the Core consists of lectures team teaching and seminar classes. The college also offers a wide range of courses from art to mathematics to psychology. Notable alumni include late best-selling author Molly Ivins and former White House chief counsel Beth Nolan. The college was founded in 1926 by Ellen Browning Scripps a newspaper publisher and philanthropist.

	Annual Growth	06/08	06/09	06/10	06/11	06/13
Sales ($ mil.)	–	–	–	(828.4)	55.9	97.6
Net income ($ mil.)	5810.0%	–	–	0.0	8.3	23.5
Market value ($ mil.)	–	–	–	–	–	–
Employees	–	–	–	–	–	180

SCRIPPS HEALTH

10140 CAMPUS POINT DR AX415
SAN DIEGO, CA 921211520
Phone: 800-727-4777
Fax: –

CEO: Christopher D. Van Gorder
CFO: Richard K. Rothberger
HR: Vic Buzachero
FYE: September 30
Type: Private

Scripps Health houses many a script-writing physician in its hospitals. The not-for-profit health system serves the San Diego area through five acute-care hospitals. Altogether the health system is home to approximately 1700 inpatient beds and a network of outpatient clinics. The system also offers home health care and operates community outreach programs. Its hospitals along with several outpatient Scripps Clinic and Scripps Coastal Medical Center locations employ some 3000 affiliated general practice and specialty physicians.

	Annual Growth	09/05	09/06	09/07	09/08	09/15
Sales ($ mil.)	6.5%	–	–	1,781.1	1,953.8	2,943.6
Net income ($ mil.)	6.5%	–	–	223.9	18.6	371.3
Market value ($ mil.)	–	–	–	–	–	–
Employees	–	–	–	–	–	13,445

SCRIPPS NETWORKS INTERACTIVE, INC.

9721 SHERRILL BLVD
KNOXVILLE, TN 379323330
Phone: 865-694-2700
Fax: –
Web: www.discovery.com

CEO: Kenneth W. (Ken) Lowe
CFO:
HR: Nello-John (NJ) Pesci
FYE: December 31
Type: Private

Lifestyle TV is a livelihood for this company. Scripps Networks Interactive operates six lifestyle cable networks including Home & Garden Television (home building and decoration) the Food Network (culinary programs) DIY - Do It Yourself Network (home repair and improvement) the Cooking Channel (culinary how-to programming) and the Travel Channel (travel and tourism). The company additionally owns music channel Great American Country and has minority interests in Asian Food Channel and regional sports network FOX Sports Net South. It also owns a 50% stake in UKTV. Trusts for the Scripps family own majority control of the company. In 2017 Discovery Communications agreed to buy Scripps Networks in a $14.6 billion deal.

	Annual Growth	12/13	12/14	12/15	12/16	12/17
Sales ($ mil.)	10.1%	–	2,665.5	3,018.2	3,401.4	3,561.8
Net income ($ mil.)	3.9%	–	726.8	778.5	847.4	814.4
Market value ($ mil.)	–	–	–	–	–	–
Employees	–	–	–	–	–	3,500

SCRYPT INC   NBB: SYPT

9050 N Capital of Texas Highway, Suite III-250
Austin, TX 78759
Phone: 512 493-6228
Fax: –
Web: www.scrypt.com

CEO: Aleksander Szymanski
CFO: Neil Burley
HR: –
FYE: December 31
Type: Public

SecureCARE Technologies (formerly eClickMD) is looking to secure more paying customers for the health of its business. The company provides Internet-based document exchange applications for doctors clinics home health care agencies hospice organizations and medical equipment providers. Its applications including its flagship Sfax enable health care providers to send receive and manage patient care documents via the Internet. As eClickMD the company filed for bankruptcy in 2003 and emerged later that year. It changed its name to SecureCARE Technologies in 2004.

	Annual Growth	12/12	12/13	12/14	12/15	12/16
Sales ($ mil.)	61.9%	1.6	2.6	3.7	8.3	11.1
Net income ($ mil.)	–	(0.6)	(0.6)	–	–	–
Market value ($ mil.)	127.3%	1.0	1.0	1.0	12.1	26.7
Employees	–	–	–	–	–	–

SCULPTOR CAPITAL MANAGEMENT — NYS: SCU

9 West 57th Street
New York, NY 10019
Phone: 212 790-0000
Fax: –
Web: www.ozm.com

CEO: Daniel S. Och
CFO: Alesia Haas
HR: –
FYE: December 31
Type: Public

Sculptor Capital Management provides a variety of alternative asset management services for more than 1200 fund investors through offices in New York and overseas in Mumbai Beijing Hong Kong and London. The company's capabilities in strategies include private equity merger arbitrage corporate credit and equity restructuring among others. With some $32.3 billion in assets under management. The hedge fund firm boasts approximately 125 investment professionals two dozen of active executive managing directors and about 50 managing directors. In 2019 Och-Ziff changed its name to Sculptor Capital Management.

	Annual Growth	12/14	12/15	12/16	12/17	12/18
Sales ($ mil.)	(24.3%)	1,542.3	1,323.0	770.4	858.3	507.2
Net income ($ mil.)	–	142.4	25.7	(124.7)	21.1	(24.3)
Market value ($ mil.)	(47.0%)	576.6	307.5	163.4	123.4	45.4
Employees	(8.6%)	595	659	524	483	416

SDB TRADE INTERNATIONAL, L.P.

11200 RICHMOND AVE # 180
HOUSTON, TX 770823178
Phone: 713-475-0048
Fax: –
Web: www.thesdbgroup.com

CEO: –
CFO: Wesley Sherer
HR: –
FYE: December 31
Type: Private

For SDB Trade International the product pipeline more than a buzzword. An international metals trading company SDB Trade International deals in steel pipe ferrous and non-ferrous scrap coils and beams. SBD Trade provide import and export services for its products sourcing its materials primarily from mills in India and China. Specializing in metal pipes for the Oil and Gas delivery and transmission industry — the company products include seamless tubing and casing electric resistance welded steel pipes seamless steel pipes and large diameter pipes. SDB Trade serves clients located around the world and provides shipping trucking storage repair and inspection services upon request.

	Annual Growth	12/08	12/09	12/11	12/12	12/17
Sales ($ mil.)	15.4%	–	29.2	4.0	51.5	91.8
Net income ($ mil.)	17.0%	–	1.7	2.0	1.1	5.9
Market value ($ mil.)	–	–	–	–	–	–
Employees	–	–	–	–	–	16

SEABOARD CORP. — ASE: SEB

9000 West, 67th Street
Merriam, KS 66202
Phone: 913 676-8800
Fax: –
Web: www.seaboardcorp.com

CEO: Steven J. Bresky
CFO: Robert L. Steer
HR: –
FYE: December 31
Type: Public

With pork and turkey from the US flour from Haiti and sugar from Argentina Seaboard has a lot on its plate. The diversified agribusiness and transportation firm has operations in some 45 countries in the Americas the Caribbean and Africa. Seaboard sells its pork and poultry in the US and abroad. Overseas it trades grain (wheat soya) operates power plants and feed and flour mills and grows and refines sugar cane. Seaboard owns a shipping service for containerized cargo between the US the Caribbean and South America; it has shipping terminals in Miami and Houston and a fleet of about 20 vessels (two owned the rest chartered) and ships to ports worldwide. Seaboard is run by descendants of founder Otto Bresky.

	Annual Growth	12/14	12/15	12/16	12/17	12/18
Sales ($ mil.)	0.4%	6,473.1	5,594.0	5,379.0	5,809.0	6,583.0
Net income ($ mil.)	–	365.3	171.0	312.0	247.0	(17.0)
Market value ($ mil.)	(4.2%)	4,908.3	3,384.6	4,620.7	5,156.2	4,136.7
Employees	4.0%	10,778	10,772	12,000	11,800	12,600

SEABROOK BROTHERS & SONS INC

85 FINLEY RD
BRIDGETON, NJ 083026078
Phone: 856-455-8080
Fax: –
Web: www.seabrookfarms.com

CEO: –
CFO: –
HR: R Scott Elliott
FYE: May 28
Type: Private

Seabrook Brothers and Sons almost has an alphabet of products. From asparagus to water chestnuts the company grows processes and freezes a harvest of vegetables. In addition to producing items for retail sale under its Seabrook Farms label the company supplies vegetables to customers in the industrial ingredients foodservice and private-label retail sectors. It serves customers throughout the US as well as in internationally in Canada Chile Israel Puerto Rico Mexico and Saudi Arabia. Seabrook also makes such value-added products as frozen skillet meals creamed spinach and butter and cheese sauces. In business since 1978 the company is still run by the founding Seabrook family.

	Annual Growth	06/12	06/13*	05/14	05/15	05/16
Sales ($ mil.)	(3.0%)	–	110.6	105.1	105.9	100.9
Net income ($ mil.)	–	–	2.3	(0.3)	3.5	(2.5)
Market value ($ mil.)	–	–	–	–	–	–
Employees	–	–	–	–	–	200

*Fiscal year change

SEACHANGE INTERNATIONAL INC. — NMS: SEAC

50 Nagog Park
Acton, MA 01720
Phone: 978 897-0100
Fax: –
Web: www.schange.com

CEO: Edward (Ed) Terino
CFO: Peter Faubert
HR: –
FYE: January 31
Type: Public

SeaChange International is taking TV and putting it on phones tablets PCs and just about any other device with a screen. The company provides software and services used by TV stations cable system operators and telecommunications companies to manage and distribute digital video. The company's back office software products allow operators to offer video-on-demand (VOD) and other interactive services to their subscribers via internet protocol TV (IPTV) while its set-top box middleware allows cable subscribers to access a variety of interactive features. SeaChange's media services business provides content aggregation and distribution. More than 40% sales come from customers in the US.

	Annual Growth	01/15	01/16	01/17	01/18	01/19
Sales ($ mil.)	(14.3%)	115.4	107.0	83.8	80.3	62.4
Net income ($ mil.)	–	(27.5)	(47.7)	(71.2)	13.5	(38.0)
Market value ($ mil.)	(31.1%)	253.5	223.3	86.9	119.6	57.1
Employees	(22.9%)	703	660	496	286	249

SEACOAST BANKING CORP. OF FLORIDA — NMS: SBCF

815 Colorado Avenue
Stuart, FL 34994
Phone: 772 287-4000
Fax: –
Web: www.seacoastbanking.com

CEO: Dennis S. (Denny) Hudson
CFO: Charles M. (Chuck) Shaffer
HR: Daniel G. (Dan) Chappell
FYE: December 31
Type: Public

Seacoast Banking Corporation is the holding company for Seacoast National Bank. It operates some 50 branches in Florida with a concentration in four large city markets. Serving individuals and businesses the bank offers a range of financial products and services including deposit accounts credit cards trust services and private banking. Commercial and residential real estate loans make up most of the bank's lending activities; to a lesser extent it also originates business and consumer loans.

	Annual Growth	12/14	12/15	12/16	12/17	12/18
Assets ($ mil.)	21.5%	3,093.3	3,534.8	4,680.9	5,810.1	6,747.7
Net income ($ mil.)	85.4%	5.7	22.1	29.2	42.9	67.3
Market value ($ mil.)	17.3%	706.2	769.4	1,133.0	1,294.8	1,336.4
Employees	11.7%	579	665	725	805	902

SEACOR HOLDINGS INC
NYS: CKH

2200 Eller Drive, P.O. Box 13038
Fort Lauderdale, FL 33316
Phone: 954 523-2200
Fax: -
Web: www.seacorholdings.com

CEO: ivind Lorentzen
CFO: Matthew R. Cenac
HR: -
FYE: December 31
Type: Public

SEACOR Holdings' diverse operations are anchored in offshore oil and gas and marine transportation. SEACOR's offerings include offshore marine inland river storage and handling distribution of petroleum chemical and agricultural commodities and shipping. The company operates one of the world's largest fleets of marine support vessels serving the offshore oil and gas industry delivering cargo and crew to offshore platforms. Its marine operations include US coastal tanker transportation of fuel and chemicals and inland river barge transportation of chemicals and bulk agricultural products. In mid-2017 the company acquired bankrupt shipper International Shipholding Corporation for roughly $50 million. That same year it spun off its Offshore Marine Services and Illinois Corn Processing businesses.

	Annual Growth	12/14	12/15	12/16	12/17	12/18
Sales ($ mil.)	(10.8%)	1,319.4	1,054.7	831.0	577.9	835.8
Net income ($ mil.)	(12.7%)	100.1	(68.8)	(215.9)	61.6	58.1
Market value ($ mil.)	(15.9%)	1,353.0	963.4	1,306.6	847.2	678.2
Employees	(15.3%)	4,901	4,849	3,716	2,264	2,518

SEALASKA CORPORATION

1 SEALASKA PLZ STE 400
JUNEAU, AK 998011276
Phone: 907-586-1512
Fax: -
Web: www.sealaska.com

CEO: Chris E. McNeil
CFO: Doug Morris
HR: -
FYE: December 31
Type: Private

Sealaska Corporation is a native-owned investment firm active in natural resources manufacturing services and gaming. The holding company owns land in southeastern Alaska home to the Tlingit Haida and Tsimshian peoples. Sealaska core holdings include Sealaska Timber Corporation Alaska Coastal Aggregates Sealaska Constructors Sealaska Environmental Services and Colorado-based information technology services provider Managed Business Solutions. Subsidiary End-to-End Enterprises manages the company's gaming business. Sealaska's subsidiaries operate throughout North America and around the world. Its companies often win government contracts for construction environmental and engineering projects.

	Annual Growth	12/14	12/15	12/16	12/17	12/18
Sales ($ mil.)	57.7%	-	109.4	145.5	293.4	429.3
Net income ($ mil.)	71.4%	-	13.7	16.0	45.8	69.1
Market value ($ mil.)	-	-	-	-	-	-
Employees	-	-	-	-	-	1,400

SEARS HOLDINGS CORP
NBB: SHLD Q

3333 Beverly Road
Hoffman Estates, IL 60179
Phone: 847 286-2500
Fax: -
Web: www.sears.com

CEO: Edward S. (Eddie) Lampert
CFO: Robert A. Riecker
HR: Megan Van Pelt
FYE: February 03
Type: Public

Once a retail giant Sears Holdings is growing smaller and leaner these days. The company is a retailer of appliances and tools as well as lawn and garden fitness and automotive repair equipment. With about 425 retail stores across the US Sears Holdings operates through subsidiaries Sears Roebuck and Co. and Kmart offering proprietary Sears brands including Kenmore and DieHard. Beyond retail Sears Holdings is a leading provider of home installation and product repair services. In response to plummeting sales in a tough retail climate Sears Holdings has been forced to sell assets and close hundreds of stores in recent years. In 2019 it emerged from Chapter 11 bankruptcy protection owned by an affiliate of hedge fund ESL Investments controlled by former Sears chairman Eddie Lampert.

	Annual Growth	02/14*	01/15	01/16	01/17*	02/18
Sales ($ mil.)	(17.6%)	36,188.0	31,198.0	25,146.0	22,138.0	16,702.0
Net income ($ mil.)	-	(1,365.0)	(1,682.0)	(1,129.0)	(2,221.0)	(383.0)
Market value ($ mil.)	(49.6%)	3,928.0	3,438.7	1,830.6	801.4	253.8
Employees	(22.7%)	249,000	196,000	178,000	140,000	89,000

*Fiscal year change

SEARS HOMETOWN & OUTLET STORES INC
NAS: SHOS

5500 Trillium Boulevard, Suite 501
Hoffman Estates, IL 60192
Phone: 847 286-7000
Fax: -
Web: www.shos.com

CEO: -
CFO: Harold Talisman
HR: -
FYE: February 03
Type: Public

Sears Hometown and Outlet (SHO) Stores are available in fewer and fewer hometowns. A spinoff of Sears Holdings Corp. the company has struggled amid a harsh retail environment and seen its store count drop below 900 (down from nearly 1300 in 2013). It sells hardware tools home appliances and lawn and garden equipment across the US Puerto Rico and Bermuda. Hometown stores offer Sears-branded products as well as a variety of national brands while Outlet stores generally stock out-of-carton discontinued reconditioned scratched and dented and other ?outlet-value? products. Each segment also sells products online. The stores are primarily operated by independent dealers and franchisees.

	Annual Growth	02/14*	01/15	01/16	01/17*	02/18
Sales ($ mil.)	(8.2%)	2,421.6	2,356.0	2,287.8	2,070.1	1,720.0
Net income ($ mil.)	-	35.6	(168.8)	(27.3)	(131.9)	(95.1)
Market value ($ mil.)	(42.5%)	476.5	257.7	158.0	86.3	52.2
Employees	(9.9%)	4,485	3,634	4,053	3,600	2,962

*Fiscal year change

SEATTLE CHILDREN'S HOSPITAL

4800 SAND POINT WAY NE
SEATTLE, WA 981053901
Phone: 206-987-2000
Fax: -
Web: www.seattlechildrens.org

CEO: Jeff Sperring
CFO: Kelly Wallace
HR: -
FYE: September 30
Type: Private

Seattle Children's Hospital which has some 325 beds serves children and infants of all ages. Its specialty units include psychiatric care neonatal intensive care and rehabilitation for children disabled by injuries illness or congenital complications. In addition to its primary campus Seattle Children's Hospital operates numerous outpatient clinics in the Puget Sound area. It also provides outreach services throughout the Pacific Northwest as well as in Alaska and Montana. Seattle Children's Hospital provides telemedicine services in Idaho.

	Annual Growth	09/11	09/12	09/13	09/14	09/15
Sales ($ mil.)	10.1%	-	814.0	1,018.0	983.4	1,086.8
Net income ($ mil.)	(0.4%)	-	150.4	192.3	177.2	148.4
Market value ($ mil.)	-	-	-	-	-	-
Employees	-	-	-	-	-	2,800

SEATTLE GENETICS INC
NMS: SGEN

21823 30th Drive SE
Bothell, WA 98021
Phone: 425 527-4000
Fax: -
Web: www.seattlegenetics.com

CEO: Clay B. Siegall
CFO: Todd E. Simpson
HR: Christopher (Chris) Pawlowicz
FYE: December 31
Type: Public

To heck with verbs Seattle Genetics is conjugating antibodies and drugs to fight cancer. The company's technologies use genetically engineered monoclonal antibodies (MAbs or single source proteins) to trigger cell death in some cancers but when they can't do it alone Seattle Genetics pairs them up with drugs using its Antibody-Drug Conjugate (ADC) technology for a one-two punch. Its first product Adcetris gained FDA approval in 2011 for the treatment of lymphoma in specific patient categories. With partner Millennium Pharmaceuticals the company is working to expand Adcetris' indications. Seattle Genetics also licenses its ADC technology to larger drugmakers to develop their own new cancer therapies.

	Annual Growth	12/14	12/15	12/16	12/17	12/18
Sales ($ mil.)	22.9%	286.8	336.8	418.1	482.3	654.7
Net income ($ mil.)	-	(76.1)	(120.5)	(140.1)	(125.5)	(222.7)
Market value ($ mil.)	15.2%	5,149.2	7,192.6	8,457.0	8,574.0	9,080.4
Employees	18.6%	657	759	890	1,100	1,302

SEATTLE UNIVERSITY

901 12TH AVE
SEATTLE, WA 981224411
Phone: 206-296-6150
Fax: –
Web: www.seattleu.edu

CEO: –
CFO: –
HR: –
FYE: June 30
Type: Private

Seattle University isn't very big but as one of 28 Jesuit universities in the US it is part of a Roman Catholic teaching legacy that spans the country and the world. With an enrollment of about 7500 students the school offers 64 undergraduate more than 35 graduate degree programs and 28 certificate programs through its eight schools (College of Arts and Sciences Albers School of Business and Economics College of Education School of Law Matteo Ricci College College of Nursing College of Science and Engineering and School of Theology and Ministry).

	Annual Growth	06/12	06/13	06/15	06/17	06/18
Sales ($ mil.)	(4.2%)	–	277.5	305.8	222.4	223.3
Net income ($ mil.)	59.6%	–	1.4	22.8	25.2	14.2
Market value ($ mil.)	–	–	–	–	–	–
Employees	–	–	–	–	–	1,100

SEAWORLD ENTERTAINMENT INC.   NYS: SEAS

6240 Sea Harbor Drive
Orlando, FL 32821
Phone: 407 226-5011
Fax: –
Web: www.seaworldentertainment.com

CEO: Joel Manby
CFO: Marc G. Swanson
HR: –
FYE: December 31
Type: Public

Swimming with the fishes takes on a whole new meaning at these parks. SeaWorld Entertainment is one of the US's largest theme park operators. The company markets its parks as family-friendly offering learning opportunities (SeaWorld and Discovery Cove where visitors can swim with dolphins and other marine life) all-ages entertainment (the Sesame Street -themed park Sesame Place) and traditional amusement parks (Busch Gardens). Previously a subsidiary of brewer Anheuser-Busch the company was sold to Blackstone for about $2.3 billion in late 2009 and became a public company in 2013.

	Annual Growth	12/14	12/15	12/16	12/17	12/18
Sales ($ mil.)	(0.1%)	1,377.8	1,371.0	1,344.3	1,263.3	1,372.3
Net income ($ mil.)	(2.7%)	49.9	49.1	(12.5)	(202.4)	44.8
Market value ($ mil.)	5.4%	1,489.8	1,638.7	1,575.5	1,129.4	1,838.5
Employees	10.8%	11,100	11,300	13,300	16,200	16,700

SECURA INSURANCE HOLDINGS INC.

2401 S. Memorial Dr.
Appleton WI 54915
Phone: 920-739-3161
Fax: 920-739-7363
Web: www.secura.net

CEO: John A Bykowski
CFO: Kathryn J Sieman
HR: –
FYE: December 31
Type: Private - Mutual Com

SECURA Insurance keeps the homestead secure. The company offers a range of personal and commercial property/casualty insurance throughout the Midwest including auto homeowners and farm-owners lines. Commercial lines include property liability workers' compensation and risk management as well as specialty coverage for niche markets such as the manufacturing restaurant and service industries. The mutual firm does business in about a dozen midwestern states and its products are marketed by independent agencies. SECURA was founded in 1900 as The Farmers Home Mutual Hail Tornado and Cyclone Insurance Company.

SECURIAN FINANCIAL GROUP INC.

400 Robert St. North
St. Paul MN 55101-2098
Phone: 651-665-3500
Fax: 651-665-4488
Web: www.securian.com

CEO: Christopher M Hilger
CFO: Warren Zaccaro
HR: –
FYE: December 31
Type: Private

After 125 years of being in business Minnesota Mutual felt secure enough to change its name to Securian Financial Group and serve the entire US. The company still operates through its subsidiary Minnesota Life which offers individual and group life and disability insurance and annuities as well as retirement services. Other subsidiaries include its brokerage network Securian Financial Services and its Allied Solutions business which distributes Securian products. Its Advantus Capital Management provides institutional asset management. It also offers a small amount of property/casualty surety coverage nationwide. The company was founded in 1880 and restructured as a mutual holding company in 2005.

SECURITIES INVESTOR PROTECTION CORPORATION

1667 K ST NW STE 1000
WASHINGTON, DC 200061620
Phone: 202-371-8300
Fax: –
Web: www.sipc.org

CEO: Stephen Harbeck
CFO: –
HR: –
FYE: December 31
Type: Private

Securities Investor Protection Corporation (SIPC) is an industry-financed insurance plan that protects clients of most broker-dealers registered with the US Securities and Exchange Commission (SEC). SIPC insures customers' securities (up to $500000 per account) against losses due to the financial failure of brokerage firms. Losses caused by fluctuations in market value are not protected. The not-for-profit membership corporation was mandated by the Securities Investor Protection Act and has more than 6000 members. Its board is appointed by the US president the treasury secretary and the Federal Reserve Board. Assessments from members and investments in government securities provide money for the SIPC Fund.

	Annual Growth	12/10	12/11	12/14	12/15	12/16
Assets ($ mil.)	12.9%	–	1,606.1	2,362.9	2,652.9	2,944.6
Net income ($ mil.)	22.4%	–	131.6	307.3	169.0	362.2
Market value ($ mil.)	–	–	–	–	–	–
Employees	–	–	–	–	–	39

SECURITY FEDERAL CORP (SC)   NBB: SFDL

238 Richland Avenue Northwest
Aiken, SC 29801
Phone: 803 641-3000
Fax: –
Web: www.securityfederalbank.com

CEO: J Chris Verenes
CFO: Jessica T Cummins
HR: –
FYE: December 31
Type: Public

Security Federal is the holding company for Security Federal Bank which has about a dozen offices in southwestern South Carolina's Aiken and Lexington counties. It expanded into Columbia South Carolina and eastern Georgia in 2007. The bank offers checking and savings accounts credit cards CDs IRAs and other retail products and services. Commercial business and mortgage loans make up more than 60% of the company's lending portfolio which also includes residential mortgages (about 25%) and consumer loans. Security Federal also offers trust services investments and life home and auto insurance.

	Annual Growth	12/14	12/15	12/16	12/17	12/18
Assets ($ mil.)	2.5%	825.4	799.7	812.7	868.8	912.6
Net income ($ mil.)	5.5%	5.8	6.1	5.9	5.9	7.2
Market value ($ mil.)	12.8%	51.7	62.8	103.4	92.5	83.6
Employees	3.3%	205	214	219	223	233

SECURITY FINANCE CORPORATION OF SPARTANBURG

181 SECURITY PL
SPARTANBURG, SC 293075450
Phone: 864-582-8193
Fax: –
Web: www.security-finance.com

CEO: –
CFO: A Greg Williams
HR: –
FYE: December 31
Type: Private

Folks looking for a little financial security just might turn to Security Finance Corporation of Spartanburg. Founded in 1955 the consumer loan company provides personal loans typically ranging from $100 to $600 (some states however allow loan amounts as high as $3000). Customers can also turn to Security Finance for credit reports and tax preparation services. The company operates approximately 900 offices in more than 15 states that are marketed under the Security Finance Sunbelt Credit and PFS banner names. A subsidiary of Security Group the financial institution also has locations operating as Security Financial Services in North Carolina and Longhorn Finance in Texas.

	Annual Growth	12/12	12/13	12/14	12/15	12/16
Assets ($ mil.)	0.5%	–	616.7	648.9	651.5	625.1
Net income ($ mil.)	4.1%	–	62.7	83.1	78.8	70.7
Market value ($ mil.)	–	–	–	–	–	–
Employees	–	–	–	–	–	2,500

SECURITY HEALTH PLAN OF WISCONSIN, INC.

1515 N SAINT JOSEPH AVE
MARSHFIELD, WI 544491343
Phone: 715-221-9555
Fax: –
Web: www.securityhealth.org

CEO: Julie Brussow
CFO: –
HR: –
FYE: December 31
Type: Private

Security Health Plan of Wisconsin provides health insurance coverage and related services to some 200000 members in more than 35 Wisconsin counties. Its managed network of providers includes more than 4000 physicians 40 hospitals and health care facilities as well as 55000 pharmacies across the US. Security Health Plan provides policies for groups and individuals. Its products include HMO coverage plans and supplemental Medicare plans as well as prescription drug and equipment coverage disease management programs and administration services for self-funded plans. Established in 1986 the company is the managed healthcare arm of Marshfield Clinic which operates medical practices across the state.

	Annual Growth	12/03	12/04	12/05	12/09	12/17
Sales ($ mil.)	9.7%	–	369.8	385.6	814.8	1,234.4
Net income ($ mil.)	(4.4%)	–	17.5	0.0	27.7	9.8
Market value ($ mil.)	–	–	–	–	–	–
Employees	–	–	–	–	–	1,006

SECURITY NATIONAL FINANCIAL CORP

NMS: SNFC A

5300 South 360 West, Suite 250
Salt Lake City, UT 84123
Phone: 801 264-1060
Fax: 801 265-9882
Web: www.securitynational.com

CEO: Scott M Quist
CFO: Garrett S Sill
HR: –
FYE: December 31
Type: Public

There are three certainties — life death and mortgage payments — and Security National Financial has you covered on all fronts. Its largest unit SecurityNational Mortgage makes residential and commercial mortgage loans through some 70 offices in more than a dozen states. Its Security National Life Memorial Insurance Company and Southern Security Life subsidiaries sell life and diving or related sports accident insurance annuities and funeral plans in about 40 states. Security National Financial also owns about 15 mortuaries and cemeteries in Utah Arizona and California. The family of chairman and CEO George Quist controls more than half of Security National Financial.

	Annual Growth	12/14	12/15	12/16	12/17	12/18
Assets ($ mil.)	11.9%	671.1	749.9	854.0	982.2	1,050.8
Net income ($ mil.)	29.3%	7.8	12.6	14.3	14.1	21.7
Market value ($ mil.)	(2.7%)	104.0	118.3	117.4	94.8	93.2
Employees	(0.8%)	1,480	1,587	1,657	1,453	1,433

SECURITY SERVICE FEDERAL CREDIT UNION

16211 La Cantera Pkwy.
San Antonio TX 78256-2419
Phone: 210-476-4000
Fax: 210-444-3000
Web: www.ssfcu.org

CEO: –
CFO: –
HR: –
FYE: December 31
Type: Private - Not-for-Pr

Security Service Federal Credit Union (SSFCU) works to keep its members' cash secure. It boasts nearly 40 branches in the San Antonio area and across South Texas plus more than 30 more in Colorado and Utah that provide such financial services as checking and savings accounts CDs credit cards insurance and investment products residential mortgages and business and consumer loans. The not-for-profit member-owned credit union was founded in 1956 to serve the US Air Force Security Service Command and today has more than 900000 members. One of the largest credit unions in the US SSFCU also has its own political action committee to participate in legislative activities related to the credit union industry.

SED INTERNATIONAL HOLDINGS, INC.

NBB: SEDN

2150 Cedars Road, Suite 200
Lawrenceville, GA 30043
Phone: 770 243-1200
Fax: –
Web: www.sedonline.com

CEO: Hesham M Gad
CFO: Juan Orlando Bravo
HR: –
FYE: June 30
Type: Public

SED International keeps North and South America computing. The company distributes PCs tablet and notebook computers components televisions small appliances and more to resellers and retailers throughout the US and Latin America. Its computer hardware products traditionally the company's primary business line include components storage devices networking equipment peripherals and systems from about 170 vendors such as Acer Dell Lenovo and Microsoft. SED also offers customized supply chain management services to its e-commerce business-to-business and business-to-consumer clients. Founded in 1980 as Southern Electronics Distributors SED International is restructuring its operations in the US.

	Annual Growth	06/10	06/11	06/12	06/13	06/14
Sales ($ mil.)	(19.1%)	541.7	607.0	577.3	517.4	232.5
Net income ($ mil.)	–	0.3	3.1	1.4	(15.7)	(18.4)
Market value ($ mil.)	(50.7%)	13.5	27.3	27.3	27.3	0.8
Employees	(5.5%)	388	402	425	327	–

SEDGWICK CLAIMS MANAGEMENT SERVICES INC.

1100 Ridgeway Loop Rd.
Memphis TN 38120
Phone: 901-415-7400
Fax: 901-415-7406
Web: www.sedgwickcms.com

CEO: David North
CFO: Henry Lyons
HR: –
FYE: December 31
Type: Private

Unlike Kyra this Sedgwick probably can't play the "Six Degrees of Kevin Bacon" game but it can help employers save a little bacon playing today's insurance game. Sedgwick Claims Management Services (Sedgwick CMS) offers insurance claims administration services to major employers focusing on workers' compensation; short- and long-term disability; and general auto and professional liability coverage. Other activities include risk management analytics worker care and absence management and Medicare compliance services. The firm serves clients in such industries as financial services health care utilities education manufacturing and retail.

SEDGWICK LLP

333 Bush St. 30th Fl.
San Francisco CA 94104-2806
Phone: 415-781-7900
Fax: 415-781-2635
Web: www.sedgwicklaw.com

CEO: -
CFO: -
HR: -
FYE: December 31
Type: Private - Partnershi

Sedgwick LLP (formerly Sedgwick Detert Moran & Arnold LLP) concentrates on corporate America. Working mainly on commercial and complex litigation matters the firm specializes in areas such as product and professional liability employment and labor antitrust intellectual property media entertainment and sports health care reinsurance and bankruptcy. Sedgwick employs more than 370 attorneys in about a dozen US offices as well as international offices in Bermuda London and Paris. Sedgwick LLP was founded in 1933 as Keith & Creede.

SEDONA CORP   NL:

1003 West 9th Avenue, Second Floor
King of Prussia, PA 19406
Phone: 610 337-8400
Fax: -
Web: www.sedonacorp.com

CEO: David R Vey
CFO: -
HR: -
FYE: December 31
Type: Public

SEDONA's software bridges the canyon between financial institutions and their customers. The company provides Web-based customer relationship management software that analyzes customer data manages marketing campaigns and generates leads for small and midsized financial institutions. Its Intarsia software also generates customer profiles that include demographic behavioral and preference information provided by third parties. Customers include community banks credit unions brokerage firms and insurance agencies.

	Annual Growth	12/11	12/12	12/13	12/14	12/15
Sales ($ mil.)	9.7%	1.3	1.5	1.6	1.6	1.9
Net income ($ mil.)	-	(0.7)	(0.6)	(0.7)	(0.7)	(0.5)
Market value ($ mil.)	(40.4%)	7.1	1.9	2.6	1.5	-
Employees	-	-	-	-	-	-

SEE'S CANDIES INC.

210 El Camino Real
South San Francisco CA 94080
Phone: 650-583-7307
Fax: 650-225-9430
Web: www.sees.com

CEO: -
CFO: -
HR: -
FYE: December 31
Type: Subsidiary

One suspects that investment guru and billionaire Warren Buffett has a sweet tooth. If we're correct he knows that See's Candies has what it takes to satisfy it. Owned by Buffett's firm Berkshire Hathaway See's Candies makes about 100 varieties of premium chocolate truffles caramels toffee and other confections including boxed assortments lollipops peppermints and licorice treats. The company sells its sweets at some 210 franchised black-and-white-decorated shops in the US primarily in California and other western states. Its products also are sold for fundraisers through its website and by mail order. A highly seasonal operation some 50% of its revenue is generated in November and December.

SEFTON RESOURCES INC.   LONDON: SER

2050 S. Oneida St. Ste. 102
Denver CO 80224
Phone: 303-759-2700
Fax: 303-759-2701
Web: www.seftonresources.com

CEO: -
CFO: -
HR: -
FYE: December 31
Type: Public

Looking to strike it rich by sifting through a number of hydrocarbon resource assets Sefton Resources explores for and produces oil and gas primarily in California and Kansas. Its core area of exploration and production is the East Ventura Basin in California where Sefton Resources owns two oil fields (Tapia Canyon and Eureka Canyon). In addition the company owns more than 40000 acres in the Forest City Basin of Eastern Kansas which has coalbed methane and conventional oil and gas deposits. The company has proved reserves of 7.6 million barrels of oil equivalent. Its operating subsidiaries are TEG Oil & Gas USA and TEG Oil & Gas MidContinent.

SEI INVESTMENTS CO   NMS: SEIC

1 Freedom Valley Drive
Oaks, PA 19456-1100
Phone: 610 676-1000
Fax: -
Web: www.seic.com

CEO: Alfred P. West
CFO: Dennis J. McGonigle
HR: -
FYE: December 31
Type: Public

SEI Investments provides outsourced investment and fund processing for roughly 11000 clients including banks trust companies investment advisors and managers and institutional investors and ultra-high-net-worth families in the US Canada the UK Europe and other locations throughout the world. Services include securities and investment processing trust accounting portfolio analysis treasury and cash management and performance measurement reporting. Its investment operations serves managers and distributors of mutual funds hedge funds and alternative investments. The company administers or manages approximately $945 billion in hedge and mutual funds and private equity comprising some $330 billion in assets under management and more than $600 billion in assets under administration.

	Annual Growth	12/14	12/15	12/16	12/17	12/18
Sales ($ mil.)	6.4%	1,266.0	1,334.2	1,401.5	1,526.6	1,624.2
Net income ($ mil.)	12.2%	318.7	331.7	333.8	404.4	505.9
Market value ($ mil.)	3.6%	6,151.5	8,050.4	7,583.4	11,040.1	7,097.9
Employees	8.1%	2,824	2,985	3,243	3,650	3,852

SEITEL INC

10811 S WESTVW CIR DR 100
HOUSTON, TX 770432748
Phone: 713-881-8900
Fax: -
Web: www.seitel.com

CEO: Robert D Monson
CFO: Marcia H Kendrick
HR: Jana Stroud
FYE: December 31
Type: Private

There aren't any "Quiet" signs in Seitel's library which consists of more than 43000 sq. miles of 3-D and about 1.1 million linear miles of 2-D seismic data. The data which is used to locate oil and gas primarily covers the Gulf of Mexico the US Gulf Coast and western Canada. The company contracts with third-party seismic crews to gather data but handles the processing itself through its Olympic Seismic Seitel Data Seitel Matrix Seitel Solutions business units. The bulk of Seitel's total revenues comes from the acquisition and licensing of seismic data. The balance is primarily generated by its Seitel Solutions subsidiary which gives customers access to the company's seismic database.

	Annual Growth	12/12	12/13	12/14	12/15	12/16
Sales ($ mil.)	(22.5%)	-	202.9	198.0	100.3	94.5
Net income ($ mil.)	-	-	113.7	9.7	(110.0)	(24.4)
Market value ($ mil.)	-	-	-	-	-	-
Employees	-	-	-	-	-	129

SELECT BANCORP INC (NEW)   NMS: SLCT

700 W. Cumberland Street
Dunn, NC 28334
Phone: 910 892-7080
Fax: –
Web: www.selectbank.com

CEO: William L Hedgepeth II
CFO: Mark A Jeffries
HR: –
FYE: December 31
Type: Public

Select Bancorp (formerly New Century Bancorp) is the holding company for the aptly named Select Bank & Trust (formerly New Century Bank). The bank has about a dozen branches across North Carolina. Targeting individuals and small to midsized businesses Select Bank & Trust offers such services as checking and savings accounts CDs IRAs and loans. Its loan book largely comprises real estate loans; the remaining portfolio includes business and consumer loans. New Century Bancorp acquired Select Bancorp in 2014 and took its name.

	Annual Growth	12/14	12/15	12/16	12/17	12/18
Assets ($ mil.)	13.2%	766.1	817.0	846.6	1,194.1	1,258.5
Net income ($ mil.)	55.5%	2.4	6.6	6.8	3.2	13.8
Market value ($ mil.)	13.9%	142.3	156.2	190.2	244.1	239.1
Employees	91.0%	154	153	150	202	2,050

SELECT INCOME REIT   NMS: SIR

Two Newton Place, 255 Washington Street, Suite 300
Newton, MA 02458-1634
Phone: 617 796-8303
Fax: –
Web: www.sirreit.com

CEO: –
CFO: –
HR: –
FYE: December 31
Type: Public

When it comes to real estate it doesn't get any more selective than Hawaii. And Select Income REIT (SIR) has amassed quite a land portfolio in the Aloha State. The externally-managed real estate investment trust owns 11 properties measuring nearly 18 million sq. ft. of single-tenant commercial and industrial properties on the island of Oahu. Tenants include an oil refinery for Tesoro and a Coca-Cola bottling plant and distribution center. On the mainland SIR owns another 37 office and warehouse properties totaling more than 8 million sq. ft. in about 20 states. The company was formed in December 2011 as a subsidiary of CommonWealth REIT. It went public in 2012.

	Annual Growth	12/12	12/13	12/14	12/15	12/16
Sales ($ mil.)	39.3%	122.8	188.3	222.7	428.4	462.0
Net income ($ mil.)	15.3%	65.9	93.1	105.9	74.7	116.3
Market value ($ mil.)	0.4%	2,215.1	2,391.3	2,182.9	1,772.5	2,253.6
Employees	–	–	–	–	–	–

SELECT MEDICAL HOLDINGS CORP   NYS: SEM

4714 Gettysburg Road, P.O. Box 2034
Mechanicsburg, PA 17055
Phone: 717 972-1100
Fax: –
Web: www.selectmedicalholdings.com

CEO: David S. Chernow
CFO: Martin F. Jackson
HR: John A. Saich
FYE: December 31
Type: Public

Learning to walk or talk again can be quite challenging but Select Medical exists to make things easier. The firm provides inpatient rehabilitation at some 100 long-term acute care hospitals (LTCH) and around 25 inpatient rehabilitation facilities in more than 25 states. These centers usually located in leased space within general hospitals specialize in treating complex medical conditions such as respiratory failure or spinal cord injury that require long-term care. Most patients are admitted as transfers from general hospitals. The company also operates more than 1600 outpatient rehab clinics in more than 35 US states and Washington DC. Additionally Select Medical offers contract rehab services at nursing homes and other locations.

	Annual Growth	12/14	12/15	12/16	12/17	12/18
Sales ($ mil.)	13.5%	3,065.0	3,742.7	4,286.0	4,443.6	5,081.3
Net income ($ mil.)	3.4%	120.6	130.7	115.4	177.2	137.8
Market value ($ mil.)	1.6%	1,947.8	1,611.0	1,792.3	2,387.4	2,076.3
Employees	10.7%	31,400	41,000	41,500	42,200	47,100

SELECTIVE INSURANCE GROUP INC   NMS: SIGI

40 Wantage Avenue
Branchville, NJ 07890
Phone: 973 948-3000
Fax: 973 948-0282
Web: www.selective.com

CEO: Gregory E. Murphy
CFO: Mark A. Wilcox
HR: Angelique Carbo
FYE: December 31
Type: Public

Property/casualty insurance holding company Selective Insurance Group's reach primarily covers the entire eastern US seaboard and much of the Midwest. Commercial policies sold by its 10 subsidiaries include workers' compensation and commercial automobile property and liability insurance. Personal lines include homeowners and automobile insurance. The company also offers federal flood insurance administration services throughout the US and some excess and surplus (E&S nonstandard) insurance. Selective Insurance Group operates through four reportable segments: Standard Commercial Lines Standard Personal Lines E&S Lines and Investments.

	Annual Growth	12/14	12/15	12/16	12/17	12/18
Assets ($ mil.)	4.8%	6,581.6	6,904.4	7,355.8	7,686.4	7,952.7
Net income ($ mil.)	6.0%	141.8	165.9	158.5	168.8	178.9
Market value ($ mil.)	22.4%	1,601.6	1,979.5	2,537.7	3,460.3	3,592.3
Employees	1.0%	2,200	2,200	2,250	2,260	2,290

SEMCO ENERGY, INC.

1411 3RD ST STE A
PORT HURON, MI 480605480
Phone: 810-987-2200
Fax: –
Web: www.semcoenergygas.com

CEO: David M Harris
CFO: Mark Moses
HR: Jenni Grimley-Smith
FYE: December 31
Type: Private

Alaska and Michigan have more in common than a cold climate. SEMCO ENERGY serves approximately 423000 natural gas consumers in both states. The company's main subsidiary is utility SEMCO ENERGY Gas which distributes gas to more than 290000 customers in 24 Michigan counties. SEMCO's ENSTAR Natural Gas unit distributes gas to more than 133000 customers in and around Anchorage Alaska. The company's unregulated operations include propane distribution in Michigan and Wisconsin; pipeline and storage facility operation; and information technology outsourcing. In 2012 SEMCO ENERGY was acquired by AltaGas.

	Annual Growth	12/11	12/12	12/13	12/14	12/16
Sales ($ mil.)	(0.3%)	–	582.3	608.1	674.0	576.0
Net income ($ mil.)	5.5%	–	41.6	48.7	51.2	51.6
Market value ($ mil.)	–	–	–	–	–	–
Employees	–	–	–	–	–	500

SEMGROUP CORP   NYS: SEMG

Two Warren Place, 6120 S. Yale Avenue, Suite 1500
Tulsa, OK 74136-4231
Phone: 918 524-8100
Fax: –
Web: www.semgroupcorp.com

CEO: Kelcy L Warren
CFO: Thomas E Long
HR: –
FYE: December 31
Type: Public

At SemGroup energy is always on the move connecting upstream producers with downstream refiners and customers. The company maintains an extensive network of pipelines processing plants refinery-connected storage facilities and deep-water marine terminals. Assets are concentrated in the US (Midwest and Gulf Coast) and Canada (Alberta). SemGroup owns 51% of White Cliffs Pipeline (links mid-continent oil producers with the Cushing terminal) and 51% of SemCams Midstream (natural gas assets in Canada's Montney play). The company sold off its UK and Mexican operations in 2018.

	Annual Growth	12/13	12/14	12/15	12/16	12/17
Sales ($ mil.)	9.9%	1,427.0	2,122.6	1,455.1	1,332.2	2,081.9
Net income ($ mil.)	–	–	48.1	29.2	30.3	2.1	(17.2)
Market value ($ mil.)	(17.5%)	5,132.6	5,381.2	2,270.8	3,285.1	2,376.3
Employees	8.2%	890	1,080	1,160	1,140	1,220

SEMINOLE ELECTRIC COOPERATIVE, INC.

16313 N DALE MABRY HWY
TAMPA, FL 336181427
Phone: 813-963-0994
Fax: –
Web: www.seminole-electric.com

CEO: Lisa Johnson
CFO: Jo Fuller
HR: –
FYE: December 31
Type: Private

This Seminole is not only a native Floridian but it has also provided electricity in the state since 1948. Seminole Electric Cooperative generates and transmits electricity for 10 member distribution cooperatives that serve 1.4 million residential and business customers in 42 Florida counties. Seminole Electric has more than 3350 MW of primarily coal-fired generating capacity. The cooperative also buys electricity from other utilities and independent power producers and it owns 350 miles of transmission lines. Some 90% of its power load uses the transmission systems of other utilities through long-term contracts.

	Annual Growth	12/15	12/16*	03/17*	12/17	12/18
Sales ($ mil.)	0.7%	–	1,068.0	1,052.4	1,067.3	1,083.5
Net income ($ mil.)	2.1%	–	20.2	33.8	23.8	21.1
Market value ($ mil.)	–	–	–	–	–	–
Employees	–	–	–	–	–	528

*Fiscal year change

SEMLER SCIENTIFIC INC

NBB: SMLR

911 Bern Court, Suite 110
San Jose, CA 95112
Phone: 877 774-4211
Fax: –
Web: www.semlerscientific.com

CEO: Douglas Murphy-Chutorian
CFO: Daniel E Conger
HR: –
FYE: December 31
Type: Public

Semler Scientific is an emerging medical device maker with a single product. The company markets the FloChec a medical device that measures arterial blood flow to the extremities (fingers and toes) quickly and easily in the doctor's office to diagnose peripheral artery disease. FloChec received FDA clearance in early 2010 and the company began commercially leasing the product in 2011. Founded in 2007 by Dr. Herbert Semler who invented the technology used in FloChec the Portland-based company went public in 2014 with an offering valued at $10 million.

	Annual Growth	12/14	12/15	12/16	12/17	12/18
Sales ($ mil.)	55.9%	3.6	7.0	7.4	12.5	21.5
Net income ($ mil.)	–	(4.5)	(8.5)	(2.6)	(1.5)	5.0
Market value ($ mil.)	104.7%	12.4	16.2	9.2	50.6	217.6
Employees	17.7%	24	37	29	37	46

SEMPRA ENERGY

NYS: SRE

488 8th Avenue
San Diego, CA 92101
Phone: 619 696-2000
Fax: –
Web: www.sempra.com

CEO: Debra L. (Debbie) Reed
CFO: Jeffrey W. Martin
HR: G. Joyce Rowland
FYE: December 31
Type: Public

Sempra Energy makes sure the lights are always on. The company provides natural gas to nearly 7 million customers and electricity to nearly 3.5 million in California via its two primary subsidiaries Southern California Gas (SoCalGas) and San Diego Gas & Electricity (SDG&E). SoCalGas operates more than 100000 miles of combined pipeline and four natural gas storage facilities while SDG&E operates 15000 miles of pipeline. Sempra also owns Oncor the largest electricity transmission firm in Texas. Sempra is selling its South America holdings which include Chilquinta Energia in Chile and Luz del Sur in Peru to focus exclusively on North America.

	Annual Growth	12/14	12/15	12/16	12/17	12/18
Sales ($ mil.)	1.4%	11,035.0	10,231.0	10,183.0	11,207.0	11,687.0
Net income ($ mil.)	(2.5%)	1,162.0	1,350.0	1,371.0	257.0	1,050.0
Market value ($ mil.)	(0.7%)	30,487.0	25,737.1	27,552.2	29,271.4	29,619.1
Employees	(30.3%)	17,046	17,387	16,575	16,046	4,015

SEMTECH CORP.

NMS: SMTC

200 Flynn Road
Camarillo, CA 93012-8790
Phone: 805 498-2111
Fax: –
Web: www.semtech.com

CEO: Mohan R. Maheswaran
CFO: Emeka N. Chukwu
HR: –
FYE: January 27
Type: Public

Semtech doesn't need a semaphore to signal its semiconductors' roles in communications. The company's analog and mixed-signal semiconductors are used by manufacturers of computers telecommunications consumer and industrial electronics. The company's chips are used for power management circuit protection transmission and other functions in a variety of devices including cellular phones and base stations notebook and desktop PCs network transmission equipment and automated test equipment. Semtech's LoRa platform for long range low power Internet of Things applications generates a growing amount of revenue for the company. About three-quarters of the company's sales are in the Asia/Pacific region.

	Annual Growth	01/15	01/16	01/17	01/18	01/19
Sales ($ mil.)	3.0%	557.9	490.2	544.3	587.8	627.2
Net income ($ mil.)	22.6%	27.9	11.5	54.7	36.4	63.1
Market value ($ mil.)	16.4%	1,766.0	1,311.3	2,198.5	2,377.9	3,246.9
Employees	(2.1%)	1,456	1,335	1,292	1,282	1,335

SENECA BIOPHARMA INC

NAS: SNCA

20271 Goldenrod Lane
Germantown, MD 20876
Phone: 301 366-4841
Fax: –
Web: www.neuralstem.com

CEO: Jim Scully
CFO: –
HR: –
FYE: December 31
Type: Public

Neuralstem is using human neural stem cells to find treatments for central nervous disorders. The company uses a proprietary technology to produce commercial quantities of brain and spinal cord stem cells that are used to develop potential treatments for Lou Gehrig's disease (also known as ALS or amyotrophic lateral sclerosis) Huntington's disease spinal cord injury and stroke. Its spinal cord stem cells are part of the first FDA-approved ALS stem cell clinical trial. Neuralstem also has a class of small molecule compounds that it is developing into oral drugs. The first NSI-189 is undergoing trials to treat major depression. These compounds may also be developed for Alzheimer's disease and schizophrenia.

	Annual Growth	12/14	12/15	12/16	12/17	12/18
Sales ($ mil.)	92.8%	0.0	0.0	0.0	0.3	0.3
Net income ($ mil.)	–	(22.6)	(20.9)	(21.1)	(15.7)	(4.9)
Market value ($ mil.)	(41.1%)	2.5	0.9	0.2	1.6	0.3
Employees	(29.3%)	24	33	11	6	6

SENECA COMPANIES INC.

4140 E. 14th St.
Des Moines IA 50313
Phone: 515-262-5000
Fax: 515-264-4360
Web: www.senecaco.com

CEO: –
CFO: –
HR: –
FYE: December 31
Type: Private

Seneca keeps cars clean in control and ready to go. The company designs and installs automobile wash systems fueling systems and other vehicle service equipment including lifts lubrication equipment and compressor systems. Seneca's data digital security camera systems and offered primarily to help secure auto dealerships. It also provides petroleum services and equipment environmental consulting remediation and waste removal general construction electrical contracting and industrial coating equipment. Seneca Companies operates from offices in Iowa Illinois and Nebraska.

SENECA FOODS CORP. NMS: SENE A

3736 South Main Street
Marion, NY 14505
Phone: 315 926-8100
Fax: –

CEO: Kraig H. Kayser
CFO: Timothy J. Benjamin
HR: –
FYE: March 31
Type: Public

Seneca Foods is one of the world's largest manufacturers and suppliers of canned vegetables. Its canned (as well as frozen and bottled) produce lineup is sold under numerous private labels and national and regional brands such as Aunt Nellie's Farm Kitchen Libby's Seneca and Green Valley that the company owns or licenses. Customers are primarily big grocery chains and some export markets and food service operators and food processors including its biggest customer Green Giant with which it has a longstanding relationship. Seneca also supplies frozen fruit and vegetables to private-label retail and food service customers. A short list of fruit and snack chip products are sold to retailers and food processors.

	Annual Growth	03/15	03/16	03/17	03/18	03/19
Sales ($ mil.)	(1.7%)	1,286.4	1,275.4	1,245.7	1,314.8	1,199.6
Net income ($ mil.)	(12.7%)	9.9	54.5	12.6	(13.8)	5.7
Market value ($ mil.)	(4.7%)	284.5	331.5	344.5	264.3	234.8
Employees	2.1%	3,400	3,500	3,600	4,300	3,700

SENOMYX INC NMS: SNMX

4767 Nexus Centre Drive
San Diego, CA 92121
Phone: 858 646-8300
Fax: –
Web: www.senomyx.com

CEO: John Poyhonen
CFO: David Humphrey
HR: –
FYE: December 31
Type: Public

Senomyx nose a good thing when it smells it. The company has identified human receptor genes related to the detection of smells and tastes and using this genetic research the company is developing sweet salty and savory flavor enhancers and bitter taste modulators. Potential products include agents that can block bitter tastes in coffee and make low-sodium snacks taste salty. Senomyx collaborates with the likes of PepsiCo Nestl-© and Firmenich. The company also works with Japan's largest flavors company Ajinomoto which has opened up the Asian market for Senomyx.

	Annual Growth	12/12	12/13	12/14	12/15	12/16
Sales ($ mil.)	(7.4%)	31.3	29.3	27.7	24.9	23.0
Net income ($ mil.)	–	(9.2)	(11.9)	(12.2)	(12.6)	(10.7)
Market value ($ mil.)	(13.0%)	76.1	229.2	272.2	170.8	43.5
Employees	(14.6%)	111	113	110	90	59

SENSIENT TECHNOLOGIES CORP. NYS: SXT

777 East Wisconsin Avenue
Milwaukee, WI 53202-5304
Phone: 414 271-6755
Fax: 414 347-4795
Web: www.sensient.com

CEO: Paul Manning
CFO: Stephen J Rolfs
HR: Amy Jones
FYE: December 31
Type: Public

Sensient Technologies makes flavors aromas and colors that are added to food beverages pharmaceuticals cosmetics and household products. It also manufactures inks for inkjet printers and specialty chemicals such as industrial dyes for the manufacture of writing instruments tinted motor-vehicle windshields and household cleaners. Flavors and food and beverage colors together account for about half Sensient's sales. The company which has facilities worldwide generates most of its revenue in North America. Its customers include global manufacturers representing many of the world's leading brands.

	Annual Growth	12/14	12/15	12/16	12/17	12/18
Sales ($ mil.)	(1.1%)	1,447.8	1,376.0	1,383.2	1,362.3	1,386.8
Net income ($ mil.)	20.9%	73.6	106.8	126.3	89.6	157.4
Market value ($ mil.)	(1.9%)	2,547.8	2,652.5	3,317.9	3,088.7	2,358.2
Employees	0.4%	4,053	4,032	4,083	4,023	4,113

SENTARA HEALTHCARE

6015 POPLAR HALL DR
NORFOLK, VA 235023819
Phone: 800-736-8272
Fax: –
Web: www.sentara.com

CEO: Howard P. Kern
CFO: Robert A. (Rob) Broerman
HR: Michael Taylor
FYE: December 31
Type: Private

Sentara Healthcare is not-for-profit operator of more than 300 health facilities in Virginia and North Carolina. The system includes a dozen acute care hospitals housing a total of more than 2000 beds including Sentara Norfolk Sentara RMH and Sentara Virginia Beach. Several of its hospitals contain specialist facilities such as the Sentara Heart Hospital the Hospital for Extended Recovery and two orthopedic hospitals. In addition the company operates medical practices urgent care clinics imaging centers rehab facilities nursing homes hospice and home health agencies and ambulance providers. Its Optima Health unit provides HMO PPO and other health insurance products to about 450000 Virginians.

	Annual Growth	12/13	12/14	12/15	12/16	12/17
Sales ($ mil.)	4.1%	–	4,694.4	4,833.9	5,083.4	5,297.9
Net income ($ mil.)	17.3%	–	359.9	139.3	329.5	580.3
Market value ($ mil.)	–	–	–	–	–	–
Employees	–	–	–	–	–	28,000

SENTARA RMH MEDICAL CENTER

2010 HEALTH CAMPUS DR
ROCKINGHAM, VA 228018679
Phone: 540-433-4100
Fax: –
Web: www.sentaracareers.com

CEO: –
CFO: –
HR: –
FYE: December 31
Type: Private

Sentara RMH Medical Center (RMH) formerly known as Rockingham Memorial Hospital serves residents in Virginia's Shenandoah Valley offering some 240 beds. In addition to emergency services and general surgeries and care procedures RMH offers specialized services including cardiovascular care cancer treatment sleep disorder diagnosis behavioral health care medical imaging orthopedic procedures obstetrics and rehabilitation as well as home health hospice and wellness services. Founded in 1912 RMH is part of the Sentara Healthcare system.

	Annual Growth	12/07	12/08	12/13	12/15	12/17
Sales ($ mil.)	5.6%	–	264.8	374.5	409.0	431.4
Net income ($ mil.)	16.4%	–	10.1	31.3	46.5	39.8
Market value ($ mil.)	–	–	–	–	–	–
Employees	–	–	–	–	–	1,892

SENTARA WILLIAMSBURG REGIONAL MEDICAL CENTER

100 SENTARA CIR
WILLIAMSBURG, VA 231885713
Phone: 757-984-6000
Fax: –

CEO: –
CFO: –
HR: –
FYE: December 31
Type: Private

History buffs flock to Colonial Williamsbug but if they get sick or injured they'd rather take a tour of Sentara Williamsburg Regional Medical Center. Part of Sentara Healthcare the center includes a 145-bed hospital that provides medical surgical and home-care services to the residents of (and visitors to) eastern Virginia. Specialized services include cardiac care pediatrics emergency medicine orthopedics pulmonary diagnostics and community health education. Additional facilities include centers for outpatient surgery and rehabilitation senior behaviorial health sleep wellness and cancer treatment. The center was founded as a 60-bed hospital in 1961.

	Annual Growth	12/13	12/14	12/15	12/16	12/17
Sales ($ mil.)	1170.6%	–	0.1	142.8	157.7	162.9
Net income ($ mil.)	601.3%	–	0.0	3.3	10.2	9.4
Market value ($ mil.)	–	–	–	–	–	–
Employees	–	–	–	–	–	1,150

SENTRY TECHNOLOGY CORPORATION OTC: SKVY

1881 Lakeland Ave. CEO: Peter L Murdoch
Ronkonkoma NY 11779 CFO: Joan E Miller
Phone: 800-645-4224 HR: –
Fax: 631-739-2117 FYE: December 31
Web: www.sentrytechnology.com Type: Public

Always on guard against pilferage Sentry Technology's surveillance products keep watch over stores and distribution centers. The company manufactures and installs electronic article surveillance (EAS) radio frequency (RF) and closed-circuit television (CCTV) systems. Its traveling SentryVision SmartTrack CCTV system is designed to pan tilt and zoom in order to provide unobstructed views. Clients include retailers wanting to deter theft and institutions wanting to protect assets and people. In addition Sentry Technology's electro-magnetic (EM) and RF identification (RFID) based Library Management systems are used by libraries to secure inventory and improve operating efficiency.

SEQUA CORPORATION

200 Park Ave. CEO: Armand F Lauzon Jr
New York NY 10166 CFO: Donna Costello
Phone: 212-986-5500 HR: –
Fax: 212-370-1969 FYE: December 31
Web: www.sequa.com Type: Private

Sequa serves the aerospace and metal coatings sectors through its two primary operating segments. Chromalloy Gas Turbine its largest unit makes and repairs jet engine parts such as major rotating parts cases frames and combustors for airlines industrial customers and other aftermarket customers. A North American industry leader Precoat Metals coats coiled steel for construction residential and industrial projects. In late 2012 its Sequa Automotive Group — which made airbag inflators for many OEMs and featured CASCO Products as a tier one automotive supplier — was sold to investment firm The Jordan Company. Sequa is owned by global private investment powerhouse The Carlyle Group.

SEQUACHEE VALLEY ELECTRIC CO-OPERATIVE INC

512 S CEDAR AVE CEO: –
SOUTH PITTSBURG, TN 373801310 CFO: Floyd Hatfield
Phone: 423-837-8605 HR: –
Fax: – FYE: June 30
Web: www.svalleyec.com Type: Private

Sequachee Valley Electric Cooperative squeezes the most efficiency out of the power distribution cooperative it manages. One of 23 rural electric cooperatives in Tennessee Sequachee Valley Electric Cooperative distributes power to more than 33000 residential commercial and industrial members in part or all of Bledsoe Coffee Grundy Hamilton Marion Rhea Sequatchie and Van Buren counties. It buys wholesale power from the Tennessee Valley Authority. Sequachee Valley Electric is governed by an 11-person board of directors directly elected by its membership.

	Annual Growth	06/10	06/11	06/12	06/13	06/16
Sales ($ mil.)	0.6%	–	81.7	78.6	81.5	84.2
Net income ($ mil.)	(1.0%)	–	2.3	3.0	2.8	2.2
Market value ($ mil.)	–	–	–	–	–	–
Employees	–	–	–	–	–	74

SEQUENOM INC NMS: SQNM

3595 John Hopkins Court CEO: Dirk Van Den Boom
San Diego, CA 92121 CFO: Carolyn D Beaver
Phone: 858 202-9000 HR: –
Fax: – FYE: December 31
Web: www.sequenom.com Type: Public

Sequenom develops and manufactures tests for the molecular diagnostics market. Its laboratory developed tests are primarily focused on prenatal and ophthalmological diseases and conditions. Tests include MaterniT21 Plus (screen for fetal chromosomal abnormalities) HerediT CF (screen for cystic fibrosis genetic mutations) and SensiGene RHD (screen for fetal Rhesus D factor) as well as RetnaGene AMD (predictive test for age-related macular degeneration). The company formerly offered technology and tools (principally based on its MassARRAY sequencing system) used by researchers but sold that business in 2014. Sequenom generates about a quarter of sales outside the US.

	Annual Growth	12/10	12/11	12/12	12/13	12/14
Sales ($ mil.)	33.7%	47.5	55.9	89.7	162.4	151.6
Net income ($ mil.)	–	(120.8)	(74.2)	(117.0)	(107.4)	1.0
Market value ($ mil.)	(17.6%)	943.0	522.6	553.1	274.8	434.5
Employees	17.3%	237	382	594	570	448

SERCO INC.

1818 Library St. Ste. 1000 CEO: David J Dacquino
Reston VA 20190 CFO: Gary A Shankman
Phone: 703-939-6000 HR: –
Fax: 866-987-3726 FYE: December 31
Web: www.serco-na.com Type: Subsidiary

Serco Inc. serves the US government by land sea and air. The US arm of UK outsourcer Serco Group plc is one of the top private contractors to the US military the federal government state agencies and corporations. Primarily an information technology (IT) services provider Serco Inc. operates in four divisions: national security and intelligence IT and professional services staffing and engineering and logistics. It has more than 200 contracts to provide program management and administrative support to the military help with border and port security and assist the Navy with hazardous waste removal. The company also manages about 65 air traffic control towers for the FAA in the US and its territories.

SERENA SOFTWARE INC.

1850 Gateway Dr. 4th Fl. CEO: Greg Hughes
San Mateo CA 94404 CFO: Robert Pender Jr
Phone: 650-481-3400 HR: Alison Edge
Fax: 650-481-3700 FYE: January 31
Web: www.serena.com Type: Private

SERENA Software isn't afraid of capitalizing on change. The company's change management software controls potentially disruptive changes during software installation migration and upgrades across multiple platforms including mainframe client/server and Web-based environments. Its applications are designed to help information technology staff manage upgrades improve productivity and reduce development costs. Customers have included American Express General Electric and IBM. The company which does much of its business in North America operates from 29 offices in 14 countries. SERENA is controlled by investment firm Silver Lake Partners which acquired the company in 2006.

SERRA AUTOMOTIVE INC.

3118 E. Hill Rd.
Grand Blanc MI 48439
Phone: 810-694-1720
Fax: 810-694-6405
Web: www.serrausa.com

CEO: –
CFO: Matthew S Daugherty
HR: –
FYE: June 30
Type: Private

Whatever will be will be and Serra Automotive will be too. The company owns more than 20 auto dealerships in California Colorado Michigan New Jersey Ohio and Tennessee where it sells BMW Buick Cadillac Honda Volkswagen Ford and other vehicle makes. All Serra Automotive locations offer parts and service and some locations including Team Chevrolet in Colorado Springs also operate body shops. Chairman president and CEO Joseph Serra owns the company. Serra's father Albert established Serra Automotive in 1973.

SERTA INC.

2600 Forbs Ave.
Hoffman Estates IL 60192
Phone: 847-645-0200
Fax: 561-640-5580
Web: www.embroidme.com

CEO: Gary T Fazio
CFO: –
HR: Jennifer Cristino
FYE: December 31
Type: Private

The #1 mattress maker in the US Serta asserts that it's also one of the world's top mattress producers (behind rival Sealy). The company is a top mattress supplier to hotels and motels such as Hilton and Waldorf. Its Perfect Sleeper line is the nation's best-selling premium mattress; its top-of-the-line collection sells under the Perfect Day name. Founded in 1931 Serta boasts nearly 30 manufacturing facilities in North America. Serta has been majority owned by Simmons Bedding owner Advent International since late 2012 when AOT Bedding Super Holdings a holding company formed in 2010 by Ares Management and the Ontario Teachers' Pension Plan reduced its ownership to a significant equity stake.

SERVCO PACIFIC INC.

2850 PUKOLOA ST STE 300
HONOLULU, HI 968194475
Phone: 808-564-1300
Fax: –
Web: www.servco.com

CEO: –
CFO: Jeffery A Bell
HR: Peter Hirano
FYE: December 31
Type: Private

Servco Pacific's business flows through an ocean's worth of enterprises. The company sells passenger vehicles (including Toyota Subaru Suzuki and Chevrolet models) and commercial trucks through dealerships in Hawaii and Australia. In addition Servco Home & Appliance wholesales kitchen and bath products to building professionals throughout the South Pacific; Servco Raynor Overhead Doors installs residential and commercial garage doors; Servco Insurance Services offers insurance coverage for businesses and individuals; and Servco School & Office Furniture outfits educational institutions and government agencies with desks seating and other furnishings. Servco Pacific was founded by Peter Fukunaga in 1919.

	Annual Growth	12/10	12/11	12/12	12/16	12/17
Sales ($ mil.)	24.9%	–	429.2	923.0	1,435.5	1,629.1
Net income ($ mil.)	30.7%	–	5.2	15.9	29.6	26.1
Market value ($ mil.)	–	–	–	–	–	–
Employees	–	–	–	–	–	925

SERVICE CORP. INTERNATIONAL NYS: SCI

1929 Allen Parkway
Houston, TX 77019
Phone: 713 522-5141
Fax: –
Web: www.sci-corp.com

CEO: Thomas L. Ryan
CFO: Eric D. Tanzberger
HR: Philip Sprick
FYE: December 31
Type: Public

Service Corporation International (SCI) is the largest funeral and cemetery services company in North America operating about 1500 funeral homes and some 480 cemeteries in 45 US states eight Canadian provinces and Puerto Rico. The company's primary services include embalming burial and cremation. As part of its business SCI also sells traditional funeral necessities including prearranged funeral services caskets burial vaults cremation receptacles flowers and burial garments. SCI operates under the Dignity Memorial and other brands. The US is the company's largest market.

	Annual Growth	12/14	12/15	12/16	12/17	12/18
Sales ($ mil.)	1.6%	2,994.0	2,986.4	3,031.1	3,095.0	3,190.2
Net income ($ mil.)	26.9%	172.5	233.8	177.0	546.7	447.2
Market value ($ mil.)	15.4%	4,119.4	4,721.9	5,153.8	6,772.5	7,306.0
Employees	0.4%	23,662	23,785	23,463	23,428	24,082

SERVICE PROPERTIES TRUST NMS: SVC

Two Newton Place, 255 Washington Street, Suite 300
Newton, MA 02458-1634
Phone: 617 964-8389
Fax: –
Web: www.hptreit.com

CEO: John G Murray
CFO: Mark L. Kleifges
HR: –
FYE: December 31
Type: Public

Real estate investment trust (REIT) Hospitality Properties Trust (HPT) owns some 325 hotels in about 45 US states Canada and Puerto Rico and around 200 full-service truck stops operating as TravelCenters of America and Petro Stopping Centers. HPT's properties are managed by or leased to companies including Marriott International Wyndham Hotels & Resorts Raddison Hospitality and Hyatt Hotels. Its properties target different markets from upscale to business and family travelers on long-term trips. HPT maintains a geographically diverse portfolio with hotels or travel centers (usually both) in nearly 45 states. In 2019 the company entered the retail property leasing business through an agreement to acquire about 775 such locations for $2.4 billion.

	Annual Growth	12/14	12/15	12/16	12/17	12/18
Sales ($ mil.)	7.2%	1,736.3	1,921.9	2,047.2	2,171.9	2,294.5
Net income ($ mil.)	(1.5%)	197.2	166.4	223.1	215.1	185.7
Market value ($ mil.)	(6.3%)	5,097.7	4,300.2	5,219.4	4,908.6	3,926.9
Employees	–	–	–	–	–	–

SERVICENOW INC NYS: NOW

2225 Lawson Lane
Santa Clara, CA 95054
Phone: 408 501-8550
Fax: –
Web: www.servicenow.com

CEO: John J. Donahoe
CFO: Michael P. Scarpelli
HR: Shelly Begun
FYE: December 31
Type: Public

ServiceNow brings self-help to the cloud. The company offers cloud-based software and services that help corporate IT organizations automate and integrate various enterprise technologies. Its main customers have been IT departments in financial services IT services and health care among other industries. Customers also use its platform to create custom automation applications for themselves. ServiceNow's software works across operating systems servers networking equipment PCs and mobile devices to facilitate workflow automation data consolidation and administration of business processes. Beyond the IT department ServiceNow has added services for human resources customer service and security.

	Annual Growth	12/14	12/15	12/16	12/17	12/18
Sales ($ mil.)	39.8%	682.6	1,005.5	1,390.5	1,933.0	2,608.8
Net income ($ mil.)	–	(179.4)	(198.4)	(451.8)	(149.1)	(26.7)
Market value ($ mil.)	27.3%	12,224.9	15,596.0	13,394.2	23,493.1	32,080.2
Employees	30.3%	2,826	3,686	4,801	6,222	8,154

SERVICESOURCE INTERNATIONAL, INC. — NMS: SREV

707 17th Street, 25th Floor
Denver, CO 80202
Phone: 720 889-8500
Fax: –
Web: www.servicesource.com

CEO: Christopher Carrington
CFO: Robert Pinkerton
HR: –
FYE: December 31
Type: Public

ServiceSource is hoping to bring a sense of renewal to its clients. Part sales professional staffer part software developer ServiceSource offers sales staff outsourcing and proprietary customer management software geared toward increasing sales contract renewals. Its software which includes data management platforms and cloud applications aggregates customer data from its clients' different enterprise systems (e.g. CRM billing order management) to facilitate customer management and analysis from a single online location. Serving clients primarily in the technology sector ServiceSource often markets its sales professionals in tandem with its software offerings.

	Annual Growth	12/14	12/15	12/16	12/17	12/18
Sales ($ mil.)	(3.3%)	272.2	252.2	252.9	239.1	238.3
Net income ($ mil.)	–	(95.2)	(40.4)	(32.1)	(29.8)	(24.9)
Market value ($ mil.)	(30.7%)	434.2	427.7	527.0	286.7	100.2
Employees	6.7%	3,017	2,745	3,145	3,269	3,914

SERVIGISTICS INC.

2300 Windy Ridge Pkwy. 450 North Tower
Atlanta GA 30339
Phone: 770-565-2340
Fax: 770-565-8767
Web: www.servigistics.com

CEO: Eric Hinkle
CFO: Peter Vlerick
HR: –
FYE: December 31
Type: Private

Servigistics makes sure companies aren't waiting on wading in or wrongly pricing parts. The company provides service lifecycle management (SLM) software and services including Web-based software that helps companies optimize parts inventory levels for their customer service operations price parts and manage field organizations (including workforce scheduling and routing). Its offerings help companies manage inventory levels and insure parts availability with the aim of improving revenue profitability and customer loyalty. Customers have included American Airlines BMW Cisco Cummins Kodak Philips Southern Company and Toshiba. In 2012 Servigistics was acquired by Parametric Technology.

SERVISFIRST BANCSHARES INC — NMS: SFBS

2500 Woodcrest Place
Birmingham, AL 35209
Phone: 205 949-0302
Fax: –
Web: www.servisfirstbank.com

CEO: Thomas A. (Tom) Broughton
CFO: William M. Foshee
HR: –
FYE: December 31
Type: Public

ServisFirst Bancshares is a bank holding company for ServisFirst Bank a regional commercial bank with about a dozen branches located in Alabama and the Florida panhandle. The bank also has a loan office in Nashville. ServisFirst Bank targets privately-held businesses with $2 million to $250 million in annual sales as well as professionals and affluent customers. The bank focuses on traditional commercial banking services including loan origination deposits and electronic banking services such as online and mobile banking. Founded in 2005 by its chairman and CEO Thomas Broughton III the bank went public in 2014 with an offering valued at nearly $57 million.

	Annual Growth	12/14	12/15	12/16	12/17	12/18
Assets ($ mil.)	18.2%	4,098.7	5,095.5	6,370.4	7,082.4	8,007.4
Net income ($ mil.)	27.2%	52.4	63.5	81.5	93.1	136.9
Market value ($ mil.)	(0.8%)	1,758.7	2,536.9	1,998.4	2,215.1	1,701.1
Employees	12.2%	298	371	420	434	473

SERVOTRONICS, INC. — ASE: SVT

1110 Maple Street
Elma, NY 14059
Phone: 716 655-5990
Fax: –
Web: www.servotronics.com

CEO: Nicholas D. Trbovich
CFO: Lisa Bencel
HR: –
FYE: December 31
Type: Public

Servotronics knows how to get things moving and cut to the chase. The company makes devices that convert electricity into mechanical movement and cutlery products. Its advanced technology products include servo-control components (torque motors electromagnetic actuators and hydraulic and pneumatic valves) which it sells mainly to clients in the aerospace industry. These include Honeywell United Technologies and the US government. Servotronics' cutlery unit makes a broad range of products from machetes and bayonets to kitchen knives and putty knives. Customers include retailers restaurants and agencies of the US government.

	Annual Growth	12/14	12/15	12/16	12/17	12/18
Sales ($ mil.)	10.9%	31.6	36.7	38.6	41.4	47.9
Net income ($ mil.)	–	(3.1)	4.6	1.8	1.3	3.5
Market value ($ mil.)	11.3%	15.5	20.0	24.1	26.6	23.8
Employees	5.8%	271	304	320	315	340

SERVPRO INTELLECTUAL PROPERTY, INC.

801 INDUSTRIAL BLVD
GALLATIN, TN 370663742
Phone: 615-451-0200
Fax: –
Web: www.servpro.com

CEO: Sue Isaacson Steen
CFO: Rick Forster
HR: –
FYE: December 31
Type: Private

If you're dealing with fire or water damage Servpro hopes you'll let the pros come to your rescue. Servpro Industries provides emergency mitigation services for water- fire- and smoke-damaged properties as well as mold and mildew situations. It operates through more than 1500 franchised locations throughout the US. Mitigation services include cleaning of carpets upholstery air ducts drapes ceilings and walls. The company also offers instruction and training on water- and fire-damage restoration. Originally established as a painting business the family-owned Servpro Industries was founded in 1967 by Ted and Doris Isaacson.

	Annual Growth	12/00	12/01	12/02	12/03	12/09
Sales ($ mil.)	–	–	–	0.0	58.5	122.5
Net income ($ mil.)	–	–	–	0.0	8.7	24.8
Market value ($ mil.)	–	–	–	–	–	–
Employees	–	–	–	–	–	111

SESEN BIO INC — NMS: SESN

245 First Street, Suite 1800
Cambridge, MA 02142
Phone: 617 444-8550
Fax: –
Web: www.elevenbio.com

CEO: Thomas Cannell
CFO: Monica Forbes
HR: –
FYE: December 31
Type: Public

After its EBI-005 treatment for dry eye disease failed in late-stage clinical trials Eleven Biotherapeutics reinvented itself as a cancer fighter. The biologics firm acquired Canadian biotech Viventia Bio in September 2016 gaining that firm's roster of development programs targeting bladder cancer (Vicinium) and head and neck cancer (Proxinium). The new company is developing Targeted Protein Therapeutics (TPTs) some in combination with immunotherapy treatments. Eleven Bio went public in 2014 on the promise of its eye disease treatments but once its most advanced candidate failed in trials it cut 70% of its workforce. It began seeking new life in other fields and found hope with the purchase of Viventia Bio. Distancing itself from its troubled past the company is now changing its name to Sesen Bio.

	Annual Growth	12/13	12/14	12/15	12/16	12/17
Sales ($ mil.)	(24.9%)	1.3	2.2	1.0	30.0	0.4
Net income ($ mil.)	–	(18.0)	(34.2)	(33.5)	1.9	(29.0)
Market value ($ mil.)	(59.2%)	–	412.3	104.5	66.3	28.1
Employees	3.2%	15	21	20	35	17

SETON HALL UNIVERSITY

400 S ORANGE AVE
SOUTH ORANGE, NJ 070792697
Phone: 973-761-9000
Fax: –
Web: www.shu.edu

CEO: –
CFO: Stephen A. Graham
HR: Ileana Farris
FYE: June 30
Type: Private

Seton Hall University is a Catholic institution with an enrollment of almost 10000 students (5500 undergraduates and 4300 graduates) who hail from 70 countries. The university offers more than 90 undergraduate and graduate degree programs as well as more than a dozen doctoral programs at eight colleges and schools including the Whitehead School of Diplomacy and International Relations Stillman School of Business and Immaculate Conception Seminary School of Theology. Seton Hall also offers degree and certificate programs online. Seton Hall is the US' oldest diocesan university and is under purview of the Archdiocese of Newark.

	Annual Growth	06/14	06/15	06/16	06/17	06/18
Sales ($ mil.)	2.5%	–	272.3	281.4	287.2	293.2
Net income ($ mil.)	31.3%	–	4.0	(12.1)	32.1	9.0
Market value ($ mil.)	–	–	–	–	–	–
Employees	–	–	–	–	–	2,700

SETON HEALTHCARE FAMILY

1201 W 38TH ST
AUSTIN, TX 787051056
Phone: 512-324-1000
Fax: –
Web: www.seton.net

CEO: –
CFO: Scott Herndon
HR: –
FYE: June 30
Type: Private

For those who work hard to Keep Austin Weird there's Seton Healthcare Network. The not-for-profit health care provider operates nearly a dozen urban and rural acute-care hospitals in Central Texas. It also offers psychiatric and children's hospitals and a network of community clinics. With a capacity of some 1800 beds Seton's facilities (known as the Seton Family of Hospitals) offer a range of services including trauma heart transplant neurological and neonatal intensive care as well as primary and specialty care services. Seton in Austin was formed in 1902 by the Daughters of Charity of St. Vincent de Paul. Today it is part of Ascension Health.

	Annual Growth	06/03	06/04	06/05	06/06	06/08
Sales ($ mil.)	9.7%	–	–	–	1,052.0	1,265.6
Net income ($ mil.)	–	–	–	–	0.0	169.7
Market value ($ mil.)	–	–	–	–	–	–
Employees	–	–	–	–	–	5,741

SETON HEALTHCARE NETWORK

1201 W. 38th St.
Austin TX 78705
Phone: 512-324-1100
Fax: 512-324-1924
Web: www.seton.net

CEO: –
CFO: Scott Herndon
HR: –
FYE: June 30
Type: Subsidiary

For those who overdo it at the Austin City Limits music festival it's a good thing Seton Healthcare Network operates within Austin's city limits. The not-for-profit health care provider operates 11 urban and rural acute-care hospitals in Central Texas as well as psychiatric and children's hospitals and a network of community clinics. With a capacity of some 1700 beds Seton's facilities (known as the Seton Family of Hospitals) offer a range of services including trauma heart transplant neurological and neonatal intensive care as well as primary and specialty care services. Seton in Austin was formed in 1902 by the Daughters of Charity of St. Vincent de Paul. Today it is part of Ascension Health.

SEVCON INC

155 Northboro Road
Southborough, MA 01772
Phone: 508 281-5510
Fax: –
Web: www.techopssevcon.com

NAS: SEV
CEO: Matthew Boyle
CFO: Paul N Farquhar
HR: –
FYE: September 30
Type: Public

You might say that Tech/Ops Sevcon prevents electric vehicles from becoming speed demons. The company makes Sevcon solid-state controllers which regulate motor speed and acceleration in battery-powered vehicles such as forklifts and coal mining equipment. Through a UK-based subsidiary Tech/Ops Sevcon also makes metalized film capacitors for power electronics signaling and audio equipment applications. Targeting manufacturers of aerial lifts forklift trucks and underground mining vehicles Tech/Ops sells directly and through a network of independent dealers in Asia Europe and the US. About 60% of sales are to customers outside the US.

	Annual Growth	09/12	09/13	09/14	09/15	09/16
Sales ($ mil.)	8.8%	35.5	32.2	37.9	41.1	49.8
Net income ($ mil.)	–	1.2	(1.1)	0.9	1.6	(5.8)
Market value ($ mil.)	16.7%	25.4	25.9	43.5	50.3	47.1
Employees	21.9%	125	119	136	152	276

SEVEN SEAS TECHNOLOGIES INC.

720 SPIRIT 40 PARK DR
CHESTERFIELD, MO 630051122
Phone: 636-778-0705
Fax: –
Web: www.s2tech.com

CEO: –
CFO: –
HR: –
FYE: December 31
Type: Private

Seven Seas Technologies which does business as S2 Tech provides IT services such as custom software development database administration and networking. Founded in 1997 the company specializes in managing Medicaid systems and HIPAA compliance with clients that have included CACI MasterCard and Sallie Mae. S2 Tech has locations in the US and India.

	Annual Growth	12/09	12/10	12/11	12/12	12/13
Sales ($ mil.)	27.5%	–	9.5	11.3	14.2	19.7
Net income ($ mil.)	5.0%	–	–	0.4	0.4	0.4
Market value ($ mil.)	–	–	–	–	–	–
Employees	–	–	–	–	–	120

SEVENTY SEVEN ENERGY LLC

777 NW 63RD ST
OKLAHOMA CITY, OK 731167601
Phone: 405-608-7777
Fax: –
Web: www.patenergy.com

CEO: William A. (Andy) Hendricks
CFO: John E. Vollmer
HR: –
FYE: December 31
Type: Private

Seventy Seven Energy (formerly Chesapeake Oilfield Services) is a company that was spun off from Chesapeake Energy one of the top onshore energy companies in the US. Chesapeake Energy reorganized six of its oilfield services subsidiaries into then Chesapeake Oilfield Services to create a new publicly traded entity that offers drilling hydraulic fracturing and trucking services as well as renting tools and manufacturing natural gas compressor equipment. It operates in onshore plays in the US. The company filed for Chapter 11 bankruptcy protection in 2016. In 2017 the company was bought by Patterson-UTI in a $1.76 billion stock deal including debt.

	Annual Growth	12/11	12/12	12/13	12/14	12/15
Sales ($ mil.)	(45.6%)	–	–	–	2,080.9	1,131.2
Net income ($ mil.)	–	–	–	–	(8.0)	(221.4)
Market value ($ mil.)	–	–	–	–	–	–
Employees	–	–	–	–	–	1,700

SEVERN BANCORP INC (ANNAPOLIS MD) — NAS: SVBI

200 Westgate Circle, Suite 200
Annapolis, MD 21401
Phone: 410 260-2000
Fax: –
Web: www.severnbank.com

CEO: Alan J Hyatt
CFO: Marc Winkler
HR: –
FYE: December 31
Type: Public

Severn Bancorp is the holding company for Severn Savings Bank which operates about five bank branches in Anne Arundel County Maryland. The thrift provides traditional retail products including checking and savings accounts CDs and IRAs. Severn uses funds from deposits to originate loans and mortgages primarily residential and commercial mortgages construction loans and business loans. The holding company also owns SBI Mortgage which originates riskier loans than Severn Savings Bank does; it also invests in real estate on its own behalf. Severn is working towards recovery after suffering real estate- and mortgage-related losses in the economic recession.

	Annual Growth	12/14	12/15	12/16	12/17	12/18
Assets ($ mil.)	5.8%	776.3	762.1	787.5	804.8	974.2
Net income ($ mil.)	31.0%	2.9	4.5	15.5	2.8	8.6
Market value ($ mil.)	15.2%	57.9	73.4	100.8	92.6	101.8
Employees	2.3%	150	152	142	141	164

SEVION THERAPEUTICS INC — NBB: SVON

10210 Campus Point Drive, Suite 150
San Diego, CA 92121
Phone: 858 909-0749
Fax: –
Web: www.senesco.com

CEO: Robert E Ward
CFO: Gregory Weaver
HR: –
FYE: June 30
Type: Public

Senesco Technologies wants to find the fountain of youth for melons tomatoes bananas and lettuce. The company does research surrounding new plant gene technologies for use in combating senescence or cell aging in fruits vegetables and flowers. Its research activities are geared toward developing plants whose crops will have longer shelf-lives and higher yields. Senesco Technologies' research work is performed by third parties primarily researchers at the University of Waterloo in Ontario Canada. The company is also investigating some of its technologies for use as treatments for inflammatory diseases and/or to delay or inhibit apoptosis i.e. cell aging in humans (for possible use in cancer treatment).

	Annual Growth	06/12	06/13	06/14	06/15	06/16
Sales ($ mil.)	(21.7%)	0.2	–	0.1	0.1	0.1
Net income ($ mil.)	–	(5.1)	(6.1)	(9.2)	(18.1)	(8.3)
Market value ($ mil.)	(48.3%)	61.5	0.6	57.4	19.7	4.4
Employees	6.5%	7	9	21	14	9

SEYFARTH SHAW LLP

233 S WACKER DR STE 8000
CHICAGO, IL 606066448
Phone: 312-460-5000
Fax: –
Web: www.seyfarth.com

CEO: Robert Saccone
CFO: Kate Kohn
HR: –
FYE: December 31
Type: Private

Every day is labor day at law firm Seyfarth Shaw which specializes in handling employment-related matters for its clients. The firm divides its numerous practices into four main areas: business services employee benefits labor and employment and litigation. Overall Seyfarth Shaw has about 800 attorneys in 14 offices — ten spread throughout the US plus four international outposts. Seyfarth Shaw draws clients from industries such as financial services life sciences and telecommunications. Henry Seyfarth Lee Shaw and Owen Fairweather founded the firm in 1945.

	Annual Growth	12/04	12/05	12/06	12/07	12/08
Sales ($ mil.)	11.7%	–	332.2	385.6	431.8	463.0
Net income ($ mil.)	5.8%	–	124.1	136.3	141.9	147.0
Market value ($ mil.)	–	–	–	–	–	–
Employees	–	–	–	–	–	1,608

SFN GROUP INC.

2050 Spectrum Blvd.
Fort Lauderdale FL 33309
Phone: 954-308-7600
Fax: 954-308-7666
Web: www.sfngroup.com

CEO: Roy G Krause
CFO: Mark W Smith
HR: Denise Zilla
FYE: December 31
Type: Subsidiary

This group seeks to circumvent your personnel problems. SFN Group (formerly Spherion) provides traditional temporary staffing along with services such as professional and executive recruitment and employee consulting and assessment. Through several subsidiaries and specialized staffing units SFN Group offers staffing and technology services in such areas as project management quality assurance and data center and network operations. It operates through a network of some 550 locations in the US and Canada serving more than 8000 clients ranging from small businesses to FORTUNE 500 companies. In September 2011 SFN Group was acquired by staffing powerhouse rival Randstad.

SFX ENTERTAINMENT, INC. — NBB: SFXE Q

902 Broadway, Fifteenth Floor
New York, NY 10010
Phone: 646 561-6400
Fax: –
Web: www.sfxii.com

CEO: –
CFO: Richard Rosenstein
HR: –
FYE: December 31
Type: Public

SFX Entertainment makes flashing strobe lights hot musical acts big crowds and a driving dance beat its business. The company founded in 2011 produces music festivals in North America and Europe that attract fans of “electronic music culture” or EDM (electronic dance music). As much as a fifth of the company's sales come from digital music sales between and around its musical events which earn revenue through sales of tickets concessions sponsorships promotion fees and advertising. In 2013 SFX went public in a $260 million IPO. In 2016 the company filed for bankruptcy.

	Annual Growth	12/10	12/11	12/12	12/13	12/14
Sales ($ mil.)	–	0.0	–	24.8	170.5	354.4
Net income ($ mil.)	–	0.0	(0.1)	(16.2)	(111.9)	(131.0)
Market value ($ mil.)	–	–	0.0	–	1,111.2	419.5
Employees	87.4%	–	–	178	450	625

SGT, LLC

7701 GREENBELT RD STE 400
GREENBELT, MD 207706521
Phone: 301-614-8600
Fax: –
Web: www.sgt-inc.com

CEO: Kam Ghaffarian
CFO: Joe Morway
HR: –
FYE: September 30
Type: Private

Like its acronym name suggests SGT (aka Stinger Ghaffarian Technologies) is used to taking military orders; in this case very specific technical ones. An engineering services firm SGT provides aerospace engineering project management IT systems development and related services to NASA the US Navy the US Air Force and other primarily military-related government entities through contracts. The company also offers science-related services such as earth climate and planetary modeling and analysis. SGT's facilities are located near airfields and other military facilities.

	Annual Growth	09/07	09/08	09/12	09/13	09/15
Sales ($ mil.)	10.0%	–	293.0	374.7	416.5	570.8
Net income ($ mil.)	16.3%	–	8.3	9.0	15.5	23.9
Market value ($ mil.)	–	–	–	–	–	–
Employees	–	–	–	–	–	2,300

SHAMROCK FOODS COMPANY

3900 E CAMELBACK RD # 300
PHOENIX, AZ 850182615
Phone: 602-477-2500
Fax: –
Web: www.shamrockfoodservice.com

CEO: –
CFO: F. Phillips (Phil) Giltner
HR: Vince Daniels
FYE: September 30
Type: Private

Shamrock Foods Company is one of the nation's leading foodservice distributors with a strong presence in the western US. It primarily serves restaurants healthcare facilities and hospitality customers by providing everyday staples such as meats produce dry goods beverages and supplies as well as ethnic foods and artisanal gourmet and other specialty foods. Proprietary brands include Gold Canyon Markon Jensen Foods and Ridegline. Through Shamrock Farms the company is also one of the largest family-owned and -operated dairies in the country. Founded in 1922 as a mom-and-pop dairy Shamrock Foods Company is still owned and operated by the founding McClelland family.

	Annual Growth	09/13	09/14	09/16	09/17	09/18
Sales ($ mil.)	12.5%	–	2,433.8	–	3,447.1	3,900.6
Net income ($ mil.)	–	–	0.0	–	0.0	0.0
Market value ($ mil.)	–	–	–	–	–	–
Employees	–	–	–	–	–	4,000

SHANDS JACKSONVILLE MEDICAL CENTER, INC.

655 W 8TH ST
JACKSONVILLE, FL 322096511
Phone: 904-244-5576
Fax: –

CEO: David S Guzick
CFO: William J Ryan
HR: –
FYE: June 30
Type: Private

Close to the shifting sands of the northern Florida coast Shands Jacksonville Medical Center (doing business as UF Health Jacksonville) offers a range of services to the 19 counties it serves in Florida and southern Georgia. The 695-bed hospital includes a cardiovascular center Level III neonatal intensive care unit and a Level I trauma center. It also operates primary and specialty clinics in the Jacksonville area. The medical center is affiliated with the University of Florida and is the largest of seven hospitals in the Shands HealthCare family.

	Annual Growth	06/08	06/09	06/10	06/15	06/16
Sales ($ mil.)	1.6%	–	591.6	593.0	480.6	663.3
Net income ($ mil.)	18.8%	–	7.1	19.2	10.3	23.6
Market value ($ mil.)	–	–	–	–	–	–
Employees	–	–	–	–	–	3,000

SHANDS TEACHING HOSPITAL AND CLINICS, INC.

1600 SW ARCHER RD
GAINESVILLE, FL 326103003
Phone: 352-265-0111
Fax: –
Web: www.shands.ufl.edu

CEO: Ed Jimenez
CFO: William J. (Bill) Robinson
HR: –
FYE: June 30
Type: Private

While its full name is Shands Teaching Hospital and Clinics most people call it UF&Shands. The network affiliated with the University of Florida Health Science Center provides health care services to patients in north-central and northeast Florida. The company is made up of seven not-for-profit acute care community and specialty hospitals as well as more than 80 physician practices and outpatient rehabilitation centers. It also operates a home health care agency. The Shands network has some 1700 licensed beds and about 1000 affiliated University of Florida doctors. Specialty services include oncology pediatrics cardiovascular transplants and neurological care.

	Annual Growth	06/08	06/09	06/10	06/14	06/15
Sales ($ mil.)	(5.4%)	–	1,735.3	1,040.4	1,244.0	1,242.6
Net income ($ mil.)	–	–	(183.5)	(67.7)	66.1	81.9
Market value ($ mil.)	–	–	–	–	–	–
Employees	–	–	–	–	–	3,071

SHARI'S MANAGEMENT CORPORATION

9400 SW GEMINI DR
BEAVERTON, OR 970087105
Phone: 503-605-4299
Fax: –
Web: www.sharis.com

CEO: Samuel Borgese
CFO: –
HR: –
FYE: January 02
Type: Private

This Shari keeps the kitchen open all day and all night. Shari's Management Corporation owns and operates more than 100 Shari's family restaurants in six states (primarily in the Northwest) that serve breakfast lunch and dinner 24 hours a day. The chain of eateries offers standard American fare such as pancakes and eggs sandwiches and burgers and beef chicken and pasta dishes as well as a selection of appetizers and desserts through a menu of about 120 items. The company is owned by a group of private investors led by Circle Peak Management. Ron and Sharon (Shari) Berquist opened the first Shari's in Hermiston Oregon in 1978.

	Annual Growth	01/04	01/05	01/06	01/07	01/08
Sales ($ mil.)	320.4%	–	–	–	40.5	170.3
Net income ($ mil.)	(99.9%)	–	–	–	1,073.7	1.5
Market value ($ mil.)	–	–	–	–	–	–
Employees	–	–	–	–	–	4,000

SHARON REGIONAL HEALTH SYSTEM INC.

740 E STATE ST
SHARON, PA 16146-3328
Phone: 724-983-5864
Fax: –
Web: www.sharonregional.com

CEO: –
CFO: Jeffrey Chrobak
HR: –
FYE: June 30
Type: Private

Ready to show some mercy to the ill in Mercer County is Sharon Regional Health System (SRHS) serving residents throughout northwestern Pennsylvania and northeastern Ohio. The not-for-profit hospital has some 240 beds and operates a network of nearly 20 outpatient clinics. Specialty services include behavioral health care cancer treatment home health and hospice care women's health services rehabilitation and speech and occupational therapy. As one of the region's primary health care providers SRHS has had to work to keep up with patient demand by opening a new $2 million diagnostic and imaging clinic expanding existing facilities and adding new care programs such as its Cancer Genetics Program.

	Annual Growth	06/08	06/09	06/10	06/11	06/12
Sales ($ mil.)	(1.5%)	–	172.5	174.6	184.5	165.1
Net income ($ mil.)	–	–	(5.5)	(6.4)	8.4	0.3
Market value ($ mil.)	–	–	–	–	–	–
Employees	–	–	–	–	–	1,850

SHARP HEALTHCARE

8695 SPECTRUM CENTER BLVD
SAN DIEGO, CA 921231489
Phone: 858-499-4000
Fax: –

CEO: Michael W. (Mike) Murphy
CFO: Staci Dickerson
HR: Ky Lewis
FYE: September 30
Type: Private

Sharp HealthCare stands on the cutting edge of health care delivery in Southern California. The system of not-for-profit hospitals and health care facilities is the largest in the San Diego area. The network includes four acute-care hospitals (Sharp Chula Vista Sharp Coronado Sharp Grossmont and Sharp Memorial) as well as three specialty hospitals for women's care psychiatry and chemical dependence. It also operates two physician medical groups and a number of urgent care and outpatient facilities and clinics. With some 2100 beds and about 2600 physicians Sharp HealthCare offers cancer and cardiac care fertility and maternity services surgical procedures and hospice care.

	Annual Growth	09/08	09/09	09/13	09/14	09/15
Sales ($ mil.)	24.8%	–	897.6	1,158.6	1,234.4	3,396.5
Net income ($ mil.)	–	–	(0.6)	(11.4)	(12.1)	355.6
Market value ($ mil.)	–	–	–	–	–	–
Employees	–	–	–	–	–	14,000

SHARP MEMORIAL HOSPITAL

7901 FROST ST
SAN DIEGO, CA 921232701
Phone: 858-939-3636
Fax: –

CEO: Tim Smith
CFO: –
HR: –
FYE: September 30
Type: Private

The docs and the scalpels are sharp at Sharp Memorial Hospital. The flagship facility of Sharp HealthCare the not-for-profit hospital has roughly 675 beds and is a designated trauma center for San Diego County. Specialties include cardiac care women's health multi-organ transplantation and cancer treatment. It also provides skilled nursing home health and hospice services. Sharp Memorial Hospital first opened in 1955. Sharp HealthCare completed reconstruction efforts on the Sharp Memorial facility in 2009; the new hospital has improved inpatient surgery emergency trauma and intensive care facilities.

	Annual Growth	09/13	09/14	09/15	09/16	09/17
Sales ($ mil.)	3.6%	–	1,042.8	1,195.6	1,200.9	1,158.9
Net income ($ mil.)	1.3%	–	227.9	240.4	290.3	237.1
Market value ($ mil.)	–	–	–	–	–	–
Employees	–	–	–	–	–	3,500

SHARPE RESOURCES CORPORATION

OTC: SHGP

3258 Mob Neck Rd.
Heathsville VA 22473
Phone: 804-580-8107
Fax: 804-580-4132
Web: www.sharperesourcescorporation.com

CEO: –
CFO: –
HR: –
FYE: December 31
Type: Public

Sharpe Resources keeps a sharp eye out for natural resource opportunities in the US. Through subsidiary Standard Energy Company it focuses on developing coal bed methane (CBM) coal and shale projects in West Virginia. Coal bed methane is natural gas trapped in coal beds; the CBM is more easily drilled and utilized than other sources of natural gas. Sharpe leases and holds options on about 17000 acres in West Virginia that it hopes to tap for CBM and coal. It is also exploring the option of creating relatively clean coal energy from underground coal gasification which allows for the coal to be used in the generation of electricity without the coal having to be mined first.

SHARPS COMPLIANCE CORP.

NAS: SMED

9220 Kirby Drive, Suite 500
Houston, TX 77054
Phone: 713 432-0300
Fax: –
Web: www.sharpsinc.com

CEO: David P Tusa
CFO: Diana P Diaz
HR: –
FYE: June 30
Type: Public

Sharps Compliance is on the cutting edge of the medical waste disposal business — and wants to make sure people don't get hurt. The company offers services to health care providers to make the disposal of medical waste safer and more efficient. It also serves customers in the pharmaceutical agricultural hospitality industrial and retail industries. Products include medical sharps (needles and other sharp objects) disposal systems disposable IV poles waste and equipment return boxes linen recovery systems and biohazardous spill clean-up kits. Sharps Compliance also provides regulatory compliant waste tracking incineration and disposal verification services as well as consulting services.

	Annual Growth	06/15	06/16	06/17	06/18	06/19
Sales ($ mil.)	9.4%	30.9	33.4	38.2	40.1	44.3
Net income ($ mil.)	(34.5%)	1.2	0.0	(1.3)	(0.7)	0.2
Market value ($ mil.)	(15.4%)	112.2	70.8	68.3	59.5	57.4
Employees	21.6%	75	109	130	152	164

SHAWMUT WOODWORKING & SUPPLY, INC.

560 HARRISON AVE STE 200
BOSTON, MA 021182632
Phone: 617-622-7000
Fax: –
Web: www.shawmut.com

CEO: Les Hiscoe
CFO: Roger C. Tougas
HR: –
FYE: November 30
Type: Private

Shawmut Woodworking & Supply which does business as Shawmut Design and Construction provides beginning-to-end construction services from preconstruction planning to post-construction quality assurance checks. The $860 million national construction management firm has experience building retail hotel gaming spa sports restaurant education banking healthcare and life science facilities. It also handles corporate interiors and high-end residential construction and boasts expertise in cultural and historical preservation projects. Founded in 1982 by Jim Ansara the employee-owned company serves clients nationwide from offices in a handful of US states.

	Annual Growth	12/04	12/05*	11/09	11/11	11/14
Sales ($ mil.)	9.0%	–	440.7	618.3	662.8	957.6
Net income ($ mil.)	9.9%	–	3.1	(21.6)	3.7	7.2
Market value ($ mil.)	–	–	–	–	–	–
Employees	–	–	–	–	–	1,476

*Fiscal year change

SHAWNEE MISSION MEDICAL CENTER, INC.

9100 W 74TH ST
SHAWNEE MISSION, KS 662044004
Phone: 913-676-2000
Fax: –
Web: www.adventhealth.com

CEO: Ken Bacon
CFO: Jack Wagnar
HR: –
FYE: December 31
Type: Private

Shawnee Mission Medical Center (SMMC) cares for Kansas City residents primarily on the Kansas-side. The health care facility located in the city's southwest suburbs has some 500 inpatient beds. It also offers outpatient surgery and other health services in areas such as pediatrics rehabilitation oncology and radiology. The medical center's emergency department receives some 50000 visits each year. SMMC also operates satellite facilities including the Shawnee Mission Outpatient Pavilion in nearby Lenexa which offers emergency and outpatient diagnostic general practice and surgical care. SMMC is part of Adventist Health System.

	Annual Growth	12/13	12/14	12/15	12/16	12/17
Sales ($ mil.)	8.4%	–	385.1	435.4	454.8	491.2
Net income ($ mil.)	29.6%	–	25.5	38.0	54.4	55.5
Market value ($ mil.)	–	–	–	–	–	–
Employees	–	–	–	–	–	1,850

SHEA HOMES LIMITED PARTNERSHIP

655 Brea Canyon Rd.
Walnut CA 91789
Phone: 909-594-9500
Fax: 909-869-0897
Web: www.sheahomes.com

CEO: –
CFO: –
HR: –
FYE: December 31
Type: Private

Building communities comes naturally for Shea Homes. The company designs builds and markets single-family homes in Arizona California Colorado the Carolinas Florida Nevada and Washington. The home builder specializes in detached and attached residences including condominiums townhomes and luxury estates Its Trilogy brand builds active adult housing. The company's SPACES brand targets younger buyers. Shea Homes touts its master-planned communities and serves entry-level move-up and luxury buyers. The average price of a Shea home is $423000. Affiliated Shea Mortgage provides mortgage financing services. Shea Homes is a member of the J.F. Shea group.

SHEARER'S FOODS INC.

692 Wabash Ave. North
Brewster OH 44613-1056
Phone: 330-767-3426
Fax: 330-767-3393
Web: www.shearers.com

CEO: C J Fraleigh
CFO: Fritz Kohmann
HR: Dianne Ford
FYE: September 30
Type: Private

Shearer's Foods' potato chips are Shearer perfection. Using Grandma Shearer's "hand-cooked" kettle recipe the snacks company produces more than 30 million pounds of potato chips each year. Shearer's also makes and markets tortilla chips cheese curls corn puffs pretzels and pork rinds as well as dips and salsa. The food maker's products are sold around the country and in the Shearer's Marketplace Factory Outlet store across the street from its headquarters in Brewster Ohio. In addition to the Shearer brand the firm makes a variety of snacks for private-label customers. Shearer's produces kettle-cooked potato chips for snack-food giant Frito-Lay.

SHELL OIL COMPANY

910 Louisiana St.
Houston TX 77002
Phone: 713-241-6161
Fax: 713-241-4044
Web: www.shell.us

CEO: –
CFO: –
HR: –
FYE: December 31
Type: Subsidiary

Shell Oil doesn't shilly-shally around as it explores for produces and markets oil and natural gas and produces and markets chemicals. The company's Shell Exploration & Production unit focuses its exploration on the deepwater plays in the Gulf of Mexico. Shell partners with Saudi Aramco in a US refining and marketing venture (Motiva) and owns Motiva's sister company Shell Oil Products US. Shell also produces petrochemicals (Shell Chemical) and liquefied natural gas (Shell US Gas & Power) and markets natural gas and electricity. Shell's parent Royal Dutch Shell vies with Exxon Mobil) to be the world's #1 integrated oil company.

SHENANDOAH TELECOMMUNICATIONS CO   NMS: SHEN

500 Shentel Way
Edinburg, VA 22824
Phone: 540 984-4141
Fax: –
Web: www.shentel.com

CEO: Christopher E. (Chris) French
CFO: Adele M. Skolits
HR: –
FYE: December 31
Type: Public

If Virginia is for lovers Shenandoah Telecommunications must carry some interesting conversations. Through subsidiaries the company (which does business as Shentel) provides telecom services in the Shenandoah Valley and beyond. Shenandoah Telephone has more than 20500 access lines in service. As a Sprint affiliate subsidiary Shenandoah Personal Communications offers wireless services to more than 262000 customers. The company's cable TV unit serves about 115000 customers while about 13000 households subscribe to its dial-up and broadband Internet access.

	Annual Growth	12/14	12/15	12/16	12/17	12/18
Sales ($ mil.)	17.9%	326.9	342.5	535.3	612.0	630.9
Net income ($ mil.)	8.3%	33.9	40.9	(0.9)	66.4	46.6
Market value ($ mil.)	9.1%	1,550.9	2,136.6	1,354.9	1,677.5	2,196.1
Employees	9.8%	708	730	1,236	1,066	1,029

SHEPHERD CENTER, INC.

2020 PEACHTREE RD NW
ATLANTA, GA 303091465
Phone: 404-352-2020
Fax: –
Web: www.shepherd.org

CEO: Gary R Ulicny
CFO: Stephen B Holleman
HR: –
FYE: March 31
Type: Private

Here to shepherd those with catastrophic injuries back to good health is Shepherd Center. The not-for-profit hospital specializes in medical treatment research and rehabilitation for people with spinal cord and brain injuries as well as patients with neuromuscular disorders (such as spina bifida) and chronic pain. Shepherd Center boasts more than 150 beds and a 10-bed intensive care unit. Of its patients who have suffered injuries about 60% have been in car accidents. The hospital conducts neurological and neuromuscular research through its Virginia C. Crawford Research Institute.

	Annual Growth	03/12	03/13	03/14	03/15	03/16
Sales ($ mil.)	5.5%	–	168.6	170.6	187.6	198.3
Net income ($ mil.)	(34.1%)	–	23.4	27.2	24.1	6.7
Market value ($ mil.)	–	–	–	–	–	–
Employees	–	–	–	–	–	800

SHEPHERD ELECTRIC COMPANY INCORPORATED

7401 PULASKI HWY
BALTIMORE, MD 212372529
Phone: 410-866-6000
Fax: –
Web: www.shepherdelec.com

CEO: Charles C Vogel III
CFO: –
HR: –
FYE: December 31
Type: Private

For well over a hundred years Shepherd Electric has steered customers through a range of electrical needs. The company supplies a variety of electrical products to wholesale and retail customers primarily to the commercial construction market but it also serves government entities industrial firms and OEMs. Shepherd Electric carries products from major manufacturers such as 3M Brady Eaton Hadco Fluke General Electric and Thomas & Betts among many others. The company was founded in 1892 by Ernest Fluharty and Henry Shepherd. Shepherd Electric is owned by the Vogel family which has had a controlling interest in the company since 1931.

	Annual Growth	12/09	12/10	12/11	12/12	12/13
Sales ($ mil.)	7.5%	–	–	163.2	183.9	188.4
Net income ($ mil.)	3.5%	–	–	2.9	5.5	3.1
Market value ($ mil.)	–	–	–	–	–	–
Employees	–	–	–	–	–	185

SHERIDAN COMMUNITY HOSPITAL (OSTEOPATHIC)

301 N MAIN ST
SHERIDAN, MI 488849235
Phone: 989-291-3261
Fax: –
Web: www.sheridanhospital.com

CEO: Bobbi McColley
CFO: Mindy Buffman
HR: –
FYE: March 31
Type: Private

Sheridan Community Hospital certainly lives up to its "community" moniker. Local volunteers are considered a mainstay of the hospital logging more than 4000 hours of service every year. The facility offers residents of Montcalm Michigan and surrounding counties emergency services occupational health cardiology orthopedics and general surgery. The hospital has begun testing the waters of 21st century technology by investing in digital imaging and high-tech scanning systems. Sheridan Community Hospital has also opened Edmore Care-West its second family practice location in Edmore.

	Annual Growth	03/09	03/10	03/11	03/12	03/13
Sales ($ mil.)	1.1%	–	14.3	13.9	16.2	14.7
Net income ($ mil.)	–	–	–	0.3	0.6	(0.3)
Market value ($ mil.)	–	–	–	–	–	–
Employees	–	–	–	–	–	153

SHERWIN-WILLIAMS CO (THE)   NYS: SHW

101 West Prospect Avenue
Cleveland, OH 44115-1075
Phone: 216 566-2000
Fax: 216 566-3310
Web: www.sherwin.com

CEO: John G. Morikis
CFO: Allen J. Mistysyn
HR: Matt Schupp
FYE: December 31
Type: Public

For roughly 150 years Sherwin-Williams has maintained its position as one of the world's top paint manufacturers (along with Akzo Nobel PPG Industries and Henkel). Sherwin-Williams' products include a variety of paints finishes coatings applicators and varnishes sold under brands such as Dutch Boy Krylon Sherwin-Williams and Valspar The company operates mostly in the US Canada Latin America and the Caribbean through about 4700 paint stores and sells automotive finishing and refinishing products through wholesale branches. Its other outlets include home centers independent dealers and automotive retailers. More than 90% of US residents live within 50 miles of one of the company's retail locations.

	Annual Growth	12/14	12/15	12/16	12/17	12/18
Sales ($ mil.)	12.0%	11,129.5	11,339.3	11,855.6	14,983.8	17,534.5
Net income ($ mil.)	6.4%	865.9	1,053.8	1,132.7	1,772.3	1,108.7
Market value ($ mil.)	10.6%	24,493.4	24,173.1	25,024.2	38,181.6	36,637.7
Employees	7.7%	39,674	40,706	42,550	52,695	53,368

SHI INTERNATIONAL CORP.

290 DAVIDSON AVE
SOMERSET, NJ 088734145
Phone: 732-764-8888
Fax: –

CEO: Thai Lee
CFO: Paul Ng
HR: –
FYE: December 31
Type: Private

Businesses that need more than boxes of hardware and software can call SHI International. The company distributes scores of computer hardware and software products from suppliers such as Adobe Cisco Microsoft VMware Symantec and Lenovo. It resells PCs networking products data storage systems printers software and keyboards among other items. SHI offers a range of professional services including software licensing asset management managed desktop services systems integration and vocational training. The company serves corporate government and health care customers from more than 30 offices across the US Canada the UK Germany France and Hong Kong. SHI was founded in 1989 by Chairman Koguan Leo.

	Annual Growth	12/14	12/15	12/16	12/17	12/18
Sales ($ mil.)	14.3%	–	6,540.1	7,268.9	8,243.6	9,767.0
Net income ($ mil.)	52.1%	–	69.9	104.6	197.7	245.7
Market value ($ mil.)	–	–	–	–	–	–
Employees	–	–	–	–	–	4,500

SHILOH INDUSTRIES, INC.   NMS: SHLO

880 Steel Drive
Valley City, OH 44280
Phone: 330 558-2600
Fax: 330 558-2666
Web: www.shiloh.com

CEO: Ramzi Y Hermiz
CFO: Lillian Etzkorn
HR: Jodi Vasil
FYE: October 31
Type: Public

When Shiloh Industries draws a blank it's a good thing. The company produces stampings modular assemblies and steel and welded blanks for the automotive heating and air-conditioning and lawn and garden equipment industries. It also makes tools and assembly equipment for its own use and to sell to OEMs and other suppliers. Shiloh's largest customer is General Motors accounting for about 20% of sales. Other customers include Ford Chrysler (15% of sales) and Toyota as well as home appliance manufacturers construction companies and steel producers. The company traces its roots back to 1950 when it was founded as Shiloh Tool & Die Manufacturing.

	Annual Growth	10/15	10/16	10/17	10/18	10/19
Sales ($ mil.)	(1.3%)	1,109.2	1,065.8	1,042.0	1,139.9	1,054.7
Net income ($ mil.)	–	8.3	3.7	(0.7)	11.5	(19.9)
Market value ($ mil.)	(16.8%)	179.4	166.3	220.8	216.3	86.1
Employees	1.4%	3,400	3,100	3,600	4,200	3,600

SHIMADZU SCIENTIFIC INSTRUMENTS INC.

7102 Riverwood Dr.
Columbia MD 21046
Phone: 410-381-1227
Fax: 410-381-1222
Web: www.ssi.shimadzu.com

CEO: –
CFO: –
HR: –
FYE: March 31
Type: Subsidiary

Shimadzu Scientific Instruments helps researchers work magic in the lab. The company develops and manufactures analytical and monitoring equipment for scientific and medical laboratories. Products include diagnostic imaging systems such as ultrasound systems and mobile X-ray systems environmental testing and inspection machinery and mass spectrometers for the biotechnology sector. Its equipment is also available for lease. The company has more than 50 offices that offer sales service and support to clients. Founded in 1975 Shimadzu Scientific Instruments is the American arm of analytical instruments manufacturer Shimadzu Corporation.

SHOE CARNIVAL, INC.   NMS: SCVL

7500 East Columbia Street
Evansville, IN 47715
Phone: 812 867-6471
Fax: –
Web: www.shoecarnival.com

CEO: Clifton E. (Cliff) Sifford
CFO: W. Kerry Jackson
HR: Sean Georges
FYE: February 02
Type: Public

Shoe Carnival works hard to make shoe shopping a toe-tappin' good time. The company operates more than 350 family footwear stores across 30-plus US states including Puerto Rico that feature bright lights and neon signs. It also sells shoes online. In line with its name in-store "barkers" bellow out specials and organize games soliciting customer participation to promote the "carnival-like" atmosphere the retailer hopes will edge out rivals. Shoe Carnival sells brand-name and private-label men's and children's footwear as well as its primary women's and athletic shoes which together generate 64% of sales. The family of Chairman J. Wayne Weaver owns 25% of Shoe Carnival's shares.

	Annual Growth	01/15	01/16	01/17*	02/18	02/19
Sales ($ mil.)	2.3%	940.2	984.0	1,001.1	1,019.2	1,029.7
Net income ($ mil.)	10.6%	25.5	28.8	23.5	18.9	38.1
Market value ($ mil.)	12.3%	357.0	356.5	388.8	342.2	567.3
Employees	(3.1%)	5,900	5,500	5,100	4,700	5,200

*Fiscal year change

SHOP 'N SAVE ST. LOUIS INC.

10461 Manchester Rd.
St. Louis MO 63122
Phone: 314-984-0900
Fax: 314-984-1350
Web: www.shopnsave.com/

CEO: –
CFO: –
HR: –
FYE: February 28
Type: Subsidiary

Shop 'N Save St. Louis operates about 40 discount supermarkets in the St. Louis metro area and several in Springfield Illinois. The regional chain is owned by SUPERVALU and is part of that company's growing retail organization which also includes Shop 'N Save Warehouse Foods and about 20 Shop 'n Save markets in Pittsburgh where along with rival Giant Eagle it is one of the city's two biggest grocery chains. Shop 'N Save supermarkets offer savings of up to 20% and bakery deli pharmacy seafood and video departments among other amenities. The stores also feature dollar sections with merchandise sourced by sister company Save-A-Lot. Shop 'N Save was founded in 1979 as a single store in Illinois.

SHORE BANCSHARES INC. NMS: SHBI

28969 Information Lane
Easton, MD 21601
Phone: 410 763-7800
Fax: -
Web: www.shorebancshares.com

CEO: Lloyd L Beatty Jr
CFO: Edward C Allen
HR: -
FYE: December 31
Type: Public

Shore Bancshares sits on the edge of the banking ocean. The institution is the holding company for Shore United Bank which operates about 20 branches serving individuals and businesses in the Maryland counties of Caroline Dorchester Kent Queen Anne and Talbot as well as in Kent County Delaware. Shore Bancshares sells insurance through subsidiary The Avon-Dixon Agency (with specialty lines Elliott Wilson Insurance trucking coverage; and Jack Martin & Associates marine products). Another subsidiary Wye Financial & Trust offers trust and wealth management services. In 2016 the company merged its former two banks Centreville National Bank and Talbot bank into the single Shore United Bank.

	Annual Growth	12/14	12/15	12/16	12/17	12/18
Assets ($ mil.)	7.7%	1,100.4	1,135.1	1,160.3	1,393.9	1,483.1
Net income ($ mil.)	49.2%	5.1	7.1	9.6	11.3	25.0
Market value ($ mil.)	11.7%	119.1	138.7	194.4	212.9	185.4
Employees	(1.4%)	309	293	305	346	292

SHORE MEMORIAL HOSPITAL

100 MEDICAL CENTER WAY
SOMERS POINT, NJ 082442389
Phone: 609-653-3500
Fax: -
Web: www.shoremedicalcenter.org

CEO: -
CFO: -
HR: -
FYE: December 31
Type: Private

You might be able to get a room with a view of the ocean at Shore Memorial Hospital. Operating as Shore Medical Center the facility is a not-for-profit community hospital with some 300 beds. It offers acute care services and more than 35 specialized care programs including oncology cardiology neurology obstetrics and orthopedic care. Shore Medical Center is affiliated with The University of Pennsylvania Health System and The Children's Hospital of Philadelphia. In addition to the hospital Shore Medical Center operates community-based health and fitness centers.

	Annual Growth	12/13	12/14	12/15	12/17	12/18
Sales ($ mil.)	0.9%	-	187.9	183.3	190.8	194.5
Net income ($ mil.)	-	-	(0.7)	2.0	0.0	23.6
Market value ($ mil.)	-	-	-	-	-	-
Employees	-	-	-	-	-	1,600

SHORETEL INC NMS: SHOR

960 Stewart Drive
Sunnyvale, CA 94085-3913
Phone: 408 331-3300
Fax: 408 331-3333
Web: www.shoretel.com

CEO: Richard D McBee
CFO: -
HR: -
FYE: June 30
Type: Public

ShoreTel's internet protocol-based telephony hardware and software offers small and midsized businesses government agencies and schools an alternative to standard phone service. It provides voice video data and mobile communications with products that include phones and switches as well as messaging and systems management software. The company provides a cloud-based subscription service and licenses its software for use in customers' data centers. It also offers communications service for call centers. ShoreTel generates most of its sales in the US. The company counts about 40000 customers in the financial services health care manufacturing nonprofit and technology industries among others.

	Annual Growth	06/12	06/13	06/14	06/15	06/16
Sales ($ mil.)	9.9%	246.6	313.5	339.8	360.7	360.3
Net income ($ mil.)	-	(20.7)	(25.7)	(1.0)	(4.3)	(4.8)
Market value ($ mil.)	11.2%	295.2	271.6	439.4	456.9	450.8
Employees	6.4%	933	965	954	1,063	1,194

SHPS INC.

9200 Shelbyville Rd. Ste. 700
Louisville KY 40222
Phone: 502-426-4888
Fax: 502-420-5590
Web: www.shps.com

CEO: -
CFO: -
HR: -
FYE: December 31
Type: Private

SHPS works to bring out the best in an employer's health plan and its employees. The company's primary subsidiary Carewise Health offers employers ways to control healthcare costs through disease management programs medical bill review and personal wellness perks that encourage employees to stay healthy and use benefits responsibly. SHPS' clients include midsized and large employer groups. The company divested its human resource and information technology operations in 2012 to focus on Carewise. Investment firm Welsh Carson Anderson & Stowe owns SHPS.

SHRINERS HOSPITALS FOR CHILDREN

12502 USF PINE DR
TAMPA, FL 336129499
Phone: 813-972-2250
Fax: -
Web: www.shrinershospitalsforchildren.org

CEO: Douglas E. Maxwell
CFO: -
HR: Amy Suarez
FYE: December 31
Type: Private

The Shriners' red fez and mini-scooter parades are the goofy side to their very serious support of the Shriners Hospitals For Children. The system operates nearly two dozen hospitals throughout North America. The majority of its hospitals specialize in orthopedic conditions while others specialize in treating serious burn injuries spinal cord injuries and cleft lips and palates. Founded by fellowship Shriners International the hospitals are supported by a multitude of fundraising events that are arranged by the organization's 340000 members. As a result Shriners Hospitals is able to treat children regardless of their families' ability to pay.

	Annual Growth	12/08	12/09	12/13	12/14	12/16
Sales ($ mil.)	(13.8%)	-	285.1	0.0	120.0	100.4
Net income ($ mil.)	-	-	(300.9)	45.6	58.4	38.0
Market value ($ mil.)	-	-	-	-	-	-
Employees	-	-	-	-	-	6,100

SHUTTERFLY INC NMS: SFLY

2800 Bridge Parkway
Redwood City, CA 94065
Phone: 650 610-5200
Fax: -
Web: www.shutterflyinc.com

CEO: Ryan O'Hara
CFO: Michael Pope
HR: -
FYE: December 31
Type: Public

Whether or not you are the consummate shutterbug you can rely on Shutterfly for digital prints. An e-commerce company specializing in digital photo products and services for the consumer and professional photography markets the company offers customers the ability to upload share store and edit digital photos through its website. In addition to traditional 4-inch by 6-inch prints Shutterfly provides prints ranging from wallet-sized to jumbo enlargements. The company also offers personalized items including mugs photo books and calendars through its personalized products and services business segment. In 2012 Shutterfly acquired Kodak Imaging Network (doing business as KODAK Gallery).

	Annual Growth	12/13	12/14	12/15	12/16	12/17
Sales ($ mil.)	11.0%	783.6	921.6	1,059.4	1,134.2	1,190.2
Net income ($ mil.)	34.2%	9.3	(7.9)	(0.8)	15.9	30.1
Market value ($ mil.)	(0.6%)	1,644.9	1,346.6	1,439.2	1,620.7	1,606.8
Employees	5.3%	1,573	1,812	2,016	2,084	1,934

SHUTTERSTOCK INC
NYS: SSTK

350 Fifth Avenue, 21st Floor
New York, NY 10118
Phone: 646 710-3417
Fax: –
Web: www.shutterstock.com

CEO: Jonathan (Jon) Oringer
CFO: Steven Berns
HR: –
FYE: December 31
Type: Public

Shutterstock brings the online marketplace mentality to the world of digital images illustrations and videos. Its 35000+ contributors have uploaded more than 19 millions bits of content perused by 550000 subscribers. The company's primary customers include marketing agencies media organizations and communications departments of businesses that subscribe to single downloads a set number of images or unlimited downloads for a month or a year; average cost per image is $3. Shutterstock's marketplace is available in 10 languages and 150 countries where its images are used for corporate communications websites ads and books and other published materials. Formed in 2007 the company went public in 2012.

	Annual Growth	12/14	12/15	12/16	12/17	12/18
Sales ($ mil.)	17.4%	328.0	425.1	494.3	557.1	623.3
Net income ($ mil.)	25.4%	22.1	19.6	32.6	16.7	54.7
Market value ($ mil.)	(15.0%)	2,422.6	1,133.8	1,666.1	1,508.6	1,262.5
Employees	19.1%	512	621	858	1,130	1,029

SI FINANCIAL GROUP INC (MD)
NMS: SIFI

803 Main Street
Willimantic, CT 06226
Phone: 860 423-4581
Fax: –
Web: www.mysifi.com

CEO: –
CFO: –
HR: –
FYE: December 31
Type: Public

Sigh. You mean you still don't know SI? SI Financial Group is the holding company for Savings Institute Bank and Trust Company a community savings bank serving eastern Connecticut and southern Rhode Island from 20-plus locations including branches within retail stores. In addition to traditional deposit services like checking and savings accounts and CDs the bank and its subsidiaries offer financial services such as trust services investment management retirement planning and life insurance. Residential and commercial mortgages dominate Savings Institute's lending portfolio which also includes commercial business and consumer loans. SI Financial Group acquired Rhode Island's Newport Bancorp. in 2013.

	Annual Growth	12/13	12/14	12/15	12/16	12/17
Assets ($ mil.)	4.1%	1,346.4	1,350.5	1,481.8	1,550.9	1,581.0
Net income ($ mil.)	–	(0.9)	4.4	4.3	11.3	5.2
Market value ($ mil.)	5.1%	147.5	138.7	167.1	188.5	180.0
Employees	(2.8%)	315	299	292	297	281

SIEBERT FINANCIAL CORP
NAS: SIEB

120 Wall Street
New York, NY 10005
Phone: 212 644-2400
Fax: –
Web: www.siebertnet.com

CEO: –
CFO: –
HR: –
FYE: December 31
Type: Public

Siebert Financial through subsidiary Muriel Siebert & Co. provides discount securities brokerage and institutional financial services. Its retail division offers equity trading mutual fund access and retirement accounts to self-directed individual investors. Customers can access their accounts and trade by phone Internet wireless device or in person at seven retail branches in California Florida New Jersey and New York. Siebert Financial provides securities trading and underwriting and other services to corporations and government entities. Nevada firm Kennedy Cabot Acquisition is buying the 90% of Siebert that is owned by the estate of its founder Muriel "Mickie" Siebert.

	Annual Growth	12/14	12/15	12/16	12/17	12/18
Sales ($ mil.)	17.4%	15.8	10.1	9.8	13.1	30.0
Net income ($ mil.)	–	(6.6)	(2.9)	(5.6)	2.2	12.0
Market value ($ mil.)	60.1%	59.7	35.0	80.9	366.6	392.7
Employees	12.2%	48	43	31	80	76

SIEMENS INDUSTRY INC.

1000 Deerfield Pkwy.
Buffalo Grove IL 60089
Phone: 847-215-1000
Fax: 847-215-1093
Web: www.siemens.com/industry

CEO: Daryl D Dulaney
CFO: –
HR: Andrea Janecek
FYE: September 30
Type: Subsidiary

Siemens Industry caters to the needs of industrial customers. Its divisions provide specialty engineering services and equipment for customers in the automotive cement chemical food and beverage mining metals and waste water industries. Siemens Industry provides automation technology and products and services for drive train systems. Its services arm provides maintenance and repair functions as well as planning and technical consulting and engineering support. Siemens Industry is part of Siemens Corporation the US holding company of German electrics and engineering giant Siemens AG.

SIERRA BANCORP
NMS: BSRR

86 North Main Street
Porterville, CA 93257
Phone: 559 782-4900
Fax: –
Web: www.bankofthesierra.com

CEO: Kevin J McPhaill
CFO: Kenneth R. (Ken) Taylor
HR: –
FYE: December 31
Type: Public

Sierra Bancorp is the holding company for the nearly $2 billion-asset Bank of the Sierra which operates approximately 30 branches in Central California's San Joaquin Valley between (and including) Bakersfield and Fresno. The bank offers traditional deposit products and loans to individuals and small and mid-size businesses. About 70% of its loan portfolio is made up of real estate loans while another 15% is made up of mortgage warehouse loans and a further 10% is tied to commercial and industrial loans (including SBA loans and direct finance leases). The bank also issues agricultural loans and consumer loans.

	Annual Growth	12/14	12/15	12/16	12/17	12/18
Assets ($ mil.)	11.4%	1,637.3	1,796.5	2,032.9	2,340.3	2,522.5
Net income ($ mil.)	18.1%	15.2	18.1	17.6	19.5	29.7
Market value ($ mil.)	8.2%	268.7	270.1	406.8	406.4	367.7
Employees	6.2%	437	431	497	576	556

SIERRA CLUB

2101 WEBSTER ST STE 1300
OAKLAND, CA 946123546
Phone: 415-977-5500
Fax: –
Web: www.sierraclub.org

CEO: –
CFO: –
HR: –
FYE: December 31
Type: Private

Wanna take a hike with the Sierra Club? The growing grassroots organization promotes outdoor activities and environmental activism on both the local and national levels through political lobbies education outings litigation and publications. The club's more than 2.4 million members are organized into state and regional chapters throughout the US and Canada. Founded in 1892 by naturalist John Muir Sierra Club publishes books calendars SIERRA magazine and activist newsletter Currents . Some of Sierra Club's current issues include smart energy solutions clean water stopping commercial logging in national forests ending sprawl and protecting wetlands.

	Annual Growth	12/07	12/08	12/09	12/13	12/17
Sales ($ mil.)	5.5%	–	87.4	97.3	98.2	141.4
Net income ($ mil.)	–	–	(14.4)	6.0	0.3	13.0
Market value ($ mil.)	–	–	–	–	–	–
Employees	–	–	–	–	–	600

SIERRA MONITOR CORP
NBB: SRMC

1991 Tarob Court
Milpitas, CA 95035
Phone: 408 262-6611
Fax: –
Web: www.investor.sierramonitor.com

CEO: Nishan J Vartanian
CFO: –
HR: –
FYE: December 31
Type: Public

If there's hazardous gas in the air Sierra Monitor wants its customers to know — fast. Sierra Monitor manufactures distributes and services gas and flame detection devices for oil and gas petrochemical transportation and wastewater treatment industries. Sierra Monitor also makes environmental and security monitoring equipment for remote telecommunications facilities along with communications bridging equipment and software (FieldServer and ProtoCessor) that allow building automation systems and gas detection systems that use different communications protocols to exchange data. Directors Richard Kramlich and Jay Last own 21% and 18% of Sierra Monitor respectively. CEO Gordon Arnold owns 11%.

	Annual Growth	12/13	12/14	12/15	12/16	12/17
Sales ($ mil.)	1.9%	18.3	19.3	20.3	19.2	19.8
Net income ($ mil.)	–	1.4	0.3	0.9	(0.1)	(0.4)
Market value ($ mil.)	(8.5%)	20.4	15.3	17.9	14.2	14.3
Employees	3.7%	71	79	79	79	82

SIERRA NEVADA CORPORATION

444 SALOMON CIR
SPARKS, NV 894349651
Phone: 775-331-0222
Fax: –
Web: www.sncorp.com

CEO: Fatih Ozmen
CFO: –
HR: Anne Bruce
FYE: December 31
Type: Private

Sierra Nevada Corporation (SNC) believes that military agility isn't just about how fast a soldier completes the obstacle course in basic training. It's also about employing technology to support the soldier. The company provides defense electronics engineering manufacturing and integration services. Its operates in three overall areas: Space Systems Commercial Solutions and National Security and Defense. SNC's Dream Chaser space vehicle was selected by NASA to provide service to the International Space Station.

	Annual Growth	12/10	12/11	12/12	12/13	12/14
Sales ($ mil.)	2.9%	–	–	1,400.1	1,623.0	1,481.0
Net income ($ mil.)	–	–	–	0.0	0.0	0.0
Market value ($ mil.)	–	–	–	–	–	–
Employees	–	–	–	–	–	3,063

SIERRA PACIFIC POWER CO.
NL:

6100 Neil Road
Reno, NV 89511
Phone: 775 834-4011
Fax: –
Web: www.sierrapacific.com

CEO: Paul J. Caudill
CFO: E. Kevin Bethel
HR: –
FYE: December 31
Type: Public

Sierra Pacific Power mitigates the effects of hot Sierra winds and moist Pacific breezes. The company is a natural gas and electricity distribution utility serving customers in towns and cities across Nevada. Sierra Pacific Power a subsidiary of NV Energy Inc does business as NV Energy. The company serves about 323000 power customers and 153000 natural gas customers. Sierra Pacific Power also owns more than 15 fossil-fueled and hydroelectric power plants with about 1510 MW of generating capacity and it sells excess energy to wholesale customers.

	Annual Growth	12/14	12/15	12/16	12/17	12/18
Sales ($ mil.)	(1.4%)	904.0	947.0	812.0	812.0	855.0
Net income ($ mil.)	1.4%	87	83	84	109	92.0
Market value ($ mil.)	–	–	–	–	–	–
Employees	0.0%	1,000	1,000	1,000	1,000	1,000

SIERRA VIEW DISTRICT HOSPITAL LEAGUE, INC.

465 W PUTNAM AVE
PORTERVILLE, CA 932573320
Phone: 559-784-1110
Fax: –
Web: www.sierra-view.com

CEO: Donna Hefner
CFO: Douglas Dickson
HR: –
FYE: June 30
Type: Private

Patients at Sierra View District Hospital (SVDH) are likely to have a bedside view of central California's San Joaquin Valley. The not-for-profit acute-care medical center offers a comprehensive range of primary specialty and emergency services serving Porterville California and surrounding areas. Divisions at the hospital's nearly 170-bed facility include oncology pediatrics diagnostics women's care and rehabilitation. SVDH which boasts a 32-station outpatient dialysis center and the Roger S. Good Cancer Treatment Center also offers laboratory wellness and counseling services. Founded in 1948 the hospital serves more than 40000 patients in its emergency room each year.

	Annual Growth	12/09	12/10*	06/15	06/16	06/18
Sales ($ mil.)	11.4%	–	62.2	–	138.3	148.0
Net income ($ mil.)	(7.4%)	–	2.0	–	0.0	1.1
Market value ($ mil.)	–	–	–	–	–	–
Employees	–	–	–	–	–	600

*Fiscal year change

SIFCO INDUSTRIES INC.
ASE: SIF

970 East 64th Street
Cleveland, OH 44103
Phone: 216 881-8600
Fax: –
Web: www.sifco.com

CEO: –
CFO: Thomas R Kubera
HR: Wendy Worthington
FYE: September 30
Type: Public

Airplanes need parts and SIFCO coats machines and produces jet engine and aerospace components. It forges parts and offers forging heat-treating and precision component machining services. Products include components for aircraft and industrial gas turbine engines structural airframe components aircraft landing gear components brakes and wheels. Aerospace components for both fixed wing aircraft and rotorcraft account for nearly 80% of its total sales. SIFCO caters to original equipment manufacturers (OEMs) for both commercial and defense aerospace applications. It also serves the energy market.

	Annual Growth	09/15	09/16	09/17	09/18	09/19
Sales ($ mil.)	0.7%	109.3	119.1	121.5	111.2	112.5
Net income ($ mil.)	–	(2.9)	(11.3)	(14.2)	(7.2)	(7.5)
Market value ($ mil.)	(29.9%)	65.2	57.3	32.9	29.2	15.7
Employees	(7.5%)	593	607	491	453	434

SIGA TECHNOLOGIES INC
NMS: SIGA

31 East 62nd Street
New York, NY 10065
Phone: 212 672-9100
Fax: –
Web: www.siga.com

CEO: Phillip L Gomez
CFO: Daniel Luckshire
HR: Annie Offutt
FYE: December 31
Type: Public

SIGA Technologies is trying to put itself on the front lines of US biodefense efforts. The drug company has a number of development programs for vaccines antivirals and antibiotics for drug resistant infections; however its main focus is on vaccines for bio-defense. Its lead product TPOXX (aka tecovirimat) was the first treatment to be approved for the treatment of smallpox in case of a bioterrorist attack; it was given approval in mid-2018. SIGA is also developing vaccines for use against hemorrhagic fevers and other infectious diseases and biothreats. Much of its work is done through funding from the NIH and the HHS. SIGA emerged from a short stint under Chapter 11 bankruptcy protection in 2016.

	Annual Growth	12/14	12/15	12/16	12/17	12/18
Sales ($ mil.)	251.1%	3.1	8.2	15.0	12.3	477.1
Net income ($ mil.)	–	(265.5)	(39.5)	(39.7)	(36.2)	421.8
Market value ($ mil.)	53.0%	116.3	33.9	232.6	391.7	638.0
Employees	4.8%	34	29	36	37	41

SIGE SEMICONDUCTOR INC.

200 Brickstone Sq. Ste. 203 — CEO: Sohail Khan
Andover MA 01810 — CFO: –
Phone: 978-327-6850 — HR: –
Fax: 978-475-0859 — FYE: December 31
Web: www.sige.com — Type: Subsidiary

SiGe Semiconductor sized up the wireless semiconductor market and made its move. The fabless chip company designs radio-frequency (RF) semiconductors used in wireless communications gear. Its WiMAX and Bluetooth power amplifiers RF front-end devices GPS receiver chips and other chip products are used to link laptops printers phones and cameras; enable wireless gaming and streaming video; and provide GPS location and mapping services. Its chips are made from silicon germanium (SiGe) which offers better performance than chips made from silicon alone. Most of its sales come from Asia. SiGe Semi filed for an IPO in 2010; it was acquired by Skyworks Solutions the following year for about $275 million.

SIGMA DESIGNS INC — NBB: SIGM

47467 Fremont Boulevard — CEO: Thinh Q. Tran
Fremont, CA 94538 — CFO: Elias Nader
Phone: 510 897-0200 — HR: –
Fax: 408 957-9740 — FYE: February 03
Web: www.sigmadesigns.com — Type: Public

Sigma Designs designs devices that control the machines that control (or will) control the home. The company's system-on-a-chip (SoC) products go into smart TVs (high-definition and ultra high-def) set-top boxes and gateways for internet protocol TVs (IPTVs) Blu-ray players media communication devices and home automation devices for security energy management and other services. Its SoCs support a variety of industry standards for audio and video in consumer entertainment devices. Sigma Designs outsources the fabrication of its chips to Taiwan Semiconductor Manufacturing. Customers include Vizio Roku Ericsson and AT&T. The majority of Sigma Designs' sales come from Asia; China is its largest market.

	Annual Growth	02/14*	01/15	01/16	01/17*	02/18
Sales ($ mil.)	(24.2%)	199.2	188.3	227.3	220.5	65.9
Net income ($ mil.)	–	(11.0)	(21.7)	0.2	(18.3)	(120.0)
Market value ($ mil.)	4.3%	185.1	251.0	261.6	252.6	219.0
Employees	(13.1%)	716	691	717	718	409

*Fiscal year change

SIGMA-ALDRICH CORP. — NMS: SIAL

3050 Spruce Street — CEO: Rakesh Sachdev
St. Louis, MO 63103 — CFO: Jan A Bertsch
Phone: 314 771-5765 — HR: –
Fax: 314 286-7874 — FYE: December 31
Web: www.sigma-aldrich.com — Type: Public

Check the shelves of any research (or mad) scientist and you'll likely find Sigma-Aldrich's chemical products. The company is a leading supplier of chemicals to research laboratories. It has more than 100000 accounts including labs involved in government and commercial research for 230000 chemical and biochemical and 45000 equipment products it offers in its Sigma Aldrich Fluka and Supelco catalogs. It makes about 110000 of the products it sells. The business derives revenues from two major areas: Research Chemicals (essentials specialties and biotech) and Fine Chemicals (commercial applications). In 2014 the company agreed to be acquired by Germany-based pharmaceutical giant Merck for $17 billion.

	Annual Growth	12/10	12/11	12/12	12/13	12/14
Sales ($ mil.)	5.2%	2,271.0	2,505.0	2,623.0	2,704.0	2,785.0
Net income ($ mil.)	6.8%	384.0	457.0	460.0	491.0	500.0
Market value ($ mil.)	19.8%	7,920.6	7,432.7	8,756.0	11,187.2	16,335.1
Employees	4.2%	7,890	8,300	9,000	9,000	9,300

SIGMATRON INTERNATIONAL INC. — NAS: SGMA

2201 Landmeier Road — CEO: Gary R Fairhead
Elk Grove Vilage, IL 60007 — CFO: Linda K Frauendorfer
Phone: 847 956-8000 — HR: –
Fax: – — FYE: April 30
Web: www.sigmatronintl.com — Type: Public

An assembly at SigmaTron International doesn't mean fraternizing over a keg. The company produces electronic components printed circuit board assemblies and box-build (completely assembled) electronic products on a contract basis for customers in the appliance automotive consumer electronics fitness equipment industrial electronics and telecommunications industries. SigmaTron also offers design testing shipping and storage services. Major customers include electronic controls manufacturer Spitfire Controls and fitness equipment maker Life Fitness together accounting for nearly half of sales. Besides its US manufacturing facilities the company boasts plants in China Mexico and Taiwan.

	Annual Growth	04/15	04/16	04/17	04/18	04/19
Sales ($ mil.)	6.0%	230.2	253.9	252.2	278.1	290.6
Net income ($ mil.)	–	0.9	2.1	1.4	(3.2)	(0.9)
Market value ($ mil.)	(23.6%)	34.1	26.1	22.9	28.7	11.6
Employees	3.5%	2,710	2,790	3,053	2,993	3,106

SIGNATURE BANK (NEW YORK, NY) — NMS: SBNY

565 Fifth Avenue — CEO: Joseph J. DePaolo
New York, NY 10017 — CFO: Vito Susca
Phone: 646 822-1500 — HR: –
Fax: – — FYE: December 31
Web: www.signatureny.com — Type: Public

Signature Bank marks the spot where some professional New Yorkers bank. The institution provides customized banking and financial services to smaller private businesses their owners and their top executives through 30 branches across the New York metropolitan area including all five boroughs Long Island and affluent Westchester County. The bank's lending activities mainly entail real estate and business loans. Subsidiary Signature Securities offers wealth management financial planning brokerage services asset management and insurance while its Signature Financial subsidiary offers equipment financing and leasing. Founded in 2001 the bank now boasts assets of roughly $29 billion.

	Annual Growth	12/14	12/15	12/16	12/17	12/18
Assets ($ mil.)	14.7%	27,318.6	33,450.5	39,047.6	43,117.7	47,364.8
Net income ($ mil.)	14.2%	296.7	373.1	396.3	387.2	505.3
Market value ($ mil.)	(5.0%)	6,932.8	8,441.4	8,266.9	7,554.7	5,658.6
Employees	8.4%	1,010	1,122	1,218	1,305	1,393

SIGNATURE CONSULTANTS LLC

200 W CYPRESS CREEK RD # 400 — CEO: Jay Cohen
FORT LAUDERDALE, FL 333092175 — CFO: Philip Monti
Phone: 954-677-1020 — HR: –
Fax: – — FYE: December 31
Web: www.sigconsult.com — Type: Private

Signature Consultants wants your John Hancock when it comes to signing up for its staffing services. The company provides information technology staffing services to clients from a variety of industries. Signature places IT professionals with expertise in areas like project management Web application development database administration storage and network security. The firm has experience placing IT professionals across such industries as aerospace automotive banking and financial services education electronics government technology pharmaceutical and manufacturing.

	Annual Growth	12/12	12/13	12/14	12/15	12/16
Sales ($ mil.)	15.8%	–	202.2	235.2	253.2	314.1
Net income ($ mil.)	14.1%	–	3.7	4.3	1.3	5.6
Market value ($ mil.)	–	–	–	–	–	–
Employees	–	–	–	–	–	1,450

SIGNATURE EYEWEAR INC.

OTC: SEYE

498 N. Oak St.
Inglewood CA 90302
Phone: 310-330-2700
Fax: 310-330-2765
Web: www.signatureeyewear.com

CEO: Michael Prince
CFO: Michael Prince
HR: –
FYE: October 31
Type: Public

Signature Eyewear views prescription eyeglasses and sunglasses as the ultimate fashion statement and an integral part of its business. Laura Ashley Nicole Miller and bebe licensed eyewear accounts for about three-fourths of the firm's sales. Signature Eyewear also licenses frames by Michael Stars Dakota Smith and Hart Schaffner Marx. Its own Signature line of frames is produced by contract manufacturers in Hong Kong China Japan and Italy and markets them to optical retailers in more than 20 countries. The company markets footwear and accessories through its Signature Fashion Group division which was formed in 2010.

SILGAN HOLDINGS INC

NMS: SLGN

4 Landmark Square
Stamford, CT 06901
Phone: 203 975-7110
Fax: –

CEO: Anthony J. (Tony) Allott
CFO: Robert B. (Bob) Lewis
HR: –
FYE: December 31
Type: Public

Silgan Holdings is one of the leading makers of metal containers in the world and in North America it holds the #1 position in metal food containers. Its containers are used by customers such as Campbell's Soup Del Monte and Nestl-© to package soups vegetables meat seafood and pet food. Through its Silgan Dispensing Systems business the company supplies highly engineered triggers pumps sprayers and dispensing closure solutions for health care garden home and beauty and food products. Silgan also makes plastic containers used by personal care pharmaceutical and other companies. About 80% of its revenue comes from North America.

	Annual Growth	12/14	12/15	12/16	12/17	12/18
Sales ($ mil.)	3.3%	3,911.8	3,764.0	3,612.9	4,089.9	4,448.9
Net income ($ mil.)	5.3%	182.4	172.4	153.4	269.7	224.0
Market value ($ mil.)	(18.5%)	5,919.0	5,932.3	5,651.8	3,245.5	2,608.3
Employees	(23.2%)	9,200	9,600	9,100	3,100	3,200

SIKA CORPORATION

201 POLITO AVE
LYNDHURST, NJ 070713601
Phone: 201-933-8800
Fax: –
Web: www.usa.sika.com

CEO: Rick Montani
CFO: Stephen Lysik
HR: –
FYE: December 31
Type: Private

When plain old mortar won't do Sika Corporation offers its construction customers specialty mortars. Sika also manufactures adhesives coatings epoxies acrylics silicones and polyurethane. Its products are used to seal bond dampen sounds reinforce and protect load-bearing structures. It markets to the construction and manufacturing industries including transportation marine and automotive. Sika's Construction Products division is based along with its headquarters in New Jersey and its Industry and Automotive divisions are based in Michigan. Sika is the US unit as well as the largest manufacturing segment of global chemicals company Sika AG.

	Annual Growth	12/11	12/12	12/13	12/14	12/15
Sales ($ mil.)	7.2%	–	744.0	761.9	842.6	915.9
Net income ($ mil.)	15.4%	–	41.4	31.7	42.6	63.7
Market value ($ mil.)	–	–	–	–	–	–
Employees	–	–	–	–	–	1,067

SILICON GRAPHICS INTERNATIONAL CORP.

940 N MCCARTHY BLVD
MILPITAS, CA 950355128
Phone: 669-900-8000
Fax: –
Web: www.hpe.com

CEO: Jorge L. Titinger
CFO: Mack Asrat
HR: –
FYE: June 24
Type: Private

Silicon Graphics International (SGI) handles computing on a large scale. The company provides high-performance computer servers that are based on the Linux operating system and designed for large-scale data center deployments. SGI also offers data storage servers as well as modular data center systems sold under the ICE brand. Its equipment is tailored to quickly access analyze process manage visualize and store large amounts of data. SGI targets the IT Internet financial services government and electronics sectors as well as scientific community. Clients have included Amazon.com (18% of sales in 2014) Microsoft Yahoo! and Deutsche Bank. In November 2016 SGI was acquired by Hewlett-Packard Enterprise.

	Annual Growth	06/12	06/13	06/14	06/15	06/16
Sales ($ mil.)	(11.4%)	–	767.2	529.9	521.3	532.9
Net income ($ mil.)	–	–	(2.8)	(52.8)	(39.1)	(11.2)
Market value ($ mil.)	–	–	–	–	–	–
Employees	–	–	–	–	–	1,100

SIKORSKY AIRCRAFT CORPORATION

6900 Main St.
Stratford CT 06615
Phone: 203-386-4000
Fax: +46-8-728-00-28
Web: www.bonnier.se

CEO: –
CFO: Mary Gallagher
HR: –
FYE: December 31
Type: Subsidiary

Russian-born helicopter pioneer Igor Sikorsky is long dead but helicopters bearing his name still soar the skies. A subsidiary of United Technologies Sikorsky Aircraft designs manufactures and services such military helicopters as the Black Hawk (combat support border security medevac); Seahawk (anti-submarine/surface warfare search/rescue); and Superhawk (military operations). Sikorsky's CH-53K helicopter is used by the US Marines for heavy lift operations. Civil aircraft include the S-76 and S-92 which are used for rescue offshore oil medical and corporate use. Sikorsky also offers fixed-wing aircraft aftermarket spare parts and MRO services for helicopters used by US and foreign governments.

SILICON IMAGE INC

NMS: SIMG

1140 East Arques Avenue
Sunnyvale, CA 94085
Phone: 408 616-4000
Fax: –
Web: www.siliconimage.com

CEO: –
CFO: Joe Bedewi
HR: –
FYE: December 31
Type: Public

It would be silly to imagine that Silicon Image's chips only produce pretty pictures. Silicon Image designs and sells a variety of integrated circuits including digital video controllers receivers transmitters and processors that are built into mobile devices digital TVs camera personal computers and DVD and Blu-ray players. The company helped create HDMI and DVI industry standards as well as MHL the standard for mobile devices and the 60GHz wireless HD video standard WirelessHD. Through subsidiary Simplay Labs it offers HDMI licensing and compliance testing services. Customers located outside the US account for about 60% of the company's sales.

	Annual Growth	12/09	12/10	12/11	12/12	12/13
Sales ($ mil.)	16.4%	150.6	191.3	221.0	252.4	276.4
Net income ($ mil.)	–	(129.1)	8.2	(11.6)	(11.2)	11.5
Market value ($ mil.)	24.3%	199.7	569.0	363.9	384.0	476.1
Employees	5.0%	526	432	521	623	640

SILICON LABORATORIES INC NMS: SLAB

400 West Cesar Chavez
Austin, TX 78701
Phone: 512 416-8500
Fax: –
Web: www.silabs.com

CEO: G. Tyson Tuttle
CFO: John C. Hollister
HR: –
FYE: December 28
Type: Public

Silicon Laboratories makes little translation machines. The company develops mixed-signal integrated circuits (ICs) which translate real-world analog signals (such as sound) into digital signals that can be processed by electronic products. Silicon Labs provides ICs used in set-top boxes game consoles portable electronics industrial monitoring and control devices and wireless handsets. Products include microcontrollers clocks and oscillators sensors and broadcast communications chips. Top customers include Cisco Huawei LG Electronics Pace Samsung Technicolor Varian Medical Systems and ZTE. About 85% of the company's sales come from customers outside the US.

	Annual Growth	01/16*	12/16	12/17	12/18	12/19
Sales ($ mil.)	9.1%	644.8	697.6	768.9	868.3	837.6
Net income ($ mil.)	(13.3%)	29.6	61.5	47.1	83.6	19.3
Market value ($ mil.)	33.9%	2,111.3	2,827.2	3,840.7	3,414.4	5,068.2
Employees	8.8%	1,199	1,252	1,279	1,505	1,545

*Fiscal year change

SILVER BAY REALTY TRUST CORP.

3300 FERNBROOK LN N
PLYMOUTH, MN 554475338
Phone: 952-358-4400
Fax: –
Web: www.silverbayrealtytrustcorp.com

CEO: Thomas W. Brock
CFO: –
HR: –
FYE: December 31
Type: Private

Silver Bay makes green on rentals in sunny locales. The real estate investment trust (REIT) is externally managed by PRCM Real Estate Advisers. It focuses on buying single-family homes in urban markets with an oversupply of housing. Silver Bay acquires properties via foreclosures auctions sales listings and bulk purchases and uses its manager's rental property experience to achieve economies of scale for property management and maintenance. The company has a portfolio of about 2250 income-generating single-family homes that it leases in Arizona California Florida Georgia Nevada North Carolina and Texas. Real estate investor Two Harbors formed Silver Bay in 2012 and it went public later that year.

	Annual Growth	12/12	12/13	12/14	12/15	12/16
Assets ($ mil.)	12.9%	–	846.1	1,002.4	1,224.4	1,218.6
Net income ($ mil.)	–	–	(24.6)	(56.7)	(10.0)	(2.6)
Market value ($ mil.)	–	–	–	–	–	–
Employees	–	–	–	–	–	5

SILVER CROSS HOSPITAL AND MEDICAL CENTERS

1900 SILVER CROSS BLVD
NEW LENOX, IL 604519509
Phone: 815-300-1100
Fax: –
Web: www.silvercross.org

CEO: Paul Pawlak
CFO: William Brownlow
HR: –
FYE: September 30
Type: Private

Silver Cross Hospital and Medical Centers serve the Illinois counties of Will Grundy and Cook through its 290-bed main hospital campus and nine satellite facilities throughout the area. Services provided by the medical facility include cardiovascular care women's health rehabilitation and behavioral health care. Its outpatient facilities provide primary and specialty care services such as medical imaging and dialysis. The Silver Cross Hospital and Medical Centers name comes from the emblem (the Maltese Cross) of the Christian organization that founded the not-for-profit hospital the International Order of The King's Daughters and Sons.

	Annual Growth	09/12	09/13	09/14	09/15	09/18
Sales ($ mil.)	4.8%	–	306.7	320.2	335.6	387.0
Net income ($ mil.)	33.9%	–	6.3	10.4	(59.4)	27.1
Market value ($ mil.)	–	–	–	–	–	–
Employees	–	–	–	–	–	1,600

SILVER SPRING NETWORKS INC NYS: SSNI

230 W. Tasman Drive
San Jose, CA 95134
Phone: 669 770-4000
Fax: –
Web: www.silverspringnet.com

CEO: –
CFO: –
HR: –
FYE: December 31
Type: Public

Silver Spring Networks helps utility companies plug into the 21st century. Its Smart Energy Platform modernizes a utility's existing power grid infrastructure into the "smart" grid i.e. one that is connected to a digital network and more energy efficient. The Smart Energy Platform is a secure Internet-based network made up of hardware such as access points communications modules bridges and relays; its UtilOS-brand network operating system; and software. It also offers managed services to maintain and regulate the network. Silver Spring sells its platform to electric gas and water utilities — FPL PG&E and OG&E account for almost 80% of service revenue. The company went public in 2013.

	Annual Growth	12/11	12/12	12/13	12/14	12/15
Sales ($ mil.)	19.9%	237.1	196.7	326.9	191.3	489.6
Net income ($ mil.)	–	(92.4)	(89.7)	(66.8)	(89.2)	80.0
Market value ($ mil.)	(17.2%)	–	–	1,063.0	426.7	729.4
Employees	4.8%	–	566	602	576	652

SILVERLEAF RESORTS INC.

1221 River Bend Dr. Ste. 120
Dallas TX 75247
Phone: 214-631-1166
Fax: 214-637-0585
Web: www.silverleafresorts.com

CEO: Thomas R Nelson
CFO: Sonya Dixon
HR: –
FYE: December 31
Type: Private

Silverleaf Resorts helps vacationers get away without going far away. The company owns and operates more than a dozen time-share resorts in six states (Florida Georgia Illinois Massachusetts Missouri and Texas). Its resorts feature amenities such as golf clubhouses and indoor water parks. Silverleaf's portfolio of properties include six "destination resorts" located near national tourist areas and seven affordable "getaway resorts" located near major metropolitan markets. The company also owns and operates a hotel near the Winter Park recreational area in Colorado. Previously a public company in 2011 SL Resort Holdings an affiliate of Cerberus Capital Management purchased Silverleaf for $94 million.

SIMMONS FIRST NATIONAL CORP NMS: SFNC

501 Main Street
Pine Bluff, AR 71601
Phone: 870 541-1000
Fax: –
Web: www.simmonsbank.com

CEO: George A. Makris
CFO: Robert A. Fehlman
HR: –
FYE: December 31
Type: Public

Simmons First National thinks it's only natural it should be one of the largest financial institutions in The Natural State. The $8.1 billion-asset holding company owns Simmons First National Bank and seven other community banks that bear the Simmons First Bank name and maintain local identities; together they operate around 150 branches throughout Arkansas and in Kansas Tennessee and Missouri. Serving consumers and area businesses the banks offer standard deposit products like checking and savings accounts IRAs and CDs. Lending activities mainly consist of commercial real estate loans single-family mortgages and consumer loans such as credit card and student loans.

	Annual Growth	12/14	12/15	12/16	12/17	12/18
Assets ($ mil.)	37.4%	4,643.4	7,559.7	8,400.1	15,055.8	16,543.3
Net income ($ mil.)	56.8%	35.7	74.4	96.8	92.9	215.7
Market value ($ mil.)	(12.2%)	3,753.9	4,743.0	5,739.4	5,273.1	2,228.3
Employees	18.8%	1,331	1,946	1,875	2,640	2,654

SIMON PROPERTY GROUP, INC.   NYS: SPG

225 West Washington Street
Indianapolis, IN 46204
Phone: 317 636-1600
Fax: 317 685-7336
Web: www.simon.com

CEO: David Simon
CFO: Andrew A. (Andy) Juster
HR: –
FYE: December 31
Type: Public

Simon Property Group is the largest shopping mall and retail center owner in the US. The self-managed self-administered real estate investment trust (REIT) owns develops and manages regional shopping malls outlet malls (under the Premium Outlet and The Mills brands) boutique malls and shopping centers. Its real estate portfolio is composed of some 230 retail properties totaling approximately 190 million sq. ft. of leasable space. Its portfolio covers 35 states and Puerto Rico though much is concentrated in the US Southeast Midwest and Northeast. The REIT also has stakes in outlet centers in Canada Mexico Europe and Asia. The company is still run by the founding family.

	Annual Growth	12/14	12/15	12/16	12/17	12/18
Sales ($ mil.)	3.8%	4,870.8	5,266.1	5,435.2	5,538.6	5,657.9
Net income ($ mil.)	14.7%	1,408.6	1,827.7	1,838.9	1,948.0	2,440.1
Market value ($ mil.)	(2.0%)	58,351.6	62,302.4	56,928.9	55,028.9	53,827.3
Employees	6.3%	5,250	5,000	5,000	5,000	6,700

SIMON WORLDWIDE INC.   PINK SHEETS: SWWI

5200 W. Century Blvd.
Los Angeles CA 90045
Phone: 310-417-4660
Fax: 858-513-1870
Web: www.aldila.com

CEO: Greg Mays
CFO: Anthony Espiritu
HR: –
FYE: December 31
Type: Public

Here is a true business tragedy a successful company brought low by the machinations of a lone employee. Simon Worldwide once offered an array of promotional marketing services but the firm was dealt a severe blow in 2001 when a Simon employee rigged McDonald's "Monopoly" game promotion by hoarding winning game pieces. (The employee pleaded guilty to embezzlement.) McDonald's a 25-year client that accounted for the bulk of Simon's sales stopped doing business with the company as did Simon's second-largest client Philip Morris. The company then shut down its promotional marketing business to focus on resolving legal issues arising from the scandal; it has no operations.

SIMPLICITY BANCORP, INC   NMS: SMPL

1359 N. Grand Avenue
Covina, CA 91724
Phone: 800 524-2274
Fax: –
Web: www.simplicitybancorp.com

CEO: –
CFO: –
HR: –
FYE: June 30
Type: Public

Simplicity Bancorp (formerly Kaiser Federal Financial) is the holding company of Simplicity Bank (formerly Kaiser Federal Bank) a community thrift operating in Southern California and the San Francisco Bay area. With about 10 full-service branches and financial services offices Simplicity Bank offers such traditional retail deposit products as checking accounts savings accounts and CDs. The company uses deposit funds to originate or purchase a variety of loans; real estate loans make up the bulk of a lending portfolio that also includes automobile home equity and other consumer loans. Simplicity Bancorp converted to a stock holding structure in 2010.

	Annual Growth	06/10	06/11	06/12	06/13	06/14
Sales ($ mil.)	(5.8%)	49.7	48.1	45.1	43.2	39.1
Net income ($ mil.)	12.3%	3.3	8.8	7.2	6.2	5.3
Market value ($ mil.)	12.3%	–	90.8	108.9	106.8	128.6
Employees	3.1%	107	117	132	130	121

SIMPSON MANUFACTURING CO., INC. (DE)   NYS: SSD

5956 W. Las Positas Blvd.
Pleasanton, CA 94588
Phone: 925 560-9000
Fax: 925 833-1496
Web: www.simpsonmfg.com

CEO: Karen W. Colonias
CFO: Brian J. Magstadt
HR: Jennifer Lutz
FYE: December 31
Type: Public

Through its subsidiaries Simpson Manufacturing makes connectors and venting systems for the building remodeling and do-it-yourself industries. Subsidiary Simpson Strong-Tie (SST) makes more than 15000 types of standard and custom products that are used to connect and reinforce joints between wood concrete and masonry building components which the company markets globally and distributes through home centers and a network of contractor and dealer distributors. The company's products are sold primarily in Canada Europe Asia the US and the South Pacific.

	Annual Growth	12/14	12/15	12/16	12/17	12/18
Sales ($ mil.)	9.4%	752.1	794.1	860.7	977.0	1,078.8
Net income ($ mil.)	18.8%	63.5	67.9	89.7	92.6	126.6
Market value ($ mil.)	11.8%	1,556.9	1,536.7	1,968.7	2,583.3	2,435.7
Employees	6.5%	2,434	2,498	2,647	2,902	3,135

SIMPSON STRONG-TIE COMPANY INC.

5956 W. Las Positas Blvd.
Pleasanton CA 94588
Phone: 925-560-9000
Fax: 925-847-1597
Web: www.strongtie.com

CEO: Karen Colonias
CFO: –
HR: –
FYE: December 31
Type: Subsidiary

Blessed be the ties that bind a building together. Simpson Strong-Tie (SST) manufactures steel connectors for wood concrete and masonry that support buildings. The company's reinforcement products include anchors angles bases caps connectors fasteners and hangers; it also offers prefabricated shearwalls powder-actuated tools and adhesives. The Home Depot is its largest customer. SST is the operating subsidiary of Simpson Manufacturing. It serves customers in the commercial and residential construction furniture and do-it-yourself (DIY) markets. The company has manufacturing and warehouse operations in North America Europe and the Asia/Pacific region; it markets its products through distributors.

SIMS LTD   NBB: SMSM Y

Suite C - 300, 555 Theodore Fremd Avenue
Rye, NY 10010
Phone: 212 604-0710
Fax: (61) 2 8113 1622
Web: www.simsmm.com

CEO: –
CFO: –
HR: –
FYE: June 30
Type: Public

Sims Metal Management provides metal recycling services primarily in Australia the UK and the US. In addition to processing steel and non-ferrous scrap Sims also provides municipal recycling services in New York City; recycles electronics materials in Africa the Asia/Pacific region Europe and North America; and distributes and trades scrap materials throughout Europe and the Americas. In Australia the company also recycles consumer and automotive plastics and owns a 50% stake in LMS Generation a pioneer in converting landfill gas to energy. Sims has grown exponentially in the latter half of the decade having acquired about two dozen businesses in Australia North America and the UK.

	Annual Growth	06/15	06/16	06/17	06/18	06/19
Sales ($ mil.)	(1.1%)	4,863.0	3,470.0	3,910.6	4,768.5	4,659.4
Net income ($ mil.)	6.1%	84.5	(161.1)	156.4	150.3	106.9
Market value ($ mil.)	(1.1%)	1,616.8	1,165.7	2,352.7	2,438.9	1,546.8
Employees	(2.1%)	5,429	4,756	4,561	5,052	4,995

SIMULATIONS PLUS INC.
NAS: SLP

42505 Tenth Street West
Lancaster, CA 93534-7059
Phone: 661 723-7723
Fax: 661 723-5524
Web: www.simulations-plus.com

CEO: Shawn M O'Connor
CFO: John R Kneisel
HR: –
FYE: August 31
Type: Public

Molecular modeling software plus applications to help individuals with disabilities equals Simulations Plus. The company is a leading provider of applications used by pharmaceutical researchers to model absorption rates for orally dosed drug compounds. Its Words+ subsidiary provides augmentative communication software and input devices that help people with disabilities use computers. Simulations Plus also provides educational software targeted to high school and college students through its FutureLab unit. Pharmaceutical giants GlaxoSmithKline and Roche are among its clients. CEO Walter Woltosz and his wife Virginia (a director) together own about 40% of the company.

	Annual Growth	08/15	08/16	08/17	08/18	08/19
Sales ($ mil.)	16.7%	18.3	20.0	24.1	29.7	34.0
Net income ($ mil.)	22.2%	3.8	5.0	5.8	8.9	8.6
Market value ($ mil.)	52.1%	118.7	151.6	255.1	366.8	635.2
Employees	16.6%	60	63	86	95	111

SINAI HEALTH SYSTEM

1500 S FAIRFIELD AVE
CHICAGO, IL 606081782
Phone: 773-542-2000
Fax: –
Web: www.sinai.org

CEO: –
CFO: Charles Weiss
HR: –
FYE: March 31
Type: Private

You don't have to scale any mountains to reach this Sinai. Sinai Health System provides medical care for the residents of West Side of Chicago. The system is comprised of its flagship Mount Sinai Hospital Holy Cross Hospital Schwab Rehabilitation Hospital and the Sinai Children's Hospital. The health system's Sinai Medical Group provides primary and specialty care through a range of clinics in the area. The Sinai Community Institute offers health wellness and educational programs for all ages and the Sinai Urban Health Institute conducts research and disease outreach programs. Altogether the system has some 700 inpatient beds and 800 physicians.

	Annual Growth	06/04	06/05	06/06	06/08*	03/15
Assets ($ mil.)	77.1%	–	4.3	9.2	9.5	1,297.6
Net income ($ mil.)	–	–	0.0	0.0	0.0	(3.2)
Market value ($ mil.)	–	–	–	–	–	–
Employees	–	–	–	–	–	6,000

*Fiscal year change

SINAI HOSPITAL OF BALTIMORE, INC.

2401 W BELVEDERE AVE
BALTIMORE, MD 212155270
Phone: 410-601-5678
Fax: –
Web: www.sscsi.com

CEO: Neil Meltzer
CFO: –
HR: –
FYE: June 30
Type: Private

Sinai Hospital of Baltimore part of the LifeBridge Health network provides medical care in northwestern Baltimore. The 470-bed hospital is a not-for-profit medical center that includes such facilities as a heart center a children's hospital a cancer institute and a rehab center. Other specialties include orthopedics neurology and women's care. Medical students from Johns Hopkins University and the University of Maryland do some of their training at the hospital. Sinai Hospital of Baltimore was founded in 1866 as the Hebrew Hospital and Asylum and became a subsidiary of LifeBridge when it merged with other area providers in 1998.

	Annual Growth	06/13	06/14	06/15	06/16	06/17
Sales ($ mil.)	2.5%	–	714.9	677.8	690.6	769.2
Net income ($ mil.)	14.9%	–	41.6	45.2	26.6	63.1
Market value ($ mil.)	–	–	–	–	–	–
Employees	–	–	–	–	–	4,497

SINGING MACHINE CO., INC.
NBB: SMDM

6301 NW 5th Way, Suite 2900
Fort Lauderdale, FL 33309
Phone: 954 596-1000
Fax: –
Web: www.singingmachine.com

CEO: Gary Atkinson
CFO: Lionel Marquis
HR: –
FYE: March 31
Type: Public

The Singing Machine Company strives to give everyone their 15 minutes of fame. It sells more than 50 different models of karaoke audio equipment from basic players to semi-professional machines. The karaoke machines primarily made in China are sold through electronics retailers and mass merchants such as Best Buy Costco and RadioShack. About a third of its sales come from outside the US. The Singing Machine Company also produces CDs and audio tapes for use in its karaoke equipment and offers a catalog of more than 2500 songs. To clear its books of liabilities The Singing Machine Company sold its Hong Kong unit in late 2006 and consolidated its Hong Kong office into Starlight International Holdings Ltd.

	Annual Growth	03/15	03/16	03/17	03/18	03/19
Sales ($ mil.)	4.3%	39.3	48.9	52.9	60.8	46.5
Net income ($ mil.)	38.8%	0.2	1.7	1.7	0.2	0.6
Market value ($ mil.)	24.9%	6.5	12.3	18.1	15.8	15.8
Employees	8.5%	26	27	38	39	36

SINO-GLOBAL SHIPPING AMERICA LTD
NAS: SINO

1044 Northern Boulevard, Suite 305
Roslyn, NY 11576-1514
Phone: 718 888-1814
Fax: –
Web: www.sino-global.com

CEO: Lei Cao
CFO: Tuo Pan
HR: –
FYE: June 30
Type: Public

Sino-Global Shipping America assists foreign companies in navigating the murky regulatory waters of China's marine shipping industry. Through subsidiaries Trans Pacific and Sino-China the company is a shipping agent for US Australian and Hong Kong companies transporting iron ore to China. (Currently freight forwarding company Beijing Shou Rong is Sino-Global's largest customer representing more than half of the company's revenues.) Trans Pacific has operations at six ports in China; however each of the country's 76 ports have different rules. CEO Cao Lei owns more than 70% of Sino-Global Shipping America and Sino-China. Sino-Global Shipping America was founded in 2001.

	Annual Growth	06/15	06/16	06/17	06/18	06/19
Sales ($ mil.)	38.6%	11.3	7.3	11.4	23.1	41.8
Net income ($ mil.)	–	0.7	(2.0)	3.6	0.5	(6.5)
Market value ($ mil.)	(17.3%)	24.1	10.8	45.7	18.8	11.3
Employees	7.8%	20	27	24	23	27

SINTX TECHNOLOGIES INC
NAS: SINT

1885 West 2100 South
Salt Lake City, UT 84119
Phone: 801 839-3500
Fax: –
Web: www.amedicacorp.com

CEO: –
CFO: B Sonny Bal
HR: Huey Hewitson
FYE: December 31
Type: Public

You can spin a disc or burn a disc but when you blow a disc (in your back) the fun stops and Amedica steps in. It develops manufactures and commercializes joint and spine implants made of silicon nitride ceramic a more durable resistant and patient-compatible alternative to traditional implant materials. Amedica's lead product candidates are its Valeo spinal implants which are intended to restore and maintain vertebrae alignment in the neck and lower back. Valeo spinal spacer implants have received FDA and EU approval for use as vertebra replacements. Amedica's other candidates include ceramic hip and knee implants with material that mimic the porous structure of natural bone. It went public in 2014.

	Annual Growth	12/14	12/15	12/16	12/17	12/18
Sales ($ mil.)	(74.6%)	22.8	19.5	15.2	11.2	0.1
Net income ($ mil.)	–	(32.6)	(23.9)	(16.6)	(9.3)	(8.7)
Market value ($ mil.)	(36.1%)	0.6	0.1	0.5	2.4	0.1
Employees	(26.8%)	66	56	35	33	19

SIRCHIE ACQUISITION COMPANY LLC

100 Hunter Place
Youngsville NC 27596-9447
Phone: 919-554-2244
Fax: 800-899-8181
Web: www.sirchie.com

CEO: –
CFO: Jennifer Walton
HR: –
FYE: September 30
Type: Private

Sirchie Acquisition Company leaves old fingerprinting methods in the dust. The company develops manufactures and sells crime-scene investigation equipment including fingerprint gathering and recording materials forensic analysis equipment DNA kits narcotic and blood alcohol test kits and software that assists in creating composite images of crime suspects. Sirchie also has a vehicle division in New Jersey that makes surveillance vehicles for law enforcement agencies. Its corporate headquarters in North Carolina includes manufacturing facilities. The company was founded in 1927 by Francis Sirchie originally specializing in fingerprint recording. It is a portfolio company of Raymond James Financial.

SIRVA INC.

700 Oakmont Ln.
Westmont IL 60559
Phone: 630-570-3047
Fax: 415-442-4803
Web: www.frogdesign.com

CEO: Tom Oberdorf
CFO: Douglas V Gathany
HR: –
FYE: December 31
Type: Private

Whether you're moving across the street across town or across the ocean SIRVA is serious about the business of packing. One of the world's largest relocation and moving services companies SIRVA operates in more than 150 countries. Its North American brands include Allied Van Lines Global Van Lines and northAmerican Van Lines. It uses brands such as Allied Pickfords and Concept Mobility Services in other regions. The company boasts 300000-plus relocations a year; outsourced moves delivered under contract with corporate employers and government and military customers to transfer personnel account for the majority of SIRVA's sales.

SIRIUS XM HOLDINGS INC   NMS: SIRI

1221 Avenue of the Americas, 35th Floor
New York, NY 10020
Phone: 212 584-5100
Fax: –
Web: www.siriusxm.com

CEO: James E. (Jim) Meyer
CFO: David J. Frear
HR: Walt Sanderson
FYE: December 31
Type: Public

You might say radio programming from this company comes from a higher plane. SIRIUS XM Holdings operating through SIRIUS XM Radio manages satellite radio systems under the SIRIUS and XM brands that together boast more than 25 million subscribers. Each service offers more than 150 channels of CD-quality music news and talk shows. Programming includes National Football League Major League Baseball and college games as well as talk shows featuring hosts Howard Stern Martha Stewart and Oprah Winfrey. The company has equipment alliances with several automakers; it also sells satellite radio equipment through its website and through such retail outlets as Best Buy and WalMart. In 2018 SiriusXM offered $3.5 billion for music streaming company Pandora.

	Annual Growth	12/15	12/16	12/17	12/18	12/19
Sales ($ mil.)	14.3%	4,570.1	5,017.2	5,425.1	5,770.7	7,794.0
Net income ($ mil.)	15.7%	509.7	745.9	647.9	1,175.9	914.0
Market value ($ mil.)	–	0.0	0.0	0.0	0.0	0.0
Employees	18.2%	2,323	2,402	2,575	2,699	4,534

SITE CENTERS CORP   NYS: SITC

3300 Enterprise Parkway
Beachwood, OH 44122
Phone: 216 755-5500
Fax: 216 755-1500
Web: www.sitecenters.com

CEO: David R. Lukes
CFO: Matthew L. Ostrower
HR: –
FYE: December 31
Type: Public

DDR (formerly Developers Diversified Realty) is a self-administered real estate investment trust (REIT) that acquires develops renovates leases and manages retail and office properties. Its portfolio includes some 500 community shopping centers malls and other retail properties in the US Brazil and Puerto Rico. All together DDR owns more than 120 million sq. ft of space and more than 1800 acres of undeveloped land. Almost half of its shopping centers are owned through joint ventures. DDR's largest tenants include Wal-Mart PetSmart TJX and Kohl's. No longer primarily a development firm the REIT changed its name to DDR in 2011.

	Annual Growth	12/14	12/15	12/16	12/17	12/18
Sales ($ mil.)	(8.0%)	985.7	1,028.1	1,005.8	921.6	707.3
Net income ($ mil.)	(0.6%)	117.3	(72.2)	60.0	(241.7)	114.4
Market value ($ mil.)	(11.9%)	3,329.4	3,053.7	2,769.0	1,624.8	2,007.4
Employees	(10.5%)	589	576	540	447	378

SIRONA DENTAL SYSTEMS INC   NMS: SIRO

30-30 47th Avenue, Suite 500
Long Island City, NY 11101
Phone: 718 482-2011
Fax: –
Web: www.sirona.com

CEO: –
CFO: –
HR: –
FYE: September 30
Type: Public

Factoid for the day: The first electric dental drill was invented in 1882 and the company that made it is now known as Sirona Dental Systems. The firm still makes handheld dental instruments as well as imaging systems dental CAD/CAM systems used in restorations and a full line of other products used by dentists and dental laboratories worldwide. Its CEREC system is a 3-D computer-aided contraption for making ceramic restorations (such as crowns and bridges) in the dentist's office rather than a lab. Its imaging systems include traditional X-ray equipment and digital radiography systems. Other products include dental chairs and instrument cleaning systems. DENTSPLY is buying Sirona for $5.5 billion.

	Annual Growth	09/11	09/12	09/13	09/14	09/15
Sales ($ mil.)	6.2%	913.9	979.4	1,101.5	1,171.1	1,161.3
Net income ($ mil.)	11.2%	121.8	133.8	146.7	175.7	186.2
Market value ($ mil.)	21.8%	2,370.5	3,183.8	3,741.1	4,286.1	5,217.3
Employees	6.3%	2,705	2,979	3,216	3,327	3,458

SIX FLAGS ENTERTAINMENT CORP   NYS: SIX

924 Avenue J East
Grand Prairie, TX 75050
Phone: 972 595-5000
Fax: –
Web: www.sixflags.com

CEO: John M. Duffey
CFO: Marshall Barber
HR: Kathy Aslin
FYE: December 31
Type: Public

For millions of people Six Flags is the standard-bearer for theme park thrills. The company is the largest regional amusement park operator in the world drawing about 32 million visitors to its parks in North America. Of its 25 regional properties 22 are in the US two are in Mexico and one is in Canada. Fancying itself a regional entertainment destination most parks operate under the Six Flags banner (including Six Flags Fiesta Texas and Six Flags Magic Mountain) offering roller coasters and other rides water slides concerts and other entertainment. Revenues come from gate receipts food and merchandise. Six Flags licenses characters from Warner Bros. and DC Entertainment such as Looney Tunes and Batman.

	Annual Growth	12/14	12/15	12/16	12/17	12/18
Sales ($ mil.)	5.6%	1,175.8	1,263.9	1,319.4	1,359.1	1,463.7
Net income ($ mil.)	38.0%	76.0	154.7	118.3	273.8	276.0
Market value ($ mil.)	6.6%	3,623.0	4,612.9	5,034.4	5,589.4	4,670.8
Employees	7.4%	40,900	43,900	47,000	48,000	54,400

SJW GROUP

NYS: SJW

110 West Taylor Street
San Jose, CA 95110
Phone: 408 279-7800
Fax: –
Web: www.sjwater.com

CEO: W. Richard (Rich) Roth
CFO: James P. Lynch
HR: –
FYE: December 31
Type: Public

It is hard to water down SJW Group's contribution in quenching America's thirst. A holding company it owns public utility services that engage in the production storage purification distribution and retail sale of water. Its two main subsidiaries the San Jose Water Company and Canyon Lake Water Service Company (CLWSC) serves nearly 1.5 million residents in California and Texas through more than 270000 water connections. The SJW Land Company is a holder of some undeveloped land in Tennessee. In March 2018 the SJW Group announced plans of a “merger of equals” with the public utility Connecticut Water Service pending regulatory approval.

	Annual Growth	12/14	12/15	12/16	12/17	12/18
Sales ($ mil.)	5.6%	319.7	305.1	339.7	389.2	397.7
Net income ($ mil.)	(7.0%)	51.8	37.9	52.8	59.2	38.8
Market value ($ mil.)	14.7%	912.3	842.2	1,590.1	1,813.0	1,579.8
Employees	1.3%	395	399	406	411	416

SKANSKA USA CIVIL INC.

7520 ASTORIA BLVD STE 200
EAST ELMHURST, NY 113701135
Phone: 718-340-0777
Fax: –
Web: www.usa.skanska.com

CEO: Salvatore Mancini
CFO: –
HR: –
FYE: December 31
Type: Private

Skanska USA Civil builds some of the world's largest cable-stayed bridges. Part of the US operations of Swedish engineering and construction giant Skanska Skanska USA Civil focuses on infrastructure projects throughout the country. Along with sister firm Skanska USA Building it is a market leader in the New York area where it has worked on the Brooklyn Bridge the AirTrain light-rail system and the Roosevelt Island Bridge. It builds roads tunnels and rail systems in addition to bridges and industrial and marine facilities such as power and water filtration plants gas-treatment plants and dry docks.

	Annual Growth	12/04	12/05	12/06	12/07	12/08
Sales ($ mil.)	8.8%	–	–	–	1,611.5	1,753.5
Net income ($ mil.)	5.2%	–	–	–	52.0	54.7
Market value ($ mil.)	–	–	–	–	–	–
Employees	–	–	–	–	–	5,200

SKECHERS USA INC

NYS: SKX

228 Manhattan Beach Blvd.
Manhattan Beach, CA 90266
Phone: 310 318-3100
Fax: –
Web: www.skechers.com

CEO: Robert Greenberg
CFO: John Vandemore
HR: –
FYE: December 31
Type: Public

Skechers USA designs and sells 3000-plus styles of lifestyle and athletic footwear for men women and children. Its products include oxfords boots sandals sneakers training shoes and dress and semi-dressy shoes. In addition to many versions of its namesake brand (Skechers Sport Skechers Performance BOBS from Skechers Skechers Kids) the company offers high-end footwear under the Mark Nason name. Its shoes are sold through more than 2000 third-party department and specialty stores in more than 170 countries as well as some 700 company-owned concept and outlet stores and ecommerce websites. Skechers generates more than half its sales outside the US.

	Annual Growth	12/14	12/15	12/16	12/17	12/18
Sales ($ mil.)	18.2%	2,386.7	3,159.1	3,577.2	4,180.8	4,662.7
Net income ($ mil.)	21.4%	138.8	231.9	243.5	179.2	301.0
Market value ($ mil.)	(19.8%)	8,481.3	4,637.5	3,773.2	5,808.7	3,513.8
Employees	12.8%	7,772	9,200	9,800	11,800	12,600

SKF USA INC.

890 FORTY FOOT RD
LANSDALE, PA 194464303
Phone: 267-436-6000
Fax: –
Web: www.skf.com

CEO: –
CFO: Drew Cross
HR: –
FYE: December 31
Type: Private

SKF USA is a subsidiary of Swedish ball bearing giant AB SKF and a global supplier of bearings seals lubricants linear motion components and condition monitoring systems. It also specializes in related services from repair and rebuilding to consulting logistics and training. Its repair stations also provide bearing inspection repair and overhaul services. With hundreds of manufacturing sales and authorized distribution locations across the US SKF USA's offerings are geared at a wide range of industries including aerospace automotive construction machine tooling and alternative energy. Brand names include Alemite Lincoln Reelcraft and S2M.

	Annual Growth	12/10	12/11	12/12	12/13	12/14
Sales ($ mil.)	14.4%	–	–	2,397.8	2,554.4	3,138.7
Net income ($ mil.)	6.0%	–	–	138.7	95.6	155.9
Market value ($ mil.)	–	–	–	–	–	–
Employees	–	–	–	–	–	4,000

SKIDMORE COLLEGE

815 N BROADWAY
SARATOGA SPRINGS, NY 128661698
Phone: 518-580-5000
Fax: –
Web: www.skidmore.edu

CEO: –
CFO: –
HR: –
FYE: May 31
Type: Private

Skidmore College offers more than 40 degree programs including majors in both traditional liberal arts disciplines and pre-professional areas. The private college grants bachelor's and master's degrees in the sciences humanities social sciences business education social work and the arts. Skidmore enrolls about 2400 students from the US and some 40 other countries and boasts a student-faculty ratio of about 9 to 1. It was founded by Lucy Skidmore Scribner in 1903 as the Young Women's Industrial Club of Saratoga.

	Annual Growth	05/12	05/13	05/15	05/16	05/17
Sales ($ mil.)	11.2%	–	140.2	216.3	229.2	214.7
Net income ($ mil.)	(26.0%)	–	32.8	19.4	65.2	9.9
Market value ($ mil.)	–	–	–	–	–	–
Employees	–	–	–	–	–	720

SKILLSOFT CORPORATION

300 INNOVATIVE WAY # 201
NASHUA, NH 030625746
Phone: 603-324-3000
Fax: –
Web: www.skillsoft.com

CEO: Bill Donoghue
CFO: Tom McDonald
HR: –
FYE: January 31
Type: Private

SkillSoft provides cloud-based training courses and software for business and information technology (IT) professionals. It offers more than 7000 courses and 65000 videos on business compliance safety and technology. The firm's SkillPort software manages corporate e-learning programs and its SkillSoft Dialogue portal helps clients create custom learning sessions. SkillSoft also offers online mentoring for some 100 IT certification exams and its Books24x7 allows customers to search more than 46000 professional reference reports and books online. SkillSoft is owned by investment firm Charterhouse Capital Partners.

	Annual Growth	01/05	01/06	01/07	01/08	01/09
Sales ($ mil.)	20.8%	–	–	225.2	281.2	328.5
Net income ($ mil.)	45.0%	–	–	24.2	60.0	50.8
Market value ($ mil.)	–	–	–	–	–	–
Employees	–	–	–	–	–	2,133

SKINVISIBLE INC
NBB: SKVI

6320 South Sandhill Road, Suite 10
Las Vegas, NV 89120
Phone: 702 433-7154
Fax: –

CEO: Terry H Howlett
CFO: Terry H Howlett
HR: –
FYE: December 31
Type: Public

Skinvisible keeps invisible substances like lotion and sunscreen from washing off your skin. The company develops topical drug delivery systems for dermatology and healthcare products including products to treat acne eczema fungal infections and inflammation as well as sunscreens anti-aging products pre-surgical preparations and various other medical treatments using its Invisicare technology. Licensing its delivery technology is the goal of the firm; its clients include dermatological and other drugmakers cosmetics companies and manufacturers of personal care items in Asia Europe and the US. Licensees include DRJ Group J.D. Nelson & Associates and Embil Pharmaceutical.

	Annual Growth	12/14	12/15	12/16	12/17	12/18
Sales ($ mil.)	6.0%	0.1	0.2	0.1	0.6	0.1
Net income ($ mil.)	–	(1.9)	(2.0)	(2.1)	(1.8)	0.2
Market value ($ mil.)	–	0.1	0.1	0.0	0.1	0.0
Employees	(5.4%)	5	4	3	4	4

SKULLCANDY INC
NMS: SKUL

1441 West Ute Boulevard, Suite 250
Park City, UT 84098
Phone: 435 940-1545
Fax: –
Web: www.skullcandy.com

CEO: Jason Hodell
CFO: –
HR: –
FYE: December 31
Type: Public

If your head craves sweet tunes Skullcandy has a treat for you. The youth-oriented firm designs and sells edgy stylish headphones ear buds docking speakers and other audio goodies as well as apparel and accessories under the Skullcandy Astro Gaming and 2XL brands. Featuring an aesthetic that appeals to its target audience of action sports enthusiasts the gear was originally sold at specialty shops but can also be found nationwide at Target and Best Buy through the company's website and in more than 80 countries where youth culture thrives. Skullcandy retains its street cred by sponsoring boarders surfers and BMX bikers. Founded in 2003 Skullcandy went public in 2011.

	Annual Growth	12/10	12/11	12/12	12/13	12/14
Sales ($ mil.)	11.5%	160.6	232.5	297.7	210.1	247.8
Net income ($ mil.)	–	(9.7)	18.6	25.8	(3.0)	7.6
Market value ($ mil.)	(9.8%)	–	353.6	220.0	203.6	259.5
Employees	10.7%	200	290	335	295	300

SKYLINE CHAMPION CORP
NYS: SKY

755 West Big Beaver Road, Suite 1000
Troy, MI 48084
Phone: 248 614-8211
Fax: –
Web: www.skylinechampion.com

CEO: Keith Anderson
CFO: Laurie Hough
HR: –
FYE: March 30
Type: Public

Skyline's idea of a beautiful skyline would probably include several rows of doublewides. The company and its subsidiaries design and make manufactured homes. It distributes them to independent dealers and manufactured housing communities throughout the US and Canada. About half of Skyline's revenues come from selling HUD-code manufactured homes (products built according to US Housing and Urban Development standards); the rest of its typically two- to four-bedroom homes are modular in design.

	Annual Growth	05/14	05/15	05/16	05/17*	03/19
Sales ($ mil.)	48.0%	191.7	187.0	211.8	236.5	1,360.0
Net income ($ mil.)	–	(11.9)	(10.4)	1.7	0.0	(58.2)
Market value ($ mil.)	31.6%	272.5	187.0	584.7	298.0	1,076.5
Employees	40.0%	1,300	1,200	1,350	1,300	7,000

*Fiscal year change

SKYWEST INC.
NMS: SKYW

444 South River Road
St. George, UT 84790
Phone: 435 634-3000
Fax: –
Web: www.skywest.com

CEO: Russell A. (Chip) Childs
CFO: Robert J. (Rob) Simmons
HR: –
FYE: December 31
Type: Public

SkyWest Inc. is the holding company for SkyWest Airlines and SkyWest Leasing. SkyWest has destinations to about 260 cities in the US Canada Mexico and the Caribbean supporting approximately 2500 daily departures. Combined SkyWest's carriers operate a fleet of over 480 aircraft consisting of Canadair regional jets (CRJs made by Bombardier) and Embraer aircraft. SkyWest also operates through code-sharing agreements with United Airlines (operating as United Express) Delta Air Lines (Delta Connection) American Airlines (American Eagle) and Alaska Airlines. (Code-sharing allows airlines to sell tickets on one another's flights.) In 2018 Wallethub ranked SkyWest Airlines the third-best overall US airline behind Alaska Airlines and Delta. In 2019 the company sold its subsidiary to United Airlines ManaAir for $70 million.

	Annual Growth	12/14	12/15	12/16	12/17	12/18
Sales ($ mil.)	(0.1%)	3,237.4	3,095.6	3,121.2	3,204.3	3,221.7
Net income ($ mil.)	–	(24.2)	117.8	(161.6)	428.9	280.4
Market value ($ mil.)	35.3%	682.4	977.4	1,873.1	2,728.7	2,285.2
Employees	(3.7%)	18,500	18,300	16,900	16,300	15,900

SKYWORKS SOLUTIONS INC
NMS: SWKS

20 Sylvan Road
Woburn, MA 01801
Phone: 781 376-3000
Fax: –
Web: www.skyworksinc.com

CEO: Liam K. Griffin
CFO: Kris Sennesael
HR: Kari Durham
FYE: September 27
Type: Public

Skyworks Solutions makes computer chips that make sure wireless devices such as smartphones don't get their signals crossed. Its flagship handset products handle amplification filtering tuning power management and audio processing in phones made by Apple Inc. Samsung Electronics Huawei HTC and ZTE. Other devices include attenuators diodes couplers phase shifters receivers and switches used in a broad array of industries. The company's non-mobile customers in the automotive industrial and health and medical businesses provide a significant portion of revenue. About 50% of the company's sales are to companies with headquarters in the US.

	Annual Growth	10/15*	09/16	09/17	09/18	09/19
Sales ($ mil.)	0.9%	3,258.4	3,289.0	3,651.4	3,868.0	3,376.8
Net income ($ mil.)	1.7%	798.3	995.2	1,010.2	918.4	853.6
Market value ($ mil.)	(2.0%)	14,298.6	12,951.4	17,333.2	15,429.8	13,177.6
Employees	7.7%	6,700	7,300	8,400	9,400	9,000

*Fiscal year change

SL GREEN REALTY CORP
NYS: SLG

420 Lexington Avenue
New York, NY 10170
Phone: 212 594-2700
Fax: –
Web: www.slgreen.com

CEO: Marc Holliday
CFO: Matthew J. DiLiberto
HR: Lynne-Courtne Hodges
FYE: December 31
Type: Public

SL Green Realty is a self-managed real estate investment trust (REIT) that acquires develops manages and leases commercial properties?primarily office buildings in the New York metropolitan area (one of the US's largest office markets). The firm has interests in some 80 consolidated and unconsolidated properties in Manhattan buildings totaling more than 30 million square feet. SL Green owns both Class B assets?buildings older than 25 years but in desirable locations and in generally good condition?and Class A assets?new properties which garner the highest rents in their markets. SL Green's largest tenants by rentable square feet are Credit Suisse Securities (USA) Viacom Sony and Debevoise & Plimpton. The REIT also provides real estate financing via structured finance originations and preferred equity investments.

	Annual Growth	12/14	12/15	12/16	12/17	12/18
Sales ($ mil.)	(5.2%)	1,520.0	1,662.8	1,864.0	1,511.5	1,227.4
Net income ($ mil.)	(16.9%)	518.1	284.1	249.9	101.4	247.3
Market value ($ mil.)	(9.7%)	9,960.1	9,454.6	9,000.2	8,446.2	6,617.7
Employees	(0.0%)	1,060	1,177	1,075	1,065	1,058

SL INDUSTRIES INC.
ASE: SLI

520 Fellowship Road, Suite A114
Mt. Laurel, NJ 08054
Phone: 856 727-1500
Fax: –
Web: www.slindustries.com

CEO: –
CFO: –
HR: –
FYE: December 31
Type: Public

SL Industries has the power to protect. Operating through four business segments SL Industries makes and markets custom and standard AC/DC and DC/DC power supplies surge suppressors conditioning and distribution units motion-control systems and power protection equipment. Products are typically married to larger systems to improve their operating performance and safety. SL sells its power electronics and systems and related products to OEMs in the aerospace computer medical wireless and wireline communications infrastructure and transportation industries as well as to US military contractors and municipal utilities.

	Annual Growth	12/10	12/11	12/12	12/13	12/14
Sales ($ mil.)	1.9%	189.8	212.3	200.6	204.7	204.4
Net income ($ mil.)	64.9%	2.6	8.2	7.8	8.2	18.9
Market value ($ mil.)	22.2%	72.5	67.1	74.6	112.3	161.6
Employees	(3.3%)	1,600	1,600	1,400	1,400	1,400

SLALOM LLC

821 2nd Ave. Ste. 1900
Seattle WA 98104
Phone: 206-438-5700
Fax: 206-438-5686
Web: www.slalom.com

CEO: –
CFO: –
HR: –
FYE: December 31
Type: Private

Slalom has both feet on the ground when it comes to helping businesses succeed. Operating as Slalom Consulting the company provides consulting services in the areas of information technology management and development (application development system analysis and design project and program management); business management (business intelligence and improving corporate processes strategies and operations); and financial (enterprise resource planning compliance and reporting). Slalom Consulting maintains a dozen offices in Atlanta Chicago Dallas Denver Los Angeles New York San Francisco Portland Oregon and other major cities. The company was founded in 2001.

SLEEP NUMBER CORP
NMS: SNBR

1001 Third Avenue South
Minneapolis, MN 55404
Phone: 763 551-7000
Fax: –
Web: www.sleepnumber.com

CEO: Shelly R. Ibach
CFO: David R. Callen
HR: –
FYE: December 29
Type: Public

Sleep Number Corporation (formerly Select Comfort) has got your number. The firm's line of Sleep Number beds which can carry hefty price tags use air-chamber technology to allow sleepers to adjust the firmness on each side of the mattress providing better sleep quality and addressing sleep-related problems such as lower back pain. Sleep Number Corporation also offers foundations frames pillows and a sofa bed. A leading bedding retailer in the US the company operates 550 company-owned stores in the US. The air-bed maker also sells through a company-operated call center its own website and on the QVC shopping channel. Sleep Number Corporation was founded in 1987 has grown to become one of the nation's leading bed makers and retailers. It changed its name from Select Comfort to Sleep Number in 2017.

	Annual Growth	01/15	01/16*	12/16	12/17	12/18
Sales ($ mil.)	9.8%	1,156.8	1,213.7	1,311.3	1,444.5	1,531.6
Net income ($ mil.)	0.8%	68.0	50.5	51.4	65.1	69.5
Market value ($ mil.)	6.1%	829.4	660.9	698.2	1,160.3	991.8
Employees	10.3%	3,149	3,484	3,768	4,099	4,220

*Fiscal year change

SLEEPMED INCORPORATED

200 CORPORATE PL STE 5
PEABODY, MA 019603840
Phone: 978-536-7400
Fax: –
Web: www.sleepmedinc.com

CEO: Sean Heyniger
CFO: Jack Fiedor
HR: –
FYE: December 31
Type: Private

SleepMed tracks your vital signs while you count sheep. The company provides diagnostic tests and treatments for patients with sleep disorders through more than 160 sleep centers located in hospitals medical clinics and freestanding clinics nationwide. SleepMed also partners with epilepsy centers to provide brain monitoring services to patients suffering from seizures or unexplained neurologic episodes. Patients who don't want to travel for treatment can make use of SleepMed's in-home diagnostic services. The company designs and produces neurological testing equipment under the DigiTrace brand. SleepMed was formed by the 1999 merger of DigiTrace Care Services and Sleep Disorder Centers of America.

	Annual Growth	12/06	12/07	12/08	12/09	12/10
Sales ($ mil.)	(54.2%)	–	–	437.3	96.0	91.9
Net income ($ mil.)	5680.4%	–	–	0.0	2.3	1.7
Market value ($ mil.)	–	–	–	–	–	–
Employees	–	–	–	–	–	945

SLM CORP.
NMS: SLM

300 Continental Drive
Newark, DE 19713
Phone: 302 451-0200
Fax: –
Web: www.salliemae.com

CEO: Raymond J. Quinlan
CFO: Steven J. McGarry
HR: –
FYE: December 31
Type: Public

If SLM doesn't seem familiar perhaps you know it by its more common moniker Sallie Mae. Holding more than $8 billion in student loans SLM's main subsidiary Sallie Mae Bank is one of the nation's largest education loan providers and specializes in originating acquiring financing and servicing private student loans which are not guaranteed by the government. The company also earns fees for its processing and administrative offerings through various subsidiaries.

	Annual Growth	12/14	12/15	12/16	12/17	12/18
Assets ($ mil.)	19.7%	12,972.2	15,214.1	18,533.0	21,779.6	26,638.2
Net income ($ mil.)	25.9%	194.2	274.3	250.3	288.9	487.5
Market value ($ mil.)	(5.0%)	4,439.6	2,840.6	4,801.2	4,923.2	3,620.5
Employees	14.2%	1,000	1,200	1,300	1,500	1,700

SLOAN IMPLEMENT COMPANY, INC.

120 N BUSINESS 51
ASSUMPTION, IL 625101120
Phone: 217-226-4411
Fax: –
Web: www.sloans.com

CEO: –
CFO: –
HR: –
FYE: December 31
Type: Private

There's no slowin' down at Sloan Implement. The company provides the tools of trade for farmers in Illinois. Headquartered in Assumption Illinois Sloan is an authorized dealer of John Deere equipment and new and used parts. Founded in 1931 the company sells and services new and used Deere equipment including combines tractors manure spreaders tillers earth moving and lawn machinery and grain-handling equipment at five locations in Wisconsin and at 11 locations in Illinois; it also ships products nationwide and to international customers.

	Annual Growth	12/03	12/04	12/05	12/06	12/07
Sales ($ mil.)	10.8%	–	159.4	150.5	146.2	217.2
Net income ($ mil.)	27.2%	–	4.6	5.2	4.3	9.4
Market value ($ mil.)	–	–	–	–	–	–
Employees	–	–	–	–	–	350

SM ENERGY CO.

NYS: SM

1775 Sherman Street, Suite 1200
Denver, CO 80203
Phone: 303 861-8140
Fax: 303 861-0934
Web: www.sm-energy.com

CEO: Javan D. (Jay) Ottoson
CFO: A. Wade Pursell
HR: –
FYE: December 31
Type: Public

SM Energy looks for energy (mainly natural gas) across the continental US. While the oil and gas exploration and production company spreads its operations across the US (the Gulf Coast the Williston Basin in North Dakota and Montana and the Permian Basin in West Texas and New Mexico the Eagle Ford shale in South Texas and the Haynesville Shale play in East Texas) it gets most of its revenues from South Texas and the Gulf Coast. In 2015 the company posted estimated proved reserves of 471.3 million barrels of oil equivalent 14% down on 2014 as the result of the sale of its Mid-Continent assets.

	Annual Growth	12/14	12/15	12/16	12/17	12/18
Sales ($ mil.)	(4.9%)	2,522.3	1,557.0	1,217.5	1,129.4	2,067.1
Net income ($ mil.)	(6.5%)	666.1	(447.7)	(757.7)	(160.8)	508.4
Market value ($ mil.)	(20.4%)	4,330.3	2,206.7	3,870.1	2,478.3	1,737.5
Employees	(9.1%)	896	786	607	635	611

SMALLBIZPROS INC.

160 Hawthorne Park
Athens GA 30606
Phone: 706-548-1040
Fax: 800-548-1040
Web: www.smallbizpros.com

CEO: Steven Rafsky
CFO: –
HR: –
FYE: May 31
Type: Private

SmallBizPros knows the pros and cons of small businesses. Through Padgett Business Services the company and its franchisees provide business advice tax consulting and preparation government compliance and financial reporting and payroll services to small businesses throughout the US and Canada. As suggested by its name SmallBizPros targets owner-operated companies with fewer than 20 employees. There are more than 400 owner-operated offices in the company's network. SmallBizPros was founded as an accounting firm in 1965 and began franchising in 1975.

SMART & FINAL INC.

600 Citadel Dr.
Commerce CA 90040
Phone: 323-869-7500
Fax: 323-869-7865
Web: www.smartandfinal.com

CEO: George Golleher
CFO: –
HR: –
FYE: December 31
Type: Private

Smart & Final caters to caterers — as well as small businesses restaurants and households in the western US. Its 235 non-membership warehouse stores stock groceries party supplies paper products cleaning supplies and more in bulk sizes and quantities. The stores operate under the Smart & Final Smart & Final Extra! and Cash & Carry banners in urban and suburban areas in Arizona California Idaho Nevada Oregon and Washington as well as northern Mexico. Founded in 1871 in Los Angeles it later took the names of owners J. S. Smart and H. D. Final. The chain's owner Apollo Management has agreed to sell a majority stake in Smart & Final to private equity firm Ares Management for about $975 million.

SMART MODULAR TECHNOLOGIES INC.

39870 Eureka Dr.
Newark CA 94560
Phone: 510-623-1231
Fax: 510-623-1434
Web: www.smartm.com

CEO: –
CFO: –
HR: –
FYE: August 31
Type: Private

SMART is smart because of its memory. The company is a top global designer and manufacturer of memory products such as flash memory cards solid-state drives (SSDs) and DRAM modules. Original equipment makers in the computer defense gaming networking telecom and other sectors use its products and supply chain services. SMART has counted HP Cisco and Dell among its largest customers. In 2011 the company was taken private by equity investors Silver Lake Partners and Silver Lake Sumeru in a deal valued at around $645 million. The move allowed it shed the regulatory and market burdens of a public company to better navigate the notoriously cyclical DRAM industry.

SMARTFINANCIAL INC

NAS: SMBK

5401 Kingston Pike, Suite 600
Knoxville, TN 37919
Phone: 865 437-5700
Fax: –
Web: www.smartfinancialinc.com

CEO: William Y Carroll Jr
CFO: C Bryan Johnson
HR: –
FYE: December 31
Type: Public

Cornerstone Bancshares is the holding company for Cornerstone Community Bank which operates about five locations in Chattanooga Tennessee and surrounding communities in addition to two loan production offices in Knoxville Tennessee and Dalton Georgia. The bank offers standard retail and commercial services including checking and savings accounts money market accounts and CDs. Its lending activities primarily consist of commercial real estate loans residential mortgages real estate construction loans and business and agricultural loans. Another subsidiary of Cornerstone Bancshares Eagle Financial purchases accounts receivable and acts as a conduit lender.

	Annual Growth	12/14	12/15	12/16	12/17	12/18
Assets ($ mil.)	52.9%	415.7	1,024.0	1,062.5	1,720.8	2,274.4
Net income ($ mil.)	82.3%	1.6	1.5	5.8	5.0	18.1
Market value ($ mil.)	53.3%	46.1	224.2	258.6	302.4	254.6
Employees	38.9%	104	225	222	343	387

SMARTPROS LTD

NAS: SPRO

12 Skyline Drive
Hawthorne, NY 10532
Phone: 914 345-2620
Fax: –
Web: www.smartpros.com

CEO: Allen S Greene
CFO: Stanley P Wirtheim
HR: –
FYE: December 31
Type: Public

SmartPros counts on accountants and engineers to keep its numbers shipshape. SmartPros offers professional development courses in online DVD and CD-ROM formats. Its classes are used by accounting finance engineering legal and business professionals to build skills keep certifications current and prepare for certification testing. The company also offers executive workshops consulting and e-learning training program development. Among its offerings are courses in auditing design compliance ethics financial reporting project management and safety. CPE (continuing professional education) credits can be earned immediately by passing tests offered at the end of accredited courses.

	Annual Growth	12/09	12/10	12/11	12/12	12/13
Sales ($ mil.)	(3.3%)	19.3	17.6	17.0	15.9	16.8
Net income ($ mil.)	(22.6%)	0.4	(0.1)	0.2	(1.9)	0.1
Market value ($ mil.)	(8.0%)	16.3	11.2	8.8	6.9	11.7
Employees	(8.2%)	100	89	82	76	71

SMARTRONIX, INC.

44150 SMARTRONIX WAY
HOLLYWOOD, MD 206363172
Phone: 301-373-6000
Fax: –
Web: www.smartronixstore.com

CEO: –
CFO: Joseph Gerczak
HR: –
FYE: December 31
Type: Private

Smartronix works an intelligent approach to electronics. Serving the US Department of Defense and other federal agencies its IT products and services include cyber security cloud computing enterprise software health IT network operations and mission-focused engineering. The company specializes in application development business management network management and systems engineering. Founded in 1995 Smartronix offers ruggedized computing and communications equipment and network diagnostic tools. The company counts the US Air Force Marine Corps and Navy among its regular clients as well as the Department of Homeland Security and the Transportation Security Administration.

	Annual Growth	10/03	10/04	10/05	10/06*	12/07
Sales ($ mil.)	0.0%	–	–	–	78.5	78.5
Net income ($ mil.)	0.0%	–	–	–	4.1	4.1
Market value ($ mil.)	–	–	–	–	–	–
Employees	–	–	–	–	–	566

*Fiscal year change

SMEAD MANUFACTURING COMPANY

600 Smead Blvd.
Hastings MN 55033
Phone: 651-437-4111
Fax: 800-959-9134
Web: www.smead.com

CEO: Sharon L Avent
CFO: –
HR: –
FYE: April 30
Type: Private

Smead Manufacturing has kept its customers' offices organized for more than a century. The company manufactures and distributes more than 1500 paper filing products in the US that are sold in office supply stores nationwide (including Office Depot) and authorized resellers (such as Amazon.com). Smead's product assortment includes folders (hanging tabbed and expandable) labels fasteners and binder and report covers. The company also provides open and secure shelving systems. The company was founded in 1906 by Charles Smead; following his death Smead Manufacturing was purchased by P. A. Hoffman an employee whose granddaughter Sharon Hoffman Avent is president and CEO.

SMG INDUSTRIES INC

710 N. Post Oak Road, Suite 315
Houston, TX 77024
Phone: 713 821-3153
Fax: –
Web: www.smgindustries.com

NBB: SMGI
CEO: Matthew C Flemming
CFO: Matthew C Flemming
HR: –
FYE: December 31
Type: Public

SMG Indium Resources has a simple plan. The company has amassed a stockpile of indium (42.5 metric tons) in a vault and plans to sit on it for a few years and ride the appreciation all the way to the bank. The group may lease lend or sell portions (or even all) of its stockpile based on market conditions but does not have any plans to actively speculate on the short-term fluctuations in the price of the metal. Number 49 on the Periodic Table indium has a number of industrial applications and its use in the manufacture of flat panel displays has created significant demand for the metal. Indium is also used in solar energy technology. SMG Indium filed an IPO in 2011 and made its first sale in 2012.

	Annual Growth	12/14	12/15	12/16	12/17	12/18
Sales ($ mil.)	(32.3%)	21.1	–	–	2.5	4.4
Net income ($ mil.)	–	4.8	(0.5)	(0.4)	(0.7)	(1.1)
Market value ($ mil.)	(28.5%)	21.4	2.1	3.2	9.5	5.6
Employees	105.0%	3	3	3	34	53

SMITH (A O) CORP

11270 West Park Place
Milwaukee, WI 53224-9508
Phone: 414 359-4000
Fax: 414 359-4115
Web: www.aosmith.com

NYS: AOS
CEO: Ajita G. Rajendra
CFO: John J. Kita
HR: Jill Franz
FYE: December 31
Type: Public

Water-heating company A.O. Smith makes equipment for residential and commercial users. Its products include home gas and electric water heaters and large-scale commercial water heating systems. Its Lochinvar subsidiary specializes in high efficiency water heaters boilers pool heaters and storage tanks. Some of A.O. Smith's most prominent brands include American Water Heaters Aquasana and GSW. A.O. Smith sells its products in North America and China where it generates the majority of its revenue through a network of more than 1300 wholesale distributors as well as large hardware and home center retail chains such as Lowe's.

	Annual Growth	12/14	12/15	12/16	12/17	12/18
Sales ($ mil.)	7.9%	2,356.0	2,536.5	2,685.9	2,996.7	3,187.9
Net income ($ mil.)	20.9%	207.8	282.9	326.5	296.5	444.2
Market value ($ mil.)	(6.7%)	9,485.9	12,882.7	7,962.3	10,304.8	7,180.4
Employees	7.1%	12,400	13,400	15,500	16,100	16,300

SMITH MICRO SOFTWARE INC

5800 Corporate Drive
Pittsburgh, PA 15237
Phone: 412 837-5300
Fax: –
Web: www.smithmicro.com

NAS: SMSI
CEO: William W Smith Jr
CFO: Timothy C Huffmyer
HR: –
FYE: December 31
Type: Public

Smith Micro Software provides wireless connectivity software designed to enhance the mobile experience for users and optimize network operations for enterprises and wireless service providers. Its primary product families include QuickLink (mobile internet connection) NetWise (data traffic management) and CommSuite (voice messaging and video). The company which operates primarily in the Americas counts wireless carriers such as Sprint and Verizon Wireless among its leading customers. In addition to wireless connectivity software Smith Micro develops productivity and graphics software for artists educators and other consumers.

	Annual Growth	12/14	12/15	12/16	12/17	12/18
Sales ($ mil.)	(8.2%)	37.0	39.5	28.2	23.0	26.3
Net income ($ mil.)	–	(11.8)	(2.6)	(14.5)	(6.7)	(2.7)
Market value ($ mil.)	16.7%	27.4	20.6	44.3	80.2	50.8
Employees	(4.4%)	183	191	173	161	153

SMITH'S FOOD & DRUG CENTERS INC.

1550 S. Redwood Rd.
Salt Lake City UT 84104
Phone: 801-974-1400
Fax: 801-974-1676
Web: www.smithsfoodanddrug.com

CEO: –
CFO: –
HR: –
FYE: January 31
Type: Subsidiary

From a small grocery store founded by Ren Smith in Brigham City Utah Smith's Food & Drug has grown into a regional powerhouse with supermarkets in Nevada New Mexico and Utah. Major markets include Las Vegas Salt Lake City and Albuquerque. Most of its 130-plus stores are conventional supermarkets with in-store pharmacy departments and many offering bakeries one-hour photo labs and other services. The regional chain also operates about a half a dozen larger Smith's Marketplace stores (154000 sq. ft. on average) in Utah that combine full-service grocery pharmacy and general merchandise departments. Smith's joined the Kroger family when Kroger the #1 US grocer bought its parent Fred Meyer in 1999.

SMITH-MIDLAND CORP.
NBB: SMID

5119 Catlett Road, P.O. Box 300
Midland, VA 22728
Phone: 540 439-3266
Fax: 540 439-1232
Web: www.smithmidland.com

CEO: Ashley B Smith
CFO: Adam J Krick
HR: –
FYE: December 31
Type: Public

Smith-Midland has cemented its reputation with stone and concrete products. The company sells its patented precast concrete products to contractors and federal state and local transportation authorities in the mid-Atlantic midwestern and northeastern US. Products include lightweight concrete and steel exterior wall systems (Slenderwall) precast concrete safety and sound barriers (J-J Hooks) roadside sound barriers (Sierra Wall) portable concrete buildings and farm products primarily cattleguards and water and feed troughs. Smith-Midland licenses its products to precast concrete makers in Australia Belgium New Zealand North America and Spain.

	Annual Growth	12/14	12/15	12/16	12/17	12/18
Sales ($ mil.)	15.7%	22.5	29.2	40.1	41.7	40.2
Net income ($ mil.)	–	(0.8)	1.0	2.8	2.7	1.7
Market value ($ mil.)	35.9%	11.2	16.7	27.4	35.0	38.2
Employees	29.0%	156	205	203	242	432

SMITHSONIAN INSTITUTION

1000 JEFFERSON DR SW
WASHINGTON, DC 205600009
Phone: 202-633-1000
Fax: –
Web: www.si.edu

CEO: Gary M Beer
CFO: Alice C Maroni
HR: –
FYE: September 30
Type: Private

The Smithsonian Institution has many hats from the one worn by Harrison Ford in the Indiana Jones movies to the one worn by Abraham Lincoln the night he was assassinated. One of the world's leading cultural institutions the Smithsonian houses some 155 million objects in 19 museums and galleries most of which are on the National Mall in Washington DC. Roughly 30 million people visit every year to view the Smithsonian's exhibits on art music TV and film science history and other subjects. Admission to all but one of the Smithsonian's facilities is free; only the Cooper-Hewitt National Design Museum in New York charges admission.

	Annual Growth	09/14	09/15	09/16	09/17	09/18
Sales ($ mil.)	3.4%	–	1,412.7	1,541.3	1,514.7	1,563.5
Net income ($ mil.)	51.8%	–	50.6	192.3	153.2	177.0
Market value ($ mil.)	–	–	–	–	–	–
Employees	–	–	–	–	–	6,100

SMUCKER (J.M.) CO.
NYS: SJM

One Strawberry Lane
Orrville, OH 44667-0280
Phone: 330 682-3000
Fax: –
Web: www.jmsmucker.com

CEO: Mark T. Smucker
CFO: Mark R. Belgya
HR: Jill Penrose
FYE: April 30
Type: Public

The J. M. Smucker Company gets its bread and butter from more than just jelly. The food and beverage company known for its namesake Smucker's fruit spread has an extended product portfolio that includes Folgers coffee (the top brand in the US) Jif peanut butter (the top brand in the US) and Milk-Bone dog snacks (the top brand in the US); other products include shortening and oils frozen sandwiches and juices. It generates roughly equal parts of its revenue from pet foods coffee and consumer foods. Smucker's generates more than 90% of its sales in the US.

	Annual Growth	04/15	04/16	04/17	04/18	04/19
Sales ($ mil.)	8.3%	5,692.7	7,811.2	7,392.3	7,357.1	7,838.0
Net income ($ mil.)	10.5%	344.9	688.7	592.3	1,338.6	514.4
Market value ($ mil.)	1.4%	13,185.0	14,443.0	14,413.4	12,975.7	13,948.2
Employees	0.1%	7,370	6,910	7,140	7,000	7,400

SNAP-ON, INC.
NYS: SNA

2801 80th Street
Kenosha, WI 53143
Phone: 262 656-5200
Fax: 262 656-5577
Web: www.snapon.com

CEO: Nicholas T. Pinchuk
CFO: Aldo J. Pagliari
HR: Jim McKibbin
FYE: December 29
Type: Public

Snap-on is a manufacturer and distributor of high-quality hand tools as well as auto diagnostic equipment and "under-car" shop implements such as hydraulic lifts and tire changers. Snap-on has built a business serving mechanics car makers and government and industrial organizations. Other products — with brand names such as Snap-on Blackhawk Lindstr- ¶m ShopKey and Sun — include collision repair equipment management software roll cabinets tool chests wheel balancers and wrenches. Founded in 1920 Snap-on originated the mobile-van tool distribution channel in the automotive repair market.

	Annual Growth	01/15	01/16*	12/16	12/17	12/18
Sales ($ mil.)	5.2%	3,492.6	3,593.1	3,711.8	4,000.3	4,070.4
Net income ($ mil.)	17.2%	421.9	478.7	546.4	557.7	679.9
Market value ($ mil.)	1.9%	7,579.2	9,533.4	9,524.5	9,693.0	8,021.9
Employees	3.4%	11,400	11,500	11,500	12,600	12,600

*Fiscal year change

SNAPPING SHOALS ELECTRIC TRUST, INC.

14750 BROWN BRIDGE RD
COVINGTON, GA 300164113
Phone: 770-786-3484
Fax: –
Web: www.ssemc.com

CEO: Bradley Kent Thomas
CFO: Carl Smith
HR: –
FYE: December 31
Type: Private

Named after a geographic area that sounds like an angler's dream Snapping Shoals Electric Membership Corporation (Snapping Shoals EMC) distributes electricity to 95000 residential commercial and industrial customers in an 8-county region in the southeastern portion of the Atlanta metropolitan area. The member-owned cooperative also provides competitive retail natural gas supply services to customers through Snapping Shoals Energy Management Company a partnership with SCANA. Snapping Shoals EMC also offers security systems surge protection services and security lighting options.

	Annual Growth	12/13	12/14	12/15	12/16	12/17
Sales ($ mil.)	1.9%	–	174.0	168.3	190.6	183.9
Net income ($ mil.)	–	–	3.2	3.4	0.0	0.0
Market value ($ mil.)	–	–	–	–	–	–
Employees	–	–	–	–	–	270

SNYDER'S-LANCE, INC.

13515 BALLANTYN CORP PL
CHARLOTTE, NC 282772706
Phone: 704-554-1421
Fax: –
Web: www.snyderslance.com

CEO: Brian J. Driscoll
CFO: Alexander W. Pease
HR: Emily Berwager
FYE: December 30
Type: Private

If you're familiar with the munchies named Toastchee Nip Chee and Captain's Wafers Snyder's-Lance (formerly Lance) has undoubtedly helped you satisfy a snack attack. The company produces single-serve multi-pack and family-sized packages of bakery products and sweet and savory snack foods including cookies crackers nuts potato chips and pretzels. Its snacks are sold under the Lance Cape Cod Tom's Archway and Snyder's brands at food retailers mass merchants and convenience and club stores in the US. International brands include Kettle Chips and Metcalfe's popcorn. The company also makes private-label and branded snacks for food makers. Snyder's-Lance agreed to its acquisition by The Campbell Soup company in 2017 in a $4.9 billion deal.

	Annual Growth	12/12	12/13*	01/15*	12/16	12/17
Sales ($ mil.)	6.0%	–	1,761.0	1,620.9	2,109.2	2,226.8
Net income ($ mil.)	17.2%	–	79.1	192.5	14.7	149.3
Market value ($ mil.)	–	–	–	–	–	–
Employees	–	–	–	–	–	5,900

*Fiscal year change

SOCIETY OF MANUFACTURING ENGINEERS

1 SME DR
DEARBORN, MI 481282408
Phone: 313-425-3000
Fax: –
Web: www.sme.org

CEO: Jeff Krause
CFO: –
HR: –
FYE: December 31
Type: Private

The Society of Manufacturing Engineer (SME) has members in more than 70 countries. The society provides manufacturing engineers and executives with ongoing information on new and improved technologies as well as professional-development resources. It also organizes expositions and other industry-related events and publishes the monthly magazine Manufacturing Engineering along with a number of peer-reviewed journals and research publications. SME was founded by 33 original members in 1932 as The Society of Tool Engineers. It adopted its current name in 1969. Along with its headquarters in Dearborn Michigan SME also has an office in Toronto.

	Annual Growth	12/00	12/01	12/09	12/10	12/13
Sales ($ mil.)	(25.9%)	–	1,994.3	0.4	26.9	55.1
Net income ($ mil.)	–	–	–	(0.2)	1.8	3.2
Market value ($ mil.)	–	–	–	–	–	–
Employees	–	–	–	–	–	200

SOCKET MOBILE INC

39700 Eureka Drive
Newark, CA 94560
Phone: 510 933-3000
Fax: –
Web: www.socketmobile.com

NAS: SCKT

CEO: Kevin J Mills
CFO: Lynn Zhao
HR: –
FYE: December 31
Type: Public

Socket Mobile plugs expansion devices. The company provides PC and CompactFlash cards for handheld and notebook computers. Its products include peripheral connection and Ethernet cards. It also offers handheld computers bar code scanners and scanner cards and cards for digital phones as well as embedded products including Bluetooth modules and interface chips. Socket Mobile's largest sales segment mobile peripheral products accounts for about half of its revenues. The segment encompasses bar code scanners data collection plug-in cards and serial interface products.The company sells worldwide through original equipment manufacturers (OEMs) resellers and distributors including Ingram Micro and Tech Data.

	Annual Growth	12/14	12/15	12/16	12/17	12/18
Sales ($ mil.)	(0.8%)	17.0	18.4	20.8	21.3	16.5
Net income ($ mil.)	–	0.4	1.8	12.1	(1.4)	(0.6)
Market value ($ mil.)	0.9%	8.5	8.5	22.6	21.1	8.8
Employees	2.9%	50	50	53	56	56

SODEXO REMOTE SITES PARTNERSHIP

5749 Susitna Dr.
Harahan LA 70123
Phone: 504-733-5761
Fax: 504-733-2017
Web: www.sodexousa.com

CEO: –
CFO: –
HR: –
FYE: August 31
Type: Subsidiary

Start building it and they will come — to feed you. Sodexo Remote Sites (formerly Universal Sodexho) provides foodservices and catering for employees working at remote locations such as construction sites mining operations and off-shore oil rigs. It also offers facilities maintenance services including janitorial and groundskeeping services procurement and logistics and vehicle maintenance. In addition the company serves some military bases primarily those in Korea. Sodexo Remote Sites is a unit of Paris-based contract foodservices provider Sodexo.

SOFT COMPUTER CONSULTANTS INC.

5400 TECH DATA DR
CLEARWATER, FL 337603116
Phone: 727-789-0100
Fax: –
Web: www.softcomputer.com

CEO: Gilbert Hakim
CFO: –
HR: –
FYE: August 31
Type: Private

Soft Computer Consultants makes sure medical labs don't have a hard time managing their information. The company (which does business as SCC Soft Computer) develops laboratory information systems (LIS) and clinical information systems for medical laboratories radiology departments genetics laboratories pharmacies and blood banks. Its software links labs to other departments in order to enable quick distribution of data and test results. The company also offers clinical accounts receivable and billing software for finance departments and consulting services to help customers improve their workflow processes. SCC was founded in 1979 by the Hakim brothers Gilbert (CEO) and Jean (President).

	Annual Growth	08/06	08/07	08/08	08/09	08/10
Sales ($ mil.)	–	–	–	(1,521.7)	97.7	107.8
Net income ($ mil.)	–	–	–	0.0	13.7	23.4
Market value ($ mil.)	–	–	–	–	–	–
Employees	–	–	–	–	–	900

SOFTECH, INC

650 Suffolk Street, Suite 415
Lowell, MA 01854
Phone: 978 513-2700
Fax: 978 458-4096
Web: www.softech.com

NBB: SOFT

CEO: –
CFO: –
HR: –
FYE: May 31
Type: Public

SofTech has designs on product manufacturers with its product lifecycle management (PLM) products. SofTech's ProductCenter suite allows users to consolidate product information automate processes such as review cycles and change orders facilitate collaboration and ensure regulatory compliance. The company also provides consulting maintenance and training services. Clients include GE Honeywell Sikorsky Aircraft Siemens and the US Army.

	Annual Growth	05/12	05/13	05/14	05/15	05/16
Sales ($ mil.)	(10.2%)	6.4	6.4	5.0	3.9	4.2
Net income ($ mil.)	–	0.4	0.4	(0.7)	(1.3)	(0.7)
Market value ($ mil.)	(2.4%)	1.1	1.5	1.5	1.0	1.0
Employees	(9.9%)	41	40	31	27	27

SOFTWARE & INFORMATION INDUSTRY ASSOCIATION

1090 Vermont Ave. NW
Washington DC 20005-4095
Phone: 202-289-7442
Fax: 202-289-7097
Web: www.siia.net

CEO: –
CFO: –
HR: –
FYE: June 30
Type: Private - Associatio

The SIIA keeps tabs on Congressional representatives and pirates alike. The Software & Information Industry Association (SIIA) is an international trade organization for the software and digital content industries. Its more than 500 corporate members include Bank of America Bloomberg Dow Jones and Sun Microsystems. SIIA offers market research access to industry information lobbying awards and conferences. It also investigates and prosecutes companies accused of using software or content illegally. SIIA was formed in 1999 by the merger of the Software Publishers Association and the Information Industry Association. The Specialized Information Publishers Association is becoming a division of SIIA.

SOLARWINDS INC
NYS: SWI

7171 Southwest Parkway, Building 400
Austin, TX 78735
Phone: 512 682-9300
Fax: –
Web: www.solarwinds.com

CEO: Kevin B Thompson
CFO: Jason Ream
HR: –
FYE: December 31
Type: Public

SolarWinds helps IT professionals improve IT infrastructure management without burning holes in their wallets. The company provides fault and performance management configuration management and compliance and troubleshooting applications. Designed to work on single devices or networks with as many as 100000 machines its downloadable software can be installed and configured without professional implementation services. The company's customers range from small businesses to large enterprises and government agencies. Its clients have included Booz Allen Hamilton FedEx Lockheed Martin Microsoft Chevron and NASA. SolarWinds gets 70% of sales from customers in the US.

	Annual Growth	12/09	12/10	12/11	12/12	12/13
Sales ($ mil.)	30.3%	116.4	152.4	198.4	269.0	335.4
Net income ($ mil.)	32.1%	29.5	44.7	62.4	81.3	89.8
Market value ($ mil.)	13.2%	1,726.0	1,443.9	2,096.5	3,934.3	2,837.6
Employees	38.7%	354	458	628	865	1,312

SOLERA HOLDINGS INC
NYS: SLH

1301 Solana Blvd. Building #2, Suite 2100
Westlake, TX 76262
Phone: 817 961-2100
Fax: –
Web: www.solerainc.com

CEO: Jeff Tarr
CFO: Renato Giger
HR: –
FYE: June 30
Type: Public

The next time you report a fender bender your adjuster might be using technology from Solera to process the claim. Solera Holdings develops software for the auto insurance industry. Its Audatex software automates such processes as auditing claims management and damage estimation. Solera serves insurance companies worldwide; other customers include auto repair shops and independent assessors. Its Hollander subsidiary provides the Hollander Interchange parts catalog in print or electronic form to car recyclers as an inventory management supplement. In Brazil and Mexico it operates an online marketplace for salvage vehicle sales. Vista Equity Partners acquired Solera in 2015.

	Annual Growth	06/11	06/12	06/13	06/14	06/15
Sales ($ mil.)	13.6%	684.7	790.2	838.1	987.3	1,140.8
Net income ($ mil.)	–	157.4	107.0	93.9	(8.7)	(100.8)
Market value ($ mil.)	(6.8%)	3,962.8	2,799.3	3,727.7	4,498.0	2,984.9
Employees	24.7%	2,247	2,483	2,767	3,638	5,442

SOLIGENIX INC
NAS: SNGX

29 Emmons Drive, Suite B-10
Princeton, NJ 08540
Phone: 609 538-8200
Fax: 609 452-6467
Web: www.soligenix.com

CEO: –
CFO: Karen Krumeich
HR: –
FYE: December 31
Type: Public

Soligenix (formerly DOR BioPharma) is opening the door to more effective biodefense. The company's BioDefense unit is focusing on the development of nasally administered vaccines for such bioterror threats as ricin and botulinum toxins. Ricin vaccine candidate RiVax is in early-stage clinical trials. Through its BioTherapeutics division Soligenix is developing lead candidate orBec an orally administered drug using the same active ingredient as GlaxoSmithKline's allergy and asthma drug Beconase; orBec is a potential therapy for intestinal graft-versus-host disease a life-threatening complication of bone marrow transplantation.

	Annual Growth	12/14	12/15	12/16	12/17	12/18
Sales ($ mil.)	(7.1%)	7.0	8.8	10.4	5.4	5.2
Net income ($ mil.)	–	(6.7)	(7.8)	(3.2)	(7.1)	(8.9)
Market value ($ mil.)	(3.2%)	17.3	20.0	39.8	39.2	15.2
Employees	(4.7%)	17	16	19	18	14

SOLITARIO EXPLORATION & ROYALTY CORP
ASE: XPL

4251 Kipling St., Suite 390
Wheat Ridge, CO 80033
Phone: 303 534-1030
Fax: –
Web: www.solitarioresources.com

CEO: Christopher E Herald
CFO: James R Maronick
HR: –
FYE: December 31
Type: Public

Solitude can be a precious resource but Solitario Exploration & Royalty is more interested in finding precious minerals. The company explores and develops gold silver platinum and zinc properties in Brazil Mexico and Peru. Solitario has formed alliances to help finance its exploration work with industry giants like Newmont Mining and Anglo Platinum. None of its properties are in development. The company changed its name from Solitario Resources in 2008. The following year it agreed to buy Metallic Ventures Gold which has properties in Nevada. Not long after International Minerals came in with its own offer for Metallic Ventures.

	Annual Growth	12/10	12/11	12/12	12/13	12/14
Sales ($ mil.)	0.0%	0.2	0.2	0.3	0.3	0.2
Net income ($ mil.)	–	(4.1)	(3.4)	(3.3)	(2.1)	(1.8)
Market value ($ mil.)	(29.1%)	142.5	56.1	65.9	33.4	36.1
Employees	(32.0%)	28	28	18	7	6

SOLITRON DEVICES, INC.
NBB: SODI

3301 Electronics Way
West Palm Beach, FL 33407
Phone: 561 848-4311
Fax: 561 863-5946
Web: www.solitrondevices.com

CEO: Tim Eriksen
CFO: Tim Eriksen
HR: –
FYE: February 29
Type: Public

Solitron Devices' tiny devices have taken some big trips — to Jupiter on the Galileo spacecraft and to Mars on the Sojourner. Used primarily in military and aerospace applications the company's solid-state semiconductor components include thin-film resistors field-effect and power transistors and hybrid circuits. Nearly all of Solitron's sales come from US government contractors including Raytheon and Lockheed Martin and the US government itself. Solitron has faced ongoing financial challenges (plus attention from the EPA in relation to some of the company's former manufacturing sites).

	Annual Growth	02/12	02/13	02/14	02/15	02/16
Sales ($ mil.)	0.3%	8.3	8.4	8.7	9.8	8.4
Net income ($ mil.)	–	0.7	0.8	0.9	0.9	(0.2)
Market value ($ mil.)	4.7%	7.0	8.4	9.1	9.6	8.4
Employees	(2.8%)	84	84	82	80	75

SOLO CUP COMPANY

150 S. Saunders Rd. Ste. 150
Lake Forest IL 60045
Phone: 847-444-5000
Fax: 847-236-6049
Web: www.solocup.com

CEO: Robert C Dart
CFO: –
HR: Julia N Gonzales
FYE: December 31
Type: Private

Solo Cup is not just the maker of the iconic red solo cup it's a major player in the disposable consumer products industry. The company makes single-use cups plates cutlery take-out containers and other similar products under the Solo Sweetheart Creative Carryouts and Bare brand names. Solo's plastic paper and foam items are sold through retailers and foodservice distributors around the world. In addition Solo makes specialty party supplies upscale disposable products and plastic and paper packaging for manufacturers of snack foods and dairy products. In mid-2012 Solo was acquired by rival Dart Container in a deal valued at $1 billion.

SOLUTIA INC.
NYSE: SOA

575 Maryville Centre Dr.
St. Louis MO 63141
Phone: 314-674-1000
Fax: 314-674-1585
Web: www.solutia.com

CEO: Jeffry N Quinn
CFO: James M Sullivan
HR: –
FYE: December 31
Type: Public

Solutia looks to provide industrial solutions by manufacturing plastics films and chemicals for the construction automotive and rubber manufacturing industries. The company operates through three segments. Its Technical Specialties unit manufactures specialty chemicals for rubber and transmission fluids customers through its Flexsys Terminol and Skydrol businesses. Its Advanced Interlayers unit produces polyvinyl butyral (PVB) sheet which is used in the manufacture of glass. Performance Films makes various plastic films for use in glass tapes and packaging products. Solutia has operations in 50 locations worldwide. In 2012 the company was acquired by Eastman Chemical in a $4.7 billion deal.

SOMERSET MEDICAL CENTER

110 REHILL AVE
SOMERVILLE, NJ 08876-2598
Phone: 908-685-2200
Fax: –
Web: www.smcfoundation.com

CEO: –
CFO: –
HR: –
FYE: December 31
Type: Private

Serving central New Jersey Somerset Medical Center provides a variety of health care services including cancer care women's health cardiology and surgical and rehabilitative services. Founded in 1899 the hospital has 355 beds as well as a medical and dental staff of approximately 650 members. The medical center is affiliated with the University of Medicine and Dentistry of New Jersey - Robert Wood Johnson Medical School campus. It also provides clinical research services in affiliation with The Cancer Institute of New Jersey. Somerset Medical Center agreed to merge with Robert Wood Johnson University Hospital in 2013.

	Annual Growth	12/07	12/08	12/08	12/11	12/12
Sales ($ mil.)	0.5%	–	240.3	260.5	260.4	245.3
Net income ($ mil.)	–	–	1.0	(1.2)	(4.5)	(1.3)
Market value ($ mil.)	–	–	–	–	–	–
Employees	–	–	–	–	–	1,743

SOMERSET TIRE SERVICE, INC.

358 SAW MILL RIVER RD
MILLWOOD, NY 105461000
Phone: 732-356-8500
Fax: –
Web: www.mavistire.com

CEO: William Caulin
CFO: Anthony Losardo
HR: –
FYE: December 31
Type: Private

Somerset Tire Service (STS) operates about 145 tire and auto centers throughout New Jersey New York and Pennsylvania. The company primarily sells tires auto parts batteries and accessories under such top brand names as Bridgestone Firestone Michelin Toyo Pirelli Goodyear Yokohama and Continental. Operating under the banner STS Tire & Auto Centers the company's locations feature a window between the store and service bays so customers can watch the work being done on their cars. STS has grown by acquiring other regional tire and service centers with hopes of saturating the Northeast before moving outside its home region. Founded in 1958 the company is employee-owned.

	Annual Growth	12/09	12/10	12/11	12/12	12/13
Sales ($ mil.)	4.4%	–	189.2	201.4	203.6	214.9
Net income ($ mil.)	(2.3%)	–	10.6	8.7	7.7	9.9
Market value ($ mil.)	–	–	–	–	–	–
Employees	–	–	–	–	–	1,000

SONESTA INTERNATIONAL HOTELS CORPORATION
NASDAQ: SNSTA

116 Huntington Ave.
Boston MA 02116
Phone: 617-421-5400
Fax: 617-421-5402
Web: www.sonesta.com

CEO: Carlos Flores
CFO: –
HR: –
FYE: December 31
Type: Public

Siesta whenever you want at Sonesta International Hotels. The company operates several hotels in the US (Boston Miami New Orleans and Orlando) and Egypt while its name is licensed to additional hotels in Chile Columbia Egypt St. Maarten Brazil and Peru. The nearly 30 luxury properties cater to upscale business and leisure travelers and are designed to showcase the history and culture of their locales. Sonesta also operates six cruise ships on the Nile. The firm was founded by "Sonny" Sonnabend in the 1940s. Members of the Sonnabend family (including executive chairman Peter and CEO Stephanie) continue to run the business. "Sonesta" is a combination of the names of Sonny and his wife Esther.

SONIC AUTOMOTIVE, INC.
NYS: SAH

4401 Colwick Road
Charlotte, NC 28211
Phone: 704 566-2400
Fax: 704 536-5116
Web: www.sonicautomotive.com

CEO: B. Scott Smith
CFO: Heath R. Byrd
HR: Raquel Cail
FYE: December 31
Type: Public

Sonic Automotive is one of the leading US auto dealers just behind rivals like AutoNation and Penske Automotive. Sonic operates 100 new and used vehicle franchises about 10 company-owned used vehicle stores and about 15 collision repair centers in major markets in more than a dozen states including California Texas the Carolinas Alabama and Tennessee. The company sells some 25 brands of cars and light trucks including Honda Ford and Subaru and offers extended aftermarket services. Chairman O. Bruton Smith is also the majority owner of Speedway Motorsports which operates eight NASCAR auto racetracks.

	Annual Growth	12/14	12/15	12/16	12/17	12/18
Sales ($ mil.)	2.0%	9,197.1	9,624.3	9,731.8	9,867.2	9,951.6
Net income ($ mil.)	(14.6%)	97.2	86.3	93.2	93.0	51.7
Market value ($ mil.)	(15.5%)	1,156.0	973.0	979.0	788.7	588.2
Employees	1.1%	9,300	9,800	9,800	9,750	9,700

SONIC CORP.

300 JOHNNY BENCH DR
OKLAHOMA CITY, OK 731042471
Phone: 405-225-5506
Fax: –
Web: www.sonicdrivein.com

CEO: J. Clifford (Cliff) Hudson
CFO: Corey R Horsch
HR: –
FYE: August 31
Type: Private

Keeping the drive-in burger joint alive sounds like a good idea to this company. Sonic Corp. operates the largest chain of quick-service drive-ins in the US with more than 3550 locations throughout the country. The chain has a significant presence in the South namely in Texas. The eateries offer a menu of hamburgers hot dogs (Coneys) onion rings tater tots and breakfast items along with specialty drinks such as cherry limeade and frozen desserts. Most locations offer drive-thru service with skating carhops and some have indoor seating. The company operates and has a majority interest in 345 Sonic locations while the rest are operated by franchisees.

	Annual Growth	08/14	08/15	08/16	08/17	08/18
Sales ($ mil.)	(11.3%)	–	606.1	606.3	477.3	423.6
Net income ($ mil.)	3.4%	–	64.5	64.1	63.7	71.2
Market value ($ mil.)	–	–	–	–	–	–
Employees	–	–	–	–	–	6,173

SONIC FOUNDRY, INC.
NBB: SOFO

222 West Washington Ave.
Madison, WI 53703
Phone: 608 443-1600
Fax: –
Web: www.sonicfoundry.com

CEO: –
CFO: Kenneth A Minor
HR: –
FYE: September 30
Type: Public

It's about more than just sound at Sonic Foundry. The company's Mediasite recorders and software enable educational institutions (more than half of sales) corporations and government agencies to capture stream and archive online multi-media presentations. Its products are used for corporate meetings media analysis distance learning and content publishing. Sonic Foundry also provides webcasting services and it offers managed communications services — including content hosting and delivery. It markets through resellers its own sales team and system integrator partnerships. The company's customers have included Thermo Fisher Scientific BAE Systems and Georgetown University.

	Annual Growth	09/15	09/16	09/17	09/18	09/19
Sales ($ mil.)	(1.2%)	36.5	38.0	36.0	34.5	34.8
Net income ($ mil.)	–	(4.5)	(3.3)	(5.0)	(12.2)	(3.6)
Market value ($ mil.)	(39.7%)	56.6	39.1	21.6	10.8	7.5
Employees	(2.4%)	202	205	188	198	183

SONICS & MATERIALS INC.

53 Church Hill Rd.
Newtown CT 06470
Phone: 203-270-4600
Fax: 203-270-4610
Web: www.sonicsandmaterials.com

CEO: Robert Soloff
CFO: Steven Bowen
HR: –
FYE: June 30
Type: Private

Acoustic sounds abound — and they're not all coming from MTV's Unplugged. Sonics & Materials makes standard and customized equipment that uses sound to bond thermoplastic components textiles and other synthetic materials. The ultrasonic process creates clean welding of metal and materials that are difficult to bond by other means; it also offers liquid processing (dispersing blending cleaning) and food cutting. The company serves a broad range of customers including appliance automotive chemical consumer products industrial medical packaging synthetic textile and toy manufacturers. President and CEO Robert Soloff founded Sonics & Materials in 1969; the company was delisted in 2002.

SONO-TEK CORP.
NBB: SOTK

2012 Route 9W
Milton, NY 12547
Phone: 845 795-2020
Fax: –
Web: www.sono-tek.com

CEO: Christopher L Coccio
CFO: Stephen J Bagley
HR: –
FYE: February 28
Type: Public

Sono-Tek wants to spray it not say it. The company makes ultrasonic liquid atomizing nozzles that can apply fluids such as flux (used with solder on electronic circuit boards) molten metals and polymeric coatings. Its SonoFlux 2000F spray fluxer product is designed for high-volume operations. SonoFlux XL applies solder flux to electronic printed circuit boards that vary from two inches up to 24 inches in width. Sono-Tek's MediCoat product is used for stent coating applying thin layers of expensive polymer and drug coating to arterial stents.

	Annual Growth	02/15	02/16	02/17	02/18	02/19
Sales ($ mil.)	1.7%	10.8	11.8	9.7	11.0	11.6
Net income ($ mil.)	(28.1%)	0.6	0.5	0.1	0.4	0.2
Market value ($ mil.)	21.1%	17.8	17.5	17.9	24.3	38.3
Employees	4.5%	57	59	58	64	68

SONOCO PRODUCTS CO.
NYS: SON

1 N. Second St.
Hartsville, SC 29550
Phone: 843 383-7000
Fax: 843 383-7008
Web: www.sonoco.com

CEO: M. Jack Sanders
CFO: Barry L. Saunders
HR: Allan H. McLeland
FYE: December 31
Type: Public

Sonoco Products is a manufacturer of industrial and consumer packaging used by the food consumer goods construction and automotive industries. The company makes composite cans for things like snack foods powdered beverages and pet foods and produces flexible and rigid packaging (paper and plastic) for food personal care items and chemicals. Sonoco also manufactures point-of-sale displays protective packaging and paperboard tubes for industrial processes. Other services include fulfillment and supply chain management. About two-thirds of Sonoco's revenues are generated in the US.

	Annual Growth	12/14	12/15	12/16	12/17	12/18
Sales ($ mil.)	1.8%	5,014.5	4,964.4	4,782.9	5,036.7	5,390.9
Net income ($ mil.)	7.0%	239.2	250.1	286.4	175.3	313.6
Market value ($ mil.)	5.0%	4,362.5	4,080.0	5,261.0	5,304.9	5,303.9
Employees	2.5%	20,800	21,000	20,000	21,000	23,000

SONOMA PHARMACEUTICALS INC
NAS: SNOA

1129 North McDowell Blvd.
Petaluma, CA 94954
Phone: 707 283-0550
Fax: –
Web: www.sonomapharma.com

CEO: Amy Trombly
CFO: John Dal Poggetto
HR: –
FYE: March 31
Type: Public

Sonoma Pharmaceuticals (formerly Oculus) uses super-agents in its fight against the evil super-bug MRSA. The company works with proprietary platform technology Microcyn a super-oxidized water-based solution designed to safely (i.e. without any known side effects) eliminate a wide range of annoying pathogens (including MRSA) attempting to infect patients with open wounds. Aside from use in wound care the solution has potential applications for use in disinfectants and sterilization as well as respiratory dermatology veterinary and dental markets. Oculus' products are primarily sold through partnerships with distributors.

	Annual Growth	03/15	03/16	03/17	03/18	03/19
Sales ($ mil.)	8.2%	13.9	15.1	12.8	16.7	19.0
Net income ($ mil.)	–	(8.2)	(10.2)	9.3	(14.3)	(11.8)
Market value ($ mil.)	2.2%	1.1	1.3	9.4	4.8	1.2
Employees	(16.9%)	132	225	75	79	63

SONOMAWEST HOLDINGS INC.
PINK SHEETS: SWHI

2064 Hwy. 116 North
Sebastopol CA 95472
Phone: 707-824-2534
Fax: 707-829-4630
Web: www.sonomawestholdings.com

CEO: Craig R Stapleton
CFO: Craig R Stapleton
HR: –
FYE: June 30
Type: Public

Formerly Vacu-dry SonomaWest sold its dehydrated fruit business in 2000 and 2001 in search of a candy apple future in real estate. The company now owns two former agricultural production properties (totaling some 90 acres) left over from its fruity past. The properties are located in Northern California's Sonoma County and are leased to multiple tenants for commercial use; Benziger Family Winery is one of its largest tenants. SonomaWest also holds an investment in telecommunications firm MetroPCS Communications. The Stapleton family including CEO Craig Stapleton acquired SonomaWest and took it private in 2011.

SONOSITE INC.

NASDAQ: SONO

21919 30th Dr. SE
Bothell WA 98021-3904
Phone: 425-951-1200
Fax: 425-951-1201
Web: www.sonosite.com

CEO: Takaaki Ueda
CFO: Marcus Y Smith
HR: Meredyth Wanink
FYE: December 31
Type: Public

Size is everything for SonoSite. The firm makes handheld ultrasonic imaging devices that health care providers can use outside traditional imaging facilities for instance in the ER at a patient's bedside or in the doctor's office. Its fourth- and fifth-generation systems include the handheld NanoMaxx tool and the M-Turbo and Edge portable consoles that produce imaging quality comparable to larger cart-based systems. Its S Series of products feature customized interfaces for different clinical applications including the ER or the ICU. SonoSite also sells some earlier-generation products and accessories used with its products. Diversified imaging company FUJIFILM Holdings acquired SonoSite in 2012.

SONUS NETWORKS, INC.

NMS: SONS

4 Technology Park Drive
Westford, MA 01886
Phone: 978 614-8100
Fax: -
Web: www.sonus.net

CEO: -
CFO: -
HR: Tracy Spirito
FYE: December 31
Type: Public

Sonus Networks has found a sound place in the voice infrastructure market. The company makes hardware and software that public network providers — including long-distance carriers ISPs and cable operators — use to provide voice and data communications services to their subscribers. Service providers use Sonus' switches session border control (SBC) products and related network software partly to transition from older circuit-based equipment to VoIP-based systems. The company also provides installation support and training services. Customers include AT&T BT Group Verizon and Deutsche Telekom; Sonus operates worldwide but generates most of its sales in the US.

	Annual Growth	12/11	12/12	12/13	12/14	12/15
Sales ($ mil.)	(1.0%)	259.7	254.1	276.7	296.3	249.0
Net income ($ mil.)	-	(12.7)	(50.2)	(22.1)	(16.9)	(31.9)
Market value ($ mil.)	31.3%	118.7	84.1	155.8	196.4	352.7
Employees	(1.1%)	1,095	1,093	1,059	1,193	1,049

SOTERA DEFENSE SOLUTIONS INC.

2121 Cooperative Way Ste. 400
Herndon VA 20171-5393
Phone: 703-738-2840
Fax: 703-883-4037
Web: www.soteradefense.com

CEO: William Weber
CFO: Michael Alber
HR: -
FYE: December 31
Type: Private

Military intelligence is no joking matter at Sotera Defense Solutions. The company formerly Global Defense Technology & Systems operates through an array of subsidiaries. It provides software system engineering and technology development to help the Department of Defense CIA Homeland Security and other government agencies fight terrorism and enforce national security. Sotera's services include design of mobile computers (called Force Mobility and Modernization Systems) for military clients. Its Intelligence business focuses on counter-terrorism and communications systems; a Cyber operation collects and analyzes information in cyberspace. The company was acquired by an Ares Management affiliate in 2011.

SOTHEBY'S

NYS: BID

1334 York Avenue
New York, NY 10021
Phone: 212 606-7000
Fax: -
Web: www.sothebys.com

CEO: Charles F Stewart
CFO: Michael Goss
HR: -
FYE: December 31
Type: Public

Sotheby's believes that one man's collection is another man's treasure — especially when that collection is a rare antique a unique collectible or a distinctive work of art. Along with rival Christie's International Sotheby's dominates the world's auction house market. It orchestrates hundreds of sales each year at its auction centers dealing mainly in fine art antiques and collectibles. Sotheby's receives commissions and fees from both the buyer and the seller on each sale. It also provides loans (secured against works of art) to clients as part of its finance services and acts as an art dealer through its Noortman Master Paintings business which specializes in Dutch Flemish and French paintings.

	Annual Growth	12/13	12/14	12/15	12/16	12/17
Sales ($ mil.)	3.8%	853.7	938.1	961.5	805.4	989.4
Net income ($ mil.)	(2.2%)	130.0	117.8	43.7	74.1	118.8
Market value ($ mil.)	(0.8%)	2,791.0	2,265.3	1,351.4	2,091.1	2,707.0
Employees	1.3%	1,577	1,550	1,596	1,617	1,662

SOTHERLY HOTELS INC

NMS: SOHO

410 West Francis Street
Williamsburg, VA 23185
Phone: 757 229-5648
Fax: -
Web: www.mhihospitality.com

CEO: Andrew M Sims
CFO: Anthony E Domalski
HR: -
FYE: December 31
Type: Public

MHI Hospitality owns seven full-service hotels operating under the Hilton Holiday Inn Sheraton and Crowne Plaza brands in the mid-Atlantic and southeastern US. The company also holds a minority stake in another hotel has two under development and owns leasehold interests in common areas of the Shell Island Resort in Wilmington North Carolina. MHI Hotel Services which spun off MHI Hospitality in 2004 manages the REIT's properties. Executive officers and board members of MHI Hospitality collectively own more than a quarter of the company.

	Annual Growth	12/14	12/15	12/16	12/17	12/18
Sales ($ mil.)	9.7%	122.9	138.5	152.8	154.3	178.2
Net income ($ mil.)	-	(0.6)	5.4	0.9	0.4	0.1
Market value ($ mil.)	(7.0%)	106.6	87.5	96.5	91.7	79.7
Employees	0.0%	13	12	12	12	13

SOUND FINANCIAL INC.

OTC: SNFL

2005 5th Ave. Ste. 200
Seattle WA 98121
Phone: 206-448-1884
Fax: 403-538-7033
Web: www.swenergy.ca

CEO: Laurie Stewart
CFO: Matthew Deines
HR: -
FYE: December 31
Type: Public

Sounds heard by Sound Financial's banks could include that of crisp $100 bills and the foghorns of passing ships. Located in the Puget Sound region surrounding Seattle Sound Financial is a bank holding company operating principally through Sound Community Bank and its five area locations. The bank offers traditional savings and checking accounts to retail and business customers as well as residential mortgages home equity loans and various secured and unsecured consumer loans. It also provides construction land commercial business and multifamily housing loans but to a lesser extent. Sound Community Bank traces it roots back to 1953 when it was founded as a credit union.

SOUTH BEND MEDICAL FOUNDATION INC

530 N LAFAYETTE BLVD
SOUTH BEND, IN 466011004
Phone: 574-234-4176
Fax: –
Web: www.sbmf.org

CEO: –
CFO: –
HR: –
FYE: December 31
Type: Private

South Bend Medical Foundation provides clinical testing and blood bank services for communities in Illinois Indiana Kentucky Michigan and Ohio. The foundation works together with local hospitals clinics and doctors' offices to provide diagnostic laboratory services for patients. It operates about a dozen lab facilities at medical facilities and independent locations. The company's forensic toxicology department conducts employee and athletic drug testing. South Bend Medical Foundation also provides public health screenings for diseases such as sickle cell anemia and prostrate cancer. The foundation was formed in 1912 by a group of physicians.

	Annual Growth	12/10	12/11	12/13	12/14	12/15
Sales ($ mil.)	(1.5%)	–	97.7	101.2	95.9	91.8
Net income ($ mil.)	–	–	–	2.3	0.8	(1.1)	(0.1)
Market value ($ mil.)	–	–	–	–	–	–
Employees	–	–	–	–	–	800

SOUTH BROWARD HOSPITAL DISTRICT

3501 JOHNSON ST
HOLLYWOOD, FL 330215421
Phone: 954-987-2000
Fax: –
Web: www.mhs.net

CEO: Frank V. Sacco
CFO: Matthew J. Muhart
HR: –
FYE: April 30
Type: Private

South Broward Hospital District (dba Memorial Healthcare System) is a community-owned health services network that provides health service to residents of Florida's Broward Dade and Palm Beach counties. The system's major hospitals include Memorial Regional Hospital Memorial Hospital Pembroke Memorial Hospital West and Memorial Hospital Miramar. The hospitals have a combined capacity of roughly 1900 licensed beds and provide services including diagnostic emergency surgical and rehabilitative care. Memorial also operates a pediatric hospital cardiac and vascular medicine institute a cancer treatment center and a center for women's health as well as nursing home facilities (120 beds) and community clinics.

	Annual Growth	04/14	04/15	04/16	04/17	04/18
Sales ($ mil.)	33.1%	–	854.7	1,897.1	1,937.6	2,014.9
Net income ($ mil.)	–	–	(649.1)	188.7	134.1	64.6
Market value ($ mil.)	–	–	–	–	–	–
Employees	–	–	–	–	–	9,200

SOUTH CAROLINA PUBLIC SERVICE AUTHORITY (INC)

1 RIVERWOOD DR
MONCKS CORNER, SC 294612998
Phone: 843-761-4121
Fax: –
Web: www.santeecooper.com

CEO: Lonnie N. Carter
CFO: Jeff Armfield
HR: –
FYE: December 31
Type: Private

This company turns the lights on in South Carolina. South Carolina Public Service Authority known as Santee Cooper (after two interconnected river systems) provides wholesale electricity to 20 cooperatives and two municipalities that serve more than 2 million customers in South Carolina. It directly retails electricity to more than 174000 customers. One of the largest US state-owned utilities Santee Cooper operates in all 46 counties in South Carolina and has stakes in power plants (fossil-fueled nuclear hydro and renewable) that give it more than 5180 MW of generating capacity. Its Santee Cooper Regional Water System also distributes water to customers in its service area.

	Annual Growth	12/11	12/12	12/13	12/15	12/17
Sales ($ mil.)	(1.4%)	–	1,887.8	1,816.6	1,879.6	1,757.0
Net income ($ mil.)	1.4%	–	84.9	65.5	34.4	90.9
Market value ($ mil.)	–	–	–	–	–	–
Employees	–	–	–	–	–	1,748

SOUTH CAROLINA STATE PORTS AUTHORITY

200 PORTS AUTHORITY DR
MOUNT PLEASANT, SC 294647998
Phone: 843-723-8651
Fax: –
Web: www.scspa.com

CEO: –
CFO: Peter N Hughes
HR: Robert Mozdean
FYE: June 30
Type: Private

Offering gateways for trade in the Palmetto State The South Carolina State Ports Authority (SCSPA) operates marine terminals at the ports in Charleston and Georgetown. The agency maintains its own container terminals at each port and provides container handling services; in addition space at the ports is leased to other terminal operators. The Port of Charleston provides services for cruise ships as well as for freight-carrying vessels including freight rail service. SCSPA is overseen by a nine-member board appointed by the governor along with the Secretaries of Transportation and Commerce. The agency which was founded in 1942 does not receive state money and is funded primarily by its operations.

	Annual Growth	06/04	06/05	06/06	06/11	06/18
Sales ($ mil.)	(10.1%)	–	1,008.7	154.0	124.6	252.0
Net income ($ mil.)	–	–	0.0	60.1	21.2	26.0
Market value ($ mil.)	–	–	–	–	–	–
Employees	–	–	–	–	–	493

SOUTH CENTRAL COMMUNICATIONS CORPORATION

20 NW 3RD ST FL 14
EVANSVILLE, IN 477081200
Phone: 812-463-7950
Fax: –
Web: www.southcentralcommunications.net

CEO: J P Engelbrecht
CFO: Randy Champion
HR: –
FYE: December 31
Type: Private

South Central Communications-, enjoys making waves in the-, central US radio market. The company owns and operates more than a dozen radio stations serving midsized and large markets in Tennessee and Indiana with a range of mostly music programming. In addition the company operates-, Muzak-, franchises (subscriber-based radio and voice services targeted to businesses) in seven states. Other operations include Dish Network installation services restaurant drive-thru intercoms and office paging systems. Its also owns Knoxville independent digital television station WMAK.-, The family-owned company was started in 1946 by John A. Engelbrecht.

	Annual Growth	12/08	12/09	12/10	12/11	12/12
Sales ($ mil.)	3.5%	–	–	38.6	40.8	41.3
Net income ($ mil.)	37.2%	–	–	3.2	4.1	6.0
Market value ($ mil.)	–	–	–	–	–	–
Employees	–	–	–	–	–	298

SOUTH CENTRAL POWER COMPANY INC

2780 COONPATH RD NE
LANCASTER, OH 431309343
Phone: 740-653-4422
Fax: –
Web: www.southcentralpower.com

CEO: Rick Lemonds
CFO: Rebecca Witt
HR: –
FYE: December 31
Type: Private

Although South Central Power Company may sound like a power plant in Watts Los Angeles it is in fact a member-owned cooperative that provides electricity to consumers and businesses in southern Ohio. An affiliate of the nationwide Touchstone Energy Cooperative network the electric cooperative provides power to more than 115570 customers over 11000 miles of power lines. In addition to distributing electricity South Central Power also provides outdoor lighting surge suppression products security systems water heater switches and other energy-related services.

	Annual Growth	12/12	12/13	12/14	12/15	12/16
Sales ($ mil.)	3.1%	–	257.7	266.9	273.9	282.1
Net income ($ mil.)	(6.7%)	–	17.8	21.4	22.3	14.4
Market value ($ mil.)	–	–	–	–	–	–
Employees	–	–	–	–	–	235

SOUTH DAKOTA STATE UNIVERSITY

2201 ADMINISTRATION LANE
BROOKINGS, SD 570070001
Phone: 605-688-6101
Fax: –
Web: www.statealum.com

CEO: –
CFO: –
HR: –
FYE: June 30
Type: Private

South Dakota State University (SDSU) is big on education in the Mount Rushmore State. The college offers undergraduate graduate and pre-professional programs to some 13000 students. Academic offerings include agriculture engineering and pharmacy courses. Its SDSU Sioux Falls Program targets non-traditional students (such as students with jobs and families) by providing evening and weekend classes. Notable SDSU alumni include former US Senator Tom Daschle and professional football players Adam Timmerman and Adam Vinatieri. SDSU a public school governed by the South Dakota Board of Regents was founded as a land grant college in 1881.

	Annual Growth	12/13	12/14*	06/16	06/17	06/18
Sales ($ mil.)	48.3%	–	44.1	209.8	213.6	213.3
Net income ($ mil.)	132.6%	–	1.5	44.3	31.6	44.3
Market value ($ mil.)	–	–	–	–	–	–
Employees		–	–	–	–	2,000

*Fiscal year change

SOUTH JERSEY GAS CO.

NL: –

1 South Jersey Plaza
Folsom, NJ 08037
Phone: 609 561-9000
Fax: –
Web: www.sjindustries.com

CEO: Jeffrey E Dubois
CFO: Stephen H Clark
HR: –
FYE: December 31
Type: Public

Atlantic City gamblers don't have to gamble on getting hot showers thanks to South Jersey Gas which transmits and distributes natural gas to more than 343560 customers in its regulated service territory in seven southern New Jersey counties. The utility a subsidiary of South Jersey Industries also provides gas transportation services and sells wholesale gas to power plant operators and other energy marketing companies. South Jersey Gas's service territory of 2500 sq. miles includes 112 towns and cities throughout Atlantic Cape May Cumberland and Salem Counties and in portions of Burlington Camden and Gloucester Counties with an estimated total population of 1.2 million. In 2017 South Jersey Gas agreed to purchase for $1.7 billion Elizabethtown Gas and Elkton Gas from a subsidiary of The Southern Co adding 300000 new gas customers.

	Annual Growth	12/14	12/15	12/16	12/17	12/18
Sales ($ mil.)	2.2%	501.9	534.3	461.1	517.3	548.0
Net income ($ mil.)	5.7%	66.5	66.6	69.0	72.6	82.9
Market value ($ mil.)	–	–	–	–	–	–
Employees	3.4%	481	483	504	530	550

SOUTH JERSEY INDUSTRIES INC

NYS: SJI

1 South Jersey Plaza
Folsom, NJ 08037
Phone: 609 561-9000
Fax: –
Web: www.sjindustries.com

CEO: Michael J Renna
CFO: Stephen H. Clark
HR: –
FYE: December 31
Type: Public

South Jersey Industries (SJI) is Atlantic City's answer to cold casino nights. In 2014 its main subsidiary South Jersey Gas (SJG) provided natural gas to 342155 residents 24253 commercial customers and 446 industrial customers in southern New Jersey including Atlantic City. The utility has more than 6000 miles of transmission and distribution mains; it also sells and transports gas. SJI's deregulated retail supplier South Jersey Energy (SJE) provides retail gas electricity and energy management services. Its South Jersey Resources (SJR) unit is a wholesale gas services provider in the Southeast US. Subsidiary Marina Energy develops on-site energy projects. In 2017 subsidiary South Jersey Gas agreed to purchase for $1.7 billion Elizabethtown Gas and Elkton Gas from a subsidiary of The Southern Co adding nearly 300000 new gas customers.

	Annual Growth	12/14	12/15	12/16	12/17	12/18
Sales ($ mil.)	16.6%	887.0	959.6	1,036.5	1,243.1	1,641.3
Net income ($ mil.)	(34.7%)	97.0	105.1	118.8	(3.5)	17.7
Market value ($ mil.)	(17.1%)	5,038.9	2,011.1	2,880.7	2,670.4	2,377.1
Employees	12.0%	700	720	750	760	1,100

SOUTH MIAMI HOSPITAL, INC.

6200 SW 73RD ST
SOUTH MIAMI, FL 331434679
Phone: 786-662-4000
Fax: –
Web: –

CEO: Lincoln S Mendez
CFO: –
HR: –
FYE: September 30
Type: Private

South Miami Hospital offers primary and tertiary health care services to the residents living near the University of Miami. The hospital has about 470 beds and is one of the largest members of Baptist Health South Florida a top regional health system. Specialty services include emergency care cardiovascular services oncology neurology women's health metabolic care and rehabilitation. It operates an addiction treatment residential facility provides home health care and provides child development diagnostic and early intervention services. South Miami Hospital was founded in 1960.

	Annual Growth	09/13	09/14	09/15	09/16	09/17
Sales ($ mil.)	(1.4%)	–	505.4	495.4	492.4	484.7
Net income ($ mil.)	(50.0%)	–	53.6	40.6	3.5	6.7
Market value ($ mil.)	–	–	–	–	–	–
Employees		–	–	–	–	2,205

SOUTH PENINSULA HOSPITALS, INC.

4300 BARTLETT ST
HOMER, AK 996037005
Phone: 907-235-0369
Fax: –
Web: –

CEO: –
CFO: Lori Meyer
HR: –
FYE: June 30
Type: Private

South Peninsula Hospital provides a variety of medical services including home health care emergency medicine surgery orthopedics and ophthalmology for the residents of the Kenai Peninsula and surrounding areas in Alaska. The hospital also provides a 25-bed long-term facility that offers physical and occupational therapy services. In addition South Peninsula Hospital provides community and staff education classes.

	Annual Growth	06/12	06/13	06/14	06/15	06/16
Sales ($ mil.)	9.4%	–	50.8	55.0	61.3	66.5
Net income ($ mil.)	(13.3%)	–	1.4	0.8	2.7	0.9
Market value ($ mil.)	–	–	–	–	–	–
Employees		–	–	–	–	300

SOUTH STATE CORP

NMS: SSB

520 Gervais Street
Columbia, SC 29201
Phone: 800 277-2175
Fax: –
Web: www.southstatebank.com

CEO: Robert R. Hill
CFO: John C. Pollok
HR: –
FYE: December 31
Type: Public

South State Corporation (formerly First Financial Holdings) is the holding company for South State Bank (formerly South Carolina Bank and Trust and South Carolina Bank and Trust of the Piedmont both known as SCBT). The bank operates branches throughout the Palmetto state as well as in select counties in Georgia and North Carolina. Serving retail and business customers the banks provide deposit accounts loans and mortgages as well as trust and investment planning services. More than half of the firm's loan portfolio is devoted to commercial mortgages while consumer real estate loans make up more than a quarter. South State plans to merge with Southeastern Bank Financial parent of Georgia Bank & Trust.

	Annual Growth	12/14	12/15	12/16	12/17	12/18
Assets ($ mil.)	17.0%	7,826.2	8,557.3	8,900.6	14,466.6	14,676.3
Net income ($ mil.)	24.1%	75.4	99.5	101.3	87.6	178.9
Market value ($ mil.)	(2.8%)	2,403.4	2,577.9	3,131.5	3,122.5	2,148.0
Employees	5.7%	2,081	2,058	2,055	2,719	2,602

SOUTHCO DISTRIBUTING COMPANY

2201 S JOHN ST
GOLDSBORO, NC 275307163
Phone: 919-735-8012
Fax: –
Web: www.southcodistributing.com

CEO: Sherwin Herring
CFO: Chris Wise
HR: –
FYE: December 28
Type: Private

This company makes sure you can get subs on the go from the convenience store. Southco Distributing is a leading convenience food supplier that distributes prepackaged sandwiches and other products to retail stores in seven states in the Southeast and Midwest. In addition to prepackaged foods Southco provides branded quick-service kiosks and equipment that allow convenience stores and other retailers to offer food on the go. Its foodservice programs are branded under the names AutoFry Pizza Primo Sub Express and Squawkers.

	Annual Growth	12/0-1	12/00	12/05	12/06	12/12
Sales ($ mil.)	5.7%	–	203.8	0.0	253.9	397.2
Net income ($ mil.)	0.0%	–	2.6	0.0	1.1	2.6
Market value ($ mil.)	–	–	–	–	–	–
Employees	–	–	–	–	–	225

SOUTHCOAST FINANCIAL CORP   NMS: SOCB

530 Johnnie Dodds Boulevard
Mt. Pleasant, SC 29464
Phone: 843 884-0504
Fax: –
Web: www.southcoastbank.com

CEO: –
CFO: –
HR: –
FYE: December 31
Type: Public

Southcoast Financial Corporation pays a great deal of interest to the Palmetto State. The institution is the holding company for Southcoast Community Bank which was established in 1998. It serves South Carolina's Berkeley Charleston and Dorchester counties through about 10 branches. Catering to individuals and local small businesses the bank offers savings checking money market and individual retirement accounts as well as certificates of deposit. Its lending activities consist of real estate mortgages (around 45% of the company's loan portfolio) commercial loans (more than one-third) and to a lesser extent consumer construction and land development loans. BNC Bancorp acquired Southcoast in 2015.

	Annual Growth	12/10	12/11	12/12	12/13	12/14
Assets ($ mil.)	(0.1%)	478.3	427.5	438.2	447.4	476.8
Net income ($ mil.)	171.4%	0.1	(16.5)	3.5	9.1	3.7
Market value ($ mil.)	23.1%	21.8	10.1	36.2	41.2	50.0
Employees	(2.4%)	98	93	92	92	89

SOUTHCOAST HOSPITALS GROUP, INC.

363 HIGHLAND AVE
FALL RIVER, MA 027203703
Phone: 508-679-3131
Fax: –
Web: www.southcoast.org

CEO: –
CFO: –
HR: –
FYE: September 30
Type: Private

When you feel more than a little physically washed up get to one of the Southcoast Hospitals Group facilities. The not-for-profit company provides medical services in the southeastern corner of Massachusetts and in Rhode Island. Its primary facilities in Massachusetts are the Charlton Memorial Hospital (with about 330 beds) in Fall River St. Luke's Hospital (420 beds) in New Bedford and Tobey Hospital (65 beds) in Wareham which provide acute medical care and specialty services including cardiology neurology orthopedics and women's care. Southcoast Hospitals Group also operates about 20 ancillary facilities including nursing and assisted-living facilities and home health and hospice agencies.

	Annual Growth	09/03	09/04	09/06	09/12	09/13
Sales ($ mil.)	4.9%	–	445.7	506.5	704.4	687.7
Net income ($ mil.)	5.4%	–	13.9	14.0	49.3	22.4
Market value ($ mil.)	–	–	–	–	–	–
Employees	–	–	–	–	–	3,853

SOUTHCROSS ENERGY PARTNERS LP   NYS: SXE

1717 Main Street, Suite 5200
Dallas, TX 75201
Phone: 214 979-3700
Fax: –
Web: www.southcrossenergy.com

CEO: James W Swent III
CFO: Michael B Howe
HR: –
FYE: December 31
Type: Public

Southcross Energy Partners transports natural gas and natural gas liquids (NGLs) across the southern US. The company operates about 2500 miles of intrastate pipeline in Alabama Mississippi and South Texas. More than half of its pipeline mileage is located in Texas where it also has two gas processing plants that can process 185 million cu. ft. per day two treating plants and one fractionator. Top customers Formosa Hydrocarbons (a subsidiary of Formosa Plastics) and Sherwin Alumina together account for about 35% of sales. Southcross Energy formed in 2009 after it bought the Alabama Mississippi and Texas pipeline from Crosstex for $220 million. It went public in late 2012 raising about $170 million.

	Annual Growth	12/13	12/14	12/15	12/16	12/17
Sales ($ mil.)	1.2%	634.7	842.7	698.5	548.7	665.9
Net income ($ mil.)	–	(16.0)	(31.3)	(51.2)	(94.9)	(67.6)
Market value ($ mil.)	(44.7%)	1,456.4	1,284.4	287.6	109.1	136.5
Employees	–	–	–	–	–	–

SOUTHEAST MISSOURI STATE UNIVERSITY

1 UNIVERSITY PLZ
CAPE GIRARDEAU, MO 637014710
Phone: 573-651-2000
Fax: –
Web: www.semo.edu

CEO: –
CFO: –
HR: –
FYE: June 30
Type: Private

Guess where this university is located. Southeast Missouri State University — located in Cape Girardeau Missouri (two hours south of St. Louis and three hours north of Memphis) — offers some 200 areas of undergraduate study through five colleges as well as graduate degrees in biology business administration history mathematics public administration and a multitude of other fields. Nearly 12000 students are enrolled at the school which has a student-to-faculty ratio of 22-to-1. Southeast Missouri State University was founded in 1873 as a teacher's college.

	Annual Growth	06/14	06/15	06/16	06/17	06/18
Sales ($ mil.)	(4.3%)	–	123.1	109.7	111.4	107.7
Net income ($ mil.)	–	–	5.0	0.7	(6.0)	(12.5)
Market value ($ mil.)	–	–	–	–	–	–
Employees	–	–	–	–	–	941

SOUTHEAST TEXAS INDUSTRIES, INC.

35911 US HIGHWAY 96 S
BUNA, TX 776124031
Phone: 409-994-3570
Fax: –
Web: www.setxind.com

CEO: –
CFO: James Parsley
HR: –
FYE: December 31
Type: Private

Southeast Texas Industries (aka STI Group) is a down home manufacturer that likes staying local but it also keeps an eye open for international opportunities. The company specializes in the fabrication of pipe plate pressure vessel sheet metal heavy structural steel and drilling rig products. Southeast Texas Industries also provides project management construction and maintenance services. Customers include companies in the oil and gas power generation pulp and paper and petrochemical industries along with engineering firms that work on industrial projects. Southeast Texas Industries was founded in 1978.

	Annual Growth	12/01	12/02	12/03	12/04	12/07
Sales ($ mil.)	5.1%	–	98.6	36.8	36.8	126.7
Net income ($ mil.)	(9.0%)	–	8.5	0.2	0.2	5.3
Market value ($ mil.)	–	–	–	–	–	–
Employees	–	–	–	–	–	850

SOUTHEASTERN BANK FINANCIAL CORP   NBB: SBFC

3530 Wheeler Road   CEO: –
Augusta, GA 30909   CFO: –
Phone: 706 738-6990   HR: –
Fax: –   FYE: December 31
Web: www.georgiabankandtrust.com   Type: Public

Southeastern Bank Financial has Georgia (and its neighbors) on its mind. It is the holding company for Georgia Bank & Trust of Augusta and Southern Bank & Trust which serve the Augusta-Richmond County metropolitan area of Georgia and South Carolina from about a dozen branches. The company also has mortgage operations in Augusta and Savannah. The banks offer standard deposit products including checking and savings accounts. Funds from deposits are primarily used to originate real estate loans which make up about 85% of its loan book. The company also offers commercial and consumer loans in addition to wealth mangement and trust services.

	Annual Growth	12/10	12/11	12/12	12/13	12/14
Assets ($ mil.)	1.9%	1,607.1	1,614.8	1,662.5	1,689.3	1,732.8
Net income ($ mil.)	24.8%	6.9	11.0	14.4	16.3	16.6
Market value ($ mil.)	27.1%	67.1	72.8	112.0	137.2	175.3
Employees	(0.7%)	349	345	344	340	340

SOUTHEASTERN FREIGHT LINES, INC.

420 DAVEGA DR   CEO: –
LEXINGTON, SC 290737485   CFO: –
Phone: 803-794-7300   HR: Peggy Lyons
Fax: –   FYE: December 31
Web: www.sefl.com   Type: Private

Less-than-truckload (LTL) carrier Southeastern Freight Lines hauls freight throughout the southern US with a fleet of about 2000 tractors and 6000 trailers. (LTL carriers consolidate freight from multiple shippers into a single truckload.) Southeastern operates from a network of about 90 terminals in a dozen states (mainly in Texas) and Puerto Rico. Clients have included Lowe's and Home Depot. Through partnerships with carriers including Quik X Transportation A. Duie Pyle Dayton Freight and Oak Harbor Freight Lines Southeastern provides service throughout the US Mexico and Canada.

	Annual Growth	06/10	06/11*	09/15	09/16*	12/17
Sales ($ mil.)	18.4%	–	409.4	–	0.8	1,126.5
Net income ($ mil.)	32.1%	–	20.7	–	0.1	109.9
Market value ($ mil.)	–	–	–	–	–	–
Employees	–	–	–	–	–	8,000

*Fiscal year change

SOUTHEASTERN PENNSYLVANIA TRANSPORTATION AUTHORITY

1234 MARKET ST FL 4   CEO: –
PHILADELPHIA, PA 191073701   CFO: Joseph M. (Joe) Casey
Phone: 215-580-7800   HR: –
Fax: –   FYE: June 30
Web: www.septa.org   Type: Private

The Southeastern Pennsylvania Transportation Authority known as SEPTA provides passenger transportation services in the Philadelphia area. The agency's operations include buses subways and elevated trains trolleys and light rail and commuter rail lines. All together SEPTA maintains more than 300 stations and bus terminals chiefly in five Pennsylvania counties (Bucks Chester Delaware Montgomery and Philadelphia) and in the neighboring states of Delaware and New Jersey. Its territory spans some 2200 sq. mi. The Pennsylvania legislature established SEPTA in 1964 and over the years the agency has acquired the assets of several for-profit transportation companies that operated in the region.

	Annual Growth	06/13	06/14	06/15	06/16	06/18
Sales ($ mil.)	(0.3%)	–	–	–	528.2	525.3
Net income ($ mil.)	3659.6%	–	–	–	0.1	120.1
Market value ($ mil.)	–	–	–	–	–	–
Employees	–	–	–	–	–	9,000

SOUTHEASTERN UNIVERSITIES RESEARCH ASSOCIATION INC

1201 NEW YORK AVE NW # 430   CEO: –
WASHINGTON, DC 200056134   CFO: Peter Bjonerud
Phone: 202-408-7872   HR: Carl Patton
Fax: –   FYE: September 30
Web: www.sura.org   Type: Private

Southeastern Universities Research Association (SURA) is sure about science. The not-for-profit association is a consortium of more than 60 universities and colleges in the southern and eastern US that helps to coordinate and sponsor research projects in engineering biology physical sciences and natural sciences. Its main areas of interest are nuclear physics information technology and coastal research. To qualify for SURA sponsorship a project must be conducted by more than one institution. SURA also operates the Thomas Jefferson National Accelerator Laboratory a lab dedicated to studying the structure of atoms. SURA was founded in 1980 and SURAnet became the first regional IT network in the mid-1980s.

	Annual Growth	09/07	09/08	09/13	09/14	09/15
Sales ($ mil.)	69.6%	–	4.0	5.1	6.6	161.4
Net income ($ mil.)	–	–	(3.6)	(1.8)	(2.1)	(2.1)
Market value ($ mil.)	–	–	–	–	–	–
Employees	–	–	–	–	–	700

SOUTHERN BANC CO., INC.   NBB: SRNN

221 South 6th Street   CEO: Gates Little
Gadsden, AL 35901   CFO: –
Phone: 256 543-3860   HR: –
Fax: 256 543-3864   FYE: June 30
                                            Type: Public

The Southern Banc Company is the holding company for The Southern Bank which operates about five branches in Etowah Cherokee and Marshall counties in northeastern Alabama. Serving both local businesses and consumers the bank offers standard deposit products including checking and savings accounts certificates of deposit and individual retirement accounts. Its loan portfolio is dominated by one-to-four family residential mortgages business loans and consumer loans but Southern Bank also writes nonresidential real estate mortgages and loans secured by savings accounts. The bank also offers "factoring" services for its business-to-business clients which conducts account receivables management.

	Annual Growth	06/14	06/15	06/16	06/17	06/18
Assets ($ mil.)	(0.1%)	94.3	97.2	97.9	96.5	94.1
Net income ($ mil.)	–	(0.3)	(0.4)	(1.4)	(0.8)	(0.6)
Market value ($ mil.)	5.0%	7.5	8.0	8.1	9.1	9.1
Employees	–	–	–	–	–	–

SOUTHERN CALIFORNIA EDISON CO.   ASE: SCE PRC

2244 Walnut Grove Avenue, P.O. Box 800   CEO: Kevin M. Payne
Rosemead, CA 91770   CFO: William M Petmecky III
Phone: 626 302-1212   HR: –
Fax: –   FYE: December 31
Web: www.sce.com   Type: Public

One of the Golden State's largest utilities Southern California Edison (SCE) distributes power to 5.1 million customers in central coastal and southern California (excluding Los Angeles and some other cities). The utility's system consists of more than 12600 miles of transmission lines and some 91400 miles of distribution lines. SCE has about 6900 MW of generating capacity from stakes in nuclear hydroelectric fossil-fueled and solar power plants. The utility also has power purchase agreements and sells excess power to wholesale customers. SCE is a unit of utility and competitive power holding company Edison International.

	Annual Growth	12/14	12/15	12/16	12/17	12/18
Sales ($ mil.)	(1.5%)	13,380.0	11,485.0	11,830.0	12,254.0	12,611.0
Net income ($ mil.)	–	1,565.0	1,111.0	1,499.0	1,136.0	(189.0)
Market value ($ mil.)	(5.1%)	9,785.0	10,402.1	10,577.3	10,480.8	7,949.8
Employees	(2.6%)	13,600	12,678	11,947	12,234	12,219

SOUTHERN CALIFORNIA GAS CO.
NBB: SOCG P

555 West Fifth Street
Los Angeles, CA 90013
Phone: 213 244-1200
Fax: –
Web: www.socalgas.com

CEO: Patricia K. (Patti) Wagner
CFO: Bruce Folkmann
HR: –
FYE: December 31
Type: Public

Southern California Gas (SoCalGas) figures being the largest gas utility in the US gives it the right to call itself "The Gas Company." The utility an indirect subsidiary of Sempra Energy distributes natural gas to 5.9 million residential commercial and industrial meters (21.6 million customers) in more than 500 communities throughout the southern half of California. SoCalGas' natural gas facilities include 2962 miles of transmission and storage pipelines 50097 miles of distribution pipelines and 47524 miles of service pipelines. It also includes 11 transmission compressor stations and 4 underground natural gas storage reservoirs with a combined working capacity of 137 billion cu. ft.

	Annual Growth	12/14	12/15	12/16	12/17	12/18
Sales ($ mil.)	0.7%	3,855.0	3,489.0	3,471.0	3,785.0	3,962.0
Net income ($ mil.)	4.8%	333.0	420.0	350.0	397.0	401.0
Market value ($ mil.)	(2.8%)	2,821.0	2,548.0	2,384.2	2,652.7	2,516.2
Employees	(2.5%)	8,324	8,438	8,042	7,546	7,523

SOUTHERN CALIFORNIA PUBLIC POWER AUTHORITY

225 S. Lake Ave. Ste. 1250
Pasadena CA 91101
Phone: 626-793-9364
Fax: 626-793-9461
Web: www.scppa.org

CEO: –
CFO: Ron Davis
HR: –
FYE: June 30
Type: Government-owned

Southern Californians soak up the sun and the energy. The latter is where Southern California Public Power Authority comes in. The power authority generates and transmits electricity for 10 municipal distribution utilities and one irrigation district in southwestern California. Members include the municipal utilities of the cities Anaheim Burbank Colton Glendale Los Angeles Pasadena and Riverside. The authority has interests in three power plants and three transmission projects in the western US. It is constructing a fourth generation project. Southern California Public Power Authority also provides legislative representation and cost efficiency services to its members.

SOUTHERN CALIFORNIA REGIONAL RAIL AUTHORITY

900 WILSHIRE BLVD # 1500
LOS ANGELES, CA 900174701
Phone: 213-452-0200
Fax: –
Web: www.metrolinktrains.com

CEO: Arthur T Leahy
CFO: Ronnie Campbell
HR: –
FYE: June 30
Type: Private

The Southern California Regional Rail Authority (SCRRA) operates Metrolink a regional rail system that offers transportation for commuters and other passengers. Metrolink trains serve more than 55 stations in the greater Los Angeles area on several regional lines including Antelope Valley Orange County Riverside San Bernardino and Ventura County. Overall Metrolink operates over a network of about 510 miles of track including lines controlled by other entities. The SCRRA was established in 1991; operations began the next year.

	Annual Growth	06/06	06/07	06/08	06/09	06/10
Sales ($ mil.)	5.7%	–	96.9	108.9	113.4	114.3
Net income ($ mil.)	29.4%	–	55.5	46.0	71.6	120.4
Market value ($ mil.)	–	–	–	–	–	–
Employees	–	–	–	–	–	275

SOUTHERN COMMUNITY FINANCIAL CORPORATION
NASDAQ: SCMF

4605 Country Club Rd.
Winston-Salem NC 27104
Phone: 336-768-8500
Fax: 336-768-2437
Web: www.smallenoughtocare.com

CEO: –
CFO: –
HR: –
FYE: December 31
Type: Public

Southern Community Financial is the holding company for Southern Community Bank and Trust which operates more than 20 branches in the Piedmont Triad region and other parts of North Carolina. Serving area individuals small and mid-sized businesses and homebuilders the bank offers such retail services as checking and savings accounts money market accounts and credit cards. The bulk of Southern Community Financial's loan portfolio is made up of commercial mortgages residential mortgages construction loans and commercial and industrial loans. The bank also offers insurance products through an agreement with The Phoenix Companies. Capital Bank Financial Corporation is buying Southern Community Financial.

SOUTHERN COMPANY (THE)
NYS: SO

30 Ivan Allen Jr. Boulevard, N.W.
Atlanta, GA 30308
Phone: 404 506-5000
Fax: 404 506-0455
Web: www.southerncompany.com

CEO: Joseph A Miller
CFO: William C Grantham
HR: –
FYE: December 31
Type: Public

Southern Power provides power for the burgeoning population in the South. The company owns builds acquires and markets energy in the competitive wholesale supply business. It develops and operates independent power plants in the southeastern US. The company which is part of Southern Company's generation and energy marketing operations has more than 10500 MW of primarily fossil-fueled facilities generating capacity operating or under construction in Alabama California Florida Georgia Nevada North Carolina Texas and New Mexico. Southern Power's electricity output is marketed to wholesale customers in the region. It is growing by acquiring and developing solar power facilities.

	Annual Growth	12/14	12/15	12/16	12/17	12/18
Sales ($ mil.)	6.2%	18,467.0	17,489.0	19,896.0	23,031.0	23,495.0
Net income ($ mil.)	2.5%	2,031.0	2,421.0	2,493.0	880.0	2,242.0
Market value ($ mil.)	(2.8%)	50,769.3	48,370.9	50,852.0	49,714.9	45,404.0
Employees	2.6%	26,369	26,703	32,020	31,344	29,192

SOUTHERN CONNECTICUT BANCORP INC.
NYSE AMEX: SSE

215 Church St.
New Haven CT 06510
Phone: 203-782-1100
Fax: 203-787-5056
Web: www.scbancorp.com

CEO: Joseph J Greco
CFO: Stephen V Ciancarelli
HR: –
FYE: December 31
Type: Public

Southern Connecticut Bancorp is the holding company for The Bank of Southern Connecticut which serves greater New Haven from about five locations. The bank offers standard deposit products such as checking and savings accounts CDs and IRAs. It is mainly a business lender with operating loans and commercial loans secured by real estate comprising about 90% of the company's loan portfolio. Construction consumer installment and home equity loans round out its lending activities. Southern Connecticut Bancorp and Naugatuck Valley Financial called off plans to merge in 2010.

SOUTHERN FIRST BANCSHARES, INC. NMS: SFST

100 Verdae Boulevard, Suite 100
Greenville, SC 29607
Phone: 864 679-9000
Fax: –
Web: www.southernfirst.com

CEO: R Arthur Seaver Jr
CFO: Michael D Dowling
HR: –
FYE: December 31
Type: Public

Southern First Bancshares operates in two markets: Greenville South Carolina where it operates under the Greenville First Bank moniker and in Columbia South Carolina as Southern First Bank. Selling itself as a local alternative to larger institutions the company which has more than five bank branches targets individuals and small to midsized businesses. It offers traditional deposit services and products including checking accounts savings accounts and CDs. The banks use funds from deposits mainly to write commercial mortgages residential mortgages and commercial business loans.

	Annual Growth	12/14	12/15	12/16	12/17	12/18
Assets ($ mil.)	16.6%	1,029.9	1,217.3	1,340.9	1,624.6	1,900.6
Net income ($ mil.)	35.4%	6.6	10.2	13.0	13.0	22.3
Market value ($ mil.)	17.2%	127.1	169.5	268.8	308.0	239.5
Employees	10.2%	155	167	179	198	229

SOUTHERN ILLINOIS HEALTHCARE ENTERPRISES, INC.

1239 E MAIN ST STE C
CARBONDALE, IL 629013176
Phone: 618-457-5200
Fax: –

CEO: Rex Budde
CFO: Mike Kasser
HR: –
FYE: March 31
Type: Private

Southern Illinois Healthcare a nonprofit health care system operates the flagship 145-bed tertiary-care Memorial Hospital of Carbondale as well as Herrin Hospital (with 114 beds) and St. Joseph Memorial Hospital (with 25 beds). The hospitals serve residents of across southern Illinois. The nearly 280-bed system provides services such as birthing cardiac cancer and emergency care as well as surgery and rehabilitation. Its cardiac care is offered through an affiliation with the Prairie Heart Institute at St. John's Hospital in Springfield Illinois. The medical school at Southern Illinois University conducts its Family Practice Residency Program at Memorial Hospital of Carbondale.

	Annual Growth	03/13	03/14	03/16	03/17	03/18
Sales ($ mil.)	349.1%	–	1.5	1.6	1.7	624.7
Net income ($ mil.)	157.9%	–	0.7	0.5	0.7	30.4
Market value ($ mil.)	–	–	–	–	–	–
Employees	–	–	–	–	–	3,493

SOUTHERN ILLINOIS UNIVERSITY INC

1400 DOUGLAS DR
CARBONDALE, IL 629014332
Phone: 618-536-3475
Fax: –
Web: www.siumed.edu

CEO: –
CFO: –
HR: –
FYE: June 30
Type: Private

Southern Illinois University (SIU) helps to train future doctors dentists and other other professionals. The university enrolls some 32000 students at its two institutions — Southern Illinois University at Carbondale (SIUC which includes medical and law schools) and Southern Illinois University at Edwardsville (SIUE which houses education dental and nursing schools) — as well as smaller satellite centers. SIU offers associate baccalaureate master's doctoral and professional degrees. It also boasts a number of study abroad partnerships with international universities. Tracing its roots back to 1869 SIU is known for its extensive research programs.

	Annual Growth	06/14	06/15	06/16	06/17	06/18
Sales ($ mil.)	(0.7%)	–	597.9	740.0	601.2	584.8
Net income ($ mil.)	72.2%	–	27.4	(104.8)	(59.7)	139.7
Market value ($ mil.)	–	–	–	–	–	–
Employees	–	–	–	–	–	9,576

SOUTHERN MAINE HEALTH CARE

1 MEDICAL CENTER DR
BIDDEFORD, ME 040059422
Phone: 207-283-7000
Fax: –
Web: www.mainehealth.org

CEO: –
CFO: Norm Belair
HR: –
FYE: September 30
Type: Private

Southern Maine Medical Center (SMMC) provides health care services to the residents of York County Maine. The central facility of the not-for-profit medical organization is its 150-bed full-service hospital. Founded in 1906 the medical center also operates a home health care service and outpatient diagnostic and therapy centers. Specialty services include pediatrics cardiology oncology and emergency care. The medical center has a staff of about 200 physicians. SMMC is a member of MaineHealth a network of area hospitals and health clinics.

	Annual Growth	09/12	09/13	09/14	09/15	09/18
Sales ($ mil.)	4.5%	–	–	–	256.9	293.0
Net income ($ mil.)	–	–	–	–	(6.0)	(5.5)
Market value ($ mil.)	–	–	–	–	–	–
Employees	–	–	–	–	–	1,000

SOUTHERN METHODIST UNIVERSITY INC

6425 BOAZ LN
DALLAS, TX 75205
Phone: 214-768-2000
Fax: –
Web: www.smu.edu

CEO: –
CFO: –
HR: –
FYE: May 31
Type: Private

What do former first lady Laura Bush actress Kathy Bates and NFL Hall-of-Famer Doak Walker have in common? They're all graduates of Southern Methodist University (SMU). Founded in 1911 by what is now The United Methodist Church SMU is a nonsectarian private institution offering undergraduate graduate and professional degrees in arts business engineering humanities law science and theology through seven schools. It's one of a handful of schools nationwide to offer an academic major in human rights. Some 11000 students attend the university which has a student-faculty ratio of 11:1. About 85% of the 700-member full-time faculty hold the doctorate or highest degree in their fields.

	Annual Growth	05/10	05/11	05/13	05/17	05/18
Sales ($ mil.)	1.1%	–	602.6	563.3	580.6	652.2
Net income ($ mil.)	7.4%	–	58.1	115.6	56.9	96.1
Market value ($ mil.)	–	–	–	–	–	–
Employees	–	–	–	–	–	2,200

SOUTHERN MICHIGAN BANCORP INC (UNITED STATES) NBB: SOMC

51 West Pearl Street
Coldwater, MI 49036
Phone: 517 279-5500
Fax: 517 279-5578
Web: www.smb-t.com

CEO: John H Castle
CFO: Danice L Chartrand
HR: –
FYE: December 31
Type: Public

Southern Michigan Bancorp is the holding company for Southern Michigan Bank & Trust which operates about 20 branches in a primarily rural area near Michigan's border with Indiana and Ohio. The bank provides standard deposit services such as checking and savings accounts money market and heath savings accounts CDs and IRAs. It originates commercial financial agricultural consumer and mortgage loans. The banks also offers trust and investment services. Southern Michigan Bank & Trust got its start in the room of a hotel named Southern Michigan Hotel in 1872.

	Annual Growth	12/14	12/15	12/16	12/17	12/18
Assets ($ mil.)	8.0%	543.3	582.8	641.5	712.3	738.8
Net income ($ mil.)	14.1%	4.8	5.8	6.1	5.4	8.1
Market value ($ mil.)	16.0%	48.7	58.7	69.2	85.9	88.2
Employees	–	–	–	–	–	–

SOUTHERN MINNESOTA BEET SUGAR COOPERATIVE

83550 COUNTY ROAD 21 — CEO: Kelvin Thompsen
RENVILLE, MN 562842319 — CFO: Ian O'connell
Phone: 320-329-8305 — HR: –
Fax: – — FYE: August 31
Web: www.smbsc.com — Type: Private

Southern Minnesota Beet Sugar Cooperative (SMBSC) offers a sweet deal to its approximately 585 member/farmers. The co-op slices about 3 million tons of Minnesota-grown sugar beets annually. Converted products include baker's sugar and fruit sugar as well as molasses beet pulp pellets and shreds and raffinate (liquid from desugaring molasses). The co-op also provides member services such as seed agronomy research farm support products and workers' compensation insurance. SMBSC's refined and liquid sugars are marketed through Cargill Sweeteners; the by-products (dried beet pulp and beet molasses for use in cattle feed) are marketed by Midwest Agri-Commodities in North American and Europe.

	Annual Growth	08/13	08/14	08/15	08/16	08/17
Sales ($ mil.)	–	–	–	0.0	350.0	465.2	418.1
Net income ($ mil.)	(7.0%)	–	–	123.1	101.2	176.5	99.1
Market value ($ mil.)	–	–	–	–	–	–	–
Employees	–	–	–	–	–	–	610

SOUTHERN MINNESOTA MUNICIPAL POWER AGENCY

500 1ST AVE SW — CEO: –
ROCHESTER, MN 559023303 — CFO: –
Phone: 507-285-0478 — HR: –
Fax: – — FYE: December 31
Web: www.smmpa.com — Type: Private

Lake Wobegon may well get its power from the Southern Minnesota Municipal Power Agency. The power provider supplies wholesale electricity to its 18 member municipal distribution utilities which in turn distribute power to more than 109000 retail customers. The agency's main power source is the 900 MW Sherco 3-power plant generating unit near Becker Minnesota. Southern Minnesota Municipal Power Agency owns 41% of the low-sulfur Western coal fueled plant in partnership Northern States Power Company the unit's operator. It also relies on a range of intermediate and peaking units owned by the agency's members.

	Annual Growth	12/11	12/12	12/13	12/14	12/15
Sales ($ mil.)	(1.3%)	–	241.3	253.0	242.2	231.6
Net income ($ mil.)	5.6%	–	8.4	13.5	9.4	9.9
Market value ($ mil.)	–	–	–	–	–	–
Employees	–	–	–	–	–	41

SOUTHERN MISSOURI BANCORP, INC. — NMS: SMBC

2991 Oak Grove Road — CEO: Greg A Steffens
Poplar Bluff, MO 63901 — CFO: Matthew T Funke
Phone: 573 778-1800 — HR: –
Fax: – — FYE: June 30
Web: www.bankwithsouthern.com — Type: Public

Southern Missouri Bancorp is the holding company for Southern Bank (formerly Southern Missouri Bank and Trust) which serves local residents and businesses in southeastern Missouri and northeastern Arkansas through more than 10 branches. Residential mortgages account for the largest percentage of the bank's loan portfolio followed by commercial mortgages and business loans. Construction and consumer loans round out its lending activities. Deposit products include checking savings and money market accounts CDs and IRAs. The bank also offers financial planning and investment services. Originally chartered in 1887 Southern Bank acquired Arkansas-based Southern Bank of Commerce in 2009.

	Annual Growth	06/15	06/16	06/17	06/18	06/19
Assets ($ mil.)	14.2%	1,300.1	1,403.9	1,707.7	1,886.1	2,214.4
Net income ($ mil.)	20.6%	13.7	14.8	15.6	20.9	28.9
Market value ($ mil.)	16.6%	175.1	218.6	299.7	362.5	323.5
Employees	9.5%	327	342	390	415	470

SOUTHERN NATIONAL BANCORP OF VIRGINIA INC — NMS: SONA

6830 Old Dominion Drive — CEO: Georgia S Derrico
McLean, VA 22101 — CFO: William H Lagos
Phone: 703 893-7400 — HR: –
Fax: – — FYE: December 31
Web: www.sonabank.com — Type: Public

Southern National Bancorp of Virginia is the holding company for Sonabank which has some 20 locations in central and northern Virginia and southern Maryland. Founded in 2005 the bank serves small and midsized businesses their owners and retail consumers. It offers standard deposit products including checking savings and money market accounts and CDs. The bank's lending is focused on commercial real estate single-family residential construction and single-family homes as well as other types of consumer and commercial loans. In 2009 Southern National Bancorp acquired the failed Greater Atlantic Bank in an FDIC-assisted transaction; in 2012 it acquired the loans and deposits of HarVest Bank of Maryland.

	Annual Growth	12/14	12/15	12/16	12/17	12/18
Assets ($ mil.)	31.0%	916.6	1,036.1	1,142.4	2,614.3	2,701.3
Net income ($ mil.)	45.7%	7.5	9.3	10.3	2.4	33.7
Market value ($ mil.)	3.9%	272.8	314.1	393.0	385.6	318.0
Employees	19.1%	173	181	162	393	348

SOUTHERN NATURAL GAS COMPANY, L.L.C.

1001 LOUISIANA ST — CEO: Norman G Holmes
HOUSTON, TX 770025089 — CFO: John R Sult
Phone: 713-420-2600 — HR: –
Fax: – — FYE: December 31
Web: www.kindermorgan.com — Type: Private

Now here's a company that pipes in the goods that keep the South fueled naturally. Southern Natural Gas operates an 7600-mile long natural gas pipeline (SNG System) which serves major markets across the southeastern US. This system transports more than 3 billion cu. ft. of natural gas per day. The SNG pipeline system has about 60 billion cu. ft. of underground working natural gas storage capacity. Major customers include Atlanta Gas Light Company Alabama Gas Southern Company and SCANA. Southern Natural Gas is a unit of El Paso Pipeline Partners.

	Annual Growth	12/13	12/14	12/15	12/16	12/17
Sales ($ mil.)	(0.6%)	–	–	–	609.6	606.1
Net income ($ mil.)	(15.2%)	–	–	–	169.6	143.8
Market value ($ mil.)	–	–	–	–	–	–
Employees	–	–	–	–	–	3

SOUTHERN NEW HAMPSHIRE MEDICAL CENTER

8 PROSPECT ST — CEO: –
NASHUA, NH 030603925 — CFO: –
Phone: 603-577-2000 — HR: –
Fax: – — FYE: September 30
Web: www.snhhealth.org — Type: Private

Southern New Hampshire Medical Center (SNHMC) provides medical care for the residents of the Nashua New Hampshire area and surrounding region through Southern New Hampshire Medical Center and Foundation Medical Partners. The two-campus hospital which has about 190 beds and is part of the Southern New Hampshire Health System offers centers for cancer treatment diabetes education fertility and childbirth obesity sleep disorders trauma and other programs. Outpatient and rehabilitation services are offered through several clinic locations. SNHMC is also affiliated with physician practice organization Foundation Medical Partners and it is a teaching facility for the Dartmouth Medical School.

	Annual Growth	09/14	09/15	09/16	09/17	09/18
Sales ($ mil.)	5.9%	–	215.7	205.8	241.2	256.5
Net income ($ mil.)	–	–	(8.4)	46.5	40.4	27.1
Market value ($ mil.)	–	–	–	–	–	–
Employees	–	–	–	–	–	1,200

SOUTHERN NUCLEAR OPERATING COMPANY, INC.

42 INVERNESS CENTER PKWY
BIRMINGHAM, AL 352424809
Phone: 205-992-5000
Fax: –

CEO: Thomas A Fanning
CFO: –
HR: Amy Self
FYE: December 31
Type: Private

The night the lights went out in Georgia they should have called Southern Nuclear Operating Company. The company a subsidiary of Southern Company since 1990 operates six nuclear power units at three plant locations which combined provide about 20% of the electricity used in Alabama and Georgia. Southern Nuclear's Joseph M. Farley Nuclear Plant began commercial operation in 1977. The Edwin I. Hatch Nuclear Plant and the Alvin W. Vogtle Electric Generating Plant are jointly owned by Southern Company's Georgia Power (50%) Oglethorpe Power (30%) the Municipal Electrical Authority of Georgia (18%) and the city of Dalton.

	Annual Growth	12/01	12/02	12/03	12/04	12/16
Sales ($ mil.)	5.2%	–	455.5	441.9	479.8	922.5
Net income ($ mil.)	–	–	0.0	0.0	0.0	0.3
Market value ($ mil.)	–	–	–	–	–	–
Employees	–	–	–	–	–	2,960

SOUTHERN PINE ELECTRIC COOPERATIVE

110 RISHER ST
TAYLORSVILLE, MS 391685555
Phone: 601-785-6511
Fax: –
Web: www.spepa.com

CEO: –
CFO: –
HR: –
FYE: December 31
Type: Private

People pine for electricity and Southern Pine Electric Power Association (Southern Pine EPA) delivers. The consumer-owned utility cooperative that serves about 65000 members in south central Mississippi. The cooperative provides power over more than 10000 miles of line to some 60400 residential meters and 4600 commercial meters. A board of directors elected by Southern Pine EPA membership sets the policies and establishes the business structure of the organization which is led on a day-to-day operational basis by a general manager. Southern Pine EPA established four district offices in 1994 to enable the cooperative to better serve its large service area.

	Annual Growth	12/04	12/05	12/06	12/13	12/14
Sales ($ mil.)	4.7%	–	149.0	0.0	223.7	226.2
Net income ($ mil.)	–	–	34.8	0.0	21.6	0.0
Market value ($ mil.)	–	–	–	–	–	–
Employees	–	–	–	–	–	260

SOUTHERN PIPE & SUPPLY COMPANY, INC.

4330 HIGHWAY 39 N
MERIDIAN, MS 393011082
Phone: 601-693-2911
Fax: –
Web: www.southernpipe.com

CEO: –
CFO: Marc Ransier
HR: Ronald Black
FYE: December 31
Type: Private

Southern Pipe and Supply Co. sells pipes and anything that connects to them. Serving everyone from contractors and homeowners to commercial real estate property owners Southern Pipe sells plumbing heating and air-conditioning supplies through more than 90 stores located throughout seven southeastern states. The company operates a central distribution center and a handful of Southern Bath & Kitchen showrooms that feature various products for homeowners. Southern Pipe's vendors include dozens of supply companies and manufacturers such as MOEN Kohler and Amana Heating and Air Conditioning. Southern Pipe and Supply Co. was founded in 1938.

	Annual Growth	12/12	12/13	12/14	12/15	12/16
Sales ($ mil.)	3.6%	–	–	–	436.1	451.8
Net income ($ mil.)	(4.5%)	–	–	–	19.9	19.0
Market value ($ mil.)	–	–	–	–	–	–
Employees	–	–	–	–	–	767

SOUTHERN POWER CO

30 Ivan Allen Jr. Boulevard, N.W.
Atlanta, GA 30308
Phone: 404 506-5000
Fax: –

CEO: Joseph A Miller
CFO: William C Grantham
HR: –
FYE: December 31
Type: Public

Southern Power provides power for the burgeoning population in the South. The company owns builds acquires and markets energy in the competitive wholesale supply business. It develops and operates independent power plants in the southeastern US. The company which is part of Southern Company's generation and energy marketing operations has more than 10500 MW of primarily fossil-fueled facilities generating capacity operating or under construction in Alabama California Florida Georgia Nevada North Carolina Texas and New Mexico. Southern Power's electricity output is marketed to wholesale customers in the region. It is growing by acquiring and developing solar power facilities.

	Annual Growth	12/14	12/15	12/16	12/17	12/18
Sales ($ mil.)	10.1%	1,501.2	1,390.0	1,577.0	2,075.0	2,205.0
Net income ($ mil.)	2.1%	172.3	215.0	338.0	1,071.0	187.0
Market value ($ mil.)	–	–	–	–	–	–
Employees	–	–	–	–	541	491

SOUTHERN RESEARCH INSTITUTE INC

2000 9TH AVE S
BIRMINGHAM, AL 352052708
Phone: 205-581-2000
Fax: –
Web: www.southernresearch.org

CEO: Arthur J Tipton
CFO: David A Rutledge
HR: –
FYE: December 29
Type: Private

Southern Research Institute performs contract research in areas such as drug development and discovery engineering and environmental and energy issues. The not-for-profit organization launched a life science R&D consulting firm BioSafety Solutions in 2008. The institute's clients have included large government agencies such as the National Institutes of Health the US Department of Defense and NASA as well as corporate clients Mercedes-Benz and Southern Company. The organization tests anti-influenza and anti-HIV drugs for NanoViricides Inc.

	Annual Growth	01/14	01/15	01/16*	12/16	12/17
Sales ($ mil.)	(10.0%)	–	81.9	67.8	72.8	66.3
Net income ($ mil.)	–	–	(1.4)	(16.3)	(4.3)	(8.4)
Market value ($ mil.)	–	–	–	–	–	–
Employees	–	–	–	–	–	535

*Fiscal year change

SOUTHERN UNION COMPANY   NYSE: SUG

5444 Westheimer Rd.
Houston TX 77056-5306
Phone: 713-989-2000
Fax: 713-989-1121
Web: www.southernunionco.com

CEO: George L Lindemann
CFO: Richard N Marshall
HR: –
FYE: December 31
Type: Subsidiary

Diversified natural gas player Southern Union (a subsidiary of Energy Transfer Equity) is looking to form a more perfect union of natural gas transportation storage gathering processing and distribution assets. Its major utilities Missouri Gas Energy and New England Gas distribute natural gas to more than 550000 customers. Southern Union has gas storage facilities and more than 15000 miles of interstate natural gas pipeline across the US (primarily through Panhandle Energy and its 50% ownership of Florida Gas). It also operates 5500 miles of gathering pipelines and one of North America's largest liquefied natural gas import terminals. In 2012 the company was acquired by Energy Transfer Equity.

SOUTHFIRST BANCSHARES INC.
OTC: SZBI

126 N. Norton Ave.
Sylacauga AL 35150
Phone: 256-245-4365
Fax: 256-245-6341
Web: www.southfirst.com

CEO: Sandra H Stephens
CFO: Janice Browning
HR: Pat Bush
FYE: September 30
Type: Public

SouthFirst Bancshares is the holding company for SouthFirst Bank which has three branches in Alabama. Deposit products include checking and savings accounts NOW and money market accounts CDs and IRAs. One- to four-family residential mortgages account for more than half of the company's loan portfolio; SouthFirst Bank also writes commercial mortgages business loans and consumer loans. Residential and commercial construction loans are offered through subsidiary SouthFirst Mortgage. SouthFirst Bancshares agreed to be acquired by Palm Financial in 2009 but Palm terminated the deal later that year and SouthFirst sued the company for breach of agreement. The case is pending in Alabama state court.

SOUTHSIDE HOSPITAL

301 E MAIN ST
BAY SHORE, NY 117068458
Phone: 631-968-3000
Fax: -

CEO: -
CFO: -
HR: -
FYE: December 31
Type: Private

One of Long Island's oldest and largest community hospitals Southside Hospital offers acute care and other services through its more than 340-bed facility. Established in 1913 Southside Hospital operates as part of North Shore-Long Island Jewish Health System (North Shore-LIJ Health System). Its facilities include a Vascular Institute the Frank Gulden Radiation Oncology Center Regional Center for Brain Injury Rehabilitation Southside Hospital Institute of Neurosciences and a Center for Wound Healing. As part of its operations Southside Hospital also provides patients with pain management cardiology outpatient surgery orthopedics and women's services.

	Annual Growth	12/13	12/14	12/15	12/16	12/17
Sales ($ mil.)	7.7%	-	357.7	381.9	419.6	447.0
Net income ($ mil.)	-	-	(10.3)	(17.0)	(8.4)	(20.9)
Market value ($ mil.)	-	-	-	-	-	-
Employees	-	-	-	-	-	1,900

SOUTHLAND INDUSTRIES

12131 WESTERN AVE
GARDEN GROVE, CA 928412914
Phone: 800-613-6240
Fax: -
Web: www.southlandind.com

CEO: Andrew A. Fimiano
CFO: Jon Spallino
HR: -
FYE: September 30
Type: Private

Southland Industries designs builds and maintains a variety of mechanical systems for facilities around North America. The employee-owned mechanical engineering firm provides design construction fabrication and maintenance of plumbing process piping fire protection HVAC and controls and automation systems. Southland Industries' clients are in the health care life sciences hospitality industrial education government and telecommunication sectors. Projects include the renovation of the Pentagon following the terrorist attacks of September 11 and the M Resort in Las Vegas. Founded in 1949 Southland Industries has offices in the Northern California Southern California Mid-Atlantic and Southwest regions.

	Annual Growth	09/05	09/06	09/07	09/08	09/11
Sales ($ mil.)	2.9%	-	-	363.8	471.6	407.3
Net income ($ mil.)	21.1%	-	-	28.5	44.4	61.1
Market value ($ mil.)	-	-	-	-	-	-
Employees	-	-	-	-	-	2,150

SOUTHWALL TECHNOLOGIES INC.
OTC: SWTX

3788 Fabian Way
Palo Alto CA 94303
Phone: 650-798-1200
Fax: 650-798-1403
Web: www.southwall.com

CEO: B Travis Smith
CFO: -
HR: -
FYE: December 31
Type: Subsidiary

Southwall Technologies has developed a thin skin. The company makes thin-film coatings for auto glass electronic displays and architectural uses. The films absorb reflect and transmit energy such as UV light rays. Customers include glass makers like Saint Gobain and Pilkington. Southwall also makes films that reduce glare on computer screens LCDs phones and ATMs. Its architectural films are used on glass to insulate and to protect interiors from UV light. Investment firms with stakes in Southwall include Needham Capital Management (50%) and Dolphin Direct Equity Partners (21%). In 2011 Solutia acquired Southwall for an estimated $113 million.

SOUTHSIDE BANCSHARES, INC.
NMS: SBSI

1201 S. Beckham Avenue
Tyler, TX 75701
Phone: 903 531-7111
Fax: -
Web: www.southside.com

CEO: Lee R. Gibson
CFO: Julie N. Shamburger
HR: -
FYE: December 31
Type: Public

Southside Bancshares is the holding company for Southside Bank which boasts nearly 65 branches across East North and Central Texas with many around the cities of Tyler and Longview. About one-third of its branches are located in supermarkets (including Albertsons and Brookshire stores) and 40% are motor bank facilities. The bank provides traditional services such as savings money market and checking accounts CDs and other deposit products as well as trust and wealth management services. Real estate loans primarily residential mortgages make up about half of the company's loan portfolio which also includes business consumer and municipal loans. The bank has total assets exceeding $4.8 billion.

	Annual Growth	12/14	12/15	12/16	12/17	12/18
Assets ($ mil.)	6.2%	4,807.3	5,162.1	5,563.8	6,498.1	6,123.5
Net income ($ mil.)	37.3%	20.8	44.0	49.3	54.3	74.1
Market value ($ mil.)	2.4%	975.0	810.1	1,270.4	1,135.8	1,070.8
Employees	0.2%	813	683	679	855	820

SOUTHWEST BANCORP, INC. (OK)
NMS: OKSB

608 South Main Street
Stillwater, OK 74074
Phone: 405 742-1800
Fax: -
Web: www.oksb.com

CEO: -
CFO: -
HR: -
FYE: December 31
Type: Public

Southwest does what it can to make its earnings charts point northeast. Southwest Bancorp is the holding company for Bank SNB (formerly Stillwater National Bank and Trust Company) which has more than 20 branches across the states of Oklahoma Texas and Kansas. The bank primarily uses the funds it collects from deposits such as CDs and checking savings and money market accounts to originate commercial mortgages construction loans and commercial loans. Southwest Bancorp specializes in serving the health care industry offering such niche services as financing to launch physicians' practices and document imaging.

	Annual Growth	12/11	12/12	12/13	12/14	12/15
Assets ($ mil.)	(0.3%)	2,382.9	2,122.3	1,981.4	1,942.0	2,357.0
Net income ($ mil.)	-	(68.3)	16.2	17.4	21.0	17.4
Market value ($ mil.)	30.9%	119.2	224.1	318.5	347.3	349.7
Employees	(1.3%)	435	422	402	359	412

SOUTHWEST GEORGIA FINANCIAL CORP.   ASE: SGB

201 First Street, S.E.
Moultrie, GA 31768
Phone: 229 985-1120
Fax: 229 985-0251
Web: www.sgb.bank

CEO: Dewitt Drew
CFO: George R Kirkland
HR: –
FYE: December 31
Type: Public

Southwest Georgia Financial is the holding company for Southwest Georgia Bank which also operates as Baker County Bank Bank of Pavo and Sylvester Banking Company. With about 10 locations the bank provides such retail services as checking and savings accounts NOW accounts CDs and credit cards as well as property/casualty life and disability insurance and trust and investment services. Bank subsidiary Empire Financial Services provides commercial mortgage banking services. Real estate loans account for some three-fourths of the company's lending portfolio. Southwest Georgia Bank was founded as Moultrie National Bank in 1928.

	Annual Growth	12/14	12/15	12/16	12/17	12/18
Assets ($ mil.)	9.3%	374.3	414.9	448.5	489.1	534.8
Net income ($ mil.)	12.5%	2.9	3.4	4.0	3.8	4.6
Market value ($ mil.)	9.0%	36.6	40.6	50.9	61.1	51.6
Employees	1.3%	116	111	113	117	122

SOUTHWEST LOUISIANA ELECTRIC MEMBERSHIP CORPORATION

3420 NE EVANGELINE TRWY
LAFAYETTE, LA 705072554
Phone: 337-896-5384
Fax: –
Web: www.slemco.com

CEO: J U Gajan
CFO: Katherine Domingue
HR: –
FYE: December 31
Type: Private

Southwest Louisiana Electric Membership Corporation (SLEMCO) is no slowpoke when it comes to serving more than 93400 power customers in eight Louisiana parishes. SLEMCO provides regulated power transmission and distribution services via 9000 miles of power lines to its residential commercial and industrial members. It also provides energy conservation and street and security lighting services. SLEMCO extended assistance to help repair the badly damaged infrastructure in parishes from New Orleans to the Mississippi border following the devastation caused by Hurricane Katrina.

	Annual Growth	12/07	12/08	12/15	12/16	12/18
Sales ($ mil.)	3.7%	–	161.8	211.9	225.4	233.4
Net income ($ mil.)	3.3%	–	9.2	2.5	(0.5)	12.8
Market value ($ mil.)	–	–	–	–	–	–
Employees	–	–	–	–	–	269

SOUTHWEST MISSISSIPPI REGIONAL MEDICAL CENTER

215 MARION AVE
MCCOMB, MS 396482705
Phone: 601-249-5500
Fax: –
Web: www.smrmc.com

CEO: Norman Price
CFO: Reece Nunnery
HR: –
FYE: September 30
Type: Private

In M-I-S-S-I-S-S-I-P-P-I health care is spelled S-M-R-M-C. Southwest Mississippi Regional Medical Center (SMRMC) provides health care services to southwestern Mississippi counties and nearby portions of Louisiana. The medical center campus established in 1969 includes a 165-bed inpatient hospital as well as cancer and cardiovascular institutes a geriatric/psychiatric unit and a home health agency. SMRMC also owns and operates a number of clinics providing family medicine services as well as outpatient rehabilitation and surgery centers. The medical center founded in 1969 has about 70 physicians on staff. Its emergency room serves as a regional level III trauma center.

	Annual Growth	09/14	09/15	09/16	09/17	09/18
Sales ($ mil.)	(3.9%)	–	139.7	141.3	139.0	124.0
Net income ($ mil.)	–	–	(0.8)	0.2	(8.7)	(14.6)
Market value ($ mil.)	–	–	–	–	–	–
Employees	–	–	–	–	–	1,100

SOUTHWEST RESEARCH INSTITUTE INC

6220 CULEBRA RD
SAN ANTONIO, TX 782385100
Phone: 210-684-5111
Fax: –
Web: www.swri.org

CEO: Adam L Hamilton
CFO: –
HR: –
FYE: September 28
Type: Private

If you're looking for research at an institute in the Southwest look no further. Founded in 1947 by oilman and rancher Thomas Slick Jr. Southwest Research Institute (SwRI) is an independent not-for-profit research and development institution that contracts to explore subjects in areas including automation and data systems applied physics space science and engineering and chemistry. SwRI has about 2700 scientists engineers and support staff at some 40 laboratories and offices in the US China and the UK. Customers include the private sector and government agencies. SwRI's Signature Science subsidiary researches national security environmental management and biotechnology.

	Annual Growth	09/14	09/15	09/16	09/17	09/18
Sales ($ mil.)	(0.5%)	–	592.4	559.8	498.1	583.7
Net income ($ mil.)	17.3%	–	23.8	6.9	11.4	38.4
Market value ($ mil.)	–	–	–	–	–	–
Employees	–	–	–	–	–	2,754

SOUTHWESTERN ELECTRIC POWER CO.   NL:

1 Riverside Plaza
Columbus, OH 43215
Phone: 614 716-1000
Fax: –

CEO: Nicholas K Akins
CFO: Brian X Tierney
HR: –
FYE: December 31
Type: Public

Southwestern Electric Power cuts a wide welcome swath through the southwestern US to help beat the sweltering heat. The utility founded in 1912 serves some 520400 electricity customers in portions of Arkansas Louisiana and Texas. Southwestern Electric Power operates 20450 miles of transmission and distribution lines. Southwestern Electric Power also has interests in fossil-fueled power plants (including 73% of the $1.7 billion Turk plant in Arkansas) that give it a generating capacity of 4850 MW and it sells power to wholesale customers. The utility is a subsidiary of American Electric Power Company (AEP).

	Annual Growth	12/14	12/15	12/16	12/17	12/18
Sales ($ mil.)	(0.3%)	1,846.4	1,780.9	1,748.0	1,779.9	1,821.9
Net income ($ mil.)	1.2%	140.4	192.3	165.6	124.7	147.2
Market value ($ mil.)	–	–	–	–	–	–
Employees	0.0%	1,468	1,483	1,486	1,479	1,469

SOUTHWESTERN ENERGY COMPANY   NYS: SWN

10000 Energy Drive
Spring, TX 77389
Phone: 832 796-1000
Fax: –
Web: www.swn.com

CEO: William J. (Bill) Way
CFO: R. Craig Owen
HR: –
FYE: December 31
Type: Public

Southwestern Energy is a gas and oil exploration and production company with natural gas gathering transportation and marketing activities. The company operates in Arkansas and Texas as well as New Brunswick Canada. Southwestern boasts estimated proved reserves of more than 14.8 trillion cu. ft. of natural gas equivalent all of which was natural gas. Southwestern's core properties include assets in the Fayetteville Shale play and the Marcellus Shale.

	Annual Growth	12/14	12/15	12/16	12/17	12/18
Sales ($ mil.)	(1.1%)	4,038.0	3,133.0	2,436.0	3,203.0	3,862.0
Net income ($ mil.)	(12.7%)	924.0	(4,556.0)	(2,643.0)	1,046.0	537.0
Market value ($ mil.)	(40.5%)	14,908.9	3,884.3	5,911.1	3,048.4	1,862.9
Employees	(23.3%)	2,781	2,597	1,469	1,575	960

SOUTHWESTERN UNIVERSITY

1001 E UNIVERSITY AVE
GEORGETOWN, TX 786266107
Phone: 512-863-6511
Fax: –
Web: www.southwestern.edu

CEO: –
CFO: –
HR: –
FYE: June 30
Type: Private

The first institution of higher learning in Texas Southwestern University was chartered by the Republic of Texas in 1840. The liberal arts university consists of The Brown College of Arts and Sciences and The Sarofim School of Fine Arts. It offers more than two-dozen undergraduate majors as well as pre-professional and certification programs and confers bachelor's degrees in arts music fine arts and science. Affiliated with The United Methodist Church Southwestern University has an enrollment of more than 1500 students. More than 80% of students live in residence halls on campus which is located on the edge of the Texas Hill Country in Georgetown Texas just north of Austin.

	Annual Growth	06/11	06/12	06/13	06/14	06/15
Sales ($ mil.)	24.7%	–	46.1	69.0	58.2	89.5
Net income ($ mil.)	–	–	(25.2)	43.3	24.4	6.2
Market value ($ mil.)	–	–	–	–	–	–
Employees						357

SP PLUS CORP
NMS: SP

200 E. Randolph Street, Suite 7700
Chicago, IL 60601-7702
Phone: 312 274-2000
Fax: –
Web: www.spplus.com

CEO: G. Marc Baumann
CFO: Vance C. Johnston
HR: Colleen Kozak
FYE: December 31
Type: Public

SP Plus (formerly Standard Parking) wants to be the driving force in the parking industry — and it likely is. The parking behemoth manages about 4200 surface and multilevel parking facilities for airports hospitals hotels local governments office buildings retail centers sports venues and universities in more than 340 cities throughout the US and Canada. Its airport facilities consist of parking and shuttle bus operations at more than 75 airports including Chicago O'Hare and Dallas/Fort Worth International. Overall SP Plus provides more than 2 million parking spaces.

	Annual Growth	12/14	12/15	12/16	12/17	12/18
Sales ($ mil.)	(0.8%)	1,514.7	1,615.9	1,615.5	1,590.5	1,468.4
Net income ($ mil.)	23.2%	23.1	17.4	23.1	41.2	53.2
Market value ($ mil.)	4.0%	574.8	544.5	641.4	845.3	673.0
Employees	(0.6%)	24,030	21,974	22,490	20,800	23,500

SPACE SYSTEMS/LORAL INC.

3825 Fabian Way
Palo Alto CA 94303-4604
Phone: 650-852-4000
Fax: 610-926-6327
Web: www.rednersmarkets.com

CEO: –
CFO: Ron Haley
HR: –
FYE: December 31
Type: Subsidiary

For Space Systems/Loral (SS/L) business is up in the air. The company makes satellites and related accessories for commercial and government customers. Its fixed satellite services supplies satellites that beam TV radio and other communications information from orbit to a fixed location on the ground. Its direct broadcast satellites send TV to DISH and DIRECTV subscribers' homes while broadband services facilitate Internet connections across North America. The mobile broadcast services and mobile satellite services groups send audio video and communications signals to cars and cell phones. SS/L is a subsidiary of Loral Space & Communications which has agreed to sell SS/L to a rival.

SPACELABS HEALTHCARE INC.

5150 220th Ave. SE
Issaquah WA 98029
Phone: 425-657-7200
Fax: 425-657-7212
Web: www.spacelabshealthcare.com

CEO: Deepak Chopra
CFO: Alan Edrick
HR: –
FYE: June 30
Type: Subsidiary

Spacelabs Healthcare launched monitoring the health of NASA astronauts; now it designs makes sells and services diagnostic and therapeutic equipment for Earth-bound patients. The company operates through four divisions: Patient Monitoring & Connectivity Anesthesia Delivery & Ventilation Diagnostic Cardiology and Clinician Education. Its Ultraview bedside patient monitor and telemetry systems monitor patient data and transmit it to caregivers through a wireless network. Its Blease anesthesia delivery systems and ventilators are used in operative and perioperative settings. Spacelabs Healthcare is owned by OSI Systems and accounts for about 30% of its parent company's sales.

SPAN-AMERICA MEDICAL SYSTEMS, INC.
NMS: SPAN

70 Commerce Center
Greenville, SC 29615
Phone: 864 288-8877
Fax: –
Web: www.spanamerica.com

CEO: James D Ferguson
CFO: Richard C Coggins
HR: –
FYE: October 1/
Type: Public

With its mattresses and cushioning products Span-America Medical Systems offers more comfort to the sick and wounded than Grandma's chicken soup. The company's medical products division makes therapeutic mattresses and mattress overlays (under the Geo-Matt and PressureGuard brand names) as well as Span-Aid patient positioners (used to elevate and support body parts) and Isch-Dish pressure-relief seat cushions to aid wound healing. Span-America also markets skin care creams for wound management and consumer bedding and industrial foam products. It sells its wares through sales staff and distributors to hospitals home health care dealers and extended-care facilities in the US and Canada.

	Annual Growth	09/12	09/13	09/14*	10/15	10/16
Sales ($ mil.)	(2.9%)	76.1	73.8	55.9	64.3	67.6
Net income ($ mil.)	(5.0%)	5.2	5.1	2.6	4.0	4.2
Market value ($ mil.)	2.4%	46.2	59.0	52.5	48.5	50.7
Employees	(8.8%)	344	275	253	261	238

*Fiscal year change

SPANISH BROADCASTING SYSTEM INC
NBB: SBSA A

7007 NW 77th Ave.
Miami, FL 33166
Phone: 305 441-6901
Fax: –
Web: www.spanishbroadcasting.com

CEO: Raul Alarcon
CFO: Jose I Molina
HR: –
FYE: December 31
Type: Public

You might say this company is turning up the volume on Spanish radio. Spanish Broadcasting System (SBS) is one of the largest Spanish-language radio broadcasters in the US (along with Univision Radio and Entravision) with 20 stations in the US and Puerto Rico. Its radio stations serve such large markets as Chicago Los Angeles New York City and Miami reaching about half the US Hispanic population with music formats ranging from regional Mexican to Spanish tropical. In addition the company operates website LaMusica.com and several TV stations that offer original and syndicated Spanish-language programming under the Mega TV brand. Chairman and CEO R- - ul Alarc- - n Jr. controls about 80% of SBS.

	Annual Growth	12/14	12/15	12/16	12/17	12/18
Sales ($ mil.)	(0.7%)	146.3	146.9	144.6	134.7	142.4
Net income ($ mil.)	–	(20.0)	(27.0)	(16.3)	19.6	16.5
Market value ($ mil.)	(48.9%)	19.1	21.3	20.4	1.8	1.3
Employees	(5.6%)	557	567	484	492	442

SPANSION INC
NYS: CODE

915 DeGuigne Drive
Sunnyvale, CA 94088
Phone: 408 962-2500
Fax: –
Web: www.spansion.com

CEO: John H Kispert
CFO: Randy W Furr
HR: –
FYE: December 29
Type: Public

Spansion favors flash expansion. The company originally formed as a joint venture between Advanced Micro Devices and Fujitsu makes and markets flash memory devices. Flash memory is used in a wide variety of electronic devices including wireless phones networking equipment and automotive subsystems. Although the flash memory market is dominated by NAND flash memory (used in MP3 players digital cameras USB flash drives) Spansion primarily sells NOR flash memory (used mainly in wireless phones). To address the NAND market the company is developing new NAND products based on its MirrorBit technology. Spansion also provides hardware development tools and production manufacturing support.

	Annual Growth	05/10*	12/10	12/11	12/12	12/13
Sales ($ mil.)	34.0%	403.6	764.7	1,069.9	915.9	971.7
Net income ($ mil.)	–	363.6	(96.7)	(55.9)	24.9	(78.3)
Market value ($ mil.)	(12.5%)	–	1,185.9	457.5	803.8	794.9
Employees	2.7%	–	–	3,400	3,375	2,838	3,685

*Fiscal year change

SPAR GROUP, INC.
NAS: SGRP

333 Westchester Avenue, Suite 204
White Plains, NY 10604
Phone: 248 364-7727
Fax: –
Web: www.sparinc.com

CEO: Christiaan M Olivier
CFO: James R Segreto
HR: –
FYE: December 31
Type: Public

SPAR Group knows how to fight for shelf space. Founded in 1967 the company provides an array of marketing and merchandising services to manufacturers and retailers. Clients include drugstore chains grocery stores and convenience stores. SPAR Group offers services such as in-store product demonstration and sampling shelf maintenance mystery shopping database marketing teleservices and market research. The company has an international presence through operations and joint ventures located in about 10 countries including Australia Canada India Japan New Zealand Romania South Africa and China.

	Annual Growth	12/14	12/15	12/16	12/17	12/18
Sales ($ mil.)	17.1%	122.0	119.3	134.3	181.4	229.2
Net income ($ mil.)	–	3.3	0.9	0.2	(0.9)	(1.6)
Market value ($ mil.)	(21.4%)	29.1	21.2	20.8	25.6	11.1
Employees	2.5%	18,000	17,100	18,500	26,100	19,900

SPARK NETWORKS INC
ASE: LOV

11150 Santa Monica Boulevard, Suite 600
Los Angeles, CA 90025
Phone: 310 893-0550
Fax: –
Web: www.spark.net

CEO: Daniel M Rosenthal
CFO: Robert W O'Hare
HR: Gabby Correa
FYE: December 31
Type: Public

Find yourself humming "Matchmaker Matchmaker make me a match" just a little too often? Spark Networks (formerly MatchNet) can help. The company owns and operates a variety of online personal sites including dating sites JDate.com (for Jewish singles) BlackSingles.com and ChristianMingle.com. Spark Networks also operates websites in English Hebrew and French. Most revenue comes from subscriptions — members pay a monthly fee to communicate with other users. (Customers are offered discounts for longer-term subscriptions.) In addition the company offers offline events and opportunities for travel (such as cruises dinners speed dating and mixers) designed to encourage live social interaction.

	Annual Growth	12/11	12/12	12/13	12/14	12/15
Sales ($ mil.)	(0.2%)	48.5	61.7	69.4	61.6	48.1
Net income ($ mil.)	–	(1.6)	(15.0)	(12.4)	(1.1)	(1.4)
Market value ($ mil.)	0.3%	98.2	201.6	159.2	92.8	99.5
Employees	6.1%	161	182	200	222	204

SPARROW HEALTH SYSTEM

1215 E MICHIGAN AVE
LANSING, MI 489121811
Phone: 517-364-1000
Fax: –
Web: www.sparrow.org

CEO: William Roeser
CFO: Paula Reichle
HR: –
FYE: December 31
Type: Private

Ailing residents of central Michigan fly to Sparrow Health System for care. The not-for-profit network's hospitals include the flagship Sparrow Hospital Sparrow Clinton Memorial Hospital Sparrow Specialty Hospital and Carson City Hospital. The health system also operates dozens of satellite clinics a long-term-care center a hospice care provider medical equipment rental unit and athletic club. Through affiliate Physicians Health Plan Sparrow Health provides health plan coverage to some 70000 Michigan residents. Its Sparrow Physicians Health Network includes some 1000 physicians in the region. The system traces its roots back to 1896.

	Annual Growth	12/13	12/14	12/16	12/17	12/18
Sales ($ mil.)	2.6%	–	1,156.8	1,286.3	1,259.2	1,281.7
Net income ($ mil.)	–	–	(53.2)	63.7	49.0	(58.0)
Market value ($ mil.)	–	–	–	–	–	–
Employees	–	–	–	–	–	3,400

SPARTA INC.

25531 Commercentre Dr. Ste. 120
Lake Forest CA 92630-8874
Phone: 949-768-8161
Fax: 949-583-9113
Web: www.sparta.com

CEO: Charles L Harrington
CFO: –
HR: –
FYE: December 31
Type: Subsidiary

SPARTA (doing business as Cobham Analytic Solutions) equips modern soldiers with something more than a spear and shield. The company provides technical products and services to the US military the Department of Defense and the Department of Homeland Security. As a prime contractor and subcontractor it contributes to the design and development of tactical and strategic weapons and defense systems including ballistic missile defense systems. The company also fabricates prototype hardware and makes composite parts for aircraft and missile systems. Parent Cobham plc sold SPARTA to Parsons Corporation in November 2011 for $350 million in cash.

SPARTAN MOTORS, INC.
NMS: SPAR

1541 Reynolds Road
Charlotte, MI 48813
Phone: 517 543-6400
Fax: –
Web: www.spartanmotors.com

CEO: Daryl M. Adams
CFO: Frederick (Rick) Sohm
HR: –
FYE: December 31
Type: Public

Spartan Motors has built itself on the foundation of its chassis. Founded in 1975 Spartan Motors (through its core Spartan Chassis unit) makes custom chassis for fire trucks motor homes and other specialty vehicles including mine resistant and light armored vehicles for the US military. The company also manufactures emergency vehicles through Spartan USA which was formed with the 2016 merger of three subsidiaries: Crimson Fire Aerials Crimson Fire and Utilimaster. Other operations manufacture chassis and other products to customer specifications for use in the package delivery one-way truck rental bakery and snack delivery utility and linen and uniform rental sectors.

	Annual Growth	12/14	12/15	12/16	12/17	12/18
Sales ($ mil.)	12.7%	506.8	550.4	590.8	707.1	816.2
Net income ($ mil.)	89.1%	1.2	(17.0)	8.6	15.9	15.0
Market value ($ mil.)	8.3%	185.8	109.8	326.7	556.3	255.4
Employees	9.9%	1,600	1,900	2,340	2,327	2,338

SPARTANNASH CO.

NMS: SPTN

850 76th Street, S.W., P.O. Box 8700
Grand Rapids, MI 49518
Phone: 616 878-2000
Fax: –
Web: www.spartannash.com

CEO: David M. (Dave) Staples
CFO: Mark E. Shamber
HR: Brian Wright
FYE: December 29
Type: Public

Grocery wholesaler and retailer SpartanNash distributes some 60000 nationally branded and private-label products to more than 2100 independent grocery retail locations across all 50 US states through some 20 distribution centers. It also services national retailers such as Family Dollar. In addition the company distributes goods to 600-plus US military commissaries and exchanges in the US and several other countries. On the retail side SpartanNash operates about 160 supermarkets under the Family Fare Supermarkets D&W Fresh Market VG's Food and Pharmacy Martin's and Sun Mart banners among others. The company traces its roots to 1917.

	Annual Growth	01/15	01/16*	12/16	12/17	12/18
Sales ($ mil.)	0.6%	7,916.1	7,652.0	7,734.6	8,128.1	8,064.6
Net income ($ mil.)	(16.9%)	58.6	62.7	56.8	(52.8)	33.6
Market value ($ mil.)	(13.2%)	928.3	778.0	1,421.5	959.2	607.2
Employees	(4.6%)	16,100	15,200	14,700	14,800	14,000

*Fiscal year change

SPARTON CORP

NYS: SPA

425 N. Martingale Road, Suite 1000
Schaumburg, IL 60173
Phone: 847 762-5800
Fax: –
Web: www.sparton.com

CEO: Joseph G McCormack
CFO: –
HR: –
FYE: July 01
Type: Public

As its name implies Sparton is big on defense. Working for aerospace defense and medical companies the company provides contract electronics manufacturing services primarily the design and production of electronic and electromechanical devices. Its products include printed circuit boards sensors and electromechanical components as well as fully built systems and devices. The company also manufactures an anti-submarine warfare device called a sonobuoy for the US Navy and foreign governments. Sparton which tracks its roots to 1900 generates most of its sales in the US.

	Annual Growth	06/14	06/15*	07/16	07/17	07/18
Sales ($ mil.)	2.8%	336.1	382.1	419.4	397.6	375.0
Net income ($ mil.)	–	13.0	11.0	(38.3)	1.3	(8.3)
Market value ($ mil.)	(9.0%)	272.8	268.7	220.8	216.3	186.8
Employees	3.7%	1,483	1,990	1,853	1,710	1,715

*Fiscal year change

SPAW GLASS CONSTRUCTION CORPORATION

13800 WEST RD
HOUSTON, TX 77041-1114
Phone: 281-970-5300
Fax: –
Web: www.spawglass.com

CEO: Joel Stone
CFO: –
HR: –
FYE: December 31
Type: Private

You don't need a spyglass to notice general contractor SpawGlass Construction Corp.'s projects. The buildings include the Cynthia Woods Mitchell Pavillion the Cockrell Butterfly Center and Wortham IMAX Theatre. SpawGlass provides design/build and preconstruction services to its clients for projects that range from office buildings special events facilities and dormitories to retail institutional and health care facilities. The company founded in 1953 is an employee-owned subsidiary of SpawGlass Holding LP which also owns general builder SpawGlass Contractors.

	Annual Growth	12/02	12/03	12/04	12/05	12/10
Sales ($ mil.)	(5.6%)	–	226.4	259.3	241.4	150.7
Net income ($ mil.)	33.9%	–	1.4	2.5	2.7	10.5
Market value ($ mil.)	–	–	–	–	–	–
Employees	–	–	–	–	–	220

SPAW GLASS HOLDING, L.P.

9331 CORPORATE DR
SELMA, TX 781541250
Phone: 210-651-9000
Fax: –
Web: www.spawglass.com

CEO: Joel Stone
CFO: Bobby Friedel
HR: –
FYE: December 31
Type: Private

Deep in the heart of Texas SpawGlass Holding is busy providing general building and construction management services for commercial and institutional projects through its SpawGlass Construction and SpawGlass Contractors subsidiaries. The group also offers design/build delivery and tenant finish-out services. Among its landmark projects is the interior restoration of the Texas State Capitol. It also worked on the NASA Shuttle Flight Training Facility near Houston and the University of Texas Health Science Center at San Antonio. Louis Spaw and Frank Glass formed SpawGlass in 1953. The company now employee-owned has offices in Austin Houston San Antonio and the Rio Grande Valley in Texas.

	Annual Growth	12/04	12/05	12/06	12/07	12/09
Sales ($ mil.)	(37.4%)	–	–	1,879.2	336.5	461.0
Net income ($ mil.)	–	–	–	0.0	5.9	8.7
Market value ($ mil.)	–	–	–	–	–	–
Employees	–	–	–	–	–	650

SPECIAL OLYMPICS, INC.

1133 19TH ST NW STE 1200
WASHINGTON, DC 200363645
Phone: 202-628-3630
Fax: –
Web: www.specialolympics.org

CEO: Mary Davis
CFO: Michael Meenan
HR: –
FYE: December 31
Type: Private

Special Olympics gives special attention to the differently abled. The organization offers year-round athletic training and competition in more than 30 team and individual sports for adults and children with intellectual disabilities. More than 4 million athletes in about 170 countries take part in the group's programs. Special Olympics believes participation in its activities helps athletes improve physical fitness and motor skills while developing self-confidence. The group's support comes mainly from contributions made in response to direct-mail campaigns and from individual and corporate sponsorships and donations. The late Eunice Kennedy Shriver organized the First International Special Olympic Games in 1968.

	Annual Growth	12/09	12/10	12/13	12/14	12/15
Sales ($ mil.)	3.9%	–	90.7	95.5	108.2	110.0
Net income ($ mil.)	–	–	0.1	(3.4)	(2.5)	(8.4)
Market value ($ mil.)	–	–	–	–	–	–
Employees	–	–	–	–	–	160

SPECTRA ENERGY CORP

5400 WESTHEIMER CT
HOUSTON, TX 770565353
Phone: 713-627-5400
Fax: –
Web: www.enbridge.com

CEO: Gregory L. (Greg) Ebel
CFO: J. Patrick (Pat) Reddy
HR: –
FYE: December 31
Type: Private

Spectra Energy covers the spectrum of natural gas activities — gathering processing transmission storage and distribution. The company now part of Enbridge operates more than 15400 miles of transmission pipeline and has 305 billion cu. ft. of storage capacity in the US and Canada. Units include U.S. Gas Transmission Texas Eastern Transmission Natural Gas Liquids Division and Market Hub Partners. It also has stakes in DCP Midstream Maritimes & Northeast Pipeline Gulfstream Natural Gas System Spectra Energy Income Fund and 75% of Spectra Energy Partners. Its Union Gas unit distributes gas to 1.5 million Ontario customers. In 2017 Spectra merged with Enbridge creating the largest energy infrastructure company in North America.

	Annual Growth	12/12	12/13	12/14	12/15	12/16
Sales ($ mil.)	(6.1%)	–	–	–	5,234.0	4,916.0
Net income ($ mil.)	121.7%	–	–	–	460.0	1,020.0
Market value ($ mil.)	–	–	–	–	–	–
Employees	–	–	–	–	–	8,700

SPECTRA ENERGY PARTNERS LP — NYS: SEP

5400 Westheimer Court
Houston, TX 77056
Phone: 713 627-5400
Fax: –
Web: www.spectraenergypartners.com

CEO: William T Yardley
CFO: Stephen J Neyland
HR: –
FYE: December 31
Type: Public

When you take one company's energy holdings and splinter them you get Spectra Energy Partners. Formed by Spectra Energy out of the former natural gas holdings of Duke Energy the company is a natural gas pipeline and storage facility operator. Its assets include a liquefied natural gas storage location in Tennessee 50% of Market Hub (two natural gas storage facilities in Texas and Louisiana) and 49% of Gulfstream Natural Gas System. All told Spectra Energy Partners has 3200 miles of natural gas transmission and gathering pipelines capable of moving about 3.6 billion cu. ft. per day. It also has 57 billion cu. ft. of gas storage capacity.

	Annual Growth	12/12	12/13	12/14	12/15	12/16
Sales ($ mil.)	80.8%	236.8	1,965.0	2,269.0	2,455.0	2,533.0
Net income ($ mil.)	56.5%	193.5	1,070.0	1,004.0	1,225.0	1,161.0
Market value ($ mil.)	10.1%	9,828.1	14,271.6	17,928.5	15,011.2	14,425.8
Employees	–	–	–	–	–	–

SPECTRANETICS CORP. (THE) — NMS: SPNC

9965 Federal Drive
Colorado Springs, CO 80921
Phone: 719 633-8333
Fax: –
Web: www.spnc.com

CEO: Scott Drake
CFO: Stacy McMahan
HR: Robert Fuchs
FYE: December 31
Type: Public

Spectranetics develops markets and distributes an excimer laser system that uses ultraviolet radiation rays to conduct minimally invasive treatment of various coronary and vascular conditions. Its CVX-300 laser unit and disposable delivery devices (fiber-optic catheters and sheaths) remove partial or total arterial blockages caused by plaque buildup; the laser system can also be used to remove lead wires from pacemakers and implantable defibrillators. The company's customers include major cardiac catheterization labs and hospitals in the US. Although its products are sold in some 65 countries Spectranetics generates nearly 85% of its sales in the US and Canada.

	Annual Growth	12/11	12/12	12/13	12/14	12/15
Sales ($ mil.)	17.9%	127.3	140.3	158.8	204.9	246.0
Net income ($ mil.)	–	0.9	2.2	(0.4)	(40.9)	(59.5)
Market value ($ mil.)	20.2%	308.0	630.1	1,066.5	1,475.2	642.4
Employees	15.3%	504	548	575	753	892

SPECTRUM BRANDS HOLDINGS INC — NYS: SPB

3001 Deming Way
Middleton, WI 53562
Phone: 608 275-3340
Fax: –
Web: www.spectrumbrands.com

CEO: David M Maura
CFO: Douglas L Martin
HR: –
FYE: September 30
Type: Public

And you will know them by their trail of brands. Spectrum Brands makes and markets products sold under some of the most recognizable names in the world. They include batteries (Rayovac and VARTA) pet foods and supplies (Tetra Marineland Dingo) personal care (Remington) and garden care (Spectracide Cutter Hot Shot). Its small appliances unit includes such notable brands as Stanley Black & Decker George Foreman Toastmaster and Farberware. A leader in the sale of rechargeable batteries and hearing aid batteries to manufacturers Spectrum Brands markets its products in more than 1 million stores spanning 160 countries. The company is 60% owned by HRG Group and 40% by publicly traded stock.

	Annual Growth	09/13	09/14	09/15	09/16	09/17
Sales ($ mil.)	5.2%	4,085.6	4,429.1	4,690.4	5,039.7	5,007.4
Net income ($ mil.)	–	(55.2)	214.1	148.9	357.1	295.8
Market value ($ mil.)	12.6%	3,792.4	5,214.5	5,271.0	7,930.9	6,101.0
Employees	5.6%	13,500	13,400	15,500	15,700	16,800

SPECTRUM BRANDS HOLDINGS INC (NEW) — NYS: SPB

3001 Deming Way
Middleton, WI 53562
Phone: 608 275-3340
Fax: –
Web: www.spectrumbrands.com

CEO: Joseph S. Steinberg
CFO: George C. Nicholson
HR: Stacey Neu
FYE: September 30
Type: Public

Spectrum Brands Holdings (formerly HRG Group) is a leading global branded consumer products company. It manufactures markets and distributes brands including Kwikset Weiser Baldwin National Hardware Pfister Remington George Foreman Russell Hobbs Black+Decker Tetra Marineland GloFish Nature?s Miracle Dingo 8-in-1 FURminator and IAMS. The company primarily serves pet stores warehouse clubs security/alarm monitoring providers hardware stores and home and garden distributors. It operates in 160 countries; about 80% of sales comes from the US. In 2018 HRG Group completed its merger with Spectrum Brands. Spectrum Brands continues as the successor to HRG Group.

	Annual Growth	09/15	09/16	09/17	09/18	09/19
Sales ($ mil.)	(10.1%)	5,815.9	5,215.4	5,008.5	3,145.9	3,802.1
Net income ($ mil.)	–	(556.8)	(198.8)	106.0	768.3	471.9
Market value ($ mil.)	45.6%	572.4	766.2	761.8	3,646.3	2,572.7
Employees	(4.9%)	15,922	16,021	17,113	13,000	13,000

SPECTRUM CONTROL INC.

8031 Avonia Rd.
Fairview PA 16415
Phone: 814-474-2207
Fax: 814-474-2208
Web: www.spectrumcontrol.com

CEO: Robert E Tavares
CFO: –
HR: –
FYE: November 30
Type: Subsidiary

Custom electronic components and systems are within the scope of Spectrum Control's product offerings. The company designs and manufactures components for many industry applications its largest being military/defense and communications equipment. It operates in four segments: advanced specialty products (antennas connectors ceramics and electromagnetic interference filters); microwave components and systems (amplifiers filters oscillators and synthesizers); power management systems (power distribution units and power strips); and sensors and controls (temperature sensors). Most of its sales are made in the US. Spectrum Control was acquired in 2011 by API Technologies for about $270 million in cash.

SPECTRUM GROUP INTERNATIONAL INC — NBB: SPGZ

1063 McGaw, Suite 250
Irvine, CA 92614
Phone: 949 748-4800
Fax: –
Web: www.spectrumgi.com

CEO: Gregory N Roberts
CFO: Paul Soth
HR: –
FYE: June 30
Type: Public

From gold bullion to fine wine and baseball memorabilia one auction house spans the spectrum of global collectibles. Spectrum Group International serves both collectors and dealers operating in two primary areas: trading (the majority of its business) and collectibles (handled through both auctions and direct sales). Its trading business operates through A-Mark Precious Metals which sells coins and other precious metals on a wholesale basis. Spectrum Group has auction houses in North America Europe and Asia. The company was founded by Greg Manning who started collecting stamps at age 7 and opened an office to market stamps in 1971 at the age of 25.

	Annual Growth	06/09	06/10	06/11	06/12	06/13
Sales ($ mil.)	14.6%	4,293.3	6,012.4	7,202.2	7,974.8	7,406.0
Net income ($ mil.)	(17.1%)	7.1	(1.1)	3.8	4.1	3.4
Market value ($ mil.)	0.0%	0.1	0.1	0.1	0.1	0.1
Employees	1.2%	142	143	177	190	149

SPECTRUM PHARMACEUTICALS INC   NMS: SPPI

11500 South Eastern Avenue, Suite 240
Henderson, NV 89052
Phone: 702 835-6300
Fax: -
Web: www.sppirx.com

CEO: Rajesh C. Shrotriya
CFO: Kurt A. Gustafson
HR: -
FYE: December 31
Type: Public

Spectrum Pharmaceuticals is a biotechnology firm focused on anti-cancer therapies. It has three late-stage candidates including poziotinib (for the treatment of non-small cell lung cancer and breast cancer) Rolontis (for chemotherapy-induced neutropenia in patients with breast cancer) and Apaziuone for bladder cancer symptoms. In 2019 the company sold its seven marketed products to Acrotech Biopharma in order to focus on its development candidates. The divestiture included Folotyn its biggest money-maker which is a treatment for patients with relapsed or refractory peripheral T-cell lymphoma. Other products included in the sale were Fusilev Zevalin Marqibo Beleodaq Evomela and Khapzory.

	Annual Growth	12/14	12/15	12/16	12/17	12/18
Sales ($ mil.)	(12.5%)	186.8	162.6	146.4	128.4	109.3
Net income ($ mil.)	-	(45.7)	(50.8)	(68.5)	(91.2)	(120.0)
Market value ($ mil.)	6.0%	765.9	666.5	489.6	2,094.5	967.1
Employees	(0.6%)	241	212	227	215	235

SPEED COMMERCE INC   NBB: SPDC

1303 E. Arapaho Road, Suite 200
Richardson, TX 75081
Phone: 866 377-3331
Fax: -
Web: www.speedcommerce.com

CEO: -
CFO: -
HR: -
FYE: March 31
Type: Public

Before there was streaming there was Speed Commerce. Speed Commerce (formerly Navarre Corporation) distributes home entertainment and multimedia software products and provides logistics for major retail chains (Best Buy Wal-Mart) and Internet-based retail channels (Amazon iTunes) throughout North America. Its smaller publishing segment is run through its Encore Software subsidiary which provides print education and family entertainment under such titles as The Print Shop Mavis Beacon Teaches Typing Hoyle PC Gaming and Punch Home Design. Founded in 1983 as an entertainment distributor Speed Commerce has diversified into a licenser and publisher of entertainment.

	Annual Growth	03/11	03/12	03/13	03/14	03/15
Sales ($ mil.)	(29.7%)	490.9	480.8	485.3	107.1	120.0
Net income ($ mil.)	-	-	11.2	(34.3)	(11.8)	(26.6)	(56.0)
Market value ($ mil.)	-	-	-	-	-	-
Employees	40.5%	413	279	819	1,123	1,609

SPEEDWAY MOTORSPORTS, INC.   NYS: TRK

5555 Concord Parkway South
Concord, NC 28027
Phone: 704 455-3239
Fax: -
Web: www.speedwaymotorsports.com

CEO: Marcus G Smith
CFO: William R Brooks
HR: -
FYE: December 31
Type: Public

Here's one sports company that lives life in the fast lane. Speedway Motorsports is the #2 operator of auto racing facilities in the US behind International Speedway Corporation (ISC) with eight motorsports facilities. Its tracks including Atlanta Motor Speedway Las Vegas Motor Speedway and Texas Motor Speedway (Fort Worth) host a number of events sanctioned by such US racing bodies as the Indy Racing League the National Hot Rod Association and the World of Outlaws; however more than 80% of the company's revenue comes from NASCAR events. Chairman and CEO Bruton Smith head of auto dealership empire Sonic Automotive owns about 70% of Speedway Motorsports.

	Annual Growth	12/13	12/14	12/15	12/16	12/17
Sales ($ mil.)	(1.4%)	480.6	484.3	496.5	512.2	453.6
Net income ($ mil.)	-	(6.5)	31.1	(34.4)	39.5	148.2
Market value ($ mil.)	(1.3%)	813.7	896.5	849.4	888.3	773.5
Employees	(1.7%)	1,077	1,070	1,087	1,071	1,005

SPELMAN COLLEGE

350 SPELMAN LN SW 589
ATLANTA, GA 303144399
Phone: 404-681-3643
Fax: -
Web: www.spelman.edu

CEO: -
CFO: Robert D Flanigan
HR: -
FYE: June 30
Type: Private

Spelman College is a private historically African American college for women. The college enrolls more than 2100 students from more than 40 states in the US and 15 countries. It offers majors in areas such as English economics mathematics music psychology art and religion. Tuition (for 12-20 credit hours) costs about $10650 and the student-faculty ratio is 12-to-1. Its alumnae include Sam's Club CEO Rosalind Brewer; former acting Surgeon General and Spelman's first alumna President Audrey Forbes Manley; author Pearl Cleage; and actress LaTanya Richardson Jackson. Spelman boasts a graduation rate of more than 80%.

	Annual Growth	06/14	06/15	06/16	06/17	06/18
Sales ($ mil.)	4.2%	-	90.4	99.6	97.2	102.2
Net income ($ mil.)	-	-	(4.8)	(11.6)	21.6	57.3
Market value ($ mil.)	-	-	-	-	-	-
Employees	-	-	-	-	-	550

SPF ENERGY, INC.

100 27TH ST NE
MINOT, ND 587035164
Phone: 701-852-1194
Fax: -

CEO: Jeffrey Farstad
CFO: Bruce Hest
HR: -
FYE: December 31
Type: Private

Super-jobber SPF Energy is also a super-pumper of petroleum. The company's Superpumper subsidiary runs a chain of about 15 convenience stores and gas stations in Minnesota Montana and North Dakota under the Cenex Conoco Exxon Sinclair Tesoro and Shell banners. Its Farstad Oil subsidiary offers bulk transportation of petroleum products including the annual distribution of about 250 million gallons of gas 20 million gallons of propane and 2.5 million gallons of lubricants. The Farstad fleet serves businesses and government agencies from Montana to eastern Minnesota and from northern Wyoming to the Canadian border. SPF Energy is owned by North American fuel wholesaler Parkland Fuel Corporation.

	Annual Growth	12/11	12/12	12/13	12/14	12/16
Sales ($ mil.)	(19.7%)	-	1,062.7	1,012.9	1,026.9	442.7
Net income ($ mil.)	7.7%	-	5.3	8.9	16.4	7.1
Market value ($ mil.)	-	-	-	-	-	-
Employees	-	-	-	-	-	300

SPHERIX INC   NAS: SPEX

One Rockefeller Plaza
New York, NY 10020
Phone: 212 745-1374
Fax: -
Web: www.spherix.com

CEO: Anthony Hayes
CFO: Anthony Hayes
HR: -
FYE: December 31
Type: Public

Spherix is sweet on health. The company's BioSpherix division is developing products from tagatose a low-calorie sweetener with possible applications for improving health. Approved for use in foods the company sold the food-use rights for tagatose to Arla Foods but hung onto the non-food rights which it then branded Naturlose. The product is in clinical trials as a possible treatment for Type 2 diabetes although patient recruitment has been slower than expected. Spherix reported it will likely need a development partner to see the product through to market. To supplement its income Spherix launched a Health Sciences division to provide regulatory and technical consulting services to other biotech firms.

	Annual Growth	12/15	12/16	12/17	12/18	12/19
Sales ($ mil.)	(27.7%)	0.0	0.9	1.2	0.0	0.0
Net income ($ mil.)	-	(51.5)	(6.5)	(3.3)	1.7	(4.2)
Market value ($ mil.)	73.9%	0.7	5.0	6.8	3.1	6.4
Employees	(6.9%)	4	5	3	6	3

SPINDLETOP OIL & GAS CO (TEX)

NBB: SPND

12850 Spurling Rd., Suite 200
Dallas, TX 75230
Phone: 972 644-2581
Fax: –
Web: www.spindletopoil.com

CEO: –
CFO: –
HR: –
FYE: December 31
Type: Public

In 1901 the discovery of oil at Spindletop marked the beginning of the modern petroleum industry. Today Spindletop Oil & Gas is keeping that tradition alive in its exploration for and production of oil and natural gas. The company has major operations throughout Texas as well as interests in oil and gas properties in more than a dozen other states. Spindletop Oil & Gas has proved reserves of more than 323000 barrels of oil and 12.5 billion cu. ft. of natural gas. The company also operates more than 26 miles of gas pipelines and an oilfield equipment rental business. It manages subsidiaries Prairie Pipeline and Spindletop Drilling. Chairman and president Chris Mazzini and his wife own 77% of the company.

	Annual Growth	12/14	12/15	12/16	12/17	12/18
Sales ($ mil.)	(15.5%)	13.2	5.9	4.5	5.6	6.7
Net income ($ mil.)	(46.4%)	3.2	(5.8)	(1.3)	(0.0)	0.3
Market value ($ mil.)	(7.9%)	35.4	13.6	19.5	25.3	25.5
Employees	(5.4%)	70	72	70	54	56

SPIRE ALABAMA INC.

2101 6TH AVE N STE 210
BIRMINGHAM, AL 352032761
Phone: 205-326-8100
Fax: –
Web: www.spireenergy.com

CEO: Steven L Lindsey
CFO: Steven P Rasche
HR: Judy Moseley
FYE: September 30
Type: Private

With all the gas a customer could possibly need Alagasco is THE gas co. in Alabama. A unit of Spire (formerly The Laclede Group) in 2015 utility Alabama Gas Corporation (Alagasco) distributed natural gas to 425000 commercial and industrial customers in about half of the counties in the state. The utility also provides gas transportation services to large end users who purchase wholesale gas from suppliers. Alagasco has seven operating districts: Anniston Birmingham Gadsden Montgomery Opelika Selma and Tuscaloosa. The Alagasco distribution system includes 11230 miles of mains and more than 12000 miles of service lines.

	Annual Growth	09/14	09/15	09/16	09/17	09/18
Sales ($ mil.)	1.5%	–	479.2	368.5	400.5	500.7
Net income ($ mil.)	(70.0%)	–	48.0	53.2	58.1	1.3
Market value ($ mil.)	–	–	–	–	–	–
Employees	–	–	–	–	–	819

SPIRE CORP.

NBB: SPIR

One Patriots Park
Bedford, MA 01730-2396
Phone: 781 275-6000
Fax: –
Web: www.spirecorp.com

CEO: Rodger W Lafavre
CFO: Robert S Lieberman
HR: –
FYE: December 31
Type: Public

Success in solar is more than an aspiration for Spire. Factories worldwide use Spire's photovoltaic solar cell manufacturing equipment including cell testers and assemblers to produce modules that convert sunlight into electricity. Its solar systems unit also uses the equipment to make solar energy modules for buildings and homes. Though Spire's roots are in solar energy the company also has a biomedical unit that provides coating services to orthopedic and other medical device makers. Its products are manufactured at its US headquarters and Spire gets almost half of its sales domestic customers. Key customers include First Solar and Stryker Orthopedics.

	Annual Growth	12/09	12/10	12/11	12/12	12/13
Sales ($ mil.)	(32.4%)	69.9	79.8	61.6	22.1	14.6
Net income ($ mil.)	–	(5.3)	(0.4)	(1.5)	(1.9)	(8.5)
Market value ($ mil.)	(43.6%)	49.4	48.0	5.8	4.6	5.0
Employees	(20.1%)	211	194	173	118	86

SPIRE INC

NYS: SR

700 Market Street
St. Louis, MO 63101
Phone: 314 342-0500
Fax: –

CEO: –
CFO: Steven P. Rasche
HR: Gerard Gorla
FYE: September 30
Type: Public

Spire is one of the top publicly-traded natural gas utilities in the US. Serving 1.7 million customers it sells regulated natural gas across the Midwest states of Missouri Alabama and Mississippi through its Spire Missouri Spire Alabama Spire Gulf and Spire Mississippi subsidiaries. The utilities have about 60000 miles of mains and service lines. Its Spire Marketing subsidiary provides energy marketing and related services to more than 120 wholesalers and 250 retail customers in the central US region. Spire also owns some gas transportation and storage assets.

	Annual Growth	09/15	09/16	09/17	09/18	09/19
Sales ($ mil.)	(0.3%)	1,976.4	1,537.3	1,740.7	1,965.0	1,952.4
Net income ($ mil.)	7.8%	136.9	144.2	161.6	214.2	184.6
Market value ($ mil.)	12.5%	2,779.6	3,249.1	3,805.2	3,749.1	4,446.9
Employees	3.5%	3,078	3,296	3,279	3,366	3,536

SPIRIT AIRLINES INC

NYS: SAVE

2800 Executive Way
Miramar, FL 33025
Phone: 954 447-7920
Fax: –
Web: www.spirit.com

CEO: Robert L. (Bob) Fornaro
CFO: Edward M Christie III
HR: Derek V Keuren
FYE: December 31
Type: Public

Ultra-low-cost carrier Spirit Airlines operates more than 600 daily flights between major US cities and popular vacation spots in South Florida the Caribbean and Latin America serving more than 75 destinations. The airline operates an all-Airbus fleet of about 130 single-aisle aircraft in the A320 family. Spirit Airlines capitalizes on an ancillary service model charging separately for baggage advanced seat selection and other travel-related upgrades. In addition to scheduled service the company partners with third-party vendors to offer a slate of vacation packages via its website. Domestic markets account for the majority of the company's sales.

	Annual Growth	12/15	12/16	12/17	12/18	12/19
Sales ($ mil.)	15.6%	2,141.5	2,322.0	2,647.7	3,323.0	3,830.5
Net income ($ mil.)	1.4%	317.2	264.9	420.6	155.7	335.3
Market value ($ mil.)	0.3%	2,727.9	3,960.8	3,070.2	3,964.9	2,759.4
Employees	16.5%	4,847	5,742	6,795	7,708	8,938

SPLUNK INC

NMS: SPLK

270 Brannan Street
San Francisco, CA 94107
Phone: 415 848-8400
Fax: –
Web: www.splunk.com

CEO: Douglas (Doug) Merritt
CFO: David F. Conte
HR: Tracy Edkins
FYE: January 31
Type: Public

Splunk loves diving for data. The company's software collects and indexes the machine-generated data produced by nearly every piece of hardware and software that contains a time-stamped record of transactions user actions security threats and other activity. With Splunk's software users can dive deep into the data analyzing monitoring and reporting for operational intelligence application management and security and compliance as well as analytics. The company partners with the likes of Microsoft and VMware to include its software in their products. Splunk counts about 17500 corporate and government customers in about 130 countries. The company relies on customers in the US for about 70% of its revenue.

	Annual Growth	01/15	01/16	01/17	01/18	01/19
Sales ($ mil.)	41.4%	450.9	668.4	950.0	1,270.8	1,803.0
Net income ($ mil.)	–	(217.1)	(278.8)	(355.2)	(259.1)	(275.6)
Market value ($ mil.)	24.7%	7,704.5	6,905.0	8,630.8	13,778.6	18,622.0
Employees	33.1%	1,400	1,400	2,700	3,200	4,400

SPOK HOLDINGS INC
NMS: SPOK

6850 Versar Center, Suite 420
Springfield, VA 22151-4148
Phone: 800 611-8488
Fax: –
Web: www.spok.com

CEO: Vincent D. (Vince) Kelly
CFO: Michael W. Wallace
HR: Bonnie Culp
FYE: December 31
Type: Public

Paging Dr. Spok? Actually it's Spok Holdings (formerly USA Mobility) doing the paging as a leading US provider of paging and other wireless services primarily for health care and large enterprises and government agencies. It offers one-way and two-way paging services nationwide over its own network while also marketing and reselling wireless voice and data services through an agreement with Sprint Nextel. Spok also provides customized wireless connectivity systems for health care government and education clients as well as telemetry systems used for asset tracking utility meter reading and other remote monitoring applications. It serves also has customers in Europe and Australia.

	Annual Growth	12/14	12/15	12/16	12/17	12/18
Sales ($ mil.)	(4.1%)	200.3	189.6	179.6	171.2	169.5
Net income ($ mil.)	–	20.7	84.2	14.0	(15.3)	(1.5)
Market value ($ mil.)	(6.5%)	336.6	355.2	402.3	303.4	257.1
Employees	0.4%	587	600	587	596	596

SPORT CHALET, INC.
NMS: SPCH A

One Sport Chalet Drive
La Canada, CA 91011
Phone: 818 949-5300
Fax: –
Web: www.sportchalet.com

CEO: –
CFO: –
HR: –
FYE: March 31
Type: Public

For those who play there's Sport Chalet. The sporting goods retailer operates 50-plus stores mostly in California but also in Arizona Nevada and Utah. It also sells its goods through its online shopping site. The stores which average about 41000 sq. ft. are known for carrying specialty products such as mountain climbing and SCUBA gear. Sport Chalet has traditionally specialized in gear for cold-weather sports such as skiing and snowboarding but its stores sell brand-name footwear apparel and equipment for many other activities too. Shoppers at Sport Chalet can sign up for SCUBA training and join dive clubs associated with the stores. Sport Chalet was founded in 1959 by the late Norbert Olberz.

	Annual Growth	03/09	03/10*	04/11	04/12*	03/13
Sales ($ mil.)	(0.8%)	372.7	353.7	362.5	349.9	360.6
Net income ($ mil.)	–	(52.2)	(8.3)	(3.0)	(5.1)	(3.3)
Market value ($ mil.)	67.7%	2.4	37.6	28.7	18.2	19.0
Employees	(1.6%)	3,200	3,000	3,100	2,900	3,000

*Fiscal year change

SPRAGUE RESOURCES LP
NYS: SRLP

185 International Drive
Portsmouth, NH 03801
Phone: 800 225-1560
Fax: –
Web: www.spragueenergy.com

CEO: David C. (Dave) Glendon
CFO: Gary A. Rinaldi
HR: –
FYE: December 31
Type: Public

Venerable but spry Sprague Resources delivers when it comes energy delivery. The company founded in 1870 as a coal and oil supplier has grown into one of the largest fuel suppliers in the northeast. Sprague Resources' products include diesel gasoline home heating oil jet fuel and residual fuels. The company distributes around 60 billion cu. ft. of natural gas some 1.5 billion gallons of petroleum products and about 2.5 million tons of bulk materials each year. It also owns or operates about 20 storage terminals that can hold more than 9 million barrels of refined products.

	Annual Growth	12/14	12/15	12/16	12/17	12/18
Sales ($ mil.)	(7.1%)	5,069.8	3,481.9	2,390.0	2,855.0	3,771.1
Net income ($ mil.)	(10.2%)	122.8	78.3	10.2	29.5	79.8
Market value ($ mil.)	(11.3%)	533.1	458.5	638.8	550.2	329.4
Employees	8.4%	580	590	600	880	800

SPRING ARBOR UNIVERSITY

106 E MAIN ST
SPRING ARBOR, MI 492839701
Phone: 517-750-1200
Fax: –
Web: www.saucougars.com

CEO: –
CFO: –
HR: –
FYE: May 31
Type: Private

Spring Arbor University is an evangelical Christian university affiliated with the Free Methodist Church. The liberal arts institution offers more than 70 undergraduate and 10 graduate degrees as well as professional programs. It has an enrollment of more than 4000 students most of which hail from Michigan. The school's main 100-acre campus in Spring Arbor Michigan is supplemented by about 20 satellite locations in Michigan and Ohio. Academic fields include business nursing and spiritual leadership. Spring Arbor University was founded as an elementary and secondary school in 1873.

	Annual Growth	05/12	05/13	05/14	05/15	05/16
Sales ($ mil.)	(0.9%)	–	67.4	69.3	67.1	65.5
Net income ($ mil.)	(28.0%)	–	3.6	2.9	1.3	1.3
Market value ($ mil.)	–	–	–	–	–	–
Employees	–	–	–	–	–	340

SPRINGFIELD HOSPITAL INC.

25 RIDGEWOOD RD
SPRINGFIELD, VT 051563057
Phone: 802-885-2151
Fax: –
Web: www.springfieldhospital.org

CEO: Michael Halstead
CFO: Andrew J Majka
HR: Janet Lyle
FYE: September 30
Type: Private

Bart Simpson might wind up in Springfield Hospital after cruising down the town's hilly roads on his skateboard. The 70-bed facility located in Springfield Vermont (also known as the Home of the Simpsons) serves 16 communities in southeastern Vermont and southwestern New Hampshire. Specialized services include adult day care emergency medicine physical therapy rehabilitation and surgery. Founded in 1913 the hospital also offers a childbirth center breast care center and inpatient and outpatient units for psychiatry neurology oncology and cardiac care. Springfield Hospital is part of the Springfield Medical Care Systems.

	Annual Growth	09/06	09/07	09/13	09/14	09/15
Sales ($ mil.)	1.3%	–	52.1	48.0	49.5	57.9
Net income ($ mil.)	–	–	2.7	0.1	(2.4)	(0.4)
Market value ($ mil.)	–	–	–	–	–	–
Employees	–	–	–	–	–	500

SPROUTS FARMERS MARKET INC
NMS: SFM

5455 East High Street, Suite 111
Phoenix, AZ 85054
Phone: 480 814-8016
Fax: –
Web: www.sprouts.com

CEO: Amin N. Maredia
CFO: Bradley S. (Brad) Lukow
HR: Gwynn Simpson
FYE: December 30
Type: Public

A fast-growing natural foods retailer Sprouts Farmers Market operates more than 310 stores in about 20 US states including Arizona California Colorado Nevada New Mexico Oklahoma Texas and Utah. The stores (ranging from 28000 to 30000 sq. ft.) sell organic and local produce baked goods all-natural meats and seafood imported cheeses bulk foods and vitamins and supplements. Stores also offer more than 450 bins of bulk rice spices nuts and grains. Sprouts also sells its own private label brand of groceries.

	Annual Growth	12/14*	01/16	01/17*	12/17	12/18
Sales ($ mil.)	15.1%	2,967.4	3,593.0	4,046.4	4,664.6	5,207.3
Net income ($ mil.)	10.2%	107.7	129.0	124.3	158.4	158.5
Market value ($ mil.)	(8.3%)	4,090.5	3,323.1	2,364.5	3,043.2	2,898.2
Employees	15.3%	17,000	20,000	24,000	27,000	30,000

*Fiscal year change

SPS COMMERCE, INC.
NMS: SPSC

333 South Seventh Street, Suite 1000
Minneapolis, MN 55402
Phone: 612 435-9400
Fax: –
Web: www.spscommerce.com

CEO: Archie C. Black
CFO: Kimberly K. (Kim) Nelson
HR: –
FYE: December 31
Type: Public

SPS Commerce answers the supply chain SOS. Founded in 1987 as St. Paul Software the company offers an Internet-based suite of supply chain management software to consumer goods suppliers retailers distributors and logistics companies in North America. Its software which is maintained and delivered as a service via the cloud is used by customers to manage place and fill orders and track the shipments of goods. Customers can electronically send invoices shipping notices and purchase orders automate shipment functions and evaluate the performance of their vendors or suppliers. Best Buy Costco and Callaway Golf are among SPS's thousands of customers.

	Annual Growth	12/14	12/15	12/16	12/17	12/18
Sales ($ mil.)	18.0%	127.9	158.5	193.3	220.6	248.2
Net income ($ mil.)	72.4%	2.7	4.6	5.7	(2.4)	23.9
Market value ($ mil.)	9.8%	1,964.6	2,435.7	2,424.6	1,685.7	2,857.9
Employees	6.9%	943	1,046	1,217	1,336	1,231

SPX CORP.
NYS: SPXC

13320-A Ballantyne Corporate Place
Charlotte, NC 28277
Phone: 980 474-3700
Fax: 704 752-4505
Web: www.spx.com

CEO: Eugene J. (Gene) Lowe
CFO: Scott W. Sproule
HR: NaTausha H. White
FYE: December 31
Type: Public

SPX Corp. blows hot and cold on a big scale. The supplies infrastructure equipment for heating ventilation and air conditioning (HVAC) detection and measurement and power transmission and generation. It makes and sells cooling towers and boilers underground pipe and cable locators power transformers and heat exchangers. SPX's brands include Berko Qmark Fahrenheat Radiodetection Pearpoint Dielectric and Waukesha. The company operates in 15 countries with a sales presence in 100 countries. Most of its sales are to customers in the US. In recent years SPX has divested non-core businesses starting with the 2015 spin-off of its flow technology operations into SPX Flow.

	Annual Growth	12/14	12/15	12/16	12/17	12/18
Sales ($ mil.)	(24.4%)	4,721.1	1,719.3	1,472.3	1,425.8	1,538.6
Net income ($ mil.)	(32.8%)	397.9	(82.7)	(67.2)	89.3	81.2
Market value ($ mil.)	(24.4%)	3,733.3	405.4	1,030.6	1,363.9	1,217.0
Employees	(26.9%)	14,000	6,000	5,000	5,000	4,000

SPX FLOW INC
NYS: FLOW

13320 Ballantyne Corporate Place
Charlotte, NC 28277
Phone: 704 752-4400
Fax: –
Web: www.spxflow.com

CEO: Marcus G. (Marc) Michael
CFO: Jeremy W. Smeltser
HR: Belinda G. Hyde
FYE: December 31
Type: Public

SPX Flow manufactures products for processing and transporting liquids that range from milk to oil. The company's products include pumps valves heat exchangers mixers metering systems air dryers filters hydraulic tools homogenizers separators and dehydration equipment. The company's products serve a wide range of end markets including food and beverage oil and gas power generation chemical mining and general industrial. A short list of its brands include Bran + Luebbe Lightnin Waukesha Cherry-Burrell and M&J Valve Products. About 35% of its revenue comes from the US.

	Annual Growth	12/14	12/15	12/16	12/17	12/18
Sales ($ mil.)	(6.8%)	2,769.6	2,388.5	1,996.0	1,951.5	2,090.1
Net income ($ mil.)	(24.4%)	134.5	87.5	(381.8)	46.4	44.0
Market value ($ mil.)	2.9%	–	1,187.4	1,363.9	2,022.9	1,294.2
Employees	(3.3%)	8,000	8,000	7,000	7,000	7,000

SPY INC
NBB: XSPY

2070 Las Palmas Drive
Carlsbad, CA 92011
Phone: 760 804-8420
Fax: –
Web: www.spyoptic.com

CEO: Seth Hamot
CFO: James McGinty
HR: –
FYE: December 31
Type: Public

SPY Inc. formerly known as Orange 21 has its sights set on the colorful Gen Y. The company designs and distributes high-end sunglasses and goggles under the Spy Spy Optic Margaritaville and O'Neill brands. SPY markets its upscale eyewear to the club kid scene for use in surfing skateboarding snowboarding and other extreme action sports. The line is available at about 3000 outlets in the US and Canada including Sunglass Hut Sport Chalet and Zumiez and internationally through around 3000 retailers. SPY also markets some apparel and accessories. In late 2010 the company refocused and sold its LEM subsidiary which made up most of SPY's eyewear and provided manufacturing services for other companies.

	Annual Growth	12/10	12/11	12/12	12/13	12/14
Sales ($ mil.)	2.2%	35.0	33.4	35.6	37.8	38.1
Net income ($ mil.)	–	(4.6)	(10.9)	(7.2)	(2.9)	(1.9)
Market value ($ mil.)	(12.3%)	18.1	24.1	20.1	19.4	10.7
Employees	0.8%	91	108	86	85	94

SPYR INC
NBB: SPYR

4643 S. Ulster St., Suite 1510
Denver, CO 80237
Phone: 303 991-8000
Fax: –
Web: www.pocketstarships.com

CEO: James R Thompson
CFO: Barry D Loveless
HR: –
FYE: December 31
Type: Public

Eat At Joe's operates a themed casual-dining restaurant at the Philadelphia airport that offers breakfast lunch and dinner. The concept features such interior appointments as 1950s-era Harley-Davidsons booths resembling 1957 Chevy interiors and tabletop jukeboxes. Patrons can choose from such menu items as hot dogs burgers and meatloaf. CEO Joseph Fiore owns more than 60% of Eat at Joe's.

	Annual Growth	12/14	12/15	12/16	12/17	12/18
Sales ($ mil.)	(28.1%)	1.5	1.6	1.6	0.1	0.4
Net income ($ mil.)	–	2.2	(8.9)	(7.4)	(16.1)	(7.1)
Market value ($ mil.)	(24.0%)	47.6	39.7	122.7	52.6	15.9
Employees	(20.5%)	10	20	24	6	4

SRAM INTERNATIONAL CORPORATION

1333 N. Kingsbury St. 4th Fl.
Chicago IL 60642
Phone: 312-664-8800
Fax: 312-664-8826
Web: www.sram.com

CEO: Ken Lousberg
CFO: Mike Herr
HR: –
FYE: December 31
Type: Private

SRAM International keeps the wheels of commerce spinning as it makes and sells bicycle shifters derailleurs brakes chains pedals power meters and other cycling parts. Its components are used by bicycle manufacturers (some 65% of sales) and sold in the aftermarket to distributors or directly to high-end US bicycle retailers. Products are marketed under the SRAM (drivetrain systems) RockShox (suspension) Avid (brakes) Truvativ (cranks) and Zipp (wheelsets) brand names. The firm's products are sold worldwide (the US accounts for only 15%). SRAM International was founded in 1987 by president and CEO Stanley Day Jr.

SRC ENERGY INC
ASE: SRCI

1675 Broadway, Suite 2600
Denver, CO 80202
Phone: 720 616-4300
Fax: 720 616-4301
Web: www.srcenergy.com

CEO: Barton R Brookman Jr
CFO: –
HR: –
FYE: December 31
Type: Public

SRC Energy (formerly Synergy Resources) is on a quest to exploit the natural energy sources found in the Denver-Julesburg Basin (D-J Basin) which spans Colorado Kansas Nebraska and Wyoming. The company is exploring the Wattenberg Field a 50-mile area north of Denver rich with oil and gas deposits. SRC Energy reports proved reserves of about 239 billion cu. ft. of natural gas and 26.4 million barrels of oil and condensate. It has about 349000 net acres under lease with more than 420 producing wells. SRC Energy was founded in 2005 and began operations three years later.

	Annual Growth	08/14	08/15*	12/15	12/16	12/17
Sales ($ mil.)	51.5%	104.2	124.8	34.1	107.1	362.5
Net income ($ mil.)	70.3%	28.9	18.0	(122.9)	(219.2)	142.5
Market value ($ mil.)	(14.1%)	3,248.8	2,592.3	2,056.4	2,150.6	2,058.8
Employees	61.4%	29	36	62	96	122

*Fiscal year change

SRI INTERNATIONAL

333 RAVENSWOOD AVE
MENLO PARK, CA 940253493
Phone: 650-859-2000
Fax: –
Web: www.sri.com

CEO: William Jeffrey
CFO: Luther Lau
HR: –
FYE: December 31
Type: Private

SRI International sometimes called "Silicon Valley's soul" is a not-for-profit think tank pondering advances in biotechnology chemicals and energy computer science electronics and public policy — and ways to commercialize those advances. It focuses on technology research and development business strategies and analysis. The organization has patents and patent applications in IT communications robotics and pharmaceuticals. SRI's clients have included Samsung General Motors and AT&T. The artificial intelligence it designed for the Department of Defense became Apple's Siri. Originally founded in 1946 as Stanford Research Institute SRI became fully independent in 1970.

	Annual Growth	12/13	12/14	12/15	12/16	12/17
Sales ($ mil.)	(9.1%)	–	539.4	513.5	504.0	405.8
Net income ($ mil.)	143.5%	–	0.1	2.7	6.8	1.3
Market value ($ mil.)	–	–	–	–	–	–
Employees	–	–	–	–	–	2,437

SRI/SURGICAL EXPRESS INC.
NASDAQ: STRC

12425 Race Track Rd.
Tampa FL 33626
Phone: 813-891-9550
Fax: 813-818-9076
Web: www.srisurgical.com

CEO: Richard Steeves
CFO: Mark R Faris
HR: –
FYE: December 31
Type: Public

SRI/Surgical Express has doctors and patients covered even when the gown opens to the back. The company which conducts business under the name SRI Surgical provides hospital and surgical centers with such reusable surgical products as gowns and towels. It also provides reprocessed surgical instruments basins and surgical accessories that it sorts sterilizes and packages at about a dozen regional facilities in the US. The company offers pick-up and delivery service as an alternative to in-house recovery programs. SRI Surgical forms multi-year or short-term agreements with such customers as Kaiser Permanenteand Novation. SRI/Surgical Express was acquired by Synergy Health in 2012.

SS&C TECHNOLOGIES HOLDINGS INC
NMS: SSNC

80 Lamberton Road
Windsor, CT 06095
Phone: 860 298-4500
Fax: –
Web: www.ssctech.com

CEO: William C. (Bill) Stone
CFO: Patrick J. Pedonti
HR: –
FYE: December 31
Type: Public

SS&C Technologies helps its clients buy low and sell high and do some of it automatically. The company develops software for managing financial portfolios alternative investments (such as hedge funds) loans real estate equity and securities trading as well as consulting outsourcing services and back-office processing. SS&C also sells software to the healthcare industry for managing information processing quality of care cost management and payment. SS&C serves asset managers insurance companies banks corporate financial offices hedge funds and government agencies among others. Clients include Fidelity Credit Suisse Pacific Life and Humana. It has offices around the world.

	Annual Growth	12/14	12/15	12/16	12/17	12/18
Sales ($ mil.)	45.3%	767.9	1,000.3	1,481.4	1,675.3	3,421.1
Net income ($ mil.)	(5.8%)	131.1	42.9	131.0	328.9	103.2
Market value ($ mil.)	(6.3%)	14,669.3	17,122.1	7,172.9	10,152.4	11,313.6
Employees	48.3%	4,674	6,089	8,001	8,287	22,600

SSI (U.S.) INC.

353 N. Clarke St. Ste. 2400
Chicago IL 60654
Phone: 312-822-0088
Fax: 312-822-0116
Web: www.spencerstuart.com

CEO: Ben Williams
CFO: –
HR: –
FYE: September 30
Type: Private

When the board of directors ousts your CEO for running the company into the ground it might look to SSI (U.S.) — more commonly known as Spencer Stuart Management Consultants — for a replacement. Founded in 1956 the firm offers leadership consulting and executive search services specializing in searches for top-level executives and board directors. Clients hire Spencer Stuart to recruit the best chief executives and functional leaders in such areas as finance human resources information technology legal and marketing. The firm operates from 50 offices worldwide. Citing the desire to protect client confidentiality the firm's partners have declined to follow rivals into the public marketplace.

SSM HEALTH CARE CORPORATION

10101 WOODFIELD LN # 100
SAINT LOUIS, MO 631322944
Phone: 314-994-7800
Fax: –
Web: www.ssmhealth.com

CEO: William P. Thompson
CFO: –
HR: Angela Schlansker
FYE: December 31
Type: Private

The mission of SSM Health began with five nuns who fled religious persecution in Germany in 1872 only to arrive in St. Louis in the midst of a smallpox epidemic. They formed their first hospital there in 1877. Today the Midwest-based not-for-profit system sponsored by the Franciscan Sisters of Mary owns some 25 acute care hospitals with about 4500 licensed beds; it also has management or affiliation agreements with a number of other area hospitals. Additionally the company offers more than 300 outpatient facilities including physicians' practices home care and hospice services post-acute facilities and an insurance company.

	Annual Growth	12/11	12/12	12/13	12/16	12/17
Sales ($ mil.)	53.3%	–	–	1,177.9	6,109.2	6,497.0
Net income ($ mil.)	65.9%	–	–	32.5	(30.9)	245.8
Market value ($ mil.)	–	–	–	–	–	–
Employees	–	–	–	–	–	24,230

SSP AMERICA INC.

19465 Deerfield Ave. Ste. 105
Lansdowne VA 20176
Phone: 703-729-2333
Fax: 703-858-7091
Web: www.foodtravelexperts.com/america

CEO: Michael Svagdis
CFO: Roger Worrell
HR: Jill Hart
FYE: September 30
Type: Subsidiary

SSP America encourages travelers to get to the airport early and to show up hungry. The company is a leading contract foodservices provider that operates food courts and concession facilities at more than 40 airports in the US Canada and the Caribbean. Most of its eateries operate under national chain brands licensed from such fast-food companies as Arby's Chick-fil-a and Quiznos. It also partners with some independent and local restaurant operators and it has proprietary brands such as bakery cafe Upper Crust. SSP America is a regional operating unit of global foodservice contractor SSP Group.

ST BARNABAS MEDICAL CENTER (INC)

94 OLD SHORT HILLS RD # 1
LIVINGSTON, NJ 070395668
Phone: 973-322-5000
Fax: –
Web: www.rwjbh.org

CEO: –
CFO: Patrick Aheran
HR: Arnie Manzo
FYE: December 31
Type: Private

Part of the Saint Barnabas Health Care System Saint Barnabas Medical Center is a 600-bed acute-care hospital that provides a full range of health services to residents of Livingston New Jersey and surrounding areas. The not-for-profit medical center provides general inpatient and outpatient care programs as well as burn and perinatal care. It also houses units specializing in organ transplant stroke care cardiac surgery and comprehensive cancer treatment. Its Institute for Reproductive Medicine and Science provides assisted reproductive technology services. Saint Barnabas Medical Center treats some 35000 inpatients and more than 85000 emergency-room patients each year.

	Annual Growth	12/14	12/15	12/16	12/17	12/18
Sales ($ mil.)	4.0%	–	728.3	760.4	818.2	818.2
Net income ($ mil.)	9.0%	–	87.6	84.2	113.4	113.4
Market value ($ mil.)	–	–	–	–	–	–
Employees	–	–	–	–	–	4,000

ST DAVID'S SOUTH AUSTIN MEDICAL CENTER

901 W BEN WHITE BLVD
AUSTIN, TX 787046903
Phone: 512-447-2211
Fax: –

CEO: Charles Laird
CFO: –
HR: –
FYE: October 31
Type: Private

South Austin baby! St. David's South Austin Medical Center provides health services in the hippest part of the "Live Music Capital of the World." Established in 1982 the acute-care hospital has more than 250 beds. St. David's South Austin Medical Center (formerly known as South Austin Hospital) has a cardiovascular center an emergency department an obstetrics unit and an outpatient surgery center along with services in diabetes education diagnostics oncology and rehabilitation among other offerings. It also operates outpatient facilities in the nearby communities. Founded in 1982 the medical center is part of St. David's Health Care System in partnership with nationwide hospital operator HCA.

	Annual Growth	12/13	12/14*	10/15	10/16	10/17
Sales ($ mil.)	1392.8%	–	0.1	260.5	289.6	328.1
Net income ($ mil.)	1717.1%	–	0.0	53.8	50.3	55.3
Market value ($ mil.)	–	–	–	–	–	–
Employees	–	–	–	–	–	1,400

*Fiscal year change

ST DAVIDS HEALTHCARE PARTNERSHIP LLP

2400 ROUND ROCK AVE
ROUND ROCK, TX 786814004
Phone: 512-341-1000
Fax: –

CEO: Deborah Ryl
CFO: –
HR: Amanda Frye
FYE: February 28
Type: Private

St. David's Round Rock Medical Center serves the growing Williamson County community located in Central Texas. The facility includes an acute care hospital with approximately 175 beds a heart center a women's center and an outpatient surgery center. Other services include respiratory therapy vascular lab work orthopedics and intermediate care. The medical center is part of St. David's HealthCare Partnership a joint venture between St. David's Health Care System and HCA. The hospital's size was almost doubled through expansion construction in 2006.

	Annual Growth	12/02	12/03	12/04	12/05*	02/17
Sales ($ mil.)	13.9%	–	–	–	40.0	190.4
Net income ($ mil.)	(0.3%)	–	–	–	36.1	34.9
Market value ($ mil.)	–	–	–	–	–	–
Employees	–	–	–	–	–	610

*Fiscal year change

ST JAMES HEALTHCARE, INC

400 S CLARK ST
BUTTE, MT 597012328
Phone: 406-723-2484
Fax: –

CEO: Chuck Wright
CFO: James Doyle
HR: –
FYE: December 31
Type: Private

St. James Healthcare provides general medical and surgical services as well as specialized care to Southwestern Montana. St. James Healthcare's specialized services include oncology women's and children's health care neurology and cardiac care. The hospital is a member of the Sisters of Charity of Leavenworth Health System. St. James Healthcare was established in 1881.

	Annual Growth	05/02	05/03	05/05*	12/08	12/13
Sales ($ mil.)	–	–	(1,229.5)	0.1	0.0	120.1
Net income ($ mil.)	–	–	0.0	0.0	(0.0)	5.0
Market value ($ mil.)	–	–	–	–	–	–
Employees	–	–	–	–	–	514

*Fiscal year change

ST JOHN FISHER COLLEGE

3690 EAST AVE OFC
ROCHESTER, NY 146183597
Phone: 585-385-8000
Fax: –
Web: www.sjfc.edu

CEO: –
CFO: –
HR: –
FYE: May 31
Type: Private

St. John Fisher College is a Catholic liberal arts institution. The independent school offers 35 academic majors in the business education humanities natural sciences and nursing as well as about a dozen pre-professional programs 10 master's programs and three doctoral programs. Its enrollment includes more than 2700 full-time undergraduate students as well as 200 part time students. The student-faculty ratio is 13:1. The college is guided by the educational philosophy of the Congregation of St. Basil. St. John Fisher College was founded in 1948 as a Catholic college for men; it did not become coeducational until 1971. The college was formed by the Congregation of St. Basil.

	Annual Growth	05/12	05/13	05/15	05/17	05/18
Sales ($ mil.)	(3.2%)	–	122.6	130.1	100.7	104.4
Net income ($ mil.)	6.6%	–	10.8	7.4	(2.7)	14.9
Market value ($ mil.)	–	–	–	–	–	–
Employees	–	–	–	–	–	574

ST JOHN'S UNIVERSITY, NEW YORK

8000 UTOPIA PKWY
JAMAICA, NY 114399000
Phone: 718-990-6161
Fax: -
Web: www.redstormsports.com

CEO: -
CFO: Sharon Hewitt Watkins
HR: -
FYE: May 31
Type: Private

No university is an island but one of St. John's campuses is on Manhattan Island. A private co-educational Roman Catholic school St. John's University offers undergraduate and graduate programs in more than 100 majors through five colleges a law school and a distance learning program. St. John's has more than 20000 students at five campuses (Queens Staten Island and Manhattan in New York City one in Oakdale New York and one graduate center in Rome). The school has a 17-to-1 student-faculty ratio. More than 80% of its graduates reside in the New York region including notable alumni such as former New York governors Hugh Carey and Mario Cuomo. The school was founded in 1870 by the Vincentian Community.

	Annual Growth	05/08	05/09	05/10	05/11	05/12
Sales ($ mil.)	4.8%	-	-	-	450.1	471.5
Net income ($ mil.)	(96.5%)	-	-	-	82.7	2.9
Market value ($ mil.)	-	-	-	-	-	-
Employees	-	-	-	-	-	3,310

ST JOSEPH'S COLLEGE NEW YORK

245 CLINTON AVE
BROOKLYN, NY 112053688
Phone: 718-940-5300
Fax: -
Web: www.sjcny.edu

CEO: -
CFO: George Ann Kelly
HR: -
FYE: June 30
Type: Private

St. Joseph's College is a liberal arts college with two locations in the metropolitan New York City area — one in Brooklyn and one in Long Island. St. Joseph's offers more than 20 undergraduate majors pre-professional and certificate programs and graduate degrees in management business and infant/toddler early childhood special education to over 5000 students. Its School of Adult and Professional Education provides adult students with certificate and degree programs in fields such as management computer information systems and health. Its Brooklyn campus also houses the Dillon Child Study Center a working preschool where child-study majors gain hands-on experience. St. Joseph's was founded in 1916.

	Annual Growth	06/12	06/13	06/14	06/15	06/16
Sales ($ mil.)	9.2%	-	80.0	106.2	103.5	104.2
Net income ($ mil.)	-	-	(4.6)	(2.2)	(5.0)	(4.1)
Market value ($ mil.)	-	-	-	-	-	-
Employees	-	-	-	-	-	800

ST JOSEPHS WAYNE HOSPITAL INC

224 HAMBURG TPKE
WAYNE, NJ 074702124
Phone: 973-942-6900
Fax: -

CEO: -
CFO: -
HR: -
FYE: December 31
Type: Private

St. Joseph's Wayne Hospital (SJWH) helps its patients get back into a healthy realm. The acute care facility serves the residents of northern New Jersey. With some 230 beds and more than 400 physicians on staff SJWH offers services including cancer care neurology radiology surgery rehabilitation and senior care. It also includes an ambulatory center that offers minor surgery infusions and other outpatient procedures as well as a sleep diagnostics center and affiliated home health and hospice agencies. Established in 1871 the Catholic hospital is part of the St. Joseph's Healthcare System which is sponsored by the Sisters of Charity of Saint Elizabeth.

	Annual Growth	12/01	12/02	12/03*	06/05*	12/08
Sales ($ mil.)	3.3%	-	66.3	73.3	73.3	80.7
Net income ($ mil.)	19.8%	-	1.1	(7.9)	0.0	3.3
Market value ($ mil.)	-	-	-	-	-	-
Employees	-	-	-	-	-	925

*Fiscal year change

ST JUDE MEDICAL INC

NYS: STJ

One St. Jude Medical Drive
St. Paul, MN 55117
Phone: 651 756-2000
Fax: 651 756-3301
Web: www.sjm.com

CEO: Michael T Rousseau
CFO: Donald J Zurbay
HR: -
FYE: January 3/
Type: Public

If your heart has trouble catching the beat St. Jude Medical's got rhythm to spare. The company is a global medical device manufacturer focused on improving the treatment of some of the world's most expensive epidemic diseases. St. Jude Medical operates in one segment producing six principal product categories: ICD (implantable cardiac defibrillator) Systems (the largest category representing 35% of total earnings) Pacemaker Systems Atrial Fibrillation Products Vascular Products Structural Heart Products and Neuromodulation Products. The company sells its products in more than 100 countries; the US is its largest market. St. Jude Medical was formed in 1976.

	Annual Growth	01/11*	12/11	12/12	12/13*	01/15
Sales ($ mil.)	2.1%	5,164.8	5,611.7	5,503.0	5,501.0	5,622.0
Net income ($ mil.)	2.5%	907.4	825.8	752.0	723.0	1,002.0
Market value ($ mil.)	11.0%	12,254.7	9,832.4	10,167.8	17,844.6	18,615.7
Employees	1.6%	15,000	16,000	15,000	16,000	16,000

*Fiscal year change

ST LAWRENCE UNIVERSITY (INC)

23 ROMODA DR 209
CANTON, NY 136171501
Phone: 315-229-5011
Fax: -
Web: www.stlawu.edu

CEO: -
CFO: -
HR: -
FYE: June 30
Type: Private

St. Lawrence University is a four-year liberal arts college that also offers graduate degrees in education. The university has an enrollment of more than 2500 students as well as 200 faculty members and a student-to-teacher ratio of 12:1. Major fields of study include biology computer science economics history psychology foreign language and religious studies. Actors Kirk Douglas and Viggo Mortensen and US Senator Susan Collins are among the school's alumni. Founded in 1856 by members of the Universalist Church (now Unitarian Universalist) St. Lawrence is the oldest continuously coeducational institution of higher learning in New York State.

	Annual Growth	06/14	06/15	06/16	06/17	06/18
Sales ($ mil.)	5.2%	-	118.7	125.9	145.0	138.2
Net income ($ mil.)	-	-	(2.9)	6.1	48.1	18.8
Market value ($ mil.)	-	-	-	-	-	-
Employees	-	-	-	-	-	700

ST MARY'S REGIONAL HEALTH CENTER

1027 WASHINGTON AVE
DETROIT LAKES, MN 565013409
Phone: 218-847-5611
Fax: -
Web: www.trustedcareforlife.org

CEO: -
CFO: Ryan Hill
HR: -
FYE: June 30
Type: Private

St. Mary's Innovis Health (formerly St. Mary's Regional Health Center) provides acute and long-term health care services to central Minnesota including general medical and surgical care cardiac rehabilitation and skilled nursing services for the elderly. The health care company's hospital has nearly 90 beds and its nursing center has about 100 beds. The organization also includes two senior housing facilities community clinics surgery centers home health providers and an affiliated physician network. St. Mary's is an affiliate of Innovis Health which operates a network of health care facilities in North Dakota and Minnesota.

	Annual Growth	06/13	06/14	06/15	06/16	06/17
Sales ($ mil.)	13.6%	-	86.1	111.1	125.7	126.3
Net income ($ mil.)	48.4%	-	2.3	4.5	10.1	7.4
Market value ($ mil.)	-	-	-	-	-	-
Employees	-	-	-	-	-	400

ST PATRICK HOSPITAL CORPORATION

500 W BROADWAY ST
MISSOULA, MT 598024008
Phone: 406-543-7271
Fax: –
Web: montana.providence.org/locations-directory/s/st-patrick-

CEO: –
CFO: Kirk Bodlovic
HR: Kerry Schultz
FYE: December 31
Type: Private

Feeling a little green? St. Patrick Hospital and Health Sciences Center is there to help. The not-for-profit hospital boasts some 250 beds (acute-care and transitional) and serves nearly 20 counties in and around Missoula Montana. Its specialty services include cancer treatment surgery and occupational health. The center also provides Life Flight air transport to critically ill or injured patients. The hospital provides outpatient primary and specialty care through a host of affiliated physician practices and clinics throughout the area. St. Patrick Hospital and Health Sciences Center is part of Providence Health & Services which has two hospitals and more than 40 clinics across Montana.

	Annual Growth	12/04	12/05	12/15	12/16	12/17
Sales ($ mil.)	4.8%	–	191.8	289.7	300.9	338.0
Net income ($ mil.)	11.4%	–	8.2	15.4	2.0	29.9
Market value ($ mil.)	–	–	–	–	–	–
Employees	–	–	–	–	–	1,460

ST. AGNES HEALTHCARE, INC.

900 S CATON AVE
BALTIMORE, MD 212295201
Phone: 667-234-6000
Fax: –
Web: www.stagnes.org

CEO: Keith Vander Kolk
CFO: Scott Furniss
HR: –
FYE: June 30
Type: Private

If you're in agony in Charm City St. Agnes HealthCare is here to help. The Catholic health system provides a spectrum of medical services to the residents of southwest Baltimore. Its flagship facility St. Agnes Hospital has 276 beds and offers a comprehensive range of medical and surgical services including treatment in areas such as oncology cardiovascular disease bariatric medicine women's health plastic surgery and orthopedics. The system also includes a multispecialty physicians group (Seton Medical Group) and a diagnostic imaging center. St. Agnes HealthCare is a member of Ascension Health. The health system traces its roots to 1862 when the Daughters of Charity set up a local infirmary in 1862.

	Annual Growth	06/08	06/09	06/10	06/15	06/16
Sales ($ mil.)	4.2%	–	336.3	400.3	438.1	447.4
Net income ($ mil.)	–	–	(11.5)	50.8	23.4	7.7
Market value ($ mil.)	–	–	–	–	–	–
Employees	–	–	–	–	–	2,506

ST. ALEXIUS MEDICAL CENTER

900 E BROADWAY AVE
BISMARCK, ND 585014520
Phone: 701-530-7000
Fax: –
Web: www.chistalexiushealth.org

CEO: Gary P Miller
CFO: Terri Donovan
HR: –
FYE: June 30
Type: Private

Established in 1885 CHI St. Alexius Health (formerly St. Alexius Medical Center) has been serving the health care needs of those who reside in the Dakotas and Montana longer than any other area hospital. The medical facility with more than 300 beds caters to central and western North Dakota and parts of South Dakota and Montana. Specialty services include cancer care trauma care geriatrics orthopedics and rehabilitation. As part of its operations the longtime hospital also owns and manages a handful of smaller regional hospitals and community clinics. In 2014 St. Alexius joined the Catholic Health Initiatives health care system.

	Annual Growth	06/12	06/13	06/14	06/15	06/16
Sales ($ mil.)	3.5%	–	291.4	308.6	289.3	323.2
Net income ($ mil.)	–	–	(2.0)	14.2	148.1	(10.1)
Market value ($ mil.)	–	–	–	–	–	–
Employees	–	–	–	–	–	1,947

ST. ANTHONY'S HOSPITAL, INC.

1200 7TH AVE N
SAINT PETERSBURG, FL 337051388
Phone: 727-825-1100
Fax: –
Web: www.stanthonysfoundation.org

CEO: –
CFO: Carl Tremonti
HR: –
FYE: December 31
Type: Private

Saint or not for those needing medical care in St. Petersburg Florida St. Anthony's Hospital has you covered. The facility offers a full array of health care services including emergency medicine surgery cancer treatment and heart care as well as services in fields including neurology orthopedics and metabolic care. The 400-bed hospital also provides outpatient services through a host of ambulatory surgery rehabilitation and imaging centers. St. Anthony's Hospital is a member of the Bay-Care Health System and as such provides home health and occupational health services through agencies affiliated with that system.

	Annual Growth	12/11	12/12	12/13	12/14	12/16
Sales ($ mil.)	13.0%	–	203.3	248.4	252.1	331.0
Net income ($ mil.)	16.1%	–	28.3	24.7	34.4	51.5
Market value ($ mil.)	–	–	–	–	–	–
Employees	–	–	–	–	–	1,076

ST. BERNARD HOSPITAL

326 W 64TH ST
CHICAGO, IL 606213146
Phone: 773-962-3900
Fax: –
Web: www.stbh.org

CEO: –
CFO: –
HR: –
FYE: December 31
Type: Private

Like a giant dog trudging through blinding snow to rescue a traveler in need St. Bernard Hospital is a powerhouse of betterment for the people it serves. St. Bernard Hospital and Health Care Center serves the residents of Chicago's south side neighborhood of Englewood. The facility has about 200 beds and its specialties include pediatrics psychiatry neurology orthopedics and cardiology services. The hospital also offers inpatient detoxification services for patients dependent on opiates or alcohol. St. Bernard has a separate nonprofit unit that takes care of south side residents' residences: Bernard Place Housing Development is a 90-unit affordable homes initiative in the Englewood neighborhood.

	Annual Growth	12/08	12/09	12/13	12/14	12/15
Sales ($ mil.)	(0.1%)	–	94.7	97.3	94.9	94.2
Net income ($ mil.)	–	–	11.8	7.3	(3.1)	(7.5)
Market value ($ mil.)	–	–	–	–	–	–
Employees	–	–	–	–	–	875

ST. CLAIR HEALTH CORPORATION

1000 BOWER HILL RD
PITTSBURGH, PA 152431873
Phone: 412-561-4900
Fax: –
Web: www.stclair.org

CEO: James Collins
CFO: –
HR: Mary Franzetta
FYE: June 30
Type: Private

St. Clair Health operates St. Clair Hospital an acute care hospital with about than 330 beds serving residents in Pittsburgh and southwestern Pennsylvania. The health care provider offers inpatient and outpatient services including specialized units for cancer treatment behavioral and mental health cardiovascular therapy physical rehabilitation pulmonary therapy women and children's health and other niche services. St. Clair Hospital was established in 1954 by members of the Pittsburgh community. St. Clair Health also operates two outpatient centers a surgical center an imaging unit and an occupational medicine division.

	Annual Growth	06/13	06/14	06/16	06/17	06/18
Sales ($ mil.)	706.2%	–	0.1	0.1	329.6	344.0
Net income ($ mil.)	523.4%	–	0.0	0.1	55.0	58.1
Market value ($ mil.)	–	–	–	–	–	–
Employees	–	–	–	–	–	1,504

ST. FRANCIS HOSPITAL, ROSLYN, NEW YORK

100 PORT WASHINGTON BLVD
ROSLYN, NY 115761347
Phone: 516-562-2000
Fax: –

CEO: Alan Guerci
CFO: William C Arms
HR: Betty Anson
FYE: December 31
Type: Private

Sure St. Francis Hospital can handle your gall bladder and sinus difficulties but it's really on top of your heart problems. The hospital's Heart Center — New York State's only specially designated cardiac center — provides surgical diagnostic and treatment services. The 365-bed St. Francis Hospital also has centers for ENT (ear nose and throat) orthopedic vascular prostate cancer gastrointestinal and general surgery services. As part of Catholic Health Services of Long Island St. Francis opened its doors in 1954 to children and adults. It was originally established as St. Francis Hospital and Sanatorium for Cardiac Children in 1936.

	Annual Growth	12/01	12/02	12/04	12/08	12/15
Sales ($ mil.)	–	–	(828.9)	366.7	385.1	614.2
Net income ($ mil.)	152.0%	–	0.0	47.4	28.5	37.9
Market value ($ mil.)	–	–	–	–	–	–
Employees	–	–	–	–	–	2,184

ST. FRANCIS" HOSPITAL POUGHKEEPSIE NEW YORK

241 NORTH RD
POUGHKEEPSIE, NY 12601-1154
Phone: 845-471-2000
Fax: –
Web: www.sfhospital.org

CEO: –
CFO: –
HR: –
FYE: December 31
Type: Private

When leaf-peepers sprain their ankles or landscape painters fall on their brushes they turn to Saint Francis for help. Saint Francis Hospital provides primary and specialty health care services to residents throughout New York's Hudson Valley area. The Poughkeepsie-based organization includes centers specializing in behavioral health home care orthopedics plastic surgery and trauma care. The hospital also operates a chemical dependency treatment program. It is licensed for 33 beds and provides medical care for more than 10000 inpatients every year.

	Annual Growth	12/01	12/02*	06/05*	12/08	12/09
Sales ($ mil.)	1.3%	–	132.7	709.0	124.7	145.5
Net income ($ mil.)	–	–	3.5	48.0	(7.5)	(4.5)
Market value ($ mil.)	–	–	–	–	–	–
Employees	–	–	–	–	–	1,490

*Fiscal year change

ST. JOE CO. (THE)

NYS: JOE

133 South Watersound Parkway
Watersound, FL 32461
Phone: 850 231-6400
Fax: –
Web: www.joe.com

CEO: –
CFO: Marek Bakun
HR: Rhea Goff
FYE: December 31
Type: Public

Wanna buy some swampland in Florida? Perhaps something a bit more upscale? St. Joe has it along with timberland and beaches. Formerly operating in paper sugar timber telephone systems and railroads St. Joe is a Florida real estate developer and one of the state's largest private landowners. It holds some 573000 acres of land located mostly in northwest Florida. Some 70% of its land holdings are within 15 miles of the Gulf of Mexico including beach frontage and other waterfront properties. The company is primarily engaged in developing residential resorts and towns commerce parks and rural property sales. St. Joe also operates a forestry segment which grows harvests and sells timber and wood fiber.

	Annual Growth	12/14	12/15	12/16	12/17	12/18
Sales ($ mil.)	(37.0%)	701.9	103.9	95.7	98.8	110.3
Net income ($ mil.)	(46.9%)	406.5	(1.7)	15.9	59.6	32.4
Market value ($ mil.)	(8.0%)	1,115.8	1,123.0	1,152.8	1,095.1	799.1
Employees	(3.5%)	61	55	47	47	53

ST. JOHN HEALTH SYSTEM, INC.

1923 S UTICA AVE
TULSA, OK 741046520
Phone: 918-744-2180
Fax: –
Web: www.stjohnhealthsystem.com

CEO: –
CFO: –
HR: –
FYE: June 30
Type: Private

St. John Health System aims to bring health into the lives of the ill. The not-for-profit system provides health care services to residents of Tulsa and surrounding areas in northeastern Oklahoma and southern Kansas. In addition to flagship facility St. John Medical Center it owns or manages eight other community hospitals as well as urgent care and long-term care facilities. St. John Health System provides primary and specialty medical care through OMNI Medical Group and offers health insurance through CommunityCare health plan. Established in 1926 by the Sisters of the Sorrowful Mother the health system is part of Marian Health.

	Annual Growth	09/09	09/10	09/11	09/12*	06/14
Sales ($ mil.)	5.7%	–	–	895.5	977.4	1,057.0
Net income ($ mil.)	64.9%	–	–	17.7	74.8	79.3
Market value ($ mil.)	–	–	–	–	–	–
Employees	–	–	–	–	–	4,011

*Fiscal year change

ST. JOHN HOSPITAL AND MEDICAL CENTER

28000 DEQUINDRE RD
WARREN, MI 480922468
Phone: 313-343-4000
Fax: –
Web: www.ascension.org

CEO: Mark Taylor
CFO: –
HR: –
FYE: June 30
Type: Private

St. John Hospital & Medical Center is part of the larger Detroit area-based St. John Health regional health care system. Besides providing acute and trauma care the 770-bed teaching hospital operates specialized cancer and pediatric centers a hip and knee center an inpatient mental health unit and a Parkinson's Disease clinic. It also operates the only emergency trauma center on Detroit's East Side. The hospital was established in 1952 and has grown to include a 200-physician medical team that specializes in more than 50 medical and surgical fields. It boasts 34000 admissions; 14500 surgical visits; and more than 126500 emergency center visits each year.

	Annual Growth	06/02	06/03	06/05	06/09	06/15
Sales ($ mil.)	(6.3%)	–	1,642.9	0.0	638.3	753.3
Net income ($ mil.)	12.0%	–	9.2	0.0	2.0	36.1
Market value ($ mil.)	–	–	–	–	–	–
Employees	–	–	–	–	–	5,000

ST. JOHN PROVIDENCE

28000 DEQUINDRE RD
WARREN, MI 480922468
Phone: 586-753-0500
Fax: –

CEO: –
CFO: –
HR: –
FYE: June 30
Type: Private

St. John Providence Health System is out to keep southeastern Michigan's denizens healthy. A subsidiary of not-for-profit group Ascension Health St. John Providence is a regional health care system founded in 1844 that consists of six hospitals with more than 2000 beds. It has more than 125 additional medical facilities including urgent care clinics outpatient centers and doctors' offices. The health system also runs St. John Home Services a home health care agency providing infusion services rehabilitative services and hospice care. Flagship hospital St. John Hospital and Medical Center is a regional referral hospital with more than 800 beds providing care in numerous medical and surgical specialties.

	Annual Growth	06/07	06/08	06/09	06/13	06/14
Sales ($ mil.)	(33.9%)	–	–	2,023.9	257.5	255.0
Net income ($ mil.)	–	–	–	(84.9)	7.8	(8.4)
Market value ($ mil.)	–	–	–	–	–	–
Employees	–	–	–	–	–	17,806

ST. JOHN'S HOSPITAL OF THE HOSPITAL SISTERS OF THE THIRD ORDER OF ST. FRANCIS

800 E CARPENTER ST
SPRINGFIELD, IL 627690002
Phone: 217-544-6464
Fax: –
Web: www.st-johns.org

CEO: Charles Lucore
CFO: Larry Ragel
HR: –
FYE: June 30
Type: Private

Truck-struck Homer Simpson might use his last gasp trying to blurt out "St. John's Hospital of the Hospital Sisters of the Third Order of St. Francis-Springfield" to his ambulance driver but he might be better off using the hospital's more common name St. John's. D'oh! The 440-bed St. John's Hospital serves residents of central and southern Illinois with general and specialized health care services. The teaching hospital affiliated with Southern Illinois University's School of Medicine has centers devoted to women and children's health trauma cardiac care cancer orthopedics and neurology. It also operates area health clinics. Founded in 1875 St. John's is part of the Hospital Sisters Health System.

	Annual Growth	06/07	06/08	06/14	06/15	06/16
Sales ($ mil.)	2.9%	–	393.2	500.5	501.1	494.4
Net income ($ mil.)	–	–	(8.7)	10.7	4.0	3.4
Market value ($ mil.)	–	–	–	–	–	–
Employees	–	–	–	–	–	3,000

ST. JOSEPH HEALTHCARE FOUNDATION

360 BROADWAY
BANGOR, ME 044013979
Phone: 207-907-1000
Fax: –
Web: www.stjoeshealing.org

CEO: Mary Prybylo
CFO: –
HR: –
FYE: December 31
Type: Private

If you have a little accident climbing trees in the Pine Tree State St. Joseph Healthcare can fix you right up. The hospital cares for the people of central Maine through St. Joseph Hospital a more than 110-bed acute care community hospital. The organization which is affiliated with Covenant Health System also operates several specialty outpatient clinics. Services include cardiology home health oncology outreach osteoporosis research and pain management. St. Joseph physician practices include specialties such as endocrinology and gastroenterology. St. Joseph Healthcare was founded in 1947 by the Felician Sisters of Enfield Connecticut.

	Annual Growth	12/11	12/12	12/13	12/14	12/15
Sales ($ mil.)	1443.3%	–	–	0.5	124.4	120.1
Net income ($ mil.)	313.7%	–	–	0.1	11.7	1.8
Market value ($ mil.)	–	–	–	–	–	–
Employees	–	–	–	–	–	900

ST. JOSEPH HOSPITAL OF ORANGE

1100 W STEWART DR
ORANGE, CA 928683891
Phone: 714-633-9111
Fax: –
Web: www.sjo.org

CEO: Larry K Ainsworth
CFO: Tina Nycroft
HR: –
FYE: June 30
Type: Private

If you're feeling green or blue in Orange County St. Joseph Hospital of Orange is there to help get back to feeling pink and rosy. The California hospital provides general medical and surgical services as well as specialty care such as women's health mental health services oncology cardiology and physical rehabilitation. Part of the St. Joseph Health System the hospital provides primary care and specialty outpatient services through a network of affiliated physician practices. It also operates low-income and mobile clinics. The hospital has about 468 beds and a medical staff of some 1000.

	Annual Growth	06/13	06/14	06/15	06/16	06/17
Sales ($ mil.)	4.9%	–	566.9	567.4	599.1	655.1
Net income ($ mil.)	–	–	(5.5)	2.8	11.8	29.7
Market value ($ mil.)	–	–	–	–	–	–
Employees	–	–	–	–	–	3,300

ST. JOSEPH'S HOSPITAL HEALTH CENTER

301 PROSPECT AVE
SYRACUSE, NY 132031899
Phone: 315-448-5882
Fax: –
Web: www.sjhsyr.org

CEO: Leslie Paul Luke
CFO: Meredith Price
HR: –
FYE: December 31
Type: Private

With about 450 inpatient beds St. Joseph's Hospital Health Center serves the residents of 16 central New York counties. The not-for-profit hospital system provides general emergency and surgical care as well as specialty services in areas such as obstetrics cardiology dialysis and wound care. In addition to its inpatient facilities the organization operates a home health agency a nursing school medical and dental residency programs and several outpatient care centers. Its Franciscan Companies affiliate offers some ancillary services including the provision of medical supplies home health equipment and senior services. St. Joseph's Hospital Health Center was founded in 1869 and became part of Trinity Health in 2015.

	Annual Growth	12/07	12/08	12/09	12/14	12/15
Sales ($ mil.)	4.5%	–	399.1	436.3	523.6	542.2
Net income ($ mil.)	–	–	6.3	5.4	0.5	(2.7)
Market value ($ mil.)	–	–	–	–	–	–
Employees	–	–	–	–	–	3,300

ST. JUDE CHILDREN'S RESEARCH HOSPITAL, INC.

262 DANNY THOMAS PL
MEMPHIS, TN 381053678
Phone: 901-595-3300
Fax: –
Web: www.stjude.org

CEO: James Downing
CFO: Pat Keel
HR: –
FYE: June 30
Type: Private

St. Jude Children's Research Hospital studies and treats catastrophic diseases in children especially pediatric cancers. The hospital which only has about 80 beds annually treats more than 7800 children most of whom are treated on an outpatient basis as part of its research efforts into finding cures and more effective treatments. The hospital not only helps children with their health it also helps their parents: It pays all expenses that are not covered by insurance and doesn't require payment from patients without insurance. St. Jude Children's Research Hospital was founded in 1962.

	Annual Growth	06/08	06/09	06/10	06/11	06/15
Sales ($ mil.)	(19.0%)	–	–	589.9	573.7	205.9
Net income ($ mil.)	–	–	–	(5.0)	(26.3)	195.4
Market value ($ mil.)	–	–	–	–	–	–
Employees	–	–	–	–	–	2,500

ST. JUDE HOSPITAL

101 E VALENCIA MESA DR
FULLERTON, CA 928353875
Phone: 714-871-3280
Fax: –
Web: www.stjudemedicalcenter.org

CEO: –
CFO: –
HR: Lisa Schoening
FYE: June 30
Type: Private

St. Jude Medical Center gets sickly Southern Californians on their feet again. The faith-based not-for-profit acute care facility with some 385 beds serves the residents of Orange County. The medical center provides an onsite cancer center (the Virginia K. Crosson Cancer Center) and a heart institute that offers cardiac surgeries and rehabilitation programs. It also provides inpatient and outpatient physical rehabilitation services and a variety of community outreach programs. Established by the Sisters of St. Joseph of Orange religious order in the 1950s St. Jude Medical Center is part of the St. Joseph Health System.

	Annual Growth	06/13	06/14	06/15	06/16	06/17
Sales ($ mil.)	4.4%	–	477.5	458.3	490.1	544.0
Net income ($ mil.)	(4.4%)	–	51.7	9.0	4.4	45.3
Market value ($ mil.)	–	–	–	–	–	–
Employees	–	–	–	–	–	2,600

ST. JUDE MEDICAL, INC.

One St. Jude Medical Drive
St. Paul, MN 55117
Phone: 651 756-2000
Fax: 651 756-3301
Web: www.sjm.com

NYS: STJ
CEO: Michael T Rousseau
CFO: Donald J Zurbay
HR: –
FYE: December 28
Type: Public

If your heart has trouble catching the beat St. Jude Medical's got rhythm to spare. The company operates through two product segments: Implantable Electronic Systems (combines the former cardiac rhythm management and neuromodulation divisions) and Cardiovascular and Ablation Technologies (combines the former cardiovascular and atrial fibrillation units). Implantable Electronics St. Jude's largest unit includes pacemakers and implantable cardiac defibrillators (ICDs) both of which use electrical impulses to shock irregularly beating hearts back into rhythm. The company sells its products in more than 100 countries; the US is its largest market. St. Jude was formed in 1976.

	Annual Growth	01/10	01/11*	12/11	12/12	12/13
Sales ($ mil.)	5.5%	4,681.3	5,164.8	5,611.7	5,503.0	5,501.0
Net income ($ mil.)	(2.4%)	777.2	907.4	825.8	752.0	723.0
Market value ($ mil.)	19.2%	10,633.7	12,359.8	9,916.7	10,255.0	17,997.6
Employees	4.6%	14,000	15,000	16,000	15,000	16,000

*Fiscal year change

ST. LUKE'S EPISCOPAL HOSPITAL INDEPENDENT PRACTICE ASSOCIATION, INC.

6720 BERTNER AVE
HOUSTON, TX 770302697
Phone: 832-355-1000
Fax: –

CEO: –
CFO: Alan F Koval
HR: –
FYE: June 30
Type: Private

St. Luke's Episcopal Hospital is deep in the hearts of Texans. Opened in 1954 by the Episcopal Diocese of Texas the Houston-area hospital is home to the Texas Heart Institute a leader in cardiovascular research and patient care. The institute is best-known as the location of the world's first artificial heart implantation as well as the first successful heart transplant in the US. In addition St. Luke's Episcopal Hospital provides general and advanced medical-surgical care across some 40 medical specialties. With more than 850 beds the hospital is the flagship facility of St. Luke's Episcopal Health System which was acquired by Catholic Health Initiatives in 2013.

	Annual Growth	06/12	06/13	06/14	06/15	06/17
Sales ($ mil.)	22.6%	–	–	100.0	114.9	184.5
Net income ($ mil.)	–	–	–	2.3	(21.5)	(12.6)
Market value ($ mil.)	–	–	–	–	–	–
Employees	–	–	–	–	–	4,500

ST. LUKE'S EPISCOPAL-PRESBYTERIAN HOSPITALS

232 S WOODS MILL RD
CHESTERFIELD, MO 630173406
Phone: 314-434-1500
Fax: –
Web: www.stlukes-stl.com

CEO: Christine Candio
CFO: –
HR: –
FYE: June 30
Type: Private

St. Luke's Episcopal-Presbyterian Hospital doing business as St. Luke's Hospital provides health care services to St. Louis residents and surrounding areas of eastern Missouri. The medical center houses more than 490 beds and offers general medical and surgical care as well as specialty services in areas such as heart disease cancer neuroscience orthopedics pediatrics and women's health. St. Luke's also operates half a dozen urgent care clinics in St. Louis and St. Charles counties providing treatment for minor emergencies such as cuts and animal bites as well as a skilled-nursing facility rehabilitation hospital and several diagnostic imaging centers. The not-for-profit hospital was founded in 1866.

	Annual Growth	06/01	06/02	06/03	06/04	06/15
Sales ($ mil.)	–	–	(1,170.2)	263.5	274.1	470.6
Net income ($ mil.)	148.2%	–	0.0	9.3	11.2	49.7
Market value ($ mil.)	–	–	–	–	–	–
Employees	–	–	–	–	–	3,000

ST. LUKE'S HEALTH NETWORK, INC.

801 OSTRUM ST
BETHLEHEM, PA 180151000
Phone: 610-954-4000
Fax: –
Web: www.stlukespawildmed.com

CEO: –
CFO: –
HR: –
FYE: June 30
Type: Private

St. Luke's University Hospital (formerly St. Luke's Hospital - Bethlehem Campus) serves residents of Pennsylvania's Lehigh Valley with primary specialty and emergency care services. The not-for-profit teaching hospital has about 480 acute-care beds. Its medical specialties include trauma oncology cardiology orthopedics neurology open-heart surgery radiology and robotic surgery. The medical center also operates outpatient surgery centers and general physician care clinics and it operates home health and community wellness programs. St. Luke's University Hospital was founded in 1872 and is part of the St. Luke's University Health Network.

	Annual Growth	06/13	06/14	06/15	06/17	06/18
Sales ($ mil.)	128.7%	–	67.4	0.0	1,521.7	1,844.7
Net income ($ mil.)	–	–	0.0	0.0	121.5	159.0
Market value ($ mil.)	–	–	–	–	–	–
Employees	–	–	–	–	–	2,958

ST. LUKE'S HEALTH SYSTEM, LTD.

190 E BANNOCK ST
BOISE, ID 837126241
Phone: 208-381-2222
Fax: –
Web: www.stlukesonline.org

CEO: David C. Pate
CFO: –
HR: –
FYE: September 30
Type: Private

To Catholics St. Luke is also known as the "beloved physician" and St. Luke's Health System strives to live up to its namesake. The regional not-for-profit health system provides a range of health services to residents of Idaho eastern Oregon and northern Nevada. St. Luke's is home to six general acute care hospitals with a total of about 860 beds. Its flagship facility is the 400-bed St. Luke's Boise Medical Center which also includes a full-service children's hospital. St. Luke's also runs a network of cancer care sites under the name Mountain States Tumor Institute as well as a number of urgent care family practice and specialty health centers.

	Annual Growth	09/08	09/09	09/16	09/17	09/18
Sales ($ mil.)	55.5%	–	49.0	1,937.2	2,327.1	2,603.0
Net income ($ mil.)	–	–	0.0	48.0	10.1	34.1
Market value ($ mil.)	–	–	–	–	–	–
Employees	–	–	–	–	–	7,891

ST. LUKE'S HOSPITAL OF DULUTH

915 E 1ST ST
DULUTH, MN 558052193
Phone: 218-726-5555
Fax: –
Web: www.slhduluth.com

CEO: John Strange
CFO: James Wuellner
HR: –
FYE: December 31
Type: Private

St. Luke's cares for colds cancers and other conditions in the chilly northern US. St. Luke's Hospital provides a variety of health care services to patients in northeastern Minnesota northwestern Wisconsin and parts of Michigan. The medical center has some 270 beds and a staff of about 370 physicians. Services include cardiology emergency medicine pediatrics oncology rehabilitation and vascular surgery. In addition to acute care services the organization offers primary and specialty health care services through a network of outpatient clinics.

	Annual Growth	12/08	12/09	12/13	12/16	12/17
Sales ($ mil.)	5.5%	–	307.1	377.9	434.4	471.9
Net income ($ mil.)	13.5%	–	8.0	3.0	9.1	22.0
Market value ($ mil.)	–	–	–	–	–	–
Employees	–	–	–	–	–	2,200

ST. MARY'S HEALTH CARE SYSTEM, INC.

1230 BAXTER ST
ATHENS, GA 306063712
Phone: 706-389-3000
Fax: –
Web: www.stmarysathens.org

CEO: Don McKenna
CFO: –
HR: Nancy Argo
FYE: June 30
Type: Private

St. Mary's Health Care System cares for the residents of northeast Georgia. Its St. Mary's Hospital has almost 200 acute-care beds. From health and wellness programs to women's and children's services the hospital also has centers dedicated to outpatient rehabilitation home health and long-term care. Specialty services include neurology cardiovascular care orthopedics and gastroenterology. It also operates the 25-bed St. Mary's Good Samaritan Hospital and a retirement village. The organization is sponsored by the Sisters of Mercy of the Americas St. Mary's Health Care System is a member of CHE Trinity Health (formed in 2013 through the consolidation of Catholic Health East and Trinity Health).

	Annual Growth	06/13	06/14	06/15	06/16	06/18
Sales ($ mil.)	12.5%	–	177.9	174.1	185.3	285.4
Net income ($ mil.)	(3.9%)	–	11.1	29.4	29.2	9.5
Market value ($ mil.)	–	–	–	–	–	–
Employees	–	–	–	–	–	1,350

ST. MARY'S HEALTH, INC.

3700 WASHINGTON AVE
EVANSVILLE, IN 477140541
Phone: 812-485-4000
Fax: –
Web: www.stvincent.org

CEO: –
CFO: –
HR: –
FYE: June 30
Type: Private

St. Mary's Medical Center of Evansville is a 433-bed hospital serving Indiana's River City. It is the primary facility in regional St. Mary's Health System which is in turn part of Ascension Health. The Evansville hospital provides emergency trauma diagnostic surgical and rehabilitative services as well as specialized cancer cardiac orthopedic and neurological services. With a total of some 750 physicians St. Mary's Health System also includes St. Mary's Hospital for Women & Children (100 beds adjacent to the main hospital) and St. Mary's Warrick (a 25-bed hospital in Boonville Indiana) as well as specialty outpatient surgical cancer and home health units in surrounding areas of southern Indiana.

	Annual Growth	06/10	06/11	06/13	06/15	06/16
Sales ($ mil.)	–	–	–	0.0	468.4	574.8	495.8
Net income ($ mil.)	–	–	–	0.0	48.9	52.7	66.2
Market value ($ mil.)	–	–	–	–	–	–
Employees	–	–	–	–	–	3,500

ST. MARY'S MEDICAL CENTER

2900 1ST AVE
HUNTINGTON, WV 257021241
Phone: 304-526-1234
Fax: –
Web: www.st-marys.org

CEO: –
CFO: Angela Swearingen
HR: Susan Robinson
FYE: September 30
Type: Private

Nobody wants to get sick but if you're ailing in West Virginia St. Mary's Medical Center wants you to know you are in good hands. The not-for-profit 395-bed medical facility serves patients in areas such as cardiac emergency neuroscience and cancer treatment. The largest health care facility in the tri-state region St. Mary's Medical Center is also a teaching facility affiliated with Joan C. Edwards Marshall University School of Medicine. St. Mary's Home Health Services administers care for patients in a six county area in Ohio and West Virginia. Services include IV therapy and occupational and physical therapies. St. Mary's Medical Center was founded in 1924.It now plans to merge with Cabell Huntington Hospital.

	Annual Growth	09/13	09/14	09/15	09/16	09/17
Sales ($ mil.)	(1.6%)	–	401.2	311.7	372.5	382.1
Net income ($ mil.)	35.2%	–	10.9	(42.1)	5.3	27.0
Market value ($ mil.)	–	–	–	–	–	–
Employees	–	–	–	–	–	2,000

ST. NORBERT COLLEGE, INC.

100 GRANT ST
DE PERE, WI 541152099
Phone: 920-337-3181
Fax: –
Web: www.snc.edu

CEO: Thomas Kunkel
CFO: –
HR: –
FYE: May 31
Type: Private

St. Norbert College is a private Catholic liberal arts institution offering undergraduate and graduate programs to approximately 2200 students. The school offers more than 40 undergraduate programs of study in the natural sciences social sciences and humanities and fine arts. It also confers Master's degrees in Science in Education and Theological Studies. The college is one of only a handful of institutions in the US that offer a Peace Corps Preparatory Program. St. Norbert College was founded in 1898 by Abbot Bernard Pennings a Dutch immigrant priest as a school to ready men for the priesthood. It became coeducational in 1952.

	Annual Growth	05/14	05/15	05/16	05/17	05/18
Sales ($ mil.)	4.0%	–	63.9	65.4	70.1	71.9
Net income ($ mil.)	92.4%	–	5.5	11.8	9.6	39.4
Market value ($ mil.)	–	–	–	–	–	–
Employees	–	–	–	–	–	490

ST. OLAF COLLEGE

1520 SAINT OLAF AVE
NORTHFIELD, MN 550571574
Phone: 507-786-2222
Fax: –
Web: www.wp.stolaf.edu

CEO: –
CFO: Janet Hanson
HR: –
FYE: May 31
Type: Private

The hills of Northfield Minnesota are alive with the sounds of St. Olaf College. The private liberal arts university offers undergraduate and pre-professional education to more than 3000 students offering degrees in about 45 academic focus areas. The school has a faculty of more than 250 teachers and is recognized for its choral and orchestral music programs as well as its mathematics department. Other popular majors include English psychology biology economics social services theology language medical science and chemistry. St. Olaf College was founded in 1874 by Norwegian immigrants and is affiliated with the Evangelical Lutheran Church of America.

	Annual Growth	05/10	05/11	05/12	05/13	05/16
Sales ($ mil.)	10.4%	–	121.3	124.6	193.0	198.5
Net income ($ mil.)	(27.7%)	–	60.3	(10.7)	22.2	11.9
Market value ($ mil.)	–	–	–	–	–	–
Employees	–	–	–	–	–	800

ST. PETER'S HEALTH PARTNERS

315 S MANNING BLVD
ALBANY, NY 122081707
Phone: 518-525-1111
Fax: –
Web: www.sphp.com

CEO: James Reed
CFO: Thomas Schuhle
HR: –
FYE: June 30
Type: Private

St. Peter's Health Partners (formerly St. Peter's Health Care Services) is a not-for-profit health care system that serves northeastern New York. It includes health networks Seton Health and Northeast Health. Its primary facility St. Peter's Hospital has more than 440 acute-care beds and a medical staff of more than 600 physicians. Specialty services include emergency medicine cancer and cardiovascular care and women's health. St. Peter's also operates community health clinics long-term care facilities mental health centers and home health and hospice agencies. Founded by the Religious Sisters of Mercy in 1869 St. Peter's operates from more than 125 locations and is a subsidiary of Catholic Health East.

	Annual Growth	12/11	12/12*	06/13	06/14	06/15
Sales ($ mil.)	5.7%	–	1,069.6	571.4	1,185.2	1,263.3
Net income ($ mil.)	(34.7%)	–	61.1	23.9	48.4	17.1
Market value ($ mil.)	–	–	–	–	–	–
Employees	–	–	–	–	–	12,000

*Fiscal year change

STAAR SURGICAL CO.

NMS: STAA

25651 Atlantic Ocean Drive
Lake Forest, CA 92630
Phone: 626 303-7902
Fax: –
Web: www.staar.com

CEO: Caren L. Mason
CFO: Deborah Andrews
HR: –
FYE: December 28
Type: Public

STAAR Surgical does what it can to help you to see more clearly. The company makes products for minimally invasive ophthalmic surgical procedures. Its primary products include Visian-branded implantable lenses (ICLs) for correcting such refractive conditions as near- and far-sightedness and astigmatism. More than 750000 of its ICLs have been implanted to date. STAAR also makes foldable intraocular lenses (IOLs) to replace natural lenses removed in cataract surgery. The company sells its products in about 75 countries. China is STAAR's largest single market.

	Annual Growth	01/15	01/16*	12/16	12/17	12/18
Sales ($ mil.)	18.2%	75.0	77.1	82.4	90.6	124.0
Net income ($ mil.)	–	(8.4)	(6.5)	(12.1)	(2.1)	5.0
Market value ($ mil.)	51.3%	399.1	315.6	479.5	685.0	1,381.5
Employees	16.6%	300	360	336	353	475

*Fiscal year change

STAFFMARK HOLDINGS INC.

435 Elm St. Ste. 300
Cincinnati OH 45202-2644
Phone: 513-651-1111
Fax: 650-230-0625
Web: www.castironsys.com

CEO: Geno A Cutolo
CFO: William E Aglinsky
HR: –
FYE: December 31
Type: Private

Staffmark Holdings (formerly CBS Personnel Services) wants to ensure your business gets its fill of people. Providing temporary and permanent staffing to about 6000 clients across the US the company fills positions in such areas as light industrial financial health care legal scientific IT and clerical. Staffmark's geographical reach extends across more than 30 states primarily concentrated in the northern US through about 200 branch offices and 90 client onsite locations. Formerly owned by middle-market investor Compass Diversified Holdings Staffmark was sold to Japan-based Recruit Co. Ltd in late 2011.

STABILIS ENERGY INC

NBB: SLNG

10375 Richmond Avenue, Suite 700
Houston, TX 77042
Phone: 832 456-6500
Fax: –
Web: www.aeti.com

CEO: Jim Reddinger
CFO: Andrew Puhala
HR: –
FYE: December 31
Type: Public

American Electric Technologies (AETI) tames wild and woolly wiring. Its technical products and services segment makes low- and medium-voltage switchgears for land- and offshore-based oil and gas drilling as well as refineries and municipal power companies. The electrical and instrumentation construction unit makes electric power delivery and control products and provides technical field services and electrical and instrumentation construction services. American Access Technologies makes zone-cabling cabinets for telephone lines data networking and security systems.

	Annual Growth	12/14	12/15	12/16	12/17	12/18
Sales ($ mil.)	(39.7%)	57.3	49.1	37.8	47.1	7.6
Net income ($ mil.)	–	(4.7)	(2.6)	(7.1)	(2.2)	(2.6)
Market value ($ mil.)	(37.1%)	6.4	2.4	1.8	1.7	1.0
Employees	(25.5%)	332	235	232	246	102

STAG INDUSTRIAL INC

NYS: STAG

One Federal Street, 23rd Floor
Boston, MA 02110
Phone: 617 574-4777
Fax: 617 574-0052
Web: www.stagindustrial.com

CEO: Benjamin S. Butcher
CFO: William R. Crooker
HR: –
FYE: December 31
Type: Public

If STAG Industrial were to show up alone at a party it would likely be on the hunt for single tenants looking to lease industrial space. The self-managed and self-administered real estate investment trust (REIT) has built a business acquiring and managing single-tenant industrial properties located across more than 35 states. The company's portfolio consists primarily of 50 million sq. ft. of leasable warehouse distribution manufacturing and office space located in secondary markets. STAG conducts most of its business through its operating partner STAG Industrial Operating Partnership. The Massachusetts-based REIT went public in 2011.

	Annual Growth	12/14	12/15	12/16	12/17	12/18
Sales ($ mil.)	19.2%	173.8	218.6	250.2	301.1	351.0
Net income ($ mil.)	–	(4.0)	(29.4)	34.5	31.3	92.9
Market value ($ mil.)	0.4%	2,748.1	2,069.5	2,677.4	3,065.5	2,790.7
Employees	7.8%	54	68	68	72	73

STAFF FORCE, INC.

419 MASON PARK BLVD
KATY, TX 774506187
Phone: 281-492-6044
Fax: –
Web: www.staff-force.com

CEO: –
CFO: Glenn T Van Dusen
HR: –
FYE: December 31
Type: Private

Companies in need of interviewing hiring or payroll expertise trust in this Force. Staff Force — which does business as Staff Force Personnel Services — provides temporary temp-to-hire and direct hire staffing and payroll services in areas such as technology light industrial and hospitality. The company also provides employee handbooks (available in both English and Spanish) employee benefits and criminal background and reference checks. Customers come from industries such as health care manufacturing transportation and consumer goods. Founded in 1989 the company has locations throughout Texas.

	Annual Growth	12/11	12/12	12/13	12/14	12/15
Sales ($ mil.)	4.6%	–	91.6	94.2	99.2	104.8
Net income ($ mil.)	20.0%	–	0.7	0.7	0.6	1.2
Market value ($ mil.)	–	–	–	–	–	–
Employees	–	–	–	–	–	20,000

STAGE STORES INC.

NYS: SSI

2425 West Loop South
Houston, TX 77027
Phone: 800 579-2302
Fax: –
Web: www.stagestoresinc.com

CEO: Michael L. Glazer
CFO: Oded Shein
HR: Stephen B. (Steve) Parsons
FYE: February 02
Type: Public

Stage Stores operates some 650 department stores mainly in rural towns across more than 40 US states. (More than a quarter of the stores are in Texas.) Through its Peebles Bealls Stage Palais Royal and Goody's Family Clothing chains the retailer offers small-town America moderately priced apparel and accessories cosmetics and footwear. Nationally recognized brands such as Adidas Calvin Klein Estee Lauder Levi's and Nike account for most of sales and are offered alongside Stage Stores' private-label merchandise. It also operates the Gordmans chain of more than 140 off-price stores located mostly in midsized midwestern US markets.

	Annual Growth	01/15	01/16	01/17*	02/18	02/19
Sales ($ mil.)	0.0%	1,638.6	1,604.4	1,442.7	1,592.3	1,641.5
Net income ($ mil.)	–	30.9	3.8	(37.9)	(37.3)	(87.7)
Market value ($ mil.)	(53.2%)	565.9	234.8	77.8	46.4	27.1
Employees	(1.2%)	14,300	13,500	12,400	14,500	13,600

*Fiscal year change

STAMFORD HEALTH SYSTEM INC.

30 Shelburne Rd.
Stamford CT 06902
Phone: 203-276-1000
Fax: 203-276-7905
Web: www.stamfordhospital.org

CEO: –
CFO: –
HR: –
FYE: September 30
Type: Private

It sounds like one of the most famous universities in the country but it's actually a comprehensive medical center located on the opposite coast. Stamford Health System provides health services to residents of Stamford Connecticut and surrounding areas through a not-for-profit 300-bed community medical center called Stamford Hospital. The hospital administers acute and specialty services that include oncology cardiology orthopedics and women's health services. It is a teaching facility for the Columbia University College of Physicians and Surgeons and a member of the New York Presbyterian Health System.

STAMPS.COM INC.   NMS: STMP

1990 E. Grand Avenue
El Segundo, CA 90245
Phone: 310 482-5800
Fax: –
Web: www.stamps.com

CEO: Kenneth (Ken) McBride
CFO: Jeff Carberry
HR: –
FYE: December 31
Type: Public

Stamps.com hopes its customers keep putting letters in the mail. Its PC Postage Service lets registered users who have downloaded Stamps.com software buy stamps online and print the postage directly onto envelopes and labels. Customers can order US Postal Service options such as registered mail certified mail and delivery confirmation as well as print custom stamps using virtually any image through its PhotoStamps.com website. Stamps.com charges a monthly fee for its service which is aimed at consumers home offices and small businesses. In addition customers can buy mailing labels scales and dedicated postage printers from Stamps.com. Postage fees are sent directly to the US Postal Service.

	Annual Growth	12/14	12/15	12/16	12/17	12/18
Sales ($ mil.)	41.3%	147.3	214.0	364.3	468.7	586.9
Net income ($ mil.)	46.2%	36.9	(4.2)	75.2	150.6	168.6
Market value ($ mil.)	34.2%	847.6	1,935.9	2,024.9	3,320.5	2,748.9
Employees	36.2%	343	600	700	825	1,179

STANADYNE LLC

92 DEERFIELD RD
WINDSOR, CT 060954200
Phone: 860-525-0821
Fax: –
Web: www.stanadyne.com

CEO: David P. Galuska
CFO: Stephen S. Langin
HR: –
FYE: December 31
Type: Private

Stanadyne's products give engines their growl. The company manufactures fuel pumps for gas and diesel engines and injectors for diesel engines. The line focuses on diesel engine components used by OEMs of agricultural and industrial off-highway equipment. The company also makes fuel heaters and oil pumps for diesel engines and related parts distributed by diesel engine aftermarkets. On an exclusive contract basis its services are tapped by businesses for precision manufacturing assembly and testing.

	Annual Growth	12/07	12/08	12/09	12/11	12/12
Sales ($ mil.)	10.6%	–	–	185.8	245.8	251.5
Net income ($ mil.)	–	–	–	(15.2)	(4.6)	(11.5)
Market value ($ mil.)	–	–	–	–	–	–
Employees	–	–	–	–	–	1,399

STANCORP FINANCIAL GROUP INC   NYS: SFG

1100 SW Sixth Avenue
Portland, OR 97204
Phone: 971 321-7000
Fax: –
Web: www.stancorpfinancial.com

CEO: J Greg Ness
CFO: Floyd F Chadee
HR: Molly Amano
FYE: December 31
Type: Public

Providing insurance and related financial services is standard operating procedure at StanCorp Financial Group. Through Standard Insurance (aka The Standard) and other divisions the company offers a range of financial products nationwide including group and individual disability coverage life and accident insurance retirement plans and supplemental group benefit plans. The insurance services segment holds approximately 42000 group policies covering 6.1 million employees throughout the US. The company's asset management segment provides investment advisory retirement planning mortgage lending and other financial services. Meiji Yasuda Life Insurance is buying StanCorp for approximately $5 billion.

	Annual Growth	12/10	12/11	12/12	12/13	12/14
Assets ($ mil.)	6.2%	17,843.3	18,433.8	19,791.3	21,393.3	22,729.9
Net income ($ mil.)	3.8%	189.0	139.3	138.5	228.5	219.3
Market value ($ mil.)	11.5%	1,899.4	1,546.4	1,543.0	2,787.7	2,939.6
Employees	(2.4%)	3,091	2,974	2,875	2,702	2,803

STAND ENERGY CORPORATION

1077 CELESTIAL ST STE 110
CINCINNATI, OH 45202-1629
Phone: 513-621-1113
Fax: –
Web: www.stand-energy.com

CEO: Judith Phillips
CFO: –
HR: –
FYE: December 31
Type: Private

Stand Energy Corporation (SEC) took a stand in the 1980s when the US government deregulated the natural gas industry. The company markets natural gas to large commercial and industrial customers in nine states (Illinois Indiana Kentucky Maryland New York Ohio Pennsylvania Virginia and West Virginia) and the District of Columbia. SEC also constructs bypass pipelines for its customers (allowing companies to bypass the local utility) and designs and builds propane backup systems to take advantage of reduced gas rates. SEC was founded in 1984 by Chairman Matth Toebben and CEO Judith Phillips. Customers include Coors and the Ohio Hospital Association.

	Annual Growth	12/08	12/09	12/09	12/11	12/12
Sales ($ mil.)	(14.1%)	–	149.3	12.7	117.4	94.6
Net income ($ mil.)	–	–	0.0	0.0	0.0	0.0
Market value ($ mil.)	–	–	–	–	–	–
Employees	–	–	–	–	–	32

STANDARD AVB FINANCIAL CORP   NAS: STND

2640 Monroeville Boulevard
Monroeville, PA 15146
Phone: 412 856-0363
Fax: –
Web: www.standardbankpa.com

CEO: Timothy K Zimmerman
CFO: Susan A Parente
HR: –
FYE: December 31
Type: Public

Standard Financial provides standard banking services and a little bit more. Standard Financial is the holding company of Standard Bank which offers traditional personal and business checking and savings accounts as well as loan products. It operates 10 branches serving southwestern Pennsylvania and northern Maryland. Its loan portfolio includes residential and mortgages home equity loans and commercial loans; to a lesser extent it provides consumer and construction loans. Brokerage services retirement planning and other investment services are offered through PrimeVest Financial. Standard Financial is combining with Allegheny Valley Bancorp in a $56.5 million merger of equals.

	Annual Growth	09/15	09/16*	12/16	12/17	12/18
Assets ($ mil.)	27.6%	468.3	495.2	488.0	972.6	971.8
Net income ($ mil.)	35.5%	3.5	3.0	0.6	4.3	8.8
Market value ($ mil.)	8.3%	113.1	109.7	121.3	144.8	143.8
Employees	9.7%	–	–	–	144	158

*Fiscal year change

STANDARD ELECTRIC COMPANY

2650 TRAUTNER DR
SAGINAW, MI 486049599
Phone: 989-497-2100
Fax: –
Web: www.standardelectricco.com

CEO: –
CFO: –
HR: –
FYE: February 28
Type: Private

Standard Electric and its affiliates distribute electrical and electronic products and supplies to customers through about 30 locations in Michigan. The company was founded in 1929 by Samuel Cohen and brothers Morris and Max Blumberg. The Blumberg brothers earlier established another Michigan-based electrical distributor Madison Electric an affiliate of Standard Electric with 10 Michigan locations. Another affiliated firm U.P. Electric/Wittock Supply Co. is a distributor of electrical and mechanical products with four locations on the upper Michigan peninsula. The company is owned by its directors and their families.

	Annual Growth	02/13	02/14	02/15	02/16	02/17
Sales ($ mil.)	6.3%	–	160.0	173.0	176.1	192.3
Net income ($ mil.)	5.8%	–	1.8	2.2	0.3	2.1
Market value ($ mil.)	–	–	–	–	–	–
Employees	–	–	–	–	–	250

STANDARD FORWARDING LLC

2925 MORTON DR
EAST MOLINE, IL 61244-1960
Phone: 309-755-4504
Fax: –

CEO: Al Toliver
CFO: Ross Resetich
HR: Dennis Blum
FYE: December 31
Type: Private

Standard Forwarding specializes in less-than-truckload (LTL) freight transportation services. (LTL carriers consolidate freight from multiple shippers into a single trailer.) The company operates a fleet of about 300 tractors and 790 trailers from a network of more than a dozen terminals in Illinois Indiana Iowa Minnesota and Wisconsin. The company also offers freight transportation in Canada through partnerships. Farm equipment manufacturer Deere is a major customer as it has been since Standard Forwarding was founded in 1934. As a result of experiencing higher-than-market operating costs in the midst of the recession the company voluntarily filed for Chapter 11 bankruptcy protection in November 2009.

	Annual Growth	12/04	12/05	12/06	12/07	12/08
Sales ($ mil.)	9.4%	–	60.6	66.2	73.9	79.3
Net income ($ mil.)	(47.6%)	–	2.0	64.0	(0.7)	0.3
Market value ($ mil.)	–	–	–	–	–	–
Employees	–	–	–	–	–	510

STANDARD MOTOR PRODUCTS, INC.   NYS: SMP

37-18 Northern Blvd.
Long Island City, NY 11101
Phone: 718 392-0200
Fax: 718 472-0122
Web: www.smpcorp.com

CEO: Eric P. Sills
CFO: James J. Burke
HR: Thomas Tesoro
FYE: December 31
Type: Public

Standard Motor Products (SMP) is a manufacturer and distributor of replacement parts for the automotive industry. The company is organized into two major operating segments. Its largest segment Engine Management makes ignition and emission parts ignition wires battery cables and fuel system parts. Its Temperature Control segment manufactures and remanufactures air conditioning compressors heating parts engine cooling system parts power window accessories and windshield washer parts. Customers include warehouse distributors CARQUEST and NAPA Auto Parts and retail chains Advance Auto Parts and AutoZone. North America is SMP's core market but a small portion of sales come from Europe.

	Annual Growth	12/14	12/15	12/16	12/17	12/18
Sales ($ mil.)	2.7%	980.4	972.0	1,058.5	1,116.1	1,092.1
Net income ($ mil.)	(0.0%)	43.0	46.0	60.4	38.0	43.0
Market value ($ mil.)	6.2%	855.1	853.6	1,193.9	1,007.5	1,086.4
Employees	6.7%	3,400	3,400	4,100	4,200	4,400

STANDARD REGISTER CO.   NYS: SR

600 Albany Street
Dayton, OH 45417
Phone: 937 221-1940
Fax: 937 221-3431
Web: www.standardregister.com

CEO: Landen Williams
CFO: Benjamin T Cutting
HR: –
FYE: December 29
Type: Public

When it comes to managing communication The Standard Register Company (SRC) helps businesses maintain a certain set of standards. SRC primarily provides print services (both digital and traditional) for healthcare manufacturing financial services and other commercial businesses helping manage their communications so that they align with corporate standards and priorities. Formerly a provider of traditional document services the company is now focused on providing market-driven communication services that help companies in specific industries build and enhance their brands and reputations reduce risk and operate more efficiently. The 100-year-old firm was founded by John Q. Sherman in 1912.

	Annual Growth	01/10	01/11	01/12*	12/12	12/13
Sales ($ mil.)	1.2%	694.0	668.4	648.1	602.0	719.8
Net income ($ mil.)	–	(12.4)	2.6	(87.7)	(9.1)	(7.4)
Market value ($ mil.)	10.6%	43.7	29.2	20.0	5.2	59.1
Employees	8.5%	2,900	2,600	2,700	2,200	3,700

*Fiscal year change

STANDEX INTERNATIONAL CORP.   NYS: SXI

11 Keewaydin Drive
Salem, NH 03079
Phone: 603 893-9701
Fax: 603 893-7324
Web: www.standex.com

CEO: –
CFO: Thomas D. DeByle
HR: Ross Mcgovern
FYE: June 30
Type: Public

Be it a rotisserie or a rocket part Standex stands and delivers. The company is a manufacturer and service provider for various industrial markets. It has five main reportable segments: Food Service Equipment a manufacturer of commercial food service equipment; Engraving a maker of molds used to produce plastic components; Engineering Technologies a provider of custom fabrication and machining services for engineered components; and Electronics and Hydraulics which consists of the Custom Hoists and Standex Electronics businesses. Standex traces its historical roots back to the 1950s.

	Annual Growth	06/15	06/16	06/17	06/18	06/19
Sales ($ mil.)	0.6%	772.1	751.6	755.3	868.4	791.6
Net income ($ mil.)	5.5%	54.7	52.1	46.5	36.6	67.9
Market value ($ mil.)	(2.2%)	985.9	1,019.2	1,118.7	1,260.6	902.2
Employees	(0.5%)	5,100	5,300	5,500	5,600	5,000

STANFORD HEALTH CARE

300 PASTEUR DR
STANFORD, CA 943052200
Phone: 650-723-4000
Fax: –

CEO: David Entwistle
CFO: David Connor
HR: –
FYE: August 31
Type: Private

Doctors patients medical students and researchers gather at Stanford Health Care (formerly Stanford Hospital and Clinics). As Stanford University's primary medical teaching facility the more than 600-bed Stanford Hospital specializes in such areas as cardiac care cancer treatment neurology surgery and organ transplant. The affiliated Stanford Clinics is a physician group practice organization that represents more than 100 specialized fields of medicine. Stanford Health Care is part of the Stanford Medicine organization which also includes the nearby Stanford University School of Medicine and the 310-bed Lucile Packard Children's Hospital (named for the wife of Hewlett-Packard co-founder David Packard).

	Annual Growth	08/09	08/10	08/15	08/17	08/18
Sales ($ mil.)	10.9%	–	2,141.8	3,570.7	4,454.4	4,910.5
Net income ($ mil.)	11.9%	–	186.2	372.4	450.4	456.6
Market value ($ mil.)	–	–	–	–	–	–
Employees	–	–	–	–	–	5,045

STANION WHOLESALE ELECTRIC CO., INC.

812 S MAIN ST
PRATT, KS 671242600
Phone: 620-672-5678
Fax: –
Web: www.stanion.com

CEO: –
CFO: –
HR: –
FYE: December 31
Type: Private

Stanion Wholesale Electric distributes electrical products and supplies to customers through nearly 20 branch locations in Kansas and Missouri. The company specializes in products for factory automation lighting telecommunications and utilities carrying items from such manufacturers as Cooper Industries General Electric Rockwell Automation and Thomas & Betts. Stanion Wholesale Electric makes all of its product catalog available over its corporate Web site along with other e-commerce functions. The family-owned company was founded in 1961 by chairman Jud Stanion and his wife Bobbe. Stanion Wholesale Electric is owned by Bill Keller (president and CEO) and his wife Cindy Stanion Keller.

	Annual Growth	12/12	12/13	12/14	12/15	12/16
Sales ($ mil.)	(2.2%)	–	86.2	0.0	84.1	80.7
Net income ($ mil.)	(13.3%)	–	3.4	3.0	(2.8)	2.2
Market value ($ mil.)	–	–	–	–	–	–
Employees	–	–	–	–	–	197

STANLEY BLACK & DECKER INC

NYS: SWK

1000 Stanley Drive
New Britain, CT 06053
Phone: 860 225-5111
Fax: 860 827-3895
Web: www.stanleyblackanddecker.com

CEO: James M. (Jim) Loree
CFO: Donald (Don) Allan
HR: Joseph Voelker
FYE: December 29
Type: Public

Stanley Black & Decker has all the tools of the trade. A leading global toolmaker the company generates more than two-thirds of sales from a plethora of tools (hand mechanics' power pneumatic hydraulic) and related accessories. In addition to its well-known namesake brands it sells other top brands such as Bostitch Mac Tools and DEWALT directly to consumers as well as through distributors home centers and mass-merchant distributors. Stanley Black & Decker also sells engineered fastening and infrastructure products to customers in the automotive manufacturing and oil & gas industries among others and designs and installs electronic security systems and automatic doors to commercial customers. It generates nearly half of sales outside the US.

	Annual Growth	01/15	01/16*	12/16	12/17	12/18
Sales ($ mil.)	7.2%	11,338.6	11,171.8	11,406.9	12,747.2	13,982.4
Net income ($ mil.)	(7.3%)	760.9	883.7	965.3	1,226.0	605.2
Market value ($ mil.)	7.4%	14,528.1	16,148.5	17,352.9	25,674.5	17,979.3
Employees	6.4%	50,400	51,250	54,023	57,765	60,767

*Fiscal year change

STANLEY STEEMER INTERNATIONAL, INC.

5800 INNOVATION DR
DUBLIN, OH 430163271
Phone: 614-764-2007
Fax: –
Web: www.stanleysteemer.com

CEO: Wesley C. Bates
CFO: Mark Bunner
HR: –
FYE: December 31
Type: Private

Carpet stains don't startle this Stanley. Stanley Steemer International provides residential and commercial carpet and upholstery cleaning through more than 300 franchise and corporate locations in 48 states. In addition to cleaning carpets the company provides cleaning services for tile and grout and air ducts as well as cars boats and RVs. The company which is known for its fleet of yellow vans sells its own brand of cleaning products through an online store. Founded by Jack Bates in 1947 when he established his own one-man carpet cleaning business Stanley Steemer is owned by his descendants including CEO Wesley Bates and President Justin Bates.

	Annual Growth	12/13	12/14	12/15	12/16	12/17
Sales ($ mil.)	3.7%	–	215.2	234.2	242.0	240.7
Net income ($ mil.)	(6.4%)	–	19.1	23.2	14.7	15.6
Market value ($ mil.)	–	–	–	–	–	–
Employees	–	–	–	–	–	2,000

STANT MANUFACTURING INC.

1620 Columbia Ave.
Connersville IN 47331-1696
Phone: 765-825-3121
Fax: 419-782-5145
Web: www.fdef.com

CEO: –
CFO: –
HR: –
FYE: April 30
Type: Subsidiary

Gentlemen "Stant" your engines. Formerly a subsidiary of Tomkins PLC Stant manufactures a broad line of automotive parts and tools. The company produces fuel radiator and oil filler caps as well as gaskets and seals. Other products include thermal products such as thermostats and thermostat housings. The company also makes testers used to measure radiator cap pressure fuel cap leakage compliance and engine vacuum pressure. Stant sells to automakers and aftermarket retailers. Tomkins sold Stant to Miami-based private equity firm H.I.G. Capital in 2008. The company filed Chapter 11 bankruptcy and emerged in 2009.

STAPLE COTTON COOPERATIVE ASSOCIATION

214 W MARKET ST
GREENWOOD, MS 389304329
Phone: 662-453-6231
Fax: –
Web: www.staplcotn.com

CEO: –
CFO: Mike Moffatt
HR: Russell Robertson
FYE: August 31
Type: Private

Referred to as Staplcotn the Staple Cotton Cooperative has been a staple of its member-producers' business lives since 1921. One of the oldest and largest cotton marketing co-ops in the US it provides domestic and export marketing cotton warehousing and agricultural financing to some 9730 members in 47 states. As of 2011 the co-op handles nearly 14000 farm accounts in 10 states. Staplcotn's inventory is consigned by member-producers and averages from 2.5 million to 3 million bales of cotton a year. The co-op operates though 15 warehouses serving the mid-south and southeastern US to supply more than 25% of the cotton consumed by the US textile industry as well as the needs of textile mills overseas.

	Annual Growth	08/09	08/10	08/11	08/12	08/13
Sales ($ mil.)	8.7%	–	–	963.4	1,236.6	1,138.3
Net income ($ mil.)	(91.7%)	–	–	875.1	8.2	6.0
Market value ($ mil.)	–	–	–	–	–	–
Employees	–	–	–	–	–	187

STAPLES INC

NMS: SPLS

Five Hundred Staples Drive
Framingham, MA 01702
Phone: 508 253-5000
Fax: 508 370-8955
Web: www.staples.com

CEO: J Alexander Douglas
CFO: Christine T Komola
HR: –
FYE: January 30
Type: Public

Staples is clipping along as the #1 office supply superstore operator in the US and as a worldwide leader in the office category. It sells office products furniture computers and other supplies through more than 1900 Staples stores in the US Canada the UK Australia Brazil and a half-dozen European countries. In addition to its retail outlets Staples sells office products via the Internet and through its catalog and direct sales operations including subsidiary Quill Corp. The company also provides document management and copying services at its stores.

	Annual Growth	01/12*	02/13	02/14*	01/15	01/16
Sales ($ mil.)	(4.2%)	25,022.2	24,380.5	23,114.3	22,492.4	21,059.0
Net income ($ mil.)	(21.2%)	984.7	(210.7)	620.1	134.5	379.0
Market value ($ mil.)	(13.6%)	10,338.0	8,723.7	8,497.7	11,009.6	5,759.9
Employees	(3.7%)	87,782	85,087	83,008	79,075	75,371

*Fiscal year change

STAR GROUP LP
NYS: SGU

9 West Broad Street, Suite 310
Stamford, CT 06902
Phone: 203 328-7310
Fax: –
Web: www.stargrouplp.com

CEO: Jeffrey M Woosnam
CFO: Richard F Ambury
HR: –
FYE: September 30
Type: Public

Those who wish for heat and power can wish upon a star — Star Gas Partners. The company is the nation's largest retail distributor of home heating oil. Its Petro Holdings subsidiary provides heating oil and propane to 416000 customers in the US Northeast and Mid-Atlantic. The company sells home heating oil gasoline and diesel fuel to 48000 customers on a delivery only basis and provides HVAC and ancillary home services including home security and plumbing to 11500 customers. Investment firm Kestrel Energy Partners controls the general partner of Star Gas Partners.

	Annual Growth	09/15	09/16	09/17	09/18	09/19
Sales ($ mil.)	1.2%	1,674.3	1,161.3	1,323.6	1,677.8	1,753.9
Net income ($ mil.)	(17.2%)	37.6	44.9	26.9	55.5	17.6
Market value ($ mil.)	2.8%	407.6	463.3	544.9	469.1	454.7
Employees	2.7%	3,101	3,140	3,362	3,403	3,446

STAR MULTI CARE SERVICES INC.

115 Broad Hollow Road Suite 275
Melville NY 11747
Phone: 631-423-6689
Fax: 631-427-5466
Web: www.starmulticare.com/

CEO: –
CFO: David Schoenberg
HR: –
FYE: May 31
Type: Private

When you wish upon this Star a nurse will come to where you are. Star Multi Care Services along with its two subsidiary companies provides home health care to the elderly infirm and disabled 24 hours a day seven days a week. The company's Extended Family Care subsidiary provides services in Pennsylvania; Central Star Home Health covers Ohio; and Star Multi Care provides services in Florida and New York. In addition to its in-home health care the company offers occupational physical respiratory and speech therapies as well as medical social services. The privately-held firm was founded in 1938 and is led by CEO Stephen Sternbach.

STAR OF THE WEST MILLING COMPANY

121 E TUSCOLA ST
FRANKENMUTH, MI 487341731
Phone: 989-652-9971
Fax: –
Web: www.starofthewest.com

CEO: –
CFO: –
HR: –
FYE: December 31
Type: Private

All hands are on the mill floor at Star of the West Milling. The company operates five flour mills in four US states an about 10 storage elevators. The mills and elevators store and process wheat corn and soybeans. Its flour milling capacity is about 20000 lbs. per day. North Star Bean a division of Star of the West processes beans such as navy pinto kidney and black beans into dry commodity products. The company also owns Eastern Michigan Grain an elevator that offers grain handling and marketing services. Star of the West Milling sells its flour and beans worldwide to canning and packaging customers the likes of Kellogg General Mills Nabisco and Pepperidge Farm.

	Annual Growth	12/12	12/13	12/14	12/15	12/16
Sales ($ mil.)	(3.0%)	–	416.9	0.0	396.8	380.1
Net income ($ mil.)	(27.3%)	–	15.6	12.9	11.2	6.0
Market value ($ mil.)	–	–	–	–	–	–
Employees	–	–	–	–	–	239

STARBUCKS CORP.
NMS: SBUX

2401 Utah Avenue South
Seattle, WA 98134
Phone: 206 447-1575
Fax: –
Web: www.starbucks.com

CEO: Howard D. Schultz
CFO: Scott H. Maw
HR: Lucy Hur
FYE: September 29
Type: Public

Wake up and smell the coffee — Starbucks is everywhere. The world's #1 specialty coffee retailer Starbucks has more than 29300 coffee shops in 80 countries. The shops offer coffee drinks and food items as well as roasted beans coffee accessories and teas. Starbucks operates more than 15300 of its own shops which are located mostly in the US while licensees and franchisees operate roughly 14000 units worldwide (including many locations in shopping centers and airports). In addition Starbucks markets its coffee through grocery stores food service customers and licenses its brand for other food and beverage products. The US accounts for the majority of Starbucks' revenue.

	Annual Growth	09/15*	10/16	10/17*	09/18	09/19
Sales ($ mil.)	8.5%	19,162.7	21,315.9	22,386.8	24,719.5	26,508.6
Net income ($ mil.)	6.9%	2,757.4	2,817.7	2,884.7	4,518.3	3,599.2
Market value ($ mil.)	11.1%	68,695.0	64,134.2	63,624.9	67,332.7	104,683.1
Employees	9.8%	238,000	254,000	277,000	291,000	346,000

*Fiscal year change

STARRETT (LS) CO (THE)
NYS: SCX

121 Crescent Street
Athol, MA 01331-1915
Phone: 978 249-3551
Fax: –
Web: www.starrett.com

CEO: Douglas A. Starrett
CFO: Francis J O'Brien
HR: –
FYE: June 30
Type: Public

L.S. Starrett has forged its business inch by inch. It makes more than 5000 products including hand measuring tools (Evans Rule tape measures steel rules combination squares micrometers) and precision instruments (vernier calipers and height and depth gauges). Starrett sells its products in more than 100 countries boasting major subsidiaries in Brazil Scotland and China. The company also makes levels vises lubricants saw blades and vocational and educational materials. Starrett caters to machinists in the metalworking industry but also serves the DIY automotive aviation construction marine and farm equipment industries. The company was founded in 1880 in Massachusetts by Laroy S. Starrett.

	Annual Growth	06/15	06/16	06/17	06/18	06/19
Sales ($ mil.)	(1.4%)	241.6	209.7	207.0	216.3	228.0
Net income ($ mil.)	3.8%	5.2	(14.1)	1.0	(3.6)	6.1
Market value ($ mil.)	(18.5%)	103.4	82.1	59.3	44.1	45.7
Employees	(2.9%)	1,804	1,694	1,647	1,572	1,603

STARTEK, INC.
NYS: SRT

6200 South Syracuse Way, Suite 485
Greenwood Village, CO 80111
Phone: 303 262-4500
Fax: –
Web: www.startek.com

CEO: Chad A. Carlson
CFO: Don Norsworthy
HR: –
FYE: December 31
Type: Public

When it comes to outsourcing this company reaches for the stars. StarTek provides business clients with outsourcing services such as customer care technical support and e-commerce fulfillment under the StarTek and Aegis brands. Other services include social media monitoring back office functions such as HR and accounting collections and research and analytics. The company operates call centers and other facilities from 58 locations in 13 countries on five continents. Most of its top clients come from high-tech industries such as telecommunications (48% of revenue) and e-commerce services. StarTek was founded in 1987. In 2018 the company acquired Aegis an outsourcing firm based in Singapore.

	Annual Growth	12/15	12/16	12/17*	03/18*	12/18
Sales ($ mil.)	14.2%	282.1	307.2	292.6	170.0	420.3
Net income ($ mil.)	–	(15.6)	0.4	(1.3)	(6.8)	(24.3)
Market value ($ mil.)	22.9%	134.1	316.4	373.3	366.2	249.0
Employees	48.5%	14,500	13,500	13,300	–	47,500

*Fiscal year change

STARWOOD HOTELS & RESORTS WORLDWIDE INC   NYS: HOT

One StarPoint
Stamford, CT 06902
Phone: 203 964-6000
Fax: –
Web: www.starwoodhotels.com

CEO: Arne M Sorenson
CFO: Kathleen K Oberg
HR: –
FYE: December 31
Type: Public

Starwood Hotels & Resorts Worldwide knows how to shine a light on hospitality. One of the world's largest hotel companies it has about 1125 properties in about 100 countries. Starwood's hotel empire consists of upscale brands such as Sheraton and Westin. It operates about 100 luxury resorts and hotels through its St. Regis and Luxury Collection units while its 40 W Hotels offer ultra-modern style. Other brands include Four Points (value-oriented) Le Méridien (European-inspired) Aloft (select-service) and Element (extended stay). Starwood Vacation Ownership operates about 15 time-share resorts. In 2015 Marriott agreed to acquire Starwood for about $12.2 billion.

	Annual Growth	12/10	12/11	12/12	12/13	12/14
Sales ($ mil.)	4.2%	5,071.0	5,624.0	6,321.0	6,115.0	5,983.0
Net income ($ mil.)	7.3%	477.0	489.0	562.0	635.0	633.0
Market value ($ mil.)	7.5%	10,496.4	8,284.1	9,905.7	13,720.6	14,000.3
Employees	5.6%	145,000	154,000	171,000	181,400	180,400

STARWOOD PROPERTY TRUST INC.   NYS: STWD

591 West Putnam Avenue
Greenwich, CT 06830
Phone: 203 422-7700
Fax: –
Web: www.starwoodpropertytrust.com

CEO: Barry S Sternlicht
CFO: Rina Paniry
HR: –
FYE: December 31
Type: Public

Starwood Property Trust hopes to shine brightly in the world of mortgages. A real estate investment trust (REIT) the company originates finances and manages US commercial and residential mortgage loans commercial mortgage-backed securities and other commercial real estate debt investments. It acquires discounted loans from failed banks and financial institutions some through the FDIC which typically auctions off large pools of loan portfolios. Starwood Property Trust is externally managed by SPT Management LLC an affiliate of Starwood Capital Group. As a REIT the trust is exempt from paying federal income tax so long as it distributes quarterly dividends to shareholders.

	Annual Growth	12/14	12/15	12/16	12/17	12/18
Assets ($ mil.)	(12.4%)	116,099.3	85,738.1	77,256.3	62,941.3	68,262.5
Net income ($ mil.)	(6.0%)	495.0	450.7	365.2	400.8	385.8
Market value ($ mil.)	(4.0%)	6,406.3	5,667.6	6,050.7	5,885.3	5,433.2
Employees	(11.3%)	468	450	340	312	290

STARZ   NMS: STRZ A

8900 Liberty Circle
Englewood, CO 80112
Phone: 720 852-7700
Fax: –
Web: www.starz.com

CEO: Christopher P Albrecht
CFO: Scott D Macdonald
HR: –
FYE: December 31
Type: Public

Starz (formerly Liberty Media Corporation) has a galaxy of premium cable properties including the Starz Encore and MoviePlex networks. The company's 17 channels across those three networks — Starz Comedy Encore Black Encore Espanol Indieplex and Retroplex among them — serve nearly 60 million subscribers. Starz also distributes content digitally and through DVDs in the US and internationally through its Anchor Bay Entertainment subsidiary and produces animated content via Film Roman. In 2013 the company spun off its other operations (the Atlanta Braves a majority stake in SIRIUS XM and other holdings) into the new Liberty Media Corporation; it then took the Starz name.

	Annual Growth	12/10	12/11	12/12	12/13	12/14
Sales ($ mil.)	(5.1%)	2,050.0	3,024.0	1,630.7	1,777.5	1,663.9
Net income ($ mil.)	(28.2%)	1,021.0	812.0	254.5	247.3	271.3
Market value ($ mil.)	(17.0%)	6,365.3	7,941.3	11,803.6	2,975.1	3,021.9
Employees	131.5%	—	77	926	959	955

STATE AUTO FINANCIAL CORP.   NMS: STFC

518 East Broad Street
Columbus, OH 43215-3976
Phone: 614 464-5000
Fax: –
Web: www.stateauto.com

CEO: Michael E. (Mike) LaRocco
CFO: Steven E. English
HR: –
FYE: December 31
Type: Public

Thanks to State Auto Financial the state of auto insurance is healthy in the Midwest. The company sells property/casualty policies through several subsidiaries writing personal commercial and specialty coverage including automobile homeowners multi-peril and workers' compensation insurance. It also participates in an insurance pool through its parent company State Auto Mutual Insurance which owns more than 60% of State Auto Financial and provides the offices for its headquarters. Subsidiary Stateco Financial Services manages the company's invested assets. State Auto Financial is the only part of State Auto Mutual that is publicly traded.

	Annual Growth	12/14	12/15	12/16	12/17	12/18
Assets ($ mil.)	1.1%	2,766.9	2,828.5	2,959.4	3,014.3	2,895.9
Net income ($ mil.)	(41.2%)	107.4	51.2	21.0	(10.7)	12.8
Market value ($ mil.)	11.3%	959.9	889.5	1,158.2	1,258.0	1,470.5
Employees	(5.0%)	2,274	2,065	2,020	1,962	1,854

STATE BANK FINANCIAL CORP   NAS: STBZ

3399 Peachtree Road N.E., Suite 1900
Atlanta, GA 30326
Phone: 404 475-6599
Fax: –

CEO: –
CFO: –
HR: –
FYE: December 31
Type: Public

State Bank Financial Corp. aspires to one day live in the center of central Georgia's banking world. The $3.5 billion-asset holding company operates through subsidiary State Bank and Trust Company a state-charted commercial bank that serves individuals and businesses through more than 25 branches and more than half a dozen mortgage origination offices in central Georgia and in the Atlanta metropolitan area. The bank offers traditional checking and savings accounts as well as commercial and residential real estate mortgages construction and commercial loans and consumer loans.

	Annual Growth	12/12	12/13	12/14	12/15	12/16
Assets ($ mil.)	12.2%	2,663.0	2,600.7	2,882.2	3,470.1	4,224.9
Net income ($ mil.)	20.3%	22.7	12.7	30.9	28.4	47.6
Market value ($ mil.)	14.0%	616.9	706.6	776.1	816.9	1,043.4
Employees	4.8%	605	577	566	664	731

STATE COMPENSATION INSURANCE FUND

333 Bush St. 8th Fl.
San Francisco CA 94104
Phone: 415-565-1234
Fax: +33-1-53-63-38-58
Web: www.atics.fr

CEO: –
CFO: Jay Stewart
HR: –
FYE: December 31
Type: Government-owned

From San Diego in the south to Eureka up north State Compensation Insurance Fund (State Fund) keeps workers in the Golden State covered. Run like a mutual company State Fund is a not-for-profit public enterprise fund. Its primary product is workers' compensation insurance but the company also offers claims management coordinated care plans and loss control services to policyholders. Employers can purchase coverage directly from the insurer or through independent brokers. It boasts some 180000 policy holders. As the insurer of last resort State Fund has prospered as other insurers have withdrawn from the workers' compensation market in California. The company was established in 1914.

STATE FARM MUTUAL AUTOMOBILE INSURANCE COMPANY

1 State Farm Plaza
Bloomington IL 61710-0001
Phone: 309-766-2311
Fax: 309-766-3621
Web: www.statefarm.com

CEO: Michael L Tipsord
CFO: –
HR: –
FYE: December 31
Type: Private - Mutual Com

Like an enormous corporation State Farm is everywhere. The leading US personal lines property/casualty company (by premiums) State Farm Mutual Automobile Insurance Company is the #1 provider of private auto insurance. It also is the leading home insurer and offers nonmedical health and life insurance through its subsidiary companies. Its products are marketed via more than 18000 agents in the US and Canada. State Farm's efforts to diversify include a federal savings bank charter (State Farm Bank) that offers consumer and business loans through its agents and by phone mail and the Internet.

STATE OF NEW YORK MORTGAGE AGENCY

641 LEXINGTON AVE FL 4
NEW YORK, NY 100224503
Phone: 212-688-4000
Fax: –
Web: www.nyshcr.org

CEO: –
CFO: Sheila Robinson
HR: –
FYE: October 31
Type: Private

The State of New York Mortgage Agency (SONYMA pronounced "Sony Mae") is a public benefit corporation of the State of New York that makes homebuying more affordable for low- and moderate-income residents of the state. SONYMA has two program divisions: Its single-family programs and financing division provides low-interest rate mortgages to first-time homebuyers with low and moderate incomes through the issuance of mortgage revenue bonds while its mortgage insurance fund provides mortgage insurance and credit support for multi-family affordable residential projects and special care facilities throughout the state.

	Annual Growth	10/08	10/09	10/16	10/17	10/18
Assets ($ mil.)	0.2%	–	5,225.1	5,187.2	5,229.0	5,324.0
Net income ($ mil.)	(1.0%)	–	162.3	63.9	34.8	148.0
Market value ($ mil.)	–	–	–	–	–	–
Employees	–	–	–	–	–	221

STATE STREET CORP.

NYS: STT

One Lincoln Street
Boston, MA 02111
Phone: 617 786-3000
Fax: –
Web: www.statestreet.com

CEO: Joseph L. (Jay) Hooley
CFO: Eric Aboaf
HR: Kathryn M. (Kathy) Horgan
FYE: December 31
Type: Public

Through its flagship State Street Bank and other subsidiaries State Street provides investment servicing (including clearing settlement payment brokerage and trading and risk and compliance analytics) and investment management services (which include core and enhanced indexing multi-asset strategies environment and social investing and ETFs). The holding company's primary clientele comprises investment managers mutual funds corporate and public retirement plans collective investment funds and other investment pools foundations endowments and insurance companies. Founded in 1792 as Union Bank State Street has some $31.6 trillion in assets under custody and administration and roughly $2.5 trillion in assets under management.

	Annual Growth	12/14	12/15	12/16	12/17	12/18
Assets ($ mil.)	(2.8%)	274,119.0	245,192.0	242,698.0	238,425.0	244,626.0
Net income ($ mil.)	6.3%	2,037.0	1,980.0	2,143.0	2,177.0	2,599.0
Market value ($ mil.)	(5.3%)	29,825.8	25,213.3	29,529.5	37,086.6	23,963.2
Employees	7.6%	29,970	32,356	33,783	36,643	40,142

STATE UNIVERSITY OF IOWA FOUNDATION

1 W PARK RD
IOWA CITY, IA 522422000
Phone: 319-335-3305
Fax: –
Web: www.uifoundation.org

CEO: –
CFO: Sherri Furman
HR: –
FYE: June 30
Type: Private

If you ever find yourself shouting "Fight! Fight! Fight! for IOWA" most likely you're a current former or honorary Hawkeye. Since 1956 The University of Iowa Foundation has been organizing University of Iowa fund-raising campaigns to get private contributions for equipment facilities fellowships professorships research and scholarships. Its endowment which is almost entirely restricted to donor-specified uses is valued at more than $690 million. Though independent of the school the not-for-profit organization is the university's preferred channel for contributions.

	Annual Growth	06/11	06/12	06/13	06/14	06/15
Sales ($ mil.)	25.5%	–	79.3	105.6	129.4	156.8
Net income ($ mil.)	–	–	(34.6)	(2.5)	14.2	36.7
Market value ($ mil.)	–	–	–	–	–	–
Employees	–	–	–	–	–	180

STATE UNIVERSITY OF NEW YORK

353 BROADWAY
ALBANY, NY 122462915
Phone: 518-320-1100
Fax: –
Web: www.suny.edu

CEO: –
CFO: Kimberly R Cline
HR: –
FYE: June 30
Type: Private

SUNY days are ahead for many New Yorkers seeking higher education. With an enrollment of more than 460000 students The State University of New York (SUNY) is vying with California State University System for the title of largest university system in the US. Most students are residents of New York State. Students come from all 50 states as well as 160 countries. SUNY maintains 64 campuses around the state including four university centers about two dozen university colleges 30 community colleges and a handful of technical colleges as well as medical centers. The system has a student-teacher ratio of about 16:1.

	Annual Growth	10/03	10/04	10/05*	06/06	06/12
Sales ($ mil.)	–	–	–	0.0	4.4	5,961.0
Net income ($ mil.)	–	–	–	0.0	(2.4)	(374.8)
Market value ($ mil.)	–	–	–	–	–	–
Employees	–	–	–	–	–	88,024

*Fiscal year change

STATEN ISLAND UNIVERSITY HOSPITAL

475 SEAVIEW AVE
STATEN ISLAND, NY 103053436
Phone: 718-226-9000
Fax: –

CEO: –
CFO: Thomas Reca
HR: –
FYE: December 31
Type: Private

Staten Island University Hospital (SIUH) ferries health care services to residents of New York City's fastest growing borough and surrounding areas at its two medical campuses. Established in 1861 SIUH maintains about 715 beds and is a teaching affiliate of the State University of New York's Brooklyn Health Science Center. Its larger north campus includes units specializing in cardiology pathology cancer blood-related diseases burn treatment trauma and women's health. The south campus site offers specialty programs such as sleep medicine geriatric psychiatry and substance abuse services. A member of Northwell Health SIUH employs approximately 1200 physicians.

	Annual Growth	12/13	12/14	12/15	12/16	12/17
Sales ($ mil.)	3.2%	–	811.8	850.1	871.8	891.5
Net income ($ mil.)	10.2%	–	51.7	41.8	57.2	69.1
Market value ($ mil.)	–	–	–	–	–	–
Employees	–	–	–	–	–	5,700

STATER BROS. HOLDINGS INC.

ASE: HGN A

301 S. Tippecanoe Avenue
San Bernardino, CA 92408
Phone: 909 733-5000
Fax: –
Web: www.staterbros.com

CEO: –
CFO: –
HR: –
FYE: September 29
Type: Public

Stater Bros. has no shortage of major-league rivals operating in the same crowded Southern California markets as Kroger-owned Ralphs and Safeway-owned Vons. Stater Bros. Holdings operates more than 165 full-service Stater Bros. Markets in six counties primarily in the Riverside and San Bernardino areas. Most of the grocery chain's stores have deli department about 45% house bakeries while another 25 host Super Rx Pharmacies. The Southern California grocery operator builds and remodels its own stores through its Stater Bros. Development subsidiary. Founded in 1936 by twin brothers Leo and Cleo Stater Stater Bros. is owned by chairman and CEO Jack Brown through La Cadena Investments.

	Annual Growth	09/09	09/10	09/11	09/12	09/13
Sales ($ mil.)	0.6%	3,766.0	3,606.8	3,693.3	3,873.2	3,859.8
Net income ($ mil.)	(3.3%)	34.8	24.6	26.3	37.7	30.4
Market value ($ mil.)	–	–	–	–	–	–
Employees	(2.1%)	17,500	16,300	16,500	16,500	16,100

STATESVILLE HMA, LLC

218 OLD MOCKSVILLE RD
STATESVILLE, NC 286251930
Phone: 704-873-0281
Fax: –
Web: www.davisregional.com

CEO: Andy Davis
CFO: –
HR: –
FYE: September 30
Type: Private

Davis Regional Medical Center (DRMC) is a 145-bed acute care hospital that serves Iredell County North Carolina and surrounding counties. The medical center has a staff of more than 200 independent physicians representing 40 specialties. DRMC offers a range of emergency general health and specialty medical services for adults children and the elderly. It is home to centers for rehabilitation wound treatment orthopedics diabetes care pain management birthing surgery and psychiatric care. Established in 1920 Davis Regional Medical Center is part of the Health Management Associates family of hospitals.

	Annual Growth	06/04	06/05*	09/13	09/14	09/15
Sales ($ mil.)	–	–	0.0	74.3	62.8	64.9
Net income ($ mil.)	–	–	0.0	15.2	4.2	1.2
Market value ($ mil.)	–	–	–	–	–	–
Employees	–	–	–	–	–	1,055

*Fiscal year change

STATIC CONTROL COMPONENTS INC.

3010 LEE AVE
SANFORD, NC 27332-6210
Phone: 919-774-3808
Fax: –
Web: www.scc-inc.com

CEO: –
CFO: –
HR: –
FYE: December 31
Type: Private

Static Control Components (SCC) isn't stuck on static cling. The company that made a name for itself by selling anti-static products has made an even greater impression by selling parts for rebuilt toner cartridges. Its Imaging Division which sells parts to recycle used printer cartridges has captured more than half of the world market. SCC also makes electrical testing tools. In 2006 Static Control Components sold its SCC Products affiliate to 3M. President and CEO Ed Swartz founded Static Control Components in 1987; the company is owned and operated by his family.

	Annual Growth	12/01	12/02	12/03	12/04	12/11
Sales ($ mil.)	(2.4%)	–	238.9	245.8	264.1	191.2
Net income ($ mil.)	8.8%	–	3.7	5.3	0.0	7.9
Market value ($ mil.)	–	–	–	–	–	–
Employees	–	–	–	–	–	1,200

STATS LLC

2775 Shermer Rd.
Northbrook IL 60062
Phone: 847-583-2100
Fax: 847-470-9140
Web: www.stats.com

CEO: Carl Mergele
CFO: Jill Hansen
HR: –
FYE: June 30
Type: Joint Venture

This company takes sports fans beyond the win-loss column. STATS LLC (formerly STATS Inc.) is the world's leading provider of sports information and statistics offering up-to-the-minute data on more than 230 sports (50000 events) a year through a network of reporters. It sells the data to news organizations magazines television sports networks and other media outlets including Yahoo! The Wall Street Journal Online and CBS. STATS also licenses its data for use in fantasy sports games trading cards and video games as well as for use on the Web sites of many professional sports teams. STATS is a 50-50 joint venture between News Corporation and The Associated Press.

STEEL CONNECT INC

NMS: STCN

1601 Trapelo Road, Suite 170
Waltham, MA 02451
Phone: 781 663-5001
Fax: –
Web: www.moduslink.com

CEO: James R. Henderson
CFO: Louis J. (Lou) Belardi
HR: –
FYE: July 31
Type: Public

ModusLink Global Solutions' modus operandi involves supply chain management services. The company through subsidiaries ModusLink Corporation and ModusLink PTS offers inventory management and distribution services for customers across the consumer electronics and packaged goods retail luxury goods communications computer hardware and software and medical device industries. ModusLink Global Solutions manages more than 470 million product shipments through 25 facilities in 15 countries across the North America Asia/Pacific region and Europe.

	Annual Growth	07/15	07/16	07/17	07/18	07/19
Sales ($ mil.)	9.9%	561.7	459.0	436.6	645.3	819.8
Net income ($ mil.)	–	(18.4)	(61.3)	(25.8)	36.7	(66.7)
Market value ($ mil.)	(14.0%)	200.9	79.1	103.8	131.0	110.0
Employees	10.7%	2,500	2,200	1,990	3,924	3,760

STEEL DYNAMICS INC.

NMS: STLD

7575 West Jefferson Blvd.
Fort Wayne, IN 46804
Phone: 260 969-3500
Fax: –
Web: www.steeldynamics.com

CEO: Mark D. Millett
CFO: Theresa E. Wagler
HR: Benjamin Eisbart
FYE: December 31
Type: Public

Steel Dynamics may operate mini-mills but it produces steel on a large scale. Steel Dynamics operates electric arc furnace mini-mills steel scrap processing and metals recycling centers and steel fabrication facilities. The company sells to companies in the automotive construction and manufacturing industries as well as to steel processors and service centers primarily in the Midwestern and eastern US. Among its mini-mill output are beams rails and other products used in the construction industrial machinery and transportation industries. Steel Dynamics' annual steel shipping capacity is 11 million tons.

	Annual Growth	12/14	12/15	12/16	12/17	12/18
Sales ($ mil.)	7.8%	8,756.0	7,594.4	7,777.1	9,538.8	11,821.8
Net income ($ mil.)	68.3%	157.0	(130.3)	382.1	812.7	1,258.4
Market value ($ mil.)	11.1%	4,446.9	4,025.6	8,015.2	9,716.0	6,767.2
Employees	1.3%	7,780	7,500	7,695	7,635	8,200

STEEL OF WEST VIRGINIA, INC.

17TH ST & 2ND AVE
HUNTINGTON, WV 25703
Phone: 304-696-8200
Fax: –
Web: www.steeldynamics.com

CEO: Timothy R Duke
CFO: –
HR: –
FYE: December 31
Type: Private

Steel of West Virginia (SWV) a subsidiary of Steel Dynamics owns and operates a steel minimill and steel fabrication facilities in West Virginia and Tennessee. The company custom-designs and manufactures finished steel products including structural beams channels and special shape sections using electric furnace steel. SWV's products are used as structural elements of trucks trailers heavy machinery and manufactured housing as well as in guardrail posts mining applications and light-rail systems. SWV's custom-finished products are intended to go directly into its customers' assembly lines. Its Tennessee-based subsidiary Marshall Steel fabricates steel cross members. SWV got its start in 1909.

	Annual Growth	12/13	12/14	12/15	12/16	12/17
Sales ($ mil.)	(4.6%)	–	357.6	341.5	319.3	310.5
Net income ($ mil.)	–	–	–	0.0	0.0	0.0	0.0
Market value ($ mil.)	–	–	–	–	–	–
Employees	–	–	–	–	–	165

STEEL PARTNERS HOLDINGS LP

590 Madison Avenue, 32nd Floor
New York, NY 10022
Phone: 212 520-2300
Fax: –
Web: www.steelpartners.com

NYS: SPLP PRA
CEO: –
CFO: Douglas B Woodworth
HR: –
FYE: December 31
Type: Public

Steel Partners Holdings is a hedge fund that rules with an iron fist. The activist fund invests in a variety of businesses from banks to hot dog restaurants. It often takes positions on those companies' boards and is not bashful about making sweeping changes within those enterprises. The firm also likes to hold on to its portfolio assets for the long term. Among its holdings is Utah-based WebBank which offers commercial consumer and mortgage loans as well as federally guaranteed USDA and SBA loans. With some $4 billion in assets under management Steel Partners also owns portions of Unisys Aerojet Rocketdyne Selectica SL Industries and Nathan's Famous. Activist investor Warren Lichtenstein heads the firm.

	Annual Growth	12/14	12/15	12/16	12/17	12/18
Sales ($ mil.)	16.9%	849.5	998.0	1,163.5	1,372.0	1,584.6
Net income ($ mil.)	–	(7.6)	136.7	6.6	(0.0)	(32.6)
Market value ($ mil.)	0.3%	–	–	–	535.2	536.7
Employees	15.0%	3,028	3,548	4,857	4,800	5,300

STEEL TECHNOLOGIES LLC

15415 Shelbyville Rd.
Louisville KY 40245-4137
Phone: 502-245-2110
Fax: 502-244-0182
Web: www.steeltechnologies.com

CEO: Michael J Carroll
CFO: –
HR: –
FYE: September 30
Type: Joint Venture

If you need sheets for a bed try a white sale; if you need sheets to make a car try Steel Technologies. Founded in 1971 Steel Technologies' lineup includes close-tolerance cold- and hot-rolled strip and sheet high-carbon hot-rolled pickle strip and sheet and alloy strip and sheet metal. The company purchases steel coils from steel mills and produces flat-rolled steel used by the agricultural appliance automotive HVAC lawn and garden machinery and office equipment industries. Automotive customers represent about half of Steel Technologies' sales. In 2010 the company's ownership changed to a 50/50 joint venture between Nucor and former parent Mitsui & Co. (U.S.A.) a subsidiary of Japan's Mitsui.

STEELCASE, INC.

901 44th Street SE
Grand Rapids, MI 49508
Phone: 616 247-2710
Fax: –
Web: www.steelcase.com

NYS: SCS
CEO: James P. (Jim) Keane
CFO: David C. (Dave) Sylvester
HR: Kelly Jarvis
FYE: February 22
Type: Public

Steelcase is a top maker of chairs and other office furniture for customers worldwide. Through its Systems and Storage business the company manufactures and sells panel-based and freestanding furniture such as storage systems tables and ergonomic work tools. Its Seating business makes casual and shared seating and specialty chairs for the health care and education markets. Steelcase also provides a variety of services including workspace planning interior construction and project management. The company's major brands include Coalesse Designtex AMQ PolyVision Steelcase and Turnstone. Founded in 1912 Steelcase has operations in North America Europe and Asia although the US accounts for most sales.

	Annual Growth	02/15	02/16	02/17	02/18	02/19
Sales ($ mil.)	3.0%	3,059.7	3,060.0	3,032.4	3,055.5	3,443.2
Net income ($ mil.)	10.0%	86.1	170.3	124.6	80.7	126.0
Market value ($ mil.)	(1.6%)	2,185.9	1,464.3	1,862.4	1,710.6	2,049.3
Employees	0.6%	12,400	11,000	13,600	13,300	12,700

STEIN MART, INC.

1200 Riverplace Blvd.
Jacksonville, FL 32207
Phone: 904 346-1500
Fax: –
Web: www.steinmart.com

NAS: SMRT
CEO: D. Hunt Hawkins
CFO: Gregory W. (Greg) Kleffner
HR: Jennifer Wellington
FYE: February 02
Type: Public

Stein Mart's style is to operate department store-like stores that feature discount prices while maintaining an upscale vibe. With about 290 shops in some 30 states as well as an online presence it sells off-price women's men's and children's brand-name clothing. Fashions range from casual to formal. Stein Mart also sells jewelry handbags linens home decor and gifts. An independent firm leases Stein Mart's shoe departments. Its target customers are mature women with household incomes of $100000 and a taste for bargains. Stein Mart tries to place stores in shopping malls in upscale areas. Chairman Jay Stein the founder's grandson controls the company.

	Annual Growth	01/15	01/16	01/17*	02/18	02/19
Sales ($ mil.)	(0.9%)	1,317.7	1,359.9	1,360.5	1,318.6	1,272.7
Net income ($ mil.)	–	26.9	23.7	0.4	(24.3)	(6.0)
Market value ($ mil.)	(46.3%)	658.8	352.4	174.7	30.9	54.6
Employees	(4.2%)	11,300	11,000	11,000	10,200	9,500

*Fiscal year change

STEINER ELECTRIC COMPANY

1250 TOUHY AVE
ELK GROVE VILLAGE, IL 600074985
Phone: 847-228-0400
Fax: –
Web: www.steinerelectric.com

CEO: –
CFO: Edward Carroll
HR: –
FYE: December 31
Type: Private

Steiner Electric electrifies Chicago by distributing electrical products and providing related supplies and services through locations in southern Wisconsin northern Illinois and northwest Indiana. Besides such standard electrical supplies as ballasts and fasteners the company's products include industrial supplies automation products motors and drives lighting products generators and bar code devices. Services include energy audits turnkey project management motor repair and electric vehicle charging. Customers purchase Steiner Electric's products for commercial construction residential and industrial applications. The founding Steiner family owns the firm.

	Annual Growth	12/09	12/10	12/11	12/12	12/13
Sales ($ mil.)	12.7%	–	–	181.0	230.0	230.0
Net income ($ mil.)	–	–	–	0.0	0.0	0.0
Market value ($ mil.)	–	–	–	–	–	–
Employees	–	–	–	–	–	480

STELLAR GROUP, INCORPORATED

2900 HARTLEY RD
JACKSONVILLE, FL 322578221
Phone: 904-260-2044
Fax: –
Web: www.stellar.net

CEO: Ronald Foster Jr
CFO: Scott V Witt
HR: –
FYE: September 30
Type: Private

Stellar Group Incorporated has risen to astral levels in the design world. The firm founded in 1985 offers architectural engineering and mechanical services via design/build general contracting and construction management delivery. It targets a cosmos of markets from education food and health care to manufacturing retail and utility among many others. Stellar's performance in designing and constructing perishable food processing and distribution facilities has elevated the company to the top tiers of its industry both domestically and internationally. Stellar has locations throughout the US in addition to offices in Mexico Puerto Rico and Brazil.

	Annual Growth	06/06	06/07	06/08*	09/09	09/10
Sales ($ mil.)	–	–	–	0.0	427.6	219.2
Net income ($ mil.)	–	–	–	0.0	8.2	12.3
Market value ($ mil.)	–	–	–	–	–	–
Employees	–	–	–	–	–	600

*Fiscal year change

STEMLINE THERAPEUTICS INC

750 Lexington Avenue, Eleventh Floor
New York, NY 10022
Phone: 646 502-2311
Fax: –
Web: www.stemline.com

NAS: STML
CEO: Ivan Bergstein
CFO: David G Gionco
HR: –
FYE: December 31
Type: Public

Stemline Therapeutics is working on ways to eradicate cancer stem cells (CSC) and tumors. The development-stage biopharmaceutical company's pipeline includes three lead clinical-stage candidates (SL-401 SL-701 and SL-801) for leukemia and brain cancer in children and adults. Its drugs work by targeting CSCs which are believed to be the seeds of tumors that often survive traditional cancer treatment. Stemline is part of the biopharma race to be the first to successfully kill CSCs and usher in a new era of cancer drugs. Once its candidates are approved the company intends to create an in-house sales and marketing team for North America and Europe.

	Annual Growth	12/14	12/15	12/16	12/17	12/18
Sales ($ mil.)	10.5%	0.3	0.7	1.0	0.9	0.5
Net income ($ mil.)	–	(28.8)	(37.2)	(38.3)	(67.8)	(85.0)
Market value ($ mil.)	(13.6%)	545.0	201.6	341.8	498.3	303.5
Employees	43.0%	22	24	29	37	92

STEPAN CO.

22 West Frontage Road
Northfield, IL 60093
Phone: 847 446-7500
Fax: –
Web: www.stepan.com

NYS: SCL
CEO: F. Quinn Stepan
CFO: Scott D. Beamer
HR: Greg Servatius
FYE: December 31
Type: Public

Stepan Company makes basic and intermediate chemicals including surfactants specialty products phthalic anhydride and polyurethane polyols. Surfactants the company's largest business are used in cleaning agents and consumer products like detergents toothpastes and cosmetics. Stepan's surfactants also have commercial and industrial applications ranging from emulsifiers for agricultural insecticides to agents used in oil recovery. The company also makes phthalic anhydride and other polymers in addition to specialty chemicals for food and pharmaceutical uses. The US is Stepan's biggest market.

	Annual Growth	12/14	12/15	12/16	12/17	12/18
Sales ($ mil.)	0.9%	1,927.2	1,776.2	1,766.2	1,925.0	1,993.9
Net income ($ mil.)	18.5%	57.1	76.0	86.2	91.6	112.8
Market value ($ mil.)	16.6%	902.0	1,118.3	1,833.8	1,777.3	1,665.4
Employees	2.7%	2,024	2,073	2,145	2,096	2,250

STEPHAN CO (THE)

6708 N. 54th Street
Tampa, FL 33610
Phone: 813 248-5761
Fax: –
Web: www.thestephanco.com

NBB: SPCO
CEO: Frank F Ferola
CFO: Robert C Spindler
HR: –
FYE: December 31
Type: Public

From hair cream to stretch mark cream The Stephan Company manages a vast portfolio of products as a maker of branded and private-label personal care items. The company's brands include Cashmere Bouquet Quinsana Medicated Balm Barr Stretch Mark Cr-"me Protein 29 Stiff Stuff Wildroot and Frances Denney. It sells them worldwide by mail order and in retail stores and salons through its subsidiaries including Morris Flamingo-Stephan Old 97 American Manicure Lee Stafford Beauty Group Williamsport Barber and Beauty Corp. and Scientific Research Products among others. Chairman president and CEO Frank Ferola owns about 21% of the firm which bought Bowman Beauty and Barber Supply Company in August 2008.

	Annual Growth	12/14	12/15	12/16	12/17	12/18
Sales ($ mil.)	0.3%	8.8	8.0	7.9	8.3	9.0
Net income ($ mil.)	–	(2.7)	(0.5)	0.7	0.9	0.6
Market value ($ mil.)	3.0%	6.3	5.0	7.1	10.3	7.1
Employees	(10.9%)	46	27	27	29	29

STEPHEN F AUSTIN STATE UNIVERSITY

1936 NORTH ST
NACOGDOCHES, TX 75965-3940
Phone: 936-468-2304
Fax: –
Web: www.sfanew.sfasu.edu

CEO: –
CFO: –
HR: –
FYE: August 31
Type: Private

Stephen F. Austin State University (SFA) is a public university located in the Pineywoods of East Texas. Its campus in the heart of Nacogdoches was part of the original homestead of Thomas J. Rusk an early Texas patriot and US senator. The school's 13000-plus enrolled students may choose from about 85 majors in study areas including business and nursing. The student-to-faculty ratio is 20:1. Stephen F. Austin also offers a number of undergraduate graduate and certification programs online or partially online. Notable alumni include former NFL coach Bum Phillips and Don Henley of the Eagles. Named for the founding father of Texas the university was created in 1923 as a teacher's college.

	Annual Growth	08/01	08/02	08/03	08/04	08/11
Sales ($ mil.)	6.0%	–	71.3	78.2	71.3	120.6
Net income ($ mil.)	(15.7%)	–	8.4	3.2	5.6	1.8
Market value ($ mil.)	–	–	–	–	–	–
Employees	–	–	–	–	–	2,914

STEPHEN GOULD CORPORATION

35 S JEFFERSON RD
WHIPPANY, NJ 079811043
Phone: 973-428-1500
Fax: –
Web: www.gouldny.com

CEO: Michael Golden
CFO: Anthony Lupo
HR: –
FYE: December 31
Type: Private

Others can worry about what's inside — Stephen Gould Corporation concentrates on the package. The company provides a full range of packaging-related design and printing services for customers worldwide. Its products include gift packaging point-of-purchase displays product merchandising and retail and industrial packaging. Stephen Gould Corporation also provides graphic design and package-engineering services as well as assembly and fulfillment. The company was originally founded in 1939 by Stephen Gould David Golden and Leonard Beckerman.

	Annual Growth	12/11	12/12	12/13	12/16	12/17
Sales ($ mil.)	5.2%	–	526.7	526.7	665.1	678.7
Net income ($ mil.)	14.7%	–	3.9	3.9	11.9	7.8
Market value ($ mil.)	–	–	–	–	–	–
Employees	–	–	–	–	–	325

STEPHENSON WHOLESALE COMPANY, INC.

230 S 22ND AVE
DURANT, OK 747015646
Phone: 580-920-0125
Fax: –
Web: www.inwsupply.com

CEO: Tammy Cross
CFO: Jerry Wheatley
HR: –
FYE: December 31
Type: Private

Buying a candy bar and a box of nails is made easier thanks to Stephenson Wholesale. Operating through subsidiaries Indian National Wholesale Company and GLC Marketing the company is a leading supplier of food and non-food goods to convenience stores and other retail outlets in Oklahoma and Texas. It also distributes goods to snack bars concessions operators and tribal smoke shops. The family-owned company was founded in 1953 by Ralphen Cross.

	Annual Growth	12/13	12/14	12/15	12/16	12/17
Sales ($ mil.)	(3.2%)	–	325.2	316.1	297.7	295.3
Net income ($ mil.)	–	–	1.2	0.8	(0.5)	(5.3)
Market value ($ mil.)	–	–	–	–	–	–
Employees	–	–	–	–	–	305

STEREOTAXIS INC

ASE: STXS

4320 Forest Park Avenue, Suite 100
St. Louis, MO 63108
Phone: 314 678-6100
Fax: 314 678-6110
Web: www.stereotaxis.com

CEO: –
CFO: Martin C Stammer
HR: David Giffen
FYE: December 31
Type: Public

Stereotaxis can drive in the fast lane through your veins because it has the road map to your heart. The company's systems are used to treat abnormal heart rhythms known as arrhythmias as well as coronary artery disease. Via digital remote control doctors steer catheters guidewires and stent delivery devices through blood vessels all the way to the chambers of the heart (and all the way back out if necessary) in a procedure that is less invasive than traditional heart surgeries. Stereotaxis markets the cardiology instrument control system to interventional surgery labs (or "cath labs") research hospitals and large commercial medical centers worldwide.

	Annual Growth	12/14	12/15	12/16	12/17	12/18
Sales ($ mil.)	(4.3%)	35.0	37.7	32.2	31.1	29.3
Net income ($ mil.)	–	(5.2)	(7.4)	(5.3)	(5.9)	0.1
Market value ($ mil.)	(7.6%)	87.4	43.9	38.4	47.2	63.8
Employees	(2.7%)	133	126	120	117	119

STERICYCLE INC.

NMS: SRCL

2355 Waukugen Road
Bannockburn, IL 60015
Phone: 847 367-5910
Fax: –
Web: www.stericycle.com

CEO: Charles A. (Charlie) Alutto
CFO: Daniel V. (Dan) Ginnetti
HR: –
FYE: December 31
Type: Public

A leading medical and pharmaceutical waste management company Stericycle serves more than 1 million clients worldwide including large waste generators (pharmaceutical manufacturers hospitals and blood banks) and small waste generators (dental and medical offices veterinary offices pharmacies and municipalities). Services include disposing of used needles and expired drugs. Through more than 250 processing and collection sites and some 300 transfer sites and almost 100 recall and returns or communication services facilities Stericycle treats waste through incineration autoclaving (using high temperature and pressure to kill pathogens) and electro-thermal-deactivation (using low-frequency radio waves to kill pathogens).

	Annual Growth	12/14	12/15	12/16	12/17	12/18
Sales ($ mil.)	8.1%	2,555.6	2,985.9	3,562.3	3,580.7	3,485.9
Net income ($ mil.)	–	326.5	267.0	206.4	42.4	(244.7)
Market value ($ mil.)	(27.3%)	11,889.0	10,938.4	6,987.5	6,166.7	3,327.8
Employees	4.8%	18,656	25,472	25,000	–	22,500

STERIS INSTRUMENT MANAGEMENT SERVICES, INC.

3316 2ND AVE N
BIRMINGHAM, AL 352221214
Phone: 205-879-3840
Fax: –
Web: www.imsready.com

CEO: Gene Robinson
CFO: David Strevy
HR: –
FYE: December 31
Type: Private

STERIS Instrument Management Services (STERIS IMS) repairs sterilizes and maintains medical and surgical equipment for health care providers. The company specializes in surgical device instrument and scope repair as well as outsourced management of sterilization departments. It also provides consulting to help hospitals and surgery centers improve their sterile processing procedures. In addition STERIS IMS sells products such as instrument cabinets and cleaning devices as well as certified pre-owned surgical equipment. The company is a subsidiary of sterilization equipment maker STERIS.

	Annual Growth	12/05	12/06	12/07	12/08	12/12
Sales ($ mil.)	10.5%	–	–	–	79.1	117.9
Net income ($ mil.)	26.7%	–	–	–	1.8	4.6
Market value ($ mil.)	–	–	–	–	–	–
Employees	–	–	–	–	–	1,155

STERLING BANCORP (DE)

NYS: STL

400 Rella Boulevard
Montebello, NY 10901
Phone: 845 369-8040
Fax: –
Web: www.sterlingbancorp.com

CEO: Jack L Kopnisky
CFO: Luis Massiani
HR: –
FYE: December 31
Type: Public

Sterling Bancorp is the holding company for Sterling National Bank a community-based thrift operating dozens of offices in New York's Hudson Valley region and Greater New York City area. Founded in 1888 the bank attracts consumers and business clients by offering traditional deposit products such as checking and savings accounts and CDs. It uses funds from deposits to originate primarily real estate loans and mortgages. Sterling Bancorp which has assets of more than $7 billion was formerly Provident New York Bancorp; Provident acquired the former Sterling Bancorp in late 2013 and changed its name as well as the name of its banking subsidiary to Sterling. In 2017 the bank agreed to acquire Astoria Financial for $2.2 billion.

	Annual Growth	12/14	12/15	12/16	12/17	12/18
Assets ($ mil.)	43.4%	7,424.8	11,956.0	14,178.4	30,359.5	31,383.3
Net income ($ mil.)	126.5%	17.0	66.1	140.0	93.0	447.3
Market value ($ mil.)	3.5%	3,109.4	3,507.2	5,059.7	5,319.2	3,569.9
Employees	23.2%	829	1,089	970	2,076	1,907

STERLING CHEMICALS INC.

333 Clay St. Ste. 3600
Houston TX 77002-4109
Phone: 713-650-3700
Fax: 713-654-9551
Web: www.sterlingchemicals.com

CEO: John V Genova
CFO: Carla E Stucky
HR: –
FYE: December 31
Type: Subsidiary

Sterling Chemicals focuses on producing a small number of products and selling those products to a small number of customers. Its core product is acetic acid (used to make vinyl acetate monomer which is an ingredient in adhesives coatings and fibers). It is also used to make purified terephthalic acid an ingredient in the production of plastic bottle resins. Sterling Chemicals supplies all of its acetic acid to BP. Although the loss of a contract forced the company to close its plasticizers facility (used to make flexible plastics such as automotive parts and shower curtains) in early 2011 it plans to manufacture non-phthalate plasticizers. Sterling Chemicals is owned by Eastman Chemical.

STERLING CONSTRUCTION CO INC

NMS: STRL

1800 Hughes Landing Blvd.
The Woodlands, TX 77380
Phone: 281 214-0800
Fax: –
Web: www.strlco.com

CEO: Joseph A Cutillo
CFO: Ronald A Ballschmiede
HR: –
FYE: December 31
Type: Public

Sterling Construction company specializes in the building reconstruction and repair of transportation and water infrastructure. It also works on specialty projects such as excavation shoring and drilling. The heavy civil construction company and its subsidiaries (Texas Sterling Construction Ralph L. Wadsworth Contractors RDI Foundation Drilling Myers and Sons Banicki Construction and Road and Highway Builders) primarily serve public sector clients throughout the Southwest and West. Transportation projects include excavation and asphalt paving as well as construction of bridges and rail systems. Water projects include work on sewers and storm drainage systems.

	Annual Growth	12/14	12/15	12/16	12/17	12/18
Sales ($ mil.)	11.5%	672.2	623.6	690.1	958.0	1,037.7
Net income ($ mil.)	–	(9.8)	(20.4)	(9.2)	11.6	25.2
Market value ($ mil.)	14.2%	170.0	161.7	225.0	433.0	289.6
Employees	1.8%	1,799	1,565	1,684	1,740	1,935

STERLING FINANCIAL CORP. (WA)

NAS: STSA

111 North Wall Street
Spokane, WA 99201
Phone: 509 358-8097
Fax: 509 458-2391
Web: www.sterlingfinancialcorporation-spokane.com

CEO: –
CFO: –
HR: –
FYE: December 31
Type: Public

Sterling Financial Corporation is the holding company for Sterling Bank (formerly Sterling Savings Bank) one of the largest regional community banks in the Pacific Northwest. The bank operates about 190 branch locations in northern California Idaho Oregon and Washington and lends throughout the West from more than 30 loan origination offices. In California it does business under the name Sonoma Bank. Real estate and construction loans account for the majority of the bank's portfolio. Its wealth management division markets stocks bonds mutual funds annuities and other investments to bank customers. Sterling Financial is regaining its luster after being hard hit by the downturn in the housing market.

	Annual Growth	12/08	12/09	12/10	12/11	12/12
Assets ($ mil.)	(7.8%)	12,790.7	10,877.4	9,493.2	9,193.2	9,236.9
Net income ($ mil.)	–	(335.5)	(838.1)	(224.3)	39.1	385.7
Market value ($ mil.)	24.1%	547.4	38.6	1,180.1	1,038.9	1,300.1
Employees	0.5%	2,481	2,641	2,498	2,496	2,532

STERLING JEWELERS INC.

375 Ghent Rd.
Fairlawn OH 44333
Phone: 330-668-5000
Fax: 330-668-5052
Web: www.sterlingjewelers.com

CEO: Virginia C Drosos
CFO: –
HR: Lynn Ahlers
FYE: January 31
Type: Subsidiary

There's more in store at Sterling Jewelers than sterling silver. The jewelry firm sells gold silver diamond and gemstone jewelry watches and gifts from more than 1300 stores in all 50 US states. Sterling Jewelers operates Kay Jewelers which has about 910 stores in shopping centers and malls nationwide as well as the off-mall format Jared the Galleria of Jewelry and some 230 regional jewelry stores under other names (Belden JB Robinson Marks & Morgan). Some 180 Jared stores sell diamond jewelry and loose diamonds as well as luxury watches such as Rolex Tag Heuer and Raymond Weil. Sterling Jewelers is the US subsidiary of London-based Signet Jewelers the world's largest jewelry retailer.

STERLING METS LP

123-01 Roosevelt Ave.
Flushing NY 11368-1699
Phone: 718-507-8499
Fax: 718-507-6395
Web: www.mets.com

CEO: –
CFO: –
HR: –
FYE: September 30
Type: Private

This team from Queens has twice been crowned king of baseball. Sterling Mets owns and operates the New York Mets professional baseball franchise which joined Major League Baseball as an expansion club in 1962. After losing a record 120 games in its first season the team earned the nickname "the Miracle Mets" when it toppled the Baltimore Orioles for the franchise's first World Series title in 1969. A second championship came in 1986 over the Boston Red Sox. The Mets faced the New York Yankees in the 2000 "Subway Series" but lost to the Bronx Bombers. CEO Fred Wilpon has controlled the Mets since 2002.

STERLING SUGARS, INC.

611 IRISH BEND RD
FRANKLIN, LA 705383345
Phone: 337-828-0620
Fax: –
Web: www.mapatout.com

CEO: Craig P Caillier
CFO: –
HR: –
FYE: July 31
Type: Private

Sterling Sugars creates splendid sweetness. The company processes sugarcane to make raw sugar cane syrup and blackstrap molasses for sale to sugar refiners and candy and other food manufacturers. Sterling Sugars owns cane cropland which supplies 35% of the company's raw material. the other 65% is purchased from other growers. It processes about 1.2 million tons of cane per year at its mill in Franklin Louisiana. Sterling also leases land for oil and natural gas exploration. The company is a subsidiary of M A Patout & Son; it was taken private by shareholders in 2005. Sterling Sugars was founded in 1807.

	Annual Growth	07/12	07/13	07/14	07/15	07/16
Sales ($ mil.)	24.4%	–	–	–	64.2	79.9
Net income ($ mil.)	(24.9%)	–	–	–	4.5	3.4
Market value ($ mil.)	–	–	–	–	–	–
Employees	–	–	–	–	–	188

STETSON UNIVERSITY, INC.

421 N WOODLAND BLVD
DELAND, FL 327238300
Phone: 386-822-7000
Fax: –
Web: www.stetson.edu

CEO: –
CFO: –
HR: –
FYE: June 30
Type: Private

Not everyone at Stetson University wears a cowboy hat but there is a connection (it was named after hat maker and benefactor John B. Stetson). The school offers Stetson offers 73 academic programs with undergraduate and graduate studies offered through its College of Arts and Sciences School of Business Administration School of Music and College of Law. The university enrolls about 2200 undergraduate students. Stetson has four campuses located in DeLand (main) Celebration (graduate degrees and continuing education) Tampa (law) and St. Petersburg/Gulfport (law). The university enrolls about 3900 students a year of which 2500 are undergraduate students and about 1400 graduate students from 43 states the District of Columbia and 47 other nations.

	Annual Growth	06/14	06/15	06/16	06/17	06/18
Sales ($ mil.)	4.1%	–	124.1	134.5	136.8	139.9
Net income ($ mil.)	122.6%	–	3.5	(4.3)	26.1	38.3
Market value ($ mil.)	–	–	–	–	–	–
Employees	–	–	–	–	–	1,033

STEVENS INDUSTRIES INC

704 W MAIN ST
TEUTOPOLIS, IL 62467-1212
Phone: 217-540-3100
Fax: –
Web: www.stevensadvantage.com

CEO: –
CFO: –
HR: Brittney West
FYE: December 31
Type: Private

What do children playing at school nurses at work in hospitals and receptionists typing away at their computers have in common? Chances are they've all used products from Stevens Industries. The company manufactures cabinets countertops workstations and other furniture for schools hospitals and medical clinics. It also produces hardware (pulls hooks) and laminated paneling for use by office furniture and shelving manufacturers. Stevens' products offer an array of decorative inlays and color finishes. The company was founded in 1956 by Chuck Stevens.

	Annual Growth	12/03	12/04	12/05	12/06	12/07
Sales ($ mil.)	(72.7%)	–	–	1,090.1	81.0	81.4
Net income ($ mil.)	13663.4%	–	–	0.0	3.5	1.4
Market value ($ mil.)	–	–	–	–	–	–
Employees	–	–	–	–	–	500

STEVENS INSTITUTE OF TECHNOLOGY (INC)

1 CASTLE POINT TER
HOBOKEN, NJ 070305906
Phone: 201-216-5000
Fax: –
Web: www.stevens.edu

CEO: –
CFO: Randy L. Greene
HR: –
FYE: June 30
Type: Private

Even before the advent of the internal combustion engine Stevens Institute of Technology was educating students in science technology and engineering. Founded in 1870 through an endowment from engineer Edwin Stevens the university offers undergraduate master's and doctoral degrees in engineering science humanities computer science and technology management. The school enrolls roughly 3100 undergraduates and some 3800 graduate students. Stevens Institute teams up with corporate and military institutions to provide students with hands-on research experience; Stevens Technologies a for-profit subsidiary of the school licenses and sells the technological fruits of these partnerships.

	Annual Growth	06/07	06/08	06/10	06/13	06/17
Sales ($ mil.)	4.4%	–	168.2	211.5	259.3	247.9
Net income ($ mil.)	–	–	(1.8)	8.5	29.2	50.6
Market value ($ mil.)	–	–	–	–	–	–
Employees	–	–	–	–	–	500

STEVENS TRANSPORT, INC.

9757 MILITARY PKWY
DALLAS, TX 752274805
Phone: 972-216-9000
Fax: –
Web: www.stevenstransport.com

CEO: –
CFO: –
HR: John Brandt
FYE: December 31
Type: Private

Staying cool is a must for Stevens Transport. An irregular-route refrigerated truckload carrier (or reefer) Stevens hauls temperature-controlled cargo throughout the US covering the 48 contiguous states. Through alliances Stevens also covers every province in Canada and every state in Mexico. The company operates a fleet of about 2000 Kenworth and Peterbuilt tractors and 3500 Thermo King refrigerated trailers from a network of more than a dozen service centers. Partnerships with railroads allow Stevens to arrange intermodal transport of temperature-controlled cargo. The company also provides third-party logistics services. Stevens Transport was founded in 1980.

	Annual Growth	12/07	12/08	12/11	12/12	12/15
Sales ($ mil.)	2.8%	–	550.0	566.9	607.4	668.7
Net income ($ mil.)	505.7%	–	0.0	76.5	85.3	87.0
Market value ($ mil.)	–	–	–	–	–	–
Employees	–	–	–	–	–	2,100

STEVENSON UNIVERSITY INC.

1525 GREENSPRING VLY RD
STEVENSON, MD 211530641
Phone: 410-486-7000
Fax: –
Web: www.stevenson.edu

CEO: –
CFO: –
HR: –
FYE: June 30
Type: Private

Stevenson University is a career-focused liberal arts college with about 4300 undergraduate and graduate students. It has more than 500 faculty members and a student-to-teacher ratio of 15:1. The school has two locations in Stevenson and Owings Mills Maryland near Baltimore. Stevenson University offers more than 20 bachelor's degree programs as well as a handful of master's degree programs at six schools in areas including business and leadership education design humanities information technologies and forensic studies. About 83% of the student body are Maryland residents.

	Annual Growth	06/12	06/13	06/14	06/15	06/16
Sales ($ mil.)	(7.3%)	–	125.0	141.4	143.7	99.5
Net income ($ mil.)	–	–	2.7	8.2	5.4	(4.0)
Market value ($ mil.)	–	–	–	–	–	–
Employees	–	–	–	–	–	550

STEWARD HEALTH CARE SYSTEM LLC

1900 N PEARL ST STE 2400
DALLAS, TX 752012470
Phone: 469-341-8800
Fax: –
Web: www.steward.org

CEO: Ralph de la Torre
CFO: Mark Rich
HR: –
FYE: September 30
Type: Private

Steward Health Care System is a steward of its patients' good health. With a total of some 7300 beds Steward Health operates 36 hospitals in 10 states including Holy Family Hospital Norwood Hospital St. Elizabeth's Medical Center The Medical Center of Southeast Texas and Pikes Peak Regional Hospital. Several of the hospitals are affiliated with Boston-area medical schools. The company also has managed operations in Arizona Utah and Massachusetts. Steward Health also includes a physician practice organization an outpatient clinic network and a home care and hospice agency. Steward which is owned by Cerberus Capital Management merged with IASIS Healthcare in 2017 to become the US' largest private for-profit hospital operator.

	Annual Growth	09/03	09/04	09/05	09/06	09/07
Sales ($ mil.)	572.6%	–	–	27.4	1,220.5	1,240.7
Net income ($ mil.)	272.9%	–	–	2.2	47.6	30.5
Market value ($ mil.)	–	–	–	–	–	–
Employees	–	–	–	–	–	37,000

STEWARDSHIP FINANCIAL CORP.

NAS: SSFN

630 Godwin Avenue
Midland Park, NJ 07432
Phone: 201 444-7100
Fax: –
Web: www.asbnow.com

CEO: –
CFO: –
HR: –
FYE: December 31
Type: Public

Like any good steward this company likes to give back to the community it lives in. Stewardship Financial is the holding company for Atlantic Stewardship Bank which serves northeastern New Jersey's Bergen Morris and Passaic counties from about a dozen branches. Catering to area consumers professionals and small to midsized businesses the bank offers standard products and services including checking and savings accounts certificates of deposit loans and credit cards. Stewardship Financial donates 10% of its pre-tax profits to Christian and civic organizations in its market area.

	Annual Growth	12/13	12/14	12/15	12/16	12/17
Assets ($ mil.)	8.4%	673.5	693.6	717.9	795.5	928.8
Net income ($ mil.)	12.4%	2.5	3.1	4.2	4.7	3.9
Market value ($ mil.)	20.6%	42.0	42.1	52.2	84.8	88.7
Employees	(1.7%)	155	151	150	144	145

STEWART & STEVENSON INC.

1000 Louisiana St., Suite 5900
Houston, TX 77002
Phone: 713 751-2700
Fax: –

CEO: John B Simmons
CFO: Jack L Pieper
HR: –
FYE: January 31
Type: Public

Houstonian Stewart & Stevenson helps its customers quench their thirst for Texas Tea. The company is a leading supplier of equipment used in oilfield services. Stewart & Stevenson operates three divisions: Equipment (oil well stimulation coil tubing engines and material handling equipment) Aftermarket Parts and Service (parts and service for customers in oil and gas marine power generation mining and construction industries) and Rental (rental of generators material handling equipment and air compressors). While the company primarily sells and markets its products directly through its own sales and service centers it also uses authorized dealers and independent overseas sales representatives.

	Annual Growth	01/08	01/09	01/10	01/11	01/12
Sales ($ mil.)	(0.2%)	1,335.4	1,217.1	688.7	861.2	1,324.0
Net income ($ mil.)	1.6%	91.8	50.6	(23.9)	(10.0)	97.9
Market value ($ mil.)	–	–	–	–	–	–
Employees	(3.7%)	3,374	2,852	2,276	2,300	2,900

STEWART BUILDERS, INC.

16575 VILLAGE DR
JERSEY VILLAGE, TX 770401124
Phone: 713-983-8002
Fax: –
Web: www.keystoneconcrete.com

CEO: –
CFO: –
HR: –
FYE: December 31
Type: Private

Concrete is the key to Stewart Builders' success in the construction industry. Stewart Builders through main subsidiaries Keystone Concrete Placement and Keystone Structural Concrete provides concrete construction services for commercial industrial and institutional facilities as well as for residential markets primarily serving working on projects in the Lone Star State. Other subsidiaries do site work and construct basements. President Don Stewart and his sons founded the firm in 1993. The company has operations in Austin Georgetown Houston and San Antonio Texas.

	Annual Growth	12/09	12/10	12/12	12/13	12/14
Sales ($ mil.)	22.0%	–	144.0	206.6	237.0	319.5
Net income ($ mil.)	–	–	0.0	5.1	10.2	19.8
Market value ($ mil.)	–	–	–	–	–	–
Employees	–	–	–	–	–	1,400

STEWART INFORMATION SERVICES CORP   NYS: STC

1360 Post Oak Blvd., Suite 100
Houston, TX 77056
Phone: 713 625-8100
Fax: 713 629-2244
Web: www.stewart.com

CEO: Matthew W. (Matt) Morris
CFO: David C. Hisey
HR: Michelle Williams
FYE: December 31
Type: Public

Real estate services company Stewart Information Services distributes residential and commercial title insurance policies and conducts closing and settlement through offices and independent agencies in the US and abroad. Unlike most insurance that covers future events or losses title insurance protects lenders and buyers against past problems with titles. Stewart offers real estate information services through PropertyInfo and a variety of mortgage origination process services through Stewart Lender Services. In 2018 the company agreed to be acquired by Fidelity National Financial the largest title insurer in the US but hit a roadblock the next year when the New York State Department of Financial Services announced its disapproval of the transaction.

	Annual Growth	12/14	12/15	12/16	12/17	12/18
Assets ($ mil.)	(0.4%)	1,392.5	1,321.6	1,341.7	1,405.9	1,372.9
Net income ($ mil.)	12.4%	29.8	(6.2)	55.5	48.7	47.5
Market value ($ mil.)	2.8%	878.6	885.4	1,093.0	1,003.3	982.0
Employees	(7.6%)	7,400	6,900	6,350	5,960	5,400

STEWART'S SHOPS CORP.

2907 STATE ROUTE 9
BALLSTON SPA, NY 120204201
Phone: 518-581-1201
Fax: –
Web: www.stewartsshops.com

CEO: –
CFO: –
HR: –
FYE: December 31
Type: Private

I scream you scream we all scream for Stewart's ice cream — especially if we live in upstate New York or Vermont home to some 330 Stewart's Shops. The chain of convenience stores sells more than 3000 products across 30-plus counties. They include dairy items groceries food to go (soup sandwiches hot entrees) beer coffee gasoline and of course ice cream. In addition to its retail business the company owns about 100 rental properties including banks hair salons and apartments near its stores. Stewart's Shops formerly known as Stewart's Ice Cream Company was established in 1945. The founding Dake family owns about two-thirds of the company; employee compensation plans own the rest.

	Annual Growth	12/12	12/13	12/14	12/16	12/17
Sales ($ mil.)	(0.6%)	–	1,577.1	1,610.6	1,405.9	1,542.7
Net income ($ mil.)	5.9%	–	73.9	60.0	80.1	93.0
Market value ($ mil.)	–	–	–	–	–	–
Employees	–	–	–	–	–	3,800

STG LLC

11091 SUNSET HILLS RD # 200
RESTON, VA 201905377
Phone: 703-691-2480
Fax: –
Web: www.stg.com

CEO: –
CFO: Charles Cosgrove
HR: –
FYE: December 31
Type: Private

STG provides technical TLC to government agencies. Serving the US Defense Department and about 50 other federal agencies the company provides information technology services such as project management application development network implementation security systems support and IT systems integration. It also offers data security assessment and compliance reporting services as well as foreign language translation and transcription. In addition to the DOD STG counts the US departments of State and Agriculture among its clients as well as Fortune 100 companies. Internationally the company has worked with NATO the Korea Airports Authority and other agencies.

	Annual Growth	12/10	12/11	12/12	12/13	12/14
Assets ($ mil.)	(3.6%)	–	80.5	91.4	83.0	72.1
Net income ($ mil.)	(40.2%)	–	20.2	5.9	3.8	4.3
Market value ($ mil.)	–	–	–	–	–	–
Employees	–	–	–	–	–	800

STIFEL FINANCIAL CORP   NYS: SF

501 North Broadway
St. Louis, MO 63102-2188
Phone: 314 342-2000
Fax: –
Web: www.stifel.com

CEO: Ronald J. (Ron) Kruszewski
CFO: James M. Zemlyak
HR: –
FYE: December 31
Type: Public

Through subsidiaries Stifel Nicolaus (founded 1890) Thomas Weisel Century Securities Associates Stifel Bank & Trust and others Stifel Financial provides asset management financial advice and banking services for private individuals corporations municipal and institutional clients in the US. Stifel also offers brokerage and mergers and acquisitions advisory services for corporate clients underwrites debt and equity and provides research on more than 1000 US and European equities. The firm boasts nearly 360 US offices with a concentration in the Midwest and mid-Atlantic regions and additional offices in the UK and the rest of Europe.

	Annual Growth	12/14	12/15	12/16	12/17	12/18
Assets ($ mil.)	26.7%	9,518.2	13,335.9	19,129.4	21,384.0	24,519.6
Net income ($ mil.)	22.3%	176.1	92.3	81.5	182.9	394.0
Market value ($ mil.)	(5.1%)	3,612.3	2,999.2	3,536.5	4,216.9	2,932.6
Employees	4.9%	6,200	7,100	7,100	7,100	7,500

STILES CORPORATION

301 E LAS OLAS BLVD
FORT LAUDERDALE, FL 333012295
Phone: 954-627-9150
Fax: –
Web: www.stiles.com

CEO: Kenneth Stiles
CFO: Robert Esposito
HR: George Bou
FYE: December 31
Type: Private

Stiles Corporation is a full-service commercial real estate development and investment firm. It provides architectural design and construction realty services and property management. The firm operates primarily throughout the southeastern US with a special interest in Florida. The company's Capital Group unit offers asset management and arranges financing for development projects. Since 1951 when the company was founded Stiles has built more than 37 million sq. ft. of office industrial retail and mixed use properties. The firm's completed projects include Fort Lauderdale's Las Olas City Centre and Trump International Tower as well as the PGA Financial Plaza at MacArthur Center in Palm Beach Gardens.

	Annual Growth	12/11	12/12	12/13	12/14	12/15
Sales ($ mil.)	8.7%	–	170.2	143.4	228.3	218.9
Net income ($ mil.)	13.4%	–	3.3	0.8	0.1	4.8
Market value ($ mil.)	–	–	–	–	–	–
Employees	–	–	–	–	–	284

STOCK BUILDING SUPPLY LLC

8020 Arco Corporate Dr.
Raleigh NC 27617
Phone: 919-431-1000
Fax: 919-431-1700
Web: www.stockbuildingsupply.com

CEO: –
CFO: James F Major Jr
HR: –
FYE: July 31
Type: Joint Venture

Stock Building Supply (SBS) has crafted itself into a leading supplier of lumber and building materials to home builders and contractors. SBS operates about 100 building supply stores (down from 200 prior to a stint in bankruptcy) in about a dozen states and Washington DC. Products include lumber plywood sheetrock tools and trusses. It also operates commercial flooring and roofing services. Founded in 1922 by B.B. Benson to sell boards and plaster base it is owned by Los Angeles-based private equity firm The Gores Group. The building supplies retailer emerged from Chapter 11 bankruptcy protection in mid-2009 and is anxiously awaiting the rebound of the US housing market.

STOCK YARDS BANCORP INC   NMS: SYBT

1040 East Main Street
Louisville, KY 40206
Phone: 502 582-2571
Fax: –
Web: www.syb.com

CEO: David P. Heintzman
CFO: Nancy B. Davis
HR: –
FYE: December 31
Type: Public

Stock Yards Bancorp is the holding company of Stock Yards Bank & Trust which operates about 35 branches mostly in Louisville Kentucky but also in Indianapolis and Cincinnati. Founded in 1904 the $3 billion-asset bank targets individuals and regional business customers offering standard retail services such as checking and savings accounts credit cards certificates of deposit and IRAs. It also provides trust services while brokerage and credit card services are offered through agreements with other banks. Commercial real estate mortgages make up 40% of the bank's loan portfolio which also includes commercial and industrial loans (30%) residential mortgages (15%) construction loans and consumer loans.

	Annual Growth	12/14	12/15	12/16	12/17	12/18
Assets ($ mil.)	6.5%	2,563.9	2,816.8	3,039.5	3,239.6	3,302.9
Net income ($ mil.)	12.4%	34.8	37.2	41.0	38.0	55.5
Market value ($ mil.)	(0.4%)	758.5	859.7	1,068.1	857.6	746.2
Employees	3.1%	524	555	578	580	591

STONE ENERGY CORP   NYS: SGY

625 E. Kaliste Saloom Road
Lafayette, LA 70508
Phone: 337 237-0410
Fax: 337 521-9880
Web: www.stoneenergy.com

CEO: –
CFO: –
HR: Denise Hebert
FYE: December 31
Type: Public

You can't squeeze blood from a stone but as Stone Energy knows you can squeeze energy. Stone Energy acquires and exploits mature oil and natural gas properties that have high potential. The company which for 2015 reported estimated proved reserves of 342 billion cu. ft. of natural gas equivalent has producing properties in the Gulf of Mexico. It has sold the bulk of its Rocky Mountain oil and gas properties in order to focus its energy on targeting reserves and production in the deep shelf and deep water areas of the Gulf of Mexico. In 2015 it had 1.2 million of gross acres of undeveloped properties. The company filed for Chapter 11 bankruptcy protection in late 2016 and emerged from it in early 2017.

	Annual Growth	12/12	12/13	12/14	12/15	12/16
Sales ($ mil.)	(20.6%)	951.5	974.2	795.5	544.6	377.4
Net income ($ mil.)	–	149.4	117.6	(189.5)	(1,090.9)	(590.6)
Market value ($ mil.)	(23.1%)	20.3	34.2	16.7	4.2	7.1
Employees	(11.1%)	386	409	384	310	241

STONEGATE MORTGAGE CORP   NYS: SGM

9190 Priority Way West Drive, Suite 300
Indianapolis, IN 46240
Phone: 317 663-5100
Fax: –
Web: www.stonegatemtg.com

CEO: –
CFO: –
HR: –
FYE: December 31
Type: Public

Stonegate Mortgage is opening doors for homeowners to finance their dream homes. The mortgage company originates acquires sells and services residential mortgage loans. It also owns a warehouse lender mortgage financing company NattyMac. Stonegate Mortgage's servicing portfolio contains more than 40000 million loans that total $7.5 billion in unpaid principal balances. The company is licensed in 45 states (excluding the West) and Washington DC. It serves customers from more than 25 retail branches in a dozen states and works with more than 950 mortgage brokers. The company went public in 2013 raising $115 million which it will use to make investments and spend on general corporate purposes.

	Annual Growth	12/11	12/12	12/13	12/14	12/15
Sales ($ mil.)	62.8%	26.0	95.5	157.9	185.6	182.7
Net income ($ mil.)	–	2.3	17.1	22.6	(30.7)	(22.3)
Market value ($ mil.)	(42.6%)	–	–	426.4	308.5	140.6
Employees	12.4%	–	652	1,219	1,294	927

STONEMOR INC   NYS: STON

3600 Horizon Boulevard
Trevose, PA 19053
Phone: 215 826-2800
Fax: –
Web: www.stonemor.com

CEO: Joseph M Redling
CFO: Mark L Miller
HR: –
FYE: December 31
Type: Public

StoneMor Partners can show you some of the best locations for an extended stay locations where you may even want to reside permanently. The company operates more than 275 cemeteries and about 90 funeral homes in more than 25 states primarily along the East Coast but also in Puerto Rico. It also owns most of its properties. StoneMor sells burial lots lawn and mausoleum crypts cremation niches and perpetual care. It offers burial vaults caskets grave markers and bases and memorials. The company has grown since its formation in 2004 when it took over more than 120 properties previously owned by CFSI (then named Cornerstone Family Services) a significant shareholder.

	Annual Growth	12/14	12/15	12/16	12/17	12/18
Sales ($ mil.)	2.3%	288.1	305.6	326.2	338.2	316.1
Net income ($ mil.)	–	(10.8)	(24.2)	(30.5)	(75.2)	(72.7)
Market value ($ mil.)	(46.6%)	978.2	1,014.6	338.2	249.0	79.7
Employees	30.8%	1,009	3,444	3,220	3,145	2,952

STONERIDGE INC.
NYS: SRI

39675 MacKenzie Drive, Suite 400
Novi, MI 48377
Phone: 248 489-9300
Fax: –
Web: www.stoneridge.com

CEO: Jonathan B. DeGaynor
CFO: Robert R. Krakowiak
HR: –
FYE: December 31
Type: Public

Stoneridge makes electrical and electronic components and systems for automobiles commercial vehicles and agricultural/off-highway vehicles. The company's Control Devices segment (51% of sales) makes products that monitor measure or activate vehicle functions including actuators sensors switches and valves. Stoneridge's Electronics unit (40% of sales) offers electronic instrument clusters driver information systems and camera-based vision systems. The PST segment (9% of sales) manufactures in-vehicle audio and video systems security alarms and tracking devices primarily for the automobile and motorcycle markets. Customers include vehicle OEMs and their suppliers distributors and aftermarket retailers. North America accounts for 55% of sales.

	Annual Growth	12/14	12/15	12/16	12/17	12/18
Sales ($ mil.)	7.0%	660.6	644.8	696.0	824.4	866.2
Net income ($ mil.)	–	(47.1)	22.8	77.5	45.2	53.8
Market value ($ mil.)	17.7%	366.4	421.6	504.0	651.2	702.2
Employees	2.3%	4,200	4,100	4,200	4,500	4,600

STORR OFFICE ENVIRONMENTS INC

10800 WORLD TRADE BLVD
RALEIGH, NC 276174200
Phone: 919-313-3700
Fax: –
Web: www.storr.com

CEO: –
CFO: Terry McGuire
HR: –
FYE: December 31
Type: Private

Change the way you store your employees with the help of Storr Office Environments. The firm is an office furniture supplier to companies in the southeastern US carrying more than 200 products under brands such as Peter Pepper and Steelcase. It offers the usual desks and seating as well as interior architecture floor coverings and office technology. Storr also provides professional space planning facility management and installation services for its clients. The company operates a warehouse showroom and distribution center in North Carolina and has offices in Florida. Storr was founded in 1914.

	Annual Growth	12/03	12/04	12/05	12/06	12/07
Sales ($ mil.)	19.6%	–	29.7	34.9	42.5	50.9
Net income ($ mil.)	36.5%	–	–	1.5	2.1	2.8
Market value ($ mil.)	–	–	–	–	–	–
Employees	–	–	–	–	–	200

STOWERS INSTITUTE FOR MEDICAL RESEARCH

1000 E 50TH ST
KANSAS CITY, MO 641102262
Phone: 816-926-4000
Fax: –
Web: www.stowers.org

CEO: David Chao
CFO: –
HR: –
FYE: December 31
Type: Private

The Stowers Institute for Medical Research is into mutant life forms. It conducts basic biomedical research on genes and proteins to study the cellular and molecular changes involved in diseases such as cancer cardiovascular disease diabetes and dementia. It carries out its research by causing mutations in mice chicken embryos zebra fish fruit flies sea urchins and yeast and by studying the results to see how normal genes function. Cancer survivors Virginia and Jim Stowers founded the organization in 1994 after deciding it was a better legacy to leave their children than a thriving mutual fund. The Stowers Institute planned to open a facility for stem cell research in 2010 but that has been delayed.

	Annual Growth	12/12	12/13	12/14	12/15	12/16
Sales ($ mil.)	(0.6%)	–	68.0	179.5	60.7	66.7
Net income ($ mil.)	–	–	(5.9)	105.3	(14.9)	(14.1)
Market value ($ mil.)	–	–	–	–	–	–
Employees	–	–	–	–	–	335

STR HOLDINGS INC.
NBB: STRI

10 Water Street
Enfield, CT 06082
Phone: 860 272-4235
Fax: –
Web: www.strsolar.com

CEO: Robert S Yorgensen
CFO: Thomas D Vitro
HR: –
FYE: December 31
Type: Public

Think of it as plastic wrap for solar cells. STR Holdings operates primarily through subsidiary Specialized Technology Resources which manufactures solar encapsulants — polymer films that hold solar modules (panels) together and protect semiconductors from exposure to the elements. The company pioneered the development of ethylene vinyl acetate- (EVA-) based encapsulants for the US Department of Energy in the 1970s. Its PhotoCap-brand encapsulants are sold worldwide to photovoltaic (PV) module makers. The company has production plants in Malaysia and Spain each with an annual production capacity of 3000 MW.

	Annual Growth	12/14	12/15	12/16	12/17	12/18
Sales ($ mil.)	(27.5%)	39.3	29.8	20.1	13.5	10.9
Net income ($ mil.)	–	(23.6)	(9.5)	(15.9)	(5.1)	(5.8)
Market value ($ mil.)	(31.7%)	27.6	7.4	3.0	4.6	6.0
Employees	(26.8%)	220	165	135	90	63

STRACK AND VAN TIL SUPER MARKET INC.

2244 45TH ST
HIGHLAND, IN 463222629
Phone: 219-924-7588
Fax: –

CEO: –
CFO: Keith Bruxvoort
HR: –
FYE: August 01
Type: Private

One of Chicagoland's leading grocery chains Strack & Van Til operates more than 35 supermarkets in and around Chicago and northern Indiana. Stores operate under the banners of Strack & Van Til Town & Country Food Market and Ultra Foods. The regional grocery chain offers fresh and packaged foods and has delicatessen and bakery divisions in each of its stores. Its websites offer weekly circulars and coupons as well as feature recipes cooking videos meal planners and food-related articles. The company is owned by Chicago-based grocery distributor Central Grocers which also operates supermarkets under the Berkot's and Key Market banners. In 2017 Central Grocers filed for Chapter 11 bankruptcy protection and put Strack & Van Til up for sale as part of the filing.

	Annual Growth	08/06	08/07	08/08	08/09	08/10
Sales ($ mil.)	(3.4%)	–	–	–	995.1	961.6
Net income ($ mil.)	16.1%	–	–	–	13.8	16.0
Market value ($ mil.)	–	–	–	–	–	–
Employees	–	–	–	–	–	2,000

STRATA SKIN SCIENCES INC
NAS: SSKN

5 Walnut Grove Drive, Suite 140
Horsham, PA 19044
Phone: 215 619-3200
Fax: –
Web: www.strataskinsciences.com

CEO: Dolev Rafaeli
CFO: Matthew C Hill
HR: Lisa Phillips
FYE: December 31
Type: Public

Strata Skin Sciences (formerly MELA Sciences) can detect whether that mole is a sign of a more serious medical condition — melanoma. The company's lead product is a hand-held imaging device called MelaFind which captures images of suspicious skin lesions compares them to other malignant and benign lesions stored in a database and provides information about whether they should be biopsied. Strata Skin Sciences markets the point-of-care product to primary care physicians dermatologists and plastic surgeons in the US. Other products include XTRAC (which produces ultraviolet light to treat psoriasis and vitiligo) and VTRAC (a system utilizing a precise wavelength excimer lamp to treat vitiligo patches).

	Annual Growth	12/14	12/15	12/16	12/17	12/18
Sales ($ mil.)	139.0%	0.9	18.5	31.8	31.4	29.9
Net income ($ mil.)	–	(14.1)	(24.9)	(3.3)	(18.8)	(4.0)
Market value ($ mil.)	21.4%	35.9	33.2	13.2	36.8	77.9
Employees	32.6%	34	106	96	98	105

STRATEGIC EDUCATION INC
NMS: STRA

2303 Dulles Station Boulevard
Herndon, VA 20171
Phone: 703 561-1600
Fax: –
Web: www.strayereducation.com

CEO: Karl McDonnell
CFO: Daniel W. Jackson
HR: Debra Sandler
FYE: December 31
Type: Public

Students who wander from traditional learning paths can turn to Strategic Education (formerly Strayer Education). The company's Strayer University offers some 90 different degree diploma and certificate programs from more than 70 campuses in 16 US states and Washington DC. Strategic Education's online Capella University offers more than 50 degrees to some 38000 students throughout the US. The company also offers an executive MBA online through Jack Welch Management Institute. Strayer Education merged with Capella Education to create Strategic Education in mid-2018.

	Annual Growth	12/14	12/15	12/16	12/17	12/18
Sales ($ mil.)	9.2%	446.0	434.4	441.1	454.9	634.2
Net income ($ mil.)	–	46.4	40.0	34.8	20.6	(15.7)
Market value ($ mil.)	11.2%	1,615.1	1,307.2	1,753.2	1,947.8	2,466.1
Employees	19.8%	1,534	1,464	1,869	1,544	3,158

STRATEGIC HOTELS & RESORTS, INC.
NYS: BEE

200 West Madison Street, Suite 1700
Chicago, IL 60606-3415
Phone: 312 658-5000
Fax: 312 658-5799
Web: www.strategichotels.com

CEO: –
CFO: –
HR: –
FYE: December 31
Type: Public

Hotels & Resorts (SHR) is a busy BEE when it comes to hospitality. The self-administered and self-managed real estate investment trust (REIT) which is traded under the symbol BEE owns or has interests in more than 15 upscale and luxury hotels (some 8200 rooms) in the US. It also has interests in two Marriott hotels in Europe and owns the Four Seasons Punta Mita resort in Mexico. In addition SHR owns land for development which is adjacent to existing hotel resorts. Affiliated brands include Four Seasons Hyatt InterContinental and Marriott. Focused on the asset management aspect of its properties SHR does not manage its hotels directly. It relies on third-party management companies to handle day-to-day operations.

	Annual Growth	12/09	12/10	12/11	12/12	12/13
Sales ($ mil.)	5.6%	723.8	686.3	763.8	808.3	900.0
Net income ($ mil.)	–	(243.9)	(231.1)	(5.2)	(55.3)	11.0
Market value ($ mil.)	50.1%	382.4	1,087.5	1,104.0	1,315.7	1,942.8
Employees	(3.0%)	43	43	42	39	38

STRATTEC SECURITY CORP.
NMS: STRT

3333 West Good Hope Road
Milwaukee, WI 53209
Phone: 414 247-3333
Fax: 414 247-3329
Web: www.strattec.com

CEO: Frank J Krejci
CFO: Patrick J Hansen
HR: –
FYE: June 30
Type: Public

STRATTEC SECURITY has your car under lock and key. The company designs and makes mechanical security locks electro-mechanical locks and keys and ignition lock housings primarily for global automakers. It also makes access control products including door handles latches power sliding doors and power lift gates. Chrysler Ford and General Motors account for the majority of STRATTEC's sales. In addition to cars and light trucks its products are used in the heavy truck and recreational vehicle markets as well as in precision die castings. With facilities in the US and Mexico STRATTEC delivers products mainly in North America but also abroad in Asia Europe and South America.

	Annual Growth	06/15*	07/16	07/17	07/18*	06/19
Sales ($ mil.)	4.3%	411.5	401.4	417.3	439.2	487.0
Net income ($ mil.)	–	20.7	9.1	7.2	12.3	(17.0)
Market value ($ mil.)	(23.5%)	259.4	156.3	130.7	112.8	89.0
Employees	5.3%	3,420	3,877	3,892	4,420	4,209

*Fiscal year change

STRATUS PROPERTIES INC.
NMS: STRS

212 Lavaca Street, Suite 300
Austin, TX 78701
Phone: 512 478-5788
Fax: –
Web: www.stratusproperties.com

CEO: William H Armstrong III
CFO: Erin D Pickens
HR: –
FYE: December 31
Type: Public

Stratus Properties is on cloud nine over real estate investments. The company develops owns and manages commercial residential and mixed-use properties primarily in Texas primarily in the Austin area where it has some 2500 acres of developed and undeveloped land. The firm's principal developments include Austin's Barton Creek subdivision and portions of the metro area's Circle C Ranch. In partnership with other developers Stratus is developing two high-profile mixed-use projects in the city. It also owns a couple of undeveloped acres in San Antonio and has completed the development and sale of a project in Plano.

	Annual Growth	12/14	12/15	12/16	12/17	12/18
Sales ($ mil.)	(1.8%)	94.1	80.9	80.3	80.3	87.6
Net income ($ mil.)	–	13.4	12.2	(6.0)	3.9	(4.0)
Market value ($ mil.)	14.8%	112.7	166.6	267.4	242.5	195.8
Employees	5.5%	113	114	123	139	140

STREAM GLOBAL SERVICES INC.
NYSE AMEX: SGS

Wellesley Office Park 20 William St. Ste. 310
Wellesley MA 02481
Phone: 781-304-1800
Fax: 781-304-1701
Web: www.stream.com

CEO: Kathryn V Marinello
CFO: Michael Henricks
HR: –
FYE: December 31
Type: Private

This company can handle a torrent of customer service calls. Stream Global Services is a leading provider of business process outsourcing (BPO) services such as customer care and technical support. The company maintains about 50 call centers in more than 20 countries from which it works with its customers' customers over the telephone via e-mail and through online chat sessions in 35 different languages. In addition to customer service Stream offers sales support and order processing. After several years as a public company Stream Global Services went private in 2012.

STREAMLINE HEALTH SOLUTIONS INC
NAS: STRM

1175 Peachtree Street, NE, 10th Floor
Atlanta, GA 30361
Phone: 888 997-8732
Fax: –
Web: www.streamlinehealth.net

CEO: Wyche T Green III
CFO: Thomas J Gibson
HR: –
FYE: January 31
Type: Public

Streamline Health Solutions (formerly LanVision Systems) helps health care providers streamline business processes. The software developer and service provider offers medical records workflow and document management software that consolidates information from existing media (paper disk X-ray film photographs video and audio) into a single database. Products include accessANYware which captures and manages medical documents; a multimedia system for accessing patient records; and hosted medical records management tools. The company also offers application hosting project management and disaster recovery services.

	Annual Growth	01/15	01/16	01/17	01/18	01/19
Sales ($ mil.)	(5.1%)	27.6	28.3	27.1	24.3	22.4
Net income ($ mil.)	–	(12.0)	(4.3)	(5.2)	(3.1)	(5.9)
Market value ($ mil.)	(25.4%)	83.5	34.5	30.5	37.0	25.8
Employees	(3.7%)	123	123	129	116	106

STRIKE, LLC

1800 HUGHES LANDING BLVD # 500
THE WOODLANDS, TX 773801684
Phone: 713-389-2400
Fax: –
Web: www.strikeconstruction.com

CEO: –
CFO: –
HR: –
FYE: December 31
Type: Private

Strike Construction aims to strike it rich by constructing installing and testing pipelines for the oil and gas industry. The family-owned contracting firm builds and repairs onshore pipelines and meter stations for customers the likes of Kinder Morgan SandRidge Energy and TransCanada. It also performs state-mandated integrity tests to ensure pipeline safety and offers remediation services in case a pipe should require repairs. Subsidiary Pickett Systems designs and installs flow measurement systems for onshore and offshore use; it also offers fabrication services. Strike Construction is licensed to work in about 30 states but the bulk of its business is concentrated in oil-rich Texas and along the Gulf Coast.

	Annual Growth	12/05	12/06	12/07	12/08	12/10
Sales ($ mil.)	–	–	–	(870.6)	114.2	192.4
Net income ($ mil.)	2547.0%	–	–	0.0	7.7	7.9
Market value ($ mil.)	–	–	–	–	–	–
Employees	–	–	–	–	–	5,140

STRIKEFORCE TECHNOLOGIES INC

1090 King Georges Post Road, Suite 603
Edison, NJ 08837
Phone: 732 661-9641
Fax: –
Web: www.strikeforcetech.com

NBB: SFOR
CEO: Mark L Kay
CFO: Philip E Blocker
HR: –
FYE: December 31
Type: Public

StrikeForce Technologies doesn't want your identity getting away from you. The company develops software that guards consumers and businesses against identity theft encompassing areas such as identity management remote access and biometric layering. StrikeForce's products guard against phishing attempts keylogging malware and spyware. StrikeForce also offers professional services such as consulting implementation maintenance and support. Its customers come from a range of industries including financial services health care and manufacturing.

	Annual Growth	12/14	12/15	12/16	12/17	12/18
Sales ($ mil.)	(7.9%)	0.3	0.3	0.4	0.3	0.2
Net income ($ mil.)	–	(3.4)	(1.8)	2.9	(3.2)	(3.3)
Market value ($ mil.)	–	0.0	0.0	0.0	0.0	0.0
Employees	10.7%	6	7	8	9	9

STRONGWELL CORPORATION

400 COMMONWEALTH AVE
BRISTOL, VA 242013800
Phone: 276-645-8000
Fax: –
Web: www.strongwell.com

CEO: G David Oakley Jr
CFO: –
HR: –
FYE: December 31
Type: Private

Strong wells and a myriad of other products can be made by Strongwell a top pultruder of fiber-reinforced polymer composites. The company's primary division is its pultrusion manufacturing operation (comprised of 65 pultrusion machines) which makes structural shapes fabricates fiberglass structures and systems and builds pultrusion equipment and tooling. It primarily has expertise in making grating panels fencing products and stair treads. It serves such markets as energy automotive construction marine and leisure. Strongwell has three pultrusion manufacturing facilities in Virginia and Minnesota. Through these locations the company maintains about 647000 sq. ft. of total manufacturing space.

	Annual Growth	12/07	12/08	12/09	12/10	12/11
Sales ($ mil.)	6.7%	–	–	84.7	70.5	96.4
Net income ($ mil.)	0.6%	–	–	2.6	1.0	2.6
Market value ($ mil.)	–	–	–	–	–	–
Employees	–	–	–	–	–	500

STRYKER CORP

2825 Airview Boulevard
Kalamazoo, MI 49002
Phone: 269 385-2600
Fax: 269 385-1062
Web: www.stryker.com

NYS: SYK
CEO: Kevin A. Lobo
CFO: Glenn Boehnlein
HR: Art Hartman
FYE: December 31
Type: Public

Is this an operating room or Dad's workshop? Stryker's surgical products include such instruments as drills saws and even cement mixers. The company operates through three primary segments — MedSurg Orthopaedic and Neurotechnology & Spine. MedSurg's products include microsurgery instruments endoscopy equipment communications systems emergency medical equipment and patient handling tools. The Orthopaedic segment makes artificial hip and knee joints trauma implants bone cement and other orthopedic supplies. The Neurotechnology & Spine segment provides rods screws and artificial discs for spinal surgeries as well as coils and stents for cerebral vascular procedures. Stryker's products are marketed globally to doctors hospitals and other health care facilities via direct sales personnel and distributors.

	Annual Growth	12/15	12/16	12/17	12/18	12/19
Sales ($ mil.)	10.6%	9,946.0	11,325.0	12,444.0	13,601.0	14,884.0
Net income ($ mil.)	9.7%	1,439.0	1,647.0	1,020.0	3,553.0	2,083.0
Market value ($ mil.)	22.6%	34,806.0	44,868.8	57,987.6	58,702.9	78,622.5
Employees	10.3%	27,000	33,000	33,000	36,000	40,000

STUART-DEAN CO. INC.

450 FASHION AVE STE 3800
NEW YORK, NY 101233801
Phone: 212-273-6900
Fax: –
Web: www.stuartdean.com

CEO: Mark Parrish
CFO: –
HR: –
FYE: December 31
Type: Private

The Stuart Dean Company provides restoration refinishing conservation and maintenance services for architectural metal stone and woodwork in residential institutional and commercial buildings. Projects include curtain wall restorations bronze statue preservation church pew refinishing and marble restorations. The company serves a variety of customers including homeowners corporations and building industry professionals such as property managers and maintenance engineers. Its diverse group of clients have included AT&T Hyatt Hotels and Resorts The Kennedy Center and Stanford University.

	Annual Growth	12/12	12/13	12/14	12/15	12/17
Sales ($ mil.)	0.9%	–	63.0	61.3	61.3	65.5
Net income ($ mil.)	48.5%	–	0.3	(1.0)	(1.0)	1.5
Market value ($ mil.)	–	–	–	–	–	–
Employees	–	–	–	–	–	450

STURDY MEMORIAL HOSPITAL, INC.

211 PARK ST
ATTLEBORO, MA 027033137
Phone: 508-222-5200
Fax: –
Web: www.sturdymemorial.org

CEO: –
CFO: Amy Posesser
HR: –
FYE: September 30
Type: Private

Sturdy Memorial Hospital has been a stalwart provider of health care to southeast Massachusetts and Rhode Island since 1913. In addition to comprehensive medical surgical and emergency care the hospital offers cardiac and pulmonary rehabilitation women's health services diagnostic imaging and a center devoted to treating multiple sclerosis patients. It also operates pain management cancer and wound care centers. In 2014 Sturdy Memorial admitted some 7000 patients facilitated around 700 births and had some 51000 emergency department visits. The not-for-profit hospital employs more than 150 physicians.

	Annual Growth	09/14	09/15	09/16	09/17	09/18
Sales ($ mil.)	5.2%	–	163.9	169.2	177.7	190.7
Net income ($ mil.)	–	–	(23.3)	15.7	18.6	27.9
Market value ($ mil.)	–	–	–	–	–	–
Employees	–	–	–	–	–	1,300

STURGIS BANCORP INC
NBB: STBI

113-125 East Chicago Road
Sturgis, MI 49091
Phone: 269 651-9345
Fax: -
Web: www.sturgisbank.com

CEO: -
CFO: Brian Hoggatt
HR: Emily Frohriep
FYE: December 31
Type: Public

Sturgis Bancorp is the holding company for Sturgis Bank & Trust which has about 10 branches in south-central Michigan. Founded in 1905 the bank offers checking and savings accounts CDs trust services and other standard banking fare. Real estate loans comprise the bulk of its lending activities: one- to four-family residential mortgages make up more than half of the company's loan portfolio. Subsidiary Oak Leaf Financial Services provides insurance and investment products and services from third-party provider Linsco/Private Ledger.

	Annual Growth	12/14	12/15	12/16	12/17	12/18
Assets ($ mil.)	8.4%	312.5	368.6	398.6	414.4	431.6
Net income ($ mil.)	23.5%	1.9	2.5	2.7	3.2	4.4
Market value ($ mil.)	22.2%	18.7	22.0	28.9	39.6	41.7
Employees	-	-	-	-	-	-

STURM, RUGER & CO., INC.
NYS: RGR

Lacey Place
Southport, CT 06890
Phone: 203 259-7843
Fax: 203 256-3367
Web: www.ruger.com

CEO: Christopher J. Killoy
CFO: Thomas A. Dineen
HR: -
FYE: December 31
Type: Public

Sturm Ruger & Co. also called Ruger is one of the nation's biggest gun makers and produces pistols revolvers rifles and shotguns. Models include hunting and target rifles single- and double-action revolvers muzzleloading guns and double-barreled shotguns. Its guns are sold by independent wholesale distributors to independent firearms retailers and chains including Academy Sports and Cabelas. Ruger also makes metal products — known as castings — for the commercial and military markets. Sturm Ruger & Company was founded in 1949 by William Ruger and Alexander Sturm.

	Annual Growth	12/14	12/15	12/16	12/17	12/18
Sales ($ mil.)	(2.3%)	544.5	551.1	664.3	522.3	495.6
Net income ($ mil.)	7.2%	38.6	62.1	87.5	52.1	50.9
Market value ($ mil.)	11.3%	604.6	1,040.7	920.0	975.0	929.1
Employees	(3.1%)	2,073	2,180	2,430	1,750	1,830

STV GROUP, INCORPORATED

205 W WELSH DR
DOUGLASSVILLE, PA 195188713
Phone: 610-385-8200
Fax: -
Web: www.stvinc.com

CEO: Milo E Riverso
CFO: Thomas Butcher
HR: -
FYE: September 30
Type: Private

STV Group helps create the systems through which SUVs LRVs and 747s can travel. Its subsidiaries and partnerships provide architectural engineering environmental construction management interior design and planning services for infrastructure projects that include airports light-rail systems ports and railroads. STV Group's security division conducts threat assessments and mitigates safety strategies for facilities. Its STV Canada Consulting joint venture is developing the Ottawa Light Rail Transit Project. The group serves public and private clients worldwide but primarily in the US. The employee-owned STV Group was founded in 1912 and taken private in 2001.

	Annual Growth	09/01	09/02	09/03	09/16	09/17
Sales ($ mil.)	2.8%	-	213.9	138.3	301.1	322.3
Net income ($ mil.)	1.8%	-	6.8	4.2	7.0	8.9
Market value ($ mil.)	-	-	-	-	-	-
Employees	-	-	-	-	-	1,700

SUBJEX CORPORATION
OTC: SBJX

3245 Hennepin Ave. South Ste. 1
Minneapolis MN 55408
Phone: 612-827-2203
Fax: 866-468-4988
Web: www.subjex.com

CEO: Andrew D Hyder
CFO: Sharon Rae Hyder
HR: -
FYE: December 31
Type: Public

Subjex is more than happy to change the subject even when it comes to business. The company was originally formed in 1999 as PageLab Network to develop Internet search engine technology but changed direction when it came up with an artificial intelligence-based program that can function as a virtual customer service representative "talking" with customers through a website interface. Subjex has since focused its efforts on developing software for individual investors that forecasts a variety of financial indexes such as the Dow Jones Industrial Average.

SUBURBAN HOSPITAL INC

8600 OLD GEORGETOWN RD
BETHESDA, MD 20814-1497
Phone: 301-896-3100
Fax: -
Web: www.suburbanhospital.org

CEO: Brian A Gragnolati
CFO: -
HR: -
FYE: June 30
Type: Private

Don't let the name fool you this hospital isn't just for big city expatriates. Suburban Hospital a member of the Johns Hopkins Medicine network is an acute-care medical-surgical hospital with about 235 beds that provides all major medical services except obstetrics to the residents of Montgomery County in Maryland. Specialized services include behavioral health cardiology cancer care home care and pediatrics. Founded in 1943 Suburban Hospital serves as the regional trauma center for the county and is equipped with a helipad. Other services include a center for sleep disorders 24-hour stroke team diagnostic pathology and radiology departments and a range of inpatient and outpatient programs.

	Annual Growth	06/08	06/09	06/10	06/11	06/12
Sales ($ mil.)	2.7%	-	243.9	240.8	256.4	263.9
Net income ($ mil.)	-	-	(5.9)	15.4	32.8	(2.5)
Market value ($ mil.)	-	-	-	-	-	-
Employees	-	-	-	-	-	1,550

SUBURBAN PROPANE PARTNERS LP
NYS: SPH

240 Route 10 West
Whippany, NJ 07981
Phone: 973 887-5300
Fax: -
Web: www.suburbanpropane.com

CEO: Michael A. Stivala
CFO: Michael A. Kuglin
HR: -
FYE: September 28
Type: Public

Suburban Propane Partners one of the top US retail propane marketers distributes propane fuel oil and other refined fuels to a million customers across the country. The company also markets natural gas and electricity in deregulated markets. It specializes in installing and servicing home comfort equipment mainly heating and ventilation. From residents to industries and agricultural customers Suburban Propane serves a wide variety of clients through its nearly 670 locations in more than 40 states.

	Annual Growth	09/15	09/16	09/17	09/18	09/19
Sales ($ mil.)	(2.7%)	1,417.0	1,046.1	1,187.9	1,344.4	1,267.7
Net income ($ mil.)	(5.0%)	84.4	14.4	38.0	76.5	68.6
Market value ($ mil.)	(8.3%)	2,074.9	2,110.7	1,610.7	1,452.6	1,467.4
Employees	(1.1%)	3,646	3,417	3,221	3,416	3,494

SUCAMPO PHARMACEUTICALS INC
NMS: SCMP

805 King Farm Boulevard, Suite 550
Rockville, MD 20850
Phone: 301 961-3400
Fax: –
Web: www.sucampo.com

CEO: –
CFO: –
HR: –
FYE: December 31
Type: Public

Sucampo Pharmaceuticals is a biopharmaceutical company with a focus on unmet medical needs around the world. Sucampo works with a group of compounds derived from fatty acids called prostones; it uses prostones in the development of therapies for the treatment of age-related gastrointestinal respiratory vascular and central nervous system disorders. It has two FDA-approved products: AMITIZA which treats chronic constipation in adults and irritable bowel syndrome in adult women and Rescula for the treatment of glaucoma and ocular hypertension. Sucampo's pipeline has other candidates in pre-clinical and early stage clinical development to treat a range of conditions.

	Annual Growth	12/11	12/12	12/13	12/14	12/15
Sales ($ mil.)	29.3%	54.8	81.5	89.6	115.5	153.2
Net income ($ mil.)	–	(17.3)	4.8	6.4	13.1	33.4
Market value ($ mil.)	40.5%	188.3	208.2	399.5	606.9	734.8
Employees	10.2%	108	128	77	80	159

SUCCESSFACTORS INC.
NASDAQ: SFSF

1500 Fashion Island Blvd. Ste. 300
San Mateo CA 94404
Phone: 650-645-2000
Fax: 650-645-2099
Web: www.successfactors.com

CEO: –
CFO: –
HR: –
FYE: December 31
Type: Public

SuccessFactors has a recipe for business success. The SAP subsidiary provides software designed to help align business strategies boost employee productivity and manage development and performance. Its Business Execution Software provides everyone from FORTUNE 500 companies to small businesses with a Software-as-a-Service (SaaS) platform that automates goal planning progress tracking and performance reviews. The company targets customers in markets ranging from financial services (Wells Fargo) and health care (Baylor Health Care System) to education (Kaplan) retail (LensCrafters) and technology (EMC). About 80% of sales comes from customers in the US. SAP acquired the company in 2012.

SUCCESSORIES LLC

2520 Diehl Rd.
Aurora IL 60502
Phone: 630-820-7200
Fax: 630-820-3599
Web: www.successories.com

CEO: –
CFO: –
HR: –
FYE: January 31
Type: Private

At a time when workplace cynicism is in vogue Successories is the anti-Dilbert. The company makes personal motivation and self-improvement items including awards books coffee mugs computer and desk accessories framed desk and wall decor greeting cards and pens. Products produced by Successories are sold through the millions of catalogs it mails each year its Web site and a handful of retail stores in Florida Indiana North Carolina and Texas. Successories was founded in 1985 by Arnold (Mac) Anderson. It published its first catalog in 1988 went public in 1990 and was taken private in 2003. TWS Partnership acquired the company in June 2009.

SUFFOLK BANCORP
NYS: SCNB

4 West Second Street, P.O. Box 9000
Riverhead, NY 11901
Phone: 631 208-2400
Fax: 631 727-3214
Web: www.scnb.com

CEO: –
CFO: –
HR: –
FYE: December 31
Type: Public

Suffice it to say that Suffolk Bancorp serves the banking needs of folks on Long Island. The holding company owns Suffolk County National Bank which serves Suffolk County New York through about 30 branches. Targeting individuals and small to midsized businesses the bank offers standard services such as checking savings and money market accounts and trust and asset management. It also provides insurance and investment products including IRAs mutual funds annuities bonds and brokerage services. Commercial mortgages account for nearly half of the company's loan portfolio; business loans make up another 20%. People's United Financial is buying Suffolk Bancorp for $402 million.

	Annual Growth	12/11	12/12	12/13	12/14	12/15
Assets ($ mil.)	9.9%	1,484.2	1,622.5	1,699.8	1,895.3	2,168.6
Net income ($ mil.)	–	(0.1)	(1.7)	12.7	15.3	17.7
Market value ($ mil.)	27.3%	127.3	154.6	245.5	268.0	334.5
Employees	(5.0%)	414	373	350	333	337

SUFFOLK CONSTRUCTION COMPANY, INC.

65 ALLERTON ST
BOSTON, MA 021192923
Phone: 617-445-3500
Fax: –
Web: www.suffolk.com

CEO: John F. Fish
CFO: Michael (Mike) Azarela
HR: –
FYE: August 31
Type: Private

Suffolk Construction Company provides construction services from top to bottom. The company kicks off the building process with pre-construction services and follows through with design/build general contracting and construction management. Suffolk Construction builds for both the public and private organizations in the science and technology health care education government and commercial sectors operating in the Northeast Mid-Atlantic Southeast and West Coast regions of the US. Founded in 1982 the privately-held firm is owned by president and CEO John Fish whose family has been in construction for four generations.

	Annual Growth	08/11	08/12	08/13	08/14	08/15
Sales ($ mil.)	17.0%	–	–	1,825.0	1,761.1	2,500.0
Net income ($ mil.)	–	–	–	0.0	0.0	0.0
Market value ($ mil.)	–	–	–	–	–	–
Employees	–	–	–	–	–	1,150

SUFFOLK COUNTY WATER AUTHORITY INC

4060 SUNRISE HWY
OAKDALE, NY 117691005
Phone: 631-563-0255
Fax: –
Web: www.scwa.com

CEO: Jeffrey W Szabo
CFO: Douglas Celiberti
HR: –
FYE: May 31
Type: Private

Sufficient to say Suffolk County Water Authority makes sure that there is potable water across Long Island in addition to the seawater that surrounds it. The utility provides water services to about 1.2 million people in New York's Suffolk County on the eastern end of Long Island. The water authority's system (the largest water system in the nation operating entirely with groundwater) includes more than 5500 miles of mains. The authority also runs the largest groundwater testing facility in the US. Suffolk County Water Authority is a public benefit corporation of the state of New York.

	Annual Growth	05/04	05/05	05/06	05/07	05/08
Sales ($ mil.)	2.7%	–	–	132.6	130.2	140.0
Net income ($ mil.)	(4.1%)	–	–	16.5	9.7	15.2
Market value ($ mil.)	–	–	–	–	–	–
Employees	–	–	–	–	–	570

SUFFOLK UNIVERSITY

73 TREMONT ST STE 200
BOSTON, MA 021083901
Phone: 617-573-8000
Fax: -
Web: www.suffolk.edu

CEO: -
CFO: -
HR: -
FYE: June 30
Type: Private

Suffolk University provides a well-rounded education around the Athens of America and abroad. From its main campus in Boston and its satellite and branch campuses across Massachusetts as well as through study abroad programs the university provides undergraduate and graduate degrees in more than 70 areas of study through the College of Arts and Sciences Sawyer Business School and Suffolk Law School. It also runs about 25 institutes and research centers. More than 7500 students attend the private university which has a 13:1 student-to-faculty ratio and offers courses taught by about 900 faculty members. The university was founded in 1906 as the Suffolk School of Law.

	Annual Growth	06/10	06/11	06/13	06/17	06/18
Sales ($ mil.)	(4.2%)	-	298.3	236.8	217.7	220.7
Net income ($ mil.)	20.8%	-	5.4	28.6	0.6	20.3
Market value ($ mil.)	-	-	-	-	-	-
Employees	-	-	-	-	-	800

SUMMA HEALTH

525 E MARKET ST
AKRON, OH 443041619
Phone: 330-375-3000
Fax: -

CEO: T. Clifford Deveny
CFO: Brian Derrick
HR: -
FYE: December 31
Type: Private

Summa Health System operates hospitals and outpatient care clinics plus a health care plan in Ohio. The not-for-profit system serves the residents of the greater Akron Ohio area through acute care hospitals rehabilitation facilities community clinics emergency rooms and physician practices. Together its hospitals are home to more than 1300 beds. In addition to general medical and surgical care Summa's key services include cardiac stroke behavioral health cancer care emergency services and women's health. Summa Health has agreed to be acquired by Detroit-based Beaumont Health.

	Annual Growth	12/05	12/06	12/07	12/08	12/09
Sales ($ mil.)	(40.4%)	-	797.1	940.8	1,264.1	168.6
Net income ($ mil.)	(52.8%)	-	61.5	71.1	(75.1)	6.5
Market value ($ mil.)	-	-	-	-	-	-
Employees	-	-	-	-	-	7,431

SUMMER INFANT INC

NAS: SUMR

1275 Park East Drive
Woonsocket, RI 02895
Phone: 401 671-6550
Fax: -
Web: www.summerinfant.com

CEO: Stuart Noyes
CFO: Paul Francese
HR: -
FYE: December 29
Type: Public

Summer Infant makes products for infants and children that can be used in any season. Through its operating subsidiaries Summer Infant develops and markets health and safety and wellness products for children from birth to 3 years old mostly under the Summer Infant and Born Free brand names. Some of its products include booster seats audio and video monitors bed rails safety gates bedding and durable bath items. Most of its products are manufactured in Asia (primarily China) and Israel. The company earns the majority of its revenue from the North American market selling through retailers such as Toys "R" Us Target Wal-Mart and Amazon.com. In Europe customers include Tesco Argos and Mothercare.

	Annual Growth	01/15	01/16*	12/16	12/17	12/18
Sales ($ mil.)	(5.4%)	205.4	205.8	194.3	189.9	173.6
Net income ($ mil.)	-	(0.2)	(8.7)	(4.3)	(2.2)	(4.3)
Market value ($ mil.)	(34.1%)	62.9	42.0	37.6	28.2	18.0
Employees	(2.0%)	203	197	209	201	191

*Fiscal year change

SUMMERLIN HOSPITAL MEDICAL CENTER, LLC

657 N TOWN CENTER DR
LAS VEGAS, NV 891446367
Phone: 702-233-7000
Fax: -
Web: www.summerlinhospital.com

CEO: Robert Freymuller
CFO: Bonny Sorensen
HR: -
FYE: December 31
Type: Private

Vegas can take its toll (and not just on your pocketbook). For those who have perhaps overindulged in all the city has to offer there is Summerlin Hospital Medical Center. The subsidiary of Universal Health Service is a 450-bed acute care hospital on a 40-acre campus in the master-planned community of Summerlin in Las Vegas. The hospital's nearly 300 physicians offer care in roughly 30 specialties including cardiology cancer OB-GYN and wound care. Summerlin Hospital has undergone a series of expansions in recent years that have added a Pediatric Intensive Care Unit and a six-story tower housing about 175 rooms.

	Annual Growth	12/00	12/01	12/15	12/16	12/17
Sales ($ mil.)	-	-	0.0	375.2	404.6	424.5
Net income ($ mil.)	-	-	0.0	47.8	61.0	80.2
Market value ($ mil.)	-	-	-	-	-	-
Employees	-	-	-	-	-	600

SUMMIT BANCSHARES INC.

OTC: SMAL

2969 Broadway
Oakland CA 94611
Phone: 510-839-8800
Fax: 510-839-8853
Web: www.summitbanking.com

CEO: -
CFO: Kikuo Nakahara
HR: -
FYE: December 31
Type: Public

Summit Bancshares wants your business to operate at peak performance. Holding company Summit Bancshares does business through its primary subsidiary Summit Bank which operates four branch offices in the East Bay communities of Emeryville Oakland and Walnut Creek California. The bank targets professionals entrepreneurs and executives and their businesses offering them standard business and personal checking and savings accounts as well as commercial loans and online banking. It also offers courier service for its busy business-owner customers. Summit Bancshares was formed in 1981.

SUMMIT CORPORATION OF AMERICA

1430 Waterbury Rd.
Thomaston CT 06787
Phone: 860-283-4391
Fax: 860-283-4010
Web: www.scact.com

CEO: -
CFO: -
HR: -
FYE: September 30
Type: Private

Summit Corporation of America is at the peak of its game. The electroplating company offers a number of services including continuous coil stock plating wire plating and continuous stampings plating. Summit Corporation also electroplates metal ribbon tape wire and individual manufactured metal parts such as pins springs washers cans and chemically etched materials. Its major customers include component manufacturers and other companies in the aerospace automotive battery computer defense marine metal distribution semiconductor and telecommunications industries. Summit Corporation offers prototypes and contract manufacturing as well as research and development and testing services.

SUMMIT ELECTRIC SUPPLY CO., INC.

2900 STANFORD DR NE
ALBUQUERQUE, NM 871071814
Phone: 505-346-2900
Fax: –
Web: www.summit.com

CEO: Victor R. Jury
CFO: Thomas Klemp
HR: Amalia Rosas
FYE: December 31
Type: Private

SUMMIT continues its ascent within the electronics distribution sector. SUMMIT Electric Supply distributes goods from manufacturers such as Dialight Eaton Fluke and Thomas & Betts. Products include cable conduits switches fuses lamps light fixtures instruments and safety equipment. The company offers in-house marine cable braiding for offshore oil and gas customers. SUMMIT also sells to electrical contractors government agencies construction firms and public utilities. It has nearly 25 branches located in New Mexico Arizona Louisiana Oklahoma and Texas and a service center in Dubai.

	Annual Growth	12/08	12/09	12/10	12/11	12/12
Sales ($ mil.)	12.9%	–	–	301.6	358.5	384.7
Net income ($ mil.)	12.8%	–	–	7.9	7.5	10.1
Market value ($ mil.)	–	–	–	–	–	–
Employees	–	–	–	–	–	675

SUMMIT FINANCIAL GROUP INC   NMS: SMMF

300 North Main Street
Moorefield, WV 26836
Phone: 304 530-1000
Fax: –
Web: www.summitfgi.com

CEO: H Charles Maddy III
CFO: Robert S Tissue
HR: –
FYE: December 31
Type: Public

Summit Financial Group is at the peak of community banking in West Virginia and northern Virginia. The company owns Summit Community Bank which operates about 20 branches that offer standard retail banking fare such as deposit accounts loans and cash management services. Commercial real estate loans including land development and construction loans account for about 40% of Summit Financial Group's loan portfolio which also includes residential mortgages and a smaller percentage of business and consumer loans. The bank's Summit Insurance Services unit sells both commercial and personal coverage.

	Annual Growth	12/14	12/15	12/16	12/17	12/18
Assets ($ mil.)	11.1%	1,443.6	1,492.4	1,758.6	2,134.2	2,200.6
Net income ($ mil.)	25.4%	11.4	16.1	17.3	11.9	28.1
Market value ($ mil.)	12.9%	146.5	146.3	339.0	324.1	237.8
Employees	13.7%	222	231	251	349	371

SUMMIT HOTEL PROPERTIES INC   NYS: INN

13215 Bee Cave Parkway, Suite B-300
Austin, TX 78738
Phone: 512 538-2300
Fax: –
Web: www.shpreit.com

CEO: Daniel P. Hansen
CFO: Greg A. Dowell
HR: –
FYE: December 31
Type: Public

From the southern states to the Mountain States Summit Hotel Properties has plenty of room for US travelers. Operating through its subsidiaries Summit Hotel is a self-advised real estate investment trust (REIT) that holds a portfolio of almost 90 midscale and upscale hotels with 11400-plus rooms across 24 states including major markets in western and southern states like Arizona California Colorado Idaho and Texas. More than 60% of its hotels operated under the Marriott International and Hilton brands during 2015 while the rest mostly operated under the Hyatt and Intercontinental Hotel brands. Summit Hotel was formed in 2010 and went public in 2011.

	Annual Growth	12/14	12/15	12/16	12/17	12/18
Sales ($ mil.)	8.9%	403.5	463.5	473.9	515.4	567.3
Net income ($ mil.)	44.5%	20.9	124.4	107.8	99.2	90.9
Market value ($ mil.)	(6.0%)	1,303.5	1,252.2	1,679.7	1,595.8	1,019.5
Employees	10.0%	39	40	44	49	57

SUMMIT STATE BANK (SANTA ROSA, CA)   NMS: SSBI

500 Bicentennial Way
Santa Rosa, CA 95403
Phone: 707 568-6000
Fax: –
Web: www.summitstatebank.com

CEO: Thomas Duryea
CFO: –
HR: –
FYE: December 31
Type: Public

Contrary to its name Summit State Bank does business in both the hills and the valleys of Sonoma County in western California. Serving consumers and small to midsized businesses the bank offers standard deposit services like checking savings and retirement accounts as well as lending services such as real estate and commercial loans. Commercial real estate loans account for about 40% of the bank's loan portfolio while commercial and agriculture loans make up about 20%. Its other lending products include single-family and multifamily mortgages construction loans and consumer loans. Summit State Bank operates about half a dozen branches in Petaluma Rohnert Park Santa Rosa and Windsor.

	Annual Growth	12/14	12/15	12/16	12/17	12/18
Assets ($ mil.)	7.9%	459.7	513.4	513.7	610.9	622.1
Net income ($ mil.)	1.5%	5.5	6.0	5.0	3.3	5.8
Market value ($ mil.)	(4.0%)	84.2	83.5	91.0	76.4	71.4
Employees	9.9%	61	67	74	78	89

SUN BANCORP INC. (NJ)   NMS: SNBC

350 Fellowship Road, Suite 101
Mount Laurel, NJ 08054
Phone: 856 691-7700
Fax: –
Web: www.sunnb.com

CEO: Thomas M O'Brien
CFO: Thomas R Brugger
HR: –
FYE: December 31
Type: Public

Sun Bancorp revolves around New Jersey. Boasting nearly $3 billion in total assets the holding company for Sun National Bank targets individuals and local businesses in central and southern New Jersey through some 60 branch locations. Sun National Bank offers standard retail services including savings accounts CDs and IRAs. The company's primary lending focus is originating industrial and commercial loans (including Small Business Administration (SBA) loans and lines of credit) which account for some 75% of its portfolio. Sun National Bank stopped providing residential mortgage and home equity loans in the second half of 2014. It offers investment services through Prosperis Financial Solutions.

	Annual Growth	12/11	12/12	12/13	12/14	12/15
Assets ($ mil.)	(8.7%)	3,183.9	3,224.0	3,087.6	2,715.3	2,210.6
Net income ($ mil.)	–	(67.5)	(50.5)	(9.9)	(29.8)	10.2
Market value ($ mil.)	70.9%	45.2	66.2	65.8	362.6	385.8
Employees	(13.7%)	713	750	690	509	395

SUN COAST RESOURCES, INC.

6405 CAVALCADE ST BLDG 1
HOUSTON, TX 770264315
Phone: 713-844-9600
Fax: –
Web: www.suncoastresources.com

CEO: Kathy Lehne
CFO: Sheila Kahanek
HR: –
FYE: December 31
Type: Private

Breaking the glass ceiling with large containers of Texas tea woman-owned Sun Coast Resources buys refined oil and sells it to more than 10000 third-party customers such airlines and construction educational energy industrial and retail companies in about 40 states. The company has an extensive truck fleet (more than 1000 vehicles) and delivers gasoline and diesel fuels marine and aviation fuels and lubricants. It also provides oilfield transportation and services onsite and fleet fueling petroleum tanks and generator fueling services. Sun Coast was founded in 1985 by president and CEO Kathy Lehne with $2000 in start-up capital.

	Annual Growth	12/03	12/04	12/05	12/06	12/07
Sales ($ mil.)	15.1%	–	697.8	867.9	864.2	1,064.1
Net income ($ mil.)	(2.7%)	–	3.0	13.9	7.2	2.8
Market value ($ mil.)	–	–	–	–	–	–
Employees	–	–	–	–	–	1,649

SUN COMMUNITIES INC
NYS: SUI

27777 Franklin Rd., Suite 200
Southfield, MI 48034
Phone: 248 208-2500
Fax: –
Web: www.suncommunities.com

CEO: –
CFO: Karen J Dearing
HR: Laura Messa
FYE: December 31
Type: Public

Sun Communities helps residents in the Sunshine State and around the US. The self-managed real estate investment trust (REIT) owns develops and operates manufactured housing communities (trailer and recreation vehicle parks) in nearly 30 states. Its portfolio includes more than 200 properties with nearly 80000 developed manufactured home and RV sites. Its Sun Home Services unit sells new and used homes for placement on its properties the majority of which are in Michigan Florida Indiana Texas and Ohio. Sun Communities also acquires at a discount and resells mobile homes that have been repossessed by lenders in its communities.

	Annual Growth	12/14	12/15	12/16	12/17	12/18
Sales ($ mil.)	24.3%	471.7	674.7	833.8	982.6	1,126.8
Net income ($ mil.)	37.3%	31.4	160.4	31.3	76.8	111.7
Market value ($ mil.)	13.9%	5,221.1	5,918.0	6,615.8	8,012.2	8,783.4
Employees	16.2%	1,525	1,790	2,679	2,727	2,784

SUN ORCHARD FRUIT COMPANY INC.

2087 TRANSIT RD
BURT, NY 140289797
Phone: 716-778-8544
Fax: –
Web: www.sunorchardapples.com

CEO: –
CFO: –
HR: –
FYE: August 31
Type: Private

Sun Orchard Fruit-, doesn't grow any fruit. Instead it gets fruit where it needs to go. The company stores packages and delivers apples grown by New York farmers. It fresh-packs some 500000 cartons of apples harvested by 60 growers in central and western New York and ships them to food wholesalers and retailers around the globe. The company handles-, 17 of the most popular Eastern varieties of eating apples including Gala Honeycrisp Jonagold and Empire. Founded in 1952 Sun Orchard Fruit is owned and operated by the Riessen family.

	Annual Growth	08/10	08/11	08/12	08/13	08/14
Sales ($ mil.)	10.8%	–	12.3	14.0	10.9	16.8
Net income ($ mil.)	330.3%	–	–	0.0	0.0	0.8
Market value ($ mil.)	–	–	–	–	–	–
Employees	–	–	–	–	–	54

SUN-MAID GROWERS OF CALIFORNIA

13525 S BETHEL AVE
KINGSBURG, CA 936319232
Phone: 559-897-6235
Fax: –
Web: www.sunmaid.com

CEO: Harry J Overly
CFO: Braden Bender
HR: Tim Renna
FYE: July 31
Type: Private

The Sun-Maid's basket runneth over. Sun-Maid Growers is the producer of Sun-Maid Raisins. Packaged in the familiar red boxes with the smiling red-sunbonneted maid Lorraine Collett Petersen offering her basket laden with grapes the brand is seen in just about every food store in the US. In addition to offering every toddler's (and moms of toddlers) favorite little-red-boxed snack the grower-owned cooperative manufactures industrial and food service products and exports to more than 50 countries. The company's other dried fruits include pitted prunes currants apricots cranberries figs dates apples fruit bits and tropical fruit mixtures. Founded in 1912 the coop is owned by 750 family farmers.

	Annual Growth	07/14	07/15	07/16	07/17	07/18
Sales ($ mil.)	(2.8%)	–	–	383.0	360.8	362.1
Net income ($ mil.)	67.9%	–	–	15.1	20.2	42.5
Market value ($ mil.)	–	–	–	–	–	–
Employees	–	–	–	–	–	800

SUNBELT BEVERAGE COMPANY LLC

60 E. 42nd St.
New York NY 10165
Phone: 212-699-7000
Fax: 212-699-7099
Web: www.charmer-sunbelt.com

CEO: Charles Merinoff
CFO: Gene D Luciana
HR: –
FYE: December 31
Type: Private

Sunbelt Beverage (doing business as The Charmer Sunbelt Group) is one of the biggest swigs in its industry. A leading US distributor of fine wines beer and spirits the company serves more than a dozen states (mostly along the East Coast) and the District of Columbia. It operates through 10 subsidiaries and eight joint ventures including Florida subsidiary Premier Beverage and Maryland subsidiary Bacchus Importers as well as joint ventures R & R Marketing (New Jersey) and Associated Distributors (Virginia). These entities link up suppliers with retailers in more than a dozen major markets. Aside from alcoholic beverages Charmer Sunbelt also offers non-alcoholic drinks such as bottled water.

SUNCOAST SCHOOLS FEDERAL CREDIT UNION

6801 E. Hillsborough Ave.
Tampa FL 33680
Phone: 813-621-7511
Fax: 813-621-8693
Web: www.suncoastfcu.org

CEO: Kevin Johnson
CFO: –
HR: –
FYE: December 31
Type: Private - Cooperativ

Suncoast Schools Federal Credit Union is Florida's largest credit union and one of the largest in the US based on assets. It serves public and private school employees municipal workers students and those working for a select group of more than 1000 employers (and their families) in about 15 western Florida counties. The credit union offers standard services such as checking and savings accounts residential mortgages credit cards and consumer loans in addition to insurance investment trust and real estate services. Founded in 1934 as Hillsborough County Teachers Credit Union the not-for-profit member-owned cooperative has about 50 locations (including a mobile branch) and some 500000 members.

SUNCOKE ENERGY INC
NYS: SXC

1011 Warrenville Road, Suite 600
Lisle, IL 60532
Phone: 630 824-1000
Fax: 630 824-1001
Web: www.suncoke.com

CEO: Frederick A. (Fritz) Henderson
CFO: Fay West
HR: –
FYE: December 31
Type: Public

If you're looking for a new soda product look elsewhere; if you're looking to produce steel SunCoke Energy's products may be right up your alley. One of North America's largest coke producers SunCoke produces metallurgical coke (a coal-derived fuel used in steel production) for steel companies. Its owned and operated plants — located in Virginia Indiana Ohio Illinois in the US Vit--ria Brazil (operated only) and India— operate about 1240 coke ovens and can produce an aggregate 4.2 million tons of coke per year. Major customers include ArcelorMittal US Steel and AK Steel.

	Annual Growth	12/14	12/15	12/16	12/17	12/18
Sales ($ mil.)	(0.4%)	1,472.7	1,362.7	1,223.3	1,331.5	1,450.9
Net income ($ mil.)	–	(126.1)	(22.0)	14.4	122.4	26.2
Market value ($ mil.)	(18.5%)	1,252.4	224.7	734.3	776.4	553.7
Employees	(5.5%)	1,480	1,398	1,174	1,179	1,180

SUNCOKE ENERGY PARTNERS LP   NYS: SXCP

1011 Warrenville Road, Suite 600   CEO: Michael G Rippey
Lisle, IL 60532   CFO: Fay West
Phone: 630 824-1000   HR: –
Fax: –   FYE: December 31
Web: www.suncoke.com   Type: Public

SunCoke Energy Partners is a master limited partnership formed by its parent and one of the largest coke producers in the Americas SunCoke Energy Inc. SunCoke Energy Partners was formed in 2012 for the purpose of owning a majority interest in SunCoke Energy's Ohio-based Haverhill and Middletown cokemaking facilities. Today the partnership owns a 65% interest in each of those facilities which make metallurgical coke a raw material used in steelmaking. Together they have 300 cokemaking ovens with a capacity of 1.7 million tons per year. The company's two main customers are AK Steel and ArcelorMittal USA. SunCoke Energy Partners went public in early 2013 with an offering worth $256.5 million.

	Annual Growth	12/13	12/14	12/15	12/16	12/17
Sales ($ mil.)	5.3%	687.3	648.4	838.5	779.7	845.6
Net income ($ mil.)	–	62.1	56.0	86.0	119.1	(18.1)
Market value ($ mil.)	(10.4%)	1,252.8	1,254.1	344.4	889.9	806.7
Employees	7.0%	431	562	606	574	565

SUNEDISON INC   NYS: SUNE

13736 Riverport Drive, Suite 180   CEO: –
Maryland Heights, MO 63043   CFO: –
Phone: 314 770-7300   HR: –
Fax: –   FYE: December 31
Web: www.sunedison.com   Type: Public

SunEdison (formerly MEMC Electronic Materials) turns sun into power. The company not only makes solar modules polysilicon and silicon wafers used in solar panels it also designs makes installs and maintains solar installations for individuals and corporate customers. The company has 2.4 gigawatts of electricity-producing panels installed and a pipeline of 5.1 ggawatts. It has also begun generating electricity from solar power and selling that electricity to utility customers. The sale of silicon wafers and solar panels are becoming less of the company's business as it focuses on solar power. SunEdison spun off 20% of its silicon wafer fabrication business and part of its solar business.

	Annual Growth	12/10	12/11	12/12	12/13	12/14
Sales ($ mil.)	2.6%	2,239.2	2,715.5	2,529.9	2,007.6	2,484.4
Net income ($ mil.)	–	34.4	(1,536.0)	(150.6)	(586.7)	(1,180.4)
Market value ($ mil.)	14.7%	3,063.8	1,072.1	873.4	3,550.9	5,308.7
Employees	2.9%	6,480	6,840	56,680	6,358	7,260

SUNESIS PHARMACEUTICALS INC   NAS: SNSS

395 Oyster Point Boulevard, Suite 400   CEO: Dayton Misfeldt
South San Francisco, CA 94080   CFO: –
Phone: 650 266-3500   HR: –
Fax: –   FYE: December 31
Web: www.sunesis.com   Type: Public

Sunesis builds drugs in miniature first before it builds them in full scale. The biotech firm's method involves building small drug fragments then examining their protein-binding ability and potential for development. Once a fragment shows potential Sunesis then builds a larger therapeutic compound based upon its model. Its drug candidates target various forms of cancer. Its lead candidate Vosaroxin (SNS-595) is in clinical trials to evaluate its effect on ovarian cancer and acute myeloid leukemia. Other candidates are being studied for treatment of solid tumors and other forms of cancer both independently and through partnerships. Milestone payments from those partnerships are Sunesis' only revenue to date.

	Annual Growth	12/14	12/15	12/16	12/17	12/18
Sales ($ mil.)	(54.9%)	5.7	3.1	2.5	0.7	0.2
Net income ($ mil.)	–	(43.0)	(36.7)	(38.0)	(35.5)	(26.6)
Market value ($ mil.)	(36.4%)	95.6	33.6	135.7	138.3	15.6
Employees	(7.1%)	39	38	37	34	29

SUNFLOWER ELECTRIC POWER CORPORATION

301 W 13TH ST   CEO: –
HAYS, KS 676013087   CFO: H Davis Rooney
Phone: 785-628-2845   HR: –
Fax: –   FYE: December 31
Web: www.sunflower.net   Type: Private

Rural Kansans bloom under the light provided by Sunflower Electric Power an electricity generation and transmission cooperative. The utility has interests in six fossil-fueled generation facilities (600 MW of capacity) and operates a more-than-1150-mile transmission system with 76 substations. Sunflower Electric Power provides electricity to its owners six member distribution cooperatives which collectively have more than 51000 customers in western Kansas; it also indirectly serves a further 10000 meters as wholesale power suppliers to regional cities and towns.

	Annual Growth	12/06	12/07	12/08	12/09	12/10
Sales ($ mil.)	(4.1%)	–	–	232.7	195.2	213.8
Net income ($ mil.)	26.0%	–	–	13.8	16.0	21.8
Market value ($ mil.)	–	–	–	–	–	–
Employees	–	–	–	–	–	215

SUNGARD AVAILABILITY SERVICES LP

680 E. Swedesford Rd.   CEO: Michael K Robinson
Wayne PA 19087   CFO: Terrence J Anderson
Phone: 610-878-2644   HR: Allie Hogman
Fax: 610-225-1132   FYE: December 31
Web: www.sungardas.com   Type: Subsidiary

SunGard Availability Services wants to be every big company's virtual IT department. The company provides managed network hosting business continuity and related consulting services via data centers located throughout the US and Europe (primarily in the UK). Areas of specialty include online backup data co-location managed hosting and disaster recovery. SunGard Availability Services serves more than 9000 clients in a wide range of industries including energy financial services healthcare and manufacturing. Its customers include Reply! Inc. and First Citizens Bank. The company is a subsidiary of software and IT services provider SunGard Data Systems.

SUNGARD DATA SYSTEMS INC.

680 E. Swedesford Rd.   CEO: Russell P Fradin
Wayne PA 19087-1586   CFO: Charles J Neral
Phone: 484-582-2000   HR: –
Fax: 610-225-1120   FYE: December 31
Web: www.sungard.com   Type: Private

Nearly every top financial services company under the sun relies on this company's data systems. A majority of Nasdaq trades pass through SunGard's investment support systems which banks stock exchanges mutual funds insurance companies governments and others use for transaction processing asset management securities and commodities trading and investment accounting. This business is part of SunGard's Financial Systems business segment which serves the 25 largest global financial services firms. Its other primary segments Public Sector and Availability Services provide software and business continuity managed IT and professional services to datacentric businesses worldwide.

SUNGARD PUBLIC SECTOR INC.

1000 Business Center Dr.
Lake Mary FL 32746
Phone: 407-304-3235
Fax: 407-304-1005
Web: www.sungardps.com

CEO: –
CFO: –
HR: –
FYE: December 31
Type: Subsidiary

Whether it's in your school your town your state or your favorite charity SunGard Public Sector thrives on bureaucracy. The company provides enterprise resource planning (ERP) and administrative software for public-sector organizations ranging from utility companies and schools to public safety departments and government agencies. Its applications include tools for state and local governments law enforcement agencies and utility companies. The company also offers consulting and other IT services. SunGard Public Sector a unit of financial services software maker SunGard Data Systems does business primarily in the US.

SUNKIST GROWERS, INC.

27770 ENTERTAINMENT DR
VALENCIA, CA 913551092
Phone: 661-290-8900
Fax: –
Web: www.sunkist.com

CEO: Russell Hanlin II
CFO: Richard G French
HR: Diane P Johnson
FYE: October 31
Type: Private

Sunkist Growers is one business that is least susceptible to an outbreak of scurvy among its employees. America's oldest continually operating citrus cooperative the company is owned by California and Arizona citrus growers who farm some 300000 acres of citrus trees. Sunkist offers traditional and organic fresh oranges lemons limes grapefruit and tangerines worldwide. The co-op which operates some 20 packing facilities also makes juice and cut fruit packaged in jars. Fruit that doesn't meet fresh market standards is turned into oils and peels for use in food products made by other manufacturers. Sunkist's customers include food retailers and manufacturers and foodservice providers worldwide.

	Annual Growth	10/14	10/15	10/16	10/17	10/18
Sales ($ mil.)	5.7%	–	1,150.4	1,207.9	1,299.2	1,359.8
Net income ($ mil.)	(20.9%)	–	5.5	7.0	9.0	2.7
Market value ($ mil.)	–	–	–	–	–	–
Employees	–	–	–	–	–	500

SUNLINK HEALTH SYSTEMS INC   ASE: SSY

900 Circle 75 Parkway, Suite 1120
Atlanta, GA 30339
Phone: 770 933-7000
Fax: –
Web: www.sunlinkhealth.com

CEO: Robert M. Thornton
CFO: Mark J. Stockslager
HR: –
FYE: June 30
Type: Public

SunLink Health Systems is hoping to shine brightly in the health care business through the management of community hospitals. Through its subsidiaries the firm operates five community hospitals with a total of more than 280 beds in Alabama Georgia Mississippi and Missouri. Each hospital is the only acute care facility in its service area. The company also operates two nursing facilities that have a collective bed count of about 170 beds to serve the geographical areas surrounding the hospitals. SunLink also operates a home health agency and SunLink ScriptsRx a specialty pharmacy business.

	Annual Growth	06/15	06/16	06/17	06/18	06/19
Sales ($ mil.)	(16.0%)	91.8	63.4	53.3	52.9	45.6
Net income ($ mil.)	–	0.2	(14.1)	2.7	(1.6)	(1.8)
Market value ($ mil.)	(0.7%)	10.6	3.5	11.6	9.0	10.3
Employees	–	–	–	–	–	–

SUNOCO LP   NYS: SUN

8111 Westchester Drive, Suite 400
Dallas, TX 75225
Phone: 214 981-0700
Fax: –
Web: www.sunocolp.com

CEO: Joseph Kim
CFO: Thomas R Miller
HR: –
FYE: December 31
Type: Public

Sunoco LP (formerly Susser Petroleum Partners) pairs with its parent to proffer petroleum. It operates about 900 convenience stores and retail fuel sites and distributes motor fuel to convenience stores independent dealers commercial customers and distributors in more than 30 US states at 6800 sites both directly and through its 32% stake in in Sunoco LLC owned in partnership with Energy Transfer Partners (ETP). Energy Transfer Equity owns 's general partner and incentive distribution rights. ETP owns a 38.4% limited partner interest in the company. In 2016 Sunoco LP bought the fuels business of Emerge Energy Services LP for $167.7 million.In 2017 Japan-based Seven & i Holdings agreed to buy 1100 convenience stores and gas stations from Sunoco LP for about $3.3 billion.

	Annual Growth	12/14	12/15	12/16	12/17	12/18
Sales ($ mil.)	73.2%	1,889.8	16,935.3	15,698.0	11,723.0	16,994.0
Net income ($ mil.)	–	35.3	237.4	(406.0)	149.0	(207.0)
Market value ($ mil.)	(14.0%)	4,931.0	3,924.4	2,664.1	2,813.8	2,693.9
Employees	–	–	–	–	–	3,622

SUNOVION PHARMACEUTICALS INC.

84 Waterford Dr.
Marlborough MA 01752
Phone: 508-481-6700
Fax: 508-357-7499
Web: www.sunovion.com

CEO: Hiroshi Nomura
CFO: –
HR: –
FYE: December 31
Type: Subsidiary

Helping people breathe easy and sleep properly are the core of Sunovion. The company focuses its drug development efforts in two main therapeutic categories: respiratory and central nervous system (CNS) disorders. Among its marketed products are asthma drug Xopenex insomnia therapy Lunesta schizophrenia treatment Latuda and chronic obstructive pulmonary disease (COPD) treatment Brovana. Sunovion markets its products to primary care physicians and some specialists in the US. Sunovion is a subsidiary of Japanese firm Dainippon Sumitomo Pharma (DSP).

SUNPOWER CORP   NMS: SPWR

77 Rio Robles
San Jose, CA 95134
Phone: 408 240-5500
Fax: –
Web: www.sunpower.com

CEO: Thomas H. (Tom) Werner
CFO: Charles D. (Chuck) Boynton
HR: –
FYE: December 30
Type: Public

SunPower is all about being a stellar provider of solar energy. The company makes solar panels and systems under the SunPower Equinox and Helix brands among others. Its solar panel brands are the P-Series and A-Series. SunPower sells its products to dealers distributors and system integrators for use by residential commercial government and utility customers around the world. The company is the top provider of solar technologies for the commercial market in the US. While the company has offices across the globe nearly 70% of revenue comes from customers in the US. SunPower was founded in 1985 and French energy company TOTAL SA bought a majority interest in 2011.

	Annual Growth	12/14*	01/16	01/17*	12/17	12/18
Sales ($ mil.)	(13.1%)	3,027.3	1,576.5	2,559.6	1,871.8	1,726.1
Net income ($ mil.)	–	245.9	(187.0)	(471.1)	(851.2)	(811.1)
Market value ($ mil.)	(33.8%)	3,715.9	4,236.8	933.2	1,190.1	714.4
Employees	(2.1%)	7,188	8,309	8,902	7,306	6,600

*Fiscal year change

SUNRISE MEDICAL INC.

7477 E. Dry Creek Pkwy.
Longmont CO 80503
Phone: 303-218-4600
Fax: 303-218-4590
Web: www.sunrisemedical.com

CEO: Thomas Julius Rossnagel
CFO: –
HR: –
FYE: June 30
Type: Private

Sunrise Medical wants its customers to greet the day on a roll. The company manufactures and supplies wheelchairs and wheelchair accessories and replacement parts. Its Quickie wheelchairs range from manual to motorized adult to child-sized and from everyday use to sports models for athletes. Its products are targeted for use in both institutional and home use. Sunrise Medical also makes Jay brand cushions and wheelchair backs. The company's A.R.T. division designs and manufactures custom configured seating and positioning equipment. Sunrise Medical markets its products in about 100 countries around the globe through an inside sales force and through distributors.

SUNSHINE SILVER MINES CORPORATION

370 17th Street Ste. 3800
Denver CO 80202
Phone: 303-784-5350
Fax: 310-214-0075
Web: www.emmausmedical.com

CEO: Stephen Orr
CFO: Roger Johnson
HR: –
FYE: December 31
Type: Private

Mining is a tight race and Sunshine Silver Mines intends to take home the silver metal. The precious metals exploration and development company is trying to become a major silver producer initially through two main projects: the Sunshine Mine in Idaho (a previously prolific producing mine) and Los Gatos in Mexico (a relatively new prospecting area). In total it owns or controls about 20 exploration properties in the US and Mexico. Formed in early 2011 after its predecessor converted from a limited liability company to a Delaware corporation Sunshine Silver Mines filed to go public mid-year in an IPO worth about $250 million.

SUNRISE SENIOR LIVING INC.   NYSE: SRZ

7900 Westpark Drive
McLean VA 22102
Phone: 703-273-7500
Fax: 703-744-1601
Web: www.sunriseseniorliving.com/

CEO: Mark S Ordan
CFO: Marc Richards
HR: –
FYE: December 31
Type: Public

From sunrise to sunset Sunrise Senior Living helps the elderly make the most of life. A top senior living services provider Sunrise operates some 300 assisted living communities with some 30000 units across the US and into Canada and the UK. Sunrise owns outright or has an interest in half of the facilities and manages the rest for third parties under long-term contracts. The company's communities offer a range of care for their residents; some provide opportunities for independent living while others offer special care for Alzheimer's patients or skilled nursing care. Sunrise is being acquired by Health Care REIT.

SUNSTONE HOTEL INVESTORS INC.   NYSE: SHO

120 Vantis Ste. 350
Aliso Viejo CA 92656
Phone: 949-330-4000
Fax: 424-288-2900
Web: www.caa.com

CEO: Ken Cruse
CFO: Jon D Kline
HR: –
FYE: December 31
Type: Public

Sunstone Hotel Investors shines brightly in the hospitality investment sector. The real estate investment trust (REIT) invests in develops and renovates mostly upscale and upper-upscale hotels in major markets around the US. The company owns more than 30 hotels with some 13000 rooms in more than a dozen states. Most of Sunstone Hotel Investors' properties are located in Southern California and have affiliations with such franchises as Hilton Worldwide Hyatt Marriott and Starwood. Sunstone's hotels are managed by third parties; a division of Interstate Hotels & Resorts operates about half of the properties.

SUNRUN INSTALLATION SERVICES INC.

775 FIERO LN STE 200
SAN LUIS OBISPO, CA 934017904
Phone: 415-580-6900
Fax: –
Web: www.sunrun.com

CEO: Lynn Jurich
CFO: Robert Komin Jr
HR: –
FYE: December 31
Type: Private

Sunrun Installation Services (formerly REC Solar) helps its customers bid farewell to fossil fuel-burning power dependence. The company designs and installs solar electric systems for more than 11000 residential customers in seven US states including Arizona California Colorado Hawaii and New Jersey. The company primarily makes rooftop panel displays for residential customers. REC Solar uses solar panels manufactured by Kyocera Mitsubishi Sanyo and Sharp and components by Satcon SMA Solar Technology and Xantrex. In 2014 Sunrun acquired REC Solar's residential division and renamed the company.

SUNSWEET GROWERS INC.

901 N WALTON AVE
YUBA CITY, CA 959939370
Phone: 800-417-2253
Fax: –
Web: www.sunsweet.com

CEO: –
CFO: –
HR: Sharon Braun
FYE: July 31
Type: Private

Being all dried up is a good thing at Sunsweet Growers. The more than 400 member/grower-owned cooperative processes and markets dried fruit. Sunsweet produces one-third of the world's prunes (it processes more than 50000 tons of prunes each year). Its other fruit products include prune and other juices as well as dried apples apricots dates cranberries blueberries mangoes peaches pears pineapples and more. Sunsweet which has gotten into dietary supplement beverages supplies its products to retail food and foodservice outlets worldwide. Sunsweet produces some 40000 cases of dried fruit products every day. The co-op was founded in 1917 as the California Prune and Apricot Growers Association.

	Annual Growth	04/03	04/04	04/05	04/06*	12/08
Sales ($ mil.)	420.8%	–	–	–	5.7	155.8
Net income ($ mil.)	–	–	–	–	1.4	(3.4)
Market value ($ mil.)	–	–	–	–	–	–
Employees	–	–	–	–	–	2,184

*Fiscal year change

	Annual Growth	07/13	07/14	07/15	07/16	07/17
Sales ($ mil.)	(2.2%)	–	261.8	277.8	301.8	244.9
Net income ($ mil.)	(8.2%)	–	81.9	103.3	112.5	63.3
Market value ($ mil.)	–	–	–	–	–	–
Employees	–	–	–	–	–	700

SUNTORY INTERNATIONAL CORP.

4141 PARKLAKE AVE STE 600
RALEIGH, NC 276122380
Phone: 917-756-2747
Fax: -

CEO: -
CFO: Tsutomu Santoki
HR: -
FYE: December 31
Type: Private

Suntory USA established in the 1960s on the other side of the globe from its parent Japanese trading giant Suntory Holdings Limited imports Suntory products to the US market from its New York headquarters. Well-known offerings include wine beer and distilled spirits such as Yamazaki Single Malt Whisky and Zen Green Tea and Midori Melon liqueurs. Other operations handled by Suntory USA include a soft drink bottling business (Pepsi Bottling Ventures) a winery various restaurants and its parent's bottled water division Suntory Water Group once the second-largest bottled water producer in the US. Altogether Suntory USA comprises 17 companies contributing 4% of its parent's 2013 revenue.

	Annual Growth	12/06	12/07	12/08	12/09	12/10
Sales ($ mil.)	5928.4%	-	-	-	13.1	790.4
Net income ($ mil.)	1002.2%	-	-	-	5.5	60.7
Market value ($ mil.)	-	-	-	-	-	-
Employees						2,199

SUNTRUST BANKS INC   NYS: STI

303 Peachtree Street, N.E.
Atlanta, GA 30308
Phone: 800 786-8787
Fax: -
Web: www.suntrust.com

CEO: -
CFO: -
HR: -
FYE: December 31
Type: Public

Through its flagship SunTrust Bank subsidiary SunTrust Banks operates some 1300 branches in about a dozen southeastern and mid-Atlantic states. With total assets of some $200 billion and total deposits of over $160 billion the bank offers standard retail and commercial services such as credit deposit and investment services. SunTrust also operates subsidiaries that offer mortgage wealth and investment management insurance investment banking and brokerage services. The namesake of the Atlanta Braves? SunTrust baseball park the company was also behind the original "Coke float" when it underwrote the public flotation of Coca-Cola in the 1920s and was one of the soda company's largest shareholders. In February 2019 SunTrust agreed to merge with financial services holding company BB&T in a $66 billion deal.

	Annual Growth	12/13	12/14	12/15	12/16	12/17
Assets ($ mil.)	4.1%	175,335.0	190,328.0	190,817.0	204,875.0	205,962.0
Net income ($ mil.)	14.0%	1,344.0	1,774.0	1,933.0	1,878.0	2,273.0
Market value ($ mil.)	15.1%	17,335.0	19,732.0	20,174.7	25,830.6	30,417.4
Employees	(2.5%)	26,281	24,638	24,043	24,375	23,785

SUNVALLEY SOLAR INC (NV)   NBB: SSOL

398 Lemon Creek Drive, Suite A
Walnut, CA 91789
Phone: 909 598-0618
Fax: -

CEO: Zhijian James Zhang
CFO: Mandy Chung
HR: -
FYE: December 31
Type: Public

Homes and businesses looking to go eco turn to companies like Sunvalley Solar. Sunvalley Solar offers solar power system design installation and maintenance services to owners builders and architecture firms in the residential commercial and government sectors primarily in California. The company also distributes solar equipment including solar panels inverters and related goods from such manufacturers as Canadian Solar and China Electric Equipment Group (CEEG). A portion of Sunvalley Solar's resources are spent on solar technology research and development. Founded in 2007 Sunvalley Solar was the first Chinese-American owned solar installation company in Southern California.

	Annual Growth	12/13	12/14	12/15	12/16	12/17
Sales ($ mil.)	8.7%	4.1	3.3	5.8	8.5	5.7
Net income ($ mil.)		0.8	(1.3)	0.2	(1.0)	(1.8)
Market value ($ mil.)	21.8%	0.5	0.4	0.7	2.0	1.1
Employees	30.6%	11	11	11	32	32

SUPER CENTER CONCEPTS INC.

15510 Carmenita Rd.
Santa Fe Springs CA 90670
Phone: 562-345-9000
Fax: +49-9342-806-150
Web: www.k-m.de

CEO: Mimi R Song
CFO:
HR: Eunice Min
FYE: December 31
Type: Private

Super Center Concepts is big on superlatives as well as groceries. One of the largest independently-owned grocery supercenter chains in the Los Angeles metropolitan area the company operates about 40 outlets under the Superior Grocers banner. The regional grocery chain has continued to expand in spite of operating in the super competitive supercenter market where it competes with national chains including Wal-Mart and Costco Wholesale. The stores sell name brand and private label merchandise in the traditional grocery departments (produce meat bakery) and offer services such as check cashing and money orders. The first Superior Super Warehouse opened in Los Angeles in 1981.

SUPER MICRO COMPUTER INC   NMS: SMCI

980 Rock Avenue
San Jose, CA 95131
Phone: 408 503-8000
Fax: -
Web: www.supermicro.com

CEO: Charles Liang
CFO: Howard Hideshima
HR: -
FYE: June 30
Type: Public

Super Micro Computer manufactures high-performance server products based on open standard components (including Intel AMD and NVIDIA processors). Its nearly 5000 offerings include motherboards blade servers rackmounts GPU systems chassis and Ethernet switches and network adaptors. The company also sells a host of subsystems and accessories. Super Micro markets its products sold directly and through distributors and resellers to customers in some 100 countries; about 40% of its sales are generated outside the US. Manufacturing is handled in-house and through contractors.

	Annual Growth	06/15	06/16	06/17	06/18	06/19
Sales ($ mil.)	15.1%	1,991.2	2,215.6	2,484.9	3,360.5	3,500.4
Net income ($ mil.)	(8.3%)	101.9	72.0	66.9	46.2	71.9
Market value ($ mil.)	(10.1%)	1,477.7	1,241.4	1,231.4	1,181.5	966.7
Employees	12.6%	2,285	2,699	2,996	3,266	3,670

SUPERCONDUCTOR TECHNOLOGIES INC   NAS: SCON

9101 Wall Street, Suite 1300
Austin, TX 78754
Phone: 512 334-8900
Fax: -
Web: www.suptech.com

CEO: Jeffrey A Quiram
CFO: William J Buchanan
HR: -
FYE: December 31
Type: Public

Superconductor Technologies Inc. (STI) can cool even the most heated conversation. The company uses high-temperature superconducting (HTS) technology in its line of communications products which combine low-noise amplifiers and filters are designed to improve the quality of radio-frequency (RF) transmissions between cellular base stations and mobile devices in wireless networks. It also makes cryogenic cooling devices used to cool HTS materials. STI relies on government contracts to fund its R&D operations; on the commercial side the company serves such top wireless network operators as AT&T Verizon Wireless Sprint Nextel and T-Mobile.

	Annual Growth	12/14	12/15	12/16	12/17	12/18
Sales ($ mil.)	25.3%	0.6	0.2	0.1	0.4	1.6
Net income ($ mil.)		(8.3)	(8.6)	(11.1)	(9.5)	(8.1)
Market value ($ mil.)	(17.6%)	9.1	0.7	4.0	3.6	4.2
Employees	(13.7%)	45	25	23	22	25

SUPERIOR BULK LOGISTICS, INC.

711 JORIE BLVD STE 101N
OAK BROOK, IL 605232285
Phone: 630-573-2555
Fax: –
Web: www.superiorbulklogistics.com

CEO: William W Stone
CFO: Timothy McCann
HR: –
FYE: December 31
Type: Private

Superior Bulk Logistics through subsidiaries Superior Carriers and Carry Transit hauls liquid and dry bulk cargo including both chemical and food-grade products. Overall the trucking units of Superior Bulk Logistics operate a fleet of some 875 tractors and 2000 trailers. The company's SuperFlo unit provides transloading services — the transfer of cargo between railcars and trucks. Superior Bulk Logistics' Sanicare Wash Systems unit cleans tank truck trailers and other bulk containers used for food products. Superior Bulk Logistics offers service between Mexico and the US and Canada through a partnership with Transpormex a division of Grupo Dexel.

	Annual Growth	12/04	12/05	12/06	12/07	12/09
Sales ($ mil.)	(5.1%)	–	–	220.5	235.0	188.2
Net income ($ mil.)	(26.0%)	–	–	5.1	7.2	2.0
Market value ($ mil.)	–	–	–	–	–	–
Employees	–	–	–	–	–	1,160

SUPERIOR ENERGY SERVICES, INC.   NYS: SPN

1001 Louisiana Street, Suite 2900
Houston, TX 77002
Phone: 713 654-2200
Fax: –
Web: www.superiorenergy.com

CEO: David D. Dunlap
CFO: Robert S. Taylor
HR: –
FYE: December 31
Type: Public

Superior Energy Services has a healthy ego when it comes to describing its specialized oil field activities. The company provides drilling completion and production-related services to major national and independent oil and natural gas companies operating in the Gulf of Mexico on the US mainland and internationally. Its international operations extend into Europe the Middle East Latin America Asia/Pacific and Africa. Superior develops specialized tools and technologies for drilling such as connecting iron drill pipe stabilizers and hole openers pressure control equipment and tubular goods. Onshore completion services include pressure pumping and fluid handling and well servicing rigs.

	Annual Growth	12/14	12/15	12/16	12/17	12/18
Sales ($ mil.)	(17.3%)	4,556.6	2,774.6	1,450.0	1,874.1	2,130.3
Net income ($ mil.)	–	257.8	(1,854.7)	(886.9)	(205.9)	(858.1)
Market value ($ mil.)	–	–	–	–	–	–
Employees	(17.6%)	14,300	8,300	6,400	6,400	6,600

SUPERIOR GROUP OF COMPANIES INC   NMS: SGC

10055 Seminole Boulevard
Seminole, FL 33772-2539
Phone: 727 397-9611
Fax: –
Web: www.superiorgroupofcompanies.com

CEO: Michael Benstock
CFO: Andrew D. Demott
HR: –
FYE: December 31
Type: Public

Superior Uniform Group works to keep its business all sewn up. The company makes work clothing and accessories for US employees in several industries. The apparel firm designs makes and markets uniforms for employees in the medical and health fields as well as those who work in hotels fast food joints and other restaurants and public safety industrial and commercial markets. About half of its products are sold under the Fashion Seal brand. The company also makes and distributes specialty labels such as Martin's Worklon Blade and UniVogue. Chairman Gerald Benstock and his son CEO Michael run company which began as Superior Surgical Mfg. Co. in 1920.

	Annual Growth	12/14	12/15	12/16	12/17	12/18
Sales ($ mil.)	15.3%	196.2	210.3	252.6	266.8	346.4
Net income ($ mil.)	10.6%	11.3	13.1	14.6	15.0	17.0
Market value ($ mil.)	(12.0%)	446.5	258.1	298.3	406.1	268.3
Employees	28.8%	1,055	1,278	1,632	2,280	2,906

SUPERIOR INDUSTRIES INTERNATIONAL, INC.   NYS: SUP

26600 Telegraph Road, Suite 400
Southfield, MI 48033
Phone: 248 352-7300
Fax: 818 780-3500
Web: www.supind.com

CEO: Donald J. (Don) Stebbins
CFO: Nadeem Moiz
HR: –
FYE: December 31
Type: Public

Superior Industries International is one of the world's largest makers of cast aluminum wheels for passenger cars and light trucks holding the #1 position in North America. The company has the capacity to make approximately 21 million wheels annually at its nine manufacturing facilities located in Arkansas Mexico Poland and Germany. It sells to the ten largest original equipment manufacturers (OEMs) in the world however sales to Ford General Motors Volkswagen and Toyota represent more than 55% of net sales. Wheels are primarily sold for factory installation but in Europe Superior sells aftermarket brands under the ATS RIAL ALUTEC and ANZIO brands. North America represents about 55% of net sales while Europe accounts for about 45%.

	Annual Growth	12/14	12/15	12/16	12/17	12/18
Sales ($ mil.)	19.1%	745.4	727.9	732.7	1,108.1	1,501.8
Net income ($ mil.)	31.0%	8.8	23.9	41.4	(6.2)	26.0
Market value ($ mil.)	(29.8%)	495.1	472.1	671.8	371.5	120.3
Employees	28.8%	3,000	3,050	4,189	8,150	8,260

SUPERIOR OIL COMPANY INC

1402 N CAPITOL AVE # 100
INDIANAPOLIS, IN 462022375
Phone: 317-781-4400
Fax: –
Web: www.superioroil.com

CEO: Robert W Andersen
CFO: Douglas P Stewart
HR: –
FYE: December 31
Type: Private

Despite the name Superior Oil actually distributes industrial products and provides chemical and waste services. Superior's solvents and chemicals division supplies manufacturers of paints and coatings pharmaceuticals fabricated metal products and adhesives. The fiberglass and resins unit sells to clients that make products ranging from parts for recreational vehicles to bathtubs and showers. Superior Oil also provides blending solvent reclamation and hazardous waste removal services. The company has nine stocking facilities and a fleet of trucks trailers and tankers. The company is owned by members of its management team.

	Annual Growth	12/13	12/14	12/15	12/16	12/17
Sales ($ mil.)	–	–	0.0	221.2	200.0	200.0
Net income ($ mil.)	–	–	0.0	0.0	7.9	7.9
Market value ($ mil.)	–	–	–	–	–	–
Employees	–	–	–	–	–	300

SUPERNUS PHARMACEUTICALS INC   NMS: SUPN

1550 East Gude Drive
Rockville, MD 20850
Phone: 301 838-2500
Fax: –
Web: www.supernus.com

CEO: Jack A. Khattar
CFO: Gregory S. Patrick
HR: –
FYE: December 31
Type: Public

Supernus Pharmaceuticals wouldn't mind being a drug-maker superhero of sorts to epileptics. As a specialty pharmaceutical company Supernus develops treatments for epilepsy and other central nervous system disorders. It has two marketed products for treating epilepsy: Oxtellar XR and Trokendi XR. In addition it is developing a number of candidates to treat such ailments as attention deficit hyperactivity disorder (ADHD) impulsive aggression in patients with ADHD autism bipolar disorder schizophrenia depression and dementia. The company utilizes third-party commercial manufacturing organizations (CMOs) for all of its manufacturing.

	Annual Growth	12/14	12/15	12/16	12/17	12/18
Sales ($ mil.)	35.3%	122.0	144.4	215.0	302.2	408.9
Net income ($ mil.)	53.7%	19.9	14.0	91.2	57.3	111.0
Market value ($ mil.)	41.4%	434.2	703.1	1,321.0	2,084.8	1,738.0
Employees	9.7%	309	344	363	422	448

SUPERTEX, INC.
NMS: SUPX

1235 Bordeaux Drive
Sunnyvale, CA 94089
Phone: 408 222-8888
Fax: –
Web: www.supertex.com

CEO: –
CFO: –
HR: –
FYE: March 30
Type: Public

In many ways Supertex is a superhero for manufacturers needing integrated circuits (ICs). The company designs and manufactures high-voltage analog and mixed-signal integrated circuits (ICs) and transistors. Its ICs are used in a variety of applications including automated test equipment industrial electronics flat-panel TV displays medical ultrasound imaging equipment printers and telecommunications gear. Supertex touts its proprietary technologies as enabling it to combine low power consumption with high-voltage output on a single chip. About two-thirds of Supertex's sales come from customers outside the US more than half from Asia/Pacific.

	Annual Growth	03/09*	04/10	04/11*	03/12	03/13
Sales ($ mil.)	(6.2%)	78.8	66.7	83.2	65.5	61.0
Net income ($ mil.)	(23.7%)	12.5	5.1	12.3	4.7	4.2
Market value ($ mil.)	(2.4%)	281.6	319.2	254.1	208.3	256.0
Employees	(1.6%)	352	350	373	361	330

*Fiscal year change

SUPERVALU INC
NYS: SVU

11840 Valley View Road
Eden Prairie, MN 55344
Phone: 952 828-4000
Fax: –
Web: www.supervalu.com

CEO: Mark Gross
CFO: Rob N Woseth
HR: –
FYE: February 25
Type: Public

SUPERVALU understands the lure of a good deal. The company offers wholesale grocery distribution and logistics services to about 1900 independent retailers and more than 180 military commissaries in the US and overseas. It supplies brand-name and private-label goods in every price range. SUPERVALU's retail operations include more than 200 regional grocery stores under the Cub Foods Shoppers Food & Pharmacy Shop 'n Save Farm Fresh Hornbachers and Rainbow banners. All told the company covers about 40 US states from nearly 20 distribution centers. In 2016 the company sold its Save-A-Lot grocery stores to investment firm Onex Corp. for $1.36 billion in cash.

	Annual Growth	02/13	02/14	02/15	02/16	02/17
Sales ($ mil.)	(7.6%)	17,097.0	17,155.0	17,820.0	17,529.0	12,480.0
Net income ($ mil.)	—	(1,466.0)	182.0	192.0	178.0	650.0
Market value ($ mil.)	0.5%	147.4	233.5	378.3	188.7	150.1
Employees	(4.6%)	35,000	35,800	38,500	38,000	29,000

SUPPORT.COM INC
NAS: SPRT

1521 Concord Pike (US 202), Suite 301
Wilmington, DE 19803
Phone: 650 556-9440
Fax: –
Web: www.support.com

CEO: Richard A Bloom
CFO: –
HR: –
FYE: December 31
Type: Public

Support.com wants to be a pillar of tech support. The company's cloud-based Nexus platform proactively identifies and repairs hardware and software problems reducing the need for technical support staffing. It also specializes in phone and Web support for a wide variety of technology issues related to computer security data recovery networking file management and software installation. Support.com serves consumers and small businesses with its offerings available through its website and through partners such as retailers broadband providers and anti-virus software providers. Nearly all sales come from customers in the Americas.

	Annual Growth	12/14	12/15	12/16	12/17	12/18
Sales ($ mil.)	(4.3%)	83.0	77.3	61.7	60.1	69.5
Net income ($ mil.)	—	(3.5)	(27.0)	(16.0)	(1.5)	(9.1)
Market value ($ mil.)	3.9%	40.0	19.1	16.3	45.9	46.6
Employees	0.1%	2,023	1,695	1,525	1,776	2,035

SUREWEST COMMUNICATIONS
NASDAQ: SURW

8150 Industrial Ave. Bldg. A
Roseville CA 95678
Phone: 916-786-6141
Fax: 916-786-7170
Web: www.surewest.com

CEO: Steven C Oldham
CFO: Steven L Childers
HR: –
FYE: December 31
Type: Public

SureWest Communications wants to be a sure bet for communications in Northern California and beyond. The company's broadband unit provides Internet access TV data and voice service to about 110000 residential customers and about 8000 business clients in the Sacramento California and Kansas City area as well as network access and exchange services to other carriers. SureWest's telecommunications segment (which includes subsidiary SureWest Telephone) is the company's incumbent local and long-distance business. In 2012 the company was acquired by Consolidated Communications Holdings in a cash and stock transaction valued at around $324 million excluding debt.

SURGE COMPONENTS INC
NBB: SPRS

95 East Jefryn Boulevard
Deer Park, NY 11729
Phone: 631 595-1818
Fax: 631 595-1283
Web: www.surgecomponents.com

CEO: Ira Levy
CFO: Ira Levy
HR: –
FYE: November 30
Type: Public

Surge Components offers a wave of components for use in all sorts of electrical and electronic gear. The company distributes capacitors and other electronic components such as diodes semiconductor rectifiers and transistors. Most of its clients are manufacturers. The company's Challenge/Surge subsidiary (also known as Challenge Electronics) deals in electronic components as a broker and distributor. Surge represents Lelon Electronics a Taiwanese manufacturer of aluminum electrolytic capacitors in North America. Surge Components was established in 1981.

	Annual Growth	11/14	11/15	11/16	11/17	11/18
Sales ($ mil.)	4.4%	27.2	29.7	29.6	29.8	32.4
Net income ($ mil.)	45.4%	0.4	0.9	(0.6)	0.4	2.0
Market value ($ mil.)	1.0%	4.7	4.0	5.4	5.0	4.9
Employees	5.6%	29	33	39	38	36

SURGE GLOBAL ENERGY INC
NBB: SRGG

75-153 Merle Drive, Suite B
Palm Desert, CA 92211
Phone: 800 284-3898
Fax: 786 923-0963
Web: www.surgeglobalenergy.com

CEO: Clark Morton
CFO: E Jamie Schloss
HR: –
FYE: December 31
Type: Public

Surge Global Energy has the urge to acquire crude oil and natural gas properties in the US and Canada. The company's portfolio includes a well in Wyoming which it is drilling for commercial production of oil and gas and the Green Springs Prospect in Nevada which it plans to tap. Surge also invests in businesses engaged in alternative fuel technologies such as biodiesel developer 11 Good Energy. Other investments include minority stakes in two Alberta-based companies Andora Energy and North Peace Energy. Surge divested its interest in an Argentina project in 2008 to focus on its core North American operations and investments. Officers and board members as a group own about one-third of the company.

	Annual Growth	12/10	12/11	12/12	12/13	12/14
Sales ($ mil.)	–	0.0	0.0	–	0.0	0.0
Net income ($ mil.)	–	0.0	0.0	(1.7)	(0.9)	(0.9)
Market value ($ mil.)	–	0.0	0.0	0.1	1.2	1.5
Employees	(20.0%)	–	–	–	5	4

SURGLINE INTERNATIONAL INC.   OTC: CNUV

319 Clematis St. Ste. 703   CEO: –
West Palm Beach FL 33401   CFO: –
Phone: 561-514-9042   HR: –
Fax: 770-751-0543   FYE: July 31
Web: www.kidsii.com   Type: Public

Holding company SurgLine International owns SurgLine and Nuvo Solar Energy. SurgLine distributes medical and surgical products at a discount. It recently expanded that business with the 2012 acquisition of Eden Surgical Technologies which distributes trauma products and the creation of subsidiary SurgLine MDC Holdings which has been tasked with forming joint ventures with orthopedic surgeons to lower the costs of surgical implants. The company's other holding Nuvo Solar Energy is a development-stage company with patent pending solar and photovoltaic related technology. The company changed its name from China Nuvo Solar Energy to SurgLine International in 2012.

SURMODICS INC   NMS: SRDX

9924 West, 74th Street   CEO: Gary R. Maharaj
Eden Prairie, MN 55344   CFO: Andrew D. C. (Andy) LaFrence
Phone: 952 500-7000   HR: –
Fax: –   FYE: September 30
Web: www.surmodics.com   Type: Public

SurModics doesn't want to scratch the surface of the medical device market — it just wants to coat it with its own special agent. The company's medical device unit makes special coatings that make the devices easier to use less traumatic to the body and even more useful in delivering drugs to patients. For example it is developing drug-coated balloons designed to treat peripheral artery disease which causes narrowing of the arteries. SurModics' in vitro diagnostics (IVD) unit handles diagnostic test and research kits and products. Three scientists formed the company in 1979.

	Annual Growth	09/15	09/16	09/17	09/18	09/19
Sales ($ mil.)	12.8%	61.9	71.4	73.1	81.3	100.1
Net income ($ mil.)	(10.7%)	11.9	10.0	3.9	(4.5)	7.6
Market value ($ mil.)	20.3%	294.9	406.3	418.6	1,008.1	617.7
Employees	21.7%	168	219	257	338	369

SURREY BANCORP (NC)   NBB: SRYB

145 North Renfro Street, P.O. Box 1227   CEO: Edward C Ashby III
Mount Airy, NC 27030   CFO: –
Phone: 336 783-3900   HR: –
Fax: –   FYE: December 31
                                                   Type: Public

This surrey doesn't have fringe on top but it does have funds inside. Surrey Bancorp is the holding company for Surrey Bank & Trust which serves northwestern North Carolina's Surry County and neighboring portions of Virginia through about five offices and a lending center. The bank offers standard retail services including checking and savings accounts CDs IRAs and credit and debit cards. Surrey Bank & Trust writes mostly commercial and industrial loans (more than two-thirds of its portfolio) followed by residential mortgages (about 20%). Subsidiary SB&T Insurance sells property/casualty coverage. The bank offers investment services through a third-party provider UVEST which is part of LPL Financial.

	Annual Growth	12/14	12/15	12/16	12/17	12/18
Assets ($ mil.)	5.1%	253.2	257.8	277.1	300.5	309.2
Net income ($ mil.)	10.3%	3.4	3.1	3.6	3.0	5.1
Market value ($ mil.)	(0.3%)	59.3	47.5	47.1	55.8	58.6
Employees	0.0%	78	78	–	–	–

SUSQUEHANNA BANCSHARES, INC   NMS: SUSQ

26 North Cedar St.   CEO: –
Lititz, PA 17543   CFO: –
Phone: 717 626-4721   HR: –
Fax: –   FYE: December 31
Web: www.susquehanna.net   Type: Public

Susquehanna Bancshares which bears the name of the river that flows through the heart of its market area is the holding company for Susquehanna Bank. The bank serves individuals and regional businesses through more than 245 branches in south-central and southeastern Pennsylvania Maryland New Jersey and West Virginia. It offers standard services such as deposits loans and credit cards. Non-banking subsidiaries provide wealth management insurance brokerage and employee benefits and vehicle leasing. Loans secured by commercial and residential real estate account for more nearly 60% of the bank's portfolio. Susquehanna Bancshares boasts assets of some $18.5 billion.

	Annual Growth	12/09	12/10	12/11	12/12	12/13
Assets ($ mil.)	7.8%	13,689.3	13,954.1	14,974.8	18,037.7	18,473.5
Net income ($ mil.)	92.4%	12.7	31.8	54.9	141.2	173.7
Market value ($ mil.)	21.5%	1,103.6	1,813.7	1,570.1	1,963.6	2,405.7
Employees	2.7%	3,055	3,039	3,122	3,464	3,395

SUSSER HOLDINGS CORP   NYS: SUSS

4525 Ayers Street   CEO: –
Corpus Christi, TX 78415   CFO: –
Phone: 361 884-2463   HR: –
Fax: 361 884-2494   FYE: December 30
Web: www.susser.com   Type: Public

Stripes are in Circles are out at Susser Holdings. The company operates about 560 Stripes convenience stores in Texas New Mexico and Oklahoma. (The company's Circle K stores were converted to the Stripes name several years ago.) The chain offers restaurant service in about 360 of its stores primarily under its proprietary Laredo Taco Company (LTC) brand. LTC serves up breakfast and lunch tacos rotisserie chicken and other hot foods. Susser Holdings is the largest independent c-store operator and non-refining motor fuel distributor through Susser Petroleum in Texas. (Fuel accounts for more than 80% of total sales.) Founded by Sam J. Susser in 1938 the company is now run by his son.

	Annual Growth	12/08*	01/10	01/11	01/12*	12/12
Sales ($ mil.)	8.2%	4,239.9	3,307.3	3,930.6	5,194.2	5,818.1
Net income ($ mil.)	29.8%	16.5	2.1	0.8	47.5	46.7
Market value ($ mil.)	26.7%	281.1	182.4	294.0	480.2	724.6
Employees	7.3%	6,567	7,211	7,165	7,584	8,697

*Fiscal year change

SUTHERLAND GLOBAL SERVICES INC.

1160 Pittsford-Victor Rd.   CEO: Dilip R Vellodi
Pittsford NY 14534   CFO: Micheal Bartusek
Phone: 585-586-5757   HR: –
Fax: 585-784-2154   FYE: June 30
Web: www.sutherlandglobal.com   Type: Private

Sutherland Global Services is willing to do all the legwork when it comes to helping your business close a sale or complete a transaction. The company offers business-process outsourcing (BPO) services primarily for clients in the airline technology retail banking and finance and telecommunications industries. It provides outsourced customer acquisition and retention technical assistance sales support functions and back-office services from more than 30 centers in Bulgaria Canada Egypt India the Philippines Mexico Nicaragua the United Arab Emirates the UK and the US. Established in 1986 Sutherland also acts as a consultant to companies looking to improve their call center operations.

SUTRON CORP.

NAS: STRN

22400 Davis Drive
Sterling, VA 20164
Phone: 703 406-2800
Fax: –
Web: www.sutron.com

CEO: –
CFO: Glen E Goold
HR: –
FYE: December 31
Type: Public

Through its Hydromet unit and other segments Sutron makes equipment that collects and transmits water and weather data. The company also provides related hydrological services. Customers use Sutron products to manage water resources obtain early warning of potentially disastrous floods or storms and help hydropower plants operate as efficiently as possible. The company's largest customer is the US government. Other customers include state and local governments engineering companies and power companies. In 2012 it acquired meterological firm IPS Meteostar for $4.2 million. Sutron sells its products globally; customers outside the US account for about 40% of sales. CEO Raul McQuivey owns 19% of the company.

	Annual Growth	12/09	12/10	12/11	12/12	12/13
Sales ($ mil.)	6.9%	20.9	23.0	20.2	25.2	27.2
Net income ($ mil.)	(22.7%)	2.2	3.0	1.5	1.1	0.8
Market value ($ mil.)	(8.1%)	36.4	33.5	25.8	25.6	26.0
Employees	8.1%	90	92	89	127	123

SUTTER BAY HOSPITALS

633 FOLSOM ST FL 5
SAN FRANCISCO, CA 941073623
Phone: 415-600-6000
Fax: –
Web: www.sutterhealth.org

CEO: Jeff Gerard
CFO: –
HR: –
FYE: December 31
Type: Private

Sutter West Bay Hospitals (doing business as California Pacific Medical Center or CPMC) is a health care complex located in the heart of hospital-heavy San Francisco. The private not-for-profit center's four area campuses (California Davies Pacific and St. Luke's) offer acute and specialty care including obstetrics and gynecology cardiovascular services pediatrics neurosciences orthopedics and organ transplantation. With more than 1300 beds between its campuses the center also conducts professional education and biomedical clinical and behavioral research. CPMC is part of the West Bay Region division of the Sutter Health hospital system.

	Annual Growth	12/06	12/07	12/08	12/09	12/11
Sales ($ mil.)	24.9%	–	–	830.0	1,245.9	1,616.0
Net income ($ mil.)	(26.5%)	–	–	168.9	159.1	67.0
Market value ($ mil.)	–	–	–	–	–	–
Employees	–	–	–	–	–	3,597

SUTTER HEALTH

2200 RIVER PLAZA DR
SACRAMENTO, CA 958334134
Phone: 916-733-8800
Fax: –
Web: www.sutterhealth.org

CEO: Sarah Krevans
CFO: Robert D. (Bob) Reed
HR: –
FYE: December 31
Type: Private

Whether you drink too much in Wine Country hit some rough waters off the Marin Headlands or trip during a hike through the redwood forest it's likely Sutter Health is just a stone's throw away. The Northern California not-for-profit health care system is one of the nation's largest with more than 4250 acute care beds. After being formed through the merger of Sutter Health and California Healthcare System Sutter Health now caters to residents of more than 100 communities from the California Bay Area to the beaches of Hawaii. Its services are provided through affiliated doctors from a host of health care facilities including acute care hospitals home health networks and skilled nursing facilities.

	Annual Growth	12/14	12/15	12/16	12/17	12/18
Sales ($ mil.)	4.9%	–	10,998.0	11,873.0	12,444.0	12,697.0
Net income ($ mil.)	–	–	84.0	422.0	1,060.0	(447.0)
Market value ($ mil.)	–	–	–	–	–	–
Employees	–	–	–	–	–	48,000

SVB FINANCIAL GROUP

NMS: SIVB

3003 Tasman Drive
Santa Clara, CA 95054-1191
Phone: 408 654-7400
Fax: –
Web: www.svb.com

CEO: Gregory W. (Greg) Becker
CFO: Daniel Beck
HR: –
FYE: December 31
Type: Public

SVB Financial Group is the holding company for Silicon Valley Bank which serves emerging and established companies involved in technology life sciences and private equity and provides customized financing to entrepreneurs executives and investors in those industries. It also offers deposit accounts loans and international banking and plays matchmaker for young firms and private investors. SVB also provides investment advisory brokerage and asset management services and markets credit and banking services to wealthy individuals. Founded in 1983 SVB has $60 billion in assets and holds $29 billion in deposits.

	Annual Growth	12/14	12/15	12/16	12/17	12/18
Assets ($ mil.)	9.7%	39,344.6	44,686.7	44,683.7	51,214.5	56,928.0
Net income ($ mil.)	38.6%	263.9	343.9	382.7	490.5	973.8
Market value ($ mil.)	13.1%	6,103.7	6,252.5	9,027.0	12,293.1	9,987.2
Employees	10.9%	1,914	2,089	2,311	2,438	2,900

SWANK INC.

PINK SHEETS: SNKI

90 Park Ave. 13th Fl.
New York NY 10016
Phone: 212-867-2600
Fax: 212-370-1039
Web: www.swankinc.com

CEO: John A Tulin
CFO: Jerold R Kassner
HR: –
FYE: December 31
Type: Public

No guy's outfit would be complete without some swank. Swank makes and distributes men's fashion accessories including leather goods (belts wallets) and jewelry (cuff links chains). The items are sold under brand names such as its namesake Swank Claiborne Kenneth Cole Tommy Hilfiger Guess? Nautica and Donald Trump. Swank also distributes products under the Pierre Cardin name as well as under its clients' private labels. Its clients are mainly US national department stores specialty stores mass merchandisers catalog retailers and some US military retail exchanges. Swank was acquired in 2012 by Randa Accessories a maker and marketer of consumer fashion must-haves for some $57 million.

SWARTHMORE COLLEGE

500 COLLEGE AVE STE 2
SWARTHMORE, PA 190811390
Phone: 610-328-8000
Fax: –
Web: www.swarthmore.edu

CEO: –
CFO: –
HR: Pamela Prescod-caesar
FYE: June 30
Type: Private

The Borough of Swarthmore Pennsylvania was established nearly three decades after its namesake Swarthmore College Founded in 1864 by the Quakers it is a private liberal arts and engineering college 11 miles southwest of Philadelphia. With a student-teacher ratio of 8:1 the college offers more than 50 academic programs and bachelor's degrees in the arts and sciences. Swarthmore enrolls about 1550 students or nearly 25% of the town's population. Notable alumni include Pulitzer Prize-winning author James Michener and former governor of Massachusetts Michael Dukakis.

	Annual Growth	06/13	06/14	06/15	06/17	06/18
Sales ($ mil.)	6.0%	–	139.2	195.5	162.9	175.4
Net income ($ mil.)	(7.4%)	–	253.5	22.5	201.9	186.3
Market value ($ mil.)	–	–	–	–	–	–
Employees	–	–	–	–	–	700

SWEDISH HEALTH SERVICES

747 BROADWAY
SEATTLE, WA 981224379
Phone: 206-386-6000
Fax: –

CEO: R. Guy Hudson
CFO: –
HR: –
FYE: December 31
Type: Private

Swedish Health Services doing business as Swedish Medical Center is the largest not-for-profit health provider in the greater Seattle area. Swedish Medical operates five acute care hospitals; it also runs two ambulatory care centers and the Swedish Medical Group physician practice organization which has more than 100 primary and specialty care offices in the greater Puget Sound region. Swedish Medical is affiliated with Providence St. Joseph Health a Catholic not-for-profit organization with 50 hospitals in seven states.

	Annual Growth	12/13	12/14	12/15	12/16	12/17
Sales ($ mil.)	29.3%	–	1,127.4	1,240.0	1,278.4	2,438.9
Net income ($ mil.)	–	–	79.9	56.5	(2.9)	(9.4)
Market value ($ mil.)	–	–	–	–	–	–
Employees	–	–	–	–	–	9,700

SWEDISH MATCH NORTH AMERICA INC.

2 James Center 1021 E. Cary St. Ste. 1600
Richmond VA 23219
Phone: 804-787-5100
Fax: 804-225-7000
Web: www.swedishmatch.com

CEO: Lars Dahlgren
CFO: Thomas Hayes
HR: –
FYE: December 31
Type: Business Segment

Business is up to snuff at Swedish Match North America — that's snuff tobacco. A subsidiary of Stockholm-based Swedish Match AB the company (SMNA) primarily makes and sells moist snuff and increasingly General-brand snus (a spit-free smokeless pouch) in the US. SMNA also ranks as the largest manufacturer of US chewing tobacco; Red Man is the country's #1 selling label. Snuff brands include Longhorn and Timber Wolf. Among other offerings SMNA makes mass market cigars sold under the ubiquitous White Owl and Garcia y Vega brands and matches and Cricket brand disposable lighters. The company expanded its presence in the tobacco space when Swedish Match acquired premium cigar maker General Cigar (2005).

SWH CORPORATION

18872 MacArthur Blvd Ste 400
Irvine CA 92612
Phone: 949-825-7000
Fax: 513-754-8778
Web: www.harrisproductsgroup.com

CEO: Daniel R Dillon
CFO: Edward T Bartholemy
HR: –
FYE: April 30
Type: Subsidiary

This company pairs the bistro life with home-style cooking. SWH Corporation owns and operates about 145 casual dining spots operating under the Mimi's Cafe banner. The New Orleans bistro-themed restaurants serve a variety of American classic dishes for breakfast lunch and dinner including chicken pot pie pancakes and eggs and pot roast as well as seafood pasta and sandwiches. The company has locations in more than 20 states mostly in California. Founded by Tom Simms and his family in 1978 SWH is owned by family-restaurant operator Bob Evans Farms.

SWIFT TRANSPORTATION CO

2200 South 75th Avenue
Phoenix, AZ 85043
Phone: 602 269-9700
Fax: –

NYS: SWFT
CEO: David A Jackson
CFO: Adam Miller
HR: –
FYE: December 31
Type: Public

Swift but within the speed limit: Truckload carrier Swift Transportation hauls freight such as building materials food paper products and retail merchandise throughout the North America. The company operates a fleet of 19800 tractors (about 75% are company-owned) and 65200 trailers via a network of more than 40 terminals. Its services include dedicated contract carriage (drivers and equipment assigned to a customer long-term). Besides standard dry vans Swift's fleet includes refrigerated flatbed and specialized trailers and about 9150 intermodal containers.

	Annual Growth	12/11	12/12	12/13	12/14	12/15
Sales ($ mil.)	6.1%	3,333.9	3,493.2	4,118.2	4,298.7	4,229.3
Net income ($ mil.)	21.5%	90.6	114.6	155.4	161.2	197.6
Market value ($ mil.)	13.8%	1,143.7	1,265.9	3,082.8	3,973.9	1,918.2
Employees	4.8%	17,400	17,600	19,600	21,274	21,000

SWIMWEAR ANYWHERE INC.

85 SHERWOOD AVE
FARMINGDALE, NY 117351717
Phone: 631-420-1400
Fax: –
Web: www.swimwearanywhere.com

CEO: –
CFO: –
HR: –
FYE: December 31
Type: Private

Life would certainly be more interesting if consumers took heed and sported their swimwear anywhere and everywhere. Swimwear Anywhere is a major North American swimwear manufacturer that makes and markets swimwear and beachwear lines under its own private labels and through licensing agreements for brands including DKNY Juicy Couture and Carmen Marc Valvo. The company's subsidiary TYR Sport (named after mythical Norse god of warriors and athletes) makes swimwear and gear designed primarily for professional athletes. Spokespeople have included Olympic swimming medalist Amanda Weir. Swimwear Anywhere was founded in 1993 by its owners Joseph and Rosemarie DiLorenzo.

	Annual Growth	06/0-1	06/00	06/03	06/04*	12/12
Sales ($ mil.)	0.0%	–	53.7	47.1	46.0	53.8
Net income ($ mil.)	(30.5%)	–	–	17.2	0.9	0.7
Market value ($ mil.)	–	–	–	–	–	–
Employees	–	–	–	–	–	150

*Fiscal year change

SWINERTON BUILDERS

260 TOWNSEND ST
SAN FRANCISCO, CA 941071761
Phone: 415-421-2980
Fax: –

CEO: –
CFO: Linda G Schowalter
HR: –
FYE: December 31
Type: Private

Swinerton Builders a subsidiary of Swinerton focuses on commercial and sustainable construction and renovation projects. Operating primarily in the western US its interiors group offers interior tenant finishes and remodeling working on such projects as high-tech and lab renovations hospitals retail facilities and seismic upgrades. The employee-owned company's building group focuses on new construction and retrofitting for such projects as the San Francisco Museum of Modern Art a Lockheed Martin launch vehicle assembly plant in Colorado and the Bay Bridge toll operations building in San Francisco. Swinerton Builders operates from offices in California Colorado Hawaii Texas New Mexico and Washington.

	Annual Growth	12/14	12/15	12/16	12/17	12/18
Sales ($ mil.)	7.8%	–	2,826.4	3,664.9	3,306.4	3,542.0
Net income ($ mil.)	9.5%	–	28.9	53.9	40.0	38.0
Market value ($ mil.)	–	–	–	–	–	–
Employees	–	–	–	–	–	900

SWINERTON INCORPORATED

260 TOWNSEND ST
SAN FRANCISCO, CA 941071761
Phone: 415-421-2980
Fax: -
Web: www.swinertonrenewable.com

CEO: Jeffrey C Hoopes
CFO: Linda G Showalter
HR: -
FYE: December 31
Type: Private

Swinerton is building up the West just as it helped rebuild San Francisco after the 1906 earthquake. One of the largest contractors in California the construction group builds commercial industrial and government facilities including resorts subsidized housing public schools soundstages hospitals and airport terminals. Through its subsidiaries (including Swinerton Builders) Swinerton offers general contracting and design/build services as well as construction and program management. The firm also provides property management for conventional subsidized and assisted living residences and is active in the renewable energy sector. The 100% employee-owned company traces its roots to 1888.

	Annual Growth	12/14	12/15	12/16	12/17	12/18
Sales ($ mil.)	8.7%	-	2,827.7	0.0	3,365.8	3,631.5
Net income ($ mil.)	18.9%	-	21.8	0.0	31.7	36.6
Market value ($ mil.)	-	-	-	-	-	-
Employees	-	-	-	-	-	900

SWISHER HYGIENE INC

NBB: SWSH

c/o Akerman LLP, Las Olas Centre II, Suite 1600, 350 East Las Olas Boulevard
Fort Lauderdale, FL 33301-2999
Phone: 203 682-8331
Fax: -
Web: www.swsh.com

CEO: William M Pierce
CFO: William T Nanovsky
HR: -
FYE: December 31
Type: Public

Swisher Hygiene sweeps away the competition in the corporate world. The company provides commercial cleaning services equipment and supplies to more than 50000 businesses in North America and abroad. Recognized for its restroom cleaning and disinfection services Swisher also sells soap cleaning chemicals and paper products and it rents facility service items (such as floor mats and mops). The company sells rents and maintains commercial dishwashers and other cleaning equipment. Swisher has expertise in serving customers in the foodservice hospitality health care industrial and retail industries. It boasts a global network of about 80 company-owned operations 10 franchises and 10 master licensees.

	Annual Growth	12/10	12/11	12/12	12/13	12/14
Sales ($ mil.)	32.1%	63.7	220.0	230.5	213.7	193.8
Net income ($ mil.)	-	(17.6)	(25.3)	(73.2)	(153.0)	(46.8)
Market value ($ mil.)	(20.8%)	83.7	65.9	30.8	9.1	32.9
Employees	2.7%	1,077	2,105	1,641	1,375	1,200

SWISS VALLEY FARMS COOPERATIVE

247 Research Pkwy.
Davenport IA 52808
Phone: 563-468-6600
Fax: 563-468-6616
Web: www.swissvalley.com

CEO: Don Boelens
CFO: Don Boelens
HR: -
FYE: September 30
Type: Private - Cooperativ

You don't need to be a mountain climber to view a Swiss valley. Just go to Iowa where Swiss Valley Farms operates a rather large and expanding dairy cooperative. The cooperative which represents more than 1000 member/farmers in the upper Midwest offers milk cheese butter yogurt dips and soft-serve and shake mixes. The organization also sells orange juice lemonade fruit drinks and bottled water. Swiss Valley's customers include retail food outlets and school lunch programs as well as other foodservice providers. As part of its operations the co-op manages several manufacturing and packaging plants in Iowa Wisconsin and Minnesota.

SWS GROUP, INC.

NYS: SWS

1201 Elm Street, Suite 3500
Dallas, TX 75270
Phone: 214 859-1800
Fax: 214 749-0810
Web: www.swsgroupinc.com

CEO: -
CFO: -
HR: -
FYE: June 30
Type: Public

Southwest Securities hopes stock prices go northeast. The primary subsidiary of SWS Group provides securities clearing and brokerage services to retail and institutional clients in the US and Canada. Accounting for some three-fourths of revenues Southwest Securities counts some 150 financial services organizations among its clients. It also serves individual investors through its private client brokerages located in California Texas Nevada and Oklahoma. Southwest Securities performs securities underwriting securities lending and public finance activities for institutional customers. Thrift subsidiary Southwest Securities FSB specializes in commercial lending and mortgage banking in Texas and New Mexico.

	Annual Growth	06/09	06/10	06/11	06/12	06/13
Assets ($ mil.)	(2.6%)	4,199.0	4,530.7	3,802.2	3,546.8	3,780.4
Net income ($ mil.)	-	23.6	(2.9)	(23.2)	(4.7)	(33.4)
Market value ($ mil.)	(20.3%)	441.5	331.8	184.0	173.9	177.8
Employees	(2.6%)	1,170	1,142	1,073	1,065	1,055

SYBRON DENTAL SPECIALTIES INC.

1717 W. Collins Ave.
Orange CA 92867-5422
Phone: 714-516-7400
Fax: +44-20-7306-8697
Web: www.channel4.com

CEO: Dan Even
CFO: -
HR: -
FYE: September 30
Type: Subsidiary

Crooked teeth may have met their match in Sybron Dental Specialties. The company makes and distributes dental and orthodontic appliances and tools through subsidiaries including Axis Dental Kerr SybronEndo and Ormco. Its product lines include braces dental implant systems cleaning tools and impression and restorative materials. The company also makes endodontic (dental surgery) supplies including hand pieces disinfectants curatives and other tools. Outside of dentistry the company has a smaller line of products for physicians. Sybron markets its products both directly through its subsidiaries and through dealers around the world. The company is a subsidiary of tools and technology giant Danaher.

SYCAMORE ENTERTAINMENT GROUP INC.

NBB: SEGI

Lexington Avenue, Suite 120
Hollywood, CA 90038
Phone: 323 790-1717
Fax: -
Web: www.imarx.com

CEO: -
CFO: -
HR: -
FYE: December 31
Type: Public

Sycamore Entertainment Group intends to grow fast and get its products up on screens across North America. The newly sprouted film marketing and distribution company went public in 2010 by acquiring the shell of a former pharmaceutical development company. Hopeful that public investors will make it rain the company is seeking to pick up market and distribute feature-length films. Sycamore Entertainment hopes to occupy a niche in the industry left vacant by the departure or demise of larger distribution companies — namely the distribution of art films independent films and foreign films.

	Annual Growth	12/10	12/11	12/12	12/13	12/14
Sales ($ mil.)	(83.4%)	-	-	0.2	0.2	0.0
Net income ($ mil.)	-	(3.5)	(1.0)	(1.8)	(0.3)	(0.6)
Market value ($ mil.)	(57.0%)	14.6	11.6	0.8	0.5	0.5
Employees						

SYKES ENTERPRISES, INC.
NMS: SYKE

400 North Ashley Drive, Suite 2800
Tampa, FL 33602
Phone: 813 274-1000
Fax: 813 273-0148
Web: www.sykes.com

CEO: Charles E. (Chuck) Sykes
CFO: John Chapman
HR: Jenna R. Nelson
FYE: December 31
Type: Public

When that software won't install Sykes can take your call. Sykes Enterprises operates about 70 technical help and customer support centers in some 20 countries across the globe. The company provides services in about 30 languages through phone e-mail social media text messaging chat and digital self-service. Sykes specializes in customer service and inbound technical support and also provides large corporations with digital marketing sales expertise technical staffing and consulting relating to customer relationship management. Sykes predominantly serves the retail communications financial services technology and healthcare industries. The company was founded in 1977 by John H. Sykes.

	Annual Growth	12/14	12/15	12/16	12/17	12/18
Sales ($ mil.)	5.2%	1,327.5	1,286.3	1,460.0	1,586.0	1,625.7
Net income ($ mil.)	(4.1%)	57.8	68.6	62.4	32.2	48.9
Market value ($ mil.)	1.3%	1,001.0	1,312.8	1,230.9	1,341.4	1,054.8
Employees	0.6%	50,450	54,550	55,525	55,000	51,600

SYMETRA FINANCIAL CORP
NYS: SYA

777 108th Avenue NE, Suite 1200
Bellevue, WA 98004
Phone: 425 256-8000
Fax: –
Web: www.symetra.com

CEO: Thomas M Marra
CFO: Margaret A Meister
HR: Jennifer Sharp
FYE: December 31
Type: Public

Symetra Financial seeks a symmetrical balance of work retirement and life insurance products. The holding company's subsidiaries offer life insurance annuities retirement plans health insurance and employee benefit plans to some 1.7 million customers throughout the US. Its workplace products include such goodies as medical stop-loss insurance disability insurance and group annuities. These products are distributed by brokers independent agents consultants financial institutions and third-party administrators. For individual consumers Symetra offers annuities individual retirement accounts and life insurance sold through banks.

	Annual Growth	12/09	12/10	12/11	12/12	12/13
Assets ($ mil.)	7.6%	22,437.5	25,636.9	28,212.7	29,460.9	30,129.5
Net income ($ mil.)	14.5%	128.3	200.9	199.6	205.4	220.7
Market value ($ mil.)	11.4%	–	1,612.9	1,067.8	1,528.1	2,232.2
Employees	2.8%	1,100	1,100	1,100	1,250	1,230

SYMMETRY MEDICAL INC.
NYS: SMA

3724 North State Road 15
Warsaw, IN 46582
Phone: 574 268-2252
Fax: –
Web: www.symmetrymedical.com

CEO: –
CFO: John Connollyn
HR: Helen Rowbottom
FYE: December 29
Type: Public

Symmetry Medical covers both sides of any orthopedic implant procedure. The company makes orthopedic implants for hips and knees and the surgical instruments used to insert such devices. In addition to its numerous products for the orthopedic implant market Symmetry sells its wares to physicians who deal with spinal injuries and general trauma dental work cardiovascular care and ophthalmology. Symmetry also makes plastic and metal cases to organize hold and transport medical devices. For a few aerospace customers the company makes aerofoils and aircraft engine parts. Symmetry's sales and marketing team promote its products to global orthopedic device makers and others.

	Annual Growth	01/09	01/10	01/11*	12/11	12/12
Sales ($ mil.)	(1.0%)	423.4	365.9	360.8	359.0	410.5
Net income ($ mil.)	(27.6%)	24.0	21.8	14.0	2.9	9.1
Market value ($ mil.)	7.9%	305.0	296.6	340.4	294.0	383.0
Employees	(2.1%)	2,688	2,357	2,797	2,520	2,520

*Fiscal year change

SYNACOR, INC.
NMS: SYNC

40 La Riviere Drive, Suite 300
Buffalo, NY 14202
Phone: 716 853-1362
Fax: –
Web: www.synacor.com

CEO: Himesh Bhise
CFO: Timothy Heasley
HR: –
FYE: December 31
Type: Public

When it comes to digital entertainment Synacor is at your service. The firm provides a technology platform to broadband service providers cable TV operators and other telecom companies that lets end-users receive digital entertainment services and apps. It builds the private label portals customers see when they log onto their telecom provider's website and makes money by selling ads on these sites. Synacor also offers premium online content e-mail and security services. It has relationships with content and service providers including CinemaNow CNN and MediaNet Digital. Synacor went public in 2011.

	Annual Growth	12/14	12/15	12/16	12/17	12/18
Sales ($ mil.)	7.8%	106.6	110.2	127.4	140.0	143.9
Net income ($ mil.)	–	(12.9)	(3.5)	(10.7)	(9.8)	(7.6)
Market value ($ mil.)	(7.2%)	78.1	68.3	121.0	89.8	57.8
Employees	12.3%	258	284	322	449	410

SYNAGEVA BIOPHARMA CORP.
NASDAQ: GEVA

128 Spring St. Ste. 520
Lexington MA 02421
Phone: 781-357-9900
Fax: 781-357-9901
Web: www.synageva.com

CEO: –
CFO: –
HR: –
FYE: December 31
Type: Public

Synageva BioPharma wants to sync up rare diseases with effective therapies. The company is focused on conducting research and development efforts into drug candidates that target rare conditions including enzyme deficiencies. Synageva also receives royalties on its sole commercial product HIV drug Fuzeon which is approved in the US and the European Union; development partner Roche markets Fuzeon worldwide. The company formerly Trimeris changed its name following a 2011 reverse-merger with the predecessor Synageva BioPharma.

SYNALLOY CORP.
NMS: SYNL

4510 Cox Road, Suite 201
Richmond, VA 23060
Phone: 804 822-3260
Fax: –
Web: www.synalloy.com

CEO: Craig C Bram
CFO: Dennis M Loughran
HR: –
FYE: December 31
Type: Public

Synalloy brings stainless steel and specialty chemicals together under one company. Operating through Bristol Metals and Ram-Fab the company manufactures welded pipe and fabricates piping systems from stainless steel and other alloys or carbon and chrome alloy. Its customers who require corrosion resistance or high purity are chiefly engaged in the chemical petrochemical water and waste water treatment and paper industries. Steel pipe branded Brismet is sold to distributors and directly to end-users. Synalloy's chemicals business Manufacturers Chemicals produces specialty chemicals and dyes (defoamers surfactants softening agents) for the textile chemical paper mining and metals industries.

	Annual Growth	01/15*	12/15	12/16	12/17	12/18
Sales ($ mil.)	12.1%	199.5	175.5	138.6	201.1	280.8
Net income ($ mil.)	33.8%	5.5	(11.5)	(7.1)	1.3	13.1
Market value ($ mil.)	(2.1%)	156.8	61.1	97.2	118.9	147.2
Employees	9.4%	464	411	412	533	607

*Fiscal year change

SYNAPTICS INC
NMS: SYNA

1251 McKay Drive
San Jose, CA 95131
Phone: 408 904-1100
Fax: –
Web: www.synaptics.com

CEO: Richard A. (Rick) Bergman
CFO: Wajid Ali
HR: –
FYE: June 29
Type: Public

Synaptics keeps you in touch with your electronics. The company's human interface products are sold to contract manufacturers for use in mobile phones (more than half of sales) notebook and handheld computers and other mobile electronic devices. Its TouchPad product can be used in peripherals such as monitors and remote controls; ClickPad replaces a mouse for notebook PCs and netbooks; and ClearPad provides touchscreen control for various mobile devices. Synaptics also relies on contract manufacturers to make its products. Most sales go to manufacturers in Asia more than two thirds in China. US customers provide 10% of sales.

	Annual Growth	06/15	06/16	06/17	06/18	06/19
Sales ($ mil.)	(3.6%)	1,703.0	1,666.9	1,718.2	1,630.3	1,472.2
Net income ($ mil.)	–	110.4	72.2	48.8	(124.1)	(22.9)
Market value ($ mil.)	(23.8%)	2,878.7	1,741.5	2,000.7	1,679.8	971.8
Employees	1.0%	1,789	1,763	1,774	1,631	1,861

SYNCHRONOSS TECHNOLOGIES INC
NMS: SNCR

200 Crossing Boulevard, 8th Floor
Bridgewater, NJ 08807
Phone: 866 620-3940
Fax: –
Web: www.synchronoss.com

CEO: Stephen G. Waldis
CFO: Lawrence R. Irving
HR: –
FYE: December 31
Type: Public

Synchronoss Technologies helps telephone companies synch up a variety of customer service efforts. The company provides hosted software and services that communications service providers use to manage tasks such as phone service activation account changes and customer transactions including credit card billing inventory management and trouble ticketing. Customers include service providers such as AT&T Mobility Level 3 Time Warner Cable Verizon and Vodafone as well as equipment manufacturers such as Apple Dell and Sony. Synchronoss was founded in 2001.

	Annual Growth	12/14	12/15	12/16	12/17	12/18
Sales ($ mil.)	(8.1%)	457.3	578.8	476.8	402.4	325.8
Net income ($ mil.)	–	38.9	40.6	19.6	(109.4)	(218.2)
Market value ($ mil.)	(38.1%)	1,786.3	1,503.4	1,634.4	381.5	262.0
Employees	(5.7%)	1,804	1,895	1,765	1,428	1,428

SYNCORA HOLDINGS LTD
NBB: SYCR F

555 Madison Avenue, 11th Floor
New York, NY 10022
Phone:
Fax: –
Web: www.syncora.com

CEO: –
CFO: –
HR: –
FYE: December 31
Type: Public

Syncora Holdings Ltd. used to be a place to get loans insured but for now new customers will have to look elsewhere. Syncora is a financial guaranty insurer — the kind of insurance which covers bonds and other investments from the risk of default. Syncora operates in the US through its subsidiary Syncora Guarantee Inc. The company has also provided reinsurance on financial guarantee insurance policies. Both lines of business were closely tied to mortgage-backed securities leaving Syncora vulnerable to increased default rates. The company is currently not writing new business.

	Annual Growth	12/14	12/15	12/16	12/17	12/18
Assets ($ mil.)	(12.6%)	2,895.8	2,625.7	2,394.4	2,385.5	1,690.4
Net income ($ mil.)	–	(102.9)	216.7	32.7	133.5	(31.3)
Market value ($ mil.)	–	–	–	–	–	–
Employees	–	–	–	–	–	–

SYNERGETICS USA, INC.

3845 CORPORATE CENTRE DR
O FALLON, MO 633688678
Phone: 636-939-5100
Fax: –
Web: www.synergeticsusa.com

CEO: J Michael Pearson
CFO: Robert L Rosiello
HR: –
FYE: July 31
Type: Private

Synergetics USA is in sync with surgeons' needs. The firm makes microsurgical instruments and electrosurgery systems used in minimally invasive surgeries primarily in the fields of ophthalmology and neurology. Among its products are forceps retractors scissors and illuminators used in vitreoretinal surgeries as well as precision neurosurgery instruments. It also makes bipolar electrosurgical generators which use electrical currents to cut tissue and seal blood vessels. Synergetics USA sells to hospitals physicians and clinics directly and through distributors; it also sells certain items through partnerships with original equipment manufacturers. Valeant acquired Synergetics USA in 2015.

	Annual Growth	07/11	07/12	07/13	07/14	07/15
Sales ($ mil.)	7.7%	–	60.0	62.8	64.8	75.0
Net income ($ mil.)	(7.1%)	–	5.6	2.6	3.1	4.5
Market value ($ mil.)	–	–	–	–	–	–
Employees	–	–	–	–	–	418

SYNERGX SYSTEMS INC.

209 Lafayette Dr.
Syosset NY 11791
Phone: 516-433-4700
Fax: 516-433-1131
Web: www.synergxsystems.com

CEO: Paul Mendez
CFO: John A Poserina
HR: –
FYE: September 30
Type: Subsidiary

Before a situation gets too hot to handle Synergx Systems sounds the alarm. The diversified technology and systems integration company formerly called Firetector makes sells and services fire alarm life safety and audio/visual communication systems. Synergx also markets security and intercom systems used in apartments hospitals schools and subways. The company conducts business through its Casey Systems subsidiary which services New York City and Long Island New York. Synergx Systems operates as a subsidiary of security monitoring equipment manufacturer Firecom.

SYNERGY PHARMACEUTICALS INC.
NASDAQ: SGYP

420 Lexington Ave. Ste. 1609
New York NY 10170
Phone: 212-297-0020
Fax: 212-297-0019
Web: www.synergypharma.com

CEO: Troy Hamilton
CFO: Gary G Gemignani
HR: –
FYE: December 31
Type: Public

Synergy Pharmaceuticals is working to sooth inflamed irritable and sluggish bowels. The development stage drug company's lead candidate plecanatide is in clinical trials as a treatment for chronic idiopathic constipation. It also has another candidate in pre-clinical development as a treatment for inflammatory bowel disease. Synergy has conducted the development of these drugs on behalf of Callisto Pharmaceuticals. Callisto which has held 40% of Synergy has agreed to let its subsidiary acquire it and take full control of its drug pipeline. Synergy raised the necessary money with additional public offerings in 2012.

SYNIVERSE HOLDINGS, INC.

8125 HIGHWOODS PALM WAY
TAMPA, FL 336471776
Phone: 813-637-5000
Fax: -
Web: www.syniverse.com

CEO: Stephen Gray
CFO: Bob Reich
HR: -
FYE: December 31
Type: Private

Syniverse Holdings opens up new worlds of communication for its clients. The company which operates as Syniverse Technologies provides business and network engineering services and software for managing and interconnecting voice and data network systems. It also offers clearing and settlement services voice and data roaming facilitation fraud management software and customer data analysis services to mobile operators fixed-line carriers and other telecommunications service providers worldwide. Customers have included Verizon Wireless and Vodafone Group. Syniverse is owned by Carlyle Group affiliate Buccaneer Holdings.

	Annual Growth	12/12	12/13	12/14	12/15	12/16
Sales ($ mil.)	(3.1%)	-	859.0	916.3	861.5	781.9
Net income ($ mil.)	-	-	(45.4)	(47.0)	(49.3)	(65.2)
Market value ($ mil.)	-	-	-	-	-	-
Employees	-	-	-	-	-	2,538

SYNNEX CORP

44201 Nobel Drive
Fremont, CA 94538
Phone: 510 656-3333
Fax: -
Web: www.synnex.com

NYS: SNX
CEO: Kevin M. Murai
CFO: Marshall Witt
HR: -
FYE: November 30
Type: Public

SYNNEX connects technology sellers with buyers and helps with customer service after the sale. The company distributes PCs peripherals software and consumer electronics from manufacturers that include HP Inc. Hewlett-Packard Enterprise Google Panasonic Lenovo Asus and Microsoft. Its Concentrix segment offers customer support services using phone chat web e-mail and digital print. The company's online services include parts catalogs configuration and ordering. In addition the company offers contract design and assembly build-to-order and configure-to-order services for manufacturers and systems integrators. SYNNEX depends on the US for 70% of sales.

	Annual Growth	11/15	11/16	11/17	11/18	11/19
Sales ($ mil.)	15.5%	13,338.4	14,061.8	17,045.7	20,053.8	23,757.3
Net income ($ mil.)	24.5%	208.5	234.9	301.2	300.6	500.7
Market value ($ mil.)	6.8%	4,784.7	5,933.8	6,912.8	4,098.0	6,233.2
Employees	35.0%	72,500	110,000	113,600	231,600	240,900

SYNOPSYS INC

690 East Middlefield Road
Mountain View, CA 94043
Phone: 650 584-5000
Fax: -
Web: www.synopsys.com

NMS: SNPS
CEO: Chi-Foon Chan
CFO: Trac Pham
HR: Kevin Syvrud
FYE: October 31
Type: Public

Synopsys is a leading provider of electronic design automation (EDA) software and services used in the making of integrated circuits. Chip designers use the company's products to develop simulate and test the physical design of ICs before production and then to test finished products for bugs and security vulnerabilities. The company also provides intellectual property (IP) products or pre-designed circuits used as part of larger chips. Moving beyond silicon Synopsys had added software testing to its portfolio. Customers come from a variety of industries but particularly the semiconductor and electronics manufacturing with Intel as its top customer. The company generates about half its sales outside the US.

	Annual Growth	10/15	10/16	10/17	10/18	10/19
Sales ($ mil.)	10.6%	2,242.2	2,422.5	2,724.9	3,121.1	3,360.7
Net income ($ mil.)	23.9%	225.9	266.8	136.6	432.5	532.4
Market value ($ mil.)	28.4%	7,513.5	8,916.1	13,006.6	13,459.1	20,407.4
Employees	7.8%	10,284	10,669	11,686	13,245	13,896

SYNOVIS LIFE TECHNOLOGIES INC.

2575 University Ave. West
St. Paul MN 55114-1024
Phone: 651-796-7300
Fax: 651-642-9018
Web: www.synovislife.com

NASDAQ: SYNO
CEO: -
CFO: Brett A Reynolds
HR: Joanie Goodhart
FYE: October 31
Type: Subsidiary

Duct tape can patch a lot of life's leaks and holes but when it comes to reconstructive surgery Synovis Life Technologies has some better options. The company makes instruments and biomaterials used to patch up soft tissue to prevent leaks of air blood or other fluids. Its products include the Peri-Strip buttress used to reinforce surgical staple lines in gastric bypass procedures. Other implant tissue lines are used to repair and replace soft tissue during reconstructive surgeries including abdominal wall breast and chest wall operations. It also makes orthopedic tissues chronic wound aids and microsurgical devices to connect vessels or nerves. Synovis was acquired by Baxter International in 2012.

SYNOVUS FINANCIAL CORP

1111 Bay Avenue, Suite 500
Columbus, GA 31901
Phone: 706 649-2311
Fax: -
Web: www.synovus.com

NYS: SNV
CEO: Kessel D. Stelling
CFO: Kevin S. Blair
HR: Ronald Carr
FYE: December 31
Type: Public

Synovus Financial has a nose for community banking. The holding company owns flagship subsidiary Synovus Bank and more than 25 locally branded banking divisions that offer deposit accounts and consumer and business loans in Alabama Florida Georgia South Carolina and Tennessee. Through more than 280 branches the bank provides checking and savings accounts loans and mortgages and credit cards. Other divisions offer insurance private banking wealth and asset management and other financial services. Nonbank subsidiaries include Synovus Mortgage Synovus Trust investment bank and brokerage Synovus Securities and GLOBALT which provides asset management and financial planning services.

	Annual Growth	12/14	12/15	12/16	12/17	12/18
Assets ($ mil.)	4.8%	27,051.2	28,792.7	30,104.0	31,221.8	32,669.2
Net income ($ mil.)	21.7%	195.2	226.1	246.8	275.5	428.5
Market value ($ mil.)	4.2%	3,138.8	3,751.7	4,759.8	5,554.6	3,706.5
Employees	0.8%	4,511	4,452	4,436	4,541	4,651

SYNTA PHARMACEUTICALS CORP

45 Hartwell Avenue
Lexington, MA 02421
Phone: 781 274-8200
Fax: 781 274-8228
Web: www.syntapharma.com

NMS: SNTA
CEO: Paul A Friedman
CFO: Marc R Schneebaum
HR: -
FYE: December 31
Type: Public

Synta Pharmaceuticals doesn't fill stockings but it might eventually fill the medical need of treating cancer. The drug development company has a handful of candidates in clinical and pre-clinical development stages. Its ganetespib and elesclomol compounds are in clinical trials as possible treatments for several types of cancer including non-small cell lung cancer (NSCLC) acute myeloid leukemia melanoma and rectal pancreatic ovarian prostate and breast cancers. Synta's preclinical research efforts include potential therapies for autoimmune diseases transplant acceptance respiratory conditions and cancerous tumors.

	Annual Growth	12/08	12/09	12/10	12/11	12/12
Sales ($ mil.)	(51.3%)	2.6	144.2	14.8	7.6	0.1
Net income ($ mil.)	-	(92.6)	79.1	(37.5)	(47.4)	(62.8)
Market value ($ mil.)	10.2%	421.9	348.8	421.9	321.9	621.7
Employees	(1.0%)	129	127	112	122	124

SYNTEL INC.

NMS: SYNT

525 E. Big Beaver Road, Suite 300
Troy, MI 48083
Phone: 248 619-2800
Fax: 248 619-2888
Web: www.syntelinc.com

CEO: Rakesh Khanna
CFO: Anil Agrawal
HR: –
FYE: December 31
Type: Public

Syntel is in the know about information technology. The IT services provider offers IT services and knowledge process outsourcing (KPO) to companies in banking and finance health care and life science insurance manufacturingretail logistics and telecommunications. Its IT services include programming system integration outsourcing and overall project management. Syntel's KPO services for back-office functions are transaction processing loan servicing retirement processing collections and payment processing. Its top clients include American Express and State Street. US customers account for 90% of its business. Co-founding spouses Bharat Desai and Neerja Sethi are the company's biggest shareholders.

	Annual Growth	12/12	12/13	12/14	12/15	12/16
Sales ($ mil.)	7.5%	723.9	824.8	911.4	968.6	966.6
Net income ($ mil.)	–	185.5	219.7	249.7	252.5	(57.4)
Market value ($ mil.)	(22.1%)	4,485.2	7,606.6	3,761.9	3,784.5	1,655.1
Employees	1.8%	21,407	23,652	24,553	24,537	23,011

SYNTHESIS ENERGY SYSTEMS INC

NAS: SES

Three Riverway, Suite 300
Houston, TX 77056
Phone: 713 579-0600
Fax: 713 579-0610
Web: www.synthesisenergy.com

CEO: Robert Rigdon
CFO: –
HR: –
FYE: June 30
Type: Public

Synthesis Energy Systems (SES) prefers it when a little waste is produced posthaste. The company owns a coal gasification plant in China that began production in 2008. (Coal gasification converts low-rank coal and coal waste into fuels such as synthetic natural gas methanol ammonia and dimethyl ether which are used to make gasoline). SES leases the technology behind the plant from the Gas Technology Institute. The company has four more coal gasification plants under development — two in China with AEI and two in the US with North American Coal Corporation and CONSOL Energy.

	Annual Growth	06/14	06/15	06/16	06/17	06/18
Sales ($ mil.)	(45.8%)	17.5	15.5	6.0	0.2	1.5
Net income ($ mil.)	–	(14.2)	(37.9)	(23.1)	(26.2)	(9.6)
Market value ($ mil.)	14.9%	20.7	15.7	11.5	7.4	36.1
Employees	(50.3%)	213	142	135	22	13

SYNTROLEUM CORP

NAS: SYNM

5416 S. Yale Suite 400
Tulsa, OK 74135
Phone: 918 592-7900
Fax: –
Web: www.syntroleum.com

CEO: –
CFO: –
HR: –
FYE: December 31
Type: Public

Syntroleum is looking for business synergies with energy companies. The company licenses its patented gas-to-liquids (GTL) process (also known as the Fischer-Tropsch process) which converts natural gas into synthetic crude oil by using air instead of pure oxygen. The liquids produced can be refined into fuels such as diesel and kerosene as well as specialty products such as synthetic lubricants waxes and chemical feed stocks. In 2007 Syntroleum formed a joint venture called Dynamic Fuels with chicken giant Tyson Foods. The JV will uses Syntroleum's biorefining technologies to process Tyson's animal fat greases and vegetable oils into synthetic fuel used for jet diesel and military applications.

	Annual Growth	12/08	12/09	12/10	12/11	12/12
Sales ($ mil.)	37.6%	4.9	27.4	8.4	4.2	17.5
Net income ($ mil.)	–	(4.1)	5.0	(9.5)	(16.9)	(1.1)
Market value ($ mil.)	(7.4%)	5.3	26.1	18.2	9.4	3.9
Employees	(3.6%)	22	19	19	21	19

SYNUTRA INTERNATIONAL INC

NMS: SYUT

2275 Research Blvd., Suite 500
Rockville, MD 20850
Phone: 301 840-3888
Fax: –
Web: www.synutra.com

CEO: Liang Zhang
CFO: Ning Cai
HR: –
FYE: March 31
Type: Public

Chinese dairy products manufacturer Synutra International knows how to pack a nutritional punch — and put it into a can. The company develops manufactures and sells enriched milk- and rice-powder products for infants and children under the Super U-Smart My Angel and Dutch Cow brands. The company also makes powdered nutritional products including chondroitin and glucosamine for joint health for adults; however most of the company's business comes from the sale of its infants' and children's powders. Synutra products are sold in some 24000 retail outlets throughout mainland China. Chairman and CEO Liang Zhang owns the majority of the Synutra's shares.

	Annual Growth	03/12	03/13	03/14	03/15	03/16
Sales ($ mil.)	1.6%	342.5	265.8	370.5	413.9	365.0
Net income ($ mil.)	4.9%	16.7	(63.9)	30.9	69.5	20.2
Market value ($ mil.)	(4.1%)	333.3	266.4	379.3	362.8	281.8
Employees	(11.6%)	4,250	3,400	3,200	2,700	2,600

SYPRIS SOLUTIONS, INC.

NMS: SYPR

101 Bullitt Lane, Suite 450
Louisville, KY 40222
Phone: 502 329-2000
Fax: –
Web: www.sypris.com

CEO: Jeffrey T Gill
CFO: Anthony C Allen
HR: –
FYE: December 31
Type: Public

Sypris Solutions provides its customers with simple solutions for their manufacturing chores. The company's Industrial Group makes heavy-duty truck components including axle shafts gear sets differential cases trailer axle beams and other components. Its Electronics Group provides circuit board and box build manufacturing services primarily for the aerospace and defense industries as well as secure communications and data storage products for government clients. Sypris' top customers have traditionally included Dana Holding ArvinMeritor Raytheon Honeywell Lockheed Martin and the US Defense Department.

	Annual Growth	12/14	12/15	12/16	12/17	12/18
Sales ($ mil.)	(29.4%)	354.8	145.3	91.8	82.3	88.0
Net income ($ mil.)	–	(1.2)	(27.2)	6.0	(10.8)	(3.5)
Market value ($ mil.)	(26.4%)	56.9	23.3	18.8	29.5	16.7
Employees	(14.4%)	1,332	735	604	607	716

SYRACUSE UNIVERSITY

900 S CROUSE AVE STE 620
SYRACUSE, NY 132444407
Phone: 315-443-1870
Fax: –
Web: www.syracuse.edu

CEO: –
CFO: –
HR: –
FYE: June 30
Type: Private

Syracuse University is a serious school with a silly mascot. While it wasn't until 1995 that Otto the Orange was officially adopted as the school's mascot Syracuse's tradition of quality higher education dates back to 1870. The school enrolls more than 21000 undergraduate and graduate students and has some 1000 full-time faculty members on its campus in central New York State. It offers about 500 degree programs in areas such as communications computer science engineering psychology art mathematics music and information. Notable alumni include Dick Clark Ted Koppel Joyce Carol Oats Joe Biden and Aaron Sorkin.

	Annual Growth	06/09	06/10	06/11	06/12	06/17
Sales ($ mil.)	0.2%	–	979.0	839.7	818.7	994.8
Net income ($ mil.)	–	–	(0.9)	145.4	(73.1)	197.6
Market value ($ mil.)	–	–	–	–	–	–
Employees	–	–	–	–	–	4,350

SYSCO CORP
NYS: SYY

1390 Enclave Parkway
Houston, TX 77077-2099
Phone: 281 584-1390
Fax: 281 584-2880
Web: www.sysco.com

CEO: William J. (Bill) DeLaney
CFO: Joel T. Grade
HR: Paul T. Moskowitz
FYE: June 29
Type: Public

Sysco is the #1 food distributor in the US. The company serves more than 650000 customer locations in the US and internationally in the restaurant (standalone and chain) healthcare and education and hotel industries among others. Its 330-plus distribution centers and some 14000 delivery vehicles deliver branded and private-label food — including fresh frozen and canned foods and specialty and meat products — as well as non-food items such as silverware and utensils. The SYGMA Network focuses on supplying specific chain restaurants. Sysco also offers technology services and management consultancy services such as menu analysis and inventory management. The US accounts for about 80% of sales.

	Annual Growth	06/15*	07/16	07/17*	06/18	06/19
Sales ($ mil.)	5.4%	48,680.8	50,366.9	55,371.1	58,727.3	60,113.9
Net income ($ mil.)	25.0%	686.8	949.6	1,142.5	1,430.8	1,674.3
Market value ($ mil.)	16.5%	19,679.1	26,018.2	25,813.1	35,024.4	36,270.7
Employees	7.5%	51,700	51,900	66,500	67,000	69,000

*Fiscal year change

SYSCO GUEST SUPPLY LLC

4301 US Hwy. One
Monmouth Junction NJ 08852-090
Phone: 609-514-9696
Fax: 609-514-2692
Web: www.guestsupply.com

CEO: –
CFO: –
HR: –
FYE: June 30
Type: Subsidiary

You know those hotel goodies we've all come to know and pack for home? Thank Sysco Guest Supply. A subsidiary of food distributing giant Sysco Corporation the company makes more than 7000 guest-room accessories and operating supplies for the hospitality industry. Its products include personal care items (mini soaps shampoos) housekeeping and laundry supplies room accessories paper products and bed bath and table linens. It offers brand-name products such as Bath & Body Works Dial and Neutrogena as well as custom and generic items and distributes them from its more than 15 facilities. Sysco Guest Supply also offers hotel furniture fixtures and equipment coffee appliances and kitchenware.

SYSTEMAX, INC.
NYS: SYX

11 Harbor Park Drive
Port Washington, NY 11050
Phone: 516 608-7000
Fax: –
Web: www.systemax.com

CEO: Lawrence P. (Larry) Reinhold
CFO: Thomas (Tex) Clark
HR: –
FYE: December 31
Type: Public

Systemax is a direct marketer of computers electronics and technology products in North America and Europe (where it operates under the Misco brand). Through catalogs websites and retail stores Systemax markets thousands of brand-name and private-label computer networking camera GPS cell phone video game and other electronic products. Systemax also sells material-handling equipment shelving storage items furniture and other industrial products. Its customers include businesses government agencies and schools as well as individual consumers. Systemax was founded in 1949 as Global Equipment Company.

	Annual Growth	12/14	12/15	12/16	12/17	12/18
Sales ($ mil.)	(28.6%)	3,442.8	1,854.7	1,680.1	1,265.4	896.9
Net income ($ mil.)	–	(37.5)	(99.8)	(32.6)	40.4	224.7
Market value ($ mil.)	15.3%	504.0	321.1	327.4	1,242.2	891.9
Employees	(26.5%)	5,300	3,300	2,800	1,900	1,550

T ROWE PRICE GROUP INC.
NMS: TROW

100 East Pratt Street
Baltimore, MD 21202
Phone: 410 345-2000
Fax: 410 752-3477
Web: www.troweprice.com

CEO: Edward C. Bernard
CFO: Kenneth V. Moreland
HR: –
FYE: December 31
Type: Public

T. Rowe Price Group administers a family of mutual funds in a variety of investment styles. Traditionally oriented toward growth investing the funds offer products in many risk and taxation profiles including small- mid- and large-cap stock funds; money market funds; and bond funds both taxable and nontaxable. Other services include asset management advisory services (including retirement plan advice for individuals) corporate retirement plan management separately managed accounts variable annuity life insurance plans discount brokerage and transfer agency and shareholder services. Founded in 1937 T. Rowe Price has almost $1.1 trillion in assets under management.

	Annual Growth	12/14	12/15	12/16	12/17	12/18
Sales ($ mil.)	7.8%	3,982.1	4,200.6	4,222.9	4,793.0	5,372.6
Net income ($ mil.)	10.6%	1,229.6	1,223.0	1,215.0	1,497.8	1,837.5
Market value ($ mil.)	1.8%	20,440.6	17,019.6	17,917.1	24,980.6	21,978.5
Employees	4.6%	5,870	5,999	6,329	6,881	7,022

T. D. WILLIAMSON, INC.

6120 S YALE AVE STE 1700
TULSA, OK 741364235
Phone: 918-493-9494
Fax: –
Web: www.tdwilliamson.com

CEO: Robert D McGrew
CFO: –
HR: David R Miller
FYE: December 31
Type: Private

Keeping onshore and offshore pipelines operating safely flowing freely is what T. D. Williamson is all about. A leading global pipeline equipment and services provider the company designs manufactures and maintains oil field machinery and systems including pipeline pigging (scraping) gas leak detection pipeline inspection plugging tapping valve and clamp and cathodic protection equipment. The company also offers general pipeline training turnkey and repair services. T. D. Williamson operates a global network of sales offices and representatives.

	Annual Growth	12/0-1	12/00	12/01	12/02	12/15
Sales ($ mil.)	12.6%	–	91.5	107.0	116.5	539.5
Net income ($ mil.)	–	–	2.3	2.6	1.7	0.0
Market value ($ mil.)	–	–	–	–	–	–
Employees	–	–	–	–	–	1,425

T. MARZETTI COMPANY

37 W. Broad St.
Columbus OH 43215
Phone: 614-846-2232
Fax: 614-848-8330
Web: www.marzetti.com

CEO: –
CFO: –
HR: –
FYE: June 30
Type: Subsidiary

Specialty food is the specialty of the house at this company. T. Marzetti is a leading maker of specialty food products including salad dressings condiments dips and other food toppings mostly sold under the Marzetti brand name. Its other product include croutons (Chatham Village) dry and frozen egg noodles (Inn Maid Amish Kitchen and Reames) and frozen baked goods (Marshall's Mamma Bella and Sister Schubert's). The food manufacturer sells its items nationwide primarily through retail grocers; however it also supplies foodservice operators. Begun by Teresa Marzetti in 1896 as a small restaurant in Columbus Ohio the company represents the specialty foods division of Lancaster Colony.

T.J.T., INC.

NBB: AXLE

843 North Washington Avenue
Emmett, ID 83617
Phone: 208 472-2500
Fax: 208 472-2525
Web: www.tjtusa.com

CEO: Larry E Kling
CFO: Nicole L Glisson
HR: –
FYE: September 30
Type: Public

The next time you pass a house being carted down the road bet that it will be riding on some of T.J.T.'s tires. T.J.T. buys used axles and tires from manufactured housing dealers inspects and reconditions them and then sells them to manufactured home builders. The company also distributes vinyl siding and skirting to manufactured housing dealers and sells vinyl siding to the site-built and manufactured housing markets. It has expanded its line of products and aftermarket accessories for these markets to include skylights adhesives and sealants foundation and other set-up materials. T.J.T. operates primarily in the western US. CEO Terrence Sheldon controls a 30% stake in the company.

	Annual Growth	09/11	09/12	09/13	09/14	09/15
Sales ($ mil.)	1.0%	6.0	4.0	4.0	6.2	6.3
Net income ($ mil.)	–	(1.1)	(1.1)	(0.3)	0.8	0.2
Market value ($ mil.)	(10.1%)	2.3	0.7	1.5	1.9	1.5
Employees	(8.3%)	35	23	24	27	–

TAB PRODUCTS CO LLC

605 4th St.
Mayville WI 53050
Phone: 888-466-8228
Fax: 800-304-4947
Web: www.tab.com

CEO: Thaddeus Jaroszewicz
CFO: John Palmer
HR: –
FYE: May 31
Type: Private

TAB Products help offices get organized. A provider of record management systems the company makes products for paper-based and automated file-tracking systems. In addition to color-coded files ranging from individual folders to complete systems TAB develops tracking and labeling computer software filing cabinets and shelving. It also provides file conversion and other records management consulting services. Customers include the legal medical pharmaceutical banking and energy industries in the US as well as in Australia Canada and Europe. TAB Products was founded in 1950 by two ex-IBM salesmen Harry LeClaire and Si Foote. Today it is owned by HS Morgan Limited Partnership.

TABLE TRAC INC.

OTC: TBTC

15612 Hwy. 7 Ste. 250
Minnetonka MN 55345
Phone: 952-548-8877
Fax: 952-938-5629
Web: www.tabletrac.com

CEO: Chad B Hoehne
CFO: Randy W Gilbert
HR: –
FYE: December 31
Type: Public

You might say this company doesn't fold under pressure when it comes to tracking money at casino tables. Table Trac markets information management systems designed to help casino operators monitor their gaming operations. Its Table Trac system records and analyzes win-loss percentages dealer performance and cash movements. It also makes self-service kiosks for customer service and administering players club promotional programs. The company's customers are located mostly in the US; it also sells to markets in Central and South America. Chairman and CEO Chad Hoehne owns nearly 30% of Table Trac.

TABLEAU SOFTWARE INC

NYS: DATA

1621 North 34th Street
Seattle, WA 98103
Phone: 206 633-3400
Fax: –
Web: www.tableau.com

CEO: Adam Selipsky
CFO: Damon Fletcher
HR: –
FYE: December 31
Type: Public

Tableau Software sets the table with pretty and informative pictures of data that help businesses understand what it means. The company develops software designed to retrieve large volumes of data and quickly generate dashboards reports and other data visualization tools with products like Tableau Desktop Tableau Online Tableau Public and Tableau Server. It serves more than 70000 businesses and government agencies including Bank of America ExxonMobil and Honeywell. Tableau was founded in 1996 by CEO Christian Chabot and chief development officer Chris Stolte. It started as a research project at Stanford University funded by the US Department of Defense.

	Annual Growth	12/13	12/14	12/15	12/16	12/17
Sales ($ mil.)	39.4%	232.4	412.6	653.6	826.9	877.1
Net income ($ mil.)	–	7.1	5.9	(83.7)	(144.4)	(185.6)
Market value ($ mil.)	0.1%	5,546.3	6,820.0	7,581.2	3,391.5	5,568.0
Employees	30.3%	1,212	1,947	3,008	3,223	3,489

TACHYON NETWORKS INC.

9339 Carroll Park Dr. #150
San Diego CA 92121
Phone: 858-882-8100
Fax: 858-882-8122
Web: www.tachyon.net

CEO: Peter A Carides
CFO: Laurence A Hinz
HR: –
FYE: April 30
Type: Private

Tachyon Networks sells speed. No. Not that kind of speed. The company takes its name from a term from physics that describes a particle that is able to travel faster than the speed of light. Tachyon provides broadband satellite services — including remote Internet access virtual private networks (VPNs) and emergency network backup — to business and government clients. Large enterprises in such industries as energy construction and real estate use its service to connect to employees customers and suppliers who are beyond the reach of traditional wired networks. The company also serves US military agencies including the Naval Criminal Investigative Service and the US Army.

TACOMA PUBLIC UTILITIES

3628 S 35TH ST
TACOMA, WA 984093192
Phone: 253-502-8600
Fax: –
Web: www.mytpu.org

CEO: Bill Gaines
CFO: Dave Rosholm
HR: –
FYE: December 31
Type: Private

City of Tacoma Department of Public Utilities (Tacoma Public Utilities) is fated to fulfill the electric and water desires of the City of Destiny's dwellers. The municipal utility's Tacoma Power unit generates transmits and distributes electricity to 160000 homes and businesses in Tacoma Washington. Tacoma Water serves more than 300000 customers; the division's water supply comes from wells and the Green River Watershed. Tacoma Public Utilities also oversees Tacoma Rail a freight-switching railroad with 75 customers and more than 200 miles of track and the Click! Network a high-speed data network that serves 23790 cable TV customers via more than 1460 miles of fiber-optic and coaxial cable.

	Annual Growth	12/09	12/10	12/11	12/13	12/15
Sales ($ mil.)	45.5%	–	63.0	364.3	414.5	410.6
Net income ($ mil.)	–	–	5.1	20.7	19.9	(1.6)
Market value ($ mil.)	–	–	–	–	–	–
Employees	–	–	–	–	–	1,407

TACONIC BIOSCIENCES, INC.

1 DISCOVERY DR STE 304
RENSSELAER, NY 121443448
Phone: 609-860-0806
Fax: –
Web: www.taconic.com

CEO: Nancy J Sandy
CFO: –
HR: –
FYE: December 31
Type: Private

Yes they are cute but Taconic Biosciences prefers that you don't pet its animals. The family-owned company provides research rodents and related products and services to pharmaceutical and biomedical companies government agencies and academic institutions in Asia Europe and North America through its facilities in Denmark Germany and the US. Taconic specially breeds rats and mice the workhorses of the biomedical industry to be disease-free or genetically modified to exhibit certain traits to help researchers develop new therapies for human disease. Other company units offer drug- and animal-safety testing and monoclonal antibody production. Private equity firm H.I.G. Capital in partnership with company management acquired Taconic Biosciences in 2019.

	Annual Growth	12/07	12/08	12/09	12/10	12/11
Sales ($ mil.)	0.8%	–	–	142.6	151.7	144.9
Net income ($ mil.)	–	–	–	5.6	1.2	(23.0)
Market value ($ mil.)	–	–	–	–	–	–
Employees	–	–	–	–	–	720

TAHOE RESOURCES INC.

NYS: TAHO

5310 Kietzke Lane, Suite 200
Reno, NV 89511
Phone: 775 448-5800
Fax: 775 398-7020
Web: www.tahoeresources.com

CEO: –
CFO: –
HR: –
FYE: December 31
Type: Public

Tahoe Resources is looking for silver a little farther south than the lake that straddles California and Nevada. The company was founded as CKM Resources in 2009 by Kevin McArthur the former CEO of Goldcorp. It changed its name to Tahoe Resources when it bought a mining property in southeastern Guatemala from affiliates of Goldcorp. The firm is developing the property known as Escobal into a silver mine. Construction on the mine began in 2012 with production expected in early 2014. Tahoe Resources which operates in Canada Guatemala and the US went public in 2010 raising C$383 ($372 million). In 2016 the company acquired Lake Shore Gold.

	Annual Growth	12/13	12/14	12/15	12/16	12/17
Sales ($ mil.)	27.9%	–	350.3	519.7	784.5	733.6
Net income ($ mil.)	–	(65.6)	90.8	(71.9)	117.9	81.8
Market value ($ mil.)	(26.8%)	5,204.6	4,338.2	2,711.8	2,946.3	1,498.2
Employees	32.6%	867	–	–	–	2,684

TAITRON COMPONENTS INC.

NAS: TAIT

28040 West Harrison Parkway
Valencia, CA 91355-4162
Phone: 661 257-6060
Fax: –
Web: www.taitroncomponents.com

CEO: Stewart Wang
CFO: David H. Vanderhorst
HR: –
FYE: December 31
Type: Public

With more than a billion components in stock Taitron Components is a superstore for a small subset of the electronic component market: discrete semiconductors. Taitron also distributes optoelectronic devices and passive components such as capacitors and resistors. Discrete semiconductors are the forefathers of complex integrated circuits and are used in most consumer industrial and military electronic devices from appliances to airplanes. Taitron distributes more than 14000 different products from about 40 suppliers including Everlight Electronics Princeton Technology Samsung Electro-Mechanics and Vishay. The company gets the bulk of its sales in the US.

	Annual Growth	12/14	12/15	12/16	12/17	12/18
Sales ($ mil.)	9.0%	5.8	5.7	6.9	7.6	8.2
Net income ($ mil.)	–	(1.1)	(0.6)	(3.1)	0.7	1.4
Market value ($ mil.)	14.7%	5.6	5.5	6.8	9.5	9.7
Employees	(4.0%)	20	20	20	18	17

TAKE-TWO INTERACTIVE SOFTWARE, INC.

NMS: TTWO

110 West 44th Street
New York, NY 10036
Phone: 646 536-2842
Fax: –
Web: www.take2games.com

CEO: Strauss Zelnick
CFO: Lainie J. Goldstein
HR: David Messenger
FYE: March 31
Type: Public

Crime might not pay in the real world but in the gaming universe it means big money for Take-Two. The company's popular mature-rated Grand Theft Auto series and other games are developed by subsidiary Rockstar Games. Its 2K Games subsidiary publishes franchises such as BioShock Borderlands and Sid Meier's Civilization; the 2K Sports unit carries titles such as Major League Baseball 2K and NBA 2K. Take-Two's games are played on Microsoft Sony and Nintendo game consoles but also on PCs and handheld devices. Its products are sold through outlets including retail chains such as GameStop and Wal-Mart and as digital downloads. More than half of its sales comes from the US.

	Annual Growth	03/15	03/16	03/17	03/18	03/19
Sales ($ mil.)	25.3%	1,082.9	1,413.7	1,779.7	1,792.9	2,668.4
Net income ($ mil.)	–	(279.5)	(8.3)	67.3	173.5	333.8
Market value ($ mil.)	38.8%	2,855.6	4,225.9	6,649.0	10,969.1	10,586.5
Employees	14.6%	2,840	2,933	3,707	4,492	4,896

TAL INTERNATIONAL GROUP INC

NYS: TAL

100 Manhattanville Road
Purchase, NY 10577-2135
Phone: 914 251-9000
Fax: 914 697-2549
Web: www.talinternational.com

CEO: Brian M Sondey
CFO: John Burns
HR: –
FYE: December 31
Type: Public

If your freight is going by truck train or ship tall odds are it might be going in a container owned by TAL International Group. The company is a leading lessor of intermodal freight containers — steel boxes that come in standard sizes and can be used to move goods over the road over the rails or over the water. Marine shipping lines are among the company's top customers. TAL maintains a fleet of more than 1250000 containers or about 2.1 million 20-foot equivalent units (TEUs) of capacity. Besides its leasing operations TAL International sells used containers. Investment firm Jordan Company through its Resolute Fund affiliate and other entities controls about a 40% stake in TAL.

	Annual Growth	12/10	12/11	12/12	12/13	12/14
Sales ($ mil.)	15.4%	366.8	516.7	589.2	642.9	650.4
Net income ($ mil.)	21.1%	57.7	109.7	130.1	143.2	124.0
Market value ($ mil.)	9.0%	1,024.2	955.1	1,207.0	1,902.7	1,445.5
Employees	(0.3%)	172	174	173	172	170

TALLAHASSEE MEMORIAL HEALTHCARE, INC.

1300 MICCOSUKEE RD
TALLAHASSEE, FL 323085054
Phone: 850-431-1155
Fax: –
Web: www.tmh.org

CEO: G. Mark O'Bryant
CFO: William (Bill) Giudice
HR: –
FYE: September 30
Type: Private

Tallahassee Memorial HealthCare (TMH) aims to take the hassle out of health care. The community health system serves residents of Florida's state capital and its surrounding communities. The system is anchored by Tallahassee Memorial Hospital a not-for-profit facility with more than 770 beds and about 560 physicians on staff who represent some 50 different specialties. TMH provides general medical and surgical care as well as specialty care in areas such as oncology rehabilitation women's and children's health obesity and diabetes. TMH also has a trauma center offers a family practice residency program and provides primary medical care through a handful of regional clinics.

	Annual Growth	09/11	09/12	09/13	09/14	09/15
Sales ($ mil.)	7.1%	–	480.0	566.2	532.8	589.6
Net income ($ mil.)	(1.4%)	–	40.2	31.5	33.1	38.5
Market value ($ mil.)	–	–	–	–	–	–
Employees	–	–	–	–	–	6,430

TALLGRASS ENERGY PARTNERS, LP
NYS: TEP

4200 W. 115th Street, Suite 350
Leawood, KS 66211
Phone: 913 928-6060
Fax: –
Web: www.tallgrassenergy.com

CEO: David G Dehaemers Jr
CFO: Gary J Brauchle
HR: Kirsten Trujillo
FYE: December 31
Type: Public

This company hopes there's plenty of green out there in the tall grass. Tallgrass Energy Partners (TEP) provides transportation and storage of natural gas in the Rocky Mountains and Midwest. It also provides natural gas processing and treating at its three facilities in Wyoming. TEP's natural gas transportation systems are located in Colorado Kansas Missouri Nebraska and Wyoming. TEP also maintains a pipeline from the Colorado and Wyoming border to Beatrice Nebraska and it provides water business to customers in Colorado and Texas. TEP was formed in early 2013 to hold the midstream assets of its parent Tallgrass Development. It became a public company a few months later.

	Annual Growth	12/12	12/13	12/14	12/15	12/16
Sales ($ mil.)	99.0%	38.6	267.7	371.6	536.2	605.1
Net income ($ mil.)	–	(2.4)	14.2	70.7	160.5	263.5
Market value ($ mil.)	22.2%	–	1,906.3	3,277.4	3,021.5	3,479.1
Employees						

TALMER BANCORP INC
NAS: TLMR

2301 West Big Beaver Rd., Suite 525
Troy, MI 48084
Phone: 248 498-2802
Fax: –
Web: www.talmerbank.com

CEO: –
CFO: –
HR: –
FYE: December 31
Type: Public

Talmer Bancorp is a bank holding company primarily serving states in the Midwest. It offers online banking and bill payment services online cash management safe deposit box rentals debit card and ATM card services. It supplies a variety of loans including loans for small and medium-sized businesses residential mortgages commercial real estate and a variety of commercial and consumer demand savings and time deposit products. The company owns three subsidiary banks: Talmer Bank and Trust a Michigan state-chartered bank; First Place Bank a federal savings association; and Talmer West Bank a Michigan state-chartered bank. Chemical Bank agreed to buy Talmer Bancorp for $1.1 billion in January 2016.

	Annual Growth	12/10	12/11	12/12	12/13	12/14
Assets ($ mil.)	40.3%	–	2,123.6	2,347.5	4,547.4	5,870.8
Net income ($ mil.)	19.4%	44.7	33.4	21.7	98.6	90.9
Market value ($ mil.)	–	–	–	–	–	990.3
Employees	(4.7%)	–	–	1,550	1,446	1,408

TALON INTERNATIONAL, INC.
NBB: TALN

21900 Burbank Boulevard, Suite 270
Woodland Hills, CA 91367
Phone: 818 444-4100
Fax: –
Web: www.talonzippers.com

CEO: Larry Dyne
CFO: Larry Dyne
HR: –
FYE: December 31
Type: Public

Talon has clawed its way to the top with some thread trim and hang tags. Formerly Tag It Pacific it develops brand-identity programs for manufacturers of fashion apparel and accessories and for specialty retailers and mass merchants. Talon's "trim packages" include items such as thread zippers labels buttons and hangers as well as printed marketing materials (hang tags bar-coded tags pocket flashers size stickers) designed to promote and sell the items. It also distributes its Talon-brand metal and synthetic zippers and other apparel components such as waistbands under its TEKFIT name. Its more than 800 customers include Abercrombie & Fitch Express PVH and Victoria's Secret.

	Annual Growth	12/12	12/13	12/14	12/15	12/16
Sales ($ mil.)	2.0%	44.6	52.4	49.3	48.4	48.3
Net income ($ mil.)	10.0%	0.7	9.7	0.6	0.5	1.0
Market value ($ mil.)	27.8%	4.5	23.1	16.6	15.7	12.0
Employees	1.7%	188	215	212	195	201

TALON THERAPEUTICS INC.
OTC: TLON

7000 Shoreline Ct. Ste. 370
South San Francisco CA 94080
Phone: 650-588-6404
Fax: 650-588-2787
Web: www.talontx.com/

CEO: Joseph W Turgeon
CFO: –
HR: –
FYE: December 31
Type: Public

Talon Therapeutics (formerly Hana Biosciences) has its claws sunk deeply into the fight against cancer. The development stage pharmaceutical company acquires and develops new drugs with a focus on cancer treatments. Specifically the company seeks to find treatments that kill tumors without damaging surrounding healthy tissue. Talon's lead product candidates include Marqibo a unique formulation of an existing cancer drug targeting forms of leukemia and melanoma and Menadione a topical lotion meant to treat rashes caused by some cancer treatments. The company has other oncology pharmaceuticals in its pipeline including therapies to treat solid tumor cancers (including lung and ovarian).

TAMIR BIOTECHNOLOGY INC.
PINK SHEETS: ACEL

300 Atrium Dr.
Somerset NJ 08873
Phone: 732-652-4525
Fax: 732-652-4575
Web: www.alfacell.com

CEO: Jamie Sulley
CFO: Joanne M Barsa
HR: –
FYE: July 31
Type: Public

Development-stage Tamir Biotechnology (formerly Alfacell) is willing to kiss a few frogs in hopes one will transform into a princely product. The biotechnology firm has isolated proteins from Northern Leopard frog eggs and embryos as possible therapies for cancerous tumors that have become resistant to chemotherapy. The company's lead drug candidate Onconase is being studied as a possible treatment for a variety of cancers including non-small cell lung cancer. Tamir Biotechnology is researching applications for Onconase and other amphibian proteins for applications in other areas of oncology as well as infectious diseases.

TANDEM DIABETES CARE INC
NMS: TNDM

11075 Roselle Street
San Diego, CA 92121
Phone: 858 366-6900
Fax: –
Web: www.tandemdiabetes.com

CEO: Kim D. Blickenstaff
CFO: John Cajigas
HR: –
FYE: December 31
Type: Public

Tandem Diabetes Care is taking insulin pumps into the 21st century. The company's primary focus is its flagship insulin pump the t:slim X2 Insulin. The t:slim pump has the look of a smartphone — not a pager — and differs from traditional syringe-and-plunger insulin pumps in that it uses a miniature pump to draw insulin from a flexible bag within the cartridge rather than a mechanical syringe. The company has shipped nearly 68000 pumps to US customers since it launched the first one in 2012. (The t:slim was one of the first products approved under the FDA's Infusion Pump Improvement Initiative.) It also sells disposable products such as cartridges and infusion sets. Tandem Diabetes Care manufactures the t:slim and its accessories at a plant in California and sells them through distributors.

	Annual Growth	12/14	12/15	12/16	12/17	12/18
Sales ($ mil.)	38.7%	49.7	72.9	84.2	107.6	183.9
Net income ($ mil.)	–	(79.5)	(72.4)	(83.4)	(73.0)	(122.6)
Market value ($ mil.)	31.5%	730.9	679.7	123.7	135.8	2,185.3
Employees	10.6%	437	482	591	574	653

TANDY BRANDS ACCESSORIES, INC.   NBB: TBAC Q

3631 West Davis, Suite A
Dallas, TX 75211
Phone: 214 519-5200
Fax: –
Web: www.tandybrands.com

CEO: –
CFO: –
HR: –
FYE: June 30
Type: Public

When it comes to waist management Tandy Brands Accessories knows how to buckle down. It designs and markets leather goods including belts and wallets and other accessories such as scarves and neckties. Although the company has licenses to make products for national brands (including Dockers Totes and Dr. Martens Airwair) most of its products are proprietary brands and private-label items made for companies such as Wal-Mart Target and J. C. Penney. Some of these proprietary brands include Amity Rolfs Canterbury and Princess Gardner. Most of Tandy Brands' finished goods are manufactured in China and the Dominican Republic. Amid declining sales Tandy Brands is restructuring.

	Annual Growth	06/09	06/10	06/11	06/12	06/13
Sales ($ mil.)	(3.0%)	129.0	141.9	123.8	117.6	114.0
Net income ($ mil.)	–	(15.1)	1.2	(13.5)	(3.7)	(19.2)
Market value ($ mil.)	(28.4%)	16.4	25.7	14.0	10.3	4.3
Employees	(11.7%)	655	570	583	539	399

TANDY LEATHER FACTORY INC   NMS: TLF

1900 Southeast Loop 820
Fort Worth, TX 76140
Phone: 817 872-3200
Fax: –
Web: www.tandyleather.com

CEO: Janet Carr
CFO: Danette Click
HR: –
FYE: December 31
Type: Public

Tandy Leather Factory (aka TLF) has built a business turning hides into a cash cow. The company makes distributes and sells leather goods and related products such as leatherworking tools buckles and belt supplies leather dyes saddle and tack hardware do-it-yourself craft kits suede lace and fringe. Its Retail Leathercraft unit which generates more than 50% of sales operates about 75 retail leathercraft stores under the Tandy Leather banner that cater to leatherworking hobbyists in the US and Canada. It also sells merchandise online. The company also operates some 30 wholesale stores across in North America. Tandy Leather Factory was founded in 1980 as Midas Leathercraft Tool Co.

	Annual Growth	12/14	12/15	12/16	12/17	12/18
Sales ($ mil.)	(0.1%)	83.4	84.2	82.9	82.3	83.1
Net income ($ mil.)	(29.0%)	7.7	6.4	6.4	4.5	2.0
Market value ($ mil.)	(10.8%)	81.5	66.5	73.4	70.2	51.5
Employees	3.2%	603	584	614	656	684

TANGER FACTORY OUTLET CENTERS, INC.   NYS: SKT

3200 Northline Avenue, Suite 360
Greensboro, NC 27408
Phone: 336 292-3010
Fax: 336 297-0931
Web: www.tangeroutlet.com

CEO: Steven B. Tanger
CFO: James F. Williams
HR: –
FYE: December 31
Type: Public

Brand name bargains are on shoppers' lists when they visit Tanger Factory Outlet Centers. One of the top outlet mall developers (along with retail giant Simon Property and its Chelsea Property Group subsidiary) Tanger is a real estate investment trust (REIT) that develops owns and manages about 45 retail outlet centers in 25 states and Canada. A typical center has 75 stores and totals at least 300000 sq. ft. housing shops from more than 400 brand name companies including The Gap Ralph Lauren Ann Taylor Phillips-Van Heusen and Nike. Tanger's outlet centers which maintain about 99% occupancy are built away from malls and shopping districts so tenants don't compete with their full-price stores.

	Annual Growth	12/14	12/15	12/16	12/17	12/18
Sales ($ mil.)	4.3%	418.6	439.4	465.8	488.2	494.7
Net income ($ mil.)	(12.4%)	74.0	211.2	193.7	68.0	43.7
Market value ($ mil.)	(14.0%)	3,472.1	3,071.9	3,361.2	2,490.4	1,899.5
Employees	0.7%	625	625	659	640	643

TANGOE, INC.   NMS: TNGO

35 Executive Boulevard
Orange, CT 06477
Phone: 203 859-9300
Fax: –
Web: www.tangoe.com

CEO: Robert Irwin
CFO: Chris Taylor
HR: –
FYE: December 31
Type: Public

Tangoe dances to a telecom tempo. The company provides communications lifecycle management (CLM) software and services enabling large and midsized businesses and other organizations to manage their fixed and mobile assets and services. Its flagship hosted software suite the Communications Management Platform includes an inventory of industry reference metrics and tools to support lifecycle functions such as service provisioning inventory contracts management billing auditing reporting and analysis. Tangoe also offers such services as consulting contract negotiation bill auditing and carrier migration. The company was founded in 2000 as TelecomRFQ by CEO Albert Subbloie and went public in 2011.

	Annual Growth	12/10	12/11	12/12	12/13	12/14
Sales ($ mil.)	32.7%	68.5	104.9	154.5	188.9	212.5
Net income ($ mil.)	–	(1.8)	(3.0)	3.0	5.0	2.9
Market value ($ mil.)	(5.4%)	–	594.8	458.4	695.6	503.2
Employees	32.6%	757	1,004	1,383	2,056	2,339

TANNER INDUSTRIES, INC.

735 DAVISVILLE RD STE 3
SOUTHAMPTON, PA 189663277
Phone: 215-322-1238
Fax: –
Web: www.tannerind.com

CEO: –
CFO: Eric R Hindawi
HR: –
FYE: December 31
Type: Private

Tanner plies the trade of chemical shipping and warehousing. The company distributes anhydrous ammonia and ammonium hydroxide by tank truck railcar drum and cylinder to US customers from 16 facilities. It makes more than 20000 deliveries per year and operates 200 trucks and 150 rail cars. The company also provides custom blending contract packaging and safety training services. Tanner's products are sold to companies in the refrigeration metal treatment agriculture personal care product pulp and paper and water treatment industries. The company which was founded in 1954 by Lawrence Tanner is run by a third generation of Tanner family members.

	Annual Growth	12/03	12/04	12/05	12/06	12/07
Sales ($ mil.)	15.5%	–	52.1	64.7	74.1	80.2
Net income ($ mil.)	69.2%	–	0.8	3.5	6.8	4.1
Market value ($ mil.)	–	–	–	–	–	–
Employees	–	–	–	–	–	130

TAOS HEALTH SYSTEMS, INC.

1397 WEIMER RD
TAOS, NM 875716253
Phone: 575-758-8883
Fax: –
Web: www.taoshospital.org

CEO: Bill Patten
CFO: Ken Verdon
HR: –
FYE: May 31
Type: Private

Whether you're skiing in the winter or hiking in the summer Taos visitors and residents can turn to Holy Cross Hospital for medical care. The medical center provides inpatient and outpatient health care services for Taos and surrounding counties in northern New Mexico. The hospital opened its doors in 1937 and has expanded its facilities to include about 50 licensed beds. Among its specialty services are emergency medicine general surgery obstetrics orthopedics cardiology urology and women's health care. Holy Cross Hospital is part of the Taos Health Systems network which includes area general care rehabilitation surgical and specialist clinics.

	Annual Growth	05/13	05/14	05/15	05/16	05/17
Sales ($ mil.)	2.2%	–	55.6	53.7	56.9	59.3
Net income ($ mil.)	–	–	(7.0)	(1.3)	1.1	0.0
Market value ($ mil.)	–	–	–	–	–	–
Employees	–	–	–	–	–	412

TAPESTRY INC
NYS: TPR

10 Hudson Yards
New York, NY 10001
Phone: 212 946-8400
Fax: 212 594-1682
Web: www.tapestry.com

CEO: Victor Luis
CFO: Kevin G. Wills
HR: –
FYE: June 29
Type: Public

Tapestry is weaving together a collection of leading premium fashion brands. Previously Coach the company designs and makes (mostly through third parties) high-end leather goods and accessories including handbags wallets and luggage under the Coach brand. It also licenses the Coach name for watches eyewear and fragrances. In addition through acquisitions Tapestry owns the Stuart Weitzman (luxury women's shoes) and Kate Spade (women's apparel and accessories) brands. The company sells its wares through department and outlet stores (in the US and globally) and websites. It also operates more than 1500 retail and factory outlet stores in North America Japan China and other countries in the Asia-Pacific region.

	Annual Growth	06/15*	07/16	07/17*	06/18	06/19
Sales ($ mil.)	9.5%	4,191.6	4,491.8	4,488.3	5,880.0	6,027.1
Net income ($ mil.)	12.4%	402.4	460.5	591.0	397.5	643.4
Market value ($ mil.)	(3.2%)	10,359.2	11,681.4	13,577.1	13,396.4	9,100.2
Employees	7.4%	15,800	15,100	14,400	20,800	21,000

*Fiscal year change

TAPIMMUNE INC.
OTC: TPIV

2815 Eastlake Ave. East Ste. 300
Seattle WA 98102
Phone: 866-359-7541
Fax: 323-436-7755
Web: www.lamodels.com

CEO: Peter L Hoang
CFO: Anthony H Kim
HR: –
FYE: December 31
Type: Public

TapImmune taps into the immune system to take out autoimmune disorders. Its research is primarily focused on the biological TAP system which triggers an immune system response in cells. The TAP system shuts down in many cancer tumor cells but the company is developing a vaccine to restore the immune function. TapImmune is also researching a vaccine adjuvant product designed to enhance the effectiveness of existing and new infectious disease vaccines. The company also has technologies that could be used to identify or screen drugs for potential effectiveness in treating cancers and viral and infectious diseases.

TARGA RESOURCES CORP
NYS: TRGP

811 Louisiana St., Suite 2100
Houston, TX 77002
Phone: 713 584-1000
Fax: 713 584-1100
Web: www.targaresources.com

CEO: Joe Bob Perkins
CFO: Mattthew J. (Matt) Meloy
HR: –
FYE: December 31
Type: Public

Targa Resources Corp. has the energy to deliver natural gas throughout its service territory of Texas Oklahoma and neighboring states. Through its Targa Resources Partners entity it gathers processes transports and sells natural gas natural gas liquids (NGLs) crude oil and refined petroleum products. It owns or operates about 27000 miles of natural gas gathering pipelines and more than 35 processing plants. It has a presence in many shale basins including the Permian Eagle Ford Barnett Anadarko Arkoma and Williston. In early 2016 Targa Resources Corp purchased all unowned shares of Targa Resources Partners securing complete control of its previously majority-owned subsidiary.

	Annual Growth	12/14	12/15	12/16	12/17	12/18
Sales ($ mil.)	5.0%	8,616.5	6,658.6	6,690.9	8,814.9	10,484.0
Net income ($ mil.)	(64.6%)	102.3	58.3	(187.3)	54.0	1.6
Market value ($ mil.)	(23.7%)	24,581.4	6,272.3	12,996.5	11,223.3	8,349.1
Employees	16.2%	1,350	1,870	1,970	2,130	2,460

TARGA RESOURCES PARTNERS LP
NYS: NGLS

1000 Louisiana St, Suite 4300
Houston, TX 77002
Phone: 713 584-1000
Fax: –
Web: www.targaresources.com

CEO: Joe Bob Perkins
CFO: –
HR: –
FYE: December 31
Type: Public

Targa Resources Partners fuels its business by producing and processing natural gas. The midstream energy company owns or operates 11300 miles of natural gas gathering pipeline (and ten processing plants) with access to gas reserves in the New Mexico West and North Texas and the Gulf Coast. Targa Resources Partners also operates natural gas liquids (NGLs) storage and transportation facilities located primarily in the southern and southwestern US. Customers include oil and gas companies and utilities. Targa Resources Corp. holds a minority limited partner stake and a 2% general partner stake in Targa Resources Partners.

	Annual Growth	12/09	12/10	12/11	12/12	12/13
Sales ($ mil.)	12.5%	4,095.6	5,460.2	6,987.1	5,883.6	6,556.2
Net income ($ mil.)	45.6%	52.0	109.1	204.5	174.6	233.5
Market value ($ mil.)	21.1%	2,760.0	3,855.6	4,232.5	4,243.9	5,937.8
Employees	–	–	–	–	–	–

TARGET CORP
NYS: TGT

1000 Nicollet Mall
Minneapolis, MN 55403
Phone: 612 304-6073
Fax: –
Web: www.target.com

CEO: Brian C. Cornell
CFO: Catherine R. (Cathy) Smith
HR: Stephanie A. Lundquist
FYE: February 02
Type: Public

Cheap-but-chic Target is the US's #2 discount chain (behind Wal-Mart). The fashion-forward discounter operates 1800-plus Target and SuperTarget stores across the US as well as an online business at Target.com. It sells a broad range of household goods food and pet supplies apparel and accessories electronics decor and other items under national brands as well as owned and exclusive brands. Target and its larger grocery-carrying incarnation SuperTarget have carved out a niche by offering more upscale trend-driven merchandise than rivals Wal-Mart and Kmart. The company also offers pharmacy and clinic services in its stores through an operating agreement with CVS Pharmacy.

	Annual Growth	01/15	01/16	01/17*	02/18	02/19
Sales ($ mil.)	0.9%	72,618.0	73,785.0	69,495.0	71,879.0	75,356.0
Net income ($ mil.)	–	(1,636.0)	3,363.0	2,737.0	2,934.0	2,937.0
Market value ($ mil.)	(0.8%)	38,112.4	37,496.3	32,981.4	37,770.7	36,849.1
Employees	0.9%	347,000	341,000	323,000	345,000	360,000

*Fiscal year change

TARLETON STATE UNIVERSITY

1333 W WASHINGTON ST
STEPHENVILLE, TX 764014168
Phone: 254-968-9000
Fax: –
Web: www.tarleton.edu

CEO: –
CFO: –
HR: –
FYE: August 31
Type: Private

Tarleton State University a member of The Texas A&M University System has an enrollment of more than 9500 students on four campuses Central and North Texas. The university confers degrees in undergraduate programs and graduate programs. It also offers a doctorate in educational administration. Tarleton State has approximately 450 full- and part-time faculty providing instruction at six colleges (agriculture and human sciences business administration education liberal and fine arts science and technology and graduate studies). It ranks as one of the most affordable four-year universities in Texas.

	Annual Growth	08/14	08/15	08/16	08/17	08/18
Sales ($ mil.)	2.9%	–	106.8	115.0	111.5	116.4
Net income ($ mil.)	106.2%	–	1.7	(1.8)	16.2	14.9
Market value ($ mil.)	–	–	–	–	–	–
Employees	–	–	–	–	–	822

TARRANT COUNTY HOSPITAL DISTRICT

1500 S MAIN ST
FORT WORTH, TX 761044917
Phone: 817-921-3431
Fax: –
Web: www.jpshealthnet.org

CEO: –
CFO: David Salsberry
HR: Nikki Sumpter
FYE: September 30
Type: Private

If Fort Worth residents are searching for health care they need look no further than Tarrant County Hospital District (dba JPS Health Network). Founded in 1906 in Fort Worth Texas the network's flagship facility John Peter Smith Hospital has approximately 540 beds and provides specialty services including orthopedics cardiology and women's health. JPS Health Network also includes behavioral health treatment center Trinity Springs Pavilion and the JPS Diagnostic & Surgery Hospital of Arlington. The company provides family medical dental and specialty care through dozens of health care centers in northern Texas.

	Annual Growth	09/13	09/14	09/15	09/16	09/18
Sales ($ mil.)	22.0%	–	285.2	557.7	576.0	632.1
Net income ($ mil.)	–	–	48.1	48.6	18.6	(3.0)
Market value ($ mil.)	–	–	–	–	–	–
Employees	–	–	–	–	–	3,000

TAS-CHFH

70 EAST ST
METHUEN, MA 018444597
Phone: 978-687-0156
Fax: –
Web: www.caritasholyfamily.org

CEO: –
CFO: –
HR: –
FYE: September 30
Type: Private

Caritas Holy Family Hospital is part of a large family of hospitals. The acute care medical facility is a more than 260-bed hospital that serves the residents of some 20 communities in northern Massachusetts and southern New Hampshire. Holy Family Hospital offers specialized services in areas including surgery diagnostics pediatrics obstetrics oncology cardiology and psychiatric care. The hospital founded in 1985 also operates an outpatient surgery center and provides community outreach services. It is a member of Steward Health Care System (formerly Caritas Christi) one of the largest health care systems in New England.

	Annual Growth	09/01	09/02	09/03	09/08	09/09
Sales ($ mil.)	2.6%	–	122.0	122.7	149.2	145.7
Net income ($ mil.)	–	–	(4.4)	(1.0)	2.0	6.0
Market value ($ mil.)	–	–	–	–	–	–
Employees	–	–	–	–	–	1,700

TAS-CNH, INC.

800 WASHINGTON ST STE 1
NORWOOD, MA 020623487
Phone: 781-769-4000
Fax: –

CEO: –
CFO: –
HR: –
FYE: September 30
Type: Private

Caritas Norwood Hospital cares for hearts (and other body parts) of people in the greater Boston area. Operating as Norwood Hospital the facility is a community hospital with some 265 beds that serves patients in Norwood Massachusetts and surrounding towns. Founded in 1902 the acute care hospital has a medical staff of more than 460 that provides area residents with emergency and general health care and medical transport services. Norwood Hospital is also home to specialized programs including behavioral health services cancer treatment cardiology obstetrics/gynecology orthopedic medicine pediatrics rehabilitation sleep disorder treatment and surgery. Norwood Hospital is part of the Steward Health Care System.

	Annual Growth	09/04	09/05	09/06	09/08	09/09
Sales ($ mil.)	1.6%	–	150.0	153.4	151.5	159.6
Net income ($ mil.)	(1.1%)	–	4.5	15.1	(3.7)	4.3
Market value ($ mil.)	–	–	–	–	–	–
Employees	–	–	–	–	–	1,800

TATA AMERICA INTERNATIONAL CORPORATION

101 PARK AVE RM 2603
NEW YORK, NY 101782604
Phone: 212-557-8038
Fax: –
Web: www.tcs.com

CEO: –
CFO: S. Mahalingam
HR: Divya Bindiganavale
FYE: March 31
Type: Private

Tata America International is the North American holding company for Indian conglomerate Tata Group. In the US the company has about a dozen subsidiaries including offices for Tata Communications IT services firm Tata Consultancy Services (with more than 20 locations) and engineering consultancy Tata Technologies. In the industrial sector Tata America owns steel manufacturing plants in Ohio and Pennsylvania and General Chemical Industrial Products a soda ash plant in Wyoming. Other holdings include hotels (The Pierre in New York the Taj Boston and the Taj Campton Place in San Francisco) and sales offices for its beverage brands Eight O'Clock Coffee Good Earth and Tetley.

	Annual Growth	03/14	03/15	03/16	03/17	03/18
Sales ($ mil.)	6.4%	–	6,800.0	755.3	845.2	8,197.5
Net income ($ mil.)	3.0%	–	111.5	118.5	168.2	121.8
Market value ($ mil.)	–	–	–	–	–	–
Employees	–	–	–	–	–	1,700

TATUNG COMPANY OF AMERICA, INC.

2850 E EL PRESIDIO ST
LONG BEACH, CA 908101119
Phone: 310-637-2105
Fax: –

CEO: Huei-Jihn Jih
CFO: Danny Huang
HR: Albert Perez
FYE: December 31
Type: Private

Tongue tied by the alphabet soup of electronics? Tatung Company of America untangles the LCDs (liquid crystal displays) from the LEDs (light-emitting diodes). It offers an array of high-tech goods and manufacturing services for PC and electronics OEMs. Its digital line ranges from signage and security surveillance tools like cameras and monitors to computer monitors for PCs point-of-sale terminals and touch screens. The company also sells home appliances such as air purifiers and rice cookers as well as hospitality conveniences like microwaves and coffee makers. The company is the US arm of Taiwan's Tatung Company.

	Annual Growth	12/03	12/04	12/05	12/07	12/08
Sales ($ mil.)	(15.1%)	–	246.9	265.4	138.3	128.5
Net income ($ mil.)	(38.8%)	–	4.3	3.0	1.3	0.6
Market value ($ mil.)	–	–	–	–	–	–
Employees	–	–	–	–	–	105

TAUBER OIL COMPANY

55 WAUGH DR STE 700
HOUSTON, TX 770075837
Phone: 713-869-8700
Fax: –
Web: www.tauberoil.com

CEO: –
CFO: –
HR: –
FYE: December 31
Type: Private

No liquid petrochemical product is taboo for oil refiner and marketer Tauber Oil. The family owned company markets refined petroleum products carbon black feedstocks liquefied petroleum gases chemicals and petrochemicals (including benzene styrene monomer and methanol). Tauber Oil is one of the US's leading suppliers of feedstocks for reforming and olefin cracking. It also has oil and gas exploration and production operations. Subsidiary Tauber Petrochemical was created in 1997 to beef up the company's international petrochemical business. Tauber Oil which is owned by David and Richard Tauber maintains a fleet of more than 500 rail cars to supply its customers.

	Annual Growth	12/10	12/11	12/12	12/13	12/14
Sales ($ mil.)	(2.6%)	–	–	5,088.2	4,769.4	4,831.2
Net income ($ mil.)	(29.0%)	–	–	21.2	16.3	10.7
Market value ($ mil.)	–	–	–	–	–	–
Employees	–	–	–	–	–	135

TAUBMAN CENTERS INC
NYS: TCO

200 East Long Lake Road, Suite 300
Bloomfield Hills, MI 48304-2324
Phone: 248 258-6800
Fax: –
Web: www.taubman.com

CEO: Robert S. Taubman
CFO: Simon J. Leopold
HR: –
FYE: December 31
Type: Public

Taubman's favorite seasonal activity is most likely holiday shopping. The real estate investment trust (REIT) through its majority-owned operating partnership acquires owns and develops shopping malls primarily in the US. Taubman owns nearly 20 properties (mostly super-regional malls with more than 800000 sq. ft. each) in urban and suburban shopping centers in 10 states. Its largest tenants have included L Brands The Gap and Forever 21. Its Taubman Asia subsidiary in Hong Kong develops malls in China and South Korea. Taubman was founded in 1950 by former chairman A. Alfred Taubman who with his family controls about one-quarter of the REIT.

	Annual Growth	12/14	12/15	12/16	12/17	12/18
Sales ($ mil.)	(1.4%)	679.1	557.2	612.6	629.2	640.9
Net income ($ mil.)	(44.7%)	893.0	134.1	132.6	80.7	83.5
Market value ($ mil.)	(12.2%)	4,666.9	4,685.2	4,514.8	3,995.8	2,778.0
Employees	(6.9%)	598	615	624	468	450

TAXUS CARDIUM PHARMACEUTICALS GROUP INC
NBB: CRXM

11750 Sorrento Valley Rd, Suite 250
San Diego, CA 92121
Phone: 858 436-1000
Fax: –
Web: www.cardiumthx.com

CEO: –
CFO: –
HR: –
FYE: December 31
Type: Public

At the heart of Cardium Therapeutics is a hope to hit it big with one of its assorted holdings. Its Cardium Biologics unit includes lead candidate Generx which is in development as a treatment for candidates ischemic heart disease (such as angina) and restoring heart functioning after a heart attack. Meanwhile its Tissue Repair Company business received FDA approval for Excellagen a topical gel intended to promote healing diabetic foot ulcers and other wounds in 2012. A third business To Go Brands develops and sells nutritional supplements and skin care products.

	Annual Growth	12/09	12/10	12/11	12/12	12/13
Sales ($ mil.)	(29.6%)	0.4	0.2	0.0	0.8	0.1
Net income ($ mil.)	–	(11.7)	(4.7)	(7.1)	(8.3)	(8.9)
Market value ($ mil.)	5.0%	6.0	3.5	2.6	1.7	7.3
Employees	(5.9%)	14	15	15	24	11

TAYLOR (CALVIN B.) BANKSHARES, INC. (MD)
NBB: TYCB

24 N. Main Street
Berlin, MD 21811
Phone: 410 641-1700
Fax: 410 641-0543
Web: www.taylorbank.com

CEO: Raymond M Thompson
CFO: William H Mitchell
HR: –
FYE: December 31
Type: Public

Calvin B. Taylor Bankshares be the holding company for Calvin B. Taylor Banking Company (aka Taylor Bank) which has about 10 branches in southeastern Maryland and another in Delaware. The bank offers standard commercial and retail services including checking and savings accounts money market accounts and credit cards. It also offers discount securities brokerage through an affiliation with correspondent bank M&T Securities. Real estate loans account for some 90% of the bank's lending portfolio including residential and commercial mortgages. The bank is named after its founder who opened a predecessor to Calvin B. Taylor Banking Company in 1890.

	Annual Growth	12/14	12/15	12/16	12/17	12/18
Assets ($ mil.)	4.2%	451.0	467.0	489.3	522.0	531.9
Net income ($ mil.)	13.2%	4.5	4.6	4.9	5.5	7.4
Market value ($ mil.)	7.1%	71.3	82.3	77.4	97.6	93.8
Employees						

TAYLOR CAPITAL GROUP, INC
NMS: TAYC

9550 West Higgins Road
Rosemont, IL 60018
Phone: 847 653-7978
Fax: –
Web: www.coletaylor.com

CEO: –
CFO: –
HR: –
FYE: December 31
Type: Public

This company is tailor-made for small and midsized business owners. Taylor Capital Group is the holding company for Cole Taylor Bank which specializes in commercial banking real estate lending and wealth management services aimed primarily at closely-held and family-run businesses in the construction manufacturing distribution transportation and professional services industries. Business loans including working capital owner-occupied real estate financing and letters and lines of credit account for approximately 90% of the bank's loan portfolio. With about 10 branches in the Chicago metropolitan area the bank also offers traditional banking services to consumers.

	Annual Growth	12/08	12/09	12/10	12/11	12/12
Assets ($ mil.)	7.2%	4,388.9	4,403.5	4,483.9	4,685.8	5,802.4
Net income ($ mil.)	–	(124.5)	(31.6)	(53.8)	91.1	61.9
Market value ($ mil.)	32.5%	168.4	327.9	378.6	279.9	519.7
Employees	20.1%	451	434	591	638	938

TAYLOR DEVICES INC
NAS: TAYD

90 Taylor Drive
North Tonawanda, NY 14120-0748
Phone: 716 694-0800
Fax: 716 695-6015
Web: www.taylordevices.com

CEO: Timothy J Sopko
CFO: Mark V McDonough
HR: –
FYE: May 31
Type: Public

Taylor Devices helps buffer buildings and other structures from the forces of earthquakes high winds and even roaring crowds. The company makes seismic dampers and other equipment used to absorb shock control vibration and store energy. Along with giant dampers used in multi-story buildings — including Safeco Field home of the Seattle Mariners baseball team — Taylor Devices produces a variety of shock absorbers liquid die springs and vibration dampers used in equipment and machinery. Taylor Devices primarily sells its products in the US and Canada.

	Annual Growth	05/15	05/16	05/17	05/18	05/19
Sales ($ mil.)	2.4%	30.6	35.7	25.5	24.4	33.6
Net income ($ mil.)	4.0%	2.2	4.2	2.3	0.4	2.5
Market value ($ mil.)	(3.7%)	44.8	58.1	46.1	35.7	38.6
Employees	0.0%	119	118	110	111	119

TAYLOR MORRISON HOME CORP (HOLDING CO)
NYS: TMHC

4900 N. Scottsdale Road, Suite 2000
Scottsdale, AZ 85251
Phone: 480 840-8100
Fax: –
Web: www.taylormorrison.com

CEO: Sheryl Palmer
CFO: C. David (Dave) Cone
HR: –
FYE: December 31
Type: Public

Taylor Morrison Home designs builds and sells single- and multi-family detached and attached homes in the US under the Taylor Morrison and Darling Homes brands. The company targets a wide demographic range of first time move-up luxury and active adult buyers. Its homes are priced between $135000 and $3.1 million and sell for an average of about $415000 in the Midwest and the eastern US; $480000 in Texas and Colorado; and $610000 in California and Arizona. Taylor Morrison's sales are divided across those three geographic segments; the Midwest and eastern states provide its greatest revenue stream. The company also offers financing and title insurance.

	Annual Growth	12/14	12/15	12/16	12/17	12/18
Sales ($ mil.)	11.8%	2,708.4	2,976.8	3,550.0	3,885.3	4,227.4
Net income ($ mil.)	30.4%	71.5	61.0	52.6	91.2	206.4
Market value ($ mil.)	(4.2%)	2,133.9	1,807.5	2,175.7	2,764.3	1,796.2
Employees	11.3%	1,498	1,600	1,800	1,800	2,300

TCF FINANCIAL CORP
NYS: TCF

200 Lake Street East
Wayzata, MN 55391-1693
Phone: 952 745-2760
Fax: –
Web: www.tcfbank.com

CEO: –
CFO: –
HR: –
FYE: December 31
Type: Public

TCF Financial agreed in January 2019 to merge with Minnesota-based Chemical Financial to form a Midwest bank with about $45 billion in assets $34 billion in total deposits and more than 500 branches in nine states. Chemical's commercial lending and wealth management activities will complement TCF's large deposit base and national wholesale lending business. The combined company which is to retain the TCF brand will have a more diversified deposit mix between retail and commercial lines and a more balanced loan portfolio across geographies asset classes and industries. Following the merger TCF shareholders will have a controlling interest in the combined company.

	Annual Growth	12/13	12/14	12/15	12/16	12/17
Assets ($ mil.)	5.8%	18,379.8	19,394.6	20,691.7	21,441.3	23,002.2
Net income ($ mil.)	15.4%	151.7	174.2	197.1	212.1	268.6
Market value ($ mil.)	6.0%	2,789.6	2,727.8	2,424.0	3,363.0	3,519.2
Employees	(4.8%)	7,449	7,023	6,755	6,427	6,116

TCF FINANCIAL CORP (NEW)
NMS: TCF

333 W. Fort Street, Suite 1800
Detroit, MI 48226
Phone: 800 867-9757
Fax: –
Web: www.chemicalbank.com

CEO: Thomas W. Kohn
CFO: Lori A. Gwizdala
HR: –
FYE: December 31
Type: Public

Chemical Financial has banking down to a science. It's the holding company for Chemical Bank which provides standard services such as checking and savings accounts CDs and IRAs credit and debit cards and loans and mortgages to individuals and businesses through nearly 190 branches in the lower peninsula of Michigan. The majority of the bank's loan portfolio is made up of commercial loans while consumer loans make up the remainder. Boasting assets of $9 billion Chemical is the second largest bank in Michigan. The company also offers trust investment management brokerage and title insurance services through subsidiaries.

	Annual Growth	12/14	12/15	12/16	12/17	12/18
Assets ($ mil.)	30.9%	7,322.1	9,188.8	17,355.2	19,280.9	21,498.3
Net income ($ mil.)	46.2%	62.1	86.8	108.0	149.5	284.0
Market value ($ mil.)	4.6%	2,189.5	2,448.9	3,871.0	3,821.0	2,616.2
Employees	11.6%	2,000	2,100	3,300	3,000	3,100

TD AMERITRADE HOLDING CORP
NMS: AMTD

200 South 108th Avenue
Omaha, NE 68154
Phone: 402 331-7856
Fax: 402 597-7789
Web: www.amtd.com

CEO: Timothy D. (Tim) Hockey
CFO: Stephen J. (Steve) Boyle
HR: Karen Ganzlin
FYE: September 30
Type: Public

Through several subsidiaries TD Ameritrade Holding provides electronic discount brokerage and related financial services that enable retail investors to trade common and preferred stocks of US companies exchange-traded funds (ETFs) mutual funds bonds options futures and foreign currencies. In addition to its online offerings the company provides services through a network of more than 360 retail branches and relationships with more than 6000 independent registered investment advisors (RIAs). TD Ameritrade holds some $1.3 trillion in client assets and supports about half a million client trades per day.

	Annual Growth	09/15	09/16	09/17	09/18	09/19
Sales ($ mil.)	16.7%	3,247.0	3,327.0	3,676.0	5,452.0	6,016.0
Net income ($ mil.)	28.4%	813.0	842.0	872.0	1,473.0	2,208.0
Market value ($ mil.)	26.3%	9,998.7	19,170.6	26,547.2	28,739.5	25,404.8
Employees	12.8%	5,690	6,010	10,412	9,183	9,226

TEAM HEALTH HOLDINGS INC
NYS: TMH

265 Brookview Centre Way, Suite 400
Knoxville, TN 37919
Phone: 865 693-1000
Fax: –

CEO: Leif Murphy
CFO: David P Jones
HR: –
FYE: December 31
Type: Public

Team Health keeps its cool in an emergency room and it runs a smooth back office. The company is a leading provider of clinical outsourcing services across the US. It provides physician staffing and administrative services to hospital emergency rooms and handles everything from doctor recruitment to billing payroll and claims management. The company provides similar services for anesthesiology inpatient care (hospitalist) and pediatric programs. Team Health contracts with civilian and military hospitals clinics and physician groups across the US.

	Annual Growth	12/10	12/11	12/12	12/13	12/14
Sales ($ mil.)	16.7%	1,519.3	1,745.3	2,069.0	2,383.6	2,819.6
Net income ($ mil.)	64.5%	13.3	65.5	63.8	87.4	97.7
Market value ($ mil.)	38.7%	1,107.7	1,573.2	2,050.8	3,246.9	4,100.9
Employees	18.9%	8,600	9,800	11,500	12,400	17,200

TEAM INC
NYS: TISI

13131 Dairy Ashford, Suite 600
Sugar Land, TX 77478
Phone: 281 331-6154
Fax: –
Web: www.teaminc.com

CEO: Ted W. Owen
CFO: Greg L. Boane
HR: –
FYE: December 31
Type: Public

Consider it the A-Team for high-pressure situations. Team provides specialized maintenance services for piping systems including repairing leaks hot tapping (adding new connections to pressurized pipelines) and detecting escaping emissions. It also offers field heat treatment and testing and inspection services. The firm makes custom equipment clamps and enclosures to augment its standard materials and sealant products. Mainly serving companies in heavy industries such as the petrochemical refining power pulp and paper pipeline and steel industries. The firm operates from more than 150 locations worldwide but its largest markets are the US and Canada.

	Annual Growth	05/15*	12/15	12/16	12/17	12/18
Sales ($ mil.)	14.0%	842.0	571.7	1,196.7	1,200.2	1,246.9
Net income ($ mil.)	–	40.1	8.9	(12.7)	(104.2)	(63.1)
Market value ($ mil.)	(28.3%)	1,201.3	964.7	1,184.7	449.7	442.2
Employees	14.5%	4,800	5,900	7,400	7,300	7,200

*Fiscal year change

TEAM INDUSTRIES HOLDING CORPORATION

105 PARK AVE NW
BAGLEY, MN 566219558
Phone: 218-694-3550
Fax: –

CEO: David Ricke
CFO: Steve Kast
HR: –
FYE: September 29
Type: Private

It takes a team TEAM Industries to make the drivetrains that and other vehicles parts. The Ricke family owned company designs tests manufacturers and assembles powertrain transmissions drivetrains gear sets and chassis components for snowmobile all-terrain vehicle lawn mowers and other vehicles through partnerships with CNH Ford Honda Ingersoll-Rand Kawasaki Textron Yamaha and other OEMs. TEAM maintains half a dozen facilities throughout Minnesota and North Carolina; its manufacturing capabilities run from ductile iron and shaft machining to aluminum die-casting and gear/spline making. The company also offers engineering R&D and testing services.

	Annual Growth	09/11	09/12	09/16	09/17	09/18
Sales ($ mil.)	2.2%	–	288.4	279.8	286.7	327.8
Net income ($ mil.)	0.9%	–	25.4	19.2	22.4	26.8
Market value ($ mil.)	–	–	–	–	–	–
Employees	–	–	–	–	–	1,100

TEARLAB CORP

NBB: TEAR

150 La Terraza Blvd., Suite 101
Escondido, CA 92025
Phone: 858 455-6006
Fax: –
Web: www.tearlab.com

CEO: Joseph Jensen
CFO: Michael Marquez
HR: –
FYE: December 31
Type: Public

TearLab (formerly OccuLogix) can read your tears. The diagnostics company has developed and commercialized the TearLab Osmolarity System a tear collection and analysis system for use at the point of care. The system detects biomarkers that indicate ophthalmic conditions; its first testing product aids in the diagnosis of dry eye disease (DED). After several failed attempts to develop medical therapies for ophthalmic ailments including glaucoma and macular degeneration the company became focused on diagnostic testing; it changed its name to TearLab in 2010.

	Annual Growth	12/14	12/15	12/16	12/17	12/18
Sales ($ mil.)	6.1%	19.7	25.2	28.0	27.1	25.0
Net income ($ mil.)	–	(23.7)	(33.2)	(19.9)	(16.1)	(2.3)
Market value ($ mil.)	(57.2%)	29.9	15.7	5.9	4.3	1.0
Employees	(25.8%)	132	118	75	42	40

TECH DATA CORP.

NMS: TECD

5350 Tech Data Drive
Clearwater, FL 33760
Phone: 727 539-7429
Fax: –
Web: www.techdata.com

CEO: Robert M. Dutkowsky
CFO: Charles V. (Chuck) Dannewitz
HR: Beth E. Simonetti
FYE: January 31
Type: Public

One of the world's largest wholesale distributors of technology products Tech Data Corp. provides thousands of items to more than 125000 resellers in 100-plus countries. Its catalog of products includes computer components (disk drives keyboards and video cards) networking equipment (routers and bridges) peripherals (printers modems and monitors) systems (PCs and servers) and software. Tech Data also offer products and services geared to data centers that include storage networking servers and cloud infrastructure. Other services are technical support configuration integration financing and logistics and product fulfillment. More than 60% of Tech Data's revenues are generated outside the US.

	Annual Growth	01/15	01/16	01/17	01/18	01/19
Sales ($ mil.)	7.7%	27,670.6	26,379.8	26,234.9	36,775.0	37,239.0
Net income ($ mil.)	18.1%	175.2	265.7	195.1	116.6	340.6
Market value ($ mil.)	13.8%	2,109.3	2,305.1	3,160.6	3,704.0	3,532.6
Employees	12.0%	8,900	9,000	9,500	14,000	14,000

TECHE HOLDING CO.

ASE: TSH

1120 Jefferson Terrace
New Iberia, LA 70560
Phone: 337 560-7151
Fax: –
Web: www.teche.com

CEO: –
CFO: –
HR: –
FYE: September 30
Type: Public

Teche Holding is the holding company for Teche Federal Bank which operates some 20 branch offices in the Lafayette metropolitan area of southern Louisiana. Targeting individuals and local business customers the bank offers such traditional retail services as checking and savings accounts NOW accounts and certificates of deposit. Real estate loans make up nearly all of the company's loan portfolio including residential mortgages (about half of all loans) commercial mortgages mobile home loans and land loans.

	Annual Growth	09/09	09/10	09/11	09/12	09/13
Assets ($ mil.)	2.9%	765.1	761.5	793.2	852.0	856.7
Net income ($ mil.)	5.2%	7.1	7.1	7.2	7.3	8.7
Market value ($ mil.)	8.4%	67.8	63.5	60.4	83.0	93.6
Employees	0.5%	317	314	310	323	323

TECHNICA CORPORATION

22970 INDIAN CREEK DR
STERLING, VA 201666739
Phone: 703-662-2000
Fax: –
Web: www.technicacorp.com

CEO: –
CFO: Mark Cabrey
HR: –
FYE: December 31
Type: Private

Founded in 1991 Technica provides information technology (IT) consulting services hardware and related software including offerings in voice and data network design installation and performance testing. Technica supplies support for technologies and platforms such as storage area networks and metro optical as well as large systems integration and network security services. The company also offers on-site support and customized training for managers engineers and technicians. Its customers include telecommunications providers government and military agencies health care and educational clients and financial markets.

	Annual Growth	12/05	12/06	12/08*	06/09*	12/12
Sales ($ mil.)	(22.4%)	–	411.8	65.1	27.9	89.7
Net income ($ mil.)	4.1%	–	–	2.2	1.7	2.6
Market value ($ mil.)	–	–	–	–	–	–
Employees	–	–	–	–	–	190

*Fiscal year change

TECHNICAL COMMUNICATIONS CORP

NAS: TCCO

100 Domino Drive
Concord, MA 01742-2892
Phone: 978 287-5100
Fax: –
Web: www.tccsecure.com

CEO: Carl H Guild Jr
CFO: Michael P Malone
HR: –
FYE: September 28
Type: Public

Technical Communications Corporation also known as TCC helps its customers keep their secrets to themselves. The company makes secure communications equiment that enables users to digitally encrypt and transmit information. It also makes receivers used to decipher the data. TCC's products protect transmissions sent by radios telephones fax machines computer networks the Internet fiber-optic cables and satellite links. The company subcontracts much of its manufacturing and caters largely to government agencies but it also serves financial institutions and other corporations. It derives the bulk of its sales from a very small number of customers including the US Army.

	Annual Growth	10/15	10/16*	09/17	09/18	09/19
Sales ($ mil.)	4.3%	5.9	2.5	4.2	3.7	7.0
Net income ($ mil.)	–	(1.8)	(2.5)	(1.4)	(1.5)	0.6
Market value ($ mil.)	(3.5%)	5.3	4.9	9.9	8.4	4.6
Employees	(5.4%)	30	28	25	25	24

*Fiscal year change

TECHNICAL CONSUMER PRODUCTS INC.

325 Campus Dr.
Aurora OH 44202
Phone: 330-995-6111
Fax: 330-995-6188
Web: www.tcpi.com

CEO: Kaj Den Daas
CFO: Brian Catlett
HR: –
FYE: December 31
Type: Subsidiary

How many people does it take to screw in one of Technical Consumer Products' light bulbs? One and they only have to change the bulb every few years. Technical Consumer Products (TCP) sells energy efficient compact fluorescent light (CFLs) bulbs light emitting diodes (LEDs) high-intensity discharge (HID) lamps and halogen bulbs in the US under the brands TCP DuraBright EcoSave Fresh2 and n:vision. It also offers linear fluorescent bulbs and fixtures exit and emergency lighting CFL fixtures and ballasts to the commercial market under the brands Eco-Vations and SpringLight. TCP is the US sales arm of Chinese manufacturer TCP International Holdings.

TECHNOLOGY RESEARCH CORPORATION

5250 140th Ave. North
Clearwater FL 33760
Phone: 727-535-0572
Fax: 727-530-4324
Web: www.trci.net

CEO: G Gary Yetman
CFO: J G Cochran
HR: –
FYE: March 31
Type: Subsidiary

Technology Research Corporation (TRC) doesn't think electrical devices should be shocking. The company makes ground fault protectors portable leakage current interrupters and other electrical safety products that protect people and equipment against electric shock and fires. Its products detect electrical leaks and cut off power to equipment such as copy machines computers and printers. While the military remains an important market for TRC it is focused on building its commercial customer base and has expanded its Fire Shield product line in response to government safety regulations relating to appliance cords. In 2011 TRC was acquired by Coleman Cable in a deal valued at about $51.5 million.

TECHNOLOGY SERVICE CORPORATION

962 WAYNE AVE
SILVER SPRING, MD 209104433
Phone: 301-576-2300
Fax: –
Web: www.tsc.com

CEO: Brandon Wolfson
CFO: –
HR: –
FYE: September 30
Type: Private

Radar sensor expert Technology Service Corporation (TSC) provides engineering consulting services and specialized products primarily for US government agencies such as the Federal Aviation Administration the Navy and the Department of Defense but also for international civil aviation agencies and major radar system suppliers. Its services encompass research and advanced concept development through integrated logistics support. TSC's products include software for radar siting geographic information services and sensor simulation. Dr. Peter Swerling founded the employee-owned company in 1966.

	Annual Growth	09/05	09/06	09/07	09/08	09/10
Sales ($ mil.)	27.1%	–	–	40.6	75.4	83.3
Net income ($ mil.)	649.1%	–	–	0.0	6.2	6.9
Market value ($ mil.)	–	–	–	–	–	–
Employees	–	–	–	–	–	404

TECHTARGET INC
NMS: TTGT

275 Grove Street
Newton, MA 02466
Phone: 617 431-9200
Fax: –
Web: www.techtarget.com

CEO: Michael (Mike) Cotoia
CFO: Daniel (Dan) Noreck
HR: Arden Port
FYE: December 31
Type: Public

TechTarget can help you hit the IT professional's bull's-eye. The company operates a network of about 150 websites that focus on information technology topics such as storage security and networking. TechTarget offers original vendor-generated and user-generated content to more than 16 million registered members many of whom are technology buyers. Websites include Whatis.com DesktopReview.com SearchCRM.com and ebizQ.net. TechTarget additionally produces industry events and digital media offerings (e-mail newsletters online white papers webcasts and podcasts) aimed at IT professionals. The company generates most of its revenue through lead-generation advertising campaigns.

	Annual Growth	12/14	12/15	12/16	12/17	12/18
Sales ($ mil.)	3.4%	106.2	111.8	106.6	108.6	121.3
Net income ($ mil.)	33.5%	4.1	7.2	2.4	6.8	13.0
Market value ($ mil.)	1.8%	316.0	223.2	237.1	386.9	339.3
Employees	(1.5%)	686	696	659	622	647

TECO ENERGY INC.
NYS: TE

TECO Plaza, 702 N. Franklin Street
Tampa, FL 33602
Phone: 813 228-1111
Fax: 813 228-1670
Web: www.tecoenergy.com

CEO: John B Ramil
CFO: Sandra W Callahan
HR: –
FYE: December 31
Type: Public

TECO Energy keeps the energy flowing in west central Florida and New Mexico. The firm's Tampa Electric unit distributes power to more than 706000 customers and has about 4668 MW of generating capacity. The company produces almost all of its electricity from coal. It also distributes power to customers in New Mexico. TECO distributes natural gas in Florida through its Peoples Gas System unit (more than 350000 customers) and in New Mexico through New Mexico Gas Co. (NMGC more than 510000 gas customers). It exited the coal mining business with the sale of TECO Coal in 2015. That year the company agreed to be bought by Emera.

	Annual Growth	12/10	12/11	12/12	12/13	12/14
Sales ($ mil.)	(7.4%)	3,487.9	3,343.4	2,996.6	2,851.3	2,566.4
Net income ($ mil.)	(14.1%)	239.0	272.6	212.7	197.7	130.4
Market value ($ mil.)	3.6%	4,181.2	4,496.0	3,936.9	4,049.7	4,813.1
Employees	1.0%	4,233	4,290	3,900	3,900	4,400

TECO-WESTINGHOUSE MOTOR COMPANY

5100 N INTERSTATE 35 A
ROUND ROCK, TX 786812461
Phone: 512-218-7448
Fax: –
Web: www.tecowestinghouse.com

CEO: –
CFO: Emily KAO
HR: –
FYE: December 31
Type: Private

TECO-Westinghouse Motor Company (TWMC) is on a power trip. The subsidiary of TECO Electric & Machinery makes induction synchronous and DC electric motors (in sizes from one-quarter horsepower to 100000 hp) as well as generators and other electrical power products. TWMC also offers motor drives and controls large-motor repair and testing replacement parts and engineering services. The company serves customers in the air conditioning electrical utility marine mining and metal petrochemical pulp and paper and water/wastewater treatment industries.

	Annual Growth	12/01	12/02	12/11	12/12	12/13
Sales ($ mil.)	10.6%	–	96.5	226.2	283.7	293.5
Net income ($ mil.)	18.9%	–	3.6	17.1	20.5	23.8
Market value ($ mil.)	–	–	–	–	–	–
Employees	–	–	–	–	–	298

TECOGEN INC
NAS: TGEN

45 First Avenue
Waltham, MA 02451
Phone: 781 466-6402
Fax: –
Web: www.tecogen.com

CEO: Benjamin M Locke
CFO: –
HR: –
FYE: December 31
Type: Public

Tecogen designs and makes natural gas-fueled commercial and industrial cooling and cogeneration systems such as chillers water heaters and other types of cooling refrigeration and co-generation systems. Its product lines include TECOCHILL 25 to 400 ton engine-driven chillers Ilios high-efficiency water heaters and Tecogen co-generation equipment. Tecogen has shipped more than 2000 units throughout the US. The company was founded in the early 1960s and was spun off from Thermo Electron Corp. (a predecessor to Thermo Fisher Scientific) in 1987. Tecogen went public in 2014 after withdrawing a previous offering in 2013. In 2016 Tecogen agreed to acquire American DG Energy.

	Annual Growth	12/14	12/15	12/16	12/17	12/18
Sales ($ mil.)	16.7%	19.3	21.4	24.5	33.2	35.9
Net income ($ mil.)	–	(3.7)	(2.7)	(1.1)	0.0	(5.7)
Market value ($ mil.)	(8.7%)	129.6	86.9	104.3	67.0	90.1
Employees	6.6%	75	76	86	95	97

TECUMSEH PRODUCTS COMPANY LLC

5683 HINES DR
ANN ARBOR, MI 481087901
Phone: 734-585-9500
Fax: –
Web: www.tecumseh.com

CEO: Harold M Karp
CFO: Janice E Stipp
HR: Roger Jackson
FYE: December 31
Type: Private

Named for the legendary Shawnee chief Tecumseh Products makes a line of hermetically sealed compressors and heat pumps for residential and commercial refrigerators and freezers water coolers air conditioners dehumidifiers and vending machines. The company's line of scroll compressor models are suited for demanding commercial refrigeration applications and consist primarily of reciprocating and rotary designs. Tecumseh sells its products to OEMs and aftermarket distributors in more than 100 countries worldwide with more than 80% of its sales generated outside of the US. In mid-2015 Tecumseh agreed to be acquired by affiliates of Mueller Industries and Atlas Holdings for $123 million.

	Annual Growth	12/10	12/11	12/12	12/13	12/14
Sales ($ mil.)	(7.9%)	–	–	854.7	823.6	724.4
Net income ($ mil.)	–	–	–	22.6	(37.5)	(32.7)
Market value ($ mil.)	–	–	–	–	–	–
Employees	–	–	–	–	–	5,800

TEJON RANCH CO

P.O. Box 1000
Tejon Ranch, CA 93243
Phone: 661 248-3000
Fax: –
Web: www.tejonranch.com

NYS: TRC
CEO: Gregory S. Bielli
CFO: Allen E. Lyda
HR: –
FYE: December 31
Type: Public

Homes and nut farming are on the range for Tejon Ranch. Once one of the largest cattle ranches in the US the company hasn't run livestock on its 270000 acres in more than a decade. Instead Tejon Ranch has focused on wine grapes almonds and pistachio farming on its land which is located 60 miles north of Los Angeles. It also leases oil and gas and other mineral royalties; develops residential and commercial real estate; and leases the land for gaming grazing and filming. The historic ranch founded in 1843 hasn't totally sold out: Tejon Ranch stuck a deal in 2008 with major environmental groups to conserve about 90% of the vast chunk of open land or about 240000 acres.

	Annual Growth	12/14	12/15	12/16	12/17	12/18
Sales ($ mil.)	(2.9%)	51.3	51.1	45.6	35.7	45.6
Net income ($ mil.)	(6.9%)	5.7	3.0	0.6	(1.6)	4.3
Market value ($ mil.)	(13.4%)	765.1	497.4	660.5	539.2	430.6
Employees	(6.1%)	157	155	152	131	122

TEKELEC

5200 Paramount Pkwy.
Morrisville NC 27560
Phone: 919-460-5500
Fax: 919-460-0877
Web: www.tekelec.com

NASDAQ: TKLC
CEO: –
CFO: –
HR: –
FYE: December 31
Type: Private

Tekelec puts calls through. The company's network signaling systems include media gateway controllers and signaling gateways that enable mobile messaging network intelligence and migration to Internet protocol (IP) connectivity. Its performance management and monitoring applications are used to improve network security troubleshoot problems and detect and remedy revenue loss. Tekelec sells directly and through distributors worldwide to telephone network operators and contact centers. AT&T is a key client. In 2012 Tekelec was taken private by a group of investors led by Siris Capital Group for $780 million; other buyers included ComVest Sankaty Advisors and ZelnickMedia.

TEKNI-PLEX INC.

1150 1st Ave. Ste. 500
King of Prussia PA 19406-1334
Phone: 484-690-1520
Fax: 256-722-7440
Web: www.bench.com/viewer/worldwide_site_huntsville

CEO: –
CFO: John Seifert
HR: Rochelle Krombolz
FYE: June 30
Type: Private

Tekni-Plex is known for mixing a pinch of complexity into its packaging. The company manufactures packaging industrial materials specialty resins as well as tubing products for the healthcare food and consumer goods industries. Its packaging arm produces egg foam cartons poultry and meat processing trays pharmaceutical blister films and aerosol and dispensing pump components. Its tubing products segment makes garden and irrigation hose pool hose and vinyl medical tubing. Tekni-Plex also churns out polyvinyl chloride (PVC) compounds and recycled polyethylene terephthalate (PET) for industrial applications.

TEKNOR APEX COMPANY

505 CENTRAL AVE
PAWTUCKET, RI 028611900
Phone: 401-725-8000
Fax: –
Web: www.teknorapex.com

CEO: –
CFO: Paul Morrisroe
HR: Laurie Meisner
FYE: July 31
Type: Private

Teknor Apex offers a wide-ranging portfolio of chemicals and synthetic polymers. The company's six business divisions provide colorants (through its Teknor Color unit) vinyl compounds thermoplastic elastomers engineering thermoplastics chemicals for the polyvinyl chloride (PVC) plasticizer market and garden hoses. The company's compounds are used for building and construction consumer products industrial manufacturing electrical and electronic devices medical tools packaging and vehicular components. Founded in 1924 by Alfred A. Fain and his son-in-law Albert Pilavin Teknor invented the first plasticized (flexible) PVC.

	Annual Growth	07/02	07/03	07/04	07/05	07/14
Sales ($ mil.)	6.3%	–	–	–	574.0	996.8
Net income ($ mil.)	–	–	–	–	0.0	50.3
Market value ($ mil.)	–	–	–	–	–	–
Employees	–	–	–	–	–	2,500

TEKSYSTEMS, INC.

7437 RACE RD
HANOVER, MD 210761112
Phone: 410-540-7700
Fax: –

CEO: –
CFO: –
HR: –
FYE: December 31
Type: Private

TEKsystems a subsidiary of staffing giant Allegis provides IT consulting and staffing services from locations in North America and Europe. Considered one of the nation's largest IT staffing firms the company places more than 80000 technical professionals each year who work in a variety of fields including biotechnology telecommunications and construction and engineering. TEKsystems has 100 offices serving about 6000 clients. In addition the company runs the thingamajob.com website which is an online job board for technical staff. Spinning off of fellow Allegis unit Aerotek TEKsystems was formed in 1994 to focus on the IT needs of clients.

	Annual Growth	12/12	12/13	12/14	12/16	12/17
Sales ($ mil.)	5.2%	–	3,551.3	3,618.6	4,132.1	4,351.0
Net income ($ mil.)	–	–	0.0	0.0	0.0	0.0
Market value ($ mil.)	–	–	–	–	–	–
Employees	–	–	–	–	–	2,900

TEL FSI INC.
NASDAQ: FSII

3455 Lyman Blvd.
Chaska MN 55318-3052
Phone: 952-448-5440
Fax: 952-448-2825
Web: www.fsi-intl.com

CEO: -
CFO: -
HR: -
FYE: August 31
Type: Public

FSI International stays focused on semiconductor wafers all around the world. The company's surface conditioning equipment performs key cleaning etching and stripping functions that remove contaminants from silicon wafers and prepare them for subsequent production steps. Its equipment is used by electronics manufacturers worldwide such as Intel Samsung Electronics (about one-third of sales) STMicroelectronics and Texas Instruments as well as by other high-tech organizations including Sandia National Laboratories. Customers outside the US account for almost three-quarters of sales. In 2012 Tokyo Electron bought FSI for some $250 million.

TEL INSTRUMENT ELECTRONICS CORP.
NBB: TIKK

One Branca Road
East Rutherford, NJ 07073
Phone: 201 933-1600
Fax: -
Web: www.telinst.com

CEO: Jeffrey C O'Hara
CFO: -
HR: -
FYE: March 31
Type: Public

Before airplanes go off into the wild blue yonder attention must be paid to their avionics. Tel-Instrument Electronics manufactures avionics test equipment for the US Army the US Navy and other military and commercial customers. Tel's instruments are used to test navigation and communications equipment installed in aircraft both on the flight line (known as ramp testers) and in the maintenance shop (bench testers). The US government and military avionics customers (such as Boeing) account for more than two-thirds of sales.

	Annual Growth	03/15	03/16	03/17	03/18	03/19
Sales ($ mil.)	(9.7%)	18.2	24.8	18.7	10.0	12.1
Net income ($ mil.)	-	(0.3)	1.0	(4.8)	(4.3)	0.2
Market value ($ mil.)	(19.0%)	20.9	14.0	17.1	7.8	9.0
Employees	(11.9%)	68	42	46	44	41

TEL OFFSHORE TRUST
NBB: TELO Z

The Bank of New York Mellon Trust Company, N.A., 919 Congress Avenue
Austin, TX 78701
Phone: 512 236-6599
Fax: -

CEO: -
CFO: -
HR: -
FYE: December 31
Type: Public

TEL Offshore Trust tells it like it is. There is money in oil and gas. The trust is a passive entity formed to distribute revenues received from TEL Offshore Trust Partnership. The partnership has interests in four major properties in the Gulf of Mexico. Chevron the managing general partner operates most of the properties. TEL Offshore Trust's properties have proved reserves of about 137500 barrels of oil and more than 869 million cu. ft. of natural gas. The trust is set to close down when estimated future revenues from partnership properties fall below $2 million.

	Annual Growth	12/11	12/12	12/13	12/14	12/15
Sales ($ mil.)	(82.7%)	1.5	0.0	1.2	0.0	0.0
Net income ($ mil.)	-	-	-	-	-	-
Market value ($ mil.)	(60.9%)	4.3	3.8	5.7	0.6	0.1
Employees	-	-	-	-	-	-

TELARIA INC
NYS: TLRA

222 Broadway, 16th Floor
New York, NY 10038
Phone: 646 723-5300
Fax: -
Web: www.telaria.com

CEO: Mark Zagorski
CFO: John Rego
HR: -
FYE: December 31
Type: Public

Tremor Video wants to leave traditional advertising formats shaking in their boots. The company is focused on online video advertising. It doesn't make video ads; its VideoHub platform analyzes them to find the best ad for the best video. For example if someone is about to watch a video for a car then a car ad plays. Its clients' video ads are shown on a network of more than 500 websites (including A&E and Viacom properties) and mobile apps that can be watched from computers mobile devices and connected TVs. Tremor Video counts almost 400 customers mostly auto companies and consumer products makers. Primarily it works for the ad agencies hired by the advertisers. Founded in 2005 Tremor Video went public in mid-2013.

	Annual Growth	12/14	12/15	12/16	12/17	12/18
Sales ($ mil.)	(23.3%)	159.5	173.8	166.8	43.8	55.2
Net income ($ mil.)	-	(23.5)	(43.2)	(20.9)	2.2	(9.4)
Market value ($ mil.)	(1.2%)	127.4	91.4	110.5	178.9	121.2
Employees	(16.2%)	339	335	328	136	167

TELCORDIA TECHNOLOGIES INC.

1 Telcordia Dr.
Piscataway NJ 08854-4151
Phone: 732-699-2000
Fax: 916-327-0489
Web: www.calottery.com

CEO: Richard Jacowleff
CFO: Jerry Fechter
HR: -
FYE: January 31
Type: Subsidiary

Telcordia Technologies wants telecommunications service carriers to call on them for support. The company provides a range of networking and operations software as well as consulting implementation and training services to phone companies worldwide. Its products are used to enable such functions as network design customer care and billing service activation number portability and workforce management. Telcordia's flagship application is known as the Next Generation OSS which is a suite of network management tools covering a variety of functions for network operators. Customers have included Cincinnati Bell and Telenor. In 2012 Ericsson acquired Telcordia for about $1.15 billion.

TELECOMMUNICATION SYSTEMS INC
NMS: TSYS

275 West Street
Annapolis, MD 21401
Phone: 410 263-7616
Fax: 410 280-4903
Web: www.telecomsys.com

CEO: Fred Kornberg
CFO: Michael D Porcelain
HR: -
FYE: December 31
Type: Public

TeleCommunication Systems (TCS) keeps businesses and government agencies connected. The company develops software and provides services for wireless telecommunications carriers Internet telephony providers and branches of the US military among other clients. Its hosted applications enable phone companies mainly in the US to deliver 9-1-1 service text messaging location information and other Internet content to wireless phones. The company provides the Defense Department (DoD) with communications systems integration and IT services through its growing government division which represented more than half of the company's revenues in 2013.

	Annual Growth	12/10	12/11	12/12	12/13	12/14
Sales ($ mil.)	(1.9%)	388.8	425.4	487.4	362.3	359.8
Net income ($ mil.)	-	15.9	7.0	(98.0)	(58.6)	(1.7)
Market value ($ mil.)	(9.6%)	279.9	140.9	148.1	139.1	187.0
Employees	(1.9%)	1,205	1,345	1,426	1,286	1,115

TELEDYNE BENTHOS

49 Edgerton Dr.
North Falmouth MA 02556
Phone: 508-563-1000
Fax: 508-563-6444
Web: www.benthos.com

CEO: –
CFO: Francis E Dunne Jr
HR: –
FYE: September 30
Type: Business Segment

Like its trademark logo — the Benthosaurus — you will find Teledyne Benthos in deep water. The company makes undersea exploration systems for oil and gas companies and oceanographic researchers. Products include underwater modems sensors glass spheres hydrophones and remotely operated vehicles. In addition the company offers contract research and custom engineering design services. Customers include the US government and Sercel. In early 2006 Teledyne Technologies acquired Benthos for about $41 million in cash. The acquisition of Benthos expanded Teledyne's portfolio of underwater acoustic instruments.

TELEDYNE LECROY INC.
NASDAQ: LCRY

700 Chestnut Ridge Rd.
Chestnut Ridge NY 10977-6499
Phone: 845-425-2000
Fax: 845-578-5985
Web: www.lecroy.com

CEO: Sean B O'Connor
CFO: –
HR: –
FYE: June 30
Type: Public

If only Teledyne LeCroy made an instrument to analyze signals exchanged between the sexes. The company (formerly LeCroy) makes high-performance real-time oscilloscopes under the WaveAce WaveExpert WaveJet WaveMaster WavePro WaveRunner and WaveSurfer brand names that capture electronic signals convert them to digital form and perform measurements and analysis. Teledyne LeCroy makes such other products as protocol analyzers arbitrary waveform generators and logic analyzers. It also provides support maintenance and recalibration services. LeCroy was acquired by Teledyne Technologies in a 2012 transaction valued at around $291 million.

TELEDYNE TECHNOLOGIES INC
NYS: TDY

1049 Camino Dos Rios
Thousand Oaks, CA 91360-2362
Phone: 805 373-4545
Fax: –

CEO: Robert Mehrabian
CFO: Susan L. (Sue) Main
HR: Jason W. Connell
FYE: December 30
Type: Public

Offerings of Teledyne Technologies are critical to products that work on land in the air and under the sea. The company makes a slew of electronic components and subsystems instruments power and communications equipment for both domestic and foreign commercial customers and US government customers. Its lineup ranges from digital imaging and software to data acquisition and communication tools for aircraft monitoring and control devices for environmental marine and industrial projects defense electronics and energy generation storage and propulsion equipment. Teledyne gets most of its sales from customers in the US.

	Annual Growth	12/14*	01/16	01/17*	12/17	12/18
Sales ($ mil.)	4.9%	2,394.0	2,298.1	2,149.7	2,603.8	2,901.8
Net income ($ mil.)	11.3%	217.7	195.8	190.9	227.2	333.8
Market value ($ mil.)	18.0%	3,775.5	3,200.9	4,438.7	6,537.2	7,317.4
Employees	2.6%	9,800	9,200	8,970	10,340	10,850

*Fiscal year change

TELEFLEX INCORPORATED
NYS: TFX

550 East Swedesford Road, Suite 400
Wayne, PA 19087
Phone: 610 225-6800
Fax: –
Web: www.teleflex.com

CEO: Benson F. Smith
CFO: Thomas E. Powell
HR: Cameron B. Hicks
FYE: December 31
Type: Public

Teleflex helps medical professionals manage fluids and oxygen in critical care settings. The company makes surgical instruments medical devices and disposable supplies for hospital procedures especially catheters for all parts of the body. It divides its medical products by use into critical care surgical care and cardiac care. Teleflex also makes custom medical instruments which it sells to original equipment manufacturers (OEMs). Although the company primarily distributes its products to hospitals and health care providers (some 85% of sales) in more than 150 countries the US accounts for more than half of sales. Teleflex manufactures its products in the US the Czech Republic Germany Malaysia and Mexico.

	Annual Growth	12/14	12/15	12/16	12/17	12/18
Sales ($ mil.)	7.4%	1,839.8	1,809.7	1,868.0	2,146.3	2,448.4
Net income ($ mil.)	1.7%	187.7	244.9	237.4	152.5	200.8
Market value ($ mil.)	22.5%	5,283.6	6,048.8	7,415.5	11,449.7	11,894.2
Employees	6.8%	11,700	12,200	12,600	14,400	15,200

TELENAV, INC.
NMS: TNAV

4655 Great America Parkway, Suite 300
Santa Clara, CA 95054
Phone: 408 245-3800
Fax: –
Web: www.telenav.com

CEO: H. P. Jin
CFO: Michael Strambi
HR: –
FYE: June 30
Type: Public

TeleNav offers a platform and suite of applications that provide mobile navigation and location-based services (LBS) to 34 million users primarily in the US. Flagship product TeleNav GPS Navigator transmits voice and onscreen driving directions to mobile phones and smartphones and is marketed to end users by leading wireless carriers such as Sprint AT&T T-Mobile and U.S. Cellular. The company also offers automotive navigation services to automobile and auto parts manufacturers including Ford and Delphi Automotive Systems. In addition it is expanding into mobile advertising services through its Scout Advertising platform.

	Annual Growth	06/15	06/16	06/17	06/18	06/19
Sales ($ mil.)	8.4%	160.2	183.3	169.6	106.2	220.9
Net income ($ mil.)	–	(23.1)	(35.3)	(47.3)	(89.1)	(32.5)
Market value ($ mil.)	(0.2%)	377.6	239.2	380.0	262.7	375.3
Employees	7.9%	579	583	746	784	784

TELEPHONE & DATA SYSTEMS INC
NYS: TDS

30 North LaSalle Street, Suite 4000
Chicago, IL 60602
Phone: 312 630-1900
Fax: 312 630-1908
Web: www.teldta.com

CEO: LeRoy T. (Ted) Carlson
CFO: Peter L Sereda
HR: –
FYE: December 31
Type: Public

Telephone and Data Systems (TDS) is one of the largest US phone companies that's not descended from Ma Bell. The company has about 6.2 million local phone wireless and cable connections in about 35 states. The company's core business unit U.S. Cellular serves about 5 million customers in more than 20 states with key markets the central US and the mid-Atlantic region. The company also offers fixed-line and broadband internet services in rural and suburban markets in some 25 states through its TDS Telecom subsidiary which provides local service to 1.2 million access lines through incumbent local-exchange carriers (ILEC). Data networking and hosted telecom services are provided to business clients through the TDS Business unit.

	Annual Growth	12/14	12/15	12/16	12/17	12/18
Sales ($ mil.)	0.5%	5,009.4	5,176.2	5,104.0	5,044.0	5,109.0
Net income ($ mil.)	–	(136.4)	219.0	43.0	153.0	135.0
Market value ($ mil.)	6.5%	2,878.5	2,951.5	3,291.2	3,169.2	3,709.6
Employees	(3.0%)	10,600	10,400	10,300	9,900	9,400

TELEPHONE ELECTRONICS CORPORATION

236 E CAPITOL ST STE 400
JACKSON, MS 392012416
Phone: 601-354-9070
Fax: –
Web: www.tec.com

CEO: –
CFO: Robert J Healea
HR: Brandi F Callison
FYE: December 31
Type: Private

Telephone Electronics Corporation or TEC provides communications services for customers in the South. The privately-owned telecommunications carrier provides wired phone cable TV and Internet services for residential and business customers through subsidiaries such as CommuniGroup. TEC's rural local-exchange service reach include areas of Alabama Louisiana Mississippi and Tennessee. The company also provides long-distance interexchange services. TEC was founded in 1923 with the purchase of local phone company Bay Springs Telephone Company which had about 100 customers tied to its switchboard.

	Annual Growth	12/06	12/07	12/08	12/09	12/13
Sales ($ mil.)	7.0%	–	–	38.8	35.1	54.4
Net income ($ mil.)	(5.3%)	–	–	2.0	2.3	1.6
Market value ($ mil.)	–	–	–	–	–	–
Employees	–	–	–	–	–	250

TELETOUCH COMMUNICATIONS, INC.   NBB: TLLE Q

5718 Airport Freeway
Fort Worth, TX 76117
Phone: 800 232-3888
Fax: 817 654-6220
Web: www.teletouch.com

CEO: Robert M McMurrey
CFO: Douglas E Sloan
HR: –
FYE: May 31
Type: Public

Teletouch Communications has its own idea of what it means to "reach out and touch someone." Through its Progressive Concepts Inc. (PCI) subsidiary the company resells mobile voice and data services provided by AT&T Mobility to customers in Texas; it has nearly 80000 consumer and commercial subscribers on its books. PCI also distributes cell phones accessories and car audio and security products through its nearly 20 Hawk Electronics retail locations. Suppliers include Kenwood and and Vertex. The bulk of its stores are located in the Dallas/Fort Worth area but it also has two locations in San Antonio. Chairman Robert McMurrey owns a controlling stake in the company.

	Annual Growth	05/08	05/09	05/10	05/11	05/12
Sales ($ mil.)	(10.9%)	54.5	45.9	52.0	40.4	34.4
Net income ($ mil.)	–	(3.1)	(1.9)	1.6	(2.5)	4.2
Market value ($ mil.)	21.5%	11.2	6.8	14.7	20.5	24.4
Employees	(16.1%)	238	246	202	126	118

TELIGENT INC (NEW)   NMS: TLGT

105 Lincoln Ave
Buena, NJ 08310
Phone: 856 697-1441
Fax: –
Web: www.teligent.com

CEO: Jason Grenfell-Gardner
CFO: Jenniffer Collins
HR: –
FYE: December 31
Type: Public

Teligent (formerly IGI) is betting big on small things. It manufactures creams liquids and other topical products for drug and cosmetics companies using its microencapsulation technology. Teligent originally licensed the technology dubbed Novasome from drug firm Novovax. The Novasome process entraps and protects the active ingredients of various skin care products moisturizers shampoos and fragrances allowing for greater stability during storage and a more controlled release when used. The firm is examining further applications of the Novasome technology in food personal care products and pharmaceuticals.

	Annual Growth	12/14	12/15	12/16	12/17	12/18
Sales ($ mil.)	18.2%	33.7	44.3	66.9	67.3	65.9
Net income ($ mil.)	–	5.3	6.7	(12.0)	(15.2)	(36.3)
Market value ($ mil.)	(37.2%)	473.2	478.6	355.4	195.2	73.7
Employees	23.6%	81	107	153	183	189

TELKONET INC.   NBB: TKOI

20800 Swenson Drive, Suite 175
Waukesha, WI 53186
Phone: 414 302-2299
Fax: –

CEO: Jason L Tienor
CFO: Richard E Mushrush
HR: –
FYE: December 31
Type: Public

Telkonet runs its own Internet of things but its things are thermostats and other energy controls for hotels campuses and other properties. The company's SmartEnergy and EcoSmart line of energy efficiency-related systems are used to manage and monitor HVAC consumption. It also provides high-speed Internet access without the high-cost network upgrades through its EthoStream product line which enables computer network and Internet access over electrical lines rather than communications cables. In addition to equipment sales it recognizes recurring support revenue from the 2300 hotels that use its EthoStream broadband Internet systems. All of its product are marketed primarily to the hospitality industry. Customers include InterContinental Marriott and Wyndham.

	Annual Growth	12/14	12/15	12/16	12/17	12/18
Sales ($ mil.)	(13.1%)	14.8	15.1	8.3	8.3	8.4
Net income ($ mil.)	–	0.0	(0.2)	(1.4)	3.7	(3.0)
Market value ($ mil.)	(5.3%)	18.9	24.9	18.7	16.8	15.2
Employees	(15.5%)	100	108	101	50	51

TELLURIAN INC   NAS: TELL

1201 Louisiana Street, Suite 3100
Houston, TX 77002
Phone: 832 962-4000
Fax: –
Web: www.magellanpetroleum.com

CEO: –
CFO: Antoine J Lafargue
HR: Margery Harris
FYE: December 31
Type: Public

Magellan Petroleum has gone around the world to explore for oil and gas. The independent oil and gas exploration and production company is focused on the development of CO2-enhanced oil recovery projects in the Rocky Mountain region. Historically active internationally Magellan also owns significant exploration acreage in the Weald Basin onshore UK and an exploration block (NT/P82) in the Bonaparte Basin offshore Northern Territory Australia. Magellan Petroleum reports proved and probable reserves of approximately 5.7 million barrels of oil equivalent. It sold some of its Weald Basin assets in 2016.

	Annual Growth	06/15	06/16*	12/16	12/17	12/18
Sales ($ mil.)	32.1%	4.5	–	–	5.4	10.3
Net income ($ mil.)	–	(43.0)	(17.6)	(96.7)	(231.5)	(125.7)
Market value ($ mil.)	154.8%	101.1	284.0	2,707.4	2,344.0	1,672.6
Employees	104.9%	20	13	–	126	172

*Fiscal year change

TELOS CORP. (MD)   NBB: TLSR P

19886 Ashburn Road
Ashburn, VA 20147-2358
Phone: 703 724-3800
Fax: –
Web: www.telos.com

CEO: John B. Wood
CFO: Michele Nakazawa
HR: –
FYE: December 31
Type: Public

Telos is tuned in to the needs of high-tech government. The company provides networking and security products and services primarily to the US Department of Defense and other federal government agencies. Its core secure networking unit offers networking hardware software advanced messaging as well as systems design and support services. Subsidiary Xacta offers automated security software and consulting services. The company also provides identity management software and services through its Telos ID subsidiary. Government clients account for 97% of the company's sales.

	Annual Growth	12/14	12/15	12/16	12/17	12/18
Sales ($ mil.)	2.0%	127.6	120.6	134.9	107.7	138.0
Net income ($ mil.)	–	(12.3)	(15.9)	(7.2)	(5.8)	(1.6)
Market value ($ mil.)	(0.9%)	664.1	499.3	492.0	651.8	639.5
Employees	3.9%	538	521	502	508	627

TELVUE CORPORATION
OTC: TEVE

16000 Horizon Way Ste. 500
Mt. Laurel NJ 08054
Phone: 856-273-8886
Fax: 856-866-7411
Web: www.telvue.com

CEO: Jesse Lerman
CFO: –
HR: –
FYE: December 31
Type: Public

TelVue knows that there is often a price to be paid for spending a lot of time in front of the television. The company's products facilitate the ordering and delivery of pay-per-view programming for cable companies. Its core business is centered around digital video systems (including Princeton-branded video server computers and software) that enable the capture storage editing and playback of broadcast video. TelVue's automatic number identification (ANI) system enables cable and satellite providers to automate telephone orders for programming by subscribers. It also offers services under the WEBUS brand among others that enable the display of programming data over a cable system's access channels.

TEMCO SERVICE INDUSTRIES, INC.

417 5TH AVE FL 9
NEW YORK, NY 100162245
Phone: 212-889-6353
Fax: –
Web: www.atalian.us

CEO: Christopher Hughes
CFO: –
HR: –
FYE: September 30
Type: Private

Temco Service Industries provides temps trees and tidiness. The company offers facility management services including building management cleaning maintenance landscaping and temporary personnel staffing. It also provides temperature control HVAC systems mechanical equipment building automation systems lighting fire and security services. To address varied client needs the company runs its business through three divisions that offer support services to commercial properties; education facilities including public school systems and universities; and corporate manufacturing and industrial properties. Temco was founded in 1917.

	Annual Growth	09/96	09/97	09/98	09/05	09/07
Sales ($ mil.)	7.7%	–	–	172.3	306.3	334.7
Net income ($ mil.)	47.8%	–	–	1.2	1.2	40.7
Market value ($ mil.)	–	–	–	–	–	–
Employees	–	–	–	–	–	2,000

TEMPLE UNIVERSITY HEALTH SYSTEM, INC.

2450 W HUNTING PARK AVE
PHILADELPHIA, PA 191291302
Phone: 215-707-2000
Fax: –
Web: www.templehealth.org

CEO: –
CFO: –
HR: –
FYE: June 30
Type: Private

Temple University Health System (TUHS) is a network of academic and community hospitals associated with the Temple University School of Medicine. It provides primary secondary and tertiary care to residents in the Philadelphia County (Pennsylvania) area. The system includes 722-bed Temple University Hospital (a Level 1 trauma center) and a pair of community-based hospitals that provide acute and emergency care as well as the Jeanes Hospital and TUH-Episcopal Campus (home to a 120-bed behavioral health unit). TUHS supports programs in pediatric and adult cardiology organ transplantation oncology and pulmonary disease. TUHS also includes a community-wide network of primary care physicians.

	Annual Growth	06/07	06/08	06/09	06/11	06/12
Sales ($ mil.)	1819.9%	–	–	0.1	994.2	1,004.9
Net income ($ mil.)	–	–	–	(0.1)	45.4	(48.8)
Market value ($ mil.)	–	–	–	–	–	–
Employees	–	–	–	–	–	7,573

TEMPLE UNIVERSITY-OF THE COMMONWEALTH SYSTEM OF HIGHER EDUCATION

1801 N BROAD ST
PHILADELPHIA, PA 191226003
Phone: 215-204-1380
Fax: –
Web: www.temple.edu

CEO: –
CFO: Ken Kaiser
HR: Karen Ward
FYE: June 30
Type: Private

Temple University's owl mascot reflects its start as a night school but the owl's sagacity also points to the school's educational credentials. More than 38000 students are enrolled in its 320 academic programs across the Philadephia university's 17 schools. Its Health Sciences Center includes Temple University Hospital and schools that teach medicine and dentistry. Part of Pennsylvania's Commonwealth System of Higher Education Temple has six different campuses in the Philadelphia area as well campuses in Tokyo and Rome and educational programs in China Greece France Israel and the UK. The system has a student-teacher ratio of about 15:1. Dr. Russell Conwell founded the university in 1884; it was incorporated as Temple University in 1907.

	Annual Growth	06/06	06/07	06/08	06/12	06/13
Sales ($ mil.)	5.3%	–	–	2,034.0	2,254.8	2,635.5
Net income ($ mil.)	(3.4%)	–	–	228.3	(37.2)	192.1
Market value ($ mil.)	–	–	–	–	–	–
Employees	–	–	–	–	–	9,061

TEMPUR SEALY INTERNATIONAL, INC.
NYS: TPX

1000 Tempur Way
Lexington, KY 40511
Phone: 800 878-8889
Fax: –
Web: www.tempursealy.com

CEO: Scott L. Thompson
CFO: Bhaskar Rao
HR: Carmen Dabiero
FYE: December 31
Type: Public

Tempur Sealy International wants to be Sweet Dreams Central providing its customers with a better night's sleep. The company manufactures premium pressure-relieving temperature-sensitive mattresses pillows and other sleep products made from viscoelastic foam technology developed by NASA during the 1970s to help cushion astronauts during liftoff. Its TEMPUR Tempur-Pedic Sealy and Stearns & Foster brands are sold in 100-plus countries through retailers such as furniture and department stores online in company-owned stores and through third-party distributors. The US accounts for about 70% of Tempur Sealy's revenue. Tempur Sealy and competitor Serta Simmons Bedding dominate the mattress market.

	Annual Growth	12/14	12/15	12/16	12/17	12/18
Sales ($ mil.)	(2.5%)	2,989.8	3,151.2	3,127.3	2,754.4	2,702.9
Net income ($ mil.)	(2.0%)	108.9	73.5	202.1	151.4	100.5
Market value ($ mil.)	(6.8%)	2,992.6	3,840.1	3,721.3	3,416.6	2,256.3
Employees	(3.3%)	7,100	7,200	7,300	7,000	6,200

TENASKA INC.

1044 N. 115th St. Ste. 400
Omaha NE 68154-4446
Phone: 402-691-9500
Fax: 402-691-9526
Web: www.tenaska.com

CEO: Jerry K Crouse
CFO: Gregory A Van Dyke
HR: –
FYE: December 31
Type: Private

Tenaska is tenacious when it comes to energy. The employee-owned company is a top natural gas marketer in North America selling or managing 2.3 trillion cu. ft. of natural gas a year through Marketing Ventures/Tenaska Marketing Canada (TMV); it is also a leading power producer trading and marketing electricity (including renewable energy). Power marketing unit Tenaska Power Services develops owns or operates eight generating plants with more than 9000 MW of capacity in the US and managed more than 21000 MW of power contracts in 2011. Other operations include fuel supply biofuels development oil and gas exploration and production power transmission and gas transportation contracting.

TENAX THERAPEUTICS INC NAS: TENX

ONE Copley Parkway, Suite 490
Morrisville, NC 27560
Phone: 919 855-2100
Fax: 919 855-2133
Web: www.oxygenbiotherapeutics.com

CEO: Anthony A Ditonno
CFO: Michael B Jebsen
HR: –
FYE: April 30
Type: Public

Oxygen Biotherapeutics prescribes some good ol' O2 for whatever ails you. The development stage biotechnology company develops products that help deliver oxygen to tissues. Its Dermacyte topical cosmetic line is designed to improve the appearance of skin. A concentrate is currently available and the company is developing Dermacyte formulas specifically for acne rosacea sunscreen and other applications. Pipeline products include Oxycyte an IV emulsion created to speed surgical and other healing being tested in Israel and Switzerland and Wundecyte gel and bandages in pre-clinical trials. Oxygen Biotherapeutics was formed through a reverse merger with Synthetic Blood International in 2008.

	Annual Growth	04/11	04/12	04/13	04/14	04/15
Sales ($ mil.)	(37.5%)	0.3	0.4	1.2	0.3	0.0
Net income ($ mil.)	–	(10.4)	(15.7)	(9.4)	(19.5)	(14.1)
Market value ($ mil.)	17.9%	49.8	50.1	7.0	137.2	96.2
Employees	(12.0%)	20	15	12	14	12

TENET HEALTHCARE CORP. NYS: THC

1445 Ross Avenue, Suite 1400
Dallas, TX 75202
Phone: 469 893-2200
Fax: –
Web: www.tenethealth.com

CEO: Ronald A. (Ron) Rittenmeyer
CFO: Bill Durham
HR: Robb Webb
FYE: December 31
Type: Public

Tenet Healthcare is a for-profit company operating about 65 acute care hospitals with some 18000 beds in about 10 US states including California Florida and Texas. Its operations range from small community facilities offering basic care to major hospitals such as the 600-bed Brookwood Baptist Medical Center in Birmingham Alabama. In addition to its acute care holdings Tenet operates outpatient centers imaging centers and other health care units that form regional networks around its main hospitals. Its United Surgical Partners International (USPI) division operates ambulatory surgery centers and surgical hospitals. Tenet is spinning off its Conifer unit which provides patient billing and communications.

	Annual Growth	12/14	12/15	12/16	12/17	12/18
Sales ($ mil.)	2.5%	16,615.0	18,634.0	19,621.0	19,179.0	18,313.0
Net income ($ mil.)	74.4%	12.0	(140.0)	(192.0)	(704.0)	111.0
Market value ($ mil.)	(23.7%)	5,195.6	3,106.9	1,521.7	1,554.5	1,757.5
Employees	1.5%	108,989	134,630	130,000	125,820	115,500

TENGASCO INC ASE: TGC

8000 E. Maplewood Ave., Suite 130
Greenwood Village, CO 80111
Phone: 720 420-4460
Fax: –
Web: www.tengasco.com

CEO: Michael J Rugen
CFO: Michael J Rugen
HR: –
FYE: December 31
Type: Public

Tengasco doesn't have the strength of 10 gas companies just yet but it's getting there. The firm is engaged in exploring for producing and transporting oil and natural gas in Kansas (in properties near Hays) and Tennessee (primarily in the Swan Creek Field). Tengasco uses 3-D seismic technology to maximize recovery of its reserves. In 2008 the company reported proved reserves of 900 million cu. ft. of natural gas and 1.3 million barrels of oil. The firm is also involved in natural gas marketing pipeline construction and related energy services. Its Tengasco Pipeline unit manages its pipeline operations. Subsidiary Manufactured Methane Corporation operates a landfill gas project in Tennessee.

	Annual Growth	12/14	12/15	12/16	12/17	12/18
Sales ($ mil.)	(19.2%)	13.8	6.2	4.7	5.3	5.9
Net income ($ mil.)	–	(0.8)	(24.7)	(4.2)	(0.6)	1.6
Market value ($ mil.)	39.1%	2.7	1.3	7.4	8.5	10.1
Employees	(8.3%)	17	17	14	14	12

TENNANT CO. NYS: TNC

701 North Lilac Drive, P.O. Box 1452
Minneapolis, MN 55440
Phone: 763 540-1200
Fax: –
Web: www.tennantco.com

CEO: H. Chris Killingstad
CFO: Thomas (Tom) Paulson
HR: –
FYE: December 31
Type: Public

Tennant is one of the world's leading manufacturers of industrial floor maintenance equipment. It makes specialty surface coatings and cleaning machines including extractors scrubbers sweepers and vacuums. Parts and supplies are also offered along with maintenance and repair services. Its products are used to clean up surfaces at airports factories offices parking garages stadiums supermarkets warehouses and other high-traffic areas. Brand names include Alfa Tennant Nobles and Orbio. The Americas account for about 60% of sales.

	Annual Growth	12/14	12/15	12/16	12/17	12/18
Sales ($ mil.)	8.1%	822.0	811.8	808.6	1,003.1	1,123.5
Net income ($ mil.)	(9.9%)	50.7	32.1	46.6	(6.2)	33.4
Market value ($ mil.)	(7.8%)	1,308.1	1,019.7	1,290.5	1,316.8	944.5
Employees	8.6%	3,087	3,164	3,236	4,300	4,300

TENNECO INC NYS: TEN

500 North Field Drive
Lake Forest, IL 60045
Phone: 847 482-5000
Fax: –
Web: www.tenneco.com

CEO: Brian Kesseler
CFO: Kenneth R. (Ken) Trammell
HR: Mike Schneider
FYE: December 31
Type: Public

Tenneco is a global auto parts manufacturer that designs and distributes ride-control and emissions control products. It makes ride control equipment such as shock absorbers struts and steering stabilizers under brands like Monroe and Quick-Strut and emissions-control systems including catalytic converters exhaust pipes and mufflers under the Walker Tru-Fit Fonos and DynoMax brands. It also makes Clevite elastomer products (bushings mounts and exhaust isolators) for vibration control in cars and heavy trucks. It supplies both the original equipment (OE) and replacement markets worldwide. Major customers Ford Motor and General Motors account for more than 10% of sales. Tenneco operates worldwide on six continents.

	Annual Growth	12/14	12/15	12/16	12/17	12/18
Sales ($ mil.)	8.7%	8,420.0	8,209.0	8,599.0	9,274.0	11,763.0
Net income ($ mil.)	(29.8%)	226.0	247.0	363.0	207.0	55.0
Market value ($ mil.)	(16.6%)	4,578.4	3,713.0	5,052.3	4,734.5	2,215.2
Employees	29.3%	29,000	30,000	31,000	32,000	81,000

TENNESSEE FARMERS COOPERATIVE

180 Old Nashville Hwy.
LaVergne TN 37086
Phone: 615-793-8011
Fax: 615-287-8859
Web: www.ourcoop.com

CEO: Bart Krisle
CFO: Shannon Huff
HR: John Cain
FYE: July 31
Type: Private - Cooperativ

Talk about multi-tasking. The Tennessee Farmers Cooperative (TFC) keeps the cows fat the bugs away and the tractors running. Through a system of about 60 local co-ops TFC supplies agricultural necessities such as animal-health products feed fertilizer outdoor power equipment seeds and tires to area farmers. Its services include finance credit and risk management. It operates about 150 retail outlets located in more than 80 of Tennessee's 95 counties and five neighboring states. The outlets are open to the public as well as co-op members. TFC was chartered in 1945.

TENNESSEE STATE UNIVERSITY

3500 JOHN A MERRITT BLVD
NASHVILLE, TN 372091561
Phone: 615-963-5000
Fax: –
Web: www.tnstate.edu

CEO: –
CFO: –
HR: –
FYE: June 30
Type: Private

Tennessee State University (TSU) covers its bases in higher learning fields including science and learning. Home to some 9000 students TSU is known for its programs in education nursing biology physical therapy computer engineering agriculture public administration and psychology. The university offers about 45 undergraduate programs and 25 graduate programs through its eight colleges and schools. It also offers doctoral degrees in education philosophy and physical therapy. It has 450 full-time faculty members and a student-to-teacher ratio of 16:1.

	Annual Growth	06/03	06/04	06/05	06/08	06/11
Sales ($ mil.)	75.0%	–	–	3.7	1.6	105.6
Net income ($ mil.)	39.1%	–	–	2.5	0.4	18.4
Market value ($ mil.)	–	–	–	–	–	–
Employees	–	–	–	–	–	1,234

TENNESSEE TECHNOLOGICAL UNIVERSITY

1 WILLIAM L JONES DR
COOKEVILLE, TN 385050001
Phone: 931-372-3101
Fax: –

CEO: –
CFO: –
HR: –
FYE: June 30
Type: Private

Tennessee Technological University (TTU or Tennessee Tech) takes on the task of providing academic education and career training services in the Volunteer State. The public university has six college divisions providing more than 60 undergraduate and graduate degrees in the areas of Agriculture and Human Sciences Arts and Sciences Business Education Engineering and Interdisciplinary Studies. it aslo offers The university has some 11500 students enrolled and a faculty of about 400 staff members and has a student-to-faculty ratio of about 22:1.

	Annual Growth	06/09	06/10	06/11	06/12	06/13
Sales ($ mil.)	9.7%	–	65.1	65.1	76.8	86.0
Net income ($ mil.)	(6.9%)	–	23.3	23.3	5.6	18.8
Market value ($ mil.)	–	–	–	–	–	–
Employees	–	–	–	–	–	1,096

TENNESSEE VALLEY AUTHORITY NYS: TVE

400 W. Summit Hill Drive
Knoxville, TN 37902
Phone: 865 632-2101
Fax: –
Web: www.tva.gov

CEO: William D. (Bill) Johnson
CFO: John M. Thomas
HR: Katherine Black
FYE: September 30
Type: Public

Tennessee Valley Authority (TVA) is a US government-owned corporation and the largest public power producer in the country. It sells wholesale electricity to more than 150 municipal and cooperative power distributors which serve nearly 10 million people in Tennessee and parts of Alabama Georgia Kentucky Mississippi North Carolina and Virginia. It also sells power directly to large industrial customers and federal agencies. In addition TVA provides flood control and land management for the Tennessee River system and assists utilities and state and local governments with economic development.

	Annual Growth	09/15	09/16	09/17	09/18	09/19
Sales ($ mil.)	0.7%	11,003.0	10,616.0	10,739.0	11,233.0	11,318.0
Net income ($ mil.)	6.3%	1,111.0	1,233.0	685.0	1,119.0	1,417.0
Market value ($ mil.)	–	0.0	0.0	0.0	0.0	0.0
Employees	(2.1%)	10,918	10,691	10,092	10,023	10,009

TERADATA CORP (DE) NYS: TDC

17095 Via Del Campo
San Diego, CA 92127
Phone: 866 548-8348
Fax: –
Web: www.teradata.com

CEO: Victor L. Lund
CFO: Mark A. Culhane
HR: Suzanne (Suzy) Zoumaras
FYE: December 31
Type: Public

Teradata designs and makes enterprise data warehousing systems that companies use to store and analyze information about customers finances and operations. Products include its Vantage analytics platform database software hardware components and applications for managing demand and supply chains marketing performance and risk. It also offers consulting support and training services. Teradata's software can be used in public private and hybrid cloud and on-premise environments. The company's customers are in data-intensive industries such as financial services communications government health care manufacturing and transportation. International customers supply more than 50% of Teradata's revenue.

	Annual Growth	12/14	12/15	12/16	12/17	12/18
Sales ($ mil.)	(5.7%)	2,732.0	2,530.0	2,322.0	2,156.0	2,164.0
Net income ($ mil.)	(46.5%)	367.0	(214.0)	125.0	(67.0)	30.0
Market value ($ mil.)	(3.2%)	5,101.8	3,085.9	3,173.5	4,492.1	4,480.4
Employees	(3.1%)	11,500	11,300	10,093	10,615	10,152

TERADYNE, INC. NMS: TER

600 Riverpark Drive
North Reading, MA 01864
Phone: 978 370-2700
Fax: –
Web: www.teradyne.com

CEO: Mark E. Jagiela
CFO: Gregory R. (Greg) Beecher
HR: Loren Eaton
FYE: December 31
Type: Public

Teradyne is a leading supplier of machines that automate testing and tasks in manufacturing. The company makes automated test equipment systems for testing semiconductors and industrial robots. Teradyne's customers are integrated device manufacturers contract electronics manufacturers and original equipment manufacturers. Its customers use Teradyne products to test and analyze integrated circuits wireless devices circuit boards automotive electronics storage devices and other products. Teradyne developed its industrial robot business mainly through acquisitions. The Massachusetts-based company has operations in Asia Europe and the Americas but it generates most of its sales from customers in Asia.

	Annual Growth	12/14	12/15	12/16	12/17	12/18
Sales ($ mil.)	6.3%	1,647.8	1,639.6	1,753.3	2,136.6	2,100.8
Net income ($ mil.)	53.5%	81.3	206.5	(43.4)	257.7	451.8
Market value ($ mil.)	12.2%	3,473.6	3,628.0	4,458.3	7,349.1	5,507.9
Employees	5.9%	3,900	4,100	4,300	4,500	4,900

TEREX CORP. NYS: TEX

200 Nyala Farm Road
Westport, CT 06880
Phone: 203 222-7170
Fax: 203 222-7976
Web: www.terex.com

CEO: John L. Garrison
CFO: John D. Sheehan
HR: Peter Rall
FYE: December 31
Type: Public

Terex Corporation makes a variety of cranes aerial platforms and materials processing equipment. The company makes aerial lifts from articulating to telescopic booms used in industrial and construction overhead jobs. It also makes all sort of cranes and specialty equipment such as wood processing biomass and recycling equipment. Terex products are sold in more than 100 countries around the globe to the construction forestry recycling and utility industries under the Terex Genie and Powerscreen brands. About 55% of Terex's sales come from North America.

	Annual Growth	12/14	12/15	12/16	12/17	12/18
Sales ($ mil.)	(8.5%)	7,308.9	6,543.1	4,443.1	4,363.4	5,125.0
Net income ($ mil.)	(22.7%)	319.0	145.9	(176.1)	128.7	113.7
Market value ($ mil.)	(0.3%)	1,940.4	1,286.2	2,194.5	3,356.1	1,918.9
Employees	(13.0%)	20,400	20,400	11,300	10,700	11,700

TERRA NITROGEN COMPANY, L.P.

4 PARKWAY NORTH BLVD # 400
DEERFIELD, IL 600152502
Phone: 847-405-2400
Fax: −
Web: www.cfindustries.com

CEO: W Anthony Will
CFO: Dennis P Kelleher
HR: −
FYE: December 31
Type: Private

Making the earth's soil produce more crops is the long term mission of Terra Nitrogen which manufactures nitrogen fertilizer products. The company operates a plant in Oklahoma that produces ammonia and urea ammonium nitrate (UAN) solutions. Farmers use the company's products to improve both the quantity and the quality of crops. It sells its products to parent company agrochemical giant CF Industries which in turn sells nitrogen products wholesale to dealers distributors and national farm retail chain outlets primarily in the central and Southern Plains and Corn Belt regions of the US. CF Industries has indirect ownership of Terra Nitrogen's general partner and controls the company.

	Annual Growth	12/13	12/14	12/15	12/16	12/17
Sales ($ mil.)	(15.1%)	−	648.3	581.7	418.3	397.2
Net income ($ mil.)	(25.4%)	−	370.0	306.9	209.3	153.9
Market value ($ mil.)	−	−	−	−	−	−
Employees	−	−	−	−	−	8

TERRACON CONSULTANTS, INC.

18001 W 106TH ST STE 300
OLATHE, KS 660616447
Phone: 913-599-6886
Fax: −

CEO: Gayle Packer
CFO: −
HR: −
FYE: December 31
Type: Private

Employee-owned Terracon Consultants provides geotechnical environmental construction material evaluation pavement engineering and construction management and facilities engineering services. One of the nation's top design firms the company serves the agriculture energy telecommunications commercial development and transportation sectors as well as government clients. The company has more than 140 offices in some 40 US states. Terracon serves more than 160 clients. It helps its customers comply with new building codes and environmental regulations assess environmental hazards and tackle the problem of aging structures.

	Annual Growth	12/11	12/12	12/13	12/14	12/15
Sales ($ mil.)	11.8%	−	380.6	419.4	478.8	531.5
Net income ($ mil.)	3.7%	−	10.4	10.7	9.8	11.6
Market value ($ mil.)	−	−	−	−	−	−
Employees	−	−	−	−	−	3,747

TERRACYCLE INC.

121 New York Ave.
Trenton NJ 08638
Phone: 609-393-4252
Fax: 609-393-4259
Web: www.terracycle.net

CEO: Tom Szaky
CFO: Javier Daly
HR: −
FYE: December 31
Type: Private

Dumpster diving has never looked so good. TerraCycle makes upcycled products out of previously non-recyclable trash. The company offers tote bags backpacks and kites made from snack food wrappers; pencils made out of newspaper; and picture frames made from bicycle chains and circuit boards among other products. More than 28 million people around the world collect waste for TerraCycle and ship it to the company free of charge. (Companies such as Kraft and Solo Cup that make packaging and wrappers foot the bill for waste collection.) TerraCycle also offers a line of eco-friendly cleaning products; all of its goods are sold at major retailers such as Target Wal-Mart and Whole Foods.

TERRAVIA HOLDINGS INC

NMS: TVIA

225 Gateway Boulevard
South San Francisco, CA 94080
Phone: 650 780-4777
Fax: −
Web: www.solazyme.com

CEO: −
CFO: −
HR: −
FYE: December 31
Type: Public

We make oil may seem like a strange statement but in the case of TerraVia Holdings (formerly Solazyme) it's true. The company manufactures a variety of oils by feeding plant sugars to microalgae. Its "tailored oils" can be created to replace fuel and chemical edible or personal skin care oil traditionally derived from petroleum or animal fats. The microbial-based oils work with existing production refining and distribution infrastructure systems. TerraVia feeds its microalgae sugarcane corn and biomass-derived sugars; its oils cost half to a third as much to produce as traditional oils. The company also sells protein fiber and other system by-products.

	Annual Growth	12/11	12/12	12/13	12/14	12/15
Sales ($ mil.)	4.3%	39.0	44.1	39.8	60.4	46.1
Net income ($ mil.)	−	(53.9)	(83.1)	(116.4)	(162.1)	(141.4)
Market value ($ mil.)	(32.4%)	972.6	642.4	890.1	210.9	202.7
Employees	8.1%	168	229	271	266	229

TERREMARK WORLDWIDE INC.

1 Biscayne Tower 2 S. Biscayne Blvd. Ste. 2800
Miami FL 33131
Phone: 305-961-3200
Fax: 305-961-8190
Web: www.terremark.com

CEO: −
CFO: −
HR: −
FYE: March 31
Type: Subsidiary

Terremark Worldwide isn't afraid to NAP on the job. The company provides colocation exchange point and managed IT infrastructure services from several network access point (NAP) locations. It also leases data center space in Europe and Latin America. Terremark markets to telecom carriers interactive entertainment providers and other businesses. In addition to its commercial customers the company counts agencies of the US federal government among its clients. The company was acquired in 2011 for $1.4 billion by Verizon Communications which is investing in the hosted Web services for corporations offered by Verizon Business.

TERRENO REALTY CORP

NYS: TRNO

101 Montgomery Street, Suite 200
San Francisco, CA 94104
Phone: 415 655-4580
Fax: −
Web: www.terreno.com

CEO: W. Blake Baird
CFO: Jaime J. Cannon
HR: −
FYE: December 31
Type: Public

Terreno Realty has its eyes set on acquiring industrial real estate. The real estate investment trust (REIT) invests in and operates industrial properties in major US coastal markets including Los Angeles San Francisco Bay Area Seattle Miami Northern New Jersey/New York City and Washington DC/Baltimore. The REIT typically invests in warehouse and distribution facilities flex buildings for light manufacturing and research and development and transportation and shipping centers. The company owns more than 125 buildings spanning 9.3 million square feet and two improved land parcels totaling 3.5 acres.

	Annual Growth	12/15	12/16	12/17	12/18	12/19
Sales ($ mil.)	15.6%	95.9	108.4	132.5	151.7	171.0
Net income ($ mil.)	39.6%	14.6	15.1	53.1	63.3	55.5
Market value ($ mil.)	24.4%	1,521.3	1,916.0	2,357.9	2,365.3	3,641.1
Employees	7.5%	18	19	22	23	24

TERRITORIAL BANCORP INC
NMS: TBNK

1132 Bishop Street, Suite 2200
Honolulu, HI 96813
Phone: 808 946-1400
Fax: –
Web: www.territorialsavings.net

CEO: Allan S. Kitagawa
CFO: –
HR: –
FYE: December 31
Type: Public

Territorial Bancorp serves its customers island-style. It is the financial holding company for Territorial Savings Bank which provides standard products and services such as checking and savings accounts money market accounts CDs IRAs and loans from its nearly 30 branch locations across Hawaii. Its Territorial Financial Services subsidiary sells insurance while LPL Financial offers Mutual funds and annuities. Territorial Savings Bank targets the territorial nature of its customers — one- to four-family residential mortgages account for 95% of its loan portfolio. Multifamily and commercial mortgages and construction and home equity loans round out its lending activities.

	Annual Growth	12/14	12/15	12/16	12/17	12/18
Assets ($ mil.)	5.2%	1,691.9	1,821.1	1,877.6	2,003.8	2,069.2
Net income ($ mil.)	8.0%	14.1	14.7	16.3	15.0	19.2
Market value ($ mil.)	4.8%	207.9	267.6	316.8	297.8	250.6
Employees	1.2%	272	280	276	283	285

TESARO INC
NMS: TSRO

1000 Winter Street, Suite 3300
Waltham, MA 02451
Phone: 339 970-0900
Fax: –
Web: www.tesarobio.com

CEO: Leon O Moulder Jr
CFO: Timothy R Pearson
HR: –
FYE: December 31
Type: Public

TESARO might not cure cancer but it could one day bring some relief. An oncology-focused biopharmaceutical company TESARO is developing rolapitant a drug candidate designed to treat nausea and vomiting associated with chemotherapy treatments. Rolapitant which the company in-licensed from Opko Health is in late-stage clinical development. In addition the company has an orally available small cell lung cancer treatment in preclinical development. Founded in 2010 by former MGI PHARMA executives TESARO intends to eventually commercialize and market rolapitant and other product candidates in North America Europe and China. Seeking funding for its efforts the company went public in 2012.

	Annual Growth	12/12	12/13	12/14	12/15	12/16
Sales ($ mil.)	14039.7%	–	–	–	0.3	44.8
Net income ($ mil.)	–	(61.8)	(92.4)	(171.0)	(251.4)	(387.5)
Market value ($ mil.)	67.8%	908.9	1,514.3	1,994.2	2,805.5	7,211.0
Employees	86.3%	37	62	108	286	446

TESLA ENERGY OPERATIONS, INC.

3055 CLEARVIEW WAY
SAN MATEO, CA 944023709
Phone: 888-765-2489
Fax: –

CEO: Lyndon R. Rive
CFO: J. Radford Small
HR: –
FYE: December 31
Type: Private

Ready to get off the grid? SolarCity can help. The company sells installs finances and monitors turnkey solar energy systems that convert sunlight into electricity. Its systems either mounted on a building's roof or the ground are used by residential commercial and government customers such as eBay Intel Wal-Mart and Homeland Security. SolarCity doesn't manufacture its systems but uses solar panels from Trina Solar Yingli Green Energy and Kyocera Solar and inverters from Power-One SMA Solar Technology and Schneider Electric. In late 2016 SolarCity was acquired by Tesla Motors in a deal worth $2.6 billion.

	Annual Growth	12/12	12/13	12/14	12/15	12/16
Sales ($ mil.)	64.6%	–	163.8	255.0	399.6	730.3
Net income ($ mil.)	–	–	(151.8)	(375.2)	(768.8)	(820.3)
Market value ($ mil.)	–	–	–	–	–	–
Employees	–	–	–	–	–	12,000

TESLA INC
NMS: TSLA

3500 Deer Creek Road
Palo Alto, CA 94304
Phone: 650 681-5000
Fax: –
Web: www.teslamotors.com

CEO: Elon Musk
CFO: Deepak Ahuja
HR: –
FYE: December 31
Type: Public

Founded in 2003 the company designs manufactures and markets high-performance technologically advanced electric cars and solar energy generation and energy storage products. Tesla sells three fully electric models: the Model S sedan and the Model X SUV and the Model 3 sedan which is among the world's top-selling electric cars. The fuel-efficient fully electric vehicles recharge their lithium-ion batteries from an outlet. Tesla's Autopilot self-driving technology hardware has been available on all Tesla models since late 2016. US customers generate about 70% of Tesla?s sales. CEO Elon Musk founded PayPal and also runs SpaceX.

	Annual Growth	12/14	12/15	12/16	12/17	12/18
Sales ($ mil.)	60.9%	3,198.4	4,046.0	7,000.1	11,758.8	21,461.3
Net income ($ mil.)	–	(294.0)	(888.7)	(674.9)	(1,961.4)	(976.1)
Market value ($ mil.)	10.6%	38,388.6	41,426.4	36,883.5	53,739.9	57,442.3
Employees	48.1%	10,161	13,058	30,025	37,543	48,817

TESSADA & ASSOCIATES INC.

8001 FORBES PL STE 310
SPRINGFIELD, VA 22151-2205
Phone: 703-564-1210
Fax: –
Web: www.mlss.tessada.com

CEO: –
CFO: –
HR: –
FYE: August 31
Type: Private

Tessada & Associates provides a wide variety of business improvement consulting services to government and private sector clients from more than 25 offices throughout the US. Services include facilities management engineering finance and accounting information technology logistics and technical support and security. The company also offers multimedia production and management services helping clients create marketing materials and business presentations. Clients have included the Department of Homeland Security the Department of Agriculture and the Department of Transportation.

	Annual Growth	08/02	08/03	08/04	08/05	08/07
Sales ($ mil.)	(3.4%)	–	–	–	70.0	65.3
Net income ($ mil.)	5.3%	–	–	–	1.8	2.0
Market value ($ mil.)	–	–	–	–	–	–
Employees	–	–	–	–	–	550

TESSCO TECHNOLOGIES, INC.
NMS: TESS

11126 McCormick Road
Hunt Valley, MD 21031
Phone: 410 229-1000
Fax: –
Web: www.tessco.com

CEO: Murray Wright
CFO: Aric M. Spitulnik
HR: –
FYE: March 31
Type: Public

TESSCO Technologies distributes communications products from hundreds of manufacturers from Agilent to ZTE. TESSCO sells network systems products (broadband radios bi-directional amplifiers); base station infrastructure equipment (towers and site hardware antennas); installation test and maintenance equipment (tools device repair parts); and mobile devices and accessories. The company also offers training services. TESSCO sells to wireless carriers as well as wireless product resellers and installers manufacturers retailers government agencies and others. While 98% of its sales are in the US the remaining 2% are made in more than 80 countries.

	Annual Growth	03/15	03/16	03/17*	04/18*	03/19
Sales ($ mil.)	2.5%	549.6	530.7	533.3	580.3	606.8
Net income ($ mil.)	(10.5%)	8.6	5.3	1.4	5.2	5.5
Market value ($ mil.)	(11.7%)	215.3	145.5	127.0	196.0	131.1
Employees	0.3%	786	786	772	768	796

*Fiscal year change

TETCO INCORPORATED

1100 NE Loop 410 Ste. 900
San Antonio TX 78217-5209
Phone: 210-821-5900
Fax: 210-826-3003
Web: www.tetco.com

CEO: –
CFO: Don Bowden
HR: –
FYE: June 30
Type: Private

TETCO is a Texas-based distributor of gasoline. TETCO was founded by Tom E. Turner (hence the "TETCO" brand) and supplies a network of more than 550 company-owned and dealer-owned gas stations in Texas and six other other states in the South and Southwest. The company supplies unbranded and branded gasoline stations with a range of products. Brands provided include RAM Phillips CITGO Shell Valero Conoco Exxon Texaco Shamrock and Chevron. The family of Tom Turner also own bulk chemical transporter Mission Petroleum Transport fuel distributor United Pump Supply construction firm V.K. Knowlton Construction & Utilities. and San Antonio grocery Green Fields Market.

TETRA TECH INC   NMS: TTEK

3475 East Foothill Boulevard
Pasadena, CA 91107
Phone: 626 351-4664
Fax: –
Web: www.tetratech.com

CEO: Dan L. Batrack
CFO: Steven M. Burdick
HR: Kevin McDonald
FYE: September 29
Type: Public

Tetra Tech is a global leader in providing consulting design and engineering services in the fields of water environment infrastructure energy and development. Its solutions span the entire life cycle of consulting and engineering projects and include applied science data analytics research engineering design construction management and operations and maintenance. The US government is one of Tetra's biggest clients along with development agencies and commercial clients in oil and gas energy utilities and mining industries. Based in the US Tetra engages in projects worldwide. The company likes to do business under time-and-materials fixed-price and cost-plus contracts.

	Annual Growth	09/15*	10/16	10/17*	09/18	09/19
Sales ($ mil.)	8.6%	1,718.7	1,929.2	2,034.0	2,200.7	2,389.6
Net income ($ mil.)	42.0%	39.1	83.8	117.9	136.9	158.7
Market value ($ mil.)	35.9%	1,359.8	1,935.4	2,540.0	3,726.8	4,634.8
Employees	11.4%	13,000	16,000	16,000	17,000	20,000

*Fiscal year change

TETRA TECHNOLOGIES, INC.   NYS: TTI

24955 Interstate 45 North
The Woodlands, TX 77380
Phone: 281 367-1983
Fax: –
Web: www.tetratec.com

CEO: Stuart M. Brightman
CFO: Elijio V Serrano
HR: –
FYE: December 31
Type: Public

TETRA Technologies is a smooth operator when it comes to discarded oil wells. The company is composed of four divisions: compression fluids offshore and product testing. The compression segment provides compression-based production enhancement services. The fluids unit makes clear brine fluids as well as dry calcium chloride that aid in drilling activities by the oil and gas industry. Its offshore segment decommissions platforms and pipelines and explores for oil and gas. In addition to production testing services for oil and gas operations the company also recycles oily residuals a byproduct of refining and exploration.

	Annual Growth	12/14	12/15	12/16	12/17	12/18
Sales ($ mil.)	(1.9%)	1,077.6	1,130.1	694.8	820.4	998.8
Net income ($ mil.)	–	(169.7)	(126.2)	(161.5)	(39.0)	(61.6)
Market value ($ mil.)	(29.2%)	839.9	945.5	631.2	536.9	211.2
Employees	(6.5%)	3,800	3,000	2,400	2,600	2,900

TETRAPHASE PHARMACEUTICALS, INC   NMS: TTPH

480 Arsenal Way
Watertown, MA 02472
Phone: 617 715-3600
Fax: –
Web: www.tphase.com

CEO: Guy Macdonald
CFO: –
HR: –
FYE: December 31
Type: Public

Tetraphase Pharmaceuticals knows you have to jump through more than one hoop to have a medication approved for use in the US. The company has developed a powerful antibiotic to treat life-threatening bacterial infections that are resistant to all other antibiotics currently on the market. Xerava (eravacycline) is a synthetic tetracycline derivative that can be taken orally or intravenously to combat multi-drug resistant bacterial infections which are considered growing threats to public health. Xerava was approved in the US in 2018 and is expected to go to market by 2019.

	Annual Growth	12/14	12/15	12/16	12/17	12/18
Sales ($ mil.)	20.1%	9.1	11.7	5.1	9.7	18.9
Net income ($ mil.)	–	(66.7)	(83.2)	(77.5)	(114.8)	(72.2)
Market value ($ mil.)	(59.0%)	106.6	26.9	10.8	16.9	3.0
Employees	21.3%	55	69	66	78	119

TEXAS A & M RESEARCH FOUNDATION INC

400 HARVEY MTCHL PKWY 3
COLLEGE STATION, TX 778454375
Phone: 979-862-6777
Fax: –
Web: www.tamu.edu

CEO: –
CFO: Linda Woodman
HR: –
FYE: August 31
Type: Private

Established in 1944 the Texas A&M Research Foundation provides administrative services and support for scientific and technical research primarily within The Texas A&M University System. Its Program Development Department helps university faculty locate and approach potential sponsors and funding opportunities. The organization also provides accounting and financing support as well as grant and contract negotiations. The foundation supports a number of projects and initiatives from the Center for Advancement and Study of Early Texas Art to vaccine research at the university system's college of medicine. It is a private not-for-profit organization.

	Annual Growth	08/12	08/13	08/14	08/15	08/16
Sales ($ mil.)	(21.4%)	–	174.2	120.8	105.5	84.6
Net income ($ mil.)	–	–	0.4	(3.5)	(0.8)	(3.3)
Market value ($ mil.)	–	–	–	–	–	–
Employees	–	–	–	–	–	483

TEXAS CAPITAL BANCSHARES INC   NMS: TCBI

2000 McKinney Avenue, Suite 700
Dallas, TX 75201
Phone: 214 932-6600
Fax: –
Web: www.texascapitalbank.com

CEO: C. Keith Cargill
CFO: Julie L. Anderson
HR: Cara McDaniel
FYE: December 31
Type: Public

Texas Capital Bancshares is the parent company of Texas Capital Bank with more than 10 branches in Austin Dallas Fort Worth Houston and San Antonio. The bank targets high-net-worth individuals and Texas-based businesses with more than $5 million in annual revenue with a focus on the real estate financial services transportation communications petrochemicals and mining sectors. Striving for personalized services for its clients the bank offers deposit accounts Visa credit cards commercial loans and mortgages equipment leasing wealth management and trust services. Its BankDirect division provides online banking services. Founded in 1998 Texas Capital Bancshares has about $11.7 billion in assets.

	Annual Growth	12/14	12/15	12/16	12/17	12/18
Assets ($ mil.)	15.5%	15,899.9	18,909.1	21,697.1	25,075.6	28,257.8
Net income ($ mil.)	21.9%	136.4	144.9	155.1	197.1	300.8
Market value ($ mil.)	(1.5%)	2,727.4	2,480.9	3,935.7	4,462.8	2,564.8
Employees	9.5%	1,142	1,329	1,442	1,564	1,641

TEXAS CHILDREN'S HOSPITAL

6621 FANNIN ST
HOUSTON, TX 770302399
Phone: 832-824-1000
Fax: –

CEO: Mark A. Wallace
CFO: Benjamin (Ben) Melson
HR: Linda Aldred
FYE: September 30
Type: Private

Texas Children's Hospital (TCH) is the flagship facility of Texas Children's Hospital Integrated Delivery System. Founded in 1954 the not-for-profit hospital provides full-service medical care for children conducts extensive research and trains pediatric medical professionals. Part of the Texas Medical Center complex it has clinical facilities for every ailment ranging from psychological troubles to surgery and physical rehabilitation as well as specialized heart cancer and neurological care. TCH is the primary pediatric training facility for Baylor College of Medicine.

	Annual Growth	09/11	09/12	09/13	09/14	09/15
Sales ($ mil.)	(8.9%)	–	2,043.9	1,229.7	1,383.8	1,546.7
Net income ($ mil.)	(30.6%)	–	289.8	78.9	70.2	96.9
Market value ($ mil.)	–	–	–	–	–	–
Employees	–	–	–	–	–	6,000

TEXAS CHRISTIAN UNIVERSITY INC

2800 S UNIVERSITY DR
FORT WORTH, TX 761290001
Phone: 817-257-7000
Fax: –
Web: www.tcu.edu

CEO: –
CFO: –
HR: Yohna Chambers
FYE: May 31
Type: Private

Home of the Horned Frogs (the school mascot) Texas Christian University (TCU) offers bachelor's master's and doctorate degrees in more than 200 fields of study. Almost 10400 undergraduate and graduate students attend the university's nine colleges and schools the cover fields of study ranging from liberal arts to engineering to business. TCU has 630 full-time faculty members and a student-to-faculty ratio of 13:1. It also has one of the NCAA's top football programs. TCU is affiliated with the Disciples of Christ a Protestant denomination.

	Annual Growth	05/11	05/12	05/14	05/17	05/18
Sales ($ mil.)	2.8%	–	441.6	637.6	499.1	521.2
Net income ($ mil.)	–	–	(4.1)	154.5	123.5	185.5
Market value ($ mil.)	–	–	–	–	–	–
Employees	–	–	–	–	–	3,400

TEXAS DEPARTMENT OF TRANSPORTATION

125 E. 11th St.
Austin TX 78701
Phone: 512-463-8585
Fax: 936-437-2123
Web: www.tdcj.state.tx.us

CEO: –
CFO: –
HR: –
FYE: August 31
Type: Government Agency

Bob Wills saw Miles and Miles of Texas and the Texas Department of Transportation (TxDOT) makes sure that we do too. TxDOT builds and maintains interstate US and state highways as well as farm-to-market roads throughout the state. It also oversees public transportation systems in the state. The aviation division assists local governments manage funds for airport development. In 2009 the agency transferred some its responsibilities including issuing license plates and vehicle titles to the newly created Texas Department of Motor Vehicles. The governor-appointed five-member Texas Transportation Commission oversees TxDOT's work. The agency dates back to the Texas Highway Department created in 1917.

TEXAS GUARANTEED STUDENT LOAN CORPORATION

301 SUNDANCE PKWY
ROUND ROCK, TX 786818004
Phone: 512-219-5700
Fax: –
Web: www.trelliscompany.org

CEO: Scott Giles
CFO:
HR:
FYE: September 30
Type: Private

TG may sound like a college fraternity but it's more about tuition and books than togas and beer. Texas Guaranteed Student Loan Corporation commonly known as TG was formed by the Texas legislature in 1979 to administer the Federal Family Education Loan Program (FFELP) in the Lone Star State. However the FFELP was eliminated in 2010 and private borrowers can no longer originate government-sponsored student loans which are now provided exclusively through the US Department of Education. TG continues to service and provide support for the approximately $26 billion worth of loans in its existing portfolio. TG is a public not-for-profit corporation that receives no state funding.

	Annual Growth	09/07	09/08	09/13	09/15	09/17
Assets ($ mil.)	(0.5%)	–	783.3	551.2	632.6	745.7
Net income ($ mil.)	–	–	(64.7)	(210.8)	84.1	62.5
Market value ($ mil.)	–	–	–	–	–	–
Employees	–	–	–	–	–	413

TEXAS HEALTH HARRIS METHODIST HOSPITAL FORT WORTH

1301 PENNSYLVANIA AVE
FORT WORTH, TX 761042122
Phone: 817-250-2000
Fax: –

CEO: –
CFO: –
HR: –
FYE: December 31
Type: Private

Harris Methodist Fort Worth Hospital is the largest and busiest hospital in Fort Worth. It is a private not-for-profit almost 730-bed tertiary care hospital serving the residents of Tarrant County and nearby communities in Texas. Harris Methodist provides both inpatient and outpatient care through its main medical center and on-site health clinics. Specialized services include emergency medicine trauma care orthopedics occupational health women's health oncology and rehabilitation. Its Harris Methodist Heart Center has about 100 beds. The hospital is the flagship facility of the Texas Health Resources hospitals system.

	Annual Growth	12/12	12/13	12/14	12/15	12/17
Sales ($ mil.)	4.6%	–	–	–	770.8	844.0
Net income ($ mil.)	0.1%	–	–	–	55.0	55.1
Market value ($ mil.)	–	–	–	–	–	–
Employees	–	–	–	–	–	3,500

TEXAS HEALTH RESOURCES

612 E LAMAR BLVD STE 400
ARLINGTON, TX 760114125
Phone: 682-236-7900
Fax: –

CEO: –
CFO: Ronald R. (Ron) Long
HR: Janelle Browne
FYE: December 31
Type: Private

Texas Health Resources (THR) provides care of the Dallas/Fort Worth and North Texas region. The not-for-profit system includes about 30 acute care and short-stay hospitals including owned managed and joint venture facilities. THR also operates outpatient and surgical centers and physicians' offices and it maintains affiliations with imaging diagnostic rehabilitation facilities and home health agencies. THR's network includes more than 5500 doctors and more than 3800 licensed beds. Its Research and Education Institute for Texas Health Resources provides clinical studies management medical device testing and medical training services.

	Annual Growth	12/05	12/06	12/09	12/13	12/17
Sales ($ mil.)	6.7%	–	2,287.5	334.9	718.3	4,688.6
Net income ($ mil.)	(8.5%)	–	2,299.1	2.8	285.7	869.8
Market value ($ mil.)	–	–	–	–	–	–
Employees	–	–	–	–	–	21,277

TEXAS HOSPITAL ASSOCIATION

6225 US Hwy. 290 E.
Austin TX 78723
Phone: 512-465-1000
Fax: 512-465-1090
Web: www.thaonline.org
CEO: Daniel Stultz
CFO: Ignacio O Zamarron
HR: –
FYE: August 31
Type: Private - Associatio

The Texas Hospital Association (THA) is like life support to a vital group of institutions. The not-for-profit organization supports more than 460 hospitals and health systems in Texas primarily through lobbying — on both state and federal levels. THA also offers it members education and training and through affiliations with other providers THA offers insurance consulting and software. The association publishes the bi-monthly Texas Hospitals which updates members on issues and trends in the hospital industry; Rural Route a bi-monthly for rural and small hospitals; and HOSPAC Notes on the group's Political Action Committee's activities. THA was founded in 1930 by a group of hospital administrators.

TEXAS INDUSTRIES INC.   NYS: TXI

1503 LBJ Freeway, Suite 400
Dallas, TX 75234-6074
Phone: 972 647-6700
Fax: 972 647-3878
Web: www.txi.com
CEO: C Howard Nye
CFO: Anne H Lloyd
HR: Michael P Collar
FYE: May 31
Type: Public

Rock on is more than a catchphrase — it's a way of life for Texas Industries. The construction materials company known as TXI produces cement aggregates and consumer building products including ready-mix concrete and other specialty aggregate products. The company also produces sand gravel crushed limestone well cements shale clay and cement-treated materials used in paving. Products are sold under the Spec Mix Durmax Envirocon Terra Tone and Proset brands. TXI's consumer products division serves construction customers mainly in the southern and southwestern US. Texas Industries has more than 80 manufacturing facilities in Texas California and four other states.

	Annual Growth	05/09	05/10	05/11	05/12	05/13
Sales ($ mil.)	(4.5%)	839.2	621.1	621.8	647.0	697.1
Net income ($ mil.)	–	(17.6)	(38.9)	(64.9)	7.5	24.6
Market value ($ mil.)	20.4%	972.3	1,037.2	1,196.9	914.3	2,040.3
Employees	(0.7%)	2,100	1,930	2,020	1,630	2,040

TEXAS INSTRUMENTS INC.   NMS: TXN

12500 TI Boulevard
Dallas, TX 75243
Phone: 214 479-3773
Fax: –
Web: www.ti.com
CEO: Richard K. (Rich) Templeton
CFO: Rafael R. Lizardi
HR: –
FYE: December 31
Type: Public

Texas Instruments sticks to basics — producing analog and embedded processors the workhorses of the industry. The company's analog chips manage power in electronic equipment and its embedded processors handle specific tasks in electronic devices. TI's customers which number about 100000 use the company's chips for applications that include autos industrial machinery consumer electronics communications devices and calculators. The company also sticks to basics in production operating its own manufacturing plants which it places around the world. International customers generate about 85% of revenue. Another TI basic: TI engineer Jack Kilby was credited as co-inventor of the integrated circuit in the late 1950s.

	Annual Growth	12/14	12/15	12/16	12/17	12/18
Sales ($ mil.)	4.9%	13,045.0	13,000.0	13,370.0	14,961.0	15,784.0
Net income ($ mil.)	18.6%	2,821.0	2,986.0	3,595.0	3,682.0	5,580.0
Market value ($ mil.)	15.3%	50,532.5	51,803.7	68,967.6	98,711.5	89,316.7
Employees	(0.9%)	31,003	29,977	29,865	29,714	29,888

TEXAS LUTHERAN UNIVERSITY

1000 W COURT ST
SEGUIN, TX 781555978
Phone: 830-372-8000
Fax: –
Web: www.tlu.edu
CEO: –
CFO: –
HR: –
FYE: May 31
Type: Private

Texas Lutheran University (TLU) formerly Texas Lutheran College is a private four-year undergraduate university of liberal arts sciences and professional studies. The coeducational school annually enrolls about 1400 students from approximately 23 US states and 8 foreign countries. About two-thirds of its student body resides on campus. TLU offers about 27 majors and more than a dozen pre-professional programs as well as study abroad programs. The institution has 77 full-time faculty members; its student-faculty ratio is 14:1. The college is affiliated with the Evangelical Lutheran Church in America.

	Annual Growth	05/02	05/03	05/05	05/06	05/13
Sales ($ mil.)	–	–	0.0	32.6	31.7	50.9
Net income ($ mil.)	(34.6%)	–	–	26.1	4.3	0.9
Market value ($ mil.)	–	–	–	–	–	–
Employees	–	–	–	–	–	275

TEXAS MUNICIPAL POWER AGENCY

12824 FM 244 RD
ANDERSON, TX 778305642
Phone: 936-873-1100
Fax: –
Web: www.texasmpa.org
CEO: –
CFO: –
HR: –
FYE: September 30
Type: Private

Power and Texas come together at the Texas Municipal Power Agency which provides electricity generation and transmission services to four municipal utilities (Bryan Denton Garland and Greenville). The joint powers agency which was created in 1975 by its member cities owns and operates the 462-MW Gibbons Creek power plant and related transmission assets. In the wake of the oil embargo the early 1970s the Texas Legislature created joint powers agencies that could perform all the duties of utilities except sell power to non-members. Bryan Denton Garland and Greenville then formed the Texas Municipal Power Agency and harnessed locally available lignite to fuel a power generation plant.

	Annual Growth	12/07	12/08*	09/15	09/16	09/18
Sales ($ mil.)	–	–	0.0	–	273.3	175.5
Net income ($ mil.)	–	–	0.0	–	(1.7)	(30.7)
Market value ($ mil.)	–	–	–	–	–	–
Employees	–	–	–	–	–	137

*Fiscal year change

TEXAS PACIFIC LAND TRUST   NYS: TPL

1700 Pacific Avenue, Suite 2900
Dallas, TX 75201
Phone: 214 969-5530
Fax: 214 871-7139
Web: www.tpltrust.com
CEO: Tyler Glover
CFO: Robert J. Packer
HR: –
FYE: December 31
Type: Public

Texas Pacific Land Trust was created to sell the Texas & Pacific Railway's land after its 1888 bankruptcy and yup they're still workin' on it. The trust began with the railroad's 3.5 million acres; today it is one of the largest private landowners in Texas with around 960000 acres in 20 counties. Texas Pacific Land Trust's sales come from oil and gas royalties (70% of sales) grazing leases easements and land sales. It has a perpetual oil and gas royalty interest under some 470000 acres in West Texas. About 8% of the trust's oil and gas royalties are from leases operated by Chevron U.S.A. Texas Pacific Land Trust uses the revenues from sales and royalties to buy and retire its own shares.

	Annual Growth	12/14	12/15	12/16	12/17	12/18
Sales ($ mil.)	52.7%	55.2	79.4	59.9	132.3	300.2
Net income ($ mil.)	56.7%	34.8	50.0	37.2	76.4	209.7
Market value ($ mil.)	46.4%	916.0	1,016.3	2,303.7	3,466.9	4,204.4
Employees	72.6%	8	8	10	32	71

TEXAS ROADHOUSE INC

NMS: TXRH

6040 Dutchmans Lane, Suite 200
Louisville, KY 40205
Phone: 502 426-9984
Fax: –

CEO: W. Kent Taylor
CFO: Scott M. Colosi
HR: –
FYE: December 25
Type: Public

Texas Roadhouse operates a leading full-service casual dining restaurant chain with about 590 company-owned and franchised locations in nearly 50 US states and 10 countries. The Southwest-themed eatery serves a variety of steaks ribs chicken pork chops and seafood entrees along with sandwiches chili starters and a selection of side dishes. The company also operates a few restaurants under the name Bubba's 33 that specializes in burgers pizza and wings. Despite its name Texas Roadhouse was founded in Clarksville Indiana in 1993.

	Annual Growth	12/14	12/15	12/16	12/17	12/18
Sales ($ mil.)	11.6%	1,582.1	1,807.4	1,990.7	2,219.5	2,457.4
Net income ($ mil.)	16.1%	87.0	96.9	115.6	131.5	158.2
Market value ($ mil.)	13.9%	2,419.2	2,582.5	3,549.4	3,873.1	4,068.6
Employees	10.6%	43,300	47,900	52,500	56,300	64,900

TEXAS SOUTHERN UNIVERSITY

3100 CLEBURNE ST
HOUSTON, TX 770044598
Phone: 713-313-7011
Fax: –
Web: www.tsu.edu

CEO: –
CFO: –
HR: –
FYE: August 31
Type: Private

Texas Southern University (TSU) is a historically black public institution. The university located on a 150-acre campus in downtown Houston offers about 40 bachelor's degree programs and more than 30 master's and doctoral degree programs. Its 11 colleges and schools include the Thurgood Marshall School of Law and the Barbara Jordan Mickey Leland School of Public Affairs. (Jordan and Leland are both former US representatives and graduates of TSU.) The university has an enrollment of more than 9500 students and a staff of about 1000 faculty members and support personnel.

	Annual Growth	08/14	08/15	08/16	08/17	08/18
Sales ($ mil.)	8.3%	–	105.8	112.5	121.4	134.3
Net income ($ mil.)	–	–	(0.8)	9.8	22.0	41.8
Market value ($ mil.)	–	–	–	–	–	–
Employees	–	–	–	–	–	1,000

TEXAS STATE UNIVERSITY

601 UNIVERSITY DR
SAN MARCOS, TX 786664684
Phone: 512-245-2111
Fax: –
Web: www.txstate.edu

CEO: –
CFO: –
HR: –
FYE: August 31
Type: Private

Texas State University-San Marcos has about 38800 students pursuing degrees in about 100 undergraduate programs 90 graduate programs and a dozen doctoral programs. Comprising eight colleges as well as a graduate school Texas State University-San Marcos is the largest school in the Texas State University system which includes Angelo State University Lamar University Sam Houston State University and Sul Ross State University. It also offers bachelor's and graduate-level courses at a campus in Round Rock. The school has 209 buildings on its San Marcos cmapus.

	Annual Growth	08/13	08/14	08/15	08/16	08/18
Sales ($ mil.)	5.0%	–	377.7	404.8	436.7	459.6
Net income ($ mil.)	(21.9%)	–	73.1	25.3	34.5	27.2
Market value ($ mil.)	–	–	–	–	–	–
Employees	–	–	–	–	–	3,156

TEXAS VANGUARD OIL CO.

NBB: TVOC

9811 Anderson Mill Rd., Suite 202
Austin, TX 78750
Phone: 512 331-6781
Fax: –

CEO: –
CFO: –
HR: –
FYE: December 31
Type: Public

In the vanguard of companies squeezing oil out of old fields Texas Vanguard Oil explores and develops oil-producing properties in Nebraska New Mexico Oklahoma Texas and Wyoming. The company's growth strategy is to acquire working interests in producing oil and natural gas properties already being operated by other oil and gas firms and to then further develop these assets. In 2008 Texas Vanguard Oil reported proved reserves of 358119 barrels of oil and 2.3 billion cu. ft. of natural gas. A pure exploration and production business the company does not refine or market its own oil and gas. It also engages independent contractors to drill its wells. Chair Linda Watson owns 74% of Texas Vanguard Oil.

	Annual Growth	12/08	12/09	12/10	12/11	12/12
Sales ($ mil.)	(9.3%)	9.7	5.0	6.4	7.2	6.6
Net income ($ mil.)	(38.9%)	2.8	0.2	0.7	1.2	0.4
Market value ($ mil.)	11.0%	9.8	8.9	12.4	13.6	14.9
Employees	0.0%	2	2	2	2	2

TEXON LP

11757 Katy Fwy. Ste. 1400
Houston TX 77079-1733
Phone: 281-531-8400
Fax: 818-837-7440
Web: www.sigue.com

CEO: Terry Looper
CFO: Leonard Russo
HR: –
FYE: December 31
Type: Private

You'd never mistake it for Texaco or Exxon but Texon is also involved in the energy business though at a much more modest level. Texon LP sells natural gas and natural gas liquids (NGLs) to the wholesale market mainly to utilities municipalities and large commercial and industrial customers. Using other companies' pipelines about 50 in all it delivers its products nationwide after buying them from some 400 independent producers. Butane propane and liquefied petroleum gas are among the NGLs that Texon markets and are delivered by truck rail and barge as well as pipeline. The company also offers weather-forecasting services to clients in colder regions of the country. Texon began operations in 1989.

TEXTRON INC

NYS: TXT

40 Westminster Street
Providence, RI 02903
Phone: 401 421-2800
Fax: –
Web: www.textron.com

CEO: Scott C. Donnelly
CFO: Frank T. Connor
HR: Cheryl H. Johnson
FYE: December 29
Type: Public

Texton's products help customers across the globe get on the move — by air land or sea. The company is known for its Beechcraft and Cessna aircraft and Bell military and commercial helicopters. It also services Hawker business jets. In addition Textron provides parts repair and other aftermarket services. The company also makes specialty vehicles (E-Z-GO golf carts Arctic Cat ATVs) fuel systems land and marine systems unmanned aerial vehicles and simulation and training products. Textron which generates about 60% of revenue from the US serves government industrial and commercial clients.

	Annual Growth	01/15	01/16*	12/16	12/17	12/18
Sales ($ mil.)	0.2%	13,878.0	13,423.0	13,788.0	14,198.0	13,972.0
Net income ($ mil.)	26.8%	600.0	697.0	962.0	307.0	1,222.0
Market value ($ mil.)	2.7%	9,936.1	9,898.4	11,441.8	13,333.8	10,756.1
Employees	1.0%	34,000	35,000	36,000	37,000	35,000

*Fiscal year change

TEXTURA CORP
NYS: TXTR

1405 Lake Cook Road
Deerfield, IL 60015
Phone: 847 457-6500
Fax: –
Web: www.texturacorp.com

CEO: Patrick Allin
CFO: –
HR: –
FYE: December 31
Type: Public

Textura brings tech solutions to one of the most concrete industries — construction. The company's Software-as-a-Service (SaaS) includes tools to facilitate connection and collaboration among commercial construction owners developers general contractors and subcontractors. Its on-demand software covers everything from the bidding process and vendor risk assessment to routing invoices and project documents to billing and documenting subcontractor default. A majority of Textura's revenue comes from customers using its invoicing document-tracking and environmental certification products and monthly subscription fees (collectively "activity-driven revenue"). Formed in 2004 the company went public in 2013.

	Annual Growth	09/10	09/11	09/12	09/13*	12/14
Sales ($ mil.)	79.8%	6.0	10.5	21.7	35.5	63.0
Net income ($ mil.)	–	(15.9)	(18.9)	(15.9)	(36.9)	(24.7)
Market value ($ mil.)	(33.9%)	–	–	–	1,102.3	728.5
Employees	32.6%	–	–	287	385	505

*Fiscal year change

TF FINANCIAL CORP.
NMS: THRD

3 Penns Trail
Newtown, PA 18940
Phone: 215 579-4000
Fax: –
Web: www.thirdfedbank.com

CEO: –
CFO: –
HR: –
FYE: December 31
Type: Public

To Find out what TF Financial does isn't Too tufF. The holding company owns Third Federal Savings Bank which operates about 15 branches in southeastern Pennsylvania's Buck and Philadelphia counties and neighboring Mercer County New Jersey. The bank offers standard deposit products including CDs IRAs and savings checking NOW and money market accounts. It also provides insurance and investment products and services. The bank's lending activities mainly consist of issuing one- to four-family residential mortgages (around half of the company's loan portfolio) multifamily and commercial real estate loans (about a quarter) and construction business and consumer loans.

	Annual Growth	12/08	12/09	12/10	12/11	12/12
Assets ($ mil.)	(0.8%)	733.7	714.1	691.8	681.9	711.8
Net income ($ mil.)	6.2%	4.2	4.5	3.4	3.9	5.4
Market value ($ mil.)	5.4%	54.8	53.8	63.3	64.5	67.6
Employees	(3.9%)	196	191	196	184	167

TFS FINANCIAL CORP
NMS: TFSL

7007 Broadway Avenue
Cleveland, OH 44105
Phone: 216 441-6000
Fax: –
Web: www.thirdfederal.com

CEO: Marc A Stefanski
CFO: Paul J Huml
HR: Christine Warfield
FYE: September 30
Type: Public

TFS Financial is the holding company for Third Federal Savings and Loan a thrift with some 45 branches and loan production offices in Ohio and southern Florida. The bank offers such deposit products as checking savings and retirement accounts and CDs. It uses funds from deposits to originate a variety of consumer loans primarily residential mortgages. Third Federal also offers IRAs annuities and mutual funds as well as retirement and college savings plans. TFS subsidiary Third Capital owns stakes in commercial real estate private equity funds and other investments. Mutual holding company Third Federal Savings and Loan Association of Cleveland owns nearly three-quarters of TFS Financial.

	Annual Growth	09/15	09/16	09/17	09/18	09/19
Assets ($ mil.)	4.1%	12,368.9	12,906.1	13,692.6	14,137.3	14,542.4
Net income ($ mil.)	2.5%	72.6	80.6	88.9	85.4	80.2
Market value ($ mil.)	1.1%	4,829.4	4,986.1	4,515.8	4,202.2	5,044.9
Employees	–	–	–	–	–	–

TG THERAPEUTICS INC
NAS: TGTX

2 Gansevoort Street, 9th Floor
New York, NY 10014
Phone: 212 554-4484
Fax: 212 554-4531
Web: www.tgtherapeutics.com

CEO: Michael S. Weiss
CFO: Sean A. Power
HR: –
FYE: December 31
Type: Public

TG Therapeutics is a drug development and commercializing firm that can change hats quickly when necessary. It is currently developing two therapies targeting hematological malignancies: Glycoengineered monoclonal antibody TG-1101 (ublituximab) targets a specific epitope on the CD20 antigen found on mature B-lymphocytes while TGR-1202 is an oral P13K delta inhibitor. While its current focus is on cancer drugs TG Therapeutics — like most drug development companies — has acquired developed and spun-off other types of candidates in an effort to build a pipeline of potentially revenue-generating commercial products. Previous candidates included a vitamin B-12 nasal spray and a treatment for involuntary tremors.

	Annual Growth	12/14	12/15	12/16	12/17	12/18
Sales ($ mil.)	(0.1%)	0.2	0.2	0.2	0.2	0.2
Net income ($ mil.)	–	(55.8)	(62.9)	(78.3)	(118.5)	(173.5)
Market value ($ mil.)	(28.7%)	1,328.5	1,000.6	390.0	687.7	343.9
Employees	44.6%	24	40	64	75	105

THE ADT CORPORATION
NYSE: ADT

1501 Yamato Rd
Boca Raton FL 33431
Phone: 561-988-3600
Fax: 561-988-3601
Web: www.adt.com

CEO: Timothy J Whall
CFO: Jeff Likosar
HR: –
FYE: September 30
Type: Public

Burglar at your window? ADT wants you to be armed and calm with its alarms. The company provides products and services used for fire protection access control alarm monitoring medical alert system monitoring video surveillance and intrusion detection. It divides its security operations across four disciplines: Residential Security (provides burglar fire carbon dioxide alarms) Small Business (intruder detection and cameras) ADT Pulse (allows users to access and control security systems remotely) and Home Health (emergency response in the case of medical emergencies). ADT was a unit of conglomerate Tyco International until late 2012 when it was spun-off as a publicly traded company.

THE AEROSPACE CORPORATION
Type: Private

2310 E EL SEGUNDO BLVD
EL SEGUNDO, CA 902454609
Phone: 310-336-5000
Fax: –
Web: www.aerospace.org

CEO: Steven J. (Steve) Isakowitz
CFO: Ellen M. Beatty
HR: Heather Laychak
FYE: September 30
Type: Private

A not-for-profit company The Aerospace Corporation provides space-related research development and advisory services primarily for US government programs. Its chief sponsor is the US Air Force and its main customers have included the Space and Missile Systems Center of Air Force Space Command and the National Reconnaissance Office. Other clients have included NASA and the National Oceanic and Atmospheric Administration as well as commercial enterprises universities and international organizations. Areas of expertise include launch certification process implementation systems engineering and technology application. The Aerospace Corporation was established in 1960 and operates through about 20 offices.

	Annual Growth	09/11	09/12	09/13	09/14	09/15
Sales ($ mil.)	0.5%	–	903.4	868.6	881.9	916.7
Net income ($ mil.)	–	–	4.6	0.2	5.4	(15.2)
Market value ($ mil.)	–	–	–	–	–	–
Employees	–	–	–	–	–	3,920

THE AMACORE GROUP INC.

OTC: ACGI

485 N. Keller Rd. Ste. 450
Maitland FL 32751
Phone: 407-805-8900
Fax: 407-805-0045
Web: www.amacoregroup.com

CEO: Jay Shafer
CFO: G Scott Smith
HR: –
FYE: December 31
Type: Public

The Amacore Group wants you to be able to see a smaller optometry bill. Amacore is a provider of non-insurance based discount plans for eyewear and eyecare services including surgery. Amacore Group's products are marketed to individuals families and businesses as well as through the company's affiliations with insurance companies and other membership groups. The company has expanded its discount program offerings to include dental hearing chiropractic and other health services. It also offers traditional health plans through partnerships with insurance providers.

THE AMALGAMATED SUGAR COMPANY LLC

1951 S SATURN WAY STE 100
BOISE, ID 837092924
Phone: 208-383-6500
Fax: –

CEO: John McCreedy
CFO: –
HR: –
FYE: December 31
Type: Private

The Amalgamated Sugar Company with roots reaching back to 1915 turns beets into sweets. It's the second-largest US sugar producer processing sugar beets grown on about 180000 acres in Idaho Oregon and Washington. The company manufactures granulated coarse powdered and brown consumer sugar products marketed under the brand White Satin. It also makes products for retail grocery chains under private labels. The sugar company produces beet pulp molasses and other beet by-products for use by food and animal-feed manufacturers. Since 1997 Amalgamated Sugar has been owned by the Snake River Sugar Company a cooperative that comprises sugar beet growers in Idaho Oregon and Washington.

	Annual Growth	12/09	12/10	12/11	12/12	12/13
Sales ($ mil.)	3.7%	–	–	886.1	907.9	953.1
Net income ($ mil.)	16.0%	–	–	46.7	14.7	62.8
Market value ($ mil.)	–	–	–	–	–	–
Employees	–	–	–	–	–	1,500

THE AMERICAN AUTOMOBILE ASSOCIATION

1000 AAA Dr.
Heathrow FL 32746
Phone: 407-444-7000
Fax: 407-444-7380
Web: www.aaa.com

CEO: Marshall Doney
CFO: Robert McKee
HR: –
FYE: December 31
Type: Private - Not-for-Pr

This isn't your great-grandfather's American Automobile Association (AAA). The not-for-profit organization is best known for providing emergency roadside assistance to its members. AAA is extending its reach into other areas however such as offering a variety of financial and travel-arrangement services (foreign currency exchange and travelers checks) as well. The organization offers its members credit cards insurance and vehicle financing. AAA operates travel agencies and publishes maps and travel guides to boot. AAA and its affiliated 50-odd auto clubs maintain about 1100 facilities to serve more than 53 million members that span the US and Canada. AAA was founded in 1902.

THE AMERICAN MUSEUM OF NATURAL HISTORY

CENTRAL PARK W AT 79TH ST
NEW YORK, NY 10024
Phone: 212-769-5000
Fax: –
Web: www.amnh.org

CEO: –
CFO: Ellen Gallagher
HR: –
FYE: June 30
Type: Private

The American Museum of Natural History is one of the world's foremost scientific museums. Its landmark building on New York's Central Park West showcases parts of its immense collections of anthropological and zoological specimens along with meteorites gemstones dinosaur fossils and a butterfly conservatory. The museum which is also home to the Rose Center for Earth and Space and the Hayden Planetarium and a top-flight research library conducts many educational programs offers an IMAX theater and publishes Natural History magazine. The American Museum of Natural History is part of the University of the State of New York. The museum was chartered by the New York legislature in 1869.

	Annual Growth	06/14	06/15	06/16	06/17	06/18
Sales ($ mil.)	(12.8%)	–	284.0	198.8	193.4	188.5
Net income ($ mil.)	(26.9%)	–	82.8	(5.3)	141.0	32.3
Market value ($ mil.)	–	–	–	–	–	–
Employees	–	–	–	–	–	1,262

THE AMERICAN SOCIETY FOR THE PREVENTION OF CRUELTY TO ANIMALS

424 E 92ND ST
NEW YORK, NY 101286804
Phone: 212-876-7700
Fax: –
Web: www.aspca.org

CEO: Matthew Bershadker
CFO: Julia Nelson
HR: Art Rios
FYE: December 31
Type: Private

This group watches out for Fidos Fluffies and other furry friends all across the country. The ASPCA (American Society for the Prevention of Cruelty to Animals) is a nonprofit organization dedicated to promoting the humane treatment of non-humans. The society's aim is to save the lives of homeless pets and help victims of animal cruelty. It engages in education public awareness and government advocacy efforts and supports the work of independent humane societies throughout the US. It provides medical services and animal placement from facilities in New York City. The privately funded organization was established in 1866 by Henry Bergh.

	Annual Growth	12/12	12/13	12/14	12/15	12/16
Sales ($ mil.)	10.1%	–	–	–	197.5	217.4
Net income ($ mil.)	20.5%	–	–	–	7.4	9.0
Market value ($ mil.)	–	–	–	–	–	–
Employees	–	–	–	–	–	350

THE ANDREW W MELLON FOUNDATION

140 E 62ND ST
NEW YORK, NY 100658124
Phone: 212-838-8400
Fax: –
Web: www.mellon.org

CEO: –
CFO: –
HR: –
FYE: December 31
Type: Private

Recipients of funds from The Andrew W. Mellon Foundation don't take the organization for granted. One of the leading charitable foundations in the US the organization provides about $280 million annually in grants including awards in five core areas: including higher education and scholarship performing arts and museums and art conservation. Recent grant recipients include the Detroit Symphony Orchestra Oberlin College and the Metropolitan Museum of Art. The foundation was created in 1969 when Paul Mellon and Ailsa Mellon Bruce the son and daughter of banking titan Andrew W. Mellon merged their charitable foundations (Old Dominion Foundation and Avalon Foundation).

	Annual Growth	12/05	12/06	12/09	12/16	12/17
Sales ($ mil.)	1.0%	–	877.0	0.0	487.6	980.1
Net income ($ mil.)	0.0%	–	655.3	0.0	151.5	655.7
Market value ($ mil.)	–	–	–	–	–	–
Employees	–	–	–	–	–	70

THE ARTHRITIS FOUNDATION INC

1355 PEACHTREE ST NE # 600
ATLANTA, GA 303092922
Phone: 404-872-7100
Fax: –
Web: www.arthritis.org

CEO: Ann M Palmer
CFO: –
HR: Pam Maynard
FYE: December 31
Type: Private

Arthritis Foundation (AF) wants the country's aches and pains to go away. The not-for-profit organization funds research advocacy and support services for various kinds of arthritis and related diseases. The foundation has about 45 chapters in 33 US states and offers programs and services including aquatic programs information about treatment breakthroughs exercise tips for people with the disease and pain management information. AF raises money through The Arthritis Walk Jingle Bell Walk/Run and Joints in Motion a program that trains participants to run a marathon or hike a tough trail and take part in a fund raising event.

	Annual Growth	12/07	12/08	12/13	12/14	12/15
Sales ($ mil.)	2.3%	–	54.4	49.1	54.5	63.8
Net income ($ mil.)	14.2%	–	1.0	1.4	7.5	2.4
Market value ($ mil.)	–	–	–	–	–	–
Employees	–	–	–	–	–	150

THE ASPEN INSTITUTE INC

2300 N ST NW STE 700
WASHINGTON, DC 200371122
Phone: 202-736-5800
Fax: –
Web: www.aspeninstitute.org

CEO: Walter Isaacson
CFO: Dolores Gorgone
HR: –
FYE: December 31
Type: Private

If you're attending one of many seminars at the Aspen Institute you really should have your thinking cap on. The Aspen Institute is an international think tank providing a place to exchange ideas about leadership and contemporary issues. The not-for-profit organization holds seminars programs and conferences emphasizing a nonpartisan and non-ideological setting. Equity in public education ethical leadership practices and global security are among the issues the institute has addressed. It is primarily funded by corporate individual and foundation donations. The Aspen Institute was founded in 1950 by Chicago businessman and philanthropist Walter Paepcke.

	Annual Growth	12/07	12/08	12/13	12/14	12/16
Sales ($ mil.)	6.3%	–	73.7	93.2	96.5	120.3
Net income ($ mil.)	(6.7%)	–	10.2	11.1	5.1	5.8
Market value ($ mil.)	–	–	–	–	–	–
Employees	–	–	–	–	–	300

THE ASSOCIATED PRESS

200 LIBERTY ST FL 19
NEW YORK, NY 102812102
Phone: 212-621-1500
Fax: –
Web: www.ap.org

CEO: Gary B. Pruitt
CFO: Ken Dale
HR: –
FYE: December 31
Type: Private

This just in: The Associated Press (AP) is reporting tonight and every night wherever news is breaking. AP is one of the world's largest news gathering organizations with news bureaus in about 100 countries. It provides news photos graphics and audiovisual services that reach people daily through print radio TV and the Web. It also offers advertising management and distribution services. The not-for-profit cooperative is owned by 1500 US daily newspaper members. A group of New York newspapers founded the AP in 1846 in order to chronicle the US-Mexican War more efficiently. Founding papers include The New York Sun The Journal of Commerce The Courier and Enquirer The New York Herald and The Express .

	Annual Growth	12/13	12/14	12/15	12/16	12/17
Sales ($ mil.)	(5.5%)	–	604.0	568.0	556.3	510.1
Net income ($ mil.)	–	–	140.8	183.6	1.6	(74.0)
Market value ($ mil.)	–	–	–	–	–	–
Employees	–	–	–	–	–	3,533

THE AVEDIS ZILDJIAN COMPANY INC.

22 Longwater Dr.
Norwell MA 02061
Phone: 781-871-2200
Fax: 781-871-9652
Web: www.zildjian.com

CEO: Craigie A Zildjian
CFO: –
HR: –
FYE: December 31
Type: Private

The centuries-old story of Avedis Zildjian is rich in cymbalism. Zildjian the world's #1 maker of cymbals is the oldest family-run firm in the US. In 1623 Turkey Armenian alchemist Avedis created an alloy for making cymbals. (A sultan named him "Zildjian" or cymbalsmith.) The company moved to America in 1929. Traditionally the father passed the secret metallurgical formula on to the eldest son but in 1976 Craigie Zildjian (named CEO in 1999) became the first female family member to be employed there. Zildjian also makes drumsticks and through subsidiary Malletech other percussion instruments. Craigie's uncle Robert owns rival cymbal-maker Sabian which also uses the secret formula.

THE BALTIMORE LIFE INSURANCE COMPANY

10075 Red Run Blvd.
Owings Mills MD 21117-4871
Phone: 410-581-6600
Fax: 410-581-6604
Web: www.baltlife.com

CEO: L John Pearson
CFO: –
HR: –
FYE: December 31
Type: Private

Baltimore Life keeps its finger on the pulse of citizens in Baltimore and beyond. The company provides a variety of life insurance products and annuities to some 300000 customers in the US including individuals families and businesses. Products include term universal and whole life policies; retirement immediate and deferred annuities; and illness coverage. Independent and affiliated agents sell the company's policies. Licensed in 49 states and Washington DC the firm operates primarily in Maryland and Pennsylvania. Baltimore Life was founded in 1882 and reorganized to a mutual insurance holding company structure in 2001.

THE BANCORP INC

NMS: TBBK

409 Silverside Road
Wilmington, DE 19809
Phone: 302 385-5000
Fax: –
Web: www.thebancorp.com

CEO: Damian Kozlowski
CFO: Paul Frenkiel
HR: –
FYE: December 31
Type: Public

The Bancorp is — what else? — the holding company for The Bancorp Bank which provides financial services in the virtual world. Targeting non-bank financial service companies across the US and Europe from start-ups to small and midsized businesses underserved by larger banks in the market The Bancorp Bank provides private-label online banking to 200 affinity groups; offers specialty lending; issues prepaid debit cards; and processes ACH and merchant credit card transactions. Its specialty lending products include securities backed lines of credit (SBLOC) auto fleet and equipment leasing SBA loans and commercial mortgage loans for sale in capital markets.

	Annual Growth	12/14	12/15	12/16	12/17	12/18
Assets ($ mil.)	(2.9%)	4,986.3	4,765.8	4,858.1	4,708.1	4,437.9
Net income ($ mil.)	11.6%	57.1	13.4	(96.5)	21.7	88.7
Market value ($ mil.)	(7.5%)	613.6	358.9	442.9	556.7	448.5
Employees	(3.7%)	684	762	589	538	589

THE BEACON MUTUAL INSURANCE COMPANY

1 Beacon Centre
Warwick RI 02886-1378
Phone: 401-825-2667
Fax: 401-825-2607
Web: www.beaconmutual.com

CEO: –
CFO: Cynthia Lee Lawlor
HR: –
FYE: December 31
Type: Private - Mutual Com

Safety's a beacon in the night (and day) at Beacon Mutual Insurance a provider of workers' compensation employers' liability insurance and claim management services in Rhode Island. It is the state's largest writer of workers' compensation where it has more than 13000 policyholders. The not-for-profit organization operates under statutory duties to provide coverage at the lowest possible cost and to serve as an insurer of last resort. It also offers loss prevention services including workplace and construction safety defensive driving and industrial ergonomics programs. Beacon Mutual Insurance was founded as the State Compensation Insurance Fund in 1990; it began writing policies in 1992.

THE BERLIN STEEL CONSTRUCTION COMPANY

76 Depot Rd.
Berlin CT 06037
Phone: 860-828-3531
Fax: 860-828-8581
Web: www.berlinsteel.com

CEO: –
CFO: –
HR: Bob Smith
FYE: December 31
Type: Private

The Berlin Steel Construction Company had nothing to do with a falling wall but it does know how to erect metal. The specialty contractor fabricates and erects structural steel for all types of buildings as well as staircases handrails and grating. It also erects precast concrete precast garages metal roofs and floor decks and steel joists and girders. In addition to fabrication and site erection Berlin Steel offers project management services. Key projects include a new terminal addition at the Bradley International Airport and structural steel work for a University of Connecticut stadium and a Rhode Island convention center. Berlin Steel serves the New England and Mid-Atlantic regions of the US.

THE BELT RAILWAY COMPANY OF CHICAGO

6900 S. Central Ave.
Bedford Park IL 60638
Phone: 708-496-4000
Fax: 708-496-2608
Web: www.beltrailway.com

CEO: –
CFO: –
HR: –
FYE: December 31
Type: Joint Venture

Belt Railway of Chicago is a railroad's railroad. Freight trains converge on its Clearing Yards facility to have their cars separated and moved from one rail line to another in order to reach their destinations. To accomplish these tasks the company operates 28 miles of mainline track and 300 miles of switching lines. Belt Railway of Chicago is owned by six of the largest North American railroads: Burlington Northern Santa Fe Canadian National Canadian Pacific CSX Norfolk Southern and Union Pacific. Customers include not only the company's owners but also other railroads that serve the Chicago area which is one of North America's primary rail hubs. Belt Railway of Chicago began operations in 1882.

THE BESSEMER GROUP INCORPORATED

630 5th Ave.
New York NY 10111
Phone: 212-708-9100
Fax: 212-265-5826
Web: www.bessemertrust.com

CEO: Marc D Stern
CFO: –
HR: –
FYE: December 31
Type: Private

Wealth is personal for Bessemer Group. The privately-owned firm manages more than $60 billion in assets for wealthy individuals and families who have at least $10 million to invest. Main subsidiary Bessemer Trust administers portfolios with holdings in domestic and international equities and bonds as well as such alternative assets as hedge funds real estate and private equity funds of funds. The group also provides trust custody tax and estate planning strategic philanthropy and financial advisory services. It also counsels family businesses. The Bessemer Group has some 15 US offices in addition to locations in London and the Cayman Islands.

THE BENECON GROUP INC

147 W AIRPORT RD
LITITZ, PA 175439260
Phone: 717-723-4600
Fax: –
Web: www.benecon.com

CEO: Samuel Lombardo
CFO: Joel E Callihan
HR: –
FYE: December 31
Type: Private

The Benecon Group helps employers create implement and manage benefits programs. Benecon operates through four divisions: Consulting and Actuarial services Broker Services Municipal Insurance and Compliance Services. The Consulting and Actuarial services division helps larger corporate clients design and implement benefits programs while the Municipal Insurance division helps municipalities in central Pennsylvania gain leverage in the benefits markets by creating health insurance cooperatives. Benecon acts as a broker for hundreds of clients including Capital Blue Cross Highmark Blue Shield and- , UnitedHealth; the Compliance division provides advice on regulations and laws related to benefits packages.

	Annual Growth	12/03	12/04	12/05	12/06	12/08
Sales ($ mil.)	15.3%	–	9.7	10.1	12.5	17.1
Net income ($ mil.)	145.0%	–	–	0.0	0.1	0.4
Market value ($ mil.)	–	–	–	–	–	–
Employees	–	–	–	–	–	70

THE BILTMORE COMPANY

1 LODGE ST
ASHEVILLE, NC 288032662
Phone: 828-225-6776
Fax: –
Web: www.biltmore.com

CEO: Bill Cecil
CFO: Stephen Watson
HR: –
FYE: December 31
Type: Private

The Biltmore Company doesn't need to build more. It oversees the Biltmore Estate which includes the 250-room home (the largest privately owned in the US) as well as two hotels a winery restaurants and retail shops and licensing rights for a line of home decor products. (Guests don't stay at the Biltmore House but at the Inn on Biltmore Estate.) Some one million visitors tour the home and grounds each year. The house sits on 8000 acres of land and encompasses four acres of floor space. It has 35 bedrooms some 40 bathrooms 65 fireplaces and three kitchens. The Biltmore is family-owned by descendants of the Vanderbilts and is one of the few National Historic Landmarks that is entirely privately funded.

	Annual Growth	12/02	12/03	12/04	12/06	12/07
Sales ($ mil.)	8.0%	–	57.0	56.8	70.6	77.6
Net income ($ mil.)	(15.0%)	–	4.4	3.0	2.5	2.3
Market value ($ mil.)	–	–	–	–	–	–
Employees	–	–	–	–	–	1,900

THE BMS ENTERPRISES INC

5718 AIRPORT FWY
HALTOM CITY, TX 761176005
Phone: 877-730-1948
Fax: –
Web: www.blackmonmooring.com

CEO: Kirk Blackmon
CFO: William G Blackmon
HR: –
FYE: December 31
Type: Private

The BMS Enterprises (doing business as Blackmon Mooring) doesn't fly in the face of disaster. The company offers disaster recovery services such as fire water and smoke damage restoration as well as mold remediation. For those who haven't experienced flooding fire hurricanes or earthquakes BMS Enterprises will also clean your carpets tile floors furniture drapes and air ducts. Its BMS CAT (Catastrophe) unit provides commercial restoration services. The family-owned BMS Enterprises was founded in 1948 by Scott Mooring Jr. and Bill Blackmon Jr. as a furniture and dye shop.

	Annual Growth	12/02	12/03	12/04	12/05	12/14
Sales ($ mil.)	(5.7%)	–	–	–	262.6	155.3
Net income ($ mil.)	(7.0%)	–	–	–	12.8	6.7
Market value ($ mil.)	–	–	–	–	–	–
Employees	–	–	–	–	–	900

THE BOLER COMPANY

500 Park Blvd. Ste. 1010
Itasca IL 60143
Phone: 630-773-9111
Fax: 630-773-9121
Web: www.hendrickson-intl.com

CEO: –
CFO: –
HR: –
FYE: December 31
Type: Private

This Boler wants the big wheels of the road to ride smoothly in their own lanes. The holding company's main subsidiary Hendrickson makes suspension systems for heavy and medium-duty trucks buses and RVs. A trailer division focuses on air ride suspensions. Auxiliary axle systems and controls are made for heavy-duty trucks and trailers. A stamping division supplies bumpers and components; its spring division makes heavy-duty steel flat-leaf and parabolic taper-leaf springs. Boler sells to heavy-duty truck and trailer OEMs in the US with distribution to countries in Latin America and Europe as well as Australia and Japan. Boler is led by founder and chairman John Boler and his son president and CEO Matthew.

THE BRANCH GROUP INC

442 RUTHERFORD AVE NE
ROANOKE, VA 240162116
Phone: 540-982-1678
Fax: –
Web: www.branchgroup.com

CEO: J William Karbach
CFO: Melanie Wheeler
HR: –
FYE: December 31
Type: Private

It's not going out on a limb to say that The Branch Group has paved a lot of roads and built a lot of structures up and down the Atlantic Seaboard. The company through its subsidiaries provides heavy/highway construction (Branch Highways and E.V. Williams) building construction (Branch & Associates and R.E. Daffan) and mechanical/electrical construction services (G.J. Hopkins). The group has paved roads for highway departments built hospitals schools factories and infrastructure projects. The employee-owned company began in 1963 as Branch & Associates Inc. but traces its roots to 1955 when Billy Branch and C. W. McAlister paired up to provide road and site construction services.

	Annual Growth	12/13	12/14	12/15	12/16	12/17
Sales ($ mil.)	(1.9%)	–	384.9	392.5	393.3	363.3
Net income ($ mil.)	–	–	–	0.0	0.0	0.0	0.0
Market value ($ mil.)	–	–	–	–	–	–
Employees	–	–	–	–	–	800

THE BRIAD GROUP

78 Okner Pkwy.
Livingston NJ 07039
Phone: 973-597-6433
Fax: 973-597-6422
Web: www.briad.com

CEO: –
CFO: –
HR: –
FYE: December 31
Type: Private

This hospitality company is thankful for Friday's. The Briad Group is the #1 operator of T.G.I. Friday's restaurants with about 70 locations in six states primarily in Arizona California and New Jersey. Franchised from Carlson Restaurants Worldwide the casual dining restaurants are popular for their appetizers and bar-like atmosphere. Briad Group is also a leading franchisee of Wendy's International (part of Wendy's/Arby's Group) with more than 40 fast food restaurants in New Jersey New York and Pennsylvania. The company also has a small number of Hilton and Marriott hotels and operates one shopping center. Founder and CEO Bradford Honigfeld leads an investment group that owns Briad Group.

THE BRICKMAN GROUP LTD.

18227D Flower Hill Way
Gaithersburg MD 20879
Phone: 301-987-9200
Fax: 240-683-2030
Web: www.brickmangroup.com

CEO: Andrew Masterman
CFO: –
HR: –
FYE: December 31
Type: Private

The Brickman Group offers landscape design and maintenance services for college campuses municipal properties sports facilities and retail establishments. It provides sports turf services such as field design and consulting irrigation mowing and field maintenance for MLB and the Olympic Games. Serving thousands of clients the company has also taken on such special projects as repairing New Orleans City Park's irrigation system after Hurricane Katrina. Founded in 1939 by Theodore Brickman the group has more than 160 branch offices in about 30 US states. Private equity firm Leonard Green & Partners owns a majority shareholding of the company.

THE BROE COMPANIES INC.

252 Clayton St. 4th Fl.
Denver CO 80206
Phone: 303-393-0033
Fax: 303-393-0041
Web: www.broe.com

CEO: –
CFO: –
HR: –
FYE: December 31
Type: Private

Million-dollar investments don't phase this Broe. The secretive Broe Companies invests in a variety of industries in the US and Canada largely funded by profits made in real estate investments. It focuses primarily on hard asset-based investment opportunities as well as distressed businesses. Broe's brotherhood of companies include a short-line railroad owner (OmniTRAX) and a Kentucky coal company (Century Coal). Broe owns interests in some 29 million sq. ft. of commercial industrial and residential real estate in several states and in Canada. Denver property investor Pat Broe controls the company which he founded in 1972.

THE BROOKINGS INSTITUTION

1775 MASSACHUSETTS AVE NW CEO: –
WASHINGTON, DC 200362103 CFO: –
Phone: 202-797-6000 HR: –
Fax: – FYE: June 30
Web: www.brookings.edu Type: Private

The Brookings Institution is a non-partisan public policy organization. The institute is comprised of more than 300 resident and non-resident scholars who research and analyze emerging issues in areas such as economics foreign policy and governance. Its experts perform research; write books papers and articles; testify in front of congressional committees; and participate in public events every year. The non-profit organization which is financed by gifts and grants is named after one of its backers — businessman Robert S. Brookings a well-known civic leader and philanthropist. Founded in 1916 it is the first private organization devoted to analyzing national public policy issues.

	Annual Growth	06/10	06/11	06/12	06/13	06/15
Sales ($ mil.)	1.5%	–	100.2	130.8	100.6	106.4
Net income ($ mil.)	–	–	11.3	36.8	3.9	(1.5)
Market value ($ mil.)	–	–	–	–	–	–
Employees	–	–	–	–	–	400

THE BROTHER'S BROTHER FOUNDATION

1200 GALVESTON AVE CEO: –
PITTSBURGH, PA 152331604 CFO: –
Phone: 412-321-3160 HR: –
Fax: – FYE: December 31
Web: www.brothersbrother.org Type: Private

He ain't heavy he's my brother's brother. The lyrics aren't quite right but the sentiment is the same. The not-for-profit Brother's Brother Foundation (BBF) provides emergency and nonemergency medical supplies textbooks food shoes and other humanitarian supplies to people in some 120 countries using a combination of gifts from the general public corporations and the US government. BBF is a gift-in-kind charity meaning the bulk of the donations are goods rather than money. The organization was established in 1958 by the renowned anesthesiologist Robert Hingson as Brother's Keeper but later changed its name. Hingson invented the jet inoculation gun used to provide 1000 inoculations per hour.

	Annual Growth	12/12	12/13	12/14	12/16	12/17
Sales ($ mil.)	(20.9%)	–	244.0	244.6	217.0	95.3
Net income ($ mil.)	–	–	5.8	9.3	23.8	(24.4)
Market value ($ mil.)	–	–	–	–	–	–
Employees	–	–	–	–	–	12

THE BUREAU OF NATIONAL AFFAIRS INC.

1801 S. Bell St. CEO: –
Arlington VA 22202 CFO: Robert P Ambrosini
Phone: 703-341-3000 HR: –
Fax: 212-290-7362 FYE: December 31
Web: www.thomaspublishing.com Type: Subsidiary

All you'll find in this bureau is legal and regulatory information. The Bureau of National Affairs (BNA) publishes advisory and research reports books and newsletters for business government and academic professionals. BNA has a staff of 600 reporters editors and legal experts who gather information on topics such as economic health care labor public policy and tax issues. The firm delivers content online and via print and electronic products some available through subscription services such as LexisNexis and Thomson Reuter's Westlaw. Founded in 1929 BNA was incorporated as an employee-owned company in 1946. It is the country's oldest fully employee-owned company. BNA is owned by Bloomberg.

THE BURTON CORPORATION

80 Industrial Pkwy. CEO: Donna Carpenter
Burlington VT 05401 CFO: –
Phone: 802-862-4500 HR: –
Fax: 802-660-3250 FYE: January 31
Web: www.burton.com Type: Private

The Burton Corporation made snowboards before boardsports became extreme. The company doing business as Burton Snowboards is the world's leading snowboard manufacturer. It also makes a growing lineup of men's women's and youth snowboarding apparel eyewear boots bindings and packs under its namesake as well as the AK Anon and RED brands. The company operates through a network of about 10 retail shops and factory outlets in the US Austria and Japan. It also sells gear through sporting goods stores and online retailers such as Altrec.com and Snow & Rock Sports. Taking to the beach Burton owns surfboard maker Channel Island Surfboards whose goods are available at surf shops worldwide.

THE C.F. SAUER COMPANY

2000 W. Broad St. CEO: –
Richmond VA 23220 CFO: –
Phone: 804-359-5786 HR: –
Fax: 804-359-2263 FYE: March 31
Web: www.cfsauer.com Type: Private

For more than a century C.F. Sauer has been adding a little spice to life. In addition to a stable of spices the company produces and wholesales seasonings extracts and flavorings. C.F. Sauer offers an increasing lineup of mixes for baking in a bag microwave steaming grilling and slow cooking. Products are sold under its namesake label as well as the Duke's Bama Spice Hunter Gold Medal and Mrs. Filbert's brands to retail food stores and foodservice operators such as restaurants and concessionaires. C.F. Sauer which operates several plants (including one that makes its packaging) also provides private-label and blending services for food processors. The company has been family-owned since 1887.

THE CADMUS GROUP LLC

100 5TH AVE STE 100 # 100 CEO: –
WALTHAM, MA 024518725 CFO: Alan V Seferian
Phone: 617-673-7000 HR: Kerri Morehart
Fax: – FYE: April 30
Web: www.cadmusgroup.com Type: Private

Drinking water protection is one of the areas of sage advice offered by The Cadmus Group. The environmental consulting firm (named after Cadmus the Phoenician prince and renowned wise man who founded the city of Thebes) provides research analytical and technical support services primarily to government agencies. Over time it has established itself as a lead contractor of the US Environmental Protection Agency). Other specialties include air quality energy conservation environmental risk assessment and regulatory support as well as marketing and public education related to environmental programs. Cadmus operates from 10 offices throughout the US.

	Annual Growth	04/13	04/14	04/15	04/16	04/17
Sales ($ mil.)	14.8%	–	68.8	66.9	80.1	104.1
Net income ($ mil.)	–	–	0.8	(1.1)	(0.7)	(0.5)
Market value ($ mil.)	–	–	–	–	–	–
Employees	–	–	–	–	–	500

THE CALIFORNIA ENDOWMENT

1000 N ALAMEDA ST
LOS ANGELES, CA 900121804
Phone: 800-449-4149
Fax: –
Web: www.chirpla.org

CEO: Robert K Ross
CFO: Dan C Deleon
HR: –
FYE: March 31
Type: Private

The California Endowment awards grants to health care providers in the Golden State. Funding is directed to not-for-profit organizations particularly those that work with the state's poor and underserved communities as well as studies of the state's health care industry. Its advocacy interests include health care access culturally competent health systems and elimination of health disparities. A private foundation The California Endowment has awarded more than $1.5 billion in grants since it was established in 1996. It has regional offices in Fresno Los Angeles Sacramento San Diego and San Francisco.

	Annual Growth	02/04	02/05	02/09*	03/12	03/16
Sales ($ mil.)	(4.8%)	–	346.0	0.0	207.0	201.1
Net income ($ mil.)	–	–	144.0	0.0	42.0	(40.4)
Market value ($ mil.)	–	–	–	–	–	–
Employees	–	–	–	–	–	110

*Fiscal year change

THE CAPITAL GROUP COMPANIES INC.

333 S. Hope St. 53rd Fl.
Los Angeles CA 90071
Phone: 213-486-9200
Fax: 213-486-9217
Web: www.capgroup.com

CEO: Philip De Toledo
CFO: –
HR: –
FYE: June 30
Type: Private

The Capital Group Companies founded in 1931 has built a business being a steady Eddy for its clients. As a rule the investment firm doesn't advertise or grant many interviews and it prides itself on providing consistent high-level service believing that investment decisions should not be taken lightly. As part of its operations The Capital Group Companies operates Capital Research and Management. The unit manages The American Funds a family of more than 30 mutual funds that ranks among the largest groups of mutual funds by assets in the US. Altogether The Capital Group Companies boasts approximately $1 trillion in assets under management.

THE CARRIAGE HOUSE COMPANIES INC.

196 Newton St.
Fredonia NY 14063
Phone: 716-673-1000
Fax: 716-679-7702
Web: www.carriagehousecos.com

CEO: –
CFO: –
HR: –
FYE: September 30
Type: Subsidiary

The Carriage House Companies gets a bit carried away when spreading the word about sauces and spreads. The company is one of the largest suppliers of storebrand grocery goods including barbecue sauce jams and jellies peanut butter and table syrup. It also produces private label mayonnaise and salad dressings salsas and sauces. Carriage House products are sold through its sales staff and a broker network to retailers such as Wal-Mart and less so foodservice contract and other customers. A subsidiary Beverage Specialties makes the Major Peter's and JERO brand non-alcoholic drink mixes. Carriage House is owned by Ralcorp which counts the subsidiary as part of its Snacks Sauces & Spreads business.

THE CARTER-JONES LUMBER COMPANY

601 TALLMADGE RD
KENT, OH 442407331
Phone: 330-673-6100
Fax: –
Web: www.carterlumber.com

CEO: Neil Sackett
CFO: Jeffrey S Donley
HR: –
FYE: December 31
Type: Private

Carter Lumber has the answer when new home construction has you hollering "timber!" The company owns and operates about 145 lumber and home improvement stores in a dozen states from Michigan to South Carolina. The company caters to both contractors and do-it-yourselfers supplying them with lumber plywood roofing windows doors plumbing and electrical products heating equipment tools siding and other products. The home improvement retailer also owns Carter-Jones Lumber which runs a 17-acre lumberyard and custom millwork facilities in Ohio. The company was founded by Warren E. Carter in 1932 and it continues to be a family-owned business.

	Annual Growth	12/06	12/07	12/08	12/09	12/10
Sales ($ mil.)	(11.2%)	–	–	424.2	314.4	334.4
Net income ($ mil.)	–	–	–	(1.5)	(4.7)	(4.6)
Market value ($ mil.)	–	–	–	–	–	–
Employees	–	–	–	–	–	1,575

THE CATHOLIC UNIVERSITY OF AMERICA

620 MICHIGAN AVE NE
WASHINGTON, DC 200640002
Phone: 202-319-5000
Fax: –
Web: www.catholic.edu

CEO: –
CFO: –
HR: –
FYE: April 30
Type: Private

The Catholic University of America (CUA) established in 1887 by US bishops has an enrollment of more than 7000 students from all 50 states and nearly 100 countries. With graduate and undergraduate programs in 13 colleges CUA offers degrees in such fields as architecture and planning arts and sciences engineering music and nursing; it's expanding into business and economics. CUA is the only US university with ecclesiastical faculties granting canonical degrees in canon law philosophy and theology. Some 80% of undergraduates and nearly 60% of graduate students are Catholic. The University's Theological College prepares men for the priesthood serving dioceses nationwide.

	Annual Growth	06/12	06/13*	04/16	04/17	04/18
Sales ($ mil.)	(7.0%)	–	342.4	232.3	217.9	238.4
Net income ($ mil.)	(2.8%)	–	57.5	2.1	30.3	49.9
Market value ($ mil.)	–	–	–	–	–	–
Employees	–	–	–	–	–	4,239

*Fiscal year change

THE CENTECH GROUP INC

6402 ARLINGTON BLVD # 1000
FALLS CHURCH, VA 220422333
Phone: 703-525-4444
Fax: –
Web: www.centechgroup.com

CEO: –
CFO: –
HR: Martin Lawyer
FYE: December 31
Type: Private

The CENTECH GROUP offers a wide range of information technology services primarily to agencies of the US federal government. The company's areas of expertise include systems engineering security business operations support network services and software development. Among its clients are the Department of Defense the Department of Transportation and the State Department. CENTECH also serves customers in fields that include financial services manufacturing retail and health care. The company's core presence is in Virginia but it operates from offices in four states and serves clients in more than 20 states across the US. CENTECH was founded in 1988 by CEO Fernando Galaviz.

	Annual Growth	12/07	12/08	12/09	12/10	12/11
Sales ($ mil.)	(39.5%)	–	–	–	152.7	92.4
Net income ($ mil.)	(54.3%)	–	–	–	7.2	3.3
Market value ($ mil.)	–	–	–	–	–	–
Employees	–	–	–	–	–	165

1303

THE CHARLES MACHINE WORKS INC.

1959 W. Fir Ave.
Perry OK 73077
Phone: 580-336-4402
Fax: 580-572-3527
Web: www.ditchwitch.com

CEO: Rick Johnson
CFO: Angela Drake
HR: –
FYE: December 31
Type: Private

Ditch Witch has cast a spell over the heavy equipment industry since 1949. Captivated by its power and efficiency The Charles Machine Works (CMW) manufactures and sells underground construction equipment and parts bearing the Ditch Witch brand name. Its signature orange lineup features trenchless machines trenchers mini-excavators and plows including tractors backhoes and saws made at the company's 30-acre plant in Oklahoma. CMW also makes a slew of electronic tools: fault locators beacons for ground directional assistance and trailers. Equipment maintenance and repair services are offered too for its roster of construction and utility customers. Founders of CMW the Malzahn family own the company.

THE CHARLES STARK DRAPER LABORATORY INC

555 TECHNOLOGY SQ
CAMBRIDGE, MA 021393539
Phone: 617-258-1000
Fax: –
Web: www.draper.com

CEO: Kaigham (Ken) Gabriel
CFO: –
HR: –
FYE: July 31
Type: Private

The Charles Stark Draper Laboratory guides research into space under water and across continents. The not-for-profit corporation develops guidance navigation and control technologies for aircraft submarines missiles and spacecraft. It works with NASA the US Department of Defense and commercial businesses to develop technologies and fabricate prototypes. The organization also solves healthcare problems with its work in biomedical engineering. The lab boasts more than 850 engineers and scientists. Originally known as the Instrument Lab the laboratory was renamed in 1970 and became an independent institution three years later.

	Annual Growth	06/11	06/12	06/13	06/14*	07/16
Sales ($ mil.)	7.1%	–	514.1	542.7	522.0	676.3
Net income ($ mil.)	–	–	(20.8)	17.2	28.3	36.9
Market value ($ mil.)	–	–	–	–	–	–
Employees	–	–	–	–	–	1,134

*Fiscal year change

THE CHARLOTTE-MECKLENBURG HOSPITAL AUTHORITY

1000 BLYTHE BLVD
CHARLOTTE, NC 282035812
Phone: 704-355-2000
Fax: –
Web: www.atriumhealth.org

CEO: –
CFO: Anthony Defurio
HR: Nehemie Owen
FYE: December 31
Type: Private

The medical facilities under the watchful eye of the Charlotte-Mecklenburg Hospital Authority care for the injured and infirmed. As the largest health care system in the Carolinas the organization operating as Carolinas HealthCare System (CHS) owns or manages more than 30 affiliated hospitals. It also operates long-term care facilities research centers rehabilitation facilities surgery centers home health agencies radiation therapy facilities and other health care operations. Collectively CHS facilities have more than 6400 beds and affiliated physician practices employ more than 1700 doctors. The network's flagship facility is the 875-bed Carolinas Medical Center in Charlotte North Carolina.

	Annual Growth	12/14	12/15	12/16	12/17	12/18
Sales ($ mil.)	4.4%	–	5,478.6	5,676.2	5,991.4	6,228.2
Net income ($ mil.)	–	–	(247.9)	493.4	829.9	(69.7)
Market value ($ mil.)	–	–	–	–	–	–
Employees	–	–	–	–	–	62,000

THE CHILDREN'S HOSPITAL CORPORATION

300 LONGWOOD AVE
BOSTON, MA 021155737
Phone: 617-355-6000
Fax: –
Web: www.childrenshospital.org

CEO: James Mandell
CFO: Doug Vanderslice
HR: –
FYE: September 30
Type: Private

The Children's Hospital Corporation dba Boston Children's Hospital is a 400-bed hospital that offers acute health care and specialty services for children from birth through age 21. The medical center is Harvard Medical School's main teaching hospital for children's health care and it is the world's largest pediatric research center. Its John F. Enders Pediatric Research facility provides research for the treatment of childhood diseases. Specialty services are offered in the fields of cardiovascular surgery digestive care neurology oncology ophthalmology orthopedics autism spectrum disorder blood diseases and fetal care. The not-for-profit hospital was founded in 1869.

	Annual Growth	06/03	06/04	06/05*	09/09	09/14
Sales ($ mil.)	89.2%	–	–	4.9	1,348.7	1,514.5
Net income ($ mil.)	77.5%	–	–	0.6	94.5	111.1
Market value ($ mil.)	–	–	–	–	–	–
Employees	–	–	–	–	–	8,000

*Fiscal year change

THE CHILDREN'S HOSPITAL OF PHILADELPHIA

34th St. & Civic Center Blvd.
Philadelphia PA 19104-4399
Phone: 215-590-1000
Fax: 503-614-4601
Web: www.normthompson.com

CEO: Steven M Altschuler
CFO: Thomas Todorow
HR: –
FYE: June 30
Type: Private - Not-for-Pr

In the City of Brotherly Love sick little boys and girls have a place to get better at the The Children's Hospital of Philadelphia (CHOP). As a leading pediatric hospital CHOP also has one of the largest pediatric research programs in the world. The nation's first hospital devoted exclusively to the care of children it has about 460 beds at its primary facility and is a leader in formal pediatric medical training pediatric emergency medicine and adolescent medicine. In addition to its main hospital facilities CHOP operates a pediatric health care network with owned or affiliated offices clinics and research facilities in Delaware New Jersey and Pennsylvania. The hospital was founded in 1855.

THE CHILDRENS HOSPITAL LOS ANGELES

4650 W SUNSET BLVD
LOS ANGELES, CA 900276062
Phone: 323-660-2450
Fax: –
Web: www.chla.org

CEO: Richard Cordova
CFO: Lannie Tonnu
HR: –
FYE: June 30
Type: Private

Childrens Hospital Los Angeles (CHLA) is dedicated to treating the youngest critical care patients in the region. The about 570-bed hospital specializes in treating seriously ill and injured children from its neonatal intensive care unit to its pediatric organ transplant center. CHLA's pediatric specialists also provide care at its ambulatory care center in Arcadia and through about 40 off-site practice sites. The hospital's pediatric specialties include cancer kidney failure and cystic fibrosis care. CHLA serves more than 107000 children every year. It is one of only 12 children's hospitals in the nation (and the only one in California) ranked in all 10 pediatric specialties by U.S. News & World Report .

	Annual Growth	06/13	06/14	06/15	06/17	06/18
Sales ($ mil.)	14.1%	–	823.0	891.3	1,035.1	1,393.4
Net income ($ mil.)	–	–	(46.4)	27.1	(14.6)	247.6
Market value ($ mil.)	–	–	–	–	–	–
Employees	–	–	–	–	–	3,000

THE CHRIST HOSPITAL

2139 AUBURN AVE
CINCINNATI, OH 452192989
Phone: 513-585-2000
Fax: –
Web: www.thechristhospital.com

CEO: Susan Croushore
CFO: Chris Bergman
HR: –
FYE: June 30
Type: Private

Perched on the hilltop of Mt. Auburn The Christ Hospital oversees the health of ailing residents throughout Greater Cincinnati. Along with the flagship 528-bed hospital the organization operates about 100 outpatient and physician practice locations throughout the area. The Christ Hospital offers specialized care in a variety of fields including cardiac care cancer treatment kidney transplantation spine treatment and orthopedics. The not-for-profit hospital also provides an internal medicine residency program a family medicine residency program and a school of nursing. The Christ Hospital conducts research through its Lindner Clinical Trial Center.

	Annual Growth	06/13	06/14	06/15	06/16	06/17
Sales ($ mil.)	–	–	0.0	647.3	681.4	929.7
Net income ($ mil.)	–	–	0.0	89.8	90.1	14.4
Market value ($ mil.)	–	–	–	–	–	–
Employees	–	–	–	–	–	4,000

THE CHRISTIAN BROADCASTING NETWORK INC

977 CENTERVILLE TPKE
VIRGINIA BEACH, VA 234631001
Phone: 757-226-3030
Fax: –
Web: www.cbn.com

CEO: Gordon Robertson
CFO: –
HR: –
FYE: March 31
Type: Private

Standards & Practices probably won't find much wrong with these TV programs. The Christian Broadcasting Network (CBN) is one of the leading producers of religious television programming in the country offering news and entertainment shows with a spiritual message. Its centerpiece is The 700 Club a daily show featuring a mix of news and commentary interviews feature stories and Christian ministry co-hosted by CBN founder Pat Robertson. The company's programs are syndicated to broadcast and cable TV outlets that reach audiences around the world. CBN generates most of its revenue through ministry donations.

	Annual Growth	03/10	03/11	03/14	03/15	03/16
Sales ($ mil.)	1.5%	–	285.3	301.8	293.8	307.6
Net income ($ mil.)	–	–	6.8	5.5	(8.9)	(7.2)
Market value ($ mil.)	–	–	–	–	–	–
Employees	–	–	–	–	–	941

THE CITADEL

171 MOULTRIE ST
CHARLESTON, SC 294090002
Phone: 843-953-5110
Fax: –
Web: www.citadel.edu

CEO: –
CFO: –
HR: –
FYE: June 30
Type: Private

A state-supported military college The Citadel traces its roots back to the 1842 founding of the South Carolina Military Academy. Today's Citadel enrolls about 2000 undergraduate cadets who reside on the campus barracks. Cadets are given military and academic instruction in addition to physical training and a strict disciplinary regime; about a third of all graduates continue on to military careers. The Citadel enrolls another 1250 civilian graduate and undergraduate students who attend evening classes. With a student-to-faculty ratio of 13:1 the institution has schools in business education engineering the humanities and social sciences and science and mathematics.

	Annual Growth	06/11	06/12	06/13	06/14	06/15
Sales ($ mil.)	7.0%	–	67.7	81.5	91.9	82.8
Net income ($ mil.)	(21.2%)	–	2.7	8.7	17.7	1.3
Market value ($ mil.)	–	–	–	–	–	–
Employees	–	–	–	–	–	637

THE CITY OF SEATTLE-CITY LIGHT DEPARTMENT

700 5TH AVE STE 3200
SEATTLE, WA 981045065
Phone: 206-684-3200
Fax: –

CEO: Jorge Carrasco
CFO: Brian Brunfield
HR: –
FYE: December 31
Type: Private

City of Seattle - City Light Department (Seattle City Light) keeps guitars humming and coffee grinders running in the Seattle metropolitan area. The US's 10th largest municipally owned power company Seattle City Light transmits and distributes electricity to almost 1 million residential commercial industrial and government customers and owns hydroelectric power plants with more than 1800 MW of generation capacity. The utility also purchases power from the Bonneville Power Administration and other generators and it sells power to wholesale customers.

	Annual Growth	12/08	12/09	12/16	12/17	12/18
Sales ($ mil.)	3.6%	–	723.1	903.0	989.7	991.6
Net income ($ mil.)	18.9%	–	34.2	85.0	120.4	162.2
Market value ($ mil.)	–	–	–	–	–	–
Employees	–	–	–	–	–	1,600

THE CLEVELAND CLINIC FOUNDATION

9500 EUCLID AVE
CLEVELAND, OH 441950002
Phone: 216-636-8335
Fax: –
Web: www.my.clevelandclinic.org

CEO: Delos M. (Toby) Cosgrove
CFO: Steven C. Glass
HR: –
FYE: December 31
Type: Private

The not-for-profit Cleveland Clinic Foundation operates about 20 hospitals in Ohio Florida Abu Dhabi Toronto and soon in London. Combined the foundation's hospitals have nearly 6000 beds. Its flagship location is its namesake Cleveland Clinic an academic medical center in Cleveland Ohio. The campus specializes in cardiac care digestive disease treatment and urological and kidney care along with education and research opportunities. It has an international care center children's hospital and an outpatient center; it also contains research and educational institutes covering clinical drug research ophthalmic studies and cancer research as well as physician and scientist training programs.

	Annual Growth	12/13	12/14	12/16	12/17	12/18
Sales ($ mil.)	20.1%	–	4,290.9	8,037.2	8,407.0	8,927.6
Net income ($ mil.)	(18.8%)	–	405.1	513.5	1,150.3	176.4
Market value ($ mil.)	–	–	–	–	–	–
Employees	–	–	–	–	–	44,000

THE CLEVELAND ELECTRIC ILLUMINATING COMPANY

76 S MAIN ST
AKRON, OH 443081812
Phone: 800-589-3101
Fax: –
Web: www.firstenergycorp.com

CEO: –
CFO: Mark T Clark
HR: –
FYE: December 31
Type: Private

The Cleveland Electric Illuminating Company (CEI) has a glowing reputation. The utility commonly referred to as The Illuminating Company distributes electricity to a base population of about 1.8 million inhabitants in a 1600 sq. ml. area of northeastern Ohio. CEI has 33210 miles of distribution lines. In 2010 the utility met 4420 MW of hourly maximum generating demand from interests in fossil-fueled and nuclear power plants (which are operated by fellow FirstEnergy subsidiaries). It also engages in wholesale energy transactions with other power companies. CEI is also a competitive retail electric service provider in Ohio alongside sister companies Ohio Edison and Toledo Edison.

	Annual Growth	12/07	12/08	12/09	12/10	12/16
Sales ($ mil.)	(8.0%)	–	1,815.9	1,676.1	1,221.4	928.4
Net income ($ mil.)	(22.4%)	–	284.5	(11.0)	73.2	37.2
Market value ($ mil.)	–	–	–	–	–	–
Employees	–	–	–	–	–	897

THE COBALT GROUP INC.

2200 1st Ave. South Ste. 400
Seattle WA 98134-1408
Phone: 206-269-6363
Fax: 206-269-6350
Web: www.cobaltgroup.com

CEO: John Holt
CFO: Jim Beach
HR: –
FYE: June 30
Type: Subsidiary

The Cobalt Group's websites and services come fully loaded. Cobalt provides Web-based marketing services to auto manufacturers and dealers to help them manage their businesses online. Services include website hosting e-commerce applications Web-based customer relationship management applications social media marketing and best practices training and consulting. The company also provides automotive Internet marketing through its Dealix unit and its IntegraLink division collects automotive data from more than 15000 auto dealerships for manufacturers direct marketing firms and others who work in the automotive industry. In mid-2010 Cobalt was acquired by payroll processing giant ADP for $400 million.

THE COLLEGE NETWORK INC

3815 RIVER CROSSING PKWY # 260
INDIANAPOLIS, IN 462407758
Phone: 800-395-3276
Fax: –
Web: www.collegenetwork.com

CEO: –
CFO: –
HR: –
FYE: December 31
Type: Private

The College Network is for students who want all the advantages of a college degree without all of that sitting in classrooms and listening to lectures. The company publishes educational materials that help its customers — typically working adults — gain college credit certificates or degrees from its university partners without attending physical class. Students use the company's online study modules to prepare for college equivalency tests earning up to 82 credit hours. They then enroll in online degree programs through the company's partner schools. Participating schools include Boston University University of Southern California and Angelo State University. The College Network was founded in 1992.

	Annual Growth	12/04	12/05	12/06	12/07	12/08
Sales ($ mil.)	13.4%	–	–	72.1	102.9	92.8
Net income ($ mil.)	–	–	–	1.0	5.2	(0.1)
Market value ($ mil.)	–	–	–	–	–	–
Employees	–	–	–	–	–	100

THE COLLEGE OF CHARLESTON

66 GEORGE ST
CHARLESTON, SC 294240001
Phone: 843-953-5570
Fax: –
Web: www.cofc.edu

CEO: –
CFO: –
HR: –
FYE: June 30
Type: Private

The College of Charleston (CofC) one of the oldest universities in the nation is a state-supported institution emphasizing areas of study in the arts and sciences education and business. The liberal arts school enrolls more than 11000 undergraduate and graduate students who study in some 60 major fields and some 20 master's degree programs. CofC boasts a student-faculty ratio of about 16:1 with an average class size of 26. Some two-thirds of students are from South Carolina. The school was founded in 1770 by a group that included three future signers of the Declaration of Independence.

	Annual Growth	06/12	06/13	06/16	06/17	06/18
Sales ($ mil.)	1.7%	–	208.6	224.8	230.6	227.3
Net income ($ mil.)	(20.4%)	–	13.3	8.4	10.6	4.2
Market value ($ mil.)	–	–	–	–	–	–
Employees	–	–	–	–	–	1,500

THE COLLEGE OF WILLIAM & MARY

261 RICHMOND RD
WILLIAMSBURG, VA 23185
Phone: 757-221-3966
Fax: –
Web: www.wm.edu

CEO: –
CFO: –
HR: –
FYE: June 30
Type: Private

Not every Tom Dick and Harry gets into The College of William & Mary. The median SAT score for incoming freshmen is about 1345 (out of 1600). The second-oldest college in the US (Harvard is the oldest) William & Mary (W&M) is a "public ivy" university with an enrollment of 8300 undergraduate and graduate students. W&M offers more than 30 undergraduate and 10 graduate programs at schools of arts and sciences business education law and marine sciences. It also conducts research programs. Among its notable alumni are The Daily Show's Jon Stewart and three US presidents: Thomas Jefferson James Monroe and John Tyler.

	Annual Growth	06/05	06/06	06/11	06/16	06/17
Sales ($ mil.)	5.7%	–	178.4	94.3	350.3	329.8
Net income ($ mil.)	–	–	(96.4)	63.6	40.8	38.2
Market value ($ mil.)	–	–	–	–	–	–
Employees	–	–	–	–	–	3,500

THE COLLEGE OF WOOSTER

1189 BEALL AVE
WOOSTER, OH 446912363
Phone: 330-263-2000
Fax: –
Web: www.wooster.edu

CEO: –
CFO: –
HR: –
FYE: June 30
Type: Private

The College of Wooster is a private college providing undergraduate education in the liberal arts and sciences. It grants Bachelor of Arts (BA) Bachelor of Music (BM) and Bachelor of Music Education (BME) degrees. It offers about 50 majors including English geology film theater dance history biology math neuroscience psychology and computer science as well as pre-law pre-engineering and pre-health programs. The school's unique curriculum includes an independent study requirement in which seniors produce original work in the form of a research project. The College of Wooster enrolls about 2000 students. The school was founded in 1866 by a group of Ohio Presbyterians.

	Annual Growth	06/10	06/11	06/15	06/16	06/17
Sales ($ mil.)	5.1%	–	76.1	177.5	97.1	102.6
Net income ($ mil.)	4.2%	–	26.2	39.1	(18.7)	33.5
Market value ($ mil.)	–	–	–	–	–	–
Employees	–	–	–	–	–	610

THE COLONIAL WILLIAMSBURG FOUNDATION

427 FRANKLIN ST RM 212
WILLIAMSBURG, VA 231854304
Phone: 757-229-1000
Fax: –
Web: www.history.org

CEO: –
CFO: –
HR: Sharon Dorsey
FYE: December 31
Type: Private

The colony of Virginia lives thanks to The Colonial Williamsburg Foundation. Boasting a notable history.org Web address the organization is responsible for the restoration preservation and interpretation of 18th-century Williamsburg Virginia. Williamsburg served as the colony's capital from 1699 to 1780. In addition to maintaining a 301-acre living history museum the not-for-profit educational foundation engages in historical research publishes scholarly and popular works and produces educational films and recordings. Preservation efforts at Williamsburg were launched by the Rev. Dr. W. A. R. Goodwin and John D. Rockefeller Jr. in 1926. The Foundation was established in 1928.

	Annual Growth	12/04	12/05	12/06	12/13	12/14
Sales ($ mil.)	(4.1%)	–	216.5	235.0	139.0	148.8
Net income ($ mil.)	2.8%	–	11.3	93.9	7.3	14.6
Market value ($ mil.)	–	–	–	–	–	–
Employees	–	–	–	–	–	3,100

THE COMMUNITY HOSPITAL GROUP INC

98 JAMES ST STE 400
EDISON, NJ 088203902
Phone: 732-321-7000
Fax: –
Web: www.jfkmc.org

CEO: John P McGee
CFO: –
HR: –
FYE: December 31
Type: Private

JFK Medical Center plays a central role in health care in central New Jersey. The medical center is an acute care facility with some 500 beds and 950 physicians providing emergency surgical trauma and other inpatient services. The hospital includes the JFK New Jersey Neuroscience Institute which treats stroke and other neurological conditions and the JFK Johnson Rehabilitation Institute which treats traumatic injuries. JFK Medical Center also offers diagnostic imaging cancer care senior and hospice care and family practice services. It is also a teaching hospital affiliated with several area universities. The hospital is part of the JFK Health System.

	Annual Growth	12/09	12/10	12/14	12/16	12/17
Sales ($ mil.)	3.7%	–	427.1	467.9	532.1	551.6
Net income ($ mil.)	–	–	(17.5)	(3.2)	28.2	(13.3)
Market value ($ mil.)	–	–	–	–	–	–
Employees	–	–	–	–	–	3,000

THE COMPUTER MERCHANT LTD

95 LONGWATER CIR
NORWELL, MA 020611635
Phone: 781-878-1070
Fax: –
Web: www.tcml.com

CEO: John R Danieli
CFO: –
HR: –
FYE: December 31
Type: Private

The Computer Merchant (TCM) provide customers with information technology assets with a pulse. The company provides IT services such as staffing and consulting primarily to Fortune 1000 companies. It places more than 10000 consultants each year. TCM provides application development infrastructure management help desk and business support and technology deployments. The IT placement firm's clients have included ePresence Unisys and Premier among others. It primarily serves IT service providers large corporations and public sector clients. A preferred vendor for many government contractors TCM was founded in 1980 by CEO and former US Marine John Danieli.

	Annual Growth	12/11	12/12	12/13	12/14	12/15
Sales ($ mil.)	6.1%	–	89.5	95.9	122.2	107.1
Net income ($ mil.)	23.5%	–	3.6	2.8	5.1	6.8
Market value ($ mil.)	–	–	–	–	–	–
Employees	–	–	–	–	–	1,500

THE COMPUTING TECHNOLOGY INDUSTRY ASSOCIATION INC

3500 LACEY RD STE 100
DOWNERS GROVE, IL 605155439
Phone: 630-678-8300
Fax: –
Web: www.comptia.org

CEO: Todd Thibodeaux
CFO: Brian Laffey
HR: –
FYE: December 31
Type: Private

Welcome to the IT club. The Computing Technology Industry Association (CompTIA) is a not-for-profit trade organization that provides research training networking and partnering services to its 2000-plus members. It serves more than 100 countries with offices in Australia Canada China Germany Hong Kong India Japan South Africa South Korea Taiwan and the UK. CompTIA also helps companies implement best practices and administers vendor-neutral IT certification exams in about a dozen areas including cloud essentials green IT security Linux and storage. Like the industry it serves CompTIA has grown dramatically since it was founded in 1982 by representatives of five computer dealerships.

	Annual Growth	12/08	12/09	12/13	12/14	12/16
Sales ($ mil.)	4.4%	–	48.0	51.5	55.0	65.1
Net income ($ mil.)	(16.2%)	–	6.8	5.3	0.0	2.0
Market value ($ mil.)	–	–	–	–	–	–
Employees	–	–	–	–	–	150

THE CONSERVATION FUND A NONPROFIT CORPORATION

1655 FORT MYER DR # 1300
ARLINGTON, VA 222093199
Phone: 703-525-6300
Fax: –
Web: www.conservationfund.org

CEO: –
CFO: –
HR: Joyce Ferrell
FYE: December 31
Type: Private

The Conservation Fund was green before green was cool. The nonprofit organization is well known for negotiating deals to protect environmentally sensitive lands. It will typically purchase property financed through a revolving land fund federal and state grants and contributions from various sources and sell it back to local groups to manage. It also invests in small businesses that show a sustainable use of natural resources as well as works with communities and other not-for-profits to plan for growth and conservation. Since its founding in 1985 the Fund and its partners have protected more than 7 million acres of wildlife habitat and watersheds working landscapes and open-spaces in all 50 US states.

	Annual Growth	12/11	12/12	12/13	12/14	12/16
Sales ($ mil.)	4.7%	–	179.4	144.6	242.6	215.5
Net income ($ mil.)	–	–	41.8	3.0	39.5	(2.3)
Market value ($ mil.)	–	–	–	–	–	–
Employees	–	–	–	–	–	95

THE CONTAINER STORE INC.

500 Freeport Pkwy.
Coppell TX 75019
Phone: 972-538-6000
Fax: 972-538-7623
Web: www.containerstore.com

CEO: Melissa Reiff
CFO: Jodi Taylor
HR: –
FYE: March 31
Type: Private

With its packets pockets and boxes The Container Store has the storage products niche well-contained. Its merchandise ranges from backpacks to recipe holders. The home-organization pioneer operates about 60 stores in more than 20 states mostly in major cities in Texas California Illinois and New York as well as the District of Columbia. It also runs an e-commerce site. The company offers shipping across the US and to Canada as well as same-day delivery in New York City. Stores carry more than 10000 items; the company's Elfa brand of wire shelving (made in Sweden) accounts for a chunk of sales. Founded in 1978 The Container Store is majority owned by private equity firm Leonard Green & Partners.

THE COOPER HEALTH SYSTEM

1 COOPER PLZ
CAMDEN, NJ 081031461
Phone: 856-342-2000
Fax: –
Web: www.cooperhealth.org

CEO: Adrienne Kirby
CFO: Douglas E. Shirley
HR: –
FYE: December 31
Type: Private

The Cooper Health System keeps folks along the Delaware River shoreline feeling fine. The not-for-profit organization includes clinics and hospitals located throughout southern New Jersey and the Delaware Valley including the 600-bed Cooper University Hospital and The Children's Regional Hospital. Cooper University Hospital is a teaching campus for the University of Medicine and Dentistry of New Jersey providing training for medical students nurses residents fellows and health professionals. Its more than 700 physicians operate in about 80 specialties. Founded in 1887 the health care system provides trauma cancer cardiology neuroscience psychiatric and orthopedic specialty centers.

	Annual Growth	12/14	12/15	12/16	12/17	12/18
Sales ($ mil.)	7.0%	–	1,055.8	1,168.1	1,197.4	1,292.7
Net income ($ mil.)	(5.3%)	–	64.2	82.6	33.5	54.6
Market value ($ mil.)	–	–	–	–	–	–
Employees	–	–	–	–	–	4,900

THE CORPORATION OF GONZAGA UNIVERSITY

502 E BOONE AVE
SPOKANE, WA 992581774
Phone: 509-328-4220
Fax: −
Web: www.gonzaga.edu

CEO: −
CFO: −
HR: −
FYE: May 31
Type: Private

Gonzaga University is a private liberal arts institution providing instruction to more than 7800 undergraduate graduate doctoral and law students. The school offers about 75 undergraduate majors two dozen master's degree programs and two leadership study doc at its six colleges and schools. The university offers a juris doctorate degree at its School of Law. The Roman Catholic university is run by the Society of Jesus — the Jesuits — and is named after a sixteenth-century Italian Jesuit Aloysius Gonzaga the patron saint of youth. The university was founded in 1887 as a men's college.

	Annual Growth	05/14	05/15	05/16	05/17	05/18
Sales ($ mil.)	4.4%	−	204.0	214.7	218.3	232.0
Net income ($ mil.)	(28.7%)	−	83.5	16.8	47.4	30.3
Market value ($ mil.)	−	−	−	−	−	−
Employees	−	−	−	−	−	1,200

THE CORPORATION OF HAVERFORD COLLEGE

370 LANCASTER AVE
HAVERFORD, PA 190411336
Phone: 610-896-1000
Fax: −
Web: www.haverford.edu

CEO: −
CFO: −
HR: Megan Fitch
FYE: June 30
Type: Private

Haverford College is one of the nation's top 10 liberal arts colleges according to US News & World Report 's 2007 annual ranking. The college is a private school located 10 miles away from Philadelphia that serves about 1200 students. Among its staff are more than 135 full-time faculty members. Haverford College has a student-faculty ratio of 9:1. The college offers more than 30 departmental majors. The school boasts such notable alumni as former Time Warner CEO Gerald Levin Time editor-in-chief Norman Pearlstine and humorist Dave Barry. Haverford College was established by Quakers in 1833 as a college of higher learning.

	Annual Growth	06/09	06/10	06/11	06/13	06/15
Sales ($ mil.)	11.4%	−	76.6	79.3	86.0	131.5
Net income ($ mil.)	(5.9%)	−	13.4	51.5	47.0	9.8
Market value ($ mil.)	−	−	−	−	−	−
Employees	−	−	−	−	−	600

THE CORPORATION OF MERCER UNIVERSITY

1501 MERCER UNIVERSITY DR
MACON, GA 312071515
Phone: 478-301-2700
Fax: −
Web: www.mercer.edu

CEO: −
CFO: −
HR: −
FYE: June 30
Type: Private

Mercer University covers a lot of Georgia with one campus in Macon another in Atlanta and a third in Savannah. The main campus in Macon includes the Walter F. George School of Law (one of the nation's oldest law schools) while The Cecil B. Day Graduate and Professional campus in Atlanta includes schools of theology pharmacy and nursing. Savannah is home to a new four-year M.D. program at the Mercer School of Medicine at Memorial University Medical Center. The university which has a total enrollment of more than 8300 students also has educational centers in Douglas County Henry County and Eastman. Mercer was founded in 1833 by Jesse Mercer a prominent Georgia Baptist.

	Annual Growth	06/10	06/11	06/13	06/15	06/18
Sales ($ mil.)	0.4%	−	270.3	297.7	341.0	277.6
Net income ($ mil.)	25.5%	−	8.0	8.4	15.8	39.3
Market value ($ mil.)	−	−	−	−	−	−
Employees	−	−	−	−	−	1,658

THE COUNCIL POPULATION INC

1 DAG HAMMARSKJOLD PLZ # 2
NEW YORK, NY 100172208
Phone: 212-339-0500
Fax: −
Web: www.popcouncil.org

CEO: −
CFO: −
HR: −
FYE: December 31
Type: Private

The Population Council is a not-for-profit organization that performs biomedical public health and social science research. The organization focuses on areas such as HIV and AIDS; poverty gender and youth; and reproductive health. Specifically it conducts research on sociological topics like gender inequality population trends and sexuality education; it also assists international governments with policy and program development as they pertain to these issues. The Population Council is typically funded by governments foundations individuals and other organizations.

	Annual Growth	12/13	12/14	12/15	12/16	12/17
Sales ($ mil.)	2.7%	−	84.3	69.4	82.7	91.4
Net income ($ mil.)	−	−	(3.4)	(15.4)	(2.7)	4.7
Market value ($ mil.)	−	−	−	−	−	−
Employees	−	−	−	−	−	603

THE CULINARY INSTITUTE OF AMERICA

1946 CAMPUS DR
HYDE PARK, NY 125381430
Phone: 845-452-9600
Fax: −
Web: www.ciachef.edu

CEO: −
CFO: −
HR: Richard Mignault
FYE: May 31
Type: Private

At this CIA they work on countertops not counterterrorism. The Culinary Institute of America (CIA) offers bachelor's and associate degrees in Culinary Arts Culinary Science and Baking and Pastry Arts fields of study. It also offers continuing education programs conferences travel programs and e-learning. The independent not-for-profit educational organization enrolls some 2800 students and employs more than 125 chef-instructors and other faculty members at campuses in the US and overseas. Notable graduates include media personalities Anthony Bourdain and Rocco DiSpirito and Stever Ellis founder of Chipotle Mexican Grill.

	Annual Growth	05/10	05/11	05/12	05/13	05/14
Sales ($ mil.)	1.3%	−	−	141.4	147.3	145.3
Net income ($ mil.)	38.4%	−	−	11.1	28.7	21.2
Market value ($ mil.)	−	−	−	−	−	−
Employees	−	−	−	−	−	750

THE DAVID AND LUCILE PACKARD FOUNDATION

300 2ND ST
LOS ALTOS, CA 940223694
Phone: 650-917-7167
Fax: −
Web: www.packard.org

CEO: Carol S Larson
CFO: −
HR: −
FYE: December 31
Type: Private

One of the wealthiest philanthropic organizations in the US The David and Lucile Packard Foundation primarily provides grants to not-for-profit entities. The foundation focuses on operating in three areas: conservation and science; children families and communities; and population. The David and Lucile Packard Foundation boasts approximately $4.6 billion in assets. In 2009 the organization committed $100 million for the expansion of the Lucile Packard Children's Hospital at Stanford. The late David Packard (co-founder of Hewlett-Packard) and his wife the late Lucile Salter Packard created the foundation in 1964. Their children run the organization.

	Annual Growth	12/04	12/05	12/06	12/09	12/10
Sales ($ mil.)	302.5%	−	0.7	809.5	398.2	701.2
Net income ($ mil.)	289.2%	−	0.5	587.9	74.8	412.6
Market value ($ mil.)	−	−	−	−	−	−
Employees	−	−	−	−	−	85

THE DAY & ZIMMERMANN GROUP INC.

1500 Spring Garden St.
Philadelphia PA 19130
Phone: 215-299-8000
Fax: 215-299-8030
Web: www.dayzim.com

CEO: Harold L Yoh III
CFO: Joseph Ritzel
HR: –
FYE: December 31
Type: Private

Day & Zimmermann offers services as distinct as day and night. Its family of companies provides: engineering construction and plant maintenance; staffing; munitions manufacturing and demilitarization; and various government services. A top global contractor Day & Zimmermann provides operations contract support and maintenance services to US and foreign governments as well as commercial customers. Its Day & Zimmermann NPS unit maintains half of nuclear plants in the US. Staffing subsidiary Yoh Services specializes in filling IT engineering and health care positions. Founded in 1901 Day & Zimmermann is owned and managed by the Yoh family which has headed the firm for three generations.

THE DCH HEALTH CARE AUTHORITY

809 UNIVERSITY BLVD E
TUSCALOOSA, AL 354012029
Phone: 205-759-7111
Fax: –
Web: www.dchsystem.com

CEO: Bryan N. Kindred
CFO: John Winfrey
HR: –
FYE: September 30
Type: Private

The DCH Healthcare Authority is concerned with the Druid City's health. The company which does business as DCH Health System provides health services to residents of Tuscaloosa and several other communities in Western Alabama. Its flagship facility is the 580-bed DCH Regional Medical Center a full-service teaching hospital located near the University of Alabama campus. DCH Health System also includes the Northport Pickens County and Fayette medical centers which together house 320 acute-care beds. The hospitals offer a full range of inpatient and outpatient services including primary diagnostic emergency surgical rehabilitative and home health care.

	Annual Growth	09/12	09/13	09/16	09/17	09/18
Sales ($ mil.)	2.4%	–	463.2	531.3	516.8	520.6
Net income ($ mil.)	(16.1%)	–	16.6	23.8	8.5	6.9
Market value ($ mil.)	–	–	–	–	–	–
Employees	–	–	–	–	–	4,683

THE DEPOSITORY TRUST & CLEARING CORPORATION

55 Water St. 22nd Fl.
New York NY 10041-0099
Phone: 212-855-1000
Fax: 212-855-8440
Web: www.dtcc.com

CEO: Michael C Bodson
CFO: Susan Cosgrove
HR: –
FYE: December 31
Type: Private

It's clear that securities trading just wouldn't be the same without The Depository Trust & Clearing Corporation (DTCC). Through subsidiaries the firm provides securities clearing settlement custody and information services. Dealing in equities bonds government and mortgage-backed securities money market instruments and over-the-counter derivatives the company typically processes around 90 million securities transactions each day or more than 20 billion per year. Its depository business provides custody and asset servicing for some $34 trillion worth of securities globally. DTCC is owned by its users which include banks brokerages and NYSE Euronext.

THE DREES COMPANY

515 S CAPTAL OF TEXAS HWY
WEST LAKE HILLS, TX 787464314
Phone: 859-578-4200
Fax: –
Web: www.dreeshomes.com

CEO: Ralph Drees
CFO: –
HR: –
FYE: March 31
Type: Private

The Drees Company is a big homebuilder in Cincinnati and one of the nation's top private builders. Drees targets first-time and move-up buyers with homes that are priced from about $100000 to more than $1 million. Drees also builds condominiums townhomes and patio homes. Its homes portfolio ranges from its former Zaring Premier Homes luxury division to the company's more financially accessible and modest Marquis Homes division. Drees is active in Florida Indiana Kentucky Maryland North Carolina Ohio Tennessee Texas Virginia and Washington DC. The family-owned firm was founded in 1928.

	Annual Growth	03/12	03/13	03/14	03/15	03/16
Sales ($ mil.)	7.3%	–	585.0	683.8	669.3	722.7
Net income ($ mil.)	17.6%	–	19.1	35.9	36.3	31.1
Market value ($ mil.)	–	–	–	–	–	–
Employees	–	–	–	–	–	549

THE DUCHOSSOIS GROUP INC.

845 Larch Ave.
Elmhurst IL 60126
Phone: 630-279-3600
Fax: 919-684-4344
Web: www.duke.edu

CEO: Craig J Duchossois
CFO: –
HR: –
FYE: December 31
Type: Private

The only thing this family of companies has in common is the Duchossois family the third-generation owners of The Duchossois Group Inc. The holding company pronounced "deshy-swa" focuses its investment interests in the consumer products technology and services sectors. The Chamberlain Group a subsidiary is the world's top maker of residential and commercial door openers and a leading maker of access control products. AMX performs systems integration while other companies offer AV equipment Internet-based access control and lighting products. The Duchossois Group also owns an early-stage IT venture capital fund and holds a minority stake in horse racetrack Churchill Downs.

THE EDELMAN FINANCIAL GROUP INC.

JP Morgan Chase Tower 600 Travis Ste. 5800
Houston TX 77002
Phone: 713-224-3100
Fax: 713-224-1101
Web: www.edelmanfinancial.com

NASDAQ: EF
CEO: –
CFO: –
HR: –
FYE: December 31
Type: Private

The Edelman Financial Group is a holding company that operates through its subsidiaries and affiliates which provide wealth management services for the mass-affluent market defined as clients with $50000 to $1 million of investable assets. Edelman Financial Group also has units that target high-net-worth clients with more than $1 million to invest. Key subsidiaries include Sanders Morris Harris Edelman Financial Services and Global Financial Services. Edelman Financial Group and its affiliates have more than 65 offices and more than $18 billion of assets under management. In 2012 Edelman was taken private by an affiliate of private equity firm Lee Equity Partners LLC.

THE EMPIRE DISTRICT ELECTRIC COMPANY

602 S JOPLIN AVE
JOPLIN, MO 648012337
Phone: 417-625-5100
Fax: –
Web: www.empiredistrict.com

CEO: Bradley P. Beecher
CFO: Laurie A. Delano
HR: –
FYE: December 31
Type: Private

Empire District Electric (EDE) light ups the middle of the US. The utility transmits and distributes electricity to a population base of more than 450000 (about 217000 customers in southwestern Missouri and adjacent areas of Arkansas Kansas and Oklahoma. It also supplies water to three Missouri towns and natural gas throughout most of the state. EDE's interests in fossil-fueled and hydroelectric power plants give it a generating capacity of 1377 MW; it also wholesales power. The company also provides fiber-optic services. In early 2017 the company was bought by an Algonquin Power & Utilities unit in a C$3.2 billion (US$2.3 billion) deal.

	Annual Growth	12/13	12/14	12/15	12/16	12/17
Sales ($ mil.)	(3.6%)	–	652.3	605.6	568.8	584.8
Net income ($ mil.)	(18.2%)	–	67.1	56.6	64.0	36.7
Market value ($ mil.)	–	–	–	–	–	–
Employees	–	–	–	–	–	749

THE ESTEE LAUDER COMPANIES INC.

767 5th Ave.
New York NY 10153-0023
Phone: 212-572-4200
Fax: 617-476-6150
Web: www.fidelity.com

NYSE: EL
CEO: Fabrizio Freda
CFO: Tracey T Travis
HR: –
FYE: June 30
Type: Public

The company's Estee and Bobbi are counted among some of the closest friends to women worldwide. Estee Lauder sells cosmetics fragrances and skin care products with brands including upscale Estee Lauder and Clinique as well as professional Bobbi Brown and luxurious Tom Ford beauty and fragrance lines. Its products are sold in upscale department stores specialty retailers online and 670 company-operated single-brand stores and 130 multi-brand stores. Estee Lauder operates a chain of freestanding retail stores (primarily for its M.A.C Origins and Aveda brands). Fabrizio Freda a veteran of Procter & Gamble heads Estee Lauder as CEO.

THE EVANGELICAL LUTHERAN GOOD SAMARITAN SOCIETY

4800 W 57TH ST
SIOUX FALLS, SD 571082239
Phone: 866-928-1635
Fax: –
Web: www.good-sam.com

CEO: –
CFO: Raye Nae Nylander
HR: Alan Hieb
FYE: December 31
Type: Private

The Evangelical Lutheran Good Samaritan Society strives to be a good neighbor to all particularly to the elderly people in need of housing and health care. The not-for-profit organization owns or leases some 200 senior living facilities including nursing homes assisted living facilities and affordable housing projects for seniors. Through its facilities it also provides home health care services outpatient rehabilitation adult day care and a variety of other services such as specialized units for people with Alzheimer's disease and related dementias. Good Samaritan Society merged with hospital system Sanford Health in early 2019.

	Annual Growth	12/05	12/06	12/07	12/13	12/15
Sales ($ mil.)	2.1%	–	836.5	841.8	979.8	1,011.8
Net income ($ mil.)	–	–	44.2	18.0	0.3	(33.8)
Market value ($ mil.)	–	–	–	–	–	–
Employees	–	–	–	–	–	24,000

THE FINISH LINE INC

3308 N MITTHOEFER RD
INDIANAPOLIS, IN 462352332
Phone: 317-899-1022
Fax: –
Web: www.finishline.com

CEO: Samuel M. (Sam) Sato
CFO: Edward W. (Ed) Wilhelm
HR: Cindy Cook
FYE: March 03
Type: Private

The Finish Line sells performance and casual footwear and apparel through some 900 Finish Line stores and branded shops inside Macy's department stores across the US. Its core Finish Line stores are bigger than those of competitors and offer a wider array of clothing accessories and other merchandise including jackets backpacks sunglasses and watches. Finish Line offers big brand names (such as adidas NIKE and Timberland) and also markets its own private-label line of T-shirts socks and other basics. The company also sells athletic shoes and apparel online. It is a subsidiary of European sports retailer JD Sports.

	Annual Growth	02/14	02/15	02/16	02/17*	03/18
Sales ($ mil.)	0.3%	–	1,820.6	1,888.9	1,844.4	1,839.0
Net income ($ mil.)	(43.5%)	–	79.7	21.8	(18.2)	14.4
Market value ($ mil.)	–	–	–	–	–	–
Employees	–	–	–	–	–	12,700

*Fiscal year change

THE FISHEL COMPANY

1366 DUBLIN RD
COLUMBUS, OH 432151093
Phone: 614-274-8100
Fax: –

CEO: John E Phillips
CFO: Paul Riewe
HR: –
FYE: December 31
Type: Private

The Fishel Company reels in revenues by laying out lines. The company (also known as Team Fishel) provides engineering construction management and maintenance services for electric and gas utility and communications infrastructure projects. The aerial and underground utility contractor designs and builds distribution networks for telecommunications cable and broadband television gas transmission and distribution and electric utilities throughout the US. It also counts municipalities state and federal agencies universities commercial building owners financial services companies health care providers manufacturers and residential real estate developers among its clients.

	Annual Growth	12/13	12/14	12/15	12/16	12/17
Sales ($ mil.)	11.8%	–	311.4	301.8	342.0	434.8
Net income ($ mil.)	50.1%	–	8.7	10.1	9.0	29.4
Market value ($ mil.)	–	–	–	–	–	–
Employees	–	–	–	–	–	1,400

THE FOOD EMPORIUM INC.

42 W. 39th St. 18th Fl.
New York NY 10018
Phone: 212-915-2202
Fax: 973-625-5130
Web: www.microstrat.com

CEO: –
CFO: –
HR: –
FYE: February 28
Type: Subsidiary

The Food Emporium operates about 15 upscale supermarkets in densely-populated Manhattan and a store in Connecticut. A division of The Great Atlantic & Pacific Tea Company which filed for bankruptcy in 2010 Food Emporium stores are small (8000 to 17000 square feet). The grocery chain also operates an online shopping service (www.thefoodemporium.com) offering pick up and home delivery service to shoppers in 33 ZIP codes in Manhattan where it competes with Internet grocer FreshDirect. Food Emporium offers free delivery with $50 purchases (with some restrictions). The Food Emporium's store count has slipped as its stores in New York State and Connecticut have been converted to other A&P banners.

THE FORD FOUNDATION

320 E 43RD ST FL 4
NEW YORK, NY 100174890
Phone: 212-573-5370
Fax: –
Web: www.fordfound.org

CEO: –
CFO: –
HR: Elsie Lopez
FYE: December 31
Type: Private

As one of the nation's largest philanthropic organizations the Ford Foundation can afford to be generous. The foundation offers grants to individuals and institutions worldwide that work to meet its goals of strengthening democratic values reducing poverty and injustice promoting international cooperation and advancing human achievement. The Ford Foundation's charitable giving has run the gamut from A (Association for Asian Studies) to Z (Zanzibar International Film Festival). The foundation has an endowment of about $10 billion. Established in 1936 by Edsel Ford whose father founded the Ford Motor Company the foundation no longer owns stock in the automaker or has ties to the founding family.

	Annual Growth	09/08	09/09	09/11*	12/14	12/15
Assets ($ mil.)	2.8%	–	10,234.9	10,344.9	12,400.5	12,114.0
Net income ($ mil.)	–	–	0.0	(5.3)	(7.5)	(270.2)
Market value ($ mil.)	–	–	–	–	–	–
Employees	–	–	–	–	–	556

*Fiscal year change

THE FOX CHASE CANCER CENTER FOUNDATION

333 COTTMAN AVE
PHILADELPHIA, PA 191112434
Phone: 215-728-6900
Fax: –
Web: www.fccc.edu

CEO: Richard I Fisher
CFO: –
HR: –
FYE: June 30
Type: Private

Fox Chase Cancer Center looks at cancer from all angles. The 100-bed not-for-profit medical center specializes in cancer research detection and treatment. Founded as one of the few US institutions dedicated exclusively to cancer Fox Chase Cancer Center provides diagnostic radiation oncology pathology robotic and laser surgery and other cancer-centric medical services. Its research center supports clinical trials of possible new treatments as well as standard care for cancer patients. Much of its work is focused on cancer prevention and identifying risk levels in populations. Fox Chase Cancer Center is part of the Temple University Health System.

	Annual Growth	06/08	06/09	06/10	06/11	06/12
Sales ($ mil.)	1.7%	–	55.9	49.3	44.1	58.8
Net income ($ mil.)	–	–	–	(7.1)	(9.5)	7.7
Market value ($ mil.)	–	–	–	–	–	–
Employees	–	–	–	–	–	1,900

THE FRESH MARKET INC

628 GREEN VALLEY RD # 500
GREENSBORO, NC 274087791
Phone: 336-272-1338
Fax: –
Web: www.thefreshmarket.com

CEO: Richard A. (Rick) Anicetti
CFO: Jeffrey (Jeff) Ackerman
HR: –
FYE: January 31
Type: Private

When it comes to food fresh is best. The Fresh Market operates about 160 full-service upscale specialty grocery stores in some 25 US states from Florida to New York. As the name suggests the chain specializes in perishable goods including fruits and vegetables meat and seafood. The stores average 20500 sq. ft. about a third to half the size of a conventional supermarket. Founded by husband-and-wife team Ray and Beverly Berry who opened their first store in 1982 The Fresh Market was acquired by Apollo Global Management in mid-2016.

	Annual Growth	01/12	01/13	01/14	01/15	01/16
Sales ($ mil.)	11.8%	–	1,329.1	1,511.7	1,753.2	1,857.0
Net income ($ mil.)	0.7%	–	64.1	50.8	63.0	65.5
Market value ($ mil.)	–	–	–	–	–	–
Employees	–	–	–	–	–	12,600

THE G W VAN KEPPEL COMPANY

5800 E BANNISTER RD
KANSAS CITY, MO 641341192
Phone: 913-281-4800
Fax: –
Web: www.vankeppel.com

CEO: –
CFO: –
HR: –
FYE: November 30
Type: Private

If you ask The G. W. Van Keppel Co. being stuck in the middle isn't half bad. The company touts its role as a middle man matching original equipment manufacturers with operators of their heavy duty workhorses. Founded in 1926 it has grown to distribute a slew of construction aggregate and material handling equipment under blue chip brands including Volvo Hyster and Champion Motor Graders. The company also offers repair and maintenance services rental equipment and aftermarket parts for its equipment. G. W. Van Keppel is led by its founder's third generation chairman and president Bill Walker.

	Annual Growth	11/01	11/02	11/04	11/05	11/07
Sales ($ mil.)	9.0%	–	106.2	115.7	139.3	163.3
Net income ($ mil.)	(41.4%)	–	19.8	2.4	20.6	1.4
Market value ($ mil.)	–	–	–	–	–	–
Employees	–	–	–	–	–	200

THE GAP INC

NYS: GPS

Two Folsom Street
San Francisco, CA 94105
Phone: 415 427-0100
Fax: –
Web: www.gapinc.com

CEO: –
CFO: Teri L. List-Stoll
HR: Brent Hyder
FYE: February 02
Type: Public

The ubiquitous clothing retailer Gap has been filling closets with jeans and khakis T-shirts button-downs and poplin for some 50 years. The company which operates about 3700 owned and franchised stores worldwide built its iconic casual brand on basics for men women and children. Over the years it has extended its namesake brand to include GapBody GapKids and babyGap (among others) and has added brands such as the urban chic Banana Republic family budgeteer Old Navy women's activewear chain Athleta designer-focused Intermix and men's clothier Hill City. The company which has announced plans to split into two generates about 80% of its revenue from the US.

	Annual Growth	01/15	01/16	01/17*	02/18	02/19
Sales ($ mil.)	0.2%	16,435.0	15,797.0	15,516.0	15,855.0	16,580.0
Net income ($ mil.)	(5.6%)	1,262.0	920.0	676.0	848.0	1,003.0
Market value ($ mil.)	(11.7%)	15,569.8	9,344.2	8,535.2	12,130.0	9,450.0
Employees	(1.1%)	141,000	141,000	135,000	135,000	135,000

*Fiscal year change

THE GAVILON GROUP LLC

11 ConAgra Dr.
Omaha NE 68102
Phone: 402-889-4000
Fax: 281-358-2443
Web: www.envirogen.com

CEO: Steven Zehr
CFO: Kevin Lewis
HR: –
FYE: December 31
Type: Private

A gavilon may be one of the world's smaller hawks but The Gavilon Group is a fast-growing operation that keeps a sharp eye on its global network of food and fuel commodities. The company provides storage and handling transport marketing and distribution for grain feed ingredients fertilizer and energy products. Customers include food manufacturers livestock producers fertilizer wholesalers oil refineries and power producers. Spun off by ConAgra Foods in 2008 the company is owned by Gavilon management investment firm General Atlantic and hedge funds Soros Fund Management and Ospraie Management.

THE GENERATION COMPANIES LLC

4208 SIX FORKS RD STE 850 — CEO: -
RALEIGH, NC 276095738 — CFO: David Cook
Phone: 919-361-9000 — HR: -
Fax: - — FYE: December 31
Web: www.generationcompanies.com — Type: Private

Generation puts out the welcome mat fluffs the pillows and generally invites you to stay. The company develops owns and manages more than 25 extended-stay hotels. Brands in the firm's portfolio include Suburban Extended Stay Hotel Candlewood Suites and Days Inn & Suites; its properties are located in eight states in the US: Arkansas Florida Georgia Kansas North Carolina Tennessee Texas and Virginia. The company is also active in real estate development with some $200 million in real estate assets under management. Generation which has been growing through acquisitions was founded in 1996 by CEO Mark Daley. His father Hugh M. Daley was one of the original Holiday Inn franchisees in 1959.

	Annual Growth	12/08	12/09	12/11	12/12	12/13
Assets ($ mil.)	(46.5%)	-	207.9	4.5	174.6	17.0
Net income ($ mil.)	-	-	-	1.5	0.6	(0.5)
Market value ($ mil.)	-	-	-	-	-	-
Employees	-	-	-	-	-	300

THE GEORGE J FALTER COMPANY

3501 BENSON AVE — CEO: Frank H Falter Jr
HALETHORPE, MD 212271098 — CFO: -
Phone: 410-644-6414 — HR: -
Fax: - — FYE: December 31
Web: www.georgejfalter.com — Type: Private

The George J. Falter Company is a leading independent wholesale distributor of food and merchandise serving grocery stores convienience stores and other retailers throughout Maryland. It supplies customers with such goods as beverages dry goods and frozen foods as well as health and beauty items tobacco products and other merchandise. In addition George J. Falter distributes candy for fund raising activities. The company has delivery operations as well as a cash & carry outlet in Baltimore. The family-owned business was founded in 1878 as a candy distributor.

	Annual Growth	06/05	06/06	06/07*	12/08	12/09
Sales ($ mil.)	4.8%	-	-	171.7	181.2	188.4
Net income ($ mil.)	222.4%	-	-	0.1	0.7	0.6
Market value ($ mil.)	-	-	-	-	-	-
Employees	-	-	-	-	-	130

*Fiscal year change

THE GEORGE WASHINGTON UNIVERSITY

1918 F ST NW — CEO: -
WASHINGTON, DC 200520042 — CFO: Mark Diaz
Phone: 202-994-6600 — HR: -
Fax: - — FYE: June 30
Web: www.gwu.edu — Type: Private

The George Washington University's name is just one more reminder of the regard the nation holds for its first president. The private coeducational university's more than 26000 students are scattered across its primary campus at Foggy Bottom as well as its campuses in Mount Vernon and Ashburn Virginia. With 1250 non-medical and 1200 medical faculty staff the school's student-teacher ratio is about 15:1. Its academic programs spread across 10 schools run the gamut from business to law to medicine. Notable alumni include former First Lady Jacqueline Kennedy Onassis actor Alec Baldwin and former US Secretary of State Colin Powell.

	Annual Growth	06/03	06/04	06/05	06/06	06/13
Sales ($ mil.)	4.4%	-	-	832.9	921.5	1,178.0
Net income ($ mil.)	(7.9%)	-	-	115.2	146.1	59.4
Market value ($ mil.)	-	-	-	-	-	-
Employees	-	-	-	-	-	5,000

THE GEORGETOWN UNIVERSITY

37TH & O ST NW — CEO: -
WASHINGTON, DC 200570001 — CFO: Christopher Augostini
Phone: 202-687-0100 — HR: -
Fax: - — FYE: June 30
Web: www.georgetown.edu — Type: Private

Georgetown University is the oldest Catholic university in the US. The institution's 17400 undergraduate and graduate students are instructed by more than 2340 faculty members (representing both full- and part-time) in nine schools ranging from the university's renowned Law Center to the Edmund A. Walsh School of Foreign Service and the Georgetown School of Medicine. The system has a student-teacher ratio of about 10:1. The university is also home to the Georgetown University Medical Center and has forged numerous ties with its neighboring institutions in the Washington DC community.

	Annual Growth	06/11	06/12	06/13	06/17	06/18
Sales ($ mil.)	3.1%	-	1,038.1	1,120.6	1,203.7	1,249.4
Net income ($ mil.)	-	-	(88.9)	188.0	185.8	130.1
Market value ($ mil.)	-	-	-	-	-	-
Employees	-	-	-	-	-	9,700

THE GETTYSBURG HOSPITAL

147 GETTYS ST — CEO: -
GETTYSBURG, PA 173252536 — CFO: -
Phone: 717-334-2121 — HR: -
Fax: - — FYE: June 30
Web: www.gettysburganimalhospital.com — Type: Private

Gettysburg Hospital serves the here-and-now sick and wounded residents of historic Gettysburg Pennsylvania Adams County and parts of northern Maryland. Specialized services include a maternity center emergency medicine and home health care. The facility is affiliated with nearby York Hospital through the regional WellSpan Health organization. In 2008 Gettysburg Hospital began work on an expansive project to increase ER capacity add new patient floors and build a new maternity center.

	Annual Growth	06/13	06/14	06/15	06/16	06/18
Sales ($ mil.)	7.5%	-	140.6	165.1	174.7	187.8
Net income ($ mil.)	4.8%	-	25.1	18.3	4.5	30.3
Market value ($ mil.)	-	-	-	-	-	-
Employees	-	-	-	-	-	800

THE GO DADDY GROUP INC.

14455 N. Hayden Rd. Ste. 226 — CEO: Blake Irving
Scottsdale AZ 85260-6947 — CFO: Scott Wagner
Phone: 480-505-8800 — HR: -
Fax: 480-505-8844 — FYE: December 31
Web: www.godaddy.com — Type: Private

Go Daddy go! Go Daddy provides individuals and businesses with Internet services such as domain name registration and website hosting along with services and software for functions that include e-mail e-commerce podcasting and website creation. Touting discounted pricing on domain names and hosting services it has become the largest global domain registrar accredited by ICANN (the regulatory body for the public Internet) with some 53 million domain names under management. It targets niche markets such as private domains and reseller programs through affiliates Domains By Proxy and Wild West Domains. In 2011 KKR and Silver Lake became partners in Go Daddy; founder Bob Parsons remains its majority shareholder.

THE GOLDEN 1 CREDIT UNION

8945 Cal Center Dr.
Sacramento CA 95826-3239
Phone: 916-732-2900
Fax: 916-451-8214
Web: www.golden1.com

CEO: Teresa Halleck
CFO: –
HR: –
FYE: December 31
Type: Private - Not-for-Pr

The Golden 1 Credit Union aims to be #1. One of the largest credit unions in California and among the top 10 in the US the member-owned organization serves communities in central and northern parts of the state through 80-plus branches; nearly half of which are in and around Sacramento. The Golden 1 has assets in excess of $7.5 billion and more than 600000 members who are residents of about 35 eligible counties are California state employees or employees of hundreds of select companies or groups. The credit union offers standard products such as checking and savings accounts and credit and check cards. It also provides residential real estate and personal loans as well as investments and insurance.

THE GOLUB CORPORATION

461 NOTT ST
SCHENECTADY, NY 123081812
Phone: 518-355-5000
Fax: –
Web: www.primebusinessdining.com

CEO: Jerel T. (Jerry) Golub
CFO: Jim Peterson
HR: Shelley Florence
FYE: April 24
Type: Private

Supermarket operator The Golub Corporation offers tasty come-ons such as table-ready meals gift certificates automatic discount cards and a hotline where cooks answer food-related queries. Golub operates about 135 Price Chopper supermarkets and market 32 stores in six states in the northeastern US (New York is its largest market.) About 80 of the locations have in-store pharmacies and some New York stores provide shopping and delivery service through the Shops4U program. The founding Golub family runs the company and owns about 45% of the regional grocery chain; employees own slightly more than 45%.

	Annual Growth	04/12	04/13	04/14	04/15	04/16
Sales ($ mil.)	(0.7%)	–	–	3,472.5	3,476.9	3,427.1
Net income ($ mil.)	(32.3%)	–	–	18.3	21.2	8.4
Market value ($ mil.)	–	–	–	–	–	–
Employees	–	–	–	–	–	19,500

THE GOOD SAMARITAN HOSPITAL OF MD INC

5601 LOCH RAVEN BLVD
BALTIMORE, MD 212392945
Phone: 443-444-8000
Fax: –
Web: www.medstargoodsam.org

CEO: Jeffrey A Matton
CFO: Deana Stout
HR: –
FYE: June 30
Type: Private

Good Samaritan Hospital of Maryland provides emergency care and promotes good health in the Baltimore area. The 300-bed hospital operating as MedStar Good Samaritan provides acute medical and specialty services including rehabilitation (50-bed ward) transitional care (30-bed sub-acute ward) orthopedics cancer care cardiology dialysis and women's health as well as serving as a community teaching facility. The hospital founded in 1968 also operates nursing and assisted-living facilities for the elderly and it provides educational seminars diagnostic screening and preventative medical care through its Good Health Center. MedStar Good Samaritan of Maryland is part of the MedStar Health system.

	Annual Growth	06/10	06/11	06/14	06/15	06/16
Sales ($ mil.)	(1.0%)	–	331.9	318.4	325.0	315.4
Net income ($ mil.)	(11.0%)	–	14.0	9.4	16.9	7.9
Market value ($ mil.)	–	–	–	–	–	–
Employees	–	–	–	–	–	2,146

THE GOOD SHEPHERD HOSPITAL INC

700 E MARSHALL AVE
LONGVIEW, TX 756015572
Phone: 903-315-2000
Fax: –

CEO: Todd Hancock
CFO: –
HR: –
FYE: September 30
Type: Private

Leading its citizens toward good health Good Shepherd Health System provides medical and surgical care to patients throughout the Piney Woods region of northeastern Texas. Its flagship facility is Good Shepherd Medical Center in Longview a more than 425-bed regional referral hospital providing specialty care in areas such as trauma cardiology neurology and pulmonology. Good Shepherd also has small inpatient facilities as well as a freestanding outpatient surgery center and several primary care Family Health Centers located throughout its service area. The hospital was established in 1935 as the 50-bed Gregg Memorial Hospital. Duke LifePoint Healthcare is buying Good Shepherd Health System.

	Annual Growth	09/12	09/13	09/14	09/15	09/16
Sales ($ mil.)	(3.0%)	–	270.0	244.6	279.6	246.7
Net income ($ mil.)	–	–	2.3	(7.3)	0.8	(17.0)
Market value ($ mil.)	–	–	–	–	–	–
Employees	–	–	–	–	–	2,200

THE GREAT ATLANTIC & PACIFIC TEA COMPANY INC.   PINK SHEETS: GAPT

2 Paragon Dr.
Montvale NJ 07645
Phone: 201-573-9700
Fax: 201-505-3054
Web: www.aptea.com

CEO: –
CFO: –
HR: –
FYE: February 28
Type: Private

Once one of the biggest baggers of groceries in the US The Great Atlantic & Pacific Tea Company (A&P) has been reduced to a shrinking portfolio of regional grocery chains. It now runs about 300 supermarkets in New Jersey New York Pennsylvania and three other eastern states. In addition to its mainstay 80-store A&P chain the company operates five banners: Pathmark Waldbaum's Superfresh Food Emporium and Food Basics. A&P acquired its longtime rival in the Northeast Pathmark Stores for about $1.4 billion but the purchase failed to reverse A&P's lagging fortunes. Indeed A&P in 2012 emerged from 15 months in Chapter 11 bankruptcy after a financial restructuring and closing 75 stores.

THE GREEN BAY PACKERS INC.

Lambeau Field Atrium 1265 Lombardi Ave.
Green Bay WI 54304
Phone: 920-569-7500
Fax: 920-569-7301
Web: www.packers.com

CEO: Mark Murphy
CFO: –
HR: –
FYE: March 31
Type: Private - Not-for-Pr

On the frozen tundra of Lambeau Field the Green Bay Packers battle for pride in the National Football League. The not-for-profit corporation owns and operates the storied franchise which was founded in 1919 by Earl "Curly" Lambeau and joined the NFL in 1921. Home to such icons as Bart Starr Ray Nitschke and legendary coach Vince Lombardi Green Bay boasts a record 13 league titles including four Super Bowl victories. The team is also the only community-owned franchise in American professional sports with more than 100000 shareholders. The shares do not increase in value nor pay dividends and can only be sold back to the team.

THE GRIFFIN HOSPITAL INC

130 DIVISION ST
DERBY, CT 064181326
Phone: 203-735-7421
Fax: –
Web: www.griffinhealth.org

CEO: Patrick Charmel
CFO: Mark O'Neill
HR: –
FYE: September 30
Type: Private

Griffin Hospital is a not-for-profit community hospital and subsidiary of Griffin Health Services Corporation. The 160-bed acute-care hospital serves residents in and around Derby Connecticut. Its specialties include cardiac and physical rehabilitation psychiatry and mental health surgical services and centers for childbirth and bladder and bowel control. The hospital is a teaching center affiliated with Yale University's School of Medicine. Griffin Hospital is the flagship hospital of consumer health care organization Planetree which implements a model of patient-centered care that encourages patients to actively participate in their treatment processes.

	Annual Growth	09/13	09/14	09/15	09/16	09/17
Sales ($ mil.)	9.4%	–	135.9	142.9	159.0	178.0
Net income ($ mil.)	19.7%	–	8.9	7.5	15.8	15.2
Market value ($ mil.)	–	–	–	–	–	–
Employees	–	–	–	–	–	1,100

THE HALLSTAR COMPANY

120 S. Riverside Plaza Ste. 1620
Chicago IL 60606
Phone: 312-554-7400
Fax: 312-554-7499
Web: www.hallstar.com

CEO: John J Paro
CFO: Scott J Hinkle
HR: –
FYE: September 30
Type: Private

Hey now it's a HallStar! The HallStar Company operates through subsidiaries CPH Solutions and RTD HallStar which make polymer and personal care product additives used to improve the quality of rubber plastics adhesives coatings cosmetics skin care items and other industrial products. It has two US manufacturing facilities and distributes products to customers in the US and abroad. It also holds a joint venture with Scandiflex to market personal care products in Brazil. The company's brands include Paraplex Plasthall Hallcote Quikote Maglite and Marinco. HallStar known as CPH Holding or the C. P. Hall Company until 2007 is owned by members of its executive staff.

THE HARVARD DRUG GROUP L.L.C.

31778 Enterprise Dr.
Livonia MI 48150
Phone: 734-743-6000
Fax: 734-743-7000
Web: www.theharvarddruggroup.com

CEO: George Barrett
CFO: Steve Bencetic
HR: –
FYE: June 30
Type: Private

Medicines not scholars are what come out of this Harvard. The Harvard Drug Group distributes branded and generic prescription and OTC drugs as well as vitamins and consumer products to more than 15000 independent and chain pharmacies hospitals nursing homes physician practices veterinarians and other purchasing groups. It markets more than 18000 items (primarily generics) through sales representatives and vendor partners in North America and other select global markets. The company is controlled by investment firm Court Square Capital Partners.

THE HEALTH CARE AUTHORITY OF THE CITY OF HUNTSVILLE

101 SIVLEY RD SW
HUNTSVILLE, AL 358014421
Phone: 256-265-1000
Fax: –
Web: www.huntsvillehospital.org

CEO: –
CFO: Kelly Towers
HR: –
FYE: June 30
Type: Private

Health Care Authority of the City of Huntsville ensures that residents get the medical attention they need. The volunteer board consists of nine members that governs the more than 880-bed Huntsville Hospital one of the largest medical centers in Alabama with a staff of more than 650 physicians as well as other medical facilities. Huntsville Hospital is also a teaching facility for the University of Alabama-Birmingham. The Health Care Authority of the City of Huntsville provides a list of nominees for board members to the City Council which decides who is appointed to the board.

	Annual Growth	06/05	06/06	06/07	06/17	06/18
Sales ($ mil.)	8.9%	–	548.6	591.3	1,407.5	1,524.4
Net income ($ mil.)	6.5%	–	25.3	49.1	46.3	53.8
Market value ($ mil.)	–	–	–	–	–	–
Employees	–	–	–	–	–	8,000

THE HEICO COMPANIES L.L.C.

5600 Three First National Plaza
Chicago IL 60602
Phone: 312-419-8220
Fax: 312-419-9417
Web: www.heicocompanies.com

CEO: E A Roskovensky
CFO: L G Wolski
HR: –
FYE: December 31
Type: Private

The Heico Companies specializes in buying distressed companies and turning them around. The firm which typically invests for the long haul has a portfolio of more than 35 companies in North America Europe and Asia active in manufacturing construction and industrial services. Holdings include Davis Wire Canadian steelmaker Ivaco and heavy industrial equipment maker Pettibone. Heico also has interests in other companies in the metals processing construction materials logistics and diversified services industries. Michael Heisley launched Heico in 1979. The privately-owned company holds controlling stakes in each of its operations.

THE HENRY FRANCIS DUPONT WINTERTHUR MUSEUM INC

5105 KENNETT PIKE
WINTERTHUR, DE 197351819
Phone: 302-888-4852
Fax: –
Web: www.winterthur.org

CEO: –
CFO: –
HR: –
FYE: June 30
Type: Private

The Henry Francis du Pont Winterthur Museum offers collections of antiques and Americana a 60-acre naturalistic garden and an 87000-volume library specializing in American culture. Into 2012 the museum showcases The John and Carolyn Grossman Collection of printed paper from the Victorian and Edwardian periods. It also promotes its Enchanted Woods fairy-tale garden aimed at the young and young-at-heart containing sites such as a faerie cottage and a troll bridge. The 979-acre estate is the former home of Henry Francis du Pont a director of chemical maker DuPont from 1915 to 1958. The Winterthur country estate was converted into a museum and opened to the public in 1951.

	Annual Growth	06/08	06/09	06/10	06/11	06/13
Sales ($ mil.)	–	–	(2,109.9)	11.6	28.1	18.1
Net income ($ mil.)	–	–	–	(22.4)	4.7	(4.2)
Market value ($ mil.)	–	–	–	–	–	–
Employees	–	–	–	–	–	160

THE HERITAGE FOUNDATION

214 MASSACHUSETTS AVE NE
WASHINGTON, DC 200024999
Phone: 202-546-4400
Fax: -
Web: www.heritage.org

CEO: -
CFO: -
HR: -
FYE: December 31
Type: Private

A conservative public policy think tank The Heritage Foundation offers research and advocacy on topics ranging from agriculture and labor to missile defense religion crime and education. The Heritage Foundation promotes a conservative agenda based on the tenets of free enterprise limited government individual freedom traditional American values and a strong national defense. The foundation is supported mainly by individuals as well as by other foundations and by corporations. Its donors number 410000 and its expense budget has reached $61 million. The late beer magnate Joseph Coors provided seed money for The Heritage Foundation which was founded in 1973.

	Annual Growth	12/08	12/09	12/14	12/15	12/16
Sales ($ mil.)	(1.0%)	-	87.9	97.0	92.0	82.2
Net income ($ mil.)	(40.7%)	-	22.8	14.9	11.3	0.6
Market value ($ mil.)	-	-	-	-	-	-
Employees	-	-	-	-	-	270

THE HIBBERT COMPANY

400 PENNINGTON AVE
TRENTON, NJ 086183105
Phone: 609-392-0478
Fax: -
Web: www.hibbertgroup.com

CEO: Timothy J Moonan
CFO: -
HR: -
FYE: December 31
Type: Private

Hibbert is handy when it comes to marketing. The Hibbert Company doing business as The Hibbert Group offers marketing support services. Its three flagship services consist of the fulfillment and distribution of marketing materials and information; sales and marketing program administration; and database management and direct marketing services. The company serves clients in industries such as pharmaceutical telecommunications finance technology electronics and advertising and marketing. Hibbert has five locations in Delaware Colorado and New Jersey. Tim and Tom Moonan and their family have owned the company since 1936.

	Annual Growth	12/04	12/05	12/06	12/08	12/09
Sales ($ mil.)	(55.1%)	-	-	871.8	78.8	78.8
Net income ($ mil.)	3876.7%	-	-	0.0	3.5	3.5
Market value ($ mil.)	-	-	-	-	-	-
Employees	-	-	-	-	-	446

THE HITE COMPANY

3101 BEALE AVE
ALTOONA, PA 166011509
Phone: 814-944-6121
Fax: -
Web: www.hiteco.com

CEO: -
CFO: -
HR: -
FYE: December 31
Type: Private

Going from a mill supply house to a 20-plus operation takes a bright idea and The Hite Company has more than a few. It is a wholesale distributor of more than 35000 lighting products and a slew of electrical supplies. The company's lineup includes data and communications equipment industrial automation and motor control devices as well as lamps and professional video and audio equipment. Hite has represented Sylvania for more than 50 years; it also stocks Square D branded products (Schneider Electric) and others by major OEMs. Hite serves electrical contractors builders and residential customers in Pennsylvania New York and West Virginia. Founded in 1949 the company is family owned and operated.

	Annual Growth	12/07	12/08	12/09	12/10	12/11
Sales ($ mil.)	0.0%	-	-	96.0	96.0	96.0
Net income ($ mil.)	-	-	-	0.0	0.0	0.0
Market value ($ mil.)	-	-	-	-	-	-
Employees	-	-	-	-	-	230

THE HUMANE SOCIETY OF THE UNITED STATES

1255 23RD ST NW STE 450
WASHINGTON, DC 200371168
Phone: 202-452-1100
Fax: -
Web: www.humanesociety.org

CEO: Kitty Block
CFO: G Thomas Waite III
HR: -
FYE: December 31
Type: Private

The Humane Society of the United States (HSUS) is a watchdog for dogs and all sorts of other domestic animals and wildlife. Founded in 1954 HSUS is the country's largest animal protection organization with 11 million members and constituents. The organization supports the work of local humane societies and implements a variety of investigative educational advocacy and legislative programs to promote animal welfare. Its campaigns have addressed such issues as animal fighting factory farming animal testing the fur trade and hunting practices. Most of HSUS's revenue comes from contributions and grants. An affiliate Humane Society International takes the cause to other countries.

	Annual Growth	12/10	12/11	12/13	12/14	12/15
Sales ($ mil.)	9.8%	-	133.6	169.9	169.9	194.2
Net income ($ mil.)	-	-	5.8	21.3	21.3	(0.8)
Market value ($ mil.)	-	-	-	-	-	-
Employees	-	-	-	-	-	600

THE IAMS COMPANY

7250 Poe Ave.
Dayton OH 45414
Phone: 937-898-7387
Fax: 937-264-7264
Web: www.iams.com

CEO: AG Losley
CFO: Brian Robson
HR: -
FYE: June 30
Type: Subsidiary

As Iams tells it Old Mother Hubbard went to the cupboard to fetch her portly pooch a bag of Eukanuba Large Breed Weight Control food. The Iams Company makes Eukanuba and Iams dry and canned versions of premium dog and cat foods and sells them in pet supply stores and veterinarians' offices in more than 70 countries. However North America accounts for the vast majority of the company's sales. Founded by Paul Iams in 1946 Iams also funds research efforts related to animal dermatology geriatrics allergies and nutrition through its Paul F. Iams Technical Center. Former chairman Clayton Mathile acquired the company in 1982 and sold it to consumer products giant Procter & Gamble in 1999.

THE INGALLS MEMORIAL HOSPITAL

1 INGALLS DR
HARVEY, IL 604263558
Phone: 708-333-2300
Fax: -
Web: www.ingalls.org

CEO: Kurt Johnson
CFO: Vince Pryor
HR: -
FYE: September 30
Type: Private

Ingalls Memorial Hospital serves Chicago's south suburbs. With more than 560 beds the main hospital offers a variety of acute and tertiary health care services including cancer treatment cardiovascular care orthopedic surgery rehabilitation services neurosurgery women's health and other clinical services. It also includes specialty centers in areas such as sleep therapy and addiction treatment. Ingalls Memorial Hospital also acts as a health system operating outpatient offices and clinics and providing home health and hospice services in the area.

	Annual Growth	09/11	09/12	09/13	09/14	09/15
Sales ($ mil.)	(0.9%)	-	293.3	290.7	292.0	285.4
Net income ($ mil.)	(41.7%)	-	37.0	34.2	26.8	7.3
Market value ($ mil.)	-	-	-	-	-	-
Employees	-	-	-	-	-	2,296

THE INLAND REAL ESTATE GROUP OF COMPANIES INC.

2901 Butterfield Rd.
Oak Brook IL 60523
Phone: 630-218-8000
Fax: 630-218-4957
Web: www.inlandgroup.com

CEO: Daniel L Goodwin
CFO: –
HR: –
FYE: June 30
Type: Private

The Inland Real Estate Group lives eats breathes and sleeps real estate. Through a number of affiliated firms the group provides commercial real estate services including property investment portfolio management lending brokerage development and property management/leasing. Through real estate investment trusts (REITs) Inland primarily invests in retail properties. Its portfolio (worth some $26 billion) includes more than 120 million sq. ft. of commercial space throughout the US. Publicly traded Inland Real Estate Corporation invests in properties in the Midwest; private REIT Inland American invest in the US and Canada.

THE INSTITUTE OF ELECTRICAL AND ELECTRONICS ENGINEERS INCORPORATED

445 HOES LN
PISCATAWAY, NJ 088544141
Phone: 212-419-7900
Fax: –
Web: www.ieee.org

CEO: Howard E. Michel
CFO: Thomas Siegert
HR: –
FYE: December 31
Type: Private

A leading technology-related professional group The Institute of Electrical and Electronics Engineers (IEEE) has almost 430000 members including 100000-plus students in 160 countries. The IEEE provides technical and professional information to members on topics such as aerospace systems biomedical engineering computers consumer electronics electric power and telecommunications. It sponsors more than 1300 annual conferences and publishes a variety of technical literature including journals magazines and conference proceedings. The IEEE was formed in 1964 in a combination of the American Institute of Electrical Engineers (founded in 1884) and the Institute of Radio Engineers (founded in 1912).

	Annual Growth	12/07	12/08	12/09	12/16	12/17
Sales ($ mil.)	–	–	0.0	338.4	480.4	494.4
Net income ($ mil.)	–	–	0.0	18.7	22.6	34.1
Market value ($ mil.)	–	–	–	–	–	–
Employees	–	–	–	–	–	1,068

THE INTEC GROUP INC.

666 S. Vermont St.
Palatine IL 60067
Phone: 847-358-0088
Fax: 847-358-4391
Web: www.intecgrp.com

CEO: Steven M Perlman
CFO: –
HR: Kristen Zelazo
FYE: September 30
Type: Private

This company uses a group approach to keep in touch with its core plastic manufacturing identity. The INTEC Group makes precision insert molded and injection-molded thermoplastic parts for the automotive electronics and telecommunication industries. The company's products include antennas and related items custom insert molded parts custom injection-molded parts and single cavity preproduction tools. The INTEC Group has a 60000-sq.-ft. manufacturing facility in the US and additional plants in Mexico and Singapore. The automotive industry accounts for more than 90% of the company's production output.

THE INTERNATIONAL ASSOCIATION OF LIONS CLUBS INCORPORATED

300 W 22ND ST
OAK BROOK, IL 605238815
Phone: 630-571-5466
Fax: –
Web: www.lionsclubs.org

CEO: –
CFO: –
HR: –
FYE: June 30
Type: Private

With a growl of great compassion The International Association of Lions Clubs offers people the opportunity to volunteer in their local areas and global community. Its more than 1 million members are involved in a range of projects from neighborhood initiatives to far-reaching international campaigns. Lions clubs conduct vision and hearing screenings sponsor youth camps build homes for the disabled provide disaster relief and develop international relations. It also promotes educational programs for diabetes and drug awareness. The group has about 45000 branches in more than 200 countries. It was founded in 1917 as a way for business organizations to better their communities and the world.

	Annual Growth	06/07	06/08	06/09	06/12	06/15
Sales ($ mil.)	–	–	(998.2)	0.1	62.0	70.8
Net income ($ mil.)	–	–	0.0	(0.0)	(11.1)	1.2
Market value ($ mil.)	–	–	–	–	–	–
Employees	–	–	–	–	–	288

THE INTERNATIONAL CITY MANAGEMENT ASSOCIATION RETIREMENT CORPORATION

777 N CAPITOL ST NE # 600
WASHINGTON, DC 200024239
Phone: 202-962-4600
Fax: –
Web: www.icmarc.org

CEO: –
CFO: Michael Guarasci
HR: Catherine Leggett
FYE: December 31
Type: Private

Because public servants need financial security too. ICMA Retirement Corporation (ICMA-RC) offers retirement planning and advisory services exclusively for public-sector employees. A not-for-profit organization it offers 401(a) 401(k) and 457 plans individual retirement accounts certificates of deposit retirement health savings plans brokerage accounts and access to long-term care insurance. The company also manages the VantageTrustfamily of funds. ICMA-RC serves some 1.2 million employees of state and local governments from more than 9000 public sector plans. Founded in 1972 by public-sector employees ICMA-RC has approximately $57 billion in plan assets under management.

	Annual Growth	12/06	12/07	12/08	12/09	12/14
Assets ($ mil.)	11.4%	–	–	–	287.7	493.9
Net income ($ mil.)	–	–	–	–	(4.8)	42.9
Market value ($ mil.)	–	–	–	–	–	–
Employees	–	–	–	–	–	850

THE IRVINE COMPANY LLC

550 Newport Center Dr.
Newport Beach CA 92660-7011
Phone: 949-720-2000
Fax: 949-720-2218
Web: www.irvinecompany.com

CEO: –
CFO: Chip Fedalen Jr
HR: –
FYE: June 30
Type: Private

At The Irvine Company everything goes according to plan — the master plan. The real estate investment company plans and designs office retail and residential developments in California. It owns some 500 office buildings and 40 retail centers as well as hotels marinas and golf courses. Its Irvine Company Apartment Communities arm manages 115 apartment communities. The star in Irvine's crown Irvine Ranch in Orange County is one of the largest planned communities in the US with some 220000 residents. It covers 93000 acres a drop from its original 120000 acres back in the mid-1800s when James Irvine bought out the debts of Mexican land-grant holders. Billionaire chairman Donald Bren owns the company.

THE J G WENTWORTH COMPANY

1200 MORRIS DR STE 300
CHESTERBROOK, PA 190875507
Phone: 484-434-2300
Fax: –
Web: www.jgwentworth.com

CEO: Randi Sellari
CFO: Dwight Perry
HR: –
FYE: December 31
Type: Private

J.G. Wentworth Co. is for those who just can't wait for the big payoff. The company purchases the rights of claimants in lawsuits insurance annuities and lotteries so that instead of receiving a series of settlement payments the claimants get a smaller lump sum payment up front. J.G. Wentworth Co. operates under the brands J.G. Wentworth and Peachtree Financial Solutions and advertises its structured settlement services heavily on TV radio and digital media. (Structured settlements became legal in 1982 with the Periodic Payment Settlement Act.) Founded in 1995 J.G. Wentworth went public in 2013. In late 2017 it filed for Chapter 11 bankruptcy protection.

	Annual Growth	12/13	12/14	12/15	12/16	12/17
Sales ($ mil.)	(4.6%)	–	494.4	296.4	324.7	428.7
Net income ($ mil.)	–	–	96.6	(197.1)	(98.0)	(210.7)
Market value ($ mil.)	–	–	–	–	–	–
Employees	–	–	–	–	–	751

THE JACKSON LABORATORY

600 MAIN ST
BAR HARBOR, ME 046091500
Phone: 207-288-6000
Fax: –
Web: www.jax.org

CEO: Edison T. Liu
CFO: S. Catherine (Katy) Longley
HR: Raymond Robledo
FYE: December 31
Type: Private

The Jackson Laboratory (JAX) was into genetics before genetics was cool. Founded in 1929 the not-for-profit organization is a leading researcher of human diseases their causes and their potential cures. Much of its research into mammalian genetics is focused on mice which share a similar genetic makeup to humans. In addition to its own research in areas such as cancer immunology and metabolic disease the organization maintains colonies of mice and supplies them under the brand name JAX to other laboratories around the globe. Additionally JAX offers educational programs — including internships workshops and predoctoral programs — for both current and future scientists.

	Annual Growth	12/13	12/14	12/15	12/16	12/18
Sales ($ mil.)	9.5%	–	274.5	304.3	327.0	394.8
Net income ($ mil.)	(22.8%)	–	76.2	22.8	46.4	27.0
Market value ($ mil.)	–	–	–	–	–	–
Employees	–	–	–	–	–	2,100

THE JAMAICA HOSPITAL

8900 VAN WYCK EXPY FL 4N
RICHMOND HILL, NY 114182897
Phone: 718-206-6290
Fax: –

CEO: Neil Foster Phillips
CFO: –
HR: –
FYE: December 31
Type: Private

Jamaica Hospital Medical Center has been operating in the Queens Borough of New York since before the nation of Jamaica even was born. The hospital serves Queens and eastern Brooklyn with general medical pediatric psychiatric and ambulatory care services. The facility has about 430 beds. Its specialty services include a coma recovery unit a dialysis center a psychiatric emergency department a rehabilitation center as well as a traumatic brain injury recovery unit. The hospital also operates a nursing home with more than 220 beds as well as family practice ambulance and home health services. Jamaica Hospital Medical Center is a subsidiary of MediSys Health Network.

	Annual Growth	12/08	12/09	12/15	12/16	12/17
Sales ($ mil.)	(0.3%)	–	447.2	422.7	439.8	436.3
Net income ($ mil.)	–	–	(2.2)	(32.7)	(7.5)	(45.5)
Market value ($ mil.)	–	–	–	–	–	–
Employees	–	–	–	–	–	3,251

THE JAY GROUP INC

700 INDIAN SPRINGS DR
LANCASTER, PA 176011266
Phone: 717-285-6200
Fax: –
Web: www.jaygroup.com

CEO: –
CFO: Craig Robinson
HR: –
FYE: December 31
Type: Private

The Jay Group provides outsourced marketing and fulfillment services to clients such as Reebok iRobot and Pfizer. The company's roster of services includes product fulfillment call center services procurement and packaging services. The Jay Group's fulfillment programs serve business-to-business and business-to-consumer clients providing literature product and catalog fulfillment as well as rebate processing incentive program management and sweepstakes management for sales promotions. The company's contact center services include order processing customer service and help desk support. It was established by J. Freeland Chryst in 1965; his daughter Dana Chryst leads the company as CEO.

	Annual Growth	12/04	12/05	12/06	12/07	12/08
Sales ($ mil.)	2.5%	–	47.5	51.1	47.3	51.2
Net income ($ mil.)	(20.4%)	–	–	2.2	2.2	1.4
Market value ($ mil.)	–	–	–	–	–	–
Employees	–	–	–	–	–	273

THE JEWISH FEDERATIONS OF NORTH AMERICA INC

25 BROADWAY FL 17
NEW YORK, NY 100041015
Phone: 212-284-6500
Fax: –
Web: www.jewishfederations.org

CEO: Eric D Fingerhut
CFO: –
HR: Misty Bonilla
FYE: June 30
Type: Private

From supporting food banks in the US to helping -©migr-©s fleeing Ethiopia for Israel The Jewish Federations of North America (formerly the United Jewish Communities) works to better Jewish life across the globe. One of North America's leading not-for-profit organizations the JFNA represents more than 150 Jewish federations and about 400 independent Jewish communities across the continent. The federation raises and distributes more than $3.5 billion annually for social welfare social services and educational needs in its effort to support Israel and Jews worldwide. The organization changed its name from United Jewish Communities to The Jewish Federations of North America in 2009.

	Annual Growth	06/10	06/11	06/12	06/15	06/17
Sales ($ mil.)	33.0%	–	47.2	48.2	338.1	261.2
Net income ($ mil.)	–	–	(0.6)	0.8	13.4	(0.3)
Market value ($ mil.)	–	–	–	–	–	–
Employees	–	–	–	–	–	150

THE JONES FINANCIAL COMPANIES L.L.L.P.

12555 Manchester Rd.
Des Peres MO 63131
Phone: 314-515-2000
Fax: 314-515-2622
Web: www.edwardjones.com

CEO: –
CFO: Kevin D Bastien
HR: –
FYE: December 31
Type: Private - Partnershi

This isn't your father's broker. Well maybe it is. The Jones Financial Companies is the parent of Edward Jones an investment brokerage network catering to individual investors. Serving some seven million clients the "Wal-Mart of Wall Street" has thousands of offices (mainly in small cities rural communities and suburbs) in all 50 states and Canada. Brokers preach a conservative buy-and-hold approach offering relatively low-risk investment vehicles such as government bonds blue-chip stocks high-quality mutual funds IRAs and annuities as well as insurance. The company also engages in investment banking underwriting and making markets for corporate securities and municipal bonds.

THE JUDGE GROUP INC

151 S WARNER RD STE 100
WAYNE, PA 190872125
Phone: 610-667-7700
Fax: -
Web: www.judge.com

CEO: Marty Judge
CFO: Robert G Alessandrini
HR: -
FYE: September 30
Type: Private

If your business requires staffing technology consulting or training services The Judge Group will be predisposed to render a verdict in your favor. The company offers temporary and permanent employee placement services in a wide variety of service and manufacturing sectors but specializes in technology staffing. The company's technology consulting services address such areas as enterprise content management and strategy. It also offers training for IT-related and other professional functions through its Berkeley division. Martin Judge founded the company in 1970.

	Annual Growth	09/12	09/13	09/15	09/16	09/17
Sales ($ mil.)	8.5%	-	274.0	323.4	342.3	380.3
Net income ($ mil.)	22.9%	-	1.1	3.7	1.2	2.5
Market value ($ mil.)	-	-	-	-	-	-
Employees	-	-	-	-	-	7,000

THE JUILLIARD SCHOOL

60 LINCOLN CENTER PLZ
NEW YORK, NY 100236588
Phone: 212-799-5000
Fax: -
Web: www.juilliard.edu

CEO: -
CFO: -
HR: -
FYE: June 30
Type: Private

The Juilliard School educates some of the top performers from around the world. Students can earn undergraduate and graduate degrees in dance drama and music. The school also has an Evening Division that is geared toward working adults as well as a Pre-College Division that meets on Saturdays between September and May. Primarily a performing arts conservatory the school also enriches the community through outreach and other special programs. Juilliard was founded in 1905 in Greenwich Village and took up residence at Lincoln Center in 1969. Famed alumni include William Hurt Val Kilmer Kevin Kline Laura Linney Winton Marsalis Christopher Reeve Ving Rhames Nadja Salerno-Sonnenberg and Robin Williams.

	Annual Growth	06/07	06/08	06/09	06/13	06/15
Sales ($ mil.)	24.3%	-	-	35.9	131.8	132.3
Net income ($ mil.)	-	-	-	0.0	21.6	9.6
Market value ($ mil.)	-	-	-	-	-	-
Employees	-	-	-	-	-	550

THE KANE COMPANY

6500 KANE WAY
ELKRIDGE, MD 210756000
Phone: 410-799-3200
Fax: -

CEO: -
CFO: -
HR: -
FYE: June 03
Type: Private

Many people do business in offices but offices are business for The Kane Company. Through its subsidiaries Kane moves office contents (Office Movers) stores office records (Office Archives) shreds offices records (Office Shredding) and installs office furniture (Office Installers). Another Kane unit offers third-party logistics services including supply chain management and warehousing and distribution; an affiliate provides printing services. Kane which operates from offices in Delaware Maryland New Jersey and Virginia has long relied on federal government agencies in the area as a major source of business. The company was founded in 1969.

	Annual Growth	12/06	12/07	12/08	12/10*	06/15
Sales ($ mil.)	(34.0%)	-	1,627.5	81.8	56.2	58.2
Net income ($ mil.)	286.2%	-	0.0	1.7	1.1	2.0
Market value ($ mil.)	-	-	-	-	-	-
Employees	-	-	-	-	-	1,500

*Fiscal year change

THE KLEINFELDER GROUP INC

550 W C ST STE 1200
SAN DIEGO, CA 921013532
Phone: 858-320-2000
Fax: -
Web: www.kleinfelder.com

CEO: Louis Armstrong
CFO: -
HR: -
FYE: March 31
Type: Private

The Kleinfelder Group isn't afraid to get its hands dirty. Since its start as a materials testing lab in 1961 the company has expanded to become one of the largest engineering consulting and design groups in the US. Kleinfelder's operating subsidiaries offer soils and materials testing geotechnical engineering construction management and environmental services. With about 50 domestic offices and locations in Australia and Guam the group targets the energy transportation water commercial/industrial government and education markets; projects run the gamut from building underground parking garages to establishing wind farms. Jim Kleinfelder who retired in 1993 founded the employee-owned company.

	Annual Growth	03/10	03/11	03/12	03/13	03/14
Sales ($ mil.)	3.0%	-	222.5	216.9	224.2	243.0
Net income ($ mil.)	(43.9%)	-	-	5.3	1.0	1.7
Market value ($ mil.)	-	-	-	-	-	-
Employees	-	-	-	-	-	1,522

THE LANCASTER GENERAL HOSPITAL

555 N DUKE ST
LANCASTER, PA 176022207
Phone: 717-544-5511
Fax: -

CEO: Thomas E. (Tom) Beeman
CFO: Dennis R. Roemer
HR: -
FYE: June 30
Type: Private

Lancaster General Health (LG Health) is a 690-bed integrated health care delivery system serving residents of Lancaster County Pennsylvania and surrounding areas. Its flagship Lancaster General Hospital (LGH) - opened in 1893 - is known for its cardiology orthopedic and intensive care specialties. A separate Women & Babies hospital cares for those just making it into the world. The not-for-profit system also includes multiple outpatient clinics a rehab hospital home care services and a nursing center and health care college as well as a medical group of more than 300 physicians operating at more than 40 practices throughout the region.

	Annual Growth	06/12	06/13	06/14	06/15	06/16
Sales ($ mil.)	5.2%	-	823.0	868.0	920.3	958.7
Net income ($ mil.)	-	-	(15.4)	(14.0)	111.0	122.3
Market value ($ mil.)	-	-	-	-	-	-
Employees	-	-	-	-	-	7,000

THE LANE CONSTRUCTION CORPORATION

90 FIELDSTONE CT
CHESHIRE, CT 064101212
Phone: 203-235-3351
Fax: -
Web: www.laneconstruct.com

CEO: -
CFO: -
HR: Adolfo Criscuolo
FYE: December 31
Type: Private

Lane likes people to be in the fast lane. For more than a century the heavy civil contractor and its affiliates have been widening paving and constructing lanes for highways bridges runways railroads dams and mass transit systems in the eastern and southern US. The group also produces bituminous and precast concrete and mines aggregates at plants and quarries in the northeastern mid-Atlantic and southern US. Additionally it sells and leases construction equipment. Founded in 1902 Lane Construction has offices in more than 20 states and is owned by descendants of Lane and employees.

	Annual Growth	12/14	12/15	12/16	12/17	12/18
Sales ($ mil.)	(8.7%)	-	1,115.4	1,196.8	1,476.3	847.9
Net income ($ mil.)	-	-	(16.1)	39.7	19.0	76.1
Market value ($ mil.)	-	-	-	-	-	-
Employees	-	-	-	-	-	3,500

THE LEGAL AID SOCIETY INC

199 WATER ST FRNT 3
NEW YORK, NY 100383526
Phone: 212-577-3346
Fax: –
Web: www.legalaidnyc.org

CEO: –
CFO: –
HR: –
FYE: June 30
Type: Private

Serving as a law firm for many of New York City's less fortunate residents The Legal Aid Society represents people who could not otherwise afford a lawyer in civil criminal and juvenile rights cases. The society has a staff of some 1100 lawyers. It also draws upon the work of more than 700 investigators social workers and paralegals who combined handle about 300000 individual cases and matters each year. A not-for-profit organization The Legal Aid Society receives government money for its work in criminal and some juvenile matters and it counts on donations to support its efforts in civil cases. The Legal Aid Society was founded in 1876.

	Annual Growth	06/10	06/11	06/12	06/13	06/14
Sales ($ mil.)	9.0%	–	–	189.1	217.8	224.7
Net income ($ mil.)	104.5%	–	–	0.2	8.6	0.7
Market value ($ mil.)	–	–	–	–	–	–
Employees		–	–	–	–	1,600

THE LONG & FOSTER COMPANIES INC.

14501 George Carter Way
Chantilly VA 20151
Phone: 703-653-8500
Fax: 703-591-6978
Web: www.longandfoster.com

CEO: Jeffrey S Detwiler
CFO: Bruce Enger
HR: –
FYE: December 31
Type: Private

Longing to find your dream home? Long & Foster will gladly help. The company's flagship subsidiary Long & Foster Real Estate is one of the largest residential real estate brokerages in the Mid-Atlantic with more than 180 offices primarily in the Washington DC/Baltimore area. The brokerage has some 12000 sales agents. Other subsidiaries offer property management commercial brokerage business relocation homeowners insurance title insurance and commercial and residential mortgage financing. Chairman and CEO Wesley Foster co-founded the company which he now owns with partner Henry Long.

THE LOS ANGELES LAKERS INC.

555 N. Nash St.
El Segundo CA 90245
Phone: 310-426-6000
Fax: 310-426-6115
Web: www.nba.com/lakers

CEO: Jeanie Buss
CFO: –
HR: –
FYE: July 31
Type: Private

These Lakers can be found navigating the choppy waters of the National Basketball Association. The Los Angeles Lakers professional basketball franchise is one of the most popular and successful teams in the NBA earning 16 championship titles since joining the league in 1949. The team was founded in 1947 as the Minnesota Lakers of the National Basketball League and moved to California in 1960. Its roster has included such Hall of Fame players as Kareem Abdul-Jabbar Wilt Chamberlain Earvin "Magic" Johnson and Jerry West. The franchise has been controlled by real estate mogul Jerry Buss since 1979; billionaire Philip Anschutz Dr. Soon-Shiong and developer Edward Roski also own minority stakes in the team.

THE LOUIS BERGER GROUP INC.

412 Mt. Kemble Ave.
Morristown NJ 07960-6654
Phone: 973-407-1000
Fax: 973-267-6468
Web: www.louisberger.com

CEO: Jim Stamatis
CFO: Margaret Lassarat
HR: –
FYE: June 30
Type: Private

The Louis Berger Group provides civil structural mechanical electrical and environmental engineering services for commercial and government projects around the world. It also provides financial services maintenance and management services. Louis Berger has worked on high-profile projects such as the Pennsylvania Turnpike the redevelopment of the World Trade Center site and the renovation of the Lincoln Memorial Reflecting Pool. Louis Berger also has has built highways airports seaports and dams and contributed to cultural and environmental preservation for projects in 140 countries. The privately-held group also has worked on reconstruction projects in Iraq and Afghanistan.

THE LUBRIZOL CORPORATION

29400 Lakeland Blvd.
Wickliffe OH 44092-2298
Phone: 440-943-4200
Fax: 440-943-5337
Web: www.lubrizol.com

CEO: James L Hambrick
CFO: Charles P Cooley
HR: –
FYE: December 31
Type: Subsidiary

Lubrizol is a smooth operator — the company is the world's #1 maker of additives for lubricants and fuels. The manufacturer operates through two business segments: Lubrizol Additives and Lubrizol Advanced Materials. The Lubrizol Additives segment includes engine oil additives that fight sludge buildup viscosity breakdown and component wear; fuel additives designed to control deposits and improve combustion; and additives for paints inks greases metalworking and other markets. Lubrizol's Advanced Materials segment (performance coatings and chemicals) delivers its products to the personal care and rubber and plastics markets.

THE MASSACHUSETTS GENERAL HOSPITAL

55 FRUIT ST
BOSTON, MA 021142696
Phone: 617-726-2000
Fax: –
Web: www.mghbiomed.com

CEO: –
CFO: Laura Wysk
HR: Jeff Davis
FYE: September 30
Type: Private

The General Hospital Corporation is no soapy daytime drama. Doing business as Massachusetts General Hospital (or Mass General) the 200-year-old acute care facility is Harvard Medical School's original and largest teaching hospital. With some 1000 beds Mass General has its main campus in Boston and operates several health centers in surrounding communities. Its specialized medical departments include cancer cardiology and heart surgery; neurology and neurosurgery; and diabetes and endocrinology. As a leading research facility Mass General hosts a number of clinical drug and device trials and has an annual research budget of more than $850 million. The hospital is a founding member of the Partners HealthCare System (along with Brigham and Women's).

	Annual Growth	09/11	09/12	09/13	09/14	09/15
Sales ($ mil.)	2.4%	–	2,281.3	2,274.6	2,201.9	2,452.0
Net income ($ mil.)	(7.6%)	–	267.9	148.3	186.8	211.3
Market value ($ mil.)	–	–	–	–	–	–
Employees		–	–	–	–	10,156

THE MATHWORKS INC.

3 Apple Hill Dr. CEO: -
Natick MA 01760-2098 CFO: -
Phone: 508-647-7000 HR: -
Fax: 508-647-7001 FYE: December 31
Web: www.mathworks.com Type: Private

If you haven't heard of MATLAB chances are you aren't a scientist or engineer. The MathWorks provides technical computing software used for data analysis visualization and mathematical computations. Its MATLAB Simulink and Polyspace products are used in such industries as aerospace automotive communications electronics financial services and industrial automation. MathWorks products are also used for teaching and research at more than 5000 universities. The company was co-founded in 1984 by majority owners Jack Little (president) Cleve Moler (chief mathematician) and Steve Bangert.

THE MCLEAN HOSPITAL CORPORATION

115 MILL ST CEO: -
BELMONT, MA 024781048 CFO: David A Lagasse
Phone: 617-855-2000 HR: -
Fax: - FYE: September 30
Web: www.mcleanhospital.org Type: Private

The researchers and teachers at McLean Hospital are into heady topics. McLean Hospital a major teaching facility of Harvard Medical School provides mental and behavioral health services to the Boston Massachusetts area and surrounding communities. McLean is home to specialized programs for the research and treatment of psychiatric and neurological illnesses including depression bipolar and psychotic disorders mood and anxiety disorders substance abuse eating disorders geriatric mental illnesses and child and adolescent psychiatric disorders. The hospital offers inpatient and residential care and a range of outpatient services. McLean is an affiliate of Partners HealthCare System.

	Annual Growth	09/07	09/08	09/09	09/13	09/15
Sales ($ mil.)	226.6%	-	-	0.1	102.8	116.5
Net income ($ mil.)	-	-	-	(0.4)	3.4	3.0
Market value ($ mil.)	-	-	-	-	-	-
Employees	-	-	-	-	-	1,213

THE MECHANICS BANK

3170 Hilltop Mall Rd. CEO: John Decero
Richmond CA 94806 CFO: Nathan Duda
Phone: 510-262-7980 HR: -
Fax: 510-262-7941 FYE: December 31
Web: www.mechbank.com Type: Private

The Mechanics Bank operates more than 30 branches serving the San Francisco Bay and greater Sacramento areas of California. It offers standard products such as checking and savings accounts CDs and Visa credit and debit cards. Commercial real estate loans account for more than half of the bank's loan portfolio followed by consumer installment commercial and industrial construction and land development and residential mortgage loans. The bank also offers investment management trust financial planning private banking brokerage and retirement plan administration services. Descendents of founder E.M. Downer control The Mechanics Bank.

THE MEDICAL UNIVERSITY OF SOUTH CAROLINA

171 ASHLEY AVE CEO: Patrick J. Cawley
CHARLESTON, SC 294258908 CFO: Patrick Wamsley
Phone: 843-792-2123 HR: -
Fax: - FYE: June 30
Web: www.musc.edu Type: Private

Established in 1824 the Medical University of South Carolina (MUSC) provides Charleston with a wide range of health-related services including medical care training and research. The 50-acre medical school has 1300 faculty members and trains about 2750 full- and part-time students and residents each year through its six schools which cover medical pharmacy nursing dental health professional and graduate training. The MUSC Health organization includes the MUSC Medical Center in Charleston which has some 700 beds and includes a children's hospital and a psychiatric institute as well as the University Medical Associates physician practice organization.

	Annual Growth	06/08	06/09	06/13	06/17	06/18
Sales ($ mil.)	1.9%	-	836.5	780.9	914.1	992.5
Net income ($ mil.)	1.8%	-	3.5	26.0	9.1	4.1
Market value ($ mil.)	-	-	-	-	-	-
Employees	-	-	-	-	-	5,500

THE MEMORIAL HOSPITAL

111 BREWSTER ST CEO: -
PAWTUCKET, RI 028604474 CFO: -
Phone: 401-729-2000 HR: -
Fax: - FYE: September 30
Web: www.mhri.org Type: Private

The Memorial Hospital known as Memorial Hospital of Rhode Island (MHRI) brings a reminder of good health to the residents of the Blackstone Valley which encompasses parts of southern Massachusetts and northern Rhode Island. Founded in 1901 the not-for-profit hospital has some 300 beds and offers general medical and surgical care as well as specialty services in oncology cardiovascular care orthopedics and hernia treatment. It is also a teaching institution for Brown University's Warren Alpert Medical School. Through a handful of satellite clinics located throughout its service area MHRI provides primary and preventive care. The hospital is part of Care of New England Health System.

	Annual Growth	09/10	09/11	09/12	09/13	09/15
Sales ($ mil.)	(3.1%)	-	-	-	142.2	133.6
Net income ($ mil.)	-	-	-	-	(35.9)	(27.1)
Market value ($ mil.)	-	-	-	-	-	-
Employees	-	-	-	-	-	1,400

THE MERCHANTS COMPANY

1100 EDWARDS ST CEO: Andrew B Mercier
HATTIESBURG, MS 394015511 CFO: Jarrod Gray
Phone: 601-353-2461 HR: -
Fax: - FYE: September 30
Web: www.merchantsfoodservice.com Type: Private

The Merchants Company which does business as Merchants Foodservice is a leading foodservice supplier that serves more than 6000 customers in 10 Southeastern states. From a handful of distribution warehouses in Alabama Georgia Mississippi and South Carolina the company supplies a wide range of food and non-food items to restaurants hospitals schools and other foodservice operations. The company was founded in 1904 as Fain Grocery Co. a wholesale grocery distributor and changed its name to Merchants Company in 1927. It began focusing on foodservice distribution in 1982 and was acquired by family owned holding company Tatum Development in 1988.

	Annual Growth	09/06	09/07	09/08	09/10	09/11
Sales ($ mil.)	18.5%	-	-	294.3	441.5	489.1
Net income ($ mil.)	24.2%	-	-	1.3	5.2	2.4
Market value ($ mil.)	-	-	-	-	-	-
Employees	-	-	-	-	-	500

THE METHODIST HOSPITAL

6565 FANNIN ST　　　　　　　　　　　　　　　　　　CEO: –
HOUSTON, TX 770302892　　　　　　　　　　　CFO: Kevin Burns
Phone: 713-790-3311　　　　　　　　　　　　　　　　HR: –
Fax: –　　　　　　　　　　　　　　　　　　　FYE: December 31
Web: www.houstonmethodist.org　　　　　　　　Type: Private

Houston Methodist (formerly The Methodist Hospital) owns and operates seven Houston-area medical centers including the flagship location which has more than 800 beds and is known for innovations in urology and neurosurgery among other specialties. Other hospitals include Houston Methodist West Houston Methodist Sugar Land Houston Methodist San Jacinto Houston Methodist Willowbrook Houston Methodist St. John and Houston Methodist St. Catherine. Together the hospitals have nearly 2000 beds and employ more than 4500 physicians. In addition to hospitals the organization operates emergency care imaging outpatient and rehab centers and manages a physician organization of nearly 400.

	Annual Growth	12/11	12/12	12/13	12/14	12/15
Sales ($ mil.)	13.5%	–	2,331.0	2,616.2	3,050.8	3,407.7
Net income ($ mil.)	(6.5%)	–	386.6	683.5	361.8	316.3
Market value ($ mil.)	–	–	–	–	–	–
Employees	–	–	–	–	–	15,000

THE METHODIST HOSPITALS INC

600 GRANT ST　　　　　　　　　　　　　　　　　　CEO: James Burg
GARY, IN 464026001　　　　　　　　　　　　　CFO: John C Diehl
Phone: 219-886-4000　　　　　　　　　　　　　　　　HR: –
Fax: –　　　　　　　　　　　　　　　　　　　FYE: December 31
Web: www.methodisthospitals.org　　　　　　　Type: Private

The Methodist Hospitals Inc. is a not-for-profit community-based health care system that provides medical care to Indiana residents. More than 580 physicians representing some 60 specialties serve its two campus hospitals which have a combined total of about 640 beds. The system provides care for a range of specialized areas from neurology and neurosurgery oncology and home health and hospice to rehabilitation and orthopedics. The emergency department treats more than 59000 patients a year. The system also provides screenings charitable care and community education programs. The Methodist Hospitals established in 1923 reinvests all of its profits to improve patient care.

	Annual Growth	12/14	12/15	12/16	12/17	12/18
Sales ($ mil.)	9.0%	–	280.0	360.2	366.2	362.5
Net income ($ mil.)	19.2%	–	1.7	4.4	8.1	2.8
Market value ($ mil.)	–	–	–	–	–	–
Employees	–	–	–	–	–	3,260

THE METROHEALTH SYSTEM

2500 METROHEALTH DR　　　　　　　　　　　CEO: Akram Boutros
CLEVELAND, OH 441091900　　　　　　　　CFO: Craig Richmond
Phone: 216-398-6000　　　　　　　　　　　　　　　　HR: –
Fax: –　　　　　　　　　　　　　　　　　　　FYE: December 31
Web: www.metrohealth.org　　　　　　　　　　　Type: Private

Helping Cleveland's metropolitan citizens stay healthy (and healing them when they aren't) is what MetroHealth System is all about. At the center of the system is MetroHealth Medical Center a level I trauma center and acute care hospital that serves as a teaching affiliate for Case Western Reserve University. Services include oncology behavioral health vascular care orthopedics burn care and pediatrics. The system also operates outpatient clinics long-term care facilities a regional rehabilitation clinic a heart and vascular center two skilled nursing centers an outpatient center and a medical helicopter program. MetroHealth is owned by Ohio's Cuyahoga County.

	Annual Growth	12/10	12/11	12/12	12/13	12/15
Sales ($ mil.)	4.5%	–	–	–	813.1	888.4
Net income ($ mil.)	(5.4%)	–	–	–	41.8	37.4
Market value ($ mil.)	–	–	–	–	–	–
Employees	–	–	–	–	–	6,000

THE METROPOLITAN MUSEUM OF ART

1000 5TH AVE　　　　　　　　　　　　　　　　　　CEO: –
NEW YORK, NY 100280198　　　　　　　　　　　　CFO: –
Phone: 212-535-7710　　　　　　　　　　　　　　　　HR: –
Fax: –　　　　　　　　　　　　　　　　　　　FYE: June 30
Web: www.metmuseum.org　　　　　　　　　　　Type: Private

You won't find too much about a certain New York baseball team at this Met. One of the world's premier cultural institutions The Metropolitan Museum of Art (also known as "the Met") acquires and exhibits artwork from around the world. Its collection of more than 2 million pieces ranges from the prehistoric era to the present day. In addition to hosting exhibits the Met loans artwork to other museums publishes books and catalogs and develops educational programs. It also displays art online. The City of New York owns the museum's 2 million-sq.-ft. complex which is located on the east side of Central Park; the museum itself owns its art collection. The Met was founded in 1870.

	Annual Growth	06/13	06/14	06/15	06/16	06/18
Sales ($ mil.)	1.8%	–	344.3	361.2	379.5	369.3
Net income ($ mil.)	(3.6%)	–	275.3	(7.7)	(247.5)	237.7
Market value ($ mil.)	–	–	–	–	–	–
Employees	–	–	–	–	–	2,372

THE MIDDLE TENNESSEE ELECTRIC MEMBERSHIP CORPORATION

555 NEW SALEM HWY　　　　　　　　　　　　　　CEO: –
MURFREESBORO, TN 371293390　　　　　　　CFO: Bernie Steen
Phone: 615-890-9762　　　　　　　　　　　　　　　　HR: –
Fax: –　　　　　　　　　　　　　　　　　　　FYE: June 30
Web: www.mtemc.com　　　　　　　　　　　　Type: Private

Middle Tennessee Electric Membership Corporation's service territory is smack dab in the middle of Tennessee. The utility cooperative distributes electricity to 190750 residential and business customers (member/owners) in four counties (Cannon Rutherford Williamson and Wilson) via more than 10470 miles of power lines connected to 34 electric distribution substations. Middle Tennessee Electric purchases its power supply from the Tennessee Valley Authority. The corporation is Tennessee's largest electric cooperative and the sixth largest in the US.

	Annual Growth	06/10	06/11	06/12	06/13	06/16
Sales ($ mil.)	–	–	(1,841.4)	510.5	524.7	542.2
Net income ($ mil.)	781.4%	–	0.0	19.4	27.8	10.1
Market value ($ mil.)	–	–	–	–	–	–
Employees	–	–	–	–	–	410

THE MITRE CORPORATION

202 BURLINGTON RD　　　　　　　　　　CEO: Jason F. Providakes
BEDFORD, MA 017301420　　　　　　　　CFO: Jean C. Milbrandt
Phone: 781-271-2000　　　　　　　　　　　　HR: Julie Gravallese
Fax: –　　　　　　　　　　　　　　　　　　　FYE: October 05
Web: www.mitre.org　　　　　　　　　　　　　Type: Private

Politicians try to engineer a better government but MITRE governs the country's best engineering. A private not-for-profit organization MITRE Corporation provides consulting engineering and technical research services primarily for agencies of the federal government. It employs more than 7000 scientists engineers and other specialists who work at primary research facilities in Massachusetts and Virginia. It also manages serveral federally funded research and development centers serving organizations such as the Department of Defense the Federal Aviation Administration the Internal Revenue Service and the Department of Veterans Affairs. MITRE was founded in 1958 by former MIT researchers.

	Annual Growth	10/04	10/05	10/06	10/07	10/08
Sales ($ mil.)	10.9%	–	–	–	1,113.7	1,234.7
Net income ($ mil.)	(4.6%)	–	–	–	23.4	22.3
Market value ($ mil.)	–	–	–	–	–	–
Employees	–	–	–	–	–	7,000

THE MOSAIC COMPANY   NYSE: MOS

3033 Campus Dr. Ste. E490   CEO: Joc O Rourke
Plymouth MN 55441   CFO: Lawrence W Stranghoener
Phone: 763-577-2700   HR: –
Fax: 763-559-2860   FYE: May 31
Web: www.mosaicco.com   Type: Public

Lots of little pieces have joined together to form The Mosaic Company's big picture. The company ranks as one of the world's largest makers of phosphate and potash crop nutrients. Mosaic's potash operations position the company at the top of the industry along with Uralkali and PotashCorp. Mosaic ranks as the second-largest potash fertilizer company in North America (behind PotashCorp). Mosaic's potash mines are located in Canada and the US. The company does about two-thirds of its business outside the US; India and Brazil are its biggest international markets.

THE MOSES H CONE MEMORIAL HOSPITAL OPERATING CORPORATION

1200 N ELM ST   CEO: –
GREENSBORO, NC 274011020   CFO: –
Phone: 336-832-7000   HR: –
Fax: –   FYE: September 30
Web: www.conehealth.com   Type: Private

Cone Health (formerly Moses Cone Health System) serves patients in central North Carolina through five acute and specialty care hospitals with a total of more than 1000 beds. Its facilities include Moses H. Cone Memorial Hospital Wesley Long Community Hospital Annie Penn Hospital Moses Cone Behavioral Health Center and the Women's Hospital of Greensboro. Specialty services include rehabilitation cancer treatment neurology and heart and vascular care. The health care provider also operates outpatient clinics and nursing homes. Founded in 1911; its flagship hospital was named after textile giant Cone Denim's founder Moses Cone (it was started in Cone's honor by his wife Bertha Cone).

	Annual Growth	09/12	09/13	09/16*	12/17*	09/18
Sales ($ mil.)	17.5%	–	893.9	1,678.3	482.0	2,002.0
Net income ($ mil.)	–	–	(14.5)	63.0	37.2	102.6
Market value ($ mil.)	–	–	–	–	–	–
Employees	–	–	–	–	–	536

*Fiscal year change

THE NATIONAL ASSOCIATION FOR THE EXCHANGE OF INDUSTRIAL RESOURCES INC

560 MCCLURE ST   CEO: Gary C Smith
GALESBURG, IL 614014286   CFO: Robert B Gilstrap
Phone: 309-343-0704   HR: –
Fax: –   FYE: June 30
Web: www.naeir.org   Type: Private

The National Association for the Exchange of Industrial Resources (NAEIR) is like a modern day Robin Hood without the stealing or tights. The non-profit organization collects excess inventory from corporations and distributes the merchandise to its members: schools churches and charities. Members pay a fee to join and shipping costs for the items but the goods are free. Donations include office supplies computer software clothing books classroom materials toys and personal care products from donors including Microsoft Kid Brands and General Electric. NAEIR has 18650 members and receives donations from several thousand corporations. Manufacturing executive Norbert Smith founded NAEIR in 1977.

	Annual Growth	06/11	06/12	06/13	06/14	06/15
Sales ($ mil.)	(3.8%)	–	88.0	86.1	56.1	78.3
Net income ($ mil.)	–	–	(8.0)	22.5	(12.1)	(28.3)
Market value ($ mil.)	–	–	–	–	–	–
Employees	–	–	–	–	–	80

THE NATURE CONSERVANCY

4245 FAIRFAX DR STE 100   CEO: Mark R. Tercek
ARLINGTON, VA 222031650   CFO: Stephen (Steve) Howell
Phone: 703-841-5300   HR: –
Fax: –   FYE: June 30
Web: www.nature.org   Type: Private

The Nature Conservancy is a nonprofit dedicated to preserving the diversity of Earth's wildlife by saving some 120 million acres of land 5000 miles of rivers and 100 marine areas in every US state and more than 35 countries worldwide. The organization boasts more than 1 million members. The Nature Conservancy originally carried out its mission by simply buying land but it has evolved to incorporate other methods to further its goals. In addition to land acquisition the organization partners with government corporate and private entities to reduce harmful use of natural areas to create conservation-friendly public policy and to increase conservation funding. The Nature Conservancy was founded in 1951.

	Annual Growth	06/12	06/13	06/14	06/16	06/17
Sales ($ mil.)	7.4%	–	859.1	950.0	804.0	1,143.8
Net income ($ mil.)	30.1%	–	106.9	201.3	(8.7)	306.5
Market value ($ mil.)	–	–	–	–	–	–
Employees	–	–	–	–	–	3,400

THE NEBRASKA MEDICAL CENTER

987400 NEBRASKA MED CTR   CEO: William S Dinsmoor
OMAHA, NE 681980001   CFO: –
Phone: 402-552-2000   HR: –
Fax: –   FYE: June 30
    Type: Private

Cornhuskers take note: If health care is what you seek The Nebraska Medical Center aims to please. The not-for-profit health system provides tertiary care at two campuses in Omaha University Hospital and Clarkson Hospital that collectively house about 680 licensed beds. The medical center the largest health care facility in Nebraska is the primary teaching facility of the University of Nebraska Medical Center (UNMC). It also serves as a designated trauma facility for eastern Nebraska and western Iowa and provides highly specialized care including organ transplantation. Its Clarkson West Medical Center campus houses outpatient surgery facilities an emergency room and doctors' offices.

	Annual Growth	06/13	06/14	06/15	06/16	06/17
Sales ($ mil.)	24.1%	–	–	–	1,119.2	1,389.4
Net income ($ mil.)	22.1%	–	–	–	60.9	74.4
Market value ($ mil.)	–	–	–	–	–	–
Employees	–	–	–	–	–	4,100

THE NEW HOME COMPANY INC   NYS: NWHM

85 Enterprise, Suite 450   CEO: H. Lawrence (Larry) Webb
Aliso Viejo, CA 92656   CFO: John M. Stephens
Phone: 949 382-7800   HR: –
Fax: –   FYE: December 31
Web: www.thenewhomecompany.com   Type: Public

The New Home Company (TNHC) is busy building new homes throughout the Golden State. Targeting first-time move-up move-down and luxury home buyers TNHC builds homes under The New Home Company brand name mostly in select growth markets in California (including San Francisco and Sacramento) and in Phoenix Arizona. Its home prices range from $300000 to $5 million and range in size from 800 sq. ft. to 5400 sq. ft. It also builds homes under its brand for third-party property owners. Since its founding in 2009 TNHC has delivered more 1400 homes since its inception via company projects unconsolidated joint ventures and fee building projects. The builder went public in early 2014.

	Annual Growth	12/14	12/15	12/16	12/17	12/18
Sales ($ mil.)	45.3%	149.7	430.1	694.5	751.2	667.6
Net income ($ mil.)	–	4.8	21.7	21.0	17.2	(14.2)
Market value ($ mil.)	(22.5%)	290.5	260.0	234.9	251.3	104.9
Employees	8.3%	234	272	289	281	322

THE NEW JERSEY TRANSIT CORPORATION

1 PENN PLZ E
NEWARK, NJ 071052245
Phone: 973-491-7000
Fax: −
Web: www.njtransit.com

CEO: −
CFO: William Viqueira
HR: −
FYE: June 30
Type: Private

Government-owned New Jersey Transit (NJ TRANSIT) provides bus rail and light rail passenger transportation services. Its systems connect major points in New Jersey and provide links to the neighboring New York City and Philadelphia metropolitan areas. Overall the NJ TRANSIT service area spans about 5325 sq. miles. One of the largest transportation companies of its kind in the US NJ TRANSIT operates a fleet of more than 2000 buses 710 commuter trains and 45 light rail vehicles. Collectively the agency's passengers make more than 220 million trips a year. NJ TRANSIT oversees public transportation programs for the elderly people with disabilities and people in rural areas.

	Annual Growth	06/01	06/02	06/03	06/04	06/18
Sales ($ mil.)	4.2%	−	542.9	569.1	583.3	1,056.3
Net income ($ mil.)	−	−	357.2	482.1	256.9	(67.6)
Market value ($ mil.)	−	−	−	−	−	−
Employees	−	−	−	−	−	1,000

THE NEW LIBERTY HOSPITAL DISTRICT OF CLAY COUNTY MISSOURI

2525 GLENN HENDREN DR
LIBERTY, MO 640689625
Phone: 816-781-7200
Fax: −
Web: www.libertyhospital.org

CEO: −
CFO: −
HR: −
FYE: June 30
Type: Private

New Liberty Hospital District which operates as Liberty Hospital hopes to liberate health care patients in northwestern Missouri. The facility is a 250-bed acute care hospital that serves communities located north of Kansas City. Founded in 1974 Liberty Hospital offers general and specialty health care services including trauma care obstetrics cancer care diagnostics surgical services vascular and cardiac medicine (including open-heart surgery) rehabilitation and pediatrics. The not-for-profit medical facility has more than 300 physicians on staff and also operates a skilled nursing facility and offers home health and hospice services.

	Annual Growth	06/14	06/15	06/16	06/17	06/18
Sales ($ mil.)	2.8%	−	180.9	179.7	185.5	196.3
Net income ($ mil.)	−	−	(2.1)	2.1	(1.8)	(5.9)
Market value ($ mil.)	−	−	−	−	−	−
Employees	−	−	−	−	−	1,700

THE NEW SCHOOL

66 W 12TH ST
NEW YORK, NY 100118871
Phone: 212-229-5600
Fax: −
Web: www.newschool.edu

CEO: −
CFO: −
HR: Irwin Kroot
FYE: June 30
Type: Private

When James Lipton asks you what your favorite swear word is you know you've made it. The New School's drama department (formerly called The Actor's Studio) was made famous by the cable show Inside the Actors Studio which features Lipton interviewing movie and television stars. The school offers degrees in theater for playwriting directing and acting and has taught "Method" acting to grads such as Marlon Brando and Robert De Niro. It is also home to Parsons The New School for Design and has schools devoted to general studies liberal arts social research management and urban policy and music. More than 10500 traditional students and 5600 continuing education students are enrolled at The New School.

	Annual Growth	06/13	06/14	06/15	06/16	06/18
Sales ($ mil.)	5.5%	−	332.8	354.1	370.1	411.6
Net income ($ mil.)	(23.0%)	−	82.4	34.1	(15.1)	28.9
Market value ($ mil.)	−	−	−	−	−	−
Employees	−	−	−	−	−	855

THE NEW YORK AND PRESBYTERIAN HOSPITAL

525 E 68TH ST
NEW YORK, NY 100654870
Phone: 212-746-5454
Fax: −

CEO: Steven J. (Steve) Corwin
CFO: Phyllis R. Lantos
HR: Lorraine Orlando
FYE: December 31
Type: Private

The New York and Presbyterian Hospital is a learned institution: The not-for-profit hospital is affiliated with both the Columbia University College of Physicians & Surgeons and the Weill Cornell Medical College of Cornell University. Known as NewYork-Presbyterian Hospital the organization includes two major medical centers Columbia University Medical Center and Weill Cornell Medical Center which conduct educational and research programs in partnership with the universities. The two facilities combined have about 2600 beds and offer specialized programs for burns digestive diseases pediatrics women's health and other conditions. NewYork-Presbyterian Hospital is part of the NewYork-Presbyterian Healthcare System.

	Annual Growth	12/13	12/14	12/16	12/17	12/18
Sales ($ mil.)	19.2%	−	4,206.2	4,935.4	5,616.5	8,483.9
Net income ($ mil.)	27.8%	−	197.7	496.1	762.7	526.7
Market value ($ mil.)	−	−	−	−	−	−
Employees	−	−	−	−	−	23,709

THE NEW YORK INDEPENDENT SYSTEM OPERATOR INC

10 KREY BLVD
RENSSELAER, NY 121449681
Phone: 518-356-6000
Fax: −
Web: www.nyiso.com

CEO: Bradley R. Jones
CFO: Cheryl Hussey
HR: −
FYE: December 31
Type: Private

Keeping the lights on in Times Square is only part of the job description of the New York Independent System Operator (New York ISO). The company which replaced the New York Power Pool manages and monitors wholesale activities on the state's transmission grid which consists of more than 11000 miles of high-voltage lines. The New York ISO is charged with providing fair access to the state's competitive wholesale power market while ensuring the reliable efficient and safe delivery of power to New York's 19.5 million residents. New York ISO had 37900 MW of generating capacity in 2013. The not-for-profit company is governed by a 10-person board of directors.

	Annual Growth	12/12	12/13	12/14	12/16	12/18
Sales ($ mil.)	1.3%	−	159.8	174.3	169.8	170.4
Net income ($ mil.)	−	−	0.0	0.0	0.0	0.0
Market value ($ mil.)	−	−	−	−	−	−
Employees	−	−	−	−	−	500

THE NEW YORK PUBLIC LIBRARY

5TH AVE & 42ND ST
NEW YORK, NY 10018
Phone: 212-592-7400
Fax: −
Web: www.nypl.org

CEO: −
CFO: −
HR: Louise Shea
FYE: June 30
Type: Private

Q: Where can you learn the names of the marble lions outside New York Public Library's main branch? A: Inside the library where Patience and Fortitude (their names) along with much more information can be found. The library's four research centers and about 90 branches in metropolitan New York contain more material than any other library in the US — about 50 million items. Each year more than 18 million people visit the library's branches which house such treasures as a Gutenberg Bible and a hand-engraved Songs of Innocence . The library was formed by the 1895 consolidation of the Astor Library the Lenox Library and the Tilden Trust and by a merger with the New York Free Circulating Library in 1901.

	Annual Growth	06/07	06/08	06/09	06/16	06/17
Sales ($ mil.)	(0.8%)	−	−	362.9	300.5	341.0
Net income ($ mil.)	−	−	−	(166.3)	(93.1)	25.0
Market value ($ mil.)	−	−	−	−	−	−
Employees	−	−	−	−	−	3,645

THE NEWARK GROUP INC.

20 Jackson Dr.
Cranford NJ 07016
Phone: 908-276-4000
Fax: 908-276-2888
Web: www.newarkgroup.com

CEO: –
CFO: –
HR: –
FYE: April 30
Type: Private

Newark is proof that one man's trash is another's cash. Through several segments the company collects secondary fibers and produces 100% recycled paperboard and paperboard products. Its Recovery and Recycling segment collects and recovers the recycled raw materials while Paperboard Mills produces more than 500000 tons of recycled paper annually. Its Paperboard Products segment makes roll finishing materials such as cores tubes spools and roll headers and Newark BCI / Graphic Board caters to the coverboard puzzle and game markets. Solidboard Products makes packaging for produce and other food goods. Newark serves the paper and packaging printing recycling and construction industries.

THE NPD GROUP INC.

900 West Shore Rd.
Port Washington NY 11050
Phone: 516-625-0700
Fax: 516-625-2347
Web: www.npd.com

CEO: Karyn Schoenbart
CFO: Tom Lynch
HR: –
FYE: September 30
Type: Private

The NPD Group helps its more than 2000 clients fatten their coffers by giving them the skinny on consumer behavior. A global market research firm the company offers retail sales tracking services partnering with some 900 retailers representing 150000 stores worldwide. It tracks consumer buying behavior through an online panel consisting of nearly 2 million consumers. It offers market insight across numerous industries including apparel consumer electronics foodservice music and software and its DisplaySearch business offers market research analysis specializing in the flat-panel display industry. Controlled by CEO Tod Johnson NPD Group operates through offices in nearly 30 cities around the world.

THE NEWTRON GROUP L L C

8183 W EL CAJON DR
BATON ROUGE, LA 708158093
Phone: 225-927-8921
Fax: –
Web: www.thenewtrongroup.com

CEO: Newton B Thomas
CFO: Tami H Misuraca
HR: –
FYE: June 30
Type: Private

Some contractors bomb but The Newtron Group keeps on ticking. Through subsidiaries The Newtron Group offers a variety of industrial electrical and other specialty construction and contracting services nationwide. Services include instrumentation and control systems installation and maintenance; fiber optic installation and testing; industrial pipe and panel fabrication; aviation services; and electrical heat tracing. Newtron serves clients in such industries as refining power generation mining petrochemical and gas transmission. Subsidiaries include electrical contractor Triad Electric & Controls fiber optics firm Com-Net Services and NGI National Constructors. Founded in 1973 The Newtron Group serves the US from offices in California Louisiana Mississippi and Texas.

	Annual Growth	06/14	06/15	06/16	06/17	06/18
Sales ($ mil.)	4.4%	–	430.4	436.3	450.0	489.9
Net income ($ mil.)	–	–	0.0	0.0	0.0	0.0
Market value ($ mil.)	–	–	–	–	–	–
Employees	–	–	–	–	–	3,500

THE OLTMANS CONSTRUCTION CO

10005 MISSION MILL RD
WHITTIER, CA 906011739
Phone: 562-948-4242
Fax: –
Web: www.oltmans.com

CEO: Joseph O Oltmans II
CFO: Dan Schlothan
HR: –
FYE: March 31
Type: Private

With projects ranging from the California Speedway to a distribution/warehouse building for TV retail giant HSN Oltmans Construction has done it all. The group offers preconstruction general contracting and design/build project delivery construction management tenant improvements and seismic retrofits among its services for commercial and industrial buildings throughout California Nevada and Arizona. The company also completes its own concrete work. Oltmans is one of the top general contractors in its home state as well as one of the top builders of distribution facilities in the US. The company was founded in 1932 and has been led by three generations of the Oltmans family.

	Annual Growth	03/04	03/05	03/06	03/07	03/08
Sales ($ mil.)	10.4%	–	242.8	317.3	315.5	326.3
Net income ($ mil.)	–	–	(0.2)	3.5	4.2	5.1
Market value ($ mil.)	–	–	–	–	–	–
Employees	–	–	–	–	–	535

THE NORTH HIGHLAND COMPANY LLC

3333 PIEDMONT RD NE # 1000
ATLANTA, GA 303051843
Phone: 404-233-1015
Fax: –
Web: www.northhighland.com

CEO: Daniel (Dan) Reardon
CFO: Beth Schiavo
HR: –
FYE: December 31
Type: Private

The North Highland Company provides consulting services for business clients seeking to improve operations. The employee-owned company provides management and technology consulting services through more than 900 professionals working out of 23 offices in 10 US states. Its services cover areas such as business strategy supply chain management marketing and customer service business process improvement and technology management. The company's partners include Big Insight Sourcing Group The Difference and True Bridge Resources.

	Annual Growth	12/02	12/03	12/04	12/05	12/08
Sales ($ mil.)	30.2%	–	–	59.5	87.3	170.9
Net income ($ mil.)	(38.8%)	–	–	57.4	2.3	8.0
Market value ($ mil.)	–	–	–	–	–	–
Employees	–	–	–	–	–	2,300

THE PARADIES SHOPS LLC

2849 PACES FERRY RD SE
ATLANTA, GA 303396201
Phone: 404-344-7905
Fax: –
Web: www.paradieslagardere.com

CEO: Gregg Paradies
CFO: Kevin Smith
HR: Nikki Harland
FYE: June 30
Type: Private

For the frequent flyer this is retail paradise. The Paradies Shops operates 550-plus shops in more than 75 airports hotels and aquariums throughout the US and Canada. It serves more than half a billion passengers annually with retail sites that include bookstores gift shops jewelry stores ladies accessory shops newsstands sunglass stores and western stores among others. Paradies Shops is also the exclusive licensee of Brooks Brothers CNBC PGA Tour and the New York Times. The firm operates several hotel properties and the retail program for the Georgia Aquarium in Atlanta. The company was founded by the Paradies family in 1960. In 2010 it sold a majority stake to Freeman Spogli & Co.

	Annual Growth	06/00	06/01	06/02	06/03	06/07
Sales ($ mil.)	10.8%	–	–	223.1	248.0	372.7
Net income ($ mil.)	–	–	–	0.0	0.0	13.7
Market value ($ mil.)	–	–	–	–	–	–
Employees	–	–	–	–	–	4,000

THE PARSONS CORPORATION

5875 TRINITY PKWY STE 300
CENTREVILLE, VA 201201971
Phone: 703-988-8500
Fax: –
Web: www.parsons.com

CEO: Charles L. (Chuck) Harrington
CFO: George L. Ball
HR: –
FYE: December 31
Type: Private

Industrial construction giant Parsons provides engineering construction and other services for corporate institutional and government projects worldwide. The company designs and builds structures such as power plants and dams; provides environmental remediation services including hazardous materials cleanup; and adds improvements to airports rail systems bridges and highways. Parsons has constructed over 10000 miles of roadways worked on more than 4500 bridges assisted on 400 airport projects and destroyed 5100 tons of chemical weapons agents. The employee-owned group was founded in 1944.

	Annual Growth	12/12	12/13	12/14	12/15	12/18
Sales ($ mil.)	61.4%	–	–	–	846.8	3,560.5
Net income ($ mil.)	102.7%	–	–	–	28.8	239.4
Market value ($ mil.)	–	–	–	–	–	–
Employees	–	–	–	–	–	15,633

THE PENN MUTUAL LIFE INSURANCE COMPANY

600 Dresher Rd.
Horsham PA 19044
Phone: 215-956-8000
Fax: 215-956-7699
Web: www.pennmutual.com

CEO: Robert E Chappel
CFO: Susan T Deakins
HR: –
FYE: December 31
Type: Private - Mutual Com

Founded in 1847 Penn Mutual Life Insurance offers life insurance annuities and investment products and services. Its core product line consists of life insurance every which way including traditional life insurance products (term life whole and universal life) and a variety of fixed variable and immediate annuities. The company sells its products throughout the US through several channels using both independent and captive agents as well as brokers. Two of its financial services subsidiaries — broker/dealer Hornor Townsend & Kent and Janney Montgomery Scott — also distribute Penn Mutual products.

THE PENNSYLVANIA HOSPITAL OF THE UNIVERSITY OF PENNSYLVANIA HEALTH SYSTEM

800 SPRUCE ST
PHILADELPHIA, PA 191076130
Phone: 215-829-3000
Fax: –
Web: www.pennmedicine.org

CEO: –
CFO: –
HR: –
FYE: June 30
Type: Private

Early to bed early to rise may have made Ben Franklin healthy wealthy and wise. But for those not so healthy he (along with Dr. Thomas Bond) found it wise to establish Pennsylvania Hospital the nation's first such medical institution. The hospital is now a part of the University of Pennsylvania Health System (UPHS) and offers a comprehensive range of medical surgical and diagnostic services to the Philadelphia County area. Housing some 520 beds Pennsylvania Hospital offers specialized care in areas such as orthopedics vascular surgery neurosurgery and obstetrics; it is also a leading teaching hospital and a center for clinical research.

	Annual Growth	06/08	06/09	06/10	06/14	06/15
Sales ($ mil.)	4.2%	–	454.0	485.5	534.4	579.8
Net income ($ mil.)	–	–	0.0	27.5	(2.3)	21.7
Market value ($ mil.)	–	–	–	–	–	–
Employees	–	–	–	–	–	2,200

THE PENNSYLVANIA LOTTERY

1200 Fulling Mill Rd. Ste. 1
Middletown PA 17057
Phone: 717-702-8000
Fax: 717-702-8024
Web: www.palottery.state.pa.us

CEO: –
CFO: –
HR: –
FYE: June 30
Type: Government-owned

Even if they don't become millionaires senior citizens in Pennsylvania can still benefit from the state lottery. Established in 1971 Pennsylvania Lottery proceeds (more than $18 billion raised since inception) are dedicated to programs geared toward seniors (property-tax relief rent rebates reduced-cost transportation co-pay prescriptions). Proceeds also fund more than 50 Area Agencies on Aging across Pennsylvania. State law mandates that at least 40% of lottery proceeds must be awarded in prizes and about 30% must be used for benefit programs. Games range from the traditional Powerball to daily-wagering game Big 4.

THE PENNSYLVANIA STATE UNIVERSITY

201 OLD MAIN
UNIVERSITY PARK, PA 168021503
Phone: 814-865-4700
Fax: –

CEO: –
CFO: –
HR: –
FYE: June 30
Type: Private

The Pennsylvania State University system is one of the largest state university systems in the US. Penn State has an enrollment of 100000 students; 15000 of them are graduate students. It offers 275 undergraduate and 200 graduate programs at about 25 campuses. The school's oldest and largest campus with about half of the system's undergraduate students is at University Park in central Pennsylvania. Other sites include the Penn State College of Medicine in Hershey Pennsylvania and the Dickinson School of Law in Carlisle Pennsylvania. Penn State contributes about $11.6 billion to the state's economy.

	Annual Growth	06/14	06/15	06/16	06/17	06/18
Sales ($ mil.)	6.3%	–	5,293.4	5,764.8	6,059.1	6,363.7
Net income ($ mil.)	55.1%	–	290.0	233.4	635.6	1,081.9
Market value ($ mil.)	–	–	–	–	–	–
Employees	–	–	–	–	–	44,000

THE PEW CHARITABLE TRUSTS

2005 MARKET ST FL 28
PHILADELPHIA, PA 191037019
Phone: 215-575-9050
Fax: –
Web: www.pewtrusts.org

CEO: –
CFO: Linda Bartlett
HR: Elaine Bowman
FYE: June 30
Type: Private

Green is the grease The Pew Charitable Trusts uses to help not-for-profits run smoothly. Among the nation's largest private foundations it was established in 1948 in memory of Sun Oil founder Joseph Pew and his wife Mary by four of their children. Seven trusts were created between 1948 and 1979 to promote public health and welfare and to strengthen communities. With more than $5 billion in assets it distributes more than $100 million in grants annually to charitable organizations in culture education environment health and human services public policy and religion. The Pew Trusts has strong ties to Philadelphia and allocates a portion of its grants to programs in that area.

	Annual Growth	06/13	06/14	06/15	06/16	06/17
Sales ($ mil.)	78.4%	–	–	–	397.1	708.5
Net income ($ mil.)	426.3%	–	–	–	77.5	407.8
Market value ($ mil.)	–	–	–	–	–	–
Employees	–	–	–	–	–	1,100

THE PHILADELPHIA PARKING AUTHORITY

701 MARKET ST STE 5400
PHILADELPHIA, PA 191062895
Phone: 215-222-0224
Fax: –
Web: www.philapark.org

CEO: Vincent J Fenerty Jr
CFO: Barry Kavtsty
HR: Carmen Jenkins
FYE: March 31
Type: Private

If you're driving into the City of Brotherly Love steer clear of getting a parking ticket because then you'll have to face the Philadelphia Parking Authority. The agency oversees 14500 on-street metered parking spaces and 17000 off-street facilities such as lots and garages throughout the city including parking spaces at Philadelphia International Airport. In addition to collecting revenue the agency enforces parking regulations by issuing tickets and when necessary disabling or towing and impounding vehicles. It also regulates taxi and limousine services and the 10 red light cameras operating within the city. The Philadelphia Parking Authority was created in 1950.

	Annual Growth	03/03	03/04*	12/08*	03/10	03/17
Sales ($ mil.)	–	–	0.0	201.6	213.0	259.5
Net income ($ mil.)	–	–	0.0	13.8	10.3	8.4
Market value ($ mil.)	–	–	–	–	–	–
Employees	–	–	–	–	–	1,100

*Fiscal year change

THE PHILHARMONIC-SYMPHONY SOCIETY OF NEW YORK INC

10 LINCOLN CENTER PLZ
NEW YORK, NY 100236912
Phone: 212-875-5900
Fax: –
Web: www.nyphil.org

CEO: Zarin Mehta
CFO: –
HR: –
FYE: August 31
Type: Private

The New York Philharmonic fills up music halls with musical harmony. In addition to the music of Beethoven and Tchaikovsky over the years the orchestra has performed the works of numerous other classical composers along with specially commissioned new music. It presents some 180 concerts annually. The New York Philharmonic's musical director Alan Gilbert is the son of two of the orchestra's violinists and the second-youngest person to hold the position in its history. The New York Philharmonic was founded in 1842 and is the oldest orchestra in the US.

	Annual Growth	12/07	12/08*	08/09	08/10	08/14
Sales ($ mil.)	–	–	0.0	48.1	60.4	70.1
Net income ($ mil.)	–	–	0.0	(18.6)	(16.9)	(3.2)
Market value ($ mil.)	–	–	–	–	–	–
Employees	–	–	–	–	–	200

*Fiscal year change

THE PICTSWEET COMPANY

10 Pictsweet Dr.
Bells TN 38006
Phone: 731-422-7600
Fax: 800-561-8810
Web: www.pictsweet.com

CEO: Wesley F Eubanks
CFO: Lissa Mullins
HR: –
FYE: February 28
Type: Private

The Pictsweet Company is a veritable veggie volcano. It grows asparagus corn okra and loads of other vegetables and then quick-freezes them for sale in supermarkets. The firm offers more than 100 products (including stir-fry blends and baby and pre-seasoned vegetables) in family-sized regular and bulk portions. Pictsweet provides vegetables nationwide under its own name and for retailers' private labels (including Kroger and Wal-Mart's Great Value brands). It also supplies foodservice operators (restaurants and hotels) and institutional customers (such as hospitals and schools); Pictsweet sells its vegetables through military commissaries worldwide.

THE PLAZA GROUP INC

1177 WEST LOOP S STE 1450
HOUSTON, TX 770279020
Phone: 713-266-0707
Fax: –
Web: www.theplazagrp.com

CEO: –
CFO: –
HR: –
FYE: September 25
Type: Private

The Plaza Group (TPG) is an international distributor of petrochemical solvents and chemical intermediates. Established in 1994 TPG is the exclusive marketer of some products from companies such as Shell Oil and Frontier Oil . The company markets to FORTUNE 500 companies major international enterprises direct consumers and chemical distributors. Its products are used in the production of resins coatings and adhesives. TPG partners with global suppliers (like SABIC Innovative Plastics Total Petrochemicals and Alon) in Asia Australia Europe and the Americas. The company is owned by president Randy Velarde.

	Annual Growth	12/09	12/10	12/11	12/12*	09/17
Sales ($ mil.)	–	–	(51.6)	271.6	288.4	105.5
Net income ($ mil.)	–	–	0.0	4.4	3.5	0.8
Market value ($ mil.)	–	–	–	–	–	–
Employees	–	–	–	–	–	32

*Fiscal year change

THE PMI GROUP INC.

NYSE: PMI

3003 Oak Rd.
Walnut Creek CA 94597-2098
Phone: 925-658-7878
Fax: 925-658-6931
Web: www.pmigroup.com

CEO: L Stephen Smith
CFO: –
HR: –
FYE: December 31
Type: Public

If Barbie couldn't afford a full 20% down payment on her Malibu dream home her mortgage lender might have brought in The PMI Group. The company was one of the largest US providers of mortgage insurance which protects lenders in case of borrower default. It also insured the bundles of existing loans known as structured finance products. In addition PMI was the primary investor in the Financial Guaranty Insurance Company which offered financial guaranty insurance on public bonds. The company's international operations provided mortgage insurance and credit enhancement services in Europe. Despite attempts to survive the real estate-market implosion the company filed Chapter 11 bankruptcy protection in 2011.

THE PORT AUTHORITY OF NEW YORK & NEW JERSEY

4 WORLD TRADE CTR 150
NEW YORK, NY 100072366
Phone: 212-435-7000
Fax: –
Web: www.panynj.gov

CEO: –
CFO: Elizabeth McCarthy
HR: –
FYE: December 31
Type: Private

The Port Authority of New York and New Jersey bridges the sometimes troubled waters between the two states and helps with many of the region's other transportation needs. The bi-state agency operates and maintains airports tunnels bridges a commuter rail system shipping terminals and other facilities within the 1500-sq.-mi. Port District surrounding New York Harbor including the World Trade Center site in Lower Manhattan. A self-supporting public agency the Port Authority receives no state or local tax money. It relies on tolls fees and rents. Airport operations account for the majority of its revenue. The two governors each appoint six of the 12 members of the agency's board and review its decisions.

	Annual Growth	12/07	12/08	12/09	12/10	12/15
Sales ($ mil.)	5.2%	–	–	3,552.2	3,634.0	4,826.6
Net income ($ mil.)	(1.4%)	–	–	846.4	346.8	779.8
Market value ($ mil.)	–	–	–	–	–	–
Employees	–	–	–	–	–	7,128

THE PRESIDENT AND TRUSTEES OF COLBY COLLEGE

4120 MAYFLOWER HL
WATERVILLE, ME 049018841
Phone: 207-859-4000
Fax: –
Web: www.colby.edu

CEO: –
CFO: –
HR: –
FYE: June 30
Type: Private

Colby College is one of the nation's oldest liberal arts colleges. The school was founded in 1813 as the Maine Literary and Theological Institution and in 1871 it became the first previously all-male college in New England to admit women. Colby College offers 500 courses 55 majors 30-plus minors and independent major options. Its two dozen academic departments and nearly 10 interdisciplinary programs serve an enrollment of approximately 1800 students. Popular majors are biology economics English government history and international studies. Besides being one of the nation's oldest Colby College is one of the most pricey: Annual tuition room and board and fees total more than $46000.

	Annual Growth	06/13	06/14	06/16	06/17	06/18
Sales ($ mil.)	5.0%	–	120.7	140.0	146.5	146.5
Net income ($ mil.)	2.2%	–	120.7	(32.5)	131.8	131.8
Market value ($ mil.)	–	–	–	–	–	–
Employees	–	–	–	–	–	844

THE PRESIDENT AND TRUSTEES OF HAMPDEN-SYDNEY COLLEGE

1 COLLEGE RD
FARMVILLE, VA 239015657
Phone: 434-223-6216
Fax: –
Web: www.hsc.edu

CEO: –
CFO: –
HR: –
FYE: June 30
Type: Private

Hampden-Sydney: Where men are men and women are guests. Hampden-Sydney College is a private four-year liberal arts college for men with a student population of more than 1000. The college offers undergraduate degrees in about 30 fields and is affiliated with the Presbyterian Church. Its campus is about 60 miles southwest of Richmond Virginia. Hampden-Sydney College was founded in 1775 and although the school is not co-educational its location places it in an area with 15 colleges and universities including four women's colleges — providing ample opportunities to interact with the opposite sex.

	Annual Growth	06/13	06/14	06/15	06/16	06/18
Sales ($ mil.)	0.9%	–	66.9	58.1	35.7	69.4
Net income ($ mil.)	(2.0%)	–	20.6	10.3	(13.3)	19.0
Market value ($ mil.)	–	–	–	–	–	–
Employees	–	–	–	–	–	350

THE QUIZNOS MASTER LLC

1001 17th St. Ste. 200
Denver CO 80202
Phone: 720-359-3300
Fax: 720-359-3399
Web: www.quiznos.com

CEO: –
CFO: –
HR: –
FYE: September 30
Type: Private

Quiznos wants to be the toast of the sandwich world. The Quiznos Master operates the #2 sub sandwich chain (behind Subway). Quiznos quick-service restaurants are popular for their made-to-order oven-toasted sandwiches. Patrons can choose from a variety of signature or custom-made subs wraps salads sub sliders and flatbreads. The company has locations in all 50 states and more than 25 countries. Quiznos started getting toasty in 1981 as a single Denver area restaurant. Avenue Capital Group became majority owners in early 2012 after a debt-for-equity deal.

THE READER'S DIGEST ASSOCIATION INC.

750 3rd Ave.
New York NY 10017
Phone: 914-238-1000
Fax: 609-261-4853
Web: www.pariscorp.com

CEO: Bonnie Kintzer
CFO: Howard Halligan
HR: –
FYE: December 31
Type: Private

The Reader's Digest Association (RDA) publishes the undersized general-interest magazine Reader's Digest which boasts 50 editions and is translated into some 20 languages. In addition to publishing its flagship title RDA operates about 80 branded websites. It leverages its extensive consumer database of more than 140 million names to market books (such as Reader's Digest Select Editions how-to guides and cookbooks) special-interest magazines music videos and financial and health products in nearly 80 countries. Suffering from a heavy debt-load amid a down economy RDA filed Chapter 11 for its US businesses which emerged from bankruptcy in 2010. It is owned by RDA Holding Co.

THE REED INSTITUTE

3203 SE WOODSTOCK BLVD
PORTLAND, OR 972028138
Phone: 503-771-1112
Fax: –
Web: www.reed.edu

CEO: –
CFO: –
HR: Diane Gumz
FYE: June 30
Type: Private

Reed College offers bachelor's degrees in nearly 30 fields and a master of arts degree in liberal studies. Its special master's degree allows students to study both liberal arts and the sciences. Each year the school enrolls more than 1400 students who become known as "Reedies." Additionally it boasts an average of 17 students in its conference-style classes and a student-to-faculty ratio of 10 to 1. Reed College which has produced more than 30 Rhodes Scholars also houses a nuclear reactor that is operated primarily by undergraduates. Founded in 1908 Reed College is named for Oregon pioneers Simeon and Amanda Reed.

	Annual Growth	06/14	06/15	06/16	06/17	06/18
Sales ($ mil.)	8.1%	–	89.2	55.0	100.0	112.6
Net income ($ mil.)	217.4%	–	1.2	(39.1)	43.7	37.0
Market value ($ mil.)	–	–	–	–	–	–
Employees	–	–	–	–	–	400

THE REGENTS OF THE UNIVERSITY OF COLORADO

3100 MARINE ST STE 48157
BOULDER, CO 803031058
Phone: 303-735-6624
Fax: –

CEO: –
CFO: –
HR: –
FYE: June 30
Type: Private

The University of Colorado System spans four campuses and some 60000 students. The Boulder campus home to about 30000 students provides more than 2500 courses in 150-plus fields through nine colleges and schools. The University of Colorado at Denver has an enrollment of more than 14000 and has 120 study programs at a dozen schools and its nearby Anschutz Medical Campus serves more than 500000 patients annually. The smallest campus University of Colorado at Colorado Springs has six colleges with about 10000 students and offers nearly 60 undergraduate graduate and doctoral degree programs. The system which began in Boulder as the University of Colorado in 1876 boasts more than 4000 faculty members.

	Annual Growth	06/09	06/10	06/16	06/17	06/18
Sales ($ mil.)	6.8%	–	2,261.4	3,451.1	3,728.5	3,833.9
Net income ($ mil.)	–	–	337.4	73.0	77.2	(197.3)
Market value ($ mil.)	–	–	–	–	–	–
Employees	–	–	–	–	–	12,980

THE RENCO GROUP INC.

1 Rockefeller Plaza 29th Fl.
New York NY 10112
Phone: 212-541-6000
Fax: 212-541-6197
Web: www.rencogroup.net

CEO: Ira Leon Rennert
CFO: –
HR: –
FYE: October 31
Type: Private

Renco Group is a holding company for a diverse group of businesses. Its AM General subsidiary (a joint venture with Ronald Perelman's MacAndrews & Forbes Holdings) makes the HUMVEE an extra-wide all-terrain vehicle used by the military. Other Renco Group companies include Doe Run which is engaged in metals mining smelting recycling and fabrication; Unarco Material Handling which makes pallet racks and systems for warehouses; Inteva Products which manufactures systems for the automotive industry; and US Magnesium the largest primary magnesium producer in North America. Renco Group is owned by billionaire Ira Rennert.

THE RESEARCH FOUNDATION FOR THE STATE UNIVERSITY OF NEW YORK

35 STATE ST
ALBANY, NY 122072826
Phone: 518-434-7000
Fax: –

CEO: –
CFO: –
HR: Christy Spadaro
FYE: June 30
Type: Private

The Research Foundation of State University of New York (The Research Foundation) collects and administers research and education grants from state and federal governments corporations and foundations on behalf of the 24-campus State University of New York known as SUNY. The foundation has formed several affiliated divisions — including Long Island High Technology Incubator and NanoTech Resources — to operate research facilities encourage scientific collaboration and otherwise facilitate research for the university. It facilitates research for studies such as engineering and nanotechnology; physical sciences and medicine; life sciences and medicine; social sciences; and computer and information sciences.

	Annual Growth	06/07	06/08	06/09	06/12	06/13
Sales ($ mil.)	2.3%	–	–	985.5	1,114.7	1,079.5
Net income ($ mil.)	–	–	–	(71.5)	13.0	42.5
Market value ($ mil.)	–	–	–	–	–	–
Employees	–	–	–	–	–	16,330

THE ROCKEFELLER FOUNDATION

420 5TH AVE FL 22
NEW YORK, NY 100182711
Phone: 212-869-8500
Fax: –
Web: www.rockefellerfoundation.org

CEO: –
CFO: –
HR: –
FYE: December 31
Type: Private

The Rockefeller Foundation established in 1913 is one of the oldest private charitable organizations in the US. It supports grants fellowships and conferences for programs that concentrate on identifying and alleviating need and suffering worldwide. These programs (or themes) include initiatives to foster fair implementation of health care job opportunities for America's urban poor creative expression through the humanities and arts and agricultural policies that ensure food distribution to people in developing countries. An additional theme — global inclusion — serves as a connection between the foundation's other programs and as a way to ensure that poor people benefit from global trade increases.

	Annual Growth	12/04	12/05	12/09	12/14	12/16
Sales ($ mil.)	(12.8%)	–	343.8	34.0	401.8	75.8
Net income ($ mil.)	–	–	188.7	(150.5)	223.6	(164.9)
Market value ($ mil.)	–	–	–	–	–	–
Employees	–	–	–	–	–	150

THE ROCKEFELLER UNIVERSITY

1230 YORK AVE
NEW YORK, NY 10065-6399
Phone: 212-327-8078
Fax: –
Web: www.rockefeller.edu

CEO: –
CFO: James H Lapple
HR: –
FYE: June 30
Type: Private

Rockefeller University sniffs out solid scientific evidence. The university is a leading US research institution and scientific graduate school providing training in biomedical and physical science fields such as biochemistry structural biology immunology neuroscience and human genetics. The university is centered around more than 70 research laboratories and a hospital and it runs M.D.-Ph.D. programs in conjunction with the Memorial Sloan-Kettering Cancer Center and the Weill Medical College at Cornell University. Rockefeller University's research is funded by entities such as the National Institutes of Health and the Howard Hughes Medical Institute as well as private gifts and endowments.

	Annual Growth	06/03	06/04	06/05	06/06	06/11
Sales ($ mil.)	5.8%	–	285.9	413.7	413.7	424.8
Net income ($ mil.)	8.4%	–	61.2	271.1	271.1	107.9
Market value ($ mil.)	–	–	–	–	–	–
Employees	–	–	–	–	–	1,700

THE ROCKEFELLER UNIVERSITY FACULTY AND STUDENTS CLUB INC

1230 YORK AVE
NEW YORK, NY 100656307
Phone: 212-327-8078
Fax: –
Web: www.rucares.org

CEO: –
CFO: James H Lapple
HR: –
FYE: June 30
Type: Private

Rockefeller University sniffs out solid scientific evidence. The university is a leading US research institution and scientific graduate school providing training in biomedical and physical science fields such as biochemistry structural biology immunology neuroscience and human genetics. The university is centered around 76 research laboratories and a hospital and it runs M.D.-Ph.D. programs in conjunction with the Memorial Sloan-Kettering Cancer Center and the Weill Medical College at Cornell University. Rockefeller University's research is funded by entities such as the National Institutes of Health and the Howard Hughes Medical Institute as well as private gifts and endowments.

	Annual Growth	06/03	06/04	06/05	06/06	06/13
Sales ($ mil.)	1.5%	–	–	413.7	413.7	466.2
Net income ($ mil.)	(6.5%)	–	–	271.1	271.1	159.0
Market value ($ mil.)	–	–	–	–	–	–
Employees	–	–	–	–	–	1,700

THE RUDOLPH/LIBBE COMPANIES INC

6494 LATCHA RD
WALBRIDGE, OH 434659788
Phone: 419-241-5000
Fax: –
Web: www.rlgbuilds.com

CEO: –
CFO: Robert Pruger
HR: –
FYE: December 31
Type: Private

The corporate model of a conglomerate composed of independent unrelated businesses is not for The Rudolph/Libbe Companies. The group of companies can build or oversee real estate projects (general contractor Rudolph/Libbe Inc.); perform mechanical electrical and structural work (GEM Industrial); and then represent those properties in the market (RLWest Properties). Operating in the Ohio/Michigan corridor the group provides site selection design/build and construction management. Its portfolio includes industrial retail municipal residential educational health care and mixed-use projects. Fritz and Phil Rudolph and their cousin Allan Libbe founded flagship subsidiary Rudolph/Libbe Inc. in 1955.

	Annual Growth	12/14	12/15	12/16	12/17	12/18
Sales ($ mil.)	10.5%	–	425.4	502.7	567.8	573.4
Net income ($ mil.)	(0.2%)	–	16.2	24.0	20.1	16.2
Market value ($ mil.)	–	–	–	–	–	–
Employees	–	–	–	–	–	600

THE RUTLAND HOSPITAL INC ACT 220

160 ALLEN ST
RUTLAND, VT 057014595
Phone: 802-775-7111
Fax: -
Web: www.rrmccareers.org

CEO: Tom Huebner
CFO: Edward Ogorzalek
HR: Ashley Markie
FYE: September 30
Type: Private

For those seeking health care in the New England region Rutland Regional Medical Center (RRMC) just might be the destination for you. Part of Rutland Regional Health Services it runs a hospital that boasts more than 120 beds and serves patients in Vermont and eastern New York. RRMC offers about 40 medical specialties including cancer care diabetes treatment and total joint replacement. The acute-care facility also has centers dedicated to cardiac rehabilitation and women's health. To meet growing community medical needs RRMC also operates a prostate care unit and a 30-bed psychiatric unit. Along with a range of specialty care options RRMC administers primary care and emergency medical transport.

	Annual Growth	09/13	09/14	09/15	09/16	09/17
Sales ($ mil.)	(7.2%)	-	-	281.1	245.8	242.2
Net income ($ mil.)	(68.8%)	-	-	42.4	10.8	4.1
Market value ($ mil.)	-	-	-	-	-	-
Employees	-	-	-	-	-	1,350

THE SALVATION ARMY NATIONAL CORPORATION

615 SLATERS LN
ALEXANDRIA, VA 223141112
Phone: 703-684-5500
Fax: -
Web: www.salvationarmyusa.org

CEO: -
CFO: -
HR: -
FYE: September 30
Type: Private

Battling to provide social services The Salvation Army is one of the world's largest faith-based charities with some 3550 officers and 3.3 million volunteers. Its Christian faith-based programs assist alcoholics drug addicts the homeless the elderly prison inmates people in crisis and the jobless through offerings such as community centers housing facilities and rehabilitation centers. The organization also provides disaster-relief services and operates more than 1300 thrift stores. Overall it serves nearly 30 million people and 58 million meals a year. The US organization is a unit of the London-based Salvation Army which oversees activities in more than 100 countries. US operations began in 1880.

	Annual Growth	09/08	09/09	09/10	09/12	09/13
Sales ($ mil.)	229.0%	-	36.8	3.7	42.1	4,315.6
Net income ($ mil.)	1394.9%	-	-	0.4	2.4	1,349.5
Market value ($ mil.)	-	-	-	-	-	-
Employees	-	-	-	-	-	60,000

THE SAVANNAH COLLEGE OF ART AND DESIGN INC

126 E GASTON ST
SAVANNAH, GA 314015604
Phone: 912-525-5000
Fax: -
Web: www.shopscad.com

CEO: -
CFO: Joseph P Manory
HR: -
FYE: June 30
Type: Private

With more than 12000 students Savannah College of Art and Design (SCAD) in Georgia is a private nonprofit accredited university with students from across the US and more than 100 countries. It has undergraduate degrees in arts and fine arts as well as master's degrees in a range of subjects. The institution offers courses of study in 40-plus majors including fields such as architecture interior and graphic design fashion film and television painting dance and art history. The school also offers certificates in digital publishing digital publishing management historic preservation interactive design and typeface design and more than 60 other minors.

	Annual Growth	06/06	06/07	06/08	06/09	06/10
Sales ($ mil.)	-	-	-	0.0	283.0	314.1
Net income ($ mil.)	32707.6%	-	-	0.0	21.8	10.0
Market value ($ mil.)	-	-	-	-	-	-
Employees	-	-	-	-	-	1,200

THE SCHWAN FOOD COMPANY

115 W. College Dr.
Marshall MN 56258
Phone: 507-532-3274
Fax: 402-342-5568
Web: www.scoular.com

CEO: Dimitrios Smyrnios
CFO: Irobin Galloway
HR: -
FYE: December 31
Type: Private

Pizza rounds out business at The Schwan Food Company. With well-known retail pizza brands like Tony's Red Baron and Freschetta the company is one of the top frozen pizza makers in the US alongside rival Nestle. But pizza isn't the only product that provides it with dough. Schwan's core business involves a fleet of 5700 Home Service trucks that deliver 350 frozen food products directly to the doorsteps of some 2.5 million customers. Home Service provides entrees breakfasts sandwiches side dishes snacks ice cream and more to homes and by mail order throughout the US mainland. Besides the US market Schwan sells food in Western Europe. The family of the late founder Marvin Schwan owns the company.

THE SCOULAR COMPANY

2027 DODGE ST STE 200
OMAHA, NE 681021229
Phone: 402-342-3500
Fax: -
Web: www.scoular.com

CEO: Paul T. Maass
CFO: Richard A. (Rick) Cogdill
HR: -
FYE: May 31
Type: Private

The Scoular Company doesn't move food from farm to table but it does handle a good portion of the trip. The company buys sells stores handles and transports agricultural products (mainly grains) worldwide. It gets the mainstays of farming — corn millet sorghum soybeans and wheat — where they need to go. The company transports these products via rail truck barge and seagoing container vessels. Scoular's other divisions offer fishmeal products for farm-animal pet and aquaculture feeds; ingredients for food manufacturers; and renewable fuels as well as a host of risk management logistics and product-related services. It has customers worldwide.

	Annual Growth	05/14	05/15	05/16	05/17	05/18
Sales ($ mil.)	167.3%	-	234.9	4,667.8	4,366.7	4,486.1
Net income ($ mil.)	17.1%	-	14.2	(10.2)	25.2	22.8
Market value ($ mil.)	-	-	-	-	-	-
Employees	-	-	-	-	-	801

THE SCRIPPS RESEARCH INSTITUTE

10550 N TORREY PINES RD
LA JOLLA, CA 920371000
Phone: 858-784-1000
Fax: -
Web: www.scripps.edu

CEO: Peter G Schultz
CFO: Cary E Thomas
HR: -
FYE: September 30
Type: Private

The Scripps Research Institute (TSRI) is a not-for-profit organization that performs basic biomedical research in molecular and cellular biology chemistry immunology neuroscience disease and vaccine development. TSRI receives the majority of its funding from federal agencies such as the National Institutes of Health. TRSI opened a second facility in Florida in 2009. Its staff includes more than 2900 scientists and lab technicians and the organization traces its history back to 1924 when philanthropist Ellen Browning Scripps founded Scripps Metabolic Clinic.

	Annual Growth	09/04	09/05	09/08	09/09	09/16
Sales ($ mil.)	(1.0%)	-	387.8	464.0	375.5	348.6
Net income ($ mil.)	-	-	63.4	137.9	(18.8)	(16.1)
Market value ($ mil.)	-	-	-	-	-	-
Employees	-	-	-	-	-	209

THE SEMINOLE TRIBE OF FLORIDA INC.

6300 Stirling Rd.
Hollywood FL 33024
Phone: 954-966-6300
Fax: 954-967-3477
Web: www.seminoletribe.com

CEO: -
CFO: Suresh Geer
HR: -
FYE: September 30
Type: Private

This tribe knows how to rock. The Seminole Tribe of Florida owns Hard Rock Cafe International which includes a chain of more than 160 Hard Rock Cafes in some 45 countries. In addition to the Hard Rock properties the Seminole Tribe owns two Seminole Hard Rock Hotels & Casinos (in Tampa and Hollywood Florida) as well as a handful of non-Hard Rock casinos also in Florida. The Seminole Tribe also operates a cultural and historical museum adjacent to its gaming facilities in Hollywood as well as various educational programs at six reservations throughout Florida (Big Cypress Brighton Ft. Pierce Hollywood Immokalee and Tampa). The tribe opened the first high stakes bingo hall and casino in the US in 1979.

THE SOLOMON-PAGE GROUP LLC

260 MADISON AVE FL 3
NEW YORK, NY 100162423
Phone: 212-403-6100
Fax: -
Web: www.solomonpage.com

CEO: -
CFO: -
HR: Lynda Fraser
FYE: September 30
Type: Private

Are your worker bees buzzing off? Solomon-Page Group (SPG) knows where to find more. The company offers temporary staffing and permanent recruitment services to clients ranging from startups to FORTUNE 500 companies. Its temporary staffing division provides personnel for positions in information technology accounting human resources and legal fields. SPG also provides executive search and permanent recruitment services for businesses in publishing health care banking fashion services and other industries. The company was founded in 1990.

	Annual Growth	09/08	09/09	09/10	09/11	09/13
Sales ($ mil.)	13.2%	-	94.1	110.8	124.7	154.4
Net income ($ mil.)	-	-	(2.5)	1.5	0.7	1.5
Market value ($ mil.)	-	-	-	-	-	-
Employees	-	-	-	-	-	265

THE SERVICEMASTER COMPANY

860 Ridge Lake Blvd.
Memphis TN 38120
Phone: 901-597-1400
Fax: 630-663-2001
Web: www.servicemaster.com

CEO: Nikhil Varty
CFO: Anthony Dilucente
HR: -
FYE: December 31
Type: Private

ServiceMaster merrily mows scrubs sprays and trims. A giant in its industry the company serves millions of commercial and residential customers in the US and around the world with housecleaning termite and pest control and landscape maintenance services. Its best-known brands include Terminix TruGreen and Merry Maids. ServiceMaster Clean cleans carpets and flooring for residential and commercial clients. Its AmeriSpec division inspects homes American Home Shield provides home warranty plans and Furniture Medic repairs and restores furniture. ServiceMaster is owned by investment firm Clayton Dubilier & Rice.

THE SOUTHERN POVERTY LAW CENTER INC

400 WASHINGTON AVE
MONTGOMERY, AL 361044344
Phone: 334-956-8200
Fax: -
Web: www.splcenter.org

CEO: Karen Baynes-Dunning
CFO: -
HR: -
FYE: October 31
Type: Private

Founded in 1971 as a small civil rights law firm the Southern Poverty Law Center (SPLC) is a non-profit organization dedicated to increasing tolerance through education and when or if that fails litigation. The center provides legal services to minorities and the poor while its Intelligence Project monitors hate groups in the US. SPLC's quarterly Intelligence Report is distributed to more than 60000 law enforcement officials. The organization also operates Tolerance.org a collection of online resources for those fighting bigotry in their own communities. SPLC is credited with weakening the financial structure of white supremacist groups the likes of the Ku Klux Klan and Aryan Nation.

	Annual Growth	10/14	10/15	10/16	10/17	10/18
Sales ($ mil.)	546.6%	-	0.4	58.9	180.3	116.5
Net income ($ mil.)	-	-	(0.2)	13.0	121.4	43.0
Market value ($ mil.)	-	-	-	-	-	-
Employees	-	-	-	-	-	225

THE SHAMROCK COMPANIES INC

24090 DETROIT RD
WESTLAKE, OH 441451513
Phone: 440-899-9510
Fax: -
Web: www.shamrockcompanies.net

CEO: Tim Connor
CFO: Gary A Lesjak
HR: -
FYE: December 31
Type: Private

Need a marketing and communications firm that offers a full range of services? It's your lucky day. The Shamrock Companies provides business communications fulfillment information technology e-commerce marketing and creative services packaging print and promotional products. Neil Bennett established the company as Shamrock Forms Inc. in Detroit in 1982. CEO Robert "Bob" Troop who bought the Cleveland division in 1989 expanded the business and changed the company's name to its present form is the company's majority shareowner. The Shamrock Companies operates from about 30 US offices.

THE SUNDT COMPANIES INC

2015 W RIVER RD STE 101
TUCSON, AZ 857041676
Phone: 520-750-4600
Fax: -
Web: www.sundt.com

CEO: Mike Hoover
CFO: Kevin M Burnett
HR: -
FYE: September 30
Type: Private

Sundt has put its stamp on the Southwest. Through Sundt Construction and other subsidiaries The Sundt Companies offers preconstruction construction management general contracting and design/build services for commercial government and industrial clients. Projects include commercial buildings military bases light rails airports and schools. It builds mostly in Arizona Nevada California New Mexico and Texas. Sundt has overseen some notable projects including the development of the top-secret town of Los Alamos New Mexico (where the first atomic bomb was built) and the relocation of the London Bridge to Arizona. Sundt Companies was formed in 1998 as a holding company for various company interests.

	Annual Growth	12/00	12/01	12/02	12/03	12/07
Sales ($ mil.)	8.2%	-	42.7	43.9	51.8	68.4
Net income ($ mil.)	11.3%	-	-	2.5	1.6	4.2
Market value ($ mil.)	-	-	-	-	-	-
Employees	-	-	-	-	-	140

	Annual Growth	06/15	06/16*	09/16	09/17	09/18
Sales ($ mil.)	-	-	0.0	813.2	1,134.0	1,432.0
Net income ($ mil.)	-	-	0.0	0.0	0.0	0.0
Market value ($ mil.)	-	-	-	-	-	-
Employees	-	-	-	-	-	1,800

*Fiscal year change

THE SUSAN G KOMEN BREAST CANCER FOUNDATION INC

5005 LYNDON B JOHNSON FWY # 250　　　　　　　　　　CEO: Judith A Salerno
DALLAS, TX 752446125　　　　　　　　　　　　　　　　CFO: Gail Marcus
Phone: 972-855-1600　　　　　　　　　　　　　　　　　HR: –
Fax: –　　　　　　　　　　　　　　　　　　　　　　FYE: March 31
Web: www.komen.org　　　　　　　　　　　　　　　　Type: Private

Susan G. Komen For the Cure is dedicated to fighting breast cancer through education research screening and treatment programs. One of its well known fundraisers is an annual 5-K foot race called the Komen Race for the Cure which is conducted in numerous locations across the US and in other countries. The organization also operates a national help line and a website. Since its founding Komen for the Cure has invested more than $1.7 billion on screening education treatment and psychosocial support programs including more than $800 million to medical research as part of a broad campaign to combat breast cancer.

	Annual Growth	03/06	03/07	03/09	03/15	03/16
Sales ($ mil.)	(1.9%)	–	307.4	159.2	118.4	258.4
Net income ($ mil.)	(6.4%)	–	38.5	3.5	(2.0)	21.2
Market value ($ mil.)	–	–	–	–	–	–
Employees	–	–	–	–	–	260

THE TIMBERLAND COMPANY

200 Domain Dr.　　　　　　　　　　　　　　　　　　　CEO: –
Stratham NH 03885　　　　　　　　　　　　　　　　　CFO: –
Phone: 603-772-9500　　　　　　　　　　　　　　　　HR: –
Fax: 908-272-9492　　　　　　　　　　　　　　　　　FYE: December 31
Web: www.tofutti.com　　　　　　　　　　　　　　　　Type: Subsidiary

Even non-hikers can get a kick out of Timberlands. Best known for making men's women's and kids' footwear Timberland manufactures hiking boots boat shoes sandals and dress and outdoor casual footwear. The company also makes apparel (outerwear shirts pants socks) and accessories such as sunglasses watches and belts. Its brands include SmartWool howies IPATH and Timberland. Timberland sells its products through about 230 company-owned stores and through department and athletic shops in Asia Canada Europe Latin America the Middle East and the US. In 2011 uber apparel maker V.F. Corporation purchased the company for more than $2 billion.

THE TOLEDO HOSPITAL

2142 N COVE BLVD　　　　　　　　　　　　　　　　　CEO: Alan Brass
TOLEDO, OH 436063896　　　　　　　　　　　　　　　CFO: Cathy Hanley
Phone: 419-291-4000　　　　　　　　　　　　　　　　HR: –
Fax: –　　　　　　　　　　　　　　　　　　　　　FYE: December 31
　　　　　　　　　　　　　　　　　　　　　　　　　Type: Private

One of the region's largest acute-care facilities The Toledo Hospital provides medical care to the residents of northwestern Ohio and southeastern Michigan. Boasting nearly 800 beds the facility offers several specialties and services including the Jobst Vascular Center which provides cardiac and vascular services in conjunction with The University of Michigan. The Toledo Hospital which shares a medical complex with the Toledo Children's Hospital also operates trauma emergency outpatient arthritis sleep disorder and women's health centers. The Toledo Hospital is a member of Toledo-based ProMedica Health System a mission-based not-for-profit healthcare organization formed in 1986.

	Annual Growth	12/07	12/08	12/09	12/14	12/17
Sales ($ mil.)	5.0%	–	548.8	635.7	745.4	854.4
Net income ($ mil.)	–	–	33.4	19.2	21.0	(115.8)
Market value ($ mil.)	–	–	–	–	–	–
Employees	–	–	–	–	–	5,586

THE TRUSTEES OF DAVIDSON COLLEGE

209 RIDGE RD　　　　　　　　　　　　　　　　　　　CEO: –
DAVIDSON, NC 280360407　　　　　　　　　　　　　　CFO: –
Phone: 704-894-2000　　　　　　　　　　　　　　　　HR: –
Fax: –　　　　　　　　　　　　　　　　　　　　　FYE: June 30
Web: www.davidson.edu　　　　　　　　　　　　　　　Type: Private

The 1850 students at Davidson College account for about a fifth of the population in the small North Carolina town with the same name. Located just north of Charlotte the liberal arts school offers more than 25 majors and 17 minors in areas such as anthropology art economics history and philosophy. It also offers pre-professional programs in medicine law business ministerial and management. Students are bound by a strict honor code that allows self-scheduled unproctored exams and prohibits students from cheating and stealing.

	Annual Growth	06/06	06/07	06/08	06/09	06/10
Sales ($ mil.)	0.9%	–	–	98.5	97.0	100.3
Net income ($ mil.)	124.1%	–	–	14.3	(137.1)	71.7
Market value ($ mil.)	–	–	–	–	–	–
Employees	–	–	–	–	–	800

THE TRUSTEES OF GRINNELL COLLEGE

733 BROAD ST　　　　　　　　　　　　　　　　　　　CEO: –
GRINNELL, IA 501122227　　　　　　　　　　　　　　CFO: –
Phone: 641-269-3500　　　　　　　　　　　　　　　　HR: Robyn Berardo
Fax: –　　　　　　　　　　　　　　　　　　　　　FYE: June 30
Web: www.grinnell.edu　　　　　　　　　　　　　　　Type: Private

Ear to ear might be pushing it but the students at Grinnell College have reason to be happy. On its 120-acre campus in rural Grinnell Iowa more than 1600 students choose from courses in some 25 major fields. Programs are centered on social studies science and the humanities at this private four-year liberal arts school. The college has an open curriculum allowing students to design their own academic programs. It also offers general literary studies and has a student-to-teacher ratio of 9:1. The college which was founded in 1846 is named after abolitionist minister Josiah Bushnell Grinnell.

	Annual Growth	06/12	06/13	06/16	06/17	06/18
Sales ($ mil.)	6.6%	–	99.8	126.9	139.6	137.2
Net income ($ mil.)	(3.8%)	–	167.8	(134.3)	236.0	137.9
Market value ($ mil.)	–	–	–	–	–	–
Employees	–	–	–	–	–	535

THE TRUSTEES OF MOUNT HOLYOKE COLLEGE

50 COLLEGE ST　　　　　　　　　　　　　　　　　　　CEO: –
SOUTH HADLEY, MA 010751448　　　　　　　　　　　　CFO: –
Phone: 413-538-2000　　　　　　　　　　　　　　　　HR: –
Fax: –　　　　　　　　　　　　　　　　　　　　　FYE: June 30
Web: www.mtholyoke.edu　　　　　　　　　　　　　　Type: Private

Mount Holyoke College was the first of the Seven Sisters — the female equivalent of the predominantly male Ivy League. The nation's oldest continuing institution of higher learning for women Mount Holyoke offers nearly 50 departmental and interdisciplinary majors to about 2300 female students. Mount Holyoke is part of the Five College Consortium which also includes Amherst Hampshire Smith and the University of Massachusetts. (Mount Holyoke students can take classes at any of these schools.) Notable alumnae include poet Emily Dickinson and Tony- and Pulitzer Prize-winning playwright Wendy Wasserstein.

	Annual Growth	06/07	06/08	06/09	06/10	06/13
Sales ($ mil.)	(0.4%)	–	–	136.6	156.3	134.4
Net income ($ mil.)	–	–	–	(31.6)	(16.2)	51.8
Market value ($ mil.)	–	–	–	–	–	–
Employees	–	–	–	–	–	1,000

THE TRUSTEES OF PRINCETON UNIVERSITY

1 NASSAU HALL
PRINCETON, NJ 085442001
Phone: 609-258-3000
Fax: –
Web: www.etcweb.princeton.edu

CEO: –
CFO: –
HR: –
FYE: June 30
Type: Private

This prince's kingdom is covered with ivy. As one of the eight elite Ivy League schools in the Northeastern US Princeton is a research university that offers students degrees across 34 departments and 47 interdisciplinary certificate programs. It boasts more than 8000 students (5300 undergraduate and 2700 graduate students). The highly selective school which enjoys an undergraduate student-faculty ratio of 6:1 admits about 8% of its total applicants. Nobel Prize winners associated with Princeton include Woodrow Wilson writer Toni Morrison and physicist Richard Feynman. One of the nation's wealthiest universities Princeton has an endowment of more than $16 billion.

	Annual Growth	06/14	06/15	06/16	06/17	06/18
Sales ($ mil.)	7.5%	–	1,621.1	1,687.8	1,813.8	2,012.6
Net income ($ mil.)	12.2%	–	1,827.8	(628.5)	2,096.1	2,582.5
Market value ($ mil.)	–	–	–	–	–	–
Employees	–	–	–	–	–	6,000

THE TRUSTEES OF THE SMITH COLLEGE

10 ELM ST COLLEGE HALL
NORTHAMPTON, MA 010630001
Phone: 413-585-2550
Fax: –
Web: www.smithpioneers.com

CEO: –
CFO: –
HR: –
FYE: June 30
Type: Private

Girl Power abounds at Smith. The nation's largest liberal arts college for women Smith College provides 1000 courses in some 50 academic areas including the arts humanities languages sciences and social sciences. It enrolls nearly 2900 undergraduate students and employs about 300 professors. Annually nearly half of Smith juniors study abroad. Founded in 1871 by Sophia Smith (who left funds in her will to create a women's college) and her minister John Greene the school also offers graduate degrees in areas such as education social work and fine arts. Smith's notable alumna include chef Julia Child author and political commentator Molly Ivins and feminist icon Gloria Steinem.

	Annual Growth	12/06	12/07	12/08*	06/11	06/12
Sales ($ mil.)	326.6%	–	–	0.7	206.7	218.3
Net income ($ mil.)	–	–	–	0.0	221.9	(37.6)
Market value ($ mil.)	–	–	–	–	–	–
Employees	–	–	–	–	–	1,300

*Fiscal year change

THE TRUSTEES OF THE UNIVERSITY OF PENNSYLVANIA

3451 WALNUT ST RM 440A
PHILADELPHIA, PA 191046205
Phone: 215-898-5000
Fax: –
Web: www.hilton.com

CEO: Robert Martin
CFO: –
HR: –
FYE: June 30
Type: Private

The University of Pennsylvania (commonly called Penn) was founded by Benjamin Franklin when he had a little down time between establishing a country and experimenting with lightning. Since opening its doors to students in 1751 the Ivy League university has accumulated a notable list of accomplishments including the creation of one of the first medical schools in the US. The university currently has a total of almost 25000 students who pursue their studies in four undergraduate schools and a dozen graduate and professional schools including the renowned Wharton School and the Annenberg School for Communications. Its student-teacher ratio is a very low 6:1.

	Annual Growth	06/07	06/08	06/09	06/10	06/17
Sales ($ mil.)	6.8%	–	5,092.5	5,221.3	4.6	9,194.2
Net income ($ mil.)	33.0%	–	133.5	(1,285.4)	0.2	1,734.8
Market value ($ mil.)	–	–	–	–	–	–
Employees	–	–	–	–	–	20,433

THE TRUSTEES OF WHEATON COLLEGE

501 COLLEGE AVE
WHEATON, IL 601875501
Phone: 630-752-5000
Fax: –
Web: www.wheaton.edu

CEO: –
CFO: –
HR: –
FYE: June 30
Type: Private

Wheaton College located in Wheaton Illinois — not to be confused with a school of the same name in Massachusetts — is a interdenominational Christian college. The private school offers dozens of liberal arts programs of study including a Ph.D. in Biblical and Theological Studies to its undergraduate and graduate students. Liberal arts programs include literature music fine arts biology economics and psychology. Wheaton College has about 3000 students and a 12:1 student-teacher ratio. Wheaton College was founded in 1860 and is named after Warren L. Wheaton who donated land to the school.

	Annual Growth	06/12	06/13	06/14	06/15	06/17
Sales ($ mil.)	2.7%	–	116.1	187.3	179.5	129.0
Net income ($ mil.)	4.7%	–	53.4	50.2	37.0	64.1
Market value ($ mil.)	–	–	–	–	–	–
Employees	–	–	–	–	–	820

THE TURNER CORPORATION

375 HUDSON ST RM 700
NEW YORK, NY 100143667
Phone: 212-229-6000
Fax: –
Web: www.turnerconstruction.com

CEO: Peter J Davoren
CFO: Karen Gould
HR: –
FYE: December 31
Type: Private

The Turner Corporation a subsidiary of German construction giant HOCHTIEF is the leading general building and construction management firm in the US (as ranked by Engineering News-Record) ahead of rivals Bechtel and Fluor. The firm operates primarily through subsidiary Turner Construction and has worked on notable projects such as Madison Square Garden the UN headquarters Yankee Stadium the Taipei 101 Tower and the 68000-seat open-air stadium for the San Francisco 49ers. Known for its large projects also offers services for midsized and smaller projects and provides interior construction and renovation services.

	Annual Growth	12/11	12/12	12/13	12/14	12/15
Sales ($ mil.)	7.1%	–	8,575.9	9,522.4	10,560.2	10,523.5
Net income ($ mil.)	12.9%	–	74.8	80.5	96.0	107.7
Market value ($ mil.)	–	–	–	–	–	–
Employees	–	–	–	–	–	5,000

THE UCLA FOUNDATION

10920 WILSHIRE BLVD # 200
LOS ANGELES, CA 90024-6502
Phone: 310-794-3193
Fax: –
Web: www.uclafoundation.org

CEO: –
CFO: –
HR: –
FYE: June 30
Type: Private

Helping to make La-La Land a little more erudite The UCLA Foundation raises manages and disperses funds to help support the tripartite education research and service mission of UCLA. With more than $1 billion in assets the organization funds the aforementioned purposes as well as campus improvements and special programs. About half of the foundation's gifts received are provided by foundations; corporations and alumni each account for some 15% of gifts. The UCLA Progress Fund predecessor of the foundation was established in 1945 by the school's alumni association.

	Annual Growth	06/0-1	06/00	06/09	06/10	06/11
Assets ($ mil.)	8.2%	–	849.2	1,308.6	1,555.2	2,022.7
Net income ($ mil.)	–	–	–	0.0	(37.0)	157.7	447.5
Market value ($ mil.)	–	–	–	–	–	–
Employees	–	–	–	–	–	317

THE UNION MEMORIAL HOSPITAL

201 E UNIVERSITY PKWY
BALTIMORE, MD 212182891
Phone: 410-554-2865
Fax: –
Web: www.medstarunionmemorial.org

CEO: Bradley S Chambers
CFO: –
HR: Holly P Adams
FYE: June 30
Type: Private

Not quite for time immemorial but MedStar Union Memorial Hospital (formerly Union Memorial Hospital) has been caring for patients for more than 160 years. The Baltimore-area facility is a specialty acute-care hospital with about 250 beds and more than 620 physicians. Areas of clinical research and expertise include cardiac care orthopedics and sports medicine. In addition it offers a range of inpatient and outpatient services including diabetes and endocrine center eye surgery center general surgery oncology and thoracic and vascular surgery. MedStar Union Memorial offers post-graduate programs orthopedic surgery residencies and hand surgery fellowships. The company is a part of MedStar Health.

	Annual Growth	06/12	06/13	06/14	06/15	06/16
Sales ($ mil.)	0.6%	–	408.8	427.6	413.7	416.5
Net income ($ mil.)	–	–	(1.3)	20.6	10.1	4.2
Market value ($ mil.)	–	–	–	–	–	–
Employees	–	–	–	–	–	2,400

THE UNITED METHODIST PUBLISHING HOUSE

201 8TH AVE S
NASHVILLE, TN 372033919
Phone: 615-749-6000
Fax: –
Web: www.umph.com

CEO: –
CFO: –
HR: –
FYE: July 31
Type: Private

The United Methodist Publishing House (UMPH) keeps Christian clergy from running out of reading material. Operated by a board of directors selected by the United Methodist Church's jurisdictional conferences and Council of Bishops the company publishes and distributes content for Christian clergy and laity. It develops produces and sells official denominational church school curriculum materials books music software and multimedia resources for homes churches and church offices. Founded in 1789 UMPH is the oldest and largest general agency of the United Methodist Church and it contributes a portion of its annual revenues to the church's clergy pension fund.

	Annual Growth	07/09	07/10	07/11	07/12	07/13
Sales ($ mil.)	(19.7%)	–	88.6	84.3	51.8	45.9
Net income ($ mil.)	–	–	–	6.5	(19.1)	(6.5)
Market value ($ mil.)	–	–	–	–	–	–
Employees	–	–	–	–	–	1,000

THE UNIVERSITY OF AKRON

302 BUCHTEL MALL
AKRON, OH 443250002
Phone: 330-972-7111
Fax: –
Web: www.uakron.edu

CEO: –
CFO: –
HR: –
FYE: June 30
Type: Private

Zip it! may be an insult some places but not at The University of Akron. The school which has an enrollment of more than 28000 students plays collegiate sports as the Zips (Zippy the Kangaroo is its mascot). It offers more than 200 undergraduate majors and 100 master's degree programs as well as certificate and associate degree programs through a handful of schools and colleges. The University operates one branch campus Wayne College in Orrville Ohio and four educational centers in Ohio: the Medina County University Center in Medina the Holmes County Higher Education Center in Millersburg UA Lakewood in Lakewood and the Midpoint Campus Center in Brunswick.

	Annual Growth	06/03	06/04	06/05	06/06	06/10
Sales ($ mil.)	5.5%	–	–	231.0	237.7	302.1
Net income ($ mil.)	19.4%	–	–	20.3	463.9	49.3
Market value ($ mil.)	–	–	–	–	–	–
Employees	–	–	–	–	–	5,445

THE UNIVERSITY OF ARIZONA FOUNDATION

1111 N CHERRY AVE
TUCSON, AZ 857210111
Phone: 520-621-5494
Fax: –
Web: www.uafoundation.org

CEO: –
CFO: –
HR: –
FYE: June 30
Type: Private

The University of Arizona Foundation keeps Wildcat funds flowing. The not-for-profit organization raises funds and manages assets for the University of Arizona. Its eight-year Campaign Arizona fund-raising program begun in 1998 garnered $1.2 billion for the school. That money went to endowing faculty positions increasing scholarships promoting research and improving facilities and technology. The Foundation's asset management duties include protecting the value of stocks bonds real estate and other university investments. It also funds and develops educational programs provides construction assistance and gives grants to faculty students and researchers. The organization was founded in 1958.

	Annual Growth	06/14	06/15	06/16	06/17	06/18
Sales ($ mil.)	8.1%	–	165.4	112.0	118.7	209.0
Net income ($ mil.)	32.6%	–	47.0	12.9	23.8	109.6
Market value ($ mil.)	–	–	–	–	–	–
Employees	–	–	–	–	–	2

THE UNIVERSITY OF CENTRAL FLORIDA BOARD OF TRUSTEES

4000 CENTRAL FLORIDA BLVD
ORLANDO, FL 328168005
Phone: 407-823-2000
Fax: –
Web: www.ucf.edu

CEO: –
CFO: William F. Merck
HR: –
FYE: June 30
Type: Private

The University of Central Florida (UCF whose mascot is a stylized knight) is part of the State University System of Florida. Boasting an enrollment of more than 64300 students UCF offers more than 210 degree programs through a dozen colleges. Areas of study include engineering optics computer science medicine business administration education hospitality management and digital media. In addition to its main campus UCF operates 10 regional campuses throughout Florida.

	Annual Growth	06/04	06/05	06/06	06/07	06/08
Sales ($ mil.)	10.2%	–	279.7	311.1	382.1	374.7
Net income ($ mil.)	19.6%	–	63.4	61.0	152.7	108.3
Market value ($ mil.)	–	–	–	–	–	–
Employees	–	–	–	–	–	6,500

THE UNIVERSITY OF CHICAGO

5801 S ELLIS AVE STE 1
CHICAGO, IL 606375418
Phone: 773-702-1234
Fax: –
Web: www.uchicago.edu

CEO: –
CFO: Donald J Reaves
HR: –
FYE: June 30
Type: Private

The University of Chicago ranks among the world's most esteemed major universities. It has an enrollment of more than 15000 students about two-thirds of which are graduate and professional students. It has a student-to-faculty ratio of about 7:1. The school's undergraduate branch offers a core curriculum based on the Great Books; students can choose from majors in about 50 areas. Among its graduate programs are the University of Chicago Law School and Booth School of Business both of which consistently rank in the top 10 according to U.S. News & World Report. The school also operates the University of Chicago Medical Center and has extensive research operations.

	Annual Growth	06/10	06/11	06/12	06/13	06/17
Sales ($ mil.)	11.5%	–	2,271.5	2,207.7	3,238.0	4,355.3
Net income ($ mil.)	28.4%	–	218.9	(93.8)	371.3	980.5
Market value ($ mil.)	–	–	–	–	–	–
Employees	–	–	–	–	–	12,120

THE UNIVERSITY OF CHICAGO MEDICAL CENTER

5841 S MARYLAND AVE
CHICAGO, IL 606371443
Phone: 773-702-1000
Fax: -
Web: www.uchicagomedicine.org

CEO: James L Maderd
CFO: James M. Watson
HR: -
FYE: June 30
Type: Private

It may have received its official dedication on Halloween but The University of Chicago Medical Center (UCMC) works hard to make visiting the hospital a little less spooky. UCMC is a complex of facilities located on The University of Chicago campus that include the acute care Bernard A. Mitchell Hospital the Comer Children's Hospital a women's health and maternity facility and an outpatient care center. Established in 1927 (and dedicated on Halloween of that year) the complex includes the affiliated University of Chicago Pritzker School of Medicine and forms the clinical arm of The University of Chicago Division of Biological Sciences. UCMC houses about 550 beds.

	Annual Growth	06/08	06/09	06/14	06/15	06/18
Sales ($ mil.)	6.1%	-	1,294.9	1,495.7	1,610.6	2,212.0
Net income ($ mil.)	-	-	(190.1)	114.7	148.4	49.3
Market value ($ mil.)	-	-	-	-	-	-
Employees	-	-	-	-	-	5,000

THE UNIVERSITY OF DAYTON

300 COLLEGE PARK AVE
DAYTON, OH 454690002
Phone: 937-229-2919
Fax: -
Web: www.udayton.edu

CEO: Dr Daniel J Curran
CFO: -
HR: -
FYE: June 30
Type: Private

More than 10000 students make the University of Dayton one of the nation's largest Catholic universities and the largest private university in Ohio. The institution offers some 80 majors. Students are recruited on a national basis and from foreign countries. The student population approximates 7500 undergraduate and 2400 graduate students. It has a student-to-faculty ratio of 16:1. Well-known alumni include the late author and columnist Erma Bombeck and Super Bowl-winning NFL coaches Jon Gruden and Chuck Noll.

	Annual Growth	06/11	06/12	06/13	06/14	06/16
Sales ($ mil.)	5.6%	-	418.9	444.3	460.4	521.6
Net income ($ mil.)	-	-	(21.2)	96.6	126.1	(11.1)
Market value ($ mil.)	-	-	-	-	-	-
Employees	-	-	-	-	-	4,500

THE UNIVERSITY OF HARTFORD

200 BLOOMFIELD AVE
WEST HARTFORD, CT 061171599
Phone: 860-768-4393
Fax: -
Web: www.hartford.edu

CEO: -
CFO: -
HR: -
FYE: June 30
Type: Private

While its roots date back to 1877 The University of Hartford wasn't officially chartered until 1957 with the merger of the Hartford Art School the Hartt School of Music and Hillyer College. The modern-day university still has a strong arts and music programs and its Museum of American Political Life is home to what has been called the country's largest private collection of political memorabilia. University of Hartford which operates three campuses in West Hartford has about 7000 students enrolled in more than 80 undergraduate and 30 graduate programs including business nursing and engineering.

	Annual Growth	06/14	06/15	06/16	06/17	06/18
Sales ($ mil.)	(0.6%)	-	179.1	181.3	179.9	176.1
Net income ($ mil.)	59.5%	-	3.2	(6.3)	25.1	12.8
Market value ($ mil.)	-	-	-	-	-	-
Employees	-	-	-	-	-	950

THE UNIVERSITY OF IOWA

5W JEFFERSON ST # 101
IOWA CITY, IA 52242
Phone: 319-335-3500
Fax: -
Web: www.uihealthcare.org

CEO: -
CFO: -
HR: -
FYE: June 30
Type: Private

The University of Iowa Hawkeyes see clearly from their perch as the state's largest university. Founded in 1847 the University of Iowa has some 30500 students (and a student-faculty ratio of about 15:1) at its Iowa City campus. It is home to nearly a dozen colleges spanning more than 100 areas of study including distinguished programs in audiology printmaking speech pathology nursing service administration and creative writing. Its Writers' Workshop was the nation's first creative writing advanced degree program. It also includes programs in law engineering teaching and medicine as well as the affiliated University of Iowa Hospitals and Clinics health care organization.

	Annual Growth	06/05	06/06	06/08	06/11	06/16
Sales ($ mil.)	6.3%	-	1,556.8	1,684.2	2,067.9	2,859.6
Net income ($ mil.)	-	-	(237.4)	150.3	253.8	253.9
Market value ($ mil.)	-	-	-	-	-	-
Employees	-	-	-	-	-	17,000

THE UNIVERSITY OF NORTH CAROLINA

910 RALEIGH RD
CHAPEL HILL, NC 275143916
Phone: 919-962-2211
Fax: -
Web: www.northcarolina.edu

CEO: L Lee Isley
CFO: Charles Perusse
HR: -
FYE: June 30
Type: Private

Tar heels can sink their feet into academia and athletics at The University of North Carolina. The system of 17 universities including the flagship University of North Carolina at Chapel Hill campus counts more than 220000 undergraduate and graduate students across its campuses. It offers degrees in more than 200 disciplines. The university system chartered in 1789 is home to medical schools a teaching hospital law schools a veterinary school at NC State a school of pharmacy nursing programs schools of education schools of engineering and a school for the arts. In addition the system also operates the NC School of Science and Mathematics a public residential high school for gifted students.

	Annual Growth	06/04	06/05	06/06	06/12	06/13
Sales ($ mil.)	79.3%	-	-	30.9	0.2	1,838.7
Net income ($ mil.)	-	-	-	(9.5)	(0.6)	267.8
Market value ($ mil.)	-	-	-	-	-	-
Employees	-	-	-	-	-	55,000

THE UNIVERSITY OF NORTH CAROLINA AT CHARLOTTE

9201 UNIVERSITY CITY BLVD
CHARLOTTE, NC 282230001
Phone: 704-687-5727
Fax: -
Web: www.publichealth.uncc.edu

CEO: -
CFO: -
HR: -
FYE: June 30
Type: Private

The University of North Carolina at Charlotte is the second-largest of 17 institution members of the University of North Carolina system. Known as UNC Charlotte the university offers about 170 undergraduate and graduate programs including education architecture business and engineering. The university spans 1000 acres across four Charlotte campuses including a research campus with programs in manufacturing opto-electronics and information technology. More than 1000 full-time faculty members serve more than 27000 students — representing 22000 undergraduates and 5000 post-graduates. UNC Charlotte founded in 1946 to serve returning WWII veterans became a member of the UNC System in 1965.

	Annual Growth	06/14	06/15	06/16	06/17	06/18
Sales ($ mil.)	5.9%	-	292.3	319.4	331.4	346.8
Net income ($ mil.)	15.4%	-	39.0	67.2	59.0	60.0
Market value ($ mil.)	-	-	-	-	-	-
Employees	-	-	-	-	-	3,030

THE UNIVERSITY OF SOUTH DAKOTA

414 E CLARK ST
VERMILLION, SD 57069-2307
Phone: 605-677-5011
Fax: –
Web: www.usd.edu

CEO: –
CFO: Greg Redlin
HR: –
FYE: June 30
Type: Private

Want to follow in former NBC "Nightly News" anchor Tom Brokaw's footsteps? Head to the University of South Dakota! Along with political science studies (Brokaw's degree) the school offers instruction to more than 10000 undergraduate and graduate students taught by more than 400 faculty members. University of South Dakota students can choose from about 130 undergraduate programs and 65 graduate programs. The university's student-faculty ratio is 17:1. The land-grant school which was founded in 1862 is the home of the only law and medical schools in the state of South Dakota.

	Annual Growth	06/0-1	06/00	06/05	06/06	06/11
Sales ($ mil.)	2.2%	–	92.6	13.4	13.4	117.8
Net income ($ mil.)	25.6%	–	2.3	5.9	5.9	28.4
Market value ($ mil.)	–	–	–	–	–	–
Employees	–	–	–	–	–	1,162

THE UNIVERSITY OF SOUTHERN MISSISSIPPI

118 COLLEGE DR
HATTIESBURG, MS 394060002
Phone: 601-266-1000
Fax: –
Web: www.usm.edu

CEO: Shelby Thames
CFO: –
HR: –
FYE: June 30
Type: Private

You don't have to be a belle to attend Southern Miss but it never hurts. The University of Southern Mississippi (USM or Southern Miss for short) was established by the state legislature in 1910 to educate Mississippi's teachers. The school has grown to boast an enrollment of more than 15000 students with a student-teacher ratio of 17:1. USM offers bachelor's master's doctoral and post-master's degrees through five colleges: College of Arts and Letters College of Business College of Education and Psychology College of Health and College of Science and Technology. Southern Miss also runs an Honors College and engages in extensive research in a range of disciplines including health and technology.

	Annual Growth	06/13	06/14	06/15	06/16	06/17
Sales ($ mil.)	1.3%	–	192.7	189.8	202.9	200.0
Net income ($ mil.)	(18.8%)	–	20.8	8.5	10.7	11.1
Market value ($ mil.)	–	–	–	–	–	–
Employees	–	–	–	–	–	4,500

THE UNIVERSITY OF THE SOUTH

735 UNIVERSITY AVE
SEWANEE, TN 373831000
Phone: 931-598-1000
Fax: –
Web: www.sewanee.edu

CEO: –
CFO: –
HR: –
FYE: June 30
Type: Private

With more than two dozen Rhodes Scholars among its alumni The University of the South known as Sewanee is ranked among America's top private liberal arts colleges. Sewanee which serves about 1600 students and boasts a student to faculty ratio of 10:1 offers more than 35 majors including computer science mathematics theology and history. It is also home to a seminary of the Episcopal Church and a School of Letters summer Master's Degree program in English and creative writing. It holds the copyrights to Tennessee Williams' body of work which was left to the school by the playwright. Sewanee traces its roots back to 1857 when Episcopal leaders from 10 southern states met to discuss the formation of the school.

	Annual Growth	06/14	06/15	06/16	06/17	06/18
Sales ($ mil.)	3.9%	–	100.3	115.8	112.3	112.6
Net income ($ mil.)	81.5%	–	3.9	(7.0)	40.2	23.3
Market value ($ mil.)	–	–	–	–	–	–
Employees	–	–	–	–	–	550

THE UNIVERSITY OF TOLEDO

2801 W BANCROFT ST
TOLEDO, OH 436063390
Phone: 419-530-4636
Fax: –
Web: www.utoledo.edu

CEO: David R. Morlock
CFO: –
HR: –
FYE: June 30
Type: Private

One of Ohio's 14 state universities The University of Toledo (UT) is the third-largest by operating budget. It enrolls about 23000 students and offers more than 350 programs of study including master's degree and doctoral programs in more than 60 instructional departments. The university has a student-to-faculty ratio of 19:1. Its 14 colleges focus on subjects ranging from visual and performing arts to business and innovation as well as education engineering law medicine nursing pharmacy languages and human services. The school also operates the University of Toledo Medical Center.

	Annual Growth	06/14	06/15	06/16	06/17	06/18
Sales ($ mil.)	(1.6%)	–	–	–	728.1	716.8
Net income ($ mil.)	–	–	–	–	(62.5)	55.7
Market value ($ mil.)	–	–	–	–	–	–
Employees	–	–	–	–	–	7,000

THE UNIVERSITY OF TULSA

800 S TUCKER DR
TULSA, OK 741049700
Phone: 918-631-2000
Fax: –
Web: www.utulsa.edu

CEO: –
CFO: –
HR: –
FYE: June 30
Type: Private

If you're "Living on Tulsa Time" and looking for an education then the home of the Golden Hurricanes is the place to be. The University of Tulsa is a private university affiliated with the Presbyterian Church (USA) with an enrollment of about 5000 students. The school offers more than 60 undergraduate and about 35 graduate programs including a dozen doctoral degree programs at colleges of arts and sciences business and engineering and natural sciences. The University of Tulsa was founded in Muskogee in 1882 as the Presbyterian School for Indian Girls and was chartered as Henry Kendall College in 1894. The school moved to Tulsa in 1907 and became The University of Tulsa in 1920.

	Annual Growth	06/11	06/12	06/13	06/14	06/15
Sales ($ mil.)	5.8%	–	173.8	271.4	307.2	206.1
Net income ($ mil.)	–	–	(23.3)	13.0	38.3	30.7
Market value ($ mil.)	–	–	–	–	–	–
Employees	–	–	–	–	–	1,033

THE UNIVERSITY OF UTAH

201 PRESIDENTS CIR RM 203
SALT LAKE CITY, UT 841129008
Phone: 801-581-7200
Fax: –

CEO: Vivian S. Lee
CFO: John E. Nixon
HR: Wayne Imbrescia
FYE: June 30
Type: Private

The University of Utah (U of U) has offered instruction since long before the Beehive State was a state. Founded in 1850 as the University of Deseret the "U of U" has a total enrollment of more than 31800 undergraduate and graduate students with a student-to-faculty ratio of some 14:1. It offers more than 70 undergraduate majors and some 90 graduate-level fields of study at about 20 colleges and schools; its business science humanities and engineering departments are the university's largest. It also offers medical nursing and pharmacy programs as well as health and social science research programs. U of U confers more than 8000 baccalaureate masters and doctoral degrees annually.

	Annual Growth	06/06	06/07	06/08*	12/08*	06/13
Sales ($ mil.)	164.4%	–	–	22.5	0.6	2,907.6
Net income ($ mil.)	–	–	–	(10.8)	0.0	186.7
Market value ($ mil.)	–	–	–	–	–	–
Employees	–	–	–	–	–	18,000

*Fiscal year change

THE UNIVERSITY OF VERMONT MEDICAL CENTER INC

111 COLCHESTER AVE
BURLINGTON, VT 054011473
Phone: 802-847-0000
Fax: -
Web: www.uvmhealth.org

CEO: John R. Brumsted
CFO: Roger Deshaies
HR: Paul Macuga
FYE: September 30
Type: Private

The University Of Vermont Medical Center (formerly Fletcher Allen Health Care) provides medical care in the Green Mountain State. The company operates an academic medical center in alliance with the University of Vermont. The not-for-profit health system serves residents of Vermont and northern New York through three primary hospital campuses and more than 130 outpatient clinics patient care sites and outreach programs. Its acute care medical centers have a combined 560-bed capacity and a medical staff of some 800 health care providers representing medical specializations including emergency/trauma care pediatrics and women's health. The health care system is a subsidiary of Fletcher Allen Partners.

	Annual Growth	09/14	09/15	09/16	09/17	09/18
Sales ($ mil.)	7.4%	-	-	1,181.7	1,246.9	1,363.5
Net income ($ mil.)	(10.0%)	-	-	85.1	129.4	68.9
Market value ($ mil.)	-	-	-	-	-	-
Employees	-	-	-	-	-	7,000

THE URBAN INSTITUTE

2100 M ST NW FL 5
WASHINGTON, DC 200371207
Phone: 202-833-7200
Fax: -
Web: www.urban.org

CEO: -
CFO: -
HR: Dawn Dangel
FYE: December 31
Type: Private

The Urban Institute is a not-for-profit economic and social policy research organization that oversees research projects in such areas as education health policy employment income and benefits housing and communities population studies poverty and judicial issues. Its Urban Institute Press publishes books and reports addressing social and economic issues from tax policy to prison reform. About three-fourths of the institution's funding comes from the federal government; most of the rest comes from foundations including The Aspen Institute and the California Endowment. The Urban Institute was established as a non-partisan research facility in 1968 by the Johnson Administration.

	Annual Growth	12/10	12/11	12/12	12/13	12/14
Sales ($ mil.)	9.9%	-	71.8	82.5	77.0	95.1
Net income ($ mil.)	-	-	(2.8)	17.6	(0.5)	9.0
Market value ($ mil.)	-	-	-	-	-	-
Employees	-	-	-	-	-	400

THE VALLEY HOSPITAL INC

223 N VAN DIEN AVE
RIDGEWOOD, NJ 074502736
Phone: 201-447-8000
Fax: -
Web: www.valleyhealthcareers.com

CEO: -
CFO: Richard D Keenan
HR: -
FYE: December 31
Type: Private

The Valley Hospital is second to none when it comes to its Same-Day Service program. More than one-third of the company's annual patients experience its long-standing continuum of one-day service; fully half the surgeries performed are same-day. The not-for-profit hospital is a 450-bed facility providing general and emergency services to residents of New Jersey's Bergen County. The hospital belongs to the Valley Health System which also includes subsidiaries Valley Home Care and Valley Health Medical Group and is an affiliate member of NewYork-Presbyterian Healthcare. The Valley Hospital New Jersey's second busiest has more than 800 physicians on its medical staff.

	Annual Growth	12/13	12/14	12/15	12/16	12/17
Sales ($ mil.)	2.8%	-	606.0	622.0	638.1	657.6
Net income ($ mil.)	12.6%	-	56.4	83.3	73.8	80.4
Market value ($ mil.)	-	-	-	-	-	-
Employees	-	-	-	-	-	2,900

THE VANDERBILT UNIVERSITY

2301 VANDERBILT PL
NASHVILLE, TN 372350002
Phone: 615-322-7311
Fax: -

CEO: -
CFO: Brett Sweet
HR: Mike Dallas
FYE: June 30
Type: Private

The house that Cornelius built Vanderbilt University was founded in 1873 with a $1 million grant from industrialist Cornelius Vanderbilt. Since then the university's endowment has grown to $4.1 billion making the Nashville school a haven for its roughly 12600 students and more than 4200 full-time faculty members. Boasting a 7:1 student-faculty ratio Vanderbilt offers undergraduate and graduate programs in areas such as education and human development divinity engineering and the arts and sciences. The university operates 10 schools and colleges. Vanderbilt's Owen Graduate School of Management and its medical school regularly rank near the top in national surveys.

	Annual Growth	06/14	06/15	06/16	06/17	06/18
Sales ($ mil.)	(30.8%)	-	4,121.8	1,270.8	1,311.5	1,366.3
Net income ($ mil.)	57.3%	-	131.3	(569.3)	374.6	511.3
Market value ($ mil.)	-	-	-	-	-	-
Employees	-	-	-	-	-	21,000

THE WALDINGER CORPORATION

2601 BELL AVE
DES MOINES, IA 503211189
Phone: 515-284-1911
Fax: -
Web: www.waldinger.com

CEO: Thomas K Koehn
CFO: -
HR: Teri Lambertz
FYE: December 31
Type: Private

The Waldinger Corporation may actually do most of its work before the walls are even up. The company is an electrical mechanical and sheet metal contractor that primarily serves US customers across the Midwest and Southeast. Through its work in more than 40 states Waldinger designs fabricates installs and maintains HVAC refrigeration electrical plumbing and piping for commercial institutional and industrial clients. Waldinger also operates a division devoted to the food service industry. The company has offices in Iowa Kansas Missouri and Nebraska. Austrian tinsmith Harry Waldinger founded the company as Capital City Tin Shop in 1906.

	Annual Growth	12/09	12/10	12/11	12/12	12/13
Sales ($ mil.)	10.0%	-	155.7	160.3	186.2	207.1
Net income ($ mil.)	-	-	-	0.0	0.0	0.0
Market value ($ mil.)	-	-	-	-	-	-
Employees	-	-	-	-	-	900

THE WALSH GROUP LTD

929 W ADAMS ST
CHICAGO, IL 606073021
Phone: 312-563-5400
Fax: -
Web: www.walshgroup.com

CEO: Matthew M. (Matt) Walsh
CFO: Tim Gerken
HR: Colleen Stack
FYE: December 31
Type: Private

Operating through subsidiaries Walsh Construction Walsh Canada and Archer Western Contractors The Walsh Group provides design/build general contracting and construction services for industrial public and commercial projects. The family-owned company offers complete project management services from demolition and planning to general contracting and finance. The company is involved in the construction of highways water treatment facilities airports hotels convention centers correctional facilities and commercial industrial and residential buildings. Walsh operates out of roughly 20 offices in North America. The company was founded in 1898 by Matthew Myles Walsh.

	Annual Growth	12/06	12/07	12/08	12/09	12/10
Sales ($ mil.)	(1.0%)	-	-	3,534.7	3,316.0	3,462.3
Net income ($ mil.)	(4.4%)	-	-	203.6	191.9	186.2
Market value ($ mil.)	-	-	-	-	-	-
Employees	-	-	-	-	-	5,000

THE WARRIOR GROUP INC

1624 FALCON DR STE 100
DESOTO, TX 751152543
Phone: 972-228-9955
Fax: –
Web: facebook.com/warrior-group-154809827874149/

CEO: –
CFO: –
HR: –
FYE: December 31
Type: Private

The Warrior Group has its work cut out for it literally. A modular construction and construction management services company Warrior Group builds permanent modular buildings — including military dormitories student housing and office buildings - from prefabricated wood and metal components. Its construction management offerings include planning design purchasing engineering and post-construction services. In recent years the company has worked on projects for the Veterans Administration in Marion Illinois; built barracks at Fort Bliss and other military installations; and managed a construction project at the University of North Texas. Warrior Group was founded in 1997 by CEO Gail Warrior-Lawrence.

	Annual Growth	12/05	12/06	12/07	12/08	12/09
Sales ($ mil.)	72.5%	–	–	41.7	0.3	124.0
Net income ($ mil.)	167.2%	–	–	1.4	0.1	9.7
Market value ($ mil.)	–	–	–	–	–	–
Employees	–	–	–	–	–	36

THE WASHINGTON AND LEE UNIVERSITY

204 W WASHINGTON ST
LEXINGTON, VA 244502554
Phone: 540-458-8400
Fax: –
Web: www.wlu.edu

CEO: –
CFO: –
HR: –
FYE: June 30
Type: Private

One of the oldest colleges in the country Washington and Lee University (W&L) was founded in 1749 and is named after George Washington (who bequeathed the school its first major endowment) and Confederate general Robert E. Lee (a former president of the institution). The highly ranked liberal arts school in Lexington Virginia is attended by more than 2300 students who take courses in about 40 major areas including public policy politics international studies physics and biochemistry. The university has more than 200 faculty and a student-to-faculty ratio of 9:1. Former US Supreme Court Justice and W&L alumni Lewis F. Powell donated his personal and professional papers to the university's prestigious law school.

	Annual Growth	06/10	06/11	06/12	06/13	06/14
Sales ($ mil.)	3.7%	–	173.9	254.1	141.1	194.0
Net income ($ mil.)	(62.1%)	–	13.6	81.3	100.7	0.7
Market value ($ mil.)	–	–	–	–	–	–
Employees	–	–	–	–	–	700

THE WASHINGTON UNIVERSITY

1 BROOKINGS DR
SAINT LOUIS, MO 631304899
Phone: 314-935-8566
Fax: –
Web: www.wustl.edu

CEO: –
CFO: Barbara A. Feiner
HR: –
FYE: June 30
Type: Private

Washington University also known as Washington University in St. Louis (WUSTL) is the gateway to higher education for more than 13000 students. Founded in 1853 the independent university offers 90 bachelor's master's and doctoral degrees and has about 3400 faculty members. It offers approximately 1500 courses in fields such as arts and sciences business design and visual arts engineering law medicine and social work. WUSTL which has multiple campuses in and near the city of St. Louis also offers associate degree and continuing education programs. The affiliated Washington University Medical Center is an acute-care hospital that also provides educational training and research services.

	Annual Growth	06/14	06/15	06/16	06/17	06/18
Sales ($ mil.)	9.4%	–	2,707.4	2,876.6	3,068.4	3,543.1
Net income ($ mil.)	55.3%	–	270.3	(303.9)	737.4	1,011.8
Market value ($ mil.)	–	–	–	–	–	–
Employees	–	–	–	–	–	9,600

THE WATER WORKS BOARD OF THE CITY OF BIRMINGHAM

3600 1ST AVE N
BIRMINGHAM, AL 352221210
Phone: 205-244-4000
Fax: –

CEO: –
CFO: –
HR: –
FYE: December 31
Type: Private

Water works like magic in the Magic City. The Birmingham Water Works Board distributes water in and around the city of Birmingham Alabama. The company serves more than 600000 customers in a five-county area. It draws water from surface sources in the Black Warrior and Cahaba river basins and maintains a system of more than 3900 miles of transmission lines. Birmingham Water Works also runs two sewage treatment facilities but most of the wastewater service in the company's territory is provided by other companies. Founded in 1951 Birmingham Water Works is an independent agency run by a board appointed by the Birmingham city government.

	Annual Growth	12/05	12/06	12/07	12/08	12/16
Sales ($ mil.)	4.1%	–	115.7	122.7	120.2	173.0
Net income ($ mil.)	2.7%	–	12.4	10.9	(7.2)	16.2
Market value ($ mil.)	–	–	–	–	–	–
Employees	–	–	–	–	–	460

THE WHITING-TURNER CONTRACTING COMPANY

300 E JOPPA RD STE 800
BALTIMORE, MD 212863047
Phone: 410-821-1100
Fax: –
Web: www.whiting-turner.com

CEO: Timothy J. Regan
CFO: –
HR: –
FYE: December 31
Type: Private

Whiting-Turner Contracting provides construction management general contracting and design/build services primarily for large commercial institutional and infrastructure projects conducted across the US. A key player in retail construction the employee-owned company also undertakes such projects as biotech cleanrooms theme parks historical restorations senior living residences educational facilities stadiums and corporate headquarters. Clients past and present include the US military AT&T General Motors and Texas A&M University. Whiting-Turner Contracting operates from more than 30 offices across the US.

	Annual Growth	12/12	12/13	12/14	12/15	12/16
Sales ($ mil.)	(6.7%)	–	–	6,347.1	5,729.8	5,522.3
Net income ($ mil.)	9.8%	–	–	75.3	80.0	90.9
Market value ($ mil.)	–	–	–	–	–	–
Employees	–	–	–	–	–	4,043

THE WICHITA STATE UNIVERSITY

1845 FAIRMOUNT ST
WICHITA, KS 672600001
Phone: 316-978-3456
Fax: –
Web: www.wichita.edu

CEO: –
CFO: –
HR: –
FYE: June 30
Type: Private

State-supported Wichita State University (WSU) enrolls about 14500 students with the bulk hailing from Kansas. Along with its main campus WSU provides classes at four additional campuses. The school offers 70 undergraduate degrees in more than 200 subjects. Its Graduate School offers more than 40 master's programs a dozen doctoral degree programs an educational specialist program and more than 20 graduate certificate programs as well as research opportunities. WSU colleges include business education engineering fine arts health professions and liberal arts and sciences. The school was founded in 1895 as a Congregational institution.

	Annual Growth	06/13	06/14	06/15	06/16	06/17
Sales ($ mil.)	1.9%	–	178.9	166.5	197.5	189.3
Net income ($ mil.)	49.6%	–	5.2	(14.7)	12.0	17.5
Market value ($ mil.)	–	–	–	–	–	–
Employees	–	–	–	–	–	3,395

THE WILL-BURT COMPANY

169 S MAIN ST
ORRVILLE, OH 446671801
Phone: 330-682-7015
Fax: –
Web: www.willburt.com

CEO: Jeffrey Evans
CFO: –
HR: –
FYE: November 13
Type: Private

It's a Roger WILCO for Will-Burt Company a manufacturer of roof- and vertical-mounted masts for use in fire and rescue police and security weather military broadcast and cellular applications. The pneumatic and mechanical telescoping masts and accessories elevate lights communication (antennae) and surveillance equipment and cameras. Military masts include vehicle mounted and portable field masts. Will-Burt also designs and develops lighting systems mobile command centers and printed circuit boards. Customers include large companies in the US as well as government and military clients worldwide. Will-Burt an employee-owned company has offices in the US the UK and Singapore.

	Annual Growth	12/06	12/07	12/08	12/09*	11/14
Sales ($ mil.)	5.1%	–	–	–	49.8	63.9
Net income ($ mil.)	0.5%	–	–	–	1.7	1.7
Market value ($ mil.)	–	–	–	–	–	–
Employees	–	–	–	–	–	275

*Fiscal year change

THE WILLAMETTE VALLEY COMPANY LLC

990 OWEN LOOP N
EUGENE, OR 974029173
Phone: 541-484-9621
Fax: –
Web: www.wilvaco.com

CEO: John R Harrison
CFO: R Larry Deck
HR: –
FYE: December 31
Type: Private

Willamette Valley makes a wide landscape of synthetic paints primers sealers and adhesives for the wood products industry. It also provides metering dispensing and application equipment. The company's divisions include Canadian Willamette Tapel Willamette (a Chilean coatings subsidiary) Idaho Milling and Grain and Eclectic Products (adhesives spackle and so forth). Willamette Valley has manufacturing operations and subsidiaries throughout the US as well as in Canada and Chile; it also provides services to European and Asian customers.

	Annual Growth	03/08	03/09	03/10	03/11*	12/12
Sales ($ mil.)	–	–	–	0.0	104.7	126.5
Net income ($ mil.)	–	–	–	0.0	0.0	0.0
Market value ($ mil.)	–	–	–	–	–	–
Employees	–	–	–	–	–	265

*Fiscal year change

THE WILLIAMS COMPANIES INC. NYSE: WMB

1 Williams Center
Tulsa OK 74172
Phone: 918-573-2000
Fax: 918-573-6714
Web: www.williams.com

CEO: Alan S Armstrong
CFO: John D Chandler
HR: Alice King
FYE: December 31
Type: Public

Williams Companies has several parts but they all add up to the delivery of energy and profits. Williams is primarily engaged in gas marketing and the gathering storing and the processing of natural gas and natural gas liquids (NGLs). It also operates refineries ethanol plants and terminals. The company owns 71% of publicly traded limited master partnership Williams Partners which has gas pipeline operations in the Northwest the Rockies the Gulf Coast and the East. The gas pipeline unit operates three major interstate pipeline companies (Transco Northwest and Gulfstream).

THE WILLS GROUP INC

6355 CRAIN HWY
LA PLATA, MD 206464267
Phone: 301-932-3600
Fax: –
Web: www.willsgroup.com

CEO: J Blacklock Wills Jr
CFO: –
HR: Mark Oliver
FYE: September 30
Type: Private

The Wills Group willingly delivers petroleum products and related products and services to its customer base in southern Maryland and adjacent areas. The family-owned company operates four business subsidiaries: Dash-In Convenience Stores (with 35 locations including 18 franchises); DMO (provider of propane heating oil and HVAC equipment); and Southern Maryland Oil (SMO) and SMO Motor Fuels (distribution of diesel gasoline and kerosene products). More than 90% of SMO's gasoline products are Shell-branded fuels. The Wills Group supplies more than 300 dealer-operated gas stations in Delaware southern Maryland and Washington DC.

	Annual Growth	09/14	09/15	09/16	09/17	09/18
Sales ($ mil.)	58.1%	–	–	–	654.8	1,035.4
Net income ($ mil.)	137.1%	–	–	–	27.9	66.0
Market value ($ mil.)	–	–	–	–	–	–
Employees	–	–	–	–	–	450

THE WISTAR INSTITUTE OF ANATOMY AND BIOLOGY

3601 SPRUCE ST
PHILADELPHIA, PA 191044265
Phone: 215-898-1570
Fax: –
Web: www.wistar.org

CEO: Russel E Kaufman
CFO: –
HR: –
FYE: December 31
Type: Private

When the ailing wish upon a star Wistar might be able to find them a cure. Founded in 1892 The Wistar Institute is a not-for-profit biomedical research institution concentrating on major diseases such as cancer immune-system disorders heart ailments and infectious diseases. The institute operates from about 30 laboratories with research programs targeting genetic molecular and cellular discoveries. The company's research has been used in the development of vaccines pharmaceuticals and biotechnology drugs. Wistar collaborates with educational and governmental partners.

	Annual Growth	12/03	12/04	12/05	12/10	12/11
Sales ($ mil.)	11.3%	–	43.7	45.5	67.1	92.3
Net income ($ mil.)	51.5%	–	–	2.7	10.7	32.3
Market value ($ mil.)	–	–	–	–	–	–
Employees	–	–	–	–	–	350

THE YANKEE CANDLE COMPANY INC.

16 Yankee Candle Way
South Deerfield MA 01373
Phone: 413-665-8306
Fax: 413-665-4815
Web: www.yankeecandle.com

CEO: Hope Margala
CFO: Lisa McCarthy
HR: –
FYE: December 31
Type: Subsidiary

While most Yankees are good at warming their homes the ones at The Yankee Candle Company (YCC) are also good at making their homes smell like Egyptian Cotton or Home Sweet Home. YCC makes and sells candles — known for their burning longevity and strong fragrances — in some 200 fragrances. It also sells candleholders accessories and dinnerware. Its products are sold by some 2900 gift shops nationwide as well as internationally in nearly 50 countries. The company operates about 550 stores in the US mostly in malls and sells online and through catalogs. With roots going back to 1969 YCC has been owned by Madison Dearborn Partners since 2007.

HOOVER'S MASTERLIST OF U.S. COMPANIES 2020

THE YORK GROUP INC.

2 NorthShore Center Ste. 100
Pittsburgh PA 15212-5851
Phone: 412-995-1600
Fax: 412-995-1690
Web: www.yorkgrp.com

CEO: –
CFO: –
HR: –
FYE: September 30
Type: Subsidiary

The York Group makes boxes nearly too beautiful to part with. The nation's #2 casket maker (after Hillenbrand's Batesville Casket) produces metal and all-wood caskets memorials and plaques and cremation containers. (Cremation is the industry's growing trend — a third of US deaths are handled this way.) York is staking its vitality on an incentive program designed to boost sales via independent funeral homes. Its caskets and funeral products are sold almost entirely in the US through company-owned and independent distributors. The firm developed the York Merchandising System (YMS) a modular display of casket materials and decorative details. Industry behemoth Matthews International owns York Group.

THE ZIEGLER COMPANIES INC.

PINK SHEETS: ZGCO

200 S. Wacker Dr. Ste. 2000
Chicago IL 60606
Phone: 312-263-0110
Fax: 312-263-4066
Web: www.ziegler.com

CEO: Thomas R Paprocki
CFO: –
HR: –
FYE: December 31
Type: Public

Health and wealth go hand-in-hand for The Ziegler Companies. The firm operating through several subsidiaries offers specialty investment banking and asset management services. Catering mainly to not-for-profit institutions such as health care providers senior living facilities charter schools and churches the company provides financing advisory services and securities underwriting sales and trading. It also serves renewable energy companies. In addition Ziegler offers brokerage financial planning and asset management services including its North Track family of mutual funds to both institutional and individual investors.

THEDACARE, INC.

122 E COLLEGE AVE STE 2A
APPLETON, WI 549115741
Phone: 920-735-5560
Fax: –

CEO: –
CFO: Tim Olson
HR: Cynthia Jenkins
FYE: December 31
Type: Private

ThedaCare is a community health system that provides a wide range of health services to residents of nine central Wisconsin counties. It consists of five hospitals including Appleton Medical Center Theda Clark Medical Center New London Family Medical Center Shawano Medical Center and Riverside Medical Center in Waupaca; more than 20 physician locations; and community health and wellness programs. The hospitals provide primary and acute care and offer many specialized diagnostic and medical services including behavioral health care and women's and children's services. ThedaCare also operates long-term care and assisted living facilities and provides occupational health and emergency transport services.

	Annual Growth	12/12	12/13	12/14	12/17	12/18
Sales ($ mil.)	6.7%	–	720.5	809.7	909.2	995.2
Net income ($ mil.)	–	–	129.8	76.2	88.2	(1.7)
Market value ($ mil.)	–	–	–	–	–	–
Employees	–	–	–	–	–	7,000

THERAPEUTICSMD INC

NMS: TXMD

951 Yamato Road, Suite 220
Boca Raton, FL 33431
Phone: 561 961-1900
Fax: –
Web: www.therapeuticsmd.com

CEO: Robert G. Finizio
CFO: Daniel A. (Dan) Cartwright
HR: –
FYE: December 31
Type: Public

Moms-to-be should check out TherapeuticsMD. The company makes over-the-counter prenatal vitamins and other supplements under the brand vitaMedMD and prescription-only prenatal vitamins under the brand BocaGreenMD. The vitaMedMD brand also offers skin creams for stretch marks and scars. Its OTC vitamins and creams are sold online through the company's website; its prescription vitamins are first offered as samples at OB/GYN offices and then at pharmacies for the full prescription. Its products are made by Rhode Island-based Lang Pharma Nutrition. In addition TherapeuticsMD is developing prescription-only hormone therapy products for women to alleviate menopause symptoms such as hot flashes.

	Annual Growth	12/14	12/15	12/16	12/17	12/18
Sales ($ mil.)	1.7%	15.0	20.1	19.4	16.8	16.1
Net income ($ mil.)	–	(54.2)	(85.1)	(89.9)	(76.9)	(132.6)
Market value ($ mil.)	(3.8%)	1,070.1	2,493.6	1,387.5	1,452.4	916.2
Employees	24.6%	100	122	159	173	241

THERM-O-DISC INCORPORATED

1320 S. Main St.
Mansfield OH 44907
Phone: 419-525-8500
Fax: 419-525-8344
Web: www.tod.com

CEO: Charles C G
CFO: –
HR: –
FYE: September 30
Type: Subsidiary

Some like it hot but in reality most like it moderate. Therm-O-Disc a subsidiary of Emerson Electric keeps indoor temperatures steady with sensor switch and control products for air-conditioning and heating systems home appliances cars and electronics. Products include thermostats toggle and snap-action switches time delay relays and thermal cutoffs. Therm-O-Disc also makes products for various automotive applications (parking brakes sunroof and wiper controls seat heaters and sliding doors). Parts are supplied directly to original equipment manufacturers. Established in 1947 Therm-O-Disc has operations throughout North America and in Asia Mexico the Netherlands South America and the UK.

THERMO FISHER SCIENTIFIC INC

NYS: TMO

168 Third Avenue
Waltham, MA 02451
Phone: 781 622-1000
Fax: 781 933-4476
Web: www.thermofisher.com

CEO: –
CFO: Stephen Williamson
HR: Mark White
FYE: December 31
Type: Public

Thermo Fisher Scientific preps the laboratory for research analysis discovery or diagnostics. The company makes and distributes analytical instruments scientific equipment consumables and other laboratory supplies. Products range from chromatographs and spectrometers to Erlenmeyer flasks and fume hoods to gene-sequencers. Moving into other areas it offers testing and manufacturing of drugs including biologicals. Thermo Fisher also provides specialty diagnostic testing products as well as clinical analytical tools. The company tallies more than 400000 customers worldwide. Its key markets are pharmaceutical and biotech diagnostics and health care academic and government and industrial and applied research.

	Annual Growth	12/14	12/15	12/16	12/17	12/18
Sales ($ mil.)	9.6%	16,889.6	16,965.4	18,274.1	20,918.0	24,358.0
Net income ($ mil.)	11.6%	1,894.4	1,975.4	2,021.8	2,225.0	2,938.0
Market value ($ mil.)	15.6%	50,381.8	57,041.0	56,739.4	76,354.9	89,990.8
Employees	8.2%	51,000	52,000	55,000	70,000	70,000

1339

THERMOENERGY CORP
NBB: TMEN

10 New Bond Street
Worcester, MA 01606
Phone: 508 854-1628
Fax: –
Web: www.thermoenergy.com

CEO: –
CFO: –
HR: –
FYE: December 31
Type: Public

You want clean air and clean water? Then ThermoEnergy Corporation's your guy. The company develops and markets wastewater treatment and clean energy technologies from its base in Little Rock Arkansas. ThermoEnergy licenses three clean water process technologies that serve different purposes along the water treatment assembly line. The company also is the owner of a clean energy technology that converts fossil fuels into electricity without producing air emissions; this process also captures CO2 in liquid form for alternative uses. ThermoEnergy is contracted to build and operate a 500000 gallon water treatment ammonia recovery plant to serve New York City.

	Annual Growth	12/09	12/10	12/11	12/12	12/13
Sales ($ mil.)	(8.5%)	4.0	2.9	5.6	7.0	2.8
Net income ($ mil.)	–	(13.0)	(9.9)	(17.3)	(7.4)	(1.6)
Market value ($ mil.)	(43.4%)	38.0	35.3	25.1	12.1	3.9
Employees	1.1%	23	25	29	26	24

THERMOGENESIS HOLDINGS INC
NAS: THMO

2711 Citrus Road
Rancho Cordova, CA 95742
Phone: 916 858-5100
Fax: –
Web: www.cescatherapeutics.com

CEO: Xiaochun Xu
CFO: Jeff Cauble
HR: –
FYE: December 31
Type: Public

ThermoGenesis makes blood run cold...really cold. The firm makes equipment that harvests freezes and thaws stem cells and other blood components taken from adult sources like umbilical cord blood placentas and bone marrow. Its core products include the AutoXpress System (AXP) a medical device that retrieves stem cells from cord blood; and the BioArchive System which freezes and stores stem cells harvested from such blood. Other products include Res-Q which processes stems cells from bone marrow. Founded in 1986 the company sells its products to cord blood banks stem cell researchers and clinical laboratories around the world.

	Annual Growth	06/15	06/16	06/17*	12/17	12/18
Sales ($ mil.)	(15.5%)	16.0	11.9	14.5	6.0	9.7
Net income ($ mil.)	–	(14.9)	(18.6)	(29.1)	(2.3)	(39.7)
Market value ($ mil.)	(30.7%)	1.8	6.3	6.9	6.5	0.6
Employees	(21.8%)	111	89	70	86	53

*Fiscal year change

THERMON GROUP HOLDINGS INC
NYS: THR

7171 Southwest Parkway, Building 300, Suite 200
Austin, TX 78735
Phone: 512 690-0600
Fax: –
Web: www.thermon.com

CEO: Bruce A. Thames
CFO: Jay C. Peterson
HR: –
FYE: March 31
Type: Public

Thermon Group's heating products are not merely pipe dreams. Through its subsidiaries Thermon provides specialized cables tubes and control systems used in electric and steam "heat tracing" which involves externally applying heat to industrial-grade pipes tanks and instrumentation. Its core customers include energy chemical and power generation companies that use Thermon's products to maintain temperatures of materials transported or stored in pipes and vessels as well as for freeze protection in harsh environments. The company's customers have included dozens of multinational giants like Exxon Dow ConocoPhillips Procter and Gamble and Kellogg.

	Annual Growth	03/15	03/16	03/17	03/18	03/19
Sales ($ mil.)	7.5%	308.6	281.9	264.1	308.6	412.6
Net income ($ mil.)	(17.6%)	49.4	23.0	14.6	11.9	22.8
Market value ($ mil.)	0.5%	785.3	572.9	679.9	731.1	799.6
Employees	14.3%	991	1,021	959	1,480	1,693

THESTREET INC
NAS: TST

14 Wall Street
New York, NY 10005
Phone: 212 321-5000
Fax: 212 321-5015
Web: www.t.st

CEO: David Callaway
CFO: Eric Lundberg
HR: –
FYE: December 31
Type: Public

If you're looking for investment advice you might want to check the word on the street. TheStreet offers financial news tools and analysis as well as community features such as online chats and message boards on both its advertising supported flagship website TheStreet.com and on its subscription-based site RealMoney.com which also features commentary from market experts. Its MainStreet.com site features content related to personal finance topics. Sales come from advertising and subscriber fees. The company also distributes content through syndication deals with sites such as Yahoo! Finance MSN Money and CNN Money and provides equity research and brokerage services to institutional clients.

	Annual Growth	12/13	12/14	12/15	12/16	12/17
Sales ($ mil.)	3.5%	54.5	61.1	67.7	63.5	62.5
Net income ($ mil.)	–	(3.8)	(3.8)	(1.5)	(17.5)	2.6
Market value ($ mil.)	(10.5%)	111.2	117.1	73.8	41.8	71.3
Employees	21.3%	276	557	651	650	597

THIRTEEN PRODUCTIONS LLC

825 8TH AVE FL 14
NEW YORK, NY 100197435
Phone: 212-560-2000
Fax: –
Web: www.thirteen.org

CEO: –
CFO: Robert Clauser
HR: –
FYE: June 30
Type: Private

You might say this broadcaster has some public appeal for New Yorkers. Educational Broadcasting Corporation (EBC) operates two public broadcasting stations serving the New York City area. Its flagship Thirteen/WNET the highest-rated public TV station in the US offers a wealth of locally produced content focused on the Big Apple as well as programming supplied by the Public Broadcasting Service (PBS). Thirteen/WNET is also a major producer of shows for PBS that are distributed to other public TV stations. Thirteen/WNET began broadcasting in 1962.

	Annual Growth	06/07	06/08	06/09	06/10	06/11
Sales ($ mil.)	(15.0%)	–	–	146.1	127.3	105.7
Net income ($ mil.)	–	–	–	(39.7)	10.0	12.2
Market value ($ mil.)	–	–	–	–	–	–
Employees	–	–	–	–	–	91

THL CREDIT, INC.
NMS: TCRD

100 Federal St., 31st Floor
Boston, MA 02110
Phone: 800 450-4424
Fax: –
Web: www.thlcreditbdc.com

CEO: Christopher J Flynn
CFO: Terrence W Olson
HR: –
FYE: December 31
Type: Public

When it comes to its investment strategy THL Credit cares less about industry type and more about investment type. A business development company and closed-end investment fund THL Credit invests in a variety of public and private middle-market companies with annual revenues between $25 million and $500 million. It provides cash for recapitalizations and acquisitions as well as for organic growth initiatives like product expansions. It invests primarily in mezzanine debt and junior capital (a subordinated form of equity); its investments range from $10 million to $50 million per transaction. THL Credit is externally managed by THL Credit Advisors an affiliate of buyout firm Thomas H. Lee Partners.

	Annual Growth	12/14	12/15	12/16	12/17	12/18
Sales ($ mil.)	(7.6%)	91.9	94.2	84.6	78.8	66.9
Net income ($ mil.)	(7.8%)	48.2	47.6	44.7	39.7	34.8
Market value ($ mil.)	(15.2%)	380.1	345.8	323.5	292.5	196.5
Employees	–					

THOMAS & BETTS CORPORATION
NYSE: TNB

8155 T&B Blvd.
Memphis TN 38125
Phone: 901-252-8000
Fax: 800-816-7810
Web: www.tnb.com

CEO: -
CFO: -
HR: -
FYE: December 31
Type: Public

Thomas & Betts (T&B) bets on its good connections. The company provides electrical connectors HVAC equipment and transmission towers to the commercial construction industrial and utility markets through thousands of distributor locations and wholesalers in North America. Its segments include electrical (electrical connectors enclosures raceways installation tools); HVAC (heaters gas-fired duct furnaces and evaporative cooling products); and steel structures (poles and transmission towers for power companies). Brands include Color-Keyed Elastimold Kindorf Red Dot Reznor and Steel City. In mid-2012 T&B was acquired by power and automation technology powerhouse ABB Ltd.

THOMAS JEFFERSON UNIVERSITY

1020 WALNUT ST STE 1
PHILADELPHIA, PA 191075567
Phone: 215-955-6000
Fax: -

CEO: Stephen K Klasko
CFO: Richard J. Schmid
HR: -
FYE: June 30
Type: Private

Thomas Jefferson University named after a founding father of diverse interests is itself diversifying the world of medical training. Its Sidney Kimmel Medical College (formerly Jefferson Medical College) boasts departments in surgery and specialized areas including obstetrics neurology and psychiatry. The Graduate Studies department offers programs in public health and biomedical studies. The College of Health Professions has programs in nursing pharmacy bioscience technologies and counseling. Founded as Jefferson Medical College in 1824 it has granted more than 30000 medical degrees. In mid-2017 the school merged with Philadelphia University a design-focused liberal arts school.

	Annual Growth	06/13	06/14	06/15	06/16	06/17
Sales ($ mil.)	2788.6%	-	-	-	136.8	3,952.0
Net income ($ mil.)	7723.4%	-	-	-	8.9	700.1
Market value ($ mil.)	-	-	-	-	-	-
Employees	-	-	-	-	-	10,625

THOMAS JEFFERSON UNIVERSITY HOSPITALS, INC.

111 S 11TH ST
PHILADELPHIA, PA 191074824
Phone: 215-955-5806
Fax: -

CEO: Stephen Klasko
CFO: -
HR: -
FYE: June 30
Type: Private

Named after the "Man of the People" Thomas Jefferson University Hospitals (dba Jefferson Health) serves the people of the Keystone State with a medical staff of more than 1200 and some 1550 beds. The system provides acute tertiary and specialty medical care from a dozen hospitals nearly 20 outpatient centers and about 10 urgent care centers. The hospital also administers cardiac care at the Jefferson Heart Institute which provides everything from minimally invasive surgical procedures to heart transplants. Additionally Jefferson Health operates as the teaching hospital for Thomas Jefferson University.

	Annual Growth	06/09	06/10	06/14	06/15	06/16
Sales ($ mil.)	3.0%	-	1,250.4	1,510.0	1,456.3	1,495.4
Net income ($ mil.)	7.7%	-	49.4	51.0	42.8	76.9
Market value ($ mil.)	-	-	-	-	-	-
Employees	-	-	-	-	-	4,701

THOMAS SAINT MIDTOWN HOSPITAL

2000 CHURCH ST
NASHVILLE, TN 372360002
Phone: 615-284-5555
Fax: -

CEO: Bernie Sherry
CFO: Ken Venuto
HR: -
FYE: June 30
Type: Private

Titans and tots can find care at Saint Thomas Midtown Hospital (formerly Baptist Hospital) in Nashville Tennessee. With more than 680 beds Saint Thomas is one of the largest not-for-profit hospitals in the area. It provides general medical and surgical care along with specialty care in areas such as cardiovascular disease cancer orthopedics and pulmonary disease. Among other things the hospital also features a neurosciences institute a weight loss surgery center and a sports medicine division that serves the Tennessee Titans. Founded in 1919 as Protestant Hospital and later renamed Baptist Hospital it is now owned by Saint Thomas Health Services a Catholic health care system that is a member of Ascension Health.

	Annual Growth	06/04	06/05	06/14	06/15	06/16
Sales ($ mil.)	-	-	0.0	407.8	414.7	434.4
Net income ($ mil.)	-	-	0.0	39.7	51.2	54.9
Market value ($ mil.)	-	-	-	-	-	-
Employees	-	-	-	-	-	4,500

THOMASVILLE BANCSHARES, INC.
NBB: THVB

301 North Broad Street
Thomasville, GA 31792
Phone: 229 226-3300
Fax: -
Web: www.tnbank.com

CEO: Stephen H Cheney
CFO: -
HR: -
FYE: December 31
Type: Public

This Thomasville is more about the money under your bed than the bed itself. Thomasville Bancshares is the holding company for Thomasville National Bank which serves area consumers and businesses from two offices in Thomasville Georgia. Established in 1995 the bank offers standard services such as deposit accounts and credit cards. Real estate mortgages comprise most of the company's loan portfolio followed by commercial financial and agricultural loans. The company provides trust asset management and brokerage services through its TNB Financial Services unit. Executive officers and directors of Thomasville Bancshares collectively own more than a quarter of the company.

	Annual Growth	12/14	12/15	12/16	12/17	12/18
Assets ($ mil.)	7.9%	650.2	753.5	780.3	806.5	880.5
Net income ($ mil.)	19.0%	8.4	9.7	11.9	12.0	16.9
Market value ($ mil.)	8.6%	175.6	171.2	208.4	238.2	244.1
Employees	-	-	-	-	-	-

THOMPSON CREEK METALS COMPANY INC.
NYSE: TC

26 West Dry Creek Cir. Ste. 810
Littleton CO 80120
Phone: 303-761-8801
Fax: 303-761-7420
Web: www.thompsoncreekmetals.com

CEO: -
CFO: -
HR: -
FYE: December 31
Type: Public

Thompson Creek Metals has branched out from only mining molybdenum at its Thompson Creek site in Idaho to holding a diversified North American portfolio that also includes copper gold and silver assets. The company still obtains most of its sales (97%) from producing molybdenum a metal used to strengthen steel and make it corrosion-resistant. It operates the Thompson Creek mine and mill in Idaho and owns 75% of the Endako mine in British Columbia (Japan's Sojitz owns 25%). Thompson Creek has a metallurgical facility in Pennsylvania and holds exploration assets in British Columbia and in the Yukon and Nunavut territories. It controls about 449 million pounds of molybdenum proved and probable reserves.

THOMPSON HOSPITALITY CORPORATION

1741 BUS CTR DR STE 200
RESTON, VA 20190
Phone: 703-757-5500
Fax: –

CEO: –
CFO: Ali Azima
HR: –
FYE: December 25
Type: Private

A side of diversity please: One of the largest minority-owned companies in the US Thompson Hospitality is a contract foodservice provider to businesses government agencies and educational institutions. The foodservice operator's clients include a number of historically black colleges and universities notably Delaware State and Norfolk State as well as institutions around Washington DC such as Walter Reed Army Hospital. Thompson Hospitality also owns a handful of chain restaurants including Austin Grill. Formed through an alliance with major food provider Compass Group Thompson Hospitality has a presence in more than 45 states and four foreign countries. The two companies still partner on contracts.

	Annual Growth	12/07	12/08	12/09	12/10	12/11
Sales ($ mil.)	6.1%	–	–	97.2	101.3	109.5
Net income ($ mil.)	25.0%	–	–	2.9	10.0	4.6
Market value ($ mil.)	–	–	–	–	–	–
Employees	–	–	–	–	–	3,000

THOMSON REUTERS (LEGAL) INC.

610 Opperman Dr.
Eagan MN 55123
Phone: 651-687-7000
Fax: 707-523-2046
Web: www.westernfg.com

CEO: –
CFO: –
HR: –
FYE: December 31
Type: Business Segment

Thomson Reuters Legal focuses on the letter of the law. The division of financial information giant Thomson Reuters publishes legal information for law students professionals and consumers. Products are available in print and electronic formats and include law encyclopedias textbooks and study aids; state and federal law books; court opinions; how-to legal guides; and law indexes. The division's flagship online platform is its Westlaw research service which contains databases of legal financial and business news and information. In addition it offers law firm marketing software through its Hubbard One subsidiary and business and practice management applications for law firms through Elite.

THOR INDUSTRIES, INC.   NYS: THO

601 East Beardsley Ave.
Elkhart, IN 46514-3305
Phone: 574 970-7460
Fax: –
Web: www.thorindustries.com

CEO: –
CFO: Colleen A. Zuhl
HR: Kenneth D. Julian
FYE: July 31
Type: Public

Thor Industries is a recreation vehicle builder that makes and sells a range of RVs from motor homes to travel trailers as well as related parts. Brands include Airstream and Dutchmen. RV manufacturing plants generally produce vehicles to dealer order; Thor's independent dealers dot the US and Canada catering to private purchasers and municipalities. The company has domestic facilities in Idaho Indiana Michigan Ohio and Oregon. The US is its largest market accounting for roughly 90% of total sales. Thor rolled out in 1980 when Wade Thompson and Peter Orthwein purchased Airstream's business.

	Annual Growth	07/15	07/16	07/17	07/18	07/19
Sales ($ mil.)	18.4%	4,006.8	4,582.1	7,247.0	8,328.9	7,864.8
Net income ($ mil.)	(9.6%)	199.4	256.5	374.3	430.2	133.3
Market value ($ mil.)	1.6%	3,076.9	4,214.6	5,800.9	5,222.8	3,281.8
Employees	20.1%	10,450	14,900	17,800	17,500	21,750

THORATEC CORP.   NMS: THOR

6035 Stoneridge Drive
Pleasanton, CA 94588
Phone: 925 847-8600
Fax: –
Web: www.thoratec.com

CEO: –
CFO: Taylor C Harris
HR: –
FYE: December 28
Type: Public

Suffering from a broken heart? Thoratec's there for the rebound. The company a world leader in mechanical circulatory support makes ventricular assist devices (VAD) for patients suffering late-stage heart failure including those awaiting a heart transplant. Thoratec offers external and implantable products that provide circulatory support for both acute and long-term needs. Its products are sold under the HeartMate CentriMag and Thoratec brands. The company works closely with hospitals and cardiac surgery centers primarily in the US and Europe.

	Annual Growth	01/10	01/11*	12/11	12/12	12/13
Sales ($ mil.)	10.4%	373.9	383.0	422.7	491.7	502.8
Net income ($ mil.)	36.9%	28.6	53.2	71.5	56.2	73.3
Market value ($ mil.)	10.3%	1,531.9	1,611.5	1,909.7	2,110.6	2,055.9
Employees	(6.4%)	1,258	714	822	934	1,030

*Fiscal year change

THRUSTMASTER OF TEXAS, INC.

6900 THRUSTMASTER DR
HOUSTON, TX 770412682
Phone: 713-937-6295
Fax: –
Web: www.thrustmaster.net

CEO: –
CFO: –
HR: –
FYE: December 31
Type: Private

Thrustmaster of Texas trades on power but it does not lack finesse. The company manufactures heavy-duty commercial marine propulsion equipment including deck-mounted propulsion units thru-hull azimuthing thrusters retractable thrusters tunnel thrusters and portable dynamic positioning systems. The company's thrusters vary in size power and design with applications that include main propulsion slow-speed maneuvering and dynamic positioning. Thrusters range in power from 35hp to more than 3000hp and find uses in barges cruise ships tugs military vessels offshore platforms and other floating structures. Thrustmaster of Texas serves a global clientele through an international sales network.

	Annual Growth	12/08	12/09	12/10	12/11	12/12
Sales ($ mil.)	39.7%	–	–	45.1	84.6	87.9
Net income ($ mil.)	118973.6%	–	–	0.0	7.4	17.0
Market value ($ mil.)	–	–	–	–	–	–
Employees	–	–	–	–	–	275

THRUWAY AUTHORITY OF NEW YORK STATE

200 SOUTHERN BLVD
ALBANY, NY 122092018
Phone: 518-436-2700
Fax: –
Web: www.thruway.ny.gov

CEO: –
CFO: John Bryan
HR: –
FYE: December 31
Type: Private

Leaving Manhattan or Brooklyn to shuffle off to Buffalo? The New York State Thruway Authority oversees a 641-mile toll road system and a 524-mile canal system. The authority's toll road system known as the Governor Thomas E. Dewey Thruway is the largest in the US. It crosses the state from New York City to Buffalo and more than 80% of the population of New York State lives along the corridor formed by the Thruway's 426-mile main line. Other arms of the Thruway connect with toll roads and other highways in neighboring states. The New York State Canal Corporation oversees the state's canal system of five lakes and four canals which connect bodies of water such as the Hudson River with Lake Champlain.

	Annual Growth	12/06	12/07	12/08	12/09	12/10
Sales ($ mil.)	6.1%	–	–	598.8	640.6	674.3
Net income ($ mil.)	–	–	–	(129.9)	(129.3)	(127.3)
Market value ($ mil.)	–	–	–	–	–	–
Employees	–	–	–	–	–	2,840

THUNDER MOUNTAIN GOLD, INC.
TVX: THM

11770 W President Dr. STE F
Boise, ID 83713-8986
Phone: 208 658-1037
Fax: –
Web: www.thundermountaingold.com

CEO: Eric T Jones
CFO: Larry Thackery
HR: –
FYE: December 31
Type: Public

Mining company Thunder Mountain Gold is looking for its next project. In 2005 the company sold its real property and mining claims in the Thunder Mountain District of Valley County Idaho to the Trust For Public Land an environmental group that buys land for conservation. No minerals had been produced on Thunder Mountain Gold's Idaho properties since the early 1990s. Currently the company operates no producing mines and owns no mining properties; it is firmly in the exploration stage. In 2007 Thunder Mountain Gold acquired South Mountain Mines. Two years later it agreed to buy Kenai Resources combining to form a new company called Thunder Mountain Resources.

	Annual Growth	12/09	12/10	12/11	12/12	12/13
Sales ($ mil.)	(11.5%)	–	–	–	0.1	0.1
Net income ($ mil.)	–	(0.6)	(1.7)	(0.3)	0.3	0.1
Market value ($ mil.)	(31.7%)	6.9	9.4	3.1	2.8	1.5
Employees	(9.6%)	3	3	3	2	2

TIB FINANCIAL CORP.
NASDAQ: TIBB

599 9th St. North Ste. 101
Naples FL 34102
Phone: 239-263-3344
Fax: 305-451-6241
Web: www.capitalbank-us.com

CEO: –
CFO: –
HR: –
FYE: December 31
Type: Public

TIB Financial was the holding company for TIB Bank which operated some 30 branches in South Florida until North American Financial Holdings (now Capital Bank Financial) acquired the bank in 2011. After acquiring TIB Bank Capital Bank Financial merged the unit into its own NAFH National Bank (now Capital Bank NA). It also merged Capital Bank a former subsidiary of Capital Bank Corporation into the unit. The company has subsequently made further acquisitions and has plans for more. TIB now serves as the holding company for private bank and trust Naples Capital Advisors and owns a 21% stake in Capital Bank NA. Capital Bank Financial which went public in 2012 plans to acquire TIB Financial.

TIBCO SOFTWARE, INC.
NMS: TIBX

3303 Hillview Avenue
Palo Alto, CA 94304
Phone: 650 846-1000
Fax: –
Web: www.tibco.com

CEO: Dan Streetman
CFO: Tom Berquist
HR: –
FYE: November 30
Type: Public

TIBCO Software develops software that enables customers to integrate manage and monitor enterprise applications and information delivery. The company's software includes tools for coordinating business processes and workflows securely exchanging information with trading partners and managing distributed systems. Its core product line comprises applications for adopting service-oriented architecture (SOA) environments where reusable services are assembled to tackle common tasks such as business process management and application integration. TIBCO's other primary segments center on business optimization and process automation.

	Annual Growth	11/09	11/10	11/11	11/12	11/13
Sales ($ mil.)	14.6%	621.4	754.0	920.2	1,024.6	1,070.0
Net income ($ mil.)	7.8%	62.3	78.1	112.4	122.0	84.0
Market value ($ mil.)	29.5%	1,403.3	3,204.6	4,470.8	4,087.4	3,943.8
Employees	16.4%	2,097	2,540	2,965	3,646	3,856

TICC CAPITAL CORP.
NASDAQ: TICC

8 Sound Shore Dr. Ste. 255
Greenwich CT 06830
Phone: 203-983-5275
Fax: 415-904-5635
Web: www.ospd.ca.gov

CEO: –
CFO: –
HR: –
FYE: December 31
Type: Public

TICC Capital Corp. (formerly Technology Investment Capital Corp.) spends most of its dough on high tech. Through a network of venture capital and private equity funds investment banks accounting and law firms and company relationships TICC invests in small and midsized private technology firms. Target acquisitions are software Internet IT services media telecommunications semiconductor and hardware service providers although the company has flexibility to invest outside the tech sector. Founded in 2003 TICC commands approximately $325 million in total investments and concentrates on target firms with less than $200 million in annual revenues. Its investments range from $5 million to $30 million.

TIDELANDS BANCSHARES INC
NBB: TDBK

875 Lowcountry Blvd.
Mount Pleasant, SC 29464
Phone: 843 388-8433
Fax: –

CEO: –
CFO: –
HR: –
FYE: December 31
Type: Public

Tidelands Bancshares does its work at the intersection of Southern charm and Coastal cool. The holding company operates Tidelands Bank which has seven branches along the coast of South Carolina. The bank offers traditional retail services and products such as checking and savings accounts money market accounts and commercial and consumer loans. Tidelands Bank grows by opening loan production offices and then when they prove successful converting them into full service locations. The company specializes in services for small businesses and entrepreneurs of which there are plenty in the tourist-laden beachfront locales it calls home. About 75% of its loan activity is in Charleston.

	Annual Growth	12/10	12/11	12/12	12/13	12/14
Assets ($ mil.)	(4.5%)	571.3	534.1	526.7	486.8	475.6
Net income ($ mil.)	–	(15.6)	(9.1)	(3.2)	(1.0)	(0.4)
Market value ($ mil.)	(23.6%)	4.4	0.3	1.3	1.6	1.5
Employees	(2.1%)	85	76	78	80	78

TIDELANDS ROYALTY TRUST B
NBB: TIRT Z

c/o The Corporate Trustee:, Simmons Bank, 2911 Turtle Creek Blvd.
Dallas, TX 75219
Phone: 855 588-7839
Fax: –
Web: www.tirtz-tidelands.com

CEO: –
CFO: –
HR: –
FYE: December 31
Type: Public

Sabine Royalty Trust owns royalty interests in oil and gas properties located on about 2.1 million gross acres (216551 net) in Florida Louisiana Mississippi New Mexico Oklahoma and Texas. The trust which was formed in 1983 receives royalties based on the amount of oil and gas produced and sold and distributes them on a monthly basis to shareholders. Although royalty trusts distribute essentially all royalties received to shareholders (at substantial tax advantage) their profitability depends on the price of oil and gas and the continued productivity of the properties. Sabine Royalty Trust's properties have proved reserves of about 5.3 million barrels of oil and 35.6 billion cu. ft. of natural gas.

	Annual Growth	12/13	12/14	12/15	12/16	12/17
Sales ($ mil.)	(28.8%)	0.7	0.7	0.4	0.2	0.2
Net income ($ mil.)	(50.8%)	0.5	0.5	0.2	0.1	0.0
Market value ($ mil.)	(30.1%)	4.6	2.2	1.7	2.2	1.1
Employees		–	–	–	–	–

TIDEWATER INC (NEW) — NYS: TDW

6002 Rogerdale Road, Suite 600
Houston, TX 77072
Phone: 713 470-5300
Fax: –
Web: www.tdw.com

CEO: Jeffrey M. (Jeff) Platt
CFO: Quinn P. Fanning
HR: David Darling
FYE: December 31
Type: Public

When the tide of offshore energy activity rises Tidewater chooses to chance the wave. The company's fleet of about 300 vessels provides oil and gas exploration field development and production support. Services encompass transporting crews and supplies to offshore platforms towing of and anchor handling for mobile rigs and aiding in offshore construction and seismic operations. Its fleet includes towing-supply and supply vessels deepwater vessels crewboats utility vessels and offshore tugs. In addition to support ships Tidewater owns Quality Shipyards which builds repairs and modifies vessels for its parent and third parties. About 70% of Tidewater's revenues are generated in international waters. In 2017 the company emerged from a brief stint in bankruptcy.

	Annual Growth	03/16	03/17*	07/17*	12/17	12/18
Sales ($ mil.)	(35.6%)	979.1	601.6	151.4	178.8	406.5
Net income ($ mil.)	–	(160.2)	(660.1)	(1,646.9)	(39.3)	(171.5)
Market value ($ mil.)	67.3%	252.6	42.5	34.4	902.3	707.4
Employees	(8.4%)	6,550	5,510	–	4,700	5,500

*Fiscal year change

TIFFANY & CO. — NYS: TIF

727 Fifth Avenue
New York, NY 10022
Phone: 212 755-8000
Fax: 212 605-4465
Web: www.tiffany.com

CEO: Alessandro Bogliolo
CFO: Mark J. Erceg
HR: Victoria Berger-Gross
FYE: January 31
Type: Public

Upscale retailer Tiffany & Co. is home to the little blue box opened round the world. The company is known for its fine jewelry packaged in the trademarked Tiffany Blue Box but also puts its name on silverware timepieces china stationery and other luxury items. To entice the budget-minded to do more than window shop Tiffany has broadened its merchandise mix to include key chains and other items that sell for less than the typical Tiffany fare. The company sells its goods exclusively through about 320 Tiffany & Co. stores and boutiques its websites business-to-business accounts wholesale distribution and catalogs. Customers outside the US account for about 60% of sales.

	Annual Growth	01/15	01/16	01/17	01/18	01/19
Sales ($ mil.)	1.1%	4,249.9	4,104.9	4,001.8	4,169.8	4,442.1
Net income ($ mil.)	4.9%	484.2	463.9	446.1	370.1	586.4
Market value ($ mil.)	0.6%	10,526.8	7,756.6	9,564.5	12,958.0	10,780.7
Employees	4.3%	12,000	12,200	11,900	13,100	14,200

TIFFIN MOTOR HOMES, INC.

105 2ND ST NW
RED BAY, AL 355823859
Phone: 256-356-8661
Fax: –
Web: www.tiffinmotorhomes.com

CEO: –
CFO: –
HR: –
FYE: February 28
Type: Private

At Tiffin Motorhomes the family that stays together makes recreational vehicles together. The family-owned manufacturer builds a line of luxury recreational vehicles (RVs) including the Allegro Allegro Bus Phaeton and Zephyr models. RVs span 35 to 44 feet in length and offer amenities from washers and dryers to garden tubs to side-by-side refrigerators. Construction features are thick glass windows added storage and reinforced steel crossbracing. Tiffin's vehicles are sold by dealers across the US and Canada as well as in Australia and New Zealand. Spotlighting its nameplates the company owns the Tiffin Allegro Club an organization of more than 7500 Tiffin owners that promotes race car rallies and RV events. Robert Tiffin founded the company in 1972.

	Annual Growth	02/02	02/03	02/04	02/05	02/07
Sales ($ mil.)	26.6%	–	–	207.0	286.0	419.6
Net income ($ mil.)	104.8%	–	–	2.9	(0.5)	24.6
Market value ($ mil.)	–	–	–	–	–	–
Employees	–	–	–	–	–	545

TIFT REGIONAL MEDICAL CENTER FOUNDATION, INC.

2406 TIFT AVE N STE 203
TIFTON, GA 317941888
Phone: 229-382-7120
Fax: –
Web: www.tiftregional.com

CEO: –
CFO: –
HR: –
FYE: September 30
Type: Private

Tift Regional Medical Center (TRMC) helps keep people healthy in the Peach State. The medical center with more than 125 physicians on staff representing some 30 specialties serves residents across a dozen counties in south central Georgia. TRMC offers its patients a wide range of services including cancer treatment cardiology neurology occupational and physical therapy obstetrics and surgical care. The not-for-profit medical center has a capacity of about 190 beds. It also operates an outpatient services clinic Cook Medical Center and Cook Senior Living Center. Tift County Hospital Authority owns and operates TRMC. The hospital is also affiliated with the Emory Healthcare network.

	Annual Growth	09/07	09/08	09/09	09/14	09/15
Sales ($ mil.)	144.2%	–	0.6	216.2	1.0	288.5
Net income ($ mil.)	–	–	0.3	30.5	0.7	(0.6)
Market value ($ mil.)	–	–	–	–	–	–
Employees	–	–	–	–	–	168

TIGERLOGIC CORP — NBB: TIGR

1532 SW Morrison Street, Suite 200
Portland, OR 97205
Phone: 503 488-6988
Fax: –
Web: www.tigerlogic.com

CEO: Bradley N Timchuk
CFO: Roger Rowe
HR: –
FYE: March 31
Type: Public

TigerLogic (formerly Raining Data) can help you catch data by the tail. The company's ChunkIt! browser-based application enhances and personalizes searches of popular search engines or Web pages. TigerLogic also provides applications that software developers use to construct a variety of software programs and build databases. Its software lets users create compile test and run programs. Customers use TigerLogic's rapid application development software to build programs that can easily be updated. The company also provides maintenance implementation technical support and training services. Through investment firm Astoria Capital Partners former CEO Carlton Baab owns about 60% of the company.

	Annual Growth	03/11	03/12	03/13	03/14	03/15
Sales ($ mil.)	(15.4%)	13.7	13.3	12.8	5.5	7.0
Net income ($ mil.)	–	(3.0)	(3.5)	(2.9)	1.3	(28.7)
Market value ($ mil.)	(45.4%)	139.3	71.2	59.4	43.6	12.4
Employees	(9.5%)	97	86	101	80	65

TIGRENT INC. — OTC: TIGE

1612 E. Cape Coral Pkwy.
Cape Coral FL 33904
Phone: 239-542-0643
Fax: 239-540-6562
Web: www.wincorporate.com

CEO: Anthony C Humpage
CFO: Anne M Donoho
HR: –
FYE: December 31
Type: Public

Tigrent (formerly Whitney Information Network) wants to help show you the money. The company sells educational materials and provides training courses that teach students strategies for success in real estate investments and financial markets. It offers about 150 educational courses and training programs per month covering dozens of subjects. Its 51%-owned Rich Dad Education subsidiary offers real estate and finance courses based on the writings of Robert Kiyosaki author of the popular Rich Dad Poor Dad series of books. Its other course brand names include Tigrent Learning (formerly Wealth Intelligence Academy) Building Wealth and Teach Me To Trade.

TII NETWORK TECHNOLOGIES INC.   NASDAQ: TIII

141 Rodeo Dr. — CEO: –
Edgewood NY 11717 — CFO: –
Phone: 631-789-5000 — HR: –
Fax: 631-789-5063 — FYE: December 31
Web: www.tiinettech.com — Type: Private

When lightening strikes Tii products ensure your power stays on. Tii Network Technologies makes overvoltage surge protection devices used by telecommunications companies to protect their equipment during lightning strikes and power surges. Products include the Totel Failsafe brand modular station protectors and In-Line brand broadband coaxial cable protectors. Its Porta Systems line makes copper connectivity and surge protection products. Tii also makes gas tubes custom network interface devices and electronic products used to test the integrity of voice and data lines remotely. In 2012 Tii was acquired by Kelta which had been the contract manufacturer for its products.

TILDEN ASSOCIATES INC.   PINK SHEETS: TLDN

300 Hempstead Tpke. Ste. 110 — CEO: Christopher Panzeca
West Hempstead NY 11552 — CFO: –
Phone: 516-746-7911 — HR: –
Fax: 516-746-1288 — FYE: December 31
Web: www.tildencarcare.com — Type: Public

Providing customers with a full line of automotive repairs and services is what drives Tilden Associates. The company franchises about 50 Tilden Your Total Car Care Centers across the country but most shops are located in New York Florida and Colorado. In addition to brake work the stores offer oil changes tune-ups and general automotive repairs. The company's Tilden Equipment Corp. sells shop equipment to franchisees and its real estate subsidiaries hold leases on store sites. The Tilden brand traces its history to a brake shop founded by Sydney G. Tilden in 1923.

TIMBERLAND BANCORP, INC.   NMS: TSBK

624 Simpson Avenue — CEO: Michael R Sand
Hoquiam, WA 98550 — CFO: Dean J Brydon
Phone: 360 533-4747 — HR: –
Fax: – — FYE: September 30
Web: www.timberlandbank.com — Type: Public

Located among the tall trees of the Pacific Northwest Timberland Bancorp is the holding company for Timberland Savings Bank which operates more than 20 branches in western Washington. The bank targets individuals and regional businesses offering checking savings and money market accounts and CDs. Timberland Savings Bank concentrates on real estate lending including commercial and residential mortgages multifamily residential loans and land develoment loans; it also writes business loans and other types of loans. Timberland Savings Bank was founded in 1915 as a savings and loan.

	Annual Growth	09/15	09/16	09/17	09/18	09/19
Assets ($ mil.)	11.2%	815.8	891.4	952.0	1,018.3	1,247.1
Net income ($ mil.)	30.5%	8.3	10.2	14.2	16.7	24.0
Market value ($ mil.)	26.1%	90.7	131.2	261.0	260.2	229.1
Employees	4.2%	253	269	274	268	298

TIMBERLINE RESOURCES CORPORATION   NYSE AMEX: TLR

101 E. Lakeside Ave. — CEO: Steven Osterberg
Coeur d?Alene ID 83814 — CFO: Ted R Sharp
Phone: 208-664-4859 — HR: –
Fax: 208-664-4860 — FYE: September 30
Web: www.timberline-resources.com — Type: Public

Timberline Resources is hoping that all (or at least some) of what glitters deep in its underground mines is gold. An exploration and development company Timberline Resources conducts underground gold mining operations on two core precious metal properties in Nevada collectively known as South Eureka Property located in the state's Battle Mountain-Eureka gold-producing area. The company also conducts gold mining operations through its Montana-based Butte Highlands Joint Venture in which it owns a 50% interest and is acquiring the rest. In addition to mining Timberline provides contract underground diamond drilling services to third-party mining companies through its Timberline Drilling subsidiary.

TIME INC   NYS: TIME

225 Liberty Street — CEO: Joseph Ceryanec
New York, NY 10281 — CFO: –
Phone: 212 522-1212 — HR: –
Fax: – — FYE: December 31
Web: www.timeinc.com — Type: Public

If this company won't give you the Time who will? Time Inc. is a leading consumer magazine publisher with more than 20 US magazines and 50 corresponding websites. In addition to Time its titles include Entertainment Weekly Food & Wine People Fortune Travel & Leisure and Sports Illustrated. Subsidiary Essence Communications publishes Essence magazine while IPC Group Limited is the UK's top magazine publisher (Now Look). The publisher accounted for nearly 15% of revenue for Time Warner before it was spun off into a separate publicly traded company in 2014.

	Annual Growth	12/11	12/12	12/13	12/14	12/15
Sales ($ mil.)	–	0.0	3,436.0	3,354.0	3,281.0	3,103.0
Net income ($ mil.)	–	0.0	263.0	201.0	87.0	(881.0)
Market value ($ mil.)	–	0.0	–	–	2,609.4	1,661.5
Employees	2.9%	–	–	–	7,000	7,200

TIME WARNER CABLE INC   NYS: TWC

60 Columbus Circle — CEO: Tom Rutledge
New York, NY 10023 — CFO: –
Phone: 212 364-8200 — HR: –
Fax: – — FYE: December 31
Web: www.timewarnercable.com — Type: Public

Time Warner Cable (TWC) makes coaxial quiver. The company is the #2 US cable company after Comcast with operations in more than two dozen states across the country. It serves more than 15.2 million mostly residential customers (about 625000 business customers) with video high-speed data (primarily through ISP brand Road Runner) and voice offerings as well as security and home management. In addition to video voice and data other business services include networking and transport outsourced IT and cloud computing. In April 2015 rival Comcast dropped its $45 billion bid to acquire TWC because of regulatory hurdles. A month after that door closed another opened. TWC accepted a $55 billion offer from Charter Communications.

	Annual Growth	12/11	12/12	12/13	12/14	12/15
Sales ($ mil.)	4.8%	19,675.0	21,386.0	22,120.0	22,812.0	23,697.0
Net income ($ mil.)	2.6%	1,665.0	2,155.0	1,954.0	2,031.0	1,844.0
Market value ($ mil.)	30.7%	18,009.4	27,533.9	38,387.2	43,078.6	52,577.6
Employees	3.9%	48,500	51,000	51,600	55,170	56,600

TIME WARNER INC
NYS: TWX

One Time Warner Center — CEO: John Stankey
New York, NY 10019-8016 — CFO: Pascal Desroches
Phone: 212 484-8000 — HR: –
Fax: 212 489-6183 — FYE: December 31
Web: www.timewarner.com — Type: Public

Even among media titans this company is a giant. Time Warner is one of the world's largest media conglomerates behind Walt Disney and News Corporation with operations spanning television and film. Through subsidiary Turner Broadcasting the company runs a portfolio of cable TV networks including CNN TBS and TNT. Time Warner also operates pay-TV channels HBO and Cinemax. Its Warner Bros. Entertainment meanwhile includes film studios (Warner Bros. Pictures New Line Cinema) TV production units (Warner Bros. Television Group) and comic book publisher DC Entertainment. In 2016 Time Warner agreed to be bought by AT&T Inc. for $85 billion.

	Annual Growth	12/12	12/13	12/14	12/15	12/16
Sales ($ mil.)	0.5%	28,729.0	29,795.0	27,359.0	28,118.0	29,318.0
Net income ($ mil.)	6.8%	3,019.0	3,691.0	3,827.0	3,833.0	3,926.0
Market value ($ mil.)	19.2%	36,924.8	53,823.8	65,944.2	49,925.2	74,521.2
Employees	(7.4%)	34,000	34,000	25,600	24,800	25,000

TIMIOS NATIONAL CORP
NBB: HOMS

4601 Fairfax Drive, Suite 1200 — CEO: Trevor Stoffer
Arlington, VA 22203 — CFO: Michael T Brigante
Phone: 703 528-7073 — HR: –
Fax: – — FYE: December 31
Web: www.timios.com — Type: Public

Homeland Security Capital stakes its financial security on the nation's security. The investment firm acquires operates and develops companies that offer homeland security services and products. It hopes to capitalize on the highly fragmented nature of the young industry which brings potential customers in the government and private sectors. The company owns Polimnatrix which provides radiation dectection and protection services. Homeland Security Capital entered the mortgage and settlement services industry when it acquired Timios a provider of paperless insurance and escrow services.

	Annual Growth	06/09	06/10	06/11*	12/11	12/12
Sales ($ mil.)	(34.8%)	79.5	97.9		9.2	22.0
Net income ($ mil.)	–	(9.5)	1.9	(4.4)	4.2	(2.8)
Market value ($ mil.)	81.7%	0.3	0.1	0.1	0.0	1.8
Employees	(33.1%)	518	476	496	94	155

*Fiscal year change

TIMKEN CO. (THE)
NYS: TKR

4500 Mount Pleasant Street NW — CEO: Richard G. Kyle
North Canton, OH 44720-5450 — CFO: Philip D. (Phil) Fracassa
Phone: 234 262-3000 — HR: –
Fax: – — FYE: December 31
Web: www.timken.com — Type: Public

The Timken Company keeps its bearings straight. The company makes bearings that find their way into products from consumer appliances to railroad cars. Timken also makes helicopter transmission systems rotor-head assemblies turbine engine components gears and housings for civil and military aircraft. Its customers include manufacturers of cars light and heavy-duty trucks railcars and locomotives and heavy-duty industrial vehicles. Process industry customers include metals oil and gas pulp and paper and food and beverage. Timken traces its roots to its founding by carriage maker Henry Timken in 1899. The US accounts for about half of sales.

	Annual Growth	12/14	12/15	12/16	12/17	12/18
Sales ($ mil.)	3.9%	3,076.2	2,872.3	2,669.8	3,003.8	3,580.8
Net income ($ mil.)	15.4%	170.8	(70.8)	152.6	203.4	302.8
Market value ($ mil.)	(3.3%)	3,241.7	2,171.5	3,015.4	3,733.1	2,834.6
Employees	1.5%	16,000	14,000	14,000	15,000	17,000

TIPTREE INC
NAS: TIPT

299 Park Avenue, 13th Floor — CEO: Jonathan Ilany
New York, NY 10171 — CFO: Sandra E. Bell
Phone: 212 446-1400 — HR: –
Fax: – — FYE: December 31
Web: www.tiptreefinancial.com — Type: Public

Tiptree Financial is a holding company for primarily financial service firms. It holds majority interests in operating companies Fortegra (insurance and insurance services) Telos (asset management and specialty finance) and Luxury Mortgage and Reliance First Capital (residential mortgage origination). The company sold in early 2018 its Care Investment Trust REIT to Invesque for US$425 million.

	Annual Growth	12/14	12/15	12/16	12/17	12/18
Sales ($ mil.)	67.1%	80.3	440.1	567.2	581.8	625.8
Net income ($ mil.)	–	(1.7)	5.8	25.3	3.6	23.9
Market value ($ mil.)	(8.9%)	290.5	220.2	220.6	213.4	200.5
Employees	(15.2%)	761	929	1,042	1,011	393

TISHMAN HOTEL CORPORATION

666 5th Ave. — CEO: –
New York NY 10103 — CFO: –
Phone: 212-399-3600 — HR: –
Fax: 212-957-9791 — FYE: December 31
Web: tishmanhotel.tishman.com — Type: Private

Hoteliers looking for a place to stay call up Tishman Hotel Corporation. The company develops and owns commercial properties that are leased to hotels and retailers in the US and Puerto Rico. Tishman Hotel has a portfolio of 13 properties including 10 hotels in Chicago Florida (at Disney World) Los Angeles New Mexico New York City and Puerto Rico; and three commercial buildings in New York City. Its hotels are operated by InterContinental Marriott Sheraton and Westin. Tishman Hotel Corporation was created in 2010 when Tishman Realty & Construction split its two divisions after Tishman Construction was sold to engineering firm AECOM and Tishman Realty took over the real estate assets.

TITAN ENERGY WORLDWIDE INC
NBB: TEWI

6321 Bury Drive, Suite 8 — CEO: Tom Vagts
Eden Prairie, MN 55346 — CFO: –
Phone: 952 960-2371 — HR: –
Fax: – — FYE: December 31
Web: www.titanenergy.com — Type: Public

Titan Energy Worldwide provides power in a pinch. The company is a distributor of standby and emergency power equipment and a manufacturer of disaster relief systems. It offers power generators from such manufacturers as Generac Power Systems. It also makes and markets the Sentry 5000 mobile utility system an all-in-one trailer unit that provides electrical power heating and cooling water purification communication and lighting. Titan Energy markets these products to first responders relief agencies defense and homeland security agencies and municipalities. Those that depend on backup power — banks data centers hospitals hotels schools and telcos — are also counted as customers.

	Annual Growth	12/08	12/09	12/10	12/11	12/12
Sales ($ mil.)	20.0%	9.3	10.6	14.0	14.1	19.2
Net income ($ mil.)	–	(1.7)	(2.9)	(3.7)	(3.4)	(1.4)
Market value ($ mil.)	(45.4%)	4.5	31.2	22.2	2.1	0.4
Employees	16.5%	25	49	60	45	46

TITAN INTERNATIONAL INC — NYS: TWI

2701 Spruce Street
Quincy, IL 62301
Phone: 217 228-6011
Fax: 217 228-7499
Web: www.titan-intl.com

CEO: Paul G. Reitz
CFO: James M. (Jim) Froisland
HR: –
FYE: December 31
Type: Public

A colossus of off-roads Titan International makes off-highway steel wheels and tires for the agricultural construction mining and consumer markets. It assembles wheel-tire systems for original equipment manufacturers and aftermarket distributors of tractors cranes combines scrapers all-terrain vehicles golf carts and utility trailers. Other operations include the manufacture and distribution of wheels rims and tires to the military for trucks tanks and personnel carriers as well as boat and trailer wheels for the consumer. Titan sells its products directly to manufactures and through dealers distributors and at its own distribution centers.

	Annual Growth	12/14	12/15	12/16	12/17	12/18
Sales ($ mil.)	(4.1%)	1,895.5	1,394.8	1,265.5	1,468.9	1,602.4
Net income ($ mil.)	–	(80.5)	(75.6)	(34.0)	(60.0)	16.1
Market value ($ mil.)	(18.6%)	636.9	236.1	671.7	771.7	279.2
Employees	(0.8%)	6,500	6,000	6,100	6,300	6,300

TITAN MACHINERY, INC. — NMS: TITN

644 East Beaton Drive
West Fargo, ND 58078-2648
Phone: 701 356-0130
Fax: –
Web: www.titanmachinery.com

CEO: David J. Meyer
CFO: Mark Kalvoda
HR: –
FYE: January 31
Type: Public

Titan Machinery owns one of North America's largest full-service networks that supply construction and agricultural equipment ? tractors and combines excavators and backhoes mowers and tillers and more. The Fargo South Dakota-based company runs more than 100 dealerships that sell and rent new and used machinery attachments and parts as well as service equipment. It represents equipment by CNH's Case IH New Holland Agriculture Case Construction and New Holland Construction. Titan's customers range from large-scale farmers and builders to home gardeners. Other products include machinery used for heavy construction and light industrial jobs in commercial or residential building roadwork forestry and mining.

	Annual Growth	01/15	01/16	01/17	01/18	01/19
Sales ($ mil.)	(9.7%)	1,900.2	1,367.8	1,213.1	1,202.9	1,261.5
Net income ($ mil.)	–	(32.2)	(37.9)	(14.2)	(7.0)	12.2
Market value ($ mil.)	7.3%	313.9	188.6	306.8	477.5	416.4
Employees	(12.1%)	2,782	2,547	2,431	2,112	1,661

TITAN PHARMACEUTICALS INC (DE) — NAS: TTNP

400 Oyster Point Blvd., Suite 505
South San Francisco, CA 94080
Phone: 650 244-4990
Fax: –
Web: www.titanpharm.com

CEO: Sunil Bhonsle
CFO: –
HR: –
FYE: December 31
Type: Public

Titan Pharmaceuticals thinks big. The development-stage firm is working on drug treatments for large pharmaceutical markets including central nervous system disorders like chronic pain Parkinson's disease and schizophrenia. On its own the company is developing Probuphine which may treat opioid addiction; Probuphine combines an already-approved chemical compound with Titan's continuous-release drug delivery technology called ProNeura. Titan is working with Vanda Pharmaceuticals on late-stage compound Iloperidone a possible treatment for schizophrenia.

	Annual Growth	12/14	12/15	12/16	12/17	12/18
Sales ($ mil.)	16.1%	3.6	1.7	15.1	0.2	6.6
Net income ($ mil.)	–	(2.4)	(11.3)	5.1	(14.3)	(9.0)
Market value ($ mil.)	(33.0%)	14.4	57.8	52.0	17.2	2.9
Employees	15.3%	13	13	14	13	23

TITAN TECHNOLOGIES INC. — OTC: TITT

3206 Candelaria Rd. NE
Albuquerque NM 87107
Phone: 505-884-0272
Fax: 505-881-7113
Web: www.titantechnologiesinc.com

CEO: –
CFO: –
HR: –
FYE: July 31
Type: Public

Titan Technologies is not an enterprise of giant primordial gods of Greek mythology but rather a company that is big on recycling tires. The company licenses its technology which uses a proprietary catalyst to reduce tires to carbon black oil and steel to tire-recycling plants. Facilities in South Korea and Taiwan that are no longer operating have used Titan's system; the company is working to find licensees in the US Europe and elsewhere in Asia. Titan also is working with R&D lab Adherent Technologies to develop new ways to recycle electronic scrap (from discarded computers) and waste plastic.

TIVITY HEALTH INC — NMS: TVTY

701 Cool Springs Boulevard
Franklin, TN 37067
Phone: 800 869-5311
Fax: –
Web: www.healthways.com

CEO: Ben R. Leedle
CFO: Alfred Lumsdaine
HR: Kevin Jenkins
FYE: December 31
Type: Public

For health insurers healthy plan members are cheap plan members; that's where Tivity Health (formerly Healthways) comes in. The health services business provides disease management and wellness programs to managed care companies self-insured employers governments and hospitals with the ultimate goals of improving members' health and lowering health care costs. Its disease management programs help members manage chronic illnesses like diabetes and emphysema making sure they keep up with treatment plans and maintain healthy behaviors. Tivity Health's wellness offerings including its SilverSneakers program for seniors encourage fitness and other positive lifestyle choices.

	Annual Growth	12/14	12/15	12/16	12/17	12/18
Sales ($ mil.)	(4.9%)	742.2	770.6	501.0	556.9	606.3
Net income ($ mil.)	–	(5.6)	(30.9)	(129.1)	63.7	98.8
Market value ($ mil.)	5.7%	816.1	528.3	933.9	1,500.4	1,018.5
Employees	(34.4%)	2,700	2,400	500	475	500

TIVO CORP — NMS: TIVO

2160 Gold Street
San Jose, CA 95002
Phone: 408 519-9100
Fax: –
Web: www.tivo.com

CEO: Thomas (Tom) Carson
CFO: Peter C. Halt
HR: Dustin K. Finer
FYE: December 31
Type: Public

Rovi wants to help roving media junkies find their fix. The company develops and licenses technology to enable and enhance video content discovery distribution and advertising. Products include interactive programming guides media recognition technology and e-commerce platforms. Clients include consumer electronics (CE) makers (Dell Samsung Panasonic) and service providers (Cox Sky plc Verizon) which together account for nearly 90% of sales; others include online retailers and portals (Best Buy Ticketmaster Sony's PlayStation) and content providers (Universal Studios Disney PBS). Geographically sales are about evenly split between US and international customers. In 2016 Rovi acquired TiVo for $1.1 billion.

	Annual Growth	12/14	12/15	12/16	12/17	12/18
Sales ($ mil.)	6.4%	542.3	526.3	649.1	826.5	695.9
Net income ($ mil.)	–	(69.7)	(4.3)	32.7	(38.0)	(349.3)
Market value ($ mil.)	(19.7%)	2,800.6	2,065.4	2,591.1	1,934.0	1,166.6
Employees	9.1%	1,200	1,100	1,700	1,700	1,700

TIVO INC
NMS: TIVO

2160 Gold Street, P.O. Box 2160
San Jose, CA 95002
Phone: 408 519-9100
Fax: 408 519-5330
Web: www.tivo.com

CEO: –
CFO: Peter Halt
HR: –
FYE: January 31
Type: Public

Prime time is anytime with TiVo. That's the idea behind TiVo and its digital video recorder (DVR). The DVR (similar to a VCR but using a hard drive instead of videocassette) allows more than 4 million subscribers to record standard- and high-definition TV (broadcast cable or satellite). The company sells DVRs online and through electronics retailers such as Best Buy. In addition to buying a DVR customers pay for TiVo's subscription service which is essentially a high-tech TV listing. TiVo reaches cable and satellite viewers by licensing its technology to DIRECTV Comcast and other service providers worldwide. TiVo is evolving from an "anytime" to an "anywhere" service to stay relevant to mobile viewers.

	Annual Growth	01/11	01/12	01/13	01/14	01/15
Sales ($ mil.)	19.7%	219.6	238.2	303.9	406.3	451.5
Net income ($ mil.)	–	(84.5)	102.2	(5.3)	271.8	30.8
Market value ($ mil.)	2.0%	930.5	998.3	1,283.6	1,192.2	1,006.5
Employees	0.6%	611	631	576	626	625

TIX CORP
NBB: TIXC

12711 Ventura Blvd., Suite 340
Studio City, CA 91604
Phone: 818 761-1002
Fax: 818 761-1072
Web: www.tixcorp.com

CEO: Mitch Francis
CFO: Steve Handy
HR: –
FYE: December 31
Type: Public

Tix Corporation has got a ticket to ride. Through its Tix4Tonight subsidiary the company sells discounted same-day tickets to Las Vegas shows from about a dozen locations in Las Vegas. Tix4Tonight also includes Tix4Dinner (discounted dinners on the Vegas strip) and Tix4Golf (discounted golf reservations in the Las Vegas area). The company's Exhibit Merchandising sells branded merchandise (souvenir posters memorabilia) related to museum exhibits and theatrical productions. Sales are made in temporary specialty stores set up in conjunction with the touring event.

	Annual Growth	12/14	12/15	12/16	12/17	12/18
Sales ($ mil.)	(13.1%)	22.7	23.4	21.4	17.4	13.0
Net income ($ mil.)	–	4.1	16.8	1.9	(4.7)	(7.6)
Market value ($ mil.)	(38.5%)	25.1	37.3	27.2	6.2	3.6
Employees	–	–	–	–	–	94

TJX COMPANIES, INC.
NYS: TJX

770 Cochituate Road
Framingham, MA 01701
Phone: 508 390-1000
Fax: 508 390-2091
Web: www.tjx.com

CEO: Ernie Herrman
CFO: Scott Goldenberg
HR: Kelli McNary
FYE: February 02
Type: Public

The TJX Companies operates more than 4300 stores worldwide under half a dozen retail brand names including the two largest off-price clothing retailers in the US: T.J. Maxx and Marshalls which operate 2300-plus stores nationwide. T.J. Maxx sells brand-name family apparel accessories shoes domestics giftware and jewelry at discount prices while Marshalls offers similar items plus a broader selection of shoes and menswear through more than 1100 stores. Its HomeGoods chain of 750-plus US stores focuses exclusively on home furnishings. It trades as T.K. Maxx in Europe with 600-plus stores in the UK Ireland Austria Germany Poland and the Netherlands. TJX keeps prices low by scooping up excess stock from manufacturers and department stores.

	Annual Growth	01/15	01/16	01/17*	02/18	02/19
Sales ($ mil.)	7.6%	29,078.4	30,944.9	33,183.7	35,864.7	38,972.9
Net income ($ mil.)	8.4%	2,215.1	2,277.7	2,298.2	2,607.9	3,059.8
Market value ($ mil.)	(7.2%)	80,261.0	86,712.1	90,388.0	95,512.3	59,520.2
Employees	8.1%	198,000	216,000	235,000	249,000	270,000

*Fiscal year change

TKS INDUSTRIAL COMPANY

901 Tower Dr. Ste. 250
Troy MI 48098-2817
Phone: 248-786-5000
Fax: 248-786-5001
Web: www.taikisha-group.com/network/usa_and_canada/

CEO: –
CFO: –
HR: –
FYE: March 31
Type: Subsidiary

TKS Industrial designs fabricates and installs paint finishing systems specialized drying ovens industrial ventilation systems and commercial clean rooms for automakers and other manufacturers. The company operates offices and plants in the US in Michigan and Ohio and it has international subsidiaries in Brazil Canada and Mexico. Customers include Toyota Motor Chrysler Ford Motor Honda and General Motors. TKS Industrial established in 1981 is the US subsidiary of Taikisha Ltd. a Japanese supplier of clean room systems electrical and mechanical equipment for buildings and paint finishing systems which was founded in 1913.

TNEMEC COMPANY, INC.

6800 CORPORATE DR
KANSAS CITY, MO 641201372
Phone: 816-483-3400
Fax: –
Web: www.tnemec.com

CEO: Albert C Bean IV
CFO: –
HR: –
FYE: December 31
Type: Private

Tnemec (pronouced tah-KNEE-mick it is cement spelled backwards) makes more than 100 different paints and coatings that can be used as primers on concrete masonry steel and flooring materials. It also provides waterproofing corrosion prevention (for wastewater facilities) and exterior finishing products. Tnemec serves customers in different markets including architectural industrial manufacturing oilfield services water and wastewater and water storage tanks. Its Chemprobe line specializes in masonry products while the company's StrataShield line focuses on floor and wall coatings.

	Annual Growth	12/13	12/14	12/15	12/16	12/17
Sales ($ mil.)	0.3%	–	123.1	120.5	118.3	124.2
Net income ($ mil.)	1.1%	–	3.3	2.5	3.3	3.4
Market value ($ mil.)	–	–	–	–	–	–
Employees	–	–	–	–	–	272

TNR TECHNICAL, INC.
NBB: TNRK

301 Central Park Drive
Sanford, FL 32771
Phone: 407 321-3011
Fax: 407 321-3208
Web: www.tnrtechnical.com

CEO: Wayne Thaw
CFO: Anne Provost
HR: –
FYE: June 30
Type: Public

Not long ago batteries were batteries: A AA AAA C D. Now there are nickel cadmium nickel metal hydride lithium and alkaline varieties and TNR Technical assembles and distributes the full gamut of modern batteries for consumer applications. Typical applications include alarms cameras door locks power tools instruments golf carts laptops medical equipment and surveying equipment. TNR sells to the OEM government military leisure and wholesale markets. The company distributes most leading brands including Duracell Energizer Panasonic SANYO and Ultralife. Members of the Thaw family own more than half of the company.

	Annual Growth	06/14	06/15	06/16	06/17	06/18
Sales ($ mil.)	0.8%	8.3	8.1	8.2	8.6	8.6
Net income ($ mil.)	(18.7%)	0.4	0.3	0.3	0.2	0.2
Market value ($ mil.)	(4.0%)	5.3	4.2	3.9	3.6	4.5
Employees	–	–	–	–	–	–

TODD SHIPYARDS CORPORATION

1801 16th Ave. SW
Seattle WA 98134-1089
Phone: 206-623-1635
Fax: 206-442-8505
Web: vigorindustrial.com/companies/vigor_shipyards/

CEO: Frank J Foti
CFO: Lon V Leneve
HR: –
FYE: March 31
Type: Subsidiary

Todd Shipyards helps keep boats afloat. The company operates a handful of Washington-based dry docks through subsidiaries Vigor Shipyards and Everett Shipyard; in the marketplace of private that is non-governmental shipyard owners it is largest in the US Pacific Northwest. Its work focuses on repair (minor jobs to major overhauls) and maintenance of federal government as well as commercial vessels that plow the region's waters. Services include new construction and industrial fabrication for a select group of customers at its shipyards. Contracts with the US Navy Coast Guard and Washington State Ferries represent about 90% of its revenues. Todd was taken over by Vigor Industrial in 2011 for $130 million.

TOFUTTI BRANDS INC

NBB: TOFB

50 Jackson Drive
Cranford, NJ 07016
Phone: 908 272-2400
Fax: –
Web: www.tofutti.com

CEO: David Mintz
CFO: Steven Kass
HR: –
FYE: December 29
Type: Public

Tofutti Brands makes Tofutti Cuties and Marry Me Bars and while the company may get silly with its brand names don't let that fool you. Its soy-based foods are aimed at lactose-intolerant kosher and health-conscious consumers. Its flagship product Tofutti frozen dessert is sold by the pint and in novelty forms. The company also offers nondairy cheeses and sour cream. Tofutti's products are developed by the company at its own labs but they do no manufacturing of their own. Instead the company contracts with co-packers to furnish its products. Chairman and CEO David Mintz owns about 50% of the firm; the Financial & Investment Management Group owns almost 8%.

	Annual Growth	12/14*	01/16*	12/16	12/17	12/18
Sales ($ mil.)	(2.3%)	14.4	13.8	14.5	14.1	13.1
Net income ($ mil.)	–	(0.2)	(0.6)	0.4	0.7	0.5
Market value ($ mil.)	(24.2%)	28.4	21.5	8.5	9.3	9.4
Employees	(6.9%)	12	9	9	8	9

*Fiscal year change

TOLL BROTHERS INC.

NYS: TOL

250 Gibraltar Road
Horsham, PA 19044
Phone: 215 938-8000
Fax: 215 938-8023
Web: www.tollbrothers.com

CEO: –
CFO: Martin P. (Marty) Connor
HR: –
FYE: October 31
Type: Public

Toll Brothers builds luxury homes in the US targeted at move-up empty nester and second-home buyers. Its single-family detached houses and condominium apartments sell for an average base price of over $850000. The company also develops communities for active adults and operates country club communities. Subsidiaries offer related services and products including architectural and engineering services title and mortgage services and landscaping. Toll Brothers has operations in about 50 markets in some 20 states. Traditionally a suburban developer Toll Brothers has branched out to mid- and high-rise condominiums in urban markets and luxury rentals.

	Annual Growth	10/15	10/16	10/17	10/18	10/19
Sales ($ mil.)	14.7%	4,171.2	5,169.5	5,815.1	7,143.3	7,224.0
Net income ($ mil.)	12.9%	363.2	382.1	535.5	748.2	590.0
Market value ($ mil.)	2.5%	5,069.5	3,867.3	6,488.8	4,744.0	5,605.1
Employees	6.9%	3,900	4,200	4,500	4,900	5,100

TOM LANGE COMPANY, INC.

755 APPLE ORCHARD RD
SPRINGFIELD, IL 627035914
Phone: 217-786-3300
Fax: –
Web: www.tomlange.com

CEO: Phil Gumpert
CFO: –
HR: –
FYE: August 31
Type: Private

Tom Lange Company wants you to eat your veggies. One of the largest purchasers and distributors of fresh fruits and vegetables in the US Tom Lange supplies its comestibles to clients in the retail wholesale and food service trades. The company also provides third party logistics services specializing in truckload freight movement. The company was founded in 1960 as a three-man operation in St. Louis Missouri Tom Lange has grown to encompass 35 offices in the US and Canada. Produce subsidiaries include Seven Seas M&M Marketing and Seven Seas Fruit.

	Annual Growth	08/13	08/14	08/15	08/16	08/17
Sales ($ mil.)	1.7%	–	447.7	441.3	466.7	471.2
Net income ($ mil.)	–	–	(19.4)	1.0	2.7	7.8
Market value ($ mil.)	–	–	–	–	–	–
Employees	–	–	–	–	–	110

TOM'S OF MAINE INC.

302 Lafayette Center
Kennebunk ME 04043
Phone: 207-985-2944
Fax: 207-985-2196
Web: www.tomsofmaine.com

CEO: Tom Obrien
CFO: –
HR: –
FYE: June 30
Type: Subsidiary

Tom's of Maine hopes that natural health will lead to corporate wealth. The company has built a business by selling the firm's flagship toothpaste (responsible for more than half of company sales) as well as mouthwash dental floss deodorant soap and shaving cream made from natural ingredients and distributing them in environmentally-friendly packaging. Tom's of Maine gives 10% of its pre-tax profits to charitable organizations and encourages its employees to use 5% of their paid time doing volunteer work. CEO Tom Chappell and his wife Kate Chappell founded the company in 1970. Seeking entry into the specialty toothpaste market Colgate-Palmolive bought Tom's of Maine for about $100 million in 2006.

TOMAX CORPORATION

224 S. 200 West
Salt Lake City UT 84101
Phone: 801-990-0909
Fax: 801-924-3400
Web: www.tomax.com

CEO: Eric Olafson
CFO: –
HR: –
FYE: June 30
Type: Private

Tomax tries to take the ailing out of retailing. The company develops and hosts software that helps retail chains simplify business processes manage marketing channels and reduce IT infrastructure costs. Clients use Tomax's Retail.net suite to manage customer transactions deal with returns streamline workflow processes and forecast staffing needs. The company also provides support and training services. Customers include 24 Hour Fitness Benjamin Moore Kroger Safeway and Trader Joe's. Eric Olafson (president and CEO) and Jaye Olafson (COO) who are husband and wife are the principal shareholders of Tomax. Oracle has a minority equity stake in the company.

TOMMY BAHAMA GROUP INC.

428 Westlake Ave. N. Ste. 388
Seattle WA 98109
Phone: 206-622-8688
Fax: 206-622-4483
Web: www.tommybahama.com

CEO: –
CFO: –
HR: –
FYE: January 31
Type: Subsidiary

Tommy Bahama Group retails the island life. The company designs and markets relaxed sportswear and other items under the Tommy Bahama name. Tommy Bahama's Fishbone pants Cayman Camp shirts and other clothing are sold through specialty stores vacation resorts and about 90 namesake stores as well as through about a dozen tropical-themed Tommy Bahama restaurants in the US. Licensees have extended the Tommy Bahama brand to such items as footwear golf bags luggage handbags eyewear home furnishings and rum. Oxford Industries owns Tommy Bahama Group which was founded in 1992 by marketing director Bob Emfield designer Lucio Dalla Gasperina and former president and CEO Tony Margolis.

TOPCO ASSOCIATES LLC

7711 Gross Point Rd.
Skokie IL 60077
Phone: 847-676-3030
Fax: 847-676-4949
Web: www.topco.com

CEO: Randall J Skoda
CFO: –
HR: –
FYE: December 31
Type: Private - Cooperativ

Topco Associates is a top company in terms of private-label procurement. Topco uses the combined purchasing clout of more than 50 member companies (mostly supermarket operators and foodservice suppliers) nationwide to wring discounts from wholesalers and manufacturers. Topco distributes more than 10000 private-label items including fresh meat and produce dairy and bakery goods and health and beauty aids to retail locations throughout the US. Its brands include Food Club Shurfine and a line of "Top" labels such as Top Crest and Top Care. In addition to procurement Topco helps its members contain costs through financial-services programs and other business services.

TOMPKINS FINANCIAL CORP   ASE: TMP

118 E. Seneca Street, P.O. Box 460
Ithaca, NY 14851
Phone: 888 503-5753
Fax: –
Web: www.tompkinsfinancial.com

CEO: Robert D. (Bob) Davis
CFO: Francis M. Fetsko
HR: Bonita Lindberg
FYE: December 31
Type: Public

Tompkins Financial is the holding company for Tompkins Trust Company The Bank of Castile and Mahopac Bank which offer traditional banking services through some 45 offices in upstate New York. It also owns the 20-branch Pennsylvania-based VIST Bank. Funds from deposit products such as checking savings and money market accounts are mainly used to originate real estate loans and mortgages as well as commercial and consumer loans. Tompkins also offers trust and estate financial and tax planning and investment management services through Tompkins Financial Advisors. Tompkins Insurance Agencies sells property/casualty coverage in central and western New York and Pennsylvania.

	Annual Growth	12/14	12/15	12/16	12/17	12/18
Assets ($ mil.)	6.4%	5,269.6	5,690.0	6,236.8	6,648.3	6,758.4
Net income ($ mil.)	12.1%	52.0	58.4	59.3	52.5	82.3
Market value ($ mil.)	7.9%	842.0	855.1	1,439.5	1,238.6	1,142.1
Employees	(0.0%)	1,037	1,038	1,046	1,041	1,035

TOR MINERALS INTERNATIONAL INC   NBB: TORM

722 Burleson Street
Corpus Christi, TX 78402
Phone: 361 883-5591
Fax: –
Web: www.torminerals.com

CEO: Olaf Karasch
CFO: Barbara Russell
HR: –
FYE: December 31
Type: Public

It doesn't make winter outerwear but TOR Minerals International is concerned about good durable coats. The company makes pigments and pigment extenders that are used in paints industrial coatings and plastics. HITOX TOR's primary product is a beige titanium dioxide pigment used to add opacity and durability to paints. Other TOR products include pigment extenders that add strength and weight to end products and pigment fillers with flame-retardant and smoke-suppressant properties. The company's customers include paint and plastics manufacturers. TOR has production facilities in Corpus Christi Texas; the Netherlands; and Malaysia. Chairman Bernard Paulson owns 34% of the company.

	Annual Growth	12/14	12/15	12/16	12/17	12/18
Sales ($ mil.)	(4.2%)	46.7	37.1	38.5	39.0	39.4
Net income ($ mil.)	–	(0.6)	(6.4)	0.4	(1.1)	(0.8)
Market value ($ mil.)	(23.5%)	26.3	16.0	21.6	20.0	9.0
Employees	(10.8%)	176	103	127	125	–

TOOTSIE ROLL INDUSTRIES INC   NYS: TR

7401 South Cicero Avenue
Chicago, IL 60629
Phone: 773 838-3400
Fax: 773 838-3534
Web: www.tootsie.com

CEO: Ellen R. Gordon
CFO: G. Howard Ember
HR: Peter Lebron
FYE: December 31
Type: Public

Neither taffy nor caramel nor chocolate Tootsie Roll Industries' success is wrapped in brown-and-white waxed paper. As one of the country's largest candy companies it makes and sells the vaguely chocolate-flavored Tootsie Roll which has been produced with the same formula and name for more than a century. The company also makes such well-known candies as Andes mints Junior Mints Charleston Chew and Sugar Daddy. Its Charms and Tootsie Pops brands make the company one of the largest lollipop producers in the world. Tootsie Roll Industries sells its candy directly and through brokers to thousands of retail customers across the US (although Walmart and Dollar Tree together account for a third of sales).

	Annual Growth	12/14	12/15	12/16	12/17	12/18
Sales ($ mil.)	(1.2%)	543.5	540.1	521.1	519.3	518.9
Net income ($ mil.)	(2.6%)	63.3	66.1	67.5	80.9	56.9
Market value ($ mil.)	2.2%	2,021.7	2,083.7	2,622.0	2,401.0	2,203.1
Employees	0.0%	2,000	2,000	2,000	2,000	2,000

TORCH ENERGY ROYALTY TRUST   NBB: TRRU

Rodney Square North, 1100 North Market Street
Wilmington, DE 19890
Phone: 302 636-6016
Fax: –
Web: www.torchroyalty.com

CEO: –
CFO: –
HR: –
FYE: December 31
Type: Public

Investors in Torch Energy Royalty Trust probably won't light an eternal flame in remembrance when the gas is all gone. The trust distributes to shareholders the royalties from natural gas properties and oil wells in which it owns stakes. The trust's gas fields are in Texas Alabama and Louisiana. As a grantor trust Torch Energy does not pay federal income tax; instead the shareholders who receive quarterly royalties are taxed directly but receive tax credits on gas extracted from some of the trust's hard-to-drill properties. Torch Energy Royalty Trust's investors have voted to wind up and liquidate the trust.

	Annual Growth	12/08	12/09	12/10	12/11	12/12
Sales ($ mil.)	(61.5%)	6.4	2.6	3.2	2.7	0.1
Net income ($ mil.)	–	3.2	1.2	2.1	1.3	(1.1)
Market value ($ mil.)	(17.3%)	12.4	40.9	31.2	18.1	5.8
Employees	–	–	–	–	–	–

TOROTEL, INC.
NBB: TTLO

520 N. Rogers Road
Olathe, KS 66062
Phone: 913 747-6111
Fax: –
Web: www.torotelinc.com

CEO: Dale H Sizemore Jr
CFO: Heath C Hancock
HR: –
FYE: April 30
Type: Public

Torotel is a military magnet. The company's Torotel Products subsidiary makes more than 32000 magnetic components used to control electrical voltages and currents in aviation missile guidance communication navigational and other systems. Products include transformers inductors chokes and toroidal coils. Subsidiary Electronika designs and sells ballast transformers to the airline industry. Torotel sells its products primarily in the US to commercial customers (including those in the health care oil public safety and financial services industries) but most of the company's sales come from the aerospace and military markets.

	Annual Growth	04/15	04/16	04/17	04/18	04/19
Sales ($ mil.)	11.0%	13.6	16.2	16.3	18.4	20.6
Net income ($ mil.)	52.1%	0.1	0.5	(0.3)	(2.0)	0.6
Market value ($ mil.)	5.2%	4.0	5.3	4.7	4.0	4.9
Employees	3.1%	153	151	166	155	173

TORRANCE MEMORIAL MEDICAL CENTER

3330 LOMITA BLVD
TORRANCE, CA 905055002
Phone: 310-325-9110
Fax: –
Web: www.lapbandsurgeryorangecounty.com

CEO: Craig Leach
CFO: –
HR: –
FYE: September 30
Type: Private

Back in 1925 Jared Sydney Torrance founded Torrance Memorial Medical Center in the southern California town that also bears his name. The not-for-profit medical center now includes about 445 beds surgical suites clinical and diagnostic labs and specialist centers for cancer metabolic heart and other conditions. It is one of three burn centers in Los Angeles. Torrance Memorial Medical Center reaches beyond its walls and into the community with hospice care and home health care. The hospital also provides nursing residency programs and it offers staffing support services to physicians offices in the area.

	Annual Growth	12/15	12/16	12/17*	03/18*	09/18
Sales ($ mil.)	(74.2%)	–	–	639.0	167.1	164.9
Net income ($ mil.)	(85.2%)	–	–	13.4	4.6	2.0
Market value ($ mil.)	–	–	–	–	–	–
Employees	–	–	–	–	–	3,500

*Fiscal year change

TOTAL HEALTH CARE, INC.

3011 W GRAND BLVD # 1600
DETROIT, MI 482023000
Phone: 313-871-2000
Fax: –
Web: www.thcmi.com

CEO: –
CFO: –
HR: –
FYE: December 31
Type: Private

Total Health Care provides health care coverage and related services to members in southeast Michigan (the greater Detroit area) and surrounding counties. Groups and individuals can choose Total Health Care for their health insurance. The HMO serves more than 80000 members through individual and group health plan policies. Total Health Care also has a contract with the State of Michigan to serve patients with coverage through Medicaid and the State's MI Child program. Pharmacy services are provided through a contracted network of pharmacy providers.

	Annual Growth	12/00	12/01	12/13	12/14	12/15
Sales ($ mil.)	–	–	0.0	224.1	272.3	322.5
Net income ($ mil.)	–	–	0.0	(6.4)	5.0	5.9
Market value ($ mil.)	–	–	–	–	–	–
Employees	–	–	–	–	–	100

TOTAL SYSTEM SERVICES, INC.
NYS: TSS

One TSYS Way, P.O. 1755
Columbus, GA 31902
Phone: 706 644-6081
Fax: 706 649-2456
Web: www.tsys.com

CEO: –
CFO: –
HR: –
FYE: December 31
Type: Public

Total System Services (TSYS) helps financial institutions go paperless. The company is one of the largest electronic payment processors in the world serving financial institutions and other companies that issue bank private-label prepaid or other types of cards. TSYS' products and services include credit authorization payment processing e-commerce services card issuance and such customer-relations services as fraud monitoring. It also provides merchant services primarily in the US. Through NetSpend TSYS also issues prepaid and payroll cards to self-bank customers.

	Annual Growth	12/13	12/14	12/15	12/16	12/17
Sales ($ mil.)	23.3%	2,132.4	2,446.9	2,779.5	4,170.1	4,928.0
Net income ($ mil.)	24.4%	244.8	322.9	364.0	319.6	586.2
Market value ($ mil.)	24.2%	6,020.5	6,143.5	9,009.0	8,869.7	14,307.6
Employees	3.5%	9,600	9,900	10,500	11,500	11,000

TOTES ISOTONER CORPORATION

9655 International Blvd.
Cincinnati OH 45246-5658
Phone: 513-682-8200
Fax: 513-682-8602
Web: www.totes-isotoner.com

CEO: Daniel S Rajczak
CFO: Donna Deye
HR: –
FYE: February 28
Type: Private

From head to toe to fingertips totes>Isotoner has the goods to keep its customers dry and comfortable. The company makes and distributes weather gear including umbrellas gloves rubber shoe covers rain hats and raincoats and water-resistant tote bags. It has extended its product line to include slippers and caps through several acquisitions in recent years. It distributes its products through department stores in the US the UK and France. totes>Isotoner also operates a network of more than 100 owned outlet mall-based stores. The company formed by the merger of totes and Isotoner in 1997 is owned by private equity firm MidOcean Partners. MidOcean acquired its majority stake for $288 million.

TOUCHSTONE BANK
NBB: TSBA

20718 First Street
McKenney, VA 23872
Phone: 804 478-4434
Fax: –
Web: www.bankofmckenney.com

CEO: James R Black
CFO: Vera H Primm
HR: –
FYE: December 31
Type: Public

This company can help you make the most of your McKenney penny or your Dinwiddie dollar. The Bank of McKenney is a community thrift serving central Virginia's Dinwiddie and Chesterfield counties the independent city of Colonial Heights and surrounding areas. The bank's six branches offer traditional deposit products including savings and checking accounts NOW accounts money markets and CDs. Commercial real estate loans make up about half of the company's lending portfolio; residential mortgages and trusts make up about 35%. Subsidiary McKenney Group provides investment services insurance products and business management services.

	Annual Growth	12/12	12/13	12/14	12/15	12/16
Assets ($ mil.)	1.3%	211.9	213.4	216.1	218.3	222.8
Net income ($ mil.)	9.3%	1.2	1.7	1.9	1.7	1.7
Market value ($ mil.)	11.9%	12.7	15.9	18.9	19.2	19.9
Employees	–	–	–	–	–	–

TOURO COLLEGE

500 7TH AVE FL 5
NEW YORK, NY 100180821
Phone: 646-565-6026
Fax: –
Web: www.tourolaw.edu

CEO: Bernard J Luskin
CFO: –
HR: –
FYE: June 30
Type: Private

Touro College is a Jewish university (the largest private Jewish-based educational institution in the US) and has sister institutions in France Germany Israel and Russia and branches in California Florida and Nevada. Some 19000 (Jewish and non-Jewish) students are enrolled in its 32 schools on 25 campuses which offer associate bachelor's and master's degrees in business education and law as well as professional degrees in osteopathic medicine pharmacy law and other fields. Touro also oversees the operations of New York Medical College. The institution claims some 75000 alumni.

	Annual Growth	06/06	06/07	06/08	06/09	06/10
Sales ($ mil.)	(63.1%)	–	–	2,037.4	145.5	277.4
Net income ($ mil.)	3009.8%	–	–	0.0	0.0	15.8
Market value ($ mil.)	–	–	–	–	–	–
Employees	–	–	–	–	–	4,600

TOWER FINANCIAL CORP. NMS: TOFC

116 East Berry Street
Fort Wayne, IN 46802
Phone: 260 427-7000
Fax: –
Web: www.towerbank.net

CEO: –
CFO: –
HR: –
FYE: December 31
Type: Public

This tower aims to be a power in Indiana. Tower Financial is the holding company for Tower Bank & Trust which was formed in 1999 to fill the void in community banking services left in the wake of the consolidation of local banks into national banking companies. Targeting individuals and small to midsized businesses the bank has some six branches and loan production offices mainly in and around Fort Wayne. It focuses mainly on commercial lending with business mortgages and operating loans making up around three-quarters of its loan portfolio. It also issues residential mortgages and personal loans. Deposit products include checking savings and money market accounts and CDs.

	Annual Growth	12/08	12/09	12/10	12/11	12/12
Assets ($ mil.)	(0.5%)	696.6	680.2	659.9	700.7	684.0
Net income ($ mil.)	32.5%	1.9	(5.6)	3.2	6.6	5.7
Market value ($ mil.)	18.5%	28.6	32.5	35.8	39.3	56.3
Employees	(2.0%)	179	151	156	155	165

TOWER INTERNATIONAL INC NYS: TOWR

17672 Laurel Park Drive North, Suite 400 E
Livonia, MI 48152
Phone: 248 675-6000
Fax: –
Web: www.towerinternational.com

CEO: –
CFO: –
HR: Denise Austin
FYE: December 31
Type: Public

Tower International has a tall order to fill: supplying chassis to most of the world's biggest carmakers. The company manufactures engineered structural metal components for vehicles such as body chassis and frame structures. It also makes welded assemblies for cars pickups and SUVs. Key customers have included noteworthy names like Volkswagen Fiat and Ford Motor. Tower has roughly 25 production manufacturing facilities in North America and Europe and six engineering and sales locations worldwide. The company divested its Asia and Latin America holdings in 2016-17.

	Annual Growth	12/13	12/14	12/15	12/16	12/17
Sales ($ mil.)	(1.4%)	2,102.0	2,067.8	1,955.7	1,913.6	1,988.0
Net income ($ mil.)	–	–	(20.3)	21.5	194.1	38.6	47.6
Market value ($ mil.)	9.3%	439.6	524.9	586.9	582.4	627.6
Employees	(2.4%)	8,700	7,800	8,300	7,900	7,900

TOWERS WATSON & CO. NYS: TW

901 N. Glebe Road
Arlington, VA 22203
Phone: 703 258-8000
Fax: –
Web: www.towerswatson.com

CEO: John J Haley
CFO: Roger F Millay
HR: –
FYE: June 30
Type: Public

This company is the result of adhering to the axiom keep your friends close and your enemies even closer. Created after the 2010 merger of rivals Towers Perrin and Watson Wyatt Towers Watson is a leading human resources consulting firm providing services related to employee benefits risk and financial services and talent and rewards. The company assists clients (many Fortune 1000 firms) in such matters as controlling health care costs employee retention and negotiating the risks and challenges of mergers and acquisitions. The estimated $4 billion stock merger between Towers Perrin and Watson Wyatt was announced in June 2009 and became effective in January 2010.

	Annual Growth	06/10	06/11	06/12	06/13	06/14
Sales ($ mil.)	9.9%	2,387.8	3,259.5	3,417.7	3,596.8	3,481.9
Net income ($ mil.)	31.4%	120.6	194.4	260.2	318.8	359.3
Market value ($ mil.)	28.0%	2,732.7	4,622.0	4,213.3	5,763.6	7,331.4
Employees	3.8%	12,750	13,100	14,500	14,500	14,800

TOWERSTREAM CORP NBB: TWER

76 Hammarlund Way
Middletown, RI 02842
Phone: 401 848-5848
Fax: –
Web: www.towerstream.com

CEO: Ernest Ortega
CFO: John Macdonald
HR: –
FYE: December 31
Type: Public

TowerStream maintains a commanding view of the wireless landscape. The company provides wireless broadband network services to businesses over its network of rooftop and tower-mounted antennas. Its networks can be accessed by customers within a 10-mile radius. The company has about 3600 business customers including retailers educational institutions and banks. Charging a monthly subscription fee TowerStream provides service in a more than a dozen US markets: Boston Chicago Dallas Houston Las Vegas/Reno Los Angeles Miami Nashville New York City Philadelphia San Francisco and Seattle as well Providence Rhode Island.

	Annual Growth	12/14	12/15	12/16	12/17	12/18
Sales ($ mil.)	(7.1%)	33.0	27.9	26.9	26.2	24.6
Net income ($ mil.)	–	(27.6)	(40.5)	(20.4)	(12.5)	(10.2)
Market value ($ mil.)	3.4%	0.7	0.1	0.1	1.2	0.8
Employees	(23.5%)	140	154	88	83	48

TOWN SPORTS INTERNATIONAL HOLDINGS INC NMS: CLUB

1001 US North Highway 1, Suite 201
Jupiter, FL 33477
Phone: 212 246-6700
Fax: –
Web: www.townsportsinternational.com

CEO: Patrick Walsh
CFO: Carolyn Spatafora
HR: –
FYE: December 31
Type: Public

Town Sports International wants to be the apple a day that keeps the doctor away in NYC. The company owns and operates some 160 full-service health clubs about two-thirds of which are in the New York City area under the New York Sports Club banner. The company also has clubs in Boston Philadelphia and Washington D.C. and claims about 510000 members. It offers various membership plans that cater to its members' usage needs. Members designate a specific "home" club they can use at any time and retain an option to upgrade and gain access to multiple clubs within a single region or pay even more to gain access to all clubs in all four regions. Town Sports also has three clubs in Switzerland.

	Annual Growth	12/14	12/15	12/16	12/17	12/18
Sales ($ mil.)	(0.6%)	453.8	424.3	396.9	403.0	443.1
Net income ($ mil.)	–	(69.0)	21.2	8.0	4.4	0.1
Market value ($ mil.)	1.8%	161.8	32.4	68.0	150.9	174.0
Employees	(1.0%)	8,000	7,500	7,600	5,900	7,700

TOWNSHIP HIGH SCHOOL DISTRICT 211 FOUNDATION

1750 S ROSELLE RD STE 100
PALATINE, IL 600677302
Phone: 708-359-3300
Fax: –
Web: www.d211.org

CEO: –
CFO: –
HR: –
FYE: June 30
Type: Private

Township High School District 211 is the largest high school district in Illinois with some 12500 students attending its five high schools (grades 9 to 12) — James B. Conant William Fremd Hoffman Estates Palatine and Schaumburg — and two special education academies. The district's student-teacher ratio is nearly 14-to-1 and serves several suburban communities 25 miles northwest of Chicago. The school district started as one school (Palatine High School) in the Palatine-Schaumburg Township area in 1875 with the first graduating class in 1877.

	Annual Growth	06/13	06/14	06/15	06/16	06/17
Sales ($ mil.)	5.7%	–	280.2	296.9	304.9	331.1
Net income ($ mil.)	–	–	(8.8)	(17.2)	(10.4)	(15.1)
Market value ($ mil.)	–	–	–	–	–	–
Employees	–	–	–	–	–	1,909

TOYOTA MOTOR CREDIT CORP.

6565 Headquarters Drive
Plano, TX 75024
Phone: 469 486-9300
Fax: –
Web: www.toyotafinancial.com

CEO: Michael R. (Mike) Groff
CFO: –
HR: –
FYE: March 31
Type: Public

Toyota Motor Credit (TMCC) is the US financing arm of Toyota Financial Services which is a subsidiary of Toyota Motor Corporation the world's largest carmaker. TMCC provides retail leasing retail and wholesale sales financing and other financial services to Toyota and Lexus dealers and their customers for the purchase of new and used cars and trucks. It offers similar services to Toyota industrial equipment dealers. TMCC which underwrites and services the finance contracts operates three regional customer service centers and some 30 dealer sales and service branches across the US and Puerto Rico.

	Annual Growth	03/15	03/16	03/17	03/18	03/19
Sales ($ mil.)	8.9%	9,142.0	10,483.0	11,246.0	11,856.0	12,836.0
Net income ($ mil.)	(9.7%)	1,197.0	932.0	267.0	3,410.0	795.0
Market value ($ mil.)	–	–	–	–	–	–
Employees	(0.4%)	3,251	3,140	3,185	3,300	3,200

TPS PARKING MANAGEMENT LLC

200 W. Monroe St.
Chicago IL 60606
Phone: 312-453-1700
Fax: 312-633-1406
Web: www.h2oplus.com

CEO: Kevin J Shrier
CFO: –
HR: –
FYE: December 31
Type: Private

TPS Parking Management doing business as The Parking Spot wants to take you the last bit of the way to the airport. The company operates off-site parking lots near more than 20 major US airports some with multiple locations. Lots have both covered and uncovered areas as well as valet parking. The Parking Spot uses conspicuous black-on-yellow polka-dot vans to shuttle customers to and from the airport terminal. The company takes reservations for parking slots and offers corporate discounts as well as its own version of a frequent flyer program. It was founded by CEO Martin Nesbitt who opened the first lot at Houston's main airport in 1998 and sold in 2011 to Green Courte Partners a private-equity REIT.

TRACK GROUP INC

NBB: TRCK

200 E. 5th Avenue Suite 100
Naperville, IL 60563
Phone: 877 260-2010
Fax: –

CEO: Derek Cassell
CFO: Peter K Poli
HR: –
FYE: September 30
Type: Public

Thanks in part to SecureAlert you can run but you can not hide. The company (formerly RemoteMDx) develops markets and sells wireless monitoring equipment and services to law enforcement and bail bond agencies. Its primary product is Tracker-PAL — tracking devices worn on the ankle to monitor the whereabouts of criminals on parole or probation. Using global positioning system and cellular technology the device features two-way voice communications alarms and Web-based location tracking in real time. The company's SecureAlert Monitoring subsidiary provides monitoring services. The company electronically monitors some 12700 offenders.

	Annual Growth	09/15	09/16	09/17	09/18	09/19
Sales ($ mil.)	13.1%	20.8	27.2	29.7	30.6	34.0
Net income ($ mil.)	–	(5.7)	(8.5)	(4.7)	(5.4)	(2.6)
Market value ($ mil.)	(48.3%)	81.0	82.1	16.3	10.3	5.8
Employees	(2.3%)	182	233	156	160	166

TRACTOR SUPPLY CO.

NMS: TSCO

5401 Virginia Way
Brentwood, TN 37027
Phone: 615 440-4000
Fax: –
Web: www.tractorsupply.com

CEO: Gregory A. (Greg) Sandfort
CFO: Kurt Barton
HR: Chad M Frazell
FYE: December 29
Type: Public

Tractor Supply Company (TSC) does a whole lot more than its name might suggest. Besides providing agricultural machine parts TSC offers animal feed fencing power tools riding mowers work clothing and pet supplies as well as tools for gardening irrigation welding and towing. TSC offers both name-brand merchandise and its own crop of private-label goods. The company has nationwide scope operating more than 1850 stores in some 49 US states under the Tractor Supply Company Del's Farm Supply and Petsense banners. Stores are concentrated in rural areas and near large cities to cater to full- and part-time farmers ranchers and contractors. TSC also sells online.

	Annual Growth	12/14	12/15	12/16	12/17	12/18
Sales ($ mil.)	8.5%	5,711.7	6,226.5	6,779.6	7,256.4	7,911.0
Net income ($ mil.)	9.5%	370.9	410.4	437.1	422.6	532.4
Market value ($ mil.)	1.7%	9,492.8	10,437.0	9,235.8	9,106.6	10,137.3
Employees	8.3%	21,100	23,000	26,000	28,000	29,000

TRADE STREET RESIDENTIAL, INC.

NMS: TSRE

19950 West Country Club Drive
Aventura, NY 33180
Phone: 786 248-5200
Fax: –
Web: www.tradestreetresidential.com

CEO: –
CFO: –
HR: –
FYE: December 31
Type: Public

Trade Street Residential shopped 'til it dropped and is now ready to go home. Formerly Feldman Mall Properties the company changed its business interests in 2012 to move from shopping malls to apartment homes. The real estate investment trust (REIT) owns and operates about 15 apartment complexes in eight states in the Southeast and Texas. (As a REIT it is exempt from paying federal income tax so long as it distributes at least 90% of its income back to shareholders.) Its apartments have an average monthly rent per of $817. In addition the trust has a land portfolio of about 45 acres in Florida and Virginia that it plans to develop into four different properties. The REIT went public in 2013.

	Annual Growth	12/06	12/07	12/11	12/12	12/13
Sales ($ mil.)	(11.0%)	65.3	55.3	9.0	14.5	29.0
Net income ($ mil.)	–	20.2	(16.2)	(3.8)	(8.6)	(16.6)
Market value ($ mil.)	(9.2%)	142.8	42.3	0.7	0.9	72.6
Employees	(8.6%)	207	167	–	–	110

TRADESTATION GROUP INC.

8050 SW 10th St. Ste. 2000
Plantation FL 33324
Phone: 954-652-7000
Fax: 954-652-7300
Web: www.tradestation.com

CEO: Salomon Sredni
CFO: Edward Codispoti
HR: –
FYE: December 31
Type: Private

TradeStation is a stop on the way to wealth or poverty depending on the skill or luck of the trader. The company offers an electronic trading platform to provide commission-based direct-access online brokerage services. The technology helps traders manage trading systems and automate the execution of orders for equities and futures. Subsidiary TradeStation Technologies offers the TradeStation platform as either a hosted subscription-based service or a licensed software package and it operates an online trading strategy community site. TradeStation Securities is an online brokerage that serves retail and some institutional traders. In 2011 the company was acquired by Japan-based Monex Group for about $400 million.

TRAILER BRIDGE INC.

10405 New Berlin Rd. East
Jacksonville FL 32226
Phone: 904-751-7100
Fax: 904-751-7444
Web: www.trailerbridge.com

NASDAQ: TRBR
CEO: Mitch Luchiano
CFO: –
HR: –
FYE: December 31
Type: Public

Traversing land and sea Trailer Bridge connects the continental US Puerto Rico and the Dominican Republic. The company's oceangoing barges designed to carry shipping containers sail between Jacksonville Florida and the two islands. Southbound shipments which represent about 75% of the freight transported include raw materials consumer goods furniture and vehicles. Trailer Bridge's land-based assets move freight within the US and abroad. Its fleet comprises some 140 tractors 500 dry van trailers and car carriers 3960 high-cube containers and 3150 chassis including two roll-on/roll-off (ro/ro) multiuse barges and two container barges. Trailer Bridge emerged from Chapter 11 proceedings in 2012.

TRAMMO, INC.

667 MADISON AVE FL 4
NEW YORK, NY 100658029
Phone: 212-223-3200
Fax: –

CEO: Ashok Kishore
CFO: Edward G. Weiner
HR: Pat Berry
FYE: December 31
Type: Private

Stockpiles of fertilizers liquefied petroleum gas (LPG) and petrochemicals are the "ammo" which international trader Trammo (formerly Transammonia) uses in its battle with competitors. The company trades distributes and transports these commodities around the world. Trammo's fertilizer business includes ammonia phosphates and urea. Its Sea-3 subsidiary imports and distributes propane to residential commercial and industrial customers in the northeastern US and Florida. The Trammochem unit trades in petrochemicals specializing in aromatics and olefins. Its Trammo Gas trades LPG and propane as well as ethane butane and natural gas in the US.

	Annual Growth	12/12	12/13	12/14	12/16	12/18
Sales ($ mil.)	(26.9%)	–	–	11,266.3	6,453.3	3,212.2
Net income ($ mil.)	–	–	–	–	31.1	(229.7)	(12.7)
Market value ($ mil.)	–	–	–	–	–	–
Employees	–	–	–	–	–	250

TRANS WORLD CORP.

545 Fifth Avenue, Suite 940
New York, NY 10017
Phone: 212 983-3355
Fax: –
Web: www.transwc.com

NBB: TWOC
CEO: Rami S Ramadan
CFO: Hung D Le
HR: –
FYE: December 31
Type: Public

American-style gambling is a global bread winner for Trans World. The company which focuses on small and midsized casinos and gaming parlors owns and operates four niche casinos that feature slot machines and gaming tables in the Czech Republic. The casinos operate under the name American Chance Casinos and feature themes from different eras of US history (Chicago in the Roaring 1920s Miami Beach in the 1950s New Orleans in the 1920s and the Pacific South Seas). The company also operates a casino in Croatia near a resort city on the coast of the Adriatic Sea. Trans World is in the process of adding hotels to its operations. An investment group led by director Timothy Ewing owns nearly 40% of the company.

	Annual Growth	12/12	12/13	12/14	12/15	12/16
Sales ($ mil.)	10.3%	36.0	36.5	38.5	42.4	53.2
Net income ($ mil.)	36.8%	1.8	2.4	2.6	3.9	6.3
Market value ($ mil.)	21.7%	23.5	21.8	28.6	22.3	51.5
Employees	3.7%	524	479	502	552	605

TRANS WORLD ENTERTAINMENT CORP.

38 Corporate Circle
Albany, NY 12203
Phone: 518 452-1242
Fax: –
Web: www.twec.com

NAS: TWMC
CEO: Michael Feurer
CFO: Edwin Sapienza
HR: –
FYE: February 02
Type: Public

Just an F.Y.I. but Trans World Entertainment operates F.Y.E. and a handful of other retail ventures. F.Y.E. (aka For Your Entertainment) stores sell CDs DVDs video games software and related products at about 390 locations throughout the US Puerto Rico and the Virgin Islands. Trans World's other bricks-and-mortar operations include about 15 video stores under the Saturday Matinee and Suncoast Motion Pictures banners. Most of the firm's retail outlets are located in shopping malls. Trans World also sells entertainment products via its e-commerce sites (including fye.com secondspin.com and wherehouse.com). Chairman and CEO Bob Higgins founded the company in 1972.

	Annual Growth	01/15	01/16	01/17*	02/18	02/19
Sales ($ mil.)	3.9%	358.5	334.7	353.5	442.9	418.2
Net income ($ mil.)	–	1.8	2.7	3.2	(42.6)	(97.4)
Market value ($ mil.)	(35.4%)	6.3	5.9	5.3	2.9	1.1
Employees	(7.5%)	3,000	2,900	3,000	2,600	2,200

*Fiscal year change

TRANS-SYSTEM, INC.

7405 S HAYFORD RD
CHENEY, WA 990049633
Phone: 509-623-4001
Fax: –
Web: www.trans-system.com

CEO: James C. (Jim) Williams
CFO: Deanna Adams
HR: –
FYE: March 31
Type: Private

Freight hauler Trans-System operates through three main units: System Transport (flatbed); TW Transport (refrigerated and dry van); and James J. Williams (bulk commodities). The Trans-System trucking companies operate from some 10 terminals in the western US. Overall the company's fleet consists of about 1000 tractors and 1500 trailers. Trans-System also offers logistics services and runs a driver training school. Jim Williams founded the company in 1972 although it got its start when Williams' grandfather began transporting petroleum products throughout northern Idaho and eastern Washington.

	Annual Growth	03/12	03/13	03/14	03/15	03/16
Sales ($ mil.)	6.2%	–	197.7	210.0	228.1	236.9
Net income ($ mil.)	(14.7%)	–	8.1	6.6	15.0	5.0
Market value ($ mil.)	–	–	–	–	–	–
Employees	–	–	–	–	–	650

TRANSACT TECHNOLOGIES INC.　　　　　　　　　　　NMS: TACT

One Hamden Center, 2319 Whitney Avenue, Suite 3B　　　CEO: Bart C Shuldman
Hamden, CT 06518　　　　　　　　　　　　　　　CFO: Steven A Demartino
Phone: 203 859-6800　　　　　　　　　　　　　　　　　　　　HR: –
Fax: –　　　　　　　　　　　　　　　　　　　　　　　FYE: December 31
Web: www.transact-tech.com　　　　　　　　　　　　　　　Type: Public

TransAct Technologies knows how to ink the deal. The company makes thermal inkjet and impact printers under the Epic EPICENTRAL and other brands that record transaction information for point-of-sale (POS) casino and gaming lottery banking food safety and e-commerce transactions. TransAct's printers and terminals produce receipts coupons lottery tickets and other printed records. TransAct also makes document transport mechanisms for ATMs and kiosks and manufactures custom printers for electronics manufacturers and oil and gas exploration companies. TransAct sells its products to OEMs VARs and other distributors as well as directly to end-users. About 75% of sales comes from customers in the US.

	Annual Growth	12/14	12/15	12/16	12/17	12/18
Sales ($ mil.)	0.7%	53.1	59.7	57.2	56.3	54.6
Net income ($ mil.)	–	(2.4)	3.1	3.6	3.2	5.4
Market value ($ mil.)	13.2%	40.6	63.7	49.0	98.3	66.6
Employees	(0.6%)	129	125	120	123	126

TRANSCAT INC　　　　　　　　　　　　　　　　　NMS: TRNS

35 Vantage Point Drive　　　　　　　　　　　　　　CEO: Lee D. Rudow
Rochester, NY 14624　　　　　　　　　　　　　　　CFO: John J. Zimmer
Phone: 585 352-7777　　　　　　　　　　　　　　HR: Jennifer Nelson
Fax: –　　　　　　　　　　　　　　　　　　　　　　　FYE: March 30
Web: www.transcat.com　　　　　　　　　　　　　　　　Type: Public

This cat helps you measure up. And calibrate. And test. Transcat distributes test measurement and calibration equipment used in industrial and scientific settings. The company sells products such as multimeters oscilloscopes recorders and temperature devices from a range of instrument manufacturers to customers primarily in North America through its catalog. The company also provides instrument calibration and repair services. Transcat targets customers in the petroleum products and chemical manufacturing industries as well as pharmaceutical and telecommunications companies. Customers have included such big names as Dow Chemical Duke Energy DuPont and Exxon Mobil.

	Annual Growth	03/15	03/16	03/17	03/18	03/19
Sales ($ mil.)	6.8%	123.6	122.2	143.9	155.1	160.9
Net income ($ mil.)	15.4%	4.0	4.1	4.5	5.9	7.1
Market value ($ mil.)	24.4%	69.2	73.1	90.3	112.9	165.7
Employees	11.5%	443	537	585	606	685

TRANSCEND SERVICES INC.　　　　　　　　　　　NASDAQ: TRCR

1 Glenlake Pkwy. Ste. 1325　　　　　　　　　　　　　　　　CEO: –
Atlanta GA 30328　　　　　　　　　　　　　　　　　　　　　CFO: –
Phone: 678-808-0600　　　　　　　　　　　　　　　　　　　　HR: –
Fax: 678-808-0601　　　　　　　　　　　　　　　　　FYE: December 31
Web: www.transcendservices.com　　　　　　　　　　　Type: Subsidiary

Transcend Services helps make sense of doctors' gibberish. The medical transcription company uses Internet-based technology to turn doctors' audio patient records into written text. Its home-based medical transcriptionists convert the physicians' recorded notes (made using either Transcend Services' proprietary BeyondTXT technology or the clients' own systems) into text documents. The company counts some 400 hospitals clinics and physician group practices among its customers. It is increasing the use of speech recognition software to automatically convert voice to text after which the documents are edited by transcriptionists. In fact in 2012 Transcend Services was acquired by software firm Nuance Communications.

TRANSCONTINENTAL GAS PIPE LINE COMPANY, LLC

2800 POST OAK BLVD　　　　　　　　　　　　　　　　　　　CEO: –
HOUSTON, TX 770566100　　　　　　　　　　　　　　　　　CFO: –
Phone: 713-215-2000　　　　　　　　　　　　　　　　　　　　HR: –
Fax: –　　　　　　　　　　　　　　　　　　　　　　　FYE: December 31
　　　　　　　　　　　　　　　　　　　　　　　　　　　　　Type: Private

As coast to coast as it name implies Transcontinental Gas Pipe Line Corporation (commonly known as Transco) is an interstate natural gas transmission company. Transco operates about 9800 miles of natural gas pipeline extending from the Gulf of Mexico to New York. The company also operates 45 gas compressor stations four underground storage fields and a liquefied natural gas (LNG) storage facility. In 2011 Transco had access to 200 billion cu. ft. of natural gas. Its customers include natural gas distributors such as Public Service Enterprise Group National Grid USA and Piedmont Natural Gas Company. Transco is a subsidiary of Williams Partners itself a subsidiary of The Williams Companies.

	Annual Growth	12/12	12/13	12/14	12/15	12/16
Sales ($ mil.)	6.0%	–	1,356.3	1,433.1	1,592.5	1,616.1
Net income ($ mil.)	11.9%	–	374.0	422.9	575.5	523.4
Market value ($ mil.)	–	–	–	–	–	–
Employees						4

TRANSCONTINENTAL REALTY INVESTORS, INC.　　　NYS: TCI

1603 Lyndon B. Johnson Freeway, Suite 800　　　　　　CEO: Daniel J Moos
Dallas, TX 75234　　　　　　　　　　　　　　　　　CFO: Gene S Bertcher
Phone: 469 522-4200　　　　　　　　　　　　　　　　　　　　HR: –
Fax: –　　　　　　　　　　　　　　　　　　　　　　　FYE: December 31
Web: www.transconrealty-invest.com　　　　　　　　　　　Type: Public

Transcontinental Realty likes to find diamonds in the rough. The company acquires develops and owns income-producing commercial and residential real estate particularly properties that it believes are undervalued. Its portfolio consists nearly 40 apartment complexes with more than 6000 units in the southern US in addition to about 7.7 million sq.ft. of rentable commercial space including nearly 8 commercial properties. Texas is its largest market by far. Additionally the company has investments in apartment projects under development and more than 4000 acres of undeveloped and partially developed land most of it also in Texas.

	Annual Growth	12/14	12/15	12/16	12/17	12/18
Sales ($ mil.)	12.4%	75.9	102.2	118.5	125.2	121.0
Net income ($ mil.)	44.5%	41.6	(7.6)	0.0	(15.8)	181.5
Market value ($ mil.)	28.8%	89.8	89.8	104.8	273.0	246.9
Employees						

TRANSDIGM GROUP INC　　　　　　　　　　　　　NYS: TDG

1301 East 9th Street, Suite 3000　　　　　　　CEO: W. Nicholas (Nick) Howley
Cleveland, OH 44114　　　　　　　　　　　　　　　　CFO: James Skulina
Phone: 216 706-2960　　　　　　　　　　　　　　　　　　　　HR: –
Fax: –　　　　　　　　　　　　　　　　　　　　　　FYE: September 30
Web: www.transdigm.com　　　　　　　　　　　　　　　　　Type: Public

TransDigm Group supplies a variety of behind-the-scenes componentry for aircraft manufacturing including audio systems pumps and valves and power conditioning devices. Operating through a plethora of subsidiaries TransDigm makes and distributes systems and components for commercial and military aircraft. Its products are found in several Boeing and Airbus airplanes Bombardier and Embraer regional jets and a number of military planes and helicopters. TransDigm is a frequent acquirer of companies recently averaging about four per year. The majority of the company's products are sold to customers in the US.

	Annual Growth	09/15	09/16	09/17	09/18	09/19
Sales ($ mil.)	17.9%	2,707.1	3,171.4	3,504.3	3,811.1	5,223.2
Net income ($ mil.)	18.8%	447.2	586.4	596.9	957.1	889.8
Market value ($ mil.)	25.1%	11,355.9	15,456.9	13,667.6	19,903.9	27,836.1
Employees	22.2%	8,200	9,300	9,200	10,100	18,300

TRANSITCENTER INC.

1065 AVENUE OF THE AMERIC
NEW YORK, NY 100181878
Phone: 212-329-2000
Fax: –
Web: www.transitchek.com

CEO: –
CFO: –
HR: –
FYE: December 31
Type: Private

TransitCenter's mission is to get commuters out of their cars and onto a bus ferry train van or cable car. The not-for-profit company is charged with encouraging greater use of public and private transit services to improve mobility reduce traffic help the environment and support the economy. Its website provides transit guides for a dozen US cities including Atlanta and Washington D.C. TransitCenter sold its TransitChek program developed to encourage businesses and their employees to use public transportation through incentives that reduce payroll taxes for employers and allow commuters to pay for daily travel using pretax dollars. It continues to advocate for public transportation.

	Annual Growth	12/04	12/05	12/06	12/07	12/09
Sales ($ mil.)	6.5%	–	17.1	17.9	19.7	22.1
Net income ($ mil.)	–	–	–	(1.8)	0.6	2.7
Market value ($ mil.)	–	–	–	–	–	–
Employees	–	–	–	–	–	74

TRANSMONTAIGNE PARTNERS LP

NYS: TLP

1670 Broadway, Suite 3100
Denver, CO 80202
Phone: 303 626-8200
Fax: 303 626-8228
Web: www.transmontaignepartners.com

CEO: Frederick W Boutin
CFO: Robert T Fuller
HR: –
FYE: December 31
Type: Public

TransMontaigne Partners an affiliate of TransMontaigne Inc. provides integrated terminaling storage and pipeline services for companies that market and distribute refined products and crude oil. TransMontaigne Partners handles light refined products (gasolines heating oils and jet and diesel fuels) heavy refined products (asphalt and residual fuel oils) and crude oil. It operates about 50 terminals (with a storage of capacity of 23.7 million barrels of oil and gas) and other facilities along the Gulf Coast and major rivers in the South and Midwest; it also operates pipelines. Customers include Marathon and a marketing and supply unit of Valero.

	Annual Growth	12/13	12/14	12/15	12/16	12/17
Sales ($ mil.)	3.6%	158.9	150.1	152.5	164.9	183.3
Net income ($ mil.)	8.7%	34.7	32.5	41.7	44.1	48.5
Market value ($ mil.)	(1.8%)	701.6	520.2	441.7	730.8	651.2
Employees	(3.6%)	584	510	450	452	504

TRANSNET CORPORATION

OTC: TRNT

45 Columbia Rd.
Somerville NJ 08876-3576
Phone: 908-253-0500
Fax: 908-253-0601
Web: www.transnet.com

CEO: –
CFO: John J Wilk
HR: –
FYE: June 30
Type: Public

TransNet sells and supports computers networking equipment peripherals and software. It provides PCs from Hewlett-Packard IBM and Apple. TransNet also supplies peripherals networking products software and telephony equipment from such manufacturers as Nortel Networks Microsoft 3Com Novell and Cisco. The company's services include network support maintenance systems integration installation and training. Its clients are located primarily in the New York City/New Jersey and Eastern Pennsylvania regions. TransNet's customers have included pharmaceutical giant Schering-Plough.

TRANSPERFECT TRANSLATIONS INTERNATIONAL INC.

3 PARK AVE FL 40
NEW YORK, NY 100165934
Phone: 212-689-5555
Fax: –
Web: www.transperfect.com

CEO: Phil Shawe
CFO: –
HR: –
FYE: December 31
Type: Private

You pick the language or languages and TransPerfect Translations International will aim to get your message through. In addition to translation and interpretation the company offers services such as document management multicultural marketing staffing subtitling and voiceover work. Its network of translators can handle more than 170 languages through offices located in 90 cities spanning six continents. TransPerfect serves a wide array of industries including advertising financial services legal life science technology retail and travel. Clients have include Sony American Airlines and Omnicom. TransPerfect was founded in 1992 by Liz Elting and Phil Shawe.

	Annual Growth	12/03	12/04	12/05	12/06	12/07
Sales ($ mil.)	45.7%	–	–	73.7	79.6	156.5
Net income ($ mil.)	58.5%	–	–	11.5	11.8	29.0
Market value ($ mil.)	–	–	–	–	–	–
Employees	–	–	–	–	–	3,500

TRANSTECTOR SYSTEMS INC.

10701 Airport Dr.
Hayden ID 83835
Phone: 208-772-8515
Fax: 208-762-6133
Web: www.transtector.com

CEO: –
CFO: –
HR: –
FYE: July 31
Type: Subsidiary

Transtector Systems makes power surge suppression equipment ranging from plug-in strips for home use to load centers for satellite tracking systems. Primary markets include wireless telecommunications and military and aerospace/space; other applications include industrial automation and control products medical and lighting equipment and manufacturing. Transtector Systems serves such customers as Motorola Raytheon and Varian Medical Systems as well as the US Department of Defense. It provides consulting engineering and training services. The company is part of the Smiths Interconnect division of Smiths Group. Transtector Systems was established in 1967 and was acquired by Smiths in 1998.

TRANZYME INC.

NASDAQ: TZYM

4819 Emperor Blvd. Ste. 400
Durham NC 27703
Phone: 919-313-4760
Fax: 816-421-6677
Web: www.fishnetsecurity.com

CEO: –
CFO: –
HR: –
FYE: December 31
Type: Public

Tranzyme has a gut feeling about its therapies. A drug discovery and development company Tranzyme is developing therapies to treat acute and chronic gastrointestinal (GI) disorders. Its lead candidate ulimorelin is an intravenously-administered treatment for GI motility problems that occur after abdominal surgery. If commercialized the therapy (which is in late clinical stages of development) could be used by hospitals to quickly restore normal intestinal function to patients. The company also has other candidates in earlier stages of development including a mid-stage oral therapy to treat chronic GI motility caused by diabetes. Founded in 1998 Tranzyme went public through a $48 million IPO in 2011.

TRAVEL AND TRANSPORT INC.

2120 S 72ND ST STE 300
OMAHA, NE 681242335
Phone: 402-399-4500
Fax: –
Web: www.travelandtransport.com

CEO: Kevin O'Malley
CFO: –
HR: –
FYE: December 31
Type: Private

Travel and Transport can get you there and back. The company provides its business clients with travel management solutions such as air hotel vacation packages and meeting planning services. Its corporate travel services include travel policy development vendor negotiation analysis and reporting. Travel and Transport is able to support international travel through its membership in RADIUS a network of 90 US travel agencies with more than 3300 offices worldwide. Travel and Transport also has a travel agent school and works with leisure travelers. The company which was founded in 1946 is 100% owned by its employees.

	Annual Growth	12/09	12/10	12/11	12/12	12/13
Sales ($ mil.)	11.2%	–	–	57.1	70.6	70.6
Net income ($ mil.)	(44.1%)	–	–	3.4	1.1	1.1
Market value ($ mil.)	–	–	–	–	–	–
Employees	–	–	–	–	–	940

TRAVELCENTERS OF AMERICA INC   NMS: TA

24601 Center Ridge Road, Suite 200
Westlake, OH 44145-5639
Phone: 440 808-9100
Fax: –
Web: www.tatravelcenters.com

CEO: Andrew J. Rebholz
CFO: William E. Myers
HR: Karen Kaminski
FYE: December 31
Type: Public

TravelCenters of America (TCA) is in it for the long haul. The company operates or franchises some 540 travel centers standalone convenience stores and standalone restaurants primarily targeting truckers and highway motorists across the US. Its brands include TravelCenters of America/TA Petro Stopping Centers/Petro Minit Mart and Quaker Steak & Lube. TCA's travel centers which account for most of sales offer diesel fuel and gas truck repair and maintenance services full- or quick-service restaurants and showers and other customer amenities. The company leases about 200 of its locations from Hospitality Properties Trust (HPT) its largest shareholder.

	Annual Growth	12/14	12/15	12/16	12/17	12/18
Sales ($ mil.)	(5.4%)	7,778.6	5,850.6	5,511.4	6,051.6	6,231.4
Net income ($ mil.)	–	61.0	27.7	(2.0)	9.3	(120.6)
Market value ($ mil.)	(26.1%)	102.0	76.0	57.4	33.1	30.4
Employees	(0.7%)	22,330	24,250	25,204	23,877	21,719

TRAVELCLICK INC.

7 Times Sq. 38th Fl.
New York NY 10036
Phone: 212-817-4800
Fax: +91-80-4143-6005
Web: centumindia.com/centumelectronics

CEO: –
CFO: –
HR: –
FYE: December 31
Type: Private

TravelCLICK helps hotels navigate the seas of online reservations. The company offers market intelligence and reservations software and services used by hotels to increase revenues and improve profitability. Its iHotelier program is a Web-based central reservation system that lets hotels manage rates and room inventory across multiple channels. Hotelligence360 uses competitive intelligence data to compare revenue and market performance of a customer's hotel against a custom list of competitors. TravelCLICK also offers online marketing and media services. The company has more than 30000 clients — including Accor Banyan Tree and Loews — in 140 countries.

TRAVELERS COMPANIES INC (THE)   NYS: TRV

485 Lexington Avenue
New York, NY 10017
Phone: 917 778-6000
Fax: –
Web: www.travelers.com

CEO: –
CFO: Jay S. Benet
HR: John P. Clifford
FYE: December 31
Type: Public

Running a business is a risk The Travelers Companies will insure. While it does offer personal auto and homeowners insurance the company's largest segment is commercial property/casualty insurance to businesses big and small. It is one of the largest business insurers in the US providing commercial auto property workers' compensation marine and general and financial liability coverage to companies in North America (the largest percentage of business) and the UK. The company also offers surety and fidelity bonds as well as professional and management liability coverage for commercial operations.

	Annual Growth	12/14	12/15	12/16	12/17	12/18
Assets ($ mil.)	0.3%	103,078.0	100,184.0	100,245.0	103,483.0	104,233.0
Net income ($ mil.)	(9.1%)	3,692.0	3,439.0	3,014.0	2,056.0	2,523.0
Market value ($ mil.)	3.1%	27,902.1	29,749.9	32,269.9	35,754.7	31,566.1
Employees	0.2%	30,200	30,900	30,900	30,800	30,400

TRAVELZOO   NMS: TZOO

590 Madison Avenue, 37th Floor
New York, NY 10022
Phone: 212 484-4900
Fax: –
Web: www.travelzoo.com

CEO: Holger Bartel
CFO: Glen Ceremony
HR: –
FYE: December 31
Type: Public

Travelzoo keeps the search for travel deals tame. On its websites users find discount offers promotions and related information provided by more than 2000 travel companies. Airlines car rental companies cruise lines hotels and travel agencies pay Travelzoo to publicize fares and promotions on its eponymous website through its newsletters and across its e-mail alert service. Travelzoo also operates SuperSearch a pay-per-click search engine specializing in travel content and Fly.com a search engine that compares flight information. Travelzoo founder Ralph Bartel owns a majority of the company's shares.

	Annual Growth	12/14	12/15	12/16	12/17	12/18
Sales ($ mil.)	(5.9%)	142.1	141.7	128.6	106.5	111.3
Net income ($ mil.)	(26.9%)	16.4	10.9	6.6	3.5	4.7
Market value ($ mil.)	(6.1%)	151.0	100.1	112.4	77.2	117.6
Employees	(0.9%)	438	473	444	442	422

TRAYLOR BROS., INC.

835 N CONGRESS AVE
EVANSVILLE, IN 477152484
Phone: 812-477-1542
Fax: –

CEO: Christopher S Traylor
CFO: –
HR: Madelyn Burk
FYE: December 31
Type: Private

At Traylor Bros Inc. (TBI) building bridges and tunnels is a family affair. The family-owned heavy/civil construction company mostly builds suspension and segmental bridges dams and ports storm sewers and transmission lines. Its Underground division works on tunneling projects while its Traylor Mining LLC subsidiary works on underground mining projects and facilities for copper gold and coal mine development in North America. TBI is perhaps best known for its work for the San Francisco's Bay Area Rapid Transit (BART) system and the I-10 span bridges over Lake Pontchartrain in Louisiana. Civil engineer William Traylor founded TBI in Indiana in 1946.

	Annual Growth	12/11	12/12	12/13	12/14	12/15
Sales ($ mil.)	0.0%	–	250.0	250.0	250.0	250.0
Net income ($ mil.)	–	–	0.0	0.0	0.0	0.0
Market value ($ mil.)	–	–	–	–	–	–
Employees	–	–	–	–	–	412

TRC COMPANIES, INC.
NYS: TRR

21 Griffin Road North
Windsor, CT 06095
Phone: 860 298-9692
Fax: –
Web: www.trcsolutions.com

CEO: Christopher P Vincze
CFO: Thomas W Bennet Jr
HR: –
FYE: June 30
Type: Public

If more people treated the environment with TLC TRC Companies would be less busy. Through its Environmental Energy Pipeline Services and Infrastructure segments the firm provides engineering construction and remediation services for commercial industrial and governmental customers. Services include energy efficiency and solid- and hazardous-waste management consulting infrastructure improvements and landfill cleanup. TRC's services also include remediation for brownfield sites discontinued industrial operations operating assets and Superfund sites. It offers an Exit Strategy Program in which it assumes complete responsibility for a contaminated site's closure and cleanup.

	Annual Growth	06/12	06/13	06/14	06/15	06/16
Sales ($ mil.)	12.3%	302.7	325.2	372.9	414.6	481.3
Net income ($ mil.)	(81.3%)	33.6	36.3	12.1	19.4	0.0
Market value ($ mil.)	1.0%	185.4	213.4	189.6	309.4	192.7
Employees	16.6%	2,600	2,800	3,000	3,700	4,800

TREATY ENERGY CORP.
NBB: TECO

317 Exchange Place
New Orleans, LA 70130
Phone: 504 301-4475
Fax: –
Web: www.treatyenergy.com

CEO: David W Shutte
CFO: –
HR: –
FYE: December 31
Type: Public

Treaty Energy (formerly Alternate Energy) sought to provide alternative methods of fuel and power production but the power of petroleum won out. The company had been involved in hydrogen production and fuel cell development. In 2008 it completed a reverse merger with Treaty Petroleum and changed its focus to oil and gas development. The company focuses on the Permian Basin of West Texas and has more than 2 million barrels of proved reserves. In 2010 it was eyeing exploration prospects in Belize. It also bought Town Oil Company in 2011 to give it about 7800 acres of oil and gas leases in Kansas. In 2011 the company also acquired C&C Petroleum Management with oil and gas properties in Texas.

	Annual Growth	12/08	12/09	12/10	12/11	12/12
Sales ($ mil.)	50.4%	0.0	0.0	0.0	0.1	0.2
Net income ($ mil.)	–	(0.2)	(1.2)	(0.8)	(7.1)	(12.2)
Market value ($ mil.)	25.3%	7.1	14.7	9.5	38.8	17.5
Employees						

TRECORA RESOURCES
NYS: TREC

1650 Hwy. 6 South, Suite 190
Sugar Land, TX 77478
Phone: 281 980-5522
Fax: –
Web: www.trecora.com

CEO: Simon Upfill-Brown
CFO: Sami Ahmad
HR: –
FYE: December 31
Type: Public

Trecora Resources (formerly Arabian American Development) is an independent refiner in Texas. Through US subsidiary Texas Oil and Chemical Co. II which owns South Hampton Resources it operates a specialty petrochemical product refinery that primarily produces high-purity solvents used in the plastics and foam industries. South Hampton subsidiary Gulf State Pipe Line owns and operates seven pipelines. It owns a minority stake in the Al Masane mineral ore project in Saudi Arabia and 55% of inactive Nevada-based mining company Pioche-Ely Valley Mines.

	Annual Growth	12/14	12/15	12/16	12/17	12/18
Sales ($ mil.)	(0.1%)	289.6	242.0	212.4	245.1	287.9
Net income ($ mil.)	–	15.6	18.6	19.4	18.0	(2.3)
Market value ($ mil.)	(14.7%)	360.2	303.6	339.3	330.8	191.1
Employees	0.8%	271	296	310	324	280

TREDEGAR CORP.
NYS: TG

1100 Boulders Parkway
Richmond, VA 23225
Phone: 804 330-1000
Fax: –
Web: www.tredegar.com

CEO: John D. Gottwald
CFO: Kevin A. O'Leary
HR: –
FYE: December 31
Type: Public

Tredegar's products can be found over under and in-between. The company manufactures primarily a variety of film products and aluminum extrusions. Its film lineup specializes in personal care materials and protective and packaging films such as liners and back sheets used in diapers feminine-hygiene products surgical masks permeable ground covers and cheesecloth. Aluminum extrusions produced by its Bonnell subsidiary are used mainly in building and construction markets. Tredegar's manufacturing facilities are located in the US the Netherlands Hungary China Brazil and India.

	Annual Growth	12/14	12/15	12/16	12/17	12/18
Sales ($ mil.)	3.8%	945.1	876.1	830.7	1,013.0	1,095.9
Net income ($ mil.)	(9.4%)	36.9	(32.1)	24.5	38.3	24.8
Market value ($ mil.)	(8.4%)	746.1	451.9	796.2	637.0	526.2
Employees	4.3%	2,700	2,800	2,800	3,200	3,200

TREE TOP, INC.

220 E 2ND AVE
SELAH, WA 989421408
Phone: 509-697-7251
Fax: –
Web: www.treetop.org

CEO: Keith Gomes
CFO: Dwaine Brown
HR: –
FYE: July 31
Type: Private

Tree Top has towered over the Pacific Northwest's apple juice market for more than 50 years. The grower-owned cooperative's 1000 members cultivate and harvest thousands of tons of apples and pears each year to make a slew of juicy products. The co-op produces the Tree Top brand of apple and blended fruit juices and applesauce among many offerings for consumers and food service vendors. It also processes dehydrated and frozen fruit products for food makers worldwide through its ingredients unit. Tree Top operates production facilities in Washington Oregon and California and distributes its products through various channels including retailers and brokers in the US and several international markets.

	Annual Growth	07/06	07/07	07/08	07/09	07/10
Sales ($ mil.)	2.0%	–	–	350.7	359.0	365.0
Net income ($ mil.)	27535.3%	–	–	0.0	37.2	27.0
Market value ($ mil.)	–	–	–	–	–	–
Employees	–	–	–	–	–	1,100

TREEHOUSE FOODS INC
NYS: THS

2021 Spring Road, Suite 600
Oak Brook, IL 60523
Phone: 708 483-1300
Fax: –
Web: www.treehousefoods.com

CEO: Sam K. Reed
CFO: Matthew J. Foulston
HR: Lori Roberts
FYE: December 31
Type: Public

TreeHouse Foods Inc. is a leading manufacturer and distributor of private label and branded packaged foods and beverages in North America. The company makes shelf stable refrigerated frozen and fresh products including baked goods (refrigerated and frozen dough cereal pretzels and snack bars); beverages (broth single serve hot beverages creamers and powdered drinks); and meal solutions (dressings hot cereal macaroni and cheese and pasta). TreeHouse makes private-label products for foodservice distributors and restaurant chains as well as for supermarkets and mass merchandisers. The company also works with co-pack business and industrial customers. With most of its revenue generated in the US the company operates more than 40 manufacturing facilities across the US Canada and Italy.

	Annual Growth	12/14	12/15	12/16	12/17	12/18
Sales ($ mil.)	18.5%	2,946.1	3,206.4	6,175.1	6,307.1	5,812.1
Net income ($ mil.)	–	89.9	114.9	(228.6)	(286.2)	(61.4)
Market value ($ mil.)	(12.3%)	4,789.7	4,393.8	4,042.6	2,769.8	2,839.8
Employees	19.7%	6,181	5,880	16,027	13,489	12,700

TRELLIS EARTH PRODUCTS INC.

9125 S.W. Ridder Rd. Ste. D
Wilsonville OR 97070
Phone: 503-582-1300
Fax: 503-582-1313
Web: www.trellisearth.com

CEO: Michael Senzaki
CFO: –
HR: –
FYE: December 31
Type: Private

Sure you can recycle that disposable plastic cup but you'll earn double points with Mother Nature if it's made from bioplastic. Trellis Earth Products' disposable cups bowls plates trays cutlery and bags are made from bioplastic a material derived from renewable sources such as soybeans corn starch wheat chaff rice hulls or sugarcane. Bioplastic is less expensive and more sustainable than petroleum-based plastic. Its products are sold to more than 500 foodservice customers primarily on the West Coast including Bunzl Distribution USA Costco Food Services of America Kroger Sysco and West Coast Paper. Trellis Earth Products filed a $22 million initial public offering in September 2011.

TREVENA INC
NMS: TRVN

955 Chesterbrook Boulevard, Suite 200
Chesterbrook, PA 19087
Phone: 610 354-8840
Fax: –
Web: www.trevenainc.com

CEO: Carrie L Bourdow
CFO: Roberto Cuca
HR: –
FYE: December 31
Type: Public

Trevena hopes to make tremendous strides in medicine. The clinical stage biopharmaceutical company's lead candidate is Phase III oliceridine (TRV130) a non-opiod pain treatment. The firm's platform of biased ligands including oliceridine target G protein coupled receptors (GPCRs); Trevena has a couple of similar candidates under development. In 2016 Trevena's former lead program TRV027 for acute heart failure did not meet its study targets. The firm then set its sights on oliceridine. Dr. Robert Lefkowitz who won the Noble Prize in Chemistry for his discoveries founded the company in 2007 to develop treatments based on his ground-breaking research. Trevena went public in 2014.

	Annual Growth	12/12	12/13	12/14	12/15	12/16
Sales ($ mil.)	46.8%	0.8	0.1	–	6.3	3.8
Net income ($ mil.)	–	(15.6)	(23.3)	(49.7)	(50.5)	(103.0)
Market value ($ mil.)	(0.8%)	–	–	333.5	585.6	327.9
Employees	23.5%	31	32	42	53	72

TREX CO INC
NYS: TREX

160 Exeter Drive
Winchester, VA 22603-8605
Phone: 540 542-6300
Fax: –
Web: www.trex.com

CEO: James E Cline
CFO: James E. Cline
HR: –
FYE: December 31
Type: Public

Trex Company is all decked out with plenty of places to go. It's the world's largest maker of wood-alternative decking and railing products which are used in the construction of residential and commercial decks rails and trims. Marketed under the Trex name products resemble wood and have the workability of wood but require less long-term maintenance. The Trex Wood-Polymer composite is made of waste wood fibers and reclaimed plastic. Trex serves professional installation contractors and do-it-yourselfers through about 90 wholesale distribution centers which in turn sell to retailers including Home Depot and Lowe's. Trex products are available in more than 5500 locations primarily in the US and Canada.

	Annual Growth	12/14	12/15	12/16	12/17	12/18
Sales ($ mil.)	15.0%	391.7	440.8	479.6	565.2	684.3
Net income ($ mil.)	34.2%	41.5	48.1	67.8	95.1	134.6
Market value ($ mil.)	8.7%	2,493.1	2,227.3	3,770.7	6,346.4	3,475.6
Employees	17.8%	630	700	830	815	1,214

TRG HOLDINGS LLC

1700 Pennsylvannia Ave. NW Ste. 560
Washington DC 20006
Phone: 202-289-9898
Fax: 770-794-8381
Web: www.ttinc.net

CEO: –
CFO: –
HR: Elizabeth Wilson
FYE: June 30
Type: Holding Company

More than 120 global clients tap into the offerings of The Resource Group (TRG). Specializing in serving companies in the business process outsourcing (BPO) sector TRG provides its clients with equity capital strategic advice custom outsourced services and technology products and services. Its iSky business offers market research analytics and consultation services. TRG has industry knowledge in sectors such as automotive financial services healthcare insurance media and pharmaceuticals. The company has invested in or acquired about 20 BPO businesses since 2002. It has operations in Brazil Pakistan the Philippines Senegal the UK and the US.

TRI POINTE HOMES LLC
NYSE: TPH

19520 Jamboree Rd. Ste. 200
Irvine CA 92612
Phone: 949-478-8600
Fax: 949-478-8601
Web: www.tripointehomes.com

CEO: –
CFO: –
HR: –
FYE: December 31
Type: Private

In a home construction market that's been trying of late Tri Pointe Homes believes it's pointing the way to a successful future. The company designs and constructs single-family homes in urban areas of California singling out communities with growing populations and economies. Tri Pointe was founded in 2009 and the following year it began a partnership with Starwood Capital Group Global to fund land acquisition. There are 13 sites in operation with nearly 700 lots in varying stages of development; home prices range between $300000 and $1.5 million for residences between 1250 and 4300 sq. ft. Tri Pointe Homes went public in early 2013 with an offering worth $232.7 million.

TRI-CITY ELECTRICAL CONTRACTORS, INC.

430 WEST DR
ALTAMONTE SPRINGS, FL 327143378
Phone: 407-788-3500
Fax: –
Web: www.tcelectric.com

CEO: –
CFO: Michael A Germana
HR: –
FYE: December 31
Type: Private

Plugged in to the electrical contracting scene Tri-City Electrical Contractors targets Florida's commercial government industrial residential and communications markets. The company designs installs and services electrical systems in apartment buildings courthouses convention centers sports arenas resorts condos single- and multi-family dwellings and more. Once part of now-bankrupt Encompass Services Tri-City Electrical Contractors was repurchased by founder and chairman Buddy Eidel in 2003. Tri-City Electrical Contractors which traces its roots to 1958 operates from its Central Florida headquarters and two divisional offices throughout the Sunshine State.

	Annual Growth	12/10	12/11	12/12	12/13	12/14
Sales ($ mil.)	–	–	0.0	87.6	126.8	141.0
Net income ($ mil.)	–	–	0.0	(1.2)	2.7	3.8
Market value ($ mil.)	–	–	–	–	–	–
Employees	–	–	–	–	–	504

TRI-CITY HOSPITAL DISTRICT (INC)

4002 VISTA WAY
OCEANSIDE, CA 920564506
Phone: 760-724-8411
Fax: –
Web: www.tricitymed.org

CEO: Casey Fatch
CFO: Robert Wardwell
HR: –
FYE: June 30
Type: Private

For those in southern California's North County the Tri-City Healthcare District is there to take care of your medical needs. The organization provides primary and acute health care services primarily through Tri-City Medical Center. The hospital which has more than 500 physicians representing 60 specialties boasts about 400 beds. In addition to the medical center Tri-City Healthcare District operates the Beatrice Riggs French Women's Center an outpatient facility that offers services to women and newborns. One of the hospital's specialties is diagnosing and treating behavioral and developmental difficulties in children. In addition Tri-City Healthcare District offers home and hospice care.

	Annual Growth	06/06	06/07	06/08	06/10	06/15
Sales ($ mil.)	2.7%	–	–	267.7	279.5	321.9
Net income ($ mil.)	(21.6%)	–	–	9.3	(11.2)	1.7
Market value ($ mil.)	–	–	–	–	–	–
Employees	–	–	–	–	–	2,121

TRI-WEST, LTD.

12005 PIKE ST
SANTA FE SPRINGS, CA 906706100
Phone: 562-692-9166
Fax: –
Web: www.triwestltd.com

CEO: –
CFO: Randy Sims
HR: –
FYE: December 31
Type: Private

Tri-West tends to floor both residential and commercial customers with its broad selection of floor coverings. Founded in 1981 the company distributes floor coverings through about half a dozen warehouse facilities located in the western US and the Hawaiian Islands. In addition Tri-West also serves customers in Texas and Guam. Tri-West offers major manufacturers' products including carpets ceramic and specialty tile hardwood flooring laminate and vinyl flooring and eco-friendly items such as recycled rubber tiles and bamboo flooring. As part of its business the company sells and distributes adhesives and tools from manufacturers such as Armstrong and California-based Taylor Adhesives.

	Annual Growth	12/09	12/10	12/11	12/12	12/13
Sales ($ mil.)	17.4%	–	–	117.7	141.9	162.3
Net income ($ mil.)	41.0%	–	–	7.1	10.2	14.2
Market value ($ mil.)	–	–	–	–	–	–
Employees	–	–	–	–	–	250

TRIA BEAUTY INC.

4160 Dublin Blvd. Ste. 200
Dublin CA 94568
Phone: 925-452-2500
Fax: 514-875-0835
Web: www.enerkem.com

CEO: Kevin J Appelbaum
CFO: Sandra Gardiner
HR: –
FYE: December 31
Type: Private

TRIA Beauty helps every woman find her inner esthetician. The company's two medical devices used to zap unwanted hair and clear up acne are designed for at-home use so no more costly trips to the medical spa. Its TRIA Hair Removal Laser is a handheld device that uses laser light to stunt hair growth while its Skin Perfecting Blue Light device treats acne by using blue light therapy to kill underlying bacteria. TRIA Beauty's devices are sold online on television via QVC and infomercials and at high-end retailer Bloomingdale's. A third device the Skin Rejuvenating Laser used to reduce the appearance of facial wrinkles is under development. TRIA Beauty filed and withdrew an initial public offering in 2012.

TRIANGLE CAPITAL CORP

3700 Glenwood Avenue, Suite 530
Raleigh, NC 27612
Phone: 919 719-4770
Fax: –

NYS: TCAP
CEO: E Ashton Poole
CFO: Steven C Lilly
HR: –
FYE: December 31
Type: Public

Triangle Capital lends to companies but they must be of a certain shape and size. An internally managed business-development company Triangle provides loans to and invests in lower-middle-market US companies with annual revenues of $20 million-$100 million. The company which likes to partner with its portfolio companies' management prefers to invest in established businesses with stable financial histories. Triangle most often invests in senior and subordinated debt securities and usually takes a equity interest; it contributes between $5 million and $15 million per transaction. The company's portfolio includes some 50 manufacturers business services food services and other types of enterprises.

	Annual Growth	12/10	12/11	12/12	12/13	12/14
Assets ($ mil.)	26.2%	388.0	583.2	794.5	814.9	984.1
Net income ($ mil.)	32.5%	20.1	40.3	57.7	61.5	62.0
Market value ($ mil.)	1.7%	626.1	630.0	839.9	911.1	668.6
Employees	10.1%	17	19	22	25	25

TRIANGLE PETROLEUM CORP

1200 17th Street, Suite 2600
Denver, CO 80202
Phone: 303 260-7125
Fax: 303 260-5080
Web: www.trianglepetroleum.com

NBB: TPLM
CEO: Ryan D McGee
CFO: –
HR: –
FYE: January 31
Type: Public

Triangle Petroleum has three business - oil and gas exploration and production oilfield services and midstream services. The company holds leasehold interests in about 94000 net acres in the Williston Basin approximately 45000 net acres are located in its core focus area in McKenzie and Williams Counties North Dakota. The assets are mainly unconventional (natural gas produced from shale deposits via hydraulic fracturing). Triangle had proved reserves of 40.3 million barrels of oil equivalent in fiscal 2014. Exploration and production account for 46% of the company's revenues; Oilfield services 54%. Sales of crude oil account for about 60% of the company's revenues. Triangle Petroleum filed for Chapter 11 bankruptcy protection in 2017.

	Annual Growth	01/12	01/13	01/14	01/15	01/16
Sales ($ mil.)	157.6%	8.1	60.7	258.7	573.0	358.1
Net income ($ mil.)	–	(23.8)	(13.8)	73.5	93.4	(822.3)
Market value ($ mil.)	(49.2%)	518.5	476.8	576.9	398.0	34.4
Employees	58.5%	61	165	332	562	385

TRIBUNE MEDIA CO

515 North State Street
Chicago, IL 60654
Phone: 646 563-8296
Fax: –
Web: www.tribune.com

NYS: TRCO
CEO: Peter M Kern
CFO: Chandler Bigelow
HR: –
FYE: December 31
Type: Public

Its roots were in print journalism but the Tribune Media Company (formerly known as Tribune Company) has evolved to embrace virtually every aspect of modern media. Tribune Media currently owns 42 TV stations in more than 30 markets cable network WGN America and a 31% stake in the Food Network. In addition Tribune Media owns a number of online media properties Tribune Studios Tribune Digital Ventures WGN-Radio and a significant number of iconic real estate properties and strategic investments. In 2014 Tribune Company spun off its cornerstone newspaper publishing business into a newly formed company called Tribune Publishing (later renamed tronc) and changed the name of the TV radio and digital business to Tribune Media. .

	Annual Growth	12/13	12/14	12/15	12/16	12/17
Sales ($ mil.)	12.7%	1,147.2	1,949.4	2,010.5	1,947.9	1,849.0
Net income ($ mil.)	(5.3%)	241.6	476.7	(319.9)	14.2	194.1
Market value ($ mil.)	(14.0%)	6,777.1	5,234.8	2,952.7	3,054.9	3,709.0
Employees	(7.6%)	–	7,600	8,000	8,200	6,000

TRICO BANCSHARES (CHICO, CA) — NMS: TCBK

63 Constitution Drive
Chico, CA 95973
Phone: 530 898-0300
Fax: –
Web: www.tcbk.com

CEO: Richard P. Smith
CFO: Thomas J. (Tom) Reddish
HR: –
FYE: December 31
Type: Public

People looking for a community bank in California's Sacramento Valley can try TriCo. TriCo Bancshares is the holding company for Tri Counties Bank which serves customers through some 65 traditional and in-store branches in 23 counties in Northern and Central California. Founded in 1974 Tri Counties Bank provides a variety of deposit services including checking and savings accounts money market accounts and CDs. Most patrons are retail customers and small to midsized businesses. The bank primarily originates real estate mortgages which account for about 65% of its loan portfolio; consumer loans contribute about 25%. TriCo has agreed to acquire rival North Valley Bancorp.

	Annual Growth	12/14	12/15	12/16	12/17	12/18
Assets ($ mil.)	12.9%	3,916.5	4,220.7	4,518.0	4,761.3	6,352.4
Net income ($ mil.)	27.2%	26.1	43.8	44.8	40.6	68.3
Market value ($ mil.)	8.1%	751.3	834.6	1,039.7	1,151.6	1,027.8
Employees	3.9%	1,009	1,011	1,063	1,023	1,174

TRIDENT SEAFOODS CORPORATION

5303 Shilshole Ave. NW
Seattle WA 98107-4000
Phone: 206-783-3818
Fax: 206-782-7195
Web: www.tridentseafoods.com

CEO: Joseph Bundrant
CFO: –
HR: Brian Parsons
FYE: August 31
Type: Private

Something's "supposed" to be fishy at Trident Seafoods. The vertically integrated seafood business hauls in salmon crab and assorted other fin- and shellfish from the icy waters of Alaska and the Pacific Northwest. It then processes and cans or freezes them for retail food and foodservice customers. Trident operates a fleet of some 30 processing boats and trawlers as well as about 20 onshore processing plants in Alaska Washington and Oregon. The company's portfolio includes Trident Louis Kemp and SeaLegs brand of surimi (crab-flavored processed fish). Trident owns Port Chatham Smoked Seafood which smokes salmon and tuna under the Portlock label. The company operates a single retail store in Seattle.

TRIHEALTH, INC.

4750 WESLEY AVE
CINCINNATI, OH 452122244
Phone: 513-569-6111
Fax: –
Web: www.healthcaresolutionsnetwork.com

CEO: Mark C. Clement
CFO: Andrew Devoe
HR: –
FYE: June 30
Type: Private

TriHealth provides health care to the trifecta of Cincinnati northern Kentucky and southeastern Indiana. The company operates four acute care and surgery hospitals including Bethesda North Hospital which has 420 beds and provides trauma birthing and heart care services; the 590-bed Good Samaritan Hospital; and Bethesda Butler Hospital a 10-bed surgical hospital. TriHealth also operates a vast network of outpatient care centers and conducts medical education and research programs. The not-for-profit organization is affiliated with Catholic Health Initiatives.

	Annual Growth	06/07	06/08	06/09	06/10	06/13
Sales ($ mil.)	159.1%	–	–	4.1	1.0	183.2
Net income ($ mil.)	–	–	–	(118.0)	(0.4)	(0.1)
Market value ($ mil.)	–	–	–	–	–	–
Employees	–	–	–	–	–	13,000

TRILOGY LEASING CO. LLC

2551 Rte. 130
Cranbury NJ 08512-3509
Phone: 609-860-9900
Fax: 609-860-9974
Web: www.trilogyleasing.com

CEO: –
CFO: David Lieberman
HR: –
FYE: December 31
Type: Private

Trilogy Leasing helps companies that need a little technology TLC. Specializing in pre-owned technology equipment the company provides leasing services to businesses in the US and Canada. It offers equipment including personal computers printing and imaging equipment mainframe computers and telecom switches from vendors such as Hewlett-Packard. Trilogy also offers capital equipment such as furniture. In addition to its leasing services the company sells equipment and purchases unwanted inventory. It also offers consulting technical support and equipment liquidation services. Founded in 1999 Trilogy was acquired by Kingsbridge Holdings in 2011.

TRIMAS CORP (NEW) — NMS: TRS

38505 Woodward Avenue, Suite 200
Bloomfield Hills, MI 48304
Phone: 248 631-5450
Fax: –
Web: www.trimascorp.com

CEO: Thomas A. (Tom) Amato
CFO: Robert J. (Bob) Zalupski
HR: –
FYE: December 31
Type: Public

Whether at work or play TriMas fits the niche. The company makes a diverse mix of products through several segments. Its Energy division makes seals bolts and gaskets used primarily in the oil and gas industry. TriMas' Packaging segment makes closures and dispensing systems for industrial and consumer packaging for customers in North America and Europe. Aerospace produces aerospace fasteners and military munitions components including shell casings. Engineered Components manufactures compressed gas pressure cylinders and precision tools. It operates through 50 manufacturing plants in 13 countries.

	Annual Growth	12/14	12/15	12/16	12/17	12/18
Sales ($ mil.)	(12.5%)	1,499.1	864.0	794.0	817.7	877.1
Net income ($ mil.)	5.0%	68.5	(33.4)	(39.8)	31.0	83.3
Market value ($ mil.)	(3.4%)	1,424.6	849.1	1,069.9	1,217.9	1,242.5
Employees	(13.1%)	7,000	4,200	4,000	4,000	4,000

TRIMBLE INC — NMS: TRMB

935 Stewart Drive
Sunnyvale, CA 94085
Phone: 408 481-8000
Fax: –

CEO: Steven W. Berglund
CFO: Robert G. Painter
HR: –
FYE: December 28
Type: Public

Trimble Inc. makes equipment to prepare a site for construction build the building manage it once built and keep track of vehicles and workers. The company makes GPS Global Navigation Satellite System laser and optical technologies and software that help guide and track machines equipment parts and people. The company's products target areas such as surveying construction site project management building information modeling mapping mobile personnel management and mobile and fixed asset management. Trimble sells to end users such as government entities farmers engineering firms as well as equipment manufacturers. North America accounts for more than half of Trimble's sales.

	Annual Growth	01/15	01/16*	12/16	12/17	12/18
Sales ($ mil.)	9.1%	2,395.5	2,290.4	2,362.2	2,654.2	3,108.4
Net income ($ mil.)	9.7%	214.1	121.1	132.4	121.1	282.8
Market value ($ mil.)	5.9%	6,751.7	5,381.8	7,564.6	10,196.6	8,013.7
Employees	11.2%	8,217	8,451	8,388	9,523	11,287

*Fiscal year change

TRIMEDYNE INC
NBB: TMED

5 Holland #223
Irvine, CA 92618
Phone: 949 951-3800
Fax: 949 855-8206
Web: www.trimedyne.com

CEO: Glenn D Yeik
CFO: –
HR: –
FYE: September 30
Type: Public

Trimedyne doesn't play tag with lasers but it does use them to help surgeons do their jobs. The company's cold-pulsed lasers and fiber-optic laser energy delivery devices (including needles and fibers) are used in gastrointestinal orthopedic urologic and general surgeries as well as gynecology arthroscopy and ear nose and throat (ENT) procedures. Trimedyne markets its products to hospitals and surgery centers in the US via direct sales and internationally through distributors. The company's Mobile Surgical Technologies unit rents lasers and provides related services to health care facilities on a "fee per use" basis.

	Annual Growth	09/11	09/12	09/13	09/14	09/15
Sales ($ mil.)	(5.4%)	6.7	6.1	6.0	5.5	5.3
Net income ($ mil.)	–	(1.5)	(0.8)	0.3	(0.4)	(0.6)
Market value ($ mil.)	–	0.0	0.0	0.0	0.0	0.0
Employees	(7.2%)	62	55	42	52	46

TRIMOL GROUP INC.
OTC: TMOL

1285 Avenue of the Americas 35th Fl.
New York NY 10019
Phone: 212-554-4394
Fax: 212-554-4395

CEO: –
CFO: –
HR: –
FYE: December 31
Type: Public

Trimol Group has a license for a mechanically rechargeable aluminum-air fuel cell for use in portable consumer electronics but the company isn't actively developing the technology. Its Intercomsoft subsidiary provides technology and consumables for producing secure government identification documents. The technology was developed by Supercom of Israel which broke off its supply agreement with Intercomsoft in early 2005. Intercomsoft continued to provide support services to the Republic of Moldova (traditionally its only customer) but the Republic of Moldova has indicated that it does not intend to renew its supply agreement. Chairman Boris Birshtein owns more than three-quarters of Trimol Group.

TRINITAS REGIONAL MEDICAL CENTER

225 WILLIAMSON ST
ELIZABETH, NJ 072023625
Phone: 908-351-0714
Fax: –
Web: www.trinitasrmc.org

CEO: –
CFO: –
HR: –
FYE: December 31
Type: Private

Trinitas Regional Medical Center (formerly Trinitas Hospital) serves eastern and central Union County in New Jersey. The Catholic teaching hospital has more than 530 beds and offers acute tertiary and long-term health care services on its two campuses. It has special centers for cancer care sleep disorders cardiovascular conditions diabetes care pediatrics and women's health. The hospital also offers inpatient behavioral health care operates a local clinic and provides educational services to students of Seton Hall University's School of Health and Medical Sciences. Trinitas Regional Medical Center is co-sponsored by the Sisters of Charity of Saint Elizabeth and the Elizabethtown Healthcare Foundation.

	Annual Growth	12/13	12/14	12/15	12/16	12/17
Sales ($ mil.)	(0.3%)	–	–	–	297.5	296.8
Net income ($ mil.)	(45.2%)	–	–	–	17.5	9.6
Market value ($ mil.)	–	–	–	–	–	–
Employees	–	–	–	–	–	2,700

TRINITY HEALTH SYSTEM

380 SUMMIT AVE
STEUBENVILLE, OH 439522667
Phone: 740-283-7000
Fax: –
Web: www.trinityhealth.com

CEO: Fred Brower
CFO: Elizabeth Allen
HR: –
FYE: December 31
Type: Private

Despite its name Trinity Health System serves eastern Ohio through a mere two facilities — Trinity Medical Center East and Trinity Medical Center West. Combined they have some 470 beds and offer patients emergency and general medical diagnostic and surgical services as well as specialty care in fields including rehabilitation skilled nursing and women's health services. Hospital specialty units also include the Tony Teramana Cancer Center a sleep center and a heart center. Trinity Health's outpatient facilities include an imaging center a school of nursing and community health clinics. The not-for-profit health system is sponsored by Tri-State Health Services and Franciscan Services organizations.

	Annual Growth	12/08	12/09	12/12	12/13	12/15
Sales ($ mil.)	6.2%	–	178.6	4.5	4.6	256.1
Net income ($ mil.)	(8.5%)	–	21.8	0.0	0.0	12.8
Market value ($ mil.)	–	–	–	–	–	–
Employees	–	–	–	–	–	1,640

TRINITY INDUSTRIES, INC.
NYS: TRN

2525 N. Stemmons Freeway
Dallas, TX 75207-2401
Phone: 214 631-4420
Fax: 214 589-8501
Web: www.trin.net

CEO: Timothy R. Wallace
CFO: James E. Perry
HR: Kathryn Collins
FYE: December 31
Type: Public

Trinity Industries manufactures auto carriers box cars gondola cars hopper cars intermodal cars and tank cars. The company also leases and manages railcar fleets. Trinity's other manufacturing operations include making highway products such as guardrails crash cushions and other highway barriers. Trinity also owns a transportation company that provides support services to Trinity as well as other industrial manufacturers. In late 2018 Trinity spun off its businesses that provide products and services to the industrial energy and construction sectors as an independent public company Arsoca. The deal also gave Arcosa control of Trinity's former Inland Barge unit a builder of barges used to transport coal grain and other commodities.

	Annual Growth	12/14	12/15	12/16	12/17	12/18
Sales ($ mil.)	(20.1%)	6,170.0	6,392.7	4,588.3	3,662.8	2,509.1
Net income ($ mil.)	(30.4%)	678.2	796.5	343.6	702.5	159.3
Market value ($ mil.)	(7.4%)	3,733.7	3,201.9	3,700.4	4,993.4	2,744.6
Employees	(14.9%)	21,950	22,030	17,680	15,605	11,515

TRINITY MOTHER FRANCES HEALTH SYSTEM FOUNDATION

800 E DAWSON ST
TYLER, TX 757012036
Phone: 903-531-5057
Fax: –
Web: www.tmfhc.org

CEO: –
CFO: William Bellenfant
HR: Candy Land
FYE: June 30
Type: Private

Trinity Mother Frances Health System Foundation (dba Trinity Mother Frances Hospitals and Clinics) has a complicated name but a simple mission: to improve patient health. Consisting of three general hospitals several specialist facilities and a large physicians' group Trinity Mother Frances serves northeastern Texas. Its largest acute-care facility is Mother Frances Hospital-Tyler with more than 400 beds offering comprehensive medical surgical trauma and cardiovascular care. Two smaller hospitals in Jacksonville and Winnsboro provide emergency diagnostic surgery and select specialty services. The Trinity Clinic is a multi-specialty physician group that includes 300 doctors in 36 community clinics.

	Annual Growth	06/08	06/09	06/10	06/13	06/14
Sales ($ mil.)	4.8%	–	562.1	603.4	653.2	711.7
Net income ($ mil.)	–	–	(27.6)	19.9	21.5	36.8
Market value ($ mil.)	–	–	–	–	–	–
Employees	–	–	–	–	–	3,551

TRINITY UNIVERSITY

1 TRINITY PL
SAN ANTONIO, TX 782127200
Phone: 210-999-7011
Fax: –
Web: www.new.trinity.edu

CEO: –
CFO: –
HR: –
FYE: May 31
Type: Private

Students at Trinity University get an education of the mind body and spirit. Trinity University offers 40-plus undergraduate degree programs in the arts and sciences as well as some 55 interdisciplinary minors. The university also offers master's degree programs in accounting education and health care administration. Trinity University has roughly 2340 undergraduate and graduate students hailing from some 45 U S states and 65 countries. The student/faculty ratio is 9:1. The university was founded by Presbyterians in 1869 in Tehuacana Texas and moved to San Antonio in 1942.

	Annual Growth	05/14	05/15	05/16	05/17	05/18
Sales ($ mil.)	(13.5%)	–	215.5	128.9	135.5	139.3
Net income ($ mil.)	18.2%	–	52.1	(67.3)	105.9	86.0
Market value ($ mil.)	–	–	–	–	–	–
Employees	–	–	–	–	–	700

TRIPADVISOR INC.

141 Needham St.
Newton MA 02464
Phone: 617-670-6300
Fax: 781-444-1146
Web: www.tripadvisor.com

NASDAQ: TRIP
CEO: –
CFO: Julie MB Bradley
HR: –
FYE: December 31
Type: Public

TripAdvisor is primed to give you advice. A subsidiary of online travel services provider Expedia until late 2011 spun off TripAdvisor offers a search engine and directory that matches hotels with flights and packages. The company provides more than 60 million consumer reviews to help travelers plan consumer-savvy trips. The global source strives to fine-tune search results to provide information that is free of bias and in a mobile format for smartphone use. TripAdvisor partners with top online travel businesses such as Hotwire Hotels.com and American Airlines and offers some 30 localized versions in France Germany Ireland Italy Spain the UK China and other countries.

TRIPPE MANUFACTURING COMPANY

1111 W 35TH ST
CHICAGO, IL 60609-1404
Phone: 773-869-1111
Fax: –
Web: www.tripplite.com

CEO: Elbert Howell
CFO: Charles Lang
HR: –
FYE: December 31
Type: Private

Trippe sells protection from power trips. Doing business as Tripp Lite the company makes over 2500 products used to protect power and connect electronic equipment. Its surge suppressors guard against surges spikes and over-voltages that can damage personal computers and other electronic equipment. Its uninterruptible power supply (UPS) systems provide battery backup power while its inverters are used to power laptops and other products when other power sources are not available. Tripp Lite products also include power strips cables and connectors laptop accessories and power-management software.

	Annual Growth	12/06	12/07	12/08	12/11	12/12
Sales ($ mil.)	–	–	0.0	0.0	300.0	350.0
Net income ($ mil.)	–	–	0.0	0.0	0.0	0.0
Market value ($ mil.)	–	–	–	–	–	–
Employees	–	–	–	–	–	450

TRIQUINT SEMICONDUCTOR, INC.

2300 N.E. Brookwood Parkway
Hillsboro, OR 97124
Phone: 503 615-9000
Fax: 503 615-8900
Web: www.triquint.com

NMS: TQNT
CEO: –
CFO: Steve Buhaly
HR: –
FYE: December 31
Type: Public

TriQuint Semiconductor fills it up with GaAs. TriQuint uses specialized materials — such as gallium arsenide (GaAs) gallium nitride and quartz — instead of silicon as the substrate for its filtering switching and amplification products. Those products are applied in radio frequency (RF) microwave and millimeter-wave settings serving mobile device network and defense and aerospace customers. Major clients have included Foxconn Technology Samsung Electronics and the US government and its contractors. TriQuint also offers contract design and fabrication services. More than three-quarters of its sales come from outside the US.

	Annual Growth	12/08	12/09	12/10	12/11	12/12
Sales ($ mil.)	9.7%	573.4	654.3	878.7	896.1	829.2
Net income ($ mil.)	–	(14.6)	16.2	190.8	48.2	(26.2)
Market value ($ mil.)	8.9%	552.5	963.7	1,877.5	782.2	775.8
Employees	4.3%	2,297	2,393	2,777	2,905	2,723

TRISTATE CAPITAL HOLDINGS INC

One Oxford Centre, 301 Grant Street, Suite 2700
Pittsburgh, PA 15219
Phone: 412 304-0304
Fax: 412 304-0391
Web: www.tristatecapitalbank.com

NMS: TSC
CEO: James F. (Jim) Getz
CFO: Mark L. Sullivan
HR: –
FYE: December 31
Type: Public

TriState Capital Holdings has found its niche right in the middle of the banking industry. The holding company owns TriState Capital Bank a regional business bank that caters to midsized businesses or those annually earning between $5 million and $300 million. TriState Capital also offers private banking services nationally to high-net-worth individuals. Its loan portfolio consists of about 50% commercial loans 30% commercial real estate loans and 20% private banking-personal loans. The bank serves clients from branches in Cleveland; New Jersey; New York City Philadelphia and Pittsburgh. Altogether it has some $2 billion in assets. TriState Capital went public in mid-2013.

	Annual Growth	12/14	12/15	12/16	12/17	12/18
Assets ($ mil.)	20.7%	2,846.9	3,302.9	3,930.5	4,777.9	6,035.7
Net income ($ mil.)	36.0%	15.9	22.5	28.6	38.0	54.4
Market value ($ mil.)	17.4%	295.7	404.0	638.2	664.2	562.0
Employees	9.0%	182	192	224	230	257

TROUT-BLUE CHELAN-MAGI, INC.

8 HOWSER RD
CHELAN, WA 98816
Phone: 509-682-2591
Fax: –
Web: www.chelanfruit.com

CEO: Reggie Collins
CFO: Todd Kammers
HR: –
FYE: August 31
Type: Private

Trout-Blue Chelan-Magi has a simpler and more apt name by which it does business — Chelan Fruit. The company is fruit growers' cooperative with some 420 member/growers located in Washington State. The co-op prepares packs and sells its members' apples pears cherries and other stone fruits including peaches apricots nectarines and plums. The fruit is shipped both domestically and internationally. Product marketing is conducted through Chelan Fresh Marketing. The co-op was formed through the 1995 merger of two cooperatives Trout and Blue Chelan; the combined company changed its name again in 2004 with the acquisition of Magi.

	Annual Growth	08/12	08/13	08/14	08/15	08/16
Sales ($ mil.)	(5.0%)	–	180.9	156.3	169.6	154.9
Net income ($ mil.)	98.0%	–	5.1	4.1	4.6	39.3
Market value ($ mil.)	–	–	–	–	–	–
Employees	–	–	–	–	–	675

TROY UNIVERSITY

600 UNIVERSITY AVE
TROY, AL 360820001
Phone: 334-670-3179
Fax: –
Web: www.troy.edu

CEO: –
CFO: –
HR: –
FYE: September 30
Type: Private

Troy University is not the topic of a Homeric poem but you'd probably find a Helen enrolled there. The school is a public institution composed of a network of campuses throughout Alabama and worldwide. The network includes campuses and teaching sites in some seven US states and four other countries. Troy University has a total student enrollment of about 23000 and offers degrees in arts and sciences business communications and fine arts education and health and human services. The school also operates the Confucius Institute to promote understanding of Chinese language and culture.

	Annual Growth	09/07	09/08	09/16	09/17	09/18
Sales ($ mil.)	1.2%	–	156.5	168.5	176.1	176.3
Net income ($ mil.)	(14.2%)	–	29.1	(2.4)	4.1	6.3
Market value ($ mil.)	–	–	–	–	–	–
Employees	–	–	–	–	–	3,000

TRUE VALUE COMPANY

8600 W BRYN MAWR AVE 100S
CHICAGO, IL 606313505
Phone: 773-695-5000
Fax: –
Web: www.truevaluecompany.com

CEO: John Hartmann
CFO: Deborah O' Connor
HR: –
FYE: December 28
Type: Private

True Value Company (TVC) is a home improvement cooperative among the likes of giants The Home Depot and Lowe's. Formed by the 1997 merger of Cotter & Company and ServiStar Coast to Coast the retailer-owned wholesale hardware cooperative serves some 4400 retail outlets in 58-plus countries. Stores offer home improvement and garden supplies as well as appliances housewares sporting goods and pet food. In addition to the flagship True Value banner members operate under the names of Taylor Rental Grand Rental Station Home & Garden Showplace Induserve Supply and Party Central among others. True Value also manufactures its own brand of paints.

	Annual Growth	01/10	01/11*	12/11	12/12	12/13
Sales ($ mil.)	(11.5%)	–	1,804.0	1,864.8	1,399.1	1,411.5
Net income ($ mil.)	(4.5%)	–	60.7	60.3	74.9	55.3
Market value ($ mil.)	–	–	–	–	–	–
Employees	–	–	–	–	–	3,000

*Fiscal year change

TRUEBLUE INC

1015 A Street
Tacoma, WA 98402
Phone: 253 383-9101
Fax: 253 383-9311
Web: www.trueblue.com

NYS: TBI
CEO: Steven C. (Steve) Cooper
CFO: Derrek L. Gafford
HR: –
FYE: December 30
Type: Public

Staffing firm TrueBlue specializes in providing general laborers on short notice for short-term jobs in fields such as construction hospitality and transportation. The company offers general labor staffing services from 620 branches throughout the US Puerto Rico and Canada mostly through its PeopleReady business. The PeopleManagement unit finds contingent labor and outsourced industrial workers while the PeopleScout group provides outsourced recruitment for permanent employees. TrueBlue mainly serves companies in the services construction transportation manufacturing retail and wholesale sectors among others.

	Annual Growth	12/14	12/15*	01/17*	12/17	12/18
Sales ($ mil.)	3.5%	2,174.0	2,695.7	2,750.6	2,508.8	2,499.2
Net income ($ mil.)	0.0%	65.7	71.2	(15.3)	55.5	65.8
Market value ($ mil.)	(0.9%)	907.2	1,061.8	987.3	1,101.5	874.0
Employees	7.6%	5,000	5,500	6,000	5,500	6,700

*Fiscal year change

TRUIST FINANCIAL CORP

200 West Second Street
Winston-Salem, NC 27101
Phone: 336 733-2000
Fax: 336 671-2399
Web: www.bbt.com

NYS: TFC
CEO: Kelly S. King
CFO: Daryl N. Bible
HR: Kristi Sullivan
FYE: December 31
Type: Public

BB&T provides traditional banking insurance investment banking and wealth management services through almost 1900 bank branches mostly in the south and southeastern US. The holding company's flagship subsidiary Branch Banking and Trust (BB&T) is the oldest North Carolina-headquartered bank and a leading originator of residential mortgages in the Southeast. Boasting assets of around $225 billion BB&T is one of the largest financial services holding companies in the US. In February 2019 BB&T agreed to merge with retail and commercial banking services company SunTrust Banks and rebrand as Truist in a $66 billion deal.

	Annual Growth	12/14	12/15	12/16	12/17	12/18
Assets ($ mil.)	4.8%	186,814.0	209,947.0	219,276.0	221,642.0	225,697.0
Net income ($ mil.)	10.8%	2,151.0	2,084.0	2,426.0	2,394.0	3,237.0
Market value ($ mil.)	2.7%	29,685.7	28,861.4	35,891.6	37,952.6	33,067.3
Employees	1.8%	33,400	37,200	37,500	36,484	35,852

TRUJILLO & SONS, INC.

3325 NW 62ND ST
MIAMI, FL 331477533
Phone: 305-696-8701
Fax: –
Web: www.trujilloandsons.com

CEO: –
CFO: –
HR: –
FYE: December 31
Type: Private

Trujillo and Sons is a leading food distributor that supplies foodservice operators and retail grocery stores with dry goods canned foods beverages and a variety of other goods. Most of its products are sold under the Alberto and Don Lucas brands; the company also provides private label packaging services through affiliated companies Trujillo Oil Plant (vegetable and cooking oils) and American Spice Company. Trujillo and Sons serves customers throughout the US and in the Caribbean and South America. The family-owned company was founded in 1966 by Lucas Trujillo Sr.

	Annual Growth	12/04	12/05	12/06	12/08	12/09
Sales ($ mil.)	(37.4%)	–	–	360.9	93.2	88.5
Net income ($ mil.)	237.4%	–	–	0.0	3.7	1.3
Market value ($ mil.)	–	–	–	–	–	–
Employees	–	–	–	–	–	100

TRUMAN ARNOLD COMPANIES

701 S ROBISON RD
TEXARKANA, TX 755016747
Phone: 903-794-3835
Fax: –
Web: www.thearnoldcos.com

CEO: Truman Arnold
CFO: Steve McMillen
HR: –
FYE: September 30
Type: Private

TAC (previously Truman Arnold Companies) is one of the largest independent fuel wholesalers and aviation service providers in the US. Its energy business markets and sells more than 1.5 billion gallons of fuel to customers in industries like energy retail trucking utilities mining and construction. The company supplies refined products like gasoline diesel biodiesel ethanol renewable fuels and Diesel Exhaust Fluid (a non-hazardous product). TAC also serves the aviation industry by selling aviation fuel and providing Fixed Base Operations (aircraft fueling hangar space and transport) through some 15 locations in the US. Providing private charter flights and aircraft maintenance services is a small part of the company's business.

	Annual Growth	09/14	09/15	09/16	09/17	09/18
Sales ($ mil.)	25.8%	–	1,595.9	1,525.8	2,119.3	3,174.3
Net income ($ mil.)	1.2%	–	17.8	18.6	18.6	18.4
Market value ($ mil.)	–	–	–	–	–	–
Employees	–	–	–	–	–	550

TRUMAN MEDICAL CENTER, INCORPORATED

2301 HOLMES ST
KANSAS CITY, MO 641082677
Phone: 816-404-1000
Fax: –
Web: www.trumed.org

CEO: Charles W. (Charlie) Shields
CFO: Allen (Al) Johnson
HR: –
FYE: June 30
Type: Private

Truman Medical Center (TMC) provides primary and mental health care at two not-for-profit hospitals in the Kansas City (Missouri) area with a combined total of about 540 beds. Its Hospital Hill runs one of the busiest emergency rooms in Kansas City and is known for treatments related to asthma diabetes obstetrics ophthalmology weight management and women's health. TMC Lakewood is a leading academic medical center providing a range of health care services to the greater Kansas City metropolitan area including uninsured patients.

	Annual Growth	06/09	06/10	06/13	06/14	06/18
Sales ($ mil.)	3.1%	–	439.2	493.4	418.7	562.3
Net income ($ mil.)	20.3%	–	5.1	(4.7)	(78.2)	22.5
Market value ($ mil.)	–	–	–	–	–	–
Employees	–	–	–	–	–	3,000

TRUMP ENTERTAINMENT RESORTS INC.

15 S. Pennsylvania Ave.
Atlantic City NJ 08401
Phone: 609-449-5866
Fax: 800-824-8329
Web: www.taitroncomponents.com

CEO: Robert F Griffin
CFO: David R Hughes
HR: –
FYE: December 31
Type: Private

Feel like craps? Trump Entertainment Resorts (TER formerly Trump Hotels & Casino Resorts) owns and manages the Trump Plaza and the Trump Taj Mahal casino hotels in Atlantic City New Jersey. The two properties house hotel rooms gaming tables and slot machines. The company also owns the right to use founder and former chairman Donald Trump's name and likeness for gambling promotions. (Unhappy with the actions of the board of directors Trump resigned in 2009.) After spending about a year and a half in Chapter 11 reorganization TER exited bankruptcy in 2010. The company sold its underperforming Trump Marina in 2011.

TRUSTCO BANK CORP. (N.Y.)

NMS: TRST

5 Sarnowski Drive
Glenville, NY 12302
Phone: 518 377-3311
Fax: 518 381-3668
Web: www.trustcobank.com

CEO: Robert J. McCormick
CFO: Michael M. Ozimek
HR: –
FYE: December 31
Type: Public

In Banking They Trust. TrustCo Bank Corp is the holding company for Trustco Bank which boasts more than 140 branches across eastern New York central and western Florida and parts of Vermont Massachusetts and New Jersey. The bank offers personal and business customers a variety of deposit products loans and mortgages and trust and investment services. It primarily originates residential and commercial mortgages which account for more than three-quarters of its loan portfolio. It also writes business construction and installment loans and home equity lines of credit.

	Annual Growth	12/14	12/15	12/16	12/17	12/18
Assets ($ mil.)	1.7%	4,644.4	4,735.0	4,868.8	4,908.0	4,958.9
Net income ($ mil.)	8.6%	44.2	42.2	42.6	43.1	61.4
Market value ($ mil.)	(1.4%)	701.7	593.5	845.8	889.3	663.1
Employees	3.8%	737	787	808	846	854

TRUSTEES OF BOSTON COLLEGE

140 COMMONWEALTH AVE
CHESTNUT HILL, MA 024673800
Phone: 617-552-8000
Fax: –
Web: www.bc.edu

CEO: –
CFO: –
HR: Leo Sullivan
FYE: May 31
Type: Private

Students at Boston College (BC) get both academic excellence and the Red Sox. Located six miles from downtown Boston the university enrolls 14100 full- and part-time students (about a third of whom are graduate students) from every state in the US and 80 other countries. It has a student-teacher ratio of 13:1. BC offers degrees in more than 50 fields of study through its schools and colleges on four campuses. The university also has more than 20 research centers including the Institute for Scientific Research and the Center for International Higher Education. BC is one of the oldest Jesuit Catholic universities in the nation and has the largest Jesuit community in the world.

	Annual Growth	05/12	05/13	05/14	05/17	05/18
Sales ($ mil.)	4.5%	–	671.1	702.7	799.0	835.6
Net income ($ mil.)	(9.0%)	–	270.5	221.2	279.1	169.1
Market value ($ mil.)	–	–	–	–	–	–
Employees	–	–	–	–	–	2,493

TRUSTEES OF CLARK UNIVERSITY

950 MAIN ST
WORCESTER, MA 016101400
Phone: 508-793-7711
Fax: –
Web: www.clarku.edu

CEO: –
CFO: –
HR: –
FYE: May 31
Type: Private

If you don't want to live in the dark get an education at Clark! Clark University is a private co-educational liberal arts university with an enrollment of more than 2200 undergraduate students and more than 1000 graduate students. It offers about 30 undergraduate majors (psychology is the most popular) and about two dozen master's degree programs. Clark University has 200 full-time faculty members of which 96% hold doctoral or terminal degrees. It has a student/faculty ratio of 10:1. The university offers 17 Varsity sports (NCAA Division III). Clark University has been a pioneer in the academic study of geography; it has awarded more doctorates in the discipline than any other US school.

	Annual Growth	05/14	05/15	05/16	05/17	05/18
Sales ($ mil.)	2.3%	–	106.6	111.4	110.7	114.1
Net income ($ mil.)	28.2%	–	15.9	(30.2)	39.2	33.5
Market value ($ mil.)	–	–	–	–	–	–
Employees	–	–	–	–	–	600

TRUSTEES OF DARTMOUTH COLLEGE

20 LEBANON ST
HANOVER, NH 037553564
Phone: 603-646-1110
Fax: –
Web: www.dartmouth.edu

CEO: –
CFO: –
HR: –
FYE: June 30
Type: Private

Part of the esteemed Ivy League Dartmouth College is a private four-year liberal arts college with an enrollment of more than 6000 students. The university has an undergraduate college (offering about 40 programs) and graduate schools of business engineering and medicine plus graduate programs in the arts and sciences. Its student-teacher ratio is about 6:1. It is also home to a number of centers and institutes including Children's Hospital at Dartmouth; Dartmouth Center on Addiction Recovery and Education; and Center for Digital Strategies. Notable alumni include Daniel Webster Robert Frost Theodore "Dr. Seuss" Geisel and Nelson Rockefeller.

	Annual Growth	06/13	06/14	06/15	06/16	06/17
Sales ($ mil.)	16.5%	–	866.7	876.2	859.6	1,370.0
Net income ($ mil.)	0.5%	–	680.3	236.5	(301.5)	691.4
Market value ($ mil.)	–	–	–	–	–	–
Employees	–	–	–	–	–	5,000

TRUSTEES OF INDIANA UNIVERSITY

BRYAN HALL 107 S IND AVE ST BRYAN HA
BLOOMINGTON, IN 47405
Phone: 812-855-4848
Fax: -
Web: www.indiana.edu

CEO: -
CFO: MaryFrances McCourt
HR: John Whelan
FYE: June 30
Type: Private

Indiana University has been schooling Hoosiers (and others) since 1820. With a population of some 115000 students from all 50 states and more than 130 countries the university offers more than 1000 associate baccalaureate master's professional and doctoral degree programs at eight campuses: flagship institution IU-Bloomington; regional campuses in Fort Wayne Gary Kokomo New Albany Richmond and South Bend; and an urban campus in Indianapolis that is operated with Purdue University. The university has about 20000 faculty and professional and support staff. It has 200 research centers and institutes and offers courses in more than 70 languages.

	Annual Growth	06/12	06/13	06/14	06/15	06/16
Sales ($ mil.)	1.7%	-	2,146.7	2,195.2	2,207.6	2,256.2
Net income ($ mil.)	(17.7%)	-	189.3	201.2	138.4	105.7
Market value ($ mil.)	-	-	-	-	-	-
Employees	-	-	-	-	-	16,000

TRUSTEES OF THE COLORADO SCHOOL OF MINES

1500 ILLINOIS ST
GOLDEN, CO 804011887
Phone: 303-273-3000
Fax: -
Web: www.mines.edu

CEO: -
CFO: -
HR: -
FYE: June 30
Type: Private

Colorado School of Mines (CSM) is the oldest public institution of higher education in Colorado. The school offers about 20 undergraduate and 20 graduate academic programs in such fields as applied science and mathematics engineering and geoscience and resource engineering. Students can minor in areas related to humanities and social sciences. In addition graduate students can pursue higher degrees in social and management science. The school claims that its "M" symbol on a nearby mountainside is the nation's largest single-letter electronically lighted school emblem. Colorado School of Mines which has an enrollment of about 5500 was founded in 1874.

	Annual Growth	06/04	06/05	06/06	06/16	06/17
Sales ($ mil.)	62.4%	-	0.7	102.3	215.7	222.1
Net income ($ mil.)	-	-	(0.2)	4.6	(2.0)	(76.8)
Market value ($ mil.)	-	-	-	-	-	-
Employees	-	-	-	-	-	1,000

TRUSTEES OF THE ESTATE OF BERNICE PAUAHI BISHOP

567 S KING ST STE 200
HONOLULU, HI 968133079
Phone: 808-523-6200
Fax: -
Web: www.ksbe.edu

CEO: -
CFO: Michael Loo
HR: Winona White
FYE: June 30
Type: Private

Kamehameha Schools provides an education fit for a king ... or queen. The private charitable trust was founded and endowed by Princess Bernice Pauahi Bishop great granddaughter and last royal descendant of Kamehameha the Great. One of the largest independent schools in the US Kamehameha educates more than 5000 elementary middle school and high school students many of whom board at one of its three Hawaii campuses. In addition it operates some 30 preschools with a total enrollment of about 1500. Kamehameha Schools is also the largest private property owner in the state of Hawaii and uses the proceeds from its real estate operations to support its schools.

	Annual Growth	06/09	06/10	06/13	06/14	06/15
Sales ($ mil.)	18.1%	-	333.8	519.1	915.0	767.2
Net income ($ mil.)	-	-	(21.9)	109.7	482.1	334.0
Market value ($ mil.)	-	-	-	-	-	-
Employees	-	-	-	-	-	1,500

TRUSTEES OF TUFTS COLLEGE

169 HOLLAND ST STE 318
SOMERVILLE, MA 021442401
Phone: 617-628-5000
Fax: -
Web: www.tufts.edu

CEO: -
CFO: -
HR: Julien Carter
FYE: June 30
Type: Private

Tufts University wants to light up the minds of New England scholars. The school offers undergraduate and graduate degrees in areas such as education engineering psychology art English music and medicine. The university enrolls some 11000 students and has 1300 faculty members and it offers classes in 70 fields at three campuses in Massachusetts (Boston Medford/Somerville and Grafton). It also has an international campus in Talloires France. Tufts University's Fletcher School of Law and Diplomacy is the oldest continuous international relations graduate program in the country. The school is also home to New England's only Veterinary School.

	Annual Growth	06/11	06/12	06/13	06/14	06/15
Sales ($ mil.)	5.9%	-	769.0	768.9	965.8	914.4
Net income ($ mil.)	-	-	(100.6)	127.8	68.1	(25.6)
Market value ($ mil.)	-	-	-	-	-	-
Employees	-	-	-	-	-	4,100

TRUSTEES OF UNION COLLEGE IN THE TOWN OF SCHENECTADY IN THE STATE OF NEW YORK

807 UNION ST
SCHENECTADY, NY 123083256
Phone: 518-388-6000
Fax: -
Web: www.union.edu

CEO: -
CFO: -
HR: -
FYE: June 30
Type: Private

Union College brings liberal arts and engineering together. Union College is a private liberal arts school that offers courses in the humanities the social sciences the sciences and engineering. Notable alumni include the father of Franklin D. Roosevelt the grandfather of Winston Churchill and former US president Chester A. Arthur (class of 1848). Founded in 1795 with a class of 16 the college is supported by an endowment of more than $270 million.

	Annual Growth	06/11	06/12	06/13	06/15	06/18
Sales ($ mil.)	(1.8%)	-	159.8	165.3	173.1	143.5
Net income ($ mil.)	25.8%	-	10.5	11.1	8.0	41.5
Market value ($ mil.)	-	-	-	-	-	-
Employees	-	-	-	-	-	870

TRUSTMARK CORP

NMS: TRMK

248 East Capitol Street
Jackson, MS 39201
Phone: 601 208-5111
Fax: 601 354-5053
Web: www.trustmark.com

CEO: Gerard R. (Jerry) Host
CFO: Louis E. Greer
HR: David Kenney
FYE: December 31
Type: Public

Trustmark Corporation is the holding company for Trustmark National Bank which has 208 locations mainly in Mississippi but also in East Texas the Florida panhandle and Tennessee where it also operates its Somerville Bank & Trust subsidiary in the Memphis area. Focusing on individuals and small businesses Trustmark offers a range of financial products and services such as checking and savings accounts certificates of deposit credit cards insurance investments and trust services. The diversified financial services firm has about $11.7 billion in assets.

	Annual Growth	12/14	12/15	12/16	12/17	12/18
Assets ($ mil.)	2.0%	12,250.6	12,678.9	13,352.3	13,798.0	13,286.5
Net income ($ mil.)	4.9%	123.6	116.0	108.4	105.6	149.6
Market value ($ mil.)	3.7%	1,615.6	1,516.8	2,347.0	2,097.5	1,871.7
Employees	(1.7%)	3,060	2,941	2,788	2,893	2,856

TRUSTWAVE HOLDINGS INC.

70 W. Madison St. Ste. 1050　　　　　　　　　　CEO: Arthur Wong
Chicago IL 60602　　　　　　　　　　　　　　　　CFO: –
Phone: 312-873-7500　　　　　　　　　　　　　　HR: Julie Nagle
Fax: 312-443-8028　　　　　　　　　　　　　FYE: December 31
Web: www.trustwave.com　　　　　　　　　　　Type: Private

Because a business can't live on cash alone Trustwave helps credit card merchants and other businesses process secure transactions. The company's TrustKeeper software is a PCI (payment card industry) compliant application that protects merchants against unauthorized access fraud and other security breaches. Its software is sold to companies that process electronic transactions such as American Express Banc of America Merchant Services Chase Paymentech Discover Visa and Wells Fargo among others. These partners in turn offer TrustKeeper subscriptions at credit card merchant locations mainly in the US and Canada. The company also tailors applications for such industries as health care and hospitality.

TRUTH INITIATIVE FOUNDATION

900 G ST NW FL 4　　　　　　　　　　　　　　CEO: Robin Koval
WASHINGTON, DC 200015332　　　　　　　　　　CFO: –
Phone: 202-454-5555　　　　　　　　　　　　　　HR: –
Fax: –　　　　　　　　　　　　　　　　　　FYE: June 30
Web: www.truthinitiative.org　　　　　　　　Type: Private

Truth Initiative formerly American Legacy Foundation tells the truth. Its "truth" anti-smoking campaign is the most public face of this not-for-profit group that seeks to reach young smokers with no-nonsense TV and print ads as well as its Web site thetruth.com. The foundation's goals are to keep young people from lighting up and smoking and to make cessation tools accessible to everyone through grants training activism and community outreach. The organization was established in 1999 as a result of the Master Settlement Agreement between the attorneys general of 46 states and the tobacco industry; the settlement is the major source of funding for the Truth Initiative.

	Annual Growth	06/09	06/10	06/14	06/15	06/17
Sales ($ mil.)	5.6%	–	46.2	117.2	42.7	67.5
Net income ($ mil.)	–	–	(32.4)	52.1	(62.5)	(46.3)
Market value ($ mil.)	–	–	–	–	–	–
Employees	–	–	–	–	–	130

TRW AUTOMOTIVE HOLDINGS CORP   NYS: TRW

12001 Tech Center Drive　　　　　　　　　　　CEO: Franz Kleiner
Livonia, MI 48150　　　　　　　　　　　　　CFO: Joseph S Cantie
Phone: 734 855-2600　　　　　　　　　　　　　　HR: –
Fax: –　　　　　　　　　　　　　　　　　FYE: December 31
Web: www.trw.com　　　　　　　　　　　　　　Type: Public

TRW Automotive makes cars stop and go around the globe in addition to keeping passengers and pedestrians safe. The company designs and makes systems components and modules primarily for major automakers. Product lines range from chassis systems (brake steering and suspension systems) to safety systems such as airbags seat belts and security and safety electronics (crash and occupant weight sensors). Other products include body controls and engine valves. TRW Automotive has more than 190 facilities in two dozen countries worldwide netting nearly 70% of its sales outside North America.

	Annual Growth	12/09	12/10	12/11	12/12	12/13
Sales ($ mil.)	10.7%	11,614.0	14,383.0	16,244.0	16,444.0	17,435.0
Net income ($ mil.)	104.9%	55.0	834.0	1,157.0	1,008.0	970.0
Market value ($ mil.)	32.9%	2,729.5	6,023.5	3,726.1	6,127.6	8,502.7
Employees	5.3%	63,600	69,800	72,700	75,200	78,200

TSR INC   NAS: TSRI

400 Oser Avenue　　　　　　　　　　　　　CEO: Christopher Hughes
Hauppauge, NY 11788　　　　　　　　　　　　　　CFO: –
Phone: 631 231-0333　　　　　　　　　　　　　　HR: –
Fax: 631 435-1428　　　　　　　　　　　　　　FYE: May 31
Web: www.tsrconsulting.com　　　　　　　　　　Type: Public

Prowling for programmers? TSR would like to help. The company provides contract computer programmers and other information technology (IT) personnel mainly to FORTUNE 1000 companies that need to augment their in-house IT staffs. TSR specializes in serving the telecommunications industry; major customers have included purchasing outsourcer ProcureStaff (primarily to fulfill a contract with AT&T) and publishing giant S&P Global. Overall TSR serves more than 80 clients in the northeastern and mid-Atlantic regions of the US. In addition to providing contract personnel TSR offers direct staffing (helping clients find people for permanent placement) and project management services.

	Annual Growth	05/15	05/16	05/17	05/18	05/19
Sales ($ mil.)	2.5%	57.4	61.0	62.6	65.0	63.3
Net income ($ mil.)	–	0.2	0.4	0.3	0.5	(1.3)
Market value ($ mil.)	5.1%	7.8	7.5	14.4	10.1	9.5
Employees	7.9%	287	320	428	417	389

TSRC, INC.

14140 WASHINGTON HWY　　　　　　　　　　　CEO: Patricia Barber
ASHLAND, VA 230057237　　　　　　　　　　CFO: John Arkesteyn
Phone: 804-798-6919　　　　　　　　　　　　　　HR: –
Fax: –　　　　　　　　　　　　　　　　　FYE: December 31
Web: www.tsrcinc.net　　　　　　　　　　　　　Type: Private

TSRC does more than stock the supply room. Operating through about 12 sales offices across Virginia the company (formerly named The Supply Room Companies) markets office products computer accessories and furniture to both the private sector and government agencies. The company has grown by acquiring other office supply dealers in the state including MEGA Office Furniture Spencer Printing Network Business Interiors and Open Plan Systems. It was formed in 1986 when CEO Yancey Jones' Meade & Company and his brother Addison Jones' Magnetic Resources merged with two other office suppliers.

	Annual Growth	12/11	12/12	12/13	12/14	12/16
Sales ($ mil.)	1.5%	–	70.8	67.3	66.6	75.1
Net income ($ mil.)	(7.0%)	–	0.2	0.0	0.0	0.1
Market value ($ mil.)	–	–	–	–	–	–
Employees	–	–	–	–	–	200

TSS INC DE   NBB: TSSI

110 E. Old Settlers Blvd　　　　　　　　　　CEO: Anthony Angelini
Round Rock, TX 78664　　　　　　　　　　　　　CFO: –
Phone: 512 310-1000　　　　　　　　　　　　　　HR: –
Fax: –　　　　　　　　　　　　　　　　　FYE: December 31
Web: www.totalsitesolutions.com　　　　　　　Type: Public

Fortress International Group Inc. (FIGI) is a bastion of security. FIGI companies design build and maintain secure temperature-controlled data centers and IT storage facilities for private companies and government agencies. FIGI offers its start-to-finish service by operating through subsidiaries that specialize in a certain function such as IT consulting design construction or engineering. Projects are either built from scratch or upgraded through renovations. While most of its customers are top secret FIGI has worked with Digital Realty Trust and Internap and is cleared to work at Department of Defense and US Army Corps of Engineers properties.

	Annual Growth	12/14	12/15	12/16	12/17	12/18
Sales ($ mil.)	(5.5%)	28.0	29.5	27.4	18.3	22.3
Net income ($ mil.)	–	(2.8)	(2.2)	(1.0)	0.8	2.4
Market value ($ mil.)	22.8%	6.2	2.2	0.7	8.7	14.1
Employees	(8.8%)	97	90	78	66	67

TTEC HOLDINGS INC

NMS: TTEC

9197 South Peoria Street
Englewood, CO 80112
Phone: 303 397-8100
Fax: –
Web: www.ttec.com

CEO: Kenneth D. Tuchman
CFO: Regina M. Paolillo
HR: –
FYE: December 31
Type: Public

TTEC Holdings (formerly TeleTech Holdings) is leading global call center operator. The company provides a range of business process outsourcing (BPO) services in four areas: customer management direct sales human capital and professional services. The company serves around 300 global clients and maintains a network of some 85 facilities in two dozen countries around the world. Customers mainly major global enterprises come from sectors such as automotive communications financial services government health care retail technology and travel and leisure. TTEC also offers management consulting services.

	Annual Growth	12/14	12/15	12/16	12/17	12/18
Sales ($ mil.)	5.0%	1,241.8	1,286.8	1,275.3	1,477.4	1,509.2
Net income ($ mil.)	(16.1%)	72.3	61.7	33.7	7.3	35.8
Market value ($ mil.)	4.8%	1,093.9	1,289.3	1,408.9	1,859.3	1,319.8
Employees	3.3%	46,000	44,000	48,000	56,000	52,400

TTM TECHNOLOGIES INC

NMS: TTMI

200 East Sandpointe, Suite 400
Santa Ana, CA 92707
Phone: 714 327-3000
Fax: –
Web: www.ttm.com

CEO: Thomas T. Edman
CFO: Todd B. Schull
HR: Shawn Powers
FYE: December 31
Type: Public

TTM Technologies provides contract printed circuit board (PCB) manufacturing services primarily for the networking communications automotive high-end computing aerospace and defense medical industrial and instrumentation markets as well as to electronics manufacturing service providers that serve those markets. TTM offers both quick-turn production — limited quantities delivered in a shortened timeframe — and standard volume production services as well as prototyping services. Its top OEM customers include Collins Aerospace Huawei Apple Inc. Raytheon and Robert Bosch GmbH. TTM customers outside the US account for about 55% of its sales.

	Annual Growth	12/14	12/15*	01/17	01/18*	12/18
Sales ($ mil.)	21.1%	1,325.7	2,095.5	2,533.4	2,658.6	2,847.3
Net income ($ mil.)	85.4%	14.7	(25.9)	34.9	124.2	173.6
Market value ($ mil.)	6.5%	782.8	706.1	1,413.3	1,624.8	1,008.9
Employees	12.5%	16,857	29,570	28,360	29,000	27,000

*Fiscal year change

TUCSON ELECTRIC POWER COMPANY

88 East Broadway Boulevard
Tucson, AZ 85701
Phone: 520 571-4000
Fax: –

CEO: David G. Hutchens
CFO: Kevin P. Larson
HR: Catherine E. Ries
FYE: December 31
Type: Public

Avoiding a run-in with a Saguaro cactus in Tucson Arizona is easier when you stick to the paths lit up by Tucson Electric Power (TEP). The utility provides electricity to about 414000 residential commercial and industrial retail customers in Tucson and surrounding areas in southeastern Arizona. With more than 2240 MW of net generating capacity (primarily coal-fired) TEP supplies most of the power it distributes and it also sells energy wholesale to utilities and power marketers in the western US. TEP is a subsidiary of UNS Energy and accounts for the bulk of that company's total revenues.

	Annual Growth	12/14	12/15	12/16	12/17	12/18
Sales ($ mil.)	3.1%	1,269.9	1,306.5	1,235.0	1,340.9	1,432.6
Net income ($ mil.)	16.5%	102.3	127.8	124.4	176.7	188.3
Market value ($ mil.)	–	–	–	–	–	–
Employees	1.4%	1,448	1,478	1,508	1,510	1,528

TUESDAY MORNING CORP

NMS: TUES

6250 LBJ Freeway
Dallas, TX 75240
Phone: 972 387-3562
Fax: –
Web: www.tuesdaymorning.com

CEO: Steven R. (Steve) Becker
CFO: Stacie R. Shirley
HR: Denise Davis
FYE: June 30
Type: Public

Tuesday Morning offers big discounts to customers every day of the week. The closeout retailer sells discontinued merchandise from name-brand manufacturers at steep discounts. Its merchandise typically includes upscale linens china cookware rugs and collectibles that are not seconds irregulars or factory rejects. Tuesday Morning's 725-plus stores in about 40 states operate seven days a week excluding holidays. The retailer keeps costs down by selling from low-rent locations and using seasonal help — only about 25% of its workers are full-time employees. Its customers are primarily from middle- and upper-income households.

	Annual Growth	06/15	06/16	06/17	06/18	06/19
Sales ($ mil.)	2.7%	906.4	956.4	966.7	1,006.3	1,007.2
Net income ($ mil.)	–	10.4	3.7	(32.5)	(21.9)	(12.4)
Market value ($ mil.)	(37.8%)	525.9	327.7	88.7	142.4	78.9
Employees	2.2%	8,820	9,067	8,878	9,062	9,634

TUFCO TECHNOLOGIES, INC.

NAS: TFCO

P.O. Box 23500
Green Bay, WI 54305
Phone: 920 336-0054
Fax: –
Web: www.tufco.com

CEO: Larry Grabowy
CFO: –
HR: Lynne Nelson
FYE: September 30
Type: Public

Tough-sounding Tufco Technologies does business with paper-thin bravado. It operates through two segments: Contract manufacturing its largest custom-converts paper tissue and polyethylene film into such necessaries as cleaning wipes and disposable table cloths. The segment also offers flexographic printing adhesive laminating and custom packaging. The company's business imaging arm operated via subsidiary Hamco Manufacturing and Distributing produces specialty paper rolls (for ATMs and cash registers) standardized and customized guest checks (for restaurants) business forms and other sheeted products. Customers are multinational consumer products businesses and less so business paper distributors.

	Annual Growth	09/09	09/10	09/11	09/12	09/13
Sales ($ mil.)	3.4%	86.8	90.6	109.9	107.0	99.3
Net income ($ mil.)	–	(0.9)	(0.4)	(0.4)	(0.1)	(4.0)
Market value ($ mil.)	14.5%	12.5	14.8	15.9	18.3	21.5
Employees	(3.6%)	306	305	302	293	264

TUFTS ASSOCIATED HEALTH PLANS INC.

705 Mt. Auburn St.
Watertown MA 02472-1508
Phone: 617-972-9400
Fax: 832-355-6182
Web: www.sleh.com

CEO: Thomas Crosswell
CFO: –
HR: –
FYE: December 31
Type: Private - Not-for-Pr

Getting good health care becomes a little less rough with Tufts. Tufts Associated Health Plans is a leading New England health insurer operating as Tufts Health Plan. The company provides medical coverage to about 1 million members in Massachusetts and (to a lesser degree) Rhode Island. Its products include HMO PPO and point-of-service plans for both employers and individuals as well as Medicare Advantage plans for retirees and managed Medicaid plans for low-income families. With partner CIGNA Tufts also offers a nationwide health network called CareLink for multi-state employers. The company was founded in 1979.

TUMI HOLDINGS INC
NYS: TUMI

1001 Durham Ave.
South Plainfield, NJ 07080
Phone: 908 756-4400
Fax: –
Web: www.tumi.com

CEO: Kyle Gendreau
CFO: Michael J Mardy
HR: –
FYE: December 31
Type: Public

Tumi helps the well-heeled get where they're going in style. The high-end designer and manufacturer named after an ancient ceremonial knife makes travel gear (including suitcases and backpacks) and caters to corporate travelers with precious cargo as the company has its own Tumi Tracer tracking system for retrieving lost bags. Tumi which makes Ducati luggage under license also offers laptop covers wallets belts phone chargers and other accessories. Its products are sold in the US and in more than 75 other countries through about 115 of its own retail stores websites and upscale department and specialty stores. A unit of investment firm Doughty Hanson Tumi went public in 2012.

	Annual Growth	12/10	12/11	12/12	12/13	12/14
Sales ($ mil.)	20.2%	252.8	330.0	398.6	467.4	527.2
Net income ($ mil.)	386.0%	0.1	16.6	36.8	54.6	58.0
Market value ($ mil.)	6.7%	–	–	1,415.1	1,530.4	1,610.5
Employees	15.5%	–	963	1,152	1,307	1,484

TUPPERWARE BRANDS CORP
NYS: TUP

14901 South Orange Blossom Trail
Orlando, FL 32837
Phone: 407 826-5050
Fax: –
Web: www.tupperwarebrands.com

CEO: E. V. (Rick) Goings
CFO: Michael S. (Mike) Poteshman
HR: Lillian D. Garcia
FYE: December 29
Type: Public

Tupperware Brands Corporation (TBC) makes and sells household products and beauty items. Product categories and brands include preparation storage and serving containers for kitchen and home uses through its well-known Tupperware brand while beauty and personal care products are presented under the Avroy Shlain Fuller NaturCare Nutrimetics and Nuvo brands. TBC deploys a salesforce of about 3.2 million people across some 100 countries to sell its products. Tupperware parties became synonymous with American suburban life in the 1950s when independent salespeople organized gatherings to sell their plasticware. Today most revenue originates outside the US. In 2018 the company named the first female CEO in its 70-year history.

	Annual Growth	12/14	12/15	12/16	12/17	12/18
Sales ($ mil.)	(5.6%)	2,606.1	2,283.8	2,213.1	2,255.8	2,069.7
Net income ($ mil.)	(7.7%)	214.4	185.8	223.6	(265.4)	155.9
Market value ($ mil.)	(16.4%)	3,099.1	2,720.0	2,560.8	3,051.4	1,517.4
Employees	(2.2%)	13,100	13,000	13,000	12,000	12,000

TURNER CONSTRUCTION COMPANY INC

375 HUDSON ST FL 6
NEW YORK, NY 100143667
Phone: 212-229-6000
Fax: –
Web: www.turnerconstruction.com

CEO: Abrar Sheriff
CFO: Karen O. Gould
HR: –
FYE: December 31
Type: Private

Turner Construction has been the mastermind for scores of head-turning projects for more than a century. The company that built Madison Square Garden has ranked among the leading general builders in the US since the early 1900s. Turner provides construction and project management services for commercial and multifamily buildings airports and stadiums as well as correctional educational entertainment and manufacturing facilities. The company is also a leader in sustainable or green building practices. Founded in 1902 by Henry Turner the company is the main operating unit of The Turner Corporation which is a subsidiary of German construction group HOCHTIEF.

	Annual Growth	12/10	12/11	12/12	12/13	12/14
Sales ($ mil.)	10.9%	–	–	8,552.1	9,488.5	10,516.1
Net income ($ mil.)	17.2%	–	–	70.4	76.6	96.7
Market value ($ mil.)	–	–	–	–	–	–
Employees	–	–	–	–	–	5,000

TURTLE & HUGHES, INC

1900 LOWER RD
LINDEN, NJ 070366586
Phone: 732-574-3600
Fax: –
Web: www.turtle.com

CEO: Jayne Millard
CFO: Chris Rausch
HR: –
FYE: September 30
Type: Private

Turtle & Hughes' longevity has demonstrated that slow and steady really does win the race when it comes to distributing electrical and industrial equipment. The company's exhaustive lineup is sold through three subsidiaries: Turtle & Hughes Integrated Supply Turtle Data (wire cable and power protection devices) and Turtle Ebay Store. Its customers include industrial and construction companies electrical contractors telecommunications servers utilities and various government agencies. Family-owned the company is led by its fourth generation Jayne Millard its third female CEO. One-third of Turtle & Hughes is employee-owned.

	Annual Growth	09/14	09/15	09/16	09/17	09/18
Sales ($ mil.)	8.5%	–	590.9	628.5	671.4	754.7
Net income ($ mil.)	5.0%	–	17.5	16.3	18.1	20.2
Market value ($ mil.)	–	–	–	–	–	–
Employees	–	–	–	–	–	900

TURTLE BEACH CORP
NMS: HEAR

11011 Via Frontera, Suite A/B
San Diego, CA 92127
Phone: 888 496-8001
Fax: –
Web: www.parametricsound.com

CEO: Juergen Stark
CFO: John T Hanson
HR: –
FYE: December 31
Type: Public

Using proprietary technology Turtle Beach (formerly Parametric Sound) makes speakers that offer focused and directional sound for an immersive experience. Its current product is the HS-3000 line of speakers for the commercial market including digital kiosks and slot machines. The company is developing its Hypersonic line for the consumer market where it hopes its thin two-speaker system will rival traditional multi-speaker setups used for surround sound and be used in computers video games and mobile devices. Turtle Beach sells its products in North America Asia and Europe to OEMs for inclusion in new and existing products.

	Annual Growth	12/14	12/15	12/16	12/17	12/18
Sales ($ mil.)	11.5%	186.2	162.7	174.0	149.1	287.4
Net income ($ mil.)	–	(15.5)	(82.9)	(87.2)	(3.2)	39.2
Market value ($ mil.)	45.4%	45.5	28.7	18.7	6.5	203.6
Employees	(1.1%)	161	221	172	135	154

TUTOR PERINI CORP
NYS: TPC

15901 Olden Street
Sylmar, CA 91342-1093
Phone: 818 362-8391
Fax: –
Web: www.tutorperini.com

CEO: Robert Band
CFO: Gary G. Smalley
HR: –
FYE: December 31
Type: Public

Construction company Tutor Perini builds projects ranging from casinos and hotels to highways and housing developments. One of the largest builders in the US the company also builds schools healthcare facilities airports and industrial buildings. Tutor Perini and its subsidiaries provide pre-construction and design-build services general contracting equipment materials subcontracting and other services. Its Civil segment builds and maintains highways bridges and mass transit. The Building segment constructs buildings in the hospitality gaming and other industries while the Specialty Contractors division builds electrical and mechanical systems. More than 90% of the company's sales come from the US.

	Annual Growth	12/14	12/15	12/16	12/17	12/18
Sales ($ mil.)	(0.2%)	4,492.3	4,920.5	4,973.1	4,757.2	4,454.7
Net income ($ mil.)	(6.2%)	107.9	45.3	95.8	148.4	83.4
Market value ($ mil.)	(9.7%)	1,204.1	837.4	1,400.7	1,268.2	798.9
Employees	(7.0%)	10,939	10,626	11,603	10,061	8,200

TVAX BIOMEDICAL INC.

8006 Reeder St.
Lenexa KS 66214-1554
Phone: 913-492-2221
Fax: 913-492-2243
Web: www.tvaxbiomedical.com

CEO: –
CFO: –
HR: –
FYE: December 31
Type: Private

TVAX may be a clever play on the company's methods but it is completely serious about killing cancer. TVAX Biomedical uses cancer cell vaccination and the introduction of killer T cells to treat cancer. Its TVAX Immunotherapy uses a process of injecting a patient with their own irradiated cancer cells producing a cancer-specific T cell immune response. The company then harvests those cells from the patient's blood turns them into killer T cells and re-injects them. The patient's own immune system does the rest killing the cancer cells and cancer stem cells which are normally resistant to treatment methods. TVAX whose lead candidates attack brain and kidney cancer withdrew its IPO in May 2012.

TW TELECOM INC

NMS: TWTC

10475 Park Meadows Drive
Littleton, CO 80124
Phone: 303 566-1000
Fax: –
Web: www.twtelecom.com

CEO: Larissa L Herda
CFO: Mark A Peters
HR: –
FYE: December 31
Type: Public

tw telecom may opt for lowercase branding but there is nothing diminutive about its ambitions in the US communications industry. Serving 75 metropolitan markets in about 30 states the company provides data networking and Internet access as well as local and long-distance voice services voice over Internet Protocol (VoIP) and other communications services to midsized and large telecom-intensive businesses in such industries as health care finance manufacturing and hospitality. Additionally tw telecom serves local state and federal government organizations and provides wholesale services to other communications carriers and ISPs.

	Annual Growth	12/08	12/09	12/10	12/11	12/12
Sales ($ mil.)	6.1%	1,159.0	1,211.4	1,273.2	1,366.9	1,470.3
Net income ($ mil.)	73.3%	8.5	27.6	271.4	57.9	76.9
Market value ($ mil.)	31.7%	1,282.3	2,596.5	2,581.3	2,934.1	3,856.1
Employees	2.6%	2,844	2,870	2,975	3,051	3,147

TWIN DISC INCORPORATED

NMS: TWIN

1328 Racine Street
Racine, WI 53403
Phone: 262 638-4000
Fax: 262 638-4481
Web: www.twindisc.com

CEO: John H. Batten
CFO: Jeffery S. Knutson
HR: Denise L. Wilcox
FYE: June 30
Type: Public

Twin Disc makes heavy-duty power transmission equipment for the marine and off-highway vehicle markets. Its lineup includes marine transmissions propellers and boat management systems power-shift transmissions hydraulic torque converters and industrial clutches and control systems. Applications for Twin Disc's products include yachts and other pleasure craft and construction and military vehicles. The company also serves the energy and natural resources and industrial markets. Twin Disc markets its products through both a direct sales force and a distributor network.

	Annual Growth	06/15	06/16	06/17	06/18	06/19
Sales ($ mil.)	3.3%	265.8	166.3	168.2	240.7	302.7
Net income ($ mil.)	(1.1%)	11.2	(13.1)	(6.3)	9.5	10.7
Market value ($ mil.)	(5.1%)	246.8	142.2	213.7	328.6	199.9
Employees	(1.3%)	921	742	672	696	873

TWIN VEE POWERCATS INC

NBB: TVPC

1800 Forest Hill Blvd., Suite A7
West Palm Beach, FL 33406
Phone: 561 827-7107
Fax: –
Web: www.twinvee.com

CEO: Joseph Visconti
CFO: –
HR: –
FYE: December 31
Type: Public

The value-add for ValueRich is to create wealth by bringing small-cap companies and investors together. The company's Web-based platform magazine and events are designed to help small-cap companies raise capital go public and attract shareholders. Its iValueRich.com site allows investors to directly connect with companies that are seeking investors. ValueRich also manages and holds regular tradeshows where attendees can highlight their prospects for investment bankers and other potential investors. The company's ValueRich quarterly magazine is distributed free to a select group of executives and investment professionals in the small-cap community. ValueRich was founded in 2003.

	Annual Growth	12/14	12/15	12/16	12/17	12/18
Sales ($ mil.)	108.7%	0.6	6.8	7.3	7.1	10.6
Net income ($ mil.)	–	(0.0)	0.4	0.9	0.4	0.7
Market value ($ mil.)	(4.7%)	11.5	10.0	12.9	13.2	9.5
Employees						

TWITTER INC

NYS: TWTR

1355 Market Street, Suite 900
San Francisco, CA 94103
Phone: 415 222-9670
Fax: –
Web: www.twitter.com

CEO: Jack Dorsey
CFO: Ned D. Segal
HR: –
FYE: December 31
Type: Public

We should describe Twitter in 280 characters but we'll probably use more. That's the number of letters (and spaces) the social media platform's users have to express themselves in each tweet. Millions of people around the world use Twitter many of them posting multiple tweets a day from PCs smartphones tablets and other mobile devices. The service has become a key real-time communication platform as major events unfold around the world. Twitter claims more than 320 million monthly users worldwide. The US is its largest market accounting for more than half of the company's revenues. It makes most of its money from advertisers trying to reach those users.

	Annual Growth	12/14	12/15	12/16	12/17	12/18
Sales ($ mil.)	21.3%	1,403.0	2,218.0	2,529.6	2,443.3	3,042.4
Net income ($ mil.)	–	(577.8)	(521.0)	(456.9)	(108.1)	1,205.6
Market value ($ mil.)	(5.4%)	27,413.9	17,684.9	12,457.4	18,349.8	21,964.7
Employees	1.9%	3,638	3,898	3,583	3,372	3,920

TWO HARBORS INVESTMENT CORP

NYS: TWO

575 Lexington Avenue, Suite 2930
New York, NY 10022
Phone: 612 629-2500
Fax: –
Web: www.twoharborsinvestment.com

CEO: –
CFO: –
HR: Beth Petersen
FYE: December 31
Type: Public

Two Harbors Investment Corp. is ready to double its money. The real estate investment trust (REIT) is managed and advised by (and was founded by) PRCM Advisers a subsidiary of Pine River Capital Management. The trust primarily invests in agency residential mortgage-backed securities (RMBS) with fixed or adjustable interest rates that are backed by government-supported enterprises Fannie Mae Freddie Mac or Ginnie Mae. About a quarter of its mortgage portfolio is made up of non-agency RMBS such as subprime mortgages which carry more risk than federally-backed securities but offer higher yields.

	Annual Growth	12/14	12/15	12/16	12/17	12/18
Assets ($ mil.)	9.3%	21,084.3	14,575.8	20,112.1	24,789.3	30,132.5
Net income ($ mil.)	–	167.1	492.2	353.3	348.6	(44.3)
Market value ($ mil.)	6.4%	2,485.8	2,009.5	2,163.3	4,033.9	3,185.4
Employees	–	–	–	–	–	–

TWO RIVER BANCORP

NMS: TRCB

766 Shrewsbury Avenue
Tinton Falls, NJ 07724
Phone: 732 389-8722
Fax: -
Web: www.tworiverbank.com

CEO: William D Moss
CFO: A Richard Abrahamian
HR: Nicole Nielsen
FYE: December 31
Type: Public

Community Partners Bancorp is the holding company for Two River Community Bank and The Town Bank (a division of Two River). Through more than a dozen total branches located in eastern New Jersey the two banks offer deposit services like checking and savings accounts as well as a variety of lending services to consumers and small to midsized businesses. The banks' combined loan portfolio consists mainly of commercial real estate loans (about 40%) commercial and industrial loans (25%) and construction loans (20%). Consumer and residential loans make up only about 10% of the portfolio. Two River's branches are located in Middletown while Town Bank's are located in Westfield and Cranford.

	Annual Growth	12/13	12/14	12/15	12/16	12/17
Assets ($ mil.)	7.8%	769.7	781.2	863.7	940.2	1,039.8
Net income ($ mil.)	6.0%	5.2	6.0	6.3	8.6	6.5
Market value ($ mil.)	25.9%	61.1	71.4	84.3	126.4	153.6
Employees	3.0%	143	141	145	151	161

TYCO FIRE & SECURITY LLC

1501 Yamato Rd
Boca Raton FL 33431
Phone: 561-988-7200
Fax: 513-851-2057
Web: www.rumpke.com

CEO: -
CFO: -
HR: -
FYE: September 30
Type: Subsidiary

Tyco Fire & Security takes a global approach to minimizing risk. A subsidiary of Tyco International the company designs sells installs and monitors electronic security systems and services to more than 7 million residential commercial industrial and government customers worldwide. It operates in North America and has a presence in Africa Asia Australia Europe and South America. The company's security systems are primarily marketed under the ADT and Sensormatic brands and are designed to detect intrusion as well as react to hazards such as fire smoke flooding and other environmental conditions.

TYLER TECHNOLOGIES, INC.

NYS: TYL

5101 Tennyson Parkway
Plano, TX 75024
Phone: 972 713-3700
Fax: -
Web: www.tylertech.com

CEO: John S. Marr
CFO: Brian K. Miller
HR: -
FYE: December 31
Type: Public

Tyler Technologies doesn't want local governments tied up in red tape. The company provides software and services intended to help state and local government offices operate more efficiently. Specializing in applications for local governments and public schools Tyler's products include software for accounting and financial management filing court documents electronically tracking and managing court cases and automating appraisals and assessments. Other products include applications that allow citizens to access utility accounts or pay traffic fines online. Tyler complements its software with hosting support and maintenance services. The company counts more than 13000 government and school customers in all 50 states Canada the Caribbean and the UK.

	Annual Growth	12/14	12/15	12/16	12/17	12/18
Sales ($ mil.)	17.4%	493.1	591.0	756.0	840.7	935.3
Net income ($ mil.)	25.8%	58.9	64.9	109.9	163.9	147.5
Market value ($ mil.)	14.2%	4,188.9	6,672.2	5,464.6	6,776.7	7,112.3
Employees	12.2%	2,856	3,586	3,831	4,069	4,525

TYMCO INC.

225 E. Industrial Blvd.
Waco TX 76705
Phone: 254-799-5546
Fax: 254-799-2722
Web: www.tymco.com

CEO: Kenneth J Young
CFO: Ron Holy
HR: -
FYE: August 31
Type: Private

TYMCO doesn't have to sweep anything under the rug. The company makes regenerative air sweepers used to clean roadways runways and related surfaces. TYMCO's patented regenerative air system is designed to prevent pollutants leaving the vehicle's hopper once they have been swept from the pavement. Some sweeper models can run on alternative fuels such as compressed natural gas or liquefied petroleum gas. TYMCO sells worldwide through dealers. Construction executive B. W. Young founded the company in the late 1960s; it is owned and run by members of his family including sons Kenneth (president) and Gary (VP). TYMCO is an acronym for The Young Manufacturing Company.

TYNDALE HOUSE PUBLISHERS, INC.

351 EXECUTIVE DR
CAROL STREAM, IL 601882420
Phone: 630-668-8300
Fax: -
Web: www.tyndale.com

CEO: -
CFO: -
HR: -
FYE: April 30
Type: Private

Christian-focused publisher Tyndale House Publishers publishes fiction non-fiction and children's books as well as bibles. One of its best-selling titles is the novel Left Behind a fictional account of the apocalypse written by Jerry B. Jenkins. The titles success inspired the Left Behind series of novels which has sole some 63 million copies as well as Left Behind comic books music and three movies. Tyndale House was founded in 1962 by Kenneth N. Taylor who wrote The Living Bible in order to translate the old English in the King James Version of the Bible into a more accessible language for his children. Taylor who died in 2005 named the company after 16th Century English translator William Tyndale.

	Annual Growth	04/14	04/15	04/16	04/17	04/18
Sales ($ mil.)	(4.5%)	-	77.9	73.6	70.2	67.8
Net income ($ mil.)	(28.8%)	-	3.6	2.9	0.3	1.3
Market value ($ mil.)	-	-	-	-	-	-
Employees	-	-	-	-	-	259

TYR SPORT INC.

15391 Springdale Ave.
Huntington Beach CA 92649
Phone: 714-897-0799
Fax: 714-897-6420
Web: www.tyr.com

CEO: Matthew Dilorenzo
CFO: -
HR: -
FYE: June 30
Type: Subsidiary

TYR (pronounced tier) Sport wants to ensure that swimmers are well suited for water play and sport. The company designs and makes men's women's and youth swimwear and related gear for professional athletes as well as for recreational use. TYR is named after the Norse god of warriors and athletes. The firm's Aqua Shift technology is said to reduce wave drag by 10% and is worn by such swimmers as double Olympic gold medalist and eight-time world champion Yana Klochkova and Olympic silver medalist and US record holder Erik Vendt. Parent company Swimwear Anywhere is the second-largest branded swimwear manufacturer in North America behind Speedo maker Warnaco Swimwear.

TYSON FOODS INC
NYS: TSN

2200 West Don Tyson Parkway
Springdale, AR 72762-6999
Phone: 479 290-4000
Fax: 479 290-7984
Web: www.tyson.com

CEO: Thomas P. (Tom) Hayes
CFO: Stewart F. Glendinning
HR: Mary A. Oleksiuk
FYE: September 28
Type: Public

Tyson Foods spreads its wings beyond the chicken coop. While it is one of the largest US chicken producers (with processing capacity of some 42 million a week) Tyson's Fresh Meats division makes it a giant in the beef and pork sectors as well. The company also offers value-added processed and pre-cooked meats and refrigerated and frozen prepared foods. Its chicken operations are vertically integrated — the company hatches the eggs supplies contract growers with the chicks and feed and brings them back for processing when ready. Tyson's brands include Tyson Jimmy Dean Hillshire Farm Ball Park Wright ibp Aidells and State Fair. Its customers include retail wholesale and food service companies worldwide although the US accounts for most sales.

	Annual Growth	10/15	10/16*	09/17	09/18	09/19
Sales ($ mil.)	0.6%	41,373.0	36,881.0	38,260.0	40,052.0	42,405.0
Net income ($ mil.)	13.5%	1,220.0	1,768.0	1,774.0	3,024.0	2,022.0
Market value ($ mil.)	17.7%	16,246.7	27,329.2	25,784.7	21,788.0	31,183.2
Employees	5.7%	113,000	114,000	122,000	121,000	141,000

*Fiscal year change

TYSON FRESH MEATS INC.

800 Stevens Port Dr.
Dakota Dunes SD 57049
Phone: 605-235-2061
Fax: 605-235-2068
Web: www.tyson.com/corporate/b2b/freshmeats

CEO: –
CFO: –
HR: –
FYE: September 30
Type: Subsidiary

No matter how you slice it steak is the main attraction at Tyson Fresh Meats. A processor of beef and pork Tyson slaughters and sells fresh beef and pork and case-ready ground beef and pork products. Its offerings are sold under brand names including Chairman's Reserve Beef and Supreme Tender Pork to mostly US food retailers foodservice operators and meat processors. Tyson does not raise cattle but has buyers who purchase livestock on the open market. It has swine buyers as well; however it does raise some pigs. Non-edible animal remains are processed and sold to manufacturers of animal feed leather and pharmaceuticals. Tyson Fresh Meats is a subsidiary of chicken and meat producer Tyson Foods.

U S CHINA MINING GROUP INC.
NBB: SGZH

15310 Amberly Drive, Suite 250
Tampa, FL 33647
Phone: 813 514-2873
Fax: –
Web: www.uschinamining.com

CEO: Hongwen LI
CFO: Xinyu Peng
HR: –
FYE: December 31
Type: Public

It's a cold coal world for U.S. China Mining Group. The company operates three coal mines in Heilongjiang Province the northeastern-most part of China. Its three mines — Tong Gong Hong Yuan and Sheng Yu — produce almost 1 million tons of coal a year. The group sells its coal to power plants cement factories wholesalers and individuals for home heating. Three customers account for the majority of sales — Heilongjiang QiQiHaEr Huadian Power Plants Co. Ltd. accounted for 60% in 2010; Heilongjiang Beihai Logistics Company and Changchun Rail Transportation Co. Ltd. together accounted for another 30%. Chairman Guoqing Yue owns a third of the company's stock.

	Annual Growth	12/09	12/10	12/11	12/12	12/13
Sales ($ mil.)	(53.6%)	65.0	69.0	54.0	30.9	3.0
Net income ($ mil.)	–	–	25.1	13.4	15.2	(31.2)	(7.7)
Market value ($ mil.)	(68.5%)	152.9	119.9	20.7	7.2	1.5
Employees	(38.8%)	655	1,017	1,186	91	92

U-SWIRL INC.
NBB: SWRL

265 Turner Dr.
Durango, CO 81303
Phone: 702 586-8700
Fax: –

CEO: Bryan J Merryman
CFO: Jeremy M Kinney
HR: –
FYE: February 28
Type: Public

This company hopes to have customers circling its frozen yogurt shops. U-Swirl (formerly Healthy Fast Food) operates and franchises a small number of U-SWIRL Frozen Yogurt outlets. The chain offers non-fat frozen yogurt treats available with more than 60 different toppings. U-SWIRL locations operate primarily in Nevada. In addition to its yogurt franchising business U-Swirl operates two franchised hamburger outlets under the EVOS banner. Before changing its name to U-Swirl in 2011 Healthy Fast Food acquired the global development rights to the U-SWIRL Frozen Yogurt concept in 2008. U-Swirl plans to build the chain through franchising.

	Annual Growth	12/11	12/12*	02/13	02/14	02/15
Sales ($ mil.)	29.9%	2.6	2.8	0.6	5.5	7.5
Net income ($ mil.)	–	(0.7)	(0.5)	(0.4)	(2.1)	(0.3)
Market value ($ mil.)	7.6%	6.5	4.4	8.1	18.5	8.7
Employees	18.2%	40	80	88	117	78

*Fiscal year change

U.G.N., INC.

18410 CROSSING DR STE C
TINLEY PARK, IL 604876209
Phone: 773-437-2400
Fax: –
Web: www.ugn.com

CEO: –
CFO: Steve Hamilton
HR: Eric Kerkhoff
FYE: December 31
Type: Private

Buying a Japanese car? Sounds good. Especially if the vehicle has acoustic molding and other sound-dampening acoustic automotive trim products made by UGN. The company produces molding from a variety of materials including cotton fiber and foam for vehicles assembled in North America by US and Japanese auto makers. UGN also makes automotive interior trim and thermal management parts. Its products are used to reduce interior noise and fine tune acoustical signals. The company's clientele has included such heavy hitters as Honda Nissan and Toyota. UGN was established in 1986 and is a joint venture between Autoneum and Nihon Tokushu Toryo (Nittoku).

	Annual Growth	12/04	12/05	12/06	12/07	12/08
Sales ($ mil.)	1.7%	–	213.9	223.1	239.0	225.0
Net income ($ mil.)	10.3%	–	8.5	13.1	0.0	11.4
Market value ($ mil.)	–	–	–	–	–	–
Employees	–	–	–	–	–	1,250

U.S. AUTO PARTS NETWORK INC
NMS: PRTS

16941 Keegan Avenue
Carson, CA 90746
Phone: 424 702-1455
Fax: –
Web: www.usautoparts.net

CEO: Aaron Coleman
CFO: David Meniane
HR: Sheila Pineda
FYE: December 29
Type: Public

U.S. Auto Parts Network puts its customers in the fast lane. The company offers about 1.5 million aftermarket auto parts for all makes and models of domestic and foreign cars and trucks. Its inventory includes replacement performance body and engine parts as well as accessories (such as seat covers alarms). U.S. Auto Parts also sells products for motorcycles all-terrain vehicles and RVs. The company generates the bulk of its revenue online; a retail store in Illinois and mail-order catalogs also bring in sales. The company ships parts to about 150 countries. It also distributes a private-label line of mirrors to auto parts stores nationwide and runs a wholesale program for body shops in Southern California.

	Annual Growth	01/15	01/16*	12/16	12/17	12/18
Sales ($ mil.)	0.7%	283.5	291.1	303.6	303.4	289.5
Net income ($ mil.)	–	(6.9)	(1.3)	0.7	24.0	(4.9)
Market value ($ mil.)	(24.9%)	77.7	103.2	123.2	88.2	32.9
Employees	2.4%	983	1,084	1,080	1,069	1,054

*Fiscal year change

U.S. NEWS & WORLD REPORT L.P.

450 W. 33rd St. 11th Fl.
New York NY 10001
Phone: 212-716-6800
Fax: 212-643-7842
Web: www.usnews.com

CEO: Mortimer B Zuckerman
CFO: –
HR: –
FYE: January 31
Type: Private

This company can report first hand: The news on traditional print journalism in the US is pretty grim. U.S. News & World Report was once the publisher of a print news magazine of the same name; today its content is available online only with special printed issues. USNews.com focuses on topics such as politics and policy education and health. In recent years the company has found more luck in print with its signature America's Best annual series of books that ranks institutions and services such as colleges hospitals and mutual funds. The magazine was founded in 1933 as United States News. Real estate and media tycoon Mort Zuckerman (co-owner of the New York Daily News) has owned the company since 1984.

U.S. PHYSICAL THERAPY, INC.   NYS: USPH

1300 West Sam Houston Parkway South, Suite 300
Houston, TX 77042
Phone: 713 297-7000
Fax: –
Web: www.usph.com

CEO: Christopher J. (Chris) Reading
CFO: Lawrance W. (Larry) McAfee
HR: –
FYE: December 31
Type: Public

U.S. Physical Therapy (USPh) through its subsidiaries lends a hand to injured workers athletes and others in need of some TLC. With some 560 outpatient clinics in more than 40 states USPh provides physical therapy services for work-related and sports injuries trauma orthopedic conditions osteoarthritis treatment and post-surgical rehabilitation. The clinics operate under a number of local or regional brands including Red River Valley Physical Therapy and Pioneer Physical Therapy. USPh also operates 22 physical therapy facilities for third parties including physician groups and hospitals.

	Annual Growth	12/14	12/15	12/16	12/17	12/18
Sales ($ mil.)	10.4%	305.1	331.3	356.5	414.1	453.9
Net income ($ mil.)	13.7%	20.9	22.3	20.6	22.3	34.9
Market value ($ mil.)	25.0%	532.2	680.9	890.5	915.8	1,298.3
Employees	9.9%	3,151	3,400	3,800	4,300	4,600

U.S. SILICA HOLDINGS INC.   NYSE: SLCA

8490 Progress Dr. Ste. 300
Frederick MD 21701
Phone: 800-345-6170
Fax: 304-258-8295
Web: www.u-s-silica.com

CEO: –
CFO: Donald Merril
HR: –
FYE: December 31
Type: Public

Life's a beach for the sand-sellers at U.S. Silica. The industrial mineral company provides silica and aplite for the glass foundry chemical and construction industries; and fine ground silica and kaolin clay used to make paint plastics and ceramics. Its "frac sand" product — currently its fastest-growing offering — is used by natural gas and oil producers in hydraulic fracturing a process to boost oil and gas production. The company supplies customers in the US and Canada. In addition to its main facility in West Virginia U S. Silica also has a dozen plants in the East. A portfolio holding of private equity firm Golden Gate Capital U.S. Silica filed to go public in 2011.

U.S. VENTURE, INC.

425 BETTER WAY
APPLETON, WI 549156192
Phone: 920-739-6101
Fax: –
Web: www.usoil.com

CEO: John Schmidt
CFO: Jay Walters
HR: –
FYE: July 31
Type: Private

Privately held U.S. Venture Inc. is a North American leader in the distribution of fuel and transportation products. U.S. Oil its largest division transports more than 2 billion gallons of fuel annually via pipelines rail light oil-barges and trucks. The division maintains around 7 million BOE in storage capacity and has access to 330 terminals. Through U.S. AutoForce the company is also a top distributor of tires and car parts to independent tire retailers auto repair shops and dealerships. The company's Lubricants division maintains a competitive business as well set up to blend and market chemical products to automotive industrial and metalworking industries. Through the GAIN Clean Fuel brand U.S. Venture also sells clean biofuels.

	Annual Growth	07/11	07/12	07/13	07/14	07/15
Sales ($ mil.)	4.9%	–	–	7,346.1	9,088.9	8,076.1
Net income ($ mil.)	91.7%	–	–	47.2	49.3	173.5
Market value ($ mil.)	–	–	–	–	–	–
Employees	–	–	–	–	–	1,182

U.S. VISION INC.

1 Harmon Dr. Glen Oaks Industrial Park
Glendora NJ 08029
Phone: 856-228-1000
Fax: 856-228-3339
Web: www.usvision.com

CEO: –
CFO: –
HR: Busayo Ola Ajayi
FYE: January 31
Type: Subsidiary

U.S. Vision sees its future in stores. A subsidiary of Refac Optical Group U.S. Vision has about 700 licensed and company-owned optical centers that operate in major department stores (such as Macy's J. C. Penney) and discount outlets (BJ's Wholesale Club) in the US and Canada. Products include prescription eyewear sunglasses designer frames and contact lenses (contacts are also sold online via jcpenneyoptical.com). U.S. Vision runs its own optical laboratory distribution and lens-grinding facilities to fill orders. In 2011 parent Refac Optical was taken over by private equity firm ACON Investments and members of the management team.

UC HEALTH, LLC.

3200 BURNET AVE
CINCINNATI, OH 452293019
Phone: 513-585-6000
Fax: –

CEO: Richard P. Lofgren
CFO: Rick Hinds
HR: Bob Griffith
FYE: June 30
Type: Private

UC Health is Cincinnati's scholarly health care provider. The medical provider is a partnership between the University of Cincinnati the 480-bed University of Cincinnati Medical Center and the University of Cincinnati Physicians organization. Additionally UC Health is home to the 160-bed West Chester Hospital (a full-service community hospital) the Drake Center long-term acute care (rehabilitation) hospital the UC Health Surgical Hospital and the Lindner Center of HOPE (mental health services). Specialized services include cancer cardiovascular neuroscience and metabolic disease treatment. The not-for-profit UC Health was formed in 1994.

	Annual Growth	06/08	06/09	06/10	06/17	06/18
Sales ($ mil.)	36.3%	–	102.5	138.5	1,586.1	1,661.9
Net income ($ mil.)	–	–	0.0	(81.4)	73.9	40.9
Market value ($ mil.)	–	–	–	–	–	–
Employees	–	–	–	–	–	10,000

UCI MEDICAL AFFILIATES INC.
PINK SHEETS: UCIA

1818 Henderson St
Columbia SC 29201
Phone: 803-782-4278
Fax: 416-935-3597
Web: www.rogers.com/web/rogers.portal?_nfpb=true&_p

CEO: Michael Stout
CFO: Joseph A Boyle
HR: –
FYE: September 30
Type: Public

UCI Medical Affiliates seeks out doctors looking to avoid paperwork. The company provides practice management services to about 60 freestanding medical clinics mostly in South Carolina. (It has one center in Tennessee.) The clinics operate primarily under the Doctors Care and Progressive Physical Therapy names. UCI provides nonmedical management and administrative services such as planning accounting insurance contracting and billing non-medical staffing and other office services. Its Doctors Care locations are urgent care clinics that handle minor emergencies and provide primary care services. Blue Cross and Blue Shield of South Carolina is the company's principal stockholder.

UCP INC
NYS: UCP

99 Almaden Boulevard, Suite 400
San Jose, CA 95113
Phone: 408 207-9499
Fax: –
Web: www.unioncommunityllc.com

CEO: –
CFO: –
HR: –
FYE: December 31
Type: Public

If you see property as an asset this company might be for you. UCP which stands for Union Community Properties is a residential land developer and homebuilder. It owns more than 5000 single-family lots in Northern California and the Puget Sound area of Washington where it sells developed lots to homebuilders. Homebuilding subsidiary Benchmark Communities has constructed nearly 50 communities in 15-plus cities. Funded by parent PICO the company has capitalized on the real estate bust by purchasing distressed properties in areas it believes exceed the national average for employment opportunities and housing demand. UCP was formed in 2004 purchased in 2008 and went public in 2013.

	Annual Growth	12/12*	05/13*	12/13	12/14	12/15
Sales ($ mil.)	68.6%	58.1	–	92.7	191.2	278.8
Net income ($ mil.)	(7.7%)	3.0	–	(1.9)	(5.0)	2.4
Market value ($ mil.)	(29.9%)	–	–	117.3	84.2	57.7
Employees	72.3%	–	63	90	173	187

*Fiscal year change

UDR INC
NYS: UDR

1745 Shea Center Drive, Suite 200
Highlands Ranch, CO 80129
Phone: 720 283-6120
Fax: –
Web: www.udrt.com

CEO: Thomas W. Toomey
CFO: Joseph D. Fisher
HR: Nellcine Ford
FYE: December 31
Type: Public

This company reigns over tenants in multi-family settings. UDR (formerly United Dominion Realty Trust) is a real estate investment trust (REIT) that owns and operates more than 140 multi-family apartment communities with more than 51000 units. Through joint ventures it owns 37 more properties with nearly 10000 units. It holdings are primarily located in fast-growing urban markets on both US coasts; more than half of its income comes from California Washington and metro Washington DC. The acquisitive REIT's strategy is to continue to increase its presence in markets that have strong job growth limited apartment supply and high single-family home prices.

	Annual Growth	12/14	12/15	12/16	12/17	12/18
Sales ($ mil.)	6.4%	818.0	894.6	959.9	995.8	1,046.9
Net income ($ mil.)	7.1%	154.3	340.4	292.7	121.6	203.1
Market value ($ mil.)	6.5%	8,492.3	10,352.3	10,051.9	10,614.0	10,917.1
Employees	(2.5%)	1,582	1,611	1,587	1,542	1,431

UFP TECHNOLOGIES INC.
NAS: UFPT

100 Hale Street
Newburyport, MA 01950
Phone: 978 352-2200
Fax: –
Web: www.ufpt.com

CEO: R. Jeffrey Bailly
CFO: Ronald J. Lataille
HR: –
FYE: December 31
Type: Public

As a maker of polyethylene polyurethane and polystyrene foam products UFP Technologies peddles the primary P's of plastics. Its engineered foam operations makes car interior parts gaskets and filters carrying cases soundproofing toys beauty products and components for medical diagnostic equipment. It also makes cushion packaging and molded fiber packaging products for automotive computer electronics industrial medical and pharmaceutical manufacturers. UFP uses cross-linked polyethylene foams to laminate fabrics for footwear backpacks and gun holsters. The company also makes recycled paper packaging for computer components medical devices and electronics.

	Annual Growth	12/14	12/15	12/16	12/17	12/18
Sales ($ mil.)	8.1%	139.3	138.9	146.1	147.8	190.5
Net income ($ mil.)	17.3%	7.6	7.6	8.0	9.2	14.3
Market value ($ mil.)	5.1%	181.6	175.9	188.0	205.3	221.9
Employees	12.4%	658	722	805	796	1,051

UGI CORP.
NYS: UGI

460 North Gulph Road
King of Prussia, PA 19406
Phone: 610 337-1000
Fax: –
Web: www.ugicorp.com

CEO: John L. Walsh
CFO: Kirk R. Oliver
HR: Erika Spott
FYE: September 30
Type: Public

UGI Corporation is a leading energy products supplier to residential commercial agricultural and wholesale customers across the US and Europe. The company stores transports and markets propane liquefied petroleum gases (LPG) and natural gas; it also generates some electricity. In the US UGI serves some 2.2 million customers thanks to its partnership with AmeriGas Partners and several subsidiaries. In addition product installation and maintenance services are available to Pennsylvania Delaware and Maryland customers of UGI. Its trade names include AmeriGas America's Propane Company and Heritage Propane.

	Annual Growth	09/15	09/16	09/17	09/18	09/19
Sales ($ mil.)	2.3%	6,691.1	5,685.7	6,120.7	7,651.2	7,320.4
Net income ($ mil.)	(2.3%)	281.0	364.7	436.6	718.7	256.2
Market value ($ mil.)	9.6%	7,277.5	9,455.4	9,794.0	11,595.6	10,506.7
Employees	(1.4%)	13,570	13,320	13,000	13,000	12,800

UHY ADVISORS INC.

30 S. Wacker Dr. Ste. 1330
Chicago IL 60606
Phone: 312-578-9600
Fax: 312-346-6500
Web: www.uhyadvisors-us.com

CEO: James B McGuire
CFO: Bill White
HR: Corey Park
FYE: December 31
Type: Private

Say "hi" to UHY. UHY Advisors offers tax financial and business consulting services to companies government entities not-for-profit organizations and wealthy individuals. Audit services are provided through the company's alternative practice structure arrangement with independent CPA firm UHY LLP. UHY Advisors and its affiliates also perform litigation valuation risk advisory turnaround and restructuring and wealth management services. The company boasts more than a dozen US offices in nearly 10 states including Illinois New York and Texas. UHY Advisors is an independent member of UHY International a global association of accounting firms.

UIL HOLDING CORP   NYS: UIL

157 Church Street
New Haven, CT 06506
Phone: 203 499-2000
Fax: –
Web: www.uil.com

CEO: –
CFO: Pablo Canales
HR: –
FYE: December 31
Type: Public

UIL Holdings parent of electric utility The United Illuminating Company (UI) hopes its well-regulated business will result in regular revenue growth. The public utility distributes electricity to 321000 customers in southwestern Connecticut. Its service area largely urban and suburban includes the principal cities of Bridgeport (population 146000) and New Haven (population 130000) and their surrounding areas. UIL Holdings has teamed up with NRG Energy to operate GenConn Energy LLC a joint venture that focuses on developing new power generation facilities in Connecticut. The company has also diversified through the acquisition of three gas utilities in New England from IBERDROLA USA for $1.3 billion.

	Annual Growth	12/09	12/10	12/11	12/12	12/13
Sales ($ mil.)	15.9%	896.6	997.7	1,570.4	1,486.5	1,618.7
Net income ($ mil.)	20.7%	54.3	54.9	99.7	103.7	115.3
Market value ($ mil.)	8.4%	1,593.6	1,700.3	2,007.4	2,032.4	2,199.2
Employees	15.5%	1,066	1,824	1,868	1,865	1,895

ULTICOM INC.

1020 Briggs Rd.
Mt. Laurel NJ 08054
Phone: 856-787-2700
Fax: 856-866-2033
Web: www.ulticom.com

CEO: Bruce D Swail
CFO: Mark A Kissman
HR: –
FYE: January 31
Type: Private

Ulticom develops signaling software used to connect switching and messaging systems and manage routing and billing information. The company's flagship Signalware software product enables communications providers to offer such services as voice-activated dialing text messaging and Internet call-waiting. It serves telecom equipment manufacturers and communications service providers. Clients have included VeriSign Alcatel-Lucent and Nokia Siemens. It maintains hardware and operating system partnerships with companies such as IBM Oracle and Red Hat. Buyout firm Platinum Equity paid some $90 million to take Ulticom private in 2010 as part of its ongoing pattern of investing in the communications and IT industries.

ULTIMATE SOFTWARE GROUP, INC.   NMS: ULTI

2000 Ultimate Way
Weston, FL 33326
Phone: 954 331-7000
Fax: –
Web: www.ultimatesoftware.com

CEO: Scott Scherr
CFO: –
HR: –
FYE: December 31
Type: Public

The Ultimate Software Group helps manage a company's ultimate resource: its employees. Customers employ its cloud-based UltiPro software suite to manage hiring human resources compliance benefits enrollment payroll appraisals and time and attendance. The company does business in the US and Canada with customers that include Bloomin? Brands Red Roof Inn and Subway. It targets the communications finance health care retail technology and transportation industries. Founded in 1990 Ultimate holds more than 37 million people records in its HCM (human capital management) cloud. In 2019 Ultimate agreed to go private in an $11 billion buyout led by Hellman & Friedman.

	Annual Growth	12/13	12/14	12/15	12/16	12/17
Sales ($ mil.)	23.0%	410.4	505.9	618.1	781.3	940.7
Net income ($ mil.)	(13.9%)	25.5	44.7	22.7	30.3	14.1
Market value ($ mil.)	9.2%	4,616.5	4,423.5	5,890.7	5,494.2	6,575.3
Employees	21.8%	1,913	2,354	2,880	3,747	4,208

ULTRA CLEAN HOLDINGS INC   NMS: UCTT

26462 Corporate Avenue
Hayward, CA 94545
Phone: 510 576-4400
Fax: –
Web: www.uct.com

CEO: James P. (Jim) Scholhamer
CFO: Sheri Brumm
HR: –
FYE: December 28
Type: Public

Ultra Clean Holdings is a pure play in helping computer chip makers keep their manufacturing conditions pristine. The company which does business as Ultra Clean Technology (UCT) designs engineers manufactures and tests customized gas liquid and catalytic steam generation delivery systems used primarily in the production of semiconductors. The company also provides third-party manufacturing services. UCT has extended its know-how in the semiconductor industry to move into flat-panel display medical research and energy markets. The company's three biggest customers account for about 85% of revenue.

	Annual Growth	12/14	12/15	12/16	12/17	12/18
Sales ($ mil.)	20.9%	514.0	469.1	562.8	924.4	1,096.5
Net income ($ mil.)	34.0%	11.4	(10.7)	10.1	75.1	36.6
Market value ($ mil.)	(3.3%)	366.4	210.2	378.9	902.0	320.7
Employees	29.0%	1,546	1,817	2,183	2,747	4,280

ULTRA PETROLEUM CORP   NBB: UPLC

116 Inverness Drive East, Suite 400
Englewood, CO 80112
Phone: 303 708-9740
Fax: –
Web: www.ultrapetroleum.com

CEO: Michael D. Watford
CFO: Garland R. Shaw
HR: –
FYE: December 31
Type: Public

Ultra Petroleum is ultra-keen in its search for petroleum products. This US independent exploration & production company recovers natural gas and crude oil from Cretaceous era deposits in the Green River Basin of southwestern Wyoming as well as in the Uinta Basin of Utah. It has stakes in 39000 gross developed acres in Wyoming and 5000 gross developed acres in Utah. Ultra Petroleum has proved reserves of 3.1 trillion cu. ft. of natural gas equivalent and has about 3030 gross and about 2140 net productive wells.

	Annual Growth	12/14	12/15	12/16	12/17	12/18
Sales ($ mil.)	(7.7%)	1,230.0	839.1	721.1	891.9	892.5
Net income ($ mil.)	(37.1%)	542.9	(3,207.2)	56.2	177.1	85.2
Market value ($ mil.)	(91.6%)	–	–	–	1,788.3	150.0
Employees	(1.4%)	160	167	166	166	151

ULTRA STORES INC.

122 S. Michigan Ave. Ste. 800
Chicago IL 60610
Phone: 312-922-3800
Fax: 312-922-3933
Web: www.ultradiamonds.com

CEO: –
CFO: –
HR: –
FYE: January 31
Type: Private

Ultra Stores goes above and beyond to sell fine jewelry for less. It's a leading seller of off-price bridal and diamond and gemstone jewelry as well as watches and gifts. It operates about 100 Ultra Diamonds outlet stores in more than 30 US states as well as licensed jewelry departments in a number of off-price department stores. It also sells jewelry online and buys used jewelry. Founded in 1991 Ultra Stores is owned by jewelry retail giant Signet Jewelers which acquired the company in late 2012 from the Chicago investment firm Crystal Capital.

ULTRAGENYX PHARMACEUTICAL INC
NMS: RARE

60 Leveroni Court
Novato, CA 94949
Phone: 415 483-8800
Fax: -
Web: www.ultragenyx.com

CEO: Emil D. Kakkis
CFO: Shalini Sharp
HR: -
FYE: December 31
Type: Public

Ultragenyx Pharmaceuticals wants to treat ultra rare diseases. The company hopes to commercialize therapies for rare debilitating metabolic diseases for which there are no approved treatments. It has in-licensed five candidates that are in various stages of approval. Acquisition is the company's preferred method of drug development. Ultragenyx divides its candidates into two categories: biologics and small-molecule substrate replacement therapies. (Substrates work with enzymes to perform normal body functions.) While the company intends to grow it recognizes that treating ultra rare diseases means it will stay small since its marketing is small. Ultragenyx was formed in 2010 and filed to go public in 2014.

	Annual Growth	12/14	12/15	12/16	12/17	12/18
Sales ($ mil.)	1867.7%	-	-	0.1	2.6	51.5
Net income ($ mil.)	-	(59.8)	(145.6)	(245.9)	(302.1)	(197.6)
Market value ($ mil.)	(0.2%)	2,231.8	5,705.5	3,576.0	2,358.9	2,211.4
Employees	54.5%	107	249	376	520	610

ULTRALIFE CORP
NMS: ULBI

2000 Technology Parkway
Newark, NY 14513
Phone: 315 332-7100
Fax: -
Web: www.ultralifecorporation.com

CEO: Michael D Popielec
CFO: Philip A Fain
HR: -
FYE: December 31
Type: Public

Maybe you could sum up Ultralife's business model as PC as in power and communications that is. The company's main business is the design and manufacture of rechargeable and non-rechargeable batteries. Accounting for about a quarter of sales its Communications Systems Division provides such products as amplified speakers and cable assemblies. Ultralife sells its products around the world to OEMs distributors and retailers. The company also sells directly to the US and foreign defense departments. Military sales (both directly and indirectly) account for about 50% of Ultralife's revenues.

	Annual Growth	12/15	12/16	12/17	12/18	12/19
Sales ($ mil.)	8.7%	76.4	82.5	85.5	87.2	106.8
Net income ($ mil.)	16.1%	2.9	3.5	7.6	24.9	5.2
Market value ($ mil.)	3.4%	102.5	78.5	103.9	107.1	117.3
Employees	(4.6%)	691	552	568	580	573

ULTRATECH INC
NMS: UTEK

3050 Zanker Road
San Jose, CA 95134
Phone: 408 321-8835
Fax: -
Web: www.ultratech.com

CEO: -
CFO: Bruce R Wright
HR: -
FYE: December 31
Type: Public

Ultratech's machines take the ultimate in high-tech baby steps. The company makes step-and-repeat photolithography systems — called steppers — that help manufacturers produce semiconductors thin-film heads for disk drives and micro-machined components. Chip makers use the steppers in photolithography a process during which device features are imprinted on semiconductor wafer surfaces through repeated exposures to patterns of light. The company's steppers expose a small section of the wafer then "step" to an adjacent site to repeat the process. Ultratech was founded in 1979.

	Annual Growth	12/11	12/12	12/13	12/14	12/15
Sales ($ mil.)	(8.4%)	212.3	234.8	157.3	150.5	149.2
Net income ($ mil.)	-	39.2	47.2	(13.8)	(19.1)	(15.1)
Market value ($ mil.)	(5.2%)	651.7	989.3	769.1	492.3	525.7
Employees	(0.8%)	322	353	351	342	312

ULURU INC
NBB: ULUR

4410 Beltway Drive
Addison, TX 75001
Phone: 214 905-5145
Fax: -
Web: www.uluruinc.com

CEO: Helmut Kerschbaumer
CFO: Terrance K Wallberg
HR: -
FYE: December 31
Type: Public

ULURU named after a giant monolith in Australia is also a specialty pharmaceutical company that develops and commercializes wound care products. Based on its Nanoflex drug delivery technology ULURU has developed marketable products including Altrazeal powder dressing to treat abrasions burns donor sites and surgical wounds and Aphthasol oral paste for canker sores. Using an FDA-approved muco-adhesive thin film technology called OraDisc ULURU is also developing a line of OraDisc disc and strip products that can be applied directly to the mucosal tissue to deliver medication or active ingredients for canker sores oral pain and teeth whitening. It is working with several licensing partners around the world.

	Annual Growth	12/13	12/14	12/15	12/16	12/17
Sales ($ mil.)	17.9%	0.4	0.9	0.9	0.4	0.7
Net income ($ mil.)	-	(3.1)	(1.9)	(2.7)	(4.5)	(1.9)
Market value ($ mil.)	(54.6%)	138.9	169.1	36.2	7.6	5.9
Employees	(26.9%)	7	7	5	2	2

UMB FINANCIAL CORP
NMS: UMBF

1010 Grand Boulevard
Kansas City, MO 64106
Phone: 816 860-7000
Fax: 816 860-7143
Web: www.umb.com

CEO: J. Mariner Kemper
CFO: Ram Shankar
HR: Shannon A. Johnson
FYE: December 31
Type: Public

UMB Financial is the holding company for four UMB-branded commercial banks serving Arizona Colorado Illinois Kansas Nebraska Oklahoma and Missouri. Through some 110 branches the banks offer standard services such as checking and savings accounts credit and debit cards and trust and investment services. Commercial loans account for more than 50% of UMB's loan portfolio. Beyond its banking business it offers insurance brokerage services leasing treasury management health savings accounts and proprietary mutual funds through its more than 20 subsidiaries. Founded in 1913 the bank ranks first in the Kansas City market (based on deposits).

	Annual Growth	12/14	12/15	12/16	12/17	12/18
Assets ($ mil.)	7.5%	17,501.0	19,094.2	20,682.5	21,771.6	23,351.1
Net income ($ mil.)	12.8%	120.7	116.1	158.8	247.1	195.5
Market value ($ mil.)	1.7%	2,794.3	2,286.4	3,787.9	3,532.5	2,994.7
Employees	(0.1%)	3,592	3,830	3,688	3,570	3,573

UMH PROPERTIES INC
NYS: UMH

Juniper Business Plaza, 3499 Route 9 North, Suite 3-C
Freehold, NJ 07728
Phone: 732 577-9997
Fax: -
Web: www.umh.reit

CEO: Samuel A. Landy
CFO: Anna T. Chew
HR: -
FYE: December 31
Type: Public

UMH Properties (formerly United Mobile Homes) is a real estate investment trust (REIT) that owns and manages more than 80 manufactured home communities containing approximately 14500 developed lots in New Jersey New York Ohio Pennsylvania and several other states. The company leases home sites to private homeowners on a monthly basis and rents a small number of homes to residents. Communities offer such amenities as swimming pools playgrounds and municipal water and sewer services. The REIT sells and finances manufactured homes through subsidiary UMH Sales and Finance and owns more than 800 acres of land for development. UMH Properties also invests in other REITs.

	Annual Growth	12/14	12/15	12/16	12/17	12/18
Sales ($ mil.)	16.1%	71.4	81.5	99.2	112.6	129.6
Net income ($ mil.)	-	4.2	2.1	11.5	12.7	(36.2)
Market value ($ mil.)	5.5%	366.0	387.8	576.7	571.0	453.7
Employees	10.0%	260	295	330	340	380

UMPQUA HOLDINGS CORP
NMS: UMPQ

One S.W. Columbia Street, Suite 1200
Portland, OR 97258
Phone: 503 727-4100
Fax: –
Web: www.umpquaholdingscorp.com

CEO: Cort O'Haver
CFO: Ronald L. (Ron) Farnsworth
HR: –
FYE: December 31
Type: Public

Umpqua Holdings thinks of itself not so much as a bank but rather a retailer that sells financial products. Consequently many of the company's 380-plus Umpqua Bank "stores" in northern California northern Nevada Idaho Oregon and Washington feature coffee bars and computer cafes. While customers sip Umpqua-branded coffee pay bills online attend a financial seminar catch a poetry reading or check out wares from local merchants staff members pitch deposit accounts mortgages loans life insurance investments and more. Subsidiary Umpqua Investments (formerly Strand Atkinson Williams & York) provides retail brokerage services through more than a dozen locations mostly inside Umpqua Bank branches.

	Annual Growth	12/14	12/15	12/16	12/17	12/18
Assets ($ mil.)	4.5%	22,613.3	23,387.2	24,813.1	25,741.4	26,939.8
Net income ($ mil.)	21.0%	147.5	222.5	232.9	246.0	316.3
Market value ($ mil.)	(1.7%)	3,746.5	3,502.1	4,136.4	4,581.3	3,502.1
Employees	(3.7%)	4,569	4,491	4,295	4,380	3,928

UNBOUND

1 ELMWOOD AVE
KANSAS CITY, KS 661032118
Phone: 913-384-6500
Fax: –
Web: www.unbound.org

CEO: Scott Wasserman
CFO: –
HR: –
FYE: December 31
Type: Private

The Christian Foundation for Children and Aging (CFCA) may seem at cross purposes but it helps the poor on both ends of the age spectrum. The lay Catholic not-for-profit organization works in about two dozen countries in Africa Asia The Americas and Caribbean. CFCA provides services for children and the elderly in areas such as education medical care clothing and nutrition. It sets up relationships between more than 270000 sponsors in the US and about 310000 who need assistance in countries like Bolivia El Salvador Guatemala India Tanzania and Uganda. CFCA was founded in 1981 by a group of missionaries including its president Bob Hentzen.

	Annual Growth	12/10	12/11	12/12	12/14	12/15
Sales ($ mil.)	2.9%	–	110.1	115.8	120.9	123.5
Net income ($ mil.)	18.3%	–	0.8	2.0	(2.4)	1.6
Market value ($ mil.)	–	–	–	–	–	–
Employees	–	–	–	–	–	160

UNDER ARMOUR INC
NYS: UAA

1020 Hull Street
Baltimore, MD 21230
Phone: 410 454-6428
Fax: –
Web: www.underarmour.com

CEO: Kevin A. Plank
CFO: David E. Bergman
HR: –
FYE: December 31
Type: Public

Under Armour makes performance clothes for doing battle on the sports field and in the gym. The company is the official footwear supplier of the National Football League (NFL) and Major League Baseball (MLB) and partners with the National Basketball Association (NBA); it outfits everyday athletes as well. Under Armour claims its products made from moisture-wicking and heat-dispersing fabrics keep athletes dry and comfortable during workouts. The company also makes technology that helps customers track their fitness. It sells online by catalog and through retail and outlet stores worldwide. Its locker room of athlete endorsers include top performers in football basketball soccer and baseball. Under Armour operates worldwide but generates most of its revenue in the US.

	Annual Growth	12/14	12/15	12/16	12/17	12/18
Sales ($ mil.)	13.9%	3,084.4	3,963.3	4,825.3	4,976.6	5,193.2
Net income ($ mil.)	–	208.0	232.6	257.0	(48.3)	(46.3)
Market value ($ mil.)	(28.6%)	30,458.7	36,160.2	13,031.3	6,473.0	7,926.4
Employees	8.8%	10,700	13,400	9,400	15,800	15,000

UNDERWRITERS LABORATORIES INC.

333 PFINGSTEN RD
NORTHBROOK, IL 600622096
Phone: 847-272-8800
Fax: –
Web: www.ul.com

CEO: Keith E Williams
CFO: –
HR: –
FYE: December 31
Type: Private

Products that pass the muster of this company get the UL symbol of approval. Underwriters Laboratories (UL) is one of the world's leading providers of product safety and certification testing services performing more than 90000 evaluations each year. Products that successfully navigate through its stringent tests are registered with the lab and can bear the UL Mark — a widely trusted symbol for product safety and assurance. Nearly 20 billion products from 72000 manufacturers bear the UL Mark each year. UL also offers commercial inspection and regulatory training services as well as consumer safety advice. William Merrill founded the not-for-profit lab in 1894.

	Annual Growth	12/04	12/05	12/06	12/07	12/08
Sales ($ mil.)	(96.5%)	–	–	792,081.9	895.5	994.1
Net income ($ mil.)	–	–	–	0.2	160.5	(23.1)
Market value ($ mil.)	–	–	–	–	–	–
Employees	–	–	–	–	–	10,876

UNICO AMERICAN CORP.
NMS: UNAM

26050 Mureau Road
Calabasas, CA 91302
Phone: 818 591-9800
Fax: –

CEO: Cary L Cheldin
CFO: Michael Budnitsky
HR: –
FYE: December 31
Type: Public

Unico American helps protect California businesses from a variety of afflictions. Its Crusader Insurance subsidiary provides commercial multiperil property/casualty insurance including liability property and workers' compensation. Sister company Unifax Insurance services Crusader's policies. Unico American subsidiaries also act as agents for non-affiliated insurers provide claims-adjusting services and premium financing and market individual and group medical dental life and accidental death coverage. All of its policies are marketed by independent insurance agencies and brokers.

	Annual Growth	12/14	12/15	12/16	12/17	12/18
Assets ($ mil.)	(2.0%)	136.0	140.2	138.2	130.3	125.6
Net income ($ mil.)	–	0.8	(1.2)	(1.4)	(8.7)	(3.2)
Market value ($ mil.)	(13.6%)	60.7	53.0	57.1	45.4	33.9
Employees	(2.2%)	83	86	80	79	76

UNIFI, INC.
NYS: UFI

7201 West Friendly Avenue
Greensboro, NC 27410
Phone: 336 294-4410
Fax: –

CEO: Kevin D. Hall
CFO: Jeffrey C. (Jeff) Ackerman
HR: –
FYE: June 30
Type: Public

Unifi textures dyes and twists multifilament polyester and nylon yarns and allied raw materials. Its polyester yarns are sold to an array of original knitting and weaving manufacturers of apparel goods industrial textiles home furnishings and auto upholstery fabrics. Unifi nylons are marketed for apparel hosiery and sock manufacture. Polyester and nylon partially oriented yarn (POY) which is also purchased from suppliers is often not sold but further treated to create blends offering a variety of performance advantages. The US is Unifi's largest market.

	Annual Growth	06/15	06/16	06/17	06/18	06/19
Sales ($ mil.)	0.8%	687.1	643.6	647.3	678.9	708.8
Net income ($ mil.)	(50.9%)	42.2	34.4	32.9	31.7	2.5
Market value ($ mil.)	(14.5%)	626.6	485.4	533.9	581.9	335.5
Employees	5.2%	2,500	2,700	3,000	3,100	3,060

1377

UNIFIEDONLINE INC
NBB: UOIP

4126 Leonard Drive
Fairfax, VA 22030
Phone: 816 979-1893
Fax: –
Web: www.unifiedonline.net

CEO: Robert M Howe III
CFO: Ellen Sondee
HR: –
FYE: June 30
Type: Public

Oh what a web IceWEB weaves when it works to secure a customer's website. The company generates most of its revenues through its IT Solutions division which provides network security products to local state and federal government agencies. The division specializes in such applications as content filtering e-mail security intrusion detection and network optimization. It implements its products with help from partners including Blue Coat Systems Cisco Systems F5 Networks McAfee and RSA Security. The company also offers data storage products through its INLINE business unit. IceWEB's online services division provides small and mid-sized businesses with hosted e-mail server and security applications.

	Annual Growth	09/11	09/12	09/13*	06/14	06/15
Sales ($ mil.)	(23.4%)	2.7	2.6	1.0	0.7	0.9
Net income ($ mil.)	–	(4.7)	(6.5)	(7.1)	(4.9)	(1.9)
Market value ($ mil.)	(48.5%)	168.8	83.9	20.9	1.3	11.9
Employees	(26.3%)	–	15	13	9	6

*Fiscal year change

UNIFIRST CORP
NYS: UNF

68 Jonspin Road
Wilmington, MA 01887
Phone: 978 658-8888
Fax: –
Web: www.unifirst.com

CEO: Steven S. Sintros
CFO: Shane O'Connor
HR: –
FYE: August 31
Type: Public

Think removing lipstick from your collar is tough? Try decontaminating radioactive clothing. As North America's top supplier and servicer of uniforms and workwear UniFirst designs makes sells or rents launders and delivers work uniforms and protective clothing (shirts pants coveralls coats smocks and aprons) as well as non-garment items (floor mats and mops) to auto service centers restaurants transportation companies and utilities operating nuclear reactors among other customers. About 90% of its revenue comes from its core laundering business. UniFirst produces about 70% of the garments it supplies enabling customization through 240 facilities in North America and Europe. UniFirst also provides first-aid cabinet services and supplies.

	Annual Growth	08/15	08/16	08/17	08/18	08/19
Sales ($ mil.)	5.6%	1,456.6	1,468.0	1,591.0	1,696.5	1,809.4
Net income ($ mil.)	9.6%	124.3	125.0	70.2	163.9	179.1
Market value ($ mil.)	16.0%	2,052.0	2,421.9	2,619.6	3,460.2	3,717.5
Employees	3.9%	12,000	13,000	14,000	14,000	14,000

UNIGROUP INC.

1 Premier Dr.
Fenton MO 63026
Phone: 636-305-5000
Fax: 636-326-1106
Web: www.unigroupinc.com

CEO: –
CFO: –
HR: –
FYE: December 31
Type: Private

Moving people's possessions has made UniGroup's family of companies a household name. It transports home and other items in more than 175 countries through subsidiaries United Van Lines and Mayflower Transit and a network of affiliates. Road operations are supported by sister subsidiaries Trans Advantage which sells and leases trucks trailers and moving supplies and UniGroup Worldwide which coordinates international moves for household and bulk goods. Subsidiary Allegiant Move Management provides relocation management. Clients range from government to corporate entities and private households. UniGroup is owned by its senior executives and agents of United Van Lines and Mayflower Transit.

UNIHEALTH FOUNDATION

800 Wilshire Blvd. Ste. 1300
Los Angeles CA 90017
Phone: 213-630-6500
Fax: 213-630-6509
Web: www.unihealthfoundation.org

CEO: David Carpenter
CFO: Kathleen Salazar
HR: –
FYE: September 30
Type: Private - Foundation

UniHealth Foundation has discovered that charity begins at home. UniHealth Foundation is what is left of what was once one of California's fastest-growing health systems. After spending some 10 years trying to build an integrated health care delivery system the company sold its eight hospitals to Catholic Healthcare West and its CliniShare home health services and ElderMed senior citizens care services to Trinity Care. UniHealth used those assets to begin its second life in 1998 as a grant-making organization with more than $42 million in assets through its Facey Medical Foundation. The foundation focuses on supporting health care education and care for the indigent.

UNILIFE CORP.
NMS: UNIS

250 Cross Farm Lane
York, PA 17406
Phone: 717 384-3400
Fax: –
Web: www.unilife.com

CEO: –
CFO: –
HR: –
FYE: June 30
Type: Public

Needle pricks are never fun but Unilife hopes its medical devices make the practice a little safer and simpler. The company develops and manufactures retractable syringes including the Unifill ready-to-fill syringe which allows pharmaceutical companies to prefill the device with an injectable drug or vaccine and the Unitract 1 mL syringe which is designed for hospital use and for patients who self administer medications like diabetes sufferers. Unilife is especially focused on the development of wearable injectors which has the potential to be the next big thing in drug delivery.

	Annual Growth	06/12	06/13	06/14	06/15	06/16
Sales ($ mil.)	28.1%	5.5	2.7	14.7	13.2	14.8
Net income ($ mil.)	–	(52.3)	(63.2)	(57.9)	(90.8)	(100.8)
Market value ($ mil.)	(0.7%)	58.9	55.2	51.5	37.4	57.3
Employees	29.4%	128	159	209	278	359

UNION BANK AND TRUST COMPANY

3643 S 48TH ST
LINCOLN, NE 685064390
Phone: 402-323-1235
Fax: –
Web: www.ubt.com

CEO: Angie Muhliesen
CFO: –
HR: –
FYE: December 31
Type: Private

Union Bank & Trust a subsidiary of financial services holding company Farmers & Merchants Investment operates more than 35 branches throughout Nebraska and in Kansas. As Nebraska's third-largest privately-owned bank it offers traditional deposit and trust services as well as insurance equipment finance and investment management services. Consumer loans account for the largest portion of the bank's portfolio followed by commercial real estate and farmland loans. Union Bank also originates business loans and residential mortgages. Affiliate company Union Investment Advisors manages the Stratus family of mutual funds. Another Farmers & Merchants unit Nelnet Capital offers brokerage services.

	Annual Growth	12/13	12/14	12/15	12/16	12/17
Assets ($ mil.)	8.1%	–	3,040.5	3,351.9	3,595.6	3,836.5
Net income ($ mil.)	15.8%	–	29.5	32.2	40.9	45.8
Market value ($ mil.)	–	–	–	–	–	–
Employees	–	–	–	–	–	800

UNION BANKSHARES, INC. (MORRISVILLE, VT)   NMS: UNB

P.O. Box 667, 20 Lower Main Street
Morrisville, VT 05661
Phone: 802 888-6600
Fax: –
Web: www.ublocal.com

CEO: David S Silverman
CFO: Karyn J Hale
HR: –
FYE: December 31
Type: Public

Union Bankshares is the holding company for Union Bank which serves individuals and small to mid-sized businesses in northern Vermont and Northwestern New Hampshire through 17 branches; it opened its first office in New Hampshire in 2006. Founded in 1891 the bank offers standard deposit products such as savings checking money market and NOW accounts as well as certificates of deposit retirement savings programs investment management and trust services. It uses fund from deposits primarily to originate commercial real estate loans and residential real estate loans. Other loan products include business consumer construction and municipal loans.

	Annual Growth	12/14	12/15	12/16	12/17	12/18
Assets ($ mil.)	6.6%	624.1	628.9	691.4	745.8	805.3
Net income ($ mil.)	(2.1%)	7.7	7.9	8.5	8.4	7.1
Market value ($ mil.)	19.1%	106.1	124.7	203.0	236.5	213.3
Employees	1.2%	186	188	191	194	195

UNION HEALTH SERVICE INC

1634 W POLK ST
CHICAGO, IL 606124352
Phone: 312-423-4200
Fax: –
Web: www.unionhealth.org

CEO: –
CFO: –
HR: Barbara Lapapa
FYE: December 31
Type: Private

Union Health Service brings together doctors and patients in the Chicago area. The company is a not-for-profit health care services provider which supplies health insurance to its members through HMO (health maintenance organization) and medical prepayment plans. Union Health Service also provides primary health care as well as vision laboratory radiology and pharmacy services to its members through about 20 group practice clinics in Aurora Chicago Norridge Oak Park and other area communities. The company was established in 1955.

	Annual Growth	12/12	12/13	12/14	12/15	12/16
Sales ($ mil.)	4.9%	–	64.2	68.5	70.2	74.1
Net income ($ mil.)	(17.8%)	–	0.4	(0.0)	0.8	0.2
Market value ($ mil.)	–	–	–	–	–	–
Employees	–	–	–	–	–	250

UNION HOSPITAL, INC.

1606 N 7TH ST
TERRE HAUTE, IN 478042780
Phone: 812-238-7000
Fax: –
Web: www.myunionhealth.org

CEO: –
CFO: Wayne R Hutson
HR: Cheryl Stearley
FYE: December 31
Type: Private

Union Hospital is the flagship facility of the Union Hospital Health Group a health care system that serves communities in western Indiana and eastern Illinois. The not-for-profit hospital has about 320 beds boasts an equal number of physicians and provides general medical and surgical care as well as specialty services in areas such as women's health newborn intensive care unit (Level II) cancer cardiovascular disease and sports medicine. It also offers occupational health and physical rehabilitation as well as medical training programs. Other facilities that comprise the Union system include Union Hospital Clinton physician practices specialty clinics and a home health agency.

	Annual Growth	12/13	12/14	12/15	12/16	12/17
Sales ($ mil.)	53.8%	–	127.8	385.0	416.3	465.1
Net income ($ mil.)	71.8%	–	3.4	6.9	(11.6)	17.2
Market value ($ mil.)	–	–	–	–	–	–
Employees	–	–	–	–	–	2,700

UNION PACIFIC CORP   NYS: UNP

1400 Douglas Street
Omaha, NE 68179
Phone: 402 544-5000
Fax: –
Web: www.up.com

CEO: Lance M. Fritz
CFO: Robert M. Knight
HR: –
FYE: December 31
Type: Public

Venerable Union Pacific Railroad (UP) has been chugging down the track since the 19th century. Owned by Union Pacific Corporation (UPC) UP is one of the nation's leading rail carriers operating about 64000 freight cars and nearly 8600 locomotives. UP transports automobiles chemicals energy and industrial agricultural and other bulk freight over a system of some 32000 rail miles in 23 states in the western two-thirds of the US. UPC owns more than 26000 route miles of its rail network; leases and trackage rights which allow it to use other railroads' tracks account for the rest. UP's customers have included such big names as automakers General Motors and Toyota.

	Annual Growth	12/15	12/16	12/17	12/18	12/19
Sales ($ mil.)	(0.1%)	21,813.0	19,941.0	21,240.0	22,832.0	21,708.0
Net income ($ mil.)	5.5%	4,772.0	4,233.0	10,712.0	5,966.0	5,919.0
Market value ($ mil.)	23.3%	54,122.3	71,757.0	92,810.7	95,669.1	125,124.9
Employees	(5.7%)	47,457	42,919	41,992	41,967	37,483

UNIONBANCAL CORPORATION

400 California St.
San Francisco CA 94104-1302
Phone: 415-765-2969
Fax: 415-765-2220
Web: www.unionbank.com

CEO: Stephen E Cummings
CFO: Johannes Worsoe
HR: –
FYE: December 31
Type: Subsidiary

Whether you're in NorCal SoCal or beyond you can call on UnionBanCal. Its Union Bank subsidiary has more than 400 branches in California Washington Oregon New York and Texas. The bank offers retail banking which provides deposits and loans to consumers and small businesses. Its corporate banking segment provides commercial financing to middle-market and corporate clients with a focus on the energy real estate health care communications and retail sectors. UnionBanCal also provides wealth planning and trust services through HighMark Capital Management. Another subsidiary Cash & Save is a chain of check-cashing stores. UnionBanCal is a subsidiary of Mitsubishi UFJ Financial Group (MUFJ).

UNIPRO FOODSERVICE, INC

2500 CUMBRLD PKWY SE 60
ATLANTA, GA 30339
Phone: 770-952-0871
Fax: –
Web: www.uniprofoodservice.com

CEO: –
CFO: –
HR: –
FYE: December 31
Type: Private

UniPro Foodservice knows there's strength in numbers. As the largest US food service cooperative its members include more than 650 independent member companies that provide food and food-related products to more than 800000 food service customers including health care and educational institutions military installations and restaurants. UniPro provides training collective purchasing and marketing materials to all distributors. Its products — which include dry groceries and frozen and refrigerated foods — are sold under the brand names CODE ComSource Nifda and Nugget. Suppliers include Kraft Foods Reynolds Food Packaging Solo Cup Tyson Foods and Unilever Foodsolutions.

	Annual Growth	12/08	12/09	12/10	12/11	12/12
Sales ($ mil.)	22.5%	–	–	657.5	881.2	987.1
Net income ($ mil.)	–	–	–	0.0	0.0	(0.2)
Market value ($ mil.)	–	–	–	–	–	–
Employees	–	–	–	–	–	140

UNIROYAL GLOBAL ENGINEERED PRODUCTS INC   NBB: UNIR

1800 2nd Street, Suite 970   CEO: Howard R Curd
Sarasota, FL 34236   CFO: Edmund C King
Phone: 941 906-8580   HR: –
Fax: –   FYE: December 30
Web: www.uniroyalglobal.com   Type: Public

Invisa develops and manufactures sensors used to ensure safety and security. The company's SmartGate safety sensors are used in traffic and parking control fence and gate access and industrial automation safety applications. The sensors are meant to keep doors and gates from closing on people or objects. Invisa's InvisaShield technology is designed to detect the presence of intruders in a monitored zone such as the area around a museum exhibit. Customer Magnetic Automation Corp. a manufacturer of barrier gates accounts for nearly 30% of product sales.

	Annual Growth	12/14*	01/16	01/17*	12/17	12/18
Sales ($ mil.)	0.3%	98.3	99.8	100.4	98.1	99.6
Net income ($ mil.)	(28.0%)	4.6	7.8	7.4	(0.1)	1.2
Market value ($ mil.)	(10.2%)	43.0	59.8	61.7	27.5	28.0
Employees	(1.1%)	410	415	420	408	393

*Fiscal year change

UNISOURCE WORLDWIDE INC.

6600 Governors Lake Pkwy.   CEO: Mary A Laschinger
Norcross GA 30071   CFO: Stephen J Smith
Phone: 770-447-9000   HR: –
Fax: 770-734-2000   FYE: December 31
Web: www.unisourceworldwide.com   Type: Private

This company has a singular mission: Distribute paper to North America. Unisource Worldwide is one of the biggest independent distributors of paper products and related supplies. Operating from 85 distribution centers in the US and Canada it offers commercial printing and business imaging paper and specialty paper products. Its short list includes Xerox ink jet and laser paper and toner cartridges and coated and uncoated commercial printing paper. Unisource also distributes packaging and cleaning supplies and some equipment. The retail stores division PaperPlus provides a similiar paper selection and digital printing services. Unisource is 60% owned by Bain Capital; paper maker Georgia-Pacific owns 40%.

UNISYS CORP   NYS: UIS

801 Lakeview Drive, Suite 100   CEO: Peter A. Altabef
Blue Bell, PA 19422   CFO: Michael M Thomson
Phone: 215 986-4011   HR: –
Fax: –   FYE: December 31
Web: www.unisys.com   Type: Public

Once a provider of large-scale computing systems Unisys Corp. now helps its customers manage their large-scale information technology operations with an emphasis on services and security. The company provides services that include security data analytics cloud and infrastructure services and application services. Its technology division develops enterprise-class servers and server software. Unisys is among the largest government IT contractors serving local state and federal agencies as well as foreign governments. Other key sectors include communications financial services and transportation. Unisys' history includes a precursor company that developed some of the first digital computers.

	Annual Growth	12/14	12/15	12/16	12/17	12/18
Sales ($ mil.)	(4.2%)	3,356.4	3,015.1	2,820.7	2,741.8	2,825.0
Net income ($ mil.)	12.8%	46.7	(109.9)	(47.7)	(65.3)	75.5
Market value ($ mil.)	(20.7%)	1,506.4	564.7	763.9	416.5	594.3
Employees	(1.3%)	23,200	23,000	21,000	20,000	22,000

UNIT CORP.   NYS: UNT

8200 South Unit Drive   CEO: Larry D. Pinkston
Tulsa, OK 74132   CFO: David T. Merrill
Phone: 918 493-7700   HR: James White
Fax: –   FYE: December 31
Web: www.unitcorp.com   Type: Public

It's oil for one and one for oil. With a single-minded focus on hydrocarbons Unit conducts onshore drilling of oil and natural gas wells for customers in the Gulf Coast Midcontinent and Rocky Mountain regions of the US. Through Unit Drilling it has a drilling fleet of almost 90 rigs. The company owns stakes in more than 8871 wells. Unit also has upstream and midstream businesses. Unit Petroleum explores for and produces oil and gas in the Anadarko and Arkoma basins of Oklahoma and Texas. In 2014 it reported proved reserves of 179 million barrels of oil equivalent (a 17% increase over the previous year). Its Superior Pipeline subsidiary buys sells gathers processes and treats natural gas.

	Annual Growth	12/14	12/15	12/16	12/17	12/18
Sales ($ mil.)	(14.4%)	1,572.9	854.2	602.2	739.6	843.3
Net income ($ mil.)	—	136.3	(1,037.4)	(135.6)	117.8	(45.3)
Market value ($ mil.)	(19.6%)	1,843.3	659.5	1,452.5	1,189.2	771.9
Employees	(16.5%)	1,880	1,179	1,216	1,375	913

UNITED AIRLINES HOLDINGS INC   NMS: UAL

233 South Wacker Drive   CEO: Oscar Munoz
Chicago, IL 60606   CFO: Andrew C. Levy
Phone: 872 825-4000   HR: Michael P. (Mike) Bonds
Fax: –   FYE: December 31
Web: www.united.com   Type: Public

United Airlines Holdings (formerly United Continental Holdings) operates through its primary United Air Lines subsidiary. United Airlines is a leading passenger and cargo airline operating more than 4800 flights a day to more than 350 airports. It serves destinations across five continents from US hubs in Newark Chicago Denver Houston Los Angeles San Francisco Washington DC and the US island of Guam. The airline which also offers regional services via subsidiary United Express operates a fleet of more than 1300 aircraft. In addition United is a member of the Star Alliance a marketing and code-sharing group (the largest in the world) that includes several international airlines. In 2019 the company dropped "Continental" from its name eliminating the reference to the 2010 merger of United Airlines and Continental Airlines.

	Annual Growth	12/14	12/15	12/16	12/17	12/18
Sales ($ mil.)	1.5%	38,901.0	37,864.0	36,556.0	37,736.0	41,303.0
Net income ($ mil.)	17.1%	1,132.0	7,340.0	2,263.0	2,131.0	2,129.0
Market value ($ mil.)	5.8%	18,054.6	15,466.1	19,671.4	18,192.3	22,600.0
Employees	2.3%	84,000	84,000	88,000	89,800	92,000

UNITED AMERICAN HEALTHCARE CORP.   NBB: UAHC

303 East Wacker Drive, Suite 1040   CEO: John M Fife
Chicago, IL 60601   CFO: Robert T Sullivan
Phone: 313 393-4571   HR: –
Fax: –   FYE: December 31
Web: www.uahc.com   Type: Public

United American Healthcare (UAHC) maintains the pulse of medical device manufacturing services. Through California-based subsidiary Pulse Systems the company provides contract manufacturing services to medical device makers. More specifically Pulse provides laser-cutting capabilities and other processing technology for cardiovascular devices. Before buying Pulse in 2010 the company operated the UAHC Health Plan of Tennessee a managed care company whose network covered some 900 physicians and 20 hospitals. However when its contract to serve Medicaid recipients in western Tennessee was not renewed in 2009 the company sought alternatives.

	Annual Growth	12/14	12/15	12/16	12/17	12/18
Sales ($ mil.)	18.4%	7.9	9.0	8.9	10.7	15.6
Net income ($ mil.)	—	(13.9)	(0.8)	1.4	10.9	(0.6)
Market value ($ mil.)	37.5%	3.8	1.0	12.3	74.5	13.6
Employees						

UNITED BANCORP, INC. (MARTINS FERRY, OH)　　　NAS: UBCP

201 South Fourth Street　　　CEO: Scott A Everson
Martins Ferry, OH 43935-0010　　　CFO: Randall M Greenwood
Phone: 740 633-0445　　　HR: –
Fax: –　　　FYE: December 31
Web: www.unitedbancorp.com　　　Type: Public

United Bancorp is the holding company of Ohio's Citizens Savings Bank which operates as Citizens Savings Bank and The Community Bank. The bank divisions together operate some 20 branches offering deposit and lending products including savings and checking accounts commercial and residential mortgages and consumer installment loans. Commercial loans and mortgages combined account for about 60% of the company's loan portfolio. In 2008 Citizens Savings Bank acquired the deposits of three failed banking offices from the FDIC.

	Annual Growth	12/14	12/15	12/16	12/17	12/18
Assets ($ mil.)	10.2%	401.8	405.1	438.0	459.3	593.2
Net income ($ mil.)	12.7%	2.7	3.2	3.6	3.5	4.3
Market value ($ mil.)	9.1%	46.3	55.0	77.5	76.0	65.6
Employees	(2.8%)	148	140	138	126	132

UNITED BANCORP, INC. (TECUMSEH, MI)　　　OTC: UBMI

2723 South State Street　　　CEO: Robert K Chapman
Ann Arbor, MI 48104　　　CFO: Randal J Rabe
Phone: 517 423-8373　　　HR: –
Fax: –　　　FYE: December 31
Web: www.ubat.com　　　Type: Public

Some folks in southeastern Michigan put their trust in United Bancorp the holding company for United Bank & Trust and United Bank & Trust - Washtenaw. Together the banks operate more than 15 branches in Lenawee Washtenaw and Monroe counties. In addition to standard products such as deposits loans and credit cards the company also offers financial planning investments and trust services. Business loans and commercial mortgages make up about 60% of the banks' loan portfolio; residential mortgages personal loans and commercial construction and development loans each account for about 15%. United Bancorp was formed in 1985 but the bank traces its roots to 1860.

	Annual Growth	12/08	12/09	12/10	12/11	12/12
Assets ($ mil.)	2.2%	832.4	909.3	861.7	885.0	907.7
Net income ($ mil.)	–	(0.0)	(8.8)	(3.7)	0.9	4.5
Market value ($ mil.)	(12.1%)	95.9	66.7	44.5	31.8	57.2
Employees	1.0%	274	248	255	282	285

UNITED BANCSHARES INC. (OH)　　　NMS: UBOH

105 Progressive Drive　　　CEO: Brian D Young
Columbus Grove, OH 45830　　　CFO: Stacy A Cox
Phone: 419 659-2141　　　HR: –
Fax: –　　　FYE: December 31
Web: www.theubank.com　　　Type: Public

United Bancshares is a blend of checks and (account) balances. The institution is the holding company for The Union Bank Company a community bank serving northwestern Ohio through about a dozen branches. The commercial bank offers such retail services and products as checking and savings accounts NOW and money market accounts IRAs and CDs. It uses funds from deposits to write commercial loans (about half of its lending portfolio) residential mortgages agriculture loans and consumer loans. The Union Bank Company was originally established in 1904.

	Annual Growth	12/14	12/15	12/16	12/17	12/18
Assets ($ mil.)	6.3%	650.2	608.7	633.1	780.5	830.3
Net income ($ mil.)	17.5%	4.3	5.9	5.5	3.8	8.2
Market value ($ mil.)	8.5%	47.2	59.6	70.0	72.6	65.5
Employees	6.0%	142	151	155	177	179

UNITED BANK CARD INC.

2202 N IRVING ST　　　CEO: –
ALLENTOWN, PA 18109-9554　　　CFO: –
Phone: 800-201-0461　　　HR: –
Fax: –　　　FYE: December 31
Web: www.harbortouchli.com　　　Type: Private

United Bank Card (UBC) CEO Jared Isaacman knows to give is to receive. UBC a payment and transaction processing company more than doubled its annual profits and set a new standard for the industry when the young innovative Isaacman and his sales team began giving away (rather than selling or leasing) the terminals merchants use to process credit debit EBT government cards and electronic gift and loyalty cards. Today UBC handles accounts for more than 100000 merchants nationwide and processes nearly $10 billion annually. Customers are primarily small to midsized business owners in the e-commerce petroleum lodging mail order supermarket and restaurant industries.

	Annual Growth	12/02	12/03	12/04	12/05	12/10
Sales ($ mil.)	30.3%	–	–	–	19.1	71.8
Net income ($ mil.)	–	–	–	–	0.0	3.5
Market value ($ mil.)	–	–	–	–	–	–
Employees	–	–	–	–	–	195

UNITED BANKSHARES INC　　　NMS: UBSI

300 United Center, 500 Virginia Street, East　　　CEO: Richard M Adams
Charleston, WV 25301　　　CFO: W. Mark Tatterson
Phone: 304 424-8716　　　HR: –
Fax: –　　　FYE: December 31
Web: www.ubsi-inc.com　　　Type: Public

United Bankshares (no relation to Ohio's United Bancshares) keeps it together as the holding company for two subsidiaries doing business as United Bank (WV) and United Bank (VA). Combined the banks boast some $12 billion in assets and operate roughly 130 branches that serve West Virginia Virginia and Washington DC as well as nearby portions of Maryland Pennsylvania and Ohio. The branches offer traditional deposit trust and lending services with a focus on residential mortgages and commercial loans. United Bankshares also owns United Brokerage Services which provides investments asset management and financial planning in addition to brokerage services.

	Annual Growth	12/14	12/15	12/16	12/17	12/18
Assets ($ mil.)	11.8%	12,328.8	12,577.9	14,508.9	19,059.0	19,250.5
Net income ($ mil.)	18.5%	129.9	138.0	147.1	150.6	256.3
Market value ($ mil.)	(4.5%)	3,832.0	3,784.9	4,732.5	3,555.7	3,183.3
Employees	7.0%	1,703	1,701	1,701	2,381	2,230

UNITED CAPITAL CORP.　　　NBB: UCAP

9 Park Place　　　CEO: –
Great Neck, NY 11021　　　CFO: Anthony J Miceli
Phone: 516 466-6464　　　HR: –
Fax: 516 829-4301　　　FYE: December 31
Web: www.unitedcapitalcorp.net　　　Type: Public

Making a profit is a capital idea that unites United Capital. The company invests in and manages real estate properties as well as manufactures and sells engineered products using knitted wire. United Capital owns and oversees about 150 retail office hotel and day care properties across the US. Subsidiary Metal Textiles makes knitted wire products and parts for a range of sealing and filtering applications. Under the AFP Transformers brand the company makes transformers for switchgear to motor starters and inverters. The lines are sold to commercial and industrial customers in the automotive electronic aerospace and process and chemical market. CEO Attilio Petrocelli and his wife own 70% of the company.

	Annual Growth	12/09	12/10	12/11	12/12	12/13
Sales ($ mil.)	18.7%	60.1	80.7	90.1	115.8	119.1
Net income ($ mil.)	21.7%	5.7	12.7	17.5	16.7	12.5
Market value ($ mil.)	8.5%	139.4	190.3	125.9	161.0	193.2
Employees	17.3%	390	470	460	630	–

UNITED CEREBRAL PALSY ASSOCIATIONS INC.

1660 L St. NW Ste. 700　　　　　　　　　　　　　CEO: Steve Bennett
Washington DC 20036　　　　　　　　　　　　　CFO: -
Phone: 202-776-0406　　　　　　　　　　　　　HR: Sue Jones
Fax: 202-776-0414　　　　　　　　　　　　　FYE: September 30
Web: www.ucp.org　　　　　　　　　　　　Type: Private - Not-for-Pr

United Cerebral Palsy (UCP) fights the good fight. The not-for-profit organization and its affiliates (about 100 chapter throughout North America Australia and Scotland) serve more than 176000 children and adults with cerebral palsy and other disabilities. Cerebral palsy is a group of conditions marked by an inability to fully control muscle movement and coordination caused by poor development or damage to the brain during fetal development birth or infancy. UCP works for the inclusion of the disabled into all facets of life by lobbying Congress providing information and funding research. Direct services include therapy individual and family support employment assistance and technology training.

UNITED CEREBRAL PALSY ASSOCIATIONS OF NEW YORK STATE, INC.

40 RECTOR ST FL 15　　　　　　　　　　　　　CEO: -
NEW YORK, NY 100061722　　　　　　　　　CFO: Thomas Mandelkow
Phone: 212-947-5770　　　　　　　　　　　　　HR: Janis Pshena
Fax: -　　　　　　　　　　　　　　　　　　　FYE: June 30
Web: www.cpofnys.org　　　　　　　　　　　　Type: Private

Cerebral Palsy Associations of New York State (CP of NYS) provides health care services for people suffering with cerebral palsy and other developmental disabilities. The organization includes 24 associations that provide day treatment programs community dwelling access and at-home residential support as well as early childhood mental health and transportation services. Serving more than 100000 patients throughout the state it also acts as an advocate for its patients through legislative involvement. CP of NYS was founded in 1946 by parents seeking health and advocacy services for their children. The organization provides services directly to patients.

	Annual Growth	06/09	06/10	06/13	06/14	06/15
Sales ($ mil.)	1.2%	-	109.1	113.4	112.7	115.5
Net income ($ mil.)	(36.1%)	-	2.7	0.2	0.0	0.3
Market value ($ mil.)	-	-	-	-	-	-
Employees	-	-	-	-	-	1,700

UNITED COMMUNITY BANCORP　　　　　　　NASDAQ: UCBA

92 Walnut St.　　　　　　　　　　　　　　　　CEO: -
Lawrenceburg IN 47025　　　　　　　　　　　CFO: -
Phone: 812-537-4822　　　　　　　　　　　　HR: -
Fax: 812-537-5769　　　　　　　　　　　　　FYE: June 30
Web: https://www.bankucb.com　　　　　　　Type: Public

United Community Bancorp is the holding company of United Community Bank a regional bank serving residents and businesses of southeastern Indiana. Through about a dozen branches in Dearborn County the bank offers savings and checking accounts IRAs and CDs as well as loans such as single-family mortgages (the largest segment of its loan portfolio) and commercial and multifamily mortgages. To a lesser extent it originates construction loans business loans and consumer loans.

UNITED COMMUNITY BANKS INC (BLAIRSVILLE, GA)　　　NMS: UCBI

125 Highway 515 East　　　　　　　　　　　　CEO: Jimmy C. Tallent
Blairsville, GA 30512　　　　　　　　　CFO: Jefferson L. Harralson
Phone: 706 781-2265　　　　　　　　　　　　HR: -
Fax: -　　　　　　　　　　　　　　　　　　　FYE: December 31
Web: www.ucbi.com　　　　　　　　　　　　　Type: Public

United Community Banks is the holding company for United Community Bank (UCB). UCB provides consumer and business banking products and services through nearly 150 branches across Georgia North Carolina Tennessee and South Carolina. Commercial loans including construction loans and mortgages account for the largest portion of UCB's loan portfolio (more than 50%); residential mortgages make up 30%. The company which boasts roughly $10 billion in assets also has a mortgage lending division and provides insurance through its United Community Insurance Services subsidiary (aka United Community Advisory Services).

	Annual Growth	12/14	12/15	12/16	12/17	12/18
Assets ($ mil.)	13.5%	7,567.0	9,626.1	10,708.7	11,915.5	12,573.2
Net income ($ mil.)	25.2%	67.6	71.6	100.7	67.8	166.1
Market value ($ mil.)	3.2%	1,500.7	1,544.3	2,346.9	2,229.6	1,700.4
Employees	11.3%	1,506	1,883	1,916	2,137	2,312

UNITED COMMUNITY FINANCIAL CORP. (OH)　　　NMS: UCFC

275 West Federal Street　　　　　　　　　　CEO: Gary M Small
Youngstown, OH 44503-1203　　　　　　　CFO: Timothy W Esson
Phone: 330 742-0500　　　　　　　　　　　HR: -
Fax: -　　　　　　　　　　　　　　　　　FYE: December 31
Web: www.ucfconline.com　　　　　　　　　Type: Public

This thrift wants to keep your savings and your loans united. United Community Financial is the holding company for The Home Savings and Loan Company of Youngstown Ohio a community bank with more than 30 full-service branches and about 10 loan production offices in Ohio and western Pennsylvania. Boasting nearly $2 billion in assets the bank offers traditional checking and savings accounts CDs retirement accounts investments and credit cards as well as a variety of loans. Residential mortgages account for over 60% of the company's loan portfolio while commercial and consumer loans split the remainder.

	Annual Growth	12/13	12/14	12/15	12/16	12/17
Assets ($ mil.)	11.1%	1,737.9	1,833.6	1,988.0	2,191.3	2,649.9
Net income ($ mil.)	21.4%	10.0	50.2	16.3	18.8	21.8
Market value ($ mil.)	26.5%	177.8	267.4	293.8	445.2	454.7
Employees	(0.5%)	514	428	428	442	503

UNITED CONCORDIA COMPANIES INC.

4401 Deer Path Rd.　　　　　　　　　　　　CEO: David L Holmberg
Harrisburg PA 17110　　　　　　　　　　　CFO: Daniel J Wright
Phone: 717-260-6800　　　　　　　　　　　HR: -
Fax: 717-260-7779　　　　　　　　　　　　FYE: December 31
Web: www.ucci.com　　　　　　　　　　　　Type: Subsidiary

Look Ma! I've got dental insurance! United Concordia Companies one of the largest dental insurers in the country provides dental benefits to more than 8 million members in the US and worldwide through corporate government agency and individual accounts. Its Advantage Plus plan includes some 75000 dentists. Through its contract with the US Department of Defense (DOD) the company provides coverage to military personnel and their family members. The company distributes its products through a network of regional sales offices. United Concordia founded in 1971 became an independent operating subsidiary of Highmark in 1992.

UNITED DAIRYMEN OF ARIZONA

2008 S HARDY DR
TEMPE, AZ 852821211
Phone: 480-966-7211
Fax: –
Web: www.uda.coop

CEO: –
CFO: –
HR: –
FYE: September 30
Type: Private

Its name says it all: United Dairymen of Arizona (UDA) is a group of Arizona-based dairy farmers united together to stabilize and strengthen the market for milk products. Supplied by some 90-member producers the cooperative's plant has the capacity to process 10 million pounds of milk per day about 90% of the milk in the state. Products include sweet cream and butter fluid and condensed skim milk and non-fat dry milk among others. Customers include onsite cheese maker Schreiber Foods fluid milk processors and supermarket chains throughout The Grand Canyon State. UDA also makes dried lactose powder for food manufacturers. Started in 1960 the co-op was formed through a merger of two dairy associations.

	Annual Growth	09/07	09/08	09/09	09/10	09/11
Sales ($ mil.)	0.8%	–	–	812.2	612.6	825.8
Net income ($ mil.)	203.7%	–	–	2.3	12.3	21.3
Market value ($ mil.)	–	–	–	–	–	–
Employees		–	–	–	–	190

UNITED ELECTRIC SUPPLY COMPANY, INC.

10 BELLECOR DR
NEW CASTLE, DE 197201763
Phone: 800-322-3374
Fax: –
Web: www.unitedelectric.com

CEO: George Vorwick
CFO: Rich Stagliano
HR: –
FYE: December 31
Type: Private

True to its name United Electric Supply distributes electrical parts such as lighting fasteners sensors wire connectors and voice data and fiber-optic products. The employee-owned company carries more than 23000 items from more than 250 manufacturers including Kyocera Panasonic Security and Schneider Electric. It sells to the building and industrial trades government and other markets. United Electric's wide range of services include design value engineering energy audits procurement training inventory management and E-commerce. It also offers value-added services such as next day delivery and Saturday-morning counter hours.

	Annual Growth	12/14	12/15	12/16	12/17	12/18
Sales ($ mil.)	2.8%	–	203.7	192.2	201.7	221.4
Net income ($ mil.)	1.2%	–	5.0	4.3	4.5	5.2
Market value ($ mil.)	–	–	–	–	–	–
Employees		–	–	–	–	343

UNITED ENERGY CORP.

OTC: UNRG

600 Meadowlands Pkwy. #20
Secaucus NJ 07094
Phone: 201-842-0288
Fax: 201-842-1307
Web: www.unitedenergycorp.net

CEO: –
CFO: James McKeever
HR: –
FYE: March 31
Type: Public

United Energy is dedicated to creating a more perfect union among environmentally friendly chemicals and customers. Its eco-friendly chemicals serve the oil industry with oil dispersants and protective coatings. Subsidiary Green Globe Industries supplies the US military with environmentally friendly solvents cleaners and paint strippers under the Qualchem brand name. United Energy top sellers are its K-Line chemical products (used in cleaning oil field equipment) and its Green Globe chemical products. Chairman Ronald Wilen owns 14% of the company.

UNITED FARMERS COOPERATIVE

705 E 4TH ST
WINTHROP, MN 553962362
Phone: 507-237-2281
Fax: –
Web: www.ufcmn.com

CEO: Jeff Nielsen
CFO: Lorie Reinarts
HR: –
FYE: August 31
Type: Private

United Farmers Cooperative has it all altogether. The agricultural cooperative supplies products and services to its members through 17 locations in eight rural communities across Minnesota. The farmer-owned co-op offers farm supplies such as energy feed seed fertilizer grain milling and blending and farm machinery as well as construction finance insurance and repair services. Originally known as the Cooperative Creamery Association United Farmers Cooperative (UFC) has been helping farmers in central Minnesota since 1915 (the creamery division was sold to Mid America Dairies in 1969).

	Annual Growth	08/03	08/04	08/05	08/06	08/07
Sales ($ mil.)	33.0%	–	–	72.0	93.9	127.4
Net income ($ mil.)	4.5%	–	–	2.2	1.4	2.4
Market value ($ mil.)	–	–	–	–	–	–
Employees		–	–	–	–	269

UNITED FINANCIAL BANCORP INC (MD)

NMS: UBNK

95 Elm Street
West Springfield, MA 01089
Phone: 413 787-1700
Fax: –
Web: www.bankatunited.com

CEO: –
CFO: –
HR: –
FYE: December 31
Type: Public

United Financial Bancorp is the holding company for United Bank which operates about 20 branches serving residents and businesses in western Massachusetts. It offers such standard deposit products as CDs and checking money market NOW retirement and savings accounts. Deposits are United Bank's primary source of funds for its lending activities which focus on residential mortgages commercial real estate loans and home equity loans. To a lesser extent the bank provides business construction and consumer loans. Its United Wealth Management Group provides investments and financial planning services.

	Annual Growth	12/08	12/09	12/10	12/11	12/12
Assets ($ mil.)	17.4%	1,263.1	1,541.0	1,584.9	1,623.8	2,402.3
Net income ($ mil.)	(16.0%)	7.3	5.8	10.0	11.2	3.6
Market value ($ mil.)	0.9%	305.1	264.2	307.7	324.2	316.8
Employees	16.7%	223	284	291	292	413

UNITED FIRE GROUP, INC.

NMS: UFCS

118 Second Avenue SE
Cedar Rapids, IA 52401
Phone: 319 399-5700
Fax: –
Web: www.ufginsurance.com

CEO: Randy A. Ramlo
CFO: Dawn M. Jaffray
HR: –
FYE: December 31
Type: Public

The United Fire Group (UFG) companies join together to offer a range of property/casualty products. The group operates through its United Fire & Casualty subsidiary which in turn holds entities that carry a variety of property/casualty offerings including fidelity and surety bonds and fire auto employee liability homeowners and workers' compensation lines. Some 1600 independent agencies in around 45 states sell its property/casualty products to businesses and individuals. In 2018 UFG sold its life insurance unit United Life Insurance Company to Kuvare US Holdings for $280 million.

	Annual Growth	12/14	12/15	12/16	12/17	12/18
Assets ($ mil.)	(7.6%)	3,856.7	3,890.4	4,054.8	4,183.4	2,816.7
Net income ($ mil.)	(17.3%)	59.1	89.1	49.9	51.0	27.7
Market value ($ mil.)	16.9%	746.1	961.5	1,234.0	1,143.9	1,391.7
Employees	4.8%	981	1,070	1,112	1,180	1,183

UNITED HARDWARE DISTRIBUTING CO

5005 NATHAN LN N
PLYMOUTH, MN 554423210
Phone: 763-559-1800
Fax: –
Web: www.rchank.com

CEO: Steven G Draeger
CFO: –
HR: –
FYE: November 30
Type: Private

United Hardware Distributing is in the business of building relationships. The member-owned distributor delivers hammers nails and all the other hardware necessities to dealers in 18 states across the central US. The company is not a franchiser but it provides retail support education buying markets and consulting services to its members. In addition to providing hardware United Hardware offers expertise in accounting store design pricing marketing purchasing and merchandising. Its client list of about 1200 member stores include Hardware Hank Trustworthy Hardware Golden Rule Lumber Ranch & Pet Supply and other independent retailers.

	Annual Growth	11/07	11/08	11/09	11/10	11/11
Sales ($ mil.)	2.6%	–	–	180.0	178.9	189.6
Net income ($ mil.)	22.7%	–	–	3.9	4.0	5.9
Market value ($ mil.)	–	–	–	–	–	–
Employees	–	–	–	–	–	330

UNITED HEALTH SERVICES HOSPITAL, INC.

10-42 MITCHELL AVE
BINGHAMTON, NY 139031617
Phone: 607-762-2200
Fax: –
Web: www.trustedhealthstats.com

CEO: –
CFO: –
HR: –
FYE: December 31
Type: Private

United Health Services Hospitals (UHS Hospitals) can service injuries from a slip in the snow or a slipped disc to health that's just plain slipping. The organization operates Binghamton General Hospital (about 200 beds) Wilson Medical Center (some 280 beds) and a group of primary and specialty care clinics in upstate New York. Specialty services include cardiology dialysis neurology rehabilitation pediatrics and psychiatry. The Wilson Medical Center serves as a teaching hospital offering residency and fellowship programs. UHS Hospitals is a subsidiary of United Health Services which operates a network of affiliated hospitals clinics long-term care centers and home health agencies in the region.

	Annual Growth	12/13	12/14	12/15	12/16	12/18
Sales ($ mil.)	7.0%	–	523.5	575.7	611.9	685.8
Net income ($ mil.)	–	–	(23.7)	13.0	21.0	(0.1)
Market value ($ mil.)	–	–	–	–	–	–
Employees	–	–	–	–	–	5,000

UNITED HEALTH SERVICES, INC.

1042 MITCHELL AVE 42
BINGHAMTON, NY 139031678
Phone: 607-762-3024
Fax: –

CEO: Mathew Salanger
CFO: –
HR: –
FYE: December 31
Type: Private

United Health Services (UHS) is a regional health system in upstate New York. The not-for-profit health care network includes seven divisions: Chenango Memorial Hospital Delaware Valley Hospital Senior Living at Ideal UHS Home Care UHS Primary Care Binghamton General Hospital and Wilson Regional Medical Center. The latter three make up the UHS Hospitals subsidiary. All together the system has almost 920 beds. Among its specialized services are oncology heart care neurology orthopedics diagnostics and emergency medicine. Other services include care centers for children and families home health care providers and an independent and assisted-living center for senior citizens.

	Annual Growth	12/04	12/05	12/06	12/09	12/14
Sales ($ mil.)	(12.3%)	–	1,575.7	344.3	6.3	482.9
Net income ($ mil.)	100.5%	–	0.0	13.3	(0.1)	0.2
Market value ($ mil.)	–	–	–	–	–	–
Employees	–	–	–	–	–	5,190

UNITED INSURANCE HOLDINGS CORP

NAS: UIHC

800 2nd Avenue S
St. Petersburg, FL 33701
Phone: 727 895-7737
Fax: –
Web: www.upcinsurance.com

CEO: John L. Forney
CFO: B. Bradford Martz
HR: –
FYE: December 31
Type: Public

United Insurance Holdings insures homeowners in the Sunshine State throughout the seasons even hurricane season. The company underwrites flood fire and homeowners insurance policies in Florida and provides property insurance for automotive service companies. It distributes its products through independent agents. United Insurance was founded in 1999 then underwent a reverse merger in 2008 when it bought the OTC-listed FMG Acquisition Corp. for $95 million ($25 million in cash and 8.75 million shares of stock.) The newly merged company has listed on the NASDAQ exchange.

	Annual Growth	12/14	12/15	12/16	12/17	12/18
Assets ($ mil.)	41.2%	584.2	740.0	999.7	2,059.9	2,321.4
Net income ($ mil.)	(71.0%)	41.0	27.4	5.7	10.1	0.3
Market value ($ mil.)	(6.7%)	943.5	735.0	650.8	741.5	714.4
Employees	25.0%	120	120	167	210	293

UNITED NATURAL FOODS INC.

NMS: UNFI

313 Iron Horse Way
Providence, RI 02908
Phone: 401 528-8634
Fax: –
Web: www.unfi.com

CEO: Steven L. (Steve) Spinner
CFO: Michael P. Zechmeister
HR: –
FYE: August 03
Type: Public

United Natural Foods Inc. (UNFI) is one of the top wholesale distributors of natural organic and specialty foods in the US and Canada. It owns around 65 distribution centers that supply more than 250000 items to 30000 unique customer locations including independently-owned retailers supernatural chain Whole Foods (its #1 customer) and conventional supermarkets. The company offers groceries supplements produce frozen foods and ethnic and kosher food as well as foodservice products and personal care items. UNFI also produces roasted nuts dried fruits and other snack items through subsidiary Woodstock Farms. It acquired rival SUPERVALU in 2018 which more than doubled its size.

	Annual Growth	08/15*	07/16	07/17	07/18*	08/19
Sales ($ mil.)	27.1%	8,185.0	8,470.3	9,274.5	10,226.7	21,387.1
Net income ($ mil.)	–	138.7	125.8	130.2	165.7	(285.0)
Market value ($ mil.)	(34.4%)	2,407.9	2,643.2	2,003.3	1,719.3	445.3
Employees	21.6%	8,700	9,554	9,700	10,000	19,000

*Fiscal year change

UNITED NEGRO COLLEGE FUND, INC.

1805 7TH ST NW STE 100
WASHINGTON, DC 200013187
Phone: 800-331-2244
Fax: –
Web: www.uncf.org

CEO: –
CFO: –
HR: Manny Diaz
FYE: March 31
Type: Private

A mind is a terrible thing to waste. In this spirit the United Negro College Fund (UNCF) offers financial assistance to students of color from low- to moderate-income families pursuing a higher education. UNCF the oldest and largest higher non-profit education assistance program for African-Americans enables some 60000 students to attend college each year. About 60% of the students are the first in their families to attend college. UNCF also provides operating funds and IT services to historically black colleges and universities such as Bethune-Cookman Morehouse Xavier and Voorhees College.

	Annual Growth	03/09	03/10	03/14	03/15	03/17
Sales ($ mil.)	(12.2%)	–	197.8	208.5	221.4	79.9
Net income ($ mil.)	–	–	51.3	40.1	50.3	(104.0)
Market value ($ mil.)	–	–	–	–	–	–
Employees	–	–	–	–	–	257

UNITED ONLINE INC
NMS: UNTD

21255 Burbank Boulevard, Suite 400
Woodland Hills, CA 91367
Phone: 818 287-3000
Fax: –
Web: www.unitedonline.com

CEO: Jeff Goldstein
CFO: Edward Zinser
HR: –
FYE: December 31
Type: Public

United Online keeps people connected. Through its subsidiaries the company operates subscription-based social networking websites including Memory Lane (historic magazines newsreels sports highlights and yearbook moments) and Classmates and StayFriends. It also operates rewards membership program MyPoints and provides Internet access under the NetZero and Juno Online brands and web hosting through MySite. In late 2013 United Online spun off its largest operation floral retailer FTD. The company was created by the 2001 merger of NetZero and Juno; in subsequent years it moved to diversify its business in light of a decline in dial-up Internet subscribers.

	Annual Growth	12/10	12/11	12/12	12/13	12/14
Sales ($ mil.)	(30.3%)	920.6	897.7	870.9	233.6	217.2
Net income ($ mil.)	–	53.7	51.7	12.5	(82.2)	(5.4)
Market value ($ mil.)	21.9%	94.3	77.7	79.9	196.6	207.9
Employees	(23.7%)	1,606	1,504	1,574	622	545

UNITED PARCEL SERVICE INC
NYS: UPS

55 Glenlake Parkway N.E.
Atlanta, GA 30328
Phone: 404 828-6000
Fax: –
Web: www.ups.com

CEO: David P. Abney
CFO: Richard N. Peretz
HR: Dan Shea
FYE: December 31
Type: Public

UPS is the world's largest package deliverer transporting nearly 21 million packages and documents per business day (more than 5 billion a year) throughout the US and in over 220 countries and territories. It deploys a fleet of approximately 123000 cars vans tractors and motorcycles and roughly 600 aircraft for pickups and deliveries. In addition to package delivery the company offers logistics and freight forwarding through UPS Supply Chain Solutions and less-than-truckload (LTL) and truckload (TL) freight transportation through UPS Freight. Nearly 80% of its revenue comes from the US.

	Annual Growth	12/14	12/15	12/16	12/17	12/18
Sales ($ mil.)	5.4%	58,232.0	58,363.0	60,906.0	65,872.0	71,861.0
Net income ($ mil.)	12.1%	3,032.0	4,844.0	3,431.0	4,910.0	4,791.0
Market value ($ mil.)	(3.2%)	95,383.9	82,565.3	98,361.1	102,230.7	83,680.7
Employees	2.5%	435,000	444,000	434,000	280,000	481,000

UNITED PERFORMING ARTS FUND INC.

301 W WSCNSIN AVE STE 600
MILWAUKEE, WI 53202
Phone: 414-273-8723
Fax: –
Web: www.upaf.org

CEO: –
CFO: William Werner
HR: –
FYE: August 31
Type: Private

The United Performing Arts Fund (UPAF) is a not-for-profit organization that does fund raising work for some 40 performing arts groups in greater Milwaukee and southeastern Wisconsin — including symphonies and orchestras ballet and opera companies theater groups dance studios and performing arts schools. Large corporate donations (more than $25000) make up about a third of UPAF's campaign revenues; other categories of giving include individual donations through company campaigns private foundations and special events. The organization was founded in 1966

	Annual Growth	08/10	08/11	08/12	08/13	08/14
Sales ($ mil.)	4.9%	–	11.8	11.2	10.8	13.6
Net income ($ mil.)	121.2%	–	–	0.2	(0.0)	1.2
Market value ($ mil.)	–	–	–	–	–	–
Employees	–	–	–	–	–	21

UNITED REGIONAL HEALTH CARE SYSTEM, INC.

1600 11TH ST
WICHITA FALLS, TX 763014300
Phone: 940-764-3211
Fax: –
Web: www.unitedregional.org

CEO: –
CFO: –
HR: –
FYE: December 31
Type: Private

If you take a fall in Wichita Falls United Regional Health Care System (URHCS) will be there. The health care provider serves the residents of northern Texas through two hospitals that combined have some 500 beds. Specialized services include emergency medicine cardiac care diagnostic imaging surgery obstetrics and pediatrics. The health care system also offers cancer treatment childbirth wound care and sleep diagnostic centers. It is the only comprehensive cardiac care facility and only Level II trauma center in the region. URHCS operates a Care Flight Helicopter to get those traumas to care quicker.

	Annual Growth	12/12	12/13	12/14	12/15	12/16
Sales ($ mil.)	4.4%	–	292.8	310.7	299.6	333.3
Net income ($ mil.)	(0.3%)	–	53.6	46.7	32.6	53.2
Market value ($ mil.)	–	–	–	–	–	–
Employees	–	–	–	–	–	1,950

UNITED RENTALS INC
NYS: URI

100 First Stamford Place, Suite 700
Stamford, CT 06902
Phone: 203 622-3131
Fax: –
Web: www.unitedrentals.com

CEO: Michael J. Kneeland
CFO: William B. Plummer
HR: –
FYE: December 31
Type: Public

No cash to buy a bulldozer? Just lease one from United Rentals. The company considers itself the #1 commercial and construction equipment renter in the world serving customers in the commercial infrastructure industrial and residential sectors. It operates through a network of nearly 1000 locations in the US and Canada and provides about 3400 equipment items — everything from general to heavy construction and industrial equipment to hand tools special-event items (such as aerial towers) power (diesel generators) and HVAC equipment and trench-safety equipment. It also sells new and used equipment as well as contractor supplies and parts. United Rentals' original equipment cost (the initial purchase value of all rental equipment) is $11.5 billion. The US accounts for more than 90% of total sales.

	Annual Growth	12/15	12/16	12/17	12/18	12/19
Sales ($ mil.)	12.6%	5,817.0	5,762.0	6,641.0	8,047.0	9,351.0
Net income ($ mil.)	19.0%	585.0	566.0	1,346.0	1,096.0	1,174.0
Market value ($ mil.)	23.1%	5,394.2	7,851.2	12,783.6	7,624.4	12,401.4
Employees	10.7%	12,700	12,500	14,800	18,500	19,100

UNITED SECURITY BANCSHARES (CA)
NMS: UBFO

2126 Inyo Street
Fresno, CA 93721
Phone: 559 248-4943
Fax: 559 248-5088
Web: www.unitedsecuritybank.com

CEO: Dennis R Woods
CFO: Bhavneet Gill
HR: –
FYE: December 31
Type: Public

United Security Bancshares (unrelated to the Alabama-based corporation of the same name) is the holding company for United Security Bank which operates about 10 branches loan offices and financial services offices in central California's San Joaquin Valley. The bank attracts deposits from area businesses and individuals by offering checking and savings accounts NOW and money market accounts certificates of deposit and IRAs. In 2007 United Security Bancshares bought Legacy Bank which had a single branch in Campbell California. A year later the company purchased ICG Financial and then formed a wealth management consulting and insurance division USB Financial Services.

	Annual Growth	12/14	12/15	12/16	12/17	12/18
Assets ($ mil.)	8.9%	663.2	725.6	788.0	805.8	933.1
Net income ($ mil.)	22.5%	6.2	6.8	7.4	8.6	14.0
Market value ($ mil.)	15.1%	92.5	90.7	131.3	186.4	162.3
Employees	(1.4%)	132	129	132	128	125

UNITED SPACE ALLIANCE, LLC

3700 BAY AREA BLVD # 100
HOUSTON, TX 770582783
Phone: 281-282-2592
Fax: –
Web: www.exporttexas.com

CEO: Scott Q Hartwig
CFO: William R Capel
HR: –
FYE: December 31
Type: Private

United Space Alliance (USA) is a space-race heavyweight; the Houston-based prime contractor has run NASA's 173000 pound Shuttles — Discovery Atlantis and Endeavour. USA a joint venture between Lockheed Martin and Boeing was formed in response to NASA's move to consolidate multiple Space Shuttle contracts under a single entity. It is now wrapping up those contracts. USA has supported mission operations astronaut and flight controller training flight software development Shuttle payload integration and vehicle processing launch and recovery. It also has led training and planning for the International Space Station. USA served the Johnson and Kennedy Space Centers and Marshall Space Flight Center.

	Annual Growth	12/03	12/04	12/05	12/06	12/07
Sales ($ mil.)	(3.2%)	–	–	–	1,920.5	1,859.8
Net income ($ mil.)	14.8%	–	–	–	146.3	168.0
Market value ($ mil.)	–	–	–	–	–	–
Employees	–	–	–	–	–	8,000

UNITED STATES ANTIMONY CORP. ASE: UAMY

P.O. Box 643
Thompson Falls, MT 59873
Phone: 406 827-3523
Fax: –
Web: www.usantimony.com

CEO: John C Lawrence
CFO: Daniel L Parks
HR: –
FYE: December 31
Type: Public

The products of United States Antimony don't span the alphabet from A to Z but they do include both antimony and zeolite. The company produces antimony oxide which is used as a flame retardant in plastics fiberglass and textiles and as a color fastener in paint. U.S. Antimony buys most of its raw antimony from China and Canada. The company has begun exploratory mining operations on a property in Mexico. U.S. Antimony also processes zeolite which is used in animal feed fertilizer water filtration and other applications.

	Annual Growth	12/14	12/15	12/16	12/17	12/18
Sales ($ mil.)	(4.3%)	10.8	13.1	11.9	10.2	9.0
Net income ($ mil.)	–	(1.6)	(0.8)	(1.3)	(1.1)	0.9
Market value ($ mil.)	(4.6%)	47.8	19.7	17.1	21.8	39.6
Employees	25.7%	83	83	103	103	207

UNITED STATES BASKETBALL LEAGUE INC OTC: USBL

183 Plains Road, Suite 2
Milford, CT 06461
Phone: 203 877-9508
Fax: –

CEO: –
CFO: Richard C Meisenheimer
HR: –
FYE: February 28
Type: Public

Basketball fans have more hardwood action to enjoy thanks to this enterprise. The United States Basketball League (USBL) operates an association of professional basketball teams that play a 30-game schedule from April through June. The league encompasses a half dozen teams including the Brooklyn Kings the Dodge City Legend and the Kansas Cagerz which compete with 11 players each. The USBL generates revenue mostly through franchise fees and marketing sponsorships. It is intended to be a development league for recent college graduates and international players to showcase their skills for scouts from National Basketball Association teams. The founding Meisenheimer family controls about 90% of the USBL.

	Annual Growth	02/11	02/12	02/13	02/14	02/15
Sales ($ mil.)	–	0.0	0.0	0.0	0.0	0.0
Net income ($ mil.)	–	0.0	(0.3)	(0.2)	(0.1)	0.1
Market value ($ mil.)	–	0.0	0.7	0.5	0.1	1.1
Employees	0.0%	–	–	1	1	1

UNITED STATES BEEF CORPORATION

4923 E 49TH ST
TULSA, OK 741357002
Phone: 918-665-0740
Fax: –
Web: www.usbeefcorp.com

CEO: John Davis
CFO: Lori Humphrey
HR: –
FYE: December 31
Type: Private

This company has carved out a sandwich empire in the middle of the country. United States Beef Corporation is the largest franchisee of Arby's fast-food restaurants in the US with more than 365 locations in half a dozen states mostly in Kansas Missouri and Oklahoma. The restaurants franchised from Arby's Restaurant Group (part of Wendy's/Arby's Group) serve the chain's signature roast beef sandwiches and curly fries as well as ham chicken and turkey subs. Bob Davis and his wife Connie opened their first Arby's in 1969 and founded United States Beef in 1974. United States Beef is now owned by Flynn Restaurant Group.

	Annual Growth	12/11	12/12	12/13	12/15	12/17
Sales ($ mil.)	8.7%	–	246.9	256.5	351.1	374.0
Net income ($ mil.)	19.8%	–	7.3	7.9	14.6	18.0
Market value ($ mil.)	–	–	–	–	–	–
Employees	–	–	–	–	–	7,000

UNITED STATES CELLULAR CORP NYS: USM

8410 West Bryn Mawr
Chicago, IL 60631
Phone: 773 399-8900
Fax: –
Web: www.uscellular.com

CEO: Kenneth R. Meyers
CFO: Steven T. Campbell
HR: Deirdre Drake
FYE: December 31
Type: Public

United States Cellular takes calls from sea to shining sea. Doing business as U.S. Cellular the company provides wireless phone service to about 5 million customers in about two dozen states in the US largely in the Midwest and the South. Its pre- and post-paid products and services — marketed directly through the Internet and from about 270 retail stores — include mobile messaging prepaid calling international long distance mobile Internet and directory assistance. U.S. Cellular service is also sold through contracts with resellers. The company offers phones from HTC LG Electronics BlackBerry and Samsung Electronics.

	Annual Growth	12/14	12/15	12/16	12/17	12/18
Sales ($ mil.)	0.5%	3,892.7	3,996.9	3,939.0	3,890.0	3,967.0
Net income ($ mil.)	–	(42.8)	241.3	48.0	12.0	150.0
Market value ($ mil.)	6.9%	3,425.4	3,509.7	3,759.9	3,236.2	4,469.4
Employees	(4.0%)	6,600	6,400	6,300	5,900	5,600

UNITED STATES DEPARTMENT OF JUSTICE

950 Pennsylvania Ave. NW
Washington DC 20530-0001
Phone: 202-514-2000
Fax: 202-501-3136
Web: www.cio.gov

CEO: –
CFO: –
HR: –
FYE: September 30
Type: Government Agency

The Department of Justice (DOJ) doesn't make the laws it just enforces them. The DOJ one of 15 federal executive departments is charged with enforcing federal law defending the rights of US citizens and representing the legal interests of the US government. The department covers both civil and criminal areas of federal law and is involved in everything from prosecuting offenders of antitrust laws to investigating organized crime. With the US Attorney General at its helm the DOJ comprises roughly 40 separate components including the FBI ATF US Marshals BOP CRS and US Attorneys. It has an annual budget in excess of $42 billion.

UNITED STATES FUND FOR UNICEF

125 MAIDEN LN FL 11
NEW YORK, NY 100384999
Phone: 800-367-5437
Fax: –
Web: www.unicefusa.org

CEO: Caryl M Stern
CFO: –
HR: –
FYE: June 30
Type: Private

The US Fund for UNICEF is one of about 40 committees in America that raises money for The United Nations Children's Fund (better known as UNICEF a not-for-profit organization that works for the human rights protection and development of children worldwide through education advocacy and fundraising. Among its dedicated programs are the five-year $100 million fundraising campaign for HIV/AIDS prevention and a campaign to protect mothers and newborns from tetanus. The US Fund for UNICEF derives revenue from public support — through its signature Trick-or-Treat for UNICEF program gifts corporate grants and the sale of greeting cards and educational materials. The organization was founded in 1947.

	Annual Growth	06/13	06/14	06/15	06/16	06/18
Sales ($ mil.)	(1.7%)	–	606.9	500.1	568.3	567.1
Net income ($ mil.)	(27.0%)	–	67.7	(29.2)	7.1	19.3
Market value ($ mil.)	–	–	–	–	–	–
Employees	–	–	–	–	–	230

UNITED STATES GOLF ASSOCIATION, INC.

77 LIBERTY CORNER RD
FAR HILLS, NJ 079312570
Phone: 908-234-2300
Fax: –
Web: www.usga.org

CEO: –
CFO: –
HR: –
FYE: November 30
Type: Private

Making sure golf stays clear of the rough is par for the course at this organization. The United States Golf Association is the governing body for golf in the US its territories and Mexico. The not-for-profit group writes and interprets the rules of the game provides handicap information offers turf consulting and funds equipment and course maintenance research and testing. It also holds several national championship events including the US Open the US Women's Open and the US Senior Open. The group generates most of its revenue from the sale of broadcast rights to championship tournaments and other matches as well as through membership fees. The USGA was founded in 1894.

	Annual Growth	11/12	11/13	11/14	11/15	11/17
Sales ($ mil.)	8.2%	–	156.6	164.7	208.9	215.0
Net income ($ mil.)	17.4%	–	6.8	(5.3)	16.5	12.9
Market value ($ mil.)	–	–	–	–	–	–
Employees	–	–	–	–	–	350

UNITED STATES HOLOCAUST MEMORIAL MUSEUM

100 ROUL WALLENBERG PL SW
WASHINGTON, DC 200242126
Phone: 202-488-0400
Fax: –
Web: www.ushmm.org

CEO: –
CFO: –
HR: –
FYE: September 30
Type: Private

The United States Holocaust Memorial Museum has a lesson to share. The museum's primary mission is to advance and disseminate knowledge about the Holocaust to preserve the memory of those who suffered and to encourage its visitors to reflect on the moral and spiritual questions raised by the tragic events of the Holocaust. The museum broadens the public understanding of the Holocaust through exhibitions; research and publications; collecting and preserving material evidence; distribution of educational materials; and through a number of other programs. Chartered by an Act of Congress in 1980 the United States Holocaust Memorial Museum is a public-private partnership relying on both federal appropriations and private donations.

	Annual Growth	09/14	09/15	09/16	09/17	09/18
Sales ($ mil.)	1.3%	–	163.5	163.1	194.0	170.1
Net income ($ mil.)	(5.6%)	–	58.9	46.8	80.3	49.5
Market value ($ mil.)	–	–	–	–	–	–
Employees	–	–	–	–	–	400

UNITED STATES LIME & MINERALS INC.

NMS: USLM

5429 LBJ Freeway, Suite 230
Dallas, TX 75240
Phone: 972 991-8400
Fax: 972 385-1340
Web: www.uslm.com

CEO: Timothy W. Byrne
CFO: M. Michael Owens
HR: –
FYE: December 31
Type: Public

Don't be crushed there's no tequila; it's not that kind of lime. Instead United States Lime & Minerals operates limestone quarries and lime plants in Arkansas Colorado Oklahoma Louisiana and Texas. It produces high-calcium quicklime and limestone pulverized limestone hydrated lime lime kiln dust and lime slurry used in the construction municipal sanitation aluminum paper glass housing agricultural and environmental sectors. The company has approximately 700 customers primarily in the central US. In addition to its lime operations United States Lime & Minerals also has natural gas interests.

	Annual Growth	12/14	12/15	12/16	12/17	12/18
Sales ($ mil.)	(0.9%)	149.8	130.8	139.3	144.8	144.4
Net income ($ mil.)	0.4%	19.4	12.9	17.8	27.1	19.7
Market value ($ mil.)	(0.6%)	408.6	308.2	424.8	432.3	398.1
Employees	(2.1%)	313	323	321	318	287

UNITED STATES OLYMPIC COMMITTEE INC

1 OLYMPIC PLZ
COLORADO SPRINGS, CO 80903
Phone: 719-632-5551
Fax: –
Web: www.teamusa.org

CEO: Scott Blackmun
CFO: Walter Glover
HR: –
FYE: December 31
Type: Private

Friendship solidarity and fair play are the watchwords for this sports organization. United States Olympic Committee (USOC) is the governing body of the Olympic movement in the US and oversees the organization selection and training of the country's Olympic athletes and teams. The not-for-profit organization operates six training and education centers around the country where athletes prepare for the Olympic Games the Paralympic Games and the Pan American Games. The USOC is funded by corporate sponsorships private contributions and sales of licensed apparel. It also receives money from the International Olympic Committee (IOC). The USOC was formed in 1978.

	Annual Growth	12/13	12/14	12/15	12/16	12/17
Sales ($ mil.)	(10.5%)	–	270.3	141.6	336.1	193.9
Net income ($ mil.)	–	–	47.9	(57.7)	78.5	(15.0)
Market value ($ mil.)	–	–	–	–	–	–
Employees	–	–	–	–	–	400

UNITED STATES POSTAL SERVICE

475 L'Enfant Plaza SW
Washington DC 20260-2200
Phone: 202-268-2500
Fax: 206-342-3000
Web: www.vulcan.com

CEO: Megan J Brennan
CFO: Joseph Corbett
HR: –
FYE: September 30
Type: Government Agency

The United States Postal Service (USPS) handles cards letters and packages sent from sea to shining sea. The USPS delivered some 168 billion pieces of mail in fiscal 2011 in the US and its territories and if that's not enough it claims to deliver more than 40% of the world's mail. The independent government agency relies on postage and fees to fund operations. Though it has a monopoly on delivering the mail the USPS faces competition for services such as package delivery. The US president appoints nine of the 11 members of the board who oversee the USPS. The presidential appointees select the postmaster general and together they name the deputy postmaster general; the two also serve on the board.

UNITED STATES SOCCER FEDERATION, INC.

1801 S PRAIRIE AVE
CHICAGO, IL 606161319
Phone: 312-808-1300
Fax: -
Web: www.ussoccer.com

CEO: -
CFO: -
HR: -
FYE: March 31
Type: Private

The U.S. Soccer Federation knows how its members like to get their kicks. The organization is the governing body for the sport of soccer (known around the world as football) in the United States. It promotes the game and organizes both recreational and professional competition overseeing such leagues as Major League Soccer United Soccer Leagues and Women's Professional Soccer. U.S. Soccer hosts World Cups and Olympic soccer and runs the National Soccer Training Center. The federation is a member of the F-©d-©ration Internationale de Football Association (FIFA) the world soccer governing body. The organization was founded in 1914 as the U.S. Football Association.

	Annual Growth	03/09	03/10	03/15	03/16	03/17
Sales ($ mil.)	19.3%	-	44.3	100.5	125.3	152.1
Net income ($ mil.)	78.6%	-	0.8	9.5	14.9	46.0
Market value ($ mil.)	-	-	-	-	-	-
Employees	-	-	-	-	-	92

UNITED STATES STEEL CORP.

600 Grant Street
Pittsburgh, PA 15219-2800
Phone: 412 433-1121
Fax: 412 433-4818
Web: www.ussteel.com

NYS: X
CEO: David B. (Dave) Burritt
CFO: Kevin P. Bradley
HR: Martin Pitorak
FYE: December 31
Type: Public

Steel crazy after all these years United States Steel (U.S. Steel) is North America's largest integrated steelmaker. The company operates mills throughout the US Midwest and in Slovakia. U.S. Steel makes a wide range of flat-rolled and tubular steel products and its annual production capacity is 22 million net tons of raw steel. Its customers are primarily in the automotive appliance construction oil and gas and petrochemical industries. In addition U.S. Steel mines iron ore and procures coke which provide the primary raw materials used in steel making. It is also engaged in railroad and barge operations and real estate. The US accounts for three-fifths of its revenue.

	Annual Growth	12/14	12/15	12/16	12/17	12/18
Sales ($ mil.)	(5.1%)	17,507.0	11,574.0	10,261.0	12,250.0	14,178.0
Net income ($ mil.)	81.8%	102.0	(1,642.0)	(440.0)	387.0	1,115.0
Market value ($ mil.)	(9.1%)	4,666.9	1,392.7	5,761.2	6,141.7	3,183.4
Employees	6.0%	23,000	33,200	29,800	29,200	29,000

UNITED STATES TENNIS ASSOCIATION INCORPORATED

70 W RED OAK LN FL 1
WHITE PLAINS, NY 106043602
Phone: 914-696-7000
Fax: -
Web: www.usta.com

CEO: -
CFO: -
HR: Maria Wuster
FYE: December 31
Type: Private

This sports group makes quite a racquet on the court. The United States Tennis Association (USTA) serves as the governing body for the sport of tennis in the US. It sets the rules of play and develops and promotes the sport at the local and professional levels. USTA also owns and operates the US Open the annual Grand Slam event held at Arthur Ashe Stadium in Flushing Meadows New York. In addition the not-for-profit organization selects players to compete in such tournaments as the Davis Cup the Fed Cup and the Olympics. Founded in 1881 as the United States National Lawn Tennis Association the USTA has grown to more than 700000 individual members and 8000 organizational members.

	Annual Growth	12/04	12/05	12/06	12/08	12/13
Sales ($ mil.)	1.5%	-	-	225.5	4.6	250.2
Net income ($ mil.)	31.4%	-	-	5.3	0.0	36.1
Market value ($ mil.)	-	-	-	-	-	-
Employees	-	-	-	-	-	350

UNITED SUPERMARKETS L.L.C.

7830 Orlando Ave.
Lubbock TX 79423
Phone: 806-791-7457
Fax: 806-791-7476
Web: www.unitedtexas.com

CEO: Robert Taylor
CFO: Suzann Kirby
HR: -
FYE: January 31
Type: Private

From Muleshoe up to Dalhart and over to Pampa United Supermarkets keeps the Texas Panhandle well fed. The grocer has about 50 supermarkets mostly in rural towns under the United Market Street Amigos and United Express banners. Its stores feature deli floral and bakery shops as well as groceries pharmacies (at most locations) and gas at some locales. Its larger Market Street format stocks more specialty and international foods. United Supermarkets runs its own distribution facility. H. D. Snell founded the firm in Sayre Oklahoma in 1916. He bucked the norms of the day by selling for cash — instead of on credit — at lower prices. United Supermarkets is owned and run by the Snell family.

UNITED SURGICAL PARTNERS INTERNATIONAL INC.

15305 Dallas Pkwy. Ste. 1600
Addison TX 75001
Phone: 972-713-3500
Fax: 972-713-3550
Web: www.unitedsurgical.com

CEO: William H Wilcox
CFO: Owen Morris
HR: -
FYE: December 31
Type: Private

United Surgical Partners International (USPI) brings together surgeons from across the US and the UK. The company owns or manages about 200 short-stay ambulatory surgery centers and surgical hospitals in the US and another six medical facilities in the UK. The company creates centers from scratch converts outpatient departments into stand-alone jointly run locations and purchases existing facilities; contract management services are also available. USPI markets its facilities to patients physicians and insurance companies. Health care investment firm Welsh Carson Anderson & Stowe owns USPI.

UNITED TECHNOLOGIES CORP

10 Farm Springs Road
Farmington, CT 06032
Phone: 860 728-7000
Fax: 860 728-7028
Web: www.utc.com

NYS: UTX
CEO: Gregory J. Hayes
CFO: Akhil Johri
HR: Elizabeth B. Amato
FYE: December 31
Type: Public

United Technologies (UTC) provides high-tech products and services for the aerospace commercial building and automated controls and security industries. It operates through engine aircraft manufacturer Pratt & Whitney; Carrier its former climate controls and security business; Collins Aerospace Systems maker of engine controls and flight systems for military and commercial aircraft; and Otis the world's largest elevator and escalator manufacturer. UTC announced in 2018 that it would split into three separate companies based on its business segments. Carrier and Otis will operate as standalone companies. In 2019 UTC said it would merge the Collins and Pratt & Whitney units with Raytheon in an all-stock deal.

	Annual Growth	12/15	12/16	12/17	12/18	12/19
Sales ($ mil.)	8.3%	56,098.0	57,244.0	59,837.0	66,501.0	77,046.0
Net income ($ mil.)	(7.6%)	7,608.0	5,055.0	4,552.0	5,269.0	5,537.0
Market value ($ mil.)	11.7%	83,039.6	94,751.8	110,267.2	92,037.7	129,447.5
Employees	5.4%	197,200	201,600	205,000	240,200	243,200

UNITED THERAPEUTICS CORP
NMS: UTHR

1040 Spring Street
Silver Spring, MD 20910
Phone: 301 608-9292
Fax: –
Web: www.unither.com

CEO: Martine A. Rothblatt
CFO: James Edgemond
HR: –
FYE: December 31
Type: Public

United Therapeutics hopes its products will be in vein. Its injectable drug Remodulin treats pulmonary hypertension which affects the blood vessels between the heart and lungs; it also treats cancer and viral illnesses. The product is marketed directly and through distributors in North America Europe and the Asia/Pacific region. Other hypertension treatments include Adcirca Tyvaso and Orenitram. The company's development pipeline includes additional treatments for cardiovascular disease as well as various cancers respiratory conditions and infectious diseases. United Therapeutics has divested its cardiac monitoring division.

	Annual Growth	12/14	12/15	12/16	12/17	12/18
Sales ($ mil.)	6.0%	1,288.5	1,465.8	1,598.8	1,725.3	1,627.8
Net income ($ mil.)	14.7%	340.1	651.6	713.7	417.9	589.2
Market value ($ mil.)	(4.2%)	5,644.3	6,826.4	6,251.9	6,448.9	4,746.8
Employees	3.8%	740	750	750	800	860

UNITED WAY WORLDWIDE

701 N FAIRFAX ST LBBY
ALEXANDRIA, VA 223142045
Phone: 703-836-7100
Fax: –

CEO: Brian A Gallagher
CFO: –
HR: –
FYE: December 31
Type: Private

Where there's a will there's a Way. Working to raise money for charitable causes United Way Worldwide unites some 1800 namesake organizations active in about 40 countries and territories. While its specific priorities are set by local entities the global organization tends to focus on helping children achieve their potential promoting financial stability and improving access to health care. Major recipients of its contributions have included the American Cancer Society Big Brothers/Big Sisters Catholic Charities Girl Scouts Boy Scouts and The Salvation Army among other worthy organizations. United Way Worldwide was formed by the merger of United Way of America and United Way International.

	Annual Growth	12/12	12/13	12/14	12/15	12/17
Sales ($ mil.)	33.3%	–	–	–	99.0	175.8
Net income ($ mil.)	87.6%	–	–	–	8.1	28.5
Market value ($ mil.)	–	–	–	–	–	–
Employees	–	–	–	–	–	204

UNITED-GUARDIAN, INC.
NMS: UG

230 Marcus Boulevard
Hauppauge, NY 11788
Phone: 631 273-0900
Fax: 631 273-0858
Web: www.u-g.com

CEO: –
CFO: Robert S Rubinger
HR: –
FYE: December 31
Type: Public

Through its Guardian Laboratories division United-Guardian makes a variety of cosmetic ingredients personal care products and pharmaceuticals. Its top-selling Lubrajel line is a moisturizer used in cosmetics and as a lubricant for medical catheters. Other cosmetic products include Klensoft surfactants used in shampoos and Unitwix a thickening agent for cosmetic oils and liquids. United-Guardian's main pharmaceutical product is Renacidin Irrigation a prescription drug used to keep urinary catheters clear. In 2007 the company sold the assets of its Eastern Chemical subsidiary which distributed organic and research chemicals dyes reagents and other chemicals.

	Annual Growth	12/14	12/15	12/16	12/17	12/18
Sales ($ mil.)	0.6%	13.4	14.0	10.8	13.0	13.8
Net income ($ mil.)	1.8%	4.1	4.6	2.6	3.8	4.4
Market value ($ mil.)	(1.9%)	91.1	88.0	71.2	85.0	84.3
Employees	(5.3%)	36	34	33	31	29

UNITEDHEALTH GROUP INC
NYS: UNH

UnitedHealth Group Center, 9900 Bren Road East
Minnetonka, MN 55343
Phone: 952 936-1300
Fax: –
Web: www.unitedhealthgroup.com

CEO: Larry C. Renfro
CFO: John Rex
HR: –
FYE: December 31
Type: Public

UnitedHealth Group is a leading US health insurer offering a variety of plans and services to group and individual customers nationwide. Its UnitedHealthcare health benefits segment manages health maintenance organization (HMO) preferred provider organization (PPO) and point-of-service (POS) plans as well as Medicare Medicaid state-funded and supplemental vision and dental options. In addition UnitedHealth's Optum health services units ? OptumHealth OptumInsight and OptumRx ? provide wellness and care management programs financial services information technology solutions and pharmacy benefit management (PBM) services to individuals and the health care industry.

	Annual Growth	12/14	12/15	12/16	12/17	12/18
Sales ($ mil.)	14.8%	130,474.0	157,107.0	184,840.0	201,159.0	226,247.0
Net income ($ mil.)	20.9%	5,619.0	5,813.0	7,017.0	10,558.0	11,986.0
Market value ($ mil.)	25.3%	97,046.4	112,934.4	153,638.4	211,641.6	239,155.2
Employees	15.3%	170,000	200,000	230,000	260,800	300,000

UNITEK GLOBAL SERVICES INC.
NMS: UNTK

1777 Sentry Parkway West, Gwynedd Hall, Suite 302
Blue Bell, PA 19422
Phone: 267 464-1700
Fax: –
Web: www.unitekglobalservices.com

CEO: John Haggerty
CFO: Andrew Herning
HR: –
FYE: December 31
Type: Public

UniTek Global Services has a variety of ways to keep the lines of communications companies open. A provider of outsourced infrastructure services UniTek offers technical engineering and design repair construction and other services to major US satellite cable wired telecom and wireless communications companies. Its services range from residential and commercial installation to design and construction of fiber optic networks. The company operates through offices in Texas Florida California and the northeastern US. It has counted Clearwire T-Mobile and Ericsson as customers. UniTek Global Services was formed in early 2010 when Berliner Communications merged with UniTek Holdings.

	Annual Growth	06/09*	12/09	12/10	12/11	12/12
Sales ($ mil.)	100.3%	54.5	42.9	402.2	432.3	437.6
Net income ($ mil.)	–	(3.4)	(5.5)	(30.6)	(15.6)	(77.7)
Market value ($ mil.)	68.8%	14.1	15.0	184.0	84.9	67.8
Employees	102.7%	432	531	5,000	6,400	3,600

*Fiscal year change

UNITIL CORP
NYS: UTL

6 Liberty Lane West
Hampton, NH 03842-1720
Phone: 603 772-0775
Fax: 603 772-4651
Web: www.unitil.com

CEO: Robert G. (Bob) Schoenberger
CFO: Mark H Collin
HR: –
FYE: December 31
Type: Public

New England electric and gas company Unitil won't be satisfied until it makes all its customers happy. The company serves about 102400 electric customers and 75900 natural gas customers. Unitil Energy Systems provides regulated electric utility services to about 73800 customers in New Hampshire and subsidiary Fitchburg Gas and Electric has some 28605 power and 15615 natural gas customers in Massachusetts. Unitil's utility units provide retail supply services to customers who don't choose to purchase energy from a third-party marketer. Indirect subsidiary Usource provides energy brokerage service to large energy users throughout the Northeast seeking competitive power or natural gas supplies.

	Annual Growth	12/15	12/16	12/17	12/18	12/19
Sales ($ mil.)	0.7%	426.8	383.4	406.2	444.1	438.2
Net income ($ mil.)	13.9%	26.3	27.1	29.0	33.0	44.2
Market value ($ mil.)	14.6%	535.7	676.9	681.1	756.1	923.0
Employees	0.6%	500	498	510	520	513

UNITY BANCORP, INC. — NMS: UNTY

64 Old Highway 22
Clinton, NJ 08809
Phone: 908 730-7630
Fax: -
Web: www.unitybank.com

CEO: James A Hughes
CFO: Alan J Bedner
HR: -
FYE: December 31
Type: Public

Unity Bancorp wants to keep you and your money united. The institution is the holding company for Unity Bank a commercial bank that serves small and midsized businesses as well as individual consumers through nearly 20 offices in north-central New Jersey and eastern Pennsylvania. Unity Bank's deposit products include checking savings money market and NOW accounts and CDs. Lending to businesses is the company's life blood: Commercial loans including Small Business Administration (SBA) and real estate loans account for about 60% of its loan portfolio which is rounded out by residential mortgage and consumer loans.

	Annual Growth	12/14	12/15	12/16	12/17	12/18
Assets ($ mil.)	11.9%	1,008.8	1,084.9	1,189.9	1,455.5	1,579.2
Net income ($ mil.)	36.0%	6.4	9.6	13.2	12.9	21.9
Market value ($ mil.)	21.8%	101.7	134.4	169.2	212.9	223.8
Employees	3.1%	183	173	194	208	207

UNIVAR INC.

17425 NE Union Hill Rd.
Redmond WA 98052
Phone: 425-889-3400
Fax: 425-889-4100
Web: www.univar.com

CEO: David C Jukes
CFO: Carl J Lukach
HR: -
FYE: December 31
Type: Private

With nearly universal coverage Univar distributes a broad range of chemicals. The company is a leading global distributor of specialty chemicals ranking #1 in the US and Canada and #2 in Europe. It operates more than 260 distribution facilities in Asia Europe Latin America and North America with sales offices in Africa and the Middle East. Subsidiaries Univar Europe Univar USA and Univar Canada handle sales marketing and logistics in those key markets. Univar's portfolio includes more than 4500 products and its storage and transportation capabilities further serve customers' chemical needs. Markets include paints and coatings energy food and household and industrial cleaning.

UNIVERSAL CORP — NYS: UVV

9201 Forest Hill Avenue
Richmond, VA 23235
Phone: 804 359-9311
Fax: -
Web: www.universalcorp.com

CEO: George C. Freeman
CFO: David C. Moore
HR: -
FYE: March 31
Type: Public

Operating mainly through its flagship subsidiary Universal Leaf Tobacco Company Universal Corporation selects buys processes packs stores and ships leaf tobacco to cigarette makers in the US and more than 30 other nations including Belgium China the Netherlands Germany and Russia. Universal also procures and processes dark tobacco used in cigars pipe tobacco and smokeless products. The firm's Universal Leaf subsidiaries are active in Africa Asia Europe South America and the US. Additional businesses include a dehydrated fruit and vegetable business and a unit that recycles waste materials from tobacco production.

	Annual Growth	03/15	03/16	03/17	03/18	03/19
Sales ($ mil.)	(0.5%)	2,271.8	2,120.4	2,071.2	2,033.9	2,227.2
Net income ($ mil.)	(2.4%)	114.6	109.0	106.3	105.7	104.1
Market value ($ mil.)	5.1%	1,178.5	1,419.7	1,768.0	1,212.0	1,440.2
Employees	0.9%	27,000	24,000	24,000	24,000	28,000

UNIVERSAL DETECTION TECHNOLOGY — NBB: UNDT

340 North Camden Drive, Suite 302
Beverly Hills, CA 90210
Phone: 310 248-3655
Fax: -
Web: www.udetection.com

CEO: Jacques Tizabi
CFO: -
HR: -
FYE: December 31
Type: Public

Universal Detection Technology (UDT) has traded in acid rain for bioterrorism. UDT has leveraged its expertise in air pollution monitoring into products to identify airborne biological and chemical hazards in bioterrorism monitoring systems. Its first product — originally called the Anthrax Smoke Detector and now known as the BSM-2000 — is intended to continuously check the air in public buildings for anthrax spores. The device is an outgrowth of an agreement with NASA's Jet Propulsion Laboratory (JPL) that called for JPL to develop its bacterial spore detection technology for integration into UDT's aerosol monitoring system.

	Annual Growth	12/10	12/11	12/12	12/13	12/14
Sales ($ mil.)	8.8%	0.0	0.2	0.1	0.1	0.0
Net income ($ mil.)	-	(2.2)	(2.6)	(1.6)	(0.4)	(0.1)
Market value ($ mil.)	-	0.0	0.0	0.5	0.1	0.1
Employees	(24.0%)	3	4	4	1	1

UNIVERSAL DISPLAY CORP — NMS: OLED

375 Phillips Boulevard
Ewing, NJ 08618
Phone: 609 671-0980
Fax: -
Web: www.oled.com

CEO: Steven V. Abramson
CFO: Sidney D. Rosenblatt
HR: -
FYE: December 31
Type: Public

Universal Display thinks the world should be flat and lit with its organic light-emitting diode (OLED) technologies and materials. With its own research and through sponsored research agreements with PPG Industries and several universities the company develops OLED technologies and materials which use less energy than other lighting technologies for screens from cell phones to large flat panel displays and solid-state lighting. Based in the US it has facilities in Europe and the Asia/Pacific region. Most of the company's revenue comes from sale to customers in Asia.

	Annual Growth	12/14	12/15	12/16	12/17	12/18
Sales ($ mil.)	6.7%	191.0	191.0	198.9	335.6	247.4
Net income ($ mil.)	8.9%	41.9	14.7	48.1	103.9	58.8
Market value ($ mil.)	35.5%	1,313.1	2,576.1	2,664.1	8,169.8	4,427.7
Employees	16.5%	145	154	203	224	267

UNIVERSAL ELECTRONICS INC. — NMS: UEIC

15147 N, Scottsdale Road, Suite H300
Scottsdale, AZ 85254-2494
Phone: 480 530-3000
Fax: -
Web: www.uei.com

CEO: Paul D. Arling
CFO: Bryan M. Hackworth
HR: -
FYE: December 31
Type: Public

Universal Electronics can help couch potatoes and TV junkies end multiple remote madness. The company makes One For All -branded universal remote controls with preprogrammed infrared codes allowing them to operate virtually any remote-capable device including TVs DVD players digital video recorders and set-top boxes. Its One For All remotes are sold by retailers worldwide. Universal Electronics also markets audiovisual accessories under the One For All name outside North America and it develops Nevo-branded wireless networking products. The company sells and licenses its technologies to consumer electronics and computer manufacturers and cable companies including DIRECTV its largest customer.

	Annual Growth	12/14	12/15	12/16	12/17	12/18
Sales ($ mil.)	4.9%	562.3	602.8	651.4	695.8	680.2
Net income ($ mil.)	(22.2%)	32.5	29.2	20.4	(10.3)	11.9
Market value ($ mil.)	(21.0%)	898.5	709.5	891.8	652.8	349.3
Employees	16.9%	1,988	2,309	3,103	3,010	3,707

UNIVERSAL FOREST PRODUCTS INC. NMS: UFPI

2801 East Beltline N.E. CEO: Matthew J. Missad
Grand Rapids, MI 49525 CFO: Michael R. Cole
Phone: 616 364-6161 HR: –
Fax: 616 364-5558 FYE: December 29
Web: www.ufpi.com Type: Public

Universal Forest Products is a leading manufacturer and distributor of engineered and composite wood and construction materials which it sells to do-it-yourself retail stores residential and mobile home builders and industrial customers. Universal is one of the largest primary source buyers of solid sawn softwood lumber in the US; it primarily uses yellow pine to make such products as roof trusses wall panels flooring pallets and shipping crates. The company has facilities worldwide but generates most of its revenue in the US.

	Annual Growth	12/14	12/15	12/16	12/17	12/18
Sales ($ mil.)	14.0%	2,660.3	2,887.1	3,240.5	3,941.2	4,489.2
Net income ($ mil.)	26.8%	57.6	80.6	101.2	119.5	148.6
Market value ($ mil.)	(16.5%)	3,215.3	4,193.7	6,221.1	2,290.4	1,564.1
Employees	18.9%	6,000	7,000	9,300	10,000	12,000

UNIVERSAL HEALTH REALTY INCOME TRUST NYS: UHT

Universal Corporate Center, 367 South Gulph Road CEO: Alan B. Miller
King of Prussia, PA 19406 CFO: Charles F. Boyle
Phone: 610 265-0688 HR: –
Fax: 610 768-3336 FYE: December 31
Web: www.uhrit.com Type: Public

Universal Health Realty Income Trust (UHT) is a real estate investment trust (REIT) that primarily invests in healthcare facilities and human services. The REIT owns more than 55 facilities in 16 states including acute care hospitals behavioral healthcare facilities rehabilitation hospitals sub-acute facilities surgery centers childcare centers and medical office buildings. McAllen Medical Center in Texas is UHT's largest facility. Many properties are owned via limited liability companies in which the trust holds an equity interest. UHT's hospitals boast some 1000 beds. Subsidiaries of Universal Health Services lease most of UHT's hospitals and provide their own maintenance and renovation services.

	Annual Growth	12/14	12/15	12/16	12/17	12/18
Sales ($ mil.)	6.3%	59.8	64.0	67.1	72.3	76.2
Net income ($ mil.)	(17.2%)	51.6	23.7	17.2	45.6	24.2
Market value ($ mil.)	6.3%	661.5	687.5	901.7	1,032.5	843.6
Employees	–	–	–	–	–	–

UNIVERSAL HEALTH SERVICES, INC. NYS: UHS

Universal Corporate Center, 367 South Gulph Road CEO: Alan B. Miller
King of Prussia, PA 19406 CFO: Steve G. Filton
Phone: 610 768-3300 HR: Cheryl Lyng
Fax: – FYE: December 31
Web: www.uhsinc.com Type: Public

With dozens of health care facilities in nearly every state Universal Health Services (UHS) isn't quite ubiquitous but it's working on it. One of the nation's largest for-profit hospital operators UHS owns or leases about 25 acute care hospitals with a total of more than 6000 beds primarily in rural and suburban communities. The system also operates outpatient surgery centers and radiation treatment facilities most located near its acute care hospitals. In addition UHS' behavioral health division operates some 500 psychiatric and substance abuse hospitals with a combined capacity of more than 23000 beds; its UK-based Cygnet unit operates about 40 more facilities. UHS is controlled by founder and CEO Alan Miller.

	Annual Growth	12/14	12/15	12/16	12/17	12/18
Sales ($ mil.)	7.5%	8,065.3	9,043.5	9,766.2	10,409.9	10,772.3
Net income ($ mil.)	9.3%	545.3	680.5	702.4	752.3	779.7
Market value ($ mil.)	1.2%	10,163.6	10,915.4	9,717.8	10,354.5	10,647.7
Employees	6.1%	68,700	74,600	75,325	76,600	87,100

UNIVERSAL INSURANCE HOLDINGS INC NYS: UVE

1110 West Commercial Blvd. CEO: Sean P. Downes
Fort Lauderdale, FL 33309 CFO: Frank C Wilcox
Phone: 954 958-1200 HR: –
Fax: – FYE: December 31
Web: www.universalinsuranceholdings.com Type: Public

While some companies shy away from insuring homes in hurricane-prone Florida Universal Insurance Holdings is right at home there. Operating through its Universal Property & Casualty Insurance Company (UPCIC) and American Platinum Property and Casualty Insurance Company (APPCIC) subsidiaries the company underwrites distributes and administers homeowners property and personal liability insurance. The company's additional subsidiaries process claims perform claims adjustments and property inspections provide administrative duties and negotiate reinsurance. All together the group services some 765000 insurance policies.

	Annual Growth	12/14	12/15	12/16	12/17	12/18
Assets ($ mil.)	19.5%	911.8	993.5	1,060.0	1,455.0	1,858.4
Net income ($ mil.)	12.5%	73.0	106.5	99.4	106.9	117.1
Market value ($ mil.)	16.7%	711.3	806.3	987.8	951.3	1,319.0
Employees	21.7%	335	392	483	558	734

UNIVERSAL LOGISTICS HOLDINGS INC NMS: ULH

12755 E. Nine Mile Road CEO: Jeffrey A. (Jeff) Rogers
Warren, MI 48089 CFO: Jude Beres
Phone: 586 920-0100 HR: –
Fax: – FYE: December 31
Web: www.universallogistics.com Type: Public

Universal Logistics Holdings (formerly Universal Truckload Services) hasn't hauled freight beyond its own galaxy but the company does cover the US and parts of Canada (Ontario and Quebec) and Mexico. As an "asset-light" provider of truckload freight transportation the company operates through a network of truck owner-operators rather than employing drivers and investing heavily in equipment. It can call upon a fleet of some 4300 tractors and 6300 trailers including standard dry vans and flatbeds; the majority of its tractors and trailers are owned by others. Its flagship transportation segment transports general commodities such as automotive parts building materials paper food consumer goods furniture steel and other metals.

	Annual Growth	12/14	12/15	12/16	12/17	12/18
Sales ($ mil.)	5.2%	1,191.5	1,128.8	1,072.8	1,216.7	1,461.7
Net income ($ mil.)	3.6%	45.4	40.0	24.2	28.2	52.2
Market value ($ mil.)	(10.7%)	809.1	398.4	464.0	674.0	513.4
Employees	2.5%	5,746	5,108	6,275	8,231	6,335

UNIVERSAL MANUFACTURING CO NBB: UFMG

1128 Lincoln Mall, Suite 301 CEO: Thomas Hance
Lincoln, NE 68508 CFO: –
Phone: 515 295-3557 HR: –
Fax: 515 295-5537 FYE: July 31
Web: www.universalmanf.com Type: Public

Parts are the best part of Universal Manufacturing. The company is a remanufacturer and distributor of automotive parts including fuel pumps engines and master cylinders. Universal Manufacturing sells its remanufactured products wholesale — under the brand name ReTech — to automotive dealers warehouse distributors and parts supply stores in the midwestern US. The firm also distributes remanufactured engines. Although specializing in the car and truck industry it also has facilities for serving the marine railroad aircraft motor sport and industrial engine markets. Universal Manufacturing was founded in 1946.

	Annual Growth	07/13	07/14	07/15	07/16	07/17
Sales ($ mil.)	17.0%	23.1	27.7	23.9	67.3	43.4
Net income ($ mil.)	–	0.8	1.7	(1.5)	0.3	(3.3)
Market value ($ mil.)	18.9%	7.0	11.9	14.3	10.5	14.0
Employees	6566.7%	–	–	3	200	–

UNIVERSAL POWER GROUP INC
NBB: UPGI

488 S. Royal Lane
Coppell, TX 75019
Phone: 469 892-1122
Fax: –
Web: www.upgi.com

CEO: Ian Colin Edmonds
CFO: –
HR: –
FYE: December 31
Type: Public

Universal Power Group (UPG) gives its customers a charge. The company is a leading distributor of sealed lead-acid batteries to manufacturers and retailers in the US. Other products include lithium and nickel-cadmium batteries portable battery-powered products including jump starters solar power generators and solar panels. UPG also supplies components used in security systems including alarm panels perimeter access controls sirens speakers cable and wire. In addition UPG provides services such as inventory management kitting and packaging and battery recycling. ADT Security Services (16% of sales) Cabelas Protection One and RadioShack are among the company's customers.

	Annual Growth	12/12	12/13	12/14	12/15	12/16
Sales ($ mil.)	(0.1%)	91.9	81.6	88.6	90.9	91.6
Net income ($ mil.)	–	0.2	(0.1)	0.8	0.6	(0.2)
Market value ($ mil.)	(6.0%)	7.7	6.7	9.9	7.3	6.0
Employees	–	108	–	–	–	–

UNIVERSAL SECURITY INSTRUMENTS, INC.
ASE: UUU

11407 Cronhill Drive, Suite A
Owings Mills, MD 21117
Phone: 410 363-3000
Fax: 410 363-2218
Web: www.universalsecurity.com

CEO: Harvey B Grossblatt
CFO: James B Huff
HR: –
FYE: March 31
Type: Public

Where there's smoke there's Universal Security Instruments. The company designs and markets (to 30 countries) smoke alarms and carbon monoxide alarms as well as other safety products such as outdoor floodlights door chimes and ground fault circuit interrupter (GFCI) units. Universal Security Instruments has warehouse facilities in Maryland and Illinois. Most of its products are sold through retail stores and are designed to be installed by consumers. Products that require professional installation such as smoke alarms for the hearing-impaired are marketed to electrical products distributors by subsidiary USI Electric. The company was founded in 1969.

	Annual Growth	03/15	03/16	03/17	03/18	03/19
Sales ($ mil.)	15.5%	9.9	13.7	14.1	14.9	17.6
Net income ($ mil.)	–	(3.7)	(2.1)	(2.1)	(2.3)	(1.3)
Market value ($ mil.)	(30.5%)	13.3	9.5	6.8	3.3	3.1
Employees	(3.5%)	15	15	14	14	13

UNIVERSAL STAINLESS & ALLOY PRODUCTS, INC.
NMS: USAP

600 Mayer Street
Bridgeville, PA 15017
Phone: 412 257-7600
Fax: –
Web: www.univstainless.com

CEO: Dennis M Oates
CFO: Ross C Wilkin
HR: –
FYE: December 31
Type: Public

At Universal Stainless & Alloy Products even if something isn't totally finished that's OK. The company makes both semi-finished and finished specialty steels including stainless tool and alloyed steels. Universal Stainless' stainless steel products are used in end products made by the automotive aerospace power generation oil and gas and heavy equipment manufacturing and medical industries; its high-temperature steel is produced mainly for the aerospace industry. Before the products get there however Universal Stainless sells them to service centers rerollers OEMs forgers and wire redrawers.

	Annual Growth	12/14	12/15	12/16	12/17	12/18
Sales ($ mil.)	5.6%	205.6	180.7	154.4	202.6	255.9
Net income ($ mil.)	27.4%	4.1	(20.7)	(5.3)	7.6	10.7
Market value ($ mil.)	(10.4%)	220.1	81.3	118.2	187.5	141.9
Employees	2.3%	714	634	645	703	781

UNIVERSAL TAX SYSTEMS INC.

6 Mathis Dr.
Rome GA 30164-2729
Phone: 706-625-7757
Fax: 706-755-7802
Web: www.taxwise.com

CEO: Jason Marx
CFO: Douglas Winterrose
HR: –
FYE: April 30
Type: Subsidiary

Universal Tax Systems wants to be a universal provider for tax-related software. Founded in 1986 Universal Tax Systems (which does business as TaxWise the name of its primary product) makes tax preparation and electronic filing software used by accountants enrolled tax agents bank product providers financial service providers and other professionals. The company's software includes modules for all federal and state tax returns for both businesses and individuals. In 2006 Universal Tax Systems was purchased by CCH a Wolters Kluwer business.

UNIVERSAL TECHNICAL INSTITUTE, INC.
NYS: UTI

16220 North Scottsdale Road, Suite 500
Scottsdale, AZ 85254
Phone: 623 445-9500
Fax: –
Web: www.uti.edu

CEO: Kimberly J. (Kim) McWaters
CFO: Bryce H. Peterson
HR: –
FYE: September 30
Type: Public

Want to make a living working on hot rods? Universal Technical Institute (UTI) offers automotive diesel collision repair motorcycle and marine technician training to around 12000 full-time students in the US. The company provides undergraduate degree and certificate programs at about a dozen campuses operating under the UTI Motorcycle Mechanics Institute and Marine Mechanics Institute (MMI) and NASCAR Technical Institute (NTI) banners. It also offers advanced manufacturer-branded training for sponsors such as BMW Daimler/Mercedes-Benz Harley-Davidson and Ford at dedicated training centers. Most undergraduate programs last between 12 and 24 months and tuition ranges from $21000 to $60000.

	Annual Growth	09/15	09/16	09/17	09/18	09/19
Sales ($ mil.)	(2.2%)	362.7	347.1	324.3	317.0	331.5
Net income ($ mil.)	–	(9.1)	(47.7)	(8.1)	(32.7)	(7.9)
Market value ($ mil.)	11.6%	90.0	45.6	88.9	68.2	139.4
Employees	(4.6%)	2,020	1,880	1,730	1,800	1,670

UNIVERSAL WEATHER AND AVIATION INC.

8787 Tallyho Rd.
Houston TX 77061-3420
Phone: 713-944-1622
Fax: 713-943-4674
Web: www.univ-wea.com

CEO: Ralph J Vasami
CFO: –
HR: –
FYE: June 30
Type: Private

You might not need a weatherman to know which way the wind blows but you might very well need the services of Universal Weather and Aviation before you taxi down a runway. Universal Weather and Aviation provides a slew of services including weather briefings international flight planning fueling programs and trip support to the general business aviation community and the airline industry. The company offers necessary planning ground handling support and incidentals for all manner of trips using private airplanes. Chairman C. Gregory Evans and his family own the company which was founded in 1959.

UNIVERSAL WILDE INC.

26 DARTMOUTH ST
WESTWOOD, MA 02090-2301
Phone: 781-251-2700
Fax: −
Web: www.universalwilde.com

CEO: William Fitzgerald
CFO: Stephen Payne
HR: −
FYE: December 31
Type: Private

Sometimes the world of direct-mail marketing can seem like a jungle but W.A. Wilde can serve as your guide. The company provides tools and services for direct marketing campaigns such as fulfillment mailing print management statement processing and telemarketing. Its offerings can be purchased as a package or a la carte. The company operate through three main units: Wilde Agency a full-service direct-marketing provider; Wilde Interactive which specializes in online campaigns; and L.W. Robbins Associates an agency catering to nonprofit organizations. Family-owned W.A. Wilde traces its roots back to 1868 when William A. Wilde began publishing books.

	Annual Growth	12/08	12/09	12/10	12/11	12/12
Sales ($ mil.)	6.6%	−	−	−	104.2	111.1
Net income ($ mil.)	−	−	−	−	(0.1)	1.3
Market value ($ mil.)	−	−	−	−	−	−
Employees	−	−	−	−	−	560

UNIVERSITY BANCORP INC. (MI)

NBB: UNIB

959 Maiden Lane
Ann Arbor, MI 48105
Phone: 734 741-5858
Fax: 734 741-5859
Web: www.university-bank.com

CEO: Stephen Lange Ranzini
CFO: −
HR: −
FYE: December 31
Type: Public

University Bancorp is the holding company for University Bank. From one branch in Ann Arbor (the home of The University of Michigan) the bank offers standard services such as deposit accounts and loans. It mainly originates residential mortgages with commercial mortgages business loans and consumer loans rounding out its lending activities. Shariah-compliant banking services (banking consistent with Islamic law) are offered through University Islamic Financial which operates within University Bank's office. University Bancorp also owns University Insurance and Investments Services and a majority of Midwest Loan Services which provides mortgage origination and subservicing to credit unions.

	Annual Growth	12/14	12/15	12/16	12/17	12/18
Assets ($ mil.)	19.5%	121.0	182.5	190.9	245.9	247.0
Net income ($ mil.)	31.1%	0.8	3.1	3.8	5.1	2.2
Market value ($ mil.)	7.5%	35.1	33.7	37.5	47.3	46.8
Employees	−	−	−	−	−	−

UNIVERSITY CALIFORNIA, MERCED

5200 N LAKE RD
MERCED, CA 953435001
Phone: 209-228-4400
Fax: −
Web: www.ucmerced.edu

CEO: Josh Becker
CFO: −
HR: −
FYE: June 30
Type: Private

The University of California at Merced is four-year educational institution in the Golden State. Opened in 2005 the tenth campus in the UC system was built on some 7000 San Joaquin Valley acres donated by the Virginia Smith Trust funded by a grant of nearly $12 million from The David and Lucile Packard Foundation. The school's inaugural class included about 1000 students. In 2009 UC Merced had some 3400 mostly undergraduate students (about 7% are graduate students). Primarily a research school UC Merced offers degree programs in such areas as engineering biology computer science history and environmental systems among others.

	Annual Growth	06/05	06/06	06/07	06/08	06/11
Sales ($ mil.)	159.9%	−	−	−	5.4	94.9
Net income ($ mil.)	32.7%	−	−	−	2.2	5.1
Market value ($ mil.)	−	−	−	−	−	−
Employees	−	−	−	−	−	66

UNIVERSITY COMMUNITY HOSPITAL, INC.

3100 E FLETCHER AVE
TAMPA, FL 336134613
Phone: 813-971-6000
Fax: −
Web: www.adventhealth.com

CEO: −
CFO: −
HR: −
FYE: December 31
Type: Private

University Community Health (doing business as Florida Hospital Tampa Bay Division) is a 1000-bed regional health care system with four locations spanning the Hillsborough Pinellas and Pasco counties of Florida. It oversees a network of eight hospitals in Florida's Tampa Bay area. Its four general hospitals — three located in Tampa and one in nearby Tarpon Springs — collectively house some 860 beds and provide emergency surgical and acute medical care as well as provide outpatient services. The system also includes a specialty heart hospital a women's hospital and a long-term acute care hospital. Florida Hospital Tampa Bay Division is part of the Adventist Health System.

	Annual Growth	12/13	12/14	12/15	12/16	12/17
Sales ($ mil.)	21.7%	−	381.8	460.5	483.2	688.2
Net income ($ mil.)	38.9%	−	24.7	38.9	39.8	66.1
Market value ($ mil.)	−	−	−	−	−	−
Employees	−	−	−	−	−	8,000

UNIVERSITY CORPORATION FOR ATMOSPHERIC RESEARCH

3090 CENTER GREEN DR
BOULDER, CO 803012252
Phone: 303-497-1000
Fax: −
Web: www.ucar.edu

CEO: −
CFO: Michael Thompson
HR: Delaine Orendorff
FYE: September 30
Type: Private

The University Corporation for Atmospheric Research (UCAR) is a not-for-profit corporation founded in 1960 to promote research in atmospheric and related environmental sciences. A consortium of more than 100 universities UCAR provides real-time weather data to universities educates weather forecasters and organizes international experiments through its Office of Programs. The organization also maintains radars aircraft and computer models for weather and climate through the National Center for Atmospheric Research (NCAR). UCAR is funded by sponsors such as the National Science Foundation the National Oceanic and Atmospheric Administration and NASA.

	Annual Growth	09/13	09/14	09/15	09/16	09/18
Sales ($ mil.)	1.2%	−	214.8	212.9	216.7	225.4
Net income ($ mil.)	14.6%	−	3.1	(0.0)	9.0	5.3
Market value ($ mil.)	−	−	−	−	−	−
Employees	−	−	−	−	−	1,565

UNIVERSITY FEDERAL CREDIT UNION

3505 Steck Ave.
Austin TX 78757
Phone: 512-467-8080
Fax: +44-207-749-7890
Web: www.asite.com

CEO: −
CFO: −
HR: Erin Brown
FYE: December 31
Type: Private - Not-for-Pr

Founded in 1936 by faculty and staff of the University of Texas at Austin University Federal Credit Union (UFCU) has about a dozen branches in Austin with other locations in the Texas communities of Galveston Cedar Park Lakeway and Round Rock. Serving UT students alumni and employees as well as other residents around Texas' capital city the member-owned institution provides such financial services as checking and savings accounts IRAs money market accounts home and consumer loans credit and debit cards investments financial planning brokerage and insurance. University Federal has more than 140000 members.

UNIVERSITY HEALTH CARE INC

5100 CMMERCE CROSSINGS DR
LOUISVILLE, KY 402292128
Phone: 502-585-7900
Fax: –
Web: www.passporthealthplan.com

CEO: –
CFO: –
HR: –
FYE: December 31
Type: Private

University Health Care wants to give patients a passport to good health. The company which does business as Passport Health Plan provides managed Medicaid insurance services to about 150000 members throughout 16 counties in Kentucky. Offerings include HMO Medicare Advantage and children's health plans. University Health Care was founded in 1997 by a group of affiliated providers including the University of Louisville Medical Center Jewish Hospital and St. Mary's HealthCare and the Louisville/Jefferson County Primary Care Association. The health plan has an administration partnership with the AmeriHealth Mercy organization a Medicaid managed care joint venture between AmeriHealth and Mercy Health System.

	Annual Growth	12/97	12/98	12/99	12/00	12/14
Sales ($ mil.)	3.0%	–	810.0	284.5	330.1	1,299.5
Net income ($ mil.)	–	–	0.0	5.8	3.8	115.0
Market value ($ mil.)	–	–	–	–	–	–
Employees	–	–	–	–	–	165

UNIVERSITY HEALTH SYSTEMS OF EASTERN CAROLINA, INC.

800 W H SMITH BLVD
GREENVILLE, NC 278343763
Phone: 252-847-6690
Fax: –
Web: www.ecu.edu

CEO: Michael Waldrum
CFO: –
HR: –
FYE: September 30
Type: Private

University Health Systems of Eastern Carolina is an integrated not-for-profit health system that serves residents of eastern North Carolina. Doing business as Vidant Health it operates nine hospitals including eight community hospitals and its tertiary care center Vidant Medical Center with 1400 beds and academic affiliation with the Brody School of Medicine at East Carolina University. Vidant Health also operates centers for surgery home health hospiceand wellness and engages in community health programs. Its physician group has more than 350 primary and specialty care providers who operate frommore than 50 locations.

	Annual Growth	09/12	09/13*	12/13*	09/14	09/15
Sales ($ mil.)	(0.6%)	–	1,601.1	400.1	1,597.2	1,581.1
Net income ($ mil.)	–	–	109.6	31.6	66.2	(6.1)
Market value ($ mil.)	–	–	–	–	–	–
Employees	–	–	–	–	–	15,000

*Fiscal year change

UNIVERSITY HOSPITALS HEALTH SYSTEM, INC.

3605 WARRENSVILLE CTR RD
SHAKER HEIGHTS, OH 441225203
Phone: 216-767-8900
Fax: –

CEO: Thomas S Zenty
CFO: Michael Szubski
HR: –
FYE: December 31
Type: Private

University Hospitals Health System (UHHS) is on a mission to teach research and administer good health throughout northeastern Ohio. Its flagship facility University Hospitals of Cleveland (UHC) which operates as University Hospitals Case Medical Center (UHCMC) is a more than 1000-bed tertiary care center serving Cleveland and other parts of northeastern Ohio. The teaching hospital which is affiliated with Case Western Reserve University is also home to Rainbow Babies & Children's Hospital Seidman Cancer Center and MacDonald Women's Hospital. the not-for-profit UHHS is also home to community hospitals outpatient health and surgery centers mental health facilities and senior care centers.

	Annual Growth	12/07	12/08	12/09	12/12	12/17
Sales ($ mil.)	(11.8%)	–	1,800.1	1,938.4	2,266.3	580.1
Net income ($ mil.)	–	–	(153.6)	110.5	54.3	33.3
Market value ($ mil.)	–	–	–	–	–	–
Employees	–	–	–	–	–	30,099

UNIVERSITY MEDICAL CENTER OF SOUTHERN NEVADA

1800 W CHARLESTON BLVD
LAS VEGAS, NV 891022329
Phone: 702-383-2000
Fax: –
Web: www.umcsn.com

CEO: Anson Van Houweling
CFO: –
HR: –
FYE: June 30
Type: Private

For those who want to learn while they heal the ill University Medical Center of Southern Nevada (UMC)— an affiliate of the University of Nevada School of Medicine might just be the place. The medical center includes a teaching hospital and a network of community and urgent care health centers. Among its specialized services are cancer treatment heart care pediatrics and rehabilitation. It also offers birthing wound and burn care neurological disorder Level II Pediatric Trauma Lions Burn Care Center and Level 1 trauma centers. UMC serves southern Nevada along with parts of Arizona California and Utah.

	Annual Growth	06/00	06/01	06/02	06/03	06/15
Sales ($ mil.)	–	–	–	0.0	412.4	530.8
Net income ($ mil.)	–	–	–	0.0	20.5	49.4
Market value ($ mil.)	–	–	–	–	–	–
Employees	–	–	–	–	–	3,700

UNIVERSITY OF ALASKA SYSTEM

910 YUKON DR
FAIRBANKS, AK 997750001
Phone: 907-450-8079
Fax: –
Web: www.alaska.edu

CEO: –
CFO: –
HR: –
FYE: June 30
Type: Private

The University of Alaska System (UA) has this education thing down cold. UA governs three major campuses: the University of Alaska Anchorage the University of Alaska Fairbanks and the University of Alaska Southeast which each anchor part of a regional system of 17 community colleges. UA enrolls about 35000 students offering some 500 degrees certificates and endorsements. Programs include science engineering education business journalism and communications aviation health occupations history English arts and humanities and others. An 11-member Board of Regents governs the system. Founded in 1917 as Alaska Agricultural College and School of Mines it was named University of Alaska in 1935.

	Annual Growth	06/14	06/15	06/16	06/17	06/18
Sales ($ mil.)	(2.6%)	–	–	–	387.4	377.2
Net income ($ mil.)	–	–	–	–	(8.7)	47.1
Market value ($ mil.)	–	–	–	–	–	–
Employees	–	–	–	–	–	6,629

UNIVERSITY OF ARIZONA

888 N EUCLID AVE RM 510
TUCSON, AZ 857194824
Phone: 520-626-6000
Fax: –
Web: www.arizona.edu

CEO: –
CFO: Lisa Rulney
HR: –
FYE: June 30
Type: Private

Where else to get a grand education than the Grand Canyon State? The University of Arizona is a public research university that offers more than 120 undergraduate degree programs about 130 graduate degree programs a handful of specialist degrees and three first professional degrees. Known as UA the educational institution serves more than 43000 students across all its degree programs. It boasts some 30 colleges and schools including an Outreach College that offers distance learning and continuing education classes. Established in 1885 nearly three decades before Arizona achieved statehood the school has a student-teacher ratio of about 12:1.

	Annual Growth	06/08	06/09	06/10	06/11	06/12
Sales ($ mil.)	6.2%	–	–	–	1,058.6	1,124.2
Net income ($ mil.)	(40.3%)	–	–	–	95.5	57.0
Market value ($ mil.)	–	–	–	–	–	–
Employees	–	–	–	–	–	15,615

UNIVERSITY OF ARKANSAS SYSTEM

2404 N UNIVERSITY AVE
LITTLE ROCK, AR 722073608
Phone: 501-686-2500
Fax: -
Web: www.uasys.edu

CEO: -
CFO: -
HR: -
FYE: June 30
Type: Private

Calling "Wooo Pig Sooie" at anyone in The University of Arkansas System (UA) is not an insult. The system encompasses more than a dozen schools institutes and campuses throughout the state including five universities a college of medicine a math and science high school and the Clinton School of Public Service started in 2004 by former president Bill Clinton and offering the only Master of Public Service degree in the country. UA which has an enrollment of more than 60000 hails the razorback or hog as its mascot. "Wooo Pig Sooie" or "hog calling" is the school's cheer at sporting events. Its student-teacher ratio is 19:1; it has about 17000 employees.

	Annual Growth	06/14	06/15	06/16	06/17	06/18
Sales ($ mil.)	6.8%	-	1,970.5	2,172.3	2,297.9	2,402.2
Net income ($ mil.)	65.6%	-	30.7	65.0	88.7	139.2
Market value ($ mil.)	-	-	-	-	-	-
Employees	-	-	-	-	-	14,025

UNIVERSITY OF CALIFORNIA, DAVIS

1 SHIELDS AVE
DAVIS, CA 956168500
Phone: 530-752-1011
Fax: -
Web: www.ucdavis.edu

CEO: Ann Madden Rice
CFO: Dave Lawlor
HR: -
FYE: June 30
Type: Private

If you want to grow grapes and make wine in Napa Valley or Sonoma County you might want to swing by the University of California Davis (UC Davis) first. The school one of 10 University of California campuses offers a wide variety of agricultural programs; its Viticulture and Enology department provides professional education for aspiring winemakers. Located between Sacramento and San Francisco UC Davis also has colleges and professional schools in biology engineering education law business medicine and veterinary medicine and it is recognized for its research programs. UC Davis enrolls more than 37400 including more than 6700 graduate students and it has a student-faculty ratio of 19:1.

	Annual Growth	06/06	06/07	06/08*	12/08*	06/11
Sales ($ mil.)	474.6%	-	-	14.2	0.5	2,697.4
Net income ($ mil.)	644.1%	-	-	0.9	0.0	360.1
Market value ($ mil.)	-	-	-	-	-	-
Employees	-	-	-	-	-	17,741

*Fiscal year change

UNIVERSITY OF CINCINNATI

2600 CLIFTON AVE
CINCINNATI, OH 452202872
Phone: 513-556-6000
Fax: -
Web: www.uc.edu

CEO: -
CFO: Robert F. (Bob) Ambach
HR: Linda Bledsoe
FYE: June 30
Type: Private

The University of Cincinnati (UC) is a research institution offering undergraduate graduate and professional education from its seven campuses in Ohio. The university enrolls more than 44000 students and has more than a dozen colleges. Academic offerings include business law medicine applied science pharmacy and music. The institution offers about 70 doctoral programs and roughly 240 other degree programs. UC was founded in 1819 and became a state university in 1977; the school has an endowment of close to $1 billion. Notable alumni include former US president William Howard Taft and architect Michael Graves.

	Annual Growth	06/04	06/05	06/06	06/07	06/11
Sales ($ mil.)	16.6%	-	-	557.1	594.3	1,198.3
Net income ($ mil.)	19.2%	-	-	20.3	112.1	48.9
Market value ($ mil.)	-	-	-	-	-	-
Employees	-	-	-	-	-	14,600

UNIVERSITY OF COLORADO FOUNDATION

1800 N GRANT ST STE 725
DENVER, CO 802031114
Phone: 303-813-7935
Fax: -
Web: www.giving.cu.edu

CEO: Jack Finlaw
CFO: -
HR: -
FYE: June 30
Type: Private

Operating independently from the University of Colorado the University of Colorado Foundation (CU Foundation) engages in not-for-profit fundraising on behalf of the University. It partners with the University to raise manage and invest private support for the University's benefit. The foundation manages more than $125 million annually from nearly 50000 donors; the funds it raises are used to support scholarships research athletics building construction and faculty and staff at the University. The CU Foundation also manages the University's Creating Futures fundraising campaign which aims to raise $1.5 billion.

	Annual Growth	06/12	06/13	06/14	06/15	06/16
Sales ($ mil.)	(12.5%)	-	236.4	317.0	204.0	158.5
Net income ($ mil.)	(34.1%)	-	95.3	186.2	61.9	27.2
Market value ($ mil.)	-	-	-	-	-	-
Employees	-	-	-	-	-	180

UNIVERSITY OF COLORADO HOSPITAL AUTHORITY

4200 E 9TH AVE
DENVER, CO 802203706
Phone: 720-848-0000
Fax: -

CEO: John P. Harney
CFO: Barbara Carveth
HR: -
FYE: June 30
Type: Private

University of Colorado Hospital Authority doing business as UCHealth operates the University of Colorado Hospital (UCH) in Aurora Colorado. The facility is a teaching institution for — you guessed it — the University of Colorado. UCH is a 400-bed community hospital that includes a number of specialty care facilities including centers specializing in oncology respiratory care and endocrinology. The facility also conducts medical training and research programs in partnership with the University of Colorado's Denver School of Medicine. In addition UCHealth operates 10 primary care clinics in the Denver metropolitan area.

	Annual Growth	06/03	06/04	06/05	06/09	06/10
Sales ($ mil.)	11.4%	-	-	464.2	1.0	796.0
Net income ($ mil.)	169.7%	-	-	1.1	0.0	151.7
Market value ($ mil.)	-	-	-	-	-	-
Employees	-	-	-	-	-	4,200

UNIVERSITY OF DELAWARE

220 HULLIHEN HALL
NEWARK, DE 197160099
Phone: 302-831-2107
Fax: -
Web: www.udel.edu

CEO: -
CFO: -
HR: Wayne Guthrie
FYE: June 30
Type: Private

Delaware brings up images of many things our first president that famous river and now the private University of Delaware (UD). The school's flagship campus in Newark has an enrollment of roughly 17000 undergraduate and close to 4000 graduate students. The school also has four auxiliary campuses around the state. UD offers almost 150 undergraduate degrees about 120 master's programs and more than 50 doctoral programs as well as associate's and dual graduate programs through seven academic schools. Among its instructors are well-known authors scientists artists and Nobel Laureates.

	Annual Growth	06/14	06/15	06/16	06/17	06/18
Sales ($ mil.)	3.2%	-	-	-	992.0	1,023.6
Net income ($ mil.)	(12.6%)	-	-	-	159.9	139.7
Market value ($ mil.)	-	-	-	-	-	-
Employees	-	-	-	-	-	3,600

UNIVERSITY OF DETROIT MERCY

4001 W MCNICHOLS RD
DETROIT, MI 482213038
Phone: 313-993-6000
Fax: –
Web: www.udmercy.edu

CEO: –
CFO: –
HR: –
FYE: June 30
Type: Private

Perhaps students taking a really tough test wish for mercy at University of Detroit Mercy (UDM). Michigan's largest and most comprehensive Catholic university is sponsored by the Society of Jesus (Jesuits) and the Religious Sisters of Mercy. UDM has an enrollment of about 5100 students at its three campuses (two located in residential northwest Detroit and one in downtown Detroit). UDM has a student-faculty ratio of 13:1. It offers 100 academic programs in fields such as architecture and psychology nursing teacher education and engineering through seven schools and colleges.

	Annual Growth	06/14	06/15	06/16	06/17	06/18
Sales ($ mil.)	(0.1%)	–	159.0	152.0	152.0	158.7
Net income ($ mil.)	(33.6%)	–	10.8	(2.2)	8.8	3.2
Market value ($ mil.)	–	–	–	–	–	–
Employees	–	–	–	–	–	950

UNIVERSITY OF EVANSVILLE

1800 LINCOLN AVE
EVANSVILLE, IN 477221000
Phone: 812-488-2000
Fax: –
Web: www.evansville.edu

CEO: –
CFO: –
HR: –
FYE: May 31
Type: Private

The University of Evansville affiliated with the United Methodist Church offers more than 80 academic areas of study for undergraduate and graduate students. The university consists of three colleges (College of Arts and Sciences College of Education and Health Sciences College of Engineering and Computer Science) and one school (Schroeder School of Business). It has an annual enrollment of more than 2600 students. Recognized for its study-abroad program the university also has a campus in the UK (Harlaxton College) in addition to its main campus in Indiana's third-largest city. The University of Evansville was founded in 1854 as Moores Hill Male and Female Collegiate Institute.

	Annual Growth	05/11	05/12	05/13	05/14	05/15
Sales ($ mil.)	0.7%	–	71.8	108.1	77.5	73.2
Net income ($ mil.)	–	–	(9.9)	49.0	12.7	(3.3)
Market value ($ mil.)	–	–	–	–	–	–
Employees	–	–	–	–	–	500

UNIVERSITY OF FLORIDA

300 SW 13TH ST
GAINESVILLE, FL 326110001
Phone: 352-392-3261
Fax: –
Web: www.uflib.ufl.edu

CEO: –
CFO: Michael V. (Mike) McKee
HR: –
FYE: June 30
Type: Private

Founded in 1853 the University of Florida (UF) is the state's oldest university and one of the largest in the country with nearly 50000 students and some 5100 faculty and library staff members. UF is a major land-grant research university encompassing 2000 acres in Gainesville Florida. The university's 16 colleges offer more than 100 undergraduate majors and about 200 graduate programs including education law medicine psychology and philosophy. It is also a member of the Association of American Universities a confederation of the top research universities in North America. A founding member of the Southeastern Conference UF's athletic teams (the Florida Gators) are typically ranked nationally.

	Annual Growth	06/08	06/09	06/12	06/15	06/17
Sales ($ mil.)	(8.5%)	–	3,846.6	3,939.6	1,735.3	1,897.7
Net income ($ mil.)	–	–	(343.6)	64.3	262.0	62.3
Market value ($ mil.)	–	–	–	–	–	–
Employees	–	–	–	–	–	5,106

UNIVERSITY OF GEORGIA

424 E BROAD ST
ATHENS, GA 306021535
Phone: 706-542-2786
Fax: –
Web: www.uga.edu

CEO: –
CFO: –
HR: –
FYE: June 30
Type: Private

Located in the quintessential college town of Athens The University of Georgia (UGA) offers a wide range of degree programs to nearly 35000 students. Forest resources veterinary medicine and law are a few of the school's academic programs. UGA which also runs 170-plus study-abroad and exchange programs administers the prestigious Peabody Awards which honors media achievements and boasts one of the nation's largest map collections. Famous alumni include former US Senator Phil Gramm TV journalist Deborah Norville and former PBS president Pat Mitchell. The University of Georgia was chartered by the State of Georgia in 1785 and graduated its first class in 1804.

	Annual Growth	06/10	06/11	06/12	06/17	06/18
Sales ($ mil.)	5.4%	–	691.5	776.6	975.8	997.9
Net income ($ mil.)	–	–	(12.3)	72.0	142.5	111.7
Market value ($ mil.)	–	–	–	–	–	–
Employees	–	–	–	–	–	17,800

UNIVERSITY OF HAWAII SYSTEMS

2444 DOLE ST STE 105
HONOLULU, HI 968222388
Phone: 808-956-8111
Fax: –

CEO: David McClain
CFO: Kalbert Young
HR: –
FYE: June 30
Type: Private

With a reach that extends across half a dozen islands the University of Hawai'i System consists of three university campuses seven community college campuses and several job training and research centers. The public higher education system has an enrollment of more than 60000 students about 85% of which are Hawaii residents. It offers more than 600 different doctorate graduate undergraduate and associate degrees as well as professional certificates in more than 200 fields of study. The University of Hawai'i was founded in 1907 as the College of Agriculture and Mechanic Arts in Honolulu incidentally while Hawaii was still a US territory.

	Annual Growth	06/05	06/06	06/16	06/17	06/18
Sales ($ mil.)	–	–	0.0	799.5	771.5	772.1
Net income ($ mil.)	–	–	0.0	(117.0)	33.1	51.9
Market value ($ mil.)	–	–	–	–	–	–
Employees	–	–	–	–	–	12,000

UNIVERSITY OF HOUSTON SYSTEM

4302 UNIVERSITY DR
HOUSTON, TX 772042011
Phone: 713-743-0945
Fax: –
Web: www.uhsystem.edu

CEO: –
CFO: –
HR: –
FYE: August 31
Type: Private

The University of Houston System can't do much about the heat or humidity but it can provide higher education in Houston. The university system serves more than 65000 students at four Houston-area universities. Flagship institution the University of Houston was founded in 1927 and offers about 300 bachelor's master's and doctoral degree programs; it also conducts a number of research programs. Also under the system's umbrella are the University of Houston-Clear Lake the University of Houston-Downtown the University of Houston-Victoria as well as a handful of learning centers in the area. The system was established in 1977.

	Annual Growth	08/11	08/12	08/13	08/14	08/15
Sales ($ mil.)	(4.2%)	–	688.2	1.3	742.5	605.5
Net income ($ mil.)	(31.9%)	–	132.7	81.1	46.4	41.9
Market value ($ mil.)	–	–	–	–	–	–
Employees	–	–	–	–	–	12,608

UNIVERSITY OF KENTUCKY HOSPITAL AUXILIARY INC.

800 ROSE ST
LEXINGTON, KY 40536-0001
Phone: 859-323-5000
Fax: –
Web: www.universityofkentuckyhospital.com

CEO: –
CFO: –
HR: –
FYE: June 30
Type: Private

For the times when there's a physical reason to be carried "back to my old Kentucky home" being lugged to University of Kentucky Chandler Hospital (UK Chandler Hospital) might be a better option. The 500-bed academic hospital is operated by the University of Kentucky Auxiliary. It is located within the University of Kentucky Medical Center complex which includes the specialized medical colleges of the University of Kentucky and their affiliated clinical treatment facilities (organized under the UK HealthCare umbrella). UK Chandler Hospital's services include oncology pediatrics cardiology orthopedics and women's health and it operates eastern Kentucky's only Level I trauma and Level III neonatal ICU units.

	Annual Growth	06/08	06/09	06/10	06/11	06/12
Sales ($ mil.)	9.0%	–	704.9	785.9	797.5	912.8
Net income ($ mil.)	–	–	(47.7)	39.4	41.3	13.1
Market value ($ mil.)	–	–	–	–	–	–
Employees	–	–	–	–	–	2,879

UNIVERSITY OF LA VERNE

1950 3RD ST
LA VERNE, CA 917504401
Phone: 909-593-3511
Fax: –
Web: www.laverne.edu

CEO: Devorah Liberman
CFO: –
HR: –
FYE: June 30
Type: Private

University of La Verne (ULV) offers more than 50 undergraduate degree programs through colleges of arts and sciences business and public management education and organizational leadership and law. It also boasts about 30 graduate and four doctoral programs in education psychology and counseling business leadership public administration health care and gerontology. In addition to the central campus in La Verne California the university operates more than half a dozen regional campuses in California. It has an annual enrollment of more than 8500 undergraduate graduate law continuing education and online students. ULV has a student/faculty ratio of 14:1. The university was founded in 1891 by members of the Church of the Brethren.

	Annual Growth	06/11	06/12	06/13	06/15	06/16
Sales ($ mil.)	7.6%	–	126.0	139.6	200.1	169.1
Net income ($ mil.)	13.6%	–	11.2	21.0	17.2	18.7
Market value ($ mil.)	–	–	–	–	–	–
Employees	–	–	–	–	–	2,200

UNIVERSITY OF LOUISVILLE

2301 S 3RD ST
LOUISVILLE, KY 402922001
Phone: 502-852-5555
Fax: –

CEO: –
CFO: –
HR: –
FYE: June 30
Type: Private

Living up to its mandate to be a leading metropolitan research university the University of Louisville (U of L) has hit a few out of the park. The U of L completed the first self-contained artificial heart implant and the first successful hand transplant at its University of Louisville Hospital. The health care focused university offers associate baccalaureate master's professional and doctorate degrees in some 170 fields of study including medicine dentistry nursing and public health as well as arts and sciences education business law music social work and engineering. It has more than 22000 students enrolled in about a dozen colleges and schools on three campuses.

	Annual Growth	06/09	06/10	06/11	06/12	06/18
Sales ($ mil.)	2.8%	–	–	591.6	559.1	717.3
Net income ($ mil.)	(28.5%)	–	–	32.2	(37.0)	3.1
Market value ($ mil.)	–	–	–	–	–	–
Employees	–	–	–	–	–	6,275

UNIVERSITY OF LYNCHBURG

1501 LAKESIDE DR
LYNCHBURG, VA 245013113
Phone: 434-544-8100
Fax: –
Web: www.lynchburg.edu

CEO: –
CFO: –
HR: –
FYE: June 30
Type: Private

In Lynchburg Tennessee they make whiskey. In Lynchburg Virginia they make graduates. Lynchburg College is an independent residential college with more than 170 full-time faculty members and about 2300 undergraduate and graduate students across some 40 majors. It consists of six schools: Business and Economics Communication and the Arts Education and Human Development Health Sciences and Human Performance Humanities and Social Sciences and Sciences. Tuition is about $14000 per semester; however virtually all students receive financial aid. The college was founded in 1903 by Dr. Josephus Hopwood a Christian Church (Disciples of Christ) minister and his wife Sarah.

	Annual Growth	06/14	06/15	06/16	06/17	06/18
Sales ($ mil.)	3.6%	–	63.5	67.5	66.8	70.7
Net income ($ mil.)	120.0%	–	0.5	(2.6)	7.9	5.5
Market value ($ mil.)	–	–	–	–	–	–
Employees	–	–	–	–	–	1,077

UNIVERSITY OF MAINE SYSTEM

5703 ALUMNI HALL STE 101
ORONO, ME 044695703
Phone: 207-973-3300
Fax: –
Web: www.umit.maine.edu

CEO: –
CFO: –
HR: –
FYE: June 30
Type: Private

University of Maine System is composed of seven public universities throughout Maine serving some 40000 students. It also operates eight regional outreach centers as well as distance education programs. The University of Maine System offers nearly 600 majors minors and concentrations; its flagship campus in Orono (UMaine) offers nearly 90 bachelor's degree programs more than 60 master's degree programs and about two dozen doctoral programs. UMaine was established in 1862 as the Maine College of Agriculture and Mechanic Arts; it adopted its current name in 1897. The University of Maine System was created in 1968 by the state legislature.

	Annual Growth	06/11	06/12	06/13	06/17	06/18
Sales ($ mil.)	(0.7%)	–	476.5	460.2	448.2	458.0
Net income ($ mil.)	(13.6%)	–	38.0	27.9	20.7	15.8
Market value ($ mil.)	–	–	–	–	–	–
Employees	–	–	–	–	–	3,000

UNIVERSITY OF MARYLAND MEDICAL SYSTEM CORPORATION

250 W PRATT ST
BALTIMORE, MD 212012423
Phone: 410-328-8667
Fax: –
Web: www.umms.org

CEO: Jeffrey A. Rivest
CFO: Henry J. Franey
HR: –
FYE: June 30
Type: Private

The 12 academic specialty and community hospitals of the University of Maryland Medical System (UMMS) dot the map of the state's eastern half on both sides of Chesapeake Bay. UMMS one of the largest employers in the Baltimore area has more than 2300 acute care beds and attends to such specialties as trauma care coma emergence kidney transplants orthopedic rehabilitation stroke intervention and pediatric care. University of Maryland Medical Center the system's teaching hub is one of the oldest academic hospitals in the US. In addition to its hospitals UMMS also includes community clinics to address mental health rehabilitation and primary care. The system was established in 1984.

	Annual Growth	06/11	06/12	06/14	06/15	06/16
Sales ($ mil.)	(14.2%)	–	2,504.7	1,824.3	1,413.1	1,358.4
Net income ($ mil.)	–	–	(17.8)	17.8	13.1	(29.2)
Market value ($ mil.)	–	–	–	–	–	–
Employees	–	–	–	–	–	12,000

UNIVERSITY OF MASSACHUSETTS

1 BEACON ST
BOSTON, MA 021083107
Phone: 617-287-7000
Fax: –
Web: www.massachusetts.edu

CEO: John Cunningham
CFO: –
HR: –
FYE: June 30
Type: Private

The University of Massachusetts (UMass) has been expanding across the commonwealth since its founding in 1863. About 72000 students are enrolled in UMass programs that range from art to journalism to engineering. The university's flagship campus in Amherst (with a student-teacher ratio of 18:1) offers its 22000 undergrad students degrees in more than 90 areas and its 6400 graduate students master's degrees in nearly 70 areas and doctorates in 50 areas. Its University of Massachusetts Medical School in Worcester has an affiliated teaching hospital and students studying medicine nursing and biomedical sciences. Other UMass campuses can be found in Boston Dartmouth and Lowell.

	Annual Growth	06/11	06/12	06/16	06/17	06/18
Sales ($ mil.)	3.1%	–	2,055.5	2,403.5	2,443.0	2,468.8
Net income ($ mil.)	(18.0%)	–	255.4	129.3	325.2	77.6
Market value ($ mil.)	–	–	–	–	–	–
Employees	–	–	–	–	–	13,196

UNIVERSITY OF MISSISSIPPI

113 FALKNER
UNIVERSITY, MS 386779704
Phone: 662-915-6538
Fax: –
Web: www.olemiss.edu

CEO: –
CFO: –
HR: –
FYE: December 31
Type: Private

They call her "Ole Miss" and she really is old: The University of Mississippi was chartered in 1844 as the first public university in the state and opened in 1848. Starting with 80 students the school's enrollment has grown to more than 23000 with most students attending the main Oxford campus. Ole Miss has additional campuses in Southaven (Desoto County) and Tupelo and it operates the University of Mississippi Medical Center in Jackson. The school is home to more than 30 research centers that specialize in business engineering law and other disciplines. Its academic institutes include the Croft Institute for International Studies and the William Winter Institute for Racial Reconciliation.

	Annual Growth	06/14	06/15	06/16	06/17*	12/17
Sales ($ mil.)	6.6%	–	401.0	436.6	681.5	455.9
Net income ($ mil.)	(8.7%)	–	101.7	90.2	15.8	84.9
Market value ($ mil.)	–	–	–	–	–	–
Employees	–	–	–	–	–	8,700

*Fiscal year change

UNIVERSITY OF MISSOURI SYSTEM

321 UNIVERSITY HALL
COLUMBIA, MO 652113020
Phone: 573-882-2712
Fax: –
Web: www.murr.missouri.edu

CEO: –
CFO: Brian D. Burnett
HR: –
FYE: June 30
Type: Private

Education isn't just for show in the Show Me State. The University of Missouri (UM) founded in 1839 educates about 76000 students at four campuses and through a statewide extension program; about a quarter of students are in graduate or professional programs. The university's campuses include flagship UM-Columbia (home to roughly 33000 students some 20 schools and colleges and the University of Missouri Health Sciences Center) UM-Kansas City UM-St. Louis and the Missouri University of Science and Technology. Nicknamed "Mizzou" the University of Missouri System has close to 6000 faculty members and a student-teacher enrollment of about 11:1.

	Annual Growth	06/11	06/12	06/13	06/16	06/18
Sales ($ mil.)	3.5%	–	–	2,404.7	2,702.4	2,851.2
Net income ($ mil.)	3.8%	–	–	222.0	108.6	267.6
Market value ($ mil.)	–	–	–	–	–	–
Employees	–	–	–	–	–	30,282

UNIVERSITY OF MONTANA

32 CAMPUS DR MAIN HALL
MISSOULA, MT 598120001
Phone: 406-243-0211
Fax: –
Web: www.umt.edu

CEO: –
CFO: –
HR: –
FYE: June 30
Type: Private

Sometimes referred to as the Harvard of the West The University of Montana's motto is Lux et Veritas (Light and Truth). The Big Sky Country certainly provides plenty of light for the university which is a leading producer of Rhodes Scholars. The University of Montana (UM) is a member of the Montana University System and offers associate's bachelor's master's first-professional and doctoral degrees as well as technical certificates. About 21000 undergraduate and graduate students enroll at UM's four campuses. Founded in 1893 UM also gets high marks for the physical beauty of its campus and nearby wilderness areas.

	Annual Growth	06/12	06/13	06/16	06/17	06/18
Sales ($ mil.)	1.9%	–	259.8	272.9	284.1	285.9
Net income ($ mil.)	–	–	(8.5)	28.4	(156.3)	20.1
Market value ($ mil.)	–	–	–	–	–	–
Employees	–	–	–	–	–	2,450

UNIVERSITY OF NEW HAVEN, INCORPORATED

300 BOSTON POST RD
WEST HAVEN, CT 065161999
Phone: 203-932-7000
Fax: –
Web: www.newhaven.edu

CEO: –
CFO: –
HR: –
FYE: June 30
Type: Private

The University of New Haven (UNH) offers more than 80 undergraduate and 30 graduate degree programs from its five colleges. Fields of study include arts and sciences business criminal justice and forensic science and engineering. The private university has about 6500 students and 500 faculty members with a student-to-teacher ratio of 16:1. The University of New Haven was founded in 1920 as the New Haven YMCA Junior College. It held classes in space rented from Yale University for nearly 40 years before its own building was constructed.

	Annual Growth	06/07	06/08	06/09	06/10	06/15
Sales ($ mil.)	11.1%	–	123.9	147.7	172.5	258.4
Net income ($ mil.)	16.5%	–	6.6	8.2	6.4	19.3
Market value ($ mil.)	–	–	–	–	–	–
Employees	–	–	–	–	–	696

UNIVERSITY OF NEW MEXICO

1800 ROMA BLVD NE
ALBUQUERQUE, NM 871310001
Phone: 505-277-0732
Fax: –
Web: www.unm.edu

CEO: –
CFO: –
HR: –
FYE: June 30
Type: Private

With more than 36630 students The University of New Mexico (UNM) based in Albuquerque is most renowned for its schools of medicine law and education. Students also attend one of the school's four branches located around the northern part of the state at Gallup Los Alamos Rio Rancho Taos and Valencia. Through its schools and colleges the university offers 96 bachelor's degrees 71 master's degrees 37 doctorate degrees as well as professional practice programs in law medicine and pharmacy. Its annual budget tops $2 billion. UNM employs more than 22000 people across the state.

	Annual Growth	06/13	06/14	06/16	06/17	06/18
Sales ($ mil.)	8.3%	–	1,325.2	1,893.2	1,807.5	1,826.2
Net income ($ mil.)	–	–	55.7	6.1	11.1	(181.9)
Market value ($ mil.)	–	–	–	–	–	–
Employees	–	–	–	–	–	18,362

UNIVERSITY OF NORTH CAROLINA AT CHAPEL HILL

104 AIRPORT DR
CHAPEL HILL, NC 275995023
Phone: 919-962-1370
Fax: –
Web: www.unc.edu

CEO: –
CFO: –
HR: –
FYE: June 30
Type: Private

The University of North Carolina at Chapel Hill (UNC-Chapel Hill) has the education market cornered. One of the three original points making up North Carolina's Research Triangle (along with Duke University and North Carolina State University) Carolina is the flagship campus of the University of North Carolina (UNC) system. The institution is consistently among the top-ranked research schools in the US. It enrolls some 29000 students and offers more than 250 undergraduate graduate and professional programs including law and medicine. It has 3200 full-time faculty members.

	Annual Growth	06/04	06/05	06/08	06/11	06/17
Sales ($ mil.)	66.3%	–	4.0	281.7	1,704.9	1,773.6
Net income ($ mil.)	36.4%	–	2.3	149.7	391.4	95.3
Market value ($ mil.)	–	–	–	–	–	–
Employees	–	–	–	–	–	12,204

UNIVERSITY OF NORTH CAROLINA AT GREENSBORO

1000 SPRING GARDEN ST
GREENSBORO, NC 274125068
Phone: 336-334-5000
Fax: –

CEO: –
CFO: –
HR: –
FYE: June 30
Type: Private

The University of North Carolina at Greensboro (UNCG) has an enrollment of about 19000 students including approximately 14000 undergraduates. The university offers 75 undergraduate degree programs (in 100 subject areas) about 75 master's degrees and 30 doctoral programs through nearly ten colleges and professional schools. It also has a Division of Continual Learning that caters to non-traditional students. Originally a women's college UNCG was established in 1891; it became coeducational in 1964 when it also became a part of the University of North Carolina system and adopted its current name.

	Annual Growth	06/09	06/10	06/14	06/16	06/17
Sales ($ mil.)	4.8%	–	127.2	18.5	10.1	176.8
Net income ($ mil.)	1.9%	–	42.2	9.3	(1.5)	48.1
Market value ($ mil.)	–	–	–	–	–	–
Employees	–	–	–	–	–	2,400

UNIVERSITY OF NORTH CAROLINA HOSPITALS

101 MANNING DR BLDG 2
CHAPEL HILL, NC 275144423
Phone: 919-966-5111
Fax: –

CEO: –
CFO: Chris Ellington
HR: –
FYE: June 30
Type: Private

University of North Carolina Hospitals (UNCH) is at the heart of the UNC Health Care System (UNC HCS). The medical center provides acute care to the Tar Heel State through North Carolina Memorial Hospital North Carolina Children's Hospital North Carolina Neurosciences Hospital and North Carolina Women's Hospital. Combined the facilities have more than 800 beds. Specialties include cancer treatment at the North Carolina Cancer Hospital organ transplantation cardiac care orthopedics wound management and rehabilitation. Not-for-profit UNC HCS is owned by the state of North Carolina and is affiliated with the UNC-Chapel Hill School of Medicine.

	Annual Growth	06/06	06/07	06/15	06/16	06/18
Sales ($ mil.)	8.3%	–	787.8	1,385.6	1,551.3	1,892.4
Net income ($ mil.)	(6.4%)	–	182.9	110.9	87.6	88.6
Market value ($ mil.)	–	–	–	–	–	–
Employees	–	–	–	–	–	6,000

UNIVERSITY OF NORTH DAKOTA

264 CENTENNIAL DR
GRAND FORKS, ND 582026059
Phone: 701-777-4321
Fax: –
Web: www.und.edu

CEO: –
CFO: –
HR: –
FYE: June 30
Type: Private

Way up in the Upper Midwest is the University of North Dakota (UND) the largest and oldest institution of higher learning in the state with an enrollment of approximately 15000 students. It offers undergraduate and graduate programs in close to 225 fields through nine colleges and schools (aerospace sciences arts and sciences business and public administration education and human development engineering and mines law medical and health sciences nursing and a graduate school). The university also has nearly 20 doctoral programs as well as certificate degree programs distance degree programs and a continuing education division. UND was founded in 1883 six years before North Dakota achieved statehood.

	Annual Growth	06/10	06/11	06/16	06/17	06/18
Sales ($ mil.)	2.3%	–	278.2	311.4	316.6	325.7
Net income ($ mil.)	(10.4%)	–	27.3	57.3	19.9	12.6
Market value ($ mil.)	–	–	–	–	–	–
Employees	–	–	–	–	–	2,756

UNIVERSITY OF NORTHERN IOWA

1227 W 27TH ST
CEDAR FALLS, IA 506140012
Phone: 319-242-7325
Fax: –
Web: www.uni.edu

CEO: –
CFO: –
HR: –
FYE: June 30
Type: Private

University of Northern Iowa (UNI) offers more than 90 majors for students in a range of fields. It provides undergraduate graduate and doctoral degree programs to more than 12000 students (about 90% of which are Iowa residents). The school is comprised of four undergraduate colleges (business administration education humanities and liberal arts and social and behavioral sciences) and one graduate college. Students are also engaged in research programs. UNI was founded as Iowa State Normal School in 1876; it gained university status in 1967 and has oversight by the state board of regents. Notable alumni include US Senator Charles Grassley and NFL quarterback Kurt Warner.

	Annual Growth	06/14	06/15	06/16	06/17	06/18
Sales ($ mil.)	0.6%	–	152.8	153.7	157.5	155.7
Net income ($ mil.)	69.4%	–	1.6	24.1	25.6	7.9
Market value ($ mil.)	–	–	–	–	–	–
Employees	–	–	–	–	–	3,071

UNIVERSITY OF OKLAHOMA

2800 VENTURE DR
NORMAN, OK 730698216
Phone: 405-325-2000
Fax: –
Web: www.universitysilkscreen.com

CEO: –
CFO: –
HR: –
FYE: June 30
Type: Private

The University of Oklahoma has a primary goal: to better the Sooner. Founded in 1890 and known as OU the university has 20 colleges that offer some 160 bachelor's degrees 170 master's degrees and about 80 doctoral degrees through three campuses in Norman Oklahoma City and Tulsa. The Norman campus is where the main academic programs reside while OU's seven health-related professional colleges are based at the Health Sciences Center in Oklahoma City. OU's enrollment has reached about 31000 students who are instructed by 1500 full-time faculty members. The university adopted the Sooner nickname in 1908 deriving the moniker from homesteaders who arrived too soon in Oklahoma's 1889 Land Run.

	Annual Growth	06/08	06/09	06/10	06/11	06/12
Sales ($ mil.)	6.7%	–	–	–	466.0	497.4
Net income ($ mil.)	3.4%	–	–	–	35.1	36.3
Market value ($ mil.)	–	–	–	–	–	–
Employees	–	–	–	–	–	6,543

UNIVERSITY OF OREGON

1585 E 13TH AVE
EUGENE, OR 974031657
Phone: 541-346-1000
Fax: -
Web: www.uoregon.edu

CEO: -
CFO: -
HR: -
FYE: June 30
Type: Private

This school's got all its ducks in a row. As one of the largest schools in the state the University of Oregon (UO) has an enrollment of more than 23600 students and some 1500 faculty members. It offers its students eight different schools and colleges plus a graduate college with fields of study range from the arts and journalism to business and law. Part of the Oregon University System UO also offers development services an honors program research institutes and continuing education courses. The school's athletic department organizes more than 15 sports activities including lacrosse and football; the teams are called The Ducks.

	Annual Growth	06/14	06/15	06/16	06/17	06/18
Sales ($ mil.)	3.4%	-	-	692.7	713.7	740.1
Net income ($ mil.)	-	-	-	(48.3)	31.9	(8.2)
Market value ($ mil.)	-	-	-	-	-	-
Employees	-	-	-	-	-	7,971

UNIVERSITY OF PITTSBURGH

4200 5TH AVE
PITTSBURGH, PA 152600001
Phone: 412-624-4141
Fax: -
Web: www.medschool.pitt.edu

CEO: Mark Nordenberg
CFO: -
HR: -
FYE: June 30
Type: Private

The University of Pittsburgh (Pitt for short) operates its flagship campus in the Oakland neighborhood of Pittsburgh. More than 35000 graduate and undergraduate students attend the main campus as well as four regional campuses. Pitt Panthers pursue degrees in about 400 disciplines including arts and sciences business law medicine and engineering. The school has a student-teacher ratio of 14:1. Pitt is also affiliated with the UPMC health system which operates about 20 hospitals numerous clinics and an insurance company. Pitt was founded in 1787 making it one of the oldest universities in the US.

	Annual Growth	06/14	06/15	06/16	06/17	06/18
Sales ($ mil.)	3.4%	-	2,060.9	2,106.8	2,169.7	2,276.0
Net income ($ mil.)	141.5%	-	27.1	(212.8)	487.4	381.7
Market value ($ mil.)	-	-	-	-	-	-
Employees	-	-	-	-	-	9,607

UNIVERSITY OF PUGET SOUND

1500 N WARNER ST
TACOMA, WA 984160005
Phone: 253-879-3100
Fax: -
Web: www.pugetsound.edu

CEO: -
CFO: -
HR: -
FYE: June 30
Type: Private

The University of Puget Sound is a private liberal arts college located in the Pacific Northwest with an enrollment of some 2600 students and a student-faculty ratio of 12:1. It boasts more than 50 traditional and interdisciplinary programs and about 1200 courses. Based south of Seattle in Tacoma Washington the school offers a wide range of undergraduate degrees as well as graduate degrees in education occupational therapy and physical therapy. Students come from nearly 50 states and 15 countries. Founded in 1888 by the Methodist Church The University of Puget Sound divested its affiliation with the church in 1980. Notable alumni include Verio founder Justin Jaschke and Alaska governor Sean Parnell.

	Annual Growth	06/13	06/14	06/15	06/16	06/17
Sales ($ mil.)	(16.3%)	-	215.6	172.9	122.9	126.2
Net income ($ mil.)	(10.0%)	-	60.6	13.7	(13.6)	44.2
Market value ($ mil.)	-	-	-	-	-	-
Employees	-	-	-	-	-	1,700

UNIVERSITY OF REDLANDS

1200 E COLTON AVE
REDLANDS, CA 923743720
Phone: 909-793-2121
Fax: -
Web: www.redlands.edu

CEO: -
CFO: -
HR: -
FYE: June 30
Type: Private

Focused on liberal arts and sciences private University of Redlands consists of a College of Arts and Sciences and a School of Education both located in Southern California's City of Redlands. Its School of Business is located on campus and in regional centers throughout Southern California. The institution offers more than 40 undergraduate majors about a dozen master's degree programs a doctorate in leadership for educational justice and professional credential and certificate programs. With an enrollment of about 2400 students University of Redlands was founded in 1907 on land donated by banker and Baptist layman Karl C. Wells; it maintains an informal relationship with the American Baptist church.

	Annual Growth	06/07	06/08	06/10	06/17	06/18
Sales ($ mil.)	(0.6%)	-	136.3	141.2	127.9	128.2
Net income ($ mil.)	42.7%	-	0.3	(4.8)	16.3	10.2
Market value ($ mil.)	-	-	-	-	-	-
Employees	-	-	-	-	-	1,017

UNIVERSITY OF RHODE ISLAND

75 LOWER COLLEGE RD
KINGSTON, RI 028811974
Phone: 401-874-1000
Fax: -
Web: www.uri.edu

CEO: -
CFO: -
HR: -
FYE: June 30
Type: Private

The University of Rhode Island (URI) offers more than 80 undergraduate majors specializing in nursing psychology communication studies kinesiology and human development. It also offers master's doctoral and professional degrees from its nine colleges at four campuses across the state. URI's main campus is located in Kingston the W. Alton Jones Campus is in West Greenwich its Graduate School of Oceanography is located on Narragansett Bay and Providence is home to the university's Alan Shawn Feinstein College of Continuing Education. URI which has an enrollment of more than 16500 students was chartered as the state's agricultural school in 1888.

	Annual Growth	06/14	06/15	06/16	06/17	06/18
Sales ($ mil.)	3.0%	-	403.1	413.7	423.4	440.0
Net income ($ mil.)	94.3%	-	6.2	16.0	33.1	45.3
Market value ($ mil.)	-	-	-	-	-	-
Employees	-	-	-	-	-	2,600

UNIVERSITY OF RICHMOND

28 WESTHAMPTON WAY
RICHMOND, VA 231730002
Phone: 804-289-8133
Fax: -
Web: www.richmond.edu

CEO: -
CFO: -
HR: Carl K Sorensen
FYE: June 30
Type: Private

Suffering from arachnophobia? You may want to steer clear of the more than 4300 Spiders who are enrolled at the University of Richmond (UR). UR consists of five schools: Jepson School of Leadership Studies Richmond School of Law Robins School of Business School of Arts and Sciences and School of Continuing Studies. The university offers some 60 undergraduate majors as well as graduate and master's programs in business accounting and law. UR also offers some 75 study-abroad programs in which more than half of its students participate. Founded in 1830 by Virginia Baptists as a seminary for men the school became Richmond College in 1840.

	Annual Growth	06/09	06/10	06/13	06/16	06/18
Sales ($ mil.)	4.9%	-	210.3	253.7	283.7	308.9
Net income ($ mil.)	8.2%	-	83.5	185.2	(190.6)	157.2
Market value ($ mil.)	-	-	-	-	-	-
Employees	-	-	-	-	-	1,400

UNIVERSITY OF SAN DIEGO

5998 ALCALA PARK FRNT
SAN DIEGO, CA 921102492
Phone: 619-260-4600
Fax: –
Web: www.sandiego.edu

CEO: –
CFO: Terry Kalfayan
HR: Amber J Koch
FYE: June 30
Type: Private

The University of San Diego (USD) is private college located close to southern California's beaches and the Mexican border. The coeducational Roman Catholic university has an enrollment of more than 7800 students USD offers more than 70 bachelor's master's and doctoral degrees in areas such as arts and sciences business administration education engineering law and nursing. It has a faculty of 440 full time staff members. The university also home to the Joan B. Kroc School of Peace Studies established in 2003 by the wife of McDonald's founder Ray Kroc.

	Annual Growth	06/12	06/13	06/15	06/17	06/18
Sales ($ mil.)	3.8%	–	303.3	453.4	350.0	365.2
Net income ($ mil.)	2.7%	–	90.5	56.7	92.6	103.2
Market value ($ mil.)	–	–	–	–	–	–
Employees	–	–	–	–	–	1,600

UNIVERSITY OF SAN FRANCISCO INC

2130 FULTON ST
SAN FRANCISCO, CA 941171050
Phone: 415-422-5555
Fax: –
Web: www.usfca.edu

CEO: Stephen A Privett
CFO: –
HR: –
FYE: May 31
Type: Private

Known for their devotion to education as well as their investment portfolio the Jesuits are evident to all who visit the University of San Francisco (USF). One of 28 Jesuit Catholic colleges and universities in the US the main USF campus sits on 55 acres near Golden Gate Park in San Francisco. The school which was formed in 1855 as St. Ignatius Academy enrolls more than 10000 students. It operates five schools and colleges including the schools of business and management education law and nursing and the colleges of arts and sciences. In addition to its main campus the university operates five satellite sites in Northern and Southern California.

	Annual Growth	05/10	05/11	05/12	05/13	05/17
Sales ($ mil.)	1.6%	–	380.8	390.4	375.7	417.8
Net income ($ mil.)	(1.5%)	–	55.3	36.5	71.3	50.4
Market value ($ mil.)	–	–	–	–	–	–
Employees	–	–	–	–	–	1,200

UNIVERSITY OF SCRANTON

800 LINDEN ST
SCRANTON, PA 185104501
Phone: 888-727-2686
Fax: –
Web: www.scranton.edu

CEO: –
CFO: –
HR: –
FYE: May 31
Type: Private

The University of Scranton is a Catholic and Jesuit liberal arts university with a student population of more than 5420 including more than 600 graduate students. Its schools and colleges include the College of Arts & Sciences Panuska College of Professional Studies and Kania School of Management. It offers programs in areas such as theology music technology athletics nursing and continuing education and has some 300 faculty members. The school offers 66 undergraduate and 29 graduate programs. The University of Scranton which is overseen by the Society of Jesus (the Jesuits) was founded in 1888 as Saint Thomas College.

	Annual Growth	05/08	05/09	05/12	05/13	05/16
Sales ($ mil.)	7.6%	–	138.7	212.9	158.7	231.5
Net income ($ mil.)	–	–	(1.9)	16.3	33.3	8.2
Market value ($ mil.)	–	–	–	–	–	–
Employees	–	–	–	–	–	1,050

UNIVERSITY OF SOUTH ALABAMA

307 N UNIVERSITY BLVD # 380
MOBILE, AL 366083074
Phone: 251-460-6101
Fax: –
Web: www.southalabama.edu

CEO: –
CFO: –
HR: –
FYE: September 30
Type: Private

When you go by the moniker USA and the campus beauty queen wins the Miss USA title year after year (the Pi Kappa Phi Miss USA pageant that is) you're standing on hallowed ground. In this case it's the ground of the University of South Alabama situated on the upper Gulf Coast. The school's crown jewel is its College of Medicine and other facilities including USA Medical Center USA Knollwood Hospital and USA Children's and Women's Hospital. USA also offers degrees in Health Arts and Sciences Business Education Engineering Nursing Computer and Information Sciences Continuing Education and Special Programs and the Graduate School. More than 14880 students call the USA home.

	Annual Growth	09/14	09/15	09/16	09/17	09/18
Sales ($ mil.)	5.5%	–	556.5	624.9	662.5	653.1
Net income ($ mil.)	–	–	9.2	25.9	47.8	(0.7)
Market value ($ mil.)	–	–	–	–	–	–
Employees	–	–	–	–	–	5,403

UNIVERSITY OF SOUTH CAROLINA

1600 HAMPTON ST 414
COLUMBIA, SC 292083403
Phone: 803-777-2001
Fax: –
Web: www.mailbox.sc.edu

CEO: –
CFO: –
HR: –
FYE: June 30
Type: Private

The Fighting Gamecocks lead the way at the University of South Carolina (USC). The university which comprises 14 colleges and schools offers more than 350 courses of study. Areas of study concentrate on medicine law business education science and math liberal arts and other fields. Nearly 2200 full-time faculty members teach a student body of some 46250 across eight campuses from South Carolina's Aiken to Union. USC's main campus is located on the site of its 1801 founding in the state's capital city of Columbia. Tuition runs about $10500 a year for residents and $27500 for out-of-state students. USC has an endowment of some $514 million.

	Annual Growth	06/05	06/06	06/07	06/13	06/17
Sales ($ mil.)	–	–	0.0	672.7	801.2	1,008.5
Net income ($ mil.)	–	–	0.0	(221.5)	10.8	23.6
Market value ($ mil.)	–	–	–	–	–	–
Employees	–	–	–	–	–	5,100

UNIVERSITY OF SOUTH FLORIDA

4202 E FOWLER AVE
TAMPA, FL 336208000
Phone: 813-974-2011
Fax: –
Web: www.usf.edu

CEO: –
CFO: Nick Trivunovich
HR: Martinez-kidde Edith
FYE: June 30
Type: Private

The University of South Florida (USF) is bullishly educational. The school has nearly 50000 students at three campuses in Tampa St. Petersburg and Sarasota/Manatee. It offers some 180 undergraduate graduate specialty and doctoral degree programs through more than a dozen colleges including Arts and Sciences Business Education Engineering Marine Science Pharmacy and Public Health. USF also offers graduate certificates continuing education courses and teacher certifications and it is a major research institution among US universities. USF was founded in 1956; its mascot is the bull.

	Annual Growth	06/05	06/06	06/07	06/09	06/18
Sales ($ mil.)	–	–	0.0	533.6	892.0	872.0
Net income ($ mil.)	–	–	0.0	148.3	42.1	36.0
Market value ($ mil.)	–	–	–	–	–	–
Employees	–	–	–	–	–	16,165

UNIVERSITY OF SOUTHERN CALIFORNIA

3720 S FLOWER ST FL 3
LOS ANGELES, CA 900894304
Phone: 213-740-7762
Fax: -
Web: www.usc.edu

CEO: -
CFO: -
HR: -
FYE: June 30
Type: Private

A Trojan horse filled with students is more than welcome at the University of Southern California (USC). Founded in 1880 the private university (with a Trojan mascot) grew up with the city of Los Angeles and is now one of the largest private employers in the city. California's oldest research university USC is recognized for distinguished programs in fields including business engineering film law medicine public administration science and theater. The university has two campuses in Los Angeles and additional centers and programs elsewhere in California Washington DC and overseas. USC has a total of some 41000 undergraduate and graduate students and almost 3790 full-time faculty members.

	Annual Growth	06/10	06/11	06/12	06/13	06/18
Sales ($ mil.)	7.3%	-	-	3,233.7	3,861.5	4,936.8
Net income ($ mil.)	38.8%	-	-	68.3	587.7	489.3
Market value ($ mil.)	-	-	-	-	-	-
Employees	-	-	-	-	-	22,700

UNIVERSITY OF ST. THOMAS

2115 SUMMIT AVE
SAINT PAUL, MN 551051096
Phone: 651-962-5000
Fax: -
Web: www.stthomas.edu

CEO: -
CFO: -
HR: Michelle Thom
FYE: June 30
Type: Private

Far from any Bahamian beaches or Caribbean hot spots sits The University of St. Thomas (UST). The school is a Catholic university with campuses in Minneapolis and St. Paul Minnesota. It offers about 90 undergraduate and 60 graduate programs in seven academic divisions: education and philosophy arts and sciences business engineering divinity law and social work. The school has an enrollment of about 11000 undergraduate and graduate students with a student-to-teacher ratio of 14:1. UST along with military prep school St. Thomas Academy grew out of St. Thomas Aquinas Seminary which was founded in 1885 by Archbishop John Ireland.

	Annual Growth	06/14	06/15	06/16	06/17	06/18
Sales ($ mil.)	2.0%	-	260.6	270.1	275.3	276.5
Net income ($ mil.)	139.2%	-	2.8	(30.2)	72.2	37.7
Market value ($ mil.)	-	-	-	-	-	-
Employees	-	-	-	-	-	1,900

UNIVERSITY OF TENNESSEE

1331 CIRCLE PARK DR
KNOXVILLE, TN 379163801
Phone: 865-974-2303
Fax: -
Web: www.utk.edu

CEO: -
CFO: -
HR: -
FYE: June 30
Type: Private

Whether you want to learn the art of aviation or get ready for a career in public service the University of Tennessee System (UT) is here to help. The 200-year-old school provides undergraduate graduate and professional academic programs to about 50000 students; programs include business engineering law pharmacy medicine and veterinary medicine. It has a student-teacher ratio of about 16:1. Campuses include the flagship Knoxville location as well as the Health Science Center at Memphis the Space Institute at Tullahoma the statewide Institute for Public Service and the Institute of Agriculture. Other UT System campuses are located in Chattanooga and Martin. UT was founded in 1794 as Blount College.

	Annual Growth	12/06	12/07	12/08*	06/11	06/12
Sales ($ mil.)	440.1%	-	-	1.3	1,034.3	1,092.9
Net income ($ mil.)	-	-	-	0.0	296.5	60.5
Market value ($ mil.)	-	-	-	-	-	-
Employees	-	-	-	-	-	12,000

*Fiscal year change

UNIVERSITY OF TEXAS AT AUSTIN

110 INNER CAMPUS DR G3400
AUSTIN, TX 787123400
Phone: 512-471-3434
Fax: -
Web: www.utexas.edu

CEO: -
CFO: -
HR: -
FYE: August 31
Type: Private

They say everything's bigger in Texas and The University of Texas at Austin (UT Austin) takes them at their word. With about 51000 students it is the flagship institution of the UT System's nine universities and six health institutions. UT Austin consistently ranks on the list of the country's largest student bodies and offers more than 100 undergraduate and 170 graduate degree programs. In addition to its 350-acre downtown Austin academic campus UT Austin maintains extensive research locations including the J.J. Pickle Research campus (also in Austin) the McDonald Observatory in West Texas and the Marine Science Institute on the Texas coast. The university was founded in 1883.

	Annual Growth	08/04	08/05	08/08	08/12	08/17
Sales ($ mil.)	-	-	0.0	5.7	1,491.4	1,669.6
Net income ($ mil.)	-	-	0.0	2.2	132.7	751.6
Market value ($ mil.)	-	-	-	-	-	-
Employees	-	-	-	-	-	21,513

UNIVERSITY OF TEXAS AT DALLAS

800 W CAMPBELL RD
RICHARDSON, TX 750803021
Phone: 972-883-2295
Fax: -
Web: www.utdallas.edu

CEO: -
CFO: -
HR: -
FYE: October 31
Type: Private

Big D has a big university presence with the University of Texas at Dallas (UT Dallas). As part of The University of Texas System the school offers more than 140 undergraduate and graduate programs to a student body of about 28000. It has a student-to-teacher ratio of about 23:1. Perhaps best known now for its computer science and business administration programs UT Dallas also operates schools of arts and humanities graphic design political science criminal justice technology engineering public affairs and natural sciences and mathematics. The university also has extensive research programs with labs and institutes present in about 50 areas of study. UT Dallas' endowment totals some $320 million.

	Annual Growth	08/06	08/07	08/08	08/09*	10/10
Sales ($ mil.)	14.4%	-	-	158.5	181.5	207.3
Net income ($ mil.)	42.8%	-	-	59.7	(23.0)	121.9
Market value ($ mil.)	-	-	-	-	-	-
Employees	-	-	-	-	-	1,500

*Fiscal year change

UNIVERSITY OF TEXAS AT EL PASO

500 W UNIVERSITY AVE
EL PASO, TX 799688900
Phone: 915-747-5000
Fax: -

CEO: -
CFO: -
HR: -
FYE: August 31
Type: Private

UTEP's Miners dig the importance of higher education. The University of Texas at El Paso (UTEP) was originally founded as a mining school but now offers about 150 bachelor's and master's degrees and some 20 doctoral degrees through six academic colleges. The university's six colleges offer education in business engineering education health sciences liberal arts and science. The school draws much of its population — a majority of which is Mexican-American — from the US-Mexico border. UTEP enrolls some 23000 students annually and is part of the Austin-based University of Texas System. It was formed in 1914 as the Texas State School of Mines and Metallurgy.

	Annual Growth	08/03	08/04	08/05	08/08	08/11
Sales ($ mil.)	9.3%	-	-	122.9	187.1	209.8
Net income ($ mil.)	-	-	-	0.0	(0.4)	50.5
Market value ($ mil.)	-	-	-	-	-	-
Employees	-	-	-	-	-	3,700

UNIVERSITY OF THE PACIFIC

3601 PACIFIC AVE
STOCKTON, CA 952110197
Phone: 209-946-2401
Fax: –
Web: www.pacific.edu

CEO: –
CFO: –
HR: –
FYE: June 30
Type: Private

Situated next to the largest body of water on earth the University of the Pacific holds a sizable body of knowledge. The school offers more than 80 undergraduate majors and about 20 graduate programs in such fields as art language biology business computer science engineering history and pharmacy. It offers undergraduate graduate and professional degree programs in nine colleges and enrolls about 7000 students at its main campus in Stockton California the McGeorge School of Law in Sacramento and the Arthur A. Dugoni School of Dentistry in San Francisco. California's first chartered institution of higher education University of the Pacific was founded in 1851.

	Annual Growth	06/10	06/11	06/12	06/13	06/15
Sales ($ mil.)	7.2%	–	317.1	330.7	447.2	418.2
Net income ($ mil.)	(1.2%)	–	43.9	20.8	147.1	41.8
Market value ($ mil.)	–	–	–	–	–	–
Employees	–	–	–	–	–	1,500

UNIVERSITY OF UTAH HEALTH HOSPITALS AND CLINICS

50 N MEDICAL DR
SALT LAKE CITY, UT 841320001
Phone: 801-581-2121
Fax: –

CEO: David Entwistle
CFO: Gordon Crabtree
HR: –
FYE: June 30
Type: Private

Whether you've broken your leg on the ski slopes or need the latest treatment for a neurological condition the University of Utah Hospitals & Clinics is here for you. Part of the University of Utah Health Care system the medical services provider operates an acute and critical care hospital that has some 550 beds as well as a network of community clinics that provide primary health care pharmacy and eye care among other services. The University Hospital provides care in areas including surgery emergency care cardiology radiology and organ transplant services; it also houses centers for medical education training and research.

	Annual Growth	06/03	06/04	06/05	06/06	06/14
Sales ($ mil.)	126.0%	–	–	0.8	0.8	1,282.5
Net income ($ mil.)	–	–	–	(0.5)	(0.5)	21.0
Market value ($ mil.)	–	–	–	–	–	–
Employees	–	–	–	–	–	4,200

UNIVERSITY OF VERMONT & STATE AGRICULTURAL COLLEGE

85 S PROSPECT ST WTRMN
BURLINGTON, VT 054050001
Phone: 802-656-3131
Fax: –
Web: www.uvm.edu

CEO: –
CFO: –
HR: –
FYE: June 30
Type: Private

The University of Vermont (UVM) boasts scenic views and comprehensive secondary education. the university offers more than 100 majors through its seven undergraduate colleges as well 46 master's programs and 21 doctoral programs at its Graduate College and College of Medicine. UVM has an enrollment of more than 12820 students including undergraduate graduate medical and continuing education program participants. The university also conducts research programs in areas including translational science cancer care and transportation. UVM a public land grant university has more than 1360 faculty members.

	Annual Growth	06/11	06/12	06/13	06/14	06/17
Sales ($ mil.)	3.1%	–	526.0	557.5	545.3	613.6
Net income ($ mil.)	–	–	(30.1)	19.1	27.6	34.6
Market value ($ mil.)	–	–	–	–	–	–
Employees	–	–	–	–	–	3,710

UNIVERSITY OF WASHINGTON INC

4311 11TH AVE NE STE 600
SEATTLE, WA 981056369
Phone: 206-543-2100
Fax: –

CEO: –
CFO: –
HR: –
FYE: June 30
Type: Private

The University of Washington (UW) is Husky indeed with an annual enrollment of more than 54000 students. Founded in 1861 as the Territorial University of Washington UW (pronounced "U-dub" by those on campus) has smaller branches in Tacoma and Bothell in addition to its main campus in downtown Seattle. The university whose mascot is a Husky offers more than 600 undergraduate graduate and professional degree programs through 16 colleges and schools. It also operates four hospitals: University of Washington Medical Center Harborview Medical Center Northwest Hospital and Valley Medical Center.

	Annual Growth	06/14	06/15	06/16	06/17	06/18
Sales ($ mil.)	5.7%	–	–	–	4,893.5	5,171.8
Net income ($ mil.)	35.1%	–	–	–	363.1	490.5
Market value ($ mil.)	–	–	–	–	–	–
Employees	–	–	–	–	–	27,228

UNIVERSITY OF WEST GEORGIA

1601 MAPLE ST
CARROLLTON, GA 301180001
Phone: 678-839-4780
Fax: –
Web: www.usg.edu

CEO: –
CFO: –
HR: –
FYE: June 30
Type: Private

Go West young men and women and join the approximately 11600 students who attend University of West Georgia (UWG). UWG students major in some 110 areas through the university's schools and colleges (Arts and Sciences Business Education and the Graduate School). UWG also allows select high school students to earn both college and high school credits simultaneously. UWG also offers a full program of distance education via the Internet through its eCore program. The school was founded in 1906 as the Fourth District Agricultural and Mechanical School in Carrollton Georgia. The school became State University of West Georgia in 1996; it dropped "State" from its name in 2005.

	Annual Growth	06/09	06/10	06/11	06/12	06/16
Sales ($ mil.)	8.3%	–	–	82.4	95.0	122.6
Net income ($ mil.)	(14.4%)	–	–	9.6	4.4	4.4
Market value ($ mil.)	–	–	–	–	–	–
Employees	–	–	–	–	–	993

UNIVERSITY OF WISCONSIN FOUNDATION

1848 UNIVERSITY AVE
MADISON, WI 537264090
Phone: 608-263-4545
Fax: –
Web: www.uwhealth.org

CEO: Michael M Knetter
CFO: –
HR: –
FYE: June 30
Type: Private

Because even Badgers need help the University of Wisconsin Foundation raises funds receives gifts and manages assets for The University of Wisconsin-Madison and other donor-designated units of The University of Wisconsin System. (Bucky Badger is the school's mascot.) The foundation supports special programs and projects including professorships fellowships scholarships research efforts and building projects. The not-for-profit organization has received more than $2.4 billion in donations since it was founded in 1945.

	Annual Growth	12/09	12/10	12/12	12/13*	06/16
Sales ($ mil.)	(11.0%)	–	444.1	434.2	595.6	221.3
Net income ($ mil.)	(26.4%)	–	206.8	183.6	323.6	33.0
Market value ($ mil.)	–	–	–	–	–	–
Employees	–	–	–	–	–	275

*Fiscal year change

UNIVERSITY OF WISCONSIN HOSPITAL AND CLINICS AUTHORITY

600 HIGHLAND AVE
MADISON, WI 537920001
Phone: 608-263-6400
Fax: –
Web: www.uwhealthkids.org

CEO: Alan Kaplan
CFO: Gary Eiler
HR: –
FYE: June 30
Type: Private

The University of Wisconsin Hospital and Clinics Authority (UW Hospital and Clinics) has the last word when it comes to the health of Badger Staters. The centerpiece of the authority is the UW Hospital and Clinics medical campus which is home to a 650-bed hospital the American Family Children's Hospital a cancer clinic and a small inpatient psychiatric ward as well as Level I adult and pediatric trauma centers. The hospital administers cancer treatment heart and stroke care organ transplantation and a host of other medical services. The UW Hospital and Clinics organization also operates area health clinics that provide general and specialty outpatient care and emergency room services.

	Annual Growth	06/04	06/05	06/06	06/07	06/16
Sales ($ mil.)	4.0%	–	1,856.5	746.5	799.0	2,860.9
Net income ($ mil.)	–	–	0.0	62.1	60.2	46.5
Market value ($ mil.)	–	–	–	–	–	–
Employees	–	–	–	–	–	17,156

UNIVERSITY OF WISCONSIN MEDICAL FOUNDATION, INC.

7974 UW HEALTH CT
MIDDLETON, WI 535625531
Phone: 608-821-4223
Fax: –
Web: www.uwmf.wisc.edu

CEO: Alan Kaplan
CFO: –
HR: –
FYE: June 30
Type: Private

UW Medical Foundation provides administrative services to faculty physicians at the University of Wisconsin School of Medicine and Public Health. The foundation a not-for-profit entity is a physician practice organization that works in cooperation with the UW Hospital and Clinics and other medical offices and clinics throughout the Badger State. The foundation coordinates clinical sites and provides technical and professional staffing services as well as administrative support for legal marketing information technology and logistics functions.

	Annual Growth	06/12	06/13	06/14	06/15	06/18
Sales ($ mil.)	–	–	0.0	724.2	766.1	784.9
Net income ($ mil.)	12.8%	–	22.3	33.2	26.2	40.7
Market value ($ mil.)	–	–	–	–	–	–
Employees	–	–	–	–	–	3,200

UNIVERSITY OF WISCONSIN SYSTEM

1220 LINDEN DR
MADISON, WI 537061525
Phone: 608-262-2321
Fax: –
Web: www.wisconsin.edu

CEO: –
CFO: –
HR: –
FYE: June 30
Type: Private

Unfortunately there is no School of Cheese in the University of Wisconsin System (UW System) but across its vast operations there are 13 four-year universities 13 two-year UW Colleges campuses and a statewide extension program that has offices in every Wisconsin county. The UW System is one of the largest public university systems in the US with more than 180000 students and 40000 faculty and staff members. Its top school is UW at Madison which offers more than 400 undergraduate majors master's degree programs and doctoral programs to some 43000 students. The system's other major campus is UW at Milwaukee with about 28000 students. The UW System has a student-teacher ratio of 17:1.

	Annual Growth	06/14	06/15	06/16	06/17	06/18
Sales ($ mil.)	(2.4%)	–	–	–	3,702.8	3,614.0
Net income ($ mil.)	–	–	–	–	(20.4)	203.5
Market value ($ mil.)	–	–	–	–	–	–
Employees	–	–	–	–	–	3,190

UNIVERSITY OF WYOMING

1000 E UNIVERSITY AVE # 3434
LARAMIE, WY 820712001
Phone: 307-766-5766
Fax: –
Web: www.uwyo.edu

CEO: –
CFO: –
HR: –
FYE: June 30
Type: Private

For folks who live in Wyoming the University of Wyoming (UW) is it — the only place offering baccalaureate and graduate degrees as well as research and outreach services that stretch across the state. The main campus is in Laramie but the school also has a campus in Casper (offering coordinated education programs with the Casper College) plus regional outreach education centers stationed throughout the state. Founded in 1887 UW has grown to serve more than 13000 students with about 200 programs of study through seven academic colleges as well as numerous schools and institutes. The university has a student-to-faculty ratio of 14:1.

	Annual Growth	06/07	06/08	06/09	06/10	06/13
Sales ($ mil.)	3.6%	–	–	195.5	195.6	225.3
Net income ($ mil.)	22.0%	–	–	52.9	31.7	117.0
Market value ($ mil.)	–	–	–	–	–	–
Employees	–	–	–	–	–	7,000

UNIVERSITY SYSTEM OF MARYLAND

3300 METZEROTT RD
ADELPHI, MD 207831600
Phone: 301-445-2740
Fax: –
Web: www.umuc.edu

CEO: –
CFO: –
HR: –
FYE: June 30
Type: Private

The University System of Maryland (USM) operates one of the largest public university systems in the country serving more than 175000 students through a dozen institutions including Towson University University of Maryland University College and Bowie State University. Its flagship university in College Park boasts about 40000 students and some of the country's top-ranked education programs. The University of Maryland is also known for its successful athletic teams (named the Terrapins) which compete in the Big Ten Conference. The system also operates the University of Maryland Center for Environmental Science. Maryland established its university system in 1988.

	Annual Growth	06/14	06/15	06/16	06/17	06/18
Sales ($ mil.)	3.1%	–	–	3,386.7	3,515.7	3,601.9
Net income ($ mil.)	(19.1%)	–	–	516.7	355.6	338.4
Market value ($ mil.)	–	–	–	–	–	–
Employees	–	–	–	–	–	28,000

UNIVERSITY SYSTEM OF NEW HAMPSHIRE

5 CHENELL DR STE 301
CONCORD, NH 033018522
Phone: 603-862-1800
Fax: –
Web: www.keene.edu

CEO: –
CFO: –
HR: –
FYE: June 30
Type: Private

The University of New Hampshire (UNH) is a liberal arts college that serves about 12600 undergraduate and more than 2200 graduate students. The institution offers more than 100 majors and academic programs of study at nine colleges and schools. The student-faculty ratio is 20:1. UNH is the flagship institution of the University System of New Hampshire. In 2007 the university graduated its first international class in Seoul under a program run by its Whittemore School of Business and Economics. Founded in 1866 as the New Hampshire College of Agriculture and the Mechanic Arts UNH is a designated land-grant sea-grant and space-grant chartered school.

	Annual Growth	06/12	06/13	06/14	06/15	06/16
Sales ($ mil.)	(4.7%)	–	800.0	0.0	681.0	692.1
Net income ($ mil.)	–	–	111.9	129.0	32.0	(9.2)
Market value ($ mil.)	–	–	–	–	–	–
Employees	–	–	–	–	–	16,000

UNIVEST FINANCIAL CORP
NMS: UVSP

14 North Main Street
Souderton, PA 18964
Phone: 215-721-2400
Fax: –
Web: www.univest.net

CEO: Jeffrey M Schweitzer
CFO: Michael S Keim
HR: –
FYE: December 31
Type: Public

Univest Corporation of Pennsylvania will keep your money close to its vest. The holding company owns $3 billion-asset Univest Bank and Trust which serves the southeastern part of the Keystone State and the broader Mid-Atlantic region online and though 30 branches and provides standard retail and commercial banking services such as checking and savings accounts CDs IRAs and credit cards. Subsidiary Univest Capital provides small-ticket commercial financing while Univest Insurance offers personal and commercial coverage. Univest Investments which boasts some $3 billion in assets under management offers brokerage and investment advisory services.

	Annual Growth	12/14	12/15	12/16	12/17	12/18
Assets ($ mil.)	22.2%	2,235.3	2,879.5	4,230.5	4,554.9	4,984.3
Net income ($ mil.)	22.8%	22.2	27.3	19.5	44.1	50.5
Market value ($ mil.)	1.6%	592.4	610.6	904.5	821.0	631.4
Employees	7.2%	638	717	840	855	841

UNIVISION COMMUNICATIONS INC.

605 3rd Ave. 12th Fl.
New York NY 10158
Phone: 212-455-5200
Fax: 212-867-6710
Web: corporate.univision.com

CEO: Vincent Sadusky
CFO: Peter H Lori
HR: –
FYE: December 31
Type: Private

This company's singular vision focuses on Hispanic audiences. Univision Communications is the leading Spanish-language broadcaster in the US with a portfolio of television and radio operations. It runs the top-rated Univision network carried by more than 1400 broadcast and cable affiliates as well as sister networks TeleFutura and Galavision. The company also owns and operates about 60 local broadcast TV stations. Its Univision Radio division boasts about 70 stations. In addition to traditional broadcasting the company distributes content online. Founded in 1961 as Spanish International Network Univision is controlled by a group of private investment firms led by TPG Capital and Thomas H. Lee Partners.

UNMC PHYSICIANS

988101 NEBRASKA MED CTR
OMAHA, NE 681980001
Phone: 402-559-9700
Fax: –
Web: www.nebraskamed.com

CEO: –
CFO: Troy Wilhelm
HR: –
FYE: June 30
Type: Private

If you're in Nebraska and your doctor suddenly tells you to "Go Big Red!" — don't be shocked he's probably just a member of the not-for-profit UNMC Physicians (formerly University Medical Associates). Many of the more than 500 physicians in the UNMC group practice were trained and now teach at the University of Nebraska Medical Center. Additionally UNMC partners with The Nebraska Medical Center and the Olson Center for Women's Health to share best practices and resources. The physicians who also operate 10 family health clinics in the area provide services in about 50 specialties such as obstetrics cancer care family medicine cardiology and pediatrics.

	Annual Growth	06/11	06/12	06/13	06/14	06/16
Sales ($ mil.)	(2.2%)	–	218.7	225.5	245.5	199.7
Net income ($ mil.)	–	–	(1.6)	7.7	11.7	(109.6)
Market value ($ mil.)	–	–	–	–	–	–
Employees	–	–	–	–	–	1,200

UNS ENERGY CORPORATION
NYSE: UNS

88 E. Broadway Blvd.
Tucson AZ 85701
Phone: 520-571-4000
Fax: 262-638-4481
Web: www.twindisc.com

CEO: David G Hutchens
CFO: Kevin P Larson
HR: –
FYE: December 31
Type: Public

UNS Energy (formerly UniSource Energy) gets most of its revenues from its energy utilities. Its Tucson Electric Power (TEP) unit generates and distributes electricity to about 404000 customers in southeastern Arizona. The unit has about 2245 MW of generating capacity. Subsidiary UniSource Energy Services (UES) provides electricity (UNS Electric Services) to 91000 customers and natural gas (UNS Gas) to 148000 customers in 30 communities in northern and southern areas of the state. UNS Energy's Millennium Energy Holdings unit invests in unregulated energy and emerging technology companies. In 2012 to make its brand more distinct UniSource Energy changed its name to UNS Energy.

UNUM GROUP
NYS: UNM

1 Fountain Square
Chattanooga, TN 37402
Phone: 423-294-1011
Fax: –
Web: www.unum.com

CEO: Richard P. (Rick) McKenney
CFO: John F. (Jack) McGarry
HR: Kristen Prophater
FYE: December 31
Type: Public

Through injury or illness Unum works to keep employees employed. A top disability insurer in the US and the UK it offers short-term and long-term disability insurance supplemental health coverage and life and accidental death and dismemberment insurance to individuals and groups. Its Colonial Life unit offers expanded cancer critical illness vision products and dental insurance. Additional subsidiaries include Unum Life Insurance Company of America Provident Life and Accident First Unum Life Colonial Life & Accident and Paul Revere Life Insurance. The company operates as Unum Limited in the UK. Unum's products are sold through field sales agents and independent brokers.

	Annual Growth	12/14	12/15	12/16	12/17	12/18
Assets ($ mil.)	(0.2%)	62,497.1	60,589.7	61,941.5	64,013.1	61,875.6
Net income ($ mil.)	6.1%	413.4	867.1	931.4	994.2	523.4
Market value ($ mil.)	(4.2%)	7,483.6	7,142.5	9,425.3	11,776.8	6,303.6
Employees	0.3%	9,500	9,400	9,400	9,400	9,600

UPMC

200 LOTHROP ST
PITTSBURGH, PA 152132536
Phone: 412-647-8762
Fax: –
Web: www.upmc.com

CEO: Jeffrey A. Romoff
CFO: Robert A. DeMichiei
HR: Gregory Peaslee
FYE: June 30
Type: Private

For University of Pittsburgh students and area residents medical care is spelled UPMC. University of Pittsburgh Medical Center (UPMC) is a leading not-for-profit health care delivery system in western Pennsylvania. The organization operates about 40 hospitals including campuses in the Pittsburgh area regional and community hospitals and specialty facilities such as Children's Hospital of Pittsburgh and the Magee-Womens Hospital. Altogether UPMC has more than 8500 inpatient beds. In addition the system provides care through hundreds of physician practices outpatient clinics cancer treatment facilities and rehab centers; it also offers health insurance home health care and long-term care through about 15 senior living facilities.

	Annual Growth	12/09	12/10	12/11*	06/13	06/15
Sales ($ mil.)	(40.0%)	–	–	4,758.1	10,188.4	614.8
Net income ($ mil.)	–	–	–	(2.5)	441.5	326.5
Market value ($ mil.)	–	–	–	–	–	–
Employees	–	–	–	–	–	80,000

*Fiscal year change

UPMC ALTOONA

620 HOWARD AVE
ALTOONA, PA 166014804
Phone: 814-889-2011
Fax: –

CEO: Jerry Murray
CFO: Charles R Zorger
HR: –
FYE: June 30
Type: Private

UPMC Altoona (formerly Altoona Regional Health System) moves patients upstream towards better health. Operating in Altoona and surrounding areas in central Pennsylvania the health system's facilities include Altoona Hospital an acute care center with 380 licensed beds that provides specialized care in areas including cardiovascular ailments cancer behavioral health and neurology as well as general emergency trauma birthing and surgery services. UPMC Altoona also offers a variety of outpatient care facilities and programs including home health care a primary care physicians' group and laboratory services. The not-for-profit system merged with Pennsylvania hospital operator University of Pittsburgh Medical Center (UPMC) in 2013.

	Annual Growth	06/11	06/12	06/13	06/14	06/15
Sales ($ mil.)	0.2%	–	–	–	393.1	394.0
Net income ($ mil.)	70.1%	–	–	–	15.0	25.5
Market value ($ mil.)	–	–	–	–	–	–
Employees	–	–	–	–	–	2,494

UPSON COUNTY HOSPITAL, INC.

801 W GORDON ST
THOMASTON, GA 302863426
Phone: 706-647-8111
Fax: –
Web: www.urmc.org

CEO: David L Castleberry
CFO: John Williams
HR: –
FYE: December 31
Type: Private

Upson Regional Medical Center is a 115-bed hospital that serves the communities in and around Thomaston Georgia. In addition to general surgery and acute care the hospital offers specialty services including occupational therapy rehabilitation pediatrics and emergency care. Upson Regional also houses a neonatal special care unit a sleep disorders center and a wound healing center. The medical center has expanded its footprint with new medical offices and dining facilities.

	Annual Growth	12/11	12/12	12/13	12/14	12/15
Sales ($ mil.)	0.5%	–	71.2	76.7	69.2	72.3
Net income ($ mil.)	(54.9%)	–	7.6	14.9	5.6	0.7
Market value ($ mil.)	–	–	–	–	–	–
Employees	–	–	–	–	–	625

UPSTATE UNIVERSITY MEDICAL ASSOCIATES AT SYRACUSE, INC.

750 E ADAMS ST
SYRACUSE, NY 132102306
Phone: 315-464-7087
Fax: –
Web: www.upstate.edu

CEO: John McCabe
CFO: Sturat Wright
HR: –
FYE: December 31
Type: Private

SUNY Upstate Medical University is on the up-and-up when it comes to medical training and care. Serving Syracuse and surrounding areas the university's medical campus features the University Hospital a 700-bed two-campus teaching and research hospital with numerous specialty departments including Level I trauma burn cancer AIDS diabetes and neurosurgery centers as well as the Golisano Children's Hospital. It also conducts community health outreach programs. As part of the State University of New York (SUNY) the medical complex also comprises four professional colleges (Medicine Nursing Health Professions and Graduate Studies) an extensive Health Sciences Library and clinical research facilities.

	Annual Growth	09/05	09/06	09/07	09/08*	12/08
Sales ($ mil.)	–	–	–	–	1.9	387.1
Net income ($ mil.)	–	–	–	–	0.9	(45.4)
Market value ($ mil.)	–	–	–	–	–	–
Employees	–	–	–	–	–	8,000

*Fiscal year change

UQM TECHNOLOGIES, INC.

ASE: UQM

4120 Specialty Place
Longmont, CO 80504
Phone: 303 682-4900
Fax: 303 682-4901
Web: www.uqm.com

CEO: Joseph R Mitchell
CFO: David I Rosenthal
HR: –
FYE: December 31
Type: Public

UQM Technologies is revving up for the electric vehicle wars. The company builds permanent magnet electric motors for hybrid and electric vehicles — and the gears and electronic controls needed to operate them. UQM developed hybrid electric powertrains for GM's Precept concept car and the US Army's Humvee vehicle (made by AM General). UQM has customers in the aerospace industrial medical and telecommunications industries but views the auto industry as having the greatest potential. Denver's Regional Transportation District accounts for 12% of sales while Lippert Components is responsible for 17%; US government agencies and their contractors account for 31%.

	Annual Growth	03/14	03/15	03/16*	12/16	12/17
Sales ($ mil.)	3.4%	7.0	4.0	5.3	4.1	7.8
Net income ($ mil.)	–	(2.8)	(6.0)	(6.9)	(13.0)	(4.8)
Market value ($ mil.)	(19.2%)	142.8	59.5	31.0	23.3	75.2
Employees	(5.3%)	60	58	49	48	51

*Fiscal year change

URANIUM ENERGY CORP.

NYSE AMEX: UEC

500 N. Shoreline Blvd. #800N
Corpus Christi TX 78471
Phone: 361-888-8235
Fax: 361-888-5041
Web: www.uraniumenergy.com

CEO: Amir Adnani
CFO: Pat Obara
HR: –
FYE: July 31
Type: Public

Maybe one day it will look on Mars but in this lifetime Uranium Energy explores for uranium on our home planet. The uranium production development and exploration company has projects in South Texas including the Palangana and Goliad in-situ recovery projects. The company has bought a Texas database of historical uranium exploration and development and is acquiring promising properties throughout the southwestern US. In 2012 it looked outside the US by acquiring Cue Resources which holds an interest in a uranium exploration property in southeastern Paraguay.

URANIUM RESOURCES INC.

NASDAQ: URRE

405 State Hwy. 121 Bypass Bldg. A Ste. 110
Lewisville TX 75067
Phone: 972-219-3330
Fax: 972-219-3311
Web: www.uraniumresources.com

CEO: Christopher M Jones
CFO: Jeffrey L Vigil
HR: –
FYE: December 31
Type: Public

Mining company Uranium Resources (URI) glows with anticipation when it thinks about the fuel needs of nuclear power plants. The company has been preparing its main uranium assets in South Texas (the Kingsville Dome and Rosita mines and processing plants) for a restart in production. It also has big plans for its exploration and development interests in New Mexico. URI holds 102.1 million pounds of in-place mineralized uranium material. In 2012 the company acquired Neutron Energy in a $38 million deal. The deal adds significantly to the company's New Mexico assets and positions it as one of the US' largest uranium developers. Neutron will operate as a URI subsidiary.

URATA & SONS CONCRETE, INC.

3430 LUYUNG DR
RANCHO CORDOVA, CA 957426871
Phone: 916-638-5364
Fax: –
Web: www.urataconcrete.com

CEO: –
CFO: Darrell Dwyer
HR: –
FYE: December 31
Type: Private

Urata & Sons is a solidly established provider of concrete contracting services including slab and curb and gutter work. The firm focuses on large scale tilt-up buildings parking structures schools hospitals public works projects multi-family residences and other commercial ventures including malls casinos and resorts and industrial complexes. Most of its projects are in California and Nevada. Urata & Sons' customers include high-profile contractors DPR Construction Turner Construction and The Walsh Group. The company was started in 1974 by Sofio Urata and his sons Charles and Frank who began by paving residential patios and driveways.

	Annual Growth	12/01	12/02	12/03	12/04	12/16
Sales ($ mil.)	3.1%	–	–	–	49.2	71.1
Net income ($ mil.)	(3.8%)	–	–	–	3.4	2.2
Market value ($ mil.)	–	–	–	–	–	–
Employees	–	–	–	–	–	125

URBAN ONE INC

NAS: UONE

1010 Wayne Avenue, 14th Floor
Silver Spring, MD 20910
Phone: 301 429-3200
Fax: –
Web: www.urban1.com

CEO: –
CFO: Peter D Thompson
HR: –
FYE: December 31
Type: Public

Radio One ranks #1 among African-American audiences. The largest radio broadcaster serving black listeners the company owns about 55 stations in 15 mostly urban markets. Its radio stations which mostly operate in market clusters offer a variety of music formats as well as news and talk shows. In addition to broadcasting Radio One has a 80% stake in Reach Media. Radio One operates several websites and the company also owns more than 50% of TV One a cable television venture with Comcast. Founder and chairperson Catherine Hughes and her son president and CEO Alfred Liggins together control more than 90% of the company.

	Annual Growth	12/14	12/15	12/16	12/17	12/18
Sales ($ mil.)	(0.1%)	441.4	450.9	456.2	440.0	439.1
Net income ($ mil.)	–	(62.7)	(74.0)	(0.4)	111.9	141.0
Market value ($ mil.)	(0.9%)	77.3	79.6	134.2	81.0	74.5
Employees	1.9%	1,359	1,306	1,348	1,466	1,466

URBAN OUTFITTERS, INC.

NMS: URBN

5000 South Broad Street
Philadelphia, PA 19112-1495
Phone: 215 454-5500
Fax: –
Web: www.urbn.com

CEO: Richard A. Hayne
CFO: Francis J. (Frank) Conforti
HR: –
FYE: January 31
Type: Public

Whether your style is edgy bohemian or modern Urban Outfitters has your outfit. The firm's about 245 namesake stores (mainly in the US but also in Canada and Europe) offer casual clothes accessories housewares and shoes. The retailer's Anthropologie brand courts women in the 28-45 demographic and has more than 225 shops. Its bohemian-style Free People brand is sold through 135 retail locations. Urban Outfitters and Anthropologie sell via catalogs and their e-commerce sites as well. The company also operates a bridal brand (Bhldn) and garden center brand (Terrain). The wholesale division makes sells and distributes clothing under its Free People Anthropologie and Urban Outfitters labels for its own stores as well as 2200 department and specialty stores worldwide including Macy's Nordstrom and Selfridge's.

	Annual Growth	01/15	01/16	01/17	01/18	01/19
Sales ($ mil.)	4.4%	3,323.1	3,445.1	3,545.8	3,616.0	3,950.6
Net income ($ mil.)	6.4%	232.4	224.5	218.1	108.3	298.0
Market value ($ mil.)	(1.9%)	3,682.7	2,417.1	2,803.7	3,603.5	3,412.2
Employees	0.0%	24,000	24,000	24,000	23,000	24,000

URIGEN PHARMACEUTICALS INC.

OTC: URGP

27 Maiden Lane Suite 595
San Francisco CA 94108
Phone: 415-781-0350
Fax: 415-781-0385
Web: www.urigen.com

CEO: William J Garner
CFO: Martin E Shmagin
HR: –
FYE: June 30
Type: Public

Urigen wants to quell the urgent urge to go go go. Urigen Pharmaceuticals holds a pipeline of investigational drugs focused on urological disorders. The publicly traded company is developing treatments for chronic pelvic pain urethral discomfort and urethritis (inflammation of the urethra). Its main product candidates target painful bladder syndrome in men and women and urinary urgency associated with overactive bladder diagnoses in women. Though the company (which is seeking development partners) doesn't have any products on the market yet it plans to market its products (once approved) in the US through an inside sales force and outside the US through distributors.

URM STORES, INC.

7511 N FREYA ST
SPOKANE, WA 992178043
Phone: 509-467-2620
Fax: –
Web: www.urmstores.com

CEO: –
CFO: Laurie Bigej
HR: –
FYE: August 02
Type: Private

URM Stores is a leading wholesale food distribution cooperative serving more than 160 grocery stores in the Northwest. Its member-owner stores operate under a variety of banners including Family Foods Harvest Foods Super 1 Foods Trading Co. Stores and Yoke's Fresh Market. It also owns the Rosauers Supermarkets chain. In addition to grocery stores URM supplies 1500-plus restaurants hotels and convenience stores; it also offers such services as merchandising store development consulting and technology purchasing. The cooperative was founded in 1921 as United Retail Merchants. The business is privately owned by its members.

	Annual Growth	07/04	07/05	07/06	07/07*	08/08
Sales ($ mil.)	8.0%	–	–	799.4	859.9	932.8
Net income ($ mil.)	41.0%	–	–	4.4	7.2	8.8
Market value ($ mil.)	–	–	–	–	–	–
Employees	–	–	–	–	–	2,100

*Fiscal year change

UROLOGIX INC.

NBB: ULGX

14405 21st Avenue North
Minneapolis, MN 55447
Phone: 763 475-1400
Fax: –
Web: www.urologix.com

CEO: Gregory J Fluet
CFO: Scott M Madson
HR: –
FYE: June 30
Type: Public

For men whose prostate has them prostrate Urologix has the answer. The company's Targis and CoolWave systems are designed to treat benign prostate hyperplasia or enlargement of the prostate. The systems use Cooled ThermoTherapy a noninvasive catheter-based therapy that applies microwave heat to the diseased areas of the prostate while cooling and protecting urethral tissue. The treatment an alternative to drug therapy does not require anesthesia or surgery and can be administered on an outpatient basis. Urologix markets its products through a direct sales force in the US as well as through international distributors.

	Annual Growth	06/10	06/11	06/12	06/13	06/14
Sales ($ mil.)	(0.9%)	14.8	12.6	17.0	16.6	14.2
Net income ($ mil.)	–	(2.2)	(3.7)	(4.7)	(4.3)	(7.6)
Market value ($ mil.)	(36.2%)	22.4	19.9	16.1	3.5	3.7
Employees	(10.7%)	96	88	94	95	61

UROPLASTY, INC.
NAS: UPI

5420 Feltl Road
Minnetonka, MN 55343
Phone: 952 426-6140
Fax: 952 426-6199
Web: www.uroplasty.com

CEO: Robert C Kill
CFO: Brett A Reynolds
HR: –
FYE: March 31
Type: Public

Uroplasty makes implants used primarily to treat urinary incontinence and overactive bladder. Its flagship product is Macroplastique a soft-tissue bulking material for the treatment of urinary incontinence that is injected during a minimally invasive outpatient procedure. Another minimally invasive device the Urgent PC uses electrical pulses to treat overactive bladder symptoms. Uroplasty's I-Stop Mid-Urethral Sling treats female incontinence. The company also sells soft-tissue bulking agents used in plastic surgery vocal cord rehabilitation and treatment of fecal incontinence. Uroplasty markets its products primarily in Europe and the US; it won FDA approval to market Macroplastique in 2006.

	Annual Growth	03/10	03/11	03/12	03/13	03/14
Sales ($ mil.)	20.0%	11.9	13.8	20.6	22.4	24.6
Net income ($ mil.)	–	(3.2)	(4.6)	(4.3)	(3.3)	(5.4)
Market value ($ mil.)	14.9%	45.1	143.1	65.2	53.9	78.6
Employees	16.5%	64	88	108	101	118

URS CORP
NYS: URS

600 Montgomery Street, 26th Floor
San Francisco, CA 94111-2728
Phone: 415 774-2700
Fax: –
Web: www.urs.com

CEO: –
CFO: –
HR: –
FYE: December 28
Type: Public

URS Corporation provides a range of engineering construction maintenance and technical services for customers around the world. Through its infrastructure and environment division URS builds manages operates and maintains projects for government agencies and private corporations. Its federal services segment provides management decommissioning and technical support services to agencies including the Department of Defense and the Department of Homeland Security. URS' energy and construction segment provides design management construction maintenance and closure services. Projects include work on power generating facilities transportation networks biotechnology labs and manufacturing plants.

	Annual Growth	01/09	01/10*	12/10	12/11	12/12
Sales ($ mil.)	2.8%	10,086.3	9,249.1	9,177.1	9,545.0	10,972.5
Net income ($ mil.)	12.2%	219.8	269.1	287.9	(465.8)	310.6
Market value ($ mil.)	(2.2%)	3,179.5	3,419.1	3,195.6	2,697.2	2,972.9
Employees	2.6%	50,000	45,000	47,000	46,000	54,000

*Fiscal year change

URSTADT BIDDLE PROPERTIES INC
NYS: UBA

321 Railroad Avenue
Greenwich, CT 06830
Phone: 203 863-8200
Fax: –
Web: www.ubproperties.com

CEO: Willing L. Biddle
CFO: John T. Hayes
HR: –
FYE: October 31
Type: Public

Urstadt Biddle Properties (UBP) provides a retail stomping ground for suburbanites. A self-administered real estate investment trust (REIT) the company invests in and operates commercial real estate primarily neighborhood and community shopping centers in the Northeast. Its target markets include Connecticut's Fairfield County New York's Westchester and Putnam counties and New Jersey's Bergen County. UBP owns a growing portfolio of about 75 properties with approximately 4.9 million square feet of space. Tenants include drugstore chain CVS off-price retailer TJX and the Stop & Shop supermarket chain. The REIT also owns a handful of office properties and bank branches.

	Annual Growth	10/15	10/16	10/17	10/18	10/19
Sales ($ mil.)	4.5%	115.3	116.8	123.6	135.4	137.6
Net income ($ mil.)	(6.7%)	49.3	33.7	52.9	37.5	37.3
Market value ($ mil.)	4.9%	801.1	856.9	866.1	793.6	969.7
Employees	21.0%	49	51	51	69	105

US 1 INDUSTRIES INC.
OTC: USOO

336 W. US Hwy. 30 Ste. 201
Valparaiso IN 46385
Phone: 219-476-1300
Fax: 219-476-1385
Web: www.uslindustries.com

CEO: Michael E Kibler
CFO: Harold E Antonson
HR: –
FYE: December 31
Type: Public

The US market is the one and only concern for US 1 Industries which partners with its subsidiaries to provide truckload transportation services in the 48 contiguous states. The company owns no trucks; instead it does business through a network of independent sales agents who arrange freight transportation via independent truck owner-operators. About 160 commission-based agents monitor shipments. US 1's contractors transport freight in temperature-controlled trailers and flatbeds as well as in standard dry vans. One of its specialties is the hauling of intermodal shipping containers which can be transported by trucks trains and ships. In 2011 US 1 agreed to be acquired by Trucking Investment Co.

US BANCORP (DE)
NYS: USB

800 Nicollet Mall
Minneapolis, MN 55402
Phone: 651 466-3000
Fax: –
Web: www.usbank.com

CEO: Andrew Cecere
CFO: Terrance R. (Terry) Dolan
HR: Jennie P. Carlson
FYE: December 31
Type: Public

Boasting more than $475 billion in assets U.S. Bancorp is the holding company for U.S. Bank (the US's fifth largest commercial bank). Through that and other subsidiaries the company provides consumer and commercial loans deposits and credit cards as well as merchant processing mortgage banking trust and investment management brokerage insurance and corporate payments. The bank has about 3000 branches and some 4700 ATMs in more than 30 states (primarily in the Midwest and West). Commercial loans account for about 35% of the holding company's loan portfolio; residential mortgages represent more than 20% of the total.

	Annual Growth	12/14	12/15	12/16	12/17	12/18
Assets ($ mil.)	3.8%	402,529.0	421,853.0	445,964.0	462,040.0	467,374.0
Net income ($ mil.)	4.9%	5,851.0	5,879.0	5,888.0	6,218.0	7,096.0
Market value ($ mil.)	0.4%	72,294.6	68,627.6	82,620.2	86,174.6	73,500.9
Employees	2.4%	66,750	65,433	71,191	72,402	73,333

US CONCRETE INC
NMS: USCR

331 N. Main Street
Euless, TX 76039
Phone: 817 835-4105
Fax: –
Web: www.us-concrete.com

CEO: William J. (Bill) Sandbrook
CFO: John E Kunz
HR: Mark Peabody
FYE: December 31
Type: Public

When things get hard U.S. Concrete's products get even harder. The company produces ready-mixed concrete precast concrete and related materials and services for commercial residential and infrastructure construction projects. U.S. Concrete has a fleet of about 1360 mixer trucks and about 145 ready-mixed concrete concrete block and 10 aggregate plants. During 2015 the company produced some 7 million cu. yd. of concrete and more than 4.9 million tons of aggregates; concrete accounts for about 90% of the company's sales. U.S. Concrete concentrates on major markets such as California New Jersey/New York and Texas. In 2017 the company agreed to purchase Polaris Materials for CAD$309 million.

	Annual Growth	12/14	12/15	12/16	12/17	12/18
Sales ($ mil.)	21.0%	703.7	974.7	1,168.2	1,336.0	1,506.4
Net income ($ mil.)	9.9%	20.6	25.5	8.9	25.5	30.0
Market value ($ mil.)	5.5%	473.2	875.8	1,089.3	1,391.2	586.7
Employees	11.4%	2,144	2,700	643	3,070	3,301

US DAIRY EXPORT COUNCIL

2101 WILSON BLVD STE 400 — CEO: Tom Super
ARLINGTON, VA 222013062 — CFO: –
Phone: 703-528-3049 — HR: –
Fax: – — FYE: December 31
Web: www.usdec.org — Type: Private

Got milk? These guys do. Lots of it. The U.S. Dairy Export Council (USDEC) is a not-for-profit organization designed to increase the volume and value of US-based dairy producers' exported products. The independent membership organization represents the interests of US milk producers dairy cooperatives export traders industry suppliers and proprietary processors. The US dairy industry exports $3.8 billion worth of product each year and USDEC helps its members maintain and hopefully increase that dollar amount through its involvement in global trade issues and building demand for US dairy products. The organization founded in 1995 has offices in 15 countries worldwide.

	Annual Growth	12/06	12/07	12/08	12/09	12/12
Sales ($ mil.)	9.7%	–	–	–	17.4	23.0
Net income ($ mil.)	16.9%	–	–	–	0.2	0.4
Market value ($ mil.)	–	–	–	–	–	–
Employees	–	–	–	–	–	20

US DATAWORKS INC

NBB: UDWK

One Sugar Creek Center Boulevard, 5th Floor — CEO: –
Sugar Land, TX 77478 — CFO: –
Phone: 281 504-8000 — HR: –
Fax: – — FYE: March 31
Web: www.usdataworks.com — Type: Public

US Dataworks keeps bank balances in check. The company provides electronic payment processing and check conversion software that helps banks credit card companies and financial services firms rapidly process financial transactions without having to rely on outsourcers. Its Clearingworks software processes remote and Internet-based automated clearing house (ACH) payments defines rules for processing payments and converts paper checks into payments for high-volume transaction processing. The company's customers have included the Federal Reserve Bank Regulus Group General Electric and Citibank.

	Annual Growth	03/08	03/09	03/10	03/11	03/12
Sales ($ mil.)	3.8%	5.7	8.0	8.5	7.3	6.6
Net income ($ mil.)	–	(11.7)	(2.0)	(0.0)	(0.6)	(0.5)
Market value ($ mil.)	(0.5%)	5.0	7.0	6.4	6.0	4.9
Employees	(1.4%)	36	35	36	32	34

US DEPARTMENT OF HOMELAND SECURITY

245 Murray Lane SW — CEO: –
Washington DC 20528 — CFO: –
Phone: 202-282-8000 — HR: –
Fax: 202-447-3543 — FYE: September 30
Web: www.dhs.gov — Type: Government Agency

The US Department of Homeland Security exists to keep America safe. Created in the wake of the 9/11 terrorist attacks the department is devoted to keeping the US safe from natural and man-made disaster. Its activities include domestic nuclear detection intelligence coordination and protection of high-level government officials. The department's structure includes agencies for citizenship and immigration services customs and border protection emergency response and recovery (FEMA) and science and technology research. The US Department of Homeland Security has more than 240000 employees and an annual budget of more than $55 billion.

US DEPARTMENT OF STATE

2201 C St. NW — CEO: –
Washington DC 20520 — CFO: –
Phone: 202-647-4000 — HR: –
Fax: 212-355-5924 — FYE: September 30
Web: www.mastersoninstitute.com/ — Type: Government Agency

Plainly stated the Department of State represents the interests of the US government around the globe. The agency operates more than 280 US embassies and consulates in more than 160 countries. State's members represent the US to the UN NATO (North American Treaty Organization) UNESCO (United Nations Educational Scientific and Cultural Organization) and the European Union. The department also issues travel warnings to US citizens publishes Congressional testimonies and offers reports on doing business with State and other nations. Its goals include achieving peace and security creating jobs helping developing nations and fostering international cooperation. The Department of State was formed in 1789.

US DEPARTMENT OF THE AIR FORCE

1690 Air Force Pentagon — CEO: –
Washington DC 20330-1690 — CFO: –
Phone: 703-695-9664 — HR: –
Fax: 703-614-9601 — FYE: September 30
Web: www.af.mil — Type: Government Agency

The mission of the US Department of the Air Force is to fly fight and win — in air space and cyberspace. Along with the Army Navy and Marine Corps the US Air Force is a major military branch of the US Department of Defense responsible for defending the US and its interests through aerial space and cyber warfare. The agency includes more than a dozen major commands including the Air Force Reserve and Air National Guard. It also consists of field operating agencies and direct reporting units which are typically assigned to specialized missions. Originally part of the US Army the US Air Force was formed as a separate branch when president Harry S. Truman signed the National Security Act of 1947.

US ECOLOGY INC (NEW)

NMS: ECOL

101 S. Capitol Blvd., Suite 1000 — CEO: Jeffrey R. (Jeff) Feeler
Boise, ID 83702 — CFO: Eric L. Gerratt
Phone: 208 331-8400 — HR: –
Fax: – — FYE: December 31
Web: www.usecology.com — Type: Public

US Ecology helps keep a lid on hazardous waste industrial waste and low-level radioactive waste. The company provides hazardous and nonhazardous waste management at sites in the US Canada and Mexico. It operates a low-level radioactive waste facility in Washington State. The company does business with private waste companies state and federal agencies and a variety of industries. Customers include nuclear plants steel mills petrochemical facilities and academic and medical institutions. US Ecology retains interests in several non-operating waste disposal facilities.

	Annual Growth	12/14	12/15	12/16	12/17	12/18
Sales ($ mil.)	6.1%	447.4	563.1	477.7	504.0	565.9
Net income ($ mil.)	6.7%	38.2	25.6	34.3	49.4	49.6
Market value ($ mil.)	11.9%	883.9	802.8	1,082.9	1,123.6	1,387.6
Employees	(1.4%)	1,800	1,400	1,450	1,550	1,700

US ENERGY CORP
NAS: USEG

950 S. Cherry St., Unit 1515
Denver, CO 80246
Phone: 303 993-3200
Fax: -
Web: www.usnrg.com

CEO: Ryan Smith
CFO: Ryan L Smith
HR: -
FYE: December 31
Type: Public

U.S. Energy (USE) has put its energy in many places including oil and gas exploration and production geothermal energy projects and molybdenum mining. It operates oil and gas wells on the coast of the Gulf of Mexico and in Texas. The company bought a quarter stake in Standard Steam Trust in 2008 giving USE entry into the geothermal energy market. It also is developing a molybdenum mining project in Colorado. U.S. Energy has an agreement with Thompson Creek Metals to fund development of the project. The company had owned almost half of Sutter Gold Mining but sold most of its stake in the gold miner in 2008.

	Annual Growth	12/14	12/15	12/16	12/17	12/18
Sales ($ mil.)	(35.7%)	32.4	10.3	5.7	6.5	5.5
Net income ($ mil.)	-	(2.1)	(92.9)	(14.1)	(1.4)	(1.0)
Market value ($ mil.)	(18.1%)	2.0	0.2	1.7	2.0	0.9
Employees	(32.0%)	14	1	2	3	3

US FOODS INC.

9399 W. Higgins Rd.
Rosemont IL 60018
Phone: 847-720-8000
Fax: 847-720-8099
Web: www.usfoods.com

CEO: Pietro Satriano
CFO: -
HR: -
FYE: December 31
Type: Private

Many restaurant-goers in the US can thank this company for the food on their plates. US Foods (formerly U.S. Foodservice) is the nation's #2 foodservice supplier (with about half the sales of rival SYSCO) distributing food and nonfood supplies to more than 250000 customers. The company operates more than 60 distribution facilities that supply thousands of items to restaurants hotels schools health care facilities and institutional foodservice operations. In addition to food items and ingredients US Foods distributes kitchen and cleaning supplies as well as restaurant equipment. Tracing its roots to 1853 the company is jointly owned by private equity firms KKR & Co. and Clayton Dubilier & Rice.

US GEOTHERMAL INC
ASE: HTM

390 E. Parkcenter Blvd., Suite 250
Boise, ID 83706
Phone: 208 424-1027
Fax: 208 424-1030
Web: www.usgeothermal.com

CEO: Douglas J Glaspey
CFO: Kerry D Hawkley
HR: -
FYE: December 31
Type: Public

U.S. Geothermal likes things bubbling just under the surface. Operating through its Idaho-based subsidiary Geo-Idaho the company runs geothermal power plants which use heat from beneath the Earth's surface to generate electricity. Its Idaho plant generates 8 MW of power for Idaho Power; the operation is a joint venture with Goldman Sachs which contributed about $34 million to plant construction. The Nevada plant produces about 2.5 MW for Sierra Pacific Power. U.S. Geothermal also has exploration and development-stage properties in Oregon Nevada Idaho and in Guatemala. In addition to power generation the company produces revenue by selling its green energy credits to other power generators (7% of sales).

	Annual Growth	12/12	12/13	12/14	12/15	12/16
Sales ($ mil.)	38.3%	8.6	27.4	31.0	31.2	31.5
Net income ($ mil.)	-	(1.3)	1.9	11.6	1.8	0.5
Market value ($ mil.)	83.1%	6.9	7.2	8.7	11.9	77.6
Employees	1.0%	47	47	49	49	49

US GLOBAL INVESTORS INC
NAS: GROW

7900 Callaghan Road
San Antonio, TX 78229
Phone: 210 308-1234
Fax: -
Web: www.usfunds.com

CEO: Frank E Holmes
CFO: Lisa C Callicotte
HR: -
FYE: June 30
Type: Public

While it may be a small world financial investment company U.S. Global Investors wants to make it a little greener after all. Primarily serving the U.S. Global Investors Funds and the U.S. Global Accolade Funds the company is a mutual fund manager providing investment advisory transfer agency broker-dealer and mailing services. It offers a family of no-load mutual funds generally geared toward long-term investing. The company also engages in corporate investment activities. U.S. Global Investors had about $724 million in assets under management in 2015.

	Annual Growth	06/15	06/16	06/17	06/18	06/19
Sales ($ mil.)	(14.9%)	9.4	5.5	6.8	6.3	4.9
Net income ($ mil.)	-	(4.0)	(3.7)	(0.5)	0.6	(3.4)
Market value ($ mil.)	(10.2%)	42.1	25.7	23.0	24.4	27.4
Employees	(13.1%)	42	25	26	25	24

US GOLD CORP (CANADA)
NAS: USAU

1910 E. Idaho Street, Suite 102-Box 604
Elko, NV 89801
Phone: 800 557-4550
Fax: -
Web: www.dataram.com

CEO: Edward M Karr
CFO: -
HR: -
FYE: April 30
Type: Public

Dataram wants you to remember your DRAMs. The company makes add-in memory boards and modules that expand the capacity of computer servers and workstations running under UNIX and Windows operating systems. Its products which use DRAM memory chips are compatible with systems from scores of companies such as HP IBM and Dell and with microprocessors made by AMD and Intel. The company sells its products to OEMs distributors value-added resellers and end-users. The company has a plant in the US & sales offices in the US Japan and Europe. Most sales come from customers in the US.

	Annual Growth	04/13	04/14	04/15	04/16	04/17
Sales ($ mil.)	(10.9%)	27.6	30.4	28.3	25.2	17.4
Net income ($ mil.)	-	(4.6)	(2.6)	(3.8)	(1.2)	(1.9)
Market value ($ mil.)	(13.5%)	2.5	3.2	2.6	0.7	1.4
Employees	(23.0%)	71	54	42	36	25

US SECURITIES AND EXCHANGE COMMISSION

100 F St. NE
Washington DC 20549
Phone: 202-942-8088
Fax: 202-772-9295
Web: www.sec.gov

CEO: -
CFO: -
HR: -
FYE: September 30
Type: Government Agency

The US Securities and Exchange Commission (SEC) is one part law enforcer protecting investors from securities fraud and enforcing securities laws; one part doctor promoting healthy capital markets and contributing to America's economic well-being; and one part rule maker maintaining fair orderly and efficient markets. The agency regulates the sale of securities as well as the people and organizations involved in selling them. It also ensures the disclosure of financial information of public companies via its online EDGAR database and is involved in personal investor education. Established in 1934 the agency is overseen by five presidentially appointed commissioners.

US SILICA HOLDINGS, INC.   NYS: SLCA

24275 Katy Freeway, Suite 600   CEO: Bryan A. Shinn
Katy, TX 77494   CFO: Donald A. Merril
Phone: 281 258-2170   HR: –
Fax: –   FYE: December 31
Web: www.ussilica.com   Type: Public

Life's a beach for the sand-sellers at U.S. Silica. While the industrial mineral company got its start making sand-based glass and other products it is now known for providing its popular "frac sand" product used by natural gas and oil producers in hydraulic fracturing a process to boost oil and gas production. Supplying customers in the US and Canada the company also provides silica and aplite for the glass foundry chemical and construction industries; and fine ground silica and kaolin clay used to make paint plastics and ceramics. Additionally U.S. Silica makes raw materials for solar panels. Beyond its main facility in West Virginia U S. Silica also has 17 plants in the East.

	Annual Growth	12/14	12/15	12/16	12/17	12/18
Sales ($ mil.)	15.8%	876.7	643.0	559.6	1,240.9	1,577.3
Net income ($ mil.)	–	121.5	11.9	(41.1)	145.2	(200.8)
Market value ($ mil.)	(20.7%)	1,879.2	1,370.1	4,146.1	2,381.7	744.7
Employees	26.7%	1,092	996	1,404	2,202	2,812

US SMALL BUSINESS ADMINISTRATION

409 3rd St. SW   CEO: –
Washington DC 20416   CFO: –
Phone: 800-827-5722   HR: –
Fax: +86-10-6437-4251   FYE: September 30
Web: www.chinacache.com   Type: Government Agency

The US Small Business Administration (SBA) has the little guy's back. As an independent agency of the federal government it provides services to independently owned for-profit small businesses including those owned by women minorities veterans and disadvantaged people in the US Guam Puerto Rico and the US Virgin Islands. Small businesses are typically defined as having fewer than 500 employees. The agency provides loans and loan guarantees contract opportunities disaster assistance business development counseling and an online library of small business information and resources. The SBA was established in 1953 largely in response to the pressures of the Great Depression and WWII.

US STEM CELL INC   NBB: USRM

1560 Sawgrass Corporate Pkwy 4th Floor   CEO: Mike Tomas
Sunrise, FL 33323   CFO: Mike Tomas
Phone: 954 835-1500   HR: –
Fax: 954 845-9976   FYE: December 31
Web: www. us-stemcell.com   Type: Public

Broken hearts are no fun but damaged hearts are worse and Bioheart aims to help. The biotech company is focused on the discovery development and commercialization of therapies treating heart damage. Because the heart does not have cells to naturally repair itself Bioheart is exploring the use of cells derived from the patient's own thigh muscle to improve cardiac function after a heart has been damaged by a heart attack. Its lead candidate MyoCell uses precursor muscle cells called myoblasts to strengthen scar tissue with living muscle tissue. The company is also developing a number of proprietary techniques and processes used to obtain and inject MyoCell.

	Annual Growth	12/14	12/15	12/16	12/17	12/18
Sales ($ mil.)	34.4%	2.1	2.2	3.1	5.5	6.7
Net income ($ mil.)	–	(2.3)	(1.6)	(2.1)	(3.5)	(2.2)
Market value ($ mil.)	10.7%	4.0	330.8	0.7	11.0	6.0
Employees	38.4%	3	5	8	11	11

US XPRESS ENTERPRISES INC   NYS: USX

4080 Jenkins Road   CEO: Eric Fuller
Chattanooga, TN 37421   CFO: Eric Peterson
Phone: 423 510-3000   HR: –
Fax: 423 267-3655   FYE: December 31
Web: www.usxpress.com   Type: Public

U.S. Xpress Enterprises' truckload transportation units led by flagship U.S. Xpress and Arnold Transportation provide medium- to long-haul service throughout North America as well as regional service in the midwestern southeastern and western US. It also offers dedicated contract carriage in which drivers and equipment are assigned to a customer long-term and expedited freight hauling. Subsidiary Xpress Global Systems provides less-than-truckload freight hauling warehousing and distribution services. Overall the company's fleet includes about 8000 trucks and 22000 trailers. Co-founders Patrick Quinn and Max Fuller own the company.

	Annual Growth	12/06	12/15	12/16	12/17	12/18
Sales ($ mil.)	1.7%	1,471.8	1,541.1	1,451.2	1,555.4	1,804.9
Net income ($ mil.)	1.8%	20.1	4.1	(16.5)	(4.1)	24.9
Market value ($ mil.)	–	–	–	–	–	271.2
Employees	(1.7%)	10,885	–	–	9,288	8,912

USA TECHNOLOGIES INC   NMS: USAT

100 Deerfield Lane, Suite 300   CEO: Stephen P Herbert
Malvern, PA 19355   CFO: Glen E Goold
Phone: 610 989-0340   HR: –
Fax: –   FYE: June 30
Web: www.usatech.com   Type: Public

Since you can't get much from a vending machine with a quarter these days USA Technologies decided to make them take plastic. Its ePort device attaches onto vending machines and its eSuds works on washing machines and clothes dryers to allow them to accept debit and credit cards. With the Business Express device hotels libraries and universities can run their business centers as self-pay operations; customers simply swipe their cards to use a PC fax machine or copier. USA Technologies also sells energy-saving devices for such "always-on" appliances as vending machines and office equipment. Information from the company's remote devices is transmitted through the company's USALive network.

	Annual Growth	06/15	06/16	06/17	06/18	06/19
Sales ($ mil.)	25.4%	58.1	77.4	104.1	132.5	143.8
Net income ($ mil.)	–	(1.1)	(6.8)	(1.9)	(11.3)	(32.0)
Market value ($ mil.)	28.8%	162.0	256.2	312.0	840.1	445.9
Employees	17.5%	66	75	101	–	126

USA TRUCK, INC.   NMS: USAK

3200 Industrial Park Road   CEO: James D. Reed
Van Buren, AR 72956   CFO: Jason Bates
Phone: 479 471-2500   HR: Donald B Weis
Fax: –   FYE: December 31
Web: www.usa-truck.com   Type: Public

Truckload carrier USA Truck moves freight not only in the US but also in Canada and through partners into Mexico. It does most of its business east of the Rocky Mountains. USA Truck has a fleet of more than 2000 tractors and 6200 trailers. It transports general commodities; customers include companies in the consumer goods industrial machinery and equipment paper products rubber and plastics and retail industries. The company provides both medium-haul (800-1200 mile) and regional (500-mile) truckload services along with dedicated contract carriage in which drivers and equipment are assigned to a customer long-term. The company's average length-of-haul is about 550-miles.

	Annual Growth	12/14	12/15	12/16	12/17	12/18
Sales ($ mil.)	(3.0%)	602.5	507.9	429.1	446.5	534.1
Net income ($ mil.)	19.3%	6.0	11.1	(7.7)	7.5	12.2
Market value ($ mil.)	(14.8%)	237.5	145.9	72.8	151.6	125.2
Employees	(2.8%)	2,800	2,300	2,000	2,000	2,500

USAA

9800 Fredericksburg Rd.
San Antonio TX 78288
Phone: 210-456-1800
Fax: 206-342-3000
Web: www.vulcan.com
CEO: Josue Robles Jr
CFO: –
HR: –
FYE: December 31
Type: Private - Mutual Com

USAA has a decidedly military bearing. The mutual insurance company serves 8.4 million member customers primarily military personnel military retirees and their families. Its products and services include property/casualty and life insurance banking discount brokerage and investment management. It offers such specialty products as life insurance for soldiers deployed in war zones and financial planning services to invest hazardous duty pay. USAA relies largely on direct marketing to sell its products reaching clients via the telephone and Internet. The company's USAA Alliance Services unit provides discount shopping (floral jewelry and safety items) and travel and delivery services to its members.

USANA HEALTH SCIENCES INC — NYS: USNA

3838 West Parkway Blvd.
Salt Lake City, UT 84120
Phone: 801 954-7100
Fax: –
Web: www.usanahealthsciences.com
CEO: Kevin G. Guest
CFO: Paul A. Jones
HR: –
FYE: December 29
Type: Public

Health is a matter of science at USANA Health Sciences. The company makes nutritional personal care and weight management products selling them through a direct-sales network marketing system of some 290000 independent distributors or associates. USANA Health Sciences also sells directly to "preferred" customers who buy its products for personal use; it has some 275000 active preferred customers. USANA's associates operate throughout North America as well as the Asia/Pacific region. The company's product portfolio includes nutritional supplements and foods sold under the USANA brand and skin and hair care products marketed under the Celavive and Sensé labels. Chairman and founder Myron Wentz controls nearly half of USANA.

	Annual Growth	01/15	01/16*	12/16	12/17	12/18
Sales ($ mil.)	14.6%	790.5	918.5	1,006.1	1,047.3	1,189.2
Net income ($ mil.)	18.1%	76.6	94.7	100.0	62.5	126.2
Market value ($ mil.)	4.0%	2,410.4	3,010.7	1,442.3	1,745.1	2,709.3
Employees	7.8%	1,527	1,664	1,788	1,810	1,911

*Fiscal year change

USDA FOREST SERVICE

1400 Independence Ave. SW
Washington DC 20250-0003
Phone: 202-205-8333
Fax: 202-205-1765
Web: www.fs.fed.us
CEO: –
CFO: –
HR: –
FYE: September 30
Type: Government Agency

Responsible for managing more than 190 million acres of national forests and grasslands the USDA Forest Service is the largest agency of the US Department of Agriculture and has the conflicting mission of both preserving public forest lands and overseeing the commercial harvesting of its timber. The National Forest System consists of 155 national forests and 20 grasslands in 44 states Puerto Rico and the Virgin Islands. Through various programs the agency which began in 1905 provides states and private landowners with technical and financial assistance to promote rural economic development and improve the natural environment of cities and communities.

USFALCON, INC.

100 REGENCY FOREST DR # 150
CARY, NC 275188598
Phone: 919-388-3778
Fax: –
Web: www.usfalcon.com
CEO: Zannie Smith
CFO: Leigh Barnhill
HR: –
FYE: September 30
Type: Private

Government contractor USfalcon has been flying high with the big boys — Booz Allen Hamilton CACI and Lockheed Martin— ever since it became a preferred contractor under the Army's S3 (Strategic Services Sourcing) program in 2006. USfalcon assists the Defense Department and other federal agencies with information technology (IT) services in the areas of aerospace national security and intelligence and defense. The company is also awarded contracts through the Navy's SeaPort and works as a subcontractor for IT giants NCI and Leidos. USfalcon operates from seven offices in the US. The veteran-owned small business was taken over by owner Col. Peter von Jess (Ret.) in 2003.

	Annual Growth	09/07	09/08	09/09	09/10	09/11
Sales ($ mil.)	–	–	–	(510.3)	102.6	105.5
Net income ($ mil.)	48891.4%	–	–	0.0	3.7	3.4
Market value ($ mil.)	–	–	–	–	–	–
Employees	–	–	–	–	–	250

USG CORP — NYS: USG

550 West Adams Street
Chicago, IL 60661-3676
Phone: 312 436-4000
Fax: –
Web: www.usg.com
CEO: Christopher R Griffin
CFO: –
HR: –
FYE: December 31
Type: Public

USG the maker of the world's top brand of wallboard is one of the largest building products manufacturers and distributors in the US. The company operates in three divisions. Its gypsum unit manufactures wallboard gypsum fiberboard and other products for finishing interior walls ceilings and floors under the SHEETROCK DUROCK AND FIBEROCK brands. The ceilings division makes ceiling systems and acoustic tile used mainly in commercial buildings. In addition the company's USG Boral Building Products operations make and distribute building products and gypsum products to customers throughout Asia Australasia and the Middle East. In 2018 USG is being acquired by German construction products manufacturer Knauf KG in a deal worth $7 billion.

	Annual Growth	12/13	12/14	12/15	12/16	12/17
Sales ($ mil.)	(2.7%)	3,570.0	3,724.0	3,776.0	3,017.0	3,204.0
Net income ($ mil.)	17.0%	47.0	37.0	991.0	510.0	88.0
Market value ($ mil.)	8.0%	3,999.9	3,945.0	3,423.5	4,070.4	5,434.7
Employees	(6.5%)	8,900	8,900	8,900	6,600	6,800

USIO INC — NAS: USIO

3611 Paesanos Parkway, Suite 300
San Antonio, TX 78231
Phone: 210 249-4100
Fax: –
Web: www.paymentdata.com
CEO: Louis A Hoch
CFO: Tom Jewell
HR: –
FYE: December 31
Type: Public

Usio Inc. (formerly Payment Data Systems) offers electronic payment processing services including automated clearinghouse (ACH) and credit/debit card transaction processing to merchants and businesses. Usio also operates billx.com an online payment processing website that allows consumers to pay anyone anywhere for a flat monthly fee. Additionally the company is developing and marketing prepaid gift cards and debit cards issued by Meta Financial Group. Usio operates solely in the US.

	Annual Growth	12/14	12/15	12/16	12/17	12/18
Sales ($ mil.)	16.9%	13.4	14.4	12.1	14.6	25.0
Net income ($ mil.)	–	3.8	1.0	(1.2)	(3.0)	(3.8)
Market value ($ mil.)	75.6%	2.8	31.9	29.7	40.6	26.6
Employees	26.1%	17	22	21	33	43

USS-POSCO INDUSTRIES, A CALIFORNIA JOINT VENTURE

900 LOVERIDGE RD
PITTSBURG, CA 945652808
Phone: 800-877-7672
Fax: –
Web: www.ussposco.com

CEO: –
CFO: –
HR: –
FYE: December 31
Type: Private

US and Korean steel manufacturing interests come together in the form of USS-POSCO Industries (UPI) a 50/50 joint venture between United States Steel (US Steel) and POSCO. The company operates a steel plant (formerly owned by US Steel) in Pittsburg Northern California. It manufactures flat-rolled steel sheets in various forms: cold-rolled steel galvanized steel and tinplate. In addition USS-POSCO churns out iron oxide which is used to make hard and soft ferrites. UPI sells its products to more than 150 customers in more than dozen states throughout the western US. End products include office furniture computer cabinets metal studs cans culverts and metal building materials.

	Annual Growth	12/05	12/06	12/07	12/08	12/15
Sales ($ mil.)	(5.1%)	–	1,034.7	998.7	1,198.0	649.0
Net income ($ mil.)	–	–	14.7	(40.1)	11.9	(4.3)
Market value ($ mil.)	–	–	–	–	–	–
Employees	–	–	–	–	–	759

UT MEDICAL GROUP, INC.

1407 UNION AVE STE 700
MEMPHIS, TN 381043641
Phone: 901-866-8864
Fax: –

CEO: Juloy Raymer
CFO: Brenda H Jeter
HR: –
FYE: June 30
Type: Private

UT Medical Group knows that a little practice can go a long way. The organization is the private physician practice affiliated with the University of Tennessee Health Science Center. The not-for-profit physician group consists of more than 100 doctors serving the greater Memphis Tennessee area. Specialized practices include emergency medicine pediatrics surgery ophthalmology and cardiology. The company was founded in 1974 as the Faculty Medical Practice Corporation; one decade later its name was changed to reflect its association with University of Tennessee.

	Annual Growth	06/09	06/10	06/13	06/14	06/15
Sales ($ mil.)	(11.5%)	–	135.8	4.5	117.4	73.7
Net income ($ mil.)	–	–	1.1	0.1	19.4	(6.6)
Market value ($ mil.)	–	–	–	–	–	–
Employees	–	–	–	–	–	1,207

UTAH ASSOCIATED MUNICIPAL POWER SYSTEMS

155 N 400 W
SALT LAKE CITY, UT 841031111
Phone: 801-566-3938
Fax: –
Web: www.uamps.com

CEO: –
CFO: –
HR: –
FYE: March 31
Type: Private

Even the hardiest citizens of the Intermountain West need access to a reliable power supply. Utah Associated Municipal Power Systems supplies power to 52 member municipal utilities primarily in Utah as well as in Arizona California Idaho Nevada and New Mexico Oregon and Wyoming. These municipal electric utilities and other local government units provide retail electric or other utility services in their respective service areas. The company obtains electricity from interests in generation facilities and through power purchase agreements with other generators; Utah Associated Municipal Power Systems also has interests in traditional power transmission facilities and in wind power generation plants.

	Annual Growth	03/14	03/15	03/16	03/17	03/18
Sales ($ mil.)	4.5%	–	170.8	187.8	191.0	194.8
Net income ($ mil.)	5.6%	–	3.7	3.7	3.0	4.4
Market value ($ mil.)	–	–	–	–	–	–
Employees	–	–	–	–	–	27

UTAH MEDICAL PRODUCTS, INC.

NMS: UTMD

7043 South 300 West
Midvale, UT 84047
Phone: 801 566-1200
Fax: 801 566-7305
Web: www.utahmed.com

CEO: Kevin L. Cornwell
CFO: Brian L Koopman
HR: –
FYE: December 31
Type: Public

Utah Medical Products (UTMD) focuses on expectant moms new moms and newborns. The company designs and makes a variety of medical products used in labor and delivery and in neonatal intensive care as well as products for gynecological and female urinary problems. Products include disposable pressure transducers to monitor blood pressure intrauterine catheters used to monitor pressure in the womb during high-risk births and a device that clamps and cuts the umbilical cord and collects a blood sample from the cord. UTMD which has manufacturing facilities in the US and Ireland sells its products around the world through a domestic sales force and more than 100 international distributors.

	Annual Growth	12/14	12/15	12/16	12/17	12/18
Sales ($ mil.)	0.4%	41.3	40.2	39.3	41.4	42.0
Net income ($ mil.)	13.0%	11.4	11.8	12.1	8.5	18.6
Market value ($ mil.)	8.5%	223.4	217.8	270.6	302.8	309.1
Employees	(0.3%)	183	180	184	180	181

UTAH STATE UNIVERSITY

1000 OLD MAIN HL
LOGAN, UT 843221000
Phone: 435-797-1000
Fax: –
Web: www.utahstateaggies.com

CEO: –
CFO: –
HR: –
FYE: June 30
Type: Private

Utah State University (USU) has more than 40 academic departments at colleges of agriculture arts business education and human services engineering science natural resources and humanities and social sciences. It offers about 170 bachelor's degree programs and more than 140 graduate degree programs. Biology elementary education mechanical and aerospace engineering and business administration are among the university's most popular majors. About 29000 students attend its main campus in northern Utah its three branch campuses or extension facilities located across the state. USU was established in 1888 as an agricultural college.

	Annual Growth	06/14	06/15	06/16	06/17	06/18
Sales ($ mil.)	6.4%	–	382.7	401.3	435.9	461.0
Net income ($ mil.)	(10.1%)	–	55.0	88.9	59.6	39.9
Market value ($ mil.)	–	–	–	–	–	–
Employees	–	–	–	–	–	6,000

UTC CLIMATE CONTROLS & SECURITY

9 Farm Springs Rd.
Farmington CT 06034-4065
Phone: 860-284-3000
Fax: +82-42-939-5001
Web: www.ktng.com

CEO: –
CFO: –
HR: –
FYE: December 31
Type: Business Segment

This unit of United Technologies (UTC) has your climate needs under control. UTC Climate Controls & Security provides heating air conditioning and refrigeration systems building controls and automation and fire and security solutions. Its lead heating cooling and refrigeration brand is Carrier while its Automated Logic is a top energy solutions provider. The business supplies fire extinguishers smoke detectors and related equipment under brands such as Chubb and Kidde and security services through GE Security Onity and Lenel units. Customers include government and financial institutions building owners architects and consultants. UTC Climate Controls & Security operates in some 35 countries.

UTG INC
NBB: UTGN

205 North Depot Street
Stanford, KY 40484
Phone: 217 241-6300
Fax: –
Web: www.utgins.com

CEO: Jesse T Correll
CFO: Theodore C Miller
HR: –
FYE: December 31
Type: Public

UTG doesn't feel the need to spell out United Trust Group anymore but it is still a life insurance holding company. Universal Guaranty Life Insurance American Capitol Insurance and other subsidiaries offer individual life insurance as well as third-party administration (TPA) services for other providers. UTG's Roosevelt Equity subsidiary provides investment brokerage services to the company's insurance customers while other subsidiaries handle UTG's real estate investments. Some 20 general agents represent the company's products and focus on retaining and expanding current customer policies. CEO Jesse Correll owns about two-thirds of the company.

	Annual Growth	12/14	12/15	12/16	12/17	12/18
Assets ($ mil.)	(0.3%)	399.9	377.2	402.1	406.4	395.5
Net income ($ mil.)	15.4%	7.0	0.9	1.2	4.8	12.4
Market value ($ mil.)	22.9%	47.0	48.6	58.5	82.4	107.1
Employees	(2.9%)	45	42	46	45	40

UTICA COLLEGE

1600 BURRSTONE RD
UTICA, NY 135024892
Phone: 315-792-3111
Fax: –
Web: www.utica.edu

CEO: –
CFO: –
HR: –
FYE: May 31
Type: Private

Utica College is a liberal arts college with an enrollment of approximately 2500 full- and part-time students. The private school was founded in 1946 by Syracuse University and became an independent institution in 1995. Utica College offers about 30 undergraduate majors and 15 graduate programs. Its students earn Syracuse baccalaureate degrees for undergrads and Utica College master's and doctorate degrees.

	Annual Growth	05/14	05/15	05/16	05/17	05/18
Sales ($ mil.)	6.5%	–	71.6	76.6	82.3	86.6
Net income ($ mil.)	–	–	(2.9)	(3.4)	3.8	11.5
Market value ($ mil.)	–	–	–	–	–	–
Employees	–	–	–	–	–	646

UWHARRIE CAPITAL CORP.
NBB: UWHR

132 North First Street
Albemarle, NC 28001
Phone: 704 983-6181
Fax: –
Web: www.uwharrie.com

CEO: Roger L Dick
CFO: R David Beaver III
HR: Mike Massey
FYE: December 31
Type: Public

Uwharrie Capital is the multibank holding company for Anson Bank & Trust Bank of Stanly and Cabarrus Bank & Trust which operate a total of about ten branches in west-central North Carolina. Serving consumers and local business customers the banks offer a variety of deposit accounts and credit cards as well as investments insurance asset management and brokerage services offered by other Uwharrie subsidiaries such as insurance agency BOS Agency securities broker-dealer Strategic Alliance mortgage brokerage Gateway Mortgage and Strategic Investment Advisors. The banks mainly write residential and commercial mortgages but also construction business and consumer loans.

	Annual Growth	12/14	12/15	12/16	12/17	12/18
Assets ($ mil.)	5.1%	518.5	532.2	548.2	576.4	632.3
Net income ($ mil.)	15.1%	1.1	1.4	1.6	1.0	1.9
Market value ($ mil.)	12.3%	24.0	30.2	39.6	41.3	38.2
Employees	3.5%	165	173	181	184	189

VAALCO ENERGY, INC.
NYS: EGY

9800 Richmond Avenue, Suite 700
Houston, TX 77042
Phone: 713 623-0801
Fax: 713 623-0982
Web: www.vaalco.com

CEO: Cary Bounds
CFO: Elizabeth D Prochnow
HR: Lilith Kirsh
FYE: December 31
Type: Public

VAALCO Energy valiantly pursues energy opportunities. The small independent is engaged in the acquisition exploration development and production of oil and gas. VAALCO Energy holds high-risk exploration assets in Angola and Gabon through participating in oil company consortia and has exploration assets Gulf Coast of Texas and Louisiana and in Montana. VAALCO's near-term production strategy is to focus on developing its reserves in Gabon through the exploitation of the Etame Marin block (the Etame Avouma South Tchibala and Ebouri fields). In 2013 the company reported proved reserves of 7.2 million barrels of crude oil (46% developed); and 1.3 million cu ft. of natural gas located in the US).

	Annual Growth	12/14	12/15	12/16	12/17	12/18
Sales ($ mil.)	(4.8%)	127.7	80.4	59.8	77.0	104.9
Net income ($ mil.)	–	(77.6)	(158.7)	(26.6)	9.7	98.2
Market value ($ mil.)	(24.7%)	271.8	95.4	62.0	41.5	87.6
Employees	(1.1%)	113	125	104	102	108

VAIL RESORTS INC
NYS: MTN

390 Interlocken Crescent
Broomfield, CO 80021
Phone: 303 404-1800
Fax: 303 404-6415
Web: www.vailresorts.com

CEO: Robert A. (Rob) Katz
CFO: Michael Z. Barkin
HR: –
FYE: July 31
Type: Public

One of North America's leading ski resort operators Vail Resorts owns or manages 15 mountain resorts primarily in the US. Half of its properties are in Colorado and Utah popular destinations for skiers and winter vacationers. Key resorts include Breckenridge Mountain Resort Crested Butte Mountain and Vail Mountain. Other properties are located in Lake Tahoe on the California/Nevada border Vermont New Hampshire and a handful of other northern states. It also owns or manages lodges condominiums and hotels as well as 15 golf courses in and around the company's resorts. In addition to its US properties Vail operates the Whistler Blackcomb Resort in British Columbia Canada and the Perisher Ski Resort in Australia.

	Annual Growth	07/15	07/16	07/17	07/18	07/19
Sales ($ mil.)	12.9%	1,399.9	1,601.3	1,907.2	2,011.6	2,271.6
Net income ($ mil.)	27.3%	114.8	149.8	210.6	379.9	301.2
Market value ($ mil.)	22.4%	4,425.0	5,771.6	8,502.3	11,169.2	9,944.9
Employees	15.5%	21,613	27,000	33,500	33,300	38,500

VALCOM INC.
PINK SHEETS: VLCO

429 Rockaway Valley Rd.
Boonton Township NJ 07005
Phone: 727-953-9778
Fax: 202-728-0845
Web: www.judydiamond.com

CEO: Anthony Barrett
CFO: –
HR: –
FYE: September 30
Type: Public

There's value in entertainment. Through its Studio division ValCom leases production facilities and sound stages to major movie studios such as Warner Bros and Universal Studios. The company's Rental division leases out personnel cameras and other production equipment to production companies. Through its TV Stations and Broadcasting unit ValCom owns a small library of TV content and has a 45% stake in ValCom Broadcasting which operates KVPS (Channel 8) an independent TV station in Palm Springs California. ValCom additionally has a Film Production division that has developed and produced TV pilots and feature films such as PCH (Pacific Coast Highway) and the 40 episode TV series AJ's Time Travelers.

VALDOSTA STATE UNIVERSITY

1500 N PATTERSON ST
VALDOSTA, GA 316980001
Phone: 229-333-5800
Fax: –
Web: www.valdosta.edu

CEO: –
CFO: –
HR: –
FYE: June 30
Type: Private

Valdosta State University (VSU) nurtures higher education students as they blossom into professionals. The school a regional university of the University System of Georgia is located in the southern Georgia town of Valdosta which is known for its flower gardens and trails. The school has two campuses less than a mile apart that house six colleges and offer about 60 undergraduate and 40 graduate degree programs as well as doctorates in education and public administration. VSU was founded in 1906 as South Georgia State Normal College. Originally a girls' school the institution became co-educational in 1950. It has some 650 faculty members and a student body of about 11200.

	Annual Growth	06/06	06/07	06/08	06/10	06/11
Sales ($ mil.)	–	–	(739.3)	80.1	92.1	101.5
Net income ($ mil.)	1311.9%	–	0.0	3.6	13.7	9.0
Market value ($ mil.)	–	–	–	–	–	–
Employees		–	–	–	–	1,956

VALENCE TECHNOLOGY, INC.

12303 Technology Blvd., Suite 950
Austin, TX 78727
Phone: 512 527-2900
Fax: –
Web: www.valence.com

NBB: VLNC Q
CEO: –
CFO: –
HR: –
FYE: March 31
Type: Public

If you charged Valence Technology with battery you'd be right. The company's rechargeable lithium polymer batteries are designed for use in industrial (forklifts) military (robotics) stationary (generators) and transportation-related (cars and boats) electrical power applications. Valence touts its U-Charge lithium iron magnesium phosphate (LiFeMgPO4) energy storage systems as having a longer life and being safer and more stable under extreme conditions than even lithium-ion batteries that use oxide-based cathode materials. In 2012 Valence filed a voluntary petition for a Chapter 11 business reorganization in US Bankruptcy Court. The company expects to complete restructuring in 2012.

	Annual Growth	03/08	03/09	03/10	03/11	03/12
Sales ($ mil.)	20.9%	20.8	26.2	16.1	45.9	44.4
Net income ($ mil.)	–	(19.4)	(21.2)	(23.0)	(12.7)	(12.7)
Market value ($ mil.)	(34.6%)	749.6	362.1	144.5	265.2	137.4
Employees	(8.7%)	490	366	349	433	340

VALERO ENERGY CORP

One Valero Way
San Antonio, TX 78249
Phone: 210 345-2000
Fax: 210 246-2646
Web: www.valero.com

NYS: VLO
CEO: Joseph W. (Joe) Gorder
CFO: Michael S. (Mike) Ciskowski
HR: –
FYE: December 31
Type: Public

Valero Energy was not only named after a mission (the Mission San Antonio de Valero) it is on a mission to be the largest independent refiner in the US. Valero churns out about 3 million barrels per day refining low-cost residual oil and heavy crude into cleaner-burning higher-margin products including low-sulfur diesels. It operates 15 refineries in the US Canada and the UK. It also has 11 ethanol plants with a combined production capacity of about 1.4 billion gallons per year. Once a more diversified company Valero has exited the retail business in order to focus on its oil refining and ethanol operations.

	Annual Growth	12/14	12/15	12/16	12/17	12/18
Sales ($ mil.)	(2.8%)	130,844.0	87,804.0	75,659.0	93,980.0	117,033.0
Net income ($ mil.)	(3.7%)	3,630.0	3,990.0	2,289.0	4,065.0	3,122.0
Market value ($ mil.)	10.9%	20,671.0	29,528.3	28,530.2	38,381.3	31,307.2
Employees	0.5%	10,065	10,103	9,996	10,015	10,261

VALERO ENERGY PARTNERS LP

One Valero Way
San Antonio, TX 78249
Phone: 210 345-2000
Fax: –
Web: www.valeroenergypartners.com

NYS: VLP
CEO: Joseph W Gorder
CFO: –
HR: –
FYE: December 31
Type: Public

Valero Energy Partners teams up with Valero Energy to bring energy in the form of petroleum products to the world. The company was formed to serve as the transportation and logistics arm of major independent US refiner Valero Energy. It makes money from fees on pipeline transportation and storage of crude oil and refined petroleum along the US Gulf Coast and eastern US. The partnership serves Valero's two plants in Port Arthur and Sunray Texas and one in Memphis. As a partnership Valero Energy Partners is exempt from paying corporate income tax. It went public in 2013. In 2016 the company bought the McKee Terminal Services Business from Valero Energy for $240 million.

	Annual Growth	12/12	12/13	12/14	12/15	12/16
Sales ($ mil.)	43.0%	86.8	94.5	129.2	243.6	362.6
Net income ($ mil.)	45.4%	42.3	50.2	68.8	101.8	188.8
Market value ($ mil.)	8.7%	–	2,370.2	2,975.7	3,550.9	3,045.9
Employees		–	–	–	–	–

VALHI, INC.

5430 LBJ Freeway, Suite 1700
Dallas, TX 75240-2620
Phone: 972 233-1700
Fax: 972 448-1445
Web: www.valhi.net

NYS: VHI
CEO: Steven L. (Steve) Watson
CFO: Bobby D. O'Brien
HR: –
FYE: December 31
Type: Public

Valhi keeps it interesting by pursuing a variety of things. The company's NL Industries unit operating through subsidiary Kronos is a leading maker of titanium dioxide pigment which is used to whiten and add opacity to fibers paper paint and plastic. Other subsidiaries include CompX (ergonomic computer support systems and office security products) Tremont (titanium metal products for the aerospace and other markets through its stake in Titanium Metals) and Waste Control Specialists (operator of hazardous-waste treatment facilities in Texas). It also has real estate assets.

	Annual Growth	12/14	12/15	12/16	12/17	12/18
Sales ($ mil.)	(0.2%)	1,904.6	1,564.9	1,606.2	1,904.6	1,889.3
Net income ($ mil.)	48.6%	53.8	(133.6)	(15.9)	207.5	262.2
Market value ($ mil.)	(25.9%)	2,192.2	458.3	1,183.3	2,110.1	660.1
Employees	(3.1%)	2,485	2,280	2,260	2,245	2,195

VALLEY FINANCIAL CORP.

36 Church Avenue, S.W.
Roanoke, VA 24011
Phone: 540 342-2265
Fax: –
Web: www.myvalleybank.com

NAS: VYFC
CEO: –
CFO: –
HR: –
FYE: December 31
Type: Public

Down in the valley valley so low ... Valley Financial has a banking business dontcha know? The financial institution is the holding company for Valley Bank which operates about 10 locations in and around Roanoke Virginia. Valley Bank offers traditional banking products and services to individuals and small to midsized businesses in its market area. Deposit products include checking and savings accounts NOW accounts and CDs. Lending operations include residential mortgages business loans construction loans and consumer loans. The bank offers investment and insurance products through subsidiary Valley Wealth Management Services.

	Annual Growth	12/09	12/10	12/11	12/12	12/13
Assets ($ mil.)	3.7%	713.7	767.6	773.5	764.6	825.3
Net income ($ mil.)	–	(5.7)	3.5	5.7	6.5	6.8
Market value ($ mil.)	31.7%	16.8	14.5	23.5	43.3	50.5
Employees	1.3%	136	130	136	139	143

VALLEY HEALTH SYSTEM

1840 AMHERST ST
WINCHESTER, VA 22601-2808
Phone: 540-536-8000
Fax: -
Web: www.valleyhealthlink.com

CEO: Mark H Merrill
CFO: Pete Gallagher
HR: -
FYE: December 31
Type: Private

Valley Health's medical centers can be found in the in the Shenandoah Valley region. The not-for-profit organization operates six hospitals in Virginia and West Virginia that house a combined total of roughly 610 beds. The facilities include the flagship Winchester Medical Center as well as Warren Memorial Hospital Shenandoah Memorial Hospital and a handful of smaller community hospitals. Valley Health also operates outpatient surgery nursing home rehabilitation urgent care and family practice centers and it offers ambulance and home health care services. The system can trace its beginnings back to the opening of Winchester Memorial Hospital in 1903.

	Annual Growth	12/03	12/04	12/05	12/06	12/07
Sales ($ mil.)	-	-	-	(1,286.6)	564.1	612.2
Net income ($ mil.)	43836.8%	-	-	0.0	76.0	52.1
Market value ($ mil.)	-	-	-	-	-	-
Employees	-	-	-	-	-	4,300

VALLEY HEALTH SYSTEM LLC

620 SHADOW LN
LAS VEGAS, NV 891064119
Phone: 702-388-4000
Fax: -
Web: www.valleyhospital.net

CEO: Sam Kaufman
CFO: -
HR: -
FYE: December 31
Type: Private

If you hit the Las Vegas Strip a bit too hard Valley Hospital Medical Center could be a site you weren't planning to see. Part of Universal Health Services' subsidiary The Valley Health System Valley Hospital has about 400 beds and offers inpatient outpatient and emergency care. Founded in 1972 it also operates a Cardiac Center and the HealthPlace for Women and Children's unit (which includes a Level III Neonatal Intensive Care Unit). Valley Medical was the first hospital in the region to receive accreditation as a Primary Stroke Center a Certified Chest Pain Center and a Heart Failure Center.

	Annual Growth	12/07	12/08	12/14	12/15	12/16
Sales ($ mil.)	(0.9%)	-	305.6	244.2	269.8	283.5
Net income ($ mil.)	(6.8%)	-	26.1	5.6	15.4	14.9
Market value ($ mil.)	-	-	-	-	-	-
Employees	-	-	-	-	-	1,350

VALLEY NATIONAL BANCORP (NJ)   NMS: VLY

One Penn Plaza
New York, NY 10119
Phone: 973 305-8800
Fax: -
Web: www.valleynationalbank.com

CEO: Gerald H. Lipkin
CFO: Alan D. Eskow
HR: Terry Gehrke
FYE: December 31
Type: Public

Valley National Bancorp is high on New Jersey and New York. The holding company owns Valley National Bank which serves commercial and retail clients through more than 200 branches in northern and central New Jersey and in the New York City boroughs of Manhattan Brooklyn and Queens as well as on Long Island. The bank provides standard services like checking and savings accounts loans and mortgages credit cards and trust services. Subsidiaries offer asset management mortgage and auto loan servicing title insurance asset-based lending and property/casualty life and health insurance. Founded as The Passaic Park Trust Company in 1927 Valley National is looking to expand in Florida.

	Annual Growth	12/14	12/15	12/16	12/17	12/18
Assets ($ mil.)	14.1%	18,793.9	21,612.6	22,864.4	24,002.3	31,863.1
Net income ($ mil.)	22.5%	116.2	103.0	168.1	161.9	261.4
Market value ($ mil.)	(2.2%)	3,218.2	3,264.6	3,857.9	3,718.7	2,943.1
Employees	2.4%	2,907	2,929	2,828	2,842	3,192

VALLEY VIEW COMMUNITY UNIT SCHOOL DISTRICT 365U

801 W NORMANTOWN RD
ROMEOVILLE, IL 604464330
Phone: 815-886-2700
Fax: -
Web: www.vvsd.org

CEO: -
CFO: -
HR: Brandy McCurrie
FYE: June 30
Type: Private

Located about 35 miles southwest of downtown Chicago Valley View School District 365U provides education to 18000 elementary middle and high school students — the district also includes one alternative school and one preschool. The 20 schools included in the district (serving Romeoville and Bolingbrook communities) total approximately 2.4 million square feet. With more than 2000 full time employees Valley View School District 365U is one of Will County's largest employers. The seven-member school board (elected for a four-year term) hires and supervises the superintendent of schools and sets district policies.

	Annual Growth	06/06	06/07	06/16	06/17	06/18
Sales ($ mil.)	5.7%	-	190.1	295.0	332.7	348.4
Net income ($ mil.)	(28.6%)	-	220.6	(8.9)	11.8	5.4
Market value ($ mil.)	-	-	-	-	-	-
Employees	-	-	-	-	-	3,000

VALMONT INDUSTRIES INC   NYS: VMI

One Valmont Plaza
Omaha, NE 68154-5215
Phone: 402 963-1000
Fax: 402 963-1198
Web: www.valmont.com

CEO: Jens Holk Nielsen
CFO: Mark C. Jaksich
HR: Tim Kennedy
FYE: December 29
Type: Public

Valmont Industries helps bring you well-lit streets orderly traffic electrical power and healthy crops. The manufacturing company operates through four primary business units. The engineered support structures unit makes metal poles and other structures for lighting traffic and wireless communications. Valmont's utility support structures division manufacturers steel and concrete poles and other structures used for electrical transmission and distribution. The irrigation unit provides agricultural irrigation equipment sold under the Valley brand. The company's coatings operations offer metal coating services including galvanizing anodizing and powder coating. Valmont which generates most of its sales in the US was established in 1946.

	Annual Growth	12/14	12/15	12/16	12/17	12/18
Sales ($ mil.)	(3.1%)	3,123.1	2,618.9	2,521.7	2,746.0	2,757.1
Net income ($ mil.)	(15.4%)	184.0	40.1	173.2	116.2	94.4
Market value ($ mil.)	(4.2%)	2,835.5	2,380.0	3,092.5	3,640.1	2,387.5
Employees	(2.3%)	11,321	10,697	10,552	10,690	10,328

VALSPAR CORP   NYS: VAL

1101 South 3rd Street
Minneapolis, MN 55415
Phone: 612 851-7000
Fax: -
Web: www.valsparglobal.com

CEO: -
CFO: -
HR: -
FYE: October 28
Type: Public

Valspar wants you to put on a coat. The firm makes a variety of coatings and paints for manufacturing automotive construction and food-packaging companies as well as for consumers. The company's industrial coatings — used by OEMs including building product appliance and furniture makers — include coatings for metal wood plastic and glass. Packaging products include coatings and inks for rigid containers such as food and beverage cans. Its consumer paints include interior and exterior paints primers stains and varnishes sold through mass merchandisers like Wal-Mart and Lowe's. Valspar also makes auto paints and colorants. In 2016 rival Sherwin-Williams agreed to buy Valspar for $11.3 billion.

	Annual Growth	10/12	10/13	10/14	10/15	10/16
Sales ($ mil.)	1.0%	4,020.9	4,103.8	4,522.4	4,392.6	4,190.6
Net income ($ mil.)	4.8%	292.5	289.3	345.4	399.5	353.0
Market value ($ mil.)	15.5%	4,365.1	5,581.8	6,525.4	6,429.3	7,762.0
Employees	3.3%	9,755	10,702	10,513	11,130	11,100

VALUE DRUG COMPANY

195 THEATER DR
DUNCANSVILLE, PA 166357144
Phone: 814-944-9316
Fax: –
Web: www.valuedrugco.com

CEO: –
CFO: Robert E Tyler
HR: –
FYE: December 31
Type: Private

Value Drug Company sees a great deal of value in keeping independent pharmacies competitive. The company is a purchasing cooperative of hundreds of independent drugstores that provides wholesale pharmaceutical distribution services to its members primarily in the central Pennsylvania area. Its products include pharmaceuticals and non-prescription medications hospital and convalescent equipment health and beauty aids nutritional supplies and other health care-related products. The company works with some of the world's largest pharmaceutical makers. Value Drug was founded in 1934 and incorporated in 1936. The company is led by president Greg Drew a former Rite-Aid executive.

	Annual Growth	12/14	12/15	12/16	12/17	12/18
Sales ($ mil.)	9.9%	–	779.8	816.5	842.9	1,034.2
Net income ($ mil.)	–	–	3.2	0.2	0.9	(0.1)
Market value ($ mil.)	–	–	–	–	–	–
Employees	–	–	–	–	–	200

VALUE LINE INC

551 Fifth Avenue
New York, NY 10176-0001
Phone: 212 907-1500
Fax: –
Web: www.valueline.com

NAS: VALU
CEO: Howard A Brecher
CFO: Stephen R Anastasio
HR: –
FYE: April 30
Type: Public

Value Line's investment-related publications are likely to be found on the bookshelves of the serious investor. Its flagship publication The Value Line Investment Survey features stock reports that incorporate objective analysis financial information and forecasts of stock performance. Its print and electronic products also include Value Line Fund Advisor which offers mutual fund evaluations and rankings and investment analysis software The Value Line Investment Analyzer . The company's electronic products are available via CD-ROM and via the company's website. All total Value Line collects data and provides analysis on some 7000 stocks; 18000 mutual funds; 200000 options; and other securities.

	Annual Growth	04/15	04/16	04/17	04/18	04/19
Sales ($ mil.)	0.5%	35.5	34.5	42.7	35.9	36.3
Net income ($ mil.)	11.2%	7.3	7.3	10.4	14.7	11.2
Market value ($ mil.)	12.5%	139.9	158.4	168.9	188.2	223.7
Employees	(4.5%)	195	178	183	171	162

VAN ARPIN LINES INC

99 JAMES P MURPHY IND HWY
WEST WARWICK, RI 028932382
Phone: 800-343-3500
Fax: –

CEO: David Arpin
CFO: Michael Killoran
HR: –
FYE: December 31
Type: Private

From the fairway to the highway and home again Arpin Van Lines provides a wide range of moving services for residential business and government customers which have included the LPGA. The company formerly known as Paul Arpin Van Lines operates through a network of independent agents throughout North America. (The agents handle local moves within assigned geographic territories.) Arpin Van Lines coordinates interstate moves.) Arpin Van Lines' fleet includes some 700 trucks. The company which is run by members of the founding Arpin family is a division of Arpin Group which also includes Arpin International Group and Arpin Moving Systems (Canada). The original Arpin moving company was founded in 1900.

	Annual Growth	12/05	12/06	12/07	12/09	12/10
Sales ($ mil.)	(2.3%)	–	–	113.5	105.8	105.7
Net income ($ mil.)	(14.9%)	–	–	0.6	1.1	0.4
Market value ($ mil.)	–	–	–	–	–	–
Employees	–	–	–	–	–	79

VAN ATLAS LINES INC

1212 SAINT GEORGE RD
EVANSVILLE, IN 477112364
Phone: 812-424-4326
Fax: –
Web: www.atlas2290.com

CEO: Glen Dunkerson
CFO: Richard J Olson
HR: –
FYE: December 31
Type: Private

The main subsidiary of Atlas World Group moving company Atlas Van Lines provides transportation of household goods throughout the US and between the US and Canada. The company is one of the largest movers in the US. Atlas Van Lines also offers specialized transportation services for such cargo as trade show materials fine art electronics pianos store fixtures and even individual cars and motorcycles. It operates through a network of some 500 agents in the US and about 150 in Canada — independent companies that use the Atlas brand in assigned geographic territories and cooperate on interstate moves. Atlas Van Lines was formed in 1948 by a group of 33 small moving companies.

	Annual Growth	12/03	12/04	12/05	12/06	12/08
Sales ($ mil.)	127.4%	–	–	59.2	58.1	696.0
Net income ($ mil.)	71.0%	–	–	3.8	2.5	19.2
Market value ($ mil.)	–	–	–	–	–	–
Employees	–	–	–	–	–	606

VAN BUDD LINES INC

24 SCHOOLHOUSE RD
SOMERSET, NJ 088731213
Phone: 732-627-0600
Fax: –
Web: www.buddvanlines.com

CEO: –
CFO: –
HR: –
FYE: December 31
Type: Private

No hothouse flower Budd Van Lines aims to be a hardy perennial of the corporate relocation business. From coast to coast the independent van line company moves the household goods of employees who are relocating at the behest of their employers about 6500 annually. It offers packing and moving services to all 48 contiguous states from branch offices in New Jersey California Wisconsin Georgia Ohio and Texas. Companies that have called upon Budd Van Lines to help employees move include Bristol-Myers Squibb Merck & Co. and PricewaterhouseCoopers. Budd Van Lines was founded in 1975.

	Annual Growth	12/05	12/06	12/07	12/08	12/10
Sales ($ mil.)	–	–	–	(1,131.5)	47.1	47.2
Net income ($ mil.)	3019.9%	–	–	0.0	0.3	1.1
Market value ($ mil.)	–	–	–	–	–	–
Employees	–	–	–	–	–	155

VAN HORN METZ & CO. INC.

201 E ELM ST
CONSHOHOCKEN, PA 194282029
Phone: 610-828-4500
Fax: –
Web: www.vanhornmetz.com

CEO: –
CFO: –
HR: –
FYE: December 31
Type: Private

|Van Horn Metz & Co. (or Van Horn Metz) distributes chemical ingredients such as pigments dyes extenders additives resins lubricants and base stocks. The company's customers include makers of plastic and rubber products inks adhesives and sealants and paints and coatings. Founded in 1950 by Harold Van Horn and Donald Metz the company serves customers throughout the eastern half of the US. Van Horn Metz operates 12 warehouses and six sales offices.

	Annual Growth	12/06	12/07	12/08	12/09	12/10
Sales ($ mil.)	–	–	–	(380.0)	35.5	39.4
Net income ($ mil.)	–	–	–	0.0	0.0	0.0
Market value ($ mil.)	–	–	–	–	–	–
Employees	–	–	–	–	–	24

VANDA PHARMACEUTICALS INC   NMS: VNDA

2200 Pennsylvania Avenue, N.W., Suite 300 E   CEO: Mihael H. Polymeropoulos
Washington, DC 20037   CFO: James P. Kelly
Phone: 202 734-3400   HR: –
Fax: –   FYE: December 31
Web: www.vandapharma.com   Type: Public

Vanda Pharmaceuticals is a pharmaceutical company that is developing several drugs for disorders of the central nervous system. The company's first commercial drug was schizophrenia treatment Fanapt (iloperidone). Another drug Hetlioz (tasimelteon) was launched in the US in 2014 for the treatment of non-24-hour sleep-wake disorder; it received European Commission approval in 2015. Other drug candidates are treatments for sleep disorders including insomnia and sleep apnea as well as anxiety and depression. Vanda typically licenses development and commercialization rights for its compounds from (and to) companies including Bristol-Myers Squibb Eli Lilly and Novartis.

	Annual Growth	12/14	12/15	12/16	12/17	12/18
Sales ($ mil.)	40.1%	50.2	109.9	146.0	165.1	193.1
Net income ($ mil.)	5.7%	20.2	(39.9)	(18.0)	(15.6)	25.2
Market value ($ mil.)	16.2%	751.5	488.6	837.0	797.7	1,371.2
Employees	43.3%	64	118	142	273	270

VANDERBILT UNIVERSITY MEDICAL CENTER

1211 MEDICAL CENTER DR   CEO: C. Wright Pinson
NASHVILLE, TN 372320004   CFO: –
Phone: 615-322-5000   HR: –
Fax: –   FYE: June 30
Web: www.vanderbilthealth.com   Type: Private

The Vanderbilt University Medical Center (VUMC) is one of the top health care organizations in the US with its network of hospitals outpatient centers clinics and specialty institutes. Its medical education programs train hundreds of doctors and nurses each year and the center's Vanderbilt Clinics receive more than 1.5 million annual patient visits. Its Vanderbilt University Hospitals together with the clinics and specialty facilities have more than 1000 beds. VUMC boasts a children's hospital a psychiatric hospital a transplant center and a rehabilitation hospital as well as a biomedical research center and the Vanderbilt-Ingram Cancer Center a National Cancer Institute-designated facility.

	Annual Growth	06/14	06/15	06/16	06/17	06/18
Sales ($ mil.)	4.9%	–	–	–	3,894.4	4,086.4
Net income ($ mil.)	(62.8%)	–	–	–	264.1	98.1
Market value ($ mil.)	–	–	–	–	–	–
Employees	–	–	–	–	–	19,000

VANGUARD NATURAL RESOURCES LLC   NBB: VNRS Q

5847 San Felipe, Suite 3000   CEO: –
Houston, TX 77057   CFO: –
Phone: 832 327-2255   HR: –
Fax: –   FYE: December 31
Web: www.vnrllc.com   Type: Public

Vanguard Natural Resources is at the forefront of oil and natural gas exploration in the Appalachian Basin the Rockies the Permian Basin and South Texas acquiring and developing oil and gas properties in these region. In Vanguard Natural Resources has estimated proved reserves of 172.2 million barrels of oil equivalent and an interest in 2551 net and 7277 gross productive wells. The company also owns a 40% working interest in 797118 acres in Appalachia. Vinland Energy Eastern owns the remaining 60% working interest of the acreage. In 2017 Vanguard Natural Resources filed for Chapter 11 bankruptcy protection.

	Annual Growth	12/11	12/12	12/13	12/14	12/15
Sales ($ mil.)	15.4%	319.6	347.2	454.5	788.1	566.6
Net income ($ mil.)	–	–	62.1	(168.8)	59.5	64.3	(1,883.2)
Market value ($ mil.)	(42.7%)	3,616.7	3,403.3	3,864.1	1,972.6	390.1
Employees	36.4%	110	122	172	260	381

VANTIV INC.   NYSE: VNTV

8500 Governor's Hill Dr.   CEO: Charles Drucker
Symmes Township OH 45249   CFO: –
Phone: 513-900-5250   HR: –
Fax: 816-464-0510   FYE: December 31
Web: smithelectric.com   Type: Public

You may not know it but every time you swipe your credit card a whole world of transactions take place in the background. And Vantiv lives to rule that world. The company which operates through subsidiary Vantiv LLC (formerly Fifth Third Processing Solutions) is a merchant acquirer - a third party payment processor operating between merchants (and their banks) and customers (and their banks). One of the largest merchant acquirers it also handles PIN transactions fraud detection and management and credit card issuing. Catering to small- to mid-size customers Vantiv sells services specific to grocers pharmacies retailers restaurants and others. Formed in 1970 the company went public in 2012.

VARIAN MEDICAL SYSTEMS INC   NYS: VAR

3100 Hansen Way   CEO: Dow R. Wilson
Palo Alto, CA 94304-1038   CFO: Gary E. Bischoping
Phone: 650 493-4000   HR: –
Fax: –   FYE: September 27
Web: www.varian.com   Type: Public

Varian Medical Systems develops manufactures and services hardware and software products for the treatment of cancer with radiotherapy stereotactic radiosurgery stereotactic body radiotherapy proton therapy and brachytherapy. Products include linear accelerators simulators and data management software primarily for use in cancer radiotherapy. Its Halcyon line of treatment systems was launched and approved for use in the US and Europe during 2017; the company has already sold more than 180 Halcyon systems. Also in 2017 Varian spun off its X-ray unit which makes imaging subsystems and X-ray-generating tubes into a new public company named Varex Imaging.

	Annual Growth	10/15*	09/16	09/17	09/18	09/19
Sales ($ mil.)	1.0%	3,099.1	3,217.8	2,668.2	2,919.1	3,225.1
Net income ($ mil.)	(8.2%)	411.5	402.3	249.6	149.9	291.9
Market value ($ mil.)	12.0%	6,827.3	9,037.3	9,085.4	10,163.2	10,728.9
Employees	8.4%	7,300	7,800	6,600	7,174	10,062

*Fiscal year change

VARIAN SEMICONDUCTOR EQUIPMENT ASSOCIATES INC.   NASDAQ: VSEA

35 Dory Rd.   CEO: Gary E Dickerson
Gloucester MA 01930   CFO: Robert J Halliday
Phone: 978-282-2000   HR: Cindy Emerzian
Fax: 978-283-6376   FYE: September 30
Web: www.vsea.com   Type: Subsidiary

Varian Semiconductor Equipment Associates (VSEA) is the ion king. The company is the world's top designer and manufacturer of ion implantation equipment and systems which beam ions into semiconductor wafers to modify their electrical properties. VSEA has a common equipment platform the VIISta single-wafer system which is designed to cover a complete range of applications such as high-current medium-current and high and ultra high-energy doses of ions. It also offers product upgrades spare parts and technical support. Customers outside North America account for more than 70% of the company's sales. In 2011 Applied Materials acquired VSEA for about $4.2 billion.

VARIETY CHILDREN'S HOSPITAL

3100 SW 62ND AVE
MIAMI, FL 331553009
Phone: 305-666-6511
Fax: –
Web: www.nicklauschildrens.org

CEO: Narendra M Kini
CFO: –
HR: –
FYE: December 31
Type: Private

Miami Children's Hospital (MCH) a not-for-profit medical center boasts some 290 beds and offers more than 40 different health care specialties and sub-specialties represented by more than 650 physicians and more than 130 pediatric sub-specialists. Some specialties include pediatric emergency care cancer treatment orthopedics and rehabilitation services. The hospital's neonatal unit treats newborns referred from other hospitals. Miami Children's Hospital operates the region's only free-standing pediatric trauma center. The MCH Research Institute conducts more than 210 clinical research studies in 26 sub-specialties.

	Annual Growth	12/13	12/14	12/16	12/17	12/18
Sales ($ mil.)	1.5%	–	618.1	625.2	674.2	656.0
Net income ($ mil.)	–	–	77.1	71.7	60.6	(23.5)
Market value ($ mil.)	–	–	–	–	–	–
Employees	–	–	–	–	–	3,700

VASCULAR SOLUTIONS INC

6464 Sycamore Court North
Minneapolis, MN 55369
Phone: 763 656-4300
Fax: 877 656-4251
Web: www.vasc.com

NMS: VASC
CEO: Howard Root
CFO: James Hennen
HR: –
FYE: December 31
Type: Public

Vascular Solutions helps interventional cardiologists intervene into veins. The company develops manufactures and markets catheters used during treatment of vascular conditions. Its product line includes the Pronto extraction catheter which removes arterial clots and other tools used to get under the skin and into blood vessels. Its hemostat products include the D-Stat a thrombin-infused bandage used to control bleeding following catheterization. It also makes the Vari-Lase a laser system for treating varicose veins. Vascular Solutions markets the devices to interventional cardiologists and radiologists through its own sales team in the US; it uses independent distributors overseas.

	Annual Growth	12/11	12/12	12/13	12/14	12/15
Sales ($ mil.)	13.1%	90.0	98.4	110.5	126.1	147.2
Net income ($ mil.)	1.8%	9.7	9.9	11.1	12.7	10.5
Market value ($ mil.)	32.6%	193.5	274.7	402.5	472.2	597.9
Employees	12.5%	355	377	406	485	568

VASO CORP

137 Commercial St., Suite 200
Plainview, NY 11803
Phone: 516 997-4600
Fax: 516 997-2299
Web: www.vasocorporation.com

NBB: VASO
CEO: –
CFO: Michael J Beecher
HR: –
FYE: December 31
Type: Public

Vasomedical's noninvasive treatments for angina and congestive heart failure get patients' blood pumping. The company's main product is the EECP (enhanced external counterpulsation) system which is also approved to treat coronary artery disease and cardiogenic shock. During the company's Medicare-covered treatments cuffs attached to the patient's calves and thighs inflate and deflate in sync with the patient's heartbeat increasing and decreasing aortic blood pressure. After about 35 treatments patients may experience years of symptomatic relief. Vasomedical sells the system to hospitals clinics and other health care providers worldwide through a direct sales force and independent distributors.

	Annual Growth	12/14	12/15	12/16	12/17	12/18
Sales ($ mil.)	20.6%	35.0	57.1	72.6	72.8	74.0
Net income ($ mil.)	–	1.1	3.8	2.4	(4.5)	(3.7)
Market value ($ mil.)	(38.0%)	28.4	33.1	21.1	8.8	4.2
Employees	9.8%	218	281	311	308	317

VASSAR COLLEGE

124 RAYMOND AVE BOX 12
POUGHKEEPSIE, NY 12604-0001
Phone: 845-437-7000
Fax: –
Web: www.vassar.edu

CEO: –
CFO: –
HR: –
FYE: June 30
Type: Private

A cool nickname and certain heritage aren't enough to assure some students entrance into Vassar College. The highly selective school enrolls some 2400 students annually most of whom graduated in the top 20% of their high school class. It has a student-faculty ratio of 8:1 and a list of alumni that includes standouts in areas from business to philanthropy. Because Vassar has no core curriculum students may concentrate in a single discipline a multidisciplinary program or design an independent major. The only universal requirements for graduation are proficiency in a foreign language a freshman composition class and a quantitative class. Vassar was founded in 1861 as a women's school; it went coed in 1969.

	Annual Growth	06/08	06/09	06/10	06/11	06/12
Sales ($ mil.)	(0.9%)	–	158.4	205.9	229.5	154.0
Net income ($ mil.)	–	–	(55.4)	(7.3)	12.5	(33.1)
Market value ($ mil.)	–	–	–	–	–	–
Employees	–	–	–	–	–	974

VASSAR COLLEGE INC

124 RAYMOND AVE BOX 12
POUGHKEEPSIE, NY 126040001
Phone: 845-437-7000
Fax: –
Web: www.admissions.vassar.edu

CEO: –
CFO: –
HR: –
FYE: June 30
Type: Private

A cool nickname and certain heritage aren't enough to assure some students entrance into Vassar College. The highly selective school enrolls some 2400 students annually most of whom graduated in the top 20% of their high school class. It has a student-faculty ratio of 8:1 and a list of alumni that includes standouts in areas from business to philanthropy. Because Vassar has no core curriculum students may concentrate in a single discipline a multidisciplinary program or design an independent major. The only universal requirements for graduation are proficiency in a foreign language a freshman composition class and a quantitative class. Vassar was founded in 1861 as a women's school; it went coed in 1969.

	Annual Growth	06/10	06/11	06/12	06/13	06/14
Sales ($ mil.)	(11.2%)	–	229.5	154.0	175.7	160.6
Net income ($ mil.)	–	–	–	(33.1)	103.1	97.3
Market value ($ mil.)	–	–	–	–	–	–
Employees	–	–	–	–	–	974

VAUGHAN-BASSETT FURNITURE COMPANY, INCORPORATED

300 E GRAYSON ST
GALAX, VA 243332964
Phone: 276-236-6161
Fax: –
Web: www.vaughan-bassett.com

CEO: John D Bassett III
CFO: Andrew Williamson
HR: Linda H Croy
FYE: November 27
Type: Private

Vaughan-Bassett Furniture Company which specializes in making bedroom and dining room furniture is counted among the leading wood furniture manufacturers in the US. It's one of the few companies that operates furniture factories in America — in Virginia and North Carolina. Vaughan-Bassett collections are made using wood solids and wood veneers from pine oak cherry maple ash beech poplar and birch trees. It also operates a One for One tree-planting program to promote sustainability. At the helm is namesake John Bassett III who comes from a family of furniture entrepreneurs. His grandfather founded industry leader Bassett Furniture Industries in 1902.

	Annual Growth	11/06	11/07	11/08	11/09	11/10
Sales ($ mil.)	–	–	–	(483.9)	85.5	78.2
Net income ($ mil.)	30023.6%	–	–	0.0	2.0	1.2
Market value ($ mil.)	–	–	–	–	–	–
Employees	–	–	–	–	–	1,564

VAXART INC
NAS: VXRT

290 Utah Ave., Suite 200
South San Francisco, CA 94080
Phone: 650 550-3500
Fax: –
Web: www.aviragentherapeutics.com

CEO: Wouter W Latour
CFO: Wouter W Latour
HR: –
FYE: December 31
Type: Public

Aviragen Therapeutics (formerly Biota Biopharmaceuticals) would like to wave bye-bye to a host of viral infections plaguing mankind. It has a handful of drugs in active clinical development including Laninamivir octanoate for the treatment of influenza vapendavir for the treatment of human rhinovirus (common cold) upper respiratory infections in asthmatics and BTA585 for the treatment and prevention of condyloma caused by human papillomavirus types 6 and 11. Its Zanamivir flu treatment is marketed by GlaxoSmithKline as Relenza while another flu treatment laninamivir octanoate is marketed by Daiichi Sankyo as Inavir in Japan. Aviragen merged with California-based oral vaccine developer Vaxart in February 2018.

	Annual Growth	06/14	06/15	06/16	06/17*	12/18
Sales ($ mil.)	(50.4%)	68.7	24.6	9.3	8.9	4.2
Net income ($ mil.)	–	(11.0)	(19.1)	(25.4)	(29.4)	(18.0)
Market value ($ mil.)	(10.0%)	20.4	14.8	10.0	4.8	13.4
Employees	(15.3%)	66	19	21	16	34

*Fiscal year change

VBI VACCINES INC
NAS: VBIV

222 Third Street, Suite 2241
Cambridge, MA 02142
Phone: 613 749-4200
Fax: –
Web: www.vbivaccines.com

CEO: –
CFO: –
HR: –
FYE: December 31
Type: Public

Paulson Capital is a financial services holding company operating through its sole subsidiary Paulson Investment Company. A full-service brokerage Paulson Investment is one of the largest independent brokerage firms in the Pacific Northwest. It acts as an agent for its customers in the purchase and sale of stocks options and debt securities. The company also offers market-making and underwriting services for small and emerging companies. Paulson Investment has more than 40 branches in about a dozen states; most are run by independent contractors. The company has agreed to sell its Paulson Investment retail operations to Tampa-based JHS Capital Advisors.

	Annual Growth	12/09	12/10	12/11	12/12	12/13
Sales ($ mil.)	(8.2%)	15.2	18.1	15.4	7.7	10.8
Net income ($ mil.)	–	(2.4)	(1.2)	(3.1)	(0.4)	(1.5)
Market value ($ mil.)	(9.6%)	1.8	1.3	0.6	0.9	1.2
Employees	(14.2%)	70	65	62	15	38

VCA INC
NMS: WOOF

12401 West Olympic Boulevard
Los Angeles, CA 90064-1022
Phone: 310 571-6500
Fax: –
Web: www.vcaantech.com

CEO: Robert L Antin
CFO: –
HR: –
FYE: December 31
Type: Public

At VCA health care doesn't go to the dogs. Dogs — cats and a boatload of other animals — go to it for health services. The company operates the nation's largest chain of animal hospitals — more than 600 in some 41 states and four Canadian provinces. Its hospitals offer basic wellness checkups dental care neutering and spaying vaccinations and specialty surgeries. With about 60 diagnostic laboratories nationwide VCA also tests blood tissue and urine samples for more than 16000 animal hospitals and practices universities and government agencies. Founded in 1986 as Veterinary Centers of America the company has grown over the years through acquisitions of other animal hospitals and veterinary product suppliers. In 2017 consumer products company Mars agreed to acquire VCA for $9.1 billion including $1.4 billion in debt.

	Annual Growth	12/11	12/12	12/13	12/14	12/15
Sales ($ mil.)	9.5%	1,485.4	1,699.6	1,803.4	1,918.5	2,133.7
Net income ($ mil.)	22.0%	95.4	45.6	137.5	135.4	211.0
Market value ($ mil.)	29.2%	1,595.1	1,700.1	2,532.8	3,938.9	4,442.0
Employees	6.4%	9,900	10,500	11,000	11,500	12,700

VCG HOLDING CORP.
NASDAQ: VCGH

390 Union Blvd. Ste. 540
Lakewood CO 80228
Phone: 303-934-2424
Fax: 303-922-0746
Web: www.vcgh.com

CEO: Troy H Lowrie
CFO: –
HR: –
FYE: December 31
Type: Private

Patrons with dollar bills might get a little extra entertainment from VCG Holding. The company operates about 20 nightclubs featuring live adult entertainment. In addition to exotic dancers the clubs offer dining and bar services as well as members-only VIP rooms intended for entertaining business clients. Alcohol sales account for more than 40% of its business. Located in about 10 states the clubs operate mainly under the names PT's and The Penthouse Club (through a licensing agreement with FriendFinder Networks the publisher of PENTHOUSE). CEO Troy Lowrie and president and COO Micheal Ocello took the company private in 2010.

VECTOR GROUP LTD
NYS: VGR

4400 Biscayne Boulevard
Miami, FL 33137
Phone: 305 579-8000
Fax: –
Web: www.vectorgroupltd.com

CEO: Howard M. Lorber
CFO: J. Bryant Kirkland
HR: –
FYE: December 31
Type: Public

Vector Group holds a strong position in the US discount tobacco market through its Liggett and Vector Tobacco subsidiaries. The companies manufacture discount cigarettes under brands including Eagle 20's Pyramid Grand Prix Liggett Select and Eve. Vector also makes discount cigarettes under partner and private-label brands including the USA brand. The company manufactures cigarettes in North Carolina and distributes them throughout the US. Vector Group's real estate unit New Valley invests in properties and owns residential real estate brokerage firm Douglas Elliman Realty.

	Annual Growth	12/14	12/15	12/16	12/17	12/18
Sales ($ mil.)	4.1%	1,591.3	1,657.2	1,690.9	1,807.5	1,870.3
Net income ($ mil.)	12.0%	37.0	59.2	71.1	84.6	58.1
Market value ($ mil.)	(17.8%)	3,153.0	3,490.4	3,364.6	3,311.4	1,439.7
Employees	9.3%	1,090	1,367	1,425	1,484	1,555

VECTOR PIPELINE L.P.

38705 7 MILE RD STE 490
LIVONIA, MI 481523990
Phone: 734-462-0231
Fax: –
Web: www.vector-pipeline.com

CEO: –
CFO: –
HR: –
FYE: December 31
Type: Private

If you were to ask "what's our vector Victor?" Vector Pipelines would include mainline natural gas transportation in its answer whereas the cast from Airplane would surely answer differently (so please don't call the company "Shirley"). In service since 2000 Vector Pipelines operates a pipeline nearly 350 miles in length with receipt and delivery points in Illinois Indiana Michigan and Ontario. Approximately 95% of the pipeline is located in the US; Vector Pipeline Limited Partnership is responsible for the 15 miles of pipeline in Canada. Calgary-based Enbridge owns a 60% stake in Vector Pipeline and Detroit-based DTE Energy Company owns 40%.

	Annual Growth	12/14	12/15	12/16	12/17	12/18
Sales ($ mil.)	5.4%	–	–	85.5	83.5	95.0
Net income ($ mil.)	35.1%	–	–	20.7	19.7	37.8
Market value ($ mil.)	–	–	–	–	–	–
Employees	–	–	–	–	–	8

VECTREN CORP

NYS: VVC

One Vectren Square
Evansville, IN 47708
Phone: 812-491-4000
Fax: 812-491-4149
Web: www.vectren.com

CEO: Scott M Prochazka
CFO: –
HR: –
FYE: December 31
Type: Public

Vectren intends to inundate Indiana and Ohio with energy. Through its utility subsidiaries Indiana Gas Company (or Vectren North) Southern Indiana Gas and Electric (SIGECO or Vectren South) and Vectren Energy Delivery of Ohio (VEDO) the company distributes natural gas to more than 1 million business and residential customers in the two states. It also distributes electricity to about 144000 customers and almost 1300 MW of primarily coal-fired generating capacity in Indiana. Vectren's other nonregulated businesses include management services and utility infrastructure construction.

	Annual Growth	12/12	12/13	12/14	12/15	12/16
Sales ($ mil.)	2.3%	2,232.8	2,491.2	2,611.7	2,434.7	2,448.3
Net income ($ mil.)	7.4%	159.0	136.6	166.9	197.3	211.6
Market value ($ mil.)	15.4%	2,437.3	2,943.0	3,832.5	3,516.6	4,323.2
Employees	1.8%	5,400	5,500	5,500	5,600	5,800

VEECO INSTRUMENTS INC (DE)

NMS: VECO

Terminal Drive
Plainview, NY 11803
Phone: 516-677-0200
Fax: –
Web: www.veeco.com

CEO: John R. Peeler
CFO: David D. Glass
HR: Robert Bradshaw
FYE: December 31
Type: Public

Veeco Instruments offers precision equipment for manufacturing components such as Light Emitting Diodes ("LEDs") for solid-state lighting and display lasers for communications and 3D sensing and radio frequency (RF) filters for mobile phones. The company is the leading provider of specialized ion beam deposition technology and it is a top provider of laser annealing lithography and etching technologies. Veeco's products are used in the hard-disk drive sensor semiconductor photomask microelectromechanical (MEMS) and coatings industries. Focus Lighting Tech and OSRAM Opto Semiconductors are among its top customers. Veeco gets more than 75% of sales from outside the US.

	Annual Growth	12/14	12/15	12/16	12/17	12/18
Sales ($ mil.)	8.4%	392.9	477.0	332.5	484.8	542.1
Net income ($ mil.)	–	(66.9)	(32.0)	(122.2)	(44.8)	(407.1)
Market value ($ mil.)	(32.1%)	1,675.1	987.4	1,399.9	713.2	355.9
Employees	6.9%	800	783	716	1,014	1,043

VEEVA SYSTEMS INC

NYS: VEEV

4280 Hacienda Drive
Pleasanton, CA 94588
Phone: 925-452-6500
Fax: 925-452-6504
Web: www.veeva.com

CEO: Peter P Gassner
CFO: Timothy S Cabral
HR: –
FYE: January 31
Type: Public

Veeva Systems is breathing new life into software for the health care industry. Its cloud-based software and mobile apps are used by pharmaceutical and biotechnology companies to manage critical business functions. Veeva Systems' customer relationship management software uses Salesforce's platform to manage sales and marketing functions. Its Veeva Vault provides content management and collaboration software for quality management in clinical trials and regulatory compliance for new drug submissions. Its software is used in 75 countries and available in more than 25 languages but North America is its largest market. Founded in 2007 Veeva Systems went public in 2013.

	Annual Growth	01/15	01/16	01/17	01/18	01/19
Sales ($ mil.)	28.8%	313.2	409.2	544.0	685.6	862.2
Net income ($ mil.)	54.5%	40.4	54.5	68.8	142.0	229.8
Market value ($ mil.)	39.5%	4,204.4	3,523.2	6,188.2	9,189.5	15,943.5
Employees	28.0%	951	1,474	1,794	2,171	2,553

VELOCITY COMMERCIAL CAPITAL INC.

30699 Russell Ranch Rd. Ste. 295
Westlake Village CA 91362
Phone: 818-532-3700
Fax: 818-575-9005
Web: www.vcc-inc.com

CEO: –
CFO: Mark Szczepaniak
HR: –
FYE: December 31
Type: Private

If you're a small business in need of some new digs Velocity Commercial Capital has a deal for you. The specialty finance company acquires and originates commercial real estate loans up to $3 million for small businesses. Its average loan is less than $400000. It currently holds mortgages for more than 300 properties 30% of which are in California. Its loan portfolio includes multi-family housing retail space mixed-use developments warehouses offices industrial complexes restaurants and mobile home parks. Velocity Commercial Capital does not make construction loans or lend for undeveloped land. The company which filed to go public in 2010 intends to qualify as a real estate investment trust (REIT).

VELOCITY EXPRESS LLC

11104 W. Airport Blvd. Ste. 130
Stafford TX 77477
Phone: 713-346-9100
Fax: +49-611-6029-305
Web: www.sglgroup.com

CEO: Ken Forster
CFO: –
HR: –
FYE: June 30
Type: Private

Fulfilling customers' need for speed Velocity Express specializes in same-day delivery services. The company offers scheduled pickup and delivery distribution logistics (in which customers' shipments are sorted for delivery to multiple locations) and expedited delivery. Customers include retailers office products manufacturers pharmaceutical wholesalers and other merchandise distributors. Velocity Express operates from approximately 80 warehouses and terminal facilities and deliveries are made by independent contractor drivers. In early 2013 Velocity Express was acquired by TransForce a large provider of transportation and logistics services based in Canada.

VENOCO INC.

NYSE: VQ

370 17th St. Ste. 3900
Denver CO 80202-1370
Phone: 303-626-8300
Fax: 303-626-8315
Web: www.venocoinc.com

CEO: –
CFO: –
HR: –
FYE: December 31
Type: Private

Santa Barbara's pristine beaches and Venoco's oil and gas exploration and production activities make for a volatile mix. Although Venoco has traditionally operated in the environmentally sensitive Santa Barbara Channel it has been expanding its geographic reach and diversifying its operations. It owns interests in more than 790 drilling locations primarily in California's Sacramento Basin and Monterey shale formation. It even has a drilling location in Beverly Hills. In 2011 Venoco reported proved reserves of 95.9 million barrels of oil equivalent (of which 49% was oil). That year the company produced about 6430 barrels of oil equivalent per day.

VENTAS INC
NYS: VTR

353 N. Clark Street, Suite 3300
Chicago, IL 60654
Phone: 877 483-6827
Fax: –
Web: www.ventasreit.com

CEO: Debra A. Cafaro
CFO: Robert F. (Bob) Probst
HR: Edmund M. Brady
FYE: December 31
Type: Public

Ventas is a real estate investment trust (REIT) with a focus on healthcare. The company owns more than 1200 health care properties including senior housing communities skilled nursing facilities hospitals and medical office buildings. The REIT's properties are located throughout the US and Canada as well as in the UK. Ventas leases more than a third of its properties to long-term care providers Brookdale Senior Living Kindred Healthcare and Ardent Health Services. The company also is a major player in medical office buildings owning or managing about 25 million sq. ft. of space. Ventas makes its money from resident fees and services at its senior living properties and from rental income.

	Annual Growth	12/14	12/15	12/16	12/17	12/18
Sales ($ mil.)	5.1%	3,075.7	3,286.4	3,443.5	3,574.1	3,745.8
Net income ($ mil.)	(3.7%)	475.8	417.8	649.2	1,356.5	409.5
Market value ($ mil.)	(4.9%)	25,566.2	20,121.4	22,292.9	21,397.9	20,891.6
Employees	1.1%	479	466	493	493	500

VENTERA CORPORATION

1881 CAMPUS COMMONS DR # 350
RESTON, VA 201911519
Phone: 703-760-4600
Fax: –
Web: www.ventera.com

CEO: Robert Acosta
CFO: –
HR: –
FYE: December 31
Type: Private

Ventera which likens itself to a bulldog in its marketing materials would like clients to take note of its tenacity as a business rather than looking for a more physical resemblance between its consultants and its mascot. The company provides information technology and management consulting services to clients in both the private and public sectors. It offers application development network design systems integration and project management services among others. Ventera serves the financial services manufacturing telecommunications and retail industries among others. Customers have included the US Department of Agriculture and Sprint Nextel. The company was founded in 1996 by CEO Robert Acosta.

	Annual Growth	12/03	12/04	12/05	12/06	12/07
Sales ($ mil.)	(84.8%)	–	–	1,077.9	30.7	24.8
Net income ($ mil.)	14979.5%	–	–	0.0	(173.4)	1.7
Market value ($ mil.)	–	–	–	–	–	–
Employees	–	–	–	–	–	100

VENTURE CONSTRUCTION COMPANY INC

5660 PEACHTREE INDUS BLVD
NORCROSS, GA 300711496
Phone: 770-441-6555
Fax: –
Web: www.ventureconstruction.com

CEO: –
CFO: –
HR: –
FYE: December 31
Type: Private

Building businesses is the primary business for Venture Construction Company. The company builds and remodels fast food and full-service restaurants retail stores (including drug stores) and office buildings. The company operates throughout the US and has divisional offices in Tennessee North Carolina Virginia Georgia and Florida. Its customers include Applebee's Chick-fil-A McDonald's Taco Bell Rite Aid Pizza Hut Walgreen Winn Dixie Blockbuster AutoZone and many more. Founded in 1969 Venture Construction Company is owned by president E. Ray Morris.

	Annual Growth	12/06	12/07	12/08	12/16	12/17
Sales ($ mil.)	–	–	0.0	198.2	292.6	284.5
Net income ($ mil.)	–	–	0.0	1.9	7.8	10.1
Market value ($ mil.)	–	–	–	–	–	–
Employees	–	–	–	–	–	177

VEOLIA ENVIRONMENTAL SERVICES NORTH AMERICA CORP.

200 E. Randolph Dr. Ste. 7900
Chicago IL 60601
Phone: 312-552-2800
Fax: 212-279-9171

CEO: Jeff Adix
CFO: –
HR: –
FYE: December 31
Type: Subsidiary

Veolia Environmental Services North America brings a French accent to environmental solutions. The company holds the regional operations of the waste management division of French company Veolia Environnement. Veolia Environmental Services North America provides liquid and hazardous waste services and industrial maintenance and cleaning. Its divisions include Veolia ES Technical Solutions (hazardous waste management) Veolia Industrial Services (on-site plant cleaning and maintenance) and Veolia Canadian Operations. In addition its Marine Services industrial services business operates a fleet of ships and provides services to offshore petroleum installations primarily in the Gulf of Mexico.

VERA BRADLEY INC.
NMS: VRA

12420 Stonebridge Road
Roanoke, IN 46783
Phone: 877 708-8372
Fax: –
Web: www.verabradley.com

CEO: Robert T. Wallstrom
CFO: Kevin J. Sierks
HR: Adriane Roberts
FYE: February 02
Type: Public

Vera Bradley designs makes and sells quilted handbags and travel bags aimed at women as well as accessories such as cosmetic bags glasses cases and wallets. Its goods are available through 2300 gift and specialty stores and about 100 Vera Bradley full-price stores in the US. It also operates about 60 factory outlet shops and an online store. In addition to its core products the company licenses its name for use on Vera Bradley-branded rugs eyewear stationery and home decor items. Founded in 1982 as Vera Bradley Designs by Patricia Miller and Barbara Bradley Baekgaard to provide stylish luggage for women the company has floated publicly since 2010.

	Annual Growth	01/15	01/16	01/17*	02/18	02/19
Sales ($ mil.)	(4.9%)	509.0	502.6	485.9	454.6	416.1
Net income ($ mil.)	(14.3%)	38.4	27.6	19.8	7.0	20.8
Market value ($ mil.)	(17.4%)	655.0	507.7	398.4	320.5	304.3
Employees	(1.6%)	2,800	2,950	3,100	2,730	2,620

*Fiscal year change

VERACYTE INC
NMS: VCYT

6000 Shoreline Court, Suite 300
South San Francisco, CA 94080
Phone: 650 243-6300
Fax: –
Web: www.veracyte.com

CEO: Bonnie H. Anderson
CFO: Keith Kennedy
HR: Andy Danforth
FYE: December 31
Type: Public

Veracyte aims to give patients a verifiable diagnosis with as little discomfort as possible. The company provides molecular cytology tests that use cell samples taken with a needle instead of tissue samples obtained through a biopsy. Its first commercial product Afirma Thyroid FNA is marketed to endocrinologists as a test to diagnose thyroid cancer. (Thyroid diagnostic tests previously required surgery and hormone replacement therapy and still gave uncertain results.) Veracyte's second product launched in 2015 is the Percepta Bronchial Genomic Classifier which can help diagnose lung cancer. In late 2016 the firm launched a test to help diagnose idiopathic pulmonary fibrosis one of the most common interstitial lung diseases.

	Annual Growth	12/14	12/15	12/16	12/17	12/18
Sales ($ mil.)	24.6%	38.2	49.5	65.1	72.0	92.0
Net income ($ mil.)	–	(29.4)	(33.7)	(31.4)	(31.0)	(23.0)
Market value ($ mil.)	6.8%	394.7	294.2	316.3	266.5	514.1
Employees	12.8%	167	192	216	246	270

VERAMARK TECHNOLOGIES INC.
OTC: VERA

1565 Jefferson Road Ste. 120
Rochester NY 14623
Phone: 585-381-6000
Fax: 585-383-6800
Web: www.veramark.com

CEO: –
CFO: –
HR: –
FYE: December 31
Type: Public

Veramark Technologies can help all sorts of companies play the "telephone game" and actually keep the information straight. The company's Web-based telecommunications expense management software enables customers to track analyze and allocate telecom-related costs as well as to maintain invoices and manage business process outsourcing. Veramark's installed base of more than 4000 customers includes FORTUNE 500 corporations small and midsized businesses and public sector organizations. The company was founded in 1983.

VERASTEM INC.
NASDAQ: VSTM

215 1st St. Ste. 440
Cambridge MA 02142
Phone: 617-252-9300
Fax: +358-20-484-181
Web: www.valmet-automotive.com

CEO: Brian Stuglik
CFO: Robert Gagnon
HR: –
FYE: December 31
Type: Public

Verastem believes the truth behind recurrent tumors lies in cancer stem cells (CSCs) aggressive tumor cells that survive conventional treatment to cause recurrence. Those CSCs are the target of its biopharmaceutical R&D efforts; the company is working to produce small molecule drugs that target the cells while conventional therapy targets the rest of the tumor. Verastem's work rests on a technology licensed from MIT's Whitehead Institute that allows it to create stable CSCs in the lab something not possible in the past. Its leading drug candidate targets a type of breast cancer with a low survival rate. The company is also developing CSC diagnostics. Formed in 2010 Verastem completed an IPO in 2012.

VERICEL CORP
NAS: VCEL

64 Sidney Street
Cambridge, MA 02139
Phone: 800 556-0311
Fax: –
Web: www.vcel.com

CEO: Dominick C Colangelo
CFO: Gerard Michel
HR: –
FYE: December 31
Type: Public

Vericel brings new life to dying tissue. The company's proprietary tissue repair technology uses a patient's own cells (harvested from bone marrow) to manufacture treatments for a number of chronic diseases. The new cells created through a sterile automated process are then used in tissue regeneration therapies for the donor patient. Vericel has two products on the market in the US: MACI which is used for the repair of knee cartilage; and Epicel a permanent skin replacement for patients with burns on 30% or more of the body.

	Annual Growth	12/14	12/15	12/16	12/17	12/18
Sales ($ mil.)	33.3%	28.8	51.2	54.4	63.9	90.9
Net income ($ mil.)	–	(19.9)	(16.3)	(19.6)	(17.3)	(8.1)
Market value ($ mil.)	54.7%	132.5	112.4	130.7	237.5	758.3
Employees	3.3%	190	190	202	205	216

VERIFONE SYSTEMS INC.
NYS: PAY

88 West Plumeria Drive
San Jose, CA 95134
Phone: 408 232-7800
Fax: –
Web: www.verifone.com

CEO: Mike Pulli
CFO: Marc E Rothman
HR: –
FYE: October 31
Type: Public

The point of VeriFone Systems' sales is the point of sale. The company makes hardware and software for conducting non-cash transactions at cash registers gas pumps on mobile devices and other devices. Users can swipe or insert cards or hold smart phones within range to conduct transactions. Its also provides smart card and check readers receipt printers and internet commerce software for large chains as well as small businesses. It also provides installation training and other services. Customers include companies in the hospitality retail and healthcare markets as well as government agencies. VeriFone generates about 60% of sales outside the US.

	Annual Growth	10/13	10/14	10/15	10/16	10/17
Sales ($ mil.)	2.4%	1,702.2	1,868.9	2,000.5	1,992.1	1,871.0
Net income ($ mil.)	–	(296.1)	(38.1)	79.1	(9.3)	(173.8)
Market value ($ mil.)	(4.2%)	2,546.2	4,186.8	3,386.7	1,739.4	2,144.0
Employees	(0.4%)	5,699	5,200	5,400	5,900	5,600

VERINT SYSTEMS, INC
NMS: VRNT

175 Broadhollow Road
Melville, NY 11747
Phone: 631 962-9600
Fax: –
Web: www.verint.com

CEO: Dan Bodner
CFO: Douglas E. (Doug) Robinson
HR: Jane O'donnell
FYE: January 31
Type: Public

Verint Systems makes software that helps some of its customers identify customer opportunities and other customers identify security threats.The company provides such "actionable intelligence" through systems for capturing and analyzing structured and unstructured data from voice video text and social media sources. Its software and services offered in on-premise and cloud-based versions are used by enterprise customers to improve customer service interactions and operations and by law enforcement and government agencies to combat crime and provide security. Verint's customers are in some 180 countries and include more than 80% of the FORTUNE 100. It generates about half of its sales outside the US.

	Annual Growth	01/15	01/16	01/17	01/18	01/19
Sales ($ mil.)	2.2%	1,128.4	1,130.3	1,062.1	1,135.2	1,229.7
Net income ($ mil.)	20.9%	30.9	17.6	(29.4)	(6.6)	66.0
Market value ($ mil.)	(2.4%)	3,487.5	2,391.8	2,440.2	2,727.7	3,160.2
Employees	6.2%	4,800	5,000	5,100	5,200	6,100

VERISIGN INC
NMS: VRSN

12061 Bluemont Way
Reston, VA 20190
Phone: 703 948-3200
Fax: –
Web: www.verisign.com

CEO: D. James (Jim) Bidzos
CFO: George E. Kilguss
HR: Ellen Petrocci
FYE: December 31
Type: Public

Verisign helps companies and consumers connect the dots with the coms and the nets. The company operates two of the world's 13 root zone servers which assign internet protocol (IP) addresses to devices communicating across the internet. VeriSign is also the only issuer of the desired .com and .net domain names that are sold to users by companies such as domain registrars Go Daddy and Register.com. The company also operates the registry for the .tv and .cc country code top-level domains and the back-end registry systems for the .gov .jobs and .edu. About 60% of sales are from the US. VeriSign sold its Security Services business in 2018.

	Annual Growth	12/14	12/15	12/16	12/17	12/18
Sales ($ mil.)	4.7%	1,010.1	1,059.4	1,142.2	1,165.1	1,215.0
Net income ($ mil.)	13.2%	355.3	375.2	440.6	457.2	582.5
Market value ($ mil.)	27.0%	6,842.1	10,486.4	9,131.2	13,737.0	17,800.3
Employees	(4.0%)	1,061	1,019	990	952	900

VERISK ANALYTICS INC NMS: VRSK

545 Washington Boulevard
Jersey City, NJ 07310-1686
Phone: 201 469-3000
Fax: –
Web: www.verisk.com

CEO: Scott G. Stephenson
CFO: Lee M. Shavel
HR: Karlyn Norton
FYE: December 31
Type: Public

Insurance is a risky business and Verisk Analytics is in the business of helping to manage that risk. The company compiles and analyzes data to detect fraud economic headwinds and catastrophe weather risk. It uses what it finds to predict losses for clients in the insurance energy and specialized markets and financial services industries. Verisk's customers include the top property/casualty insurers in the US; leading credit card issuers in North America the UK and Australia; and the world's largest energy companies. Verisk was created by subsidiary Insurance Services Office (ISO) in 2008 as a means of going public.

	Annual Growth	12/14	12/15	12/16	12/17	12/18
Sales ($ mil.)	8.2%	1,746.7	2,068.0	1,995.2	2,145.2	2,395.1
Net income ($ mil.)	10.6%	400.0	507.6	591.2	555.1	598.7
Market value ($ mil.)	14.2%	10,502.3	12,606.0	13,309.5	15,741.2	17,879.3
Employees	5.7%	6,550	7,918	6,314	7,304	8,184

VERITEQ CORP NBB: VTEQ

3333 S. Congress Avenue, Suite 401
Delray Beach, FL 33445
Phone: 561 846-7000
Fax: –
Web: www.veriteqcorp.com

CEO: –
CFO: –
HR: –
FYE: December 31
Type: Public

Digital Angel puts a British accent on two-way communication equipment. The company develops emergency identification products for use in global positioning systems and other applications and distributes them in the UK. Digital Angel's conventional radio systems provide such services as site monitoring for construction companies and manufacturers while its trunked radio systems serve the security needs of large customers such as local governments and public utilities. In mid-2012 the company announced a strategic shift toward the development of games and applications for mobile devices. It has several titles in progress.

	Annual Growth	12/10	12/11	12/12	12/13	12/14
Sales ($ mil.)	(74.8%)	37.7	3.7	–	0.0	0.2
Net income ($ mil.)	–	(5.8)	(10.3)	(6.3)	(15.1)	(3.9)
Market value ($ mil.)	–	0.1	0.1	0.0	0.7	0.0
Employees	(47.2%)	167	36	15	13	13

VERIZON COMMUNICATIONS INC NYS: VZ

1095 Avenue of the Americas
New York, NY 10036
Phone: 212 395-1000
Fax: –
Web: www.verizon.com

CEO: Lowell C. McAdam
CFO: Matthew D. (Matt) Ellis
HR: –
FYE: December 31
Type: Public

Verizon Communications is the #1 wireless phone service in the US (ahead of rival AT&T) serving more than 118 million connections. Verizon's wireline unit provides local telephone long-distance internet access corporate networking and digital TV services to consumers carriers business and government customers. In addition Verizon offers a wide range of telecom managed network security and IT services to commercial and government clients in more than 150 countries. The company also sells device such as phones tablets and wearables. Verizon has expanded its video and advertising capabilities with the acquisitions of AOL and Yahoo assets.

	Annual Growth	12/14	12/15	12/16	12/17	12/18
Sales ($ mil.)	0.7%	127,079.0	131,620.0	125,980.0	126,034.0	130,863.0
Net income ($ mil.)	12.7%	9,625.0	17,879.0	13,127.0	30,101.0	15,528.0
Market value ($ mil.)	–	0.0	0.0	0.0	0.0	0.0
Employees	(5.0%)	177,300	177,700	160,900	155,400	144,500

VERMILLION INC. NASDAQ: VRML

47350 Fremont Blvd.
Fremont CA 94538
Phone: 510-226-2800
Fax: 510-226-2801
Web: www.vermillion.com

CEO: Valerie B Palmieri
CFO: Robert Beechey
HR: –
FYE: December 31
Type: Public

Vermillion is enabling the next step in biotechnology — deciphering proteins. The company is using a process called translational proteomics to develop diagnostic tests that take multiple protein biomarkers into account thus making the tests more sensitive and test results more specific. Its development efforts target therapeutic areas such as oncology hematology cardiology and women's health. It is working on some tests with Quest Diagnostics (which owns a minority stake in Vermillion) and has additional collaborations with academic and research institutions such as Johns Hopkins and M.D. Anderson. Vermillion emerged from Chapter 11 bankruptcy protection in early 2010.

VERMONT GAS SYSTEMS INC.

85 Swift St.
South Burlington VT 05403
Phone: 802-863-4511
Fax: 802-863-8872
Web: www.vermontgas.com

CEO: Donald J Rendall
CFO: –
HR: –
FYE: September 30
Type: Subsidiary

Vermont Gas Systems pumps gas through the veins of the Vermont mountains and the mains of its towns and cities. A subsidiary of Canadian utility Gaz Metro Vermont Gas Systems distributes natural gas to more than 40000 homes and businesses in the counties of Chittenden and Franklin. Its natural gas is transported through the TransCanada Pipeline which links the gas fields in Alberta Canada to the company's main pipeline at Highgate Vermont on the Canadian border. The company supplies gas to its customers through a more than 650-mile network of underground transmission and distribution lines.

VERSAR INC. ASE: VSR

6850 Versar Center
Springfield, VA 22151
Phone: 703 750-3000
Fax: 703 642-6825
Web: www.versar.com

CEO: Dwane Stone
CFO: Christine B Tarrago
HR: –
FYE: June 26
Type: Public

Environmental engineering company Versar is well-versed in keeping the homeland clean and secure. The company's infrastructure and management services business which accounts for most of Versar's sales helps clients with six main tasks: compliance with environmental regulations conservation of natural resources construction oversight engineering and design pollution prevention and restoration of contaminated sites. Major customers include the US Department of Defense and the US Environmental Protection Agency. Subsidiary GEOMET Technologies which constitutes Versar's national defense business segment makes biohazard suits for agencies involved in emergency response and counterterrorism efforts.

	Annual Growth	07/11*	06/12	06/13	06/14	06/15
Sales ($ mil.)	3.8%	137.6	119.0	102.6	110.3	159.9
Net income ($ mil.)	(20.1%)	3.4	4.2	2.4	(0.3)	1.4
Market value ($ mil.)	6.6%	30.7	29.5	44.5	33.7	39.7
Employees	0.3%	550	550	450	450	556

*Fiscal year change

VERSO CORP
NYS: VRS

8450 Gander Creek Drive
Miamisburg, OH 45342
Phone: 877 855-7243
Fax: –
Web: www.versoco.com

CEO: B. Christopher DiSantis
CFO: Allen J. Campbell
HR: –
FYE: December 31
Type: Public

Verso produces coated and supercalendered paper and pulp for publishers commercial printers specialty retail merchandisers and paper merchants throughout North America. It also makes coated groundwood and coated freesheet paper products along with specialty paper offerings. Its products are used for media and marketing purposes from magazines to catalogs brochures annual reports and direct-mail advertising. The company operates through seven mills located in Maine Maryland Michigan Minnesota and Wisconsin. Sales of graphic papers account for about 60% of the company's revenue.

	Annual Growth	12/15*	07/16*	12/16	12/17	12/18
Sales ($ mil.)	(4.9%)	3,122.0	1,417.0	1,224.0	2,461.0	2,682.0
Net income ($ mil.)	–	(422.0)	1,178.0	(32.0)	(30.0)	171.0
Market value ($ mil.)	77.6%	–	–	244.8	605.9	772.4
Employees	(5.4%)	5,200	–	4,500	4,200	4,400

*Fiscal year change

VERST GROUP LOGISTICS, INC.

300 SHORLAND DR
WALTON, KY 410949328
Phone: 859-485-1212
Fax: –
Web: www.verstgroup.net

CEO: Paul T Verst
CFO: James Stadtmiller
HR: –
FYE: December 31
Type: Private

Verst wants to be first when it comes to storing its customers' items. A warehousing and distribution specialist Verst Group Logistics maintains over 5 million sq. ft. of warehouse space. The company operates from facilities in the Cincinnati metropolitan area and in northern Kentucky. Verst Group Logistics uses its own trucking fleet to provide freight transportation services through subsidiary Zenith Logistics and a network of carriers to arrange long-distance transportation of customers' freight. It serves customers residing in the food and beverage retail and consumer products paper and automotive industries. William Verst the father of president and CEO Paul Verst founded the company in 1968.

	Annual Growth	12/10	12/11	12/12	12/13	12/16
Sales ($ mil.)	–	–	(137.2)	148.8	157.7	59.2
Net income ($ mil.)	822.7%	–	0.0	0.0	0.0	1.7
Market value ($ mil.)	–	–	–	–	–	–
Employees	–	–	–	–	–	1,300

VERTEX PHARMACEUTICALS, INC.
NMS: VRTX

50 Northern Avenue
Boston, MA 02210
Phone: 617 341-6100
Fax: –
Web: www.vrtx.com

CEO: Jeffrey M. (Jeff) Leiden
CFO: Thomas (Tom) Graney
HR: Carla Poulson
FYE: December 31
Type: Public

Vertex Pharmaceuticals is focused on developing treatments for cystic fibrosis (CF) and other life-threatening diseases. The biotechnology firm has three commercial drugs — Orkambi Kalydeco and Symdeko/Symkevi — used to treat CF. Vertex has other drugs in development including additional CF treatments and medications addressing sickle cell disease beta thalassemia alpha-1 antitrypsin deficiency and pain. The company's medicines are sold in North America Europe and Australia; the US accounts for more than three-fourths of revenue.

	Annual Growth	12/14	12/15	12/16	12/17	12/18
Sales ($ mil.)	51.4%	580.4	1,032.3	1,702.2	2,488.7	3,047.6
Net income ($ mil.)	–	(738.6)	(556.5)	(112.1)	263.5	2,096.9
Market value ($ mil.)	8.7%	30,314.5	32,108.3	18,798.5	38,240.1	42,284.6
Employees	8.1%	1,830	1,950	2,150	2,300	2,500

VERTICAL COMMUNICATIONS, INC.

3900 FREEDOM CIR STE 110
SANTA CLARA, CA 950541222
Phone: 408-404-1600
Fax: –
Web: www.vertical.com

CEO: Peter Bailey
CFO: Kenneth M Clinebell
HR: –
FYE: June 30
Type: Private

Vertical Communications hopes that Internet protocol telephony can keep its top line from going horizontal. The company focuses on its software-based phone systems which provide unified communications functions such as call control message forwarding e-mail integration and call routing and screening. Its products also include applications for managing call center operations including agent monitoring coaching and recording. Vertical targets operations with less than 1000 employees in markets such as retail financial services health care and education. It sells through a global network of 1800 business partners. Its customers have included CVS Health Staples and Apria Healthcare.

	Annual Growth	06/03	06/04	06/05	06/06	06/07
Sales ($ mil.)	(70.1%)	–	–	885.0	55.5	79.1
Net income ($ mil.)	–	–	–	0.0	(16.0)	(16.0)
Market value ($ mil.)	–	–	–	–	–	–
Employees	–	–	–	–	–	243

VERTICAL COMPUTER SYSTEMS, INC.
NBB: VCSY

101 West Renner Road, Suite 300
Richardson, TX 75082
Phone: 972 437-5200
Fax: –
Web: www.vcsy.com

CEO: Richard S Wade
CFO: –
HR: –
FYE: December 31
Type: Public

Vertical Computer Systems develops Web services development applications and administrative software. The company's SiteFlash software enables Web content management e-commerce and workflow functions. Other Web service-related offerings include ResponseFlash an emergency communications system and the Emily XML scripting language. Its administrative software line includes emPath a Web-based human resources management and payroll application that it offers using the software-as-a-service (SaaS) model. Vertical Computer Systems markets emPath through its NOW Solutions subsidiary.

	Annual Growth	12/13	12/14	12/15	12/16	12/17
Sales ($ mil.)	(11.2%)	6.1	7.4	4.3	3.8	3.8
Net income ($ mil.)	–	(2.5)	(1.5)	(2.6)	(5.3)	(3.1)
Market value ($ mil.)	(27.5%)	70.1	13.8	25.2	28.0	19.4
Employees	(1.1%)	24	29	28	27	23

VERU INC
NAS: VERU

48 NW 25th Street, Suite 102
Miami, FL 33127
Phone: 305 509-6897
Fax: –
Web: www.veruhealthcare.com

CEO: Mitchell S Steiner
CFO: Michele Greco
HR: –
FYE: September 30
Type: Public

Move over Trojan Man! Business at The Female Health Company (FHC) maker of condoms for women is gaining momentum. The female condom is the only female contraceptive that is FDA-approved for preventing both pregnancy and sexually transmitted diseases including HIV/AIDS. The firm's condoms are sold in 140-plus countries worldwide (under the FC2 name) mostly in South Africa Brazil and Uganda. Outside the US many of its products bear the Femidom name among others. FHC also provides low-cost female condoms in Africa through an agreement with the Joint United Nations Programme on HIV/AIDS (UNAIDS). It sponsors the Female Health Foundation which provides women with health education.

	Annual Growth	09/15	09/16	09/17	09/18	09/19
Sales ($ mil.)	(0.6%)	32.6	22.1	13.7	15.9	31.8
Net income ($ mil.)	–	4.3	0.3	(6.6)	(23.9)	(12.0)
Market value ($ mil.)	8.1%	102.8	79.3	172.4	92.4	140.5
Employees	20.8%	181	156	175	171	386

VESCO OIL CORPORATION

16055 W 12 MILE RD
SOUTHFIELD, MI 480762979
Phone: 800-527-5358
Fax: –
Web: www.acculube.com

CEO: Donald R Epstein
CFO: Cheryl R Reitzloff
HR: –
FYE: December 31
Type: Private

Vesco Oil gives motorists a hand in the Upper Hand and elsewhere in the state of Michigan. The company is a wholesale distributor of Valvoline and Exxon Mobil brand lubricants to automotive and industrial customers in Michigan. It also provides environmental services such as bulk and hazardous waste management. Vesco Oil has warehouse and distribution facilities in Detroit Grand Rapids Mancelona and Zilwaukee. It has expanded its warehouse and distribution center in Mancelona to better serve its northern Michigan customers. Vesco Oil is managed by president and CEO Donald Epstein the great-grandson of the company's founder Eugene Epstein.

	Annual Growth	12/06	12/07	12/08	12/09	12/10
Sales ($ mil.)	(4.7%)	–	–	119.2	100.8	108.2
Net income ($ mil.)	40.9%	–	–	1.6	(0.3)	3.3
Market value ($ mil.)	–	–	–	–	–	–
Employees	–	–	–	–	–	210

VETERANS OF FOREIGN WARS OF THE UNITED STATES

406 W 34TH ST
KANSAS CITY, MO 641112721
Phone: 816-756-3390
Fax: –
Web: www.vfw.org

CEO: –
CFO: Jr H Vander Clute
HR: –
FYE: August 31
Type: Private

The Veterans of Foreign Wars of the United States (VFW) serves those who served. The membership organization is an advocacy group for former members of any branch of the US military who have served honorably in conflicts. Services provided by the group include helping veterans secure benefits and entitlements and advocating legislation in support of veterans and their needs. The VFW also provides flag education citizenship classes and other mentoring services to young people. The organization which was chartered by Congress in 1936 serves as a visible reminder of the contributions of all veterans by marching in parades and holding public services on national holidays.

	Annual Growth	08/10	08/11	08/12	08/13	08/14
Sales ($ mil.)	(5.8%)	–	–	103.8	100.5	92.1
Net income ($ mil.)	9.9%	–	–	4.9	23.4	5.9
Market value ($ mil.)	–	–	–	–	–	–
Employees	–	–	–	–	–	185

VF CORP.

8505 E. Orchard Road
Greenwood Village, CO 80111
Phone: 720 778-4000
Fax: –
Web: www.vfc.com

NYS: VFC
CEO: Steven E. (Steve) Rendle
CFO: Scott A. Roe
HR: Ronald Lawrence
FYE: March 30
Type: Public

VF Corp. has stitched together a lineup of apparel brands that range from denim to Northface. The company is a leading manufacturer and retailer in the outdoor and action sports apparel industry owning brands in specialist product categories: Timberland and The North Face (outdoor-oriented brands) and Vans (skateboard-inspired footwear. VF also makes the jeans scene owning the Lee Wrangler and Rock & Republic brands. The company sells directly to consumers online and through more than 1500 VF-operated retail stores worldwide. It also sells wholesale to department and specialty stores and mass merchants. In 2018 VF announced it would spin off the jeans business into a separate public company to concentrate on the outdoor and footwear brands.

	Annual Growth	01/16*	12/16	12/17*	03/18	03/19
Sales ($ mil.)	3.8%	12,376.7	12,019.0	11,811.2	3,045.4	13,848.7
Net income ($ mil.)	0.8%	1,231.6	1,074.1	614.9	252.8	1,259.8
Market value ($ mil.)	11.8%	24,702.3	21,170.6	29,365.0	29,412.6	34,488.0
Employees	5.4%	64,000	69,000	69,000	–	75,000

*Fiscal year change

VHS ACQUISITION SUBSIDIARY NUMBER 3, INC.

4646 N MARINE DR
CHICAGO, IL 606405759
Phone: 773-878-8700
Fax: –
Web: www.weisshospital.com

CEO: –
CFO: –
HR: –
FYE: May 31
Type: Private

Vanguard Weiss Memorial Hospital serves the residents of Chicago's North Side. The facility has about 240 beds and some 450 physicians covering more than 40 specialties. It conducts medical research and education programs through its affiliation with the University of Chicago Medical Center. Generally known as Weiss Memorial Hospital the center offers full acute care including orthopedics cardiology vascular rehabilitation cancer geriatrics and women's health care. Specialty divisions provide laboratory radiology wound and hospice care. Tenet Healthcare owns 80% of the hospital (gained through its 2013 acquisition of Vanguard Health Systems) and the University of Chicago Medical Center owns the rest.

	Annual Growth	06/00	06/01	06/02	06/03*	05/15
Sales ($ mil.)	0.4%	–	106.0	280.1	110.3	112.1
Net income ($ mil.)	–	–	(7.4)	(10.8)	0.6	(2.8)
Market value ($ mil.)	–	–	–	–	–	–
Employees	–	–	–	–	–	1,100

*Fiscal year change

VHS OF ILLINOIS, INC.

1445 ROSS AVE STE 1400
DALLAS, TX 752022703
Phone: 708-783-9100
Fax: –
Web: www.macnealhospital.org

CEO: Charles Martin Jr
CFO: Emmy Cleary
HR: –
FYE: September 30
Type: Private

University of Illinois medical students wanting to learn family medicine can find their home-away-from-home through the residency program at MacNeal Hospital a full-service facility serving the suburbs of Chicago. Among its specialty services are behavioral health occupational health home and hospice care and radiology. With some 430 beds the teaching hospital has about 400 physicians on staff. By offering specialty care services like open heart surgery MacNeal is able to hang on to many patients who would otherwise travel from the suburbs into the Windy City itself for care. MacNeal is owned by Tenet Healthcare (gained through Tenet's 2013 purchase of Vanguard Health Systems).

	Annual Growth	09/12	09/13	09/14	09/15	09/16
Sales ($ mil.)	4.2%	–	–	255.2	265.5	277.2
Net income ($ mil.)	43.9%	–	–	24.3	48.2	50.3
Market value ($ mil.)	–	–	–	–	–	–
Employees	–	–	–	–	–	2,500

VIA CHRISTI HEALTH, INC.

2622 W CENTRAL AVE # 102
WICHITA, KS 672034970
Phone: 316-858-4900
Fax: –
Web: www.viachristi.org

CEO: –
CFO: –
HR: Marianne Moore
FYE: June 30
Type: Private

How do the sick become well? Via Christi Health of course. Via Christi Health is a Catholic not-for-profit health care system that provides a range of medical services to residents of Kansas and northern Oklahoma through a network of hospitals medical centers and health service organizations. The system's facilities include four hospitals about a dozen senior living communities nearly 20 medical clinics and specialized facilities for behavioral health and rehabilitative care. The system is affiliated with Marian Health System and Ascension Health. Via Christi Health was formed in 1995 when the Sisters of the Sorrowful Mother and the Sisters of St. Joseph of Wichita merged their health care ministries.

	Annual Growth	06/11	06/12	06/13	06/14	06/15
Sales ($ mil.)	13.7%	–	–	–	131.6	149.6
Net income ($ mil.)	–	–	–	–	(23.5)	(31.0)
Market value ($ mil.)	–	–	–	–	–	–
Employees	–	–	–	–	–	11,970

VIACOM INC
NMS: VIAB

1515 Broadway
New York, NY 10036
Phone: 212 258-6000
Fax: –
Web: www.viacom.com

CEO: –
CFO: –
HR: –
FYE: September 30
Type: Public

Viacom is a leading media conglomerate with an extensive portfolio of cable TV and film production assets. Its MTV Networks unit runs such cable networks as Comedy Central Nickelodeon and the family of MTV channels (MTV MTV2 VH1). Viacom also owns Black Entertainment Television which airs programming on BET BET Gospel and BET Hip Hop. In the film business Viacom operates through Paramount Pictures which includes imprints Paramount Pictures and Paramount Vantage. Viacom has a presence in more than 180 countries and territories primarily in North America Europe and Asia.

	Annual Growth	09/14	09/15	09/16	09/17	09/18
Sales ($ mil.)	(1.6%)	13,783.0	13,268.0	12,488.0	13,263.0	12,943.0
Net income ($ mil.)	(7.9%)	2,391.0	1,922.0	1,438.0	1,874.0	1,719.0
Market value ($ mil.)	(18.6%)	31,014.5	17,393.8	15,358.1	11,222.3	13,608.7
Employees	1.2%	9,900	9,200	9,300	11,650	10,400

VIACOMCBS INC
NMS: VIAC

51 W. 52nd Street
New York, NY 10019
Phone: 212 975-4321
Fax: –
Web: www.cbscorporation.com

CEO: Leslie (Les) Moonves
CFO: –
HR: Anthony G. Ambrosio
FYE: December 31
Type: Public

You might say this company has a real eye for broadcasting. CBS Corporation known by some as the "Eye Network" due to its eye logo is a leading mass media conglomerate with television radio online content and publishing operations. Its portfolio is anchored by CBS Broadcasting which operates the #1 rated CBS television network along with a group of local TV stations. CBS also owns cable network Showtime and produces and distributes TV programming through CBS Television Studios and CBS Television Distribution. Other operations include CBS Interactive and book publisher Simon & Schuster. Chairman Emeritus Sumner Redstone controls CBS Corporation through National Amusements. CBS agreed to merge with Viacom its National Amusements sibling in 2019.

	Annual Growth	12/14	12/15	12/16	12/17	12/18
Sales ($ mil.)	1.3%	13,806.0	13,886.0	13,166.0	13,692.0	14,514.0
Net income ($ mil.)	(9.8%)	2,959.0	1,413.0	1,261.0	357.0	1,960.0
Market value ($ mil.)	(5.7%)	20,641.8	17,579.5	23,730.3	22,007.0	16,307.6
Employees	(0.8%)	17,310	16,260	21,270	16,730	16,730

VIAD CORP.
NYS: VVI

1850 North Central Avenue, Suite 1900
Phoenix, AZ 85004-4565
Phone: 602 207-1000
Fax: –
Web: www.viad.com

CEO: Steven W Moster
CFO: Ellen M. Ingersoll
HR: –
FYE: December 31
Type: Public

Viad (pronounced VEE-ahd) offers convention and event services exhibit design and construction and travel and recreation services. Its primary business GES (Global Experience Specialists) produces exhibitions conferences corporate events and consumer events for a global marketplace of event organizers and corporate brand managers. Viad's other business Pursuit offers tourism packages to national parks in Canada and Iceland that include lodging sightseeing food and drink and transportation. Pursuit is smaller than GES but more profitable. Viad has operations across North America Europe the Middle East and Australia but most of its revenue is generated in the US.

	Annual Growth	12/14	12/15	12/16	12/17	12/18
Sales ($ mil.)	5.0%	1,065.0	1,089.0	1,205.0	1,307.0	1,296.2
Net income ($ mil.)	(1.6%)	52.4	26.6	42.3	57.7	49.2
Market value ($ mil.)	17.1%	538.4	570.1	890.5	1,118.7	1,011.5
Employees	8.1%	3,810	4,285	3,436	3,521	5,196

VIASAT INC
NMS: VSAT

6155 El Camino Real
Carlsbad, CA 92009
Phone: 760 476-2200
Fax: –
Web: www.viasat.com

CEO: Mark D. Dankberg
CFO: Shawn Duffy
HR: Melinda Del Toro
FYE: March 31
Type: Public

Viasat provides digital satellite networking and signal processing equipment for government and commercial clients. It makes secure networking products for tactical communications and mobile satellite communications systems designed for military use. For the commercial market Viasat produces satellite broadband systems for consumer applications as well as antenna systems and mobile satellite systems. The company provides technology for Wi-Fi connections on more than 1300 commercial aircraft with American Airlines and JetBlue among its customers. Consumer satellite internet services are provided through subsidiary Viasat Internet (formerly known as WildBlue).

	Annual Growth	04/15*	03/16	03/17	03/18	03/19
Sales ($ mil.)	10.6%	1,382.5	1,417.4	1,559.3	1,594.6	2,068.3
Net income ($ mil.)	–	40.4	21.7	23.8	(67.3)	(67.6)
Market value ($ mil.)	6.6%	3,632.4	4,449.2	3,864.3	3,979.4	4,692.6
Employees	13.3%	3,400	3,800	4,300	5,200	5,600

*Fiscal year change

VIASYSTEMS GROUP INC
NMS: VIAS

101 South Hanley Road
St. Louis, MO 63105
Phone: 314 727-2087
Fax: –
Web: www.viasystems.com

CEO: –
CFO: –
HR: –
FYE: December 31
Type: Public

Viasystems thinks its systems are the way to go. The company is a contract manufacturer for printed circuit boards (PCBs) and electro-mechanical (E-M) assemblies. It also offers design prototyping full system assembly testing and supply chain management services. Viasystems' products are used in automotive data networking equipment computer storage equipment flight control systems telecom switching equipment technical instruments in various sectors and wind and solar energy. Its customers total about 800 manufacturers including GE Alcatel-Lucent Continental AG and its largest customer Bosch. Its ten manufacturing facilities include two in the US one in Mexico and seven in China.

	Annual Growth	12/09	12/10	12/11	12/12	12/13
Sales ($ mil.)	23.9%	496.4	929.3	1,057.3	1,159.9	1,171.0
Net income ($ mil.)	–	(54.7)	15.6	30.3	(62.2)	(27.6)
Market value ($ mil.)	(12.1%)	–	418.1	351.2	253.3	284.0
Employees	2.2%	13,783	14,842	14,099	14,128	15,057

VIAVI SOLUTIONS INC
NMS: VIAV

6001 America Center Drive
San Jose, CA 95002
Phone: 408 404-3600
Fax: –

CEO: Oleg Khaykin
CFO: Amar Maletira
HR: –
FYE: June 29
Type: Public

Viavi Solutions formerly a part of JDS Uniphase (JDSU) facilitates better communication. The company develops test and measurement instruments and test tools that are used to build and improve communications equipment and broadband networks. Formerly operated as JDSU's Network and Service Enablement unit Viavi develops instruments and software and provides product support that helps customers build and maintain communication equipment and broadband networks. It also provides test products and services for private enterprise networks. The break up of JDSU occurred in August 2015. The former optical security and performance unit of JDSU now operates as Lumentum.

	Annual Growth	06/15*	07/16	07/17*	06/18	06/19
Sales ($ mil.)	(9.8%)	1,709.1	906.3	811.4	880.4	1,130.3
Net income ($ mil.)	–	–	(88.1)	(99.2)	166.9	(46.0)	5.4
Market value ($ mil.)	2.6%	2,747.9	1,512.4	2,409.3	2,342.9	3,040.8
Employees	(7.4%)	4,900	3,000	2,700	3,500	3,600

*Fiscal year change

VICOR CORP
NMS: VICR

25 Frontage Road
Andover, MA 01810
Phone: 978 470-2900
Fax: —
Web: www.vicorpower.com

CEO: Patrizio Vinciarelli
CFO: James A. Simms
HR: Nancy L Grava
FYE: December 31
Type: Public

Vicor makes converters that tame and transfer raw electricity into the stable DC voltages needed to power electronic circuits. The company's zero current and zero voltage switching technologies which allow its converters to operate at high frequencies with relatively little noise are designed to be mounted on a printed circuit board. Customers — including global OEMs and small manufacturers of specialized electronics devices — incorporate the converters into all sorts of electronic equipment ranging from fiber-optic systems to military radar. Vicor derives some 40% of its sales from customers in the US.

	Annual Growth	12/14	12/15	12/16	12/17	12/18
Sales ($ mil.)	6.6%	225.7	220.2	200.3	227.8	291.2
Net income ($ mil.)	—	(13.9)	4.9	(6.2)	0.2	31.7
Market value ($ mil.)	32.9%	486.3	366.5	606.9	840.0	1,518.7
Employees	(0.2%)	1,014	985	971	980	1,007

VICTOR TECHNOLOGIES GROUP INC.

16052 Swingley Ridge Rd. Ste. 300
Chesterfield MO 63017
Phone: 636-728-3000
Fax: 636-728-3011
Web: www.thermadyne.com

CEO: Martin Quinn
CFO: Jeffrey S Kulka
HR: Sylvette De Jesus
FYE: December 31
Type: Private

Victor Technologies formerly Thermadyne has a hold on men of steel (and other metals). The company makes cutting and welding equipment used in fabricating (cutting joining and reinforcing) metal. Victor sells gas (air and oxy-fuel) torches and related products to OEMs as well as construction and foundry customers in such industries as aerospace oil and gas and shipbuilding. Its lineup includes arc accessories (automatic welding guns) plasma power systems and various welders sold under the Cigweld Victor Stoody Thermal Dynamics and other brands. Victor operates worldwide; the US represents more than 50% of sales. Private equity Irving Place Capital acquired Victor Technologies in 2010.

VICTORIA'S SECRET DIRECT LLC

5 Limited Pkwy. East
Reynoldsburg OH 43068
Phone: 201-802-3000
Fax: 201-782-9601
Web: www.sys-con.com

CEO: —
CFO: —
HR: —
FYE: January 31
Type: Subsidiary

Too busy or shy to shop in person for ladies' unmentionables? Victoria's Secret Direct affords shoppers the luxury privacy and convenience of ordering from home. As the direct sales arm of Victoria's Secret Stores it mails more than 390 million catalogs worldwide annually offering bras and panties sleepwear clothing shoes swimwear beauty products and a look at some of the world's top models. It also operates the website — VictoriasSecret.com — for its bricks-and-mortar sister chain. Both Victoria's Secret Direct (VSD) and Victoria's Secret Stores are owned by Limited Brands.

VICTORIA'S SECRET STORES LLC

4 Limited Pkwy. East
Reynoldsburg OH 43068
Phone: 614-577-7111
Fax: 614-577-7844
Web: www.victoriassecret.com

CEO: Lori Greeley
CFO: —
HR: —
FYE: January 31
Type: Subsidiary

Victoria's Secret Stores is not hush-hush but it is unmentionable(s). The largest subsidiary of Limited Brands (more than 40% of sales) is also North America's #1 specialty retailer of women's intimate apparel operating about 1035 mostly mall-based Victoria's Secret and Victoria's Secret Pink shops throughout the US and Canada. Bras panties hosiery swimwear shoes and more are sold under the Victoria's Secret brand and grouped in collections such as Angels and Very Sexy. Many Victoria's Secret lingerie stores also sell beauty products. The chain's youth-oriented PINK brand targets teens and younger women with less-racy bras and panties as well as sweats and hoodies and beauty products.

VIDEO DISPLAY CORP
NBB: VIDE

1868 Tucker Industrial Road
Tucker, GA 30084
Phone: 770 938-2080
Fax: —
Web: www.videodisplay.com

CEO: Ronald D Ordway
CFO: Gregory L Osborn
HR: —
FYE: February 28
Type: Public

Video may have killed the radio star but it's been pretty good to Video Display. The company makes and distributes flat-panel projection and cathode-ray tube (CRT) display systems. Its products — both new and reconditioned — are often customized for specific needs such as space limitations or being ruggedized for adverse environments. They are targeted at niche settings such as military training and simulation displays among other applications. Its data display business (about 10% of sales) focuses on CRTs for uses such as medical monitoring equipment and computer terminals. Its largest customer is the US government primarily the Department of Defense (more than 40% of sales).

	Annual Growth	02/15	02/16	02/17	02/18	02/19
Sales ($ mil.)	4.0%	12.8	11.6	19.6	11.9	15.0
Net income ($ mil.)	—	(6.0)	(6.1)	(1.0)	(2.9)	0.1
Market value ($ mil.)	(22.0%)	15.9	4.1	6.5	6.0	5.9
Employees	(8.6%)	119	121	106	86	83

VIDEO GAMING TECHNOLOGIES INC

308 MALLORY STATION RD
FRANKLIN, TN 37067-8210
Phone: 615-372-1000
Fax: —
Web: www.vgt.net

CEO: Jayme Sevigny
CFO: —
HR: —
FYE: December 31
Type: Private

It takes more than pencil and paper to make a good video game. Video Gaming Technologies (VGT) is a leading manufacturer of Class II-based gaming machines which mostly include bingo-style platforms found outside the Las Vegas market. The company additionally makes video terminals for skill-based games. It serves primarily the Native American gaming industry and its Live-Call Bingo game is the top-earning bingo based Class II platform for Native American casinos. VGT also serves emerging gaming markets. The company has manufacturing research and development marketing and support services. It does business in Oklahoma Washington Kansas California and Texas. CEO Jon Yarbrough founded VGT in 1991.

	Annual Growth	12/03	12/04	12/05	12/06	12/08
Sales ($ mil.)	(42.8%)	—	—	1,063.5	180.1	199.3
Net income ($ mil.)	28904.0%	—	—	0.0	6.0	24.4
Market value ($ mil.)	—	—	—	—	—	—
Employees	—	—	—	—	—	600

VIDEON CENTRAL INC.

2171 SANDY DR
STATE COLLEGE, PA 168032283
Phone: 814-235-1111
Fax: –
Web: www.videon-central.com

CEO: Todd Erdley
CFO: Paul Brown
HR: Joan Potter
FYE: June 30
Type: Private

Video Central wants to put high performance video in the center of your world. The consumer electronics maker develops digital audio and video technology components including Blu-Ray and DVD players and 3D systems used in in-flight entertainment centers and home theater systems. It also provides engineering design development integration and testing services to OEMs. Videon's Advanced Technology Group creates Blu-ray Disc and DVD software used for control navigation and playback features. The company manufacturers its products at its facility in Pennsylvania. It was established in 1997 and it is owned by its officers.

	Annual Growth	06/03	06/04	06/06	06/12	06/13
Sales ($ mil.)	13.6%	–	4.3	8.0	14.2	13.6
Net income ($ mil.)	–	–	–	0.3	0.3	(0.1)
Market value ($ mil.)	–	–	–	–	–	–
Employees	–	–	–	–	–	63

VIENNA BEEF LTD.

2501 N. Damen Ave.
Chicago IL 60647
Phone: 773-278-7800
Fax: 773-278-4759
Web: www.viennabeef.com

CEO: –
CFO: Richard Steele
HR: –
FYE: April 30
Type: Private

Don't confuse the products of Vienna Beef (formerly Vienna Sausage Manufacturing) with those soggy little wieners packed in jars. Its beef wieners are the hot dogs Chicago calls its own. The company first unveiled its frankfurters (made from a secret Viennese recipe) at the 1893 World's Fair in Chicago. In addition to sausages and deli meats Vienna Sausage also makes cheesecake on a stick (WunderBar) other desserts (Pie Piper) pickles (Chipico Pickles) soups (Bistro Soups) and kosher foods (King Kold). Vienna Beef's products are available worldwide. The company sells to outside distributors grocery stores restaurants sports and other entertainment venues club stores and hot-dog stands.

VIETNAM VETERANS OF AMERICA INC.

8719 COLESVILLE RD # 100
SILVER SPRING, MD 209103919
Phone: 301-585-4000
Fax: –
Web: www.avva.org

CEO: –
CFO: Joe Sternburg
HR: –
FYE: February 28
Type: Private

Vietnam Veterans of America (VVA) has a Congressional charter to care. The not-for-profit group provides support for Vietnam veterans and their families and is the only such agency sanctioned by the US government. It promotes Vietnam veterans' issues including homelessness and health care — Agent Orange exposure is one key issue — and has about 50000 members and 635 local chapters throughout the US Puerto Rico the Virgin Islands and Guam. VVA seeks to eliminate discrimination toward Vietnam Veterans. It has programs specifically for women and minorities scholarships government benefit assistance and government advocacy. Founded in 1978 VVA is funded completely by private donations.

	Annual Growth	02/08	02/09	02/11	02/12	02/14
Sales ($ mil.)	120.2%	–	0.2	8.5	6.9	9.2
Net income ($ mil.)	(7.1%)	–	–	1.3	(0.5)	1.0
Market value ($ mil.)	–	–	–	–	–	–
Employees	–	–	–	–	–	300

VIEW SYSTEMS, INC.   NBB: VSYM

7833 Walker Drive, Suite 520
Greenbelt, MD 20770
Phone: 410 236-8200
Fax: 410 242-0765
Web: www.viewsystems.com

CEO: Gunther Than
CFO: –
HR: –
FYE: December 31
Type: Public

View Systems keeps a systematic eye out for potential dangers. The company's ViewMaxx digital video system captures and stores closed-circuit television images on computer disks for efficient monitoring. Its View Scan system offers walk-through weapons detectors under the SecureScan brand name. View Systems' wireless video camera system Visual First Responder allows emergency response teams to size up a situation before heading into harm's way. View Systems also offers biometric verification systems that can be integrated with its SecureScan and ViewMaxx products. The company acquired Colorado-based electronics manufacturing company Wytan in 2008.

	Annual Growth	12/14	12/15	12/16	12/17	12/18
Sales ($ mil.)	(46.3%)	0.4	0.2	0.1	0.1	0.0
Net income ($ mil.)	–	(1.3)	(0.4)	(0.2)	(0.2)	0.9
Market value ($ mil.)	(27.4%)	3.6	1.2	0.7	0.5	1.0
Employees	(5.4%)	10	8	8	8	8

VIKING YACHT COMPANY

ON THE BASS RIV RR 9
NEW GRETNA, NJ 08224
Phone: 609-296-6000
Fax: –
Web: www.vikingyachts.com

CEO: Robert T Healey
CFO: Gerard D Straub Sr
HR: –
FYE: July 31
Type: Private

Leif Eriksson's oceangoing Viking explorers could only dream of vessels like those made by the Viking Yacht Company. Viking Yacht can build more than 100 semi-custom fiberglass pleasure boats primarily used for sport fishing. About 90% of each yacht is made in-house. Its line of yachts vary in length from approximately 42 to 92 feet and include convertible and enclosed-bridge convertible vessels open sportfish models and a 52-foot sport yacht. The luxury boats are sold through a network of more than 40 dealers six of which are based outside the US. Founders and brothers Bob and Bill Healey own Viking Yacht Company.

	Annual Growth	07/12	07/13	07/14	07/15	07/16
Sales ($ mil.)	22.0%	–	154.1	194.1	245.1	280.0
Net income ($ mil.)	22.3%	–	10.3	16.3	17.6	18.8
Market value ($ mil.)	–	–	–	–	–	–
Employees	–	–	–	–	–	775

VILLAGE BANK & TRUST FINANCIAL CORP   NAS: VBFC

13319 Midlothian Turnpike
Midlothian, VA 23113
Phone: 804 897-3900
Fax: –
Web: www.villagebank.com

CEO: William G Foster
CFO: C Harril Whitehurst Jr
HR: –
FYE: December 31
Type: Public

Does it take a village to raise a bank? Village Bank & Trust is the holding company for Village Bank which has about a dozen branches in the suburbs of Richmond Virginia. It offers standard services including deposit accounts loans and credit cards. Deposit funds are used to write loans for consumers and businesses in the area; commercial real estate loans mainly secured by owner-occupied businesses account for about half of the bank's lending portfolio which also includes business construction residential mortgage and consumer loans. In 2008 Village Bank & Trust acquired the three-branch River City Bank in a transaction worth more than $20 million.

	Annual Growth	12/14	12/15	12/16	12/17	12/18
Assets ($ mil.)	4.4%	434.0	419.9	444.8	477.0	514.9
Net income ($ mil.)	–	(1.0)	0.6	13.5	(3.1)	3.0
Market value ($ mil.)	8.4%	31.6	27.3	38.3	44.0	43.7
Employees	(5.1%)	185	166	178	161	150

VILLAGE SUPER MARKET, INC.
NMS: VLGE A

733 Mountain Avenue
Springfield, NJ 07081
Phone: 973 467-2200
Fax: -
Web: www.shoprite.com

CEO: Robert Sumas
CFO: John L Van Orden
HR: -
FYE: July 27
Type: Public

It may take a village to raise a child but it takes the Sumases to raise and run the Village. Run by the Sumas family since its founding in 1937 Village Super Market operates some 30 ShopRite supermarkets throughout New Jersey northeastern Pennsylvania and Maryland. It is a member of Wakefern Food the largest retailer-owned food cooperative in the US and owner of the ShopRite brand name. The affiliation gives Village Super Market economies of scale in purchasing distribution and advertising. Most outlets are superstores measuring more than 60000 sq. ft. Its Power Alley store format features high-margin fresh and convenience foods such as baked goods sushi and salad bars and take-home hot-meal sections.

	Annual Growth	07/15	07/16	07/17	07/18	07/19
Sales ($ mil.)	0.9%	1,583.8	1,634.9	1,604.6	1,612.0	1,643.5
Net income ($ mil.)	(4.4%)	30.6	25.0	22.9	25.1	25.5
Market value ($ mil.)	(3.1%)	407.2	455.1	348.8	418.7	359.0
Employees	(0.1%)	6,750	6,544	6,552	6,742	6,731

VILLANOVA UNIVERSITY IN THE STATE OF PENNSYLVANIA

800 E LANCASTER AVE
VILLANOVA, PA 190851603
Phone: 610-519-4500
Fax: -
Web: www1.villanova.edu

CEO: -
CFO: -
HR: -
FYE: May 31
Type: Private

The oldest and largest Roman Catholic institution of higher learning in Pennsylvania Villanova University offers more than 50 academic undergraduate programs at its six main colleges: Business Engineering Liberal Arts and Sciences Professional Studies and Nursing. The university also has a School of Law and it offers graduate programs in most of its disciplines. Villanova has an enrollment of more than 10730 full and part-time undergraduate and graduate students. It also reports a student-to-faculty ratio of 12:1. Average tuition is $45376 million per year.

	Annual Growth	05/10	05/11	05/12	05/13	05/18
Sales ($ mil.)	4.5%	-	-	385.9	401.5	502.3
Net income ($ mil.)	-	-	-	(4.5)	102.0	150.2
Market value ($ mil.)	-	-	-	-	-	-
Employees	-	-	-	-	-	2,022

VINCE HOLDING CORP
NYS: VNCE

500 5th Avenue - 20th Floor
New York, NY 10110
Phone: 212 944-2600
Fax: -
Web: www.vince.com

CEO: Jill Granoff
CFO: Lisa K. Klinger
HR: -
FYE: February 02
Type: Public

If you want to keep up with Kim Kardashian or boast the same look as Beyonc-© you need to meet Vince. Upscale apparel company Vince Holding sells its pricey leather and knit clothing outerwear and shoes for women (mostly) in understated tones of gray and black at more than 2100 upscale department stores including Nordstrom Saks Fifth Avenue Neiman Marcus and Bloomingdale's. The company also operates about 30 Vince stores in 10 states and one in Japan. Its target market is affluent style-savvy women between the ages of 18 and 50. The company was formed in 2013 when majority shareholder Sun Capital split up the business of its portfolio company apparel-maker Kellwood.

	Annual Growth	01/15	01/16	01/17*	02/18	02/19
Sales ($ mil.)	(4.9%)	340.4	302.5	268.2	272.6	279.0
Net income ($ mil.)	-	35.7	5.1	(162.7)	58.6	(2.0)
Market value ($ mil.)	(15.8%)	272.6	60.1	34.9	89.3	137.3
Employees	4.7%	498	565	597	568	599

*Fiscal year change

VIOLIN MEMORY INC
NBB: VMEM Q

4555 Great America Parkway
Santa Clara, CA 95054
Phone: 650 396-1500
Fax: -
Web: www.vmem.com

CEO: -
CFO: -
HR: -
FYE: January 31
Type: Public

Violin Memory plays with more than a dash of flash in orchestrating computer memory. The company designs and sells flash memory arrays and memory cards used in enterprise-level servers that offer more storage than hard disk drives. It pitches its products for use in cloud Big Data analytics and virtualized environments. More than 350 companies use Violin Memory products in markets that include financial services health care Internet government media and entertainment and telecommunications. Its products are sold directly in 30 countries and through resellers such as Dell ePlus and IBM. Violin doesn't manufacture its storage devices; contract manufacturer Flextronics does the heavy lifting.

	Annual Growth	01/12	01/13	01/14	01/15	01/16
Sales ($ mil.)	(1.4%)	53.9	73.8	107.7	79.0	50.9
Net income ($ mil.)	-	(44.8)	(109.1)	(149.8)	(108.9)	(99.1)
Market value ($ mil.)	(51.5%)	-	-	93.2	94.7	21.9
Employees	(10.6%)	-	445	437	329	318

VIRCO MANUFACTURING CORP.
NMS: VIRC

2027 Harpers Way
Torrance, CA 90501
Phone: 310 533-0474
Fax: -
Web: www.virco.com

CEO: Robert A Virtue
CFO: Robert E Dose
HR: Carol Tennis
FYE: January 31
Type: Public

Have childhood memories of metal-legged folding tables upholstered auditorium seats or molded plastic chairs with attached wooden desks designed mostly for right-handers? Thank Virco Mfg. for the memories. The company makes a broad range of furniture and fixtures for the education market including student and teacher desks chairs tables computer furniture mobile pedestals and tables with combined seating for cafeterias A/V equipment and filing and storage cabinets. It also offers seating tables media units and other furniture for hotels government agencies churches and convention centers. Founded in 1950 Virco provides delivery and installation services as well.

	Annual Growth	01/15	01/16	01/17	01/18	01/19
Sales ($ mil.)	5.2%	164.1	168.6	173.4	189.3	200.7
Net income ($ mil.)	-	0.8	4.5	22.8	(3.2)	(1.6)
Market value ($ mil.)	15.1%	37.5	48.2	68.4	73.0	65.9
Employees	5.2%	685	695	735	750	840

VIRGINIA COMMONWEALTH UNIVERSITY

912 W FRANKLIN ST
RICHMOND, VA 232849040
Phone: 804-828-0100
Fax: -
Web: www.vcu.edu

CEO: -
CFO: -
HR: Cindy Andrews
FYE: June 30
Type: Private

Virginia Commonwealth University (VCU) serves the common interests of its more than 30000 enrolled students. The university offers more than 200 certificate undergraduate graduate and doctoral programs through its 15 schools. Spread across two campuses in Richmond: Monroe Park and Medical College of Virginia (MCV) which includes the Schools of Allied Health Dentistry Medicine Nursing Pharmacy and Public Health. Specialty facilities include the VCU Medical Center and a branch campus of the School of the Arts in Qatar. Founded in 1917 as the Richmond School of Social Work and Public Health in 1968 the school merged with the Medical College of Virginia to form VCU.

	Annual Growth	06/10	06/11	06/16	06/17	06/18
Sales ($ mil.)	(14.7%)	-	2,319.1	737.9	760.6	763.2
Net income ($ mil.)	(37.1%)	-	328.7	37.8	84.4	12.8
Market value ($ mil.)	-	-	-	-	-	-
Employees	-	-	-	-	-	11,000

VIRGINIA ELECTRIC & POWER CO.   NL:

120 Tredegar Street
Richmond, VA 23219
Phone: 804 819-2000
Fax: –

CEO: Thomas F Farrell II
CFO: Mark F McGettrick
HR: –
FYE: December 31
Type: Public

Virginia Electric and Power Company (Virginia Power) operates under the Dominion Virginia Power and Dominion North Carolina Power brands and provides regulated electric delivery services to about 2.4 million homes and businesses. Power generation is derived by means of coal gas oil hydro and nuclear plants. The utility's power plants (with 24300 MW of generating capacity) are managed by the Dominion Generation unit of parent Dominion Energy. Control of Virginia Power's transmission facilities is maintained by PJM Interconnection. Dominion Virginia Power also sells wholesale power to other users.

	Annual Growth	12/14	12/15	12/16	12/17	12/18
Sales ($ mil.)	0.1%	7,579.0	7,622.0	7,588.0	7,556.0	7,619.0
Net income ($ mil.)	10.6%	858.0	1,087.0	1,218.0	1,540.0	1,282.0
Market value ($ mil.)	–	–	–	–	–	–
Employees	0.0%	6,800	6,800	6,800	6,900	6,800

VIRGINIA HOSPITAL CENTER ARLINGTON HEALTH SYSTEM

1701 N GEORGE MASON DR
ARLINGTON, VA 222053610
Phone: 703-558-5668
Fax: –
Web: www.virginiahospitalcenter.com

CEO: James Cole
CFO: –
HR: –
FYE: December 31
Type: Private

Virginia Hospital Center-Arlington Health Systems is a general medical-surgical facility providing health care services to residents of northern Virginia. The hospital has about 350 beds and boasts all-private rooms. The acute medical center includes emergency cardiology neurology orthopedics respiratory urology cancer care and women's health divisions as well as radiology and diagnostic imaging facilities. In addition Virginia Hospital Center provides outpatient rehabilitation services and runs an urgent care clinic that furnishes primary care for minor emergencies. The hospital is a teaching facility for the Georgetown University School of Medicine.

	Annual Growth	10/07	10/08	10/09*	12/10	12/17
Sales ($ mil.)	190.3%	–	–	0.1	0.1	524.9
Net income ($ mil.)	–	–	–	(0.0)	(0.0)	54.3
Market value ($ mil.)	–	–	–	–	–	–
Employees	–	–	–	–	–	2,000

*Fiscal year change

VIRGINIA HOUSING DEVELOPMENT AUTHORITY

601 S BELVIDERE ST
RICHMOND, VA 232206504
Phone: 804-780-0789
Fax: –
Web: www.vhda.com

CEO: –
CFO: –
HR: –
FYE: June 30
Type: Private

Though Virginia is famous for its Civil War-era plantations these historic estates represent a lifestyle out of reach for most. For Virginians seeking a more modest homestead there's the Virginia Housing Development Authority (VHDA). The not-for-profit quasi-government agency founded by the Virginia General Assembly in 1972 provides developers of rental properties and low- to moderate-income borrowers with low interest rate loans to renovate or purchase houses and apartments across the state. Its loan products are offered by more than 140 authorized lenders throughout Virginia. The VHDA is self-supporting issuing bonds to raise capital.

	Annual Growth	06/13	06/14	06/15	06/16	06/18
Assets ($ mil.)	(2.3%)	–	8,014.9	8,070.7	8,024.9	7,292.9
Net income ($ mil.)	(0.1%)	–	132.8	176.7	171.7	132.3
Market value ($ mil.)	–	–	–	–	–	–
Employees	–	–	–	–	–	300

VIRGINIA INTERNATIONAL TERMINALS, LLC

601 WORLD TRADE CTR
NORFOLK, VA 23510
Phone: 757-440-7120
Fax: –
Web: www.portofvirginia.com

CEO: Joseph P Ruddy
CFO: –
HR: –
FYE: June 30
Type: Private

Virginia International Terminals (VIT) operates marine terminals and an inland port on behalf of the Virginia Port Authority (VPA) a state agency. Established in 1982 VIT's marine terminals handle containerships and other vessels in Newport News Norfolk and Portsmouth. The terminals are linked by rail to the Virginia Inland Port in Front Royal which serves as an intermodal container transfer facility conveying cargo from ships to trucks and vice versa. CenterPoint Properties investment firm The Carlyle Group and terminal operator Carrix Inc. bid to create a public-private partnership with VIT. The Transportation Secretary dismissed the bids in late 2010 after cargo activity started improving.

	Annual Growth	06/07	06/08	06/10	06/17	06/18
Sales ($ mil.)	7.4%	–	254.1	203.5	478.6	521.1
Net income ($ mil.)	–	–	(6.7)	2.1	(7.8)	16.1
Market value ($ mil.)	–	–	–	–	–	–
Employees	–	–	–	–	–	400

VIRGINIA POLYTECHNIC INSTITUTE & STATE UNIVERSITY

300 TURNER ST NW STE 4200
BLACKSBURG, VA 240616100
Phone: 540-231-6000
Fax: –

CEO: John E. Dooley
CFO: M. Dwight Shelton
HR: –
FYE: June 30
Type: Private

Virginia Polytechnic Institute and State University more commonly known as Virginia Tech is the state's largest university enrolling more than 32000 students. The university offers more than 200 undergraduate graduate and professional degree programs through eight academic colleges. It has a student-teacher ratio of 16 to 1. The school's most popular majors include agriculture business biology animal sciences and engineering. Virginia Tech which was formed in 1872 serves the surrounding community through outreach and education programs.

	Annual Growth	06/14	06/15	06/16	06/17	06/18
Sales ($ mil.)	4.2%	–	1,129.9	1,020.6	1,031.5	1,279.5
Net income ($ mil.)	16.6%	–	114.8	121.6	64.0	181.9
Market value ($ mil.)	–	–	–	–	–	–
Employees	–	–	–	–	–	6,866

VIRGINIA WEST UNIVERSITY FOUNDATION INCORPORATED

1 WATERFRONT PL FL 7
MORGANTOWN, WV 265015978
Phone: 304-282-4000
Fax: –
Web: www.wvuf.org

CEO: Cindi Roth
CFO: Michael Augustine
HR: –
FYE: June 30
Type: Private

The West Virginia University Foundation provides fund raising services and manages the financial assets of West Virginia University. The Foundation seeks support for faculty programs services equipment and facilities that the state of West Virginia might not be able to fund though other fiscal sources. The Foundation obtains funds from individuals corporations and philanthropic foundations in support of West Virginia University and its non-profit affiliates. The university founded the organization in 1954 as an independent non-profit corporation.

	Annual Growth	06/14	06/15	06/16	06/17	06/18
Assets ($ mil.)	5.5%	–	–	–	1,690.9	1,783.3
Net income ($ mil.)	(83.4%)	–	–	–	42.9	7.1
Market value ($ mil.)	–	–	–	–	–	–
Employees	–	–	–	–	–	115

VIRGINIA WEST UNIVERSITY HOSPITALS INC

1 MEDICAL CENTER DR
MORGANTOWN, WV 265061200
Phone: 304-598-4000
Fax: –
Web: www.wvucancer.org

CEO: Albert L Wright Jr
CFO: –
HR: John Bihun
FYE: December 31
Type: Private

West Virginia University Hospitals (WVUH) has West Virginians covered. The health care system's 530-bed main campus includes the Ruby Memorial Hospital the WVU Children's Hospital and the behavioral health Chestnut Ridge Center as well as out-patient care centers. Other services include centers for eye and dental care cancer treatment and family medicine. WVUH's facilities serve as the primary teaching locations for the West Virginia University's health professions schools. Cheat Lake Physicians is the physicians group associated with the health system. WVUH is a member of the West Virginia United Health System.

	Annual Growth	12/04	12/05	12/06	12/12	12/18
Sales ($ mil.)	–	–	–	0.0	1,386.7	1,193.9
Net income ($ mil.)	–	–	–	0.0	96.1	(39.8)
Market value ($ mil.)	–	–	–	–	–	–
Employees	–	–	–	–	–	6,267

VIRNETX HOLDING CORP   ASE: VHC

308 Dorla Court, Suite 206
Zephyr Cove, NV 89448
Phone: 775 548-1785
Fax: –
Web: www.virnetx.com

CEO: Kendall S. Larsen
CFO: Richard Nance
HR: –
FYE: December 31
Type: Public

VirnetX is involved in a net of legal battles. The company owns more than 70 US technology patents for establishing secure mobile internet communications over the 4G LTE network but it claims several major tech firms including Apple and Cisco Systems are giving away its patented internet security software for free. VirnetX bought the core patents from federal IT contractor Leidos in 2006 and has been working to commercialize its mobile communications software branded as GABRIEL Connection Technology as well as a secure domain name registry service. Before the company can convince customers to license its software it must resolve about 10 patent infringement lawsuits against Apple and Cisco.

	Annual Growth	12/14	12/15	12/16	12/17	12/18
Sales ($ mil.)	(52.6%)	1.2	1.6	1.6	1.5	0.1
Net income ($ mil.)	–	(9.9)	(29.2)	(28.6)	(17.3)	(25.4)
Market value ($ mil.)	(18.7%)	367.2	171.9	147.1	247.5	160.5
Employees	10.7%	14	20	20	21	21

VIRTUA MEMORIAL HOSPITAL BURLINGTON COUNTY, INC

175 MADISON AVE
MOUNT HOLLY, NJ 080602099
Phone: 609-267-0700
Fax: –
Web: www.susanbarnesfineart.com

CEO: Richard P Miller
CFO: –
HR: –
FYE: December 31
Type: Private

Virtua Memorial Hospital of Burlington County provides acute care to patients in southern New Jersey and the Philadelphia metropolitan area. Part of the Virtua Health network the hospital has more than 430 beds and is well-known for its women's and children's health services and stroke care. Other specialty programs include a sleep center cardiac rehabilitation diabetes treatment and wound care. Virtua Memorial provides a full range of cancer treatments through its collaboration with Philadelphia's Fox Chase Cancer Center and operates an in-hospital hospice center for terminally ill patients through a partnership with Samaritan Hospice.Strategy

	Annual Growth	12/03	12/04	12/05	12/06	12/08
Sales ($ mil.)	–	–	–	0.0	283.9	328.0
Net income ($ mil.)	–	–	–	0.0	39.1	26.0
Market value ($ mil.)	–	–	–	–	–	–
Employees	–	–	–	–	–	1,450

VIRTUALSCOPICS INC   NAS: VSCP

500 Linden Oaks
Rochester, NY 14625
Phone: 585 249-6231
Fax: –
Web: www.virtualscopics.com

CEO: Eric Converse
CFO: James Groff
HR: –
FYE: December 31
Type: Public

VirtualScopics makes medical imaging analysis tools that help clinical researchers speed up the drug development process. Its patented algorithms let researchers analyze data from computed tomography MRI PET and ultrasound scans with the aim of helping pharmaceutical biotech and medical device companies determine how an investigational drug is working (or not working). The company also hopes its products can be used to develop diagnostic tools to help with disease treatment and surgery. VirtualScopics provides services for many large pharmaceutical companies including GlaxoSmithKline and Johnson & Johnson; its largest customer is Pfizer (which also holds a minority stake).

	Annual Growth	12/10	12/11	12/12	12/13	12/14
Sales ($ mil.)	(6.0%)	13.4	14.3	13.0	11.2	10.5
Net income ($ mil.)	–	(0.6)	0.7	(1.5)	(2.7)	(3.4)
Market value ($ mil.)	10.4%	6.4	2.7	1.7	10.4	9.5
Employees	(14.3%)	176	104	104	81	95

VIRTUS INVESTMENT PARTNERS INC   NMS: VRTS

One Financial Plaza
Hartford, CT 06103
Phone: 800 248-7971
Fax: –
Web: www.virtus.com

CEO: –
CFO: Michael A. (Mike) Angerthal
HR: Mardelle Null Pena
FYE: December 31
Type: Public

Virtus Investment Partners provides investment management services to wealthy individuals corporations pension funds endowments and foundations and insurance companies. Boasting more than $47 billion in assets under management it operates through affiliated advisors including Duff & Phelps Kayne Anderson Rudnick and Newfleet Asset Management as well as outside subadvisors. Virtus markets diverse investment products such as wrap fee programs open- and closed-end funds and managed account services to high-net-worth individuals. It also manages institutional accounts for corporations and other investors. The firm was formed in 1995 through a reverse merger with Duff & Phelps.

	Annual Growth	12/14	12/15	12/16	12/17	12/18
Sales ($ mil.)	5.2%	450.6	382.0	322.6	425.6	552.2
Net income ($ mil.)	(6.2%)	97.7	35.1	48.5	37.0	75.5
Market value ($ mil.)	(17.4%)	1,193.0	821.9	826.0	805.0	555.8
Employees	8.9%	410	426	406	543	577

VIRTUSA CORP   NMS: VRTU

132 Turnpike Rd
Southborough, MA 01772
Phone: 508 389-7300
Fax: –
Web: www.virtusa.com

CEO: Kris A. Canekeratne
CFO: Ranjan Kalia
HR: Sundararajan (Sundar) Narayanan
FYE: March 31
Type: Public

Virtusa believes that virtually any business can improve its technology. The company provides a variety of offshore-based software development and information technology services including digitization cloud computing software engineering application development application outsourcing maintenance systems integration and legacy asset management. Virtusa's customers come from industries such as banking financial services insurance telecommunications entertainment media and healthcare. Customers in North America generate about 70% of Virtusa's revenue.

	Annual Growth	03/15	03/16	03/17	03/18	03/19
Sales ($ mil.)	27.0%	479.0	600.3	858.7	1,020.7	1,247.9
Net income ($ mil.)	(21.5%)	42.4	44.8	11.9	1.3	16.1
Market value ($ mil.)	6.6%	1,246.9	1,128.8	910.6	1,460.2	1,610.6
Employees	23.8%	9,247	18,226	17,750	20,491	21,745

VISA INC
NYS: V

P.O. Box 8999
San Francisco, CA 94128-8999
Phone: 650 432-3200
Fax: –
Web: www.corporate.visa.com

CEO: Charlotte M. Hogg
CFO: Vasant M. Prabhu
HR: –
FYE: September 30
Type: Public

Paper or plastic? Visa hopes you choose the latter. Visa operates the world's largest global consumer payment system (ahead of rivals MasterCard and American Express) and boasts more than 3.3 billion credit and other payment cards in circulation across more than 200 countries. As part of its business the company licenses the Visa name to member institutions which issue and market their own Visa products and participate in the VisaNet payment system that provides authorization processing and settlement services. The company also offers debit cards internet payment systems value-storing smart cards and traveler's checks. Visa's network connects thousands of financial institutions worldwide.

	Annual Growth	09/15	09/16	09/17	09/18	09/19
Sales ($ mil.)	13.4%	13,880.0	15,082.0	18,358.0	20,609.0	22,977.0
Net income ($ mil.)	17.5%	6,328.0	5,991.0	6,699.0	10,301.0	12,080.0
Market value ($ mil.)	25.4%	137,508.8	163,249.8	207,743.8	296,277.7	339,547.7
Employees	14.6%	11,300	–	15,000	17,000	19,500

VISHAY INTERTECHNOLOGY, INC.
NYS: VSH

63 Lancaster Avenue
Malvern, PA 19355-2143
Phone: 610 644-1300
Fax: –

CEO: Gerald Paul
CFO: Lori Lipcaman
HR: Werner Gebhardt
FYE: December 31
Type: Public

Vishay Intertechnology is a power player except when it's not. The company is a leader in the market for discrete semiconductor components (which require power to function) including diodes infrared optoelectronic components and MOSFETs (metal-oxide semiconductor field-effect transistors) which function as solid-state switches in power control applications. Vishay is also one of the world's top makers of passive electronic components (which don't require power to function) such as inductors capacitors and resistors. The company's components are used in everything from electric cars to spacecraft to wireless phones and laptops. The US-based company operates worldwide and gets most of its sales from international customers.

	Annual Growth	12/14	12/15	12/16	12/17	12/18
Sales ($ mil.)	5.0%	2,493.3	2,300.5	2,323.4	2,603.5	3,034.7
Net income ($ mil.)	30.9%	117.6	(108.5)	48.8	(20.3)	345.8
Market value ($ mil.)	6.2%	2,040.6	1,737.8	2,336.3	2,992.5	2,597.3
Employees	1.6%	22,600	22,400	22,100	23,000	24,100

VISHAY PRECISION GROUP INC.
NYS: VPG

3 Great Valley Parkway, Suite 150
Malvern, PA 19355
Phone: 484 321-5300
Fax: 484 321-5301
Web: www.vpgsensors.com

CEO: Ziv Shoshani
CFO: William M. Clancy
HR: –
FYE: December 31
Type: Public

Vishay Precision Group (VPG) likes to weigh in on important measurements and the company takes pleasure in getting foiled. The spinoff of Vishay Intertechnology aggregates a series of acquisitions made by Vishay in weighing modules and systems. VPG also specializes in foil resistors (electronic components that regulate electrical current and voltage) precision sensors strain gauges and other precision measurement equipment employed in process control systems. The company's products are used in industrial applications including military agricultural aerospace medical and construction. European customers account for 40% of sales.

	Annual Growth	12/14	12/15	12/16	12/17	12/18
Sales ($ mil.)	4.6%	250.8	232.2	224.9	254.4	299.8
Net income ($ mil.)	57.4%	3.9	(13.0)	6.4	14.3	23.6
Market value ($ mil.)	15.2%	231.2	152.5	254.7	338.9	407.3
Employees	0.6%	2,536	2,352	2,100	2,250	2,600

VISITING NURSE SERVICE OF NEW YORK

220 E 42ND ST FL 6
NEW YORK, NY 100175831
Phone: 212-609-6100
Fax: –
Web: www.vnsny.org

CEO: Mary Ann Christopher
CFO: Samuel Heller
HR: –
FYE: December 31
Type: Private

When you're laid up in bed Visiting Nurse Service of New York (VNSNY) can give you something besides Netflix binging to look forward to. VNSNY is one of the largest not-for-profit home health care providers in the US. The company provides a wide range of home health services to some 150000 patients throughout New York City as well as on Long Island. Visitation programs include senior care rehabilitation therapy mental health hospice and pediatrics as well as Medicare/Medicaid programs. The company's 15000 care providers make more than 2 million professional home visits each year.

	Annual Growth	12/98	12/99	12/00	12/01	12/17
Sales ($ mil.)	(10.0%)	–	663.8	740.1	725.0	100.4
Net income ($ mil.)	2.4%	–	44.7	0.0	(61.1)	69.0
Market value ($ mil.)	–	–	–	–	–	–
Employees	–	–	–	–	–	11,780

VISKASE COMPANIES INC.
PINK SHEETS: VKSC

8205 S. Cass Ave. Ste. 115
Darien IL 60561
Phone: 630-874-0700
Fax: 630-874-0179
Web: www.viskase.com

CEO: –
CFO: Mark Cole
HR: –
FYE: December 31
Type: Public

Viskase Companies forces hot dogs sausages and salami to shape up and ship out. The company is one of the world's leading producers of non-edible cellulosic fibrous and plastic casings used to prepare and package processed meat and poultry products. Viskase's casings are sold under brand names such as NOJAX (skinless hot dogs have "no jackets") VISFLEX and VISMAX. It also makes SEALFLEX SILVER heat-shrinkable plastic bags for the meat poultry and deli industries. In the nonfood arena Viskase makes MEMBRA-CEL for use in dialysis. Viskase has production facilities in Brazil Canada France Germany Italy Mexico Poland and the US. More than two-thirds of the company's sales originate outside the US

VISTA GOLD CORP.
NYSE AMEX: VGZ

7961 Shaffer Pkwy. Ste. 5
Littleton CO 80127
Phone: 720-981-1185
Fax: 720-981-1186
Web: www.vistagold.com

CEO: Frederick H Earnest
CFO: Douglas Tobler
HR: –
FYE: December 31
Type: Public

When it views its holdings Vista Gold hopes its prospects for gold are good. Since 2001 the company has acquired five gold projects with the expectation that gold prices would increase. It is developing the Mt. Todd gold project in Australia's Northern Territories and the Concordia gold project in Mexico's Baja California Sur. It also holds a 30% stake in Midas Gold Corp. which has projects in Idaho including the Yellow Pine property once held by Vista. Other holdings by Vista are the Guadelupe de los Reyes gold and silver mining complex in Mexico the Awak Mas gold mine in Indonesia and the Long Valley gold project in California. Vista has proven and probable reserves of 5.4 million ounces of gold.

VISTA INTERNATIONAL TECHNOLOGIES INC
NBB: VVIT

4835 Monaco St
Commerce City, CO 80022
Phone: 303 690-8300
Fax: 970 535-4784
Web: www.vvit.us

CEO: Timothy D Ruddy
CFO: Thomas P Pfisterer
HR: –
FYE: December 31
Type: Public

Vista International Technologies sees itself as a potential leader in renewable energy technology on a global scale. The company is working to develop and market its Thermal Gasifier Technology and to build and operate small power plants. Colorado-based Vista has operations in waste-to-energy gassification low-wind-speed generators alternative fuels and energy-saving lighting. Its primary operation is a facility in Texas that converts used tires into fuel. The company is looking for partners to build own and operate small waste-to-energy plants or utilize the company's technology under license. Investor Richard Strain owns just under 50% of Vista while board member Timothy Ruddy owns a 10% stake.

	Annual Growth	12/10	12/11	12/12	12/13	12/14
Sales ($ mil.)	11.0%	0.6	0.5	0.7	0.8	0.9
Net income ($ mil.)	–	(0.9)	(1.1)	(0.4)	(0.8)	(0.3)
Market value ($ mil.)	7.5%	0.6	0.9	1.5	1.7	0.8
Employees	(19.1%)	7	7	3	3	3

VISTEON CORP
NMS: VC

One Village Center Drive
Van Buren Township, MI 48111
Phone: 734 710-8349
Fax: –
Web: www.visteon.com

CEO: Sachin S. Lawande
CFO: Christian A. Garcia
HR: –
FYE: December 31
Type: Public

One of the largest auto parts makers in the US Visteon Corporation operates across one chief business group?Electronic Products. The company is focused on cockpit electronics such as instrument clusters information displays infotainment systems audio systems telematics solutions and head-up displays. Its customers are global vehicle manufacturers including Ford which represents around 25% of sales. The company has more than 40 manufacturing engineering and customer support facilities in nearly 20 countries. Nearly 80% of its sales are made outside the US.

	Annual Growth	12/14	12/15	12/16	12/17	12/18
Sales ($ mil.)	(20.6%)	7,509.0	3,245.0	3,161.0	3,146.0	2,984.0
Net income ($ mil.)	–	(295.0)	2,284.0	75.0	176.0	164.0
Market value ($ mil.)	(13.3%)	2,992.1	3,206.0	2,249.5	3,503.9	1,687.8
Employees	(20.9%)	25,500	11,000	10,000	10,000	10,000

VITACOST.COM INC
NMS: VITC

5400 Broken Sound Blvd.-N.W., Suite 500
Boca Raton, FL 33487-3521
Phone: 561 982-4180
Fax: –
Web: www.vitacost.com

CEO: Jeffrey J Horowitz
CFO: Brian D Helman
HR: –
FYE: December 31
Type: Public

Vitacost.com aims to capitalize on consumer preoccupation with health and wellness. The online retailer offers some 34000 items including dietary supplements from algae to zinc health food and personal and pet care products at discount prices. In addition to 1600-plus name brands such as Atkins and J?SON the company sells Vitacost-label nutritional products supplied by contract manufacturers. Customers shop by in large online. The company has a contact center a third-party center for late-night calls and two distribution hubs in the US. Founded in 1994 Vitacost is almost 20% controlled by Great Hill Equity; Vitacost chairman Michael Kumin and Christopher Gaffney a director are the firm's partners.

	Annual Growth	12/08	12/09	12/10	12/11	12/12
Sales ($ mil.)	23.2%	143.6	191.8	220.7	260.5	330.7
Net income ($ mil.)	–	0.0	5.9	(15.2)	(14.8)	(19.2)
Market value ($ mil.)	(13.4%)	–	349.1	191.0	208.4	227.1
Employees	26.0%	266	292	415	631	671

VITALANT

6210 E OAK ST
SCOTTSDALE, AZ 852571101
Phone: 602-414-3819
Fax: –
Web: www.vitalant.org

CEO: David Green
CFO: Susan L. Barnes
HR: –
FYE: December 31
Type: Private

Vitalant (formerly Blood Systems) collects blood and provides blood products and services to more than 1000 hospitals in about 40 states. One of the largest US not-for-profit blood service companies Vitalant operates about 125 donation centers and conducts 30000 mobile blood drives each year. The company's BioCare division distributes plasma derivative products used in medical procedures while Vitalant Research Institute conducts blood-related research studies. Vitalant also provides blood donor testing services through its Creative Testing Solutions (CTS) venture (owned with American Red Cross and OneBlood).

	Annual Growth	12/12	12/13	12/14	12/15	12/16
Sales ($ mil.)	15.0%	–	743.0	0.0	966.9	1,129.4
Net income ($ mil.)	(71.6%)	–	65.3	(62.7)	2.5	1.5
Market value ($ mil.)	–	–	–	–	–	–
Employees	–	–	–	–	–	5,000

VITAMIN SHOPPE INC
NYS: VSI

300 Harmon Meadow Blvd.
Secaucus, NJ 07094
Phone: 201 868-5959
Fax: –
Web: www.vitaminshoppe.com

CEO: Sharon M Leite
CFO: Charles D Knight
HR: Teresa Orth
FYE: December 30
Type: Public

Vitamin Shoppe helps vitamin-takers meet their recommended daily requirements. The fast-growing company sells vitamins supplements and minerals as well as herbal homeopathic and sports nutrition and wellness products at more than 750 company-operated The Vitamin Shoppe stores located in some 45 US states the District of Columbia Puerto Rico and Canada. It also sells directly via catalog and the websites VitaminShoppe.com and BodyTech.com. Stores offer about 20000 items including food and beverages and pet products under more than 800 national and private-label brands. Vitamin Shoppe was founded in 1977.

	Annual Growth	12/13	12/14	12/15	12/16	12/17
Sales ($ mil.)	2.0%	1,087.5	1,213.6	1,266.5	1,289.2	1,178.7
Net income ($ mil.)	–	66.5	61.2	53.2	25.0	(252.2)
Market value ($ mil.)	(45.9%)	1,235.7	1,133.1	805.0	570.5	105.7
Employees	3.6%	4,842	5,583	5,686	5,503	5,573

VITAS HEALTHCARE CORPORATION

100 S. Biscayne Blvd. Ste. 1300
Miami FL 33131
Phone: 305-374-4143
Fax: 305-350-6797
Web: www.vitas.com

CEO: Nick Westfall
CFO: –
HR: –
FYE: December 31
Type: Subsidiary

VITAS Healthcare is a vital provider of hospice services in the US. The firm a subsidiary of Chemed is a top national provider serving patients in more than 15 states and Washington DC. The company provides 50 hospice care programs for terminally ill patients in their homes nursing homes hospitals and at its 36 company-owned inpatient facilities. Its services — provided by teams of nurses doctors aides clergy and social workers — focus on managing pain and symptoms providing personal care helping with financial arrangements handling equipment and medications and offering emotional and spiritual support. The company also provides bereavement services and grief counseling to patients' families.

VITESSE SEMICONDUCTOR CORP.

NMS: VTSS

4721 Calle Carga
Camarillo, CA 93012
Phone: 805 388-3700
Fax: –
Web: www.vitesse.com

CEO: Christopher R Gardner
CFO: Martin S McDermut
HR: –
FYE: September 30
Type: Public

Swiftness and finesse come together in Vitesse Semiconductor's chips. Vitesse (French for "speed") is a leading supplier of high-speed integrated circuits; most of its chips are made with CMOS silicon processes. The company also develops silicon germanium (SiGe) compound semiconductors which are much harder to work with than ordinary silicon (and thus more expensive). But the fancier chips are much faster (electrons travel through the advanced compounds more swiftly) and consume less energy than silicon-based chips of equal size. Vitesse's chips are primarily used in communications gear particularly in networking equipment.

	Annual Growth	09/10	09/11	09/12	09/13	09/14
Sales ($ mil.)	(10.1%)	166.0	141.0	119.5	103.8	108.5
Net income ($ mil.)	–	(20.1)	(14.8)	(1.1)	(22.1)	(18.1)
Market value ($ mil.)	(0.1%)	244.4	199.7	165.2	205.8	243.7
Employees	(6.6%)	467	362	336	331	356

VIVEVE MEDICAL INC

NAS: VIVE

345 Inverness Drive South, Building B, Suite 250
Englewood, CO 80112
Phone: 720 696-8100
Fax: –
Web: www.viveve.com

CEO: Scott Durbin
CFO: –
HR: –
FYE: December 31
Type: Public

PLC Systems guards kidneys against ill effects of dehydration and toxic medicines. Its RenalGuard system marketed in Europe is a fluid balancing device that helps physicians monitor and maintain kidney fluid levels during medical imaging procedures. The company also developed the Heart Laser System a carbon dioxide laser system that performs Transmyocardial Revascularization (or TMR) as an alternative to such conventional therapies as bypass surgery and balloon angioplasty. PLC sold the TMR business to Novadaq in 2011 for $1.6 million to focus on development of RenalGuard for the US market.

	Annual Growth	12/14	12/15	12/16	12/17	12/18
Sales ($ mil.)	278.7%	0.1	1.4	7.1	15.3	18.5
Net income ($ mil.)	–	(6.2)	(12.4)	(20.1)	(37.0)	(50.0)
Market value ($ mil.)	25.7%	0.2	0.4	2.4	2.3	0.5
Employees	47.2%	–	21	42	103	67

VIVUS INC

NMS: VVUS

900 E. Hamilton Avenue, Suite 550
Campbell, CA 95008
Phone: 650 934-5200
Fax: –
Web: www.vivus.com

CEO: John P Amos
CFO: Mark K Oki
HR: –
FYE: December 31
Type: Public

Pharmaceutical company VIVUS has several therapeutic products in development to treat a variety of conditions including metabolic and sexual health ailments. Its two commercial-stage products obesity drug Qsymia and erectile dysfunction (ED) drug Stendra are FDA-approved; Stendra is also approved by the European Commission under the brand name Spedra. VIVUS commercialization strategies include selling its products through direct sales methods or through distribution partnership agreements in the US and abroad. Drug candidates in the company's pipeline include potential treatments for sleep apnea and diabetes.

	Annual Growth	12/14	12/15	12/16	12/17	12/18
Sales ($ mil.)	(13.1%)	114.2	95.4	124.3	65.4	65.1
Net income ($ mil.)	–	(82.6)	(93.1)	23.3	(30.5)	(37.0)
Market value ($ mil.)	(6.2%)	30.6	10.8	12.2	5.3	23.7
Employees	(11.8%)	94	82	65	52	57

VIZIO, INC.

39 TESLA
IRVINE, CA 926184603
Phone: 949-428-2525
Fax: –
Web: www.vizio.com

CEO: William Wang
CFO: Kurt Binder
HR: –
FYE: December 31
Type: Private

VIZIO has done for HDTVs what Dell did for PCs: sell them for less. Best known for its sticker-friendly flat panel and plasma LCD HDTVs VIZIO also makes and sells Blue-Ray players sound bars and speakers headphones Internet routers PCs and other consumer electronics through retailers and wholesalers across North America. Sourcing its products from China and Taiwan VIZIO sells many of its low-priced electronics through top discount chains including Amazon Best Buy BJ's Wholesale Costco Wholesale Sam's Club Target and Walmart. Thanks to its low prices VIZIO ranked as the #1 sound bar seller and the #2 Smart HDTV seller in the US market by unit sales in 2014. The proposed acquisition of Vizio by Chinese tech company LeEco was called off in 2017.

	Annual Growth	12/03	12/04	12/06	12/07	12/08
Sales ($ mil.)	155.8%	–	46.9	671.3	1,929.2	2,006.3
Net income ($ mil.)	115.7%	–	0.5	1.3	7.6	10.3
Market value ($ mil.)	–	–	–	–	–	–
Employees	–	–	–	–	–	225

VMWARE INC

NYS: VMW

3401 Hillview Avenue
Palo Alto, CA 94304
Phone: 650 427-5000
Fax: –
Web: www.vmware.com

CEO: Patrick P. (Pat) Gelsinger
CFO: Zane C. Rowe
HR: –
FYE: February 01
Type: Public

VMware develops software used to create and manage virtual machines — computer functions spread across multiple systems. Companies use its cloud-based and on-premise applications to more efficiently integrate and manage server storage and networking functions which reduces their IT costs. VMware also offers software maintenance and support training consulting services and hosted services. The company has marketing relationships with top computer hardware vendors including Hewlett Packard Enterprise IBM and Cisco Systems. VMware has strong geographic distribution with international customers accounting for more than half of its sales. Dell Technologies holds a controlling stake in VMware through its acquisition of EMC.

	Annual Growth	12/15	12/16*	02/17	02/18	02/19
Sales ($ mil.)	8.1%	6,571.0	7,093.0	496.0	7,922.0	8,974.0
Net income ($ mil.)	24.8%	997.0	1,186.0	(8.0)	570.0	2,422.0
Market value ($ mil.)	27.7%	23,234.1	32,335.6	36,533.1	50,402.9	61,816.7
Employees	6.2%	19,000	19,900	–	21,700	24,200

*Fiscal year change

VOCERA COMMUNICATIONS, INC.

NYS: VCRA

525 Race Street
San Jose, CA 95126
Phone: 408 882-5100
Fax: –
Web: www.vocera.com

CEO: Brent D. Lang
CFO: Justin R. Spencer
HR: Lori Stahl
FYE: December 31
Type: Public

Vocera Communications makes high-tech walkie talkies for hospital employees who have their hands full. Its digital voice communication system works over wireless computer networks and includes a communications badge worn around the neck and server software. The company also offers an optional standard-size phone handset. Its systems support text messaging and can be configured to make and receive telephone calls using smartphones and other mobile devices. Vocera markets its products primarily to health care facilities; it counts more than 1150 hospitals as customers and about 270 other customers in hospitality retail and libraries.

	Annual Growth	12/14	12/15	12/16	12/17	12/18
Sales ($ mil.)	17.1%	95.4	104.1	127.7	162.5	179.6
Net income ($ mil.)	–	(28.3)	(17.1)	(17.3)	(14.2)	(9.7)
Market value ($ mil.)	39.4%	320.0	374.6	567.8	928.0	1,208.4
Employees	13.8%	375	387	581	590	630

VOCUS INC
NMS: VOCS

12051 Indian Creek Court
Beltsville, MD 20705
Phone: 301 459-2590
Fax: -
Web: www.vocus.com

CEO: -
CFO: -
HR: -
FYE: December 31
Type: Public

For this company PR is no hocus-pocus just Vocus. It provides hosted cloud-based software that helps automate a variety of public relations duties including social search and email marketing. It also organizes media contacts and analyzes public relations effectiveness. Its government relations software manages state and federal contacts and offers lobbying analysis tools. Vocus' 120000 users vary from not-for-profits and the government to corporations and public relations professionals. The company also offers a proprietary information database of journalists analysts media outlets and publicity opportunities. Vocus has offices in North America Europe and Asia and offers its tools in seven languages.

	Annual Growth	12/08	12/09	12/10	12/11	12/12
Sales ($ mil.)	21.8%	77.5	84.6	96.8	114.9	170.8
Net income ($ mil.)	-	6.9	(2.0)	(3.7)	(14.6)	(23.6)
Market value ($ mil.)	(1.2%)	358.2	354.1	544.1	434.5	341.9
Employees	28.8%	463	518	687	808	1,273

VOLCANO CORPORATION
NMS: VOLC

3661 Valley Centre Drive, Suite 200
San Diego, CA 92130
Phone: 800 228-4728
Fax: -
Web: www.volcanocorp.com

CEO: R Scott Huennekens
CFO: John T Dahldorf
HR: Samantha Pacheco
FYE: December 31
Type: Public

Volcano creates its own sound and light show to get your heart's blood flowing. The company develops manufactures and sells medical imaging devices for cardiovascular care and other specialties. Its products include intravascular ultrasound (IVUS) and fractional flow reserve (FFR) consoles and imaging catheters that provide information about the condition of arteries as well as plaque and lesions. Its functional management (FM) consoles and single-use pressure and flow guidewires measure characteristics of blood around plaque in arteries. Volcano sells its products to physicians hospitals and other health care providers worldwide through a direct sales force and distributors.

	Annual Growth	12/08	12/09	12/10	12/11	12/12
Sales ($ mil.)	22.2%	171.5	227.9	294.1	343.5	381.9
Net income ($ mil.)	-	(13.7)	(29.0)	5.2	38.1	8.0
Market value ($ mil.)	12.0%	809.2	937.5	1,473.2	1,283.3	1,273.6
Employees	15.4%	883	969	1,144	1,289	1,565

VOLT INFORMATION SCIENCES INC
ASE: VOLT

50 Charles Lindbergh Boulevard
Uniondale, NY 11553
Phone: 516 228-6700
Fax: -
Web: www.volt.com

CEO: Linda Perneau
CFO: Paul R. Tomkins
HR: -
FYE: November 03
Type: Public

A jolt from Volt can discharge your personnel needs. Volt Information Sciences operates staffing services to clients in a range of industries including aerospace automotive banking and finance pharmaceutical technology and utilities. The company provides contingent workers personnel recruitment services and managed staffing services programs. Volt staffs administrative and light industrial ("commercial") workers as well as technical IT and engineering ("professional") positions. While Volt has business in approximately 85 locations in Asia Europe and North and South America about 88% of revenues are generated in the US. Brothers William and Jerome Shaw founded the business in 1950.

	Annual Growth	11/15*	10/16	10/17	10/18*	11/19
Sales ($ mil.)	(9.7%)	1,496.9	1,334.7	1,194.4	1,039.2	997.1
Net income ($ mil.)	-	(24.6)	(14.6)	27.1	(32.7)	(15.2)
Market value ($ mil.)	(22.8%)	184.2	136.5	83.3	77.8	65.4
Employees	(11.1%)	27,400	25,800	21,300	20,100	17,100

*Fiscal year change

VOLTARI CORP
NBB: VLTC

767 Fifth Avenue, Suite 4700
New York, NY 10153
Phone: 212 388-5500
Fax: -
Web: www.voltari.com

CEO: -
CFO: -
HR: -
FYE: December 31
Type: Public

Voltari sees big opportunity in mobile advertising. The company's Voltari Connect software provides customer analytics for mobile sales and marketing campaigns. Consumer brands such as McDonalds Starbucks and Toyota and ad agencies use it to track who looks at a brand's advertisements and when in order to lure them from being passive browsers to active buyers. In 2013 the company merged with Motricity which provided branded content to mobile subscribers until it lost its two top customers AT&T and Verizon. Voltari took the technology behind Motricity to develop Voltari Connect as a digital media and marketing application. Voltari operates from offices in Canada the UK and the US.

	Annual Growth	12/13	12/14	12/15	12/16	12/17
Sales ($ mil.)	(57.9%)	10.3	12.2	0.0	0.3	0.3
Net income ($ mil.)	-	(10.3)	(29.3)	(6.6)	(3.1)	(1.9)
Market value ($ mil.)	(28.2%)	30.9	5.9	45.0	20.1	8.2
Employees	(62.6%)	102	64	6	2	2

VOLUNTEER ENERGY COOPERATIVE

18359 STATE HIGHWAY 58 N
DECATUR, TN 373227825
Phone: 423-334-1020
Fax: -
Web: www.vec.org

CEO: -
CFO: -
HR: -
FYE: June 30
Type: Private

In the strong tradition of volunteering in Tennessee Volunteer Energy Cooperative is voluntarily cooperating with its members to serve their energy needs. The distribution utility serves more than 109000 customers (who also own the cooperative) in 17 central and eastern Tennessee counties. It operates more than 9000 miles of power lines. Volunteer Energy purchases its power supply from the Tennessee Valley Authority. The company also provides metered natural gas and propane service and offers telecommunications (Internet access and long-distance phone) services. In addition Volunteer Energy offers its customer surge protection and security equipment.

	Annual Growth	06/11	06/12	06/14	06/15	06/16
Sales ($ mil.)	0.5%	-	228.5	244.3	243.7	232.7
Net income ($ mil.)	(8.2%)	-	15.6	12.3	7.4	11.1
Market value ($ mil.)	-	-	-	-	-	-
Employees	-	-	-	-	-	175

VOLUNTEERS OF AMERICA, INC.

1660 DUKE ST STE 100
ALEXANDRIA, VA 223143427
Phone: 703-341-5000
Fax: -

CEO: Michael King
CFO: -
HR: -
FYE: June 30
Type: Private

There's a volunteer everywhere you look at Volunteers of America a national faith-based organization that provides community-level human services to more than 2 million people a year. It works to help abused and neglected children at-risk youth disabled people the homeless people with substance abuse problems the elderly and prisoners and former prisoners. The group operates from about 33 offices across the US and Puerto Rico and counts some 55000 volunteers in its ranks. It receives government grants as well as support from the public. Volunteers of America was organized in 1896 by Ballington and Maud Booth. Ballington's father William Booth founded the Salvation Army.

	Annual Growth	06/07	06/08	06/13	06/14	06/17
Sales ($ mil.)	54.1%	-	6.4	239.0	0.0	315.3
Net income ($ mil.)	20.9%	-	5.7	13.4	(0.0)	31.6
Market value ($ mil.)	-	-	-	-	-	-
Employees	-	-	-	-	-	3,000

VON MAUR INC.

6565 Brady St.
Davenport IA 52806
Phone: 563-388-2200
Fax: 563-388-2242
Web: www.vonmaur.com

CEO: –
CFO: Robert L Larsen
HR: –
FYE: January 31
Type: Private

Family-owned and -operated Von Maur runs nearly 30 upscale department stores in about a dozen midwestern states offering its customers amenities such as an interest-free credit card free gift wrapping and free shipping within the US. The stores range in size from 42000 to 203000 sq. ft. and offer clothing from brands such as Burberry Kenneth Cole and Tommy Bahama. Distinguishing itself from the rest of the pack the Von Maur chain has avoided advertising and big blowout sales; it even closes up shop on traditional retailer high-dollar days such as the Fourth of July. The von Maur family opened its first store in Davenport Iowa in 1872.

VONAGE HOLDINGS CORP   NMS: VG

23 Main Street
Holmdel, NJ 07733
Phone: 732 528-2600
Fax: –
Web: www.vonage.com

CEO: Alan Masarek
CFO: David T. Pearson
HR: –
FYE: December 31
Type: Public

Vonage Holdings helped ring in a new era of communications by providing telephone service over the internet to consumers. Now the company is building cloud-based communications services for businesses. Its Voice-Over-Internet Protocol (VoIP) service enables some 2.5 million consumer subscribers to turn their high-speed Internet connections into long-distance phone lines for domestic or international calls. On the business side Vonage has relied on acquisitions to build out its Unified Communications offerings. The company offers two services with voice text video data and mobile facets for commercial customers. Vonage Essentials targets small and medium-sized businesses while Vonage Premier goes after the enterprise field.

	Annual Growth	12/14	12/15	12/16	12/17	12/18
Sales ($ mil.)	4.8%	869.0	895.1	955.6	1,002.3	1,048.8
Net income ($ mil.)	15.2%	20.3	22.7	17.9	(33.9)	35.7
Market value ($ mil.)	23.0%	913.4	1,376.1	1,642.5	2,438.2	2,093.0
Employees	12.6%	1,400	1,752	1,883	1,780	2,248

VORNADO REALTY TRUST   NYS: VNO

888 Seventh Avenue
New York, NY 10019
Phone: 212 894-7000
Fax: –
Web: www.vno.com

CEO: Steven Roth
CFO: Joseph Macnow
HR: –
FYE: December 31
Type: Public

Vornado Realty Trust is a real estate investment trust (REIT) with holdings in office retail hospitality and residential space. The company's commercial property holdings total more than 22 million sq. ft. of space primarily in New York City. The REIT also owns the 1700-room Hotel Pennsylvania in Manhattan the 3.7 million sq. ft. theMART (formerly Merchandise Mart) office building in Chicago and a controlling stake in San Francisco's 1.8 million sq. ft. office complex 555 California Street. In addition Vornado owns about a third of New York retail property owner Alexander's.

	Annual Growth	12/14	12/15	12/16	12/17	12/18
Sales ($ mil.)	(4.8%)	2,635.9	2,502.3	2,506.2	2,084.1	2,163.7
Net income ($ mil.)	(15.1%)	864.9	760.4	906.9	227.4	450.0
Market value ($ mil.)	(14.8%)	22,427.9	19,045.9	19,886.2	14,896.1	11,818.9
Employees	(3.4%)	4,503	4,089	4,225	3,989	3,928

VOXWARE INC.

300 American Metro Blvd. Ste. 155
Hamilton NJ 08619
Phone: 609-514-4100
Fax: 609-514-4101
Web: www.voxware.com

CEO: Keith Phillips
CFO: Roger Maloch
HR: –
FYE: June 30
Type: Private

Voxware has a hands-free approach to information management. The company makes speech recognition systems that include voice recognition software a portable computer and a headset microphone. The systems enables workers to enter data by voice keeping their hands and eyes free to pick receive and sort materials; take inventory; and run inspections. Voxware also offers stationary systems for less mobile applications such as mail and package sorting. The company targets distribution centers and warehouses in such markets as consumer goods grocery logistics and retail. Customers have included retailer 7-Eleven vehicle glass repair specialist Belron and U.S. Foodservice.

VOXX INTERNATIONAL CORP   NMS: VOXX

2351 J. Lawson Boulevard
Orlando, FL 32824
Phone: 800 645-7750
Fax: –
Web: www.voxxintl.com

CEO: Patrick M. (Pat) Lavelle
CFO: Charles M. Stoehr
HR: –
FYE: February 28
Type: Public

Through more than a dozen subsidiaries and some 30 brands VOXX International makes and sells consumer premium audio and automobile electronics. Its products include HDTV and WiFi antennas power cords universal remotes a plethora of speakers and music systems auto security and remote start systems and power lift gates. The company counts Acoustic Research Audiovox Car Link Omega Prestige Rosen and Schwaiger among its brands. VOXX markets its products to original equipment manufacturers (OEMs) as well as mass merchants specialty retailers distributors and others. It generates nearly 90% of sales in the US.

	Annual Growth	02/15	02/16	02/17	02/18	02/19
Sales ($ mil.)	(12.4%)	757.5	680.7	681.0	507.1	446.8
Net income ($ mil.)	–	(0.9)	(2.7)	4.4	35.3	(46.1)
Market value ($ mil.)	(12.7%)	208.1	96.6	119.8	130.7	121.0
Employees	(19.4%)	2,100	2,100	2,060	972	885

VOYAGER ENTERTAINMENT INTERNATIONAL INC.   OTC: VEII

4483 W. Reno Ave.
Las Vegas NV 89118
Phone: 702-221-8070
Fax: 702-221-8059
Web: www.voyager-ent.com

CEO: Richard L Hannigan
CFO: –
HR: –
FYE: December 31
Type: Public

Voyager Entertainment International aims to have the world's tallest observation attractions. Modeled after the Ferris wheel the Voyager attraction will consist of 30 cabs called Orbiters that hold about 20 passengers each and revolve to a height of 600 feet for a view of the surrounding area. Plans are to have Voyager attractions in Las Vegas and Dubai. The company is seeking financing and attempting to acquire proper locations in Las Vegas and Dubai.

VRATSINAS CONSTRUCTION COMPANY

216 LOUISIANA ST
LITTLE ROCK, AR 72201-2706
Phone: 501-376-0017
Fax: –
Web: www.vccusa.com

CEO: Sam K Alley
CFO: –
HR: Donna Bean
FYE: December 31
Type: Private

Malls and more — office buildings retail shopping centers theater complexes and lodging facilities — are the focus of commercial builder Vratsinas Construction Company (VCC). The company is registered and licensed in all 50 states in the US and builds and renovates large scale commercial buildings such as a hotel and mixed use property for Simon Property Group shopping malls for General Growth Properties and movie theaters for AMC Entertainment. Engineer News-Record ranks the company as one of the top 100 contractors in the US and it operates through offices in Little Rock; Irvine California; Atlanta; Phoenix; and Dallas. Chairman and CEO Gus Vratsinas founded the company in 1987.

	Annual Growth	12/06	12/07	12/07	12/11	12/12
Sales ($ mil.)	(35.2%)	–	663.7	554.6	54.7	75.5
Net income ($ mil.)	–	–	0.0	9.1	0.0	0.0
Market value ($ mil.)	–	–	–	–	–	–
Employees	–	–	–	–	–	300

VSB BANCORP INC (NY)

NBB: VSBN

4142 Hylan Boulevard
Staten Island, NY 10308
Phone: 718 979-1100
Fax: –
Web: www.victorystatebank.com

CEO: Raffaele M Branca
CFO: Raffaele M Branca
HR: –
FYE: December 31
Type: Public

To the victor belongs the spoils. VSB Bancorp is the holding company for Victory State Bank which serves New York City's Staten Island from about five offices. It collects deposits from local residents and businesses offering standard products such as checking and savings accounts money market accounts and CDs. Commercial real estate business and construction loans make up almost all of the bank's loan portfolio. Victory State Bank generally does not write residential mortgages. Merton Corn CEO of the bank from its 1997 founding until his 2007 retirement owns approximately 10% of VSB.

	Annual Growth	12/14	12/15	12/16	12/17	12/18
Assets ($ mil.)	7.4%	281.0	306.4	333.1	349.8	373.8
Net income ($ mil.)	26.5%	1.3	1.6	2.3	2.6	3.3
Market value ($ mil.)	14.0%	21.4	24.0	28.8	35.1	36.1
Employees	–	–	–	–	–	–

VSE CORP.

NMS: VSEC

6348 Walker Lane
Alexandria, VA 22310
Phone: 703 960-4600
Fax: 703 960-2688
Web: www.vsecorp.com

CEO: Maurice A. Gauthier
CFO: Thomas R. (Tom) Loftus
HR: Bradley Smith
FYE: December 31
Type: Public

VSE brings military hand-me-downs back into fashion. The company provides engineering testing and logistics services for the US Army the US Navy and other government agencies on a contract basis. VSE operates through various subsidiaries and divisions that comprise its core federal group segment (engineering logistics communications and management services) and its international group (fleet maintenance and foreign military sales). Other segments include IT energy and management consulting (technical and consulting services for civilian government) and infrastructure (engineering and construction services). VSE generates about half of its revenues from the Department of Defense (DOD).

	Annual Growth	12/14	12/15	12/16	12/17	12/18
Sales ($ mil.)	13.2%	424.1	534.0	691.8	760.1	697.2
Net income ($ mil.)	16.0%	19.4	24.9	26.8	39.1	35.1
Market value ($ mil.)	(17.9%)	717.4	676.9	422.8	527.2	325.6
Employees	8.8%	1,589	2,057	2,523	2,306	2,228

VSOFT CORPORATION

6455 E JOHNS XING STE 450
DULUTH, GA 300971559
Phone: 770-840-0097
Fax: –
Web: www.vsoftcorp.com

CEO: Murthy Veeraghanta
CFO: –
HR: Devon Hill
FYE: March 31
Type: Private

Turning real checks into virtual checks is money in the bank at VSoft Corporation. Serving primarily financial institutions the company offers check and payment processing software and imaging technologies used to scan and change paper checks into electronic images; the images effectively replace and are processed faster than paper checks. VSoft offers these technologies — teller/branch capture (for financial institution use) and remote capture products (for merchant and financial institution customer use) — to more than 1700 credit unions banks and other financial institutions around the world.

	Annual Growth	03/08	03/09	03/10	03/12	03/13
Sales ($ mil.)	(3.0%)	–	–	17.7	16.4	16.2
Net income ($ mil.)	18.7%	–	–	0.7	0.5	1.2
Market value ($ mil.)	–	–	–	–	–	–
Employees	–	–	–	–	–	85

VU1 CORPORATION

OTC: VUOC

469 7th Avenue Suite 356
New York NY 10018
Phone: 212-359-9503
Fax: 760-476-1355
Web: www.chuaochocolatier.com

CEO: –
CFO: Matthew J Devries
HR: –
FYE: December 31
Type: Public

Vu1 Corporation has a bright idea and it takes the form of a light bulb. Parting ways with existing florescent LED and incandescent light bulb technologies Vu1 (pronounced "view one") is developing a new type of light bulb that it boasts is energy efficient and mercury-free unlike florescent lights which contain trace amounts of the element. Its proprietary technology Electron Stimulated Luminescence or ESL uses cathode ray tube (CRT) technologies to produce light. (CRTs were commonly used in older-style TVs). In 2010 Vu1 received UL certification for its first product a R30 floodlight-style bulb for use in recessed ceiling lighting and subsequently began selling the bulb in the US.

VULCAN MATERIALS CO (HOLDING COMPANY)

NYS: VMC

1200 Urban Center Drive
Birmingham, AL 35242
Phone: 205 298-3000
Fax: 205 298-2963
Web: www.vulcanmaterials.com

CEO: J. Thomas (Tom) Hill
CFO: John R. McPherson
HR: Robert Domitrovich
FYE: December 31
Type: Public

The road to just about everywhere in the southern tier of the US is paved with Vulcan Materials' materials. The company is one of the largest producers of construction aggregates in the US. Vulcan produces and distributes aggregates (crushed stone gravel and sand) asphalt mix calcium and ready-mixed concrete from some 375 facilities in about 20 states as well as the Bahamas and Mexico. Its aggregates are primarily used to build and maintain infrastructure such as highways bridges railways airports utilities and other public works projects; they're also used in residential commercial and industrial construction. Dig this: The company has 16 billion tons of proven and probable aggregates reserves.

	Annual Growth	12/14	12/15	12/16	12/17	12/18
Sales ($ mil.)	10.0%	2,994.2	3,422.2	3,592.7	3,890.3	4,382.9
Net income ($ mil.)	26.0%	204.9	221.2	419.5	601.2	515.8
Market value ($ mil.)	10.7%	8,660.7	12,513.4	16,490.0	16,914.3	13,018.1
Employees	6.1%	6,598	7,187	7,149	7,900	8,373

VUZIX CORP
NAS: VUZI

25 Hendrix Road, Suite A
West Henrietta, NY 14586
Phone: 585 359-5900
Fax: –
Web: www.vuzix.com

CEO: Paul J Travers
CFO: Grant Russell
HR: –
FYE: December 31
Type: Public

Virtual reality is in the eye of the beholder. Or in Vuzix's case the eyewear of the beholder. The company designs manufactures and sells video eyewear that simulates viewing a large-screen TV or computer monitor. Its products are used to view high-resolution video and digital information from mobile devices such as cell phones laptops and media players. These wearable devices are marketed to consumers (gaming enthusiasts in particular) as well as defense and industrial markets which account for about half of its revenues. Military products include personal head-mounted displays for night-vision applications. Founded in 1997 Vuzix went public in late 2009.

	Annual Growth	12/14	12/15	12/16	12/17	12/18
Sales ($ mil.)	27.8%	3.0	2.8	2.1	5.5	8.1
Net income ($ mil.)	–	(7.9)	(13.4)	(19.3)	(19.6)	(21.9)
Market value ($ mil.)	2.5%	120.3	209.4	187.6	172.4	132.7
Employees	23.0%	35	44	55	61	80

VWR FUNDING INC.

100 Matsonford Rd.
Radnor PA 19087
Phone: 610-386-1700
Fax: +44-1932-224-214
Web: www.kbcat.com

CEO: Manuel Brocke-Benz
CFO: Gregory L Cowan
HR: –
FYE: December 31
Type: Private

VWR Funding has all the tools that a lab rat requires. The company through principal operating subsidiary VWR International LLC is a global distributor of scientific and technical laboratory supplies including chemicals glassware instruments protective clothing and production supplies. It also provides technical services on-site storeroom services and lab and furniture design and installation. With operations in roughly 25 countries its primary customers are research labs in North America and Europe within pharmaceutical biotech and chemical companies government agencies and universities and research institutes. VWR Funding is a portfolio company of private equity firm Madison Dearborn Partners.

VYSTAR CORP
NBB: VYST

101 Aylesbury Rd.
Worcester, MA 01609
Phone: 508 791-9114
Fax: 770 965-0162
Web: www.vytex.com

CEO: Steven Rotman
CFO: –
HR: –
FYE: December 31
Type: Public

Vystar is vying to be a health care star. The company makes Vytex a natural rubber latex product that retains the positive properties of latex (strength comfort availability good barrier) without producing the allergic reaction that plagues about 20% of health care workers and more than 70% of patients. Vytex is used in health care supplies including surgical and exam gloves probe covers catheters tubing and adhesives. Other uses include sponges balloons condoms threads and mattresses. Vystar's goods are made by Revertex Malaysia. In 2012 Vystar entered the sleep disorder market by acquiring Georgia-based SleepHealth. Vystar plans to market its foam bedding products through the company.

	Annual Growth	12/14	12/15	12/16	12/17	12/18
Sales ($ mil.)	(14.9%)	0.7	0.4	0.0	0.0	0.3
Net income ($ mil.)	–	(1.4)	(1.2)	(1.2)	(1.2)	(5.4)
Market value ($ mil.)	(61.6%)	22.9	36.6	68.2	18.4	0.5
Employees	(38.5%)	7	6	1	1	1

VYSTAR CREDIT UNION

4949 Blanding Blvd.
Jacksonville FL 32210
Phone: 904-777-6000
Fax: 904-908-2488
Web: www.vystarcu.org

CEO: Terry R West
CFO: John H Turpish
HR: –
FYE: December 31
Type: Private - Not-for-Pr

VyStar offers a galaxy of financial services from Northeastern Florida. The credit union boasts more than two dozen locations a handful of high school branches a pair of drive-thru branches and a call center in Jacksonville. It provides traditional retail banking services such as checking and savings accounts CDs credit cards home mortgages and personal loans. Its VyStar Financial Group subsidiary specializes in financial management and investment services for members and non-members alike. Real estate agency VyStar Real Estate Services and VyStar Title Agency are also part of VyStar Financial Group. Membership in VyStar Credit Union is available to all who live or work in one of 17 area counties.

W & T OFFSHORE INC
NYS: WTI

Nine Greenway Plaza, Suite 300
Houston, TX 77046-0908
Phone: 713 626-8525
Fax: 713 626-8527
Web: www.wtoffshore.com

CEO: Tracy W. Krohn
CFO: J. Daniel (Danny) Gibbons
HR: –
FYE: December 31
Type: Public

W&T Offshore knows Gulf of Mexico to the T. An independent oil and natural gas company it engages in acquisition exploration development and production in the Outer Continental Shelf off the coasts of Louisiana Texas Mississippi and Alabama. With approximately 700000 gross acres under company lease W&T has working interests in about 50 offshore fields and in 135 offshore structures in federal and state waters. It reports proved reserves of 445.3 billion cu. ft. of gas equivalent.

	Annual Growth	12/14	12/15	12/16	12/17	12/18
Sales ($ mil.)	(11.5%)	948.7	507.3	400.0	487.1	580.7
Net income ($ mil.)	–	(11.7)	(1,044.7)	(249.0)	79.7	248.8
Market value ($ mil.)	(13.4%)	1,032.3	324.9	389.6	465.5	579.5
Employees	(4.5%)	339	297	302	298	282

W M KECK FOUNDATION INC

550 S HOPE ST STE 2500
LOS ANGELES, CA 900712617
Phone: 213-680-3833
Fax: –
Web: www.wmkeck.org

CEO: –
CFO: Alison Keller
HR: –
FYE: December 31
Type: Private

The W. M. Keck Foundation offers grants to research education and civic institutions primarily in the areas of medical research science and engineering. Established by William Myron Keck (founder of Superior Oil Company) in 1954 the foundation's assets now exceed $1 billion dollars. The foundation has established five broad grant areas: Liberal Arts Medical Research Science and Engineering Research Southern California and Undergraduate Science and Engineering. The Southern California program offers support in the areas of civic and community services healthcare education and the arts.

	Annual Growth	12/08	12/09	12/13	12/14	12/15
Assets ($ mil.)	0.8%	–	1,069.0	1,254.5	1,234.4	1,122.7
Net income ($ mil.)	–	–	0.0	(22.0)	8.1	29.3
Market value ($ mil.)	–	–	–	–	–	–
Employees	–	–	–	–	–	23

W. B. DONER & COMPANY

25900 Northwestern Hwy.
Southfield MI 48075
Phone: 248-354-9700
Fax: 248-827-0880
Web: www.doner.com

CEO: David Demuth
CFO: Lawrence A Kempa
HR: -
FYE: February 28
Type: Private

Doner knows how many licks it takes to get to the center of a Tootsie Roll Pop. W. B. Doner & Company doing business as Doner is one of the largest independent advertising agencies in the US. Responsible for the famous Tootsie Roll Pop owl campaign it provides creative ad development and campaign management services along with media planning and buying. The firm also created iconic campaigns for clients such as Timex ("Takes a licking and keeps on ticking") and Klondike Bar ("What would you do for a Klondike Bar?").

W. E. AUBUCHON CO., INC.

95 AUBUCHON DR
WESTMINSTER, MA 014731470
Phone: 978-874-0521
Fax: -
Web: www.hardwarestore.com

CEO: -
CFO: Jeffrey M Aubuchon
HR: Steve Gasco
FYE: December 31
Type: Private

Old houses in New England get a facelift with assistance from W.E. Aubuchon. The company operates more than 125 hardware stores throughout New England and New York as well as e-commerce site HardwareStore.com and in-store kiosks. Stores stock about 50000 products including appliances plumbing camping gear hardware housewares paint and tools. W.E. Aubuchon carries such name brands as Delta Faucet Honeywell Stanley and Weber. Store services include rug cleaner rentals propane tank filling free assembling and delivery and key cutting among many other services. Founded in 1908 by William Aubuchon a French-Canadian immigrant the company is still owned by the Aubuchon family.

	Annual Growth	12/12	12/13	12/14	12/15	12/16
Sales ($ mil.)	3.2%	-	146.3	154.4	159.2	160.6
Net income ($ mil.)	-	-	(3.3)	1.9	2.7	(0.1)
Market value ($ mil.)	-	-	-	-	-	-
Employees	-	-	-	-	-	1,252

W. K. KELLOGG FOUNDATION

1 MICHIGAN AVE E
BATTLE CREEK, MI 490174012
Phone: 269-968-1611
Fax: -
Web: www.wkkf.org

CEO: Sterling K Speirn
CFO: -
HR: -
FYE: August 31
Type: Private

Charitable grants from W.K. Kellogg Foundation are grrrrrrrrrreat! Founded in 1930 by cereal industry pioneer Will Keith Kellogg the foundation provides more than $300 million in grants annually to programs focused on youth and education health food systems and rural development and philanthropy and volunteerism. About two-thirds of its grants go to initiatives in the US (mostly in Michigan Mississippi and New Mexico) although it also serves others through grants in Latin America Mexico the Caribbean Brazil and South Africa. The work of the W.K. Kellogg Foundation is supported by a related trust; together they have assets of more than $9 billion — mainly in Kellogg Company stock.

	Annual Growth	08/11	08/12	08/13	08/15	08/16
Sales ($ mil.)	3.0%	-	359.4	329.1	350.9	404.3
Net income ($ mil.)	-	-	(106.6)	92.0	(5.9)	(75.7)
Market value ($ mil.)	-	-	-	-	-	-
Employees	-	-	-	-	-	200

W. L. BUTLER CONSTRUCTION, INC.

204 FRANKLIN ST
REDWOOD CITY, CA 940631929
Phone: 650-361-1270
Fax: -
Web: www.wlbutler.com

CEO: William L Butler
CFO: -
HR: -
FYE: December 31
Type: Private

W. L. Butler Construction is building up its reputation in the western region. The general contractor caters to customers needing commercial and light industrial construction services in Arizona California Colorado Idaho Montana Nevada and Washington. W. L. Butler Construction also has the capability to complete electrical and HVAC services. Projects include car dealerships retail centers medical offices industrial warehouses corporate headquarters and not-for-profit facilities. Commercial clients include Aetna Life Insurance Cisco Systems Home Depot Target and Walgreen's. W. L. Butler Construction was founded in 1975 by CEO William Butler as a residential remodeling contracting operation.

	Annual Growth	12/06	12/07	12/08	12/09	12/10
Sales ($ mil.)	-	-	-	(553.3)	160.5	129.5
Net income ($ mil.)	862.9%	-	-	0.0	2.6	1.5
Market value ($ mil.)	-	-	-	-	-	-
Employees	-	-	-	-	-	150

W.P. CAREY INC

50 Rockefeller Plaza
New York, NY 10020
Phone: 212 492-1100
Fax: -
Web: www.wpcarey.com

NYS: WPC
CEO: Jason E Fox
CFO: Toniann Sanzone
HR: -
FYE: December 31
Type: Public

Need help managing your property portfolio? Keep calm and Carey on. W. P. Carey invests in and manages commercial real estate including office distribution retail and industrial facilities. The company owns more than 1000 properties mainly in the US and Europe and manages properties for several non-traded real estate investment trusts (REITs). Its management portfolio totals some $15 billion. W. P. Carey typically acquires properties and then leases them back to the sellers/occupants on a long-term basis. It also provides build-to-suit financing for investors worldwide. W. P. Carey is converting to a REIT a corporate structure that comes with tax benefits and more flexibilty in investing in real estate.

	Annual Growth	12/14	12/15	12/16	12/17	12/18
Sales ($ mil.)	(0.6%)	906.2	938.4	941.5	848.3	885.7
Net income ($ mil.)	14.5%	239.8	172.3	267.7	277.3	411.6
Market value ($ mil.)	(1.7%)	11,586.1	9,751.5	9,766.4	11,387.8	10,799.4
Employees	(6.7%)	272	314	281	207	206

W.S. BADCOCK CORPORATION

205 NW 2ND ST
MULBERRY, FL 338602405
Phone: 863-425-4921
Fax: -
Web: www.badcock.com

CEO: -
CFO: -
HR: -
FYE: June 30
Type: Private

W.S. Badcock furnishes homes down in Dixie and beyond. As one of the largest privately-owned furniture retailers in the US the company sells furniture for every room in the house. It sells its furniture and accessories through more than 300 stores that operate under the banner names Badcock Home Furnishing Centers and Badcock &more. Aside from its e-commerce site Badcock's stores network extends to nearly 10 southeastern states. Stores also carry appliances lawn equipment electronics mattresses rugs bedding lighting wall art and other decorative accessories. The company was founded by Henry S. Badcock in 1904 as a general mercantile store. Today it is in its fourth generation of family management.

	Annual Growth	06/14	06/15	06/16	06/17	06/18
Sales ($ mil.)	10.1%	-	600.8	681.3	692.3	802.4
Net income ($ mil.)	19.5%	-	19.5	25.7	27.2	33.3
Market value ($ mil.)	-	-	-	-	-	-
Employees	-	-	-	-	-	1,500

WABASH COLLEGE

301 W WABASH AVE STE A
CRAWFORDSVILLE, IN 479332484
Phone: 765-361-6100
Fax: –
Web: www.wabash.edu

CEO: –
CFO: Larry Griffith
HR: –
FYE: June 30
Type: Private

Wabash College is a private all-male liberal arts school that confers Bachelor of Arts degrees in 22 majors. Engineering programs are offered in conjunction with Purdue University Washington University in St. Louis and Columbia University. Other programs range from art and biochemistry to Latin and philosophy as well as economics music psychology and religion. With an enrollment of about 900 students Wabash College is an independent and non-sectarian college founded in 1832. The school is one of the few remaining all-male colleges in the US.

	Annual Growth	06/12	06/13	06/14	06/15	06/16
Sales ($ mil.)	(2.9%)	–	63.7	75.4	71.6	58.3
Net income ($ mil.)	–	–	(0.4)	9.6	2.9	(12.1)
Market value ($ mil.)	–	–	–	–	–	–
Employees	–	–	–	–	–	225

WABASH NATIONAL CORP

NYS: WNC

1000 Sagamore Parkway South
Lafayette, IN 47905
Phone: 765 771-5300
Fax: –
Web: www.wabashnational.com

CEO: Richard J. (Dick) Giromini
CFO: Jeffery L. Taylor
HR: –
FYE: December 31
Type: Public

Wabash National is one of North America's top manufacturers of dry freight and refrigerated vans flatbed and drop deck trailers and intermodal equipment. Trailers are marketed under such brands as DuraPlate and RoadRailer through network of factory-direct sales representatives independent dealers and company-owned retail outlets. Customers have included Averitt Express FedEx and Swift. The company also makes stainless steel and aluminum tank trailers for liquid transport and engineered stainless steel tanks for use in the food beverage pharmaceutical and chemical industries. Additional products include composite panels used in truck bodies and containment and isolation systems for the pharmaceutical chemical and nuclear industries. Wabash sells mostly in the US.

	Annual Growth	12/14	12/15	12/16	12/17	12/18
Sales ($ mil.)	5.0%	1,863.3	2,027.5	1,845.4	1,767.2	2,267.3
Net income ($ mil.)	3.3%	60.9	104.3	119.4	111.4	69.4
Market value ($ mil.)	1.4%	681.5	652.3	872.2	1,196.4	721.2
Employees	8.6%	5,100	5,300	5,100	6,500	7,100

WACCAMAW BANKSHARES INC.

NASDAQ: WBNK

110 N. J.K. Powell Blvd.
Whiteville NC 28472
Phone: 910-641-0044
Fax: 910-642-2280
Web: www.waccamawbank.com

CEO: –
CFO: –
HR: –
FYE: December 31
Type: Public

Waccamaw Bancshares is the holding company for the Waccamaw Bank which operates about 15 branches in the coastal Carolina region. The bank provides traditional products such as checking and savings accounts and IRAs. It primarily uses funds from deposits to write commercial loans and mortgages including business loans construction loans and land development loans. Hit by an increase in bad loans the company is working with regulators to raise its capital holdings. It is also tightening up its lending practices. In order to raise capital Waccamaw Bankshares is selling 11 branches to First Bancorp.

WACHOVIA PREFERRED FUNDING CORP

NYS: WNA PR

90 South 7th Street, 13th Floor
Minneapolis, MN 55402
Phone: 855 825-1437
Fax: –
Web: www.wellsfargo.com

CEO: Scott C Arves
CFO: Mark J Emmen
HR: –
FYE: December 31
Type: Public

Truckload carrier Transport America delivers the goods on time for manufacturers and retailers in the US and Mexico. Long- and short-haul freight carried by Transport America includes department store merchandise furniture and recreational equipment as well as consumer grocery industrial and paper products. The company operates a fleet of about 1500 tractors and 4400 trailers; its trailer inventory is made up primarily of standard 53-foot dry vans but also includes some refrigerated units. The company also provides third-party logistics services. Owned by investment firm Goldner Hawn Johnson & Morrison Transport America filed to go public in late 2013.

	Annual Growth	12/08	12/09	12/10	12/11	12/12
Assets ($ mil.)	(7.0%)	18,836.9	18,410.1	18,178.1	13,534.4	14,068.8
Net income ($ mil.)	(6.7%)	767.3	867.7	769.4	795.6	581.9
Market value ($ mil.)	7.0%	2,016.0	2,223.0	2,559.0	2,582.0	2,641.0
Employees	(2.4%)	11	11	10	10	10

WADA FARMS MARKETING GROUP LLC

2155 PROVIDENCE WAY
IDAHO FALLS, ID 834044951
Phone: 208-542-2898
Fax: –
Web: www.wadafarms.com

CEO: Bryan Wada
CFO: –
HR: –
FYE: December 31
Type: Private

The Wada Farms folk grow pack and supply Idaho potatoes all of us meat-and-potatoes folks. And in addition to everyone's favorite starchy tuber Wada Farms does the same with sweet potatoes and onions. It also offers value-added items such as Easy-Bakers and Easy-Steamers — potatoes packaged in special plastic that can be cooked right in their packaging. The company cultivates more than 30000 acres of farmland and operates a 140000-sq.-ft. processing facility; its customers include retail wholesaler and foodservice companies across the US. Wada Farms was founded in 1943 by Frank Wada whose family moved inland during WWII to avoid the internment imposed on Japanese-Americans on the West Coast.

	Annual Growth	12/08	12/09	12/10	12/11	12/12
Sales ($ mil.)	4.8%	–	–	150.9	201.7	165.8
Net income ($ mil.)	13.4%	–	–	1.5	2.0	1.9
Market value ($ mil.)	–	–	–	–	–	–
Employees	–	–	–	–	–	39

WADDELL & REED FINANCIAL, INC.

NYS: WDR

6300 Lamar Avenue
Overland Park, KS 66202
Phone: 913 236-2000
Fax: –
Web: www.waddell.com

CEO: Philip J. (Phil) Sanders
CFO: Brent K. Bloss
HR: –
FYE: December 31
Type: Public

Waddell & Reed Financial is one of the oldest mutual fund managers in the US. Subsidiaries administer and distribute about 90 mutual funds under the names Waddell & Reed Advisors Funds (the company's longest-running and largest fund complex) Ivy Funds (administered by Ivy Investment Management) and Waddell & Reed InvestEd Portfolios; they also manage accounts for institutional investors and private clients. The firm sells annuities and insurance through agreements with third-party providers. Waddell & Reed has 160-plus registered offices nationwide usually in small cities and rural areas. Founded in 1937 the firm now boasts $105 billion in assets under management.

	Annual Growth	12/14	12/15	12/16	12/17	12/18
Sales ($ mil.)	(7.7%)	1,597.8	1,516.6	1,239.0	1,157.1	1,160.3
Net income ($ mil.)	(12.5%)	313.3	245.5	146.9	141.3	183.6
Market value ($ mil.)	(22.4%)	3,825.7	2,200.8	1,498.2	1,715.5	1,388.4
Employees	(5.2%)	1,648	1,691	1,447	1,430	1,332

WADLEY REGIONAL MEDICAL CENTER

1000 PINE ST
TEXARKANA, TX 755015100
Phone: 903-798-8000
Fax: -
Web: www.wadleyhealth.org

CEO: Thomas Gilbert
CFO: -
HR: Debby Butler
FYE: December 31
Type: Private

Wadley Regional Medical Center is a general hospital serving patients from the Ark-La-Tex region — that is Arkansas Louisiana and Texas. It also offers in-patient geriatric behavioral health cancer treatment cardiac rehabilitation and surgical services. The center founded in 1900 has about 370 beds and operates clinics dedicated to areas such as pediatric care and women's health. Citing lower patient counts the hospital filed for Chapter 11 bankruptcy protection in early 2009 but was quickly purchased by hospital management firm Brim Holdings. In 2010 however Brim Holdings and Wadley Regional were acquired by hospital operator IASIS Healthcare.

	Annual Growth	12/11	12/12	12/13	12/14	12/15
Sales ($ mil.)	10.7%	-	-	-	116.6	129.0
Net income ($ mil.)	-	-	-	-	(0.2)	10.7
Market value ($ mil.)	-	-	-	-	-	-
Employees	-	-	-	-	-	1,285

WAGEWORKS INC

1100 Park Place, 4th Floor
San Mateo, CA 94403
Phone: 650 557-5200
Fax: -
Web: www.wageworks.com

NYS: WAGE
CEO: Edgar Montes
CFO: Colm Callan
HR: -
FYE: December 31
Type: Public

WageWorks wants to make administration of tax-advantaged spending accounts easier. The company helps some 5000 clients — including more than 50% of the Fortune 100 companies — implement and manage flexible spending accounts used for health wellness and dependent care as well as commuting and tuition expenses. The WageWorks SaaS (software as a service) platform also can be used for health savings accounts and other health care reimbursement programs. Its online tools provide real-time visibility into account activity and the ability to work with any combination of insurance carrier or financial institution. Founded in 2000 WageWorks operates through about 10 offices across the US. It went public in 2012.

	Annual Growth	12/12	12/13	12/14	12/15	12/16
Sales ($ mil.)	19.8%	177.3	219.3	267.8	334.3	364.7
Net income ($ mil.)	17.8%	10.5	21.7	18.2	23.0	20.2
Market value ($ mil.)	42.1%	656.9	2,193.4	2,382.7	1,674.2	2,675.4
Employees	21.1%	1,007	1,200	1,675	1,480	2,167

WAGNER INDUSTRIES INC.

1201 E 12TH AVE
NORTH KANSAS CITY, MO 641164306
Phone: 816-474-1110
Fax: -
Web: www.wagnerlogistics.com

CEO: Brian Smith
CFO: Kevin Service
HR: -
FYE: December 31
Type: Private

When freight needs to stop between origin and destination Wagner Industries can offer the hospitality of its distribution facilities. The company maintains-, about-, 4-, million sq. ft. of warehouse space largely in the Kansas City metropolitan area but also in several states in the southeastern and western US.-, Overall the company operates-, a dozen distribution centers. In addition to warehousing and distribution Wagner Industries offers packaging and transportation management services. Customers include companies from the consumer products paper and retail industries. Owned by the Wagner family including company president John Wagner Jr. Wagner Industries was founded in 1946.

	Annual Growth	12/04	12/05	12/06	12/07	12/08
Sales ($ mil.)	(8.3%)	-	58.7	51.4	52.0	45.2
Net income ($ mil.)	-	-	-	0.3	40.8	(0.3)
Market value ($ mil.)	-	-	-	-	-	-
Employees	-	-	-	-	-	300

WAKE FOREST UNIVERSITY

1834 WAKE FOREST RD # 7326
WINSTON SALEM, NC 271096054
Phone: 336-758-5000
Fax: -
Web: www.wfu.edu

CEO: -
CFO: B Hofler Milan
HR: Melissa R Mickles
FYE: June 30
Type: Private

Demon Deacons may sound like a weary clergyman's nightmare but at Wake Forest they're something to cheer about. Wake Forest University (WFU) home of the Demon Deacon mascot is a private liberal arts institution that operates through about half a dozen colleges and schools: law medicine arts and sciences business and accountancy management and divinity. WFU provides more than 35 majors and offers a low student-faculty ratio of 11:1. Its 7700 students can also study abroad in France Spain Japan and Cuba among other countries. WFU was established in 1834 in Wake Forest North Carolina. It moved to its present location in Winston-Salem in 1956.

	Annual Growth	06/09	06/10	06/11	06/13	06/16
Sales ($ mil.)	2.5%	-	1,155.6	459.5	496.8	1,340.0
Net income ($ mil.)	(38.3%)	-	97.8	77.8	82.3	5.4
Market value ($ mil.)	-	-	-	-	-	-
Employees	-	-	-	-	-	4,860

WAKE FOREST UNIVERSITY BAPTIST MEDICAL CENTER

MEDICAL CENTER BLVD
WINSTON SALEM, NC 271570001
Phone: 336-748-8843
Fax: -
Web: www.wakehealth.edu

CEO: -
CFO: -
HR: -
FYE: June 30
Type: Private

Wake Forest University Baptist Medical Center (WFUBMC) promotes health in the thick of tobacco country. The not-for-profit system operates Wake Forest University Health Sciences with its School of Medicine Wake Forest University Physicians 16 dialysis centers and Piedmont Triad Research Park. It also operates the North Carolina Baptist Hospital with facilities devoted to geriatrics cancer pediatrics and more. The system has about 20 subsidiary or affiliate hospitals and operates about 120 regional outreach activities from satellite clinics to health fairs. WFUBMC offers rehab skilled nursing and home health services; it also has a unit that coordinates special services for international patients.

	Annual Growth	06/07	06/08	06/09	06/10	06/13
Sales ($ mil.)	-	-	(1,236.5)	0.2	758.4	84.9
Net income ($ mil.)	-	-	-	(0.0)	12.4	74.2
Market value ($ mil.)	-	-	-	-	-	-
Employees	-	-	-	-	-	11,000

WAKEFERN FOOD CORP.

5000 RIVERSIDE DR
KEASBEY, NJ 088321209
Phone: 908-527-3300
Fax: -
Web: www.wakefern.shoprite.com

CEO: Joseph Colalillo
CFO: Douglas Wille
HR: -
FYE: September 27
Type: Private

Grocery stores getting supplies from this co-op may be on the "Rite" track. Wakefern Food is the largest member-owned wholesale distribution cooperative in the US supplying groceries and other merchandise to more than 250 supermarkets under the ShopRite and The Fresh Grocer banners in New Jersey New York Connecticut Delaware Maryland Pennsylvania and Virginia. It also operates more than 50 PriceRite stores in these states plus Rhode Island and Massachusetts. Beyond supplying its member-owned stores Wakerfern distributes products to other supermarkets across the northeastern US and Bermuda. Founded by seven grocers in 1946 the coop now boasts 50 members 70000-plus employees and over $15 billion in annual sales.

	Annual Growth	09/10	09/11	09/12	09/13	09/14
Sales ($ mil.)	3.8%	-	-	11,010.2	11,456.0	11,871.4
Net income ($ mil.)	0.0%	-	-	5.0	0.1	5.0
Market value ($ mil.)	-	-	-	-	-	-
Employees	-	-	-	-	-	3,500

WAKEMED

3000 NEW BERN AVE G100
RALEIGH, NC 276101231
Phone: 919-350-8000
Fax: –
Web: www.wakemed.org

CEO: Donald R Gintzig
CFO: Michael De Vaughn
HR: –
FYE: September 30
Type: Private

If you wake up in a hospital in Wake County North Carolina you may be at one of WakeMed health system's facilities. WakeMed is a network of medical centers including two hospitals outpatient and emergency clinics rehabilitation facilities skilled nursing centers laboratories physicians' offices and home care service agencies. Its hospitals the WakeMed Raleigh Campus and the WakeMed Cary Hospital include specialty divisions such as heart care stroke trauma critical care diabetes asthma and children's and women's centers. Combined its facilities offer more than 900 beds. WakeMed also conducts research and medical training programs.

	Annual Growth	09/06	09/07	09/08	09/09	09/15
Sales ($ mil.)	3.5%	–	–	837.0	883.8	1,065.2
Net income ($ mil.)	–	–	–	12.8	0.0	(33.0)
Market value ($ mil.)	–	–	–	–	–	–
Employees	–	–	–	–	–	16,933

WALBRIDGE ALDINGER COMPANY

777 Woodward Ave. Ste. 300
Detroit MI 48226
Phone: 313-963-8000
Fax: 313-963-8150
Web: www.walbridge.com

CEO: Michael R Haller
CFO: –
HR: –
FYE: December 31
Type: Private

The Motor City has been home to Motown Madonna and one Walbridge Aldinger. The US construction company provides construction management design/build and general contracting services for industrial commercial and government facilities. It's a major builder of airports and steel and nonferrous metal plants in the US. Through different divisions it also offers specialty contracting services in the areas of structural concrete equipment installation and facilities management. Although most of its work is done in the US it also has operations and projects in Canada the Middle East and Latin America. Founded in 1916 the business is privately owned and part of The Walbridge Group family of companies.

WALGREENS BOOTS ALLIANCE INC   NMS: WBA

108 Wilmot Road
Deerfield, IL 60015
Phone: 847 315-2500
Fax: –
Web: www.walgreensbootsalliance.com

CEO: Stefano Pessina
CFO: George R. Fairweather
HR: Kathleen Wilson-Thompson
FYE: August 31
Type: Public

Whether you get your drugs from the pharmacist or the chemist Walgreens Boots Alliance has you covered. The company formed when US-based Walgreen Co. bought its European counterpart Alliance Boots includes more than 13200 retail pharmacies (or chemists in some parts of the world) in 11 countries mostly the US and its territories and the UK selling prescription and OTC drugs along with health and beauty products and general merchandise. The Alliance Boots part of the company also includes wholesale operations serving more than 230000 pharmacies hospitals and clinics in upwards of 20 countries. Walgreens Alliance Boots was formed in 2014.

	Annual Growth	08/15	08/16	08/17	08/18	08/19
Sales ($ mil.)	7.3%	103,444.0	117,351.0	118,214.0	131,537.0	136,866.0
Net income ($ mil.)	(1.4%)	4,220.0	4,173.0	4,078.0	5,024.0	3,982.0
Market value ($ mil.)	(12.3%)	77,495.8	72,266.7	72,974.1	61,387.8	45,834.9
Employees	(1.3%)	360,000	360,000	345,000	354,000	342,000

WALKER & DUNLOP INC   NYS: WD

7501 Wisconsin Avenue, Suite 1200E
Bethesda, MD 20814
Phone: 301 215-5500
Fax: –
Web: www.walkerdunlop.com

CEO: William M. (Willy) Walker
CFO: Stephen P. Theobald
HR: –
FYE: December 31
Type: Public

When it comes to its commercial real estate loans Walker & Dunlop has the government on its side. The company provides commercial real estate financial services — mainly multifamily loans for apartments health care properties and student housing — to real estate owners and developers across the US. It originates and sells its products (e.g. mortgages supplemental financing construction loans and mezzanine loans) primarily through government-sponsored enterprises (GSEs) like Fannie Mae and Freddie Mac as well as through HUD. To a lesser extent the company originates loans for insurance companies banks and institutional investors.

	Annual Growth	12/14	12/15	12/16	12/17	12/18
Sales ($ mil.)	19.1%	360.8	468.2	575.3	711.9	725.2
Net income ($ mil.)	33.1%	51.4	82.1	113.9	211.1	161.4
Market value ($ mil.)	25.3%	517.4	849.8	920.3	1,401.1	1,275.7
Employees	11.7%	465	504	550	623	723

WALKER DIE CASTING INC.

1125 HIGGS RD
LEWISBURG, TN 370914408
Phone: 931-359-6206
Fax: –
Web: www.walkerdiecasting.com

CEO: –
CFO: –
HR: –
FYE: December 31
Type: Private

Walker Die Casting doesn't leave things to chance. The company is a producer of high-pressure aluminum castings for industrial applications. Walker Die Casting provides custom die fabrication services to customers in the automotive appliance lawn and garden marine and power tool industries. Products include parts such as adapter plates brackets oil pans gear cases and housings for transmissions engines axles and flywheels. Walker Die Casting also offers product design finishing testing machining and warehousing services. The company was founded in 1958 by Robert Walker.

	Annual Growth	12/09	12/10	12/11	12/12	12/13
Sales ($ mil.)	0.0%	–	54.9	126.9	54.9	54.9
Net income ($ mil.)	–	–	–	0.0	0.0	0.0
Market value ($ mil.)	–	–	–	–	–	–
Employees	–	–	–	–	–	655

WALMART INC   NYS: WMT

702 S.W. 8th Street
Bentonville, AR 72716
Phone: 479 273-4000
Fax: –
Web: www.stock.walmart.com

CEO: Gregory S. (Greg) Foran
CFO: Michael P. Dastugue
HR: Marty Autrey
FYE: January 31
Type: Public

Walmart is an unstoppable retail force that has yet to meet any immovable object. It is the world's #1 retailer as well as the world's largest company by revenue and largest employer with 2.2 million associates. Walmart sells groceries and general merchandise operating some 5400 stores in the US including about 4800 Walmart stores and 600 Sam's Club membership-only warehouse clubs. Walmart's international division numbers about 6000 locations; operating through regional subsidiaries it's the #1 retailer in Canada and Mexico and has operations in Asia Africa Europe and Latin America. Some 275 million customers visit Walmart's stores and websites each week.

	Annual Growth	01/15	01/16	01/17	01/18	01/19
Sales ($ mil.)	1.4%	485,651.0	482,130.0	485,873.0	500,343.0	514,405.0
Net income ($ mil.)	(20.1%)	16,363.0	14,694.0	13,643.0	9,862.0	6,670.0
Market value ($ mil.)	–	0.0	0.0	0.0	0.0	0.0
Employees	0.0%	2,200,000	2,200,000	2,300,000	2,300,000	2,200,000

1443

WALSH BROTHERS, INCORPORATED

210 COMMERCIAL ST STE 1
BOSTON, MA 021091381
Phone: 617-878-4800
Fax: -
Web: www.walshbrothers.com

CEO: -
CFO: -
HR: -
FYE: December 31
Type: Private

This pair of Boston brothers has been building Beantown for more than a century. Walsh Brothers Incorporated a Boston-based construction management and contracting company that specializes in building cultural educational medical and research facilities throughout New England is known for its work on iconic projects such as Boston's Fenway Park and Faneuil Hall. The firm also offers historic renovation services and has refurbished places such as the Boston Symphony Orchestra and New England Conservatory of Music. Its clients have included Harvard University Dana-Faber Cancer Institute Amgen Novartis and Proctor & Gamble. Founded in 1901 by brothers James and Thomas Walsh the builder continues to be run by the Walsh family.

	Annual Growth	12/05	12/06	12/07	12/08	12/09
Sales ($ mil.)	10.3%	-	-	335.8	545.8	408.4
Net income ($ mil.)	30.2%	-	-	3.7	9.2	6.3
Market value ($ mil.)	-	-	-	-	-	-
Employees		-	-	-	-	91

WALTER ENERGY, INC.   NBB: WLTG Q

3000 Riverchase Galleria, Suite 1700
Birmingham, AL 35244
Phone: 205-745-2000
Fax: -
Web: www.walterenergy.com

CEO: -
CFO: -
HR: -
FYE: December 31
Type: Public

Walter Energy has renewed energy for exploiting natural resources. Its subsidiaries include Jim Walter Resources (coal production) and Walter Coke (foundry and furnace coke). Its primary business is the mining and exporting of hard coking coal for the steel industry through its US Operations segment which accounts for more than 70% of Walter Energy's total sales. The company also develops also produces thermal coal anthracite metallurgical coke and coal bed methane gas (found in coal seams). Formerly a diversified company that included water products homebuilding and financing units Walter Energy has divested itself of all but its natural resources and energy businesses. It declared bankruptcy in 2015.

	Annual Growth	12/10	12/11	12/12	12/13	12/14
Sales ($ mil.)	(3.0%)	1,587.7	2,571.4	2,399.9	1,860.6	1,407.3
Net income ($ mil.)	-	385.8	349.2	(1,060.4)	(359.0)	(470.6)
Market value ($ mil.)	(67.8%)	9,201.7	4,359.0	2,582.6	1,197.0	99.3
Employees	6.3%	2,100	4,200	4,100	3,600	2,680

WALTON ELECTRIC MEMBERSHIP CORPORATION

842 HIGHWAY 78 NW
MONROE, GA 306554475
Phone: 770-267-2505
Fax: -
Web: www.waltonemc.com

CEO: D Ronnie Lee
CFO: Marsha L Shumate
HR: -
FYE: June 30
Type: Private

Good night John-Boy. This Walton family serves more than 118400 residential agricultural commercial and industrial customers in northeastern Georgia. The Walton Electric Membership Corporation (Walton EMC) operates 6840 miles of power lines spanning across all or portions of ten counties (Athens-Clarke Barrow DeKalb Greene Gwinnett Morgan Newton Oconee Rockdale and Walton). Subsidiary Walton EMC Natural Gas competes in the state's deregulated retail gas supply market and has about 64000 customers. Other operations include security systems installation and monitoring appliance sales and rebates and outdoor lighting services.

	Annual Growth	12/06	12/07	12/08	12/09*	06/18
Sales ($ mil.)	(1.9%)	-	469.8	215.8	227.1	381.8
Net income ($ mil.)	159.7%	-	0.0	17.3	6.2	19.4
Market value ($ mil.)	-	-	-	-	-	-
Employees		-	-	-	-	273

*Fiscal year change

WALTON SIGNAGE CORPORATION

3419 E. Commerce
San Antonio TX 78220
Phone: 210-886-0644
Fax: +972-3-693-6328
Web: www.credit-suisse.com/il

CEO: -
CFO: -
HR: -
FYE: December 31
Type: Private

Big stores need big signs. That's where Walton Signage comes in. The commercial signage maker designs and installs storefront streetside and interior signs for major US retailers and leading brands including Old Navy 24 Hour Fitness Verizon and Wells Fargo. Walton Signage's signs are for sale or lease and the company oversees all phases of a project including permitting site surveying sign design manufacturing shipping and installation. Its services also include mass re-branding capable of rolling out hundreds of signs both domestically and abroad under a newly designed corporate identity. Walton Signage was founded in 1980.

WAR MEMORIAL HOSPITAL INC.

1 HEALTHY WAY
BERKELEY SPRINGS, WV 254117463
Phone: 304-258-1234
Fax: -
Web: www.valleyhealthlink.com

CEO: -
CFO: Christine Lowman
HR: -
FYE: December 31
Type: Private

|Morgan County War Memorial Hospital provides a wide range of inpatient and outpatient medical services including acute emergency and long-term health services for the residents of Morgan County West Virginia and surrounding areas. The not-for-profit hospital has about 25 beds as well as a 16-bed long-term care unit. War Memorial was founded in 1934 as a treatment center for post-paralysis care.

	Annual Growth	12/09	12/10	12/11	12/12	12/13
Sales ($ mil.)	14.1%	-	14.5	25.4	17.4	21.6
Net income ($ mil.)	(83.1%)	-	-	23.1	(1.2)	0.7
Market value ($ mil.)	-	-	-	-	-	-
Employees		-	-	-	-	150

WARD TRUCKING, LLC

1436 WARD TRUCKING DR
ALTOONA, PA 166027110
Phone: 814-944-0803
Fax: -
Web: www.wardtlctools.com

CEO: -
CFO: -
HR: -
FYE: December 31
Type: Private

Less-than-truckload (LTL) carrier Ward Trucking operates primarily in the northeastern and mid-Atlantic US. (LTL carriers consolidate freight from multiple shippers into a single truckload.) In addition to its LTL business the company offers full truckload and logistics services through the Ward Transport & Logistics brand name. Ward Trucking operates a fleet of about 450 tractors 60 trucks and 1180 trailers from a network of terminals stretching from New York to Illinois. William W. Ward founded the company in 1931 to haul freight from central Pennsylvania to New York City. Ward Trucking is run by members of the Ward family.

	Annual Growth	12/10	12/11	12/12	12/13	12/14
Sales ($ mil.)	1.1%	-	-	149.5	140.0	152.7
Net income ($ mil.)	78.6%	-	-	1.2	2.0	3.8
Market value ($ mil.)	-	-	-	-	-	-
Employees		-	-	-	-	1,057

WARNER MUSIC GROUP CORP.

1633 BROADWAY
NEW YORK, NY 100196708
Phone: 212-275-2000
Fax: –
Web: www.wmg.com

CEO: Stephen Cooper
CFO: Eric Levin
HR: –
FYE: September 30
Type: Private

These records were made to be listened to not broken. Warner Music Group (WMG) is one of the world's largest recording companies ranking #3 in terms of US market share (behind Universal Music Group and Sony Music Entertainment). It operates through two businesses: Recorded Music and Music Publishing. Its Recorded Music catalog includes best-selling albums The Eagles: Their Greatest Hits 1971-1975 and Led Zeppelin IV. Its Music Publishing business holds more than one million copyrights from some 65000 songwriters. In mid-2011 WMG was acquired by diversified business group Access Industries.

	Annual Growth	09/12	09/13	09/14	09/15	09/16
Sales ($ mil.)	4.2%	–	2,871.0	3,027.0	2,966.0	3,246.0
Net income ($ mil.)	–	–	(194.0)	(303.0)	(88.0)	30.0
Market value ($ mil.)	–	–	–	–	–	–
Employees	–	–	–	–	–	4,211

WARREN EQUITIES INC.

27 Warren Way
Providence RI 02905
Phone: 401-781-9900
Fax: 401-461-7160
Web: www.warreneq.com

CEO: –
CFO: –
HR: –
FYE: May 31
Type: Private

Warren Equities fills car tanks and stomachs in the US Northeast. The holding company sells fuel and groceries from more than 200 XtraMart brand service stations and convenience stores in nine states from Maine to Virginia. Its Warex Terminals unit (which has a network of long term supply arangements with terminals throughout the Northeast) is one of the largest independent distributors of heating oil gasoline and diesel fuel in Connecticut New Jersey New York and Pennsylvania. Drake Petroleum distributes gasoline and diesel in New England. Drake offers petroleum products from a wide range of branded suppliers including BP CITGO Exxon Mobil Gulf Shell Sunoco and Valero.

WARREN RESOURCES INC (MD)   NL:

5420 LBJ Freeway, Suite 600
Dallas, TX 75240
Phone: 214 393-9688
Fax: –
Web: www.warrenresources.com

CEO: James A Watt
CFO: Frank T Smith
HR: –
FYE: December 31
Type: Public

Warren Resources believes that its heavy investment in oil and gas is warranted. The independent exploration and production company is focused on waterflood oil recovery programs in tar fields in California's Los Angeles Basin and the development of coalbed methane natural gas properties located in the Washakie Basin in the Greater Green River Basin in southwestern Wyoming. Warren Resources also owns oil and gas properties in New Mexico and Texas. In 2012 the company reported proved reserves of 51.2 billion cu. ft. of natural gas ans 24.9 million barrels of oil. In 2016 Warren Resources filed for Chapter 11 bankruptcy protection.

	Annual Growth	12/13	12/14	12/15*	09/16*	12/16
Sales ($ mil.)	(48.3%)	128.8	150.7	88.4	42.9	17.8
Net income ($ mil.)	–	30.4	24.0	(620.0)	(150.5)	(167.1)
Market value ($ mil.)	–	–	–	–	–	–
Employees	2.1%	62	87	75	–	66

*Fiscal year change

WARREN RURAL ELECTRIC COOPERATIVE CORPORATION

951 FAIRVIEW AVE
BOWLING GREEN, KY 421014937
Phone: 270-842-6541
Fax: –
Web: www.wrecc.com

CEO: W Scott Ramsey
CFO: Roxanne Gray
HR: Greg D Vp of
FYE: June 30
Type: Private

This Warren needs no commission just a cooperative in order to deliver electric results to the people. Warren Rural Electric Cooperative Corporation (Warren RECC) provides its member customers with electricity security systems and surge suppression equipment as well as with floodlighting and street lighting. It offers propane through non-affiliated Propane Energy Partners. The co-op serves more than 55300 customers in an eight-county service area (Barren Butler Edmonson Grayson Logan Ohio Simpson and Warren counties) in rural south-central Kentucky. Warren RECC is affiliated with the Tennessee Valley Authority and a member of Touchstone Energy a 600-member alliance of electricity co-ops.

	Annual Growth	06/12	06/13	06/14*	12/14*	06/15
Sales ($ mil.)	1.4%	–	177.3	184.1	187.4	182.2
Net income ($ mil.)	6.9%	–	4.7	5.0	5.7	5.4
Market value ($ mil.)	–	–	–	–	–	–
Employees	–	–	–	–	–	165

*Fiscal year change

WASHINGTON BANKING CO. (OAK HARBOR, WA)   NMS: WBCO

450 SW Bayshore Drive
Oak Harbor, WA 98277
Phone: 360 679-3121
Fax: –
Web: www.wibank.com

CEO: –
CFO: –
HR: –
FYE: December 31
Type: Public

Washington Banking is the holding company for Whidbey Island Bank which serves individuals and businesses through some 30 branches in northwestern Washington. The bank offers standard deposit services such as checking and savings accounts CDs and IRAs. It primarily originates commercial mortgages and consumer and construction loans. To a lesser extent the bank offers one- to four-family residential mortgages and business loans. Whidbey Island Bank sells investment and insurance products through agreements with third-party providers. The bank added about a dozen branches in 2010 from the acquisitions of failed financial institutions City Bank and North County Bank in separate FDIC-assisted transactions.

	Annual Growth	12/08	12/09	12/10	12/11	12/12
Assets ($ mil.)	17.0%	899.6	1,045.9	1,704.5	1,670.6	1,687.7
Net income ($ mil.)	19.2%	8.3	6.2	25.6	16.0	16.8
Market value ($ mil.)	11.9%	134.7	184.9	212.3	184.4	210.9
Employees	16.0%	258	281	448	450	467

WASHINGTON FEDERAL INC   NMS: WAFD

425 Pike Street
Seattle, WA 98101
Phone: 206 624-7930
Fax: –
Web: www.wafdbank.com

CEO: Roy M. Whitehead
CFO: Vincent L. Beatty
HR: –
FYE: September 30
Type: Public

Washington Federal is the holding company for Washington Federal Savings which operates about 190 branches in eight western states. The thrift which was founded in 1917 collects deposits from consumers and business by offering standard products such as CDs IRAs and checking savings and money market accounts. With these funds the bank mainly originates single-family residential mortgages which account for nearly three-quarters of its loan portfolio. The bank also writes business consumer construction land and multifamily residential loans. Washington Federal sells life home and auto coverage to individuals and businesses through its First Insurance Agency subsidiary.

	Annual Growth	09/15	09/16	09/17	09/18	09/19
Assets ($ mil.)	3.1%	14,568.3	14,888.1	15,253.6	15,865.7	16,474.9
Net income ($ mil.)	7.0%	160.3	164.0	173.5	203.9	210.3
Market value ($ mil.)	12.9%	1,793.6	2,103.5	2,653.0	2,522.9	2,916.3
Employees	1.8%	1,838	1,806	1,818	1,877	1,971

WASHINGTON HOSPITAL CENTER CORPORATION

110 IRVING ST NW
WASHINGTON, DC 200103017
Phone: 855-546-1686
Fax: –
Web: www.medstarwashington.org

CEO: Kent Samet
CFO: William Gayne
HR: –
FYE: June 30
Type: Private

Washington Hospital Center (doing business as MedStar Washington Hospital Center) may be the official hospital of the Washington Redskins but you don't have to be a professional football player to make use of the facility's services. The hospital at the heart of the MedStar Health system serves some 500000 patients living in and around the nation's capital each year. Washington Hospital Center has 912 beds and includes specialized care centers for cancer cardiovascular conditions and stroke. Other offerings include organ transplantation a regional burn treatment center and emergency air transportation. MedStar Washington also conducts clinical research and offers educational residency and fellowship programs.

	Annual Growth	06/07	06/08	06/14	06/15	06/16
Sales ($ mil.)	1.6%	–	1,028.6	1,107.7	1,121.4	1,166.1
Net income ($ mil.)	12.3%	–	14.3	22.8	23.4	36.0
Market value ($ mil.)	–	–	–	–	–	–
Employees	–	–	–	–	–	5,637

WASHINGTON METROPOLITAN AREA TRANSIT AUTHORITY

600 5TH ST NW
WASHINGTON, DC 200012610
Phone: 202-962-1000
Fax: –
Web: www.washington.org

CEO: Paul J Wiedefeld
CFO: –
HR: –
FYE: June 30
Type: Private

Washington Metropolitan Area Transit Authority (WMATA or the Metro) operates the second largest rail transit system (Metrorail) and one of the largest bus networks (Metrobus) in the US. Transporting roughly a third of federal government employees to work and millions of tourists its transit service zone covers Washington DC and neighboring counties and suburbs in Maryland and Virginia. The authority's rail system consists of about 90 stations served by more than 115 miles of track both underground and aboveground. It operates a fleet of about 1400 buses. WMATA also offers MetroAccess paratransit service for eligible people with disabilities.

	Annual Growth	06/02	06/03	06/04	06/08	06/16
Sales ($ mil.)	5.1%	–	451.1	500.0	0.7	859.2
Net income ($ mil.)	1.9%	–	239.4	(76.2)	(0.2)	305.6
Market value ($ mil.)	–	–	–	–	–	–
Employees	–	–	–	–	–	11,790

WASHINGTON REAL ESTATE INVESTMENT TRUST   NYS: WRE

1775 Eye Street, NW, Suite 1000
Washington, DC 20006
Phone: 202 774-3200
Fax: –
Web: www.writ.com

CEO: Paul T. McDermott
CFO: Stephen E. Riffee
HR: Brian Guttman
FYE: December 31
Type: Public

Capital-area real estate is writ large on the mission statement of Washington Real Estate Investment Trust (WRIT). The self-administered and self-managed real estate investment trust (REIT) owns and manages commercial real estate in the Mid-Atlantic mainly in the greater Washington/Baltimore corridor. WRIT owns a diversified property portfolio spanning more than 6 million sq. ft. which includes about 20 office buildings some 15 retail centers and over a dozen apartment communities as well as land held for development. The REIT generates more than 55% of its revenue from office properties.

	Annual Growth	12/14	12/15	12/16	12/17	12/18
Sales ($ mil.)	3.9%	288.6	306.4	313.3	325.1	336.9
Net income ($ mil.)	(30.8%)	111.6	89.7	119.3	19.7	25.6
Market value ($ mil.)	(4.5%)	2,210.3	2,162.4	2,612.3	2,486.8	1,837.9
Employees	(4.7%)	181	174	153	149	149

WASHINGTON REGIONAL MEDICAL CENTER

3215 N NORTHHILLS BLVD
FAYETTEVILLE, AR 727034424
Phone: 479-463-6000
Fax: –
Web: www.wregional.com

CEO: William L Bradley
CFO: Dan Eckels
HR: –
FYE: December 31
Type: Private

Washington Regional Medical System (formerly Washington Regional Medical Center) provides acute care services to the people of northwestern Arkansas. The system's main hospital has about 370 beds in Fayetteville and also includes assisted living facilities home health and hospice services and general practice and specialty clinics. Specialty services at the medical center include cardiac and vascular care (Walker Family Heart and Vascular Institute) emergency medicine kidney dialysis women's health services (Johnelle Hunt Women's Center) cancer treatment and rehabilitation.

	Annual Growth	12/13	12/14	12/15	12/16	12/18
Sales ($ mil.)	12.5%	–	213.3	245.3	300.4	341.5
Net income ($ mil.)	–	–	34.8	45.4	58.5	(9.9)
Market value ($ mil.)	–	–	–	–	–	–
Employees	–	–	–	–	–	2,000

WASHINGTON SUBURBAN SANITARY COMMISSION (INC)

14501 SWEITZER LN
LAUREL, MD 207075901
Phone: 301-206-8000
Fax: –
Web: www.wsscwater.com

CEO: –
CFO: Yvette Downs
HR: –
FYE: June 30
Type: Private

Used water in clean water out is the job description of the Washington Suburban Sanitary Commission (WSSC). The utility provides water and wastewater services in Maryland's Montgomery and Prince George's counties just outside the nation's capital. WSSC serves 460000 customers representing 1.8 million residents in an area of about 1000 square miles. The agency draws water from the Potomac and Patuxtent rivers and maintains three reservoirs. The commission also operates two water filtration plants six wastewater treatment plants and some 11000 miles of sewer and water main lines including a network of nearly 5600 miles of fresh water pipeline and over 5400 miles of sewer pipeline.

	Annual Growth	06/14	06/15	06/16	06/17	06/18
Sales ($ mil.)	4.0%	–	645.6	649.0	725.8	725.2
Net income ($ mil.)	(14.7%)	–	192.9	214.0	179.5	119.6
Market value ($ mil.)	–	–	–	–	–	–
Employees	–	–	–	–	–	2,000

WASHINGTON TRUST BANCORP, INC.   NMS: WASH

23 Broad Street
Westerly, RI 02891
Phone: 401 348-1200
Fax: –
Web: www.washtrust.com

CEO: Joseph J. (Joe) MarcAurele
CFO: David V. Devault
HR: –
FYE: December 31
Type: Public

Without seeming naive Washington Trust Bancorp can utter Washington and trust in the same breath. The holding company owns The Washington Trust Company one of the oldest and largest banks in Rhode Island and one of the oldest banks in the entire US. Chartered in 1800 the bank boasts over $3.5 billion in assets and operates nearly 20 branches in the state and one in southeastern Connecticut. Washington Trust offers standard services such as deposit accounts CDs and credit cards. The company's commercial mortgages and loans account for more than half of its loan portfolio while residential mortgages and consumer loans make up most of the rest. The bank also offers wealth management services.

	Annual Growth	12/14	12/15	12/16	12/17	12/18
Assets ($ mil.)	8.7%	3,586.9	3,771.6	4,381.1	4,529.9	5,010.8
Net income ($ mil.)	13.8%	40.8	43.5	46.5	45.9	68.4
Market value ($ mil.)	4.3%	695.2	683.8	969.8	921.3	822.4
Employees	1.4%	590	582	596	600	623

WASTE CONNECTIONS, INC.
NYS: WCN

3 Waterway Square Place, Suite 110
The Woodlands, TX 77380
Phone: 832 442-2200
Fax: –
Web: www.wasteconnections.com

CEO: Ronald J Mittelstaedt
CFO: Worthing F Jackman
HR: –
FYE: December 31
Type: Public

Waste Connections does the dirty work so you don't have to. It provides solid waste collection transfer disposal and recycling services to more than 2 million commercial industrial and residential customers in 32 US states. The integrated solid waste services company does business mainly in smaller markets. Waste Connections owns or operates about 148 solid waste collection operations 69 transfer stations 58 landfills and 35 recycling facilities. It operates 22 liquid exploration and production (E&P) waste injection wells 17 E&P waste treatment facilities and 20 oil recovery facilities. In 2016 Waste Connections agreed to buy Canada-based Progressive Waste for $2.7 billion.

	Annual Growth	12/11	12/12	12/13	12/14	12/15
Sales ($ mil.)	8.9%	1,505.4	1,661.6	1,928.8	2,079.2	2,117.3
Net income ($ mil.)	–	165.2	159.1	195.7	232.5	(95.8)
Market value ($ mil.)	14.2%	4,055.5	4,135.1	5,339.3	5,383.3	6,892.2
Employees	5.2%	5,909	6,606	6,633	6,777	7,227

WASTE CONTROL SPECIALISTS LLC

Three Lincoln Centre 5430 LBJ Freeway Ste. 1700
Dallas TX 75240
Phone: 972-715-9800
Fax: +44-1977-662-450
Web: www.tunstall.co.uk

CEO: –
CFO: William Bambarger
HR: –
FYE: December 31
Type: Subsidiary

Everything's bigger in Texas including its capacity to store nuclear waste. Waste Control Specialists (WCS) operates a disposal facility for hazardous toxic and low-level radioactive waste in Andrews County in far West Texas on the border of southeast New Mexico. The 1300-acre site can store up to 1.8 million cu. ft. of class A B and C low-level radioactive waste more than 100 feet underground. It is licensed to accept waste from nuclear power plants in Texas and Vermont and for treatment and storage from commercial and federal generators such as the Dept. of Energy. WCS a subsidiary of Valhi is one of only three private companies in the US licensed to handle nuclear waste.

WASTE MANAGEMENT, INC. (DE)
NYS: WM

1001 Fannin Street
Houston, TX 77002
Phone: 713 512-6200
Fax: –
Web: www.wm.com

CEO: James C. (Jim) Fish
CFO: Devina A. Rankin
HR: –
FYE: December 31
Type: Public

Holding company Waste Management tops the heap in the US solid-waste industry. Through subsidiaries the company serves millions of residential industrial municipal and commercial customers in the US and Canada. Waste Management provides waste collection transfer recycling and resource recovery and disposal services. Its sites include more than 250 owned or operated landfills (the industry's largest network) more than 300 transfer stations and around 100 material recovery facilities. Collection services account for more than 50% of sales.

	Annual Growth	12/14	12/15	12/16	12/17	12/18
Sales ($ mil.)	1.6%	13,996.0	12,961.0	13,609.0	14,485.0	14,914.0
Net income ($ mil.)	10.4%	1,298.0	753.0	1,182.0	1,949.0	1,925.0
Market value ($ mil.)	14.8%	21,758.8	22,628.0	30,064.6	36,589.7	37,730.3
Employees	2.4%	39,800	40,600	41,200	42,300	43,700

WATERFURNACE RENEWABLE ENERGY INC

9000 CONSERVATION WAY
FORT WAYNE, IN 468099794
Phone: 260-478-5667
Fax: –
Web: www.waterfurnace.com

CEO: –
CFO: –
HR: –
FYE: December 31
Type: Private

WaterFurnace Renewable Energy relies on the heat within the earth to energize its products. The company also doing business as WaterFurnace International makes and sells geothermal HVAC systems that utilize heat stored in the ground for residential commercial and institutional applications. Its cooling systems work in reverse extracting heat from indoors. Touting its systems as more efficient safer and more environmentally friendly than HVAC systems that use fossil fuels the company has installed more than 300000 units. Other operations install geothermal loops that heat and cool homes and businesses by circulating pressurized water through hundreds of feet of looped pipe that is buried on-site.

	Annual Growth	06/05	06/06	06/07*	12/08	12/09
Sales ($ mil.)	–	–	–	(1,709.2)	137.8	129.1
Net income ($ mil.)	–	–	–	0.0	15.4	0.0
Market value ($ mil.)	–	–	–	–	–	–
Employees	–	–	–	–	–	270

*Fiscal year change

WATERS CORP.
NYS: WAT

34 Maple Street
Milford, MA 01757
Phone: 508 478-2000
Fax: 508 872-1990
Web: www.waters.com

CEO: Christopher J. (Chris) O'Connell
CFO: Sherry L. Buck
HR: Elizabeth B. Rae
FYE: December 31
Type: Public

Waters Corp. makes high-performance liquid chromatography instruments used by researchers scientists and engineers to separate and identify chemicals. Waters also makes mass spectrometers that help identify chemical compounds. Its products are used in applications that include drug development food testing and air and water quality testing. Waters' TA Instruments Division makes thermal analyzers and rheometry instruments used to determine the physical characteristics of polymers and other materials. Customers are in the academic government and industrial sectors. About 70% of the company's sales are to international markets. Jim Waters founded the company in 1958.

	Annual Growth	12/14	12/15	12/16	12/17	12/18
Sales ($ mil.)	5.0%	1,989.3	2,042.3	2,167.4	2,309.1	2,419.9
Net income ($ mil.)	8.3%	431.6	469.1	521.5	20.3	593.8
Market value ($ mil.)	13.7%	8,241.5	9,839.8	9,825.9	14,125.1	13,793.1
Employees	3.8%	6,200	6,600	6,900	7,000	7,200

WATKINS AND SHEPARD TRUCKING, INC.

N6400 HWY 10 W
MISSOULA, MT 59801
Phone: 406-532-6121
Fax: –
Web: www.wksh.com

CEO: Ray Kuntz
CFO: –
HR: –
FYE: December 31
Type: Private

Watkins & Shepard Trucking offers less-than-truckload (LTL) and truckload freight hauling throughout the US from about 20 terminals mainly west of the Rockies. (LTL carriers consolidate cargo from multiple shippers into a single trailer.) The company's fleet consists of about 850 tractors and 2500 trailers. Standard dry vans account for the majority of the company's trailers; Watkins & Shepard also uses flatbed trailers. In addition the company arranges intermodal transportation which involves hauling freight by multiple methods such as road and rail. In the summer of 2016 Watkins & Shepard was acquired by Schneider National.

	Annual Growth	12/98	12/99	12/00	12/12	12/13
Sales ($ mil.)	3.8%	–	95.7	102.4	157.9	160.6
Net income ($ mil.)	(0.0%)	–	2.6	0.9	3.1	2.5
Market value ($ mil.)	–	–	–	–	–	–
Employees	–	–	–	–	–	1,300

WATONWAN FARM SERVICE, INC

233 W CIRO ST
TRUMAN, MN 560882018
Phone: 507-776-1244
Fax: –

CEO: Ed Bosanko
CFO: –
HR: –
FYE: July 31
Type: Private

Watonwan Farm Service which does business as WFS helps out its south central Minnesota and north central Iowa member-farmers with complete farm-management services and products. Offering marketing opportunities financial services and farming supplies such as chemicals fertilizers livestock feed petroleum products and seed the agricultural cooperative serves more than 4000 producers from its 22 locations. The primary crops of its members include corn soybean and specialty canning crops; most of its livestock farmers raise hogs and cattle. The co-op was called the Consumers Cooperative Oil Company of St. James when it was founded in 1937.

	Annual Growth	07/11	07/12	07/13	07/14	07/15
Sales ($ mil.)	(15.4%)	–	592.5	701.2	468.3	358.6
Net income ($ mil.)	(7.9%)	–	6.7	7.7	7.7	5.2
Market value ($ mil.)	–	–	–	–	–	–
Employees	–	–	–	–	–	255

WATTS WATER TECHNOLOGIES INC NYS: WTS

815 Chestnut Street
North Andover, MA 01845
Phone: 978 688-1811
Fax: –
Web: www.wattswater.com

CEO: Robert J. (Bob) Pagano
CFO: Todd A. Trapp
HR: –
FYE: December 31
Type: Public

Watts Water Technologies manufactures a number of valves used to maintain the quality conservation and flow control of water be it in a residential commercial industrial or municipal setting. It also makes water quality products such as backflow preventers and filtration systems water pressure regulators and drainage devices. The lineup is sold under brands Brae FEBCO Flo Safe Orion Powers and Sea Tech. Watts' operations are found in North America Europe and to a lesser extent China. Almost 70% of its sales rely on plumbing heating and mechanical wholesale distributors. Do-it-yourself retail chains and OEMs account for the balance.

	Annual Growth	12/14	12/15	12/16	12/17	12/18
Sales ($ mil.)	0.8%	1,513.7	1,467.7	1,398.4	1,456.7	1,564.9
Net income ($ mil.)	26.3%	50.3	(112.9)	84.2	73.1	128.0
Market value ($ mil.)	0.4%	2,155.4	1,687.6	2,215.2	2,580.5	2,192.5
Employees	(5.8%)	6,100	5,000	4,800	4,800	4,800

WAUKESHA MEMORIAL HOSPITAL, INC.

725 AMERICAN AVE
WAUKESHA, WI 531885099
Phone: 262-928-1000
Fax: –
Web: www.prohealthcare.org

CEO: –
CFO: Robert W Mlynarek
HR: –
FYE: September 30
Type: Private

Waukesha Memorial Hospital is a 300-bed teaching hospital that provides health care services for Wisconsin's Milwaukee Waukesha and Dane counties. With about 670 physicians representing several specialties and 2700 employees the hospital operates centers for excellence focused on cardiology oncology neurology women's health and orthopedics as well as emergency neonatal and family practice services. Additionally Waukesha Memorial Hospital conducts a physician residency program. Established in 1914 the medical facility is a subsidiary of not-for-profit ProHealth Care a medical network that serves southeastern Wisconsin with acute care and specialty health services.

	Annual Growth	09/14	09/15	09/16	09/17	09/18
Sales ($ mil.)	4.2%	–	460.1	457.9	470.2	520.1
Net income ($ mil.)	(2.0%)	–	29.1	37.9	59.2	27.4
Market value ($ mil.)	–	–	–	–	–	–
Employees	–	–	–	–	–	2,071

WAUKESHA-PEARCE INDUSTRIES, INC.

12320 MAIN ST
HOUSTON, TX 770356206
Phone: 713-723-1050
Fax: –
Web: www.wpi.com

CEO: Al H Bentley
CFO: –
HR: –
FYE: March 31
Type: Private

Waukesha-Pearce Industries (WPI) wants its customers to start their engines. Through its Engine Division the company designs and packages engine-driven equipment such as power generators pumps blowers control panels and switchgear. WPI also offers a slate of heavy construction and mining products including earth movers and demolition equipment made by such OEMs as Komatsu and Gradall Industries through its Construction Machinery Division. As part of its business the company sells used equipment and leases heavy earth-moving equipment. Founded as Portable Rotary Rig Co. in 1924 by Louis M. Pearce Sr. the company is owned and run by the Pearce family.

	Annual Growth	03/09	03/10	03/11	03/15	03/16
Sales ($ mil.)	13.5%	–	197.8	248.7	461.1	423.7
Net income ($ mil.)	3.2%	–	1.7	4.7	8.8	2.0
Market value ($ mil.)	–	–	–	–	–	–
Employees	–	–	–	–	–	600

WAUSAU PAPER CORP NYS: WPP

100 Paper Place
Mosinee, WI 54455-9099
Phone: 715 693-4470
Fax: 715 692-2082
Web: www.wausaupaper.com

CEO: –
CFO: –
HR: –
FYE: December 31
Type: Public

With more than 110 years experience Wausau Paper has proficiency in selling paper and tissue products. The company produces Bay West branded towel tissue soap and dispensing products for hotels hospitals schools and office buildings. Other paper brands include DublSoft EcoSoft OptiCore Revolution and Dubl Nature. Its products are primarily sold within the US and Canada. Most of its US customers are regional and national sanitation supply distributors and paper merchants. In 2013 Wausau Paper sold its specialty paper business to Expera Specialty Solutions.

	Annual Growth	12/09	12/10	12/11	12/12	12/13
Sales ($ mil.)	(23.8%)	1,032.1	1,055.7	1,034.6	822.2	348.6
Net income ($ mil.)	–	20.6	36.9	(21.7)	0.7	(97.3)
Market value ($ mil.)	2.2%	573.7	425.8	408.5	428.3	627.1
Employees	(20.9%)	2,300	2,400	2,300	1,900	900

WAVE SYSTEMS CORP NBB: WAVX Q

480 Pleasant Street
Lee, MA 01238
Phone: 413 243-1600
Fax: 413 243-0045
Web: www.wave.com

CEO: –
CFO: –
HR: –
FYE: December 31
Type: Public

Wave Systems develops software to contend with a very particular sort of crime wave. Designed to work with security chips from such manufacturers as Broadcom and STMicroelectronics the company's digital security applications enable information encryption and identity protection to reduce the risk of data theft or unauthorized network access. Its flagship suite of EMBASSY products is used in devices including PCs made by Dell (the company's largest customer) and computer hard drives from Seagate Technology. Wave's Tel Aviv-based Safend subsidiary (acquired in 2011) provides endpoint data loss protection products and services. Founded in 1988 as Indata Corp. the company became Wave Systems in 1993.

	Annual Growth	12/10	12/11	12/12	12/13	12/14
Sales ($ mil.)	(10.2%)	26.1	36.1	28.8	24.4	17.0
Net income ($ mil.)	–	(4.1)	(10.8)	(34.0)	(20.3)	(12.9)
Market value ($ mil.)	(32.8%)	18.1	10.0	3.3	4.2	3.7
Employees	0.4%	133	249	215	150	135

WAVE SYSTEMS CORP.
NAS: WAVX

480 Pleasant Street
Lee, MA 01238
Phone: 413 243-1600
Fax: 413 243-0045
Web: www.wave.com

CEO: –
CFO: –
HR: –
FYE: December 31
Type: Public

Wave Systems develops software to contend with a very particular sort of crime wave. Designed to work with security chips from such manufacturers as Broadcom and STMicroelectronics the company's digital security applications enable information encryption and identity protection to reduce the risk of data theft or unauthorized network access. Its flagship suite of EMBASSY products is used in devices including PCs made by Dell (the company's largest customer) and computer hard drives from Seagate Technology. Wave's Tel Aviv-based Safend subsidiary (acquired in 2011) provides endpoint data loss protection products and services. Founded in 1988 as Indata Corp. the company became Wave Systems in 1993.

	Annual Growth	12/09	12/10	12/11	12/12	12/13
Sales ($ mil.)	6.6%	18.9	26.1	36.1	28.8	24.4
Net income ($ mil.)	–	(3.3)	(4.1)	(10.8)	(34.0)	(20.3)
Market value ($ mil.)	(10.5%)	49.7	138.0	76.0	25.1	31.9
Employees	9.3%	105	133	249	215	150

WAYFAIR LLC

177 Huntington Ave.
Boston MA 02115
Phone: 617-532-6100
Fax: 212-421-6292
Web: www.genesis10.com

CEO: Niraj Shah
CFO: Michael Fleisher
HR: Kelley Burke
FYE: December 31
Type: Private

Online shoppers navigating the Web's vast offering of home goods need only stop at Wayfair (formerly CSN Stores). The company is a leading online retailer of more than 5000 brands of products including cookware home and office furniture and decor lighting strollers and more. Seeking to become the Amazon.com of home goods the e-tailer in 2011 merged some 200 specialty e-commerce sites such as AllModern.com Cookware.com Luggage.com SimplyDesks.com and Strollers.com all under the Wayfair.com brand. Founded in 2002 by CEO Niraj Shah and chairman Steve Conine as a single shopping destination (RacksandStands.com) the company changed its name from CSN Stores to Wayfair in 2011.

WAYLAND BAPTIST UNIVERSITY INC

1900 W 7TH ST
PLAINVIEW, TX 790726998
Phone: 806-291-1000
Fax: –
Web: www.wbu.edu

CEO: –
CFO: Lezlie Hukill
HR: –
FYE: June 30
Type: Private

You gotta have faith to attend Wayland Baptist University. The private co-educational Baptist institution offers more than 40 undergraduate majors about a dozen pre-professional programs and graduate programs in fields such as business administration Christian ministry counseling education management public administration religion and science. It has an enrollment of approximately 7000 students at some 15 campuses in Alaska Arizona Hawaii New Mexico Oklahoma and Texas as well as Kenya. The university was founded in 1906 by Dr. and Mrs. Henry Wayland and the Staked Plains Baptist Association.

	Annual Growth	06/13	06/14	06/15	06/17	06/18
Sales ($ mil.)	0.2%	–	–	58.3	62.7	58.6
Net income ($ mil.)	(72.6%)	–	–	7.5	2.9	0.2
Market value ($ mil.)	–	–	–	–	–	–
Employees	–	–	–	–	–	281

WAYNE J. GRIFFIN ELECTRIC, INC.

116 HOPPING BROOK RD
HOLLISTON, MA 017461455
Phone: 508-429-8830
Fax: –
Web: www.waynejgriffinelectric.com

CEO: Wayne J. Griffin
CFO: –
HR: –
FYE: December 31
Type: Private

Wayne J. Griffin Electric brings a certain spark to New England and the Southeast. With offices in Massachusetts Georgia North Carolina and Alabama the electrical contractor offers construction and installation services on hospitals hotels industrial and high-tech buildings offices prisons research laboratories retirement communities and schools. The company's service division provides small project management and facility maintenance while its telecom division designs and installs fiber optics fire alarm and security systems as well as systems that control energy use from lighting to heating ventilation and air conditioning (HVAC). Founded in 1978 Wayne J. Griffin Electric is privately held.

	Annual Growth	12/13	12/14	12/15	12/16	12/17
Sales ($ mil.)	6.6%	–	293.1	303.8	333.6	355.5
Net income ($ mil.)	2.6%	–	27.4	22.6	27.3	29.6
Market value ($ mil.)	–	–	–	–	–	–
Employees	–	–	–	–	–	1,100

WAYNE MEMORIAL HEALTH SYSTEM, INC.

601 PARK ST
HONESDALE, PA 184311445
Phone: 570-253-8100
Fax: –
Web: www.wmh.org

CEO: –
CFO: –
HR: –
FYE: June 30
Type: Private

Wayne Memorial Health System provides general medical and surgical health services primary care and family medicine long-term and intermediate care and assisted living services to communities in northeastern Pennsylvania. It also offers home health care nutritional counseling and wellness programs. The Wayne Memorial Hospital has about 100 beds.

	Annual Growth	06/11	06/12	06/15	06/16	06/18
Sales ($ mil.)	91.1%	–	2.1	2.3	94.0	100.5
Net income ($ mil.)	46.5%	–	0.5	0.5	(3.0)	4.7
Market value ($ mil.)	–	–	–	–	–	–
Employees	–	–	–	–	–	600

WAYNE SAVINGS BANCSHARES INC
NBB: WAYN

151 North Market Street
Wooster, OH 44691
Phone: 800 414-1103
Fax: –
Web: www.waynesavings.com

CEO: James Rvansickle II
CFO: Myron L Swartzentruber
HR: –
FYE: December 31
Type: Public

Holy bank vaults Batman! Wayne Savings Bancshares is the holding company for Wayne Savings Community Bank which serves individuals and local businesses through about a dozen locations in north-central Ohio. Serving Ashland Holmes Medina Stark and Wayne counties the bank offers checking and savings accounts retirement and education savings accounts certificates of deposit and debit cards. One- to four-family residential mortgages make up more than half of the company's loan portfolio. To a lesser extent the bank writes business commercial mortgage land and consumer loans. It offers investments insurance and brokerage accounts through a agreement with third-party provider Infinex.

	Annual Growth	12/14	12/15	12/16	12/17	12/18
Assets ($ mil.)	3.2%	417.7	433.6	454.8	439.8	472.9
Net income ($ mil.)	18.3%	2.6	1.6	2.2	3.1	5.1
Market value ($ mil.)	8.6%	36.1	35.6	44.5	49.8	50.3
Employees	0.0%	110	114	110	–	–

WAYNE STATE UNIVERSITY

656 W KIRBY ST
DETROIT, MI 482023622
Phone: 313-577-2230
Fax: –
Web: www.wayne.edu

CEO: –
CFO: Rick Nork
HR: Adrienne Mitchell
FYE: September 30
Type: Private

Wayne State University is a public university with an annual enrollment of more than 27000 students and a student-to-teacher ratio of 16:1. It offers more than 350 bachelor's master's and doctoral degree programs as well as certificate specialist and professional programs through about a dozen colleges and schools. Located in midtown Detroit WSU traces its heritage back to 1868 with the founding of the Detroit Medical College now part of its School of Medicine. Prominent alumni include US Congressman John Conyers radio DJ Casey Kasem and actor Tom Sizemore.

	Annual Growth	09/03	09/04	09/05	09/11	09/17
Sales ($ mil.)	3.3%	–	418.8	445.9	520.9	640.4
Net income ($ mil.)	–	–	(3.2)	37.6	(15.7)	46.3
Market value ($ mil.)	–	–	–	–	–	–
Employees	–	–	–	–	–	8,500

WAYSIDE TECHNOLOGY GROUP INC

NMS: WSTG

4 Industrial Way West, Suite 300
Eatontown, NJ 07724
Phone: 732 389-8950
Fax: –
Web: www.waysidetechnology.com

CEO: Michael Vesey
CFO: –
HR: –
FYE: December 31
Type: Public

Wayside Technology connects developers with users of IT products. A leading reseller for software developers the firm's TechXtend (formerly Programmer's Paradise) business markets software hardware and services to IT professionals government agencies and educational institutions in the US and Canada. Wayside's Lifeboat Distribution subsidiary provides software to resellers consultants and systems integrators worldwide. (Software accounts for about 95% of the company's sales.) Wayside Technology sells products through its catalogs and e-commerce sites and its suppliers include Quest Software Intel Flexera TechSmith and Vmware among others.

	Annual Growth	12/14	12/15	12/16	12/17	12/18
Sales ($ mil.)	(14.6%)	340.8	382.1	418.1	449.4	181.4
Net income ($ mil.)	(11.5%)	5.8	5.8	5.9	5.1	3.5
Market value ($ mil.)	(12.7%)	77.4	82.5	84.1	75.1	45.0
Employees	5.2%	125	132	142	140	153

WBI ENERGY TRANSMISSION, INC

1250 W CENTURY AVE
BISMARCK, ND 585030911
Phone: 701-530-1601
Fax: –
Web: www.wbienergy.com

CEO: –
CFO: –
HR: –
FYE: December 31
Type: Private

This company likes to keep gas in its pipes. Williston Basin Interstate Pipeline provides customers in the Upper Midwest region of the US with natural gas gathering transportation and underground storage services. It operates 3350 miles of natural gas transmission pipeline nearly 350 miles of gathering pipeline and 30 compressor stations capable of holding more than 193 billion cu. ft. of natural gas. Williston Basin Interstate Pipeline's system connects major natural gas suppliers with markets between Canada and the Central region of the US. The company is an indirect subsidiary of MDU Resources.

	Annual Growth	12/95	12/96	12/97	12/16	12/17
Sales ($ mil.)	1.3%	–	78.6	0.0	102.2	102.7
Net income ($ mil.)	9.0%	–	3.4	0.0	22.1	20.6
Market value ($ mil.)	–	–	–	–	–	–
Employees	–	–	–	–	–	277

WCA WASTE CORPORATION

NASDAQ: WCAA

1 Riverway Ste. 1400
Houston TX 77056
Phone: 713-292-2400
Fax: 713-292-2455
Web: www.wcawaste.com

CEO: William K Caesar
CFO: Dianna Cervantes
HR: –
FYE: December 31
Type: Private

Some might see a garbage dump but WCA Waste sees a pile of money. The firm provides collection transfer and disposal of nonhazardous solid waste for 441000 commercial industrial and residential customers and 7000 landfill and transfer station customers in the US Southeast and Midwest. It operates some 25 landfills 29 collection businesses and 29 transfer stations and materials recovery facilities. Most sales come from collection and landfill disposal services provided to residential commercial and roll-off (disposal of large waste containers) customers. Macquarie Infrastructure Partners II part of the Macquarie Group through its Cod Intermediate unit bought WCA Waste for $526 million in 2012.

WCI COMMUNITIES INC

NYS: WCIC

24301 Walden Center Drive
Bonita Springs, FL 34134
Phone: 239 947-2600
Fax: –
Web: www.wcicommunities.com

CEO: Keith E Bass
CFO: Russell Devendorf
HR: –
FYE: December 31
Type: Public

WCI Communities develops luxury residential communities and homes in Florida. Founded in 1946 it caters primarily to retirement and second-home buyers offering single-family homes vacation homes villas and high-rise condominiums ranging in price from about $150000 to $1.3 million. WCI's 14 master-planned communities typically offer such amenities as golf courses tennis courts dining and entertainment facilities and nature trails. The company also offers architectural and design services as well as financing and title services. Its real estate brokerage Berkshire Hathaway HomeServices boasts 40-plus locations that serve 18 Florida counties. WCI Communities went public in 2013.

	Annual Growth	12/08	12/11	12/12	12/13	12/14
Sales ($ mil.)	(5.1%)	556.1	144.3	241.0	317.3	407.0
Net income ($ mil.)	–	(936.8)	(47.1)	50.8	146.6	21.6
Market value ($ mil.)	2.6%	–	–	–	492.9	505.3
Employees	(12.1%)	1,450	–	–	598	667

WD-40 CO

NMS: WDFC

9715 Businesspark Avenue
San Diego, CA 92131
Phone: 619 275-1400
Fax: –
Web: www.wd40company.com

CEO: Garry O. Ridge
CFO: Jay W. Rembolt
HR: –
FYE: August 31
Type: Public

Squeaky hinges are the stuff horror movie nightmares — and WD-40's dreams — are made of. The company's WD-40 product used as a lubricant rust preventative and penetrant is a staple in many homes. As well as unsticking locks and loosening rusted bolts the omnipresent blue-and-yellow aerosol can contains the slippery stuff of myth said to combat arthritis and attract fish. Its WD-40 3-IN-ONE Oil and Blue Works lubricants account for most of the company's sales. It also makes household cleaning and deodorizing products under the brands X-14 Carpet Fresh No Vac 1001 and 2000 Flushes and heavy-duty hand cleaners Lava and Solvol. WD-40 contracts with various companies to manufacture its products.

	Annual Growth	08/15	08/16	08/17	08/18	08/19
Sales ($ mil.)	2.9%	378.2	380.7	380.5	408.5	423.4
Net income ($ mil.)	5.7%	44.8	52.6	52.9	65.2	55.9
Market value ($ mil.)	21.5%	1,148.8	1,623.6	1,494.6	2,434.4	2,500.9
Employees	3.4%	433	445	448	480	495

WEATHERFORD INTERNATIONAL PLC
NBB: WFTI Q

2000 St. James Place
Houstan, TX 77056
Phone: 713 836 4000
Fax: -
Web: www.weatherford.com

CEO: Mark A. McCollum
CFO: Christoph Bausch
HR: -
FYE: December 31
Type: Public

Weatherford International can weather the natural and economic storms that affect the oil and gas market. The company which is domiciled in Switzerland but operationally based in Houston supplies a wide range of equipment and services used in the oil and gas drilling industry and operates in 100 countries. Weatherford provides well installation and completion systems equipment rental and fishing services (removing debris from wells). It provides pipeline services and oil recovery and hydraulic lift and electric submersible pumps to the oil and gas industry. The company also offers contract land drilling services.

	Annual Growth	12/14	12/15	12/16	12/17	12/18
Sales ($ mil.)	(21.2%)	14,911.0	9,433.0	5,749.0	5,699.0	5,744.0
Net income ($ mil.)	-	(584.0)	(1,985.0)	(3,392.0)	(2,813.0)	(2,811.0)
Market value ($ mil.)	-	-	-	-	-	-
Employees	(17.1%)	56,000	39,500	30,000	29,200	26,500

WEB.COM GROUP, INC.
NMS: WEB

12808 Gran Bay Parkway West
Jacksonville, FL 32258
Phone: 904 680-6600
Fax: -
Web: www.web.com

CEO: David L Brown
CFO: Kevin M Carney
HR: -
FYE: December 31
Type: Public

Web.com Group has everything a growing business needs to create a presence on the Internet. The company provides website building custom design consulting and Web hosting services. Its Register.com business provides domain name registration and its eWorks! XL product offers initial site-design setup and online marketing and technical report services. SmartClicks also offers search engine optimization and local pay-per click advertising services. The company sells to almost 3 million small and midsized US businesses mostly on a subscription basis. In late 2011 Web.com significantly expanded its customer base through the purchase of Network Solutions a website services and domain-names registration firm.

	Annual Growth	12/12	12/13	12/14	12/15	12/16
Sales ($ mil.)	14.9%	407.6	492.3	543.9	543.5	710.5
Net income ($ mil.)	-	(122.2)	(65.7)	(12.5)	90.0	4.0
Market value ($ mil.)	9.3%	744.1	1,598.3	954.8	1,006.1	1,063.4
Employees	17.3%	1,900	2,000	2,100	2,200	3,600

WEBCO INDUSTRIES INC.
NBB: WEBC

9101 West 21st Street
Sand Springs, OK 74063
Phone: 918 241-1000
Fax: -
Web: www.webcotube.com

CEO: Dana S. Weber
CFO: Michael P. Howard
HR: Daphne Applegate
FYE: July 31
Type: Public

Making carbon steel and stainless steel tubes is a competitive business and Webco Industries is working hard to keep up with its rivals. Facing stiff competition from larger US and foreign tubing suppliers Webco Industries aims to succeed by targeting niche industry markets. The company's primary products include mechanical tubing heat exchanger and boiler tubing and stainless steel tube and pipe. Subsidiary Phillips & Johnston makes tubular products from aluminum brass copper and carbon steel. Webco Industries' customers include customers in the agricultural automotive beverage oil and gas and refrigeration industries. The family of founder William Weber controls Webco Industries.

	Annual Growth	07/15	07/16	07/17	07/18	07/19
Sales ($ mil.)	7.3%	414.1	330.3	384.9	500.4	548.6
Net income ($ mil.)	128.9%	0.9	(3.2)	5.6	23.3	25.6
Market value ($ mil.)	18.9%	57.0	38.2	71.2	99.7	113.9
Employees	-	-	1,001	-	-	-

WEBER STATE UNIVERSITY

1235 VILLAGE DR
OGDEN, UT 844083701
Phone: 801-626-6606
Fax: -
Web: www.weber.edu

CEO: -
CFO: Steven E Nabor
HR: Cherrie Nelson
FYE: June 30
Type: Private

There may be more well-known universities in Utah but none with more choices. Weber State University (WSU) boasts more than 250 undergraduate certificate and degree programs which it claims is the most in the state. It also grants 11 graduate degrees in fields including accounting athletic training business administration criminal justice education English health administration and nursing. The school also offers online distance and evening courses. Some 27000 students attend the university which has campuses Ogden and Layton Utah. It was founded as Weber Stake Academy in 1889 and officially became WSU in 1991.

	Annual Growth	06/08	06/09	06/10	06/14	06/15
Sales ($ mil.)	4.9%	-	76.8	84.8	101.7	102.4
Net income ($ mil.)	(3.7%)	-	15.4	27.4	23.7	12.2
Market value ($ mil.)	-	-	-	-	-	-
Employees	-	-	-	-	-	3,500

WEBMD HEALTH CORP
NMS: WBMD

395 Hudson Street
New York, NY 10014
Phone: 212 624-3700
Fax: -
Web: www.webmd.com

CEO: Steven L Zatz
CFO: Blake Desimone
HR: -
FYE: December 31
Type: Public

House calls are a browser click away thanks to this online doctor. WebMD Health Corp. is a leading Web publisher of health information for consumers and health care professionals. Its WebMD.com portal gives consumers information on common health ailments as well as articles and features on staying healthy through diet and exercise. WebMD's Medscape is a Web portal with clinical information for doctors and other health care professionals. All total The WebMD Health Network (including WebMD.com Medscape.com and third-party sites) attracts about 185 million unique users per month. The company also operates private portals for employers and health plans.

	Annual Growth	12/11	12/12	12/13	12/14	12/15
Sales ($ mil.)	3.3%	558.8	469.9	515.3	580.4	636.4
Net income ($ mil.)	(3.7%)	74.6	(20.3)	15.1	42.1	64.0
Market value ($ mil.)	6.5%	1,382.5	528.0	1,454.3	1,456.1	1,778.3
Employees	0.6%	1,700	1,500	1,600	1,700	1,740

WEBSTER FINANCIAL CORP (WATERBURY, CONN)
NYS: WBS

145 Bank Street
Waterbury, CT 06702
Phone: 203 578-2202
Fax: -
Web: www.websterbank.com

CEO: James C. (Jim) Smith
CFO: Glenn I. MacInnes
HR: Bernard M. Garrigues
FYE: December 31
Type: Public

Webster Financial is the holding company for Webster Bank which operates about 170 branches in southern New England primarily in Connecticut but also in Massachusetts New York and Rhode Island. The bank provides commercial and retail services such as deposit accounts loans and mortgages and consumer finance as well as government and institutional banking services. It performs asset-based lending through its Webster Business Credit subsidiary and equipment financing through Webster Capital Finance. The company's HSA Bank division offers health savings accounts nationwide. Webster Bank provides brokerage and investment services through an agreement with UVEST a division of LPL Financial.

	Annual Growth	12/14	12/15	12/16	12/17	12/18
Assets ($ mil.)	5.2%	22,533.0	24,677.8	26,072.5	26,487.6	27,610.3
Net income ($ mil.)	15.9%	199.8	206.3	207.1	255.4	360.4
Market value ($ mil.)	10.9%	2,998.5	3,428.1	5,003.4	5,176.7	4,543.4
Employees	4.3%	2,764	2,946	3,168	3,302	3,265

WEBSTER UNIVERSITY

470 E LOCKWOOD AVE
SAINT LOUIS, MO 631193194
Phone: 314-968-6900
Fax: -
Web: www.webster.edu

CEO: -
CFO: Ken Creehan
HR: -
FYE: May 31
Type: Private

They have more than dictionaries at this Webster. Webster University is a private school that serves about 22000 undergraduate and graduate students through an international network of more than 100 campuses. Its main campus in St. Louis Missouri has an enrollment of more than 8000 students and 700 faculty and staff members. Other locations span the US and are also present in Europe Asia and other regions; many campuses are on military bases. Alumni include former shuttle commander Eileen Collins actress Marsha Mason and Indonesia's first democratically elected president Susilo Bambang Yudhoyono. Webster University was founded as a small Catholic women's college in 1915.

	Annual Growth	05/11	05/12	05/13	05/14	05/16
Sales ($ mil.)	(0.1%)	-	213.3	209.8	202.7	212.2
Net income ($ mil.)	21.4%	-	7.4	22.7	9.4	16.0
Market value ($ mil.)	-	-	-	-	-	-
Employees		-	-	-	-	4,500

WEC ENERGY GROUP INC
NYS: WEC

231 West Michigan Street, P.O. Box 1331
Milwaukee, WI 53201
Phone: 414 221-2345
Fax: 414 221-2172
Web: www.wecenergygroup.com

CEO: Allen L. Leverett
CFO: Scott J. Lauber
HR: Joan M. Shafer
FYE: December 31
Type: Public

WEC Energy Group keeps the lights illuminated and the gas fires burning for 4.4 million customers in four upper Midwest states. The utility holding company serves energy through its seven regulated utilities. It is one of the largest natural gas distributors in the US and even provides steam (for heating) to a few hundred customers in Milwaukee WI. It owns 8600 MW of electric generation capacity and thousands of miles of natural gas distribution and electrical transmission lines. The former Wisconsin Energy acquired for $9 billion Integrys Energy in mid-2015 and renamed the combined entity WEC Energy Group.

	Annual Growth	12/14	12/15	12/16	12/17	12/18
Sales ($ mil.)	11.3%	4,997.1	5,926.1	7,472.3	7,648.5	7,679.5
Net income ($ mil.)	15.9%	588.3	640.3	940.2	1,204.9	1,060.5
Market value ($ mil.)	7.0%	16,640.7	16,189.5	18,505.4	20,960.2	21,853.1
Employees	16.7%	4,248	8,443	8,164	8,129	7,878

WEDBUSH SECURITIES INC.

1000 Wilshire Blvd.
Los Angeles CA 90017
Phone: 213-688-8000
Fax: 213-688-6652
Web: www.wedbush.com

CEO: Edward W Wedbush
CFO: Peter Allman-Ward
HR: -
FYE: June 30
Type: Private

Operating from the famed Wilshire Boulevard in L.A. brokerage firm Wedbush Securities offers investment banking and a range of financial services including financial planning sales and trading and clearing services. The firm which targets mid-market growth companies and entrepreneurs in California and the western US also provides research to institutional clients in the consumer products retail health care and other sectors. Its ClientLink service provides clients access to account information and reports via the Internet. Wedbush Securities is affiliated with investment firm Wedbush Capital Partners; both entities are controlled by holding company Wedbush Inc.

WEEKS MARINE, INC.

4 COMMERCE DR FL 2
CRANFORD, NJ 070163520
Phone: 908-272-4010
Fax: -
Web: www.weeksmarine.com

CEO: Richard S Weeks
CFO: Arthur Smeding
HR: -
FYE: December 31
Type: Private

Weeks Marine doesn't drag its feet when it comes to dredging. The company is one of the largest providers of dredging services in the Gulf of Mexico where a majority of all US dredging occurs. (Dredging involves the moving of sand and sediment to maintain and often deepen navigation channels at shipping ports.) One of Weeks Marine's main clients is the US Army Corps of Engineers for whom it has done dredging work on many projects. The family-owned company also performs construction and demolition of bridges piers jetties pipelines and offshore platforms throughout North and South America. It is also one of the largest stevedoring (cargo handling) companies on the US's East Coast.

	Annual Growth	12/05	12/06	12/07	12/08	12/10
Sales ($ mil.)	4.3%	-	-	472.1	439.7	536.1
Net income ($ mil.)	23.7%	-	-	53.1	61.7	100.4
Market value ($ mil.)	-	-	-	-	-	-
Employees		-	-	-	-	1,500

WEGENER CORP.
NBB: WGNR

11350 Technology Circle
Johns Creek/Atlanta, GA 30097-1502
Phone: 770 623-0096
Fax: 770 623-0698
Web: www.wegener.com

CEO: C Troy Woodbury Jr
CFO: James Traicoff
HR: -
FYE: September 01
Type: Public

Wegener doesn't mind broadcasting its business. The company through its Wegener Communications subsidiary makes transmission and receiving equipment primarily for the broadcast and data communications markets. Its products include digital and analog compression equipment that increases satellite channel capacity cue and control products that enable cable networks to insert local commercials devices that feed data to news and weather services and equipment that transmits background music to businesses. Customers include MUZAK and Roberts Communications.

	Annual Growth	08/13	08/14	08/15*	09/16	09/17
Sales ($ mil.)	(6.9%)	4.5	3.2	3.2	3.5	3.4
Net income ($ mil.)		(2.1)	(1.6)	1.6	(0.2)	(0.1)
Market value ($ mil.)	0.0%	0.2	0.6	0.2	0.2	0.2
Employees	(6.1%)	27	22	23	21	21

*Fiscal year change

WEGMANS FOOD MARKETS, INC.

1500 BROOKS AVE
ROCHESTER, NY 146243589
Phone: 585-328-2550
Fax: -
Web: www.rocwiki.org

CEO: Colleen Wegman
CFO: James J Leo
HR: -
FYE: December 26
Type: Private

One name strikes fear in the hearts of supermarket owners in New York New Jersey Pennsylvania Virginia Maryland and Massachusetts: Wegmans Food Markets. The regional grocery chain owns almost 90 stores but they are hardly typical. Much larger than most supermarkets (up to 140000 sq. ft.) each store offers up to 70000 products and house huge in-store cafes cheese shops with some 300 different varieties sub shops and French-style pastry shops. The company is known for its gourmet cooking classes and an extensive employee-training program. Founded in 1916 Wegmans now boasts revenues of nearly $8 billion and is one of the largest private companies in the US. The grocery chain is owned and run by the family of founder John Wegman.

	Annual Growth	12/08	12/09	12/10	12/14	12/15
Sales ($ mil.)	7.5%	-	5,193.2	5,687.0	7,560.5	8,005.8
Net income ($ mil.)	-	-	85.3	93.1	114.8	0.0
Market value ($ mil.)	-	-	-	-	-	-
Employees		-	-	-	-	45,000

WEINGARTEN REALTY INVESTORS — NYS: WRI

2600 Citadel Plaza Drive, P.O. Box 924133
Houston, TX 77292-4133
Phone: 713 866-6000
Fax: –
Web: www.weingarten.com

CEO: Andrew M. Alexander
CFO: Stephen C. (Steve) Richter
HR: –
FYE: December 31
Type: Public

Weingarten Realty Investors is landlord to some of the nation's largest retailers including Kroger Safeway and The Home Depot. The real estate investment trust (REIT) owns develops manages and leases commercial real estate in some two dozen US states mainly in the South and West. The firm has interests in more than 230 developed income-producing properties and about a dozen projects at various stages of construction and development. Most of Weingarten's properties are community shopping centers anchored by major food retail or discount stores. The company pursues a shopping center-centric strategy.

	Annual Growth	12/14	12/15	12/16	12/17	12/18
Sales ($ mil.)	0.8%	514.4	512.8	549.6	573.2	531.1
Net income ($ mil.)	3.3%	288.0	174.4	238.9	335.3	327.6
Market value ($ mil.)	(8.2%)	4,481.4	4,437.8	4,593.0	4,218.3	3,183.9
Employees	(5.2%)	315	312	304	281	254

WEIRTON MEDICAL CENTER, INC.

601 COLLIERS WAY
WEIRTON, WV 260625014
Phone: 304-797-6000
Fax: –
Web: www.weirtonmedical.com

CEO: Charles M O'Brien Jr
CFO: Robert Frank
HR: Michael Burskey
FYE: June 30
Type: Private

There's nothing weird about Weirton Medical Center. The 240-bed not-for-profit hospital provides a wide range of health services to the tri-state region of West Virginia Ohio and Pennsylvania. Inpatient services include pediatrics obstetrics and other acute care services. Founded in 1953 the hospital also offers clinical and diagnostic care services such as emergency medicine home health care rehabilitation and occupational therapy. Weirton Medical Center has seen a steady decrease in patient volumes in recent years forcing the hospital to enact a number of cost-saving measures including cutting back on some services and laying off employees.

	Annual Growth	06/12	06/13	06/14	06/15	06/16
Sales ($ mil.)	11.2%	–	101.9	127.0	123.0	140.3
Net income ($ mil.)	32.1%	–	4.5	6.8	4.6	10.5
Market value ($ mil.)	–	–	–	–	–	–
Employees	–	–	–	–	–	1,100

WEIS MARKETS, INC. — NYS: WMK

1000 S. Second Street, P.O. Box 471
Sunbury, PA 17801-0471
Phone: 570 286-4571
Fax: –
Web: www.weismarkets.com

CEO: Jonathan H. Weis
CFO: Scott F. Frost
HR: James Marcil
FYE: December 29
Type: Public

Weis (pronounced "Wise") Markets owns more than 200 grocery stores mostly in Pennsylvania but also in about half a dozen other northern and northeastern US states. The stores range from 8000 to 71000 sq. ft. (with an average size of about 48500 sq. ft.) and offer a host of traditional grocery items — dairy products frozen foods general merchandise baked deli products — as well as pharmacy and fuel services. Weis Markets was established in 1912 by Harry and Sigmund Weis in Sunbury Pennsylvania. The Weis family still controls about 65% of the company's voting power.

	Annual Growth	12/14	12/15	12/16	12/17	12/18
Sales ($ mil.)	6.0%	2,776.7	2,876.7	3,136.5	3,466.8	3,509.3
Net income ($ mil.)	3.3%	55.2	59.3	87.2	98.4	62.7
Market value ($ mil.)	(0.2%)	1,272.8	1,235.4	1,797.9	1,113.3	1,260.2
Employees	6.0%	18,200	19,000	23,000	23,000	23,000

WELCH FOODS INC., A COOPERATIVE

300 BAKER AVE STE 101
CONCORD, MA 017422131
Phone: 978-371-1000
Fax: –
Web: www.welchs.com

CEO: Bradley C. Irwin
CFO: Michael Perda
HR: –
FYE: August 31
Type: Private

Welch Foods has a taste for the grape. An operating subsidiary of the National Grape Cooperative (owned by some 900 farmers) Welch produces the Welch's brand grape and white grape juices and jellies. Its beverage line includes refrigerated and sparkling juices and cocktails frozen and shelf-stable concentrates and single-serve drinks. Welch supplies fresh grapes and snacks as well as preserved offerings (jellies jams and spreads). The co-op licenses the Welch's name to other manufactures of frozen fruit confections dried fruit and carbonated beverages among many. Its products are purchased by grocery retailers and food service operators in the US and some 50 other countries.

	Annual Growth	08/12	08/13	08/14	08/15	08/16
Sales ($ mil.)	(0.5%)	–	608.5	609.9	609.1	600.2
Net income ($ mil.)	8.8%	–	65.1	76.9	81.3	83.9
Market value ($ mil.)	–	–	–	–	–	–
Employees	–	–	–	–	–	1,000

WELLCARE HEALTH PLANS INC — NYS: WCG

8735 Henderson Road, Renaissance One
Tampa, FL 33634
Phone: 813 290-6200
Fax: –
Web: www.wellcare.com

CEO: Kenneth A Burdick
CFO: Andrew L Asher
HR: –
FYE: December 31
Type: Public

WellCare Health Plans provides managed-care administrative services to government-funded health care programs that provide benefits via Medicaid Medicare and various State Children's Health Insurance Programs (SCHIPs). Its services include benefits management and claims processing. WellCare administers its Medicaid plans under various brands such as Care1st in Arizona Staywell in Florida; WellCare in Georgia Kentucky New York New Jersey and South Carolina; Harmony in Illinois; Missouri Care in Missouri; and 'Ohana in Hawaii. The company's Medicare prescription-drug and Medicare Advantage (MA) plans operate primarily under the WellCare brand. Altogether WellCare serves some 4.4 million customers throughout the US.

	Annual Growth	12/13	12/14	12/15	12/16	12/17
Sales ($ mil.)	15.6%	9,527.9	12,959.9	13,890.2	14,237.1	17,007.2
Net income ($ mil.)	20.8%	175.3	63.7	118.6	242.1	373.7
Market value ($ mil.)	30.0%	3,135.3	3,653.6	3,482.1	6,103.2	8,954.0
Employees	14.4%	5,200	6,700	6,900	7,400	8,900

WELLCO ENTERPRISES INC.

150 Westwood Cir.
Waynesville NC 28786
Phone: 828-456-3545
Fax: 828-456-3547
Web: www.wellco.com

CEO: –
CFO: –
HR: –
FYE: June 30
Type: Private

Wellco Enterprises keeps in step with US military footwear needs. The company makes rugged footwear primarily for the US military under firm fixed-price contracts. Sales to the military accounts for most of Wellco's sales. The company's boots include general-issue all-leather boots hot-weather (tropical) boots intermediate cold/wet boots desert boots (used in the Persian Gulf War) and antipersonnel mine blast protective boots. The estate of former director James Emerson owned about 57% of Wellco until it was bought by Golden Gate Capital and Integrity Brands in May 2007 and taken private.

WELLESLEY COLLEGE

106 CENTRAL ST
WELLESLEY, MA 024818203
Phone: 781-283-1000
Fax: -
Web: www.wellesley.edu

CEO: -
CFO: -
HR: -
FYE: June 30
Type: Private

Wellesley College is a liberal arts women's college (one of the famed "Seven Sisters" schools) that offers majors in more than 50 fields of study including anthropology computer science education physics and sociology. It has a three-college collaboration with Massachusetts' Babson and Olin Colleges to provide additional opportunities for its students and also has cross-registration agreements with MIT and Brandeis. Wellesley's Davis Degree program is geared toward women beyond traditional college age. The college has a student enrollment of some 2500 and a student-faculty ratio of about 7 to 1.

	Annual Growth	06/12	06/13	06/16	06/17	06/18
Sales ($ mil.)	(5.1%)	-	295.4	221.7	237.4	227.1
Net income ($ mil.)	21.8%	-	48.8	(92.5)	172.1	131.1
Market value ($ mil.)	-	-	-	-	-	-
Employees						2,000

WELLMONT HEALTH SYSTEM

1905 AMERICAN WAY
KINGSPORT, TN 376605882
Phone: 423-230-8200
Fax: -
Web: www.balladhealth.org

CEO: David L. Brash
CFO: Beth Ward
HR: -
FYE: June 30
Type: Private

At Wellmont Health System wellness is paramount. Wellmont Health System provides general and advanced medical-surgical care to residents of northeastern Tennessee and southwestern Virginia. The health system consists of about a dozen owned and affiliated hospitals that collectively have more than 1000 licensed beds. One of its facilities is a rehabilitation hospital operated in partnership with HealthSouth. The system's Holston Valley Medical Center features a level I trauma center and a level III neonatal intensive care unit (NICU). Wellmont also operates numerous ancillary facilities including an assisted living center a mental health clinic home health care and hospice agencies and outpatient centers.

	Annual Growth	06/07	06/08	06/09	06/10	06/17
Sales ($ mil.)	104.4%	-	-	3.0	622.0	908.1
Net income ($ mil.)	-	-	-	0.0	33.9	53.7
Market value ($ mil.)	-	-	-	-	-	-
Employees						6,114

WELLS ENTERPRISES INC.

1 Blue Bunny Dr.
Le Mars IA 51031
Phone: 712-546-4000
Fax: 712-548-3011
Web: www.wellsenterprisesinc.com

CEO: Michael C Wells
CFO: -
HR: -
FYE: December 31
Type: Private

You scream I scream we all scream for Wells Enterprises. The family-owned and operated manufacturer is best known for Blue Bunny brand ice cream and frozen novelties like Bunny Tracks (vanilla ice cream with fudge and peanut butter caramel ribbons and other goodies) and red-white-and-blue Bomb Pop. Wells also makes frozen dairy desserts under license including Cadbury ice cream bars and Yoplait frozen yogurt pints. It sells the lineup through supermarkets discount retailers convenience stores and vending machines nationwide. A foodservice division supplies dairy desserts to restaurants schools and ice cream shops. Wells has a retail presence too through the Blue Bunny Ice Cream Parlor and Museum.

WELLS FINANCIAL CORP

53 First Street, S.W., P.O. Box 310
Wells, MN 56097
Phone: 507 553-3151
Fax: 507 553-6295
Web: www.wellsfinancialcorp.com

NBB: WEFP
CEO: -
CFO: -
HR: -
FYE: December 31
Type: Public

Wells Financial doesn't want you to get tapped out. It's the holding company for Wells Federal Bank which serves southern Minnesota and northern Iowa through 10 branches and a loan production office. Founded in 1934 the bank offers standard deposit services and credit cards. Mortgages secured by agricultural real estate and one- to four-family residences comprise most of the bank's lending activities; consumer business and construction loans round out its loan portfolio. Bank subsidiary Wells Insurance Agency sells property/casualty life and health insurance and mutual funds and Greater Minnesota Mortgage originates home loans for resale through referrals from other community banks.

	Annual Growth	12/04	12/12	12/13	12/14	12/15
Assets ($ mil.)	1.3%	239.4	244.2	243.8	251.8	274.8
Net income ($ mil.)	7.7%	2.2	1.6	1.2	1.3	4.9
Market value ($ mil.)	(0.1%)	26.1	14.3	17.9	21.7	25.7
Employees	-	-	-	-	-	-

WELLSTAR HEALTH SYSTEM, INC.

805 SANDY PLAINS RD
MARIETTA, GA 300666340
Phone: 770-956-7827
Fax: -
Web: www.wellstar.org

CEO: Reynold J Jennings
CFO: A James Budzinski
HR: -
FYE: June 30
Type: Private

With WellStar in your corner you won't need to wish upon a star for good health and wellness. The not-for-profit WellStar Health System is Georgia's largest health system with about a dozen hospitals two health parks a pediatric center and more than 200 medical office locations. The network's hospitals specialize in cardiac and cancer care diabetes treatments and women's health. WellStar's physician group includes more than 1100 providers. The network is also home to hospice and home care programs; Atherton Place an independent living center for senior citizens; and about 10 urgent care facilities.

	Annual Growth	06/06	06/07	06/08	06/09	06/15
Sales ($ mil.)	105.2%	-	-	5.4	397.7	823.9
Net income ($ mil.)	60.9%	-	-	1.8	0.0	49.8
Market value ($ mil.)	-	-	-	-	-	-
Employees						11,985

WELLTOWER INC

4500 Dorr Street
Toledo, OH 43615
Phone: 419 247-2800
Fax: -
Web: www.welltower.com

NYS: WELL
CEO: Thomas J. (Tom) DeRosa
CFO: John Goodey
HR: -
FYE: December 31
Type: Public

Welltower invests in senior living and healthcare properties primarily skilled nursing and assisted-living facilities designed for older people needing help with everyday living. The real estate investment trust (REIT) also has investments in independent living facilities medical office buildings and specialty care facilities. Its portfolio includes around 1500 properties leased to healthcare operators in more than 45 states in the US?its largest market. The company also operates in Canada the UK and Luxembourg.

	Annual Growth	12/14	12/15	12/16	12/17	12/18
Sales ($ mil.)	8.9%	3,343.5	3,859.8	4,281.2	4,316.6	4,700.5
Net income ($ mil.)	12.0%	512.2	883.8	1,077.8	522.8	805.0
Market value ($ mil.)	(2.1%)	29,032.7	26,101.4	25,679.3	24,466.9	26,630.9
Employees	(3.2%)	438	476	466	392	384

WENDY'S CO (THE)   NMS: WEN

One Dave Thomas Blvd.
Dublin, OH 43017
Phone: 614 764-3100
Fax: –
Web: www.aboutwendys.com

CEO: Todd A. Penegor
CFO: Gunther Plosch
HR: –
FYE: December 30
Type: Public

The Wendy's Company operates the Wendy's fast food chain. The company is the #2 hamburger chain in the US behind #1 McDonald's and just in front of #3 chain Burger King. The Wendy's chain consists of about 6535 restaurants located in the US and about 30 other countries. Besides burgers and fries the restaurants serve chicken sandwiches wraps and a variety of salads. Instead of milkshakes Wendy's serves its famously thick Frosty. Most of the company's locations are franchised and it generates most of its sales in the US (a little more than 95%). In 2014 the company was purchased by Global Food Retail Group for about $10 million.

	Annual Growth	12/14*	01/16	01/17*	12/17	12/18
Sales ($ mil.)	(6.3%)	2,061.1	1,870.3	1,435.4	1,223.4	1,589.9
Net income ($ mil.)	39.5%	121.4	161.1	129.6	194.0	460.1
Market value ($ mil.)	15.1%	2,062.6	2,490.4	3,126.3	3,796.8	3,614.2
Employees	(20.4%)	31,200	21,200	12,100	12,100	12,500

*Fiscal year change

WERNER ENTERPRISES, INC.   NMS: WERN

14507 Frontier Road, P.O. Box 45308
Omaha, NE 68145-0308
Phone: 402 895-6640
Fax: –
Web: www.werner.com

CEO: Derek J. Leathers
CFO: John J. Steele
HR: Stefanie Christensen
FYE: December 31
Type: Public

Transportation and logistics is Werner Enterprises' game; hauling truckload shipments — both interstate and intrastate — is its fame. One of the largest truckload carriers in the US Werner operates some 7400 tractors and over 24000 trailers. Its trailer fleet consists of dry vans as well as temperature-controlled vans and flatbeds. Werner's truckload transportation offerings include dedicated contract carriage in which drivers and equipment are assigned to a customer. It also offers freight brokerage intermodal freight transportation and other value-added logistic services as well as freight forwarding. The company was founded in 1958.

	Annual Growth	12/14	12/15	12/16	12/17	12/18
Sales ($ mil.)	3.5%	2,139.3	2,093.5	2,009.0	2,116.7	2,457.9
Net income ($ mil.)	14.3%	98.7	123.7	79.1	202.9	168.1
Market value ($ mil.)	(1.3%)	2,194.3	1,647.6	1,898.4	2,722.6	2,080.9
Employees	0.0%	12,828	13,140	12,533	12,784	12,852

WESBANCO INC   NMS: WSBC

1 Bank Plaza
Wheeling, WV 26003
Phone: 304 234-9000
Fax: –
Web: www.wesbanco.com

CEO: Todd F. Clossin
CFO: Robert H. Young
HR: Anthony F. Pietranton
FYE: December 31
Type: Public

WesBanco wants to be the "BesBanco" for its customers. The holding company owns WesBanco Bank which has about 210 branches in Indiana Kentucky Ohio Pennsylvania and West Virginia. In addition to providing traditional services such as deposits and loans the bank operates a wealth management department with offices in West Virginia and Ohio and some $4.7 billion of assets under management and custody including the company's proprietary WesMark mutual funds. Other units include brokerage firm WesBanco Securities and multi-line insurance provider WesBanco Insurance Services.

	Annual Growth	12/14	12/15	12/16	12/17	12/18
Assets ($ mil.)	18.6%	6,296.6	8,470.3	9,790.9	9,816.2	12,458.6
Net income ($ mil.)	19.6%	70.0	80.8	86.6	94.5	143.1
Market value ($ mil.)	1.3%	1,900.0	1,639.0	2,351.0	2,219.4	2,003.2
Employees	13.3%	1,448	1,633	1,928	1,940	2,383

WESCO AIRCRAFT HOLDINGS INC.   NYS: WAIR

24911 Avenue Stanford
Valencia, CA 91355
Phone: 661 775-7200
Fax: –
Web: www.wescoair.com

CEO: Todd S Renehan
CFO: Kerry A Shiba
HR: –
FYE: September 30
Type: Public

Planes may fly around the world but they can't leave the ground without Wesco Aircraft Holdings. One of the largest logistics and supply chain companies serving the aerospace industry it provides distribution vendor relationship management just-in-time (JIT) delivery quality assurance and kitting. Operating through Wesco Aircraft Hardware and other subsidiaries the company stocks about 565000 different pieces of hardware bearings tools electronic components and machined parts from more than 5000 suppliers. Boeing Airbus and Bombardier are among its largest customers.

	Annual Growth	09/14	09/15	09/16	09/17	09/18
Sales ($ mil.)	3.7%	1,355.9	1,497.6	1,477.4	1,429.4	1,570.5
Net income ($ mil.)	(24.8%)	102.1	(154.7)	91.4	(237.3)	32.7
Market value ($ mil.)	(10.3%)	1,732.3	1,214.6	1,337.1	935.8	1,120.0
Employees	2.5%	2,785	2,670	2,724	2,978	3,069

WESCO FINANCIAL LLC

301 E. Colorado Blvd. Ste. 300
Pasadena CA 91101-1901
Phone: 626-585-6700
Fax: 626-449-1455
Web: www.wescofinancial.com

CEO: –
CFO: –
HR: –
FYE: December 31
Type: Subsidiary

Wesco Financial is sort of like Berkshire Hathaway Lite. Charlie Munger Berkshire vice chairman and a confidante of Warren Buffett leads Wesco. And like Berkshire the investment firm provides insurance and reinsurance; in Wesco's case it does so through subsidiaries Wesco-Financial Insurance Company and Kansas Bankers Surety. It also holds shares in some of the same companies as Berkshire like Coca-Cola Kraft Procter & Gamble and Wells Fargo. Other prominent holdings include CORT Business Services and Precision Steel Warehouse which has steel service centers in Chicago and Charlotte North Carolina. In 2011 Berkshire Hathaway acquired the 20% of Wesco that it didn't already own.

WESCO INTERNATIONAL, INC.   NYS: WCC

225 West Station Square Drive, Suite 700
Pittsburgh, PA 15219
Phone: 412 454-2200
Fax: –
Web: www.wesco.com

CEO: John J. Engel
CFO: David S (Dave) Schulz
HR: Kimberly G. Windrow
FYE: December 31
Type: Public

When contractors and manufacturers need parts it's WESCO to the rescue. The company distributes general and electrical supplies (fuses terminals connectors enclosures circuit breakers transformers switchboards tools abrasives filters safety equipment) lighting (lamps fixtures ballasts) wire and conduit materials (wire cable raceway metallic and non-metallic conduit) and automation controls and motors (relays timers and interconnects). WESCO offers more than a million products from some 30000 suppliers with about 70000 customers worldwide. The company generates 75% of its sales in the US.

	Annual Growth	12/14	12/15	12/16	12/17	12/18
Sales ($ mil.)	0.9%	7,889.6	7,518.5	7,336.0	7,679.0	8,176.6
Net income ($ mil.)	(4.7%)	275.9	210.7	101.6	163.5	227.3
Market value ($ mil.)	(10.9%)	3,437.5	1,970.2	3,001.8	3,074.0	2,165.1
Employees	(0.8%)	9,400	9,300	9,000	9,100	9,100

WESCOM CREDIT UNION

123 S. Marengo Ave.
Pasadena CA 91101
Phone: 626-535-1000
Fax: 925-687-2122

CEO: –
CFO: –
HR: –
FYE: December 31
Type: Private - Not-for-Pr

At Wescom you're welcome. Through about 30 branches in Southern California Wescom Credit Union provides checking savings and money market accounts IRAs savings certificates home loans reverse mortgages auto loans and Visa credit cards to approximately 250000 member-owners in seven counties. Its Wescom Financial Services division offers trust investment online trading and financial planning services while Wescom Insurance Services sells auto and home coverage. The credit union's Wescom Resources Group unit develops technology services including online banking statements bill payment and mobile applications for other credit unions.

WESLEYAN UNIVERSITY

45 WYLLYS AVE
MIDDLETOWN, CT 064593211
Phone: 860-685-2000
Fax: –
Web: www.wesleyan.edu

CEO: –
CFO: –
HR: –
FYE: June 30
Type: Private

Wesleyan University is a private institution offering liberal arts and sciences education from its 360-acre campus in Middleton Connecticut. Some 3500 undergraduate and graduate students attend the university which has programs in academic areas including American studies film studies and psychology. Notable alumni include television producer Joss Whedon and educational writer Ted Fiske. Founded in 1831 Wesleyan was the first of several US colleges and universities to be named after John Wesley founder of the Methodist church; it ended its formal affiliation with the church in 1937.

	Annual Growth	06/05	06/06	06/07	06/17	06/18
Sales ($ mil.)	2.3%	–	172.2	179.8	221.2	225.0
Net income ($ mil.)	1.0%	–	95.0	90.3	130.7	107.3
Market value ($ mil.)	–	–	–	–	–	–
Employees	–	–	–	–	–	900

WEST BANCORPORATION, INC. NMS: WTBA

1601 22nd Street
West Des Moines, IA 50266
Phone: 515 222-2300
Fax: –
Web: www.westbankstrong.com

CEO: David D. (Dave) Nelson
CFO: Douglas R. (Doug) Gulling
HR: –
FYE: December 31
Type: Public

West Bancorporation is the holding company for West Bank which serves individuals and small to midsized businesses through about a dozen branches mainly in the Des Moines and Iowa City Iowa areas. Founded in 1893 the bank offers checking savings and money market accounts CDs Visa credit cards and trust services. The bank's lending activities primarily consist of commercial mortgages; construction land and land development loans; and business loans such as revolving lines of credit inventory and accounts receivable financing equipment financing and capital expenditure loans to borrowers in Iowa.

	Annual Growth	12/14	12/15	12/16	12/17	12/18
Assets ($ mil.)	9.2%	1,615.8	1,748.6	1,854.2	2,114.4	2,296.6
Net income ($ mil.)	9.2%	20.0	21.7	23.0	23.1	28.5
Market value ($ mil.)	2.9%	277.3	321.8	402.5	409.8	311.1
Employees	(2.2%)	178	174	165	162	163

WEST COAST NOVELTY CORPORATION

2401 MONARCH ST
ALAMEDA, CA 945017513
Phone: 510-748-4248
Fax: –
Web: www.westcoastnovelty.com

CEO: Brian T McCroden
CFO: –
HR: –
FYE: August 31
Type: Private

|West Coast Novelty Corp. founded in the 1920s doesn't make concessions as one of the largest suppliers of licensed sports merchandise in the US. The firm has grown from its beginnings as a souvenir and concession operator to a nationwide distributor of licensed items such as jerseys T-shirts and headwear. West Coast Novelty boasts a vast portfolio of team licenses based on its agreements with the NFL MLB NBA WWF and the Collegiate Licensing Company. To extend its reach into the Eastern and Southern US the company operates a distribution center in Memphis Tennessee to supplement operations at its Alameda California facility.

	Annual Growth	08/06	08/07	08/08	08/09	08/10
Sales ($ mil.)	(86.6%)	–	–	2,104.9	45.0	37.6
Net income ($ mil.)	–	–	–	0.0	(0.5)	(0.0)
Market value ($ mil.)	–	–	–	–	–	–
Employees	–	–	–	–	–	80

WEST CORP. NMS: WSTC

11808 Miracle Hills Drive
Omaha, NE 68154
Phone: 402 963-1200
Fax: –

CEO: John Shlonsky
CFO: Nancy Disman
HR: Alexandra S Russman
FYE: December 31
Type: Public

If it's communication services you need why not go West? West Corporation provides technology-driven voice-oriented services through call centers and automated voice and data centers. It offers inbound and outbound call handling (including 911 support through its Intrado subsidiary) for services such as customer support technical assistance and order processing. It also provides automated and Web-based customer care programs through its West Interactive division and lead management team selling and sales management services through West Business Services. West additionally offers conference call services through its Intercall operations and it is a leading debt collections agency in the US.

	Annual Growth	12/11	12/12	12/13	12/14	12/15
Sales ($ mil.)	(2.2%)	2,491.3	2,638.0	2,685.9	2,218.6	2,280.3
Net income ($ mil.)	17.4%	127.5	125.5	143.2	158.4	241.8
Market value ($ mil.)	(8.4%)	–	–	2,143.4	2,751.1	1,798.2
Employees	(26.5%)	36,500	35,700	35,100	9,700	10,630

WEST MARINE, INC. NMS: WMAR

500 Westridge Drive
Watsonville, CA 95076-4100
Phone: 831 728-2700
Fax: –
Web: www.westmarine.com

CEO: Matthew L Hyde
CFO: Jeffrey L Lasher
HR: –
FYE: January 2/
Type: Public

West Marine has the goods to keep your boat shipshape. It is the nation's #1 boating supplies retailer operating through some 260 company-owned stores as well as a port supply wholesale business and direct-to-customer website catalog and call center. Its stores known by the West Marine banner dot 38 US states Canada and Puerto Rico. Five stores are franchised in Turkey. Its direct-to-consumer arm offers about 100000 boating products worldwide. The port supply business provides wholesaling and distribution to commercial government and industrial customers. West Marine's distribution centers are in California and South Carolina. The company was founded by Randolph Repass in 1975 as West Coast Ropes.

	Annual Growth	12/11	12/12	12/13*	01/15	01/16
Sales ($ mil.)	1.8%	643.4	675.3	663.2	675.8	704.8
Net income ($ mil.)	(31.4%)	29.7	15.5	7.8	1.9	4.5
Market value ($ mil.)	(6.1%)	287.6	264.4	349.7	309.2	210.0
Employees	(1.3%)	4,043	3,955	3,783	3,642	3,796

*Fiscal year change

WEST PENN ALLEGHENY HEALTH SYSTEM INC.

4800 Friendship Ave.
Pittsburgh PA 15224
Phone: 412-578-5000
Fax: 610-649-1798
Web: www.hajoca.com

CEO: John Paul
CFO: David Samuel
HR: Martha Clister
FYE: June 30
Type: Private - Not-for-Pr

West Penn Allegheny Health System (WPAHS) makes wellness a priority for Steel Town residents. The health system which operates with some 1600 beds is a network of affiliated hospitals serving the greater Pittsburgh area including Allegheny General Hospital Allegheny Valley Hospital Canonsburg General Hospital The Western Pennsylvania Hospital (West Penn) and the West Penn-Forbes Regional Campus. Among its specialty services are cancer treatment emergency medicine and orthopedics. The system's clinical campuses are affiliated with Drexel University and Temple University. WPAHS handles some 200000 emergency visits each year.

WEST PHARMACEUTICAL SERVICES, INC.   NYS: WST

530 Herman O. West Drive
Exton, PA 19341-0645
Phone: 610 594-2900
Fax: –
Web: www.westpharma.com

CEO: Eric M. Green
CFO: William J. Federici
HR: Brian Stocker
FYE: December 31
Type: Public

West Pharmaceutical Services makes the bits and pieces of health care products that you may not notice but you'd have a hard time doing without. The firm makes drug packaging seals and stoppers for blood collection syringe components and injection systems. It also provides contract manufacturing services including product design and commercialization injection molding and complex assemblies for pharmaceutical diagnostic and medical device customers. The company was founded in 1923 and has grown to have a worldwide presence. The US is West's largest single market.

	Annual Growth	12/14	12/15	12/16	12/17	12/18
Sales ($ mil.)	4.8%	1,421.4	1,399.8	1,509.1	1,599.1	1,717.4
Net income ($ mil.)	13.0%	127.1	95.6	143.6	150.7	206.9
Market value ($ mil.)	16.5%	3,945.1	4,462.3	6,285.9	7,311.4	7,264.0
Employees	2.4%	7,000	7,100	7,300	7,500	7,700

WEST TEXAS GAS, INC.

211 N COLORADO ST
MIDLAND, TX 797014607
Phone: 432-682-4349
Fax: –
Web: www.westtexasgas.com

CEO: –
CFO: –
HR: –
FYE: December 31
Type: Private

With a deep understanding the utility of natural gas natural gas utility West Texas Gas distributes more than 25 billion cu. ft. of natural gas propane and other petroleum products to more than 25000 residential commercial agricultural and governmental customers in Texas and Oklahoma Panhandle region. The company the fourth-largest investor-owned public utility in Texas also operates retail gasoline stations and convenience stores and has gas gathering production transmission and marketing operations. West Texas Gas is 100%-owned by CEO J. L. Davis.

	Annual Growth	12/06	12/07	12/16	12/17	12/18
Sales ($ mil.)	(16.8%)	–	889.3	103.2	109.0	117.5
Net income ($ mil.)	1.1%	–	40.3	18.7	13.7	45.7
Market value ($ mil.)	–	–	–	–	–	–
Employees	–	–	–	–	–	600

WEST VIRGINIA UNITED HEALTH SYSTEM, INC.

1 MEDICAL CENTER DR
MORGANTOWN, WV 265061200
Phone: 304-598-4000
Fax: –
Web: www.wvumedicine.org

CEO: Christopher Colenda
CFO: –
HR: –
FYE: December 31
Type: Private

West Virginia United Health System (WVUHS) helps residents in the Mountain State stay on top of their health. The system operates United Hospital Center (in Clarksburg) as well as hospitals in the West Virginia University Hospitals (WVUH) system including City Hospital (Martinsburg) Jefferson Memorial Hospital (Ranson) and WVUH's home hospital in Morgantown. In addition WVUHS operates WVUH's Cheat Lake physicians ambulatory center as well as a network of about a dozen primary care clinics located throughout central and northern West Virginia. Combined the system's hospitals and clinics have more than 1000 beds and treat approximately 1.4 million patients annually.

	Annual Growth	12/13	12/14	12/15	12/16	12/17
Sales ($ mil.)	507.8%	–	9.7	1,651.7	1,877.3	2,172.7
Net income ($ mil.)	–	–	(0.0)	24.0	103.2	132.6
Market value ($ mil.)	–	–	–	–	–	–
Employees	–	–	–	–	–	7,000

WEST VIRGINIA UNIVERSITY

103 STEWART HL
MORGANTOWN, WV 26506
Phone: 304-293-2545
Fax: –

CEO: –
CFO: –
HR: –
FYE: June 30
Type: Private

West Virginia University (WVU) is the intellectual home of more than 29000 Mountaineers (the school's mascot) and the state's preeminent institution of higher learning. WVU offers more than 180 bachelor's master's doctoral and professional degree programs through some 15 colleges and schools. The university's clinical psychology and forestry programs have been recognized nationally and it boasts 100% post-graduate job placement for its nursing pharmacy and mining engineering majors. WVU also runs a two-year residential school Potomac State College in Keyser West Virginia.

	Annual Growth	06/14	06/15	06/16	06/17	06/18
Sales ($ mil.)	3.2%	–	–	–	783.2	808.1
Net income ($ mil.)	390.3%	–	–	–	8.4	41.1
Market value ($ mil.)	–	–	–	–	–	–
Employees	–	–	–	–	–	6,245

WESTAMERICA BANCORPORATION   NMS: WABC

1108 Fifth Avenue
San Rafael, CA 94901
Phone: 707 863-6000
Fax: –
Web: www.westamerica.com

CEO: David L. Payne
CFO: Robert A. Thorson
HR: –
FYE: December 31
Type: Public

Annie get your checkbook? Maybe not as wild as Buffalo Bill's West but Westamerica Bancorporation still shoots high with its subsidiary Westamerica Bank. The bank operates almost 100 branches in Northern and Central California. It offers individuals and businesses such standard fare as checking and savings accounts as well as electronic banking trust services and credit cards. It focuses on the banking needs of small businesses; business loans and commercial mortgages together account for more than half of the company's loan portfolio. Westamerica Bank chartered in 1884 also originates construction residential mortgage and consumer loans.

	Annual Growth	12/14	12/15	12/16	12/17	12/18
Assets ($ mil.)	2.5%	5,035.7	5,168.9	5,366.1	5,513.0	5,568.5
Net income ($ mil.)	4.2%	60.6	58.8	58.9	50.0	71.6
Market value ($ mil.)	3.2%	1,310.3	1,249.6	1,682.1	1,591.8	1,488.3
Employees	(2.9%)	858	813	783	785	762

WESTAR ENERGY INC

NYS: WR

818 South Kansas Avenue
Topeka, KS 66612
Phone: 785 575-6300
Fax: –
Web: www.westarenergy.com

CEO: Terry Bassham
CFO: Anthony D Somma
HR: –
FYE: December 31
Type: Public

Westar Energy helps shines a light upon the people and businesses of eastern Kansas. It serves more than 700000 electricity customers in the region. Westar generates over 6200 MW of electricity distributes it through more than 35000 miles of transmission and distribution lines. It sells roughly a third of it to each of residential commercial and industrial customers. In 2017 the company agreed to a merger-of-equals transaction with its neighboring utility Great Plains Energy and expects the union to complete in the first half of 2018.

	Annual Growth	12/12	12/13	12/14	12/15	12/16
Sales ($ mil.)	3.2%	2,261.5	2,370.7	2,601.7	2,459.2	2,562.1
Net income ($ mil.)	5.9%	275.1	292.5	313.3	291.9	346.6
Market value ($ mil.)	18.5%	4,058.1	4,561.4	5,847.5	6,013.4	7,989.9
Employees	(0.6%)	2,313	2,302	2,411	2,330	2,254

WESTAT, INC.

1600 RESEARCH BLVD
ROCKVILLE, MD 208503129
Phone: 301-251-1500
Fax: –
Web: www.westat.com

CEO: –
CFO: –
HR: Joseph Hunt
FYE: December 31
Type: Private

Survey the market research business and you'll find Westat among the leaders of the pack. A statistical survey organization the company provides research and consulting services including study design and analysis data collection program evaluation and communications campaign development. It has technical expertise in survey and analytical methods computer systems technology biomedical science and clinical trials. Westat serves US state and local government clients in addition to businesses and foundations. It has offices in five US states as well as international locations around the world. The company was founded in 1963 and is employee-owned.

	Annual Growth	12/12	12/13	12/14	12/15	12/16
Sales ($ mil.)	(4.3%)	–	582.5	517.4	509.9	510.7
Net income ($ mil.)	0.2%	–	23.8	22.4	20.6	24.0
Market value ($ mil.)	–	–	–	–	–	–
Employees	–	–	–	–	–	2,000

WESTCON GROUP INC.

520 White Plains Rd.
Tarrytown NY 10591-5167
Phone: 914-829-7000
Fax: 914-829-7137
Web: www.westcongroup.com

CEO: Dolph Westerbos
CFO: Cathy Jessup
HR: –
FYE: February 28
Type: Subsidiary

The Westcon Group sees more pros than cons in networking equipment. The company distributes networking unified communications and security products to resellers and systems integrators worldwide. It operates through vendor-focused units such as Comstor (Cisco Systems) and ConvergencePoint (Avaya and Polycom). The company's Westcon Security division counts Blue Coat ArcSight RSA Palo Alto Networks and Trend Micro among its suppliers. South Africa-based IT services company Datatec owns Westcon Group which has operations in some 35 countries across six continents.

WESTELL TECHNOLOGIES INC

NAS: WSTL

750 North Commons Drive
Aurora, IL 60504
Phone: 630 898-2500
Fax: –
Web: –

CEO: Timothy Duitsman
CFO: Thomas P Minichiello
HR: –
FYE: March 31
Type: Public

Westell Technologies knows the value of the great outdoors for communication service providers. The company makes outside plant equipment used by telecommunications providers for digital transmission remote monitoring power distribution and other functions that link customer locations with central office facilities. Its products include outdoor passively cooled equipment enclosures mountings and fuse panels. The company also provides services such as design assembly and testing. It generates most of its sales from major US telecommunications service providers.

	Annual Growth	03/15	03/16	03/17	03/18	03/19
Sales ($ mil.)	(15.2%)	84.1	88.2	63.0	58.6	43.6
Net income ($ mil.)	–	(58.0)	(16.2)	(15.9)	0.0	(11.4)
Market value ($ mil.)	11.7%	20.2	18.0	10.8	51.6	31.4
Employees	(14.0%)	232	228	123	115	127

WESTERN & SOUTHERN FINANCIAL GROUP, INC.

400 BROADWAY ST
CINCINNATI, OH 452023312
Phone: 866-832-7719
Fax: –
Web: www.westernsouthern.com

CEO: John F Barrett
CFO: James N Clark
HR: –
FYE: December 31
Type: Private

While its heritage may be Western and Southern Western & Southern Financial Group covers the northern and eastern US as well. The company offers a variety of life insurance products and annuities accident and supplemental health coverage mutual funds and other investment management products and services. Western & Southern's financial services include mutual fund administration trust services financial advisory and real estate development; it owns or manages some $68 billion in assets. The company is licensed in most states and in Washington DC.

	Annual Growth	12/05	12/06	12/08	12/15	12/16
Assets ($ mil.)	106.2%	–	32.2	13.6	42.3	44,749.6
Net income ($ mil.)	104.3%	–	0.3	(3.8)	0.4	387.7
Market value ($ mil.)	–	–	–	–	–	–
Employees	–	–	–	–	–	4,000

WESTERN ALLIANCE BANCORPORATION

NYS: WAL

One E. Washington Street, Suite 1400
Phoenix, AZ 85004
Phone: 602 389-3500
Fax: –
Web: www.westernalliancebancorporation.com

CEO: Robert G. Sarver
CFO: Dale M. Gibbons
HR: –
FYE: December 31
Type: Public

Western Alliance Bancorporation and its flagship Western Alliance Bank (WAB) have an alliance with several bank brands in the West operating as the Alliance Bank of Arizona; Bank of Nevada; First Independent Bank (Nevada); as well as Bridge Bank and Torrey Pines Bank which are both located across California. Combined the banks operate nearly 50 branches that provide standard consumer and business deposit and loan products. About half of the Western Alliance's loan portfolio is made up of commercial and industrial loans while another 40% is made up of commercial real estate loans. It also makes land development loans and consumer residential mortgages and other lines of credit.

	Annual Growth	12/14	12/15	12/16	12/17	12/18
Assets ($ mil.)	21.5%	10,600.5	14,275.1	17,200.8	20,329.1	23,109.5
Net income ($ mil.)	31.0%	148.0	194.2	259.8	325.5	435.8
Market value ($ mil.)	9.2%	2,917.6	3,763.5	5,112.0	5,942.2	4,144.4
Employees	12.1%	1,131	1,446	1,557	1,725	1,787

WESTERN AREA POWER ADMINISTRATION

12155 W Alameda Pkwy.
Lakewood CO 80228-8213
Phone: 720-962-7000
Fax: 720-962-7200
Web: www.wapa.gov

CEO: –
CFO: –
HR: –
FYE: September 30
Type: Government-owned

There's power in the West thanks to Western Area Power Administration. One of four power marketing agencies of the US Department of Energy the enterprise operates 57 hydroelectric power plants and one fossil-fueled power generation facility with a combined generating capacity of about 10480 MW. It also manages and maintains more than 17100 miles of transmission lines. Western Area Power Administration sells wholesale power to investor-owned government-owned and cooperative utilities power marketers federal agencies native American tribes and other electricity users (more than 680 direct customers with a total of 11.4 million end users) in 15 western states over a 1.3-million-sq.-mi. service area.

WESTERN EXPRESS HOLDINGS INC.

7135 Centennial Pl.
Nashville TN 37209
Phone: 615-259-9920
Fax: 615-350-9957
Web: www.westernexp.com

CEO: Paul L Weick
CFO: Richard L Prickett
HR: –
FYE: December 31
Type: Private

Pick a point on the compass — Western Express Holdings isn't limited to a single direction when it comes to hauling customers' freight. The company's main subsidiary truckload carrier Western Express will go west but it does most of its business in the eastern and midwestern US concentrating on short to medium-length hauls of between 500 and 1000 miles. The Western Express fleet consists of about 2500 tractors and 4500 trailers including dry vans and flatbeds which haul cargo for a diverse customer base. President and CEO Wayne Wise and his wife Donna Wise own a controlling stake in Western Express Holdings.

WESTERN CONNECTICUT HEALTH NETWORK, INC.

24 HOSPITAL AVE
DANBURY, CT 068106099
Phone: 203-739-7000
Fax: –
Web: www.westernconnecticuthealthnetwork.org

CEO: –
CFO: –
HR: –
FYE: September 30
Type: Private

Nuvance Health is a not-for-profit health system serving New York's Hudson Valley and western Connecticut. The system has about a half-dozen hospitals including Connecticut's Danbury Hospital and New Milford Hospital and New York's Northern Dutchess Hospital and Putnam Hospital Center. It also includes a network of primary care and specialty practices. Altogether the system has more than 2600 aligned physicians. Nuvance Health was established through the 2019 merger of Western Connecticut Health Network and New York-based Health Quest.

WESTERN FAMILY FOODS INC.

6700 SW Sandburg St.
Tigard OR 97223
Phone: 503-639-6300
Fax: 503-684-3469
Web: www.westernfamily.com

CEO: –
CFO: –
HR: –
FYE: April 30
Type: Private

From mayo to mops Western Family Foods supplies private-label products to more than 3500 independent grocery retailers in about two-dozen US states including Alaska and Hawaii. It coordinates with manufacturers and wholesalers to produce more than 6000 products including dry grocery frozen deli household and heath and beauty-care items. The company's flagship brands include Western Family and Shurfine (no relation to competitor Shurfine International which merged with Topco Associates) as well as Better Buy Market Choice and Shur Saving. Established in 1963 Western Family Foods is owned by a consortium that includes Affiliated Foods Associated Food Stores and United Western Grocers.

	Annual Growth	09/09	09/10	09/15	09/16	09/18
Sales ($ mil.)	8.4%	–	625.0	23.4	1.0	1,195.4
Net income ($ mil.)	2.1%	–	48.7	12.3	(3.4)	57.5
Market value ($ mil.)	–	–	–	–	–	–
Employees	–	–	–	–	–	3,000

WESTERN DIGITAL CORP

NMS: WDC

5601 Great Oaks Parkway
San Jose, CA 95119
Phone: 408 717-6000
Fax: –
Web: www.westerndigital.com

CEO: Stephen D. (Steve) Milligan
CFO: Mark P. Long
HR: Jacqueline M. DeMaria
FYE: June 28
Type: Public

When it comes to data storage Western Digital has drive and more than a splash of flash. The company is one of the largest independent makers of hard-disk drives (HDDs) which record store and recall volumes of data. It is also active in the fast-growing area of solid-state drives (SSDs). Drives for PCs account for a major portion of Western Digital's sales although the company also makes devices used in servers cloud computing data centers and home entertainment products such as set-top boxes and video game consoles. The company sells to manufacturers and through retailers and distributors. It generates more than half its sales from the Asia/Pacific region.

WESTERN FARMERS ELECTRIC COOPERATIVE

701 NE 7TH ST
ANADARKO, OK 730052297
Phone: 405-247-3351
Fax: –
Web: www.wfec.com

CEO: Gary Roulet
CFO: –
HR: –
FYE: December 31
Type: Private

Power also comes sweeping down the plain in Oklahoma thanks to the Western Farmers Electric Cooperative. Led by its coal- and natural gas-fueled generating plants — three in Anadarko one in Mooreland and one in Hugo (all in Oklahoma) — the generation and transmission co-op produces more than 1845 MW of capacity. It pipes power over 3700 miles of transmission lines to two-thirds of rural Oklahoma and parts of New Mexico. It also operates 264 substations and 59 switch stations. Western Farmers Electric Cooperative which is owned by its member distribution cooperatives supplies 22 distribution co-ops and Altus Air Force base which serve a total of a half million members.

	Annual Growth	07/15	07/16*	06/17	06/18	06/19
Sales ($ mil.)	3.3%	14,572.0	12,994.0	19,093.0	20,647.0	16,569.0
Net income ($ mil.)	–	1,465.0	242.0	397.0	675.0	(754.0)
Market value ($ mil.)	(12.4%)	23,856.7	13,708.7	26,137.0	22,836.0	14,027.3
Employees	(5.2%)	76,449	72,878	68,000	71,600	61,800

*Fiscal year change

	Annual Growth	12/14	12/15	12/16	12/17	12/18
Sales ($ mil.)	2.2%	–	671.5	655.1	686.6	715.9
Net income ($ mil.)	(22.8%)	–	31.2	24.0	13.5	14.3
Market value ($ mil.)	–	–	–	–	–	–
Employees	–	–	–	–	–	378

WESTERN GAS PARTNERS LP   NYS: WES

1201 Lake Robbins Drive   CEO: –
The Woodlands, TX 77380   CFO: Jaime R Casas
Phone: 832 636-6000   HR: –
Fax: 832 636-6001   FYE: December 31
Web: www.westerngas.com   Type: Public

Western Gas Partners' style is to gather and go. The company gathers and transports natural gas for its largest customer and parent Anadarko Petroleum and delivers natural gas and natural gas liquids (NGLs) to end-users. It handles gathering processing and throughput of about 2.2 billion cu. ft. of gas a day through eleven natural gas gathering systems seven treating facilities one natural gas liquids pipeline and one interstate pipeline (totaling more than 8820 miles across Wyoming Utah Texas Oklahoma and Kansas). Operating principally under long-term contracts the company gathers natural gas from individual wells after which it is compressed treated and delivered to customers.

	Annual Growth	12/13	12/14	12/15	12/16	12/17
Sales ($ mil.)	22.0%	1,053.5	1,331.6	1,632.6	1,883.0	2,333.6
Net income ($ mil.)	19.8%	275.1	376.5	(73.5)	591.3	567.5
Market value ($ mil.)	(6.0%)	10,390.4	12,303.7	8,005.4	9,896.9	8,099.8
Employees	–	–	–	–	–	–

WESTERN ILLINOIS UNIVERSITY INC

1 UNIVERSITY CIR   CEO: –
MACOMB, IL 614551390   CFO: –
Phone: 309-298-1800   HR: –
Fax: –   FYE: June 30
Web: www.wiu.edu   Type: Private

Western Illinois University (WIU) is exactly where you think it is. And it's a public school that has an annual enrollment of some 14000 students at its main campus in Macomb a commuter campus in Moline and at extension sites throughout the state. With a student-to-faculty ratio of 15:1 the university offers about 65 undergraduate majors 40 graduate degree programs and about a dozen pre-professional degrees at colleges of arts and sciences business and technology education and human services and fine arts and communication. The bill to establish the university then called Western Illinois Normal School was passed in 1899 by the Illinois General Assembly.

	Annual Growth	06/14	06/15	06/16	06/17	06/18
Sales ($ mil.)	(7.5%)	–	142.1	135.3	126.7	112.5
Net income ($ mil.)	89.9%	–	3.3	(39.2)	(10.1)	22.4
Market value ($ mil.)	–	–	–	–	–	–
Employees	–	–	–	–	–	2,048

WESTERN MASSACHUSETTS ELECTRIC CO.   NBB: WMAS N

300 Cadwell Drive   CEO: Werner J Schweiger
Springfield, MA 01104   CFO: James J Judge
Phone: 800 286-5000   HR: –
Fax: –   FYE: December 31
                                                         Type: Public

Western Massachusetts Electric shines a light on the masses in western Mass. The company provides electric power services to more than 200000 customers in about 60 towns and cities in a 1490-sq.-mi. service area in Massachusetts. Western Massachusetts Electric purchases its electricity from affiliate Select Energy. It is an operating subsidiary of Eversource Energy one of the largest utility companies in New England. The company operates 4200 miles of distribution lines and 415 miles of transmission lines. It also has 45 substations and 35200 transformer locations.

	Annual Growth	12/12	12/13	12/14	12/15	12/16
Sales ($ mil.)	2.4%	441.2	472.7	493.4	518.1	484.2
Net income ($ mil.)	1.6%	54.5	60.4	57.8	56.5	58.1
Market value ($ mil.)	–	–	–	–	–	–
Employees	(3.9%)	348	308	310	291	297

WESTERN MEDICAL CENTER AUXILIARY

1301 N TUSTIN AVE   CEO: Dan Brothman
SANTA ANA, CA 927058619   CFO: –
Phone: 714-835-3555   HR: –
Fax: –   FYE: March 31
Web: www.ihhioc.com   Type: Private

Western Medical Center makes sure that The OC keeps health issues out of its drama. Western Medical Center - Santa Ana serves the residents of California's Orange County through an acute care facility that houses some 280 beds. It also boasts doctors who are able to perform heart lung liver and kidney transplants. The hospital is one of three major trauma centers in the county. Tenet sold the facility (as part of a restructuring) to Integrated Healthcare Holdings (based in Costa Mesa California). After taking over Western Medical Center IHHI met with some rough financial times and bleeding capital faced the possibility of having to sell the center.

	Annual Growth	03/03	03/04	03/05	03/12	03/13
Sales ($ mil.)	–	–	–	0.0	0.0	161.4
Net income ($ mil.)	–	–	–	0.0	(0.0)	17.3
Market value ($ mil.)	–	–	–	–	–	–
Employees	–	–	–	–	–	1,300

WESTERN MICHIGAN UNIVERSITY

1903 W MICHIGAN AVE   CEO: –
KALAMAZOO, MI 490085200   CFO: Jan Van Der Kley
Phone: 269-387-1000   HR: Warren Hills
Fax: –   FYE: June 30
Web: www.wmich.edu   Type: Private

WMU (Western Michigan University) provides an education to more than 23500 students at its main campus in Kalamazoo and branch campuses in Battle Creek Benton Harbor-St. Joseph Grand Rapids Holland Lansing Muskegon South Haven and Traverse City Michigan. The public university offers almost 150 undergraduate programs and more than 70 master's programs as well as 30 doctoral degree programs through nine colleges. WMU's medieval studies program is internationally recognized; its annual conference on the Middle Ages draws scholars from 25 countries and every US state. WMU was founded in 1903.

	Annual Growth	06/08	06/09	06/10	06/11	06/13
Sales ($ mil.)	4.2%	–	–	340.8	363.1	385.1
Net income ($ mil.)	48.2%	–	–	6.8	30.2	22.3
Market value ($ mil.)	–	–	–	–	–	–
Employees	–	–	–	–	–	861

WESTERN MIDSTREAM PARTNERS LP   NYS: WES

1201 Lake Robbins Drive   CEO: Michael P Ure
The Woodlands, TX 77380   CFO: Jaime R Casas
Phone: 832 636-6000   HR: –
Fax: –   FYE: December 31
Web: www.westerngas.com   Type: Public

Western Gas Equity Partners LP (WGEP) is taking stock of a fellow energy concern. The entity formed in September 2012 as an investment vehicle for Western Gas Partners LP (WGP). WGEP's sole purpose is to buy a stake in WGP specifically a limited partner interest of almost 45% and a general partner interest of about 2%. As a shareholder of WGP the entity will receive cash distributions at the end of every fiscal quarter from WGP and as a limited partnership WGEP will distribute its profits back to its own shareholders. It will also be exempt from paying federal income taxes. WGEP filed an IPO seeking up to $362.25 million in November 2012 and plans to use the proceeds raised to begin buying shares in WGP.

	Annual Growth	12/14	12/15	12/16	12/17	12/18
Sales ($ mil.)	11.8%	1,273.8	1,561.4	1,804.3	2,248.4	1,990.3
Net income ($ mil.)	13.6%	221.9	87.9	345.8	376.6	369.4
Market value ($ mil.)	(17.6%)	13,186.6	7,945.3	9,272.0	8,135.7	6,071.1
Employees	–	–	–	–	–	–

WESTERN NEW ENGLAND BANCORP INC　　　　　　NMS: WNEB

141 Elm Street　　　　　　　　　　　　　　　　CEO: James C Hagan
Westfield, MA 01086　　　　　　　　　　　　　CFO: Guida R Sajdak
Phone: 413 568-1911　　　　　　　　　　　　　　　　　　　　HR: –
Fax: –　　　　　　　　　　　　　　　　　　　　FYE: December 31
Web: www.westfieldbank.com　　　　　　　　　　　　　Type: Public

Westfield Financial is the holding company for Westfield Bank which serves western Massachusetts' Hampden County and surrounding areas from more than 20 branch locations. Founded in 1853 the bank has traditionally been a community-oriented provider of retail deposit accounts and loans but it is placing more emphasis on serving commercial and industrial clients. Commercial real estate loans account for approximately 45% of the company's loan portfolio and business loans are more than 25%. The bank also makes a smaller number of consumer and home equity loans. In 2016 Westfield Financial merged with Chicopee Bancorp the holding company of Chicopee Savings Bank (another bank serving Hampden County).

	Annual Growth	12/14	12/15	12/16	12/17	12/18
Assets ($ mil.)	12.6%	1,320.1	1,339.9	2,076.0	2,083.1	2,118.8
Net income ($ mil.)	27.7%	6.2	5.7	4.8	12.3	16.4
Market value ($ mil.)	8.1%	208.4	238.5	265.5	309.5	285.1
Employees	12.5%	200	195	310	317	320

WESTERN PENNSYLVANIA HOSPITAL

4800 FRIENDSHIP AVE　　　　　　　　　　　　CEO: Dtephen M Patz
PITTSBURGH, PA 152241722　　　　　　　　　　　　　　　　CFO: –
Phone: 412-578-5000　　　　　　　　　　　　　　　　　　　　HR: –
Fax: –　　　　　　　　　　　　　　　　　　　　　　FYE: June 30
Web: www.ahn.org　　　　　　　　　　　　　　　　　Type: Private

When you really feel like the pits visit The Western Pennsylvania Hospital. Based in Pittsburgh The Western Pennsylvania Hospital is a part of the West Penn Allegheny Health System. The 512-bed teaching hospital is affiliated with Clarion University Indiana University of Pennsylvania Pennsylvania State University and Temple University. It offers specialized services such as emergency medicine heart care breast disease treatment cancer treatment orthopedics and surgery (including microscopic surgery). Special facilities include an area burn center cancer treatment center and a hospice facility.

	Annual Growth	06/12	06/13	06/14	06/15	06/16
Sales ($ mil.)	18.5%	–	–	–	336.0	398.2
Net income ($ mil.)	107.3%	–	–	–	32.0	66.4
Market value ($ mil.)	–	–	–	–	–	–
Employees	–	–	–	–	–	37

WESTERN REFINING INC　　　　　　　　　　　　　　NYS: WNR

123 W. Mills Ave., Suite 200　　　　　　　　　CEO: Jeff A Stevens
El Paso, TX 79901　　　　　　　　　　　　　　CFO: Karen B Davis
Phone: 915 534-1400　　　　　　　　　　　　　　　　　　　　HR: –
Fax: –　　　　　　　　　　　　　　　　　　　　FYE: December 31
Web: www.wnr.com　　　　　　　　　　　　　　　　　Type: Public

It's the quality and volumes of its refined products that makes Western Refining a major player in the West. The independent oil refiner operates primarily in the Southwest region of the US. Western Refining's refineries (one in El Paso one in the Four Corners region of northern New Mexico and one in Minnesota) have a crude oil refining capacity of 246500 barrels per day. More than 90% of its refined products are made up of light transportation fuels including diesel and gasoline. It owns a wholesale division that complements the refining operations. Western Refining also owns about 260 retail outlets in the Southwest. In 2016 the company agreed to by acquired by Tesoro in a $6.4 billion deal.

	Annual Growth	12/11	12/12	12/13	12/14	12/15
Sales ($ mil.)	1.9%	9,071.0	9,503.1	10,086.1	15,153.6	9,787.0
Net income ($ mil.)	32.3%	132.7	398.9	276.0	559.9	406.8
Market value ($ mil.)	27.9%	1,245.1	2,641.0	3,973.1	3,539.4	3,337.0
Employees	19.5%	3,600	3,800	3,800	5,700	7,347

WESTERN REFINING LOGISTICS LP　　　　　　　　　NYS: WNRL

123 W. Mills Avenue, Suite 200　　　　　　　　　　　　　　CEO: –
El Paso, TX 79901　　　　　　　　　　　　　　　　　　　　CFO: –
Phone: 915 534-1400　　　　　　　　　　　　　　　　　　　　HR: –
Fax: –　　　　　　　　　　　　　　　　　　　　FYE: December 31
Web: www.wnrl.com　　　　　　　　　　　　　　　　　Type: Public

Western Refining Logistics holds the midstream assets of Western Refining. The company owns and operates 300 miles of crude oil pipelines and crude oil storage facilities with a capacity of almost 7 million barrels. Its pipeline and storage facilities serve Western Refining's two refineries in Texas and New Mexico. It also provides asphalt terminalling and processing services for Western Refining's asphalt plants in Arizona New Mexico and Texas. Western Refining formed Western Refining Logistics in 2013 as a limited partnership or an investment vehicle that is exempt from paying federal income tax. The company raised $303 million in its IPO which it will use to pay off Western Refining in exchange for the pipelines and storage facilities.

	Annual Growth	12/11	12/12	12/13	12/14	12/15
Sales ($ mil.)	424.7%	3.4	3.8	30.8	3,501.9	2,599.9
Net income ($ mil.)	–	(40.4)	(71.0)	(59.5)	71.8	63.6
Market value ($ mil.)	(2.6%)	–	–	1,224.6	1,443.8	1,161.2
Employees	–	–	–	–	850	780

WESTERN STATES FIRE PROTECTION COMPANY INC

7026 S TUCSON WAY　　　　　　　　　　　　　CEO: Gene Postma
CENTENNIAL, CO 801123921　　　　　　　　　　　　　　　　CFO: –
Phone: 303-792-0022　　　　　　　　　　　　　　　　　　　HR: –
Fax: –　　　　　　　　　　　　　　　　　　　　FYE: December 31
Web: www.wsfp.com　　　　　　　　　　　　　　　　Type: Private

Western States Fire Protection (WSFP) is sprinkling its own brand of safety west of the Mississippi. The company a division of APi Group installs water-based fire sprinklers and other fire suppression systems for the commercial residential and industrial markets primarily in the western US. It designs installs and maintains fire protection systems at defense gaming high-tech institutional medical processing and sports facilities. Specific projects include installing systems at the Colorado Convention Center and Microsoft's data storage facility in Washington. WSFP also manufactures fire sprinklers at its own fabrication workshops. The company was founded in 1985.

	Annual Growth	12/14	12/15	12/16	12/17	12/18
Sales ($ mil.)	7.3%	–	274.1	292.6	307.6	338.4
Net income ($ mil.)	18.1%	–	31.8	40.8	44.0	52.3
Market value ($ mil.)	–	–	–	–	–	–
Employees	–	–	–	–	–	1,429

WESTERN UNION CO　　　　　　　　　　　　　　　　NYS: WU

7001 East Belleview Avenue　　　　　　　　　　CEO: Hikmet Ersek
Denver, CO 80237　　　　　　　　　　　CFO: Rajesh K. (Raj) Agrawal
Phone: 866 405-5012　　　　　　　　　　　HR: Richard L. Williams
Fax: –　　　　　　　　　　　　　　　　　　　　FYE: December 31
Web: www.westernunion.com　　　　　　　　　　　　　Type: Public

Though the joy of receiving a singing telegram is mired in the dusty past of yesteryear you may still jump for joy at the receipt of a Western Union money transfer. The company provides in-person and electronic means to swiftly send remittances within and across country borders managing currency exchanges as needed. It achieves this with a global network of some 550000 agent locations in more than 200 countries and territories. Western Union agents work out of kiosks located in a variety of businesses including post offices banks and grocery stores. About 40% of its total sales comes from US.

	Annual Growth	12/14	12/15	12/16	12/17	12/18
Sales ($ mil.)	(0.1%)	5,607.2	5,483.7	5,422.9	5,524.3	5,589.9
Net income ($ mil.)	(0.0%)	852.4	837.8	253.2	(557.1)	851.9
Market value ($ mil.)	(1.2%)	7,901.9	7,901.9	9,582.9	8,387.2	7,526.9
Employees	4.7%	10,000	10,000	10,700	11,500	12,000

WESTERN WASHINGTON UNIVERSITY

516 HIGH ST
BELLINGHAM, WA 982255996
Phone: 360-650-3720
Fax: -
Web: www.wwu.edu

CEO: -
CFO: -
HR: -
FYE: June 30
Type: Private

If you're in the West and you're looking for a liberal arts education look no further than Western Washington University. The university is located in northwest Washington state and is one of a handful of state-funded four-year institutions of higher education in Washington. The school has an enrollment of about 15000 students; roughly 95% of those are undergraduate students. Western Washington University has a student-teacher ratio of roughly 21:1. The university has students from almost every other state and from three dozen other countries. Western which began as a teachers college accepting its first students in 1899 became a full university in 1977.

	Annual Growth	06/12	06/13	06/14	06/15	06/16
Sales ($ mil.)	2.4%	-	196.9	200.6	207.0	211.3
Net income ($ mil.)	39.4%	-	5.5	3.8	1.3	14.8
Market value ($ mil.)	-	-	-	-	-	-
Employees	-	-	-	-	-	466

WESTINGHOUSE AIR BRAKE TECHNOLOGIES CORPORATION NYSE: WAB

1001 Air Brake Ave.
Wilmerding PA 15148
Phone: 412-825-1000
Fax: 412-825-1019
Web: www.wabtec.com

CEO: Rafael O Santana
CFO: Patrick D Dugan
HR: -
FYE: December 31
Type: Public

More powerful than a speeding locomotive Westinghouse Air Brake Technologies pulls out all the stops. The company (dba Wabtec) manufactures braking equipment and other parts for locomotives freight cars and passenger railcars. Products made by Wabtec's Freight group include air brake systems draft gears hand brakes slack adjusters heat exchanges railroad electronics and monitoring and control equipment. Wabtec's Transit business supplies replacement parts and repair services to operators of passenger transit systems. Major customers include Electro-Motive Diesel General Electric Transportation Union Pacific and CSX Transportation. North America generates almost 70% of sales.

WESTLAKE CHEMICAL CORP NYS: WLK

2801 Post Oak Boulevard, Suite 600
Houston, TX 77056
Phone: 713 960-9111
Fax: -
Web: www.westlake.com

CEO: Albert Chao
CFO: M. Steven (Steve) Bender
HR: M Joel Gray
FYE: December 31
Type: Public

Westlake Chemical produces petrochemicals and plastics. Its plastics offerings include polyvinyl chloride (PVC) and polyethylene both of which are common in packaging products and grocery bags. Its PVC pipe products are sold under the North American Pipe and Royal Building Products brands. Westlake also produces the chlorine used in PVC as well as caustic soda. Its petrochemicals include ethylene ethyl benzene and styrene?which are building blocks in plastics. Westlake produces about 40 billion pounds of product each year and is the third largest producer of both PVC and chlor-alkali in the world. TTWF which is controlled by the Chao family (Westlake's founders) owns more than 70% of Westlake. The US accounts for about 70% of company's total sales.

	Annual Growth	12/14	12/15	12/16	12/17	12/18
Sales ($ mil.)	18.3%	4,415.4	4,463.3	5,075.5	8,041.0	8,635.0
Net income ($ mil.)	10.1%	678.5	646.0	398.9	1,304.0	996.0
Market value ($ mil.)	2.0%	7,848.1	6,978.4	7,192.9	13,685.7	8,500.7
Employees	25.7%	3,550	4,225	8,870	8,800	8,870

WESTMINSTER COLLEGE

1840 S 1300 E
SALT LAKE CITY, UT 841053697
Phone: 801-484-7651
Fax: -
Web: www.westminstercollege.edu

CEO: -
CFO: -
HR: -
FYE: June 30
Type: Private

Westminster College is a private liberal arts school that offers more than 70 academic programs including undergraduate bachelor of arts (BA) and bachelor of science (BS) degrees as well as select graduate degrees. Its programs are offered through four schools devoted to arts and sciences business education and nursing and health sciences. The school has an enrollment of approximately 2300 undergraduate students and 800 graduate students and has more than 400 full- and part-time faculty members. Westminster College was founded in 1875 as a preparatory school called the Salt Lake Collegiate Institute. It first offered college classes in 1897 (as Sheldon Jackson College) and adopted its current name in 1902.

	Annual Growth	06/14	06/15	06/16	06/17	06/18
Sales ($ mil.)	(6.6%)	-	96.6	64.9	76.8	78.7
Net income ($ mil.)	-	-	(0.6)	(3.1)	9.8	11.7
Market value ($ mil.)	-	-	-	-	-	-
Employees	-	-	-	-	-	500

WESTMORELAND COAL CO NBB: WLBA Q

9540 South Maroon Circle, Suite 300
Englewood, CO 80112
Phone: 855 922-6463
Fax: -
Web: www.westmoreland.com

CEO: Kevin A. Paprzycki
CFO: Gary Kohn
HR: -
FYE: December 31
Type: Public

Westmoreland Coal produces more than 53 million tons of coal annually from mines in Montana New Mexico North Dakota Texas Wyoming Ohio North Carolina Saskatchewan and Alberta. It controls more than 1222 million tons of proved and probable coal reserves. Most of the company's coal is sold to power producers. Some of Westmoreland's customers maintain power generation facilities adjacent to its mines. In addition to its coal business Westmoreland owns North Carolina's Roanoke Valley (or ROVA) coal-fired power plants which have a capacity of 230 MW and supply power under long-term agreements with Dominion Virginia Power.

	Annual Growth	12/13	12/14	12/15	12/16	12/17
Sales ($ mil.)	19.7%	674.7	1,116.0	1,411.0	1,478.0	1,384.6
Net income ($ mil.)	-	-	(4.7)	(172.3)	(203.3)	(27.1)	(71.3)
Market value ($ mil.)	(50.0%)	362.1	623.4	110.4	331.7	22.7
Employees	21.1%	1,370	3,440	3,248	3,200	2,950

WESTMORELAND RESOURCE PARTNERS LP NBB: WMLP Q

9540 South Maroon Circle, Suite 300
Englewood, CO 80112
Phone: 855 922-6463
Fax: -
Web: www. westmorelandmlp.com

CEO: Martin Purvis
CFO: -
HR: -
FYE: December 31
Type: Public

Oxford Resource Partners strives to get its customers steamed. An operator and acquirer of surface coal mines the company produces steam coal used by power plants and other energy producers to fire steam boilers. It owns and operates about 19 surface mines in the Northern Appalachia region and the Illinois Basin. In 2009 the company which has assets that include more than 91 million tons of proved and probable reserves produced 5.8 million tons of coal. It serves markets in Illinois Indiana Kentucky Ohio Pennsylvania and West Virginia and has counted AEP Duke Energy and East Kentucky Power as major customers. Formed in 2008 Oxford Resource Partners filed an initial public offering (IPO) in 2010.

	Annual Growth	12/14	12/15	12/16	12/17	12/18
Sales ($ mil.)	(11.0%)	-	384.7	349.3	315.6	271.0
Net income ($ mil.)	-	(4.4)	(33.7)	(31.6)	(31.8)	(139.2)
Market value ($ mil.)	(41.4%)	22.9	91.5	129.1	63.8	2.7
Employees	(1.1%)	602	658	640	570	576

WESTWOOD HOLDINGS GROUP, INC.   NYS: WHG

200 Crescent Court, Suite 1200 — CEO: Brian O Casey
Dallas, TX 75201 — CFO: Tiffany B. Kice
Phone: 214 756-6900 — HR: –
Fax: – — FYE: December 31
Web: www.westwoodgroup.com — Type: Public

Westwood Holdings Group provides investment management services to institutions mutual funds and high-net-worth clients. The asset manager operates through its subsidiaries. Westwood Trust handles trust custody and account management for companies institutions and high-net-worth individuals. Westwood Management is the group's institutional investment management unit overseeing accounts for corporations municipalities and charitable organizations with at least $10 million in investable assets. The firm is also the administrator of the Westwood family of mutual funds WHG Funds. Westwood Holdings Group boasts around $21 billion in assets under management.

	Annual Growth	12/14	12/15	12/16	12/17	12/18
Sales ($ mil.)	1.9%	113.2	130.9	123.0	133.8	122.3
Net income ($ mil.)	(0.5%)	27.2	27.1	22.6	20.0	26.8
Market value ($ mil.)	(13.9%)	550.5	463.9	534.2	589.6	302.8
Employees	8.8%	130	168	174	181	182

WET SEAL, INC. (THE)   NMS: WTSL

26972 Burbank — CEO: –
Foothill Ranch, CA 92610 — CFO: –
Phone: 949 699-3900 — HR: –
Fax: – — FYE: February 1/
Web: www.wetsealinc.com — Type: Public

Pubescent mall rats are likely to get hooked at The Wet Seal. The company operates about 530 shops across the US and Puerto Rico (down from some 600 stores in 2004) that sell moderate- to value-priced casual clothing and accessories under brand names and private labels. Most of the 475 Wet Seal stores are mall-based and target teenage girls. A contemporary fashion Arden B chain (11% of sales) runs about 55 stores that cater to women age 24 to 34 years old. The Wet Seal also sells apparel through its two banner websites. Amid intense competition from value-priced fast-fashion chains such as Forever 21 and H&M and slumping sales and profits the company is cutting jobs and trimming its store count.

	Annual Growth	01/10	01/11	01/12*	02/13	02/14
Sales ($ mil.)	(1.4%)	560.9	581.2	620.1	580.4	530.1
Net income ($ mil.)	–	93.4	12.6	15.1	(113.2)	(38.4)
Market value ($ mil.)	(8.1%)	283.7	299.0	307.4	234.6	202.4
Employees	4.8%	6,148	6,982	7,283	7,012	7,413

*Fiscal year change

WEX INC   NYS: WEX

1 Hancock Street — CEO: Melissa D. Smith
Portland, ME 04101 — CFO: Roberto R. Simon
Phone: 207 773-8171 — HR: –
Fax: – — FYE: December 31
Web: www.wexinc.com — Type: Public

WEX (formerly Wright Express) provides payment processing and information management services to commercial and government vehicle fleets through a network that tracks purchases made on fleet charge cards throughout the US Canada Australia New Zealand and Europe. The company provides clients with transaction data analysis tools and purchase control capabilities for every vehicle in their fleets. Data collected at the point of sale include expenditures lists of items purchased odometer readings and driver vehicle and vendor identification. Around 12.5 million vehicles use WEX for fleet management. The company also offers health and employee benefits payment platforms in Brazil and corporate purchasing and payment products.

	Annual Growth	12/14	12/15	12/16	12/17	12/18
Sales ($ mil.)	16.2%	817.6	854.6	1,018.5	1,250.5	1,492.6
Net income ($ mil.)	(4.5%)	202.2	111.3	60.6	160.3	168.3
Market value ($ mil.)	9.1%	4,266.3	3,812.6	4,813.2	6,091.1	6,040.6
Employees	16.6%	2,004	2,265	2,600	3,300	3,700

WEXFORD HEALTH SOURCES, INC.

501 HOLIDAY DR FOSTER — CEO: –
PITTSBURGH, PA 15220 — CFO: John Froehlich
Phone: 888-633-6468 — HR: Elaine Gedman
Fax: – — FYE: December 31
Web: www.wexfordhealth.com — Type: Private

Wexford Health Sources provides health care services to inmates doing time in the big house. The company has contracts at more than 100 government-run facilities including county jails state and federal prisons juvenile detention centers substance abuse treatment centers psychiatric hospitals and correctional centers for sex offenders. Wexford Health staffs professionals that perform medical and mental health care dentistry pharmacy services and administration services and serves about 90000 inmates and patients through contracts in five states — Illinois Mississippi Ohio Pennsylvania and West Virginia. Wexford Health was founded in 1992.

	Annual Growth	12/0-1	12/00	12/01	12/05	12/08
Sales ($ mil.)	4.3%	–	–	119.4	160.6	160.0
Net income ($ mil.)	43.8%	–	–	1.3	6.4	16.6
Market value ($ mil.)	–	–	–	–	–	–
Employees	–	–	–	–	–	1,525

WEYCO GROUP, INC   NMS: WEYS

333 W. Estabrook Boulevard, P.O. Box 1188 — CEO: Thomas W. (Tom) Florsheim
Milwaukee, WI 53201 — CFO: John F. Wittkowske
Phone: 414 908-1600 — HR: –
Fax: – — FYE: December 31
Web: www.weycogroup.com — Type: Public

Weyco Group has him — or at least his feet — covered. The company imports men's footwear including mid-priced leather dress and casual shoes sold under the Florsheim Nunn Bush and Stacy Adams brands. It also offers casual footwear for women and children under the BOGS Rafters and Umi labels. Weyco sells its shoes to more than 10000 shoe clothing and department stores. The company also operates about two dozen Florsheim retail stores in the US and markets shoes online. In addition it licenses the Stacy Adams name for men's clothing and accessories. Founded in 1906 as Weyenberg Shoe Manufacturing the company changed its name to Weyco Group in 1990 and stopped manufacturing shoes in 2003.

	Annual Growth	12/14	12/15	12/16	12/17	12/18
Sales ($ mil.)	(1.8%)	320.5	320.6	296.9	283.7	298.4
Net income ($ mil.)	1.9%	19.0	18.2	16.5	16.5	20.5
Market value ($ mil.)	(0.4%)	298.4	269.1	314.8	298.9	293.4
Employees	(0.6%)	640	662	661	626	626

WEYERHAEUSER CO   NYS: WY

220 Occidental Avenue South — CEO: Doyle R. Simons
Seattle, WA 98104-7800 — CFO: Russell S. Hagen
Phone: 206 539-3000 — HR: Denise M. Merle
Fax: – — FYE: December 31
Web: www.weyerhaeuser.com — Type: Public

Forest products company Weyerhaeuser produces a variety of softwood lumber and other building materials in North America. One of the world's largest private owners of timberland the company harvests trees for its products from 12 million acres of forest that it owns in the US and 14 million acres that it manages in Canada. Exports account for about 15% of the company's sales. Incorporated in 1900 as Weyerhaeuser Timber Co. the company operates as a real estate investment trust (REIT) because of its vast land holdings. The company merged with rival Plum Creek in a deal worth $10 billion bringing together the two biggest owners of timberland in the US; shortly after that deal Weyerhaeuser spun off its cellulose fibers business for $2.5 billion.

	Annual Growth	12/14	12/15	12/16	12/17	12/18
Sales ($ mil.)	0.2%	7,403.0	7,082.0	6,365.0	7,196.0	7,476.0
Net income ($ mil.)	(20.0%)	1,826.0	506.0	1,027.0	582.0	748.0
Market value ($ mil.)	(11.7%)	26,788.0	22,376.8	22,458.9	26,317.7	16,316.1
Employees	(7.7%)	12,800	12,600	10,400	9,300	9,300

WGBH EDUCATIONAL FOUNDATION

1 GUEST ST
BOSTON, MA 021352104
Phone: 617-300-2000
Fax: –
Web: www.wgbh.org

CEO: Jonathan C Abbott
CFO: –
HR: –
FYE: June 30
Type: Private

Public broadcasting forms the basis of this organization. WGBH Educational Foundation owns and operates the WGBH public TV and radio stations that serve the Boston area. Its television operations include several digital channels (WGBH Create WGBH World) as well as an on-demand service. WGBH is also one of the largest producers of programming for the Public Broadcasting Service including such shows as Antiques Roadshow Arthur Curious George Frontline Masterpiece and Nova. The foundation gets funding from corporate grants and individual contributions as well as from PBS and the Corporation for Public Broadcasting.

	Annual Growth	08/07	08/08	08/09	08/10*	06/14
Sales ($ mil.)	(5.8%)	–	278.8	190.9	141.4	195.4
Net income ($ mil.)	(18.7%)	–	54.7	(18.3)	(45.9)	15.8
Market value ($ mil.)	–	–	–	–	–	–
Employees	–	–	–	–	–	1,100

*Fiscal year change

WGI HEAVY MINERALS INCORPORATED
TORONTO: WG

810 Sherman Ave.
Coeur d'Alene ID 83814
Phone: 208-666-6000
Fax: 208-666-4000
Web: www.wgiheavyminerals.com

CEO: Greg S Emerson
CFO: Persela Reynolds
HR: –
FYE: December 31
Type: Public

OK we get it. They're heavy you're strong. WGI Heavy Minerals produces industrial minerals chiefly garnet but also ilmenite leucoxene rutile and zircon. The company markets these industrial minerals that are sourced primarily from India. It also produces industrial-grade garnet from mining and processing operations in Germany and the US (in Idaho). Subsidiary International Waterjet Parts makes replacement parts for ultra-high pressure waterjet machine tool systems. In 2012 Opta Minerals acquired 94% of WGI and plans to buy the remaining shares.

WGL HOLDINGS, INC.

1000 MAINE AVE SW
WASHINGTON, DC 200243494
Phone: 703-750-2000
Fax: –
Web: www.wglholdings.com

CEO: Terry D. McCallister
CFO: Vincent L. Ammann
HR: –
FYE: September 30
Type: Private

WGL Holdings owners of the regulated Washington Gas Light Company sells natural gas to more than 1 million customers in the District of Columbia Maryland and Virginia. It has about 600 miles of transmission mains more than 13000 miles of distribution mains and some 12500 miles of distribution lines. The company's unregulated segment also provides energy marketing clean-energy products and services and midstream asset management. In July 2018 WGL Holdings was bought by Canada-based AltaGas for $6.4 billion deal.

	Annual Growth	09/14	09/15	09/16	09/17	09/18
Sales ($ mil.)	(4.2%)	–	2,659.8	2,349.6	2,354.7	2,341.8
Net income ($ mil.)	(45.8%)	–	132.6	168.4	177.9	21.1
Market value ($ mil.)	–	–	–	–	–	–
Employees	–	–	–	–	–	1,586

WHALLEY COMPUTER ASSOCIATES, INC.

1 WHALLEY WAY
SOUTHWICK, MA 010779222
Phone: 413-569-4200
Fax: –
Web: www.wca.com

CEO: –
CFO: –
HR: Nicole Dejesus
FYE: December 31
Type: Private

Whalley Computer Associates (WCA) provides information technology products distribution consulting and technical support services primarily in Massachusets. The company sells and distributes computer hardware software and peripherals from such vendors as Hewlett-Packard 3Com and Cisco. Other services include systems integration maintenance network design project management and remote monitoring. WCA's customers come from a variety of industries including manufacturing consumer goods and retail as well as the public sector. The company was founded in 1979 by president John Whalley.

	Annual Growth	12/03	12/04	12/05	12/06	12/07
Sales ($ mil.)	14.9%	–	67.2	73.4	87.8	101.9
Net income ($ mil.)	22.9%	–	2.4	3.0	3.9	4.5
Market value ($ mil.)	–	–	–	–	–	–
Employees	–	–	–	–	–	104

WHATABURGER RESTAURANTS LP

300 Concord Plaza
San Antonio TX 78216
Phone: 210-476-6000
Fax: 212-354-8113
Web: www.whitecase.com

CEO: Preston Atkinson
CFO: Ed Nelson
HR: –
FYE: September 30
Type: Private

Fans of this chain know they can get quite a burger at the place with the orange and white roof. Whataburger Restaurants is a leading regional hamburger chain with nearly 700 outlets in Texas and about 10 other states in the South and Southwest. The restaurants are open 24 hours a day and serve burgers and fries along with chicken sandwiches salads and a breakfast menu. About 600 of the restaurants are company-owned. Loyal Whataburger fans can also don the company's line of apparel sporting the chain's logo. The late Harmon Dobson founded the family-owned chain in Corpus Christi Texas in 1950 with a single roadside burger stand.

WHEATON FRANCISCAN SERVICES, INC.

400 W RIVER WOODS PKWY
GLENDALE, WI 532121060
Phone: 414-465-3000
Fax: –

CEO: John D Oliverio
CFO: –
HR: –
FYE: June 30
Type: Private

Wheaton Franciscan Services Inc. (WFSI) is the not-for-profit parent company for more than 100 health care housing and social service organizations in Colorado Illinois Iowa and Wisconsin. Also known as Wheaton Franciscan Healthcare WFSI operates about 15 hospitals including Affinity Health System Rush Oak Park Hospital and United Hospital System with more than 1600 beds total. WFSI also includes long-term care centers home health agencies and physician offices. Its Franciscan Ministries division provides affordable housing units including assisted-living facilities and low-income dwellings. The health system is sponsored by The Franciscan Sisters Daughters of the Sacred Hearts of Jesus and Mary.

	Annual Growth	06/11	06/12	06/13	06/14	06/15
Sales ($ mil.)	1.6%	–	1,723.5	1,763.4	1,754.2	1,809.2
Net income ($ mil.)	–	–	(112.6)	177.5	128.7	18.6
Market value ($ mil.)	–	–	–	–	–	–
Employees	–	–	–	–	–	18,000

WHEATON VAN LINES INC

8010 CASTLETON RD
INDIANAPOLIS, IN 462502005
Phone: 317-849-7900
Fax: –
Web: www.wheatonworldwide.com

CEO: Mark Kirschner
CFO: –
HR: –
FYE: December 31
Type: Private

Wheaton Van Lines which operates under the Wheaton World Wide Moving and Bekins Van Lines brands provides interstate and international transportation and relocation services for individuals businesses and government agencies. Wheaton also provides relocation services for US military personnel. The company's specialties include transportation of medical equipment computers new furniture store fixtures and Steinway pianos. Wheaton Van Lines operates through a network of about 370 agents in the US. The company is owned by its employees.

	Annual Growth	12/05	12/06	12/07	12/08	12/09
Sales ($ mil.)	(4.4%)	–	–	104.2	99.3	95.2
Net income ($ mil.)	9.0%	–	–	6.3	7.8	7.5
Market value ($ mil.)	–	–	–	–	–	–
Employees	–	–	–	–	–	725

WHEELER REAL ESTATE INVESTMENT TRUST INC   NAS: WHLR

2529 Virginia Beach Blvd., Suite 200
Virginia Beach, VA 23452
Phone: 757 627-9088
Fax: –
Web: www.whlr.us

CEO: David Kelly
CFO: Wilkes J Graham
HR: –
FYE: December 31
Type: Public

Wheeler Real Estate Investment Trust develops and manages shopping centers and other real estate properties. The REIT owns eight properties including five shopping centers two stand-alone buildings and one office building. Most are in Virginia but the company plans to target the Mid-Atlantic Southeast and Southwest. It will develop and manage strip centers and free-standing retail properties with a specific focus on revamping properties in secondary and tertiary markets. Wheeler Real Estate Investment Trust will be managed by WHLR Management a company owned by company founder chairman and president Jon Wheeler. The REIT was formed in early 2011 and filed to go public later that year.

	Annual Growth	12/14	12/15	12/16	12/17	12/18
Sales ($ mil.)	39.9%	17.2	27.7	44.2	58.5	65.7
Net income ($ mil.)	–	(10.6)	(17.5)	(11.2)	(12.1)	(16.5)
Market value ($ mil.)	(36.0%)	–	–	223.5	191.2	91.6
Employees	1.0%	48	61	55	53	50

WHEELING & LAKE ERIE RAILWAY COMPANY

100 1ST ST SE
BREWSTER, OH 446131202
Phone: 330-767-3401
Fax: –

CEO: Jane Villard
CFO: Michael D. Mokodean
HR: –
FYE: June 30
Type: Private

Wheeling & Lake Erie Railway operates over a network of about 950 miles of track between the Ohio River and Lake Erie passing through parts of Maryland Ohio Pennsylvania and West Virginia. The company's system links the coal fields of West Virginia (Wheeling) with industrial Cleveland and its docks (Lake Erie). In addition to coal the railroad hauls cargo including aggregates iron ore steel products agricultural products plastic resins. Wheeling & Lake Erie Railway owns some 575 miles of track; trackage rights over other railroads account for the rest of the company's network. The railroad traces its roots back to 1871 but took its current form in 1990.

	Annual Growth	06/03	06/04	06/05	06/06	06/14
Sales ($ mil.)	(25.3%)	–	1,860.8	61.6	73.0	100.7
Net income ($ mil.)	180.2%	–	0.0	6.4	7.7	17.8
Market value ($ mil.)	–	–	–	–	–	–
Employees	–	–	–	–	–	415

WHEELING-NISSHIN, INC.

400 PENN ST
FOLLANSBEE, WV 260371412
Phone: 304-527-2800
Fax: –
Web: www.wheeling-nisshin.com

CEO: Tetsuhiko Okano
CFO: Patstuzo Shiotsuka
HR: –
FYE: December 31
Type: Private

Wheeling-Nisshin a subsidiary of Nisshin Steel produces a variety of hot-dip coated steels such as stainless steel. The company's output includes 400000 tons produced at its aluminizing and galvanizing line facility and 300000 tons produced at its continuous galvanizing line facility. Both of the facilities are located at the company's headquarters site in West Virginia. Its primary customers are in the automotive appliance and construction industries. Wheeling-Nisshin was founded in 1986. It had been a joint venture between Nisshin and US steel producer Wheeling Pitt (now operating as Severstal Wheeling) until the Japanese steel company bought out its partner in early 2008.

	Annual Growth	12/10	12/11	12/12	12/13	12/14
Sales ($ mil.)	23.5%	–	–	–	391.2	483.1
Net income ($ mil.)	100.5%	–	–	–	2.9	5.8
Market value ($ mil.)	–	–	–	–	–	–
Employees	–	–	–	–	–	175

WHIRLPOOL CORP   NYS: WHR

2000 North M-63
Benton Harbor, MI 49022-2692
Phone: 269 923-5000
Fax: –
Web: www.whirlpoolcorp.com

CEO: Marc R. Bitzer
CFO: James W. (Jim) Peters
HR: Kimberly Thompson
FYE: December 31
Type: Public

With brand names recognized by just about anyone who has ever separated dark colors from light Whirlpool is the world's top home appliance maker. It sells around 70 million laundry appliances refrigerators and freezers cooking appliances dishwashers and compressors each year under a bevy of brand names including Whirlpool Amana KitchenAid Maytag Jenn-Air and Roper. The company markets and distributes these major home appliances in North America Latin America EMEA (Europe the Middle East and Africa) and Asia. It has manufacturing operations in more than a dozen countries. Major customers include retailers Lowe's Home Depot and Best Buy.

	Annual Growth	12/14	12/15	12/16	12/17	12/18
Sales ($ mil.)	1.4%	19,872.0	20,891.0	20,718.0	21,253.0	21,037.0
Net income ($ mil.)	–	650.0	783.0	888.0	350.0	(183.0)
Market value ($ mil.)	(13.8%)	12,399.4	9,399.7	11,633.3	10,793.0	6,839.7
Employees	(2.1%)	100,000	97,000	93,000	92,000	92,000

WHITE COUNTY MEDICAL CENTER

3214 E RACE AVE
SEARCY, AR 721434810
Phone: 501-268-6121
Fax: –
Web: www.unity-health.org

CEO: Ray Montgomery
CFO: Stuart Hill
HR: Katye Ledbetter
FYE: September 30
Type: Private

If you're sick in Searcy you may want to visit White County Medical Center (WCMC). The organization provides health care to Central Arkansas' residents. It has about 440 licensed inpatient beds on two hospital campuses (WCMC North and WCMC South) as well as a number of outpatient surgery centers primary care clinics and a retirement community called River Oaks Village. The WCMC South campus features an inpatient rehabilitation center that helps patients recover from injury and illness as well as a long-term acute care hospital for patients needing extended general care. In addition WCMC provides home health care services and runs a training program for certified nurse assistants. WCMC operates under the Unity Health brand.

	Annual Growth	09/13	09/14	09/15	09/16	09/17
Sales ($ mil.)	6.7%	–	188.6	198.1	218.2	229.1
Net income ($ mil.)	8.1%	–	18.6	10.0	16.1	23.6
Market value ($ mil.)	–	–	–	–	–	–
Employees	–	–	–	–	–	3,010

WHITE MOUNTAINS INSURANCE GROUP LTD.   NYSE: WTM

80 S. Main St.
Hanover NH 03755-2053
Phone: 603-640-2200
Fax: 603-643-4592
Web: www.whitemountains.com

CEO: John J Byrne
CFO: Danielle Courchaine
HR: –
FYE: December 31
Type: Public

Incorporated in Bermuda White Mountains Insurance Group enjoys the island's tax-mild climate but slogs out the winters from its corporate headquarters in New Hampshire. The company provides insurance and reinsurance products and services through its US operating office's two main divisions: majority-owned OneBeacon Insurance (specialty and commercial property/casualty policies sold through independent agents in the US) and Sirius Group (domestic and international property/casualty insurance and reinsurance). In 2011 the company sold its Esurance unit (personal auto insurance sold online) to Allstate in a deal worth about $1 billion.

WHITE RIVER CAPITAL INC.   NYSE AMEX: RVR

1445 Brookville Way Ste. I
Indianapolis IN 46239
Phone: 317-806-2166
Fax: 317-806-2167
Web: www.whiterivercap.com

CEO: John M Eggemeyer
CFO: Martin J Szumski
HR: –
FYE: December 31
Type: Public

White River Capital is a holding company that specializes in auto finance. Subsidiary Coast Credit offers subprime auto financing in more than 20 states. The company acquires the subprime receivables from franchise and independent auto dealers. Another unit Union Acceptance oversees a portfolio of non-prime automobile receivables. In 2005 UAC was bankrupt and stockholders were looking for a way to squeak out value in their investment. The shareholders agreed to exchange UAC for shares of White River. After the swap White River bought the similar yet more successful Coast Credit. The holding-company-hat-trick allowed UAC to carry its business forward even after it declared bankruptcy in 2002.

WHITE RIVER HEALTH SYSTEM, INC.

1710 HARRISON ST
BATESVILLE, AR 725017303
Phone: 870-262-1200
Fax: –
Web: www.whiteriverhealthsystem.com

CEO: –
CFO: –
HR: –
FYE: September 30
Type: Private

White River Health System offers health care services to residents of north central Arkansas. The not-for-profit organization operates two hospitals the flagship White River Medical Center and acute care facility Stone County Medical Center which provides health care services to rural communities. Combined the two hospitals have about 225 beds and provide a range of emergency surgical medical and diagnostic services. The system also includes outpatient facilities primary care and specialty physician offices long-term care facilities for the elderly and those unable to live independently.

	Annual Growth	09/14	09/15	09/16	09/17	09/18
Sales ($ mil.)	8.2%	–	183.7	185.4	205.0	232.6
Net income ($ mil.)	(54.0%)	–	7.3	8.4	1.1	0.7
Market value ($ mil.)	–	–	–	–	–	–
Employees	–	–	–	–	–	1,500

WHITEGLOVE HEALTH INC.

5300 Bee Cave Rd. Bldg. I Ste. 100
Austin TX 78746
Phone: 512-329-9223
Fax: 512-329-8281
Web: www.whiteglove.com

CEO: Nick Balog
CFO: William J Kerley
HR: –
FYE: December 31
Type: Private

You've heard of doctors making house calls but what about nurses? WhiteGlove House Call provides patients with mobile primary and chronic care including physicals lab work vaccines generic and over-the-counter medications and "well-kits" (i.e. chicken noodle soup and Kleenex) delivered by nurse practitioners. Unlike similar companies WhiteGlove does not file insurance claims. Instead it offers services via membership to employers and the self-insured (often as a benefit of high-deductible plans) as well as through insurance firms like Aetna Humana and UnitedHealth. It operates in major markets in Texas Massachusetts and Arizona. WhiteGlove was founded in 2006.

WHITEHEAD INSTITUTE FOR BIOMEDICAL RESEARCH

455 MAIN ST
CAMBRIDGE, MA 021421025
Phone: 617-258-5000
Fax: –
Web: www.wi.mit.edu

CEO: –
CFO: –
HR: Dilly Wilson
FYE: June 30
Type: Private

The Whitehead Institute for Biomedical Research blazes new trails in bioscience. The organization funded by both the public and private sectors investigates such diseases as Parkinson's and cancer and dives into the depths of biology genomics and genetics to gain new understanding about disease and health. The Whitehead Institute contributed to the international effort to map the human genome and is actively researching stem cells. Other achievements include discovering a system for multiplying adult stem cells and creating the first genetically defined human cancer cell. The enterprise draws researchers from nearby MIT (with which it is affiliated in its teaching activities) and from all over the world.

	Annual Growth	06/09	06/10	06/13	06/15	06/18
Sales ($ mil.)	0.1%	–	67.2	71.6	74.0	68.0
Net income ($ mil.)	–	–	(9.5)	(1.2)	(1.9)	22.3
Market value ($ mil.)	–	–	–	–	–	–
Employees	–	–	–	–	–	550

WHITESTONE REIT   NYS: WSR

2600 South Gessner, Suite 500
Houston, TX 77063
Phone: 713 827-9595
Fax: 713 465-8847
Web: www.whitestonereit.com

CEO: James C. Mastandrea
CFO: David K. Holeman
HR: –
FYE: December 31
Type: Public

Whitestone REIT is out to make a name for itself in real estate. The self-managed real estate investment trust owns leases and operates around 70 retail office and warehouse properties in Texas (Houston is the company's largest market) Illinois and Arizona totaling 6 million sq. ft. Whitestone focuses on what it calls community-centered properties or high-visibility properties in established or developing culturally diverse neighborhoods. It recruits retail grocery financial services and other tenants to its Whitestone branded commercial centers. Some of its top tenants include Safeway Dollar Tree Wells Fargo Walgreens University of Phoenix and Alamo Drafthouse.

	Annual Growth	12/14	12/15	12/16	12/17	12/18
Sales ($ mil.)	13.4%	72.4	93.4	104.4	126.0	119.9
Net income ($ mil.)	29.6%	7.6	6.7	7.9	8.3	21.4
Market value ($ mil.)	(5.1%)	601.0	477.7	572.0	573.2	487.7
Employees	4.9%	81	95	106	103	98

WHITEWAVE FOODS COMPANY

12002 AIRPORT WAY
BROOMFIELD, CO 800212546
Phone: 303-635-4500
Fax: –
Web: www.whitewave.com

CEO: Gregg L. Engles
CFO: Greg S. Christenson
HR: Thomas N. Zanetich
FYE: December 31
Type: Private

WhiteWave Foods rides a wave of dietary changes as consumers seek alternatives to conventional foods. The company is best known for its refrigerated Silk soymilk in the US and Alpro brand soy products in Europe. WhiteWave also produces organic dairy products under the Horizon Organic label and dairy related foods including International Delight coffee creamers and LAND O'LAKES-branded creamers and dairy dessert toppings (licensed from dairy co-op Land O'Lakes). WhiteWave products are sold through natural food and grocery stores as well as mass merchandisers and restaurants and food service businesses in the US and Canada and parts of Europe. WhiteWave has been part of French dairy giant Danone since 2017.

	Annual Growth	12/11	12/12	12/13	12/14	12/15
Sales ($ mil.)	23.3%	–	–	2,542.1	3,436.6	3,866.3
Net income ($ mil.)	30.4%	–	–	99.0	140.2	168.4
Market value ($ mil.)	–	–	–	–	–	–
Employees	–	–	–	–	–	5,800

WHITING PETROLEUM CORP

NYS: WLL

1700 Lincoln Street, Suite 4700
Denver, CO 80203-4547
Phone: 303 837-1661
Fax: 303 861-4023
Web: www.whiting.com

CEO: Bradley J. (Brad) Holly
CFO: Michael J. Stevens
HR: Heather M Duncan
FYE: December 31
Type: Public

Focusing on US onshore properties Whiting Petroleum is attracted to the lure of oil and gas plays. The company engages in oil and natural gas exploration and production activities mainly in the North and Central Rocky Mountains regions in North Dakota and Colorado. It boasts reported estimated proved reserves of 615 million barrels of oil equivalent (of which some two-thirds is oil). Its average daily production is in the region of 130 thousand barrels of oil equivalent per day. The oil and gas company sells oil and gas production to end users marketers and other purchasers that have access to nearby pipeline facilities.

	Annual Growth	12/14	12/15	12/16	12/17	12/18
Sales ($ mil.)	(9.4%)	3,085.1	2,050.8	1,285.0	1,481.4	2,081.4
Net income ($ mil.)	51.6%	64.8	(2,219.2)	(1,339.1)	(1,237.6)	342.5
Market value ($ mil.)	(8.9%)	3,003.6	859.2	1,094.0	2,410.2	2,065.2
Employees	(12.4%)	1,282	1,200	850	830	755

WHITMAN COLLEGE

345 BOYER AVE
WALLA WALLA, WA 993622083
Phone: 509-527-5111
Fax: –
Web: www.whitman.edu

CEO: –
CFO: –
HR: –
FYE: June 30
Type: Private

Students attending this Walla Walla school hope to get more Bing Bang for their educational buck. Whitman College located in Walla Walla Washington is an independent co-educational non-sectarian undergraduate school. It offers bachelor's degrees in more than 40 liberal arts and sciences areas including education environmental studies biology English music mathematics and religion. Whitman College also offers extensive study abroad programs. It has about 1500 students and a 9:1 student-to-faculty ratio. About two-thirds of Whitman students live on campus.

	Annual Growth	06/13	06/14	06/15	06/16	06/18
Sales ($ mil.)	2.0%	–	81.8	80.5	87.8	88.7
Net income ($ mil.)	(9.1%)	–	68.7	7.2	(40.2)	46.9
Market value ($ mil.)	–	–	–	–	–	–
Employees	–	–	–	–	–	1,095

WHITNEY MUSEUM OF AMERICAN ART

945 MADISON AVE
NEW YORK, NY 100212790
Phone: 212-249-1749
Fax: –
Web: www.whitney.org

CEO: –
CFO: Alice Pratt Burns
HR: Angie Salerno
FYE: June 30
Type: Private

The Whitney Museum of American Art houses some 12000 works of 20th- and 21st-century American art including paintings sculptures drawings photographs and prints by about 2000 artists. It contains the entirety of Edward Hopper's artistic estate as well as pieces by artists such as Georgia O'Keefe Kiki Smith Louise Nevelson and Andy Warhol. The museum also offers public programs including lectures seminars and performances. The museum is housed in a large granite building at the corner of Madison Avenue and 75th Street designed by the Hungarian-born Bauhaus-trained architect Marcel Breuer. Whitney Museum of American Art was founded in 1930 by sculptor and art patron Gertrude Vanderbilt Whitney.

	Annual Growth	06/07	06/08	06/09	06/10	06/13
Sales ($ mil.)	–	–	(1,168.6)	28.1	33.9	91.3
Net income ($ mil.)	–	–	–	0.0	(8.2)	50.8
Market value ($ mil.)	–	–	–	–	–	–
Employees	–	–	–	–	–	167

WHOLE FOODS MARKET, INC.

550 BOWIE ST
AUSTIN, TX 787034644
Phone: 512-477-4455
Fax: –
Web: www.wholefoodsmarket.com

CEO: John P. Mackey
CFO: Keith Manbeck
HR: –
FYE: September 24
Type: Private

Whole Foods Market is the world's largest natural foods grocery chain. Founded in 1980 it pioneered the supermarket concept in natural and organic foods retailing. The company operates some 500 stores throughout the US Canada and the UK and focuses on organic perishable and prepared products. It sells private-label items through its 365 Organic Everyday Value and Allegro Coffee lines among others and offers a variety of non-GMO vegan and gluten-free foods. Whole Foods was acquired by Amazon.com for $13.7 billion in 2017.

	Annual Growth	09/13	09/14	09/15	09/16	09/17
Sales ($ mil.)	4.1%	–	14,194.0	15,389.0	15,724.0	16,030.0
Net income ($ mil.)	(24.9%)	–	579.0	536.0	507.0	245.0
Market value ($ mil.)	–	–	–	–	–	–
Employees	–	–	–	–	–	89,000

WHYY INC.

150 N 6TH ST
PHILADELPHIA, PA 191061521
Phone: 215-351-1200
Fax: –
Web: www.whyy.org

CEO: –
CFO: –
HR: –
FYE: June 30
Type: Private

WHYY provides the media landscape with a little Fresh Air. The company operates public radio station WHYY 90.9 FM which produces the popular NPR talk show with host Terry Gross. It also runs public television stations WHYY-TV and WDPB-TV. All three serve parts of Pennsylvania Delaware and New Jersey. Its Learning Lab offers multimedia journalism and video production training to WHYY members as well as to teens teachers and seniors. The company-, planted its roots in the 1950s when The Metropolitan Philadelphia Educational Radio and Television Corporation began broadcasting cultural and educational radio programming.-, About 100000 members — along with corporations and government agencies-, — fund WHYY.

	Annual Growth	06/07	06/08	06/09	06/10	06/11
Sales ($ mil.)	(4.1%)	–	30.6	25.7	27.8	27.0
Net income ($ mil.)	–	–	–	(3.9)	1.7	0.3
Market value ($ mil.)	–	–	–	–	–	–
Employees	–	–	–	–	–	160

WICHITA, CITY OF (INC)

455 N MAIN ST FL 5
WICHITA, KS 672021601
Phone: 316-268-4351
Fax: –
Web: www.wichita.gov

CEO: –
CFO: –
HR: –
FYE: December 31
Type: Private

What do Wyatt Earp Cessna and the first sub-four minute mile have in common? The City of Wichita. known as Cow Town and the Air Capital of the World was incorporated in 1870. The city has a population of more than 380000 occupying a little more than 163 sq. mi. Wichita State and 14 other campuses of higher education provide technical skills for leading employers. Boeing Learjet Raytheon Cargill and Koch are major companies with operations in the city.

	Annual Growth	12/08	12/09	12/15	12/16	12/17
Sales ($ mil.)	1.0%	–	387.1	392.1	408.7	419.3
Net income ($ mil.)	–	–	37.2	(8.4)	(3.1)	(9.4)
Market value ($ mil.)	–	–	–	–	–	–
Employees	–	–	–	–	–	2,200

WIDENER UNIVERSITY

1 UNIVERSITY PL
CHESTER, PA 190135792
Phone: 610-499-4000
Fax: –
Web: www.widener.edu

CEO: –
CFO: Joseph J Baker
HR: –
FYE: June 30
Type: Private

You probably won't find any narrow-minded students at Widener. A private co-educational liberal arts college Widener University offers a curriculum that emphasizes academic excellence career preparation and civic engagement. It has an enrollment of more than 6000 students and a student-to-faculty ratio of 12:1. The university grants undergraduate degrees in about 45 majors and graduate degrees in more than a dozen fields; its programs are divided into eight schools and colleges that cover areas including arts and sciences business education engineering law hospitality human services and nursing. Widener University has had its current name since 1979 but its roots reach back to 1821 when it was founded as a Quaker school for boys.

	Annual Growth	06/12	06/13	06/15	06/17	06/18
Sales ($ mil.)	–	–	0.0	206.8	149.8	150.7
Net income ($ mil.)	14.1%	–	8.5	(4.6)	11.4	16.5
Market value ($ mil.)	–	–	–	–	–	–
Employees	–	–	–	–	–	1,021

WIDEPOINT CORP

11250 Waples Mill Road, South Tower 210
Fairfax, VA 22030
Phone: 703 349-2577
Fax: –
Web: www.widepoint.com

ASE: WYY
CEO: Jin Kang
CFO: Kellie Kim
HR: –
FYE: December 31
Type: Public

WidePoint stretches to provide a variety of IT services to government and enterprise customers. The company provides wireless telecom management and business process outsourcing (BPO) services. Its cybersecurity segment provides identity management services including identity proofing credential issuing and public key infrastructure. The company also provides more traditional IT services such as architecture and planning integration services and vulnerability testing. WidePoint focuses its operations toward US federal government clients including the Department of Homeland Security (more than a quarter of sales) the TSA (nearly a quarter) the FBI Customs and Border Protection and the Justice department.

	Annual Growth	12/14	12/15	12/16	12/17	12/18
Sales ($ mil.)	11.9%	53.3	70.8	78.4	75.9	83.7
Net income ($ mil.)	–	(8.4)	(5.5)	(4.1)	(3.5)	(1.5)
Market value ($ mil.)	(25.8%)	116.1	58.5	68.1	54.7	35.1
Employees	(6.4%)	296	300	279	247	227

WIKIMEDIA FOUNDATION, INC.

149 NEW MONTGOMERY ST # 6
SAN FRANCISCO, CA 941053739
Phone: 415-839-6885
Fax: –
Web: www.wikimediafoundation.org

CEO: –
CFO: Jaime Villagomez
HR: –
FYE: June 30
Type: Private

Want free access to the sum of all human knowledge? Wikimedia Foundation can give it to you. The not-for-profit organization has produced a plethora of free-content wiki projects including one of the most visited sites on the Internet online collaborative encyclopedia Wikipedia (the foundation's first project). The term wiki (a Hawaiian word for "fast") describes a collection of Web pages designed to enable anyone with Internet access to contribute or modify content. Wikimedia has a paid staff of about 280 while hundreds of thousands of volunteers contribute content. The Wikimedia Foundation is funded primarily through donations and grants and was founded by Internet entrepreneur Jimmy Wales and philosopher Lawrence Sanger in 2001.

	Annual Growth	06/11	06/12	06/13	06/14	06/15
Sales ($ mil.)	26.6%	–	38.5	48.6	52.8	78.1
Net income ($ mil.)	40.7%	–	9.2	10.3	8.3	25.7
Market value ($ mil.)	–	–	–	–	–	–
Employees	–	–	–	–	–	240

WILBUR SMITH ASSOCIATES, INC.

1301 GERVAIS ST STE 1600
COLUMBIA, SC 292013361
Phone: 803-758-4500
Fax: –
Web: www.wilbursmith.com

CEO: –
CFO: –
HR: –
FYE: December 25
Type: Private

For many cities around the world where there's a Wilbur there's a roadway. Wilbur Smith Associates provides engineering design planning construction and economic consulting services for municipal works and infrastructure jobs including highways bridges railroads waterways airports and public buildings. Wilbur Smith is active throughout the US Europe Central America the UK the Middle East and Asia. Pioneer transportation engineer Wilbur Smith founded the firm in 1952. The company was acquired by Camp Dresser & McKee (CDM) in 2011. The deal helped broaden both firms' service capabilities and geographic reach.

	Annual Growth	12/05	12/06	12/07	12/08	12/09
Sales ($ mil.)	–	–	–	(436.9)	183.4	182.4
Net income ($ mil.)	789.0%	–	–	0.0	3.3	1.3
Market value ($ mil.)	–	–	–	–	–	–
Employees	–	–	–	–	–	1,217

WILBUR-ELLIS HOLDINGS II, INC.

345 CALIFORNIA ST FL 27
SAN FRANCISCO, CA 941042644
Phone: 415-772-4000
Fax: –
Web: www.wilburellis.com

CEO: John P. Thacher
CFO: James D. Crawford
HR: –
FYE: December 31
Type: Private

Seed 'em weed 'em and feed 'em could be the motto of San Francisco's Wilbur-Ellis Co. (aka WECO). Through its agribusiness division WECO sells fertilizer herbicides insecticides seed and farm machinery in North America. The Connell Bros. unit exports and distributes food ingredients and specialty chemicals throughout the Pacific Rim. Its feed division serves international customers in the livestock pet food and aquaculture industries. Additionally WECO provides consulting pesticide application and other agriculture-related services. Beyond North America WECO has operations in about 15 countries in the Asia/Pacific Region. WECO was founded in 1921 by Brayton Wilbur Sr. and Floyd Ellis.

	Annual Growth	12/0-1	12/00	12/09	12/10	12/11
Sales ($ mil.)	8.9%	–	1,100.0	0.0	2,342.5	2,812.0
Net income ($ mil.)	–	–	0.0	0.0	0.0	0.0
Market value ($ mil.)	–	–	–	–	–	–
Employees	–	–	–	–	–	4,600

WILCOHESS LLC

5446 University Pkwy.
Winston-Salem NC 27105
Phone: 336-767-6280
Fax: 336-767-6283
Web: www.wilcousa.com

CEO: –
CFO: –
HR: –
FYE: December 31
Type: Joint Venture

WilcoHess owns and operates more than 360 convenience stores and travel plazas as well as about 50 restaurants mostly in North Carolina and Virginia but also in Alabama Georgia Pennsylvania South Carolina and Tennessee. Many locations house quick-serve restaurants (Arby's Dairy Queen Wendy's). The company's travel plazas cater to truckers with fuel programs and rewards programs. The joint venture company was formed in 2001 by partners A.T. Williams Oil Company and Hess Corporation (formerly Amerada Hess) a leading independent oil company along the East Coast. President Steve Williams is the son of the founder of A.T. Williams Oil Co. A. Tab Williams. Jr.

WILDLIFE CONSERVATION SOCIETY

2300 SOUTHERN BLVD
BRONX, NY 104601090
Phone: 718-220-5100
Fax: –
Web: www.wcs.org

CEO: –
CFO: Laura Stolzenthaler
HR: Herman Smith
FYE: June 30
Type: Private

From Congo gorillas to humpback whales off the coast of Gabon all life is worth conserving to the Wildlife Conservation Society (WCS). The group founded in 1895 works to protect wildlife and lands throughout the world and to instill in humans a concern about nature. The not-for-profit organization operates New York City's Bronx Zoo New York Aquarium Central Park Zoo Prospect Park Zoo and the Queens Zoo. WCS's environmental education programs are used in US schools as well as those in other nations. The society has ongoing efforts in more than 60 countries to protect endangered species and ecosystems. About a quarter of the funding for its work comes from visitors at its handful of parks.

	Annual Growth	06/13	06/14	06/15	06/16	06/18
Sales ($ mil.)	7.3%	–	253.7	327.9	260.3	336.1
Net income ($ mil.)	6.3%	–	24.6	61.9	(23.8)	31.4
Market value ($ mil.)	–	–	–	–	–	–
Employees	–	–	–	–	–	4,000

WILEY (JOHN) & SONS INC.

NYS: JW A

111 River Street
Hoboken, NJ 07030
Phone: 201 748-6000
Fax: –
Web: www.wiley.com

CEO: Stephen M. (Steve) Smith
CFO: John A. Kritzmacher
HR: Patricia Peters
FYE: April 30
Type: Public

John Wiley & Sons (known as Wiley for short) publishes scientific technical and medical works including more than 7 million articles from 1700 journals as well as 19000 online books and hundreds of multi-volume reference works laboratory protocols and databases. Journal subscriptions are primarily licensed through contracts for digital content available via its Literatum platform (formerly the Wiley Online Library). The firm also produces professional and nonfiction trade books such as the For Dummies how-to series and is a publisher of college textbooks. Wiley has operations in North America Europe Asia and Australia. Most revenue comes from the US.

	Annual Growth	04/15	04/16	04/17	04/18	04/19
Sales ($ mil.)	(0.3%)	1,822.4	1,727.0	1,718.5	1,796.1	1,800.1
Net income ($ mil.)	(1.2%)	176.9	145.8	113.6	192.2	168.3
Market value ($ mil.)	(5.1%)	3,221.1	2,808.3	2,984.4	3,734.8	2,615.2
Employees	3.9%	4,900	4,700	5,100	5,000	5,700

WILHELMINA INTERNATIONAL, INC.

NAS: WHLM

200 Crescent Court, Suite 1400
Dallas, TX 75201
Phone: 214 661-7488
Fax: –

CEO: William J Wackermann
CFO: James A McCarthy
HR: –
FYE: December 31
Type: Public

Wilhelmina International has a new face. Formerly a billing services and software provider serving the telecommunications industry New Century Equity Holdings reinvented itself as a holding company and in 2009 acquired Wilhelmina International — the company responsible for the iconic modeling agency Wilhelmina Models. The $30 million transaction also included affiliates Wilhelmina Miami Wilhelmina Film & TV and Wilhelmina Artist Management. Upon the deal's closure New Century changed its name to Wilhelmina International reflecting its new primary business focus. The Wilhelmina deal came after more than four years of scouting new investment opportunities.

	Annual Growth	12/14	12/15	12/16	12/17	12/18
Sales ($ mil.)	0.3%	76.8	83.8	82.2	73.2	77.9
Net income ($ mil.)	(8.1%)	1.2	1.5	0.1	0.2	0.9
Market value ($ mil.)	(0.6%)	31.2	37.0	45.6	33.7	30.4
Employees	5.1%	96	118	121	121	117

WILL COUNTY

302 N CHICAGO ST
JOLIET, IL 604324078
Phone: 815-740-4602
Fax: –

CEO: –
CFO: –
HR: –
FYE: November 30
Type: Private

Will County is a rapidly growing county in Illinois. The regional government based in Joliet (about 45 miles southwest of Chicago) provides a multitude of services including animal control health programs highway planning and maintenance veterans assistance and workforce training to about 670000 citizens in about 40 municipalities and 24 townships. The Will County Board consists of elected officials from nine districts who establish policies and the county executive who oversees day-to-day operations. The county was formed in 1836 and is named after a salt production businessman named Dr. Conrad Will.

	Annual Growth	11/12	11/13	11/14	11/15	11/17
Sales ($ mil.)	1.4%	–	297.7	0.0	303.1	314.8
Net income ($ mil.)	–	–	(1.6)	0.0	5.0	(45.6)
Market value ($ mil.)	–	–	–	–	–	–
Employees	–	–	–	–	–	2,000

WILLAMETTE UNIVERSITY

900 STATE ST
SALEM, OR 973013930
Phone: 503-370-6728
Fax: –
Web: www.willamette.edu

CEO: –
CFO: –
HR: –
FYE: May 31
Type: Private

Willamette University's claim to fame is its status as the first university in the West. About 3000 students are enrolled in the private co-educational liberal arts school that offers undergraduate and graduate degrees. Undergraduate degrees encompass nearly 50 fields — politics biology English psychology and economics are among the most pursued majors — and graduate degrees in business law and education. The university has a student-to-faculty ratio of 10:1. Founded in the early days of the Oregon Territory by missionary Jason Lee as a school for Native American children Willamette University was established in 1842.

	Annual Growth	05/14	05/15	05/16	05/17	05/18
Sales ($ mil.)	(1.7%)	–	101.5	138.2	100.2	96.5
Net income ($ mil.)	15.8%	–	9.3	(11.5)	8.1	14.5
Market value ($ mil.)	–	–	–	–	–	–
Employees	–	–	–	–	–	700

WILLAMETTE VALLEY VINEYARD INC.   NAS: WVVI

8800 Enchanted Way S.E.
Turner, OR 97392
Phone: 503 588-9463
Fax: -
Web: www.wvv.com
CEO: James W Bernau
CFO: John Ferry
HR: -
FYE: December 31
Type: Public

Willamette Valley Vineyards is a leading producer of premium varietal wines including chardonnay dry riesling and pinot gris along with its flagship pinot noir. In addition to Willamette Valley it also makes wine under the Tualatin Estates and Griffin Creek labels. The winemaker owns leases or contracts almost 800 acres of vineyards and produced about 121000 cases of wine during 2008. Its wines are sold in Oregon through its Bacchus Fine Wines distribution operation and are available elsewhere in the US through other distributors and brokers. Founder and CEO Jim Bernau owns 12% of the company.

	Annual Growth	12/14	12/15	12/16	12/17	12/18
Sales ($ mil.)	11.1%	15.2	17.9	19.4	20.9	23.1
Net income ($ mil.)	7.2%	2.2	1.9	2.6	3.0	2.9
Market value ($ mil.)	4.4%	28.8	35.1	39.8	41.0	34.2
Employees	16.5%	122	141	146	166	225

WILLBROS GROUP INC (DE)   NYS: WG

4400 Post Oak Parkway, Suite 1000
Houston, TX 77027
Phone: 713 403-8000
Fax: -
Web: www.willbros.com
CEO: David King
CFO: Peter J Moerbeek
HR: -
FYE: December 31
Type: Public

Willbros Group develops infrastructure worldwide but primarily in North America. A construction and engineering contractor targeting oil gas and power industries the firm specializes in projects in emerging nations. Willbros has completed major pipeline systems oil and gas production plants piers and bridges. Engineering services include design feasibility studies and project management. It also offers specialty services such as dredging and pipeline. Willbros' inventory features a large fleet of company-owned and leased equipment such as camp equipment marine vessels and pipe-laying and transportation equipment. The company also offers utility transmission and distribution services.

	Annual Growth	12/12	12/13	12/14	12/15	12/16
Sales ($ mil.)	(22.3%)	2,004.2	2,018.8	2,026.7	909.0	731.7
Net income ($ mil.)	-	(30.2)	(15.9)	(79.8)	31.5	(47.8)
Market value ($ mil.)	(11.8%)	335.8	590.2	392.8	168.5	203.0
Employees	(28.4%)	12,054	9,399	7,959	3,579	3,165

WILLDAN GROUP INC   NMS: WLDN

2401 East Katella Avenue, Suite 300
Anaheim, CA 92806
Phone: 800 424-9144
Fax: -
Web: www.willdan.com
CEO: Thomas D Brisbin
CFO: Stacy B McLaughlin
HR: -
FYE: December 28
Type: Public

Willdan Group can and will do what it takes to meet its customers' numerous engineering needs. The company has four operating service segments: engineering (Willdan Engineering) energy efficiency (Willdan Energy Solutions) public finance (Willdan Financial Services) and homeland security (Willdan Homeland Solutions). Clients include federal and local governments school districts public utilities and some private industries. Willdan focuses on small- to mid-sized clients that may fall below the radar of larger competitors. The company was founded in 1964.

	Annual Growth	01/15	01/16*	12/16	12/17	12/18
Sales ($ mil.)	36.1%	108.1	135.1	208.9	273.4	272.3
Net income ($ mil.)	2.1%	9.4	4.3	8.3	12.1	10.0
Market value ($ mil.)	32.9%	159.0	91.9	247.8	262.6	372.9
Employees	23.6%	637	688	831	882	1,202

*Fiscal year change

WILLIAM MARSH RICE UNIVERSITY INC

10300 TOWN PARK DR
HOUSTON, TX 770725236
Phone: 713-348-4055
Fax: -
Web: www.rice.edu
CEO: -
CFO: -
HR: -
FYE: June 30
Type: Private

You have to be as wise as an owl to attend Rice University and have really good SAT scores. Often referred to as the "Ivy League of the South" Rice — with mascot "Sammy the Owl" — consistently appears at the top of college academic rankings including those published by U.S. News & World Report. The private university has an enrollment of more than 6000 and about 1100 full-time part-time and adjunct faculty members (giving it a student-teacher ratio of about 6:1). Rice offers programs through eight schools in areas such as engineering computer science economics music and architecture. The university opened in 1912 with funds from the estate of William Marsh Rice.

	Annual Growth	06/10	06/11	06/12	06/13	06/14
Sales ($ mil.)	2.8%	-	551.0	551.0	568.3	599.1
Net income ($ mil.)	-	-	-	(34.0)	460.0	657.6
Market value ($ mil.)	-	-	-	-	-	-
Employees	-	-	-	-	-	2,600

WILLIAM PATERSON UNIVERSITY

300 POMPTON RD
WAYNE, NJ 074702103
Phone: 973-720-2000
Fax: -
Web: www.wpupioneers.com
CEO: -
CFO: -
HR: Allison Boucher Jarvis
FYE: June 30
Type: Private

William Paterson University has evolved into a fully accredited liberal-arts university. William Paterson which has more than 400 full-time faculty members enrolls about 11000 undergraduate and graduate students and offers more than offers 45 undergraduate 22 masters one doctoral and three post-baccalaureate certificate programs through five colleges. The university has a 370-acre campus with some 40 major buildings and other facilities including the David and Lorraine Cheng Library which boasts more than 350000 bound volumes. William Paterson is accredited by the Middle States Association of Colleges and Secondary Schools. William Paterson was founded in 1855 as a normal school (teacher's college).

	Annual Growth	06/14	06/15	06/16	06/17	06/18
Sales ($ mil.)	(0.5%)	-	150.7	151.7	150.1	148.3
Net income ($ mil.)	-	-	8.0	(7.8)	(14.3)	(15.0)
Market value ($ mil.)	-	-	-	-	-	-
Employees	-	-	-	-	-	1,300

WILLIAMS CONTROLS INC.   NASDAQ: WMCO

14100 SW 72nd Ave.
Portland OR 97224
Phone: 503-684-8600
Fax: 503-624-3812
Web: www.wmco.com
CEO: -
CFO: Dennis E Bunday
HR: -
FYE: September 30
Type: Public

You want the truck driver behind you on the highway to be able to control his speed and so does Williams Controls. The company's primary business is the manufacture of electronic throttle controls for commercial trucks buses RVs off-highway equipment and military applications. Williams Controls also makes pneumatic throttle controls for diesel heavy-duty vehicles. Most of the company's products are sold directly to heavy-duty truck transit bus and off-road OEMs. However it also sells through a network of independent distributors which sell to smaller OEMs. The company makes more than half of its sales in the US. In late 2012 the company agreed to be acquired by Curtiss-Wright Corporation.

WILLIAMS INDUSTRIAL SERVICES GROUP INC — NBB: WLMS

100 Crescent Centre Parkway, Suite 1240
Tucker, GA 30084
Phone: 770 879-4400
Fax: –
Web: www.wisgrp.com

CEO: –
CFO: Randall R Lay
HR: Monte McDowell
FYE: December 31
Type: Public

Global Power Equipment Group keeps its customers in power. Through its subsidiaries the company designs and manufactures power generation equipment for OEMs engineering construction and power generation customers. Its products sold under its Braden Manufacturing Consolidated Fabricators TOG and Koontz-Wagner brands include auxiliary parts for steam and gas turbines electric transmission systems and controls and custom components. Additionally subsidiary Williams Industrial Services offers upgrades and maintenance services to industrial and utility companies and nuclear and hydroelectric power plants while its Hetsco unit provides welding and fabrication services. The company was formed in 1998.

	Annual Growth	12/14	12/15	12/16	12/17	12/18
Sales ($ mil.)	(23.0%)	538.5	589.0	418.6	187.0	188.9
Net income ($ mil.)	–	11.1	(78.7)	(43.6)	(56.5)	(25.4)
Market value ($ mil.)	(37.7%)	289.2	289.2	88.1	74.1	43.7
Employees	(22.1%)	1,244	1,449	877	366	457

WILLIAMS PARTNERS L.P. — NYS: WPZ

One Williams Center
Tulsa, OK 74172-0172
Phone: 918 573-2000
Fax: –
Web: www.williamslp.com

CEO: –
CFO: –
HR: –
FYE: December 31
Type: Public

Fractionating natural gas liquids (NGLs) is only a fraction of what Williams Partners does. The company is also engaged in the gathering and processing of natural gas and the storage of NGLs and the operation of three major interstate natural gas pipelines. (These pipelines deliver 14% of the natural gas consumed in the US.) Williams Partners assets include a 3800-mile natural gas gathering system in the San Juan Basin; 60% of Discovery Producer Services and Carbonate Trend (gas gathering systems); and the 9800-mile Transco intestate natural gas pipeline. The Williams Companies has merged its Williams Pipeline Partners (pipelines) unit into Williams Partners (which had focused on midstream operations).

	Annual Growth	12/08	12/09	12/10	12/11	12/12
Sales ($ mil.)	84.1%	637.1	470.2	5,715.0	6,729.0	7,320.0
Net income ($ mil.)	59.3%	191.4	152.5	1,085.0	1,378.0	1,232.0
Market value ($ mil.)	42.1%	4,751.7	12,205.5	18,565.0	23,873.8	19,364.9
Employees	–	–	–	–	–	–

WILLIAMS PARTNERS LP (NEW) — NYS: WPZ

One Williams Center
Tulsa, OK 74172-0172
Phone: 918 573-2000
Fax: –
Web: www.williamslp.com

CEO: Alan Armstrong
CFO: John D Chandler
HR: –
FYE: December 31
Type: Public

Williams Partners (formerly Access Midstream Partners) is a midstream gathering company that owns operates develops and acquires natural gas natural gas liquids (NGLs) and oil gathering assets in the US. It gathers about 3.9 billion cu. ft. of natural gas per day via some 5800 miles of gathering and transmission lines. The company also has processing facilities that provide services to thousands of wells. Its assets are located in a dozen states with operations in the Barnett Eagle Ford Haynesville Marcellus Niobrara and Utica shales and several unconventional plays in the Mid-Continent region.

	Annual Growth	12/12	12/13	12/14	12/15	12/16
Sales ($ mil.)	87.3%	608.4	1,073.2	1,378.9	7,331.0	7,491.0
Net income ($ mil.)	24.7%	178.5	336.0	398.1	(1,449.0)	431.0
Market value ($ mil.)	3.2%	20,920.7	35,292.0	33,807.5	17,371.6	23,721.4
Employees	45.4%	1,255	1,411	6,742	6,578	5,604

WILLIAMS SAUSAGE COMPANY INC.

5132 OLD TROY HICKMAN RD
UNION CITY, TN 382617702
Phone: 731-885-5841
Fax: –
Web: www.williams-sausage.com

CEO: –
CFO: –
HR: –
FYE: March 31
Type: Private

Union City Tennessee-headquartered Williams Sausage is a regional meat processor that makes sausage ham and bacon products for both retail and wholesale food customers. Its product lines include several varieties of pork sausage cured hams and smoked bacon. The company also markets microwavable pork biscuit sandwiches and smoked pork sausages. Most of its meat products are sold under the Williams brand but it also markets sausage and bacon under the Ole South label. The family-owned company was founded by Harold Williams in 1958.

	Annual Growth	03/03	03/04	03/05	03/06	03/07
Sales ($ mil.)	–	–	–	(77.8)	49.3	46.6
Net income ($ mil.)	27946.8%	–	–	0.0	6.8	3.1
Market value ($ mil.)	–	–	–	–	–	–
Employees	–	–	–	–	–	250

WILLIS LEASE FINANCE CORP. — NMS: WLFC

4700 Lyons Technology Parkway
Coconut Creek, FL 33073
Phone: 561 349-9989
Fax: –
Web: www.willislease.com

CEO: Charles F Willis IV
CFO: Scott B Flaherty
HR: –
FYE: December 31
Type: Public

Hey buddy got any spare Pratt & Whitneys? Willis Lease Finance buys and sells aircraft engines that it leases to commercial airlines air cargo carriers and maintenance/repair/overhaul organizations in some 30 countries. Its portfolio includes about 180 aircraft engines and related equipment made by Pratt & Whitney Rolls-Royce CFMI GE Aviation and International Aero. The engine models in the company's portfolio are used on popular Airbus and Boeing aircraft. The Willis Lease portfolio also includes four de Havilland DHC-8 commuter aircraft. Customers include Island Air Alaska Airlines American Airlines and Southwest Airlines. Almost 80% of the company's engines are leased and operated outside the US.

	Annual Growth	12/14	12/15	12/16	12/17	12/18
Sales ($ mil.)	18.9%	174.3	199.6	207.3	274.8	348.3
Net income ($ mil.)	56.3%	7.2	7.4	14.1	62.2	43.2
Market value ($ mil.)	12.1%	135.3	124.1	158.0	154.2	213.7
Employees	15.3%	99	104	147	155	175

WILMER CUTLER PICKERING HALE AND DORR LLP

1875 Pennsylvania Ave. NW
Washington DC 20006
Phone: 202-663-6000
Fax: 202-663-6363
Web: www.wilmerhale.com

CEO: –
CFO: –
HR: –
FYE: December 31
Type: Private - Partnershi

Wilmer Cutler Pickering Hale and Dorr known as WilmerHale has more than 1000 lawyers in a dozen cities in the US Europe and Asia. Major practice areas include antitrust and competition; corporate transactions; bankruptcy and financial restructuring; government regulation; intellectual property; securities and government contract litigation; and labor and employment. It has conducted legal work for such business big wigs as Boeing Deutsche Bank Procter & Gamble and Citigroup. WilmerHale was formed in the 2004 merger of Washington DC-based Wilmer Cutler & Pickering and Boston-based Hale and Dorr.

WILSHIRE BANCORP INC NMS: WIBC

3200 Wilshire Blvd.
Los Angeles, CA 90010
Phone: 213-387-3200
Fax: 213-427-6584
Web: www.wilshirebank.com

CEO: -
CFO: -
HR: -
FYE: December 31
Type: Public

Wilshire Bancorp is the holding company for Wilshire Bank where ethnic minorities are the banking majority. Based in the Koreatown section of Los Angeles the commercial bank boasts $4.2 billion in assets nearly 35 branches and a handful of lending offices mainly across California but also in New Jersey New York and Texas. Wilshire Bank targets small to midsized minority-owned businesses and ethnic groups underserved by many national banking institutions. Beyond standard deposit services (including checking and savings accounts CDs and IRAs) the bank also offers Small Business Administration (SBA) real estate and consumer loans and import/export financing services. Korean-American rival BBCN Bancorp agreed to acquire Wilshire Bancorp for $1 billion in late 2015.

	Annual Growth	12/10	12/11	12/12	12/13	12/14
Assets ($ mil.)	8.8%	2,970.5	2,696.9	2,750.9	3,617.7	4,155.5
Net income ($ mil.)	-	(34.8)	(30.3)	92.3	45.4	59.0
Market value ($ mil.)	7.4%	596.8	284.3	459.8	856.1	793.4
Employees	6.8%	405	382	415	547	527

WILSHIRE ENTERPRISES INC. PINK SHEETS: WLSE

1 Gateway Center Ste. 1030
Newark NJ 07102
Phone: 201-420-2796
Fax: 201-420-6012
Web: www.wilshireenterprisesinc.com

CEO: S Wilzig Izak
CFO: Francis Elenio
HR: -
FYE: December 31
Type: Public

Wilshire Enterprises invests in and operates commercial real estate and land. It owns a portfolio of more than a dozen multifamily retail and office properties and land tracts in Arizona Florida New Jersey and Texas. The company has shed some of its non-core and other properties and has upgraded other properties. Its land holdings (parcels of land totaling about 20 acres all located in New Jersey) have either been put up for sale or are under contract for sale already. Wilshire Enterprises is seeking sale or merger opportunities. In 2008 it entered an acquisition deal with property investment and redevelopment firm NWJ Companies but the agreement was later terminated.

WILSON ELSER MOSKOWITZ EDELMAN & DICKER LLP

150 E. 42nd St.
New York NY 10017
Phone: 212-490-3000
Fax: 212-490-3038
Web: www.wilsonelser.com

CEO: -
CFO: -
HR: -
FYE: December 31
Type: Private - Partnershi

Law firm Wilson Elser Moskowitz Edelman & Dicker maintains a broad range of practice areas and a considerable geographic scope. Wilson Elser's more than 800 attorneys work out of 20 offices in the US and one in the UK; the firm also maintains affiliations with counterparts in France Germany and Mexico. It has won recognitions for specialties such as lobbying in New York state and professional liability insurance defense; other practice areas include aviation environmental law and intellectual property. Thomas Wilson John Elser Harold Moskowitz Max Edelman and Herbert Dicker founded the firm in 1978.

WILSON SONSINI GOODRICH & ROSATI

650 Page Mill Rd.
Palo Alto CA 94304-1050
Phone: 650-493-9300
Fax: 650-493-6811
Web: www.wsgr.com

CEO: Steven E Bochner
CFO: -
HR: -
FYE: January 31
Type: Private - Partnershi

You might say these lawyers can get downright technical. Wilson Sonsini Goodrich & Rosati (WSGR) is one of the largest law firms in the US specializing in representing high-tech corporations. Its client roster has included several big Silicon Valley names such as Google Cisco Salesforce.com Hewlett-Packard Jive Software Oracle and Bazaarvoice. WSGR has advised hundreds of clients on their IPOs and has been involved in more than 500 merger and acquisition transactions (valued at more than $150 billion) in the last five years. WSGR has litigated hundreds of patent lawsuits over the years. The firm was originally founded in 1961.

WILSONART INTERNATIONAL HOLDING LLC

2400 Wilson Place
Temple TX 76503
Phone: 254-207-7000
Fax: 254-207-2545
Web: www.wilsonart.com

CEO: -
CFO: -
HR: -
FYE: December 31
Type: Private

Countertops and other surfaces are like blank canvases for Wilsonart International. The company manufacturers high pressure laminates and other surfaces used for furniture office and retail space countertops worktops and other uses. Its products are marketed under the Wilsonart Resopal Polyrey Ralph Wilson and Arborite brands. Wilsonart sells its products through a network of company-owned and independent distributors across North America; it also works through independent international distributors. The company was a subsidiary of mega tool supplies maker Illinois Tool Works until 2012 when 51% of its stock was sold to investment firm Clayton Dubilier & Rice.

WILTON BRANDS INC.

2240 W. 75th St.
Woodridge IL 60517
Phone: 630-963-1818
Fax: 630-963-7196
Web: www.wilton.com

CEO: Sue Buchta
CFO: -
HR: -
FYE: July 31
Type: Private

Wilton Brands takes the cake — then shows you how to decorate it. The company's Wilton Enterprises subsidiary founded in 1929 is a leading maker of food crafting products offering cake decorating items and bakeware under the Performance Pans Candy Melts and Cupcakes 'N More brands. It also holds classes in cake decoration and makes teakettles and cookware through its Copco division. Wilton is also home to EK Success Brands which produces scrapbooking supplies and crafting products under the Jolee's Martha Stewart Crafts Paintworks Inkadinkado Dimensions Crafts and K&Company names. Wilton Brands is a subsidiary of Wilton Holdings which is owned by TowerBrook Capital.

WINCHESTER HEALTHCARE MANAGEMENT, INC.

41 HIGHLAND AVE — CEO: –
WINCHESTER, MA 018901446 — CFO: –
Phone: 781-756-2126 — HR: –
Fax: – — FYE: September 30
Web: www.winhosp.org — Type: Private

Winchester Healthcare Management provides a variety of health care services to patients in the Boston area. The not-for-profit company owns and operates Winchester Hospital a 230-bed acute care medical center. The hospital is a leading area facility for pediatric and women's health services and it offers specialty services including diagnostics cardiology oncology pulmonary and orthopedic medical care. Winchester Healthcare also operates about 20 community family health and specialty clinics as well as a home care agency. The flagship hospital was founded in 1912.

	Annual Growth	09/14	09/15	09/16	09/17	09/18
Sales ($ mil.)	(2.5%)	–	–	–	316.7	308.7
Net income ($ mil.)	228.1%	–	–	–	6.4	21.1
Market value ($ mil.)	–	–	–	–	–	–
Employees	–	–	–	–	–	2,113

WINCHESTER MEDICAL CENTER AUXILIARY, INC.

1840 AMHERST ST — CEO: –
WINCHESTER, VA 226012808 — CFO: J Craig Lewis
Phone: 540-536-8000 — HR: –
Fax: – — FYE: December 31
Web: www.valleyhealthlink.com — Type: Private

Winchester Medical Center is the flagship facility of Valley Health System a not-for-profit health care organization serving the residents of Virginia's Shenandoah Valley. The full-service general hospital which has more than 400 inpatient beds serves as a regional referral center for the system's smaller community hospitals. It provides medical services across a number of specialties (including neuroscience heart disease and cancer) and offers surgical diagnostic and rehabilitative care. The hospital's campus also features outpatient diagnostic and surgical facilities an adult psychiatric facility and doctors' offices. Winchester Medical Center opened its doors in 1903.

	Annual Growth	12/03	12/04	12/05	12/06	12/07
Sales ($ mil.)	8.9%	–	–	382.8	413.3	453.7
Net income ($ mil.)	(6.6%)	–	–	55.9	61.7	48.8
Market value ($ mil.)	–	–	–	–	–	–
Employees	–	–	–	–	–	2,046

WIND RIVER SYSTEMS INC.

500 Wind River Way — CEO: Jim Douglas
Alameda CA 94501-1171 — CFO: Jane Bon
Phone: 510-748-4100 — HR: –
Fax: 510-749-2010 — FYE: January 31
Web: www.windriver.com — Type: Subsidiary

Wind River Systems' sails are billowing with embedded systems. The company provides software operating systems and development tools for embedded systems (composed of a microprocessor and related software) used in such diverse products as auto braking systems Internet traffic routers jet fighter control panels and traffic signals. Wind River is looking increasingly to set-top boxes mobile phones and other consumer electronics for growth opportunities. The company serves customers in such industries as aerospace automotive IT and health care from offices worldwide. Clients have included Northrop Grumman Huawei and Varian Medical Systems. The company is a subsidiary of Intel.

WINDOW TO THE WORLD COMMUNICATIONS INC.

5400 N SAINT LOUIS AVE — CEO: Daniel J Schmidt
CHICAGO, IL 606254623 — CFO: –
Phone: 773-509-1111 — HR: –
Fax: – — FYE: June 30
Web: www.wttw.com — Type: Private

|Window To The World Communications (WTTW) broadcasts arts children's current events humanities and science programming via its Chicago television station (WTTW Channel 11 with the nation's largest viewer base) and radio station (98.7 WFMT). The company's programming focuses on events and issues that effect the Chicago metropolitan area and special emphasis is given to cultural and educational topics. WTTW is a nonprofit governed by about 50 trustees representing the greater Chicago community. It is licensed by the FCC as a public TV station and is funded and governed by the community it serves. The station started by Inland Steel chairman Edward Ryerson began broadcasting in 1955.

	Annual Growth	06/08	06/09	06/10	06/12	06/13
Sales ($ mil.)	(3.1%)	–	49.9	45.7	47.9	44.1
Net income ($ mil.)	–	–	–	(7.5)	3.0	(1.1)
Market value ($ mil.)	–	–	–	–	–	–
Employees	–	–	–	–	–	192

WINDSTREAM HOLDINGS INC

NBB: WINM Q

4001 Rodney Parham Road — CEO: Anthony W. (Tony) Thomas
Little Rock, AR 72212 — CFO: Robert E. (Bob) Gunderman
Phone: 501 748-7000 — HR: John P. Fletcher
Fax: – — FYE: December 31
Web: www.windstream.com — Type: Public

Windstream Holdings offers a range of telecommunications services to consumers carriers and businesses over a fiber optic network measures nearly 150000 route miles. The company's business services include multi-site networking internet access cloud computing colocation online backup and other managed services. For residential customers Windstream offers high-speed internet (including gigabit speed in several markets) and voice services as well as video and bundles of services. The company provides infrastructure services such as call connection and backhaul connections to wireless carriers. In 2019 Windstream Holdings filed for Chapter 11 bankruptcy after a court ruling against it.

	Annual Growth	12/14	12/15	12/16	12/17	12/18
Sales ($ mil.)	(0.5%)	5,829.5	5,765.3	5,387.0	5,852.9	5,713.1
Net income ($ mil.)	–	(39.5)	27.4	(383.5)	(2,116.6)	(723.0)
Market value ($ mil.)	(29.0%)	353.5	276.3	314.5	79.4	89.7
Employees	(1.4%)	12,626	12,326	11,870	1,223	11,945

WINDTREE THERAPEUTICS INC

NBB: WINT

2600 Kelly Road, Suite 100 — CEO: Craig Fraser
Warrington, PA 18976-3622 — CFO: John A Tattory
Phone: 215 488-9300 — HR: –
Fax: – — FYE: December 31
Web: www.windtreex.com — Type: Public

If you're waiting to exhale Windtree Therapeutics may be able to help. Formerly named Discovery Laboratories the biotechnology company focuses on treatments for respiratory disorders. It bases its therapies on surfactants which are naturally produced by the lungs and essential for breathing. The firm's only product Surfaxin gained FDA approval in 2012 for the prevention of respiratory distress syndrome (RDS) in premature infants. Another candidate Aerosurf (licensed from Philip Morris) will allow for the delivery of RDS surfactant medicine in aerosol form and is being developed as an alternative to endotracheal intubation and conventional mechanical ventilation. The firm also makes respiratory drug delivery devices.

	Annual Growth	12/14	12/15	12/16	12/17	12/18
Sales ($ mil.)	(10.9%)	2.8	1.0	2.0	1.5	1.8
Net income ($ mil.)	–	(44.1)	(55.2)	(39.5)	(18.4)	(20.5)
Market value ($ mil.)	44.1%	37.3	6.9	40.2	135.0	160.7
Employees	(26.0%)	110	58	49	28	33

WINLAND HOLDINGS CORP
NBB: WELX

1950 Excel Drive
Mankato, MN 56001
Phone: 507 625-7231
Fax: 507 387-2488
Web: www.winland.com

CEO: -
CFO: Brian D Lawrence
HR: -
FYE: December 31
Type: Public

Winland Electronics has gone from good sleep to loud beeps. Formerly a contract manufacturer of electronics for such products as the Sleep Number bed Winland sold that division in order to focus on its own line of environmental monitoring products including sensors and alarms that check for changes in temperature humidity water leakage and power failure. It also makes a driveway warning system that detects when a vehicle enters a driveway or road. Winland Electronics gets almost all of its sales in the US. The company sold its electronics manufacturing services (EMS) business which made electronic controls and circuit board assemblies to Nortech in early 2011.

	Annual Growth	12/14	12/15	12/16	12/17	12/18
Sales ($ mil.)	(0.5%)	3.8	3.7	3.6	3.6	3.8
Net income ($ mil.)	(46.7%)	0.3	0.3	0.1	0.2	0.0
Market value ($ mil.)	5.1%	3.6	7.9	7.6	6.1	4.4
Employees	-	-	-	-	-	-

WINMARK CORP
NMS: WINA

605 Highway 169 North, Suite 400
Minneapolis, MN 55441
Phone: 763 520-8500
Fax: -
Web: www.winmarkcorporation.com

CEO: Brett D. Heffes
CFO: Anthony D. (Tony) Ishaug
HR: Leah Goff
FYE: December 29
Type: Public

Winmark Corporation franchises retail chains that buy sell and consign used goods (and some new items) at more than 1200 stores across the US as well as in Canada. The chains sell teen and young adult apparel (Plato's Closet) children's items (Once Upon A Child) sporting goods (Play It Again Sports) women's apparel and accessories (Style Encore) and musical instruments and electronics (Music Go Round). In addition the company leases IT equipment to midsized and large businesses through its Winmark Capital unit and it offers financing services to small businesses through its Wirth Business Credit subsidiary. Winmark generates most its revenue from the US.

	Annual Growth	12/14	12/15	12/16	12/17	12/18
Sales ($ mil.)	4.3%	61.2	69.4	66.6	69.7	72.5
Net income ($ mil.)	10.7%	20.1	21.8	22.2	24.6	30.1
Market value ($ mil.)	17.4%	326.6	359.4	493.0	505.7	620.9
Employees	(0.2%)	108	108	103	107	107

WINN-DIXIE STORES INC.
NASDAQ: WINN

5050 Edgewood Ct.
Jacksonville FL 32254-3699
Phone: 904-783-5000
Fax: 904-370-7224
Web: www.winn-dixie.com

CEO: R Randall Onstead
CFO: -
HR: -
FYE: June 30
Type: Subsidiary

Winn-Dixie Stores has found — as Jefferson Davis did long ago — that winning Dixie ain't easy. The Deep South supermarket chain operates about 480 combination food and drug stores throughout Alabama Florida Georgia Louisiana and Mississippi under the Winn-Dixie and Winn-Dixie Marketplace banners. Most of Winn-Dixie's supermarkets have pharmacies about 75 house liquor stores and several sell gas. The company's brands include Thrifty Maid Winn & Lovett and Winn-Dixie. Founded in 1925 Winn-Dixie Stores is a subsidiary of BI-LO Holding which merged Winn-Dixie and South Carolina-based BI-LO in 2012 and took them private.

WINNEBAGO INDUSTRIES, INC.
NYS: WGO

P.O. Box 152
Forest City, IA 50436
Phone: 641 585-3535
Fax: 641 585-6966
Web: www.winnebagoind.com

CEO: Michael J. Happe
CFO: Bryan Hughes
HR: -
FYE: August 31
Type: Public

A pioneer in the world of recreational vehicles Winnebago Industries makes products intended to encourage exploration. Almost all the company's sales come from its motor homes and towables which are sold via independent dealers throughout the US and Canada under brands including Winnebago Adventurer Sightseer Grand Design and Minnie Winnie. Winnebago Industries also sells RV parts and provides related services. The company also builds custom specialty vehicles for uses including mobile law enforcement command centers and mobile medical units. In 2018 Winnebago purchased Chris-Craft a manufacturer of recreational power boats. More than 90% of the company's sales are in the US. Winnebago traces its roots back to the 1950s.

	Annual Growth	08/15	08/16	08/17	08/18	08/19
Sales ($ mil.)	19.4%	976.5	975.2	1,547.1	2,016.8	1,985.7
Net income ($ mil.)	28.3%	41.2	45.5	71.3	102.4	111.8
Market value ($ mil.)	11.9%	643.5	753.5	1,088.8	1,175.5	1,009.1
Employees	11.6%	2,900	3,050	4,060	4,700	4,500

WINSTON & STRAWN LLP

35 W WACKER DR STE 4200
CHICAGO, IL 60601-1695
Phone: 312-558-5600
Fax: -
Web: www.winstonandstrawn.com

CEO: -
CFO: -
HR: -
FYE: January 31
Type: Private

Over the years Winston & Strawn has developed a reputation for its work in litigation and labor and employment law but the firm's practices encompass a wide range of specialties from antitrust to intellectual property to tax. The firm has around 1000 lawyers in about 15 offices in the US Europe and Asia. Clients have included Abbott Laboratories McDonald's Yahoo Wells Fargo and Philip Morris USA. Winston & Strawn was founded in 1853; since 2000 it has expanded by taking in firms such as New York-based Whitman Breed Abbott & Morgan and San Francisco-based Murphy Sheneman Julian & Rogers.

	Annual Growth	01/07	01/08	01/09	01/11	01/12
Sales ($ mil.)	2.0%	-	697.4	0.0	717.0	754.2
Net income ($ mil.)	3.2%	-	228.1	0.0	238.6	258.3
Market value ($ mil.)	-	-	-	-	-	-
Employees	-	-	-	-	-	1,928

WINTER HAVEN HOSPITAL, INC.

200 AVENUE F NE
WINTER HAVEN, FL 338814193
Phone: 863-293-1121
Fax: -
Web: www.baycare.org

CEO: Steve Nierman
CFO: -
HR: -
FYE: December 31
Type: Private

Winter Haven Hospital serves eastern Polk County in central Florida with general medical surgical and emergency care. The health care facility also offers specialty care in areas such as cancer heart disease stroke and a memory clinic for patients suffering from dementia and other memory disorders. The hospital's Regency Medical Center provides maternity and other health care services for women and newborns. Outpatient care is provided through an ambulatory surgery and diagnostic center and several community clinics. Winter Haven Hospital is owned by Tampa-based BayCare Health System; it was founded in 1926 as a charter hospital.

	Annual Growth	12/12	12/13	12/14	12/15	12/16
Sales ($ mil.)	5.7%	-	-	262.3	257.2	293.1
Net income ($ mil.)	167.3%	-	-	4.2	2.0	30.2
Market value ($ mil.)	-	-	-	-	-	-
Employees	-	-	-	-	-	1,480

WINTHROP NYU HOSPITAL

259 1ST ST
MINEOLA, NY 115013957
Phone: 516-663-0333
Fax: –
Web: www.winthrop.org

CEO: John F Collins
CFO: –
HR: –
FYE: December 31
Type: Private

From providing it to teaching it Winthrop-University Hospital is focused on health care. The medical center boasts some 590 beds and offers a full range of acute and tertiary health care services. Services include pediatric women's health and cancer care as well as home health services. Winthrop-University Hospital is also a leading provider of cardiovascular surgeries in the region. The hospital is a member of Winthrop-South Nassau University Health System along with sister facility South Nassau Communities Hospital. Winthrop-University Hospital serves as a teaching hospital for the SUNY at Stony Brook School of Medicine.

	Annual Growth	12/06	12/07	12/08	12/14	12/15
Sales ($ mil.)	7.9%	–	669.0	725.4	1,136.1	1,230.5
Net income ($ mil.)	–	–	0.2	(134.5)	(106.9)	(9.4)
Market value ($ mil.)	–	–	–	–	–	–
Employees	–	–	–	–	–	6,000

WINTHROP REALTY TRUST

7 Bulfinch Place, Suite 500
Boston, MA 02114
Phone: 617 570-4614
Fax: –
Web: www.winthropreit.com

NYS: FUR
CEO: –
CFO: –
HR: –
FYE: December 31
Type: Public

Winthrop Realty Trust thinks real estate loans can be just as profitable as the real thing. The externally managed real estate investment trust (REIT) invests in property real estate-related collateralized debt and other REITs. Its property portfolio consists of more than a dozen office buildings a handful of retail properties and seven apartment buildings across 15 states totaling 3.5 million square feet. Top commercial tenants include Spectra Energy's Houston headquarters grocer Kroger and e-tailer Football Fanatics' 500000-sq.-ft. distribution center. As a REIT the trust is exempt from paying federal income tax so long as it makes quarterly dividends to shareholders.

	Annual Growth	12/09	12/10	12/11	12/12	12/13
Sales ($ mil.)	13.5%	47.9	55.4	70.1	72.5	79.6
Net income ($ mil.)	–	(84.3)	16.5	10.9	24.6	28.8
Market value ($ mil.)	0.4%	395.3	465.6	370.2	402.2	402.2
Employees	–	–	–	–	–	–

WINTRUST FINANCIAL CORP (IL)

9700 W. Higgins Road, Suite 800
Rosemont, IL 60018
Phone: 847 939-9000
Fax: 847 615-4091
Web: www.wintrust.com

NMS: WTFC
CEO: Edward J. Wehmer
CFO: David A. Dykstra
HR: Janet Huffman
FYE: December 31
Type: Public

Wintrust Financial is a holding company for 15 subsidiary banks (mostly named after the individual communities they serve) with more than 150 branches primarily in the metropolitan Chicago and southern Wisconsin (including Milwaukee) markets. Boasting assets of more than $23 billion the banks offer personal and commercial banking wealth management and specialty lending services with business and commercial real estate loans making up 60% of the company's loan portfolio. Wintrust's banks target small business customers though some of Wintrust's banks also provide niche lending for homeowners associations medical practices franchisees and municipalities.

	Annual Growth	12/14	12/15	12/16	12/17	12/18
Assets ($ mil.)	11.8%	20,010.7	22,917.2	25,668.6	27,916.0	31,244.8
Net income ($ mil.)	22.7%	151.4	156.7	206.9	257.7	343.2
Market value ($ mil.)	9.2%	2,637.6	2,736.9	4,093.5	4,646.3	3,750.5
Employees	7.9%	3,491	3,770	3,878	4,075	4,727

WIRELESS TELECOM GROUP, INC.

25 Eastmans Road
Parsippany, NJ 07054
Phone: 973 386-9696
Fax: –
Web: www.wirelesstelecomgroup.com

ASE: WTT
CEO: Timothy (Tim) Whelan
CFO: Michael Kandell
HR: –
FYE: December 31
Type: Public

In an industry that prefers signal over noise Wireless Telecom Group sure makes a lot of racket. The company which markets products under the brand name Noisecom makes electronic noise generators for wireless telecommunications systems. Its products are used to test whether such systems can receive transmitted information. Its noise emulator products also operate in radar and satellite systems to continually monitor and test receivers or to jam signals. Wireless Telecom's Boonton Electronics subsidiary makes radio-frequency (RF) and microwave test equipment. Its Microlab subsidiary makes high-power passive microwave components. Wireless Telecom Group gets one-quarter of sales from outside the Americas region.

	Annual Growth	12/14	12/15	12/16	12/17	12/18
Sales ($ mil.)	7.0%	40.3	33.1	31.3	46.1	52.8
Net income ($ mil.)	(65.3%)	2.4	0.4	(1.8)	(4.5)	0.0
Market value ($ mil.)	(9.4%)	55.6	36.5	40.5	51.5	37.5
Employees	5.9%	124	113	111	154	156

WIRTZ BEVERAGE GROUP LLC

680 N. Lakeshore Dr. Ste. 1900
Chicago IL 60611
Phone: 312-943-7000
Fax: 610-370-3495
Web: www.boscovs.com

CEO: –
CFO: –
HR: –
FYE: June 30
Type: Private

Wirtz Beverage Group does it best on ice. The group owns and operates liquor distributorships and offers a full line of spirits wine and beer in the Midwest. Wirtz Beverage owns the rights to distribute some key Diageo brands such as Crown Royal Johnnie Walker J&B and Tanqueray; it also carries imported and domestic wines including labels from California's Fetzer and France's Baron Philippe de Rothschild Chateau. The company's beers include MillerCoors and Sam Adams from the US and imports the likes of as Corona. The grandson of company founder Arthur Wirtz W. Rockwell (Rocky) is the president of Wirtz Beverage Group.

WISDOMTREE INVESTMENTS, INC.

245 Park Avenue, 35th Floor
New York, NY 10167
Phone: 212 801-2080
Fax: –
Web: www.wisdomtree.com

NMS: WETF
CEO: Jonathan L. (Jono) Steinberg
CFO: Amit Muni
HR: –
FYE: December 31
Type: Public

Asset management firm WisdomTree Investments specializes in exchange-traded funds (ETFs). (ETFs are funds that track indexes such as the S&P 500 or DJIA.) Through subsidiaries WisdomTree Trust and WisdomTree Asset Management the company manages more than 90 ETFs that invest in domestic and international equities currencies fixed-income and alternatives. It provides an alternative to funds weighted by market capitalization by focusing on fundamentals such as earnings dividends and industry. Serving both individual and institutional investors fast-growing WisdomTree Investments has about $46 billion in ETF assets under management about 65% of which are tied to international hedged equities (as of early 2016).

	Annual Growth	12/14	12/15	12/16	12/17	12/18
Sales ($ mil.)	10.5%	183.8	298.9	219.4	237.4	274.1
Net income ($ mil.)	(12.0%)	61.1	80.1	26.2	27.2	36.6
Market value ($ mil.)	(19.3%)	2,401.4	2,402.2	1,706.7	1,922.7	1,018.8
Employees	16.4%	124	177	209	204	228

WISTAR INSTITUTE OF ANATOMY & BIOLOGY

3601 SPRUCE ST
PHILADELPHIA, PA 19104-4265
Phone: 215-898-3700
Fax: –
Web: www.wistar.org

CEO: Russel E Kaufman
CFO: –
HR: –
FYE: December 31
Type: Private

Founded in 1892 The Wistar Institute is a not-for-profit biomedical research institution concentrating on major diseases such as cancer cardiovascular disease autoimmune disorders and infectious diseases. The institute operates from 26 laboratories with research programs in immunology gene expression and regulation and molecular and cellular oncogenesis (process that causes formation tumors). The company has helped in the development of vaccines for rabies and rubella as well as the identification of genes associated with breast lung and prostrate cancer.

	Annual Growth	12/03	12/04	12/04	12/10	12/11
Sales ($ mil.)	11.3%	–	43.7	45.5	67.1	92.3
Net income ($ mil.)	30.5%	–	5.0	2.7	10.7	32.3
Market value ($ mil.)	–	–	–	–	–	–
Employees	–	–	–	–	–	350

WITHLACOOCHEE RIVER ELECTRIC COOPERATIVE INC

14651 21ST ST
DADE CITY, FL 335232920
Phone: 352-567-5133
Fax: –
Web: www.wrec.net

CEO: –
CFO: –
HR: Connie Hobbs
FYE: December 31
Type: Private

Withlacoochee River Electric Cooperative keeps the power flowing to the residences and businesses of more than 200360 member-owners in five counties along the central Florida Gulf Coast. The power distribution utility which was originally set up in 1941 receives wholesale generation and transmission services from the Seminole Electric Cooperative. Withlacoochee River Electric a non-profit organization returns any funds remaining at the end of each year to its membership. The cooperative has returned more than $190 million to its member-owners.

	Annual Growth	12/12	12/13	12/14	12/15	12/16
Sales ($ mil.)	1.9%	–	433.3	459.6	474.1	458.3
Net income ($ mil.)	16.6%	–	16.6	28.5	24.3	26.4
Market value ($ mil.)	–	–	–	–	–	–
Employees	–	–	–	–	–	458

WOLVERINE PIPE LINE COMPANY

8075 CREEKSIDE DR STE 210
PORTAGE, MI 490246303
Phone: 269-323-2491
Fax: –
Web: www.wolverinepipeline.com

CEO: –
CFO: –
HR: –
FYE: December 31
Type: Private

Named after a powerful weasel (the mascot of the University of Michigan) Wolverine Pipe Line transports a range of refined petroleum products across the US Midwest. It operates more than 630 miles of six-inch to 18-inch diameter pipeline which stretches through Illinois Indiana and Michigan. Wolverine Pipe Line's system also includes 12 pumping stations and transports more than 350000 barrels (or 14.7 million gallons) of refined products a day. The company also supplies about 30% of Michigan's refined petroleum products. Wolverine Pipe Line was incorporated in 1952.

	Annual Growth	12/14	12/15	12/16	12/17	12/18
Sales ($ mil.)	9.4%	–	95.3	99.5	108.4	124.8
Net income ($ mil.)	12.9%	–	32.1	33.5	50.2	46.2
Market value ($ mil.)	–	–	–	–	–	–
Employees	–	–	–	–	–	75

WOLVERINE POWER SUPPLY COOPERATIVE, INC.

10125 W WATERGATE RD
CADILLAC, MI 496018458
Phone: 231-775-5700
Fax: –
Web: www.wolverinepowercooperative.com

CEO: Eric Baker
CFO: Janet Kass
HR: –
FYE: December 31
Type: Private

Named after a voracious carnivore Wolverine Power Supply Cooperative makes sure that that voracious consumer of electricity — the American public — gets the power its needs. The non-profit company is an electric generation and transmission utility that provides services to five member distribution cooperatives in Michigan. Wolverine Power Supply Cooperative monitors and operates 1600 miles of bulk transmission lines and owns five power plants that generate 200 megawatts of capacity. It also maintains about 130 distribution substations and 36 transmission stations as well as purchases power (including windpower energy) from other utilities and marketers to distribute to its customers.

	Annual Growth	12/14	12/15	12/16	12/17	12/18
Sales ($ mil.)	7.0%	–	389.2	431.8	433.5	476.4
Net income ($ mil.)	(5.4%)	–	23.4	27.1	18.5	19.8
Market value ($ mil.)	–	–	–	–	–	–
Employees	–	–	–	–	–	110

WOLVERINE WORLD WIDE, INC.

NYS: WWW

9341 Courtland Drive N.E.
Rockford, MI 49351
Phone: 616 866-5500
Fax: –
Web: www.wolverineworldwide.com

CEO: Blake W. Krueger
CFO: Michael D. Stornant
HR: Amy Klimek
FYE: December 29
Type: Public

Wolverine World Wide makes Hush Puppies casual shoes as well as boots sandals and related apparel and accessories. In addition to Hush Puppies top footwear brands include Merrell Bates HyTest Keds Sperry Saucony Stride Rite and Wolverine; footwear is made under private labels. Wolverine also boasts several licenses from Caterpillar ("Cat") and Harley-Davidson to make branded footwear. The company licenses its Stride Rite brand under a global license arrangement. Its footwear is sold worldwide through department and specialty stores independent distributors Internet retailers and about 80 company-owned retail stores in the US and Canada. Wolverine also maintains about 40 consumer-direct e-commerce sites. About two-thirds of company total sales comes from US.

	Annual Growth	01/15	01/16*	12/16	12/17	12/18
Sales ($ mil.)	(6.7%)	2,761.1	2,691.6	2,494.6	2,350.0	2,239.2
Net income ($ mil.)	14.6%	133.1	122.8	87.7	0.3	200.1
Market value ($ mil.)	3.7%	2,662.2	1,532.4	2,012.9	2,923.5	2,972.1
Employees	(17.5%)	6,600	6,550	5,905	3,700	3,700

*Fiscal year change

WOMAN'S HOSPITAL FOUNDATION INC

100 WOMANS WAY
BATON ROUGE, LA 708175100
Phone: 225-927-1300
Fax: –
Web: www.womans.org

CEO: Teri G. Fontenot
CFO: Greg Smith
HR: Theresa M Gibson
FYE: September 30
Type: Private

Woman's Hospital is a 168-bed hospital catering to the needs of women and infants in southern Louisiana. Founded in 1968 the hospital was one of the nation's first women's specialty hospitals. Services include breast and gynecologic oncology genetics counseling neonatal intensive care and speech therapy. The not-for-profit hospital offers women's health classes as well as other educational resources and delivers about 8600 babies each year. In addition to the main hospital facility the company operates a child development center a wellness center a physician office a cancer pavilion and an ambulatory surgery center.

	Annual Growth	09/10	09/11	09/12	09/15	09/16
Sales ($ mil.)	5.7%	–	219.1	217.7	503.3	288.6
Net income ($ mil.)	0.4%	–	46.1	22.5	36.2	47.0
Market value ($ mil.)	–	–	–	–	–	–
Employees	–	–	–	–	–	1,850

WOODMEN OF THE WORLD LIFE INSURANCE SOCIETY

1700 Farnam St.   CEO: James Mounce
Omaha NE 68102   CFO: –
Phone: 402-342-1890   HR: –
Fax: 402-997-7948   FYE: December 31
Web: www.woodmen.com   Type: Insurance Society

Count the rings on Woodmen and you'll get back to 1890. Woodmen of the World Life Insurance Society is a life insurance company formed to benefit the members of Woodmen of the World a fraternal organization with some 750000 members across the US. The company provides its members with traditional life insurance as well as annuities for both individuals and small businesses. It also offers mutual funds variable annuities and 529 college savings accounts through its Woodmen Financial Services subsidiary. Additionally members have access to major medical coverage and disability insurance via marketing agreements with some third-party insurers.

WOODS HOLE, MARTHA'S VINEYARD AND NANTUCKET STEAMSHIP AUTHORITY

1 COWDRY RD   CEO: –
WOODS HOLE, MA 025431039   CFO: –
Phone: 508-548-5011   HR: Robert Davis
Fax: –   FYE: December 31
Web: www.steamshipauthority.com   Type: Private

Woods Hole Martha's Vineyard and Nantucket Steamship Authority known to owners of summer homes and year-round residents as the Steamship Authority provides ferry service from the Massachusetts ports of Woods Hole and Hyannis to the islands of Martha's Vineyard and Nantucket off the coast of Massachusetts. The company operates a fleet of nine vessels designed to carry passengers vehicles and other cargo. In 2014 it ferried 2.5 million passengers 460000 automobiles and 166500 trucks. The Steamship Authority is a quasi-public agency created by the Massachusetts legislature that competes with other private ferries but also oversees and licenses their operations.

	Annual Growth	12/13	12/14	12/15	12/16	12/17
Sales ($ mil.)	–	–	0.0	100.1	103.9	102.9
Net income ($ mil.)	7.4%	–	8.3	12.6	10.4	10.3
Market value ($ mil.)	–	–	–	–	–	–
Employees	–	–	–	–	–	750

WOODSTOCK HOLDINGS INC   NBB: WSFL

117 Towne Lake Parkway, Suite 200   CEO: –
Woodstock, GA 30188   CFO: Melissa L Whitley
Phone: 770 516-6996   HR: –
Fax: 877 431-5727   FYE: December 31
Web: www.woodstockholdingsinc.com   Type: Public

Woodstock Financial Group offers up financial advice but just don't expect to hear about hippie stock picks. The company formerly Raike Financial Group brokers support services for brokers. Founded in 1995 the company provides licensing clearing IT support education and various administrative services to a network of independent financial planners insurance agents and traditional and discount securities brokers. Woodstock handles a range of investment products including stocks bonds mutual funds annuities and life insurance. Online trading is offered through its Woodstock Discount Brokerage division. Founder and CEO William Raike owns about 80% of the company.

	Annual Growth	12/14	12/15	12/16	12/17	12/18
Sales ($ mil.)	(11.6%)	10.1	7.9	6.9	6.7	6.2
Net income ($ mil.)	–	0.2	(0.2)	(0.3)	(0.2)	(0.4)
Market value ($ mil.)	62.7%	0.1	0.1	0.2	0.7	0.7
Employees	(44.6%)	85	11	9	9	8

WOODWARD, INC.   NMS: WWD

1081 Woodward Way   CEO: Thomas A. Gendron
Fort Collins, CO 80524   CFO: Robert F. (Bob) Weber
Phone: 970 482-5811   HR: Kody Braisted
Fax: –   FYE: September 30
Web: www.woodward.com   Type: Public

Woodward Inc. is a controlling presence in many a machine. The Fort Collins Colorado-based company manufactures and services energy control and optimization systems that keep fluids gasses and electricity flowing through aircraft vehicles turbine and piston engines and electrical power equipment. Its products ? valves nozzles actuators sensors and more ? go to OEMs and prime contractors around the world for use in commercial and military aerospace power generation and distribution and transportation applications. Customers include GE and Boeing. Woodward makes its products primarily in the US which accounts for more than half of its sales.

	Annual Growth	09/15	09/16	09/17	09/18	09/19
Sales ($ mil.)	9.2%	2,038.3	2,023.1	2,098.7	2,325.9	2,900.2
Net income ($ mil.)	9.4%	181.5	180.8	200.5	180.4	259.6
Market value ($ mil.)	27.6%	2,511.6	3,855.6	4,789.2	4,989.8	6,654.1
Employees	6.9%	6,900	6,800	6,900	8,300	9,000

WOOLRICH INC.

2 MILL ST   CEO: –
WOOLRICH, PA 17779   CFO: –
Phone: 570-769-6464   HR: Dave Machamer
Fax: –   FYE: January 02
Web: www.woolrich.com   Type: Private

Woolrich has branched out beyond woolen textiles. As the US's oldest continuously operating apparel manufacturer and woolen mill the outdoor apparel maker's products include men's and women's sportswear and outerwear woolen fabrics blankets and home furnishings. Woolrich also licenses its name for the sale of furniture and accessories. Its branded products are marketed domestically and internationally. In addition Woolrich supplies woolen yard goods to apparel and home furnishings makers. The firm distributes several million catalogs per year and sells via the Internet. The Rich family founded Woolrich in 1830.

	Annual Growth	12/05	12/06	12/07*	01/09	01/10
Sales ($ mil.)	–	–	–	(1,608.9)	114.4	99.4
Net income ($ mil.)	2152.6%	–	–	0.0	(1.9)	0.8
Market value ($ mil.)	–	–	–	–	–	–
Employees	–	–	–	–	–	200

*Fiscal year change

WORKDAY INC   NMS: WDAY

6110 Stoneridge Mall Road   CEO: Aneel Bhusri
Pleasanton, CA 94588   CFO: Robynne Sisco
Phone: 925 951-9000   HR: Spence Harrell
Fax: –   FYE: January 31
Web: www.workday.com   Type: Public

Workday wants to make every day better for the folks in HR and finance. The computer software company makes cloud-based enterprise applications to manage financial and human capital resources as well as planning and analytics tools. Workday's products are designed to replace on-site legacy systems with a more collaborative mobile and intuitive interface and a frequently updated product that includes regulatory changes. Customers include Abbott Amazon Bank of America Bill Gosling Outsourcing CHC and Choice. Workday touts its workplace culture and its No. 4 ranking on Fortune's 100 Best Companies to Work For list.

	Annual Growth	01/15	01/16	01/17	01/18	01/19
Sales ($ mil.)	37.6%	787.9	1,162.3	1,569.4	2,143.1	2,822.2
Net income ($ mil.)	–	(248.0)	(289.9)	(408.3)	(321.2)	(418.3)
Market value ($ mil.)	22.9%	17,644.3	13,991.6	18,450.3	26,621.8	40,309.1
Employees	29.4%	3,750	5,200	6,600	8,200	10,500

WORKSTREAM USA INC.

OTC: WSTM

2200 Lucien Way Ste. 201
Maitland FL 32751
Phone: 407-475-5500
Fax: 407-475-5517
Web: www.workstreaminc.com

CEO: David Kennedy
CFO: –
HR: Ginger Simpson
FYE: May 31
Type: Public

Workstream puts an oar in the workforce placement and productivity waters to help clients keep their employee ships floating along. The company provides software that automates the hiring process and helps businesses manage human resources operations. Workstream's Software-as-a-Service (SaaS) offerings include recruitment systems for hiring new employees; performance management tools for measuring competencies setting goals and providing feedback; compensation management tools for planning rewards programs; and employee portal applications. The company also offers recruitment research applicant sourcing career transition and outplacement services. Canada accounts for 13% of sales.

WORLD ACCEPTANCE CORP.

NMS: WRLD

108 Frederick Street
Greenville, SC 29607
Phone: 864 298-9800
Fax: –
Web: www.loansbyworld.com

CEO: A. Alexander (Sandy) McLean
CFO: John L. Calmes
HR: Kevin Gross
FYE: March 31
Type: Public

Who in the world will accept your poor credit? World Acceptance Corp just might. The consumer finance company offers short-term and medium-term loans and credit insurance to individuals with limited access to other credit sources. Borrowers use the loans of $300 to $4000 to meet temporary or unanticipated cash needs such as car repairs and medical bills filling a void left by banks and credit unions which typically don't make loans of less than $5000. Convenience comes at a price: World Acceptance often charges the maximum interest rates and related fees allowed by law. The fast-growing company has more than 1300 offices in 15 states in the US South and Midwest as well as in Mexico.

	Annual Growth	03/15	03/16	03/17	03/18	03/19
Sales ($ mil.)	(2.8%)	610.2	557.5	531.7	548.7	544.5
Net income ($ mil.)	(23.9%)	110.8	87.4	73.6	53.7	37.2
Market value ($ mil.)	12.6%	677.0	352.1	480.7	977.6	1,087.4
Employees	(6.0%)	4,643	4,436	3,621	3,419	3,624

WORLD ENERGY SOLUTIONS, INC. (DE)

NAS: XWES

100 Front Street
Worcester, MA 01608
Phone: 508 459-8100
Fax: –
Web: www.worldenergy.com

CEO: Philip V Adams
CFO: James F Parslow
HR: –
FYE: December 31
Type: Public

World Energy Solutions offers its customers some protection from the world of hurt that is rising energy prices. The company offers energy procurement market analysis and risk management services for industrial and commercial customers and government entities in deregulated regions of the US. World Energy Solutions analyzes clients' energy needs and provides savings on electricity and natural gas supply contracts through its online reverse auction platforms; it also manages bill payments and monitors energy usage after the auction process. The company's more than 300 customers include Cargill Energy Marketing Ford Leidos and the US Postal Service.

	Annual Growth	12/08	12/09	12/10	12/11	12/12
Sales ($ mil.)	26.4%	12.4	14.6	18.0	21.1	31.8
Net income ($ mil.)	–	(6.8)	(2.3)	(0.1)	0.5	5.3
Market value ($ mil.)	84.9%	4.5	34.8	33.9	36.1	52.6
Employees	23.0%	55	54	60	82	126

WORLD FINER FOODS, LLC

1455 BROAD ST STE 4
BLOOMFIELD, NJ 070033039
Phone: 973-338-0300
Fax: –
Web: www.worldfiner.com

CEO: –
CFO: William Flynn
HR: –
FYE: December 31
Type: Private

Fine food is quite a find for this company and its customers. World Finer Foods distributes more than 900 specialty food items to US supermarkets and gourmet food stores. Its inventory boasts some 40 brands including Blanchard & Blanchard La Vie Mrs. Leeper's Pasta and Panni. The company also markets its own food products under such names as DaVinci London Pub Pritikin and Reese. Its InterNatural Foods unit represents its natural foods division while its Liberty Richter division distributes domestic and imported gourmet food items. Founded as VIP Foods in 1971 World Finer Foods is a cooperative owned by food distributors Millbrook Distribution (a unit of United Natural Foods) and Kehe Food.

	Annual Growth	12/05	12/06	12/07	12/08	12/10
Sales ($ mil.)	13.2%	–	–	–	126.0	161.4
Net income ($ mil.)	(68.7%)	–	–	–	0.7	0.1
Market value ($ mil.)	–	–	–	–	–	–
Employees	–	–	–	–	–	85

WORLD FUEL SERVICES CORP.

NYS: INT

9800 Northwest 41st Street
Miami, FL 33178
Phone: 305 428-8000
Fax: 305 392-5621
Web: www.wfscorp.com

CEO: Michael J. Kasbar
CFO: Ira M. Birns
HR: Sue Rider
FYE: December 31
Type: Public

World Fuel Services can't yet affect the earth's spin but it plays a part in moving mostly everything else across its surface. The company sells fuel and fuel handling services to small-to-midsized air carriers cargo and charter carriers and private aircraft. as well as support activities such as flight planning weather reports and card payment services. It is also a marine fuel reseller on hand to deliver marine fuel to the shipping industry and commercial vessels and supplies land transport markets via hundreds of terminals in the US and Watson Fuels in the UK. It has almost 50 offices around the world and does business or virtually every country. The company was founded in 1985 as a marine fuel brokerage firm.

	Annual Growth	12/14	12/15	12/16	12/17	12/18
Sales ($ mil.)	(2.2%)	43,386.4	30,379.7	27,015.8	33,695.5	39,750.3
Net income ($ mil.)	(12.9%)	221.7	186.9	126.5	(170.2)	127.7
Market value ($ mil.)	(17.8%)	3,144.3	2,576.8	3,076.0	1,885.4	1,434.5
Employees	5.5%	4,041	4,700	5,000	5,000	5,000

WORLD SURVEILLANCE GROUP INC

NBB: WSGI

State Road 405, Building M6-306A, Room 1400, Kennedy Space Center
Merritt Island, FL 32815
Phone: 321 452-3545
Fax: –
Web: www.wsgi.com

CEO: Glenn D Estrella
CFO: W Jeffrey Sawyers
HR: –
FYE: December 31
Type: Public

Sanswire isn't known for a down-to-earth approach to product development. The company (formerly known as GlobeTel Communications) is developing airship "stratellites" (essentially blimps equipped with wireless gear that float in the stratosphere) to enable its planned wireless broadband network. Other intended uses for Sanswire's unmanned aerial vehicles include security and surveillance (Skysat) and payload transport and delivery (PADD). The company is developing its products in conjunction with Stuttgart Germany-based TAO Technologies GmbH.

	Annual Growth	12/09	12/10	12/11	12/12	12/13
Sales ($ mil.)	95.1%	–	0.3	0.2	1.1	1.9
Net income ($ mil.)	–	(9.4)	(9.8)	(1.1)	(3.4)	(3.4)
Market value ($ mil.)	(39.8%)	48.8	56.2	25.4	8.9	6.4
Employees	15.0%	4	4	5	5	7

WORLD VISION INTERNATIONAL

800 W. Chestnut Ave.
Monrovia CA 91016-3106
Phone: 626-303-8811
Fax: 626-301-7786
Web: www.wvi.org

CEO: –
CFO: –
HR: –
FYE: September 30
Type: Private - Partnershi

World Vision International sees a world where all children are fed sheltered educated valued and loved. The Christian relief organization advocates for children and the poor and the development of families and communities around the globe. Operating in about 100 countries from some 40 offices worldwide it focuses on education health care economic and agricultural development and emergency relief efforts; its donors sponsor more than 3 million children. While the organization prohibits proselytizing 60% of its budget goes to programs that include "domestic ministry." The group receives its contributions mainly from private sources. World Vision was founded in 1950 by the Rev. Bob Pierce.

WORLD WIDE TECHNOLOGY, LLC

1 WORLD WIDE WAY
SAINT LOUIS, MO 631463002
Phone: 314-569-7000
Fax: –

CEO: James P. (Jim) Kavanaugh
CFO: Thomas W. (Tom) Strunk
HR: –
FYE: December 31
Type: Private

World Wide Technology (WWT) has a broad view of its business. The company primarily provides such IT services as network design and installation systems and application integration and procurement. It also offers a range of Web-based products and services including e-commerce systems development order tracking and catalog management. WWT serves businesses in the automotive retail and telecommunications industries as well as government agencies. Top clients have included Dell the State of Missouri and the State of Alaska. WWT was founded in 1990.

	Annual Growth	12/11	12/12	12/13	12/14	12/15
Sales ($ mil.)	20.4%	–	3,396.3	4,545.7	5,057.3	5,927.7
Net income ($ mil.)	18.3%	–	57.5	77.6	95.0	95.1
Market value ($ mil.)	–	–	–	–	–	–
Employees	–	–	–	–	–	1,052

WORLD WILDLIFE FUND, INC.

1250 24TH ST NW FL 2
WASHINGTON, DC 200371193
Phone: 202-293-4800
Fax: –
Web: www.worldwildlife.org

CEO: Neville Isdell
CFO: –
HR: –
FYE: June 30
Type: Private

A fuzzy-wuzzy with kung fu strength the panda embodies mission of the World Wildlife Fund (WWF). The conservation organization has worked on more than 13000 projects in about 100 countries to save endangered species and natural areas as well as to address threats such as global warming and the exploitation of forests. By 2020 WWF aims to conserve 15 of the world's more ecologically important regions. Its work crosses Africa Asia Latin America North America and Eurasia through national affiliates in about 100 countries. The group publishes data on wildlife wild places and global environmental challenges. Founded in 1961 WWF is joined by 1.1 million members in the US and some 5 million overseas.

	Annual Growth	06/11	06/12	06/13	06/14	06/16
Sales ($ mil.)	11.6%	–	208.5	229.2	227.7	323.5
Net income ($ mil.)	–	–	16.9	25.5	6.9	(0.5)
Market value ($ mil.)	–	–	–	–	–	–
Employees	–	–	–	–	–	400

WORLD WRESTLING ENTERTAINMENT INC   NYS: WWE

1241 East Main Street
Stamford, CT 06902
Phone: 203 352-8600
Fax: –
Web: www.wwe.com

CEO: Vincent K McMahon
CFO: George A Barrios
HR: –
FYE: December 31
Type: Public

The action might be fake but the business of World Wrestling Entertainment (WWE) is very real. The company is a leading producer and promoter of wrestling matches for TV and live audiences exhibiting more than 350 matches each year across the globe. Its WWE Network available on a variety of digital streaming and mobile devices has more than 1.5 million paying subscribers. Its most famous live pay-per-view event is its flagship program WrestleMania. Other core content includes RAW and SmackDown Live. WWE also licenses characters for merchandise and sells videos and DVDs. Two-time WWE world champion Vince McMahon has about 80% voting control of the company.

	Annual Growth	12/14	12/15	12/16	12/17	12/18
Sales ($ mil.)	14.4%	542.6	658.8	729.2	801.0	930.2
Net income ($ mil.)	–	(30.1)	24.1	33.8	32.6	99.6
Market value ($ mil.)	56.9%	962.8	1,392.0	1,435.7	2,386.0	5,830.0
Employees	4.7%	761	840	870	850	915

WORLDPAY INC   NYS: WP

8500 Governor's Hill Drive
Symmes Township, OH 45249
Phone: 513 900-5250
Fax: –
Web: www.worldpay.com

CEO: Charles D Drucker
CFO: Stephanie Ferris
HR: –
FYE: December 31
Type: Public

This company's goal is to usher in a cashless world. Worldpay (formerly Vantiv) provides businesses large and small with card payment facilities including card machines and terminals online card payments and email mail and phone payments. Its systems accept credit debt and pre-paid cards and provide additional security and fraud management. The largest merchant acquirer (the bridge between merchants customers and their banks) in the US Worldpay processes around 23 billion payments each year and counts 11 of the top-25 US retailers as customers. Formed in 1970 Vantiv acquired Worldpay Group plc the UK's biggest payments processor in 2018 for $10 billion and assumed the Worldpay name.

	Annual Growth	12/13	12/14	12/15	12/16	12/17
Sales ($ mil.)	17.6%	2,108.1	2,577.2	3,159.9	3,579.0	4,026.5
Net income ($ mil.)	(0.7%)	133.6	125.3	147.9	213.2	130.1
Market value ($ mil.)	22.5%	5,799.6	6,032.6	8,433.6	10,603.3	13,080.8
Employees	(22.6%)	2,791	3,299	3,313	3,526	1,000

WORLDWIDE MEDIA SERVICES GROUP INC.

1350 E NEWPRT CTR DR 20
DEERFIELD BEACH, FL 33442
Phone: 561-989-1342
Fax: –
Web: www.americanmediainc.com

CEO: David Pecker
CFO: Chris Polimeni
HR: –
FYE: March 31
Type: Private

Worldwide Media Services is a publisher of tabloid newspapers and magazines including National Enquirer and Star. The company also publishes women's health magazine Shape as well as a number of other magazines including Flex Men's Fitness and Natural Health. In addition to publishing its own titles Worldwide Media also distributes and markets other publishers' periodicals. The company is owned by a group of investment firms including Angelo Gordon & Co.

	Annual Growth	03/11	03/12	03/13	03/14	03/15
Sales ($ mil.)	(28.8%)	–	–	–	344.2	245.2
Net income ($ mil.)	–	–	–	–	(53.3)	(25.9)
Market value ($ mil.)	–	–	–	–	–	–
Employees	–	–	–	–	–	14,375

WORTHINGTON INDUSTRIES, INC.   NYS: WOR

200 Old Wilson Bridge Road
Columbus, OH 43085
Phone: 614 438-3210
Fax: 614 438-3256
Web: www.worthingtonindustries.com

CEO: John P. McConnell
CFO: B. Andrew (Andy) Rose
HR: Terry Dyer
FYE: May 31
Type: Public

Worthington Industries is one of the largest steel processors in the US processing flat-rolled steel and related products for industrial customers including automotive appliance and machinery companies. The company also forms flat-rolled steel to exact customer specifications filling a niche not usually served by steelmakers with limited processing capabilities. Worthington's subsidiaries make products such as pressure cylinders metal framing and automotive panels. Through joint ventures the company also makes steel products such as metal ceiling grid systems and laser-welded blanks.

	Annual Growth	05/15	05/16	05/17	05/18	05/19
Sales ($ mil.)	2.7%	3,384.2	2,819.7	3,014.1	3,581.6	3,759.6
Net income ($ mil.)	18.9%	76.8	143.7	204.5	194.8	153.5
Market value ($ mil.)	5.8%	1,509.3	2,072.3	2,328.0	2,659.7	1,893.7
Employees	3.4%	10,500	10,000	10,000	12,000	12,000

WPX ENERGY INC   NYS: WPX

3500 One Williams Center
Tulsa, OK 74172-0172
Phone: 855 979-2012
Fax: –
Web: www.wpxenergy.com

CEO: Richard E. (Rick) Muncrief
CFO: J. Kevin Vann
HR: –
FYE: December 31
Type: Public

WPX Energy searches across the US for lucrative hydrocarbon assets. The oil and gas exploration production and marketing company owns producing oil natural gas and natural gas liquids (NGL) properties in the Permian and Williston basins in North Dakota Texas and New Mexico. WPX boasts total proved reserves of 480 million barrels of oil equivalent. The company is focusing on acquiring and developing large continuous blocks of land to build its acreage position and achieve economies of scale. Recent years have seen WPX dispose all its assets outside the Permian and Williston basins.

	Annual Growth	12/14	12/15	12/16	12/17	12/18
Sales ($ mil.)	(9.8%)	3,493.0	1,888.0	693.0	1,336.0	2,310.0
Net income ($ mil.)	(2.0%)	164.0	(1,727.0)	(601.0)	(16.0)	151.0
Market value ($ mil.)	(0.6%)	4,891.6	2,414.2	6,128.1	5,917.8	4,773.8
Employees	(14.1%)	1,100	1,040	650	650	600

WRIGHT INVESTORS' SERVICE HOLDINGS, INC.   NBB: WISH

177 West Putnam Avenue
Greenwich, CT 06830
Phone: 914 242-5700
Fax: –
Web: www.corporateinformation.com

CEO: Harvey P Eisen
CFO: Ira J Sobotko
HR: –
FYE: December 31
Type: Public

National Patent Development (NPD) is a shell company that holds stakes in plastics molding and precision coatings manufacturer MXL Industries and Endo International which is developing treatments for pain overactive bladder prostate cancer and the early onset of puberty. The scaled-down NPD also owns real estate in Connecticut. In 2010 the company sold its home improvement products wholesaler Five Star Products a core unit that had represented 100% of its 2009 sales to The Merit Group for more than $30 million; NPD netted about $10 million from the deal. Investment management and financial advisory firm The Winthrop Corporation bought NPD in late 2012.

	Annual Growth	12/13	12/14	12/15	12/16	12/17
Sales ($ mil.)	(1.9%)	5.9	5.8	6.0	5.7	5.4
Net income ($ mil.)	–	(6.8)	(2.2)	(2.4)	(2.1)	(1.3)
Market value ($ mil.)	(28.5%)	38.3	32.3	38.1	12.1	10.0
Employees	(6.9%)	40	40	32	30	30

WRIGHT MEDICAL GROUP INC.   NMS: WMGI

1023 Cherry Road
Memphis, TN 38117
Phone: 901 867-9971
Fax: –
Web: www.wmt.com

CEO: Robert J Palmisano
CFO: Lance A Berry
HR: Ken Duda
FYE: December 31
Type: Public

Wright Medical Group makes replacement parts for humans. The company makes reconstructive implants for the foot ankle hand elbow shoulder and other defective joints. Product lines include the INBONE CLAW and ORTHOLOC systems for feet and ankles MICRONAIL implants to repair wrist fractures. Wright Medical makes an injectable putty for bone defects as well as bone graft and tissue substitute materials such as OSTEOSET pellets used to regenerate bone. The company sold its hip and knee implant business OrthoRecon in 2014. Wright Medical's products are sold in more than 60 countries although the US is its largest market.

	Annual Growth	12/09	12/10	12/11	12/12	12/13
Sales ($ mil.)	(16.0%)	487.5	519.0	512.9	483.8	242.3
Net income ($ mil.)	–	12.1	17.8	(5.1)	5.3	(273.9)
Market value ($ mil.)	12.8%	909.0	745.3	791.9	1,007.4	1,473.9
Employees	(9.2%)	1,320	1,390	1,290	1,400	898

WRIGHT STATE UNIVERSITY

3640 COLONEL GLENN HWY
DAYTON, OH 454350002
Phone: 937-775-3333
Fax: –
Web: www.wright.edu

CEO: –
CFO: Jeff Ulliman
HR: –
FYE: June 30
Type: Private

Wright State University named after aviation pioneers the Wright Brothers has an enrollment of more than 17770 students and offers more than 230 undergraduate graduate and professional degrees. It consists of eight colleges (including education and human services business engineering and computer science liberal arts nursing and health and science and mathematics) and three schools (graduate studies medicine professional psychology). Wright State has more than 900 full-time faculty members. Originally a branch campus of Ohio State University and Miami University Wright State became an independent university in 1967.

	Annual Growth	06/13	06/14	06/15	06/16	06/17
Sales ($ mil.)	(0.8%)	–	235.9	233.5	238.2	230.3
Net income ($ mil.)	–	–	(3.3)	(22.0)	(37.4)	(47.1)
Market value ($ mil.)	–	–	–	–	–	–
Employees	–	–	–	–	–	2,748

WRITERS GUILD OF AMERICA WEST INC.

7000 W 3RD ST
LOS ANGELES, CA 900484321
Phone: 323-951-4000
Fax: –
Web: www.wga.org

CEO: David Young
CFO: –
HR: Mary Casey
FYE: March 31
Type: Private

The Writers Guild of America west puts the H in Hollywood the T in TV and the N in new media. It's the West Coast version of the Writers Guild of America and-, a labor union-, that-, represents-, more than 7000 writers in the motion picture broadcast cable and new technologies industries. The union which began in 1921-, backs members in contract negotiations and enforcement oversees credits for films and TV shows collects and distributes payments for the reuse of movies and TV shows and conducts educational events.-, It does not-, act as an employment agency-, for writers or recommend them. The WGAw-, also-, maintains-, a registry that covers-, some 55000 written works each year protecting the authors from plagiarism.

	Annual Growth	03/08	03/09	03/10	03/11	03/14
Sales ($ mil.)	–	–	(257.7)	23.9	24.2	27.8
Net income ($ mil.)	22.3%	–	–	2.1	0.2	4.6
Market value ($ mil.)	–	–	–	–	–	–
Employees	–	–	–	–	–	160

WSFS FINANCIAL CORP
NMS: WSFS

500 Delaware Avenue
Wilmington, DE 19801
Phone: 302 792-6000
Fax: -
Web: www.wsfsbank.com

CEO: Mark A. Turner
CFO: Dominic Canuso
HR: Robert Silwa
FYE: December 31
Type: Public

WSFS isn't a radio station but it is tuned to the banking needs of Delaware. WSFS Financial is the holding company for Wilmington Savings Fund Society (WSFS Bank) a thrift with nearly $5 billion in assets and more than 75 branches mostly in Delaware and Pennsylvania. Founded in 1832 WSFS Bank attracts deposits from individuals and local businesses by offering standard products like checking and savings accounts CDs and IRAs. The bank uses funds primarily to lend to businesses: Commercial loans and mortgages account for about 85% of its loan portfolio. Bank subsidiaries Christiana Trust Cypress Capital Management and WSFS Wealth Investment provide trust and investment advisory services to wealthy clients and institutional investors.

	Annual Growth	12/14	12/15	12/16	12/17	12/18
Assets ($ mil.)	10.5%	4,853.3	5,586.0	6,765.3	6,999.5	7,248.9
Net income ($ mil.)	25.8%	53.8	53.5	64.1	50.2	134.7
Market value ($ mil.)	(16.2%)	2,412.4	1,015.3	1,454.2	1,501.3	1,189.4
Employees	8.8%	841	947	1,116	1,159	1,177

WSI INDUSTRIES, INC.
NAS: WSCI

213 Chelsea Road
Monticello, MN 55362
Phone: 763 295-9202
Fax: -
Web: www.wsiindustries.com

CEO: Michael J Pudil
CFO: Paul D Sheely
HR: -
FYE: August 27
Type: Public

WSI Industries likes to metal in the affairs of others. The precision contract machining company manufactures metal components. Through the Taurus Numeric Tool division WSI Industries provides contract machining services. Most of the company's revenues are derived from machining work for the aerospace/avionics/military industries and recreational vehicles (all-terrain vehicles and motorcycles) markets. WSI Industries has a plant in Monticello Minnesota. The firm's principal customer ATV maker Polaris Industries represents more than half of the company's sales. National Oilwell Varco accounts for about one-third of sales.

	Annual Growth	08/13	08/14	08/15	08/16	08/17
Sales ($ mil.)	(2.5%)	34.0	42.7	43.0	35.2	30.6
Net income ($ mil.)	-	0.7	1.2	1.0	0.2	(0.8)
Market value ($ mil.)	(15.7%)	18.4	22.5	16.6	10.7	9.3
Employees	1.7%	85	95	89	91	91

WVS FINANCIAL CORP.
NMS: WVFC

9001 Perry Highway
Pittsburgh, PA 15237
Phone: 412 364-1911
Fax: -
Web: www.wvsbank.com

CEO: David J Bursic
CFO: -
HR: -
FYE: June 30
Type: Public

WVS Financial is the holding company for West View Savings Bank which serves Pittsburgh's North Hills suburbs from about a half-dozen offices. The bank which opened in 1908 offers standard deposit products such as checking and savings accounts CDs and IRAs. Its lending activities primarily consist of real estate loans including construction loans and commercial multifamily and single-family mortgages. West View Savings Bank also writes consumer (mainly home equity) and business loans. Interest from investments in securities such as US government agency securities municipal and corporate bonds and mortgage-backed securities account for about half of WVS Financial's revenue.

	Annual Growth	06/15	06/16	06/17	06/18	06/19
Assets ($ mil.)	1.9%	329.7	335.7	351.6	352.3	355.8
Net income ($ mil.)	20.0%	1.3	1.3	1.6	2.1	2.8
Market value ($ mil.)	10.5%	22.8	21.6	31.3	32.2	34.0
Employees	(4.0%)	46	41	40	39	39

WW INTERNATIONAL INC
NMS: WW

675 Avenue of the Americas, 6th Floor
New York, NY 10010
Phone: 212 589-2700
Fax: -
Web: www.weightwatchersinternational.com

CEO: Mindy Grossman
CFO: Nicholas P. (Nick) Hotchkin
HR: -
FYE: December 29
Type: Public

Weight Watchers (which now goes by WW) offers one of the world's leading weight management programs hosting more than 31000 weekly meetings worldwide facilitated by some 8500 leaders. Meetings cover nutritional advice and lifestyle tips to help more than a million members lose weight and ultimately reach lifetime membership status. Another 2 million members subscribe to the company's online program. WW also sells magazine subscriptions recipe books food vitamins and activity monitors among other products. It generates most of its revenue from North America. Jean Nidetch and Al and Felice Lippert started Weight Watchers in 1963. Talk show host and entrepreneur Oprah Winfrey owns about 11% of the company.

	Annual Growth	01/15	01/16*	12/16	12/17	12/18
Sales ($ mil.)	0.8%	1,479.9	1,164.4	1,164.9	1,306.9	1,514.1
Net income ($ mil.)	31.4%	98.6	32.9	67.7	163.5	223.7
Market value ($ mil.)	24.2%	1,441.6	1,526.6	766.6	2,964.8	2,764.6
Employees	(5.0%)	21,000	19,000	18,000	18,000	18,000

*Fiscal year change

WYCKOFF HEIGHTS MEDICAL CENTER

374 STOCKHOLM ST
BROOKLYN, NY 112374006
Phone: 718-963-7272
Fax: -
Web: www.wyckoffhospital.org

CEO: Dominick Gio
CFO: -
HR: -
FYE: December 31
Type: Private

Wyckoff Heights is taking health care to new levels. Serving the New York boroughs of Brooklyn and Queens Wyckoff Heights Medical Center maintains some 350 beds and provides a comprehensive range of specialized services including diagnostics radiology cardiology obstetrics pediatrics surgery and rehabilitative care. The hospital also provides educational services through a partnership with the Weill Medical College of Cornell University and it offers outpatient services through several family health clinics in the area. The not-for-profit medical center is governed by an independent board of trustees.

	Annual Growth	12/11	12/12	12/13	12/14	12/15
Sales ($ mil.)	(2.4%)	-	246.2	276.7	249.7	229.0
Net income ($ mil.)	(47.2%)	-	4.7	1.0	2.1	0.7
Market value ($ mil.)	-	-	-	-	-	-
Employees	-	-	-	-	-	1,900

WYLE LABORATORIES INC.

1960 E. Grand Ave. Ste. 900
El Segundo CA 90245-5023
Phone: 310-563-6800
Fax: 310-563-6850
Web: www.wyle.com

CEO: George R Melton
CFO: Dana Dorsey
HR: -
FYE: December 31
Type: Private

Wyle Laboratories is wild about the technical expertise it offers. The firm provides engineering testing life cycle management clinical health services operations support and other technical support services to clients in such industries as aerospace life sciences telecommunications and transportation. Besides serving commercial and industrial clients the company is also a large government contractor working with various branches of the Department of Defense and NASA. Founded in 1949 as a testing laboratory Wyle Laboratories operates more than 50 facilities around the country with about 4800 employees. It owns fellow government contractor Wyle Information Systems Group.

WYNDHAM DESTINATIONS INC
NYS: WYND

6277 Sea Harbor Drive
Orlando, FL 32821
Phone: 407 626-5200
Fax: –
Web: www.wyndhamdestinations.com

CEO: –
CFO: Michael Hug
HR: Kimberly A. Marshall
FYE: December 31
Type: Public

Wyndham Destinations (formerly Wyndham Worldwide) is one of the world's largest timeshare vacation companies. Its portfolio includes more than 220 vacation ownership resorts offered under the Club Wyndham WorldMark by Wyndham Margaritaville Vacation Club by Wyndham and Shell Vacations Club brands. The company also manages some 4300 affiliated vacation exchange and rental properties through Resort Condominiums International (RCI). All told Wyndham Destinations is present in more than 110 countries. In 2018 the company spun off its hotel business including top franchise brands Days Inn Howard Johnson Ramada and Super 8. Its Wyndham Vacation Rentals (900 rental properties) business is up for sale.

	Annual Growth	12/14	12/15	12/16	12/17	12/18
Sales ($ mil.)	(7.1%)	5,281.0	5,536.0	5,599.0	5,076.0	3,931.0
Net income ($ mil.)	6.2%	529.0	612.0	611.0	871.0	672.0
Market value ($ mil.)	(19.6%)	8,145.7	6,900.5	7,253.8	11,005.7	3,404.2
Employees	(8.1%)	34,400	37,700	37,800	39,200	24,500

WYNN RESORTS LTD
NMS: WYNN

3131 Las Vegas Boulevard South
Las Vegas, NV 89109
Phone: 702 770-7555
Fax: –
Web: www.wynnresorts.com

CEO: Stephen A. Wynn
CFO: Craig S. Billings
HR: Troy Mitchum
FYE: December 31
Type: Public

Wynn Resorts operates a handful of luxury casino resorts including the Wynn Las Vegas in Las Vegas and the Wynn Macau and the Wynn Palace in Macau China the only place in China where gambling is legal. It opened its first US resort and casino outside Vegas the $2.6 billion Encore Boston Harbor in June 2019. The company's properties integrate luxury hotel rooms high-end retail an array of dining and entertainment options meeting and convention space and gaming. Most revenue comes from China. The firm works to attract international customers through marketing offices in Hong Kong Singapore Japan Taiwan and Canada. The Wynn brand is the brainchild of gaming mogul and former Mirage Resorts chairman Steve Wynn.

	Annual Growth	12/14	12/15	12/16	12/17	12/18
Sales ($ mil.)	5.4%	5,433.7	4,075.9	4,466.3	6,306.4	6,717.7
Net income ($ mil.)	(5.9%)	731.6	195.3	242.0	747.2	572.4
Market value ($ mil.)	(9.7%)	15,951.8	7,419.4	9,276.6	18,078.2	10,606.3
Employees	11.5%	16,800	20,800	24,600	25,200	26,000

WYOMING MEDICAL CENTER, INC.

1233 E 2ND ST
CASPER, WY 826012988
Phone: 307-577-7201
Fax: –
Web: www.wyomingmedicalcenter.org

CEO: Pam Fulks
CFO: Edmond Renenmas
HR: Lindee Zespy
FYE: June 30
Type: Private

Wyoming Medical Center is The Cowboy State's largest medical facility. The hospital founded in 1911 offers those who live in and around Wyoming's Natrona County more than 50 medical specialties thanks to its 150 physicians. The health care services provider boasts nearly 1300 skilled staff members and more than 190 beds. It offers services such as an emergency air transport system trauma care diagnostic services diabetes care center nephrology and surgical care. The facility is a community-owned not-for-profit hospital.that also operates the Heart Center of Wyoming the Wyoming Neuroscience and Spine Institute and a network of about a dozen community clinics throughout Wyoming.

	Annual Growth	06/14	06/15	06/16	06/17	06/18
Sales ($ mil.)	0.7%	–	224.2	205.9	220.3	228.7
Net income ($ mil.)	50.2%	–	8.0	1.1	34.9	26.9
Market value ($ mil.)	–	–	–	–	–	–
Employees	–	–	–	–	–	1,149

X-RITE INCORPORATED
NASDAQ: XRIT

4300 44th St. SE
Grand Rapids MI 49512
Phone: 616-803-2100
Fax: 616-534-0723
Web: www.x-rite.com

CEO: Thomas J Vacchiano Jr
CFO: Rajesh K Shah
HR: –
FYE: December 31
Type: Public

X-Rite has an eye for color. Its products help manufacturers retailers distributors printers and graphic designers achieve a consistent color appearance. Using spectrophotometers and colorimeters its color measurement products check that fabrics paints and plastics are the correct shade. Its color standards product line uses densitometers to measure optical and photographic density and control color for processing textiles film and inks. Products include paint matching systems for retailers sensitometers for manipulating photographic film exposure and color formulation software for PCs. More than two-thirds of sales come from outside the US. In 2012 Danaher bought X-Rite for about $625 million.

XAVIER UNIVERSITY

3800 VICTORY PKWY UNIT 1
CINCINNATI, OH 452071092
Phone: 513-961-0133
Fax: –
Web: www.xavier.edu

CEO: –
CFO: Maribeth Amyot
HR: –
FYE: June 30
Type: Private

Xavier University is a not-for-profit Jesuit Catholic institution that operates from a single campus located in Cincinnati Ohio. The private school which has recently grown its enrollment numbers to about 7000 students offers nearly 90 undergraduate programs and about 20 graduate programs. Xavier University's programs range from arts and sciences to social sciences and business. Boasting small class sizes the university's student-to-faculty ratio is a noteworthy 12:1. Known among sports circles as having a highly respected men's basketball program Xavier University also manages to graduate every member of its men's Musketeers group. Xavier University was founded in 1831.

	Annual Growth	06/09	06/10	06/11	06/12	06/13
Sales ($ mil.)	(1.3%)	–	–	167.9	166.9	163.5
Net income ($ mil.)	(20.7%)	–	–	22.7	(22.5)	14.3
Market value ($ mil.)	–	–	–	–	–	–
Employees	–	–	–	–	–	940

XCEL ENERGY INC
NMS: XEL

414 Nicollet Mall
Minneapolis, MN 55401
Phone: 612 330-5500
Fax: –
Web: www.xcelenergy.com

CEO: Benjamin G. S. (Ben) Fowke
CFO: Robert C. (Bob) Frenzel
HR: –
FYE: December 31
Type: Public

Xcel Energy is a utility holding company distributing electricity to 3.6 million customers and natural gas to 2 million in eight states through its four regulated utilities: Northern States Power Minnesota Northern States Power Wisconsin the Public Service Company of Colorado and Southwestern Public Service. Colorado and Minnesota account for most of the company's customers. Xcel owns power plants that have combined capacity of more than 18200 MW of electricity. It also owns transmission and distribution lines as well as natural gas assets. It is investing in wind power and operates wind farms in Colorado Minnesota and a half-a-dozen other states. The company traces its roots back to 1881.

	Annual Growth	12/14	12/15	12/16	12/17	12/18
Sales ($ mil.)	(0.3%)	11,686.1	11,024.5	11,106.9	11,404.0	11,537.0
Net income ($ mil.)	5.4%	1,021.3	984.5	1,123.4	1,148.0	1,261.0
Market value ($ mil.)	8.2%	18,464.2	18,459.1	20,921.3	24,730.3	25,326.6
Employees	(1.3%)	11,691	11,687	11,512	11,134	11,092

XCERRA CORP
NMS: XCRA

825 University Avenue
Norwood, MA 02062
Phone: 781 461-1000
Fax: 408 635-4985
Web: www.xcerra.com

CEO: David G Tacelli
CFO: Mark J Gallenberger
HR: –
FYE: July 31
Type: Public

Xcerra puts semiconductors to the test to make sure that your smartphone works. The company makes automated test equipment (ATE) that chip makers use to test semiconductors as they're manufactured and as part of the final package test. The company's equipment also tests printed circuit boards (PCBs). Its equipment runs tests on devices used in smartphones modems PCs TVs imaging instruments and a variety of others. The company sells through four brands: atg-Luther & Maelzer Everett Charles Technologies LTX-Credence and Multitest. Xcerra handles some of its manufacturing but outsources most of it to Jabil Circuit. In April 2017 Xcerra agreed to be bought by Sino IC Capital for $580 million.

	Annual Growth	07/13	07/14	07/15	07/16	07/17
Sales ($ mil.)	26.6%	152.0	330.9	398.0	324.2	390.8
Net income ($ mil.)	–	(12.1)	0.8	28.2	11.2	22.6
Market value ($ mil.)	16.0%	291.1	507.9	341.4	331.3	527.4
Employees	26.1%	649	2,059	1,722	1,676	1,640

XENCOR, INC
NMS: XNCR

111 West Lemon Avenue
Monrovia, CA 91016
Phone: 626 305-5900
Fax: –
Web: www.xencor.com

CEO: Bassil I Dahiyat
CFO: –
HR: –
FYE: December 31
Type: Public

Xencor is a biopharmaceutical company developing new types of antibodies to treat autoimmune diseases severe asthma and allergies and cancer. Its XmAb technology platform differs from other antibodies in that it interacts with multiple parts of the immune system not just the target antigens. Xencor is developing three drugs to treat rheumatoid arthritis and lupus severe asthma and allergic diseases and leukemia and non-Hodgkin lymphoma. It also licenses its technology to four major pharmaceutical companies - Boehringer Ingelheim CSL Janssen and Merck. Founded in 1997 Xencor went public in 2013. It raised about $70 million and plans to use the proceeds to further fund clinical development.

	Annual Growth	12/14	12/15	12/16	12/17	12/18
Sales ($ mil.)	43.7%	9.5	27.8	87.5	35.7	40.6
Net income ($ mil.)	–	(16.4)	(17.6)	23.6	(48.9)	(70.4)
Market value ($ mil.)	22.5%	902.7	822.8	1,481.3	1,233.6	2,035.1
Employees	41.4%	39	53	83	114	156

XENITH BANKSHARES INC
NAS: XBKS

One James Center, 901 E. Cary Street, Suite 1700
Richmond, VA 23219
Phone: 804 433-2200
Fax: –
Web: www.xenithbank.com

CEO: –
CFO: –
HR: –
FYE: December 31
Type: Public

Xenith Bankshares formerly First Bankshares is the holding company of Suffolk-First Bank a community bank with a handful of offices in southeastern Virginia. The bank targets commercial customers wealthy individuals and investors. It offers traditional products and services including checking and savings accounts CDs debit cards and merchant card processing. Its lending portfolio is primarily made up of real estate loans namely residential and commercial mortgages. Xenith Bankshares was created in late 2009 through the merger of the six-year-old First Bankshares and Xenith Corporation which had originally been established to open a new banking institution. Hampton Roads Bankshares agreed to buy Xenith for $197 million in February 2016.

	Annual Growth	12/10	12/11	12/12	12/13	12/14
Assets ($ mil.)	38.3%	251.2	477.5	563.2	679.9	918.1
Net income ($ mil.)	–	(5.9)	4.4	7.4	2.0	1.3
Market value ($ mil.)	3.9%	71.1	48.2	59.9	76.2	82.8
Employees	10.7%	78	105	104	102	117

XENONICS HOLDINGS INC
NBB: XNNH

3186 Lionshead Avenue
Carlsbad, CA 92010
Phone: 760 477-8900
Fax: –
Web: www.xenonics.com

CEO: Alan P Magerman
CFO: Richard S Kay
HR: –
FYE: September 30
Type: Public

Xenonics Holdings says fiat lux ("Let there be light"). Its NightHunter high-intensity portable lighting products are used worldwide by American military forces and by law enforcement agencies to illuminate dark areas. The SuperVision high-definition night-vision product is aimed at the commercial market and represents a growing portion of the company's sales. Xenonics' products are also used as part of security systems for facilities. Military customers — including the US Air Force US Army US Marine Corps US Navy and military equipment resellers — account for about 90% of the company's sales.

	Annual Growth	09/10	09/11	09/12	09/13	09/14
Sales ($ mil.)	(34.1%)	4.4	7.2	2.2	2.4	0.8
Net income ($ mil.)	–	(1.8)	(0.1)	(2.2)	(1.5)	(2.6)
Market value ($ mil.)	(11.6%)	8.5	9.5	10.0	3.3	5.2
Employees	(12.4%)	17	17	15	10	10

XENOPORT INC
NMS: XNPT

3410 Central Expressway
Santa Clara, CA 95051
Phone: 408 616-7200
Fax: –
Web: www.xenoport.com

CEO: Vincent J Angotti
CFO: William G Harris
HR: –
FYE: December 31
Type: Public

XenoPort sounds like something straight out of science fiction but there's nothing fictional about XenoPort's job of improving drugs' ability to be absorbed by tissues in the body. The development firm uses genomics to identify transporter proteins. It then designs oral drug molecules to find and ride these transporters through the gastrointestinal tract to their destinations. In 2011 XenoPort received FDA approval for Horizant (gabapentin enacarbil) its first drug which it markets in the US for the treatment of restless legs syndrome (RLS). It first marketed this drug in tandem with GlaxoSmithKline (GSK). In 2012 XenoPort and Astellas Pharma jointly launched gabapentin enacarbil tablets under the name Regnite in Japan.

	Annual Growth	12/10	12/11	12/12	12/13	12/14
Sales ($ mil.)	100.9%	2.9	43.5	21.6	8.0	46.9
Net income ($ mil.)	–	(82.5)	(33.4)	(30.8)	(85.9)	(49.3)
Market value ($ mil.)	0.7%	532.3	238.0	485.4	359.2	547.9
Employees	8.9%	108	112	88	92	152

XERIUM TECHNOLOGIES INC
NYS: XRM

14101 Capital Boulevard
Youngsville, NC 27596
Phone: 919 526-1400
Fax: –
Web: www.xerium.com

CEO: Mark Staton
CFO: Clifford E Pietrafitta
HR: –
FYE: December 31
Type: Public

Xerium Technologies makes clothing but not the kind that people wear. The company manufactures and supplies clothing and roll covers used on paper-making machinery. Xerium's clothing rolls are used as belts to convey paper through paper-making machines and its roll covers are used on the machines' steel cylinders; both products are consumed during paper production. The company operates about 30 manufacturing facilities in about a dozen countries primarily in North and South America Europe and Asia and nets more than 60% of sales outside North America.

	Annual Growth	12/12	12/13	12/14	12/15	12/16
Sales ($ mil.)	(3.3%)	538.7	546.9	542.9	477.2	471.3
Net income ($ mil.)	–	(18.0)	4.2	(7.4)	(4.4)	(21.6)
Market value ($ mil.)	16.5%	49.3	266.4	254.9	191.4	90.8
Employees	(2.6%)	3,279	3,200	3,100	3,000	2,950

XEROX HOLDINGS CORP NYS: XRX

P.O. Box 4505, 201 Merritt 7
Norwalk, CT 06851-1056
Phone: 203 968-3000
Fax: –
Web: www.xerox.com

CEO: Jeffrey (Jeff) Jacobson
CFO: William F. (Bill) Osbourn
HR: Darrell L. Ford
FYE: December 31
Type: Public

Xerox Corp. is not a copy of its former self. The company whose name has been a synonym for "to copy" remains a leading seller of copiers and printers from basic black-and-white output to high-end color systems. These days Xerox makes most of its revenue from its post-sale services such as document management maintenance supplies and paper and financing. Xerox also sells software for automating and integrating print jobs from start to finish. Its products are used in offices of large and small- and medium-sized businesses and in production plants of commercial printing companies. US customers account for about 60% of revenue.

	Annual Growth	12/14	12/15	12/16	12/17	12/18
Sales ($ mil.)	(15.8%)	19,540.0	18,045.0	10,771.0	10,265.0	9,830.0
Net income ($ mil.)	(21.9%)	969.0	474.0	(477.0)	195.0	361.0
Market value ($ mil.)	9.3%	3,182.6	2,440.9	2,004.6	6,693.5	4,537.4
Employees	(31.5%)	147,500	143,600	37,600	35,300	32,400

XETA TECHNOLOGIES INC.

1814 W. Tacoma St.
Broken Arrow OK 74012
Phone: 918-664-8200
Fax: 918-664-6876
Web: www.xeta.com

CEO: Kristi M Moody
CFO: Robert Wagner
HR: –
FYE: October 31
Type: Subsidiary

The next time you reach for that phone in the conference room XETA Technologies might be there with you. The company designs distributes and installs phone messaging videoconferencing data networking and contact management systems from such hardware and software vendors as Avaya Mitel Networks Polycom and Hewlett-Packard. It sells communications equipment to the hospitality industry including a line of call accounting products capable of tracking phone usage data. XETA also provides network consulting and installation services and offers managed services for maintenance and upgrades to legacy systems made by bankrupt telecom equipment maker Nortel. XETA was acquired by PAETEC acquired in 2011 for about $61 million.

XFONE INC. NYSE AMEX: XFN

5307 W. Loop 289
Lubbock TX 79414-1610
Phone: 806-771-5212
Fax: 806-788-3398
Web: www.xfone.com

CEO: –
CFO: –
HR: –
FYE: December 31
Type: Public

Xfone can help you get your lines of communications crossed but in a good way. The company offers a variety of telecommunications services including local long-distance and international phone services as well as broadband Internet access and email service. Other offerings include cellular services and prepaid calling cards; the company also resells equipment (phone systems modems etc.) and sells its various telecom services through resellers which buy access at wholesale rates. Targeting both residential and business customers Xfone operates primarily in the southern US but also offers services in Israel.

XILINX, INC. NMS: XLNX

2100 Logic Drive
San Jose, CA 95124
Phone: 408 559-7778
Fax: –
Web: www.xilinx.com

CEO: Victor Peng
CFO: Lorenzo A. Flores
HR: Marilyn Stiborek Meyer
FYE: March 30
Type: Public

Xilinx gives chip control to the programmer on the ground. The company is a top supplier of field-programmable gate arrays (FPGAs) and complex programmable logic devices (CPLDs). Customers program — and reprogram — these integrated circuits (ICs) to perform specific functions providing greater design flexibility and cutting time to market. Xilinx also offers a broad range of design software and intellectual property used to customize its chips. The company which contracts with third-party manufacturers for production sells to the automotive aerospace broadcast consumer data processing and wired and wireless communications markets. About three-quarters of revenue comes from international customers.

	Annual Growth	03/15*	04/16	04/17*	03/18	03/19
Sales ($ mil.)	6.5%	2,377.3	2,213.9	2,349.3	2,539.0	3,059.0
Net income ($ mil.)	8.2%	648.2	550.9	622.5	512.4	889.8
Market value ($ mil.)	31.6%	10,744.7	12,090.3	14,697.8	18,341.1	32,190.8
Employees	6.5%	3,451	3,458	3,831	4,014	4,433

*Fiscal year change

XO GROUP INC NYS: XOXO

195 Broadway, 25th Floor
New York, NY 10007
Phone: 212 219-8555
Fax: 212 219-1929
Web: www.xogroupinc.com

CEO: Michael Steib
CFO: Gillian Munson
HR: –
FYE: December 31
Type: Public

Here comes the bride surfing online. Where is the groom? He's in a chat room. XO Group (formerly The Knot) is a leading online publisher serving the wedding newlywed and new parent markets. Its TheKnot.com and WeddingChannel.com sites offer wedding-related content on topics from engagement to honeymoon as well as wedding planning tools (budget planner gown finder) chat rooms a directory of local resources and online registry services. Other XO Group websites target newlyweds (TheNest.com) and pregnant women and their partners (TheBump.com). The firm also produces branded video and mobile content and magazines as well as books on lifestyle topics (published by Random House and Chronicle Books).

	Annual Growth	12/12	12/13	12/14	12/15	12/16
Sales ($ mil.)	4.2%	129.1	133.8	143.7	141.6	152.1
Net income ($ mil.)	8.6%	8.7	5.8	0.5	5.5	12.1
Market value ($ mil.)	20.3%	244.6	390.9	479.0	422.5	511.6
Employees	1.8%	677	705	641	660	727

XO HOLDINGS INC.

13865 Sunrise Valley Dr.
Herndon VA 20171
Phone: 703-547-2000
Fax: 703-547-2881
Web: www.xo.com

CEO: Chris Ancell
CFO: –
HR: –
FYE: December 31
Type: Private

XO Holdings gets down to the Xs and Os of business telecom services. Through its operational subsidiary XO Communications the company provides telecommunications services to large corporations small and midsized businesses government agencies and other telecom carriers via a network of about 1 million miles of metropolitan fiber. XO Communications offers local and long-distance voice dedicated Internet access private networking data transport and managed services such as Web hosting and bundled voice and data services. The company has customers in about 85 US markets and internationally. Billionaire financier Carl Icahn owns the company through his ACF Industries.

XOMA CORP

NMS: XOMA

2200 Powell Street, Suite 310
Emeryville, CA 94608
Phone: 510 204-7200
Fax: -
Web: www.xoma.com

CEO: James R. (Jim) Neal
CFO: Thomas (Tom) Burns
HR: Charles C. (Chris) Wells
FYE: December 31
Type: Public

XOMA Corporation doesn't want to toil in anonymity. Instead the company pairs with larger drug firms to develop and market its products primarily monoclonal antibodies (biotech drugs based on cloned proteins). It's developing lead candidate gevokizumab with French drugmaker Servier. The firm partners on therapeutics for infectious disease inflammatory ailments and autoimmune conditions and receives royalties on drugs developed from licensing its technologies. XOMA has collaborative agreements with pharma companies Takeda Pharmaceutical and Novartis; it also has metabolic and oncology candidates.

	Annual Growth	12/14	12/15	12/16	12/17	12/18
Sales ($ mil.)	(27.2%)	18.9	55.4	5.6	52.7	5.3
Net income ($ mil.)	-	(38.3)	(20.6)	(53.5)	14.6	(13.3)
Market value ($ mil.)	37.0%	31.2	11.6	36.7	309.4	109.9
Employees	(50.5%)	183	86	18	12	11

XORIANT CORPORATION

1248 REAMWOOD AVE
SUNNYVALE, CA 940892225
Phone: 408-743-4400
Fax: -
Web: www.xoriantconnect.com

CEO: Girish Gaitonde
CFO: Mahesh Nalavade
HR: -
FYE: December 31
Type: Private

Xoriant is not exorbitant about offering IT services. The firm provides outsourced application development engineering and consulting services to technology start-ups such as software developers as well as banks telecommunications companies and health care providers among other businesses. The company specializes in implementing technology to enable cloud Web social networking payment embedded media and mobile applications and services. Other services included testing and technical support. Xoriant's customers have included TIBCO Software.

	Annual Growth	12/12	12/13	12/14	12/16	12/17
Sales ($ mil.)	17.9%	-	92.1	125.2	150.6	178.0
Net income ($ mil.)	(19.1%)	-	7.3	3.7	6.7	3.1
Market value ($ mil.)	-	-	-	-	-	-
Employees	-	-	-	-	-	134

XPEDX

6285 Tri-Ridge Blvd.
Loveland OH 45140
Phone: 513-965-2900
Fax: +45-4574-8888
Web: www.chr-hansen.com

CEO: -
CFO: -
HR: -
FYE: December 31
Type: Business Segment

International Paper makes a lot of paper and paper products; xpedx distributes that paper across North America — along with packaging supplies and equipment janitorial products and office furniture. (The company stopped distributing graphic imaging prepress equipment by Agfa Graphics and Ryobi in 2011). Typical customers include commercial printers publishers government agencies manufacturers retailers and creative professionals. The distribution division of International Paper xpedx operates more than 200 distribution centers 120 warehouses and about 130 retail stores in the US Canada and Mexico. It accounts for about a quarter of its parent's sales.

XPLORE TECHNOLOGIES CORP.

8601 RR 2222 BLDG 2
AUSTIN, TX 787302304
Phone: 512-637-1100
Fax: -
Web: www.xploretech.com

CEO: -
CFO: -
HR: -
FYE: March 31
Type: Private

Xplore Technologies ensures that you can take your computer with you no matter what difficult terrain you're exploring. The company manufactures and sells ruggedized tablet PCs and handheld computers. The company primarily targets manufacturers distributors and systems integrators that supply field service personnel factory workers public safety officials military personnel and other customers that require durable mobile computers. Its products incorporate wireless networking technology and can be mounted in vehicles such as carts and forklifts. Xplore was founded in 1996. The company agreed to be bought by Zebra Technologies for about $66 million in 2018.

	Annual Growth	03/14	03/15	03/16	03/17	03/18
Sales ($ mil.)	26.8%	-	42.6	100.5	77.9	86.9
Net income ($ mil.)	6.4%	-	0.2	(0.4)	(2.6)	0.3
Market value ($ mil.)	-	-	-	-	-	-
Employees	-	-	-	-	-	95

XPO LOGISTICS, INC.

NYS: XPO

Five American Lane
Greenwich, CT 06831
Phone: 855 976-6951
Fax: -
Web: www.xpologistics.com

CEO: Bradley S. Jacobs
CFO: John J. Hardig
HR: Meghan A. Henson
FYE: December 31
Type: Public

XPO Logistics is a global provider of transportation and supply chain solutions. It is one of the top five providers of freight brokerage and managed transportation services in the world. It also provides less-than-truckload (LTL) services where carriers consolidate freight from multiple shippers into a single truckload. Through its Logistics segment XPO offers services such as warehousing and distribution e-commerce fulfillment and reverse logistics (moving goods backward from their final destination for the purpose of reuse or disposal). Its customers include companies in the retail and e-commerce food and beverage consumer packaged goods and industrial markets. XPO operates more than 1500 locations in over 30 countries primarily in North America and Europe. The US is its largest market generating almost 60% of revenue.

	Annual Growth	12/14	12/15	12/16	12/17	12/18
Sales ($ mil.)	64.6%	2,356.6	7,623.2	14,619.4	15,380.8	17,279.0
Net income ($ mil.)	-	(63.6)	(191.1)	69.0	340.2	422.0
Market value ($ mil.)	8.7%	4,729.1	3,152.4	4,992.9	10,595.4	6,598.6
Employees	77.8%	10,000	89,000	87,000	95,000	100,000

XPRESSPA GROUP INC

NAS: XSPA

780 Third Avenue, 12th Floor
New York, NY 10017
Phone: 212 309-7549
Fax: -
Web: www.formholdings.com

CEO: Douglas Satzman
CFO: Janine Canale
HR: -
FYE: December 31
Type: Public

Vringo is brinnggg brinnggg bringing its video ringtones to consumer mobile phones. The upstart company is riding the next wave in mobile ringtone technology beyond just audio clips with video clips that users can upload to their phones. Subscribers of Vringo's service can browse and purchase content from its Web site which houses a library of more than 4000 video ringtones as well as tools to create customize and share them through social media networks. The company reaches subscribers through partnerships with certain mobile carriers in Armenia Malaysia Turkey and the United Arab Emirates with hopes to establish more throughout the world. Vringo filed to go public in January 2010.

	Annual Growth	12/14	12/15	12/16	12/17	12/18
Sales ($ mil.)	143.5%	1.4	22.7	19.0	48.8	50.1
Net income ($ mil.)	-	(109.7)	(11.2)	(24.0)	(28.8)	(37.2)
Market value ($ mil.)	(26.0%)	1.0	4.4	3.8	2.4	0.3
Employees	171.2%	13	27	763	845	703

XRS CORP
NAS: XRSC

965 Prairie Center Drive
Eden Prairie, MN 55344
Phone: 952 707-5600
Fax: 952 894-2463
Web: www.xrscorp.com

CEO: John J Coughlan
CFO: Michael Weber
HR: –
FYE: September 30
Type: Public

XRS (formerly Xata) helps companies keep track of their truck fleets. The company's Web-based XRS and Turnpike applications help fleet operators automate driver logs and fuel tax reporting manage vehicle and driver performance track assets and enable two-way messaging. Aimed at the for-hire segment of the transportation sector (as opposed to private fleets) its MobileMax Fleet Management System provides similar functionality. XRS markets to customers in the manufacturing distribution and petroleum markets primarily in the US. More than 115000 trucks in North America have a subscription to XRS' products. Customers have included CVS Caremark Harley-Davidson United Rentals Safeway and UPS.

	Annual Growth	09/09	09/10	09/11	09/12	09/13
Sales ($ mil.)	(3.7%)	65.3	70.7	63.0	63.1	56.2
Net income ($ mil.)	–	(2.1)	(1.3)	(2.8)	(10.3)	0.9
Market value ($ mil.)	(0.7%)	31.6	27.3	18.2	6.3	30.7
Employees	(1.6%)	176	200	210	174	165

XTANT MEDICAL HOLDINGS INC
ASE: XTNT

664 Cruiser Lane
Belgrade, MT 59714
Phone: 406 388-0480
Fax: 406 388-1354
Web: www.xtantmedical.com

CEO: Sean Browne
CFO: John P Gandolfo
HR: –
FYE: December 31
Type: Public

Xtant Medical Holdings has your back(bone). Formerly named Bacterin International the company develops manufactures and markets biomedical devices including orthopedic biomaterials used for bone grafts joint surgery and other skeletal reconstructive procedures. Its biologics products include OsteoSponge a bone void filler made of 100% human bone; OsteoLock a stabilization dowel for spinal procedures; and BacFast a dowel with demineralization technology to aid in bone grafting. Additionally the company makes implants and surgical instruments under the Axle IRIX-C Calix Xpress and Silex brand names. The company was founded in 1998.

	Annual Growth	12/14	12/15	12/16	12/17	12/18
Sales ($ mil.)	19.6%	35.3	59.3	90.0	82.6	72.2
Net income ($ mil.)	–	(10.5)	(2.2)	(19.5)	(52.4)	(70.1)
Market value ($ mil.)	(14.6%)	39.9	36.9	7.2	7.5	21.2
Employees	2.6%	150	255	257	174	166

XURA INC
NMS: MESG

200 Quannapowitt Parkway
Wakefield, MA 01880
Phone: 781 246-9000
Fax: –
Web: www.xura.com

CEO: Philippe Tartavull
CFO: Jacky Wu
HR: –
FYE: January 31
Type: Public

Comverse is conversant with communications technology. The company provides communication software and systems that handle messaging billing and accounts call management and data delivery services. It also provides related services such as consulting design implementation interoperability testing maintenance support and training. Its services are sold to more than 450 wireline wireless and cable network providers in more than 125 countries. Top customer Verizon accounts for about 18% of sales. Comverse has offices in about 40 countries and generates most of its revenues in the EMEA (Europe Middle East and Africa) region.

	Annual Growth	01/11	01/12	01/13	01/14	01/15
Sales ($ mil.)	(13.8%)	862.8	771.2	677.8	652.5	477.3
Net income ($ mil.)	–	(90.9)	(15.5)	5.1	18.7	(22.1)
Market value ($ mil.)	(22.8%)	–	–	630.5	786.8	376.1
Employees	(2.7%)	–	2,500	2,500	2,500	2,300

XYLEM INC
NYS: XYL

1 International Drive
Rye Brook, NY 10573
Phone: 914 323-5700
Fax: 914 323-5800
Web: www.xyleminc.com

CEO: Patrick K. Decker
CFO: E. Mark Rajkowski
HR: –
FYE: December 31
Type: Public

Xylem makes fluid-handling and related products used across the entire water cycle from the delivery and measurement of drinking water to the testing and treatment of wastewater. The company serves customers in the water sector as well as the electric and gas industries. Its products include water and wastewater pumps filtration and disinfection equipment heat exchangers and sensors and meters to name a few. Xylem's products are sold under about 35 different brands including Flygt Goulds and Pure. About 45% of its sales comes from the US.

	Annual Growth	12/14	12/15	12/16	12/17	12/18
Sales ($ mil.)	7.4%	3,916.0	3,653.0	3,771.0	4,707.0	5,207.0
Net income ($ mil.)	13.0%	337.0	340.0	260.0	331.0	549.0
Market value ($ mil.)	15.1%	6,842.1	6,559.9	8,899.9	12,257.2	11,991.2
Employees	8.0%	12,500	12,700	16,000	16,200	17,000

YADKIN FINANCIAL CORP
NYS: YDKN

3600 Glenwood Avenue, Suite 300
Raleigh, NC 27612
Phone: 919 659-9000
Fax: –

CEO: –
CFO: –
HR: –
FYE: December 31
Type: Public

Yadkin Financial Corporation is the holding company for Yadkin Bank (formerly Yadkin Valley Bank and Trust) which serves customers from more than 70 branches across North Carolina and upstate South Carolina. In addition to its standard loans SBA loans and deposit products including checking and savings accounts money market accounts CDs and IRAs Yadkin Bank and its subsidiaries provide mortgage banking investment and insurance services to more than 80000 business and individual customers. Founded in 1968 Yadkin Bank now boasts nearly $1.5 billion in total assets. F.N.B. Corporation is buying Yadkin for $1.4 billion.

	Annual Growth	12/11	12/12	12/13	12/14	12/15
Assets ($ mil.)	22.4%	1,993.2	1,923.4	1,806.0	4,266.3	4,474.1
Net income ($ mil.)	–	(14.4)	(8.7)	18.8	21.7	44.6
Market value ($ mil.)	98.8%	51.1	93.3	540.6	623.5	798.6
Employees	15.1%	481	481	511	882	845

YAKIMA VALLEY MEMORIAL HOSPITAL ASSOCIATION INC

2811 TIETON DR
YAKIMA, WA 989023761
Phone: 509-249-5129
Fax: –
Web: www.yakimamemorial.org

CEO: Russ Myers
CFO: –
HR: –
FYE: December 31
Type: Private

Whether you're a major yakker or quiet as a mouse Yakima Valley Memorial Hospital serves the health care needs of patients of all types. The health provider's acute-care hospital skilled-nursing facilities and outpatient specialty treatment facilities serve patients in and around Yakima in Washington State. The hospital has about 225 beds and provides a variety of services such as heart care orthopedics pediatrics cancer treatment women's health and mental health care. It also offers sleep and wound care and provides home health and hospice services. The organization is a not-for-profit group governed by a board of directors.

	Annual Growth	10/11	10/12*	12/16	12/17	12/18
Sales ($ mil.)	7.2%	–	309.8	424.5	457.3	470.1
Net income ($ mil.)	–	–	(6.6)	83.0	0.4	(12.6)
Market value ($ mil.)	–	–	–	–	–	–
Employees	–	–	–	–	–	1,150

*Fiscal year change

YALE NEW HAVEN HEALTH SERVICES CORPORATION

789 HOWARD AVE
NEW HAVEN, CT 065191300
Phone: 888-461-0106
Fax: –

CEO: Frank A. Corvino
CFO: James M. Staten
HR: –
FYE: September 30
Type: Private

Yale New Haven Health System is a health care haven for residents of Southern Connecticut Southwestern Rhode Island and parts of New York's Westchester County. The company operates Yale-New Haven Hospital Greenwich Hospital Bridgeport Hospital and Lawrence & Memorial Hospital and has a contract relationship with The Westerly Hospital in Rhode Island (Northeast Medical Group) as well as children's cancer psychiatric care hospitals. In addition Yale New Haven Health Services operates outpatient facilities and provides such managed care services as network contracting as well as disease management programs. The system is affiliated with Yale University's medical school and has a grand total of about 2560 beds.

	Annual Growth	09/10	09/11	09/12	09/13	09/15
Sales ($ mil.)	2.6%	–	–	–	427.4	449.9
Net income ($ mil.)	(25.4%)	–	–	–	35.2	19.6
Market value ($ mil.)	–	–	–	–	–	–
Employees	–	–	–	–	–	22,490

YALE UNIVERSITY

105 WALL ST
NEW HAVEN, CT 065118917
Phone: 203-432-2550
Fax: –

CEO: –
CFO: –
HR: –
FYE: June 30
Type: Private

What do former President George W. Bush and actress Meryl Streep have in common? They are Yalies. Yale University is one of the nation's most prestigious private liberal arts institutions as well as one of its oldest (founded in 1701). Yale comprises an undergraduate college a graduate school and more than a dozen professional schools. Programs of study include architecture law medicine and drama. Its 12 residential colleges (a system borrowed from Oxford) serve as dormitory dining hall and social center. The school has around 12000 students and nearly 4000 faculty members.

	Annual Growth	06/12	06/13	06/16	06/17	06/18
Sales ($ mil.)	5.6%	–	2,936.9	3,450.0	3,647.6	3,848.3
Net income ($ mil.)	10.7%	–	1,965.2	(846.7)	2,447.7	3,271.0
Market value ($ mil.)	–	–	–	–	–	–
Employees	–	–	–	–	–	11,000

YALE-NEW HAVEN HOSPITAL, INC.

20 YORK ST
NEW HAVEN, CT 065103220
Phone: 203-688-4242
Fax: –
Web: www.ynhh.org

CEO: Marna P Borgstrom
CFO: Vincent Tammaro
HR: –
FYE: September 30
Type: Private

Yale-New Haven supports its community and the brainiacs at Yale. Yale-New Haven Hospital (YNHH) is the flagship member of the Yale New Haven Health System. It provides tertiary care in more than 100 medical specialties to residents of southwestern Connecticut. The not-for-profit hospital has more than 1500 beds on two campuses. Its main location includes the Yale-New Haven Children's Hospital and the Yale-New Haven Psychiatric Hospital. Smilow Cancer Hospital with 170 beds is also part of the hospital complex. YNHH provides cardiac and cancer care performs organ transplants and offers a variety of outpatient clinics. The medical center serves as the primary teaching hospital for Yale University's medical school.

	Annual Growth	09/08	09/09	09/13	09/14	09/15
Sales ($ mil.)	11.6%	–	1,237.1	2,360.9	2,360.9	2,389.0
Net income ($ mil.)	12.5%	–	52.9	120.6	120.6	107.5
Market value ($ mil.)	–	–	–	–	–	–
Employees	–	–	–	–	–	22,000

YASH TECHNOLOGIES, INC

605 17TH AVE
EAST MOLINE, IL 612442045
Phone: 309-755-0433
Fax: –

CEO: –
CFO: –
HR: –
FYE: December 31
Type: Private

YASH Technologies hashes out all sorts of technological issues. The company provides information technology (IT) services such as consulting systems integration and network design as well as software development and business process outsourcing. It has expertise in business software from leading providers including IBM Microsoft Oracle and SAP. YASH primarily targets corporations in such fields as automotive chemicals education financial services health care manufacturing and retail. The company's customers have included Cox Interactive Hasbro and Winstar Communications. YASH has offices in India Hong Kong Singapore the UK and the US.

	Annual Growth	12/0-1	12/00	12/01	12/06	12/08
Sales ($ mil.)	–	–	0.0	23.0	39.4	79.8
Net income ($ mil.)	–	–	0.0	0.0	0.5	7.1
Market value ($ mil.)	–	–	–	–	–	–
Employees	–	–	–	–	–	3,500

YATES GROUP, INC.

2015 GALLERIA OAKS DR
TEXARKANA, TX 755034618
Phone: 903-832-6502
Fax: –
Web: www.ezmart.com

CEO: –
CFO: Stacy Yates
HR: –
FYE: December 31
Type: Private

E-Z Mart Stores aims to make filling gas tanks and stomachs EZR for small-town America. The regional convenience store chain operates about 295 stores across four neighboring states including Arkansas Louisiana Oklahoma and Texas. Rather than build its own stores the company usually expands through acquisitions. In addition to the standard hot dogs sodas coffee and cigarettes most E-Z Mart locations also offer Shell Conoco Phillips 66 or CITGO gasoline. E-Z Mart was founded in 1970 by Jim Yates in Nashville Arkansas. Yates died in 1998 when the plane he was piloting crashed leaving his daughter Sonja Hubbard at the company's helm as CEO.

	Annual Growth	12/12	12/13	12/14	12/15	12/16
Sales ($ mil.)	(7.8%)	–	1,003.8	1,026.3	827.8	786.1
Net income ($ mil.)	3.2%	–	15.2	19.3	16.8	16.7
Market value ($ mil.)	–	–	–	–	–	–
Employees	–	–	–	–	–	2,100

YELLOWBOOK INC.

398 RXR Plaza
Uniondale NY 11556
Phone: 516-730-1900
Fax: 615-329-9627
Web: www.sesac.com

CEO: Mike Pocock
CFO: Jim Haddad
HR: –
FYE: March 31
Type: Subsidiary

Let your fingers do the walking through Yellowbook. Founded in 1930 Yellowbook is one of the country's oldest and largest independent publishers of yellow pages with more than 1000 directories that serve small and medium-sized businesses nationwide. The company has grown through acquisitions and new product launches today offering not just free and paid print advertising in Yellowbook but an array of digital and mobile marketing tools and services for small businesses including custom video ads on Yellowbook.com customer lead tracking hosting and optimization search engine marketing and website design. Yellowbook is part of hibu's US operations.

YELP INC

NYS: YELP

140 New Montgomery Street, 9th Floor
San Francisco, CA 94105
Phone: 415 908-3801
Fax: –
Web: www.yelp.com

CEO: Jeremy Stoppelman
CFO: Charles C. (Lanny) Baker
HR: –
FYE: December 31
Type: Public

Yelp offers user-generated reviews and information on local businesses and service providers through its website and mobile app. Its content covers restaurants and bars spas and salons doctors and retail establishments as well as a host of other business and consumer service providers. It includes more than 177 million consumer reviews and is primarily ad-supported. The site has a social media-friendly interface — users can create and maintain profiles (complete with friend networks and photos) where they can blog on experiences with businesses. Yelp has a presence in cities across the US Canada and Europe. The firm was founded in 2004 by former PayPal engineers Jeremy Stoppelman and Russel Simmons.

	Annual Growth	12/14	12/15	12/16	12/17	12/18
Sales ($ mil.)	25.7%	377.5	549.7	713.1	846.8	942.8
Net income ($ mil.)	11.0%	36.5	(32.9)	(4.7)	152.9	55.4
Market value ($ mil.)	(10.6%)	4,487.7	2,361.5	3,126.5	3,440.6	2,869.1
Employees	22.1%	2,711	2,220	4,256	5,323	6,030

YESHIVA UNIVERSITY

500 W 185TH ST
NEW YORK, NY 100333299
Phone: 212-960-5400
Fax: –
Web: www.yu.edu

CEO: –
CFO: –
HR: –
FYE: June 30
Type: Private

Yeshivas are traditional Jewish schools and Yeshiva University believes strongly in following tradition. The Jewish higher education institution serves more than 7000 undergraduate and graduate students at four campuses in New York City. Subjects taught include liberal arts sciences medicine law business social work and psychology. It also has extensive Jewish studies and education programs including study abroad opportunities. Yeshiva University also known as YU has an undergraduate student-to-teacher ratio of 6:1. Its graduate programs include medicine law psychology and Jewish education.

	Annual Growth	06/10	06/11	06/13	06/15	06/16
Sales ($ mil.)	(18.4%)	–	674.3	704.9	583.2	244.6
Net income ($ mil.)	–	–	(85.7)	(98.1)	(206.2)	(589.3)
Market value ($ mil.)	–	–	–	–	–	–
Employees	–	–	–	–	–	4,500

YIELD10 BIOSCIENCE INC

NAS: YTEN

19 Presidential Way
Woburn, MA 01801
Phone: 617 583-1700
Fax: –
Web: www.yield10bio.com

CEO: Joseph Shaulson
CFO: –
HR: –
FYE: December 31
Type: Public

Yield10 Bioscience (formerly Metabolix) is an agricultural bioscience company focused on developing disruptive technologies to improve crop yield for food and feed crops in order to enhance global food security. Yield10 is targeting new agricultural biotechnology approaches to improve fundamental elements of plant metabolism through enhanced photosynthetic efficiency and directed carbon utilization. In particular Yield10 is working to develop validate and commercialize new traits and identify gene editing targets in canola soybean corn and other key crops. Yield10 was launched in 2015. In 2016 Metabolix sold its biopolymer intellectual property (the company's former key asset) for $10 million.

	Annual Growth	12/14	12/15	12/16	12/17	12/18
Sales ($ mil.)	(33.2%)	2.8	2.6	1.2	0.9	0.6
Net income ($ mil.)	–	(29.5)	(23.7)	(7.6)	(9.4)	(9.2)
Market value ($ mil.)	18.9%	0.1	0.4	0.1	0.4	0.2
Employees	(24.6%)	68	68	20	20	22

YORK HOSPITAL

1001 S GEORGE ST
YORK, PA 174033645
Phone: 717-851-2345
Fax: –
Web: www.wellspanmedicaleducation.org

CEO: Donald B Dellinger
CFO: Michael F O'Connor
HR: –
FYE: June 30
Type: Private

York Hospital operating as WellSpan York Hospital takes its name from the community whose health it seeks to preserve. Part of WellSpan Health the medical center has about 570 beds and serves residents of York and surrounding area of south-central Pennsylvania. It is a regional leader in cardiovascular and orthopedic care and has programs in other specialty areas including oncology behavioral health and geriatrics. Additionally WellSpan York Hospital operates a Level 1 trauma center offers outpatient surgery emergency home health and diagnostic imaging services. It is also has teaching and research programs. The hospital was founded in 1880.

	Annual Growth	06/13	06/14	06/15	06/16	06/18
Sales ($ mil.)	5.7%	–	853.3	925.9	990.5	1,063.5
Net income ($ mil.)	7.3%	–	136.5	82.9	17.9	181.2
Market value ($ mil.)	–	–	–	–	–	–
Employees	–	–	–	–	–	6,200

YORK PENNSYLVANIA HOSPITAL COMPANY LLC

325 S BELMONT ST
YORK, PA 174032608
Phone: 717-843-8623
Fax: –
Web: www.mhyork.org

CEO: –
CFO: –
HR: –
FYE: June 30
Type: Private

Memorial Hospital serves the York County region of southeastern Pennsylvania in the midst of Amish country. The hospital offers emergency critical care diagnostic surgery and rehabilitation services as well as specialty cardiovascular orthopedic and obstetric services. In addition to the 100-bed acute care facility Memorial Hospital operates Greenbriar Medical Center (a diagnostic imaging and rehabilitation center) the Surgical Center of York (outpatient surgery facility) home health and hospice agencies and primary and specialist care clinics. Memorial Hospital is part of the Community Health Systems (CHS) network.

	Annual Growth	06/08	06/09	06/10	06/12	06/15
Sales ($ mil.)	(0.6%)	–	100.7	100.8	102.0	97.2
Net income ($ mil.)	–	–	0.0	2.1	(5.9)	(1.7)
Market value ($ mil.)	–	–	–	–	–	–
Employees	–	–	–	–	–	900

YORK WATER CO

NMS: YORW

130 East Market Street
York, PA 17401
Phone: 717 845-3601
Fax: –
Web: www.yorkwater.com

CEO: Jeffrey R. Hines
CFO: Matthew E. Poff
HR: Bruce C. McIntosh
FYE: December 31
Type: Public

The York Water Company goes with the flow as long as its water flows primarily within York County Pennsylvania. The regulated water utility distributes more than 18.6 million gallons of water daily to 39 communities in York County and to seven communities in nearby Adams County. It serves about 63780 residential and business customers in a service territory with a population of 189000. York Water obtains its water primarily from two reservoirs that together hold about 2.2 billion gallons. It gets an additional 12 million gallons of untreated water per day from the Susquehanna River.

	Annual Growth	12/14	12/15	12/16	12/17	12/18
Sales ($ mil.)	1.4%	45.9	47.1	47.6	48.6	48.4
Net income ($ mil.)	3.9%	11.5	12.5	11.8	13.0	13.4
Market value ($ mil.)	8.4%	300.4	322.8	494.4	438.8	415.0
Employees	0.7%	106	104	105	102	109

YOUNG BROADCASTING, LLC

599 LEXINGTON AVE
NEW YORK, NY 100226030
Phone: 517-372-8282
Fax: –
Web: www.news8000.com

CEO: –
CFO: James A Morgan
HR: –
FYE: December 31
Type: Private

New Young Broadcasting Holding Co. (formerly known as Young Broadcasting) is a television broadcaster that owns 10 TV stations throughout the country. Five of its stations are affiliated with Walt Disney's ABC network and serve small and midsized markets. Three of its stations are affiliated with CBS and it has one station operating in San Francisco affiliated with News Corporation's MyNetworkTV and an NBC station in Iowa. New Young Broadcasting also operates a national television sales representation firm Adam Young Inc. In mid-2013 the company agreed to merge with Media General.

	Annual Growth	12/03	12/04	12/05	12/06	12/07
Sales ($ mil.)	(30.9%)	–	–	–	225.2	155.7
Net income ($ mil.)	–	–	–	–	(56.6)	(72.7)
Market value ($ mil.)	–	–	–	–	–	–
Employees	–	–	–	–	–	1,097

YOUNG LIFE

420 N CASCADE AVE
COLORADO SPRINGS, CO 809033352
Phone: 719-381-1800
Fax: –
Web: www.younglife.org

CEO: –
CFO: –
HR: Troy Mulder
FYE: September 30
Type: Private

Young Life is focused on promoting Christianity among teenagers in the US and in more than 50 other countries. Founded in 1941 the not-for-profit organization provides activities and support for junior high middle school and high school students located in rural and urban communities. Young Life also operates week-long summer camp programs at about 20 locations throughout North America as well as retreats held throughout the year. The group has grown throughout the years from a single club in Texas to about 600 international Young Life ministries dotting the globe. The organization boasts about 3000 staffers and more than 27000 volunteers.

	Annual Growth	09/12	09/13	09/14	09/15	09/16
Sales ($ mil.)	7.6%	–	276.1	311.2	331.4	343.5
Net income ($ mil.)	1.4%	–	18.0	31.9	29.9	18.7
Market value ($ mil.)	–	–	–	–	–	–
Employees	–	–	–	–	–	3,100

YOUNGSTOWN STATE UNIVERSITY INC

1 UNIVERSITY PLZ
YOUNGSTOWN, OH 445550002
Phone: 330-941-3000
Fax: –
Web: www.ysu.edu

CEO: –
CFO: –
HR: –
FYE: June 30
Type: Private

Youngstown State University (YSU) offers about 100 undergraduate majors more than 30 graduate programs and doctorate programs in education and physical therapy. The university has an enrollment of approximately 14000 students in its six undergraduate colleges (business administration; education; health and human services; fine and performing arts; liberal arts and social sciences; and science technology engineering and mathematics) as well as a school of graduate studies and research. Its tuition is the lowest among Ohio's major public universities. Its athletic teams are known as the Penguins.

	Annual Growth	06/01	06/02	06/05	06/06	06/17
Sales ($ mil.)	(14.1%)	–	1,141.2	92.9	98.5	116.3
Net income ($ mil.)	–	–	0.0	(6.6)	(4.1)	(1.2)
Market value ($ mil.)	–	–	–	–	–	–
Employees	–	–	–	–	–	2,105

YOUR COMMUNITY BANKSHARES INC

NAS: YCB

101 West Spring Street
New Albany, IN 47150
Phone: 812 944-2224
Fax: –
Web: www.yourcommunitybank.com

CEO: –
CFO: –
HR: –
FYE: December 31
Type: Public

Community Bank Shares of Indiana is the holding company for Your Community Bank and Scott County State Bank. The banks serve customers from about 20 locations in southern Indiana and Louisville Kentucky. Both banks offer deposit products such as checking money market and savings accounts as well as IRAs and CDs. Their lending activities center on commercial mortgages and residential real estate loans (each around 25% of the company's loan portfolio) but also include business construction and consumer (including home equity home improvement and auto) loans and credit cards. Community Bank Shares of Indiana is focused on organic growth within existing markets.

	Annual Growth	12/10	12/11	12/12	12/13	12/14
Assets ($ mil.)	2.6%	801.5	797.4	819.5	846.7	888.7
Net income ($ mil.)	6.6%	7.0	7.4	7.7	8.7	9.0
Market value ($ mil.)	29.6%	33.2	32.4	44.8	67.0	93.8
Employees	1.0%	205	201	202	209	213

YRC WORLDWIDE INC

NMS: YRCW

10990 Roe Avenue
Overland Park, KS 66211
Phone: 913 696-6100
Fax: –
Web: www.yrcw.com

CEO: James L. Welch
CFO: Stephanie D. Fisher
HR: –
FYE: December 31
Type: Public

YRC Worldwide stands for more than Your Regional Carrier. The company has one of the largest less-than-truckload (LTL) networks in North America with local regional national and international capabilities. YRC Worldwide is a holding company that operates through such subsidiaries as YRC Freight and YRC Reimer which transport goods for manufacturing wholesale retail and government customers in the US Canada and certain international markets as well as YRC Regional Transportation which provides regional next-day ground services in the US Canada Mexico and Puerto Rico through subsidiaries New Penn USF Holland and USF Reddaway. The company dates back to 1924.

	Annual Growth	12/14	12/15	12/16	12/17	12/18
Sales ($ mil.)	0.1%	5,068.8	4,832.4	4,697.5	4,891.0	5,092.0
Net income ($ mil.)	–	(67.7)	0.7	21.5	(10.8)	20.2
Market value ($ mil.)	(38.8%)	744.2	469.2	439.4	475.8	104.2
Employees	(22.3%)	33,000	32,000	32,000	32,000	12,000

YTB INTERNATIONAL INC.

OTC: YTBLA

1901 E. Edwardsville Rd.
Wood River IL 62095
Phone: 618-655-9477
Fax: 618-659-9607
Web: www.ytb.com

CEO: Andrew Cauthen
CFO: Steven Boyd
HR: –
FYE: December 31
Type: Public

YTB International wants its travel business to be your travel business. The company provides an online platform for individuals to set up home-based travel agency businesses. Customers pay monthly fees to have their online travel agencies hosted through YTB's ZamZuu subsidiary. YTB's Travel Network subsidiary processes and handles the transactions derived from additional hosted client websites. The company provides services for home-based travel agents in the US Canada the Bahamas and Bermuda. Reflecting the economy's impact on travel YTB announced plans in 2012 to merge with LTS Nutraceuticals. Before it does YTB has eliminated about a third of its headquarters staff including its president and CEO.

YUM! BRANDS INC
NYS: YUM

1441 Gardiner Lane
Louisville, KY 40213
Phone: 502 874-8300
Fax: -
Web: www.yum.com

CEO: Greg Creed
CFO: David W. Gibbs
HR: -
FYE: December 31
Type: Public

For those who find chicken pizza and tacos especially yummy there's only one place to turn. YUM Brands is the largest fast-food operator in the world in terms of number of locations with more than 48000 KFC Pizza Hut and Taco Bell outlets in some 140 countries. (It trails only hamburger giant McDonald's in sales.) The company's flagship chains are #1 chicken fryer KFC (with more than 22600 units) top pizza joint Pizza Hut (more than 18400) and quick-service Mexican leader Taco Bell (more than 7000). Franchisees affiliates and licensed operators run about 98% of the company's restaurants. More than 60% are located outside the US.

	Annual Growth	12/14	12/15	12/16	12/17	12/18
Sales ($ mil.)	(19.1%)	13,279.0	13,105.0	6,366.0	5,878.0	5,688.0
Net income ($ mil.)	10.1%	1,051.0	1,293.0	1,619.0	1,340.0	1,542.0
Market value ($ mil.)	5.9%	22,380.8	22,644.0	19,379.0	24,972.7	28,127.5
Employees	(49.8%)	537,000	505,000	90,000	60,000	34,000

YUMA ENERGY INC (NEW)
ASE: YUMA

1177 West Loop South, Suite 1825
Houston, TX 77027
Phone: 713 968-7000
Fax: -
Web: www.yumaenergyinc.com

CEO: Anthony C Schnur
CFO: -
HR: -
FYE: December 31
Type: Public

Not as ancient as Egypt's pyramids but quite venerable in its own right Pyramid Oil has been in business for more than a century focusing on the exploration development and production of crude oil and natural gas. The company's major operations and all of its income-producing assets are located in Kern and Santa Barbara counties in Southern California where it owns and operates about 30 oil and gas leases. Pyramid Oil also holds minority stakes in some oil and gas leases in New York Texas and Wyoming. In 2008 Pyramid Oil reported proved reserves of more than 470000 barrels of oil and 330 million cu. ft. of natural gas. Company chairman Michael Herman owns about 36% of Pyramid Oil.

	Annual Growth	12/14	12/15	12/16	12/17	12/18
Sales ($ mil.)	(16.1%)	43.3	23.7	14.8	25.4	21.5
Net income ($ mil.)	-	(20.2)	(11.0)	(41.6)	(5.4)	(15.6)
Market value ($ mil.)	(48.3%)	2.8	0.3	5.3	1.8	0.2
Employees	(13.5%)	41	30	30	31	23

YUMA REGIONAL MEDICAL CENTER INC

2400 S AVENUE A
YUMA, AZ 853647170
Phone: 928-344-2000
Fax: -
Web: www.yumaregional.org

CEO: Camie Overton
CFO: David Willer
HR: -
FYE: September 30
Type: Private

Yuma Regional Medical Center (YRMC) is an acute care hospital that provides medical services for Yuma Arizona and its surrounding communities. The not-for-profit hospital which has more than 400 beds and 400 doctors provides general medical surgical and emergency services. YRMC also operates about 30 additional facilities around Yuma including a rehabilitation hospital laboratories a wound care clinic primary care clinics and diagnostic imaging centers.

	Annual Growth	09/14	09/15	09/16	09/17	09/18
Sales ($ mil.)	9.2%	-	371.4	410.3	442.5	483.2
Net income ($ mil.)	-	-	(8.3)	37.6	50.7	66.1
Market value ($ mil.)	-	-	-	-	-	-
Employees	-	-	-	-	-	2,400

YUME INC
NYS: YUME

1204 Middlefield Road
Redwood City, CA 94063
Phone: 650 591-9400
Fax: 650 591-9401
Web: www.yume.com

CEO: -
CFO: Ed Reginelli
HR: Stephanie Parks
FYE: December 31
Type: Public

YuMe is hoping more people like you and me turn to the Internet to watch videos. The company's technology enables video advertisements to display on personal computers smartphones tablets set-top boxes game consoles and Internet-connected TVs. YuMe makes money by selling on a cost-per-click basis and its technology matches the viewer with the most appropriate ad so that an ad for acne cream won't appear on a video targeting an older demographic. Advertising agencies such as Omnicom use YuMe to power digital ads on behalf of some 880 customers including American Express AT&T GlaxoSmithKline Home Depot and McDonald's. The company went public in 2013 raising $46 million in its IPO.

	Annual Growth	12/11	12/12	12/13	12/14	12/15
Sales ($ mil.)	26.1%	68.6	116.7	151.1	177.8	173.3
Net income ($ mil.)	-	(11.1)	6.3	0.3	(8.7)	(16.7)
Market value ($ mil.)	(31.4%)	-	-	256.7	173.7	120.9
Employees	15.6%	-	357	457	531	552

Z GALLERIE, LLC

1855 W 139TH ST
GARDENA, CA 902493013
Phone: 800-358-8288
Fax: -
Web: www.zgallerie.com

CEO: -
CFO: -
HR: Mara Roitman
FYE: December 31
Type: Private

Cain and Abel they're not! Brothers and executives Joe and Mike Zeiden founded Z Gallerie in 1979 using their parents' garage for a warehouse and production facility. Initially Z Gallerie (later joined by sister Carole Malfatti) sold poster art but in the 1980s the trio added home furnishings and accessories to the merchandising mix. Today Z Gallerie stores which span some 10000 sq. ft. on average feature bedding and pillows dinnerware glassware rugs lamps candleholders clocks frames and albums games and gifts. The company's eclectic pieces are sold through its website and about 55 US retail locations in nearly 20 states. Z Gallerie is privately owned.

	Annual Growth	03/08	03/09	03/10*	12/11	12/12
Sales ($ mil.)	139.4%	-	-	30.8	154.4	176.4
Net income ($ mil.)	176.5%	-	-	3.3	20.6	25.5
Market value ($ mil.)	-	-	-	-	-	-
Employees	-	-	-	-	-	950

*Fiscal year change

ZAGG INC
NMS: ZAGG

910 West Legacy Center Way, Suite 500
Midvale, UT 84047
Phone: 801 263-0699
Fax: -
Web: www.zagg.com

CEO: Randall L. Hales
CFO: Bradley J. Holiday
HR: -
FYE: December 31
Type: Public

ZAGG makes items to protect power and improve mobile products. It generates more than half its revenue from smart phone and tablet screen protectors and cases marketed primarily under the InvisibleShield name. The company's other products include power stations and wireless chargers; earbuds headphones and speakers; and keyboards and other accessories. ZAGG sells its products primarily through big-box retailers electronics stores and other indirect channels; it also operates e-commerce websites and works with third-party franchisees. The US is the company's largest market.

	Annual Growth	12/14	12/15	12/16	12/17	12/18
Sales ($ mil.)	19.8%	261.6	269.3	401.9	519.5	538.2
Net income ($ mil.)	39.1%	10.5	15.6	(15.6)	15.1	39.2
Market value ($ mil.)	9.6%	186.5	300.6	195.1	506.9	268.7
Employees	29.5%	220	234	431	543	618

ZALE CORP.

NYS: ZLC

901 West Walnut Hill Lane
Irving, TX 75038-1003
Phone: 972 580-4000
Fax: –
Web: www.zalecorp.com

CEO: Mark Light
CFO: –
HR: –
FYE: July 31
Type: Public

Zale is multifaceted. One of North America's largest specialty jewelry retailers Zale sells diamond colored stone and gold jewelry (diamond fashion rings semi-precious stones earrings gold chains); watches; and gift items at some 1065 stores and 630 kiosks mostly in malls throughout the US Canada and Puerto Rico. The firm which targets the value-oriented customer has a trio of large chains aimed at different jewelry markets: Gordon's Jewelers flagship chain Zales Jewelers and Piercing Pagoda. Zale also operates about 125 jewelry outlet stores runs more than 200 stores in Canada under the Peoples Jewellers and Mappins Jewellers names sells online and offers jewelry insurance.

	Annual Growth	07/09	07/10	07/11	07/12	07/13
Sales ($ mil.)	1.5%	1,779.7	1,616.3	1,742.6	1,866.9	1,888.0
Net income ($ mil.)	–	(189.5)	(93.7)	(112.3)	(27.3)	10.0
Market value ($ mil.)	11.9%	193.2	57.4	183.1	98.6	302.9
Employees	(4.8%)	14,500	12,800	12,600	12,500	11,900

ZANETT INC.

NASDAQ: ZANE

635 Madison Ave. 15th Fl.
New York NY 10022
Phone: 212-583-0300
Fax: 212-244-3075
Web: www.zanettinc.com

CEO: Claudio M Guazzoni
CFO: Dennis Harkins
HR: –
FYE: December 31
Type: Public

Zanett is in the business of collecting companies. The company selects and acquires IT consulting firms that serve commercial and government clients including FORTUNE 500 and mid-market businesses and government agencies that operate in the defense and homeland security sectors. Services offered include consulting systems integration supply chain management implementation support and network design. Its commercial clients come from a variety of industries such as financial services health care and manufacturing. Founder Claudio Guazzoni and his uncle Bruno Guazzoni own about 24% and 28% of Zanett respectively.

ZAP

NBB: ZAAP

2 West 3rd Street
Santa Rosa, CA 95401
Phone: 707 525-8658
Fax: –
Web: www.zapworld.com

CEO: –
CFO: –
HR: –
FYE: December 31
Type: Public

ZAP is driving the future. An acronym for "zero air pollution" ZAP provides efficient alternative-energy vehicles and products for corporate and government fleets security and environmentally conscious consumers around the globe. Products include the Xebra Sedan and Truck Zappy 3 and Zapino scooters ZAP Taxi electric bicycles. The company has two primary businesses — ZAP Automotive (alternative energy vehicles) and ZAP Power Systems (personal transporters and ATVs) — to manufacture products that meet the growing demands of eco-friendly consumers.

	Annual Growth	12/12	12/13	12/14	12/15	12/16
Sales ($ mil.)	(32.0%)	50.3	51.5	28.7	29.5	10.8
Net income ($ mil.)	–	(21.8)	(15.0)	(17.6)	(14.1)	(23.5)
Market value ($ mil.)	(36.9%)	47.9	60.6	58.2	37.9	7.6
Employees	(3.7%)	506	405	402	400	435

ZAREBA SYSTEMS INC.

13705 26th Ave. North Ste. 102
Minneapolis MN 55441
Phone: 763-551-1125
Fax: 763-509-7450
Web: www.zarebasystemsinc.com

CEO: Dale A Nordquist
CFO: Jeffrey S Mathiesen
HR: –
FYE: June 30
Type: Private

Zareba Systems makes electrical fence and access control systems for animal containment (such as horses and livestock) and humans (for security applications at locations such as airports oil refineries remote utility sites and high value storage sites). The company provides perimeter security products for several prisons. Brands include Blitzer Garden Protector Guard Tower and Pet Controller. Its Zareba Systems Europe subsidiary is a maker of electric fencing for the farming equestrian and defense markets in the UK with products sold under the Rutland Electric Fencing Electric Shepherd and Induced Pulse brands. The company merged with Woodstream Corp. in 2010; Zareba owners received $9.00 per share.

ZAZA ENERGY CORP.

NBB: ZAZA

1301 McKinney St Suite 2800
Houston, TX 77010
Phone: 713 595-1900
Fax: –
Web: www.zazaenergy.com

CEO: Todd A Brooks
CFO: Paul F Jansen
HR: –
FYE: December 31
Type: Public

Despite the current economic downturn Toreador Resources is hopeful that a future bull market in oil prices will lift its revenues and its long term prospects. The oil and gas explorer owns royalty and mineral interests in properties located in France (in the Paris Basin Oil Shale) where it has 340000 net acres of primarily undeveloped land. Toreador sells its oil and production to France-based oil giant TOTAL which accounts for 98% of total revenues. Once a global player the company has shifted all its attention to its France. In 2012 the company merged its operations with US oil and gas explorer ZaZa Energy LCC. The expanded company was named ZaZa Energy Corporation.

	Annual Growth	12/10	12/11	12/12	12/13	12/14
Sales ($ mil.)	2.3%	10.5	17.6	205.2	8.9	11.5
Net income ($ mil.)	–	6.5	(2.9)	(106.2)	(67.6)	(8.2)
Market value ($ mil.)	10.9%	–	–	26.9	12.6	33.1
Employees	(36.2%)	–	123	70	29	32

ZEBRA TECHNOLOGIES CORP.

NMS: ZBRA

3 Overlook Point
Lincolnshire, IL 60069
Phone: 847 634-6700
Fax: –
Web: www.zebra.com

CEO: Anders Gustafsson
CFO: Olivier C. Leonetti
HR: –
FYE: December 31
Type: Public

Zebra Technologies knows where your stripes are and what that means. The company's array of technologies which includes bar codes readers help customers keep track of inventory supplies trucks and even football players. Zebra brings that information together for analysis so customers can better deploy their assets. The company also makes and sells devices that print and read bar codes ATM cards drivers' licenses labels tickets and receipts. Zebra's customers are in the retail transportation and logistics manufacturing healthcare and hospitality industries. Another customer is the National Football League which uses tags placed on shoulder pads to track players around the field.

	Annual Growth	12/14	12/15	12/16	12/17	12/18
Sales ($ mil.)	26.1%	1,670.6	3,652.0	3,574.0	3,722.0	4,218.0
Net income ($ mil.)	89.8%	32.4	(137.0)	(137.0)	17.0	421.0
Market value ($ mil.)	19.8%	4,170.2	3,752.1	4,620.0	5,591.8	8,577.9
Employees	2.1%	6,800	7,000	6,500	7,000	7,400

ZEELAND COMMUNITY HOSPITAL

8333 FELCH ST STE 202
ZEELAND, MI 494642609
Phone: 616-772-4644
Fax: –
Web: www.spectrumhealth.org

CEO: –
CFO: –
HR: –
FYE: June 30
Type: Private

Zeeland Community Hospital provides acute medical services for the residents of western Michigan. The hospital has nearly 60 beds and provides emergency diagnostic inpatient and outpatient services. Its specialty services include diabetes care orthopedics cardiology pain management rehabilitation and surgery. Zeeland Community Hospital has some 200 physicians on its medical staff which includes its two affiliated physician groups Zeeland Physicians and Georgetown Physicians. Zeeland Community Hospital was founded in 1928 as a 10-bed hospital.

	Annual Growth	09/04	09/05	09/09*	06/12	06/13
Sales ($ mil.)	4.4%	–	36.5	47.8	54.2	51.6
Net income ($ mil.)	14.7%	–	–	1.8	1.7	3.1
Market value ($ mil.)	–	–	–	–	–	–
Employees	–	–	–	–	–	–

*Fiscal year change

ZELTIQ AESTHETICS, INC.

4410 ROSEWOOD DR
PLEASANTON, CA 945883050
Phone: 925-474-2500
Fax: –
Web: www.coolsculpting.com

CEO: Mark J. Foley
CFO: Taylor C. Harris
HR: –
FYE: December 31
Type: Private

ZELTIQ Aesthetics is winning the battle of the bulge. The company's CoolSculpting device offers a non-invasive alternative to liposuction to knock out fat cells. The treatment uses controlled cooling to reduce the temperature of fat cells and melt fat without causing scar tissue or skin damage. ZELTIQ sells the CoolSculpting device and related consumables in the US for use on targeted areas of the torso and thighs but it is also used more freely in about 45 other international markets. The CoolSculpting system is sold to dermatologists plastic surgeons and aesthetic specialists such as medical spas. The company was incorporated in 2005 as Juniper Medical. Allergan bought ZELTIQ for $2.5 billion in 2017.

	Annual Growth	12/11	12/12	12/13	12/14	12/15
Sales ($ mil.)	51.3%	–	–	111.6	174.5	255.4
Net income ($ mil.)	–	–	–	(19.3)	1.5	41.8
Market value ($ mil.)	–	–	–	–	–	–
Employees	–	–	–	–	–	686

ZEP INC

NYS: ZEP

1310 Seaboard Industrial Boulevard
Atlanta, GA 30318-2825
Phone: 404 352-1680
Fax: –
Web: www.zepinc.com

CEO: William E Redmond Jr
CFO: Mark R Bachmann
HR: –
FYE: August 31
Type: Public

Zep hates a mess. A manufacturer of commercial industrial institutional and consumer chemical products it makes such brand lines as Enforcer (fertilizer pest control and drain cleaners) Selig (environmentally friendly hand cleaners and degreasers and equipment used to clean aerospace and automotive parts) and Zep (automotive and janitorial supplies such as hand cleaners degreasers and floor polish). Through its Niagara National unit it provides truck and fleet washing systems and products. The company operates eight manufacturing sites in Europe and North America. It generates more than 80% of sales from the US. Zep began trading publicly in 2007 after a spinoff from former parent Acuity Brands.

	Annual Growth	08/10	08/11	08/12	08/13	08/14
Sales ($ mil.)	5.2%	568.5	646.0	653.5	689.6	696.5
Net income ($ mil.)	(11.2%)	13.5	17.4	21.9	15.2	8.4
Market value ($ mil.)	(2.1%)	387.7	394.8	324.1	315.3	355.7
Employees	(0.5%)	2,350	2,300	2,400	2,400	2,300

ZIMMER BIOMET HOLDINGS INC

NYS: ZBH

345 East Main Street
Warsaw, IN 46580
Phone: 574 267-6131
Fax: –
Web: www.zimmer.com

CEO: Daniel P. (Dan) Florin
CFO: James T Crines
HR: –
FYE: December 31
Type: Public

Zimmer Biomet is the top global manufacturer of reconstructive implants used in knee or hip replacement surgery. It makes a variety of other orthopedic devices including shoulder implants bone and tissue grafting materials sports medicine products dental implant systems spinal implants and trauma products for broken bones (such as plates screws and pins). Additionally Zimmer Biomet makes medical equipment used in orthopedic surgeries including tourniquets and devices for wound cleansing. The firm's products are sold around the globe primarily in the Americas.

	Annual Growth	12/14	12/15	12/16	12/17	12/18
Sales ($ mil.)	14.1%	4,673.3	5,997.8	7,683.9	7,824.1	7,932.9
Net income ($ mil.)	–	720.1	147.0	305.9	1,813.8	(379.2)
Market value ($ mil.)	(2.2%)	23,137.7	20,928.4	21,052.8	24,616.7	21,158.9
Employees	17.4%	10,000	17,500	18,500	18,200	19,000

ZIMMER GUNSUL FRASCA ARCHITECTS LLP

1223 SW WASHINGTON ST # 200
PORTLAND, OR 972052360
Phone: 503-224-3860
Fax: –
Web: www.zgf.com

CEO: –
CFO: –
HR: –
FYE: December 31
Type: Private

Zimmer Gunsul Frasca may not be a household name but the firm has created homes for businesses and institutions on both coasts. The company which is among the nation's top 10 green design firms provides architectural planning and interior and urban design services for customers through its offices in Los Angeles Portland Seattle New York and Washington D.C. Zimmer Gunsul Frasca (ZGF) works on civic corporate academic health care and research facilities and has designed for such clients as the Environmental Protection Agency Microsoft Iowa State University and The University of Arizona. The firm was established in 1942 by Norman Zimmer.

	Annual Growth	12/05	12/06	12/07	12/08	12/09
Sales ($ mil.)	31.0%	–	–	65.8	149.0	112.9
Net income ($ mil.)	4827.8%	–	–	0.0	8.5	39.8
Market value ($ mil.)	–	–	–	–	–	–
Employees	–	–	–	–	–	600

ZION OIL AND GAS INC.

NASDAQ: ZN

6510 Abrams Rd. Ste. 300
Dallas TX 75231
Phone: 214-221-4610
Fax: 214-221-6510
Web: www.zionoil.com

CEO: John M Brown
CFO: Michael B Croswell Jr
HR: –
FYE: December 31
Type: Public

Zion Oil and Gas is on a mission in Israel. As an oil and gas exploration company Zion has exploration operations primarily on two onshore properties that cover about 162000 acres between Tel-Aviv and Haifa. The company operates through two licenses that were issued by the State of Israel and it owns 100% of the working interest in both licenses. When it eventually discovers oil and gas Zion has stated that it will focus its production operations on helping Israel become a more energy-independent country. The company which was founded in 2000 by chairman John M. Brown went public in 2007.

ZIONS BANCORPORATION, N.A.   NMS: ZION

One South Main
Salt Lake City, UT 84133
Phone: 801 844-7637
Fax: –
Web: www.zionsbancorporation.com

CEO: A. Scott (Scott) Anderson
CFO: Paul E. Burdiss
HR: Dianne R. James
FYE: December 31
Type: Public

Originally formed at the behest of Brigham Young Zions Bancorporation outgrew its early roots to become one of the largest banks in the US. The corporation is a holding company for ZB National Association Nevada State Bank National Bank of Arizona Vectra Bank Colorado The Commerce Bank of Washington California Bank & Trust and Texas-based Amegy Bank. Combined they operate some 430 bank branches in 11 mostly Western US states. The Zion banks focus on commercial and retail banking as well as mortgage and construction lending deposit accounts home mortgages credit cards and trust and wealth management services.

	Annual Growth	12/14	12/15	12/16	12/17	12/18
Assets ($ mil.)	4.7%	57,208.9	59,669.5	63,239.2	66,288.0	68,746.0
Net income ($ mil.)	22.0%	398.5	309.5	469.1	592.0	884.0
Market value ($ mil.)	9.3%	5,347.2	5,120.2	8,072.3	9,533.4	7,641.0
Employees	(0.6%)	10,462	10,200	10,057	10,083	10,201

ZIOPHARM ONCOLOGY INC   NMS: ZIOP

One First Avenue, Parris Building 34, Navy Yard Plaza
Boston, MA 02129
Phone: 617 259-1970
Fax: –
Web: www.ziopharm.com

CEO: Laurence J. N. Cooper
CFO: Satyavrat Shukla
HR: –
FYE: December 31
Type: Public

Biopharmaceutical company ZIOPHARM Oncology develops DNA-based drugs for different types of cancer. The company has three cancer drugs currently in various stages of clinical development. Its most promising candidate is palifosfamide (Zymafos) which targets cancers of bone muscle fat and other types of tissues. Others include indibulin (Zybulin which disrupts cancer cell division and migration) and darinaparsin (Zinapar an arsenic-based drug that treats blood and solid cancers). ZIOPHARM's roots go back to 2004 when CEO and co-founder Jonathan J. Lewis started ZIOPHARM Inc.; the next year the company merged with EasyWeb changed its name and went public.

	Annual Growth	12/14	12/15	12/16	12/17	12/18
Sales ($ mil.)	(42.9%)	1.4	4.3	6.9	6.4	0.1
Net income ($ mil.)	–	(31.8)	(120.1)	(165.3)	(54.3)	(53.1)
Market value ($ mil.)	(22.1%)	816.6	1,338.5	861.7	666.8	301.2
Employees	15.5%	27	28	36	46	48

ZIPREALTY INC   NMS: ZIPR

2000 Powell Street, Suite 300
Emeryville, CA 94608
Phone: 510 735-2600
Fax: –
Web: www.ziprealty.com

CEO: Lanny Baker
CFO: Eric L Mersch
HR: Pat Navarro
FYE: December 31
Type: Public

Whether you're on the go or sitting in the comfort of your home ZipRealty wants to help you close the deal. The residential real estate brokerage firm maintains an online searchable database of homes in some 20 major markets around the US. Buyers are able to streamline their house hunt narrowing searches by location price range and size; sellers can advertise on multiple real estate websites and listing services and post online tours of their homes. In addition to offering personalized tools such as saved searches and automated notifications on its website the company provides mobile access to home listings through a smart phone application.

	Annual Growth	12/08	12/09	12/10	12/11	12/12
Sales ($ mil.)	(9.0%)	107.5	123.1	118.7	85.1	73.8
Net income ($ mil.)	–	(13.3)	(12.9)	(15.6)	(9.7)	(9.7)
Market value ($ mil.)	1.4%	54.8	77.8	53.8	22.8	57.9
Employees	(53.0%)	3,068	3,346	161	126	150

ZIX CORP   NMS: ZIXI

2711 North Haskell Avenue, Suite 2200, LB 36
Dallas, TX 75204-2960
Phone: 214 370-2000
Fax: 214 370-2070
Web: www.zixcorp.com

CEO: David Wagner
CFO: David Rockvam
HR: –
FYE: December 31
Type: Public

Zix wants to nix unauthorized clicks or any other untoward use of your e-mail. The company offers a full-range of email security products and services that include email encryption advanced threat protection archiving Bring-Your-Own-Device security and data loss prevention. Customers can buy them as standalone products or in bundles. Zix targets customers in the health care financial services insurance and government sectors (including financial regulatory agencies). Zix delivers more than 1.5 million encrypted messages on a usual business day. The company built out its email security portfolio through acquisitions made in 2017.

	Annual Growth	12/14	12/15	12/16	12/17	12/18
Sales ($ mil.)	8.8%	50.3	54.7	60.1	65.7	70.5
Net income ($ mil.)	39.3%	4.1	5.0	5.8	(8.1)	15.4
Market value ($ mil.)	12.3%	195.1	275.3	267.7	237.3	310.5
Employees	7.6%	198	192	201	233	265

ZOETIS INC   NYS: ZTS

10 Sylvan Way
Parsippany, NJ 07054
Phone: 973 822-7000
Fax: –
Web: www.zoetis.com

CEO: Juan R. Alaix
CFO: Glenn C. David
HR: Roxanne Lagano
FYE: December 31
Type: Public

Whether you have cats or cattle Zoetis has medicines to keep them healthy. The company manufactures and sells veterinary products such as parasiticides (to protect against fleas ticks and worms) anti-infectives medicated feed additives vaccines and other pharmaceuticals for companion and farm animals. Zoetis boasts more than 300 product lines sold in more than 100 countries around the world making it one of the world's largest animal health businesses. In addition to medications and vaccines Zoetis offers diagnostics genetic tests devices and services such as dairy data management and consulting.

	Annual Growth	12/14	12/15	12/16	12/17	12/18
Sales ($ mil.)	5.0%	4,785.0	4,765.0	4,888.0	5,307.0	5,825.0
Net income ($ mil.)	25.1%	583.0	339.0	821.0	864.0	1,428.0
Market value ($ mil.)	18.7%	20,635.6	22,980.6	25,671.0	34,547.7	41,021.8
Employees	0.0%	10,000	9,000	9,000	9,200	10,000

ZOGENIX INC.   NMS: ZGNX

5858 Horton Street, Suite 455
Emeryville, CA 94608
Phone: 510 550-8300
Fax: –
Web: –

CEO: Stephen J Farr
CFO: Michael P Smith
HR: –
FYE: December 31
Type: Public

Zogenix wants to help the pain go away faster. The pharmaceutical company is developing and commercializing central nervous system (CNS) and therapeutic pain medications. Zohydro ER its second marketed product (launched in 2014) is an extended-release oral formulation of hydrocodone without acetaminophen for daily pain management. Other drugs under development include Reld017 an injectable form of risperidone to treat schizophrenia and bipolar symptoms. Zogenix's first marketed product Sumavel DosePro which combined the company's DosePro needle-free drug delivery technology with migraine drug sumatriptan was sold in 2014.

	Annual Growth	12/13	12/14	12/15	12/16	12/17
Sales ($ mil.)	(26.1%)	33.0	40.5	27.2	28.9	9.8
Net income ($ mil.)	–	(80.9)	8.6	26.1	(69.7)	(126.8)
Market value ($ mil.)	84.7%	119.7	47.7	513.1	422.9	1,394.1
Employees	(12.1%)	114	201	62	67	68

ZOLL MEDICAL CORPORATION
NASDAQ: ZOLL

269 Mill Rd.
Chelmsford MA 01824-4105
Phone: 978-421-9655
Fax: 978-421-0025
Web: www.zoll.com

CEO: Richard A Packer
CFO: -
HR: -
FYE: September 30
Type: Public

ZOLL Medical knows how to get your heart pounding. The medical equipment firm makes noninvasive cardiac defibrillators and pacing devices used in emergency situations to resuscitate hearts that have stopped beating during sudden cardiac arrest. ZOLL Medical also makes disposable electrodes for use with its products as well as related information technology software. The company's products are used by hospitals paramedics and other emergency medical personnel and are sold through a direct sales force in the US and via representatives and distributors in some 140 countries worldwide. ZOLL Medical manufactures its products at five facilities in the US. Japanese firm Asahi Kasei acquired ZOLL in 2012.

ZOLTEK COMPANIES INC
NMS: ZOLT

3101 McKelvey Road
St. Louis, MO 63044
Phone: 314 291-5110
Fax: -
Web: www.zoltek.com

CEO: Yoshihiro Takeuchi
CFO: Andrew W Whipple
HR: -
FYE: September 30
Type: Public

Zoltek Companies wants to lighten your load. The advanced materials company makes carbon fibers that can be used in a variety of applications due to their lightweight high-strength conductive and corrosion-resistant properties. Carbon fibers are most common in aircraft brakes but Zoltek has been expanding their use by employing them in composites for wind turbine blades as well as for use by energy and automotive markets. Zoltek has two segments: heat- and flame-resistant acrylic or technical fibers (under the brand Pyron) and carbon fibers (under the brand Panex). Its carbon fibers business accounts for most of its sales. Founder and CEO Zsolt Rumy is Zoltek's largest shareholder with an 18% stake.

	Annual Growth	09/09	09/10	09/11	09/12	09/13
Sales ($ mil.)	0.3%	138.8	128.5	151.7	186.3	140.5
Net income ($ mil.)	-	(4.2)	(6.3)	(3.6)	22.9	5.2
Market value ($ mil.)	12.3%	361.1	334.3	221.1	264.5	574.0
Employees	1.0%	1,136	1,095	1,282	1,380	1,183

ZOOLOGICAL SOCIETY OF SAN DIEGO

2920 ZOO DR
SAN DIEGO, CA 921011646
Phone: 619-231-1515
Fax: -
Web: www.sandiegozoo.org

CEO: -
CFO: Paula S Brock
HR: -
FYE: December 31
Type: Private

Talk about animal magnetism! The Zoological Society of San Diego is a not-for-profit organization that operates the 100-acre San Diego Zoo which cares for more than 3500 individual animals representing more than 650 species and subspecies as well as a collection of some 3500 species of plants. The Zoological Society also manages the 1800-acre San Diego Zoo Safari Park and the center for Conservation and Research. The zoo entertains all with its daily shows in-park restaurants guided tours and special events. The society also supports conservation education and efforts such as planned travel adventure-tours to exotic destinations in Mexico and Africa.

	Annual Growth	12/12	12/13	12/14	12/15	12/17
Sales ($ mil.)	7.1%	-	259.7	295.0	274.6	342.1
Net income ($ mil.)	25.3%	-	29.8	68.7	29.7	73.4
Market value ($ mil.)	-	-	-	-	-	-
Employees	-	-	-	-	-	2,300

ZOOM TELEPHONICS, INC.
NBB: ZMTP

225 Franklin Street
Boston, MA 02110
Phone: 617 423-1072
Fax: -
Web: www.zoomtel.com

CEO: Frank B Manning
CFO: -
HR: -
FYE: December 31
Type: Public

Even though it offers a variety of communications products Zoom Telephonics' primary mode is modems. Selling under its Hayes and Global Village brands the company specializes in the design and production of hardware used to move data over the Internet including DSL cable and dial-up modems as well as VoIP (Voice over Internet Protocol) and Bluetooth products. It sells its products in the US Europe South America and other markets through retailers like Best Buy Staples and Wal-Mart; it also sells through distributors and to OEMs (original equipment manufacturers). Founded in 1977 Zoom Telephonics was spun off from Zoom Technologies in 2009.

	Annual Growth	12/14	12/15	12/16	12/17	12/18
Sales ($ mil.)	28.4%	11.9	10.8	17.8	29.4	32.3
Net income ($ mil.)	-	0.1	(0.8)	(2.9)	(1.4)	(0.1)
Market value ($ mil.)	56.8%	4.0	37.4	37.9	35.5	24.2
Employees	6.1%	26	32	30	33	33

ZOOMAWAY TRAVEL INC
TVX: ZMA

960 Matley Lane, Suite 4
Reno, NV 89502
Phone: 866 848-3427
Fax: -
Web: www.zoomaway.ca

CEO: -
CFO: -
HR: -
FYE: December 31
Type: Public

Multivision Communications Corp. operates a subscription television service in Bolivia through wholly owned subsidiary Multivision S.A. The company's service which has more than 60 channels is available in four main cities in Bolivia (Cochabamba La Paz Santa Cruz and Sucre) and about 30 channels in Tarija. Multivision delivers its service via wireless MMDS technology (Multi-channel Multi-point Distribution System) so it isn't tethered to coaxial cables. The company also provides Wi-Fi Internet access and other data services in a joint-venture arrangement with South American telecom company Entel. Multivision Communications was formed in 1987.

	Annual Growth	12/14	12/15	12/16	12/17	12/18
Sales ($ mil.)	295.3%	-	-	0.0	0.3	0.2
Net income ($ mil.)	-	(0.2)	(0.4)	(3.5)	(1.5)	(0.5)
Market value ($ mil.)	(67.7%)	-	-	9.6	3.7	1.0
Employees	-	-	-	-	-	-

ZOVIO INC
NMS: ZVO

1811 E. Northrop Blvd.
Chandler, AZ 85286
Phone: 858 668-2586
Fax: -
Web: www.bridgepointeducation.com

CEO: Andrew S. Clark
CFO: Kevin S. Royal
HR: -
FYE: December 31
Type: Public

Bridgepoint Education invites students from all walks of life to cross on over to the higher-education side. The for-profit company offers some 1850 courses and about 80 graduate and undergraduate degree programs online and at its bricks-and-mortar campuses: Ashford University in Iowa and University of the Rockies in Colorado. Academic disciplines include education business psychology and health and social sciences. Most of the company's campus-based revenues are derived from federal financial aid. About 99% of Bridgepoint Education's more than 93000 students are enrolled exclusively online.

	Annual Growth	12/14	12/15	12/16	12/17	12/18
Sales ($ mil.)	(8.7%)	638.7	561.7	527.1	478.4	443.4
Net income ($ mil.)	(16.8%)	9.7	(70.5)	(30.0)	10.5	4.6
Market value ($ mil.)	(11.3%)	307.5	206.7	275.2	225.5	190.4
Employees	(11.1%)	7,660	6,960	6,615	5,600	4,790

ZUMIEZ INC
NMS: ZUMZ

4001 204th Street SW
Lynnwood, WA 98036
Phone: 425 551-1500
Fax: –
Web: www.zumiez.com

CEO: Richard M. Brooks
CFO: Christopher C. Work
HR: –
FYE: February 02
Type: Public

Zumiez's young customers like to zoom. The fast-growing retailer outfits action sports enthusiasts offering apparel footwear accessories and sports equipment for young men and women into board sports BMX biking and surfing. It stocks such brands as Billabong Burton Quiksilver Vans and Spy Optic as well as private-label goods. Zumiez operates about 700 mall-based stores across North America Europe and Australia as well as an online store. Alongside their action sports merchandise stores also feature couches video games and sales clerks who really use the gear — all designed to encourage shoppers to chill. It trades under three banners Zumiez Blue Tomato and Fast Times. Zumiez was founded in 1978 by chairman Thomas Campion.

	Annual Growth	01/15	01/16	01/17*	02/18	02/19
Sales ($ mil.)	4.8%	811.6	804.2	836.3	927.4	978.6
Net income ($ mil.)	1.1%	43.2	28.8	25.9	26.8	45.2
Market value ($ mil.)	(9.4%)	951.7	462.2	481.1	524.5	641.6
Employees	8.8%	6,500	7,000	7,300	8,900	9,100

*Fiscal year change

ZYGO CORP
NMS: ZIGO

Laurel Brook Road
Middlefield, CT 06455
Phone: 860 347-8506
Fax: –
Web: www.zygo.com

CEO: –
CFO: –
HR: –
FYE: June 30
Type: Public

Zygo knows how to measure precisely what its customers need. The company makes high-precision electro-optical inspection and measurement equipment automation systems and optical components. One of its main products is the interferometer which measures surface shape roughness and other characteristics by means of two light beams ("zygo" is Greek for "pair") used to produce 3D surface profiles for comparing test objects with control samples. Zygo also offers optical design testing certification and assembly services. Its products are used primarily for quality control in the semiconductor and industrial manufacturing markets.

	Annual Growth	06/09	06/10	06/11	06/12	06/13
Sales ($ mil.)	6.5%	116.0	101.3	150.1	166.8	149.4
Net income ($ mil.)	–	(66.1)	(6.3)	19.1	43.0	7.9
Market value ($ mil.)	35.8%	86.4	150.3	245.0	331.0	293.6
Employees	7.1%	484	454	553	609	637

ZYLA LIFE SCIENCES
NBB: ZCOR

600 Lee Road, Suite 100
Wayne, PA 19087
Phone: 610 833-4200
Fax: –
Web: www.egalet.com

CEO: Todd N Smith
CFO: Stan Musial
HR: –
FYE: December 31
Type: Public

Egalet wants to get the pain while skipping the abuse. The development stage pharmaceutical company is working on specially formulated pain pills designed to be more difficult to crush or dissolve ineffective in the presence of alcohol or otherwise abuse-resistant. It uses a hard plastic case that dissolves in stomach acid but becomes a gel when it contacts water. Egalet's two lead candidates are based on morphine and oxycodone but it believes its deterrence technology can be used in other products. It has licensed development of abuse-deterrent hydrocodone products to Shionogi. Once it has an approved product Egalet intends to hire its own sales force. The company was formed in 2013 and went public in 2014.

	Annual Growth	12/14	12/15	12/16	12/17	12/18
Sales ($ mil.)	99.4%	1.9	22.8	17.0	26.1	30.4
Net income ($ mil.)	–	(43.2)	(57.9)	(90.6)	(69.4)	(95.5)
Market value ($ mil.)	–	–	–	–	–	–
Employees	31.1%	44	78	154	131	130

ZYNGA INC
NMS: ZNGA

699 Eighth Street
San Francisco, CA 94103
Phone: 855 449-9642
Fax: –
Web: www.zynga.com

CEO: Frank D. Gibeau
CFO: Gerard Griffin
HR: Meg Makalou
FYE: December 31
Type: Public

Zynga puts people in touch with their inner vocabularian farmer and gambler. The company is a leading social game developer with titles such as Words with Friends FarmVille and Zynga Poker. It offers the games online for free primarily through the app stores of Apple and Google as well as social networking sites such as Facebook. Zynga claims more than 80 million monthly active users with about 90% of them on mobile devices. Players use a credit card or a service such as PayPal to buy virtual currency to purchase in-game virtual goods that enhance extend or accelerate gameplay. The company generates about two-thirds of its revenue from the US. Zynga founder Mark Pincus fashioned the name after his late dog Zinga.

	Annual Growth	12/14	12/15	12/16	12/17	12/18
Sales ($ mil.)	7.1%	690.4	764.7	741.4	861.4	907.2
Net income ($ mil.)	–	(225.9)	(121.5)	(108.2)	26.6	15.5
Market value ($ mil.)	10.2%	2,290.6	2,307.8	2,213.1	3,444.4	3,384.2
Employees	(2.6%)	1,974	1,669	1,681	1,555	1,777

Hoover's MasterList of U.S. Companies

Indexes

COMPANIES LISTED ALPHABETICALLY

1 Source Consulting Inc. 2
1-800 Contacts Inc. 2
1-800 Flowers.com, Inc. 2
1105 Media Inc. 2
180 Degree Capital Corp 2
1mage Software Inc. 2
1st Century Bancshares, Inc. 3
1st Colonial Bancorp Inc 3
1st Constitution Bancorp 3
1st Franklin Financial Corp. 3
1st Source Corp 3
1st United Bancorp, Inc. 3
1sync Inc. 4
21st Century North America Insurance Company 4
24/7 Real Media Inc. 4
30dc Inc 4
360i Llc 4
3d Systems Corp. (de) 4
3m Co 5
3m Cogent Inc. 5
3m Purification Inc. 5
454 Life Sciences 5
4licensing Corp 5
5linx Holdings Inc. 5
7-eleven Inc. 6
800-jr Cigar Inc. 6
84 Lumber Company 6
8x8 Inc 6
99 Cents Only Stores 6
A & H Sportswear Co. Inc. 6
A & K Railroad Materials, Inc. 7
A&e Television Networks Llc 7
A&r Logistics Inc. 7
A&w Restaurants Inc. 7
A. B. Boyd Company 7
A. Duie Pyle Inc. 7
A. Eicoff & Company 8
A. Finkl & Sons Company 8
A. P. Hubbard Wholesale Lumber Corporation 8
A.c. Moore Arts & Crafts Inc. 8
A.v. Thomas Produce, Inc. 8
A2d Technologies 8
Aaa Cooper Transportation 9
Aac Group Holding Corp. 9
Aamco Transmissions Inc. 9
Aaon, Inc. 9
Aar Corp 9
Aaron And Company, Inc. 9
Aaron's Inc 10
Aarp 10
Aastra Intecom Inc. 10
Abatix Corp. 10
Abaxis, Inc. 10
Abbott Laboratories 10
Abbvie Inc 11
Abc Appliance Inc. 11
Abc Cable Networks Group 11
Abc Inc. 11
Abdon Callais Offshore, Llc 11
Abeona Therapeutics Inc 11
Abercrombie & Fitch Co 12
Abf Freight System Inc. 12
Abilene Christian University Inc 12
Abington Memorial Hospital Inc 12
Abiomed, Inc. 12
Abm Industries, Inc. 12
Abm Security Services 13
Abp Corporation 13
Abra Inc. 13
Abs Capital Partners L.p. 13
Abt Associates Inc. 13
Acacia Research Corp 13
Acacia Technologies Llc 14
Academy Ltd. 14
Academy Of Motion Picture Arts & Sciences 14
Academy Of Television Arts & Sciences Inc. 14
Acadia Healthcare Company Inc. 14
Acadia Pharmaceuticals Inc 14
Acadia Realty Trust 15
Acadian Ambulance Service, Inc. 15
Accel Partners 15
Accelerate Diagnostics Inc 15
Acceleron Pharma, Inc. 15
Accelpath Inc 15

Accelrys Inc 16
Accentia Biopharmaceuticals Inc 16
Access Business Group Llc 16
Access National Corp 16
Access Systems Americas Inc. 16
Accesslex Institute 16
Accident Fund Holdings Inc. 17
Acco Brands Corp 17
Accor North America 17
Accredo Health Incorporated 17
Accucode Inc. 17
Accuray Inc (ca) 17
Accuride Corp 18
Accuride International Inc. 18
Accuvant, Inc. 18
Ace Hardware Corporation 18
Ace Parking Management Inc. 18
Ace Relocation Systems, Inc. 18
Ace Usa 19
Acelrx Pharmaceuticals Inc 19
Acento Advertising Incorporated 19
Acer America Corporation 19
Acer Therapeutics Inc 19
Aceto Corp 19
Acf Industries Llc 20
Ach Food Companies Inc. 20
Achillion Pharmaceuticals Inc 20
Aci Worldwide Inc 20
Acmat Corp. 20
Acme Communications Inc 20
Acme Markets Inc. 21
Acme United Corp. 21
Acnb Corp 21
Aco Hardware Inc. 21
Acorda Therapeutics Inc 21
Acorn Energy Inc 21
Acosta Inc. 22
Acquity Group L.l.c. 22
Acre Realty Investors Inc 22
Acsis Inc. 22
Act, Inc. 22
Actavis U.s. 22
Actelis Networks Inc. 23
Action For Boston Community Development, Inc. 23
Actionet, Inc. 23
Actiontec Electronics, Inc. 23
Active Day Inc. 23
Active Media Services Inc. 23
Activecare Inc 24
Activevideo Networks Inc. 24
Actividentity Corporation 24
Activision Blizzard, Inc. 24
Acts Retirement-life Communities, Inc. 24
Actua Corp 24
Actuate Corp. 25
Acuative Corporation 25
Acuity A Mutual Insurance Company 25
Acuity Brands Inc (holding Company) 25
Acumen Solutions Inc. 25
Acura Pharmaceuticals Inc 25
Acushnet Company 26
Ada-es Inc. 26
Adac Plastics, Inc. 26
Adamis Pharmaceuticals Corp. 26
Adams Fairacre Farms, Inc. 26
Adams Golf Inc. 26
Adams Media 27
Adams Resources & Energy, Inc. 27
Adams-columbia Electric Cooperative 27
Adb Airfield Solutions Llc 27
Addus Homecare Corp 27
Addvantage Technologies Group, Inc. 27
Adelphi University 28
Adena Health System 28
Adeona Pharmaceuticals Inc. 28
Adept Technology Inc. 28
Adexa Inc. 28
Adherex Technologies Inc. 28
Adirondack Park Agency 29
Adm Investor Services Inc. 29
Adm Tronics Unlimited, Inc. 29
Adobe Inc 29
Adt Corp 29
Adtalem Global Education Inc 29

Adtran, Inc. 30
Advance America Cash Advance Centers Inc. 30
Advance Auto Parts Inc 30
Advance Display Technologies Inc. 30
Advance Magazine Publishers Inc. 30
Advance Publications Inc. 30
Advanced Analogic Technologies Incorporated 31
Advanced Emissions Solutions Inc 31
Advanced Energy Industries Inc 31
Advanced Environmental Recycling Technologies, Inc. 31
Advanced Health Media Llc 31
Advanced Lighting Technologies Inc. 31
Advanced Micro Devices Inc 32
Advanced Mp Technology Inc. 32
Advanced Photonix, Inc. 32
Advanced Proteome Therapeutics Inc. 32
Advancepierre Foods Inc. 32
Advansource Biomaterials Corp 32
Advant-e Corporation 33
Advantage Sales And Marketing Llc 33
Advantego Corp 33
Advanzeon Solutions Inc 33
Advaxis Inc 33
Advent International Corporation 33
Advent Software, Inc. 34
Adventist Health System/west 34
Adventist Healthcare, Inc. 34
Adventrx Pharmaceuticals Inc. 34
Adventureland Park 34
Advisory Board Company (the) 34
Advizex Technologies Llc 35
Advocate Health And Hospitals Corporation 35
Aea Investors Lp 35
Aearo Technologies Llc 35
Aecom 35
Aegerion Pharmaceuticals Inc 35
Aegion Corp 36
Aegis Communications Group Inc. 36
Aegon Usa Llc 36
Aehr Test Systems 36
Aeolus Pharmaceuticals Inc 36
Aeon Global Health Corp 36
Aero Systems Engineering Inc. 37
Aerocentury Corp. 37
Aeroflex Holding Corp. 37
Aerogroup International Llc 37
Aerogrow International, Inc. 37
Aerojet-general Corporation 37
Aerokool Aviation Corporation 38
Aeronet, Inc. 38
Aerotek, Inc. 38
Aerovironment, Inc. 38
Aerus Llc 38
Aes Corp. 38
Aetea Information Technology Inc. 39
Aeterna Zentaris Inc 39
Aetna Inc. 39
Affiliated Computer Services Inc. 39
Affiliated Foods Midwest Cooperative, Inc. 39
Affiliated Foods, Inc. 39
Affiliated Managers Group Inc. 40
Affinia Group Holdings Inc. 40
Affinion Group Holdings Inc 40
Affirmative Insurance Holdings Inc 40
Affymax Inc 40
Affymetrix, Inc. 40
Aflac Inc 41
Ag Interactive Inc. 41
Ag Mortgage Investment Trust Inc 41
Ag Processing Inc A Cooperative 41
Ag&e Holdings Inc 41
Agar Supply Co. Inc. 41
Agc America Inc. 42
Agc Flat Glass North America Inc. 42
Agco Corp. 42
Age Group Ltd. 42
Ageagle Aerial Systems Inc (new) 42
Agent Information Software Inc 42
Agenus Inc 43
Agfirst Farm Credit Bank 43
Agilysys Inc 43
Agios Pharmaceuticals Inc 43
Agl Resources Inc. 43

Agnc Investment Corp 43
Agnes Scott College, Inc. 44
Agree Realty Corp. 44
Agri-mark Inc. 44
Agribank Fcb 44
Agritech Worldwide Inc 44
Agtegra Cooperative 44
Agy Holding Corp. 45
Ah Belo Corp 45
Ahold U.s.a. Inc. 45
Ahs Hillcrest Medical Center, Llc 45
Ahs Medical Holdings Llc 45
Aim Immunotech Inc 45
Aimco Properties, L.p. 46
Air Lease Corp 46
Air Methods Corporation 46
Air Products & Chemicals Inc 46
Air T Inc 46
Air Transport Services Group, Inc. 46
Air2web Inc. 47
Airband Communications Holdings Inc. 47
Aircastle Ltd. 47
Aircraft Service International Inc. 47
Airgas, Inc. 47
Airtran Airways Inc. 47
Airvana Inc. 48
Ak Steel Holding Corp. 48
Akal Security, Inc. 48
Akamai Technologies Inc 48
Akela Pharma Inc. 48
Akers Biosciences Inc. 48
Akibia Inc. 49
Akorn Inc 49
Akron General Medical Center Inc 49
Alabama Farmers Cooperative, Inc. 49
Alabama Power Co 49
Alacra Inc. 49
Alameda Corridor Transportation Authority 50
Alamo Community College District 50
Alamo Group, Inc. 50
Alanco Technologies Inc 50
Alaska Air Group, Inc. 50
Alaska Communications Systems Group Inc 50
Alaska Conservation Foundation 51
Alaska Native Tribal Health Consortium 51
Alaska Pacific Bancshares, Inc. 51
Alaska Railroad Corporation 51
Alaska Usa Federal Credit Union 51
Albany College Of Pharmacy And Health Sciences 51
Albany International Corp 52
Albany Medical Center 52
Albany Molecular Research Inc 52
Albemarle Corp. 52
Alberici Corporation 52
Albertson's Llc 52
Albertsons Companies, Inc. 53
Albireo Pharma Inc 53
Alcatel-lucent Usa Inc. 53
Alco Stores Inc 53
Alda Office Properties Inc. 53
Aldagen Inc. 53
Aldridge Electric, Inc. 54
Alere Inc. 54
Aleris Corp 54
Alex Lee, Inc. 54
Alexander & Baldwin Inc (reit) 54
Alexander's Inc 54
Alexandria Extrusion Company 55
Alexandria Inova Hospital 55
Alexandria Real Estate Equities Inc 55
Alexian Brothers Health System 55
Alexion Pharmaceuticals Inc. 55
Alexza Pharmaceuticals Inc 55
Alfa Corporation 56
Alfred University 56
Alico, Inc. 56
Alienware Corporation 56
Align Aerospace Llc 56
Align Technology Inc 56
Alimera Sciences Inc 57
Alion Science And Technology Corporation 57
Alixpartners Llp 57
Alj Regional Holdings Inc 57
All American Containers, Llc 57

All American Group Inc. 57
All American Semiconductor Llc 58
All Points Cooperative 58
All-american Sportpark Inc. 58
Allan Myers, Inc. 58
Alleghany Corp. 58
Allegheny College 58
Allegheny General Hospital Inc 59
Allegheny Technologies, Inc 59
Allegiant Travel Company 59
Allegis Group, Inc. 59
Allegro Microsystems, Llc 59
Allen & Company Llc 59
Allen Communication Learning Services Inc. 60
Allen Harim Foods Llc 60
Allen Lund Company, Llc 60
Allen Organ Company 60
Allen-edmonds Shoe Corporation 60
Allergan, Inc 60
Allete Inc 61
Alley-cassetty Companies, Inc. 61
Alliance Bancorp Inc. Of Pennsylvania 61
Alliance Data Systems Corp. 61
Alliance Entertainment Llc 61
Alliance Fiber Optic Products Inc. 61
Alliance Healthcare Services Inc 62
Alliance Holdings Group Lp 62
Alliance Laundry Holdings Llc 62
Alliance Of Professionals & Consultants, Inc. 62
Alliance Resource Partners Lp 62
Alliant Credit Union 62
Alliant Energy Corp 63
Alliant International University, Inc. 63
Allianz Life Insurance Company Of North America 63
Allied Building Products Corp. 63
Allied Healthcare International Inc. 63
Allied Healthcare Products Inc 63
Allied International Corporation Of Virginia 64
Allied Motion Technologies Inc 64
Allied Nevada Gold Corp 64
Allied Resources Inc 64
Allied Security Holdings Llc 64
Allied Systems Holdings Inc. 64
Allina Health System 65
Allis-chalmers Energy Inc. 65
Allison Transmission Holdings Inc 65
Allos Therapeutics Inc. 65
Alloy Inc. 65
Allscripts Healthcare Solutions, Inc. 65
Allstate Corp 66
Allsteel Inc. 66
Allways Health Partners, Inc. 66
Ally Bank 66
Ally Commercial Finance Llc 66
Ally Financial Inc 66
Alnylam Pharmaceuticals Inc 67
Aloha Petroleum Ltd. 67
Alon Usa Energy Inc 67
Alon Usa Partners Lp 67
Alorica Inc. 67
Alpha Associates Inc. 67
Alpha Natural Resources Inc 68
Alpha-en Corporation 68
Alphabet Inc 68
Alphatec Holdings Inc 68
Alpine Air Express Inc. 68
Alps Holdings Inc. 68
Alro Steel Corporation 69
Alsco Inc. 69
Alseres Pharmaceuticals Inc 69
Alston & Bird Llp 69
Alston Construction Company, Inc. 69
Alta Bates Summit Medical Center 69
Alta Mesa Holdings Lp 70
Altadis U.s.a. Inc. 70
Altair Nanotechnologies Inc 70
Altarum Institute 70
Altec Lansing Llc 70
Altegrity Inc. 70
Altera Corp. 71
Alternet Systems Inc. 71
Alteva 71
Altex Industries, Inc. 71

Alticor Inc. 71
Altigen Communications Inc 71
Altimmune Inc 72
Altra Industrial Motion Corp 72
Altria Group Inc 72
Altru Health System 72
Altum Incorporated 72
Alvarez & Marsal Holdings Llc 72
Alvernia University 73
Alyeska Pipeline Service Company 73
Alzheimer"s Disease And Related Disorders Association Inc. 73
Am-mex Products Inc. 73
Amag Pharmaceuticals, Inc. 73
Amalgamated Life Insurance Company 73
Amarillo Biosciences Inc. 74
Amazon.com Inc 74
Amb Financial Corp 74
Ambac Financial Group, Inc. 74
Ambarella, Inc. 74
Ambassadors Group Inc 74
Ambient Corp. 75
Amc Entertainment Holdings Inc. 75
Amc Networks Inc 75
Amcol International Corp. 75
Amcon Distributing Company 75
Amedisys, Inc. 75
Amen Properties Inc 76
Ameralia Inc. 76
Ameramex International Inc. 76
Amerco 76
Ameren Corp 76
Ameren Illinois Co 76
Ameresco Inc 77
Ameriana Bancorp 77
America Chung Nam (group) Holdings Llc 77
America First Credit Union 77
America's Body Company Inc. 77
America's Car-mart Inc 77
America's Home Place, Inc. 78
American Academy Of Pediatrics 78
American Agip Company Inc. 78
American Air Liquide Inc. 78
American Airlines Federal Credit Union 78
American Airlines Group Inc 78
American Apparel, Inc. 79
American Arbitration Association Inc 79
American Assets Trust, Inc. 79
American Association For The Advancement Of Science 79
American Axle & Manufacturing Holdings Inc 79
American Bank Inc (pa) 79
American Bankers Association Inc 80
American Baptist Homes Of The West 80
American Bar Association 80
American Biltrite Inc. 80
American Bio Medica Corp. 80
American Buildings Company 80
American Bureau Of Shipping 81
American Campus Communities Inc 81
American Cannabis Co Inc 81
American Capital Ltd. 81
American Caresource Holdings Inc 81
American Chartered Bancorp Inc. 81
American Chemical Society 82
American City Business Journals Inc. 82
American Civil Liberties Union Foundation, Inc. 82
American Commerce Solutions Inc 82
American Commercial Lines Inc. 82
American Community Mutual Insurance Company 82
American Crystal Sugar Company 83
American Defense Systems Inc. 83
American Dental Association 83
American Dental Partners Inc. 83
American Dg Energy Inc 83
American Diabetes Association 83
American Eagle Outfitters, Inc. 84
American Electric Power Co Inc 84
American Equity Investment Life Holding Co 84
American Eurocopter Corporation 84
American Express Co. 84
American Express Publishing Corporation 84

American Federation Of Labor & Congress Of Industrial Organzation 85
American Federation Of State County & Municipal Employees 85
American Fiber Green Products Inc 85
American Fidelity Assurance Company 85
American Financial Group Inc 85
American Foods Group Llc 85
American Fruit & Produce Corp. 86
American Furniture Manufacturing Inc. 86
American Furniture Warehouse Co Inc 86
American General Life Insurance Company 86
American Golf Corporation 86
American Heritage Life Insurance Company 86
American Homepatient Inc. 87
American Homestar Corporation 87
American Honda Finance Corporation 87
American Hospital Association 87
American Hotel Register Company 87
American Independence Corp 87
American Institute Of Architects, Inc 88
American Institute Of Certified Public Accountants 88
American Institute Of Physics Incorporated 88
American Institutes For Research In The Behavioral Sciences 88
American International Industries Inc 88
American Italian Pasta Company 88
American Jewish World Service, Inc. 89
American Lafrance Llc 89
American Land Lease Inc. 89
American Leather 89
American Licorice Company 89
American Life Insurance Company 89
American Locker Group, Inc. 90
American Management Association International 90
American Management Services West Llc 90
American Medical Alert Corp. 90
American Medical Association Inc 90
American Medical Response Ambulance Service Inc. 90
American Medical Systems Holdings Inc. 91
American Midstream Partners Lp 91
American Municipal Power, Inc. 91
American National Bankshares, Inc. (danville, Va) 91
American National Insurance Co. (galveston, Tx) 91
American Natural Energy Corp. 91
American Nutrition Inc. 92
American Oil & Gas Inc. 92
American Outdoor Brands Corp 92
American Pacific Corp. 92
American Petroleum Institute Inc 92
American Plastic Toys Inc. 92
American Pop Corn Company 93
American Power Group Corp 93
American Psychological Association, Inc. 93
American Public Education Inc 93
American Railcar Industries Inc 93
American Realty Capital Trust Inc. 93
American Realty Investors, Inc. 94
American Residential Services L.l.c. 94
American Restaurant Group Inc. 94
American River Bankshares 94
American Savings Bank Fsb 94
American Science & Engineering Inc 94
American Seafoods Group Llc 95
American Shared Hospital Services 95
American Snuff Company Llc 95
American Society For Testing And Materials 95
American Software Inc 95
American Soil Technologies Inc 95
American Spectrum Realty, Inc. 96
American Standard Energy Corp 96
American States Water Co 96
American Superconductor Corp. 96
American Systems Corporation 96
American Technical Ceramics Corp. 96
American Terrazzo Company Ltd. 97
American Tire Distributors Holdings, Inc. 97
American Tower Corp (new) 97
American Transmission Company, Llc 97
American Trim Llc 97
American Tv & Appliance Of Madison Inc. 97
American University 98

American Vanguard Corp. 98
American Water Works Co, Inc. 98
American Woodmark Corp. 98
Americares Foundation, Inc. 98
Americo Life Inc. 98
Americus Mortgage Corporation 99
Ameriflight Llc 99
Amerigas Partners Lp 99
Amerigroup Corporation 99
Ameripath Inc. 99
Ameriprise Financial Inc 99
Ameriquest Transportation Services Inc. 100
Ameris Bancorp 100
Amerisafe Inc 100
Ameriserv Financial Inc. 100
Amerisourcebergen Corp. 100
Amerisure Mutual Insurance Company 100
Ameritas Mutual Holding Company 101
Ameritrans Capital Corporation 101
Amerityre Corporation 101
Ameron International Corporation 101
Ames Construction, Inc. 101
Ames National Corp. 101
Ames True Temper Inc. 102
Ametek Inc 102
Amexdrug Corp. 102
Amgen Inc 102
Amicus Therapeutics Inc 102
Amkor Technology Inc. 102
Aml Communications Inc. 103
Amn Healthcare Services Inc 103
Amos Press Inc. 103
Ampacet Corporation 103
Ampco Services, L.l.c. 103
Ampco-pittsburgh Corp. 103
Amphenol Corp. 104
Ampio Pharmaceuticals Inc 104
Amplify Energy Corp (new) 104
Ampliphi Biosciences Corp 104
Amreit Inc. 104
Amrep Corp. 104
Amron International, Inc. 105
Ams Health Sciences Inc. 105
Amscan Holdings Inc. 105
Amsted Industries Incorporated 105
Amsurg Corp 105
Amtec Precision Products Inc. 105
Amtech Systems, Inc. 106
Amtrust Financial Services Inc 106
Amway International Inc. 106
Amx Llc 106
Amy's Kitchen Inc. 106
Amylin Pharmaceuticals Inc. 106
Amyris Inc 107
Anacor Pharmaceuticals Inc 107
Anadarko Petroleum Corp 107
Anadigics Inc 107
Anadigics, Inc. 107
Anadys Pharmaceuticals Inc. 107
Analog Devices Inc 108
Analogic Corp 108
Ancestry.com Inc. 108
Anchin Block & Anchin Llp 108
Anchor Bancorp Wisconsin Inc (de) 108
Anchor Glass Container Corporation 108
Andalay Solar Inc 109
Andeavor 109
Andeavor Logistics Lp 109
Andersen Construction Company 109
Andersen Corporation 109
Anderson And Dubose, Inc. 109
Anderson Kill & Olick P.c. 110
Anderson Trucking Service Inc. 110
Andrea Electronics Corp. 110
Angelica Corporation 110
Angelo Iafrate Construction Company 110
Angelo State University 110
Angels Baseball Lp 111
Angie's List Inc. 111
Angiodynamics Inc 111
Angstrom Graphics Inc. 111
Anheuser-busch Companies Inc. 111
Ani Pharmaceuticals Inc 111
Anika Therapeutics Inc. 112

Anixa Biosciences Inc 112
Ann & Robert H. Lurie Children's Hospital Of Chicago 112
Ann Inc 112
Annaly Capital Management Inc 112
Anne Arundel Medical Center, Inc. 112
Annie's Inc 113
Anomatic Corporation 113
Anr Pipeline Company 113
Anschutz Company 113
Ansen Corporation 113
Ansys Inc. 113
Antares Pharma Inc. 114
Antero Resources Corp 114
Anthelio Healthcare Solutions Inc. 114
Anthem Inc 114
Anthera Pharmaceuticals Inc 114
Anthony & Sylvan Pools Corporation 114
Anthony Forest Products Company, Llc 115
Ants Software Inc. 115
Anvil International Inc. 115
Anworth Mortgage Asset Corp. 115
Anxebusiness Corp. 115
Aol Advertising Inc. 115
Aol Inc. 116
Aon Benfield Inc. 116
Aoxing Pharmaceutical Co Inc 116
Apac Customer Services Inc. 116
Apache Corp 116
Apache Design Solutions Inc. 116
Apartment Investment & Management Co 117
Apelon Inc. 117
Apex Global Brands Inc 117
Apex Tool Group Llc 117
Api Group Inc. 117
Api Technologies Corp 117
Apollo Commercial Real Estate Finance Inc. 118
Apollo Education Group, Inc. 118
Apollo Global Management Inc 118
Apollo Residential Mortgage, Inc. 118
Appalachian Power Co. 118
Appalachian Regional Healthcare, Inc. 118
Appalachian State University Inc 119
Applabs Inc. 119
Apple American Group Llc 119
Apple Financial Holdings Inc. 119
Apple Inc 119
Appleton Coated Llc 119
Appleton Papers Inc. 120
Applied Card Systems Inc. 120
Applied Concepts Inc. 120
Applied Discovery Inc. 120
Applied Dna Sciences Inc 120
Applied Energetics Inc 120
Applied Industrial Technologies, Inc. 121
Applied Materials, Inc. 121
Applied Micro Circuits Corp. 121
Applied Minerals Inc 121
Applied Molecular Evolution Inc. 121
Applied Optoelectronics Inc 121
Applied Research Associates, Inc. 122
Applied Systems Inc. 122
Applied Visual Sciences Inc. 122
Appriss Inc. 122
Approach Resources Inc 122
Apptech Corp 122
Apptis Inc. 123
Apria Healthcare Group Inc. 123
Apricus Biosciences Inc 123
Apriso Corporation 123
Aps Healthcare Inc. 123
Aptalis Pharma Inc. 123
Aptargroup Inc. 124
Aptify 124
Aptimus Inc. 124
Aptina Llc 124
Aptium Oncology Inc. 124
Apyx Medical Corp 124
Aramark 125
Aramark Refreshment Services Llc 125
Aramark Uniform And Career Apparel Llc 125
Aratana Therapeutics, Inc 125
Arbella Mutual Insurance Company 125
Arbinet Corporation 125

Arbitech, Llc 126
Arbor Commercial Mortgage Llc 126
Arbor Networks Inc. 126
Arbor Realty Trust Inc 126
Arborgen Inc. 126
Arbutus Biopharma Corp 126
Arc Document Solutions, Inc. 127
Arc Group Worldwide Inc 127
Arc Logistics Partners Lp 127
Arca Biopharma Inc. 127
Arcbest Corp 127
Arch Chemicals Inc. 127
Arch Coal Inc 128
Arch Venture Partners 128
Archemix Corp. 128
Archer Daniels Midland Co. 128
Archie Comic Publications Inc. 128
Archipelago Learning Inc. 128
Archon Corporation 129
Archon Group L.p. 129
Archrock Inc 129
Archrock Partners Lp 129
Archway Marketing Services Inc. 129
Arconic Inc 129
Arcsight Llc 130
Arctic Cat Inc 130
Arctic Slope Regional Corporation 130
Arcturus Therapeutics Holdings Inc 130
Ardea Biosciences Inc. 130
Arden Group, Inc. 130
Arena Pharmaceuticals Inc 131
Ares Capital Corporation 131
Argan Inc 131
Argo International Corporation 131
Argo-tech Corporation 131
Argon St Inc. 131
Argosy Education Group Inc. 132
Ari Network Services, Inc. 132
Aria Health 132
Ariad Pharmaceuticals, Inc. 132
Ariba Inc. 132
Arinc Incorporated 132
Aristocrat Technologies Inc. 133
Ariva Distribution Inc. 133
Arizona Chemical Holdings Corporation 133
Arizona Instrument Llc 133
Arizona Professional Baseball Lp 133
Arizona Public Service Co. 133
Arizona State University 134
Ark Restaurants Corp 134
Arkansas Children's Hospital 134
Arkansas Electric Cooperative Corporation 134
Arkansas Heart Hospital Llc 134
Arkansas State University 134
Arkansas Tech University 135
Arlington Asset Investment Corp 135
Arlington Industries, Inc. 135
Armanino Foods Of Distinction, Inc. 135
Armco Metals Holdings Inc 135
Armed Forces Benefit Association 135
Armour Residential Reit Inc. 136
Armstrong Energy Inc. 136
Armstrong World Industries Inc 136
Army & Air Force Exchange Service 136
Arnold & Porter Llp 136
Arnold Machinery Company 136
Arnold Worldwide Llc 137
Aro Liquidation Inc 137
Arotech Corp 137
Arqule Inc. 137
Array Biopharma Inc. 137
Arris Group Inc. (new) 137
Arrow Electronics, Inc. 138
Arrow Financial Corp. 138
Arrow Financial Services L.l.c. 138
Arrowhead Pharmaceuticals Inc 138
Arrowhead Regional Medical Center 138
Art Center College Of Design Inc 138
Artech Information Systems L.l.c. 139
Artesian Resources Corp. 139
Arthrocare Corp. 139
Artisan Partners Asset Management Inc 139
Artisanal Brands Inc. 139
Arts Way Manufacturing Co Inc 139

Aruba Networks Inc 140
Arup Laboratories Inc. 140
Arvest Bank Group Inc. 140
Arxan Technologies Inc. 140
Asahi/america Inc. 140
Asarco Llc 140
Asb Financial Corp. 141
Asbury Automotive Group Inc 141
Ascena Retail Group Inc 141
Ascena Retail Group Inc. 141
Ascend Holdings Llc 141
Ascension Borgess Hospital 141
Ascension Health 142
Ascension Providence Hospital 142
Ascension Providence Rochester Hills Hospital 142
Ascent Healthcare Solutions Inc. 142
Ascent Solar Technologies Inc 142
Asg Technologies Group, Inc. 142
Asgn Inc 143
Ashford Hospitality Trust Inc 143
Ashland Inc 143
Asi Computer Technologies Inc 143
Asics America Corporation 143
Ask.com 143
Aspen Marketing Services Inc. 144
Aspen Technology Inc 144
Aspirus, Inc. 144
Asplundh Tree Expert Co. 144
Asrc Energy Services 144
Assembly Biosciences Inc 144
Assertio Therapeutics Inc 145
Asset Protection & Security Services, Lp 145
Associated Banc-corp 145
Associated Catholic Charities Inc. 145
Associated Electric Cooperative, Inc. 145
Associated Entertainment Releasing 145
Associated Estates Realty Corp. 146
Associated Food Stores, Inc. 146
Associated Grocers Of New England, Inc. 146
Associated Materials Llc 146
Associated Milk Producers Inc. 146
Associated Wholesale Grocers, Inc. 146
Association Of Universities For Research In Astronomy, Inc. 147
Assurant Inc 147
Asta Funding, Inc. 147
Astar Usa Llc 147
Astea International, Inc. 147
Astec Industries, Inc. 147
Astellas Pharma Us Inc. 148
Astoria Financial Corp. 148
Astoria Software Inc. 148
Astral Health & Beauty Inc. 148
Astrazeneca Pharmaceuticals Lp 148
Astronautics Corporation Of America 148
Astronics Corp 149
Astronova Inc 149
Asure Software Inc. 149
Asurion Corporation 149
At&t Inc 149
At&t Mobility Llc 149
Atalanta Corporation 150
Athenahealth Inc 150
Athens Bancshares Corp 150
Atherotech Inc. 150
Athersys Inc 150
Ati Ladish Llc 150
Ati Titanium Llc 151
Atlanta Clark University Inc 151
Atlanta Falcons Football Club Llc 151
Atlanta Hardwood Corporation 151
Atlanta National League Baseball Club Inc. 151
Atlantic American Corp. 151
Atlantic City Electric Co 152
Atlantic Coast Financial Corp 152
Atlantic Diving Supply, Inc. 152
Atlantic Health System Inc. 152
Atlantic Power Corp 152
Atlantic Premium Brands Ltd. 152
Atlantic Records Group 153
Atlantic Southeast Airlines Inc. 153
Atlantic Union Bankshares Corp 153
Atlanticare Health System Inc. 153
Atlanticus Holdings Corp 153

Atlanticus Holdings Corporation 153
Atlas Air Worldwide Holdings, Inc. 154
Atlas Copco Usa Holdings Inc. 154
Atlas Pipeline Partners Lp 154
Atlas World Group, Inc. 154
Atmel Corporation 154
Atmi, Inc. 154
Atmos Energy Corp. 155
Atn International Inc 155
Atria Senior Living Inc. 155
Atricure Inc 155
Atrion Corp. 155
Atrius Health, Inc. 155
Atrix International Inc. 156
Atrm Holdings Inc 156
Ats Corporation 156
Attorney General, Texas 156
Attronica Computers, Inc. 156
Atwell, Llc 156
Atwood Oceanics, Inc. 157
Atx Group Inc. 157
Auburn National Bancorp, Inc. 157
Auburn University 157
Audible Inc. 157
Audiencescience Inc. 157
Augustana College 158
Auntie Anne's Inc. 158
Aura Minerals Inc (british Virgin Islands) 158
Aura Systems Inc 158
Auraria Higher Education Center 158
Aurora Capital Partners L.p. 158
Aurora Casket Company Inc. 159
Aurora Diagnostics Inc. 159
Aurora Flight Sciences Corp 159
Aurora Networks Inc. 159
Aurora Organic Dairy Corp. 159
Aurora Wholesalers Llc 159
Austin College 160
Austin Community College 160
Austin Industries Inc. 160
Austin Powder Company 160
Austin Ribbon & Computer Supplies Inc. 160
Authentec Inc. 160
Auto-owners Insurance Company 161
Autoalliance International Inc. 161
Autocam Corporation 161
Autodesk Inc 161
Autogrill Group Inc. 161
Autoliv Asp Inc. 161
Automobile Protection Corporation 162
Automotive Finance Corporation 162
Autonation, Inc. 162
Autotrader Group Inc. 162
Autoweb Inc 162
Autozone, Inc. 162
Auvil Fruit Company Inc. 163
Auxilium Pharmaceuticals Inc 163
Av Homes Inc 163
Avalon Holdings Corp. 163
Avalonbay Communities, Inc. 163
Avanade Inc. 163
Avanir Pharmaceuticals, Inc. 164
Avantair Inc 164
Avaya Government Solutions Inc. 164
Avaya Holdings Corp. 164
Avaya Inc. 164
Aveo Pharmaceuticals Inc 164
Avera Health 165
Avera St. Marys 165
Averitt Express, Inc. 165
Avery Dennison Corp 165
Avery Weigh-tronix Llc 165
Avi Systems, Inc. 165
Avi-spl Inc. 166
Aviall Inc. 166
Aviat Networks, Inc. 166
Avid Bioservices Inc 166
Avid Technology, Inc. 166
Avis Budget Group Inc 166
Avis Rent A Car System Llc 167
Avista Corp 167
Avistar Communications Corporation 167
Aviv Reit Inc. 167
Avnet Inc 167

COMPANIES LISTED ALPHABETICALLY

Avnet Technology Solutions 167
Avstar Aviation Group Inc. 168
Avx Corp. 168
Aware Inc. (ma) 168
Axa Equitable Life Insurance Company 168
Axa Financial Inc. 168
Axa Rosenberg Investment Managment Llc 168
Axcelis Technologies Inc 169
Axcess International Inc. 169
Axel Johnson Inc. 169
Axesstel Inc 169
Axiall Corp 169
Axion International Holdings Inc 169
Axis Construction Corp. 170
Axogen Inc 170
Axon Enterprise Inc 170
Axos Financial Inc 170
Axsun Technologies Inc. 170
Axt Inc 170
Azure Midstream Partners Lp 171
Azusa Pacific University 171
Azz Galvanizing Services 171
Azz Inc 171
B&g Foods Inc 171
B&r Stores Inc. 171
B&w Technical Services Y-12 Llc 172
B. Braun Medical Inc. 172
B/e Aerospace, Inc 172
Bab Inc 172
Babson College 172
Babycenter L.l.c. 172
Back Yard Burgers Inc. 173
Backus Corporation 173
Bactolac Pharmaceutical Inc. 173
Badger Meter Inc 173
Badgerland Meat And Provisions Llc 173
Bae Systems Inc. 173
Bae Systems Norfolk Ship Repair Inc. 174
Baer's Furniture Co., Inc. 174
Bain Capital Llc 174
Baird & Warner Holding Company 174
Bakemark Usa Llc 174
Baker & Hostetler Llp 174
Baker & Mckenzie Llp 175
Baker Book House Company 175
Baker Botts L.l.p. 175
Baker Boyer Bancorp 175
Baker Capital 175
Baker Commodities Inc. 175
Baker Donelson Bearman Caldwell & Berkowitz Pc 176
Baker Hughes Inc. 176
Baker Michael International Inc 176
Baldor Electric Company 176
Baldwin Filters Inc. 176
Baldwin Piano Inc. 176
Baldwin Richardson Foods Co. 177
Baldwin Technology Company Inc. 177
Balfour Beatty Construction Group, Inc. 177
Balfour Beatty Infrastructure, Inc. 177
Balkamp Inc. 177
Ball Corp 177
Ball Horticultural Company 178
Ball State University 178
Ballantyne Strong, Inc. 178
Ballard Spahr Llp 178
Bally Technologies Inc 178
Baltic Trading Limited 178
Baltimore Orioles L.p. 179
Baltimore Ravens Limited Partnership 179
Banc Of America Merchant Services Llc 179
Banc Of California Inc 179
Bancfirst Corp. (oklahoma City, Okla) 179
Bancinsurance Corporation 179
Banco Popular North America Inc. 180
Bancorp Of New Jersey, Inc. 180
Bancorpsouth Bank (tupelo, Ms) 180
Banctec Inc. 180
Bancwest Corporation 180
Band-it-idex Inc. 180
Bandai America Incorporated 181
Bank Leumi Usa 181
Bank Mutual Corp 181
Bank Of America Corp 181

Bank Of Commerce Holdings (ca) 181
Bank Of Hawaii Corp 181
Bank Of Kentucky Financial Corp. 182
Bank Of Marin Bancorp 182
Bank Of New York Mellon Corp 182
Bank Of South Carolina Corp 182
Bank Of The Carolinas Corp 182
Bank Of The James Financial Group Inc 182
Bank Of The West 183
Bank Of Virginia 183
Bank Ozk 183
Bankers Financial Corporation 183
Bankfinancial Corp 183
Bankrate Inc (de) 183
Bankunited Inc. 184
Banner Corp. 184
Banner Health 184
Banner Pharmacaps Inc. 184
Banner-university Medical Center Tucson Campus Llc 184
Baptist Health 184
Baptist Health Care 185
Baptist Health South Florida, Inc. 185
Baptist Health System, Inc. 185
Baptist Healthcare System, Inc. 185
Baptist Hospital Of Miami, Inc. 185
Baptist Memorial Health Care System, Inc. 185
Baptist Memorial Hospital 186
Bar Harbor Bankshares 186
Baran Telecom Inc. 186
Barcelo Crestline Corporation 186
Barclays Bank Delaware 186
Bard (cr) Inc 186
Bard College 187
Bare Escentuals Inc. 187
Barkley Inc. 187
Barnes & Noble College Booksellers Llc 187
Barnes & Noble Inc 187
Barnes & Thornburg Llp 187
Barnes Group Inc. 188
Barnesandnoble.com Llc 188
Barneys New York Inc. 188
Barnhill Contracting Company 188
Barnwell Industries, Inc. 188
Barracuda Networks Inc 188
Barrett (bill) Corp 189
Barrett Business Services, Inc. 189
Barry (r.g.) Corp. 189
Barry University, Inc. 189
Barry-wehmiller Group, Inc. 189
Barton Malow Company 189
Basf Catalysts Llc 190
Bashas' Inc. 190
Basic American Inc. 190
Basic Energy Services Inc 190
Basin Electric Power Cooperative 190
Basis Technology Corporation 190
Bass Pro Inc. 191
Batesville Tool & Die Inc. 191
Bath & Body Works Llc 191
Bath Iron Works Corporation 191
Baton Rouge General Medical Center 191
Batson-cook Company 191
Battalia Winston International 192
Battelle Memorial Institute Inc 192
Battle Creek Farmers Cooperative, Non-stock 192
Bauer Built, Inc. 192
Bauer Publishing Usa 192
Bausch & Lomb Incorporated 192
Baxano Surgical Inc 193
Baxter County Regional Hospital, Inc. 193
Baxter International Inc 193
Bay Bancorp Inc 193
Bay Cities Paving & Grading, Inc. 193
Bay County Health System, Llc 193
Bay Regional Medical Center 194
Baycare Health System, Inc. 194
Bayer Corporation 194
Bayer Healthcare Pharmaceuticals Inc. 194
Baylake Corp. (wi) 194
Baylor Health Care System 194
Baylor University 195
Baylor University Medical Center 195
Bayou City Exploration Inc 195

Bayside Fuel Oil Depot Corp 195
Baystate Health Inc. 195
Baystate Health System Health Services, Inc. 195
Bazaarvoice Inc. 196
Bbdo Worldwide Inc. 196
Bbq Holdings Inc 196
Bbx Capital Corp 196
Bbx Capital Corp (new) 196
Bcb Bancorp Inc 196
Bct International Inc. 197
Bdo Usa Llp 197
Bdp International Inc. 197
Beacon Capital Partners Llc 197
Beacon Medical Group, Inc. 197
Beacon Power Corporation 197
Beacon Roofing Supply Inc 198
Bead Industries Inc. 198
Beal Bank S.s.b. 198
Beall's, Inc. 198
Beam Inc 198
Bear State Financial Inc 198
Bearing Distributors, Inc. 199
Beasley Broadcast Group Inc 199
Beaufort County Memorial Hospital 199
Beaumont Health 199
Beauticontrol Inc. 199
Beauty Systems Group Llc 199
Beaver Dam Community Hospitals, Inc. 200
Beaver Street Fisheries, Inc. 200
Beazer Homes Usa, Inc. 200
Bebe Stores Inc 200
Bechtel Group Inc. 200
Beck Suppliers, Inc. 200
Becton, Dickinson & Co 201
Bed, Bath & Beyond, Inc. 201
Beebe Medical Center, Inc. 201
Beech-nut Nutrition Corporation 201
Behlen Mfg. Co. 201
Behrman Capital L.p. 201
Bekaert Corporation 202
Bekins Holding Corp. 202
Bel Fuse Inc 202
Belcan Corporation 202
Belden & Blake Corporation 202
Belden Inc 202
Belfor Usa Group Inc. 203
Belk Inc (de) 203
Belkin International Inc. 203
Bell Helicopter Textron Inc. 203
Bell Partners Inc. 203
Beloit College 203
Beloit Health System, Inc. 204
Bemis Co Inc 204
Benchmark Electronics, Inc. 204
Benco Dental Supply Co. 204
Benderson Development Company Llc 204
Benedictine College 204
Benedictine Health System 205
Beneficial Life Insurance Company 205
Beneficial Mutual Bancorp Inc 205
Benefit Cosmetics Llc 205
Benefit Software Inc. 205
Benefitmall Inc. 205
Benjamin Moore & Co. 206
Bentley Systems Incorporated 206
Bentley University 206
Berea College 206
Bergelectric Corp. 206
Bergen Community College 206
Berkeley Farms Llc 207
Berklee College Of Music, Inc. 207
Berkley (wr) Corp 207
Berkley Insurance Company 207
Berkshire Bancorp Inc (de) 207
Berkshire Hathaway Inc 207
Berkshire Health Systems Inc. 208
Berkshire Income Realty Inc 208
Berkshire Partners Llc 208
Berlin Packaging L.l.c. 208
Berlitz Languages Inc. 208
Bernard Chaus Inc. 208
Bernard Hodes Group Inc. 209
Bernatello"s Pizza Inc 209
Berner Food & Beverage, Llc 209

Berry Companies, Inc. 209
Berry Global Films, Llc 209
Berry Global Group Inc 209
Bertucci's Corporation 210
Best Brands Corp. 210
Best Buy Inc 210
Best Friends Pet Care Inc. 210
Best Medical International Inc. 210
Best Western International, Inc. 210
Best Wings Usa Inc. 211
Bet Interactive Llc 211
Beth Israel Deaconess Medical Center, Inc. 211
Beth Israel Medical Center 211
Bethesda Hospital, Inc. 211
Bethune-cookman University Inc. 211
Betsey Johnson Llc 212
Bexar County Hospital District 212
Bg Medicine Inc 212
Bgc Partners Inc 212
Bhe Environmental Inc. 212
Bi-lo Holding Llc 212
Bi-rite Restaurant Supply Co., Inc. 213
Bidz.com Inc. 213
Big 5 Sporting Goods Corp 213
Big Lots, Inc. 213
Big West Oil, Llc 213
Big Y Foods Inc. 213
Big-d Construction Corp. 214
Biglari Holdings Inc (new) 214
Bill & Melinda Gates Foundation 214
Billing Services Group Ltd. 214
Billings Clinic 214
Bimini Capital Management Inc 214
Bind Therapeutics Inc 215
Bingham Mccutchen Llp 215
Bio-key International Inc 215
Bio-rad Laboratories Inc 215
Bio-reference Laboratories, Inc. 215
Bio-solutions Manufacturing Inc. 215
Bio-techne Corp 216
Bioanalytical Systems, Inc. 216
Biocardia Inc 216
Biocept Inc 216
Bioclinca 216
Biocryst Pharmaceuticals Inc 216
Biodelivery Sciences International Inc 217
Biogen Inc 217
Biohorizons Inc. 217
Bioject Medical Technologies Inc. 217
Biola University, Inc. 217
Biolargo Inc 217
Biolase Inc 218
Biolife Solutions Inc 218
Biomed Realty Trust Inc 218
Biomerica Inc 218
Biomet Inc. 218
Biomimetic Therapeutics Inc. 218
Bion Environmental Technologies, Inc. 219
Biophan Technologies Inc. 219
Bioreliance Corporation 219
Biospecifics Technologies Corp. 219
Biosynergy, Inc. 219
Biotelemetry Inc 219
Birds Eye Foods Llc 220
Birkenstock Usa Gp Llc 220
Birmingham-southern College Inc 220
Birner Dental Management Services Inc 220
Biscom Inc. 220
Bison Building Materials Ltd. 220
Bissell Homecare Inc. 221
Bitco Corporation 221
Bitstream Inc. 221
Bj's Restaurants Inc 221
Bj's Wholesale Club Inc. 221
Bjt, Inc. 221
Bk Technologies Corp 222
Bkf Capital Group Inc 222
Black & Veatch Corporation 222
Black Box Corp. (de) 222
Black Entertainment Television Llc 222
Black Hills Corporation 222
Black Hills Power Inc. 223
Black Raven Energy Inc. 223
Blackbaud, Inc. 223

Blackboard Inc. 223
Blackfoot Telephone Cooperative Inc. 223
Blackhawk Bancorp Inc 223
Blackhawk Network Holdings Inc 224
Blackrock Inc 224
Blackstone Group Inc (the) 224
Blackstone Mortgage Trust Inc 224
Blair Corporation 224
Blank Rome Llp 224
Blarney Castle Oil Co. 225
Blessing Hospital 225
Blish-mize Co. 225
Blizzard Entertainment Inc. 225
Block (h & R), Inc. 225
Blockbuster L.l.c. 225
Blonder Tongue Laboratories, Inc. 226
Bloodworks 226
Bloomberg L.p. 226
Bloomin' Brands Inc 226
Blount International, Inc. 226
Blount Memorial Hospital, Incorporated 226
Blucora, Inc. 227
Blue Bird Corporation 227
Blue Buffalo Pet Products, Inc. 227
Blue Care Network Of Michigan 227
Blue Cross & Blue Shield Association 227
Blue Cross & Blue Shield Of Mississippi 227
Blue Cross & Blue Shield Of Rhode Island 228
Blue Cross And Blue Shield Of Alabama 228
Blue Cross And Blue Shield Of Arizona, Inc. 228
Blue Cross And Blue Shield Of Massachusetts Inc. 228
Blue Cross And Blue Shield Of Minnesota 228
Blue Cross And Blue Shield Of Montana 228
Blue Cross And Blue Shield Of North Carolina 229
Blue Cross And Blue Shield Of Texas 229
Blue Cross And Blue Shield Of Vermont 229
Blue Cross Blue Shield Of Georgia Inc 229
Blue Cross Blue Shield Of Michigan 229
Blue Cross Of California 229
Blue Cross Of Idaho Health Service Inc. 230
Blue Dolphin Energy Co. 230
Blue Nile Inc 230
Blue Ridge Healthcare Hospitals, Inc. 230
Blue Ridge Healthcare System, Inc.. 230
Blue Sky Studios Inc. 230
Blue Tee Corp. 231
Blue Valley Ban Corp (ks) 231
Bluearc Corporation 231
Bluebird Bio Inc 231
Bluebonnet Electric Cooperative, Inc. 231
Bluechoice Healthplan Of South Carolina Inc. 231
Bluecross Blueshield Of Tennessee Inc. 232
Blueknight Energy Partners Lp 232
Bluelinx Holdings Inc 232
Bluepoint Solutions Inc. 232
Bluestar Energy Services Inc. 232
Bluestem Brands Inc. 232
Blyth, Inc. 233
Bmc Stock Holdings Inc 233
Bmo Financial Corp. 233
Bmw Of North America Llc 233
Bnc Bancorp 233
Bnccorp Inc 233
Bns Holding Inc. 234
Bnsf Railway Company 234
Board Of Regents Of The University Of Nebraska 234
Board Of Trustees Of Community College District 508 (inc) 234
Board Of Trustees Of Illinois State University 234
Boardriders, Inc. 234
Boardwalk Pipeline Partners Lp 235
Bob Evans Farms Inc 235
Bob Ross Buick, Inc. 235
Boddie-noell Enterprises, Inc. 235
Body Central Corp. 235
Boeing Capital Corp 235
Boeing Co. (the) 236
Boeing Employees' Credit Union 236
Boeing Satellite Systems International Inc. 236
Bogen Communications International Inc. 236
Boingo Wireless Inc 236
Boise Cascade Co. (de) 236
Boise State University 237

Bojangles' Restaurants Inc. 237
Bok Financial Corp 237
Bollinger Shipyards Inc. 237
Bollore Logistics Usa Inc. 237
Bolt Technology Corp. 237
Bon Secours - Richmond Community Hospital, Incorporated 238
Bon Secours Mercy Health, Inc. 238
Bon-ton Stores Inc 238
Bonanza Creek Energy Inc 238
Bonitz, Inc. 238
Bonneville Power Administration 238
Bonnier Corporation 239
Booking Holdings Inc 239
Books-a-million, Inc. 239
Bookspan 239
Boone Hospital Center 239
Booz Allen Hamilton Holding Corp. 239
Borghese Inc. 240
Borgwarner Inc 240
Bosch Communications Systems 240
Bosch Security Systems Inc. 240
Boss Holdings, Inc. 240
Bosselman Inc. 240
Boston Acoustics Inc. 241
Boston Beer Co Inc (the) 241
Boston Medical Center Corporation 241
Boston Mutual Life Insurance Company 241
Boston Private Financial Holdings, Inc. 241
Boston Properties Inc 241
Boston Red Sox Baseball Club Limited Partnership 242
Boston Restaurant Associates Inc. 242
Boston Scientific Corp. 242
Boston Symphony Orchestra, Inc. 242
Bostoncoach 242
Bottomline Technologies (delaware) Inc 242
Boulder Brands Inc 243
Bowdoin College 243
Bowen Engineering Corporation 243
Bowl America Inc. 243
Bowlin Travel Centers Inc. 243
Boy Scouts Of America 243
Boyd Coffee Company 244
Boyd Gaming Corp. 244
Boys & Girls Clubs Of America 244
Bozzuto's, Inc. 244
Bpz Resources, Inc. 244
Bradford Soap Works Inc. 244
Bradford White Corporation 245
Bradley University 245
Brady Corp 245
Brake Parts Inc. 245
Branch & Associates, Inc. 245
Brandeis University 245
Brandywine Realty Trust 246
Brant Industries Inc. 246
Brasfield & Gorrie L.l.c. 246
Bravo Brio Restaurant Group Inc 246
Bravo Media Llc 246
Brazos Electric Power Cooperative, Inc. 246
Bre Properties, Inc. 247
Breeze-eastern Corp 247
Breitburn Energy Partners Lp 247
Brentwood Industries, Inc. 247
Brg Sports, Inc. 247
Brickell Biotech Inc 247
Bridge Bancorp, Inc. (bridgehampton, Ny) 248
Bridge Capital Holdings 248
Bridgeline Digital Inc 248
Bridgeport Hospital & Healthcare Services Inc 248
Bridgestone Retail Operations Llc 248
Bridgford Foods Corp. 248
Briggs & Stratton Corp. 249
Briggs & Stratton Power Products Group Llc 249
Brigham Exploration Company 249
Brigham Young University 249
Bright Horizons Family Solutions Inc. 249
Bright House Networks Llc 249
Brightcove Inc 250
Brightpoint Inc. 250
Brightstar Corp. 250
Brillstein Entertainment Partners Llc 250
Brinker International, Inc. 250

Brinks Co (the) 250
Bristol Hospital Incorporated 251
Bristol-myers Squibb Co. 251
Bristow Group Inc 251
Britton & Koontz Capital Corp. 251
Brixmor Property Group Inc 251
Broadcast International Inc 251
Broadcast Music Inc. 252
Broadcom Corp. 252
Broadcom Inc (de) 252
Broadridge Financial Solutions Inc 252
Broadsoft Inc 252
Broadview Institute Inc 252
Broadview Networks Holdings Inc. 253
Broadvision Inc 253
Broadway Bancshares Inc. 253
Broadway Financial Corp. (de) 253
Broadwind Energy, Inc. 253
Broan-nutone Llc 253
Brocade Communications Systems, Inc. 254
Brockton Hospital, Inc. 254
Broder Bros., Co. 254
Bromley Communications 254
Bronson Battle Creek Hospital 254
Bronson Health Care Group, Inc. 254
Bronson Methodist Hospital Inc 255
Bronxcare Health System 255
Brookdale Senior Living Inc 255
Brookfield Property Reit Inc 255
Brookhaven Memorial Hospital Medical Center, Inc. 255
Brookline Bancorp Inc (de) 255
Brooklyn Hospital Center 256
Brooklyn Navy Yard Development Corporation 256
Brookmount Explorations Inc. 256
Brooks Automation Inc 256
Brooks Tropicals Holding Inc. 256
Brookstone Inc. 256
Brother International Corporation 257
Brown & Brown Inc 257
Brown Brothers Harriman & Co. 257
Brown Jordan International Inc. 257
Brown Printing Company 257
Brown University In Providence In The State Of Rhode Island And Providence Plantations 257
Brown-forman Corp 258
Browning Arms Company 258
Broyhill Furniture Industries Inc. 258
Brt Apartments Corp 258
Bruce Foods Corporation 258
Bruce Oakley, Inc. 258
Bruker Axs Inc. 259
Bruker Corp 259
Bruker Daltonics Inc. 259
Bruker Energy & Supercon Technologies Inc. 259
Bruno Independent Living Aids Inc. 259
Brunswick Corp. 259
Bryan Cave Llp 260
Bryan Medical Center 260
Bryce Corporation 260
Bryn Mawr Bank Corp 260
Bryn Mawr College 260
Bsb Bancorp Inc. (md) 260
Bsd Medical Corp. 261
Bsh Home Appliances Corporation 261
Bsquare Corp 261
Bt Conferencing 261
Btu International, Inc. 261
Bubba Gump Shrimp Co. Restaurants Inc. 261
Buckeye Partners Lp 262
Buckeye Pipe Line Company, L P 262
Buckeye Power, Inc. 262
Buckhead Life Restaurant Group Inc. 262
Buckle, Inc. (the) 262
Bucknell University 262
Budget Rent A Car System Inc. 263
Buffalo Bills Inc. 263
Buffalo Wild Wings Inc 263
Build-a-bear Workshop Inc 263
Builders Firstsource Inc. 263
Builders Firstsource-southeast Group Llc 263
Bulldog Solutions Inc. 264
Bulova Corporation 264
Bulova Technologies Group, Inc 264

Bunge Milling Inc. 264
Burger King Worldwide Inc. 264
Burgett Inc. 264
Burkhart Dental Supply Co. 265
Burlington Northern & Santa Fe Railway Co. (the) 265
Burlington Northern Santa Fe Llc 265
Burlington Stores Inc 265
Burrell Communications Group Llc 265
Burrill & Company Llc 265
Burroughs & Chapin Company Inc. 266
Burson-marsteller Inc. 266
Burst Media Corporation 266
Burton Lumber & Hardware Co. 266
Bush Industries Inc. 266
Bushnell Inc. 266
Busken Bakery Inc. 267
Busy Beaver Building Centers Inc. 267
Butler Health System, Inc. 267
Butler Manufacturing Company 267
Butler National Corp. 267
Buzzi Unicem Usa Inc. 267
Bway Holding Company 268
Bwx Technologies Inc 268
Bycor General Contractors, Inc. 268
C & F Financial Corp. 268
C & K Market, Inc. 268
C&a Industries Inc. 268
C&d Zodiac Inc. 269
C&s Wholesale Grocers Inc. 269
C. B. Fleet Company Incorporated 269
C.d. Smith Construction Inc. 269
C.h. Guenther & Son Inc. 269
C.r. England, Inc. 269
Ca Inc 270
Cabela's Inc 270
Cable Manufacturing And Assembly Co. Inc. 270
Cable News Network Inc. 270
Cable One Inc 270
Cablevision Systems Corp. 270
Cablexpress Corporation 271
Cabot Microelectronics Corp 271
Cabot Oil & Gas Corp. 271
Cache Inc 271
Caci International Inc 271
Cactus Feeders Inc. 271
Cadence Mcshane Construction Company Llc 272
Cadence Pharmaceuticals Inc 272
Cadiz Inc 272
Cadus Corporation 272
Cadwalader Wickersham & Taft Llp 272
Caesars Entertainment Corp 272
Cafe Enterprises Inc. 273
Cafepress Inc 273
Cahill Gordon & Reindel Llp 273
Cai International Inc 273
Caithness Corporation 273
Cajun Industries, Llc 273
Cal Dive International Inc 274
Cal-maine Foods Inc 274
Caladrius Biosciences Inc 274
Calamos Asset Management Inc 274
Calamp Corp 274
Calatlantic Group Inc 274
Calavo Growers, Inc. 275
Calcot, Ltd. 275
Calendar Holdings Llc 275
Caleres Inc 275
Calgon Carbon Corporation 275
Calibre Systems, Inc. 275
Calient Networks Inc. 276
California Bank & Trust 276
California Coastal Communities Inc. 276
California Community Foundation 276
California Dairies Inc. 276
California First National Bancorp 276
California Independent System Operator Corporation 277
California Institute Of Technology 277
California Physicians' Service 277
California Pizza Kitchen Inc. 277
California Products Corporation 277
California Public Employees' Retirement System 277
California Steel Industries, Inc. 278

California Water Service Group (de) 278
California Wellness Foundation 278
Caliper Life Sciences Inc. 278
Calix Inc 278
Call Now Inc. 278
Callidus Software Inc. 279
Callisonrtkl Inc. 279
Callon Petroleum Co. (de) 279
Calloway's Nursery, Inc. 279
Calmare Therapeutics Inc 279
Calnet Inc. 279
Calpine Corp 280
Calportland Company 280
Calumet Specialty Product Partners Lp 280
Calvary Hospital, Inc. 280
Calvert Company Inc. 280
Calverthealth Medical Center, Inc. 280
Calypso Technology Inc. 281
Calypte Biomedical Corporation 281
Camber Energy Inc 281
Cambium Learning Group, Inc. 281
Cambrex Corp 281
Cambridge Bancorp 281
Cambridge Heart Inc. 282
Cambridge Public Health Commission 282
Cambridge Soundworks Inc. 282
Camco Financial Corp 282
Camden National Corp. (me) 282
Camden Property Trust 282
Camelot Entertainment Group Inc. 283
Cameron International Corporation 283
Cameron Mitchell Restaurants Llc 283
Campagna-turano Bakery Inc. 283
Campbell Mithun Inc. 283
Campbell Soup Co 283
Campbell-ewald Company 284
Campus Crest Communities Inc 284
Campus Crest Communities, Inc. 284
Camstar Systems Inc. 284
Can-cal Resources Ltd. 284
Canaan Management Inc. 284
Canaccord Genuity Inc. 285
Canandaigua National Corp. 285
Cancer Genetics, Inc. 285
Candela Corporation 285
Candlewick Press Inc. 285
Cannondale Bicycle Corporation 285
Canon U.s.a. Inc. 286
Canon Virginia Inc. 286
Cantel Medical Corp 286
Canterbury Park Holding Corp (new) 286
Cantor Entertainment Technology Inc. 286
Cantor Fitzgerald L.p. 286
Capcom U.s.a. Inc. 287
Cape Bancorp, Inc. 287
Cape Cod Healthcare, Inc. 287
Cape Cod Hospital 287
Cape Environmental Management Inc. 287
Capella Education Company 287
Capgemini North America Inc. 288
Capital Bank Corporation 288
Capital Bank Financial Corp 288
Capital Bluecross 288
Capital City Bank Group, Inc. 288
Capital District Physicians' Health Plan, Inc. 288
Capital Health System Inc. 289
Capital One Financial Corp 289
Capital Properties, Inc. 289
Capital Senior Living Corp. 289
Capital Southwest Corp. 289
Capitalsource Inc. 289
Capitol Federal Financial Inc 290
Capri Capital Partners Llc 290
Capricor Therapeutics Inc 290
Caprius Inc. 290
Caprock Communications Inc. 290
Capsonic Group Llc 290
Capstead Mortgage Corp. 291
Capstone Turbine Corp 291
Captain D's Llc 291
Captech Ventures Inc. 291
Cara Therapeutics Inc 291
Caraco Pharmaceutical Laboratories Ltd. 291
Carahsoft Technology Corp. 292

Caraustar Recovered Fiber Group Inc. 292
Carbo Ceramics Inc. 292
Carbonite Inc 292
Cardean Learning Group Llc 292
Cardiac Science Corporation 292
Cardinal Bankshares Corp. 293
Cardinal Financial Corp 293
Cardinal Health Pharmacy Solutions 293
Cardinal Health, Inc. 293
Cardinal Logistics Management Corporation 293
Cardington Yutaka Technologies Inc. 293
Cardiogenesis Corporation 294
Cardiovascular Systems, Inc 294
Cardone Industries Inc. 294
Cardtronics Plc 294
Care New England Health System Inc 294
Care.com Inc 294
Carealliance Health Services 295
Carecentric Inc. 295
Carefirst Inc. 295
Carefusion Corp 295
Caregroup, Inc. 295
Carey International Inc. 295
Carhartt Inc. 296
Carilion Clinic 296
Carl Buddig & Company 296
Carle Foundation Hospital 296
Carle Physician Group 296
Carleton College 296
Carlisle Brake & Friction Inc. 297
Carlisle Companies Inc. 297
Carlisle Foodservice Products Incorporated 297
Carlisle Tire & Wheel Company 297
Carlson Companies Inc. 297
Carlson Hotels Worldwide Inc. 297
Carlson Restaurants Worldwide Inc. 298
Carlton Fields P.a. 298
Carlyle Group Inc (the) 298
Carma Laboratories Inc. 298
Carmax Inc. 298
Carmike Cinemas, Inc. 298
Carnegie Institution Of Washington 299
Carnegie Mellon University 299
Carnival Corp 299
Carolina Power & Light Company 299
Carolina Bank Holdings Inc 299
Carolina Care Plan Inc. 299
Carolina Handling, Llc 300
Carolina Trust Bancshares Inc 300
Carolinas Medical Center-lincoln 300
Caromont Health, Inc. 300
Carpenter Contractors Of America, Inc. 300
Carpenter Technology Corp. 300
Carquest Corporation 301
Carr-gottstein Foods Co. 301
Carriage Services, Inc. 301
Carrizo Oil & Gas, Inc. 301
Carrols Restaurant Group Inc 301
Carson Tahoe Regional Healthcare 301
Carter & Associates Enterprises Inc. 302
Carter's Inc 302
Cartesian Inc 302
Carus Publishing Company 302
Carvel Corporation 302
Carver Bancorp Inc. 302
Cas Medical Systems Inc 303
Cascade Bancorp 303
Cascade Engineering, Inc. 303
Cascade Microtech Inc 303
Cascade Natural Gas Corporation 303
Case Financial Inc. 303
Case Western Reserve University 304
Casella Waste Systems, Inc. 304
Casey's General Stores, Inc. 304
Cash America International, Inc. 304
Cash-wa Distributing Co. Of Kearney, Inc. 304
Casi Pharmaceuticals, Inc. 304
Casio America Inc. 305
Caspian Services Inc 305
Cass Information Systems Inc. 305
Castle (am) & Co 305
Castle Brands Inc. 305
Castle Rock Entertainment Inc. 305
Castlerock Security Holdings Inc. 306

Catalent Pharma Solutions Inc. 306
Catalina Marketing Corporation 306
Catalina Restaurant Group Inc. 306
Catalyst Biosciences Inc 306
Catalyst Health Solutions Inc. 306
Catalyst Pharmaceutical Partners Inc. 307
Catamount Constructors, Inc. 307
Catasys Inc 307
Catchmark Timber Trust Inc 307
Caterpillar Financial Services Corp 307
Cathay General Bancorp 307
Catholic Health East 308
Catholic Health Services Of Long Island 308
Catholic Health System, Inc. 308
Catholic Medical Center 308
Cato Corp. 308
Cavalier Telephone Llc 308
Cavium Inc 309
Cazenovia College 309
Cbeyond Inc 309
Cbiz Inc 309
Cbl & Associates Properties Inc 309
Cboe Global Markets Inc 309
Cbre Group Inc 310
Cbs Broadcasting Inc. 310
Cbs Radio Inc. 310
Cc Industries Inc. 310
Cca Industries, Inc. 310
Ccc Group Inc. 310
Ccc Information Services Group Inc. 311
Ccfnb Bancorp Inc. 311
Cch Incorporated 311
Ccom Group Inc 311
Ccur Holdings Inc 311
Cd International Enterprises Inc 311
Cdc Supply Chain 312
Cdi Contractors, Llc 312
Cdti Advanced Materials Inc 312
Cdw Corporation 312
Cecil Bancorp, Inc. 312
Ceco Environmental Corp. 312
Cedar Fair Lp 313
Cedar Realty Trust Inc 313
Cedarburg Hauser Pharmaceuticals Inc. 313
Cedars-sinai Medical Center 313
Cegedim Relationship Management 313
Cel-sci Corporation 313
Celadon Group, Inc. 314
Celanese Corp (de) 314
Celebrate Interactive Holdings Inc. 314
Celera Corporation 314
Celgene Corp 314
Cellco Partnership 314
Celldex Therapeutics, Inc. 315
Celsion Corp 315
Celsius Holdings Inc 315
Cem Holdings Corporation 315
Cenama Inc. 315
Centaur Technology Inc. 315
Centegra Health System Foundation 316
Centene Corp 316
Center For Creative Leadership Inc 316
Centerbeam Inc. 316
Centerline Capital Group Inc. 316
Centerplate Inc. 316
Centerpoint Energy Houston Electric Llc 317
Centerpoint Energy, Inc 317
Centerpoint Properties Trust 317
Centers For Disease Control And Prevention 317
Centers For Medicare & Medicaid Services 317
Centerstate Bank Corp 317
Centimark Corporation 318
Centra Health, Inc. 318
Centra Inc. 318
Central Dupage Hospital Association 318
Central Federal Corp 318
Central Freight Lines Inc. 318
Central Garden & Pet Co 319
Central Grocers, Inc. 319
Central Michigan University 319
Central Mutual Insurance Company 319
Central Pacific Financial Corp 319
Central Refrigerated Service, Llc 319
Central Steel And Wire Company 320

Central Suffolk Hospital 320
Central Valley Community Bancorp 320
Central Vermont Public Service Corporation 320
Centrastate Healthcare System Inc 320
Centre College Of Kentucky 320
Centria Inc. 321
Centric Brands Inc 321
Centric Group L.l.c. 321
Centrus Energy Corp 321
Century 21 Real Estate Llc 321
Century Aluminum Co. 321
Century Bancorp, Inc. 322
Century Casinos Inc. 322
Century Energy Ltd. 322
Century Foods International Llc 322
Centurylink Inc 322
Cenveo Inc 322
Cephalon Inc. 323
Cephas Holding Corp 323
Cepheid 323
Cequel Communications Holdings I Llc 323
Ceradyne Inc 323
Cereplast Inc 323
Ceres Inc 324
Ceres Solutions, Llp 324
Cerner Corp. 324
Cerritos Community College District 324
Certainteed Corporation 324
Certco, Inc. 324
Cerus Corp. 325
Cessna Aircraft Company 325
Ceva Inc 325
Cf Industries Holdings Inc 325
Cfc International Inc. 325
Cgb Enterprises, Inc. 325
Ch2m Hill Companies, Ltd. 326
Cha Hollywood Medical Center Lp 326
Chadbourne & Parke Llp 326
Champion Industries Inc (wv) 326
Champion Laboratories Inc. 326
Champions Oncology Inc 326
Chancelight, Inc. 327
Channeladvisor Corp 327
Chaparral Energy L.l.c. 327
Chapman University 327
Chargers Football Company Llc 327
Charles & Colvard Ltd 327
Charles C Parks Co Inc 328
Charles Industries Ltd. 328
Charles Pankow Builders Ltd. 328
Charles Regional Medical Center Foundation Inc. 328
Charles River Laboratories International Inc. 328
Charles River Systems Inc. 328
Charleston Area Medical Center, Inc. 329
Charleston Hospital, Inc. 329
Charlies Holdings Inc 329
Chart Industries Inc 329
Charter Manufacturing Company, Inc. 329
Chartis Inc 329
Chase Corp. 330
Chase General Corporation 330
Chatham Lodging Trust 330
Chatham Search International Inc. 330
Chatham University 330
Chattanooga Bakery Inc. 330
Chattem Inc. 331
Chca Conroe, L.p. 331
Checkpoint Systems Inc 331
Cheesecake Factory Inc. (the) 331
Chefs International Inc. 331
Chefs' Warehouse Inc (the) 331
Chegg Inc 332
Chelsea & Scott Ltd. 332
Chelsea Property Group Inc. 332
Chemed Corp 332
Chemocentryx, Inc. 332
Chemtura Corp 332
Chemung Financial Corp. 333
Chenega Corporation 333
Cheniere Energy Inc. 333
Cheniere Energy Partners L P 333
Cheniere Energy Partners Lp Holdings Llc 333
Chep International Inc. 333

Cherry Bekaert Llp 334
Cherry Central Cooperative, Inc. 334
Cherry Hill Mortgage Investment Corp 334
Chesapeake Energy Corp. 334
Chesapeake Lodging Trust 334
Chesapeake Oilfield Services Inc. 334
Chesapeake Utilities Corp. 335
Cheviot Financial Corp 335
Chevron Corporation 335
Chevron Phillips Chemical Company Llc 335
Chevron Pipe Line Company 335
Chevys Restaurants Llc 335
Chicago Airport System 336
Chicago Bears Football Club Inc. 336
Chicago Blackhawk Hockey Team Inc. 336
Chicago Community Trust 336
Chicago Meat Authority Inc. 336
Chicago National League Ball Club Inc. 336
Chicago Rivet & Machine Co. 337
Chicago Transit Authority 337
Chicago White Sox Ltd. 337
Chickasaw Holding Company 337
Chico's Fas Inc 337
Chicopee Bancorp Inc 337
Chief Industries Inc. 338
Childfund International, Usa 338
Children's Health System 338
Children's Health System Inc. 338
Children's Hospital & Research Center At Oakland 338
Children's Hospital And Health System, Inc. 338
Children's Hospital Colorado 339
Children's Hospital Medical Center 339
Children's Hospital Of Pittsburgh Of Upmc Health System 339
Children's Medical Center Of Dallas 339
Children's National Medical Center 339
Children's Place Inc (the) 339
Children's Specialized Hospital Inc 340
Childrens Hospital & Medical Center 340
Childrens Hospital Medical Center Of Akron 340
Childress Klein Properties Inc. 340
Chilton Hospital 340
Chimera Investment Corp 340
Chimerix Inc. 341
Chindex International Inc 341
Chipotle Mexican Grill Inc 341
Chippewa Valley Bean Company Inc. 341
Chiquita Brands International, Inc. 341
Choice Hotels International, Inc. 341
Choiceone Financial Services, Inc. 342
Christian Hospital Northeast - Northwest 342
Christiana Care Health System 342
Christopher & Banks Corp. 342
Christopher Ranch, Llc 342
Christus Health Central Louisiana 342
Christus Health International 343
Christus St. Catherine Hospital 343
Christy Sports L.l.c. 343
Chromadex Corp 343
Chrysler Group Llc 343
Chs Inc 343
Chs Mcpherson Refinery Inc. 344
Chubb Corp. 344
Chugach Alaska Corporation 344
Chugach Electric Association, Inc. 344
Church & Dwight Co Inc 344
Church Pension Group Services Corporation 344
Churchill Downs, Inc. 345
Chuy's Holdings Inc 345
Chyronhego Corp 345
Cianbro Corporation 345
Cib Marine Bancshares Inc 345
Ciber, Inc. 345
Cic Group, Inc. 346
Cicero Inc 346
Ciena Corp 346
Cifc Corp. 346
Cim Commercial Trust Corp 346
Cimarex Energy Co 346
Cincinnati Bell Inc 347
Cincinnati Bengals Inc. 347
Cincinnati Financial Corp. 347
Cinedigm Corp 347

Ciner Resources Lp 347
Cintas Corporation 347
Cipherloc Corp 348
Circor International Inc 348
Cirrus Logic Inc 348
Cirtran Corp. 348
Cisco Systems Inc 348
Cit Group Inc (new) 348
Citation Oil & Gas Corp. 349
Citgo Petroleum Corporation 349
Citi Trends Inc 349
Citigroup Inc 349
Citizens & Northern Corp 349
Citizens Bancshares Corp. (ga) 349
Citizens Community Bancorp Inc (md) 350
Citizens Energy Group 350
Citizens Equity First Credit Union 350
Citizens Financial Corp. (wv) 350
Citizens Financial Group Inc (new) 350
Citizens Financial Services Inc 350
Citizens First Corp. 351
Citizens Holding Co 351
Citizens, Inc. (austin, Tx) 351
Citrix Systems Inc 351
Citrus Valley Health Partners, Inc. 351
City Harvest, Inc. 351
City Holding Co. 352
City National Corp. (beverly Hills, Ca) 352
City Of Alexandria 352
City Of Boston 352
City Of Denton 352
City Of Houston Texas 352
City Of Laredo 353
City Of Long Beach 353
City Of Lubbock 353
City Of Mesa 353
City Of Salinas 353
City Utilities Of Springfield Mo 353
Cityservicevalcon, Llc 354
Civista Bancshares Inc 354
Ckx Inc. 354
Ckx Lands Inc 354
Clarcor Inc. 354
Clare Rose, Inc. 354
Claremont Graduate University 355
Claremont Mckenna College Foundation 355
Clark Construction Group Llc 355
Clark Enterprises Inc. 355
Clarkson University 355
Clarocity Corp 355
Clarus Corp (new) 356
Classified Ventures Llc 356
Clay Electric Cooperative, Inc. 356
Clayco, Inc. 356
Clean Energy Fuels Corp 356
Clean Harbors Inc 356
Cleannet U.s.a., Inc. 357
Clear Channel Communications Inc. 357
Clear Channel Outdoor Holdings Inc (new) 357
Clearfield Inc 357
Clearone Inc 357
Clearsign Technologies Corp 357
Clearwater Paper Corp 358
Clearway Energy Inc 358
Cleary Gottlieb Steen & Hamilton Llp 358
Cleary University 358
Cleco Corp. 358
Cleveland Biolabs Inc 358
Cleveland Browns Football Company Llc 359
Cleveland Construction, Inc. 359
Cleveland State University 359
Cleveland-cliffs Inc (new) 359
Clicker, Inc. 359
Client Network Services, Llc 359
Client Services Inc. 360
Clifton Savings Bancorp Inc 360
Cliftonlarsonallen Llp 360
Clinch Valley Medical Center, Inc. 360
Clopay Corporation 360
Clorox Co (the) 360
Cloud Peak Energy Inc 361
Cloudcommerce Inc 361
Clover Technologies Group Llc 361
Clovis Oncology Inc 361

Clubcorp Holdings Inc 361
Cme Group Inc 361
Cms Bancorp Inc 362
Cms Energy Corp 362
Cna Financial Corp 362
Cna Surety Corporation 362
Cnb Corp (mi) 362
Cnb Financial Corp. (clearfield, Pa) 362
Cno Financial Group Inc 363
Cnx Resources Corp 363
Co Holdings, Llc 363
Coast Citrus Distributors 363
Coast Distribution System 363
Coast Electric Power Association 363
Coastal Banking Co Inc 364
Coastal Carolina University 364
Coastal Pacific Food Distributors, Inc. 364
Coates International Ltd 364
Cobalt International Energy L.p. 364
Cobank, Acb 364
Cobb Electric Membership Corporation 365
Cobiz Financial Inc 365
Coborn's, Incorporated 365
Cobra Electronics Corp. 365
Coca-cola Co (the) 365
Coca-cola Consolidated Inc 365
Coca-cola Enterprises Inc 366
Codexis Inc 366
Codorus Valley Bancorp, Inc. 366
Coe College 366
Coeur Mining Inc 366
Coffee Holding Co Inc 366
Cogent Communications Holdings, Inc. 367
Cogentix Medical Inc 367
Cognex Corp 367
Cognizant Technology Solutions Corp. 367
Cohen & Company Inc (new) 367
Cohen & Steers Inc 367
Coherent Inc 368
Cohu Inc 368
Colavita Usa L.l.c. 368
Coldwater Creek Inc. 368
Cole Haan 368
Colfax Corp 368
Colgate University 369
Colgate-palmolive Co. 369
Collabera Inc. 369
Collectors Universe Inc 369
College Entrance Examination Board 369
College Of Saint Benedict 369
College Of The Holy Cross (inc) 370
Colombo Bank 370
Colonial Financial Services, Inc. 370
Colonial Pipeline Company 370
Colony Bankcorp, Inc. 370
Colony Capital Inc 370
Colony Financial Inc. 371
Colorado College 371
Colorado Interstate Gas Company Llc 371
Colorado Mesa University 371
Colorado Seminary 371
Colorado Springs Utilities 371
Colorado State University 372
Colquitt Electric Membership Corporation 372
Colsa Corporation 372
Columbia Banking System Inc 372
Columbia College Chicago 372
Columbia Gas Of Ohio, Inc. 372
Columbia Gulf Transmission, Llc 373
Columbia Ogden Medical Center, Inc. 373
Columbia Sportswear Co. 373
Columbia St. Mary's Inc. 373
Columbus Mckinnon Corp. (ny) 373
Comarco Inc. 373
Combe Incorporated 374
Combimatrix Corp 374
Comenity Bank 374
Comerica, Inc. 374
Comfort Systems Usa Inc 374
Command Security Corp 374
Commerce Bancshares Inc 375
Commerce Group Corp. 375
Commercial Bancshares, Inc. (oh) 375
Commercial National Financial Corp. (pa) 375

Commercial Vehicle Group Inc 375
Commonspirit Health 375
Commonwealth Health Corporation Inc. 376
Communications Systems, Inc. 376
Communications Test Design, Inc. 376
Communications Workers Of America, Afl-cio, Clc 376
Community Asphalt Corp. 376
Community Bancorp. (derby, Vt) 376
Community Bank Shares Of Indiana, Inc. 377
Community Bank System Inc 377
Community Bankers Trust Corp 377
Community Capital Bancshares Inc 377
Community Choice Financial Inc 377
Community Financial Corp (the) 377
Community First Bancorporation 378
Community Health Group 378
Community Health Network, Inc. 378
Community Health Systems, Inc. 378
Community Hospital Of Anderson And Madison County, Incorporated 378
Community Hospital Of San Bernardino 378
Community Hospital Of The Monterey Peninsula 379
Community Hospitals Of Central California 379
Community Investors Bancorp, Inc 379
Community Shores Bank Corp 379
Community Trust Bancorp, Inc. 379
Community West Bancshares 379
Communityone Bancorp 380
Commvault Systems Inc 380
Comp-view Inc. 380
Compass Diversified Holdings 380
Compass Group Usa Inc. 380
Compass Minerals International Inc 380
Complete Production Services Inc. 381
Compsych Corporation 381
Compucom Systems Inc. 381
Compumed Inc 381
Computer Programs & Systems Inc 381
Computer Sciences Corporation 381
Computer Task Group, Inc. 382
Compuware Corp. 382
Compx International, Inc. 382
Comscore Inc 382
Comstock Holding Companies, Inc 382
Comstock Resources Inc 382
Comtech Telecommunications Corp. 383
Comtex News Network Inc. 383
Comverge Inc. 383
Con-way Freight Inc. 383
Con-way Inc 383
Conagra Brands Inc 383
Conatus Pharmaceuticals Inc 384
Concert Pharmaceuticals Inc 384
Concho Resources Inc 384
Concord Hospital, Inc. 384
Concord Litho Group 384
Concur Technologies Inc 384
Concurrent Technologies Corporation 385
Condor Hospitality Trust Inc 385
Conmed Corp. 385
Connecticare Inc. 385
Connecticut Children's Medical Center 385
Connecticut College 385
Connecticut Light & Power Co 386
Connecticut State University System 386
Connecticut Water Service Inc 386
Connectone Bancorp Inc (new) 386
Connectria Corporation 386
Connexus Energy 386
Connor Co. 387
Conns Inc 387
Conolog Corp. 387
Conrad Industries Inc 387
Conservation International Foundation 387
Consolidated Communications Holdings Inc 387
Consolidated Edison Co. Of New York, Inc. 388
Consolidated Edison Inc 388
Consolidated Pipe & Supply Company, Inc. 388
Consolidated-tomoka Land Co. 388
Constant Contact Inc 388
Constellation Brands Inc 388
Constellation Energy Group Inc. 389
Consumer Portfolio Services, Inc. 389

Consumer Product Distributors, Inc. 389
Consumer Reports, Inc. 389
Consumers Bancorp, Inc. (minerva, Oh) 389
Consumers Energy Co. 389
Container Store Group, Inc 390
Contango Oil & Gas Co. 390
Conti Enterprises, Inc. 390
Continental Airlines Inc. 390
Continental Building Products Inc 390
Continental Materials Corp. 390
Continental Resources Inc. 391
Continucare Corporation 391
Contractors Steel Company 391
Control4 Corp 391
Convaid Products Inc. 391
Convergent Outsourcing, Inc. 391
Convergint Technologies Llc 392
Convergys Corp 392
Conversant Inc 392
Converse Inc. 392
Convio Inc. 392
Conway Hospital, Inc. 392
Conway Regional Medical Center, Inc. 393
Cook Children's Health Care System 393
Cool Holdings Inc 393
Cooper Communities Inc. 393
Cooper Companies, Inc. (the) 393
Cooper Tire & Rubber Co. 393
Cooper-standard Holdings Inc 394
Cooperative Elevator Co. 394
Cooperative For Assistance And Relief Everywhere, Inc. (care) 394
Cooperative Regions Of Organic Producer Pools 394
Copart Inc 394
Coram Llc 394
Corcept Therapeutics Inc 395
Cordis Corporation 395
Core Construction, Inc. 395
Core Mark Holding Co Inc 395
Core Molding Technologies Inc 395
Corecivic Inc 395
Corenergy Infrastructure Trust Inc 396
Coresite Realty Corp 396
Coresource Inc. 396
Corgenix Medical Corp. 396
Corinthian Colleges, Inc. 396
Cormedix Inc 396
Cornell University 397
Cornerstone Bancorp 397
Cornerstone Building Brands Inc 397
Cornerstone Ondemand, Inc. 397
Corning Inc 397
Corporate Office Properties Trust 397
Corporate Travel Consultants Inc 398
Corporation For Public Broadcasting 398
Corsair Components Inc. 398
Cortland Bancorp (oh) 398
Corvel Corp 398
Cosco Fire Protection, Inc. 398
Cosi Inc 399
Coskata Inc. 399
Costar Group, Inc. 399
Costco Wholesale Corp 399
Cotton Incorporated 399
Coty, Inc. 399
Council Of Better Business Bureaus Inc. 400
Council On Foreign Relations, Inc. 400
Counterpart International Inc 400
County Bank Corp.(lapeer, Mi) 400
Courier Corp. 400
Cousins Properties Inc 400
Covance Inc. 401
Covanta Holding Corp 401
Covenant Health 401
Covenant Health System 401
Covenant Medical Center, Inc. 401
Covenant Transportation Group Inc 401
Cover-all Technologies, Inc. 402
Coverall North America, Inc. 402
Covisint Corporation 402
Cowan Systems, Llc 402
Cowen Inc 402
Cox Communications Inc. 402
Cpa2biz Inc. 403

Cpg International Inc. 403
Cpi Aerostructures, Inc. 403
Cpi International Inc. 403
Cps Energy 403
Cps Technologies Corp 403
Cra International Inc 404
Cracker Barrel Old Country Store, Inc. 404
Craft Brew Alliance Inc 404
Craftmade International Inc. 404
Crane Co. 404
Crawford & Co. 404
Crawford United Corp 405
Cray Inc 405
Creative Group Inc. 405
Creative Realities Inc 405
Credit Acceptance Corp (mi) 405
Credit Suisse (usa) Inc 405
Creditriskmonitor.com, Inc. 406
Credo Petroleum Corporation 406
Cree Inc 406
Creighton Alegent Health 406
Creighton University 406
Crescent Financial Bancshares Inc. 406
Crest Operations, Llc 407
Crested Butte Llc 407
Crestwood Midstream Partners Lp 407
Crete Carrier Corporation 407
Crexendo Inc 407
Crista Ministries 407
Crocs Inc 408
Croghan Bancshares, Inc. 408
Cropking Incorporated 408
Cross Border Resources Inc. 408
Cross Country Healthcare Inc 408
Cross Timbers Royalty Trust 408
Crossamerica Partners Lp 409
Crossland Construction Company, Inc. 409
Crossroads Systems Inc (new) 409
Crosstex Energy Inc 409
Crowder Construction Company Inc 409
Crowley Maritime Corporation 409
Crown Battery Manufacturing Company 410
Crown Crafts, Inc. 410
Crown Gold Corporation 410
Crown Holding Company 410
Crown Holdings Inc 410
Crown Media Holdings Inc 410
Crozer-keystone Health System 411
Crst International, Inc. 411
Crum & Forster Holdings Corp. 411
Cryo-cell International Inc 411
Cryolife, Inc. 411
Crystal Flash, Inc. 411
Crystal Rock Holdings Inc 412
Csg Systems International Inc. 412
Csi Leasing, Inc. 412
Csl Behring Llc 412
Csp Inc 412
Css Industries, Inc. 412
Cssi Inc. 413
Cst Brands Inc 413
Csu Fullerton Auxiliary Services Corporation 413
Cti Biopharma Corp 413
Cti Group Holdings Inc. 413
Cti Industries Corp 413
Ctpartners Executive Search Inc 414
Ctpartners Executive Search Llc 414
Cts Corp 414
Cts Valpey Corporation 414
Ctsc Llc 414
Cubesmart 414
Cubic Corp 415
Cubic Simulation Systems Inc. 415
Cubist Pharmaceuticals Inc. 415
Cui Global Inc 415
Cuivre River Electric Cooperative, Inc. 415
Cullen/frost Bankers, Inc. 415
Culp Inc 416
Culver Franchising System, Inc. 416
Cumberland County Hospital System, Inc. 416
Cumberland Farms Inc. 416
Cumberland Pharmaceuticals Inc 416
Cumulus Media Inc 416
Cupertino Electric Inc. 417

Curaegis Technologies Inc 417
Curis Inc 417
Curtiss-wright Corp. 417
Cuso Financial Services, L.p. 417
Customers Bancorp Inc 417
Customink Llc 418
Cutera Inc 418
Cutter & Buck Inc. 418
Cvb Financial Corp 418
Cvd Equipment Corp. 418
Cvent, Inc 418
Cvr Energy Inc 419
Cvr Partners Lp 419
Cvr Refining Lp 419
Cvs Health Corporation 419
Cyalume Technologies Holdings, Inc 419
Cyanotech Corp. 419
Cyberdefender Corporation 420
Cybernet Software Systems Inc. 420
Cyberonics, Inc. 420
Cyberoptics Corp. 420
Cyclacel Pharmaceuticals Inc 420
Cycle Country Accessories Corp. 420
Cyios Corporation 421
Cynergistek Inc 421
Cynosure Inc 421
Cyoptics Inc. 421
Cypress Energy Partners Lp 421
Cypress Semiconductor Corp. 421
Cys Investments, Inc. 422
Cystic Fibrosis Foundation 422
Cytec Industries, Inc. 422
Cytokinetics Inc 422
Cytosorbents Corporation 422
Cytrx Corp 422
D W W Co., Inc. 423
D'agostino Supermarkets Inc. 423
D. C. Taylor Co. 423
D/l Cooperative Inc. 423
Daegis Inc 423
Daily Express, Inc. 423
Daily Journal Corporation 424
Dairy Farmers Of America, Inc. 424
Dairyland Power Cooperative 424
Dais Corp 424
Dakota Electric Association 424
Dakota Gasification Company Inc 424
Dakota Supply Group, Inc. 425
Daktronics Inc. 425
Dale Carnegie & Associates Inc. 425
Dale Jarrett Racing Adventure Inc 425
Dallas County Hospital District 425
Dallas Cowboys Football Club Ltd. 425
Dallas/fort Worth International Airport 426
Dana-farber Cancer Institute, Inc. 426
Danaher Corp 426
Dancker, Sellew & Douglas, Inc. 426
Danis Building Construction Company 426
Dara Biosciences, Inc. 426
Darden Restaurants, Inc. 427
Darling Ingredients Inc 427
Dartmouth-hitchcock Clinic 427
Dasan Zhone Solutions Inc 427
Data I/o Corp. 427
Datacolor Inc. 427
Datalink Corp 428
Datatrak International Inc. 428
Datawatch Corp. 428
Dats Trucking, Inc. 428
Dave & Busters Entertainment Inc 428
Davenport University 428
Davey Tree Expert Co. (the) 429
David's Bridal Inc. 429
Davidson Companies 429
Daviess County Hospital 429
Davita Inc 429
Dawson Geophysical Co (new) 429
Dawson Geophysical Co. 430
Dawson Metal Company Inc. 430
Daxor Corporation 430
Day Kimball Healthcare, Inc. 430
Daylight Donut Flour Company Llc 430
Daystar Technologies Inc. 430
Dcb Financial Corp 431

Dcp Midstream Lp 431
Dct Industrial Trust Inc 431
Ddi Corp. 431
De Paul University 431
Deacon Industrial Supply Co. Inc. 431
Deaconess Health System, Inc. 432
Deaconess Hospital Inc 432
Dealers Supply Company Inc. 432
Dealertrack Technologies, Inc. 432
Dean & Deluca Incorporated 432
Dean Foods Co. 432
Debt Resolve Inc 433
Decatur Memorial Hospital 433
Decision Diagnostics Corp 433
Deckers Outdoor Corp. 433
Deco, Inc. 433
Deep Down Inc 433
Deffenbaugh Industries Inc. 434
Defoe Corp. 434
Dekalb Medical Center, Inc. 434
Del Frisco's Restaurant Group Inc 434
Del Monaco Specialty Foods Inc. 434
Del Monte Corporation 434
Delaware North Companies Inc. 435
Delaware River Port Authority 435
Delaware State University 435
Delaware Valley University 435
Delcath Systems Inc 435
Delek Logistics Partners Lp 435
Delhaize America Llc 436
Deli Management, Inc. 436
Delmarva Power & Light Co. 436
Deloitte & Touche Llp 436
Deloitte Consulting Llp 436
Deloitte Llp 436
Deloitte Touche Tohmatsu Services Inc. 437
Delphi Financial Group Inc. 437
Delta Air Lines Inc (de) 437
Delta Apparel Inc. 437
Delta Community Credit Union 437
Delta Dental Of California 437
Delta Mutual Inc. 438
Delta Natural Gas Co Inc 438
Delta Regional Medical Center 438
Delta Tucker Holdings, Inc. 438
Deltathree Inc 438
Deltek Inc. 438
Deltic Timber Corp. 439
Deluxe Corp 439
Deluxe Entertainment Services Group Inc. 439
Demandware Inc 439
Demoulas Super Markets Inc. 439
Denbury Resources, Inc. (de) 439
Dendreon Corp 440
Denison University 440
Denmark Bancshares Inc 440
Denny's Corp 440
Denso International America Inc. 440
Denton County Electric Cooperative, Inc. 440
Denver Board Of Water Commissioners 441
Denver Health And Hospitals Authority Inc 441
Depauw University 441
Derma Sciences Inc 441
Desales University 441
Deseret Generation And Transmission Co-operative 441
Desert Schools Federal Credit Union 442
Desert Springs Hospital Medical Center 442
Designer Brands Inc 442
Destination Maternity Corp 442
Destination Xl Group Inc 442
Determine Inc 442
Detrex Corp. 443
Detroit Pistons Basketball Company 443
Detroit Tigers Inc. 443
Deutsche Bank Securities Inc. 443
Devcon Construction Incorporated 443
Devereux Foundation 443
Devon Energy Corp. 444
Dewey & Leboeuf Llp 444
Dewey Electronics Corp. 444
Dexcom Inc 444
Dextera Surgical Inc 444
Dfb Pharmaceuticals, Llc 444

Dfc Global Corp. 445
Dgt Holdings Corp 445
Dhi Group Inc 445
Diagnostic Laboratory Services, Inc. 445
Diakon 445
Dialogic Inc 445
Dialysis Clinic, Inc. 446
Diamond Discoveries International Corp. 446
Diamond Foods Inc 446
Diamond Hill Investment Group Inc. 446
Diamond Offshore Drilling, Inc. 446
Diamond Resorts Holdings Llc 446
Diamondback Energy Inc. 447
Diamondback Energy, Inc. 447
Diamondrock Hospitality Co. 447
Dicerna Pharmaceuticals Inc 447
Dick Clark Productions Inc. 447
Dick's Sporting Goods, Inc 447
Dickinson College 448
Diebold Nixdorf Inc 448
Diedrich Coffee Inc. 448
Digerati Technologies Inc 448
Digi International Inc 448
Digimarc Corp 448
Digirad Corp 449
Digital Ally Inc 449
Digital Cinema Destinations Corp. 449
Digital Federal Credit Union 449
Digital Realty Trust Inc 449
Digital River, Inc. 449
Digital Turbine Inc 450
Digitalglobe Inc 450
Digitas Inc. 450
Dignity Health 450
Dillard's Inc. 450
Dillon Companies Inc. 450
Dime Community Bancshares, Inc 451
Dimensions Health Corporation 451
Dimeo Construction Company 451
Dine Brands Global Inc 451
Diodes, Inc. 451
Dionex Corporation 451
Direct Relief 452
Directv 452
Disabled American Veterans 452
Discovery Inc 452
Dish Network Corp 452
Ditech Holding Corp 452
Diversified Chemical Technologies, Inc. 453
Diversified Healthcare Trust 453
Diversified Restaurant Holdings Inc. 453
Dixie Gas And Oil Corporation 453
Dixie Group Inc. 453
Dixon Ticonderoga Company 453
Dlh Holdings Corp 454
Dlt Solutions Llc 454
Dmc Global Inc 454
Dnb Financial Corp. 454
Do It Best Corp. 454
Doall Company 454
Doc's Drugs, Ltd. 455
Doctor's Associates Inc. 455
Doctors Hospital Of Augusta, Llc 455
Doctors' Hospital, Inc. 455
Document Capture Technologies Inc 455
Document Security Systems Inc 455
Dolan Company (the) 456
Dollar Bank Fsb 456
Dollar General Corp 456
Dollar Thrifty Automotive Group Inc. 456
Dollar Tree Inc 456
Dominion Energy Inc (new) 456
Dominion Resources Black Warrior Trust 457
Dominos Pizza Inc. 457
Donaldson Co. Inc. 457
Donegal Group Inc. 457
Donnelley (rr) & Sons Company 457
Dorchester Minerals Lp 457
Dorman Products Inc 458
Dorsey & Whitney Llp 458
Dot Foods Inc. 458
Dot Hill Systems Corp. 458
Dougherty's Pharmacy Inc 458
Douglas Dynamics, Inc. 458

Douglas Emmett Inc 459
Dover Corp 459
Dover Motorsports, Inc. 459
Dover Saddlery Inc 459
Dow Chemical Co. 459
Dowling College 459
Doylestown Hospital Health And Wellness Center, Inc. 460
Dpl Inc. 460
Dpr Construction, Inc. 460
Dpw Holdings Inc 460
Drake University 460
Dreams Inc. 460
Dreamworks Animation Skg Inc 461
Dresser-rand Group Inc. 461
Drew University 461
Drexel University 461
Dri Corporation 461
Dril-quip Inc 461
Drive Shack Inc 462
Drivetime Automotive Group, Inc. 462
Dropcar Inc 462
Drugstore.com Inc. 462
Dsc Logistics Inc. 462
Dsp Group, Inc. 462
Dte Electric Company 463
Dte Energy Co 463
Dts Inc 463
Ducks Unlimited, Inc. 463
Ducommun Inc. 463
Ducommun Labarge Technologies 463
Duke Energy Corp 464
Duke Energy Florida Llc 464
Duke Energy Indiana, Inc. 464
Duke Realty Corp 464
Duke University 464
Duke University Health System, Inc. 464
Dun & Bradstreet Corp (de) 465
Duncan Energy Partners L.p. 465
Duncan Equipment Company 465
Dundee Precious Metals Inc 465
Dune Energy, Inc. 465
Dunkin' Brands Group Inc 465
Dunkin' Brands Group Inc. 466
Dupont Fabros Technology Inc 466
Duquesne Light Company 466
Duquesne University Of The Holy Spirit 466
Dura Automotive Systems Llc 466
Dura Coat Products Inc. 466
Durata Therapeutics Inc. 467
Durect Corp 467
Dusa Pharmaceuticals Inc. 467
Dxp Enterprises, Inc. 467
Dyadic International Inc 467
Dyax Corp 467
Dycom Industries, Inc. 468
Dynacq Healthcare Inc 468
Dynamex Inc. 468
Dynamic Offshore Resources Llc 468
Dynamix Group, Inc 468
Dynasil Corp Of America 468
Dynatronics Corp. 469
Dynavax Technologies Corp 469
Dynavox Inc. 469
Dyncorp International Inc. 469
Dynegy Inc (new) (de) 469
Dynex Capital, Inc. 469
Dyntek Inc. 470
E Z Loader Boat Trailers Inc. 470
E*trade Financial Corp 470
E. C. Barton & Company 470
E.digital Corp. 470
E.n.m.r. Telephone Cooperative 470
Ea Engineering, Science, And Technology, Inc., Pbc 471
Eaco Corp 471
Eagle Bancorp Inc (md) 471
Eagle Bancorp Montana, Inc. 471
Eagle Bulk Shipping Inc 471
Eagle Materials Inc 471
Eagle Pharmaceuticals, Inc. 472
Eagle Rock Energy Partners Lp 472
Earl L. Henderson Trucking Company 472
Earlham College 472

Earthstone Energy Inc 472
East Alabama Health Care Authority 472
East Bay Municipal Utility District, Water System 473
East Orange General Hospital (inc) 473
East Tennessee Children's Hospital Association, Inc. 473
East Tennessee State University 473
East Texas Medical Center Regional Healthcare Syst 473
East West Bancorp, Inc 473
Easter Seals, Inc. 474
Eastern American Natural Gas Trust 474
Eastern Bag And Paper Company, Incorporated 474
Eastern Bank Corporation 474
Eastern Co. 474
Eastern Kentucky University 474
Eastern Maine Healthcare Systems 475
Eastern Michigan University 475
Eastern Mountain Sports Inc. 475
Eastern Virginia Bankshares, Inc 475
Eastern Virginia Medical School 475
Eastern Washington University Inc 475
Eastgroup Properties Inc 476
Eastman Chemical Co 476
Eastman Kodak Co. 476
Easylink Services International Corporation 476
Eaton Vance Corp 476
Eau Technologies Inc 476
Ebay Inc. 477
Ebix Inc 477
Ebsco Industries Inc. 477
Eby Corporation 477
Eby-brown Company Llc 477
Echelon Corp. 477
Echo Global Logistics Inc 478
Echo Therapeutics Inc 478
Echostar Corp 478
Eckerd College, Inc. 478
Eckerd Youth Alternatives, Inc. 478
Eclinicalworks Llc 478
Ecolab Inc 479
Ecology And Environment, Inc. 479
Ecotality Inc 479
Ecova Inc. 479
Ecs Federal, Llc 479
Edelbrock Llc 479
Edgewell Personal Care Co 480
Edison International 480
Edison Mission Energy 480
Edp Renewables North America Llc 480
Education Management Corp 480
Education Realty Trust Inc 480
Educational & Institutional Cooperative Service Inc. 481
Educational Development Corp. 481
Educational Funding Of The South, Inc. 481
Educational Testing Service Inc 481
Edwards Lifesciences Corp 481
Eei Holding Corporation 481
Egain Corp 482
Egpi Firecreek Inc 482
Ehealth Inc 482
Eide Bailly Llp 482
Eileen Fisher, Inc. 482
Einstein Noah Restaurant Group Inc 482
Eisai Inc. 483
Eisenhower Medical Center 483
Eisneramper Llp 483
El Dorado Furniture Corp 483
El Paso Corporation 483
El Paso County Hospital District 483
El Paso Electric Company 484
El Paso Pipeline Partners Lp 484
Elah Holdings Inc 484
Eldorado Artesian Springs Inc 484
Elecsys Corp. 484
Electric Power Board Of Chattanooga 484
Electric Power Board Of The Metropolitan Government Of Nashville & Davidson County 485
Electric Power Research Institute, Inc. 485
Electric Reliability Council Of Texas, Inc. 485
Electro Rent Corp. 485
Electro Scientific Industries Inc 485

Electro-matic Ventures, Inc. 485
Electro-sensors, Inc. 486
Electromed, Inc. 486
Electronic Arts, Inc. 486
Electronic Control Security Inc. 486
Electronic Systems Technology, Inc. 486
Electronics For Imaging, Inc. 486
Element Solutions Inc 487
Elevance Renewable Sciences Inc. 487
Elite Pharmaceuticals Inc 487
Elixir Industries 487
Elizabeth Arden Inc. 487
Elkhart General Hospital, Inc. 487
Elkins Constructors, Inc. 488
Ellie Mae Inc 488
Ellington Financial Inc 488
Ellington Residential Mortgaging Real Estate Investment Trust 488
Elliot Hospital Of The City Of Manchester 488
Ellis (perry) International Inc 488
Ellis Hospital 489
Ellsworth Cooperative Creamery 489
Elma Electronic Inc. 489
Elmhurst Memorial Hospital Inc 489
Elmira Savings Bank (ny) 489
Eloqua Limited 489
Elvis Presley Enterprises Inc. 490
Elwyn 490
Elxsi Corp 490
Emagin Corp 490
Embarcadero Technologies Inc. 490
Emblemhealth Inc. 490
Embree Construction Group, Inc. 491
Embry-riddle Aeronautical University Inc. 491
Emc Corp. (ma) 491
Emc Insurance Group Inc. 491
Emclaire Financial Corp. 491
Emcor Group, Inc. 491
Emcore Corp. 492
Emdeon Inc. 492
Emerald Dairy Inc. 492
Emerald Oil, Inc 492
Emerge Energy Services Lp 492
Emergent Biosolutions Inc 492
Emergent Capital Inc 493
Emergent Group Inc. 493
Emerging Vision Inc. 493
Emeritus Corp. 493
Emerson College 493
Emerson Hospital 493
Emerson Network Power-embedded Computing Inc. 494
Emerson Radio Corp. 494
Emisphere Technologies, Inc. 494
Emj Corporation 494
Emkay Inc. 494
Emmis Communications Corp 494
Empire Resorts Inc 495
Empire Resources, Inc. 495
Empire Southwest, Llc 495
Empire State Realty Trust Inc 495
Empirix Inc. 495
Employers Holdings Inc 495
Emporia State University 496
Emrise Corp 496
Ems Technologies Inc. 496
Emtec Inc. 496
Emulex Corporation 496
Enable Midstream Partners L.p. 496
Enanta Pharmaceuticals Inc 497
Enbridge Energy Management Llc 497
Enbridge Energy Partners, L.p. 497
Encision Inc. 497
Encompass Health Corp 497
Encore Bancshares Inc. 497
Encore Capital Group Inc 498
Encore Energy Partners Lp 498
Encore Nationwide Inc. 498
Encore Wire Corp. 498
Endeavour International Corp 498
Endo Health Solutions Inc 498
Endocyte Inc 499
Endologix Inc 499
Endurance International Group Holdings Inc 499

Enel Green Power North America Inc. 499
Energen Corp. 499
Energy & Environmental Services Inc 499
Energy & Exploration Partners Inc. 500
Energy Conversion Devices Inc. 500
Energy Focus Inc 500
Energy Future Holdings Corp 500
Energy Recovery Inc 500
Energy Services Of America Corp. 500
Energy Services Providers, Inc. 501
Energy Transfer Lp 501
Energy Transfer Operating Lp 501
Energyunited Electric Membership Corporation 501
Enernoc Inc 501
Enerpac Tool Group Corp 501
Enersys 502
Enervest Ltd. 502
Engelberth Construction, Inc. 502
Engility Holdings Inc (new) 502
Englefield Oil Company 502
Englewood Hospital And Medical Center Foundation Inc. 502
Englobal Corp. 503
Enlink Midstream Partners Lp 503
Ennis Inc 503
Enova Systems Inc 503
Enphase Energy Inc. 503
Enpro Industries Inc 503
Enservco Corp 504
Ensign Group Inc 504
Ensync Inc 504
Ent Federal Credit Union 504
Entech Sales And Service, Llc 504
Entech Solar Inc. 504
Entegee, Inc. 505
Entegris Inc 505
Entercom Communications Corp 505
Entergy Arkansas Inc 505
Entergy Corp 505
Entergy Gulf States Louisiana Llc 505
Entergy Louisiana Llc (new) 506
Entergy Mississippi Inc 506
Entergy New Orleans Inc 506
Enterprise Bancorp, Inc. (ma) 506
Enterprise Diversified Inc 506
Enterprise Electric, Llc 506
Enterprise Financial Services Corp 507
Enterprise Products Partners L.p. 507
Entravision Communications Corp. 507
Entropic Communications, Inc. 507
Entrust Inc. 507
Entrx Corporation 507
Envela Corp 508
Envestnet Inc 508
Enviro Technologies Inc 508
Environmental Defense Fund, Incorporated 508
Environmental Tectonics Corp. 508
Envision Healthcare Holdings Inc 508
Enzo Biochem, Inc. 509
Enzon Pharmaceuticals Inc 509
Eog Resources, Inc. 509
Ep Energy Corp. 509
Epam Systems, Inc. 509
Epicore Bionetworks Inc. 509
Epiq Systems Inc 510
Epitec, Inc. 510
Epizyme Inc. 510
Epl Oil & Gas Inc 510
Eplus Inc 510
Epr Properties 510
Epsilon Systems Solutions, Inc. 511
Eqt Corp 511
Equifax Inc 511
Equilar Inc. 511
Equinix Inc 511
Equinor Marketing & Trading (us) Inc. 511
Equinox Payments Llc 512
Equity Commonwealth 512
Equity Lifestyle Properties Inc 512
Equity Residential 512
Era Group Inc 512
Erba Diagnostics 512
Eresearchtechnology Inc. 513
Erhc Energy Inc. 513

Erickson Inc 513
Erie Indemnity Co. 513
Eroom System Technologies Inc 513
Eros International Plc 513
Escalade, Inc. 514
Escalera Resources Co 514
Escalon Medical Corp 514
Esco Corporation 514
Esco Technologies, Inc. 514
Escreen Inc. 514
Esl Federal Credit Union 515
Espey Manufacturing & Electronics Corp. 515
Espn Inc. 515
Essa Bancorp Inc 515
Essendant Inc 515
Essential Utilities Inc 515
Essex Property Trust Inc 516
Essex Rental Corp 516
Estee Lauder International Inc. 516
Esterline Technologies Corp 516
Estes Express Lines, Inc. 516
Ethan Allen Interiors, Inc. 516
Etna Distributors, Llc 517
Ets-lindgren Lp 517
Eugene Water & Electric Board 517
Eureka Financial Corp (md) 517
Eurofins Lancaster Laboratories, Inc 517
Euromarket Designs Inc. 517
Euronet Worldwide Inc. 518
Evangelical Community Hospital 518
Evans & Sutherland Computer Corp. 518
Evans Bancorp, Inc. 518
Event Network, Inc. 518
Everbank Financial Corp 518
Evercore Inc 519
Evergreen Fs Inc 519
Evergreen State College 519
Everi Holdings Inc 519
Eversource Energy 519
Eversource Energy Service Company 519
Evi Industries Inc 520
Evolution Petroleum Corp 520
Evolving Systems, Inc. 520
Evonik Corporation 520
Ewing Irrigation Products, Inc. 520
Exa Corp 520
Exact Sciences Corp. 521
Exactech, Inc. 521
Examworks Group Inc 521
Exantas Capital Corp 521
Exar Corp. 521
Excel Trust Inc. 521
Exchange Bank (santa Rosa, Ca) 522
Exco Resources Inc 522
Exel Inc. 522
Exelis Inc. 522
Exelixis Inc 522
Exelon Corp 522
Exelon Generation Co Llc 523
Exide Technologies 523
Exlservice Holdings Inc 523
Exone Co. (the) 523
Expedia Group Inc 523
Expeditors International Of Washington, Inc. 523
Experian Information Solutions Inc. 524
Experience Works, Inc. 524
Exponent Inc. 524
Exponential Interactive Inc. 524
Export-import Bank Of The United States 524
Express Inc 524
Express Scripts Holding Co 525
Express Services Inc 525
Extended Stay America Inc 525
Extra Space Storage Inc 525
Extreme Networks Inc 525
Exxon Mobil Corp 525
Exxonmobil Pipeline Company 526
Ezcorp, Inc. 526
F & M Bank Corp. 526
F&b Manufacturing Company 526
F&s Produce Company, Inc. 526
F5 Networks, Inc. 526
Fab Universal Corp 527
Facebook Inc 527

Factset Research Systems Inc. 527
Fairchild Semiconductor International, Inc. 527
Fairfield Medical Center 527
Fairfield University 527
Fairleigh Dickinson University 528
Fairpoint Communications Inc 528
Fairview Health Services 528
Fairway Group Holdings Corp 528
Faith Technologies, Inc. 528
Falconstor Software Inc 528
Famc Subsidiary Company 529
Family Dollar Stores, Inc. 529
Family Express Corporation 529
Family Health International Inc 529
Fannie Mae 529
Far East Energy Corp 529
Farm Credit Bank Of Texas 530
Farm Credit Services Of Mid-america Aca 530
Farm Service Cooperative 530
Farmer Bros. Co. 530
Farmers Capital Bank Corp. 530
Farmers Co-operative Society, Sioux Center, Iowa 530
Farmers Cooperative Company 531
Farmers National Banc Corp. (canfield,oh) 531
Farmers Telephone Cooperative, Inc. 531
Farmington Foods Inc. 531
Faro Technologies Inc. 531
Farstad Oil Inc. 531
Fashion Institute Of Technology 532
Fastenal Co. 532
Fatburger Corporation 532
Fate Therapeutics Inc 532
Fatwire Corporation 532
Fauquier Bankshares, Inc. 532
Fayette Community Hospital, Inc. 533
Fayetteville Public Works Commission 533
Fbl Financial Group Inc 533
Fbr & Co 533
Fci Constructors Inc. 533
Federal Agricultural Mortgage Corp 533
Federal Aviation Administration 534
Federal Home Loan Bank Boston 534
Federal Home Loan Bank New York 534
Federal Home Loan Bank Of Atlanta 534
Federal Home Loan Bank Of Chicago 534
Federal Home Loan Bank Of Pittsburgh 534
Federal Home Loan Bank Of San Francisco 535
Federal Home Loan Bank Topeka 535
Federal Prison Industries Inc. 535
Federal Realty Investment Trust (md) 535
Federal Reserve Bank Of Atlanta, Dist. No. 6 535
Federal Reserve Bank Of Boston, Dist. No. 1 535
Federal Reserve Bank Of Chicago, Dist. No. 7 536
Federal Reserve Bank Of Cleveland, Dist. No. 4 536
Federal Reserve Bank Of Dallas, Dist. No. 11 536
Federal Reserve Bank Of Kansas City, Dist. No. 10 536
Federal Reserve Bank Of Minneapolis, Dist. No. 9 536
Federal Reserve Bank Of New York, Dist. No. 2 536
Federal Reserve Bank Of Philadelphia, Dist. No. 3 537
Federal Reserve Bank Of Richmond, Dist. No. 5 537
Federal Reserve Bank Of San Francisco, Dist. No. 12 537
Federal Reserve Bank Of St. Louis, Dist. No. 8 537
Federal Reserve System 537
Federal Screw Works 537
Federal Signal Corp. 538
Federal-mogul Holdings Corp 538
Federated Hermes Inc 538
Federated Insurance Companies 538
Fedex Corp 538
Fedex Custom Critical Inc. 538
Fedex Ground Package System Inc. 539
Fedex Office And Print Services Inc. 539
Fedfirst Financial Corporation 539
Fednat Holding Co 539
Feed The Children Inc. 539
Fei Co. 539
Felcor Lodging Trust Inc 540
Feld Entertainment Inc. 540
Fender Musical Instruments Corporation 540
Fentura Financial Inc 540

Ferguson Enterprises Inc. 540
Ferrellgas Partners Lp 540
Ferris State University 541
Ferro Corp 541
Ffd Financial Corp 541
Ffw Corp. 541
Fhi Services 541
Fiberlink Communications Corporation 541
Fibertower Corporation 542
Fibrocell Science Inc 542
Fidelitone Inc. 542
Fidelity & Guaranty Life 542
Fidelity & Guaranty Life Insurance Company 542
Fidelity D&d Bancorp Inc 542
Fidelity National Financial Inc 543
Fidelity National Information Services Inc 543
Fidelity Southern Corp 543
Fidus Investment Corporation 543
Field Museum Of Natural History 543
Fieldpoint Petroleum Corp 543
Fiesta Mart Inc. 544
Fiesta Restaurant Group, Inc 544
Fifth Third Bancorp (cincinnati, Oh) 544
Filemaker Inc. 544
Financial Engines Inc 544
Financial Executives International 544
Financial Industry Regulatory Authority, Inc. 545
Financial Institutions Inc. 545
Findex.com Inc. 545
Finisar Corp 545
Finjan Holdings Inc 545
Fireeye Inc 545
Firelands Regional Health System 546
First Acceptance Corp 546
First Advantage Bancorp 546
First American Financial Corp 546
First Aviation Services, Inc. 546
First Bancorp (nc) 546
First Bancorp Inc (me) 547
First Bancorp Of Indiana Inc 547
First Bancshares Inc (ms) 547
First Bancshares Inc. (mo) 547
First Banctrust Corp 547
First Banks, Inc. (mo) 547
First Busey Corp 548
First Business Financial Services, Inc. 548
First Capital Bancorp Inc (va) 548
First Capital Inc. 548
First Century Bankshares, Inc. 548
First Citizens Bancshares Inc (nc) 548
First Clover Leaf Financial Corp 549
First Commonwealth Financial Corp (indiana, Pa) 549
First Community Bankshares Inc (va) 549
First Community Corp (sc) 549
First Connecticut Bancorp Inc. (md) 549
First Defiance Financial Corp 549
First Electric Co-operative Corporation 550
First Federal Of Northern Michigan Bancorp Inc 550
First Financial Bancorp (oh) 550
First Financial Bankshares, Inc. 550
First Financial Corp. (in) 550
First Financial Northwest Inc 550
First Financial Service Corp 551
First Hartford Corp 551
First Hawaiian Bank 551
First Horizon National Corp 551
First Independence Corporation 551
First Industrial Realty Trust Inc 551
First Internet Bancorp 552
First Interstate Bancsystem Inc 552
First Keystone Corp 552
First Marblehead Corp 552
First Mariner Bancorp. 552
First Merchants Corp 552
First Mid Bancshares Inc 553
First Midwest Bancorp, Inc. (naperville, Il) 553
First National Bank Alaska 553
First National Corp. (strasburg, Va) 553
First Nbc Bank Holding Co. 553
First Niagara Financial Group, Inc. 553
First Niles Financial Inc. 554
First Northern Community Bancorp 554
First Of Long Island Corp 554

First Physicians Capital Group Inc 554
First Potomac Realty Trust 554
First Republic Bank (san Francisco, Ca) 554
First Robinson Financial Corp. 555
First Savings Financial Group Inc 555
First Security Group Inc 555
First Solar Inc 555
First South Bancorp Inc (va) 555
First Tech Federal Credit Union 555
First United Corporation (md) 556
First Us Bancshares Inc 556
First West Virginia Bancorp Inc 556
Firstbank Corp. (mi) 556
Firstcash Inc 556
Firstenergy Corp 556
Firstfleet, Inc. 557
Firsthealth Of The Carolinas, Inc. 557
Firstmerit Corp 557
Fiserv Inc 557
Fiskars Brands Inc. 557
Five Below Inc 557
Five Prime Therapeutics, Inc 558
Five Star Cooperative 558
Five Star Senior Living Inc 558
Flagstaff Medical Center, Inc. 558
Flagstar Bancorp, Inc. 558
Flanders Corporation 558
Flanigan's Enterprises, Inc. 559
Flatbush Federal Bancorp Inc. 559
Fleetcor Technologies Inc 559
Fleming Gannett Inc 559
Fletcher Music Centers Inc. 559
Flexera Software Llc 559
Flexion Therapeutics, Inc. 560
Flexsteel Industries, Inc. 560
Flint Electric Membership Corporation 560
Flint Telecom Group Inc 560
Flir Systems, Inc. 560
Florida Atlantic University 560
Florida Gaming Corp. 561
Florida Gas Transmission Company, Llc 561
Florida Health Sciences Center Inc 561
Florida Hospital Heartland Medical Center 561
Florida Hospital Waterman, Inc 561
Florida Housing Finance Corp 561
Florida International University 562
Florida Municipal Power Agency 562
Florida Power & Light Co. 562
Florida State University 562
Florida's Natural Growers 562
Florstar Sales, Inc. 562
Flotek Industries Inc 563
Flowers Foods, Inc. 563
Flowserve Corp 563
Floyd Healthcare Management, Inc. 563
Fluidigm Corp (de) 563
Fluor Corp. 563
Flushing Financial Corp. 564
Flying Food Group Llc 564
Fmc Corp. 564
Fmc Technologies, Inc. 564
Fnb Bancorp (ca) 564
Fnb Corp 564
Fnbh Bancorp, Inc. 565
Fncb Bancorp Inc 565
Fogo De Chao, Inc. 565
Foley & Lardner Llp 565
Fonar Corp 565
Food For The Poor, Inc. 565
Food Technology Service Inc. 566
Foot Locker, Inc. 566
Football Northwest Llc 566
Forbes Energy Services Ltd 566
Force 3, Llc 566
Force Protection Inc. 566
Ford Motor Co. (de) 567
Ford Motor Credit Company Llc 567
Fordham University 567
Foremost Groups, Inc. 567
Forest City Enterprises, Inc. 567
Forest Laboratories, Inc. 567
Forest Snavely Products Inc 568
Forestar Group Inc (new) 568
Forever 21 Inc. 568

Forevergreen Worldwide Corp 568
Forge Industries, Inc. 568
Formfactor Inc 568
Forms & Supply, Inc. 569
Forrest County General Hospital (inc) 569
Forrester Research Inc. 569
Forsythe Technology Inc. 569
Fortegra Financial Corp 569
Fortinet Inc 569
Fortis Construction, Inc. 570
Fortress Investment Group Llc 570
Fortune Brands Home & Security, Inc. 570
Forum Energy Technologies Inc 570
Forward Air Corp 570
Forward Industries, Inc. 570
Fossil Group Inc 571
Foster (l.b.) Co 571
Foundation Healthcare, Inc 571
Foundation Medicine Inc 571
Four Oaks Fincorp, Inc. 571
Fox Broadcasting Company 571
Fox Chase Bancorp, Inc. 572
Fox Factory Holding Corp 572
Fox Head, Inc. 572
Fox News Network Llc 572
Fox Searchlight Pictures Inc. 572
Foxworth-galbraith Lumber Company 572
Fpb Bancorp Inc. 573
Fpic Insurance Group Inc. 573
Franchise Group Inc 573
Francis Saint Medical Center 573
Franciscan Alliance, Inc. 573
Franciscan Health System 573
Franciscan University Of Steubenville 574
Frank's International Inc. 574
Franklin And Marshall College 574
Franklin Community Health Network 574
Franklin Covey Co 574
Franklin Credit Holding Corporation 574
Franklin Electric Co., Inc. 575
Franklin Financial Services Corp 575
Franklin Hospital 575
Franklin Resources Inc 575
Franklin Square Hospital Center, Inc. 575
Franklin Street Properties Corp 575
Franklin Wireless Corp 576
Fraser/white Inc. 576
Frazier Industrial Company 576
Fred Meyer Stores Inc. 576
Fred's Inc. 576
Freddie Mac 576
Frederick Memorial Hospital, Inc. 577
Frederick's Of Hollywood Group Inc 577
Frederick's Of Hollywood Inc. 577
Freedom From Hunger 577
Freedom Resources Enterprises Inc. 577
Freedomroads Llc 577
Freeman Health System 578
Freeport Regional Health Care Foundation 578
Freeport-mcmoran Inc 578
Freese And Nichols, Inc. 578
Freightcar America Inc 578
Freightquote.com Inc. 578
Fremont Bancorporation 579
Fremont Contract Carriers, Inc. 579
Fremont Health 579
Frequency Electronics Inc 579
Fresh Mark, Inc. 579
Freshpoint Inc. 579
Fried Frank Harris Shriver & Jacobson Llp 580
Friedman Industries, Inc. 580
Friendfinder Networks Inc 580
Frisbie Memorial Hospital 580
Frisch's Restaurants, Inc. 580
Frito-lay North America Inc. 580
Froedtert Memorial Lutheran Hospital, Inc. 581
Frontier Communications Corp 581
Frontier Oilfield Services Inc. 581
Frontrange Solutions Inc. 581
Frost Brown Todd Llc 581
Frozen Specialties Inc. 581
Frp Holdings Inc 582
Fruit Growers Supply Company Inc 582
Fruth, Inc. 582

COMPANIES LISTED ALPHABETICALLY

Fry's Food And Drug Stores 582
Fs Bancorp Inc (washington) 582
Ftd Companies Inc 582
Fti Consulting Inc. 583
Fts International Inc. 583
Fuel Systems Solutions Inc 583
Fuel Tech Inc 583
Fuelcell Energy Inc 583
Fuelstream, Inc. 583
Fulcrum Bioenergy Inc. 584
Full Circle Capital Corp 584
Full Compass Systems Ltd. 584
Fuller (hb) Company 584
Fuller Theological Seminary 584
Fullnet Communications Inc 584
Fulton Financial Corp. (pa) 585
Furiex Pharmaceuticals Inc 585
Furman Foods, Inc. 585
Furman University 585
Furman University Foundation Inc. 585
Furmanite Corp 585
Fusion Connect Inc 586
Fusion-io Inc. 586
Fusionstorm 586
Fusionstorm Global Inc. 586
Future Tech Enterprise, Inc. 586
Futurefuel Corp 586
Fx Alliance Inc. 587
Fx Energy Inc. 587
G&k Services Inc 587
G&p Trucking Company, Inc. 587
G-i Holdings Inc. 587
G-iii Apparel Group Ltd. 587
G.s.e. Construction Company Inc. 588
Gabriel Brothers Inc. 588
Gadsden Properties Inc 588
Gadsden Regional Medical Center, Llc 588
Gaia Inc (new) 588
Gain Capital Holdings Inc 588
Gainesville Regional Utilities (inc) 589
Galectin Therapeutics Inc. 589
Galena Biopharma Inc 589
Gallagher (arthur J.) & Co. 589
Gallaudet University 589
Gallery Model Homes, Inc. 589
Gallery Of History Inc. 590
Gallup, Inc. 590
Gamco Investors Inc 590
Gamefly Inc. 590
Gamestop Corp 590
Gaming Partners International Corp 590
Gander Mountain Company 591
Gannett Co Inc (new) 591
Garden Fresh Restaurant Corp. 591
Garden Ridge Corporation 591
Gartner Inc 591
Gary Rabine & Sons Inc. 591
Gas Depot Oil Company 592
Gas Transmission Northwest Llc 592
Gasco Energy Inc. 592
Gateway Energy Corporation 592
Gateway Health Plan Inc. 592
Gatx Corp 592
Gct Semiconductor Inc. 593
Gee Group Inc 593
Geeknet Inc 593
Gehan Homes, Ltd. 593
Geico Corporation 593
Geisinger Health 593
Gelber Group, Llc 594
Gen-probe Incorporated 594
Genasys Inc 594
Genco Distribution System Inc. 594
Genco Shipping & Trading Ltd 594
Gencor Industries Inc 594
Genelink Inc 595
General Bearing Corporation 595
General Cable Corp (de) 595
General Communication Inc 595
General Dynamics Corp 595
General Electric Capital Corporation 595
General Electric Co 596
General Finance Corp 596
General Health System 596

General Magnaplate Corporation 596
General Maritime Corporation 596
General Microwave Corporation 596
General Mills Inc 597
General Moly Inc. 597
General Motors Co 597
General Motors Financial Company Inc. 597
Generex Biotechnology Corp (de) 597
Genesco Inc. 597
Genesee & Wyoming Inc. 598
Genesee Valley Group Health Association 598
Genesis Corp. 598
Genesis Energy L.p. 598
Genesis Health Inc. 598
Genesis Health System 598
Genesis Healthcare Inc 599
Genesis Healthcare Llc 599
Genesis Healthcare System 599
Genesys Regional Medical Center 599
Genethera Inc. 599
Genica Corporation 599
Genie Energy Ltd 600
Genmark Diagnostics, Inc. 600
Genocea Biosciences Inc 600
Genomic Health Inc 600
Gentex Corp. 600
Gentherm Inc 600
Gentiva Health Services Inc 601
Genuine Parts Co. 601
Genvec Inc (de) 601
Genworth Financial, Inc. (holding Co) 601
Genzyme Corporation 601
Geo Group Inc (the) (new) 601
Geobio Energy Inc. 602
Geomet Inc (de) 602
Geopetro Resources Co 602
George E. Warren Corporation 602
George Foreman Enterprises Inc. 602
Georgetown Memorial Hospital 602
Georgia Lottery Corporation 603
Georgia Power Co 603
Georgia Southern University 603
Georgia Transmission Corporation 603
Georgia-carolina Bancshares, Inc. 603
Geospace Technologies Corp 603
Geosyntec Consultants, Inc. 604
Gerber Childrenswear Llc 604
Gerber Scientific Inc. 604
German American Bancorp Inc 604
Gerrity's Super Market, Inc. 604
Getty Realty Corp. 604
Gettysburg College 605
Gevo Inc 605
Gfi Group Inc 605
Ggnsc Holdings Llc 605
Giant Eagle Inc. 605
Gibbs Die Casting Corporation 605
Gibraltar Industries Inc 606
Gibraltar Packaging Group Inc. 606
Gibson Dunn & Crutcher Llp 606
Giga-tronics Inc 606
Gigamon Inc 606
Gigpeak Inc 606
Gilbane Building Company 607
Gilbane Inc. 607
Gilbert May, Inc. 607
Gilead Sciences Inc 607
Gillette Children's Specialty Healthcare 607
Ginkgo Residential Trust Inc. 607
Girl Scouts Of The United States Of America 608
Glacier Bancorp, Inc. 608
Glacier Water Services Inc. 608
Gladstone Capital Corporation 608
Gladstone Commercial Corp 608
Gladstone Investment Corp 608
Gladstone Land Corp 609
Glassbridge Enterprises Inc 609
Glasshouse Technologies Inc. 609
Gleacher & Co, Inc. (de) 609
Glen Burnie Bancorp 609
Glendale Adventist Medical Center Inc 609
Glenn O. Hawbaker Inc. 610
Glimcher Realty Trust 610
Global Axcess Corp. 610

Global Brass & Copper Holdings Inc 610
Global Brass And Copper Holdings Inc. 610
Global Brokerage Inc 610
Global Communication Semiconductors Inc. 611
Global Custom Commerce L.p. 611
Global Diversified Industries Inc. 611
Global Earth Energy Inc. 611
Global Entertainment Corporation 611
Global Geophysical Services Inc 611
Global Pacific Produce Inc. 612
Global Partners Lp 612
Global Payments Inc 612
Global Telecom & Technology Inc. 612
Global Traffic Network Inc. 612
Globaloptions Group Inc. 612
Globalscape Inc 613
Globalstar Inc 613
Globe Life Inc 613
Globe Specialty Metals Inc 613
Globeimmune, Inc 613
Globus Medical Inc 613
Glori Energy Inc. 614
Glowpoint Inc 614
Glu Mobile Inc 614
Glycomimetics Inc 614
Gnc Holdings Inc 614
Godfather's Pizza Inc. 614
Gold Reserve Inc 615
Gold Resource Corp 615
Gold's Gym International Inc. 615
Gold-eagle Cooperative 615
Golden Enterprises, Inc. 615
Golden Entertainment Inc 615
Golden Gate National Parks Conservancy 616
Golden Grain Energy, Llc 616
Golden Minerals Co 616
Golden Star Enterprises Ltd 616
Goldfield Corp. 616
Goldman Sachs Group Inc 616
Goldrich Mining Co 617
Golf Galaxy Llc 617
Golfsmith International Holdings Inc. 617
Golub Capital Bdc Inc. 617
Good Sam Enterprises Llc 617
Good Samaritan Hospital 617
Good Samaritan Hospital 618
Good Samaritan Hospital 618
Good Samaritan Hospital Medical Center 618
Good Samaritan Hospital, L.p. 618
Good Times Restaurants Inc. 618
Good360 618
Goodfellow Bros. Inc. 619
Goodman Networks Incorporated 619
Goodrich Corporation 619
Goodrich Petroleum Corp 619
Goodwill Industries International, Inc. 619
Goodwill Industries Of Central Texas 619
Goodwin Procter Llp 620
Goodyear Tire & Rubber Co. 620
Gordmans Stores Inc 620
Gordon College 620
Gordon Food Service, Inc. 620
Gorman-rupp Company (the) 620
Gottlieb Memorial Hospital 621
Goya Foods Inc. 621
Gpm Investments, Llc 621
Grace (wr) & Co 621
Graceland Fruit Inc. 621
Gradall Industries Inc. 621
Graebel Companies, Inc. 622
Graftech International Ltd 622
Graham Corp. 622
Graham Holdings Co. 622
Graham Packaging Company L.p. 622
Grainger (w.w.) Inc. 622
Gramercy Property Trust Inc 623
Grand Canyon Education Inc 623
Grand Piano & Furniture Co. 623
Grand River Dam Authority 623
Grand Strand Regional Medical Center, Llc 623
Grand Valley State University 623
Grand View Hospital 624
Granite City Food & Brewery Ltd 624
Granite Construction Inc 624

1513

Granite Telecommunications Llc 624
Graphic Packaging Holding Co 624
Gray Television Inc 624
Graybar Electric Co., Inc. 625
Graycor Inc. 625
Great American Bancorp Inc 625
Great Elm Capital Group Inc 625
Great Lakes Aviation Ltd. 625
Great Lakes Cheese Company Inc. 625
Great Lakes Dredge & Dock Corp 626
Great Northern Iron Ore Properties 626
Great Plains Energy Inc 626
Great Plains Manufacturing Incorporated 626
Great River Energy 626
Great Southern Bancorp, Inc. 626
Great West Life & Annuity Insurance Co - Insurance Products 627
Great Wolf Resorts Inc. 627
Greater Baltimore Medical Center Inc. 627
Greater Lafayette Health Services Inc. 627
Greater Orlando Aviation Authority 627
Greater Washington Educational Telecommunications Association, Inc. 627
Greatwide Logistics Services Llc 628
Green Brick Partners Inc 628
Green Dot Corp 628
Green Energy Group (new) 628
Green Mountain Power Corporation 628
Green Plains Inc. 628
Greenberg Traurig P.a. 629
Greene County Bancorp Inc 629
Greenhill & Co Inc 629
Greenhunter Resources, Inc 629
Greenshift Corp 629
Greenstone Farm Credit Services Aca 629
Greenville Utilities Commission 630
Greenway Medical Technologies Inc. 630
Griffin Industrial Realty Inc 630
Griffith Laboratories Inc. 630
Griffon Corp. 630
Grill Concepts Inc. 630
Groen Brothers Aviation Inc 631
Groove Botanicals Inc 631
Grossmont Hospital Corporation 631
Group 1 Automotive, Inc. 631
Group Health Cooperative 631
Group O, Inc. 631
Groupon Inc 632
Growmark, Inc. 632
Gruma Corporation 632
Grunley Construction Co., Inc. 632
Gse Holding Inc. 632
Gse Systems Inc 632
Gsi Commerce Inc. 633
Gsi Technology Inc 633
Gt Advanced Technologies Inc. 633
Gtsi Corp. 633
Gtt Communications, Inc 633
Gtx Inc 633
Guadalupe Valley Telephone Cooperative, Inc. 634
Guarantee Electrical Company 634
Guaranty Bancorp (de) 634
Guaranty Bancshares Inc 634
Guardian Life Insurance Co. Of America (nyc) 634
Guardsmark Llc 634
Guess ?, Inc. 635
Guest Services, Inc. 635
Guidance Software Inc 635
Guided Therapeutics Inc 635
Guidewire Software Inc 635
Guilford Mills Inc. 635
Guitar Center Inc. 635
Gulf Coast Project Services, Inc. 636
Gulf Island Fabrication, Inc. 636
Gulf Oil Limited Partnership 636
Gulf Power Co 636
Gulf States Toyota Inc. 636
Gulf United Energy Inc. 637
Gulfmark Offshore Inc 637
Gulfport Energy Corp. 637
Gulfstream Natural Gas System, L.l.c. 637
Gundersen Lutheran Medical Center, Inc. 637
Gustavus Adolphus College 637
Guthrie Healthcare System 638

Gyrodyne Co. Of America, Inc. 638
H. E. Butt Grocery Company 638
H. J. Russell & Company 638
H. Lee Moffitt Cancer Center And Research Institute Hospital, Inc. 638
H.c. Schmieding Produce Company, Llc 638
Habasit America 639
Habitat For Humanity International, Inc. 639
Hackett Group Inc 639
Hackley Hospital 639
Haemonetics Corp. 639
Haggar Clothing Co. 639
Haggen, Inc. 640
Hahn Automotive Warehouse Inc. 640
Hain Celestial Group Inc 640
Halcon Resources Corp 640
Hallador Energy Co 640
Halliburton Company 640
Hallmark Financial Services Inc. 641
Hallwood Group Inc. 641
Halozyme Therapeutics Inc 641
Hamilton Chattanooga County Hospital Authority 641
Hamilton College 641
Hampden Bancorp Inc 641
Hampshire Group, Ltd. 642
Hampton University 642
Hancock Fabrics, Inc. 642
Hancock Whitney Corp 642
Handy & Harman Ltd 642
Hanesbrands Inc 642
Hanger Inc 643
Hanmi Financial Corp. 643
Hannon Armstrong Sustainable Infrastructure Capital Inc 643
Hanover College 643
Hanover Foods Corporation 643
Hanover Insurance Group Inc 643
Hansen Medical Inc 644
Harbor Biosciences Inc. 644
Harbor Hospital 644
Hardee's Food Systems Inc. 644
Hardinge Inc 644
Hargrove, Llc 644
Harland Clarke Corp. 645
Harland M. Braun & Co., Inc. 645
Harley-davidson Inc 645
Harleysville Financial Corp 645
Harleysville Group Inc. 645
Harman International Industries Inc 645
Harmonic, Inc. 646
Harrington Memorial Hospital, Inc. 646
Harris Teeter Inc. 646
Harry & David Holdings Inc. 646
Harry Winston Inc. 646
Harte Hanks Inc 646
Hartford Financial Services Group Inc. 647
Hartford Healthcare Corporation 647
Harvard Bioscience Inc. 647
Harvard Pilgrim Health Care Inc. 647
Harvest Natural Resources Inc. 647
Harvest Oil & Gas Corp 647
Harvey Mudd College 648
Hasbro, Inc. 648
Hastings Entertainment, Inc. 648
Hat World Corporation 648
Hatteras Financial Corp 648
Hauppauge Digital, Inc. 648
Hawai I Pacific Health 649
Hawaii Pacific University 649
Hawaiian Electric Industries Inc 649
Hawaiian Macadamia Nut Orchards Lp 649
Hawaiian Telcom Holdco Inc 649
Hawkins Construction Company 649
Hawkins Inc 650
Haworth Inc. 650
Hawthorne Machinery Co. 650
Hay House Inc. 650
Hayes Lemmerz International Inc. 650
Haynes International, Inc. 650
Hays Medical Center, Inc. 651
Haywood Health Authority 651
Hazen And Sawyer, D.p.c. 651
Hc2 Holdings Inc 651

Hca Healthcare Inc 651
Hcc Insurance Holdings, Inc. 651
Hci Group Inc 652
Hcr Manorcare Inc. 652
Hcsb Financial Corp 652
Hdr, Inc. 652
Headwaters Inc 652
Health First, Inc. 652
Health Net, Inc. 653
Health Partners Plans, Inc. 653
Health Research, Inc. 653
Healthcare Distribution Management Association 653
Healthcare Partners Llc 653
Healthcare Realty Trust, Inc. 653
Healthcare Services Group, Inc. 654
Healtheast St John's Hospital 654
Healthmarkets Inc. 654
Healthpeak Properties Inc 654
Healthspring Inc. 654
Healthstream Inc 654
Healthwarehouse.com, Inc. 655
Heartland Express, Inc. 655
Heartland Financial Usa, Inc. (dubuque, Ia) 655
Heartland Health 655
Heartland Payment Systems, Llc 655
Heartware International Inc 655
Heaven Hill Distilleries Inc. 656
Hecla Mining Co 656
Heery International Inc. 656
Heico Corp 656
Heidrick & Struggles International, Inc. 656
Heidtman Steel Products Inc. 656
Heifer Project International Inc 657
Helen Keller International 657
Helicos Biosciences Corporation 657
Helios & Matheson Analytics Inc 657
Helios Technologies Inc 657
Helix Biomedix Inc. 657
Helix Energy Solutions Group Inc 658
Hella Corporate Center Usa Inc. 658
Helmerich & Payne, Inc. 658
Helmsman Management Services Llc 658
Hemacare Corp. 658
Hemagen Diagnostics Inc 658
Hemmings Motor News 659
Henricksen & Company, Inc. 659
Henry County Memorial Hospital 659
Henry Ford Health System 659
Henry Mayo Newhall Memorial Hospital 659
Henry Modell & Company, Inc. 659
Hensel Phelps Construction Co. 660
Herbert Mines Associates Inc. 660
Herc Holdings Inc 660
Hercules Offshore Inc 660
Hercules Technology Growth Capital Inc. 660
Heritage Bankshares, Inc. (norfolk, Va) 660
Heritage Commerce Corp 661
Heritage Financial Corp (wa) 661
Heritage Financial Group Inc. 661
Heritage Global Inc 661
Heritage Oaks Bancorp 661
Heritage Southeast Bancorporation Inc 661
Heritage Valley Health System, Inc. 662
Heritage-crystal Clean Inc 662
Heron Therapeutics Inc 662
Herschend Family Entertainment Corporation 662
Hersha Hospitality Trust 662
Hershey Company (the) 662
Hershey Entertainment & Resorts Company 663
Hertz Global Holdings Inc (new) 663
Heska Corp. 663
Hess Corp 663
Hewlett Packard Enterprise Co 663
Hewlett, William And Flora Foundation (inc) 663
Hexcel Corp. 664
Hexion Inc 664
Hf Financial Corp. 664
Hfb Financial Corp. 664
Hff Inc 664
Hg Holdings Inc 664
Hhgregg Inc 665
Hi-shear Technology Corporation 665
Hi-tech Pharmacal Co., Inc. 665

Hibbett Sports Inc 665
Hickman, Williams & Company 665
Hickory Farms Inc. 665
Hickory Tech Corp. 666
High Concrete Group Llc 666
High Country Bancorp, Inc. 666
High Industries Inc. 666
High Performance Technologies Inc. 666
High Point Regional Health 666
High Point Solutions Inc. 667
High Steel Structures Llc 667
Higher One Holdings Inc. 667
Highlands Bankshares Inc (va) 667
Highlands Bankshares Inc. 667
Highmark Bcbsd Inc. 667
Highwoods Properties, Inc. 668
Hiland Dairy Foods Company., Llc 668
Hilite International, Inc. 668
Hill Country Memorial Hospital 668
Hill International Inc 668
Hill Physicians Medical Group, Inc. 668
Hill-rom Holdings, Inc. 669
Hillenbrand Inc 669
Hills Bancorporation 669
Hillsborough County Aviation Authority 669
Hillshire Brands Co 669
Hilltop Holdings, Inc. 669
Hilton Worldwide Holdings Inc 670
Hines Interests Limited Partnership 670
Hingham Institution For Savings 670
Hinshaw & Culbertson Llp 670
Hirequest Inc 670
Hitchiner Manufacturing Co., Inc. 670
Hitt Contracting, Inc. 671
Hittite Microwave Corp 671
Hkn Inc 671
Hks, Inc. 671
Hmg/courtland Properties, Inc. 671
Hmh Hospitals Corporation 671
Hmi Industries Inc. 672
Hmn Financial Inc. 672
Hms Holdings Corp 672
Hni Corp 672
Hntb Corporation 672
Ho-chunk, Inc. 672
Hoag Hospital Foundation 673
Hoag Memorial Hospital Presbyterian 673
Hobart And William Smith Colleges 673
Hobby Lobby Stores, Inc. 673
Hofstra University 673
Holiday Builders, Inc. 673
Holiday Wholesale, Inc. 674
Holland Community Hospital Auxiliary, Inc. 674
Hollingsworth Oil Co. Inc. 674
Holly Energy Partners Lp 674
Hollyfrontier Corp 674
Hollywood Media Corp 674
Holmes Lumber & Building Center Inc. 675
Holmes Regional Medical Center, Inc. 675
Hologic Inc 675
Holophane 675
Holy Cross Hospital, Inc. 675
Holy Spirit Hospital Of The Sisters Of Christian Charity 675
Homasote Co. 676
Home Bancorp Inc 676
Home Bancshares Inc 676
Home City Financial Corp 676
Home Depot Inc 676
Home Federal Bancorp Inc. 676
Home Financial Bancorp 677
Home Loan Financial Corp 677
Home Properties Inc 677
Homeaway, Inc. 677
Homefed Corp. 677
Homestreet Inc 677
Honda North America Inc. 678
Honeywell International Inc 678
Hooker Furniture Corp 678
Hooper Holmes Inc 678
Hoosier Energy Rural Electric Cooperative Inc. 678
Hoover's Inc. 678
Hopfed Bancorp, Inc. 679
Hopto Inc 679

Horace Mann Educators Corp. 679
Horizon Bancorp Inc 679
Horizon Health Corporation 679
Horizon Lines Inc 679
Horizon Pharma Inc 680
Hormel Foods Corp. 680
Hornbeck Offshore Services Inc 680
Hornblower Yachts, Llc 680
Horne International Inc 680
Horry Telephone Cooperative, Inc. 680
Horsehead Holding Corp 681
Horton (dr) Inc 681
Hospice Of Michigan Inc. 681
Hospira Inc 681
Hospital Authority Of Valdosta And Lowndes County, Georgia 681
Hospital Of Central Connecticut 681
Hospital Service District 1 Of East Baton Rouge Parish 682
Hospital Service District No. 1 682
Hospital Sisters Health System 682
Hoss's Steak & Sea House, Inc. 682
Host Hotels & Resorts Inc 682
Houchens Industries, Inc. 682
Houghton Mifflin Harcourt Co. 683
Houghton Mifflin Harcourt Publishing Company 683
Houston American Energy Corp. 683
Houston Community College, Inc. 683
Houston County Healthcare Authority 683
Houston Wire & Cable Co 683
Hovnanian Enterprises, Inc. 684
Howard Hughes Corp 684
Howard University (inc) 684
Hp Hood Llc 684
Hp Inc 684
Hsbc Usa, Inc. 684
Hsn Inc (de) 685
Hub Group, Inc. 685
Hub International Limited 685
Hubbell Inc. 685
Hudson City Bancorp Inc 685
Hudson Global Inc 685
Hudson Pacific Properties Inc 686
Hudson Technologies Inc 686
Hudson Valley Federal Credit Union 686
Hudson Valley Holding Corp. 686
Hughes Communications Inc. 686
Hughes Telematics Inc. 686
Hugoton Royalty Trust (tx) 687
Hulu Llc 687
Human Genome Sciences Inc. 687
Human Pheromone Sciences Inc. 687
Human Rights Watch, Inc. 687
Humana Inc. 687
Humax Usa, Inc 688
Hunt (j.b.) Transport Services, Inc. 688
Hunt Memorial Hospital District 688
Hunter Douglas Inc. 688
Huntington Bancshares Inc 688
Huntington Hospital Dolan Family Health Center, Inc. 688
Huntington Ingalls Industries, Inc. 689
Hunton & Williams Llp 689
Huntsman Corp 689
Hurco Companies Inc 689
Hurley Medical Center 689
Huron Consulting Group Inc 689
Husson University 690
Hutcheson Medical Center Inc. 690
Hutchinson Technology Inc. 690
Huttig Building Products, Inc. 690
Hy-vee, Inc. 690
Hyatt Hotels Corp 690
Hycroft Mining Corp 691
Hydromer, Inc. 691
Hydron Technologies Inc. 691
Hyperdynamics Corporation 691
Hypertension Diagnostics, Inc. 691
Hyster-yale Materials Handling Inc 691
I/omagic Corporation 692
Ia Global Inc. 692
Iap Worldwide Services, Inc. 692
Iasis Healthcare Corporation 692
Iaso Pharma Inc. 692

Iberdrola Usa Inc. 692
Iberiabank Corp 693
Ic Compliance Llc 693
Icad Inc 693
Icagen Inc. 693
Icahn Enterprises Lp 693
Icf International Inc 693
Icims.com Inc 694
Icon Health & Fitness Inc. 694
Icon Identity Solutions, Inc. 694
Iconix Brand Group Inc 694
Iconma L.l.c. 694
Icu Medical Inc 694
Idacorp Inc 695
Idaho Power Co 695
Idaho State University 695
Idealab 695
Idemia Identity & Security Usa Llc 695
Idenix Pharmaceuticals Inc 695
Ideo Llc 696
Idera Pharmaceuticals Inc 696
Idex Corporation 696
Idexx Laboratories, Inc. 696
Idt Corp 696
Idw Media Holdings Inc 696
Iec Electronics Corp. 697
Ies Holdings Inc 697
Igate Corp 697
Ignite Restaurant Group Inc 697
Igo Inc 697
Iheartmedia Inc 697
Ihs Inc 698
Ikano Communications Inc. 698
Ikanos Communications Inc 698
Ikonics Corp 698
Ilg Inc 698
Illinois Institute Of Technology 698
Illinois Tool Works, Inc. 699
Illinois Wesleyan University 699
Illumina Inc 699
Image Protect Inc 699
Image Sensing Systems, Inc. 699
Imagetrend Inc. 699
Imageware Systems Inc 700
Imagine Entertainment 700
Imaging Diagnostic Systems Inc 700
Imedia Brands Inc 700
Immersion Corp 700
Immixgroup, Inc. 700
Immucell Corp. 701
Immucor Inc. 701
Immune Pharmaceuticals Inc 701
Immunocellular Therapeutics Ltd. 701
Immunogen, Inc. 701
Immunomedics, Inc. 701
Impac Mortgage Holdings, Inc. 702
Imperial Industries Inc. 702
Imperial Irrigation District 702
Imperial Petroleum Recovery Corporation 702
Imperial Sugar Company 702
Imperva Inc 702
Impinj Inc. 703
Implant Sciences Corp 703
Impreso Inc. 703
In-q-tel Inc 703
Inc.jet Holding Inc 703
Income Opportunity Realty Investors Inc. 703
Incontact, Inc. 704
Incyte Corporation 704
Independence Holding Company 704
Independent Bank Corp (ma) 704
Independent Bank Corporation (ionia, Mi) 704
Independent Bank Group Inc. 704
Index Fresh, Inc. 705
India Globalization Capital Inc 705
Indiana Botanic Gardens Inc 705
Indiana Harbor Belt Railroad Co 705
Indiana Municipal Power Agency 705
Indiana University Foundation, Inc. 705
Indiana University Health Bloomington, Inc. 706
Indiana University Health, Inc. 706
Indiana University Of Pennsylvania 706
Indianapolis Colts Inc. 706
Indus Corporation 706

Industrial Scientific Corporation 706
Industrial Services Of America Inc (fl) 707
Industrial Turnaround Corporation 707
Indyne, Inc. 707
Infinera Corp 707
Infinite Energy, Inc. 707
Infinite Group, Inc. 707
Infinity Energy Resources Inc. 708
Infinity Pharmaceuticals Inc 708
Infinity Property & Casualty Corp 708
Infoblox Inc. 708
Infogain Corporation 708
Infor Global Solutions Inc. 708
Inforeliance Corporation 709
Informatica Corp. 709
Information Analysis Inc. 709
Information Services Group Inc 709
Infovision Inc. 709
Ing Bank Fsb 709
Ing U.s. Inc. 710
Ingersoll Machine Tools, Inc. 710
Ingles Markets Inc 710
Ingram Micro Inc. 710
Ingredion Inc 710
Inksure Technologies Inc. 710
Innerworkings Inc 711
Innodata Inc 711
Innophos Holdings Inc 711
Innospec Inc 711
Innovaro Inc. 711
Innovation Ventures Llc 711
Innovative Solutions And Support Inc 712
Innoviva Inc 712
Innsuites Hospitality Trust 712
Inogen, Inc 712
Inova Health System Foundation 712
Inova Technology Inc 712
Inovio Pharmaceuticals Inc. 713
Inphi Corp 713
Inrad Optics Inc 713
Inseego Corp 713
Insight Enterprises Inc. 713
Insight Health Services Holdings Corp. 713
Insignia Systems, Inc. 714
Insite Vision Inc. 714
Insituform Technologies Inc. 714
Insmed Incorporated 714
Inspire Pharmaceuticals Inc. 714
Installed Building Products Inc 714
Instant Web Inc. 715
Insteel Industries, Inc. 715
Institute For Defense Analyses Inc 715
Institute Of Gas Technology 715
Insulet Corp 715
Insys Therapeutics Inc 715
Insys Therapeutics Inc. 716
Intcomex Inc. 716
Integer Holdings Corp 716
Integra Lifesciences Holdings Corp 716
Integra Telecom Inc. 716
Integral Systems Inc. 716
Integral Technologies Inc. 717
Integral Vision Inc. 717
Integramed America Inc. 717
Integrated Biopharma Inc 717
Integrated Device Technology Inc 717
Integrated Silicon Solution, Inc. 717
Integrated Surgical Systems Inc. 718
Integris Baptist Medical Center, Inc. 718
Integris Health, Inc. 718
Integrys Energy Group Inc 718
Intel Corp 718
Inteliquent Inc 718
Intellicorp Inc. 719
Intellidyne L.l.c. 719
Intelligent Software Solutions Inc. 719
Intelligent Systems Corp. 719
Inter Parfums, Inc. 719
Inter-american Development Bank 719
Interactive Brokers Group Inc 720
Interactive Intelligence Group Inc. 720
Interactive Intelligence Inc. 720
Interbond Corporation Of America 720
Intercept Pharmaceuticals Inc 720

Intercloud Systems Inc 720
Intercontinentalexchange Inc. 721
Interdigital Inc (pa) 721
Interface Inc. 721
Interface Security Systems L.l.c. 721
Intergroup Corp. (the) 721
Interim Healthcare Inc. 721
Interleukin Genetics Inc 722
Interline Brands Inc. 722
Interlink Electronics Inc 722
Intermatic Incorporated 722
Intermetro Communications, Inc. (nv) 722
Intermolecular Inc 722
Intermountain Health Care Inc 723
Intermune Inc. 723
Internap Corp 723
International Association Of Amusement Parks & Attractions Inc 723
International Baler Corp 723
International Bancshares Corp. 723
International Brotherhood Of Electrical Workers 724
International Brotherhood Of Teamsters 724
International Building Technologies Group Inc. 724
International Business Machines Corp 724
International Card Establishment Inc. 724
International Creative Management Inc. 724
International Finance Corp. (world Corporations Gov't) 725
International Flavors & Fragrances Inc. 725
International Fleet Sales Inc. 725
International Isotopes Inc 725
International Lease Finance Corp. 725
International Lottery & Totalizator Systems, Inc. 725
International Minerals Corporation 726
International Monetary Systems Ltd. 726
International Paper Co 726
International Rectifier Corp. 726
International Shipholding Corp 726
International Speedway Corp 726
International Textile Group, Inc. 727
International Wire Group, Inc. 727
Internet America Inc. 727
Internet Corporation For Assigned Names And Numbers 727
Interpace Biosciences Inc 727
Interpore Spine Ltd. 727
Interpublic Group Of Companies Inc. 728
Intersections Inc 728
Interstate Power & Light Co 728
Intersystems Corporation 728
Intervest Bancshares Corp. 728
Intest Corp. 728
Intevac, Inc. 729
Intl Fcstone Inc. 729
Intralinks Holdings Inc 729
Intrawest Resorts Holdings Inc 729
Intrepid Potash Inc 729
Intricon Corp 729
Intrusion Inc 730
Intrust Financial Corporation 730
Intuit Inc 730
Intuitive Surgical Inc 730
Inuvo Inc 730
Invacare Corp 730
Invensense Inc 731
Inventergy Global Inc 731
Inventure Foods Inc. 731
Invesco Ltd. 731
Invesco Mortgage Capital Inc 731
Investment Technology Group Inc. 731
Investors Bancorp Inc (new) 732
Investors Capital Holdings, Ltd. 732
Investors Heritage Capital Corp. 732
Investors Real Estate Trust 732
Investors Title Co. 732
Ion Geophysical Corp 732
Ionis Pharmaceuticals Inc 733
Iowa Health System 733
Iowa State University Of Science And Technology 733
Ipass Inc 733
Ipayment Inc. 733
Ipc Healthcare, Inc. 733
Ipc Systems Inc. 734

Ipg Photonics Corp 734
Iqvia Holdings Inc 734
Irc Retail Centers Llc 734
Iridex Corp. 734
Iridium Communications Inc 734
Iridium Communications Inc. 735
Iris International Inc. 735
Irobot Corp 735
Iron Mountain Inc (new) 735
Ironplanet Inc. 735
Isc8 Inc 735
Isg Technology Llc 736
Isign Solutions Inc 736
Isle Of Capri Casinos Inc 736
Iso New England Inc. 736
Isola Group Ltd. 736
Isomet Corp. 736
Isoray, Inc. 737
Israel Discount Bank Of New York 737
Isramco, Inc. 737
Ista Pharmaceuticals Inc. 737
Istar Inc 737
Ita Group, Inc 737
Itc Holdings Corp 738
Itc^deltacom Inc. 738
Iteris Inc 738
Itex Corp 738
Itron Inc 738
Itt Educational Services Inc 738
Ivci, Llc 739
Ivey Mechanical Company, Llc 739
Iwatt Inc. 739
Ixia 739
Ixys Corp. 739
J & D Produce, Inc. 739
J M Smith Corporation 740
J&j Snack Foods Corp. 740
J. Crew Group Inc. 740
J. D. Streett & Company, Inc. 740
J. F. White Contracting Company 740
J. H. Findorff & Son, Inc. 740
J.d. Abrams, L.p. 741
J.e. Dunn Construction Company 741
J.e. Dunn Construction Group, Inc. 741
J.m. Huber Corporation 741
J.r. Simplot Company 741
Jabil Inc 741
Jack Henry & Associates, Inc. 742
Jack In The Box, Inc. 742
Jackson County Memorial Hospital Authority 742
Jackson Electric Membership Corporation 742
Jackson Energy Authority 742
Jackson Healthcare, Llc 742
Jackson Hewitt Tax Service Inc. 743
Jackson Hospital & Clinic, Inc 743
Jackson State University 743
Jacksonville Bancorp Inc (fl) 743
Jacksonville Bancorp Inc (md) 743
Jacksonville University 743
Jaclyn Inc. 744
Jaco Oil Company 744
Jacobs Engineering Group, Inc. 744
Jacobs Financial Group Inc 744
Jacobs, Malcolm & Burtt 744
Jacuzzi Brands Corp. 744
Jagged Peak Inc. 745
Jakks Pacific Inc. 745
Jamba Inc 745
James Madison University 745
James River Coal Co 745
Janel Corp 745
Janone Inc 746
Janus Capital Group Inc 746
Javelin Mortgage Investment Corp 746
Jayco Inc. 746
Jda Software Group Inc. 746
Jea 746
Jefferies Financial Group Inc 747
Jefferson Bancshares Inc (tn) 747
Jefferson Homebuilders, Inc. 747
Jefferson Hospital Association, Inc. 747
Jefferson Regional Medical Center 747
Jeffersonville Bancorp 747
Jennifer Convertibles Inc. 748

COMPANIES LISTED ALPHABETICALLY

Jerry Biggers Chevrolet Inc. 748
Jersey Central Power & Light Company 748
Jersey City Medical Center (inc) 748
Jetblue Airways Corp 748
Jewel-osco 748
Jewett-cameron Trading Co. Ltd. 749
Jive Software Inc 749
Jlg Industries Inc. 749
Jlm Couture Inc. 749
Jm Family Enterprises Inc. 749
Jmp Group Llc 749
John Bean Technologies Corp 750
John C. Lincoln Health Network 750
John Carroll University 750
John D And Catherine T Macarthur Foundation 750
John D. Oil And Gas Company 750
John F Kennedy Center For The Performing Arts 750
John Hine Pontiac 751
John Morrell & Co. 751
John Muir Health 751
John T. Mather Memorial Hospital Of Port Jefferson, New York, Inc. 751
John Wieland Homes And Neighborhoods Inc. 751
Johns Hopkins All Children's Hospital, Inc. 751
Johns Hopkins Bayview Medical Center, Inc. 752
Johns Hopkins Health Sys Corp 752
Johns Hopkins Medicine International L.l.c. 752
Johns Hopkins University 752
Johnson & Johnson 752
Johnson & Wales University Inc 752
Johnson Controls Fire Protection Lp 753
Johnson Matthey Inc. 753
Johnson Outdoors Inc 753
Johnson Supply And Equipment Corporation 753
Johnsonville Sausage Llc 753
Johnston Enterprises, Inc. 753
Joie De Vivre Hospitality Inc. 754
Joint Commission On Accreditation Of Healthcare Organizations 754
Jones Group Inc 754
Jones Lang Lasalle Inc 754
Jones Soda Co. 754
Jordan Cf Investments Llp 754
Jos. A. Bank Clothiers, Inc. 755
Journal Communications Inc 755
Joy Global Inc 755
Joyce Leslie Inc 755
Jpmorgan Chase & Co 755
Jps Industries Inc. 755
Jth Holding Inc. 756
Jth Tax Inc. 756
Jtm Provisions Company Inc. 756
Judlau Contracting, Inc. 756
Jujamcyn Theaters Llc 756
Juniata College 756
Juniata Valley Financial Corp 757
Juniper Group Inc. 757
Juniper Networks Inc 757
Juniper Pharmaceuticals Inc 757
Jupiter Medical Center, Inc. 757
K&g Men's Company Inc 757
K-sea Transportation Partners L.p. 758
K-tron International Inc. 758
K-va-t Food Stores Inc. 758
K12 Inc 758
Kadant Inc 758
Kadlec Regional Medical Center 758
Kaiser Aluminum Corp. 759
Kaiser Foundation Hospitals Inc 759
Kaiser-francis Oil Company 759
Kaleida Health 759
Kalobios Pharmaceuticals Inc. 759
Kaman Corp. 759
Kana Software Inc. 760
Kansas City Board Of Public Utilities 760
Kansas City Chiefs Football Club Inc. 760
Kansas City Life Insurance Co (kansas City, Mo) 760
Kansas City Southern 760
Kansas Electric Power Cooperative, Inc. 760
Kansas State University 761
Kapstone Paper & Packaging Corp 761
Kar Auction Services Inc. 761
Karyopharm Therapeutics Inc 761
Kate Spade Llc 761

Katy Industries, Inc. 761
Kaz Inc. 762
Kb Home 762
Kbr Inc 762
Kbs, Inc. 762
Kearny Financial Corp 762
Keck Graduate Institute 762
Keenan, Hopkins, Schmidt And Stowell Contractors, Inc. 763
Kehe Distributors Llc 763
Keithley Instruments Inc. 763
Kellogg Co 763
Kellstrom Aerospace, Llc 763
Kellwood Company 763
Kemet Corp. 764
Kemira Chemicals Inc. 764
Kemper Corp (de) 764
Ken's Foods Inc. 764
Kenergy Corp. 764
Kenexa Corporation 764
Kennametal Inc. 765
Kennedy Krieger Institute, Inc. 765
Kennedy-wilson Holdings Inc 765
Kennesaw State University 765
Kennestone Hospital At Windy Hill, Inc. 765
Kenneth Cole Productions Inc. 765
Kensey Nash Corporation 766
Kensington Publishing Corp. 766
Kent County Memorial Hospital 766
Kent Financial Services Inc. 766
Kent State University 766
Kentucky First Federal Bancorp 766
Kentucky Medical Services Foundation, Inc. 767
Kentucky Power Company 767
Kenyon College 767
Keryx Biopharmaceuticals Inc. 767
Kettering Adventist Healthcare 767
Kettering University 767
Keurig Green Mountain Inc 768
Kewaunee Scientific Corporation 768
Key City Furniture Company Inc 768
Key Energy Services Inc (de) 768
Key Food Stores Co-operative, Inc. 768
Key Technology Inc 768
Key Tronic Corp 769
Keycorp 769
Keyw Holding Corp 769
Kforce Inc. 769
Kgbo Holdings, Inc 769
Kid Brands, Inc. 769
Killbuck Bancshares, Inc. 770
Kilroy Realty Corp 770
Kimball Electronics Group Inc. 770
Kimball International, Inc. 770
Kimball Medical Center Inc. 770
Kimberly-clark Corp. 770
Kimco Realty Corp 771
Kimpton Hotel & Restaurant Group Llc 771
Kinder Morgan Energy Partners, L.p. 771
Kinder Morgan Inc. 771
Kindred Healthcare Inc 771
Kinecta Federal Credit Union 771
Kinetic Concepts Inc. 772
Kinetic Systems, Inc. 772
King Kullen Grocery Co. Inc. 772
King's College 772
Kingsbrook Jewish Medical Center Inc 772
Kingstone Companies Inc 772
Kior, Inc. 773
Kips Bay Medical Inc. 773
Kirby Corp. 773
Kirby Risk Corporation 773
Kirkland & Ellis Llp 773
Kirkland's Inc 773
Kish Bancorp Inc. 774
Kissimmee Utility Authority (inc) 774
Kitchell Corporation 774
Kite Realty Group Trust 774
Kiwanis International 774
Kiwibox.com, Inc. 774
Kkr & Co. L.p. 775
Kkr Financial Holdings Llc 775
Kmart Corporation 775
Kmg Chemicals, Inc. 775

Knape & Vogt Manufacturing Company 775
Knight Transportation Inc. 775
Knights Of Columbus 776
Knoll Inc 776
Knouse Foods Cooperative, Inc. 776
Knowles Corp 776
Knoxville Utilities Board 776
Koch Enterprises Inc. 776
Koch Foods Incorporated 777
Koch Industries Inc. 777
Kodiak Oil & Gas Corp. 777
Kohlberg Capital Corporation 777
Kohn Pedersen Fox Associates, Pc 777
Kohr Brothers Inc. 777
Kona Grill Inc 778
Kopin Corp. 778
Koppers Holdings Inc 778
Korn Ferry 778
Korn/ferry International Futurestep Inc. 778
Korte Construction Company 778
Kosmos Energy Ltd (de) 779
Koss Corp 779
Kph Healthcare Services Inc. 779
Kpmg L.l.p. 779
Kqed Inc. 779
Kraft Foods Group Inc 779
Kraft Heinz Co (the) 780
Kraton Corp 780
Kratos Defense & Security Solutions, Inc. 780
Kreisler Manfacturing Corp. 780
Krispy Kreme Doughnuts Inc 780
Kroger Co (the) 780
Krones, Inc. 781
Kronos Incorporated 781
Kronos Worldwide Inc 781
Krueger International, Inc. 781
Ksw Inc. 781
Kuakini Health System 781
Kurt Manufacturing Company Inc. 782
Kvh Industries, Inc. 782
Kwik Trip, Inc. 782
L & S Electric, Inc. 782
L Brands, Inc 782
L&l Energy Inc 782
L. & R. Distributors Inc. 783
L3harris Technologies Inc 783
La France Corp. 783
La Jolla Pharmaceutical Co. 783
La Madeleine Of Texas Inc. 783
La-z-boy Inc. 783
Laboratory Corporation Of America Holdings 784
Lacks Enterprises Inc. 784
Lacrosse Footwear Inc. 784
Ladder Capital Corp 784
Ladenburg Thalmann Financial Services Inc 784
Ladies Professional Golf Association 784
Lafayette College 785
Lafayette General Medical Center, Inc. 785
Laird Technologies Inc. 785
Lake Area Corn Processors Co-operative 785
Lake Forest College 785
Lake Hospital System, Inc. 785
Lake Shore Bancorp Inc 786
Lake Sunapee Bank Group 786
Lakeland Bancorp, Inc. 786
Lakeland Financial Corp 786
Lakeland Industries, Inc. 786
Lakeland Regional Medical Center, Inc. 786
Lakeside Foods Inc. 787
Lakeside Industries, Inc. 787
Lam Research Corp 787
Lamar Advertising Co (new) 787
Lamb Weston Holdings Inc 787
Lancaster Colony Corp. 787
Land O' Lakes Inc 788
Landauer, Inc. 788
Landec Corp. 788
Landmark Bancorp Inc 788
Landry's Inc. 788
Landstar System, Inc. 788
Lane Bryant Inc. 789
Lane Powell Pc 789
Langston Snyder L P 789
Lanier Parking Holdings Inc. 789

1517

Lannett Co., Inc. 789
Lansing Board Of Water And Light 789
Lantronix Inc. 790
Lapolla Industries Inc 790
Laredo Petroleum Holdings Inc. 790
Larkin Community Hospital, Inc. 790
Las Vegas Sands Corp 790
Las Vegas Valley Water District 790
Lasalle Hotel Properties 791
Lasalle University 791
Laserlock Technologies Inc. 791
Lastar Inc. 791
Latham & Watkins Llp 791
Lattice Inc 791
Lattice Semiconductor Corp 792
Lauren Engineers & Constructors, Inc. 792
Lawnwood Medical Center, Inc. 792
Lawrence + Memorial Hospital, Inc. 792
Lawson Products, Inc. 792
Layne Christensen Co 792
Lca-vision Inc. 793
Lci Industries 793
Lcnb Corp 793
Ldr Holding Corp 793
Le Moyne College 793
Leaf Group Ltd 793
Leap Wireless International Inc 794
Leapfrog Enterprises Inc 794
Lear Corp. 794
Learjet Inc. 794
Learning Tree International Inc 794
Lee County Electric Cooperative, Inc. 794
Lee Enterprises, Inc. 795
Lee Lewis Construction, Inc. 795
Lee Memorial Health System Foundation, Inc. 795
Lee University 795
Legacy Emanuel Hospital & Health Center 795
Legacy Farmers Cooperative 795
Legacy Health 796
Legacy Reserves Inc 796
Legacytexas Financial Group Inc 796
Legal Services Corporation 796
Legalshield 796
Legalzoom.com Inc. 796
Legend Oil & Gas Ltd 797
Legg Mason, Inc. 797
Leggett & Platt, Inc. 797
Lehigh University 797
Lehigh Valley Health Network, Inc. 797
Lehman Trikes Usa Inc. 797
Leidos Holdings Inc 798
Leland Stanford Junior University 798
Lemaitre Vascular Inc 798
Lendingtree Inc (new) 798
Lennar Corp 798
Lennox International Inc 798
Lenox Corporation 799
Leo A. Daly Company 799
Lescarden Inc 799
Lester E. Cox Medical Centers 799
Level 3 Communications, Inc. 799
Levi Strauss & Co. 799
Levi Strauss & Co. 800
Levindale Hebrew Geriatric Center And Hospital, Inc. 800
Lewis & Clark College 800
Lexicon Pharmaceuticals, Inc. 800
Lexington Medical Center 800
Lexington Realty Trust 800
Lexmark International, Inc. 801
Lgi Homes, Inc. 801
Lgl Group Inc (the) 801
Lhc Group Inc 801
Lhh Corporation 801
Libbey Inc. 801
Liberty Bancorp Inc (mo) 802
Liberty Diversified International Inc. 802
Liberty Homes Inc 802
Liberty Mutual Holding Company Inc. 802
Liberty Orchards Company Inc. 802
Liberty Property Trust 802
Licking Memorial Health Systems 803
Lict Corp 803
Liebert Corporation 803

Life Care Centers Of America Inc. 803
Life Partners Holdings Inc 803
Life Storage Inc 803
Life-time Fitness Inc 804
Lifebridge Health, Inc. 804
Lifecore Biomedical Inc. 804
Lifelock Inc 804
Lifepoint Health Inc 804
Lifequest World Corp 804
Lifespan Corporation 805
Lifestore Financial Group 805
Lifetime Brands Inc 805
Lifeway Christian Resources Of The Southern Baptist Convention 805
Lifeway Foods, Inc. 805
Ligand Pharmaceuticals Inc 805
Lightbridge Corp 806
Lighthouse Computer Services, Inc. 806
Lighting Science Group Corp 806
Lightpath Technologies, Inc. 806
Lilly (eli) & Co 806
Lime Energy Co 806
Limelight Networks Inc 807
Limestone Bancorp Inc 807
Limetree Bay Terminals Llc 807
Limoneira Co 807
Linc Logistics Company 807
Lincare Holdings Inc. 807
Lincoln Center For The Performing Arts, Inc. 808
Lincoln Educational Services Corp 808
Lincoln Electric Holdings, Inc. 808
Lincoln Industries 808
Lincoln National Corp. 808
Lincoln Provision Inc. 808
Lineage Cell Therapeutics Inc 809
Lineage Power Corporation 809
Linear Technology Corp 809
Linkedin Corp 809
Linkshare Corporation 809
Linnco Llc 809
Linux Foundation 810
Lionbridge Technologies Inc. 810
Lipscomb University 810
Liquefied Natural Gas Ltd 810
Liquid Investments, Inc. 810
Liquidity Services Inc 810
Liquidmetal Technologies Inc 811
Liro Program And Construction Management P.c. 811
Litehouse, Inc. 811
Lithia Motors Inc 811
Littelfuse Inc 811
Little Lady Foods Inc. 811
Little Sioux Corn Processors Llc 812
Littler Mendelson P.c. 812
Live Nation Entertainment Inc 812
Live Ventures Inc 812
Liveperson Inc 812
Liveramp Holdings Inc 812
Liveworld, Inc. 813
Lkq Corp 813
Lmi Aerospace, Inc. 813
Lnb Bancorp, Inc. 813
Local Corp 813
Loeb & Loeb Llp 813
Loeber Motors, Inc. 814
Loehmann's Holdings Inc. 814
Loews Corp. 814
Logansport Financial Corp. 814
Logic Devices Incorporated 814
Logicalis, Inc. 814
Logicquest Technology Inc 815
Logisticare Solutions, Llc 815
Logistics Management Solutions L.c. 815
Logmein Inc 815
Lojack Corporation 815
Loma Linda University Medical Center 815
Long Beach Medical Center 816
Long Beach Memorial Medical Center 816
Long Island Jewish Medical Center 816
Long Island Power Authority 816
Long Island University 816
Looksmart Ltd. 816
Loop Llc 817

Loopnet Inc. 817
Lorillard, Inc. 817
Los Angeles County Department Of Health Services 817
Los Angeles County Metropolitan Transportation Authority 817
Los Angeles Department Of Water And Power 817
Los Angeles Philharmonic Association 818
Louis Vuitton North America Inc. 818
Louisiana Bancorp Inc 818
Louisiana Tech University 818
Louisiana-pacific Corp 818
Love's Travel Stops & Country Stores Inc. 818
Low Temp Industries Inc. 819
Lowe's Companies Inc 819
Lowe's Food Stores Inc. 819
Lower Colorado River Authority 819
Loyola Marymount University 819
Loyola University Maryland, Inc. 819
Loyola University New Orleans Inc 820
Loyola University Of Chicago Inc 820
Lpl Financial Holdings Inc. 820
Lri Holdings Inc. 820
Lrr Energy, L.p. 820
Lsb Financial Corp. 820
Lsb Industries, Inc. 821
Lsi Corp 821
Lsi Industries Inc. 821
Ltc Properties, Inc. 821
Luby's, Inc. 821
Lucasfilm Entertainment Company Ltd. 821
Lucid Inc. 822
Luckey Farmers, Inc. 822
Lucy Webb Hayes National Training School For Deaconesses And Missionaries 822
Lumber Liquidators Holdings Inc 822
Luminex Corp 822
Lumos Networks Corp 822
Luna Innovations Inc 823
Luther College 823
Lutheran Medical Center 823
Lydall, Inc. 823
Lyntegar Electric Cooperative, Inc. 823
Lynuxworks Inc. 823
Lyon (william) Homes 824
Lyric Opera Of Chicago 824
Lyris, Inc. 824
M & F Bancorp Inc 826
M & F Worldwide Corp. 826
M & H Enterprises Inc. 826
M & M Merchandisers Inc. 826
M & T Bank Corp 826
M Financial Holdings Incorporated 826
M. B. Kahn Construction Co., Inc. 827
M. F. A. Oil Company 827
M.a. Patout & Son Limited, L.l.c. 827
M.d.c. Holdings, Inc. 827
M/i Homes Inc 827
Mabvax Therapeutics Holdings Inc 827
Mac Beath Hardwood Company 828
Macalester College 828
Macatawa Bank Corp. 828
Macdonald Mott Group Inc 828
Mace Security International, Inc. 828
Macerich Co (the) 828
Mach 1 Global Services, Inc. 829
Machado/garcia-serra Publicidad Inc. 829
Mack Cali Realty Corp 829
Mackinac Financial Corp 829
Macom Technology Solutions Holdings Inc 829
Macomb Oakland Regional Center Inc 829
Macquarie Infrastructure Corp 830
Macrogenics, Inc 830
Madden (steven) Ltd. 830
Madison Area Technical College District 830
Madison Electric Company 830
Madonna Rehabilitation Hospital 830
Magee Rehabilitation Hospital Foundation 831
Magellan Health Inc. 831
Magellan Midstream Partners Lp 831
Magma Design Automation Inc. 831
Magneco/metrel Inc. 831
Magnetek, Inc. 831
Magnum Construction Management, Llc 832

COMPANIES LISTED ALPHABETICALLY

HOOVER'S MASTERLIST OF U.S. COMPANIES 2020

Magnum Hunter Resources Corp (de) 832
Magyar Bancorp Inc 832
Maimonides Medical Center 832
Main Line Health Inc. 832
Main Line Health System 832
Main Line Hospitals, Inc. 833
Main Street America Group Inc. 833
Main Street Capital Corp 833
Maine Coast Regional Health Facilities Inc 833
Mainegeneral Health 833
Mainehealth 833
Mainsource Financial Group Inc 834
Mainstreet Bankshares Inc 834
Make-a-wish Foundation Of America 834
Malvern Bancorp Inc. 834
Mammatech Corporation 834
Management & Training Corporation 834
Manatee Memorial Hospital, L.p. 835
Maner Builders Supply Company, Llc 835
Mango Capital Inc. 835
Manhattan Associates, Inc. 835
Manhattan Bridge Capital, Inc. 835
Manhattan College Corp 835
Manhattan School Of Music Inc 836
Manhattanville College 836
Manitex International Inc 836
Mannatech Inc 836
Manning & Napier Inc. 836
Mannkind Corp 836
Mantech International Corp 837
Manufactured Housing Enterprises Inc. 837
Mar-jac Poultry, Inc. 837
Marathon Oil Corp. 837
Marathon Petroleum Corp. 837
March Of Dimes Inc. 837
Marchex Inc 838
Marcum Llp 838
Marcus Corp. (the) 838
Marian University, Inc. 838
Marin General Hospital 838
Marin Software Inc 838
Marina Biotech Inc 839
Marine Products Corp 839
Marine Toys For Tots Foundation 839
Marinemax Inc 839
Marion Community Hospital Inc 839
Marist College 839
Maritz Holdings Inc. 840
Mark Iv Llc 840
Markel Corp (holding Co) 840
Market & Johnson, Inc. 840
Market America, Inc. 840
Marketaxess Holdings Inc. 840
Marketo Inc 841
Markwest Energy Partners L.p. 841
Marlin Business Services Corp 841
Marquette University 841
Marriott International, Inc. 841
Marriott Vacations Worldwide Corp. 841
Marrone Bio Innovations Inc 842
Mars Incorporated 842
Marsh & Mclennan Companies Inc. 842
Marsh Supermarkets Inc. 842
Marsh Usa Inc. 842
Marshall University 842
Marshfield Clinic Health System, Inc. 843
Marten Transport Ltd 843
Martha Stewart Living Omnimedia, Inc. 843
Martin & Bayley, Inc. 843
Martin Midstream Partners Lp 843
Martin Resource Management Corporation 843
Marubeni America Corporation 844
Marvin Engineering Co., Inc. 844
Mary Kay Holding Corporation 844
Mary Kay Inc. 844
Mary Washington Healthcare 844
Maryland And Virginia Milk Producers Cooperative Association, Incorporated 844
Maryland Department Of Transportation 845
Maryland Southern Electric Cooperative Inc 845
Marymount Manhattan College 845
Masco Corp. 845
Mascoma Corporation 845
Masergy Communications Inc. 845

Masimo Corp. 846
Massachusetts Higher Education Assistance Corporation 846
Massachusetts Institute Of Technology 846
Massachusetts Medical Society Inc 846
Massachusetts Municipal Wholesale Electric Company 846
Massachusetts Mutual Life Insurance Company 846
Massachusetts Port Authority 847
Mast Industries Inc. 847
Mastec Inc. (fl) 847
Mastech Digital Inc 847
Mastercard Inc 847
Matador Resources Company 847
Matanuska Telephone Association Incorporated 848
Material Sciences Corp. 848
Materion Advanced Materials Technologies And Services Inc 848
Materion Corp 848
Matrix Service Co. 848
Matrixx Initiatives Inc. 848
Matson Inc 849
Mattel Inc 849
Mattersight Corp 849
Matteson-ridolfi Inc. 849
Matthews International Corp 849
Mattingly Foods, Inc. 849
Mattress Firm Holding Corp 850
Mattson Technology Inc 850
Mattson Technology, Inc. 850
Maui Land & Pineapple Co., Inc. 850
Maxim Healthcare Services, Inc. 850
Maxim Integrated Products, Inc. 850
Maximus Inc. 851
Maxlinear Inc 851
Maxor National Pharmacy Services Llc 851
Maxus Realty Trust Inc 851
Maxwell Technologies Inc 851
Mayer Brown Llp 851
Mayer Electric Supply Company, Inc. 852
Mayflower Bancorp Inc. 852
Mayo Clinic Health System-northwest Wisconsin Region, Inc. 852
Mayo Clinic Hospital-rochester 852
Mayo Clinic Jacksonville (a Nonprofit Corporation) 852
Mays (j.w.), Inc. 852
Mayville Engineering Co Inc 853
Mb Financial Inc 853
Mbc Holdings, Inc. 853
Mbia Inc. 853
Mbt Financial Corp. 853
Mc Neese State University 853
Mcafee Inc. 854
Mccarter & English Llp 854
Mccarthy Building Companies, Inc. 854
Mcclatchy Co (the) 854
Mccormick & Co Inc 854
Mccormick & Schmick's Seafood Restaurants Inc. 854
Mccoy-rockford, Inc. 855
Mcdaniel College, Inc 855
Mcdermott International Inc (panama) 855
Mcdonald's Corp 855
Mcdonough County Hospital District 855
Mcg Capital Corp 855
Mcgladrey Llp 856
Mcgrath Rentcorp 856
Mckee Foods Corporation 856
Mckesson Corp 856
Mckinstry Co. Llc 856
Mclane Company, Inc. 856
Mclaren Health Care Corporation 857
Mcmaster-carr Supply Company 857
Mcnaughton-mckay Electric Co. 857
Mcneilus Companies Inc. 857
Mcnichols Company 857
Mcphee Electric, Ltd 857
Mcrae Industries, Inc. 858
Mdc Partners Inc 858
Mdu Resources Group Inc 858
Mead Johnson Nutrition Co 858
Meadowbrook Insurance Group Inc 858
Meadwestvaco Corp. 858

Measurement Specialties, Inc. 859
Mechanical Technology, Inc. 859
Mecklermedia Corp 859
Meco Corporation 859
Medallion Financial Corp 859
Medassets Inc 859
Media General Inc (new) 860
Media Sciences International Inc. 860
Media Storm, Llc 860
Mediamind Technologies Inc. 860
Medical Action Industries, Inc. 860
Medical Information Technology, Inc. 860
Medical Properties Trust Inc 861
Medicine Shoppe International Inc. 861
Medicines Co (the) 861
Medicinova Inc 861
Medicis Pharmaceutical Corporation 861
Medidata Solutions, Inc. 861
Medifast Inc 862
Medivation Inc 862
Mediware Information Systems Inc. 862
Medline Industries Inc. 862
Mednax, Inc. 862
Medseek Inc. 862
Medstar Health, Inc. 863
Medstar-georgetown Medical Center, Inc. 863
Medtox Scientific Inc. 863
Medtronic Sofamor Danek Usa Inc. 863
Meenan Oil Co. L.p. 863
Meet Group Inc (the) 863
Mei Technologies, Inc. 864
Meijer Inc. 864
Meineke Car Care Centers Inc. 864
Melinta Therapeutics Inc 864
Memorial Health Services 864
Memorial Health System 864
Memorial Health System Of East Texas 865
Memorial Hermann Healthcare System 865
Memorial Hospital 865
Memorial Hospital Corporation 865
Memorial Medical Center 865
Memorial Sloan-kettering Cancer Center 865
Memry Corporation 866
Menard Inc. 866
Menasha Corporation 866
Menil Foundation Inc. 866
Menno Travel Service, Inc. 866
Mentor Graphics Corporation 866
Mera Pharmaceuticals Inc. 867
Mercantile Bancorp Inc. 867
Mercantile Bank Corp. 867
Mercer Inc. 867
Mercer Insurance Group Inc. 867
Merchants Bancshares, Inc. (burlington, Vt) 867
Merck & Co Inc 868
Mercury General Corp. 868
Mercury Systems Inc 868
Mercy Care 868
Mercy Children's Hospital 868
Mercy College 868
Mercy Corps 869
Mercy Gwynedd University 869
Mercy Health 869
Mercy Health - St. Rita's Medical Center, Llc 869
Mercy Hospital 869
Mercy Hospital And Medical Center 869
Mercy Hospital South 870
Mercy Hospital Springfield 870
Mercy Medical Center 870
Mercy Medical Center, Inc. 870
Mercy Ships International 870
Merge Healthcare Inc 870
Merial Inc. 871
Meridian Bancorp Inc 871
Meridian Bioscience Inc. 871
Merit Medical Systems, Inc. 871
Meritage Homes Corp 871
Meritage Hospitality Group Inc 871
Meriter Health Services, Inc. 872
Meritor Inc 872
Meritus Health Inc. 872
Merkle Group Inc. 872
Merle Norman Cosmetics, Inc. 872
Merrill Corporation 872

1519

Merrill Lynch And Co. Inc. 873
Merrimack Pharmaceuticals Inc 873
Merriman Holdings Inc. 873
Meru Networks Inc. 873
Merz Pharmaceuticals Inc. 873
Mesa Air Group Inc 873
Mesa Laboratories, Inc. 874
Mesa Royalty Trust 874
Mesabi Trust 874
Mesirow Financial Holdings Inc. 874
Messer Construction Co. 874
Messiah College 874
Mestek Inc. 875
Meta Financial Group Inc 875
Metalico Inc 875
Methes Energies International Ltd. 875
Methode Electronics Inc 875
Methodist Hospital Of Southern California 875
Methodist Hospitals Of Dallas Inc 876
Methodist Le Bonheur Healthcare 876
Metlife Inc 876
Metro Bancorp Inc Pa 876
Metro Packaging & Imaging Inc 876
Metro-north Commuter Railroad Co Inc 876
Metroplex Adventist Hospital, Inc. 877
Metropolitan Airports Commission 877
Metropolitan Edison Company 877
Metropolitan Health Networks Inc. 877
Metropolitan Opera Association, Inc. 877
Metropolitan Security Services, Inc. 877
Metropolitan St. Louis Sewer District 878
Metropolitan State University Of Denver 878
Metropolitan Transit Authority Of Harris County 878
Metropolitan Transportation Authority 878
Metropolitan Utilities District 878
Mettler-toledo International, Inc. 878
Metwood Inc 879
Mexco Energy Corp. 879
Mexican American Opportunity Foundation 879
Mexican Restaurants, Inc. 879
Meyer & Wallis Inc. 879
Mfa Financial, Inc. 879
Mfa Incorporated 880
Mgc Diagnostics Corp 880
Mge Energy Inc 880
Mgic Investment Corp. (wi) 880
Mgm Resorts International 880
Mgt Capital Investments Inc 880
Miami Jewish Health Systems, Inc. 881
Miami University 881
Miami Valley Hospital 881
Michael Foods Group Inc. 881
Michels Corporation 881
Michigan Milk Producers Association 881
Michigan State University 882
Michigan Technological University 882
Micrel, Inc. 882
Micro Imaging Technology Inc. 882
Microbot Medical Inc 882
Microchip Technology Inc 882
Microfinancial, Inc. 883
Micron Solutions Inc (de) 883
Micron Technology Inc. 883
Micronetics Inc. 883
Micropac Industries, Inc. 883
Micros Systems, Inc. 883
Microsemi Corp 884
Microstrategy Inc. 884
Microtechnologies Llc 884
Microvision Inc. 884
Microwave Filter Co., Inc. 884
Microwave Transmission Systems, Inc 884
Micrus Endovascular Corporation 885
Mid America Clinical Laboratories Llc 885
Mid Penn Bancorp Inc 885
Mid-america Apartment Communities Inc 885
Mid-con Energy Partners Lp 885
Midamerican Energy Holdings Company 885
Midas Inc. 886
Midasplus Inc. 886
Midcoast Energy Partners, L.p. 886
Midcontinent Independent System Operator, Inc. 886
Middle Tennessee State University 886

Middleburg Financial Corp 886
Middleby Corp 887
Middlefield Banc Corp. 887
Middlesex Water Co. 887
Midland Financial Co. 887
Midland States Bancorp Inc 887
Midsouth Bancorp, Inc. 887
Midstate Medical Center 888
Midwest Energy, Inc. 888
Midwestone Financial Group, Inc. 888
Mikart Inc. 888
Milacron Llc 888
Milaeger"s Inc. 888
Miles Health Care, Inc 889
Milestone Scientific Inc. 889
Milford Regional Medical Center, Inc. 889
Milken Family Foundation 889
Millennial Media Inc 889
Millennium Prime Inc 889
Miller (herman) Inc 890
Miller Electric Company 890
Miller Electric Construction Inc 890
Miller Energy Resources, Inc. 890
Miller Industries Inc. (tn) 890
Miller Transportation Services, Inc. 890
Millercoors Llc 891
Mills-peninsula Health Services 891
Minden Bancorp Inc. 891
Mindwireless 891
Minerals Technologies, Inc. 891
Miners Incorporated 891
Mines Management, Inc. 892
Ministry Health Care Inc. 892
Minitab Inc. 892
Minn-dak Farmers Cooperative 892
Minnesota Vikings Football Club L.l.c. 892
Minnkota Power Cooperative, Inc. 892
Mintz Levin Cohn Ferris Glovsky And Popeo P.c. 893
Minuteman Press International Inc. 893
Miracle Software Systems Inc. 893
Miramax Film Corp. 893
Mirapoint Software Inc. 893
Mirati Therapeutics Inc 893
Mirenco Inc. 894
Misonix, Inc. 894
Mission Community Bancorp 894
Mission Hospital, Inc. 894
Mission Pharmacal Company 894
Mississippi County Electric Cooperative, Inc. 894
Mississippi Power Co 895
Mississippi State University 895
Missouri Higher Education Loan Authority 895
Missouri State University 895
Mistras Group Inc 895
Mitcham Industries Inc 895
Mitchell Silberberg & Knupp Llp 896
Mitek Systems, Inc. 896
Mks Instruments Inc 896
Mktg, Inc. 896
Mma Capital Holdings Inc 896
Mmodal Inc. 896
Mmr Group, Inc. 897
Mmrglobal Inc 897
Mnp Corporation 897
Mobile Area Networks Inc 897
Mobile Mini, Inc. 897
Mobitv Inc. 897
Mocon Inc. 898
Model N, Inc 898
Modern Woodmen Of America 898
Modesto Irrigation District (inc) 898
Modine Manufacturing Co 898
Modsys International Ltd 898
Mohawk Industries, Inc. 899
Mohegan Tribal Gaming Authority 899
Molecular Templates Inc 899
Molina Healthcare Inc 899
Moller International Inc. 899
Molloy College 899
Molson Coors Brewing Company 900
Molycorp Inc. (de) 900
Momenta Pharmaceuticals Inc 900
Momentive Performance Materials Inc. 900
Monarch Casino & Resort, Inc. 900

Monarch Cement Co. 900
Monarch Community Bancorp Inc 901
Monarch Financial Holdings Inc 901
Mondelez International Inc 901
Moneygram International Inc 901
Monmouth Medical Center Inc. 901
Monmouth Real Estate Investment Corp 901
Monmouth University Inc 902
Monogram Food Solutions, Llc 902
Monolithic Power Systems Inc 902
Monongahela Power Company 902
Monotype Imaging Holdings Inc 902
Monro Inc 902
Monsanto Co 903
Monster Worldwide Inc 903
Montage Resource Corp 903
Montana State University, Inc 903
Montclair State University 903
Montefiore Medical Center 903
Monumental Sports & Entertainment 904
Moody's Corp. 904
Moog Inc 904
Moorefield Construction, Inc. 904
Moravian College 904
Moredirect Inc. 904
Morehead Memorial Hospital Inc 905
Morehouse College (inc.) 905
Morgan Lewis & Bockius Llp 905
Morgan Properties Trust 905
Morgan Stanley 905
Morgan Stanley Smith Barney Llc 905
Morgan's Foods, Inc. 906
Morgans Hotel Group Co 906
Morningstar Inc 906
Moro Corp. 906
Moroso Performance Products Inc. 906
Morris Business Development Co 906
Morris Hospital 907
Morris Publishing Group Llc 907
Morrow-meadows Corporation 907
Morse Operations, Inc. 907
Morton's Restaurant Group Inc. 907
Mosaic 907
Mosaic Co (the) 908
Mosaic Life Care 908
Mosys Inc 908
Mother Murphy's Laboratories, Inc. 908
Motion Industries Inc. 908
Motorcar Parts Of America Inc 908
Motorola Mobility Holdings Inc. 909
Motorola Solutions Inc 909
Motorsports Authentics Llc 909
Mount Carmel Health System 909
Mount Clemens Regional Medical Center 909
Mount Sinai Medical Center Of Florida, Inc. 909
Mountain Valley Spring Company Llc 910
Mountaire Corporation 910
Movado Group, Inc. 910
Move Inc 910
Mozilla Foundation 910
Mphase Technologies Inc. 910
Mplx Lp 911
Mpw Industrial Services Group Inc. 911
Mrc Global Inc 911
Mri Interventions Inc 911
Mriglobal 911
Mrv Communications, Inc. 911
Msb Financial Corp 912
Msc Industrial Direct Co Inc 912
Msci Inc 912
Msg Network Inc 912
Msgi Technology Solutions Inc. 912
Mtge Investment Corp 912
Mtm Technologies, Inc. 913
Mtr Gaming Group, Inc. 913
Mts Systems Corp 913
Mueller (paul) Co 913
Mueller Industries Inc 913
Mueller Water Products Inc 913
Mulesoft, Inc. 914
Multi-color Corp. 914
Multi-fineline Electronix Inc 914
Multicare Health System 914
Multicell Technologies Inc 914

COMPANIES LISTED ALPHABETICALLY

Multimedia Games Holding Company, Inc. 914
Municipal Electric Authority Of Georgia 915
Munroe Regional Medical Center, Inc. 915
Munson Healthcare 915
Murphy Company Mechanical Contractors And Engineers 915
Murphy Oil Corp 915
Murphy Oil Usa Inc. 915
Murphy Usa Inc 916
Murphy-brown Llc 916
Muscular Dystrophy Association, Inc. 916
Museum Of Fine Arts 916
Mustang Fuel Corporation 916
Mutual Of America Life Insurance Company 916
Mutual Of Enumclaw Insurance Company 917
Mutual Of Omaha Insurance Co. (ne) 917
Mutualfirst Financial Inc 917
Mv Oil Trust 917
Mv Transportation, Inc. 917
Mvp Health Plan, Inc. 917
Mwh Global, Inc. 918
Mwi Veterinary Supply Inc 918
Myers Industries Inc. 918
Myr Group Inc 918
Myrexis Inc. 918
Myriad Genetics, Inc. 918
N-viro International Corp 919
Nacco Industries Inc 919
Nalco Holding Company 919
Nan Ya Plastics Corporation U.s.a. 919
Nanophase Technologies Corp. 919
Nanosphere Inc 919
Nanostring Technologies Inc 920
Napco Security Technologies, Inc. 920
Narus Inc. 920
Nasb Financial Inc 920
Nasdaq Inc 920
Nassau Health Care Corporation 920
Nathan's Famous, Inc. 921
National Academy Of Recording Arts & Sciences Inc 921
National Alliance To End Homelessness Inc. 921
National American University Holdings Inc. 921
National Association Of Broadcasters 921
National Audubon Society, Inc. 921
National Automobile Dealers Association 922
National Bancshares Corp. (ohio) 922
National Bank Holdings Corp 922
National Bankshares Inc. (va) 922
National Beverage Corp. 922
National Cable Satellite Corp 922
National Cinemedia Inc 923
National Collegiate Athletic Association 923
National Council Of Young Men's Christian Associations Of The United States Of America 923
National Education Association Of The United States 923
National Football League Players Association 923
National Frozen Foods Corporation 923
National Fuel Gas Co. (nj) 924
National Gallery Of Art 924
National Grape Co-operative Association, Inc. 924
National Head Start Association 924
National Health Investors, Inc. 924
National Healthcare Corp. 924
National Heritage Academies Inc. 925
National Holdings Corp 925
National Instruments Corp. 925
National Interstate Corp 925
National Life Insurance Company 925
National Multiple Sclerosis Society 925
National Park Foundation (inc) 926
National Penn Bancshares Inc. 926
National Presto Industries, Inc. 926
National Public Radio, Inc. 926
National Railroad Passenger Corporation 926
National Research Corp 926
National Restaurants Management Inc. 927
National Retail Federation, Inc. 927
National Retail Properties Inc 927
National Rifle Association Of America 927
National Rural Electric Cooperative Association 927
National Rural Utilities Cooperative Finance Corp 927

National Safety Council 928
National Security Group, Inc 928
National Trust For Historic Preservation In The United St 928
National University 928
National Van Lines, Inc. 928
National Western Life Insurance Co. (austin, Tx) 928
National Wildlife Federation Inc 929
Nationstar Mortgage Holdings Inc 929
Nationstar Mortgage Holdings Inc. 929
Nationwide Children's Hospital 929
Nationwide Mutual Insurance Company 929
Native Environmental L.l.c. 929
Natural Alternatives International, Inc. 930
Natural Gas Services Group Inc 930
Natural Grocers By Vitamin Cottage Inc 930
Natural Resource Partners Lp 930
Natural Resources Defense Council Inc. 930
Nature's Sunshine Products, Inc. 930
Natus Medical Inc. 931
Naugatuck Valley Financial Corporation 931
Nautica Apparel Inc. 931
Nautilus Inc 931
Navarro Research And Engineering Inc. 931
Navidea Biopharmaceuticals Inc 931
Navient Corp 932
Navigant Consulting, Inc. 932
Navigators Group Inc (the) 932
Navisite Inc. 932
Navy Federal Credit Union 932
Nb&t Financial Group, Inc. 932
Nbcuniversal Media Llc 933
Nbhx Trim Usa Corporation 933
Nbl Permian Llc 933
Nbt Bancorp. Inc. 933
Nbty Inc. 933
Nch Corporation 933
Nch Healthcare System Inc. 934
Nci Inc 934
Ncs Technologies, Inc. 934
Neace Lukens Inc. 934
Nebraska Book Company Inc. 934
Nebraska Public Power District 934
Neenah Inc 935
Neffs Bancorp Inc. 935
Neighborhood Reinvestment Corporation 935
Nektar Therapeutics 935
Nelnet Inc 935
Nemours Foundation 935
Neogen Corp 936
Neogenomics Inc 936
Neomagic Corporation 936
Neomedia Technologies, Inc. 936
Neophotonics Corp 936
Nephros Inc 936
Nes Rentals Holdings, Inc. 937
Nestle Waters North America Inc. 937
Net Medical Xpress Solutions Inc 937
Netezza Corporation 937
Netflix Inc 937
Netgear Inc 937
Netiq Corporation 938
Netlist Inc 938
Netscout Systems Inc 938
Netsol Technologies Inc 938
Netsuite Inc 938
Network Engines Inc. 938
Network Management Resources Inc. 939
Networkfleet Inc. 939
Neumann Systems Group Inc. 939
Neurocrine Biosciences, Inc. 939
Neurometrix Inc 939
Neustar, Inc. 939
Neutron Energy Inc. 940
Nevada Gold & Casinos, Inc. 940
Nevada Power Co. 940
Nevada State Bank 940
Nevada System Of Higher Education 940
New Braunfels Utilities 940
New Bridge Medical Center 941
New Cam Commerce Solutions Llc 941
New Concept Energy, Inc. 941
New England Realty Associates L.p. 941
New Hampshire Electric Cooperative Inc 941

New Hampshire Thrift Bancshares, Inc. 941
New Hanover Regional Medical Center 942
New Jersey Housing And Mortgage Finance Agency 942
New Jersey Institute Of Technology 942
New Jersey Mining Co. 942
New Jersey Natural Gas Company 942
New Jersey Resources Corp 942
New Jersey Turnpike Authority Inc 943
New Mexico State University 943
New Milford Hospital Inc. 943
New Mountain Finance Corp 943
New Prime, Inc. 943
New Source Energy Corporation 943
New Source Energy Partners Lp 944
New Tangram, Llc 944
New York Blood Center, Inc. 944
New York City Health And Hospitals Corporation 944
New York City Transit Authority 944
New York City Transitional Finance Authority 944
New York Community Bancorp Inc. 945
New York Convention Center Operating Corporation 945
New York Football Giants Inc. 945
New York Jets Llc 945
New York Life Insurance Company 945
New York Medical College 945
New York Mortgage Trust Inc 946
New York Power Authority 946
New York Public Radio 946
New York State Catholic Health Plan, Inc. 946
New York State Lottery 946
New York State Teachers' Retirement System 946
New York Times Co. 947
New York University 947
New York Yankees Partnership 947
Newark Beth Israel Medical Center Inc. 947
Newark Corporation 947
Neways Inc. 947
Newbridge Bancorp 948
Newegg Inc. 948
Newell Brands Inc 948
Newesco Inc. 948
Newfield Exploration Co 948
Newgistics Inc. 948
Newlink Genetics Corp 949
Newly Weds Foods Inc. 949
Newmark & Company Real Estate, Inc. 949
Newmarket Corp 949
Newmarket Technology Inc. 949
Newmont Corp 949
Newpage Group Inc. 950
Newpark Resources, Inc. 950
Newport Corporation 950
News America Marketing Fsi Llc 950
News Corp (new) 950
Newsmax Media, Inc. 950
Newstar Financial Inc 951
Newtek Business Services Corp 951
Newton Memorial Hospital Inc 951
Newton Wellesley Hospital Corp 951
Newyork-presbyterian/brooklyn Methodist 951
Newyork-presbyterian/queens 951
Nexsan Corporation 952
Nexstar Media Group Inc 952
Nextec Group 952
Nextera Energy Inc 952
Nextgen Healthcare Inc 952
Nfinanse Inc. 952
Nfp Corp. 953
Ngas Resources Inc. 953
Ngl Energy Partners Lp 953
Nhl Enterprises, Inc. 953
Nhs Human Services, Inc. 953
Nic Inc. 953
Nice-pak Products Inc. 954
Nicholas Financial Inc (bc) 954
Nicolon Corporation 954
Nii Holdings Inc. 954
Nimble Storage, Inc. 954
Nintendo Of America Inc. 954
Ninyo & Moore Geotechnical & Environmental Sciences Consultants 955
Nisource Inc. (holding Co.) 955

Nixon Peabody Llp 955
Nl Industries, Inc. 955
Nmi Health Inc 955
Nmi Holdings Inc 955
Nn, Inc 956
Nobel Learning Communities Inc. 956
Nobility Homes, Inc. 956
Noble Energy Inc 956
Noble Roman's, Inc. 956
Noblis, Inc. 956
Nocopi Technologies, Inc. 957
Non-invasive Monitoring Systems Inc. 957
Nonpareil Corporation 957
Noodles & Co 957
Noranda Aluminum Holding Corp 957
Nordstrom, Inc. 957
Norfolk Southern Corp 958
Norfolk State University 958
Norkus Enterprises, Inc. 958
Norman Regional Hospital Authority 958
Nortech Systems Inc. 958
Nortek Inc 958
North American Electric Reliability Corporation 959
North American Lighting, Inc. 959
North Broward Hospital District 959
North Carolina Electric Membership Corporation 959
North Central Bancshares Inc. 959
North Central Farmers Elevator 959
North Dakota Mill & Elevator Association 960
North Dakota State University 960
North European Oil Royalty Trust 960
North Florida Regional Medical Center, Inc. 960
North Memorial Health Care 960
North Mississippi Health Services, Inc. 960
North Mississippi Medical Center, Inc. 961
North Pacific Paper Company, Llc 961
North Park University 961
North Shore Medical Center, Inc. 961
North Shore University Hospital 961
North Valley Bancorp (redding, Ca) 961
North Wind Inc. 962
Northeast Bank (me) 962
Northeast Community Bancorp Inc 962
Northeast Georgia Health System, Inc. 962
Northeast Health Systems Inc. 962
Northeast Indiana Bancorp Inc 962
Northeastern Supply, Inc. 963
Northeastern University 963
Northern Arizona Healthcare Corporation 963
Northern Arizona University 963
Northern Indiana Public Service Company 963
Northern Inyo Healthcare District 963
Northern Natural Gas Company 964
Northern Oil & Gas Inc (mn) 964
Northern States Financial Corp. (waukegan, Il) 964
Northern Technologies International Corp. 964
Northern Tier Energy Inc. 964
Northern Tier Energy Lp 964
Northern Tier Energy Lp 965
Northern Trust Corp 965
Northern Utah Healthcare Corporation 965
Northern Virginia Electric Cooperative 965
Northfield Bancorp Inc. 965
Northrim Banccorp Inc 965
Northrop Grumman Corp 966
Northshore University Healthsystem 966
Northside Hospital 966
Northside Hospital, Inc. 966
Northstar Aerospace Inc. 966
Northstar Realty Finance Corp 966
Northway Financial, Inc. 967
Northwest Bancorporation Inc 967
Northwest Bancshares Inc. 967
Northwest Biotherapeutics Inc 967
Northwest Community Hospital Inc 967
Northwest Dairy Association 967
Northwest Farm Credit Services 968
Northwest Indiana Bancorp 968
Northwest Natural Holding Co 968
Northwest Pipe Co. 968
Northwest Texas Healthcare System, Inc. 968
Northwestern Corp. 968
Northwestern Lake Forest Hospital 969

Northwestern Memorial Healthcare 969
Northwestern University 969
Norton Community Hospital Auxiliary Inc. 969
Nortonlifelock Inc 969
Norwegian Cruise Line Holdings Ltd. 969
Norwich University 970
Norwood Financial Corp. 970
Notify Technology Corporation 970
Nova Southeastern University, Inc. 970
Novabay Pharmaceuticals Inc 970
Novant Health, Inc. 970
Novanta Inc 971
Novation Companies Inc 971
Novavax, Inc. 971
Novelis Inc. 971
Npc International Inc. 971
Npc Restaurant Holdings, Llc 971
Nps Pharmaceuticals Inc. 972
Nrg Energy Inc 972
Nstar Electric Co 972
Ntelos Holdings Corp 972
Ntn Buzztime Inc 972
Nts Inc 972
Nts Realty Holdings Ltd Partnership 973
Nu Horizons Electronics Corp. 973
Nu Skin Enterprises, Inc. 973
Nuance Communications Inc 973
Nuco2 Inc. 973
Nucor Corp. 973
Nuo Therapeutics Inc 974
Nustar Energy Lp 974
Nustar Gp Holdings Llc 974
Nutra Pharma Corp 974
Nutraceutical International Corp. 974
Nutrisystem Inc 974
Nutrition 21 Llc 975
Nutrition Management Services Company 975
Nutroganics Inc 975
Nuvasive Inc 975
Nuveen Investments Inc. 975
Nuvera Communications Inc 975
Nuvilex Inc. 976
Nv5 Global Inc 976
Nve Corp 976
Nvidia Corp 976
Nvr Inc. 976
Nxstage Medical Inc 976
Nyack Hospital Foundation, Inc. 977
Nypro Inc. 977
O P I Products Inc. 977
O'brien & Gere Limited 977
O'charley's Inc. 977
O'melveny & Myers Llp 977
O'neil Industries, Inc. 978
O'reilly Automotive, Inc. 978
O-i Glass Inc 978
O. C. Tanner Company 978
O.f. Mossberg & Sons Inc. 978
Oak Valley Bancorp 978
Oak Valley Bancorp (oakdale, Ca) 979
Oakland University 979
Oakridge Energy Inc. 979
Oakridge Global Energy Solutions Inc 979
Oakridge Holdings Inc 979
Oaktree Capital Group Llc 979
Oaktree Specialty Lending Corp 980
Oakwood Healthcare Inc. 980
Oasis Petroleum Inc. 980
Oba Financial Services Inc 980
Oberlin College 980
Ocata Therapeutics Inc 980
Occidental College 981
Occidental Petroleum Corp 981
Ocean Beauty Seafoods Llc 981
Ocean Bio-chem, Inc. 981
Ocean Duke Corporation 981
Ocean Power Technologies Inc 981
Ocean Shore Holding Co 982
Ocean Spray Cranberries, Inc. 982
Oceaneering International, Inc. 982
Oceanfirst Financial Corp 982
Ocera Therapeutics Inc 982
Oci Partners Lp 982
Oclaro Inc 983

Oclc, Inc. 983
Oconee Regional Health Systems, Inc. 983
Ocwen Financial Corporation 983
Ocz Technology Group Inc 983
Odom Corporation 983
Odyssey Marine Exploration, Inc. 984
Oec Business Interiors Inc. 984
Office Depot, Inc. 984
Office Properties Income Trust 984
Official Payments Holdings Inc. 984
Oge Energy Corp. 984
Oglethorpe Power Corp 985
Ohio Edison Company 985
Ohio Legacy Corp 985
Ohio Living 985
Ohio Power Company 985
Ohio Turnpike And Infrastructure Commission 985
Ohio Valley Banc Corp 986
Ohio Valley Electric Corporation 986
Ohio Valley General Hospital 986
Ohio Valley Medical Center Incorporated 986
Ohiohealth Corporation 986
Oil States International, Inc. 986
Oil-dri Corp. Of America 987
Oiltanking Partners Lp 987
Okeechobee Hospital, Inc. 987
Oklahoma State University 987
Old Dominion Electric Cooperative 987
Old Dominion Freight Line, Inc. 987
Old Line Bancshares Inc 988
Old National Bancorp (evansville, In) 988
Old Navy Inc. 988
Old Point Financial Corp 988
Old Republic International Corp. 988
Old Second Bancorp., Inc. (aurora, Ill.) 988
Old Time Pottery Inc. 989
Oldcastle Inc. 989
Ole' Mexican Foods, Inc. 989
Olin Corp. 989
Olmsted Medical Center 989
Olympic Pipe Line Company 989
Olympic Steel Inc. 990
Om Group, Inc. 990
Omagine Inc. 990
Omaha Public Power District 990
Omega Flex Inc 990
Omega Healthcare Investors, Inc. 990
Omega Protein Corp. 991
Omeros Corp 991
Omni Cable Corporation 991
Omniamerican Bancorp, Inc. 991
Omnicare Inc. 991
Omnicell Inc 991
Omnicom Group, Inc. 992
Omnicomm Systems Inc 992
Omnivision Technologies Inc 992
Omnova Solutions Inc 992
On Semiconductor Corp 992
On-site Fuel Service, Inc. 992
Oncologix Tech Inc 993
Oncomed Pharmaceuticals Inc. 993
Onconova Therapeutics Inc 993
Oncor Electric Delivery Co Llc 993
Oncothyreon Inc. 993
One Gas, Inc. 993
One Liberty Properties, Inc. 994
One Stop Systems Inc. 994
Onebeacon Insurance Group Ltd. 994
Oneida Ltd. 994
Onemain Holdings Inc 994
Oneok Inc 994
Oneok Partners, L.p. 995
Onespan Inc 995
Online Vacation Center Holdings Corp 995
Onstream Media Corp 995
Onto Innovation Inc 995
Onvia Inc 995
Op-tech Environmental Services Inc. 996
Open Solutions Inc. 996
Openlink Financial Llc 996
Opentable Inc. 996
Operating Engineers Funds Inc. 996
Operation Smile, Inc. 996
Opko Health Inc 997

Oplink Communications Inc. 997
Opnext Inc. 997
Oppenheimer Holdings Inc 997
Optical Cable Corp. 997
Optimumbank Holdings Inc 997
Option Care Health Inc 998
Optionsxpress Holdings Inc. 998
Optumrx Inc. 998
Oragenics Inc 998
Orange And Rockland Utilities Inc 998
Orange County Transportation Authority 998
Orasure Technologies Inc. 999
Orbcomm Inc 999
Orbit International Corp. 999
Orbit/fr, Inc. 999
Orbital Atk Inc 999
Orbital Sciences Corp. 999
Orbitz Worldwide Inc 1000
Orca Bay Seafoods, Inc. 1000
Orchid Cellmark Inc. 1000
Orchid Island Capital, Inc. 1000
Orchids Paper Products Co. (de) 1000
Oregon Health & Science University 1000
Oregon State Lottery 1001
Oregon State University 1001
Orexigen Therapeutics Inc 1001
Organically Grown Company 1001
Orion Energy Systems Inc 1001
Orion Group Holdings Inc 1001
Orlando Health, Inc. 1002
Orlando Utilities Commission 1002
Ormat Technologies Inc 1002
Orrstown Financial Services, Inc. 1002
Ortholgic Corp. 1002
Osage Bancshares Inc. 1002
Osborn & Barr Communications Inc. 1003
Osc Sports, Inc. 1003
Oscar De La Renta, Llc 1003
Osf Healthcare System 1003
Osi Group Llc 1003
Osi Systems, Inc. (de) 1003
Osiris Therapeutics Inc 1004
Otelco Inc 1004
Otsuka America Inc 1004
Otter Products, Llc 1004
Otter Tail Corp. 1004
Our Lady Of Lourdes Medical Center, Inc 1004
Our Lady Of Lourdes Regional Medical Center, Inc. 1005
Our Lady Of The Lake Hospital, Inc. 1005
Our Lady Of The Lake University Of San Antonio 1005
Ourpet's Company 1005
Outerwall Inc 1005
Overlake Hospital Medical Center 1005
Overland Contracting Inc. 1006
Overland Storage, Inc. 1006
Overseas Shipholding Group Inc (new) 1006
Overstock.com Inc (de) 1006
Owens & Minor, Inc. 1006
Owens Corning 1006
Owensboro Municipal Utilities Electric Light & Power System 1007
Oxbow Corporation 1007
Oxford Global Resources Inc. 1007
Oxford Industries, Inc. 1007
Oxford University Press Inc. 1007
Oxigene, Inc. 1007
Oxis International Inc. 1008
Ozarks Electric Cooperative Corporation 1008
P & F Industries, Inc. 1008
P&g-clairol Inc. 1008
P.a.m. Transportation Services, Inc. 1008
P.f. Chang's China Bistro Inc. 1008
P10 Holdings Inc 1009
Pabst Brewing Company 1009
Paccar Inc. 1009
Pace University 1009
Pacer International Inc 1009
Pacific Biosciences Of California Inc 1009
Pacific Building Group 1010
Pacific Coast Producers 1010
Pacific Continental Corp 1010
Pacific Dental Services Inc. 1010

Pacific Ethanol Inc 1010
Pacific Financial Corp. 1010
Pacific Hide & Fur Depot 1011
Pacific Mercantile Bancorp 1011
Pacific Mutual Holding Co. 1011
Pacific National Group 1011
Pacific Northwest National Laboratory 1011
Pacific Office Properties Trust Inc 1011
Pacific Sands Inc 1012
Pacific Sunwear Of California, Inc. 1012
Pacific Theatres Corporation 1012
Pacific Webworks, Inc. 1012
Pacifichealth Laboratories Inc. 1012
Pacificorp 1012
Pacira Biosciences Inc 1013
Packaging Corp Of America 1013
Pacwest Bancorp 1013
Paetec Holding Corp. 1013
Page Southerland Page L.l.p. 1013
Paid Inc 1013
Pain Therapeutics Inc 1014
Palatin Technologies Inc 1014
Pall Corp. 1014
Palladium Equity Partners Llc 1014
Palmetto Bancshares, Inc. (sc) 1014
Palmetto Health 1014
Palms West Hospital Limited Partnership 1015
Palo Alto Medical Foundation For Health Care Research And Educat 1015
Palo Alto Networks, Inc 1015
Palomar Health 1015
Pamida Stores Operating Company Llc 1015
Panavision Inc. 1015
Pandora Media Inc 1016
Panduit Corp. 1016
Panera Bread Co 1016
Panhandle Eastern Pipe Line Company, Lp 1016
Panhandle Oil & Gas Inc 1016
Pantry Inc. (the) 1016
Papa John's International, Inc. 1017
Paper Converting Machine Company 1017
Paperworks Industries Inc. 1017
Par Pacific Holdings Inc 1017
Par Pharmaceutical Companies Inc. 1017
Par Technology Corp. 1017
Paradigm Holdings Inc. 1018
Paradise Valley Hospital 1018
Paradise, Inc. 1018
Paragon Development Systems, Inc. 1018
Paragon Real Estate Equity & Investment Trust 1018
Paragon Technologies Inc 1018
Paramount Gold & Silver Corp 1019
Paratek Pharmaceuticals Inc 1019
Paratek Pharmaceuticals Inc. 1019
Parature Inc. 1019
Parexel International Corporation 1019
Park Aerospace Corp 1019
Park Bancorp, Inc. 1020
Park City Group Inc 1020
Park National Corp (newark, Oh) 1020
Park Nicollet Health Services 1020
Park Nicollet Methodist Hospital 1020
Park Sterling Corp 1020
Park-ohio Holdings Corp. 1021
Parkdale Mills Incorporated 1021
Parke Bancorp Inc 1021
Parker Drilling Co 1021
Parker Hannifin Corp 1021
Parkervision Inc 1021
Parkridge Medical Center, Inc. 1022
Parkway Properties Inc. 1022
Parkwest Medical Center 1022
Parlux Fragrances Llc 1022
Parma Community General Hospital 1022
Parron-hall Corporation 1022
Parsons Environment & Infrastructure Group Inc. 1023
Partners Healthcare System, Inc. 1023
Pasadena Area Community College District 1023
Pasadena Hospital Association, Ltd. 1023
Passur Aerospace, Inc. 1023
Patapsco Bancorp Inc. 1023
Patelco Credit Union 1024
Patheon Inc. 1024

Pathfinder Bancorp, Inc. 1024
Pathfinder Cell Therapy Inc. 1024
Pathfinder International 1024
Pathmark Stores Inc. 1024
Patient Safety Technologies Inc. 1025
Patrick Cudahy Incorporated 1025
Patrick Industries Inc 1025
Patriot Coal Corp 1025
Patriot National Bancorp Inc 1025
Patriot Scientific Corporation 1025
Pattern Energy Group Inc 1026
Patterson Companies Inc 1026
Patterson-uti Energy Inc. 1026
Paul Hastings Janofsky & Walker Llp 1026
Pavilion Energy Resources Inc. 1026
Paxton Media Group, Llc 1026
Paybox Corp 1027
Paychex Inc 1027
Payment Alliance International Inc. 1027
Paypal Inc. 1027
Pbf Energy Inc 1027
Pbf Energy Inc. 1027
Pc Connection, Inc. 1028
Pc Group Inc. 1028
Pc-tel Inc 1028
Pcl Construction Enterprises, Inc. 1028
Pcm, Inc 1028
Pcre L.l.c 1028
Pcs Edventures! Inc 1029
Pdc Energy Inc 1029
Pdf Solutions Inc. 1029
Pdl Biopharma Inc 1029
Pds Tech, Inc. 1029
Peabody Energy Corp (new) 1029
Peacehealth 1030
Peak Resorts Inc 1030
Peapack-gladstone Financial Corp. 1030
Pebblebrook Hotel Trust 1030
Pedernales Electric Cooperative, Inc. 1030
Pedevco Corp 1030
Pediatric Services Of America Inc. 1031
Peerless Systems Corp. 1031
Peet's Coffee & Tea Inc. 1031
Pegasystems Inc 1031
Pen Inc 1031
Pendrell Corp 1031
Penford Corp. 1032
Penguin Computing, Inc. 1032
Penn National Gaming Inc 1032
Penn Virginia Corp (new) 1032
Pennantpark Investment Corporation 1032
Penney (j.c.) Co.,inc. (holding Co.) 1032
Pennichuck Corporation 1033
Pennoni Associates Inc. 1033
Penns Woods Bancorp, Inc. (jersey Shore, Pa) 1033
Pennsylvania - American Water Company 1033
Pennsylvania Electric Company 1033
Pennsylvania Higher Education Assistance Agency 1033
Pennsylvania Housing Finance Agency 1034
Pennsylvania Power Company Inc 1034
Pennsylvania Real Estate Investment Trust 1034
Pennymac Financial Services Inc (new) 1034
Pennymac Mortgage Investment Trust 1034
Pension Benefit Guaranty Corporation 1034
Penske Automotive Group Inc 1035
Pentagon Federal Credit Union 1035
Pentair Ltd. 1035
People For The Ethical Treatment Of Animals, Inc. 1035
People's United Financial Inc 1035
Peoples Bancorp Inc (auburn, In) 1035
Peoples Bancorp Inc (marietta, Oh) 1036
Peoples Bancorp Of North Carolina Inc 1036
Peoples Bancorp, Inc. (md) 1036
Peoples Educational Holdings, Inc. 1036
Peoples Federal Bancshares, Inc. 1036
Peoples Financial Corp (biloxi, Ms) 1036
Peoples Financial Services Corp 1037
Peoples-sidney Financial Corp. 1037
Pep Boys-manny, Moe & Jack 1037
Pepco Holdings Inc. 1037
Pepper Construction Group, Llc 1037
Pepperdine University 1037

Pepsi-cola Bottling Co Of Central Virginia 1038
Pepsico Inc 1038
Perceptron, Inc. 1038
Perdoceo Education Corp 1038
Peregrine Semiconductor Corporation 1038
Perez Trading Company, Inc. 1038
Perfection Bakeries Inc. 1039
Perficient Inc 1039
Performance Food Group Inc. 1039
Performance Technologies, Inc. 1039
Performant Financial Corp 1039
Perfumania Holdings Inc 1039
Pericom Semiconductor Corp. 1040
Perkinelmer, Inc. 1040
Perkins Coie Llp 1040
Perma-fix Environmental Services, Inc. 1040
Perma-pipe International Holdings Inc 1040
Permian Basin Royalty Trust 1040
Pernix Group Inc 1041
Perseon Corp 1041
Persian Arts Society Incorporated 1041
Pervasip Corp 1041
Pet Supermarket Inc. 1041
Petco Animal Supplies Inc. 1041
Peter Kiewit Sons', Inc. 1042
Peter Pan Bus Lines Inc. 1042
Petmed Express Inc 1042
Petro Holdings Inc. 1042
Petro Star Inc. 1042
Petrocelli Electric Co. 1042
Petrohawk Energy Corporation 1043
Petroleum Marketers Incorporated 1043
Petroleum Traders Corporation 1043
Petrologistics Lp 1043
Petroquest Energy Inc (new) 1043
Petsmart, Inc. 1043
Pfizer Inc 1044
Pfsweb Inc 1044
Pg&e Corp (holding Co) 1044
Pga Tour, Inc. 1044
Pgt Innovations Inc 1044
Ph Glatfelter Co 1044
Pharmaceutical Product Development Inc. 1045
Pharmacyclics, Inc. 1045
Pharmerica Corp 1045
Pharmos Corporation 1045
Phelps Dunbar L.l.p. 1045
Phelps Memorial Hospital Association 1045
Phh Corp 1046
Phi Group Inc. 1046
Phi Inc 1046
Phibro Animal Health Corporation 1046
Philadelphia Consolidated Holding Corp. 1046
Philadelphia North Health System 1046
Philadelphia Workforce Development Corporation 1047
Philip Morris International Inc 1047
Philips Electronics North America Corporation 1047
Phillips 66 1047
Phillips 66 Company 1047
Phillips 66 Partners Lp 1047
Phillips And Jordan, Incorporated 1048
Phillips-medisize Corporation 1048
Phoebe Putney Memorial Hospital, Inc. 1048
Phoenix Children's Hospital, Inc. 1048
Phoenix Companies, Inc. (the) 1048
Phoenix Footwear Group, Inc. 1048
Phoenix Technologies Ltd. 1049
Photronics, Inc. 1049
Physicians Formula Holdings Inc. 1049
Physicians Realty Trust 1049
Pico Holdings Inc. 1049
Piedmont Athens Regional Medical Center, Inc. 1049
Piedmont Hospital, Inc. 1050
Piedmont Municipal Power Agency 1050
Piedmont Natural Gas Co Inc 1050
Piedmont Natural Gas Co., Inc. 1050
Piedmont Office Realty Trust Inc 1050
Pier 1 Imports Inc. 1050
Pierce Manufacturing Inc. 1051
Pike Corp 1051
Pikeville Medical Center, Inc. 1051
Pilgrims Pride Corp. 1051
Pilkington North America, Inc. 1051

Pilot Corporation 1051
Pine Grove Manufactured Homes Inc. 1052
Piney Woods Healthcare System, L.p. 1052
Pinnacle Bancshares, Inc. 1052
Pinnacle Bankshares Corp 1052
Pinnacle Data Systems Inc. 1052
Pinnacle Entertainment Inc 1052
Pinnacle Financial Partners Inc 1053
Pinnacle Foods Finance Llc 1053
Pinnacle Foods Inc. 1053
Pinnacle Frames And Accents Inc. 1053
Pinnacle Health System 1053
Pinnacle West Capital Corp 1053
Pioneer Bankshares Inc 1054
Pioneer Energy Services Corp 1054
Pioneer Natural Resources Co 1054
Pioneer Railcorp 1054
Piper Sandler Companies 1054
Pismo Coast Village, Inc. 1054
Piston Automotive L.l.c. 1055
Pitney Bowes Inc 1055
Pitt County Memorial Hospital, Incorporated 1055
Pitt-ohio Express, Llc 1055
Pixelworks Inc 1055
Pjm Interconnection, L.l.c. 1055
Placid Refining Company Llc 1056
Plains All American Pipeline Lp 1056
Plains Cotton Cooperative Association 1056
Planar Systems Inc. 1056
Planet Payment, Inc. 1056
Plangraphics Inc. 1056
Planned Parenthood Federation Of America, Inc. 1057
Plantation Pipe Line Company 1057
Plante & Moran Pllc 1057
Plantronics, Inc. 1057
Planview Inc. 1057
Plastipak Packaging Inc. 1057
Platinum Energy Solutions Inc. 1058
Platte River Power Authority (inc) 1058
Players Network (the) 1058
Plexus Corp. 1058
Plug Power Inc 1058
Plum Creek Timber Co., Inc. 1058
Plumas Bancorp Inc 1059
Plumb Supply Company 1059
Plus Therapeutics Inc 1059
Plx Technology Inc 1059
Ply Gem Holdings, Inc. 1059
Pmc-sierra Inc. 1059
Pmfg, Inc. 1060
Pnm Resources Inc 1060
Poage Bankshares Inc 1060
Pocono Health System 1060
Point Loma Nazarene University 1060
Point.360 (new) 1060
Pokertek Inc 1061
Polaris Inc 1061
Polarityte Inc 1061
Polycom Inc. 1061
Polymer Group Inc. 1061
Polyone Corp. 1061
Polypore International Inc 1062
Polyvision Corporation 1062
Pomona College 1062
Pomp's Tire Service, Inc. 1062
Pool Corp 1062
Pope Resources Lp 1062
Popeyes Louisiana Kitchen, Inc. 1063
Poplar Bluff Regional Medical Center, Inc. 1063
Popular Inc. 1063
Population Services International 1063
Port Of Corpus Christi Authority Of Nueces County, Texas 1063
Port Of Houston Authority 1063
Port Of New Orleans 1064
Port Of Seattle 1064
Portage Inc. 1064
Portion Pac Inc. 1064
Portland General Electric Co. 1064
Portland State University 1064
Portola Pharmaceuticals, Inc. 1065
Portsmouth Square, Inc. 1065
Positiveid Corp 1065

Positron Corp 1065
Positron Corp. 1065
Post Holdings Inc 1065
Post Properties, Inc. 1066
Postrock Energy Corp 1066
Potbelly Corp 1066
Potlatchdeltic Corp 1066
Potomac Bancshares, Inc. 1066
Potomac Hospital Corporation Of Prince William 1066
Poudre Valley Health Care, Inc. 1067
Powell Electronics Inc. 1067
Powell Industries, Inc. 1067
Powell's Books Inc. 1067
Power Construction Company Llc 1067
Power Integrations Inc. 1067
Powerfleet Inc 1068
Powersecure International, Inc. 1068
Powersouth Energy Cooperative 1068
Powertech Uranium Corp. 1068
Powerverde Inc 1068
Ppg Industries Inc 1068
Ppl Corp 1069
Ppl Electric Utilities Corp 1069
Pra Group Inc 1069
Prairie Farms Dairy, Inc. 1069
Prairie View A&m University 1069
Pratt Industries, Inc. 1069
Precigen Inc 1070
Precipio Inc 1070
Precision Auto Care, Inc. 1070
Precision Castparts Corp. 1070
Precision Optics Corp Inc (ma) 1070
Precyse Solutions Llc 1070
Preferred Apartment Communities Inc. 1071
Preferred Bank (los Angeles, Ca) 1071
Preformed Line Products Co. 1071
Premier Ag Co-op, Inc. 1071
Premier Entertainment Iii, Llc 1071
Premier Exhibitions Inc 1071
Premier Financial Bancorp, Inc. 1072
Premier Health Partners 1072
Premiere Global Services Inc 1072
Premio, Inc. 1072
Premium Beers Of Oklahoma, L.l.c. 1072
President & Trustees Of Bates College 1072
President & Trustees Of Williams College 1073
President And Board Of Trustees Of Santa Clara College 1073
President And Fellows Of Middlebury College 1073
Presidential Life Corporation 1073
Presidential Realty Corp. 1073
Presonus Audio Electronics Inc. 1073
Presstek Inc. 1074
Pressure Biosciences Inc 1074
Prestige Consumer Healthcare Inc 1074
Prestige Travel Inc 1074
Pretium Packaging Llc 1074
Prgx Global, Inc. 1074
Pricesmart Inc 1075
Pricewaterhousecoopers Llp 1075
Pridgeon & Clay, Inc 1075
Prime Healthcare Services - Garden City, Llc 1075
Prime Healthcare Services - Shasta, Llc 1075
Primeenergy Resources Corp 1075
Primex International Trading Corp 1076
Primo Water Corp 1076
Primoris Services Corp 1076
Primus Builders Inc. 1076
Princeton Community Hospital Association, Inc. 1076
Principal Financial Group Inc 1076
Principal Global Investors Llc 1077
Priority Aviation Inc 1077
Priority Health Managed Benefits Inc. 1077
Prisma Health-upstate 1077
Prison Rehabilitative Industries And Diversified Enterprises, Inc. 1077
Privatebancorp Inc 1077
Pro-dex Inc. (co) 1078
Proassurance Corp 1078
Probuild Holdings Inc. 1078
Procera Networks Inc 1078
Processa Pharmaceuticals Inc 1078

COMPANIES LISTED ALPHABETICALLY

Procter & Gamble Company (the) 1078
Procyon Corporation 1079
Producers Rice Mill, Inc. 1079
Production Tool Supply Company, Llc 1079
Professional Diversity Network Inc 1079
Professional Golfers Association Of America Inc 1079
Professional Project Services Inc. 1079
Progenics Pharmaceuticals, Inc. 1080
Proginet Corporation 1080
Progress Energy Inc. 1080
Progress Software Corp 1080
Progressive Corp. (oh) 1080
Prohealth Care Inc 1080
Project Enhancement Corp 1081
Project Leadership Associates Inc. 1081
Prologis Inc 1081
Promega Corporation 1081
Prometheus Laboratories Inc. 1081
Promise Technology Inc. 1081
Proofpoint Inc 1082
Prophase Labs Inc 1082
Prophotonix Ltd 1082
Pros Holdings Inc 1082
Prosek Partners 1082
Prospect Capital Corporation 1082
Prospect Medical Holdings Inc. 1083
Prospect Waterbury, Inc. 1083
Prosperity Bancshares Inc. 1083
Protalex Inc 1083
Protective Insurance Corp 1083
Protective Life Corp. 1083
Protective Life Insurance Co 1084
Protestant Memorial Medical Center, Inc. 1084
Protext Mobility Inc 1084
Proto Labs Inc 1084
Provectus Pharmaceuticals Inc. 1084
Provide Commerce Inc. 1084
Providence & Worcester Railroad Co. 1085
Providence College 1085
Providence Resources Inc. 1085
Providence Service Corp 1085
Provident Community Bancshares, Inc. 1085
Provident Financial Holdings, Inc. 1085
Provident Financial Services Inc 1086
Prudential Annuities Life Assurance Corp 1086
Prudential Financial Inc 1086
Prudential Overall Supply 1086
Prwt Services, Inc. 1086
Ps Business Parks Inc 1086
Psb Holdings Inc 1087
Pscu Incorporated 1087
Pseg Power Llc 1087
Psychemedics Corp. 1087
Ptc Inc 1087
Ptc Therapeutics Inc 1087
Public Broadcasting Service 1088
Public Communications Services, Inc. 1088
Public Health Solutions 1088
Public Health Trust Of Miami Dade County 1088
Public Service Company Of Oklahoma 1088
Public Service Enterprise Group Inc 1088
Public Storage 1089
Public Utilities Board Of The City Of Brownsville 1089
Public Utility District 1 Of Clark County 1089
Public Utility District 1 Of Snohomish County 1089
Public Utility District No 1 Of Cowlitz County 1089
Public Utility District No. 1 Of Chelan County 1089
Publix Super Markets, Inc. 1090
Publix Super Markets, Inc. 1090
Puerto Rico Electric Power Authority 1090
Puget Energy, Inc. 1090
Pulaski Financial Corp 1090
Pulaski Financial Corp. 1090
Pulse Electronics Corp 1091
Pultegroup Inc 1091
Puradyn Filter Technologies Inc 1091
Purdue University 1091
Pure Bioscience Inc 1091
Pure Cycle Corp. 1091
Purple Communications, Inc. 1092
Pvh Corp 1092
Pvr Partners Lp 1092
Pvs Technologies Inc. 1092

Pyco Industries, Inc. 1092
Pyxus International Inc 1092
Pzena Investment Management Inc 1093
Q.e.p. Co., Inc. 1093
Qad, Inc. 1093
Qc Holdings Inc 1093
Qcr Holdings Inc 1093
Qep Resources Inc 1093
Qhg Of South Carolina, Inc. 1094
Qlik Technologies Inc. 1094
Qlogic Corp. 1094
Qnb Corp. 1094
Qorvo Inc 1094
Qr Energy Lp 1094
Qts Realty Trust Inc 1095
Quad/graphics, Inc. 1095
Quaker Chemical Corporation 1095
Quaker Valley Foods, Inc. 1095
Qualcomm Atheros Inc. 1095
Qualcomm Inc 1095
Quality Distribution Inc (fl) 1096
Quality Food Centers Inc. 1096
Quality Oil Company, Llc 1096
Qualserv Corporation 1096
Qualstar Corp 1096
Qualys, Inc. 1096
Quanex Building Products Corp 1097
Quanta Services, Inc. 1097
Quantum Corp 1097
Quantum Fuel Systems Technologies Worldwide Inc. 1097
Queen Of The Valley Medical Center 1097
Quest Diagnostics, Inc. 1097
Quest Media & Supplies, Inc. 1098
Quest Software Inc. 1098
Questar Corp. 1098
Questar Gas Co. 1098
Questcor Pharmaceuticals Inc 1098
Quick-med Technologies Inc. 1098
Quicken Loans Inc. 1099
Quicklogic Corp 1099
Quicksilver Production Partners Lp 1099
Quicksilver Resources, Inc. 1099
Quidel Corp. 1099
Quiktrip Corporation 1099
Quill Corporation 1100
Quinn Emanuel Urquhart & Sullivan Llp 1100
Quinnipiac University 1100
Quinstreet, Inc. 1100
Qumu Corp 1100
Qurate Retail Inc 1100
Qvc, Inc. 1101
R. E. Michel Company, Llc 1101
R. L. Jordan Oil Company Of North Carolina, Inc. 1101
R.c. Willey Home Furnishings 1101
R.s. Hughes Company, Inc. 1101
R1 Rcm Inc 1101
Rabobank N.a. 1102
Racetrac Petroleum, Inc. 1102
Rackspace Hosting Inc 1102
Radian Group, Inc. 1102
Radiant Logistics, Inc. 1102
Radiant Systems Inc. 1102
Radisys Corp. 1103
Radius Health Inc 1103
Radnet Inc 1103
Rady Children's Hospital-san Diego 1103
Rae Systems Inc. 1103
Railamerica Inc. 1103
Rainmaker Systems Inc. 1104
Rait Financial Trust 1104
Ralcorp Frozen Bakery Products Inc. 1104
Raley's 1104
Ralph Lauren Corp 1104
Rambus Inc. (de) 1104
Ramtron International Corporation 1105
Rand Logistics Inc 1105
Random House Inc. 1105
Range Resources Corp 1105
Rapid City Regional Hospital, Inc. 1105
Rappahannock Electric Cooperative 1105
Raptor Networks Technology Inc. 1106
Raptor Pharmaceuticals Corp. 1106

Raritan Bay Medical Center, A New Jersey Nonprofit Corporation 1106
Raritan Valley Community College 1106
Rave Restaurant Group Inc 1106
Raven Industries, Inc. 1106
Rayburn Country Electric Cooperative, Inc 1107
Raymond James & Associates Inc 1107
Raymond James Financial, Inc. 1107
Raymours Furniture Company, Inc. 1107
Rayonier Inc. 1107
Raytheon Applied Signal Technology Inc. 1107
Raytheon Co. 1108
Raytheon Technical Services Company Llc 1108
Rb Rubber Products Inc. 1108
Rbc Bearings Inc 1108
Rbc Life Sciences Inc 1108
Rbs Global Inc. 1108
Rc2 Corporation 1109
Rci Hospitality Holdings Inc 1109
Rcm Technologies, Inc. 1109
Rcs Capital Corp 1109
Rdo Equipment Co. 1109
Reachlocal Inc. 1109
Reading Hospital 1110
Reading International Inc 1110
Ready Capital Corp 1110
Real Goods Solar Inc 1110
Reald Inc. 1110
Realogy Holdings Corp 1110
Realpage Inc 1111
Realty Income Corp 1111
Recall Corporation 1111
Recology Inc. 1111
Rector & Visitors Of The University Of Virginia 1111
Recyclenet Corporation 1111
Red Blossom Sales, Inc. 1112
Red Gold Inc. 1112
Red Hat Inc 1112
Red Lions Hotels Corp 1112
Red River Commodities, Inc. 1112
Red River Computer Co. Inc. 1112
Red Robin Gourmet Burgers Inc 1113
Redmond Park Hospital, Llc 1113
Redner's Markets, Inc. 1113
Redpoint Bio Corporation 1113
Redwood Trust Inc 1113
Reed & Barton Corporation 1113
Reeds Inc 1114
Refac Optical Group 1114
Regal Beloit Corp 1114
Regal Entertainment Group 1114
Regency Centers Corp 1114
Regency Energy Partners Lp 1114
Regeneron Pharmaceuticals, Inc. 1115
Regenerx Biopharmaceuticals Inc 1115
Regents Of The University Of Idaho 1115
Regents Of The University Of Michigan 1115
Regional Health Properties Inc 1115
Regional Management Corp 1115
Regional Transportation District 1116
Regions Financial Corp (new) 1116
Regions Hospital Foundation 1116
Regis Corp 1116
Rei Systems, Inc. 1116
Reinsurance Group Of America, Inc. 1116
Reis, Inc 1117
Relax The Back Corporation 1117
Reliability Incorporated 1117
Reliance Steel & Aluminum Co. 1117
Reliv' International Inc 1117
Remy International Inc. 1117
Renaissance Learning Inc. 1118
Renasant Corp 1118
Renesas Electronics America Inc. 1118
Renewable Energy Group Inc. 1118
Renewable Energy Group, Inc. 1118
Renfro Corporation 1118
Rennova Health Inc 1119
Reno Contracting Inc. 1119
Rensselaer Polytechnic Institute 1119
Rent-a-center Inc. 1119
Rentech Inc 1119
Rentrak Corp. 1119
Replacement Parts, Inc. 1120

Replacements, Ltd. 1120
Repligen Corp. 1120
Repro Med Systems, Inc. 1120
Repros Therapeutics Inc 1120
Republic Airways Holdings Inc 1120
Republic Bancorp, Inc. (ky) 1121
Republic First Bancorp, Inc. 1121
Republic Services Inc 1121
Res-care Inc. 1121
Research Frontiers Inc. 1121
Research Incorporated 1121
Research Triangle Institute Inc 1122
Reserve Petroleum Co. 1122
Reshape Lifesciences Inc 1122
Resmed Inc. 1122
Resolute Energy Corp 1122
Resource America, Inc. 1122
Resources Connection Inc 1123
Respirerx Pharmaceuticals Inc 1123
Restaurant Technologies Inc. 1123
Restorgenex Corp 1123
Retail Opportunity Investments Corp 1123
Retail Properties Of America Inc 1123
Retailmenot Inc 1124
Retractable Technologies Inc 1124
Reval Holdings Inc. 1124
Revance Therapeutics Inc 1124
Revett Mining Co Inc 1124
Revlon Inc 1124
Revolution Lighting Technologies Inc 1125
Rex American Resources Corp 1125
Rex Energy Corp 1125
Rex Healthcare, Inc. 1125
Rexahn Pharmaceuticals Inc. 1125
Rexford Industrial Realty Inc 1125
Rexford Industrial Realty, Inc. 1126
Rexnord Corp (new) 1126
Reynolds American Inc 1126
Rf Industries Ltd. 1126
Rf Micro Devices, Inc. 1126
Rf Monolithics Inc. 1126
Rgc Resources, Inc. 1127
Rh 1127
Rhe Hatco Inc. 1127
Rhino Resource Partners Lp 1127
Rhode Island Housing 1127
Rhode Island School Of Design Inc 1127
Rhodes College 1128
Rib-x Pharmaceuticals Inc. 1128
Rice Energy Inc 1128
Ricebran Technologies 1128
Riceland Foods, Inc. 1128
Rich Products Corporation 1128
Richard J. Caron Foundation 1129
Richardson Electronics Ltd 1129
Ridge Tool Company 1129
Ridgewood Savings Bank 1129
Rigel Pharmaceuticals Inc 1129
Rignet Inc 1129
Ringcentral Inc 1130
Rio Holdings, Inc. 1130
Riot Blockchain Inc 1130
Rip Griffin Truck Service Center, Inc. 1130
Risk George Industries Inc 1130
Rite Aid Corp 1130
River Valley Bancorp 1131
Riverbed Technology Inc 1131
Riverside Healthcare Association, Inc. 1131
Riverside Hospital, Inc. 1131
Riverview Bancorp, Inc. 1131
Riverview Hospital 1131
Riviera Holdings Corporation 1132
Rli Corp 1132
Roadrunner Transportation Services Holdings Inc. 1132
Roadrunner Transportation Systems Inc 1132
Roan Resources Inc 1132
Robert Bosch Llc 1132
Robert Half International Inc. 1133
Robert Morris University 1133
Robert W. Baird & Co. Incorporated 1133
Robert Wood Johnson University Hospital At Rahway 1133
Robert Wood Johnson University Hospital, Inc. 1133

Roberts Dairy Company, Llc 1133
Robinson (c.h.) Worldwide, Inc. 1134
Robinson Health System, Inc. 1134
Robinson Oil Corporation 1134
Rochester Gas And Electric Corporation 1134
Rochester Institute Of Technology (inc) 1134
Rock Creek Pharmaceuticals Inc 1134
Rock Energy Resources Inc. 1135
Rock-tenn Co. 1135
Rocket Fuel Inc 1135
Rockview Dairies, Inc. 1135
Rockwell Collins Inc 1135
Rockwell Medical, Inc 1135
Rockwood Holdings Inc 1136
Rocky Brands Inc 1136
Rocky Mountain Chocolate Factory Inc (de) 1136
Rofin Sinar Technologies Inc. 1136
Rogers Corp. 1136
Rollins College 1136
Rollins, Inc. 1137
Ronco Acquisition Corporation 1137
Ronile, Inc. 1137
Roofing Wholesale Co., Inc. 1137
Roomlinx Inc 1137
Root Learning Inc. 1137
Root9b Holdings Inc 1138
Roper Technologies Inc 1138
Rose Acre Farms Inc. 1138
Rose International, Inc. 1138
Rose Paving Co. 1138
Rose Rock Midstream L P 1138
Rose's Southwest Papers, Inc. 1139
Rosen Hotels And Resorts Inc. 1139
Rosen's Diversified Inc. 1139
Rosetta Resources, Inc. 1139
Rosetta Stone Inc 1139
Ross Stores Inc 1139
Ross-simons Of Warwick Inc. 1140
Rotary International 1140
Roth Capital Partners Llc 1140
Roth Produce Co. 1140
Roth Staffing Companies, L.p. 1140
Roundy's Inc. 1140
Rouse Properties, Inc. 1141
Rowan Companies Inc. 1141
Rowan Regional Medical Center, Inc. 1141
Rowland Coffee Roasters Inc. 1141
Royal Bancshares Of Pennsylvania Inc 1141
Royal Caribbean Cruises Ltd 1141
Royal Gold Inc 1142
Royale Energy Inc 1142
Rpc, Inc. 1142
Rpm International Inc (de) 1142
Rpt Realty 1142
Rpx Corp 1142
Rsa Security Llc 1143
Rsm Mcgladrey Inc. 1143
Rsp Permian Inc 1143
Rti International Metals, Inc. 1143
Rti Surgical Holdings Inc 1143
Rtw Retailwinds Inc 1143
Rubicon Technology Inc 1144
Ruby Tuesday, Inc. 1144
Ruckus Wireless Inc 1144
Rudolph And Sletten, Inc. 1144
Rudolph Technologies, Inc. 1144
Rumsey Electric Company 1144
Rush Enterprises Inc. 1145
Rush-copley Medical Center, Inc. 1145
Russell Sigler, Inc. 1145
Ruth's Hospitality Group Inc 1145
Rutherford Electric Membership Corporation 1145
Rvue Holdings Inc 1145
Rw Stearns Inc. 1146
Ryan Building Group, Inc. 1146
Ryan, Llc 1146
Ryder System, Inc. 1146
Ryerson Holding Corp 1146
Ryland Group, Inc. 1146
Ryman Hospitality Properties Inc 1147
Ryman Hospitality Properties, Inc. 1147
S & B Engineers And Constructors, Ltd. 1147
S & T Bancorp Inc (indiana, Pa) 1147
S&me, Inc. 1147

S&p Global Inc 1147
S&w Seed Co. 1148
S. D. Warren Company 1148
S.c. Johnson & Son Inc. 1148
Sabine Royalty Trust 1148
Sabra Health Care Reit Inc 1148
Sabre Industries Inc. 1148
Sacramento Municipal Utility District 1149
Sacred Heart Health System, Inc. 1149
Sacred Heart Hospital Of Allentown 1149
Sacred Heart Hospital Of The Hospital Sisters Of The Third Order Of St. Francis 1149
Saddleback Memorial Medical Center 1149
Safe Ride Services Inc. 1149
Safeguard Scientifics Inc. 1150
Safenet Inc. 1150
Safety Insurance Group, Inc. 1150
Safety-kleen Inc. 1150
Safeway Inc. 1150
Safra National Bank Of New York 1150
Saga Communications Inc 1151
Sagarsoft Inc. 1151
Sage Software Inc. 1151
Sagent Pharmaceuticals Inc 1151
Saia Inc 1151
Saint Agnes Medical Center 1151
Saint Alphonsus Regional Medical Center, Inc. 1152
Saint Anselm College 1152
Saint Edward's University, Inc. 1152
Saint Elizabeth Medical Center, Inc. 1152
Saint Elizabeth Regional Medical Center 1152
Saint Francis Health System, Inc. 1152
Saint Francis Hospital And Medical Center Foundation, Inc. 1153
Saint Francis University 1153
Saint Joseph Hospital, Inc 1153
Saint Joseph's University 1153
Saint Louis University 1153
Saint Luke's Health System, Inc. 1153
Saint Mary's University Of Minnesota 1154
Saint Peter's University Hospital, Inc. 1154
Saint Tammany Parish Hospital Service District 1 1154
Saint Thomas Rutherford Hospital 1154
Sajan Inc. 1154
Saks Fifth Avenue Inc. 1154
Salary.com Inc. 1155
Salem Health 1155
Salem Media Group, Inc. 1155
Salesforce.com Inc 1155
Salinas Valley Memorial Healthcare Systems 1155
Saline Memorial Hospital Auxiliary 1155
Salisbury Bancorp, Inc. 1156
Salix Pharmaceuticals Ltd 1156
Sally Beauty Holdings Inc 1156
Salon Media Group Inc. 1156
Salt Lake Community College 1156
Salt River Project Agricultural Improvement And Power District 1156
Salve Regina University 1157
Sam Ash Music Corporation 1157
Sam Houston State University 1157
Sam Levin Inc. 1157
Samaritan Regional Health System 1157
Sammons Enterprises Inc. 1157
Samsung C&t America, Inc. 1158
Samsung Electronics America Inc. 1158
Samuels Jewelers 1158
San Antonio Water System 1158
San Diego State University Foundation 1158
San Diego Unified Port District 1158
San Francisco Bay Area Rapid Transit District 1159
San Joaquin Refining Co. Inc. 1159
San Jose Water Company 1159
San Juan Basin Royalty Trust 1159
Sanchez Energy Corp. 1159
Sanchez Midstream Partners Lp 1159
Sanderson Farms Inc 1160
Sandia National Laboratories 1160
Sandisk Corp. 1160
Sandridge Energy Inc 1160
Sandston Corporation 1160
Sandy Spring Bancorp Inc 1160
Sanfilippo (john B) & Son Inc 1161

COMPANIES LISTED ALPHABETICALLY

Sanford 1161
Sanford Burnham Prebys Medical Discovery Institute 1161
Sanford Health Of Northern Minnesota 1161
Sanmina Corp 1161
Sanofi-aventis U.s. Llc 1161
Santa Cruz Seaside Company Inc 1162
Santa Fe Financial Corp. 1162
Santa Fe Gold Corp 1162
Santa Monica Community College District 1162
Santander Consumer Usa Holdings Inc 1162
Santander Holdings Usa Inc. 1162
Sap America Inc. 1163
Sapient Corp. 1163
Sapp Bros. Petroleum Inc. 1163
Sapp Bros., Inc. 1163
Sarah Bush Lincoln Health Center 1163
Sarah Lawrence College 1163
Sarasota County Public Hospital District 1164
Saratoga Resources Inc 1164
Sarepta Therapeutics Inc 1164
Sargent Electric Company 1164
Sas Institute Inc. 1164
Satmetrix Systems Inc. 1164
Satterfield And Pontikes Construction, Inc. 1165
Saul Centers Inc 1165
Savannah Health Services, Llc 1165
Save The Children Federation, Inc. 1165
Savient Pharmaceuticals Inc 1165
Savvis Inc. 1165
Sawnee Electric Membership Corporation 1166
Sb Financial Group Inc 1166
Sb One Bancorp 1166
Sba Communications Corp (new) 1166
Sc Fuels 1166
Scai Holdings, Llc 1166
Scana Corp 1167
Schawk, Inc. 1167
Scheid Vineyards Inc. 1167
Schein (henry) Inc 1167
Schewel Furniture Company Incorporated 1167
Schlumberger Limited 1167
Schmitt Industries Inc (or) 1168
Schmitt Music Company 1168
Schnitzer Steel Industries Inc 1168
Schnuck Markets Inc. 1168
Scholastic Corp 1168
School Employees Retirement System Of Ohio 1168
Schoolsfirst Fcu 1169
Schottenstein Realty Trust Inc. 1169
Schreiber Foods Inc. 1169
Schulman (a) Inc 1169
Schumacher Electric Corporation 1169
Schwab (charles) Corp (the) 1169
Schweitzer-mauduit International Inc 1170
Sciclone Pharmaceuticals, Inc. 1170
Science Applications International Corp (new) 1170
Scientific Industries Inc 1170
Scientific Learning Corp. 1170
Scientific Research Corp 1170
Sciquest Inc 1171
Scl Health - Front Range, Inc. 1171
Scott & White Health Plan 1171
Scott Equipment Company, L.l.c. 1171
Scott's Liquid Gold, Inc. 1171
Scotts Miracle-gro Co (the) 1171
Scottsdale Healthcare Corp. 1172
Scripps (ew) Company (the) 1172
Scripps College 1172
Scripps Health 1172
Scripps Networks Interactive, Inc. 1172
Scrypt Inc 1172
Sculptor Capital Management 1173
Sdb Trade International, L.p. 1173
Seaboard Corp. 1173
Seabrook Brothers & Sons Inc 1173
Seachange International Inc. 1173
Seacoast Banking Corp. Of Florida 1173
Seacor Holdings Inc 1174
Sealaska Corporation 1174
Sears Holdings Corp 1174
Sears Hometown & Outlet Stores Inc 1174
Seattle Children's Hospital 1174
Seattle Genetics Inc 1174

Seattle University 1175
Seaworld Entertainment Inc. 1175
Secura Insurance Holdings Inc. 1175
Securian Financial Group Inc. 1175
Securities Investor Protection Corporation 1175
Security Federal Corp (sc) 1175
Security Finance Corporation Of Spartanburg 1176
Security Health Plan Of Wisconsin, Inc. 1176
Security National Financial Corp 1176
Security Service Federal Credit Union 1176
Sed International Holdings, Inc. 1176
Sedgwick Claims Management Services Inc. 1176
Sedgwick Llp 1177
Sedona Corp 1177
See's Candies Inc. 1177
Sefton Resources Inc. 1177
Sei Investments Co 1177
Seitel Inc 1177
Select Bancorp Inc (new) 1178
Select Income Reit 1178
Select Medical Holdings Corp 1178
Selective Insurance Group Inc 1178
Semco Energy, Inc. 1178
Semgroup Corp 1178
Seminole Electric Cooperative, Inc. 1179
Semler Scientific Inc 1179
Sempra Energy 1179
Semtech Corp. 1179
Seneca Biopharma Inc 1179
Seneca Companies Inc. 1179
Seneca Foods Corp. 1180
Senomyx Inc 1180
Sensient Technologies Corp. 1180
Sentara Healthcare 1180
Sentara Rmh Medical Center 1180
Sentara Williamsburg Regional Medical Center 1180
Sentry Technology Corporation 1181
Sequa Corporation 1181
Sequachee Valley Electric Co-operative Inc 1181
Sequenom Inc 1181
Serco Inc. 1181
Serena Software Inc. 1181
Serra Automotive Inc. 1182
Serta Inc. 1182
Servco Pacific Inc. 1182
Service Corp. International 1182
Service Properties Trust 1182
Servicenow Inc 1182
Servicesource International, Inc. 1183
Servigistics Inc. 1183
Servisfirst Bancshares Inc 1183
Servotronics, Inc. 1183
Servpro Intellectual Property, Inc. 1183
Sesen Bio Inc 1183
Seton Hall University 1184
Seton Healthcare Family 1184
Seton Healthcare Network 1184
Sevcon Inc 1184
Seven Seas Technologies Inc. 1184
Seventy Seven Energy Llc 1184
Severn Bancorp Inc (annapolis Md) 1185
Sevion Therapeutics Inc 1185
Seyfarth Shaw Llp 1185
Sfn Group Inc. 1185
Sfx Entertainment, Inc. 1185
Sgt, Llc 1185
Shamrock Foods Company 1186
Shands Jacksonville Medical Center, Inc. 1186
Shands Teaching Hospital And Clinics, Inc. 1186
Shari's Management Corporation 1186
Sharon Regional Health System Inc. 1186
Sharp Healthcare 1186
Sharp Memorial Hospital 1187
Sharpe Resources Corporation 1187
Sharps Compliance Corp. 1187
Shawmut Woodworking & Supply, Inc. 1187
Shawnee Mission Medical Center, Inc. 1187
Shea Homes Limited Partnership 1187
Shearer's Foods Inc. 1188
Shell Oil Company 1188
Shenandoah Telecommunications Co 1188
Shepherd Center, Inc. 1188
Shepherd Electric Company Incorporated 1188
Sheridan Community Hospital (osteopathic) 1188

Sherwin-williams Co (the) 1189
Shi International Corp. 1189
Shiloh Industries, Inc. 1189
Shimadzu Scientific Instruments Inc 1189
Shoe Carnival, Inc. 1189
Shop 'n Save St. Louis Inc. 1189
Shore Bancshares Inc. 1190
Shore Memorial Hospital 1190
Shoretel Inc 1190
Shps Inc. 1190
Shriners Hospitals For Children 1190
Shutterfly Inc 1190
Shutterstock Inc 1191
Si Financial Group Inc (md) 1191
Siebert Financial Corp 1191
Siemens Industry Inc. 1191
Sierra Bancorp 1191
Sierra Club 1191
Sierra Monitor Corp 1192
Sierra Nevada Corporation 1192
Sierra Pacific Power Co. 1192
Sierra View District Hospital League, Inc. 1192
Sifco Industries Inc. 1192
Siga Technologies Inc 1192
Sige Semiconductor Inc. 1193
Sigma Designs Inc 1193
Sigma-aldrich Corp. 1193
Sigmatron International Inc. 1193
Signature Bank (new York, Ny) 1193
Signature Consultants Llc 1193
Signature Eyewear Inc. 1194
Sika Corporation 1194
Sikorsky Aircraft Corporation 1194
Silgan Holdings Inc 1194
Silicon Graphics International Corp. 1194
Silicon Image Inc 1194
Silicon Laboratories Inc 1195
Silver Bay Realty Trust Corp. 1195
Silver Cross Hospital And Medical Centers 1195
Silver Spring Networks Inc 1195
Silverleaf Resorts Inc. 1195
Simmons First National Corp 1195
Simon Property Group, Inc. 1196
Simon Worldwide Inc. 1196
Simplicity Bancorp, Inc 1196
Simpson Manufacturing Co., Inc. (de) 1196
Simpson Strong-tie Company Inc. 1196
Sims Ltd 1196
Simulations Plus Inc. 1197
Sinai Health System 1197
Sinai Hospital Of Baltimore, Inc. 1197
Singing Machine Co., Inc. 1197
Sino-global Shipping America Ltd 1197
Sintx Technologies Inc 1197
Sirchie Acquisition Company Llc 1198
Sirius Xm Holdings Inc 1198
Sirona Dental Systems Inc 1198
Sirva Inc. 1198
Site Centers Corp 1198
Six Flags Entertainment Corp 1198
Sjw Group 1199
Skanska Usa Civil Inc. 1199
Skechers Usa Inc 1199
Skf Usa Inc. 1199
Skidmore College 1199
Skillsoft Corporation 1199
Skinvisible Inc 1200
Skullcandy Inc 1200
Skyline Champion Corp 1200
Skywest Inc. 1200
Skyworks Solutions Inc 1200
Sl Green Realty Corp 1200
Sl Industries Inc. 1201
Slalom Llc 1201
Sleep Number Corp 1201
Sleepmed Incorporated 1201
Slm Corp. 1201
Sloan Implement Company, Inc. 1201
Sm Energy Co. 1202
Smallbizpros Inc. 1202
Smart & Final Inc. 1202
Smart Modular Technologies Inc. 1202
Smartfinancial Inc 1202
Smartpros Ltd 1202

Smartronix, Inc. 1203
Smead Manufacturing Company 1203
Smg Industries Inc 1203
Smith (a O) Corp 1203
Smith Micro Software Inc 1203
Smith's Food & Drug Centers Inc. 1203
Smith-midland Corp. 1204
Smithsonian Institution 1204
Smucker (j.m.) Co. 1204
Snap-on, Inc. 1204
Snapping Shoals Electric Trust, Inc. 1204
Snyder's-lance, Inc. 1204
Society Of Manufacturing Engineers 1205
Socket Mobile Inc 1205
Sodexo Remote Sites Partnership 1205
Soft Computer Consultants Inc. 1205
Softech, Inc 1205
Software & Information Industry Association 1205
Solarwinds Inc 1206
Solera Holdings Inc 1206
Soligenix Inc 1206
Solitario Exploration & Royalty Corp 1206
Solitron Devices, Inc. 1206
Solo Cup Company 1206
Solutia Inc. 1207
Somerset Medical Center 1207
Somerset Tire Service, Inc. 1207
Sonesta International Hotels Corporation 1207
Sonic Automotive, Inc. 1207
Sonic Corp. 1207
Sonic Foundry, Inc. 1208
Sonics & Materials Inc. 1208
Sono-tek Corp. 1208
Sonoco Products Co. 1208
Sonoma Pharmaceuticals Inc 1208
Sonomawest Holdings Inc. 1208
Sonosite Inc. 1209
Sonus Networks, Inc. 1209
Sotera Defense Solutions Inc. 1209
Sotheby's 1209
Sotherly Hotels Inc 1209
Sound Financial Inc. 1209
South Bend Medical Foundation Inc 1210
South Broward Hospital District 1210
South Carolina Public Service Authority (inc) 1210
South Carolina State Ports Authority 1210
South Central Communications Corporation 1210
South Central Power Company Inc 1210
South Dakota State University 1211
South Jersey Gas Co. 1211
South Jersey Industries Inc 1211
South Miami Hospital, Inc. 1211
South Peninsula Hospitals, Inc. 1211
South State Corp 1211
Southco Distributing Company 1212
Southcoast Financial Corp 1212
Southcoast Hospitals Group, Inc. 1212
Southcross Energy Partners Lp 1212
Southeast Missouri State University 1212
Southeast Texas Industries, Inc. 1212
Southeastern Bank Financial Corp 1213
Southeastern Freight Lines, Inc. 1213
Southeastern Pennsylvania Transportation Authority 1213
Southeastern Universities Research Association Inc 1213
Southern Banc Co., Inc. 1213
Southern California Edison Co. 1213
Southern California Gas Co. 1214
Southern California Public Power Authority 1214
Southern California Regional Rail Authority 1214
Southern Community Financial Corporation 1214
Southern Company (the) 1214
Southern Connecticut Bancorp Inc. 1214
Southern First Bancshares, Inc. 1215
Southern Illinois Healthcare Enterprises, Inc. 1215
Southern Illinois University Inc 1215
Southern Maine Health Care 1215
Southern Methodist University Inc 1215
Southern Michigan Bancorp Inc (united States) 1215
Southern Minnesota Beet Sugar Cooperative 1216
Southern Minnesota Municipal Power Agency 1216
Southern Missouri Bancorp, Inc. 1216
Southern National Bancorp Of Virginia Inc 1216

Southern Natural Gas Company, L.l.c. 1216
Southern New Hampshire Medical Center 1216
Southern Nuclear Operating Company, Inc. 1217
Southern Pine Electric Cooperative 1217
Southern Pipe & Supply Company, Inc. 1217
Southern Power Co 1217
Southern Research Institute Inc 1217
Southern Union Company 1217
Southfirst Bancshares Inc. 1218
Southland Industries 1218
Southside Bancshares, Inc. 1218
Southside Hospital 1218
Southwall Technologies Inc. 1218
Southwest Bancorp, Inc. (ok) 1218
Southwest Georgia Financial Corp. 1219
Southwest Louisiana Electric Membership Corporation 1219
Southwest Mississippi Regional Medical Center 1219
Southwest Research Institute Inc 1219
Southwestern Electric Power Co. 1219
Southwestern Energy Company 1219
Southwestern University 1220
Sp Plus Corp 1220
Space Systems/loral Inc. 1220
Spacelabs Healthcare Inc. 1220
Span-america Medical Systems, Inc. 1220
Spanish Broadcasting System Inc 1220
Spansion Inc 1221
Spar Group, Inc. 1221
Spark Networks Inc 1221
Sparrow Health System 1221
Sparta Inc. 1221
Spartan Motors, Inc. 1221
Spartannash Co. 1222
Sparton Corp 1222
Spaw Glass Construction Corporation 1222
Spaw Glass Holding, L.p. 1222
Special Olympics, Inc. 1222
Spectra Energy Corp 1222
Spectra Energy Partners Lp 1223
Spectranetics Corp. (the) 1223
Spectrum Brands Holdings Inc 1223
Spectrum Brands Holdings Inc (new) 1223
Spectrum Control Inc. 1223
Spectrum Group International Inc 1223
Spectrum Pharmaceuticals Inc 1224
Speed Commerce Inc 1224
Speedway Motorsports, Inc. 1224
Spelman College 1224
Spf Energy, Inc. 1224
Spherix Inc 1224
Spindletop Oil & Gas Co (tex) 1225
Spire Alabama Inc. 1225
Spire Corp. 1225
Spire Inc 1225
Spirit Airlines Inc 1225
Splunk Inc 1225
Spok Holdings Inc 1226
Sport Chalet, Inc. 1226
Sprague Resources Lp 1226
Spring Arbor University 1226
Springfield Hospital Inc. 1226
Sprouts Farmers Market Inc 1226
Sps Commerce, Inc. 1227
Spx Corp. 1227
Spx Flow Inc 1227
Spy Inc 1227
Spyr Inc 1227
Sram International Corporation 1227
Src Energy Inc 1228
Sri International 1228
Sri/surgical Express Inc. 1228
Ss&c Technologies Holdings Inc 1228
Ssi (u.s.) Inc. 1228
Ssm Health Care Corporation 1228
Ssp America Inc. 1229
St Barnabas Medical Center (inc) 1229
St David's South Austin Medical Center 1229
St Davids Healthcare Partnership Llp 1229
St James Healthcare, Inc 1229
St John Fisher College 1229
St John's University, New York 1230
St Joseph's College New York 1230
St Josephs Wayne Hospital Inc 1230

St Jude Medical Inc 1230
St Lawrence University (inc) 1230
St Mary's Regional Health Center 1230
St Patrick Hospital Corporation 1231
St. Agnes Healthcare, Inc. 1231
St. Alexius Medical Center 1231
St. Anthony's Hospital, Inc. 1231
St. Bernard Hospital 1231
St. Clair Health Corporation 1231
St. Francis Hospital, Roslyn, New York 1232
St. Francis" Hospital Poughkeepsie New York 1232
St. Joe Co. (the) 1232
St. John Health System, Inc. 1232
St. John Hospital And Medical Center 1232
St. John Providence 1232
St. John's Hospital Of The Hospital Sisters Of The Third Order Of St. Francis 1233
St. Joseph Healthcare Foundation 1233
St. Joseph Hospital Of Orange 1233
St. Joseph's Hospital Health Center 1233
St. Jude Children's Research Hospital, Inc. 1233
St. Jude Hospital 1233
St. Jude Medical, Inc. 1234
St. Luke's Episcopal Hospital Independent Practice Association, Inc. 1234
St. Luke's Episcopal-presbyterian Hospitals 1234
St. Luke's Health Network, Inc. 1234
St. Luke's Health System, Ltd. 1234
St. Luke's Hospital Of Duluth 1234
St. Mary's Health Care System, Inc. 1235
St. Mary's Health, Inc. 1235
St. Mary's Medical Center 1235
St. Norbert College, Inc. 1235
St. Olaf College 1235
St. Peter's Health Partners 1235
Staar Surgical Co. 1236
Stabilis Energy Inc 1236
Staff Force, Inc. 1236
Staffmark Holdings Inc. 1236
Stag Industrial Inc 1236
Stage Stores Inc. 1236
Stamford Health System Inc. 1237
Stamps.com Inc. 1237
Stanadyne Llc 1237
Stancorp Financial Group Inc 1237
Stand Energy Corporation 1237
Standard Avb Financial Corp 1237
Standard Electric Company 1238
Standard Forwarding Llc 1238
Standard Motor Products, Inc. 1238
Standard Register Co. 1238
Standex International Corp. 1238
Stanford Health Care 1238
Stanion Wholesale Electric Co., Inc. 1239
Stanley Black & Decker Inc 1239
Stanley Steemer International, Inc. 1239
Stant Manufacturing Inc. 1239
Staple Cotton Cooperative Association 1239
Staples Inc 1239
Star Group Lp 1240
Star Multi Care Services Inc. 1240
Star Of The West Milling Company 1240
Starbucks Corp. 1240
Starrett (ls) Co (the) 1240
Startek, Inc. 1240
Starwood Hotels & Resorts Worldwide Inc 1241
Starwood Property Trust Inc. 1241
Starz 1241
State Auto Financial Corp. 1241
State Bank Financial Corp 1241
State Compensation Insurance Fund 1241
State Farm Mutual Automobile Insurance Company 1242
State Of New York Mortgage Agency 1242
State Street Corp. 1242
State University Of Iowa Foundation 1242
State University Of New York 1242
Staten Island University Hospital 1242
Stater Bros. Holdings Inc. 1243
Statesville Hma, Llc 1243
Static Control Components Inc. 1243
Stats Llc 1243
Steel Connect Inc 1243
Steel Dynamics Inc. 1243

Steel Of West Virginia, Inc. 1244
Steel Partners Holdings Lp 1244
Steel Technologies Llc 1244
Steelcase, Inc. 1244
Stein Mart, Inc. 1244
Steiner Electric Company 1244
Stellar Group, Incorporated 1245
Stemline Therapeutics Inc 1245
Stepan Co. 1245
Stephan Co (the) 1245
Stephen F Austin State University 1245
Stephen Gould Corporation 1245
Stephenson Wholesale Company, Inc. 1246
Stereotaxis Inc 1246
Stericycle Inc. 1246
Steris Instrument Management Services, Inc. 1246
Sterling Bancorp (de) 1246
Sterling Chemicals Inc. 1246
Sterling Construction Co Inc 1247
Sterling Financial Corp. (wa) 1247
Sterling Jewelers Inc. 1247
Sterling Mets Lp 1247
Sterling Sugars, Inc. 1247
Stetson University, Inc. 1247
Stevens Industries Inc 1248
Stevens Institute Of Technology (inc) 1248
Stevens Transport, Inc. 1248
Stevenson University Inc. 1248
Steward Health Care System Llc 1248
Stewardship Financial Corp. 1248
Stewart & Stevenson Inc. 1249
Stewart Builders, Inc. 1249
Stewart Information Services Corp 1249
Stewart's Shops Corp. 1249
Stg Llc 1249
Stifel Financial Corp 1249
Stiles Corporation 1250
Stock Building Supply Llc 1250
Stock Yards Bancorp Inc 1250
Stone Energy Corp 1250
Stonegate Mortgage Corp 1250
Stonemor Inc 1250
Stoneridge Inc. 1251
Storr Office Environments Inc 1251
Stowers Institute For Medical Research 1251
Str Holdings Inc. 1251
Strack And Van Til Super Market Inc. 1251
Strata Skin Sciences Inc 1251
Strategic Education Inc 1252
Strategic Hotels & Resorts, Inc. 1252
Strattec Security Corp. 1252
Stratus Properties Inc. 1252
Stream Global Services Inc. 1252
Streamline Health Solutions Inc 1252
Strike, Llc 1253
Strikeforce Technologies Inc 1253
Strongwell Corporation 1253
Stryker Corp 1253
Stuart-dean Co. Inc. 1253
Sturdy Memorial Hospital, Inc. 1253
Sturgis Bancorp Inc 1254
Sturm, Ruger & Co., Inc. 1254
Stv Group, Incorporated 1254
Subjex Corporation 1254
Suburban Hospital Inc 1254
Suburban Propane Partners Lp 1254
Sucampo Pharmaceuticals Inc 1255
Successfactors Inc. 1255
Successories Llc 1255
Suffolk Bancorp 1255
Suffolk Construction Company, Inc. 1255
Suffolk County Water Authority Inc 1255
Suffolk University 1256
Summa Health 1256
Summer Infant Inc 1256
Summerlin Hospital Medical Center, Llc 1256
Summit Bancshares Inc. 1256
Summit Corporation Of America 1256
Summit Electric Supply Co., Inc. 1257
Summit Financial Group Inc 1257
Summit Hotel Properties Inc 1257
Summit State Bank (santa Rosa, Ca) 1257
Sun Bancorp Inc. (nj) 1257
Sun Coast Resources, Inc. 1257

Sun Communities Inc 1258
Sun Orchard Fruit Company Inc. 1258
Sun-maid Growers Of California 1258
Sunbelt Beverage Company Llc 1258
Suncoast Schools Federal Credit Union 1258
Suncoke Energy Inc 1258
Suncoke Energy Partners Lp 1259
Sunedison Inc 1259
Sunesis Pharmaceuticals Inc 1259
Sunflower Electric Power Corporation 1259
Sungard Availability Services Lp 1259
Sungard Data Systems Inc. 1259
Sungard Public Sector Inc. 1260
Sunkist Growers, Inc. 1260
Sunlink Health Systems Inc 1260
Sunoco Lp 1260
Sunovion Pharmaceuticals Inc. 1260
Sunpower Corp 1260
Sunrise Medical Inc. 1261
Sunrise Senior Living Inc. 1261
Sunrun Installation Services Inc. 1261
Sunshine Silver Mines Corporation 1261
Sunstone Hotel Investors Inc. 1261
Sunsweet Growers Inc. 1261
Suntory International Corp. 1262
Suntrust Banks Inc 1262
Sunvalley Solar Inc (nv) 1262
Super Center Concepts Inc. 1262
Super Micro Computer Inc 1262
Superconductor Technologies Inc 1262
Superior Bulk Logistics, Inc. 1263
Superior Energy Services, Inc. 1263
Superior Group Of Companies Inc 1263
Superior Industries International, Inc. 1263
Superior Oil Company Inc 1263
Supernus Pharmaceuticals Inc 1263
Supertex, Inc. 1264
Supervalu Inc 1264
Support.com Inc 1264
Surewest Communications 1264
Surge Components Inc 1264
Surge Global Energy Inc 1264
Surgline International Inc. 1265
Surmodics Inc 1265
Surrey Bancorp (nc) 1265
Susquehanna Bancshares, Inc 1265
Susser Holdings Corp 1265
Sutherland Global Services Inc. 1265
Sutron Corp. 1266
Sutter Bay Hospitals 1266
Sutter Health 1266
Svb Financial Group 1266
Swank Inc. 1266
Swarthmore College 1266
Swedish Health Services 1267
Swedish Match North America Inc. 1267
Swh Corporation 1267
Swift Transportation Co 1267
Swimwear Anywhere Inc. 1267
Swinerton Builders 1267
Swinerton Incorporated 1268
Swisher Hygiene Inc 1268
Swiss Valley Farms Cooperative 1268
Sws Group, Inc. 1268
Sybron Dental Specialties Inc. 1268
Sycamore Entertainment Group Inc. 1268
Sykes Enterprises, Inc. 1269
Symetra Financial Corp 1269
Symmetry Medical Inc. 1269
Synacor, Inc. 1269
Synageva Biopharma Corp. 1269
Synalloy Corp. 1269
Synaptics Inc 1270
Synchronoss Technologies Inc 1270
Syncora Holdings Ltd 1270
Synergetics Usa, Inc. 1270
Synergx Systems Inc. 1270
Synergy Pharmaceuticals Inc. 1270
Syniverse Holdings, Inc. 1271
Synnex Corp 1271
Synopsys Inc 1271
Synovis Life Technologies Inc. 1271
Synovus Financial Corp 1271
Synta Pharmaceuticals Corp 1271

Syntel Inc. 1272
Synthesis Energy Systems Inc 1272
Syntroleum Corp 1272
Synutra International Inc 1272
Sypris Solutions, Inc. 1272
Syracuse University 1272
Sysco Corp 1273
Sysco Guest Supply Llc 1273
Systemax, Inc. 1273
T Rowe Price Group Inc. 1273
T. D. Williamson, Inc. 1273
T. Marzetti Company 1273
T.j.t., Inc. 1274
Tab Products Co Llc 1274
Table Trac Inc. 1274
Tableau Software Inc 1274
Tachyon Networks Inc. 1274
Tacoma Public Utilities 1274
Taconic Biosciences, Inc. 1275
Tahoe Resources Inc. 1275
Taitron Components Inc. 1275
Take-two Interactive Software, Inc. 1275
Tal International Group Inc 1275
Tallahassee Memorial Healthcare, Inc. 1275
Tallgrass Energy Partners, Lp 1276
Talmer Bancorp Inc 1276
Talon International, Inc. 1276
Talon Therapeutics Inc. 1276
Tamir Biotechnology Inc. 1276
Tandem Diabetes Care Inc 1276
Tandy Brands Accessories, Inc. 1277
Tandy Leather Factory Inc 1277
Tanger Factory Outlet Centers, Inc. 1277
Tangoe, Inc. 1277
Tanner Industries, Inc. 1277
Taos Health Systems, Inc. 1277
Tapestry Inc 1278
Tapimmune Inc. 1278
Targa Resources Corp 1278
Targa Resources Partners Lp 1278
Target Corp 1278
Tarleton State University 1278
Tarrant County Hospital District 1279
Tas-chfh 1279
Tas-cnh, Inc. 1279
Tata America International Corporation 1279
Tatung Company Of America, Inc. 1279
Tauber Oil Company 1279
Taubman Centers Inc 1280
Taxus Cardium Pharmaceuticals Group Inc 1280
Taylor (calvin B.) Bankshares, Inc. (md) 1280
Taylor Capital Group, Inc 1280
Taylor Devices Inc 1280
Taylor Morrison Home Corp (holding Co) 1280
Tcf Financial Corp 1281
Tcf Financial Corp (new) 1281
Td Ameritrade Holding Corp 1281
Team Health Holdings Inc 1281
Team Inc 1281
Team Industries Holding Corporation 1281
Tearlab Corp 1282
Tech Data Corp. 1282
Teche Holding Co. 1282
Technica Corporation 1282
Technical Communications Corp 1282
Technical Consumer Products Inc. 1282
Technology Research Corporation 1283
Technology Service Corporation 1283
Techtarget Inc 1283
Teco Energy Inc. 1283
Teco-westinghouse Motor Company 1283
Tecogen Inc 1283
Tecumseh Products Company Llc 1284
Tejon Ranch Co 1284
Tekelec 1284
Tekni-plex Inc. 1284
Teknor Apex Company 1284
Teksystems, Inc. 1284
Tel Fsi Inc. 1285
Tel Instrument Electronics Corp. 1285
Tel Offshore Trust 1285
Telaria Inc 1285
Telcordia Technologies Inc. 1285
Telecommunication Systems Inc 1285

Teledyne Benthos 1286
Teledyne Lecroy Inc. 1286
Teledyne Technologies Inc 1286
Teleflex Incorporated 1286
Telenav, Inc. 1286
Telephone & Data Systems Inc 1286
Telephone Electronics Corporation 1287
Teletouch Communications, Inc. 1287
Teligent Inc (new) 1287
Telkonet Inc. 1287
Tellurian Inc 1287
Telos Corp. (md) 1287
Telvue Corporation 1288
Temco Service Industries, Inc. 1288
Temple University Health System, Inc. 1288
Temple University-of The Commonwealth System Of Higher Education 1288
Tempur Sealy International, Inc. 1288
Tenaska Inc. 1288
Tenax Therapeutics Inc 1289
Tenet Healthcare Corp. 1289
Tengasco Inc 1289
Tennant Co. 1289
Tenneco Inc 1289
Tennessee Farmers Cooperative 1289
Tennessee State University 1290
Tennessee Technological University 1290
Tennessee Valley Authority 1290
Teradata Corp (de) 1290
Teradyne, Inc. 1290
Terex Corp. 1290
Terra Nitrogen Company, L.p. 1291
Terracon Consultants, Inc. 1291
Terracycle Inc. 1291
Terravia Holdings Inc 1291
Terremark Worldwide Inc. 1291
Terreno Realty Corp 1291
Territorial Bancorp Inc 1292
Tesaro Inc 1292
Tesla Energy Operations, Inc. 1292
Tesla Inc 1292
Tessada & Associates Inc. 1292
Tessco Technologies, Inc. 1292
Tetco Incorporated 1293
Tetra Tech Inc 1293
Tetra Technologies, Inc. 1293
Tetraphase Pharmaceuticals, Inc 1293
Texas A & M Research Foundation Inc 1293
Texas Capital Bancshares Inc 1293
Texas Children's Hospital 1294
Texas Christian University Inc 1294
Texas Department Of Transportation 1294
Texas Guaranteed Student Loan Corporation 1294
Texas Health Harris Methodist Hospital Fort Worth 1294
Texas Health Resources 1294
Texas Hospital Association 1295
Texas Industries Inc. 1295
Texas Instruments Inc. 1295
Texas Lutheran University 1295
Texas Municipal Power Agency 1295
Texas Pacific Land Trust 1295
Texas Roadhouse Inc 1296
Texas Southern University 1296
Texas State University 1296
Texas Vanguard Oil Co. 1296
Texon Lp 1296
Textron Inc 1296
Textura Corp 1297
Tf Financial Corp. 1297
Tfs Financial Corp 1297
Tg Therapeutics Inc 1297
The Adt Corporation 1297
The Aerospace Corporation 1297
The Amacore Group Inc. 1298
The Amalgamated Sugar Company Llc 1298
The American Automobile Association 1298
The American Museum Of Natural History 1298
The American Society For The Prevention Of Cruelty To Animals 1298
The Andrew W Mellon Foundation 1298
The Arthritis Foundation Inc 1299
The Aspen Institute Inc 1299
The Associated Press 1299

The Avedis Zildjian Company Inc. 1299
The Baltimore Life Insurance Company 1299
The Bancorp Inc 1299
The Beacon Mutual Insurance Company 1300
The Belt Railway Company Of Chicago 1300
The Benecon Group Inc 1300
The Berlin Steel Construction Company 1300
The Bessemer Group Incorporated 1300
The Biltmore Company 1300
The Bms Enterprises Inc 1301
The Boler Company 1301
The Branch Group Inc 1301
The Briad Group 1301
The Brickman Group Ltd. 1301
The Broe Companies Inc. 1301
The Brookings Institution 1302
The Brother's Brother Foundation 1302
The Bureau Of National Affairs Inc. 1302
The Burton Corporation 1302
The C.f. Sauer Company 1302
The Cadmus Group Llc 1302
The California Endowment 1303
The Capital Group Companies Inc. 1303
The Carriage House Companies Inc. 1303
The Carter-jones Lumber Company 1303
The Catholic University Of America 1303
The Centech Group Inc 1303
The Charles Machine Works Inc. 1304
The Charles Stark Draper Laboratory Inc 1304
The Charlotte-mecklenburg Hospital Authority 1304
The Children's Hospital Corporation 1304
The Children's Hospital Of Philadelphia 1304
The Childrens Hospital Los Angeles 1304
The Christ Hospital 1305
The Christian Broadcasting Network Inc 1305
The Citadel 1305
The City Of Seattle-city Light Department 1305
The Cleveland Clinic Foundation 1305
The Cleveland Electric Illuminating Company 1305
The Cobalt Group Inc. 1306
The College Network Inc 1306
The College Of Charleston 1306
The College Of William & Mary 1306
The College Of Wooster 1306
The Colonial Williamsburg Foundation 1306
The Community Hospital Group Inc 1307
The Computer Merchant Ltd 1307
The Computing Technology Industry Association Inc 1307
The Conservation Fund A Nonprofit Corporation 1307
The Container Store Inc. 1307
The Cooper Health System 1307
The Corporation Of Gonzaga University 1308
The Corporation Of Haverford College 1308
The Corporation Of Mercer University 1308
The Council Population Inc 1308
The Culinary Institute Of America 1308
The David And Lucile Packard Foundation 1308
The Day & Zimmermann Group Inc. 1309
The Dch Health Care Authority 1309
The Depository Trust & Clearing Corporation 1309
The Drees Company 1309
The Duchossois Group Inc. 1309
The Edelman Financial Group Inc. 1309
The Empire District Electric Company 1310
The Estee Lauder Companies Inc. 1310
The Evangelical Lutheran Good Samaritan Society 1310
The Finish Line Inc 1310
The Fishel Company 1310
The Food Emporium Inc. 1310
The Ford Foundation 1311
The Fox Chase Cancer Center Foundation 1311
The Fresh Market Inc 1311
The G W Van Keppel Company 1311
The Gap Inc 1311
The Gavilon Group Llc 1311
The Generation Companies Llc 1312
The George J Falter Company 1312
The George Washington University 1312
The Georgetown University 1312
The Gettysburg Hospital 1312
The Go Daddy Group Inc. 1312

The Golden 1 Credit Union 1313
The Golub Corporation 1313
The Good Samaritan Hospital Of Md Inc 1313
The Good Shepherd Hospital Inc 1313
The Great Atlantic & Pacific Tea Company Inc. 1313
The Green Bay Packers Inc. 1313
The Griffin Hospital Inc 1314
The Hallstar Company 1314
The Harvard Drug Group L.l.c. 1314
The Health Care Authority Of The City Of Huntsville 1314
The Heico Companies L.l.c. 1314
The Henry Francis Dupont Winterthur Museum Inc 1314
The Heritage Foundation 1315
The Hibbert Company 1315
The Hite Company 1315
The Humane Society Of The United States 1315
The Iams Company 1315
The Ingalls Memorial Hospital 1315
The Inland Real Estate Group Of Companies Inc. 1316
The Institute Of Electrical And Electronics Engineers Incorporated 1316
The Intec Group Inc. 1316
The International Association Of Lions Clubs Incorporated 1316
The International City Management Association Retirement Corporation 1316
The Irvine Company Llc 1316
The J G Wentworth Company 1317
The Jackson Laboratory 1317
The Jamaica Hospital 1317
The Jay Group Inc 1317
The Jewish Federations Of North America Inc 1317
The Jones Financial Companies L.l.l.p. 1317
The Judge Group Inc 1318
The Juilliard School 1318
The Kane Company 1318
The Kleinfelder Group Inc 1318
The Lancaster General Hospital 1318
The Lane Construction Corporation 1318
The Legal Aid Society Inc 1319
The Long & Foster Companies Inc. 1319
The Los Angeles Lakers Inc. 1319
The Louis Berger Group Inc. 1319
The Lubrizol Corporation 1319
The Massachusetts General Hospital 1319
The Mathworks Inc. 1320
The Mclean Hospital Corporation 1320
The Mechanics Bank 1320
The Medical University Of South Carolina 1320
The Memorial Hospital 1320
The Merchants Company 1320
The Methodist Hospital 1321
The Methodist Hospitals Inc 1321
The Metrohealth System 1321
The Metropolitan Museum Of Art 1321
The Middle Tennessee Electric Membership Corporation 1321
The Mitre Corporation 1321
The Mosaic Company 1322
The Moses H Cone Memorial Hospital Operating Corporation 1322
The National Association For The Exchange Of Industrial Resources Inc 1322
The Nature Conservancy 1322
The Nebraska Medical Center 1322
The New Home Company Inc 1322
The New Jersey Transit Corporation 1323
The New Liberty Hospital District Of Clay County Missouri 1323
The New School 1323
The New York And Presbyterian Hospital 1323
The New York Independent System Operator Inc 1323
The New York Public Library 1323
The Newark Group Inc. 1324
The Newtron Group L L C 1324
The North Highland Company Llc 1324
The Npd Group Inc. 1324
The Oltmans Construction Co 1324
The Paradies Shops Llc 1324
The Parsons Corporation 1325

COMPANIES LISTED ALPHABETICALLY

The Penn Mutual Life Insurance Company 1325
The Pennsylvania Hospital Of The University Of Pennsylvania Health System 1325
The Pennsylvania Lottery 1325
The Pennsylvania State University 1325
The Pew Charitable Trusts 1325
The Philadelphia Parking Authority 1326
The Philharmonic-symphony Society Of New York Inc 1326
The Pictsweet Company 1326
The Plaza Group Inc 1326
The Pmi Group Inc. 1326
The Port Authority Of New York & New Jersey 1326
The President And Trustees Of Colby College 1327
The President And Trustees Of Hampden-sydney College 1327
The Quiznos Master Llc 1327
The Reader's Digest Association Inc. 1327
The Reed Institute 1327
The Regents Of The University Of Colorado 1327
The Renco Group Inc. 1328
The Research Foundation For The State University Of New York 1328
The Rockefeller Foundation 1328
The Rockefeller University 1328
The Rockefeller University Faculty And Students Club Inc 1328
The Rudolph/libbe Companies Inc 1328
The Rutland Hospital Inc Act 220 1329
The Salvation Army National Corporation 1329
The Savannah College Of Art And Design Inc 1329
The Schwan Food Company 1329
The Scoular Company 1329
The Scripps Research Institute 1329
The Seminole Tribe Of Florida Inc. 1330
The Servicemaster Company 1330
The Shamrock Companies Inc 1330
The Solomon-page Group Llc 1330
The Southern Poverty Law Center Inc 1330
The Sundt Companies Inc 1330
The Susan G Komen Breast Cancer Foundation Inc 1331
The Timberland Company 1331
The Toledo Hospital 1331
The Trustees Of Davidson College 1331
The Trustees Of Grinnell College 1331
The Trustees Of Mount Holyoke College 1331
The Trustees Of Princeton University 1332
The Trustees Of The Smith College 1332
The Trustees Of The University Of Pennsylvania 1332
The Trustees Of Wheaton College 1332
The Turner Corporation 1332
The Ucla Foundation 1332
The Union Memorial Hospital 1333
The United Methodist Publishing House 1333
The University Of Akron 1333
The University Of Arizona Foundation 1333
The University Of Central Florida Board Of Trustees 1333
The University Of Chicago 1333
The University Of Chicago Medical Center 1334
The University Of Dayton 1334
The University Of Hartford 1334
The University Of Iowa 1334
The University Of North Carolina 1334
The University Of North Carolina At Charlotte 1334
The University Of South Dakota 1335
The University Of Southern Mississippi 1335
The University Of The South 1335
The University Of Toledo 1335
The University Of Tulsa 1335
The University Of Utah 1335
The University Of Vermont Medical Center Inc 1336
The Urban Institute 1336
The Valley Hospital Inc 1336
The Vanderbilt University 1336
The Waldinger Corporation 1336
The Walsh Group Ltd 1336
The Warrior Group Inc 1337
The Washington And Lee University 1337
The Washington University 1337
The Water Works Board Of The City Of Birmingham 1337
The Whiting-turner Contracting Company 1337

The Wichita State University 1337
The Will-burt Company 1338
The Willamette Valley Company Llc 1338
The Williams Companies Inc. 1338
The Wills Group Inc 1338
The Wistar Institute Of Anatomy And Biology 1338
The Yankee Candle Company Inc. 1338
The York Group Inc. 1339
The Ziegler Companies Inc. 1339
Thedacare, Inc. 1339
Therapeuticsmd Inc 1339
Therm-o-disc Incorporated 1339
Thermo Fisher Scientific Inc 1339
Thermoenergy Corp 1340
Thermogenesis Holdings Inc 1340
Thermon Group Holdings Inc 1340
Thestreet Inc 1340
Thirteen Productions Llc 1340
Thl Credit, Inc. 1340
Thomas & Betts Corporation 1341
Thomas Jefferson University 1341
Thomas Jefferson University Hospitals, Inc. 1341
Thomas Saint Midtown Hospital 1341
Thomasville Bancshares, Inc. 1341
Thompson Creek Metals Company Inc. 1341
Thompson Hospitality Corporation 1342
Thomson Reuters (legal) Inc. 1342
Thor Industries, Inc. 1342
Thoratec Corp. 1342
Thrustmaster Of Texas, Inc. 1342
Thruway Authority Of New York State 1342
Thunder Mountain Gold, Inc. 1343
Tib Financial Corp. 1343
Tibco Software, Inc. 1343
Ticc Capital Corp. 1343
Tidelands Bancshares Inc 1343
Tidelands Royalty Trust B 1343
Tidewater Inc (new) 1344
Tiffany & Co. 1344
Tiffin Motor Homes, Inc. 1344
Tift Regional Medical Center Foundation, Inc. 1344
Tigerlogic Corp 1344
Tigrent Inc. 1344
Tii Network Technologies Inc. 1345
Tilden Associates Inc. 1345
Timberland Bancorp, Inc. 1345
Timberline Resources Corporation 1345
Time Inc 1345
Time Warner Cable Inc 1345
Time Warner Inc 1346
Timios National Corp 1346
Timken Co. (the) 1346
Tiptree Inc 1346
Tishman Hotel Corporation 1346
Titan Energy Worldwide Inc 1346
Titan International Inc 1347
Titan Machinery, Inc. 1347
Titan Pharmaceuticals Inc (de) 1347
Titan Technologies, Inc. 1347
Tivity Health Inc 1347
Tivo Corp 1347
Tivo Inc 1348
Tix Corp 1348
Tjx Companies, Inc. 1348
Tks Industrial Company 1348
Tnemec Company, Inc. 1348
Tnr Technical, Inc. 1348
Todd Shipyards Corporation 1349
Tofutti Brands Inc 1349
Toll Brothers Inc. 1349
Tom Lange Company, Inc. 1349
Tom's Of Maine Inc. 1349
Tomax Corporation 1349
Tommy Bahama Group Inc. 1350
Tompkins Financial Corp 1350
Tootsie Roll Industries Inc 1350
Topco Associates Llc 1350
Tor Minerals International Inc 1350
Torch Energy Royalty Trust 1350
Torotel, Inc. 1351
Torrance Memorial Medical Center 1351
Total Health Care, Inc. 1351
Total System Services, Inc. 1351
Totes Isotoner Corporation 1351

Touchstone Bank 1351
Touro College 1352
Tower Financial Corp. 1352
Tower International Inc 1352
Towers Watson & Co. 1352
Towerstream Corp 1352
Town Sports International Holdings Inc 1352
Township High School District 211 Foundation 1353
Toyota Motor Credit Corp. 1353
Tps Parking Management Llc 1353
Track Group Inc 1353
Tractor Supply Co. 1353
Trade Street Residential, Inc. 1353
Tradestation Group Inc. 1354
Trailer Bridge Inc. 1354
Trammo, Inc. 1354
Trans World Corp. 1354
Trans World Entertainment Corp. 1354
Trans-system, Inc. 1354
Transact Technologies Inc. 1355
Transcat Inc 1355
Transcend Services Inc. 1355
Transcontinental Gas Pipe Line Company, Llc 1355
Transcontinental Realty Investors, Inc. 1355
Transdigm Group Inc 1355
Transitcenter Inc. 1356
Transmontaigne Partners Lp 1356
Transnet Corporation 1356
Transperfect Translations International Inc. 1356
Transtector Systems Inc. 1356
Tranzyme Inc. 1356
Travel And Transport Inc. 1357
Travelcenters Of America Inc 1357
Travelclick Inc. 1357
Travelers Companies Inc (the) 1357
Travelzoo 1357
Traylor Bros., Inc. 1357
Trc Companies, Inc. 1358
Treaty Energy Corp. 1358
Trecora Resources 1358
Tredegar Corp. 1358
Tree Top, Inc. 1358
Treehouse Foods Inc 1358
Trellis Earth Products Inc. 1359
Trevena Inc 1359
Trex Co Inc 1359
Trg Holdings Llc 1359
Tri Pointe Homes Llc 1359
Tri-city Electrical Contractors, Inc. 1359
Tri-city Hospital District (inc) 1360
Tri-west, Ltd. 1360
Tria Beauty Inc. 1360
Triangle Capital Corp 1360
Triangle Petroleum Corp 1360
Tribune Media Co 1360
Trico Bancshares (chico, Ca) 1361
Trident Seafoods Corporation 1361
Trihealth, Inc. 1361
Trilogy Leasing Co. Llc 1361
Trimas Corp (new) 1361
Trimble Inc 1361
Trimedyne Inc 1362
Trimol Group Inc. 1362
Trinitas Regional Medical Center 1362
Trinity Health System 1362
Trinity Industries, Inc. 1362
Trinity Mother Frances Health System Foundation 1362
Trinity University 1363
Tripadvisor Inc. 1363
Trippe Manufacturing Company 1363
Triquint Semiconductor, Inc. 1363
Tristate Capital Holdings Inc 1363
Trout-blue Chelan-magi, Inc. 1363
Troy University 1364
True Value Company 1364
Trueblue Inc 1364
Truist Financial Corp 1364
Trujillo & Sons, Inc. 1364
Truman Arnold Companies 1364
Truman Medical Center, Incorporated 1365
Trump Entertainment Resorts Inc. 1365
Trustco Bank Corp. (n.y.) 1365
Trustees Of Boston College 1365

Trustees Of Clark University 1365
Trustees Of Dartmouth College 1365
Trustees Of Indiana University 1366
Trustees Of The Colorado School Of Mines 1366
Trustees Of The Estate Of Bernice Pauahi Bishop 1366
Trustees Of Tufts College 1366
Trustees Of Union College In The Town Of Schenectady In The State Of New York 1366
Trustmark Corp 1366
Trustwave Holdings Inc. 1367
Truth Initiative Foundation 1367
Trw Automotive Holdings Corp 1367
Tsr Inc 1367
Tsrc, Inc. 1367
Tss Inc De 1367
Ttec Holdings Inc 1368
Ttm Technologies Inc 1368
Tucson Electric Power Company 1368
Tuesday Morning Corp 1368
Tufco Technologies, Inc. 1368
Tufts Associated Health Plans Inc. 1368
Tumi Holdings Inc 1369
Tupperware Brands Corp 1369
Turner Construction Company Inc 1369
Turtle & Hughes, Inc 1369
Turtle Beach Corp 1369
Tutor Perini Corp 1369
Tvax Biomedical Inc. 1370
Tw Telecom Inc 1370
Twin Disc Incorporated 1370
Twin Vee Powercats Inc 1370
Twitter Inc 1370
Two Harbors Investment Corp 1370
Two River Bancorp 1371
Tyco Fire & Security Llc 1371
Tyler Technologies, Inc. 1371
Tymco Inc. 1371
Tyndale House Publishers, Inc. 1371
Tyr Sport Inc. 1371
Tyson Foods Inc 1372
Tyson Fresh Meats Inc. 1372
U S China Mining Group Inc. 1372
U-swirl Inc. 1372
U.g.n., Inc. 1372
U.s. Auto Parts Network Inc 1372
U.s. News & World Report L.p. 1373
U.s. Physical Therapy, Inc. 1373
U.s. Silica Holdings Inc. 1373
U.s. Venture, Inc. 1373
U.s. Vision Inc. 1373
Uc Health, Llc. 1373
Uci Medical Affiliates Inc. 1374
Ucp Inc 1374
Udr Inc 1374
Ufp Technologies Inc. 1374
Ugi Corp. 1374
Uhy Advisors Inc. 1374
Uil Holding Corp 1375
Ulticom Inc. 1375
Ultimate Software Group, Inc. 1375
Ultra Clean Holdings Inc 1375
Ultra Petroleum Corp 1375
Ultra Stores Inc. 1375
Ultragenyx Pharmaceutical Inc 1376
Ultralife Corp 1376
Ultratech Inc 1376
Uluru Inc 1376
Umb Financial Corp 1376
Umh Properties Inc 1376
Umpqua Holdings Corp 1377
Unbound 1377
Under Armour Inc 1377
Underwriters Laboratories Inc. 1377
Unico American Corp. 1377
Unifi, Inc. 1377
Unifiedonline Inc 1378
Unifirst Corp 1378
Unigroup Inc. 1378
Unihealth Foundation 1378
Unilife Corp. 1378
Union Bank And Trust Company 1378
Union Bankshares, Inc. (morrisville, Vt) 1379
Union Health Service Inc 1379

Union Hospital, Inc. 1379
Union Pacific Corp 1379
Unionbancal Corporation 1379
Unipro Foodservice, Inc 1379
Uniroyal Global Engineered Products Inc 1380
Unisource Worldwide Inc. 1380
Unisys Corp 1380
Unit Corp. 1380
United Airlines Holdings Inc 1380
United American Healthcare Corp. 1380
United Bancorp, Inc. (martins Ferry, Oh) 1381
United Bancorp, Inc. (tecumseh, Mi) 1381
United Bancshares Inc. (oh) 1381
United Bank Card Inc. 1381
United Bankshares Inc 1381
United Capital Corp. 1381
United Cerebral Palsy Associations Inc. 1382
United Cerebral Palsy Associations Of New York State, Inc. 1382
United Community Bancorp 1382
United Community Banks Inc (blairsville, Ga) 1382
United Community Financial Corp. (oh) 1382
United Concordia Companies Inc. 1382
United Dairymen Of Arizona 1383
United Electric Supply Company, Inc. 1383
United Energy Corp. 1383
United Farmers Cooperative 1383
United Financial Bancorp Inc (md) 1383
United Fire Group, Inc. 1383
United Hardware Distributing Co 1384
United Health Services Hospital, Inc. 1384
United Health Services, Inc. 1384
United Insurance Holdings Corp 1384
United Natural Foods Inc. 1384
United Negro College Fund, Inc. 1384
United Online Inc 1385
United Parcel Service Inc 1385
United Performing Arts Fund Inc. 1385
United Regional Health Care System, Inc. 1385
United Rentals Inc 1385
United Security Bancshares (ca) 1385
United Space Alliance, Llc 1386
United States Antimony Corp. 1386
United States Basketball League Inc 1386
United States Beef Corporation 1386
United States Cellular Corp 1386
United States Department Of Justice 1386
United States Fund For Unicef 1387
United States Golf Association, Inc. 1387
United States Holocaust Memorial Museum 1387
United States Lime & Minerals Inc. 1387
United States Olympic Committee Inc 1387
United States Postal Service 1387
United States Soccer Federation, Inc. 1388
United States Steel Corp. 1388
United States Tennis Association Incorporated 1388
United Supermarkets L.l.c. 1388
United Surgical Partners International Inc. 1388
United Technologies Corp 1388
United Therapeutics Corp 1389
United Way Worldwide 1389
United-guardian, Inc. 1389
Unitedhealth Group Inc 1389
Unitek Global Services Inc. 1389
Unitil Corp 1389
Unity Bancorp, Inc. 1390
Univar Inc. 1390
Universal Corp 1390
Universal Detection Technology 1390
Universal Display Corp 1390
Universal Electronics Inc. 1390
Universal Forest Products Inc. 1391
Universal Health Realty Income Trust 1391
Universal Health Services, Inc. 1391
Universal Insurance Holdings Inc 1391
Universal Logistics Holdings Inc 1391
Universal Manufacturing Co 1391
Universal Power Group Inc 1392
Universal Security Instruments, Inc. 1392
Universal Stainless & Alloy Products, Inc. 1392
Universal Tax Systems Inc. 1392
Universal Technical Institute, Inc. 1392
Universal Weather And Aviation Inc. 1392
Universal Wilde Inc. 1393

University Bancorp Inc. (mi) 1393
University California, Merced 1393
University Community Hospital, Inc. 1393
University Corporation For Atmospheric Research 1393
University Federal Credit Union 1393
University Health Care Inc 1394
University Health Systems Of Eastern Carolina, Inc. 1394
University Hospitals Health System, Inc. 1394
University Medical Center Of Southern Nevada 1394
University Of Alaska System 1394
University Of Arizona 1394
University Of Arkansas System 1395
University Of California, Davis 1395
University Of Cincinnati 1395
University Of Colorado Foundation 1395
University Of Colorado Hospital Authority 1395
University Of Delaware 1395
University Of Detroit Mercy 1396
University Of Evansville 1396
University Of Florida 1396
University Of Georgia 1396
University Of Hawaii Systems 1396
University Of Houston System 1396
University Of Kentucky Hospital Auxiliary Inc. 1397
University Of La Verne 1397
University Of Louisville 1397
University Of Lynchburg 1397
University Of Maine System 1397
University Of Maryland Medical System Corporation 1397
University Of Massachusetts 1398
University Of Mississippi 1398
University Of Missouri System 1398
University Of Montana 1398
University Of New Haven, Incorporated 1398
University Of New Mexico 1398
University Of North Carolina At Chapel Hill 1399
University Of North Carolina At Greensboro 1399
University Of North Carolina Hospitals 1399
University Of North Dakota 1399
University Of Northern Iowa 1399
University Of Oklahoma 1399
University Of Oregon 1400
University Of Pittsburgh 1400
University Of Puget Sound 1400
University Of Redlands 1400
University Of Rhode Island 1400
University Of Richmond 1400
University Of San Diego 1401
University Of San Francisco Inc 1401
University Of Scranton 1401
University Of South Alabama 1401
University Of South Carolina 1401
University Of South Florida 1401
University Of Southern California 1402
University Of St. Thomas 1402
University Of Tennessee 1402
University Of Texas At Austin 1402
University Of Texas At Dallas 1402
University Of Texas At El Paso 1402
University Of The Pacific 1403
University Of Utah Health Hospitals And Clinics 1403
University Of Vermont & State Agricultural College 1403
University Of Washington Inc 1403
University Of West Georgia 1403
University Of Wisconsin Foundation 1403
University Of Wisconsin Hospital And Clinics Authority 1404
University Of Wisconsin Medical Foundation, Inc. 1404
University Of Wisconsin System 1404
University Of Wyoming 1404
University System Of Maryland 1404
University System Of New Hampshire 1404
Univest Financial Corp 1405
Univision Communications Inc. 1405
Unmc Physicians 1405
Uns Energy Corporation 1405
Unum Group 1405
Upmc 1405
Upmc Altoona 1406

Upson County Hospital, Inc. 1406
Upstate University Medical Associates At Syracuse, Inc. 1406
Uqm Technologies, Inc. 1406
Uranium Energy Corp. 1406
Uranium Resources Inc. 1406
Urata & Sons Concrete, Inc. 1407
Urban One Inc 1407
Urban Outfitters, Inc. 1407
Urigen Pharmaceuticals Inc. 1407
Urm Stores, Inc. 1407
Urologix Inc. 1407
Uroplasty, Inc. 1408
Urs Corp 1408
Urstadt Biddle Properties Inc 1408
Us 1 Industries Inc. 1408
Us Bancorp (de) 1408
Us Concrete Inc 1408
Us Dairy Export Council 1409
Us Dataworks Inc 1409
Us Department Of Homeland Security 1409
Us Department Of State 1409
Us Department Of The Air Force 1409
Us Ecology Inc (new) 1409
Us Energy Corp 1410
Us Foods Inc. 1410
Us Geothermal Inc 1410
Us Global Investors Inc 1410
Us Gold Corp (canada) 1410
Us Securities And Exchange Commission 1410
Us Silica Holdings, Inc. 1411
Us Small Business Administration 1411
Us Stem Cell Inc 1411
Us Xpress Enterprises Inc 1411
Usa Technologies Inc 1411
Usa Truck, Inc. 1411
Usaa 1412
Usana Health Sciences Inc 1412
Usda Forest Service 1412
Usfalcon, Inc. 1412
Usg Corp 1412
Usio Inc 1412
Uss-posco Industries, A California Joint Venture 1413
Ut Medical Group, Inc. 1413
Utah Associated Municipal Power Systems 1413
Utah Medical Products, Inc. 1413
Utah State University 1413
Utc Climate Controls & Security 1413
Utg Inc 1414
Utica College 1414
Uwharrie Capital Corp. 1414
Vaalco Energy, Inc. 1414
Vail Resorts Inc 1414
Valcom Inc. 1414
Valdosta State University 1415
Valence Technology, Inc. 1415
Valero Energy Corp 1415
Valero Energy Partners Lp 1415
Valhi, Inc. 1415
Valley Financial Corp. 1415
Valley Health System 1416
Valley Health System Llc 1416
Valley National Bancorp (nj) 1416
Valley View Community Unit School District 365u 1416
Valmont Industries Inc 1416
Valspar Corp 1416
Value Drug Company 1417
Value Line Inc 1417
Van Arpin Lines Inc 1417
Van Atlas Lines Inc 1417
Van Budd Lines Inc 1417
Van Horn Metz & Co. Inc. 1417
Vanda Pharmaceuticals Inc 1418
Vanderbilt University Medical Center 1418
Vanguard Natural Resources Llc 1418
Vantiv Inc. 1418
Varian Medical Systems Inc 1418
Varian Semiconductor Equipment Associates Inc. 1418
Variety Children's Hospital 1419
Vascular Solutions Inc 1419
Vaso Corp 1419
Vassar College 1419

Vassar College Inc 1419
Vaughan-bassett Furniture Company, Incorporated 1419
Vaxart Inc 1420
Vbi Vaccines Inc 1420
Vca Inc 1420
Vcg Holding Corp. 1420
Vector Group Ltd 1420
Vector Pipeline L.p. 1420
Vectren Corp 1421
Veeco Instruments Inc (de) 1421
Veeva Systems Inc 1421
Velocity Commercial Capital Inc. 1421
Velocity Express Llc 1421
Venoco Inc. 1421
Ventas Inc 1422
Ventera Corporation 1422
Venture Construction Company Inc 1422
Veolia Environmental Services North America Corp. 1422
Vera Bradley Inc. 1422
Veracyte Inc 1422
Veramark Technologies Inc. 1423
Verastem Inc. 1423
Vericel Corp 1423
Verifone Systems Inc. 1423
Verint Systems, Inc 1423
Verisign Inc 1423
Verisk Analytics Inc 1424
Veriteq Corp 1424
Verizon Communications Inc 1424
Vermillion Inc. 1424
Vermont Gas Systems Inc. 1424
Versar Inc. 1424
Verso Corp 1425
Verst Group Logistics, Inc. 1425
Vertex Pharmaceuticals, Inc. 1425
Vertical Communications, Inc. 1425
Vertical Computer Systems, Inc. 1425
Veru Inc 1425
Vesco Oil Corporation 1426
Veterans Of Foreign Wars Of The United States 1426
Vf Corp. 1426
Vhs Acquisition Subsidiary Number 3, Inc. 1426
Vhs Of Illinois, Inc. 1426
Via Christi Health, Inc. 1426
Viacom Inc 1427
Viacomcbs Inc 1427
Viad Corp. 1427
Viasat Inc 1427
Viasystems Group Inc 1427
Viavi Solutions Inc 1427
Vicor Corp 1428
Victor Technologies Group Inc. 1428
Victoria's Secret Direct Llc 1428
Victoria's Secret Stores Llc 1428
Video Display Corp 1428
Video Gaming Technologies Inc 1428
Videon Central Inc. 1429
Vienna Beef Ltd. 1429
Vietnam Veterans Of America Inc. 1429
View Systems, Inc. 1429
Viking Yacht Company 1429
Village Bank & Trust Financial Corp 1429
Village Super Market, Inc. 1430
Villanova University In The State Of Pennsylvania 1430
Vince Holding Corp 1430
Violin Memory Inc 1430
Virco Manufacturing Corp. 1430
Virginia Commonwealth University 1430
Virginia Electric & Power Co. 1431
Virginia Hospital Center Arlington Health System 1431
Virginia Housing Development Authority 1431
Virginia International Terminals, Llc 1431
Virginia Polytechnic Institute & State University 1431
Virginia West University Foundation Incorporated 1431
Virginia West University Hospitals Inc 1432
Virnetx Holding Corp 1432
Virtua Memorial Hospital Burlington County, Inc 1432

Virtualscopics Inc 1432
Virtus Investment Partners Inc 1432
Virtusa Corp 1432
Visa Inc 1433
Vishay Intertechnology, Inc. 1433
Vishay Precision Group Inc. 1433
Visiting Nurse Service Of New York 1433
Viskase Companies Inc. 1433
Vista Gold Corp. 1433
Vista International Technologies Inc 1434
Visteon Corp 1434
Vitacost.com Inc 1434
Vitalant 1434
Vitamin Shoppe Inc 1434
Vitas Healthcare Corporation 1434
Vitesse Semiconductor Corp. 1435
Viveve Medical Inc 1435
Vivus Inc 1435
Vizio, Inc. 1435
Vmware Inc 1435
Vocera Communications, Inc. 1435
Vocus Inc 1436
Volcano Corporation 1436
Volt Information Sciences Inc 1436
Voltari Corp 1436
Volunteer Energy Cooperative 1436
Volunteers Of America, Inc. 1436
Von Maur Inc. 1437
Vonage Holdings Corp 1437
Vornado Realty Trust 1437
Voxware Inc. 1437
Voxx International Corp 1437
Voyager Entertainment International Inc. 1437
Vratsinas Construction Company 1438
Vsb Bancorp Inc (ny) 1438
Vse Corp. 1438
Vsoft Corporation 1438
Vu1 Corporation 1438
Vulcan Materials Co (holding Company) 1438
Vuzix Corp 1439
Vwr Funding Inc. 1439
Vystar Corp 1439
Vystar Credit Union 1439
W & T Offshore Inc 1439
W M Keck Foundation Inc 1439
W. B. Doner & Company 1440
W. E. Aubuchon Co., Inc. 1440
W. K. Kellogg Foundation 1440
W. L. Butler Construction, Inc. 1440
W.p. Carey Inc 1440
W.s. Badcock Corporation 1440
Wabash College 1441
Wabash National Corp 1441
Waccamaw Bankshares Inc. 1441
Wachovia Preferred Funding Corp 1441
Wada Farms Marketing Group Llc 1441
Waddell & Reed Financial, Inc. 1441
Wadley Regional Medical Center 1442
Wageworks Inc 1442
Wagner Industries Inc. 1442
Wake Forest University 1442
Wake Forest University Baptist Medical Center 1442
Wakefern Food Corp. 1442
Wakemed 1443
Walbridge Aldinger Company 1443
Walgreens Boots Alliance Inc 1443
Walker & Dunlop Inc 1443
Walker Die Casting Inc. 1443
Walmart Inc 1443
Walsh Brothers, Incorporated 1444
Walter Energy, Inc. 1444
Walton Electric Membership Corporation 1444
Walton Signage Corporation 1444
War Memorial Hospital Inc. 1444
Ward Trucking, Llc 1444
Warner Music Group Corp. 1445
Warren Equities Inc. 1445
Warren Resources Inc (md) 1445
Warren Rural Electric Cooperative Corporation 1445
Washington Banking Co. (oak Harbor, Wa) 1445
Washington Federal Inc 1445
Washington Hospital Center Corporation 1446
Washington Metropolitan Area Transit Authority 1446

Washington Real Estate Investment Trust 1446
Washington Regional Medical Center 1446
Washington Suburban Sanitary Commission (inc) 1446
Washington Trust Bancorp, Inc. 1446
Waste Connections, Inc. 1447
Waste Control Specialists Llc 1447
Waste Management, Inc. (de) 1447
Waterfurnace Renewable Energy Inc 1447
Waters Corp. 1447
Watkins And Shepard Trucking, Inc. 1447
Watonwan Farm Service, Inc 1448
Watts Water Technologies Inc 1448
Waukesha Memorial Hospital, Inc. 1448
Waukesha-pearce Industries, Inc. 1448
Wausau Paper Corp 1448
Wave Systems Corp 1448
Wave Systems Corp. 1449
Wayfair Llc 1449
Wayland Baptist University Inc 1449
Wayne J. Griffin Electric, Inc. 1449
Wayne Memorial Health System, Inc. 1449
Wayne Savings Bancshares Inc 1449
Wayne State University 1450
Wayside Technology Group Inc 1450
Wbi Energy Transmission, Inc 1450
Wca Waste Corporation 1450
Wci Communities Inc 1450
Wd-40 Co 1450
Weatherford International Plc 1451
Web.com Group, Inc. 1451
Webco Industries Inc. 1451
Weber State University 1451
Webmd Health Corp 1451
Webster Financial Corp (waterbury, Conn) 1451
Webster University 1452
Wec Energy Group Inc 1452
Wedbush Securities Inc. 1452
Weeks Marine, Inc. 1452
Wegener Corp. 1452
Wegmans Food Markets, Inc. 1452
Weingarten Realty Investors 1453
Weirton Medical Center, Inc. 1453
Weis Markets, Inc. 1453
Welch Foods Inc., A Cooperative 1453
Wellcare Health Plans Inc 1453
Wellco Enterprises Inc. 1453
Wellesley College 1454
Wellmont Health System 1454
Wells Enterprises Inc. 1454
Wells Financial Corp 1454
Wellstar Health System, Inc. 1454
Welltower Inc 1454
Wendy's Co (the) 1455
Werner Enterprises, Inc. 1455
Wesbanco Inc 1455
Wesco Aircraft Holdings Inc. 1455
Wesco Financial Llc 1455
Wesco International, Inc. 1455
Wescom Credit Union 1456
Wesleyan University 1456
West Bancorporation, Inc. 1456
West Coast Novelty Corporation 1456
West Corp. 1456
West Marine, Inc. 1456
West Penn Allegheny Health System Inc. 1457
West Pharmaceutical Services, Inc. 1457
West Texas Gas, Inc. 1457
West Virginia United Health System, Inc. 1457
West Virginia University 1457
Westamerica Bancorporation 1457
Westar Energy Inc 1458
Westat, Inc. 1458
Westcon Group Inc. 1458
Westell Technologies Inc 1458
Western & Southern Financial Group, Inc. 1458
Western Alliance Bancorporation 1458
Western Area Power Administration 1459
Western Connecticut Health Network, Inc. 1459
Western Digital Corp 1459
Western Express Holdings Inc. 1459
Western Family Foods Inc. 1459
Western Farmers Electric Cooperative 1459
Western Gas Partners Lp 1460

Western Illinois University Inc 1460
Western Massachusetts Electric Co. 1460
Western Medical Center Auxiliary 1460
Western Michigan University 1460
Western Midstream Partners Lp 1460
Western New England Bancorp Inc 1461
Western Pennsylvania Hospital 1461
Western Refining Inc 1461
Western Refining Logistics Lp 1461
Western States Fire Protection Company Inc 1461
Western Union Co 1461
Western Washington University 1462
Westinghouse Air Brake Technologies Corporation 1462
Westlake Chemical Corp 1462
Westminster College 1462
Westmoreland Coal Co 1462
Westmoreland Resource Partners Lp 1462
Westwood Holdings Group, Inc. 1463
Wet Seal, Inc. (the) 1463
Wex Inc 1463
Wexford Health Sources, Inc. 1463
Weyco Group, Inc 1463
Weyerhaeuser Co 1463
Wgbh Educational Foundation 1464
Wgi Heavy Minerals Incorporated 1464
Wgl Holdings, Inc. 1464
Whalley Computer Associates, Inc. 1464
Whataburger Restaurants Lp 1464
Wheaton Franciscan Services, Inc. 1464
Wheaton Van Lines Inc 1465
Wheeler Real Estate Investment Trust Inc 1465
Wheeling & Lake Erie Railway Company 1465
Wheeling-nisshin, Inc. 1465
Whirlpool Corp 1465
White County Medical Center 1465
White Mountains Insurance Group Ltd. 1466
White River Capital Inc. 1466
White River Health System, Inc. 1466
Whiteglove Health Inc. 1466
Whitehead Institute For Biomedical Research 1466
Whitestone Reit 1466
Whitewave Foods Company 1467
Whiting Petroleum Corp 1467
Whitman College 1467
Whitney Museum Of American Art 1467
Whole Foods Market, Inc. 1467
Whyy Inc. 1467
Wichita, City Of (inc) 1468
Widener University 1468
Widepoint Corp 1468
Wikimedia Foundation, Inc. 1468
Wilbur Smith Associates, Inc. 1468
Wilbur-ellis Holdings Ii, Inc. 1468
Wilcohess Llc 1469
Wildlife Conservation Society 1469
Wiley (john) & Sons Inc. 1469
Wilhelmina International, Inc. 1469
Will County 1469
Willamette University 1469
Willamette Valley Vineyard Inc. 1470
Willbros Group Inc (de) 1470
Willdan Group Inc 1470
William Marsh Rice University Inc 1470
William Paterson University 1470
Williams Controls Inc. 1470
Williams Industrial Services Group Inc 1471
Williams Partners L.p. 1471
Williams Partners Lp (new) 1471
Williams Sausage Company Inc. 1471
Willis Lease Finance Corp. 1471
Wilmer Cutler Pickering Hale And Dorr Llp 1471
Wilshire Bancorp Inc 1472
Wilshire Enterprises Inc. 1472
Wilson Elser Moskowitz Edelman & Dicker Llp 1472
Wilson Sonsini Goodrich & Rosati 1472
Wilsonart International Holding Llc 1472
Wilton Brands Inc. 1472
Winchester Healthcare Management, Inc. 1473
Winchester Medical Center Auxiliary, Inc. 1473
Wind River Systems Inc 1473
Window To The World Communications Inc. 1473
Windstream Holdings Inc 1473
Windtree Therapeutics Inc 1473

Winland Holdings Corp 1474
Winmark Corp 1474
Winn-dixie Stores Inc. 1474
Winnebago Industries, Inc. 1474
Winston & Strawn Llp 1474
Winter Haven Hospital, Inc. 1474
Winthrop Nyu Hospital 1475
Winthrop Realty Trust 1475
Wintrust Financial Corp (il) 1475
Wireless Telecom Group, Inc. 1475
Wirtz Beverage Group Llc 1475
Wisdomtree Investments, Inc. 1475
Wistar Institute Of Anatomy & Biology 1476
Withlacoochee River Electric Cooperative Inc 1476
Wolverine Pipe Line Company 1476
Wolverine Power Supply Cooperative, Inc. 1476
Wolverine World Wide, Inc. 1476
Woman's Hospital Foundation Inc 1476
Woodmen Of The World Life Insurance Society 1477
Woods Hole, Martha's Vineyard And Nantucket Steamship Authority 1477
Woodstock Holdings Inc 1477
Woodward, Inc. 1477
Woolrich Inc. 1477
Workday Inc 1477
Workstream Usa Inc. 1478
World Acceptance Corp. 1478
World Energy Solutions, Inc. (de) 1478
World Finer Foods, Llc 1478
World Fuel Services Corp. 1478
World Surveillance Group Inc 1478
World Vision International 1479
World Wide Technology, Llc 1479
World Wildlife Fund, Inc. 1479
World Wrestling Entertainment Inc 1479
Worldpay Inc 1479
Worldwide Media Services Group Inc. 1479
Worthington Industries, Inc. 1480
Wpx Energy Inc 1480
Wright Investors' Service Holdings, Inc. 1480
Wright Medical Group Inc. 1480
Wright State University 1480
Writers Guild Of America West Inc. 1480
Wsfs Financial Corp 1481
Wsi Industries, Inc. 1481
Wvs Financial Corp. 1481
Ww International Inc 1481
Wyckoff Heights Medical Center 1481
Wyle Laboratories Inc. 1481
Wyndham Destinations Inc 1482
Wynn Resorts Ltd 1482
Wyoming Medical Center, Inc. 1482
X-rite Incorporated 1482
Xavier University 1482
Xcel Energy Inc 1482
Xcerra Corp 1483
Xencor, Inc 1483
Xenith Bankshares Inc 1483
Xenonics Holdings Inc 1483
Xenoport Inc 1483
Xerium Technologies Inc 1483
Xerox Holdings Corp 1484
Xeta Technologies Inc. 1484
Xfone Inc 1484
Xilinx, Inc. 1484
Xo Group Inc 1484
Xo Holdings Inc. 1484
Xoma Corp 1485
Xoriant Corporation 1485
Xpedx 1485
Xplore Technologies Corp. 1485
Xpo Logistics, Inc. 1485
Xpresspa Group Inc 1485
Xrs Corp 1486
Xtant Medical Holdings Inc 1486
Xura Inc 1486
Xylem Inc 1486
Yadkin Financial Corp 1486
Yakima Valley Memorial Hospital Association Inc 1486
Yale New Haven Health Services Corporation 1487
Yale University 1487
Yale-new Haven Hospital, Inc. 1487
Yash Technologies, Inc 1487

Yates Group, Inc. 1487
Yellowbook Inc. 1487
Yelp Inc 1488
Yeshiva University 1488
Yield10 Bioscience Inc 1488
York Hospital 1488
York Pennsylvania Hospital Company Llc 1488
York Water Co 1488
Young Broadcasting, Llc 1489
Young Life 1489
Youngstown State University Inc 1489
Your Community Bankshares Inc 1489
Yrc Worldwide Inc 1489
Ytb International Inc. 1489
Yum! Brands Inc 1490
Yuma Energy Inc (new) 1490
Yuma Regional Medical Center Inc 1490
Yume Inc 1490
Z Gallerie, Llc 1490
Zagg Inc 1490
Zale Corp. 1491
Zanett Inc. 1491
Zap 1491
Zareba Systems Inc. 1491
Zaza Energy Corp. 1491
Zebra Technologies Corp. 1491
Zeeland Community Hospital 1492
Zeltiq Aesthetics, Inc. 1492
Zep Inc 1492
Zimmer Biomet Holdings Inc 1492
Zimmer Gunsul Frasca Architects Llp 1492
Zion Oil And Gas Inc. 1492
Zions Bancorporation, N.a. 1493
Ziopharm Oncology Inc 1493
Ziprealty Inc 1493
Zix Corp 1493
Zoetis Inc 1493
Zogenix Inc. 1493
Zoll Medical Corporation 1494
Zoltek Companies Inc 1494
Zoological Society Of San Diego 1494
Zoom Telephonics, Inc. 1494
Zoomaway Travel Inc 1494
Zovio Inc 1494
Zumiez Inc 1495
Zygo Corp 1495
Zyla Life Sciences 1495
Zynga Inc 1495

Index by Headquarters

ALABAMA

ANDALUSIA
Powersouth Energy Cooperative 1068

Auburn
Auburn National Bancorp, Inc. 157
Auburn University 157

Birmingham
Alabama Power Co 49
Aptalis Pharma Inc. 123
Atherotech Inc. 150
Biohorizons Inc. 217
Birmingham-southern College Inc 220
Blue Cross And Blue Shield Of Alabama 228
Books-a-million, Inc. 239
Brasfield & Gorrie L.l.c. 246
Children's Health System 338
Consolidated Pipe & Supply Company, Inc. 388
Ebsco Industries Inc. 477
Encompass Health Corp 497
Energen Corp. 499
First Us Bancshares Inc 556
Golden Enterprises, Inc. 615
Hibbett Sports Inc 665
Infinity Property & Casualty Corp 708
Mayer Electric Supply Company, Inc. 852
Medical Properties Trust Inc 861
Motion Industries Inc. 908
Proassurance Corp 1078
Protective Life Corp. 1083
Protective Life Insurance Co 1084
Regions Financial Corp (new) 1116
Servisfirst Bancshares Inc 1183
Southern Nuclear Operating Company, Inc. 1217
Southern Research Institute Inc 1217
Spire Alabama Inc. 1225
Steris Instrument Management Services, Inc 1246
The Water Works Board Of The City Of Birmingham 1337
Vulcan Materials Co (holding Company) 1438
Walter Energy, Inc. 1444

DECATUR
Alabama Farmers Cooperative, Inc. 49

DOTHAN
Aaa Cooper Transportation 9
Houston County Healthcare Authority 683

Elba
National Security Group, Inc 928

Eufaula
American Buildings Company 80

GADSDEN
Gadsden Regional Medical Center, Llc 588
Southern Banc Co., Inc. 1213

HOOVER
Medseek Inc. 862

Huntsville
Adtran, Inc. 30
Colsa Corporation 372
Itc^deltacom Inc. 738
The Health Care Authority Of The City Of Huntsville 1314

Jasper
Pinnacle Bancshares, Inc. 1052

Mobile
Computer Programs & Systems Inc 381
International Shipholding Corp 726
University Of South Alabama 1401

Montgomery
Alfa Corporation 56
Jackson Hospital & Clinic, Inc 743
The Southern Poverty Law Center Inc 1330

Oneonta
Otelco Inc 1004

OPELIKA
East Alabama Health Care Authority 472

RED BAY
Tiffin Motor Homes, Inc. 1344

Sylacauga
Southfirst Bancshares Inc. 1218

TROY
Troy University 1364

TUSCALOOSA
The Dch Health Care Authority 1309

ALASKA

Anchorage
Alaska Communications Systems Group Inc 50
Alaska Conservation Foundation 51
Alaska Native Tribal Health Consortium 51
Alaska Railroad Corporation 51
Alaska Usa Federal Credit Union 51
Alyeska Pipeline Service Company 73
Arctic Slope Regional Corporation 130
Asrc Energy Services 144
Carr-gottstein Foods Co. 301
Chenega Corporation 333
Chugach Alaska Corporation 344
Chugach Electric Association, Inc. 344
First National Bank Alaska 553
General Communication Inc 595
Northrim Bancorp Inc 965
Petro Star Inc. 1042

FAIRBANKS
University Of Alaska System 1394

HOMER
South Peninsula Hospitals, Inc. 1211

Juneau
Alaska Pacific Bancshares, Inc. 51
Sealaska Corporation 1174

PALMER
Matanuska Telephone Association Incorporated 848

ARIZONA

Chandler
Arizona Instrument Llc 133
Bashas' Inc. 190
Insys Therapeutics Inc 715
Isola Group Ltd. 736
Microchip Technology Inc 882
Rogers Corp. 1136
Zovio Inc 1494

FLAGSTAFF
Flagstaff Medical Center, Inc. 558
Northern Arizona Healthcare Corporation 963
Northern Arizona University 963

MESA
City Of Mesa 353
Empire Southwest, Llc 495

Phoenix
Apollo Education Group, Inc. 118
Arizona Professional Baseball Lp 133
Arizona Public Service Co. 133
Ascent Healthcare Solutions Inc. 142
Avnet Inc 167
Banner Health 184
Best Western International, Inc. 210
Blue Cross And Blue Shield Of Arizona, Inc. 228
Cable One Inc 270
Core Construction, Inc. 395
Desert Schools Federal Credit Union 442
Ewing Irrigation Products, Inc. 520
F&b Manufacturing Company 526
Freeport-mcmoran Inc 578
Grand Canyon Education Inc 623
Innsuites Hospitality Trust 712
Insys Therapeutics Inc. 716
Inventure Foods Inc. 731
John C. Lincoln Health Network 750
Kitchell Corporation 774
Knight Transportation Inc. 775
Make-a-wish Foundation Of America 834
Matrixx Initiatives Inc. 848
Mercy Care 868
Mesa Air Group Inc 873
Mobile Mini, Inc. 897
Native Environmental L.l.c. 929
On Semiconductor Corp 992
Petsmart, Inc. 1043
Phoenix Children's Hospital, Inc. 1048
Pinnacle West Capital Corp 1053
Republic Services Inc 1121
Roofing Wholesale Co., Inc. 1137
Safe Ride Services Inc. 1149
Shamrock Foods Company 1186
Sprouts Farmers Market Inc 1226
Swift Transportation Co 1267
Viad Corp. 1427
Western Alliance Bancorporation 1458

Scottsdale
Alanco Technologies Inc 50
American Standard Energy Corp 96
Av Homes Inc 163
Axon Enterprise Inc 170
Carlisle Companies Inc. 297
Delta Mutual Inc. 438
Egpi Firecreek Inc 482
Equinox Payments Llc 512
Fender Musical Instruments Corporation 540
Gadsden Properties Inc 588
Igo Inc 697
International Minerals Corporation 726
Jda Software Group Inc. 746
Kona Grill Inc 778
Limelight Networks Inc 807
Magellan Health Inc. 831
Medicis Pharmaceutical Corporation 861
Meritage Homes Corp 871
P.f. Chang's China Bistro Inc. 1008
Scottsdale Healthcare Corp. 1172
Taylor Morrison Home Corp (holding Co) 1280
The Go Daddy Group Inc. 1312
Universal Electronics Inc. 1390
Universal Technical Institute, Inc. 1392
Vitalant 1434

Tempe
Amkor Technology Inc. 102
Amtech Systems, Inc. 106
Arizona State University 134
Avnet Technology Solutions 167
Benchmark Electronics, Inc. 204
Crexendo Inc 407
Drivetime Automotive Group, Inc. 462

INDEX BY HEADQUARTERS LOCATION

Emerson Network Power-embedded Computing Inc. 494
First Solar Inc 555
Global Entertainment Corporation 611
Insight Enterprises Inc. 713
Lifelock Inc 804
Mach 1 Global Services, Inc. 829
Northern Tier Energy Lp 964
Nortonlifelock Inc 969
Orthologic Corp. 1002
Salt River Project Agricultural Improvement And Power District 1156
United Dairymen Of Arizona 1383

Tolleson
Fry's Food And Drug Stores 582
Russell Sigler, Inc. 1145

Tucson
Accelerate Diagnostics Inc 15
Applied Energetics Inc 120
Asarco Llc 140
Association Of Universities For Research In Astronomy, Inc. 147
Banner-university Medical Center Tucson Campus Llc 184
Midasplus Inc. 886
The Sundt Companies Inc 1330
The University Of Arizona Foundation 1333
Tucson Electric Power Company 1368
University Of Arizona 1394
Uns Energy Corporation 1405

Yuma
Yuma Regional Medical Center Inc 1490

ARKANSAS

BATESVILLE
White River Health System, Inc. 1466

BENTON
Saline Memorial Hospital Auxiliary 1155

Bentonville
America's Car-mart Inc 77
Arvest Bank Group Inc. 140
Walmart Inc 1443

BLYTHEVILLE
Mississippi County Electric Cooperative, Inc. 894

CONWAY
Conway Regional Medical Center, Inc. 393
Home Bancshares Inc 676

EL DORADO
Anthony Forest Products Company, Llc 115
Deltic Timber Corp. 439
Murphy Oil Corp 915
Murphy Oil Usa Inc. 915
Murphy Usa Inc 916

FAYETTEVILLE
Ozarks Electric Cooperative Corporation 1008
Washington Regional Medical Center 1446

Fort Smith
Abf Freight System Inc. 12
Arcbest Corp 127
Baldor Electric Company 176
Ggnsc Holdings Llc 605
Qualserv Corporation 1096

Hot Springs National
Mountain Valley Spring Company Llc 910

JACKSONVILLE
First Electric Co-operative Corporation 550

JONESBORO
Arkansas State University 134
E. C. Barton & Company 470

LITTLE ROCK
Arkansas Children's Hospital 134
Arkansas Electric Cooperative Corporation 134
Arkansas Heart Hospital Llc 134
Bank Ozk 183
Baptist Health 184
Bear State Financial Inc 198
Cdi Contractors, Llc 312
Dillard's Inc. 450
Entergy Arkansas Inc 505
Heifer Project International Inc 657
Inuvo Inc 730
Replacement Parts, Inc. 1120
University Of Arkansas System 1395
Vratsinas Construction Company 1438
Windstream Holdings Inc 1473

Lowell
Hunt (j.b.) Transport Services, Inc. 688

MOUNTAIN HOME
Baxter County Regional Hospital, Inc. 193

NORTH LITTLE ROCK
Bruce Oakley, Inc. 258
Mountaire Corporation 910

PINE BLUFF
Jefferson Hospital Association, Inc. 747
Simmons First National Corp 1195

ROGERS
Cooper Communities Inc. 393

RUSSELLVILLE
Arkansas Tech University 135

SEARCY
White County Medical Center 1465

SPRINGDALE
Advanced Environmental Recycling Technologies, Inc. 31
H.c. Schmieding Produce Company, Llc 638
Tyson Foods Inc 1372

STUTTGART
Producers Rice Mill, Inc. 1079
Riceland Foods, Inc. 1128

Tontitown
P.a.m. Transportation Services, Inc. 1008

Van Buren
Usa Truck, Inc. 1411

CALIFORNIA

Alameda
Celera Corporation 314
Exelixis Inc 522
Insite Vision Inc. 714
West Coast Novelty Corporation 1456
Wind River Systems Inc. 1473

Alhambra
Emcore Corp. 492

Aliso Viejo
Avanir Pharmaceuticals, Inc. 164
Microsemi Corp 884
Qlogic Corp. 1094
Quest Software Inc. 1098
Sunstone Hotel Investors Inc. 1261
The New Home Company Inc 1322

Anaheim
Angels Baseball Lp 111
Bridgford Foods Corp. 248
Ddi Corp. 431
Eaco Corp 471
Pacific Sunwear Of California, Inc. 1012
Questcor Pharmaceuticals Inc 1098
Willdan Group Inc 1470

ARCADIA
Methodist Hospital Of Southern California 875

ATWATER
A.v. Thomas Produce, Inc. 8

AZUSA
Azusa Pacific University 171
Physicians Formula Holdings Inc. 1049

BAKERSFIELD
Calcot, Ltd. 275
Jaco Oil Company 744
San Joaquin Refining Co. Inc. 1159

Belmont
Ringcentral Inc 1130

Berkeley
Alta Bates Summit Medical Center 69
Andalay Solar Inc 109
Annie's Inc 113

BEVERLY HILLS
Academy Of Motion Picture Arts & Sciences 14
Brillstein Entertainment Partners Llc 250
Capricor Therapeutics Inc 290
Castle Rock Entertainment Inc. 305
First Physicians Capital Group Inc 554
Imagine Entertainment 700
Kennedy-wilson Holdings Inc 765
Live Nation Entertainment Inc 812
Pacwest Bancorp 1013
Pavilion Energy Resources Inc. 1026
Reald Inc. 1110
Universal Detection Technology 1390

BISHOP
Northern Inyo Healthcare District 963

Brisbane
Bebe Stores Inc 200
Bi-rite Restaurant Supply Co., Inc. 213
Cutera Inc 418
Intermune Inc. 723

Burbank
Abc Cable Networks Group 11
Ameriflight Llc 99
Aramark Uniform And Career Apparel Llc 125

Burlingame
Aerocentury Corp. 37
Innoviva Inc 712
Mills-peninsula Health Services 891

Calabasas Hills
Cheesecake Factory Inc. (the) 331

Calabasas
Asgn Inc 143

Dts Inc 463
Ixia 739
Netsol Technologies Inc 938
Unico American Corp. 1377

Camarillo
Aml Communications Inc. 103
International Card Establishment Inc. 724
Qualstar Corp 1096
Red Blossom Sales, Inc. 1112
Salem Media Group, Inc. 1155
Semtech Corp. 1179
Vitesse Semiconductor Corp. 1435

Campbell
Barracuda Networks Inc 188
Iwatt Inc. 739
Rainmaker Systems Inc. 1104
Vivus Inc 1435

Carlsbad
Alphatec Holdings Inc 68
Apptech Corp 122
Bergelectric Corp. 206
Case Financial Inc. 303
Catalina Restaurant Group Inc. 306
Clarocity Corp 355
Genmark Diagnostics, Inc. 600
Hay House Inc. 650
Homefed Corp. 677
Ionis Pharmaceuticals Inc 733
Lineage Cell Therapeutics Inc 809
Maxlinear Inc 851
Natural Alternatives International, Inc. 930
Ntn Buzztime Inc 972
Patriot Scientific Corporation 1025
Phoenix Footwear Group, Inc. 1048
Spy Inc 1227
Viasat Inc 1427
Xenonics Holdings Inc 1483

Carson
U.s. Auto Parts Network Inc 1372

Chatsworth
1105 Media Inc. 2
Align Aerospace Llc 56
Iris International Inc. 735
Mrv Communications, Inc. 911

Chico
Ameramex International Inc. 76
Trico Bancshares (chico, Ca) 1361

Chino Hills
Jacuzzi Brands Corp. 744

Chowchilla
Global Diversified Industries Inc. 611

CHULA VISTA
Community Health Group 378

CITY OF INDUSTRY
America Chung Nam (group) Holdings Llc 77
International Building Technologies Group Inc. 724
Morrow-meadows Corporation 907
Newegg Inc. 948
Premio, Inc. 1072

CLAREMONT
Claremont Graduate University 355
Claremont Mckenna College Foundation 355
Harvey Mudd College 648
Keck Graduate Institute 762
Pomona College 1062
Scripps College 1172

COLTON
Arrowhead Regional Medical Center 138

INDEX BY HEADQUARTERS LOCATION

Commerce
Amexdrug Corp. 102
Smart & Final Inc. 1202

Compton
Arden Group, Inc. 130

CONCORD
Bay Cities Paving & Grading, Inc. 193
Cerus Corp. 325

Corte Madera
Rh 1127

Costa Mesa
Ceradyne Inc. 323
Charlies Holdings Inc 329
Emulex Corporation 496
Experian Information Solutions Inc. 524
Isc8 Inc 735
Pacific Mercantile Bancorp 1011

COVINA
Citrus Valley Health Partners, Inc. 351
Simplicity Bancorp, Inc 1196

Culver City
Reading International Inc 1110

Cupertino
Affymax Inc 40
Apple Inc 119
Arcsight Llc 130
Durect Corp 467
Inventergy Global Inc 731

Cypress
Bandai America Incorporated 181
Chevys Restaurants Llc 335

Davis
Freedom From Hunger 577
Marrone Bio Innovations Inc 842
Moller International Inc. 899
University Of California, Davis 1395

DEL MAR
Liquid Investments, Inc. 810

Dixon
First Northern Community Bancorp 554

DOWNEY
Rockview Dairies, Inc. 1135

DUARTE
Pacific National Group 1011

DUBLIN
Callidus Software Inc. 279
Giga-tronics Inc 606
Ross Stores Inc 1139
Tria Beauty Inc. 1360

East Palo Alto
Finjan Holdings Inc 545

El Cajon
Royale Energy Inc 1142

El Centro
Rabobank N.a. 1102

El Segundo
Big 5 Sporting Goods Corp 213
Boeing Satellite Systems International Inc. 236
Directv 452
International Rectifier Corp. 726
Mattel Inc 849
Pcm, Inc 1028
Stamps.com Inc. 1237
The Aerospace Corporation 1297
The Los Angeles Lakers Inc. 1319
Wyle Laboratories Inc. 1481

Emeryville
Amyris Inc 107
Dynavax Technologies Corp 469
Exponential Interactive Inc. 524
Leapfrog Enterprises Inc 794
Lyris, Inc. 824
Mobitv Inc. 897
Nmi Holdings Inc 955
Novabay Pharmaceuticals Inc 970
Peet's Coffee & Tea Inc. 1031
Xoma Corp 1485
Ziprealty Inc 1493
Zogenix Inc. 1493

ESCONDIDO
One Stop Systems Inc. 994
Palomar Health 1015
Tearlab Corp 1282

FOLSOM
California Independent System Operator Corporation 277

FONTANA
California Steel Industries, Inc. 278

Foothill Ranch
Kaiser Aluminum Corp. 759
Wet Seal, Inc. (the) 1463

Foster City
Aoxing Pharmaceutical Co Inc 116
Gilead Sciences Inc 607
Ic Compliance Llc 693
Qualys, Inc. 1096
Quinstreet, Inc. 1100
Sciclone Pharmaceuticals, Inc. 1170

FOUNTAIN VALLEY
Memorial Health Services 864
New Cam Commerce Solutions Llc 941

Fremont
Actelis Networks Inc. 23
Actividentity Corporation 24
Aehr Test Systems 36
Asi Computer Technologies Inc 143
Axt Inc 170
Corsair Components Inc. 398
Electronics For Imaging, Inc. 486
Elma Electronic Inc. 489
Enphase Energy Inc. 503
Exar Corp. 521
Fremont Bancorporation 579
Ikanos Communications Inc 698
Lam Research Corp 787
Mattson Technology Inc 850
Mattson Technology, Inc. 850
Oplink Communications Inc. 997
Opnext Inc. 997
Penguin Computing, Inc. 1032
Procera Networks Inc 1078
Sigma Designs Inc 1193
Synnex Corp 1271
Vermillion Inc. 1424

Fresno
Central Valley Community Bancorp 320
Community Hospitals Of Central California 379
Saint Agnes Medical Center 1151
United Security Bancshares (ca) 1385

FULLERTON
Csu Fullerton Auxiliary Services Corporation 413
St. Jude Hospital 1233

GARDEN GROVE
Southland Industries 1218

GARDENA
Encore Nationwide Inc. 498

Z Gallerie, Llc 1490

GILROY
Christopher Ranch, Llc 342

Glendale
Avery Dennison Corp 165
Dine Brands Global Inc 451
Dreamworks Animation Skg Inc 461
Glendale Adventist Medical Center Inc 609
Legalzoom.com Inc. 796
Ps Business Parks Inc 1086
Public Storage 1089

Glendora
Calportland Company 280

Goleta
Community West Bancshares 379
Deckers Outdoor Corp. 433
Inogen, Inc 712

Hawthorne
Osi Systems, Inc. (de) 1003

Hayward
Anthera Pharmaceuticals Inc 114
Armanino Foods Of Distinction, Inc. 135
Berkeley Farms Llc 207
Ultra Clean Holdings Inc 1375

Hercules
Bio-rad Laboratories Inc 215

Hollywood
Deluxe Entertainment Services Group Inc. 439
Frederick's Of Hollywood Inc. 577
Sycamore Entertainment Group Inc. 1268

Huntington Beach
Bj's Restaurants Inc 221
Boardriders, Inc. 234
Bsh Home Appliances Corporation 261
C&d Zodiac Inc. 269
Tyr Sport Inc. 1371

IMPERIAL
Imperial Irrigation District 702

INGLEWOOD
Marvin Engineering Co., Inc. 844
Signature Eyewear Inc. 1194

Irvine
Acacia Research Corp 13
Advantage Sales And Marketing Llc 33
Aeronet, Inc. 38
Allergan, Inc 60
Alorica Inc. 67
Arbitech, Llc 126
Asics America Corporation 143
Biolase Inc 218
Biomerica Inc 218
Blizzard Entertainment Inc. 225
Broadcom Corp. 252
Calamp Corp 274
Calatlantic Group Inc 274
California Coastal Communities Inc. 276
California First National Bancorp 276
Camelot Entertainment Group Inc. 283
Cardiogenesis Corporation 294
Combimatrix Corp 374
Corvel Corp 398
Diedrich Coffee Inc. 448
Edwards Lifesciences Corp 481
Endologix Inc 499
Fox Head, Inc. 572
Healthpeak Properties Inc 654
I/omagic Corporation 692

Impac Mortgage Holdings, Inc. 702
Ingram Micro Inc. 710
Interpore Spine Ltd. 727
Ista Pharmaceuticals Inc. 737
Langston Snyder L P 789
Lantronix Inc. 790
Local Corp 813
Masimo Corp. 846
Mri Interventions Inc 911
Multi-fineline Electronix Inc 914
Netlist Inc 938
Newport Corporation 950
Nextgen Healthcare Inc 952
Optumrx Inc. 998
Pacific Dental Services Inc. 1010
Pro-dex Inc. (co) 1078
Prudential Overall Supply 1086
Resources Connection Inc 1123
Sabra Health Care Reit Inc 1148
Sage Software Inc. 1151
Spectrum Group International Inc 1223
Swh Corporation 1267
Tri Pointe Homes Llc 1359
Trimedyne Inc 1362
Vizio, Inc. 1435

KENTFIELD
Marin General Hospital 838

KINGSBURG
Sun-maid Growers Of California 1258

LA CANADA FLINTRIDGE
Allen Lund Company, Llc 60

La Canada
Sport Chalet, Inc. 1226

La Jolla
Medicinova Inc 861
National University 928
Orexigen Therapeutics Inc 1001
Sanford Burnham Prebys Medical Discovery Institute 1161
The Scripps Research Institute 1329

LA MESA
Grossmont Hospital Corporation 631

LA MIRADA
Biola University, Inc. 217

La Palma
Relax The Back Corporation 1117

LA VERNE
University Of La Verne 1397

LAGUNA HILLS
Saddleback Memorial Medical Center 1149

Lake Forest
Apria Healthcare Group Inc. 123
Comarco Inc. 373
Insight Health Services Holdings Corp. 713
Liquidmetal Technologies Inc 811
Quantum Fuel Systems Technologies Worldwide Inc. 1097
Sparta Inc. 1221
Staar Surgical Co. 1236

Lancaster
Simulations Plus Inc. 1197

Livermore
Formfactor Inc 568
G.s.e. Construction Company Inc. 588
Kinetic Systems, Inc. 772
Mcgrath Rentcorp 856
Performant Financial Corp 1039

LODI
Pacific Coast Producers 1010

INDEX BY HEADQUARTERS LOCATION

LOMA LINDA
Loma Linda University Medical Center 815

LONG BEACH
Alameda Corridor Transportation Authority 50
Apriso Corporation 123
City Of Long Beach 353
Long Beach Memorial Medical Center 816
Molina Healthcare Inc 899
Tatung Company Of America, Inc. 1279

Los Altos
American Restaurant Group Inc. 94
The David And Lucile Packard Foundation 1308

Los Angeles
1st Century Bancshares, Inc. 3
99 Cents Only Stores 6
Acento Advertising Incorporated 19
Adexa Inc. 28
Aecom 35
Air Lease Corp 46
Alda Office Properties Inc. 53
American Apparel, Inc. 79
Aptium Oncology Inc. 124
Associated Entertainment Releasing 145
Aurora Capital Partners L.p. 158
Baker Commodities Inc. 175
Boingo Wireless Inc 236
Breitburn Energy Partners Lp 247
Broadway Financial Corp. (de) 253
Cadiz Inc 272
California Community Foundation 276
California Pizza Kitchen Inc. 277
Capitalsource Inc. 289
Cathay General Bancorp 307
Cbre Group Inc 310
Cha Hollywood Medical Center Lp 326
Chromadex Corp 343
City National Corp. (beverly Hills, Ca) 352
Colony Capital Inc 370
Compumed Inc 381
Cyberdefender Corporation 420
Cytrx Corp 422
Daily Journal Corporation 424
Dick Clark Productions Inc. 447
Forever 21 Inc. 568
Fox Broadcasting Company 571
Fox Searchlight Pictures Inc. 572
Fraser/white Inc. 576
Gamefly Inc. 590
Gibson Dunn & Crutcher Llp 606
Good Samaritan Hospital 618
Guess ?, Inc. 635
Hanmi Financial Corp. 643
Harland M. Braun & Co., Inc. 645
Hudson Pacific Properties Inc 686
Hulu Llc 687
Intergroup Corp. (the) 721
International Creative Management Inc. 724
International Lease Finance Corp. 725
Internet Corporation For Assigned Names And Numbers 727
Kb Home 762
Kilroy Realty Corp 770
Korn Ferry 778
Korn/ferry International Futurestep Inc. 778
Latham & Watkins Llp 791
Loeb & Loeb Llp 813
Los Angeles County Department Of Health Services 817
Los Angeles County Metropolitan Transportation Authority 817
Los Angeles Department Of Water And Power 817
Los Angeles Philharmonic Association 818
Loyola Marymount University 819
Mercury General Corp. 868
Merle Norman Cosmetics, Inc. 872
Mitchell Silberberg & Knupp Llp 896
Mmrglobal Inc 897
O'melveny & Myers Llp 977
Oaktree Capital Group Llc 979
Oaktree Specialty Lending Corp 980
Occidental College 981
Pabst Brewing Company 1009
Pacific Theatres Corporation 1012
Paul Hastings Janofsky & Walker Llp 1026
Persian Arts Society Incorporated 1041
Point.360 (new) 1060
Portsmouth Square, Inc. 1065
Preferred Bank (los Angeles, Ca) 1071
Primex International Trading Corp 1076
Prospect Medical Holdings Inc. 1083
Public Communications Services, Inc. 1088
Quinn Emanuel Urquhart & Sullivan Llp 1100
Radnet Inc 1103
Reliance Steel & Aluminum Co. 1117
Restorgenex Corp 1123
Rexford Industrial Realty Inc 1125
Rexford Industrial Realty, Inc. 1126
Santa Fe Financial Corp. 1162
Simon Worldwide Inc. 1196
Southern California Gas Co. 1214
Southern California Regional Rail Authority 1214
Spark Networks Inc 1221
The California Endowment 1303
The Capital Group Companies Inc. 1303
The Childrens Hospital Los Angeles 1304
The Ucla Foundation 1332
Unihealth Foundation 1378
University Of Southern California 1402
Vca Inc 1420
W M Keck Foundation Inc 1439
Wedbush Securities Inc. 1452
Wilshire Bancorp Inc 1472
Writers Guild Of America West Inc. 1480

Los Gatos
Bns Holding Inc. 234
Infogain Corporation 708
Netflix Inc 937

MALIBU
Pepperdine University 1037

Manhattan Beach
Kinecta Federal Credit Union 771
Skechers Usa Inc 1199

Menlo Park
Corcept Therapeutics Inc 395
Exponent Inc. 524
Facebook Inc 527
Hewlett, William And Flora Foundation (inc) 663
Pacific Biosciences Of California Inc 1009
Robert Half International Inc. 1133
Sri International 1228

MERCED
University California, Merced 1393

Mill Valley
Redwood Trust Inc 1113

MILPITAS
Devcon Construction Incorporated 443
Dialogic Inc 445
Fireeye Inc 545
Integrated Silicon Solution, Inc. 717
Ixys Corp. 739
Linear Technology Corp 809
Pericom Semiconductor Corp. 1040
Phoenix Technologies Ltd. 1049
Promise Technology Inc. 1081
Renesas Electronics America Inc. 1118
Sandisk Corp. 1160
Sierra Monitor Corp 1192
Silicon Graphics International Corp. 1194

Mission Viejo
Aeolus Pharmaceuticals Inc 36
Elixir Industries 487

Modesto
A. B. Boyd Company 7
Modesto Irrigation District (inc) 898

Moffett Field
Msgi Technology Solutions Inc. 912

Monrovia
World Vision International 1479
Xencor, Inc 1483

MONTEBELLO
Mexican American Opportunity Foundation 879

MONTEREY
Community Hospital Of The Monterey Peninsula 379

Morgan Hill
Coast Distribution System 363
Del Monaco Specialty Foods Inc. 434

Mountain View
Alexza Pharmaceuticals Inc 55
Alphabet Inc 68
Ceva Inc 325
Chemocentryx, Inc. 332
Hansen Medical Inc 644
Intuit Inc 730
Iridex Corp. 734
Linkedin Corp 809
Mozilla Foundation 910
Omnicell Inc 991
Synopsys Inc 1271

NAPA
Queen Of The Valley Medical Center 1097

NATIONAL CITY
Paradise Valley Hospital 1018

NEWARK
Bioclinca 216
Revance Therapeutics Inc 1124
Smart Modular Technologies Inc. 1202
Socket Mobile Inc 1205

Newport Beach
Acacia Technologies Llc 14
Alliance Healthcare Services Inc 62
American Vanguard Corp. 98
Chipotle Mexican Grill Inc 341
Clean Energy Fuels Corp 356
Dpw Holdings Inc 460
Dyntek Inc. 470
Hoag Hospital Foundation 673
Hoag Memorial Hospital Presbyterian 673
Lyon (william) Homes 824
Morris Business Development Co 906
Pacific Mutual Holding Co. 1011
Roth Capital Partners Llc 1140
The Irvine Company Llc 1316

North Hollywood
Academy Of Television Arts & Sciences Inc. 14
Ipc Healthcare, Inc. 733
O P I Products Inc. 977

Northridge
American Soil Technologies Inc 95

NORWALK
Cerritos Community College District 324

Novato
Bank Of Marin Bancorp 182
Birkenstock Usa Gp Llc 220
Raptor Pharmaceuticals Corp. 1106
Ultragenyx Pharmaceutical Inc 1376

Oakdale
Oak Valley Bancorp 978
Oak Valley Bancorp (oakdale, Ca) 979

Oakland
Ask.com 143
Children's Hospital & Research Center At Oakland 338
Clorox Co (the) 360
Dasan Zhone Solutions Inc 427
East Bay Municipal Utility District, Water System 473
Kaiser Foundation Hospitals Inc 759
Pandora Media Inc 1016
San Francisco Bay Area Rapid Transit District 1159
Scientific Learning Corp. 1170
Sierra Club 1191
Summit Bancshares Inc. 1256

OCEANSIDE
Tri-city Hospital District (inc) 1360

Ontario
Cvb Financial Corp 418

ORANGE
Chapman University 327
D W W Co., Inc. 423
Orange County Transportation Authority 998
Roth Staffing Companies, L.p. 1140
Sc Fuels 1166
St. Joseph Hospital Of Orange 1233
Sybron Dental Specialties Inc. 1268

Orinda
Axa Rosenberg Investment Managment Llc 168

Oxnard
Cdti Advanced Materials Inc 312

Palm Desert
Surge Global Energy Inc 1264

Palo Alto
Accel Partners 15
Anacor Pharmaceuticals Inc 107
Electric Power Research Institute, Inc. 485
First Tech Federal Credit Union 555
Hercules Technology Growth Capital Inc. 660
Hp Inc 684
Ideo Llc 696
Jive Software Inc 749
Ocera Therapeutics Inc 982
Palo Alto Medical Foundation For Health Care Research And Educat 1015

Southwall Technologies Inc. 1218
Space Systems/loral Inc. 1220
Tesla Inc 1292
Tibco Software, Inc. 1343
Varian Medical Systems Inc 1418
Vmware Inc 1435
Wilson Sonsini Goodrich & Rosati 1472

Pasadena
3m Cogent Inc. 5
Alexandria Real Estate Equities Inc 55
Ameron International Corporation 101
Arrowhead Pharmaceuticals Inc 138
Art Center College Of Design Inc 138
California Institute Of Technology 277
Charles Pankow Builders Ltd. 328
East West Bancorp, Inc 473
Fuller Theological Seminary 584
General Finance Corp 596
Green Dot Corp 628
Guidance Software Inc 635
Idealab 695
Operating Engineers Funds Inc. 996
Pasadena Area Community College District 1023
Pasadena Hospital Association, Ltd. 1023
Southern California Public Power Authority 1214
Tetra Tech Inc 1293
Wesco Financial Llc 1455
Wescom Credit Union 1456

Paso Robles
Heritage Oaks Bancorp 661

Petaluma
Amy's Kitchen Inc. 106
Sonoma Pharmaceuticals Inc 1208

Pico Rivera
Bakemark Usa Llc 174

Pismo Beach
Pismo Coast Village, Inc. 1054

PITTSBURG
Uss-posco Industries, A California Joint Venture 1413

Playa Vista
Belkin International Inc. 203

Pleasanton
Adept Technology Inc. 28
American Baptist Homes Of The West 80
Blackhawk Network Holdings Inc 224
Cooper Companies, Inc. (the) 393
Ellie Mae Inc 488
Frontrange Solutions Inc. 581
Fulcrum Bioenergy Inc. 584
Ironplanet Inc. 735
Natus Medical Inc. 931
Safeway Inc. 1150
Simpson Manufacturing Co., Inc. (de) 1196
Simpson Strong-tie Company Inc. 1196
Thoratec Corp. 1342
Veeva Systems Inc 1421
Workday Inc 1477
Zeltiq Aesthetics, Inc. 1492

Porterville
Sierra Bancorp 1191
Sierra View District Hospital League, Inc. 1192

Poway
Cohu Inc 368

Quincy
Plumas Bancorp Inc 1059

Rancho Cordova
Aerojet-general Corporation 37
American River Bankshares 94
Thermogenesis Holdings Inc 1340
Urata & Sons Concrete, Inc. 1407

Rancho Cucamonga
Agent Information Software Inc 42
Pure Bioscience Inc 1091

RANCHO MIRAGE
Eisenhower Medical Center 483

Redding
North Valley Bancorp (redding, Ca) 961
Prime Healthcare Services - Shasta, Llc 1075

REDLANDS
University Of Redlands 1400

Redondo Beach
Aura Systems Inc 158
Bidz.com Inc. 213

Redwood City
Acelrx Pharmaceuticals Inc 19
Broadvision Inc 253
Codexis Inc 366
Dextera Surgical Inc 444
Dpr Construction, Inc. 460
Electronic Arts, Inc. 486
Equilar Inc. 511
Equinix Inc 511
Genomic Health Inc 600
Informatica Corp. 709
Oncomed Pharmaceuticals Inc. 993
Rocket Fuel Inc 1135
Shutterfly Inc 1190
W. L. Butler Construction, Inc. 1440
Yume Inc 1490

Redwood Shores
Imperva Inc 702
Ipass Inc 733

Richmond
The Mechanics Bank 1320

RIVERSIDE
Dura Coat Products Inc. 466
Index Fresh, Inc. 705
Provident Financial Holdings, Inc. 1085

ROCKLIN
Purple Communications, Inc. 1092

Rosemead
Edison International 480
Southern California Edison Co. 1213

ROSEVILLE
Adventist Health System/west 34
Quest Media & Supplies, Inc. 1098
Surewest Communications 1264

SACRAMENTO
Alston Construction Company, Inc. 69
Bank Of Commerce Holdings (ca) 181
Burgett Inc. 264
California Public Employees' Retirement System 277
Integrated Surgical Systems Inc. 718
Mcclatchy Co (the) 854
Pacific Ethanol Inc 1010
Sacramento Municipal Utility District 1149
Sutter Health 1266
The Golden 1 Credit Union 1313

SALINAS
City Of Salinas 353
Salinas Valley Memorial Healthcare Systems 1155
Scheid Vineyards Inc. 1167

SAN BERNARDINO
Community Hospital Of San Bernardino 378
Stater Bros. Holdings Inc. 1243

San Carlos
Biocardia Inc 216
Rudolph And Sletten, Inc. 1144

SAN CLEMENTE
Advanced Mp Technology Inc. 32
Bubba Gump Shrimp Co. Restaurants Inc. 261
Icu Medical Inc 694
Image Protect Inc 699
Micro Imaging Technology Inc. 882
Reshape Lifesciences Inc 1122

San Diego
Acadia Pharmaceuticals Inc 14
Accelrys Inc 16
Ace Parking Management Inc. 18
Ace Relocation Systems, Inc. 18
Adamis Pharmaceuticals Corp. 26
Adventrx Pharmaceuticals Inc. 34
Alliant International University, Inc. 63
American Assets Trust, Inc. 79
Amn Healthcare Services Inc 103
Ampliphi Biosciences Corp 104
Amylin Pharmaceuticals Inc. 106
Anadys Pharmaceuticals Inc. 107
Applied Molecular Evolution Inc. 121
Apricus Biosciences Inc 123
Arcturus Therapeutics Holdings Inc 130
Ardea Biosciences Inc. 130
Arena Pharmaceuticals Inc 131
Axesstel Inc 169
Biocept Inc 216
Biomed Realty Trust Inc 218
Brickell Biotech Inc 247
Bycor General Contractors, Inc. 268
Cadence Pharmaceuticals Inc 272
California Bank & Trust 276
Carefusion Corp 295
Chargers Football Company Llc 327
Coast Citrus Distributors 363
Conatus Pharmaceuticals Inc 384
Cubic Corp 415
Cuso Financial Services, L.p. 417
Dexcom Inc 444
E.digital Corp. 470
Encore Capital Group Inc 498
Entropic Communications, Inc. 507
Epsilon Systems Solutions, Inc. 511
Event Network, Inc. 518
Excel Trust Inc. 521
Fate Therapeutics Inc 532
Franklin Wireless Corp 576
Garden Fresh Restaurant Corp. 591
Gen-probe Incorporated 594
Genasys Inc 594
Halozyme Therapeutics Inc 641
Harbor Biosciences Inc. 644
Hawthorne Machinery Co. 650
Heritage Global Inc 661
Heron Therapeutics Inc 662
Iaso Pharma Inc. 692
Illumina Inc 699
Imageware Systems Inc 700
Jack In The Box, Inc. 742
John Hine Pontiac 751
Kratos Defense & Security Solutions, Inc. 780
La Jolla Pharmaceutical Co. 783
Leap Wireless International Inc 794
Ligand Pharmaceuticals Inc 805
Mabvax Therapeutics Holdings Inc 827
Maxwell Technologies Inc 851
Mirati Therapeutics Inc 893
Mitek Systems, Inc. 896
Networkfleet Inc. 939
Neurocrine Biosciences, Inc. 939
Ninyo & Moore Geotechnical & Environmental Sciences Consultants 955
Nuvasive Inc 975
Overland Storage, Inc. 1006
Pacific Building Group 1010
Parron-hall Corporation 1022
Peregrine Semiconductor Corporation 1038
Petco Animal Supplies Inc. 1041
Plus Therapeutics Inc 1059
Point Loma Nazarene University 1060
Pricesmart Inc 1075
Prometheus Laboratories Inc. 1081
Provide Commerce Inc. 1084
Pulse Electronics Corp 1091
Qualcomm Inc 1095
Quidel Corp. 1099
Rady Children's Hospital-san Diego 1103
Realty Income Corp 1111
Reno Contracting Inc. 1119
Resmed Inc. 1122
Retail Opportunity Investments Corp 1123
Rf Industries Ltd. 1126
San Diego State University Foundation 1158
San Diego Unified Port District 1158
Scripps Health 1172
Sempra Energy 1179
Senomyx Inc 1180
Sequenom Inc 1181
Sevion Therapeutics Inc 1185
Sharp Healthcare 1186
Sharp Memorial Hospital 1187
Tachyon Networks Inc. 1274
Tandem Diabetes Care Inc 1276
Taxus Cardium Pharmaceuticals Group Inc 1280
Teradata Corp (de) 1290
The Kleinfelder Group Inc 1318
Turtle Beach Corp 1369
University Of San Diego 1401
Volcano Corporation 1436
Wd-40 Co 1450
Zoological Society Of San Diego 1494

San Dimas
American States Water Co 96

San Francisco
Advent Software, Inc. 34
American Shared Hospital Services 95
Ants Software Inc. 115
Aptimus Inc. 124
Astoria Software Inc. 148
Babycenter L.l.c. 172
Bancwest Corporation 180
Bank Of The West 183
Bare Escentuals Inc. 187
Bechtel Group Inc. 200
Benefit Cosmetics Llc 205
Bre Properties, Inc. 247
Burrill & Company Llc 265
Cai International Inc 273
California Physicians' Service 277
Calypso Technology Inc. 281
Del Monte Corporation 434
Delta Dental Of California 437
Diamond Foods Inc 446
Digital Realty Trust Inc 449
Dignity Health 450
Ecotality Inc 479
Embarcadero Technologies Inc. 490
Federal Home Loan Bank Of San Francisco 535

INDEX BY HEADQUARTERS LOCATION

Federal Reserve Bank Of San Francisco, Dist. No. 12 537
Fibertower Corporation 542
First Republic Bank (san Francisco, Ca) 554
Fusionstorm 586
Geopetro Resources Co 602
Glu Mobile Inc 614
Golden Gate National Parks Conservancy 616
Hornblower Yachts, Llc 680
Ia Global Inc. 692
Jmp Group Llc 749
Joie De Vivre Hospitality Inc. 754
Kimpton Hotel & Restaurant Group Llc 771
Kkr Financial Holdings Llc 775
Kqed Inc. 779
Levi Strauss & Co. 799
Levi Strauss & Co. 800
Linux Foundation 810
Littler Mendelson P.c. 812
Liveramp Holdings Inc 812
Looksmart Ltd. 816
Loopnet Inc. 817
Lucasfilm Entertainment Company Ltd. 821
Mac Beath Hardwood Company 828
Marin Software Inc 838
Medivation Inc 862
Merriman Holdings Inc. 873
Mulesoft, Inc. 914
Nektar Therapeutics 935
Old Navy Inc. 988
Opentable Inc. 996
Otsuka America Inc 1004
Patelco Credit Union 1024
Pattern Energy Group Inc 1026
Pg&e Corp (holding Co) 1044
Prologis Inc 1081
Recology Inc. 1111
Riverbed Technology Inc 1131
Rpx Corp 1142
Rw Stearns Inc. 1146
Salesforce.com Inc 1155
Salon Media Group Inc. 1156
Schwab (charles) Corp (the) 1169
Sedgwick Llp 1177
Splunk Inc 1225
State Compensation Insurance Fund 1241
Sutter Bay Hospitals 1266
Swinerton Builders 1267
Swinerton Incorporated 1268
Terreno Realty Corp 1291
The Gap Inc 1311
Twitter Inc 1370
Unionbancal Corporation 1379
University Of San Francisco Inc 1401
Urigen Pharmaceuticals Inc. 1407
Urs Corp 1408
Visa Inc 1433
Wikimedia Foundation, Inc. 1468
Wilbur-ellis Holdings Ii, Inc. 1468
Yelp Inc 1488
Zynga Inc 1495

San Jose
8x8 Inc 6
Acer America Corporation 19
Activevideo Networks Inc. 24
Adobe Inc 29
Align Technology Inc 56
Altera Corp. 71
Altigen Communications Inc 71
Anixa Biosciences Inc 112
Apache Design Solutions Inc. 116
Aptina Llc 124
Atmel Corporation 154
Bluearc Corporation 231
Bridge Capital Holdings 248
Broadcom Inc (de) 252

Brocade Communications Systems, Inc. 254
Calient Networks Inc. 276
California Water Service Group (de) 278
Calix Inc 278
Cavium Inc 309
Centerbeam Inc. 316
Cisco Systems Inc 348
Cupertino Electric Inc. 417
Cybernet Software Systems Inc. 420
Cypress Semiconductor Corp. 421
Document Capture Technologies Inc 455
Dsp Group, Inc. 462
Ebay Inc. 477
Extreme Networks Inc 525
Fairchild Semiconductor International, Inc. 527
Gct Semiconductor Inc. 593
Gigpeak Inc 606
Good Samaritan Hospital, L.p. 618
Harmonic, Inc. 646
Heritage Commerce Corp 661
Hewlett Packard Enterprise Co 663
Human Pheromone Sciences Inc. 687
Immersion Corp 700
Integrated Device Technology Inc 717
Intermolecular Inc 722
Invensense Inc 731
Isign Solutions Inc 736
Liveworld, Inc. 813
Lsi Corp 821
Lynuxworks Inc. 823
Magma Design Automation Inc. 831
Maxim Integrated Products, Inc. 850
Micrel, Inc. 882
Micrus Endovascular Corporation 885
Mosys Inc 908
Move Inc 910
Neophotonics Corp 936
Netgear Inc 937
Nimble Storage, Inc. 954
Notify Technology Corporation 970
Oclaro Inc 983
Ocz Technology Group Inc 983
Paypal Inc. 1027
Pixelworks Inc 1055
Polycom Inc. 1061
Power Integrations Inc. 1067
Qualcomm Atheros Inc. 1095
Quantum Corp 1097
Quicklogic Corp 1099
Rae Systems Inc. 1103
San Jose Water Company 1159
Sanmina Corp 1161
Semler Scientific Inc 1179
Silver Spring Networks Inc 1195
Sjw Group 1199
Sunpower Corp 1260
Super Micro Computer Inc 1262
Synaptics Inc 1270
Tivo Corp 1347
Tivo Inc 1348
Ucp Corp 1374
Ultratech Inc 1376
Verifone Systems Inc. 1423
Viavi Solutions Inc 1427
Vocera Communications, Inc. 1435
Western Digital Corp 1459
Xilinx, Inc. 1484

SAN JUAN CAPISTRANO
Cosco Fire Protection, Inc. 398
Ensign Group Inc 504

San Leandro
Energy Recovery Inc 500
International Fleet Sales Inc. 725

San Luis Obispo
Mission Community Bancorp 894

Sunrun Installation Services Inc. 1261

San Mateo
Actuate Corp. 25
Armco Metals Holdings Inc 135
Avistar Communications Corporation 167
Capcom U.s.a. Inc. 287
Essex Property Trust Inc 516
Franklin Resources Inc 575
Guidewire Software Inc 635
Marketo Inc 841
Model N, Inc 898
Netsuite Inc 938
Satmetrix Systems Inc. 1164
Serena Software Inc. 1181
Successfactors Inc. 1255
Tesla Energy Operations, Inc. 1292
Wageworks Inc 1442

San Rafael
Autodesk Inc 161
Westamerica Bancorporation 1457

San Ramon
Arc Document Solutions, Inc. 127
Chevron Corporation 335
Galena Biopharma Inc 589
Hill Physicians Medical Group, Inc. 668
Jacobs, Malcolm & Burtt 744

Santa Ana
Acme Communications Inc 20
Banc Of California Inc 179
Collectors Universe Inc 369
Corinthian Colleges, Inc. 396
Ducommun Inc. 463
Edison Mission Energy 480
First American Financial Corp 546
Iteris Inc 738
Moorefield Construction, Inc. 904
Raptor Networks Technology Inc. 1106
Schoolsfirst Fcu 1169
Ttm Technologies Inc 1368
Western Medical Center Auxiliary 1460

Santa Barbara
Benefit Software Inc. 205
Direct Relief 452
Qad, Inc. 1093

SANTA CLARA
Actiontec Electronics, Inc. 23
Advanced Analogic Technologies Incorporated 31
Advanced Micro Devices Inc 32
Affymetrix, Inc. 40
Ambarella, Inc. 74
Applied Materials, Inc. 121
Applied Micro Circuits Corp. 121
Aurora Networks Inc. 159
Avaya Holdings Corp. 164
Chegg Inc 332
Coherent Inc 368
Daystar Technologies Inc. 430
Echelon Corp. 477
Ehealth Inc 482
Filemaker Inc. 544
Gigamon Inc 606
Infoblox Inc. 708
Inphi Corp 713
Intel Corp 718
Intellicorp Inc. 719
Intevac Inc. 729
Landec Corp. 788
Mcafee Inc. 854
Neomagic Corporation 936
Nvidia Corp 976
Omnivision Technologies Inc 992
Palo Alto Networks, Inc 1015

Pdf Solutions Inc. 1029
President And Board Of Trustees Of Santa Clara College 1073
Robinson Oil Corporation 1134
Servicenow Inc 1182
Svb Financial Group 1266
Telenav, Inc. 1286
Vertical Communications, Inc. 1425
Violin Memory Inc 1430
Xenoport Inc 1483

Santa Cruz
Plantronics, Inc. 1057
Santa Cruz Seaside Company Inc 1162

Santa Fe Springs
Accuride International Inc. 18
New Tangram, Llc 944
Super Center Concepts Inc. 1262
Tri-west, Ltd. 1360

Santa Monica
Activision Blizzard, Inc. 24
American Golf Corporation 86
Anworth Mortgage Asset Corp. 115
Catasys Inc 307
Colony Financial Inc. 371
Cornerstone Ondemand, Inc. 397
Douglas Emmett Inc 459
Entravision Communications Corp. 507
Fatburger Corporation 532
Jakks Pacific Inc. 745
Leaf Group Ltd 793
Macerich Co (the) 828
Milken Family Foundation 889
Miramax Film Corp. 893
National Academy Of Recording Arts & Sciences Inc 921
Santa Monica Community College District 1162

Santa Paula
Calavo Growers, Inc. 275
Limoneira Co 807

Santa Rosa
Cpi International Inc. 403
Exchange Bank (santa Rosa, Ca) 522
Summit State Bank (santa Rosa, Ca) 1257
Zap 1491

Sebastopol
Sonomawest Holdings Inc. 1208

Sherman Oaks
Apex Global Brands Inc 117

Simi Valley
Aerovironment, Inc. 38
Intermetro Communications, Inc. (nv) 722

South San Francisco
Catalyst Biosciences Inc 306
Cytokinetics Inc 422
Five Prime Therapeutics, Inc 558
Fluidigm Corp (de) 563
Fnb Bancorp (ca) 564
Kalobios Pharmaceuticals Inc. 759
Oxigene, Inc. 1007
Portola Pharmaceuticals, Inc. 1065
Rigel Pharmaceuticals Inc 1129
See's Candies Inc. 1177
Sunesis Pharmaceuticals Inc 1259
Talon Therapeutics Inc. 1276
Terravia Holdings Inc 1291
Titan Pharmaceuticals Inc (de) 1347
Vaxart Inc 1420
Veracyte Inc 1422

Stamford
Peerless Systems Corp. 1031

INDEX BY HEADQUARTERS LOCATION

STANFORD
Leland Stanford Junior University 798
Stanford Health Care 1238

STOCKTON
Coastal Pacific Food Distributors, Inc. 364
University Of The Pacific 1403

Studio City
Crown Media Holdings Inc 410
Tix Corp 1348

Sun Valley
Emergent Group Inc. 493

Sunnyvale
Access Systems Americas Inc. 16
Accuray Inc (ca) 17
Alliance Fiber Optic Products Inc. 61
Ariba Inc. 132
Aruba Networks Inc 140
Cepheid 323
Dionex Corporation 451
Egain Corp 482
Financial Engines Inc 544
Finisar Corp 545
Fortinet Inc 569
Gsi Technology Inc 633
Infinera Corp 707
Intuitive Surgical Inc 730
Juniper Networks Inc 757
Kana Software Inc. 760
Logic Devices Incorporated 814
Meru Networks Inc. 873
Mirapoint Software Inc. 893
Narus Inc. 920
Pharmacyclics, Inc. 1045
Plx Technology Inc 1059
Pmc-sierra Inc. 1059
Proofpoint Inc 1082
R.s. Hughes Company, Inc. 1101
Rambus Inc. (de) 1104
Raytheon Applied Signal Technology Inc. 1107
Ruckus Wireless Inc 1144
Shoretel Inc 1190
Silicon Image Inc 1194
Spansion Inc 1221
Supertex, Inc. 1264
Trimble Inc 1361
Xoriant Corporation 1485

Sylmar
Tutor Perini Corp 1369

Tejon Ranch
Tejon Ranch Co 1284

TEMECULA
Genica Corporation 599
Patient Safety Technologies Inc. 1025

Thousand Oaks
Amgen Inc 102
Blue Cross Of California 229
Ceres Inc 324
Nexsan Corporation 952
Teledyne Technologies Inc 1286

TORRANCE
American Honda Finance Corporation 87
Convaid Products Inc. 391
Edelbrock Llc 479
Enova Systems Inc 503
Global Communication Semiconductors Inc. 611
Healthcare Partners Llc 653
Hi-shear Technology Corporation 665
Honda North America Inc. 678
Motorcar Parts Of America Inc 908
Ocean Duke Corporation 981
Torrance Memorial Medical Center 1351

Virco Manufacturing Corp. 1430

Tustin
Avid Bioservices Inc 166
Humax Usa, Inc 688

UNION CITY
Abaxis, Inc. 10

VALENCIA
Fruit Growers Supply Company Inc 582
Henry Mayo Newhall Memorial Hospital 659
Sunkist Growers, Inc. 1260
Taitron Components Inc. 1275
Wesco Aircraft Holdings Inc. 1455

Van Nuys
Capstone Turbine Corp 291
Electro Rent Corp. 485
Hemacare Corp. 658

Ventura
Good Sam Enterprises Llc 617

Visalia
California Dairies Inc. 276

VISTA
Amron International, Inc. 105
Bluepoint Solutions Inc. 232
Glacier Water Services Inc. 608
International Lottery & Totalizator Systems, Inc. 725

Walnut Creek
Basic American Inc. 190
Central Garden & Pet Co 319
John Muir Health 751
The Pmi Group Inc. 1326

Walnut
Shea Homes Limited Partnership 1187
Sunvalley Solar Inc (nv) 1262

Watsonville
Granite Construction Inc 624
West Marine, Inc. 1456

WEST HOLLYWOOD
Cedars-sinai Medical Center 313

WEST SACRAMENTO
Raley's 1104

Westlake Village
Bkf Capital Group Inc 222
Conversant Inc 392
Decision Diagnostics Corp 433
Guitar Center Inc. 636
Interlink Electronics Inc 722
Ltc Properties, Inc. 821
Mannkind Corp 836
Pennymac Financial Services Inc (new) 1034
Pennymac Mortgage Investment Trust 1034
Ryland Group, Inc. 1146
Velocity Commercial Capital Inc. 1421

Westminster
Biolargo Inc 217

WHITTIER
The Oltmans Construction Co 1324

WOODLAND HILLS
California Wellness Foundation 278
Grill Concepts Inc. 630
Health Net, Inc. 653
Immunocellular Therapeutics Ltd. 701
Panavision Inc. 1015
Reachlocal Inc. 1109
Talon International, Inc. 1276
United Online Inc 1385

YUBA CITY
Sunsweet Growers Inc. 1261

COLORADO

AURORA
Children's Hospital Colorado 339
Graebel Companies, Inc. 622

Boulder
Aerogrow International, Inc. 37
Array Biopharma Inc. 137
Aurora Organic Dairy Corp. 159
Boulder Brands Inc 243
Clovis Oncology Inc 361
Encision Inc. 497
Neomedia Technologies, Inc. 936
The Regents Of The University Of Colorado 1327
University Corporation For Atmospheric Research 1393

Breckenridge
Altex Industries, Inc. 71

Broomfield
Arca Biopharma Inc. 127
Ball Corp 177
Corgenix Medical Corp. 396
Dmc Global Inc 454
Level 3 Communications, Inc. 799
Mwh Global, Inc. 918
Noodles & Co 957
Vail Resorts Inc 1414
Whitewave Foods Company 1467

Castle Rock
Riot Blockchain Inc 1130

Centennial
Accucode Inc. 17
Advance Display Technologies Inc. 30
Arrow Electronics, Inc. 138
National Cinemedia Inc 923
Penford Corp. 1032
Performance Food Group Inc. 1039
Western States Fire Protection Company Inc 1461

Colorado Springs
Century Casinos Inc. 322
Colorado College 371
Colorado Springs Utilities 371
Ent Federal Credit Union 504
Gold Resource Corp 615
Intelligent Software Solutions Inc. 719
Memorial Hospital Corporation 865
Neumann Systems Group Inc. 939
Ramtron International Corporation 1105
Root9b Holdings Inc 1138
Spectranetics Corp. (the) 1223
United States Olympic Committee Inc 1387
Young Life 1489

Commerce City
Vista International Technologies Inc 1434

Crestone
Bion Environmental Technologies, Inc. 219

Denver
Accuvant Inc. 18
Advantego Corp 33
Aimco Properties, L.p. 46
Alps Holdings Inc. 68
American Cannabis Co Inc 81
American Oil & Gas Inc. 92
Anschutz Company 113

Antero Resources Corp 114
Apartment Investment & Management Co 117
Auraria Higher Education Center 158
Band-it-idex Inc. 180
Barrett (bill) Corp 189
Birner Dental Management Services Inc 220
Black Raven Energy Inc. 223
Bonanza Creek Energy Inc 238
Cimarex Energy Co 346
Cobiz Financial Inc 365
Colorado Seminary 371
Coram Llc 394
Coresite Realty Corp 396
Credo Petroleum Corporation 406
Davita Inc 429
Dcp Midstream Lp 431
Dct Industrial Trust Inc 431
Denver Board Of Water Commissioners 441
Denver Health And Hospitals Authority Inc 441
Emerald Oil, Inc 492
Enservco Corp 504
Escalera Resources Co 514
Gasco Energy Inc. 592
Glowpoint Inc 614
Guaranty Bancorp (de) 634
Intrawest Resorts Holdings Inc 729
Intrepid Potash Inc 729
Janus Capital Group Inc 746
Kodiak Oil & Gas Corp. 777
M.d.c. Holdings, Inc. 827
Markwest Energy Partners L.p. 841
Metropolitan State University Of Denver 878
Molson Coors Brewing Company 900
Pcl Construction Enterprises, Inc. 1028
Pdc Energy Inc 1029
Probuild Holdings Inc. 1078
Qep Resources Inc 1093
Real Goods Solar Inc 1110
Red Lions Hotels Corp 1112
Regional Transportation District 1116
Resolute Energy Corp 1122
Royal Gold Inc 1142
Saint Joseph Hospital, Inc 1153
Scott's Liquid Gold, Inc. 1171
Sefton Resources Inc. 1177
Servicesource International, Inc. 1183
Sm Energy Co. 1202
Spyr Inc 1227
Src Energy Inc 1228
Sunshine Silver Mines Corporation 1261
The Broe Companies Inc. 1301
The Quiznos Master Llc 1327
Transmontaigne Partners Lp 1356
Triangle Petroleum Corp 1360
University Of Colorado Foundation 1395
University Of Colorado Hospital Authority 1395
Us Energy Corp 1410
Venoco Inc. 1421
Western Union Co 1461
Whiting Petroleum Corp 1467

Durango
Rocky Mountain Chocolate Factory Inc (de) 1136
U-swirl Inc. 1372

Englewood
1mage Software Inc. 2
American Furniture Warehouse Co Inc 86
Ampio Pharmaceuticals Inc 104
Blockbuster L.l.c. 225
Ch2m Hill Companies, Ltd. 326

INDEX BY HEADQUARTERS LOCATION

Dish Network Corp 452
Echostar Corp 478
Evolving Systems, Inc. 520
Gevo Inc 605
Ihs Inc 698
Innospec Inc 711
Neutron Energy Inc. 940
Qurate Retail Inc 1100
Starz 1241
Ttec Holdings Inc 1368
Ultra Petroleum Corp 1375
Viveve Medical Inc 1435
Westmoreland Coal Co 1462
Westmoreland Resource Partners Lp 1462

Fort Collins
Advanced Energy Industries Inc 31
Colorado State University 372
Otter Products, Llc 1004
Platte River Power Authority (inc) 1058
Poudre Valley Health Care, Inc. 1067
Woodward, Inc. 1477

Golden
Golden Minerals Co 616
Trustees Of The Colorado School Of Mines 1366

GRAND JUNCTION
Colorado Mesa University 371
Fci Constructors Inc. 533

GREELEY
Hensel Phelps Construction Co. 660
Pilgrims Pride Corp. 1051

GREENWOOD VILLAGE
Air Methods Corporation 46
American Medical Response Ambulance Service Inc. 90
Ciber, Inc. 345
Cobank, Acb 364
Csg Systems International Inc. 412
Envision Healthcare Holdings Inc 508
Great West Life & Annuity Insurance Co - Insurance Products 627
Molycorp Inc. (de) 900
National Bank Holdings Corp 922
Newmont Corp 949
Powertech Uranium Corp. 1068
Red Robin Gourmet Burgers Inc 1113
Startek, Inc. 1240
Tengasco Inc 1289
Vf Corp. 1426

Highlands Ranch
Advanced Emissions Solutions Inc 31
Udr Inc 1374

LAKEWOOD
Catamount Constructors, Inc. 307
Christy Sports L.l.c. 343
Einstein Noah Restaurant Group Inc 482
General Moly Inc. 597
Good Times Restaurants Inc. 618
Mesa Laboratories, Inc. 874
Natural Grocers By Vitamin Cottage Inc 930
Vcg Holding Corp. 1420
Western Area Power Administration 1459

Littleton
Ada-es Inc. 26
Thompson Creek Metals Company Inc. 1341
Tw Telecom Inc 1370
Vista Gold Corp. 1433

Lone Tree
Ameralia Inc. 76

Longmont
Dot Hill Systems Corp. 458
S&w Seed Co. 1148
Sunrise Medical Inc. 1261
Uqm Technologies, Inc. 1406

Louisville
Eldorado Artesian Springs Inc 484
Gaia Inc (new) 588
Globeimmune, Inc 613

Loveland
Heska Corp. 663

Mt. Crested Butte
Crested Butte Llc 407

Niwot
Crocs Inc 408

Salida
High Country Bancorp, Inc. 666

Thornton
Ascent Solar Technologies Inc 142

Watkins
Pure Cycle Corp. 1091

Westminster
Allos Therapeutics Inc. 65
Digitalglobe Inc 450

Wheat Ridge
Genethera Inc. 599
Scl Health - Front Range, Inc. 1171
Solitario Exploration & Royalty Corp 1206

CONNECTICUT

Berlin
Connecticut Light & Power Co 386
The Berlin Steel Construction Company 1300

Bethel
Cannondale Bicycle Corporation 285
Memry Corporation 866

Bloomfield
Kaman Corp. 759

Branford
454 Life Sciences 5
Cas Medical Systems Inc 303

BRIDGEPORT
Bridgeport Hospital & Healthcare Services Inc 248
People's United Financial Inc 1035

Bristol
Barnes Group Inc. 188
Bristol Hospital Incorporated 251
Espn Inc. 515

Brookfield
Photronics, Inc. 1049

CHESHIRE
Bozzuto's, Inc. 244
The Lane Construction Corporation 1318

Clinton
Connecticut Water Service Inc 386

Cromwell
Chatham Search International Inc. 330

Danbury
Atmi, Inc. 154
Ethan Allen Interiors, Inc. 516
Fuelcell Energy Inc 583

Western Connecticut Health Network, Inc. 1459

Darien
Genesee & Wyoming Inc. 598

DERBY
The Griffin Hospital Inc 1314

Enfield
Str Holdings Inc. 1251

Fairfield
Acme United Corp. 21
Calmare Therapeutics Inc 279
Fairfield University 527
Prosek Partners 1082
Save The Children Federation, Inc. 1165

Farmington
Acmat Corp. 20
Connecticare Inc. 385
First Connecticut Bancorp Inc. (md) 549
Mcphee Electric, Ltd 857
United Technologies Corp 1388
Utc Climate Controls & Security 1413

Glastonbury
Open Solutions Inc. 996
Sagarsoft Inc. 1151

Greenwich
Berkley (wr) Corp 207
Berkley Insurance Company 207
Blue Sky Studios Inc. 230
Blyth, Inc. 233
Brant Industries Inc. 246
Full Circle Capital Corp 584
Interactive Brokers Group Inc 720
Starwood Property Trust Inc. 1241
Ticc Capital Corp. 1343
Urstadt Biddle Properties Inc 1408
Wright Investors' Service Holdings, Inc. 1480
Xpo Logistics, Inc. 1485

Guilford
Moroso Performance Products Inc. 906

HAMDEN
Quinnipiac University 1100
Transact Technologies Inc. 1355

Hartford
Aetna Inc. 39
Connecticut Children's Medical Center 385
Connecticut State University System 386
Eversource Energy Service Company 519
Hartford Financial Services Group Inc. 647
Hartford Healthcare Corporation 647
Phoenix Companies, Inc. (the) 1048
Saint Francis Hospital And Medical Center Foundation, Inc. 1153
Virtus Investment Partners Inc 1432

Lakeville
Salisbury Bancorp, Inc. 1156

Manchester
First Hartford Corp 551
Lydall, Inc. 823

Meriden
3m Purification Inc. 5
Midstate Medical Center 888

Middlefield
Zygo Corp 1495

MIDDLETOWN
Wesleyan University 1456

Milford
Bead Industries Inc. 198
Doctor's Associates Inc. 455
Eastern Bag And Paper Company, Incorporated 474
United States Basketball League Inc 1386

Naugatuck
Eastern Co. 474
Naugatuck Valley Financial Corporation 931

NEW BRITAIN
Hospital Of Central Connecticut 681
Stanley Black & Decker Inc 1239

New Haven
Achillion Pharmaceuticals Inc 20
Higher One Holdings Inc. 667
Knights Of Columbus 776
Precipio Inc 1070
Rib-x Pharmaceuticals Inc. 1128
Southern Connecticut Bancorp Inc. 1214
Uil Holding Corp 1375
Yale New Haven Health Services Corporation 1487
Yale University 1487
Yale-new Haven Hospital, Inc. 1487

NEW LONDON
Connecticut College 385
Lawrence + Memorial Hospital, Inc. 792

NEW MILFORD
New Milford Hospital Inc. 943

Newtown
Sonics & Materials Inc. 1208

North Haven
O.f. Mossberg & Sons Inc 978

Norwalk
Arch Chemicals Inc. 127
Best Friends Pet Care Inc. 210
Bolt Technology Corp. 237
Booking Holdings Inc 239
Emcor Group, Inc. 491
Factset Research Systems Inc. 527
Frontier Communications Corp 581
General Electric Capital Corporation 595
Mecklermedia Corp 859
Media Storm, Llc 860
Mphase Technologies Inc. 910
Reeds Inc 1114
Xerox Holdings Corp 1484

Norwich
Backus Corporation 173
Inc.jet Holding Inc 703

Old Greenwich
Ellington Financial Inc 488
Ellington Residential Mortgaging Real Estate Investment Trust 488
Hudson Global Inc 685

Orange
Tangoe, Inc. 1277

Oxford
Rbc Bearings Inc 1108

PUTNAM
Day Kimball Healthcare, Inc. 430
Psb Holdings Inc 1087

Ridgefield
Apelon Inc. 117
Chefs' Warehouse Inc (the) 331

INDEX BY HEADQUARTERS LOCATION

Northern Tier Energy Inc. 964
Northern Tier Energy Lp 965

Shelton
Baldwin Technology Company Inc. 177
Edgewell Personal Care Co 480
Hubbell Inc. 685
Prudential Annuities Life Assurance Corp 1086

Southport
Sturm, Ruger & Co., Inc. 1254

Stamford
Affinion Group Holdings Inc 40
Aircastle Ltd. 47
Americares Foundation, Inc. 98
Cara Therapeutics Inc 291
Cenveo Inc 322
Crane Co. 404
Eagle Bulk Shipping Inc 471
Equinor Marketing & Trading (us) Inc. 511
Gartner Inc 591
Harman International Industries Inc 645
Hexcel Corp. 664
Idw Media Holdings Inc 696
Independence Holding Company 704
Information Services Group Inc 709
Navigators Group Inc (the) 932
Nestle Waters North America Inc. 937
Passur Aerospace, Inc. 1023
Patriot National Bancorp Inc 1025
Petro Holdings Inc. 1042
Pitney Bowes Inc 1055
Revolution Lighting Technologies Inc 1125
Silgan Holdings Inc 1194
Stamford Health System Inc. 1237
Star Group Lp 1240
Starwood Hotels & Resorts Worldwide Inc 1241
United Rentals Inc 1385
World Wrestling Entertainment Inc 1479

Stratford
Sikorsky Aircraft Corporation 1194

Thomaston
Summit Corporation Of America 1256

Tolland
Gerber Scientific Inc. 604

UNCASVILLE
Mohegan Tribal Gaming Authority 899

Wallingford
Amphenol Corp. 104
Pcre L.l.c 1028

WATERBURY
Prospect Waterbury, Inc. 1083
Webster Financial Corp (waterbury, Conn) 1451

Watertown
Crystal Rock Holdings Inc 412

WEST HARTFORD
The University Of Hartford 1334

WEST HAVEN
University Of New Haven, Incorporated 1398

Westport
Canaan Management Inc. 284
Compass Diversified Holdings 380
First Aviation Services, Inc. 546
Terex Corp. 1290

Willimantic
Si Financial Group Inc (md) 1191

WILTON
Blue Buffalo Pet Products, Inc. 227

Windsor
Ss&c Technologies Holdings Inc 1228
Stanadyne Llc 1237
Trc Companies, Inc. 1358

DELAWARE

Dover
Chesapeake Utilities Corp. 335
Delaware State University 435
Dover Motorsports, Inc. 459
Premier Entertainment Iii, Llc 1071

LEWES
Beebe Medical Center, Inc. 201

NEW CASTLE
United Electric Supply Company, Inc. 1383

Newark
Artesian Resources Corp. 139
Atlantic City Electric Co 152
Delmarva Power & Light Co. 436
Slm Corp. 1201
University Of Delaware 1395

Seaford
Allen Harim Foods Llc 60

Wilmington
21st Century North America Insurance Company 4
Acorn Energy Inc 21
American Life Insurance Company 89
Astrazeneca Pharmaceuticals Lp 148
Barclays Bank Delaware 186
Christiana Care Health System 342
Comenity Bank 374
Delphi Financial Group Inc. 437
Highmark Bcbsd Inc. 667
Incyte Corporation 704
Ing Bank Fsb 709
Interdigital Inc (pa) 721
Navient Corp 932
Support.com Inc 1264
The Bancorp Inc 1299
Torch Energy Royalty Trust 1350
Wsfs Financial Corp 1481

WINTERTHUR
The Henry Francis Dupont Winterthur Museum Inc 1314

DISTRICT OF COLUMBIA

WASHINGTON
Aarp 10
Advisory Board Company (the) 34
American Association For The Advancement Of Science 79
American Bankers Association Inc 80
American Chemical Society 82
American Federation Of Labor & Congress Of Industrial Organzation 85
American Federation Of State County & Municipal Employees 85
American Institute Of Architects, Inc 88
American Institutes For Research In The Behavioral Sciences 88
American Petroleum Institute Inc 92
American Psychological Association, Inc. 93
American University 98

Carlyle Group Inc (the) 298
Carnegie Institution Of Washington 299
Children's National Medical Center 339
Cogent Communications Holdings, Inc. 367
Colombo Bank 370
Communications Workers Of America, Afl-cio, Clc 376
Corporation For Public Broadcasting 398
Costar Group, Inc. 399
Cssi Inc. 413
Danaher Corp 426
Dupont Fabros Technology Inc 466
Fannie Mae 529
Federal Agricultural Mortgage Corp 533
Federal Reserve System 537
Financial Industry Regulatory Authority, Inc. 545
Fti Consulting Inc. 583
Gallup, Inc. 590
Howard University (inc) 684
International Brotherhood Of Electrical Workers 724
International Brotherhood Of Teamsters 724
International Finance Corp. (world Corporations Gov't) 725
John F Kennedy Center For The Performing Arts 750
Legal Services Corporation 796
Lucy Webb Hayes National Training School For Deaconesses And Missionaries 822
Medstar-georgetown Medical Center, Inc. 863
National Association Of Broadcasters 921
National Cable Satellite Corp 922
National Education Association Of The United States 923
National Football League Players Association 923
National Gallery Of Art 924
National Park Foundation (inc) 926
National Public Radio, Inc. 926
National Railroad Passenger Corporation 926
National Retail Federation, Inc. 927
Neighborhood Reinvestment Corporation 935
Pepco Holdings Inc. 1037
Population Services International 1063
Rentech Inc 1119
Securities Investor Protection Corporation 1175
Smithsonian Institution 1204
Southeastern Universities Research Association Inc 1213
Special Olympics, Inc. 1222
The Aspen Institute Inc 1299
The Brookings Institution 1302
The Catholic University Of America 1303
The George Washington University 1312
The Georgetown University 1312
The Heritage Foundation 1315
The Humane Society Of The United States 1315
The International City Management Association Retirement Corporation 1316
The Urban Institute 1336
Truth Initiative Foundation 1367
United Negro College Fund, Inc. 1384
United States Holocaust Memorial Museum 1387

Vanda Pharmaceuticals Inc 1418
Washington Hospital Center Corporation 1446
Washington Metropolitan Area Transit Authority 1446
Washington Real Estate Investment Trust 1446
Wgl Holdings, Inc. 1464
World Wildlife Fund, Inc. 1479

DISTRICT OF COLUMBI

1 Source Consulting Inc. 2
Aptify 124
Arnold & Porter Llp 136
Bet Interactive Llc 211
Black Entertainment Television Llc 222
Blackboard Inc. 223
Carey International Inc. 295
Cyios Corporation 421
Export-import Bank Of The United States 524
Federal Aviation Administration 534
Federal Prison Industries Inc. 535
Inter-american Development Bank 719
Monumental Sports & Entertainment 904
National Alliance To End Homelessness Inc. 921
National Trust For Historic Preservation In The United St 928
Pension Benefit Guaranty Corporation 1034
Software & Information Industry Association 1205
Trg Holdings Llc 1359
United Cerebral Palsy Associations Inc. 1382
United States Department Of Justice 1386
United States Postal Service 1387
Us Department Of Homeland Security 1409
Us Department Of State 1409
Us Department Of The Air Force 1409
Us Securities And Exchange Commission 1410
Us Small Business Administration 1411
Usda Forest Service 1412
Wilmer Cutler Pickering Hale And Dorr Llp 1471

FLORIDA

Alachua
Axogen Inc 170

ALTAMONTE SPRINGS
Florida Hospital Waterman, Inc 561
Tri-city Electrical Contractors, Inc. 1359

Bartow
American Commerce Solutions Inc 82

Bay Harbor Islands
Clicker, Inc. 359

Boca Raton
1st United Bancorp, Inc. 3
Adt Corp 29
Applied Card Systems Inc. 120
Celsius Holdings Inc 315
Cross Country Healthcare Inc 408
Emergent Capital Inc 493
Florida Atlantic University 560
Friendfinder Networks Inc 580
Geo Group Inc (the) (new) 601

HOOVER'S MASTERLIST OF U.S. COMPANIES 2020

1545

INDEX BY HEADQUARTERS LOCATION

Geosyntec Consultants, Inc. 604
Hollywood Media Corp 674
Johnson Controls Fire Protection Lp 753
Juniper Group Inc. 757
Metropolitan Health Networks Inc. 877
Moredirect Inc. 904
Newsmax Media, Inc. 950
Office Depot, Inc. 984
Q.e.p. Co., Inc. 1093
Sba Communications Corp (new) 1166
The Adt Corporation 1297
Therapeuticsmd Inc 1339
Tyco Fire & Security Llc 1371
Vitacost.com Inc 1434

Bonita Springs
Herc Holdings Inc 660
Wci Communities Inc 1450

Boynton Beach
Puradyn Filter Technologies Inc 1091

BRADENTON
Beall's, Inc. 198
Manatee Memorial Hospital, L.p. 835

BRANDON
Prison Rehabilitative Industries And Diversified Enterprises, Inc. 1077

CAPE CANAVERAL
Iap Worldwide Services, Inc. 692

Cape Coral
Tigrent Inc. 1344

Clearwater
American Land Lease Inc. 89
Apyx Medical Corp 124
Avantair Inc 164
Baycare Health System, Inc. 194
Eckerd Youth Alternatives, Inc. 478
Fletcher Music Centers Inc. 559
Lincare Holdings Inc. 807
Marinemax Inc 839
Nicholas Financial Inc (bc) 954
Procyon Corporation 1079
Soft Computer Consultants Inc. 1205
Tech Data Corp. 1282
Technology Research Corporation 1283

COCONUT CREEK
Food For The Poor, Inc. 565
Willis Lease Finance Corp. 1471

Coconut Grove
Hmg/courtland Properties, Inc. 671

Coral Gables
Catalyst Pharmaceutical Partners Inc. 307
Machado/garcia-serra Publicidad Inc. 829
Mastec Inc. (fl) 847

Coral Springs
Alliance Entertainment Llc 61
Nutra Pharma Corp 974

DADE CITY
Withlacoochee River Electric Cooperative Inc 1476

DAVIE
Nova Southeastern University, Inc. 970

DAYTONA BEACH
Bethune-cookman University Inc. 211
Brown & Brown Inc 257
Consolidated-tomoka Land Co. 388
Embry-riddle Aeronautical University Inc. 491

International Speedway Corp 726
Ladies Professional Golf Association 784

DEERFIELD BEACH
Coverall North America, Inc. 402
Jm Family Enterprises Inc. 749
Worldwide Media Services Group Inc. 1479

Deland
Arc Group Worldwide Inc 127
Stetson University, Inc. 1247

DELRAY BEACH
Morse Operations, Inc. 907
Petmed Express Inc 1042
Positiveid Corp 1065
Protext Mobility Inc 1084
Veriteq Corp 1424

Estero
Hertz Global Holdings Inc (new) 663

Fernandina Beach
Coastal Banking Co Inc 364

Fort Lauderdale
Altadis U.s.a. Inc. 70
Autonation, Inc. 162
Bbx Capital Corp 196
Bbx Capital Corp (new) 196
Bct International Inc. 197
Citrix Systems Inc 351
Cyalume Technologies Holdings, Inc 419
Element Solutions Inc 487
Enviro Technologies Inc 508
Flanigan's Enterprises, Inc. 559
Holy Cross Hospital, Inc. 675
Imaging Diagnostic Systems Inc 700
Inksure Technologies Inc. 710
Kemet Corp. 764
National Beverage Corp. 922
North Broward Hospital District 959
Ocean Bio-chem, Inc. 981
Omnicomm Systems Inc 992
Online Vacation Center Holdings Corp 995
Optimumbank Holdings Inc 997
Parlux Fragrances Llc 1022
Paybox Corp 1027
Seacor Holdings Inc 1174
Sfn Group Inc. 1185
Signature Consultants Llc 1193
Singing Machine Co., Inc. 1197
Stiles Corporation 1250
Swisher Hygiene Inc 1268
Universal Insurance Holdings Inc 1391

Fort Myers
Alico, Inc. 56
Chico's Fas Inc 337
Lee County Electric Cooperative, Inc. 794
Lee Memorial Health System Foundation, Inc. 795
Neogenomics Inc 936

FORT PIERCE
Lawnwood Medical Center, Inc. 792

Gainesville
Exactech, Inc. 521
Gainesville Regional Utilities (inc) 589
Infinite Energy, Inc. 707
Mammatech Corporation 834
North Florida Regional Medical Center, Inc. 960
Quick-med Technologies Inc. 1098
Shands Teaching Hospital And Clinics, Inc. 1186
University Of Florida 1396

Heathrow
The American Automobile Association 1298

HIALEAH
Aerokool Aviation Corporation 38

Hollywood
Angstrom Graphics Inc. 111
Heico Corp 656
Interbond Corporation Of America 720
Nv5 Global Inc 976
South Broward Hospital District 1210
The Seminole Tribe Of Florida Inc. 1330

HOMESTEAD
Brooks Tropicals Holding Inc. 256

Jacksonville
Acosta Inc. 22
American Heritage Life Insurance Company 86
Arizona Chemical Holdings Corporation 133
Atlantic Coast Financial Corp 152
Baptist Health System, Inc. 185
Beaver Street Fisheries, Inc. 200
Body Central Corp. 235
Crowley Maritime Corporation 409
Elkins Constructors, Inc. 488
Everbank Financial Corp 518
Fidelity National Financial Inc 543
Fidelity National Information Services Inc 543
Fortegra Financial Corp 569
Fpic Insurance Group Inc. 573
Frp Holdings Inc 582
Gee Group Inc 593
Genesis Health Inc. 598
Global Axcess Corp. 610
Interline Brands Inc. 722
International Baler Corp 723
Jacksonville Bancorp Inc (fl) 743
Jacksonville University 743
Jea 746
Landstar System, Inc. 788
Main Street America Group Inc. 833
Mayo Clinic Jacksonville (a Nonprofit Corporation) 852
Miller Electric Company 890
Nemours Foundation 935
Parkervision Inc 1021
Railamerica Inc. 1103
Regency Centers Corp 1114
Shands Jacksonville Medical Center, Inc. 1186
Stein Mart, Inc. 1244
Stellar Group, Incorporated 1245
Trailer Bridge Inc. 1354
Vystar Credit Union 1439
Web.com Group, Inc. 1451
Winn-dixie Stores Inc. 1474

Juno Beach
Florida Power & Light Co. 562
Nextera Energy Inc 952

Jupiter
Dyadic International Inc 467
Green Energy Group (new) 628
Jupiter Medical Center, Inc. 757
Town Sports International Holdings Inc 1352

KEYSTONE HEIGHTS
Clay Electric Cooperative, Inc. 356

KISSIMMEE
Kissimmee Utility Authority (inc) 774

LAKE MARY
Dixon Ticonderoga Company 453
Faro Technologies Inc. 531

Sungard Public Sector Inc. 1260

Lake Wales
Florida's Natural Growers 562

LAKELAND
Lakeland Regional Medical Center, Inc. 786
Publix Super Markets, Inc. 1090
Publix Super Markets, Inc. 1090

LAKEWOOD RANCH
Gulf Coast Project Services, Inc. 636

Largo
Bulova Technologies Group, Inc 264

LOXAHATCHEE
Palms West Hospital Limited Partnership 1015

Maitland
The Amacore Group Inc. 1298
Workstream Usa Inc. 1478

MEDLEY
All American Containers, Llc 57
Community Asphalt Corp. 376

Melbourne
Authentec Inc. 160
Goldfield Corp. 616
Holiday Builders, Inc. 673
Holmes Regional Medical Center, Inc. 675
L3harris Technologies Inc 783

Merritt Island
World Surveillance Group Inc 1478

Miami Beach
Millennium Prime Inc 889
Mount Sinai Medical Center Of Florida, Inc. 909

MIAMI GARDENS
El Dorado Furniture Corp 483

Miami Lakes
Bankunited Inc. 184
Erba Diagnostics 512
Kellstrom Aerospace, Llc 763

MIAMI SHORES
Barry University, Inc. 189

Miami
Alienware Corporation 56
All American Semiconductor Llc 58
Alternet Systems Inc. 71
Astar Usa Llc 147
Aura Minerals Inc (british Virgin Islands) 158
Baptist Hospital Of Miami, Inc. 185
Brightstar Corp. 250
Burger King Worldwide Inc. 264
Carnival Corp 299
Continucare Corporation 391
Cool Holdings Inc 393
Ellis (perry) International Inc 488
Evi Industries Inc 520
Florida Gaming Corp. 561
Florida International University 562
Globe Specialty Metals Inc 613
Greenberg Traurig P.a. 629
Hackett Group Inc 639
Ilg Inc 698
Intcomex Inc. 716
Ladenburg Thalmann Financial Services Inc 784
Lennar Corp 798
Miami Jewish Health Systems, Inc. 881
Non-invasive Monitoring Systems Inc. 957
Norwegian Cruise Line Holdings Ltd. 969

1546   HOOVER'S MASTERLIST OF U.S. COMPANIES 2020

INDEX BY HEADQUARTERS LOCATION

Opko Health Inc 997
Perez Trading Company, Inc. 1038
Popeyes Louisiana Kitchen, Inc. 1063
Powerverde Inc 1068
Public Health Trust Of Miami Dade County 1088
Rowland Coffee Roasters Inc. 1141
Royal Caribbean Cruises Ltd 1141
Ryder System, Inc. 1146
Spanish Broadcasting System Inc 1220
Terremark Worldwide Inc. 1291
Trujillo & Sons, Inc. 1364
Variety Children's Hospital 1419
Vector Group Ltd 1420
Veru Inc 1425
Vitas Healthcare Corporation 1434
World Fuel Services Corp. 1478

Miramar
Elizabeth Arden Inc. 487
Energy Services Providers, Inc. 501
Generex Biotechnology Corp (de) 597
Spirit Airlines Inc 1225

Mulberry
Food Technology Service Inc. 566
W.s. Badcock Corporation 1440

Naples
Aci Worldwide Inc 20
Asg Technologies Group, Inc. 142
Beasley Broadcast Group Inc 199
Nch Healthcare System Inc. 934
Tib Financial Corp. 1343

North Venice
Pgt Innovations Inc 1044

Ocala
Aim Immunotech Inc 45
Marion Community Hospital Inc 839
Munroe Regional Medical Center, Inc. 915
Nobility Homes, Inc. 956

Odessa
Dais Corp 424

OKEECHOBEE
Okeechobee Hospital, Inc. 987

Oldsmar
Cryo-cell International Inc 411

OPA LOCKA
American Fruit & Produce Corp. 86

Orlando
Aircraft Service International Inc. 47
Airtran Airways Inc. 47
Api Technologies Corp 117
Chep International Inc. 333
Cubic Simulation Systems Inc. 415
Darden Restaurants, Inc. 427
Elxsi Corp 490
Florida Municipal Power Agency 562
Gencor Industries Inc 594
Genelink Inc 595
Greater Orlando Aviation Authority 627
Lgl Group Inc (the) 801
Lightpath Technologies, Inc. 806
Marriott Vacations Worldwide Corp. 841
National Retail Properties Inc 927
Orlando Health, Inc. 1002
Orlando Utilities Commission 1002
Parkway Properties Inc. 1022
Rosen Hotels And Resorts Inc. 1139
Seaworld Entertainment Inc. 1175
The University Of Central Florida Board Of Trustees 1333
Tupperware Brands Corp 1369
Voxx International Corp 1437

Wyndham Destinations Inc 1482

Palm Bay
Oakridge Global Energy Solutions Inc 979

Palm Beach Gardens
Ameripath Inc. 99
Aurora Diagnostics Inc. 159
Dycom Industries, Inc. 468
Professional Golfers Association Of America Inc 1079

PANAMA CITY
Bay County Health System, Llc 193

Pensacola
Baptist Health Care 185
Gulf Power Co 636
Sacred Heart Health System, Inc. 1149

Plant City
Paradise, Inc. 1018

Plantation
Cd International Enterprises Inc 311
Dreams Inc. 460
Tradestation Group Inc. 1354

POMPANO BEACH
Baer's Furniture Co., Inc. 174
Imperial Industries Inc. 702
Onstream Media Corp 995

PONTE VEDRA BEACH
Pga Tour, Inc. 1044

Port St. Lucie
Fpb Bancorp Inc. 573

ROCKLEDGE
Health First, Inc. 652

SAINT PETERSBURG
Eckerd College, Inc. 478
Johns Hopkins All Children's Hospital, Inc. 751
Northside Hospital 966
Pscu Incorporated 1087
Raymond James & Associates Inc 1107
St. Anthony's Hospital, Inc. 1231

Sanford
Mobile Area Networks Inc 897
Tnr Technical, Inc. 1348

Sarasota
Helios Technologies Inc 657
Rock Creek Pharmaceuticals Inc 1134
Roper Technologies Inc 1138
Sarasota County Public Hospital District 1164
Uniroyal Global Engineered Products Inc 1380

SEBRING
Florida Hospital Heartland Medical Center 561

Seminole
Superior Group Of Companies Inc 1263

SOUTH MIAMI
Baptist Health South Florida, Inc. 185
Larkin Community Hospital, Inc. 790
Magnum Construction Management, Llc 832
South Miami Hospital, Inc. 1211

St. Augustine
Brown Jordan International Inc. 257

St. Petersburg
Bankers Financial Corporation 183
Catalina Marketing Corporation 306

Duke Energy Florida Llc 464
Hsn Inc (de) 685
Hydron Technologies Inc. 691
Jabil Inc 741
Raymond James Financial, Inc. 1107
United Insurance Holdings Corp 1384

Stuart
Nuco2 Inc. 973
Seacoast Banking Corp. Of Florida 1173

Sunrise
Fednat Holding Co 539
Interim Healthcare Inc. 721
Mednax, Inc. 862
Pet Supermarket Inc. 1041
Us Stem Cell Inc 1411

Tallahassee
Capital City Bank Group, Inc. 288
Florida Housing Finance Corp 561
Florida State University 562
Tallahassee Memorial Healthcare, Inc. 1275

Tampa
Accentia Biopharmaceuticals Inc 16
Advanzeon Solutions Inc 33
American Fiber Green Products Inc 85
Anchor Glass Container Corporation 108
Autoweb Inc 162
Avi-spl Inc. 166
Bloomin' Brands Inc 226
Carlton Fields P.a. 298
Florida Health Sciences Center Inc 561
Gulfstream Natural Gas System, L.l.c. 637
H. Lee Moffitt Cancer Center And Research Institute Hospital, Inc. 638
Hci Group Inc 652
Hillsborough County Aviation Authority 669
Innovaro Inc. 711
Jagged Peak Inc. 745
Keenan, Hopkins, Schmidt And Stowell Contractors, Inc. 763
Kforce Inc. 769
Mcnichols Company 857
Mosaic Co (the) 908
Nfinanse Inc. 952
Odyssey Marine Exploration, Inc. 984
Oragenics Inc 998
Overseas Shipholding Group Inc (new) 1006
Oxis International Inc. 1008
Quality Distribution Inc (fl) 1096
Seminole Electric Cooperative, Inc. 1179
Shriners Hospitals For Children 1190
Sri/surgical Express Inc. 1228
Stephan Co (the) 1245
Suncoast Schools Federal Credit Union 1258
Sykes Enterprises, Inc. 1269
Syniverse Holdings, Inc. 1271
Teco Energy Inc. 1283
U S China Mining Group Inc. 1372
University Community Hospital, Inc. 1393
University Of South Florida 1401
Wellcare Health Plans Inc 1453

University Park
Benderson Development Company Llc 204

Vero Beach
Armour Residential Reit Inc. 136
Bimini Capital Management Inc 214
George E. Warren Corporation 602

Javelin Mortgage Investment Corp 746
Orchid Island Capital, Inc. 1000

Watersound
St. Joe Co. (the) 1232

Wellington
B/e Aerospace, Inc 172

West Melbourne
Bk Technologies Corp 222

West Palm Beach
Affiliated Managers Group Inc. 40
Chatham Lodging Trust 330
Forward Industries, Inc. 570
Oxbow Corporation 1007
Rennova Health Inc 1119
Solitron Devices, Inc. 1206
Surgline International Inc. 1265
Twin Vee Powercats Inc 1370

Weston
Ultimate Software Group, Inc. 1375

Wildlight
Rayonier Inc. 1107

WINTER HAVEN
Carpenter Contractors Of America, Inc. 300
Centerstate Bank Corp 317
Winter Haven Hospital, Inc. 1474

Winter Park
Bonnier Corporation 239
Rollins College 1136
Ruth's Hospitality Group Inc 1145

GEORGIA

Albany
Community Capital Bancshares Inc 377
Heritage Financial Group Inc. 661
Phoebe Putney Memorial Hospital, Inc. 1048

Alpharetta
Agc America Inc. 42
Agc Flat Glass North America Inc. 42
Agilysys Inc 43
Alimera Sciences Inc 57
Angelica Corporation 110
Colonial Pipeline Company 370
Greenshift Corp 629
Inseego Corp 713
Jackson Healthcare, Llc 742
Legend Oil & Gas Ltd 797
Medassets Inc 859
Neenah Inc 935
Plantation Pipe Line Company 1057
Radiant Systems Inc. 1102
Schweitzer-mauduit International Inc 1170

ATHENS
Piedmont Athens Regional Medical Center, Inc. 1049
Smallbizpros Inc. 1202
St. Mary's Health Care System, Inc. 1235
University Of Georgia 1396

Atlanta
360i Llc 4
Aaron's Inc 10
Acuity Brands Inc (holding Company) 25
Agl Resources Inc. 43
Air2web Inc. 47
Allied Systems Holdings Inc. 64
Alston & Bird Llp 69
American Caresource Holdings Inc 81

INDEX BY HEADQUARTERS LOCATION

American Software Inc 95
Ameris Bancorp 100
Astral Health & Beauty Inc. 148
At&t Mobility Llc 149
Atlanta Clark University Inc 151
Atlanta National League Baseball Club Inc. 151
Atlantic American Corp. 151
Atlantic Southeast Airlines Inc. 153
Atlanticus Holdings Corp 153
Atlanticus Holdings Corporation 153
Autotrader Group Inc. 162
Axiall Corp 169
Balfour Beatty Infrastructure, Inc. 177
Beazer Homes Usa, Inc. 200
Blue Cross Blue Shield Of Georgia Inc 229
Boys & Girls Clubs Of America 244
Buckhead Life Restaurant Group Inc. 262
Bway Holding Company 268
Cable News Network Inc. 270
Carecentric Inc. 295
Carter & Associates Enterprises Inc. 302
Carter's Inc 302
Carvel Corporation 302
Catchmark Timber Trust Inc 307
Cbeyond Inc 309
Centers For Disease Control And Prevention 317
Ciner Resources Lp 347
Citizens Bancshares Corp. (ga) 349
Coca-cola Co (the) 365
Coca-cola Enterprises Inc 366
Cooperative For Assistance And Relief Everywhere, Inc. (care) 394
Cousins Properties Inc 400
Cox Communications Inc. 402
Cumulus Media Inc 416
Delta Air Lines Inc (de) 437
Delta Community Credit Union 437
Dlh Holdings Corp 454
Equifax Inc 511
Examworks Group Inc 521
Federal Home Loan Bank Of Atlanta 534
Federal Reserve Bank Of Atlanta, Dist. No. 6 535
Fidelity Southern Corp 543
Gentiva Health Services Inc 601
Genuine Parts Co. 601
Georgia Lottery Corporation 603
Georgia Power Co 603
Global Payments Inc 612
Graphic Packaging Holding Co 624
Gray Television Inc 624
H. J. Russell & Company 638
Habitat For Humanity International, Inc. 639
Heartland Payment Systems, Llc 655
Heery International Inc. 656
Home Depot Inc 676
Hughes Telematics Inc. 686
Intercontinentalexchange Inc. 721
Interface Inc. 721
Invesco Ltd. 731
Invesco Mortgage Capital Inc 731
John Wieland Homes And Neighborhoods Inc. 751
K&g Men's Company Inc 757
Lanier Parking Holdings Inc. 789
Logisticare Solutions, Llc 815
Manhattan Associates, Inc. 835
Marine Products Corp 839
Mikart Inc. 888
Morehouse College (inc.) 905
Mueller Water Products Inc 913
Municipal Electric Authority Of Georgia 915
Newell Brands Inc 948

North American Electric Reliability Corporation 959
Northside Hospital, Inc. 966
Novelis Inc. 971
Ocwen Financial Corporation 983
Oldcastle Inc. 989
Oxford Industries, Inc. 1007
Perma-fix Environmental Services, Inc. 1040
Piedmont Hospital, Inc. 1050
Piedmont Office Realty Trust Inc 1050
Post Properties, Inc. 1066
Preferred Apartment Communities Inc. 1071
Premier Exhibitions Inc 1071
Premiere Global Services Inc 1072
Prgx Global, Inc. 1074
Providence Service Corp 1085
Pultegroup Inc 1091
Racetrac Petroleum, Inc. 1102
Rollins, Inc. 1137
Rpc, Inc. 1142
Scientific Research Corp 1170
Servigistics Inc. 1183
Shepherd Center, Inc. 1188
Southern Company (the) 1214
Southern Power Co 1217
Spelman College 1224
State Bank Financial Corp 1241
Streamline Health Solutions Inc 1252
Sunlink Health Systems Inc 1260
Suntrust Banks Inc 1262
The Arthritis Foundation Inc 1299
The North Highland Company Llc 1324
The Paradies Shops Llc 1324
Transcend Services Inc. 1355
Unipro Foodservice, Inc 1379
United Parcel Service Inc 1385
Zep Inc 1492

AUGUSTA
Doctors Hospital Of Augusta, Llc 455
Georgia-carolina Bancshares, Inc. 603
Morris Publishing Group Llc 907
Southeastern Bank Financial Corp 1213

Austell
Caraustar Recovered Fiber Group Inc. 292

Ball Ground
Chart Industries Inc 329

Blairsville
United Community Banks Inc (blairsville, Ga) 1382

Braselton
Fox Factory Holding Corp 572

Calhoun
Mohawk Industries, Inc. 899

Carrollton
Greenway Medical Technologies Inc. 630
University Of West Georgia 1403

Columbus
Aflac Inc 41
Carmike Cinemas, Inc. 298
Synovus Financial Corp 1271
Total System Services, Inc. 1351

CONYERS
Pratt Industries, Inc. 1069

COVINGTON
Snapping Shoals Electric Trust, Inc. 1204

Cumming
Baran Telecom Inc. 186

Sawnee Electric Membership Corporation 1166

Dalton
Dixie Group Inc. 453

DECATUR
Agnes Scott College, Inc. 44
Dekalb Medical Center, Inc. 434

Duluth
Agco Corp. 42
Asbury Automotive Group Inc 141
Ccur Holdings Inc 311
Merial Inc. 871
Vsoft Corporation 1438

FAYETTEVILLE
Fayette Community Hospital, Inc. 533

Fitzgerald
Colony Bankcorp, Inc. 370

Flowery Branch
Atlanta Falcons Football Club Llc 151

FOREST PARK
Dealers Supply Company Inc. 432

FORT OGLETHORPE
Hutcheson Medical Center Inc. 690

Fort Valley
Blue Bird Corporation 227

Gainesville
Aeon Global Health Corp 36
America's Home Place, Inc. 78
Mar-jac Poultry, Inc. 837
Northeast Georgia Health System, Inc. 962

JEFFERSON
Jackson Electric Membership Corporation 742

Johns Creek/Atlanta
Wegener Corp. 1452

Johns Creek
Ebix Inc 477
Saia Inc 1151

Jonesboro
Heritage Southeast Bancorporation Inc 661
Low Temp Industries Inc. 819

Kennesaw
Cryolife, Inc. 411
Eau Technologies Inc 476
Kemira Chemicals Inc. 764
Kennesaw State University 765

Lawrenceville
Sed International Holdings, Inc. 1176

MABLETON
Atlanta Hardwood Corporation 151

MACON
The Corporation Of Mercer University 1308

Marietta
Bluelinx Holdings Inc 232
Cobb Electric Membership Corporation 365
Kennestone Hospital At Windy Hill, Inc. 765
Wellstar Health System, Inc. 1454

MARTINEZ
Maner Builders Supply Company, Llc 835

MILLEDGEVILLE
Oconee Regional Health Systems, Inc. 983

Milton
Exide Technologies 523

MONROE
Walton Electric Membership Corporation 1444

MOULTRIE
Colquitt Electric Membership Corporation 372
Southwest Georgia Financial Corp. 1219

Norcross
Automobile Protection Corporation 162
Cape Environmental Management Inc. 287
Comverge Inc. 383
Easylink Services International Corporation 476
Ems Technologies Inc. 496
Guided Therapeutics Inc 635
Herschend Family Entertainment Corporation 662
Immucor Inc. 701
Intelligent Systems Corp. 719
Ole' Mexican Foods, Inc. 989
Pediatric Services Of America Inc. 1031
Recall Corporation 1111
Rock-tenn Co. 1135
Unisource Worldwide Inc. 1380
Venture Construction Company Inc 1422

Peachtree Corners
Crawford & Co. 404
Fleetcor Technologies Inc 559

PENDERGRASS
Nicolon Corporation 954

REYNOLDS
Flint Electric Membership Corporation 560

ROME
Floyd Healthcare Management, Inc. 563
Redmond Park Hospital, Llc 1113
Universal Tax Systems Inc. 1392

ROSWELL
Dynamix Group, Inc 468

Savannah
Citi Trends Inc 349
Savannah Health Services, Llc 1165
The Savannah College Of Art And Design Inc 1329

STATESBORO
Georgia Southern University 603

Suwanee
Arris Group Inc. (new) 137
Digirad Corp 449
Habasit America 639
Polyvision Corporation 1062
Regional Health Properties Inc 1115

THOMASTON
Upson County Hospital, Inc. 1406

Thomasville
Flowers Foods, Inc. 563
Thomasville Bancshares, Inc. 1341

TIFTON
Tift Regional Medical Center Foundation, Inc. 1344

Toccoa
1st Franklin Financial Corp. 3

INDEX BY HEADQUARTERS LOCATION

TUCKER
Georgia Transmission Corporation 603
Oglethorpe Power Corp 985
Video Display Corp 1428
Williams Industrial Services Group Inc 1471

VALDOSTA
Hospital Authority Of Valdosta And Lowndes County, Georgia 681
Valdosta State University 1415

West Point
Batson-cook Company 191

WOODSTOCK
Primus Builders Inc. 1076
Woodstock Holdings Inc 1477

HAWAII

AIEA
Diagnostic Laboratory Services, Inc. 445

Hilo
Hawaiian Macadamia Nut Orchards Lp 649

Honolulu
Alexander & Baldwin Inc (reit) 54
Aloha Petroleum Ltd. 67
American Savings Bank Fsb 94
Bank Of Hawaii Corp 181
Barnwell Industries, Inc. 188
Central Pacific Financial Corp 319
First Hawaiian Bank 551
Hawai I Pacific Health 649
Hawaii Pacific University 649
Hawaiian Electric Industries Inc 649
Hawaiian Telcom Holdco Inc 649
Kuakini Health System 781
Matson Inc 849
Pacific Office Properties Trust Inc 1011
Servco Pacific Inc. 1182
Territorial Bancorp Inc 1292
Trustees Of The Estate Of Bernice Pauahi Bishop 1366
University Of Hawaii Systems 1396

Kailua-Kona
Cyanotech Corp. 419
Mera Pharmaceuticals Inc. 867

Maui
Maui Land & Pineapple Co., Inc. 850

IDAHO

Blackfoot
Nonpareil Corporation 957

Boise
Albertson's Llc 52
Albertsons Companies, Inc. 53
Boise Cascade Co. (de) 236
Boise State University 237
Idacorp Inc 695
Idaho Power Co 695
J.r. Simplot Company 741
Micron Technology Inc. 883
Mwi Veterinary Supply Inc 918
Pcs Edventures! Inc 1029
Saint Alphonsus Regional Medical Center, Inc. 1152
St. Luke's Health System, Ltd. 1234
The Amalgamated Sugar Company Llc 1298
Thunder Mountain Gold, Inc. 1343
Us Ecology Inc (new) 1409

Us Geothermal Inc 1410

Coeur d'Alene
Hecla Mining Co 656
New Jersey Mining Co. 942
Wgi Heavy Minerals Incorporated 1464

Coeur d?Alene
Timberline Resources Corporation 1345

Eagle
Lamb Weston Holdings Inc 787

Emmett
T.j.t., Inc. 1274

Hayden
Transtector Systems Inc. 1356

Idaho Falls
International Isotopes Inc 725
North Wind Inc. 962
Portage Inc. 1064
Wada Farms Marketing Group Llc 1441

Meridian
Blue Cross Of Idaho Health Service Inc. 230

MOSCOW
Regents Of The University Of Idaho 1115

Nampa
Home Federal Bancorp Inc. 676

POCATELLO
Idaho State University 695

Sandpoint
Coldwater Creek Inc. 368
Litehouse, Inc. 811

ILLINOIS

Abbott Park
Abbott Laboratories 10

ADDISON
Magneco/metrel Inc. 831

Albion
Champion Laboratories Inc. 326

Alsip
Griffith Laboratories Inc. 630

Arlington Heights
Castlerock Security Holdings Inc. 306
Northwest Community Hospital Inc 967

ASSUMPTION
Sloan Implement Company, Inc. 1201

Aurora
Cabot Microelectronics Corp 271
Old Second Bancorp., Inc. (aurora, Ill.) 988
Osi Group Llc 1003
Rush-copley Medical Center, Inc. 1145
Successories Llc 1255
Westell Technologies Inc 1458

Bannockburn
Apac Customer Services Inc. 116
Option Care Health Inc 998
Stericycle Inc. 1246

Bedford Park
Northstar Aerospace Inc. 966
The Belt Railway Company Of Chicago 1300

BELLEVILLE
Protestant Memorial Medical Center, Inc. 1084

Bensenville
Rubicon Technology Inc 1144

BERWYN
Campagna-turano Bakery Inc. 283

Bloomingdale
Bridgestone Retail Operations Llc 248
Pc-tel Inc 1028

BLOOMINGTON
Evergreen Fs Inc 519
Growmark, Inc. 632
Illinois Wesleyan University 699
State Farm Mutual Automobile Insurance Company 1242

BRAIDWOOD
Doc's Drugs, Ltd. 455

Bridgeview
Manitex International Inc 836
Rose Paving Co. 1138

BROADVIEW
National Van Lines, Inc. 928
Robert Bosch Llc 1132

Buffalo Grove
Essex Rental Corp 516
Siemens Industry Inc. 1191

Burr Ridge
Bankfinancial Corp 183

CARBONDALE
Southern Illinois Healthcare Enterprises, Inc. 1215
Southern Illinois University Inc 1215

CARMI
Martin & Bayley, Inc. 843

CAROL STREAM
Tyndale House Publishers, Inc. 1371

CASEYVILLE
Earl L. Henderson Trucking Company 472

Champaign
First Busey Corp 548
Great American Bancorp Inc 625

Chicago Heights
Cfc International Inc. 325

Chicago
A. Eicoff & Company 8
A. Finkl & Sons Company 8
Acquity Group L.l.c. 22
Adm Investor Services Inc. 29
Adtalem Global Education Inc 29
Alliant Credit Union 62
Allscripts Healthcare Solutions, Inc. 65
Alzheimer"s Disease And Related Disorders Association Inc. 73
American Bar Association 80
American Dental Association 83
American Hospital Association 87
American Medical Association Inc 90
Amsted Industries Incorporated 105
Ann & Robert H. Lurie Children's Hospital Of Chicago 112
Aon Benfield Inc. 116
Arch Venture Partners 128
Archer Daniels Midland Co. 128
Argosy Education Group Inc. 132
Aviv Reit Inc. 167
Baird & Warner Holding Company 174
Baker & Mckenzie Llp 175

Bdo Usa Llp 197
Berlin Packaging L.l.c. 208
Blue Cross & Blue Shield Association 227
Bluestar Energy Services Inc. 232
Bmo Financial Corp. 233
Board Of Trustees Of Community College District 508 (inc) 234
Boeing Co. (the) 236
Burrell Communications Group Llc 265
Capri Capital Partners Llc 290
Cardean Learning Group Llc 292
Carus Publishing Company 302
Cboe Global Markets Inc 309
Cc Industries Inc. 310
Ccc Information Services Group Inc. 311
Central Steel And Wire Company 320
Century Aluminum Co. 321
Chicago Airport System 336
Chicago Blackhawk Hockey Team Inc. 336
Chicago Community Trust 336
Chicago Meat Authority Inc. 336
Chicago National League Ball Club Inc. 336
Chicago Transit Authority 337
Chicago White Sox Ltd. 337
Classified Ventures Llc 356
Clayco, Inc. 356
Cme Group Inc 361
Cna Financial Corp 362
Cna Surety Corporation 362
Cobra Electronics Corp. 365
Coeur Mining Inc 366
Columbia College Chicago 372
Commonspirit Health 375
Compsych Corporation 381
Conagra Brands Inc 383
Continental Materials Corp. 390
De Paul University 431
Donnelley (rr) & Sons Company 457
Easter Seals, Inc. 474
Echo Global Logistics Inc 478
Envestnet Inc 508
Equity Commonwealth 512
Equity Lifestyle Properties Inc 512
Equity Residential 512
Exelon Corp 522
Federal Home Loan Bank Of Chicago 534
Federal Reserve Bank Of Chicago, Dist. No. 7 536
Field Museum Of Natural History 543
First Industrial Realty Trust Inc 551
First Midwest Bancorp, Inc. (naperville, Il) 553
Flying Food Group Llc 564
Freightcar America Inc 578
Gatx Corp 592
Gelber Group, Llc 594
Golub Capital Bdc Inc. 617
Groupon Inc 632
Heidrick & Struggles International, Inc. 656
Hill-rom Holdings, Inc. 669
Hillshire Brands Co 669
Hinshaw & Culbertson Llp 670
Hub International Limited 685
Huron Consulting Group Inc 689
Hyatt Hotels Corp 690
Illinois Institute Of Technology 698
Innerworkings Inc 711
Integrys Energy Group Inc 718
Inteliquent Inc 718
John Bean Technologies Corp 750
John D And Catherine T Macarthur Foundation 750
Jones Lang Lasalle Inc 754
Kemper Corp (de) 764
Kirkland & Ellis Llp 773

INDEX BY HEADQUARTERS LOCATION

Lawson Products, Inc. 792
Lincoln Provision Inc. 808
Littelfuse Inc 811
Lkq Corp 813
Loyola University Of Chicago Inc 820
Lyric Opera Of Chicago 824
Mattersight Corp 849
Mayer Brown Llp 851
Mb Financial Inc 853
Mcdonald's Corp 855
Mcgladrey Llp 856
Mercy Hospital And Medical Center 869
Merge Healthcare Inc 870
Mesirow Financial Holdings Inc. 874
Methode Electronics Inc 875
Millercoors Llc 891
Morningstar Inc 906
Motorola Solutions Inc 909
Muscular Dystrophy Association, Inc. 916
National Council Of Young Men's Christian Associations Of The United States Of America 923
Navigant Consulting, Inc. 932
Nes Rentals Holdings, Inc. 937
Newark Corporation 947
Newly Weds Foods Inc. 949
North Park University 961
Northern Trust Corp 965
Northwestern Memorial Healthcare 969
Nuveen Investments Inc. 975
O'neil Industries, Inc. 978
Oakridge Holdings Inc 979
Oil-dri Corp. Of America 987
Old Republic International Corp. 988
Onespan Inc 995
Optionsxpress Holdings Inc. 998
Orbitz Worldwide Inc 1000
Park Bancorp, Inc. 1020
Pepper Construction Group, Llc 1037
Potbelly Corp 1066
Privatebancorp Inc 1077
Professional Diversity Network Inc 1079
Project Leadership Associates Inc. 1081
R1 Rcm Inc 1101
Ryerson Holding Corp 1146
Seyfarth Shaw Llp 1185
Sinai Health System 1197
Sp Plus Corp 1220
Sram International Corporation 1227
Ssi (u.s.) Inc. 1228
St. Bernard Hospital 1231
Strategic Hotels & Resorts, Inc. 1252
Telephone & Data Systems Inc 1286
The Hallstar Company 1314
The Heico Companies L.l.c. 1314
The University Of Chicago 1333
The University Of Chicago Medical Center 1334
The Walsh Group Ltd 1336
The Ziegler Companies Inc. 1339
Tootsie Roll Industries Inc 1350
Tps Parking Management Llc 1353
Tribune Media Co 1360
Trippe Manufacturing Company 1363
True Value Company 1364
Trustwave Holdings Inc. 1367
Uhy Advisors Inc. 1374
Ultra Stores Inc. 1375
Union Health Service Inc 1379
United Airlines Holdings Inc 1380
United American Healthcare Corp. 1380
United States Cellular Corp 1386
United States Soccer Federation, Inc. 1388
Usg Corp 1412
Ventas Inc 1422

Veolia Environmental Services North America Corp. 1422
Vhs Acquisition Subsidiary Number 3, Inc. 1426
Vienna Beef Ltd. 1429
Window To The World Communications Inc. 1473
Winston & Strawn Llp 1474
Wirtz Beverage Group Llc 1475

Cicero
Broadwind Energy, Inc. 253

Collinsville
Ameren Illinois Co 76

Crystal Lake
Aptargroup Inc. 124
Centegra Health System Foundation 316

DAKOTA
Berner Food & Beverage, Llc 209

Darien
Viskase Companies Inc. 1433

DECATUR
Decatur Memorial Hospital 433

Deerfield
Bab Inc 172
Baxter International Inc 193
Beam Inc 198
Cf Industries Holdings Inc 325
Essendant Inc 515
Fortune Brands Home & Security, Inc. 570
Horizon Pharma Inc 680
Mondelez International Inc 901
Rti Surgical Holdings Inc 1143
Scai Holdings, Llc 1166
Terra Nitrogen Company, L.p. 1291
Textura Corp 1297
Walgreens Boots Alliance Inc 1443

DES PLAINES
Brg Sports, Inc. 247
Dsc Logistics Inc. 462
Institute Of Gas Technology 715
Schawk, Inc. 1167

Downers Grove
Dover Corp 459
Ftd Companies Inc 582
Ralcorp Frozen Bakery Products Inc. 1104
Roadrunner Transportation Systems Inc 1132
The Computing Technology Industry Association Inc 1307

EAST MOLINE
Standard Forwarding Llc 1238
Yash Technologies, Inc 1487

Edwardsville
First Clover Leaf Financial Corp 549
Prairie Farms Dairy, Inc. 1069

Effingham
Midland States Bancorp Inc 887

Elgin
Amtec Precision Products Inc. 105
Capsonic Group Llc 290
Heritage-crystal Clean Inc 662
Jerry Biggers Chevrolet Inc. 748
Middleby Corp 887
Sanfilippo (john B) & Son Inc 1161

Elk Grove Vilage
Sigmatron International Inc. 1193

Elk Grove Village
Biosynergy, Inc. 219
Little Lady Foods Inc. 811

Material Sciences Corp. 848
Newesco Inc. 948
Steiner Electric Company 1244

ELMHURST
Elmhurst Memorial Hospital Inc 489
Mcmaster-carr Supply Company 857
Oec Business Interiors Inc. 984
The Duchossois Group Inc. 1309

Evanston
Fidus Investment Corporation 543
Northshore University Healthsystem 966
Northwestern University 969
Rotary International 1140

FOREST PARK
Farmington Foods Inc. 531

Frankfort
Baldwin Richardson Foods Co. 177

FREEPORT
Freeport Regional Health Care Foundation 578

GALESBURG
The National Association For The Exchange Of Industrial Resources Inc 1322

Glenview
Illinois Tool Works, Inc. 699
Mead Johnson Nutrition Co 858
Ryan Building Group, Inc. 1146

Glenwood
Landauer, Inc. 788

HARVEY
The Ingalls Memorial Hospital 1315

Hillside
Bekins Holding Corp. 202

Hoffman Estates
Amcol International Corp. 75
Clover Technologies Group Llc 361
Kmart Corporation 775
Sears Holdings Corp 1174
Sears Hometown & Outlet Stores Inc 1174
Serta Inc. 1182

Homewood
Carl Buddig & Company 296

ITASCA
American Academy Of Pediatrics 78
Emkay Inc. 494
Flexera Software Llc 559
Henricksen & Company, Inc. 659
Jewel-osco 748
Knowles Corp 776
Midas Inc. 886
National Safety Council 928
The Boler Company 1301

Jacksonville
Jacksonville Bancorp Inc (md) 743

JOLIET
Central Grocers, Inc. 319
Will County 1469

Kewanee
Boss Holdings, Inc. 240

LaFox
Richardson Electronics Ltd 1129

Lake Barrington
Cti Industries Corp 413

Lake Bluff
Chelsea & Scott Ltd. 332

Lake Forest
Akorn Inc 49
Assertio Therapeutics Inc 145
Chicago Bears Football Club Inc. 336
Coresource Inc. 396
Grainger (w.w.) Inc. 622
Hospira Inc 681
Idex Corporation 696
Lake Forest College 785
Northwestern Lake Forest Hospital 969
Packaging Corp Of America 1013
Solo Cup Company 1206
Tenneco Inc 1289

Lake Zurich
Acco Brands Corp 17

LIBERTYVILLE
Aldridge Electric, Inc. 54
Motorola Mobility Holdings Inc. 909

Lincolnshire
Freedomroads Llc 577
Quill Corporation 1100
Zebra Technologies Corp. 1491

LINCOLNWOOD
Loeber Motors, Inc. 814

LISLE
Alexian Brothers Health System 55
Cts Corp 414
Suncoke Energy Inc 1258
Suncoke Energy Partners Lp 1259

Lombard
Pernix Group Inc 1041

MACOMB
Mcdonough County Hospital District 855
Western Illinois University Inc 1460

Mattoon
Consolidated Communications Holdings Inc 387
First Mid Bancshares Inc 553
Sarah Bush Lincoln Health Center 1163

McHenry
Brake Parts Inc. 245

MELROSE PARK
Gottlieb Memorial Hospital 621

Mettawa
Brunswick Corp. 259

MILAN
Group O, Inc. 631

Moline
Qcr Holdings Inc 1093

Morris
A&r Logistics Inc. 7
Morris Hospital 907

Morton Grove
Gas Depot Oil Company 592
Lifeway Foods, Inc. 805

MOUNT PROSPECT
Schumacher Electric Corporation 1169

Mt. Sterling
Dot Foods Inc. 458

Mundelein
Medline Industries Inc. 862

Naperville
Calamos Asset Management Inc 274
Chicago Rivet & Machine Co. 337
Corporate Travel Consultants Inc 398

INDEX BY HEADQUARTERS LOCATION

Eby-brown Company Llc 477
Nalco Holding Company 919
Track Group Inc 1353

NEW LENOX
Silver Cross Hospital And Medical Centers 1195

New York
Dgt Holdings Corp 445

Niles
Arrow Financial Services L.l.c. 138
Perma-pipe International Holdings Inc 1040

NORMAL
Board Of Trustees Of Illinois State University 234

North Chicago
Abbvie Inc 11

Northbrook
Allstate Corp 66
Astellas Pharma Us Inc. 148
Atlantic Premium Brands Ltd. 152
Euromarket Designs Inc. 517
Kapstone Paper & Packaging Corp 761
Nanosphere Inc 919
Stats Llc 1243
Underwriters Laboratories Inc. 1377

Northfield
Kraft Foods Group Inc 779
Stepan Co. 1245

OAK BROOK
Ace Hardware Corporation 18
Castle (am) & Co 305
Centerpoint Properties Trust 317
Federal Signal Corp. 538
Great Lakes Dredge & Dock Corp 626
Hub Group, Inc. 685
Irc Retail Centers Llc 734
Rc2 Corporation 1109
Retail Properties Of America Inc 1123
Superior Bulk Logistics, Inc. 1263
The Inland Real Estate Group Of Companies Inc. 1316
The International Association Of Lions Clubs Incorporated 1316
Treehouse Foods Inc 1358

Oakbrook Terrace
Graycor Inc. 625
Joint Commission On Accreditation Of Healthcare Organizations 754
Rvue Holdings Inc 1145

Palatine
Acura Pharmaceuticals Inc 25
The Intec Group Inc. 1316
Township High School District 211 Foundation 1353

Paris
First Banctrust Corp 547
North American Lighting, Inc. 959

PARK RIDGE
Advocate Health And Hospitals Corporation 35
Koch Foods Incorporated 777

PEORIA
Bradley University 245
Citizens Equity First Credit Union 350
Connor Co. 387
Osf Healthcare System 1003
Pioneer Railcorp 1054
Rli Corp 1132

QUINCY
Blessing Hospital 225
Mercantile Bancorp Inc. 867

Titan International Inc 1347

Riverwoods
Cch Incorporated 311

Robinson
First Robinson Financial Corp. 555

ROCK ISLAND
Augustana College 158
Bitco Corporation 221
Modern Woodmen Of America 898

ROCKFORD
Ingersoll Machine Tools, Inc. 710

Rolling Meadows
Charles Industries Ltd. 328
Gallagher (arthur J.) & Co. 589
Icon Identity Solutions, Inc. 694
Myr Group Inc 918

ROMEOVILLE
Florstar Sales, Inc. 562
Kehe Distributors Llc 763
Nanophase Technologies Corp. 919
Valley View Community Unit School District 365u 1416

Rosemont
Banco Popular North America Inc. 180
Taylor Capital Group, Inc 1280
Us Foods Inc. 1410
Wintrust Financial Corp (il) 1475

Schaumburg
American Chartered Bancorp Inc. 81
Convergint Technologies Llc 392
Gary Rabine & Sons Inc. 591
Global Brass & Copper Holdings Inc 610
Global Brass And Copper Holdings Inc. 610
Perdoceo Education Corp 1038
Power Construction Company Llc 1067
Sagent Pharmaceuticals Inc 1151
Sparton Corp 1222

Skokie
Forsythe Technology Inc. 569
Topco Associates Llc 1350

SPRING GROVE
Intermatic Incorporated 722

SPRINGFIELD
Eei Holding Corporation 481
Horace Mann Educators Corp. 679
Hospital Sisters Health System 682
Memorial Health System 864
Memorial Medical Center 865
St. John's Hospital Of The Hospital Sisters Of The Third Order Of St. Francis 1233
Tom Lange Company, Inc. 1349

TEUTOPOLIS
Stevens Industries Inc 1248

TINLEY PARK
Panduit Corp. 1016
U.g.n., Inc. 1372

University Park
Applied Systems Inc. 122

URBANA
Carle Foundation Hospital 296
Carle Physician Group 296

Vernon Hills
American Hotel Register Company 87
Cdw Corporation 312

Warrenville
Coskata Inc. 399

Fuel Tech Inc 583

Wauconda
Fidelitone Inc. 542

Waukegan
Northern States Financial Corp. (waukegan, Il) 964

West Chicago
Aspen Marketing Services Inc. 144
Ball Horticultural Company 178

Westchester
Ingredion Inc 710

Westmont
Positron Corp 1065
Positron Corp. 1065
Sirva Inc. 1198

WHEATON
The Trustees Of Wheaton College 1332

Wheeling
Doall Company 454

WINFIELD
Central Dupage Hospital Association 318

Wood Dale
Aar Corp 9

Wood River
Ytb International Inc. 1489

Woodridge
Elevance Renewable Sciences Inc. 487
Wilton Brands Inc. 1472

INDIANA

ANDERSON
Community Hospital Of Anderson And Madison County, Incorporated 378

Auburn
Peoples Bancorp Inc (auburn, In) 1035

Aurora
Aurora Casket Company Inc. 159

Batesville
Batesville Tool & Die Inc. 191
Hillenbrand Inc 669

BLOOMINGTON
Hoosier Energy Rural Electric Cooperative Inc. 678
Indiana University Foundation, Inc. 705
Indiana University Health Bloomington, Inc. 706
Trustees Of Indiana University 1366

Carmel
Assembly Biosciences Inc 144
Automotive Finance Corporation 162
Cno Financial Group Inc 363
Determine Inc 442
Indiana Municipal Power Agency 705
Itt Educational Services Inc 738
Kar Auction Services Inc. 761
Midcontinent Independent System Operator, Inc. 886
Protective Insurance Corp 1083

Clarksville
First Savings Financial Group Inc 555

Connersville
Stant Manufacturing Inc. 1239

Corydon
First Capital Inc. 548

CRAWFORDSVILLE
Ceres Solutions, Llp 324
Wabash College 1441

Elkhart
All American Group Inc. 57
Elkhart General Hospital, Inc. 487
Lci Industries 793
Patrick Industries Inc 1025
Thor Industries, Inc. 1342

Evansville
Accuride Corp 18
Atlas World Group, Inc. 154
Berry Global Group Inc 209
Deaconess Health System, Inc. 432
Deaconess Hospital Inc 432
Escalade, Inc. 514
First Bancorp Of Indiana Inc 547
Koch Enterprises Inc. 776
Old National Bancorp (evansville, In) 988
Onemain Holdings Inc 994
Shoe Carnival, Inc. 1189
South Central Communications Corporation 1210
St. Mary's Health, Inc. 1235
Traylor Bros., Inc. 1357
University Of Evansville 1396
Van Atlas Lines Inc 1417
Vectren Corp 1421

Fishers
First Internet Bancorp 552

FORT WAYNE
Do It Best Corp. 454
Franklin Electric Co., Inc. 575
Perfection Bakeries Inc. 1039
Petroleum Traders Corporation 1043
Steel Dynamics Inc. 1243
Tower Financial Corp. 1352
Waterfurnace Renewable Energy Inc 1447

GARY
The Methodist Hospitals Inc 1321

GOSHEN
Liberty Homes Inc 802

GREENCASTLE
Depauw University 441

Greensburg
Mainsource Financial Group Inc 834

HAMMOND
Indiana Harbor Belt Railroad Co 705

HANOVER
Hanover College 643

HIGHLAND
Strack And Van Til Super Market Inc. 1251

HOBART
Indiana Botanic Gardens Inc 705

Huntington
Northeast Indiana Bancorp Inc 962

Indianapolis
Aearo Technologies Llc 35
Allison Transmission Holdings Inc 65
Angie's List Inc. 111
Anthem Inc 114
Balkamp Inc. 177
Barnes & Thornburg Llp 187
Bowen Engineering Corporation 243
Brightpoint Inc. 250
Calumet Specialty Product Partners Lp 280
Celadon Group, Inc. 314
Citizens Energy Group 350

INDEX BY HEADQUARTERS LOCATION

Community Health Network, Inc. 378
Cti Group Holdings Inc. 413
Duke Realty Corp 464
Emmis Communications Corp 494
Hat World Corporation 648
Hhgregg Inc 665
Hurco Companies Inc 689
Indiana University Health, Inc. 706
Indianapolis Colts Inc. 706
Interactive Intelligence Group Inc. 720
Interactive Intelligence Inc. 720
Kite Realty Group Trust 774
Kiwanis International 774
Lilly (eli) & Co 806
Marian University, Inc. 838
Marsh Supermarkets Inc. 842
Mid America Clinical Laboratories Llc 885
National Collegiate Athletic Association 923
Noble Roman's, Inc. 956
Republic Airways Holdings Inc 1120
Simon Property Group, Inc. 1196
Stonegate Mortgage Corp 1250
Superior Oil Company Inc 1263
The College Network Inc 1306
The Finish Line Inc 1310
Wheaton Van Lines Inc 1465
White River Capital Inc. 1466

Jasper
German American Bancorp Inc 604
Kimball Electronics Group Inc. 770
Kimball International, Inc. 770

Jeffersonville
American Commercial Lines Inc. 82

Kokomo
Haynes International, Inc. 650

LAFAYETTE
Greater Lafayette Health Services Inc. 627
Kirby Risk Corporation 773
Lsb Financial Corp. 820
Wabash National Corp 1441

Lawrenceburg
United Community Bancorp 1382

Logansport
Logansport Financial Corp. 814
Memorial Hospital 865

Madison
River Valley Bancorp 1131

Merrillville
Nisource Inc. (holding Co.) 955
Northern Indiana Public Service Company 963

Michigan City
Horizon Bancorp Inc 679

Middlebury
Jayco Inc. 746

MISHAWAKA
Franciscan Alliance, Inc. 573

MUNCIE
Ball State University 178
First Merchants Corp 552
Mutualfirst Financial Inc 917

Munster
Amb Financial Corp 74
Northwest Indiana Bancorp 968

New Albany
Community Bank Shares Of Indiana, Inc. 377
Your Community Bankshares Inc 1489

New Castle
Ameriana Bancorp 77
Henry County Memorial Hospital 659

NOBLESVILLE
Riverview Hospital 1131

Orestes
Red Gold Inc. 1112

Pendleton
Remy International Inc. 1117

Plainfield
Duke Energy Indiana, Inc. 464

RICHMOND
Earlham College 472

Roanoke
Vera Bradley Inc. 1422

Seymour
Cereplast Inc 323
Premier Ag Co-op, Inc. 1071
Rose Acre Farms Inc. 1138

South Bend
1st Source Corp 3
Beacon Medical Group, Inc. 197
South Bend Medical Foundation Inc 1210

Spencer
Home Financial Bancorp 677

Terre Haute
First Financial Corp. (in) 550
Hallador Energy Co 640
Union Hospital, Inc. 1379

VALPARAISO
Family Express Corporation 529
Us 1 Industries Inc. 1408

VINCENNES
Good Samaritan Hospital 617

Wabash
Ffw Corp. 541

Warsaw
Biomet Inc. 218
Lakeland Financial Corp 786
Symmetry Medical Inc. 1269
Zimmer Biomet Holdings Inc 1492

WASHINGTON
Daviess County Hospital 429

West Lafayette
Bioanalytical Systems, Inc. 216
Endocyte Inc 499
Purdue University 1091

IOWA

Algona
American Power Group Corp 93

Altoona
Adventureland Park 34

Ames
Ames National Corp. 101
Iowa State University Of Science And Technology 733
Newlink Genetics Corp 949
Renewable Energy Group Inc. 1118
Renewable Energy Group, Inc. 1118

Ankeny
Casey's General Stores, Inc. 304

Armstrong
Arts Way Manufacturing Co Inc 139

CEDAR FALLS
University Of Northern Iowa 1399

Cedar Rapids
Aegon Usa Llc 36
Coe College 366
Crst International, Inc. 411
D. C. Taylor Co. 423
Interstate Power & Light Co 728
Rockwell Collins Inc 1135
United Fire Group, Inc. 1383

DAVENPORT
Genesis Health System 598
Lee Enterprises, Inc. 795
Swiss Valley Farms Cooperative 1268
Von Maur Inc. 1437

DECORAH
Luther College 823

DES MOINES
Drake University 460
Emc Insurance Group Inc. 491
Fidelity & Guaranty Life 542
Midamerican Energy Holdings Company 885
Plumb Supply Company 1059
Principal Financial Group Inc 1076
Principal Global Investors Llc 1077
Seneca Companies Inc. 1179
The Waldinger Corporation 1336

Dubuque
Flexsteel Industries, Inc. 560
Heartland Financial Usa, Inc. (dubuque, Ia) 655

FARNHAMVILLE
Farmers Cooperative Company 531

Forest City
Winnebago Industries, Inc. 1474

Fort Dodge
North Central Bancshares Inc. 959

GOLDFIELD
Gold-eagle Cooperative 615

GRINNELL
The Trustees Of Grinnell College 1331

HARLAN
Farm Service Cooperative 530

Hills
Hills Bancorporation 669

IOWA CITY
Act, Inc. 22
Midwestone Financial Group, Inc. 888
State University Of Iowa Foundation 1242
The University Of Iowa 1334

Le Mars
Wells Enterprises Inc. 1454

MARCUS
Little Sioux Corn Processors Llc 812

MASON CITY
Golden Grain Energy, Llc 616

Muscatine
Allsteel Inc. 66
Hni Corp 672

NEW HAMPTON
Five Star Cooperative 558

North Liberty
Heartland Express, Inc. 655

Radcliffe
Mirenco Inc. 894

SIOUX CENTER
Farmers Co-operative Society, Sioux Center, Iowa 530

Sioux City
American Pop Corn Company 93

Spencer
Cycle Country Accessories Corp. 420

West Des Moines
American Equity Investment Life Holding Co 84
Fbl Financial Group Inc 533
Hy-vee, Inc. 690
Iowa Health System 733
Ita Group, Inc 737
West Bancorporation, Inc. 1456

KANSAS

ATCHISON
Benedictine College 204
Blish-mize Co. 225

COLUMBUS
Crossland Construction Company, Inc. 409

EMPORIA
Emporia State University 496

HAYS
Hays Medical Center, Inc. 651
Midwest Energy, Inc. 888
Sunflower Electric Power Corporation 1259

Humboldt
Monarch Cement Co. 900

Hutchinson
Dillon Companies Inc. 450

Independence
First Independence Corporation 551

KANSAS CITY
Associated Wholesale Grocers, Inc. 146
Dairy Farmers Of America, Inc. 424
Deffenbaugh Industries Inc. 434
Epiq Systems Inc 510
Kansas City Board Of Public Utilities 760
Unbound 1377

Leawood
Amc Entertainment Holdings Inc. 75
Aratana Therapeutics, Inc 125
Euronet Worldwide Inc. 518
Tallgrass Energy Partners, Lp 1276

Lenexa
Digital Ally Inc 449
Mediware Information Systems Inc. 862
Tvax Biomedical Inc. 1370

MANHATTAN
Kansas State University 761
Landmark Bancorp Inc 788

MCPHERSON
Chs Mcpherson Refinery Inc. 344

Merriam
Seaboard Corp. 1173

Neodesha
Ageagle Aerial Systems Inc (new) 42

Olathe
Butler National Corp. 267
Elecsys Corp. 484
Hooper Holmes Inc 678

Nic Inc. 953
Terracon Consultants, Inc. 1291
Torotel, Inc. 1351
OVERLAND PARK
Black & Veatch Corporation 222
Blue Valley Ban Corp (ks) 231
Bushnell Inc. 266
Cartesian Inc 302
Compass Minerals International Inc 380
Escreen Inc. 514
Ferrellgas Partners Lp 540
Flint Telecom Group Inc 560
Infinity Energy Resources Inc. 708
Npc International Inc. 971
Npc Restaurant Holdings, Llc 971
Qc Holdings Inc 1093
Qts Realty Trust Inc 1095
Waddell & Reed Financial, Inc. 1441
Yrc Worldwide Inc 1489
PRATT
Stanion Wholesale Electric Co., Inc. 1239
Salina
Great Plains Manufacturing Incorporated 626
Isg Technology Llc 736
SHAWNEE MISSION
Shawnee Mission Medical Center, Inc. 1187
Topeka
Capitol Federal Financial Inc 290
Federal Home Loan Bank Topeka 535
Kansas Electric Power Cooperative, Inc. 760
Westar Energy Inc 1458
WICHITA
Berry Companies, Inc. 209
Cessna Aircraft Company 325
Dean & Deluca Incorporated 432
Eby Corporation 477
Intrust Financial Corporation 730
Koch Industries Inc. 777
Learjet Inc. 794
The Wichita State University 1337
Via Christi Health, Inc. 1426
Wichita, City Of (inc) 1468

KENTUCKY
Ashland
Poage Bankshares Inc 1060
Bardstown
Heaven Hill Distilleries Inc. 656
BEREA
Berea College 206
Bowling Green
Bayou City Exploration Inc 195
Citizens First Corp. 351
Commonwealth Health Corporation Inc. 376
Houchens Industries, Inc. 682
Warren Rural Electric Cooperative Corporation 1445
COLD SPRING
Disabled American Veterans 452
Covington
Ariva Distribution Inc. 133
Ashland Inc 143
Crestview Hills
Bank Of Kentucky Financial Corp. 182

DANVILLE
Centre College Of Kentucky 320
EDGEWOOD
Saint Elizabeth Medical Center, Inc. 1152
Elizabethtown
First Financial Service Corp 551
Florence
Healthwarehouse.com, Inc. 655
Frankfort
Farmers Capital Bank Corp. 530
Investors Heritage Capital Corp. 732
Plangraphics Inc. 1056
Hazard
Kentucky First Federal Bancorp 766
HENDERSON
Gibbs Die Casting Corporation 605
Kenergy Corp. 764
Highland Heights
General Cable Corp (de) 595
Hopkinsville
Hopfed Bancorp, Inc. 679
Lexington
A&w Restaurants Inc. 7
Appalachian Regional Healthcare, Inc. 118
Kentucky Medical Services Foundation, Inc. 767
Lexmark International, Inc. 801
Ngas Resources Inc. 953
Rhino Resource Partners Lp 1127
Tempur Sealy International, Inc. 1288
University Of Kentucky Hospital Auxiliary Inc. 1397
Louisville
Appriss Inc. 122
Atria Senior Living Inc. 155
Banc Of America Merchant Services Llc 179
Baptist Healthcare System, Inc. 185
Brown-forman Corp 258
Cafepress Inc 273
Churchill Downs, Inc. 345
Creative Realities Inc 405
Farm Credit Services Of Mid-america Aca 530
Humana Inc. 687
Industrial Services Of America Inc (fl) 707
Kindred Healthcare Inc 771
Limestone Bancorp Inc 807
Neace Lukens Inc. 934
Nts Realty Holdings Ltd Partnership 973
Papa John's International, Inc. 1017
Payment Alliance International Inc. 1027
Pharmerica Corp 1045
Republic Bancorp, Inc. (ky) 1121
Res-care Inc. 1121
Shps Inc. 1190
Steel Technologies Llc 1244
Stock Yards Bancorp Inc 1250
Sypris Solutions, Inc. 1272
Texas Roadhouse Inc 1296
University Health Care Inc 1394
University Of Louisville 1397
Yum! Brands Inc 1490
Middlesboro
Hfb Financial Corp. 664
OWENSBORO
Owensboro Municipal Utilities Electric Light & Power System 1007

PADUCAH
Paxton Media Group, Llc 1026
Pikeville
Community Trust Bancorp, Inc. 379
Pikeville Medical Center, Inc. 1051
RICHMOND
Eastern Kentucky University 474
Stanford
Utg Inc 1414
WALTON
Verst Group Logistics, Inc. 1425
Winchester
Delta Natural Gas Co Inc 438

LOUISIANA
ALEXANDRIA
Christus Health Central Louisiana 342
Baton Rouge
Amedisys, Inc. 75
Baton Rouge General Medical Center 191
Cajun Industries, Llc 273
Entergy Gulf States Louisiana Llc 505
General Health System 596
Lamar Advertising Co (new) 787
Mmr Group, Inc. 897
Our Lady Of The Lake Hospital, Inc. 1005
Presonus Audio Electronics Inc. 1073
The Newtron Group L L C 1324
Woman's Hospital Foundation Inc 1476
COVINGTON
Cgb Enterprises, Inc. 325
Globalstar Inc 613
Hornbeck Offshore Services Inc 680
Loop Llc 817
Pool Corp 1062
Saint Tammany Parish Hospital Service District 1 1154
DeRidder
Amerisafe Inc 100
FRANKLIN
Sterling Sugars, Inc. 1247
GOLDEN MEADOW
Abdon Callais Offshore, Llc 11
Gonzales
Crown Crafts, Inc. 410
Harahan
Sodexo Remote Sites Partnership 1205
HOUMA
Hospital Service District No. 1 682
Houston
Epl Oil & Gas Inc 510
JEANERETTE
M.a. Patout & Son Limited, L.l.c. 827
Jefferson
Entergy Louisiana Llc (new) 506
LAFAYETTE
Acadian Ambulance Service, Inc. 15
Home Bancorp Inc 676
Iberiabank Corp 693
Lafayette General Medical Center, Inc. 785
Lhc Group Inc 801
Midsouth Bancorp, Inc. 887

Our Lady Of Lourdes Regional Medical Center, Inc. 1005
Petroquest Energy Inc (new) 1043
Phi Inc 1046
Southwest Louisiana Electric Membership Corporation 1219
Stone Energy Corp 1250
Lake Charles
Ckx Lands Inc 354
Mc Neese State University 853
Lockport
Bollinger Shipyards Inc. 237
Metairie
Louisiana Bancorp Inc 818
Minden
Minden Bancorp Inc. 891
Monroe
Centurylink Inc 322
Scott Equipment Company, L.l.c. 1171
Morgan City
Conrad Industries Inc 387
New Iberia
Teche Holding Co. 1282
New Orleans
Entergy Corp 505
Entergy New Orleans Inc 506
First Nbc Bank Holding Co. 553
Loyola University New Orleans Inc 820
Phelps Dunbar L.l.p. 1045
Port Of New Orleans 1064
Pineville
Cleco Corp. 358
Crest Operations, Llc 407
RUSTON
Louisiana Tech University 818
St. Martinville
Bruce Foods Corporation 258
ZACHARY
Hospital Service District 1 Of East Baton Rouge Parish 682

MAINE
AUGUSTA
Mainegeneral Health 833
BANGOR
Husson University 690
St. Joseph Healthcare Foundation 1233
Bar Harbor
Bar Harbor Bankshares 186
The Jackson Laboratory 1317
Bath
Bath Iron Works Corporation 191
BIDDEFORD
Southern Maine Health Care 1215
BREWER
Eastern Maine Healthcare Systems 475
BRUNSWICK
Bowdoin College 243
Camden
Camden National Corp. (me) 282
Damariscotta
First Bancorp Inc (me) 547
Miles Health Care, Inc 889

INDEX BY HEADQUARTERS LOCATION

ELLSWORTH
Maine Coast Regional Health Facilities Inc 833

FARMINGTON
Franklin Community Health Network 574

Kennebunk
Tom's Of Maine Inc. 1349

Lewiston
Northeast Bank (me) 962
President & Trustees Of Bates College 1072

New Gloucester
Iberdrola Usa Inc. 692

ORONO
University Of Maine System 1397

PITTSFIELD
Cianbro Corporation 345

Portland
Immucell Corp. 701
Mainehealth 833
Mercy Hospital 869
Wex Inc 1463

WATERVILLE
The President And Trustees Of Colby College 1327

Westbrook
Idexx Laboratories, Inc. 696
Osc Sports, Inc. 1003

Yarmouth
Cole Haan 368

MARYLAND

ADELPHI
University System Of Maryland 1404

Annapolis Junction
Colfax Corp 368

ANNAPOLIS
Anne Arundel Medical Center, Inc. 112
Arinc Incorporated 132
Hannon Armstrong Sustainable Infrastructure Capital Inc 643
Severn Bancorp Inc (annapolis Md) 1185
Telecommunication Systems Inc 1285

Baltimore
Abs Capital Partners L.p. 13
Aol Advertising Inc. 115
Associated Catholic Charities Inc. 145
Baltimore Orioles L.p. 179
Callisonrtkl Inc. 279
Centers For Medicare & Medicaid Services 317
Constellation Energy Group Inc. 389
Cowan Systems, Llc 402
Fidelity & Guaranty Life Insurance Company 542
First Mariner Bancorp. 552
Franklin Square Hospital Center, Inc. 575
Greater Baltimore Medical Center Inc. 627
Harbor Hospital 644
Johns Hopkins Bayview Medical Center, Inc. 752
Johns Hopkins Health Sys Corp 752
Johns Hopkins Medicine International L.l.c. 752
Johns Hopkins University 752
Kennedy Krieger Institute, Inc. 765

Legg Mason, Inc. 797
Levindale Hebrew Geriatric Center And Hospital, Inc. 800
Lifebridge Health, Inc. 804
Loyola University Maryland, Inc. 819
Medifast Inc 862
Millennial Media Inc 889
Mma Capital Holdings Inc 896
Northeastern Supply, Inc. 963
Shepherd Electric Company Incorporated 1188
Sinai Hospital Of Baltimore, Inc. 1197
St. Agnes Healthcare, Inc. 1231
T Rowe Price Group Inc. 1273
The Good Samaritan Hospital Of Md Inc 1313
The Union Memorial Hospital 1333
The Whiting-turner Contracting Company 1337
Under Armour Inc 1377
University Of Maryland Medical System Corporation 1397

Belcamp
Safenet Inc. 1150

Beltsville
Vocus Inc 1436

Berlin
Taylor (calvin B.) Bankshares, Inc. (md) 1280

Bethesda
Agnc Investment Corp 43
American Capital Ltd. 81
Arxan Technologies Inc. 140
Autogrill Group Inc. 161
Centrus Energy Corp 321
Chindex International Inc 341
Clark Construction Group Llc 355
Clark Enterprises Inc. 355
Condor Hospitality Trust Inc 385
Cystic Fibrosis Foundation 422
Diamondrock Hospitality Co. 447
Eagle Bancorp Inc (md) 471
First Potomac Realty Trust 554
Host Hotels & Resorts Inc 682
Lasalle Hotel Properties 791
Liquidity Services Inc 810
Marriott International, Inc. 841
Mtge Investment Corp 912
Northwest Biotherapeutics Inc 967
Pebblebrook Hotel Trust 1030
Saul Centers Inc 1165
Suburban Hospital Inc 1254
Walker & Dunlop Inc 1443

Bowie
Old Line Bancshares Inc 988

Chestertown
Peoples Bancorp, Inc. (md) 1036

CHEVERLY
Dimensions Health Corporation 451

Chevy Chase
Geico Corporation 593

COLLEGE PARK
American Institute Of Physics Incorporated 88

Columbia
Bay Bancorp Inc 193
Cleannet U.s.a., Inc. 357
Corporate Office Properties Trust 397
Grace (wr) & Co 621
Hemagen Diagnostics Inc 658
Integral Systems Inc. 716
Maxim Healthcare Services, Inc. 850
Medstar Health, Inc. 863
Merkle Group Inc. 872
Micros Systems, Inc. 883

Osiris Therapeutics Inc 1004
Shimadzu Scientific Instruments Inc. 1189

CROFTON
Force 3, Llc 566

Dundalk
Patapsco Bancorp Inc. 1023

Easton
Shore Bancshares Inc. 1190

ELKRIDGE
The Kane Company 1318

Elkton
Cecil Bancorp, Inc. 312

FREDERICK
Frederick Memorial Hospital, Inc. 577
U.s. Silica Holdings Inc. 1373

GAITHERSBURG
Adventist Healthcare, Inc. 34
Altimmune Inc 72
Attronica Computers, Inc. 156
Broadsoft Inc 252
Emergent Biosolutions Inc 492
Genvec Inc (de) 601
Novavax, Inc. 971
The Brickman Group Ltd. 1301

Germantown
Hughes Communications Inc. 686
Nutroganics Inc 975
Oba Financial Services Inc 980
Precigen Inc 1070
Project Enhancement Corp 1081
Seneca Biopharma Inc 1179

GLEN BURNIE
Allied International Corporation Of Virginia 64
Glen Burnie Bancorp 609
R. E. Michel Company, Llc 1101

GREENBELT
Sgt, Llc 1185
View Systems, Inc. 1429

Hagerstown
Jlg Industries Inc. 749
Meritus Health Inc. 872

HALETHORPE
The George J Falter Company 1312

Hampstead
Jos. A. Bank Clothiers, Inc. 755

HANOVER
Aerotek, Inc. 38
Allegis Group, Inc. 59
Ciena Corp 346
Keyw Holding Corp 769
Maryland Department Of Transportation 845
Processa Pharmaceuticals Inc 1078
Teksystems, Inc. 1284

HOLLYWOOD
Smartronix, Inc. 1203

HUGHESVILLE
Maryland Southern Electric Cooperative Inc 845

HUNT VALLEY
Ea Engineering, Science, And Technology, Inc., Pbc 471
Mccormick & Co Inc 854
Omega Healthcare Investors, Inc. 990
Tessco Technologies, Inc. 1292

LA PLATA
Charles Regional Medical Center Foundation Inc. 328

The Wills Group Inc 1338

LANHAM
Doctors' Hospital, Inc. 455
Hargrove, Llc 644

LAUREL
Washington Suburban Sanitary Commission (inc) 1446

MARRIOTTSVILLE
Bon Secours Mercy Health, Inc. 238

National Harbor
Accelpath Inc 15

Oakland
First United Corporation (md) 556

Olney
Sandy Spring Bancorp Inc 1160

Owings Mills
Active Day Inc. 23
Baltimore Ravens Limited Partnership 179
Carefirst Inc. 295
The Baltimore Life Insurance Company 1299
Universal Security Instruments, Inc. 1392

Potomac
India Globalization Capital Inc 705

PRINCE FREDERICK
Calverthealth Medical Center, Inc. 280

ROCKVILLE
Aetea Information Technology Inc. 39
Argan Inc 131
Bioreliance Corporation 219
Casi Pharmaceuticals, Inc. 304
Catalyst Health Solutions Inc. 306
Choice Hotels International, Inc. 341
Client Network Services, Llc 359
Federal Realty Investment Trust (md) 535
Glycomimetics Inc 614
Goodwill Industries International, Inc. 619
Grunley Construction Co., Inc. 632
Human Genome Sciences Inc. 687
Macrogenics, Inc 830
Paradigm Holdings Inc. 1018
Regenerx Biopharmaceuticals Inc 1115
Rexahn Pharmaceuticals Inc. 1125
Sucampo Pharmaceuticals Inc 1255
Supernus Pharmaceuticals Inc 1263
Synutra International Inc 1272
Westat, Inc. 1458

Silver Spring
Discovery Inc 452
Technology Service Corporation 1283
United Therapeutics Corp 1389
Urban One Inc 1407
Vietnam Veterans Of America Inc. 1429

Sparks
Apex Tool Group Llc 117

STEVENSON
Stevenson University Inc. 1248

Sykesville
Gse Systems Inc 632

Waldorf
Community Financial Corp (the) 377

WESTMINSTER
Mcdaniel College, Inc 855

INDEX BY HEADQUARTERS LOCATION

MASSACHUSETTS

Acton
Insulet Corp 715
Psychemedics Corp. 1087
Seachange International Inc. 1173

Allston
New England Realty Associates L.p. 941

Andover
California Products Corporation 277
Cambridge Soundworks Inc. 282
Enel Green Power North America Inc. 499
Mercury Systems Inc 868
Mks Instruments Inc 896
Navisite Inc. 932
Philips Electronics North America Corporation 1047
Sige Semiconductor Inc. 1193
Vicor Corp 1428

Athol
Starrett (ls) Co (the) 1240

ATTLEBORO
Sturdy Memorial Hospital, Inc. 1253

Auburndale
Alseres Pharmaceuticals Inc 69
Atrius Health, Inc. 155

Avon
Adams Media 27

Ayer
American Superconductor Corp. 96

BABSON PARK
Babson College 172

Bedford
Anika Therapeutics Inc. 112
Aspen Technology Inc 144
Aware Inc. (ma) 168
Cambridge Heart Inc. 282
Datawatch Corp. 428
Irobot Corp 735
Novanta Inc 971
Progress Software Corp 1080
Rsa Security Llc 1143
Spire Corp. 1225
The Mitre Corporation 1321

Belmont
Bsb Bancorp Inc. (md) 260
The Mclean Hospital Corporation 1320

Beverly
Atn International Inc 155
Axcelis Technologies Inc 169
Northeast Health Systems Inc. 962
Oxford Global Resources Inc. 1007

Billerica
American Science & Engineering Inc 94
Axsun Technologies Inc. 170
Bruker Corp 259
Bruker Daltonics Inc. 259
Bruker Energy & Supercon Technologies Inc. 259
Empirix Inc. 495
Entegris Inc 505

Boston
Abp Corporation 13
Action For Boston Community Development, Inc. 23
Advanced Proteome Therapeutics Inc. 32
Advent International Corporation 33
Albireo Pharma Inc 53
Alexion Pharmaceuticals Inc. 55
American Tower Corp (new) 97
Arnold Worldwide Llc 137
Bain Capital Llc 174
Beacon Capital Partners Llc 197
Berklee College Of Music, Inc. 207
Berkshire Income Realty Inc 208
Berkshire Partners Llc 208
Beth Israel Deaconess Medical Center, Inc. 211
Bingham Mccutchen Llp 215
Blue Cross And Blue Shield Of Massachusetts Inc. 228
Boston Beer Co Inc (the) 241
Boston Medical Center Corporation 241
Boston Private Financial Holdings, Inc. 241
Boston Properties Inc 241
Boston Red Sox Baseball Club Limited Partnership 242
Boston Symphony Orchestra, Inc. 242
Brightcove Inc 250
Brookline Bancorp Inc (de) 255
Canaccord Genuity Inc. 285
Carbonite Inc 292
Caregroup, Inc. 295
City Of Boston 352
Cosi Inc 399
Cra International Inc 404
Dana-farber Cancer Institute, Inc. 426
Digitas Inc. 450
Eastern Bank Corporation 474
Eaton Vance Corp 476
Emerson College 493
Enernoc Inc 501
Federal Home Loan Bank Boston 534
Federal Reserve Bank Of Boston, Dist. No. 1 535
General Electric Co 596
Goodwin Procter Llp 620
Haemonetics Corp. 639
Helmsman Management Services Llc 658
Houghton Mifflin Harcourt Co. 683
Houghton Mifflin Harcourt Publishing Company 683
Iron Mountain Inc (new) 735
Juniper Pharmaceuticals Inc 757
Keryx Biopharmaceuticals Inc. 767
Liberty Mutual Holding Company Inc. 802
Logmein Inc 815
Lpl Financial Holdings Inc. 820
Massachusetts Higher Education Assistance Corporation 846
Massachusetts Port Authority 847
Mintz Levin Cohn Ferris Glovsky And Popeo P.c. 893
Museum Of Fine Arts 916
Newstar Financial Inc 951
Northeastern University 963
Nstar Electric Co 972
Paratek Pharmaceuticals Inc 1019
Paratek Pharmaceuticals Inc 1019
Partners Healthcare System, Inc. 1023
Ptc Inc 1087
S. D. Warren Company 1148
Safety Insurance Group, Inc. 1150
Santander Holdings Usa Inc. 1162
Sapient Corp. 1163
Shawmut Woodworking & Supply, Inc. 1187
Sonesta International Hotels Corporation 1207
Stag Industrial Inc 1236
State Street Corp. 1242
Suffolk Construction Company, Inc. 1255
Suffolk University 1256
The Children's Hospital Corporation 1304
The Massachusetts General Hospital 1319
Thl Credit, Inc. 1340
University Of Massachusetts 1398
Vertex Pharmaceuticals, Inc. 1425
Walsh Brothers, Incorporated 1444
Wayfair Llc 1449
Wgbh Educational Foundation 1464
Winthrop Realty Trust 1475
Ziopharm Oncology Inc 1493
Zoom Telephonics, Inc. 1494

Braintree
Altra Industrial Motion Corp 72

Brighton
Peoples Federal Bancshares, Inc. 1036

BROCKTON
Brockton Hospital, Inc. 254

Burlington
Arqule Inc. 137
Avid Technology, Inc. 166
Bridgeline Digital Inc 248
Burst Media Corporation 266
Charles River Systems Inc. 328
Circor International Inc 348
Demandware Inc 439
Dyax Corp 467
Endurance International Group Holdings Inc 499
Exa Corp 520
Flexion Therapeutics, Inc. 560
Lemaitre Vascular Inc 798
Microfinancial, Inc. 883
Nuance Communications Inc 973

Cambridge
Abt Associates Inc. 13
Acceleron Pharma, Inc. 15
Acer Therapeutics Inc 19
Aegerion Pharmaceuticals Inc 35
Agios Pharmaceuticals Inc 43
Akamai Technologies Inc 48
Alnylam Pharmaceuticals Inc 67
Archemix Corp. 128
Ariad Pharmaceuticals, Inc. 132
Aveo Pharmaceuticals Inc 164
Basis Technology Corporation 190
Bind Therapeutics Inc 215
Biogen Inc 217
Bluebird Bio Inc 231
Cambridge Bancorp 281
Cambridge Public Health Commission 282
Dicerna Pharmaceuticals Inc 447
Epizyme Inc. 510
Forrester Research Inc. 569
Foundation Medicine Inc 571
Genocea Biosciences Inc 600
Genzyme Corporation 601
Helicos Biosciences Corporation 657
Idenix Pharmaceuticals Inc 695
Infinity Pharmaceuticals Inc 708
Intersystems Corporation 728
Massachusetts Institute Of Technology 846
Merrimack Pharmaceuticals Inc 873
Momenta Pharmaceuticals Inc 900
Pathfinder Cell Therapy Inc. 1024
Pegasystems Inc 1031
Sarepta Therapeutics Inc 1164
Sesen Bio Inc 1183
The Charles Stark Draper Laboratory Inc 1304
Vbi Vaccines Inc 1420
Verastem Inc. 1423
Vericel Corp 1423
Whitehead Institute For Biomedical Research 1466

Canton
Boston Mutual Life Insurance Company 241
Destination Xl Group Inc 442
Dunkin' Brands Group Inc 465
Dunkin' Brands Group Inc. 466
Lojack Corporation 815
Network Engines Inc. 938

Chelmsford
Airvana Inc. 48
Arbor Networks Inc. 126
Biscom Inc. 220
Brooks Automation Inc 256
Hittite Microwave Corp 671
Kronos Incorporated 781
Zoll Medical Corporation 1494

CHESTNUT HILL
Trustees Of Boston College 1365

Chicopee
Chicopee Bancorp Inc 337
Consumer Product Distributors, Inc. 389

CLINTON
Nypro Inc. 977

CONCORD
Emerson Hospital 493
Technical Communications Corp 1282
Welch Foods Inc., A Cooperative 1453

Danvers
Abiomed, Inc. 12

Dedham
Atlantic Power Corp 152

Everett
Bostoncoach 242

Fairhaven
Acushnet Company 26

FALL RIVER
Southcoast Hospitals Group, Inc. 1212

Fitchburg
Micron Solutions Inc (de) 883

Framingham
Ameresco Inc 77
Cumberland Farms Inc. 416
Glasshouse Technologies Inc. 609
Gulf Oil Limited Partnership 636
Heartware International Inc 655
J. F. White Contracting Company 740
Staples Inc 1239
Tjx Companies, Inc. 1348

Gardner
Precision Optics Corp Inc (ma) 1070

Gloucester
Varian Semiconductor Equipment Associates Inc. 1418

Hanover
Independent Bank Corp (ma) 704

Hingham
Hingham Institution For Savings 670
Microbot Medical Inc 882

Holliston
Harvard Bioscience Inc. 647
Wayne J. Griffin Electric, Inc. 1449

HOLYOKE
Iso New England Inc. 736

Hopkinton
Caliper Life Sciences Inc. 278
Cts Valpey Corporation 414
Emc Corp. (ma) 491

INDEX BY HEADQUARTERS LOCATION

HYANNIS
Cape Cod Healthcare, Inc. 287
Cape Cod Hospital 287

Lawrence
Nxstage Medical Inc 976

Lee
Wave Systems Corp 1448
Wave Systems Corp. 1449

Lexington
Agenus Inc 43
Concert Pharmaceuticals Inc 384
Cubist Pharmaceuticals Inc. 415
Curis Inc 417
Synageva Biopharma Corp. 1269
Synta Pharmaceuticals Corp 1271

Littleton
Dover Saddlery Inc 459

Lowell
Csp Inc 412
Enterprise Bancorp, Inc. (ma) 506
Macom Technology Solutions Holdings Inc 829
Softech, Inc 1205

LUDLOW
Massachusetts Municipal Wholesale Electric Company 846

Lynnfield
Boston Restaurant Associates Inc. 242
Hp Hood Llc 684
Investors Capital Holdings, Ltd. 732

Malden
Asahi/america Inc. 140

Marlborough
Bitstream Inc. 221
Boston Scientific Corp. 242
Digital Federal Credit Union 449
Hologic Inc 675
Ken's Foods Inc. 764
Netezza Corporation 937
Ocata Therapeutics Inc 980
Paid Inc 1013
Sunovion Pharmaceuticals Inc. 1260

Medford
Century Bancorp, Inc. 322
First Marblehead Corp 552

Methuen
Agri-mark Inc. 44
Tas-chfh 1279

Middleboro
Mayflower Bancorp Inc. 852
Ocean Spray Cranberries, Inc. 982

MILFORD
Milford Regional Medical Center, Inc. 889
Waters Corp. 1447

Natick
Cognex Corp 367
The Mathworks Inc. 1320

Needham
Salary.com Inc. 1155

Newburyport
Ufp Technologies Inc. 1374

Newton
Ambient Corp. 75
Diversified Healthcare Trust 453
Dynasil Corp Of America 468
Five Star Senior Living Inc 558
Galectin Therapeutics Inc. 589
Karyopharm Therapeutics Inc 761
Newton Wellesley Hospital Corp 951
Office Properties Income Trust 984

Select Income Reit 1178
Service Properties Trust 1182
Techtarget Inc 1283
Tripadvisor Inc. 1363

North Andover
Converse Inc. 392
Watts Water Technologies Inc 1448

North Billerica
Btu International, Inc. 261
Entegee, Inc. 505

North Chelmsford
Courier Corp. 400

North Falmouth
Teledyne Benthos 1286

North Quincy
Bt Conferencing 261

North Reading
Teradyne, Inc. 1290

NORTHAMPTON
The Trustees Of The Smith College 1332

Northborough
Bertucci's Corporation 210

Norton
Cps Technologies Corp 403

Norwell
Clean Harbors Inc 356
The Avedis Zildjian Company Inc. 1299
The Computer Merchant Ltd 1307

Norwood
Analog Devices Inc 108
Tas-cnh, Inc. 1279
Xcerra Corp 1483

Oxford
Ipg Photonics Corp 734

Peabody
Analogic Corp 108
Boston Acoustics Inc. 241
Meridian Bancorp Inc 871
Sleepmed Incorporated 1201

Pittsfield
Berkshire Health Systems Inc. 208

Quincy
Arbella Mutual Insurance Company 125
Granite Telecommunications Llc 624

SALEM
North Shore Medical Center, Inc. 961

SOMERVILLE
Allways Health Partners, Inc. 66
Candlewick Press Inc. 285
Trustees Of Tufts College 1366

South Deerfield
The Yankee Candle Company Inc. 1338

South Easton
Pressure Biosciences Inc 1074

SOUTH HADLEY
The Trustees Of Mount Holyoke College 1331

Southborough
Sevcon Inc 1184
Virtusa Corp 1432

SOUTHBRIDGE
Harrington Memorial Hospital, Inc. 646

SOUTHWICK
Whalley Computer Associates, Inc. 1464

Springfield
American Outdoor Brands Corp 92
Baystate Health Inc. 195
Baystate Health System Health Services, Inc. 195
Big Y Foods Inc. 213
Eversource Energy 519
Hampden Bancorp Inc 641
Massachusetts Mutual Life Insurance Company 846
Peter Pan Bus Lines Inc. 1042
Western Massachusetts Electric Co. 1460

Taunton
Agar Supply Co. Inc. 41
Reed & Barton Corporation 1113

Tewksbury
Demoulas Super Markets Inc. 439

Tyngsboro
Beacon Power Corporation 197

Wakefield
American Dental Partners Inc. 83
Franklin Street Properties Corp 575
Xura Inc 1486

Waltham
Alere Inc. 54
Amag Pharmaceuticals, Inc. 73
American Dg Energy Inc 83
Bentley University 206
Bg Medicine Inc 212
Brandeis University 245
Care.com Inc 294
Constant Contact Inc 388
Cys Investments, Inc. 422
Global Partners Lp 612
Great Elm Capital Group Inc 625
Immunogen, Inc. 701
Interleukin Genetics Inc 722
Lionbridge Technologies Inc. 810
Massachusetts Medical Society Inc 846
Neurometrix Inc 939
Parexel International Corporation 1019
Perkinelmer, Inc. 1040
Radius Health Inc 1103
Raytheon Co. 1108
Repligen Corp. 1120
Steel Connect Inc 1243
Tecogen Inc 1283
Tesaro Inc 1292
The Cadmus Group Llc 1302
Thermo Fisher Scientific Inc 1339

Watertown
Athenahealth Inc 150
Bright Horizons Family Solutions Inc. 249
Enanta Pharmaceuticals Inc 497
Pathfinder International 1024
Tetraphase Pharmaceuticals, Inc 1293
Tufts Associated Health Plans Inc. 1368

Wayland
Candela Corporation 285

Wellesley Hills
American Biltrite Inc. 80

Wellesley
Harvard Pilgrim Health Care Inc. 647
Stream Global Services Inc. 1252
Wellesley College 1454

WENHAM
Gordon College 620

West Springfield
United Financial Bancorp Inc (md) 1383

Westborough
Akibia Inc. 49
Bj's Wholesale Club Inc. 221
Eclinicalworks Llc 478
Kopin Corp. 778

Westfield
Mestek Inc. 875
Western New England Bancorp Inc 1461

Westford
Cynosure Inc 421
Kadant Inc 758
Netscout Systems Inc 938
Sonus Networks, Inc. 1209

WESTMINSTER
W. E. Aubuchon Co., Inc. 1440

Weston
Monster Worldwide Inc 903

Westwood
Chase Corp. 330
Medical Information Technology, Inc. 860
Universal Wilde Inc. 1393

WILLIAMSTOWN
President & Trustees Of Williams College 1073

Wilmington
Advansource Biomaterials Corp 32
Charles River Laboratories International Inc. 328
Dusa Pharmaceuticals Inc. 467
Implant Sciences Corp 703
Onto Innovation Inc 995
Rudolph Technologies, Inc. 1144
Unifirst Corp 1378

WINCHESTER
Winchester Healthcare Management, Inc. 1473

Woburn
Fusionstorm Global Inc. 586
Monotype Imaging Holdings Inc 902
Skyworks Solutions Inc 1200
Yield10 Bioscience Inc 1488

WOODS HOLE
Woods Hole, Martha's Vineyard And Nantucket Steamship Authority 1477

WORCESTER
College Of The Holy Cross (inc) 370
Hanover Insurance Group Inc 643
Providence & Worcester Railroad Co. 1085
Thermoenergy Corp 1340
Trustees Of Clark University 1365
Vystar Corp 1439
World Energy Solutions, Inc. (de) 1478

MICHIGAN

ADA
Access Business Group Llc 16
Alticor Inc. 71
Amway International Inc. 106
Baker Book House Company 175

INDEX BY HEADQUARTERS LOCATION

ALLENDALE
Grand Valley State University 623

Alma
Firstbank Corp. (mi) 556

Alpena
First Federal Of Northern Michigan Bancorp Inc 550

Ann Arbor
Adeona Pharmaceuticals Inc. 28
Advanced Photonix, Inc. 32
Affinia Group Holdings Inc. 40
Altarum Institute 70
Arotech Corp 137
Cleary University 358
Con-way Freight Inc. 383
Con-way Inc 383
Dominos Pizza Inc. 457
Regents Of The University Of Michigan 1115
Tecumseh Products Company Llc 1284
United Bancorp, Inc. (tecumseh, Mi) 1381
University Bancorp Inc. (mi) 1393

Auburn Hills
Borgwarner Inc 240
Chrysler Group Llc 343
Detroit Pistons Basketball Company 443
Dura Automotive Systems Llc 466

BATTLE CREEK
Bronson Battle Creek Hospital 254
Kellogg Co 763
W. K. Kellogg Foundation 1440

BAY CITY
Bay Regional Medical Center 194

BEAR LAKE
Blarney Castle Oil Co. 225

Benton Harbor
Whirlpool Corp 1465

BIG RAPIDS
Ferris State University 541

Birmingham
Belfor Usa Group Inc. 203

Bloomfield Hills
Agree Realty Corp. 44
Penske Automotive Group Inc 1035
Sandston Corporation 1160
Taubman Centers Inc 1280
Trimas Corp (new) 1361

CADILLAC
Wolverine Power Supply Cooperative, Inc. 1476

Charlotte
Spartan Motors, Inc. 1221

Cheboygan
Cnb Corp (mi) 362

CLINTON TOWNSHIP
Macomb Oakland Regional Center Inc 829

Coldwater
Monarch Community Bancorp Inc 901
Southern Michigan Bancorp Inc (united States) 1215

COMSTOCK PARK
Nbhx Trim Usa Corporation 933

Dearborn
Carhartt Inc. 296
Ford Motor Co. (de) 567
Ford Motor Credit Company Llc 567
Oakwood Healthcare Inc. 980
Society Of Manufacturing Engineers 1205

Detroit
Ally Financial Inc 66
American Axle & Manufacturing Holdings Inc 79
Blue Cross Blue Shield Of Michigan 229
Caraco Pharmaceutical Laboratories Ltd. 291
Compuware Corp. 382
Detroit Tigers Inc. 443
Diversified Chemical Technologies, Inc. 453
Dte Electric Company 463
Dte Energy Co 463
General Motors Co 597
Henry Ford Health System 659
Hospice Of Michigan Inc. 681
Pvs Technologies Inc. 1092
Quicken Loans Inc. 1099
Tcf Financial Corp (new) 1281
Total Health Care, Inc. 1351
University Of Detroit Mercy 1396
Walbridge Aldinger Company 1443
Wayne State University 1450

EAST LANSING
Greenstone Farm Credit Services Aca 629
Michigan State University 882

Eden Prairie
Titan Energy Worldwide Inc 1346

Farmington Hills
Aco Hardware Inc. 21
Amerisure Mutual Insurance Company 100
Electro-matic Ventures, Inc. 485
Innovation Ventures Llc 711

Fenton
Fentura Financial Inc 540

Flat Rock
Autoalliance International Inc. 161

FLINT
Hurley Medical Center 689
Kettering University 767

Florida
Pen Inc 1031

FRANKENMUTH
Star Of The West Milling Company 1240

FRANKFORT
Graceland Fruit Inc. 621

GARDEN CITY
Prime Healthcare Services - Garden City, Llc 1075

GRAND BLANC
Genesys Regional Medical Center 599
Mclaren Health Care Corporation 857
Serra Automotive Inc. 1182

GRAND RAPIDS
Adac Plastics, Inc. 26
Bissell Homecare Inc. 221
Cascade Engineering, Inc. 303
Crystal Flash, Inc. 411
Davenport University 428
Etna Distributors, Llc 517
Independent Bank Corporation (ionia, Mi) 704
Knape & Vogt Manufacturing Company 775
Lacks Enterprises Inc. 784

Meijer Inc. 864
Mercantile Bank Corp. 867
Meritage Hospitality Group Inc 871
National Heritage Academies Inc. 925
Oncologix Tech Inc 993
Pridgeon & Clay, Inc 1075
Priority Health Managed Benefits Inc. 1077
Spartannash Co. 1222
Steelcase, Inc. 1244
Universal Forest Products Inc. 1391
X-rite Incorporated 1482

Grosse Pointe Farms
Saga Communications Inc 1151

Holland
Haworth Inc. 650
Holland Community Hospital Auxiliary, Inc. 674
Macatawa Bank Corp. 828

HOUGHTON
Michigan Technological University 882

Howell
Fnbh Bancorp, Inc. 565

JACKSON
Alro Steel Corporation 69
Cms Energy Corp 362
Consumers Energy Co. 389

KALAMAZOO
Ascension Borgess Hospital 141
Bronson Health Care Group, Inc. 254
Bronson Methodist Hospital Inc 255
Stryker Corp 1253
Western Michigan University 1460

Kentwood
Autocam Corporation 161

Lansing
Accident Fund Holdings Inc. 17
Auto-owners Insurance Company 161
Lansing Board Of Water And Light 789
Neogen Corp 936
Sparrow Health System 1221

Lapeer
County Bank Corp.(lapeer, Mi) 400

Livonia
American Community Mutual Insurance Company 82
Contractors Steel Company 391
Masco Corp. 845
The Harvard Drug Group L.l.c. 1314
Tower International Inc 1352
Trw Automotive Holdings Corp 1367
Vector Pipeline L.p. 1420

MADISON HEIGHTS
Mcnaughton-mckay Electric Co. 857

Manistique
Mackinac Financial Corp 829

Midland
Dow Chemical Co. 459

Monroe
La-z-boy Inc. 783
Mbt Financial Corp. 853

MOUNT CLEMENS
Mount Clemens Regional Medical Center 909

MOUNT PLEASANT
Central Michigan University 319

Muskegon
Community Shores Bank Corp 379
Hackley Hospital 639

Northville
Genthern Inc 600
Hayes Lemmerz International Inc. 650

Novi
Cooper-standard Holdings Inc 394
Itc Holdings Corp 738
Michigan Milk Producers Association 881
Miracle Software Systems Inc. 893
Stoneridge Inc. 1251

PIGEON
Cooperative Elevator Co. 394

Plymouth
Hella Corporate Center Usa Inc. 658
Perceptron, Inc. 1038
Plastipak Packaging Inc. 1057
Rofin Sinar Technologies Inc. 1136

Pontiac
Abc Appliance Inc. 11

PORT HURON
Semco Energy, Inc. 1178

PORTAGE
Wolverine Pipe Line Company 1476

REDFORD
Piston Automotive L.l.c. 1055

RIVERVIEW
Matteson-ridolfi Inc. 849

Rochester Hills
Energy Conversion Devices Inc. 500

ROCHESTER
Ascension Providence Rochester Hills Hospital 142
Oakland University 979

Rockford
Wolverine World Wide, Inc. 1476

Romulus
Federal Screw Works 537

ROYAL OAK
Beaumont Health 199

SAGINAW
Covenant Medical Center, Inc. 401
Standard Electric Company 1238

SHERIDAN
Sheridan Community Hospital (osteopathic) 1188

Southfield
Alixpartners Llp 57
Ally Commercial Finance Llc 66
Anxebusiness Corp. 115
Ascension Providence Hospital 142
Atwell, Llc 156
Barton Malow Company 189
Blue Care Network Of Michigan 227
Covisint Corporation 402
Credit Acceptance Corp (mi) 405
Denso International America Inc. 440
Detrex Corp. 443
Epitec, Inc. 510
Federal-mogul Holdings Corp 538
Lear Corp. 794
Meadowbrook Insurance Group Inc 858
Plante & Moran Pllc 1057
Sun Communities Inc 1258
Superior Industries International, Inc. 1263
Vesco Oil Corporation 1426
W. B. Doner & Company 1440

INDEX BY HEADQUARTERS LOCATION

Sparta
Choiceone Financial Services, Inc. 342
SPRING ARBOR
Spring Arbor University 1226
Sturgis
Sturgis Bancorp Inc 1254
TRAVERSE CITY
Cherry Central Cooperative, Inc. 334
Munson Healthcare 915
Troy
Diversified Restaurant Holdings Inc. 453
Flagstar Bancorp, Inc. 558
Iconma L.l.c. 694
Meritor Inc 872
Skyline Champion Corp 1200
Syntel Inc. 1272
Talmer Bancorp Inc 1276
Tks Industrial Company 1348
UTICA
Mnp Corporation 897
Van Buren Township
Visteon Corp 1434
WALLED LAKE
American Plastic Toys Inc. 92
WARREN
Angelo Iafrate Construction Company 110
Campbell-ewald Company 284
Centra Inc. 318
Linc Logistics Company 807
Madison Electric Company 830
Production Tool Supply Company, Llc 1079
St. John Hospital And Medical Center 1232
St. John Providence 1232
Universal Logistics Holdings Inc 1391
Wixom
Integral Vision Inc. 717
WYOMING
Gordon Food Service, Inc. 620
YPSILANTI
Eastern Michigan University 475
Zeeland
Gentex Corp. 600
Miller (herman) Inc 890
Zeeland Community Hospital 1492

MINNESOTA

ALEXANDRIA
Alexandria Extrusion Company 55
Arden Hills
Intricon Corp 729
Land O' Lakes Inc 788
Austin
Hormel Foods Corp. 680
BAGLEY
Team Industries Holding Corporation 1281
Baudette
Ani Pharmaceuticals Inc 111
Bayport
Andersen Corporation 109
Bemidji
Sanford Health Of Northern Minnesota 1161

Bloomington
Granite City Food & Brewery Ltd 624
Rsm Mcgladrey Inc. 1143
Brooklyn Center
Abra Inc. 13
Brooklyn Park
Clearfield Inc 357
BURNSVILLE
Ames Construction, Inc. 101
Atrix International Inc. 156
Bosch Communications Systems 240
CHAMPLIN
Deco, Inc. 433
Chanhassen
Instant Web Inc. 715
Life-time Fitness Inc 804
Chaska
Lifecore Biomedical Inc. 804
Tel Fsi Inc. 1285
Circle Pines
Northern Technologies International Corp. 964
DETROIT LAKES
St Mary's Regional Health Center 1230
Dodge Center
Mcneilus Companies Inc. 857
Duluth
Allete Inc 61
Benedictine Health System 205
Ikonics Corp 698
St. Luke's Hospital Of Duluth 1234
Eagan
Blue Cross And Blue Shield Of Minnesota 228
Thomson Reuters (legal) Inc. 1342
EDEN PRAIRIE
Avi Systems, Inc. 165
Bluestem Brands Inc. 232
Datalink Corp 428
Imedia Brands Inc 700
Minnesota Vikings Football Club L.l.c. 892
Mts Systems Corp 913
Nve Corp 976
Research Incorporated 1121
Robinson (c.h.) Worldwide, Inc. 1134
Supervalu Inc 1264
Surmodics Inc 1265
Xrs Corp 1486
Edina
Regis Corp 1116
Fairmont
Avery Weigh-tronix Llc 165
Rosen's Diversified Inc. 1139
FARMINGTON
Dakota Electric Association 424
Fergus Falls
Otter Tail Corp. 1004
Hastings
Smead Manufacturing Company 1203
HERMANTOWN
Miners Incorporated 891
Hopkins
Digi International Inc 448
Hutchinson
Hutchinson Technology Inc. 690

Hypertension Diagnostics, Inc. 691
Inver Grove Heights
Chs Inc 343
LAKEVILLE
Imagetrend Inc. 699
Mankato
Hickory Tech Corp. 666
Winland Holdings Corp 1474
MAPLE GROVE
Great River Energy 626
Nortech Systems Inc. 958
MAPLE LAKE
Bernatello"s Pizza Inc 209
Maple Plain
Proto Labs Inc 1084
Marshall
The Schwan Food Company 1329
Medina
Polaris Inc 1061
Mendota Heights
Restaurant Technologies Inc. 1123
Minneapolis
Allianz Life Insurance Company Of North America 63
Allina Health System 65
Ameriprise Financial Inc 99
Arctic Cat Inc 130
Bio-techne Corp 216
Buffalo Wild Wings Inc 263
Campbell Mithun Inc. 283
Capella Education Company 287
Cliftonlarsonallen Llp 360
Cyberoptics Corp. 420
Dolan Company (the) 456
Donaldson Co. Inc. 457
Dorsey & Whitney Llp 458
Entrx Corporation 507
Fairview Health Services 528
Federal Reserve Bank Of Minneapolis, Dist. No. 9 536
General Mills Inc 597
Groove Botanicals Inc 631
Insignia Systems, Inc. 714
Kips Bay Medical Inc. 773
Kurt Manufacturing Company Inc. 782
Metropolitan Airports Commission 877
Mocon Inc. 898
North Memorial Health Care 960
Park Nicollet Health Services 1020
Pentair Ltd. 1035
Piper Sandler Companies 1054
Qumu Corp 1100
Schmitt Music Company 1168
Sleep Number Corp 1201
Sps Commerce, Inc. 1227
Subjex Corporation 1254
Target Corp 1278
Tennant Co. 1289
Urologix Inc. 1407
Us Bancorp (de) 1408
Valspar Corp 1416
Vascular Solutions Inc 1419
Wachovia Preferred Funding Corp 1441
Winmark Corp 1474
Xcel Energy Inc 1482
Zareba Systems Inc. 1491
Minnetonka
American Medical Systems Holdings Inc. 91
Bbq Holdings Inc 196

Best Brands Corp. 210
Carlson Companies Inc. 297
Carlson Hotels Worldwide Inc. 297
Cogentix Medical Inc 367
Communications Systems, Inc. 376
Digital River, Inc. 449
Electro-sensors, Inc. 486
G&k Services Inc 587
Michael Foods Group Inc. 881
Northern Oil & Gas Inc (mn) 964
Onebeacon Insurance Group Ltd. 994
Table Trac Inc. 1274
Unitedhealth Group Inc 1389
Uroplasty, Inc. 1408
Monticello
Wsi Industries, Inc. 1481
Moorhead
American Crystal Sugar Company 83
New Hope
Liberty Diversified International Inc. 802
New Prague
Electromed, Inc. 486
New Ulm
Associated Milk Producers Inc. 146
Nuvera Communications Inc 975
NORTHFIELD
Carleton College 296
St. Olaf College 1235
Oakdale
Atrm Holdings Inc 156
Glassbridge Enterprises Inc 609
Owatonna
Federated Insurance Companies 538
Plymouth
Christopher & Banks Corp. 342
Silver Bay Realty Trust Corp. 1195
The Mosaic Company 1322
United Hardware Distributing Co 1384
RAMSEY
Connexus Energy 386
RENVILLE
Southern Minnesota Beet Sugar Cooperative 1216
Richfield
Best Buy Inc 210
Rochester
Hmn Financial Inc. 672
Mayo Clinic Hospital-rochester 852
Olmsted Medical Center 989
Southern Minnesota Municipal Power Agency 1216
Rogers
Archway Marketing Services Inc. 129
Roseville
Hawkins Inc 650
SAINT CLOUD
Coborn's, Incorporated 365
SAINT JOSEPH
College Of Saint Benedict 369
SAINT LOUIS PARK
Park Nicollet Methodist Hospital 1020
SAINT PAUL
Api Group Inc. 117
Gillette Children's Specialty Healthcare 607
Great Northern Iron Ore Properties 626
Healtheast St John's Hospital 654

INDEX BY HEADQUARTERS LOCATION

Macalester College 828
Merrill Corporation 872
Mgc Diagnostics Corp 880
Regions Hospital Foundation 1116
University Of St. Thomas 1402

SAINT PETER
Gustavus Adolphus College 637

Shakopee
Canterbury Park Holding Corp (new) 286

Shoreview
Deluxe Corp 439

St. Cloud
Anderson Trucking Service Inc. 110

St. Paul
3m Co 5
Aero Systems Engineering Inc. 37
Agribank Fcb 44
Cardiovascular Systems, Inc 294
Ecolab Inc 479
Fuller (hb) Company 584
Gander Mountain Company 591
Image Sensing Systems, Inc. 699
Medtox Scientific Inc. 863
Patterson Companies Inc 1026
Securian Financial Group Inc. 1175
St Jude Medical Inc 1230
St. Jude Medical, Inc. 1234
Synovis Life Technologies Inc. 1271

TRUMAN
Watonwan Farm Service, Inc 1448

Waseca
Brown Printing Company 257

Wayzata
Tcf Financial Corp 1281

Wells
Wells Financial Corp 1454

Winona
Fastenal Co. 532
Saint Mary's University Of Minnesota 1154

WINTHROP
United Farmers Cooperative 1383

Woodbury
Broadview Institute Inc 252

MISSISSIPPI

Baldwyn
Hancock Fabrics, Inc. 642

Biloxi
Peoples Financial Corp (biloxi, Ms) 1036

BRANDON
On-site Fuel Service, Inc. 992

Ecru
American Furniture Manufacturing Inc. 86

Flowood
Blue Cross & Blue Shield Of Mississippi 227

GREENVILLE
Delta Regional Medical Center 438

GREENWOOD
Staple Cotton Cooperative Association 1239

Gulfport
Hancock Whitney Corp 642
Mississippi Power Co 895

HATTIESBURG
First Bancshares Inc (ms) 547
Forrest County General Hospital (inc) 569
The Merchants Company 1320
The University Of Southern Mississippi 1335

Jackson
Cal-maine Foods Inc 274
Entergy Mississippi Inc 506
Jackson State University 743
Miller Transportation Services, Inc. 890
Telephone Electronics Corporation 1287
Trustmark Corp 1366

KILN
Coast Electric Power Association 363

KOSCIUSKO
Ivey Mechanical Company, Llc 739

Laurel
Sanderson Farms Inc 1160

MCCOMB
Southwest Mississippi Regional Medical Center 1219

MERIDIAN
Southern Pipe & Supply Company, Inc. 1217

MISSISSIPPI STATE
Mississippi State University 895

Natchez
Britton & Koontz Capital Corp. 251

Philadelphia
Citizens Holding Co 351

Ridgeland
Eastgroup Properties Inc 476

TAYLORSVILLE
Southern Pine Electric Cooperative 1217

Tupelo
Bancorpsouth Bank (tupelo, Ms) 180
North Mississippi Health Services, Inc. 960
North Mississippi Medical Center, Inc. 961
Renasant Corp 1118

UNIVERSITY
University Of Mississippi 1398

MISSOURI

CAPE GIRARDEAU
Francis Saint Medical Center 573
Southeast Missouri State University 1212

Carthage
Leggett & Platt, Inc. 797

Chesterfield
Aegion Corp 36
Insituform Technologies Inc. 714
Kellwood Company 763
Mercy Health 869
Missouri Higher Education Loan Authority 895
Pretium Packaging Llc 1074
Reinsurance Group Of America, Inc. 1116
Reliv' International Inc 1117
Rose International, Inc. 1138
Savvis Inc. 1165
Seven Seas Technologies Inc. 1184

St. Luke's Episcopal-presbyterian Hospitals 1234
Victor Technologies Group Inc. 1428

Clayton
Enterprise Financial Services Corp 507
First Banks, Inc. (mo) 547
Olin Corp. 989

COLUMBIA
Boone Hospital Center 239
M. F. A. Oil Company 827
Mfa Incorporated 880
University Of Missouri System 1398

Des Peres
The Jones Financial Companies L.l.lp. 1317

Earth City
Interface Security Systems L.l.c. 721
Laird Technologies Inc. 785
Medicine Shoppe International Inc. 861

FENTON
Maritz Holdings Inc. 840
Unigroup Inc. 1378

Grandview
Nasb Financial Inc 920

JOPLIN
Freeman Health System 578
The Empire District Electric Company 1310

Kansas City
American Italian Pasta Company 88
Americo Life Inc. 98
Barkley Inc. 187
Block (h & R), Inc. 225
Butler Manufacturing Company 267
Commerce Bancshares Inc 375
Corenergy Infrastructure Trust Inc 396
Epr Properties 510
Federal Reserve Bank Of Kansas City, Dist. No. 10 536
Great Plains Energy Inc 626
Hntb Corporation 672
J.e. Dunn Construction Company 741
J.e. Dunn Construction Group, Inc. 741
Kansas City Chiefs Football Club Inc. 760
Kansas City Life Insurance Co (kansas City, Mo) 760
Kansas City Southern 760
Mercy Children's Hospital 868
Mriglobal 911
Novation Companies Inc 971
Saint Luke's Health System, Inc. 1153
Stowers Institute For Medical Research 1251
The G W Van Keppel Company 1311
Tnemec Company, Inc. 1348
Truman Medical Center, Incorporated 1365
Umb Financial Corp 1376
Veterans Of Foreign Wars Of The United States 1426

LENEXA
Freightquote.com Inc. 578

Liberty
Liberty Bancorp Inc (mo) 802
The New Liberty Hospital District Of Clay County Missouri 1323

MARYLAND HEIGHTS
J. D. Streett & Company, Inc. 740
Sunedison Inc 1259

Monett
Jack Henry & Associates, Inc. 742

Mountain Grove
First Bancshares Inc. (mo) 547

North Kansas City
Cerner Corp. 324
Maxus Realty Trust Inc 851
Wagner Industries Inc. 1442

O FALLON
Synergetics Usa, Inc. 1270

POPLAR BLUFF
Poplar Bluff Regional Medical Center, Inc. 1063
Southern Missouri Bancorp, Inc. 1216

SAINT CHARLES
Client Services Inc. 360

SAINT JOSEPH
Heartland Health 655
Mosaic Life Care 908

SAINT LOUIS
Alberici Corporation 52
Ascension Health 142
Barry-wehmiller Group, Inc. 189
Christian Hospital Northeast - Northwest 342
Cic Group, Inc. 346
Connectria Corporation 386
Csi Leasing, Inc. 412
Guarantee Electrical Company 634
Isle Of Capri Casinos Inc 736
Korte Construction Company 778
Logistics Management Solutions L.c. 815
Mccarthy Building Companies, Inc. 854
Mercy Hospital South 870
Metropolitan St. Louis Sewer District 878
Murphy Company Mechanical Contractors And Engineers 915
Osborn & Barr Communications Inc. 1003
Perficient Inc 1039
Saint Louis University 1153
Ssm Health Care Corporation 1228
The Washington University 1337
Webster University 1452
World Wide Technology, Llc 1479

SPRINGFIELD
Associated Electric Cooperative, Inc. 145
Bass Pro Inc. 191
City Utilities Of Springfield Mo 353
Great Southern Bancorp, Inc. 626
Hiland Dairy Foods Company., Llc 668
Lester E. Cox Medical Centers 799
Mercy Hospital Springfield 870
Missouri State University 895
Mueller (paul) Co 913
New Prime, Inc. 943
O'reilly Automotive, Inc. 978

St. Charles
Acf Industries Llc 20
American Railcar Industries Inc 93
Lmi Aerospace, Inc. 813

St. Joseph
Chase General Corporation 330

St. Louis
Allied Healthcare Products Inc 63
Ameren Corp 76
Anheuser-busch Companies Inc. 111
Arch Coal Inc 128
Armstrong Energy Inc. 136
Belden Inc 202

INDEX BY HEADQUARTERS LOCATION

Bryan Cave Llp 260
Build-a-bear Workshop Inc 263
Bunge Milling Inc. 264
Caleres Inc 275
Cass Information Systems Inc. 305
Centene Corp 316
Centric Group L.l.c. 321
Cequel Communications Holdings I Llc 323
Ducommun Labarge Technologies 463
Esco Technologies, Inc. 514
Express Scripts Holding Co 525
Federal Reserve Bank Of St. Louis, Dist. No. 8 537
Futurefuel Corp 586
Graybar Electric Co., Inc. 625
Hardee's Food Systems Inc. 644
Huttig Building Products, Inc. 690
Katy Industries, Inc. 761
Monsanto Co 903
Panera Bread Co 1016
Patriot Coal Corp 1025
Peabody Energy Corp (new) 1029
Post Holdings Inc 1065
Pulaski Financial Corp 1090
Pulaski Financial Corp. 1090
Schnuck Markets Inc. 1168
Shop 'n Save St. Louis Inc. 1189
Sigma-aldrich Corp. 1193
Solutia Inc. 1207
Spire Inc 1225
Stereotaxis Inc 1246
Stifel Financial Corp 1249
Viasystems Group Inc 1427
Zoltek Companies Inc 1494

TROY
Cuivre River Electric Cooperative, Inc. 415

Wildwood
Peak Resorts Inc 1030

MONTANA

Belgrade
Xtant Medical Holdings Inc 1486

BILLINGS
Billings Clinic 214
First Interstate Bancsystem Inc 552

BOZEMAN
Montana State University, Inc 903

BUTTE
St James Healthcare, Inc 1229

Great Falls
Davidson Companies 429
Pacific Hide & Fur Depot 1011

Helena
Blue Cross And Blue Shield Of Montana 228
Eagle Bancorp Montana, Inc. 471

KALISPELL
Cityservicevalcon, Llc 354
Glacier Bancorp, Inc. 608

MISSOULA
Blackfoot Telephone Cooperative Inc. 223
St Patrick Hospital Corporation 1231
University Of Montana 1398
Watkins And Shepard Trucking, Inc. 1447

Thompson Falls
United States Antimony Corp. 1386

NEBRASKA

BATTLE CREEK
Battle Creek Farmers Cooperative, Non-stock 192

Columbus
Behlen Mfg. Co. 201
Nebraska Public Power District 934

FREMONT
Fremont Contract Carriers, Inc. 579
Fremont Health 579

GOTHENBURG
All Points Cooperative 58

Grand Island
Bosselman Inc. 240
Chief Industries Inc. 338

Hastings
Gibraltar Packaging Group Inc. 606

Kearney
Baldwin Filters Inc. 176
Buckle, Inc. (the) 262
Cash-wa Distributing Co. Of Kearney, Inc. 304

Kimball
Risk George Industries Inc 1130

Lincoln
Ameritas Mutual Holding Company 101
B&r Stores Inc. 171
Board Of Regents Of The University Of Nebraska 234
Bryan Medical Center 260
Crete Carrier Corporation 407
Lincoln Industries 808
Madonna Rehabilitation Hospital 830
National Research Corp 926
Nebraska Book Company Inc. 934
Nelnet Inc 935
Saint Elizabeth Regional Medical Center 1152
Union Bank And Trust Company 1378
Universal Manufacturing Co 1391

NORFOLK
Affiliated Foods Midwest Cooperative, Inc. 39

OMAHA
Ag Processing Inc A Cooperative 41
Amcon Distributing Company 75
Berkshire Hathaway Inc 207
C&a Industries Inc. 268
Childrens Hospital & Medical Center 340
Creighton Alegent Health 406
Creighton University 406
Findex.com Inc. 545
Godfather's Pizza Inc. 614
Gordmans Stores Inc 620
Green Plains Inc. 628
Hawkins Construction Company 649
Hdr, Inc. 652
Leo A. Daly Company 799
Metropolitan Utilities District 878
Mosaic 907
Mutual Of Omaha Insurance Co. (ne) 917
Northern Natural Gas Company 964
Omaha Public Power District 990
Pamida Stores Operating Company Llc 1015
Peter Kiewit Sons', Inc. 1042
Roberts Dairy Company, Llc 1133
Sapp Bros. Petroleum Inc. 1163
Sapp Bros., Inc. 1163
Td Ameritrade Holding Corp 1281
Tenaska Inc. 1288
The Gavilon Group Llc 1311
The Nebraska Medical Center 1322
The Scoular Company 1329
Travel And Transport Inc. 1357
Union Pacific Corp 1379
Unmc Physicians 1405
Valmont Industries Inc 1416
Werner Enterprises, Inc. 1455
West Corp. 1456
Woodmen Of The World Life Insurance Society 1477

Sidney
Cabela's Inc 270

WINNEBAGO
Ho-chunk, Inc. 672

NEVADA

Boulder City
Ameritrye Corporation 101

CARSON CITY
Carson Tahoe Regional Healthcare 301
Pico Holdings Inc. 1049

Elko
Us Gold Corp (canada) 1410

HENDERSON
Global Pacific Produce Inc. 612
Spectrum Pharmaceuticals Inc 1224

Incline Village
Pdl Biopharma Inc 1029

Las Vegas
All-american Sportpark Inc. 58
Allegiant Travel Company 59
American Pacific Corp. 92
Aristocrat Technologies Inc. 133
Axos Financial Inc 170
Bally Technologies Inc 178
Bio-solutions Manufacturing Inc. 215
Boyd Gaming Corp. 244
Caesars Entertainment Corp 272
Can-cal Resources Ltd. 284
Cantor Entertainment Technology Inc. 286
Consumer Portfolio Services, Inc. 389
Desert Springs Hospital Medical Center 442
Diamond Resorts Holdings Llc 446
Everi Holdings Inc 519
Gallery Of History Inc. 590
Golden Entertainment Inc 615
Golden Star Enterprises Ltd 616
Inova Technology Inc 712
Janone Inc 746
Las Vegas Sands Corp 790
Las Vegas Valley Water District 790
Live Ventures Inc 812
M & H Enterprises Inc. 826
Methes Energies International Ltd. 875
Mgm Resorts International 880
Nevada Gold & Casinos, Inc. 940
Nevada Power Co. 940
Nevada State Bank 940
Phi Group Inc. 1046
Pinnacle Entertainment Inc 1052
Players Network (the) 1058
Prestige Travel Inc 1074
Riviera Holdings Corporation 1132
Skinvisible Inc 1200
Summerlin Hospital Medical Center, Llc 1256
University Medical Center Of Southern Nevada 1394
Valley Health System Llc 1416
Voyager Entertainment International Inc. 1437
Wynn Resorts Ltd 1482

North Las Vegas
Archon Corporation 129
Gaming Partners International Corp 590

Reno
Allied Nevada Gold Corp 64
Altair Nanotechnologies Inc 70
Amerco 76
Crown Gold Corporation 410
Employers Holdings Inc 495
Hycroft Mining Corp 691
Monarch Casino & Resort, Inc. 900
Nevada System Of Higher Education 940
Nmi Health Inc 955
Ormat Technologies Inc 1002
Sierra Pacific Power Co. 1192
Tahoe Resources Inc. 1275
Zoomaway Travel Inc 1494

SPARKS
Sierra Nevada Corporation 1192

Winnemucca
Paramount Gold & Silver Corp 1019

Zephyr Cove
Virnetx Holding Corp 1432

NEW HAMPSHIRE

Berlin
Northway Financial, Inc. 967

Claremont
Red River Computer Co. Inc. 1112

CONCORD
Concord Hospital, Inc. 384
Concord Litho Group 384
Hopto Inc 679
University System Of New Hampshire 1404

Hampton
Unitil Corp 1389

HANOVER
Trustees Of Dartmouth College 1365
White Mountains Insurance Group Ltd. 1466

Hudson
Micronetics Inc. 883
Presstek Inc. 1074

Keene
C&s Wholesale Grocers Inc. 269
Co Holdings, Llc 363
North European Oil Royalty Trust 960

LEBANON
Dartmouth-hitchcock Clinic 427
Mascoma Corporation 845

MANCHESTER
Allegro Microsystems, Llc 59
Catholic Medical Center 308
Elliot Hospital Of The City Of Manchester 488
Saint Anselm College 1152

Merrimack
Brookstone Inc. 256
Pc Connection, Inc. 1028
Pennichuck Corporation 1033

MILFORD
Hitchiner Manufacturing Co., Inc. 670

INDEX BY HEADQUARTERS LOCATION

Nashua
Gt Advanced Technologies Inc. 633
Icad Inc 693
Skillsoft Corporation 1199
Southern New Hampshire Medical Center 1216

Newport
Lake Sunapee Bank Group 786
New Hampshire Thrift Bancshares, Inc. 941

PEMBROKE
Associated Grocers Of New England, Inc. 146

Peterborough
Eastern Mountain Sports Inc. 475

PLYMOUTH
New Hampshire Electric Cooperative Inc 941

Portsmouth
Anvil International Inc. 115
Bottomline Technologies (delaware) Inc 242
Sprague Resources Lp 1226

Rochester
Albany International Corp 52
Frisbie Memorial Hospital 580

Salem
Prophotonix Ltd 1082
Standex International Corp. 1238

Stratham
The Timberland Company 1331

NEW JERSEY

ALLENTOWN
United Bank Card Inc. 1381

Atlantic City
Trump Entertainment Resorts Inc. 1365

Basking Ridge
Avaya Inc. 164
Barnes & Noble College Booksellers Llc 187
Cellco Partnership 314

Bayonne
Bcb Bancorp Inc 196

Bedminster
Cegedim Relationship Management 313
Gain Capital Holdings Inc 588
Nps Pharmaceuticals Inc. 972
Peapack-gladstone Financial Corp. 1030

Berkeley Heights
Cormedix Inc 396
Cyclacel Pharmaceuticals Inc 420

Berlin
A.c. Moore Arts & Crafts Inc. 8

BLOOMFIELD
World Finer Foods, Llc 1478

Boonton Township
Valcom Inc. 1414

BRANCHBURG
Dancker, Sellew & Douglas, Inc. 426
Hydromer, Inc. 691
Raritan Valley Community College 1106

Branchville
Selective Insurance Group Inc 1178

BRIDGETON
Seabrook Brothers & Sons Inc 1173

Bridgewater
Advanced Health Media Llc 31
Brother International Corporation 257
Cordis Corporation 395
Igate Corp 697
Sanofi-aventis U.s. Llc 1161
Savient Pharmaceuticals Inc 1165
Synchronoss Technologies Inc 1270

Buena
Teligent Inc (new) 1287

Burlington
Burlington Stores Inc 265

Camden
American Water Works Co, Inc. 98
Campbell Soup Co 283
Delaware River Port Authority 435
Our Lady Of Lourdes Medical Center, Inc 1004
The Cooper Health System 1307

Cape May Court House
Cape Bancorp, Inc. 287

Cedar Knolls
Artech Information Systems L.l.c. 139

Cherry Hill
1st Colonial Bancorp Inc 3
Ameriquest Transportation Services Inc. 100
Nuvilex Inc. 976

Clifton
Clifton Savings Bancorp Inc 360
Electronic Control Security Inc. 486

Clinton
Unity Bancorp, Inc. 1390

Cranbury
1st Constitution Bancorp 3
Amicus Therapeutics Inc 102
Innophos Holdings Inc 711
Palatin Technologies Inc 1014
Trilogy Leasing Co. Llc 1361

Cranford
Enzon Pharmaceuticals Inc 509
Metalico Inc 875
The Newark Group Inc. 1324
Tofutti Brands Inc 1349
Weeks Marine, Inc. 1452

Dover
Casio America Inc. 305

East Brunswick
K-sea Transportation Partners L.p. 758

EAST HANOVER
Foremost Groups, Inc. 567

EAST ORANGE
East Orange General Hospital (inc) 473

East Rutherford
Allied Building Products Corp. 63
Cambrex Corp 281
New York Football Giants Inc. 945
Tel Instrument Electronics Corp. 1285

Eastampton
Epicore Bionetworks Inc. 509

Eatontown
Wayside Technology Group Inc 1450

Edison
Aerogroup International Llc 37
Colavita Usa L.l.c. 368
Conti Enterprises, Inc. 390
Hmh Hospitals Corporation 671
J.m. Huber Corporation 741
Strikeforce Technologies Inc 1253
The Community Hospital Group Inc 1307

EGG HARBOR TOWNSHIP
Atlanticare Health System Inc. 153

ELIZABETH
Atalanta Corporation 150
Trinitas Regional Medical Center 1362

Elmwood Park
Bio-reference Laboratories, Inc. 215
Kreisler Manfacturing Corp. 780

Englewood Cliffs
Asta Funding, Inc. 147
Bauer Publishing Usa 192
Connectone Bancorp Inc (new) 386

ENGLEWOOD
Englewood Hospital And Medical Center Foundation Inc. 502

Ewing
Antares Pharma Inc. 114
Church & Dwight Co Inc 344
Redpoint Bio Corporation 1113
Universal Display Corp 1390

FAIRFIELD
Acuative Corporation 25
Kearny Financial Corp 762

FAR HILLS
United States Golf Association, Inc. 1387

Farmingdale
Cherry Hill Mortgage Investment Corp 334

Florham Park
New York Jets Llc 945
Protalex Inc 1083

Folsom
South Jersey Gas Co. 1211
South Jersey Industries Inc 1211

Fort Lee
Bancorp Of New Jersey, Inc. 180
Empire Resources, Inc. 495
Refac Optical Group 1114

Franklin Lakes
Becton, Dickinson & Co 201

FREEHOLD
Centrastate Healthcare System Inc 320
Umh Properties Inc 1376

Glen Rock
Respirerx Pharmaceuticals Inc 1123

Glendora
U.s. Vision Inc. 1373

Hackensack
Champions Oncology Inc 326
Rockwell Medical, Inc 1135
Roomlinx Inc 1137

Hamilton
Voxware Inc. 1437

Hammonton
Ag&e Holdings Inc 41

Hampton
Celldex Therapeutics, Inc. 315

Hawthorne
Ccom Group Inc 311

HILLSBOROUGH
Joyce Leslie Inc 755

Hillside
Integrated Biopharma Inc 717

HOBOKEN
Stevens Institute Of Technology (inc) 1248
Wiley (john) & Sons Inc. 1469

Holmdel
Monmouth Real Estate Investment Corp 901
Vonage Holdings Corp 1437

Iselin
Basf Catalysts Llc 190
Echo Therapeutics Inc 478
Macdonald Mott Group Inc 828
Middlesex Water Co. 887
Pharmos Corporation 1045

Jersey City
Bel Fuse Inc 202
Franklin Credit Holding Corporation 574
Ipc Systems Inc. 734
Jersey City Medical Center (inc) 748
Mack Cali Realty Corp 829
Provident Financial Services Inc 1086
Rand Logistics Inc 1105
Verisk Analytics Inc 1424

KEASBEY
Wakefern Food Corp. 1442

Kenilworth
Merck & Co Inc 868

Lakewood
Eroom System Technologies Inc 513
Kimball Medical Center Inc. 770

Lawrence
Datacolor Inc. 427

Lawrenceville
1sync Inc. 4
Celsion Corp 315

Liberty Corner
Caladrius Biosciences Inc 274

Linden
General Magnaplate Corporation 596
Turtle & Hughes, Inc 1369

Little Falls
Cantel Medical Corp 286

Livingston
Milestone Scientific Inc. 889
Nan Ya Plastics Corporation U.s.a. 919
St Barnabas Medical Center (inc) 1229
The Briad Group 1301

LONG BRANCH
Monmouth Medical Center Inc. 901

LONG VALLEY
Frazier Industrial Company 576

LYNDHURST
Argo International Corporation 131
Cca Industries, Inc. 310
Sika Corporation 1194

MADISON
Drew University 461
Realogy Holdings Corp 1110

Mahwah
Ascena Retail Group Inc 141

HOOVER'S MASTERLIST OF U.S. COMPANIES 2020

INDEX BY HEADQUARTERS LOCATION

Marlton
Acsis Inc. 22

Matawan
Hovnanian Enterprises, Inc. 684
Icims.com Inc 694
Pacifichealth Laboratories Inc. 1012

Maywood
Jaclyn Inc. 744

Midland Park
Stewardship Financial Corp. 1248

Millington
Msb Financial Corp 912

Monmouth Junction
Cytosorbents Corporation 422
Sysco Guest Supply Llc 1273

Monroe Township
Ocean Power Technologies Inc 981

Montclair
180 Degree Capital Corp 2
Montclair State University 903

Montvale
Benjamin Moore & Co. 206
Berry Global Films, Llc 209
Kpmg L.l.p. 779
Pathmark Stores Inc. 1024
The Great Atlantic & Pacific Tea Company Inc. 1313

Moorestown
Destination Maternity Corp 442

Morris Plains
Honeywell International Inc 678
Immunomedics, Inc. 701

Morristown
Actavis U.s. 22
Atlantic Health System Inc. 152
Collabera Inc. 369
Covanta Holding Corp 401
Cover-all Technologies, Inc. 402
Crum & Forster Holdings Corp. 411
Durata Therapeutics Inc. 467
Financial Executives International 544
Melinta Therapeutics Inc 864
The Louis Berger Group Inc. 1319

MOUNT HOLLY
Virtua Memorial Hospital Burlington County, Inc 1432

Mount Laurel
Marlin Business Services Corp 841
Sun Bancorp Inc. (nj) 1257

Mountain Lakes
Pinnacle Foods Finance Llc 1053

MOUNTAINSIDE
Children's Specialized Hospital Inc 340

Mt. Laurel
Intest Corp. 728
Phh Corp 1046
Sl Industries Inc. 1201
Telvue Corporation 1288
Ulticom Inc. 1375

Murray Hill
Alcatel-lucent Usa Inc. 53
Bard (cr) Inc 186

New Brunswick
Johnson & Johnson 752
Magyar Bancorp Inc 832
Robert Wood Johnson University Hospital, Inc. 1133
Saint Peter's University Hospital, Inc. 1154

NEW GRETNA
Viking Yacht Company 1429

Newark
Audible Inc. 157
Genie Energy Ltd 600
Idt Corp 696
Lime Energy Co 806
Mccarter & English Llp 854
New Jersey Institute Of Technology 942
Newark Beth Israel Medical Center Inc. 947
Prudential Financial Inc 1086
Pseg Power Llc 1087
Public Service Enterprise Group Inc 1088
The New Jersey Transit Corporation 1323
Wilshire Enterprises Inc. 1472

NEWTON
Newton Memorial Hospital Inc 951

Northvale
Adm Tronics Unlimited, Inc. 29
Elite Pharmaceuticals Inc 487
Inrad Optics Inc 713

Oak Ridge
Lakeland Bancorp, Inc. 786

Oakland
Dewey Electronics Corp. 444
Media Sciences International Inc. 860

Ocean City
Ocean Shore Holding Co 982

Old Bridge
Blonder Tongue Laboratories, Inc. 226

Paramus
Alexander's Inc 54
Bergen Community College 206
Caprius Inc. 290
Hudson City Bancorp Inc 685
Movado Group, Inc. 910
New Bridge Medical Center 941
Sb One Bancorp 1166

Parsippany
Avis Budget Group Inc 166
Avis Rent A Car System Llc 167
B&g Foods Inc 171
Budget Rent A Car System Inc. 263
Century 21 Real Estate Llc 321
Emerson Radio Corp. 494
Evonik Corporation 520
Interpace Biosciences Inc 727
Jackson Hewitt Tax Service Inc. 743
Medicines Co (the) 861
Pacira Biosciences Inc 1013
Pbf Energy Inc 1027
Pbf Energy Inc. 1027
Pinnacle Foods Inc. 1053
Wireless Telecom Group, Inc. 1475
Zoetis Inc 1493

Pennington
Mercer Insurance Group Inc. 867

Pennsauken
J&j Snack Foods Corp. 740
Lattice Inc 791
Rcm Technologies, Inc. 1109

PERTH AMBOY
Raritan Bay Medical Center, A New Jersey Nonprofit Corporation 1106

Pine Brook
Atlas Copco Usa Holdings Inc. 154

PISCATAWAY
Aaron And Company, Inc. 9
Telcordia Technologies Inc. 1285
The Institute Of Electrical And Electronics Engineers Incorporated 1316

Pitman
K-tron International Inc. 758

Plainsboro
Integra Lifesciences Holdings Corp 716

Point Pleasant Beach
Chefs International Inc. 331
Norkus Enterprises, Inc. 958

POMPTON PLAINS
Chilton Hospital 340

Princeton Junction
Mistras Group Inc 895

Princeton
Advaxis Inc 33
Berlitz Languages Inc. 208
Clearway Energy Inc 358
Covance Inc. 401
Derma Sciences Inc 441
Educational Testing Service Inc 481
Nrg Energy Inc 972
Orchid Cellmark Inc. 1000
Rockwood Holdings Inc 1136
Soligenix Inc 1206
The Trustees Of Princeton University 1332

RAHWAY
Robert Wood Johnson University Hospital At Rahway 1133

Ramsey
Bogen Communications International Inc. 236

Red Bank
Oceanfirst Financial Corp 982

Ridgefield Park
Innodata Inc 711
Lifequest World Corp 804
Samsung C&t America, Inc. 1158
Samsung Electronics America Inc. 1158

RIDGEWOOD
The Valley Hospital Inc 1336

Rochelle Park
Orbcomm Inc 999

Roseland
Chelsea Property Group Inc. 332
Emisphere Technologies, Inc. 494

Rutherford
Cancer Genetics, Inc. 285
Kid Brands, Inc. 769

Saddle Brook
Peoples Educational Holdings, Inc. 1036

Secaucus
Children's Place Inc (the) 339
Eros International Plc 513
Goya Foods Inc. 621
Quest Diagnostics, Inc. 1097
United Energy Corp. 1383
Vitamin Shoppe Inc 1434

Short Hills
Dun & Bradstreet Corp (de) 465
Investors Bancorp Inc (new) 732

Shrewsbury
Intercloud Systems Inc 720

SOMERS POINT
Shore Memorial Hospital 1190

Somerset
Catalent Pharma Solutions Inc. 306
Shi International Corp. 1189
Tamir Biotechnology Inc 1276
Van Budd Lines Inc 1417

Somerville
Conolog Corp. 387
Somerset Medical Center 1207
Transnet Corporation 1356

South Orange
Nephros Inc 936
Seton Hall University 1184

South Plainfield
Ptc Therapeutics Inc 1087
Tumi Holdings Inc 1369

SPARTA
High Point Solutions Inc. 667

Springfield
Emtec Inc. 496
Village Super Market, Inc. 1430

Summit
Celgene Corp 314

SWEDESBORO
Powell Electronics Inc. 1067

Teaneck
Cognizant Technology Solutions Corp. 367
Fairleigh Dickinson University 528
Phibro Animal Health Corporation 1046

Thorofare
Akers Biosciences Inc. 48
Checkpoint Systems Inc 331

Tinton Falls
Commvault Systems Inc 380
Two River Bancorp 1371

TRENTON
Capital Health System Inc. 289
New Jersey Housing And Mortgage Finance Agency 942
Terracycle Inc. 1291
The Hibbert Company 1315

Union
Bed, Bath & Beyond, Inc. 201

Vineland
Colonial Financial Services, Inc. 370
F&s Produce Company, Inc. 526

Wall Township
Coates International Ltd 364

Wall
Bio-key International Inc 215
New Jersey Natural Gas Company 942
New Jersey Resources Corp 942

Warren
Anadigics Inc 107
Anadigics, Inc. 107
Chubb Corp. 344

Washington Township
Parke Bancorp Inc 1021

Wayne
Bayer Healthcare Pharmaceuticals Inc. 194
G-i Holdings Inc. 587
Metro Packaging & Imaging Inc 876
St Josephs Wayne Hospital Inc 1230
William Paterson University 1470

INDEX BY HEADQUARTERS LOCATION

WEST LONG BRANCH
Monmouth University Inc 902

West New York
Deltathree Inc 438

West Orange
Lincoln Educational Services Corp 808

West Trenton
Homasote Co. 676

Westfield
Digital Cinema Destinations Corp. 449

Whippany
800-jr Cigar Inc. 6
Breeze-eastern Corp 247
Stephen Gould Corporation 1245
Suburban Propane Partners Lp 1254

Woodbridge
Alpha Associates Inc. 67
New Jersey Turnpike Authority Inc 943
Northfield Bancorp Inc. 965

Woodcliff Lake
Bmw Of North America Llc 233
Eagle Pharmaceuticals, Inc. 472
Eisai Inc. 483
Par Pharmaceutical Companies Inc. 1017
Powerfleet Inc 1068

Woodland Park
Cytec Industries, Inc. 422

NEW MEXICO

ALBUQUERQUE
Applied Research Associates, Inc. 122
Bowlin Travel Centers Inc. 243
Net Medical Xpress Solutions Inc 937
Pnm Resources Inc 1060
Rose's Southwest Papers, Inc. 1139
Sandia National Laboratories 1160
Santa Fe Gold Corp 1162
Summit Electric Supply Co., Inc. 1257
Titan Technologies Inc. 1347
University Of New Mexico 1398

CLOVIS
E.n.m.r. Telephone Cooperative 470

ESPANOLA
Akal Security, Inc. 48

LAS CRUCES
New Mexico State University 943

TAOS
Taos Health Systems, Inc. 1277

NEW YORK

ALBANY
Albany College Of Pharmacy And Health Sciences 51
Albany Medical Center 52
Albany Molecular Research Inc 52
Capital District Physicians' Health Plan, Inc. 288
Mechanical Technology, Inc. 859
Momentive Performance Materials Inc. 900
New York State Teachers' Retirement System 946
St. Peter's Health Partners 1235
State University Of New York 1242

The Research Foundation For The State University Of New York 1328
Thruway Authority Of New York State 1342
Trans World Entertainment Corp. 1354

ALFRED
Alfred University 56

Amherst
Allied Motion Technologies Inc 64
Mark Iv Llc 840

Amityville
Hi-tech Pharmacal Co., Inc. 665
Napco Security Technologies, Inc. 920

Amsterdam
Beech-nut Nutrition Corporation 201

Ann Arbor
Cephas Holding Corp 323

ANNANDALE ON HUDSON
Bard College 187

Ardsley
Acorda Therapeutics Inc 21

Armonk
International Business Machines Corp 724

Aventura
Trade Street Residential, Inc. 1353

BALLSTON SPA
Stewart's Shops Corp. 1249

Batavia
Graham Corp. 622

BAY SHORE
Southside Hospital 1218

Bellport
Perfumania Holdings Inc 1039

Bethpage
Cablevision Systems Corp. 270
King Kullen Grocery Co. Inc. 772

BINGHAMTON
United Health Services Hospital, Inc. 1384
United Health Services, Inc. 1384

Bohemia
Andrea Electronics Corp. 110
Scientific Industries Inc 1170

Brentwood
Medical Action Industries, Inc. 860

Bridgehampton
Bridge Bancorp, Inc. (bridgehampton, Ny) 248

BRONX
Bronxcare Health System 255
Calvary Hospital, Inc. 280
Fordham University 567
Loehmann's Holdings Inc. 814
Manhattan College Corp 835
Montefiore Medical Center 903
New York Yankees Partnership 947

BRONXVILLE
Sarah Lawrence College 1163

BRONX
Wildlife Conservation Society 1469

Brooklyn
Applied Minerals Inc 121
Bayside Fuel Oil Depot Corp 195
Brooklyn Hospital Center 256
Brooklyn Navy Yard Development Corporation 256

Dime Community Bancshares, Inc 451
Flatbush Federal Bancorp Inc. 559
Kingsbrook Jewish Medical Center Inc 772
L. & R. Distributors Inc. 783
Lutheran Medical Center 823
Maimonides Medical Center 832
Mays (j.w.), Inc. 852
Newyork-presbyterian/brooklyn Methodist 951
St Joseph's College New York 1230
Wyckoff Heights Medical Center 1481

BUFFALO
Catholic Health System, Inc. 308
Cleveland Biolabs Inc 358
Computer Task Group, Inc. 382
Delaware North Companies Inc. 435
First Niagara Financial Group, Inc. 553
Gibraltar Industries Inc 606
Global Earth Energy Inc. 611
Kaleida Health 759
M & T Bank Corp 826
Materion Advanced Materials Technologies And Services Inc 848
Rich Products Corporation 1128
Synacor, Inc. 1269

BURT
Sun Orchard Fruit Company Inc. 1258

CAMDEN
International Wire Group, Inc. 727

Canandaigua
Canandaigua National Corp. 285

CANTON
St Lawrence University (inc) 1230

Carle Place
1-800 Flowers.com, Inc. 2

Catskill
Greene County Bancorp Inc 629

CAZENOVIA
Cazenovia College 309

Central Islip
Cvd Equipment Corp. 418

Chester
Repro Med Systems, Inc. 1120

Chestnut Ridge
Teledyne Lecroy Inc. 1286

CLINTON
Hamilton College 641

Corning
Corning Inc 397

Deer Park
Pc Group Inc. 1028
Surge Components Inc 1264

DeWitt
Community Bank System Inc 377

DOBBS FERRY
Mercy College 868

Dunkirk
Lake Shore Bancorp Inc 786

E. Syracuse
Bright House Networks Llc 249

East Aurora
Astronics Corp 149

EAST ELMHURST
Skanska Usa Civil Inc. 1199

EAST MEADOW
Nassau Health Care Corporation 920

EAST PATCHOGUE
Brookhaven Memorial Hospital Medical Center, Inc. 255

EAST SYRACUSE
D/l Cooperative Inc. 423
Microwave Filter Co., Inc. 884

EAST YAPHANK
Clare Rose, Inc. 354

Edgewood
Cpi Aerostructures, Inc. 403
Tii Network Technologies Inc. 1345

Elma
Servotronics, Inc. 1183

Elmira
Chemung Financial Corp. 333
Elmira Savings Bank (ny) 489
Hardinge Inc 644

Elmsford
Amscan Holdings Inc. 105

Fairport
Bosch Security Systems Inc. 240
Manning & Napier Inc. 836
Paetec Holding Corp. 1013

Farmingdale
General Microwave Corporation 596
Minuteman Press International Inc. 893
Misonix, Inc. 894
Swimwear Anywhere Inc. 1267

FLUSHING
Judlau Contracting, Inc. 756
Newyork-presbyterian/queens 951
Sterling Mets Lp 1247

Fredonia
The Carriage House Companies Inc. 1303

GARDEN CITY
Adelphi University 28
Bookspan 239
Lifetime Brands Inc 805
Proginet Corporation 1080

GENEVA
Hobart And William Smith Colleges 673

Getzville
Columbus Mckinnon Corp. (ny) 373

Glen Head
First Of Long Island Corp 554

Glens Falls
Arrow Financial Corp. 138

Glenville
Trustco Bank Corp. (n.y.) 1365

GOUVERNEUR
Kph Healthcare Services Inc. 779

Great Neck
Brt Apartments Corp 258
Manhattan Bridge Capital, Inc. 835
One Liberty Properties, Inc. 994
United Capital Corp. 1381

GREENVALE
Long Island University 816

Hamburg
Evans Bancorp, Inc. 518

HAMILTON
Colgate University 369

HOOVER'S MASTERLIST OF U.S. COMPANIES 2020

INDEX BY HEADQUARTERS LOCATION

HAUPPAUGE
Axis Construction Corp. 170
Bactolac Pharmaceutical Inc. 173
Dale Carnegie & Associates Inc. 425
Hauppauge Digital, Inc. 648
Ivci, Llc 739
Orbit International Corp. 999
Tsr Inc 1367
United-guardian, Inc. 1389

Hawthorne
Smartpros Ltd 1202

HEMPSTEAD
Hofstra University 673

Hicksville
Sam Ash Music Corporation 1157

HOLBROOK
Future Tech Enterprise, Inc. 586

Hollywood
Frederick's Of Hollywood Group Inc 577

Hopewell Junction
Emagin Corp 490

Huntington Station
American Technical Ceramics Corp. 96

HUNTINGTON
Huntington Hospital Dolan Family Health Center, Inc. 688

HYDE PARK
The Culinary Institute Of America 1308

IRVINGTON
Eileen Fisher, Inc. 482

ITHACA
Cornell University 397
Tompkins Financial Corp 1350

JAMAICA
Bollore Logistics Usa Inc. 237
St John's University, New York 1230

Jamestown
Bush Industries Inc. 266
Dawson Metal Company Inc. 430

Jeffersonville
Jeffersonville Bancorp 747

JERICHO
Educational & Institutional Cooperative Service Inc. 481
Getty Realty Corp. 604
Nathan's Famous, Inc. 921

Kinderhook
American Bio Medica Corp. 80

Kingston
Kingstone Companies Inc 772

Lake Success
Astoria Financial Corp. 148
Broadridge Financial Solutions Inc 252
Canon U.s.a. Inc. 286
Dealertrack Technologies, Inc. 432
Hain Celestial Group Inc 640
Newtek Business Services Corp 951

Lancaster
Ecology And Environment, Inc. 479

Larchmont
D'agostino Supermarkets Inc. 423

Latham
Angiodynamics Inc 111
Plug Power Inc 1058

LIVERPOOL
Raymours Furniture Company, Inc. 1107

LONG BEACH
Long Beach Medical Center 816
Planet Payment, Inc. 1056

Long Island City
Jetblue Airways Corp 748
Ksw Inc. 781
Madden (steven) Ltd. 830
Petrocelli Electric Co. Inc. 1042
Sirona Dental Systems Inc 1198
Standard Motor Products, Inc. 1238

Lynbrook
Biospecifics Technologies Corp. 219
Janel Corp 745

Mamaroneck
Archie Comic Publications Inc. 128

MANHASSET
North Shore University Hospital 961

Marion
Seneca Foods Corp. 1180

Melville
Chyronhego Corp 345
Comtech Telecommunications Corp. 383
Fonar Corp 565
Msc Industrial Direct Co Inc 912
Nu Horizons Electronics Corp. 973
P & F Industries, Inc. 1008
Schein (henry) Inc 1167
Star Multi Care Services Inc. 1240
Verint Systems, Inc 1423

MENANDS
Health Research, Inc. 653

MILLWOOD
Somerset Tire Service, Inc. 1207

Milton
Sono-tek Corp. 1208

Mineola
Fatwire Corporation 532
Winthrop Nyu Hospital 1475

Mitchel Field
Frequency Electronics Inc 579

Montebello
Sterling Bancorp (de) 1246

Monticello
Empire Resorts Inc 495

MOUNT VERNON
Defoe Corp. 434

New Hartford
Par Technology Corp. 1017

New Hyde Park
Kimco Realty Corp 771
Long Island Jewish Medical Center 816

New York City
Emerging Vision Inc. 493

New York
24/7 Real Media Inc. 4
30dc Inc 4
4licensing Corp 5
A&e Television Networks Llc 7
Abc Inc. 11
Abeona Therapeutics Inc 11
Abm Industries, Inc. 12
Acre Realty Investors Inc 22
Advance Magazine Publishers Inc. 30
Aea Investors Lp 35
Ag Mortgage Investment Trust Inc 41
Age Group Ltd. 42
Agritech Worldwide Inc 44
Alacra Inc. 49
Alj Regional Holdings Inc 57
Alleghany Corp. 58
Allen & Company Llc 59
Allied Healthcare International Inc. 63
Alloy Inc. 65
Alvarez & Marsal Holdings Llc 72
Ambac Financial Group, Inc. 74
Amc Networks Inc 75
American Agip Company Inc. 78
American Arbitration Association Inc 79
American Civil Liberties Union Foundation, Inc. 82
American Express Co. 84
American Express Publishing Corporation 84
American Independence Corp 87
American Jewish World Service, Inc. 89
American Management Association International 90
Ameritrans Capital Corporation 101
Amtrust Financial Services Inc 106
Anchin Block & Anchin Llp 108
Anderson Kill & Olick P.c. 110
Ann Inc 112
Annaly Capital Management Inc 112
Aol Inc. 116
Apollo Commercial Real Estate Finance Inc. 118
Apollo Global Management Inc 118
Apollo Residential Mortgage, Inc. 118
Apple Financial Holdings Inc. 119
Arc Logistics Partners Lp 127
Ares Capital Corporation 131
Ark Restaurants Corp 134
Aro Liquidation Inc 137
Artisanal Brands Inc. 139
Assurant Inc 147
Atlantic Records Group 153
Axa Equitable Life Insurance Company 168
Axa Financial Inc. 168
Axel Johnson Inc. 169
Baker Capital 175
Baltic Trading Limited 178
Bank Leumi Usa 181
Bank Of New York Mellon Corp 182
Bankrate Inc (de) 183
Barnes & Noble Inc 187
Barnesandnoble.com Llc 188
Barneys New York Inc. 188
Battalia Winston International 192
Bbdo Worldwide Inc. 196
Behrman Capital L.p. 201
Berkshire Bancorp Inc (de) 207
Bernard Chaus Inc. 208
Bernard Hodes Group Inc. 209
Beth Israel Medical Center 211
Betsey Johnson Llc 212
Bgc Partners Inc 212
Blackrock Inc 224
Blackstone Group Inc (the) 224
Blackstone Mortgage Trust Inc 224
Bloomberg L.p. 226
Blue Tee Corp. 231
Borghese Inc. 240
Bravo Media Llc 246
Bristol-myers Squibb Co. 251
Brixmor Property Group Inc 251
Broadcast Music Inc. 252
Brookfield Property Reit Inc 255
Brown Brothers Harriman & Co. 257
Burson-marsteller Inc. 266
Ca Inc 270
Cache Inc 271
Cadus Corporation 272
Cadwalader Wickersham & Taft Llp 272
Cahill Gordon & Reindel Llp 273
Caithness Corporation 273
Cantor Fitzgerald L.p. 286
Capgemini North America Inc. 288
Carver Bancorp Inc. 302
Castle Brands Inc. 305
Cbs Broadcasting Inc. 310
Cbs Radio Inc 310
Centerline Capital Group Inc. 316
Centric Brands Inc 321
Chadbourne & Parke Llp 326
Chartis Inc. 329
Chimera Investment Corp 340
Church Pension Group Services Corporation 344
Cifc Corp. 346
Cinedigm Corp 347
Cit Group Inc (new) 348
Citigroup Inc 349
City Harvest, Inc. 351
Ckx Inc. 354
Cleary Gottlieb Steen & Hamilton Llp 358
Cohen & Steers Inc 367
Colgate-palmolive Co. 369
College Entrance Examination Board 369
Consolidated Edison Co. Of New York, Inc. 388
Consolidated Edison Inc 388
Coty, Inc. 399
Council On Foreign Relations, Inc. 400
Cowen Inc 402
Cpa2biz Inc. 403
Credit Suisse (usa) Inc 405
Ctpartners Executive Search Inc 414
Ctpartners Executive Search Llc 414
Daxor Corporation 430
Delcath Systems Inc 435
Deloitte & Touche Llp 436
Deloitte Consulting Llp 436
Deloitte Llp 436
Deloitte Touche Tohmatsu Services Inc. 437
Deutsche Bank Securities Inc. 443
Dewey & Leboeuf Llp 444
Dhi Group Inc 445
Diamond Discoveries International Corp. 446
Drive Shack Inc 462
Dropcar Inc 462
E*trade Financial Corp 470
Eisneramper Llp 483
Emblemhealth Inc. 490
Empire State Realty Trust Inc 495
Environmental Defense Fund, Incorporated 508
Enzo Biochem, Inc. 509
Estee Lauder International Inc. 516
Evercore Inc 519
Exantas Capital Corp 521
Exlservice Holdings Inc 523
Fairway Group Holdings Corp 528
Fashion Institute Of Technology 532
Federal Home Loan Bank New York 534
Federal Reserve Bank Of New York, Dist. No. 2 536
Foot Locker, Inc. 566
Forest Laboratories, Inc. 567
Fortress Investment Group Llc 570
Fox News Network Llc 572
Fried Frank Harris Shriver & Jacobson Llp 580
Fuel Systems Solutions Inc 583
Fusion Connect Inc 586
Fx Alliance Inc. 587
G-iii Apparel Group Ltd. 587
Gannett Co Inc (new) 591

INDEX BY HEADQUARTERS LOCATION

Genco Shipping & Trading Ltd 594
General Maritime Corporation 596
Genesis Corp. 598
Gfi Group Inc 605
Girl Scouts Of The United States Of America 608
Gleacher & Co, Inc. (de) 609
Global Brokerage Inc 610
Global Traffic Network Inc. 612
Globaloptions Group Inc. 612
Goldman Sachs Group Inc 616
Gramercy Property Trust Inc 623
Greenhill & Co Inc 629
Griffin Industrial Realty Inc 630
Griffon Corp. 630
Guardian Life Insurance Co. Of America (nyc) 634
Guardsmark Llc 634
Hampshire Group, Ltd. 642
Harry Winston Inc. 646
Hazen And Sawyer, D.p.c. 651
Hc2 Holdings Inc 651
Helen Keller International 657
Helios & Matheson Analytics Inc 657
Henry Modell & Company, Inc. 659
Herbert Mines Associates Inc. 660
Hess Corp 663
Hsbc Usa, Inc. 684
Human Rights Watch, Inc. 687
Icahn Enterprises Lp 693
Iconix Brand Group Inc 694
Immune Pharmaceuticals Inc 701
Infor Global Solutions Inc. 708
Ing U.s. Inc. 710
Inter Parfums, Inc. 719
Intercept Pharmaceuticals Inc 720
International Flavors & Fragrances Inc. 725
Interpublic Group Of Companies Inc. 728
Intervest Bancshares Corp. 728
Intl Fcstone Inc. 729
Intralinks Holdings Inc 729
Investment Technology Group Inc. 731
Israel Discount Bank Of New York 737
Istar Inc 737
J. Crew Group Inc. 740
Jefferies Financial Group Inc 747
Jlm Couture Inc. 749
Jones Group Inc 754
Jpmorgan Chase & Co 755
Jujamcyn Theaters Llc 756
Kate Spade Llc 761
Kaz Inc. 762
Kenneth Cole Productions Inc. 765
Kensington Publishing Corp. 766
Kiwibox.com, Inc. 774
Kkr & Co. L.p. 775
Kohlberg Capital Corporation 777
Kohn Pedersen Fox Associates, Pc 777
Ladder Capital Corp 784
Lescarden Inc 799
Lexington Realty Trust 800
Lhh Corporation 801
Lincoln Center For The Performing Arts, Inc. 808
Linkshare Corporation 809
Liveperson Inc 812
Loews Corp. 814
Logicalis, Inc. 814
Logicquest Technology Inc 815
Louis Vuitton North America Inc. 818
M & F Worldwide Corp. 826
Macquarie Infrastructure Corp 830
Manhattan School Of Music Inc 836
Marcum Llp 838
Marketaxess Holdings Inc. 840
Marsh & Mclennan Companies Inc. 842
Marsh Usa Inc. 842

Martha Stewart Living Omnimedia, Inc. 843
Marubeni America Corporation 844
Marymount Manhattan College 845
Mdc Partners Inc 858
Medallion Financial Corp 859
Mediamind Technologies Inc. 860
Medidata Solutions, Inc. 861
Memorial Sloan-kettering Cancer Center 865
Mercer Inc. 867
Mesabi Trust 874
Metlife Inc 876
Metro-north Commuter Railroad Co Inc 876
Metropolitan Opera Association, Inc. 877
Metropolitan Transportation Authority 878
Mfa Financial, Inc. 879
Minerals Technologies, Inc. 891
Mktg, Inc. 896
Moody's Corp. 904
Moog Inc 904
Morgan Stanley 905
Morgans Hotel Group Co 906
Msci Inc 912
Msg Network Inc 912
Mutual Of America Life Insurance Company 916
Nasdaq Inc 920
National Audubon Society, Inc. 921
National Holdings Corp 925
National Multiple Sclerosis Society 925
National Restaurants Management Inc. 927
Natural Resources Defense Council Inc. 930
Nautica Apparel Inc. 931
Nbcuniversal Media Llc 933
New Mountain Finance Corp 943
New York Blood Center, Inc. 944
New York City Health And Hospitals Corporation 944
New York City Transit Authority 944
New York City Transitional Finance Authority 944
New York Convention Center Operating Corporation 945
New York Life Insurance Company 945
New York Mortgage Trust Inc 946
New York Public Radio 946
New York Times Co. 947
New York University 947
Newmark & Company Real Estate, Inc. 949
News America Marketing Fsi Llc 950
News Corp (new) 950
Nfp Corp. 953
Nhl Enterprises, Inc. 953
Northstar Realty Finance Corp 966
Omagine Inc. 990
Omnicom Group, Inc. 992
Oppenheimer Holdings Inc 997
Oscar De La Renta, Llc 1003
Oxford University Press Inc. 1007
Pace University 1009
Palladium Equity Partners Llc 1014
Pennantpark Investment Corporation 1032
Pfizer Inc 1044
Philip Morris International Inc 1047
Planned Parenthood Federation Of America, Inc. 1057
Presidential Realty Corp. 1073
Pricewaterhousecoopers Llp 1075
Priority Aviation Inc 1077
Progenics Pharmaceuticals, Inc. 1080
Prospect Capital Corporation 1082
Public Health Solutions 1088

Pvh Corp 1092
Pzena Investment Management Inc 1093
Ralph Lauren Corp 1104
Random House Inc. 1105
Rcs Capital Corp 1109
Ready Capital Corp 1110
Reis, Inc 1117
Reliability Incorporated 1117
Reval Holdings Inc. 1124
Revlon Inc 1124
Ronco Acquisition Corporation 1137
Rouse Properties, Inc. 1141
Rpt Realty 1142
Rtw Retailwinds Inc 1143
S&p Global Inc 1147
Safra National Bank Of New York 1150
Saks Fifth Avenue Inc. 1154
Scholastic Corp 1168
Sculptor Capital Management 1173
Sequa Corporation 1181
Sfx Entertainment, Inc. 1185
Shutterstock Inc 1191
Siebert Financial Corp 1191
Siga Technologies Inc 1192
Signature Bank (new York, Ny) 1193
Sirius Xm Holdings Inc 1198
Sl Green Realty Corp 1200
Sotheby's 1209
Spherix Inc 1224
State Of New York Mortgage Agency 1242
Steel Partners Holdings Lp 1244
Stemline Therapeutics Inc 1245
Stuart-dean Co. Inc 1253
Sunbelt Beverage Company Llc 1258
Swank Inc. 1266
Syncora Holdings Ltd 1270
Synergy Pharmaceuticals Inc. 1270
Take-two Interactive Software, Inc. 1275
Tapestry Inc 1278
Tata America International Corporation 1279
Telaria Inc 1285
Temco Service Industries, Inc. 1288
Tg Therapeutics Inc 1297
The American Museum Of Natural History 1298
The American Society For The Prevention Of Cruelty To Animals 1298
The Andrew W Mellon Foundation 1298
The Associated Press 1299
The Bessemer Group Incorporated 1300
The Council Population Inc 1308
The Depository Trust & Clearing Corporation 1309
The Estee Lauder Companies Inc. 1310
The Food Emporium Inc. 1310
The Ford Foundation 1311
The Jewish Federations Of North America Inc 1317
The Juilliard School 1318
The Legal Aid Society Inc 1319
The Metropolitan Museum Of Art 1321
The New School 1323
The New York And Presbyterian Hospital 1323
The New York Public Library 1323
The Philharmonic-symphony Society Of New York Inc 1326
The Port Authority Of New York & New Jersey 1326
The Reader's Digest Association Inc. 1327
The Renco Group Inc. 1328

The Rockefeller Foundation 1328
The Rockefeller University 1328
The Rockefeller University Faculty And Students Club Inc 1328
The Solomon-page Group Llc 1330
The Turner Corporation 1332
Thestreet Inc 1340
Thirteen Productions Llc 1340
Tiffany & Co. 1344
Time Inc 1345
Time Warner Cable Inc 1345
Time Warner Inc 1346
Tiptree Inc 1346
Tishman Hotel Corporation 1346
Touro College 1352
Trammo, Inc. 1354
Trans World Corp. 1354
Transitcenter Inc. 1356
Transperfect Translations International Inc. 1356
Travelclick Inc. 1357
Travelers Companies Inc (the) 1357
Travelzoo 1357
Trimol Group Inc. 1362
Turner Construction Company Inc 1369
Two Harbors Investment Corp 1370
U.s. News & World Report L.p. 1373
United Cerebral Palsy Associations Of New York State, Inc. 1382
United States Fund For Unicef 1387
Univision Communications Inc. 1405
Valley National Bancorp (nj) 1416
Value Line Inc 1417
Verizon Communications Inc 1424
Viacom Inc 1427
Viacomcbs Inc 1427
Vince Holding Corp 1430
Visiting Nurse Service Of New York 1433
Voltari Corp 1436
Vornado Realty Trust 1437
Vu1 Corporation 1438
W.p. Carey Inc 1440
Warner Music Group Corp. 1445
Webmd Health Corp 1451
Whitney Museum Of American Art 1467
Wilson Elser Moskowitz Edelman & Dicker Llp 1472
Wisdomtree Investments, Inc. 1475
Ww International Inc 1481
Xo Group Inc 1484
Xpresspa Group Inc 1485
Yeshiva University 1488
Young Broadcasting, Llc 1489
Zanett Inc. 1491

Newark
Iec Electronics Corp. 697
Ultralife Corp 1376

North Tonawanda
Taylor Devices Inc 1280

Norwich
Nbt Bancorp. Inc. 933

NYACK
Nyack Hospital Foundation, Inc. 977
Presidential Life Corporation 1073

OAKDALE
Dowling College 459
Suffolk County Water Authority Inc 1255

Oceanside
American Medical Alert Corp. 90

Ogdensburg
Ansen Corporation 113

Oneida
Oneida Ltd. 994

INDEX BY HEADQUARTERS LOCATION

Orangeburg
Nice-pak Products Inc. 954

Orchard Park
Buffalo Bills Inc. 263

Oswego
Pathfinder Bancorp, Inc. 1024

Pearl River
Active Media Services Inc. 23
Hudson Technologies Inc 686
Hunter Douglas Inc. 688
Orange And Rockland Utilities Inc 998

Pittsford
Biophan Technologies Inc. 219
Infinite Group, Inc. 707
Sutherland Global Services Inc. 1265

Plainview
Aeroflex Holding Corp. 37
Vaso Corp 1419
Veeco Instruments Inc (de) 1421

PORT JEFFERSON
John T. Mather Memorial Hospital Of Port Jefferson, New York, Inc. 751

Port Washington
Aceto Corp 19
Cedar Realty Trust Inc 313
Pall Corp. 1014
Systemax, Inc. 1273
The Npd Group Inc. 1324

POTSDAM
Clarkson University 355

POUGHKEEPSIE
Adams Fairacre Farms, Inc. 26
Hudson Valley Federal Credit Union 686
Marist College 839
St. Francis" Hospital Poughkeepsie New York 1232
Vassar College 1419
Vassar College Inc 1419

Purchase
Atlas Air Worldwide Holdings, Inc. 154
Integramed America Inc. 717
Manhattanville College 836
Mastercard Inc 847
Mbia Inc. 853
Morgan Stanley Smith Barney Llc 905
Mtm Technologies, Inc. 913
Nutrition 21 Llc 975
Pepsico Inc 1038
Tal International Group Inc 1275

Ray Brook
Adirondack Park Agency 29

REGO PARK
New York State Catholic Health Plan, Inc. 946

RENSSELAER
Taconic Biosciences, Inc. 1275
The New York Independent System Operator Inc 1323

RICHMOND HILL
The Jamaica Hospital 1317

Ridgewood
Ridgewood Savings Bank 1129

RIVERHEAD
Central Suffolk Hospital 320
Suffolk Bancorp 1255

ROCHESTER
5linx Holdings Inc. 5
Bausch & Lomb Incorporated 192
Birds Eye Foods Llc 220
Curaegis Technologies Inc 417
Document Security Systems Inc 455
Eastman Kodak Co. 476
Esl Federal Credit Union 515
Genesee Valley Group Health Association 598
Hahn Automotive Warehouse Inc. 640
Home Properties Inc 677
Lucid Inc. 822
Monro Inc 902
Nixon Peabody Llp 955
Paychex Inc 1027
Performance Technologies, Inc. 1039
Rochester Gas And Electric Corporation 1134
Rochester Institute Of Technology (inc) 1134
St John Fisher College 1229
Transcat Inc 1355
Veramark Technologies Inc. 1423
Virtualscopics Inc 1432
Wegmans Food Markets, Inc. 1452

Rockville Centre
Catholic Health Services Of Long Island 308
Mercy Medical Center 870
Molloy College 899

Ronkonkoma
Lakeland Industries, Inc. 786
Nbty Inc. 933
Sentry Technology Corporation 1181

Roslyn
Sino-global Shipping America Ltd 1197
St. Francis Hospital, Roslyn, New York 1232

Rye Brook
Broadview Networks Holdings Inc. 253
Xylem Inc 1486

Rye
Acadia Realty Trust 15
Gamco Investors Inc 590
Lict Corp 803
Sims Ltd 1196

Saratoga Springs
Espey Manufacturing & Electronics Corp. 515
Skidmore College 1199

SCHENECTADY
Ellis Hospital 489
Mvp Health Plan, Inc. 917
New York State Lottery 946
The Golub Corporation 1313
Trustees Of Union College In The Town Of Schenectady In The State Of New York 1366

SLEEPY HOLLOW
Phelps Memorial Hospital Association 1045

Somers
Mango Capital Inc. 835

St. James
Gyrodyne Co. Of America, Inc. 638

Staten Island
Advance Publications Inc. 30
Coffee Holding Co Inc 366
Key Food Stores Co-operative, Inc. 768
Staten Island University Hospital 1242
Vsb Bancorp Inc (ny) 1438

Stony Brook
Applied Dna Sciences Inc 120

Suffern
Ascena Retail Group Inc. 141

SYOSSET
Liro Program And Construction Management P.c. 811
Synergx Systems Inc. 1270

SYRACUSE
Cablexpress Corporation 271
Carrols Restaurant Group Inc 301
Le Moyne College 793
O'brien & Gere Limited 977
Op-tech Environmental Services Inc. 996
St. Joseph's Hospital Health Center 1233
Syracuse University 1272
Upstate University Medical Associates At Syracuse, Inc. 1406

Tarrytown
Alpha-en Corporation 68
Ampacet Corporation 103
Prestige Consumer Healthcare Inc 1074
Regeneron Pharmaceuticals, Inc. 1115
Westcon Group Inc. 1458

TROY
Rensselaer Polytechnic Institute 1119

Uniondale
Arbor Commercial Mortgage Llc 126
Arbor Realty Trust Inc 126
Flushing Financial Corp. 564
Long Island Power Authority 816
Openlink Financial Llc 996
Volt Information Sciences Inc 1436
Yellowbook Inc. 1487

Utica
Conmed Corp. 385
Utica College 1414

VALHALLA
New York Medical College 945

Valley Cottage
Creditriskmonitor.com, Inc. 406

VALLEY STREAM
Franklin Hospital 575

Victor
Constellation Brands Inc 388

Wantagh
Meenan Oil Co. L.p. 863

Warsaw
Financial Institutions Inc. 545

West Hempstead
Tilden Associates Inc. 1345

West Henrietta
Vuzix Corp 1439

WEST ISLIP
Good Samaritan Hospital Medical Center 618

West Nyack
General Bearing Corporation 595

Westbury
New York Community Bancorp Inc. 945
Park Aerospace Corp 1019

WESTFIELD
National Grape Co-operative Association, Inc. 924

White Plains
Amalgamated Life Insurance Company 73
Aps Healthcare Inc. 123
Cms Bancorp Inc 362
Combe Incorporated 374
Debt Resolve Inc 433
Handy & Harman Ltd 642
New York Power Authority 946
Northeast Community Bancorp Inc 962
Pervasip Corp 1041
Spar Group, Inc. 1221
United States Tennis Association Incorporated 1388

Williamsville
Life Storage Inc 803
National Fuel Gas Co. (nj) 924

Woodbury
Jennifer Convertibles Inc. 748
Research Frontiers Inc. 1121

Woodside
Bulova Corporation 264

YONKERS
Consumer Reports, Inc. 389
Hudson Valley Holding Corp. 686

NORTH CAROLINA

Albemarle
Uwharrie Capital Corp. 1414

ASHEVILLE
Mission Hospital, Inc. 894
The Biltmore Company 1300

Black Mountain
Ingles Markets Inc 710

BOONE
Appalachian State University Inc 119

Burlington
Laboratory Corporation Of America Holdings 784

Cary
Cicero Inc 346
Cornerstone Building Brands Inc 397
Cotton Incorporated 399
Pantry Inc. (the) 1016
Ply Gem Holdings, Inc. 1059
Sas Institute Inc. 1164
Usfalcon, Inc. 1412

Chapel Hill
Adherex Technologies Inc. 28
Investors Title Co. 732
The University Of North Carolina 1334
University Of North Carolina At Chapel Hill 1399
University Of North Carolina Hospitals 1399

Charlotte
Albemarle Corp. 52
American City Business Journals Inc. 82
Ballantyne Strong, Inc. 178
Bank Of America Corp 181
Belk Inc (de) 203
Bojangles' Restaurants Inc. 237
Campus Crest Communities Inc 284
Campus Crest Communities, Inc. 284
Camstar Systems Inc. 284
Capital Bank Financial Corp 288
Carolina Handling, Llc 300
Cato Corp. 308
Childress Klein Properties Inc. 340

INDEX BY HEADQUARTERS LOCATION

Chiquita Brands International, Inc. 341
Coca-cola Consolidated Inc 365
Communityone Bancorp 380
Compass Group Usa Inc. 380
Crowder Construction Company Inc 409
Duke Energy Corp 464
Enpro Industries Inc 503
Extended Stay America Inc 525
Fairpoint Communications Inc 528
Forms & Supply, Inc. 569
Ginkgo Residential Trust Inc. 607
Goodrich Corporation 619
Hg Holdings Inc 664
Horizon Lines Inc 679
Lendingtree Inc (new) 798
Meineke Car Care Centers Inc. 864
Merrill Lynch And Co. Inc. 873
Nn, Inc 956
Nucor Corp. 973
Park Sterling Corp 1020
Parsons Environment & Infrastructure Group Inc. 1023
Piedmont Natural Gas Co Inc 1050
Piedmont Natural Gas Co., Inc. 1050
Polymer Group Inc. 1061
Polypore International Inc 1062
Snyder's-lance, Inc. 1204
Sonic Automotive, Inc. 1207
Spx Corp. 1227
Spx Flow Inc 1227
The Charlotte-mecklenburg Hospital Authority 1304
The University Of North Carolina At Charlotte 1334

CLYDE
Haywood Health Authority 651

Concord
Cardinal Logistics Management Corporation 293
Motorsports Authentics Llc 909
Speedway Motorsports, Inc. 1224

Davidson
Curtiss-wright Corp. 417
The Trustees Of Davidson College 1331

Denver
Air T Inc 46

Dunn
Select Bancorp Inc (new) 1178

Durham
Aldagen Inc. 53
American Institute Of Certified Public Accountants 88
Biocryst Pharmaceuticals Inc 216
Blue Cross And Blue Shield Of North Carolina 229
Chimerix Inc. 341
Cree Inc 406
Duke University 464
Duke University Health System, Inc. 464
Emrise Corp 496
Family Health International Inc 529
Icagen Inc. 693
Iqvia Holdings Inc 734
M & F Bancorp Inc 826
Mgt Capital Investments Inc 880
Patheon Inc. 1024
Research Triangle Institute Inc 1122
Tranzyme Inc. 1356

EDEN
Morehead Memorial Hospital Inc 905

FAYETTEVILLE
Cumberland County Hospital System, Inc. 416

Fayetteville Public Works Commission 533

FOREST CITY
Rutherford Electric Membership Corporation 1145

Four Oaks
Four Oaks Fincorp, Inc. 571

GARNER
Overland Contracting Inc. 1006

GASTONIA
Caromont Health, Inc. 300
Parkdale Mills Incorporated 1021

GOLDSBORO
Southco Distributing Company 1212

GREENSBORO
A. P. Hubbard Wholesale Lumber Corporation 8
Bell Partners Inc. 203
Carolina Bank Holdings Inc 299
Center For Creative Leadership Inc 316
International Textile Group, Inc. 727
Lorillard, Inc. 817
Market America, Inc. 840
Merz Pharmaceuticals Inc. 873
Mother Murphy's Laboratories, Inc. 908
Newbridge Bancorp 948
Qorvo Inc 1094
Rf Micro Devices, Inc. 1126
Tanger Factory Outlet Centers, Inc. 1277
The Fresh Market Inc 1311
The Moses H Cone Memorial Hospital Operating Corporation 1322
Unifi, Inc. 1377
University Of North Carolina At Greensboro 1399

GREENVILLE
Greenville Utilities Commission 630
Pitt County Memorial Hospital, Incorporated 1055
University Health Systems Of Eastern Carolina, Inc. 1394

HICKORY
Alex Lee, Inc. 54
Dale Jarrett Racing Adventure Inc 425

High Point
Banner Pharmacaps Inc. 184
Bnc Bancorp 233
Culp Inc 416
High Point Regional Health 666

HUNTERSVILLE
American Tire Distributors Holdings, Inc. 97

Lenoir
Broyhill Furniture Industries Inc. 258

Lillington
American Defense Systems Inc. 83

Lincolnton
Carolina Trust Bancshares Inc 300
Carolinas Medical Center-lincoln 300

Matthews
Cem Holdings Corporation 315
Family Dollar Stores, Inc. 529
Harris Teeter Inc. 646
Pokertek Inc 1061

MC LEANSVILLE
Replacements, Ltd. 1120

Mocksville
Bank Of The Carolinas Corp 182

Mooresville
Lowe's Companies Inc 819

MORGANTON
Blue Ridge Healthcare Hospitals, Inc. 230
Blue Ridge Healthcare System, Inc.. 230

Morrisville
Channeladvisor Corp 327
Charles & Colvard Ltd 327
Furiex Pharmaceuticals Inc 585
Pyxus International Inc 1092
Sciquest Inc 1171
Tekelec 1284
Tenax Therapeutics Inc 1289

Mount Airy
Insteel Industries, Inc. 715
Pike Corp 1051
Renfro Corporation 1118
Surrey Bancorp (nc) 1265

Mount Gilead
Mcrae Industries, Inc. 858

Newton
Peoples Bancorp Of North Carolina Inc 1036

PINEHURST
Firsthealth Of The Carolinas, Inc. 557

Raleigh
Advance Auto Parts Inc 30
Alliance Of Professionals & Consultants, Inc. 62
Baxano Surgical Inc 193
Biodelivery Sciences International Inc 217
Bjt, Inc. 221
Bmc Stock Holdings Inc 233
Capital Bank Corporation 288
Carolina Power & Light Company 299
Carquest Corporation 301
Crescent Financial Bancshares Inc. 406
Dara Biosciences, Inc. 426
First Citizens Bancshares Inc (nc) 548
Highwoods Properties, Inc. 668
Inspire Pharmaceuticals Inc. 714
Kent Financial Services Inc. 766
North Carolina Electric Membership Corporation 959
Progress Energy Inc. 1080
Red Hat Inc 1112
Rex Healthcare, Inc. 1125
S&me, Inc. 1147
Salix Pharmaceuticals Ltd 1156
Stock Building Supply Llc 1250
Storr Office Environments Inc 1251
Suntory International Corp. 1262
The Generation Companies Llc 1312
Triangle Capital Corp 1360
Wakemed 1443
Yadkin Financial Corp 1486

ROCKY MOUNT
Boddie-noell Enterprises, Inc. 235

Salisbury
Delhaize America Llc 436
Rowan Regional Medical Center, Inc. 1141

SANFORD
Static Control Components Inc. 1243

Southern Pines
First Bancorp (nc) 546

STATESVILLE
Energyunited Electric Membership Corporation 501

Kewaunee Scientific Corporation 768
Statesville Hma, Llc 1243

Tarboro
Barnhill Contracting Company 188

Thomasville
Old Dominion Freight Line, Inc. 987

Wake Forest
Powersecure International, Inc. 1068

Warsaw
Murphy-brown Llc 916

Washington
First South Bancorp Inc (va) 555
Flanders Corporation 558

Waynesville
Wellco Enterprises Inc. 1453

West Jefferson
Lifestore Financial Group 805

Whiteville
Waccamaw Bankshares Inc. 1441

WILKESBORO
Key City Furniture Company Inc 768

Wilmington
Cenama Inc. 315
Guilford Mills Inc. 635
New Hanover Regional Medical Center 942
Pharmaceutical Product Development Inc. 1045

Winston Salem
Hatteras Financial Corp 648
Novant Health, Inc. 970
Quality Oil Company, Llc 1096
Wake Forest University 1442
Wake Forest University Baptist Medical Center 1442

Winston-Salem
Hanesbrands Inc 642
Krispy Kreme Doughnuts Inc 780
Lowe's Food Stores Inc. 819
Primo Water Corp 1076
Reynolds American Inc 1126
Southern Community Financial Corporation 1214
Truist Financial Corp 1364
Wilcohess Llc 1469

Youngsville
Sirchie Acquisition Company Llc 1198
Xerium Technologies Inc 1483

NORTH DAKOTA

BEULAH
Dakota Gasification Company Inc 424

BISMARCK
Basin Electric Power Cooperative 190
Bnccorp Inc 233
Mdu Resources Group Inc 858
St. Alexius Medical Center 1231
Wbi Energy Transmission, Inc 1450

FARGO
Dakota Supply Group, Inc. 425
Eide Bailly Llp 482
North Dakota State University 960
Rdo Equipment Co. 1109
Red River Commodities, Inc. 1112
Sanford 1161

GRAND FORKS
Altru Health System 72
Minnkota Power Cooperative, Inc. 892

INDEX BY HEADQUARTERS LOCATION

North Dakota Mill & Elevator
Association 960
University Of North Dakota 1399
MINOT
Farstad Oil Inc. 531
Investors Real Estate Trust 732
Spf Energy, Inc. 1224
Wahpeton
Minn-dak Farmers Cooperative 892
West Fargo
Titan Machinery, Inc. 1347

OHIO

AKRON
Akron General Medical Center Inc 49
Bekaert Corporation 202
Childrens Hospital Medical Center Of
Akron 340
Firstenergy Corp 556
Firstmerit Corp 557
Goodyear Tire & Rubber Co. 620
Jersey Central Power & Light
Company 748
Metropolitan Edison Company 877
Myers Industries Inc. 918
Ohio Edison Company 985
Pennsylvania Electric Company 1033
Pennsylvania Power Company
Inc 1034
Summa Health 1256
The Cleveland Electric Illuminating
Company 1305
The University Of Akron 1333
ARCHBOLD
Mbc Holdings, Inc. 853
ASHLAND
Samaritan Regional Health
System 1157
Aurora
Technical Consumer Products
Inc. 1282
Avon Lake
Polyone Corp. 1061
Batavia
Multi-color Corp. 914
Beachwood
Omnova Solutions Inc 992
Site Centers Corp 1198
Beavercreek
Advant-e Corporation 33
Berea
Cleveland Browns Football Company
Llc 359
Ohio Turnpike And Infrastructure
Commission 985
BLUE ASH
Belcan Corporation 202
Bolivar
Cable Manufacturing And Assembly
Co. Inc. 270
Brewster
Shearer's Foods Inc. 1188
Wheeling & Lake Erie Railway
Company 1465
Brooklyn Heights
Graftech International Ltd 622
BRYAN
Manufactured Housing Enterprises
Inc. 837

Bucyrus
Community Investors Bancorp,
Inc 379
Cambridge
Camco Financial Corp 282
Canfield
Farmers National Banc Corp.
(canfield,oh) 531
CANTON
Mercy Medical Center, Inc. 870
Cardington
Cardington Yutaka Technologies
Inc. 293
CHILLICOTHE
Adena Health System 28
Cincinnati
Advancepierre Foods Inc. 32
American Financial Group Inc 85
Bethesda Hospital, Inc. 211
Bhe Environmental Inc. 212
Busken Bakery Inc. 267
Chemed Corp 332
Cheviot Financial Corp 335
Children's Hospital Medical
Center 339
Cincinnati Bell Inc 347
Cincinnati Bengals Inc. 347
Cintas Corporation 347
Convergys Corp 392
Fifth Third Bancorp (cincinnati,
Oh) 544
First Financial Bancorp (oh) 550
Frisch's Restaurants, Inc. 580
Frost Brown Todd Llc 581
Hickman, Williams & Company 665
John Morrell & Co. 751
Kgbo Holdings, Inc 769
Kroger Co (the) 780
Lca-vision Inc. 793
Lsi Industries Inc. 821
Meridian Bioscience Inc. 871
Messer Construction Co. 874
Milacron Llc 888
Omnicare Inc. 991
P&g-clairol Inc. 1008
Procter & Gamble Company
(the) 1078
Scripps (ew) Company (the) 1172
Staffmark Holdings Inc. 1236
Stand Energy Corporation 1237
The Christ Hospital 1305
Totes Isotoner Corporation 1351
Trihealth, Inc. 1361
Uc Health, Llc. 1373
University Of Cincinnati 1395
Western & Southern Financial Group,
Inc. 1458
Xavier University 1482
Cleveland
Ag Interactive Inc. 41
Aleris Corp 54
Applied Industrial Technologies,
Inc. 121
Argo-tech Corporation 131
Athersys Inc 150
Austin Powder Company 160
Baker & Hostetler Llp 174
Bearing Distributors, Inc. 199
Case Western Reserve University 304
Cbiz Inc 309
Cleveland State University 359
Cleveland-cliffs Inc (new) 359
Crawford United Corp 405
Federal Reserve Bank Of Cleveland,
Dist. No. 4 536
Forest City Enterprises, Inc. 567

Hyster-yale Materials Handling
Inc 691
Keycorp 769
Lincoln Electric Holdings, Inc. 808
Mace Security International, Inc. 828
Morgan's Foods, Inc. 906
Nacco Industries Inc 919
Om Group, Inc. 990
Park-ohio Holdings Corp. 1021
Parker Hannifin Corp 1021
Sherwin-williams Co (the) 1189
Sifco Industries Inc. 1192
Tfs Financial Corp 1297
The Cleveland Clinic Foundation 1305
The Metrohealth System 1321
Transdigm Group Inc 1355
Columbus Grove
United Bancshares Inc. (oh) 1381
Columbus
Adb Airfield Solutions Llc 27
Alliance Data Systems Corp. 61
America's Body Company Inc. 77
American Electric Power Co Inc 84
American Municipal Power, Inc. 91
Appalachian Power Co. 118
Bancinsurance Corporation 179
Battelle Memorial Institute Inc 192
Big Lots, Inc. 213
Bravo Brio Restaurant Group Inc 246
Buckeye Power, Inc. 262
Cameron Mitchell Restaurants
Llc 283
Columbia Gas Of Ohio, Inc. 372
Core Molding Technologies Inc 395
Designer Brands Inc 442
Diamond Hill Investment Group
Inc. 446
Express Inc 524
Glimcher Realty Trust 610
Hexion Inc 664
Huntington Bancshares Inc 688
Installed Building Products Inc 714
Kentucky Power Company 767
L Brands, Inc 782
Lane Bryant Inc. 789
Liebert Corporation 803
M/i Homes Inc 827
Mast Industries Inc. 847
Mettler-toledo International, Inc. 878
Mount Carmel Health System 909
Nationwide Children's Hospital 929
Nationwide Mutual Insurance
Company 929
Ohio Living 985
Ohio Power Company 985
Ohiohealth Corporation 986
Public Service Company Of
Oklahoma 1088
Roth Produce Co. 1140
School Employees Retirement System
Of Ohio 1168
Schottenstein Realty Trust Inc. 1169
Southwestern Electric Power
Co. 1219
State Auto Financial Corp. 1241
T. Marzetti Company 1273
The Fishel Company 1310
Worthington Industries, Inc. 1480
Cortland
Cortland Bancorp (oh) 398
Coshocton
Home Loan Financial Corp 677
Cuyahoga Falls
Associated Materials Llc 146
DAYTON
Bob Ross Buick, Inc. 235
Dpl Inc. 460
Good Samaritan Hospital 618

Kettering Adventist Healthcare 767
Miami Valley Hospital 881
Premier Health Partners 1072
Rex American Resources Corp 1125
Standard Register Co. 1238
The Iams Company 1315
The University Of Dayton 1334
Wright State University 1480
Defiance
First Defiance Financial Corp 549
Sb Financial Group Inc 1166
Dover
Ffd Financial Corp 541
Dublin
Cardinal Health, Inc. 293
Community Choice Financial Inc 377
Navidea Biopharmaceuticals Inc 931
Oclc, Inc. 983
Pacer International Inc 1009
Stanley Steemer International,
Inc. 1239
Wendy's Co (the) 1455
Elyria
Invacare Corp 730
Ridge Tool Company 1129
Fairfield
Cincinnati Financial Corp. 347
Fairlawn
Schulman (a) Inc 1169
Sterling Jewelers Inc. 1247
Fairport Harbor
Ourpet's Company 1005
Findlay
Andeavor Logistics Lp 109
Cooper Tire & Rubber Co. 393
Legacy Farmers Cooperative 795
Marathon Petroleum Corp. 837
Mplx Lp 911
FREMONT
Beck Suppliers, Inc. 200
Croghan Bancshares, Inc. 408
Crown Battery Manufacturing
Company 410
Gallipolis
Ohio Valley Banc Corp 986
GAMBIER
Kenyon College 767
GRANVILLE
Denison University 440
Holophane 675
Groveport
Pinnacle Data Systems Inc. 1052
Harrison
Jtm Provisions Company Inc. 756
Heath
Englefield Oil Company 502
Hebron
Mpw Industrial Services Group
Inc. 911
Highland Hills
Olympic Steel Inc. 990
Hiram
Great Lakes Cheese Company Inc. 625
Independence
Advizex Technologies Llc 35
Apple American Group Llc 119
Kent
Davey Tree Expert Co. (the) 429
Kent State University 766

INDEX BY HEADQUARTERS LOCATION

The Carter-jones Lumber Company 1303
Killbuck
Killbuck Bancshares, Inc. 770
LANCASTER
Fairfield Medical Center 527
South Central Power Company Inc 1210
Lebanon
Lcnb Corp 793
Lewis Center
Dcb Financial Corp 431
Lima
American Trim Llc 97
Mercy Health - St. Rita's Medical Center, Llc 869
Lodi
Cropking Incorporated 408
Lorain
Lnb Bancorp, Inc. 813
Loveland
Xpedx 1485
Mansfield
Gorman-rupp Company (the) 620
Therm-o-disc Incorporated 1339
Marietta
Integral Technologies Inc. 717
Peoples Bancorp Inc (marietta, Oh) 1036
Martins Ferry
United Bancorp, Inc. (martins Ferry, Oh) 1381
Marysville
Scotts Miracle-gro Co (the) 1171
Mason
Atricure Inc 155
Clopay Corporation 360
Portion Pac Inc. 1064
MASSILLON
Fresh Mark, Inc. 579
Maumee
Hickory Farms Inc. 665
Mayfield Heights
Datatrak International Inc. 428
Ferro Corp 541
Materion Corp 848
Mayfield Village
Anthony & Sylvan Pools Corporation 114
Preformed Line Products Co. 1071
Progressive Corp. (oh) 1080
Medina
Rpm International Inc (de) 1142
MENTOR
Cleveland Construction, Inc. 359
John D. Oil And Gas Company 750
MIAMISBURG
Danis Building Construction Company 426
Newpage Group Inc. 950
Verso Corp 1425
Middlefield
Middlefield Banc Corp. 887
MILLERSBURG
Holmes Lumber & Building Center Inc. 675

Minerva
Consumers Bancorp, Inc. (minerva, Oh) 389
MORAINE
Lastar Inc. 791
Nelsonville
Rocky Brands Inc 1136
New Albany
Abercrombie & Fitch Co 12
Bob Evans Farms Inc 235
Commercial Vehicle Group Inc 375
New Philadelphia
Gradall Industries Inc. 621
Newark
Anomatic Corporation 113
Licking Memorial Health Systems 803
Park National Corp (newark, Oh) 1020
Niles
First Niles Financial Inc. 554
North Canton
Diebold Nixdorf Inc 448
Ohio Legacy Corp 985
Timken Co. (the) 1346
OBERLIN
Oberlin College 980
Orrville
National Bancshares Corp. (ohio) 922
Smucker (j.m.) Co. 1204
The Will-burt Company 1338
OXFORD
Miami University 881
PAINESVILLE
Lake Hospital System, Inc. 785
PARMA
Parma Community General Hospital 1022
PERRYSBURG
Frozen Specialties Inc. 581
O-i Glass Inc 978
Pickerington
Barry (r.g.) Corp. 189
PIKETON
Ohio Valley Electric Corporation 986
Portsmouth
Asb Financial Corp. 141
RAVENNA
Robinson Health System, Inc. 1134
Reynoldsburg
Bath & Body Works Llc 191
Victoria's Secret Direct Llc 1428
Victoria's Secret Stores Llc 1428
Richfield
National Interstate Corp 925
Richmond Hts.
Associated Estates Realty Corp. 146
Sandusky
Cedar Fair Lp 313
Civista Bancshares Inc 354
Firelands Regional Health System 546
SHAKER HEIGHTS
University Hospitals Health System, Inc. 1394
Sidney
Amos Press Inc. 103
Peoples-sidney Financial Corp. 1037

Solon
Advanced Lighting Technologies Inc. 31
Aurora Wholesalers Llc 159
Carlisle Brake & Friction Inc. 297
Energy Focus Inc 500
Keithley Instruments Inc. 763
Springfield
Home City Financial Corp 676
STEUBENVILLE
Franciscan University Of Steubenville 574
Trinity Health System 1362
Strongsville
Hmi Industries Inc. 672
Sylvania
Root Learning Inc. 1137
Symmes Township
Vantiv Inc. 1418
Worldpay Inc 1479
Toledo
Hcr Manorcare Inc. 652
Heidtman Steel Products Inc. 656
Libbey. Inc. 801
N-viro International Corp 919
Owens Corning 1006
Pilkington North America, Inc. 1051
The Toledo Hospital 1331
The University Of Toledo 1335
Welltower Inc 1454
Uniontown
Fedex Custom Critical Inc. 538
UNIVERSITY HEIGHTS
John Carroll University 750
Upper Sandusky
Commercial Bancshares, Inc. (oh) 375
Valley City
Shiloh Industries, Inc. 1189
Van Wert
Central Mutual Insurance Company 319
WALBRIDGE
The Rudolph/libbe Companies Inc 1328
WARREN
Anderson And Dubose, Inc. 109
Avalon Holdings Corp. 163
West Chester
Ak Steel Holding Corp. 48
Westerville
Exel Inc. 522
Lancaster Colony Corp. 787
WESTLAKE
The Shamrock Companies Inc 1330
Travelcenters Of America Inc 1357
Wickliffe
The Lubrizol Corporation 1319
Wilmington
Air Transport Services Group, Inc. 46
Nb&t Financial Group, Inc. 932
WOODVILLE
Luckey Farmers, Inc. 822
WOOSTER
The College Of Wooster 1306
Wayne Savings Bancshares Inc 1449
Worthington
Central Federal Corp 318

YOUNGSTOWN
Forge Industries, Inc. 568
United Community Financial Corp. (oh) 1382
Youngstown State University Inc 1489
Zanesville
Axion International Holdings Inc 169
Genesis Healthcare System 599
Mattingly Foods, Inc. 849

OKLAHOMA

Ada
Legalshield 796
ALTUS
Jackson County Memorial Hospital Authority 742
ANADARKO
Western Farmers Electric Cooperative 1459
Broken Arrow
Xeta Technologies Inc. 1484
DURANT
Stephenson Wholesale Company, Inc. 1246
Edmond
Energy & Environmental Services Inc 499
ENID
Johnston Enterprises, Inc. 753
NORMAN
Norman Regional Hospital Authority 958
University Of Oklahoma 1399
Oklahoma City
American Fidelity Assurance Company 85
Ams Health Sciences Inc. 105
Bancfirst Corp. (oklahoma City, Okla) 179
Carlisle Foodservice Products Incorporated 297
Chaparral Energy L.l.c. 327
Chesapeake Energy Corp. 334
Chesapeake Oilfield Services Inc. 334
Continental Resources Inc. 391
Devon Energy Corp. 444
Duncan Equipment Company 465
Enable Midstream Partners L.p. 496
Express Services Inc 525
Feed The Children Inc. 539
Foundation Healthcare, Inc 571
Fullnet Communications Inc 584
Gulfport Energy Corp. 637
Hobby Lobby Stores, Inc. 673
Integris Baptist Medical Center, Inc. 718
Integris Health, Inc. 718
Love's Travel Stops & Country Stores Inc. 818
Lsb Industries, Inc. 821
Midland Financial Co. 887
Mustang Fuel Corporation 916
New Source Energy Corporation 943
New Source Energy Partners Lp 944
Oge Energy Corp. 984
Panhandle Oil & Gas Inc 1016
Postrock Energy Corp 1066
Premium Beers Of Oklahoma, L.l.c. 1072
Reserve Petroleum Co. 1122
Sandridge Energy Inc 1160
Seventy Seven Energy Llc 1184
Sonic Corp. 1207

INDEX BY HEADQUARTERS LOCATION

Oklahoma

Oklahoma
Roan Resources Inc 1132

Pawhuska
Osage Bancshares Inc. 1002

Perry
The Charles Machine Works Inc. 1304

Pryor
Orchids Paper Products Co. (de) 1000

Sand Springs
Webco Industries Inc. 1451

STILLWATER
Oklahoma State University 987
Southwest Bancorp, Inc. (ok) 1218

SULPHUR
Chickasaw Holding Company 337

Tulsa
Aaon, Inc. 9
Ahs Hillcrest Medical Center, Llc 45
Alliance Holdings Group Lp 62
Alliance Resource Partners Lp 62
American Natural Energy Corp. 91
Blueknight Energy Partners Lp 232
Bok Financial Corp 237
Cypress Energy Partners Lp 421
Daylight Donut Flour Company Llc 430
Dollar Thrifty Automotive Group Inc. 456
Educational Development Corp. 481
Helmerich & Payne, Inc. 658
Kaiser-francis Oil Company 759
Laredo Petroleum Holdings Inc. 790
Magellan Midstream Partners Lp 831
Matrix Service Co. 848
Mid-con Energy Partners Lp 885
Ngl Energy Partners Lp 953
One Gas, Inc. 993
Oneok Inc 994
Oneok Partners, L.p. 995
Quiktrip Corporation 1099
Rose Rock Midstream L P 1138
Saint Francis Health System, Inc. 1152
Semgroup Corp 1178
St. John Health System, Inc. 1232
Syntroleum Corp 1272
T. D. Williamson, Inc. 1273
The University Of Tulsa 1335
The Williams Companies Inc. 1338
Unit Corp. 1380
United States Beef Corporation 1386
Williams Partners L.p. 1471
Williams Partners Lp (new) 1471
Wpx Energy Inc 1480

VINITA
Grand River Dam Authority 623

ONTARIO

Toronto
Dundee Precious Metals Inc 465

OREGON

Albany
Ati Titanium Llc 151

Beaverton
Cascade Microtech Inc 303
Comp-view Inc. 380
Digimarc Corp 448
Planar Systems Inc. 1056
Shari's Management Corporation 1186

Bend
American Licorice Company 89
Cascade Bancorp 303

CORVALLIS
Oregon State University 1001

EUGENE
Eugene Water & Electric Board 517
Organically Grown Company 1001
Pacific Continental Corp 1010
The Willamette Valley Company Llc 1338
University Of Oregon 1400

Hillsboro
Fei Co. 539
Lattice Semiconductor Corp 792
Radisys Corp. 1103
Triquint Semiconductor, Inc. 1363

KEIZER
Gallaudet University 589

McMinnville
Rb Rubber Products Inc. 1108

MEDFORD
C & K Market, Inc. 268
Harry & David Holdings Inc. 646
Lithia Motors Inc 811

North Plains
Jewett-cameron Trading Co. Ltd. 749

PORTLAND
Andersen Construction Company 109
Blount International, Inc. 226
Bonneville Power Administration 238
Boyd Coffee Company 244
Calypte Biomedical Corporation 281
Columbia Sportswear Co. 373
Craft Brew Alliance Inc 404
Electro Scientific Industries Inc 485
Erickson Inc 513
Esco Corporation 514
Fortis Construction, Inc. 570
Fred Meyer Stores Inc. 576
Integra Telecom Inc. 716
Lacrosse Footwear Inc. 784
Legacy Emanuel Hospital & Health Center 795
Legacy Health 796
Lewis & Clark College 800
M Financial Holdings Incorporated 826
Mccormick & Schmick's Seafood Restaurants Inc. 854
Mercy Corps 869
Northwest Natural Holding Co 968
Oregon Health & Science University 1000
Pacificorp 1012
Portland General Electric Co. 1064
Portland State University 1064
Powell's Books Inc. 1067
Precision Castparts Corp. 1070
Rentrak Corp. 1119
Schmitt Industries Inc (or) 1168
Schnitzer Steel Industries Inc 1168
Stancorp Financial Group Inc 1237
The Reed Institute 1327
Tigerlogic Corp 1344
Umpqua Holdings Corp 1377
Williams Controls Inc. 1470
Zimmer Gunsul Frasca Architects Llp 1492

SALEM
Oregon State Lottery 1001
Salem Health 1155
Willamette University 1469

Tigard
Western Family Foods Inc. 1459

Tualatin
Bioject Medical Technologies Inc. 217
Cui Global Inc 415

Turner
Willamette Valley Vineyard Inc. 1470

Wilsonville
Flir Systems, Inc. 560
Mentor Graphics Corporation 866
Trellis Earth Products Inc. 1359

PENNSYLVANIA

ABINGTON
Abington Memorial Hospital Inc 12

Allentown
Air Products & Chemicals Inc 46
American Bank Inc (pa) 79
Crossamerica Partners Lp 409
Lehigh Valley Health Network, Inc. 797
Ppl Corp 1069
Ppl Electric Utilities Corp 1069
Sacred Heart Hospital Of Allentown 1149

ALLISON PARK
Miller Electric Construction Inc 890

ALTOONA
The Hite Company 1315
Upmc Altoona 1406
Ward Trucking, Llc 1444

Ambler
Bradford White Corporation 245

Audubon
Globus Medical Inc 613

Bala Cynwyd
Laserlock Technologies Inc. 791
Philadelphia Consolidated Holding Corp. 1046
Royal Bancshares Of Pennsylvania Inc 1141

BEAVER
Heritage Valley Health System, Inc. 662

Belleville
Kish Bancorp Inc. 774

Bensalem
Healthcare Services Group, Inc. 654

Berwick
First Keystone Corp 552

Berwyn
Ametek Inc 102
Dfc Global Corp. 445

Bethlehem
B. Braun Medical Inc. 172
Buzzi Unicem Usa Inc. 267
Lehigh University 797
Moravian College 904
Orasure Technologies Inc. 999
St. Luke's Health Network, Inc. 1234

Bloomsburg
Ccfnb Bancorp Inc. 311

BLUE BELL
Fiberlink Communications Corporation 541
Unisys Corp 1380
Unitek Global Services Inc. 1389

Boyertown
National Penn Bancshares Inc. 926

Breinigsville
Cyoptics Inc. 421

Bridgeville
Universal Stainless & Alloy Products, Inc. 1392

BRISTOL
Lenox Corporation 799

Broomall
Alliance Bancorp Inc. Of Pennsylvania 61

Bryn Mawr
Bryn Mawr Bank Corp 260
Bryn Mawr College 260
Essential Utilities Inc 515
Main Line Health Inc. 832
Main Line Hospitals, Inc. 833

BUTLER
Butler Health System, Inc. 267

Camp Hill
Ames True Temper Inc. 102
Fleming Gannett Inc 559
Holy Spirit Hospital Of The Sisters Of Christian Charity 675
Rite Aid Corp 1130

Canonsburg
Ansys Inc. 113
Centimark Corporation 318
Cnx Resources Corp 363
Rice Energy Inc 1128

Carlisle
Ahold U.s.a. Inc. 45
Daily Express, Inc. 423
Dickinson College 448

Carnegie
Ampco-pittsburgh Corp. 103

CENTER VALLEY
Desales University 441

Chambersburg
Franklin Financial Services Corp 575

Chesterbrook
Amerisourcebergen Corp. 100
Auxilium Pharmaceuticals Inc 163
The J G Wentworth Company 1317
Trevena Inc 1359

CHESTER
Widener University 1468

CLAIRTON
Jefferson Regional Medical Center 747

Clearfield
Cnb Financial Corp. (clearfield, Pa) 362

Colmar
Dorman Products Inc 458

CONCORDVILLE
La France Corp. 783

CONSHOHOCKEN
Allied Security Holdings Llc 64
American Society For Testing And Materials 95
David's Bridal Inc. 429
Quaker Chemical Corporation 1095
Rumsey Electric Company 1144
Van Horn Metz & Co. Inc. 1417

Coraopolis
Dick's Sporting Goods, Inc 447
Fedex Ground Package System Inc. 539
Robert Morris University 1133

INDEX BY HEADQUARTERS LOCATION

DANVILLE
Geisinger Health 593
DENVER
High Concrete Group Llc 666
DOUGLASSVILLE
Stv Group, Incorporated 1254
Downingtown
Dnb Financial Corp. 454
DOYLESTOWN
Delaware Valley University 435
Doylestown Hospital Health And Wellness Center, Inc. 460
Prophase Labs Inc 1082
DUNCANSVILLE
Hoss's Steak & Sea House, Inc. 682
Value Drug Company 1417
Dunmore
Fidelity D&d Bancorp Inc 542
Fncb Bancorp Inc 565
East Greenville
Knoll Inc 776
East Stroudsburg
Pocono Health System 1060
EASTON
Lafayette College 785
Paragon Technologies Inc 1018
Eighty Four
84 Lumber Company 6
Emlenton
Emclaire Financial Corp. 491
EMMAUS
Buckeye Pipe Line Company, L P 262
EPHRATA
Menno Travel Service, Inc. 866
Erie
Erie Indemnity Co. 513
Exton
Bentley Systems Incorporated 206
Fibrocell Science Inc 542
Idera Pharmaceuticals Inc 696
Innovative Solutions And Support Inc 712
Kensey Nash Corporation 766
Omega Flex Inc 990
West Pharmaceutical Services, Inc. 1457
Fairview
Spectrum Control Inc. 1223
Fort Washington
Ditech Holding Corp 452
Nutrisystem Inc 974
Gettysburg
Acnb Corp 21
Gettysburg College 605
The Gettysburg Hospital 1312
GWYNEDD VALLEY
Mercy Gwynedd University 869
Hanover
Hanover Foods Corporation 643
HARLEYSVILLE
Deacon Industrial Supply Co. Inc. 431
Harleysville Financial Corp 645
Harleysville Group Inc. 645
Harrisburg
Capital Bluecross 288
Hersha Hospitality Trust 662
Metro Bancorp Inc Pa 876

Pennsylvania Higher Education Assistance Agency 1033
Pennsylvania Housing Finance Agency 1034
Pinnacle Health System 1053
United Concordia Companies Inc. 1382
Hatboro
Fox Chase Bancorp, Inc. 572
HAVERFORD
The Corporation Of Haverford College 1308
Hershey
Hershey Company (the) 662
Hershey Entertainment & Resorts Company 663
Pennsylvania - American Water Company 1033
Honesdale
Norwood Financial Corp. 970
Wayne Memorial Health System, Inc. 1449
Horsham
Aamco Transmissions Inc. 9
Astea International, Inc. 147
Orbit/fr, Inc. 999
Strata Skin Sciences Inc 1251
The Penn Mutual Life Insurance Company 1325
Toll Brothers Inc. 1349
HUNTINGDON
Juniata College 756
Indiana
First Commonwealth Financial Corp (indiana, Pa) 549
Indiana University Of Pennsylvania 706
S & T Bancorp Inc (indiana, Pa) 1147
Jenkintown
American Realty Capital Trust Inc. 93
Johnstown
Ameriserv Financial Inc. 100
Concurrent Technologies Corporation 385
Crown Holding Company 410
Kennett Square
Exelon Generation Co Llc 523
Genesis Healthcare Inc 599
Genesis Healthcare Llc 599
Kimberton
Nutrition Management Services Company 975
King of Prussia
Amerigas Partners Lp 99
Csl Behring Llc 412
Gsi Commerce Inc. 633
Morgan Properties Trust 905
Nocopi Technologies, Inc. 957
Sedona Corp 1177
Tekni-plex Inc. 1284
Ugi Corp. 1374
Universal Health Realty Income Trust 1391
Universal Health Services, Inc. 1391
LAFAYETTE HILL
Nhs Human Services, Inc. 953
Lancaster
Armstrong World Industries Inc 136
Auntie Anne's Inc. 158
Eurofins Lancaster Laboratories, Inc 517
Franklin And Marshall College 574
Fulton Financial Corp. (pa) 585

High Industries Inc. 666
High Steel Structures Llc 667
The Jay Group Inc 1317
The Lancaster General Hospital 1318
LANSDALE
Skf Usa Inc. 1199
Latrobe
Commercial National Financial Corp. (pa) 375
Lawrence
Black Box Corp. (de) 222
LEWISBURG
Bucknell University 262
Evangelical Community Hospital 518
Lititz
Susquehanna Bancshares, Inc 1265
The Benecon Group Inc 1300
LORETTO
Saint Francis University 1153
Macungie
Allen Organ Company 60
Malvern
Acme Markets Inc. 21
Biotelemetry Inc 219
Cephalon Inc. 323
Cubesmart 414
Endo Health Solutions Inc 498
Usa Technologies Inc 1411
Vishay Intertechnology, Inc. 1433
Vishay Precision Group Inc. 1433
Mansfield
Citizens Financial Services Inc 350
Marietta
Donegal Group Inc. 457
MC KEES ROCKS
Ohio Valley General Hospital 986
MEADVILLE
Allegheny College 58
MECHANICSBURG
Messiah College 874
Select Medical Holdings Corp 1178
MEDIA
Elwyn 490
Middletown
The Pennsylvania Lottery 1325
Mifflintown
Juniata Valley Financial Corp 757
Milford
Altec Lansing Llc 70
Millersburg
Mid Penn Bancorp Inc 885
Monessen
Fedfirst Financial Corporation 539
Monroeville
Standard Avb Financial Corp 1237
MOON TOWNSHIP
Calgon Carbon Corporation 275
Centria Inc. 321
Mastech Digital Inc 847
Neffs
Neffs Bancorp Inc. 935
New Hope
Meet Group Inc (the) 863
NEWTOWN SQUARE
Catholic Health East 308
Sap America Inc. 1163

Newtown
Epam Systems, Inc. 509
Onconova Therapeutics Inc 993
Tf Financial Corp. 1297
NORRISTOWN
Pjm Interconnection, L.l.c. 1055
North Huntingdon
Exone Co. (the) 523
North Wales
Sabre Industries Inc. 1148
NORTHUMBERLAND
Furman Foods, Inc. 585
OAKDALE
Industrial Scientific Corporation 706
Oaks
Sei Investments Co 1177
Paoli
Malvern Bancorp Inc. 834
PEACH GLEN
Knouse Foods Cooperative, Inc. 776
Pen Argyl
A & H Sportswear Co. Inc. 6
Philadelphia
Ace Usa 19
Alteva 71
Aramark 125
Aramark Refreshment Services Llc 125
Aria Health 132
Ballard Spahr Llp 178
Bdp International Inc. 197
Beneficial Mutual Bancorp Inc 205
Blank Rome Llp 224
Brandywine Realty Trust 246
Cardone Industries Inc. 294
Carpenter Technology Corp. 300
Chemtura Corp 332
Cohen & Company Inc (new) 367
Drexel University 461
Entercom Communications Corp 505
Eresearchtechnology Inc. 513
Federal Reserve Bank Of Philadelphia, Dist. No. 3 537
Five Below Inc 557
Fmc Corp. 564
Health Partners Plans, Inc. 653
Hill International Inc 668
Lannett Co., Inc. 789
Lasalle University 791
Magee Rehabilitation Hospital Foundation 831
Morgan Lewis & Bockius Llp 905
Paperworks Industries Inc. 1017
Pennoni Associates Inc. 1033
Pennsylvania Real Estate Investment Trust 1034
Pep Boys-manny, Moe & Jack 1037
Philadelphia North Health System 1046
Philadelphia Workforce Development Corporation 1047
Prwt Services, Inc. 1086
Quaker Valley Foods, Inc. 1095
Radian Group, Inc. 1102
Rait Financial Trust 1104
Republic First Bancorp, Inc. 1121
Resource America, Inc. 1122
Saint Joseph's University 1153
Southeastern Pennsylvania Transportation Authority 1213
Temple University Health System, Inc. 1288
Temple University-of The Commonwealth System Of Higher Education 1288

INDEX BY HEADQUARTERS LOCATION

The Children's Hospital Of
  Philadelphia 1304
The Day & Zimmermann Group
  Inc. 1309
The Fox Chase Cancer Center
  Foundation 1311
The Pennsylvania Hospital Of The
  University Of Pennsylvania Health
  System 1325
The Pew Charitable Trusts 1325
The Philadelphia Parking
  Authority 1326
The Trustees Of The University Of
  Pennsylvania 1332
The Wistar Institute Of Anatomy And
  Biology 1338
Thomas Jefferson University 1341
Thomas Jefferson University Hospitals,
  Inc. 1341
Urban Outfitters, Inc. 1407
Whyy Inc. 1467
Wistar Institute Of Anatomy &
  Biology 1476

PINE GROVE
Pine Grove Manufactured Homes
  Inc. 1052

PITTSBURGH
Allegheny General Hospital Inc 59
Allegheny Technologies, Inc 59
American Eagle Outfitters, Inc. 84
Arconic Inc 129
Atlas Pipeline Partners Lp 154
Baker Michael International Inc 176
Bayer Corporation 194
Busy Beaver Building Centers
  Inc. 267
Carnegie Mellon University 299
Chatham University 330
Children's Hospital Of Pittsburgh Of
  Upmc Health System 339
Dollar Bank Fsb 456
Duquesne Light Company 466
Duquesne University Of The Holy
  Spirit 466
Dynavox Inc. 469
Education Management Corp 480
Eqt Corp 511
Eureka Financial Corp (md) 517
Fab Universal Corp 527
Federal Home Loan Bank Of
  Pittsburgh 534
Federated Hermes Inc 538
Fnb Corp 564
Forest Snavely Products Inc 568
Foster (l.b.) Co 571
Gateway Health Plan Inc. 592
Genco Distribution System Inc. 594
Giant Eagle Inc. 605
Gnc Holdings Inc 614
Golf Galaxy Llc 617
Horsehead Holding Corp 681
Kennametal Inc. 765
Koppers Holdings Inc 778
Kraft Heinz Co (the) 780
Matthews International Corp 849
Pitt-ohio Express, Llc 1055
Ppg Industries Inc 1068
Rti International Metals, Inc. 1143
Sargent Electric Company 1164
Smith Micro Software Inc 1203
St. Clair Health Corporation 1231
The Brother's Brother
  Foundation 1302
The York Group Inc. 1339
Tristate Capital Holdings Inc 1363
United States Steel Corp. 1388
University Of Pittsburgh 1400
Upmc 1405
Wesco International, Inc. 1455

West Penn Allegheny Health System
  Inc. 1457
Western Pennsylvania Hospital 1461
Wexford Health Sources, Inc. 1463
Wvs Financial Corp. 1481

PITTSTON
Benco Dental Supply Co. 204

Plymouth Meeting
Amrep Corp. 104
Css Industries, Inc. 412
Inovio Pharmaceuticals Inc. 713

Quakertown
Qnb Corp. 1094

Radnor
Actua Corp 24
Airgas, Inc. 47
Lincoln National Corp. 808
Main Line Health System 832
Pvr Partners Lp 1092
Qlik Technologies Inc. 1094
Vwr Funding Inc. 1439

READING
Alvernia University 73
Brentwood Industries, Inc. 247
Enersys 502
Reading Hospital 1110
Redner's Markets, Inc. 1113

SAYRE
Guthrie Healthcare System 638

SCRANTON
Arlington Industries, Inc. 135
Cpg International Inc. 403
Gerrity's Super Market, Inc. 604
Peoples Financial Services Corp 1037
University Of Scranton 1401

SELLERSVILLE
Grand View Hospital 624

Sharon
Best Wings Usa Inc. 211
Sharon Regional Health System
  Inc. 1186

Shippensburg
Orrstown Financial Services,
  Inc. 1002

SMITHTON
Sam Levin Inc. 1157

Souderton
Univest Financial Corp 1405

Southampton
Environmental Tectonics Corp. 508
Tanner Industries, Inc. 1277

SPRINGFIELD
Crozer-keystone Health System 411

STATE COLLEGE
Glenn O. Hawbaker Inc. 610
Minitab Inc. 892
Rex Energy Corp 1125
Videon Central Inc. 1429

Stroudsburg
Essa Bancorp Inc 515

Sunbury
Weis Markets, Inc. 1453

SWARTHMORE
Swarthmore College 1266

TOPTON
Diakon 445

TREVOSE
Broder Bros., Co. 254
Stonemor Inc 1250

UNIVERSITY PARK
The Pennsylvania State
  University 1325

Valley Forge
Certainteed Corporation 324

VILLANOVA
Devereux Foundation 443
Villanova University In The State Of
  Pennsylvania 1430

Warminster
Arbutus Biopharma Corp 126

Warren
Blair Corporation 224
Northwest Bancshares Inc. 967

Warrington
Windtree Therapeutics Inc 1473

Wayne
Escalon Medical Corp 514
Johnson Matthey Inc. 753
Kenexa Corporation 764
Liberty Property Trust 802
Moro Corp. 906
Precyse Solutions Llc 1070
Safeguard Scientifics Inc. 1150
Sungard Availability Services Lp 1259
Sungard Data Systems Inc. 1259
Teleflex Incorporated 1286
The Judge Group Inc 1318
Zyla Life Sciences 1495

Wellsboro
Citizens & Northern Corp 349

WERNERSVILLE
Richard J. Caron Foundation 1129

West Chester
A. Duie Pyle Inc. 7
Accesslex Institute 16
Communications Test Design,
  Inc. 376
Nobel Learning Communities Inc. 956
Omni Cable Corporation 991
Qvc, Inc. 1101

WEST POINT
Acts Retirement-life Communities,
  Inc. 24

WILKES BARRE
King's College 772

Wilkes-Barre
George Foreman Enterprises Inc. 602

Williamsport
Penns Woods Bancorp, Inc. (jersey
  Shore, Pa) 1033

Willow Grove
Asplundh Tree Expert Co. 144

Wilmerding
Westinghouse Air Brake Technologies
  Corporation 1462

WOOLRICH
Woolrich Inc. 1477

WORCESTER
Allan Myers, Inc. 58

Wyomissing
Customers Bancorp Inc 417
Penn National Gaming Inc 1032

Yardley
Crown Holdings Inc 410

York
Bon-ton Stores Inc 238
Codorus Valley Bancorp, Inc. 366
Graham Packaging Company L.p. 622

Ph Glatfelter Co 1044
Unilife Corp. 1378
York Hospital 1488
York Pennsylvania Hospital Company
  Llc 1488
York Water Co 1488

PUERTO RICO

San Juan
Popular Inc. 1063

Santurce
Puerto Rico Electric Power
  Authority 1090

RHODE ISLAND

Cranston
Ross-simons Of Warwick Inc. 1140

KINGSTON
University Of Rhode Island 1400

LINCOLN
Lighthouse Computer Services,
  Inc. 806

Middletown
Kvh Industries, Inc. 782
Towerstream Corp 1352

NEWPORT
Salve Regina University 1157

Pawtucket
Hasbro, Inc. 648
Teknor Apex Company 1284
The Memorial Hospital 1320

Providence
Blue Cross & Blue Shield Of Rhode
  Island 228
Brown University In Providence In The
  State Of Rhode Island And
  Providence Plantations 257
Capital Properties, Inc. 289
Care New England Health System
  Inc 294
Citizens Financial Group Inc
  (new) 350
Dimeo Construction Company 451
Gilbane Building Company 607
Gilbane Inc. 607
Johnson & Wales University Inc 752
Lifespan Corporation 805
Nortek Inc 958
Providence College 1085
Rhode Island Housing 1127
Rhode Island School Of Design
  Inc 1127
Textron Inc 1296
United Natural Foods Inc. 1384
Warren Equities Inc. 1445

WARWICK
Kent County Memorial Hospital 766
The Beacon Mutual Insurance
  Company 1300

West Warwick
Astronova Inc 149
Bradford Soap Works Inc. 244
Lighting Science Group Corp 806
Van Arpin Lines Inc 1417

Westerly
Washington Trust Bancorp, Inc. 1446

Woonsocket
Cvs Health Corporation 419
Multicell Technologies Inc 914
Summer Infant Inc 1256

INDEX BY HEADQUARTERS LOCATION

SOUTH CAROLINA

Aiken
Agy Holding Corp. 45
Carlisle Tire & Wheel Company 297
Security Federal Corp (sc) 1175

BEAUFORT
Beaufort County Memorial Hospital 199

Cayce
Scana Corp 1167

Charleston
Bank Of South Carolina Corp 182
Blackbaud, Inc. 223
Carealliance Health Services 295
The Citadel 1305
The College Of Charleston 1306
The Medical University Of South Carolina 1320

COLUMBIA
Agfirst Farm Credit Bank 43
Bluechoice Healthplan Of South Carolina Inc. 231
Bonitz, Inc. 238
Carolina Care Plan Inc 299
M. B. Kahn Construction Co., Inc. 827
Palmetto Health 1014
South State Corp 1211
Uci Medical Affiliates Inc. 1374
University Of South Carolina 1401
Wilbur Smith Associates, Inc. 1468

CONWAY
Coastal Carolina University 364
Conway Hospital, Inc. 392
Horry Telephone Cooperative, Inc. 680

Easley
Cornerstone Bancorp 397

FLORENCE
Qhg Of South Carolina, Inc. 1094

Fountain Inn
Avx Corp. 168

GASTON
G&p Trucking Company, Inc. 587

GEORGETOWN
Georgetown Memorial Hospital 602

Goose Creek
Hirequest Inc 670

Greenville
Bi-lo Holding Llc 212
Delta Apparel Inc. 437
Furman University 585
Furman University Foundation Inc. 585
Gerber Childrenswear Llc 604
Jps Industries Inc. 755
Palmetto Bancshares, Inc. (sc) 1014
Prisma Health-upstate 1077
Southern First Bancshares, Inc. 1215
Span-america Medical Systems, Inc. 1220
World Acceptance Corp. 1478

GREER
Piedmont Municipal Power Agency 1050
Regional Management Corp 1115

Hartsville
Sonoco Products Co. 1208

KINGSTREE
Farmers Telephone Cooperative, Inc. 531

Lexington
First Community Corp (sc) 549
Southeastern Freight Lines, Inc. 1213

Loris
Hcsb Financial Corp 652

MONCKS CORNER
South Carolina Public Service Authority (inc) 1210

MOUNT PLEASANT
South Carolina State Ports Authority 1210
Tidelands Bancshares Inc 1343

Mt. Pleasant
Southcoast Financial Corp 1212

Myrtle Beach
Burroughs & Chapin Company Inc. 266
Grand Strand Regional Medical Center, Llc 623

Rock Hill
3d Systems Corp. (de) 4
Provident Community Bancshares, Inc. 1085

Seneca
Community First Bancorporation 378

Spartanburg
Advance America Cash Advance Centers Inc. 30
Centerplate Inc. 316
Denny's Corp 440
J M Smith Corporation 740
R. L. Jordan Oil Company Of North Carolina, Inc. 1101
Security Finance Corporation Of Spartanburg 1176

Summerville
Aeterna Zentaris Inc 39
American Lafrance Llc 89
Arborgen Inc. 126
Force Protection Inc. 566

Taylors
Cafe Enterprises Inc. 273

WEST COLUMBIA
Lexington Medical Center 800

SOUTH DAKOTA

ABERDEEN
Agtegra Cooperative 44

Brookings
Daktronics Inc. 425
South Dakota State University 1211

Dakota Dunes
Tyson Fresh Meats Inc. 1372

IPSWICH
North Central Farmers Elevator 959

PIERRE
Avera St. Marys 165

Rapid City
Black Hills Corporation 222
Black Hills Power Inc. 223
National American University Holdings Inc. 921
Rapid City Regional Hospital, Inc. 1105

SIOUX FALLS
Avera Health 165
Hf Financial Corp. 664
Meta Financial Group Inc 875

Northwestern Corp. 968
Raven Industries, Inc. 1106
The Evangelical Lutheran Good Samaritan Society 1310

Spearfish
Lehman Trikes Usa Inc. 797

VERMILLION
The University Of South Dakota 1335

WENTWORTH
Lake Area Corn Processors Co-operative 785

TENNESSEE

Athens
Athens Bancshares Corp 150

Bells
The Pictsweet Company 1326

Brentwood
American Homepatient Inc. 87
Brookdale Senior Living Inc 255
Corecivic Inc 395
Delek Logistics Partners Lp 435
Kirkland's Inc 773
Lifepoint Health Inc 804
Tractor Supply Co. 1353

Chattanooga
Astec Industries, Inc. 147
Bluecross Blueshield Of Tennessee Inc. 232
Cbl & Associates Properties Inc 309
Chattanooga Bakery Inc. 330
Chattem Inc. 331
Covenant Transportation Group Inc 401
Electric Power Board Of Chattanooga 484
Emj Corporation 494
First Security Group Inc 555
Hamilton Chattanooga County Hospital Authority 641
Metropolitan Security Services, Inc. 877
Parkridge Medical Center, Inc. 1022
Unum Group 1405
Us Xpress Enterprises Inc 1411

Clarksville
First Advantage Bancorp 546

CLEVELAND
Lee University 795
Life Care Centers Of America Inc. 803

Collegedale
Mckee Foods Corporation 856

Collierville
Mueller Industries Inc 913

COOKEVILLE
Averitt Express, Inc. 165
Tennessee Technological University 1290

DECATUR
Volunteer Energy Cooperative 1436

Franklin
Acadia Healthcare Company Inc. 14
Biomimetic Therapeutics Inc. 218
Clarcor Inc. 354
Community Health Systems, Inc. 378
Famc Subsidiary Company 529
Healthspring Inc. 654
Iasis Healthcare Corporation 692
Mmodal Inc. 896
Noranda Aluminum Holding Corp 957

Tivity Health Inc 1347
Video Gaming Technologies Inc 1428

GALLATIN
Charles C Parks Co Inc 328
Servpro Intellectual Property, Inc. 1183

Germantown
Mid-america Apartment Communities Inc 885

Goodlettsville
Dollar General Corp 456

Greeneville
Forward Air Corp 570
Meco Corporation 859

JACKSON
Jackson Energy Authority 742

JOHNSON CITY
East Tennessee State University 473

Kingsport
Eastman Chemical Co 476
Wellmont Health System 1454

KNOXVILLE
Covenant Health 401
East Tennessee Children's Hospital Association, Inc. 473
Educational Funding Of The South, Inc. 481
Knoxville Utilities Board 776
Miller Energy Resources, Inc. 890
Parkwest Medical Center 1022
Phillips And Jordan, Incorporated 1048
Pilot Corporation 1051
Provectus Pharmaceuticals Inc. 1084
Regal Entertainment Group 1114
Scripps Networks Interactive, Inc. 1172
Smartfinancial Inc 1202
Team Health Holdings Inc 1281
Tennessee Valley Authority 1290
University Of Tennessee 1402

LaVergne
Tennessee Farmers Cooperative 1289

Lebanon
Cracker Barrel Old Country Store, Inc. 404

LEWISBURG
Walker Die Casting Inc. 1443

MARYVILLE
Blount Memorial Hospital, Incorporated 226
Ruby Tuesday, Inc. 1144

Memphis
Accredo Health Incorporated 17
Ach Food Companies Inc. 20
American Residential Services L.l.c. 94
American Snuff Company Llc 95
Autozone, Inc. 162
Baker Donelson Bearman Caldwell & Berkowitz Pc 176
Baptist Memorial Health Care System, Inc. 185
Baptist Memorial Hospital 186
Bryce Corporation 260
Ducks Unlimited, Inc. 463
Education Realty Trust Inc 480
Elvis Presley Enterprises Inc. 490
Fedex Corp 538
First Horizon National Corp 551
Fred's Inc. 576
Gtx Inc. 633
International Paper Co 726

INDEX BY HEADQUARTERS LOCATION

Medtronic Sofamor Danek Usa Inc. 863
Methodist Le Bonheur Healthcare 876
Monogram Food Solutions, Llc 902
Rhodes College 1128
Sedgwick Claims Management Services Inc. 1176
St. Jude Children's Research Hospital, Inc. 1233
The Servicemaster Company 1330
Thomas & Betts Corporation 1341
Ut Medical Group, Inc. 1413
Wright Medical Group Inc. 1480

Morristown
Jefferson Bancshares Inc (tn) 747

MURFREESBORO
Firstfleet, Inc. 557
Middle Tennessee State University 886
National Health Investors, Inc. 924
National Healthcare Corp. 924
Old Time Pottery Inc. 989
Saint Thomas Rutherford Hospital 1154
The Middle Tennessee Electric Membership Corporation 1321

Nashville
Ahs Medical Holdings Llc 45
Alley-cassetty Companies, Inc. 61
Amsurg Corp 105
Asurion Corporation 149
Back Yard Burgers Inc. 173
Baldwin Piano Inc. 176
Captain D's Llc 291
Caterpillar Financial Services Corp 307
Chancelight, Inc. 327
Cumberland Pharmaceuticals Inc 416
Dialysis Clinic, Inc. 446
Electric Power Board Of The Metropolitan Government Of Nashville & Davidson County 485
Emdeon Inc. 492
Enterprise Electric, Llc 506
First Acceptance Corp 546
Genesco Inc. 597
Hca Healthcare Inc 651
Healthcare Realty Trust, Inc. 653
Healthstream Inc 654
Ipayment Inc. 733
Lifeway Christian Resources Of The Southern Baptist Convention 805
Lipscomb University 810
Louisiana-pacific Corp 818
Lri Holdings Inc. 820
O'charley's Inc. 977
Pinnacle Financial Partners Inc 1053
Ryman Hospitality Properties Inc 1147
Ryman Hospitality Properties, Inc. 1147
Tennessee State University 1290
The United Methodist Publishing House 1333
The Vanderbilt University 1336
Thomas Saint Midtown Hospital 1341
Vanderbilt University Medical Center 1418
Western Express Holdings Inc. 1459

Oak Ridge
B&w Technical Services Y-12 Llc 172
Navarro Research And Engineering Inc. 931
Professional Project Services Inc. 1079

Ooltewah
Miller Industries Inc. (tn) 890

SEWANEE
The University Of The South 1335

SOUTH PITTSBURG
Sequachee Valley Electric Co-operative Inc 1181

SPRINGFIELD
Hollingsworth Oil Co. Inc. 674

UNION CITY
Williams Sausage Company Inc. 1471

TEXAS

ABILENE
Abilene Christian University Inc 12
First Financial Bankshares, Inc. 550
Lauren Engineers & Constructors, Inc. 792

Addison
Affirmative Insurance Holdings Inc 40
Axcess International Inc. 169
Cadence Mcshane Construction Company Llc 272
Gehan Homes, Ltd. 593
Guaranty Bancshares Inc 634
Mary Kay Holding Corporation 844
Mary Kay Inc. 844
Uluru Inc 1376
United Surgical Partners International Inc. 1388

Alice
Forbes Energy Services Ltd 566

Allen
Atrion Corp. 155
Pfsweb Inc 1044

AMARILLO
Affiliated Foods, Inc. 39
Amarillo Biosciences Inc. 74
Cactus Feeders Inc. 271
Hastings Entertainment, Inc. 648
Maxor National Pharmacy Services Llc 851
Northwest Texas Healthcare System, Inc. 968

ANDERSON
Texas Municipal Power Agency 1295

Arlington
Forestar Group Inc (new) 568
Horton (dr) Inc 681
Texas Health Resources 1294

Austin
Aac Group Holding Corp. 9
Akela Pharma Inc. 48
American Campus Communities Inc 81
Arthrocare Corp. 139
Asure Software Inc. 149
Attorney General, Texas 156
Austin Community College 160
Austin Ribbon & Computer Supplies Inc. 160
Aviat Networks, Inc. 166
Bazaarvoice Inc. 196
Brigham Exploration Company 249
Bulldog Solutions Inc. 264
Calendar Holdings Llc 275
Centaur Technology Inc. 315
Chuy's Holdings Inc 345
Cirrus Logic Inc 348
Citizens, Inc. (austin, Tx) 351
Convio Inc. 392
Cynergistek Inc 421
Digital Turbine Inc 450
Eastern American Natural Gas Trust 474
Electric Reliability Council Of Texas, Inc. 485
Falconstor Software Inc 528
Farm Credit Bank Of Texas 530
Fieldpoint Petroleum Corp 543
Golfsmith International Holdings Inc. 617
Goodwill Industries Of Central Texas 619
Hanger Inc 643
Harte Hanks Inc 646
Homeaway, Inc. 677
Hoover's Inc. 678
J.d. Abrams, L.p. 741
Ldr Holding Corp 793
Lower Colorado River Authority 819
Luminex Corp 822
Mindwireless 891
Molecular Templates Inc 899
Multimedia Games Holding Company, Inc. 914
National Instruments Corp. 925
National Western Life Insurance Co. (austin, Tx) 928
Newgistics Inc. 948
Pain Therapeutics Inc 1014
Pinnacle Frames And Accents Inc. 1053
Planview Inc. 1057
Providence Resources Inc. 1085
Retailmenot Inc 1124
Rio Holdings, Inc. 1130
Saint Edward's University, Inc. 1152
Samuels Jewelers 1158
Scrypt Inc 1172
Seton Healthcare Family 1184
Seton Healthcare Network 1184
Silicon Laboratories Inc 1195
Solarwinds Inc 1206
St David's South Austin Medical Center 1229
Stratus Properties Inc. 1252
Summit Hotel Properties Inc 1257
Superconductor Technologies Inc 1262
Tel Offshore Trust 1285
Texas Department Of Transportation 1294
Texas Hospital Association 1295
Texas Vanguard Oil Co. 1296
Thermon Group Holdings Inc 1340
University Federal Credit Union 1393
University Of Texas At Austin 1402
Valence Technology, Inc. 1415
Whiteglove Health Inc. 1466
Whole Foods Market, Inc. 1467
Xplore Technologies Corp. 1485

BASTROP
Bluebonnet Electric Cooperative, Inc. 231

BEAUMONT
Deli Management, Inc. 436

BROWNSVILLE
Public Utilities Board Of The City Of Brownsville 1089

Buda
Cipherloc Corp 348

BUNA
Southeast Texas Industries, Inc. 1212

Carrollton
Accor North America 17
Beauticontrol Inc. 199
Carlson Restaurants Worldwide Inc. 298
Hilite International, Inc. 668

Cedar Park
Ets-lindgren Lp 517

COLLEGE STATION
Texas A & M Research Foundation Inc 1293

CONROE
Chca Conroe, L.p. 331

Coppell
Alco Stores Inc 53
Container Store Group, Inc 390
Craftmade International Inc. 404
Impreso Inc. 703
Nationstar Mortgage Holdings Inc 929
The Container Store Inc. 1307
Universal Power Group Inc 1392

CORINTH
Denton County Electric Cooperative, Inc. 440

CORPUS CHRISTI
Asset Protection & Security Services, Lp 145
Port Of Corpus Christi Authority Of Nueces County, Texas 1063
Susser Holdings Corp 1265
Tor Minerals International Inc 1350
Uranium Energy Corp. 1406

Dallas
7-eleven Inc. 6
Aerus Llc 38
Affiliated Computer Services Inc. 39
Ah Belo Corp 45
Airband Communications Holdings Inc. 47
Alon Usa Energy Inc 67
Alon Usa Partners Lp 67
American Leather 89
American Realty Investors, Inc. 94
Anthelio Healthcare Solutions Inc. 114
Archipelago Learning Inc. 128
Army & Air Force Exchange Service 136
Ashford Hospitality Trust Inc 143
At&t Inc 149
Atmos Energy Corp. 155
Austin Industries Inc. 160
Azure Midstream Partners Lp 171
Balfour Beatty Construction Group, Inc. 177
Baylor Health Care System 194
Baylor University Medical Center 195
Benefitmall Inc. 205
Brinker International, Inc. 250
Builders Firstsource Inc. 263
Builders Firstsource-southeast Group Llc 263
Cambium Learning Group, Inc. 281
Capital Senior Living Corp. 289
Capital Southwest Corp. 289
Capstead Mortgage Corp. 291
Ceco Environmental Corp. 312
Children's Medical Center Of Dallas 339
Cim Commercial Trust Corp 346
Clubcorp Holdings Inc 361
Comerica, Inc. 374
Compucom Systems Inc. 381
Compx International, Inc. 382
Copart Inc 394
Cross Border Resources Inc. 408
Cross Timbers Royalty Trust 408
Crossroads Systems Inc (new) 409
Crosstex Energy Inc 409
Dallas County Hospital District 425
Dave & Busters Entertainment Inc 428
Dean Foods Co. 432
Dominion Resources Black Warrior Trust 457
Dorchester Minerals Lp 457

INDEX BY HEADQUARTERS LOCATION

Dougherty's Pharmacy Inc 458
Dri Corporation 461
Dynamex Inc. 468
Eagle Materials Inc 471
Elah Holdings Inc 484
Energy Future Holdings Corp 500
Energy Transfer Lp 501
Energy Transfer Operating Lp 501
Enlink Midstream Partners Lp 503
Entech Sales And Service, Llc 504
Entrust Inc. 507
Envela Corp 508
Exco Resources Inc 522
Federal Reserve Bank Of Dallas, Dist. No. 11 536
Fedex Office And Print Services Inc. 539
Fiesta Restaurant Group, Inc 544
Frontier Oilfield Services Inc. 581
Gilbert May, Inc. 607
Greatwide Logistics Services Llc 628
Haggar Clothing Co. 639
Hallmark Financial Services Inc. 641
Hallwood Group Inc. 641
Hff Inc 664
Hilltop Holdings, Inc. 669
Hks, Inc. 671
Holly Energy Partners Lp 674
Hollyfrontier Corp 674
Howard Hughes Corp 684
Hugoton Royalty Trust (tx) 687
Income Opportunity Realty Investors Inc. 703
Jacobs Engineering Group, Inc. 744
Kimberly-clark Corp 770
Kosmos Energy Ltd (de) 779
Kronos Worldwide Inc 781
La Madeleine Of Texas Inc. 783
Matador Resources Company 847
Methodist Hospitals Of Dallas Inc 876
Modsys International Ltd 898
Moneygram International Inc 901
Mv Transportation, Inc. 917
New Concept Energy, Inc. 941
Newmarket Technology Inc. 949
Nl Industries, Inc. 955
Oncor Electric Delivery Co Llc 993
P10 Holdings Inc 1009
Panhandle Eastern Pipe Line Company, Lp 1016
Permian Basin Royalty Trust 1040
Placid Refining Company Llc 1056
Pmfg, Inc. 1060
Primoris Services Corp 1076
Regency Energy Partners Lp 1114
Rf Monolithics Inc. 1126
Rsp Permian Inc 1143
Ryan, Llc 1146
Sabine Royalty Trust 1148
Sammons Enterprises Inc. 1157
Santander Consumer Usa Holdings Inc 1162
Silverleaf Resorts Inc. 1195
Southcross Energy Partners Lp 1212
Southern Methodist University Inc 1215
Spindletop Oil & Gas Co (tex) 1225
Stevens Transport, Inc. 1248
Steward Health Care System Llc 1248
Sunoco Lp 1260
Sws Group, Inc. 1268
Tandy Brands Accessories, Inc. 1277
Tenet Healthcare Corp. 1289
Texas Capital Bancshares Inc 1293
Texas Industries Inc. 1295
Texas Instruments Inc. 1295
Texas Pacific Land Trust 1295
The Susan G Komen Breast Cancer Foundation Inc 1331
Tidelands Royalty Trust B 1343
Transcontinental Realty Investors, Inc. 1355

Trinity Industries, Inc. 1362
Tuesday Morning Corp 1368
United States Lime & Minerals Inc. 1387
Valhi, Inc. 1415
Vhs Of Illinois, Inc. 1426
Warren Resources Inc (md) 1445
Waste Control Specialists Llc 1447
Westwood Holdings Group, Inc. 1463
Wilhelmina International, Inc. 1469
Zion Oil And Gas Inc. 1492
Zix Corp 1493

Denton
Beauty Systems Group Llc 199
City Of Denton 352
Sally Beauty Holdings Inc 1156

DESOTO
The Warrior Group Inc 1337

DFW Airport
American Locker Group, Inc. 90
Aviall Inc. 166
Dallas/fort Worth International Airport 426

EDINBURG
J & D Produce, Inc. 739

EL PASO
El Paso County Hospital District 483
El Paso Electric Company 484
Jordan Cf Investments Llp 754
University Of Texas At El Paso 1402
Western Refining Inc 1461
Western Refining Logistics Lp 1461

Euless
Us Concrete Inc 1408

Farmers Branch
Addvantage Technologies Group, Inc. 27

Flower Mound
Mannatech Inc 836

Fort Worth
American Airlines Federal Credit Union 78
American Airlines Group Inc 78
Approach Resources Inc 122
Azz Galvanizing Services 171
Azz Inc 171
Basic Energy Services Inc 190
Bnsf Railway Company 234
Burlington Northern & Santa Fe Railway Co. (the) 265
Burlington Northern Santa Fe Llc 265
Calloway's Nursery, Inc. 279
Cash America International, Inc. 304
Cook Children's Health Care System 393
Dfb Pharmaceuticals, Llc 444
Emerge Energy Services Lp 492
Encore Energy Partners Lp 498
Energy & Exploration Partners Inc. 500
Entech Solar Inc. 504
Firstcash Inc 556
Freese And Nichols, Inc. 578
Fts International Inc. 583
General Motors Financial Company Inc. 597
Kmg Chemicals, Inc. 775
M & M Merchandisers Inc. 826
Omniamerican Bancorp, Inc. 991
Pier 1 Imports Inc. 1050
Quicksilver Production Partners Lp 1099
Quicksilver Resources, Inc. 1099
Range Resources Corp 1105
San Juan Basin Royalty Trust 1159
Tandy Leather Factory Inc 1277

Tarrant County Hospital District 1279
Teletouch Communications, Inc. 1287
Texas Christian University Inc 1294
Texas Health Harris Methodist Hospital Fort Worth 1294

FREDERICKSBURG
Hill Country Memorial Hospital 668

Frisco
Aastra Intecom Inc. 10
Addus Homecare Corp 27
Comstock Resources Inc 382
Goodman Networks Incorporated 619
Jamba Inc 745

Galveston
American National Insurance Co. (galveston, Tx) 91

GARLAND
American Terrazzo Company Ltd. 97
Micropac Industries, Inc. 883
Rhe Hatco Inc. 1127

GEORGETOWN
Embree Construction Group, Inc. 491
Southwestern University 1220

Grand Prairie
American Eurocopter Corporation 84
Six Flags Entertainment Corp 1198

Grapevine
Gamestop Corp 590
Greenhunter Resources, Inc 629

GREENVILLE
Hunt Memorial Hospital District 688

HALTOM CITY
The Bms Enterprises Inc 1301

Houstan
Weatherford International Plc 1451

Houston
Abm Security Services 13
Adams Resources & Energy, Inc. 27
Allis-chalmers Energy Inc. 65
Alta Mesa Holdings Lp 70
American Air Liquide Inc. 78
American General Life Insurance Company 86
American Midstream Partners Lp 91
American Spectrum Realty, Inc. 96
Americus Mortgage Corporation 99
Ampco Services, L.l.c. 103
Amplify Energy Corp (new) 104
Amreit Inc. 104
Anr Pipeline Company 113
Apache Corp 116
Archrock Inc 129
Archrock Partners Lp 129
Atwood Oceanics, Inc. 157
Avstar Aviation Group Inc. 168
Baker Botts L.l.p. 175
Baker Hughes Inc. 176
Belden & Blake Corporation 202
Bison Building Materials Ltd. 220
Blue Dolphin Energy Co. 230
Boardwalk Pipeline Partners Lp 235
Bpz Resources, Inc. 244
Bristow Group Inc 251
Buckeye Partners Lp 262
Cabot Oil & Gas Corp. 271
Cal Dive International Inc 274
Callon Petroleum Co. (de) 279
Calpine Corp 280
Camber Energy Inc 281
Camden Property Trust 282
Cameron International Corporation 283
Caprock Communications Inc. 290
Carbo Ceramics Inc. 292

Cardinal Health Pharmacy Solutions 293
Cardtronics Plc 294
Carriage Services, Inc. 301
Carrizo Oil & Gas, Inc. 301
Centerpoint Energy Houston Electric Llc 317
Centerpoint Energy, Inc 317
Century Energy Ltd. 322
Cheniere Energy Inc. 333
Cheniere Energy Partners L P 333
Cheniere Energy Partners Lp Holdings Llc 333
Chevron Pipe Line Company 335
Citation Oil & Gas Corp. 349
Citgo Petroleum Corporation 349
City Of Houston Texas 352
Cobalt International Energy L.p. 364
Colorado Interstate Gas Company Llc 371
Columbia Gulf Transmission, Llc 373
Comfort Systems Usa Inc 374
Complete Production Services Inc. 381
Contango Oil & Gas Co. 390
Continental Airlines Inc. 390
Crestwood Midstream Partners Lp 407
Cyberonics, Inc. 420
Deep Down Inc 433
Diamond Offshore Drilling, Inc. 446
Dresser-rand Group Inc. 461
Dril-quip Inc 461
Duncan Energy Partners L.p. 465
Dune Energy, Inc. 465
Dxp Enterprises, Inc. 467
Dynamic Offshore Resources Llc 468
Dynegy Inc (new) (de) 469
Eagle Rock Energy Partners Lp 472
Edp Renewables North America Llc 483
El Paso Corporation 483
El Paso Pipeline Partners Lp 484
Enbridge Energy Management Llc 497
Enbridge Energy Partners, L.p. 497
Encore Bancshares Inc. 497
Endeavour International Corp 498
Enervest Ltd. 502
Englobal Corp. 503
Enterprise Products Partners L.p. 507
Eog Resources, Inc. 509
Ep Energy Corp. 509
Era Group Inc 512
Erhc Energy Inc. 513
Evolution Petroleum Corp 520
Far East Energy Corp 529
Fiesta Mart Inc. 544
Florida Gas Transmission Company, Llc 561
Flotek Industries Inc 563
Fmc Technologies, Inc. 564
Forum Energy Technologies Inc 570
Frank's International Inc. 574
Freshpoint Inc 579
Furmanite Corp 585
Gallery Model Homes, Inc. 589
Garden Ridge Corporation 591
Gas Transmission Northwest Llc 592
Gateway Energy Corporation 592
Genesis Energy L.p. 598
Geomet Inc (de) 602
Geospace Technologies Corp 603
Global Custom Commerce L.p. 611
Glori Energy Inc. 614
Goodrich Petroleum Corp 619
Group 1 Automotive, Inc. 631
Gse Holding Inc. 632
Gulf Island Fabrication, Inc. 636
Gulf States Toyota Inc. 636
Gulf United Energy Inc. 637
Gulfmark Offshore Inc 637
Halcon Resources Corp 640

INDEX BY HEADQUARTERS LOCATION

Halliburton Company 640
Harvest Natural Resources Inc. 647
Harvest Oil & Gas Corp 647
Hcc Insurance Holdings, Inc. 651
Helix Energy Solutions Group Inc 658
Hercules Offshore Inc 660
Hines Interests Limited Partnership 670
Houston American Energy Corp. 683
Houston Community College, Inc. 683
Houston Wire & Cable Co 683
Ies Holdings Inc 697
Ignite Restaurant Group Inc 697
Internet America Inc. 727
Ion Geophysical Corp 732
Isramco, Inc. 737
Johnson Supply And Equipment Corporation 753
Kbr Inc 762
Key Energy Services Inc (de) 768
Kinder Morgan Energy Partners, L.p. 771
Kinder Morgan Inc. 771
Kirby Corp. 773
Kraton Corp 780
Landry's Inc. 788
Lapolla Industries Inc 790
Linnco Llc 809
Liquefied Natural Gas Ltd 810
Lrr Energy, L.p. 820
Luby's, Inc. 821
Main Street Capital Corp 833
Marathon Oil Corp. 837
Mattress Firm Holding Corp 850
Mccoy-rockford, Inc. 855
Mcdermott International Inc (panama) 855
Mei Technologies, Inc. 864
Memorial Hermann Healthcare System 865
Menil Foundation Inc. 866
Mesa Royalty Trust 874
Metropolitan Transit Authority Of Harris County 878
Mexican Restaurants, Inc. 879
Midcoast Energy Partners, L.p. 886
Morton's Restaurant Group Inc. 907
Mrc Global Inc 911
Mv Oil Trust 917
Natural Resource Partners Lp 930
Nbl Permian Llc 933
Netiq Corporation 938
Nextec Group 952
Noble Energy Inc 956
Nuo Therapeutics Inc 974
Oasis Petroleum Inc. 980
Occidental Petroleum Corp 981
Oceaneering International, Inc. 982
Oil States International, Inc. 986
Oiltanking Partners Lp 987
Omega Protein Corp. 991
Orion Group Holdings Inc 1001
Page Southerland Page L.l.p. 1013
Par Pacific Holdings Inc 1017
Paragon Real Estate Equity & Investment Trust 1018
Parker Drilling Co 1021
Patterson-uti Energy Inc. 1026
Pedevco Corp 1030
Penn Virginia Corp (new) 1032
Petrohawk Energy Corporation 1043
Petrologistics Lp 1043
Phillips 66 1047
Phillips 66 Company 1047
Phillips 66 Partners Lp 1047
Plains All American Pipeline Lp 1056
Platinum Energy Solutions Inc. 1058
Port Of Houston Authority 1063
Powell Industries, Inc. 1067
Primeenergy Resources Corp 1075
Pros Holdings Inc 1082

Prosperity Bancshares Inc. 1083
Qr Energy Lp 1094
Quanex Building Products Corp 1097
Quanta Services, Inc. 1097
Rci Hospitality Holdings Inc 1109
Rignet Inc 1129
Rock Energy Resources Inc. 1135
Rosetta Resources, Inc. 1139
Rowan Companies Inc. 1141
S & B Engineers And Constructors, Ltd. 1147
Sanchez Energy Corp. 1159
Sanchez Midstream Partners Lp 1159
Saratoga Resources Inc 1164
Satterfield And Pontikes Construction, Inc. 1165
Schlumberger Limited 1167
Sdb Trade International, L.p. 1173
Seitel Inc 1177
Service Corp. International 1182
Sharps Compliance Corp. 1187
Shell Oil Company 1188
Smg Industries Inc 1203
Southern Natural Gas Company, L.l.c. 1216
Southern Union Company 1217
Spaw Glass Construction Corporation 1222
Spectra Energy Corp 1222
Spectra Energy Partners Lp 1223
St. Luke's Episcopal Hospital Independent Practice Association, Inc. 1234
Stabilis Energy Inc 1236
Stage Stores Inc. 1236
Sterling Chemicals Inc. 1246
Stewart & Stevenson Inc. 1249
Stewart Information Services Corp 1249
Sun Coast Resources, Inc. 1257
Superior Energy Services, Inc. 1263
Synthesis Energy Systems Inc 1272
Sysco Corp 1273
Targa Resources Corp 1278
Targa Resources Partners Lp 1278
Tauber Oil Company 1279
Tellurian Inc 1287
Texas Children's Hospital 1294
Texas Southern University 1296
Texon Lp 1296
The Edelman Financial Group Inc. 1309
The Methodist Hospital 1321
The Plaza Group Inc 1326
Thrustmaster Of Texas, Inc. 1342
Tidewater Inc (new) 1344
Transcontinental Gas Pipe Line Company, Llc 1355
U.s. Physical Therapy, Inc. 1373
United Space Alliance, Llc 1386
Universal Weather And Aviation Inc. 1392
University Of Houston System 1396
Vaalco Energy, Inc. 1414
Vanguard Natural Resources Llc 1418
W & T Offshore Inc 1439
Waste Management, Inc. (de) 1447
Waukesha-pearce Industries, Inc. 1448
Wca Waste Corporation 1450
Weingarten Realty Investors 1453
Westlake Chemical Corp 1462
Whitestone Reit 1466
Willbros Group Inc (de) 1470
William Marsh Rice University Inc 1470
Yuma Energy Inc (new) 1490
Zaza Energy Corp. 1491

Humble
A2d Technologies 8

HUNTSVILLE
Sam Houston State University 1157

Hurst
Bell Helicopter Textron Inc. 203

Irving
Aegis Communications Group Inc. 36
Archon Group L.p. 129
Atx Group Inc. 157
Banctec Inc. 180
Blucora, Inc. 227
Boy Scouts Of America 243
Celanese Corp (de) 314
Christus Health International 343
Daegis Inc 423
Dallas Cowboys Football Club Ltd. 425
Darling Ingredients Inc 427
Del Frisco's Restaurant Group Inc 434
Exxon Mobil Corp 525
Felcor Lodging Trust Inc 540
Flowserve Corp 563
Fluor Corp. 563
Gold's Gym International Inc. 615
Gruma Corporation 632
Hms Holdings Corp 672
Magnum Hunter Resources Corp (de) 832
Mckesson Corp 856
Montage Resource Corp 903
Nch Corporation 933
Nexstar Media Group Inc 952
Pds Tech, Inc. 1029
Pioneer Natural Resources Co 1054
Rbc Life Sciences Inc 1108
Zale Corp. 1491

JERSEY VILLAGE
Stewart Builders, Inc. 1249

JOHNSON CITY
Pedernales Electric Cooperative, Inc. 1030

Katy
Academy Ltd. 14
Christus St. Catherine Hospital 343
Staff Force, Inc. 1236
Us Silica Holdings, Inc. 1411

Kemah
American International Industries Inc 88

Kilgore
Martin Midstream Partners Lp 843
Martin Resource Management Corporation 843

KILLEEN
Foxworth-galbraith Lumber Company 572
Metroplex Adventist Hospital, Inc. 877

LAREDO
City Of Laredo 353
International Bancshares Corp. 723

LEAGUE CITY
American Homestar Corporation 87

Lewisville
Horizon Health Corporation 679
Nationstar Mortgage Holdings Inc. 929
Uranium Resources Inc. 1406

LINDALE
Mercy Ships International 870

Little Elm
Retractable Technologies Inc 1124

Longview
Friedman Industries, Inc. 580

The Good Shepherd Hospital Inc 1313

LUBBOCK
City Of Lubbock 353
Covenant Health System 401
Lee Lewis Construction, Inc. 795
Nts Inc 972
Plains Cotton Cooperative Association 1056
Pyco Industries, Inc. 1092
Rip Griffin Truck Service Center, Inc. 1130
United Supermarkets L.l.c. 1388
Xfone Inc. 1484

LUFKIN
Memorial Health System Of East Texas 865
Piney Woods Healthcare System, L.p. 1052

McAllen
Am-mex Products Inc. 73

McKinney
Encore Wire Corp. 498
Globe Life Inc 613
Independent Bank Group Inc. 704

MESQUITE
Abatix Corp. 10

Midland
Concho Resources Inc 384
Dawson Geophysical Co (new) 429
Dawson Geophysical Co. 430
Diamondback Energy Inc. 447
Diamondback Energy, Inc. 447
Legacy Reserves Inc 796
Mexco Energy Corp. 879
Natural Gas Services Group Inc 930
West Texas Gas, Inc. 1457

Midlothian
Ennis Inc 503

Missouri City
Global Geophysical Services Inc 611

NACOGDOCHES
Stephen F Austin State University 1245

Nederland
Oci Partners Lp 982

NEW BRAUNFELS
Guadalupe Valley Telephone Cooperative, Inc. 634
New Braunfels Utilities 940
Rush Enterprises Inc. 1145

New Orleans
Treaty Energy Corp. 1358

North Richland Hills
Healthmarkets Inc. 654

Northlake
Farmer Bros. Co. 530

Pasadena
Dynacq Healthcare Inc 468
Kior, Inc. 773

PLAINVIEW
Wayland Baptist University Inc 1449

Plano
Adams Golf Inc. 26
Applied Concepts Inc. 120
Beal Bank S.s.b. 198
Denbury Resources, Inc. (de) 439
Diodes, Inc. 451
Fogo De Chao, Inc. 565
Frito-lay North America Inc. 580
Green Brick Partners Inc 628
Integer Holdings Corp 716

INDEX BY HEADQUARTERS LOCATION

Legacytexas Financial Group Inc 796
Lineage Power Corporation 809
Masergy Communications Inc. 845
Penney (j.c.) Co.,inc. (holding Co.) 1032
Rent-a-center Inc. 1119
Toyota Motor Credit Corp. 1353
Tyler Technologies, Inc. 1371

PRAIRIE VIEW
Prairie View A&m University 1069

Richardson
Amen Properties Inc 76
Amx Llc 106
Blue Cross And Blue Shield Of Texas 229
Fossil Group Inc 571
Infovision Inc. 709
Intrusion Inc 730
Lennox International Inc 798
Microwave Transmission Systems, Inc 884
Realpage Inc 1111
Safety-kleen Inc. 1150
Speed Commerce Inc 1224
University Of Texas At Dallas 1402
Vertical Computer Systems, Inc. 1425

ROCKWALL
Rayburn Country Electric Cooperative, Inc 1107

Rollingwood
Ezcorp, Inc. 526

ROUND ROCK
St Davids Healthcare Partnership Llp 1229
Teco-westinghouse Motor Company 1283
Texas Guaranteed Student Loan Corporation 1294
Tss Inc De 1367

SAN ANGELO
Angelo State University 110

SAN ANTONIO
Alamo Community College District 50
Andeavor 109
Bexar County Hospital District 212
Biglari Holdings Inc (new) 214
Billing Services Group Ltd. 214
Broadway Bancshares Inc. 253
Bromley Communications 254
C.h. Guenther & Son Inc. 269
Ccc Group Inc. 310
Clear Channel Communications Inc. 357
Clear Channel Outdoor Holdings Inc (new) 357
Cloudcommerce Inc 361
Cps Energy 403
Cst Brands Inc 413
Cullen/frost Bankers, Inc. 415
Digerati Technologies Inc 448
Globalscape Inc 613
H. E. Butt Grocery Company 638
Harland Clarke Corp. 645
Iheartmedia Inc 697
Kinetic Concepts Inc. 772
Mission Pharmacal Company 894
Nustar Energy Lp 974
Nustar Gp Holdings Llc 974
Our Lady Of The Lake University Of San Antonio 1005
Pioneer Energy Services Corp 1054
Rackspace Hosting Inc 1102
San Antonio Water System 1158
Security Service Federal Credit Union 1176
Southwest Research Institute Inc 1219

Tetco Incorporated 1293
Trinity University 1363
Us Global Investors Inc 1410
Usaa 1412
Usio Inc 1412
Valero Energy Corp 1415
Valero Energy Partners Lp 1415
Walton Signage Corporation 1444
Whataburger Restaurants Lp 1464

SAN MARCOS
Texas State University 1296

Seguin
Alamo Group, Inc. 50
Texas Lutheran University 1295

Selma
Call Now Inc. 278
Spaw Glass Holding, L.p. 1222

SHERMAN
Austin College 160

Southlake
Hkn Inc 671

SPRING
American Bureau Of Shipping 81
Exxonmobil Pipeline Company 526
Southwestern Energy Company 1219

Stafford
Velocity Express Llc 1421

STEPHENVILLE
Tarleton State University 1278

Sugar Land
Applied Optoelectronics Inc 121
Cvr Energy Inc 419
Cvr Partners Lp 419
Cvr Refining Lp 419
Hyperdynamics Corporation 691
Imperial Sugar Company 702
Team Inc 1281
Trecora Resources 1358
Us Dataworks Inc 1409

TAHOKA
Lyntegar Electric Cooperative, Inc. 823

TEMPLE
Mclane Company, Inc. 856
Scott & White Health Plan 1171
Wilsonart International Holding Llc 1472

TEXARKANA
Truman Arnold Companies 1364
Wadley Regional Medical Center 1442
Yates Group, Inc. 1487

The Colony
Rave Restaurant Group Inc 1106

The Woodlands
Anadarko Petroleum Corp 107
Chevron Phillips Chemical Company Llc 335
Conns Inc 387
Earthstone Energy Inc 472
Huntsman Corp 689
Imperial Petroleum Recovery Corporation 702
Layne Christensen Co 792
Lexicon Pharmaceuticals, Inc. 800
Lgi Homes, Inc. 801
Mitcham Industries Inc 895
Newfield Exploration Co 948
Newpark Resources, Inc. 950
Repros Therapeutics Inc 1120
Ricebran Technologies 1128
Sterling Construction Co Inc 1247
Strike, Llc 1253
Tetra Technologies, Inc. 1293

Waste Connections, Inc. 1447
Western Gas Partners Lp 1460
Western Midstream Partners Lp 1460

TYLER
East Texas Medical Center Regional Healthcare Syst 473
Southside Bancshares, Inc. 1218
Trinity Mother Frances Health System Foundation 1362

WACO
Baylor University 195
Brazos Electric Power Cooperative, Inc. 246
Central Freight Lines Inc. 318
Life Partners Holdings Inc 803
Tymco Inc. 1371

WEST LAKE HILLS
The Drees Company 1309

Westlake
Core Mark Holding Co Inc 395
Solera Holdings Inc 1206

Wichita Falls
Oakridge Energy Inc. 979
United Regional Health Care System, Inc. 1385

UTAH

CENTERVILLE
Management & Training Corporation 834

Cottonwood Heights
Dynatronics Corp. 469

Draper
1-800 Contacts Inc. 2
Fuelstream, Inc. 583

HURRICANE
Dats Trucking, Inc. 428

Lehi
Nature's Sunshine Products, Inc. 930

Lindon
Forevergreen Worldwide Corp 568

Logan
Icon Health & Fitness Inc. 694
Utah State University 1413

MIDVALE
Ally Bank 66
Freedom Resources Enterprises Inc. 577
Overstock.com Inc (de) 1006
Utah Medical Products, Inc. 1413
Zagg Inc 1490

Morgan
Browning Arms Company 258

Murray
Park City Group Inc 1020

North Salt Lake
Ascend Holdings Llc 141
Big West Oil, Llc 213

Odgen
American Nutrition Inc. 92

Ogden
Autoliv Asp Inc. 161
Columbia Ogden Medical Center, Inc. 373
Weber State University 1451

Orem
Activecare Inc 24

Park City
Nutraceutical International Corp. 974
Skullcandy Inc 1200

Provo
Alpine Air Express Inc. 68
Ancestry.com Inc. 108
Brigham Young University 249
Nu Skin Enterprises, Inc. 973

Riverdale
America First Credit Union 77

SALT LAKE CITY
A & K Railroad Materials, Inc. 7
Allen Communication Learning Services Inc. 60
Allied Resources Inc 64
Alsco Inc. 69
Arnold Machinery Company 136
Arup Laboratories Inc. 140
Associated Food Stores, Inc. 146
Beneficial Life Insurance Company 205
Big-d Construction Corp. 214
Broadcast International Inc 251
Bsd Medical Corp. 261
Burton Lumber & Hardware Co. 266
C.r. England, Inc. 269
Caspian Services Inc 305
Clarus Corp (new) 356
Clearone Inc 357
Control4 Corp 391
Evans & Sutherland Computer Corp. 518
Extra Space Storage Inc 525
Franklin Covey Co 574
Fusion-io Inc. 586
Fx Energy Inc. 587
Groen Brothers Aviation Inc 631
Ikano Communications Inc. 698
Incontact, Inc. 704
Intermountain Health Care Inc 723
Myrexis Inc. 918
Myriad Genetics, Inc. 918
Northern Utah Healthcare Corporation 965
O. C. Tanner Company 978
Pacific Webworks, Inc. 1012
Perseon Corp 1041
Polarityte Inc 1061
Questar Corp. 1098
Questar Gas Co. 1098
R.c. Willey Home Furnishings 1101
Recyclenet Corporation 1111
Salt Lake Community College 1156
Security National Financial Corp 1176
Sintx Technologies Inc 1197
Smith's Food & Drug Centers Inc. 1203
The University Of Utah 1335
Tomax Corporation 1349
University Of Utah Health Hospitals And Clinics 1403
Usana Health Sciences Inc 1412
Utah Associated Municipal Power Systems 1413
Westminster College 1462
Zions Bancorporation, N.a. 1493

SOUTH JORDAN
Deseret Generation And Transmission Co-operative 441
Headwaters Inc 652
Merit Medical Systems, Inc. 871

Springville
Neways Inc. 947

St. George
Skywest Inc. 1200

WEST VALLEY CITY
Central Refrigerated Service, Llc 319

INDEX BY HEADQUARTERS LOCATION

Cirtran Corp. 348

VERMONT

Bennington
Hemmings Motor News 659

Berlin
Blue Cross And Blue Shield Of Vermont 229

Burlington
The Burton Corporation 1302
The University Of Vermont Medical Center Inc 1336
University Of Vermont & State Agricultural College 1403

COLCHESTER
Engelberth Construction, Inc. 502
Green Mountain Power Corporation 628

Derby
Community Bancorp. (derby, Vt) 376

MIDDLEBURY
President And Fellows Of Middlebury College 1073

Montpelier
National Life Insurance Company 925

Morrisville
Union Bankshares, Inc. (morrisville, Vt) 1379

NORTHFIELD
Norwich University 970

Rutland
Casella Waste Systems, Inc. 304
Central Vermont Public Service Corporation 320
The Rutland Hospital Inc Act 220 1329

South Burlington
Merchants Bancshares, Inc. (burlington, Vt) 867
Vermont Gas Systems Inc. 1424

SPRINGFIELD
Springfield Hospital Inc. 1226

Waterbury
Keurig Green Mountain Inc 768

VIRGIN ISLANDS

CHRISTIANSTED
Limetree Bay Terminals Llc 807

VIRGINIA

Abingdon
Highlands Bankshares Inc (va) 667
K-va-t Food Stores Inc. 758

ALEXANDRIA
Alexandria Inova Hospital 55
Armed Forces Benefit Association 135
Bowl America Inc. 243
Calibre Systems, Inc. 275
City Of Alexandria 352
Comtex News Network Inc. 383
Good360 618
Institute For Defense Analyses Inc 715
International Association Of Amusement Parks & Attractions Inc 723
National Head Start Association 924
Pentagon Federal Credit Union 1035

The Salvation Army National Corporation 1329
United Way Worldwide 1389
Volunteers Of America, Inc. 1436
Vse Corp. 1438

Altavista
Pinnacle Bankshares Corp 1052

Arlington
Aes Corp. 38
American Diabetes Association 83
Avalonbay Communities, Inc. 163
Bae Systems Inc. 173
Caci International Inc 271
Chesapeake Lodging Trust 334
Conservation International Foundation 387
Council Of Better Business Bureaus Inc. 400
Counterpart International Inc 400
Experience Works, Inc. 524
Fbr & Co 533
Graham Holdings Co. 622
Greater Washington Educational Telecommunications Association, Inc. 627
Healthcare Distribution Management Association 653
In-q-tel Inc 703
March Of Dimes Inc. 837
Mcg Capital Corp 855
National Rural Electric Cooperative Association 927
Public Broadcasting Service 1088
Rosetta Stone Inc 1139
The Bureau Of National Affairs Inc. 1302
The Conservation Fund A Nonprofit Corporation 1307
The Nature Conservancy 1322
Timios National Corp 1346
Towers Watson & Co. 1352
Us Dairy Export Council 1409
Virginia Hospital Center Arlington Health System 1431

Ashburn
Telos Corp. (md) 1287

ASHLAND
Tsrc, Inc. 1367

Blacksburg
National Bankshares Inc. (va) 922
Virginia Polytechnic Institute & State University 1431

Bluefield
First Community Bankshares Inc (va) 549

Boones Mill
Metwood Inc 879

Bristol
Alpha Natural Resources Inc 68
Strongwell Corporation 1253

CENTREVILLE
The Parsons Corporation 1325

CHANTILLY
American Systems Corporation 96
Apptis Inc. 123
Engility Holdings Inc (new) 502
Intersections Inc 728
Network Management Resources Inc. 939
Rei Systems, Inc. 1116
The Long & Foster Companies Inc. 1319

CHARLOTTESVILLE
Kohr Brothers Inc. 777

Pepsi-cola Bottling Co Of Central Virginia 1038
Rector & Visitors Of The University Of Virginia 1111

Chesapeake
Dollar Tree Inc 456
Monarch Financial Holdings Inc 901

CHESTER
Industrial Turnaround Corporation 707

CULPEPER
Jefferson Homebuilders, Inc. 747

Danville
American National Bankshares, Inc. (danville, Va) 91

Dulles
National Rural Utilities Cooperative Finance Corp 927
Orbital Atk Inc 999
Orbital Sciences Corp. 999
Raytheon Technical Services Company Llc 1108

Edinburg
Shenandoah Telecommunications Co 1188

Fairfax
Argon St Inc. 131
Avaya Government Solutions Inc. 164
Barcelo Crestline Corporation 186
Customink Llc 418
Ecs Federal, Llc 479
Geeknet Inc 593
Guest Services, Inc. 635
Horne International Inc 680
Icf International Inc 693
Inforeliance Corporation 709
Information Analysis Inc. 709
National Rifle Association Of America 927
Unifiedonline Inc 1378
Widepoint Corp 1468

Falls Church
Altegrity Inc. 70
Applabs Inc. 119
Dyncorp International Inc. 469
Hitt Contracting, Inc. 671
Inova Health System Foundation 712
Intellidyne L.l.c. 719
Northrop Grumman Corp 966
The Centech Group Inc 1303

FARMVILLE
The President And Trustees Of Hampden-sydney College 1327

Floyd
Cardinal Bankshares Corp. 293

FREDERICKSBURG
Mary Washington Healthcare 844
Rappahannock Electric Cooperative 1105

GAINESVILLE
Ncs Technologies, Inc. 934

GALAX
Vaughan-bassett Furniture Company, Incorporated 1419

Glen Allen
Dynex Capital, Inc. 469
Eastern Virginia Bankshares, Inc 475
First Capital Bancorp Inc (va) 548
Markel Corp (holding Co) 840
Old Dominion Electric Cooperative 987

HAMPTON
Hampton University 642
Measurement Specialties, Inc. 859
Old Point Financial Corp 988

HARRISONBURG
James Madison University 745

Heathsville
Sharpe Resources Corporation 1187

Herndon
Applied Visual Sciences Inc. 122
Arbinet Corporation 125
Beacon Roofing Supply Inc 198
Command Security Corp 374
Continental Building Products Inc 390
Deltek Inc. 438
Dlt Solutions Llc 454
Eplus Inc 510
Gtsi Corp. 633
K12 Inc 758
Learning Tree International Inc 794
Mantech International Corp 837
Parature Inc. 1019
Sotera Defense Solutions Inc. 1209
Strategic Education Inc 1252
Xo Holdings Inc. 1484

Lansdowne
Ssp America Inc. 1229

Leesburg
Precision Auto Care, Inc. 1070

LEXINGTON
The Washington And Lee University 1337

LORTON
Ctsc Llc 414

Lynchburg
Bank Of The James Financial Group Inc 182
Bwx Technologies Inc 268
C. B. Fleet Company Incorporated 269
Centra Health, Inc. 318
Schewel Furniture Company Incorporated 1167
University Of Lynchburg 1397

MANASSAS
Aurora Flight Sciences Corp 159
Northern Virginia Electric Cooperative 965

Martinsville
Hooker Furniture Corp 678
Mainstreet Bankshares Inc 834

MC LEAN
Delta Tucker Holdings, Inc. 438
Immixgroup, Inc. 700
National Automobile Dealers Association 922

McKenney
Touchstone Bank 1351

McLean
Acumen Solutions Inc. 25
Alion Science And Technology Corporation 57
Arlington Asset Investment Corp 135
Ats Corporation 156
Booz Allen Hamilton Holding Corp. 239
Capital One Financial Corp 289
Cardinal Financial Corp 293
Exelis Inc. 522
Freddie Mac 576
Gladstone Capital Corporation 608
Gladstone Commercial Corp 608
Gladstone Investment Corp 608

INDEX BY HEADQUARTERS LOCATION

Gladstone Land Corp 609
Global Telecom & Technology Inc. 612
Gtt Communications, Inc 633
Hilton Worldwide Holdings Inc 670
Iridium Communications Inc 734
Iridium Communications Inc. 735
Mars Incorporated 842
Southern National Bancorp Of Virginia Inc 1216
Sunrise Senior Living Inc. 1261

Mechanicsville
Owens & Minor, Inc. 1006

Middleburg
Middleburg Financial Corp 886

Midland
Smith-midland Corp. 1204

Midlothian
Bank Of Virginia 183
Village Bank & Trust Financial Corp 1429

Newport News
Canon Virginia Inc. 286
Ferguson Enterprises Inc. 540
Huntington Ingalls Industries, Inc. 689
Riverside Healthcare Association, Inc. 1131
Riverside Hospital, Inc. 1131

Norfolk
Bae Systems Norfolk Ship Repair Inc. 174
Children's Health System Inc. 338
Eastern Virginia Medical School 475
Heritage Bankshares, Inc. (norfolk, Va) 660
Norfolk Southern Corp 958
Norfolk State University 958
People For The Ethical Treatment Of Animals, Inc. 1035
Pra Group Inc 1069
Sentara Healthcare 1180
Virginia International Terminals, Llc 1431

NORTON
Norton Community Hospital Auxiliary Inc. 969

Reston
Access National Corp 16
Altum Incorporated 72
Calnet Inc 279
Carahsoft Technology Corp. 292
Comscore Inc 382
Comstock Holding Companies, Inc 382
Emerald Dairy Inc. 492
General Dynamics Corp 595
High Performance Technologies Inc. 666
Idemia Identity & Security Usa Llc 695
Internap Corp 723
Leidos Holdings Inc 798
Lightbridge Corp 806
Maryland And Virginia Milk Producers Cooperative Association, Incorporated 844
Maximus Inc. 851
National Wildlife Federation Inc 929
Nci Inc 934
Nii Holdings Inc. 954
Noblis, Inc. 956
Nvr Inc. 976
Official Payments Holdings Inc. 984
Science Applications International Corp (new) 1170
Serco Inc. 1181

Stg Llc 1249
Thompson Hospitality Corporation 1342
Ventera Corporation 1422
Verisign Inc 1423

RICHLANDS
Clinch Valley Medical Center, Inc. 360

Richmond
Altria Group Inc 72
Atlantic Union Bankshares Corp 153
Bon Secours - Richmond Community Hospital, Incorporated 238
Brinks Co (the) 250
Captech Ventures Inc. 291
Carmax Inc. 298
Cavalier Telephone Llc 308
Cherry Bekaert Llp 334
Childfund International, Usa 338
Community Bankers Trust Corp 377
Dominion Energy Inc (new) 456
Enterprise Diversified Inc 506
Estes Express Lines, Inc. 516
Federal Reserve Bank Of Richmond, Dist. No. 5 537
Genworth Financial, Inc. (holding Co) 601
Gpm Investments, Llc 621
Hunton & Williams Llp 689
Insmed Incorporated 714
James River Coal Co 745
Kbs, Inc. 762
Meadwestvaco Corp. 858
Media General Inc (new) 860
Newmarket Corp 949
Swedish Match North America Inc. 1267
Synalloy Corp. 1269
The C.f. Sauer Company 1302
Tredegar Corp. 1358
Universal Corp 1390
University Of Richmond 1400
Virginia Commonwealth University 1430
Virginia Electric & Power Co. 1431
Virginia Housing Development Authority 1431
Xenith Bankshares Inc 1483

ROANOKE
Branch & Associates, Inc. 245
Carilion Clinic 296
Grand Piano & Furniture Co. 623
Luna Innovations Inc 823
Optical Cable Corp. 997
Petroleum Marketers Incorporated 1043
Rgc Resources, Inc. 1127
The Branch Group Inc 1301
Valley Financial Corp. 1415

ROCKINGHAM
Sentara Rmh Medical Center 1180

ROCKY MOUNT
Ronile, Inc. 1137

Springfield
Best Medical International Inc. 210
Isomet Corp. 736
Spok Holdings Inc 1226
Tessada & Associates Inc. 1292
Versar Inc. 1424

Stanley
Pioneer Bankshares Inc. 1054

STERLING
Indyne, Inc. 707
Neustar, Inc. 939
Sutron Corp. 1266
Technica Corporation 1282

Strasburg
First National Corp. (strasburg, Va) 553

Timberville
F & M Bank Corp. 526

Toano
Lumber Liquidators Holdings Inc 822

TRIANGLE
Marine Toys For Tots Foundation 839

Tysons Corner
Cvent, Inc 418
Microstrategy Inc. 884

TYSONS
Computer Sciences Corporation 381

VERONA
Dixie Gas And Oil Corporation 453

VIENNA
Actionet, Inc. 23
Cel-sci Corporation 313
Eloqua Limited 489
Feld Entertainment Inc. 540
Indus Corporation 706
Microtechnologies Llc 884
Navy Federal Credit Union 932

Virginia Beach
Amerigroup Corporation 99
Atlantic Diving Supply, Inc. 152
Franchise Group Inc 573
Jth Holding Inc. 756
Jth Tax Inc. 756
Operation Smile, Inc. 996
The Christian Broadcasting Network Inc 1305
Wheeler Real Estate Investment Trust Inc 1465

Warrenton
Fauquier Bankshares, Inc. 532
Fhi Services 541

Waynesboro
Lumos Networks Corp 822
Ntelos Holdings Corp 972

West Point
C & F Financial Corp. 268

WILLIAMSBURG
Sentara Williamsburg Regional Medical Center 1180
Sotherly Hotels Inc 1209
The College Of William & Mary 1306
The Colonial Williamsburg Foundation 1306

Winchester
American Woodmark Corp. 98
Trex Co Inc 1359
Valley Health System 1416
Winchester Medical Center Auxiliary, Inc. 1473

WOODBRIDGE
Potomac Hospital Corporation Of Prince William 1066

WASHINGTON

Aberdeen
Pacific Financial Corp. 1010

Bellevue
Applied Discovery Inc. 120
Audiencescience Inc. 157
Bsquare Corp 261
Concur Technologies Inc 384
Drugstore.com Inc. 462
Esterline Technologies Corp 516

Expedia Group Inc 523
Itex Corp 738
Odom Corporation 983
Outerwall Inc 1005
Overlake Hospital Medical Center 1005
Paccar Inc. 1009
Puget Energy, Inc. 1090
Quality Food Centers Inc. 1096
Radiant Logistics, Inc. 1102
Symetra Financial Corp 1269

BELLINGHAM
Haggen, Inc. 640
Western Washington University 1462

Bothell
Biolife Solutions Inc 218
Cardiac Science Corporation 292
Helix Biomedix Inc. 657
Marina Biotech Inc 839
Seattle Genetics Inc 1174
Sonosite Inc. 1209

CASHMERE
Liberty Orchards Company Inc. 802

CHELAN
Trout-blue Chelan-magi, Inc. 1363

CHENEY
Eastern Washington University Inc 475
Trans-system, Inc. 1354

Enumclaw
Mutual Of Enumclaw Insurance Company 917

EVERETT
Public Utility District 1 Of Snohomish County 1089

Ferndale
Brookmount Explorations Inc. 256

Hoquiam
Timberland Bancorp, Inc. 1345

Issaquah
Costco Wholesale Corp 399
Lakeside Industries, Inc. 787
Spacelabs Healthcare Inc. 1220

Kennewick
Electronic Systems Technology, Inc. 486

Kirkland
Celebrate Interactive Holdings Inc. 314
Monolithic Power Systems Inc 902
Pendrell Corp 1031

Liberty Lake
Itron Inc 738

LONGVIEW
North Pacific Paper Company, Llc 961
Public Utility District No 1 Of Cowlitz County 1089

Lynnwood
Zumiez Inc 1495

Mountlake Terrace
Fs Bancorp Inc (washington) 582

Oak Harbor
Washington Banking Co. (oak Harbor, Wa) 1445

OLYMPIA
Evergreen State College 519
Heritage Financial Corp (wa) 661

ORONDO
Auvil Fruit Company Inc. 163

HOOVER'S MASTERLIST OF U.S. COMPANIES 2020

INDEX BY HEADQUARTERS LOCATION

Poulsbo
Pope Resources Lp 1062
Redmond
Data I/o Corp. 427
Microvision Inc. 884
Nintendo Of America Inc. 954
Univar Inc. 1390
Renton
Boeing Capital Corp 235
Convergent Outsourcing, Inc. 391
First Financial Northwest Inc 550
Football Northwest Llc 566
Olympic Pipe Line Company 989
Richland
Isoray, Inc. 737
Kadlec Regional Medical Center 758
Pacific Northwest National Laboratory 1011
Seattle
Alaska Air Group, Inc. 50
Amazon.com Inc 74
American Management Services West Llc 90
American Seafoods Group Llc 95
Avanade Inc. 163
Bill & Melinda Gates Foundation 214
Bloodworks 226
Blue Nile Inc 230
Cascade Natural Gas Corporation 303
Clearsign Technologies Corp 357
Cray Inc 405
Cti Biopharma Corp 413
Cutter & Buck Inc. 418
Dendreon Corp 440
Emeritus Corp. 493
Expeditors International Of Washington, Inc. 523
F5 Networks, Inc. 526
Geobio Energy Inc. 602
Group Health Cooperative 631
Homestreet Inc 677
Impinj Inc. 703
Jones Soda Co. 754
L&l Energy Inc 782
Lane Powell Pc 789
Marchex Inc 838
Mckinstry Co. Llc 856
Nanostring Technologies Inc 920
National Frozen Foods Corporation 923
Nordstrom, Inc. 957
Northwest Dairy Association 967
Ocean Beauty Seafoods Llc 981
Omeros Corp 991
Oncothyreon Inc. 993
Onvia Inc 995
Orca Bay Seafoods, Inc. 1000
Perkins Coie Llp 1040
Plum Creek Timber Co., Inc. 1058
Port Of Seattle 1064
Seattle Children's Hospital 1174
Seattle University 1175
Slalom Llc 1201
Sound Financial Inc. 1209
Starbucks Corp. 1240
Swedish Health Services 1267
Tableau Software Inc 1274
Tapimmune Inc. 1278
The City Of Seattle-city Light Department 1305
The Cobalt Group Inc. 1306
Todd Shipyards Corporation 1349
Tommy Bahama Group Inc. 1350
Trident Seafoods Corporation 1361
University Of Washington Inc 1403
Washington Federal Inc 1445
Weyerhaeuser Co 1463

SELAH
Tree Top, Inc. 1358
SHORELINE
Crista Ministries 407
Spokane Valley
Key Tronic Corp 769
Revett Mining Co Inc 1124
Spokane
Ambassadors Group Inc 74
Avista Corp 167
Clearwater Paper Corp 358
E Z Loader Boat Trailers Inc. 470
Ecova Inc 479
Gold Reserve Inc 615
Goldrich Mining Co 617
Mines Management, Inc. 892
Northwest Bancorporation 967
Northwest Farm Credit Services 968
Potlatchdeltic Corp 1066
Sterling Financial Corp. (wa) 1247
The Corporation Of Gonzaga University 1308
Urm Stores, Inc. 1407
TACOMA
Burkhart Dental Supply Co. 265
Columbia Banking System Inc 372
Franciscan Health System 573
Multicare Health System 914
Tacoma Public Utilities 1274
Trueblue Inc 1364
University Of Puget Sound 1400
Tukwila
Boeing Employees' Credit Union 236
Vancouver
Barrett Business Services, Inc. 189
Calvert Company Inc. 280
Nautilus Inc 931
Northwest Pipe Co. 968
Peacehealth 1030
Public Utility District 1 Of Clark County 1089
Riverview Bancorp, Inc. 1131
Walla Walla
Baker Boyer Bancorp 175
Banner Corp. 184
Key Technology Inc 768
Whitman College 1467
WENATCHEE
Goodfellow Bros. Inc. 619
Public Utility District No. 1 Of Chelan County 1089
YAKIMA
Yakima Valley Memorial Hospital Association Inc 1486

WEST VIRGINIA

BERKELEY SPRINGS
War Memorial Hospital Inc. 1444
Bluefield
First Century Bankshares, Inc. 548
Charles Town
American Public Education Inc 93
Potomac Bancshares, Inc. 1066
CHARLESTON
Charleston Area Medical Center, Inc. 329
Charleston Hospital, Inc. 329
City Holding Co. 352
Jacobs Financial Group Inc 744
United Bankshares Inc 1381

Chester
Mtr Gaming Group, Inc. 913
Elkins
Citizens Financial Corp. (wv) 350
FAIRMONT
Monongahela Power Company 902
FOLLANSBEE
Wheeling-nisshin, Inc. 1465
Huntington
Champion Industries Inc (wv) 326
Energy Services Of America Corp. 500
Marshall University 842
Premier Financial Bancorp, Inc. 1072
St. Mary's Medical Center 1235
Steel Of West Virginia, Inc. 1244
Moorefield
Summit Financial Group Inc 1257
Morgantown
Gabriel Brothers Inc. 588
Virginia West University Foundation Incorporated 1431
Virginia West University Hospitals Inc 1432
West Virginia United Health System, Inc. 1457
West Virginia University 1457
Petersburg
Highlands Bankshares Inc. 667
POINT PLEASANT
Fruth, Inc. 582
PRINCETON
Princeton Community Hospital Association, Inc. 1076
WEIRTON
Weirton Medical Center, Inc. 1453
Wheeling
First West Virginia Bancorp Inc 556
Ohio Valley Medical Center Incorporated 986
Wesbanco Inc 1455

WISCONSIN

Appleton
Appleton Papers Inc. 120
Creative Group Inc. 405
Pierce Manufacturing Inc. 1051
Secura Insurance Holdings Inc. 1175
Thedacare, Inc. 1339
U.s. Venture, Inc. 1373
BEAVER DAM
Beaver Dam Community Hospitals, Inc. 200
BELOIT
Beloit College 203
Beloit Health System, Inc. 204
Blackhawk Bancorp Inc 223
Regal Beloit Corp 1114
Brookfield
Cib Marine Bancshares Inc 345
Fiserv Inc 557
Paragon Development Systems, Inc. 1018
Brownsville
Michels Corporation 881
Cudahy
Ati Ladish Llc 150
Patrick Cudahy Incorporated 1025
Roadrunner Transportation Services Holdings Inc. 1132

DE PERE
St. Norbert College, Inc. 1235
Denmark
Denmark Bancshares Inc 440
DURAND
Bauer Built, Inc. 192
Eau Claire
Citizens Community Bancorp Inc (md) 350
Market & Johnson, Inc. 840
Mayo Clinic Health System-northwest Wisconsin Region, Inc. 852
Menard Inc. 866
National Presto Industries, Inc. 926
Sacred Heart Hospital Of The Hospital Sisters Of The Third Order Of St. Francis 1149
ELLSWORTH
Ellsworth Cooperative Creamery 489
FITCHBURG
Certco, Inc. 324
Promega Corporation 1081
FOND DU LAC
C.d. Smith Construction Inc. 269
FRANKLIN
Carma Laboratories Inc. 298
Krones, Inc. 781
FRIENDSHIP
Adams-columbia Electric Cooperative 27
GLENDALE
Wheaton Franciscan Services, Inc. 1464
Grafton
Cedarburg Hauser Pharmaceuticals Inc. 313
Green Bay
American Foods Group Llc 85
Associated Banc-corp 145
Krueger International, Inc. 781
Paper Converting Machine Company 1017
Pomp's Tire Service, Inc. 1062
Schreiber Foods Inc. 1169
The Green Bay Packers Inc. 1313
Tufco Technologies, Inc. 1368
Hartford
Broan-nutone Llc 253
Hudson
Phillips-medisize Corporation 1048
Kenosha
Pacific Sands Inc 1012
Snap-on, Inc. 1204
Kimberly
Appleton Coated Llc 119
LA CROSSE
Dairyland Power Cooperative 424
Gundersen Lutheran Medical Center, Inc. 637
Kwik Trip, Inc. 782
LA FARGE
Cooperative Regions Of Organic Producer Pools 394
Madison
Alliant Energy Corp 63
American Tv & Appliance Of Madison Inc. 97
Anchor Bancorp Wisconsin Inc (de) 108

Badgerland Meat And Provisions Llc 173
Bruker Axs Inc. 259
Exact Sciences Corp. 521
First Business Financial Services, Inc. 548
Fiskars Brands Inc. 557
Full Compass Systems Ltd. 584
Great Wolf Resorts Inc. 627
J. H. Findorff & Son, Inc. 740
Madison Area Technical College District 830
Meriter Health Services, Inc. 872
Mge Energy Inc 880
Sonic Foundry, Inc. 1208
University Of Wisconsin Foundation 1403
University Of Wisconsin Hospital And Clinics Authority 1404
University Of Wisconsin System 1404

Manitowoc
Lakeside Foods Inc. 787
Orion Energy Systems Inc 1001

MARSHFIELD
Marshfield Clinic Health System, Inc. 843
Security Health Plan Of Wisconsin, Inc. 1176

MAYVILLE
Mayville Engineering Co Inc 853
Tab Products Co Llc 1274

MENASHA
Faith Technologies, Inc. 528

Menomonee Falls
Enerpac Tool Group Corp 501
Ensync Inc 504
Magnetek, Inc. 831

MENOMONIE
Chippewa Valley Bean Company Inc. 341

MEQUON
Charter Manufacturing Company, Inc. 329

Middelton
Spectrum Brands Holdings Inc (new) 1223

Middleton
Spectrum Brands Holdings Inc 1223
University Of Wisconsin Medical Foundation, Inc. 1404

Milwaukee
Ari Network Services, Inc. 132
Artisan Partners Asset Management Inc 139
Astronautics Corporation Of America 148
Badger Meter Inc 173
Bank Mutual Corp 181
Brady Corp 245
Cdc Supply Chain 312
Children's Hospital And Health System, Inc. 338
Columbia St. Mary's Inc. 373
Commerce Group Corp. 375
Douglas Dynamics, Inc. 458
Foley & Lardner Llp 565
Froedtert Memorial Lutheran Hospital, Inc. 581
Harley-davidson Inc 645
Journal Communications Inc 755
Joy Global Inc 755
Koss Corp 779
Marcus Corp. (the) 838
Marquette University 841
Meyer & Wallis Inc. 879

Mgic Investment Corp. (wi) 880
Ministry Health Care Inc. 892
Physicians Realty Trust 1049
Rbs Global Inc. 1108
Rexnord Corp (new) 1126
Robert W. Baird & Co. Incorporated 1133
Roundy's Inc. 1140
Sensient Technologies Corp. 1180
Smith (a O) Corp 1203
Strattec Security Corp. 1252
United Performing Arts Fund Inc. 1385
Wec Energy Group Inc 1452
Weyco Group, Inc 1463

Mondovi
Marten Transport Ltd 843

Mosinee
Wausau Paper Corp 1448

Neenah
Bemis Co Inc 204
Menasha Corporation 866
Plexus Corp. 1058

New Berlin
International Monetary Systems Ltd. 726

Oconomowoc
Bruno Independent Living Aids Inc. 259

Port Washington
Allen-edmonds Shoe Corporation 60

PRAIRIE DU SAC
Culver Franchising System, Inc. 416

Racine
Johnson Outdoors Inc 753
Milaeger"s Inc. 888
Modine Manufacturing Co 898
S.c. Johnson & Son Inc. 1148
Twin Disc Incorporated 1370

RIPON
Alliance Laundry Holdings Llc 62

River Falls
Sajan Inc. 1154

SCHOFIELD
L & S Electric, Inc. 782

Sheboygan Falls
Johnsonville Sausage Llc 753

Sheboygan
Acuity A Mutual Insurance Company 25

Sparta
Century Foods International Llc 322

Sturgeon Bay
Baylake Corp. (wi) 194

Sussex
Quad/graphics, Inc. 1095

WAUKESHA
American Transmission Company, Llc 97
Prohealth Care Inc 1080
Telkonet Inc. 1287
Waukesha Memorial Hospital, Inc. 1448

WAUSAU
Aspirus, Inc. 144

Wauwatosa
Briggs & Stratton Corp. 249
Briggs & Stratton Power Products Group Llc 249

WISCONSIN DELLS
Holiday Wholesale, Inc. 674

Wisconsin Rapids
Renaissance Learning Inc. 1118

WYOMING

CASPER
Wyoming Medical Center, Inc. 1482

Cheyenne
Great Lakes Aviation Ltd. 625

Gillette
Cloud Peak Energy Inc 361

LARAMIE
University Of Wyoming 1404

This Page left intentionally blank